SOCIAL SECURITY LEGISLATION 2019/20

VOLUME I:
NON MEANS TESTED BENEFITS AND EMPLOYMENT AND SUPPORT ALLOWANCE

SOCIAL SECURITY LEGISLATION 2019/20

General Editor
Nick Wikeley, M.A. (Cantab)

VOLUME I:
NON MEANS TESTED BENEFITS AND EMPLOYMENT AND SUPPORT ALLOWANCE

Commentary By

Ian Hooker, LL.B.
Formerly Lecturer in Law, University of Nottingham,
Formerly Chairman, Social Security Tribunals

John Mesher, B.A., B.C.L. (Oxon), LL.M. (Yale)
Formerly Judge of the Upper Tribunal

Edward Mitchell, LL.B.
Judge of the Upper Tribunal

Richard Poynter, B.C.L., M.A. (Oxon)
Judge of the Upper Tribunal

Christopher Ward, M.A. (Cantab)
Judge of the Upper Tribunal

Nick Wikeley, M.A. (Cantab)
Judge of the Upper Tribunal,
Emeritus Professor of Law, University of Southampton

Consultant Editor
Child Poverty Action Group

SWEET & MAXWELL

THOMSON REUTERS

Published in 2019 by Thomson Reuters, trading as Sweet & Maxwell.
Registered in England & Wales, Company No.1679046.
Registered Office and address for service: 5 Canada Square,
Canary Wharf, London, E14 5AQ.

For further information on our products and services, visit
http://www.sweetandmaxwell.co.uk.

Typeset by Servis Filmsetting Ltd, Stockport, Cheshire
Printed and bound by CPI Group (UK) Ltd, Croydon, CR0 4YY

Thomson Reuters, the Thomson Reuters Logo and
Sweet & Maxwell® are trademarks of Thomson Reuters.

No natural forests were destroyed to make this product.
Only farmed timber was used and re-planted.

A CIP catalogue record for this book is available from the British Library.

ISBN 978-0-41407-196-4

Thomson Reuters, the Thomson Reuters Logo and
Sweet & Maxwell® are trademarks of Thomson Reuters.

CHILD POVERTY ACTION GROUP

The Child Poverty Action Group (CPAG) is a charity, founded in 1965, which campaigns for the relief of poverty in the United Kingdom. It has a particular reputation in the field of welfare benefits law derived from its legal work, publications, training and parliamentary and policy work, and is widely recognised as the leading organisation for taking test cases on social security law.

CPAG is therefore ideally placed to act as Consultant Editor to this 5-volume work—**Social Security Legislation 2019/20**. CPAG is not responsible for the detail of what is contained in each volume, and the authors' views are not necessarily those of CPAG. The Consultant Editor's role is to act in an advisory capacity on the overall structure, focus and direction of the work.

For more information about CPAG, its rights and policy publications or training courses, its address is 30 Micawber Street, London, N1 7TB (telephone: 020 7837 7979—website: *http://www.cpag.org.uk*).

FOREWORD

The First-tier Tribunal has, over many years, been a beneficiary of the immense learning and experience of those who compile the Social Security Legislation series, and we are tremendously grateful for the easy access and concentrated learning that the accompanying commentary affords. Together they provide a crucial contribution towards the means by which we seek to deliver access to justice to thousands of people each year and I am happy to recommend them to anyone who might have an interest in this important area of the law.

Judge John Aitken
Chamber President, Social Entitlement Chamber
Social Security and Child Support,
Criminal Injuries Compensation,
Asylum Support

PREFACE

Non-Means Tested Benefits and Employment and Support Allowance is Volume I of *Social Security Legislation 2019/20*. The companion volumes are Volume II: *Income Support, Jobseeker's Allowance, State Pension Credit and the Social Fund*; Volume III: *Administration, Adjudication and the European Dimension*; Volume IV: *Tax credits and HMRC-administered Social Security Benefits*; and *Volume V: Universal Credit*. The "year" in the title of the works relates to the tax/contribution year, and conveys the period the books (and the Supplement) are designed to cover.

Each of the volumes in the series provides the text of benefits legislation in Great Britain, clearly showing the form and date of amendments, and is up to date to April 8, 2019. This year has seen relatively little change to primary legislation, with Parliament preoccupied on other matters. However, this edition includes the usual plethora of miscellaneous amendments made by secondary legislation to the scope of social security provision.

Where possible, the commentary includes references to some later case law since April 8, 2019. More generally, so far as developments in the case law since the previous edition are concerned, the jurisprudence of the Upper Tribunal continues to provide clarification in respect of the meaning and application of the various descriptors for both personal independence payment (PIP) and employment and support allowance (ESA). The commentary provides extensive and in-depth analysis of such developments as well as coverage of the Upper Tribunal's decision on the HRA discrimination challenge to the rules on so-called 'polygamous widows' (*NA v SSWP (BB)* [2019] UKUT 144 (AAC)), along with a series of decisions on the 'competent state' and exportability of disability-related benefits under EU law (see e.g. *JG v SSWP (CA)* [2019] UKUT 83 (AAC) and *SSWP v MC (DLA)* [2019] UKUT 84 (AAC)).

As we noted last year, neither the outcome of the EU referendum of June 23, 2016 nor the Prime Minister's letter of March 29, 2017 triggering art.50 of the Treaty on European Union immediately alters the United Kingdom's membership of the Union. The United Kingdom will remain a Member State and European Union law will continue to apply until such time as the exit arrangements provided for in art.50 are completed. Readers will appreciate this Preface may (or may not) be overtaken by events.

As always, revising and updating the legislative text and commentary has required considerable flexibility on the part of the publisher and a great deal of help from a number of sources, including CPAG as advisory editor to the series. We remain grateful for this assistance in our task of providing an authoritative reflection on the current state of the law. To maximise space for explanatory commentary in books which seem to grow in size year on year, we have provided lists of definitions only where the commentary on the provision is substantial, or where reference to definitions is essential for a proper understanding. Users of the books should always check whether particular words or phrases they are called upon to apply have a particular meaning ascribed to them in legislation. Generally the first or second regulation in each set of regulations contains definitions of key terms (check the "Arrangement of Regulations" at the beginning of each set for an indication of the subject matter covered by each regulations). There are also definition or "interpretation" sections in primary legislation.

Users of the series, and its predecessor works, have over the years contributed to their effectiveness by providing valuable comments on our commentary, as well as pointing out where the text of some provision has been omitted in error, or become garbled, or not been brought fully up to date. In some cases, this has drawn attention to an error which might otherwise have gone unnoticed. In providing such feedback, users of the work have helped to shape the content and ensure the accuracy of our material. We hope that users of the work will continue to provide such helpful input and feedback. Please write to the General Editor of the series, Professor Nick Wikeley, c/o School of Law, University of Southampton, Highfield, Southampton SO17 1BJ, e-mail njw@soton.ac.uk, and he will pass on any comments received to the appropriate commentator.

Our gratitude also goes to the Chamber President of the Social Entitlement Chamber of the First-tier Tribunal and his colleagues there for continuing the now long tradition of help and encouragement in our endeavours.

August 2019

Ian Hooker
John Mesher
Ed Mitchell
Richard Poynter
Christopher Ward
Nick Wikeley

CONTENTS

	Page
Foreword	vii
Preface	ix
Using this book: An Introduction to Legislation and Case Law	xvii
Change of Name from Department of Social Security to Department for Work and Pensions	xxix
Changes in Terminology Consequent upon the Entry into Force of the Treaty of Lisbon	xxxi
The Marriage (Same Sex Couples) Act 2013	xxxiii
Table of Cases	xxxv
Table of Commissioners' Decisions 1948–2009	liii
Table of Abbreviations used in this Series	lxiii

PART I
STATUTES

	Paras
Vaccine Damage Payments Act 1979 (c.17)	1.1
Pneumoconiosis etc. (Workers' Compensation) Act 1979 (c.41)	1.31
Social Security Contributions and Benefits Act 1992 (c.4)	1.35
Social Security (Consequential Provisions) Act 1992 (c.6)	1.641
Pensions Schemes Act 1993 (c.48)	1.642
Social Security (Incapacity for Work) Act 1994 (c.18)	1.651
Pensions Act 1995 (c.26)	1.652
Welfare Reform and Pensions Act 1999 (c.30)	1.670
Gender Recognition Act 2004 (c.7)	1.676
Welfare Reform Act 2007 (c.5)	1.709
Child Maintenance and Other Payments Act 2008 (c.6)	1.856
Welfare Reform Act 2009 (c.24)	1.883
Welfare Reform Act 2012 (c.5)	1.897
Mesothelioma Act 2014 (c.1)	1.944
Pensions Act 2014 (c.19)	1.964
Welfare Reform and Work Act 2016	1.1071

REGULATIONS

PART II
CONTRIBUTION CREDITS AND HOME RESPONSIBILITIES PROTECTION

SI		Paras
1975/556	The Social Security (Credits) Regulations 1975	2.1
1994/704	The Social Security Pensions (Home Responsibilities) Regulations 1994	2.47

Contents

1974/2010 The Social Security (Benefit) (Married Women and
Widows Special Provisions) Regulations 1974 2.51
2001/769 The Social Security (Crediting and Treatment of
Contributions, and National Insurance Numbers)
Regulations 2001 2.54
2010/19 The Social Security (Contributions Credits for Parents
and Carers) Regulations 2010 2.69

PART III
REGULATIONS COMMON TO SEVERAL BENEFITS

SI *Paras*
1996/2745 The Social Security Benefit (Computation of
Earnings) Regulations 1996 3.1
1977/343 The Social Security Benefit (Dependency)
Regulations 1977 3.39
2005/3360 The Social Security (Hospital In-Patients)
Regulations 2005 3.74
1979/597 The Social Security (Overlapping Benefits)
Regulations 1979 3.80
1975/563 The Social Security Benefit (Persons Abroad)
Regulations 1975 3.106
1977/956 The Social Security Benefit (Persons Residing
Together) Regulations 1977 3.146
1975/561 The Social Security and Family Allowances
(Polygamous Marriages) Regulations 1975 3.154

PART IV
DISABILITY BENEFITS

SI *Paras*
1991/2740 The Social Security (Attendance Allowance)
Regulations 1991 4.1
1991/2890 The Social Security (Disability Living Allowance)
Regulations 1991 4.31
1976/409 The Social Security (Invalid Care Allowance)
Regulations 1976 4.123
1984/1303 The Social Security (Severe Disablement Allowance)
Regulations 1984 4.160
2013/377 The Social Security (Personal Independence
Payment) Regulations 2013 4.161
2013/387 The Personal Independence Payment (Transitional
Provisions) Regulations 2013 4.261

PART V
MATERNITY BENEFITS

SI *Paras*
1987/416 The Social Security (Maternity Allowance)
Regulations 1987 5.1
1987/417 The Social Security (Maternity Allowance) (Work
Abroad) Regulations 1987 5.6

2000/688   The Social Security (Maternity Allowance)
            (Earnings) Regulations 2000   5.9
2014/3053   The Maternity Allowance (Curtailment)
            Regulations 2014   5.16

PART VI
PENSIONS, SURVIVORS' BENEFITS AND GRADUATED
RETIREMENT BENEFIT

SI   *Paras*
2005/453   The Social Security (Deferral of Retirement Pensions)
            Regulations 2005   6.1
2005/2677   The Social Security (Deferral of Retirement Pensions,
            Shared Additional Pension and Graduated
            Retirement Benefit) (Miscellaneous Provisions)
            Regulations 2005   6.8
1978/393   The Social Security (Graduated Retirement Benefit)
            (No.2) Regulations 1978   6.15
2001/1323   The Additional Pension and Social Security Pensions
            (Home Responsibilities) (Amendment) Regulations
            2001   6.29
2005/454   The Social Security (Graduated Retirement Benefit)
            Regulations 2005   6.39
2010/426   The Social Security (Maximum Additional Pension)
            Regulations 2010   6.74
2005/469   The Social Security (Retirement Pensions etc.)
            (Transitional Provisions) Regulations 2005   6.80
1979/642   The Social Security (Widow's Benefit and
            Retirement Pensions) Regulations 1979   6.85
1979/643   The Social Security (Widow's Benefit, Retirement
            Pensions and Other Benefits) (Transitional)
            Regulations 1979   6.126
2010/2818   The Rate of Bereavement Benefits Regulations
            2010   6.152
2014/3229   The Marriage and Civil Partnership (Scotland) Act
            2014 and Civil Partnership Act 2004
            (Consequential Provisions and Modifications)
            Order 2014   6.156
2015/134   The Pensions Act 2014 (Commencement No.4)
            Order 2015   6.164
2015/173   The State Pension Regulations 2015   6.167
2016/39   The Pensions Act 2014 (Pension Sharing on
            Divorce etc.) (Transitional Provision) Order 2016   6.211
2016/408   The Pensions Act 2014 (Transitional and
            Transitory Provisions) Order 2016   6.214
2017/410   The Bereavement Support Payment Regulations
            2017   6.218

PART VII
UNEMPLOYMENT, SICKNESS AND INVALIDITY BENEFIT

Contents

PART VIII
INCAPACITY BENEFIT AND INCAPACITY FOR WORK

PART IX
"OLD STYLE" EMPLOYMENT AND SUPPORT ALLOWANCE

SI		*Paras*
2008/794	The Employment and Support Allowance Regulations 2008	9.1
2008/794	*Schs 2 and 3 to the Employment and Support Allowance Regulations 2008 as in force at March 27, 2011 (the original LCWA and LCWRA)*	9.507
2008/795	The Employment and Support Allowance (Transitional Provisions) Regulations 2008	9.508
2008/3195	The Social Security (Housing Costs Special Arrangements) (Amendment and Modification) Regulations 2008	9.520
2010/1907	The Employment and Support Allowance (Transitional Provisions, Housing Benefit and Council Tax Benefit) (Existing Awards) (No. 2) Regulations 2010	9.528
2011/1349	The Employment and Support Allowance (Work-Related Activity) Regulations 2011	9.596
2012/3096	The Employment and Support Allowance (Amendment) Regulations 2012	9.612
2015/1647	The Social Security (Housing Costs Amendments) Regulations 2015	9.616
2017/204	The Employment and Support Allowance and Universal Credit (Miscellaneous Amendments and Transitional and Savings Provisions) Regulations 2017	9.619
2017/581	The Employment and Support Allowance (Miscellaneous Amendments and Transitional and Savings Provision) Regulations 2017	9.630

PART X
INDUSTRIAL INJURIES AND PRESCRIBED DISEASES

SI		*Paras*
1979/628	The Social Security (Claims and Payments) Regulations 1979	10.1
1982/1408	The Social Security (General Benefit) Regulations 1982	10.15
1985/967	The Social Security (Industrial Injuries) (Prescribed Diseases) Regulations 1985	10.57
1986/1561	The Social Security (Industrial Injuries and Diseases) Miscellaneous Provisions Regulations 1986	10.209
1987/415	The Social Security (Industrial Injuries) (Reduced Earnings Allowance and Transitional) Regulations 1987	10.220

1990/256	The Social Security (Industrial Injuries) (Regular Employment) Regulations 1990	10.237
1993/1985	The Social Security (Industrial Injuries) (Prescribed Diseases) Amendment (No. 2) Regulations 1993	10.244
1996/425	The Social Security (Industrial Injuries and Diseases) (Miscellaneous Amendments) Regulations 1996	10.248
2000/1588	The Social Security (Industrial Injuries) (Prescribed Diseases) Amendment Regulations 2000	10.252
2003/270	The Social Security (Industrial Injuries) (Prescribed Diseases) Amendment Regulations 2003	10.260
2003/2190	The Social Security (Industrial Injuries) (Prescribed Diseases) Amendment (No. 2) Regulations 2003	10.267
2005/324	The Social Security (Industrial Injuries) (Prescribed Diseases) Amendment Regulations 2005	10.273
2007/811	The Social Security (Industrial Injuries) (Prescribed Diseases) Amendment Regulations 2007	10.278
2007/1753	The Social Security (Industrial Injuries) (Prescribed Diseases) Amendment (No. 2) Regulations 2007	10.282
2012/2743	The Industrial Injuries Benefit (Injuries arising before 5th July 1948) Regulations 2012	10.287
2013/2540	The Industrial Injuries Benefit (Employment Training Schemes and Courses) Regulations 2013	10.292

PART XI
VACCINE DAMAGE PAYMENTS

SI		*Paras*
1979/432	The Vaccine Damage Payments Regulations 1979	11.1
1990/623	The Vaccine Damage Payments (Specified Disease) Order 1990	11.13
1995/1164	The Vaccine Damage Payments (Specified Disease) Order 1995	11.16
2001/1652	The Vaccine Damage Payments (Specified Disease) Order 2001	11.19
2006/2066	The Vaccine Damage Payments (Specified Disease) Order 2006	11.23
2008/2103	The Vaccine Damage Payments (Specified Disease) Order 2008	11.26
2009/2516	The Vaccine Damage Payments (Specified Disease) Order 2009	11.30
2010/1988	The Vaccine Damage Payments (Specified Disease) (Revocation and Savings) Order 2010	11.35
2015/47	The Vaccine Damage Payments (Specified Disease) Order 2015	11.40
2016/454	The Vaccine Damage Payments (Specified Disease) Order 2016	11.44
2007/1931	The Vaccine Damage Payments Act 1979 Statutory Sum Order 2007	11.49

Contents

PART XII
MESOTHELIOMA LUMP SUM PAYMENTS

SI		Paras
2008/1595	The Mesothelioma Lump Sum Payments (Claims and Reconsiderations) Regulations 2008	12.1
2008/1963	The Mesothelioma Lump Sum Payments (Conditions and Amounts) Regulations 2008	12.13
2014/916	The Diffuse Mesothelioma Payment Scheme Regulations 2014	12.22
2014/2904	The Diffuse Mesothelioma Payment Scheme (Levy) Regulations 2014	12.64

PART XIII
"NEW STYLE" EMPLOYMENT AND SUPPORT ALLOWANCE

SI		Paras
	Welfare Reform Act 2012 (c.5) (as applicable in "Pathfinder" cases and areas)	13.1
	Welfare Reform Act 2007 (c.5) (as applicable in "Pathfinder" cases and areas)	13.4
2013/379	The Employment and Support Allowance Regulations 2013	13.103

	Page
Index	1773

USING THIS BOOK: AN INTRODUCTION TO
LEGISLATION AND CASE LAW

Introduction

This book is not a general introduction to, or general textbook on, the law relating to social security but it is nonetheless concerned with both of the principal sources of social security law—*legislation* (both primary and secondary) and *case law*. It sets out the text of the most important legislation, as currently in force, and then there is added commentary that refers to the relevant case law. Lawyers will be familiar with this style of publication, which inevitably follows the structure of the legislation.

This note is designed primarily to assist readers who are not lawyers to find their way around the legislation and to understand the references to case law, but information it contains about how to find social security case law is intended to be of assistance to lawyers too.

Primary legislation

Primary legislation of the United Kingdom Parliament consists of *Acts of Parliament* (also known as *Statutes*). They will have been introduced to Parliament as *Bills*. There are opportunities for Members of Parliament and peers to debate individual clauses and to vote on amendments before a Bill is passed and becomes an Act (at which point the clauses become sections). No tribunal or court has the power to disapply, or hold to be invalid, an Act of Parliament unless it is inconsistent with European Union law.

An Act is known by its "short title", which incorporates the year in which it was passed (e.g. the Social Security Contributions and Benefits Act 1992), and is given a chapter number (abbreviated as, for instance, "c.4" indicating that the Act was the fourth passed in that year). It is seldom necessary to refer to the chapter number but it appears in the running heads in this book.

Each *section* (abbreviated as "s." or, in the plural, "ss.") of an Act is numbered and may be divided into *subsections* (abbreviated as "subs." and represented by a number in brackets), which in turn may be divided into *paragraphs* (abbreviated as "para." and represented by a lower case letter in brackets) and *subparagraphs* (abbreviated as "subpara." and represented by a small roman numeral in brackets). Subparagraph (ii) of para.(a) of subs. (1) of s.72 will usually be referred to simply as "s.72(1)(a)(ii)". Upper case letters may be used where additional sections or subsections are inserted by amendment and additional lower case letters may be used where new paragraphs and subparagraphs are inserted. This accounts for the rather ungainly s.109B(2A)(aa) of the Social Security Adminstation Act 1992.

Sections of a large Act may be grouped into a numbered *Part*, which may even be divided into *Chapters*. It is not usual to refer to a Part or a Chapter unless referring to the whole Part or Chapter.

Where a section would otherwise become unwieldy because it is necessary to include a list or complicated technical provisions, the section may simply refer to a *Schedule* at the end of the Act. A Schedule (abbreviated as "Sch.") may be divided into paragraphs and subparagraphs and further divided into heads and subheads. Again, it is usual to refer simply to, say, "para.23(3)(b)(ii) of Sch.3". Whereas it is conventional to speak of a section *of* an Act, it is usual to speak of a Schedule *to* an Act.

When Parliament wishes to change the law, it may do so by passing a new Act that amends a previous Act or it may do so by passing a freestanding Act, although even then consequential amendments to other legislation are usually required. Thus, for instance, when incapacity benefit was introduced by the Social Security (Incapacity for Work) Act 1994, the changes were largely made by inserting sections 30A to 30E and Part XIIA into the Social Security Contributions and Benefits Act 1992 and repealing the provisions in that Act dealing with sickness and invalidity benefit. In contrast, when jobseeker's allowance was introduced by the Jobseekers Act 1995, it was decided that the main provisions relating to the new benefit would be found in the 1995 Act itself and the 1992 Act was amended only so as to repeal, or amend, the provisions dealing with, or referring to, unemployment benefit.

When there has been a proliferation of Acts or Acts have been very substantially amended, the legislation may be consolidated in a new Act, for which there is a fast track procedure in Parliament. Only limited amendments may be made by a consolidation Act but such an Act reorganises and tidies up the legislation. Because social security law is so frequently amended, it used to be consolidated every decade or two. However, the last consolidation Acts relevant to this book were the Social Security Contributions and Benefits Act 1992 (in Vols I, II and IV) and the Social Security Administration Act 1992 (in this volume). Perhaps there will be a further consolidation if and when universal credit is brought fully into force.

Secondary legislation

Secondary legislation (also known as *subordinate legislation* or *delegated legislation*) is made by *statutory instrument* in the form of a set of *Regulations* or a set of *Rules* or an *Order*. The power to make such legislation is conferred on ministers and other persons or bodies by Acts of Parliament. To the extent that a statutory instrument is made beyond the powers (in Latin, ultra vires) conferred by primary legislation, it may be held by a tribunal or court to be invalid and ineffective. Secondary legislation must be laid before Parliament. However, most secondary legislation is not debated in Parliament and, even when it is, it cannot be amended although an entire statutory instrument may be rejected.

A set of Regulations or Rules or an Order has a name indicating its scope and the year it was made and also a number, as in the Social Security (Disability Living Allowance) Regulations 1991 (SI 1991/2890) (the 2890th statutory instrument issued in 1991). Because there are over 3,000 statutory instruments each year, the number of a particular statutory instrument is important as a means of identification and it should usually be cited the first time reference is made to that statutory instrument.

Sets of Regulations or Rules are made up of individual *regulations* (abbreviated as "reg.") or *rules* (abbreviated as "r." or, in the plural, "rr."). An Order is made up of *articles* (abbreviated as "art."). Regulations, rules and articles may be divided into paragraphs, subparagraphs and heads. As in Acts, a set of Regulations or Rules or an Order may have one or more Schedules attached to it. The style of numbering used in statutory instruments is the same as in sections of, and Schedules to, Acts of Parliament. As in Acts, a large statutory instrument may have regulations or rules grouped into Parts and, occasionally, Chapters. Statutory instruments may be amended in the same sort of way as Acts.

Northern Ireland legislation

Most of the legislation set out in this series applies only in Great Britain, social security not generally being an excepted or reserved matter in relation to Northern Ireland. However, Northern Irish legislation—both primary legislation, most relevantly in the form of *Orders in Council* (which, although statutory instruments, had the effect of primary legislation in Northern Ireland while there was direct rule from Westminster and still do when made under the Northern Ireland (Welfare Reform) Act 2015) and *Acts of the Northern Ireland Assembly*, and subordinate legislation, in the form of *statutory rules*—largely replicates legislation in Great Britain so that much of the commentary in this book will be applicable to equivalent provisions in Northern Ireland legislation. Although there has latterly been a greater reluctance in Northern Ireland to maintain parity with Great Britain, which led to some delay in enacting legislation equivalent to the Welfare Reform Act 2012, this has partially been resolved for the time being by the allocation of funds to allow the effects of some of the reforms to be mitigated in Northern Ireland while the broad legislative structure remains similar.

European Union legislation

The United Kingdom is a Member State of the European Union, and European Union legislation has effect within the United Kingdom. The outcome of the EU referendum of June 23, 2016 does not immediately alter the United Kingdom's membership of the Union; the United Kingdom will remain a Member State and European Union law will continue to apply until such time as the exit arrangements provided for in art.50 of the Treaty on European Union are completed. Moreover, if it is brought fully into force, the effect of the European Union (Withdrawal Act) 2018 will broadly be that European Union law (except for the Charter of Fundamental Rights) that was in force immediately before "exit day" will form part of United Kingdom law thereafter, until it is amended or repealed by domestic legislation.

European Union primary legislation is in the form of the *Treaties* agreed by the Member States. Relevant subordinate legislation is in the form of *Regulations,* adopted to give effect to the provisions of the Treaties, and *Directives,* addressed to Member States and requiring them to incorporate certain provisions into their domestic laws. Directives are relevant because, where a person brings proceedings against an organ of the State, as is invariably the case where social security is concerned, that person may rely on the Directive as having direct effect if the Member State has failed to comply with it. European Union Treaties, Regulations and Directives are divided into *Articles* (abbreviated as "Art.") United Kingdom legislation that is inconsistent with European Union legislation may be disapplied. The most relevant provisions of the European Communities Act 1972 and of European Union legislation are set out in Part III of this volume.

Finding legislation in this book

If you know the name of the piece of legislation for which you are looking, use the list of contents at the beginning of each volume of this series which lists the pieces of legislation contained in the volume. That will give you the paragraph reference to enable you to find the beginning of the piece of legislation. Then, it is easy to find the relevant section, regulation, rule, article or Schedule by using the running heads on the right hand pages. If you do not know the name of the piece of legislation, you will probably need to use the index at the end of the volume in order to find the relevant paragraph number but will then be taken straight to a particular provision.

The legislation is set out as amended, the amendments being indicated by numbered sets of square brackets. The numbers refer to the numbered entries under the heading "AMENDMENTS" at the end of the relevant section, regulation, rule, article or Schedule, which identify the amending statute or statutory instrument. Where an Act has been consolidated, there is a list of "DERIVATIONS" identifying the provisions of earlier legislation from which the section or Schedule has been derived.

Finding other legislation

Legislation in both its amended and its unamended form may now be found on *http://www.legislation.gov.uk*. Northern Ireland social security legislation may also be found at *https://eur-lex.europa.eu/homepage.html*. European Union legislation may be found at *http://eur-lex.europa.eu/collection/eu-law.html*.

Interpreting legislation

Legislation is written in English and generally means what it says. However, more than one interpretation is often possible. Most legislation itself contains definitions. Sometimes these are in the particular provision in which a word occurs but, where a word is used in more than one place, any definition will appear with others. In an Act, an interpretation section is usually to be found towards the end of the Act or of the relevant Part of the Act. In a statutory instrument, an interpretation provision usually appears near the beginning of the statutory instrument or the relevant Part of it. In the more important pieces of legislation in this series, there is included after every section, regulation, rule, article or Schedule a list of "DEFINITIONS", showing where definitions of words used in the provision are to be found.

However, not all words are statutorily defined and there is in any event more to interpreting legislation than merely defining its terms. Decision-makers and tribunals need to know how to apply the law in different types of situations. That is where case law comes in.

Case law and the commentary in this book

In deciding individual cases, courts and tribunals interpret the relevant law and incidentally establish legal principles. Decisions on questions of legal principle of the superior courts and appellate tribunals are said to be binding on decision-makers and the First-tier Tribunal, which means that decision-makers and the First-tier Tribunal must apply those principles. Thus the judicial decisions of the superior courts and appellate tribunals form part of the law. The commentary to the legislation in this series, under the heading "GENERAL NOTE" after a section, regulation, rule, article or Schedule, refers to this *case law*.

Much case law regarding social security benefits is still in the form of decisions of Social Security Commissioners and Child Support Commissioners. However, while there are still Commissioners in Northern Ireland, which has a largely separate judiciary and tribunal system, the functions of Commissioners in Great Britain were transferred to the Upper Tribunal and allocated to the Administrative Appeals Chamber of that tribunal on November 3, 2008. Consequently, social security case law is increasingly to be found in decisions of the Upper Tribunal.

The commentary in this series is not itself binding on any decision-maker or tribunal because it is merely the opinion of the author. It is what is actually said in the legislation or in the judicial decision that is important. The legislation is set out in this series, but it will generally be necessary to look elsewhere for the precise words used in judicial decisions. The way that decisions are cited in the commentary enables that to be done.

The reporting of decisions of the Upper Tribunal and Commissioners

About 50 of the most important decisions of the Administrative Appeals Chamber of the Upper Tribunal are selected to be "reported" each year in the Administrative Appeals Chamber Reports (AACR), using the same criteria as were formerly used for reporting Commissioners' decisions in Great Britain. The selection is made by an editorial board of judges and decisions are selected for reporting only if they are of general importance and command the assent of at least a majority of the relevant judges. The term "reported" simply means that they are published in printed form as well as on the Internet (see *Finding case law*, below) with headnotes (i.e. summaries) and indexes, but there are two other important consequences of a decision being reported. Reported decisions are available in all tribunal venues and can be consulted in local social security offices and some main libraries. They also have a greater precedential status than ordinary decisions (see *Judicial precedent* below).

A handful of Northern Ireland Commissioners' decisions are also selected for reporting in the Administrative Appeals Chamber Reports each year, the selection being made by the Chief Social Security Commissioner in Northern Ireland.

Citing case law

As has been mentioned, much social security case law is still to be found in decisions of Social Security Commissioners and Child Support Commissioners, even though the Commissioners have now effectively been abolished in Great Britain.

Reported decisions of Commissioners were known merely by a number or, more accurately, a series of letters and numbers beginning with an "R". The type of benefit in issue was indicated by letters in brackets (e.g. "IS" was income support, "P" was retirement pension, and so on) and the year in which the decision was selected for reporting or, from 2000, the year in which it was published as a reported decision, was indicated by the last two digits, as in *R(IS) 2/08*. In Northern Ireland there was a similar system until 2009, save that the type of benefit was identified by letters in brackets after the number, as in *R 1/07 (DLA)*.

Unreported decisions of the Commissioners in Great Britain were known simply by their file numbers, which began with a "C", as in *CIS/2287/2008*. The letters following the "C" indicated the type of benefit in issue in the case. Scottish and, at one time, Welsh cases were indicated by a "S" or "W" immediately after the "C", as in *CSIS/467/2007*. The last four digits indicated the calendar year in which the case was registered, rather than the year it was decided. A similar system operated in Northern Ireland until 2009, save that the letters indicating the type of benefit appeared in brackets after the numbers and, from April 1999, the financial year rather than the calendar year was identified, as in *C 10/06-07 (IS)*.

Decisions of the Upper Tribunal, of courts and, since 2010, of the Northern Ireland Commissioners are generally known by the names of the parties (or just two of them in multi-party cases). Individuals are anonymised through the use of initials in the names of decisions of the Upper Tribunal and the Northern Ireland Commissioners and occasionally in the names of decisions of courts. In this series, the names of official bodies may also be abbreviated (e.g. "SSWP" for the Secretary of State for Work and Pensions, "HMRC" for Her Majesty's Revenue and Customs, "CMEC" for the Child Maintenance and Enforcement Commission and "DSD" for the Department for Social Development in Northern Ireland). Since 2010, decisions of the Upper Tribunal and of Northern Ireland Commissioners have also been given a "flag" in brackets to indicate the subject matter of the decision, which in social security cases indicates the principal benefit in issue in the case. Thus, the name of one jobseeker's allowance case is *SSWP v JB (JSA)*.

Any decision of the Upper Tribunal, of a court since 2001 or of a Northern Ireland Commissioner since 2010 that has been intended for publication has also given a *neutral citation number* which enables the decision to be more precisely identified. This indicates, in square brackets, the year the decision was made (although in relation to decisions of the courts it sometimes merely indicates the year the number was issued) and also indicates the court or tribunal that made the decision (e.g. "UKUT" for the Upper Tribunal, "NICom" for a Northern Ireland Commissioner, "EWCA Civ" for the Civil Division of the Court of Appeal in England and Wales, "NICA" for the Court of Appeal in Northern Ireland, "CSIH" for the Inner House of the Court of Session (in Scotland), "UKSC" for the Supreme Court and so on). A number is added so that the reference is unique and finally, in the case of the Upper Tribunal or the High Court in England and Wales, the relevant chamber of the Upper Tribunal or the relevant division or other part of the High Court is identified (e.g."(AAC)" for the Administrative Appeals Chamber, "(Admin)" for the Administrative Court and so on). Examples of decisions of the Upper Tribunal and a Northern Ireland Commissioner with their neutral citation numbers are *SSWP v JB (JSA)* [2010] UKUT 4 (AAC) and *AR v DSD (IB)* [2010] NICom 6.

If the case is reported in the Administrative Appeals Chamber Reports or another series of law reports, a reference to the report usually follows the neutral citation number. Conventionally, this includes either the year the case was decided (in round brackets) or the year in which it was reported (in square brackets), followed by the volume number (if any), the name of the series of reports (in abbreviated form, so see the Table of Abbreviations at the beginning of each volume of this series) and either the page number or the case number. However, before 2010, cases reported in the Administrative Appeals Chamber Reports or with Commissioners' decisions were numbered in the same way as reported Commissioners' decisions. *Abdirahman v Secretary of State for Work and Pensions* [2007] EWCA Civ 657; [2008] 1 W.L.R. 254 (also reported as *R(IS) 8/07*) is a Court of Appeal decision, decided in 2007 but reported in 2008 in volume 1 of the Weekly Law Reports at page 254 and also in the 2007 volume of reported Commissioners' decisions. *NT v SSWP* [2009] UKUT 37 (AAC), *R(DLA) 1/09* is an Upper Tribunal case decided in 2009 and reported in the Administrative Appeals Chamber Reports in the same year. *Martin v SSWP* [2009] EWCA Civ 1289; [2010] AACR 9 is a decision of the Court of Appeal that was decided in 2009 and was the ninth decision reported in the Administrative Appeals Chamber Reports in 2010.

It is usually necessary to include the neutral citation number or a reference to a series of reports only the first time a decision is cited in any document. After that, the name of the case is usually sufficient.

All decisions of the Upper Tribunal that are on their website have neutral citation numbers. If you wish to refer a tribunal or decision-maker to a decision of the Upper Tribunal that does not have a neutral citation number, contact the office of the Administrative Appeals Chamber (*adminappeals@ justice.gsi.gov.uk*) who will provide a number and add the decision to the website.

Decision-makers and claimants are entitled to assume that judges of both the First-tier Tribunal and the Upper Tribunal have immediate access to reported decisions of Commissioners or the Upper Tribunal and they need not provide copies, although it may sometimes be helpful to do so. However, where either a decision-maker or a claimant intends to rely on an unreported decision, it will be necessary to provide a copy of the decision to the judge and other members of the tribunal. A copy of the decision should also be provided to the other party before the hearing because otherwise it may be necessary for there to be an adjournment to enable that party to take advice on the significance of the decision.

Finding case law

The extensive references described above are used so as to enable people easily to find the full text of a decision. Most decisions of any significance since the late 1990s can be found on the Internet.

Decisions of the Upper Tribunal and of the Commissioners in Great Britain may be found at *https://www.gov.uk/administrative-appeals-tribunal-decisions*. This includes reported decisions since 1991 and other decisions considered likely to be of interest to tribunals and tribunal users since about 2000, together with a few older decisions. Decisions of Commissioners in Northern Ireland may be found on *https://www.communities-ni.gov.uk/services/northern-ireland-digest-case-law*.

The Administrative Appeals Chamber Reports. They are also published by the Stationery Office in bound volumes which follow on from the bound volumes of Commissioners' decisions published from 1948.

Copies of decisions of the Administrative Appeals Chamber of the Upper Tribunal or of Commissioners that are otherwise unavailable may be obtained from the offices of the Upper Tribunal (Administrative Appeals Chamber) or, in Northern Ireland, from the Office of the Social Security and Child Support Commissioners.

Decisions of a wide variety of courts and tribunals in the United Kingdom may be found on the free website of the British and Irish Legal Information Institute, *http://www.bailii.org*. It includes all decisions of the Supreme Court and provides fairly comprehensive coverage of decisions given since about 1996 by the House of Lords and Privy Council and most of the higher courts in England and Wales, decisions given since 1998 by the Court of Session and decisions given since 2000 by the Court of Appeal and High Court in Northern Ireland. Some earlier decisions have been included, so it is always worth looking and, indeed, those decisions dating from 1873 or earlier and reported in the English Reports may be found through a link to *http://www.commonlii.org/uk/cases/EngR/*.

Decisions of the Court of Justice of the European Union are all to be found at *https://curia.europa.eu*.

Decisions of the European Court of Human Rights are available at *https://www.echr.coe.int*.

Most decisions of the courts in social security cases, including decisions of the European Court of Justice on cases referred by United Kingdom courts and tribunals, are reported in the Administrative Appeals Chamber Reports or with the reported decisions of Commissioners and may therefore be found on the same websites and in the same printed series of reported decisions. So, for example, *R(I) 1/00* contains Commissioner's decision *CSI/12/1998*, the decision of the Court of Session upholding the Commissioner's decision and the decision of the House of Lords in *Chief Adjudication Officer v Faulds*, reversing the decision of the Court of Session. The most important decisions of the courts can also be found in the various series of law reports familiar to lawyers (in particular, in the *Law Reports*, the *Weekly Law Reports*, the *All England Law Reports*, the *Public and Third Sector Law Reports*, the *Industrial Cases Reports* and the *Family Law Reports*) but these are not widely available outside academic or other law libraries, although the *All England Law Reports* are occasionally to be found in the larger public libraries. See the Table of Cases at the beginning of each volume of this series for all the places where a decision mentioned in that volume is reported.

If you know the name or number of a decision and wish to know where in a volume of this series there is a reference to it, use the Table of Cases or the Table of Commissioners' Decisions 1948–2009 in the relevant volume to find the paragraph(s) where the decision is mentioned.

Judicial precedent

As already mentioned, decisions of the Upper Tribunal, the Commissioners and the higher courts in Great Britain become *case law* because they set binding precedents which must be followed by decision-makers and the First-tier Tribunal in Great Britain. This means that, where the Upper Tribunal, Commissioner or court has decided a point of legal principle, decision-makers and appeal tribunals must make their decisions in conformity with the decision of the Upper Tribunal, Commissioner or court, applying the same principle and accepting the interpretation of the law contained in the decision. So a decision of the Upper Tribunal, a Commissioner or a superior court explaining what a term in a particular regulation means, lays down the definition of that term in much the same way as if the term had been defined in the regulations themselves. The decision may also help in deciding what the same term means when it is used in a different set of regulations, provided that the term appears to have been used in a similar context.

Only decisions on points of law set precedents that are binding and, strictly speaking, only decisions on points of law that were necessary to the overall conclusion reached by the Upper Tribunal, Commissioner or court are binding. Other parts of a decision (which used to be known as obiter dicta) may be regarded as helpful guidance but need not be followed if a decision-maker or the First-tier Tribunal is persuaded that there is a better approach. It is particularly important to bear this in mind in relation to older decisions of Social Security Commissioners because, until 1987, the right of appeal to a Commissioner was not confined to points of law.

Where there is a conflict between precedents, a decision-maker or the First-tier Tribunal is generally free to choose between decisions of equal status. For these purposes, most decisions of the Upper Tribunal and decisions of Commissioners are of equal status. However, a decision-maker or First-tier Tribunal should generally prefer a reported decision to an unreported one unless the unreported decision was the later decision and the Commissioner or Upper Tribunal expressly decided not to follow the earlier reported decision. This is simply because the fact that a decision has been reported shows that at least half of the relevant judges of the Upper Tribunal or the Commissioners agreed with it at the time. A decision of a Tribunal of Commissioners (i.e. three Commissioners sitting together) or a decision of a three-judge panel of the Upper Tribunal must be preferred to a decision of a single Commissioner or a single judge of the Upper Tribunal.

A single judge of the Upper Tribunal will normally follow a decision of a single Commissioner or another judge of the Upper Tribunal, but is not bound to do so. A three-judge panel of the Upper Tribunal will generally follow a decision of another such panel or of a Tribunal of Commissioners, but similarly is not bound to do so, whereas a single judge of the Upper Tribunal will always follow such a decision.

Strictly speaking, the Northern Ireland Commissioners do not set binding precedent that must be followed in Great Britain but their decisions are relevant, due to the similarity of the legislation in Northern Ireland, and are usually regarded as highly persuasive with the result that, in practice, they are generally given as much weight as decisions of the Great Britain Commissioners. The same approach is taken in Northern Ireland to decisions of the Upper Tribunal on social security matters and to decisions of the Great Britain Commissioners.

Decisions of the superior courts in Great Britain and Northern Ireland on questions of legal principle are almost invariably followed by decision-makers, tribunals and the Upper Tribunal, even when they are not strictly binding because the relevant court was in a different part of the United Kingdom or exercised a parallel – but not superior – jurisdiction.

Decisions of the European Court of Justice come in two parts: the Opinion of the Advocate General and the decision of the Court. It is the decision of the Court which is binding. The Court is assisted by hearing the Opinion of the Advocate General before itself coming to a conclusion on the issue before it. The Court does not always follow its Advocate General. Where it does, the Opinion of the Advocate General often elaborates the arguments in greater detail than the single collegiate judgment of the Court. Decision-makers, tribunals and Commissioners must apply decisions of the European Court of Justice, where relevant to cases before them, in preference to other authorities binding on them.

The European Court of Human Rights in Strasbourg is quite separate from the European Court of Justice in Luxembourg and serves a different purpose: interpreting and applying the European Convention on Human Rights, which is incorporated into United Kingdom law by the Human Rights Act 1998. Since October 2, 2000, public authorities in the United Kingdom, including courts, Commissioners, tribunals and decision-makers have been required to act in accordance with the incorporated provisions of the Convention, unless statute prevents this. They must take into account the Strasbourg case law and are required to interpret domestic legislation, so far as it is possible to do so, to give effect to the incorporated Convention rights. Any court or tribunal may declare secondary legislation incompatible with those rights and, in certain circumstances, invalidate it. Only the higher courts can declare a provision of primary legislation to be incompatible with those rights, but no court, tribunal or Upper Tribunal can invalidate primary legislation. The work of the Strasbourg Court and the impact of the Human Rights Act 1998 on social security are discussed in the commentary in Part IV of this volume.

See the note to s.3(2) of the Tribunals, Courts and Enforcement Act 2007 in Part V of this volume for a more detailed and technical consideration of the rules of precedent.

Other sources of information and commentary on social security law

For a comprehensive overview of the social security system in Great Britain, CPAG's *Welfare Benefits and Tax Credits Handbook*, published annually each spring, is unrivalled as a practical introduction from the claimant's viewpoint.

From a different perspective, the Department for Work and Pensions publishes the 14-volume *Decision Makers' Guide* at *https://www.gov.uk/government/collections/decision-makers-guide-staff-guide* and the new *Advice for Decision Making*, which covers personal independence payment, universal credit and the "new" versions of Jobseeker's Allowance and Employment and Support Allowance, at *https://www.gov.uk/government/publications/advice-for-decision-making-staff-guide*. Similarly, Her Majesty's Revenue and Customs publish manuals relating to tax credits, child benefit and guardian's allowance, which they administer, see *https://www.gov.uk/government/collections/hmrc-manuals*. (Note that the *Child Benefit Technical Manual* also covers guardian's allowance.) These guides and manuals are extremely useful but their interpretation of the law is not binding on tribunals and the courts, being merely internal guidance for the use of decision-makers.

There are a number of other sources of valuable information or commentary on social security case law: see in particular publications such as the *Journal of Social Security Law*, CPAG's *Welfare Rights Bulletin*, *Legal Action* and the *Adviser*. As far as online resources go there is little to beat *Rightsnet* (*https://www.rightsnet.org.uk*). This site contains a wealth of resources for people working in the welfare benefits field but of special relevance in this context are Commissioners'/Upper Tribunal Decisions section of the "Toolkit" area and also the "Briefcase" area which contains summaries of the decisions (with links to the full decisions). Sweet and Maxwell's online subscription service *Westlaw* is another valuable source (*https://legalsolutions. thomsonreuters.co.uk/en/products-services/westlaw-uk.html*), as is LexisNexis Lexis (*https://www.lexisnexis.co.uk*).

Conclusion

The internet provides a vast resource but a search needs to be focused. Social security schemes are essentially statutory and so in Great Britain the legislation which is set out in this series forms the basic structure of social security law. However, the case law shows how the legislation should be interpreted and applied. The commentary in this series should point the way to the case law relevant to each provision and the Internet can then be used to find it where that is necessary.

CHANGE OF NAME FROM DEPARTMENT OF SOCIAL SECURITY TO DEPARTMENT FOR WORK AND PENSIONS

The Secretaries of State for Education and Skills and for Work and Pensions Order 2002 (SI 2002/1397) makes provision for the change of name from the Department of Social Security to Department for Work and Pensions. Article 9(5) provides:

"(5) Subject to article 12 [which makes specific amendments], any enactment or instrument passed or made before the coming into force of this Order shall have effect, so far as may be necessary for the purposes of or in consequence of the entrusting to the Secretary of State for Work and Pensions of the social security functions, as if any reference to the Secretary of State for Social Security, to the Department of Social Security or to an officer of the Secretary of State for Social Security (including any reference which is to be construed as such as reference) were a reference to the Secretary of State for Work and Pensions, to the Department for Work and Pensions or, as the case may be, to an officer of the Secretary of State for Work and Pensions."

CHANGES IN TERMINOLOGY CONSEQUENT UPON THE ENTRY INTO FORCE OF THE TREATY OF LISBON

The Treaty of Lisbon (Changes in Terminology) Order 2011 (SI 2011/1043) (which came into force on April 22, 2011) makes a number of changes to terminology used in primary and secondary legislation as a consequence of the entry into force of the Treaty of Lisbon on December 1, 2009. The Order accomplishes this by requiring certain terms in primary and secondary legislation to be read in accordance with the requirements of the Order. No substantive changes to the law are involved.

The changes are somewhat complex because of the different ways in which the term "Community" is used, and the abbreviations "EC" or "EEC" are used. References to the "European Community", "European Communities", "European Coal and Steel Communities", "the Community", "the EC", and "the EEC" are generally to be read as references to the "European Union".

The following table shows the more common usages involving the word "Community" in the first column which are now to be read in the form set out in the second column:

Original term	To be read as
Community treaties	EU treaties
Community institution	EU institution
Community instrument	EU instrument
Community obligation	EU obligation
Enforceable Community right	Enforceable EU right
Community law, or European Community law	EU law
Community legislation, or European Community legislation	EU legislation
Community provision, or European Community provision	EU provision

Provision is also made for changes to certain legislation relating to Wales in the Welsh language.

Relevant extracts from the Order can be found in Vol.III, *Administration, Adjudication and the European Dimension.*

THE MARRIAGE (SAME SEX COUPLES) ACT 2013

The Marriage (Same Sex Couples) Act 2013 (c.30) provides in s.3 and Schedules 3 and 4 that the terms 'marriage', 'married couple' and being 'married' in existing and future legislation in England and Wales are to be read as references to a marriage between persons of the same sex. The same approach is taken to any legislation about couples living together as if married. This is subject to certain specified exclusions contained in Sch.4, and in any Order providing for a contrary approach to be taken.

Sch.2 to The Marriage (Same Sex Couples) Act 2013 (Consequential and Contrary provisions and Scotland) Order 2014 (SI 2014/560) contains a substantial list of contrary provisions to s.11(1) and (2) and paras 1 to 3 of Sch.3 to the 2013 Act. Most of these relate to specific enactments, but note that Pt 2 of the Schedule provides that s.11(1) and (2) do not apply to "EU instruments". This term is defined in Sch.1 to the European Communities Act 1972 (as amended) as "any instrument issued by an EU institution". It refers mainly to regulations, directives, decisions, recommendations and opinions issued by the institutions.

TABLE OF CASES

AA v Secretary of State for Work and Pensions (PIP) [2018] UKUT 339 (AAC)..........4.256
AB v Secretary of State for Work and Pensions (ESA) [2012] UKUT 151 (AAC)........**9.415**
AB v Secretary of State for Work and Pensions (ESA) [2016] UKUT 96 (AAC) **9.421**
AB v Secretary of State for Work and Pensions (PIP) [2017] UKUT 217 (AAC)........4.176,
4.252
AB v Secretary of State for Work and Pensions [2015] UKUT 522 (AAC) **1.230**
AB v Secretary of State for Work and Pensions [2015] UKUT 89 (AAC)....................1.907
AC v Secretary of State for Work and Pensions [2009] UKUT 83 (AAC)....................1.201
AD v Secretary of State for Work and Pensions [2011] UKUT 307 (AAC) 1.202, 9.47
AD v Secretary of State for Work and Pensions [2017] UKUT 29 (AAC) **1.199**
Adjudication Officer v Bath R(G) 1/00..1.1010
AF v Secretary of State for Work and Pensions (ESA) [2011] UKUT 61 (AAC)...........9.403
AG v Secretary of State for Work and Pensions (ESA) [2013] UKUT 77 (AAC) 9.403
AG v Secretary of State for Work and Pensions (ESA) [2017] UKUT 413 (AAC) 9.407
AG v Secretary of State for Work and Pensions (ESA) [2018] UKUT 137 (AAC) 9.410
AH v Secretary of State for Work and Pensions (DLA) [2012] UKUT 387 (AAC) 1.239,
4.93, 4.94, 4.238
AH v Secretary of State for Work and Pensions (ESA) [2011] UKUT 333 (AAC) 9.47,
9.399, 9.416
AH v Secretary of State for Work and Pensions (ESA) [2013] UKUT 118 (AAC);
[2013] AACR 32 ....**9.110**, 9.407, **9.429**
AH v Secretary of State for Work and Pensions (PIP) [2016] UKUT 276 (AAC) 4.234,
4.251
AH v Secretary of State for Work and Pensions (PIP) [2016] UKUT 541 (AAC) **4.183**
AH v Secretary of State for Work and Pensions [2017] UKUT 55 (AAC) 1.193
AI v Secretary of State for Work and Pensions (PIP) [2016] UKUT 322 (AAC)... **4.239**, 4.236
AI v Secretary of State for Work and Pensions (PIP) [2016] UKUT 512 (AAC)...........4.241
AI v Secretary of State for Work and Pensions (PIP) [2019] UKUT 103 (AAC)...........4.187
AI v Secretary of State for Work and Pensions [2015] UKUT 176 (AAC) 1.223, 4.239
AJ v Secretary of State for Work and Pensions (ESA) [2013] UKUT 279 (AAC).............**9.85**
AJ v Secretary of State for Work and Pensions (II) [2012] UKUT 209 ....1.574
AK v Secretary of State for Work and Pensions (CSPIP) [2016] UKUT 256 (AAC)....4.171,
4.244
AK v Secretary of State for Work and Pensions (ESA) [2013] UKUT 435 (AAC) 9.111
AK v Secretary of State for Work and Pensions (PIP) [2015] UKUT 620 (AAC) 4.183
Akhter v Khan and the Attorney General. *See* NA v MSK
AL v Secretary of State for Work and Pensions (ESA) [2011] UKUT 512 (AAC)..9.58, 9.61
AM v Secretary of State for Work and Pensions (ESA) [2013] UKUT 458 (AAC) 9.401
AM v Secretary of State for Work and Pensions (PIP) [2017] UKUT 7 (AAC) 4.251
AM v Secretary of State for Work and Pensions [2015] UKUT 215 (AAC)........**4.240**, **4.252**
AM v Secretary of State for Work and Pensions. *See* Mathieson v Secretary of State for
Work and Pensions
AP v Secretary of State for Work and Pensions (ESA) [2013] UKUT 293 (AAC).........**9.423**
AP v Secretary of State for Work and Pensions (ESA) [2013] UKUT 553 (AAC).........9.111
AP v Secretary of State for Work and Pensions (ESA) [2014] UKUT 35 (AAC)...........9.111
AP v Secretary of State for Work and Pensions (PIP) [2016] UKUT 416 (AAC) 4.173,
4.185
AP v Secretary of State for Work and Pensions (PIP) [2016] UKUT 501 (AAC) **4.171**,
4.247, 4.258
Appleby v Chief Adjudication Officer R(I)5/99...10.149
AR v Secretary of State for Work and Pensions (ESA) [2013] UKUT 358 (AAC) 9.345
AR v Secretary of State for Work and Pensions (ESA) [2013] UKUT 417 (AAC) 9.407
AR v Secretary of State for Work and Pensions (ESA) [2013] UKUT 446 (AAC) **9.422**

AR v Secretary of State for Work and Pensions (II) [2016] UKUT 111 (AAC) ...**10.20**, 10.25
AR v Secretary of State for Work and Pensions (PIP) [2018] UKUT 313 (AAC).........4.173,
4.257
AR v Secretary of State for Work and Pensions [2012] UKUT 467 (AAC).................1.1012
AR v Secretary of State for Work and Pensions [2013] UKUT 463 (AAC)...................**1.261**
Arthur v Revenue and Customs Commissioners [2017] EWCA Civ 1756; [2018]
S.T.C. 1; [2017] 11 WLUK 55; [2017] B.T.C. 33; [2017] S.T.I. 2271 ....3.124
AS v Secretary of State for Work and Pensions (DLA) [2010] UKUT 482 (AAC)..........9.65
AS v Secretary of State for Work and Pensions (ESA) [2013] UKUT 587 (AAC)........**9.403**,
9.407, 9.423
AS v Secretary of State for Work and Pensions (PIP) [2017] UKUT 104 (AAC); [2017]
AACR 31 .... **4.244, 4.246**, 4.253
AS v Secretary of State for Work and Pensions [2010] UKUT 482 (AAC) **4.56**
AT and VC v Secretary of State for Work and Pensions (ESA) [2015] UKUT 445
(AAC); [2016] AACR 8..**9.412**, 9.430
Autoclenz Ltd v Belcher [2011] UKSC 41; [2011] 4 All E.R. 745; [2011] 7 WLUK
790; [2011] I.C.R. 1157; [2011] I.R.L.R. 820; (2011) 161 N.L.J. 1099; (2011)
155(30) S.J.L.B. 31 ....1.40
Aviva Insurance v Secretary of State for Work and Pensions [2015] UKUT 613 (AAC);
[2016] AACR 29 ....1.34
AW v Secretary of State for Work and Pensions (ESA) [2011] UKUT 75 (AAC) 9.407
AW v Secretary of State for Work and Pensions (PIP) [2018] UKUT 76 (AAC)...........4.173
AY v Secretary of State for Work and Pensions (RP) [2011] UKUT 324 (AAC)...........**3.124**
Ballantine v Newalls Insulation Co Ltd [2000] 6 WLUK 391; [2001] I.C.R. 25; [2000]
P.I.Q.R. Q327; (2000) 97(26) L.S.G. 36 CA (Civ Div) 1.857
Bartlett v Secretary of State for Work and Pensions (C-537/09) EU:C:2011:278; [2012]
P.T.S.R. 535; [2011] 5 WLUK 50; [2011] 3 C.M.L.R. 9; (2011) 120 B.M.L.R.
123; [2012] UKUT 26 (AAC) 1.195
Batty v Secretary of State for Work and Pensions [2005] EWCA Civ 1746; [2005] 12
WLUK 382; (2006) 103(4) L.S.G. 31; R(A) 1/06...**1.213**
BB v Secretary of State for Work and Pensions (ESA) [2011] UKUT 158 (AAC);
[2012] AACR 2 ....9.415
BB v Secretary of State for Work and Pensions (ESA) [2015] UKUT 545 (AAC).........**9.117**
BB v Secretary of State for Work and Pensions (PIP) [2017] UKUT 506 (AAC).........1.907,
4.173
BB v South London and Maudsley NHS Trust and Ministry of Justice [2009] UKUT
157 (AAC) 1.401
BC v Secretary of State for Work and Pensions [2014] UKUT 237 (AAC).................1.1018
BG v Secretary of State for Work and Pensions (ESA) [2013] UKUT 504 (AAC) 9.407
Bibi v Chief Adjudication Officer [1997] 6 WLUK 416; [1998] 1 F.L.R. 375; [1998] 1
F.C.R. 301; [1997] Fam. Law 793; (1997) 94(27) L.S.G. 22; (1997) 141 S.J.L.B.
162 CA (Civ Div); R(G) 1/97...1.1015
BK v Secretary of State for Work and Pensions and Secretary of State for Work and
Pensions v MM [2016] UKUT 547 (AAC)..4.37, 4.149, **4.209**
BM v Secretary of State for Work and Pensions (CDLA) [2015] UKUT 18 (AAC);
[2015] AACR 29 .... 1.211, **1.242**, 1.266
BM v Secretary of State for Work and Pensions (PIP) [2017] UKUT 486 (AAC)........4.191,
4.259
Board of Management of Trim Joint District School v Kelly; sub nom, Trim Joint
District School Board of Management v Kelly [1914] A.C. 667; [1914] 4 WLUK
10 HL... 1.337, 1.338
Botchett v Chief Adjudication Officer R(IS) 10/96...4.56
BP v Secretary of State for Work and Pensions [2009] UKUT 90 (AAC) 1.268
Britnell v Secretary of State for Social Security. *See* R. v Secretary of State for Social
Services Ex p. Britnell
BS v Secretary of State for Work and Pensions (PIP) [2016] UKUT 456 (AAC) 4.246
BTC v Secretary of State for Work and Pensions [2015] UKUT 155 (AAC) 1.907
CA v Secretary of State for Work and Pensions (ESA) [2013] UKUT 442 (AAC) 9.401
CA v Secretary of State for Work and Pensions (ESA) [2016] UKUT 523 (AAC) 9.401
Cassinelli v Secretary of State for Social Services R(M) 2/92 ....4.82
CB v Secretary of State for Work and Pensions (ESA) [2015] UKUT 287 (AAC) 9.415
CC v Secretary of State for Work and Pensions (ESA) [2015] UKUT 62 (AAC)...........9.89,
9.408, 9.413

CC v Secretary of State for Work and Pensions (PIP) [2017] UKUT 429 (AAC) 4.248
CD v Secretary of State for Work and Pensions (ESA) [2012] UKUT (AAC) 289;
    [2013] AACR 12 ....**9.428**
CD v Secretary of State for Work and Pensions [2013] UKUT 68 (AAC) 4.91
CE v Secretary of State for Work and Pensions (PIP) [2015] UKUT 643 (AAC)..........4.176
CF v Secretary of State for Work and Pensions (ESA) [2012] UKUT 29 (AAC) 9.82,
    9.88
CG v Secretary of State for Work and Pensions (ESA) [2011] UKUT 167 (AAC) **9.515**
CG v Secretary of State for Work and Pensions (ESA) [2011] UKUT 384 (AAC) **9.343**
CH and KN v Secretary of State for Work and Pensions (PIP) [2018] UKUT 330
    (AAC) 4.173, 4.185
CH and KN v SSWP (PIP) [2018] UKUT 330 (AAC)..1.198
CH v Secretary of State for Work and Pensions (ESA) [2013] UKUT 207 (AAC) 9.105,
    9.432, 9.433
CH v Secretary of State for Work and Pensions (ESA) [2014] UKUT 11 (AAC)........... 9.85
CH v Secretary of State for Work and Pensions (ESA) [2017] UKUT 6 (AAC).............9.60
CH v Secretary of State for Work and Pensions [2009] UKUT 54 (AAC) 1.244
Chard v Chard; Chard v Chard (also known as Chard v Northcott) [1956] P. 259;
    [1955] 3 W.L.R. 954; [1955] 3 All E.R. 721; [1955] 11 WLUK 70; (1955) 99 S.J.
    890 PDA...1.1016
Charlton v Secretary of State for Work and Pensions [2009] EWCA Civ 42; [2009] 2
    WLUK 139; R(IB) 2/09 ....**9.82**, 9.84, 9.85, 9.86, 9.87, 9.89, 9.109,
    9.110, 9.111, 9.403, 9.407
Chatterton v Chief Adjudication Officer, 8 July 1993; R(I) 1/94 ....1.424, 10.73, 10.109
Chief Adjudication Officer v Astle [1999] 6 J.S.S.L. 203 CA............................ 1.832, 9.337
Chief Adjudication Officer v Belmer and Ahmed, *Guardian*, April 18, 1994 CA (Civ
    Div); R(S) 1/96...3.112
Chief Adjudication Officer v Creighton [2000] N.I. 222 ....4.22
Chief Adjudication Officer v Faulds [2000] 1 W.L.R. 1035; [2000] 2 All E.R. 961;
    2000 S.C. (H.L.) 116; 2000 S.L.T. 712; 2000 S.C.L.R. 713; [2000] 5 WLUK
    239; [2000] I.C.R. 1297; (2000) 97(22) L.S.G. 46; 2000 G.W.D. 17-703 HL; R(I)
    1/00 .... 1.338, **1.339**, 1.341, 1.344, 1.345, **1.346**, 1.347
Chief Adjudication Officer v Maguire R(I) 3/99 ....1.600
Chief Adjudication Officer v McKiernon unreported 8 July 1993 CA; R(I) 2/94 ....10.109
Chief Adjudication Officer v Pearse R(P) 2/93..6.95
Chief Adjudication Officer v Rhodes R(I) 1/99 .... 1.350, 1.354, 1.355, 1.356,
    1.360, 1.361
Chief Adjudication Officer v White R(IS) 18/94 .... 4.20, 4.54, 4.56
Chief Supplementary Benefit Officer v Cunningham [1984] 7 WLUK 210; [1985]
    I.C.R. 660 CA (Civ Div)..3.17
CJ v Secretary of State for Work and Pensions (ESA) [2012] UKUT 201 (AAC) 9.65
CL v Secretary of State for Work and Pensions (ESA) [2013] UKUT 434 (AAC) **9.411**
CL v Secretary of State for Work and Pensions (ESA) [2015] UKUT 375 (AAC) 9.84,
    9.111
CL v Secretary of State for Work and Pensions (ESA) [2019] UKUT 39 (AAC) 9.414
Clover Clayton & Co Ltd v Hughes [1910] A.C. 242; [1910] 3 WLUK 55 HL 1.346
CM (by appointee Mr CM) v Secretary of State for Work and Pensions (DLA) [2013]
    UKUT 27 (AAC) **4.62**
CM (deceased) by his father CM. *See* AM v Secretary of State for Work and Pensions
CM v Secretary of State for Work and Pensions [2016] UKUT 242 (AAC)....... 9.412, 9.430
CMcC v Secretary of State for Work and Pensions (ESA) [2014] UKUT 176 (AAC);
    [2015] AACR 9 .... 9.111, **9.115**
CN v Secretary of State for Work and Pensions (ESA) [2014] UKUT 286 (AAC)........**9.428**
CO v Secretary of State for Work and Pensions (II) [2011] UKUT 105 (AAC) 1.610
Cockburn v Chief Adjudication Officer; Secretary of State for Social Security v Fairey
    (also known as Halliday) [1997] 1 W.L.R. 799; [1997] 3 All E.R. 844; [1997] 5
    WLUK 404; (1997) 94(24) L.S.G. 32; (1997) 147 N.L.J. 794; (1997) 141 S.J.L.B.
    122 HL; R(A) 2/98 .... 1.200, **1.205**, 1.208, 1.212, 1.213, 1.214,
    1.216, 4.176, 4.259, 4.246
Cotton v Secretary of State for Works and Pensions [2009] EWCA Civ 1333; [2009]
    12 WLUK 415; [2010] AACR 17... **3.13, 3.17**
CP v Secretary of State for Work and Pensions (ESA) [2011] UKUT 507 (AAC).........9.414
CP v Secretary of State for Work and Pensions (PIP) [2018] UKUT 5 (AAC) 4.236

CS v Secretary of State for Work and Pensions (ESA) [2014] UKUT 519 (AAC).........9.407
CS v Secretary of State for Work and Pensions [2009] UKUT 257 (AAC) 1.155
CT v Secretary of State for Work and Pensions (ESA) [2013] UKUT 414 (AAC) 9.58
Culpeck v Orient Steam Navigation Co Ltd (1922) 12 Ll. L. Rep. 248; [1922] 7 WLUK
    25 CA 1.386
Customs and Excise Commissioners v Top Ten Promotions [1969] 1 W.L.R. 1163;
    [1969] 3 All E.R. 39; [1969] 6 WLUK 83; (1969) 113 S.J. 725; (1969) 113 S.J.
    568 HL **9.429**
CW v Secretary of State for Work and Pensions (ESA) [2011] UKUT 386 (AAC) 9.401
CW v Secretary of State for Work and Pensions (PIP) [2016] UKUT 197 (AAC);
    [2016] AACR 44 ....**4.171, 4.236, 4.240**, 4.245, 4.247
CW v Secretary of State for Work and Pensions [2016] UKUT 197 (AAC); [2016]
    AACR 44 ....**4.171, 4.236, 4.247**
DA v Secretary of State for Work and Pensions (PIP) [2015] UKUT 344 (AAC) 4.256
Davis v Secretary of State for Social Security R(I) 2/01 .... 10.140, 10.164
DB v Secretary of State for Work and Pensions (DLA) [2016] UKUT 205 (AAC) **4.114**
DB v Secretary of State for Work and Pensions (ESA) [2014] UKUT 41 (AAC) 9.88
DB v Secretary of State for Work and Pensions (ESA) [2014] UKUT 471 (AAC) 9.407
DB v Secretary of State for Work and Pensions (ESA) [2016] UKUT 493 (AAC) **9.89**
DB v Secretary of State for Work and Pensions (ESA) [2017] UKUT 251 (AAC) **9.89**
DB v Secretary of State for Work and Pensions (II) [2010] UKUT 144 (AAC) 1.401
DC v Secretary of State for Work and Pensions (PIP) [2016] UKUT 117 (AAC) 4.185
DC v Secretary of State for Work and Pensions (PIP) [2016] UKUT 11 (AAC) 4.243,
                                                                                                    4.244, 4.265
DC v Secretary of State for Work and Pensions [2008] UKUT 23 (AAC) **3.13, 3.17**
DC v Secretary of State for Work and Pensions [2009] UKUT 45 (AAC) **4.77**
Dennis v AJ White & Co [1917] A.C. 479; [1917] 6 WLUK 29 HL.............................1.352
DF v Secretary of State for Work and Pensions (CSPIP) [2017] UKUT 160 (AAC).....**4.241**
DF v Secretary of State for Work and Pensions (ESA) [2014] UKUT 129 (AAC) 9.407
DG v Secretary of State for Work and Pensions (ESA) [2014] UKUT 100 (AAC)........9.411
DG v Secretary of State for Work and Pensions (ESA) [2015] UKUT 370 (AAC)........9.414
DG v Secretary of State for Work and Pensions [2009] UKUT 41 (AAC)..... 10.161, 10.286
DG v Secretary of State for Work and Pensions [2013] UKUT 351 (AAC) 1.227
DH v Secretary of State for Work and Pensions (ESA) [2013] UKUT 573 (AAC)........9.111
Diment v Chief Adjudication Officer R(DLA) 6/99..4.71, 4.83
DJ v Secretary of State for Work and Pensions (ESA) [2015] UKUT 342 (AAC) 9.444,
                                                                                                                9.535
DJ v Secretary of State for Work and Pensions (ESA) [2016] UKUT 93 (AAC) **9.407**
DJ v Secretary of State for Work and Pensions [2016] UKUT 169 (AAC)..........**1.238, 1.240**
DM v Department for Social Development (ESA) [2013] NI Com 17.........................9.415
DM v Secretary of State for Work and Pensions (DLA) [2015] UKUT 87 (AAC) **4.91**
DM v Secretary of State for Work and Pensions (II) [2010] UKUT 198 (AAC) 10.170,
                                                                                                                10.173
DM v Secretary of State for Work and Pensions (II) [2010] UKUT 318 (AAC) **10.140**
DMcK v Secretary of State for Work and Pensions (ESA) [2014] UKUT 45 (AAC).......**9.46**
DN v Secretary of State for Work and Pensions (DLA) [2016] UKUT 233 (AAC).......**1.218**
DO v Secretary of State for Work and Pensions (PIP) [2017] UKUT 115 (AAC).........**4.183**
Dorset Healthcare NHS Foundation Trust v MH [2009] UKUT 4 (AAC)....................4.94
DP v Secretary of State for Work and Pensions (PIP) [2017] UKUT 156 (AAC) 4.247,
                                                                                                                4.254
DR v Secretary of State for Work and Pensions (ESA) [2014] UKUT 188 (AAC);
    [2014] AACR 38 ....9.79, **9.115, 9.425, 9.433**
DR v Secretary of State for Work and Pensions (PIP) [2018] UKUT 209 (AAC) 4.171,
                                                                                                    4.236, 4.240
Drake v Chief Adjudication Officer (C-150/85) EU:C:1986:257; [1987] Q.B. 166;
    [1986] 3 W.L.R. 1005; [1986] 3 All E.R. 65; [1986] E.C.R. 1995; [1986] 6
    WLUK 231; [1986] 3 C.M.L.R. 43; (1987) 84 L.S.G. 264; (1986) 130 S.J.
    923 .... 1.178, 1.185
DS v Secretary of State for Work and Pensions (PIP) [2016] UKUT 538 (AAC); [2017]
    AACR 19 .... 4.173, 4.191
DS v Secretary of State for Work and Pensions [2018] UKUT 270 (AAC)........ 1.712, 9.535
DT v Secretary of State for Work and Pensions (ESA) [2013] UKUT 224 (AAC)........9.408
DT v Secretary of State for Work and Pensions (PIP) [2016] UKUT 240 (AAC) **4.258**

Dunbar v Plant [1998] Ch. 412; [1997] 3 W.L.R. 1261; [1997] 4 All E.R. 289; [1997] 7 WLUK 487; [1998] 1 F.L.R. 157; [1997] 3 F.C.R. 669; [1998] Fam. Law 139; (1997) 94(36) L.S.G. 44; (1997) 141 S.J.L.B. 191 CA (Civ Div) 1.1017
DV v Secretary of State for Work and Pensions (PIP) [2017] UKUT 244 (AAC); [2017] AACR 38 ....4.251
DW v Secretary of State for Work and Pensions (ESA) [2010] UKUT 245 (AAC) 9.411
DW v Secretary of State for Work and Pensions (ESA) [2011] UKUT 79 (AAC) **9.421**
DW v Secretary of State for Work and Pensions (ESA) [2014] UKUT 20 (AAC) 9.422
DW v Secretary of State for Work and Pensions (ESA) [2016] UKUT 179 (AAC) 9.58, 9.61
EB v Secretary of State for Work and Pensions (PIP) [2017] UKUT 311 (AAC) 4.306
EC (by SC) v Secretary of State for Work and Pensions (DLA) [2017] UKUT 391 (AAC) 4.94
EC v Secretary of State for Work and Pensions (ESA) [2015] UKUT 618 (AAC) **9.408**
EG v Secretary of State for Work and Pensions (PIP) [2015] UKUT 275 (AAC) 4.240, 4.248, 4.251
EG v Secretary of State for Work and Pensions (PIP) [2017] UKUT 101 (AAC) 4.176, **4.248, 4.253**
EG v Secretary of State for Work and Pensions [2009] UKUT 112 (AAC) 1.218
EH v Department for Communities (PIP) [2018] NI Comm 55 ....4.237, 4.242
EH v Secretary of State for Work and Pensions (ESA) [2011] UKUT 21 (AAC) 9.427
EH v Secretary of State for Work and Pensions (ESA) [2014] UKUT 473 (AAC) 9.112
EI v Secretary of State for Work and Pensions (ESA) [2016] UKUT 397 (AAC) ...9.92, 9.94
EJ v Secretary of State for Work and Pensions (ESA) [2014] UKUT 551 (AAC) ...9.86, **9.89**
EM v Secretary of State for Work and Pensions (ESA) [2014] UKUT 34 (AAC) **9.414**
ES v Secretary of State for Work and Pensions (MA) [2010] UKUT 200 (AAC) 1.1009
ET v Secretary of State for Work and Pensions (PIP) [2017] UKUT 478 (AAC) 1.907
European Parliament v Commission of the European Communities (C-299/05) EU:C:2007:608; [2007] E.C.R. I–8695 ECJ........................... 1.157, 1.186, 1.195, 4.43
EW v Secretary of State for Work and Pensions (ESA) [2013] UKUT 228 (AAC)........9.408
Falmouth Docks and Engineering Co Ltd v Treloar [1933] A.C. 481; [1933] 1 WLUK 60 HL 1.346
Faulkner v Chief Adjudication Officer [1994] 3 WLUK 281; [1994] P.I.Q.R. P244 CA (Civ Div); R(I) 8/94 .... 1.354, 1.355, **1.359**, 1.361
Fawcett Properties Ltd v Buckingham CC [1961] A.C. 636; [1960] 3 W.L.R. 831; [1960] 3 All E.R. 503; [1960] 10 WLUK 124; (1961) 125 J.P. 8; 59 L.G.R. 69; (1961) 12 P. & C.R. 1; (1960) 104 S.J. 912 HL...10.148
FE v Secretary of State for Work & Pensions (RP) [2019] UKUT 61 (AAC) 1.1031
Fenton v J Thorley & Co Ltd [1903] A.C. 443; [1903] 8 WLUK 16 HL........... **1.337**, 1.346
FH v HMRC and Secretary of State for Work and Pensions (HRP) [2015] UKUT 672 (AAC)..2.50
FJ v Secretary of State for Work and Pensions (PIP) [2019] UKUT 27 (AAC) 4.173
FK v Secretary of State for Work and Pensions (PIP) [2017] UKUT 375 (AAC)..........4.246
Flemming v Secretary of State for Work and Pensions [2002] EWCA Civ 641; [2002] 1 W.L.R. 2322; [2002] 5 WLUK 251; [2002] E.L.R. 477; R(IS) 5/02 ....4.134
FM v Secretary of State for Work and Pensions (DLA) [2017] UKUT 380 (AAC).........4.35
FN v Secretary of State for Work and Pensions (ESA) [2015] UKUT 670 (AAC); [2016] AACR 24 ....1.198, 4.173, 9.401
FR v Secretary of State for Work and Pensions (ESA) [2015] UKUT 175 (AAC)...........9.46
FR v Secretary of State for Work and Pensions (ESA) [2015] UKUT 151 (AAC)........9.401, **9.414**
FR v Secretary of State for Work and Pensions [2008] UKUT 12 (AAC) 10.168
Francovich v Italy (C-6/90); Bonifacti v Italy (C-9/90) EU:C:1991:428; [1991] E.C.R. I-5357; [1991] 11 WLUK 237; [1993] 2 C.M.L.R. 66; [1995] I.C.R. 722; [1992] I.R.L.R. 84...1.188
FY v Secretary of State for Work & Pensions (RP) [2018] UKUT 146 (AAC)..............1.118
GA v Secretary of State for Work and Pensions (PIP) [2017] UKUT 416 (AAC) 4.173
GB v Secretary of State for Work and Pensions (DLA) [2016] UKUT 566 (AAC) **4.88**
GB v Secretary of State for Work and Pensions (ESA) [2015] UKUT 200 (AAC) 9.112, 9.113
GB v Secretary of State for Work and Pensions (PIP) [2015] UKUT 546 (AAC) **4.171**, 4.240
GC v Secretary of State for Work and Pensions (ESA) [2013] UKUT 271 (AAC).........9.77

GC v Secretary of State for Work and Pensions (ESA) [2013] UKUT 405 (AAC).......**9.420,
9.422**
GC v Secretary of State for Work and Pensions (ESA) [2014] UKUT 117 (AAC).......9.407,
9.429
GD v Secretary of State for Work and Pensions (PIP) [2017] UKUT 415 (AAC)........4.173,
4.185, 4.187
GG v Secretary of State for Work and Pensions (PIP) [2016] UKUT 194 (AAC)........**4.237,
4.239**
GJ v Secretary of State for Work and Pensions (PIP) [2016] UKUT 8 (AAC) **4.248**
GK v Secretary of State for Work and Pensions (CA) [2019] UKUT 87 (AAC) 1.187
GL v Secretary of State for Work and Pensions (ESA) [2015] UKUT 503 (AAC) 9.407
Glasgow Coal Co Ltd v Welsh; sub nom. Welsh v Glasgow Coal Co Ltd [1916] 2 A.C.
    1; 1916 S.C. (H.L.) 141; 1916 1 S.L.T. 272; [1916] 3 WLUK 1 HL 1.346
Goodwin v United Kingdom (28957/95) [2002] 7 WLUK 347; [2002] I.R.L.R. 664;
    [2002] 2 F.L.R. 487; [2002] 2 F.C.R. 577; (2002) 35 E.H.R.R. 18; 13 B.H.R.C.
    120; (2002) 67 B.M.L.R. 199; [2002] Fam. Law 738; (2002) 152 N.L.J. 1171
    ECtHR...1.677
GP v Secretary of State for Work and Pensions (PIP) [2015] UKUT 498 (AAC)..........**4.246**
GP v Secretary of State for Work and Pensions (PIP) [2016] UKUT 444 (AAC).........**4.176,
4.178**, 4.240
Gray v Barr [1971] 2 Q.B. 554; [1971] 2 W.L.R. 1334; [1971] 2 All E.R. 949; [1971]
    2 Lloyd's Rep. 1; [1971] 3 WLUK 134; (1971) 115 S.J. 364 CA (Civ Div)..........1.1017
GS v Secretary of State for Work and Pensions (ESA) [2010] UKUT 244 (AAC) 9.411,
9.427
GS v Secretary of State for Work and Pensions (ESA) [2014] UKUT 16 (AAC) 9.82,
9.85, 9.87, 9.114
GS v Secretary of State for Work and Pensions [2016] UKUT 687 (AAC)....................**1.280**
GT v Secretary of State for Work and Pensions (PIP) [2019] UKUT 30 (AAC) 1.933
GV v Secretary of State for Work and Pensions [2012] UKUT 208 (AAC) **10.172,**
10.173
GW v Secretary of State for Work and Pensions [2015] UKUT 570 (AAC) **4.246**
GZ v Secretary of State for Work and Pensions (ESA) [2017] UKUT 447 (AAC) 9.408
H (Minors) (Sexual Abuse: Standard of Proof), Re; sub nom. H and R (Child Sexual
    Abuse: Standard of Proof), Re; H (Minors) (Child Abuse: Threshold Conditions),
    Re [1996] A.C. 563; [1996] 2 W.L.R. 8; [1996] 1 All E.R. 1; [1995] 12 WLUK
    274; [1996] 1 F.L.R. 80; [1996] 1 F.C.R. 509; [1996] Fam. Law 74; (1995) 145
    N.L.J. 1887; (1996) 140 S.J.L.B. 24 HL...4.176
HA v Secretary of State for Work and Pensions (PIP) [2018] UKUT 56 (AAC) 4.251
Hagan v Secretary of State for Social Security [2001] EWCA Civ 1452; [2001] 7
    WLUK 763; R(I) 2/02 ....1.415, **1.603**, 1.604
Hampshire CC v JP [2009] UKUT 239 (ACAC); [2010] AACR 15 ....1.401
Harrison v Secretary of State for Social Services R(M) 1/88 ....4.71, 4.72
HB v Secretary of State for Work and Pensions (PIP) [2016] UKUT 160 (AAC) 4.248
HB v Secretary of State for Work and Pensions [2015] UKUT 346 (AAC) 4.173
HD v Secretary of State for Work and Pensions (ESA) [2014] UKUT 72 (AAC) 9.407,
9.429
Hepple v Chief Adjudication Officer (C–196/98) EU:C:2000:278; [2000] E.C.R.
    I-3701; [2000] 5 WLUK 661; [2000] 3 C.M.L.R. 271; [2000] All E.R. (EC) 513;
    [2000] C.E.C. 351; R(I) 2/00..1.624
Hewitt v Chief Adjudication Officer; Diment v Chief Adjudication Officer. *See* R(DLA)
    6/99 ....4.71, 4.83
HH v Secretary of State for Work and Pensions (PIP) [2015] UKUT 558 (AAC).........4.244
Hickey v Secretary of State for Work and Pensions [2018] EWCA Civ 851; [2018] 4
    W.L.R. 71; [2018] 3 All E.R. 563; [2018] 4 WLUK 330......................................4.251
HJ v Secretary of State for Work and Pensions (PIP) [2016] UKUT 487 (AAC) **4.252**
HJ v Secretary of State for Work and Pensions [2013] UKUT 613 (AAC)...................1.223
HL v Secretary of State for Work and Pensions (PIP) [2015] UKUT 694 (AAC) **4.256**
HL v Secretary of State for Work and Pensions [2011] UKUT 183 (AAC)...................**1.203**
HMRC v HEH and Secretary of State for Work and Pensions (TC and CHB) [2018]
    UKUT 237 (AAC) 1.439
Hooper v Secretary of State for Work and Pensions [2007] EWCA Civ 495; [2007] 5
    WLUK 619; R(IB) 4/07 ....1.907
HP v Secretary of State for Work and Pensions [2013] UKUT 248 (AAC)....................4.66

HR v Secretary of State for Work and Pensions (ESA) [2013] UKUT 55 (AAC)............**9.82**
HS v Secretary of State for Work and Pensions (ESA) [2013] UKUT 591 (AAC) 9.111
HT v Secretary of State for Work and Pensions (ESA) [2018] UKUT 174 (AAC)..........9.86
I v United Kingdom (25680/94) [2002] 7 WLUK 345; [2002] 2 F.L.R. 518; [2002]
    2 F.C.R. 613; (2003) 36 E.H.R.R. 53; [2002] Fam. Law 740; (2002) 152 N.L.J.
    1171 ECtHR..1.677
I.O. v McCaffrey. *See* Insurance Officer v McCaffrey
IC v Secretary of State for Work and Pensions (ESA) [2015] UKUT 615 (AAC) **9.433**
IE v Secretary of State for Work and Pensions (II) [2011] UKUT 383 (AAC)..............1.606
IG v Secretary of State for Work and Pensions [2016] UKUT 176 (AAC); [2016]
    AACR 41 .... 1.164, 1.187
IJ v Secretary of State for Work and Pensions (IB) [2010] UKUT 408 (AAC) 9.82, 9.83,
                                                                                                9.86
IM v Secretary of State for Work and Pensions (ESA) [2014] UKUT 412 (AAC);
    [2015] AACR 10 ....9.111, 9.115, 9.117
IM v Secretary of State for Work and Pensions (PIP) [2015] UKUT 680 (AAC).........4.243,
                                                                                                4.244
Insurance Officer v McCaffrey [1984] 1 W.L.R. 1353; [1985] 1 All E.R. 5; [1984] 11
    WLUK 196; (1985) 82 L.S.G. 203; (1984) 128 S.J. 836 HL..............................1.188
IP v Secretary of State for Work and Pensions [2013] UKUT 235 (AAC) **4.85**
JA-K v Secretary of State for Work and Pensions (DLA) [2017] UKUT 420
    (AAC)...4.87
Janicki v Secretary of State for Social Security; sub nom. Janicki v Secretary of State for
    the Home Department [2000] 12 WLUK 120; [2001] I.C.R. 1220 CA (Civ Div);
    R(I) 1/01 ....10.167
Jayawardhana v Secretary of State for Work and Pensions [2006] EWCA Civ 1865 ......1.100
JB v Secretary of State for Work and Pensions (ESA) [2013] UKUT 518 (AAC)............9.89
JB v Secretary of State for Work and Pensions (ESA) [2017] UKUT 20 (AAC)............9.407
JB v Secretary of State for Work and Pensions [2015] UKUT 361 (AAC) 1.155, 1.280
JC v DSD (IB) [2011] NICom 177; [2014] AACR 30..9.401
JC v Secretary of State for Work and Pensions (ESA) [2014] UKUT 257 (AAC) 9.407
JC v Secretary of State for Work and Pensions (ESA) [2014] UKUT 352 (AAC); [2015]
    AACR 6 ....**9.86**, 9.423, 9.433
JC v Secretary of State for Work and Pensions (PIP) [2016] UKUT 533 (AAC)...........4.173
JC v Secretary of State for Work and Pensions [2015] UKUT 144 (AAC)....................4.183
JF v Secretary of State for Work and Pensions (IB) [2011] UKUT 385 (AAC) ...**9.401, 9.416**
JF v Secretary of State for Work and Pensions [2012] UKUT 335 (AAC) 1.204, 1.225
JG v Secretary of State for Work and Pensions (CA) [2019] UKUT 83 (AAC)..............1.187
JG v Secretary of State for Work and Pensions (ESA) [2013] UKUT 37 (AAC); [2013]
    AACR 23 .... 1.202, 4.235, 9.46, 9.47, **9.79**, 9.80, 9.115, 9.425, 9.433
JG v Secretary of State for Work and Pensions (ESA) [2013] UKUT 496 (AAC) **9.415**
JH v Secretary of State for Work and Pensions (DLA) [2010] UKUT 456 (AAC) 1.239,
                                                                                                4.93, 4.94
JH v Secretary of State for Work and Pensions (ESA) [2013] UKUT 269 (AAC) 9.401,
                                                                                                9.416
JH(S) v Secretary of State for Work and Pensions (ESA) [2015] UKUT 567 (AAC).......9.89
JL and DO v Secretary of State for Work and Pensions (II) [2011] UKUT 294 (AAC);
    [2012] AACR 15 ....1.400, 10.172, 10.173
JL v Secretary of State for Work and Pensions (ESA) [2018] UKUT 346 (AAC)..........9.109
JM v Secretary of State for Work and Pensions (ESA) [2013] UKUT 234 (AAC).........**9.532**
JM v Secretary of State for Work and Pensions (ESA) [2014] UKUT 22 (AAC)...........**9.423**
JM v Secretary of State for Work and Pensions (IB) [2010] UKUT 386 (AAC).............9.401
JM v Secretary of State for Work and Pensions (PIP) [2016] UKUT 296 (AAC)..........**4.246**
JM v Secretary of State for Work and Pensions (PIP) [2016] UKUT 542 (AAC).........4.171,
                                                                                                4.247
JM v Secretary of State for Work and Pensions and HMRC [2018] UKUT 2 (AAC)......2.50
John (A Minor: Vaccine Damage Payment scheme), Re. *See* Secretary of State for Work
    and Pensions v G
Johnson v Chief Adjudication Officer (No.2) R(S) 1/95 ....1.188
Jones v Chief Adjudication Officer [1991] 1 All E.R. 353; [1990] 7 WLUK 411; [1990]
    I.R.L.R. 533 CA (Civ Div); R(G) 2/91 ....3.95
Jones v Secretary of State for Social Services; Hudson v Secretary of State for Social
    Services; sub nom. R. v National Insurance Commissioner Ex p. Lloyd-Jones;

R. v National Insurance Commissioner Ex p. Jones; R. v National Insurance Commissioner Ex p. Hudson [1972] A.C. 944; [1972] 2 W.L.R. 210; [1972] 1 All E.R. 145; [1971] 12 WLUK 111; (1971) 116 S.J. 57 HL; R(I) 3/69 .... **1.345**, 1.347, **1.398**, 1.400

JP v Secretary of State for Work and Pensions (PIP) [2015] UKUT 529 (AAC) **4.258**

JP v Secretary of State for Work and Pensions [2013] UKUT 524 (AAC) **4.56**

JR v Secretary of State for Work and Pensions (II) [2011] UKUT 450 (AAC) 1.578

JR v Secretary of State for Work and Pensions (II) [2013] UKUT 317 (AAC) 1.600

JS v Secretary of State for Work and Pensions (ESA) [2011] UKUT 243 (AAC) 9.416

JS v Secretary of State for Work and Pensions (ESA) [2013] UKUT 635 (AAC) 9.114

JS v Secretary of State for Work and Pensions (ESA) [2014] UKUT 428 (AAC); [2015] AACR 12 .... **9.89**, 9.90

JS v Secretary of State for Work and Pensions [2012] AACR 7 .... 1.195

JT v Secretary of State for Work and Pensions (DLA) [2013] UKUT 221 (AAC)........... 4.77

JT v Secretary of State for Work and Pensions (ESA) [2018] UKUT 124 (AAC)... 9.83, 9.84

JT v Secretary of State for Work and Pensions (PIP) [2018] UKUT 101 (AAC)............ 4.176, 4.237, 4.240

JW v Secretary of State for Work and Pensions (ESA) [2011] UKUT 416 (AAC)........... 9.75, 9.85, 9.87

JW v Secretary of State for Work and Pensions (ESA) [2016] UKUT 207 (AAC)............ 9.60

JW v Secretary of State for Work and Pensions (ESA) [2016] UKUT 208 (AAC)............ 9.60

JW v Secretary of State for Work and Pensions (PIP) [2018] UKUT 169 (AAC).......... 4.241

JW v Secretary of State for Work and Pensions [2012] UKUT 336 (AAC) 1.257

Kavanagh v Secretary of State for Work and Pensions [2019] EWCA Civ 272; [2019] 3 WLUK 70; *Times*, 7 May 2019 .... 4.7, 4.37

KB v Secretary of State for Work and Pensions (ESA) [2013] UKUT 152 (AAC) **9.105**, **9.110**, **9.422**, 9.423, **9.433**

KB v Secretary of State for Work and Pensions (ESA) [2014] UKUT 126 (AAC) 9.414, 9.429

KB v Secretary of State for Work and Pensions (ESA) [2014] UKUT 126 (AAC) **9.407**

KB v Secretary of State for Work and Pensions (ESA) [2014] UKUT 303 (AAC) 9.88

KB v Secretary of State for Work and Pensions (ESA) [2015] UKUT 179 (AAC) 9.114

KB v Secretary of State for Work and Pensions (PIP) [2016] UKUT 0537 (AAC)........ **4.191**

KB v Secretary of State for Work and Pensions (PIP) [2016] UKUT 537 (AAC) 4.173, 4.191

KC and MC v Secretary of State for Work and Pensions (ESA) [2017] UKUT 94 (AAC)... **9.113**

KC-MS v Secretary of State for Work and Pensions [2015] UKUT 284 (AAC)............ **1.266**

KE v Department for Social Development (ESA) [2013] NI Com 59............................ 9.411

KE v Secretary of State for Work and Pensions (ESA) [2013] UKUT 370 (AAC) **9.425**

KG v Secretary of State for Work and Pensions [2012] UKUT 222 (AAC) 1.204, 1.211

KH v Secretary of State for Work and Pensions (DLA) [2015] UKUT 8 (AAC)........... 1.261

KH v Secretary of State for Work and Pensions (ESA) [2014] UKUT 455 (AAC)....... 9.410, **9.411**

KH v Secretary of State for Work and Pensions [2014] UKUT 138 (AAC) 1.138, 1.560

KJ v Secretary of State for Work and Pensions (CA) [2011] AACR 8 .... **3.21**

KK v Secretary of State for Work and Pensions [2012] UKUT 356 (AAC) 1.155, **1.204**

KKL v Secretary of State for Work and Pensions (PIP) [2018] UKUT 17 (AAC)......... 1.907

KL v Secretary of State for Work and Pensions (PIP) [2015] UKUT 612 (AAC) **4.258**

KL v Secretary of State for Work and Pensions (PIP) [2016] UKUT 545 (AAC) 4.176, 4.258

KM v Secretary of State for Work and Pensions (PIP) [2018] UKUT 296 (AAC) 1.907, 4.231, 4.234

KM v Secretary of State for Work and Pensions [2013] UKUT 159 (AAC); [2014] AACR 2 .... **1.204**, 1.211, 1.240

KN v Secretary of State for Work and Pensions (ESA) [2011] UKUT 229 (AAC)......... 9.47, 9.399, 9.416

KN v Secretary of State for Work and Pensions (ESA) [2016] UKUT 521 (AAC)....... 9.116, **9.401**

KN v Secretary of State for Work and Pensions [2016] UKUT 261 (AAC) 4.259

KO v Secretary of State for Work and Pensions (PIP) [2018] UKUT 78 (AAC)........... 4.246

KP v Secretary of State for Work and Pensions (ESA) [2011] UKUT 216 (AAC); [2012] AACR 5 .... 9.47, 9.399, 9.416

KP v Secretary of State for Work and Pensions (PIP) [2017] UKUT 30 (AAC)............4.250
KR v Secretary of State for Work and Pensions (DLA) [2019] UKUT 85 (AAC) 1.195
KR v Secretary of State for Work and Pensions (ESA) [2013] UKUT 637 (AAC) 9.77
KR v Secretary of State for Work and Pensions (PIP) [2015] UKUT 547 (AAC) **4.171,**
4.244
KS v Secretary of State for Work and Pensions (DLA) [2013] UKUT 390 (AAC).......1.271,
4.71
KS v Secretary of State for Work and Pensions [2011] UKUT 29 (AAC)....................1.226
KW v Secretary of State for Work and Pensions (ESA) [2015] UKUT 131 (AAC) **9.112,**
9.113
KW v Secretary of State for Work and Pensions (PIP) [2017] UKUT 54 (AAC) 4.171
KW v Secretary of State for Work and Pensions [2012] UKUT 181 (AAC).................**10.20**
LB v Secretary of State for Work and Pensions (DLA) [2018] UKUT 445 (AAC)........1.236
LB v Secretary of State for Work and Pensions (ESA) [2013] UKUT 352 (AAC).........**9.414**
LB v Secretary of State for Work and Pensions (PIP) [2017] UKUT 436 (AAC).........4.238
LC v Secretary of State for Work and Pensions (DLA) [2015] UKUT 32 (AAC) 1.198
LC v Secretary of State for Work and Pensions (ESA) [2015] UKUT 664 (AAC) 9.408
LC v Secretary of State for Work and Pensions (PIP) [2016] UKUT 150 (AAC).........**4.240,**
4.247
LD v Secretary of State for Work and Pensions (ESA) [2014] UKUT 131 (AAC) 9.87
LD v Secretary of State for Work and Pensions [2009] UKUT 208 (AAC)...................9.407
Lees v Secretary of State for Social Services; sub nom. Lees v Department of Health
& Social Security [1985] A.C. 930; [1985] 2 W.L.R. 805; [1985] 2 All E.R. 203;
[1985] 4 WLUK 170; (1985) 82 L.S.G. 1944; (1985) 135 N.L.J. 437; (1985) 129
S.J. 316 HL; R(M) 1/84..1.257, 4.71, 4.76, 4.80, 4.81, 4.84
LH v Secretary of State for Work and Pensions (ESA) [2014] UKUT 480 (AAC);
[2015] AACR 14 .... **1.712, 9.535**
LH v Secretary of State for Work and Pensions (ESA) [2015] UKUT 154 (AAC) 9.109
LM v Secretary of State for Work and Pensions (ESA) [2013] UKUT 552 (AAC).......9.105,
9.421, **9.422, 9.423**
LM v Secretary of State for Work and Pensions (ESA) [2013] UKUT 553 (AAC).......9.433
LM v Secretary of State for Work and Pensions (ESA) [2016] UKUT 360 (AAC).......9.598,
9.601, 9.604, 9.606
LM v Secretary of State for Work and Pensions [2008] UKUT 24 (AAC).....................4.94
LS v Secretary of State for Work and Pensions [2019] UKUT 3 (AAC) 4.173
M (A Child) v Chief Adjudication Officer R(DLA) 1/00 .... 1.265, 4.91
M v Secretary of State for Work and Pensions (ESA) [2012] UKUT 376 (AAC).........9.407
M's Guardian v Advocate General for Scotland; sub nom SM v Advocate General for
Scotland [2010] CSOH 15; 2010 S.L.T. 621...1.252
MA v Secretary of State for Work and Pensions (ESA) [2014] UKUT 185 (AAC) 9.407
MA v Secretary of State for Work and Pensions (ESA) [2015] UKUT 290 (AAC) 9.401,
9.407
MA v Secretary of State for Work and Pensions (PIP) [2017] UKUT 351 (AAC)........4.173,
4.185
Maguire v Harland & Wolff Plc [2005] EWCA Civ 1; [2005] 1 WLUK 439; [2005]
P.I.Q.R. P21; (2005) 102(12) L.S.G. 26; (2005) 149 S.J.L.B. 144 ....1.858
Mallinson v Secretary of State for Social Security [1994] 1 W.L.R. 630; [1994] 2 All
E.R. 295; [1994] 4 WLUK 142; (1994) 144 N.L.J. 604; (1994) 138 S.J.L.B. 112;
R(A) 3/94 HL...................................... 1.204, 1.207, 1.208, 1.209, 1.212, 1.218, 4.95
Margereson v JW Roberts Ltd; Hancock v JW Roberts Ltd; Hancock v T&N Plc [1996]
4 WLUK 21; [1996] Env. L.R. 304; [1997] 6 Re. L.R. 74; [1996] P.I.Q.R. P358;
(1996) 93(22) L.S.G. 27 CA (Civ Div)..1.858
Mathieson v Secretary of State for Work and Pensions; sub nom. AM v Secretary of
State for Work and Pensions [2015] UKSC 47; [2015] 1 W.L.R. 3250; [2016] 1
All E.R. 779; [2015] 7 WLUK 232; 39 B.H.R.C. 372; (2015) 146 B.M.L.R. 1;
[2015] AACR 19 ....4.54, 4.59, 4.62, 4.223
MB v Secretary of State for Work and Pensions (C-451/16) EU:C:2018:492; 26 June
2018...1.677
MB v Secretary of State for Work and Pensions (ESA) [2012] UKUT 228 (AAC)........ **9.82,**
9.85
MB v Secretary of State for Work and Pensions (PIP) [2018] UKUT 139 (AAC).........4.245
MC and JH v Secretary of State for Work and Pensions (ESA) [2014] UKUT 125
(AAC)..1.723

MC v Secretary of State for Work and Pensions (ESA) [2012] UKUT 324 (AAC); [2013] AACR 13 .... 9.408, 9.411

MC v Secretary of State for Work and Pensions (ESA) [2015] UKUT 646 (AAC) **9.47,** 9.421

MC v Secretary of State for Work and Pensions [2012] UKUT 337 (AAC) 1.178, 1.198

McKiernon v Secretary of State for Social Security [1989] 1 WLUK 519; (1989-90) 2 Admin. L.R. 133; (1990) 87(15) L.S.G. 39 CA (Civ Div) 1.424, 10.73, 10.109, 10.125

McLaughlin's Application for Judicial Review, Re [2018] UKSC 48; [2018] 1 W.L.R. 4250; [2019] 1 All E.R. 471; [2018] 8 WLUK 268; [2018] H.R.L.R. 21; 46 B.H.R.C. 268 .... 1.1009, 1.1010

McNeice v Singer Sewing Machine Co Ltd, 1911 S.C. 12; 1910 2 S.L.T. 210; [1910] 10 WLUK 22 IH (1 Div) 1.352

MD v Secretary of State for Work and Pensions (II) [2011] UKUT 137 (AAC) 10.172

MF v Secretary of State for Work and Pensions (ESA) [2014] UKUT 523 (AAC)..........**9.89**

MF v Secretary of State for Work and Pensions (PIP) [2015] UKUT 554 (AAC); [2016] AACR 20 ....4.243, 4.244, 4.246

MG v Department for Social Development (ESA) [2013] NI Com 359.......................9.407

MH v Secretary of State for Work and Pensions (ESA) [2011] UKUT 492 (AAC).......9.410

MH v Secretary of State for Work and Pensions (ESA) [2018] UKUT 194 (AAC).......9.407

MH v Secretary of State for Work and Pensions (PIP) [2016] UKUT 531 (AAC); [2018] AACR 12 ....4.176, **4.234**, 4.256

MH v Secretary of State for Work and Pensions (PIP) [2017] UKUT 424 (AAC); [2018] AACR 15 .... 1.929, 4.223

MH v Secretary of State for Work and Pensions [2009] UKUT 94 (AAC) **4.90**

MH v Secretary of State for Work and Pensions [2014] UKUT 113 (AAC) 1.648

MI v Secretary of State for Work and Pensions (ESA) [2013] UKUT 447 (AAC).........9.407

Miller v Chief Adjudication Officer R(A) 4/94 .... 1.205, 1.206

Minister of Health v General Committee of the Royal Midland Counties Home for Incurables at Leamington Spa [1954] Ch. 530; [1954] 2 W.L.R. 755; [1954] 1 All E.R. 1013; [1954] 3 WLUK 121; (1954) 98 S.J. 250 CA 4.56

MK v Secretary of State for Work and Pensions (ESA) [2016] UKUT 74 (AAC) **9.410**

ML v Secretary of State for Work and Pensions (DLA) [2016] UKUT 323 (AAC); [2017] AACR 2 ....**4.59**

ML v Secretary of State for Work and Pensions (ESA) [2013] UKUT 174 (AAC); [2013] AACR 33 ....**9.110**, 9.111, 9.407

ML v Secretary of State for Work and Pensions (PIP) [2017] UKUT 171 (AAC).........4.247

MM and BJ v Secretary of State for Work and Pensions (PIP) [2016] UKUT 490 (AAC)...**4.241**

MM and DM v Secretary of State for Work and Pensions [2013] UKUT 259 (AAC) 9.55, 9.396

MM and SI v Secretary of State for Work and Pensions (DLA) [2016] UKUT 149 (AAC); [2016] AACR 3 .... **4.5, 4.35, 4.143, 4.201**

MM v Department for Social Development (ESA) [2014] NI Com 48 ....9.408

MM v Secretary of State for Work and Pensions (ESA) [2017] UKUT 236 (AAC) 9.408

MM v Secretary of State for Work and Pensions (PIP) [2018] UKUT 193 (AAC).......4.243, 4.248

MM v Secretary of State for Work and Pensions; sub nom Secretary of State for Work and Pensions v The Queen [2013] EWCA Civ 1565; [2014] 1 W.L.R. 1716; [2014] 2 All E.R. 289; [2013] 12 WLUK 110; [2014] Eq. L.R. 34; [2016] AACR 11 ....9.55

MMcG v Department for Social Development (DLA) 4.93

MMcK v Secretary of State for Work and Pensions (PIP) [2016] UKUT 191 (AAC); [2017] AACR 38 ....**4.251**

MMF v Secretary of State for Work and Pensions [2012] UKUT 312 (AAC)...............4.83

MN v Bury Council and Secretary of State for Work and Pensions (HB) [2014] UKUT 187 (AAC) 9.495

MN v Secretary of State for Work and Pensions (ESA) [2013] UKUT 262 (AAC); [2014] AACR 6 .... **9.110**, 9.111

Mongan v Department of Social Development [2005] NICA 16; R3/05 (DLA) 1.261

Moore v Manchester Liners Ltd [1910] A.C. 498 HL...**1.354**

Moran v Secretary of State for Social Services [1987] 3 WLUK 156; *Times* 14 March 1987, CA; R(A) 1/88 ....1.157, 1.207, 1.231, 1.259, 4.176

Moyna v Secretary of State for Work and Pensions; sub nom. Moyna v Secretary of State for Social Security [2003] UKHL 44; [2003] 1 W.L.R. 1929; [2003] 4 All E.R. 162; [2003] 7 WLUK 992; (2003) 73 B.M.L.R. 201; R(DLA) 7/03... **1.199**, 1.222, 1.223, 1.229, **1.252**, 1.268, 4.183, 9.411, 9.419

MP v Secretary of State for Work and Pensions (DLA) [2014] UKUT 426 (AAC) **4.91**

MP v Secretary of State for Work and Pensions (ESA) [2015] UKUT 458 (AAC)........**9.419**

MP v Secretary of State for Work and Pensions (ESA) [2016] UKUT 502 (AAC)........**9.116**

MP v Secretary of State for Work and Pensions [2010] UKUT 231 (AAC) 4.22

MR v Secretary of State for Work and Pensions (PIP) [2017] UKUT 86 (AAC)..........**4.171**, 4.234

MS v Secretary of State for Work and Pensions (DLA) [2016] UKUT 42 (AAC)...........4.35

MT v Secretary of State for Work and Pensions (ESA) [2013] UKUT 545 (AAC) **9.86**, 9.111, **9.116**

MT v Secretary of State for Work and Pensions (ESA) [2014] UKUT 548 (AAC)..**9.410**

Mullen v Secretary of State for Work and Pensions, 2002 S.C. 2512002 S.C. 251; 2002 S.L.T. 149; 2002 S.C.L.R. 475; [2002] 1 WLUK 210; 2002 G.W.D. 3-121 IH (2 Div) 1.343, 1.344

Murrell v Secretary of State for Social Services. *See* R(I) 3/84....................................10.23

MW v Secretary of State for Work and Pensions (ESA) [2012] UKUT 31 (AAC) **9.81**

MW v Secretary of State for Work and Pensions (ESA) [2014] UKUT 112 (AAC) **9.419**

MW v Secretary of State for Work and Pensions (ESA) [2015] UKUT 665 (AAC) 9.83, 9.85

MW v Secretary of State for Work and Pensions (ESA) [2018] UKUT 304 (AAC) 9.42, 9.102

MW v Secretary of State for Work and Pensions (PIP) [2016] UKUT 540 (AAC)........4.173

MW v Secretary of State for Work and Pensions [2013] UKUT 158 (AAC)...............1.194, 1.203

NA (by ST) v Secretary of State for Work and Pensions (ESA) [2012] UKUT 428 (AAC)..9.88

NA v MSK [2018] EWFC 54; [2019] 2 W.L.R. 771; [2018] 7 WLUK 745; [2019] 1 F.L.R. 575; [2019] 1 F.C.R. 24; [2018] W.T.L.R. 729 ....1.1010

NA v Secretary of State for Work and Pensions (BB) [2019] UKUT 144 (AAC) 1.1010, 3.157

NA v Secretary of State for Work and Pensions (ESA) [2014] UKUT 305 (AAC) 9.111

NA v Secretary of State for Work and Pensions (ESA) [2018] UKUT 399 (AAC) 9.411

NA v Secretary of State for Work and Pensions (PIP) [2015] UKUT 572 (AAC) **4.171**, **4.236**, **4.245**, **4.247**

NA v Secretary of State for Work and Pensions (PIP) [2016] UKUT 572 (AAC) **4.171**

Nancollas v Insurance Officer; Ball v Insurance Officer [1985] 1 All E.R. 833; [1985] 3 WLUK 3 CA (Civ Div); R(I) 7/85..................................... 1.355, 1.359, 1.361, 1.379

NC v Secretary of State for Work and Pensions (DLA) [2012] UKUT 384 (AAC).........4.87

NC v Secretary of State for Work and Pensions (ESA) [2015] UKUT 147 (AAC).........9.348

NC v Secretary of State for Work and Pensions (ESA) [2016] UKUT 401 (AAC)..........9.47

NH v Secretary of State for Work and Pensions (ESA) [2011] UKUT 82 (AAC) **9.414**

NH v Secretary of State for Work and Pensions (ESA) [2014] UKUT 114 (AAC)........**9.402**

NK v Secretary of State for Work and Pensions (PIP) [2016] UKUT 146 (AAC)........4.235, 4.257

NL v Secretary of State for Work and Pensions (ESA) [2017] UKUT 397 (AAC) 9.414

NMcM v Secretary of State for Work and Pensions (DLA) [2014] UKUT 312 (AAC)..**4.91**

NN-K v Secretary of State for Work and Pensions (ESA) [2015] UKUT 385 (AAC)....**9.117**

NS v Secretary of State for Work and Pensions (ESA) [2014] UKUT 115 (AAC); [2014] AACR 33 ....9.83, **9.88, 9.89**

NS v Secretary of State for Work and Pensions (ESA) [2014] UKUT 149 (AAC) **9.114**, 9.115

NT v Secretary of State for Work and Pensions (DLA) [2009] UKUT 37 (AAC); R(DLA) 1/09...1.155, **1.280**, 4.87

NT v Secretary of State for Work and Pensions (ESA) [2013] UKUT 360 (AAC)........9.407

O'Neill v Department for Communities [2018] NICA 29 ....9.403

OM v Secretary of State for Work and Pensions (PIP) [2017] UKUT 458 (AAC) 4.187

P v Secretary of State for Work and Pensions (PIP) [2018] UKUT 359 (AAC) 4.270

P v Secretary of State for Work and Pensions (PIP) [2018] UKUT 376 (AAC) 4.248

P v Secretary of State for Work and Pensions (PIP) [2019] UKUT 82 (AAC) 4.173
PB v Secretary of State for Work and Pensions (DLA) [2016] UKUT 280 (AAC)..........**4.37**
PB v Secretary of State for Work and Pensions (PIP) [2017] UKUT 493 (AAC) 1.906
PC v Secretary of State for Work and Pensions (ESA) [2014] UKUT 1 (AAC) 9.88
PC v Secretary of State for Work and Pensions (ESA) [2015] UKUT 285 (AAC)........9.414
PC v Secretary of State for Work and Pensions (ESA) [2015] UKUT 531 (AAC)........**9.421**
PC v Secretary of State for Work and Pensions (II) [2017] UKUT 409 (AAC)...........10.195
PC v Secretary of State for Work and Pensions (PIP) [2015] UKUT 622 (AAC)..........4.243
PD v Secretary of State for Work and Pensions (ESA) [2012] UKUT 255 (AAC) **9.420**
PD v Secretary of State for Work and Pensions (ESA) [2014] UKUT 148 (AAC) **9.84,**
9.86, 9.116
PE v Secretary of State for Work and Pensions (PIP) [2015] UKUT 309 (AAC)..........4.244
PE v Secretary of State for Work and Pensions (PIP) [2015] UKUT 309 (AAC); [2016]
    AACR 10 .... 4.246, **4.247**
Pearse v Secretary of State for Social Security [1992] Pens. L.R. 117 CA (Civ Div) 3.95
Pepper (Inspector of Taxes) v Hart; sub nom. Pepper v Hart [1993] A.C. 593; [1992]
    3 W.L.R. 1032; [1993] 1 All E.R. 42; [1992] S.T.C. 898; [1992] 11 WLUK 389;
    [1993] I.C.R. 291; [1993] I.R.L.R. 33; [1993] R.V.R. 127; (1993) 143 N.L.J. 17;
    [1992] N.P.C. 154 HL 4.171
PF v Secretary of State for Work and Pensions (ESA) [2013] UKUT 634 (AAC).........9.111
PH v Secretary of State for Work and Pensions (ESA) [2014] UKUT 502 (AAC) **9.89**
PH v Secretary of State for Work and Pensions (ESA) [2016] UKUT 119 (AAC) **9.60**
PH v Secretary of State for Work and Pensions (II) [2016] UKUT 94 (AAC) ... 10.67, **10.72**
Pimlico Plumbers v Smith [2018] UKSC 29; [2018] 4 All E.R. 641; [2018] 6 WLUK
    224; [2018] I.C.R. 1511; [2018] I.R.L.R. 872 ....1.40
Plummer v Hammond R(I) 2/99; R(I) 2/99
PM v Secretary of State for Work and Pensions (PIP) [2017] UKUT 154 (AAC)........**4.176,**
4.234, 4.253, 4.259
PM v Secretary of State for Work and Pensions (PIP) [2017] UKUT 37 (AAC)..........4.173,
4.191
PM v Secretary of State for Work and Pensions (PIP) [2017] UKUT 502 (AAC).........4.237
PM v Secretary of State for Work and Pensions (PIP) [2018] UKUT 138 (AAC).........4.243
PR v Secretary of State for Work and Pensions (PIP) [2015] UKUT 584 (ACC)..........**4.251**
Pridding v Secretary of State for Work and Pensions [2002] EWCA Civ 306; [2002] 3
    WLUK 35; [2002] C.P.L.R. 315; (2002) 99(15) L.S.G. 35; (2002) 146 S.J.L.B.
    77; R(G) 1/0..4.132
PS v Secretary of State for Work and Pensions (PIP) [2016] UKUT 326 (AAC) 4.259
Quashie v Stringfellow Restaurants Ltd; sub nom. Stringfellow Restaurants Ltd v
    Quashie [2012] EWCA Civ 1735; [2012] 12 WLUK 805; [2013] I.R.L.R. 99;
    (2013) 157(1) S.J.L.B. 31 ....1.40
R (Iran) v Secretary of State for the Home Department; T (Eritrea) v Secretary of State
    for the Home Department; T (Afghanistan) v Secretary of State for the Home
    Department; M (Afghanistan) v Secretary of State for the Home Department; A
    (Afghanistan) v Secretary of State for the Home Department; sub nom. R. (on the
    application of R) v Secretary of State for the Home Department [2005] EWCA Civ
    982; [2005] Imm. A.R. 535; [2005] I.N.L.R. 633 ....1.574
R v Secretary of State for Work and Pensions [2018] UKUT 326 (AAC) 9.411
R. (MM and DM) v Secretary of State for Work and Pensions [2015] UKUT 107
    (AAC); [2016] AACR 11 ....**9.55**
R. (on the application of C) v Secretary of State for Work and Pensions [2017] UKSC
    72; [2017] 1 W.L.R. 4127; [2018] 2 All E.R. 391; [2017] P.T.S.R. 1476; [2017]
    11 WLUK 3; [2017] H.R.L.R. 17; 44 B.H.R.C. 209..1.678
R. (on the application of D) v Secretary of State for Work and Pensions. See R. (on the
    application of RD) v Secretary of State for Work and Pensions
R. (on the application of M) v Secretary of State for Work and Pensions. See R. (on the
    application of RD) v Secretary of State for Work and Pensions
R. (on the application of National Association of Colliery Overmen Deputies and
    Shotfirers) v Secretary of State for Work and Pensions [2003] EWHC 607
    (Admin); [2003] 5 WLUK 14; [2004] A.C.D. 14 .... 10.161, 10.162
R. (on the application of RD) v Secretary of State for Work and Pensions; R. (on the
    application of EM) v Secretary of State for Work and Pensions [2010] EWCA Civ
    18; [2010] 1 W.L.R. 1782; [2010] 1 WLUK 509; [2010] H.R.L.R. 19; (2010) 112
    B.M.L.R. 140; [2010] M.H.L.R. 72; (2010) 154(4) S.J.L.B. 30 .... 1.438, **3.75**

R. (on the application of RF) v Secretary of State for Work and Pensions [2017] EWHC 3375 (Admin); [2018] P.T.S.R. 1147; [2017] 12 WLUK 636; [2018] AACR 13 ....4.176, 4.234, 4.256
R. (on the application of Sumpter) v Secretary of State for Work and Pensions [2015] EWCA Civ 1033; [2015] 10 WLUK 410...**4.180**
R. (on the application of ToTel Ltd) v First-tier Tribunal (Tax Chamber) [2012] EWCA Civ 1401; [2013] Q.B. 860; [2013] 2 W.L.R. 1136; [2013] S.T.C. 1557; [2012] 10 WLUK 960; [2012] B.V.C. 333; [2012] S.T.I. 3230............................9.533
R. v Barnet LBC Ex p. Shah; Akbarali v Brent LBC; Abdullah v Shropshire CC; Shabpar v Barnet LBC; Shah (Jitendra) v Barnet LBC; Ablack v Inner London Education Authority; R. v Shropshire CC Ex p. Abdullah [1983] 2 A.C. 309; [1983] 2 W.L.R. 16; [1983] 1 All E.R. 226; [1982] 12 WLUK 164; 81 L.G.R. 305; (1983) 133 N.L.J. 61; (1983) 127 S.J. 36 HL **3.124**, 4.35
R. v Chief National Insurance Commissioner Ex p. Connor [1981] Q.B. 758; [1981] 2 W.L.R. 412; [1981] 1 All E.R. 769; [1980] 5 WLUK 23; [1980] Crim. L.R. 579; (1980) 124 S.J. 478 QBD 1.1016
R. v Deputy Industrial Injuries Commissioner Ex p. Humphreys; sub nom. R. v Deputy National Insurance Commissioner Ex p. Humphreys [1966] 2 Q.B. 1; [1966] 2 W.L.R. 63; [1965] 3 All E.R. 885; [1965] 11 WLUK 81; (1965) 109 S.J. 934 CA 1.607, 1.611
R. v Industrial Injuries Commissioner Ex p. Amalgamated Engineering Union (No.2) [1966] 2 Q.B. 31; [1966] 2 W.L.R. 97; [1966] 1 All E.R. 97; [1965] 11 WLUK 78; (1965) 109 S.J. 934 CA; R(I) 4/66..**1.354, 1.358**
R. v Medical Appeal Tribunal Ex p. Cable R(I) 11/66 ....1.400, 1.576, 10.24
R. v National Insurance (Industrial Injuries) Commissioner Ex p. Richardson [1958] 1 W.L.R. 851; [1958] 2 All E.R. 689; [1958] 7 WLUK 9; (1958) 102 S.J. 563 DC; R(I) 21/58 ....**1.363**
R. v National Insurance Commissioner Ex p Secretary of State for Social Services [1974] 1 W.L.R. 1290; [1974] 3 All E.R. 522; [1974] 7 WLUK 28; (1974) 118 S.J. 598 DC; R(A) 4/74...1.220, 1.228, 1.234
R. v National Insurance Commissioner Ex p. East [1975] 10 WLUK 113; [1976] I.C.R. 206 QBD; R(I) 16/75...1.357
R. v National Insurance Commissioner Ex p. McMenemey R(S) 2/69.........................3.114
R. v National Insurance Commissioner Ex p. Mellors [1971] 2 Q.B. 401; [1971] 2 W.L.R. 593; [1971] 1 All E.R. 740; [1971] 1 WLUK 469; 10 K.I.R. 109; (1971) 115 S.J. 156 CA (Civ Div); R(I) 7/69 ....**1.610**, 1.618
R. v National Insurance Commissioner Ex p. Michael [1977] 1 W.L.R. 109; [1977] 2 All E.R. 420; [1976] 11 WLUK 174; [1977] I.C.R. 121; (1976) 120 S.J. 856 CA (Civ Div); R(I) 5/75..1.359
R. v National Insurance Commissioner Ex p. Secretary of State for Social Services [1981] 1 W.L.R. 1017; [1981] 2 All E.R. 738; [1981] 4 WLUK 142; R(A) 2/80...**1.208**, 1.228, **1.230, 1.237**
R. v Secretary of State for Social Security Ex p. Armstrong [1996] 6 WLUK 9; (1996) 8 Admin. L.R. 626; (1996) 32 B.M.L.R. 32 CA (Civ Div) 1.222, 4.239
R. v Secretary of State for Social Security Ex p. Perry and Ex p. McGillivray [1998] C.L.Y. 4513 CA (Civ Div) **4.98**
R. v Secretary of State for Social Services Ex p. Britnell; sub nom. Britnell v Secretary of State for Social Security [1991] 1 W.L.R. 198; [1991] 2 All E.R. 726; [1991] 3 WLUK 197; (1991) 135 S.J. 412 HL 4.306
R. v Social Security Commissioner Ex p. Akbar [1991] 10 WLUK 385; (1992) 4 Admin. L.R. 602; [1992] C.O.D. 245; (1992) 89(4) L.S.G. 34; (1991) 135 S.J.L.B. 214 QBD..3.152
R. v Social Security Commissioner Ex p. Dobie unreported 26 October 1999 QBD......9.401
R. v Soneji (Kamlesh Kumar); R. v Bullen (David Frederick); sub nom. R. v Soneiji (Kamalesh Kumar) [2005] UKHL 49; [2006] 1 A.C. 340; [2005] 3 W.L.R. 303; [2005] 4 All E.R. 321; [2005] 7 WLUK 669; [2006] 2 Cr. App. R. 20; [2006] 1 Cr. App. R. (S.) 79; [2006] Crim. L.R. 167; (2005) 102(31) L.S.G. 26; (2005) 155 N.L.J. 1315; (2005) 149 S.J.L.B. 924..**9.532**
R. v Woodling. *See* Woodling v Secretary of State for Social Services
RA v Secretary of State for Work and Pensions (ESA) [2010] UKUT 301 (AAC) 9.47, 9.415
Ramsden v Secretary of State for Work and Pensions [2003] EWCA Civ 32; [2003] 1 WLUK 740; R(DLA) 2/03................................... 1.213, **1.214**, 1.220, 1.228, 1.234

RB v Secretary of State for Work and Pensions (ESA) [2012] UKUT 431 (AAC)..........9.75, 9.87, 9.88
RB v Secretary of State for Work and Pensions (ESA) [2016] UKUT 384 (AAC)........9.274, 9.282
RB v Secretary of State for Work and Pensions (PIP) [2016] UKUT 304 (AAC)..........**4.257**
RB v Secretary of State for Work and Pensions (PIP) [2016] UKUT 393 (AAC)..........**4.254**
RB v Secretary of State for Work and Pensions (PIP) [2016] UKUT 556 (AAC).........4.171, **4.244**
RC v Secretary of State for Work and Pensions (PIP) [2015] UKUT 386 (AAC) **4.256**
RC v Secretary of State for Work and Pensions (PIP) [2017] UKUT 352 (AAC) 4.252
RF v Secretary of State for Work and Pensions. *See* R. (on the application of RF) v Secretary of State for Work and Pensions
RH v Secretary of State for Work and Pensions (PIP) [2015] UKUT 281 (AAC) **4.239**, **4.242, 2.243**
Richards v Secretary of State for Work and Pensions R(P) 1/07.....................................1.680
RJ v Secretary of State for Work and Pensions (PIP) [2017] UKUT 105 (AAC); [2017] AACR 32 ....4.176, **4.183**, 4.238, 4.245, 4.259
RK v Secretary of State for Work and Pensions (ESA) [2015] UKUT 549 (AAC) **9.89**
RM v Secretary of State for Work and Pensions (ESA) [2011] UKUT 454 (AAC) **9.47**, 9.399, 9.416
RO v Secretary of State for Work and Pensions (ESA) [2016] UKUT 402 (AAC)..........**9.60**
Roberts v Dorothea Slate Quarries Ltd [1948] 2 All E.R. 201; [1948] 6 WLUK 75; [1948] W.N. 246; [1948] L.J.R. 1409; (1948) 92 S.J. 513 HL.............................**1.342**
RP v Secretary of State for Work and Pensions (ESA) [2011] UKUT 449 (AAC) ...**9.48**, 9.414
RR v Secretary of State for Work and Pensions (ESA) [2018] UKUT 143 (AAC) 9.417
RR v Secretary of State for Work and Pensions [2009] UKUT 272 (AAC) 1.257
RS v Secretary of State for Work and Pensions (ESA) [2016] UKUT 85 (AAC) **1.933**
RS-G v Secretary of State for Work and Pensions (PIP) [2017] UKUT 152 (AAC) 4.176
RU v Secretary of State for Work and Pensions (ESA) [2014] UKUT 77 (AAC).............**9.88**
RV v Secretary of State for Work and Pensions (ESA) [2014] UKUT 56 (AAC) **9.114**
RVS v Secretary of State for Work and Pensions (ESA) [2019] UKUT 102 (AAC); [2019] 3 WLUK 697 ....9.34, 9.40
S (on behalf of S, deceased) v Secretary of State for Work and Pensions [2016] UKUT 485 (AAC) 1.461, **10.186**
SA v Secretary of State for Work and Pensions (ESA) [2013] UKUT 616 (AAC).........**9.401**
SA v Secretary of State for Work and Pensions (ESA) [2019] UKUT 118 (AAC).........9.60
SA v Secretary of State for Work and Pensions (PIP) [2015] UKUT 512 (AAC) **4.241**
SA v Secretary of State for Work and Pensions [2013] UKUT 436 (AAC) 1.1012
SAG v Department for Social Development (ESA) [2012] AACR 6 ....9.403
Sandhu v Secretary of State for Work and Pensions [2010] EWCA Civ 962; [2010] 6 WLUK 118 ....4.76
SB v Secretary of State for Work and Pensions (ESA) [2015] UKUT 88 (AAC).............**9.89**
SB v Secretary of State for Work and Pensions (PIP) [2016] UKUT 219 (AAC) 4.238
SB v Secretary of State for Work and Pensions (PIP) [2018] UKUT 122 (AAC) 4.248
SB v Secretary of State for Work and Pensions [2010] UKUT 219 (AAC) 1.1013
SB v Secretary of State for Work and Pensions [2014] UKUT 495 (AAC); [2015] AACR 15 ....1.1011
SC v Secretary of State for Work and Pensions (DLA) [2010] UKUT 76 (AAC)... 4.74, **4.91**
SC v Secretary of State for Work and Pensions (PIP) [2017] UKUT 317 (AAC).........4.238, 4.239
SD v Secretary of State for Work and Pensions (ESA) [2014] UKUT 240 (AAC) 9........9.82
SD v Secretary of State for Work and Pensions (ESA) [2016] UKUT 100 (AAC); [2016] AACR 35 .... 1.202, 4.235, 9.47, **9.80**
SD v Secretary of State for Work and Pensions (PIP) [2017] UKUT 310 (AAC)..........4.235
SE v Secretary of State for Work and Pensions (ESA) [2012] UKUT 469 (AAC) 9.401
Secretary of State for Social Security v Davies R(I) 2/01................................. 10.140, 10.164
Secretary of State for Social Security v Fairey. *See* Cockburn v Chief Adjudication Officer
Secretary of State for Social Security v Thomas (C-328/91); sub nom. Thomas v Chief Adjudication Officer (C328/91) EU:C:1993:117; [1993] Q.B. 747; [1993] 3 W.L.R. 581; [1993] 4 All E.R. 556; [1993] E.C.R. I-1247; [1993] 3 WLUK 443; [1993] 3 C.M.L.R. 880; [1993] I.C.R. 673; [1993] I.R.L.R. 292 ....1.188
Secretary of State for Work and Pensions v Adams [2003] EWCA Civ 796; [2003] 6 WLUK 462; R(G) 1/03...3.49

Secretary of State for Work and Pensions v AI (rule 17) (ESA) [2017] UKUT 346
(AAC)...9.413
Secretary of State for Work and Pensions v AM (PIP) [2015] UKUT 215 (AAC).........4.252
Secretary of State for Work and Pensions v AT (ESA) [2017] UKUT 338 (AAC) 9.417,
9.431
Secretary of State for Work and Pensions v Brade [2014] CSIH 39; 2014 S.C. 742;
2014 S.L.T. 680; 2014 S.C.L.R. 737; [2014] 5 WLUK 42; 2014 G.W.D. 16-303;
[2014] AACR 29 .... 9.105, 9.422, 9.423, 9.433
Secretary of State for Work and Pensions v Cattrell [2011] EWCA Civ 572; [2011]
AACR 35 ....**9.87**
Secretary of State for Work and Pensions v CO'C (ESA) [2011] UKUT 447 (AAC) 9.515
Secretary of State for Work and Pensions v CS (II) [2010] UKUT 198 (AAC); [2011]
AACR 5 ....10.141
Secretary of State for Work and Pensions v DA [2009] UKUT 214 (AAC) **4.22**
Secretary of State for Work and Pensions v DC (DLA) [2011] UKUT 235 (AAC).........4.96,
4.256
Secretary of State for Work and Pensions v Deane; sub nom. Deane v Secretary of
State for Work and Pensions [2010] EWCA Civ 699; [2011] 1 W.L.R. 743; [2011]
P.T.S.R. 289; [2010] 6 WLUK 537; [2010] E.L.R. 662; (2010) 107(27) L.S.G.
17; [2010] AACR 42.. 4.134, 4.135
Secretary of State for Work and Pensions v DM (DLA) [2010] UKUT 318 (AAC) 4.93,
4.93
Secretary of State for Work and Pensions v Doyle; sub nom. Doyle v Secretary of State
for Work and Pensions [2006] EWCA Civ 466; [2006] 4 WLUK 468; (2006)
103(19) L.S.G. 27; (2006) 156 N.L.J. 761; R(IB) 1/06 ....3.7, 3.30
Secretary of State for Work and Pensions v DT (PIP) [2017] UKUT 272 (AAC) 4.240
Secretary of State for Work and Pensions v EK (deceased) (II) [2016] UKUT 458
(AAC)..10.195
Secretary of State for Work and Pensions v ER (II) [2012] UKUT 204 (AAC)........... **10.195**
Secretary of State for Work and Pensions v G (VDP) [2015] UKUT 321 (AAC); [2017]
AACR 20 ....**1.3**, 1.9, **1.13, 1.15**, 1.17, **1.20**
Secretary of State for Work and Pensions v G [2017] EWCA Civ 61; [2017] 1 W.L.R.
1956; [2017] 2 WLUK 259; (2017) 154 B.M.L.R. 100... 1.3
Secretary of State for Work and Pensions v Garland [2014] EWCA Civ 1550; [2014]
12 WLUK 122; [2015] 1 C.M.L.R. 56..1.288
Secretary of State for Work and Pensions v GM (PIP) [2017] UKUT 268 (AAC) 4.236
Secretary of State for Work and Pensions v GS (WB) [2015] UKUT 33 (AAC) **1.648**
Secretary of State for Work and Pensions v HY and LO (RP) [2017] UKUT 303
(AAC)...1.680
Secretary of State for Work and Pensions v IV (PIP) [2016] UKUT 420 (AAC)..........4.250,
4.257
Secretary of State for Work and Pensions v JG (RP) [2013] UKUT 300 (AAC) 1.288
Secretary of State for Work and Pensions v JL (ESA) [2018] UKUT 291 (AAC)..........4.427
Secretary of State for Work and Pensions v JL [2011] UKUT 293; [2012] AACR 14.....**4.22**,
4.58
Secretary of State for Work and Pensions v JS [2008] UKUT 35 (AAC) 10.183
Secretary of State for Work and Pensions v KJ (PIP) [2017] UKUT 358 (AAC)...........4.240
Secretary of State for Work and Pensions v KM [2009] UKUT 85 (AAC) 3.23
Secretary of State for Work and Pensions v KS (PIP) [2018] UKUT 102 (AAC).........4.183,
4.241, 4.244
Secretary of State for Work and Pensions v LB (PIP) [2016] UKUT 530 (AAC).........4.176,
4.231, **4.234**, 4.242, **4.254**
Secretary of State for Work and Pensions v LC (ESA) [2014] UKUT 268 (AAC) 9.423
Secretary of State for Work and Pensions v LH (ESA) [2017] UKUT 475 (AAC) 9.411
Secretary of State for Work and Pensions v LT [2012] UKUT 282 (AAC) 1.157, 1.195,
4.211
Secretary of State for Work and Pensions v M; sub nom. Secretary of State for Work
and Pensions v MMcK [2017] CSIH 57; 2018 S.C. 1; 2017 S.L.T. 1045; [2017]
8 WLUK 269; 2017 G.W.D. 29-468; [2017] AACR 38 ....4.251
Secretary of State for Work and Pensions v MC (DLA) [2019] UKUT 84 (AAC) 1.195
Secretary of State for Work and Pensions v MG (DLA) [2012] UKUT 429 (AAC) .. **4.92**, 4.94
Secretary of State for Work and Pensions v MMcK. *See* Secretary of State for Work
and Pensions v M

Secretary of State for Work and Pensions v MN (BB) [2018] UKUT 68 (AAC) 1.1010, 1.1013, 3.157

Secretary of State for Work and Pensions v MS (DLA) [2013] UKUT 267 (AAC) 4.87

Secretary of State for Work and Pensions v NC (ESA) [2013] UKUT 477 (AAC) **9.12**

Secretary of State for Work and Pensions v Nelligan; sub nom. Secretary of State for Work and Pensions v Nelligan [2003] EWCA Civ 555; [2004] 1 W.L.R. 894; [2003] 4 All E.R. 171; [2003] 4 WLUK 464; (2003) 100(26) L.S.G. 38; (2003) 153 N.L.J. 667; R(P) 2/03..1.131

Secretary of State for Work and Pensions v NF (PIP) [2017] UKUT 480 (AAC) 4.257

Secretary of State for Work and Pensions v NH (II) [2010] UKUT 84 (AAC)..1.624, **10.243**

Secretary of State for Work and Pensions v NH (PIP) [2017] UKUT 258 (AAC)........4.183, 4.246

Secretary of State for Work and Pensions v PA [2010] UKUT 401 (AAC) 1.258

Secretary of State for Work and Pensions v PD (ESA) [2014] UKUT 549 (AAC); [2015] AACR 24 ....**9.533**

Secretary of State for Work and Pensions v Pridding. *See* Pridding v Secretary of State for Work and Pensions

Secretary of State for Work and Pensions v PT (ESA) [2011] UKUT 317 (AAC); [2012] AACR 17 ....1.731, **1.740**, 9.347

Secretary of State for Work and Pensions v PW [2011] UKUT 3 (AAC) **4.135**

Secretary of State for Work and Pensions v Queen, The (on the application of MM and DM). *See* MM v Secretary of State for Work and Pensions

Secretary of State for Work and Pensions v RD (II) [2018] UKUT 481 (AAC) 1.606

Secretary of State for Work and Pensions v RM [2014] UKUT 42 (AAC).....................9.12

Secretary of State for Work and Pensions v Robertson [2015] CSIH 82; 2016 S.C. 725; 2016 S.L.T. 52; 2016 S.C.L.R. 522; [2015] 11 WLUK 611; 2016 G.W.D. 1-1 ....1.254, 4.87

Secretary of State for Work and Pensions v Scullion [2010] EWCA Civ 310; [2010] 3 WLUK 604; (2010) 107(14) L.S.G. 18; [2015] AACR 29 .... 1.338, 1.339, 1.345, **1.347**

Secretary of State for Work and Pensions v SH (PIP) [2017] UKUT 301 (AAC)..........4.250

Secretary of State for Work and Pensions v SK [2014] UKUT 12 (AAC) 3.30

Secretary of State for Work and Pensions v Slavin [2011] EWCA Civ 1515; [2012] P.T.S.R. 692; [2011] 12 WLUK 320; (2012) 15 C.C.L. Rep. 354; [2012] AACR 30 ....**4.56**

Secretary of State for Work and Pensions v SS (PIP) [2015] UKUT 240 (AAC) **4.257**

Secretary of State for Work and Pensions v TG (DLA) [2019] UKUT 86 (AAC) 1.195

Secretary of State for Work and Pensions v Tolley (C-430/15); sub nom. Tolley v Secretary of State for Work and Pensions (C-430/15) EU:C:2017:74; EU:C:2017:74; [2017] 1 W.L.R. 1261; [2017] 2 WLUK 26; [2017] AACR 40.....................1.157, 1.195, 4.211

Secretary of State for Work and Pensions v Tolley (Deceased) [2015] UKSC 55; [2016] 1 All E.R. 40; [2015] 7 WLUK 917; [2016] 1 C.M.L.R. 23 ....1.195

Secretary of State for Work and Pensions v TR (DLA) [2013] UKUT 622 (AAC) **4.55**

Secretary of State for Work and Pensions v Whalley; Whalley v Secretary of State for Work and Pensions [2003] EWCA Civ 166; [2003] 2 WLUK 433; *Times*, 3 March 2003; R(I) 2/03... 1.600, 1.601, 10.71, 10.72

Secretary of State for Work and Pensions v Yates [2009] EWCA Civ 479; [2010] P.T.S.R. 493; [2009] 6 WLUK 231; [2009] Pens. L.R. 217 ....**3.124**

Secretary of State for Work and Pensions v ZC [2011] UKUT 2 (AAC); [2011] AACR 28 ....**4.135**

Secretary of State v Scully R(S) 5/93 ....1.492

SF v Secretary of State for Work and Pensions (PIP) [2016] UKUT 481 (AAC) **4.173**

SF v Secretary of State for Work and Pensions (PIP) [2016] UKUT 543 (AAC) 4.251

SF v Secretary of State for Work and Pensions [2010] UKUT 78 (AAC) **1.204**, 1.245

SF v Secretary of State for Work and Pensions and HM Revenue and Customs (HRP) [2013] UKUT 175 (AAC) **2.50**

SG v Secretary of State for Work and Pensions (ESA) [2018] UKUT 34 (AAC) 9.407

SH v Secretary of State for Work and Pensions (ESA) [2014] UKUT 574 (AAC) **9.58**, 9.61

SH v Secretary of State for Work and Pensions (PIP) [2018] UKUT 251 (AAC).........4.176, 4.245

Shackell v United Kingdom (45851/99) unreported 27 April 2000 ECtHR.... 1.1008, 1.1009

Shephard, Re; sub nom. George v Thyer [1904] 1 Ch. 456; [1904] 2 WLUK 38 Ch D 1.1010

SI v Secretary of State for Work and Pensions (ESA) [2013] UKUT 453 (AAC) **9.66**
SI v Secretary of State for Work and Pensions (ESA) [2014] UKUT 308 (AAC); [2015]
    AACR 5 ....**9.407**
SJ v Secretary of State for Work and Pensions (ESA) [2015] UKUT 180 (AAC) ...9.65, 9.67
SJ v Secretary of State for Work and Pensions [2009] UKUT 37 (AAC) **4.140**
SJ v Secretary of State for Work and Pensions [2014] UKUT 222 (AAC)......................1.218
SK v Secretary of State for Work and Pensions (ESA) [2018] UKUT 267 (AAC)........9.535
SK v Secretary of State for Work and Pensions [2009] UKUT 121 (AAC) 9.347
SL v Secretary of State for Work and Pensions (ESA) [2016] UKUT 170 (AAC) 9.113
SL v Secretary of State for Work and Pensions (PIP) [2016] UKUT 147 (AAC) 4.251
SM v Advocate General for Scotland. *See* M's Guardian v Advocate General for Scotland
SM v Secretary of State for Work and Pensions (CA) [2016] UKUT 406 (AAC)..........4.135
SM v Secretary of State for Work and Pensions (ESA) [2014] UKUT 241 (AAC)..........9.84
SM v Secretary of State for Work and Pensions (ESA) [2015] UKUT 617 (AAC)........**9.411**
SM v Secretary of State for Work and Pensions (PIP) [2018] UKUT 314 (AAC) 4.173
Smith v Stages [1989] A.C. 928; [1989] 2 W.L.R. 529; [1989] 1 All E.R. 833; [1989]
    2 WLUK 296; [1989] I.C.R. 272; [1989] I.R.L.R. 177; (1989) 86(15) L.S.G. 42;
    (1989) 139 N.L.J. 291; (1989) 133 S.J. 324 HL; R(I) 8/94..............1.352, 1.354, 1.355,
                                                                            1.361, **1.379**
SP v Secretary of State for Work and Pensions (ESA) [2014] UKUT 10 (AAC) 9.88
SP v Secretary of State for Work and Pensions (ESA) [2014] UKUT 278 (AAC) 9.88
SP v Secretary of State for Work and Pensions (ESA) [2014] UKUT 522 (AAC)....9.82, **9.86**
SP v Secretary of State for Work and Pensions (ESA) [2018] UKUT 205 (AAC)....9.89, 9.90
SP v Secretary of State for Work and Pensions (PIP) [2016] UKUT 190 (AAC); [2016]
    AACR 43 ....**4.245**
SP v Secretary of State for Work and Pensions [2012] UKUT 156 (AAC)....................1.680
SP v Secretary of State for Work and Pensions (RP) [2013] UKUT 156 (AAC) 1.680
SR v Secretary of State for Work and Pensions [2009] UKUT 39 (AAC) 10.161
SS v Secretary of State for Work and Pensions (ESA) [2015] UKUT 101 (AAC) 9.86,
                                                                                    9.88, 9.89
SSWP v PT (ESA) [2011] UKUT 317 (AAC) 1.731
ST and GF v Secretary of State for Work and Pensions (ESA) [2014] UKUT 547
    (AAC); [2015] AACR 23 ....**9.401, 9.416**
St Helens Colliery Co Ltd v Hewitson [1924] A.C. 59; [1923] 11 WLUK 81 HL.........1.355
ST v Secretary of State for Work and Pensions (ESA) [2012] UKUT 469 (AAC).........9.401
Stewart v Secretary of State for Work and Pensions (C–503/09) EU:C:2011:500;
    [2012] P.T.S.R. 1; [2011] 7 WLUK 629; [2012] 1 C.M.L.R. 13; [2012] C.E.C.
    479; [2012] AACR 8.. 4.149, 4.209
Stringfellow Restaurants Ltd v Quashie. *See* Quashie v Stringfellow Restaurants Ltd
Swan v Secretary of State for Work and Pensions (C3/2016/0431) unreported..............1.648
SY v Secretary of State for Work and Pensions (ESA) [2016] UKUT 378 (AAC).........9.415
SY v Secretary of State for Work and Pensions (PIP) [2017] UKUT 363 (AAC) 4.187
TA v Secretary of State for Work and Pensions (II) [2010] UKUT 101 (AAC)..............1.625
TA v Secretary of State for Work and Pensions (II) [2014] UKUT 127 (AAC)..............1.623
TB v Secretary of State for Work and Pensions (ESA) [2013] UKUT 408 (AAC) 9.407
TC v Secretary of State for Work and Pensions (No.2) (PIP) [2018] UKUT 286
    (AAC)..4.187
TC v Secretary of State for Work and Pensions (PIP) [2016] UKUT 550 (AAC) 4.249
TF v Secretary of State for Work and Pensions (PIP) [2015] UKUT 661 (AAC)..........4.259
TH v Secretary of State for Work and Pensions (PIP) [2017] UKUT 231 (AAC) 4.173,
                                                                                    4.191
Thlimmenos v Greece (34369/97) (2001) 31 E.H.R.R. 15; 9 B.H.R.C. 12 ECtHR 4.87
Timbrell v Secretary of State for Work and Pensions [2010] EWCA Civ 701; [2010]
    6 WLUK 445; [2010] 3 C.M.L.R. 42; [2010] Eu. L.R. 739; [2010] I.C.R. 1369;
    [2011] 1 F.L.R. 332; [2010] Pens. L.R. 245; [2010] Fam. Law 921; (2010)
    107(27) L.S.G. 15; [2011] AACR 13 ....1.680
TM v Secretary of State for Work and Pensions (ESA) [2018] UKUT 9 (AAC) 9.48,
                                                                                9.417, 9.421
TO'B v Secretary of State for Work and Pensions (ESA) [2011] UKUT 461 (AAC).....9.410
Tolley v SSWP. *See* Secretary of State for Work and Pensions v Tolley
TR v Secretary of State for Work and Pensions (PIP) [2015] UKUT 626 (AAC); [2016]
    AACR 23 .... 4.176, **4.183**
TW v Secretary of State for Work and Pensions (PIP) [2017] UKUT 25 (AAC) 4.265

TW v Secretary of State for Work and Pensions [2012] UKUT 152 (AAC)..................9.343
V (A Child) v Secretary of State for Social Security unreported 23 February 2001 CA ..1.261
Vandyk v Minister of Pensions and National Insurance [1955] 1 Q.B. 29; [1954] 3
    W.L.R. 342; [1954] 2 All E.R. 723; (1954) 98 S.J. 541 QBD 1.39
Vandyk v Fender; sub nom. Vandyke v Fender and Reddington Foundries [1970] 2
    Q.B. 292; [1970] 2 W.L.R. 929; [1970] 2 All E.R. 335; [1970] 1 Lloyd's Rep. 320;
    [1970] 3 WLUK 14; [1970] R.T.R. 236; 8 K.I.R. 854; (1970) 114 S.J. 205 CA
    (Civ Div) **1.352**, 1.355
VH v Secretary of State for Work and Pensions (ESA) [2018] UKUT 290 (AAC) 9.414,
                                                                                           9.419
VT v Secretary of State for Work and Pensions (ESA) [2016] UKUT 241 (AAC) 9.46
W Da-C v Secretary of State for Work and Pensions (ESA) [2015] UKUT 158 (AAC)...**9.53**
Wallis v Bristol Water Plc [2009] EWHC 3432 (Admin); [2010] P.T.S.R. 1986; [2009]
    12 WLUK 309; [2010] Env. L.R. 16 DC **4.176**
WC v Secretary of State for Work and Pensions (ESA) [2014] UKUT 363 ....**9.425**
WC v Secretary of State for Work and Pensions (ESA) [2015] UKUT 304 (AAC);
    [2016] AACR 1 ....9.433
Welsh v Glasgow Coal. *See* Glasgow Coal Co Ltd v Welsh
Westgate v Secretary of State for Work and Pensions [2006] EWCA Civ 725; [2006] 4
    WLUK 72; R(I) 1/06 ....**10.165**
Whalley v Secretary of State for Work and Pensions. *See* Secretary of State for Work
    and Pensions v Whalley
White v W&T Avery Ltd, 1916 S.C. 209; 1915 2 S.L.T. 374; [1915] 12 WLUK 12 IH
    (1 Div) 1.352
Woodling v Secretary of State for Social Services; sub nom. Woodling, Re [1984] 1
    W.L.R. 348; [1984] 1 All E.R. 593; [1984] 2 WLUK 102; (1984) 81 L.S.G. 740;
    (1984) 134 N.L.J. 236; (1984) 128 S.J. 130 HL; R(A) 2/80 ....1.208, 1.216, 1.222
Worley v Secretary of State for Work and Pensions [2019] EWCA Civ 15; [2019] 1
    WLUK 280 ....4.265
Wright-Turner [2001] C.A.R.C. 3567 (CA of NI); R1/02 CA (NI)............................4.134
WT v Secretary of State for Work and Pensions (ESA) [2013] UKUT 556 (AAC) **9.105,
                                                                                       9.425, 9.433**
WT v Secretary of State for Work and Pensions (ESA) [2016] UKUT 472 (AAC);
    [2017] AACR 16 ....9.407
XT v Secretary of State for Work and Pensions (ESA) [2015] UKUT 581 (AAC) 9.113
YA and SA v Secretary of State for Work and Pensions (ESA) [2017] UKUT 80
    (AAC) **9.115**, 9.116
YD v Secretary of State for Work and Pensions (IB) [2010] UKUT 290 (AAC) 9.406
YM v Secretary of State for Work and Pensions (PIP) [2018] UKUT 16 (AAC)...........4.173
Young and Woods v West [1980] I.R.L.R. 201 CA (Civ Div) 1.40
Young v Bristol Aeroplane Co Ltd [1944] K.B. 718; [1944] 2 All E.R. 293; (1945) 78
    Ll. L. Rep. 6; [1944] 7 WLUK 50 CA..4.251
YR v Secretary of State for Work and Pensions [2014] UKUT 80 (AAC)............ 1.254, 4.87
YW v Secretary of State for Work and Pensions (PIP) [2017] UKUT 42 (AAC)..........**4.171**
ZI v Secretary of State for Work and Pensions (PIP) [2016] UKUT 572 (AAC); [2018]
    AACR 1 ....4.240

TABLE OF SOCIAL SECURITY COMMISSIONERS' DECISIONS

C1/95 (IB) 9.403, 9.405
C46/97 (IB) 9.406
C19/98 (DLA) 1.261
C1/04–05 (REA) 10.72
C5/00–01 (IB).................................9.77
C1/06–07(II) **1.347**
C1/07–08 (IB)................................9.60
C11/03–04 (IB)..............................9.61
C38/03–04..9.47
CA/6/72..1.207
CA/96/84 ....1.204
CA/137/1984 .... 1.200, 4.241
CA/147/84...........................1.228, 1.233
CA/1140/85 ....1.228
CA/281/89 ....1.228
CA/780/91 ....1.216
CA/92/92 ....1.242
CA/233/95 ....1.233
CA/1474/97 ....1.163
CA/2985/97.......................................4.59
CA/3800/2006 ....4.22
CA/3943/2006 ....1.204
CA/2574/2007 .... 1.155, 1.211
CDLA/58/93...................................1.221
CDLA/20/94...................................1.227
CDLA/42/94.............1.231, 1.258, 1.261
CDLA/52/94....................... 1.193, 1.259
CDLA/156/1994 ....4.74
CDLA/267/94.................................1.205
CDLA/393/94....................................4.91
CDLA/608/94....................................4.78
CDLA/805/94....................................4.78
CDLA/899/1994 .... 1.204, **1.233**
CDLA/2267/95 .... 1.223, 4.239
CDLA/2293/95 ....1.224
CDLA/2364/95 ....1.261
CDLA/3711/95 ....1.212
CDLA/7980/95 .... 4.20, 4.54
CDLA/8167/95 ....1.212
CDLA/8462/95 ....4.81
CDLA/11099/95 .... 4.20, 4.54
CDLA/12150/1996 .... 1.228, 1.229
CDLA/12381/96 ....1.212
CDLA/15884/96 ....1.216
CDLA/16129/96 ....1.206
CDLA/16668/96 ....1.216
CDLA/16996/96 .... 1.205, 1.206
CDLA/17189/96 ....1.216
CDLA/17329/96 ....1.226
CDLA/17611/1996 ....4.93
CDLA/835/97...................................1.261
CDLA/1148/97 ....1.215

CDLA/1389/97 .... 4.78, 4.82
CDLA/1678/97....................................4.91
CDLA/2457/97................................1.222
CDLA/3925/97....................................4.83
CDLA/5153/97....................................4.91
CDLA/5183/1997 ....4.74
CDLA/5494/1997 ....4.85
CDLA/5183/97....................................4.74
CDLA/717/98......................................4.78
CDLA/1465/98....................................4.59
CDLA/2054/98......................... 4.92, **4.93**
CDLA/5216/1998 ....1.206
CDLA/433/99..................................1.194
CDLA/1361/99....................................4.83
CDLA/1463/99.................................1.220
CDLA/2973/1999 ....4.85
CDLA/3433/1999 ....1.218
CDLA/4388/1999 ....4.78
CDLA/5686/1999 ....1.224
CDLA/7090/1999 ....4.88
CDLA/754/2000 .... 1.280, 4.113
CDLA/770/2000 ....1.224
CDLA/778/2000 ....1.202
CDLA/948/2000 ....4.72
CDLA/1534/00................................1.218
CDLA/2878/2000 ....1.245
CDLA/4486/2000 ....4.74
CDLA/97/2001 ....4.76
CDLA/944/2001 ....9.47
CDLA/1000/2001 ....1.193
CDLA/5106/2001 ....4.22
CDLA/1338/02....................................4.98
CDLA/3542/2002 ....1.202
CDLA/3737/2002 .... 1.199, 1.240
CDLA/997/2003 ....1.235
CDLA/2751/2003 ....3.59
CDLA/3323/2003 ....4.72
CDLA/3781/2003 ....1.261
CDLA/4565/2003 ....4.81
CDLA/829/2004 ....1.243
CDLA/0902/2004 .... 1.203, 4.82
CDLA/1471/2004 .... 1.227, 4.240
CDLA/1721/2004 ....1.243
CDLA/2089/2004 ....3.112
CDLA/2367/2004 ....1.226
CDLA/2495/2004 .... 1.205, 1.246
CDLA/2974/2004 .... 1.209, 1.214
CDLA/3525/2004 ....1.242
CDLA/3779/2004 ....1.243
CDLA/3831/2004 ....1.257
CDLA/4100/2004 ....1.242
CDLA/4333/2004 .... 1.215, 4.66

CDLA/4475/2004 ....1.200
CDLA/205/2005 ....1.220
CDLA/301/05 .... 1.280, 4.109
CDLA/313/2005 ....4.83
CDLA/1534/2005 ....4.237
CDLA/1572/2005 ....1.227
CDLA/2142/2005 ....1.268
CDLA/2333/2005 ....1.218
CDLA/3376/2005 ....1.213
CDLA/3420/2005 ....4.74
CDLA/3941/2005 ....4.85
CDLA/618/2006 ....1.215
CDLA/1639/2006 .... 1.269, 4.71
CDLA/2470/2006 .... 4.92, 4.93, 4.94
CDLA/2747/2006 ....1.203
CDLA/2955/2006 ....4.94
CDLA/3461/2006 ....1.244
CDLA/3896/2006 ....4.83
CDLA/3898/2006 ....4.84
CDLA/4351/2006 .... 1.225, 4.239
CDLA/304/07 ....1.204
CDLA/2084/2007 ....1.193
CDLA/2423/2007 ....4.77
CDLA/3292/2007 ....4.82
CDLA/3839/2007 ....4.81
CDLA/4051/2007 ....1.225
CDLA/496/2008 ....1.252, 1.268, 1.269
CDLA/1525/2008 ....4.74
CDLA/1984/2008 ....1.227
CDLA/2195/2008 ....4.78
CDLA/2955/2008 ....4.94
CDLA/509/2009 ....4.55
CDLA/2714/2009 ....4.93
CDLA/2167/2010 .... 4.92, 4.93, 4.94
CDLA/2617/2010 ....**4.93**
CDLA/1498/2011 ....**4.94**
CFG/4622/03 ....1.1018
CFP/4349/2004 ....1.116
CFP/2688/2004 ....1.1017
CG/006/1990 .... 1.179, 4.130
CG/012/1991 .... 1.179, 4.130
CG/058/92 ....1.181
CG/068/1993 ....1.180
CG/5425/95 ....1.188
CG/75/96 ....1.1016
CG/6329/1997 ....4.139
CG/1822/1998 ....1.1013
CG/4024/2001 ....3.26
CG/4172/2001 .... 3.13, 3.16
CG/173/2002 ....2.50
CG/2309/2002 ....1.495
CG/734/2003 ....4.139
CG/2611/2003 ....3.157
CG/2902/2003 ....2.13
CG/4941/2003 ....3.20
CG/3189/2004 ....4.134
CG/4018/2005 ....4.139
CG/1752/2006 ....3.34
CG/4139/2006 ....3.5
CG/0607/2008 .... 3.21, 4.140
CG/0645/2008 ....3.23
CI/129/49 ....1.349
CI/257/49 ....1.344

CI/280/49 .... 1.385, 1.386
CI/285/49 ....10.69
CI/83/50 ....1.344
CI/210/50 ....1.376
CI/228/50 ....1.359
CI/443/50 (KL) 1.611
CI/444/50 (KL) 1.611
CI/445/50 (KL) 1.611
CI/446/50 (KL) 1.611
CI/447/50 (KL) 1.611
CI/448/50 (KL) 1.611
CI/789/70 ....1.341
CI/7/71 .... 1.340, 1.341
CI/71/1987 ....1.344
CI/72/1987 ....1.343
CI/114/1987 ....1.357
CI/207/1987 ....1.363
CI/37/1988 ....10.150
CI/110/1988 ....1.379
CI/163/1988 ....1.379
CI/246/1988 ....10.150
CI/276/1988 ....10.109
CI/387/1988 ....1.351
CI/203/1989 .... 10.226, 10.230
CI/308/1989 .... 10.151, 10.193
CI/309/1989 ....10.154
CI/365/89 ....1.356
CI/373/89 ....10.165
CI/550/89 ....10.151
CI/105/1990 .... 1.357, 1.361
CI/175/90 .... 10.154, 10.193
CI/16/91 .... 10.109, 10.169
CI/22/91 .... 10.140, 10.165
CI/209/1991 ....1.623
CI/226/91 ....10.148
CI/245/1991 ....10.148
CI/43/92 ....10.154
CI/383/92 ....10.193
CI/554/1992 ....1.340, 1.343, 1.344
CI/17/93 ....10.149
CI/34/93 ....10.22
CI/141/93 ....10.165
CI/156/1993 ....1.343
CI/278/1993 ....1.342
CI/636/93 .... 1.333, 1.403, 10.28, 10.138
CI/73/94 ....10.193
CI/160/94 ....10.167
CI/227/94 ....10.167
CI/289/1994 ....1.351
CI/319/94 ....10.163
CI/362/94 ....10.163
CI/402/1994 ....1.415
CI/420/94 ....1.397, 1.415, 1.424
CI/514/94 ....10.167
CI/540/1994 ....10.150
CI/737/1994 .... 1.343, 1.344
CI/56/95 .... 10.169, 10.179
CI/136/95 ....10.167
CI/268/95 ....10.143
CI/286/95 .... 10.109, 10.113,
                                              10.125, 10.143
CI/474/95 ....10.167
CI/808/95 .... 10.140, 10.150

CI/1195/1995...................... 1.343, 1.344
CI/2879/1995................................10.153
CI/4987/1995................................10.193
CI/5249/95 .... 1.337, 1.340
CI/6872/95 ....1.397
CI/11015/1995................................1.623
CI/15408/1995..............................10.167
CI/12311/1996................................1.415
CI/13232/1996..............................10.188
CI/13238/1996.................... 10.150, 10.151
CI/13664/96 ....10.139
CI/14532/1996..............................10.162
CI/15589/1996............1.333, 1.338, 1.403,
                           10.28, 10.138
CI/15803/1996................................1.606
CI/16202/96 ....10.243
CI/17220/1996................................10.70
CI/3284/97 ....10.164
CI/3924/1997................................10.163
CI/5009/97 ....10.168
CI/105/1998 ....1.341, 1.343, 1.347
CI/110/1998 ....1.355
CI/1446/98 ....10.61
CI/1589/1998................................1.611
CI/2414/98 ....1.340, 1.341, 1.343
CI/1307/1999..............1.333, 1.403, 10.28,
                                 10.138
CI/3370/1999................................1.344
CI/3521/1999................................1.578
CI/4478/1999................................1.603
CI/4567/1999.........10.145, 10.146, 10.147
CI/5972/99 ....10.63
CI/6027/1999...................... 10.20, 10.70
CI/6207/1999................................1.600
CI/7507/1999...................... 1.446, 1.449
CI/499/2000 ....1.574, 1.575, 1.576
CI/2012/2000.................... 10.146, 10.147
CI/3038/2000................................1.606
CI/3261/2000................................10.140
CI/226/2001 ....10.72
CI/349/2001 ....10.142
CI/1052/2001................................1.604
CI.1720/2001................................10.162
CI/1802/2001.................... 1.574, 1.575
CI/2517/01 ....10.243
CI/2531/2001...................... 1.601, 10.71
CI/2553/2001...............1.574, 1.576, 10.26
CI/3596/2001.................... 10.161, 10.163
CI/4708/2001...............1.341, 1.342, 1.347
CI/4874/2001................................10.161
CI/4940/01 ....1.601
CI/1/2002 ....10.147
CI/126/2002 ....10.198
CI/1714/2002................................1.342
CI/1763/2002................................10.162
CI/1807/2002................................10.161
CI/2286/2002................................10.155
CI/2393/02 ....10.193
CI/2543/2002................................10.193
CI/2668/2002................................10.140
CI/2746/2002................................10.22
CI/3379/2002................................1.606
CI/3511/2002...............1.341, 1.344, 1.347

CI/5029/2002...................... 10.148, 10.158
CI/5092/2002................................1.574
CI/5138/2002................................1.599
CI/5270/2002................................10.72
CI/5271/2002................................10.72
CI/5331/2002................................10.155
CI/3178/2003........................... 1.599, 1.600
CI/3463/2003................................10.72
CI/3625/2003................................10.178
CI/3178/2003........................... 1.613, 1.614
CI/3758/2003........................... 1.574, 1.576
CI/3759/2003........................... 1.574, 1.576
CI/4249/2003................................1.601
CI/207/2004 ....10.165
CI/1098/2004................................1.361
CI/1160/2004................................10.200
CI/1884/2004...................... 10.140, 10.184
CI/2683/2004...................... 10.198, 10.199
CI/3224/04 ....10.243
CI/3225/2004................................10.240
CI/3565/2004................................10.194
CI/3600/2004................................1.343
CI/0293/2005................................1.446
CI/535/2005 ....10.162
CI/564/2005 .... 10.193, 10.194
CI/2930/2005....................... 1.398, 10.20
CI/3696/2005................................1.341
CI/3729/2005................................10.193
CI/142/2006 ....1.341
CI/421/2006 ....10.162
CI/954/2006 ....1.402
CI/2842/2006...................... 1.338, 1.347
CI/3384/2006................................10.20
CI/3745/2006.........10.20, 10.144, 10.166
CI/732/2007 ....1.338
CI/1654/2008...................... 1.353, 1.390
CI/1961/2008................................10.168
CI/1737/2015................................10.186
CIB/1959/1977 ....9.94
CIB/2811/1995 ....9.409
CIB/3968/1996 ....9.401
CIB/13039/1996 ....9.401
CIB/13161/96 .... 9.403, 9.405
CIB/13508/96 .... 9.403, 9.405
CIB/14202/1996 .... 9.406, 9.416
CIB/14332/96 ....9.414
CIB/14442/96 ....9.406
CIB/14499/1996 ....9.411, 9.413, 9.414
CIB/14587/1996 ....9.405
CIB/14656/96 ....9.131
CIB/15482/1996 ....9.71
CIB/15663/1996 ....9.401
CIB/16572/96 ....9.406
CIB/17257/1996 ....9.401
CIB/309/1997 ....9.401
CIB/911/1997 ....9.405
CIB/969/97 ....9.60
CIB/1959/1997 ....9.93, 9.94, 9.347
CIB/2198/1997 .... 9.93, 9.94, 9.347
CIB/5298/1997 ....9.131
CIB/5361/1997 ....9.402
CIB/5797/1997 ....9.402
CIB/6244/1997 .... 9.71, 9.405

CIB/243/1998 ....9.71
CIB/3512/1998 .... 9.57, 9.60, 9.61
CIB/3620/1998 ....9.401
CIB/4497/1998 ....9.406
CIB/2645/99 .... 9.60, 9.61
CIB/4306/1999 ....9.411
CIB/5586/1999 ....9.401
CIB/6777/1999 ....9.131
CIB/1031/2000 .... 9.343, 9.347
CIB/2161/2000 ....1.495
CIB/2338/00 ....1.495
CIB/2620/2000 ....9.405
CIB/849/2001 ....9.60
CIB/1956/2001 ....3.116
CIB/2011/2001 .... 9.60, 9.61
CIB/2308/2001 ....9.401
CIB/2858/2001 ....9.202
CIB/2859/2001 ....9.202
CIB/2864/2001 ....9.202
CIB/2913/2001 ....9.401
CIB/4506/01 ....9.76
CIB/21/2002 ....9.401
CIB/3507/2002 ....9.132
CIB/3519/2002 ....9.81
CIB/3645/2002 ....1.439
CIB/3734/2002 .... 1.495, 1.502
CIB/4512/2002 ....9.60
CIB/4841/2002 ....9.46
CIB/399/2003 ....9.71
CIB/1381/2003 ....9.60
CIB/3074/2003 ....9.401
CIB/3106/2003 .... 9.343, 9.347
CIB/4684/2003 ....9.132
CIB/26/2004 ....9.47
CIB/155/2004 ....9.76
CIB/2767/2004 ....9.81
CIB/3327/2004 .... 1.493, 1.494, 2.5, 2.7,
                2.11, 2.13, 2.15, 2.17, 2.19,
                2.21, 2.24, 2.26, 2.33, 2.35,
                             2.37, 2.39, 2.41
CIB/3589/2004 ....9.402
CIB/4012/2004 .... 9.58, 9.61
CIB/476/2005 ....9.401
CIB/511/2005 ....9.401
CIB/0664/2005 ....9.401
CIB/1410/2005 ....9.24
CIB/1522/2005 ....9.401
CIB/1602/2006 ....1.493, 1.494, 2.5,
                2.7, 2.11, 2.13, 2.15, 2.17,
                2.19, 2.21, 2.22, 2.24, 2.26,
                2.33, 2.35, 2.37, 2.39,
                                       2.41
CIB/2248/2006 ....1.680
CIB/2445/2006 ....2.24
CIB/143/2007 ....9.82
CIB/360/2007 ....9.83
CIB/1296/2007 ....9.47
CIB/2576/2007 ....9.60
CIB/3950/2007 ....9.401
CIB/4232/2007 ....9.401
CIB/1006/2008 ....9.401
CIS/17020/1996 ....3.34
CJSA/2028/2000 ....9.480

CM/125/1983 ....4.79
CM/39/84 ....4.78
CM/23/1985 ....4.85
CM/186/1985 ....4.80
CM/47/86 ....4.78
CM/145/88 ....4.78
CM/98/1989 ....4.81
CM/364/92 ....4.79
CM/158/94 ....4.85
CP/068/1989 ....3.59
CP/037/1991 ....6.94
CP/14276/1996 ....1.138
CP/3017/2004 .... 3.23, 3.59
CP/3108/2004 ....1.1014
CP/4062/2004 ....1.1012
CP/271/2005 ....1.131
CP/3638/2006 ....3.124
CP/4017/2006 ....2.50
CP/4205/2006 ....1.495
CP/98/2007 ....1.694
CP/1792/2007 .... 1.494, 2.5
CP/891/2008 ....1.1012
CPIP/1861/2015 ....4.251
CS/58/49 ....3.44
CS/65/49 ....3.150
CS/221/49 ....9.46
CS/317/1949 (KL) 3.116
CS/01/1971 ....3.116
CS/02/1976 ....1.439
CS/5/76 ....3.113
CS/1/81 ....9.46
CS/7/82 ....9.46
CS/57/82 ....9.46
CS/130/1987 ....3.44
CS/229/1988 ....3.45
CS/299/1988 ....3.44
CS/002/1990 ....9.362
CS/207/1990 ....3.112
CS/202/1991 ....3.152
CS/061/1992 ....3.115
CS/143/1993 ....3.117
CS/7934/95 ....9.202
CSA/68/89 ....1.251
CSA/164/2004 ....4.22
CSA/469/2005 ....4.22
CSA/694/2007 ....1.213
CSDLA/29/94 ....1.221
CSDLA/252/94 ....4.78
CSDLA/160/95 ....1.216
CSDLA/281/1996 ....1.212
CSDLA/265/97 .... 4.72, 4.74
CSDLA/314/97 .... 1.206, 1.212
CSDLA/867/1997 .... 1.209, 1.231
CSDLA/24/1998 ....1.229
CSDLA/678/99 ....4.82
CSDLA/832/1999 ....1.209
CSDLA/388/2000 .... 1.280, 4.109
CSDLA/590/2000 .... 1.228, 1.230
CSDLA/860/2000 ....1.209
CSDLA/552/2001 ....1.241, 1.243, 9.47
CSDLA/590/00 ....1.228
CSDLA/1282/01 ....4.54
CSDLA/12/2003 .... 1.261, 1.268

CSDLA/91/2003 .... 1.266
CSDLA/854/2003 .... 1.227
CSDLA/430/2004 .... 4.96
CSDLA/725/2004 .... 1.227
CSDLA/399/2005 .... 4.74
CSDLA/567/2005 .... 1.215, 1.240
CSDLA/427/2006 .... 1.204
CSDLA/202/2007 .... 1.265, 4.92, 4.93
CSDLA/535/2007 .... 1.243
CSDLA/2349/2010 .... 1.204
CSE/422/2013 .... 9.401
CSE/435/2013 .... 9.401
CSE/19/2014 .... 9.401
CSG/6/95 .... 1.188
CSI/54/89 .... 1.386
CSI/84/89 .... 10.109
CSI/154/89 .... 1.352
CSI/22/91 .... 10.109
CSI/65/94 .... 10.153
CSI/82/94 .... 10.166
CSI/26/96 .... 1.338, 1.346
CSI/89/96 .... 10.109, 10.113, 10.125
CSI/524/1999 .... 10.156
CSI/382/2000 .... 10.70
CSI/371/2001 .... 1.344
CSI/1180/2001 .... 9.46
CSI/248/2003 .... 10.156
CSIB/12/96 .... 9.401, 9.405, 9.406
CSIB/14/1996 .... 9.415
CSIB/17/96 .... 9.403
CSIB/60/1996 .... 9.407
CSIB/324/97 .... 9.406
CSIB/459/1997 .... 9.401, 9.405
CSIB/684/1997 .... 9.401
CSIB/848/1997 .... 9.401
CSIB/389/1998 .... 9.406
CSIB/889/1999 .... 9.414
CSIB/880/2003 .... 9.414
CSIB/721/2004 .... 9.60
CSPIP/203/2015 .... 4.251, 4.253
CSPIP/210/2015 .... 4.251
CSPIP/229/2015 .... 4.257
CSPIP/386/2015 .... 4.244
CSS/71/1949 .... 3.116
CSS/18/88 .... 3.151
CSS/617/97 .... 4.20
CU/108/1993 .... 3.45
DMG 18/15 .... 4.87
R1/00 (FC) 4.94
R1/01 (IB) (T) 9.401
R1/02 (IB) (T) 9.405
R1/03 (IB) 9.411
R1/07 (DLA) 1.257
R2/60 (SB) 9.364
R2/99 (IB) 9.47
R4/99 (IB) 9.401
R(A) 1/72 .... 1.574
R(A) 1/73 .... 1.204, 1.232
R(A) 2/74 .... 1.160, 1.199, 1.237, 9.405
R(A) 3/74 .... 1.207
R(A) 4/74 .... 1.234
R(A) 1/78 .... 1.235
R(A) 2/80 .... 1.237

R(A) 1/81 .... 1.232
R(A) 5/81 .... 1.232
R(A) 2/83 .... 4.173
R(A) 11/83 ....
     1.232 ....
R(A) 1/87 .... 1.216
R(A) 1/88 .... 1.157, 1.207
R(A) 2/89 .... 1.232
R(A) 3/89 .... 1.205, 1.233
R(A) 5/90 .... 1.205, 1.233
R(A) 2/91 .... 1.233
R(A) 2/92 .... 1.200, 1.233
R(A) 3/92 .... 1.232
R(A) 1/94 .... .1.167, 1.245
R(A) 3/94 .... 1.207
R(A) 4/94 .... 1.205, 1.206
R(A) 2/98 .... 1.205, 1.208, 1.212,
                               1.213, 4.176, 4.259
R(A) 1/02 .... 4.22
R(A) 1/03 .... 1.218
R(A) 1/04 .... 1.236
R(A) 1/06 .... 1.213
R(DLA) 2/95 .... 1.223, 1.224, 1.226
R(DLA) 3/95 .... 4.88
R(DLA) 2/96 .... 4.91
R(DLA) 1/97 .... 1.227, 4.240
R(DLA) 2/97 .... 1.193
R(DLA) 2/98 .... 4.246
R(DLA) 3/98 .... 4.91
R(DLA) 4/98 .... 4.82
R(DLA) 1/99 .... 1.243
R(DLA) 6/99 .... 4.71, 4.83
R(DLA) 1/00 .... 1.265, 4.91
R(DLA) 2/01 .... 1.245, 9.77, 9.416
R(DLA) 3/01 .... 9.77, 9.416
R(DLA) 4/01 .... 1.218, 1.260, 4.95
R(DLA) 7/01 .... 4.35
R(DLA) 1/02 .... 1.216
R(DLA) 2/02 .... 1.216
R(DLA) 3/02 .... 1.217
R(DLA) 4/02 .... 4.77
R(DLA) 5/02 .... 1.280
R(DLA) 7/02 .... 1.265, 4.92, 4.93, 4.94
R(DLA) 9/02 .... 4.93
R(DLA) 10/02 .... 1.201
R(DLA) 11/02 .... 1.245, 1.270
R(DLA) 2/03 .... 1.213, 1.214, 1.220,
                               1.234
R(DLA) 3/03 .... 1.209, 1.211
R(DLA) 4/03 .... 4.82
R(DLA) 5/03 .... 1.194
R(DLA) 6/03 .... 1.261
R(DLA) 7/03 .... 1.222, 1.252
R(DLA) 1/04 .... 1.199, 4.84
R(DLA) 3/04 .... 1.258, 4.96
R(DLA) 4/04 .... 4.83
R(DLA) 6/04 .... 4.59
R(DLA) 1/05 .... 1.202, 1.241, 1.243
R(DLA) 2/05 .... 1.223
R(DLA) 5/05 .... 1.229
R(DLA) 6/05 .... 1.227
R(DLA) 2/06 .... 1.241, 3.78, 4.54,
                               4.55, 4.58

R(DLA) 3/06 .... 1.200, 1.201, 1.202, 1.209, 1.257, 1.910, 4.72, 4.234, 4.241
R(DLA) 4/06 .... 1.202, 4.72
R(DLA) 6/06 .... 1.202, 4.235, 9.47, 9.79, 9.115, 9.425, 9.433
R(DLA) 6/06(T) 9.47
R(DLA) 7/06 .... 1.272
R(DLA) 1/07 .... 1.208, 1.211, 1.257
R(DLA) 1/07T 1.213
R(DLA) 2/07 .... 4.93, 4.94
R(DLA) 1/08 .... 1.227
R(DLA) 2/08 .... **1.257**
R(DLA) 1/09 .... 1.155, 1.280, 4.87
R(F) 2/79 .... 3.150
R(FG) 1/04 .... 1.1018
R(FP) 1/05 .... 1.1017
R(G) 8/55 .... 1.59
R(G) 4/56 .... 1.58
R(G) 12/59 .... 1.58
R(G) 2/70 .... 1.1010
R(G) 1/82(T) 1.492
R(G) 1/83 .... 1.1018
R(G) 3/84 .... 1.1016, 1.1018
R(G) 1/85 .... 1.1015
R(G) 1/90 .... 1.1018
R(G) 1/91 .... 1.1018
R(G) 2/91 .... 3.95
R(G) 3/91 .... 4.130
R(G) 1/93 .... 1.1013
R(G) 4/93 .... 1.1011
R(G) 1/94 .... 1.1011
R(G) 2/94 .... 1.188
R(G) 1/95 .... 1.1012
R(G) 1/98 .... 1.1018
R(G) 1/00 .... 1.1010
R(G) 2/00 .... 1.1011
R(G) 1/02 .... 4.132
R(G) 1/03 .... 3.49
R(G) 1/04 .... 1.1009
R(G) 1/09 .... 4.140
R(I) 1/51 .... 10.34
R(I) 2/51 .... 9.401
R(I) 4/51 .... 1.359
R(I) 10/51 .... 3.43, 3.150
R(I) 11/51 .... 1.386
R(I) 13/51 .... 1.359
R(I) 14/51 .... 1.348
R(I) 42/51 .... 1.344
R(I) 59/51 .... 1.349
R(I) 60/51 .... 10.143
R(I) 62/51 .... 1.386
R(I) 67/51 .... 1.381
R(I) 68/51 .... 1.359
R(I) 73/51 .... 1.348
R(I) 77/51 .... 1.344
R(I) 5/52 .... 1.607, 10.92
R(I) 12/52 .... 1.348
R(I) 20/52 .... 10.176
R(I) 22/52 .... 1.606
R(I) 29/52 .... 1.610, 1.611
R(I) 38/52 .... 10.65
R(I) 39/52 .... 1.611

R(I) 42/52 .... 1.608, 1.610
R(I) 73/52 .... 1.610
R(I) 4/53 .... 10.139
R(I) 6/53 .... 1.358
R(I) 21/53 .... 1.358
R(I) 22/53 .... 1.357
R(I) 31/53 .... 1.359
R(I) 49/53 .... 1.381
R(I) 56/53 .... 1.601
R(I) 62/53 .... 1.351, 1.352
R(I) 67/53 .... 1.351
R(I) 69/53 .... 10.34
R(I) 81/53 .... 10.34
R(I) 93/53 .... 10.34
R(I) 1/54 .... 1.610
R(I) 11/54 .... 1.357
R(I) 18/54 .... 1.344
R(I) 24/54 .... 1.344
R(I) 32/54 .... 1.386
R(I) 37/54 .... 3.43
R(I) 52/54 .... 1.352, 1.386, 1.387
R(I) 58/54 .... 1.608
R(I) 65/54 .... 1.607
R(I) 72/54 .... 1.357
R(I) 78/54 .... 10.143
R(I) 11/55 .... 1.358
R(I) 24/55 .... 1.608
R(I) 35/55 .... 10.34
R(I) 39/55 .... 1.611
R(I) 43/55 .... 1.343, 1.344
R(I) 2/56 .... 1.604
R(I) 3/56 .... 1.349
R(I) 7/56 .... 1.336
R(I) 11/56 .... 1.386
R(I) 14/56 .... 3.150
R(I) 17/56 .... 10.187
R(I) 19/56 .... 1.344
R(I) 22/56 .... 1.357
R(I) 42/56 .... 1.381
R(I) 1/57 .... 3.44, 3.45
R(I) 1/57(T) 3.44
R(I) 3/57 .... 1.359
R(I) 8/57 .... 10.139
R(I) 15/57 .... 1.381
R(I) 35/57 .... 10.34
R(I) 40/57 .... 10.61
R(I) 5/58 .... 1.611
R(I) 7/58 .... 1.610
R(I) 21/58 .... 1.363
R(I) 26/58 .... 10.187
R(I) 33/58 .... 1.608
R(I) 35/58 .... 10.34
R(I) 3/59 .... 1.381
R(I) 10/59 .... 1.611
R(I) 22/59 .... 1.351
R(I) 24/59 .... 1.610
R(I) 4/60 .... 1.608
R(I) 5/60 .... 1.381
R(I) 18/60 .... 1.607
R(I) 19/60 .... 1.336
R(I) 20/60 .... 3.44
R(I) 46/60 .... 1.386, 1.387
R(I) 6/61 .... 1.403

R(I) 12/61......................................1.376
R(I) 14/61......................................1.357
R(I) 15/61......................................1.338
R(I) 16/61......................................1.363
R(I) 20/61......................................1.358
R(I) 22/61......................................1.610
R(I) 23/61......................................10.23
R(I) 30/61..........................1.574, 1.578
R(I) 34/61......................................10.27
R(I) 43/61......................................1.344
R(I) 3/62..1.357
R(I) 4/62..1.344
R(I) 8/62..1.381
R(I) 13/62......................................1.608
R(I) 6/63..1.387
R(I) 17/63......................................1.352
R(I) 1/64..1.363
R(I) 10/65......................................1.608
R(I) 1/66..1.376
R(I) 6/66..1.611
R(I) 7/66..1.344
R(I) 11/66..................1.400, 1.576, 10.24
R(I) 13/66......................................1.359
R(I) 14/66......................................1.400
R(I) 3/67............................1.392, 1.393
R(I) 4/67..1.358
R(I) 8/67..1.609
R(I) 6/68..1.618
R(I) 1/69..10.34
R(I) 2/69..1.359
R(I) 3/69..1.400
R(I) 1/70..1.376
R(I) 2/70..1.608
R(I) 1/72............................1.610, 1.618
R(I) 8/73..1.609
R(I) 1/74..1.610
R(I) 2/74............................10.22, 10.23
R(I) 11/74................1.342, 1.344, 10.144
R(I) 15/74......................................1.606
R(I) 5/75..1.359
R(I) 6/75..1.608
R(I) 12/75............................4.94, 9.411
R(I) 13/75......................................10.22
R(I) 15/75......................................10.172
R(I) 15/75(T) 10.140
R(I) 1/76............................1.336, 1.610
R(I) 3/76............................1.402, 10.22
R(I) 5/76..10.149
R(I) 6/76..1.358
R(I) 7/76..10.148
R(I) 8/76..10.149
R(I) 2/77..10.139
R(I) 4/77..1.611
R(I) 6/77..1.610
R(I) 3/78.....10.139, 10.140, 10.172, 10.173
R(I) 1/79..10.23
R(I) 2/79............................10.109, 10.169
R(I) 2/79(T) 10.60, 10.138,
                                      10.172, 10.173
R(I) 4/79..1.358
R(I) 1/80..10.149
R(I) 2/80..1.359
R(I) 3/80..10.149

R(I) 5/80..1.381
R(I) 7/80..1.358
R(I) 11/80......................................1.345
R(I) 13/80......................................10.149
R(I) 1/81..10.22
R(I) 2/81..1.606
R(I) 3/81..1.359
R(I) 4/81..1.359
R(I) 5/81............................1.336, 1.358
R(I) 10/81......................................1.358
R(I) 11/81(T) 10.138
R(I) 12/81......................................1.609
R(I) 13/81......................................10.153
R(I) 14/81......................................1.379
R(I) 1/82..1.336
R(I) 6/82....................1.346, 1.353, 1.363
R(I) 5/83.......................... 10.138, 10.150
R(I) 6/83..10.149
R(I) 3/84..10.23
R(I) 4/84..10.151
R(I) 1/85.............................. 10.61, 10.188
R(I) 2/85.............................. 10.138, 10.148
R(I) 7/85..1.379
R(I) 8/85..10.148
R(I) 11/86......................................1.576
R(I) 1/88............................. 1.355, 1.379
R(I) 1/89..10.119
R(I) 1/90..1.402
R(I) 1/91..1.379
R(I) 3/91..10.25
R(I) 6/91..1.343
R(I) 1/92..10.109
R(I) 2/92............. 10.151, 10.154, 10.193
R(I) 531/92....................................10.176
R(I) 1/93..1.355
R(I) 2/93....................1.623, 10.240, 10.242
R(I) 3/93............................. 1.623, 10.242
R(I) 1/94....................1.424, 10.73, 10.109
R(I) 2/94..10.109
R(I) 4/94..10.21
R(I) 6/94..10.139
R(I) 8/94....................1.354, 1.355, 1.359
R(I) 1/95....................10.20, 10.21, 10.23
R(I) 2/95..10.160
R(I) 3/95............... 10.138, 10.166, 10.167
R(I) 5/95....................1.333, 1.403, 1.576,
                                      10.28, 10.138
R(I) 1/96..10.186
R(I) 2/96........................... 10.166, 10.167
R(I) 3/96..1.402
R(I) 4/96....... 10.20, 10.69, 10.138, 10.199
R(I) 5/96........................... 10.163, 10.164
R(I) 2/97..10.156
R(I) 3/97........................... 10.138, 10.141
R(I) 2/98..10.119
R(I) 4/98..10.192
R(I) 5/98..10.143
R(I) 6/98..10.167
R(I) 7/98..10.186
R(I) 8/98..10.167
R(I) 1/99....................1.350, 1.354, 1.360
R(I) 2/99....................1.599, 1.624, 10.242
R(I) 3/99..1.600

R(I) 4/99................. 10.138, 10.157, 10.172
R(I) 5/99...10.149
R(I) 1/00............. 1.338, 1.339, 1.344, 1.346
R(I) 2/00...1.624
R(I) 3/00...1.402
R(I) 1/01...10.167
R(I) 2/01.................... 10.138, 10.164
R(I) 1/02.................... 10.160, 10.161
R(I) 2/02...1.603
R(I) 3/02................. 10.160, 10.161, 10.162
R(I) 6/02................. 10.145, 10.146, 10.147
R(I) 7/02...10.189
R(I) 8/02...10.193
R(I) 2/03.................... 1.600, 10.71
R(I) 3/03...10.186
R(I) 4/03.................... 1.402, 1.415
R(I) 1/04...10.28
R(I) 2/04.................... 1.601, 10.72
R(I) 3/04...10.161
R(I) 4/04...10.26
R(I) 5/04................1.601, 10.67, 10.72
R(I) 1/06...10.165
R(I) 2/06................1.574, 10.28, 10.161
R(I) 2/06(T) 1.574
R(I) 2/09...10.168
R(IB) 2/98 .... 9.46, 9.416
R(IB) 3/98 ....9.49
R(IB) 2/99 .... 9.405, 9.427
R(IB) 2/99(T) 9.71, 9.405
R(IB) 1/00 ....9.57
R(IB) 2/00 ....9.60
R(IB) 1/01 ....9.60
R(IB) 2/01 ....9.61
R(IB) 3/01 ....9.202
R(IB) 3/02 ....9.411
R(IB) 2/03 ....9.408
R(IB) 5/03 ....9.410
R(IB) 1/04 ....1.735
R(IB) 6/04 ....9.408
R(IB) 8/04 .... 9.343, 9.347
R(IB) 1/05 ....1.735
R(IB) 7/05 ....9.402
R(IB) 1/06 .... 3.7, 3.30
R(IB) 2/06 ....9.401
R(IB) 2/07(T) 9.415
R(IB) 3/07 ....3.30
R(IB) 1/09 .... 1.492, 1.493
R(IB) 2/09 ....9.403
R(IS) 18/94.................... 4.20, 4.54, 4.56
R(IS) 10/96...4.56
R(JSA) 8/02 ....1.493
R(M) 1/78 .... 4.78, 4.79
R(M) 2/78 .... 4.71, 4.74, 4.80
R(M) 3/78 .... 4.76, 4.85
R(M) 1/80 ....4.71
R(M) 1/81 ....4.82
R(M) 2/81 ....4.81
R(M) 1/83 .... 4.71, 4.76, 4.80
R(M) 2/83 .... 1.268, 1.269
R(M) 1/84 .... 1.257, 4.80
R(M) 1/85 ....3.124
R(M) 3/86 .... 4.71, 4.80, 4.81
R(M) 4/86 ....4.41

R(M) 5/86 ....4.78
R(M) 1/88 .... 4.71, 4.72
R(M) 2/89 .... 4.76, 4.90
R(M) 1/91 ....4.77
R(M) 2/92 ....4.82
R(M) 1/95 ....4.90
R(M) 1/96 .... 1.907, 4.173
R(P) 2/67..3.124
R(P) 4/67..1.180
R(P) 1/78..3.124
R(P) 1/90..**3.152**
R(P) 2/93..6.95
R(P) 3/93..3.59
R(P) 1/02..1.438
R(P)2/03...1.131
R(P) 2/06..1.1014
R(P) 1/08..1.150
R(P) 1/09..1.680
R(P) 2/09..1.680
R(S) 2/51..3.114
R(S) 8/51..3.150
R(S) 9/51.................... 9.362, 9.364
R(S) 10/51..3.114
R(S) 16/51..3.114
R(S) 21/52.................... 9.365, 9.366
R(S) 1/53..9.401
R(S) 2/53..9.363
R(S) 6/55..9.366
R(S) 9/55..3.112
R(S) 3/57.................... 9.364, 9.365
R(S) 6/59..9.46
R(S) 5/61..3.114
R(S) 6/61.................... 3.114, 3.116
R(S) 10/62..3.114
R(S) 1/65..3.114
R(S) 1/66..1.437
R(S) 1/69..3.114
R(S) 2/69..3.114
R(S) 3/74.................... 3.47, 3.55
R(S) 1/75.................... 3.114, 3.116
R(S) 1/77..3.116
R(S) 8/79..1.438
R(S) 4/80..3.114
R(S) 6/81..3.114
R(S) 7/83.................... 9.362, 9.366
R(S) 8/83..3.113
R(S) 10/83..3.112
R(S) 12/83.................... 3.44, 3.45, 3.51
R(S) 4/84..4.20
R(S) 1/85..3.112
R(S) 2/85..3.44
R(S) 7/85..1.610
R(S) 2/86..3.114
R(S) 1/87.................... 9.362, 9.366
R(S) 2/89..1.189
R(S) 7/89..3.44
R(S) 7/89(T)..3.44
R(S) 1/90..3.116
R(S) 1/93..1.439
R(S) 4/93..9.46
R(S) 5/93..1.492
R(S) 5/94..3.95
R(S) 1/95..1.188

Table of Social Security Commissioners' Decisions

R(S) 1/96...3.112
R(S) 1/00...1.439
R(U) 16/52..1.623
R(U) 18/60..1.437
R(U) 11/62..3.150
R(U) 16/62......................... 1.437, 3.112
R(U) 3/66...3.43
R(U) 2/71..9.362

R(U) 2/74...1.623
R(U) 8/74(T)..9.362
R(U) 3/78...3.55
R(U) 6/79...3.55
R(U) 4/87..9.362
R(U) 1/89..1.339
R(U) 6/89..1.492

TABLE OF ABBREVIATIONS USED IN THIS SERIES

1975 Act	Social Security Act 1975
1977 Act	Marriage (Scotland) Act 1977
1979 Act	Pneumoconiosis (Workers' Compensation) Act 1979
1986 Act	Social Security Act 1986
1996 Act	Employment Rights Act 1996
1998 Act	Social Security Act 1998
2002 Act	Tax Credits Act 2002
2004 Act	Gender Recognition Act 2004
2006 Act	Armed Forces Act 2006
2008 Act	Child Maintenance and Other Payments Act 2008
2013 Act	Marriage (Same Sex Couples) Act 2013
2014 Act	Marriage and Civil Partnership (Scotland) Act 2014
A1P1	Art.1 of Protocol 1 to the European Convention on Human Rights
AA	Attendance Allowance
AA 1992	Attendance Allowance Act 1992
AAC	Administrative Appeals Chamber
AACR	Administrative Appeals Chamber Reports
A.C.	Law Reports, Appeal Cases
A.C.D.	Administrative Court Digest
Admin	Administrative Court
Admin L.R.	Administrative Law Reports
Administration Act	Social Security Administration Act 1992
Administration Regulations	Statutory Paternity Pay and Statutory Adoption Pay (Administration) Regulations 2002
AIP	assessed income period
All E.R.	All England Reports
All E.R. (E.C.)	All England Reports (European Cases)
AMA	Adjudicating Medical Authorities
AO	Adjudication Officer
AOG	*Adjudication Officers Guide*
art.	article
Art.	Article
ASD	Autistic Spectrum Disorder
ASPP	Additional Statutory Paternity Pay
A.T.C.	Annotated Tax Cases

Attendance Allowance Regulations	Social Security (Attendance Allowance) Regulations 1991
AWT	All Work Test
BA	Benefits Agency
Benefits Act	Social Security Contributions and Benefits Act 1992
B.H.R.C.	Butterworths Human Rights Cases
B.L.G.R.	Butterworths Local Government Reports
Blue Books	*The Law Relating to Social Security*, Vols 1–11
B.P.I.R.	Bankruptcy and Personal Insolvency Reports
B.T.C.	British Tax Cases
BTEC	Business and Technology Education Council
B.V.C.	British Value Added Tax Reporter
B.W.C.C.	Butterworths Workmen's Compensation Cases
c.	chapter
C	Commissioner's decision
C&BA 1992	Social Security Contributions and Benefits Act 1992
CAA 2001	Capital Allowances Act 2001
CAB	Citizens Advice Bureau
CAO	Chief Adjudication Officer
CB	Child Benefit
CBA 1975	Child Benefit Act 1975
CBJSA	Contribution-Based Jobseeker's Allowance
C.C.L. Rep.	Community Care Law Reports
CCM	HMRC *New Tax Credits Claimant Compliance Manual*
C.E.C.	European Community Cases
CERA	cortical evoked response audiogram
CESA	Contribution-based Employment and Support Allowance
CFS	chronic fatigue syndrome
Ch.	Chancery Division Law Reports; Chapter
Citizenship Directive	Directive 2004/38/EC of the European Parliament and of the Council of April 29, 2004
CJEC	Court of Justice of the European Communities
CJEU	Court of Justice of the European Union
Claims and Payments Regulations	Social Security (Claims and Payments) Regulations 1987
Claims and Payments Regulations 1979	Social Security (Claims and Payments) Regulations 1979
Claims and Payments Regulations 2013	Universal Credit, Personal Independence Payment, Jobseeker's Allowance and Employment and Support Allowance (Claims and Payments) Regulations 2013
CM	Case Manager
CMA	Chief Medical Adviser

CMEC	Child Maintenance and Enforcement Commission
C.M.L.R.	Common Market Law Reports
C.O.D.	Crown Office Digest
COLL	*Collective Investment Schemes Sourcebook*
Community, The	European Community
Computation of Earnings Regulations	Social Security Benefit (Computation of Earnings) Regulations 1978
Computation of Earnings Regulations 1996	Social Security Benefit (Computation of Earnings) Regulations 1996
Consequential Provisions Act	Social Security (Consequential Provisions) Act 1992
Contributions and Benefits Act	Social Security Contributions and Benefits Act 1992
Contributions Regulations	Social Security (Contributions) Regulations 2001
COPD	chronic obstructive pulmonary disease
CP	Carer Premium; Chamber President
CPAG	Child Poverty Action Group
CPR	Civil Procedure Rules
Cr. App. R.	Criminal Appeal Reports
CRCA 2005	Commissioners for Revenue and Customs Act 2005
Credits Regulations 1974	Social Security (Credits) Regulations 1974
Credits Regulations 1975	Social Security (Credits) Regulations 1975
Crim. L.R.	Criminal Law Review
CRU	Compensation Recovery Unit
CSA 1995	Children (Scotland) Act 1995
CSIH	Inner House of the Court of Session (Scotland)
CSM	Child Support Maintenance
CS(NI)O 1995	Child Support (Northern Ireland) Order 1995
CSOH	Outer House of the Court of Session (Scotland)
CSPSSA 2000	Child Support, Pensions and Social Security Act 2000
CTA	Common Travel Area
CTA 2009	Corporation Tax Act 2009
CTA 2010	Corporation Tax Act 2010
CTB	Council Tax Benefit
CTC	Child Tax Credit
CTC Regulations	Child Tax Credit Regulations 2002
CTF	child trust fund
CTS	Carpal Tunnel Syndrome
DAC	Directive 2011/16/ EU (Directive on administrative co-operation in the field of taxation)
DAT	Disability Appeal Tribunal
dB	decibels

DCA	Department for Constitutional Affairs
DCP	Disabled Child Premium
Decisions and Appeals Regulations 1999	Social Security Contributions (Decisions and Appeals) Regulations 1999
Dependency Regulations	Social Security Benefit (Dependency) Regulations 1977
DfEE	Department for Education and Employment
DHSS	Department of Health and Social Security
Disability Living Allowance Regulations	Social Security (Disability Living Allowance) Regulations
DIY	do it yourself
DLA	Disability Living Allowance
DLA Regs 1991	Social Security (Disability Living Allowance) Regulations 1991
DLAAB	Disability Living Allowance Advisory Board
DLADWAA 1991	Disability Living Allowance and Disability Working Allowance Act 1991
DM	Decision Maker
DMA	Decision-making and Appeals
DMG	*Decision Makers' Guide*
DMP	Delegated Medical Practitioner
DP	Disability Premium
DPT	diffuse pleural thickening
DPTC	Disabled Person's Tax Credit
DRO	Debt Relief Order
DSD	Department for Social Development (Northern Ireland)
DSM IV; DSM-5	Diagnostic and Statistical Manual of Mental Disorders of the American Psychiatric Association
DSS	Department of Social Security
DTI	Department of Trade and Industry
DWA	Disability Working Allowance
DWP	Department for Work and Pensions
DWPMS	Department for Work and Pensions Medical Service
EAA	Extrinsic Allergic Alveolitis
EAT	Employment Appeal Tribunal
EC	European Community
ECHR	European Convention on Human Rights
ECJ	European Court of Justice
E.C.R.	European Court Reports
ECSC	European Coal and Steel Community
ECSMA	European Convention on Social and Medical Assistance
EEA	European Economic Area
EEC	European Economic Community

EESSI	Electronic Exchange of Social Security Information
E.G.	Estates Gazette
E.G.L.R.	Estates Gazette Law Reports
EHC plan	education, health and care plan
EHIC	European Health Insurance Card
EHRC	European Human Rights Commission
E.H.R.R.	European Human Rights Reports
EL	employers' liability
E.L.R	Education Law Reports
EMA	Education Maintenance Allowance
EMP	Examining Medical Practitioner
Employment and Support Allowance Regulations	Employment and Support Allowance Regulations 2008
EPS	extended period of sickness
Eq. L.R.	Equality Law Reports
ERA	evoked response audiometry
ERA scheme	Employment, Retention and Advancement scheme
ES	Employment Service
ESA	Employment and Support Allowance
ESA Regs 2013	Employment and Support Allowance Regulations 2013
ESA Regulations	Employment and Support Allowance Regulations 2008
ESA WCAt	Employment and Support Allowance Work Capability Assessment
ESC	employer supported childcare
ESE Scheme	Employment, Skills and Enterprise Scheme
ESE Regulations	Jobseeker's Allowance (Employment, Skills and Enterprise Scheme) Regulations 2011
ESES Regulations	Jobseeker's Allowance (Employment, Skills and Enterprise Scheme) Regulations 2011
ETA 1973	Employment and Training Act 1973
ETA(NI) 1950	Employment and Training Act (Northern Ireland) 1950
ETS	European Treaty Series
EU	European Union
Eu.L.R.	European Law Reports
EWCA Civ	Civil Division of the Court of Appeal (England and Wales)
EWHC Admin	Administrative Court Division of the High Court (England and Wales)
FA 1993	Finance Act 1993
FA 1996	Finance Act 1996
FA 2004	Finance Act 2004
Fam. Law	Family Law

FAS	Financial Assistance Scheme
F.C.R.	Family Court Reporter
FEV	forced expiratory volume
FIS	Family Income Supplement
FISMA 2000	Financial Services and Markets Act 2000
F.L.R.	Family Law Reports
FME	further medical evidence
F(No.2)A 2005	Finance (No.2) Act 2005
FOTRA	Free of Tax to Residents Abroad
FRAA	flat rate accrual amount
FRS Act 2004	Fire and Rescue Services Act 2004
FSCS	Financial Services Compensation Scheme
FTT	First-tier Tribunal
General Benefit Regulations 1982	Social Security (General Benefit) Regulations 1982
General Regulations	Statutory Shared Parental Pay (General) Regulations 2014
GMCA	Greater Manchester Combined Authority
GMFRA	Greater Manchester Fire and Rescue Authority
GMP	Guaranteed Minimum Pension
GMWDA	Greater Manchester Waste Disposal Authority
GNVQ	General National Vocational Qualification
GP	General Practitioner
GRA	Gender Recognition Act 2004
GRB	Graduated Retirement Benefit
GRP	Graduated Retirement Pension
HB	Housing Benefit
HB (WSP) R (NI) 2017	Housing Benefit (Welfare Social Payment) Regulations (Northern Ireland) 2017
HBRB	Housing Benefit Review Board
HCA	Homes and Communities Agency
HCD	House of Commons Debates
HCP	healthcare professional
HCV	Hepatitis C virus
Health Service Act	National Health Service Act 2006
Health Service (Wales) Act	National Health Service (Wales) Act 2006
HIV	Human Immunodeficiency Virus
HL	House of Lords
H.L.R.	Housing Law Reports
HMIT	Her Majesty's Inspector of Taxes
HMRC	Her Majesty's Revenue and Customs
HMSO	Her Majesty's Stationery Office
Hospital In-Patients Regulations 1975	Social Security (Hospital In-Patients) Regulations 1975
HP	Health Professional

HPP	Higher Pensioner Premium
HRA 1998	Human Rights Act 1998
H.R.L.R.	Human Rights Law Reports
HRP	Home Responsibilities Protection
HSE	Health and Safety Executive
IAC	Immigration and Asylum Chamber
IAP	Intensive Activity Period
IB	Incapacity Benefit
IB PCA	Incapacity Benefit Personal Capability Assessment
IB Regs	Social Security (Incapacity Benefit) Regulations 1994
IB Regulations	Social Security (Incapacity Benefit) Regulations 1994
IB/IS/SDA	Incapacity Benefits Regime
IBJSA	Income-Based Jobseeker's Allowance
IBS	Irritable Bowel Syndrome
ICA	Invalid Care Allowance
I.C.R.	Industrial Cases Reports
ICTA 1988	Income and Corporation Taxes Act 1988
IFW Regulations	Incapacity for Work (General) Regulations 1995
IH	Inner House of the Court of Session
I.I.	Industrial Injuries
IIAC	Industrial Injuries Advisory Council
IIDB	Industrial Injuries Disablement Benefit
ILO	International Labour Organization
Imm. A.R.	Immigration Appeal Reports
Incapacity for Work Regulations	Social Security (Incapacity for Work) (General) Regulations 1995
Income Support General Regulations	Income Support (General) Regulations 1987
IND	Immigration and Nationality Directorate of the Home Office
I.N.L.R.	Immigration and Nationality Law Reports
I.O.	Insurance Officer
IPPR	Institute of Public Policy Research
IRESA	Income-Related Employment and Support Allowance
I.R.L.R.	Industrial Relations Law Reports
IS	Income Support
IS Regs	Income Support Regulations
IS Regulations	Income Support (General) Regulations 1987
ISA	Individual Savings Account
ISBN	International Standard Book Number
ITA 2007	Income Tax Act 2007
ITEPA 2003	Income Tax, Earnings and Pensions Act 2003

I.T.L. Rep.	International Tax Law Reports
I.T.R.	Industrial Tribunals Reports
ITS	Independent Tribunal Service
ITTOIA 2005	Income Tax (Trading and Other Income) Act 2005
IVB	Invalidity Benefit
IW (General) Regs	Social Security (Incapacity for Work) (General) Regulations 1995
IW (Transitional) Regs	Incapacity for Work (Transitional) Regulations
Jobseeker's Allowance Regulations	Jobseeker's Allowance Regulations 1996
Jobseeker's Regulations 1996	Jobseeker's Allowance Regulations 1996
JSA	Jobseeker's Allowance
JSA 1995	Jobseekers Act 1995
JSA (NI) Regulations	Jobseeker's Allowance (Northern Ireland) Regulations 1996
JSA (Transitional) Regulations	Jobseeker's Allowance (Transitional) Regulations 1996
JSA Regs 1996	Jobseeker's Allowance Regulations 1996
JSA Regs 2013	Jobseeker's Allowance Regulations 2013
JS(NI)O 1995	Jobseekers (Northern Ireland) Order 1995
J.S.S.L.	Journal of Social Security Law
J.S.W.L.	Journal of Social Welfare Law
K.B.	Law Reports, King's Bench
L.& T.R.	Landlord and Tenant Reports
LCW	limited capability for work
LCWA	Limited Capability for Work Assessment
LCWRA	limited capability for work-related activity
LDEDC Act 2009	Local Democracy, Economic Development and Construction Act 2009
LEA	local education authority
LEL	Lower Earnings Limit
LET	low earnings threshold
L.G. Rev.	Local Government Review
L.G.L.R.	Local Government Reports
L.J.R.	Law Journal Reports
LRP	liable relative payment
L.S.G.	Law Society Gazette
Luxembourg Court	Court of Justice of the European Union (also referred to as CJEC and ECJ)
MA	Maternity Allowance
MAF	Medical Assessment Framework
Maternity Allowance Regulations	Social Security (Maternity Allowance) Regulations 1987
MDC	Mayoral development corporation
ME	myalgic encephalomyelitis

Medical Evidence Regulations	Social Security (Medical Evidence) Regulations 1976
MEN	Mandatory Employment Notification
Mesher and Wood	*Income Support, the Social Fund and Family Credit: the Legislation* (1996)
M.H.L.R.	Mental Health Law Reports
MHP	mental health problems
MIF	minimum income floor
MIG	minimum income guarantee
Migration Regulations	Employment and Support Allowance (Transitional Provisions, Housing Benefit and Council Tax Benefit (Existing Awards) (No.2) Regulations 2010
MP	Member of Parliament
MRSA	methicillin-resistant Staphylococcus aureus
MS	Medical Services
MWA Regulations	Jobseeker's Allowance (Mandatory Work Activity Scheme) Regulations 2011
MWAS Regulations	Jobseeker's Allowance (Mandatory Work Activity Scheme) Regulations 2011
NCB	National Coal Board
NDPD	Notes on the Diagnosis of Prescribed Diseases
NHS	National Health Service
NI	National Insurance
N.I..	Northern Ireland Law Reports
NICA	Northern Ireland Court of Appeal
NICom	Northern Ireland Commissioner
NICs	National Insurance Contributions
NINO	National Insurance Number
NIRS 2	National Insurance Recording System
N.L.J.	New Law Journal
NMC	Nursing and Midwifery Council
Northern Ireland Contributions and Benefits Act	Social Security Contributions and Benefits (Northern Ireland) Act 1992
N.P.C.	New Property Cases
NRCGT	non-resident capital gains tax
NTC Manual	Clerical procedures manual on tax credits
NUM	National Union of Mineworkers
NUS	National Union of Students
OCD	obsessive compulsive disorder
Ogus, Barendt and Wikeley	A. Ogus, E. Barendt and N. Wikeley, *The Law of Social Security* (1995)
Old Cases Act	Industrial Injuries and Diseases (Old Cases) Act 1975
OPB	One Parent Benefit
O.P.L.R.	Occupational Pensions Law Reports

OPSSAT	Office of the President of Social Security Appeal Tribunals
Overlapping Benefits Regulations	Social Security (Overlapping Benefits) Regulations 1975
P	retirement pension case
P. & C.R.	Property and Compensation Reports
para.	paragraph
Pay Regulations	Statutory Paternity Pay and Statutory Adoption Pay (General) Regulations 2002; Statutory Shared Parental Pay (General) Regulations 2014
PAYE	Pay As You Earn
PC	Privy Council
PCA	Personal Capability Assessment
PCC	Police and Crime Commissioner
PD	Practice Direction; prescribed disease
Pens. L.R.	Pensions Law Reports
Pensions Act	Pension Schemes Act 1993
PEP	Personal Equity Plan
Persons Abroad Regulations	Social Security Benefit (Persons Abroad) Regulations 1975
Persons Residing Together Regulations	Social Security Benefit (Persons Residing Together) Regulations 1977
PIE	Period of Interruption of Employment
PILON	pay in lieu of notice
Pilot Scheme Regulations	Universal Credit (Work-Related Requirements) In Work Pilot Scheme and Amendment Regulations 2015
PIP	Personal Independence Payment
P.I.Q.R.	Personal Injuries and Quantum Reports
Polygamous Marriages Regulations	Social Security and Family Allowances (Polygamous Marriages) Regulations 1975
PPF	Pension Protection Fund
Prescribed Diseases Regulations	Social Security (Industrial Injuries) (Prescribed Diseases) Regulations 1985
PSCS	Pension Service Computer System
Pt	Part
PTA	pure tone audiometry
P.T.S.R.	Public and Third Sector Law Reports
PTWR 2000	Part-time Workers (Prevention of Less Favourable Treatment) Regulations 2000
PVS	private and voluntary sectors
Q.B.	Queen's Bench Law Reports
QBD	Queen's Bench Division
QCS Board	Quality Contract Scheme Board
QEF	qualifying earnings factor
QYP	qualifying young person

r.	rule
R	Reported Decision
R.C.	Rules of the Court of Session
REA	Reduced Earnings Allowance
reg.	regulation
RIPA	Regulation of Investigatory Powers Act 2000
RMO	Responsible Medical Officer
rr.	rules
RR	reference rate
RSI	repetitive strain injury
RTI	Real Time Information
R.V.R.	Rating & Valuation Reporter
s.	section
S	Scottish Decision
SAP	Statutory Adoption Pay
SAPOE Regulations	Jobseeker's Allowance (Schemes for Assisting Persons to Obtain Employment) Regulations 2013
SAWS	Seasonal Agricultural Work Scheme
SAYE	Save As You Earn
SB	Supplementary Benefit
SBAT	Supplementary Benefit Appeal Tribunal
SBC	Supplementary Benefits Commission
S.C.	Session Cases
S.C. (H.L.)	Session Cases (House of Lords)
S.C. (P.C.)	Session Cases (Privy Council)
S.C.C.R.	Scottish Criminal Case Reports
S.C.L.R.	Scottish Civil Law Reports
Sch.	Schedule
SDA	Severe Disablement Allowance
SDP	Severe Disability Premium
SEC	Social Entitlement Chamber
SEN	special educational needs
SERPS	State Earnings Related Pension Scheme
ShPP	statutory shared parental pay
ShPP Regulations	Statutory Shared Parental Pay (General) Regulations 2014
SI	Statutory Instrument
SIP	Share Incentive Plan
S.J.	Solicitors Journal
S.J.L.B.	Solicitors Journal Law Brief
SLAN	statement like an award notice
S.L.T.	Scots Law Times
SMP	Statutory Maternity Pay

SMP (General) Regulations 1986	Statutory Maternity Pay (General) Regulations 1986
SPC	State Pension Credit
SPC Regulations	State Pension Credit Regulations 2002
SPCA 2002	State Pension Credit Act 2002
SPL Regulations	Shared Parental Leave Regulations 2014
SPP	Statutory Paternity Pay
ss.	sections
SS (No.2) A 1980	Social Security (No.2) Act 1980
SSA 1975	Social Security Act 1975
SSA 1977	Social Security Act 1977
SSA 1978	Social Security Act 1978
SSA 1979	Social Security Act 1979
SSA 1981	Social Security Act 1981
SSA 1986	Social Security Act 1986
SSA 1988	Social Security Act 1988
SSA 1989	Social Security Act 1989
SSA 1990	Social Security Act 1990
SSA 1998	Social Security Act 1998
SSAA 1992	Social Security Administration Act 1992
SSAC	Social Security Advisory Committee
SSAT	Social Security Appeal Tribunal
SSCBA 1992	Social Security Contributions and Benefits Act 1992
SSCB(NI)A 1992	Social Security Contributions and Benefits (Northern Ireland) Act 1992
SSCPA 1992	Social Security (Consequential Provisions) Act 1992
SSD	Secretary of State for Defence
SSHBA 1982	Social Security and Housing Benefits Act 1982
SSHD	Secretary of State for the Home Department
SSI	Scottish Statutory Instrument
SS(MP)A 1977	Social Security (Miscellaneous Provisions) Act 1977
SSP	Statutory Sick Pay
SSP (General) Regulations	Statutory Sick Pay (General) Regulations 1982
SSPA 1975	Social Security Pensions Act 1975
SSPP	statutory shared parental pay
SSWP	Secretary of State for Work and Pensions
State Pension Credit Regulations	State Pension Credit Regulations 2002
S.T.C.	Simon's Tax Cases
S.T.C. (S.C.D.)	Simon's Tax Cases: Special Commissioners' Decisions
S.T.I.	Simon's Tax Intelligence
STIB	Short-Term Incapacity Benefit
subpara.	subparagraph

Table of Abbreviations used in this Series

subs.	subsection
T	Tribunal of Commissioners' Decision
T.C.	Tax Cases
TCA 1999	Tax Credits Act 1999
TCA 2002	Tax Credits Act 2002
TCC	Technology and Construction Court
TCEA 2007	Tribunals, Courts and Enforcement Act 2007
TCGA 1992	Taxation of Chargeable Gains Act 2002
TCTM	*Tax Credits Technical Manual*
TEC	Treaty Establishing the European Community
TENS	transcutaneous electrical nerve stimulation
TEU	Treaty on European Union
TFC	tax-free childcare
TFEU	Treaty on the Functioning of the European Union
TIOPA 2010	Taxation (International and Other Provisions) Act 2010
TMA 1970	Taxes Management Act 1970
T.R.	Taxation Reports
Transfer of Functions Act	Social Security Contributions (Transfer of Functions etc.) Act 1999
Tribunal Procedure Rules	Tribunal Procedure (First-tier Tribunal)(Social Entitlement Chamber) Rules 2008
UB	Unemployment Benefit
UC	Universal Credit
UC Regs 2013	Universal Credit Regulations 2013
UCITS	Undertakings for Collective Investments in Transferable Securities
UKAIT	UK Asylum and Immigration Tribunal
UKBA	UK Border Agency of the Home Office
UKCC	United Kingdom Central Council for Nursing, Midwifery and Health Visiting
UKFTT	United Kingdom First-tier Tribunal Tax Chamber
UKHL	United Kingdom House of Lords
U.K.H.R.R.	United Kingdom Human Rights Reports
UKSC	United Kingdom Supreme Court
UKUT	United Kingdom Upper Tribunal
UN	United Nations
Universal Credit Regulations	Universal Credit Regulations 2013
URL	uniform resource locator
USI Regs	Social Security (Unemployment, Sickness and Invalidity Benefit) Regulations 1983
USI Regulations	Social Security (Unemployment, Sickness and Invalidity Benefit) Regulations 1983
UT	Upper Tribunal
VAT	Value Added Tax

VCM	vinyl chloride monomer
Vol.	Volume
VWF	Vibration White Finger
W	Welsh Decision
WCA	Work Capability Assessment
WCAt	limited capability for work assessment
WFHRAt	Work-Focused Health-Related Assessment
WFI	work-focused interview
WFTC	Working Families Tax Credit
Wikeley, Annotations	N. Wikeley, "Annotations to Jobseekers Act 1995 (c.18)" in *Current Law Statutes Annotated* (1995)
Wikeley, Ogus and Barendt	Wikeley, Ogus and Barendt, *The Law of Social Security* (2002)
W.L.R.	Weekly Law Reports
WLUK	Westlaw UK
Workmen's Compensation Acts	Workmen's Compensation Acts 1925 to 1945
WP	Widow's Pension
WPS	War Pensions Scheme
WRA 2007	Welfare Reform Act 2007
WRA 2009	Welfare Reform Act 2009
WRA 2012	Welfare Reform Act 2012
W-RA Regulations	Employment and Support Allowance (Work-Related Activity) Regulations 2011
WRAAt	Work-Related Activity Assessment
WRPA 1999	Welfare Reform and Pensions Act 1999
WRP(NI)O 1999	Welfare Reform and Pensions (Northern Ireland) Order 1999
WRWA 2016	Welfare Reform and Work Act 2016
WSP (LCP) R (NI) 2016	Welfare Supplementary Payment (Loss of Carer Payments) Regulations (Northern Ireland) 2016
WSP (LDRP) R (NI) 2016	Welfare Supplementary Payment (Loss of Disability-Related Premiums) Regulations (Northern Ireland) 2016
WSPR (NI) 2016	Welfare Supplementary Payment Regulations (Northern Ireland) 2016
WTC	Working Tax Credit
WTC Regulations	Working Tax Credit (Entitlement and Maximum Rate) Regulations 2002

PART I
STATUTES

Vaccine Damage Payments Act 1979

(1979 c.17)

1.   Payments to persons severely disabled by vaccination.   1.1
2.   Conditions of entitlement.
3.   Determination of claims.
3A.   Decisions reversing earlier decisions.
4.   [Appeals to appeal tribunals.]
5.   Reconsideration of determinations and recovery of payments in certain cases.
6.   Payments to or for the benefit of disabled persons.
7.   Payments, claims, etc. made prior to the Act.
7A.   Correction of errors and setting aside of decisions.
7B.   Finality of decisions.
8.   Regulations.
9.   Fraudulent statements etc.
10.–11. *Omitted.*
12.   Financial provisions.
13.   Short title and extent.

An Act to provide for payments to be made out of public funds in cases where severe disablement occurs as a result of vaccination against certain diseases or of contact with a person who has been vaccinated against any of those diseases; to make provision in connection with similar payments made before the passing of this Act; and for purposes connected therewith.
[22nd March 1979]

Payments to persons severely disabled by vaccination

1.—(1) If, on consideration of a claim, the Secretary of State is   1.2
satisfied—

   (a) that a person is, or was immediately before his death, severely disa-
       bled as a result of vaccination against any of the diseases to which
       this Act applies; and
   (b) that the conditions of entitlement which are applicable in accordance
       with section 2 below are fulfilled,

he shall in accordance with this Act make a payment of [¹the relevant
       statutory sum] to or for the benefit of that person or to his personal
       representatives.

       [¹(1A) In subsection (1) above "statutory sum" means £10,000 or
such other sum as is specified by the Secretary of State for the purposes
of this Act by order made by statutory instrument with the consent of the
Treasury; and the relevant statutory sum for the purposes of that subsection
is the statutory sum at the time when a claim for payment is first made.]

       (2) The diseases to which this Act applies are–
   (a) diphtheria,
   (b) tetanus,
   (c) whooping cough,
   (d) poliomyelitis,
   (e) measles,
   (f) rubella,

(g) tuberculosis,

(h) smallpox, and

(i) any other disease which is specified by the Secretary of State for the purposes of this Act by order made by statutory instrument.

(3) Subject to section 2(3) below, this Act has effect with respect to a person who is severely disabled as a result of a vaccination given to his mother before he was born as if the vaccination had been given directly to him and, in such circumstances as may be prescribed by regulations under this Act, this Act has effect with respect to a person who is severely disabled as a result of contracting a disease through contact with a third person who was vaccinated against it as if the vaccination had been given to him and the disablement resulted from it.

(4) For the purposes of this Act, a person is severely disabled if he suffers disablement to the extent of [²60] per cent. or more, assessed as for the purposes of section 57 of the Social Security Act 1975 or the Social Security (Northern Ireland) Act 1975 (disablement gratuity and pension).

[¹(4A) No order shall be made by virtue of subsection (1A) above unless a draft of the order has been laid before Parliament and been approved by a resolution of each House.]

(5) A statutory instrument under subsection (2)(i) above shall be subject to annulment in pursuance of a resolution of either House of Parliament.

AMENDMENTS

1. Social Security Act 1985 s.23.

2. Regulatory Reform (Vaccine Damage Payments Act 1979) Order 2002 (SI 2002/1592) art.2 (June 16, 2002).

GENERAL NOTE

1.3   The 1979 Act is subject to detailed analysis in *SSWP v G (VDP)* [2015] UKUT 321 (AAC). The Secretary of State appealed to the Court of Appeal against the Upper Tribunal's decision in *G*. The Court dismissed the appeal. Davis LJ, who gave the principal judgment, said "I would endorse the decision of the [Upper Tribunal Judge] in all respects" (*John (A Minor: Vaccine Damage Payments scheme), Re* ([2017] AACR 20; [2017] EWCA Civ 61; [2017] EWCA Civ 61, [2017] 1 W.L.R. 1956; [2017] W.L.R.(D) 118). A child ("John") had a vaccination against pandemic influenza A (H1N1, or swine flu) when aged 7, and later developed narcolepsy and cataplexy. John's mother made a claim under the 1979 Act. Causation was not in dispute, but the Secretary of State disputed that John met the disablement threshold of 60 per cent. In particular, the Secretary of State argued that future developments should be discounted and John should simply be compared with a boy of the same age in normal health at the date of assessment. The First-tier Tribunal rejected that argument and decided that John's mother was entitled to the statutory award of £120,000, taking into account future disability.

Judge Mitchell noted that s.1(1)(a) essentially set out three fundamental conditions of entitlement, namely:

"(a) causation must be established. A person must be disabled 'as a result of' vaccination; and

(b) a disability threshold must be reached: the disability must be 'severe' and

(c) the vaccination must have been against a disease to which the Act applies" (para.44).

There are then the further conditions set out in s.1(1)(b) and (2) relating to the place and date of vaccination (in the UK after July 5, 1948), the age of the disabled person at vaccination (where relevant) and their age at date of claim (at least 2).

The assessment of disablement is governed by subs.(4), the effect of which is that s.103 of the SSCBA 1992 applies with any necessary modifications (see Judge Mitchell at paras 75-77; thus Sch.6 para.6(2) and (3) of the SSCBA do not apply – see paras 103-104). Having reviewed the principles from the industrial injuries scheme, Judge Mitchell held as follows:

"81...In order, therefore, to comply with the requirement in section 1(4) of the VDPA 1979 to assess disablement 'as for the purposes of' section 103, the VDPA 1979 assessment should reflect these elements. This calls for:
  (a) identification of an event akin to a relevant accident that has caused personal injury. That is if course the vaccination;
  (b) identification of a loss of physical or mental faculty (or both) because of the vaccination;
  (c) identification of disability or disabilities incurred as a result of the loss of faculty;
  (c) a judgement to be made as to the extent of disablement, expressed as a percentage which represents the sum of the person's disabilities."

This also requires the relevant principles from Schedule 6 of the SSCBA 1992 to be imported:

"86. If this is dissected, it shows:
  (a) Schedule 6(1)(a) is about identifying the disabilities to be taken into account in assessing the extent of a person's disablement. Its role in the overall assessment is limited to that;
  (b) the assessment is over a particular period (the 'period taken into account by the assessment') although this period is not fixed by paragraph (a);
  (c) unless excluded by sub-paragraphs (b) to (d), the disabilities to be taken into account are 'all disabilities so incurred' (as a result of the loss of faculty) to which the individual 'may be expected to be subject during the period taken into account'. This requires, therefore, the assessor to make predictions about what is likely to happen during the period taken into account;
  (d) in identifying the disabilities to which the person may be expected to be subject over the period taken into account, regard must be had to the individual's 'physical and mental condition at the date of the assessment';
  (e) in identifying the disabilities expected during the period taken into account, a comparison is to be made with 'a person of the same age and sex whose physical and mental condition is normal'."

See also, on the application of reg.11 of the Social Security (General) Benefit) Regulations 1982, Judge Mitchell's decision at paras 106–114.

Based on this careful analysis, Judge Mitchell concluded that the assessment of disablement under the 1979 Act is not a snapshot, restricted to the presenting disablement at the time of the assessment, but rather could take into account future disability (paras 116–121). The Court of Appeal agreed with that conclusion, dismissing the Secretary of State's principal ground of appeal (at paras 34–42); Davis LJ was "in no real doubt that the FTT was justified in looking (as it did) to the future prognosis, on the balance of probabilities, in assessing whether the threshold was crossed for the necessary 60% disablement" (at para.42). In the Upper Tribunal decision Judge Mitchell gave the following general guidance about the assessment of disablement (at para.149):

  "(a) the need to identify something akin to an accident. This is straightforward because it is, of course, is the vaccination;
  (b) the need to identify a loss of faculty, which is generally taken to mean 'an impairment of the proper functioning of part of the body or mind';
  (c) the need to identify the period to be taken into account by the assessment. In many cases, the nature of vaccine damage is that this is the disabled

person's lifetime because that will be the period during which the person is expected to suffer from the loss of faculty;

(d) the need to identify the disabilities, resulting from the vaccination, that may be expected during that period. A disability is generally taken to mean 'partial or total failure of power to perform normal bodily or mental processes';

(e) the need to understand how the prescribed scale of disablement functions and the extent to which it is legitimate to rely on it. I think it is clear that vaccine damage would be most unlikely to take the form of an injury on the prescribed scale because prescribed injuries all tend to be various types of physical trauma. Therefore, it will be used for comparative purposes only. A meaningful comparison is only likely to be made between disabilities, rather than injuries. To do that effectively calls for the disabilities associated with the prescribed injury to be compared with those associated with disabilities resulting from vaccination;

(f) the final stage in the process is to express the sum of disabilities in terms of overall disablement, using a percentage. At this stage, I think it is important to note that vaccine damage, tending often to be systemic in nature, may well result in a constellation of disabilities. These should be carefully identified;

(g) it should be remembered that personal factors may not be taken into account, other than age, sex, physical and mental condition. However, evidence about personal activities is perfectly acceptable if it says something relevant about disability or disablement."

Finally, Judge Mitchell was also highly critical of the conduct of the appeal by the Vaccine Damage Unit, in particular with regard to the poor quality of the appeal papers (paras 13, 28–29 and 145) and failure to send a presenting officer to the First-tier Tribunal hearing (para.30). The Court of Appeal subsequently affirmed Judge Mitchell's "observation that *disabilities* themselves are but a stepping-stone towards the assessment of *disablement*" (per Davis LJ at para.46, emphasis in the original).

Subsection (1A)

1.4   The statutory sum was increased to £120,000 by the Vaccine Damage Payments Act 1979 Statutory Sum Order 2007 (SI 2007/1931) with effect from July 12, 2007.

Subsection (2)

1.5   Mumps is added to the lists of diseases by the Vaccine Damage Payments (Specified Disease) Order 1990 (SI 1990/623) and haemophilus influenza type b infection was added by the Vaccine Damage Payments (Specified Disease) Order 1995 (SI 1995/1164).

Meningococcal Group C was added to the list by the Vaccine Damage Payments (Specified Disease) Order 2001 (SI 2001/1652).

With effect from September 4, 2006, pneumococcal infection was added to the list of diseases by the Vaccine Damage Payments (Specified Disease) Order 2006 (SI 2006/2066).

With effect from September 1, 2008, human papillomavirus was added to the list of diseases by the Vaccine Damage Payments (Specified Disease) Order 2008 (SI 2008/2103).

With effect from September 1, 2010, influenza caused by the pandemic influenza A (H1N1) 2009 virus ("swine flu") was removed from the list of diseases to which the Act applies by the Vaccine Damage Payments (Specified Disease) (Revocation and Savings) Order 2010 (SI 2010/1988). Article 4 of the Order ensures, however, that protection under the Act remains applicable to anyone who received the vaccination prior to September 1, 2010.

With effect from February 28, 2015, rotavirus and influenza, other than influenza caused by a pandemic influenza virus, were added to the list of diseases by the Vaccine Damage Payments (Specified Disease) Order 2015 (SI 2015/47). The addition of influenza (other than influenza caused by a pandemic influenza virus) does not, however, affect any entitlement arising under the Vaccine Damage Payments (Specified Disease) Order 2009 (SI 2009/2516), which added pandemic influenza A (H1N1 virus), and references in the 2015 Order to pandemic influenza are to be construed accordingly.

Subsection (4)

The substitution of 60 per cent for 80 per cent applies to claims made on or after June 16, 2002 (the specified date). There is transitional provision in Art.4 and the Schedule to the Order. Art.4 provides:

"Transitional claims

4. The provisions in the Schedule to this Order shall have effect and are designäted as subordinate provisions for the purposes of section 4(3) of the Regulatory Reform Act 2001."

The Schedule to the Order deals with Transitional Claims (defined in paragraph 3(1) of the Schedule) and provides as follows:

Article 4   SCHEDULE

TRANSITIONAL CLAIMS

1.—A transitional claim may be made in the cases specified in paragraph 3(1).   1.6

2. In this Schedule—
  (a) references to sections are to sections of the Act;
  (b) "advised" means—
      (i) informed in written form; or
      (ii) informed orally where there is a record in written form created by the adviser at the time when, or shortly after the time when, that advice was given;
  (c) "in written form" means in a manner which is in, or which is capable of being reproduced in, legible form;
  (d) "the amended section 1(4)" means section 1(4) as it is in force on or after the specified date;
  (e) "the amended section 3(1)(c)" means section 3(1)(c) as it is in force on or after the specified date;
  (f) "the extra-statutory scheme" means the non-statutory scheme of payments referred to in section 7;
  (g) "the previous section 1(4)" means section 1(4) as it was in force prior to the specified date;
  (h) "the previous section 3(1)(c)" means section 3(1)(c) as it was in force prior to the specified date;
  (i) "the specified date" means the date this Order comes into force; and
  (j) "transitional claim" has the meaning given in paragraph 4.
3.—(1) Subject to sub-paragraph (2), the specified cases are those where—
  (a) a claim for a payment under section 1(1) was made prior to the specified date and—
      (i) the Secretary of State refused to consider the application for a claim on the ground that the previous section 3(1)(c) was not satisfied but the amended section 3(1)(c) would have been satisfied had it been in force at the time of that refusal; or
      (ii) it was determined that no payment was due under section 1(1) on the basis that the previous section 1(4) was not satisfied;
  (b) a claim for a payment was made under the extra-statutory scheme and it was determined that no payment was due on the basis that the disabled person did not suffer disablement to the extent of 80 per cent. or more;
  (c) no claim for a payment under section 1(1) was made prior to the specified date and the Secretary of State is satisfied that—
      (i) the reason such a claim was not made was that the disabled person, those acting on his behalf or, as the case may be, his personal representatives had been advised prior to the specified date that either the previous section 1(4) or the previous section 3(1)(c) would not be satisfied if such a claim were made; and
      (ii) the amended section 3(1)(c) would have been satisfied had it been in force at the date the advice referred to in paragraph (i) was given; or
  (d) no claim for a payment under the extra-statutory scheme was made whilst it was in force and the Secretary of State is satisfied that the reason such a claim was not made was

that the disabled person, those acting on his behalf or, as the case may be, his personal representatives had been advised whilst the extra-statutory scheme was in force that the requirement in the extra-statutory scheme that the disabled person suffers disablement to the extent of 80 per cent. or more would not be satisfied if such a claim were made.

(2) The Secretary of State shall not be satisfied for the purposes of sub-paragraph (1)(c) or (d) unless there has been produced to him the written form of the advice referred to in those paragraphs or a copy of it.

4.—A "transitional claim" is a claim for a payment under section 1 (1) which is made—

   (a) by or on behalf of the disabled person concerned or, as the case may be, by his personal representatives;

   (b) in the manner prescribed by regulations under the Act for a claim under section 3; and

   (c) within 3 years after the date on which this Order came into force.

5.—(1) Where sub-paragraph (2) or (3) applies, a transitional claim shall be determined on the basis that the disabled person is, or was immediately before his death, disabled as a result of vaccination against any of the diseases to which the Act applies and whether he is, or was, severely disabled shall be determined in accordance with the amended section 1(4).

(2) This sub-paragraph applies where—

   (a) a case is a specified case by virtue of paragraph 3(1)(a)(ii); and

   (b) at the time of the claim referred to in paragraph 3(1)(a) it was determined that the condition that the person was disabled as a result of vaccination against any of the diseases to which the Act applies was satisfied but the condition that he was severely disabled in accordance with the previous section 1(4) was not satisfied.

(3) This sub-paragraph applies where—

   (a) a case is a specified case by virtue of paragraph 3(1)(b); and

   (b) at the time of the claim referred to in paragraph 3(1)(b) it was determined that the condition that the person was disabled as a result of vaccination against any of the diseases to which the extra-statutory scheme applied was satisfied but the condition that he suffered disablement to the extent of 80 per cent. or more was not satisfied.

6.—Subject to paragraph 5, a transitional claim shall be treated for the purposes of the Act as a claim which satisfies the conditions in section 3(1).

GENERAL NOTE

1.7   Note that the method of assessing the percentage degree of disablement is the same as that for industrial injuries disablement pension: see further SSCBA 1992 s.103 and commentary thereto.

Conditions of entitlement

1.8   **2.**—(1) Subject to the provisions of this section, the conditions of entitlement referred to in section 1(1)(b) above are—

   (a) that the vaccination in question was carried out—

      (i) in the United Kingdom or the Isle of Man, and

      (ii) on or after 5th July 1948, and

      (iii) in the case of vaccination against smallpox, before 1st August 1971;

   (b) except in the case of vaccination against poliomyelitis or rubella, that the vaccination was carried out either at a time when the person to whom it was given was under the age of eighteen or at the time of an outbreak within the United Kingdom or the Isle of Man of the disease against which the vaccination was given; and

   (c) that the disabled person was over the age of two on the date when the claim was made or, if he died before that date, that he died after 9th May 1978 and was over the age of two when he died.

(2) An order under section 1(2)(i) above specifying a disease for the purposes of this Act may provide that, in relation to vaccination against that disease, the conditions of entitlement specified in subsection (1) above

shall have effect subject to such modifications as may be specified in the order.

(3) In a case where this Act has effect by virtue of section 1(3) above, the reference in subsection (1)(b) above to the person to whom a vaccination was given is a reference to the person to whom it was actually given and not to the disabled person.

(4) With respect to claims made after such date as may be specified in the order and relating to vaccination against such disease as may be so specified, the Secretary of State may by order made by statutory instrument—

(a) provide that, in such circumstances as may be specified in the order, one or more of the conditions of entitlement appropriate to vaccination against that disease need not be fulfilled; or

(b) add to the conditions of entitlement which are appropriate to vaccination against that disease, either generally or in such circumstances as may be specified in the order.

(5) Regulations under this Act shall specify the cases in which vaccinations given outside the United Kingdom and the Isle of Man to persons defined in the regulations as serving members of Her Majesty's forces or members of their families are to be treated for the purposes of this Act as carried out in England.

(6) The Secretary of State shall not make an order containing any provision made by virtue of paragraph (b) of subsection (4) above unless a draft of the order has been laid before Parliament and approved by a resolution of each House; and a statutory instrument by which any other order is made under that subsection shall be subject to annulment in pursuance of a resolution of either House of Parliament.

GENERAL NOTE

See generally *SSWP v G (VDP)* [2015] UKUT 321 (AAC) at paras 42–51.   1.9

Subsection (1)(a)(ii), (2)

This stipulates that the vaccination was carried out on or after July 5, 1948. As regards vaccination against rotavirus, that date is changed to July 1, 2013, while for vaccination against influenza (other than influenza caused by a pandemic influenza virus) the relevant date is September 1, 2013. See Vaccine Damage Payments (Specified Disease) Order 2015 (SI 2015/47) art.3.   1.10

Subsection (1)(b), (2)

The condition in subs.(1)(b) (age or time at which vaccination was carried out) does not apply to vaccination against the following diseases: 1.11

● Meningococcal Group C (Vaccine Damage Payments (Specified Disease) Order 2001 (SI 2001/1652) art.3);

● Human papillomavirus (Vaccine Damage Payments (Specified Disease) Order 2008 (SI 2008/2103) art.3);

● Influenza caused by the pandemic influenza A (H1N1) 2009 virus (Vaccine Damage Payments (Specified Disease) Order 2009 (SI 2009/2516) art.3).

Moreover, as regards vaccination against rotavirus or influenza (other than influenza caused by a pandemic influenza virus) subs.(1)(b) as set out in the statutory text above does not apply and is substituted by the Vaccine Damage Payments (Specified Disease) Order 2015 (SI 2015/47) art.3(c) to read as follows:

"(b) that the vaccination was carried out at a time when the person to whom it was given was under the age of eighteen; and".

9

Determination of claims

1.12   **3.**—(1) Any reference in this Act, other than section 7, to a claim is a reference to a claim for a payment under section 1(1) above which is made—

(a) by or on behalf of the disabled person concerned or, as the case may be, by his personal representatives; and

(b) in the manner prescribed by regulations under this Act; and

[²(c) on or before whichever is the later of—

(i) the date on which the disabled person attains the age of 21, or where he has died, the date on which he would have attained the age of 21; and

(ii) the end of the period of six years beginning with the date of the vaccination to which the claim relates;]

and, in relation to a claim, any reference to the claimant is a reference to the person by whom the claim was made and any reference to the disabled person is a reference to the person in respect of whose disablement a payment under subsection (1) above is claimed to be payable.

(2) As soon as practicable after he has received a claim, the Secretary of State shall give notice in writing to the claimant of his determination whether he is satisfied that a payment is due under section 1(1) above to or for the benefit of the disabled person or to his personal representatives.

(3) If the Secretary of State is not satisfied that a payment is due as mentioned in subsection (2) above, the notice in writing under that subsection shall state the grounds on which he is not so satisfied.

(4) If, in the case of any claim, the Secretary of State—

(a) is satisfied that the conditions of entitlement which are applicable in accordance with section 2 above are fulfilled, but

(b) is not satisfied that the disabled person is or, where he has died, was immediately before his death severely disabled as a result of vaccination against any of the diseases to which this Act applies,

the notice in writing under subsection (2) above shall inform the claimant [¹of the right of appeal conferred by section 4 below.]

(5) If in any case a person is severely disabled, the question whether his severe disablement results from vaccination against any of the diseases to which this Act applies shall be determined for the purposes of this Act on the balance of probability.

AMENDMENTS

1. Social Security Act 1998, Sch.7 para.5 (October 18, 1999).
2. Regulatory Reform (Vaccine Damage Payments Act 1979) Order 2002 (SI 2002/1592) art.3 (June 16, 2002).

GENERAL NOTE

1.13   Section 3(1) creates a time limit for claiming by defining a claim as being a claim for payment made on or before the later of two dates, being (i) the date on which the disabled person attains 21 and (ii) the end of six years starting with the date of vaccination. As Judge Mitchell noted in *SSWP v G (VDP)* [2015] UKUT 321 (AAC):

> "54. If a 'claim' is made outside this window, it is not a claim at all. The Secretary of State's duty to make a payment under section 1(1) VDPA 1979 can only arise 'on consideration of a claim'. The duty cannot be triggered, therefore, by a non-claim which is why the definition of 'claim' effectively imposes a time-limit for claiming. In this case, the claim was in-time."

[¹ Decisions reversing earlier decisions

3A.—(1) Subject to subsection (2) below, any decision of the Secretary   1.14
of State under section 3 above or this section, and any decision of [² a tri-
bunal] under section 4 below, may be reversed by a decision made by the
Secretary of State—

   (a) either within the prescribed period or in prescribed cases or circum-
       stances; and
   (b) either on an application made for the purpose or on his own initiative.

(2) In making a decision under subsection (1) above, the Secretary of
State need not consider any issue that is not raised by the application or, as
the case may be, did not cause him to act on his own initiative.

(3) Regulations may prescribe the procedure by which a decision may be
made under this section.

(4) Such notice as may be prescribed by regulations shall be given of a
decision under this section.

(5) Except as provided by section 5(4) below, no payment under section
1(1) above shall be recoverable by virtue of a decision under this section.

(6) In this section and sections 4 and 8 below "appeal tribunal" means an
appeal tribunal constituted under Chapter I of Part I of the Social Security
Act 1998.]

AMENDMENTS

1. Social Security Act 1998 s.45 (October 18, 1999).
2. Transfer of Tribunal Functions Order 2008 (SI 2008/2833) art.6 and Sch.3
para.31 (November 3, 2008).

GENERAL NOTE

In *SSWP v G (VDP)* [2015] UKUT 321 (AAC), Judge Mitchell explained the   1.15
position as regards the reversal of previous decisions as follows:

"65. Drawing the reversal strings together, the upshot, so far as unsuccessful
claimants are concerned, is that, if they go to tribunal and lose, they have a
limited period in which to apply for reversal. This is either two years from notification of the tribunal's decision or six years from notification of the original
decision of the Secretary of State, whichever is later. But if they keep their powder
dry, as it were, and do not appeal, there is no time limit and an application for
reversal may be made at any time. However, the Secretary of State's power to
reverse on his own initiative expires six years after notification of his original decision (unless he wishes to reverse due to misrepresentation of or failure to disclose
a material fact which I imagine means converting a decision to award a payment
into a decision to refuse)."

[¹ Appeals to appeal tribunals

4.—(1) The claimant may appeal to [²the First-tier Tribunal] against any   1.16
decision of the Secretary of State under section 3 or 3A above.

[³(1B) If the claimant's address is not in Northern Ireland, regulations
may provide that, in such cases or circumstances as may be prescribed,
there is a right of appeal only if the Secretary of State has considered
whether to reverse the decision under section 3A.

(1C) The regulations may in particular provide that that condition is met
only where–

(a) the consideration by the Secretary of State was on an application,

(b) the Secretary of State considered issues of a specified description, or

(c) the consideration by the Secretary of State satisfied any other condition specified in the regulations.]

(2) Regulations may make–

(a) provision as to the manner in which, and the time within which, appeals are to be brought; [[2]...]

[[3](c) provision that, where in accordance with regulations under subsection (1B) there is no right of appeal against a decision, any purported appeal may be treated as an application to reverse the decision under section 3A.]

(3) The regulations may in particular make any provision of a kind mentioned in Schedule 5 to the Social Security Act 1998.

(4) In deciding an appeal under this section, [[2]the First-tier Tribunal] shall consider all the circumstances of the case (including any not obtaining at the time when the decision appealed against was made).]

AMENDMENTS

1. This version of s.4 (October 18, 1999) was substituted by Social Security Act 1998 s.46.

2. Transfer of Tribunal Functions Order 2008 (SI 2008/2833) art.6 and Sch.3 para.32 (November 3, 2008).

3. Welfare Reform Act 2012 s.102(6) and Sch.11 paras 1, 2 (February 25, 2013).

GENERAL NOTE

1.17   Note that there is no time limit for bringing an appeal (*SSWP v G (VDP)* [2015] UKUT 321 (AAC) at para.68). Judge Mitchell also noted that by virtue of s.4(4) the "default position" for social security appeals in s.12(8) of the Social Security Act 1988 does not apply to appeals under the 1979 Act. "Accordingly, all relevant circumstances up to the date of the appeal hearing are to be taken into account. This is consistent with the absence of a time limit for bringing an appeal because, in theory, many years might elapse between decision and appeal hearing" (at para.69).

The non-sequential numbering is to accommodate a new subs. (1A) inserted by the Welfare Reform Act 2007 s.57(2), which has not yet been brought into effect.

Reconsideration of determinations and recovery of payments in certain cases

1.18   **5.**—[[1] *Subss. (1)–(3) Repealed.*]

(4) If, whether fraudulently or otherwise, any person misrepresents or fails to disclose any material fact and in consequence of the misrepresentation or failure a payment is made under section 1(1) above, the person to whom the payment was made shall be liable to repay the amount of that payment to the Secretary of State unless he can show that the misrepresentation or failure occurred without his connivance or consent.

(5) [[1] *Repealed*]

AMENDMENT

1. Social Security Act 1998 Sch.7 para.6 (October 18, 1999).

Payments to or for the benefit of disabled persons

6.—(1) Where a payment under section 1(1) above falls to be made in respect of a disabled person who is over eighteen and capable of managing his own affairs, the payment shall be made to him.

1.19

(2) Where such a payment falls to be made in respect of a disabled person who has died, the payment shall be made to his personal representatives.

(3) Where such a payment falls to be made in respect of any other disabled person, the payment shall be made for his benefit by paying it to such trustees as the Secretary of State may appoint to be held by them upon such trusts or, in Scotland, for such purposes and upon such conditions as may be declared by the Secretary of State.

(4) The making of a claim for, or the receipt of, a payment under section 1(1) above does not prejudice the right of any person to institute or carry on proceedings in respect of disablement suffered as a result of vaccination against any disease to which this Act applies; but in any civil proceedings brought in respect of disablement resulting from vaccination against such a disease, the court shall treat a payment made to or in respect of the disabled person concerned under section 1(1) above as paid on account of any damages which the court awards in respect of such disablement.

GENERAL NOTE

As Judge Mitchell explained in *Secretary of State for Work and Pensions v G* [2015] UKUT 321 (AAC) (at para.72), s.6(4) means that "a payment under the VDPA 1979 does not affect any rights to bring proceedings but, where civil proceedings are brought in respect of disablement, the payment will reduce the damages received by the claimant."

1.20

Payments, claims etc. made prior to the Act

7.—(1) Any reference in this section to an extra-statutory payment is a reference to a payment of £10,000 made by the Secretary of State to or in respect of a disabled person after 9th May 1978 and before the passing of this Act pursuant to a non-statutory scheme of payments for severe vaccine damage.

1.21

(2) No such claim as is referred to in section 3(1) above shall be entertained if an extra-statutory payment has been made to or for the benefit of the disabled person or his personal representatives.

(3) For the purposes of [¹section 3A above], a determination that an extra-statutory payment should be made shall be treated as a determination that a payment should be made under section 1(1) above [¹ . . .].

(4) [¹ Section 5(4) above] and section 6(4) above shall apply in relation to an extra-statutory payment as they apply in relation to a payment made under section 1(1) above.

(5) For the purposes of this Act (other than this section) regulations under this Act may—

(a) treat claims which were made in connection with the scheme referred to in subsection (1) above and which have not been disposed of at the commencement of this Act as claims falling within section 3(1) above; and

(b) treat information and other evidence furnished and other things done before the commencement of this Act in connection with any

13

such claim as is referred to in paragraph (a) above as furnished or done in connection with a claim falling within section 3(1) above.

AMENDMENT

1. Social Security Act 1998 Sch.7 para.7 (October 18, 1999).

[¹ Correction of errors and setting aside of decisions

1.22   **7A.**—(1) Regulations may make provision with respect to—
        (a) the correction of accidental errors in any decision or record of a decision under section [² 3 or 3A] of this Act; [² . . .].
        (2) Nothing in subsection (1) shall be construed as derogating from any power to correct errors [² . . .] which is exercisable apart from regulations made by virtue of that subsection.]

AMENDMENTS

1. Inserted by Social Security Act 1998 s.47 (October 18, 1999).
2. Transfer of Tribunal Functions Order 2008 (SI 2008/2833) art.6 and Sch.3 para.34 (November 3, 2008).

[¹Finality of decisions

1.23   **7B.**—(1) Subject to the provisions of this Act [² and article 4 of, and the Schedule to, the Regulatory Reform (Vaccine Damage Payments Act 1979) Order 2002 (modifications of this Act in relation to transitional claims)], any decision made in accordance with the foregoing provisions of this Act shall be final.
        (2) If and to the extent that regulations so provide, any finding of fact or other determination embodied in or necessary to such a decision, or on which such a decision is based, shall be conclusive for the purposes of—
        (a) further such decisions;
        (b) decisions made in accordance with sections 8 to 16 of the Social Security Act 1998, or with regulations under section 11 of that Act; and
        (c) decisions made under the Child Support Act 1991.]

AMENDMENTS

1. Inserted by Social Security Act 1998 Sch.7 para.8 (October 18, 1999).
2. Regulatory Reform (Vaccine Damage Payments Act 1979) Order 2002 (SI 2002/1592) art.5 (June 16, 2002).

GENERAL NOTE

Subsection (1)
1.24   Article 4 of and the Schedule to the Order are reproduced in the annotation to s.1(4), above.

Regulations

1.25   **8.**—(1) Any reference in the preceding provisions of this Act to regulations under this Act is a reference to regulations made by the Secretary of State.
        (2) Any power of the Secretary of State under this Act to make regulations—
        (a) shall be exercisable by statutory instrument [²...]; and

(b) includes power to make such incidental or supplementary provision as appears to the Secretary of State to be appropriate.

[²(2A) A statutory instrument containing regulations made by the Secretary of State under this Act–
- (a) except in the case of an instrument containing regulations under section 4(1B), is subject to annulment in pursuance of a resolution of either House of Parliament;
- (b) in the case of an instrument containing regulations under section 4(1B), may not be made unless a draft of the instrument has been laid before and approved by a resolution of each House of Parliament.]

(3) Regulations made by the Secretary of State may contain provision—
- (a) with respect to the information and other evidence to be furnished in connection with a claim;
- (b) requiring disabled persons to undergo medical examination before their claims are determined or for the purposes of [¹a decision under section 3A above];
- (c) restricting the disclosure of medical evidence and advice tendered in connection with a claim or [¹a decision under section 3A above]; and
- (d) conferring functions on [¹appeal tribunals] with respect to the matters referred to in paragraphs (a) to (c) above.

[²(5) The power to make regulations under section 4(1B) may be exercised–
- (a) in relation to all cases to which it extends, in relation to those cases but subject to specified exceptions or in relation to any specified cases or classes of case;
- (b) so as to make, as respects the cases in relation to which it is exercised–
  - (i) the full provision to which it extends or any lesser provision (whether by way of exception or otherwise);
  - (ii) the same provision for all cases, different provision for different cases or classes of case or different provision as respects the same case or class of case but for different purposes of this Act;
  - (iii) provision which is either unconditional or is subject to any specified condition.]

AMENDMENTS

1. Social Security Act 1998 Sch.7 para.9.
2. Welfare Reform Act 2012 s.102(6) and Sch.11 paras 1, 2 (February 25, 2013).

GENERAL NOTE

The non-sequential numbering is to accommodate a new subs. (4) inserted by the Welfare Reform Act 2007 Sch.7 para.1(7), relating only to Northern Ireland, which has not yet been brought into effect.

1.26

Fraudulent statements etc.

9.—(1) Any person who, for the purpose of obtaining any payment under this Act, whether for himself or some other person,—
- (a) knowingly makes any false statement or representation, or
- (b) produces or furnishes or causes or knowingly allows to be produced or furnished any document or information which he knows to be false in a material particular,

1.27

15

shall be liable on summary conviction to a fine not exceeding [¹ level 5 on the standard scale]

(2) In the application of subsection (1) above to the Isle of Man, for the words following "liable" there shall be substituted the words "on summary conviction, within the meaning of the Interpretation Act 1976 (an Act of Tynwald), to a fine of £400 and on conviction on information to a fine".

AMENDMENT

1. Words substituted by virtue of Criminal Justice Act 1982 (c.48) s.46, Criminal Procedure (Scotland) Act 1975 (c.21) s.289G, and for Northern Ireland by SI 1984/703 (NI3) arts 5, 6.

1.28   *Sections 9A, 10 and 11 omitted.*

Financial provisions

1.29   **12.**—(1) [² *Repealed*].

(2) The Secretary of State shall pay such fees as he considers appropriate to medical practitioners, as defined in [¹ section 191 of the Social Security Administration Act 1992] who provide information or other evidence in connection with claims.

(3) The Secretary of State shall pay such travelling and other allowances as he may determine—

(a) to persons required under this Act to undergo medical examinations; [³ . . .] and

(c) in circumstances where he considers it appropriate, to any person who accompanies a disabled person to such a medical examination [³ . . .].

(4) There shall be paid out of moneys provided by Parliament—

(a) any expenditure incurred by the Secretary of State in making payments under section 1(1) above;

(b) any expenditure incurred by the Secretary of State by virtue of subsections (1) to (3) above; and

(c) any increase in the administrative expenses of the Secretary of State attributable to this Act.

(5) Any sums repaid to the Secretary of State by virtue of section 5(4) above shall be paid into the Consolidated Fund.

AMENDMENTS

1. Social Security (Consequential Provisions) Act 1992 Sch.2 para.54 (July 1, 1992).

2. Social Security Act 1998 Sch.7 para.10 (October 18, 1999).

3. Transfer of Tribunal Functions Order 2008 (SI 2008/2833) art.6 and Sch.3 para.36 (November 3, 2008).

Short title and extent

1.30   **13.**—(1) This Act may be cited as the Vaccine Damage Payments Act 1979.

(2) This Act extends to Northern Ireland and the Isle of Man.

Pneumoconiosis etc. (Workers' Compensation) Act 1979

(1979 C.41)

ARRANGEMENT OF SECTIONS

1–2   *Omitted.*
3   Dependants
4–9   *Omitted.*
10   Short title, construction, commencement and extent
Schedule *Omitted.*

1.31

An Act to make provision for lump sum payments to or in respect of certain persons who are, or were immediately before they died, disabled by pneumoconiosis, byssinosis or diffuse mesothelioma; and for connected purposes.

[4th April 1979]

Dependants

3. — (1) In this Act "dependant", in relation to a person who, immediately before he died, was disabled by a disease to which this Act applies, means—

1.32

   (a) if he left a spouse [¹ or civil partner] who was residing with him or was receiving or entitled to receive from him periodical payments for her maintenance, that spouse [¹ or civil partner];

   (b) if paragraph (a) above does not apply but he left a child or children who fall within subsection (2) below, that child or those children;

[¹ (c) if neither of the preceding paragraphs applies but he left a person who was residing with him and with whom he was in a qualifying relationship, that person;]

   (d) if none of the preceding paragraphs applies, any relative or relatives of his who fall within subsection (2) below and who were, in the opinion of the Secretary of State, wholly or mainly dependent on him at the date of his death.

(2) A person falls within this subsection if, at the relevant date, he was—

   (a) under the age of 16;

   (b) under the age of 21 and not gainfully employed full-time; or

   (c) permanently incapable of self-support;

and in this subsection "relevant date" means the date of the deceased's death or the date of the coming into force of this Act, whichever is the later.

[²(2A) For the purposes of subsection (1)(c) two persons are in a qualifying relationship if they are living together as a married couple.]

AMENDMENTS

1. Welfare Reform Act 2007 s.59 (July 3, 2007).
2. Marriage (Same Sex Couples) Act 2013 (Consequential and Contrary Provisions and Scotland) Order 2014 (SI 214/560) art.2 and Sch.1 para.18 (March 13, 2014) (as regards England and Wales only) and Marriage and Civil Partnership (Scotland) Act 2014 and Civil Partnership Act 2004 (Consequential Provisions and Modifications) Order 2014 (SI 2014/3229) art.29, Sch.5 para.7(a) (December 16, 2014) (Scotland only).

Short title, construction, commencement and extent

1.33   **10.**—(1) This Act may be cited as the Pneumoconiosis etc (Workers' Compensation) Act 1979.

(2) Except where the context otherwise requires, any expression to which a meaning is assigned by [¹ the Social Security Contributions and Benefits Act 1992 or the Social Security Administration Act 1992], or by any regulations made under [¹ either of those Acts], has that meaning also for the purposes of this Act.

(3) This Act shall come into force on the expiration of a period of three months beginning with the day on which it is passed.

(4) This Act does not extend to Northern Ireland.

AMENDMENT

1. Social Security (Consequential Provisions) Act 1992 s.4, Sch.2 para.57 (July 1, 1992).

GENERAL NOTE

1.34   Sections 3 and 10 of the Pneumoconiosis etc (Workers' Compensation) Act 1979 have been included in this volume as the definitions therein have been incorporated by reference into the 2008 Diffuse Mesothelioma Scheme. On the scheme of the 1979 Act generally, see the decision by Judge Mitchell in the compensation recovery appeal case, *Aviva Insurance v SSWP* [2015] UKUT 613 (AAC).

Social Security Contributions and Benefits Act 1992

(1992 c.4)

ARRANGEMENT OF SECTIONS

PART I

CONTRIBUTIONS

Preliminary

1.35   1.   Outline of contributory system.
2.   Categories of earners.
3.   "Earnings" and "earner".
4.   Payments treated as remuneration and earnings.
5–19.   *Omitted.*

PART II

CONTRIBUTORY BENEFITS

Preliminary

20.   Descriptions of contributory benefits.

21.   Contribution conditions.
22.   Earnings factors.
23.   *Omitted.*
23A.   Contributions credits for relevant parents and carers
24.   *Omitted.*

Unemployment benefit

25–30. *Repealed.*

Incapacity benefit

30A.–30E.   *Omitted.*
For the text of these sections, see the 2011/12 edition of this Volume.

Sickness benefit

31.   *Omitted.*
32.   *Omitted.*

Invalidity benefits

33.   *Omitted.*
34.   *Omitted.*

Maternity

35.   State maternity allowance.

*Bereavement benefits: deaths before the day on which section 30
of the Pensions Act 2014 comes into force*

36.   *Bereavement payment (repealed).*
36A.   *Cases in which sections 37 to 41 apply (repealed).*
37.   Widowed mother's allowance: deaths before April 9, 2001.
38.   Widow's pension.
39.   Rate of widowed mother's allowance and widow's pension.
39A.   Widowed parent's allowance.
39B.   Bereavement allowance where no dependent children.
39C.   Rate of widowed parent's allowance and bereavement allowance.
40.   Long-term incapacity benefit for widows.
41.   Long-term incapacity benefit for widowers.
42.   Entitlement under section 40 or 41 after period of employment or training
            for work.

Retirement pensions (Categories A and B)

43.   Persons entitled to more than one retirement pension.
44.   Category A retirement pension.
45.   The additional pension in a Category A retirement pension.
45A.   Effect of working families' tax credit and disabled persons' tax credit on
            earnings factor.

45B. Reduction of additional pension in Category A retirement pension: pension sharing.

46. Modifications of section 45 for calculating the additional pension in certain benefits.

47. Increase of Category A retirement pension for invalidity.

48. Use of former spouse's contributions.

48A. Category B retirement pension for married person or civil partner.

48AA. Category B retirement pension for divorcee or former civil partner.

48B. Category B retirement pension for widows and widowers.

48BB. Category B retirement pension: entitlement by reference to benefits under section 39A or 39B.

48C. Category B retirement pension: general.

49. *Repealed.*

50. *Repealed.*

51. Category B retirement pension for widows, widowers and surviving civil partners who attained pensionable age before 6 April 2010.

51ZA. Special provision for married person whose spouse changed gender.

51A. Special provision for married people.

52. Special provision for surviving spouses.

53. *Repealed.*

54. Category A and Category B retirement pensions: supplemental provisions.

55. Increase of retirement pension where entitlement is deferred.

55A. Shared additional pension.

55AA. Shared additional pension because of a new state scheme pension credit.

55B. Reduction of shared additional pension: pension sharing.

55C. Increase of shared additional pension where entitlement is deferred.

Child's special allowance

56. Child's special allowance—existing beneficiaries.

Provisions relating to unemployment benefit, sickness benefit and invalidity benefit

57. *Repealed.*

58. *Repealed.*

Invalidity benefit-disqualifications etc.

59. *Repealed.*

Complete or partial failure to satisfy contribution conditions

60.–61A. *Omitted.*

Graduated retirement benefit

62. Graduated retirement benefit.

PART III

NON-CONTRIBUTORY BENEFITS

63.   Descriptions of non-contributory benefits.

Attendance allowance

64.   Entitlement.
65.   Period and rate of allowance.
66.   Attendance allowance for the terminally ill.
67.   Exclusions by regulation.

Severe disablement allowance

68.   Entitlement and rate.
69.   Severe disablement allowance: age related addition.

Invalid care allowance

70.   Invalid care allowance.

Disability living allowance

71.   Disability living allowance.
72.   The care component.
73.   The mobility component.
74.   Mobility component for certain persons eligible for invalid carriages.
75.   Persons 65 or over.
76.   Disability living allowance-supplementary.

Guardian's allowance

77.   Omitted. See *Vol.IV: Tax Credits and HMRC–administered Social Security Benefits.*

Benefits for the aged

78.   Category C and Category D retirement pensions and other benefits for the aged.
79.   Age addition.

PART IV

INCREASES FOR DEPENDANTS

Child dependants

80. Beneficiary's dependent children.
81. Restrictions on increase—child not living with beneficiary, etc.

Adult dependants

82. Short-term benefit: increase for adult dependants.
83. Pension increase (wife).
84. Pension increase (husband).
85. Pension increase (person with care of children).
86. *Repealed.*
86A. Incapacity benefit: increase for adult dependants.
87. Rate of increase where associated retirement pension is attributable to reduced contributions.
88. Increases to be in respect of only one adult dependant.

Miscellaneous

89. Earnings to include occupational and personal pensions for purposes of provisions relating to increases of benefits in respect of child or adult dependants.
90. Beneficiaries under sections 68 and 70.
91. Effect of trade disputes on entitlement to increases.
92. Dependency increases: continuation of awards in cases of fluctuating earnings.
93. Dependency increases on termination of employment after period of entitlement to disability working allowance.

PART V

BENEFIT FOR INDUSTRIAL INJURIES

General provisions

94. Right to industrial injuries benefit.
95. Relevant employments.
96. Persons treated as employers for certain purposes.
97. Accidents in course of illegal employments.
98. Earner acting in breach of regulations, etc.
99. Earner travelling in employer's transport.
100. Accidents happening while meeting emergency.
101. Accident caused by another's misconduct etc.

Sickness benefit

102.   *Repealed.*

Disablement pension

103.   Disablement pension.
104.   Increase where constant attendance needed.
105.   Increase for exceptionally severe disablement.

Other benefits and increases

106.   Benefits and increases subject to qualifications as to time.

Successive accidents

107.   Adjustments for successive accidents.

Prescribed industrial diseases, etc.

108.   Benefit in respect of prescribed industrial diseases, etc.
109.   General provisions relating to benefit under section 108.
110.   Respiratory diseases.

Old cases

111.   Workmen's compensation etc.

Part VI

Miscellaneous Provisions Relating to Parts I to V

Earnings

112.   Certain sums to be earnings.

Disqualification and suspension

113.   General provisions as to disqualification and suspension.

Persons maintaining dependants etc.

114.   Persons maintaining dependants, etc.

Special cases

115.   Crown employment—Parts I to VI.
116.   Her Majesty's forces.
117.   Mariners, airmen, etc.
118.   Married women and widows.
119.   Persons outside Great Britain.
120.   Employment at sea (continental shelf operations).
121.   Treatment of certain marriages.

Interpretation

122.   Interpretation of Parts I to VI and supplementary provisions.

PART VII

INCOME-RELATED BENEFITS

Omitted.

See *Vol. II: Income Support, Jobseeker's Allowance, State Pension Credit and the Social Fund.*

PART VIII

THE SOCIAL FUND

Omitted.

See *Vol. II: Income Support, Jobseeker's Allowance, State Pension Credit and the Social Fund.*

PART IX

CHILD BENEFIT

141.–147. *Omitted.* See *Vol. IV Tax Credits and HMRC–administered Social Security Benefits.*

PART X

CHRISTMAS BONUS FOR PENSIONERS

148.   Entitlement of pensioners to Christmas bonus.
149.   Provisions supplementary to section 148.
150.   Interpretation of Part X.

PART XI

STATUTORY SICK PAY

151.–163.   *Omitted.*
See Vol.IV: Tax Credits and HMRC-administered Social Security Benefits.

PART XII

STATUTORY MATERNITY PAY

164.–171.   *Omitted.*
See Vol.IV: Tax Credits and HMRC-administered Social Security Benefits.

PART XIIZA

STATUTORY PATERNITY PAY

171ZA.–171ZK.   *Omitted.*
See Vol.IV: Tax Credits and HMRC-administered Social Security Benefits.

PART XIIZB

STATUTORY ADOPTION PAY

171ZL.–171ZT.   *Omitted.*
See Vol.IV: Tax Credits and HMRC-administered Social Security Benefits.

PART XIIZC

STATUTORY SHARED PARENTAL PAY

171ZU.– 171ZZ5.   *Omitted.*
See Vol.IV: Tax Credits and HMRC-administered Social Security Benefits.

PART XIIA

INCAPACITY FOR WORK

171A.–171G. *Omitted.*
For the text of these sections see the 2011/12 edition of this Volume.

PART XIII

GENERAL

Interpretation

172.   Application of Act in relation to territorial waters.
173.   Age.
174.   References to Acts.

Subordinate legislation

175.   Regulations, orders and schemes.
176.   Parliamentary control.

Short title, commencement and extent

177.   Short title, commencement and extent.

SCHEDULES

Schedule 1—*Omitted.*
Schedule 2—*Omitted.*
Schedule 3—Contribution conditions for entitlement to benefit.
    Part I—The conditions.
    Part II—Satisfaction of conditions in early years of contribution.
Schedule 4—Rates of benefits, etc.
    Part I—Contributory periodical benefits.
    Part II—Widow's payment.
    Part III—Non-contributory periodical benefits.
    Part IV—Increases for dependants.
    Part V—Rates of industrial injuries benefit.
Schedule 5—*Omitted.*
Schedule 6—Assessment of extent of disablement.
Schedule 7—Industrial injuries benefits.
    Part I—Unemployability supplement.
    Part II—Disablement gratuity.
    Part III—Increase of disablement pension during hospital treatment.
    Part IV—Reduced earnings allowance.
    Part V—Retirement allowance.
    Part VI—*Omitted.*
Schedule 8—*Omitted.*
Schedule 9—Exclusions from entitlement to child benefit.

Schedule 10—Priority between persons entitled to child benefit.
Schedule 11—*Omitted.*
Schedule 12—Relationship of statutory sick pay with benefits and other payments, etc.
Schedule 13—Relationship of statutory maternity pay with benefits and other payments, etc.
An Act to consolidate certain enactments relating to social security contributions and benefits with amendments to give effect to recommendations of the Law Commission and the Scottish Law Commission.

[13TH FEBRUARY 1992]

PART I

CONTRIBUTIONS

Preliminary

Outline of contributory system

1.36

1.—(1) The funds required—
  (a) for paying such benefits under this Act [¹⁶ or any other Act] as are payable out of the National Insurance Fund and not out of other public money; and
  (b) for the making of payments under section 162 of the Administration Act towards the cost of the National Health Service,
shall be provided by means of contributions payable to the [¹ Inland Revenue] by earners, employers and others, together with the additions under subsection (5) below [² and amounts payable under section 2 of the Social Security Act 1993].
  (2) Contributions under this Part of this Act shall be of the following [³[¹⁹. . .]] classes—
  (a) Class 1, earnings-related, payable under section 6 below, being—
    (i) primary Class 1 contributions from employed earners; and
    (ii) secondary Class 1 contributions from employers and other persons paying earnings;
  (b) Class 1A, payable under section 10 below [⁴. . .] by persons liable to pay secondary Class 1 contributions and certain other persons;
  [⁵(bb) Class 1B, payable under section 10A below by persons who are accountable to the Inland Revenue in respect of income tax on [⁶ general earnings] in accordance with a PAYE settlement agreement;]
  (c) Class 2, flat-rate, payable [¹⁷. . .] under section 11 below by self-employed earners;
  (d) Class 3, payable under section 13 [¹⁴ or 13A] below by earners and others voluntarily with a view to providing entitlement to benefit, or making up entitlement; [¹⁹. . .]
  [¹⁹(da) Class 3A, payable by eligible people voluntarily under section 14A with a view to obtaining units of additional pension; and]
  (e) Class 4, payable under section 15 below in respect of the profits or gains of a trade, profession or vocation, or under section 18 below in respect of equivalent earnings.
  (3) The amounts and rates of contributions in this Part of this Act and the other figures in it which affect the liability of contributions shall—

(a) be subject to regulations under sections 19(4) and 116 to 120 below; and

(b) to the extent provided for by Part IX of the Administration Act be subject to alteration by orders made by the [⁷ Treasury] from year to year under that Part

[⁸ . . .].

(4) Schedule 1 to this Act—

(a) shall have effect with respect to the computation, collection and recovery of contributions of Classes 1, 1A, [⁹ 1B,] 2, 3, [¹⁹ and 3A] and otherwise with respect to contributions of those classes; and

(b) shall also, to the extent provided by regulations made under section 18 below, have effect with respect to the computation, collection and recovery of Class 4 contributions, and otherwise with respect to such contributions [¹⁰ . . .].

(5) For each financial year there shall, by way of addition to contributions, be paid out of money provided by Parliament, in such manner and at such times as the Treasury may determine, amounts the total of which for any such year is equal to the aggregate of all statutory sick pay [¹¹, statutory maternity pay], [¹⁵statutory paternity pay][¹¹ statutory adoption pay] [¹⁸ and statutory shared parental pay] recovered by employers and others in that year, as estimated by the Government Actuary or the Deputy Government Actuary.

(6) No person shall—

(a) be liable to pay Class 1, Class 1A [¹², Class 1B] or Class 2 contributions unless he fulfils prescribed conditions as to residence or presence in Great Britain;

(b) be entitled to pay Class 3 contributions unless he fulfils such conditions; or

(c) be entitled to pay Class 1, Class 1A [¹², Class 1B] or Class 2 contributions other than those which he is liable to pay, except so far as he is permitted by regulations to pay them.

[¹³ (7) Regulations under subsection (6) above shall be made by the Treasury.]

AMENDMENTS

1. Social Security Contributions (Transfer of Functions, etc.) Act 1999 Sch.1 para.5(2) (February 25, 1999 for the purpose of enabling the Secretary of State to make subordinate legislation conferring functions on the Commissioners of Inland Revenue; April 1, 1999 otherwise).

2. Social Security Act 1993 s.2(9) (January 29, 1993).

3. Social Security Act 1998 Sch.7 para.56(1) (September 8, 1998 for the purpose of authorising the making of regulations or orders; April 6, 1999 otherwise).

4. Child Support, Pensions and Social Security Act 2000 Sch.9 (Part VIII), para.1 (April 6, 2000: repeal has effect in relation to the tax year beginning April 6, 2000 and subsequent tax years).

5. Social Security Act 1998 Sch.7 para.56(1) (September 8, 1998 for the purpose of authorising the making of regulations or orders; April 6, 1999 otherwise).

6. Income Tax (Earnings and Pensions) Act 2003 Sch.6(2) para.170 (April 6, 2003 subject to transitional provisions and savings specified in 2003 c.1 Sch.7).

7. Social Security Contributions (Transfer of Functions, etc.) Act 1999 Sch.3 para.1(2) (April 1, 1999).

8. Pensions Act 2014 Sch.13 para.49 (April 6, 2016).

9. Social Security Act 1998 Sch.7 para.56(2) (September 8, 1998 for the purpose of authorising the making of regulations or orders; April 6, 1999 otherwise).

10. Social Security Contributions (Transfer of Functions, etc.) Act 1999 Sch.1 para.5(3) (February 25, 1999 for the purpose of enabling the Secretary of State to make subordinate legislation conferring functions on the Commissioners of Inland Revenue; April 1, 1999 otherwise).

11. Employment Act 2002 Pt 1, s.6(3) (December 8, 2002 subject to transitional provisions specified in SI 2002/2866 Sch.3; not yet in force otherwise).

12. Social Security Act 1998 Sch.7, para.56(3) (September 8, 1998 for the purpose of authorising the making of regulations or orders; April 6, 1999 otherwise).

13. Social Security Contributions (Transfer of Functions, etc.) Act 1999 Sch.3, para.1(3) (April 1, 1999).

14. Pensions Act 2008 s.135(3) (April 6, 2009).

15. Children and Families Act 2014 s.126, Sch.7, para.7(a) (April 5, 2015).

16. Pensions Act 2014 Sch.12 para.3 (April 6, 2016).

17. National Insurance Contributions Act 2015 s.2 Sch.1 para.2 (April 6, 2015).

18. Children and Families Act 2014 Sch.7, para.7(b) (December 1, 2014).

19. Pensions Act 2014 Sch.15(1) para.2 (October 12, 2015).

Categories of earners

2.—(1) In this Part of this Act and Parts II to V below—   1.37

(a) "employed earner" means a person who is gainfully employed in Great Britain either under a contract of service, or in an office (including elective office) with [² [³ . . .] earnings]; and

(b) "self-employed earner" means a person who is gainfully employed in Great Britain otherwise than in employed earner's employment (whether or not he is also employed in such employment).

(2) Regulations may provide—

(a) for employment of any prescribed description to be disregarded in relation to liability for contributions otherwise arising from employment of that description;

(b) for a person in employment of any prescribed description to be treated, for the purposes of this Act, as falling within one or other of the categories of earner defined in subsection (1) above, notwithstanding that he would not fall within that category apart from the regulations.

[⁴(2ZA) Regulations under subsection (2)(b) may make provision treating a person ("P") as falling within one or other of the categories of earner in relation to an employment where arrangements have been entered into the main purpose, or one of the main purposes, of which is to secure—

(a) that P is not treated by other provision in regulations under subsection (2)(b) as falling within that category of earner in relation to the employment, or

(b) that a person is not treated as the secondary contributor in respect of earnings paid to or for the benefit of P in respect of the employment.

(2ZB) In subsection (2ZA) "arrangements" include any scheme, transaction or series of transactions, agreement or understanding, whether or not legally enforceable, and any associated operations.]

[¹ (2A) Regulations under subsection (2) above shall be made by the Treasury and, in the case of regulations under paragraph (b) of that subsection, with the concurrence of the Secretary of State.]

(3) Where a person is to be treated by reference to any employment of his as an employed earner, then he is to be so treated for all purposes of this Act; and references throughout this Act to employed earner's employment shall be construed accordingly.

(4) Subsections (1) to (3) above are subject to the provision made by section 95 below as to the employments which are to be treated, for the purposes of industrial injuries benefit, as employed earner's employments.

(5) For the purposes of this Act, a person shall be treated as a self-employed earner as respects any week during any part of which he is such an earner (without prejudice to his being also treated as an employed earner as respects that week by reference to any other employment of his).

AMENDMENTS

1. Welfare Reform and Pensions Act 1999 Sch.11 para.2 (April 6, 2000), replacing an earlier amendment made by the Transfer of Functions Act 1999, Sch.3 para.2 (April 1, 1999).
2. Income Tax (Earnings and Pensions) Act 2003 s.722, Sch.6 paras 169 and 171 (April 6, 2003).
3. National Insurance Contributions Act 2014, s.15(1) (May 13, 2014).
4. National Insurance Contributions Act 2015 s.6(3) (December 12, 2015)

DERIVATION

1.38   SSA 1975 s.2.

DEFINITIONS

"contract of service"—s.122.
"employment"—s.122.
"prescribed"—s.122.

GENERAL NOTE

1.39   The definitions in this section are primarily of importance in determining liability to pay contributions of a particular class, which is a matter for Her Majesty's Revenue and Customs. Their importance for tribunals is that the definition of "earnings" in s.3 refers back to this section.

The definition of employed earners refers to a person being "gainfully employed". This notion has caused some difficulty but it appears that it refers to cases where there is an obligation by an employer to pay remuneration to an employee for those tasks the employee is bound to perform for the employer under the contract of employment: see Slade J. in *Vandyk v Minister of Pensions and National Insurance* [1955] 1 Q.B. 29 at 38.

"Contract of service"

1.40   This is broadly defined by the Act to include any contract of service or apprenticeship, whether written or oral and whether express or implied. The existence of an employer/employee relationship may not always be obvious. The trend of a complex general case law on the issue is that in determining whether a person is self-employed or employed, particular regard will be had to whether the person has risked his or her own capital in the enterprise: *Young and Woods v West* [1980] I.R.L.R. 201 at 209. For a detailed discussion of the question see *Wikeley Ogus & Barendt*, pp.96–109, and see now *Autoclenz Ltd v Belcher* [2011] UKSC 41; [2011] I.C.R. 1157 and *Stringfellow Restaurants Ltd v Quashie* [2012] EWCA Civ 1735; [2013] I.R.L.R. 99; see further *Pimlico Plumbers v Smith* [2018] UKSC 29.

"Earnings" and "earner"

1.41   **3.**—(1) In this Part of this Act and Parts II to V below—
(a) "earnings" includes any remuneration or profit derived from an employment; and
(b) "earner" shall be construed accordingly.

(2) For the purposes of this Part of this Act and of Parts II to V below other than those of Schedule 8—

(a) the amount of a person's earnings for any period; or

(b) the amount of his earnings to be treated as comprised in any payment made to him or for his benefit,

shall be calculated or estimated in such manner and on such basis as may be prescribed [¹ by regulations made by the Treasury with the concurrence of the Secretary of State.]

[² (2A) Regulations made for the purposes of subsection (2) above may provide that, where a payment is made or a benefit provided to or for the benefit of two or more earners, a proportion (determined in such manner as may be prescribed) of the amount or value of the payment or benefit shall be attributed to each earner.]

(3) Regulations made for the purposes of subsection (2) above may prescribe that payments of a particular class or description made or falling to be made to or by a person shall, to such extent as may be prescribed, be disregarded or, as the case may be, be deducted from the amount of that person's earnings.

[³ (4) Subsection (5) below applies to regulations made for the purposes of subsection (2) above which make special provision with respect to the earnings periods of directors and former directors of companies.

(5) Regulations to which this subsection applies may make provisions—

(a) for enabling companies, and directors and former directors of companies, to pay on account of any earnings-related contributions that may become payable by them such amounts as would be payable by way of such contributions if the special provision had not been made; and

(b) for requiring any payments made in accordance with the regulations to be treated, for prescribed purposes, as if they were the contributions on account of which they were made.]

AMENDMENTS

1. Transfer of Functions Act 1999 Sch.3 para.3 (April 1, 1999).
2. Social Security Act 1998 s.48 (September 8, 1998).
3. Social Security Act 1998 s.49(1) (September 8, 1998).

DERIVATION

SSA 1975 s.3(1)–(3).   1.42

DEFINITIONS

"employment"—s.122.
"prescribed"—s.122.

GENERAL NOTE

The computation of earnings is required in connection with a number of benefits: 1.43

(1) to calculate reduced earnings allowance;

(2) in disregarding casual or subsidiary work producing small sums in relation to entitlement to benefits based on incapacity for work, unemployment or retirement, and allowance;

(3) to determine entitlement to increases of benefit for children and dependants; and

(4) to determine any reduction of retirement pensions by reason of earnings.

The rules on computation are to be found in the Computation of Earnings Regulations and in Commissioners' decisions. The Computation of Earnings Regulations 1996 take an approach to the calculation of earnings in relation to non-means tested benefits which closely parallels that which has applied for some time to the calculation of earnings for income-related benefits.

Payments treated as remuneration, and earnings

1.44   **4.**—(1) For the purposes of section 3 above there shall be treated as remuneration derived from employed earner's employment—

    (a) any sum paid to or for the benefit of a person in satisfaction (whether in whole or in part) of any entitlement of that person to—

        (i) statutory sick pay; or

        (ii) statutory maternity pay;

    [6 (iii) [8 . . .] statutory paternity pay];

        (iv) [9 . . .]

    [6 (v) statutory adoption pay];

[9 or (vi) statutory shared parental pay; and]

    (b) any sickness payment made—

        (i) to or for the benefit of the employed earner; and

        (ii) in accordance with arrangements under which the person who is the secondary contributor in relation to the employment concerned has made, or remains liable to make, payments towards the provision of that sickness payment.

(2) Where the funds for making sickness payments under arrangements of the kind mentioned in paragraph (b) of subsection (1) above are attributable in part to contributions to those funds made by the employed earner, regulations may make provision for disregarding, for the purposes of that subsection, the prescribed part of any sum paid as a result of the arrangements.

(3) For the purposes of subsections (1) and (2) above "sickness payment" means any payment made in respect of absence from work due to incapacity for work, [1 . . .].

[2 (4) For the purposes of section 3 above there shall be treated as remuneration derived from an employed earner's employment—

    [7 (a) the amount of any gain calculated under section 479 or 480 of ITEPA 2003 in respect of which an amount counts as employment income of the earner under section 476 or 477 of that Act (charge on exercise, assignment or release of share option);]

    (b) any sum paid (or treated as paid) to or for the benefit of the earner which is chargeable to tax by virtue of [section 225 or 226 of ITEPA 2003] (taxation of consideration for certain restrictive undertakings).]

(5) For the purposes of section 3 above regulations may make provision for treating as remuneration derived from an employed earner's employment any payment made by a body corporate to or for the benefit of any of its directors where that payment would, when made, not be earnings for the purposes of this Act.

[3 (6) Regulations may make provision for the purposes of this Part—

    (a) for treating any amount on which an employed earner is chargeable to income tax under [7 the employment income Parts of ITEPA 2003] as remuneration derived from the earner's employment; and

(b) for treating any amount which in accordance with regulations under paragraph (a) above constitutes remuneration as an amount of remuneration paid, at such time as may be determined in accordance with the regulations, to or for the benefit of the earner in respect of his employment.]

[⁴ (7) Regulations under this section shall be made by the Treasury with the concurrence of the Secretary of State.]

AMENDMENTS

1. Incapacity for Work Act 1994 Sch.1 para.1 (April 13, 1995).
2. Social Security Act 1998 s.50(1) (September 8, 1998).
3. Child Support, Pensions and Social Security Act 2000 s.74(3) (April 6, 2000).
4. Transfer of Functions Act 1999 Sch.3 para.5 (April, 1999).
5. Employment Act 2002 s.53 and Sch.7 paras 2 and 3 (December 8, 2002).
6. Work and Families Act 2006 Sch.1, para. 3 (April 6, 2010).
7. Income Tax (Earnings and Pensions) Act 2003 s.722, Sch.6 paras 169 and 172 (April 5, 2003).
8. Children and Families Act 2014 s.126, Sch.7, para.8(a) (April 5, 2015).
9. Children and Families Act 2014 Sch.7, paras 8(b) & (c) (December 1, 2014).

DERIVATION

SSA 1975 s.3(1A)–(1D) and (4).   1.45

Sections 5–19 omitted.   1.46

PART II

CONTRIBUTORY BENEFITS

Preliminary

Descriptions of contributory benefits

20.—(1) Contributory benefits under this Part of this Act are of the fol-   1.47
lowing descriptions, namely—
  (a) [⁴ . . .]
[³ (b) incapacity benefit, comprising—
        (i) short-term incapacity benefit, and
        (ii) long-term incapacity benefit;]
  (c) [³ . . .]
  (d) maternity allowance [¹⁰ . . .];
  (e) widow's benefit, comprising—
        (i)   [⁵ . . .]
        (ii) widowed mother's allowance [⁸ . . .]
        (iii) widow's pension;
[¹² (ea) widowed parent's allowance;]
  (f) retirement pensions of the following categories—
        (i) Category A, payable to a person by virtue of his own contribu-
             tions (with increase for adult [⁸ . . .] dependants); and
      [³(ii) Category B, payable to a person by virtue of the contributions
             of a spouse [⁸ . . .] [⁹or civil partner];]

33

[⁶ (fa) shared additional pensions]
   (g) for existing beneficiaries only, child's special allowance.
   (2) In this Act—
"long-term benefit" means—
   [² (a) long-term incapacity benefit;]
      (b) a widowed mother's allowance;
[⁷ (ba) widowed parent's allowance;
[¹² (bb) . . ..]]
         (c) a widow's pension; [⁶ . . ..]
         (d) a Category A or Category B retirement pension; and
   [¹²(e) a shared additional pension under section 55A below].
"short-term benefit" means—
         (a) [⁴ . . .]
   [² (b) short-term incapacity benefit; and]
         (c) maternity allowance.
   (3) The provisions of this Part of this Act are subject to the provisions
of [¹Chapter II of Part III of the Pensions Act [¹¹ (reduction in benefits for
members of schemes that were contracted-out)]].

AMENDMENTS

   1. Pensions Schemes Act 1993 Sch.8 para.35 (February 7, 1994).
   2. Social Security (Incapacity for Work) Act 1994 Sch.1 para.2 (April 13, 1995).
   3. Pensions Act 1995 Sch.4 para.21 (July 19, 1995).
   4. Jobseekers Act 1995 Sch.3 para.1 (October 7, 1996).
   5. Welfare Reform and Pensions Act 1999 Sch.13 para.1 (April 24, 2000).
   6. Welfare Reform and Pensions Act 1999 Sch.8 para.3 (December 1, 2000).
   7. Welfare Reform and Pensions Act 1999 Sch.8 para.3 (April 9, 2001).
   8. Tax Credits Act 2002 Sch.6 para.1 (April 6, 2003).
   9. Civil Partnership Act 2004 Sch.24 para.13 (December 5, 2005).
   10. Welfare Reform Act 2009 Sch.7 para.1 (April 6, 2010).
   11. Pensions Act 2014 Sch.13 para.53 (April 6, 2016).
   12. Pensions Act 2014 Sch.16 para.3 (April 6, 2017).

Contribution conditions

1.48   **21.**—(1) Entitlement to any of the benefits specified in section 20(1)
above, [¹ other than [² short-term incapacity benefit under subsection (1)(b)
of section 30A below] long-term incapacity benefit under [² subsection (5)
of that section] [³ maternity allowance under section 35 [¹⁴ or 35B] below]
or short-term or long-term incapacity benefit under 40 or 41 below], [⁴ or a
shared additional pension under section 55A [¹⁵ or 55AA] below] depends
on contribution conditions being satisfied (either by the claimant or by
some other person, according to the particular benefit).
   (2) The class or classes of contribution which, for the purposes of subsection (1) above, are relevant in relation to each of those benefits are as
follows—

Short-term benefit

[⁵ . . .]
[¹ short-term incapacity benefit under section [⁶ 30A(1)(a)] below. Class 1
or 2
[⁷ . . .]

Other benefits

[8 [16 . . .]
Widowed mother's allowance Class 1, 2 or 3
[8 Widowed parent's allowance Class 1, 2 or 3
[16 . . .]
Widow's pension Class 1, 2 or 3
Category A retirement pension Class 1, 2 or 3
Category B retirement pension Class 1, 2 or 3
Child's special allowance Class 1, 2 or 3

(3) The relevant contribution conditions in relation to the benefits specified in subsection (2) above are those specified in Part I of Schedule 3 to this Act.

(4) [16 . . .]

(5) In subsection (4) above and Schedule 3 to this Act—

(a) "the contributor concerned" for the purposes of any contribution condition, means the person by whom the condition is to be satisfied.

(b) "a relevant class", in relation to any benefit, means a class of contributions specified in relation to that benefit in subsection (2) above;

(c) "the earnings factor"—

(i) where the year in question is 1987–88 or any subsequent tax year, means, in relation to a person, the aggregate of his earnings factors derived from [12 so much of his earnings as did not exceed the upper earnings limit] upon which primary Class 1 contributions have been paid or treated as paid and from his Class 2 and Class 3 contributions; and

(ii) where the year in question is any earlier tax year, means, in relation to a person's contributions of any class or classes, the aggregate of his earnings factors derived from all those contributions;

(d) except in the expression "benefit year", "year" means a tax year.

[9 (5A) Where primary Class 1 contributions have been paid or treated as paid on any part of a person's earnings, the following provisions, namely—

(a) subsection (5)(c) above;

(b) sections 22(1)(a) [10 (2A)] and (3)(a), 23(3)(a), 24(2)(a), [10 44(6) (za) and (a)] [11 . . .] below; and

(c) paragraphs 2(4)(a) and (5)(a), 4(2)(a), 5(2)(b) and 4(a) [13 5A(3) (a)] and 7(a) of Schedule 3 to this Act,

shall have effect as if such contributions had been paid or treated as paid on so much of the earnings as did not exceed the upper earnings limit.]

(6) In this Part of this Act "benefit year", means a period—

(a) beginning with the first Sunday in January in any calendar year, and

(b) ending with the Saturday immediately preceding the first Sunday in January in the following calendar year;

but for any prescribed purposes of this Part of this Act "benefit year" may by regulations be made to mean such other period (whether or not a period of 12 months) as may be specified in the regulations.

AMENDMENTS

1. Social Security (Incapacity for Work) Act 1994 Sch.1 para.3 (April 13, 1995).
2. Welfare Reform and Pensions Act 1999 s.70 (April 6, 2001).
3. Welfare Reform and Pensions Act 1999 Sch.8 para.31(2) (April 2, 2000).

4. Welfare Reform & Pensions Act 1999 Sch.12 para.15(16) (December 1, 2000).
5. Jobseekers Act 1995 Sch.3 (October 10, 1996).
6. Welfare Reform and Pensions Act 1999 s.88 (April 6, 2001).
7. Welfare Reform and Pensions Act 1999 Sch.8 para.31(3) & (4) (April 2, 2000).
8. Welfare Reform and Pensions Act 1999 s.70 (April 8, 2001).
9. Social Security Act 1998 Sch.7, para.61 (April 6, 1999).
10. Child Support, Pensions and Social Security Act 2000 s.35(2) (April 6, 2002).
11. Tax Credits Act 2002 Sch.6 (April 6, 2003).
12. National Insurance Contributions Act 2002 Sch.1 para.6 (April 6, 2003).
13. Pensions Act 2008 Sch.4 para.2 (January 3, 2012).
14. Social Security (Maternity Allowance) (Participating Wife or Civil Partner of Self-employed Earner) Regulations 2014 Social Security (Maternity Allowance) (Participating Wife or Civil Partner of Self-employed Earner) Regulations 2014 (SI 2014/606) reg.2(1) and (2) (April 1, 2014).
15. Pensions Act 2014 s.15 and Sch.11 paras 2 and 3 (April 6, 2016).
16. Pensions Act 2014 Sch.16 para.4 (April 6, 2017).

Earnings factors

1.49　　**22.**—(1) A person shall, for the purposes specified in subsection (2) below, be treated as having annual earnings factors derived—
　　(a) in the case of 1987–88 or any subsequent tax year, from [³so much of his earnings as did not exceed the upper earnings limit and] upon which primary Class 1 contributions have been paid or treated as paid and from Class 2 and Class 3 contributions; and
　　(b) in the case of any earlier tax year, from his contributions of any of Classes 1, 2 and 3;
but subject to the following provisions of this section and those of section 23 below.
　　(2) The purposes referred to in subsection (1) above are those of—
　　(a) establishing, by reference to the satisfaction of contribution conditions, entitlement to [¹a contribution-based jobseeker's allowance [¹⁰, to a contributory employment and support allowance] or to] any benefit specified in section 20(1) above, other than maternity allowance; [¹¹...]
　　(b) calculating the additional pension in the rate of a long-term benefit [¹¹; and]
　　[¹¹ (c) establishing entitlement to a state pension under Part 1 of the Pensions Act 2014 and, where relevant, calculating the rate of a state pension under that Part [¹² and]]
　　[¹² (d) establishing entitlement to bereavement support payment under section 30 of the Pensions Act 2014.]
　　[³(2A) For the purposes specified in subsection (2)(b) above, in the case of the first appointed year or any subsequent tax year a person's earnings factor shall be treated as derived only from [⁴so much of his earnings as did not exceed [⁵the applicable limit] and] on which primary Class 1 contributions have been paid or treated as paid.] [⁵This subsection does not affect the operation of sections 44A and 44B (deemed earnings factors).]
　　[⁵(2B) "The applicable limit" means—
　　(a) in relation to a tax year before [⁹2009–10], the upper earnings limit;
　　(b) in relation to [⁹2009–10] or any subsequent tax year, the upper accrual point.]
　　(3) Separate earnings factors may be derived for 1987–88 and subsequent tax years—

(a) from earnings [⁴not exceeding the upper earnings limit] upon which primary Class 1 contributions have been paid or treated as paid.

(b) from earnings which have been credited;

(c) from contributions of different classes paid or credited in the same tax year;

(d) by any combination of the methods mentioned in paragraphs (a) to (c) above,

and may be derived for any earlier tax year from contributions of different classes paid or credited in the same tax year, and from contributions which have actually been paid, as opposed to those not paid but credited.

(4) Subject to regulations under section 19(4) to (6) above, no earnings factor shall be derived–

(a) for 1987–88 or any subsequent tax year, from earnings [² in respect of which] primary Class 1 contributions are paid at the reduced rate, or

(b) for any earlier tax year, from primary Class 1 contributions paid at the reduced rate or from secondary Class 1 contributions.

(5) Regulations may provide for crediting—

(a) for 1987–88 or any subsequent tax year, earnings or Class 2 or Class 3 contributions, or

(b) for any earlier tax year, contributions of any class,

for the purpose of bringing a person's earnings factor for that tax year to a figure which will enable him to satisfy contribution conditions of entitle-ment to [¹a contribution based jobseeker's allowance or to] any prescribed description of benefit (whether his own entitlement or another person's).

[¹¹ (5ZA) Regulations may provide for crediting—

(a) for 1987-88 or any subsequent tax year, earnings or Class 2 or Class 3 contributions, or

(b) for any earlier tax year, contributions of any class,

for the purpose of bringing an earnings factor for that tax year to a figure which will make that year a "qualifying year", "pre-commencement quali-fying year" or "post-commencement qualifying year" of a person for the purposes of Part 1 of the Pensions Act 2014 (see sections 2(4) and 4(4) of that Act).

(5ZB) Regulations under subsection (5ZA) must provide for crediting a person with such contributions as may be specified in respect of periods on or after 6 April 1975 during which the person was—

(a) a spouse or civil partner of a member of Her Majesty's forces,

(b) accompanying the member on an assignment outside the United ` Kingdom, and

(c) not of a description specified in the regulations.]

[⁷(5A) Section 23A makes provision for the crediting of Class 3 contribu-tions for the purpose of determining entitlement to the benefits to which that section applies.]

(6) Regulations may impose limits with respect to the earnings factors which a person may have or be treated as having in respect of any one tax year.

(7) The power to amend regulations made before 30th March 1977 (the passing of the Social Security (Miscellaneous Provisions) Act 1977) under subsection (5) above may be so exercised as to restrict the circumstances in which and the purposes for which a person is entitled to credits in respect of weeks before the coming into force of the amending regulations; but not

so as to affect any benefit for a period before the coming into force of the amending regulations if it was claimed before 18th March 1977.

[¹⁰(8) In this section, "contributory employment and support allowance" means a contributory allowance under Part 1 of the Welfare Reform Act 2007 (employment and support allowance).]

[⁸ (9) References in this Act or any other Act to earnings factors derived from so much of a person's earnings as do not exceed the upper accrual point or the upper earnings limit are to be read, in relation to earners paid otherwise than weekly, as references to earnings factors derived from so much of those earnings as do not exceed the prescribed equivalent.]

AMENDMENTS

1. Jobseekers Act 1995 Sch.2 para.22 (October 7, 1996).
2. Social Security Act 1998 Sch.7 para.61 (April 6, 1999).
3. Child Support, Pensions and Social Security Act 2000 s.30(1) (April 6, 2002).
4. National Insurance Contributions Act 2002 Sch.1 para.7 (April 6, 2002).
5. Pensions Act 2007 s.12 (September 26, 2007).
6. Pensions Act 2007 Sch.1 para.33 (September 26, 2007).
7. Pensions Act 2007 Sch.1 para.9 (September 26, 2007).
8. National Insurance Contributions Act 2008 Sch.1 para.2 (September 22, 2008).
9. National Insurance Contributions Act 2008 s.3(2) (September 22, 2008).
10. Welfare Reform Act 2007 Sch.3 para.9 (October 27, 2008).
11. Pensions Act 2014 s.23 and Sch.12 paras 2 and 6 (April 6, 2016).
12. Pensions Act 2014 Sch.16 para.5 (April 6, 2017).

1.50   **Section 23** *omitted because the province of HMRC*

[¹ **Contributions credits for relevant parents and carers**

1.51   **23A.**—(1) This section applies to the following benefits—
  (a) a Category A retirement pension in a case where the contributor concerned attains pensionable age on or after 6th April 2010;
  (b) a Category B retirement pension payable by virtue of section 48A [² or 48AA] below in a case where the contributor concerned attains pensionable age on or after that date;
  (c) a Category B retirement pension payable by virtue of section 48B below in a case where the contributor concerned dies on or after that date without having attained pensionable age before that date;
  (d) a widowed parent's allowance payable in a case where the contributor concerned dies on or after that date.
  (e) [⁴ . . .]
  (2) The contributor concerned in the case of a benefit to which this section applies shall be credited with a Class 3 contribution for each week falling after 6th April 2010 in respect of which the contributor was a relevant carer.
  (3) A person is a relevant carer in respect of a week if the person—
  (a) is awarded child benefit for any part of that week in respect of a child under the age of 12,
  (b) is a foster parent for any part of that week, or
  (c) is engaged in caring, within the meaning given by regulations, in that week.

(4) Regulations may make provision for a person's entitlement to be credited with Class 3 contributions by virtue of falling within subsection (3) (b) or (c) above to be conditional on the person—

(a) applying to be so credited in accordance with the prescribed requirements, and

(b) complying with the prescribed requirements as to the provision of information to the Secretary of State.

(5) The contributor concerned in the case of a benefit to which this section applies shall be credited with 52 Class 3 contributions for each tax year ending before 6th April 2010 in which the contributor was precluded from regular employment by responsibilities at home within the meaning of regulations under paragraph 5(7) of Schedule 3.

(6) But the maximum number of tax years for which a person can be credited with contributions under subsection (5) above is—

(a) in the case of a benefit mentioned in subsection (1)(a) to (c) above, 22;

(b) in the case of a benefit mentioned in subsection (1)(d) [⁴. . .] above, half the requisite number of years of the person's working life.

(7) The table in paragraph 5(5) of Schedule 3 (requisite number of years of a working life of given duration) applies for the purposes of subsection (6)(b) above as it applies for the purposes of the second condition set out in paragraph 5(3)of that Schedule.

(8) For the purpose of determining entitlement to a benefit to which this section applies, a week that falls partly in one tax year and partly in another is to be treated as falling in the year in which it begins and not in the following year.

[³ (8A) Where this section, or regulations made under it, have the effect that the contributor concerned is credited, on or after 6 April 2016, with contributions for a tax year starting before that date, the contributions are to be treated for the purposes of calculating the rate under paragraph 3 of Schedule 1 to the Pensions Act 2014 as having been credited before 6 April 2016.]

(9) In this section—

"the contributor concerned" has the meaning given in section 21(5)(a) above;

"foster parent" has the meaning given by regulations.]

AMENDMENTS

1. Pensions Act 2007 s.3(1) (September 2, 2007).
2. Pensions Act 2014 Sch.11 para.58 (April 6, 2016).
3. Pensions Act 2014 (Consequential and Supplementary Amendments) Order 2016 (SI 2016/224) art.2(2) (April 6, 2016).
4. Pensions Act 2014 Sch.16 para.6 (April 6, 2017).

DEFINITIONS

"engaged in caring"—see reg.5 Social Security (Contributions Credits for Parents and Carers) Regulations 2010.

"foster parent"—see reg.4, Social Security (Contributions Credits for Parents and Carers) Regulations 2010.

"relevant carer"—see subs.(3).

"the contributor concerned"—see s.21(5)(a).

GENERAL NOTE

1.52   This section introduces weekly National Insurance credits (which replace Home Responsibilities Protection for periods of caring from April 6, 2010) for parents (including foster-parents) and carers in respect of their caring activities.

Although awarding these credits in cases dependent on the award of child benefit has been transferred to HMRC, their administration is done on behalf of the Secretary of State and appeals still lie to the First-tier Tribunal (Social Entitlement Chamber) and the Upper Tribunal (Administrative Appeals Chamber) rather than to the tax tribunals: see the National Insurance Contribution Credits (Transfer of Functions) Order 2009 (SI 2009/1377). The regulations governing the award of these credits are the Social Security (Contributions Credits for Parents and Carers) Regulations 2010 (SI 2010/19): see Pt II of this book.

The section applies to the benefits listed in subs.(1) where the determining event (attainment of pensionable age or death) occurs on or after April 6, 2010. In respect of such benefits, the contributor concerned (see subs.(9) and s.21(5)(a)) is to be credited with a Class 3 contribution for each week falling after April 6, 2010 in respect of which the contributor was a "relevant carer". Subsection (3) stipulates that someone is a "relevant carer" in respect of a week) if he is awarded child benefit for any part of that week in respect of a child under the age of 12, or is a foster parent for any part of that week, or is in that week engaged in caring, within the meaning given by regulations (see reg.5 of the Social Security (Contributions Credits for Parents and Carers) Regulations 2010). Under subs.(5), the contributor concerned is to be credited with 52 Class 3 contributions for each tax year ending before April 6, 2010 in which the contributor was precluded from regular employment by responsibilities at home within the meaning of regulations under para.5(7) of Sch.3 (see further the Social Security Pensions (Home Responsibilities Regulations 1994 in Pt II of this book). But subs.(6) sets maximum limits on the number of tax years in respect of which home responsibilities credits under subs.(5) can be used. The limits are 22 years (Category A or B retirement pensions) or half the requisite number of years of the person's working life (widowed parent's allowance or bereavement allowance).

1.53   **Section 24** *omitted because the province of HMRC.*

Unemployment benefit

Unemployment benefit

1.54   [¹ *Sections 25–30 repealed.*]

REPEAL

1. Jobseekers Act 1995 Sch.3 (October 7, 1996).

[Incapacity Benefit]

1.55   **30A.—30E.**   *Omitted.*
For the text of and commentary to these sections see the 2011/12 edition of this Volume.

Maternity

State maternity allowance [⁷ for employed or self-employed earner]

35.—[¹ (1) A woman shall be entitled to a maternity allowance [⁷ under this section], at the appropriate weekly rate determined under section (35A) below if—

    (a) she has become pregnant and has reached, or been confined before reaching, the commencement of the 11th week before the expected week of confinement; and

    (b) she has been engaged in employment as an employed or self-employed earner for any part of the week in the case of at least 26 of the 66 weeks immediately preceding the expected week of confinement; and

    [⁶(c) her average weekly earnings (within the meaning of section 35A below) are not less than the maternity allowance threshold for the tax year in which the beginning of the period of 66 weeks mentioned in paragraph (b) above falls;]

    (d) she is not entitled to statutory maternity pay for the same week in respect of the same pregnancy].

(2) Subject to the following provisions of this section, a maternity allowance [⁷under this section] shall be payable for the period ("the maternity allowance period") which, if she were entitled to statutory maternity pay, would be the maternity pay period under section 165 below.

(3) Regulations may provide—

    (a) for disqualifying a woman for receiving a maternity allowance [⁷under this section] if—

        [⁵(i) during the maternity allowance period, except in prescribed cases, she does any work in employment as an employed or self-employed earner;

        (ia) during the maternity allowance period she fails without good cause to observe any prescribed rules of behaviour; or]

        (ii) at any time before she is confined she fails without good cause to attend for, or submit herself to, any medical examination required in accordance with the regulations;

    (b) that this section and [¹ Section 35A below] shall have effect subject to prescribed modifications in relation to cases in which a woman has been confined and—

        (i) has not made a claim for a maternity allowance [⁷under this section] in expectation of that confinement (other than a claim which has been disallowed); or

        (ii) has made a claim for a maternity allowance [⁷under this section] in expectation of that confinement (other than a claim which has been disallowed), but she was confined more than 11 weeks before the expected week of confinement.

    [²(c) that subsection (2) above shall have effect subject to prescribed modifications in relation to cases in which a woman fails to satisfy the conditions referred to in subsection (1)(b) [¹[⁶ or (c) above]] at the commencement of the 11th week before the expected week of confinement, but subsequently satisfies those conditions at any time before she is confined.]

1.56

[⁸ (3A) Regulations may provide for the duration of the maternity allowance period as it applies to a woman to be reduced, subject to prescribed restrictions and conditions.

(3B) Regulations under subsection (3A) are to secure that the reduced
period ends at a time—

  (a) after a prescribed period beginning with the day on which the
woman is confined, and

  (b) when at least a prescribed part of the maternity allowance period
remains unexpired.

(3C) Regulations under subsection (3A) may, in particular, prescribe
restrictions and conditions relating to—

  (a) the end of the woman's entitlement to maternity leave;

  (b) the doing of work by the woman;

  (c) the taking of prescribed steps by the woman or another person as
regards leave under section 75E of the Employment Rights Act
1996 in respect of the child;

  (d) the taking of prescribed steps by a person other than the woman as
regards statutory shared parental pay in respect of the child.

(3D) Regulations may provide for a reduction in the duration of the
maternity allowance period as it applies to a woman to be revoked,
or to be treated as revoked, subject to prescribed restrictions and
conditions.

(3E) A woman who would, but for the reduction in duration of a maternity
pay period by virtue of section 165(3A), be entitled to statutory maternity pay for a week is not entitled to a maternity allowance for that
week.]

(4) A woman who has become entitled to a maternity allowance [⁷under
this section] shall cease to be entitled to it if she dies before the beginning
of the maternity allowance period; and if she dies after the beginning, but
before the end, of that period, the allowance shall not be payable for any
week subsequent to that in which she dies.

(5) Where for any purpose of this Part of this Act or of regulations it is
necessary to calculate the daily rate of a maternity allowance [⁷under this
section] [⁴the amount payable by way of that allowance for any day shall be
taken as one seventh of the weekly rate of that allowance.]

(6) In this section "confinement" means—

  (a) labour resulting in the issue of a living child, or

  (b) labour after [³24 weeks] of pregnancy resulting in the issue of a child
whether alive or dead,

and "confined" shall be construed accordingly; and where a woman's
labour begun on one day results in the issue of a child on another day she
shall be taken to be confined on the day of the issue of the child or, if labour
results in the issue of twins or a greater number of children, she shall be
taken to be confined on the day of the issue of the last of them.

[⁶ (6A) In this section 'the maternity allowance threshold', in relation to a
tax year, means (subject to subsection (6B) below) £30.

(6B) The Secretary of State may, in relation to any tax year after 2001-
2002, by order increase the amount for the time being specified in
subsection (6A) above to such amount as is specified in the order.

(6C) When deciding whether, and (if so) by how much, to increase the
amount so specified the Secretary of State shall have regard to the
movement, over such period as he thinks fit, in the general level of

prices obtaining in Great Britain (estimated in such manner as he thinks fit).

(6D) The Secretary of State shall in each tax year carry out such a review of the amount for the time being specified in subsection (6A) above as he thinks fit.]

(7) The fact that the mother of a child is being paid maternity allowance [[7]under this section] shall not be taken into consideration by any court in deciding whether to order payment of expenses incidental to the birth of the child.

AMENDMENTS

1. Welfare Reform and Pensions Act 1999 s.53 (April 2, 2000).
2. Maternity Allowance and Statutory Maternity Pay Regulations 1994 (SI 1994/ 1230) reg.2 (October 16, 1994).
3. Still Birth (Definition) Act 1992 s.2(1)(a) (October 1, 1992).
4. Social Security Act 1998 s.67 (October 1, 2006).
5. Work and Families Act 2006 Sch.1 para.6 (October 1, 2006).
6. Employment Act 2002 Sch.7 para.4 (April 6, 2003).
7. Social Security (Maternity Allowance) (Participating Wife or Civil Partner of Self-Employed Earner) Regulations 2014 (SI 2014/606) (April 1, 2014).
8. Children and Families Act 2014 s.120 (June 30, 2014).

DERIVATION

SSA 1978 s.22.   1.57

DEFINITIONS

"Confinement"—see subs.(6).
"Confined"—*ibid.*

GENERAL NOTE

State Maternity Allowance, MA, is a benefit equivalent to Statutory Maternity Pay.   1.58
It is paid chiefly to women who have been self-employed. It will also cover women whose service with their current employer does not qualify them for SMP; and women who have been in employment and whose job ended more than 15 weeks before their expected date of confinement and for a reason other than their pregnancy.

From April 2000 this benefit is no longer a contributory benefit. When the claimant's expected week of confinement is on or after April 2, 2000, entitlement will depend upon her showing involvement in work as either an employee or as a self-employed person for a total of 26 weeks out of the preceding 66 weeks. As well, she will have to show a certain level of earnings depending upon which she will qualify for benefit and be paid either standard rate MA, or a lower variable rate MA.

The allowance is payable when the claimant has become pregnant and has been confined, or has reached a stage in her pregnancy, which is the beginning of the 11th week before her expected week of confinement (s.165). There is no definition of pregnancy in the legislation but sufficient proof of that condition will normally follow from the need to prove an expected confinement. Confinement is defined in subs.6 as labour resulting in a living child, or labour after 24 weeks of pregnancy resulting in the issue of a child whether alive or dead. The only dispute that is likely to arise is whether a woman has been pregnant for 24 weeks, or more, before she gives birth to a still-born child. In one case, the Commissioner fixed the date that the pregnancy would be assumed to have commenced by calculating back from the estimated date of confinement for the period of a normal pregnancy *(R(G) 4/56)*. In another, he accepted medical evidence of the duration of the pregnancy from an examination of the foetus *(R(G) 12/59)*.

Subsection (2)

1.59   The maternity allowance period is defined by reference to the SMP period. This is defined in s.165 of this Act (and extended by reg.2 of SMP (General) Regulations). Generally it is for a continuous period of 39 weeks beginning not earlier than the 11th week before the expected week of confinement. What is important for this purpose is the correct expected week of confinement rather than the actual week of confinement, even though the confinement may have taken place by the time the decision-maker comes to make a decision (see *R(G) 8/55*). But where regulations alter the allowance period by reference to when a woman is confined it is the date of confinement that applies. Regulation 3 of the Maternity Allowance Regulations permits the shifting of the allowance period where a woman is not entitled at the date of the 11th week before her expected date of confinement, but becomes entitled before she is confined. The allowance period is altered also in the case of a woman who gives birth unexpectedly early. This is because the allowance period is determined by reference to what would have been the Statutory Maternity Pay period had she been entitled to SMP and then by reference to reg.2(3) of the Statutory Maternity Pay Regulations.

Subsection (3)

1.60   Regulations may also provide for the claimant to be disqualified if at any time during the allowance period, she does any work as an employed or self-employed earner. She is not disqualified if she merely does her own housework. Regulations that provided for disqualification of a woman who failed to take care of her health were repealed with effect from 2015, but she may still be disqualified if she fails, without good cause, to attend for a medical examination that has been required on behalf of the Secretary of State. See Maternity Allowance Regulations 1987.

Subsection 3A

1.61   Subsection (3A) was added, with effect from June 30, 2014, by the Children and Families Act 2014. The regulations made in furtherance of it are the Maternity Allowance (Curtailment) Regulations (SI 2014/3053). These regulations permit a woman to curtail her maternity allowance period so as to allow her partner (which can be either her spouse or the father of her child) to claim statutory shared parental pay and statutory shared parental leave for the balance of the period that remains.

Subsection (5)

1.62   With effect from October 1, 2006 s.35(5) was amended by the Social Security Act 1998 (Commencement No. 14) Order 2006 (SI 2006/2376). This brought into force s.67 of Social Security Act 1998 which provides for the daily rate of Maternity Allowance to be calculated at the rate of one-seventh of the weekly rate. This amount will apply to a woman whose date of confinement falls on or after April 1, 2007. A woman whose date of confinement is earlier will be covered by the earlier version of s.35 which provided for a Sunday to be disregarded as a day of entitlement, and any other day to be paid at a rate of one-sixth of the weekly rate. (For the original version of s.35 see earlier editions of the main volume of this work).

[¹ Appropriate weekly rate of maternity allowance [⁵under section 35]

1.63   **35A.**—[² (1) For the purposes of section 35(1) above the appropriate weekly rate is (subject to subsection (5A) below) whichever is the lower rate of—

   (a) a weekly rate equivalent to 90 per cent of the woman's average weekly earnings; and

   (b) the weekly rate for the time being prescribed under section 166(1)(b) below.]

   (2) [. . .]

(3) [. . .]

(4) For the purposes of this section a woman's "average weekly earnings" shall be taken to be the average weekly amount (as determined in accordance with regulations) of specified payments which—

(a) were made to her or for her benefit as an employed earner, or

(b) are (in accordance with regulations) to be treated as made to her or for her benefit as a self-employed earner,

during the specified period.

(5) Regulations may, for the purposes of subsection (4) above, provide—

(a) for the amount of any payments falling within paragraph (a) or (b) of that subsection to be calculated or estimated in such manner and on such basis as may be prescribed;

(b) for a payment made outside the specified period to be treated as made during that period where it was referable to that period or any part of it;

(c) for a woman engaged in employment as a self-employed earner to be treated as having received a payment in respect of a week—

   (i) equal to [⁴ an amount 90 per cent of which is equal to the weekly rate prescribed under section 166(1)(b) below that is] in force on the last day of the week, if she [⁶ has] paid a Class 2 contribution in respect of the week, or

   (ii) equal to the maternity allowance threshold in force on that day, if she [⁶ could have paid, but has not paid,] such a contribution in respect of the week;

(d) for aggregating payment made or treated as made to or for the benefit of a woman where, either in the same week or in different weeks, she was engaged in two or more employments (whether, in each case, as an employed earner or a self-employed earner).

[² (5A) Where subsection (5B) below applies the appropriate weekly rate is the weekly rate for the time being prescribed under section 166(1)(b) below.

(5B) This subsection applies where a woman is treated by virtue of regulations under sub-paragraph (i) of paragraph (c) of subsection (5) above as having received a payment in respect of each week in the specified period equal to the amount mentioned in that sub-paragraph.]

[³ (6) In this section "the maternity allowance threshold" has the same meaning as in section 35 above and "specified" means prescribed by or determined in accordance with regulations.]

AMENDMENTS

1. Welfare Reform and Pensions Act 1999 s.53 (April 2, 2000).

2. Employment Act 2002 s.48 (April 6, 2003).

3. Employment Act 2002 Sch.7 (April 6, 2003).

4. Employment Act 2002 s.48(1)(b) (November 24, 2004).

5. Social Security (Maternity Allowance) (Participating Wife or Civil Partner of Self Employed Earner) Regulations 2014 (SI 2014/606) reg.2 (April 1, 2014).

6. National Insurance Contributions Act 2015 s.2 Sch.1 para.6 (April 6, 2015).

GENERAL NOTE

This section will apply when the woman's expected week of confinement begins on or after August 20, 2000.

1.64

[¹ State maternity allowance for participating wife or civil partner of self-employed earner

1.65   **35B.** (1) A woman (W) shall be entitled to a maternity allowance under this section, at the weekly rate given by subsection (3) below, if—

   (a) W has become pregnant and has reached, or been confined before reaching, the commencement of the 11th week before the expected week of confinement; and

   (b) for any part of the week in the case of at least 26 of the 66 weeks immediately preceding the expected week of confinement, W has worked with a person (S) who at the time of her doing so—
     (i) was her spouse or civil partner, and
     (ii) was engaged in employment as a self-employed earner; and

   (c) S [² has paid] a Class 2 contribution in respect of the 26 weeks referred to in paragraph (1)(b); and

   (d) W is not entitled to a maternity allowance under section 35 above, or statutory maternity pay, for the same week in respect of the same pregnancy.

   (2) In this section—

   (a) a reference to W working with S is a reference to W participating in the activities engaged in by S as a   self-employed earner, performing the same tasks or ancillary tasks, without being employed by S or being in partnership with S;

   (b) a reference to W ceasing to work with S is a reference to W ceasing to do so either permanently or until after her confinement.

   (3) The rate of allowance under this section for any particular week is 90 per cent of the amount of the maternity allowance threshold for the tax year in which the week ends.

   (4) Subject to subsections (10) and (11) below, a maternity allowance under this section shall be payable for the period of 14 weeks ("the 14-week period") beginning as set out in subsection (5), (6), (7) or (8) below (whichever applies).

   (5) If W ceases to work with S before the commencement of the 11th week before the expected week of confinement, the 14-week period begins with the commencement of the 11th week before the expected week of confinement.

   (6) If W ceases to work with S on a day that falls within the period beginning with the commencement of the 11th week before the expected week of confinement and ending with the end of the fifth week before the expected week of confinement, the 14-week period begins immediately after that day.

   (7) If on a day that falls within the period beginning with the commencement of the fourth week before the expected week of confinement and ending with the date of confinement—

   (a) W ceases to work with S, or

   (b) she refrains from working with S wholly or partly because of her pregnancy or confinement, the 14-week period begins immediately after the day on which she ceases or refrains.

   (8) If none of subsections (5) to (7) above applies, the 14-week period begins immediately after the date of confinement.

   (9) In relation to maternity allowance under this section, a reference in a provision contained in or made under any enactment to the

46

maternity allowance period shall be read as a reference to the 14-week period.

(10) Subsections (4) to (7) of section 35 above have effect for the purposes of this section as they have effect for the purposes of that section (reading references to the maternity allowance period as references to the 14-week period).

(11) Regulations under section 35 above may make provision for the purposes of this section corresponding or similar to the provision that may be made by virtue of subsection (3)(a), (b) or (c) of that section.]

AMENDMENTS

1. Social Security (Maternity Allowance) (Participating Wife or Civil Partner of Self Employed Earner) Regulations 2014 (SI 2014/606) reg.2 (April 1, 2014).
2. National Insurance Contributions Act 2015 s.2 Sch.1 para.7 (April 6, 2015).

GENERAL NOTE

This section will apply when a woman's expected week of confinement begins on or after July 27, 2014.

1.66

Bereavement benefits: deaths before the day on which section 30 of the Pensions Act 2014 comes into force

[¹ Bereavement payment

36.—(1) A person whose spouse [² or civil partner] dies on or after the appointed day shall be entitled to a bereavement payment if—

1.67

(a) either that person was under pensionable age at the time when the spouse [² or civil partner] died or the spouse [² or civil partner] was then not entitled to a category A retirement pension under section 44 below; and

(b) the spouse [² or civil partner] satisfied the contribution condition for a bereavement payment specified in Schedule 3, Part I, paragraph 4.

(2) [³ A bereavement payment shall not be payable to a person if that person and a person whom that person was not married to, or in a civil partnership with, were living together as a married couple at the time of the spouse's or civil partner's death.]

(3) In this section "the appointed day" means the day appointed for the coming into force of sections 54 to 56 of the Welfare Reform and Pensions Act 1999.]

AMENDMENTS

1. Welfare Reform and Pensions Act 1999 s.54 (April 9, 2001).
2. Civil Partnership Act 2004 Sch.24 (December 5, 2005).
3. Marriage (Same Sex Couples) Act 2013 (Consequential and Contrary Provisions and Scotland) Order 2014 (SI 2014/560) art.2 and Sch.1 (March 13, 2014).

DEFINITION

"pensionable age"—see s.122.

GENERAL NOTE

1.68   This section was repealed with effect from April 6, 2017 by para.8 of Sch.16 of Pensions Act 2014. Bereavement payments replaced Widow's Payment from April 9, 2001. They have been replaced in turn by Bereavement Support Payment, under Part 5 of the Pensions Act 2014, with effect from April 6, 2017. Claimants whose spouse or partner died before that date will still qualify for this benefit and not for the new benefit. For further comments on this benefit please refer to Vol.I of the edition for 2016/17 of this work.

[¹ Cases in which sections 37 to 41 apply

1.69   *36A.—(1) Sections 37 to 39 and section 40 below apply only in cases where a woman's husband has died before the appointed day, and section 41 below applies only in cases where a man's wife has died before that day.*

(2) Sections 39A to 39C below apply in cases where a person's spouse [² or civil partner] dies on or after the appointed day, but section 39A also applies (in accordance with subsection (1)(b) of that section) in cases where a man's wife has died before that day.

(3) In this section, and in sections 39A and 39B below, "the appointed day" means the day appointed for the coming into force of sections 54 to 56 of the Welfare Reform and Pensions Act 1999.]

AMENDMENTS

1. Welfare Reform and Pensions Act 1999 s.55 (April 9, 2001).
2. Civil Partnership Act 2004 Sch.24 (December 5, 2005).

GENERAL NOTE

1.70   The "appointed day" for these provisions was April 9, 2001. This section was repealed with effect from April 6, 2017 by the Pensions Act 2014 Sch.16 para.9. It will still be effective in respect of claims that are made following the death of a spouse or partner that occurred before that date.

Widowed mother's allowance [⁷: deaths before 9 April 2001]

1.71   37.— [⁷ (A1) This section applies only in cases where a woman's husband has died before 9 April 2001.]

(1) A woman who has been widowed shall be entitled to a widowed mother's allowance at the rate determined in accordance with section 39 below if her late husband satisfied the contribution conditions for a widowed mother's allowance specified in Schedule 3, Part I, paragraph 5 and either—

 (a) the woman is entitled to child benefit in respect of a child [³ or qualifying young person] falling within subsection (2) below; or
 (b) the woman is pregnant by her late husband; or
 (c) if the woman and her late husband were residing together immediately before the time of his death, the woman is pregnant as the result of being artificially inseminated before that time with the semen of some person other than her husband, or as the result of the placing in her before that time of an embryo, of an egg in the process of fertilisation, or of sperm and eggs.

(2) A child [³ or qualifying young person] falls within this subsection if [⁴ [⁵ . . .]] the child [³ or qualifying young person] is either—

 (a) a son or daughter of the woman and her late husband; or
 (b) a child [³ or qualifying young person] in respect of whom her late husband was immediately before his death entitled to child benefit; or

48

(c) if the woman and her late husband were residing together immediately before his death, a child [³ or qualifying young person] in
respect of whom she was then entitled to child benefit.

(3) The widow shall not be entitled to the allowance for any period after
she remarries [² or forms a civil partnership], but, subject to that, she shall
continue to be entitled to it for any period throughout which she satisfies
the requirements of subsection (1)(a), (b) or (c) above.

(4) A widowed mother's allowance shall not be payable—
(a) for any period falling before the day on which the widow's entitlement is to be regarded as commencing for that purpose by virtue of
section 5(1)(k) of the Administration Act; [² [⁶ or
(b) for any period during which she and a person whom she is not
married to, or in a civil partnership with, are living together as a
married couple.]]

AMENDMENTS

1. Tax Credits Act 2003 Sch.3 (April 6, 2003).
2. Civil Partnership Act 2004 Sch.24 (December 5, 2005).
3. Child Benefit Act 2005 Sch.1 (April 10, 2006).
4. Welfare Reform Act 2007 s.50 and art.2(3)(a) of the Welfare Reform Act
2007 (Commencement No.7, Transitional and Savings Provisions) Order 2008 (SI
2008/2101) (October 7, 2008).
5. Welfare Reform Act 2007 s.67 and art.2(b) of the Welfare Reform Act 2007
(Commencement No.10, Transitional and Savings Provisions) Order 2009 (SI
2009/775) (March 27, 2009).
6. Marriage (Same Sex Couples) Act 2013 (Consequential and Contrary
Provisions and Scotland) Order 2014 (SI 2014/560) art.2 and Sch.1 (March 13,
2014).
7. Pensions Act 2014 Sch.16 para.10 (April 6, 2017).

DERIVATION

SSA 1975 s.25.   1.72

DEFINITION

"late husband"—see s.122 below.

GENERAL NOTE

This benefit is payable only to a widow whose husband died before April 9, 2001   1.73
and who is the mother of children for whom she is entitled to claim Child Benefit.
For further commentary on this section please refer to Vol.I of the edition of this
work for 2016/17.

Widow's pension [⁴: deaths before 9 April 2001]

38.— [⁴ (A1) This section applies only in cases where a woman's husband   1.74
has died before 9 April 2001.]

(1) A woman who has been widowed shall be entitled to a widow's
pension at the rate determined in accordance with section 39 below if her
late husband satisfied the contribution conditions for a widow's pension
specified in Schedule 3, Part I, paragraph 5 and either—
(a) she was, at the husband's death, over the age of 45 but under the age
of 65; or
(b) she ceased to be entitled to a widowed mother's allowance at a time
when she was over the age of 45 but under the age of 65.

(2) The widow shall not be entitled to the pension for any period after she remarries [¹ or forms a civil partnership], but, subject to that, she shall continue to be entitled to it until she attains [² pensionable age].

(3) A widow's pension shall not be payable—

(a) for any period falling before the day on which the widow's entitlement is to be regarded as commencing for that purpose by virtue of section 5(1)(k) of the Administration Act;

(b) for any period for which she is entitled to a widowed mother's allowance; [² [³ or

(c) for any period during which she and a person whom she is not married to, or in a civil partnership with, are living together as a married couple.]]

(4) In the case of a widow whose late husband died before 11th April 1988 and who either—

(a) was over the age of 40 but under the age of 55 at the time of her husband's death; or

(b) is over the age of 40 but under the age of 55 at the time when she ceases to be entitled to a widowed mother's allowance,

subsection (1) above shall have effect as if for "45" there were substituted "40".

AMENDMENT

1. Civil Partnership Act 2004 Sch.24 (December 5, 2005).

2. Pension Act 2007 Sch.1 Pt.8 para.40. This amendment was originally not to have effect until April 6, 2024, but now has had effect from April 6, 2018—see Pensions Act 2011 s.1.

3. Marriage (Same Sex Couples) Act 2013 (Consequential and Contrary Provisions and Scotland) Order 2014 (SI 2014/560) art.2 and Sch.1 (March 13, 2014).

4. Pensions Act 2014 Sch.16 para.11 (April 6, 2017).

DERIVATION

1.75   SSA 1975 s.26.

DEFINITION

"late husband"—see s.122.

GENERAL NOTE

1.76   Note: the amendment to subs.(1) and (2) above to "pensionable age" did not have effect until April 6, 2018. Until that time the section should be read as if it retained the words "the age of 65".

This benefit is payable only to a widow whose husband died before April 9, 2001. For further commentary on this section please refer to Vol.I of the edition of this work for 2016/17.

Rate of widowed mother's allowance and widow's pension

1.77   **39.**—(1) The weekly rate of—

(a) a widowed mother's allowance,

(b) a widow's pension,

shall be determined in accordance with the provisions of sections [¹ 44 to [² 45B]] [³ [⁵. . .]] below as they apply in the case of a Category A retirement pension, but subject, in particular, to the following provisions of this section and section [⁷46] below.

(2) In the application of sections [¹ 44 to [² 45B]] [³ [⁵. . .]] below by virtue of subsection (1) above—

   (a) where the woman's husband was over pensionable age when he died, references in those sections to the pensioner shall be taken as references to the husband, and

   (b) where the husband was under pensionable age when he died, references in those sections to the pensioner and the tax year in which he attained pensionable age shall be taken as references to the husband and the tax year in which he died.

[⁴ (2A) In its application by virtue of subsection (1) above, section 44(4) below is to be read as if for the first amount specified in that provision there were substituted a reference to the amount prescribed for the purposes of this subsection.]

(3) [⁶ omitted]

(4) Where a widow's pension is payable to a woman who was under the age of 55 at the time when the applicable qualifying condition was fulfilled, the weekly rate of the pension shall be reduced by 7 per cent. of what it would be apart from this subsection multiplied by the number of years by which her age at that time was less than 55 (any fraction of a year being counted as a year).

(5) For the purposes of subsection (4) above, the time when the applicable qualifying condition was fulfilled is the time when the woman's late husband died or, as the case may be, the time when she ceased to be entitled to a widowed mother's allowance.

(6) In the case of a widow whose late husband died before 11th April 1988 and who either—

   (a) was over the age of 40 but under the age of 55 at the time of her husband's death; or

   (b) is over the age of 40 but under the age of 55 at the time when she ceases to be entitled to a widowed mother's allowance, subsection (4) above shall have effect as if for "55" there were substituted "50" in both places where it occurs.

AMENDMENTS

   1. Pensions Act 1995 s.127(2) where ss.127(3)–(5) of that Act apply.
   2. Welfare Reform and Pensions Act 1999 Sch.12 (April 9, 2001).
   3. Child Support, Pensions and Social Security Act 2000 s.35 (April 6, 2002).
   4. Pensions Act 2007 s.6(5) (July 26, 2007).
   5. Pensions Act 2007 Sch.7 Pt 5 (September 26, 2007).
   6. Pensions Act 2007 Sch.2 Pt 3 para.3 (September 26, 2007).
   7. Pensions Act 2008 Sch.4 para.3 (January 3, 2012).

DERIVATIONS

SSA 1975 s.13 and s.26.   **1.78**
SSA 1986 s.19 and s.36.

[¹ Widowed parent's allowance

39A.—[⁸ (1) This section applies where—   **1.79**

   (a) a person's spouse or civil partner has died before the day on which section 30 of the Pensions Act 2014 comes into force (but see subsection (1A)),

   (b) the person has not married or formed a civil partnership after the death but before that day, and

(c) the person is under pensionable age on that day.

(1A) This section does not apply in cases where a woman's husband has died before 9 April 2001.]

(2) The surviving spouse [³ or civil partner] shall be entitled to a widowed parent's allowance at the rate determined in accordance with section 39C below if the deceased spouse [³ or civil partner] satisfied the contribution conditions for a widowed parent's allowance specified in Schedule 3, Part I, paragraph 5 and—

(a) the surviving spouse [³ or civil partner] is entitled to child benefit in respect of a child [⁴ or qualifying young person] falling within subsection (3) below;

(b) the surviving spouse is a woman who either—
  (i) is pregnant by her late husband, or
  (ii) if she and he were residing together immediately before the time of his death, is pregnant in circumstances falling within section 37(1)(c) above. [³ or

(c) the surviving civil partner is a woman who—
  (i) was residing together with the deceased civil partner immediately before the time of the death, and
  (ii) is pregnant as the result of being artificially inseminated before that time with the semen of some person, or as a result of the placing in her before that time of an embryo, of an egg in the process of fertilisation, or of sperm and eggs].

(3) A child [⁴ or qualifying young person] falls within this subsection if [⁵[⁶. . .]]the child [⁴ or qualifying young person] is either—

(a) a son or daughter of the surviving spouse [³ or civil partner] and the deceased spouse [³ or civil partner]; or

(b) a child in respect of whom the deceased spouse [³ or civil partner] was immediately before his or her death entitled to child benefit; or

(c) if the surviving spouse and the deceased spouse were residing together immediately before his or her death, a child [⁴ or qualifying young person] in respect of whom the surviving spouse [³ or civil partner] was then entitled to child benefit.

(4) The surviving spouse [³ or civil partner] shall not be entitled to the allowance for any period after she or he remarries [³ or forms a civil partnership], but, subject to that, the surviving spouse shall continue to be entitled to it for any period throughout which she or he—

(a) satisfied the requirements for subsection (2)(a) or (b) above; and

(b) is under pensionable age.

[³ (4A) The surviving civil partner shall not be entitled to the allowance for any period after she or he forms a subsequent civil partnership or marries, but, subject to that, the surviving civil partner shall continue to be entitled to it for any period throughout which she or he—

(a) satisfies the requirements of subsection (2)(a) or (b) above; and

(b) is under pensionable age].

(5) A widowed parent's allowance shall not be payable—

(a) for any period falling before the day on which the surviving spouse's [³ or civil partner's] entitlement is to be regarded as commencing by virtue of section 5(1)(k) of the Administration Act; [³ [⁷ or

(b) for any period during which the surviving spouse or civil partner and a person whom she or he is not married to, or in a civil partnership with, are living together as a married couple.]]

AMENDMENTS

1. Welfare Reform and Pension Act 1999 s.55 (April 9, 2001).
2. Tax Credits Act 2003 Sch.3, (April 6, 2003).
3. Civil Partnership Act 2004 Sch.24 (December 5, 2005).
4. Child Benefit Act 2005 Sch.1 (April 10, 2006).
5. Welfare Reform Act 2007 s.51 and art.2(3)(b) of the Welfare Reform Act 2007 (Commencement No.7, Transitional and Savings Provisions) Order 2008 (SI 2008/2101) (October 7, 2008).
6. Welfare Reform Act 2007 s.67 and art.2(b) of the Welfare Reform Act 2007 (Commencement No. 10, Transitional and Savings Provisions) Order 2009 (SI 2009/775) (March 27, 2009).
7. Marriage (Same Sex Couples) Act 2013 (Consequential and Contrary Provisions and Scotland) Order 2014 (SI 2014/560) art.2 and Sch.1 (March 13, 2014).
8. Pensions Act 2014 Sch.16 para.12 (April 6, 2017).

GENERAL NOTE

For commentary on this section please refer to Vol.I of the edition of this work for 2016/17.   1.80

Bereavement allowance where no dependent children

[¹ **39B.**—*(1) This section applies where a person whose spouse [² or civil partner] dies on or after the appointed day is over the age of 45 but under pensionable age at the spouse's [² or civil partner's] death.*   1.81

(2) The surviving spouse [² or civil partner] shall be entitled to a bereavement allowance at the rate determined in accordance with section 39C below if the deceased spouse [² or civil partner] satisfied the contribution conditions for a bereavement allowance specified in Schedule 3, Part I, paragraph 5.

(3) A bereavement allowance shall be payable for not more than 52 weeks beginning with the date of the spouse's [² or civil partner's] death or (if later) the day on which the surviving spouse's [² or civil partner's] entitlement is to be regarded as commencing by virtue of section 5 (1)(k) of the Administration Act.

(4) The surviving spouse shall not be entitled to the allowance for any period after she or he remarries [² or forms a civil partnership], but, subject to that, the surviving spouse shall continue to be entitled to it until—

(a) she or he attains pensionable age, or
(b) the period of 52 weeks mentioned in subsection (3) above expires, whichever happens first.

[² *(4A) The surviving civil partner shall not be entitled to the allowance for any period after she or he forms a subsequent civil partnership or marries, but, subject to that, the surviving civil partner shall continue to be entitled to it until*

(a) she or he attains pensionable age, or
(b) the period of 52 weeks mentioned in subsection (3) above expires, whichever happens first].

(5) The allowance shall not be payable—

(a) for any period which the surviving spouse [² or civil partner] is entitled to a widowed parent's allowance; [² [³ or
(b) for any period during which the surviving spouse or civil partner and a person whom she or he is not married to, or in a civil partnership with, are living together as a married couple.]] [² or
(c) for any period during which the surviving spouse or civil partner and a person of the same sex who is not his or her civil partner are living together as if they were civil partners].

AMENDMENTS

    1. *Welfare Reform and Pension Act 1999 s.55 (April 9, 2001).*
    2. *Civil Partnership Act 2004 Sch.24 (December 5, 2005).*
    3. *Marriage (Same Sex Couples) Act 2013 (Consequential and Contrary Provisions and Scotland) Order 2014 (SI 2014/560) art.2 and Sch.1 (March 13, 2014).*

GENERAL NOTE

1.82   This section was repealed by the Pensions Act 2014 Sch.16 para.13 with effect from April 6, 2017.

[¹ Rate of widowed parent's allowance [⁹ . . .]

1.83   **39C.**—(1) The weekly rate of a widowed parent's allowance shall be determined in accordance with the provisions of section 44 to [⁷[⁸ 45AA and Schedules 4A and 4B below as they apply]] in the case of a Category A retirement pension, but subject, in particular, to the following provisions of this section [⁷46] below.

    [⁵ (1A) In its application by virtue of subsection (1) above, section 44(4) below is to be read as if for the first amount specified in that provision there were substituted a reference to the amount prescribed for the purposes of this subsection.

    (2) [⁹. . .]]

    (3) In the application of sections 44 to [⁷[⁸ 45AA and Schedules 4A and 4B below by virtue of subsection (1) above]]

    (a) where the deceased spouse [⁴ or civil partner] was over pensionable age at his or her death, references in those [⁶ provisions] to the pensioner shall be taken as references to the deceased spouse [⁴ or civil partner], and

    (b) where the deceased spouse [⁴ or civil partner] was under pensionable age at his or her death, references in those [⁶ provisions] to the pensioner and the tax year in which he attained pensionable age shall be taken as references to the deceased spouse [⁴ or civil partner] and the tax year in which he or she died.

    (4) Where a widowed parent's allowance is payable to a person whose spouse [⁴ or civil partner] dies after 5th April 2000, the additional pension falling to be calculated under sections 44 to [⁷[⁸ 45AA and Schedules 4A and 4B below]] by virtue of subsection (1) above shall be one half of the amount which it would be apart from this subsection.

    (5) [⁹. . .]]

AMENDMENTS

1.84   1. Welfare Reform and Pension Act 1999 s.55 (April 9, 2001).
    2. Child Support, Pensions and Social Security Acbt 2000 s.35 (April 6, 2002).
    3. Tax Credit Act 2002 Sch.3 (April 6, 2003).
    4. Civil Partnership Act 2004 Sch.24 (December 5, 2005).
    5. Pensions Act 2007 s.6(6) (July 26, 2007).
    6. Pensions Act 2007 Sch.2 Pt 3 (July 26, 2007).
    7. Pensions Act 2008 Sch.4 para.2 (January 3, 2012) (except in relation to 4C).
    8. Pensions Act 2014 Sch.12 para.93 (April 6, 2016).
    8. Pensions Act 2014 Sch.16 para.14 (April 6, 2017).

General Note For Sections 36–39C.

For commentary on ss.36-39C please refer to the notes following s.39C in Vol.I of the edition of this work for 2016/17.

1.85

Long-term incapacity benefit for widows

[¹ **40.**—(1) Subject to subsection (2) below, this section applies to a woman who—

1.86

(a) on her late husband's death is not entitled to a widowed mother's allowance or subsequently ceases to be entitled to such an allowance;

(b) is incapable of work at the time when he dies or when she subsequently ceases to be so entitled;

(c) either—

    (i) would have been entitled to a widow's pension if she had been over the age of 45 when her husband died or when she ceased to be entitled to a widowed mother's allowance; or

    (ii) is entitled to such a pension with a reduction under section 39(4) above; and

(d) is not entitled to incapacity benefit apart from this section.

(2) This section does not apply to a woman unless—

(a) her husband died after 5th April 1979; or

(b) she ceased to be entitled to a widowed mother's allowance after that date (whenever her husband died).

(3) A woman to whom this section applies is entitled to long-term incapacity benefit under this section for any day of incapacity for work which—

(a) falls in a period of incapacity for work that began before the time when her late husband died or she subsequently ceased to be entitled to a widowed mother's allowance; and

(b) is after that time and after the first 364 days of incapacity for work in that period.

(4) A woman to whom this section applies who is not entitled to long-term incapacity benefit under subsection (3) above, but who is terminally ill, is entitled to short-term incapacity benefit under this section for any day of incapacity for work which—

(a) falls in a period of incapacity for work that began before the time when her late husband died or she subsequently ceased to be entitled to a widowed mother's allowance, and

(b) is after that time and after the first 196 days of incapacity for work in that period

For the purposes of this subsection a woman is terminally ill if she suffers from a progressive disease and her death in consequence of that disease can reasonably be expected within 6 months.

(5) The weekly rate of incapacity benefit payable under this section is—

(a) if the woman is not entitled to a widow's pension, that which would apply if she were entitled to long-term incapacity benefit under section 30A above; and

(b) if she is entitled to a widow's pension with a reduction under section 39(4) above, the difference between the weekly rate of that pension and the weekly rate referred to in paragraph (a) above.

(6) A woman is not entitled to incapacity benefit under this section if she is over pensionable age; but if she has attained pensionable age and

55

the period of incapacity for work mentioned in subsection (3)(a) or (4)(a) above did not terminate before she attained that age—

(a) she shall, if not otherwise entitled to a Category A retirement pension, be entitled to such a pension, and

(b) the weekly rate of the Category A retirement pension to which she is entitled (whether by virtue of paragraph (a) above or otherwise) shall be determined in the prescribed manner.

(7) Where a woman entitled to short-term incapacity benefit under subsection (4) above attains pensionable age and defers her entitlement to a Category A pension or makes an election under section 54(1) below, the days of incapacity for work falling within the period of incapacity for work mentioned in that subsection shall, for the purpose of determining any subsequent entitlement to incapacity benefit under section 30A above or the rate of that benefit, be treated as if they had been days of entitlement to short-term incapacity benefit.

(8) References to short-term incapacity benefit at the higher rate shall be construed as including short-term incapacity benefit payable under subsection (4) above.]

AMENDMENT

1. Social Security (Incapacity for Work) Act 1994 Sch.1 (April 13, 1995).

DERIVATION

1.87 SSA 1975 s.15.
Substituted by Social Security (Incapacity for Work) Act 1994.

DEFINITIONS

"entitled"—see s.122.
"day of incapacity for work"—see s.57.
"period of interruption of employment"—see s.57.

GENERAL NOTE

1.88 This benefit will in appropriate circumstances, be affected by the Gender Recognition Act 2004. A person in receipt of benefit by virtue of this section who obtains a gender recognition certificate will cease to be entitled to benefit (and will lose, as well, the right to transfer to Category A Retirement Pension in due course). This is surprising because s.41 that follows makes an equivalent provision for widowers. See the notes to the Gender Recognition Act in Vol.III of this work.

Long-term incapacity benefit for widowers

1.89 [¹ 41.—(1) This section applies to a man whose wife has died on or after 6th April 1979 and who either—

(a) was incapable of work at the time when she died, or
(b) becomes incapable of work within the prescribed period after that time,
and is not entitled to incapacity benefit apart from this section.

(2) A man to whom this section applies is entitled to long-term incapacity benefit under this section for any day of incapacity for work which—

(a) falls in a period of incapacity for work that began before the time when his wife died or within the prescribed period after that time, and
(b) is after that time and after the first 364 days of incapacity for work in that period.

(3) A man to whom this section applies who is not entitled to longterm

incapacity benefit under subsection (2) above, but who is terminally ill, is entitled to short-term incapacity benefit under this section for any day of incapacity for work which—

(a) falls in a period of incapacity for work that began before the time when his wife died or within the prescribed period after that time, and

(b) is after that time and after the first 196 days of incapacity for work in that period.

For the purposes of this subsection a man is terminally ill if he suffers from a progressive disease and his death in consequence of that disease can reasonably be expected within 6 months.

(4) The weekly rate of incapacity benefit payable under this section is that which would apply if he were entitled to long-term incapacity benefit under section 30A above.

(5) A man is not entitled to incapacity benefit under this section if he is over pensionable age; but if he has attained pensionable age, and the period of incapacity for work mentioned in subsection (2)(a) or (3)(a) above did not terminate before he attained that age—

(a) he shall, if not otherwise entitled to a Category A retirement pension and also not entitled to a Category B retirement pension by virtue of [² the contributions of his wife] be entitled to Category A retirement pension; and

(b) the weekly rate of the Category A retirement pension to which he is entitled (whether by virtue of paragraph (a) above or otherwise) shall be determined in the prescribed manner.

(6) Where a man entitled to short-term incapacity benefit under subsection (3) above attains pensionable age and defers his entitlement to a Category A pension or makes an election under section 54(1) below, the days of incapacity for work falling within the period of incapacity for work mentioned in that subsection shall, for the purpose of determining any subsequent entitlement to incapacity benefit under section 30A above or the rate of that benefit, be treated as if they had been days of entitlement to short-term incapacity benefit.

(7) References to short-term incapacity benefit at the higher rate shall be construed as including short-term incapacity benefit payable under subsection (3) above.]

AMENDMENTS

1. Social Security (Incapacity for Work) Act 1994 Sch.1 para.9 (April 13, 1995).
2. Pensions Act 1995 Sch.4, para.21(4) (July 19, 1995).

DERIVATIONS

SSPA 1975 s.16.   1.90
SSA 1977 s.4.
SSA 1979 s.5.
SSA 1986 s.19.
SSA 1989 s.7.
SSA 1990 s.4.
Substituted by Social Security (Incapacity for Work) Act 1994.

GENERAL NOTE

This benefit will in appropriate circumstances, be affected by the Gender   1.91
Recognition Act 2004. A person in receipt of benefit by virtue of this section who

obtains a gender recognition certificate will cease to be entitled to benefit (and will lose, as well, the right to transfer to Category A Retirement Pension in due course). This is surprising because Section 40 above makes an equivalent provision for widows. See the notes to the Gender Recognition Act in Vol.III of this work.

Entitlement under s.40 or 41 after period of employment or training for work

1.92

42.—[2(1) Where a person claims incapacity benefit under section 40 or 41 above for a period commencing after he has ceased to be in qualifying remunerative work (within the meaning of Part 1 of the Tax Credits Act 2002) and—

(a) the day following that on which he so ceased was a day of incapacity for work for him,

(b) he has been entitled to incapacity benefit under that section within the period of two years ending with that day of incapacity for work, and

(c) he satisfied the relevant tax credit conditions on the day before he so ceased,

every day during that period on which he satisfied those conditions is to be treated for the purposes of the claim as a day of incapacity for work for him.

(1A) A person satisfies the relevant tax credit conditions on a day if—

(a) he is entitled for the day to the disability element of working tax credit (on a claim made by him or by him jointly with another) or would be so entitled but for the fact that the relevant income (within the meaning of Part 1 of the Tax Credits Act 2002) in his or their case is such that he is not so entitled, and

(b) either working tax credit or any element of child tax credit other than the family element is paid in respect of the day on such a claim.]

(2) Where—

(a) a person becomes engaged in training for work, and

(b) he was entitled to incapacity benefit under section 40 or 41 above for one or more of the 56 days immediately before he became so engaged, and

(c) the first day after he ceases to be so engaged is for him a day of incapacity for work and falls not later than the end of the period of two years beginning with the last day for which he was entitled to incapacity benefit under that section,

any day since that day in which he was engaged in training for work shall be treated for the purposes of any claim for incapacity benefit under that section for a period commencing after he ceases to be so engaged as having been a day of incapacity for work.

In this subsection "training for work" means training for work in pursuance of arrangements made under section 2(1) of the Employment and Training Act 1973 or section 2(3) of the Enterprise and New Towns (Scotland) Act 1990 or training of such other description as may be prescribed.

(3) For the purposes of this section "week" means any period of 7 days.]

AMENDMENTS

1. Social Security (Incapacity for Work) Act 1994 Sch.1 para.10 (April 13, 1995).
2. Tax Credits Act 2002 Sch.3 para.30 (April 6, 2003).

DERIVATIONS

1.93

SSPA 1975 s.16A.
DLA and DWAA 1991 s.9.
Substituted by Social Security (Incapacity for Work) Act 1994.

GENERAL NOTE

1.94

Note that in respect of someone who claims incapacity benefit on or before April 6, 2005 under s.40 or 41, s.42 has effect as if, after subs.(1A) there were inserted

"(1B) A person also satisfies the relevant tax credit conditions on any day before 7th April 2003 if that day falls within a week for which he is entitled to a disabled person's tax credit."

See Tax Credits Act 2002 (Commencement No.4, Transitional Provisions and Savings) Order SI 2003/962, art.5(3).

Retirement pensions (Categories A and B)

Persons entitled to more than one retirement pension

43.—(1) A person shall not be entitled for the same period to more than one retirement pension under this Part of this Act except as provided by subsection (2) below[⁴ and section 61ZC below (which deals with unusual cases involving units of additional pension)].

1.95

(2) A person who, apart from subsection (1) above, would be entitled for the same period to both—

(a) a Category A or a Category B retirement pension under this Part; and
(b) a Category C or a Category D retirement pension under Part III below,

shall be entitled to both of those pensions for that period, subject to any adjustment of them in pursuance of regulations under section 73 of the Administration Act.

(3) A person who, apart from subsection (1) above, would be entitled—

[² (a) to both a Category A retirement pension and one or more Category B retirement pensions under this Part for the same period,
(aa) to more than one Category B retirement pension (but not a Category A retirement pension) under this Part for the same period, or]
(b) to both a Category C and a Category D retirement pension under Part III below for the same period,

may from time to time give notice in writing to the Secretary of State specifying which of the pensions referred to in [² paragraph (a), (aa) or (b) (as the case may be)] he wishes to receive.

(4) If a person gives such a notice, the pension so specified shall be the one to which he is entitled in respect of any week commencing after the date of the notice.

(5) If no such notice is given, the person shall be entitled to whichever of the pensions is from time to time the most favourable to him (whether it is the pension which he claimed or not).

[¹ (6) For the purpose of this section a provision under section 55A [³ or 55AA] below is not a retirement pension.]

1. Welfare Reform and Pensions Act 1999 Sch.12 para.18 (April 9, 2001).
2. Pensions Act 2004 s.296 (November 18, 2004).
3. Pensions Act 2014 Sch.11 para. 4 (April 6, 2016).
4. Pensions Act 2014 Sch.15 para.15 (October 12, 2015).

GENERAL NOTE

1.96   Section 43 was the key section for all claims to state retirement pensions for those reaching state pensionable age up to and including April 5, 2016. From April 6, 2016 no new claim can be made under this section and the sections that follow. Claims for those reaching state pensionable age on or after April 6, 2016 must be made for a state pension under the Pensions Act 2014. See the general note to s.1 of that Act below. This and the following provisions of the 1992 Act are preserved both for past cases where pensions are already in payment and in relation to transitional cases preserved by the Pensions Act 2014.

The Pensions Act 2014 introduces major changes to the structure of the state pension including the introduction of a single tier pension, the abolition (subject to transitional provisions) of pensions based on a spouse's or partner's contributions (Category B pensions), the abolition of the state second pension or additional pension, and the abolition of Category C pensions. Much of the detailed comment on these sections in previous editions of this work is therefore of no continuing relevance to current and future new claims and is therefore not repeated here. See the 2015/16 edition (or other previous editions) of this work for a full explanation and analysis.

Category A retirement pension

1.97   **44.**—(1) A person shall be entitled to a Category A retirement pension if—

[14 (a) the person attained pensionable age before 6 April 2016,] and
[10(b) he satisfies the relevant conditions or condition].

and, subject to the provisions of this Act, he shall become so entitled on the day on which he attains pensionable age and his entitlement will continue throughout his life.

[10(1A) In subsection (1)(b) above "the relevant conditions or condition" means—

(a) in a case where the person attains pensionable age before 6th April 2010, the conditions specified in Schedule 3, Part I, paragraph 5;

(b) in a case where the person attains pensionable age on or after that date, the condition specified in Schedule 3, Part I, paragraph 5A.]

(2) A Category A retirement pension shall not be payable in respect of any period falling before the day on which the pensioner's entitlement is to be regarded as commencing for that purpose by virtue of section 5(1)(k) of the Administration Act.

(3) A Category A retirement pension shall consist of—

(a) a basic pension payable at a weekly rate; and

(b) an additional pension payable where there are one or more surpluses in the pensioner's earnings factors for the relevant years [15 or where the pensioner has one or more units of additional pension.

For units of additional pension, see section 14A.]

[16 (4) The weekly rate of the basic pension shall be [1 £129.20] except that, so far as the sum is relevant for the purpose of calculating the [2 rate of short-term incapacity benefit under section 30B(3) above] it shall be [1 £107.65].

In this subsection "the lower rate" means the rate payable for the first 196 days of entitlement in any period of incapacity for work]

(5) For the purposes of this section and section 45 below—

(a) there is a surplus in the pensioner's earnings factor for a relevant year if that factor exceeds the qualifying earnings factor for the final relevant year; and

(b) the amount of the surplus is the amount of that excess; and for the purposes of paragraph (a) above the pensioner's earnings factor for any relevant year shall be taken to be that factor as increased by the last order under section 148 of the Administration Act to come into force before the end of the final relevant year.

[³ (5A) For the purposes of this section and section 45 [⁸ and [¹¹ Schedules 4A and 4B]] below—

(a) there is a surplus in the pensioner's earnings factor for a relevant year if that factor exceeds the qualifying earnings factor for [⁸that year,

(b) the amount of the surplus is the amount of that excess, and

(c) for the purposes of section 45(1) and (2)(a) and (b) below, the adjusted amount of the surplus] is the amount of that excess, as increased by the last order under section 148 of the Administration Act to come into force before the end of the final relevant year.

(6) [⁴ [⁵Subject to subsection (7A) below] any reference in this section or section 45 [⁸ or [¹¹ Schedule 4A or 4B]] below to the pensioner's earnings factor for any relevant year is a reference—

[⁷ (za)] where the relevant year is the first appointed year or any subsequent year, to the aggregate of his earnings factors derived from [⁹ so much of his earnings as did not exceed [¹² the applicable limit]] upon which primary Class 1 contributions have been paid or treated as paid in respect of that year;

(a) where the relevant year is 1987–88 or any subsequent tax year [⁷ before the first appointed year], to the aggregate of—

(i) his earnings factors derived from earnings upon which primary Class 1 contributions were paid or treated as paid in respect of that year, and

(ii) his earnings factors derived from Class 2 and Class 3 contributions actually paid in respect of that year, or, if less, the qualifying earnings factor for that year; and

(b) where the relevant year is an earlier tax year, to the aggregate of—

(i) his earnings factors derived from Class 1 contributions actually paid by him in respect of that year, and

(ii) his earnings factors derived from Class 2 and Class 3 contributions actually paid by him in respect of that year, or, if less, the qualifying earnings factor for that year.]

(7) In this section—

(a) "relevant year" means 1978–79 or any subsequent tax year in the period between—

(i) (inclusive) the tax year in which the pensioner attained the age of 16, and

(ii) (exclusive) the tax year in which he attained pensionable age;

(b) "final relevant year" means the last tax year which is a relevant year in relation to the pensioner.

[¹⁰ (c) "the applicable limit" means—

(i) in relation to a tax year before [¹³2009–10] the upper earnings limit;

(ii) in relation to [¹³2009–10] or any subsequent tax year, the upper accrual point.]

[⁵ (7A) The Secretary of State may prescribe circumstances in which pensioners' earnings factors for any relevant year may be calculated in such manner as may be prescribed.]

(8) For the purposes of this section any order under [⁶ section 21 of the Social Security Pensions Act 1975] (which made provision corresponding to section 148 of the Administration Act) shall be treated as an order under section 148 (but without prejudice to sections 16 and 17 of the Interpretation Act 1978).

AMENDMENTS

1. Social Security Benefits Up-rating Order 2019 (SI 2019/480) art.4(3) (April 8, 2019).
2. Social Security (Incapacity for Work) Act 1994 Sch.1 para.11 (April 13, 1995).
3. Pensions Act 1995 s.128(1), subs.(5A) applies in substitution for subs.(5) where ss.128(4)–(6) of that Act apply.
4. Pension Act 1995 s.128. This version of subs.(6) takes effect where the relevant person reaches pensionable age, or dies, after April 5, 2000.
5. Social Security (Consequential Provisions) Act 1992 Sch.4 para.3.
6. Pensions Schemes Act 1993 Sch.8 para.38 (February 7, 1994).
7. Child Support, Pensions and Social Security Act 2000 s.30 (April 6, 2002).
8. Child Support, Pensions and Social Security Act 2000 s.35 (April 6, 2002).
9. National Insurance Contributions Act 2002 Sch.1 para.8 (April 6, 2002).
10. Pensions Act 2007 Sch.1 para.1 (September 26, 2007).
11. Pensions Act 2007 Sch.2 Pt 3, para.5 (September 26, 2007).
12. Pensions Act 2007 s.12 (September 26, 2007).
13. National Insurance Contributions Act 2008 s.3(3) (September 21, 2008).
14. Pensions Act 2014 Sch.12 para.55 (April 6, 2016).
15. Pensions Act 2014 Sch.15 para.6 (October 12, 2015).
16. Social Security Act 1998 s.68 (September 8, 1988).

DEFINITION

"pensionable age"—see s.122.

GENERAL NOTE

1.98   The amendment to subs.(1)(a) of this section closes it to those reaching state pensionable age after April 5, 2016. This is because they can now make claims only under the Pensions Act 2014 s.1 and following for a state pension. See the general note to that Act below.

While this section remains relevant to those already of state pensionable age and claiming a pension by that date and in connection with some transitional cases, no new claims can therefore be made under this section. As noted to s.43 above, much of the detail of the state pension has changed. See the 2015/16 edition (or other previous editions) of this work for a full explanation and analysis of this section as it applies to existing pensioners and transitional cases.

Deemed earnings factors

1.99   **44A.** [³ (A1) Subsections (1) to (4) below apply to the first appointed year or any subsequent tax year before 2010–11.]

(1) For the purposes of section 44(6)(za) above, if any of the conditions in subsection (2) below is satisfied for a relevant year [³ to which this

subsection applies], a pensioner is deemed to have an earnings factor for that year which—

(a) is derived from [² so much of his earnings as did not exceed [⁴ the applicable limit] and] on which primary Class 1 contributions were paid; and

(b) is equal to the amount which, when added to any other earnings factors taken into account under that provision, produces an aggregate of earnings factors equal to the low earnings threshold.

(2) The conditions referred to in subsection (1) above are that—

(a) the pensioner would, apart from this section, have an earnings factor for the year—

    (i) equal to or greater than the qualifying earnings factor for the year; but

    (ii) less than the low earnings threshold for the year;

(b) [¹ carer's allowance]—

    (i) was payable to the pensioner throughout the year; or

    (ii) would have been so payable but for the fact that under regulations the amount payable to him was reduced to nil because of his receipt of other benefits;

(c) for the purposes of paragraph 5(7)(b) of Schedule 3, the pensioner is taken to be precluded from regular employment by responsibilities at home throughout the year by virtue of—

    (i) the fact that child benefit was payable to him in respect of a child under the age of six; or

    (ii) his satisfying such other condition as may be prescribed;

(d) the pensioner is a person satisfying the requirement in subsection (3) below to whom long-term incapacity benefit [⁵ or qualifying employment and support allowance] was payable throughout the year, or would have been so payable but for the fact that—

    (i) he did not satisfy the contribution conditions in paragraph 2 of Schedule 3 [⁵ or, as the case may be, [⁶ in paragraphs 1 and 2] of Schedule 1 to the Welfare Reform Act [⁶ 2007]].; or

    (ii) under regulations the amount payable to him was reduced to nil because of his receipt of other benefits or of payments from an occupational pension scheme or personal pension scheme.

(3) The requirement referred to in subsection (2)(d) above is that—

(a) for one or more relevant years the pensioner has paid, or (apart from this section) is treated as having paid, primary Class 1 contributions on earnings equal to or greater than the qualifying earnings factor; and

(b) the years for which he has such a factor constitute at least one tenth of his working life.

(4) For the purposes of subsection (3)(b) above—

(a) a pensioner's working life shall not include—

    (i) any tax year before 1978–79; or

    (ii) any year in which he is deemed under subsection (1) above to have an earnings factor by virtue of fulfilling the condition in subsection (2)(b) or (c) above; and

(b) the figure calculated by dividing his working life by ten shall be rounded to the nearest whole year (and any half year shall be rounded down).

[³ (4A) The following do not apply to a pensioner attaining pensionable age on or after 6th April 2010—

(a) the requirement referred to in subsection (2)(d) above, and

(b) subsections (3) and (4) above.]

(5) The low earnings threshold for the first appointed year and subsequent tax years shall be £9,500 (but subject to section 148A of the Administration Act).

[⁴ (5A) In subsection (1)(a) "the applicable limit" has the same meaning as in section 44.]

(6) In subsection (2)(d)(ii) above, "occupational pension scheme" and "personal pension scheme" have the meanings given by subsection (6) of section 30DD above for the purposes of subsection (5) of that section.]

[⁵ (7) In subsection (2)(d) "qualifying employment and support allowance" means contributory employment and support allowance where—

(a) that allowance was payable for a continuous period of 52 weeks;

(b) that allowance included the support component under section 2(2) of the Welfare Reform Act [2007]; or

(c) in the case of—

(i) a man born between 6th April 1944 and 5th April 1947; or

(ii) a woman born between 6th April 1949 and 5th April 1951, that allowance was payable for a continuous period of 13 weeks immediately following a period throughout which statutory sick pay was payable.]

AMENDMENTS

1. Regulatory Reform (Carer's Allowance) Order 2002 (SI 2002/1457), art.2 (April 1, 2003).

2. National Insurance Contributions Act 2002 Sch.1 para.11 (April 6, 2003).

3. Pensions Act 2007 Sch.1 para.34 (September 26, 2007).

4. National Insurance Contributions Act 2008 Sch.1 para.4 (September 21, 2008).

5. Employment and Support Allowance (Consequential Provisions) (No. 2) Regulations 2008 (SI 2008/1554) (October 27, 2008).

6. Social Security (Miscellaneous Amendment) (No.3) Regulations 2010 (SI 2010/840) (June 6, 2010).

GENERAL NOTE

1.100   This section introduced what is sometimes known as the second state pension. In *Jayawardhana v Secretary of State for Work and Pensions* [2006] EWCA Civ 1865, 19.12.06, it was held that the effect of this and the preceding section could apply only prospectively and not retrospectively. Where, therefore, the claimant had reached retirement age in the tax year 2002/03, (which year could not be counted under s.44(7)(a)(ii)) and the amended version of this section became effective only from April 2002, it could have no application to him.

Regulations made under subsection (2)(c)(ii) specify an additional means by which a pensioner is to be taken as precluded from regular employment throughout the year. See regulation 6 of the Additional Pension and Social Security Pensions (Home Responsibilities) (Amendment) Regulations 2001 (SI 2001/1323).

Subsection (5)

1.101   *Low earnings threshold:* this annual figure currently stands at £15,300, having been raised to that level for 2015/16 and successive tax years (see Social Security Pensions (Low Earnings Threshold) Order 2015 (SI 2015/186) art.2), and has not been increased since.

[¹ 44B. Deemed earnings factors: 2010–11 onwards

(1) This section applies to 2010–11 and subsequent tax years.

1.102

(2) For the purposes of section 44(6)(za) above, if any of Conditions A to C in subsections (3) to (5) below is satisfied for a relevant year to which this section applies, a pensioner is deemed to have an earnings factor for that year which—

  (a) is derived from so much of his earnings as did not exceed [¹the upper accrual point] and on which primary Class 1 contributions were paid; and

  (b) is equal to the amount which, when added to any other earnings factors taken into account under that provision, produces an aggregate of earnings factors equal to the low earnings threshold.

(3) Condition A is that the pensioner would, apart from this section, have an earnings factor for the year—

  (a) equal to or greater than the qualifying earnings factor ("the QEF") for the year, but

  (b) less than the low earnings threshold for the year.

(4) Condition B is that the pensioner—

  (a) would, apart from this section and section 44C below, have an earnings factor for the year less than the QEF for the year, but

  (b) is entitled to an aggregate amount of earnings factor credits for that year under section 44C below equal to the difference between the QEF for the year and the earnings factor mentioned in paragraph (a) above.

(5) Condition C is that the pensioner is entitled to 52 earnings factor credits for that year under section 44C below.

(6) This section has effect in relation to the flat rate introduction year and any subsequent tax year as if—

  (a) subsection (2)(b) referred to an aggregate of earnings factors greater than the QEF, but less than the low earnings threshold, for the year (rather than to one equal to that threshold); and

  (b) Condition A in subsection (3) (and the reference to it in subsection (2)) were omitted.

(7) In this section—

  (a) [² *Repealed*]

  (b) "the low earnings threshold" means the low earnings threshold for the year concerned as specified in section 44A above; and

  (c) in subsections (3) and (4), any reference to the pensioner's earnings factor for a relevant year is to be construed in accordance with section 44(6)(za) above.

AMENDMENTS

1. National Insurance Contributions Act 2008 Sch.1 para.5 (September 21, 2008).
2. National Insurance Contributions Act 2008 Sch.2 (September 21, 2008).

MODIFICATION

Section 44B is modified by Sch.2 para.46 of the Employment and Support Allowance (Transitional Provisions, Housing Benefit and Council Tax Benefit) (Existing Awards) (No. 2) Regulations 2010 (SI 2010/1907) (as amended) for the purposes specified in reg.6(1). For details of the modification, see the text of those Regulations below.

44C. Earnings factor credits

1.103 (1) This section applies, for the purposes of Conditions B and C in section 44B(4) and (5) above, to 2010–11 and subsequent tax years.

(2) In respect of each week—

(a) which falls in a relevant year to which this section applies, and

(b) in respect of which a pensioner is eligible for earnings factor enhancement,

the pensioner is entitled to an earnings factor credit equal to 1/52 of the QEF for that year.

This is subject to subsection (5) below.

(3) A pensioner is eligible for earnings factor enhancement in respect of a week if one or more of the following apply—

(a) he was a relevant carer in respect of that week for the purposes of section 23A above (see section 23A(3));

(b) carer's allowance was payable to him for any part of that week, or would have been so payable but for the fact that under regulations the amount payable to him was reduced to nil because of his receipt of other benefits;

(c) severe disablement allowance was payable to him for any part of that week;

(d) long-term incapacity benefit was payable to him for any part of that week or would have been so payable but for the fact that—

(i) he did not satisfy the contribution conditions in paragraph 2 of Schedule 3, or

(ii) under regulations the amount payable to him was reduced to nil because of his receipt of other benefits or of payments from an occupational pension scheme or personal pension scheme;

(e) he satisfies such other conditions as may be prescribed.

(4) In subsection (3)(d)(ii) above "occupational pension scheme" and "personal pension scheme" have the meanings given by subsection (6) of section 30DD above for the purposes of subsection (5) of that section.

(5) For the purposes of Condition B in section 44B(4) above a person is not entitled to an aggregate amount of earnings factor credits in respect of a year that is greater than the difference referred to in that Condition.

(6) For the purposes of this section a week that falls partly in one tax year and partly in another is to be treated as falling in the year in which it begins and not in the following year.

(7) In section 44B above and this section—

(a) "the QEF" means the qualifying earnings factor, and

(b) any reference to a person being entitled to an earnings factor credit of a particular amount (or to an aggregate amount of earnings factor credits) for a year is a reference to the person being treated as having for that year an earnings factor (within the meaning of section 44(6)(za) above) of the amount in question by virtue of subsection (2) above.]

AMENDMENT

1. Pensions Act 2007 s.9(1) (September 26, 2007).

The additional pension in a Category A retirement pension

1.104 **45.**—(1) The weekly rate of the additional pension in a Category A retirement pension in any case where the pensioner attained pensionable age in a tax year before 6th April 1999 shall be [⁴ the sum of the following—

    (a) in relation to any surpluses in the pensioner's earnings factors, weekly equivalent of 1¼ per cent. of the [¹ adjusted] amount of the surpluses mentioned in section 44(3)(b) above; and

    (b) if the pensioner has one or more units of additional pension, a specified amount for each of those units.]

(2) The weekly rate of the additional pension in a Category A retirement pension in any case where the pensioner attained pensionable age in a tax year after 5th April 1999 shall be [² the sum of the following]

    (a) in relation to any surpluses in the pensioner's earnings factors for the tax years in the period beginning with 1978–79 and ending with 1987–88, the weekly equivalent of 25/N per cent. of the [¹ adjusted] amount of those surpluses; and

    (b) in relation to any surpluses in the pensioner's earnings factors in a tax year after 1987–88 [² but before the first appointed year], the weekly equivalent of the relevant percentage of the [¹ adjusted] amount of those surpluses.

[² (c) in relation to any tax years falling within subsection (3A) below, the weekly equivalent of the amount calculated in accordance with Schedule 4A to this Act.]

[³ and

    (d) in relation to the flat rate introduction year and subsequent tax years, the weekly equivalent of the amount calculated in accordance with Schedule 4B to this Act.] [⁴ ; and

    (e) if the pensioner has one or more units of additional pension, a specified amount for each of those units.]

[⁴ (2A) For the purposes of subsections (1)(b) and (2)(e) the "specified amount" is an amount to be specified by the Secretary of State in regulations.]

(3) In subsection (2)(b) above, "relevant percentage" means—

    (a) 20/N per cent., where the pensioner attained pensionable age in 2009–10 or any subsequent tax year;

    (b) (20 + X)/N per cent., where the pensioner attained pensionable age in a tax year falling within the period commencing with 1999–2000 and ending with 2008–9.

[² (3A) The following tax years fall within this subsection—

    (a) the first appointed year;

    (b) subsequent tax years] [³ before the flat rate introduction year.]

(4) In this section—

    (a) X = 0.5 for each tax year by which the tax year in which the pensioner attained pensionable age precedes 2009–10; and

    (b) N = the number of tax years in the pensioner's working life which fall after 5th April 1978;

but paragraph (b) above is subject, in particular, to subsection (5) and, where applicable, section 46 below.

(5) Regulations may direct that in prescribed cases or classes of cases any tax year shall be disregarded for the purpose of calculating N under subsection (4)(b) above, if it is a tax year after 5th April 1978 in which the pensioner—

    (a) was credited with contributions or earnings under this Act by virtue of regulations under section 22(5) above, or

    (b) was precluded from regular employment by responsibilities at home, or

(c) in prescribed circumstances, would have been treated as falling within paragraph (a) or (b) above,

but not so as to reduce the number of years below 20.

(6) For the purposes of subsections (1) and (2) above, the weekly equivalent of [¹ any amount] shall be calculated by dividing that amount by 52 and rounding the result to the nearest whole penny, taking any ½p as nearest to the next whole penny.

(7) Where the amount falling to be rounded under subsection (6) above is a sum less than ½p, the amount calculated under that subsection shall be taken to be zero, notwithstanding any other provision of this Act or the Administration Act.

(8) The sums which are the weekly rate of the additional pension in a Category A retirement pension are subject to alteration by orders made by the Secretary of State under section 150 of the Administration Act.

AMENDMENTS

1. Child Support, Pensions and Social Security Act 2000 s.35 (April 6, 2002).
2. Child Support, Pensions and Social Security Act 2000 s.31 (April 6, 2002).
3. Pensions Act 2007 s.11 (September 26, 2007).
4. Pensions Act 2014 Sch.15 para.7 (October 12, 2015).

DERIVATION

SSPA 1975 s.6.

GENERAL NOTE

1.105   The Social Security Class 3A Contributions (Units of Additional Pension) Regulations 2014 (SI 2014/3240) contain the "specified amount" for the purposes of subsections (1b) and (2A). It is £1.

1.106   [**45A.**—[¹ *Repealed*]

REPEALS

1. Tax Credits Act 2002 Sch.6 (April 1, 2003).

[¹ **Effect of working families' tax credit and disabled person's tax credit on earnings factor**

1.107   **45AA.**—(1) For the purposes of calculating additional pension under sections 44 and 45 where, in the case of any relevant year, working families' tax credit is paid in respect of any employed earner, or disabled person's tax credit is paid to any employed earner, section 44(6)(a)(i) shall have effect as if—

(a) where that person had earnings of not less than the qualifying earnings factor for that year, being earnings upon which primary class 1 contributions were paid or treated as paid ("qualifying earnings") in respect of that year, the amount of those qualifying earnings were increased by the aggregate amount ("AG") of working families' tax credit, or, as the case may be, disabled person's tax credit paid in respect of that year, and

(b) in any other case, that person had qualifying earnings in respect of that year and the amount of those qualifying earnings were equal to AG plus the qualifying earnings factor for that year.

(2) The reference in subsection (1) to the person in respect of whom working families' tax credit is paid—
(a) where it is paid to one of a couple, is a reference to the prescribed member of the couple, and
(b) in any other case, is a reference to the person to whom it is paid.

(3) A person's qualifying earnings in respect of any year cannot be treated by virtue of subsection (1) as exceeding the upper earnings limit for that year multiplied by 53.

(4) Subsection (1) does not apply to any woman who has made, or is treated as having made, an election under regulations under section 19(4), which has not been revoked, that her liability in respect of primary Class 1 contributions shall be at a reduced rate.

(5) In this section—
"couple" has the same meaning as in Part 7 (see section 137);
"relevant year" has the same meaning as in section 44.]

AMENDMENT

1. Pensions Act 2008 Sch.4 para.5(1) (January 3, 2012).

GENERAL NOTE

The insertion of s.45AA (and consequent amendments are together referred to below as "the relevant provisions") have effect in relation to a pensioner who attains pensionable age after April 5, 1999 and, in relation to widowed mother's allowance and widow's pension, to a widow whose husband dies after that date and, in relation to a claim based on a spouse's contributions, to a claimant whose spouse dies after that date, in accordance with subparas (2), (3), (4), and (5) of para.5 of Sch.4 of Pensions Act 2008 as follows:

"(3) Subject to sub-paragraphs (4) and (5), the relevant provisions apply to a person ("the pensioner") who attains pensionable age after 5 April 1999 and, in relation to such a person—
(a) have effect for 1995-96 and subsequent tax years, and
(b) are deemed so to have had effect (with the necessary modifications) during the period—
(i) beginning with 6 April 2003, and
(ii) ending with the coming into force of this paragraph.

(4) Where the pensioner is a woman, the relevant provisions have effect in the case of additional pension falling to be calculated under sections 44 and 45 of the Social Security Contributions and Benefits Act 1992 (c. 4) by virtue of section 39 of that Act (widowed mother's allowance and widow's pension), including Category B retirement pension payable under section 48B(4), if her husband—
(a) dies after 5 April 1999, and
(b) has not attained pensionable age on or before that date.

(5) The relevant provisions have effect, where additional pension falls to be calculated under sections 44 and 45 of the Social Security Contributions and Benefits Act 1992 as applied by section 48A or 48B(2) of that Act (other Category B retirement pension) if—
(a) the pensioner attains pensionable age after 5 April 1999, and
(b) the pensioner's spouse has not attained pensionable age on or before that date."

For claims based upon an earlier period see previous editions of this work.

1.108

[¹ Reduction of additional pension in Category A retirement pension: pension sharing

1.109   **45B.**—(1) The weekly rate of the additional pension in a Category A retirement pension shall be reduced as follows in any case where—

(a) the pensioner has become subject to a state scheme pension debit, and

(b) the debit is to any extent referable to the additional pension.

(2) If the pensioner became subject to the debit in or after the final relevant year, the weekly rate of the additional pension shall be reduced by the appropriate weekly amount.

(3) If the pensioner became subject to the debit before the final relevant year, the weekly rate of the additional pension shall be reduced by the appropriate weekly amount multiplied by the relevant revaluation percentage.

(4) The appropriate weekly amount for the purposes of subsections (2) and (3) above is the weekly rate, expressed in terms of the valuation day, at which the cash equivalent, on that day, of the pension mentioned in subsection (5) below is equal to so much of the debit as is referable to the additional pension.

(5) The pension referred to above is a notional pension for the pensioner by virtue of section 44(3)(b) above which becomes payable on the later of—

(a) his attaining pensionable age, and

(b) the valuation day.

(6) For the purposes of subsection (3) above, the relevant revaluation percentage is the percentage specified, in relation to earnings factors for the tax year in which the pensioner became subject to the debit, by the last order under section 148 of the Administration Act to come into force before the end of the final relevant year.

[²(7) The Secretary of State may by regulations make provision about the calculation and verification of cash equivalents for the purposes of this section.

(7A) The power conferred by subsection (7) above includes power to provide—

(a) for calculation or verification in such manner as may be approved by or on behalf of the Government Actuary, and

(b) for things done under the regulations to be required to be done in accordance with guidance from time to time prepared by a person prescribed by the regulations.]

(8) In this section—

"final relevant year" means the tax year immediately preceding that in which the pensioner attains pensionable age;

"state scheme pension debit" means a debit under section 49(1)(a) of the Welfare Reform and Pensions Act 1999 (debit for the purposes of this Part of this Act);

"valuation day" means the day on which the pensioner became subject to the state scheme pension debit.]

AMENDMENTS

1. Welfare Reform and Pensions Act 1999 Sch.6 para.2 (December 1, 2001).
2. Child Support, Pensions and Social Security Act s.41(2) (September 29, 2000).

GENERAL NOTE

The Sharing of State Scheme Rights (Provision of Information and Valuation) (No.2) Regulations 2000 (SI 2000/2914) are made under subsection (7).   **1.110**

Modifications of section 45 for calculating the additional pension in certain benefits

46.—(1) *Omitted.*   **1.111**
(2) For the purpose of determining the additional pension falling to be calculated under section 45 above by virtue of section 39(1) [¹ or 39C(1)] above or section [² [⁷...] [⁶ 48B(2)] [¹ ...]] below in a case where the deceased spouse died under pensionable age [⁴ or by virtue of section 39C(1) above or section [⁷...] 48BB(2) below in a case where the deceased civil partner died under pensionable age], the following definition shall be substituted for the definition of "N" in section 45(4)(b) above—
[² "N" =
(a) the number of tax years which begin after 5th April 1978 and end before the date when the entitlement to the additional pension commences, or
(b) the number of tax years in the period—
  (i) beginning with the tax year in which the deceased spouse ("S") [⁴ or civil partner]attained the age of 16 or if later 1978–79, and
  (ii) ending immediately before the tax year in which S would have attained pensionable age if S had not died earlier,
  whichever is the smaller number].
[³ (3) For the purpose of determining the additional pension falling to be calculated under section 45 above by virtue of section 48BB below in a case where the deceased spouse [⁴ or civil partner] died under pensionable age, the following definition shall be substituted for the definition of "N" in section 45(4)(b) above—
" 'N' =
(a) the number of tax years which begin after 5th April 1978 and end before the date when the deceased spouse [⁴ or civil partner] dies, or
(b) the number of tax years in the period—
  (i) beginning with the tax year in which the deceased spouse [⁴ or civil partner] ('S') attained the age of 16 or, if later, 1978–79, and
  (ii) ending immediately before the tax year in which S would have attained pensionable age if S had not died earlier,
  whichever is the smaller number."]
[⁵ (4) For the purpose of determining the additional pension falling to be calculated under section 45 above by virtue of section 39C(1) above in a case where the deceased spouse or civil partner died under pensionable age, section 45 has effect subject to the following additional modifications—
(a) the omission of subsection (2)(d), and
(b) the omission in subsection (3A)(b) of the words "before the flat rate introduction year".]

AMENDMENTS

1. Welfare Reform and Pensions Act 1999 Sch.8 (April 9, 2001).
2. Pensions Act 1995 Sch.4 (July 19, 1995).

3. Child Support, Pensions and Social Security Act 2000 s.32 (April 9, 2001).
4. Civil Partnership Act 2004 Sch.24 (December 5, 2005).
5. Pensions Act 2007 Sch.2 Pt 3, para.46 (September 26, 2007).
6. Pensions Act 2008 Sch.4 para.6(3) (January 3, 2012).
7. Pensions Act 2014 Sch.12 para.59 (April 6, 2016).

Increase of Category A retirement pension for incapacity

1.112
47.—(1) Subject to section 61 below, the weekly rate of a Category A retirement pension shall be increased if the pensioner was entitled to an [¹ age addition to long-term incapacity benefit by virtue of regulations under section 30B(7) above] in respect of—

(a) any day falling within the period of 8 weeks ending immediately before the day on which he attains pensionable age; or

(b) the last day before the beginning of that period;

and the increase shall, subject to subsection (2) below, be of an amount equal to the appropriate weekly rate of the [¹ age addition to long-term incapacity benefit by virtue of regulations under section 30B(7) above on that day.]

(2) Where for any period the weekly rate of a Category A retirement pension includes an additional pension, for that period the relevant amount shall be deducted from the amount that would otherwise be the increase under subsection (1) above and the pensioner shall be entitled to an increase under that subsection only if there is a balance remaining after that deduction and, if there is such a balance, of an amount equal to it.

(3) In subsection (2) above the "relevant amount" means an amount equal to the additional pension, reduced by the amount of any reduction in the weekly rate of the Category A retirement pension made by virtue of [² section 46] of the Pensions Act.

[³ (3A) In subsections (2) and (3) above references to additional pension do not include any amount of additional pension attributable to units of additional pension.

(3B) For units of additional pension, see section 14A.]

(4) In this section any reference to an additional pension is a reference to that pension after any increase under section 52(3) below but without any increase under paragraphs 1 and 2 of Schedule 5 to this Act.

(5) In ascertaining for the purposes of subsection (1) above the rate of a pensioner's [¹ age addition to long-term incapacity benefit by virtue of regulations under section 30B(7) above] regard shall be had to the rates in force from time to time.

(6) Regulations may provide that subsection (1) above shall have effect as if for the reference to 8 weeks there were substituted a reference to a larger number of weeks specified in the regulations.

AMENDMENTS

1. Social Security (Incapacity for Work) Act 1994 Sch.1 (April 13, 1995).
2. Pensions Schemes Act 1993 Sch.8 (February 7, 1994).
3. Pensions Act (Consequential Amendments)(Unit of Additional Pensions) Order 2014 (SI 2014/3213) art.2 (October 12, 2015).

GENERAL NOTE

1.113
Note that under s.46 of the Pensions Schemes Act 1993, the amount of any retirement pension is reduced by the guaranteed minimum pension to which the claimant may be entitled. See notes to that section.

Regulation 23 of the Social Security (Incapacity Benefit) (Transitional) Regulations 1995 (SI 1995/310) is made under subsection (6). It provides:

"23. Increase of Category A retirement pension for incapacity
(1) Where a person has been entitled to invalidity allowance or transitional invalidity allowance at any time during a period of 57 days before attaining pensionable age, sections 47 and 61 of the 1992 Act shall continue to have effect as though section 11 of, and paragraph 13 of Schedule 1 to, the 1994 Act had not come into force and as though any reference to invalidity allowance in section 47 were a reference to transitional invalidity allowance or invalidity allowance.
(2) In the case of a person who is a welfare to work beneficiary in accordance with regulation 13A of the Social Security (Incapacity for Work) (General) Regulations 1995, the reference in paragraph (1) to a period of 57 days shall be treated as a reference to a period of 104 weeks."

Use of former spouse's contributions

48.—(1) Where a person [³ who attained pensionable age before 6 April 2016]— 1.114
  (a) has been [¹ in a relevant relationship], and
  (b) in respect of the tax year in which the [¹ relationship] terminated or any previous tax year, does not with his own contributions satisfy the contribution conditions for a Category A retirement pension,
then, for the purpose of enabling him to satisfy those conditions (but only in respect of any claim for a Category A retirement pension), the contributions of his former spouse may to the prescribed extent be treated as if they were his own contributions.

(2) Subsection (1) above shall not apply in relation to any person who attained pensionable age before 6th April 1979 if the termination of his [¹ relevant relationship] also occurred before that date.

[³ (2A) Regulations under subsection (1) may not provide for contributions of a person in respect of times on or after 6 April 2016 to be treated as contributions of another person.]

(3) [¹ (3) Where a person has been in a relevant relationship more than once, this section applies only to the last relevant relationship and the references to his relevant relationship and his former spouse or civil partner shall be construed accordingly.

(4) In this section, "relevant relationship" means a marriage or civil partnership].

[² (5) For the purposes of this section, a civil partnership is not to be treated as having terminated by reason of its having been—
  (a) converted into a marriage under section 9 of the Marriage (Same Sex Couples) Act 2013;
  (b) changed into a marriage under the Marriage (Scotland) Act 1977;
  (c) changed into a marriage in accordance with provision made under section 10 of the Marriage and Civil Partnership (Scotland) Act 2014; or
  (d) changed into a marriage under Part 5 of the Marriage and Civil Partnership (Scotland) Act 2014 and Civil Partnership Act 2004 (Consequential Provisions and Modifications) Order 2014.]

AMENDMENTS

1. Civil Partnership Act 2004 Sch.24 (December 5, 2005).
2. Marriage and Civil Partnership (Scotland) Act 2014 and Civil Partnership Act

2004 (Consequential Provisions and Modifications) Order 2014 (SI 2014/3229) Sch.4 para.2 (December 12, 2014).

3. Pensions Act 2014 Sch.12 para. 56 (April 6, 2016)

DERIVATIONS

1.115   SSPA 1975 s.20.
             SSA 1979 s.5.

GENERAL NOTE

1.116   The principle of forfeiture will apply in a case where the death of the former spouse is the result of homicide committed by the claimant. An example of its application and the exercise of discretion by the Commissioner is *CFP/4349/2004*. There the claimant had pleaded guilty to the manslaughter of her husband on the grounds of diminished responsibility and was sentenced to a term of probation. She made no claim to widows' benefits for the next 13 years, but then claimed retirement pension relying, in part, on her husband's contribution record. It was held that the forfeiture rule applied, but that relief should be granted with effect from the time of the claim for retirement pension.

The amendment in 2016 made by the Pensions Act 2014 ensures that the section does not apply to any contributions made after the introduction of the single state pension (see the note to s.44 above). This follows the decision to abolish Category B pensions from that date save for existing pensioners and transitional cases.

[¹ Category B retirement pension for married person or civil partner

1.117   **48A.**–(1) A married person is entitled to a Category B retirement pension by virtue of the contributions of his or her spouse if—

(a) the person attained pensionable age before 6 April 2016, and

(b) the spouse—

(i) has attained pensionable age, and

(ii) satisfies the relevant contribution condition.

(2) But subsection (1) does not confer a right to a Category B retirement pension on—

(a) a man whose spouse was born before 6 April 1950, or

(b) a woman whose wife was born before 6 April 1950.

(3) A person who is a civil partner is entitled to a Category B retirement pension by virtue of the contributions of his or her civil partner ("the contributing civil partner") if—

(a) the person attained pensionable age before 6 April 2016, and

(b) the contributing civil partner—

(i) was born on or after 6 April 1950,

(ii) has attained pensionable age, and

(iii) satisfies the condition in paragraph 5A of Schedule 3.

(4) A Category B retirement pension payable under this section is payable at the weekly rate specified in paragraph 5 of Part 1 of Schedule 4.

(5) A person ceases to be entitled to a Category B retirement pension under this section if—

(a) the person's spouse or civil partner dies (but see sections 48B and 51), or

(b) the person otherwise ceases to be married or in the civil partnership (but see section 48AA).

(6) In subsection (1)(b)(ii) "the relevant contribution condition" means—

(a) in a case where the spouse was born before 6 April 1945, the conditions in paragraph 5 of Schedule 3;

(b) in any other case, the condition in paragraph 5A of Schedule 3.

(7) For the purposes of any provision of this Act as it applies in relation to this section, no account is to be taken of any earnings factors of the spouse or contributing civil partner for the tax year beginning with 6 April 2016 or any later tax year.]

AMENDMENT

1. Pensions Act 2014 Sch.12 para 60 (April 6, 2016).

GENERAL NOTE

The new ss.48A and 48AA replace the previous s.48A in consequence of the general changes introduced by Pensions Act 2016. The new sections prevent anyone who reaches state pensionable age on or after April 6, 2016 from claiming entitlement to a Category B pension in respect of any marriage or civil partnership. The rights of those who reach that age before that date are, however, protected subject to the provisions of the sections. For a fuller analysis of the previous provisions under which protected claims could be made see the commentary to the previous s.48A in previous editions of this volume.   **1.118**

An attempted challenge to s.48A's general exclusion of those who attained pensionable age on or after April 6, 2016 was made in *FY v Secretary of State for Work & Pensions* (RP) [2018] UKUT 146 (AAC). The appellant attained pensionable age on April 21, 2016 and his wife, for whom the appellant wished to secure a category B pension, would attain pensionable age on January 11, 2021. The condition in s.48A(1)(a) was not met because the wife had not attained pensionable age by April 6, 2016. While the wife's entitlement to a Category B pension was in issue, the proceedings were brought by the husband and followed the Secretary of State's decision on his own claim for retirement pension. Upper Tribunal Judge Wikeley held that no decision had been made about the wife's entitlement to a category B pension. In the absence of such a decision, there was nothing to be challenged before the First-tier Tribunal and, in turn, the Upper Tribunal. The Upper Tribunal could not, therefore, consider the Appellant's substantive arguments.

In *FY*, the Appellant husband did, in fact, apply without success to the First-tier Tribunal for his wife to be made a party to the proceedings. Judge Wikeley rejected the husband's challenge to the First-tier Tribunal's refusal to make his wife a party to the proceedings. In the absence of a decision as to her entitlement to a Category B pension, the First-tier Tribunal rightly refused to make the wife to a party to the proceedings. Judge Wikeley went on to observe that, in advance of a decision as to the wife's entitlement to a Category B pension, which could not possibly be given before 2021 when she attained pensionable age, the only potential means of challenging what the Appellant described as the 'abolition' of Category B pensions was a claim for judicial review in the High Court.

[¹ **Category B retirement pension for divorcee or former civil partner**

48BAA.–(1) A person who has been in a marriage that has been dissolved is entitled to a Category B retirement pension by virtue of the contributions of his or her former spouse if—   **1.119**

(a) the person attained pensionable age—

  (i) before 6 April 2016, and

  (ii) before the marriage was dissolved, and

(b) the former spouse—

(i) attained pensionable age before the marriage was dissolved, and

(ii) satisfied the relevant contribution condition.

(2) But subsection (1) does not confer a right to a Category B retirement pension on—

(a) a man whose former spouse was born before 6 April 1950, or

(b) a woman whose former wife was born before 6 April 1950.

(3) A person who has been in a civil partnership that has been dissolved is entitled to a Category B retirement pension by virtue of the contributions of his or her former civil partner if—

(a) the person attained pensionable age—

(i) before 6 April 2016, and

(ii) before the civil partnership was dissolved, and

(b) the former civil partner—

(i) was born on or after 6 April 1950,

(ii) attained pensionable age before the civil partnership was dissolved, and

(iii) satisfied the condition in paragraph 5A of Schedule 3.

(4) During any period when the person's former spouse or civil partner is alive, a Category B retirement pension payable under this section is payable at the weekly rate specified in paragraph 5 of Part 1 of Schedule 4.

(5) During any period after the person's former spouse or civil partner is dead, a Category B retirement pension payable under this section is payable at the weekly rate of the basic pension specified in section 44(4).

(6) In subsection (1)(b)(ii) "the relevant contribution condition" means—

(a) in a case where the former spouse was born before 6 April 1945, the conditions in paragraph 5 of Schedule 3;

(b) in any other case, the condition in paragraph 5A of Schedule 3.

(7) For the purposes of any provision of this Act as it applies in relation to this section, no account is to be taken of any earnings factors of the former spouse or civil partner for the tax year beginning with 6 April 2016 or any later tax year.

(8) A voidable marriage or civil partnership which has been annulled is to be treated for the purposes of this section as if it had been a valid marriage or civil partnership which was dissolved at the date of annulment.

(9) Section 51ZA contains special rules for cases involving changes in gender.]

AMENDMENT

1. Pensions Act 2014 Sch.12 para.60 (April 6, 2016).

GENERAL NOTE

1.120   See General Note to s.48A.

Category B retirement pension for widows and widowers

1.121   [¹ **48B.**—[¹⁰ (1) A person ("the pensioner") whose spouse died while they were married is entitled to a Category B retirement pension by virtue of the contributions of his or her spouse if—

(a) the pensioner attained pensionable age—

(i) before 6 April 2016, and

(ii) before the spouse died, and

(b) the spouse satisfied the relevant contribution condition.

(1ZA) But subsection (1) does not confer a right to a Category B retirement pension on—
(a) a man who attained pensionable age before 6 April 2010, or
(b) a woman who attained pensionable age before 6 April 2010 and whose spouse was a woman.
(1ZB) In subsection (1)(b) "the relevant contribution condition" means—
(a) in a case where the spouse—
(i) died before 6 April 2010, or
(ii) died on or after that date having attained pensionable age before that date,
the conditions in paragraph 5 of Schedule 3, and
(b) in any other case, the condition in paragraph 5A of Schedule 3.
(1A) A person ("the pensioner") whose civil partner died while they were civil partners of each other is entitled to a Category B retirement pension by virtue of the contributions of his or her civil partner if—
(a) the pensioner attained pensionable age—
(i) on or after 6 April 2010 but before 6 April 2016, and
(ii) before the civil partner died, and
(b) the civil partner satisfied the relevant contribution condition.
(1B) In subsection (1A)(b) "the relevant contribution condition" means—
(a) in a case where the deceased civil partner attained pensionable age before 6 April 2010, the conditions in paragraph 5 of Schedule 3, and
(b) in any other case, the condition in paragraph 5A of Schedule 3.]
(2) A Category B retirement pension payable by virtue of subsection (1) [⁵ or (1A)] above shall be payable at a weekly rate corresponding to—
(a) the weekly rate of the basic pension, plus
(b) half of the weekly rate of the additional pension,
determined in accordance with the provisions of sections 44 to [² 45B] [³ and [⁶ Schedules 4A and 4B below] above as they apply in relation to a Category A retirement pension, but subject to section [⁸ 46 . . .] above and the modifications in subsection (3) below and section 48C(4) below.
(3) Where the spouse [⁵ or civil partner] died under pensionable age, references in the provisions of sections 44 to [³ 45B] [² and Schedule 4A below] above as applied by subsection (2) above to the tax year in which the pensioner attained pensionable age shall be taken as references to the tax year in which the spouse [⁵ or civil partner] died.
[¹⁰ (3A) For the purposes of any provision of this Act as it applies in relation to this section, no account is to be taken of any earnings factors of the deceased for the tax year beginning with 6 April 2016 or any later tax year.]
[¹⁰(4) A woman ("the pensioner") whose husband died before she attained pensionable age is entitled to a Category B retirement pension by virtue of the contributions of her husband if—
(a) she attained pensionable age before 6 April 2016, and
(b) the condition in subsection (5) is satisfied.
(4A) A man ("the pensioner") whose wife died before he attained pensionable age is entitled to a Category B retirement pension by virtue of the contributions of his wife if—
(a) he attained pensionable age on or after 6 April 2010 but before 6 April 2016, and

77

(b) the condition in subsection (5) would have been satisfied on the assumption mentioned in subsection (7).]

(5) The condition is that the pensioner—

(a) is entitled (or is treated by regulations as entitled) to a widow's pension by virtue of section 38 above, and

(b) became entitled to that pension in consequence of the spouse's death.

(6) A Category B retirement pension payable by virtue of subsection (4) [¹⁰ or (4A)] above shall be payable—

(a) where the pensioner is a woman, at the same weekly rate as her widow's pension, and

(b) where the pensioner is a man, at the same weekly rate as that of the pension to which he would have been entitled by virtue of section 38 above on the assumption mentioned in subsection (7) below.

(7) The assumption referred to in subsections [¹⁰(4A)] and (6) above is that a man is entitled to a pension by virtue of section 38 above on the same terms and conditions, and at the same rate, as a woman.]

[⁴ (8) Nothing in subsections (4) to (7) above applies in a case where the spouse dies on or after [¹² 9 April 2001],]

[¹⁰ (9) Section 51ZA contains special rules for cases involving changes in gender.]

[¹¹ (10) Subsection (11) applies in the case of a pensioner entitled to a Category B retirement pension by virtue of subsection (1) or (1A) whose spouse or civil partner—

(a) attained pensionable age on or after 6 April 2016, and

(b) died after attaining pensionable age.

(11) Where this subsection applies, the amount determined in accordance with subsection (2) as the weekly rate of the additional pension payable to the pensioner must be increased by such percentage as equals the overall percentage by which, had the pension been in payment as from the date when the spouse or civil partner reached pensionable age until the spouse's or civil partner's death, that weekly rate would have increased during that period by virtue of orders under section 150 of the Administration Act (annual uprating of benefits).]

AMENDMENTS

1. Pensions Act 1995 Sch.4 (July 19, 1995).
2. Welfare Reform and Pensions Act 1999 Sch.12 para.00 (April 9, 2001).
3. Child Support, Pensions and Social Security Act 2000 s.35 (April 6, 2002).
4. Welfare Reform and Pensions Act 1999 Sch.8 para.00 (April 9, 2001).
5. Civil Partnership Act 2004 Sch.24 (December 5, 2005).
6. Pensions Act 2007 Sch.1 (September 26, 2007).
7. Pensions Act 2007 Sch.2 Pt 3, para.8 (September 26, 2007).
8. Pensions Act 2014 Sch.4 para.96 repealing amendments made by Pensions Act 2008 (October 1, 2014).
9. Marriage (Same Sex Couples) Act 2013 Sch.4 Pt.5, para.12(3) (March 13, 2014). (Provisions that relate to a claim based on a gender recognition certificate will come into force at a later date-see Marriage (Same Sex Couples) Act 2013 (Commencement No.2 and Transitional Provisions Order 2014 (SI 2014/93) art.3.See also Marriage and Civil Partnership (Scotland) Act 2014 and Civil Partnership Act 2004 (Consequential Provisions and Modifications) Order 2014 (SI 2014/3229) Sch.4 para.2 (with effect from December 12, 2014).

10. Pensions Act 2014 Sch.12 para.61 (April 6, 2016).
11. Pensions Act 2014 (Consequential and Supplementary Amendments) Order 2016 (SI 2016/44) art.2(3) (April 6, 2016).
12. Pensions Act 2014 Sch.16 para.15 (April 6, 2017).

GENERAL NOTE

The amendments to this section made by and under the Pensions Act 2016   **1.122**
follow through the policy of that Act by closing entitlement to Category B pensions to anyone reaching state pensionable age on or after April 6, 2016. See subs. (1), (1A),(4) and (4A). Existing rights for those reaching pensionable age before that date are protected by the amended legislation. For a comment on those rights see the note to s.48B in previous editions of this work.

Regulation 7A of the Social Security (Widow's Benefit and Retirement Pensions) Regulations 1979 (SI 1979/643) sets out when a person is to be treated as entitled to a widow's pension for the purposes of subsection (5)(a).

[¹ Category B retirement pension: entitlement by reference to benefits under section 39A or 39B

48BB.—(1) Subsection (2) below applies where a person ("the pen-   **1.123**
sioner") [⁸ who attained pensionable age before 6 April 2016]—
  (a) was, immediately before attaining that age, entitled to a widowed parent's allowance in consequence of the death of his or her spouse [⁵ or civil partner]; and
  (b) has not [⁵ following the death, married or formed a civil partnership].

(2) The pensioner shall be entitled to a Category B retirement pension by virtue of the contributions of the spouse [⁵ or civil partner], which shall be payable at the same weekly rate as the widowed parent's allowance.

(3) Subsections (4) to (10) below apply where a person ("the pensioner") [⁸ who attained pensionable age before 6 April 2016]—
  (a) was in consequence of the death of his or her spouse [⁵ or civil partner] either—
    (i) entitled to a bereavement allowance [⁹ under section 39B (before that section was repealed)] at any time prior to attaining that age, or
    (ii) entitled to a widowed parent's allowance at any time when over the age of 45 (but not immediately before attaining pensionable age); and
  (b) has not [⁵ following the death, married or formed a civil partnership].

(4) The pensioner shall be entitled to a Category B retirement pension by virtue of the contributions of the spouse [⁵ or civil partner].

(5) A Category B retirement pension payable by virtue of subsection (4) above shall be payable at a weekly rate corresponding to the weekly rate of the additional pension determined in accordance with the provisions of sections 44 to [⁷ 45] above [² and [⁶ Schedules 4A [⁷ and 4B]] below] as they apply in relation to a Category A retirement pension, but [⁶ subject to section [⁷ 46] above and to the following provisions of this section and the modification in section 48C(4) below.]

(6) Where the spouse [⁵ or civil partner] died under pensionable age, references in the provisions of sections 44 to [⁷ 45AA and 45B] above [² and Schedule 4A below], as applied by subsection (5) above, to the tax year in which the pensioner attained pensionable age shall be taken as references to the tax year in which the spouse [⁵ or civil partner] died.

(7) Where the spouse [⁵ or civil partner] dies after [¹⁰ 5ᵗʰ October 2002], the pension payable by virtue of subsection (4) above shall (before making any reduction required by subsection (8) below) be one half of the amount which it would be apart from this subsection.

(8) Where the pensioner was under the age of 55 at the relevant time, the weekly rate of the pension shall be reduced by 7 per cent. of what it would be apart from this subsection multiplied—

(a) by the number of years by which the pensioner's age at that time was less than 55 (any fraction of a year being counted as a year), or

(b) by ten, if that number exceeds ten.

(9) In subsection (8) above "the relevant time" means—

(a) where the pensioner became entitled to a widowed parent's allowance in consequence of the death of the spouse [⁵ or civil partner], the time when the pensioner's entitlement to that allowance ended; and

(b) otherwise, the time of the spouse's [⁵ or civil partner's] death.

(10) The amount determined in accordance with subsections (5) to (9) above as the weekly rate of the pension payable to the pensioner by virtue of subsection (4) above shall be increased by such percentage as equals the overall percentage by which, had the pension been in payment as from the date of the spouse's [⁵ or civil partner's] death until the date when the pensioner attained pensionable age, that weekly rate would have been increased during that period by virtue of any orders under section 150 of the Administration Act (annual up-rating of benefits).]

AMENDMENTS

1. Welfare Reform and Pensions Act 1999 s.56 (April 9, 2001).
2. Child Support Pensions and Social Security Act 2000 s.35 (April 6, 2002).
3. Child Support Pensions and Social Security Act 2000 s.32(2) (April 9, 2001).
4. Tax Credit Act 2002 Sch.3 (April 6, 2003).
5. Civil Partnership Act 2004 Sch.24 (December 5, 2005).
6. Pensions Act 2007 Sch.2, Pt 3, para.9 (September 26, 2007).
7. Pensions Act 2014 Sch.14, para.96 repealing amendments earlier made by the Pensions Act 2008 (October 1, 2014).
8. Pensions Act 2014 Sch.12 para.62 (April 6, 2016).
9. Pensions Act 2014 Sch.16 para.16 (April 6, 2017).
10. Child Support, Pensions and Social Security Act 2000 s.39, which provides that this amendment has retrospective effect.

GENERAL NOTE

1.124   The amendments made by Pensions Act 2014 close entitlement to include only those who reached state pensionable age on or before April 5, 2016. See the note to s.48B above.

Category B retirement pension: general

1.125   [¹ 48C.—(1) Subject to the provisions of this Act, a person's entitlement to a Category B retirement pension shall begin on the day on which the conditions of entitlement become satisfied and shall continue for life.

(2) In any case where—

(a) a person would, apart from section 43(1) above, be entitled both to a Category A and to a Category B retirement pension, and

(b) section 47(1) above would apply for the increase of the Category A retirement pension, section 47(1) above shall be taken as applying also for the increase of the Category B retirement pension, subject to reduction or extinguishment of the increase by the application of section 47(2) above or section 46(5) of the Pensions Act.

(3) In the case of a pensioner whose spouse died on or before [⁹ 5th October 2002], [⁸ section] 48B(2)(b) above shall have effect with the omission of the words "half of".

(4) In the application of the provisions of sections 44 to [² 45B] [³ and [⁵ Schedules 4A [⁶ and 4B]] below] above by virtue of sections [⁸...] 48B(2) [⁴ or 48BB(5) above, references in those provisions to the pensioner shall be taken as references to the spouse [⁷ or civil partner].]

AMENDMENTS

1. Pensions Act 1995 Sch.4 (July 19, 1995).
2. Welfare Reform and Pensions Act 1999 Sch.12 (April 9, 2001).
3. Child Support Pensions and Social Security Act 2000 s.35 (April 6, 2002).
4. Welfare Reform and Pensions Act 1999 Sch.8 (April 9, 2001).
5. Pensions Act 2007 Sch.2 Pt 3, para.10 (September 26, 2007).
6. Pensions Act 2014 Sch.14 para.96 repealing amendments earlier made by the Pensions Act 2008 (October 1, 2014).
7. Civil Partnership (Pensions and Benefits Payments) (Consequential, etc. Provisions) Order 2005 (SI 2005/2053) (December 5, 2005).
8. Pensions Act 2014 Sch.12 para.63 (April 6, 2016).
9. Child Support, Pensions and Social Security Act 2000 s.39, which provides that this amendment has retrospective effect.

Sections 49 and 50 repealed.   1.126

[¹ Category B retirement pension for widows, widowers and surviving civil partners who attained pensionable age before 6 April 2010

51.–(1) A person ("the pensioner") whose spouse died while they were   1.127
married is entitled to a Category B retirement pension if—
 (a) they were both over pensionable age at the time of the death,
 (b) the pensioner attained pensionable age before 6 April 2010,
and
 (c) the spouse satisfied the relevant contribution condition.
(2) But subsection (1) does not confer a right to a Category B retirement pension on—
 (a) a woman whose husband has died, or
 (b) a man whose wife died before 6 April 1979.
(3) In subsection (1)(c) "the relevant contribution condition" means—
 (a) in a case where the spouse attained pensionable age before 6 April 2010, the conditions in paragraph 5 of Schedule 3, and
 (b) in a case where the spouse attained pensionable age on or after 6 April 2010, the condition in paragraph 5A of Schedule 3.
(4) A person ("the pensioner") whose civil partner died while they were civil partners of each other is entitled to a Category B retirement pension if—
 (a) they were both over pensionable age at the time of the death,
 (b) the pensioner attained pensionable age before 6 April 2010, and
 (c) the deceased civil partner satisfied the relevant contribution condition.

(5) In subsection (4)(c) "the relevant contribution condition" means—

    (a) in a case where the deceased civil partner attained pensionable age before 6 April 2010, the conditions in paragraph 5 of Schedule 3, and

    (b) in a case where the deceased civil partner attained pensionable age on or after 6 April 2010, the condition in paragraph 5A of Schedule 3.

(6) The weekly rate of a person's Category B retirement pension under this section is to be determined in accordance with sections 44 to 45AA and [² Schedule 4A and 4B] as they apply in the case of a Category A retirement pension taking references in those sections to the pensioner as references to the spouse or deceased civil partner.

(7) But in the case of—

    (a) a man whose wife dies after 5 October 2002,

    (b) a surviving party to a marriage of a same sex couple, or

    (c) a surviving civil partner,

any amount of additional pension falling to be calculated under subsection (6) is to be halved.

(8) For the purposes of any provision of this Act as it applies in relation to this section, no account is to be taken of any earnings factors of the spouse or deceased civil partner for the tax year beginning with 6 April 2016 or any later tax year.

(9) Subject to the provisions of this Act, a person becomes entitled to a Category B retirement pension under this section on the day on which the conditions of entitlement become satisfied and the entitlement continues throughout the person's life.

(10) Section 51ZA contains special rules for cases involving changes in gender.]

[²(11) Subsection (12) applies in the case of a pensioner whose spouse or civil partner—

    (a) attained pensionable age on or after 6 April 2016, and

    (b) died after attaining pensionable age.

(12) Where this subsection applies, the amount determined in accordance with this section as the weekly rate of the additional pension payable to the pensioner must be increased by such percentage as equals the overall percentage by which, had the pension been in payment as from the date when the spouse or civil partner reached pensionable age until the spouse's or civil partner's death, that weekly rate would have increased during that period by virtue of orders under section 150 of the Administration Act (annual uprating of benefits).]

AMENDMENTS

    1. Pensions Act 2014 Sch.12 para.64 (April 6, 2016).

    2. Pensions Act 2014 (Consequential and Supplementary Amendments) Order 2016 (SI 2016/224) art. 2(4) (April 6, 2016).

DEFINITION

    "pensionable age"—see s.122.

GENERAL NOTE

1.128   This section and s.51ZA below tidy up the existing legislation providing for Category B pensions, while at the same time following the policy of the Pensions

Act 2014 in preventing anyone reaching state pensionable age on or after April 6, 2016 from claiming a Category B pension (save in transitional cases). In those cases the section again confirms the policy of the Act in excluding from any such claim any contributions paid after the Pensions Act 2014 took effect.

[¹ Special provision for married person whose spouse changed gender

51ZA.–(1) Section 48A(2)(b) does not prevent a woman from being entitled to a Category B retirement pension under that section in a case where—

  (a) her spouse is a woman by virtue of a full gender recognition certificate having been issued under the Gender Recognition Act 2004, and

  (b) the marriage subsisted before the time when that certificate was issued.

(2) Section 48AA(2)(b) does not prevent a woman from being entitled to a Category B retirement pension under that section in a case where—

  (a) her former spouse was, at the time the marriage was dissolved, a woman by virtue of a full gender recognition certificate having been issued under the Gender Recognition Act 2004, and

  (b) the marriage subsisted before the time when that certificate was issued.

(3) Section 48B(1ZA)(b) does not prevent a woman from being entitled to a Category B retirement pension under that section in a case where—

  (a) her dead spouse was, at the time of death, a woman by virtue of a full gender recognition certificate having been issued under the Gender Recognition Act 2004, and

  (b) the marriage subsisted before the time when that certificate was issued,

and in such a case the reference in section 48B(1ZB)(a)(ii) to the spouse having attained pensionable age before 6 April 2010 is to be read as a reference to the spouse having been born before 6 April 1945.

(4) Section 51(1) does not confer a right to a Category B retirement pension on a woman if—

  (a) her dead spouse was, at the time of death, a woman by virtue of a full gender recognition certificate having been issued under the Gender Recognition Act 2004, and

  (b) the marriage subsisted before the time when that certificate was issued.]

1.129

AMENDMENT

1. Pensions Act 2014 Sch.12 para.65 (April 6, 2016).

Special provision for married people

[¹ **51A.**—This section has effect where, apart from section 43(1) above, a married person [² or civil partner] would be entitled both—

  (a) to a Category A retirement pension, and

  (b) to a Category B retirement pension by virtue of the contributions of the other party to the marriage [² or civil partnership].

(2) If by reason of a deficiency of contributions the basic pension in the Category A retirement pension falls short of the weekly rate specified in

1.130

Schedule 4, Part I, paragraph 5, that basic pension shall be increased by the lesser of—

(a) the amount of the shortfall, or

(b) the amount of the weekly rate of the Category B retirement pension.

(3) This section does not apply in any case where both parties to the marriage [² or civil partnership] attained pensionable age before 6th April 1979].

AMENDMENTS

1. Pensions Act 1995 Sch.4, para.21(6) (July 19, 1995).
2. Civil Partnership Act 2004 Sch.4 (December 5, 2005).

GENERAL NOTE

1.131   The effect of *Secretary of State for Work and Pensions v Nelligan, R(P)2/03* is extended to include s.51A in *CP/271/2005*. The claimant's wife had, like that in *Nelligan*, qualified for a Category A pension of her own on reaching age 60, but at a reduced rate. Subsequently, her husband qualified for his pension at the full rate at which point the claimant could have qualified for an increased pension on the basis of s.51A. Unfortunately the claimant did not discover this until some two years later and when she then claimed, she was allowed backdating for only the usual three month period.

The claimant argued that *Nelligan* did not apply to s.51A, and that if it did, then *Nelligan* was decided per incuriam since no reference there had been made to s.51A. That section, it was argued, should be read as creating entitlement without the need for a claim to be made. It was contended, on her behalf, that her increased entitlement arose under s.51A as a result of a decision to supersede her existing award of Category A pension and without a fresh claim being made.

This argument failed, however, because, as the Commissioner points out, the supersession takes effect only from the date of a relevant change of circumstances which, for the purpose of s.51A, could only be by her becoming entitled to a Category B pension, and as *Nelligan* had held, that entitlement depended upon a claim having been made.

Special provision for surviving spouses

1.132   **52.**—(1) This section has effect where, apart from section 43(1) above, a person would be entitled both—

(a) to a Category A retirement pension; and

[¹ (b) to a Category B retirement pension by virtue of the contributions of a spouse [² or civil partner] who has died]

(2) If by reason of a deficiency of contributions the basic pension in the Category A retirement pension falls short of the full amount, that basic pension shall be increased by the lesser of—

(a) the amount of the shortfall, or

(b) the amount of the basic pension in the rate of the Category B retirement pension,

"full amount" meaning for this purpose the sum specified in section 44(4) above as the weekly rate of the basic pension in a Category A retirement pension.

(3) If the additional pension in the Category A retirement pension falls short of the [³ maximum amount specified in regulations], that additional pension shall be increased by the lesser of—

(a) the amount of the shortfall, or

(b) the amount of the additional pension in the Category B retirement pension.

[⁴ (3A) In subsection (3) the references to additional pension in a

Category A or Category B retirement pension do not include any amount of additional pension attributable to units of additional pension.

(3B) If an amount of additional pension in the Category B retirement pension is attributable to units of additional pension, the additional pension in the Category A retirement pension is increased by that amount (in addition to any increase under subsection (3)).]

(4) This section does not apply in any case where the death of the wife or husband, as the case may be, occurred before 6th April 1979 and the surviving spouse had attained pensionable age before that date.

AMENDMENTS

1. Pensions Act 1995 Sch.4, para.21(7) (July 19, 1995).
2. Civil Partnership Act 2004 Sch.24 (December 5, 2005).
3. Pensions Act 2014 Sch.12 para.66 (April 6, 2016).
4. Pensions Act 2014 Sch.15 para.8 (October 12, 2015).

GENERAL NOTE

As with the sections above, this section now only applies to those who reached state pensionable age before April 6, 2016 or have a transitional entitlement after that date. For a comment on this section see the previous (2015/16) edition of this volume.   1.133

Section 53 repealed.   1.134

Category A and Category B retirement pensions: supplemental provisions

54. [*This section, so far as not previously repealed, is a regulation making power linked to s.52 and has now been superseded by the equivalent powers by and under the Pensions Act 2014. See regs.4 &ff of the State Pensions Regulations 2015 below.*]   1.135

[² Pension increase or lump sum where entitlement to retirement pension is deferred

55.—(1) Where a person's entitlement to a Category A or Category B retirement pension is deferred, Schedule 5 to this Act has effect.   1.136

(2) In that Schedule—

paragraph A1 makes provision enabling an election to be made where the pensioner's entitlement is deferred

paragraphs 1 to 3 make provision about increasing pension where the pensioner's entitlement is deferred

paragraphs 3A and 3B make provision about lump sum payments where the pensioner's entitlement is deferred

paragraph 3C makes provision enabling an election to be made where the pensioner's deceased spouse [⁴ or civil partner] has deferred entitlement

paragraphs 4 to 7 make provision about increasing pension where the pensioner's deceased spouse [⁴ or civil partner] has deferred entitlement

paragraphs 7A and 7B make provision about lump sum payments where the pensioner's deceased spouse [⁴ or civil partner] has deferred entitlement

paragraphs 7C to 9 make supplementary provision.

(3) For the purposes of this Act a person's entitlement to a Category A or Category B retirement pension is deferred if and so long as that person—

[³ (a) does not become entitled to that pension by reason only of not satisfying the conditions of section 1 of the Administration Act (entitlement to benefit dependent on claim), or]

(b) in consequence of an election under section 54(1), falls to be treated as not having become entitled to that pension,

and, in relation to any such pension, "period of deferment" shall be construed accordingly.]

AMENDMENTS

1. Pensions Act 1995 s.134(3) (July 19, 1995).
2. Pensions Act 2004 s.297 (April 6, 2005, subs.(3) from November 18, 2004).
3. Pensions Act 2007 Sch.1 para.7 (September 26, 2007).
4 Civil Partnership (Pensions and Benefits Payments) (Consequential, etc. Provisions) Order 2005 art.2, Sch. para.3 (SI 2005/2053) (December 5, 2005).

DERIVATIONS

1.137   SSPA 1975 s.12.
         SSA 1989 s.7.

GENERAL NOTE

1.138   Note that the increase in pension does not depend upon the claimant having decided to defer his claim. As subs.(2)(a)(i) makes clear, it applies equally to a person making a late claim for pension where the delay is the result of ignorance of entitlement, or otherwise. In *CP/14276/1996* the claimant had been resident in China and made her claim five years after she reached pensionable age. Although her claim could be backdated only one year (see SSAA 1992, s.1), it was paid at an enhanced rate to reflect the effective period of delay—four years.

In *KH v SSWP* [2014] UKUT 138 (AAC) Judge Wikeley held that the calculation of the increase in pension entitlement occurred only once when a decision on the claim to a pension was made; thereafter payment of the pension was made, with that increase, and adjusted by the annual up-rating procedure. The claimant had argued that because of the words used in a departmental booklet, that he was entitled to have his pension calculated afresh each year and then have the percentage increase that had been earned by deferment applied to that new annual total. The judge found that whatever the booklet might have suggested (and he did not find that it was necessarily misleading) that the meaning of the provisions in Sch.5 to this act that govern the calculation could admit of only one meaning—the claim was determined at the outset and the percentage increase then applied to the pension; the percentage increase so earned then remained as a part of his pension for life. The provisions for calculating the amount of the increase are found in Sch.5 to this Act and any increases provided for in the annual up-rating of Benefits Order. Note that from April 2005, benefit that is deferred for a year or more may be taken in the form of a lump sum.

This section may be affected, in appropriate cases, by the operation of the Gender Recognition Act 2004.

[¹ Shared additional pension

1.139   **55A.** [⁴ (1) A person is entitled to a shared additional pension under this section

if—
    (a) the person attained pensionable age before 6 April 2016, and
    (b) the person is entitled to an old state scheme pension credit.]

(2) A person's entitlement to a shared additional pension shall continue throughout his life.

(3) The weekly rate of a shared additional pension [⁴ under this section] shall be the appropriate weekly amount, unless the pensioner's entitlement to the [⁴ old] state scheme pension credit arose before the final relevant year, in which case it shall be that amount multiplied by the relevant revaluation percentage.

(4) The appropriate weekly amount for the purposes of subsection (3) above is the weekly rate, expressed in terms of the valuation day, at which the cash equivalent, on that day, of the pensioner's entitlement, or prospective entitlement, to the shared additional pension [⁴ under this section] is equal to the [⁴ old] state scheme pension credit.

(5) The relevant revaluation percentage for the purposes of that subsection is the percentage specified, in relation to earnings factors for the tax year in which the entitlement to the [⁴ old] state scheme pension credit arose, by the last order under section 148 of the Administration Act to come into force before the end of the final relevant year.

[² (6) The Secretary of State may by regulations make provision about the calculation and verification of cash equivalents for the purposes of this section.

(6A) The power conferred by subsection (6) above includes power to provide—
    (a) for calculation or verification in such manner as may be approved by or on behalf of the Government Actuary, and
    (b) for things done under the regulations to be required to be done in accordance with guidance from time to time prepared by a person prescribed by the regulations.]

(7) In this section—
"final relevant year" means the tax year immediately preceding that in which the pensioner attains pensionable age;
"[⁴ old] state scheme pension credit" means a credit under section 49(1)(b) of the Welfare Reform and Pensions Act 1999 (credit for the purposes of this Part of this Act);
"valuation day" means the day on which the pensioner becomes entitled to the state scheme pension credit.]

AMENDMENTS

1. Welfare Reform and Pensions Act 1999 Sch.6 para.3 (April 9, 2001).
2. Child Support, Pensions and Social Security Act 2000 s.41 (September 29, 2000).
3. Pensions Act 2007 Sch.1 para.7 (September 26, 2007).
4. Pensions Act 2014 Sch.11 para.5 (April 6, 2016).

GENERAL NOTE

Note the special provisions made for persons claiming a shared additional   **1.140** pension between April 6, 2005 and April 5, 2006 in reg.10 of the Shared Additional Pensions (Miscellaneous Amendments) Regulations 2005 (S1 2005/ 1551).

The sums which are shared additional pensions under this section were increased, with effect from April 8, 2019, by 2.4 per cent: see art.4(5) of the Social Security Benefits Up-rating Order 2019 (SI 2019/480).

[¹ Shared additional pension because of a new state scheme pension credit

1.141   **55AA** .–(1) A person is entitled to a shared additional pension under this section if—

(a) the person reached pensionable age before 6 April 2016, and

(b) the person is entitled to a new state scheme pension credit.

(2) A person's entitlement to a shared additional pension under this section continues throughout his or her life.

(3) The weekly rate of a shared additional pension under this section is equal to the amount of the new state scheme pension credit.

(4) In this section "new state scheme pension credit" means a credit under section 49A(2)(b) of the Welfare Reform and Pensions Act 1999.]

AMENDMENTS

1. Pensions Act 2014 Sch.11 para.6 (April 6, 2016).

GENERAL NOTE

1.142   The sums which are shared additional pensions under this section were increased, with effect from April 8, 2019, by 2.4 per cent: see art.4(5) of the Social Security Benefits Up-rating Order 2019 (SI 2019/480).

[¹ Reduction of shared additional pension: pension sharing

1.143   **55B.**—(1) The weekly rate of a shared additional pension shall be reduced as follows in any case where—

(a) the pensioner has become subject to [³ an old] state scheme pension debit, and

(b) the debit is to any extent referable to the pension.

(2) If the pensioner became subject to the debit in or after the final relevant year, the weekly rate of the pension shall be reduced by the appropriate weekly amount.

(3) If the pensioner became subject to the debit before the final relevant year, the weekly rate of the additional pension shall be reduced by the appropriate weekly amount multiplied by the relevant revaluation percentage.

(4) The appropriate weekly amount for the purposes of subsections (2) and (3) above is the weekly rate, expressed in terms of the valuation day, at which the cash equivalent, on that day, of the pension mentioned in subsection (5) below is equal to so much of the debit as is referable to the shared additional pension.

(5) The pension referred to above is a notional pension for the pensioner by virtue of section [³ 55A or 55AA (as the case may be)] which becomes payable on the later of—

(a) his attaining pensionable age, and

(b) the valuation day.

(6) For the purposes of subsection (3) above, the relevant revaluation percentage is the percentage specified, in relation to earnings factors for the tax year in which the pensioner became subject to the debit, by the last order under section 148 of the Administration Act to come into force before the end of the final relevant year.

[² (7) The Secretary of State may by regulations make provision about the calculation and verification of cash equivalents for the purposes of this section.

(7A) The power conferred by subsection (7) above includes power to provide—

(a) for calculation or verification in such manner as may be approved by or on behalf of the Government Actuary, and

(b) for things done under the regulations to be required to be done in accordance with guidance from time to time prepared by a person prescribed by the regulations.]

(8) In this section—

"final relevant year" means the tax year immediately preceding that in which the pensioner attains pensionable age;

"[³ old] state scheme pension debit" means a debit under section 49(1)(a) of the Welfare Reform and Pensions Act 1999 (debit for the purposes of this Part of this Act);

"valuation day" means the day on which the pensioner became subject to the state scheme pension debit.]

AMENDMENTS

1. Welfare Reform and Pensions Act 1999 Sch.6 para.3 (April 9, 2001).
2. Child Support, Pensions and Social Security Act 2000 s.41 (September 29, 2000).
3. Pensions Act 2014 Sch.11 para.7 (April 6, 2016).

[¹ Pension increase or lump sum where entitlement to shared additional pension is deferred

55C.—(1) Where a person's entitlement to a shared additional pension is deferred, Schedule 5A to this Act has effect.　　　　1.144

(2) In that Schedule—

paragraph 1 makes provision enabling an election to be made where the person's entitlement is deferred

paragraphs 2 and 3 make provision about increasing pension where the person's entitlement is deferred

paragraphs 4 and 5 make provision about lump sum payments where the person's entitlement is deferred.

(3) For the purposes of this Act, a person's entitlement to a shared additional pension is deferred—

(a) where he would be entitled to a Category A or Category B retirement pension but for the fact that his entitlement is deferred, if and so long as his entitlement to such a pension is deferred, and

(b) otherwise, if and so long as he does not become entitled to the shared additional pension by reason only of not satisfying the conditions of section 1 of the Administration Act (entitlement to benefit dependent on claim),

and, in relation to a shared additional pension, "period of deferment" shall be construed accordingly.]

AMENDMENTS

1. Pensions Act 2004 s.297 (April 6, 2005).

Child's special allowance—existing beneficiaries

1.145   **56.**—*Omitted.*

1.146   *Sections 57 to 59 repealed.*

1.147   *Sections 60, 60A, 61 and 61A omitted.*

Graduated retirement benefit

1.148   **62.**—(1) So long as sections 36 and 37 of the National Insurance
Act 1965 (graduated retirement benefit) continue in force by virtue of
regulations made under Schedule 3 to the Social Security (Consequential
Provisions) Act 1975 or under Schedule 3 to the Consequential Provisions
Act, regulations may make provision—

  (a) for [¹ amending section 36(2) of the National Insurance Act 1965
      (value of unit of graduated contributions) so that the value is the
      same for women as it is for men and for replacing section 36(4)
      of that Act] (increase of graduated retirement benefit in cases of
      deferred retirement) with provisions corresponding to those of para-
      graphs [⁶ A1 to 3B and 7C] of Schedule 5 to this Act;

[² (aa) for amending section 36(7) of that Act (persons to be treated as
      receiving nominal retirement pension) so that where a person has
      claimed a Category A or Category B retirement pension but—
          (i) because of an election under section 54(1) above, or
          (ii) because he has withdrawn his claim for the pension,
      he is not entitled to such a pension, he is not to be treated for the pur-
      poses of the preceding provisions of that section as receiving such a
      pension at a nominal weekly rate;]

[⁵ (ab) for extending section 37 of that Act (increase of woman's retirement
      pension by reference to her late husband's graduated retirement
      benefit) to civil partners [⁷ and their late civil partners] and for that
      section (except subsection (5)) so to apply as it applies to women
      and their late husbands;]

[⁴ (ac) for extending section 37 of that Act (increase of woman's retirement
      pension by reference to her late husband's graduated retirement
      benefit) to civil partners and their late civil partners who attain
      pensionable age before 6th April 2010 and for that section (except
      subsection (5)) so to apply as it applies to men and their late wives;]

[⁸ (ad) for extending section 37 of that Act (increase of woman's retirement
      pension by reference to her late husband's graduated retirement
      benefit) to—
          (i) men and their late husbands, and
          (ii) women and their late wives,
      and for that section (except subsection (5)) so to apply as it applies to
      women and their late husbands;

  (ae) for extending section 37 of that Act (increase of woman's retirement
      pension by reference to her late husband's graduated retirement
      benefit) to—
          (i) men and their late husbands, and
          (ii) women and their late wives,

who attained pensionable age before 6th April 2010 and for that section (except subsection (5)) so to apply as it applies to men and their late wives;]
  (b) for extending section 37 of that Act (increase of woman's retirement pension by reference to her late husband's graduated retirement benefit) to men and their late wives [³ and for that section (except subsection (5)) so to apply as it applies to women and their late husbands].
[⁶ (c) for amending that section in order to make provisions corresponding to those of paragraphs 3C, 4(1) and (1A) and 7A to 7C of Schedule 5 to this Act enabling a widowed person [⁷ or surviving civil partner] to elect to receive a lump sum, rather than an increase in the weekly rate of retirement pension, in respect of the graduated retirement benefit of his or her deceased spouse [⁷ or civil partner].]
  (2) This section is without prejudice to any power to modify the said sections 36 and 37 conferred by Schedule 3 to the Consequential Provisions Act.
  [⁸ (3) In relevant gender change cases, women and their late wives are to be treated for the purposes of sections 36 and 37 of the National Insurance Act 1965 in the same way as women and their late husbands.
  (4) For that purpose "relevant gender change case", in relation to a woman ("the pensioner") and her late wife, means a case where—
  (a) the late wife was, at the time of her death, a woman by virtue of a full gender recognition certificate having been issued under the Gender Recognition Act 2004, and
  (b) the marriage of the pensioner and her late wife subsisted before the time when the certificate was issued.]

AMENDMENTS

  1. Pensions Act 1995 Sch.4 para.7(a). (July 19, 1995).
  2. Pensions Act 1995 s.131(1) (July 19, 1995).
  3. Pensions Act 1995 Sch.4 para.7(b) (July 19, 1995).
  4. Civil Partnership (Miscellaneous and Consequential Provisions) Order 2005 (SI 2005/3029) Sch.1, (October 29, 2005).
  5. Civil Partnership Act 2004 Sch.24 (December 5, 2005).
  6. Pensions Act 2004 Sch.11 (April 4, 2005).
  7. Civil Partnership (Pensions and Benefits Payments) (Consequential, etc. Provisions) Order 2005 (SI 2005/2053) (December 5, 2005).
  8. Marriage (Same Sex Couples) Act 2013 Sch.4 Pt. 5 para.14. See also the Marriage and Civil Partnership (Scotland) Act 2014 and Civil Partnership Act 2004 (Consequential Provisions and Modifications) Order 2014 (SI 2014/3229) Sch.4 para.2 (with effect from December 12, 2014).

DERIVATION

  SSPA 1975 s.24.   1.149

GENERAL NOTE

  R(P) 1/08 Commissioner Williams demonstrated the complexity that arises in relation to claims for GRB and to appeals from those decisions. Unlike other contributory benefits no part of the functions of the Secretary of State for Work and Pensions has been transferred to Her Majesty's Revenue and Customs. Yet HMRC are still responsible for recording and providing any information necessary in relation to a claimant's contribution record. This means that officers of HMRC must do so as agents acting on behalf of the SSWP, and any decision made by them becomes one for which the SSWP is legally responsible. This means, in turn, that all such decisions are appealable to the tribunal system. This decision also contains useful guidance for tribunals on the correct approach to questions that arise from the contribution record.   1.150

PART III

NON-CONTRIBUTORY BENEFITS

Descriptions of non-contributory benefits

1.151   **63.**—Non-contributory benefits under this Part of this Act are of the following descriptions, namely—

(a) attendance allowance;

(b) severe disablement allowance (with age related addition and increase for adult and child dependants);

(c) [¹ carer's allowance] (with increase for adult [² . . .] dependants);

(d) disability living allowance;

(e) guardian's allowance;

(f) retirement pensions of the following categories—

(i) Category C, [³ payable in certain cases to a widow whose husband was over pensionable age on 5 July 1948 or to a woman whose marriage to a husband who was over pensionable age on that date was terminated otherwise than by his death] (with increase for adult [² . . .] dependants), and

(ii) Category D, payable to persons over the age of 80;

(g) age addition payable, in the case of persons over the age of 80, by way of increase of a retirement pension of any category [³ under this Act] or of some other pension or allowance from the Secretary of State.

AMENDMENTS

1. Regulatory Reform (Carer's Allowance) Order 2002 (SI 2002/1457) art.2 (April 1, 2003).

2. Tax Credits Act 2002 Sch.6 (April 6, 2003).

3. Pensions Act 2014 Sch.12 paras.79 and 85 (April 6, 2016)

DERIVATION

1.152   SSA 1975 s.34.

Attendance allowance

Entitlement

1.153   **64.**—(1) A person shall be entitled to an attendance allowance if he [² has attained pensionable age], he is not entitled to [³ an allowance within subsection (1A)] and he satisfies either—

(a) the condition specified in subsection (2) below ("the day attendance condition"), or

(b) the condition specified in subsection (3) below ("the night attendance condition"),

and prescribed conditions as to residence and presence in Great Britain.

[³ (1A) The following allowances are within this subsection—

(a) personal independence payment;

(b) the care component of a disability living allowance.]

(2) A person satisfies the day attendance condition if he is so severely

disabled physically or mentally that, by day, he requires from another person either—

(a) frequent attention throughout the day in connection with his bodily functions, or

(b) continual supervision throughout the day in order to avoid substantial danger to himself or others.

(3) A person satisfies the night attendance condition if he is so severely disabled physically or mentally that, at night,—

(a) he requires from another person prolonged or repeated attention in connection with his bodily functions, or

(b) in order to avoid substantial danger to himself or others he requires another person to be awake for a prolonged period or at frequent intervals for the purpose of watching over him.

[[1] (4) Circumstances may be prescribed in which a person is to be taken to satisfy or not to satisfy such of the conditions mentioned in subsections (2) and (3) above as may be prescribed.]

AMENDMENT

1. Welfare Reform and Pensions Act 1999 s.66 (January 12, 2000).
2. Pensions Act 2007 Sch.1 Pt 8 para.41. This amendment was orginally not to have effect until April 6, 2024, but now has had effect from April 6, 2018—see Pensions Act 2011 s.1.
3. Welfare Law Reform 2012 Sch.9 (April 8, 2013).

DERIVATION

SSA 1975 s.35(1).   1.154

GENERAL NOTE

Note: the amendment to subs.(1) above to "pensionable age" did not have effect   1.155
until April 6, 2018. Until that time the section should be read as if it retained the words "is aged 65 or over".

Attendance Allowance is a weekly benefit paid to those who are disabled so as to need a sufficient level of care and attention from someone else. The benefit is usually paid to the claimant rather than to the carer. It is not necessary that the claimant is actually paying for the care (or, in theory, even that he is receiving the care). What is necessary is that he should *need* the care.

See the discussion of this point in relation to DLA where the wording is the same. In *KK v SSWP* [2012] UKUT 356 (AAC) Judge Jacobs held that there was an error of law where the FTT failed to explain to the claimant that he may be entitled to benefit even though he chose not spend it on acquiring care; he had said that he would not want a carer entering his home and intruding on his privacy. The FTT treated this as withdrawing his claim for the care component. The UT affirms that the question to be decided is whether the claimant *needs* care (though not obtaining care may be some evidence that it is not required) and the FTT has a duty, in its inquisitorial role, to explain that to the claimant.

Attendance Allowance was originally introduced in 1970 and was then payable at just one rate to those who needed attention or supervision both day and night. In 1972, the lower rate was introduced for those who required attention or supervision by day or at night but not both.

Attendance Allowance is payable to those persons who become disabled after they attain pensionable age or who first claim this allowance after that age even though they may have been disabled earlier. The allowance is not payable to anyone who is in receipt of the care component of Disability Living Allowance and who turned 65 before April 2013. Nor is it payable to someone in receipt of Personal Independence

Payment. Attendance Allowance is less generous than the care component of Disability Living Allowance in two respects. First, it has a six-month qualifying period (s.65(1)(b)) as opposed to the three-month period for the care component (s.72(2)(a)) although neither qualifying period applies in the case of a person who is terminally ill. Secondly, there are only two rates of Attendance Allowance, which are the same as the highest and middle rate of the care component. There is no equivalent to the lowest rate of the care component.

The lack of an equivalent lowest rate of benefit in Attendance Allowance was attacked by the claimant in *CS v SSWP* [2009] UKUT 257 (AAC). He was aged 71 and, therefore, excluded from making a claim for DLA. He argued that the absence of benefit at the lowest rate was discrimination on the ground of age contrary to the Human Rights Act. Judge Lane rejected that argument, though she accepted that his right to a social security benefit was within art.1 of Protocol 1 and that the difference in treatment was discrimination on the ground of age. She held that this discrimination was justified because in her view it was rational and proportionate, she said, to distinguish those who were affected by disability at a younger age and whose earning capacity was thus reduced. Retirement pension, she said, was there to make provision, at least in part, for those over retiring age. (cf. *NT v SSWP* [2009] UKUT 37 (AAC); *R(DLA) 1/09*, in relation to the mobility component of DLA).

The limitations that these conditions impose are shown by the decision in *CA/2574/2007*. The claimant was a widow who was agoraphobic, anorexic and depressed, and had lived as a recluse since the death of her husband. She was visited daily by her daughter who supplied all her physical needs and remained each day for a period of several hours to stimulate and encourage her mother. A report by a consultant psychiatrist suggested that the claimant was being kept alive by the services and the visits of her daughter. This much was accepted as true by the Commissioner, but still could not qualify her for AA. The services such as shopping and housekeeping supplied by the daughter could not qualify as they were not sufficiently "personal" (see notes that follow s.72) and, although the Commissioner was prepared to accept that the time spent stimulating her mother might qualify as attention in connection with the bodily functioning of the brain, it was neither "frequent" nor "continual" throughout the day so as to satisfy the conditions of subs.(2). Had the claimant been able to claim DLA (she could not because of her age) she might have succeeded in a claim for the lowest rate of that benefit on the basis that the attention was for a "significant portion of the day".

Note that although Attendance Allowance has no equivalent to the mobility component provided under DLA, or as in PIP, it is possible for a claimant who requires assistance in moving about to include that help in the assessment of their need for attention in connection with their bodily functions—in this case, the bodily function of mobilising whether within doors, or out of doors. Thus, for someone in a wheelchair who requires another person to push them about, that assistance can count towards the frequency and extent of the assistance that they require: see *JB v SSWP* [2015] UKUT 361 (AAC).

Subsection (1)

1.156   For the circumstances in which a person over 65 is entitled to the care component of a disability living allowance, see s.75 and also reg.3 of and Sch.1 to the Disability Living Allowance Regulations. For prescribed conditions as to residence and presence, see reg.2 of the Social Security (Attendance Allowance) Regulations 1991.

Subsections (2) and (3)

1.157   Subs.(3) contains two alternative "day" conditions and subs.(3) contains two alternative "night" conditions. Subject to the waiting period imposed by s.65(1)(b), attendance allowance is paid at the higher rate if both a "day" and a "night" condition are satisfied and at the lower rate if the conditions are satisfied only for the day or the night (s.65(3)).

The attendance conditions in subss.(2) and (3) are the same as those in paras (b) and (c) of s.72(1) and reference should be made to the notes to that subsection.

Note that both conditions may be deemed to be satisfied in the case of a person who is terminally ill and can reasonably be expected to die within six months (s.66).

Note also that reg.5 of the Attendance Allowance Regulations provides that certain people undergoing renal dialysis are deemed to satisfy either the day or the night attention condition so as to qualify them for attendance allowance at the lower rate. There is no reason why they should not satisfy another condition for other reasons and so qualify for the higher rate.

Before March 15, 1988, the night condition was different. Under the earlier version it was possible for supervision to be provided by someone who was "on call", though not necessarily awake, so as to be ready to render assistance as necessary (*Moran v Secretary of State for Social Services* reported as appendix to *R(A) 1/88*). After that date it has been necessary for the carer to be awake and watching over the claimant.

Since May 5, 2005 Attendance Allowance can be claimed by those who have gone to live in another European Union country. This is because the decision of the European Court in Case C-299/05, *Commission v European Parliament and Council* [2007] ECR I-8695 held that this benefit, together with Carer's Allowance and the care component of Disability Living Allowance, were not properly excluded from entitlement and could be claimed as a form of sickness benefits.

And note too the decision in *SSWP v LT* [2012] UKUT 282 (AAC). This is a decision of a three judge panel which holds that the care component of DLA is exportable even when the claimant had ceased all employment or self-employment before she left the UK. It was sufficient that she had been employed and had preserved benefits in the form of an entitlement to a retirement pension when she reached retirement age.

That decision was appealed but has ultimately been confirmed by the answers to questions put to the EUECJ by the Supreme Court: see *SSWP v Tolley* [2017] EUECJ C-430/15). They confirm that the care component is a "sickness benefit" and that the claimant's past contribution record made her an "employed person" and therefore within the protection of the regulation. This case is concerned with the old Regulation 1408/71 but it is likely that the same result would follow under the current Regulation 883/04.

Period and rate of allowance

65.—(1) Subject to the following provisions of this Act, the period for which a person is entitled to an attendance allowance shall be—   1.158

(a) a period throughout which he has satisfied or is likely to satisfy the day or the night attendance condition or both; and

(b) a period preceded immediately, or within such period as may be prescribed, by one of not less than six months throughout which he satisfied, or is likely to satisfy, one or both of those conditions.

(2) For the purposes of subsection (1) above a person who suffers from renal failure and is undergoing such form of treatment as may be prescribed shall, in such circumstances as may be prescribed, be deemed to satisfy or to be likely to satisfy the day or the night attendance condition or both.

(3) The weekly rate of the attendance allowance payable to a person for any period shall be the higher rate specified in Schedule 4, Part III, paragraph 1, if both as regards that period and as regards the period of six months mentioned in subsection (1)(b) above he has satisfied or is likely to satisfy both the day and the night attendance conditions, and shall be the lower rate in any other case.

(4) A person shall not be entitled to an attendance allowance for any period preceding the date on which he makes or is treated as making a claim for it.

(5) Notwithstanding anything in subsection (4) above, provision may be made by regulations for a person to be entitled to an attendance allowance for a period preceding the date on which he makes or is treated as making a claim for it if such an allowance has previously been paid to or in respect of him.

(6) Except in so far as regulations otherwise provide and subject to section 66(1) below—

(a) a claim for an attendance allowance may be made during the period of six months immediately preceding the period for which the person to whom the claim relates is entitled to the allowance; and

(b) an award may be made in pursuance of a claim so made, subject to the condition that, throughout that period of six months, that person satisfies—

(i) both the day and the night attendance conditions, or

(ii) if the award is at the lower rate, one of those conditions.

[¹ (7) A person to whom either Regulation (EC) No 1408/71 or Regulation/(EC) No 883/2004 applies shall not be entitled to an attendance allowance for a period unless during that period the UK is competent for payment of sickness benefits in cash to the person for the purposes of Chapter 1 of Title III of the Regulation in question.]

DERIVATION

1.159   SSA 1975 ss.35(2), (2A), (3), (4) and (4A).

AMENDMENTS

1. Social Security (Disability Living Allowance, Attendance Allowance and Carer's Allowance) (Miscellaneous Amendments) Regulations 2011, reg.5(3). (SI 2011/2426) (October 31, 2011).

GENERAL NOTE

Subsection (1)

1.160   Paragraph (a) has the effect that an award of attendance allowance should be for the period for which the claimant has satisfied or is *likely* to satisfy one or both of the attendance conditions. An award may be for life or for a specified period. There is no minimum period specified but it will seldom be appropriate to make an award for less than six months which is the minimum period for an award of the care component of a disability living allowance (see s.72(2)(b)). In this case, "likely" can be read as "more likely than not" since the subsection is concerned with the continued satisfaction of the conditions of entitlement. If the prognosis is uncertain, the award should be limited in time.

It is not necessary that the conditions are likely to be satisfied in respect of every day. *R(A) 2/74* concerned a claimant who had to undergo renal dialysis for 10 hours on three nights a week, at a time before any specific provision was made for such claimants (see now reg.5 of the Social Security (Attendance Allowance) Regulations 1991). The Commissioner held that it was wrong to take a purely arithmetical approach and that the claimant was not, as a matter of law, excluded from entitlement. Variations in a claimant's condition present greater problems because they are irregular and difficult to predict. "These are matters for the good sense and judgment of the [decision-maker]."

Both attendance conditions are deemed to be satisfied for the remainder of the life of a person suffering from a progressive disease and likely to die within six months (s.66(1)(a)(i)).

Paragraph (b) provides for the six-month qualifying period. A person is not entitled to attendance allowance until he or she has satisfied an attendance condition for six months. The combined effect of this subsection and subs.(3) is that, if a person has been receiving the lower rate because he or she satisfies only, say, the day attendance condition and then his or her condition deteriorates so that he or she also satisfies the night condition, he or she does not become entitled to the higher rate until six months have elapsed. This six-month qualifying period is waived in the case of a person who is suffering from a progressive disease and likely to die within six months (s.66(1)(a)(ii)). Other claimants may make their claims during the qualifying period so that a decision can be made straightaway and payment can start as soon as the qualifying period has been completed (subs.(4)(a)).

Usually the six-month qualifying period immediately precedes the period of entitlement but it may fall within such other period as may be prescribed. Reg.3 of the Social Security (Attendance Allowance) Regulations 1991 prescribes the period of two years.

Subsection (2)

This enables regulations to be made so that a person who undergoes renal dialysis **1.161** is deemed to satisfy either or both of the day and the night attendance conditions. Reg.5 of the Social Security (Attendance Allowance) Regulations 1991 allows a person having such treatment at least twice a week to be deemed, in some circumstances, to satisfy one, but not both, of the attendance conditions. Any question whether a person suffers renal failure is determined by an appeal tribunal which includes a medically qualified member and one with a disability qualification on appeal from the Secretary of State.

Subsections (4) and (5)

Awards of attendance allowance cannot usually be made in respect of a period **1.162** before the date of claim. For details affecting the date a claim is treated as made see reg.6 of Claims and Payments Regulations in Vol.I of this work.

Regulation 4 of the Social Security (Attendance Allowance) Regulations 1991, treated as made under subs.(5), allowed an award to be made from the end of a previous period of entitlement if the renewal claim was made within six months but that regulation was revoked from September 1, 1997.

Subsection (6)

A claim may be made in advance during the six-month waiting period. The **1.163** award is, of course, conditional on the claimant continuing to satisfy the attendance conditions. In *CA/1474/97*, the Commissioner held that a tribunal who found that the attendance conditions had been satisfied for a period of less than six months could make a prospective award. However, they were not bound to do so and could decline to reach any firm conclusion as to whether the attendance conditions had been satisfied for that period although, if they took that course, they were obliged to tell the claimant that he or she could make another claim so as to have the question determined. Since the coming into force of para.3(2) of Sch.6 to the Social Security Act 1998 on May 21, 1998, it is possible to make a prospective award only if the attendance conditions were satisfied at the date of the decision-maker's decision so that the decision-maker could have made a prospective award.

Subsection (7)

Subsection (7) was held to be valid in *IG v SSWP* [2016] UKUT 176 (AAC); **1.164** [2016] AACR 41. Judge Jacobs held that attendance allowance was a sickness benefit and that the UK was entitled under Regulation (EC) 883/2004 to make this regulation which had the effect of denying benefit where a foreign state was the competent state in respect of sickness benefits.

Attendance allowance for the terminally ill

66.—(1) If a terminally ill person makes a claim expressly on the ground **1.165** that he is such a person then—
    (a) he shall be taken—

      (i) to satisfy, or to be likely to satisfy, both the day attendance condition and the night attendance condition [¹ for so much of the period for which he is terminally ill as does not fall before the date of claim.] and

      (ii) to have satisfied those conditions for the period of six months immediately preceding [¹ the date of the claim or, if later, the first date on which he is terminally ill.] (so however that no allowance shall be payable by virtue of this sub-paragraph for any period preceding that date); and

    (b) the period for which he is entitled to attendance allowance shall be [¹ so much of the period for which he is terminally ill as does not fall before the date of the claim].

(2) For the purposes of subsection (1) above—

    (a) a person is "terminally ill" at any time if at that time he suffers from a progressive disease and his death in consequence of that disease can reasonably be expected within six months; and

    (b) where a person purports to make a claim for an attendance allowance by virtue of that subsection on behalf of another, that other shall be regarded as making the claim, notwithstanding that it is made without his knowledge or authority.

AMENDMENT

1. Welfare Reform and Pensions Act 1999 s.66 (January 12, 2000).

DERIVATION

1.166   SSA 1975 ss.35(2B), (2C).

GENERAL NOTE

1.167   Terminally ill patients are deemed to satisfy both attendance conditions and therefore qualify for benefit at the higher rate. Furthermore, in order to meet the criticism that such patients sometimes died before they could complete the normal six-month qualifying period, the benefit is paid under this section from the date of claim. (The claimant is deemed to satisfy the conditions for the remainder of his life and to have done so in the six months preceding his claim.) Nor is it necessary for the claimant to show that he requires attention, etc.; this is assumed to be the case for those who are terminally ill.

    Subs.(2)(a) provides the definition of when a person is "terminally ill". A person is terminally ill when he suffers from a progressive disease and his death from the cause can "reasonably be expected within six months".

    This phrase, though potentially of uncertain meaning, does not seem to have given rise to difficulty. It is fairly clear that someone whose death is more likely than not is "reasonably expected" to die. Equally, where the doctor says that his patient is likely to survive beyond six months it would seem true to say his death is not "expected" within that period. But what of those cases where the outcome is simply very uncertain? Could death be "reasonably expected" when it is "quite possible", though not yet "probable"? Note that some of this difficulty will be obviated by the need to show that death is expected from a "progressive disease". This will include conditions such as cancer but in most cases will not cover other common causes of death such as heart attacks.

    It is important to note that the question to be considered by the decision-maker, and a tribunal on appeal, is prospective in the sense that what must be determined is whether death is reasonably to be expected within six months of the date of claim. Medical evidence in the form of the doctor's opinion must relate to that question regardless of what may have transpired since the claim was made. In *R(A)*

1/94 a claim had been made for a baby born with brain damage. The award was made from a date six months after the baby's birth. The baby's mother applied for review of the award to run from the date of birth and a consultant was asked to answer the question as above. However, by the time he came to answer the baby had already survived for more than a year and he felt unable to answer, given what was now known. The AO decided that death was not to be expected, etc. The Commissioner allowed an appeal, holding that the survival of the baby was irrelevant to the question that had to be answered, *viz.* what was reasonably to be expected at the date the review was requested, and he allowed the appeal. This did not avail the mother, however, as this claim was made under the old legislation for attendance allowance. Those provisions required a claimant to have been present in Great Britain for six months. In the case of a baby the Commissioner held that this meant an award could not begin until six months after its birth. In the case of disability living allowance, for which a claim of this sort would now be made, this requirement is expressly removed (reg.2(4) of the Disability Living Allowance Regulations) and benefit would be paid from birth, or from the time the baby left an NHS hospital.

In any event, death must be expected as a result of a progressive disease, rather than some other cause. This may be a significant qualification for a few very elderly people. A question whether a person is terminally ill is decided by the Secretary of State with appeal to an appeal tribunal which includes a medically qualified member and one with a disability qualification. Although a claim must be made expressly on the ground that the claimant is terminally ill, the Secretary of State may accept any notification that a person is terminally ill as being sufficient to amount to a claim (reg.4 of the Social Security (Claims and Payments) Regulations 1987). Presumably, in the case of a claimant with an existing award of attendance allowance at the lower rate, an application for a review on this ground counts as a claim for the purposes of s.66. In any case this decision will now be made by the Secretary of State. Subs.(2)(b) allows someone else to make a claim on this basis on behalf of the claimant, which enables a claim to be made in a case where the claimant's prognosis is being kept from him or her.

Exclusions by regulation

67.—(1) Regulations may provide that, in such circumstances, and for such purposes as may be prescribed, a person who is, or is treated under the regulations as, undergoing treatment for renal failure in a hospital or other similar institution otherwise than as an in-patient shall be deemed not to satisfy or to be unlikely to satisfy the day attendance condition or the night attendance condition or both of them.

[³ (2) Regulations may provide that an attendance allowance shall not be payable in respect of a person for a period when he is a resident of a care home in circumstances in which any of the costs of any qualifying services provided for him are borne out of public or local funds under a specified enactment.

(3) The reference in subsection (2) to a care home is to an establishment that provides accommodation together with nursing or personal care.

(4) The following are qualifying services for the purposes of subsection (2)—
  (a) accommodation,
  (b) board, and
  (c) personal care.

(5) The reference in subsection (2) to a specified enactment is to an enactment which is, or is of a description, specified for the purposes of that subsection by regulations.

1.168

(6) The power to specify an enactment for the purposes of subsection (2) includes power to specify it only in relation to its application for a particular purpose.

(7) In this section, "enactment" includes an enactment comprised in, or in an instrument made under, an Act of the Scottish Parliament.]

AMENDMENTS

1. Mental Health (Care and Treatment) (Scotland) Act 2003 (Consequential Provisions) Order (SI 2005/2078) Sch.1 para.4 (October 5, 2005).
2. National Health Service (Consequential Provisions) Act 2006 Sch.1 para.143 (March 1, 2007).
3. Welfare Reform Act 2007 s.60(1) (October 29, 2007).

DERIVATION

1.169   SSA 1975 ss.35(5A), (6).

GENERAL NOTE

Subsection (1)
1.170   See reg.5(3) and 5(4) of the Social Security (Attendance Allowance) Regulations 1991.

Subsection (2)
1.171   See regs 6–8 of the Social Security (Attendance Allowance) Regulations 1991.

Severe disablement allowance

1.172   [The entry into force on April 6, 2001 of s.65 of the Welfare Reform and Pensions Act means that ss.68 and 69 ceased to have effect on that date. However, certain existing entitlements continue under a transitional provision in art.4 of the Welfare Reform and Pensions Act 1999 (Commencement No. 9, and Transitional and Savings Provisions) Order 2000 (SI 2000/2958) in respect of any entitlement to SDA for a day of incapacity on or after April 6, 2001 forming part of a period of incapacity beginning before April 6, 2001. Art.4 of the Order provides:

"Saving for existing severe disablement allowance beneficiaries

1.173   4.—Notwithstanding the commencement of the provisions referred to in article 2(3)(d), (f) and (g) and (6)(b) ("severe disablement allowance provisions"), the provisions referred to in paragraphs 26 *[SSCBA 1992, s. 90]* and 27 of Schedule 8 and Part IV of Schedule 13 *[SSCBA 1992, ss. 68, 69]* shall continue to have effect, in the period of incapacity for work beginning before 6th April 2001 which would have continued, whether or not by virtue of section 30C or 68(10) or (10A) of the Contributions and Benefits Act or regulations made thereunder, on or after that date but for the commencement of the severe disablement allowance provisions, as if those provisions had not been commenced—

(a) in relation to a person, to whom paragraph (b) does not apply, who

is entitled to severe disablement allowance under section 68 or 69 of the Contributions and Benefits Act on any day of incapacity for work in that period of incapacity for work; or
(b) until the beginning of 6th April 2002, in relation to a person who —

  (i) was under the age of 20 years on 6th April 2001, and
  (ii) is entitled to severe disablement allowance under section 68(1) of the Contributions and Benefits Act on any day of incapacity for work in that period of incapacity for work." (Provisions in italics added by commentator.)

Accordingly, ss.68 and 69 can be found in the 2005 edition of this volume for the purposes of those continued entitlements, which cover those over 20 on April 6, 2001 until SDA entitlement ceases under the preserved SDA rules. Those under 20 on April 6, 2001 who remain entitled to, or are receiving, SDA in that period of incapacity until on or immediately before April 5, 2002, will on April 6, 2002, if still incapable of work, be transferred to long-term incapacity benefit without having to satisfy the contribution conditions, and without that entitlement being subject to reduction for pension payments under s.30DD. So will those aged under 20 on April 6, 2001, then entitled to SDA, whose period of incapacity for work covers the period on or immediately after April 5, 2002. See SSCBA s.30A(1)(b), (2A), and IB Regs, Pt IV, reg.19.

Entitlement and rate

68.—*Section 68 omitted*   1.174
69.—*Section 69 omitted*   1.175

Invalid Care Allowance

70.—(1) A person shall be entitled to [² a carer's allowance] for any day   1.176
on which he is engaged in caring for a severely disabled person if—
(a) he is regularly and substantially engaged in caring for that person;
(b) he is not gainfully employed; and
(c) the severely disabled person is either such relative of his as may be prescribed or a person of any such other description as may be prescribed.

[² (1A) A person who was entitled to an allowance under this section immediately before the death of the severely disabled person referred to in subsection (1) shall continue to be entitled to it, even though he is no longer engaged in caring for a severely disabled person (and the requirements of subsection (1)(a) and (c) are not satisfied), until—
(a) the end of the week in which he ceases to satisfy any other requirement as to entitlement to the allowance; or
(b) the expiry of the period of eight weeks beginning with the Sunday following the death (or beginning with the date of the death if the death occurred on a Sunday), whichever occurs first].

(2) In this section, "severely disabled person" means a person in respect of whom there is payable either an attendance allowance or a disability living allowance by virtue of entitlement to the care component at the highest or middle rate [⁵ or personal independence payment by virtue of entitlement to the daily living component at the standard or enhanced rate] [⁶ or armed forces independence payment under the Armed Forces and Reserve Forces

(Compensation Scheme) Order 2011] or such other payment out of public funds on account of his need for attendance as may be prescribed.

(3) A person shall not be entitled to an allowance under this section if he is under the age of 16 or receiving full-time education.

(4) A person shall not be entitled to an allowance under this section unless he satisfies prescribed conditions as to residence or presence in Great Britain.

[[4] (4A) A person to whom either Regulation (EC) No 1408/71 or Regulation (EC) No 883/2004 applies shall not be entitled to an allowance under this section for a period unless during that period the UK is competent for payment of sickness benefits in cash to the person for the purposes of Chapter 1 of Title III of the Regulation in question.]

(5) [[2] . . .]

(6) [[2] . . .]

(7) No person shall be entitled for the same day to more than one allowance under this section; and where, apart from this subsection, two or more persons [[7] have a relevant entitlement for the same day] in respect of the same severely disabled person, one of them only [[7] shall have that entitlement] and that shall be such one of them—

(a) as they may jointly elect in the prescribed manner, or

(b) as may, in default of such an election, be determined by the Secretary of State in his discretion.

[[7] (7A) For the purposes of subsection (7) a person has a "relevant entitlement" if—

(a) the person is entitled to a carer's allowance, or

(b) the person is entitled under section 12 of the Welfare Reform Act 2012 to the inclusion in an award of universal credit of an amount in respect of the fact that the person has regular and substantial caring responsibilities for a severely disabled person.]

(8) Regulations may prescribe the circumstances in which a person is or is not to be treated for the purposes of this section as engaged, or regularly and substantially engaged, in caring for a severely disabled person, as gainfully employed or as receiving full-time education.

(9) [[3] A carer's allowance] shall be payable at the weekly rate specified in Schedule 4, Part III, paragraph 4.

(10)[[1] . . .]

AMENDMENTS

1. Social Security (Severe Disablement Allowance and Invalid Care Allowance) Amendment Regulations 1994 (SI 1994/2556) reg.2(3) (October 28, 1994).

2. Regulatory Reform (Carer's Allowance) Order 2002 (SI 2002/1457) art.3 (April 1, 2003).

3. Regulatory Reform (Carer's Allowance) Order 2002 (SI 2002/1457) art.2 (October 28, 2002).

4. Social Security (Disability Living Allowance, Attendance Allowance and Carer's Allowance) (Miscellaneous Amendments) Regulations 2011 reg.5(3) (SI 2011/2426) (October 31, 2011).

5. Personal Independence Payment (Supplementary, Provisional and Consequential) Regulations 2013 Sch., para.5 (SI 2013/388) April 8, 2013.

6. Armed Forces and Reserve Forces (Compensation Scheme) (Consequential Provisions: Primary Legislation) Order 2013 art.2 (SI 2013/796) (April 8, 2013).

7. Universal Credit and Miscellaneous Amendment Regulations 2015 (SI 2015/1754) reg.11, (November 5, 2015).

Derivation

SSA 1975 s.37.   **1.177**

General Note

Until April 2003 Carer's Allowance (CA) was known as Invalid Care Allowance
(ICA). The side-note to s.70 remains unchanged, but for all other purposes ICA
has become CA and will be so referred to in this note. Note too, that the regulations
that were made for ICA have also never been renamed and therefore references to
the regulations that cover CA remain as references to the Invalid Care Allowance
Regulations.

    Carer's Allowance is a weekly benefit payable to those who spend at least 35   **1.178**
hours per week caring for another person who is in receipt of a relevant benefit.
Those benefits that qualify for this purpose are: attendance allowance, the care
component of disability allowance at the middle or the higher rate, constant attendance allowance under the industrial injuries or the war disablement schemes, armed
forces independence payment under the Armed Forces and Reserve Forces scheme
and either rate of the daily living allowance of personal independence payment.

    Where the person who is being cared for dies so that the claimant is no longer
caring, subs.(1A) now provides that the carer's entitlement will continue for a
period of 8 weeks following the death, but only so long as the claimant satisfies the
remaining conditions of entitlement. When first enacted, s.37 of the Social Security
Act 1975 excluded married or cohabiting women from entitlement. In Case 150/85
Drake v Chief Adjudication Officer [1987] Q.B. 166 that exclusion was held to be
contrary to Council Directive 79/7 so the offending words were removed from subs.
(3) retrospectively by the Social Security Act 1986.

    Note that there is nothing in the rules defining entitlement to CA, or in those
defining entitlement to the benefit of the person who is cared for, that prevents a
claimant receiving both CA and also one of those benefits in respect of their own
disablement. It is simply a question of the claimant's ability to perform the tasks of
caring while being disabled themselves and that will turn upon the facts of each case
(see *MC v SSWP* UKUT [2012] 337 (AAC)).

Subsection (1)(a)
    Neither this section nor the Regulations define what is meant by "caring".   **1.179**
Given the degree of disablement that has to be shown in the patient, it is likely
that the statutory authorities have accepted any period in which the claimant is
present for the purpose of company and supervision, as well as actual assistance,
as qualifying.

    Two unreported Commissioners' decisions throw some light on the meaning
of caring. In the first, a starred decision, *CG/012/91*, the claimant received CA
in respect of her brother who was tetraplegic. Notwithstanding his condition he
went abroad on holiday with friends for four months. The claimant remained
in the UK and continued to draw CA. When the absence became known to the
DSS they sought to recover the CA paid beyond the usual four-week period of
absence (see ICA Regulations). The claimant resisted recovery using two arguments: first, that in respect of the whole period she continued to care for her
brother because she had to be ready on "stand-by" to fly immediately to his aid.
His condition was such that he could very quickly suffer major problems in the
hands of inexperienced nurses or assistants. Secondly, that in respect of at least
the final month of absence she was engaged for long hours each week (in excess
of 35) in trying to arrange sufficient nursing care for her brother upon his return.
The Commissioner rejected both arguments. He points to the connection
between CA of the claimant and AA (or DLA) of the patient. This connection,
he says, supports the view that caring presupposes the more or less continuous
presence of the person cared for. Some degree of absence might be acceptable,
for example shopping for the patient, or the patient's absence for treatment, and

dealing with the affairs of the patient might be seen as caring. But the claimant could not be caring, he said, when the patient was not "from day to day available to be cared for". Even the month spent in making arrangements therefore, did not count as caring.

This contrasts, though is not necessarily inconsistent with the other decision, *CG/006/1990*. This case arose through the question of whether the claimant could satisfy the 35 hours per week which is defined by regulation as "regularly and substantially caring". The claimant's son was normally resident in a special school for severely disabled patients. He returned to the claimant's home every other weekend, Friday evening to Monday morning—approximately 60 hours. The claimant said she spent at least five hours of the Friday preparing for his visit in shopping, cooking and other matters that related solely to his visit. She also spent at least another five hours cleaning up and washing on the Monday after his visit. When aggregated this gave at least 35 hours of caring in each week. The Commissioner accepted that all of this time qualifies as time spent in caring.

The difference between the cases is one of degree. A month spent in preparation and making arrangements cannot be seen as caring "on a day to day basis" as required in the starred decision, while preparation (and cleaning up) on the day of presence can.

The meaning of "regularly and substantially engaged" in caring is provided for in reg.4 of the ICA Regulations.

Subsection (1)(b)

1.180   What amounts to gainful employment is defined in reg.8 of the ICA Regulations. This fixes a limit on earnings, but higher sums may be earned in weeks while the claimant is on holiday.

Several unreported Commissioners' decisions have highlighted the problem of claimants who have been paid a "salary" usually from a firm owned by their husband or in which they are partners, with little or nothing having been required from them by way of work. In such circumstances they have claimed CA not realising that the sum received may disqualify them on the grounds that they are "gainfully employed" and claims to recover substantial overpayments have resulted.

In such a case it is important to ascertain that the claimant is in fact employed by that employer, or working as a self-employed person. As decision *CG/068/1993* makes clear it is not enough that the claimant's name appears on the company's books as receiving a salary, if, as was claimed in this case, she does not realise that she is being paid as an employee. The claimant, whose husband was a solicitor, was, at first, paid a personal cheque each month for housekeeping. Later, when he became a partner in the firm, she was paid by a cheque drawn on the firm's account and appeared in the books as an employee, but she claimed to know nothing of her new status. The Commissioner held that she could not become an employee without her knowledge and consent, and directed that the appeal be re-heard to make further findings of fact. Earlier cases such as *R(P) 4/67* have referred to the undesirability of allowing claimants to "blow hot and cold" in their dealings with different departments of state (namely the HM Revenue and Customs). But that does not answer the question as to which of the inconsistent statements is inaccurate. In any case, the claimant here could not be treated as adopting the role of employee unless she herself had assented to it in a tax return, rather than a return made by her husband or his firm.

1.181   The difficulties presented by the definition of "gainful employment" (reg.8) are highlighted by a further unreported Commissioner's decision. In *CG/058/92*, the claimant who looked after her disabled daughter had, with her husband, purchased a seaside hotel. Annual accounts submitted to the Inland Revenue disclosed the business to be run as a partnership and in four out of the five relevant years, the claimant's share of profits had clearly exceeded the limit prescribed by reg.8. The tribunal which had heard her appeal accepted that the claimant did not work to any appreciable extent in the business and that she did not draw any share of the profits at all. Nevertheless because of the width of the definition in reg.8 the claimant was disqualified from receiving CA and an overpayment was recoverable from her.

Regulation 8 refers to "earnings" which in turn is defined in s.3. The essence of earnings is that it is reward from employment or self-employment but not income from investment (see General Note to s.3). In this case, the Commissioner holds that the tribunal was correct to find that the claimant was a partner in the hotel business, that she was entitled to a half share of the profits, and that she was, therefore, not entitled to CA. But what of the true "sleeping partner". Someone whose only interest is to put capital into a business and to draw on income in the form of a share of profit, if there is any, should be regarded as receiving an investment income. It would be unfortunate if entitlement to CA, (and liability to repay an overpayment) were to turn upon the precise legal forms used by an investor as to whether he is partner or a creditor or a shareholder.

It should also be noted that Statutory Sick Pay or Statutory Maternity Pay qualify as "earnings" (see Contributions and Benefits Act, s.4) and therefore, under reg. 8 of the ICA Regulations, mean that a person is in gainful employment for the purposes of the section.

Subsection (1)(c)

This creates no limit on the persons who may claim because reg.6 of the ICA Regulations prescribes for this purpose, all persons who are in fact caring for a severely disabled person. **1.182**

Subsection (1A)

A person entitled to a CA will continue to receive the benefit for a period of eight weeks if they cease caring because their patient has died. If they cease to care because they are no longer providing care for 35 hours per week then (unless that is because the patient has entered hospital) the entitlement will end forthwith. **1.183**

Subsection (2)

The person cared for is classed as "severely disabled" under this subsection if they are in receipt of one of the qualifying benefits. These are: **1.184**
(i) Attendance allowance;
(ii) Disability Living allowance at either the middle or the highest rate;
(iii) Personal Independence Payment of the care component at either the standard or the enhanced rate;
(iv) Armed Forces Independence Payment; or
(v) Constant attendance allowance under either the industrial injuries or war pensions disablement schemes (see reg.3 of the CA regulations).
In the past problems have arisen in relation to overpayments that occurred when people in receipt over DLA had their entitlement reduced to the lowest level. For discussion of these cases see an earlier edition of this work.

Subsection (3)

A claimant must be at least 16 years of age and not in full-time education. For the meaning of full-time education in this context, see reg.5 of the ICA Regulations and the notes to that regulation. The former restriction on married women, and women cohabiting with a man as his wife, no longer applies (following the decision on the European Court of Justice in Case 150/85 *Drake v Chief Adjudication Officer* [1987] Q.B. 166). **1.185**

Subsection (4)

Benefit is payable only if the claimant is present and ordinarily resident in Great Britain but regulations provide for some absences (reg.9 of the ICA Regulations). **1.186**

Since May 5, 2005 it has been possible for a claimant who has moved to another European Union country to continue claiming Carer's Allowance. This is because the decision of the European Court in Case C-299/05, *Commission v European Parliament and Council* [2007] E.C.R. I-8695 held that this benefit, together with Attendance Allowance and the care component of Disability Living Allowance, were not properly excludable from payment and could be claimed as a form of sickness benefits.

For questions that involve persons either coming from or going to another country that is a part of the European Union reference should be made to the relevant sections of Vol.III of this Work.

Subsection (4A)

1.187   The effect of this provision has been considered by Judge Jacobs in a series of cases, two of which apply to CA (*JG v SSWP (CA)* [2019] UKUT 83 (AAC) and at *GK v SSWP (CA)* [2019] UKUT 87 (AAC)). The claimant in both cases had become habitually resident in France and while there commenced caring for another who was in receipt of a qualifying benefit (AA) that they had exported when they had moved to France. Judge Jacobs holds that although CA and the qualifying benefit are closely related, they are separate benefits and that entitlement must depend upon determining which is the competent state in respect of the claim to CA. In both cases he holds that must be France. For a more detailed account of these issues, please refers to Vol III of this work.

Paragraph (7) of subs.(4A) was held to be valid in *IG v SSWP* [2016] UKUT 176 (AAC); [2016] AACR 41. Judge Jacobs held that attendance allowance was a sickness benefit and that the UK was entitled under Regulation (EC) 883/2004 to make this regulation which had the effect of denying benefit where a foreign state was the competent state in respect of a sickness benefit. Carer's allowance is also a classed as a sickness benefit.

Subsections (5) and (6)

1.188   These subsections were repealed with effect from October 28, 2002 so that a claim may now be made by a person over 65. The effect of this change will be strictly limited because CA is covered by the Overlapping Benefits Regulations so that it will overlap with Retirement Pensions. It seems likely that most claimants will be entitled to one or other category of RP and if that is paid at a higher rate than CA then only the higher benefit will be paid.

Under the previous regulations a person could not claim over the age of 65, but if they were already in receipt of benefit when they reached that age their entitlement continued for life even if they ceased to care for their patient—e.g. if their patient died. This will no longer be the case. A claimant whose patient dies loses entitlement after six weeks. See subs.(1A) above. There is, however, a saving for claimants who were over 65 on October 28, 2002 under art.4 of Regulatory Reform (Carer's Allowance) Order 2002 (2002/1457).

Prior to October 1994, CA was not payable to a claimant over pensionable age. This meant a cut-off age for women of 60 years and for men of 65 years. That discrimination was held to be unlawful under the Equal Treatment Directive (79/7) in *Secretary of State v Thomas* [1993] Q.B. 747 and *R(G) 2/94*. The UK law should have been amended to provide equality from 1984, when the Equal Treatment Directive should have been implemented. The United Kingdom law was so amended, but not until October 1994. In the meantime many women had been refused benefit, or discouraged from making a claim for benefit, because of the continued insistence on differential ages. Art.4(1) of Directive 79/7 (which imposes the requirement of equal treatment) has been held to be sufficiently clear and precise for those rights to be directly enforceable within the Member States by those persons entitled to rely upon them. A Commissioner's decision, *CG/5425/95*, has helped to clarify a number of points that may arise in such claims.

The claimant had cared for her invalid mother for a number of years but attendance allowance and hence entitlement to CA became payable in respect of her mother only from a time about six months after the claimant's 60th birthday. She became aware that she may have had a valid claim under European law only in 1989 (when she did make a claim), by which time she was already over 65 years. At about that time, too, her mother died, but under subs.(6) the claimant would have remained entitled to CA for the rest of her life.

Clearly, under UK law the claimant became entitled by virtue of reg.10A of the ICA Regulations, but only from October 1994. Could she use her rights under European law to claim from some other earlier point in time?

In the case of this particular claimant, the Commissioner decided that she could not. But that was because she did not form a part of the "working population" to whom the rights under art.4 are confined. The claimant had last worked in 1949 when she left work to commence a family. She had never re-entered the workforce or sought paid employment and she could not therefore claim under European law. However, the Commissioner did go on to consider what the position would have been had she been so qualified. The Department argued that because she did not claim until after she was 65, she could not now be entitled (as neither would a man) even under European law. The Commissioner held that her failure to claim before reaching 65 years of age was because the legislation, the department's publications and its officers all then said that she could not do so. To accept its argument would be to perpetuate their own failure to implement the Directive. In his view the claimant would have been entitled to benefit from when it was claimed (1989) and back-dated for 12 months from that date (*i.e.* 1988). Further back-dating would be prevented by the SS(A) Act s.1. Such limitation is not a breach of Directive 79/7: *Johnson v CAO (No.2) (R(S) 1/95)*. Before leaving the case the Commissioner made one further observation. Since the claimant had plainly been deprived of benefit since at least 1988 by the United Kingdom Government's failure to implement equal treatment, he suggested that the minister might consider an *ex gratia* payment of an equivalent amount rather than put the claimant and her legal advisers to the trouble and expense of pursuing a claim under the principle of *Francovich v Republic of Italy* [1991] E.C.R. 5357—though whether the *Francovich* claim should start at 1988 rather than 1984 is another matter.

A different approach on the question of late claims made by women past retirement age has been taken in decision *CSG/6/95*. The Commissioner there rejects the robust approach adopted, *obiter*, in *CG/5425/95*, but reaches a similar conclusion, at least on the facts of the new case, by another route. The claimant had given up work in 1979 in order to care for her husband. She reached the retirement age for women (60) in December 1982, but under Directive 79/7 (which came into force in December 1984) would have remained entitled to claim until December 1987. In the meantime (September 1985) the UK law had been changed to require a claim to be made for entitlement to benefit to begin. The claimant eventually made her claim in November 1993 well past her 65th birthday. The Commissioner rejected the argument that had found favour in *CG/5425/95*, namely that the requirement to claim before that age could be ignored because of the continued non-compliance of UK domestic law. Instead, he held that the claimant had, in 1984, become "entitled" to benefit in accordance with *I.O. v McCaffrey* [1985] 1 All E.R. 5 and that entitlement had not been removed by the introduction of the need for a claim to be made in 1985. It followed that the claimant could satisfy the conditions for entitlement in accordance with reg.10 of the CA Regulation prior to her 65th birthday and was accordingly entitled to payment of that benefit from the time that she did claim (1993) though back-dating was limited to one year.

Subsection (7)

This makes it clear that a claimant can receive only one payment of CA no matter how many patients he may be caring for, and that each patient can provide the basis

1.189

for payment to only one carer at a time. Furthermore, reg.4 of the ICA Regulations has been amended to ensure that a claimant must qualify for the benefit by looking after a single patient for the requisite number of hours each week and cannot aggregate the hours spent looking after two or more patients. It should be noted as well that CA overlaps with several other benefits. (See reg.4 of the Overlapping Benefits Regulations.)

In *R(S)2/89* a widow who gave up work to care for her invalid daughter was refused CA (then ICA) because she was already in receipt of a widow's pension. She argued that this was discriminatory, contrary to Art.4 of European Community Directive 79/7, in that a man would not be refused CA. The Commissioner rejected that argument on the ground that the difference in treatment did not arise from discrimination in relation to that benefit, but because a man could not qualify for widow's pension at all; the regulations were therefore not discriminatory in terms of the European Community Directive.

Disability living allowance

Disability living allowance

1.190   **71.**—(1) Disability living allowance shall consist of a care component and a mobility component.

(2) A person's entitlement to a disability living allowance may be an entitlement to either component or to both of them.

(3) A person may be awarded either component for a fixed period or [¹ for an indefinite period], but if his award of a disability living allowance consists of both components, he may not be awarded the components for different fixed periods.

(4) The weekly rate of a person's disability living allowance for a week for which he has only been awarded one component is the appropriate weekly rate for that component as determined in accordance with this Act or regulations under it.

(5) The weekly rate of a person's disability living allowance for a week for which he has been awarded both components is the aggregate of the appropriate weekly rates for the two components as so determined.

(6) A person shall not be entitled to a disability living allowance unless he satisfies prescribed conditions as to residence and presence in Great Britain.

AMENDMENT

1. Welfare Reform and Pensions Act 1999 s.67(1) (January 12, 2000).

DERIVATION

1.191   SSA 1975 s.37ZA.

GENERAL NOTE

1.192   In general terms Disability Living Allowance (DLA) is a non-contributory benefit paid to those people who are so disabled as to need assistance in leading a normal life, or so disabled as to be unable to walk properly. From April 8, 2013 DLA is replaced by Personal Independence Payments (PIP) in accordance with Pt 4 of the Welfare Reform Act 2012. PIP will apply to claimants of working age and has been introduced for new claims throughout the country. Existing DLA claimants who were born after April 8, 1948 will be transferred to PIP. DLA will remain for claimants who are under the age of 16 until their sixteenth birthday and for those who were in receipt of DLA when they reached retirement age. Where a claimant has an existing award of DLA when they reach retirement age that award can continue, but where a new claim is made by a person over 65 the claim can only be for Attendance Allowance, apart from certain exceptions—see Sch.1 to the DLA Regulations). Until the retirement age for women advanced to 65 it was possible for a woman who was over the current retirement age, but not yet 65, to make a new claim for DLA. DLA was introduced in 1992 and replaced two separate benefits—attendance allowance, and mobility allowance. Attendance Allowance remains for those first claiming for their disability when they are over pension age (see ss.64–67).

DLA consists of two components. The care component (s.72) is similar to attendance allowance but includes a third lower rate of payment for those requiring a lesser degree of care. The mobility component (s.73) is paid at two rates. For both components there is a qualifying period of three months, rather than the six months for attendance allowance, and the disability must be one which is likely to continue for at least six months.

Subsections (2)–(5)

Although a person may be awarded either just one component or both, the com-   **1.193**
ponents are not entirely separate benefits. In *R(DLA) 2/97*, it was held:

> "Where a claim under appeal relates only to one component and there is no award of the other component and no evidence of substance relating to that other component, a tribunal may safely accept, record and proceed upon a restriction of the appeal to the component claimed."

Although DLA consists of two components it is paid as only a single allowance. It is not uncommon, however, for decisions on the two components to be taken separately. It should be noted that where the separate components are each awarded for a fixed period, that must be for the same period. In other words, the issue of "limping" awards can arise only where one component has been awarded for an indefinite period and the other for a fixed period.

There is now (under the Social Security Act 1998) no special protection for awards for life. (For discussion of the problems that did arise under the older system of review & revision of awards in the SSAA 1992, see earlier editions of this work.) In *CDLA/1000/2001*, the Commissioner held that an appeal under s.12 of the SSA 1998 raised anything that was covered by the substance of the information provided by the appellant and was not confined to the specific point against which he had appealed. This means that where the claimant appeals against an award of benefit at, say, the lower or middle rate on the ground that it is too low, it is open to a tribunal to find, on the contrary, that it is too high, and reduce the award accordingly. But where a tribunal is minded to do this it may do so only deliberately and consciously and, furthermore, it can do so only after giving a clear warning to the claimant that such may be the outcome of the appeal so that the claimant has a chance then to abandon the appeal. See *CDLA/2084/2007*.

Where the claimant is appealing against a refusal or a reduction of benefit on a renewal award the tribunal should be provided with a copy of the paperwork in respect of the previous claim—see r.24 of the Tribunal Procedure (First-tier Tribunal) (Social Entitlement Chamber) Rules 2008. Where that has not been done the FTT should consider whether to adjourn and call for the documentation to be provided. They will not be compelled always to do so, but should be cautious about proceeding without doing so: see *AH v SSWP* [2017] UKUT 55 (AAC).

If a person is awarded both components, there is one award of DLA at a rate calculated by aggregating the appropriate rates of the components and the award, if for a fixed period, must be for one common period and not different periods for the different components. It follows that, if one component has been awarded and the claimant appeals against refusal of the other, the tribunal must be informed of the period of the award (*CDLA/52/94*).

1.194   In determining whether a claimant qualifies for these benefits, a tribunal, must reach its conclusion in accordance with the restrictions imposed upon it by s.20(3) of the SSA 1998. This section prevents the tribunal from making a physical examination of the claimant and it precludes a physical test for the purposes of the mobility component of DLA. It does not, however, prevent the tribunal from reaching a conclusion based upon their observation of the claimant's physical abilities, or based upon his response to questions that test what he is capable of doing and, except in relation to mobility, it does not prevent the tribunal asking the claimant to carry out a simple physical task e.g. to pick an object up from the floor. The claimant may refuse, but in that case the tribunal may draw an inference from his refusal provided that in doing so they make due allowance for any reason he may give for that refusal. (See *R(DLA)5/03* and commentary to s.20 in *Vol.III: Administration, Adjudication and the European Dimension.*

In case *CDLA/433/99* the Commissioner holds that a tribunal which has, contrary to s.55(2)(a) of AA 1992, conducted an examination of the claimant does not make an error of law that requires the decision to be set aside unless the evidence obtained by that examination has influenced the tribunal's decision. In this case he held that it did not. The claimant had appealed against the disallowance of DLA care component in respect of eczema on her hands. The note of evidence recorded that the medical member had "examined" her hands, but the decisions, and the reasons for decision, made clear that the tribunal had not regarded the condition as viewed on the day, as being indicative of her condition generally, which was said to vary from time to time. The Commissioner also suggested that a distinction could be drawn between an "examination" and a general observation as, for example, when the claimant might show her hands to the tribunal.

Decision makers and tribunals are frequently faced with a conflict of opinion as to the extent of a claimant's disablement. This is often between information provided by the claimant, and sometimes their own medical adviser, and the EMP who has been appointed by the department to examine the claimant.. Where there is such a conflict in the evidence brought before a FTT there is a duty to consider all of the evidence without giving any particular preference given to the evidence of the EMP for the reason, for example, that it is "independent" or "unbiased"—see *MW v SSWP* [2013] UKUT 158 (AAC).

Subsection (6)

1.195   See reg.2 of the DLA Regulations.

The European Court of Justice has held that the care component of this and other care benefits (Attendance Allowance and Carer's Allowance) are exportable within the European Community. See *Commission of the European Communities v European Parliament and the Council of the European Union* (C-299/05), October 18, 2007. This decision has been applied in *JS v Secretary of State for Work and Pensions* [2012] AACR 7.

In *Secretary of State for Work and Pensions v LT (DLA)* [2012] UKUT 282 (AAC) a three judge panel of the Upper Tribunal has decided that the care component is exportable even where the claimant ceased all employment and self employment before she left the United Kingdom for permanent residence in another member state. They have concluded that the claimant is an "employed or self employed person" for this purpose so long as she is entitled to some preserved benefit by virtue of her past contributions in the UK system—in this case to a reduced retirement pension when she would have reached retirement age. The Secretary of State's appeal to the Court of Appeal (reported as *Tolley v SSWP* [2013] EWCA Civ 1471) was dismissed, but that decision has been appealed further to the Supreme Court. That Court has referred certain questions to the CJEU (see report at [2015] UKSC 55).

This decision, and therefore that of the UT, has been upheld by the answers provided by the EUECJ: see *SSWP v Tolley* [2017] EUECJ C-430/15; [2017] AACR

40 (CJEU only). They confirm that the care component is a "sickness benefit" and that the claimant's past contribution record made her an "employed person" and therefore within the protection of the regulation. This case is concerned with the old Regulation 1408/71 but it is likely that the same result would follow under the current Regulation 883/04.

The mobility component has been held to be not exportable in Case C-537/09, *Bartlett, Ramos and Taylor v Secretary of State for Work and Pensions* [2012] UKUT 26 (AAC).

Three cases concern the export of DLA to other EU member countries. All are decisions by Judge Jacobs. In the first, *SSWP v MC (DLA)* [2019 UKUT 84 (AAC), the claimant while in receipt of the benefit had moved to Germany where he took up employment. In those circumstances the judge held that Germany had become the competent state for the payment of sickness benefits and hence the claimant had not been entitled to the payment of DLA while he worked there. In the second, *KR v SSWP (DLA)* [2019] UKUT 85 (AAC), the claimant had moved to Finland and became habitually resident there but not employed. In this case it was held that she retained her right to export the benefit as the UK remained the competent state for sickness benefits.

In a third case, *SSWP v TG (DLA)* [2019] UKUT 86 (AAC), where the claimant had become habitually resident (though not employed) in Cyprus before making his claim for DLA, the judge held that Cyprus had become the competent state in respect of sickness benefits and therefore the claimant was not entitled.

For more detail of these and other cases involving a European dimension, please see the relevant material in Vol III of this work.

The care component

72.—(1) Subject to the provisions of this Act, a person shall be entitled to the care component of a disability living allowance for any period throughout which—   **1.196**

(a) he is so severely disabled physically or mentally that—

    (i) he requires in connection with his bodily functions attention from another person for a significant portion of the day (whether during a single period or a number of periods); or

    (ii) he cannot prepare a cooked main meal for himself if he has the ingredients; or

(b) he is so severely disabled physically or mentally that, by day, he requires from another person—

    (i) frequent attention throughout the day in connection with his bodily functions; or

    (ii) continual supervision throughout the day in order to avoid substantial danger to himself or others; or

(c) he is so severely disabled physically or mentally that, at night,—

    (i) he requires from another person prolonged or repeated attention in connection with his bodily functions; or

    (ii) in order to avoid substantial danger to himself or others he requires another person to be awake for a prolonged period or at frequent intervals for the purpose of watching over him.

[⁴ (1A) In its application to a person in relation to so much of a period as falls before the day on which he reaches the age of 16, subsection (1) has effect subject to the following modifications—

(a) the condition mentioned in subsection (1)(a)(ii) shall not apply, and

(b) none of the other conditions mentioned in subsection (1) shall be taken to be satisfied unless—

    (i) he has requirements of a description mentioned in the condition

substantially in excess of the normal requirements of persons of
his age, or

    (ii) he has substantial requirements of such a description which
younger persons in normal physical and mental health may also
have but which persons of his age and in normal physical and
mental health would not have.]

(2) Subject to the following provisions of this section, a person shall not
be entitled to the care component of a disability living allowance unless—

  (a) throughout—

    (i) the period of three months immediately preceding the date on
which the award of that component would begin; or

    (ii) such other period of three months as may be prescribed,

he has satisfied or is likely to satisfy one or other of the conditions
mentioned in subsection (1)(a) to (c) above; and

  (b) he is likely to continue to satisfy one or other of those conditions
throughout—

    (i) the period of six months beginning with that date; or

    (ii) (if his death is expected within the period of six months begin-
ning with that date) the period so beginning and ending with his
death.

[4 (2A) The modifications mentioned in subsection (1A) shall have effect
in relation to the application of subsection (1) for the purposes of subsection (2), but only—

  (a) in the case of a person who is under the age of 16 on the date on
which the award of the care component would begin, and

  (b) in relation to so much of any period mentioned in subsection (2) as
falls before the day on which he reaches the age of 16.]

(3) Three weekly rates of the care component shall be prescribed.

(4) The weekly rate of the care component payable to a person for
each week in the period for which he is awarded that component shall be—

  (a) the highest rate, if he falls within subsection (2) above by virtue
of having satisfied or being likely to satisfy both the conditions
mentioned in subsection (1)(b) and (c) above throughout both the
period mentioned in paragraph (a) of subsection (2) above and that
mentioned in paragraph (b) of that subsection;

  (b) the middle rate, if he falls within that subsection by virtue of having
satisfied or being likely to satisfy one or other of those conditions
throughout both those periods; and

  (c) the lowest rate in any other case.

(5) For the purposes of this section, a person who is terminally ill, as
defined in section 66(2) above, and makes a claim expressly on the ground
that he is such a person, shall [4 (notwithstanding subsection (1A)(b))] be
taken—

  (a) to have satisfied the conditions mentioned in subsection (1)(b) and
(c) above for the period of three months immediately preceding the
date of the claim, or, if later, the first date on which he is terminally
ill (so however that the care component shall not be payable by
virtue of this paragraph for any period preceding that date); and

  (b) to satisfy or to be likely to satisfy those conditions [1 for so much of
the period for which he is terminally ill as does not fall before the
date of the claim.]

  (6) [5 *repealed*]

(7) Subject to [⁴ subsection (5)] above, circumstances may be prescribed in which a person is to be taken to satisfy or not to satisfy such of the conditions mentioned in subsection (1)(a) to (c) above as may be prescribed.

[⁴ (7A) Subsection (1A) has effect subject to regulations made under subsection (7) (except as otherwise prescribed).]

[⁷ (7B) A person to whom either Regulation (EC) No 1408/71 or Regulation (EC) No 883/2004 applies shall not be entitled to the care component of a disability living allowance for a period unless during that period the United Kingdom is competent for payment of sickness benefits in cash to the person for the purposes of Chapter 1 of Title III of the Regulation in question.]

[⁶ (8) Regulations may provide that no amount in respect of a disability living allowance which is attributable to entitlement to the care component shall be payable in respect of a person for a period when he is a resident of a care home in circumstances in which any of the costs of any qualifying services provided for him are borne out of public or local funds under a specified enactment.

(9) The reference in subsection (8) to a care home is to an establishment that provides accommodation together with nursing or personal care.

(10) The following are qualifying services for the purposes of subsection (8)—

(a) accommodation,

(b) board, and

(c) personal care.

(11) The reference in subsection (8) to a specified enactment is to an enactment which is, or is of a description, specified for the purposes of that subsection by regulations.

(12) The power to specify an enactment for the purposes of subsection (8) includes power to specify it only in relation to its application for a particular purpose.

(13) In this section, "enactment" includes an enactment comprised in, or in an instrument made under, an Act of the Scottish Parliament.]

AMENDMENTS

1. Welfare Reform and Pension Act 1999 s.67(2) (January 12, 2000).

2. Mental Health (Care and Treatment) (Scotland) Act 2003 (Consequential Provisions) Order 2005 (SI 2005/2078) Sch.1 para.4 (October 5, 2005).

3. National Health Service (Consequential Provisions) Act 2006 Sch.1 para.144 (March 1, 2007).

4. Welfare Reform Act 2007 s.52 (October 1, 2007).

5. Welfare Reform Act 2007 Sch.8 (October 1, 2007).

6. Welfare Reform Act 2007 s.60(2) (October 29, 2007).

7. Social Security (Disability Living Allowance, Attendance Allowance and Carer's Allowance)(Miscellaneous Amendments) Regulations 2011 reg.5(5). (SI 2011/2426) (October 31, 2011).

DERIVATION

SSA 1975 s.37ZB.   **1.197**

GENERAL NOTE

This section defines the conditions for the care component of DLA. Subsection   **1.198**
(1) provides for three levels of benefit according to different requirements for care. Para.(a) specifies two alternative conditions by which some form of attention is

required; para.(b) specifies one condition of attention and one alternative condition for supervision, both during the day; and para.(c) has one condition for attention and an alternative one for supervision, both by night. Benefit is paid at the lowest rate if the patient satisfies only para.(a); at the middle rate if they satisfy either paras (b) or (c); and at the highest rate if they satisfy both (b) and (c). There is no increase if the claimant satisfies (a) and another paragraph.

Note that reg.7 of the DLA Regulations deems certain people undergoing renal dialysis to satisfy either the day or the night attention condition and so qualify for the middle rate of the care component.

Note also that, under subs.(5), terminally ill claimants may be deemed to satisfy both the day and night conditions and so qualify for the highest rate of the care component for the rest of their lives.

Note that there is nothing in the law relating to either Carer's Allowance or DLA (even of the care component) which would preclude a claimant from being entitled to both benefits—though, of course, the Carer's Allowance must depend upon the claimant caring for another person who is in receipt of DLA. Whether the claimant does qualify for both benefits will depend upon the facts found in relation to each claim. See *MC v Secretary of State for Work and Pensions* [2012] UKUT 337 (AAC).

In *LC v SSWP* (DLA) [2015] UKUT 32 (AAC) Judge Hemingway has addressed the issue of the relationship between the finding of an FTT on a claim for DLA and a contemporaneous claim in respect of ESA. It is perhaps surprising that this matter has not been considered before. The claimant in this instance was a woman who had made a new claim for DLA that had been refused. At the hearing of her appeal the tribunal had been provided with a copy of the decision of an ESA tribunal, issued only the day before, in which it had been accepted that she scored 9 points in respect of 2 of the descriptors, social interaction and getting about. The FTT hearing the case for DLA rejected her appeal on the ground that she was not at all a creditable witness—they said "Quite frankly we do not believe her"—but they then made no reference at all to the ESA decision. Judge Hemingway held that in the circumstances of this case not to do so was an error of law. Clearly the decision of neither tribunal is binding on the other—they are applying different tests on possibly different evidence— yet to reach an entirely different conclusion on matters that are very similar and addressed at a similar time, should require some explanation. By the time the appeal came before the UT only the mobility component of DLA was in issue; the judge explains his decision as follows:

"33. [. . .] Certainly I would accept that the F-tT hearing the disability living allowance appeal was not bound in any way by the decision of the ESA tribunal. I accept that entitlement to different benefits based on different statutory tests was in issue. I accept that there was no obligation upon the F-tT to follow any of the ESA tribunal's reasoning and, indeed, there was very little evidence contained within the decision notice about what the ESA tribunal's reasoning was. In this context it is perhaps unlikely that the ESA tribunal produced a statement of reasons for decision unless that was requested by the respondent and there is no indication that it was. Even if it had been then, of course, it would not have been produced within sufficient time for it to have been available to this F-tT.

34. Having said all of the above, the decision notice issued by the ESA tribunal was, at the least, an indication that that tribunal had found, after consideration of the appeal and whatever evidence was before it, that the appellant was, as at the same date this F-tT was concerned with, unable to get to a specified place with which she is familiar without being accompanied. Whilst it does not necessarily follow that such a conclusion would lead to satisfaction of the statutory test for lower rate mobility I would take the view that it certainly suggests it might be. There is, it seems to me, a considerable interrelationship between the two statutory tests. So, potentially, the award made by the ESA tribunal was a matter of some significance. It merited the paying of some attention to it by the F-tT. Had the F-tT not effectively overlooked the award, which is what it appears to have

done given the absence of any mention of it at all, it might have (I do not say it would have) taken a different view regarding her credibility. It might have asked her some questions about the ESA tribunal's decision and, in particular, whether she had attended an oral hearing and had given oral evidence to that tribunal. It might have enquired as to whether there was some documentary evidence before the ESA tribunal which was not before it. It might have considered adjourning in order to ascertain what documentary evidence had been before the ESA tribunal in case it impacted upon the issues it had to decide with respect to lower rate mobility. It might have been more cautious about rejecting the entirety of the claims made by the appellant given the knowledge that the ESA tribunal had resolved at least some matters of significance, in the context of that particular benefit, in her favour.

35. In light of all the above and, in particular, in light of the relationship between the sorts of factors that might give entitlement to lower rate mobility and the sorts of factors that might give entitlement to 9 points under descriptor 15(b) I conclude that the F-tT was obliged to consider the decision of the ESA tribunal as recorded in the decision notice and address it in some way. It would have been open to it to have gone on to make the decision it did make so long as it properly took that decision into account. However, it did not appear to take it into account at all. That does, to my mind, constitute an error of law. This is because the F-tT has failed to consider a relevant matter. I cannot say that the error is immaterial in the sense that the F-tT would inevitably have reached the same conclusion had it taken account of the ESA tribunal's decision. It might have adjusted its approach in the various ways I have suggested above and that might, though I do not by any means say it would, have led to a different outcome. In light of the above, therefore, I conclude that the F-tT's decision although in many respects an admirably straightforward one, must be set aside."

And note the extensive consideration that has been given to this issue in the context of appeals for personal independence payment – see *FN v SSWP (ESA)* [2015] UKUT 670 (AAC); [2016] AACR 24 and *CH and KN v SSWP (PIP)* [2018[UKUT 330 (AAC), discussed in the notes following reg.3 of the PIP regulations.

Certain phrases in this section will apply to all claims:

For any period throughout which: These words require some consistency in the claimant's need for attendance over the whole period of an award but they do not require that the conditions should be satisfied on every day. The former Attendance Allowance Board's *Handbook for Delegated Medical Practitioners* suggested that a man satisfies the night attention condition if he "invariably requires prolonged or repeated attention on more nights of the week than he does not". Although DLA is a weekly benefit, there does not seem to be any particular reason for requiring that it should *invariably* be the case that a person should satisfy the statutory criteria in the majority of the days of a week. In *R(A) 2/74*, the Commissioner said: 1.199

"I think that the delegate should take a broad view of the matter, asking himself some such question as whether in the whole circumstances the words of the statute do or do not as a matter of the ordinary usage of the English language cover or apply to the facts. These are matters for the good sense and judgment of the delegate."

Thus, it may be appropriate in some cases to make an award covering a substantial period notwithstanding that there may be expected to be periods of remission in the claimant's condition lasting longer than a week. Both the length of the periods of remission and their frequency are likely to be relevant considerations as, perhaps, is the severity of the disablement during other periods. If the disability is one from which a substantial period of remission is quite likely, an award for a short period may be appropriate. If at the end of that period the claimant no longer satisfies the conditions for an award, or an award at the same rate, but the period of remission lasts less than two years, reg.6 of the DLA Regulations enables the claimant to qualify again without having to wait the usual three months (or six months if the claimant is over 65).

The test to be applied in assessing whether attention is required throughout any period for "prolonged or repeated attention" at night has been explained again by Judge Brunner QC in *AD v SSWP* [2017] UKUT 29 (AAC). This was another case in which a child suffered from a medical condition that caused him frequently to soil himself at night and at other times suffered prolonged pain so that he required attention, sometimes for hours, at night. The FTT had refused an appeal after finding that he did not need this attention "most of the time," and that they regarded this as requiring attention on more than half of the nights of the week. Judge Brunner held that this was the wrong approach. She refers to *SSWP v Moyna* [2003] UKHL 44 in which it was emphasised that the decision should involve a broad approach, was not a matter of arithmetical calculation, and was a matter of judgment for the tribunal.

A different problem in the application of this phrase has been considered in *CDLA/3737/2002*. The claimant was a child who was partially sighted. Her care needs at home were found by a tribunal to be insufficient to qualify for an award of the care component and they gave no account to her needs while at school. The Commissioner allowed an appeal and awarded the middle rate of care component. He accepted that she required extra attention in connection with her bodily function of seeing whilst learning at school and, applying the principles above, accepted that these needs could be said to apply "throughout the period", notwithstanding that the needs at school would not exist during vacation period. The Secretary of State appealed against this decision but the Court of Appeal *R(DLA) 1/04*, refused to consider the appeal because the way in which the appeal had been argued before the Commissioner meant that, effectively, there was now no point of law to be considered by the CA, or, at any rate, no point on which the considered views of the Commissioner had been expressed. The court stressed the importance of having such issues fully considered before they reach the court. It seems likely that this issue will be considered again. The claimant would probably do well to emphasise that the attention provided by a teacher in term time would be replaced by extra parental attention in keeping a child occupied and entertained in vacation.

1.200   *So severely disabled mentally or physically:* There has been a difference of opinion between Commissioners on the significance of these words. On the one hand the view has sometimes been taken that they act as a prerequisite by which a claimant must show a disability in a medical sense that is recognised and labelled as such by a doctor; on the other hand the words are regarded simply as a complement to the need for care so that if it is shown that the claimant requires care and that it is something to do with their mental or physical condition they succeed.

This issue has been resolved by a decision of a Tribunal of Commissioners in *R(DLA)3/06*. They held that the words do not require the finding of a specific disease or medical condition that is identifiable as the cause of the claimant's disability. All that is necessary is to identify some functional lack of ability that can be traced to a physical or mental cause in the claimant. This means that a medical condition will often be a relevant piece of evidence to support the claim (see e.g. *CDLA/4475/2004*), but it is not an essential prerequisite. For example, where the claimant is a child, as in the present case, behavioural difficulties may cause a need for care, so as to satisfy the conditions necessary for the care component, and for the mobility component too if the child may not be trusted to walk out alone. In that case the child may need the care etc. to compensate for a functional inability, without having to prescribe a medical condition. But this conclusion still requires two matters to be satisfied: first, does the inability have some physical or mental cause? This would be satisfied where the child suffers from arrested development or from a very low I.Q., or where they do suffer from some diagnosable medical condition, but not where their conduct is simply wilful or irresponsible misbehaviour, and cases, like those in the past where that may have been the cause of the claimant's inability, would still fail. (See, for example *R(A)2/92*, where the Commissioners suggest that the correct approach would have been to ask whether the claimant could desist from his aggressive and irresponsible behaviour.)

Apart from the element of volition, however, the Commissioners otherwise found it difficult to envisage a situation in which a disability that expressed a need for care etc. was not the result of some physical or mental cause. Those words, they thought, were intended to be inclusive rather than exclusive so as to include any psychological as well as physical cause. But they do confirm the decision in *CA/137/1984*. That was the case in which the claimant, a Muslim child who had a disabled right hand, had claimed on the basis that he needed assistance in eating. In his religion all food must be handled only with the right hand because the left is used for washing after defecating. The claim failed because the Commissioner took the view that his need arose from his culture rather than his disability. The Tribunal here confirm that decision, though they do not explain how it is to be reconciled with the decision in *Fairey* (see below) where the emphasis is on allowing the claimant to lead a normal life which should presumably mean normal in his own culture.

The second requirement of this phrase is that the disability must be "severe". **1.201** Here the tribunal of Commissioners confirms that the test of severity does not condition the degree of disability other than by reference to the scale of requirements that the section provides for. The words of the section, they point out, are "so severely disabled . . . that." In other words the test of severity is satisfied by the claimant proving the requisite level of need according to the particular claim he has made, (adopting the approach used in *R(DLA) 10/02*). The commissioners therefore conclude:

> "in our view, section 72 raises two issues. (i) Does the claimant have a disability, i.e. does he have a functional deficiency, physical or mental? (ii) If so, do the care needs to which the functional deficiency give rise satisfy any of paragraphs (i) or (ii) of section 72 (1)(a) to (c),and if so which? Section 73 (1)(d) gives rise to similar questions in relation to mobility".

Although this question appeared to have been resolved in *R (DLA) 3/06*, the matter has been opened again, at least in relation to a very young child, by Judge May. The case concerned a three-year-old child who was described as exhibiting behavioural difficulties, but in respect of whom there was no medical diagnosis of any mental condition or abnormality. The judge makes clear his disagreement with the decision in *R (DLA) 3/06*, but accepts that he must follow it. In doing so, however, he distinguishes the case of a very young child, as here— (the child in *R(DLA)3/06* was aged 12). In the case of a very young child he says there must still be a medical diagnosis because behaviour (for which read misbehaviour) alone, cannot be a disability.

That much was accepted by the Tribunal of commissioners in *R(DLA)3/06*, but they go on to say that behaviour may be evidence of a mental deficiency of some sort such that the claimant was incapable of controlling his behaviour, and that could be a disability. The trouble with this, says Judge May in *AC v SSWP* [2009] UKUT 83 (AAC), is that young children generally are incapable of controlling their behaviour by the standards of adult society and that is what they all learn to do, as a process of maturing by growing up. He upheld the decision of the First-tier Tribunal to refuse benefit.

It is not clear that it was necessary for him to go so far as to distinguish *R(DLA) 3/06* in order to do so; the absence of any medical diagnosis could certainly be taken account of as a part of the totality of the evidence before the tribunal and without it, there was very little else to support a finding of disability.

The decision in *R(DLA)3/06* will affect the approach to be adopted in a number of **1.202** other analogous situations. In relation to alcoholism there has already been a decision by another Tribunal of Commissioners in *R(DLA)6/06*. There the Tribunal apply the decision above so that the question becomes one essentially of the claimant's need for assistance etc., rather than of its cause. However, its cause is not irrelevant because the tribunal accept that voluntary intoxication cannot be said, of itself, to produce a state of disablement in the sense required for the legislation, any more than a claimant who had requested that his legs be bound would be said to be disabled so as to require care and attention. So the question of whether the claimant can be said to be disabled as a result of alcoholism will involve, at least to some extent, his ability to choose to remain (or become) sober. The test, according to the Tribunal, should be whether the claimant can be expected realistically to stop drinking. If he cannot, because of a medical condition (physical or mental), then any attention and supervision he might require should be taken into account to determine his entitlement to this benefit. (Though if the cause of his alcohol dependence is only mental, then in accordance with *R(DLA)4/06* any claim for higher rate mobility component would fail.) (See s.73 and reg.12 below.) The Tribunal suggests a number of other limiting devices that would affect a claim based upon the needs of someone suffering from alcoholism. As suggested by Commissioner Fellner in *CDLA/778/2000* the claimant should be encouraged to control his alcoholism either with or without professional assistance, and any award of benefit should be time limited to take account of such a possibility. Furthermore, the care needs of an alcoholic will vary through the day on the assumption that his day may commence with relative sobriety. This means that some levels of care component will not be appropriate, if, for example they require "continual" supervision, or attention "throughout" the day, or even for a "significant portion" of the day. Again the Tribunal confirms a point made in *CDLA/3542/2002* that assistance can only be said to be properly required if it could serve some useful purpose. Thus supervision designed to prevent the claimant drinking, or even to assist him when he has done so, would not be "required" if it were impossible or impractical to achieve that end.

The problems presented by alcohol and drug dependency have also been considered in cases relating to Incapacity Benefit and Employment Support Allowance— see *AD v Secretary of State for Work and Pensions* [2011] UKUT 307 (AAC) where the DLA decision was relied upon. And see too the decision in *JG v SSWP* [2013] UKUT 37 (AAC) where the UT judge has regard to the Diagnostic and Statistical Manual of Mental Disorders of the American Psychiatric Association- DSM- IV and the subsequent decision in *SD v SSWP* [2016] UKUT 100 (AAC); [2016] AACR 35 which updates to the later version of DSM-5. Both of these cases are useful in establishing the evidence that might be brought to a tribunal to establish the claimant's mental condition that is relevant to determining his capability for work when claiming ESA and equally for DLA.

In relation to the problem of bed wetting which has also caused a divergence of decisions among Commissioners it will no longer (in accordance with *R(DLA)3/06*) be necessary to find some medical reason for the incontinence. However, it will still remain necessary to establish that the claimant is suffering from a disability. This means that the incontinence must at least, be something that is not normal for a person of his age, and, in the case of a young child, that he has requirements that are substantially in excess of what is normal for a child of that age. (See subs.(6), and *R(DLA)1/05*.)

1.203   Similar reasoning will now apply to cases of chronic fatigue syndrome and psychosomatic pain. The only question should be whether the claimant suffers the fatigue or pain, genuinely and is thereby disabled so as to need the care, without any need to provide a medical diagnosis.

In many cases the claimant's disablement will be defined by the extent to which they can do things without experiencing pain or discomfort to an unacceptable extent. Detailed advice for tribunals on the matter of pain is given by Commissioner Jacobs in *CDLA/0902/2004*.

Tribunals sometimes have a difficult task in determining whether a claim of disablement involving pain or discomfort is genuine. Medical examiners sometimes remark upon inappropriate responses made by patients during examination that might tend to suggest that they are exaggerating their condition—the so-called "Waddell signs" (named after Prof. Waddell). In *CDLA/2747/2006* the tribunal had dismissed an appeal on the grounds that the claimant had displayed those signs and his claim could then be taken, for that reason, to be unjustified. The Commissioner allowed an appeal. It was an error of law he said, to reach such a conclusion on the basis of Waddell signs alone. That evidence, he says, might be indicative of exaggeration, but could equally indicate that the claimant has both physical and mental components in his disablement. The correct approach, he says, is to look at that evidence within the context of the evidence as a whole that is before the tribunal, and reach a conclusion on the whole of the evidence.

The information upon which a tribunal will rely when hearing an appeal will generally be derived from three sources: the claimant themselves (including that provided on the claim form); the claimant's GP; and an examining health practitioner (when a report has been requested by the DWP). The approach to be adopted to information from each of these sources has been considered in *HL v Secretary for State for Work and Pensions* [2011] UKUT 183 (AAC) where Judge Jacobs remarks:

> "All too often, judges present the tribunal's reasons as if the tribunal had a choice between accepting the evidence of the GP or of the examining medical practitioner. There may be cases where that is so, but in many cases the reports each have their strengths and each their limitations as an assessment of the claimant's disablement. In those cases, what a proper analysis usually requires is for the tribunal to show a balance between the value that can be distilled from each report and its limitations."

In *MW v SSWP* [2013] UKUT 158 (AAC) Judge Bano has reminded FTT that they should not regard a conflict of medical evidence as a contest between the claimant's own advisers and the EMP and in particular should not simply prefer that of the EMP on the ground that it was "independent". The evidence, he says, must be looked at as a whole and such evidence as was relevant taken from each.

Requires: This means reasonably requires not medically requires (see *Mallinson*). In *CA/96/84* it was suggested that an eight-year-old girl who suffered from enuresis would suffer no harm if left in her wet bedding for the rest of the night. The Commissioner held that attention was reasonably required simply to make her comfortable again and added that otherwise a person unable to dress themselves could be said to have no need for attention because they could stay in a dressing gown all day.

1.204

The section provides that care must be required; it does not have to be shown that care is in fact provided. But if care, whether by attention or supervision, is in fact provided, that may be strong evidence that the care is required. As one Commissioner put it "mothers would be unlikely to exhaust themselves by providing it for years" (*R(A) 1/73*). On the other hand if the claimant chooses to do without care, that may be a clear indication that care is not required (*CDLA/899/1994*). Tribunals should consider why the claimant does not use the care and whether their life can be considered normal without it (see below).

In *KK v Secretary of State for Work and Pensions* [2012] UKUT 356 (AAC) Judge Jacobs held that a First-tier Tribunal had made an error of law when they failed to explain to the claimant that he could be entitled to the benefit even though he might choose not to spend the benefit by acquiring any assistance. The claimant had claimed both the mobility and the care components, but said that he would not want anyone coming into his home and invading his privacy. The FTT treated that as abandonment of any claim for the care component. The judge examines the obligation of a tribunal to explore the inquisitorial aspect of its jurisdiction by making it clear to the claimant that his entitlement depended upon his need and not upon how he chose to spend the benefit.

Where care is provided there has been some difference of opinion about the source of that care. In two cases, *CSDLA/427/2006* and *CSDLA/2349/2010* (now [2012] UKUT 222 (AAC)) Judge May had decided that the care provided, in the first case, by teachers at school and in the other, by a district nurse, could not be included in the claim for DLA because both forms of care were provided through publicly funded arrangements and to include it in the claim would mean "double funding" at public expense. This argument has been disapproved by a tribunal of judges in

KM v SSWP (DLA) [2013] UKUT 159 (AAC); [2014] AACR 2. The judges there decide that there is no reason to read the words of the statute with such a gloss put upon them. Indeed, they argue that the provisions of the DLA Regulations suggest that there could have been no such intention when the statute was passed because regs 8 and 9 remove the payability of benefit when the claimant is in publicly funded accommodation thereby implying that otherwise he is entitled. An alternative argument advanced by Judge May, that care provided by medical staff could not qualify was also not approved, though because that point did not arise on the facts of the case before them they confined themselves to general comments. What they say, however, is consistent with the view they expressed above—that there is no reason to limit the words of the statute in this way. It could also be argued that reg.7 of the DLA Regulations (which qualifies a renal patient for DLA) supports that conclusion because it specifically excludes a claimant who has dialysis in an NHS hospital unless no member of the staff is assisting him; the specific exclusion in this instance suggests that it is not applicable in other circumstances.

The question of whether a claimant "requires" attention will be affected by whether some aid or device might assist the claimant so as to eliminate the need for attention. This matter was considered by Judge Ward in the case of *SF v SSWP* [2010] UKUT 78 (AAC). There, the claim had been refused by the First-tier Tribunal on the ground that the claimant's need for assistance in bathing could be obviated by the provision of a bath-board, or by the fitting of a bath with showering facilities. Judge Ward followed an earlier decision in *CDLA/304/07* in holding that it must be found to be reasonable for the claimant to obtain such devices. He remitted the case to a new tribunal for further findings to be made as to the availability of such measures and consideration of the timing, as well as the cost, with which they might be accomplished within the six-month qualifying period of that claim. In the instant case it was argued that major alterations might not have been reasonable because the claimant was moving house at that time. In *CA/3943/2006*, the Deputy Commissioner held that it would be difficult ever to conclude that the use of a bucket in the kitchen, as a substitute for a lavatory, could be regarded as acceptable so as to render assistance that was needed to climb the stairs, no longer "reasonably required". The question of whether the use of a commode downstairs, if that were available, would be acceptable, she decided, should be left to a subsequent tribunal. And see also *JF v SSWP* [2012] UKUT 335 (AAC) where Judge Rowland considered the size of the claimant's kitchen in relation to the use of a high stool to assist her when preparing food.

Though in *CDLA/2495/2004* the Commissioner held that the claimant, who had mental health problems and required prompting by his mother before he would do anything more than get out of bed, did not qualify for benefit at the middle rate—frequent attention—because some of the tasks for which he needed to be prompted, such as shaving, were performed only every four days, and the Commissioner suggested that as the claimant rarely went out, even help with dressing did not necessarily require her attention every day.

1.205   It is sometimes suggested, particularly in relation to supervision, that the claimant could avoid the need for care by adapting their lifestyle to avoid that risk. The scope for this suggestion now seems strictly limited.

In *R(A) 3/89* the Commissioner ridiculed the suggestion by asking whether the claimant was expected to remain chairbound to avoid the risk of falling and in *R(A) 5/90* a Tribunal of Commissioners said that any tribunal adopting the argument that the claimant could avoid a danger should identify the precautions to be taken and explain how they were compatible with normal domestic arrangements. The leading case on this point must now be *Secretary of State v Fairey* [1997] 1 W.L.R. 799 (reported as *R(A) 2/98*) in which the House of Lords held that the claimant who was profoundly deaf was entitled to care on the basis that she needed the assistance of an interpreter by way of sign language to assist her in travelling and carrying out other social activities. Lord Slynn of Hadley said at 815:

"In my opinion the yardstick of a 'normal life' is important; it is a better approach than adopting the test as to whether something is 'essential' or 'desirable.' Social life in the sense of mixing with others, taking part in activities with others, undertaking recreation and cultural activities can be part of normal life. It is not in any way unreasonable that the severely disabled person should wish to be involved in them despite his disability. What is reasonable will depend on the age, sex, interests of the applicant and other circumstances. To take part in such activities sight and hearing are normally necessary and if they are impaired attention is required in connection with the bodily functions of seeing and hearing to enable the person to overcome his disability. As Swinton Thomas L.J. in the Court of Appeal said: 'Attention given to a profoundly deaf person to enable that person to carry on, so far as possible in the circumstances, an ordinary life is capable of being attention that is reasonably required.'

How much attention is reasonably required and how frequently it is required are questions of fact for the adjudication officer."

But it may not yet be possible to say that the claimant should be put in exactly the same position as if they had no disability. In *CDLA/267/94* it was suggested that a claimant who was blind and needed assistance to find anything he had lost, might reasonably be expected to wait for periods of attention by finding. This would affect the issue of whether his need was "frequent" (see below).

In *Miller v Chief Adjudication Officer* (reported as *R(A) 4/94*), the claimant and her husband were both disabled and in receipt of attendance allowance. The Court of Appeal held that the claimant's requirements arising out of her attending to the needs of her husband had been rightly ignored because otherwise there would be "double recovery" for the needs of the husband or an aggregation of his needs with those of the claimant. The court expressly reserved the question whether there might be taken into account requirements arising from a claimant attending to an infant daughter not in receipt of attendance allowance. That question has not received a uniform answer from Commissioners. In *CDLA/16996/96*, the Commissioner dismissed an appeal against a tribunal who had said:

"The majority of the tribunal decided that there was no more fundamental a social activity than that of a mother bringing up young children. It was essential to her well-being that she did, as far as possible, as much as any other mother would do for a young family. Playing with children, supervising their behaviour, washing and dressing them, taking them out to play, reading their school work and generally performing all the functions which a sighted mother would perform for herself were all activities which required a third party's assistance, either to carry them out in safety or at all. [The claimant] needed help, not for someone to do these things for her, but with the function of seeing to do these things herself: she needed someone to act as her eyes."

But in *CSDLA/314/97*, another case of a blind mother, the Commissioner expressly disagreed with the earlier decision. He questioned whether the attention required was sufficiently closely related to the claimant's bodily function of sight. (But as to this, see below.) He also found that the evidence was not clear on whether the attention was provided as assistance for the mother to care for the children herself, or whether it was provided as a substitute for the mother's caring. This point was regarded as crucial in *CDLA/16996/96* and was adopted in the third case of a blind mother (*CDLA/16129/96*) in which the Commissioner preferred to follow the first case. It has also been found to be critical in *CDLA/5216/1998*. In this case the claimant suffered from arthritis and hearing loss in one ear. She was caring for her twin babies, themselves also disabled. The Commissioner allowed the claimant's appeal against refusal of benefit and sent the case back to be determined by a fresh tribunal but with extensive directions as to how they should proceed. The Commissioner considers all three of the previous decisions on this point. Although he accepts the conclusion reached on the facts in *CSDLA/314/97*

1.206

he finds some of the statements there to be too broad. In principle he agrees with the reasoning of the other cases. First, that it is possible for a claimant to require supervision to ensure the safety of others, i.e. her children. In this case it seems unlikely that the claimant would succeed on the basis of supervision, because, by day, it was unlikely that the requirement would be "continual", and by night, she did not need "watching over", but only that someone could wake her when she could not hear the babies' crying. Secondly, that attention given to the claimant to enable her to care for her children could qualify so long as the attention was given to *her* to enable her to do the activity rather than the assitance being a substitute for the claimant's own caring. Furthermore the assistance has to be personal and intimate to the bodily functions of the claimant. Thus the Commissioner envisaged that a mother who was deaf and needs to be told always when the baby cried, or a mother whose arms were impaired and needed help to hold the baby might qualify, but a mother whose hands were arthritic and could not manage the fastenings on the babies' clothes, so that someone else had to dress the baby for her, would not. By the same reasoning taking the children to the park for their mother would not be attention to her bodily functions, but taking the mother in a wheelchair to the park to be with her children would be. Finally, the Commissioner noted that by the time the case had reached him an award of DLA had been made to each of the children for their own care needs. He directed the fresh tribunal that from the date of that award they could not include any help that the claimant needed to look after her children as being assistance required in her claim. To do so would be to allow double recovery for the children's needs (see *Miller v CAO*, reported as *R(A) 4/94*).

1.207   *Attention and Supervision:* The difference between these terms has been explored in *CA/6/72 (approved in R(A) 3/74)*. Attention was taken to involve personal service of an active nature, such as bathing or feeding, while supervision was more passive, such as being present to warn or give guidance and to intervene when necessary. This distinction was accepted by the Court of Appeal in *Moran v Secretary of State for Social Services* (reported as appendix *R(A) 1/88*) and approved in *Mallinson v Secretary of State for Social Security* [1994] 1 W.L.R. 630, also reported as appendix to *R(A) 3/94* where the point was made that the concepts were not necessarily mutually exclusive—a person might be supervising a blind person while at the same time providing attention by way of guidance.

1.208   *Attention in connection with bodily functions:* From the start it has been recognised that these words hold the key to qualification for most claimants. In *R. v National Insurance Commissioner Ex. p. the Secretary of State for Social Services (Packer's case)* [1981] 1 W.L.R. 1017 Lord Denning M.R. said bodily functions:

> "include breathing, hearing, seeing, eating, drinking, walking, sitting, sleeping, getting out of bed, dressing, undressing, eliminating waste products—and the like—all of which an ordinary person—who is not suffering from any disability— does for himself. But they do not include cooking, shopping or other things which a wife or daughter does as part of her domestic duties: or generally which one member of the household normally does for the rest of the family".

Although he accepted that cooking could be said to be "connected with" the function of eating, it was, he thought, too remote. In subsequent cases (*R. v Woodling* [1984] 1 W.L.R. 348; *Cockburn* (reported as *R(A) 2/98*): and *Fairey*) this distinction between activities that are close and intimate to the claimant and those which are not has been sustained. It has, however, created a complex and often conflicting path between Commissioners' decisions.

The concept of "bodily functions" has been examined by a tribunal of Commissioners in *R(DLA) 1/07*. The case concerned a child claimant whose mother described her as having behavioural problems, memory loss, difficulty concentrating and other problems, as well as being hyperactive. It was clear that at school she required special attention to motivate her and to aid in integrating with her peers, while at home her mother said she had to be with her all the time to control her behaviour and to ensure her safety. While there was no medical diagnosis of the condition a report by a paediatric neuropsychologist described her as "having significant learning difficulties with prominent language processing disorder and associated behavioural problems". The claimant's need for attention could probably be summed up as requiring help with motivation, communication and social integration. Her claim for the mobility component of DLA at the lower rate, and for care component at the middle rate, was refused and her appeal to a tribunal dismissed on the ground that the assistance she needed was not help in relation to her bodily functions.

The Tribunal of Commissioners allowed an appeal. They begin their reasons by facing the issue squarely and deciding: "Firstly, the functions of the brain are included within the term 'bodily functions'. They found authority for that proposition in a series of cases including *Packer's Case, Mallinson, Cockburn,* and *Fairey.*

In accepting that cognitive functioning (thinking) can be a bodily function they expressly overrule a line of cases (*CSDLA/867/1997, CSDLA/832/1999* and *CSDLA/860/2000*) asserting that it was not. The Commissioners also refer to *R(DLA) 3/03*, which had been relied on by the appeal tribunal, but they distinguished it as deciding only that the claimant there did not need the assistance for which he was claiming—the evidence suggested that he was able to communicate adequately without assistance—and did not decide that communication could never be a bodily function.   1.209

The Commissioners in the present case made no reference to *CDLA/2974/2004,* a decision of Mr Commissioner Rowland, in which he accepted that the defective cognitive processes of a 16-year-old autistic boy could amount to a defective bodily function.

The problem that the Commissioners then faced in their decision was to make any distinction between what has been known as activities and bodily functions. Here they break new ground by suggesting that what may be regarded as activities should be broken down into the parts that are contributed by individual organs of the body. If such organs are defective so as to need assistance then that may be help in connection with a bodily function for the purposes of a claim to DLA. The Tribunal express their reasons for this as follows:

"33. As identified by Dunn LJ in *Packer's Case,* a 'bodily function' primarily refers to the normal action of any organ of the body. For example, the function or a function of the lower jaw is to move up and down, i.e. its normal action. By way of extension, we consider it quite appropriate to extend this reference to the organ's immediate purpose: in our example, the purpose of the lower jaw moving up and down is to masticate food, and we do not consider it would be incorrect to refer to such mastication as a 'bodily function', i.e. a function of the lower jaw. It appears to us that the term is sufficiently wide to cover this extension.

34. Such functions might be voluntarily controlled (e.g. the lower jaw, as in our example), or involuntary (e.g. it is the function of the kidneys to filter waste products from the blood, which it does without any voluntary instigating action).

35. Furthermore, as Dunn LJ indicated in *Packer's Case* (see paragraph 30 above), 'bodily functions' includes not only the action of one organ of the body, but also those of any set of such organs in concert. Therefore, when the lower jaw is looked at with the mouth and various internal organs including the stomach and alimentary tract, it can properly be said of that set of organs of which the jaw is a part that the bodily function (in the sense of purpose as described above) is eating. We see no inconsistency between the proposition that it is a function of the lower jaw to move up and down and masticate food, and, as part of a set of organs, its function is also eating. Indeed, far from there being a strict dichotomy between 'microfunctions' and 'macrofunctions'—and to be fair to Mr Collins he did not submit that there was such a clear and absolute dichotomy—in terms of the organs of the body, there is complex web of functionality that requires acknowledgment.

36. However, of course, there are limits. Not every activity performed by the body is a 'bodily function', because it cannot properly be said that that activity is either a normal action or purpose of that organ or set of organs. Shopping is one example which falls clearly on the wrong side of the line: whilst no doubt involving various functions of the body, shopping could not properly be said itself to be a function (in terms of either simple actions or purpose) of any organ or set of organs of the body. Similarly, it was not suggested by any of the judges in *Packer's Case* that cooking could itself be a 'bodily function'. There may be difficult, borderline cases; but, like Lord Slynn (and with respect to Lord Denning's obiter dicta in *Packer's Case* and those of subsequent judges, to which we have referred: see paragraph 31 above), we do not consider that getting in and out of bed, or dressing and undressing, are 'bodily functions', because (in our respectful view) it cannot properly be said that it is the normal action or purpose of any organ or sets of organs to perform these exercises. These are not functions of organs of the body, but merely things which a body can do if the relevant bodily functions (e.g. movement of the limbs) are working normally.

37. However, given that activities such as shopping, dressing and undressing, getting in and out of bed necessarily involve bodily functions of one sort or another (which can be specifically identified, if necessary), why does the relevant 'bodily function' matter in any specific case? The answer to this lies in looking at the wording of the statutory provisions as a whole, as has been urged by the House of Lords (see paragraph 16 above) and in the approach to those provisions of Lord Woolf in *Mallinson* and the tribunal of Commissioners in *R(DLA) 3/06*. As already indicated (paragraphs 8–11), the focus of these provisions is on the disablement (i.e. functional deficiency) of the claimant. Even where such a disablement is shown, the relevant attention is that *reasonably required* by virtue of that functional deficiency. On the issue of relevant attention, it may therefore be necessary to focus upon the functional deficiency with some particularity. It may not be crucial whether the bodily function impaired in someone who cannot move his legs and consequently walk is looked at as (i) movement of the legs, or (ii) walking. We consider both have equal validity for the reasons we give above. However the function is viewed, the necessary attention to address the claimant's reasonable care requirements will be the same. But in other cases it may be of importance, because it will be necessary to identify the bodily function that is impaired with some precision so that the attention reasonably required to address the impairment can be properly identified and assessed.

38. For example, Mr Mallinson was blind, and was consequently unable to walk in unfamiliar surroundings because (as Lord Woolf put it, at page 639H) he did not know where to walk or (e.g. when crossing the road) when to walk. As Lord Woolf pointed out (at page 639G), to say whether the attention he received in the form of being guided was 'in connection with his bodily functions' (i.e. reasonably necessary as the result of an impairment to those functions), it was necessary to identify the bodily function or functions to which the attention relates. We consider that in substance this is no more than ensuring that the relevant attention is reasonably necessary—because, as indicated above (paragraphs 8–9), the severity of the functional disablement is in fact defined by that attention. Therefore, although in one sense it could be said that Mr Mallinson's ability to walk was impaired (in the ways identified by Lord Woolf), in considering this question, as Mr Mallinson's legs were working normally—but his eyesight was not—of the interwoven bodily functions involved, 'it is preferable to focus on that function [i.e. his deficient ability to see]' (per Lord Woolf at page 641A). The relevant 'bodily function' that is impaired (i.e. the disablement) must therefore be identified with sufficient particularity so that the assistance reasonably required can be identified and assessed; and this is why 'bodily function' cannot be given a definition so wide as to include all human activity or indeed any particularly complex activity. This is therefore another reflection of the close relationship

between functional disablement and the assistance reasonably required to cope with that disablement referred to in paragraph 9 above of identifying the relevant bodily functions given above.

39. However, even where an activity is such that it cannot itself properly be described as a bodily function, that will not be the end of the matter—because recourse will then have to be had to the discrete bodily functions which are involved in the activity and the extent to which they are impaired, and particularly as to whether the functions or any of them are so impaired that assistance to the level of any of the provisions of section 72 is required in respect of the disablement. In these circumstances, the relevant discrete bodily functions will have to be identified and 'unbundled', considered and assessed. Indeed, given the purpose 36–37), in functionally complex activities which may be borderline, we regard this 'unbundling' exercise as the correct approach in any event, and warn against the temptation of considering in very fine detail whether the complex activity can truly be described as a single bodily function or not. We consider the potential dangers of such an arid exercise are well illustrated in this very case. As the various House of Lords opinions referred to above (but notably that of Lord Slynn in *Cockburn*) make clear, in borderline cases it cannot be incorrect to unbundle functions in this way, and it is likely to be helpful in approaching the issue of assistance reasonably required."

The Commissioners then go on to point out that just identifying a bodily function that is deficient so as to need assistance, is not a sufficient condition to qualify for DLA. It will remain necessary, as well, to show that the assistance has the requisite degree of intimacy, and also that it satisfies one of the tests as to frequency, constancy, etc.

Applying all this to the facts of the present case the Commissioners found it to be an error of law to say that communication was not a bodily function. It was necessary, they say, to "unbundle" that word and examine what the claimant's difficulty in communicating was caused by. Clearly elements such as hearing, seeing and speaking can qualify for assistance and now we can say also, in the light of their decision above, comprehending, thinking and concentrating. Cases that have held to the contrary were disapproved. Similarly, social integration needed to be unbundled so as to analyse the parts with which the claimant required assistance. Where these could be identified as requiring assistance in the form of close personal care and attention to particular mental processes the claimant may be regarded as requiring assistance with bodily functions. The case was referred to a fresh tribunal for further consideration of the evidence.

1.210

The cases that were overruled in *R(DLA)1/07* concerned claimants who were described as having Asperger's syndrome. It seems now that that condition may qualify for benefit if the assistance given can be identified as relating to a bodily function when communicating and social integration are appropriately unbundled and if that assistance otherwise satisfies the statutory requirements. Decision *R(DLA) 3/03*, in which an Asperger's claimant had also been refused, was distinguished on the ground that there the claimant was capable of communicating without assistance and the fact that he did so in a manner that might be different, did not qualify the assistance given as being assistance in connection with a bodily function.

1.211

A three judge court of the UT has resolved the differences that had arisen in cases concerning claimants who suffered from dyslexia. In several cases such claims had succeeded while in others they were rejected. In some of the successful cases the bodily function for which attention was necessary was said to be "seeing" while in others it was held to be a malfunction of the brain. Those claims which had failed, did so on the ground either, that the attention given was for education rather than assistance with any disability, or that it was attention that was provided already out of public funds and could not, therefore, have been intended by parliament to qualify for an award of DLA. All of these points have been dealt with by the UT in *KM v SSWP (DLA)* [2013] UKUT 159 (AAC); [2014] AACR 2. The claimant was a child who was dyslexic, but also suffered from a syndrome that causes difficulty in dealing with fine visual tasks.

The UT quote extensively from the earlier decisions and give detailed advice to the FTT to whom the case would be returned, but in essence they confirm that there is no need to distinguish between the function of seeing and other brain functions—the important point is to determine whether the claimant requires the requisite level of attention because of some mental or physical disability whatever the label that might be attached to it. They reject the argument that attention given in helping the claimant to learn to read cannot qualify for DLA. It will all depend upon the basis of facts that are found by the FTT. It may be necessary to distinguish between the claimant and a slow learner, but that will depend upon finding the necessary disability in the functioning of his seeing/brain processes as well as making a comparison with help that may be required by children of a similar age but without that disability.

The UT rejects the suggestion that care provided by publicly funded bodies cannot be included in the DLA claim. They refer to regs 8 and 9 of the DLA Regulations (which remove the *payability* of benefit when the claimant is in a publicly funded care-home or a hospital) as demonstrating that he otherwise is *entitled*. They point out that much of the care that is received by claimants must come from care workers provided by the social services departments of local authorities because not all claimants will have family and friends able and willing to provide necessary help.

In *BM v SSWP (DLA)* [2015] UKUT 18 (AAC); [2015] AACR 29 (discussed more fully below—see *Subs 1A*) Judge Markus has made clear that the decision in *KM* is applicable in all cases of learning disability. In the case of *BM* the FTT had declined to consider the extra attention required by a child in learning at school because, they said, it was not a case of dyslexia as *KM* had been. Judge Markus explains that the reasoning of that case must apply in any case where the child's deficiency can be said to be associated with a bodily function. In *KM* it was the function of the brain in learning to read; in *BM*, where the child had difficulties with speech, it was the bodily function of speaking or, again, the function of the brain.

KM and *BM* emphasise the care that must be taken by DM and tribunals in finding the facts that are relevant before proceeding to the task of measuring them against the criteria for awarding DLA of either component and at any of the rates.

The UT in *KM* deals also with an associated argument that had been advanced by Judge May in *KG v SSWP* [2012] UKUT 222 (AAC). There he suggested that attention given by a medically qualified person could not be included in a claim for DLA. In that case the claimant had ulcers on his legs which were dressed daily by the district nurse. The UT in *KM* dealt with this argument only in general terms because it was not relevant to the case of the dyslexic child, but they do say that they see no reason in applying the words of the statute to make this distinction. Rather, they say, the matter should be determined by a careful consideration of the facts and the application then of the DLA criteria. Thus in the case of *KG* it appeared that the need for care arose because the ulcers required attention by a medically skilled person. There was no evidence that the claimant could not reach the ulcers himself (though he did need help with socks and shoes) and it followed that his need for care of the ulcers did not arise from his disability, but from lack of medical skill.

The activity of the brain as a bodily function was considered by Commissioner Mesher in *CA/2574/2007*. The claimant was an elderly widow who suffered from agoraphobia, anorexia and depression and had lived as a recluse since the death of her husband three years earlier. She was visited daily by her daughter who, in addition to taking care of all her mother's physical needs by way of shopping, housekeeping etc., also spent several hours each day providing stimulation and encouragement to her mother. The Commissioner allowed an appeal against the decision of a tribunal, who had failed to consider the latter involvement as attention in connection with the bodily function of brain activity, though he then went on to reject the claim in entering his own decision on the ground that she could not satisfy the more restricted requirements for AA. A claim for DLA at lowest rate (had she been younger) might have been successful.

1.212

After *Mallinson* and *Fairey* it is clear that a sense of physical intimacy will suffice and that physical contact is not necessary. Thus in the case of a blind man, guidance by words is sufficient and interpreting by sign language is sufficient for the deaf. In the case of *Cockburn* (reported as *R(A) 2/98*) it was accepted that some attention might even be given without the claimant being present so long as it was a continuance of attention that began in person (though this will now be limited by reg.10c of the DLA Regulations). In that case the claimant was both incontinent and arthritic. Help that was given in changing her bedclothes and wringing out wet sheets was all a part of the attention to her bodily functions, though this did not extend to doing her laundry for her the next day. Many services such as shopping, cooking and cleaning done for another would not count as attention, being too remote, but if these same activities are attempted by the claimant in person, with the carer providing assistance to them, for example reading labels to a blind claimant, or reaching items on the shelf for a physically disabled one, then they should qualify as attention in connecting with seeing and lifting respectively (*CDLA/3711/95* and *CDLA/12381/96* though there are conflicting Commissioners' decisions in *CSDLA/281/1996* and *CSDLA/314/1997*).

It needs to be borne in mind that there is still a distinction between attention in the sense of any assistance that is given to a disabled person to enable them to lead a normal life and "attention in connection with a bodily function". It is only that help which has the sufficient degree of closeness and intimacy with the claimant's person that will qualify. A useful examination of the criteria was made in *CDLA/8167/95*. There the claimant was a blind woman who was in receipt of the care component at the lowest rate. She applied for a review of her entitlement claiming the middle rate. In order to demonstrate the frequency with which she needed help from others she listed at least 17 occasions daily when she needed such assistance. These included checking that the food in her kitchen was fit to eat, that her appearance was acceptable and that her clothing was appropriate, as well as help with public transport, shopping, dealing with correspondence, domestic chores, gardening and, finally, cleaning up after her guide dog. The commissioner, allowing an appeal, rejected her claim on the basis that many of these actions were not sufficiently closely related to her bodily function of seeing. As he put it;

"If you have to tell another person they have gravy on their chin this is not an act of close personal contact or intimacy, whether they are sighted and have forgotten to look in the mirror or are blind and unable to do so. The required closeness of contact or intimacy only comes if the degree and nature of the disability means that you also have to do something like guiding their arm or standing over them to help with the applying of a wet cloth to their face, without which they could not reasonably cope with such a personal thing for themselves. Steering a blind person across the road or on to a bus or helping them to read their own correspondence all count, as these actions have been accepted by the House of Lords to involve the required degree of contact or intimacy beyond what is ordinary between adult human beings apart from the disability. So has enabling a deaf person to conduct a conversation with someone else by taking part in it for them as an interpreter. Again the help involves what would ordinarily be an intrusion into the personal space and privacy of the individual. On the other hand merely telling a blind person about their appearance, helping them choose matching clothes to put on, helping them locate things they have put down somewhere, telling them whether the carpet is hovered properly, a picture hung straight or the windows smeary, all things readily acceptable as reasonably required to help deal with their disability in the course of leading a normal life, are not things that appear to me self-evidently to have the special character of personal contact or intimacy which the House of Lords has expressly confirmed is essential for 'attention'."

The distinction is not, he says, between household duties and other tasks—even **1.213** help with domestic duties may qualify—but what is important, in his words, is that the attention should be given to the blind person so as to enable them to do the housework, rather than that housework is done for them. But the importance of a close enough connection between the claimant's disability and the assistance needed has been reasserted by the Court of Appeal in *Secretary of State for Work and Pensions v Batty* [2005] EWCA Civ 1746 *R(A) 1/06*. The claimant, who was severely restricted by arthritis, could not carry a drink of any kind from a place where it was prepared to a place where it might conveniently be consumed. She therefore needed someone's assistance every time she wished to have a drink both at home and at work, where she was able to work at her desk. The Commissioner who had found in her favour did so on the basis that, short of standing at the sink every time she needed a drink, she could not live a reasonably normal life without such assistance. The Court of Appeal, however, returned to the basics of earlier decisions such as Packer and decided that while helping a claimant to drink was clearly attention in connection with a bodily function, bringing a drink to them was not. And see too *CSA/694/2007* where it was held that assistance given to a blind claimant with her correspondence could qualify whereas assistance in driving her to social and other events would not.

A more recent attempt to extend the scope of assistance to include any support that might enable the claimant to lead a normal life was rejected in *CDLA/3376/2005*, but the decision still demonstrates the breadth of activities for which assistance may be required and can qualify the claimant for the care component. It also demonstrates the correct approach to be adopted to the question by tribunals. The claimant, who was blind from birth, had been allowed mobility component at the lower rate and care component at the lowest rate. She appealed against a refusal to grant the care component at a higher rate. The appeal tribunal, who rejected that appeal, did so by approaching the list of activities for which she claimed she needed assistance as falling into a category of domestic activities for which no assistance could qualify. The decision of Commissioner Jacobs demonstrates the error in this approach. The decisions of the House of Lords in *Cockburn* (reported as *R(A) 2/98*) and the Court of Appeal in *Ramsden (R(DLA) 2/03)* make clear that the only limiting device on the range of activities to be considered is whether it is reasonable for the claimant to experience that as part of a normal family and community life. (Together with the fact that the assistance given must be sufficiently intimate and personal to qualify.) In this case the Commissioner accepted that help given to the claimant to assist her in doing her own shopping, laundry and housework could all qualify for the benefit. This decision was made before the decision in *R(DLA)1/07T*, and it may be useful to counter the impression that could be given by that decision that shopping, dressing etc could not be considered as the subject of assistance (see paras36 and 37 above). What is said there is that shopping, for example, should not itself be regarded as a bodily function for which assistance is given. Quite so, but the bodily function, in this case, would be seeing, for which assistance is given in connection with the reasonable activity of shopping.

In the case of the claimants who are mentally disabled the appropriate "bodily function" is of course, thinking; this is confirmed in *CDLA/2974/2004*.

1.214   The Court of Appeal gave further consideration to this phrase in *Ramsden v Secretary of State for Work and Pensions* [2003] EWCA Civ 32, R(DLA) 2/03. The claimant, aged twelve, was faecally incontinent as a result of spina bifida, but for psychological reasons did not wear incontinence pads. He soiled himself once or twice a day and required attention from his mother in cleaning him up in a bath and shower, and also cleaning up the clothes, towels, bedding, carpets, furniture and other surfaces that had been fouled. On a renewal claim the AO refused to renew and that decision was upheld by a tribunal. The tribunal took into account the washing of the claimant, and the rinsing of his soiled clothing, bedding, etc, but specifically excluded any time spent in laundering the clothing etc as required, in their view, by the decision in *Cockburn*. The tribunal made no overt reference to the time spent cleaning carpets, furniture, and other surfaces, though, in the proceedings that followed, it was assumed that that time, too, was excluded on the basis that it was not sufficiently closely connected with the child's bodily function. A Commissioner upheld the tribunal decision.

The Court of Appeal, in allowing the appeal, reviewed thoroughly the speeches in *Cockburn*. That case, they concluded, recognised that certain acts of attendance performed by way of cleaning-up after an incident of incontinence could qualify as acts of attendance for the purpose of this benefit. Potter L.J., giving the first judgment continued:

> "Within the constraints of the requirement that such cleaning-up should take place in the presence or the vicinity of the applicant, I consider that steps taken for the **immediate** removal of soiling from clothes, towels or bed linen or adjacent surfaces are apt to qualify under this head. In a case of faecal incontinence which results in the soiling of clothes, towels or bed linen, or the dropping or smearing of faeces on carpets or furniture, it is at the very least in the interests of hygiene that such occurrences be rectified immediately as a part and parcel of the cleaning-up operation necessary following the incident of incontinence giving rise to such soiling. If that is done, then, even if the operation concerned is one of thorough washing rather than merely 'rinsing', the criteria of immediacy and intimacy are sufficiently satisfied and the time spent in cleaning-up should be taken into account when assessing whether or not the attention given amounts to a significant portion of the day".

The court returned the case to a fresh tribunal to consider whether the attention amounted to "a significant portion of the day". On that point, too, they take a flexible view of what is meant by "significant". (See below.)   1.215

Giving support and encouragement to someone who is severely disabled by phobias, depression and paranoid illnesses has now been held to be attention in connection with bodily functions. With that support the claimant was able to get up from bed, to cook, to eat properly, and generally to take care of herself so as to create a reasonable quality of life (*CDLA/1148/97*). This was a re-hearing of the case after an appeal to the Court of Appeal. The other point held by the Commissioner in this case, that such care could be provided over the telephone, has been short lived. Its effect was reversed by reg.10c of DLA regulations (and reg.8BA of the AA regulations). But see *CDLA/4333/2004* noted after that regulation. Support and encouragement has also been held to qualify as attention when it is given to a person suffering from obsessive compulsive disorder (OCD), to encourage him to desist from his behaviour. In *CDLA/618/2006* the claimant had been awarded the lowest rate of care component because his obsessive need to wash and clean himself, or his equipment, effectively prevented him from accomplishing the task of cooking a meal. But the Commissioner considered that, as well, he might qualify for care component at the middle rate, if he could show that encouragement for the purpose of dissuading him from his compulsive behaviour was necessary. On the facts of this case, however, he held that there was no evidence that such encouragement would have assisted him. Attention in soothing a person to sleep (at least in the case of a child) has been held to be attention in connection with a bodily function so long as the difficulty in sleeping is connected with a physical or mental disability (*CSDLA/567/2005*).

There are conflicting decisions on whether the preparation of meals that involve a   1.216 special diet with careful control of the ingredients for illnesses such as pheylketonuria, or even diabetes, could qualify as attention in connection with a bodily function. In *R(A) 1/87* the Commissioner held that the extra care and attention required over and above that of normal cooking made a difference, but in *CSDLA/160/95* that decision was disapproved of on the ground that it had not referred to the concept of intimacy as required in *Woodling*.

With regard to the attention that is given to a deaf person by someone using sign language when the *Fairey* case was before Commissioner Sanders (*CA/780/91*) he drew a distinction between someone communicating with a claimant who is deaf by the use of sign language when they are acting as an interpreter to a third party, and when they are not. In the former, the interpreter is clearly providing attention to the claimant in connection with the bodily function of hearing and speaking; in the latter he may be merely holding a conversation with the claimant in the language in which they are both comfortable. The Commissioner seems to have been saying that merely because the signing might be slower or involve more effort than oral communication for both of them, it could not, for that reason alone, be regarded as "attention". Thus a conversation between the claimant and his wife using sign language about ordinary domestic matters would not be "attention" but his wife communicating those matters to a visitor would be. What subsequently emerged in the Court of Appeal, and was not criticised in the House of Lords, was that this did not preclude the possibility that an attendant who had to use physical contact to make the claimant aware, or "if the person giving the attention . . . has to do extra work, or take extra time, away from the attendant's ordinary duties to help the disabled person that may, as a question of fact, qualify as attention". This much seems clear from two decisions of Commissioner Sanders, himself (*CDLA/17189/96* and *CDLA/15884/96*), where he draws these conclusions from what was said in the Court of Appeal. The same formulation has been approved by another Commissioner in *CDLA/16668/96* and again, after a very full consideration, in *R(DLA) 1/02*. In a similar case (*R(DLA) 2/02*) Commissioner Levenson, after careful consideration of all the authorities, has suggested the following propositions as representing the current law:

- the operation of the senses is a bodily function and a defect in the senses leads to disability in connection with which attention might be required;
- the test is whether the attention is reasonably required to enable the severely disabled person as far as reasonably possible to live a normal life;
- the aggregate of attention that is reasonably required includes such attention as may enable the claimant to carry out a reasonable level of social activity;
- what is reasonable will depend on the age, sex, interests of the applicant and other circumstances;
- how much attention is reasonably required and how frequently it is required are questions of fact;
- attention in connection with bodily functions includes unusual efforts reasonably required to attract the attention of the deaf person in order to communicate with her. Unusual in this context means steps that are not or would not be required in respect of attracting the attention of a person in the same environment who is not deaf;
- a person is not providing attention when communicating with a deaf claimant by means of reasonably fluent signing unless communication is particularly slow and difficult;
- if communicating through an interpreter is significantly more efficient or effective than communicating through writing, or trying to converse with a person who has to shout loudly, then it might well be that the services of an interpreter are reasonably required even if initiating the communication or conducting a two-way conversation does not itself constitute attention;
- help required to undertake activities other than those "concerned with the relatively mundane everyday activities of functioning as a human being in ordinary life" does not count as attention for these purposes;
- although, in order to count as attention, any service provided must be of a close and intimate nature involving personal contact carried out in the presence of a disabled person, in the case of a deaf person this includes communication between that person and an interpreter;
- for these purposes there is no significant difference between the interpretation of the written word and the interpretation of speech.

With the possible proviso that a decision-maker must remember that "communicating with" is not the same thing as "interpreting for" (which will always be attention) these points seem unexceptionable.

1.217

Two Commissioners' decisions return to the question of the extra effort required
to communicate with a deaf person, and the extra effort that may be required to
initiate communication with them. In *R(DLA) 3/02*, Commissioner Fellner had
to consider the case of a pre-lingually deaf person, now of middle age, who had
completed City & Guilds qualifications, and worked as a foreman joiner on building sites and other places. She allowed an appeal against a decision awarding only
lowest rate care component (on the grounds of inadequate facts and reasons) but
substituted her own decision also at the lowest rate.

In doing so she accepted the law developed in the decisions cited above, including, generally, the points made by Commissioner Levenson, but with the *caveat*
that the extra effort involved both in effecting two-person communication, and
in attracting the attention of a person for that communication must be something
more than de minimis. It must also be more than would be required to communicate with a hearing person in like circumstances. While she emphasises that these
matters must always be ones for the decision-maker on the basis of the particular
facts found by them, she suggests that tapping the shoulder, stamping a foot,
flashing a light or throwing a paper ball, might all be regarded as so minimal as not
to count on this basis. Similarly, though the claimant probably required people to
go to him to communicate in the workplace, the same would be true of a hearing
person doing that job because of the general level of noise on a building site. The
Commissioner suggests the same may be true of many instances of initiating communication in the home—even hearing-able people may need to be contacted
by going to them when they are cooking, watching television or doing DIY. The
Commissioner suggested that the fact-finding stage of the decision process should
begin with the claimant's need for attention in relation to his current level of activity, and then go on to explore further needs for attention based upon the "wish
list" suggested by the claimant. But in doing so the decision-maker must approach
the claimant's declared aspirations with a robust sense of what would be feasible,
realistic and practicable as well as the established (but not very helpful) test of what
is reasonable.

In this case, for example, she thought it would not be feasible for the claimant
to have someone read the newspaper and magazines to him, given the time that it
would take and the pattern of his existing daily life. Again, she thought it would be
unrealistic to suggest that the claimant might accept the presence of an interpreter in
the home, every evening, to help him watch television programmes without subtitles,
and impractical to suggest that an interpreter could assist at the cinema (because of
darkness) or on a building site (because of danger and unfamiliarity). She did not
accept that an interpreter could attend work site meetings and that his services would
be justified to replace the extra time and effort that was currently spent in communicating with the claimant. This is a useful case for decision-makers because it goes a
long way to explore some of the practical application of the legal principles.

1.218

In the other case, *R(A) 1/03*, Commissioner Parker allowed an appeal against
refusal of the lower rate of Attendance Allowance. (The claimant was over 65 at
the date of his first claim although he was pre-lingually deaf, probably from birth.)
The appeal was allowed for more than one reason, one of them being that the
tribunal had discounted the assistance that the claimant already received from a
centre for sensory impaired people. Commissioner Parker follows both the decision of Commissioner Levenson, *CDLA/3433/1999*, and that of Commissioner
Fellner, *CDLA/1534/00*, above. In doing so she accepts the latter's constraint that
the extra effort involved either in communication or attracting attention must be
more than *de minimus*, but she reconciles this to some extent with Commissioner
Levenson by drawing attention to his point that the extra effort in communicating,
once it is significant, may justify a need for an interpreter which then will qualify
as attention.

In *EG* v *SSWP* [2009] UKUT 112 (AAC) Judge Ward upheld the appeal of a deaf claimant who could lip-read, but only in Polish, and who therefore required the services of a translator in order to communicate. The First-tier Tribunal had rejected her appeal on the ground that her need arose from a language difficulty rather than from her hearing difficulty. The judge held that this was wrong; her inability to communicate arose at least for a reasonable period, from her inability to hear. Until such time as she might reasonably be expected to develop the skill of lip-reading in English, she would need the services of a translator. (The judge recognises that there might be a real difficulty in learning to associate the movements of the mouth with the meaning of words in English.)

It is also clear from *Mallinson* that a claimant may receive attention in connection with a bodily function even though that bodily function is completely inoperative. A person who is totally blind, for example, receives attention in connection with the bodily function of sight when his guide provides a substitute method of seeing and assistance given to a person by pushing them in a manual wheelchair when they are unable to walk or to move the wheelchair by themselves, is attention given in connection with the function of walking—see *SJ* v *SSWP* [2014] UKUT 222 (AAC).

In *CDLA/2333/2005* Commissioner Mesher holds that care in the form of supervision for the purpose of walking outside (mobility component) counts also for the purpose of attention or supervision of the bodily function of walking in the care components. This is not surprising because it is simply the converse of *R(DLA) 4/01*, but is a point that deserves to be noted.

And see too the decision in *DN v SSWP (DLA)* [2016] 233 (AAC), where the claimant's age of only four years precluded attention given to him when walking outside qualifying in respect of the lower rate of the mobility component, but should nevertheless have been taken into account when considering his entitlement to the care component.

THE LOWEST RATE CONDITIONS

1.219   In order to claim benefit at the lowest rate the claimant must show that he satisfies one or other, or both, of the conditions in subs.(1)(a).

1.220   *Attention for a significant portion of the day:* To qualify under para.(a)(i) the claimant must show that he requires attention in connection with his bodily functions for a *significant portion of the day*. In *CDLA/205/2005* it appeared to the Commissioner that the tribunal had before it evidence of how long it took the claimant to do things for himself, but not how long it might have taken, were assistance to be given. The Commissioner points out that it is the latter which is relevant to the question of whether attention is for a significant portion of the day. How long things took for the claimant to do for himself might, however, be relevant to the question of whether he required assistance in the first place. This phrase has now been considered by the Court of Appeal in *Ramsden v Secretary of State for Work and Pensions* [2003] EWCA Civ 32 reported as *R(DLA) 2/03*. This case determines that the meaning of the word "day" is to be consistent with the time remaining as a residue of 24 hours when the "night" has been accounted for as in *R. v National Insurance Commissioner Ex p. Secretary of State for Social Services* [1974] 1 W.L.R. 1290; in other words it is the period between the time when the household becomes active in the morning and when its members finally retire to bed at night. The earlier suggestion in *CDLA/1463/99* that "day" should mean the whole 24 hour period is thus overruled. While this undoubtedly is the better interpretation of the section it does seem to work unjustly in the case of a claimant who requires some, though not significant, attention, during the day and one, far more disruptive, event at night, because, unless the night time attention is prolonged or repeated, it appears that that attention cannot be accounted for at all. On the other hand, of course, by limiting the time period of day it does become easier for the claimant to show that his day time attention is significant as a proportion of that period.

The Court of Appeal also considers what should be regarded as a "significant portion" of a day and they endorse the view that the phrase should be interpreted so as to make a "broad determination" of the question. Lord Justice Potter, giving the leading judgment, accepts that the task for the tribunal is principally a mathematical exercise involving comparison of the aggregate of time spent in giving attention, with the day as a whole. But he continues,

> "However it is also likely to be affected by the total time available in the day, by the extent to which the relevant tasks become a matter of routine, and the concentration and intensity of the activity comprised in those tasks. Thus while in broad terms it seems to me that a period of one hour, made up of two half-hour periods [of] concentrated activity, would reasonably be regarded as a significant portion of a day, in different circumstances there may well be room for a different view".

This passage is followed by one in which Potter L.J. expressly approves the reasoning in *CSDLA/29/94* in which Commissioner Walker puts forward the view that the day, and the "significant portion" of it, must be assessed from the position of the attender. In that case the Commissioner had held that even a lesser period than an hour might be significant if it consisted of many short periods that so broke up the day of the attender that for *them* the total, represented a greater inconvenience that the arithmetic sum of time might suggest. He also suggested that the tribunal should take a broad determination to record the total portion or percentage of the normal day that was involved for this household. Combining this with the decision of the Court of Appeal it would seem now possible to argue that, for an attender with an especially long and busy day, the time spent attending does become significant when it might not be for someone who was otherwise largely idle. For the busy attender, the time spent attending is significant because without it their day might seem already full, or, again, if the tasks required are arduous and physically or mentally demanding the time spent becomes significant because the effect of those tasks may be to exhaust the attender. For him or her their "day" (in the sense of what is achievable) would be largely used up. On the other hand if the tasks become routine and can be fitted in to the attender's regular daily pattern of life they will offer less inconvenience and may become a less than significant part of their "day". 1.221

As to the "one-hour" rule of thumb used by many tribunals and referred to in the Parlimentary debates, this case makes clear that there is no such minimum period–*CDLA/58/93* must to that extent be overruled. While, no doubt, tribunals may still choose to centre their thinking around a total time period of an hour, it is now clear that they must reach their decision on the basis of their own common sense and judgment of what is significant and explain that in their reasoning.

The Cooking Test

With the introduction of PIP the need for this test will diminish. It is not available as a basis of qualification by persons under 16 and will remain viable only for those who are in receipt of DLA when they reach retirement age or, in the case of a new claim, a woman who claims between that age and when she reaches 65. 1.222

To qualify under para.(a)(ii) the claimant has to show that he cannot prepare a cooked main meal for himself. This enables some claimants to qualify who are otherwise excluded from the care component because the provision of meals by another is not attention in connection with a bodily function (*Re Woodling*). Note that the claimant is assumed to have the ingredients to hand, which eliminates any need for help with planning and shopping. It is not sufficient for the claimant to say that he has never cooked and is unwilling to learn (see *R. v Secretary of State for Social Security Ex p. Armstrong*, (1996) 8 Admin. L.R. 626, CA) but a claimant cannot be expected to learn to cook if his mental condition is such that he is incapable of learning (*CDLA/2457/97*).

In *Moyna v Secretary of State for Work and Pensions* [2003] 4 All E.R. 162, *R(DLA) 7/03*, the House of Lords have confirmed that the cooking test is one of overall impression to be reached by tribunals by a general approach rather than by fixed rules. The case dealt with the vexed question of claimants whose ability to cook was sporadic. In that case the claimant was unable to prepare herself a main meal on at least one day every week, and in some weeks she was incapable on as many as three days. A tribunal had found that this did not mean that she was unable to cook for herself and the Commissioner, to whom she appealed, upheld that decision because he could find no error of law in it. The Court of Appeal disagreed. They thought that someone who could not prepare a meal on a regular and not infrequent basis could not be said to be capable of cooking, and to decide that they were, would be an error of law. The House of Lords restored the decision of the Commissioner; the test, they say, is a general one of overall impression and whilst others might disagree with the conclusion reached, that would not be an error of law.

But this does leave us in some difficulty, for if the tribunal had found initially that Mrs Moyna was not capable of cooking then, it would seem, that that too, would have been a decision that was properly made and could not be reviewed as an error of law. This does nothing to assist tribunals hearing appeals in the case of claimants whose abilities fluctuate within the nine month period for qualification. The House of Lords make clear that the test is not one of frequency (only the claim form for the benefit introduces the matter of the number of days on which the claimant is unable to cook a meal) and they make clear also that it never has been the case that a claimant's inability to cook must be total throughout the qualifying period, but beyond that their Lordships leave it to the good sense of tribunals to decide whether a claimant is capable of cooking, by "taking 'a broad view' of the matter and making a judgment". It is, they say "an exercise in judgment rather than in arithmetical calculation of frequency".

1.223   Past cases on the cooking test must all now be approached with some caution. The emphasis of the House of Lords reasoning makes these decisions essentially ones of fact for the tribunal. The approach to be adopted is demonstrated in *R(DLA) 2/05*. The Commissioner there upholds a decision by the tribunal in which they assessed her ability to cook, directly from what she told them of what she did do, and, indirectly from what they concluded she could not do on the basis of her evidence, and inferences drawn from her general condition. In that case the tribunal had decided that the claimant was capable of cooking a meal.

The "cooking test" was considered at length in *R(DLA) 2/95*, where the Commissioner said:

". . . In my view the 'cooking test' is a hypothetical test to be determined objectively. Factors such as the type of facilities or equipment available and a claimant's cooking skills are irrelevant.

8. The nature of the 'cooked main meal' which the claimant 'cannot prepare' is crucial. In my view it is a labour intensive reasonable main daily meal freshly cooked on a traditional cooker. What is reasonable is a question of fact to be determined by reference to what is reasonable for a member of the community to which the claimant belongs, e.g. a vegetarian meal as opposed to one which is not. The use of the phrase 'for himself' shows that the meal is intended to be just for one person, not for the whole family. The 'main meal' at issue is therefore a labour intensive, main reasonable daily meal for one person, not a celebration meal or a snack. The main meal must be cooked on a daily basis and it is irrelevant that a claimant may prepare, cook and freeze a number of main meals on the days that help is provided and then defrost and heat them in a microwave on subsequent days. The test depends on what a claimant cannot do without help on each day. Because the main meal has to be cooked, the test includes all activities auxiliary to the cooking such as reaching for a saucepan, putting water in it and lifting it on and off the cooker. All cooking utensils must of course be placed in a reasonable position.

9. The word 'prepare' emphasises a claimant's ability to make all the ingredients ready for cooking. This includes the peeling and chopping of fresh vegetable as opposed to frozen vegetables, which require no real preparation. However in my

view a chop, a piece of fish or meat ready minced does not fall in the category of 'convenience foods' and are permissible as basic ingredients. I should add for completeness that because the test is objective it is irrelevant that a claimant may never wish to cook such a meal or that it is considered financially impossible."

The phrase used in this decision "what is reasonable for a member of the community to which the claimant belongs" has been criticised in *AI v SSWP* [2015] UKUT 176 (AAC). It was argued in that case that allowance should be made for the fact that it would take longer for the claimant to cook a meal of Nigerian style food that would be appropriate for the community to which he belonged. This argument was rejected by Judge Mitchell in the UT; he thought the nature of the meal must be the same for all claimants for, otherwise, "different claimants would face different disability thresholds". In his view that could not have been the intention of Parliament. He thought that a standard which took account of ethnic or religious differences was inconsistent with what had been said in *Moyna* where the emphasis had been placed on a "notional test, a thought experiment, to calibrate the severity of the disability". Although Judge Mitchell concedes that there could be different notional meals for different communities he rejects that idea because the test is simply to "calibrate disability" rather than to ensure "access to a reasonable daily meal". He also went on to reject an argument that a single standard discriminated against the claimant under the Human Rights Act. Although the emphasis on a single standard is understandable it could be argued that a decision that requires the claimant to adopt a diet that is quite unknown to him, because that is all that he is capable of cooking, is also objectionable. Section 72(1)(a)(ii) does require that the claimant is unable to cook a meal "for himself"- that could be said to mean not only that it is a meal for one person, but that it is a meal that is suitable for that person. Taking account of the claimant's community will not necessarily mean that a lower standard of disability is adopted; it might, in an appropriate case, mean that the claimant is capable of cooking the food that is appropriate for their ethnic community when they were, at the same time, incapable of cooking what has been regarded in this country as "traditional food". The test in *Moyna* laid emphasis on a broad common-sense approach to be adopted by tribunals. Perhaps the answer lies in that approach- it is hard to see that a person well accustomed to their own cuisine could not, by appropriate adjustments and adaptations, manage to cook those meals when disabled only to the same extent as those who qualified in other communities.

The meaning of "preparing" a main meal has been explored further in *HJ v SSWP* [2013] UKUT 613 (AAC). The claimant suffered from several conditions one of which prevented her from peeling and cutting root vegetables. The question that arose (amongst other points) was whether that meant that she was incapable of cooking a main meal. On behalf of the secretary of state it was argued that modern habits of retailing fresh vegetables included the presentation of ready-prepared vegetables which could be used by the claimant. Presumably this argument sought to equate ready-prepared vegetables with the minced meat mentioned in *R/DLA 2/95*, rather than a packet of frozen peas, but Judge Jupp rejected it on the basis that to adopt the change in modern marketing methods as a sufficient explanation could open the door to a whole range of ready prepared meals that would require only to be heated before eating. Instead the judge sidestepped this argument by holding (a) that not all meals need involve the use of root vegetables—what is required is a reasonable variety of wholesome foods, and (b) that in any case root vegetables could be cooked first, in their skins, and cut up afterwards when they were softened by the cooking process. The case was returned to the FTT for a new decision on this and other points.

In *CDLA/2267/95*, the Commissioner said:

"It cannot be overstressed that the 'main meal' at issue is a main reasonable daily meal for *one* person. It follows that the use of heavy pans or dishes is not necessary for the preparation of such a meal. Nor is it necessary to use the oven. If the claimant is unable to stand for any length of time, such a meal can be prepared and cooked while sitting on a high stool or chair if necessary. It is all a question of what is reasonable in the circumstances of the case."

1.224   Two Commissioners' decisions give further consideration to the "cooking test". The first (*CDLA/5686/1999*) is a decision of Mr Commissioner Rowland. In it he confirms that the test is abstract in the sense of being unrelated to the claimant's ability, inclination or even need to cook a meal, but that it may take account of devices and stratagems that the claimant might have available to him. This was a case where the claimant used sticks to get about the home, and was unable to bend. The Commissioner confirmed earlier decisions to the effect that it was unnecessary to be able to use the oven by bending. The adjudication officer had allowed the claim on the basis that the claimant could not manage safely in lifting pans of hot water, etc. The claimant appealed in an attempt to get the middle rate of benefit and the tribunal decided that he was not entitled to even the lowest rate because he could use a slotted spoon to remove food from a hot pan and empty the pan safely when it had cooled. The Commissioner's decision upholds this reasoning although he did allow the appeal on the facts of this case.

The other decision, *CDLA/770/2000*, is a decision of Commissioner Fellner, and makes a thorough investigation of the background and application, to date, of the cooking test. The claimant in this case was a middle-aged man who had been injured in a road accident and left with an unstable knee joint on which he had to wear a brace and walked with the support of a stick. Although he assisted his wife in the kitchen she would not leave him to prepare and cook a main meal because she thought there was a danger of him stumbling, dropping hot containers, and injuring himself.

The claimant had been refused benefit on a renewal decision and the tribunal that heard his appeal also concluded that he did not satisfy the cooking test. They said he could use the microwave and sit down while cooking. The Commissioner seems to have regarded these reasons as inadequate and the appeal was allowed and sent back for re-hearing by a fresh tribunal. The Commissioner's survey of the decisions on cooking begins by pointing to the divergence that has arisen between those Commissioners who have regarded the test as almost entirely objective (e.g. *R(DLA) 2/95* and *CDLA/2293/95* where a wheelchair user whose kitchen had been specially adapted so that she could cook her own meals, nevertheless qualified on the basis that she could not have cooked in an ordinary kitchen) and those Commissioners who have admitted subjective elements so that the use of special devices and adaptations, if available to the claimant, may deprive them of benefit by showing that the claimant is in fact able to cook a main meal.

1.225   The Commissioner accepted the invitation of the parties to look at parliamentary material in determining the "intention" of Parliament in inventing the cooking test. She accepted that this material showed that what was intended was a purely objective test akin to that adopted subsequently for Incapacity Benefit. Nevertheless, she rejected this interpretation because in her view the wording of s.72 was not ambiguous so as to require, or entitle, her to have regard to the parliamentary material.

Without it she was clear that the words of the statute, "cannot prepare a cooked main meal", meant a test that took account of what the claimant could in fact do for himself given the provision of reasonably available special devices and the adoption of special stratagems. The touchstone, she thought, was a reasonable compromise between what able cooks might do and what a disabled claimant might be expected to do. Thus, sitting to prepare food could be expected even though an able cook might prefer to stand; the use of food from tins and jars and the use of reasonable devices to open them was also acceptable (though the use of frozen vegetables and the reheating of meals previously prepared by, or with the help of, others had been rejected in earlier decisions and remains outside the range of acceptable stratagems). The disabled cook could be expected to avoid particularly dangerous procedures, such as deep fat frying; oven chips were a reasonable alternative. The kitchen should be organised so that items and utensils were readily to hand. Where the claimant suffered from achondroplasia, a condition that restricted his height and meant that he had especially short arms and legs, it was held (in *CDLA/4351/2006*) that the availability of a "Baby Belling" cooker and a microwave, on which he could cook a main meal, meant the claim should fail.

The time taken by the claimant over preparing a meal may also be relevant in deciding whether they are capable of cooking themselves a meal (*CDLA/4051/2007*). But this too must now be taken to be a matter of judgment for a tribunal to say whether a claimant can fairly be described as capable, and a strategy of resting between stages of meal preparation has been adopted as a sensible and acceptable mode of preparing a meal.

In *JF v SSWP (DLA)* [2012] UKUT 335 (AAC) Judge Rowland held that the size of the claimant's kitchen might be a relevant factor in applying this test. The claimant had said she was not able to sustain her weight on an arthritic knee for sufficient time to prepare a meal, to which the First-tier Tribunal had suggested that she should use a chair or "perching stool" in her kitchen. The claimant said her kitchen was too small to include such a device. The FTT rejected her appeal saying that the size of her kitchen was irrelevant to the question of whether she was capable of cooking a main meal. The judge allowed her appeal on the ground that the test must be applied in the context of the claimant's home, allowing for any modifications that were made, but allowing also for the limitations that it imposed.

There remains some doubt about the use of special devices—the Commissioner accepted that devices designed specially for the disabled would be outside the spirit of the legislation. But at what point does an ergonomically designed tin opener become one that is intended only for those who suffer from arthritis? Only the common sense of tribunals can save us! And finally what about the microwave? Microwaves used to reheat food as described above do not count, but (assuming the claimant does in fact have one) they may be taken account of when used to cook fresh vegetables, and otherwise as an ordinary cooking appliance. The use of a microwave oven as an ordinary means of cooking food that has been prepared by the claimant, rather than as a means of reheating meals prepared by others, has been accepted in *CDLA/2367/2004*.   1.226

Note too, the consideration given by Judge Rowland in *KS v SSWP* [2011] UKUT 29 (AAC) to the use of a slow-cooker as a means of preparing a meal. He explains that the use of a "traditional cooker" is not a requirement of the legislation. What is required is that the claimant is capable of producing a "cooked main meal" which might be described as a traditional meal (i.e. by preparing and cooking from raw ingredients) and a reasonable variety of meals, on the equipment that is available to him.

It is sufficient if the claimant can cook a sufficient number of dishes to provide a reasonable degree of variety to his diet (*CDLA/17329/96*). The test assumes the claimant will use the equipment available to him—devices and appliances that he does not have should be ignored (*R(DLA) 2/95*)—but where the claimant has such equipment there is no reason why the test should not assume that he will use them (*CDLA/17329/96*).

In *R(DLA) 1/97* it was held that the claimant was not entitled where he was capable of cooking a main meal (and did so) even though it involved risk to himself. The claimant could have succeeded only if that risk became unreasonable. The claimant was a haemophiliac for whom the process of preparing and cooking clearly presented extra risk. The Commissioner said: 1.227

"Clearly it takes the claimant rather longer to prepare a meal than it would for most people and clearly also he suffers some anxiety when he does so, but the fact remains that he can and does prepare traditional cooked main meals. To say that he acts unreasonably in doing so would be to imply that a person in his position acts reasonably only if he or she gives up traditional meals or cooking methods or has someone else cook such meals. It is not unreasonable for a person with a disability to try and pursue as normal a life as possible unless the risks involved in carrying out a particular task make it so. I do not think that the additional risk and associated anxiety involved in cooking, over and above the risk attending all the claimant's activities, justifies a finding that it is unreasonable to expect him to prepare a cooked main meal."

On the other hand where the claimant was prevented from cooking because heat from the cooker brought on an attack of asthma he was entitled to the benefit (*CDLA/20/94*). It was not suggested that his main meal might always be a cold meal of raw ingredients!

In *CDLA/1471/2004*, Commissioner Jacobs had to consider whether a risk of self-harming could cause the claimant to be unable to cook a main meal for himself, presumably because he could not be trusted to be in possession of sharp knives or, possibly, to have access to hot surfaces. An argument was put on behalf of the Secretary of State that, as the cooking test was of an hypothetical ability to cook, it was sufficient that the claimant could have been able to cook were he able to have the means to do so. The Commissioner rejects this argument. The test, he says, was hypothetical only in the sense that the claimant's need to cook, or his inclination to do so, were irrelevant in determining his ability to cook a main meal. In other words anything that derives from the claimant's mental or physical condition and prevents him from cooking can be a disability for this purpose and that includes the safety risk arising from a propensity for self-harm.

Where the claimant is unable to cook because of nausea brought on by the smell of cooking the claim should succeed so long as the nausea makes it unreasonable to expect the claimant to endure that experience. See *R(DLA) 1/08* in which the contrary view expressed in *CSDLA/854/2003* (discussed in earlier editions of this book) was rejected. A claimant who has lost their sense of smell, (and in this case their sense of taste also), is not for that reason to be regarded as unable to cook a main meal for themselves. In *CDLA 1984/2008* Judge Rowland thought that while such a person might have to adapt their behaviour by, for example, remaining in the kitchen to watch what was cooking rather than relying upon the smell of burning, and while they might also have to store food for less time to avoid the risk of using things that were unfit and could not be detected by their smell, he thought that such stratagems as these were a reasonable adaptation of a normal cook's behaviour so that a claimant would remain capable of cooking.

An inability to concentrate sufficiently to accomplish cooking tasks safely has been accepted, at least in principle, to be sufficient in *R(DLA) 6/05* and in *CSDLA/725/2004* Commissioner Parker has held that a lack of motivation to cook a main meal, if it derives from the claimant's physical or mental disability (and is not simply a manifestation of laziness), may be a basis upon which to award the benefit. In *DG v SSWP* [2013] UKUT 351 (AAC) the claimant suffered from several conditions one of which was chronic fatigue syndrome (CFS). The claimant was in work- it is unclear where he worked; it is possible that he worked at home. The claim under this heading was based upon the fact that although the claimant was capable of cooking a main meal, that by the time he had completed his work, he lacked the energy to do so. The FTT held that he was not incapable of cooking. In their view he should have prioritised his life so that he took care of himself first and devoted time and energy to his work afterwards. As the UT judge pointed out this came close to deciding that it was unreasonable for this claimant to work! The appeal was allowed and returned to a new FTT for rehearing. The judge accepted the argument advanced on behalf of the Secretary of State that the claimant might be expected to moderate his working effort to conserve energy for self care and that the new FTT would have to explore the nature and extent of the claimant's working arrangements, before deciding what was a proper work/care balance for him. Note that this is another case that demonstrates that although the cooking test is a test only of the claimant's hypothetical ability to cook, this means only that his willingness and his need to cook can be it ignored; it remains necessary to show that it is reasonable for that claimant, in his circumstances, to undertake the tasks of cooking.

In *CDLA/1572/2005* the claimant objected to the use, as evidence of his ability to cook, of the fact that he was capable of driving his motor car. While the Commissioner agreed that an ability to drive might not be much evidence of the claimant's grip and manual dexterity, he affirmed that it could be evidence of other relevant factors such as an ability to concentrate and to co-ordinate physical movements. Note that the cooking test route for qualification is not available to a person under 16 (subs.(6)(a)).

THE DAY CONDITIONS

In order to qualify for benefit at the middle rate a claimant must show that he qualifies under at least one of the conditions in subs.(1)(b) (the day conditions) or, at least one of the conditions under subs.(1)(c) (the night conditions) see below. Subsection (1)(b) provides two conditions either of which must be satisfied "throughout the day".

1.228

Frequent attention throughout the day: To satisfy para.(b)(i) the claimant must be shown to require "frequent attention throughout the day."

The meaning of "day" has been determined by the Court of Appeal in *Ramsden v SSWP* [2003] EWCA Civ 32 to mean that part of a period of 24 hours as is remaining after the "night" has been accounted for in relation to subs.(1)(c) below in accordance with *R v National Insurance Commissioner Ex p. Secretary of State for Social Services* [1974] 1 W.L.R. 1290. In other words "day" means that period between the time that the household becomes active in the morning and when its members retire to bed at night.

Frequent attention has been said to be "several times—not once or twice" (*per* Lord Denning M.R., *R. v National Insurance Commissioner Ex. p. the Secretary of State for Social Services*) and in *CA/281/89* the Commissioner held that the need should be "at intervals spread over the day".

In *CA/147/84* a child who required attention on four occasions spread approximately equally across the day was held not to qualify, but in *CA/1140/85* the Chief Commissioner stressed that even a person whose main attention was required at the beginning and end of each day could qualify so long as there were other events that required some brief attention during the day. The claimant was blind, and help in making tea, eating meals, putting on his coat and outdoor shoes qualified him even though he was largely self reliant once he had been got up and dressed each morning.

Commissioner's decision *CSDLA/590/00* considers the relationship between frequency of attention and the duration of that attention. It holds (as had *CDLA/12150/1996*) that the proper approach to frequency takes no account of the duration of attention, either in aggregate, or separately—except to exclude the instance of attention that is *de minimis* in the latter respect.

In this case the claimant was a five-year-old child with talipes of one foot. This caused him to fall between 5 and 10 times each day. In addition his mother had to manipulate his foot "several times" each day. The tribunal had rejected the claim on the basis that the need for attention did not amount to frequent attention throughout the day because it would amount to only, approximately, one hour in total during the day. Both representatives and the Commissioner thought this wrong. But the representative of the Secretary of State drew on *CSDLA/24/98* to suggest that the aggregate of attention time could be considered a factor in determining frequency. This seems to be a misinterpretation of that case where it seems the Commissioner was willing to uphold the decision because the tribunal had given its attention specifically to frequency as a separate issue in holding that four or five attendances were not frequent (although other cases have held that they can be).

In the present case the Commissioner accepts that entitlement depends solely

1.229

upon pattern and frequency and not the total duration. It may be that the thinking of the tribunal in this case, and in *CSDLA/24/1998*, was inspired by the thought that if attention amounting to no more than one hour per day could not qualify a claimant for the lowest rate of care component, it might seem odd that it should, nevertheless, qualify him for the middle rate if it were spread in small periods frequently throughout the day. This point is answered effectively in *CDLA/12150/1996* (and quoted again in this decision). In the first place it is the inevitable outcome of giving the different words their natural meaning and secondly it would be supported as a rational outcome if the cost of providing numerous instances of attention spread over the whole day were greater than fewer points at either end of it, as would seem likely to be the case.

But all this must now be considered in the light of *R(DLA) 5/05*. Judge G. R. Hickinbottom, the Chief Commissioner, has carried the approach to interpretation that was set by the House of Lords in *Moyna* across to the rest of the criteria for qualification for DLA care component in s.72(1). This means, he says, that decision makers and tribunals must take a broad view of the matter, reading the words of the section in their context so as to identify the correct legal test and then deciding each case as a question of fact according to whether it falls on one side or of that line of the other. Thereafter, an appeal on points of law could only interfere with their decision if either they have identified the wrong legal line or if they have reached a conclusion which is "outside the bounds of reasonable judgment", *i.e.* irrational.

1.230   Judge Hickinbottom goes on to point out that the oft quoted guidance taken from the judgment of Lord Denning in *R. v National Insurance Commissioner, Ex p. Secretary of State for Social Services* [1981] 1 W.L.R. 1017, on the meaning of these phrases, was not only obiter, but was only a limited attempt to identify some fairly obvious characteristics of the words used, and must not be regarded as providing anything like definitions—as he suggests commentators appear to have done. He also takes to task certain Commissioners for attempting to paraphrase the sections in alternative words to explain their meaning.

The test of "frequently throughout the day", he suggests, is not to be approached in two stages—how often and over what period—but is to be treated as a single composite impression. Again, frequency is not just a question of number, but may be affected by the nature and duration of the occurrences, thus disagreeing with Commissioner Parker in *CSDLA/590/2000*. By way of example he contrasts the meaning of frequent when used in relation to an ice age with its use in relation to a train timetable; or again, a long distance train service every hour might be regarded as frequent when an hourly local service was not. As well, he points out that, although the scheme of s.72(1) is not necessarily one of gradation, in as much as the qualifying conditions in each of the three paragraphs are quite distinct and different, the context requires a recognition that Parliament can hardly have intended that a claimant should qualify for the middle-rate benefit on a lesser requirement for care than was necessary to gain the lowest rate of benefit.

All of this makes good sense. But it may make things difficult for tribunals for two reasons. First, tribunals must give reasons to support their decision. Often, an attempt to explain a decision will consist of rephrasing the statute to explain the line the tribunal is taking. If tribunals are not to rephrase the section to explain what they take to be its meaning, will it suffice for a tribunal to say, e.g. "we find this to be frequent attention because we think it is"? Secondly, decisions that are treated as findings of fact and appealable to a Commissioner only when they are grossly unreasonable may result in inequitable chaos. For example, in one of the cases that was considered in this appeal the Judge concluded, as had the tribunal, that an epileptic claimant who regularly required attention, at night, once or twice a week for up to 20 minutes on each occasion, did not satisfy the test of requiring "prolonged attention" throughout the period of his claim. Taking a broad view of the matter, and in particular the length of the fits and the pattern on an unpredictable but regular basis, he concluded that the claimant's need did not constitute prolonged attention throughout the relevant period. But what if a more generously inclined tribunal on a similar case were to conclude that it did? Would that be so unreasonable as to be appealable? (It could not be said to be out of line with the treatment of a lowest-rate claimant because the drafting of the section envisages that night-time care will be treated differently.) But if it is not appealable, then will it not be inequitable for the first claimant?

But note it is still possible to find an example where an error of law has occurred by the application of the wrong legal test to the facts found by the FTT. In *AB v SSWP* [2015] UKUT 522 (AAC) the claimant was a person who required stimulation to her mental processes at several points during the day on about half of the days each week, although the claimant did not require someone to be with her all of the day and could safely be left on her own for part of each day. The FTT held on the facts as found by them that this qualified her for benefit at only the lower rate—attention needed for a significant portion of the day. They held that that she did not qualify at the middle rate because, it seemed, they required the attention to have been necessary not only frequently, but also throughout the day—meaning that she might require someone to be with her all day. Judge Gray held that this was a mistake in the law as explained by Judge Hickinbottom, and that on the facts found by the FTT she was able to make the award at the middle rate without requiring a rehearing.

Continual supervision—in order to avoid danger: To satisfy para.(b)(ii) the claimant must show that he requires "continual supervision . . . in order to avoid danger to himself or others". Note the point made by Commissioner May (as he then was) in *CSDLA/867/97* that supervision by the teachers at school to protect the claimant from bullying could not qualify because it served to prevent danger to the claimant from others, whereas, in his view, the subsection envisages protection of the claimant (and others) from himself. This decision has been disapproved on other grounds but without reference to this point.   **1.231**

Supervision may be of two kinds. It can be precautionary or anticipatory, as when a carer watches over his patient ready to intervene when necessary; or, it may be ancillary to a series of acts of attention, as when the carer accompanies a blind person on a walk and offers guidance both physical and verbal. (In either case where the intervention becomes frequent the claimant may qualify anyway under para.(b)(i).)

Supervision is more passive than attention, but even supervision of the precautionary kind must be something more than mere presence (*CDLA/42/94*). It requires a degree of monitoring by the carer so that they do more than merely respond to a call from the claimant. Even so, it has been held in *Moran v Secretary of State for Social Services* (*The Times*, March 14, 1987, CA) that a supervisor could be in another room and even may be asleep, if they are so attuned to the needs of their patient that they would respond immediately by sensing the onset of, in that case, a fit.

In order to be *substantial* the danger must be "considerable, solid or big" (*R(A) 1/73*) but it need not be life threatening. In *R(A) 11/83* a Tribunal of Commissioners felt that the risk of a claimant biting his tongue in an epileptic fit was a substantial danger to him and in *CSA/68/89* the risk of impulsive suicide was a substantial danger even though it was not determined and was unlikely to succeed.   **1.232**

The danger is also substantial if the risk of harm is high. Although the language used by Commissioners in a number of decisions is sometimes inconsistent it is clear that risk is a factor of both the degree of harm that is possible, and the likelihood of a harmful event occurring. Thus although the likelihood of a house catching fire might be low, the consequence to a tetraplegic who was caught within it, would be fatal and the danger to him would therefore be substantial (see *R(A) 2/89*). Likewise in *R(A) 1/81* and *R(A) 5/81* the point is made that it only takes a child to run out into traffic once to present a substantial danger to himself and others.

In *R(A) 1/73* the Commissioner said that the word "continual" was not synonymous with continuous. This means that supervision may be continual notwithstanding some short breaks. In order to "avoid" substantial danger it is not necessary to eliminate the risk altogether; it is enough to effect a real reduction in the risk. In *R(A) 3/92* the Commissioner accepted that no amount of supervision could prevent a determined suicide but it could substantially reduce the risk that it would succeed.

1.233 Many cases on supervision involve the risk of falling. In *R(A) 3/89* a Commissioner proposed that in such cases the following questions should be determined.

> "(i) Are the situations in which the claimant may fall predictable or unpredictable? That is to say, does the claimant have a liability to fall anywhere at any time? Or does he fall only in certain circumstances or situations? This is, of course, a matter of medical opinion: but the opinion must be based on evidence.
>
> (ii) If the falling is predictable, can the claimant reasonably be expected to avoid the risk of falling or to place himself at such risk only when adequately supervised? That again is a matter of medical opinion. If the claimant cannot reasonably be expected either to avoid the risk or to place himself at risk only when adequately supervised, the DMP should treat the case as one in which the falling was unpredictable.
>
> (iii) If the falling is unpredictable, will the falling give rise to substantial danger to himself? This is again, of course, a matter of medical opinion. Nevertheless it must be borne in mind that a person, particularly a disabled person, may when falling hit his head on the corner of a cupboard or on a fire kerb or radiator; and whether or not he is injured in the course of falling, he may by reason of his disability be unable to rise or be unable to summon help. Or he may be of such an age that a fall will be likely to have serious consequences. Clearly such matters ought in an appropriate case to be taken into account.
>
> (iv) Is the substantial danger too remote? In the present case, the DMP stated that in his medical opinion the risk of substantial danger arising from a fall 'is so remote a possibility that it ought to be reasonably disregarded.' But he has failed to give any indication why he reached that conclusion or to indicate on what evidence he relied to support that conclusion. Although, as I have said, those questions are matters of medical opinion, it is incumbent upon a DMP to consider all the evidence, including the evidence of the claimant, to make the relevant findings of fact and to give adequate reasons for the conclusions which he reaches upon those findings of fact so that the claimant 'looking at the decision should be able to discern on the face of it the reasons why' the evidence failed to satisfy the DMP: *R(A) 1/72* at paragraph 8. In my judgment the DMP has failed to do so in the present case."

In *R(A) 5/90* a Tribunal of Commissioners cautioned against treating these questions as a statutory requirement and said that it was not an error of law if the DMP failed to answer them. But they also said that his failure to do so might well reflect an insufficiency of reasons for his decision. A single instance of falling does not show a propensity to fall (*CA/233/95*) and even where there is a propensity to fall it does not follow that there is a need for continual supervision to avoid danger. In *CDLA/899/94* the Commissioner said:

> "10. . . . This is not a case of a person who is so unsteady that he requires to be supported whenever he stands, which may have been the case in *R(A) 3/89*. It is always possible that a person who falls may suffer some injury. However, that is far more likely in the case of a person who falls due to a fit or loss of consciousness and therefore cannot take any steps to mitigate the effects of the fall. In the present case, the risk of falling at home is slight and the risk of serious injury when falling at home is even slighter. This is not the case of an elderly person who is particularly frail. It really cannot be said that the claimant reasonably requires

someone to be so close to him the whole time as to be able to catch him should he fall.

11. It is of course theoretically possible that a person falls and the effects of the fall are made worse by the lack of immediate response. Supervision may be required in some case in order to avoid the risk of danger arising after a fall. However, one must have regard to the relative frequency of falls and the likelihood of serious injury, *of a type that might be avoided if there were supervision*, arising from them."

But it is not necessary that the supervision should be able to prevent the fall—it is enough that supervision will reduce the risk of serious harm as a consequence of falling (*R(A) 2/92*).

Where the need for supervision is based upon the claimant's mental disablement some medical evidence may be necessary (*CA/147/84*), though it is possible that a history of previous suicide attempts may suffice. In *R(A) 2/91* the Commissioner held that a view expressed by the consultant psychiatrist that "the claimant was at times significantly depressed and potentially at risk to herself" was sufficient to justify supervision.

THE NIGHT CONDITIONS

In order to qualify for benefit at the highest rate a claimant must show that they satisfy at least one of the conditions in subs.(1)(c) (the night conditions) and, at least one, of the conditions in subs.(1)(b) (the day conditions)—see above.   1.234

Subs.(1)(c) provides two conditions either of which must be satisfied "at night".

Night was defined in *R. v National Insurance Commissioner Ex p. Secretary of State for Social Services* [1974] 1 W.L.R. 1290, Appendix to *R(A) 4/74*, as being:

"that period of inactivity or that principal period of inactivity through which each household goes in the dark hours and to measure the beginning of the night from the time at which the household as it were, closed down for the night".

This case has probably been credited with deciding more than it did. The Court of Appeal were considering an appeal from a Commissioner who had himself allowed an appeal from an Attendance Allowance Board. Then, as now, the Commissioner was limited to allowing an appeal on a point of law. The decision of the Court was simply that in their view no error of law could be seen in the decision of the Board and that the Commissioner had therefore been wrong in allowing an appeal. Any definition that they gave was strictly speaking *obiter*, but in any case they expressly eschew any attempt to provide any general definition. Nevertheless they did adopt the formulae that had been agreed by counsel which formed the test above and which has since been adopted and applied elsewhere (see e.g. *Ramsden R(DLA) 2/03*). But that is not the end of the matter. The definition of night which the Court of Appeal commended was no different from that of the Commissioner in that case, nor so far as can be seen, from the Board. Where they differed was in the application of that test to the facts. The particular point of contention was whether assistance given to the claimant, (a paraplegic) in undressing and getting into bed, and in getting up and dressing the morning, should be regarded as assistance rendered by night. The Board had regarded both as being given by day. The Commissioner thought that at least the process of getting to bed should be part of his night attention-in his view, applying the words of the test, getting undressed and into bed is a part of the process of "closing down" for the night. All that the Court of Appeal decided was that there was no error of law in the decision of the Board that undressing etc was accomplished as a part of the day, but they make equally clear that the decision on the point, in their view, was one of fact to be decided in accordance with the common sense of the Board and, it follows, that were the Board, (or a tribunal now) to decide that going to bed was part of what one does at night, there would be, equally, nothing wrong with that decision.

For the past thirty years, however, tribunals have accepted that night begins only when the claimant has got into bed and ends when he climbs out. It may be too late for such a revolutionary change.   1.235

While this definition seems to address itself to the habits of the particular household there should be room to take account of a more objective, typical household. Thus if one (possibly the only other) member of the household remains up late to undertake what is a regular attention need that should be regarded as a night time need because otherwise the household would, as a whole, have been retired to bed. Conversely, when children have gone to bed, but their parents have not, any attention prior to the parents normal bed time will be attention by day, and any attention to the child before the parents' usual time of rising will be attention at night. The first part of this approach was confirmed in *R(A) 1/78* (rejecting another part of Lord Widgery's judgment in the case above).

In *CDLA/997/2003*, the child who, because of his disabilities, had to be attended to whenever he was awake, woke regularly every morning at about 5.00 am. His mother had to rise then to give continual supervision. Had the child not woken at that time she would not have risen until 7.00 am. The Commissioner accepted the argument that the night of the household should be defined by what the household would normally do. In this case the household as a whole would not have risen before 7.00 am and therefore the period of supervision between 5.00 am and 7.00 am should count as being given at night.

1.236   Again, in *R(A)1/04*, the claimant frequently got up at 4.30 am and then went for a walk. The Commissioner held that a tribunal was wrong to fix the end of the night by reference to what that particular claimant did; the distinction should have a more objective element to reflect what ordinary households did. In this case it would probably be fair to say that the ordinary use of language would be to describe the claimant as going out for a walk in the night. The Commissioner suggests that a normal period of night, as identified in accordance with the test above, would be something like the hours between 11.00 pm and 7.00 am.

This approach has been confirmed again in *LB v SSWP (DLA)* [2018] UKUT 445 (AAC), where Judge Hemingway, in giving guidance to the FTT to whom the case was returned, said it should take account of time when the claimant's mother stayed up later than she might otherwise have done, even when just remaining awake beside the child could be regarded as time spent caring for the claimant at night.

1.237   *Prolonged or repeated attention:* In order to satisfy para.(c)(i) the claimant must show that he requires, by night, "prolonged or repeated attention".

"Prolonged", seems to be accepted by decision-makers to mean 20 minutes or more. In *R. v National Insurance Commissioners Ex p. Secretary of State for Social Services*, [1981], W.L.R. 1017, CA, *R(A) 2/80*, Lord Denning said "repeated means more than once at any rate". Since the decision of the Court was that the Attendance Allowance Board had been correct in finding that the claimant satisfied only the day conditions it would seem that anything said as to the meaning of the night conditions was obiter, but as a minimum, it must mean at least twice.. It is therefore open to a tribunal to require more than two acts of attention during the night, but current experience suggests that generally twice per night has sufficed.

It is not necessary that the care is needed every night. If the need is there on most nights the claim should succeed and in *R(A) 2/74* the Commissioner suggested that decision-makers should take a broad view of the matter and consider whether, in all of the circumstances, their good sense indicates that the words of the statute are satisfied. This might suggest care that is needed several times a week without focusing on counting nights every week.

1.238   In *DJ v SSWP* [2016] UKUT 169 (AAC) Judge Hemingway dealt with the case of a five-year-old child whose medical condition caused him to require attention when he woke at night suffering acute pain. The evidence recorded by the FTT showed typically that on three nights of the week he would wake several times for an hour or more at a time, and on the other four nights he would wake only once, usually for between 30 and 60 minutes. The FTT had refused an appeal on the ground that on most nights he did not require prolonged or repeated attention. This conclusion seems to have been reached by conflating the requirements of s.72(1) with those of s.72(1A)—see below. The judge had little difficulty in concluding that, looked at broadly and not arithmetically, the claimant could be described as requiring prolonged attention most of the time.

Awake for a prolonged period or at frequent intervals for the purpose of watching over: **1.239**
In order to satisfy para.(c)(ii) the claimant must show that, by night, he requires someone to be "awake for a prolonged period or at frequent intervals for the purpose of watching over him" in order to avoid substantial danger to himself or others.

For the meaning of "prolonged", see above under para.(c)(i). For the meaning of "frequent", see above under para.(b)(i)—though it is possible that fewer occurrences should be spread throughout the night (cf. the wording of para.(b)(i)).

Under this paragraph it is no longer possible for the carer to be asleep "on call". They must be awake and watching over the claimant. It is suggested that, as with supervision, the carer might be watching over, without actually looking at, the claimant at the time, e.g. they could be watching television in a room nearby. But as to the requirement of being awake there can be no compromise.

There has been some consideration of the use of CCTV and baby-minder devices as a means of watching over in *JH v SSWP* [2010] UKUT 456, but that case was a decision on para.(6) of reg.12 of the Disability Living Allowance Regulations and that provision requires that the carer is "present" when watching over the claimant.

This point has been considered again in *AH v Secretary of State for Work and Pensions* [2012] UKUT 387, another case on reg.12, where the judge suggests that use of CCTV may be a suitable way of watching over. He observes also that a person may be "watching over" without having the patient in view all of the time. It is significant, he suggests, that the expression, in both contexts, is "watching over" and not "looking at".

Subsection (1A)
A child (being for this purpose someone under 16) cannot qualify under the   **1.240**
cooking test (subs.(1A)(a)), but otherwise there is no lower age limit for the care component. However, since all young children need a certain amount of attention and supervision, a disabled child qualifies for the care component only if he or she requires more attention or supervision than children of the same age who are not disabled. Note that the child is the claimant although an adult will be appointed to act on his or her behalf. In *CSDLA/567/2005* it was held that even attention given in soothing a child to sleep could be attention in connection with their bodily functions but only if the difficulty in sleeping were caused by a disability and, under this subsection, would qualify only if it were substantially in excess of that which would be normal for a child of that age. In *DJ v SSWP* [2016] UKUT 169 (AAC) the FTT had remarked of a child who needed attention at night for 30–60 minutes on four nights of the week that "This would not be unusual for some five year olds". In allowing an appeal, Judge Hemingway doubted the correctness of that statement, but in any case was able to point out that the test is one of comparison with "normal" children of that age, which must relate to children generally and would not be satisfied only if some children required that attention.

In *CDLA/3737/2002* the Commissioner held that attention provided to a partially sighted child by her teachers at school to assist her in the bodily function of seeing and so learning could qualify her for the middle rate of care component. The amount of attention she required was considerably in excess of that which was required by a normally sighted child. There is nothing in the legislation to suggest that this sort of care should not be taken into account even if it is provided by a publicly funded institution.

This point has now been confirmed in the decision of a tribunal of judges—see *KM v SSWP (DLA)* [2013] UKUT 159 (AAC); [2014] AACR 2.

Where a claim is made on behalf of a child, and it is based on the care and   **1.241**
attention necessary to clean and wash as a result of the child not having developed

control over their bowel or bladder, it may seem that the most obvious question is whether the child satisfies the requirement set in this subsection namely, is that attention substantially in excess of the normal requirements for a child of his age. But, as has been pointed out in *CSDLA/552/01*, and now again in *R(DLA)1/05*, there is another question that needs to be decided first—is there evidence that the child's condition is the result of any physical or mental disability? The fact that a child is late in developing control of the bowels, etc. is not, in itself, evidence of disability, and nocturnal enuresis may continue in a normal child for several years. In this case a claim for a child of six failed because the evidence did not necessarily show a disability even though she wet and sometimes fouled herself on most nights of the week. But the Commissioner did add that as she grew older a continuing failure to develop control might become some evidence of disability that might then be supported by medical evidence, though the need to find a medical condition will no longer apply since the decision in *R(DLA)2/06*.

Paragraph (a) provides that a claim for the lowest rate cannot be based on a child's inability to prepare a main meal, even if the child is 15.

Paragraph (b) defines the extra requirement that must be shown for a child claimant to succeed. This is either, under sub-para.(i) that they have care requirements of the kind defined in subs.(1) which are substantially in excess of the requirements of a normal child of that age; or, under sub-para.(ii) that they have extra such care requirements that would be common to younger children, but which children of their age would normally have grown out of. Obviously the younger a child is the more difficult it will be to show these conditions have been satisfied.

1.242   In *CA/92/92* the Deputy Commissioner made the following points:

"5. In the case of a child, it is to be noted that the attention or supervision required must be 'substantially in excess of that normally required by a child of the same age and sex.' Attention or supervision may be required 'substantially in excess of that normally required' either by virtue of the time over which it is required or by virtue of the quality or degree of attention or supervision which is required.

6. The idea of a greater quality or degree of attention can be illustrated by considering meal times. A young child may require attention in connection with eating because he or she requires the food to be cut up. A disabled child of the same age may require attention in excess of that normally required by a child of the same age because he or she not only requires the food to be cut up but also requires it to be spooned into the mouth. The fact that the child will be supervised anyway is irrelevant: there is still an additional requirement for attention. Whether such additional attention, taken with any other additional attention requirements, is 'substantial' and 'frequent . . . throughout the day' are matters of judgement to be determined in each case where the condition in section [72(1)(b)(i)] is being considered. Those may be significant limiting factors.

7. When considering the condition in section [72(1)(b)(ii)], the additional condition that the supervision required must be substantially in excess of that normally required by a child of the same age is indeed 'stringent' as it was described in *CA/21/88*. Because young children normally require continual supervision throughout the day in order to avoid substantial danger to themselves, the focus will be on the quality or degree of supervision. Thus a very young immobile baby or an older child might normally be regarded as being adequately supervised by a person who was getting on with his or her own chores in a different part of the home. On the other hand, a disabled child of the same age may need much closer supervision amounting, perhaps, to being watched over. That would be supervision in excess of that normally required. Again, it is necessary to consider whether such additional supervision is 'substantial' and 'continual . . . throughout the day' and those may be significant limiting factors.

8. Similar considerations apply to the night conditions in section [72(1)(c)],

although it may in practice be more difficult for claimants to qualify on the basis of the additional quality or degree of attention or watching over rather than on the basis of the additional frequency or length of time for which attention or watching over is required.

9. The other general question raised by this appeal is how one judges what attention of supervision is normally required by a child of the same age and sex. Children vary considerably in their requirements for attention and supervision, particularly when they are young. At any age, there is a range of requirements for attention or supervision. It is significant that the legislation does not speak of attention or supervision substantially in excess of that which would be required by the particular child being considered were he not physically or mentally disabled. So that, if it were possible to ascribe tantrums to frustration arising out of a disability, that would not be enough for the child to qualify unless the attention or supervision was substantially in excess of that normally required by a child of the same age and sex. It seems to me that the legislation contemplates a yardstick of an average child, neither particularly bright or well behaved nor particularly dull or badly behaved, and then the attention or supervision required by the child whose case is being considered must be judged to decide whether it is 'substantially' more than would normally be required by the average child. That, I think, comes to much the same thing as saying that the attention or supervision required must be substantially more than that normally required by *most* children, which is the way the delegated medical practitioner put it in paragraph 4 of his decision in this case. Attention or supervision is not to be regarded as 'substantially' in excess of that normally required unless it is outside the whole range of attention or supervision that would normally be required by the average child. However, it need not necessarily be substantially in excess of that which would be required by a particularly dull or badly behaved, but not physically or mentally disabled, child. I appreciate that all this is pitched at a fairly theoretical level and that there may be significant evidential problems and problems of judgement in individual cases, but it seems desirable to provide some sort of theoretical framework within which the present case can be considered."

The distinction between the tests posed by subpara.(i) and that of subpara.(ii) has been considered in *BM v SSWP (DLA)* [2015] UKUT 18 (AAC); [2015] AACR 29. The child in this case suffered from several conditions all of which contributed to his developmental delay. The FTT that heard an appeal brought on his behalf for both the care component and the mobility component held that he did not satisfy the requirements of subpara. (i) – they gave no consideration to subpara.(ii). In the UT it was at first argued on behalf of the Secretary of State that there was effectively no difference in practice between the two tests, though subsequently it was accepted that the two tests were different. Judge Markus concedes that the difference in practice is not easy to see, but she explains that in subpara.(i) the focus is upon the question whether the claimant requires more attention though of the same kind as that which a non-disabled child of the same age might need; whereas subpara.(ii) is focused on the need for attention that is different from that required by children of the same age, though it might be the same as that required by children of a younger age. On this basis a claim might succeed so long as the different attention required is "substantial", but would not necessarily have to be overall "substantially in excess" of that required by a child of the same age. She puts it thus:

"34. Once it has been determined that a claimant has requirements falling within section 72(1) (which I have assumed to be the case in the above hypothetical examples), the issues which arise for determination under section 72(1A)(b) (i) are: (a) what the relevant requirements are of normally healthy children of the same age; and (b) whether the claimant's requirements are substantially in excess of those in (a). Under section 72(1A)(b)(ii) the issues which arise are: (a) whether the claimant's requirements are substantial; (b) whether the claimant's requirements are different from those of children of the claimant's age in normal physical and mental health; (c) whether younger children in normal physical and mental health would have those requirements."

An example of how *subs.(1A)* is to be applied in the case of a very young child (there a matter of six months) is provided by *CDLA/3525/2004*. The child required a special diet and careful supervision. The majority of the tribunal found this extra care did not amount to care substantially in excess of what would be required for such a young child anyway. The Commissioner held that the tribunal had applied the right test and the conclusion they reached, essentially a finding of fact, could not be said to show any error of law.

The care needs of a very young child were considered in *CDLA/4100/2004*. The claimant was a child of 17 months who was profoundly deaf. She was provided with hearing aids which gave limited hearing ability, but it was claimed still required considerably more attention and supervision than a normal child of that age. Commissioner Rowland allowed her appeal and awarded the middle rate care component on the basis of the written evidence before him.

1.243　　Further consideration of a child's claim is given by Commissioner Parker in *CDLA/829/2004* where she extends to three stages the test she suggested earlier in *CSDLA/552/01*. In these cases it is necessary, she suggests, to decide first; whether the claimant has a mental or physical disability (as now explained in *CDLA/1721/2004*), secondly whether they satisfy one or more of the care requirements, and then thirdly whether that amount of care substantially exceeds that required for a normal child of that age. For the question of what is normal, she adopts the approach of Commissioner Rowland in *R(DLA)1/05* as being a matter of quality as well as quantity, frequency, duration etc. A useful resume of these cases can be found again in *CSDLA/535/2007*, another decision of Commissioner Parker.

In *CDLA/3779/2004* the Commissioner points out that evidence from the school of supervision, or rather, lack of any extra supervision that is required for the claimant, may be misleading because the school may find it necessary to supervise all the children together, and that supervision may suffice for the claimant. But that is not to say that at other times, and away from school, that the claimant does not need supervision in circumstances (e.g. playing on his own) when a normal child would not.

A child who is terminally ill is taken to satisfy para.(b) and (c) of subs.(1) by virtue of subs.(5). Subsection (6)(b) has no application in such a case (*R(DLA)1/99*).

Subsection (2)

1.244　　Paragraph (a) imposes the three-month qualifying period but this is deemed to be satisfied in the case of a person who is terminally ill (see subs.(5)). If a person's condition deteriorates so that he or she satisfies a further condition and would qualify for a higher rate of the care component, the effect of subs.(4) is that the claimant must still wait three months before qualifying for the higher rate unless terminally ill. See *KH v SSWP* [2009] UKUT 54 (AAC) where the claimant had applied for her benefit to be increased from a certain date, but the increased rate could be paid only from a date three months later because there was no evidence that the claimant had qualified for the higher rate before the application for supersession was received. Under s.76(1), an award cannot usually be made before the date of claim but this does not prevent the three-month qualifying period imposed by s.72(2)(a) from being satisfied as at the date of claim if the conditions were met during the three months before the date of claim. The date of claim is determined in accordance with Reg.6 of the Social Security (Claims and Payments) Regulations—see Vol.III of this work. Reg.6 of the DLA Regulations prescribes, for the purpose of para.(a)(ii), a period of three months ending on the day on which the claimant was last entitled to the component or to attendance allowance if that was not more than two years before the current period of entitlement would otherwise begin. This has the practical effect in most cases that the three-month qualifying period is deemed to be satisfied if the current claim is within two years of a previous period of entitlement at the relevant rate.

Under paras 3(2) and 7(2) of Sch.1 to the DLA Regulations, a period of six months is substituted for the period of three months in subs.(2) in the case of a person over the age of 65 who makes a renewal claim for DLA or whose entitlement is to be revised on review.

Paragraph (b) requires that a person should be expected to satisfy the conditions for the component for six months, unless he or she is expected to die sooner. In *CDLA/3461/2006*, it was held that this requirement applies equally to a renewal claim as much as to a new claim. Thus where, on the medical evidence provided, it was reasonable to expect that the claimant would be recovered within the next six months, even though he may not have recovered yet, the claim was properly refused.

Although this means that six months will normally be the minimum period for which an award will be made this section does not prevent an award for a lesser period when that is appropriate. In *R(DLA) 11/02* the claimant had applied unsuccessfully and then appealed. Before that appeal could be heard her condition had deteriorated and she made a fresh claim that was allowed. The Commissioner held that an award of less than six months could be made to fill the gap between the date when she was now regarded as qualifying and the date when the existing award commenced even though that was less than six months. This period of six months begins as the three-month (or six-month for those over 65) qualifying period ends and both conditions are intended to ensure that only the chronically disabled are entitled to DLA.   1.245

As the need for assistance may also depend upon the facilities and adaptations that are available to the claimant it will be necessary for the DM to decide what it is reasonable for a claimant to acquire and how quickly he may be expected to do that. In *SF v SSWP* [2010] UKUT 78 (AAC) a tribunal was directed to make enquiries as to the fitting of a shower for the claimant which matter would itself require information about the claimant's accommodation and his resources. If it was reasonable for him to have the shower within six months, that might preclude the basis of a claim.

On an appeal the claimant's disability must be judged on the basis of his condition at the time of claim and up to the time of the DM decision. Information that only becomes available after that time is still admissible before a tribunal provided that it relates to the claimant's condition within that period–see *R(DLA) 2/01*. Where, however the question relates to the claimant's prospective condition it must be evidence as to what might then have been expected to happen, rather than what has in fact happened by the time of the tribunal determination.

This was the conclusion reached in *CDLA/2878/2000*. The claimant (who was a nurse) developed a condition of her back as a result of which she became unable to care for herself and suffered restricted mobility. She claimed both components of DLA, but less than three months later, and, according to her, quite unexpectedly she was operated on successfully and had recovered sufficiently to return to work within six months of her date of claim. The tribunal, which heard an appeal several weeks after that, held that she could not be entitled because events had proved the condition not to have lasted the requisite period. The Commissioner allowed her appeal for the reasons stated above after making a full review of authorities across a wide range of ex post facto situations. He drew a distinction between those cases where the subsequent event is relevant to establish a fact that might be shown to have pre-existed, and those cases, such as this (and the situation in *R(A) 1/94*), where the decision-maker must decide what was then a likely outcome.

Subsections (3) and (4)

Regulation 4(1) of the DLA Regulations provides for three rates of benefit.   1.246

Despite the strange use of the words "in any other case" in subs.(4)(c) it is plain that it is intended that the lowest rate is applicable only if a claimant satisfies the condition mentioned in subs.(1)(a) without also satisfying the condition in either subs.(1)(b) or (1)(c) If he or she were to satisfy the conditions in, say, both subs.(1)(a) and (1)(c), the middle rate would be applicable. see *CDLA/2495/2004.*

Subsection (5)

1.247　　　Under s.66(2), a person is "terminally ill" if "he suffers from a progressive disease and his death in consequence of that disease can reasonably be expected within six months". See the notes to that section. Note also that someone may make a claim on this ground on behalf of the claimant without the claimant's knowledge or authority (s.76(3)).

The effect of this subsection is that a terminally ill person is deemed to satisfy the three-month (or six-month in the case of a person over 65) qualifying period and is entitled to an award of the highest rate of the care component for the remainder of his or her life, subject only to satisfying presence and residence conditions and the rules about people in hospital and other accommodation. Even those are relaxed. Reg.2(4) of the DLA Regulations relaxes the presence conditions for terminally ill claimants so that it is not necessary for them to have been in Great Britain before the day in respect of which the claim is made. Reg.9(3) also enables such claimants to receive the care component even though they are in accommodation where the cost could be, but is not, borne wholly or partly out of public or local funds.

Subsection (7)

1.248　　　Regulation 7 of the DLA Regulations deems people undergoing renal dialysis to satisfy the condition of either subs.(1)(b) or (1)(c).

Subsection (8)

1.249　　　See regs 8–10 of the DLA Regulations.

The mobility component

1.250　　　**73.**—(1) Subject to the provisions of this Act, a person shall be entitled to the mobility component of a disability living allowance for any period in which he is over [¹ the relevant age] and throughout which—

(a) he is suffering from physical disablement such that he is either unable to walk or virtually unable to do so; or

[⁶ (ab) he falls within subsection (1AB) below; or

(b) he does not fall within that subsection but does fall within subsection (2) below; or]

(c) he falls within subsection (3) below; or

(d) he is able to walk but is so severely disabled physically or mentally that, disregarding any ability he may have to use routes which are familiar to him on his own, he cannot take advantage of the faculty out of doors without guidance or supervision from another person most of the time.

[¹ (1A) In subsection (1) above "the relevant age" means—

(a) in relation to the conditions mentioned in paragraph (a), [⁶(ab),] (b) or (c) of that subsection, the age of 3;

(b) in relation to the conditions mentioned in paragraph (d) of that subsection, the age of 5.]

[⁶(1AB) A person falls within this subsection if—

(a) he has such severe visual impairment as may be prescribed; and

(b) he satisfies such other conditions as may be prescribed.]

(2) A person falls within this subsection if—

(a) he is both blind and deaf; and

(b) he satisfies such other conditions as may be prescribed.

(3) A person falls within this subsection if—

(a) he is severely mentally impaired; and

(b) he displays severe behavioural problems; and

(c) he satisfies both the conditions mentioned in section 72(1)(b) and (c) above.

[³ (4A) In its application to a person in relation to so much of a period as falls before the day on which he reaches the age of 16, subsection (1) has effect subject to the modification that the condition mentioned in paragraph (d) shall not be taken to be satisfied unless—

(a) he requires substantially more guidance or supervision from another person than persons of his age in normal physical and mental health would require, or

(b) persons of his age in normal physical and mental health would not require such guidance or supervision

(5) [⁴ . . .], circumstances may be prescribed in which a person is to be taken to satisfy or not to satisfy a condition mentioned in subsection (1)(a) or (d) or subsection (2)(a) above.

[³ (5A) Subsection (4A) has effect subject to regulations made under subsection (5) (except as otherwise prescribed).]

(6) Regulations shall specify the cases which fall within subsection (3)(a) and (b) above.

(7) A person who is to be taken for the purposes of section 72 above to satisfy or not to satisfy a condition mentioned in subsection (1)(b) or (c)of that section is to be taken to satisfy or not to satisfy it for the purposes of subsection (3)(c) above.

(8) A person shall not be entitled to the mobility component for a period unless during most of that period his condition will be such as permits him from time to time to benefit from enhanced facilities for locomotion.

(9) A person shall not be entitled to the mobility component of a disability living allowance unless—

(a) throughout—

(i) the period of three months immediately preceding the date on which the award of that component would begin; or

(ii) such other period of three months as may be prescribed, he has satisfied or is likely to satisfy one or other of the conditions mentioned in subsection (1) [⁵ (a) to (d)] above; and

(b) he is likely to continue to satisfy one or other of those conditions throughout—

(i) the period of six months beginning with that date; or

(ii) (if his death is expected within the period of six months beginning with that date) the period so beginning and ending with his death.

[³ (9A) The modifications mentioned in subsection (4A) shall have effect in relation to the application of subsection (1) for the purposes of subsection (9), but only—

(a) in the case of a person who is under the age of 16 on the date on which the award of the mobility component would begin, and

(b) in relation to so much of any period mentioned in subsection (9) as falls before the day on which he reaches the age of 16.]

(10) Two weekly rates of the mobility component shall be prescribed.

(11) The weekly rate of the mobility component payable to a person for each week in the period for which he is awarded that component shall be—

(a) the higher rate, if he falls within subsection (9) above by virtue of having satisfied or being likely to satisfy one or other of the conditions mentioned in subsection (1)(a), [⁶ (ab),] (b) and (c) above throughout both the period mentioned in paragraph (a) of subsection (9) above and that mentioned in paragraph (b) of that subsection; and

(b) the lower rate in any other case.

(12) For the purposes of this section in its application to a person who is terminally ill, as defined in section 66(2) above, and who makes a claim expressly on the ground that he is such a person—

(a) subsection (9)(a) above shall be omitted; and

(b) subsection (11)(a) above shall have effect as if for the words from "both" to "subsection", in the fourth place where it occurs, there were substituted the words "the period mentioned in subsection (9) (b) above".

(13) Regulations may prescribe cases in which a person who has the use—

(a) of an invalid carriage or other vehicle provided by [²the Welsh Ministers under paragraph 9 of Schedule 1 to the National Health Service (Wales) Act 2006, or the Secretary of State under paragraph 9 of Schedule 1 to the National Health Service Act 2006] or under section 46 of the National Health Service (Scotland) Act 1978 or provided under Article 30(1) of the Health and Personal Social Services (Northern Ireland) Order 1972; or

(b) of any prescribed description of appliance supplied under the enactments relating to the National Health Service being such an appliance as is primarily designed to afford a means of personal and independent locomotion out of doors,

is not to be paid any amount attributable to entitlement to the mobility component or is to be paid disability living allowance at a reduced rate in so far as it is attributable to that component.

(14) A payment to or in respect of any person which is attributable to his entitlement to the mobility component, and the right to receive such a payment, shall (except in prescribed circumstances and for prescribed purposes) be disregarded in applying any enactment or instrument under which regard is to be had to a person's means.

AMENDMENTS

1. Welfare Reform and Pensions Act 1999 s.67 (April 9, 2001).
2. National Health Service (Consequential Provisions) Act 2006 Sch.1 para.145 (March 1, 2007).
3. Welfare Reform Act 2007 s.53(2) (October 1, 2007).
4. Welfare Reform Act 2007 Sch.8 (October 1, 2007).
5. Welfare Reform Act 2007 Sch.7 para.2(2) (October 1, 2007).
6. Welfare Reform Act 2009 s.14 (October 15, 2010).

DERIVATION

1.251   SSA 1975 s.37ZC.

GENERAL NOTE

Subsection (1)

1.252   The mobility component of DLA is a benefit paid to claimants who experience difficulty, to the requisite extent, in getting about on foot. It is paid at two levels.

From April 2001 a claimant may qualify for benefit at the higher level from the age of three, but for the lower level only from the age of five. In respect of the lower rate infant claimants have to satisfy an extra requirement test until they reach the age of 16. An attempt to have the lower age restriction declared to be in breach of Convention Rights failed in *SM v Advocate General for Scotland* [2010] CSOH 15. S.75 imposes an upper limit of 65, though claimants who have been entitled before reaching that age can continue to be entitled for the remainder of their life. It is no longer possible for a person to first claim for benefit over the age of 65 except in the case of someone moving from a previous entitlement under the invalid carriage scheme (DLA Regulations, Sch.2).

Note that the inability to walk or virtual inability to walk must exist throughout the period on which the claim is based. This has been interpreted, in *CDLA/496/2008*, as having the same meaning as the same words in s.72 have been given in *Secretary of State for Work and Pensions v Moyna* [2003] UKHL 44; [2003] 1 W.L.R. 1929; and *R(DLA) 7/03*. There, it was explained as being a matter of judgment, rather than arithmetical calculation, whether a person could fairly be described as being unable to cook themselves a main meal throughout the period in question, and the same will be said of their ability to walk. In this case the claimant suffered from epilepsy and sometimes had seizures when she was out walking. Commissioner Rowland held that her walking ability needed to be considered in three phases; one when she was out walking normally (for which she was entitled to mobility component at the lower rate because she needed to be supervised in case she had a seizure); another when she was unable to walk immediately after a seizure and when she could benefit from facilities for enhanced locomotion by being transported home in a car; and thirdly when she needed to sleep for a period of hours and sometimes days, to recover after the seizure. During this third period he felt she could not benefit from enhanced locomotion because she needed to remain resting and usually asleep (see subs.(8)). On this basis it was only the relatively short period during which she was travelling home that could qualify for benefit at the higher rate (unable to walk), and this, even if repeated, was insufficient to constitute an inability to walk throughout the period.

Paragraph (a)

This was the original basis upon which a mobility benefit was paid and still forms the basis of most claims. Note that claims under this paragraph are limited to ones in which the claimant has a *physical* disability; claims based on a mental disability may be considered under para.(d), or under subs.(3) below. For a detailed consideration of this distinction see the notes to reg.12 of the DLA regulations below. The circumstances in which a person can be taken to be "unable to walk or virtually unable to do so" are set out in reg.12 of the DLA regulations made under subs.(5) of this section. For a detailed discussion of those circumstances and the meaning of "physical disablement", see the notes to that Regulation.

1.253

Paragraph (ab)

The claimant will qualify under this paragraph if they satisfy the conditions prescribed in reg.12(1A) of the DLA regulations.

Regulation 12(1A) was held to be ultra vires, though not a nullity, by Judge Agnew in *YR v SSWP* [2014] UKUT 80 (AAC). That decision was appealed to the Court of Session (*SSWP v Robertson* [2015] CSIH 82), but the court found the appeal to be incompetent, presumably on the ground that the judge's finding had been unnecessary to his decision and therefore an *obiter dictum*. The consequence has been that the Secretary of State has continued to apply the regulation as drafted.

1.254

Paragraph (b)

The claimant qualifies under this paragraph if he satisfies the conditions of subs. (2)—see below.

1.255

Paragraph (c)

1.256   The claimant qualifies under this paragraph if he satisfies the conditions of subs. (3)—see below.

Paragraph (d)

1.257   The phrase "so severely disabled physically or mentally" is to be treated in the same way as the identical phrase in s.72. It does not require the claimant to show that they suffer from some medically prescribed condition and that it is severe, but only that they have a disability, mental or physical, that severely affects their ability in relation to walking. (See *CDLA/3831/2004* and *R(DLA) 3/06.*)

This paragraph which qualifies a claimant for benefit at the lower rate only, is designed to help those who do not qualify under the paragraphs above, yet still need assistance to enable them to walk normally out of doors. It was passed in consequence of the decision of the House of Lords in *Lees v Secretary of State for Social Services* [1985] 1 A.C. 930, also reported as appendix to *R(M) 1/84*. In that case the claimant was blind but suffered as well from a severe impairment of her capacity for spatial orientation. This meant that she could walk outside only with someone to guide her—otherwise she had no idea in which direction to move. An argument that this meant she was virtually unable to walk was not accepted. Under this paragraph, however, she would clearly qualify on the grounds that she needed guidance from another most of the time. The paragraph applies in cases of mental disability as well as physical disability in cases where mere supervision is required in order for the claimant to take advantage of the ability to walk. Thus a mentally handicapped adult who requires supervision before he or she can safely be allowed to walk near traffic would appear to qualify. This approach is reinforced by subs. (4) which makes it an additional condition in the case of a child under 16 that he or she should require substantially more guidance or supervision than a child of the same age in normal health. That makes it clear that the sort of supervision normally required by children may well be sufficient to enable an adult to qualify. Note that ability to use familiar routes is to be ignored so that the fact that a claimant can get to and from a local shop may not be a bar to entitlement. But, although the ability to use familiar routes is to be ignored in applying this test, such ability may still be relevant in an evidential sense in determining whether the claimant has shown at least some aspects of an inability when using unfamiliar routes. That is the approach suggested by Commissioner Parker in *R (DLA) 2/08* as follows:

"11. In *CSDLA/12/03*, cited by the representative, at paragraph 28 I gave the two usual questions relevant to entitlement to lower mobility:
'(a) First of all, [a tribunal] must determine whether, through disablement, the appellant is unable to walk on familiar routes without guidance or supervision, in which case he satisfies;
(b) However, if the appellant does not qualify in this way, the tribunal must then ask if it is different if the routes are unfamiliar viz. is the appellant unable to walk on such routes without guidance or supervision? If he is not so able, he satisfies.'
12. If a claimant is unable to walk even on familiar routes without guidance or supervision, then it logically follows that he will also be unable to do so on unfamiliar ones; but the converse does not apply. It will depend upon the nature of the claimant's condition. If the complaint is of a bad left knee causing falls, then the difficulties are likely to be the same whether the route is familiar or unfamiliar; however if, for example, a claimant has genuine anxiety and panic, then what he is able to do on a familiar route does not necessarily govern his capacity on an unfamiliar one.
13. The present tribunal, in effect, ran together the two stage process; however, that is not a problem provided the relevant issues are in substance addressed, and the tribunal did so. It first of all explained (when rejecting entitlement to the higher rate of the mobility component) why it refused to accept the claimed

physical difficulties in the present case (particularly the asserted collapses of the appellant's left knee), which were in the circumstances relevant also to an ability both on familiar and unfamiliar routes. It then turned to the assertion about anxiety and panic attacks, which had greater significance with respect to unfamiliar routes. For reasons it fully explained, the tribunal refused to accept that any of these claims were other than exaggerated. No error is demonstrated in the way the tribunal weighed the evidence and it was entitled to rely, if it wished, on the EMP's report.

14. In consideration of the *legal* criteria for entitlement to lower mobility, there must be ignored any ability to use familiar routes, albeit not an inability. However, when considering whether the claimant is unable to walk on unfamiliar routes without guidance or supervision, it may be *evidentially* relevant to that question as a matter of fact what, if any, are his difficulties with familiar routes. When a claimant does not differentiate between problems on familiar and unfamiliar routes, and there is nothing inherent in his condition to suggest a relevant distinction, then if he is unable to satisfy a tribunal that he has the required difficulty on familiar routes, in a context where the onus of proof on all matters lies on him, a tribunal may legitimately infer that he therefore would not need guidance or supervision on unfamiliar routes either. It is not that an adjudicating authority is requiring as a matter of law that he has difficulties on familiar routes before it will accept entitlement to lower mobility but rather that, from all the evidence, when considering his capacity on unfamiliar routes, it makes deductions from the information about his ability on familiar ones. A tribunal usually has to so reason because a claimant often says that he never walks on unfamiliar routes, which is entirely understandable.

15. In the present case, the tribunal correctly considered that, if the claimant genuinely suffered from anxiety and panic, this could make a material difference to his capacity on unfamiliar routes when compared with familiar ones. This is the clear implication of its reasoning. However, the tribunal was not satisfied of the genuine nature of his alleged problems, whether physical or mental; it neither applied the wrong legal approach nor, having regard to the evidence, drew any irrational conclusions and its explanation of which evidence was accepted, and which rejected, and why, was impeccable. It is apparent from the tribunal's whole reasoning that it answered 'no' to both the sequential questions posed in my paragraph 11 above."

Evidence as to whether a claimant has need of guidance or supervision can be derived in a number of ways. In *R 1/07(DLA)* the commissioner in Northern Ireland held that evidence of the claimant's ability to drive a motor car, was properly accepted as showing the claimant's "clear headedness and competency" which could be relevant to that aspect of her ability to walk on an unfamiliar route without the need for guidance or supervision.

The decision in *R1/07(DLA)* using the claimant's ability to drive as evidence of his ability to go out on foot without guidance or supervision has been approved in two more recent UT decisions, though with a word of caution. The caution has been to remind first-tier tribunals that such information is evidence of that ability, but is not necessarily decisive. It is suggested, for example, that the claimant's disability may be in the nature of anxiety about being outside-something that might not affect him when in his own motor car, but still be overpowering when on foot. See *JW v Secretary of State for Work and Pensions* [2012] UKUT 336 (AAC).

In *RR v SSWP* [2009] UKUT 272 (AAC) Judge Levenson considered the case of a claimant who, because of his mental state, frequently found himself in strange places not knowing how he came to be there. The fact that he could then get himself back home safely by asking for assistance and by using his mobile phone was not relevant, said the judge, because the test was whether he needed supervision to avoid getting into strange places to begin with.

1.258   The meaning of "guidance" and "supervision" in this context was considered in *CDLA/42/94* in which the Commissioner summarised his conclusions as follows:

"(i) The meaning of guidance or supervision must be considered within the context of action which is aimed at enabling the claimant to take advantage of the faculty of walking despite the limits imposed by her physical or mental condition. It is not a condition that guidance or supervision should be necessary to avoid a risk of danger to the claimant or others.

(j) Guidance means the action of directing or leading. It may, for example, be constituted by physically directing or leading the claimant or by oral direction, persuasion or suggestion.

(k) Supervision, in the context of section 73(1)(d), means accompanying the claimant and at the least monitoring the claimant or the circumstances for signs of a need to intervene so as to prevent the claimant's ability to take advantage of the faculty of walking being compromised. Other, more active, measures may also amount to supervision. The monitoring does not cease to fall within the meaning of supervision by reason only that intervention by the person accompanying the claimant has not in the past actually been necessary.

(l) The fact that the claimant derives reassurance from the presence of the other person does not prevent action which would otherwise fall within point (j) or (k) from being guidance or supervision."

In *R(DLA) 3/04* Commissioner Rowland considered the case of a claimant who, because of her state of anxiety and depression, suffered severe panic attacks if she tried to walk out on her own. She could only walk for any significant distance if she was accompanied by one of her family who would provide continuous reassurance and encouragement. The Commissioner held that this level of support could constitute guidance and supervision. He went on to hold that her claim was not precluded by reg.12(7) of the Disability Living Allowance Regulations because her state of anxiety was a symptom of a mental disability provided for under reg.12(8).

In *SSWP v PA* [2010] UKUT 401 (AAC) Judge Mark upheld a decision in favour of a claimant for lower rate mobility component who suffered severely from Crohn's Disease which made him unexpectedly and urgently incontinent. The judge held, that on the evidence that had been before the tribunal and before the Upper Tribunal, that the claimant had shown a sufficient need for supervision in assisting him to find a public toilet and assisting him in cleaning himself.

1.259   In *CDLA/52/94* the claimant suffered from epilepsy and the Commissioner said:

"7. Where a person has only occasional fits, the expression 'most of the time' focuses attention on the needs of the claimant between fits, rather than during or immediately after them. Therefore, so far as epilepsy is concerned, guidance may be of little relevance. The question then arises whether a person who is accompanying the claimant is thereby exercising 'supervision'. . . .

8. It is likely that a claimant who, due to epilepsy, satisfies the condition of section 72(1)(b)(ii) and is entitled to the care component of disability living allowance on the ground that he or she 'requires from another person . . . continual supervision throughout the day in order to avoid substantial danger to himself or others' will also satisfy the condition of section 73(i)(d). What is less clear is whether a person who fails to satisfy the condition of section 72(1)(b)(ii), because he or she merely needs a person to be nearby, will also fail to satisfy the condition of section 73(1)(d), because all that can be shown is a need to be accompanied when walking. Is a person accompanying such a claimant out walking in any different position from that of a person 'who keeps himself available to be called' while the claimant is at home?

9. It is, I think, important to bear in mind that Nicholls L.J. [in *Moran*—see note to s.72(1), above] did not exclude the possibility that a person 'who keeps himself available to be called' *might* be exercising supervision. 'It will all depend on the facts of the case.' In my view, the most significant factor is that a person who is keeping himself available while the claimant is at home (or at work) is likely to be able to get on with his or her own activities, whereas having to accompany a claimant is likely to preclude that and, unless he or she wishes to go on the same journey anyway, there is inevitably an element of service involved. It is that element of service that is significant. In my view, the use of the word 'monitoring' by the Commissioner in *CDLA/42/94* reflects the facts of the case before the Commissioner and the need for there to be some element of service rather than mere presence. In a case where a claimant can give warning to a person who is accompanying him or her, I do not think that it can reasonably be said that the accompanying person is 'monitoring' the claimant. However, even though there may be an absence of monitoring, I take the view that a need to be accompanied when walking may amount to a need for supervision. In practice, where epilepsy is concerned, the focus is likely to be on the reasonableness of the claim that there is a *need* to be accompanied when walking a modest distance. Relevant issues will be the likelihood of a fit occurring when the claimant is out walking and the risk of substantial danger if one does occur then. There may well be a greater risk of danger when the claimant has a fit out in the street than when he or she is at home."

In other cases, however, it had been suggested that if supervision were of a kind that might have qualified the claimant under s.72(1)(b) for the care component, it could not at the same time be used as part of a claim under this section. That difference of opinion was put to rest by the decision of a Tribunal of Commissioners in four joined appeals reported as *R(DLA) 4/01*.

1.260

The Tribunal finds nothing in the law to prevent the same type of assistance enabling the claimant to qualify for both parts of the benefit. On the other hand the Commissioners reject the suggestion that a claimant who qualifies for the care condition should be passported automatically to the other. While they accept that many such claimants are likely to succeed to both components, they emphasise that the test applicable to each component must be considered separately and applied by the decision-maker to the facts found in respect of each claim.

The decision will enable many claimants who are mentally ill, or epileptic, or deaf or blind to qualify for the mobility component. Three of the cases joined in this appeal, and several of those in which Commissioners had previously disagreed dealt with deaf claimants. In this decision the Commissioners dealt specifically with the problems of pre-lingually deaf claimants. In such cases, they thought, it would be quite appropriate to find that the claimant required guidance (or possibly supervision) all of the time he was walking over unfamiliar routes because without that company he would not attempt that route for fear of becoming lost and being unable to communicate effectively with anyone. They accept that supervision must require something more than just keeping another company, but they hold that a person who is present to lend assistance whenever that may become necessary is supervising in the sense of being ancillary to an episode of attention. In any case where the claimant is unable to communicate and is undertaking unfamiliar routes such attention may be frequent enough to be guidance. The Commissioners emphasise that such cases depend upon clear findings of fact as to the claimant's ability to communicate by writing, or lip reading and to his ability to read maps and other directions.

The Tribunal in *R(DLA) 4/01* also took the opportunity of considering whether the words "cannot take advantage of " should be read as conditioned by some word such as "reasonably" so that a claimant need not show that, without assistance, he is totally unable to take advantage of outdoor walking. The Commissioners held it is unnecessary to read in any such words because the paragraph as a whole makes it apparent that some outside walking ability is assumed, for example, the claimant's inability need apply only to unfamiliar routes, and to most of the time. The Tribunal felt that it could safely be left to the good sense of decision-makers to decide when a claimant might otherwise require assistance over unfamiliar routes.

1.261   This does not however resolve the difference between Commissioners over whether it must be shown that the claimant is capable of walking out of doors when given the benefit of guidance and supervision. Commissioners have differed as to whether guidance or supervision will only be relevant if it will enable the claimant to overcome his or her inability to make use of the faculty of walking. In *CDLA/42/94* the Commissioner said that "it would be absurd if a claimant whose disablement was so severe that she was not able to take advantage of the faculty of walking on unfamiliar routes out of doors even with guidance or supervision was excluded from s.73(1)(d). Because of the negative formulation of the provision, a claimant does not necessarily have to show an ability to take advantage of that faculty with guidance or supervision." However, in *CDLA/2364/95* (followed in *CSDLA/12/2003*), the Commissioner rejected that approach and decided that a person who suffered from claustrophobia and agoraphobia and who could not be persuaded to walk outdoors would not be entitled to the lower rate of the mobility component. These latter decisions have been upheld by the Court of Appeal in NI in *Mongan v Department of Social Development* [2005] NICA 16. That court holds that a claimant must show that the guidance or supervision will enhance the claimant's walking ability. But a person can qualify for mobility component at the lower rate under paragraph (d) even though they may never undertake to walk on unfamiliar routes. The test is hypothetical in the sense that the claimant is entitled if they could not walk that route without guidance or supervision — it matters not that they would not walk there anyway. In *R(DLA)6/03* the tribunal had found that the claimant (to whom they had already refused mobility allowance at the higher rate) would not have gone walking on unfamiliar routes (or seemingly on familar routes) because of the danger of falling. It seems that the claimant must have said that the provision of supervision would have made no difference to her because the chairman went on to remark "There is no point in making an award if its purpose is frustrated". The Commissioner allowed the appeal remarking that the element of an award being frustrated is provided for in subs.(8), but that provision requires that the claimant be *unable to* benefit from locomotion not merely that he chooses not to. Notice that in this case the claimant *could* have walked on unfamiliar routes with supervision—it was simply that she chose not to, whereas in *CDLA/2364/95* the claimant was unable to walk outside because their medical condition prevented them from doing so even with supervision.

The decision in *CDLA/2364/95* has been followed and that in *Mongan v Department of Social Development* applied in *KH v SSWP (DLA)* [2015] UKUT 8 (AAC). This was another case where the claimant had for many years refused to leave her home. Evidence suggested that no amount of persuasion would encourage her to do so. Although the decision of the FTT seemed to swing between an approach based on *para. (d)* and one based on *subs. (8)* (claimant able to benefit from facilities for enhanced locomotion) Judge Hemingway holds that their decision was correctly decided on the basis that a claimant should succeed under *para. (d)* only if it can be shown that with guidance or supervision they would be able to walk out of doors. Note, however that this is exactly the sort of claim which may now succeed under the Personal Independence Payment provisions. (See descriptor (e) in the Mobility Activities in Sch.1 of those regulations).

In *CDLA/835/97*, the Commissioner directed that, in considering entitlement to the lower rate of the mobility component under s.73(1)(d), the tribunal to whom he was referring the case should exclude any supervision required to stop the claimant from "going off and getting into trouble shoplifting and the like." He held that supervision to prevent a claimant getting himself into criminal activity or moral danger was outside the scope of the subsection. This part of the decision was, however, set aside (by consent) by the Court of Appeal in *V (a child) v Secretary of State for Social Security* (February 23, 2001), and *CDLA/3781/2003* holds that this has the effect of rendering all of *CDLA/835/97* of no legal effect.

In *AR v SSWP* [2013] UKUT 463 (AAC) the claimant suffered from hyperacusis—an extreme intolerance to noise. In his claim form he said that exposure to noise made him anxious and aggressive. He had been arrested on several occasions as a result of confrontational behaviour resulting from this medical condition. He claimed mobility component on the ground that he needed someone to accompany him to provide reassurance and supervision when walking outside most of the time. The FTT that heard his appeal against refusal of benefit held, in a carefully reasoned decision, that a person accompanying him would not be providing "guidance or supervision" and that any guidance or supervision that was available would, in any case, make no difference to him. In the UT Judge Wikeley expressed his sympathy with the FTT in dealing with a difficult and novel case only on the paper record before them, however, he held that on both these points there was an error of law and directed that the case be reheard before a fresh tribunal. The representative of the Secretary of State had supported the appeal on both grounds, though she argued too, that mobility allowance could not be awarded if the purpose of supervision were to prevent or dissuade the claimant from engaging in criminal activity. Judge Wikeley says this proposition must be approached with caution in the light of cases referred to above. It is possible that benefit might be available, he suggests, if the supervision is needed to prevent a person with a psychiatric condition engaging in criminal or at least anti-social behaviour.

In *C19/98(DLA)*, the Northern Ireland Commissioner holds that the use of suitable aids and appliances can be taken into account when considering s.73(1)(d) even though there is no specific provision to that effect.

Subsection (1A)

This means that a child can qualify for the higher rate of mobility component from the age of three years, but for the lower rate only from the age of five years. 1.262

Subsection (1AB)

The level of visual impairment is specified in subs.(1A) of reg.12 of the DLA regulations. 1.263

Subsection (2)

Regulation 12(2) of the DLA Regulations 1991, made under subs.(5), defines blindness and deafness for the purposes of para.(a). It is not necessary for the claimant to have total loss of vision and hearing (see the note to that regulation). Reg.12(3), made under para.(b), makes it a further condition of entitlement that the combined effects of the claimant's blindness and deafness should make him unable, without the assistance of another, to walk to any intended or required destination while out of doors. 1.264

Subsection (3)

This provision is intended to reduce the immense difficulties caused in mobility allowance cases by the fact that only virtual inability to walk due to *physical* disablement could be taken into account. Some of those who would qualify under this subsection would also qualify under subs.(1)(a) but adjudication in such cases is made much simpler by this new provision. The conditions imposed by this subsection are quite stringent but those who fail to qualify may be able to qualify under subs.(1)(a) for the higher rate (if they can show physical disablement) or under subs.(1)(d) for the lower rate. 1.265

Regulations 12(5) and 12(6) of the DLA Regulations 1991, made under subs.(6), specify who falls within paras (a) and (b) as suffering from mental impairment and displaying severe behavioural problems. A person falls within para.(a) if "he suffers from a state of arrested development or incomplete physical development of the brain, which results in severe impairment of intelligence and social functioning". In *M (A child) v Chief Adjudication Officer*, reported as *R(DLA) 1/00*, the Court of Appeal held that an I.Q. test of the claimant was not conclusive of whether the claimant satisfied this test. It has been usual to look for a score of less than 55 as indicative of a severe impairment of intelligence. In this case the claimant was autistic and had an I.Q. score considerably above that level. The Court of Appeal hold that the claimant's I.Q. is only one of several factors that are relevant. It is a useful starting point, but a full evaluation of intelligence and social functioning should include other elements of social interaction, "sagacity" and "insight". A person falls within para. (b) if the disruptive behaviour "(a) is extreme, (b) regularly requires another person to intervene and physically restrain him in order to prevent him causing physical injury to himself or another, or damage to property, and (c) is so unpredicable that he requires another person to be present and watching over him whenever he is awake." In *CSDLA/202/2007*, a claim for higher rate mobility component made on behalf of a child of 3, who was autistic, was returned for consideration by a new tribunal because the first appeal tribunal had failed to consider both of the possible routes by which such a claim might succeed; *viz.* either under s.73(1)(a) (temporary paralysis as to walking resulting from the autism), or, by s.73(1)(c) (severely mentally impaired and severe behavioural problems, etc.). In doing so, Commissioner Parker adopts both *R(DLA) 1/00* and *R(DLA) 7/02*. Both of these routes now have age limitations in respect of a child—see subs.(1A) above.

Under para.(c), it is also necessary for the claimant to satisfy the conditions for the highest rate of the care component. It is not clear why entitlement to an allowance in respect of mobility outdoors should require satisfaction of the night attendance condition for the care component, and this may be a major obstacle for some claimants. Subs.(7) has the effect that those who are deemed to satisfy one or both of the attendance conditions for the care component because they undergo renal dialysis or are terminally ill may rely on the same provisions for the purpose of satisfying para.(c)

Subsection (4A)

1.266
Subsection (4A) imposes similar conditions on a claim made under s.73(1)(d) in respect of a child, to those that are provided in s.72(1A). A recent decision of Commissioner Parker (*CSDLA/91/2003*) applies the same reasoning to the conditions for mobility as that adopted for the care component. When guidance and supervision is required it must be substantially more than would be required for a child of that age of normal physical and mental development. In judging what is substantially more, account must be taken of both the quality and the quantity of the supervision. Thus where all children might need to be accompanied on a certain route, a disabled child who required support, or restraint, or encouragement, or even constant surveillance should qualify. This has been confirmed by the decision in *KC-MS v SSWP* [2015] UKUT 284 (AAC). The FTT had rejected an appeal by the mother of a six-year-old child in respect of the middle rate of benefit. In doing so they observed that no six-year-old would be permitted to go out on unfamiliar routes without supervision. Judge Gray allowed an appeal pointing out that the test was not whether all such children would require supervision, but whether this disabled child required substantially more supervision, or a different kind of supervision, than that required by a normal child of that age.

Note too, the decision in *BM v SSWP* (CDLA) [2014] UKUT 18 (AAC); [2015] AACR 29 where Judge Markus has given a careful analysis of the provisions in s.72 (1A). Although the wording is not identical the approach adopted should be the same.

1.267
Subsections (5) and (6)
See regs 12 to 12c of the DLA Regulations, 1991.

Subsection (8)

This is in the same terms as s.37A(2)(b) of the Social Security Act 1975 relating   **1.268**
to mobility allowance which was considered by a Commissioner in *R(M) 2/83*. He
approved a passage in the second edition of Ogus and Barendt, *The Law of Social
Security*, in which they said:

> "This obviously excludes human vegetables and those whom it is unsafe to move,
> but it is arguable that of the remainder there will be few who will not receive some
> benefit from the occasional sortie, and it is not easy to draw a line between the
> deserving and the undeserving except on some arbitrary basis."

The Commissioner pointed out that the word "benefit" was a wide one and that the
provision contained the words "from time to time" but he added a further category
of excluded persons, "that is persons so severely mentally deranged that a high
degree of supervision and restraint would be required to prevent them either injuring themselves or others."

Although the claimant need show only that he will benefit from locomotion "from
time to time" during "most" of the period in respect of which his claim is made it is
necessary, as well, to satisfy *subs (1)* of this section that the claimant can be said to
be unable to walk "throughout" that period.

This has been given a meaning consistent with the approach adopted in *Secretary
of State v Moyna* [2003] UKHL 44, (that it is a matter of judgement rather than
arithmetical calculation), but unless the need for help is more than brief and more
frequent than occasional, it will not satisfy this test- see the decision of Judge
Rowland in *CDLA/496/2008* noted above in relation to *subs (1)*. Whereas the
words in these two subsections might appear to be inconsistent they should not be
so if proper regard is given to their respective purposes. *Subs (1)* sets the standard
to qualify for the benefit; *subs (8)* deprives an otherwise qualified claimant of his
benefit if he cannot make sufficient use of it.

The expression "from time to time" conditions the claimant's ability to benefit
in the sense that he might enjoy even just an occasional outing, though his need for
assistance to achieve locomotion might be constant. But even if the claimant's need
for assistance does apply throughout the period his claim would still fail if his ability
to benefit from locomotion is only on rare occasions because then he would not be
able to do so "most" of the time.

In *CDLA/2142/2005* the Commissioner agrees with the decision in *CSDLA/12/2003*
that the claimant, who was agoraphobic, must be willing to make use of the assistance by walking out of doors so as to show that she would benefit from enhanced
locomotion. But he returned the case to a new tribunal with the suggestion to consider whether walking within the confines of the claimant's own back garden, which
was all that she could be persuaded to do, could satisfy that test if it were beneficial
to the health, both mental and physical, of the claimant.

This matter has been considered again by Judge Wikeley in the Upper Tribunal.
See *BP v SSWP* [2009] UKUT 90 (AAC). The claimant was a middle-aged man
who suffered from chronic fatigue syndrome and ME. He described himself in the
claim papers as "bedridden and housebound" and had not in fact been further than
his bedroom and the bathroom on the upper floor of his home for several years. He
had been in receipt of the mobility component at the higher rate, but on a renewal
claim the DM took the view that subs.(8) applied and refused the claim. This decision was upheld by the First-tier Tribunal. Judge Wikeley allowed an appeal. He
draws attention to the lack of any evidence that the claimant was prevented from
leaving his house (or going downstairs) because of any mental state that prevented
him from doing so. The limitation on the claimant's going out seemed to stem from
the weakness of his legs and consequent inability to get down stairs; indeed, his
wife gave evidence that if there were a man to carry him down to a wheelchair, she
could certainly take him out in the car with her. The judge reiterated the point that
the operation of this subsection should be limited to those claimants for whom it
would be impossible to be taken out and those for whom it would present a danger

to their health. On that basis the cases of patients suffering from agoraphobia would be explicable either on the basis that their refusal to leave the home was an instance of impossibility, (they could hardly be forced to leave even if for their own good), or, of creating a danger to their mental health, again, if they were forced to leave.

1.269   The Judge deals with two other points. First, that the argument presented on behalf of the claimant that because he lived in a country location he needed his car so that his wife could collect medicines for him was not sufficient for him to show that he would benefit by "enhanced facilities for locomotion." Judge Wikeley holds that the enhanced facility must refer to the claimant's own locomotion to be of benefit to him.

Secondly, the Judge draws attention also to the caveat that Commissioner Morcom had added to his decision in *R (M) 2/83*. The commissioner had suggested that there might be a further category of excluded claimants—those who were so mentally deranged that they would require a high degree of supervision and security to avoid danger to themselves and others. Judge Wikeley suggests that this qualification might need to be reconsidered in light of the fact that mobility component, (as distinct from the old Mobility Benefit that was in force at the time of the earlier case) extends now to those who are "severely mentally impaired" and those who display "severe behavioural problems".

This case is useful also in demonstrating the importance of the difference between a decision that records the evidence, and one that makes findings of fact. An extensive, even verbatim, record of the evidence is no substitute for a statement of the facts as found by the tribunal.

In *CDLA/1639/2006* the Commissioner held that a tribunal which allowed a claim for higher rate mobility component in respect of a claimant suffering from severe attacks of migraine had erred in law by overlooking the effects of s.73(8). As the commissioner pointed out the only time that the claimant would have had any need for attention was during the time he was suffering a migraine attack; at that same time however, on his own evidence, he was compelled to sit or to lie down, so no amount of assistance could aid his mobility.

And see too *CDLA/496/2008* noted above in relation to *subs.(1),* where it was held that the period for which the claimant required to be resting and usually asleep, could not be included as part of the time in which she could benefit from facilities for enhanced locomotion.

Subsection (9)
1.270   Paragraph (a) imposes the three-month qualifying period but this is deemed to be satisfied in the case of a person who is terminally ill (see subs.(12)). If a person is entitled to the lower rate of the mobility component by virtue of satisfying the condition in subs.(1)(d) and his or her condition deteriorates so that he or she would satisfy one or other of the conditions in subs.(1)(a), (b) or (c) the effect of subs.(11)(a) is that the claimant must still wait three months before qualifying for the higher rate unless terminally ill. Under s.76(1), an award cannot usually be made before the date of claim which is determined in accordance with reg.6(1) and (5) of the Social Security (Claims and Payments) Regulations 1987 (see Vol.III of this work). Reg.11 of the DLA Regulations prescribes, for the purpose of para.(a)(ii) a period of three months ending on the day on which the claimant was last entitled to the component if that was not more than two years before the current period of entitlement would otherwise begin. This has the practical effect in most cases that the three-month qualifying period is deemed to be satisfied if the current claim is within two years of a previous period of entitlement at the relevant rate.

Under para.4(2) of Sch.1 to the DLA Regulations, a period of six months is substituted for the period of three months in para.(a) in the case of a person over the age of 65 who makes a claim for the mobility component and is entitled to do so because he or she was formerly entitled to a car or other assistance under an invalid vehicle scheme.

Paragraph (b) requires that a person should be expected to satisfy the conditions for the component for six months, unless he or she is expected to die sooner.

Although this means that six months will normally be the minimum period for which an award will be made, this section does not prevent an award for a lesser period when that is appropriate. In *R(DLA)11/02* the claimant had applied unsuccessfully and then appealed. Before that appeal could be heard her condition had deteriorated and she made a fresh claim that was allowed. The Commissioner held that an award of less than six months could be made to fill the gap between the date when she was now regarded as qualifying and the date when the existing award commenced even though that was less than six months. This period of six months begins as the three-month (or six-month for those over 65) qualifying period ends and both conditions are intended to ensure that only the chronically disabled are entitled to DLA.

Note that since the condition is prospective the matter must be determined on the basis of the information available and the prognosis at the time of the claim. For the effect of this, see note to s.72(2)(b) above.

Subsections (10) and (11)

The higher rate is payable if one or other of the conditions in subs. (a), (ab), (b), or (c) is satisfied and the lower rate is payable in any other case. In *KS v SSWP* [2013] UKUT 390 (AAC) it was argued that the limitation of the higher rate of the mobility component to conditions having a physical cause was overruled by the provisions of the Equality Act 2010 as being discriminatory on the grounds of mental disablement. The argument failed because the terms of that act specify that nothing is unlawful if that action is required by the terms of legislation (see Sch.22, para.(1) of that Act). To be entitled at the higher rate, it is not necessary that the *same* condition should have been satisfied throughout the qualifying period and the period of the award.

1.271

Subsection (12)

Under s.66(2), a person is "terminally ill" if "he suffers from a progressive disease and his death in consequence of that disease can reasonably be expected within six months". See the notes to that section.

1.272

The effect of this subsection is that a terminally ill person is deemed to satisfy the three-month qualifying period (or the six-month period in the case of a person over 65 formerly entitled to an invalid vehicle). Note also that reg.2(4) of the DLA Regulations relaxes the presence conditions for terminally ill claimants so that it is not necessary for them to have been in Great Britain before the day in respect of which the claim is made. However, while terminally ill claimants are deemed to satisfy the conditions for the highest rate of the care component, they are not deemed to satisfy any of the conditions for the mobility component except subs.(3) (c) (see subs.(7)). This is confirmed in *R(DLA)7/06*.

Subsection (13)

Sch.2 to the DLA Regulations makes provision allowing former invalid vehicle scheme beneficiaries to be deemed to satisfy the conditions for the higher rate of the mobility component and Sch.1, para.4 permits them to claim the mobility component even if they are aged over 65.

1.273

Subsection (14)

There is specific provision in the legislation governing disability working allowance which ensures that disability living allowance is not to be treated as income (Sch.3, para.4 to the Disability Working Allowance (General) Regulations 1991). But *quaere* whether para.8(a) of Sch.4 to those Regulations (which allows arrears of disability living allowance to be disregarded as capital only for 52 weeks and so implies it should be taken into account after that) is overridden by this subsection

1.274

so that the arrears may continue to be disregarded for longer. The power to make regulations under this subsection is not referred to in the preamble to those Regulations. This provision also applies to any local authority scheme applying a means test where there is a statutory power to make charges for services, e.g. charges for home helps under para.3 of Sch.8 to the National Health Service Act 1977.

Mobility component for certain persons eligible for invalid carriages

1.275

74.—(1) Regulations may provide for the issue, variation and cancellation of certificates in respect of prescribed categories of persons to whom this section applies; and a person in respect of whom such a certificate is issued shall, during any period while the certificate is in force, be deemed for the purposes of section 73 above to satisfy the condition mentioned in subsection (1)(a) of that section and to fall within paragraphs (a) and (b) of subsection (9) by virtue of having satisfied or being likely to satisfy that condition throughout both the periods mentioned in those paragraphs.

(2) This section applies to any person whom the Secretary of State considers—

(a) was on 1st January 1976 in possession of an invalid carriage or other vehicle provided in pursuance of section 33 of the Health Services and Public Health Act 1968 (which related to vehicles for persons suffering from physical defect or disability) or receiving payments in pursuance of subsection (3) of that section; or

(b) had at that date, or at a later date specified by the Secretary of State, made an application which the Secretary of State approved for such a carriage or vehicle or for such payments; or

(c) was, both at some time during a prescribed period before that date and at some time during a prescribed period after that date, in possession of such a carriage or vehicle or receiving such payments; or

(d) would have been, by virtue of any of the preceding paragraphs, a person to whom this section applies but for some error or delay for which in the opinion of the Secretary of State the person was not responsible and which was brought to the attention of the Secretary of State within the period of one year beginning with 30th March 1977 (the date of the passing of the Social Security (Miscellaneous Provisions) Act 1977, section 13 of which made provisions corresponding to the provision made by this section).

DERIVATION

1.276

SS(MP)A 1977 s.13.

GENERAL NOTE

1.277

For regulations, see reg.13 of, and Sch.2 to, the Social Security (Disability Living Allowance) Regulations 1991, which are treated by s.2(2) of the Social Security (Consequential Provisions) Act 1992 as having been made under this section.

Mobility allowance (which was introduced by s.22 of the Social Security Pensions Act 1975 and was later replaced by the higher rate of the mobility component of disability living allowance) was intended to replace the provision of invalid vehicles and the alternative system of paying for vehicles. Those who were already entitled to vehicles or payments under the Health Services and Public Health Act 1968 on

January 1, 1976, have retained the right to them but may at any time exchange them for the higher rate of the mobility component of disability living allowance, even if they are over the usual maximum age of 65.

[¹ Persons who have attained pensionable age]

75.—(1) Except to the extent to which regulations provide otherwise, no person shall be entitled to either component of a disability living allowance for any period after he attains [¹ pensionable age] otherwise than by virtue of an award made before he attains that age.

(2) Regulations may provide in relation to persons who are entitled to a component of a disability living allowance by virtue of subsection (1) above that any provisions of this Act which relates to disability living allowance, other than section 74 above, so far as it so relates, and any provision of the Administration Act which is relevant to disability living allowance—

    (a) shall have effect subject to modifications, additions or amendments; or

    (b) shall not have effect.

1.278

AMENDMENT

1. Pensions Act 2007 Sch.1 Pt 8 para.42. This amendment was originally not to have effect until April 6, 2024, but now has had effect from April 6, 2018—see Pensions Act 2011 s.1.

DERIVATION

SSA 1975 s.37ZD

1.279

GENERAL NOTE

Note: the amendment to subs.(1) above to "pensionable age" did not have effect until April 6, 2018. Until that time the section should be read as if it retained the words "the age of 65".

1.280

The general rule established by this subsection is that a person is not entitled to DLA for any period after reaching the age of 65 unless entitled by virtue of an award made before he or she reaches that age. Reg.3 of, Sch.1 to, the DLA Regulations are made under this section.

Note that the age of 65 is to be replaced by the phrase "pensionable age" by Pensions Act 2007 s.13, but the effect of this amendment was postponed until April 2024. That date is now due to be brought forward to December 6, 2018. (Pensions Act 2011 Sch.1).

An attempt was made in *NT v SSWP* [2009] UKUT 37(AAC); *R(DLA) 1/09* to show that the denial of mobility component to those over pensionable age was unlawful as a denial of the claimant's human rights by reason of discriminating on the ground of age. The judge of the Upper Tribunal, Judge Levenson, found that a claim to mobility component did engage the rights of the claimant under Article 1 of the First Protocol, and her rights under Article 8. He found, as well, that a distinction based upon age was capable of being discrimination under Article 14, but even so, the judge disallowed the appeal. He accepted that the DWP had demonstrated a rational and proportionate justification for the difference in treatment because the mobility component of DLA had always been intended to benefit those of working age who found that their earning capacity, as well as their life style, was affected adversely by their disability. When the claimant reached an age at which earning could be assumed to be replaced by entitlement to other benefits, such as retirement pension, the reason for mobility component had largely ceased.

And note too *GS v SSWP* [2016] UKUT 687 (AAC). The claimant had previously been in receipt of a mobility component when he lived in this country, but that entitlement ceased when he emigrated to another EU country. He returned to live here after he had attained the age of 65 and his claim was refused. His argument in the UT that refusal on the ground of his age was a denial of the freedom of movement was rejected.

Regulation 3 originally provided for two exceptions to the general rule. First, a person who would have qualified at the age of 65 could be awarded DLA provided a claim was made before he or she reached the age of 66. That provision was revoked from October 6, 1997. Secondly, if a claimant reaches the age of 65 during the three-month qualifiying period for either component, having claimed before reaching that age, then the claimant is not prejudiced by the fact that the award is not made, or effective, until after his or her 65th birthday. There is a further exception under para.4 of Sch.1 of the DLA Regulations allowing a former invalid vehicle scheme beneficiary to qualify for the mobility component. Sch.1 to the DLA Regulations also enables further awards to be made to those people who have established entitlement to DLA beyond the age of 65, although there are some restrictions.

Where the claimant's entitlement to DLA is revised after reaching the age of 65 and it is concluded that he is no longer entitled to the care component at the higher or middle rate, or the mobility component at the higher rate, it is not possible for him to qualify then for the lowest rate of the care component, nor for the lower rate of mobility component, if the review is based upon a change of circumstances occurring after he has reached the age of 65 (see *R(DLA) 5/02*). Where, however, the revision is based upon a change of circumstances that occurred before he reached that age (or is based upon a mistake of law or fact made at the initial award, or a subsequent renewal, before that age), the claimant may be entitled to an award at the lowest rate for care and for the lower rate of mobility where his condition would justify such an award from the appropriate date before the age of 65. See reg.3 and Sch.1 the Disability Living Allowance Regulations 1991 and the decision of Commissioner Parker, *CSDLA/388/2000* and see too *CDLA/754/2000* where the Commissioner draws attention, for the benefit of a new tribunal, to the effect of paras 3 and 5 of Sch.1 which is that in an appropriate case a claimant whose entitlement to the DLA components ceases even when he is over the age of 65 may have those entitlements restored if his condition then deteriorates again. See also the decisions in *CDLA/301/05* noted after Sch.1, in which the Commissioner also holds that a claim for the lowest rate of DLA may succeed even if the need for that care developed after the age of 65, so long as the basis of the review was something that occurred before that age.

People over 65 who are not entitled to DLA may instead qualify for attendance allowance under s.64. Note that although attendance allowance has no equivalent to the mobility component provided under DLA it is possible for a claimant who requires assistance in moving about to include that help in the assessment of their need for attention in connection with their bodily functions—in that case the bodily function of mobilising, whether within doors or out of doors. Thus, for someone in a wheelchair who requires another person to push them about, that assistance can count towards the frequency and extent of the assistance that they require: see *JB v SSWP* [2015] UKUT 361 (AAC).

Disability living allowance—supplementary

1.281   **76.**—(1) Subject to subsection (2) below, a person shall not be entitled to a disability living allowance for any period preceding the date on which a claim for it is made or treated as made by him or on his behalf.

(2) Notwithstanding anything in subsection (1) above, provision may be

made by regulations for a person to be entitled to a component of a disability living allowance for a period preceding the date on which a claim for such an allowance is made or treated as made by him or on his behalf if he has previously been entitled to that component.

(3) For the purposes of sections 72(5) and 73(12) above where—

(a) a person purports to make a claim for a disability living allowance on behalf of another; and

(b) the claim is made expressly on the ground that the person on whose behalf it purports to be made is terminally ill,

that person shall be regarded as making the claim notwithstanding that it is made without his knowledge or authority.

DERIVATION

SSA 1975 s.37ZE.   1.282

GENERAL NOTE

This section makes provision for claims to DLA.   1.283

Subsections (1) and (2)

This states the general rule that claims for DLA cannot be backdated to cover a   1.284
period before the date on which a claim is made or *is treated as made*. The general rule has been criticised as unduly severe. Claims for most other social security benefits can be backdated, including benefits in respect of incapacity for work which suggests that the gathering of medical evidence in respect of past periods is not an insuperable problem. It should, however, be noted that the three-month qualifying period (six months for people over 65) is normally before the date of claim, so to that extent, claims can be regarded as being backdated over that period. There is also some further flexibility. Reg.6(1)(a) of the Claims and Payments Regulations 1987 provides that a claim shall be treated as made on the date it is received in an appropriate office of the Department of Social Security. Reg.4(1) requires a claim to be made in writing either on a claim form or in such other manner as the Secretary of State may accept as suffcient. If the Secretary of State does not accept a document as a claim, he may ask the claimant to complete a proper claim form or simply to give further information. If that is done within a reasonable period, the claim is then treated as having been made when the original document was received (regs 4(7) and 6(1)(b)). More specific provision is made in respect of DLA and attendance allowance in reg.6(8) under which a claim is treated as having been made when a request for a claim form is received by the Department, provided that the claimant duly completes and returns the claim form within six weeks or such longer period as the Secretary of State considers reasonable. Leaflets widely available to claimants include requests for claim forms rather than claim forms themselves which are bulky documents. If a claim is delayed in the post owing to industrial action, it is treated as having been made on the date it would have arrived in the ordinary course of post (reg.6(7)). Until October 6, 1997, reg.5 of the DLA Regulations, made under subs.(2), allowed a claim to be backdated to the end of a previous period of entitlement to the same component of DLA, provided that the renewal claim was made within six months of the end of that period of entitlement and the claimant satisfied the conditions of entitlement throughout the intervening period. For these purposes, a previous period of entitlement to attendance allowance was treated as a period of entitlement to the care component and a previous period of entitlement to mobility allowance was treated as a period of entitlement to the mobility component.

Subsection (3)
1.285   This is necessary to enable a person to make a claim for DLA on behalf of someone who is terminally ill in a case when the claimant is not to be told of the prognosis in his case.

Guardian's allowance

Guardian's allowance

1.286   **77.** *Omitted. See Vol.IV: Tax Credits and HMRC-administered Social Security Benefits.*

Benefits for the aged

Category C and Category D retirement pensions and other benefits for the aged

1.287   **78.**—(1) [³...]

(2) [³...]

(3) A person who is over the age of 80 [³ , who reached pensionable age before 6 April 2016 and who satisfies] such conditions as may be prescribed shall be entitled to a Category D retirement pension at the appropriate weekly rate if—

(a) he is not entitled to a Category A, Category B or Category C retirement pension; or

(b) he is entitled to such a pension, but it is payable at a weekly rate which, disregarding those elements specified in subsection (4) below, is less than the appropriate weekly rate.

(4) The elements referred to in subsection (3)(b) above are—

(a) any additional pension;

(b) any increase so far as attributable to—

(i) any additional pension, or

(ii) any increase in a guaranteed minimum pension;

(c) any graduated retirement benefit; and

(d) [² . . .]

(5) [³...]

(6) The appropriate weekly rate of a Category D retirement pension shall be that specified in Schedule 4, Part III, paragraph 7.

(7) Entitlement to a [³...] Category D retirement pension shall continue throughout the pensioner's life.

(8) A [³...] Category D retirement pension shall not be payable for any period falling before the day on which the pensioner's entitlement is to be regarded as commencing for that purpose by virtue of section 5(1)(k) of the Administration Act.

(9) Regulations may provide for the payment—

(a) to a widow whose husband was over pensionable age on 5th July 1948; or

(b) to a woman whose marriage to a husband who was over pensionable age on that date was terminated otherwise than by his death.

of a Category C retirement pension or of benefit corresponding to a widow's pension or a widowed mother's allowance; and any such retirement pension or any such benefit shall be at the prescribed rate.

AMENDMENTS

1. Tax Credits Act 2002 Sch.6 (April 6, 2003).
2. Pensions Act 2007 Sch.1 para.13 (September 26, 2007).
3. Pensions Act 2014 Sch.12 para.84 (April 6, 2016)

GENERAL NOTE

The repeal of subss.(1), (2) and (5) remove entitlement to Category C pensions **1.288**
generally, following the policy of the Pensions Act 2014, leaving only existing pensions and transitional cases to be dealt with under that legislation. The amendments
also close off Category D pensions to those reaching state pensionable age on or
after April 6, 2016.

In *Secretary of State for Work and Pensions v JG (RP)* [2013] UKUT 300 (AAC)
Judge White of the Upper Tribunal discussed the application of the section to a
claim for a category D pension in the context of a claimant who spent considerable periods of his life outside the United Kingdom in various countries including
Gibraltar and the Isle of Man. That decision was over-ruled by the Court of Appeal
as *Secretary of State for Work and Pensions v Garland* [2014] EWCA Civ 1550.

Age addition

79.—(1) A person who is over the age of 80 and entitled to a retirement **1.289**
pension of any category [¹ under this Act] shall be entitled to an increase of
the pension, to be known as "age addition".

(2) Where a person is in receipt of a pension or allowance payable by
the Secretary of State by virtue of any prescribed enactment or instrument
(whether passed or made before or after this Act) and—

(a) he is over the age of 80; and
(b) he fulfils such other conditions as may be prescribed, he shall be
    entitled to an increase of that pension or allowance, also known as
    age addition.

(3) Age addition shall be payable for the life of the person entitled, at the
weekly rate specified in Schedule 4, Part III, paragraph 8.

AMENDMENT

1. Pensions Act 2014 Sch.12 para.85 (April 6, 2016). **1.290**

GENERAL NOTE

The amendment to this section by the Pensions Act 2014 restricts entitlement to **1.291**
pensions awarded or claimed under this Act and excludes any pension entitlement
under the 2014 Act.

PART IV

INCREASES FOR DEPENDANTS

Child dependants

Beneficiary's dependent children

80. [¹ . . .] **1.292**

1. Repealed by the Tax Credits Act 2002 s.60 and Sch.6 (April 6, 2003).

SAVING

Art.3 of The Tax Credits Act 2002 (Commencement No. 3 and Transitional Provisions and Savings) Order 2003 (SI 2003/938) provides:

"Saving provision

1.293   **3.**—(1) Notwithstanding the coming into force of the specified provisions, the Contributions and Benefits Act and the Administration Act shall, in cases to which paragraph (2) applies, subject to paragraph (3), continue to have effect from the commencement date as if those provisions had not come into force.

(2) This paragraph applies where a person—

(a) is entitled to a relevant increase on the day before the commencement date; or

(b) claims a relevant increase on or after the commencement date and it is subsequently determined that he is entitled to a relevant increase in respect of a period which includes the day before the commencement date.

(3) The provisions saved by paragraph (1) shall continue to have effect until—

(a) subject to sub-paragraph (c), where a relevant increase ceases to be payable to a person to whom paragraph (2) applies for a period greater than 58 days beginning with the day on which it was last payable, on the day 59 days after the day on which it was last payable; or

(b) in any other case, subject to sub-paragraph (c), on the date on which entitlement to a relevant increase ceases;

(c) where regulation 6(19) or (23) of the Social Security (Claims and Payments) Regulations 1987 applies to a further claim for a relevant increase, on the date on which entitlement to that relevant increase ceases.

(4) In this article—

"the commencement date" means 6th April 2003;

"a relevant increase" means an increase under section 80 or 90 of the Contributions and Benefits Act;

"the specified provisions" means the provisions of the 2002 Act which are brought into force by article 2."

GENERAL NOTE

1.294   The operation of section 80 is preserved in the circumstances specified in this savings provision. See, further, Welfare Reform Act 2009 s.37(1). Section 80(4) set out income limits above which no child dependency increase are payable. The figures in that subsection are uprated for those cases where the savings provision applies.

From the first day of the first benefit week to start for a particular beneficiary on or after April 1, 2019, the relevant figures are earnings of £240.00 per week in respect of the first child, and in respect of a further child for each complete £32 by which the earnings exceed £240: The Social Security Benefits Up-rating Order 2019 (SI 2019/480) art.8.

Restrictions on increase—child not living with beneficiary etc.

1.295   **81.** [¹ . . .]

AMENDMENT

1. Repealed by the Tax Credits Act 2002 s.60 and Sch.6 (April 6, 2003).

SAVING

Art.3 of The Tax Credits Act 2002 (Commencement No.3 and Transitional Provisions and Savings) Order 2003 (SI 2003/938) (and see, further, Welfare Reform Act 2009 s.37(1)) provides:

"Saving provision

3.—(1) Notwithstanding the coming into force of the specified provisions, the Contributions and Benefits Act and the Administration Act shall, in cases to which paragraph (2) applies, subject to paragraph (3), continue to have effect from the commencement date as if those provisions had not come into force.

(2) This paragraph applies where a person—

(a) is entitled to a relevant increase on the day before the commencement date; or

(b) claims a relevant increase on or after the commencement date and it is subsequently determined that he is entitled to a relevant increase in respect of a period which includes the day before the commencement date.

(3) The provisions saved by paragraph (1) shall continue to have effect until—

(a) subject to sub-paragraph (c), where a relevant increase ceases to be payable to a person to whom paragraph (2) applies for a period greater than 58 days beginning with the day on which it was last payable, on the day 59 days after the day on which it was last payable; or

(b) in any other case, subject to sub-paragraph (c), on the date on which entitlement to a relevant increase ceases;

(c) where regulation 6(19) or (23) of the Social Security (Claims and Payments) Regulations 1987 applies to a further claim for a relevant increase, on the date on which entitlement to that relevant increase ceases.

(4) In this article—

"the commencement date" means 6th April 2003;

"a relevant increase" means an increase under section 80 or 90 of the Contributions and Benefits Act;

"the specified provisions" means the provisions of the 2002 Act which are brought into force by article 2."

Adult dependants

Short-term benefit: increase for adult dependants

82. [¹ . . .]

AMENDMENT

1. Repealed by the Welfare Reform Act 2009 s.15 (April 6, 2010).

SAVING

Section 15(2)(a) of the Welfare Reform Act 2009 provides:

"(2) Nothing in subsection (1) or Part 2 of Schedule 7 applies in relation to—

(a) the amount of a maternity allowance payable for a maternity allowance period (within the meaning of section 35(2) of the Benefits Act) which begins before 6 April 2010 but ends on or after that date, ..."

Pension increase (wife)

83.—[. . .]

1.296

1.297

1.298

1.299

GENERAL NOTE

1.300   This section ceased to have effect on April 6, 2010 under s.4 of the Pensions Act 2007.

SAVING

1.301   Section 4(5)–(8) of the Pensions Act 2007 provides:

"(5) Nothing in–

    (a) the repeals in subsection (1),
    (b) the amendments in Part 4 of Schedule 1, or
    (c) the repeals in Part 2 of Schedule 7,

applies in relation to a qualifying person at any time falling on or after 6th April 2010 but before the appropriate date.

(6) In subsection (5) a "qualifying person" means a person who–

    (a) has, before 6th April 2010, made a claim for a relevant increase in accordance with section 1 of the Administration Act; and
    (b) immediately before that date is either–

        (i) entitled to the increase claimed, or
        (ii) a beneficiary to whom section 92 of the SSCBA (continuation of awards where fluctuating earnings) applies in respect of that increase.

(7) In subsection (5) "the appropriate date" means the earlier (or earliest) of–

    (a) 6th April 2020;
    (b) the date when the qualifying person ceases to be either entitled to the relevant increase or a beneficiary to whom section 92 of the SSCBA applies in respect of it;
    (c) where the relevant increase is payable to the qualifying person under section 83 of that Act, the date on which his wife attains pensionable age.

(8) In this section "relevant increase" means an increase in a Category A or Category C retirement pension under section 83, 84 or 85 of the SSCBA."

GENERAL NOTE

1.302   Note that s.83, where applicable, does not cease to apply because of a change of gender and accordingly references to a man or to his wife are to be construed accordingly. (Marriage (Same Sex Couples) Act 2013 Sch.4 Pt 5, para.15(1)).

With effect from December 16, 2014 art.11(1) of the Marriage and Civil Partnership (Scotland) Act 2014 and Civil Partnership Act 2004 (Consequential Provisions and Modifications Order 2001 (SI 2014/3229) provides:

"In a case where a full gender recognition certificate is issued to a person under the 2004 Act—

    (a) section 83 of the 1992 Act (pension increase (wife)) does not cease to apply by virtue of the change of gender; and
    (b) in the continued application of section 83 in such a case, references to a pension payable to a man, or references to his wife, are to be construed accordingly."

Pension increase (husband)

1.303   **84.**—[. . .]

GENERAL NOTE

1.304   This section ceased to have effect on April 6, 2010 under s.4, Pensions Act 2007. The saving referred to in the annotations to s.83 also applies to this section.

Note also that in relation to cases under s.84 where that section is still applicable it does not cease to apply because of a change of gender and references in that case to a woman and to her husband are to be construed accordingly. (Marriage (Same Sex Couples) Act 2013 Sch.4 Pt 5, para.15(2)).

With effect from December 16, 2014 art.11(2) of the Marriage and Civil   1.305
Partnership (Scotland) Act 2014 and Civil Partnership Act 2004 (Consequential Provisions and Modifications Order 2001 (SI 2014/3229) provides:

"In a case where a full gender recognition certificate is issued to a person under the 2004 Act—

(a) section 84 of the 1992 Act (pension increase (husband)) does not cease to apply by virtue of the change of gender; and

(b) in the continued application of section 83 in such a case, references to a pension payable to a woman, or references to her husband, are to be construed accordingly."

Pension increase (person with care of children [¹ or qualifying young person])

85.—[. . .]   1.306

GENERAL NOTE

This section ceased to have effect on April 6, 2010 under s.4 of the Pensions Act   1.307
2007. The saving referred to in the annotations to s.83 also applies to this section.

Incapacity benefit—increases for adult dependants

[¹ **86A.**—(1) The weekly rates of short-term and long-term incapacity   1.308
benefit shall, in such circumstances as may be prescribed, be increased for adult dependants by the appropriate amounts specified in relation to benefit of that description in Schedule 4, Part IV, column (3).

(2) Regulations may provide that where the person in respect of whom an increase of benefit is claimed has earnings in excess of such amount as may be prescribed there shall be no increase in benefit under this section.]

AMENDMENT

1. Social Security (Incapacity for Work) Act 1994 s.2(5) (November 18, 1994 for regulation-making purposes; April 13, 1995 for other purposes).

Rate of increase where associated retirement pension is attributable to reduced contributions

87.—(1) Where a person—   1.309
[¹ (a) is entitled to a short-term incapacity benefit under section 30A(2)
  (b); and]

(b) would have been entitled only by virtue of section 60(1) above to the retirement pension by reference to which the rate of that benefit [² . . .] is determined,

the amount of any increase of the benefit attributable to sections 82 to [³ 85] above shall be determined in accordance with regulations under this section.

(2) The regulations shall not provide for any such increase in a case where the retirement pension by reference to which the rate of the said benefit [² . . .] or invalidity pension is determined—

(a) would have been payable only by virtue of section 60 above; and
(b) would, in consequence of a failure to satisfy a contribution condition, have contained no basic pension.

AMENDMENTS

1. Jobseekers Act 1995 Sch.2 para.26 (October 7, 1996).
2. Social Security (Incapacity for Work) Act 1994 Sch.1, para.24(3) and Sch.2 (April 13, 1995).
3. Welfare Reform Act 2007 s.28 and Sch.3 para.9(7) (October 27, 2008).

DERIVATION

1.310   SSA 1975 s.47A as amended.

GENERAL NOTE

1.311   See reg.13 of the Dependency Regulations.

Increases to be in respect of only one adult dependant

1.312   [¹ **88.** A person shall not [² by virtue of section 86A] above be entitled for the same period to an increase of benefit in respect of more than one person.]

AMENDMENTS

1. Social Security (Incapacity for Work) Act 1994 Sch.1 para.25 (April 13, 1995).
2. Pensions Act 2007 Sch.1 para.14 (September 26, 2007).

DERIVATION

1.313   SSA 1975 s.48.

Miscellaneous

Earnings to include occupational and personal pensions [³ etc.] for purposes of provisions relating to increases of benefits in respect of [¹. . .] adult dependants

1.314   **89.**—(1) Except as may be prescribed, in [¹ . . .] [² [⁴ sections 82 and 86A]] above, any reference to earnings includes a reference to payments by way of occupational or personal pension.

[³ (1A) Except as may be prescribed, in [⁴ sections 82 and 86A] above, and in regulations under section 86A above, any reference to earnings includes a reference to payments by way of PPF periodic payments.]

(2) For the purposes of the provisions mentioned in [³ subsections (1) and (1A) above], the Secretary of State may by regulations provide, in relation to cases where payments by way of occupational or personal pension [³ or PPF periodic payments] are made otherwise than weekly, that any necessary apportionment of the payments shall be made in such manner and on such basis as may be prescribed.

[³ (3) In this section "PPF periodic payments" means—
(a) any periodic compensation payments made in relation to a person, payable under the pension compensation provisions as specified in section 162(2) of the Pensions Act 2004 or Article 146(2) of the

Pensions (Northern Ireland) order 2005 (the pension compensation provisions); or

(b) any periodic payments made in relation to a person, payable under section 166 of the Pensions Act 2004 or Article 150 of the Pensions (Northern Ireland) Order 2005 (duty to pay scheme benefits unpaid at assessment date etc.),

other than payments made to a surviving dependant of a person entitled to such compensation.]

AMENDMENTS

1. Tax Credits Act 2002 s.60 and Sch.6 (April 6, 2003).
2. Social Security (Incapacity for Work) Act 1994 Sch.1 para.26 (April 13, 1995).
3. The Pensions Act 2004 (PPF Payments and FAS Payments) (Consequential Provisions) Order 2006 (SI 2006/343) (February 14, 2006).
4. Pensions Act 2007 Sch.1 para.15 (September 26, 2007).
5. Welfare Reform Act 2007 s.28 and Sch.3 para.9(8) (October 27, 2008).

DERIVATION

SSA 1975 s.47B as amended.   1.315

GENERAL NOTE

In *R(U) 1/89* it was held that payments under a Civil Service pension have suffi-   1.316
cient cognate features with payments under ordinary occupational pensions to bring
them within the ambit of the term "payments by way of occupational pension" in s.5
of the SS (No.2) A 1980. By analogy they will fall to be treated as payments by way
of occupational pension under the provisions of this Part of this Act.

Beneficiaries under sections 68 and 70

90 [¹ . . .]   1.317

AMENDMENT

1. Repealed by the Welfare Reform Act 2009 s.15 (April 6, 2010).

SAVING

Section 15(2)(b) of the Welfare Reform Act 2009 provides: 1.318

"(2) Nothing in subsection (1) or Part 2 of Schedule 7 applies in relation to—

(a) . . .
(b) the amount of a carer's allowance payable to a qualifying person at any time on or after 6 April 2010 but before the appropriate date."

Section 15(3) of the same Act defines the relevant terms as follows: 1.319

""a qualifying person" means a person who—

(a) has, before 6 April 2010, made a claim for an increase in a carer's allowance under section 90 of the Benefits Act; and
(b) immediately before that date is either entitled to the increase claimed or a beneficiary to whom section 92 of the Benefits Act applies in respect of that increase (continuation of awards where fluctuating earnings);

"the appropriate date" means whichever is the earlier of—

(a) 6 April 2020; and

(b) the date when the qualifying person ceases to be either entitled to that increase or a beneficiary to whom section 92 of the Benefits Act applies in respect of that increase."

Effect of trade disputes on entitlement to increases

1.320 **91.**—(1) A beneficiary shall not be entitled—

(a) to an increase in any benefit [¹ under or by virtue of sections 82 to 88 above]; or

(b) to an increase in benefit [² . . .] by virtue of regulations under section 90 above,

if the person in respect of whom he would be entitled to the increase falls within subsection (2) below.

[³(2) A person falls within this subsection if—

(a) he is prevented from being entitled to a jobseeker's allowance by section 14 of the Jobseekers Act 1995 (trade disputes); or

(b) he would be so prevented if he were otherwise entitled to that benefit.]

AMENDMENTS

1. Social Security (Incapacity for Work) Act 1994 Sch.1 para.27 (April 13, 1995).
2. Tax Credits Act 2002 s.60 and Sch.6.
3. Jobseekers Act 1995 Sch.2 para.27 (October 7, 1996).

DERIVATION

1.321 SSA 1975 s.49A as amended.

GENERAL NOTE

1.322 This section provides that no increases of benefit are payable in respect of any person caught by the disqualification for receiving jobseeker's allowance under s.14 of the Jobseekers Act 1995 or who would be so disqualified if otherwise entitled to that benefit.

See annotations to s.14 of the Jobseekers Act 1995 in *Vol.II: Income Support, Jobseeker's Allowance, State Pension Credit and the Social Fund.*

SAVING

In relation to the deletion of the words "for an adult dependant" in subs.(1)(b), there is a saving provided in art.3 of The Tax Credits Act 2002 (Commencement No. 3 and Transitional Provisions and Savings) Order 2003 (SI 2003/938) which provides:

"Saving provision

1.323 3.—(1) Notwithstanding the coming into force of the specified provisions, the Contributions and Benefits Act and the Administration Act shall, in cases to which paragraph (2) applies, subject to paragraph (3), continue to have effect from the commencement date as if those provisions had not come into force.

(2) This paragraph applies where a person—

(a) is entitled to a relevant increase on the day before the commencement date; or

(b) claims a relevant increase on or after the commencement date and it is subsequently determined that he is entitled to a relevant increase in respect of a period which includes the day before the commencement date.

(3) The provisions saved by paragraph (1) shall continue to have effect until—

(a) subject to sub-paragraph (c), where a relevant increase ceases to be payable to a person to whom paragraph (2) applies for a period greater than 58 days beginning with the day on which it was last payable, on the day 59 days after the day on which it was last payable; or

(b) in any other case, subject to sub-paragraph (c), on the date on which entitlement to a relevant increase ceases;

(c) where regulation 6(19) or (23) of the Social Security (Claims and Payments) Regulations 1987⁴] applies to a further claim for a relevant increase, on the date on which entitlement to that relevant increase ceases.

(4) In this article—

"the commencement date" means 6th April 2003;

"a relevant increase" means an increase under section 80 or 90 of the Contributions and Benefits Act;

"the specified provisions" means the provisions of the 2002 Act which are brought into force by article 2."

Dependency increases: continuation of awards in cases of fluctuating earnings

92.—(1) Where a beneficiary—   1.324

(a) has been awarded an increase of benefit under this Part of this Act, but

(b) ceases to be entitled to the increase by reason only that the weekly earnings of some other person ("the relevant earner") exceed the amount of the increase or, as the case may be, some specified amount,

then, if and so long as the beneficiary would have continued to be entitled to the increase, disregarding any such excess of earnings, the award shall continue in force but the increase shall not be payable for any week if the earnings relevant to that week exceed the amount of the increase or, as the case may be, the specified amount.

(2) In this section the earnings which are relevant to any week are those earnings of the relevant earner which, apart from this section, would be taken into account in determining whether the beneficiary is entitled to the increase in question for that week.

DERIVATION

SSA 1975 s.84A as amended.   1.325

GENERAL NOTE

The meaning of this section is obscure. Nor is its relationship with reg.8(3)   1.326
of the Computation of Earnings Regulations entirely clear. The difficulty arises because of the use of the term "fluctuating earnings" in the title of the section and the reference to fluctuating earnings in reg.8(3). Correspondence with the Department for Work and Pensions has revealed that its operation in practice is very different from that set out in the commentary in earlier editions. The Department's view is that the notion of fluctuating earnings in s.92 is different from the notion of earnings which fluctuate in reg.8(3). The view of the Department is that s.92 is intended to cover the situation where an award of a dependency increase is made where the dependent person is either not earning or is earning under the earnings limit for the award, and on a later date becomes an earner with earnings over the earnings limit. This is what is intended by the reference in the title to the section to fluctuating. In such a situation entitlement continues but payment will cease for the period in which the earnings limit is exceeded, but can be resurrected when the earnings fall below the limit (presumably without the need for a fresh claim).

The practice of the Department is described in the correspondence as follows.

"In terms of section 92 . . . we have always operated on the basis that, for dependency benefit purposes, entitlement, once established, always exists and it is only the payment which is disqualified for the weeks following any periods during which the dependant's earnings exceeds the specified amount. In this event any change in earnings which takes the earnings over the limit or reduces them to under the limit will be grounds to review (supersede) the award to either disqualify or reinstate payment. The date of change will be that determined under the [Computation of Earnings] Regulations. In cases of actual fluctuating earnings there can be no continuation of payment until a permanent change can be established. The weekly rate of earnings are established under the provisions of regulation 8 of the above Regulations and the date on which a particular payment of earnings is due determines the date on which a disqualification of payment of dependency increase is imposed or removed."

Dependency increases on termination of employment after period of entitlement to disability working allowance

1.327
93.—Where—
(a) [¹ a person becomes entitled—
    (i) to the higher rate of short-term incapacity benefit, or to long-term incapacity benefit, by virtue of section 30C(5) or (6) or section 42 above,] [² . . .]
(b) when he was last entitled to that [³ benefit] [² . . .], it was increased in respect of a dependant by virtue of—
    (i) regulation 8(6) of the Social Security Benefit (Dependency) Regulations 1977;
    (ii) regulation 2 of the Social Security (Savings for Existing Beneficiaries) Regulations 1984;
    (iii) regulation 3 of the Social Security Benefit (Dependency) Amendment Regulations 1984; or
    (iv) regulation 4 of the Social Security Benefit (Dependency and Computation of Earnings) Amendment Regulations 1989,

for the purpose of determining whether his [³ benefit] [² . . .] should be increased by virtue of that regulation for any period beginning with the day on which he again becomes entitled to his [³ benefit] [² . . .] the increase in respect of that dependant shall be treated as having been payable to him on each day between the last day on which his [³ benefit] [² . . .] was previously payable and the day on which he again becomes entitled to it.

AMENDMENTS

1. Social Security (Incapacity for Work) Act 1994 Sch.1 para.28(a) (April 13, 1995).
2. Welfare Reform and Pensions Act 1999 Sch.13 Pt IV (April 6, 2001).
3. Social Security (Incapacity for Work) Act 1994 Sch.1 para.28(b) (April 13, 1995).

DERIVATION

1.328
DLADWAA 1991 s.9(5).

GENERAL NOTE

Disability working allowance (subsequently disabled person's tax credit) was a   1.329
benefit modelled on family credit designed to top up low pay received by people
who are disabled. In order to encourage those who are disabled to engage in work,
a special rule concerning requalification for a benefit connected with the disability
is provided in s.42 if they leave that work within a two-year period. They become
immediately qualified to receive the benefit they were receiving before becoming in
receipt of disability working allowance.

The rule in this section simply allows such persons to receive any increases of the
benefit in respect of dependants.

The section has not yet been amended on the introduction of disabled person's
tax credit to replace disability working allowance, nor on its replacement by the disability component of working tax credit.

PART V

BENEFIT FOR INDUSTRIAL INJURIES

General provisions

Right to industrial injuries benefit

94.—(1) Industrial injuries benefit shall be payable where an employed   1.330
earner suffers personal injury caused [¹ . . .] by accident arising out of and
in the course of his employment, being employed earner's employment.

(2) Industrial injuries benefit consists of the following benefits—

(a) disablement benefit payable in accordance with sections 103 to 105
below, paragraphs 2 and 3 of Schedule 7 below and Parts II and III
of that Schedule;

(b) reduced earnings allowance payable in accordance with Part IV;

(c) retirement allowance payable in accordance with Part V; and

(d) industrial death benefit, payable in accordance with Part VI.

(3) For the purposes of industrial injuries benefit an accident arising
in the course of an employed earner's employment shall be taken, in the
absence of evidence to the contrary, also to have arisen out of that employment.

(4) Regulations may make provision as to the day which, in the case of
night workers and other special cases, is to be treated for the purposes of
industrial injuries benefit as the day of the accident.

(5) Subject to sections 117, 119 and 120 below, industrial injuries benefit
shall not be payable in respect of an accident happening while the earner is
outside Great Britain.

(6) In the following provisions of this Part of this Act "work" in the contexts "incapable of work" and "incapacity for work" means work which the
person in question can be reasonably expected to do.

AMENDMENT

1. Welfare Reform Act 2012 s.64 (December 5, 2012).

DERIVATION

1.331   SSA 1975 s.50 as amended.

DEFINITIONS

"employed earner"—see s.2(1)(a), above.
"employed earner's employment"—see s.95, below.
"work"—see subs.(6).

GENERAL NOTE

1.332   This section contains the basic elements of the industrial injuries scheme. The scheme has undergone significant change. Injury benefit was abolished in 1982; death benefit was abolished (in respect of deaths occurring on or after April 11, 1988) in April 1988; title to disablement benefit was substantially diminished by provisions in the SSA 1986 which are dealt with below.

The system for decision-making and appeals for claims to industrial injuries benefits has undergone several reforms over the years. However, one constant throughout this period of change is that the question of whether a claimant is an employed or self-employed earner, and whether a specific employment is, or is not, employed earner's employment, is to be decided not by the Secretary of State, but by officers of HMRC (Social Security Contributions (Transfer of Functions, etc.) Act 1999 s.8(1)). Accordingly, such decisions are not matters of appeal for the FTT Social Entitlement Chamber but rather for appeal to the FTT Tax Chamber. Such decisions and appeals are regulated by the Social Security Contributions (Decisions and Appeals) Regs 1999 (SI 1999/1027).

Historically, for all other industrial injuries matters, there was a distinction between medical issues (the disablement questions), decided by the medical adjudicating authorities, including on appeal the former MAT, and non-medical issues, decided by insurance officers (and later adjudication officers), with appeals to the former SSAT (or its predecessor). However, on July 5, 1999, the functions of adjudication officers with respect to industrial injuries benefits and the making of industrial accident declarations were transferred to the Secretary of State (SSA 1998, ss.1, 8 and Commencement Order No.8). He or she may, however, refer certain issues for report to a medical practitioner (now a health care professional) who has experience of the issues. The issues so referable are: (a) the extent of a personal injury for the purposes of s.94; (b) whether the claimant has a prescribed industrial disease and the extent of the resulting disablement; and (c) whether, for disablement benefit purposes, the claimant has a disablement and its extent (Decisions and Appeals Regs 1999 reg.12(1)).

1.333   After 1999 decisions by the Secretary of State on industrial injuries benefits, including those on prescribed industrial diseases, and on the matter of an industrial accident declaration, were appealable to the so-called "unified" appeal tribunal, composed of a legally qualified member and up to two medically qualified members (SSA 1998 ss.4, 12, Schs 2 and 3). Like the Secretary of State, that tribunal was competent to deal with the both the medical and non-medical aspect of industrial injuries matters. Since November 3, 2008, and as a result of the Tribunals, Courts and Enforcement Act 2007, the FTT Social Entitlement Chamber has assumed these appellate functions.

The key point from all this for industrial injuries matters is that the historic distinction between medical issues and non-medical issues is no longer relevant. Consequently both the FTT and the Upper Tribunal now have jurisdiction over both medical and non-medical matters. So, an Upper Tribunal judge, allowing an appeal on a point of law, can now take his or her own decision on the facts rather than remitting it to another tribunal. Commissioner Williams did so in *CI/1307/1999* giving a staged assessment of disablement in respect of post-traumatic stress disorder. The decision considers the medical aspects of the claimant's case found to be an industrial accident in *CI/15589/ 1996*, noted below. In paras 15–17,

Commissioner Williams distinguished 'diagnosis' and 'disablement' decisions. The former is essentially "a question of medical expertise". A "disablement" decision in contrast is not dissimilar to the tasks performed by judges in assessing common law damages or in applying the tariff of the Criminal Injuries Compensation Authority. In assessing disablement for industrial injuries benefits, however, that Criminal Injuries tariff is not an appropriate yardstick. Instead, supplementing SSCBA 1992 s.103 and Sch.6, regard should be had also to reg.11 and Sch.2 to the General Benefit Regulations, below. Nonetheless, the import of para.37 of the decision is that exercise of the Commissioner's (and now the Upper Tribunal's) power to decide on the facts available, rather than remitting to another tribunal, may well be rare. Even so, the decision contrasts markedly with the traditional view of such matters as ones for medical rather than legal judgment (see, for example, Commissioner Howell in *CI/636/93*). Note that the suitability of cross-reference to Sch.2 was also advocated in *R(I) 5/95*, where Commissioner Rowland stated that "assessment of disablement should be brought into line with those prescribed in the Schedule", with assessment also reflecting any intermittent or episodic character of the disablement (para.16).

Subsection (1)

Whilst it is possible to divide this subsection conveniently for explanation, there is some overlap between the various conditions of entitlement and the temptation to categorise issues *too* rigidly should be avoided. To qualify for benefit: (i) the claimant must be an employed earner . . . [in] employed earner's employment; (ii) the claimant must suffer personal injury caused by accident; (iii) [the accident] must be arising out of and in the course of his [employed earner's] employment.

1.334

"Employed earner . . . employed earner's employment"

The definition of employed earner in s.2(1)(a), above, applies. Power is given to the Secretary of State to make regulations providing that certain employment shall (or shall not) be treated as employed earner's employment (see note to s.95, below). Whether a specific employment is, or is not, employed earner's employment is determined solely by the Commissioners for Her Majesty's Revenue and Customs.

1.335

The employment that the accident occurs in must be employed earner's employment.

"Suffers personal injury caused by accident"

Suffers personal injury: The injury must be to the living body of a human being. Damage to some artificial appendage of the body (spectacles, false teeth, etc.) is not enough (*R(I) 7/56, R(I) 1/82*), unless the appendage is so intimately linked with the body so as to form a part of it (*R(I) 5/81*—damage to artificial hip joint held to be personal injury). Damage to an artificial limb *may* constitute personal injury depending on the circumstances. (How should damage to a heart pacemaker be treated?) This situation is less likely to be significant given the abolition of injury benefit because of the short-term nature of damage of this kind. However, the question may arise where the damage causes incapacity for work which lasts longer than 15 weeks (is there entitlement to disablement benefit?), or where the claimant does not meet the contribution conditions for sickness benefit (is the incapacity for work the result of a personal injury?). Despite the demise of sickness benefit on April 13, 1995, the matter retains importance for those who transferred from it or from invalidity benefit to the replacement incapacity benefit, and who are covered by the IW (Transitional) Regulations, below.

1.336

The injury must be sufficiently severe to constitute a discernible physiological change for the worse so that a "strain" or an "increase of pain" will not constitute injury unless there is such a change (*R(I) 19/60, R(I) 1/76*). If incapacity is caused by increased or aggravated pain, or the gradual worsening of an existing condition it is also relevant to consider whether the claimant has suffered an accident (see *R(I) 1/76* and notes on "accident" below).

1.337   *By accident:* Leaving the question of causation to the last, the claimant must show that his injury resulted from an identifiable *accident*. Problems arise in defining "accident"; in distinguishing between accident and process; and in cases where suffering the injury is alleged to constitute the accident.

The usual definition of accident is that of Lord MacNaughten in *Fenton v Thorley* [1903] A.C. 443, ". . . an unlooked-for mishap or an untoward event which is neither expected or designed". "Designed" means planned by the claimant and does not exclude him from benefit where the accident has been planned by others (*Trim Joint District School Board v Kelly* [1914] A.C. 667). In *CI/365/89*, Commissioner Skinner, upholding the SSAT's decision that the incidents and events in that case did not constitute an "accident", stated:

"The question of the existence of the personal injury and of its cause or causes is one of fact, but the question as to whether such cause or causes amounts to an accident within the meaning of the [legislation] is a question of law; *Fenton v. Thorley* . . . so decided in relation to the Workmen's Compensation Act and in my judgment that principle is equally applicable to the question which was before the tribunal." (para.6).

The width and imprecision of the principles on "accident" in *Fenton v Thorley* (above) and *Trim Joint District Schoolboard v Kelly* (above) are apt to cause problems if not approached with a commonsense understanding of the natural everyday sense of the word "accident" (*per* Commissioner Rice in *CI/5249/95*). Hence in *CI/5249/95*, Commissioner Rice rejected the claim that someone, suffering a nervous breakdown on being suspended from work by his employer, had suffered injury through "accident". While the suspension may have been "unexpected" (from the point of view of the claimant), it would fly in the face of the ordinary use of the English language and be regarded as absurd by the man in the street to regard it as an "accident" in the sense used in s.94.

1.338   Focusing on the "untoward" aspect of *Trim* and its deployment in respect of vaccinations in *R(I)15/61*, Commissioner Mesher in *CI/732/2007* was of the opinion that a vaccination, administered in the course of employment, to which the claimant had consented, was not an "accident" for the purposes of this section (see paras 14–17). Since she could also not show a personal injury (which might have constituted the accident) flowing from the vaccination, her claim for an industrial accident declaration was rightly rejected by the appeal tribunal.

The "not expected" or "unforeseen" aspect has given some difficulties, in so far as there are some occupations where the risk of some injury might be said to be foreseeable, for example, prison officer, fireman or policeman. The matter has been considered recently in two cases: in *CI/15589/96*, a decision of Commissioner Goodman; and in *CAO v Faulds*, in which the issue was pronounced on both by the Inner House of the Scottish Court of Session and, on appeal, by the House of Lords. Both courts emphatically rejected the notion that the nature of such employments precludes incidents being regarded as accidents. In approaching the matter the emphasis needs to be on the perspective of the "victim"; the incident must not have been wanted or intended by him. But the focus must be on the identifiable incident said to rank as the "accident"; it is not enough that the injury was an unexpected untoward event. As noted below, following *Faulds* and *SSWP v Scullion* [2010] EWCA Civ 310, in which the Court of Appeal found erroneous in law the decision of Commissioner Bano in *CI/2842/2006* conflating injury and accident, although the injury and accident can overlap, they cannot merge indistinguishably.

In *CAO v Faulds* 1998 S.L.T. 1203, 1998 S.C.L.R. 719 (judgments included in *R(I) 1/00*), the Inner House of the Scottish Court of Session (the equivalent of the Court of Appeal in England and Wales) affirmed Commissioner Walker's decision in *CSI/26/96* reported as part of *R(I) 1/00*, that a fireman who suffered post-traumatic stress disorder after having attended a series of horrific fatalities in the course of his employment had suffered "accidents". The Inner House rejected the argument that, given his special training and the nature of his job, these horrific events did not constitute "accidents".

The Secretary of State appealed to the House of Lords. In *CAO v Faulds* [2000] 2 All E.R. 961, reported as *R(I) 1/00*, their Lordships held (Lord Hutton dissenting) that the Inner House had erred in law by not identifying the precise incidents that ranked as accidents. Rather harshly perhaps, the majority considered the Inner House to have erroneously based their decision on the notion that the post-traumatic stress disorder had arisen "accidentally". In essence they referred the case back down the line for evidential findings which would enable resolution of the accident/process issue. But their Lordships all stressed that something which happens as an ordinary element in, or an incident of, an employment can still be an "accident". Lord Hope expressly approved that part of the judgment of the Inner House, in which it rejected the CAO's argument "that an injury could not be said to have been sustained 'by accident' where the event or events causing it were foreseeable . . . the sustaining of an *unexpected* personal injury by an *expected* event or incident may itself amount to an accident" ([2000] 2 All E.R. 961 at 969). Lord Clyde (with whose opinion Lords Browne-Wilkinson, Mackay and Hope concurred), referring to Lord Macnaghten's definition and the *Trim* case, said: 1.339

> "The decision in the *Trim* case is important not only in stressing that Lord Macnaghten's formulation is to be taken as descriptive and not definitive, but also in pointing out that the question whether there has been an accident requires particular consideration to be paid to the victim. At least the accident cannot be something he intended to happen. Where his injury came about through the operation of some external force, that operation must have been something that he did not intend to happen. Where his injury has followed on some action or activity of his own, then the consequences of his doing what he did cannot have been intended by him. The mischance or the mishap was something which was not in any way wanted or intended. It was not meant to happen. . . . Indeed even where it may be foreseen that a person may possibly suffer physical injury in the ordinary course of his work when the incident occurs and injury is sustained it is still proper to recognise that event as an accident. Lord Shaw of Dunfermline gave the examples in this context of prison warders, lunatic asylum attendants and gamekeepers, and the same may hold true of their modern equivalents" ([2000] 2 All E.R. 961 at 978–979).

Lord Hutton, supporting the decision of the Inner House, stated that "the authorities establish that an accident may happen in the ordinary course of the employee's work" ([2000] 2 All E.R. 961, at 983).

This need for a definition of "accident" and the overall requirement that the accident should be identifiable as something distinct from the injury to which it gives rise (*Faulds*, above; *SSWP v Scullion* [2010] EWCA Civ 310, below) both reflect the crucial importance (for purposes of establishing title to benefit) of distinguishing between:

- Injury caused by "accident" (within s.94(1)) and injury caused by "process" (outside s.94(1)); and

- Injury caused by accident happening *because of* the claimant's work (within the scheme) and injury merely happening *at* work but brought about by some non-work-related cause (e.g. a stress disorder because of acute problems in a marital or other close relationship; a cardiac arrest suffered at work but the pure product of a congenital defect such that the arrest might have happened anywhere, at any time) (outside the scheme).

Title to industrial injuries benefits through s.94 will depend on decision-makers, tribunals and judges grappling with some difficult distinctions and problems of causation (*Scullion*).

1.340   While most diseases will tend to arise by process rather than accident—and thus be covered under the scheme only if a prescribed industrial disease—this will not invariably be the case. So where a workman was burnt on the lip by a splash of hot metal and the burn became cancerous, that cancer would arise "by accident". Similarly, a stress-related illness can be the product of an industrial accident. Distinguishing *CI/5249/95* on the facts, Commissioner Williams in *CI/2414/98* was not prepared to say that an SSAT had no basis for finding that a claimant who had suffered extreme post-traumatic stress after a particular conversation with a senior colleague had suffered an industrial accident for the purposes of the scheme. The conversation related to a situation which had brought about a period of post-traumatic stress and depression. That situation concerned an industrial dispute during which the claimant, a team leader and deputy manager at an office of the Employment Service, had been given the job of manning the office entrance from early morning to ensure the well-being of non-striking staff crossing the picket-line to come into work. She suffered a high level of abuse from those on the picket-line and was worried by their aggressive behaviour. When she returned to work after her illness she transferred to another job at another office. In the conversation found to be an "accident" she was told by the senior colleague, wrongly as it turned out, that no disciplinary action was to be taken against those abusive and aggressive former colleagues. Commissioner Williams considered the argument that words cannot be, or cause, an industrial accident, with *CI/7/71* being cited in support of the proposition that the phrase "suffers personal injury by accident" cannot cover the use of language alone. Commissioner Williams commented that:

> "while that observation may apply to most situations, I do not agree with those views as applied to all forms of personal injury in all circumstances. Given that 'accident' includes deliberate actions, and that words can constitute assault or other crimes to the person, the statement in *CI/7/71* is too general. For example verbal sexual harassment at work might be such in extreme cases as to amount to an accident or series of accidents, as might misinformation designed to shock or causing shock. I note that in the recent decision of *CI/4642/97* and linked cases, the Commissioner reaches the same conclusion. Any claim that words cause an accident must also be taken in context. This conversation reopened an issue that had clearly traumatised the claimant. That is relevant in considering its effect on her. It was not just the words by themselves that must be considered, but the context of those words and what the words concerned" (para.8).

Commissioner Williams pointed out that the incident alleged to constitute an "accident" need not be the sole or main cause of all injury suffered (para.12). Nor was the stressful nature of the claimant's job a relevant factor. This was an unusual case. An appeal to the Court of Appeal by the adjudication officer was not pursued. See also *CI/554/1992*, noted later in this annotation.

1.341   In *CI/105/1998*, Commissioner Rowland considered the case of a senior member of the teaching staff of a further education college who suffered from depression following what the tribunal found to be three aggressive and bullying interviews with the principal and vice-principal over a six-month period. The Commissioner declined to find erroneous in law the tribunal's finding that the injury arose through accident rather than process. Accepting *CI/7/71* (on file as *CI/789/70*) as correctly decided on its facts, he, like Commissioner Williams in *CI/2414/98*, disagreed with its broader *obiter* propositions. Given that a physical assault during an interview would rank as personal injury caused by accident, Commissioner Rowland found:

> "it very difficult to see why a person who suffers psychological injury having been caused, by words from a superior, to apprehend immediate and unlawful violence, should not be said to have suffered personal injury caused by accident.

Such a person would have been the victim of an unlawful assault at common law by the superior and it seems obvious that he or she should be covered by the industrial injuries scheme just as the schoolmaster was covered by the Workmen's Compensation Acts in *Trim* . . . But coverage by the scheme does not depend on someone having done something unlawful; it is enough that the conversation was an untoward event. I agree with the view expressed in *CI/5249/95* that a perfectly proper conversation cannot itself constitute an accident because it seems to me that it may be an event but it cannot be an untoward event. However, I do not agree with the suggestion in *CI/7/71* that use of language alone can never *constitute* an accident. In my view the tribunal in the present case were quite entitled to regard the three material interviews as being sufficient to amount to accidental causes of any injury that flowed from them. On the tribunal's findings, those interviews were quite untoward" (para.17).

However, it is the conversation itself, rather than suspension, dismissal or criticism, which must cause the injury; one looks to the *manner* of dismissal rather than dismissal itself (para.18); or, in the context of a claim in respect of the effects of an unexpected interview, said to have brought on the claimant's depression and chronic anxiety, to the manner and context of the interview (*CI/142/2006*). So the less outrageous the employer's behaviour, the more difficult will be the claimant's task. Injury arising from a series of events can rank as 'accident' rather than 'process'; the tribunal's conclusion that it so ranked here was not such that no tribunal, acting judicially and properly instructed as to the law, could have reached on the material before it (paras 22, 23). As Commissioner Fellner noted in *CI/3511/2002*, on balance, stress illnesses are more likely to arise through process rather than accident (para.14). Stress illnesses are not currently listed as Prescribed Industrial Diseases, and, in a recently published paper—Position Paper no.13, *Stress at Work* [found at URL *http://www.iiac.org.uk/papers/13.pdf*]—the Industrial Injuries Advisory Council considered itself unable to recommend extending the schedule of prescription to include adverse health outcomes ascribed to stress at work, but is to keep the area under review (para.56). However, as Commissioner Howell made clear in *CI/4708/2001*, work related stress can arise through accident where one can identify an event which produced a pathological change for the worse in the claimant's condition. Referring the tribunal to which he remitted the case to *CI/105/1998* noted above, he further emphasised that

"in the light of present more up-to-date knowledge about the way people can suffer breakdowns and stress reactions to particular events, it should no longer be taken to be the law, if ever it was, that words alone can never give rise to an 'accident' for this purpose" (para.11).

As *CAO v Faulds* (above) makes clear, however, there must be something describable as an accident. In *CI/3696/2005*, Commissioner Levenson, summarising and applying the principles in *Faulds* (see para.11) upheld a tribunal decision that the claimant, suffering from stress as a result of allegations made against him of false expenses claims, had not suffered an accident: neither being suspended nor receiving the letter of suspension could properly be regarded as an accident in the ordinary sense of the word (paras 12, 13).

Where the injury appears to result from a general deterioration of the claimant's   **1.342** condition over a period of time it may not be possible to identify a precise moment when there was a discernible physiological change for the worse, nor to identify a particular incident which occasioned the deterioration. In these circumstances, the claimant may have difficulty in establishing personal injury (see above) and/or in proving that there was an accident. Describing the distinction between accident and process, Lord Porter said,

". . . two types of case have not always been sufficiently differentiated. In one type there is to be found a simple accident followed by a resultant injury . . . or a series of specific and ascertainable accidents followed by an injury which may be the consequence of any or all of them . . . In the other type of case there is a continuous process going on substantially from day to day though not necessarily from hour to hour, which gradually and over a period of years produces incapacity. In the first of these types of cases the resulting incapacity is held to be injury by accident; in the second it is not . . . There must come a time when the indefinite number of so-called accidents and the length of time over which they occur take away the element of accident and substitute that of process." (*Roberts v Dorothea Slate Quarries Ltd* [1948] 2 All E.R. 201).

Although an accident denotes a moment at which an injury occurred, so long as such a moment can be identified, uncertainty (years after the event) as to the precise date, does not prevent a finding of accident (*CI/278/1993*). In *CI/1714/2002* Commissioner Rowland stressed that it is not necessary for the claimant to identify when the accident took place more precisely than necessary for the determination of the claim, so that there "the summer of 1978" sufficed (para.10). The key point is rather that the tribunal should be satisfied that an accident occurred, and on this aspect it is important to note that the law does not require corroboration of the claimant's evidence if the tribunal believe that evidence (para.11).

Whether the injury is caused by accident(s) or process is an important question of fact for the decision-maker or tribunal. A number of Commissioners decisions have given guidance on the principles to be applied in reaching a decision but the facts of each case will be crucial. Modern authority has directed attention away from the length of the period over which the injury developed as the most significant factor (as Lord Porter seemed to suggest) and emphasised that it is a question of fact and degree in each case (see *R(I) 11/74* and Appendix). Attention must be given to the nature of the injury, the nature of the work, and the nature of the incidents which are alleged to constitute the accident when reaching a decision. As always where fine distinctions need to be made, it is not easy to reconcile all the cases. As Commissioner Howell put it in *CI/4708/2001*, it is a difficult and invidious line for decision-makers and tribunals to have to draw (paras 6, 11).

1.343 An examination of the accident/process distinction was undertaken by Commissioner Goodman in *CI/72/1987*. In that case, an oboeist in a world famous orchestra sought a declaration that he had suffered an industrial accident in the course of playing the oboe which had caused hernia of the throat. The Commissioner observed that the question of accident or process is one of fact and laid emphasis on medical evidence which referred to a series of incidents causing the conditions. He held that there had by a specific date (the date on which the condition had been diagnosed) been an accident or accidents which would have occurred on a distinct occasion or occasions. The decision of the adjudication officer and the unanimous decision of the local tribunal was reversed. *R(I) 6/91* affirms that usually harm suffered (e.g. asthma, bronchial complaints) because of "passive smoking" (the inhalation of the smoke from other people's smoking) will not be attributable to accident but to process. However, in the particular circumstances of that case, where the claimant was able to point to six separate and isolated incidents involving her being moved into smoky environments, the Commissioner granted her six accident declarations under SSA 1975 s.107 (now SSA 1998 s.29, formerly AA 1992 s.44). In *CI/156/1993* the claimant was unsuccessful in her claim for an accident declaration in respect of harm suffered through passive smoking, thus indicating the exceptional nature of the decision in *R(I) 6/91*. Nor had her claim in respect of prescribed disease D7 (occupational asthma) been successful. In most cases, a claimant suffering mental or physical injury because of stress at work would rightly be regarded as having suffered it through process, rather than through accident, putting the matter outside s.94. Although Commissioner Goodman was careful to characterise his decision as dependent on its "highly individual facts and on the detailed nature of the medical evidence given in the High Court action [against his employer for damages]", and while he was anxious to deny that his decision constituted a precedent "for any other case where it may be asserted that stress at work has caused a claimant mental or physical injury" (para.16), nonetheless his decision in *CI/554/1992*, granting the claimant an accident declaration, is a welcome reminder that, in circumstances which may well be rare, mental injury through stress can arise through accident. Tribunals should thus take great care in any such case with the evidence, and not assume that any case of injury through stress inevitably *must* be through process. In *CI/554/1992*, Commissioner Goodman noted *R(I) 43/55* (explosions leading to psychoneurotic disorder, an identifiable series of accidents) and decided that the medical evidence showed that the claimant was "more or less all right at one moment and severely ill the next" and that the stressful situation at work in September/October 1974 was an industrial "accident" which tipped him over the edge into depression. The fact that he was abnormally sensitive to stress did not prevent this finding: the "egg shell skull" principle noted in para.11 of *R(I) 6/91* (the passive smoking case) applied. See also *CI/2414/98*, noted earlier.

CI/737/1994 and CI/1195/1995, two decisions of Commissioner Henty, both apply *R(I) 6/91* (the "passive smoking" case) and contain useful reviews of the major authorities on the difficult accident/process distinction. In *CI/737/1994*, the Commissioner made a declaration that on each occasion between 1973 and 1983 when the claimant suffered temporary deafness/tinnitus after a shooting practice session as part of his police firearms training, he suffered an accident. Although not as well documented as in *R(I) 6/91*, the evidence was clear that there were such occasions (para.14). Furthermore, despite the fact that the permanent condition only manifested itself some four years after the claimant fired his last shot, the Commissioner declared also that the permanent injury was caused by accident (para.15). In *CI/3600/2004*, Commissioner Fellner considered the case of a school care assistant, who had to give up work, suffering from a major depressive disorder, post-traumatic stress disorder and a number of physical or somatic manifestations. It was argued that this had arisen through process, since she had become increasingly concerned at the nature of physical restraint applied by school staff, and the tribunal had so decided. There was, indeed, that backdrop, but Commissioner Fellner, taking account of *Mullen* noted below, considered that the evidence established that the "trigger" incident was one some three weeks before she left, when she witnessed a pupil being inappropriately restrained by another teacher, and granted an industrial accident declaration (see esp. paras 14–18). In contrast, in *CI/1195/1995*, Commissioner Henty could point to no particular incidents triggering off the claimant's heart attack; it came about as a result of a cumulative process (para.9).

The following situations are only illustrative—the tribunal must decide each case upon its facts: **1.344**

(i) The period of development may be too short to indicate process:

R(I) 18/54   (two months, but there was also an identifiable point at which the injury was first noticed)

R(I) 43/61   (less than three days' use of scissors causing digital neuritis—but compare *R(I) 19/56*)

R(I) 4/62   (about two weeks' welding causing ganglion)

(ii) There may be an identifiable series of individual accidents:

R(I) 77/51   (repeated operation of stiff levers)

R(I) 24/54   (repeated burns and pricks on hands)

R(I) 43/55   (explosions leading to psychoneurotic disorder) (see note above)

CI/71/1987   (oboe playing and rehearsal leading to laryngoceles) (see note above)

CI/737/1994   (shooting practice leading to temporary deafness/tinnitus) (see note above)

CAO v Faulds   1998 S.L.T. 1203 (remitted for further evidence by the House of Lords (see [2000] 2 All E.R. 961))

CI/3370/1999   (the case of a teacher who claimed that her injury (nodules on her bilateral vocal chords) had resulted from a series of interacting incidents, constituting "accident", at school. The decision-maker had already given an accident declaration in respect of one such incident when she was trapped in a stock cupboard by a pupil and had to shout before escaping. Commissioner remitted to tribunal for further consideration but implying support for the "accident" view')

Mullen v Secretary of State for Work and Pensions, 2002 S.L.T. 149   (the Court of Session Second Division in a Scottish case held that a former assistant care officer incapacitated by back pain brought about through lifting patients had suffereda series of accidents over a seven year period, and had thus suffered injury caused by accident, even though it was not possible to identify the date of each of the accidents or to state which of them, if not all, caused or contributed to the back condition.)

(iii) There may be a process:

CI/257/49   (development of "Raynaud's phenomenon" as a result of operating a grinding machine for five years)

CI/83/50   (doctor developing tuberculosis after two years of treating persons suffering from it)

R(I) 42/51   (strained chest muscles over two-month period)

R(I) 19/56   (osteoarthritis of the fingers was the "cumulative result" of three days of leather stitching and had come on gradually during that period)

R(I) 7/66   (prolonged exposure to nitro-glycerine resulting in death)

R(I) 11/74   (condition of left elbow developing over five months' work with heavy electrical boring machine)

CI/1195/1995   (cumulative process leading to heart attack) (see note above)

CAO v Faulds   [2000] 2 All E.R. 961, reported as R(I) 1/00 (post-traumatic stress disorder remitted by House of Lords to Court of Session for further evidence on the issue).

CSI/371/2001   (not available on the Commissioners' website) placed on the process side of the line a case where a civil servant had suffered stress and anxiety because of excessive workload and a number of incidents of friction with his line manager, whom he saw as unreasonable. The tribunal had not there been prepared to find that the claimant's appreciation of excessive workload was the sort of triggering event that had enabled success in CI/554/1992, noted above, one of the rare cases where mental injury through stress resulted from accident)

CI/3511/2002   (Commissioner Fellner considered the case of an ambulance technician incapacitated because of work-related stress. The single person tribunal erred in law by holding that the claimant was entitled to an industrial accident declaration because this was a case of accident by process. Commissioner Fellner held that the case fell on the 'process' side of the line—there was no identifiable accident or series of accidents).

The claimant who develops a disease or other condition as a result of his work may be entitled to benefit notwithstanding that there is no accident so long as the disease or condition is one which is "prescribed" for his employment (see s.108, below).

Decision-makers, tribunals and judges will also have to make a difficult decision where the claimant, in common-parlance terms, alleges that the personal injury suffered at work constitutes the "accident" for the purposes of the section. The supermarket shelf-stacker who strains his back muscles when picking up a case of baked beans is likely to say that he has had an "accident" at work. But since he was doing nothing other than he was accustomed to, he is thus likely to see the "injury" as the "accident".

Legally speaking, the leading authorities (*Faulds*, above; *Scullion*, below) decide   **1.345**
that the wording of s.94(1) requires that the two be clearly distinguished. The wording is "personal injury caused by accident" rather than the Workmen's Compensation Acts' formula, "personal injury by accident", so that broad statements in House of Lords' authorities on those Acts need to be approached very cautiously to avoid falling into the error of applying the industrial injuries benefits scheme too widely to take in any "accidental injury". "Injury" and "accident" cannot legally merge indistinguishably, so that a cardiac arrest suffered at work cannot be both the injury and the accident. It constitutes the requisite "injury", but to be brought within the scheme there must be identified some incident or small series of incidents (the "accident") which caused the cardiac arrest, and that this occurred both at and through work ("arising out of and in the course of employment"). Thus the authorities suggest that s.94(1) covers the standard case where the accident and injury are clearly distinct (the forklift truck drives over and breaks the employee's legs) and the more difficult case where, on a common-parlance approach, there is a degree of overlap between the accident and the injury (the supermarket shelf-stacker straining his back because of lifting the case of baked beans). This more difficult class of case will be within the section so long as there is an internal physiological change for the worse (e.g. the strained muscles; a cardiac arrest; post traumatic stress disorder) which is partly caused by the work activity which the claimant is performing at the time (e.g. lifting the case of baked beans or heavy papers; wrestling with a jammed filing cabinet drawer) or by the act of another, performed at and connected with the claimant's work (e.g. a teacher's heart attack at school caused by being threatened or struck there by an irate pupil or parent).

In *Jones v Secretary of State for Social Services* [1972] A.C. 944, the claimant suffered a heart attack some days after he had been doing heavy lifting at work. A tribunal held that the heart attack had been brought on by the heavy work and the House of Lords decided that there had been an accident within the terms of the section. Lord Diplock said that he would call a perfectly ordinary part of a man's work (here the heavy lifting) an accident if it had the effect of causing injury. It would appear that the only injuries excluded will be those which would have happened whether the claimant was at work or not. Such injuries are not attributable to the work done but are risks of everyday activity.

The law was stated thus in *R(I)11/80* (where the claimant sustained a head injury by banging his head after an unexplained fall):

> "where (in what is sometimes called an internal accident) a physiological or pathological change for the worse occurs while a person is at work, such as a fit or a heart attack or a dislocation, that change for the worse is, if caused by the work that is being done itself, injury by accident for the purposes of the section; but that, on the other hand, where one of these happens while a person is at work but not because of his work the change is not itself injury by accident . . . But in any case if the internal accident causes the person concerned to fall and injure himself that injury may be injury by accident arising out of and in the course of employment even if the change itself was not."

This statement was approved in *R(I) 6/82* where the claimant had broken his ankle   **1.346**
while carrying out his duties as a maintenance engineer in a bakery. In holding that the claimant had not had an accident, the Commissioner said,

"walking, standing, sitting etc. are all part of everyday human activity and unless they represent a special danger to a claimant because of some inherent, idiopathic, characteristic of the individual claimant, accidents happening during those activities, even in the course of employment cannot be said to arise out of the employment unless there is the additional factor of an injury by contact with the employer's premises etc. There is no distinction in my view between a heart attack suffered by a sedentary employee and an unexplained bone fracture or dislocation suffered by a walking employee. Neither will constitute an industrial accident unless some aspect of the employment caused the heart attack, the fracture or the dislocation or they were caused by the employee coming into contact with the employer's plant, premises, or machinery."

In *CAO v Faulds* 1998 S.L.T. 1203, 1998 S.C.L.R. 719, reported with *R(I) 1/00*, the Inner House of the Scottish Court of Session (the equivalent of the Court of Appeal in England and Wales) affirmed Commissioner Walker's decision in *CSI/26/96* (reported as part of *R(I) 1/00*), that a fireman who suffered post-traumatic stress disorder after having attended a series of horrific fatalities in the course of his employment had suffered "accidents" (a series of "accidents", not a "process") (see above). Lord McCluskey said in giving the opinion of the court:

"in a case like the present just as in *R(I) 22/59*, *CI/15589/1996* and *R(I) 43/55*, also quoted to us, the accidental cause is found in the exposure of the employee on one or several—or even many—occasions to shocking sights or other such phenomena, resulting in his suffering a severe—and unintended— nervous reaction. We do not consider that the wording of the Act requires that there be found a separable 'accident' in the form of a distinct event separate from the injury and preceding it in point of time. In circumstances in which the horror of the exposure triggers a response which takes the form of nervous trauma, the injury and its cause may merge indistinguishably, but the injury may still be properly said to be caused by accident" (1998 S.L.T. 1203 at 1210).

In *CAO v Faulds* [2000] 2 All E.R. 961, reported as *R(I) 1/00* the majority of the House of Lords (Lord Hutton dissenting) rather harshly read this passage as failing sufficiently to identify, as was necessary, particular incidents, constituting accidents, which produced the injury (the post-traumatic stress disorder) and as erroneously tending to suggest that it sufficed for purposes of the industrial injuries scheme that the injury had arisen "accidentally" (see Lord Hope at 969, Lord Clyde at 973). In short, their Lordships considered that there was insufficient evidence for SSAT, Commissioner and the Inner House to find "accident" rather than "process" and remitted the matter back to the Inner House (doubtless to pass on to the Commissioner and to a differently constituted appeal tribunal) for further consideration. Lord Hutton took the view that the Inner House had identified a series of incidents producing and aggravating the post-traumatic stress disorder and was entitled to find as it did. The House of Lords, while unhappy with its precise application in the particular case of psychological injury before them in *Faulds,* approved a line of cases involving physical injury held to be within the scheme in which the distinction between "accident" and "injury" becomes blurred: *Fenton v Thorley* [1903] A.C. 443 (rupture when turning an unexpectedly resistant wheel); *Welsh v Glasgow Coal* 1916 S.C. (HL) 141 (workman immersed in water developed rheumatism); *Clover, Clayton & Co. Ltd v Hughes* [1910] A.C. 242 (death from burst aneurism when tightening a nut with a spanner); *Falmouth Docks and Engineering Co. Ltd v Treloar* [1933] A.C. 481 (man suffering from heart disease dropped dead when lifting his hand, holding a hook, above his head) (see Lord Clyde [2000] 2 All E.R. 961 at 976–977). The key point is the need to identify some causative event or small series of events, remembering, in Lord Hope's words, "that the sustaining of an *unexpected* personal injury caused by an *expected* event or incident may itself amount to an accident" ([2000] 2 All E.R. 961 at 969). In the context of injury through shock or stress, there is still need to:

"identify the accident of which notice would require to be given, and the injury which was caused by it. The principle established in the cases of physical injury should in that respect be applicable to cases of psychological injury. In cases of shock and stress the activity which triggers the accident may only consist of the claimant confronting an horrific spectacle. It may involve some additional activity, such as the handling or the close examination of something particularly gruesome or distressing. But in every case, although the concepts may overlap, it should be possible to identify an accident as well as the consequent injury. But the identification of the accident and the establishment of a causal connection between the incident and the injury may well call for a very careful investigation of the circumstances of the case and the nature of the condition" ([2000] 2 All E.R. 961 at 979, *per* Lord Clyde).

Commissioner Parker, sitting as a Deputy Commissioner in Northern Ireland, in broader context, encapsulated the matter well:

1.347

"although the majority of the House of Lords recognises that there are cases where the elements of accident and injury overlap, it is nevertheless stressed that there is a distinction between the two which must be observed. A physiological or psychological change for the worse can only constitute an accident if it is, at least partly, caused by the work which the claimant is doing at the time; if there is no causal link to the relevant work and the injury would have happened whether the claimant was at work or not then the internal accident does not count as amounting to accidental injury in the sense of the statute. A claimant must identify some causative event or events which produced the physiological or pathological change for the worse, such as turning a wheel or a screw or lifting his hand, and that such trigger was *because* of his ordinary work not merely *at* his work. That in such case it is hardly possible to distinguish in time between "accident" and "injury" does not negate the distinction. The reasoning of the House of Lords stressed the essential requirement of identifying an incident which brought about the physiological injury which constitutes, in effect, the required accident/injury. It is only when there is a triggering work event for an injury that it can be accepted that the very injury suffered constitutes the necessary accident for the purposes of the section" *(C1/06-07(II)*, para.30).

Accordingly, accepting this, Commissioner Bano in *CI/2842/2006*, held that, since his cardiologist accepted that the claimant's work conditions might have contributed to his condition, it was more likely than not that the exceptional work pressures, to which he was subject immediately prior to his suffering a cardiac arrest at work, contributed to that cardiac arrest and that this was properly to be regarded as an accident, "even though it occurred in the normal course of the claimant's duties and was not preceded by any [separate] abnormal event" (paras 13, 16).

The Court of Appeal, however, unanimously allowed the Secretary of State's appeal against Commissioner Bano's decision (*SSWP* v *Scullion* [2010] EWCA Civ 310; [2010] AACR 29). The Court undertook a thorough review of the authorities on Workmen's Compensation and the post-1948 industrial injuries scheme, but particularly *Faulds*. In the light of that, it held that Commissioner Bano had erred in law in treating the "injury" (the cardiac arrest")—being improbable, sudden and an unlooked for mishap or untoward event—as also constituting the "accident", so that the only issue for him was the "out of employment" aspect, the "necessary causal connection with his work" (the stressful situation). Having dealt with step one (identifying the "injury") he ought also to have dealt with step two (specifying the identifiable "accident") and considered:

"what external event or series of events (allied or not to some action by the claimant) had some physiological or psychological effect on the claimant .. [T]he

191

plain fact here is that there is no evidence that any external event, even if allied to some action by Mr Scullion, such as lifting a very heavy pile of papers, opening a file drawer which had stuck, or even lifting an arm to get heavy papers from a shelf, caused the cardiac arrest. Therefore, the claimant failed to prove that his personal injury, viz. the cardiac arrest and all that followed from it, was "caused by accident" within the meaning of section 94(1) of the 1992 Act" (paras 53, 54, per Aikens L.J.).

As Pill L.J. stressed, "the statements of principle [in *Faulds*] are inconsistent with the assertion that the cardiac arrest was itself an accident within the meaning of [s. 94(1)]" (para.20). In such cases, decision-makers, tribunal and judges need to identify the precipitating external event(s). On that basis, the fact that a work environment or a mode of work may be stressful and produce a deleterious effect (the "injury") such as a mental disorder, a breakdown or a cardiac arrest will not suffice; a precipitating cause within the notion "accident" must also be present, as, for example, in cases such as *Jones* or *CI/4708/2001* or *CI/105/1998*, noted earlier in this annotation; otherwise the injury (as perhaps in most cases of stress illness: see *CI/3511/2002*) appears rather as the result of "process".

1.348   *Caused by accident:* The meaning of "accident" has been discussed above.

The injury must be *caused* by the accident. Three situations should be noted: (i) where the claimant is predisposed to the injury suffered because of disease or constitutional weakness; (ii) where the injury suffered renders the claimant susceptible to other forms of injury; (iii) where the injury suffered is aggravated by a further non-industrial accident.

If the claimant is predisposed to injury it will still be proper to say that the accident caused the injury if it would not have happened but for the accident *(R(I) 12/52*—a bus conductor with abnormally fragile bones; *R(I) 14/51*—a miner with an existing heart condition; *R(I) 73/51*—a labourer suffering from Paget's disease). Note that there must still be something which can be termed an accident occurring as a result of the particular duties of the employment (see above).

1.349   Where the claimant can show that the original industrial injury was an effective cause of the eventual non-industrial injury he will also succeed in his claim. In *R(I) 3/56*, a Tribunal of Commissioners allowed a claim by a man who had been injured in a fall on the way to work as a result of a previous accident at work. The Tribunal said,

". . . if the immediate cause of his incapacity is an injury by non-industrial accident the claimant will be entitled to injury benefit if he can prove that a previous injury by industrial accident was an effective cause of the injury by non-industrial accident which was the immediate cause of his incapacity."

Similar successful claims may be found in *CI/129/49* and *R(I) 59/51*.

The same principle is relevant to determine cases where the non-industrial injury is an aggravation of the industrial injury but is not related to it. Illness following upon an injury or a completely unrelated non-industrial accident which incapacitates the claimant will not be taken into account except in so far as the industrial injury continues to be an effective cause of the claimant's incapacity.

Provision is made for taking into account a combination of industrial and non-industrial accidents in assessing the extent of disablement for the purposes of disablement benefit. See ss.103, 107, and General Benefit Regs below.

"arising out of and in the course of employment"

1.350   This phrase first appeared in the Workmen's Compensation Act 1897 to limit compensation paid under the original scheme to injuries which were suffered through work and not merely at work.

The two tests, "in the course of" and "out of", look to different things. The former embraces time, place and activity. The latter requires a causal nexus between the injury and the employment. The separateness of the two tests is affirmed by the statutory presumption in s.94(3), readily defeasible if there is any evidence to the contrary, that an accident "in the course of" also arises "out of" the employment (*Chief Adjudication Officer v Rhodes,* reported as *R(I) 1/99*). The distinct nature of the two tests is also manifest in the deeming provision in s.101 (an accident arising "in the course of" employment will be deemed to arise "out of" it in a bewildering range of situations whose only common factor consists of their being situations which courts or commissioners had ruled as not arising out of the employment applying general principles). A person may satisfy one test but not secure benefit because failing to meet the other. So, in *Rhodes,* above, in the case of the civil servant assaulted on her drive by a neighbour because of her work (she had reported him as claiming benefit whilst working), the work nexus satisfied the "out of" test, but her claim failed. While all the other requisites of s.94(1) were met, she was not "in the course of" her employment because when assaulted she was at home on sick leave, returning from a visit to her doctor, and not engaged at the material time in performing any work tasks.

Arising out of . . . employment: The first part of the phrase confines the industrial   1.351
injuries scheme to those injuries which are work-related and seeks to exclude those which result from the ordinary risks which affect everybody. To give two examples, in *R(I) 62/53* a lorry driver suffered a corneal abrasion when something went into his eye whilst he was driving. The Commissioner held that he was not entitled to benefit because the accident did not arise out of the employment—the risk was general and not particular to his employment. By contrast, a policeman on motor-bike patrol duty who was similarly injured *was* entitled to benefit because the risk of eye injury whilst riding a motor-bike on duty was greater than normal (*R(I) 67/53*).

There is a further interesting comparison between *R(I) 22/59* and unreported decision *CI/387/1988*. In the former case, a miner suffered nervous debility resulting from the shock of hearing of his son's death in an accident at the same mine; in the latter case, a worker suffered anxietal depression after seeing a colleague in the terminal stages of angiosarcoma of the liver, a disease to which his own work exposed him.

In *R(I) 22/59*, the accident (hearing of the death) was held not to have arisen out of employment; in *CI/387/1988*, the accident (sighting the colleague) was held to have arisen out of the employment. The distinction taken was that the father could have been shocked at the son's death wherever he worked; the latter claimant would not have suffered shock unless he had been working at the particular place where industrial conditions created the hazard which threatened him. *CI/387/1988* was distinguished by Commissioner Goodman in *CI/289/1994* when he upheld the decision of an SSAT (which applied *R(I) 22/59* and *R(I) 62/53*) that the post-traumatic stress disorder suffered by a lorry driver when he learned over the radio in his cab of the Zeebrugge ferry disaster did not arise out of his employment:

> "In [*CI/387/1988*], the claimant himself had worked for many years with vinyl chloride monomer and therefore was at potential risk of developing cancer of the liver . . . But that is not the same as the facts of the present case. Admittedly the claimant had had to use the same ferry crossing but he had successfully made the trips. Any danger that there might have been from the ferry sailing [which had been on a different vessel] had gone as soon as the claimant had driven off the ferry. There was no continuing risk such as the continuing risk of cancer [in *CI/387/1988*] nor was there necessarily any such risk in the future, particularly as the claimant could reasonably assume that the occurrence of the disaster would cause further safety precautions to be taken" (para.10).

It is thus crucial for the "out of" employment issue properly to analyse the nature of   1.352
the risk in the case. *CSI/154/89*, a decision of Commissioner Walker shows the difficulties of drawing a line between injuries resulting from the ordinary risks to which everyone is exposed, whether employed or not (not arising out of employment) and those injuries resulting from risks created by the employment (which do arise out of the employment as being work-related). The case takes a more generous approach

193

than some other decisions (e.g. *R(I) 62/53* and *R(I) 52/54*). Indeed the case is strikingly similar on its facts to *R(I) 52/54*, but it is an approach which draws on leading authorities on the interpretation of the same phraseology in the Workmen's Compensation legislation (*White v W & T Avery*, 1916 S.C. 209, *McNeice v Singer Sewing Machine Co Ltd* 1911 S.C. 12 and the House of Lords' decision, *Dennis v AJ White & Co.* [1917] A.C. 479). In *Dennis*, Lord Finlay L.C. said:

> "If a servant in the course of his master's business has to pass along the public street, whether it be on foot or on a bicycle, or on an omnibus or car, and he sustains an accident by reason of the risks incidental to the street, the accident arises out of as well as in the course of his employment. The frequency or infrequency of the occasions on which the risk is incurred has nothing to do with the question whether an accident resulting from that risk arose out of the employment . . . but as soon as it is established that the work itself involves exposure to the perils of the streets the workmen can recover for any injury so occasioned.
>
> Where the risk is one shared by all men, whether in or out of employment, it must be established that special exposure to it is involved. But when a workman is sent into the street on his master's business, whether it be occasionally or habitually, his employment necessarily involves exposure to the risks of the streets, and injury from such a cause arises out of his employment." (cited in para.17).

Further, Commissioner Walker recalls Lord Denning's exhortation in *Vandyke v Fender* [1970] 2 Q.B. 292 that this phraseology be given the same interpretation whether used in industrial injuries legislation, road traffic legislation or employer's liability policies. One can here note that something like that approach is inherent in the way Commissioners, dealing with "travelling cases" under the industrial injuries scheme, have drawn on the tests in the House of Lords' decision in *Smith v Stages* [1989] 1 All E.R. 833, dealing with similar issues in the law of torts. Commissioner Walker then noted, looking to *Smith v Stages*, that what is incidental to the employment appears to be relevant to the issue "out of" as well as that of "in the course of" with which that case dealt. The court decisions he had cited persuaded him that the SSAT had adopted an incorrect analysis of the claimant's situation, and was thus erroneous in law:

> "The question which they should have asked themselves was whether the claimant was exposed to the risk by the job or whether the risk was one that could have affected her whether or not in the employment at that time. That raises the question as to what was the risk. In this case I conclude that it was the risk of falling, as evidenced by the finding of fact that she fell on the pavement. That is a normal risk of the streets but it was a risk to which she became exposed only because her employment put her in the relevant place at the relevant time. And so I come at last to the question whether the fact that Mrs Falconer was reacting there and then to an emergency [trying to save a child who had run into the road] yet takes her out of the scope and/or course of her employment.
>
> I approach these two questions separately. 'In the course of' is simple. The Commissioner in *R(I) 52/54* would have taken it for granted. The claimant was where she was at the time of the accident because so required or at least permitted by her employment. She had not deviated nor gone deliberately out of her way. The employment was not interrupted. So I hold that Mrs Falconer's accident occurred in the course of her employment. As to whether it arose 'out of' that employment I am persuaded by the language quoted above from *White v Avery*, *McNeice* and *Dennis v AJ White & Co.* that it is the risk that has to be considered rather than what brought it to pass. How it came to pass might affect liability in a damages claim but not for present purposes—*cf.* the potato picker's case [*R(I) 17/63*]. It was not outwith the nature and type of risk that might befall a messenger. That seems to me to be enough. I think that the word 'emergency' is misleading in, and inappropriate to this case. I have therefore to add that I am unable to agree with the decision *R(I) 52/54*. So I hold that the accident here arose 'out of' the

claimant's employment as well." (paras 19 and 20; words in brackets added by commentator).

In *CI/1654/2008* Commissioner Jacobs considered the case of an employee who   **1.353**
slipped and was injured while showering at a hotel before attending a training
session there. He held that the accident befell her when in the course of her employment; her actions in making herself presentable were reasonably incidental to her
duties and she was where she was because of her work. But it did not arise "out" of
the employment:

> "The risk was not created by her employment. It was inherent in the nature of
> a shower. It was a risk that anyone would run who took a shower. Indeed, it
> was not limited to the shower. There was a similar risk in the bathroom outside
> the shower. The claimant's employment did not expose her to any hazard that
> was additional to, or exceptional when compared with, the risk that anyone else
> would run who was taking a shower or using a hotel bathroom" (paras 36, 37).

Nor did SSCBA 1992 s.101 operate so as to treat this accident arising in the course
of employment as also arising out of it; there was "no evidence that the accident was
caused by someone else's misconduct, skylarking or negligence" (para.28).

Note the relationship between this concept and the question of whether an accident has occurred, in circumstances where the claimant merely suffers injury at
work which might have happened anywhere, e.g. a heart attack, a fit or a dislocation.
In *R(I) 6/82* (above), the Commissioner held that there was no accident, but, even
if there had been, it would not have arisen out of the course of employment unless
there had been an injury caused by contact with the employer's plant, premises or
machinery or unless some aspect of the employment caused the injury.

The claimant is assisted by the provision in subs.(3) of this section (noted below)
that an accident which occurs in the course of employment shall be deemed to have
arisen out of the employment unless there is evidence to the contrary. Note also, for
cases of any doubt, the role of s.101 (deemed "out of").

Arising . . . in the course of employment: This looks to matters of time, place and activ-   **1.354**
ity. As Lord Loreburn put it in *Moore v Manchester Liners Ltd* [1910] A.C. 498 at
500–501:

> "An accident befalls a man 'in the course of' his employment if it occurs while he
> is doing what a man so employed may reasonably do within a time during which
> he is employed, and at a place where he may reasonably be during that time to
> do that thing".

The test requires a focus on what the claimant is doing rather than on what was
done to the claimant. In *Chief Adjudication Officer v Rhodes*, reported as *R(I) 1/99*),
Schiemann L.J. (with whose judgment Roch L.J. concurred to give the majority
in the case) approved Hoffmann L.J.'s statement in *Faulkner v Chief Adjudication
Officer* [1994] P.I.Q.R. 244 at 256; *The Times*, April 8, 1994 (one citing as authority
Smith v Stages [1989] A.C. 928) reported as *R(I) 8/94* and adapted it so as to read
(adaptation in square brackets):

> "An office or employment involves a legal relationship: it entails the existence of
> specific duties on the part of the employee. An act or event happens 'in the course
> of employment' if [what the employee is doing] constitutes the discharge of one
> of those duties or is reasonably incidental thereto".

One must first ascertain what the employee is employed to do and then consider
whether what the employee was doing at the material time constitutes the discharge
of one of those duties or something reasonably incidental thereto.

This "back to basics" approach in *Rhodes* is firmly located within the structure of this statutory regime and within the mass of authority since the tests were first included in the Workmen's Compensation Act 1897 (see R. Lewis, *Compensation for Industrial Injury* (1987), p.51). So, for example, the approach meshes with the general formulation found in the headnote to an earlier Court of Appeal decision, *R. v Industrial Injuries Commissioner Ex p. A.E.U. (No. 2)* [1966] 2 Q.B. 31 (*Culverwell's* case):

"The test whether a man is acting 'in the course of his employment' is not the strict test of whether he is at the relevant time performing a duty for his employer, for he may be 'in the course of his employment' when he acts casually, negligently or even disobediently, so long as it is something reasonably incidental to his contract of employment".

With respect to the dissenting Swinton Thomas L.J. in *Rhodes*, above, matters of time and place are important: those injured away from the employer's premises during a lunch break, unless performing tasks for their employer, are not "in the course of employment". The system has always been predicated on there being a difference between injuries suffered at work during working hours and those suffered while resting at home or when travelling to or from a fixed point of work. Were that not so, the justifications for a separate system of compensation for work injuries would be further called into question. Crucial lines drawn by a raft of previous authority (e.g. on travelling to and from a fixed place of work generally being outside the scheme [*Lewis*, pp.76, 77] and, by implication, the deeming provision in s.99 (passengers travelling in employer provided transport)) would respectively be rendered nugatory and unnecessary.

1.355   The matter of the proper approach to "in the course of employment" had been thrown into some disarray by the Court of Appeal decision in *Nancollas v Insurance Officer* [1985] 1 All E.R. 833. That case dealt with the issue of whether two claimants injured in motor accidents were injured in the course of employment. In the case, Lord Donaldson M.R. went so far as to suggest that there were no legal rules (other than the plain statutory language) for courts or tribunals to follow, merely factors pointing one way or the other. Hence the proper approach was for tribunals to look at the factual picture as a whole, rejecting any approach based on the fallacious concept that any one factor is conclusive. The Court of Appeal decision in *Rhodes*, above, is a firm affirmation of the trend (see *Smith v Stages* [1989] A.C. 928, especially Lord Lowry at 948, 955–956, and the Court of Appeal in *Faulkner v Chief Adjudication Officer* [1994] P.I.Q.R. 244 reported as *R(I) 8/94*), of effectively relegating the *Nancollas* impressionistic "factor" approach to the secondary issue of the characterisation of particular acts once the central questions have been posed: what was the claimant employed to do and was s/he doing it, or something reasonably incidental to it, when the accident occured. This is both right in principle and, by more clearly establishing parameters, enables an expert body of Commissioners more closely to scrutinise decisions of appeals tribunals, the better to ensure a degree of "horizontal equity between claimants" (see Wikeley, Ogus and Barendt, *The Law of Social Security*, p.728), since it is submitted that the "back to basics" approach in *Rhodes* offers a framework of analysis relatively more certain and consistent than the impressionist, artistic brushwork of Lord Donaldson M.R. in *Nancollas*. Whilst part of his judgment in *Nancollas* was approved by Lord Goff in *Smith v Stages*, it is clear that the House of Lords did not approve the proposition that there are no rules. Indeed, Lord Lowry set out six propositions designed to assist with the question whether a person travelling could be regarded as being in the course of employment (see annotations to s.99, below, "Introduction"). Although *Smith v Stages* was not concerned with a social security question, but rather with the matter of an employer's vicarious liability for the acts of his employee in the law of torts, the same phrase, "acting in the course of employment" was under consideration. Moreover, their Lordships reverted to older authorities for guidance, relying particularly on *St Helens Colliery Limited v Hewitson* [1924] A.C. 59, and stated that *Vandyke v Fender* [1970] 2 Q.B. 292

is still good law. Indeed in *R(I) 1/88* (see further the annotations to s.99, below, "Introduction"), the Commissioner held that *Nancollas* did not remove the well-accepted distinction betwen acts done under an obligation to an employer and acts merely done with his permission: in the former case it almost necessarily follows that the employee was acting in the course of his employment, but this does not equally necessarily follow from the fact that the employee was doing what was authorised by the employer.

Rightly, however, given the immense variety of the world of work, the post-*Nancollas* reappraisal culminating in *Rhodes* nonetheless requires the application of broad principle to the facts of individual cases rather than proceeding on the basis that a similar fact case *dictates* the result. Tribunals should not rely too heavily on previous decisions without relating them to a detailed consideration of the facts of the particular case *(R(I) 1/93; CI 110/98)*. In *R(I) 1/93*, Commissioner Johnson set aside an SSAT decision as erroneous in law because it failed to look at the factual picture as a whole:

> "the tribunal clearly relied on apparently similar cases [Commissioners' decisions] in reaching their decisions, whereas they should have given primary consideration to the particular facts of the case before them" (para.6).

In the particular case the claimant was injured when she tripped and fell during a site meeting, held on her employer's premises, but not at her usual workplace. The purpose of the meeting was to discuss the pending actions brought against the company by the claimant and others with respect to repetitive strain injury (RSI). The factor which tipped the balance for the Commissioner, who held that the accident befell her out of and in the course of her employment, was "the company's interest in her attending the site meeting" which might well save time and costs in the litigation even if it did not secure a settlement of the claims (paras 10, 11).

"In the course of employment" and the tests noted above have a good degree of **1.356** elasticity. That, as held in *Rhodes* above (see further below, "(iv) Flexible working and employees on sick leave"), those incapable of work, and thus not as such "in the course of their employment", can still be protected if injured while performing one of their work tasks (the performance bringing them back within the course of their employment) amply illustrates the flexibility of application inherent in the central tests, adherence to which is essential in a compensation system for accidents suffered at or during work and because of it.

There are four statutory "extensions" in ss.98–101 bringing certain accidents, which would otherwise not arise in the course of [ss.98–100], or out of [s.101], employment, within the scope of the scheme. Travelling accidents, a continual problem, are dealt with in the note to s.99. Three other common types of claim illustrate the difficulty of determining the course of employment when applying s.94.

(i) Beginnings and endings

When does the course of employment start and finish on the normal working day? **1.357** Clocking in and out? Getting into and out of working clothes? Getting onto and off the employer's premises? The terms of employment may be part of the answer but all the facts must be considered and weighed, perhaps with a view to asking whether at the point at which the accident happened the employee was exposed to the risks of the workplace or merely those risks which he would run as a member of the general public. By way of example of successful claims:

R. v N.I. Commissioner Ex p. East [1976] I.C.R. 206 (accident suffered by claimant in works canteen prior to clocking-on)

R(I) 3/62 (employee habitually arriving very early at work to avoid rush-hour travel)

R(I) 22/56 (miner suffering accident on colliery road after visiting colliery canteen at the end of work to avoid the rush for the first bus)

R(I) 72/54 (miner suffering accident on way to collect replacement for bootlace broken whilst changing into working clothes)

CI/105/1990 (employee injured while getting into taxi to have her injury checked and, if necessary, treated, in hospital: see below).

Unsuccessful claims:

R(I) 22/53 (railwayman injured on his way from home to work—on railway land but half a mile from the depot where he worked)

R(I) 11/54 (miner visiting canteen before his shift to buy sandwiches to eat during shift—injured on canteen steps)

R(I) 14/61 (part-time clerk completing work at 1.00pm then taking lunch in the canteen and suffering injury on leaving)

CI/114/1987 (employee going in to work on day off for sole purpose of collecting pay and suffering injury outside the wages office).

(ii) Taking a break

1.358   Is the course of employment interrupted where the claimant takes a break in the working day? Again, a matter of fact for the decision-maker or tribunal, but it may be useful to discover whether the break was imposed by the employer, permitted, condoned, provided for in the terms of employment, or proscribed. Were any particular activities required (or prohibited) during the break? Was the claimant still on duty, or on call during the break? *R. v Industrial Injuries Commissioner Ex p. A.E.U. (No.2)* [1996] 2 Q.B. 31 (*Culverwell's* case) concerned an accident happening during a break. The claimant was only permitted to smoke in a designated booth. Throughout a permitted break the booth was occupied and the claimant was injured by a fork-lift truck as he waited outside the booth after the end of the permitted break. The Court of Appeal held that he was not in the course of employment because he had overstayed the permitted break and was doing something for his own purposes quite unconnected with his employment.

As examples of successful claims:

R(I) 21/53, R(I) 11/55, R(I) 20/61 and *R(I) 4/67* (all concern bus drivers or conductors injured during a break from duty and observing the instructions or permission of their employer about the way the break should be spent)

R(I) 7/80 (police sergeant in charge of station permitted to take meal break at home whilst remaining on call—injured on journey back to station).

Unsuccessful claims:

R(I) 6/53 and *R(I) 4/79* (bus crews)

R(I) 6/76 (interruption of work due to bomb scare)

R(I) 5/81 (fire officer travelling from office to home to begin on-call period)

R(I) 10/81 (merchant seaman going ashore for his own purposes during an official break).

(iii) Recreational activity

1.359   Some employments have recreational activity as a part of the work; some offer facilities for recreation; some offer periods of inactivity during which employees may take recreation. Whether an accident occurring during recreational activity has arisen in the course of employment must be a question of mixed fact and law, but whereas one type of claim has generally been successful, two other types have not. This may indicate the important questions to ask in such a case.

The successful claims have been in cases where the employee is required to take part in the activity:

CI/228/50 (apprentice injured during compulsory physical training as part of day class he was required to attend—see also *R(I) 4/51, R(I) 31/53*)

R(I) 13/51 (male nurse at mental hospital injured whilst playing football with patients—see also *R(I) 3/57*)

R(I) 68/51 (fireman injured playing volleyball during compulsory fitness training period—see also *R(I) 13/66*)

R(I) 3/81 (police cadet injured whilst travelling back from National Swimming Championships in which she had been detailed to take part).

The unsuccessful claims have been in cases where the recreational activity is merely encouraged (even strongly encouraged) rather than compulsory (*R . v N.I. Commissioners Ex p. Michael* [1977] 1 W.L.R. 109, Appendix to *R(I) 5/75*); or where the employee takes recreation during an off-duty period or during an enforced break in employment:

R(I) 2/69 (laboratory technician playing football during the lunch-hour)

R(I) 2/80 (fireman attending residential college injured playing football in the evening)

R(I) 4/81 (airline stewardess injured playing tennis during a stop-over between flights).

R. v N.I. Commissioners Ex p. Michael has been followed by the Court of Appeal, in preference to *Nancollas*, in *Faulkner v Chief Adjudication Officer, The Times*, April 8, 1994 reported as *R(I) 8/94*. In *Faulkner*, the claimant policeman sustained personal injury while playing football for his police football team. The SSAT held this to have arisen in the course of his employment but their decision was set aside as erroneous in law on September 30, 1990 by Commissioner Johnson. The Court of Appeal upheld the Commissioner's decision; there was no evidence before the SSAT which could justify such a conclusion. Following *Michael*, the question was whether the claimant was doing his job when injured and not whether he was doing something reasonably incidental to it. The court considered that the implication of a contractual term was not to be made because it seemed sensible or reasonable that such a term should be implied or because the chief police officer, the Police Federation representative, or the claimant regarded community policing as a good and useful policy, but in accordance with the ordinary legal principle that an obligation could be read into a contract if it was such as the nature of the contract itself implicitly required. The claimant had sought to rely on *Nancollas* to argue that *Michael* should be reconsidered in the light of changing social circumstances. The Court decided that *Nancollas* gave no basis for distinguishing *Michael*.

(iv) Flexible working and employees on sick leave

In *R(I) 1/99*, Commissioner Goodman held that "in the course of employment"   1.360
embraced the employee, a Benefits Agency clerical officer at home on sick leave, incapable of work and, by rights, doing none, who was assaulted in her drive by her neighbour for reasons clearly connected with and the product of her employment (she had reported the neighbour to the appropriate Benefits Agency authorities for claiming benefits whilst working). While the injury undoubtedly arose out of the employment, it is difficult, applying factors of time, place and activity, to regard such a claimant as properly being in the course of her employment (see further D. Bonner, "Compensation for Assault: an Unusual Dimension to the Industrial Injuries System" (1998) 5 J.S.S.L. 68). The Court of Appeal, by majority (Schiemann and Roch L.JJ., Swinton Thomas L.J. dissenting), upheld the appeal against Commissioner Goodman's decision: *Chief Adjudication Officer v Rhodes*, reported as *R(I) 1/99*; see further Bonner (1999) 6 J.S.S.L. 33). Commissioner Goodman had erred in law. While Mrs Rhodes at the time of the assault was clearly still employed as an employed earner, and while the work-connected reason for the assault undoubtedly rendered this "accident" one arising "out of" of the employment, the reason for the assault could not of itself bring her within "the course of employment". "Out of" and "in the course of" are distinct conditions *both* of which must be satisifed to render the accident an industrial one. "In the course of" requires a focus on what the claimant was doing rather than on what was done to her. There was no basis for saying that at the material time Mrs Rhodes was doing something she was employed to do or something reasonably incidental thereto, that being the established test (see above). Commissioner Goodman had instead concentrated in effect (though not in form) on whether or not she was an employed

earner. Undoubtedly she was, even when on sick leave. But so too would be a claimant injured when on a skiing holiday. Merely being still an employed earner does not render one in the course of employment. Roch L.J. rejected Commissioner Goodman's view that, being still employed and on sick leave, she was thus at home only with the consent and authority of her employer, in so far as that view misleadingly suggested that the employer required her to be at home. Hence, merely being on permitted sick leave does not bring a claimant within the course of employment. Roch L.J. saw the Commissioner's decision and the points made in support of Mrs Rhodes (and by implication Swinton Thomas L.J.'s dissent?) as foundering "on the ground that they elide the two requirements into a single requirement, namely has the accident arisen out of the claimant's employment". The two are separate, something affirmed as Parliament's intention by the presumption in s.94(3) that accidents in the course of also arise out of employment in the absence of any evidence to the contrary. "In the course of" requires examination of *the activity of* the claimant, not of *what is being done to* the claimant. Schiemann L.J. considered, however, (and Roch L.J. agreed with his reasoning) that someone on sick leave can still be in the course of employment if performing duties required of him (and similar propositions must apply to those working at home under flexible working arrangements). For example someone in hospital with a broken leg in traction but whose mental faculties are unimpaired could be given files to read and would be in the course of employment when doing that. Similarly if Mrs Rhodes had actually been working on material from the office. If, when off sick, she had been assaulted while using a mobile phone to report a fraudulent claimant, that, for Schiemann L.J., would be something reasonably incidental to what she was employed to do. He might also have so held, though he saw lesser force in this situation, if the assault had occurred just after she had ended the telephone conversation. But none of this could avail Mrs Rhodes whose information was given days, if not weeks, before. Although she sometimes did work at home under the Agency's flexi-time system, there was no material before the Commissioner for him to find as a fact that at the relevant time Mrs Rhodes was working at home. The matters the claimant drew to the court's attention—the fact that she was sometimes sent material to help her to keep up to date with the law and practice in the field in which she was employed:

> "did not suggest that on that particular day she was actually doing anything, although she could have been required to do something . . . simply as a matter of construction of the relevant section [SSCBA, s.94(1)], the twin test is not satisfied.
> One of the pillars is fulfilled, the accident did arise out of the employment, but it does not seem to me that it arose in the course of the employment. To say that something was causally linked to something which has been done in the course of employment does not seem to me to be good enough".

However, had Mrs Rhodes been assaulted on her drive while giving advice in her official capacity to her neighbour on benefit matters, one might surely agree with the dissenting Swinton Thomas L.J. that such an accident arose not only "out of" but also "in the course of" her employment.

1.361   In *CI/1098/2004*, Commissioner Howell was faced with an application for an accident declaration from a hospital staff nurse, who argued that he had suffered psychological damage because of what he was told in the course of a telephone conversation he made to his Directorate Manager when at home on sick leave, having earlier been telephoned from work and asked to call his Directorate Manager. Commissioner Howell directed the tribunal to which he remitted the application for an accident declaration that for that purpose the telephone conversation was one made in the course of and out of the applicant's employment

> "but that it is for the claimant to establish to the satisfaction of the tribunal that he did in fact suffer something in the course of or as the immediate consequence of that conversation which is identifiable as an 'accident' before he can be granted the declaration he seeks. This is something the tribunal must determine for itself,

the apparent departmental acceptance that he has suffered some form of personal injury being insufficient" (para.2).

It cannot be emphasised too strongly that the whole of this note on the course of employment should be read in the light of the comments in the *Nancollas* case, *Smith v Stages*, *Faulkner v Chief Adjudication Officer* and *CAO v Rhodes* (above) about the proper approach to determining the question of whether a claimant is, or is not, in the course of his employment. In starred decision *CI/105/1990*, Commissioner Goodman considered how one should approach the case in which several accidents (in this instance two on the same day) are each said to be industrial accidents:

"[I]n deciding whether or not first, second or subsequent accidents are of themselves industrial accidents, each must be looked at in isolation, though what happened in one accident may have some bearing on whether or not when a subsequent accident occurred the claimant was still within the course of employment. *But* it must still be established independently that the second accident did arise out of and in the course of employment, as that is required imperatively by section 50(1) of the Social Security Act 1975 [now s.94(1)]" (para.13).

In *CI/105/1990*, the claimant home carer (home help) slipped on an icy pavement on her way to her first visit of the day, incurring what was later established to be a hairline fracture of the fibula. She nevertheless continued work and undertook a number of tasks at and in relation to her first call. Being still in pain, she informed her supervisor that she was going to hospital to have her leg checked and, if necessary, treated. "It was either expressed or implied that if all was well she would be carrying on with her schedule of visits for the day." Unfortunately, she slipped on the icy pavement when the taxi came, suffering a "potts fracture" of the right ankle, so severe that she had not at the time of the Commissioner's hearing been able to resume work as a home carer. The SSAT upheld her appeal against the AO's refusal to grant any declaration of industrial accident, but only in relation to the first incident. On appeal by the claimant from the SSAT, Commissioner Goodman considered the proper course was to regard there as having been two separate decisions by the SSAT, so that he was only concerned with the second incident. He considered that when it occurred, the claimant was still in the course of her employment, acting as an employee would if there was continued pain in the leg, namely to obtain some medical investigation of it, in her case in the only way open to a peripatetic worker, that is, by going to hospital. In this case, dependent on this point entirely on its own facts, the line dividing the course of employment and its cessation for that day was to be drawn only when it was clear that the claimant would not be coming back to work that day, something which only became clear when investigations took place in the hospital (see paras 10 and 11).

Subsection (2)

Industrial death benefit is no longer payable except in respect of deaths occurring before April 11, 1988. On reduced earnings allowance and retirement allowance, see commentary to Sch.7, Pts IV and V.

1.362

Subsection (3)

This provision has been referred to in the note on subs.(1) above. The so-called presumption created by this subsection has no operation where all the facts are known—it can only help the claimant where there is some doubt about the circumstances of the accident.

In *R. v N.I. (Industrial Injuries) Commissioner Ex p. Richardson* [1958] 1 W.L.R. 851 (Appendix to *R(I) 21/58*), the Divisional Court considered the equivalent provision in an earlier statute:

1.363

"if . . . there is no other evidence except that [the claimant] suffered an accident in the course of his employment, then it is to be deemed, it is taken to be proved, that it arose out of the employment. But if there is evidence to the contrary by whoever it is given, that is to say, the facts which are before the Commissioner can amount to evidence to the contrary, then the presumption or the deeming disappears, and if once that deeming disappears it is then for [the claimant] to prove that the accident did arise not only in the course of but also out of his employment."

In *R(I) 16/61*, a Tribunal of Commissioners said that, ". . . as the facts are known and it is a question of applying the law to them it seems to us that there is no room for the application of [the presumption]."

In *R(I) 1/64*, the Commissioner suggested that "evidence to the contrary" in the subsection meant something more than speculative inference, but something less than proof. All the authorities were considered in *R(I) 6/82* (maintenance engineer in bakery suffering unexplained fracture to ankle whilst walking round a milling machine) where the subsection was held to be inapplicable because all the circumstances of the accident were known.

The presumption was considered again recently in *CI/207/1987*, where Commissioner Hoolahan considered the nature of the evidence required to rebut the presumption. He rejected the proposition that an inference could amount to evidence, since an inference may only be drawn from an established fact. If no clear inference can be drawn from the established facts, there is no evidence "to the contrary" for the purposes of this section.

Subsection (5)

1.364   Except for the special groups of workers referred to, industrial injuries benefit is not payable in respect of accidents happening outside Great Britain, notwithstanding that the victim may be carrying out his job abroad. This apparent anomaly was rectified by an amendment to the Persons Abroad Regulations which permits a claim for benefit in respect of accidents happening abroad to an employed earner, with effect from October 1, 1986.

Subsection (6)

1.365   For "incapable of work" and "incapacity for work" see the notes to s.57 (pp.180–182, and 187–194 of Bonner, Hooker and White, *Non Means Tested Benefits: The Legislation* (1994)). The new tests of incapacity in Pt XIIA do not apply for the purposes of industrial injuries benefits (s.171G(1)(a), below).

Relevant employments

1.366   **95.**—(1) In section 94 above, this section and sections 98 and 109 below "employed earner's employment" shall be taken to include any employment by virtue of which a person is, or is treated by regulations as being for the purposes of industrial injuries benefit, an employed earner.

(2) Regulations may provide that any prescribed employment shall not be treated for the purposes of industrial injuries benefit as employed earner's employment notwithstanding that it would be so treated apart from the regulations.

(3) For the purposes of the provisions of this Act mentioned in subsection (1) above an employment shall be an employed earner's employment in relation to an accident if (and only if) it is, or is treated by regulations as being, such an employment when the accident occurs.

(4) Any reference in the industrial injuries and diseases provisions to an "employed earner" or "employed earner's employment" is to be construed, in relation to any time before 6th April 1975, as a reference respectively to

an "insured person" or "insurable employment" within the meaning of the provisions relating to industrial injuries and diseases which were in force at that time.

(5) In subsection (4) above "the industrial injuries and diseases provisions" means—

(a) this section and sections 96 to 110 below;

(b) any other provisions of this Act so far as they relate to those sections; and

(c) [¹ any provisions of the Administration Act, Chapter II of Part I of the Social Security Act 1998 or Part II of the Social Security Contributions (Transfer of Functions, etc.) Act 1999, so far as they so relate.]

AMENDMENT

1. Social Security Act 1998 Sch.7 para.64 and Social Security Contributions (Transfer of Functions, etc.) Act 1999 Sch.7 para.4 (July 5, 1999).

DERIVATION

SSA 1975 s.51 as amended; SS(MP)A 1977 s.17(3).   **1.367**

GENERAL NOTE

The regulations referred to in this section are the Social Security (Employed   **1.368** Earner's Employments for Industrial Injuries Purposes) Regulations 1975 (SI 1975/467) (as amended). Decisions on whether a person is, or was, employed in employed earner's employment so as to bring him within the scheme were until April 1, 1999 solely for the Secretary of State (SSAA 1992 s.17). From April 1, 1999, such decisions became matters for officers of the Board of Revenue and Customs (see Social Security Contributions (Transfer of Functions, etc.) Act 1999 s.8(1)(b), below) and are now the province of the Commissions for Her Majesty's Revenue and Customs (see Commissioners for Revenue and Customs Act 2005 s.5(2)).

[¹Employment training schemes etc

95A.—(1) In the industrial injuries and diseases provisions any reference   **1.369** to employed earner's employment shall be taken to include participation in an employment training scheme or employment training course of a prescribed description (and "employed earner" shall be construed accordingly).

(2) In those provisions, a reference to an employer, in relation to any such participation, shall be taken to be a prescribed person.

(3) In this section "industrial injuries and diseases provisions" has the same meaning as in s.95(4) above.]

AMENDMENT

1. Welfare Reform Act 2012 s.66 (October 31, 2013).   **1.370**

GENERAL NOTE

As part of the simplification of benefits schemes, this applies the industrial inju-   **1.371** ries scheme to cover accidents and prescribed diseases resulting from participation in an employment training scheme or employment training course of a prescribed description, rather than, as previously, having participants covered under the Analogous Industrial Injuries Scheme (AIIS). Such participation is treated as employed earner's employment, participants as employed earner's (for II purposes) and "a prescribed person" is treated as the employer of such participants. See the Industrial Injuries Benefit (Employment Training Schemes and Courses) Regulations 2013 (SI 2013/2540). The "employers" for industrial injuries benefit purposes are persons providing an employment training scheme or employment training course of a description prescribed in reg.2 of those Regulations (reg.3).

Persons treated as employers for certain purposes

1.372 **96.**—In relation to—

(a) a person who is an employed earner for the purposes of this Part of this Act otherwise than by virtue of a contract of service or apprenticeship; or

(b) any other employed earner—

(i) who is employed for the purpose of any game or recreation and is engaged or paid through a club; or

(ii) in whose case it appears to the Secretary of State there is special difficulty in the application of all or any of the provisions of this Part of this Act relating to employers,

regulations may provide for a prescribed person to be treated in respect of industrial injuries benefit and its administration as the earner's employer.

Accidents in course of illegal employments

1.373 **97.**—(1) Subsection (2) below has effect in any case where—

(a) a claim is made for industrial injuries benefit in respect of an accident, or of a prescribed disease or injury; or

(b) [¹ an application is made under section 29 of the Social Security Act 1998 for a declaration that an accident was an industrial accident, or for a corresponding declaration as to a prescribed disease or injury.]

(2) The Secretary of State may direct that the relevant employment shall, in relation to that accident, disease or injury, be treated as having been employed earner's employment notwithstanding that by reason of a contravention of, or non-compliance with, some provision contained in or having effect under an enactment passed for the protection of employed persons or any class of employed persons, either—

(a) the contract purporting to govern the employment was void; or

(b) the employed person was not lawfully employed in the relevant employment at the time when, or in the place where, the accident happened or the disease or injury was contracted or received.

(3) In subsection (2) above "relevant employment" means—

(a) in relation to an accident, the employment out of and in the course of which the accident arises, and

(b) in relation to a prescribed disease or injury, the employment to the nature of which the disease or injury is due.

AMENDMENT

1. Social Security Act 1998 Sch.7 para.64 (July 5, 1999).

Earner acting in breach of regulations, etc.

1.374 **98.**—An accident shall be taken to arise out of and in the course of an employed earner's employment, notwithstanding that he is at the time of the accident acting in contravention of any statutory or other regulations applicable to his employment, or of any orders given by or on behalf of his employer, or that he is acting without instructions from his employer, if—

   (a) the accident would have been taken so to have arisen had the act not been done in contravention of any such regulations or orders, or without such instructions, as the case may be; and

   (b) the act is done for the purposes of and in connection with the employer's trade or business.

DERIVATION

SSA 1975 s.52.   1.375

GENERAL NOTE

This is the first of four successive sections which extend the scheme to situations   1.376 in which, on general principle, the accident would not be regarded as arising out of, or in the course of, employment. For three of the four sections it is still necessary to consider the question of whether, on a given hypothesis, the accident happened in the course of employment and reference must, therefore, be made to the general discussion in the note to s.94(1) above.

If an accident happens to an employee who is acting contrary to regulations, or without the permission of or contrary to the instructions of his employer it would not be difficult to conclude that he had taken himself out of the course of employment by virtue of his acts. This section *deems* the accident to have arisen out of and in the course of employment provided two conditions are fulfilled. In *CI/210/50*, where a miner had (contrary to the Coal Mines Act 1911) jumped on a tram to ride back to the shaft bottom and was injured when it was derailed, the Commissioner formulated the following approach to the application of the equivalent section of the National Insurance (Industrial Injuries) Act 1946:

   (a) looking at the facts as a whole, including any regulations or orders affecting the claimant, was the accident one which arose out of and in the course of employment?

   (b) if the answer to the first question is "no"—is that because the claimant was acting in contravention of some regulation or order?

   (c) if the answer to the second question is "yes"—was the claimant's act done for the purposes of and in connection with the employer's business?

Following through the reasoning, if the answer to the first question is "yes", the claimant will have proved that part of his case without recourse to the section. The approach recommended by the Commissioner demonstrates that it is still necessary to determine whether the accident arose in the course of employment, either taking account of or ignoring the breach of regulation or instruction. That question must be answered on general principles.

Particular difficulty has been encountered in cases where the claimant has done something unauthorised which was outside his normal duties. In *R(I) 12/61*, a repairer in a colliery was injured in an explosion occurring as he illegally connected up detonators—a job reserved for shotfirers, and in *R(I) 1/66*, a dock labourer was killed when, to expedite the loading of a ship, he attempted to use a fork-lift truck which he drove off the dock—driving being a job reserved for authorised fork-lift drivers. Both claims for benefit failed because the Commissioner held that the victim had been doing something which was not part of his job and, therefore, was not in the course of his employment. The victim was not doing his job in an unauthorised way—he was not doing *his* job. This restrictive approach was relaxed somewhat in *R(I) 1/70* where a wider view was taken of what amounted to the claimant's "job".

Earner travelling in employer's transport

1.377   **99.**—(1) An accident happening while an employed earner is, with the express or implied permission of his employer, travelling as a passenger by any vehicle to or from his place of work shall, notwithstanding that he is under no obligation to his employer to travel by that vehicle, be taken to arise out of and in the course of his employment if—

(a) the accident would have been taken so to have arisen had he been under such an obligation; and

(b) at the time of the accident, the vehicle—

(i) is being operated by or on behalf of his employer or some other person by whom it is provided in pursuance of arrangements made with his employer; and

(ii) is not being operated in the ordinary course of a public transport service.

(2) In this section references to a vehicle include a ship, vessel, hovercraft or aircraft.

DERIVATION

1.378   SSA 1975, s.53.

GENERAL NOTE

1.379   *(1) Introduction: looking at "travelling" accidents within the general principles set out in s.94*

Accidents occurring in the course of travel cause many problems. A person whose work requires travel (the sales representative, the fireman, the lorry driver, etc.) should be able to show that an accident happening during such travelling arose in the course of his employment, although there may be the same uncertainty about when the course of employment begins and ends as in other jobs. Equally, a person who is merely travelling to his work is unlikely to be able to show that the course of his employment has begun until, at least, he has reached work.

There are a mass of decisions on travelling accidents which attempt to distinguish significant features to place the accident inside or outside the course of employment. Some of them are considered in *Nancollas v Insurance Officer* [1985] 1 All E.R. 833 and others in the later House of Lords decision *Smith v Stages* [1989] 1 All E.R. 833, considered further, below. The *Nancollas* decision deals with two appeals from the Commissioner *(R(I) 14/81* and *R(I) 7/85)* which had both been decided against the claimant concerned. In the former, N was in a job (disablement resettlement officer) based at Worthing which required him to call in at other centres and to make home visits throughout Sussex and Surrey. He did not work fixed hours and determined his own itinerary. On the day in question he had to visit Aldershot and set out to travel there direct from home without first going into the office at Worthing. He was injured in a motor accident. In the other appeal, B was a police finger-print expert living, and normally working, at Wakefield. He was also a sailing instructor and, as part of his police duties, gave sailing courses to police cadets at a reservoir 40 miles from Wakefield. He was injured in an accident whilst travelling on his motorcycle to the reservoir to give a course. In both cases the Commissioner held that the accident did not arise in the course of employment, but the Court of Appeal allowed both appeals. The impressionistic, total factor, no rules, no binding precedents approach in *Nancollas* has been considered in the annotations to "arising in the course of employment" in s.94. Subsequent decisions seem to have relegated it to the secondary characterisation of particular acts once the principal questions have been posed: what was the claimant employed to do and was s/he doing it, or something reasonably incidental to it, when the accident occurred. But in *R(I) 1/88* (decided before this reappraisal), the Commissioner had in any event held that *Nancollas* did not remove the well-accepted distinction between acts done under an obligation to an employer and acts merely done with his permission: in the former case it almost necessarily follows that the employee was acting in the course of his employment, but this does not equally necessarily follow from the fact that the employee was doing what was authorised by the employer. So that in *R(I) 1/88*, a British Telecom employee, who usually travelled by train, was given the use of a company vehicle to enable him to work overtime on a specific project, and was given specific permission, subject to strict rules, to use the vehicle to return home when the job was completed later than expected. The Commissioner held that the accident suffered on the journey home arose in the course of the man's employment.

The House of Lords decision in *Smith v Stages* was not concerned specifically with s.99, nor even with the industrial injuries legislation generally, but it is instructive to set out the propositions formulated by Lord Lowry since they have general application to the interpretation of the phrase "arising in the course of employment" and specific application to travelling.

In *Smith v Stages* there had been a motor accident causing injury which had occurred whilst the employees were on their way home from a job away from their normal place of work. There were, of course, specific circumstances which led to the particular decision, but Lord Lowry attempted a more general analysis. He said (at [1989] 1 All E.R. at 851):

> "It is impossible to provide for every eventuality and foolish, without the benefit of argument, to make the attempt, but some prima facie propositions may be stated with reasonable confidence. (1) An employee travelling from his ordinary residence to his regular place of work, whatever the means of transport and even if it is provided by his employer, is not on duty and is not acting in the course of his employment, but, if he is obliged by his contract of service to use the employer's transport, he will normally, in the absence of an express condition to the contrary, be regarded as acting in the course of his employment while doing so. (2) Travelling in the employer's time between workplaces (one of which may be the regular workplace) or in the course of a peripatetic occupation whether accompanied by goods or tools or simply in order to reach a succession of workplaces (as an inspector of gas meters might do), will be in the course of employment. (3) Receipt of wages (though not receipt of a travelling allowance) will indicate that the employee is travelling in the employer's time and for his benefit and is acting in the course of his employment, and in such a case the fact that the employee may have discretion as to the mode and time of travelling will not take the journey out of the course of his employment. (4) An employee travelling *in the employer's time* from his ordinary residence to a work-place other than his regular workplace or in the course of a peripatetic occupation or to the scene of an emergency (such as a fire, an accident or a mechanical breakdown of plant) will be acting in the course of his employment. (5) A deviation from or interruption of a journey undertaken in the course of employment (unless the deviation or interruption is merely incidental to the journey) will for the time being (which may include an overnight interruption) take the employee out of the course of his employment. (6) Return journeys are to be treated on the same footing as outward journeys."

These remarks were said expressly not to refer to salaried employees and there are, of course, some observations which are not entirely appropriate to a social security context. Nonetheless, the case was quickly referred to with approval in two unreported decisions, *CI/110/1988* and *CI/163/1988*. In *R(I)1/91*, Commissioner Rice considered the above quoted statement of Lord Lowry in *Smith v Stages* in upholding the tribunal's decision that the claimant, severely injured in a motor accident 10 minutes after finishing work, was not still in the course of his employment when the accident occurred. On the facts, the Commissioner rejected the view that the claimant was being paid by the employer to travel to and from the place of work, but went on to say that, even if he had been, "it did not necessarily follow that this in itself meant that he was in the course of his employment" (para.9). Here the Commissioner cited Lord Goff in *Smith v Stages* [1989] 2 W.L.R. 529 at 534:

". . . the fact that a man is being paid by his employer in respect of the relevant period of time is often important, but cannot of itself be decisive. A man is usually paid nowadays during his holidays; and it often happens that an employer may allow a man to take the afternoon off, or even a whole day off, without affecting his wages. In such circumstances, he would ordinarily, not be acting in the course of his employment despite the fact that he is being paid. Indeed, any rule that payment at the relevant time is decisive would be very difficult to apply in the case of a salaried man. Let me however give an example concerned with travelling to work. Suppose that a man is applying for a job, and it turns out that he would have a pretty arduous journey between his home and his new place of work, lasting about an hour each way, which is deterring him from taking the job. His prospective employer may want to employ him, and may entice him by offering an extra hour's pay at each end of the day—say 10 hours' pay instead of eight. In those circumstances he would not I think, be acting in the course of his employment when travelling to or from work. This is because he would not be employed to make the journey: the extra pay would simply be given to him in recognition of the fact that his journey to and from work was an arduous one."

(2) The effect of s.99

1.380   The provisions of this section extend the course of employment to include an accident occurring on transport provided by the employer for the benefit of his workers, but which is not obligatory. (If use of the transport *is* obligatory, as with building contractors taking employees to a site by lorry from an arranged pick-up point, then the course of employment is likely to begin when the employee boards the transport.)

Subsection (1)

1.381   The extension is limited by the conditions which are attached by the section.

(a) The claimant must be travelling with the express or implied permission of his employer. Implied permission is sufficient (*R(I) 8/62*—bus conductress on her way to work picked up by empty bus returning to depot, a practice condoned by the employer), but must normally be given in advance. If permission is given retrospectively it must be express (*R(I) 5/80*—no permission given by employer for bus journey to be continued in the private car of the bus driver);

(b) The accident would have been in the course of employment if the claimant had been under an obligation to use the transport.
      This again involves a consideration of the general principles in the note to s.94(1) and "Introduction", above. The nature of the accident and its relationship to the claimant's employment and his presence on the transport will be relevant.

(c) The transport is operated by or on behalf of the employer, *or* is operated as a result of arrangements made by the employer. These are alternative conditions. It should not be difficult to ascertain whether the transport is provided by the employer or on his behalf—so long as there is some measure of control exercised by the employer over the transport that should be enough (*R(I) 42/56*). The meaning of "arrangements" is less clear, but a similar concept of control has been used to determine what sort of transport service should fall within the section. It is not necessary that there should be a contract between the employer and the person who provides the transport, but there must be something more than a mere request or suggestion from the employer.
      In *R(I) 67/51*, the Commissioner said,

"The 'arrangements' would normally be made by contract between the employer and the provider of the vehicle but in the absence of a contract one would expect to find at least some definite ascertainable engagement between the employer and the provider of the service whereby the employer 'arranged' for it to be provided. One would expect to find also that the employer had the exclusive use of the vehicle and that members of the public travelling as ordinary fare-paying passengers would not be carried."

Acquiescence in a scheme made by another employer is sufficient *(R(I) 49/53)*, but a purely private agreement under which an employee was given the use of a company car to get to work whilst his own was under repair is not, even though he was in the habit of bringing other employees to work in his own car *(R(I) 5/60)*.

(d) The transport is not being operated in the ordinary course of a public transport service.

This condition may already have been taken into account in deciding whether the employer had sufficient control over the provision of the transport for it to be said that it was provided under an arrangement with him, but it is a separate statutory requirement. In *R(I) 15/57* it was regarded as significant that the bus bore no destination indicator, did not stop to pick up members of the public, did not appear on published timetables, did not run during factory closures, and finished the journey on a private road to the factory. It was suggested in *R(I) 3/59* that once members of the public were permitted to ride on the bus it would lose its "private" status, but this may be too restrictive given the words "operated in the ordinary course of . . .".

Subsection (2)
Special provision is made for mariners and airmen by SI 1975/470 and SI 1975/469 respectively.   1.382

Accidents happening while meeting emergency

100.—An accident happening to an employed earner in or about any premises at which he is for the time being employed for the purposes of his employer's trade or business shall be taken to arise out of and in the course of his employment if it happens while he is taking steps, on an actual or supposed emergency at those premises, to rescue, succour or protect persons who are, or are thought to be or possibly to be, injured or imperilled, or to avert or minimise serious damage to property.   1.383

DERIVATION

SSA 1975 s.54.   1.384

GENERAL NOTE

Prior to 1946, when the forerunner of this section first appeared in the National Insurance (Industrial Injuries) Act, the courts had decided that accidents sustained in responding to an "emergency" could be regarded as "arising out of and in the course of employment" so long as the response was broadly incidental to the employee's duties. Since 1946, the Commissioners have taken the same line and this section need only be considered when, on general principle, the accident has not arisen in the course of employment *(CI/280/49)*.   1.385

Emergencies under general principle (i.e. within s.94)
Once the Court of Appeal had decided that a ship's baker, injured on remonstrating with an Egyptian who had used foul language to two lady passengers, had suffered an accident arising out of and in the course of his employment   1.386

(*Culpeck v Orient Steam Navigation Co. Ltd* (1922) B.W.C.C. 187), the way was clear for a reasonable response to any unexpected occurrence to be within the course of employment so long as the acts done were within the general nature of the claimant's employment. Hence, an employee assisting a fellow employee in difficulties (*CI/280/49*); a lorry driver assisting a stranded motorist (*R(I) 11/51*); a security guard assisting a policeman to investigate suspicious circumstances in another building (*R(I) 62/51*); a delivery driver assisting in moving an obstructing concrete mixer (*R(I) 11/56*); and an Admiralty policeman stopping an inhabited runaway push-chair (*R(I) 46/60*), were all acting in the course of their employment.

There seem to have been relatively few unsuccessful claims on this ground. In *R(I) 32/54*, the response of climbing through a first-floor window to enter a locked factory rather than waiting for the key was held to be unreasonable, and in *R(I) 52/54*, a civil servant was held not to be in the course of his employment when rescuing a child on a runaway tricycle on his way to make an interview visit to a private house. For a different approach to a similar situation to *R(I) 52/54* see *CSI/54/89*, noted above in the annotation to s.94(1) ("arising out of the employment").

Emergencies under the section

1.387   The section has only been considered extensively in *R(I) 6/63*. It is clear from that decision that the section can operate where the acts done were no part of the general duties of the employee, nor done for the employer's purposes. However, some of the phrases in the section may be restrictive.

"in or about premises"—does not include the highway generally (*R(I) 52/54*), but does include the road adjacent to particular premises (*R(I) 46/60*).

"rescue, succour or protect"—should be wide enough to cover most circumstances where there is actual or supposed danger to the person, but note that if steps are taken to protect property the damage to be averted or minimised must be "serious".

Note that the "emergency" must be "*at* these premises".

Accident caused by another's misconduct, etc.

1.388   **101.**—An accident happening after 19th December 1961 shall be treated for the purposes of industrial injuries benefit, where it would not apart from this section be so treated, as arising out of an employed earner's employment if—

    (a) the accident arises in the course of the employment; and

    (b) the accident either is caused—

        (i) by another person's misconduct, skylarking or negligence, or

        (ii) by steps taken in consequence of any such misconduct, skylarking or negligence, or

        (iii) by the behaviour or presence of an animal (including a bird, fish or insect), or is caused by or consists in the employed earner being struck by any object or by lightning; and

    (c) the employed earner did not directly or indirectly induce or contribute to the happening of the accident by his conduct outside the employment or by any act not incidental to the employment.

DERIVATION

1.389   SSA 1975 s.55.

GENERAL NOTE

1.390   This deeming provision brings within the scheme some accidents which happen *at* work, rather than *through* work. It was a response to some apparent injustices in the operation of the scheme and was first introduced in 1961. For a rare case where this was considered, see *CI/1654/2008*, noted in the commentary to s.94, above ("out of . . . the employment"). It did not there assist the claimant.

Subsection 1(a)

The accident must still arise in the course of employment (see note to s.94(1), above). The "deeming" effect of the section applies only to the "out of employment" aspect.

1.391

Subsection 1(b)

R(I) 3/67 seems to be the only reported decision on this section and it concerned "skylarking" and its aftermath. The claimant, whilst having a permitted smoking break in the appointed place, was hit by a snowball thrown by a fellow-employee. He followed the snowballer towards the cloak-room to remonstrate. As he reached the cloakroom, the door was slammed on him and his hand went through it. Was he still in the course of his employment? The Commissioner held that remonstration was reasonably incidental to his employment.

1.392

Subsection 1(c)

R(I) 3/67 (above) also considered whether the claimant had fallen foul of this subsection, but the Commissioner held that whereas remonstration was incidental to employment, retaliation would not have been. Note also that conduct outside employment which induces or contributes to the happening of the accident may debar the claimant.

1.393

Sickness benefit

Section 102 repealed from April 13, 1995 by the Social Security (Incapacity for Work) Act 1994 Sch.1, para.29.

1.394

Disablement pension

Disablement pension

103.—(1) Subject to the provisions of this section, an employed earner shall be entitled to disablement pension if he suffers as the result of the relevant accident from loss of physical or mental faculty such that the assessed extent of the resulting disablement amounts to not less than 14 per cent. or, on a claim made before 1st October 1986, 20 per cent.

1.395

(2) In the determination of the extent of an employed earner's disablement for the purposes of this section there may be added to the percentage of the disablement resulting from the relevant accident the assessed percentage of any present disablement of his—

(a) which resulted from any other accident [1 . .] arising out of and in the course of his employment, being employed earner's employment, and

(b) in respect of which a disablement gratuity was not paid to him after a final assessment of his disablement,

(as well as any percentage which may be so added in accordance with regulations under subsection (2) of section 109 below made by virtue of subsection (4)(b) of that section).

211

(3) Subject to subsection (4) below, where the assessment of disablement is a percentage between 20 and 100 which is not a multiple of 10, it shall be treated—

  (a) if it is a multiple of 5, as being the next higher percentage which is a multiple of 10, and

  (b) if it is not a multiple of 5, as being the nearest percentage which is a multiple of 10,

and where the assessment of disablement on a claim made on or after 1st October 1986 is less than 20 per cent., but not less than 14 per cent., it shall be treated as 20 per cent.

(4) Where subsection (2) above applies, subsection (3) above shall have effect in relation to the aggregate percentage and not in relation to any percentage forming part of the aggregate.

(5) In this Part of this Act "assessed", in relation to the extent of any disablement, means assessed in accordance with Schedule 6 to this Act; and for the purposes of that Schedule there shall be taken to be no relevant loss of faculty when the extent of the resulting disablement, if so assessed, would not amount to 1 per cent.

(6) A person shall not be entitled to a disablement pension until after the expiry of the period of 90 days (disregarding Sundays) beginning with the day of the relevant accident.

(7) Subject to subsection (8) below, where disablement pension is payable for a period, it shall be paid at the appropriate weekly rate specified in Schedule 4, Part V, paragraph 1.

(8) Where the period referred to in subsection (7) above is limited by reference to a definite date, the pension shall cease on the death of the beneficiary before that date.

AMENDMENT

  1. Welfare Reform Act 2012 s.64 (December 5, 2012).

DERIVATION

1.396   SSA 1975 s.57 as amended.

DEFINITIONS

  "employed earner"—s.2(1)(a), above.
  "relevant accident"—s.122(1).
  "loss of physical faculty"—*ibid*.

GENERAL NOTE

Subsection (1)

1.397   Disablement benefit is payable in respect of disablement even if the claimant's capacity for work is unimpaired. The practice of the Department has been to require a separate claim for disablement benefit in respect of each industrial accident. However, in *CI/6872/95*, following the approach he had taken in *CI/420/94*, the Commissioner held that, where disablement benefit had been claimed in respect of one accident but had not been finally determined, a further claim in respect of another accident was not required. If disablement benefit is already in payment in respect of one accident, a further "claim" in respect of another accident is really an application for review. Equally, if there is in existence an assessment of disablement but disablement benefit is not payable because the assessment is below 14 per cent, an application for review of the assessment must be treated as a claim for disablement benefit if benefit is to be paid.

A useful checklist of questions

In *CI/2930/2005*, Commissioner Williams applied a key statement (definitions **1.398** and cautions) of Lord Simon in *Jones v Secretary of State for Social Services* [1972] A.C. 944 at p.1019:

"although in particular cases the concepts may overlap, the statute envisages them as separate — in order for 'disablement' benefit to be payable, the 'accident' must result in 'injury', which must result in 'loss of faculty', which must result in 'disability' . . . my understanding of the terminology is as follows: . . . 'injury' is hurt to body or mind . . . 'loss of faculty' is impairment of the proper functioning of part of the body or mind . . . 'disability' is partial or total failure of power to perform normal bodily or mental processes . . . 'disablement' is the sum of disabilities which, by contrast with the powers of a normal person, can be expressed as a percentage."

He then set out in para.36 a useful framework of questions to be answered and the order of the rules to be applied under s.103:

"Reading that vocabulary into the statutory issues that I must consider, the questions to be answered are:

(a) Did the claimant 'suffer personal injury ['hurt to body or mind'] caused' by the relevant accident?
Social Security Contributions and Benefits Act 1992 ('1992 Act'), section 94(1)

(b) If so, did the claimant 'suffer as a result of the relevant accident from loss of physical or mental faculty' ['impairment of the proper functioning of part of the body or mind'] during the period relevant to this assessment?
1992 Act, section 103(1)

(c) If so, what were 'the disabilities ['the partial or total failure of power to perform normal bodily or mental functions'] incurred by the claimant as a result of the relevant loss of faculty ['impairment of the proper functioning']'?
1992 Act, Schedule 6, paragraph 1. Paragraph 1(a) requires that 'the disabilities to be taken into account shall be all disabilities so incurred (whether or not involving loss of earning power or additional expense) to which the claimant may be expected, having regard to his physical and mental condition at the date of the assessment, to be subject during the period taken into account by the assessment as compared with a person of the same age and sex whose physical and mental condition is normal'

(d) Do those disabilities ['failure of power to perform . . .'] take into account 'disabilities which, though resulting from the relevant loss of faculty ['impairment of the proper functioning . . .'], also result, or without the relevant accident might be expected to result, from a cause other than the relevant accident', if there are any?
This is required by 1992 Act, Schedule 6, paragraph 1(b) and Social Security (General Benefit) Regulations 1982 (SI 1982 No 1408 as amended) ("1982 Regulations"), regulation 11.

(e) What is the total percentage of the 'assessed extent of the resulting disablement' ['the sum of disabilities', or of 'failure of power to perform . . .'] —

(i) by reference to those disabilities ['failure of power to perform . . .'] without reference to the particular circumstances of the claimant other than age, sex and physical and mental condition, and

(ii) adding 'to the percentage of the disablement ['the sum of disabilities . . .'] . . . the assessed percentage of any present disablement" of the claimant resulting from any other industrial accident or any prescribed disease?

1992 Act, section 103(1), (2), and Schedule 6, paragraph 1(c)

(f) If the answers to (d) and (e) include disabilities ['failure of power to perform. . .'] resulting from the loss of faculty ['impairment of the proper functioning. . .'] both from the relevant accident and from any effective cause other than the relevant accident (whether congenital defect, injury or disease) that predate the accident, then what is the extent of disablement ['the sum of disabilities'] 'to which the claimant would have been subject . . . if the relevant accident had not occurred'?

1992 Act, Schedule 6, paragraph 1(c) and 1982 Regulations, regulation 11(3). Regulation 11(5) requires that where there are two or more industrial accidents (or disease) then the disablement resulting from both or all "shall only be taken into account in assessing the extent of disablement resulting from . . . the one which occurred or developed last in point of time".

(g) If the answers to (d) and (e) include disabilities ['failure of power to perform . . .'] resulting from the loss of faculty ['impairment of the proper functioning . . .'] both from the relevant accident and from any effective cause that postdates the accident and are not directly attributable to it, then what is the extent of disablement if that other effective cause had not arisen?

1982 Regulations, regulation 11(4). That requires that if the answer to (g) is not less than 11 per cent, then the answer to (e) 'shall also take account of any disablement to which the claimant may be subject as a result of that other effective cause except to the extent to which the claimant would have been subject thereto in the relevant accident had not occurred'. See also regulation 11(5) noted to question (f)".

1.399   *Employed earner:* See the note to s.94.

Accident: See the note to s.94. S.108 has the effect that disablement benefit is also payable in respect of prescribed diseases and prescribed personal injuries not caused by accident.

1.400   *Loss of physical or mental faculty as a result of the relevant accident:* "Loss of faculty" means "an impairment of the proper functioning of part of the body or mind" (*Jones v Secretary of State for Social Services* [1972] A.C. 944 at 1009 also reported as an appendix to *R(I) 3/69*). Thus a loss of a kidney by a claimant, which necessarily results in a loss of useful function, must, as a matter of law, mean he or she has suffered a loss of faculty even if the claimant can live normally in every way (*R(I) 14/66*). It was pointed out in *R(I) 14/66* that it does not follow that there is any resulting disablement. Nevertheless, adjudicating medical authorities have been advised to assess a "loss of reserve function" which in the case of a kidney is usually put at between 5 and 10 per cent. It is doubtful whether that is correct since that seems to be an assessment of loss of faculty rather than an assessment of disablement. The Deputy Commissioner in *R(I) 14/66* expressed concern that a claimant's assessment of disablement could not be increased if he or she lost the other kidney owing to a non-industrial disease or accident. Although *R(I) 11/66*, to which he referred, was overturned in the Court of Appeal (*R. v Medical Appeal Tribunal Ex p. Cable*, appendix to *R(I) 11/66*), reg.11(4) of the Social Security (General Benefit) Regulations 1982 appears to limit the effect of *Cable* to cases where the assessment of disablement before the loss of the second kidney has been assessed at not less than 11 per cent.

In *JL and DO v SSWP (II)* [2011] UKUT 294 (AAC); [2012] AACR 15, in the context of PD A14 (osteoarthritis of the knee), Judge Ward considered whether it made any difference where a claimant's osteoarthritis resulted in knee replacement surgery. He held that, where the original loss of faculty was osteoarthritis of the knee, the knee replacement surgery did not break the chain of causation so as to substitute a new cause of ongoing loss of faculty. The relevance of the knee replacement surgery went rather to the stage of assessment of the degree of disablement.

The definition of "loss of physical faculty" in s.122(1) makes special provision so that it includes disfigurement whether or not accompanied by any actual loss of faculty.

Dealing with differences of expert medical opinion: Where medical experts differ on   **1.401**
whether there is loss of faculty or whether it was the result of the relevant industrial accident(s), the First-tier Tribunal must give sufficient reasons for preferring the view of one expert and rejecting that of the other(s). See Judge Wikeley in *DB v SSWP (II)* [2010] UKUT 144 (AAC), paras 40–51, citing statements by different three judge panels of the Upper Tribunal in *Hampshire CC v JP* [2009] UKUT 239 (AAC) (now reported as [2010] AACR 15) and *BB v South London & Maudsley NHS Trust and Ministry of Justice* [2009] UKUT 157 (AAC). The relevant factors for a tribunal to consider are set out in Judge Edward Jacobs's *Tribunal Practice and Procedure* (4th edn., 2016), at paras.11.120-11.131. They relate to "the expert(s), the area of expertise and the evidence" (para.44). As respects the experts, matters to consider are each expert's qualifications, expertise and experience on the issue material to the appeal. On expertise, the tribunal must "bear in mind the limits to which the doctors' areas of expertise can actually provide answers to the issue in the appeal" (para.46). On the expert evidence itself, it is a question of examining the "factual basis and soundness of the experts' respective reasoned opinions" (para.47). This may be difficult where, as in this case, there was a clash between the "majority view" of the "medical establishment" and the "minority view" provided by one of the experts. As Judge Wikeley noted, experience in hindsight of changes in medical opinion indicates that the fact that an expert is in the minority does not mean that his/her opinion is thereby necessarily wrong. Lacking hindsight, the tribunal, drawing on the expertise of its medical members in full compliance with the rules of natural justice and fairness, "will have to form its own best judgment today on the soundness of the science and reasons underpinning [the minority expert's evidence] in this appeal" (para.50).

Resulting disablement amounts to not less than 14 per cent: It is disablement which must   **1.402**
be assessed and not loss of faculty. In *R(I) 3/76*, it was held that:

> " 'disability' means inability to do something which persons of the same age and sex and normal physical and mental powers can do; 'disablement' means a collection of disabilities, that is to say the sum total of all the relevant disabilities found present in a given case."

"14 per cent" was substituted for "one per cent" in s.57(1) of the Social Security Act 1975 from October 1, 1986 (SSA 1986, Sch.3, para.3). Before that date, disablement benefit was paid in the form of a gratuity if the assessment was less than 20 per cent and in the form of a pension if the assessment was 20 per cent or more. That remains the case where a claim was made before that date (Social Security (Industrial Injuries and Diseases) Miscellaneous Provisions Regulations 1986 reg.14). Any pension is payable under this section and any gratuity is payable under Sch.7, para.9. This remains important where, on a claim made before October 1, 1986, there have been a series of provisional assessments. If a claim is made after October 1, 1986 in respect of a period before that date, the new legislation applies (*R(I) 1/90, R(I)/3/96*).

Disablement benefit is also payable where the assessment is less than 14 per cent, but at least one per cent, if it is due to pneumoconiosis, byssinosis or diffuse mesothelioma (Prescribed Diseases Regulations reg.20(1)).

The provisions for aggregating assessments of disablement have been considered in *R(I) 3/00*. The claimant had received a disablement gratuity in respect of prescribed disease A11 giving rise to disablement assessed at 7 per cent from April 1, 1985 for life. In May 1992, he claimed disablement benefit in respect of prescribed disease D4 and the disablement owing to that disease was assessed at 8 per cent from January 1, 1960 for life. He then applied for a review of the assessment of disablement in respect of prescribed disease A11 on the ground of unforeseen aggravation and the consequent disablement was assessed at 8 per cent from May 3, 1995 for life.

The Commissioner considered the way in which disablement gratuities were calculated and, in particular, the way further gratuities payable following reviews had been calculated under reg.85 of the Social Security (Adjudication) Regulations 1984. He concluded that disablement in respect of which a gratuity had been awarded did not fall to be aggregated under s.103 for the first seven years of the period of the assessment but did thereafter and that, following a review on the ground of unforeseen aggravation, the whole of the new assessment fell to be aggregated and not just the difference between the old and the new assessments. Accordingly, no disablement pension was payable to the claimant in respect of the period before April 1, 1992 (because only the 8 per cent in respect of prescribed disease D4 could be taken into account) but disablement pension was payable to the claimant thereafter on the basis that his aggregated disablement was 15 per cent from April 1, 1992 and 16 per cent from May 3, 1995.

Following *R(I) 4/03*, Commissioner Rowland in *CI/954/2006* agreed that aggregation is a mere alternative to a separate award of disablement pension (para.16). It can be set in motion by an application for supersession.

Subsection (5)

1.403   There is deemed to be no loss of faculty if the resulting disablement is assessed at less than 1 per cent. In *R(I) 6/61*, the Commissioner held that it was desirable that a medical appeal tribunal should indicate whether they have concluded that there is *no* loss of faculty or whether they have concluded that there *is* a loss of faculty, but that the resulting disablement does not amount to 1 per cent. Note that, under s.110(3), a person suffering from pneumoconiosis *shall* be treated as suffering from a loss of faculty such that the assessed extent of disablement amounts to not less than 1 per cent.

For notes on the assessment of disablement, see the annotations to Sch.6 to the Act and to reg.11 of the General Benefit Regulations 1982.

Both the unified tribunal and the Commissioners now have jurisdiction over medical and non-medical matters. A Commissioner, allowing an appeal on a point of law, can now take his or her own decision on the facts available rather than remitting it to another tribunal. Commissioner Williams did so in *CI/1307/1999* giving a staged assessment of disablement in respect of post-traumatic stress disorder. The decision considers the medical aspects of the claimant's case found to be an industrial accident in *CI/15589/1996*, noted in the annotation to "accident" in respect of SSCBA 1992 s.94. In paras 15–17, Commissioner Williams distinguished "diagnosis" and "disablement" decisions. The former is essentially "a question of medical expertise". A "disablement" decision in contrast is not dissimilar to the tasks performed by judges in assessing common law damages or in applying the tariff of the Criminal Injuries Compensation Authority. In assessing disablement for industrial injuries benefits, however, that Criminal Injuries tariff is not an appropriate yardstick. Instead, supplementing SSCBA 1992 s.103 and Sch.6, regard should be had also to reg.11 and Sch.2 to the General Benefit Regulations below. Nonetheless, the import of para.37 of the decision is that exercise of the Commissioner's power to decide on the facts, rather than remitting to another tribunal, may well be rare. Even so, the decision contrasts markedly with the traditional view of such matters as ones for medical rather than legal judgment (see, for example, Commissioner Howell in *CI/636/93*). Note that the suitability of cross-reference to Sch.2 was also advocated in *R(I) 5/95*, where Commissioner Rowland stated that "assessment of disablement should be brought into line with those prescribed in the Schedule", with assessment also reflecting any intermittent or episodic character of the disablement (para.16).

Subsection (6)

1.404   This does not apply where a person is awarded disablement benefit in respect of occupational deafness (reg.28 of the Prescribed Diseases Regulations) or where a claim is made in respect of diffuse mesothelioma, see *ibid.* reg.20(4).

Under Sch.4, the amount of the pension depends on whether the claimant is   **1.405**
over 18 and on the extent of disablement. A person over 18 whose disablement is
assessed at 100 per cent receives £174.80 per week. The amount paid to people
with lower assessments is proportionately less.

Increase where constant attendance needed

104.—(1) Where a disablement pension is payable in respect of an assess-   **1.406**
ment of 100 per cent, then, if as the result of the relevant loss of faculty the
beneficiary requires constant attendance, the weekly rate of the pension
shall be increased by an amount, not exceeding the appropriate amount
specified in Schedule 4, Part V, paragraph 2 determined in accordance with
regulations by reference to the extent and nature of the attendance required
by the beneficiary.

(2) An increase of pension under this section shall be payable for such
period as may be determined at the time it is granted, but may be renewed
from time to time.

(3) The Secretary of State may by regulations direct that any provision of
sections 64 to 67 above shall have effect, with or without modifications, in
relation to increases of pension under this section.

(4) In subsection (3) above, "modifications" includes additions and
omissions.

DERIVATION

SSA 1975 s.61.   **1.407**

DEFINITIONS

"beneficiary" and "relevant loss of faculty"—see s.122(1).
"modifications"—see subs.(4).

GENERAL NOTE

See regs 19–21 of the Social Security (General Benefit) Regulations 1982 for   **1.408**
further provisions relating to constant attendance allowance. Note that, under
para.5 of Sch.1 to the Overlapping Benefits Regulations, constant attendance allowance overlaps with attendance allowance under s.35 and the care component of
disability living allowance.

The Secretary of State's decision on constant attendance allowance is not appealable (Decisions and Appeals Regulations 1999 Sch.2, para.14(a)).

Increase for exceptionally severe disablement

105.—(1) Where a disablement pension is payable to a person—   **1.409**
  (a) who is or, but for having received medical or other treatment as an
      in patient in a hospital or similar institution, would be entitled to an
      increase of the weekly rate of the pension under section 104 above,
      and the weekly rate of the increase exceeds the amount specified in
      Schedule 4, Part V, paragraph 2(a); and
  (b) his need for constant attendance of an extent and nature qualifying
      him for such an increase at a weekly rate in excess of that amount is
      likely to be permanent,
the weekly rate of the pension shall, in addition to any increase under
section 104 above, be further increased by the amount specified in Schedule
4, Part V, paragraph 3.

(2) An increase under this section shall be payable for such period as may be determined at the time it is granted, but may be renewed from time to time.

DERIVATION

1.410   SSA 1975 s.63.

DEFINITIONS

"medical treatment"—see s.122(1).

GENERAL NOTE

1.411   The Secretary of State's decision on exceptionally severe disablement allowance is not appealable (Decisions and Appeals Regulations 1999 Sch.2 para.14(b)).

Other benefits and increases

Benefits and increases subject to qualifications as to time

1.412   **106.**—Schedule 7 to this Act shall have effect in relation—
(a) to unemployability supplement;
(b) to disablement gratuity;
(c) to increases of disablement pension during hospital treatment;
(d) to reduced earnings allowance;
(e) to retirement allowance; and
(f) to industrial death benefit,
for all of which the qualifications include special qualifications as to time.

Successive accidents

Adjustments for successive accidents

1.413   **107.**—(1) Where a person suffers two or more successive accidents arising out of and in the course of his employed earner's employment—
(a) he shall not for the same period be entitled (apart from any increase of benefit mentioned in subsection (2) below) to receive industrial injuries benefit by way of two or more disablement pensions at an aggregate weekly rate exceeding the appropriate amount specified in Schedule 4, Part V, paragraph 4; and
(b) regulations may provide for adjusting—
(i) disablement benefit, or the conditions for the receipt of that benefit, in any case where he has received or may be entitled to a disablement gratuity;
(ii) any increase of benefit mentioned in subsection (2) below, or the conditions for its receipt.

(2) The increases of benefit referred to in subsection (1) above are those under the following provisions of this Act—
section 104,
section 105,
paragraph 2, 4 or 6 of Schedule 7.

DERIVATION

SSA 1975 s.91.
1.414

DEFINITIONS

"employed earner"—see ss.2 and 95(4).
"employed earner's employment"—see ss.95 and 97.
"entitled", "employment" and "industrial injuries benefit"—see s.122(1).

GENERAL NOTE

In *CI/402/1994*, the Commissioner stated that the 1986 amendments to the   1.415
industrial injuries scheme "stopped the making of separate awards" so from then on
there could only ever be one award of disablement benefit in respect of any period.
On that view, it appeared that this section was only of relevance where the last claim
was made before October 1, 1986. Commissioner Howell in *R(I)4/03* makes it clear
that this is not in fact so:

" . . . unfortunately the continued provision in the post-1986 legislation for a
person to have two or more disablement pensions for successive accidents (section
107(1)(a) above, and its predecessor section 91 Social Security Act 1975), was not
drawn to the Commissioner's attention in that case. Moreover the later decision
in *CI/12311/1996* above plainly holds otherwise, and a similar line of reasoning on
separate claims for reduced earnings allowance has since been overruled by the
Court of Appeal, in *Hagan v. Secretary of State* [2001] EWCA Civ 1452, 30 July
2001. I do not therefore think what was said in *CI/420/1994* should be taken as a
ground for depriving claimants of the benefit of the normal prescribed time for
claiming a new entitlement in the way that happened here" (para.34).

Regulations 38 and 39 of the General Benefit Regulations 1982 are treated as
made under this section (SSCBA 1992 s.2(2)).

Prescribed industrial diseases, etc.

Benefit in respect of prescribed industrial diseases, etc

108.—(1) Industrial injuries benefits shall, in respect of a person who has   1.416
been in employed earner's employment, be payable in accordance with this
section and sections 109 and 110 below in respect of—
  (a) any prescribed disease, or
  (b) any prescribed personal injury (other than an injury caused by acci-
      dent arising out of and in the course of his employment),
which is a disease or injury due to the nature of that employment [[1] . . .].
  (2) A disease or injury may be prescribed in relation to any employed
earners if the Secretary of State is satisfied that—
  (a) it ought to be treated, having regard to its causes and incidence and
      any other relevant considerations, as a risk of their occupations and
      not as a risk common to all persons; and
  (b) it is such that, in the absence of special circumstances, the attribu-
      tion of particular cases to the nature of the employment can be estab-
      lished or presumed with reasonable certainty.
  (3) Regulations prescribing any disease or injury for those purposes
may provide that a person who developed the disease or injury on or at
any time after a date specified in the regulations (being a date before the

regulations come into force [¹ . . .]) shall be treated, subject to any pre-scribed modifications of this section or section 109 or 110 below, as if the regulations had been in force when he developed the disease or injury.

(4) Provision may be made by regulations for determining—

(a) the time at which a person is to be treated as having developed any prescribed disease or injury; and

(b) the circumstances in which such a disease or injury is, where the person in question has previously suffered from it, to be treated as having recrudesced or as having been contracted or received afresh.

(5) Notwithstanding any other provision of this Act, the power conferred by subsection (4)(a) above includes power to provide that the time at which a person shall be treated as having developed a prescribed disease or injury shall be the date on which he first makes a claim which results in the payment of benefit by virtue of this section or section 110 below in respect of that disease or injury.

(6) Nothing in this section or in section 109 or 110 below affects the right of any person to benefit in respect of a disease which is a personal injury by accident within the meaning of this Part of this Act, except that a person shall not be entitled to benefit in respect of a disease as being an injury by accident arising out of and in the course of any employment if at the time of the accident the disease is in relation to him a prescribed disease by virtue of the occupation in which he is engaged in that employment.

AMENDMENT

1. Welfare Reform Act 2012 s.64 (December 5, 2012).

DERIVATION

1.417   SSA 1975 s.76.

DEFINITIONS

"employed earner"—see ss.2 and 95(4).
"employed earner's employment"—see ss.95 and 97.
"entitled", "employment", "industrial injuries benefit" and "prescribe"—see s.122(1).

GENERAL NOTE

1.418   This section makes general provision for payment of industrial injuries benefits to employed earners who are suffering from a disease or personal injury which was *not* caused by accident and so could not give rise to entitlement under s.94. S.109 makes more detailed provision. For the prescribed diseases, see col.1 of Sch.1 to the Social Security (Industrial Injuries) (Prescribed Diseases) Regulations 1985. Each disease is prescribed in relation to a fairly narrowly defined occupation.

Subsection (3)
1.419   See reg.43 of, and Sch.4 to, the Prescribed Diseases Regulations 1985.

Subsections (4) and (5)
1.420   See regs 6 and 7 of the Prescribed Diseases Regulations 1985.

Subsection (6)
1.421   This makes it clear that a person who develops, as the result of an accident, a disease which *is not* prescribed in relation to him or her remains entitled to benefit under s.94. On the other hand, if the disease *is* prescribed in relation to the

220

claimant, he or she must rely on the provisions relating to prescribed diseases and cannot claim benefit in respect of it under s.94.

General provisions relating to benefit under section 108

109.—(1) Subject to the power to make different provision by regulations, and to the following provisions of this section and section 110 below—

1.422

(a) the benefit payable under section 108 above in respect of a pre-scribed disease or injury, and

(b) the conditions for receipt of benefit,

shall be the same as in the case of personal injury by accident arising out of and in the course of employment.

[¹ (2) In relation to prescribed diseases and injuries, regulations may provide—

(a) for modifying any provisions contained in this Act, the Administra-tion Act or Chapter II of Part I of the Social Security Act 1998 which relate to disablement benefit or reduced earnings allowance or their administration; and

(b) for adapting references in this Act, that Act and that Chapter to accidents,

and for the purposes of this subsection the provisions of that Act and that Chapter which relate to the administration of disablement benefit or reduced earnings allowance, shall be taken to include section 1 of that Act and any provision which relates to the administration of both the benefit in question and other benefits.]

(3) Without prejudice to the generality of subsection (2) above, regula-tions under that subsection may in particular include provision—

(a) for presuming any prescribed disease or injury—

(i) to be due, unless the contrary is proved, to the nature of a per-son's employment where he was employed in any prescribed occupation at the time when, or within a prescribed period or for a prescribed length of time (whether continuous or not) before, he developed the disease or injury,

(ii) not to be due to the nature of person's employment unless he was employed in some prescribed occupation at the time when, or within a prescribed period or for a prescribed length of time (whether continuous or not) before, he developed the disease or injury;

(b) for such matters as appear to the Secretary of State to be incidental to or consequential on provisions included in the regulations by virtue of subsection (2) and paragraph (a) above.

(4) Regulations under subsection (2) above may also provide—

(a) that, in the determination of the extent of an employed earner's disablement resulting from a prescribed disease or injury, the appropriate percentage may be added to the percentage of that disa-blement; and

(b) that, in the determination of the extent of an employed earner's disablement for the purposes of section 103 above, the appropriate percentage may be added to the percentage of disablement resulting from the relevant accident.

(5) In subsection (4)(a) above "the appropriate percentage" means the assessed percentage of any present disablement of the earner which resulted—

(a) from any accident [² . . .] arising out of and in the course of his employment, being employed earner's employment, or

(b) from any other prescribed disease or injury due to the nature of that employment [² . . .],

and in respect of which a disablement gratuity was not paid to him after a final assessment of his disablement.

(6) In subsection (4)(b) above "the appropriate percentage" means the assessed percentage of any present disablement of the earner—

(a) which resulted from any prescribed disease or injury due to the nature of his employment [² . . .], and

(b) in respect of which a disablement gratuity was not paid to him after a final assessment of his disablement.

(7) Where regulations under subsection (2) above—

(a) make provision such as is mentioned in subsection (4) above, and

(b) also make provision corresponding to that in section 103(3) above,

they may also make provision to the effect that those corresponding provisions shall have effect in relation to the aggregate percentage and not in relation to any percentage forming part of the aggregate.

AMENDMENT

1. Social Security Act 1998 Sch.7 para.65 (July 5, 1999).
2. Welfare Reform Act 2012 s.64 (December 5, 2012).

DERIVATION

1.423   SSA 1975 s.77.

DEFINITIONS

"employed earner"—see ss.2 and 95(4).
"employed earner's employment"—see ss.95 and 97.
"assessed"—see s.103(5).
"employment", "employed", "prescribe" and "relevant accident"—see s.122(1).

GENERAL NOTE

1.424   In general the same benefits are payable in respect of prescribed diseases as are payable in respect of injuries caused by accident. For regulations, see the Prescribed Diseases Regulations 1985. The practice of the Department has been to require a separate claim for disablement benefit in respect of each disease. However, in *CI/420/94*, it was held that, where disablement benefit was in payment in respect of one disease, a "claim" in respect of another disease was really an application for review. The concluding words of subs.(2) were added to s.77(2) of the Social Security Act 1975 in order to reverse the effect of *McKiernon v Secretary of State for Social Security, The Times*, November 1, 1989 in which reg.25 of the 1985 Regulations had been held to be ultra vires. In *Chatterton v Chief Adjudication Officer, McKiernon v Chief Adjudication Officer* (reported in *R(I) 1/94*), the Court of Appeal held that the amendment did have the intended effect.

Respiratory diseases

1.425   **110.**—(1) As respects pneumoconiosis, regulations may further provide that, where a person is found to be suffering from pneumoconiosis accompanied by tuberculosis, the effects of the tuberculosis shall be treated for the purposes of this section and sections 108 and 109 above as if they were effects of the pneumoconiosis.

(2) Subsection (1) above shall have effect as if after "tuberculosis" (in both places) there were inserted "emphysema or chronic bronchitis", but only in relation to a person the extent of whose disablement resulting from pneumoconiosis, or from pneumoconiosis accompanied by tuberculosis, would (if his physical condition were otherwise normal) be assessed at not less than 50 per cent.

(3) A person found to be suffering from pneumoconiosis shall be treated for the purposes of this Act as suffering from a loss of faculty such that the assessed extent of the resulting disablement amounts to not less than 1 per cent.

(4) In respect of byssinosis, a person shall not (unless regulations otherwise provide) be entitled to disablement benefit unless he is found to be suffering, as the result of byssinosis, from loss of faculty which is likely to be permanent.

DERIVATION

SSA 1975 s.78.   1.426

DEFINITIONS

"assessed"—see s.103(5).
"pneumoconiosis"—see s.122(1).

GENERAL NOTE

Subsections (1) and (2)
See regs 21 and 22 of the Prescribed Diseases Regulations 1985.   1.427

Subsection (3)
This requires that a person suffering from pneumoconiosis *shall* be treated as   1.428
being disabled to the extent of at least 1 per cent, even if the disablement is in fact
negligible. Under reg.20(1) of the Prescribed Diseases Regulations 1985 a person
suffering from pneumoconiosis is entitled to disablement benefit if the resulting
disablement is at least 1 per cent.

Subsection (4)
This subsection is disapplied by reg.20(2) of the Prescribed Diseases Regulations   1.429
1985.

Section 111 repealed by Welfare Reform Act 2012 s.64 (December 5, 2012).   1.430

PART VI

MISCELLANEOUS PROVISIONS RELATING TO PARTS I TO V

Earnings

Certain sums to be earnings

112.—(1) [¹ The Treasury may by regulations made with the concurrence   1.431
of the Secretary of State] provide—
  (a) that any employment protection entitlement shall be deemed for
      the purposes of this Act and the Administration Act to be earnings payable by and to such persons as are prescribed and to be so
      payable in respect of such periods as are prescribed; and

(b) that those periods shall, so far as they are not periods of employment, be deemed for those purposes to be periods of employment.

(2) In subsection (1) above "employment protection entitlement" means—

(a) any sum, or a prescribed part of any sum, mentioned in subsection (3) below; and

(b) prescribed amounts which the regulations provide are to be treated as related to any of those sums.

[¹(2A) Regulations under subsection (2) above shall be made by the Treasury with the concurrence of the Secretary of State.]

(3) The sums referred to in subsection (2) above are the following—

(a) a sum payable in respect of arrears of pay in pursuance of an order for reinstatement or re-engagement under [² the Employment Rights Act 1996],

(b) a sum payable by way of pay in pursuance of an order under that Act [³ or the Trade Union and Labour Relations (Consolidation) Act 1992] for the continuation of a contract of employment,

(c) a sum payable by way of remuneration in pursuance of a protective award under [⁴ the Trade Union and Labour Relations (Consolidation) Act 1992].

AMENDMENTS

1.432
1. Transfer of Functions Act 1999 Sch.3 para.21 (April 1, 1999).
2. Employment Rights Act 1996 Sch.1 para.51(4)(a) (August 22, 1996).
3. Employment Rights Act 1996 Sch.1 para.51(4)(b) (August 22, 1996).
4. Employment Rights Act 1996 Sch.1 para.51(4)(c) (August 22, 1996).

DERIVATION

1.433
SS(MP)A 1977 s.18.

Disqualification and suspension

General provisions as to disqualification and suspension

1.434
113.—(1) Except where regulations otherwise provide, a person shall be disqualified for receiving any benefit under Parts II to V of this Act, and an increase of such benefit shall not be payable in respect of any person as the beneficiary's [² wife, husband or civil partner], for any period during which the person—

(a) is absent from Great Britain; or

(b) is undergoing imprisonment or detention in legal custody.

(2) Regulations may provide for suspending payment of such benefit to a person during any period in which he is undergoing medical or other treatment as an in-patient in a hospital or similar institution.

(3) Regulations may provide for a person who would be entitled to any such benefit but for the operation of any provision of this Act [¹, the Administration Act or Chapter II of Part I of the Social Security Act 1998] to be treated as if entitled to it for the purposes of any rights or obligations (whether his own or another's) which depend on his entitlement, other than the right to payment of the benefit.

AMENDMENTS

1. Social Security Act 1998 Sch.7 para.66 (July 5, 1999).
2. Civil Partnership Act 2004 s.254 and Sch.24 para.38 (December 5, 2005).

DERIVATION

SSA 1975 s.82(5)–(6) and s.83 as amended.   1.435

DEFINITION

"Great Britain"—by art.1 of the Union with Scotland Act 1706, this means England, Scotland and Wales and see s.172.

GENERAL NOTE

Subs.(1) states two general disqualifications for receiving benefit: absence from   1.436
Great Britain and undergoing imprisonment or detention in legal custody.
A Tribunal of Commissioners has clarified that this provision stops the payment of benefit rather than entitlement: *CIB/3645/2002.*

Absence from Great Britain
Absence means "not physically present" in England, Scotland or Wales; it does   1.437
not necessitate the presence of the person in the past in England, Scotland or Wales: *R(U) 18/60* and *R(U) 16/62.* To be absent from Great Britain, a person must be absent throughout a whole day: *R(S) 1/66.* For the impact of absence from Great Britain on particular benefits, see the Persons Abroad Regulations, which are largely concerned with displacing the disqualification either permanently or temporarily. Very broadly speaking, the disqualification is displaced where the benefit is not related to the ability to work; some temporary relief is given where the benefit arises by reason of incapacity or confinement; and no relief at all is given where the benefit arises by reason of unemployment.

Undergoing imprisonment or detention in legal custody
Although the wording of subs.(1)(b) makes no reference to imprisonment   1.438
being connected with criminal proceedings, there is now authority for reading in such a requirement. The history of the controversy is well summarised by the Commissioner in *R(S) 8/79* where the Commissioner concludes,

"I am bound by these decisions to hold that a person is not disqualified under section 82(5)(b) of the Social Security Act 1975 by reason of undergoing detention in legal custody which has nothing to do with a criminal offence" (para.5). "The decisions that I am following are all based on the proposition that imprisonment in the section means imprisonment imposed by a court exercising criminal jurisdiction . . ." (para.8).

So imprisonment for non-payment of maintenance did not disqualify the claimant from receiving invalidity benefit.
See also regs 2 and 3 of the General Benefit Regulations.
In *R(P) 1/02* the Commissioner upholds a decision to disqualify the claimant while in prison from entitlement to any part of his retirement pension. In particular, he holds that the disqualification extends to additional pension under SERPS and to graduated retirement pension. The disqualification is also held to be compatible with the requirements of the Human Rights Act 1998.
For a decision of the Administrative Court on the eligibility of post-tariff life prisoners to income support on transfer from prison to a mental health hospital, see *R. (RD and PM) v Secretary of State for Work and Pensions* [2008] EWHC 2635 (Admin), which confirmed that there was no such entitlement.

Reciprocal agreements

1.439   When considering benefit entitlement for persons from abroad, you should first consider whether they are assisted by European Union rules, which apply to nationals of the 28 Member States, plus nationals of the three European Economic Area countries (Iceland, Liechtenstein and Norway) and Swiss nationals. Material on the European Union rules can be found in *Vol III: Administration, Adjudication and the European Dimension.*

There are also Association or Co-operation Agreements with a number of countries bordering the Mediterranean in the Middle East and North Africa which extend entitlement to social security benefits to nationals of those countries. For a decision on the EEC–Morocco agreement, see *R(S) 1/00* and *HMRC v HEH and SSWP (TC and CHB)* [2018] UKUT 237 (AAC).

You will also need to consider whether there is a reciprocal agreement which may smooth the way to benefit entitlement for a particular claimant. There are currently reciprocal agreements with the following non-EEA countries or territories: Barbados, Bermuda, Canada, Guernsey, Isle of Man, Israel, Jamaica, Jersey, Mauritius, New Zealand, Phillipines, Switzerland, Turkey, USA, and Yugoslavia (which relates to the republics of the former Yugoslavia). The text of the Conventions and the Orders bringing them into effect in national law can be found on Vol.10 of the Law Volumes maintained by the Department for Work and Pensions (the so-called "Blue Books"). For a decision that explores the GB/Jamaica agreement, and the lack of appeal rights in respect of Secretary of State decisions made thereunder, see *CIB/3645/2002.*

Note too that there remain some reciprocal agreements with EEA countries, which may assist in some circumstances where the Community rules do not, though most of these agreements have been superseded by the Community rules. Reciprocal agreements also exist with Northern Ireland, which although part of the United Kingdom has its own, largely parallel, social security system.

In addition, there are a number of reciprocal agreements orders of more general application, including specific rules for refugees.

R(S) 1/93 illustrates the need to take care to look at the definitions contained in each set of relevant regulations requiring to be considered in determining a question arising on appeal and to distinguish between points of legal principle and distinctions of fact. In this case the tribunal had correctly concluded that a claimant who had been resident in Malta for nearly seven years, because he found relief in the warm climate for the symptoms of his multiple sclerosis, was not temporarily absent from Great Britain under reg.2 of the Persons Abroad Regulations. The tribunal nevertheless went on to hold that the claimant was "temporarily" in Malta under Art.9A of the Order establishing reciprocal arrangements with Malta, because it felt bound by the decision in *CS/02/1976* in which the immigration status of the claimant, described in that case as being that of a "temporary visitor", was regarded as powerful evidence for consideration even though the claimant had been in Malta for two years with no foreseeable prospect of leaving unless required to do so by the immigration authorities. The fact remained that for immigration purposes the claimant's presence was "on sufferance without a right of permanent residence".

Commissioner Johnson held that *CS/02/1976* turned on a question of fact and degree and that the conclusion in *CS/02/1976* was not binding upon the tribunal. Commissioner Johnson says the facts of the two cases are "plainly distinguishable" whereas the tribunal had described them as "virtually indistinguishable". The outcome was that the expressed inclination (as distinct from the decision) of the tribunal that the claimant was not temporarily in Malta was correct.

The result is that there are now two decisions of Commissioners which place differing emphasis on the immigration status of the individual. *CS/02/1976* suggests that it is powerful evidence of status, whereas *R(S) 1/93* (paras 13–15) suggests that it is just one factor which can be displaced by other facts present in the case.

1.440   The Social Security (Reciprocal Agreements) Order 1995 (SI 1995/767) amends the reciprocal agreements listed in Sch.2 to the Order (which includes all the agreements mentioned in these annotations) by deeming references to sickness and invalidity benefits to include references to incapacity benefit. References to the calculation of benefit under the law of the UK are to be read so as to apply to short-term and long-term incapacity benefit: see further SI 2012/360 (below).

The Social Security (Reciprocal Agreements) Order 1996 (SI 1996/1928) provides for certain reciprocal agreements listed in its Sch.2 to be modified to take account of changes made by the Jobseekers Act 1995.

The Social Security (Reciprocal Agreements) Order 2001 (SI 2001/407) entering into force on April 9, 2001, provided for social security legislation to be modified or adapted in the reciprocal agreements listed in the Order to accommodate changes made by the Welfare Reform and Pensions Act 1999 in introducing new bereavement benefits; see further SI 2007/159 (below).

Note that the Social Security (Reciprocal Agreements) Order 2005 (SI 2005/2765) makes provision for the Social Security Contributions and Benefits Act 1992 and the Social Security Administration Act 1992 to be modified to reflect changes made to the benefit entitlement of spouses and civil partners by the Welfare Reform and Pensions Act 1999 and the Civil Partnership Act 2004 in relation to the Orders in Council referred to in Sch.2 to the Order.

1.441

The Social Security (Reciprocal Agreements) Order 2012 (SI 2012/360), which entered into force on February 22, 2012, makes provision for the Social Security Contributions and Benefits Act 1992, the Social Security Administration Act 1992, and Pt I of the Welfare Reform Act 2007 to be modified to reflect the transition from incapacity benefit to employment and support allowance in relation to the Orders in Council specified in Sch.2 to the Order.

See also The Social Security (Application of Reciprocal Agreements with Australia, Canada and New Zealand) (EEA States and Switzerland) Regulations 2015 (SI 2015/349) in force from April 1, 2015.

The Social Security (Reciprocal Agreements) Order 2017 (SI 2017/159) makes provision for the Social Security Administration Act 1992, the Social Security Contributions and Benefits Act 1992 and Part 5 (bereavement support payment) of the Pensions Act 2014 and regulations made under those Acts or section 30 of the Pensions Act 2014 to be modified to reflect the replacement of various bereavement benefits by bereavement support payment.

Persons maintaining dependants, etc.

Persons maintaining dependants, etc.

114.—(1) Regulations may provide for determining the circumstances in which a person is or is not to be taken, for the purposes of Parts II to V of this Act—

1.442

(a) to be wholly or mainly, or to a substantial extent, maintaining, or to be contributing at any weekly rate to the maintenance of, another person; or

(b) to be, or have been, contributing at any weekly rate to the cost of providing for a child [² or qualifying young person].

(2) Regulations under this section may provide, for the purposes of the provisions relating to an increase of benefit under Parts II to V of this Act in respect of a [¹ wife, civil partner] or other adult dependant, that where—

(a) a person is partly maintained by each of two or more beneficiaries, each of whom would be entitled to such an increase in respect of that person if he were wholly or mainly maintaining that person, and

(b) the contributions made by those two or more beneficiaries towards the maintenance of that person amount in the aggregate to sums

which would, if they had been contributed by one of those beneficiaries, have been sufficient to satisfy the requirements of regulations
under this section.

that person shall be taken to be wholly or mainly maintained by such of
those beneficiaries as may be prescribed.

(3) Regulations may provide for any sum or sums paid by a person
by way of contribution towards either or both the following, that is to
say—

    (a) the maintenance of his or her spouse [[1] or civil partner], and

    (b) the cost of providing for one or more children [[2] or qualifying
persons], to be treated for the purposes of any of the provisions of
this Act specified in subsection (4) below as such contributions, of
such respective amounts equal in the aggregate to the said sum or
sums, in respect of such persons, as may be determined in accordance with the regulations so as to secure as large a payment as
possible by way of benefit in respect of the dependants.

(4) The provisions in question are [[3] sections 56, 86 and paragraphs 5
and 6 of Schedule 7] to this Act.

AMENDMENTS

    1. Civil Partnership Act 2004 s.254 and Sch.24 para.39 (December 5, 2005).
    2. Child Benefit Act 2005 Sch.1 para.7 (April 10, 2006).
    3. Welfare Reform Act 2009 Sch.7(2) para.1 (April 6, 2010).

DERIVATION

1.443   SSA 1975 s.84 as amended.

Special cases

Crown employment—Parts I to VI

1.444   **115.**—(1) Subject to the provisions of this section, Parts I to V and this
Part of this Act apply to persons employed by or under the Crown in like
manner as if they were employed by a private person.

(2) Subsection (1) above does not apply to persons serving as members
of Her Majesty's forces in their capacity as such.

(3) Employment as a member of Her Majesty's forces and any other
prescribed employment under the Crown are not, and are not to be treated
as, employed earner's employment for any of the purposes of Part V of this
Act.

(4) The references to Parts I to V of this Act in this section and sections 116,
117, 119, 120 and 121 below do not include references to section 111 above.

DERIVATION

1.445   SSA 1975 s.127.

GENERAL NOTE

1.446   In *CI/7507/1999*, the Commissioner notes that s.115(1) is designed to reverse the
common law rule that persons serving the Crown in whatever capacity are not "in a
master and servant" relationship with the Crown (para.13). But the reversal of the

common law rule in s.115(1) is made subject to exceptions in subs.(2) and (3) in relation to persons serving as members of Her Majesty's forces in their capacity as such. So, during a period of service in the Royal Air Force, a person is not treated as being employed by the Crown for the purpose of being in employed earner's employment for industrial injuries purposes.

The preclusion covers service in the Territorial Army (see subs.(3) and Social Security (Contribution) Regulation 2001 Sch.6 Pt I item 6). Exemptions in the Social Security (Benefit) (Members of the Forces) Regulations, reg.2, do not embrace industrial injuries benefits. Accordingly, in *CI/0293/2005*, Commissioner Fellner held that a Territorial Army cook, injured through slipping when cooking, was not entitled to those benefits.

Her Majesty's forces

116.—(1) Subject to section 115(2) and (3) above and to this section, a person who is serving as a member of Her Majesty's forces shall, while he is so serving, be treated as an employed earner, in respect of his membership of those forces, for the purposes—

    (a) of Parts I to V and this Part of this Act; and

    (b) of any provision of the Administration Act in its application to him as an employed earner.

(2) [¹ The Treasury may with the concurrence of the Secretary of State] make regulations modifying Parts I to V and this Part of this Act, [² and Part II of the Social Security Contributions (Transfer of Functions, etc.) Act 1999] and any [³ provisions of Chapter II of Part I of the Social Security Act 1998 which correspond to] provisions of Part III of the 1975 Act, in such matter as [¹ the Treasury think] proper, in their application to persons who are or have been members of Her Majesty's forces; and regulations under this section may in particular provide [⁴, in the case of persons who are employed earners in respect of their membership of those forces, for reducing the rate of the contributions payable in respect of their employment and determining—

    (a) the amounts payable on account of those contributions by the Secretary of State and the time and manner of payment, and

    (b) the deduction (if any) to be made on account of those contributions from the pay of those persons;]

(3) For the purposes of Parts I to V and this Part of this Act, Her Majesty's forces shall be taken to consist of such establishments and organisation as may be prescribed, [¹ by regulations made by the Treasury with the concurrence of the Secretary of State] being establishments and organisations in which persons serve under the control of the Defence Council.

1.447

AMENDMENTS

    1. Transfer of Functions Act 1999 Sch.3 para.22 (April 1, 1999).
    2. Transfer of Functions Act 1999 Sch.7 paras 5–6 (April 1, 1999).
    3. Social Security Act 1998 Sch.7 paras 67–68 (July 5, 1999).
    4. Jobseekers Act 1995 Sch.2 para.28

DERIVATION

    SSA 1975 s.128.

1.448

GENERAL NOTE

    In *CI/7507/1999*, the Commissioner notes that s.116 is "dealing largely with the question of the payment of contributions" (para.13) and so there is no real contradiction between the wording of ss.115 and 116.

1.449

Mariners, airmen, etc.

1.450   **117.**—[¹ (1) The Treasury may with the concurrence of the Secretary of State] make regulations modifying provisions of Parts I to V and this Part of this Act, [² and Part II of the Social Security Contributions (Transfer of Functions, etc.) Act 1999] and any [³ provisions of Chapter II of Part I of the Social Security Act 1998 which correspond to] provisions of Part III of the 1975 Act, in such manner as [¹ the Treasury think] proper, in their application to persons who are or have been, or are to be, employed on board any ship, vessel, hovercraft or aircraft.

(2) Regulations under subsection (1) above may in particular provide—

(a) for any such provision to apply to such persons, notwithstanding that it would not otherwise apply;

(b) for excepting such persons from the application of any such provision where they neither are domiciled nor have a place of residence in any part of Great Britain;

(c) for requiring the payment of secondary Class 1 contributions in respect of such persons, whether or not they are (within the meaning of Part I of this Act) employed earners;

(d) for the taking of evidence, for the purposes of any claim to benefit, in a country or territory outside Great Britain, by a British consular official or such other person as may be prescribed;

(e) for enabling persons who are or have been so employed to authorise the payment of the whole or any part of any benefit to which they are or may become entitled to such of their dependants as may be prescribed.

AMENDMENTS

1. Transfer of Functions Act 1999 Sch.3 para.23 (April 1, 1999).
2. Transfer of Functions Act 1999 Sch.7 paras 5–6 (April 1, 1999).
3. Social Security Act 1998 ss.116–17 (July 5, 1999).

DERIVATION

1.451   SSA 1975 s.129.

Married women and widows

1.452   **118.** [¹ The Treasury may with the concurrence of the Secretary of State] make regulations modifying any of the following provisions of this Act, namely—

(a) Part I;

(b) Part II (except section 60); and

(c) Parts III and IV, in such manner as [¹ the Treasury think] proper, in their application to women who are or have been married.

AMENDMENT

1. Transfer of Functions Act 1999 Sch.3 para.24 (April 1, 1999).

DERIVATION

1.453   SSA 1975 s.130.

Persons outside Great Britain

1.454   **119.**—[¹ The Treasury may with the concurrence of the Secretary of State] make regulations modifying Parts I to V of this Act [² and Part II of the Social Security Contributions (Transfer of Functions, etc.) Act 1999] and any [³ provisions of Chapter II of Part I of the Social Security Act 1998 which corresponds to] provisions of Part III of the 1975 Act, in such manner as [¹ the Treasury think] proper, in their application to persons who are or have been outside Great Britain at any prescribed time or in any prescribed circumstances.

AMENDMENTS

1. Transfer of Functions Act 1999 Sch.3 para.25 (April 1, 1999).
2. Transfer of Functions Act 1999 Sch.7 paras 7–8 (April 1, 1999).
3. Social Security Act 1998 Sch.7 paras 69–70.

DERIVATION

SSA 1975 s.131.

1.455

Employment at sea (continental shelf operations)

120.—(1) [¹ The Treasury may with the concurrence of the Secretary of State] make regulations modifying Parts I to V and this Part of this Act [² and Part II of the Social Security Contributions (Transfer of Functions, etc.) Act 1999], and any [³ provisions of Chapter II of Part I of the Social Security Act 1998 which corresponds to] provisions of Part III of the 1975 Act, in such manner as [¹ the Treasury think] proper, in their application to persons in any prescribed employment (whether under a contract of service or not) in connection with continental shelf operations.

1.456

(2) "Continental shelf operations" means any activities which, if paragraphs (a) and (d) of [⁴ subsection 18) of section 11 of the Petroleum Act 1998] (application of civil law to certain offshore activities) were omitted, would nevertheless fall within subsection (2) of that section.

(3) In particular (but without prejudice to the generality of subsection (1) above), the regulations may provide for any prescribed provision of Parts I to V and this Part of this Act to apply to any such person notwithstanding that he does not fall within the description of an employed or self-employed earner, or does not fulfil the conditions prescribed under section 1(6) above as to residence or presence in Great Britain.

[⁵ (4) The Treasury may also, by regulations, make provision for, and in connection with, the issue by Her Majesty's Revenue and Customs of certificates to prescribed persons who are, by virtue of regulations under subsection (1), to be treated as the secondary contributor in relation to the payment of earnings to or for the benefit of one or more continental shelf workers—

(a) confirming that the prescribed person's liabilities to pay contributions in respect of the continental shelf workers specified or described in the certificate are being met by another person, and

(b) discharging the prescribed person, while the certificate is in force, from liability to make any payments in respect of the contributions, in the event that the other person fails to pay them in full.

(5) Regulations under subsection (4) may, in particular, make provision about—

(a) applying for a certificate;

(b) the circumstances in which a certificate may, or must, be issued or cancelled;

(c) the form and content of a certificate;

    (d) the effect of a certificate (including provision modifying the effect mentioned in subsection (4)(b) or specifying further effects;

    (e) the effect of cancelling a certificate.]

AMENDMENTS

  1. Transfer of Functions Act 1999 Sch.3 para.26 (April 1, 1999).
  2. Transfer of Functions Act 1999 Sch.7 paras 7–8 (April 1, 1999).
  3. Social Security Act 1998 Sch.7 paras 69–70.
  4. Petroleum Act 1998 Sch.4 para.30 (February 15, 1999).
  5. National Insurance Contributions Act 2014 s.12(4) (March 13, 2014).

DERIVATION

1.457   SSA 1975 s.132 as amended.

Treatment of certain marriages

1.458   **121.**—(1) Regulations [¹ made by the Treasury with the concurrence of the Secretary of State] may provide—

    (a) for a voidable marriage which has been annulled, whether before or after the date when the regulations come into force, to be treated for the purposes of the provisions to which this subsection applies as if it had been a valid marriage which was terminated by divorce at the date of annulment;

[³ (aa) for a voidable civil partnership which has been annulled, whether before or after the date when the regulations come into force, to be treated for the purposes of the provisions to which this subsection applies as if it had been a valid civil partnership which was dissolved at the date of annulment;]

    (b) as to the circumstances in which, for the purposes of the enactments to which this section [² applies, a marriage during the subsistence of which a party to it is at any time married to more than one person is to be treated as having, or as not having, the same consequences as any other marriage.]

  (2) Subsection (1) above applies—

    (a) to any enactment contained in Parts I to V or this Part of this Act; and

    (b) to regulations under any such enactment.

AMENDMENTS

  1. Transfer of Functions Act 1999 Sch.3 para.27 (April 1, 1999).
  2. Private International Law (Miscellaneous Provisions) Act 1995 Sch. para.4(2) (January 8, 1996).
  3. Civil Partnership Act 2004 s.254 and Sch.24 para.40 (December 5, 2005).

DERIVATION

1.459   SSA 1975 s.162.

Interpretation

Interpretation of Parts I to VI and supplementary provisions

1.460   **122.**—(1) In Parts I to V above and this Part of this Act, unless the context otherwise requires—

[¹ "additional Class 4 percentage" is to be construed in accordance with section 15(3ZA)(b) above;

"additional primary percentage" is to be construed in accordance with section 8(2)(b) above;]

[³⁰ "age-related secondary percentage" is to be construed in accordance with section 9A(2) above;]

[¹⁹ "Bank of England base rate" means—

    (a) the rate announced from time to time by the Monetary Policy Committee of the Bank of England as the official dealing rate, being the rate at which the Bank is willing to enter into transactions for providing short term liquidity in the money markets, or

    (b) where an order under section 19 of the Bank of England Act 1998 is in force, any equivalent rate determined by the Treasury under that section;]

"beneficiary", in relation to any benefit, means the person entitled to that benefit;

"benefit" means—

    (a) benefit under Parts II to V of this Act other than Old Cases payments;

    (b) as respects any period before 1st July 1992 but not before 6th April 1975, benefit under Part II of the 1975 Act; or

    (c) as respects any period before 6th April 1975, benefit under—

        (i) the National Insurance Act 1946 or 1965; or

        (ii) The National Insurance (Industrial Injuries) Act 1946 or 1965;

[²⁹ (For the meaning of "benefit" in Part 1, see also section 19B)]

[¹² "the benefits code" has the meaning given by section 63(1) of ITEPA 2003;]

[¹⁵ "child" has the same meaning as in Part 9 of this Act;]

"claim" is to be construed in accordance with "claimant";

"claimant", in relation to benefit other than industrial injuries benefit, means a person who has claimed benefit;

"claimant", in relation to industrial injuries benefit, means a person who has claimed industrial injuries benefit;

"contract of service" means any contract of service or apprenticeship whether written or oral and whether express or implied;

[² "contribution-based jobseeker's allowance" has the same meaning as in the Jobseeker's Act 1995];

"current", in relation to the lower and upper earnings limits [³ and primary and secondary thresholds] under section 5(1) above, means for the time being in force;

[⁴ "day of interruption of employment" has the meaning given by section 25A(1)(c) above];

"deferred" and "period of deferment" have the meanings assigned to them by section 55 above;

"earner" and "earnings" are to be construed in accordance with sections 3, 4 and 112 above;

"employed earner" has the meaning assigned to it by section 2 above;

"employment" includes any trade, business, profession, office or vocation and "employed" has a corresponding meaning;

[²⁰ "the employment income parts of ITEPA 2003" means Parts 2 to 7 of that Act;]

233

"entitled", in relation to any benefit, is to be construed in accordance with—

    (a) the provisions specifically relating to that benefit;

    (b) in the case of a benefit specified in section 20(1) above, section 21 above; and

    (c) sections 1 to 3 of the Administration Act [5 and section 27 of the Social Security Act 1998];

[12 . . .]

[6 "first appointed year" means such tax year, no earlier than 2002–03, as may be appointed by order, and "second appointed year" means such subsequent tax year as may be so appointed;]

[21 "the flat rate introduction year" means such tax year as may be designated by order;]

[12 "general earnings" has the meaning given by section 7 of ITEPA 2003 and accordingly sections 3 and 112 of this Act do not apply in relation to the word "earnings" when used in the expression "general earnings"]

"industrial injuries benefit" means benefit under Part V of this Act, other than under Schedule 8;

[7 . . .]

"the Inland Revenue" means the Commissioners of Inland Revenue;

[12 "ITEPA 2003" means the Income Tax (Earnings and Pensions) Act 2003;]

"late husband", in relation to a woman who has been more than once married, means her last husband;

"long-term benefit" has the meaning assigned to it by section 20(2) above;

"loss of physical faculty" includes disfigurement whether or not accompanied by any loss of physical faculty;

[8 "lower earnings limit" and "upper earnings limit" [3 . . .] [3 "primary threshold" and "secondary threshold"] are to be construed in accordance with subsection (1) of section 5 above, and references to the lower or upper earnings limit, or to [3 . . .] [3 the primary or secondary] threshold, of a tax year are to whatever is (or was) for that year the limit or threshold in force under that subsection;]

[7 . . .]

[31"lower-paid employment as a minister of religion" has the meaning given by section 290D of ITEPA 2003;]

[1 "main Class 4 percentage" is to be construed in accordance with section 15(3ZA) above;

"main primary percentage" is to be construed in accordance with section 8(2)(b) above;]

"medical examination" includes bacteriological and radiographical tests and similar investigations, and "medically examined" has a corresponding meaning;

"medical treatment" means medical, surgical or rehabilitative treatment (including any course or diet or other regimen), and references to a person receiving or submitting himself to medical treatment are to be construed accordingly;

"the Northern Ireland Department" means the Department of Health and Social Services for Northern Ireland;

"Old Cases payments" means payments under Part I or II of Schedule 8 to this Act;

[² "PAYE settlement agreement" has the same meaning as in [¹² Chapter 5 of Part 11 of ITEPA 2003];]

"payments by way of occupational or personal pension" means, in relation to a person, periodical payments which, in connection with the coming to an end of an employment of his, fall to be made to him—

(a) out of money provided wholly or partly by the employer or under arrangements made by the employer; or

(b) out of money provided under an enactment or instrument having the force of law in any part of the United Kingdom or elsewhere; or

(c) under a personal pension scheme as defined in section 84(1) of the 1986 Act; or

[²² (d) under a pension scheme registered under section 153 of the Finance Act 2004;]

and such other payments as are prescribed.

[⁴ "pensionable age" has the meaning given by the rules in paragraph 1 to Schedule 4 to the Pensions Act 1995];

[¹⁶ "PPF periodic payments" means—

(a) any periodic compensation payments made in relation to a person, payable under the pension compensation provisions as specified in section 162(2) of the Pensions Act 2004 or Article 146(2) of the Pensions (Northern Ireland) order 2005 (the pension compensation provisions); OR

(b) any periodic payments made in relation to a person, payable under section 166 of the Pensions Act 2004 or Article 150 of the Pensions (Northern Ireland) Order 2005 (duty to pay scheme benefits unpaid at assessment date etc.);

"pneumoconiosis" means fibrosis of the lungs due to silica dust, asbestos dust, or other dust, and includes the condition of the lungs known as dust-reticulation;

"prescribe" means prescribe by regulations;

[. . .]

"qualifying earnings factor" means an earnings factor equal to the lower earnings limit for the tax year in question multiplied by 52;

[¹⁵ "qualifying young person" has the same meaning as in Part 9 of this Act;]

[²⁵ "Regulation (EC) No 1408/71" means Council Regulation (EC) No 1408/71 of 14 June 1971 [³² as amended from time to time] on the application of social security schemes to employed persons, to self-employed persons and to members of their families moving within the Community;

"Regulation (EC) No 883/2004" means Regulation (EC) No 883/2004 of the European Parliament and of the Council of 29 April 2004 [³² as amended from time to time] on the coordination of social security systems;]

"relative" includes a person who is a relative by marriage [¹⁴ or civil partnership];

"relevant accident" means the accident in respect of which industrial injuries benefit is claimed or payable;

"relevant injury" means the injury in respect of which industrial injuries benefit is claimed or payable;

"relevant loss of faculty" means—

[⁹ . . .]

(b) in relation to industrial injuries benefit, the loss of faculty resulting from the relevant injury;

[[1] "secondary percentage" is to be construed in accordance with section 9(2) above;]

"self-employed earner" has the meaning assigned to it by section 2 above;

"short-term benefit" has the meaning assigned to it by section 20(2) above;

"tax week" means one of the successive periods in a tax year beginning with the first day of that year and every seventh day thereafter, the last day of a tax year (or, in the case of a tax year ending in a leap year, the last two days) to be treated accordingly as a separate tax week;

"tax year" means the 12 months beginning with 6th April in any year, the expression "1978–79" meaning the tax year beginning with 6th April 1978, and any correspondingly framed reference to a pair of successive years being construed as a reference to the tax year beginning with 6th April in the earlier of them;

[[18] "[24] the upper accrual point" is £770;]]

"trade or business" includes, in relation to a public or local authority, the exercise and performance of the powers and duties of that authority;

"trade union" means an association of employed earners;

[[28] "unit of additional pension" means a unit of additional pension for which a person has paid a Class 3A contribution under section 14A;]

"week", [[13] . . .], means a period of 7 days beginning with Sunday.

[[2] "working life" has the meaning given by paragraph 5(8) of Schedule 3 to this Act].

[1A] . . . [[26,27]]

(2) Regulations [[11] made by the Treasury with the concurrence of the Secretary of State] may make provision modifying the meaning of "employment" for the purposes of any provision of Parts I to V and this Part of this Act.

(3) Provision may be made [[11] by the Treasury by regulations made with the concurrence of the Secretary of State] as to the circumstances in which a person is to be treated as residing or not residing with another person for any of the purposes of Parts I to V and this Part of this Act and as to the circumstances in which persons are to be treated for any of those purposes as residing or not residing together.

(4) A person who is residing with his spouse shall be treated for the purposes of Parts I to V and this Part of this Act as entitled to any child benefit to which his spouse is entitled.

(5) Regulations may, for the purposes of any provision of those Parts under which the right to any benefit or increase of benefit depends on a person being or having been entitled to child benefit, make provision whereby a person is to be treated as if he were or had been so entitled or as if he were not or had not been so entitled.

(6) For the purposes of Parts I to V and this Part of this Act a person is "permanently incapable of self-support" if (but only if) he is incapable of supporting himself by reason of physical or mental infirmity and is likely to remain so incapable for the remainder of his life.

[[23] (6A) The Treasury may by regulations prescribe an equivalent of the upper accrual point in relation to earners paid otherwise than weekly (and references in this or any other Act to "the prescribed equivalent", in the context of the upper accrual point, are to the equivalent prescribed under this subsection in relation to such earners).

(6B) The power conferred by subsection (6A) includes power to prescribe an amount which exceeds by not more than £1 the amount which is the arithmetical equivalent of the upper accrual point.]

[[23]. . .]

AMENDMENTS

1. National Insurance Contributions Act 2002 s.6 and Sch.1 para.12 (has effect in relation to the tax year beginning April 6, 2003 and subsequent tax years: see National Insurance Contributions Act 2002, s.8(2)).

2. Jobseekers Act 1995 Sch.2 para.29 (October 7, 1996).

3. Welfare Reform and Pensions Act 1999 Sch.12 para.77 (April 6, 2000).

4. Social Security (Incapacity for Work) Act 1994 Sch.1 para.30 (April 13, 1995).

5. Social Security Act 1998 Sch.7 para.71(a) (July 5, 1999).

6. Child Support, Pensions and Social Security Act 2000 s.35 (January 8, 2001).

7. Social Security Act 1998 Sch.7 para.71(b) (July 5, 1999).

8. Social Security Act 1998 Sch.7 para.71(c) (July 5, 1999).

9. Welfare Reform and Pensions Act 1999 Sch.13 Pt IV (April 6, 2001).

10. Tax Credits Act 1999 Sch.1 para.2 (October 5, 1999).

11. Transfer of Functions Act 1999 Sch.3 para.28 (April 1, 1999).

12. Finance Act 2015 c.11 Sch.1(2) para.23(4)(a) (March 26, 2015).

13. Tax Credits Act 2002 Sch.6 (April 6, 2003).

14. Civil Partnership Act 2004 s.254 and Sch.24 para.41 (December 5, 2005).

15. Child Benefit Act 2005 c.6 Sch.1 Part, para.8 (April 10, 2006).

16. The Pensions 2004 (PPF Payments and FAS Payments)(Consequential Provisions) Order 2006 (SI 2006/343) (February 14, 2006).

17. Pensions Act 2007 s.11 (September 26, 2007).

18. Pensions Act 2007 s.12 (September 26, 2007).

19. Pensions Act 2004 Sch.11(2) para.18(a) (November 18, 2004 for enabling the making of regulations; April 6, 2005 otherwise).

20. Income Tax (Earnings and Pensions) Act 2003 Sch.6(2) para.178(2) (April 6, 2003 subject to transitional provisions and savings specified in 2003 c.1 Sch.7).

21. Pensions Act 2007 Pt 1, s.11(4) (September 26, 2007).

22. Taxation of Pension Schemes (Consequential Amendments) Order 2006 (SI 2006/745) Pt 1 art.4(3) (April 6, 2006).

23. National Insurance Contributions Act 2008 Sch.2 para.1 (September 22, 2008 for purposes specified in 2008 c.16 s.6(1); shall come into force on the commencement of 2007 c.22, Sch.4 para.45(2) otherwise).

24. National Insurance Contributions Act 2008 s.3(4) (September 21, 2008).

25. The Social Security (Disability Living Allowance, Attendance Allowance and Carer's Allowance) (Miscellaneous Amendments) Regulations 2011 (SI 2011/2426) (October 31, 2011).

26. The Marriage (Same Sex Couples) Act 2013 (Consequential and Contrary Provisions and Scotland) Order 2014 (SI 2014/560) art.22(7) (March 13, 2014).

27. The Marriage and Civil Partnership (Scotland) Act 2014 and Civil Partnership Act 2004 (Consequential Provisions and Modifications) Order 2014 (SI 2014/3229) Sch.4 para.2(12) (December 12, 2014).

28. Pensions Act 2014 Sch.15 para.10 (October 12, 2015).

29. Pensions Act 2014 Sch.12 para.7 (April 6, 2016).

30. National Insurance Contributions Act 2014 s.9(4) (April 6, 2015).

31. Finance Act 2015 c.11 Sch.1(2) para.23(4)(b) (March 26, 2015).

32. Social Security (Updating of EU References) (Amendment) Regulations 2018 (SI 2018/1084) reg.2 (November 15, 2018).

GENERAL NOTE

On the meaning of "dust-reticulation" in the definition of pneumoconiosis see *S (on behalf of S, deceased) v SSWP* [2016] UKUT 485 (AAC); see further the anno-   **1.461** tation to Sch.1 of the Social Security (Industrial Injuries) (Prescribed Diseases) Regulations 1985 (SI 1985/967).

1.462   *For Pts VI and VII see Vol.II.*

PART IX

CHILD BENEFIT

Child benefit

1.463   **141.—147.** *Omitted. See Vol.IV: Tax Credits and HMRC-administered Social Security Benefits.*

PART X

CHRISTMAS BONUS FOR PENSIONERS

Entitlement of Pensioners to Christmas Bonus

1.464   **148.**—(1) Any person who in any year—

  (a) is present or ordinarily resident in the United Kingdom or any other member State at any time during the relevant week; and

  (b) is entitled to a payment of a qualifying benefit in respect of a period which includes a day in that week or is to be treated as entitled to a payment of a qualifying benefit in respect of such a period,

shall, subject to the following provisions of this Part of this Act and to section 1 of the Administration Act, be entitled to payment under this subsection in respect of that year.

(2) Subject to the following provisions of this Part of this Act, any person who is a member of a couple and is entitled to a payment under subsection (1) above in respect of a year shall also be entitled to payment under this subsection in respect of that year if—

  (a) both members have attained pensionable age not later than the end of the relevant week; and

  (b) the other member satisfies the condition mentioned in subsection (1)(a) above; and

  (c) either—

    (i) he is entitled or treated as entitled, in respect of the other member, to an increase in the payment of the qualifying benefit; or

    (ii) the only qualifying benefit to which he is entitled is [² state pension credit].

[⁴ (2ZA) In a case where a person is entitled to a payment of armed forces independence payment, the reference in subsection (1) to section 1 of the Administration Act is to be read as a reference to article 43 of the Armed Forces and Reserve Forces (Compensation Scheme) Order 2011 (SI 2011/517)].

[² (2A) In a case falling within paragraph (c)(ii) of subsection (2) above, paragraph (a) of that subsection has effect with the substitution of "qualifying age for state pension credit" for "pensionable age".]

(3) A payment under subsection (1) and (2) above—
(a) is to be made by the Secretary of State; and
(b) is to be of [³ £ 70]or such larger sum as the Secretary of State may
by order specify.
    [² . . .]
(4) [² . . .]
(5) Only one sum shall be payable in respect of any person.

AMENDMENTS

1. Pensions Act 1995 Sch.4 (July 19, 1995).
2. State Pension Credit Act 2002 Sch.2(1) para.5(2) (July 2, 2002 for the purposes
of exercising powers to make regulations or orders; October 6, 2003 otherwise).
3. Christmas Bonus (Specified Sum) Order 2008 (SI 2008/3255) para.2
(December 19, 2008).
4. The Armed Forces and Reserve Forces (Compensation Scheme) (Consequential
Provisions: Primary Legislation) Order 2013 (SI 2013/796) art.3 (April 8, 2013).

GENERAL NOTE

A decision whether a person is entitled to payment of a Christmas Bonus is a   1.465
decision against which no appeal lies to the First-tier Tribunal: Social Security Act
1998 s.12(1), Sch.2 para.2.

Provisions supplementary to section 148

149.— (1) For the purposes of section 148 above the Channel Islands,   1.466
the Isle of Man and Gibraltar shall be treated as though they were part of
the United Kingdom.
(2) A person shall be treated for the purposes of section 148(1)(b) above
as entitled to a payment of a qualifying benefit if he would be so entitled—
(a) in the case of a qualifying benefit [² other than state pension credit],
but for the fact that he or, if he is a member of a couple, the other
member is entitled to receive some other payment out of public funds;
(b) in the case of [² state pension credit], but for the fact that his income
or, if he is a member of a couple, the income of the other member
was exceptionally of an amount which resulted in his having ceased
to be entitled to [² state pension credit]
(3) A person shall be treated for the purpose of section 148(2)(c)(i)
above as entitled in respect of the other member of the couple to an increase
in a payment of a qualifying benefit if he would be so entitled—
(a) but for the fact that he or the other member is entitled to receive
some other payment out of public funds;
(b) but for the operation of any provision of [¹ . . .] paragraph 6(4) of
Schedule 7 to this Act or any regulations made under paragraph 6(3)
of that Schedule whereby entitlement to benefit is affected by the
amount of a person's earnings in a given period.
(4) For the purposes of section 148 above a person shall be taken not to
be entitled to a payment of a war disablement pension unless not later than
the end of the relevant week he has attained [³[⁴ pensionable age]].
(5) A sum payable under section 148 above shall not be treated as benefit
for the purposes of any enactment or instrument under which entitlement
to the relevant qualifying benefit arises or is to be treated as arising.
(6) A payment and the right to receive a payment—

(a) under section 148 above or any enactment corresponding to it in Northern Ireland; or

(b) under regulations relating to widows which are made by the Secretary of State under any enactment relating to police and which contain a statement that the regulations provide for payments corresponding to payments under that section,

shall be disregarded for all purposes of income tax and for the purposes of any enactment or instrument under which regard is had to a person's means.

AMENDMENTS

1. Pensions Act 2007 Sch.1 para.17 (September 26, 2007).
2. State Pension Credit Act 2002 Sch.2(1) para.6(2) (July 2, 2002 for the purposes of exercising powers to make regulations or orders; October 6, 2003 otherwise).
3. Pensions Act 1995 Sch.4(II) para.8 (July 19, 1995).
4. Pensions Act 2007 Sch.1 para. 43 (April 6, 2018).

Interpretation of Part X

1.467

150.—(1) In this Part of this Act "qualifying benefit" means—

(a) a retirement pension;

[¹ (b)   long-term incapacity benefit;]

[² (ba) a qualifying employment and support allowance;]

[³ (bb) personal independence payment;]

[¹³ (bc) armed forces independence payment;]

(c) a widowed mother's allowance [⁴ , widowed parent's allowance] or widow's pension;

(d) [⁵ . . .]

(e) [⁶ a carer's allowance;]

(f) industrial death benefit;

(g) an attendance allowance;

(h) an unemployability supplement or allowance;

(i) a war disablement pension;

(j) a war widow's pension;

(k) [⁷ state pension credit;]

[⁸ (l) a mobility supplement].

(2)   in this Part of this Act—

[¹³ "armed forces independence payment" means armed forces independence payment under the Armed Forces and Reserve Forces (Compensation Scheme) Order 2011 (SI 2011/517)];

"attendance allowance" means—

(a) an attendance allowance;

(b) a disability living allowance;

(c) an increase of disablement pension under section 104 or 105 above;

(d) a payment under regulations made in exercise of the powers in section 159(3)(b) of the 1975 Act or paragraph 7(2) of Schedule 8 to this Act;

(e) an increase of allowance under article 8 of the Pneumoconiosis, Byssinosis and Miscellaneous Diseases Benefit Scheme 1983 (constant attendance allowance for certain persons to whom that scheme applies) or under the corresponding provision of any Scheme which may replace that Scheme;

(f) an allowance in respect of constant attendance on account of disablement for which a person is in receipt of a war disablement pension, including an allowance in respect of exceptionally severe disablement;

[⁸ "mobility supplement" means a supplement awarded in respect of disablement which affects a person's ability to walk and for which the person is in receipt of a war disablement pension;]

[⁹ "pensionable age" has the meaning given by the rules in paragraph 1 of Schedule 4 to the Pensions Act 1995];

[⁷ "the qualifying age for state pension credit" is (in accordance with section 1(2)(b) and (6) of the State Pension Credit Act 2002)—

(a) in the case of a woman, pensionable age; or

(b) in the case of a man, the age which is pensionable age in the case of a woman born on the same day as a man;]

[² "qualifying employment and support allowance" means [¹⁰ a contributory allowance] under Part 1 of the Welfare Reform Act 2007 the calculation of the amount of which includes an addition in respect of the support component or the work-related activity component.]

[¹⁴ "retirement pension" means—

(a) a state pension under Part 1 of the Pensions Act 2014,

(b) a retirement pension under this Act, or

(c) graduated retirement benefit.] [⁸ . . .];

[⁷ "state pension credit" means state pension credit under the State Pension Credit Act 2002;]

"unemployability supplement or allowance" means—

(a) an unemployability supplement payable under Part 1 of Schedule 7 to this Act; or

(b) any corresponding allowance payable—

   (i) by virtue of paragraph 6(4)(a) of Schedule 8 to this Act⁶;

   (ii) by way of supplement to retired pay or pension exempt from income tax under [¹¹ section 641 of the Income Tax (Earnings and Pensions) Act 2003;]

   (iii) under the Personal Injuries (Emergency Provisions) Act 1939; [⁸ . . .]

   (iv) by way of supplement to retired pay or pension under the Polish Resettlement Act 1947;

   (v) [¹¹ . . .];

"war disablement pension" means—

(a) any retired pay, pension or allowance granted in respect of disablement under powers conferred by or under the Air Force (Contribution) Act 1917, the Personal Injuries (Emergency Provisions) Act 1939; the Pensions (Navy, Army, Air Force and Mercantile Marine Act 1939, the Polish Resettlement Act 1947, or Part VII or section 151 of the Reserve Forces Act 1980;

(b) without prejudice to paragraph (a) of this definition, any retired pay or pension to which [¹¹ any of paragraphs (a) to (f) of section 641(1) of the Income Tax (Earnings and Pensions) Act 2003] applies;

"war widow's pension" means any widow's [¹² or surviving civil partner's] pension or allowance granted in respect of a death due to service or war injury and payable by virtue of any enactment mentioned in paragraph (a) of the preceding definition or a pension or allowance for a widow [¹² or surviving civil partner] granted under any scheme mentioned in [¹¹ section 641(1)(e) or (f) of the Income Tax (Earnings and Pensions) Act 2003];

and each of the following expressions, namely "attendance allowance", "unemployability supplement or allowance", "war disablement pension" and "war widow's pension", includes any payment which the Secretary of State accepts as being analogous to it.

[[12] (3) In this Part of this Act, "couple" has the meaning given by section 137(1) above].

(4) In this Part of this Act "the relevant week", in relation to any year, means the week beginning with the first Monday in December or such other week as may be specified in an order made by the Secretary of State.

AMENDMENTS

1. Social Security (Incapacity for Work) Act 1994 Sch.1 para.33 (April 13, 1995).
2. Welfare Reform Act 2007 Sch.3 para.9(11) (October 27, 2008).
3. Welfare Reform Act 2012 Sch.9 para.6 (April 8, 2013).
4. Welfare Reform and Pensions Act 1999 s.70 (April 9, 2001).
5. Welfare Reform and Pensions Act 1999 s.88 (April 6, 2001).
6. Regulatory Reform (Carer's Allowance) Order 2002 (SI 2002/1457) Sch.1 para.2(e) (September 1, 2002).
7. State Pension Credit Act 2002 Sch.2 para.7 (July 2, 2002).
8. Pensions Act 1995 s.132 (July 19, 1995).
9. Pensions Act 1995 Sch.4 para.13 (July 19, 1995).
10. Welfare Reform Act 2007 s.37(3) (November 12, 2009).
11. Income Tax (Earnings and Pensions) Act 2003 Sch.6 para.180 (April 6, 2003).
12. Civil Partnership Act 2004 Sch.24 para.49 (December 5, 2005).
13. Armed Forces and Reserve Forces (Compensation Scheme) (Consequential Provisions: Primary Legislation) Order 2013 (SI 2013/796) art.3 (April 8, 2013).
14. Pensions Act 2014 Sch.12 para.86. (April 6, 2016).

PART XI

STATUTORY SICK PAY

1.468 *Omitted as the province of the Board of Inland Revenue. See Vol.IV.*

PART XII

STATUTORY MATERNITY PAY

164.–171. *Omitted.*
See Vol. IV: Tax Credits and HMRC-administered Social Security Benefits

PART XIIZA

STATUTORY PATERNITY PAY

171ZA.–171ZK. *Omitted.*
See Vol. IV: Tax Credits and HMRC-administered Social Security Benefits

PART XIIZB

STATUTORY ADOPTION PAY

171ZL.–171ZT.   *Omitted.*
See Vol. IV: Tax Credits and HMRC-administered Social Security Benefits

PART XIIZC

STATUTORY SHARED PARENTAL PAY

171ZU.–171ZZ5.   *Omitted.*
See Vol. IV: Tax Credits and HMRC-administered Social Security Benefits

PART XIIA

INCAPACITY FOR WORK

171A.–171G.   *Omitted.*   1.469
For the text of and commentary to these sections see the 2011/12 edition of this Volume.

PART XIII

GENERAL

Interpretation

Application of Act in relation to territorial waters

172.—In this Act—   1.470
(a) any reference to Great Britain includes a reference to the territorial
waters of the United Kingdom adjacent to Great Britain;
(b) any reference to the United Kingdom includes a reference to the territorial waters of the United Kingdom.

DERIVATION
SSHBA 1982 s.26 as amended.   1.471

Age

173.—For the purposes of this Act a person—   1.472
(a) is over or under a particular age if he has or, as the case may be, has
not attained that age; and

(b) is between two particular ages if he has attained the first but not the second;

and in Scotland (as in England and Wales) the time at which a person attains a particular age expressed in years is the commencement of the relevant anniversary of the date of his birth.

DERIVATION

1.473   SSA 1975 s.168(1) and Sch.20 as amended.

References to Act

1.474   **174.**—In this Act—
"the 1975 Act" means the Social Security Act 1975;
"the 1986 Act" means the Social Security Act 1986;
"the Administration Act" means the Social Security Administration Act 1991;
"the Consequential Provisions Act" means the Social Security (Consequential Provisions) Act 1991;
"the Northern Ireland Contributions and Benefits Act" means the Social Security Contributions and Benefits (Northern Ireland) Act 1991;
"the Old Cases Act" means the Industrial Injuries and Diseases (Old Cases) Act 1975; and
"the Pensions Act" means the [¹ Pension Schemes Act 1993].

AMENDMENT

1. Pension Schemes Act 1993 Sch.8 para.41 (February 7, 1994).

Subordinate legislation

Regulations, orders and schemes

1.475   **175.**—(1) Subject to [¹ subsection 1(A) below] regulations and orders under this Act shall be made by the Secretary of State.
[¹ (1A) Subsection (1) above has effect subject to—
(a) any provision [⁴ . . .] providing for regulations or an order to be made by the Treasury or by the Commissioners of the Inland Revenue,
(b) [⁴ . . .]]
(2) Powers under this Act to make regulations, orders or schemes shall be exercisable by statutory instrument.
(3) Except in the case of an order under section 145(3) above and in so far as this Act otherwise provides, any power under this Act to make regulations or an order may be exercised—
(a) either in relation to all cases to which the power extends, or in relation to those cases subject to specified exceptions, or in relation to any specified cases or classes of case;
(b) so as to make, as respects the cases in relation to which it is exercised—
(i) the full provision to which the power extends or any less provision (whether by way of exception or otherwise),
(ii) the same provision for all cases in relation to which the power is exercised, or different provision for different cases or different

classes of case or different provision as respects the same case or class for different purposes of this Act,

(iii) any such provision either unconditionally or subject to any specified condition;

and where such a power is expressed to be exercisable for alternative purposes it may be exercised in relation to the same case for any or all of those purposes; and powers to make regulations or an order for the purposes of any one provision of this Act are without prejudice to powers to make regulations or an order for the purposes of any other provision.

(4) Without prejudice to any specific provision in this Act, any power conferred by this Act to make regulations or an order (other than the power conferred in section 145(3) above) includes power to make thereby such incidental, supplementary, consequential or transitional provision as appears to the [¹ person making the regulations or order] to be expedient for the purposes of the regulations or order.

(5) Without prejudice to any specific provisions in this Act, a power conferred by any provision of this Act except—

(a) sections 30, 47(6), [² 25B(2)(a)] and 145(3) above and paragraph 3(9) of Schedule 7 to this Act;

(b) section 122(1) above in relation to the definition of "payments by way of occupational or personal pension"; and

(c) Part XI,

to make regulations or an order includes power to provide for a person to exercise a discretion in dealing with any matter.

(6) [⁵ . . .]

(7) Any power of the Secretary of State under any provision of this Act, except the provisions mentioned in subsection (5)(a) and (b) above and Part IX, to make any regulations or order, where the power is not expressed to be exercisable with the consent of the Treasury, shall if the Treasury so direct be exercisable only in conjunction with them.

(8) Any power under any of sections 116 to 120 above to modify provisions of this Act or the Administration Act extends also to modifying so much of any other provision of this Act or that Act as re-enacts provisions of the 1975 Act which replace provisions of the National Insurance (Industrial Injuries) Act 1965 to 1974.

(9) A power to make regulations under any of sections 116 to 120 above shall be exercisable in relation to any enactment passed after this Act which is directed to be construed as one with this Act; but this subsection applies only so far as a contrary intention is not expressed in the enactment so passed, and is without prejudice to the generality of any such direction.

(10) Any reference in this section or section 176 below to an order or regulations under this Act includes a reference to an order or regulations made under any provision of an enactment passed after this Act and directed to be construed as one with this Act; but this subsection applies only so far as a contrary intention is not expressed in the enactment so passed, and without prejudice to the generality of any such direction.

AMENDMENTS

1. Transfer of Functions Act 1999 Sch.3 para.29 (April 1, 1999).
2. Social Security (Incapacity for Work) Act 1994 Sch.1 para.36 (April 13, 1995).
3. Local Government Finance Act 1992 Sch.9 para.10 (March 6, 1992).

4. Tax Credits Act 2002 Sch.6 (April 1, 2003).

5. Welfare Reform Act 2012 Sch.14(1) para.1 (April 1, 2013, subject to certain transitional provisions and savings in SI 2013/358).

DERIVATION

1.476   SSA 1975 ss.162, 166 and 168 as amended.

GENERAL NOTE

1.477   By virtue of Sch.2 Pt V para.20 and with effect from October 5, 1999, s.175 is to be construed, in relation to tax credit, as if references to the Secretary of State were references to the Treasury or, as the case maybe, the Board of the Inland Revenue now Her Majesty's Revenue and Customs.

Parliamentary control

1.478   **176.**—(1) Subject to the provisions of this section, a statutory instrument containing (whether alone or with other provisions)—

[1 (za) regulations under section 5 specifying the lower earnings limit for the tax year following the designated tax year (see section 5(4) of the Pensions Act 2007) or any subsequent tax year;]

[2 (zb) regulations under section 5 specifying the upper earnings limit;]

(a) regulations made by virtue of—
[3 section 4B(2);
section 4C;]
[27 section 9A(7)]
[28 section 9B(4), (8) or (10)]
[4 section 10ZC;]
[29 section 11(8) or (9)]
[26 section 14A]
section 18;
[30 section 18A;]
section 19(4) to (6);
section 28(3);
[5 section 30DD(5)(b) or (c);]
[26 section 45(2A)]
[6 . . .]
section 104(3);
section 117;
section 118;
[7 . . .]
section 145;
[8 section 171ZE(1)];
[24 . . .]
[30 . . .]
[31 any of sections 171ZU to 171ZY;]
[9 . . .]
[10 (aa) the first regulations made by virtue of section 23A(3)(c);]
[25 (ab) the first regulations made by virtue of section 130A(5) or (6);]

(b) regulations prescribing payments for the purposes of the definition of "payments by way of occupational or personal pension" in section 122(1) above;

[11 (bb) regulations prescribing a percentage rate for the purposes of–
  (i) paragraph 3B(3) or 7B(3) of Schedule 5, or
  (ii) paragraph 5(3) of Schedule 5A;]
(c) an order under—
  [12 section 25B(1);]
  section 28(2);
  [13 section 35A(7);]
  [14 . . .]
  [15 . . .]
  [6 . . .]
  section 148(3)(b);
  section 157(2);
  [16 . . .]
  [17 section 159A(1),]
shall not be made unless a draft of the instrument has been laid before Parliament and been approved by a resolution of each House.

(2) Subsection (1) above does not apply to a statutory instrument by reason only that it contains—
(a) regulations under section 117 which the instrument states are made for the purpose of making provision consequential on the making of an order under section 141, 143, 145, 146 or 162 of the Administration Act;
(b) regulations under powers conferred by any provision mentioned in paragraph (a) of that subsection [18 . . .] which are to be made for the purpose of consolidating regulations to be revoked in the instrument;
(c) regulations which, in so far as they are made under powers conferred by any provision mentioned in paragraph (a) of that subsection (other than [19 section 145]), only replace provisions of previous regulations with new provisions to the same effect.

[20 (2A) In the case of a statutory instrument containing (whether alone or with other provisions) regulations made by virtue of section 4B(2) to which subsection (1) above applies, the draft of the instrument must be laid before Parliament before the end of the period of 12 months beginning with the appropriate date.

(2B) For the purposes of subsection (2A), the "appropriate date" means–
(a) where the corresponding retrospective tax provision was passed or made before the day on which the National Insurance Contributions Act 2006 was passed, the date upon which that Act was passed, and
(b) in any other case, the date upon which the corresponding retrospective tax provision was passed or made.

(2C) For the purposes of subsection (2B), "the corresponding retrospective tax provision" in relation to the regulations means–
(a) the retrospective tax provision mentioned in subsection (1) of section 4B in relation to which the regulations are to be made by virtue of subsection (2) of that section, or
(b) where there is more than one such tax provision, whichever of those provisions was the first to be passed or made.]

(3) A statutory instrument—
(a) which contains (whether alone or with other provisions) any order, regulations or scheme made under this Act by the Secretary of State,

[²¹ the Treasury or the Commissioners of Inland Revenue] other than an order under section 145(3) above; and

(b) which is not subject to any requirement that a draft of the instrument shall be laid before and approved by a resolution of each House of Parliament,

shall be subject to annulment in pursuance of a resolution of either House of Parliament.

[³² (4) Subsection (3) above does not apply to a statutory instrument by reason only that it contains an order appointing the first or second appointed year [²³ or designating the flat rate introduction year] (within the meanings given by section 122(1) above).]

AMENDMENTS

1. Pensions Act 2007 Pt 1 s.7(5) (September 26, 2007).
2. National Insurance Contributions Act 2008 s.1(2) (September 22, 2008: insertion has effect in relation to regulations specifying the upper earnings limit for 2009-10 or any subsequent tax year).
3. National Insurance Contributions Act 2006 s.1(2)(a) (March 30, 2006).
4. National Insurance Contributions Act 2006 s.3(2) (March 30, 2006).
5. Welfare Reform and Pensions Act 1999 Sch.8(II) para.25 (November 3, 2000).
6. Social Security (Incapacity for Work) Act 1994 Sch.2 para.1 (April 13, 1995).
7. Welfare Reform Act 2007 Pt 2, s.31(3).
8. Employment Act 2002 Sch.7 para.7 (December 8, 2002).
9. Statutory Sick Pay Percentage Threshold Order 1995 (SI 1995/512), art.6(1)(a)(i) (April 6, 1995).
10. Pensions Act 2007 Sch.1(3) para.10 (September 26, 2007).
11. Pensions Act 2004 Sch.11(2) para.19 (November 18, 2004 for enabling the making of regulations; April 6, 2005 otherwise).
12. Social Security (Incapacity for Work) Act 1994 Sch.1(I) para.37(b) (April 13, 1995).
13. Welfare Reform and Pensions Act 1999 Sch.8(VI) para.32 (January 12, 2000 for the purpose of making regulations; April 2, 2000 otherwise).
14. National Insurance Contributions Act 2008 Sch.2 para.1 (September 22, 2008 for purposes specified in 2008 c.16, s.6(1); shall come into force on the commencement of 2007 c.22, Sch.4 para.45(2) otherwise).
15. Welfare Reform Act 2007 Pt 2, s.31(3).
16. Statutory Sick Pay Percentage Threshold Order 1995 (SI 1995/512) art.6(1)(a)(ii) (April 6, 1995).
17. Statutory Sick Pay Act 1994 s.3(2) (February 10, 1994).
18. Statutory Sick Pay Percentage Threshold Order 1995 (SI 1995/512) art.6(1)(a)(iii) (April 6, 1995).
19. Statutory Sick Pay Percentage Threshold Order 1995 (SI 1995/512) art.6(1)(a)(iv) (April 6, 1995).
20. National Insurance Contributions Act 2006 s.1(2)(b) (March 30, 2006).
21. Social Security Contributions (Transfer of Functions, etc.) Act 1999 Sch.3 para.30 (April 1, 1999).
22. Child Support, Pensions and Social Security Act 2000 s.35(15) (April 6, 2002).
23. Pensions Act 2007 Sch.1 Pt 7 para.35(b) (September 26, 2007).
24. Children and Families Act 2014 Sch.7, para.22 (April 5, 2015)
25. Welfare Reform Act 2012 s.69(4) (January 1, 2013).
26. Pensions Act 2014 s.15 and Sch.15 para.11 (October 13, 2014).
27. National Insurance Contributions Act 2014, s.9(5) (May 13, 2014).
28. National Insurance Contributions Act 2015, s.1(5) (April 6, 2016).
29. National Insurance Contributions Act 2015, s.2 and Sch. 1, para. 8 (April 6, 2015).

30. Children and Families Act 2014 s.124(2) (April 5, 2015).

31. Children and Families Act 2014 s.119(2) (June 30, 2014).

32. Child Support, Pensions and Social Security Act 2000, s.35(15) (January 8, 2001 for regulation and order-making purposes, January 25, 2001 for certain other purposes–see SI 2001/153, art.2(a)(i)–and April 6, 2002 for all other purposes).

DERIVATION

SSA 1975 s.167 as amended.   **1.479**

GENERAL NOTE

By virtue of Sch.2 Pt V, para.20 and with effect from October 5, 1999, s.176(3)   **1.480**
is to be construed, in relation to tax credit, as if references to the Secretary of State were references to the Treasury or, as the case may be, the Board of the Revenue and Customs.

Short title, commencement and extent

177.—(1) This Act may be cited as the Social Security Contributions and   **1.481**
Benefits Act 1992.

(2) This Act is to be read, where appropriate, with the Administration Act and the Consequential Provisions Act.

(3) The enactments consolidated by this Act are repealed, in consequence of the consolidation, by the Consequential Provisions Act.

(4) Except as provided in Schedule 4 to the Consequential Provisions Act, this Act shall come into force on 1st July 1992.

(5) The following provisions extend to Northern Ireland—

section 16 and Schedule 2;

section 116(2); and this section.

(6) Except as provided by this section, this Act does not extend to Northern Ireland.

SCHEDULES

Schedules 1 and 2 *Omitted because the province of the Board of Inland Revenue.*

SCHEDULE 3

CONTRIBUTION CONDITIONS FOR ENTITLEMENT TO BENEFIT

PART I

THE CONDITIONS

[¹ Unemployment benefit

1.—. . .]   **1.482**

[² Short-term incapacity benefit]

2.—(1) The contribution conditions for [² short-term incapacity benefit] are the following.   **1.483**

(2) The first condition is that—

[³

  (a) the claimant must have actually paid contributions of a relevant class in respect of one of the last three complete years before the beginning of the relevant benefit year, and those contributions must have been paid before the relevant time; and]

  (b) the earnings factor derived as mentioned in sub-paragraph (4) below

must be not less than that year's lower earnings limit multiplied by 25.

(3) The second condition is that—

    (a) the claimant must in respect of the last two complete years before the beginning of the relevant benefit year have either paid or been credited with contributions of a relevant class or been credited (in the case of 1987–88 or any subsequent year) with earnings; and

    (b) the earnings factor derived as mentioned in sub-paragraph (5) below must be not less in each of those years than the year's lower earnings limit multiplied by 50.

(4) The earnings factor referred to in paragraph (b) of sub-paragraph (2) above is that which is derived—

    (a) if the year in question is 1987–88 or any subsequent year—

        (i) from [18 so much of the claimant's earnings as did not exceed the upper earnings limit and] upon which primary Class 1 contributions have been paid or treated as paid; or

        (ii) from Class 2 contributions; and

    (b) if the year in question is an earlier year, from the contributions paid as mentioned in paragraph (a) of that sub-paragraph.

(5) The earnings factor referred to in paragraph (b) of sub-paragraph (3) above is that which is derived—

    (a) if the year in question is 1987–88 or any subsequent year—

        (i) from [18 so much of the claimant's earnings as did not exceed the upper earnings limit and] upon which primary Class 1 contributions have been paid or treated as paid or from earnings credited; or

        (ii) from Class 2 contributions; and

    (b) if the year in question is an earlier year, from the contributions referred to in paragraph (a) of that sub-paragraph.

(6) For the purposes of these conditions—

    (a) "the relevant time" is the day in respect of which benefit is claimed;

    (b) "the relevant benefit year" is the benefit year in which there falls the beginning of the [4 period of incapacity for work] which includes the relevant time.

[5 (7) Where a person makes a claim for incapacity benefit and does not satisfy [6 the first contribution condition (specified in sub-paragraph (2) above) or, as the case may be,] the second contribution condition (specified in sub-paragraph (3) above) and, in a later benefit year in which he would satisfy that condition had no such claim been made, he makes a further claim for incapacity benefit, the previous claim shall be disregarded.]

[6 (8) Regulations may—

    (a) provide for the first contribution condition (specified in sub-paragraph (2) above) to be taken to be satisfied in the case of persons who have been entitled to any prescribed description of benefit during any prescribed period or at any prescribed time;

    (b) with a view to securing any relaxation of the requirements of that condition (as so specified) in relation to persons who have been so entitled, provide for that condition to apply in relation to them subject to prescribed modifications.

(9) In sub-paragraph (8)—

"benefit" includes (in addition to any benefit under Parts II to V of this Act)—

    (a) any benefit under Parts VII to XII of this Act, and

    (b) credits under regulations under section 22(5) above;

"modifications" includes additions, omissions and amendments.]

Maternity Allowance

1.484   **3.**—[7 . . .]

[8 [22 . . .]]

1.485   **4.**—[22 . . .]

Widowed mother's allowance [9, widowed parent's allowance, bereavement allowance,] and widow's pension; retirement pensions (Categories A and B)

1.486   **5.**—[21 (1) This paragraph sets out the contribution conditions for–

    (a) a widowed mother's allowance, a widowed parent's allowance or a widow's pension;

    (b) a Category A retirement pension (other than one in relation to which paragraph 5A applies);

    (c) a Category B retirement pension in the cases provided for by any of sections 48A to 51ZA.]

(2) The first condition is that—

    (a) the contributor concerned must in respect of any one relevant year have actually paid contributions of a relevant class; and

(b) the earnings factor derived—
   (i) if that year is 1987–88 or any subsequent year, from [[18] so much of the claimant's earnings as did not exceed the upper earnings limit and] upon which such
   of those contributions as are primary Class 1 contributions were paid or treated
   as paid and any Class 2 or Class 3 contributions, or
   (ii) if that year is an earlier year, from the contributions referred to in paragraph (a)
   above,
must be not less than the qualifying earnings factor of that year.

(3) The second condition is that—
   (a) the contributor concerned must, in respect of each of not less than the requisite
   number of years of his working life, have paid or been credited with contributions of
   a relevant class [[10] or been credited (in the case of 1987–88 or any subsequent year)
   with earnings]; and
   (b) in the case of each of those years, the earnings factor derived as mentioned in sub-
   paragraph (4) below must be not less than the qualifying earnings factor for that year.

(4) For the purposes of paragraph (b) of sub-paragraph (3) above, the earnings factor—
   (a) in the case of 1987–88 or any subsequent year, is that which is derived from—
   (i) [[18] so much of the claimant's earnings as did not exceed the upper earnings limit
   and] upon which such of the contributions mentioned in paragraph (a) of that
   sub-paragraph as are primary Class 1 contributions were paid or treated as paid
   or earnings credited; and
   (ii) any Class 2 or Class 3 contributions for the year; or
   (b) in the case of any earlier year, is that which is derived from the contributions
   mentioned in paragraph (a) of that sub-paragraph.

(5) For the purposes of the first condition, a relevant year is any year ending before that
in which the contributor concerned attained pensionable age or died under that age; and the
following table shows the requisite number of years for the purpose of the second condition,
by reference to a working life of a given duration—

Duration of working life	Requisite number of years
10 years or less	The number of years of the working life, minus 1.
20 years or less (but more than 10)	The number of years of the working life, minus 2.
30 years or less (but more than 20)	The number of years of the working life, minus 3.
40 years or less (but more than 30)	The number of years of the working life, minus 4.
More than 40 years	The number of years of the working life, minus 5.

(6) The first condition shall be taken to be satisfied if the contributor concerned was entitled
to [[11] long-term incapacity benefit] at any time during—
   (a) the year in which he attained pensionable age or died under that age, or
   (b) the year immediately preceding that year.

[[20] (6A) The first condition shall be taken to be satisfied if the contributor concerned was
entitled to main phase employment and support allowance at any time during–
   (a) the year in which he attained pensionable age or died under that age, or
   (b) the year immediately preceding that year.

(6B) The reference in sub-paragraph (6A) to main phase employment and support allowance is to an employment and support allowance in the case of which the calculation of the
amount payable in respect of the claimant includes an addition under section 2(1)(b) or 4(2)
(b) of the Welfare Reform Act 2007 (addition where conditions of entitlement to support
component or work-related activity component satisfied).]

(7) The second condition shall be taken to be satisfied notwithstanding that paragraphs (a)
and (b) of sub-paragraph (3) above are not complied with as respects each of the requisite
number of years if—
   (a) those paragraphs are complied with as respects at least half that number of years [[12] (or
   at least 20 of them, if that is less than half)]; and
   (b) in each of the other years the contributor concerned was, within the meaning of regulations, precluded from regular employment by responsibilities at home.

[[23] But nothing in this sub-paragraph applies in relation to any benefit to which section 23A
above applies.]

[[13] (7A) Regulations may provide that a person is not to be taken for the purposes of sub-
paragraph (7)(b) above as precluded from regular employment by responsibilities at home
unless he meets the prescribed requirements as to the provision of information to the Secretary
of State.]

(8) For the purposes of [[14]] Parts I to VI of this Act] a person's working life is the period between—

    (a) (inclusive) the tax year in which he attained the age of 16; and

    (b) (exclusive) the tax year in which he attained pensionable age or died under that age.

1.487

[[19]] 5A—(1) This paragraph applies to—

    (a) a Category A retirement pension in a case where the contributor concerned attains pensionable age on or after 6th April 2010;

[[21]] (b) a Category B retirement pension in the cases provided for by any of sections 48A to 51ZA.]

(2) The contribution condition for a Category A or Category B retirement pension in relation to which this paragraph applies is that—

    (a) the contributor concerned must, in respect of each of not less than 30 years of his working life, have paid or been credited with contributions of a relevant class or been credited (in the case of 1987–88 or any subsequent year) with earnings; and

    (b) in the case of each of those years, the earnings factor derived as mentioned in sub-paragraph (3) below must be not less than the qualifying earnings factor for that year.

(3) For the purposes of paragraph (b) of sub-paragraph (2) above, the earnings factor—

    (a) in the case of 1987–88 or any subsequent year, is that which is derived from—

        (i) so much of the contributor's earnings as did not exceed the upper earnings limit and upon which such of the contributions mentioned in paragraph (a) of that sub-paragraph as are primary Class 1 contributions were paid or treated as paid or earnings credited; and

        (ii) any Class 2 or Class 3 contributions for the year; or

    (b) in the case of any earlier year, is that which is derived from the contributions mentioned in paragraph (a) of that sub-paragraph.

(4) Regulations may modify sub-paragraphs (2) and (3) above for the purposes of their application in a case where—

    (a) the contributor concerned has paid, or been credited with, contributions, or

    (b) contributions have been deemed to be, or treated as, paid by or credited to him, under the National Insurance Act 1946 or the National Insurance Act 1965.]

Child's special allowance

1.488

6.—(1) The contribution condition for a child's special allowance is that—

    (a) the contributor concerned must in respect of any one relevant year have actually paid contributions of a relevant class; and

    (b) the earnings factor derived from those contributions must be not less than that year's lower earnings limit multiplied by 50.

(2) For the purposes of this condition, a relevant year is any year ending before the date on which the contributor concerned attained pensionable age or died under that age.

PART II

SATISFACTION OF CONDITIONS IN EARLY YEARS OF CONTRIBUTION

1.489

7.—[[22]] . . .]

8. Where a person claims [[16]] short-term incapacity benefit], he shall be taken to satisfy the first contribution condition for the benefit if on a previous claim for any short-term benefit he has satisfied the first contribution condition for that benefit, by virtue of paragraph 8 of Schedule 3 to the 1975 Act, with contributions of a class relevant to [[16]] short-term incapacity benefit].

    9. [[22]] . . .]

REPEALS AND AMENDMENTS

1. Repealed by Jobseekers Act 1995 Sch.3 para.1 (October 10, 1996).

2. Social Security (Incapacity for Work) Act 1994 s.1(2) (April 13, 1995).

3. Welfare Reform and Pensions Act 1999 s.62(2) (April 6, 2001).

4. Social Security (Incapacity for Work) Act 1994 Sch.1 para.38(2) (April 13, 1995).

5. Social Security (Incapacity for Work) Act 1994 s.3(2) (April 13, 1995).

6. Welfare Reform and Pensions Act 1999 ss.62(3), (4) (April 6, 2001).

7. Welfare Reform and Pensions Act 1999 Sch.13 Pt V (April 2, 2000).

8. Welfare Reform and Pensions Act 1999 Sch.8 Pt I, para.13(2) (April 9, 2001).

9. Welfare Reform and Pensions Act 1999 Sch.8 Pt I, para.13(3) (April 9, 2001).

10. Pensions Act 1995 s.129 (July 19, 1995).

11. Social Security (Incapacity for Work) Act 1994 Sch.1 para.38(3) (April 13, 1995).

12. These words are deleted as regards any person reaching pensionable age after April 5, 2010, by the Pensions Act 1995 Sch.4 para.4 and Sch.7 Pt II.

13. Child Support, Pensions and Social Security Act 2000 s.40 (January 8, 2001).

14. Pensions Act 1995 s.134(5) (July 19, 1995).

15. Welfare Reform and Pensions Act 1999 Sch.8 Pt I, para.13(4) (April 24, 2000).

16. Social Security (Incapacity for Work) Act 1994 Sch.1 para.38(4) (April 13, 1995).

17. Welfare Reform and Pensions Act 1999 Sch.8 Pt I, para.13(5)(b) (April 24, 2000).

18. National Insurance Contributions Act 2002 Sch.1 para.14 (April 6, 2003).

19. Pensions Act 2007 s.1 (September 26, 2007).

20. Welfare Reform Act 2007 s.40 and Sch.5 para.9(13) (October 27, 2008).

21. Pensions Act 2014 s.23 and Sch.12 paras 57 and 67 (April 6, 2016).

22. Pensions Act 2014 Sch.16 para.18 (April 6, 2017).

23. Pensions Act 2007 s.3(2) (September 26, 2007).

DERIVATIONS

SSA 1975 Sch.3.   1.490
SSPA 1975 Sch.1.

DEFINITIONS

"benefit" (in para.2(8))—see para.2(9).
"benefit"—see s.122(1).
"benefit year"—see s.21(6).
"claimant"—see s.122(1).
"contributor concerned"—see s.21(5)(a).
"earnings"—see s.122(1).
"earnings factor"—see s.21(5)(c).
"lower earnings limit"—see s.122(1).
"modifications" (in para.2(8))—see para.2(9).
"period of incapacity for work"—see s.30C(1).
"qualifying earnings factor"—see s.122(1).
"relevant benefit year"—see para.2(6)(b).
"relevant class"—see s.21(5)(a).
"relevant time"—see para.2(6)(a).
"relevant year" (in para.6)—see para.6(2).
"short-term benefit"—see ss.122(1), 20(2).
"working life"—see para.5(8).
"year"—see s.21(5)(d).

GENERAL NOTE

What the Schedule covers
  By their nature, certain "contributory benefits" require, as a precondition of   1.491
entitlement, that the claimant, or in certain cases, the claimant's husband or,
sometimes, spouse, have a valid contribution record in terms of national insurance
contributions. Pt I of this Schedule sets out the contribution conditions which must
be met for entitlement to certain "contributory benefits":

● short-term incapacity benefit (s.30A);

● bereavement payment (s.36);

- widowed mothers allowance (s.37);
- widowed parent's allowance (s.39A);
- bereavement allowance (s.39B);
- widow's pension (s.38);
- categories A and B retirement pensions (ss.43–54);
- child's special allowance (s.59).

Pt II of the Schedule, deals with the matter of satisfaction of conditions in early years of contribution in respect of bereavement payment and of short-term incapacity benefit.

Contributions matters: a division of responsibility

1.492   Since the coming into force of the SSA 1998, contribution conditions are more directly relevant to appeals tribunals and the Commissioners, although cases raising them are likely relatively to be rare. The position is also complicated because some relevant matters are ones for HM Revenue and Customs (not appealable to appeals tribunals or social security commissioners) while others are ones for the Secretary of State and are appealable to unified appeals tribunals and to the social security commissioners (now the First-tier Tribunal and the Upper Tribunal respectively).

Prior to the implementation of the decision-making and appeals changes in that Act, whether the contribution conditions were satisfied or not was a "Secretary of State's question" rather than a matter of decision for the AO. It was, accordingly, not as such appealable to an SSAT (SSAA 1992 s.17(1)(b), (2), set out with commentary in Bonner, Hooker and White, *Non Means Tested Benefits: Legislation 1999*, pp.16–19). It was thought at one time that the terms of section 17 were, however, to be narrowly construed, so that while a tribunal could not properly deal with whether the claimant should have been credited with contributions (*R(U) 6/89*), the "statutory authorities" (AO, SSAT and Commissioner) were the ones with jurisdiction over certain phrases in the contribution conditions: over establishing the date of claim ("the relevant time"), over identifying the pertinent benefit year (the one in which there falls the first day of the period of incapacity for work of which the day of claim forms part) and thus over identifying the appropriate past tax/contribution years to be considered with regard to the question (determinable by the Secretary of State and not appealable to an SSAT) of whether in the relevant tax years the requisite level of paid contributions (the first contribution condition) or paid and/or credited contributions (the second contribution condition) had been reached (see *R(G) 1/82(T)*). But the approach in *R(G) 1/82(T)* was rejected by the Court of Appeal in *Secretary of State v Scully* (reported as *R(S) 5/93*). The section (then SSA 1975 s.93) was to be read according to its "plain and natural meaning" and left it to the Secretary of State to make all determinations relevant to the contribution conditions.

After the implementation of the SSA 1998 changes, as regards all contributory benefits, whether someone satisfies the contribution conditions for the benefit is a decision of the Secretary of State and now appealable to a tribunal, and onwards to the Commissioners, as a decision on a claim or award of benefit not otherwise rendered non-appealable (SSA 1998 s.12 and Sch.2; Decisions and Appeals Regs, reg.27 and Sch.2). See further *Vol.III: Administration, Adjudication and the European Dimension*. In *R(IB) 1/09*, Commissioner Williams held that disputes about the interpretation of the Earnings factor regulations lay within the jurisdiction of the Secretary of State, rather than HMRC, and that appeal about that interpretation lay to the social security (now First-tier) tribunal. See para.7 for his summary of the proper procedure.

1.493   Some contributions matters are ones, however, for officers of HM Revenue and Customs, and appealable through a different system (Social Security Contributions

(Transfer of Functions) Act 1999 ss.8(1)(a)–(e), 11, 12). The matters in question are those of the categorisation of earners, which class of contributions a person is liable or entitled to pay, and whether they have been paid (or should be treated as having been paid: see *R(JSA) 8/02*) in respect of any period. Decisions on such matters will impact to some degree on the Secretary of State's (and thus an appeal tribunal's or a Commissioner's) decisions on whether the contribution conditions for a benefit are met. There is a special procedure for the Secretary of State or the appeal tribunal to refer relevant questions to HM Revenue and Customs (SSA 1998, ss.10A, 24A; Decisions and Appeals Regs, regs.11A, 38A). Note that under s.8(1)(m) of that Transfer of Functions Act, regulations can transfer further issues relating to contributions. So the decision-maker on particular issues could change (see further *Vol. III: Administration, Adjudication and the European Dimension*).

The administrative process on the matter of referring to HM Revenue and Customs [formerly Board of Inland Revenue] questions on whether contributions have been paid has been subjected to scathing criticism by two Commissioners. In *CIB/1602/2006*, Commissioner Williams, like Commissioner Rowland in interim decision *CIB/3327/2004*, criticised the process as set out in the DMG guidance (Vol.3, ch.3, paras 03230–03233). Reading it with the more accurate guidance in Vol.1, ch.1, he thought the guidance to be:

"internally inconsistent. Compare 01055 and 01056 with 56014. And it also guides administrators to make assumptions about contribution issues rather than decide them. See 01055 and 03231. And it does not tell the administrators to make it clear that their decisions depend on assumptions about a claimant's NI record rather than decisions about it. In my view the instruction to officials to make undisclosed assumptions about contribution issues combined with the failure to make it clear that there has been no decision on a contribution question have contributed to the systems failure to which Commissioner Rowland draws attention. In particular, there is a recurring failure to make a clear appealable decision on a question of credited earnings and a system in place that enables administrators to avoid the need to make the required decisions. This may explain why, even in this case where there was a decision, it has been assumed that there was no decision." (Para.19.)

He also considered DMG, paras 56014 and 56015 to "contain errors of law" (para.16).

In *CIB/1602/2006*, the matter in dispute was whether the claimant had sufficient credited earnings in tax/contribution year 2002–2003 to meet the second contribution condition. This turned on a much neglected area: in this case the complicated provisions of the Credits Regulations 1974 regs 3 and 8A. Commissioner Williams' decision on that is noted in the commentary to those regs, below. In *R(IB)1/09*, he set out the proper procedure for determining issues in a dispute about the application of the Social Security (Earnings Factor) Regulations 1979 to a claim for incapacity benefit:

"(a) It is for the National Insurance Contributions Office of Her Majesty's Revenue and Customs to decide any question about the contribution record of a claimant for incapacity benefit.

(b) Any challenge to that decision on either an issue of fact or a question of law goes to a tax tribunal, not a social security tribunal. If an appeal involving a question about a claimant's contributions comes before a social security tribunal, then the social security tribunal must apply regulation 38A of the Social Security and Child Support (Decisions and Appeals) Regulations 1999. This requires it to adjourn the appeal and refer the matter to the Secretary of State for onward reference to Her Majesty's Revenue and Customs for decision. The tribunal may decide the appeal only after a decision has been received from Her Majesty's Revenue and Customs.

(c) It is for the Secretary of State for Work and Pensions to decide any question about the interpretation and application of the Social Security (Earnings Factor) Regulations 1979 to the individual contribution record of any claimant for incapacity benefit.

(d) If a claimant disputes the decision of the Secretary of State on any issue of fact or law arising under the 1979 Regulations, then that dispute is to be decided by a social security tribunal. This includes any dispute about calculating the earnings factor attributable to a claimant under those regulations. If necessary, it is the task of the tribunal itself to check any disputed calculations" (para.7).

1.494   For further consideration of some of the difficulties arising where records have been destroyed as part of normal administrative processes and for the text of the regulations on unemployment credits covering 1977-89, see Commissioner Williams' decision in *CP/1792/2007*.

Commissioner Rowland's interim decision in *CIB/3327/2004* delineated the effect on a claimant's claim and appeals of the confusion generated by changes in jurisdiction on contributions matters (paras 2–4) and on the matter of awarding credits for spells of unemployment, a situation in which she was passed from pillar to post, a process during which Commissioner Rowland considered that there had been no actual decision on the award of credits for those spells, but only on non-entitlement to JSA (paras 19–21). This resulted in part from the changes on decision-making, appeals and jurisdictions wrought by the 1998 and 1999 legislation. But Commissioner Rowland rightly drew to attention for remedial action "some more fundamental flaws in the way in which the Department functions" in respect of these matters. Essentially, the key flaw was that no system had been put in place for informing the claimant that credits for unemployment had not been awarded. In the Commissioner's view, what was needed, "above all" was the establishment of:

"a system . . . to ensure that challenges to refusals of credits result in formal decisions that comply with regulation 28 of the [Decisions and Appeals Regs] and inform the contributor of his or her right of appeal. That is so whether credits decisions are to be made during the relevant contribution year or after it has ended" (para.29).

Commissioner Williams considered in *CIB/1602/2006* that he had to reiterate that call for action:

"That decision was made a year ago. It was an interim decision. I understand that as a result of later proceedings in the appeal the matter has now ceased to be an active appeal and that therefore the Commissioner will not be issuing a final decision. I have also seen no offcial response to that decision beyond the specific case. I therefore consider that I should adopt and repeat some of that analysis as it applies to this case in order to make clear why I entirely agree with him that the existing situation does not accord with the law. I depart from the approach of Commissioner Rowland in taking the view that in this case there is an appealable decision. But his criticisms of the lack of system are clearly part of the explanation for the confusion on the part of the secretary of state's representatives and the tribunal in this case" (para.14).

To that, this commentator can only add his support. This is a crucial area for contribution-based benefits and claimants and tribunals are entitled to expect at least as much decision-making clarity here as elsewhere in the benefits system. So far it is conspicuously lacking.

1.495   Some problems, of course, have arisen because of the mismatch in data on credits in the respective departments' computer and recording systems: the DWP's Pension Service Computer System (PSCS) and the National Insurance

Recording System (NIRS 2) system. Work is in hand to reconcile the latter with the former. It appears that up to 30,000 people may have been underpaid and about 90,000 may have been overpaid as a result of incorrect records. Overpayments are dealt with in amendments to the Credits Regulations 1975. Underpayments are to be made good by administrative action. See further the Explanatory Memorandum to the amending regulations (SI 2007/2582) at *http:// www.opsi.gov.uk/si/si200725.htm.*

Whether a person's contributions record should be *credited* with contributions/ earnings remains, however, one for the Secretary of State and is now appealable to an appeal tribunal (SSA 1998 Sch.3, para.17; *CIB/2338/00, CG2309/2002, CIB/2161/2000*). So does the question whether a person was (within the meaning of regulations) precluded from regular employment by responsibilities at home (SSA 1998 Sch.3, para.16). On when contributions may be credited, see s.22, above, and the Social Security (Credits) Regulations 1975, below. On entitlement to home responsibilities protection, see para.5(7) of this Schedule and the Social Security Pensions (Home Responsibilities) Regulations 1994.

On difficulties arising where the periods to be considered predate the abolition of sickness benefit and unemployment benefit and the re-allocation of functions and jurisdictions, see the decision of Commissioner Williams in *CIB/3734/2002*. On the complexities split jurisdiction can produce in pensions' entitlement cases, see his decision in *CP/4205/2006*.

With that division of responsibilities in mind, it is useful to give a brief outline of the contributory system as regards payments and credits, the better to understand the contributions conditions for entitlement to a contributory benefit.

An outline of the contributory system: payments, credits and the earnings factor (the amount added to the contribution record)

The contributory system embraces distinct classes of contribution: Class 1 (primary and secondary), Class 1A, Class 1B, Class 2, Class 3, Class 3A and Class 4. This last category—a levy on the profits of the self-employed—is irrelevant in respect of title to benefit. So are secondary Class 1 contributions and Class 1A and 1B contributions.   **1.496**

Class 1 contributions—capable of establishing entitlement to all the contributory   **1.497**
benefits listed in s.21(2) and to bereavement support payment—are paid by employed earners (see s.2(1)(a)), that is by persons employed under a contract of service (employees) and by certain office holders (e.g. constables, MPs). They are earnings-related, and are paid on weekly/ monthly earnings between a lower and an upper earnings limit. Those limits change for each tax (contribution) year. Where earnings fall below the relevant lower limit for the tax (contribution) year, there is no liability or ability to pay— for the period in question the contribution record will be blank in terms of Class 1. Primary Class 1 contributions are also the only class of contribution relevant for title to contribution-based jobseeker's allowance (see Jobseekers Act 1995 s.2 and commentary in *Vol.II: Income Support, Jobseeker's Allowance, State Pension Credit and the Social Fund*). Secondary Class 1 contributions and Class IA or 1B contributions are paid by the primary contributor's employer and are not relevant to title to benefit.

Basically, each primary Class 1 contribution paid generates an earnings factor, that is puts into the person's contribution record for the year an amount equivalent to the weekly/monthly earnings (but only up to the relevant upper earnings limit for that year) in respect of which it is paid. So in each week in tax (contribution) year 1999/2000, a weekly paid person earning £300 per week would each week have that amount added to his record.

Class 2 contributions—also capable of establishing entitlement to all the contribu-   **1.498**
tory benefits listed in s.21(2) and bereavement support payment—are paid by self-employed earners (see s.2(1)(b)), basically those employed under a contract for

services. A Class 2 contribution generates an *earnings factor*, that is puts into the person's contribution record for the year a weekly amount equivalent to the lower earnings limit for that year for Class 1 contributions' liability. Even where a person is not liable to pay them, s/he can pay voluntarily so as to maintain their contribution record.

1.499   *Class 3 contributions* cannot generate title to incapacity benefit, but can in respect of the other contributory benefits listed in s.21(2): bereavement payment; widowed mother's allowance, widowed parent's allowance, bereavement allowance, widow's pension, category A and B retirement pensions. There is no liability, only an ability, to pay—they are always voluntary, paid to remedy deficiencies in the contribution record for particular years. Each Class 3 contribution paid generates an earnings factor, that is puts into the person's contribution record for the year a weekly amount equivalent to the lower earnings limit for that year for Class 1 contributions' liability.

Certain married women and widows could before April 5, 1977 elect to pay Class 1 contributions at a *reduced rate*, or not to pay a Class 2 contribution. Non-payment of the latter means no earnings factor, no amount added to the contribution record. Payment of Class 1 at the reduced rate generates no earnings factor, produces no amount to add to the contribution record (see s.22(4)).

The scheme recognises that in certain situations, for socially valid reasons someone may not be able to pay contributions, and protects that person's contribution record by crediting a certain amount to the person's contribution account (see s.22(5), Social Security (Credits) Regulations 1975). The weekly amount generated (the earnings factor) is one equivalent to the lower earnings limit for purposes of Class 1 contributions' liability. Where someone is precluded from working because of responsibilities at home, the scheme gives protection by a different route; it provides a degree of home responsibilities protection for the contribution record by, in certain circumstances, treating the second contribution condition (the one that can be satisfied by paid and/ or credited contributions) as fulfilled in any year in which the person "was, within the meaning of regulations, precluded from regular employment by responsibilities at home" (Sch.3, para.5(7); Social Security Pensions (Home Responsibilities) Regulations 1994). This applies only in respect of bereavement payment (s.36); widowed mothers allowance (s.37); widowed parent's allowance (s.39A); bereavement allowance (s.39B); widow's pension (s.38); and categories A and B retirement pensions (ss. 43–54).

1.500   *Class 3A contributions:* Between October 2015 and April 5, 2017, it was possible for people with entitlement to a State Pension, and who had reached their state pension age before April 6, 2016, to pay voluntary Class 3A contributions to purchase additional State Pension.

With that outline in mind, the particular contribution conditions for each of the benefits listed in s.21 can now be examined in more detail.

PART I

THE CONDITIONS

Paragraph 2 read with s.30A(2)(a): short-term incapacity benefit for claimants under pensionable age

1.501   Unless he is a person incapacitated in youth (before 20 or sometimes 25) (see s.30A(1)(b), (2A)) a claimant must fulfil the requirements of this paragraph. There are two contribution conditions. The first can be met only by *paid* contributions of the relevant class (primary Class 1 or Class 2) reaching the requisite level in a tax year. The second can be satisfied by *paid and/or credited* contributions in a tax year.

This aspect of title to short-term incapacity benefit has been rendered more complex in that the first condition was altered substantially from April 6, 2001 to require for those under pensionable age a more recent connection with the world of work in terms of paid contributions than had previously been the case, whether with incapacity benefit or its predecessors, sickness and invalidity benefits. However, the rigour of the new rule is relaxed in certain situations (para.2(8), (9), IB Regulations, Pt IA, reg.2B) and by the fact that the change is not retrospective so that those whose continuing period of incapacity began before April 6, 2001 remain subject to the previous contribution condition first until that period of incapacity ends.

In order to appreciate the requirements of para.2, and the terms and operation of the contribution conditions, take first, as an illustrative example, the position of someone claiming incapacity benefit for the very first time in May 2001 (that is, with no link back to any previous period of incapacity for work) and never having claimed or received any other benefit. He must meet *both of the two contribution conditions* set out in para.2. The first step is to identify the relevant benefit year, the one which includes the first day of the period of incapacity of which his claim is part (para.2(6)). This identification of the relevant benefit year is the real substantive matter for the Secretary of State or the appeal tribunal to focus on, since that determines the tax/ contribution years in which the requisite record must be fulfilled. His first day of claim—the relevant time (para.2(6))—in May 2001 falls in benefit year 2001–2002 (the relevant benefit year: see s.21(6)). "Year", standing alone, means tax/contribution year (s.21(5)(d). The tax/contribution years in *one of which* the first contribution condition (sub-para.(2)) must be fulfilled are the last three tax/contribution years (April 6–April 5) complete before the start of the relevant benefit year (early January 2001). The tax/contribution years to which to have regard are thus 1999/2000, 1998/1999, and 1997/1998. The contribution record in tax/ contribution year 2000/2001 cannot be taken into account because it was not complete at the start of the relevant benefit year (early January 2001). The first contribution condition (sub-para.(2)) can only be met with paid contributions of the relevant class—Class 1 (employed earners) or Class 2 (self-employed earners)—reaching the requisite level (an earnings factor of 25 times the lower earnings limit (LEL) for Class 1 contributions purposes for the tax year in question — remember that each Class 2 contribution generates an earnings factor equal to the LEL pertinent to the tax/contribution year in question, while the amount of earnings on which Class 1 contributions are paid generates the earnings factor for an employed earner claimant. See further, s.21, and the "outline of the contributory system" earlier in this annotation.

The second contribution condition (sub-para.(3)) requires examination of the last two tax years complete before the start of the relevant benefit year (early January 2001), that is 1999/2000 and 1998/1999. The claimant's contribution record in each of those tax/contribution years must attain 50 times the lower earnings limit for the year. But the condition can be met through paid and/or credited contributions (a Class 1 credit can be received, for example, for each week of unemployment; see further Social Security (Credits) Regulations 1975). On difficulties arising where the periods to be considered predate the abolition of sickness benefit and unemployment benefit and the re-allocation of functions and jurisdictions, see the decision of Commissioner Williams in *CIB/3734/2002*.

1.502

From May 5, 2003, the definition of "relevant benefit year" is different in the case of someone discharged from Her Majesty's forces and in respect of whom days of sickness absence from duty recorded by the Secretary of State for Defence are, under s.30D, included in calculating the number of days for which he has been entitled to short-term incapacity benefit. In such a case, the "relevant benefit year" is that in which there falls the beginning of the period to which the claim for incapacity benefit relates. See reg.4 of the Social Security Contributions and Benefits Act 1992 (Modifications for Her Majesty's Forces and Incapacity Benefit) Regulations 2003, below. See also annotations to s.30A(3) and s.30D.

Note that sub-para.(8) enables regulations to relax the rules set out above which apply to all claims in a period of incapacity for work commencing on or after April 6, 2001. So a claim in principle subject to these rules, is not just the first ever claim for incapacity benefit as used in the illustrative example, above. A "new" claim subject to those rules, could, for instance, just as well come from someone on incapacity benefit during 2000 whose "period of incapacity" came to an end in December 2000. If such a person claims again in, say, August 2001, he would, in principle, be subject to those rules, because his two spells of incapacity do not "link" to form one under the "linking rule" in s.30C. Note that the relaxation afforded applies not just to benefits under Pts II–V and VII–XII of the SSCBA 1992 but also to contributions credits (sub-paras(8), (9)). The "relaxation" rules are contained in IB Regulations, Pt 1A, reg.2B, and are annotated there.

Various groups will have difficulty meeting these contribution conditions:

(a) *those who have never been employed*: The requirement in the first contribution condition for payment of contributions effectively excludes those who, whether through unemployment, incapacity or disability, have been unable to build a contribution record in terms of paid contributions.

(b) *some of the long-term unemployed* (last employed in a tax year earlier than the first of the three on which the first contribution condition focuses).

(c) *very low-paid, probably part-time, employees*: those whose weekly or monthly earnings fall below the lower earnings limit for the whole or main part of the relevant tax years will not satisfy the contribution conditions since there is no liability or ability to pay Class 1 contributions where earnings fall below that limit, and, because they are in work, no Class 1 credits are generated from unemployment.

(d) *certain married women and widows paying reduced rate contributions*: these do not generate any earnings factor (and so do not count) for incapacity benefit purposes (s.22(4)).

Severe Disablement Allowance (SDA) was introduced in 1984 to cater for those who were incapacitated below the age of 20, or, if incapacitated later, were also assessed as 80 per cent disabled (see ss.68, 69). SDA was abolished on April 2, 2001 for new claims. Of course, some of the above, if incapacitated in youth (before 20 or sometimes 25) (s.30A(1)(b), (2A); IB Regulations, Pt IV, regs14–19), will be able to take advantage of the intended counter-balancing measure for those more likely than others to have been unable to build up a contribution record—the non-contributory route into incapacity benefit (see commentary to subs.(2A)). Those incapacitated, even through severe disability, later in life, will have to look to income support, with all its disability premiums, to underwrite their incapacity for work. While they may well be eligible for various components of disability living allowance, that is a benefit designed to provide for the extra costs that disability, as opposed to incapacity for work, brings with it. The transitional provisions protect existing recipients and those whose period of incapacity (without receipt of SDA) spans April 6, 2001. See further the prefatory commentary to ss.68 and 69, preserved in force for those individuals.

Paragraph 3: maternity allowance

1.503   There are now no contribution conditions in respect of maternity allowance. See s.35.

Paragraph 5: widowed mother's allowance, widowed parent's allowance, bereavement allowance, widow's pension, category A and B retirement pensions

1.504   These long-term benefits (where available) all require satisfaction of the same contribution conditions. Like the short-term benefits there are two conditions to be satisfied. The first requires actual payment of contributions; the second may be satisfied by payments or by credits.

The person whose contribution record is to be tested will depend upon the benefit claimed. For a Category A Retirement Pension it will be the claimant's own record. For a Category B Retirement Pension it will be the record of the claimant's spouse. For a Widowed Parent's Allowance and a Bereavement Allowance it is the late spouse's contribution record; and for a Widowed Mother's Allowance or Widow's Pension her late husband's record. (For the various widow's and bereavement benefits the condition may also be satisfied if the contributor has died as a result of an industrial injury or disease.)

The first condition for these benefits requires that the contributor has actually paid contributions (either Class 1, Class 2 or Class 3) in any one year to produce an earnings factor of at least 52 times the lower earnings limit for that year (the "qualifying earnings factor": see s.122(1)). The year can be any year that ends before the year in which that person retires or dies. The condition is also deemed to be satisfied if that person was in receipt of long-term incapacity benefit in the year in which they reached retirement age or died, or if they were in receipt of that benefit in the preceding year. Before 1975, Class 1 contributions were paid as a flat rate "stamp" each week. This condition will also be satisfied by 50 flat rate contributions in any year.

The second condition must be fulfilled in each of what may be a much longer period of years. The requisite period is defined by reference to the length of the person's working life (the years between that in which they reach the age of 16 and the last complete tax year before they reach retirement age or die under that age), but subject to a reduction in the total number of years according to the scale that appears in App.3, para.5, sub-para.5 above. Once the "requisite number of years" has been defined the contributor must be shown to have paid, or been credited with, payments that produce an earnings factor equal to at least 52 times the lower earnings limit for each of those years. (For years before 1975 the number of satisfied years is calculated by counting all the weekly payments made over those years and dividing by 50. The answer is rounded up to the next whole number.)

1.505

The requisite number of years may also be reduced by years of home responsibility as explained above. Such years are deducted from the working life and may reduce the requisite number of years to 20 or to half of what they would otherwise have been, whichever is the lower.

Where the second condition is satisfied the long-term benefits will be paid at their full rate. Where the condition is only partially satisfied, benefit will be paid at a percentage of that rate corresponding to the percentage of satisfied years, so long as at least 25 per cent of those years are so satisfied.

Paragraph 5A: Category A retirement pensions where the contributor attains pensionable age on or after April 6, 2010 and certain Category B retirement pensions

For people reaching state pension age (a term interchangeable with 'pensionable age') from April 6, 2010, the previous contribution conditions for Category A and B pensions were replaced with a single contribution condition. The same condition applies to the spouse or civil partner of a claimant of a Category B pension (within sections 48A to 51ZA) where the spouse or civil partner reaches state pension age on or after April 6, 2010 (or dies on or after that date without having reached that age).

1.506

For those reaching state pension age from April 6, 2010, the number of years needed to qualify for a full Category A or B pension was reduced from 44 years for a man and 39 years for a woman to 30 qualifying years for men and women alike. A person who has less than 30 qualifying years is entitled to a proportion of the full basic state pension for each qualifying year they have built up.

The position must however now be considered in the light of the changes made by the Pensions Act 2014.

Paragraph 6: child's special allowance

This has only one contribution condition (sub-para(1)), satisfiable only by contributions of the relevant class—(Class 1, 2 or 3, separately or combined (s.21(2))—paid by the contributor concerned in respect of any one relevant tax (contribution) year to a level not less than 50 times that year's lower earnings limit. A "relevant year" is any one ending before the date on which the contributor concerned attained

1.507

pensionable age or died under that age (sub-para.(2)). The claimant for child's special allowance is a woman whose marriage has been terminated by divorce, and the "contributor concerned" is the deceased husband of that marriage who was contributing to the cost of providing for the child or from whom she was entitled to receive, under a court order, a trust or agreement, maintenance for the child (s.56).

PART II

SATISFACTION OF CONDITIONS IN EARLY YEARS OF CONTRIBUTION

Paragraph 8
1.508   This applies only to short-term incapacity benefit, and seems to protect previous recipients of the contributory maternity allowance. It enables a claimant for short-term incapacity benefit to be treated as satisfying its first contribution condition (see para. 2(2)) if on a previous claim for any short-term benefit (defined in s.20(2) to cover short-term incapacity benefit and maternity allowance) he satisfied the first contribution condition for that shortterm benefit by virtue of SSA 1975, Sched. 3, para. 8, with contributions of the class relevant to short-term incapacity benefit (Class 1 or 2 and their predecessors). Paragraph 8 in the 1975 Act dealt with aggregation of contributions as regards early years of contribution in a similar way to para. 7 of this Schedule and bereavement payment.

SCHEDULE 4

RATES OF BENEFIT ETC.

[¹PART I

CONTRIBUTORY PERIODICAL BENEFITS

1.509

Description of benefit	*Weekly rate*	
2. Short-term incapacity benefit.	(a) lower rate	£84.65
	(b) higher rate	£100.20
2A. Long-term incapacity benefit.		£112.25
5. Category B retirement pension where [³ section 48A(4) or 48AA(4)] applies.		£77.45

PART II

BEREAVEMENT PAYMENT

1.510   [⁵. . .]

PART III

NON-CONTRIBUTORY PERIODICAL BENEFITS

1.511

Description of benefit	*Weekly rate*	
1. Attendance allowance.	(a) higher rate	£87.65
	(b) lower rate	£58.70

Description of benefit	Weekly rate	
	(the appropriate rate being determined in accordance with section 65(3)).	
2. Severe disablement allowance.		£79.50
3. Age related addition.	(a) higher rate	£11.90
	(b) middle rate	£6.60
	(c) lower rate	£6.60
	(the appropriate rate being determined in accordance with section 69(1)).	
4. Carer's allowance.		£66.15
5. Guardian's allowance.		[²£17.60]
6. [⁴ . . .]	[⁴ . . .]	[⁴ . . .]
7. Category D retirement pension.	[⁴ the amount specified in paragraph 6 as the higher rate for a Category C retirement pension immediately before 6 April 2016].	£77.45
8. Age addition (to a pension of any category, and otherwise under section 79).		£0.25.

PART IV

INCREASES FOR DEPENDANTS

Benefit to which increase applies (1)	Increase for qualifying child (2)	Increase for adult dependant (3)
	£	£
1A. Short-term incapacity benefit—		
(a) where the beneficiary is under pensionable age;	11.35	50.80
(b) where the beneficiary is over pensionable age.	11.35	62.75
2. Long-term incapacity benefit.	11.35	65.20

1.512

Benefit to which increase applies (1)		Increase for qualifying child (2)	Increase for adult dependant (3)
4.	Widowed mother's allowance.	11.35	—
4A.	Widowed parent's allowance.	11.35	—
5.	Category A or B retirement pension.	11.35	70.00
6.	Category C retirement pension.	11.35	41.90
8.	Severe disablement allowance.	11.35	39.10
9.	Carer's allowance.	11.35	38.90

1.513

PART V

RATES OF INDUSTRIAL INJURIES BENEFIT

1.514

Description of benefit, *etc.*		Rate
1.	Disablement pension (weekly rates).	For the several degrees of disablement set out in column (1) of the following Table, the respective amounts in column (2) of that Table.

TABLE

Degree of Disablement	Amount
(1)	(2)
Per cent.	£
100	179.00
90	161.10
80	143.20
70	125.30
60	107.40
50	89.50
40	71.60
30	53.70
20	35.80

2.	Maximum increase of weekly rate of disablement pension where constant attendance needed.	(a)	except in cases of exceptionally severe disablement	£71.60;
		(b)	in any case	£143.20

264

Description of benefit, *etc.*	Rate		
3. Increase of weekly rate of disablement pension (exceptionally severe disablement).			£71.60.
4. Maximum of aggregate of weekly benefit payable for successive accidents.			£179.00
5. Unemployability supplement under paragraph 2 of Schedule 7.			£110.65
6. Increase under paragraph 3 of Schedule 7 of weekly rate of unemployability supplement.	(a)	if on the qualifying date the beneficiary was under the age of 35 or if that date fell before 5th July 1948	£22.90;
	(b)	if head (a) above does not apply and on the qualifying date the beneficiary was under the age of 40 and he had not attained pensionable age before 6th April 1979	£22.90;
	(c)	if heads (a) and (b) above do not apply and on the qualifying date the beneficiary was under the age of 45	£14.70
	(d)	if heads (a), (b) and (c) above do not apply and on the qualifying date the beneficiary was under the age of 50 and had not attained pensionable age before 6th April 1979	£14.70
	(e)	in any other case	£7.35
7. Increase under paragraph 4 of Schedule 7 of weekly rate of disablement pension.			£11.35.
8. Increase under paragraph 6 of Schedule 7 of weekly rate of disablement pension.			£66.15
9. Maximum disablement gratuity under paragraph 9 of Schedule 7.			£11,880.00

Description of benefit, *etc.*	Rate		
10. Widow's pension (weekly rates).			
	(b)	higher permanent rate	£129.20
	(c)	lower permanent rate 30 per cent of the first sum specified in section 44(4) (Category A basic retirement pension) (the appropriate rate being determined in accordance with paragraph 16 of Schedule 7)	
11. Widower's pension (weekly rate).			£129.20
12. Weekly rate of allowance in respect of children and qualifying young persons under paragraph 18 of Schedule 7.	In respect of each child or qualifying young person		£11.35.

AMENDMENTS

1. The whole Schedule was substituted by the Social Security Benefits Up-rating Order 2019 (SI 2019/480) art.3 and Sch.1 to take effect on April 8, 2019.

2. The amount in para.5 of Pt III was amended by the Tax Credits and Guardians Allowance Up-rating Regulations 2019 (SI 2019/252) reg.4 (April 8, 2019). But where a question arises as to the entitlement to Guardian's Allowance by virtue of the Up-rating Regulations, or whether conditions for the receipt of benefit at that rate are satisfied, the altered rates will not apply until the question has been decided by HM Revenue and Customs, or the First-tier or Upper Tribunal (see the Guardian's Allowance Up-rating Regulations 2019 (SI 2019/525) reg.2 (April 8, 2019)).

3. Pensions Act 2014 s.23 and Sch.12 paras 57 and 68 (April 6, 2016).

4. Pensions Act 2014 s.23 and Sch.12 paras 78 and 81 (April 6, 2016).

6. Pensions Act 2014 Sch.16 para.19 (April 6, 2017).

[1 SCHEDULE 4A

[2 ADDITIONAL PENSION ACCRUAL RATES FOR PURPOSES OF SECTION 45 (2)(C)]

PART I

THE AMOUNT

1.516   1.—(1) The amount referred to in section 45(2)(c) above is to be calculated as follows—
(a) take for each tax year concerned the amount for the year which is found under the following provisions of this Schedule;
(b) add the amounts together;
(c) divide the sum of the amounts by the number of relevant years;
(d) the resulting amount is the amount referred to in section 45(2)(c) above, except that if the resulting amount is a negative one the amount so referred to is nil.

(2) For the purpose of applying sub-paragraph (1) above in the determination of the rate of any additional pension by virtue of section [² . . .], 39C(1)[⁵. . .] or 48B(2) above, in a case where the deceased spouse died under pensionable age, [³ or by virtue of section 39C(1) [⁵ ...] or 48B(2) above, in a case where the deceased civil partner died under pensionable age,] the divisor used for the purposes of sub-paragraph (1)(c) above shall be whichever is the smaller of the alternative numbers referred to below (instead of the number of relevant years).

(3) The first alternative number is the number of tax years which begin after 5th April 1978 and end before the date when the entitlement to the additional pension commences.

(4) The second alternative number is the number of tax years in the period—
   (a) beginning with the tax year in which the deceased spouse [³ or civil partner] attained the age of 16 or, if later, 1978–79; and
   (b) ending immediately before the tax year in which the deceased spouse [³ or civil partner] would have attained pensionable age if he had not died earlier.

(5) For the purpose of applying sub-paragraph (1) above in the determination of the rate of any additional pension by virtue of section 48BB(5) above, in a case where the deceased spouse [³ or civil partner] died under pensionable age, the divisor used for the purposes of sub-paragraph (1)(c) above shall be whichever is the smaller of the alternative numbers referred to below (instead of the number of relevant years).

(6) The first alternative number is the number of tax years which begin after 5th April 1978 and end before the date when the deceased spouse [³ or civil partner] dies.

(7) The second alternative number is the number of tax years in the period—
   (a) beginning with the tax year in which the deceased spouse [³ or civil partner] attained the age of 16 or, if later, 1978–79; and
   (b) ending immediately before the tax year in which the deceased spouse [³ or civil partner] would have attained pensionable age if he had not died earlier.

(8) In this paragraph "relevant year" has the same meaning as in section 44 above.

PART II

SURPLUS EARNINGS FACTOR

2.—(1) This Part of this Schedule applies if for the tax year concerned there is a surplus in the pensioner's earnings factor. **1.517**

(2) The amount for the year is to be found as follows—
   (a) calculate the part of the surplus for that year falling into each of the bands specified in the appropriate table below;
   (b) multiply the amount of each such part in accordance with the last order under section 148 of the Administration Act to come into force before the end of the final relevant year;
   (c) multiply each amount found under paragraph (b) above by the percentage specified in the appropriate table in relation to the appropriate band;
   (d) add together the amounts calculated under paragraph (c) above

(3) The appropriate table for persons attaining pensionable age after the end of the first appointed year but before 6th April 2009 is as follows—

TABLE 1 **1.518**

Amount of surplus	Percentage
Band 1. Not exceeding LET	40 + 2N
Band 2. Exceeding LET but not exceeding 3LET–2QEF	10 + N/2
Band 3. Exceeding 3LET–2QEF	20 + N

(4) The appropriate table for persons attaining pensionable age on or after April 6th 2009 [² where the tax year concerned falls before 2010–11] is as follows—

TABLE 2 **1.519**

Amount of surplus	Percentage
Band 1. Not exceeding LET	40
Band 2. Exceeding LET but not exceeding 3LET–2QEF	10
Band 3. Exceeding 3LET–2QEF	20

[² (4A) The appropriate table for persons attaining pensionable age on or after 6th April 2009 where the tax year concerned is 2010–11 or a subsequent tax year is as follows—

1.520 **TABLE 2A**

Amount of surplus	Percentage
Band 1. Not exceeding LET	40
Band 2. Exceeding LET [⁴ . . .]	10]

(5) Regulations may provide, in relation to persons attaining pensionable age after such date as may be prescribed, that the amount found under this Part of this Schedule for the second appointed year or any subsequent tax year is to be calculated using only so much of the surplus in the pensioner's earnings factor for that year as falls into Band 1 in the table in sub-paragraph (4) above.

(6) For the purposes of the tables in this paragraph—

    (a) the value of N is 0.5 for each tax year by which the tax year in which the pensioner attained pensionable age precedes 2009–10;

    (b) "LET" means the low earnings threshold for that year as specified in section 44A above;

    (c) "QEF" means the qualifying earnings factor for the tax year concerned.

[² [⁴ . . .]]

(7) In the calculation of "2QEF" the amount produced by doubling QEF shall be rounded to the nearest whole £100 (taking any amount of £50 as nearest to the previous whole £100).

(8) In this paragraph "final relevant year" has the same meaning as in section 44 above.

PART III

Contracted-Out Employment

Introduction

1.521 **3.**—(1) This Part of this Schedule applies if the following condition is satisfied in relation to each tax week in the tax year concerned.

(2) The condition is that any earnings paid to or for the benefit of the pensioner in the tax week in respect of employment were in respect of employment qualifying him for a pension provided by a salary related contracted-out scheme or by a money purchase contracted-out scheme or by an appropriate personal pension scheme.

(3) If the condition is satisfied in relation to one or more tax weeks in the tax year concerned, Part II of this Schedule does not apply in relation to the year.

The amount

1.522 **4.**—The amount for the year is amount C where—

    (a) amount C is equal to amount A minus amount B, and

    (b) amounts A and B are calculated as follows.

Amount A

1.523 **5.**—(1) Amount A is to be calculated as follows.

(2) If there is an assumed surplus in the pensioner's earnings factor for the year—

    (a) calculate the part of the surplus for that year falling into each of the bands specified in the appropriate table below;

    (b) multiply the amount of each such part in accordance with the last order under section 148 of the Administration Act to come into force before the end of the final relevant year;

    (c) multiply each amount found under paragraph (b) above by the percentage specified in the appropriate table in relation to the appropriate band;

    (d) add together the amounts calculated under paragraph (c) above

(3) The appropriate table for persons attaining pensionable age after the end of the first appointed year but before 6th April 2009 is as follows—

1.524 **TABLE 3**

Amount of surplus	Percentage
Band 1. Not exceeding LET	40 + 2N
Band 2. Exceeding LET but not exceeding 3LET–2QEF	10 + N/2
Band 3. Exceeding 3LET–2QEF	20 + N

(4) The appropriate table for persons attaining pensionable age on or after 6th April 2009 [² where the tax year concerned falls before 2010–11] is as follows—

TABLE 4   1.525

Amount of surplus	*Percentage*
Band 1. Not exceeding LET	40
Band 2. Exceeding LET but not exceeding 3LET–2QEF	10
Band 3. Exceeding 3LET–2QEF	20

[² (4A) The appropriate table for persons attaining pensionable age on or after 6th April 2009 where the tax year concerned is 2010–11 or a subsequent tax year is as follows—

TABLE 4A   1.526

Amount of surplus	*Percentage*
Band 1. Not exceeding LET	40
Band 2. Exceeding LET [⁴ . . .]	10]

Amount B (first case)

6.—(1) Amount B is to be calculated in accordance with this paragraph if the pensioner's   1.527
employment was entirely employment qualifying him for a pension provided by a salary related contracted-out scheme or by a money purchase contracted-out scheme.

(2) If there is an assumed surplus in the pensioner's earnings factor for the year—
  (a) multiply the amount of the assumed surplus in accordance with the last order under section 148 of the Administration Act to come into force before the end of the final relevant year;
  (b) multiply the amount found under paragraph (a) above by the percentage specified in sub-paragraph (3) below.

(3) The percentage is—
  (a) 20 + N if the person attained pensionable age after the end of the first appointed year but before 6th April 2009;
  (b) 20 if the person attained pensionable age on or after 6th April 2009.

Amount B (second case)

7.—(1) Amount B is to be calculated in accordance with this paragraph if the pensioner's   1.528
employment was entirely employment qualifying him for a pension provided by an appropriate personal pension scheme.

(2) If there is an assumed surplus in the pensioner's earnings factor for the year—
  (a) calculate the part of the surplus for that year falling into each of the bands specified in the appropriate table below;
  (b) multiply the amount of each such part in accordance with the last order under section 148 of the Administration Act to come into force before the end of the final relevant year;
  (c) multiply each amount found under paragraph (b) above by the percentage specified in the appropriate table in relation to the appropriate band;
  (d) add together the amounts calculated under paragraph (c) above.

(3) The appropriate table for persons attaining pensionable age after the end of the first appointed year but before April 6th 2009 is as follows—

TABLE 5   1.529

Amount of surplus	*Percentage*
Band 1. Not exceeding LET	40 + 2N
Band 2. Exceeding LET but not exceeding 3LET–2QEF	10 + N/2
Band 3. Exceeding 3LET–2QEF	20 + N

(4) The appropriate table for persons attaining pensionable age on or after April 6th 2009 [² where the tax year concerned falls before 2010–11] is as follows—

TABLE 6   1.530

Amount of surplus	*Percentage*
Band 1. Not exceeding LET	40
Band 2. Exceeding LET but not exceeding 3LET–2QEF	10
Band 3. Exceeding 3LET–2QEF	20

[² (4A) The appropriate table for persons attaining pensionable age on or after 6th April 2009 where the tax year concerned is 2010–11 or a subsequent tax year is as follows—

1.531   **TABLE 6A**

Amount of surplus	Percentage
Band 1. Not exceeding LET	40
Band 2. Exceeding LET [⁴ . . .]	10.]

Interpretation

1.532   8.—(1) In this Part of this Schedule "salary related contracted-out scheme", "money purchase contracted-out scheme" and "appropriate personal pension scheme" have the same meanings as in the Pension Schemes Act 1993.

(2) For the purposes of this Part of this Schedule the assumed surplus in the pensioner's earnings factor for the year is the surplus there would be in that factor for the year if section 48A(1) of the Pension Schemes Act 1993 (no primary Class 1 contributions deemed to be paid) did not apply in relation to any tax week falling in the year.

(3) Section 44A above shall be ignored in applying 44(6) above for the purpose of calculating amount B.

(4) For the purposes of this Part of this Schedule—

    (a) the value of N is 0.5 for each tax year by which the tax year in which the pensioner attained pensionable age precedes 2009–10;

    (b) "LET" means the low earnings threshold for that year as specified in section 44A above;

    (c) "QEF" is the qualifying earnings factor for the tax year concerned.

[² [⁴ . . .]]

(5) In the calculation of "2QEF" the amount produced by doubling QEF shall be rounded to the nearest whole £100 (taking any amount of £50 as nearest to the previous whole £100).

(6) In this Part of this Schedule "final relevant year" has the same meaning as in section 44 above.

PART IV

OTHER CASES

1.533   9.—The Secretary of State may make regulations containing provisions for finding the amount for a tax year in—

    (a) cases where the circumstances relating to the pensioner change in the course of the year;

    (b) such other cases as the Secretary of State thinks fit.]

AMENDMENTS

1. Sch.4A inserted by Child Support, Pensions and Social Security Act 2000 s.31 and Sch.4 (April 6, 2002).

2. Pensions Act 2007 s.10 and Sch.7 Pt 5 (September 26, 2007).

3. Civil Partnership Act 2004 s 254(1) Sch.24 Pt 3 para.51 (December 5, 2005).

4. National Insurance Contributions Act 2008 Sch.2 (September 21, 2008).

5. Pensions Act 2014 Sch.12 para.69 (April 6, 2016).

GENERAL NOTE

1.534   The Additional Pension and Social Security Pensions (Home Responsibilities) (Amendment) Regulations 2001 (SI 2001/1323) are made under para.9.

[1 SCHEDULE 4B

ADDITIONAL PENSION: ACCRUAL RATES FOR PURPOSES OF SECTION 45(2)(D)

PART I

AMOUNT FOR PURPOSES OF SECTION 45(2)(D)

1.535   1 (1) The amount referred to in section 45(2)(d) is to be calculated as follows—

    (a) calculate the appropriate amount for each of the relevant years within section 45(2)(d) to which Part 2 of this Schedule applies;

(b) calculate the appropriate amount for each of the relevant years within section 45(2)(d) to which Part 3 of this Schedule applies; and

(c) add those amounts together.

(2) But if the resulting amount is a negative one, the amount referred to in section 45(2) (d) is nil.

PART II

NORMAL RULES: EMPLOYMENT NOT CONTRACTED-OUT

Application

2 This Part applies to a relevant year if [³—   **1.536**

(a)] the contracted-out condition is not satisfied in respect of any tax week in the year [³ and

(b) there is a surplus in the pensioner's earnings factor for the year.]

Appropriate amount for year

3 The appropriate amount for the year for the purposes of paragraph 1 is either—   **1.537**

(a) the flat rate amount for the year (if [³ the pensioner's earnings factor for the year] does not exceed the LET), or

(b) the sum of the flat rate amount and the earnings-related amount for the year (if [³ that earnings factor] exceeds the LET).

4 [⁴ (1) Where the final relevant year is 2015–16 or an earlier tax year,] the flat rate amount for the year is calculated by multiplying the FRAA in accordance with the last order under section 148AA of the Administration Act to come into force before the end of the final relevant year.

[⁴ (2) Otherwise, the flat rate amount is calculated by increasing the FRAA by the percentage by which earnings factors for 2015-16 are directed to be increased by the last order under section 148 of the Administration Act to come into force before the end of the final relevant year.]

5 The earnings-related amount for the year is calculated as follows—

(a) take the part of the [³ earnings factor] for the year which exceeds the LET [²*repealed*]

(b) multiply that amount in accordance with the last order under section 148 of the Administration Act to come into force before the end of the final relevant year;

(c) multiply the amount found under paragraph (b) by 10%;

(d) divide the amount found under paragraph (c) by 44.

PART III

CONTRACTED-OUT EMPLOYMENT

Application

6 This Part applies to a relevant year if [³—   **1.538**

(a)] the contracted-out condition is satisfied in respect of each tax week in the year[³ and

(b) there would be a surplus in the pensioner's earnings factor for the year if section 48A of the Pensions Schemes Act 1993 did not apply in relation to any tax week falling in the year.]

Appropriate amount for year

7 The appropriate amount for the year for the purposes of paragraph 1 is calculated as   **1.539**
follows—

(a) calculate amounts A and B in accordance with paragraphs 8 to 10;

(b) subtract amount B from amount A.

Amount A: assumed [³ earnings factor] not exceeding LET

8 (1) Amount A is calculated in accordance with this paragraph if [³ the pensioner's assumed   **1.540**
earnings factor for the year] does not exceed the LET.

(2) In such a case, amount A is the flat rate amount for the year.

(3) [⁴ Where the final relevant year is 2015–16 or an earlier tax year,] the flat rate amount for the year is calculated by multiplying the FRAA in accordance with the last order under section 148AA of the Administration Act to come into force before the end of the final relevant year.

271

[⁴ (4) Otherwise, the flat rate amount is calculated by increasing the FRAA by the percentage by which earnings factors for 2015–16 are directed to be increased by the last order under section 148 of the Administration Act to come into force before the end of the final relevant year.]

Amount A: assumed [³ earnings factor] exceeding LET

1.541 9 (1) Amount A is calculated in accordance with this paragraph if [³ the pensioner's assumed earnings factor for the year] exceeds the LET.

(2) In such a case, amount A is calculated as follows—

(a) take the part of the [³ assumed earnings factor] for the year which exceeds the LET [²repealed]

(b) multiply that amount in accordance with the last order under section 148 of the Administration Act to come into force before the end of the final relevant year;

(c) multiply the amount found under paragraph (b) by 10%;

(d) divide the amount found under paragraph (c) by 44;

(e) add the amount found under paragraph (d) to the flat rate amount for the year.

(3) [⁴ Where the final relevant year is 2015–16 or an earlier tax year,] the flat rate amount for the year is calculated by multiplying the FRAA in accordance with the last order under section 148AA of the Administration Act to come into force before the end of the final relevant year.

[⁴ (4) Otherwise, the flat rate amount is calculated by increasing the FRAA by the percentage by which earnings factors for 2015–16 are directed to be increased by the last order under section 148 of the Administration Act to come into force before the end of the final relevant year.]

Amount B

1.542 10 (1) Amount B is calculated as follows—

(a) take the part of the [³ pensioner's assumed earnings factor] for the year which exceeds the QEF [²repealed];

(b) multiply that amount in accordance with the last order under section 148 of the Administration Act to come into force before the end of the final relevant year;

(c) multiply the amount found under paragraph (b) by 20%;

(d) divide the amount found under paragraph (c) by the number of relevant years in the pensioner's working life.

(2) Section 44B is to be ignored in applying section 44(6) for the purposes of this paragraph.

PART IV

OTHER CASES

1.543 11 The Secretary of State may make regulations containing provision for finding for a tax year the amount referred to in section 45(2)(d)—

(a) in cases where the circumstances relating to the pensioner change in the course of the year, and

(b) in such other cases as the Secretary of State thinks fit.

PART 5

INTERPRETATION

1.544 12 In this Schedule—
* [³ omitted]
* "the contracted-out condition", in relation to a tax week, means the condition that any earnings paid to or for the benefit of the pensioner in that week in respect of employment were in respect of employment qualifying him for a pension provided by a salary related contracted-out scheme (within the meaning of the Pension Schemes Act 1993);
* "the FRAA" has the meaning given by paragraph 13;
* "the LET", in relation to a tax year, means the low earnings threshold for the year as specified in section 44A above;
* "the QEF", in relation to a tax year, means the qualifying earnings factor for the year;
* [³ "the pensioner's assumed earnings factor", in relation to a year, means the earnings factor that the pensioner would have for the year if section 48A(1) of the Pension Schemes Act 1993 did not apply in relation to any tax week falling in the year;];

- "relevant year" and "final relevant year" have the same meanings as in section 44 above;
- [²*repealed*]

13 (1) "The FRAA" means the flat rate accrual amount.

(2) [⁴ Where the final relevant year is 2015–16 or an earlier tax year,] that amount is £72.80 for the flat rate introduction year and subsequent tax years (but subject to section 148AA of the Administration Act).]

[⁴ (3) Otherwise, that amount is £93.60 for the flat rate introduction year and subsequent tax years.]

AMENDMENTS

1. Schedule 4B was added by Sch.2 of the Pensions Act 2007 (September 26, 2007).
2. National Insurance Contributions Act 2008 Sch.3 (September 21, 2008).
3. Pensions Act 2008 Sch.4, para.12 (January 3, 2012).
4. Pensions Act 2014 (Consequential and Supplementary Amendments) Order 2016 (SI 2016/224) art.2(5)–(8) (April 6, 2016).

GENERAL NOTE

The flat rate accrual rate was raised to £93.60 for the 2015/16 tax year and subse-   **1.545**
quent years (see Social Security Pensions (Flat Rate Accrual Amount) Order 2015 (SI 2015/185)) and has not been increased since.

SCHEDULE 5

[⁵ PENSION INCREASE OR LUMP SUM WHERE ENTITLEMENT TO RETIREMENT PENSION IS DEFERRED]

[⁵ *Choice between increase of pension and lump sum where pensioner's entitlement is deferred*

A1.—(1) Where a person's entitlement to a Category A or Category B retirement pension   **1.546**
is deferred and the period of deferment is at least 12 months, the person shall, on claiming his pension or within a prescribed period after claiming it, elect in the prescribed manner either—
- (a) that paragraph 1 (entitlement to increase of pension) is to apply in relation to the period of deferment, or
- (b) that paragraph 3A (entitlement to lump sum) is to apply in relation to the period of deferment.

(2) If no election under sub-paragraph (1) is made within the period prescribed under that sub-paragraph, the person is to be treated as having made an election under sub-paragraph (1)(b).

(3) Regulations—
- (a) may enable a person who has made an election under sub-paragraph (1) (including one that the person is treated by sub-paragraph (2) as having made) to change the election within a prescribed period and in a prescribed manner, if prescribed conditions are satisfied, and
- (b) if they enable a person to make an election under sub-paragraph (1)(b) in respect of a period of deferment after receiving any increase of pension under paragraph 1 by reference to that period, may for the purpose of avoiding duplication of payment—
  - (i) enable an amount determined in accordance with the regulations to be recovered from the person in a prescribed manner and within a prescribed period, or
  - (ii) provide for an amount determined in accordance with the regulations to be treated as having been paid on account of the amount to which the person is entitled under paragraph 3A.

(4) Where the Category A or Category B retirement pension includes any increase under [⁶ paragraphs 5 to 6A], no election under sub-paragraph (1) applies to so much of the pension as consists of that increase (an entitlement to an increase of pension in respect of such an increase after a period of deferment being conferred either by paragraphs 1 and 2 or by paragraph 2A).]

Increase of pension where pension entitlement is deferred.

[⁵ **1.**— (1) This paragraph applies where a person's entitlement to a Category A or Category   **1.547**
B retirement pension is deferred and one of the following conditions is met—
- (a) the period of deferment is less than 12 months, or
- (b) the person has made an election under paragraph A1(1)(a) in relation to the period of deferment.

(2) The rate of the person's Category A or Category B retirement pension shall be increased by an amount equal to the aggregate of the increments to which he is entitled under paragraph 2, but only if that amount is enough to increase the rate of the pension by at least 1 per cent.]

2.—(1) Subject to paragraph 3 below, a person is entitled to an increment under this paragraph for each complete incremental period in his period of enhancement.

(2) In this Schedule—

"incremental period" means any period of six days which are treated by regulations as days of increment for the purposes of this Schedule in relation to the person and the pension in question: and

"the period of enhancement", in relation to that person and that pension, means the period which—

(a) begins on the same day as the period of deferment in question; and

(b) ends on the same day as that period or, if earlier, on the day before the 5th anniversary of the beginning of that period.

(3) Subject to paragraph 3 below, the amount of the increment for any such incremental period shall be 1/7 per cent. of the weekly rate of the Category A or Category B retirement pension to which that person would have been entitled for the period if his entitlement had not been deferred.

(4) Where an amount is required to be calculated in accordance with the provisions of sub-paragraph (3) above

(a) the amount so calculated shall be rounded to the nearest penny, taking any 1/2p as nearest to the next whole penny above; and

(b) where the amount so calculated would, apart from this sub-paragraph, be a sum less than 1/2p, that amount shall be taken to be zero, notwithstanding any other provision of this Act, the Pensions Act or the Administration Act.

(5) For the purposes of sub-paragraph (3) above the weekly rate of pension for any period shall be taken—

(a) to include any increase under section 47(1) above and any increase under [6 paragraphs 4, 5, 5A, 6 or 6A] below, but

(b) not to include any increase under section [1 . . .], [583A or] 85 above or any graduated retirement benefit.

(6) The reference in sub-paragraph (5) above to any increase under subsection (1) of section 47 above shall be taken as a reference to any increase that would take place under that subsection if subsection (2) of that section and [4section 46(5)] of the Pensions Act were disregarded.

(7) Where one or more orders have come into force under section 150 [7 or 150A] of the Administration Act during the period of enhancement, the rate for any incremental period shall be determined as if the order or orders had come into force before the beginning of the period of enhancement.

(8) Where a pension's rights premium is paid in respect of a person who is, or if his entitlement had not been deferred would be, entitled to a Category A or Category B retirement pension, then, in calculating any increment under this paragraph which falls to be paid to him in respect of such a pension after the date on which the premium is paid there shall be disregarded any guaranteed minimum pension to which the pensioner was entitled in connection with the employment to which the premium relates.

[5 **2A.**—(1) This paragraph applies where—

(a) a person's entitlement to a Category A or Category B retirement pension is deferred,

(b) the pension includes an increase under [6 paragraphs 5 to 6A], and

(c) the person has made (or is treated as having made) an election under paragraph A1(1)(b) in relation to the period of deferment.

(2) The rate of the person's Category A or Category B retirement pension shall be increased by an amount equal to the aggregate of the increments to which he is entitled under sub-paragraph (3).

(3) For each complete incremental period in the person's period of deferment, the amount of the increment shall be 1/5th per cent. of the weekly rate of the increase to which the person would have been entitled under [6 paragraphs 5 to 6A] for the period if his entitlement to the Category A or Category B retirement pension had not been deferred.]

3.—(1) Regulations may provide that sub-paragraphs (1) to (3) of paragraph 2 above shall have effect with such additions, omissions and amendments as are prescribed in relation to a person during whose period of enhancement there has been a change, other than a change made by such an order as is mentioned in sub-paragraph (7) of that paragraph, in the rate of the Category A or Category B retirement pension to which he would have been entitled if his entitlement to the pension had commenced on attaining pensionable age.

(2) Any regulations under this paragraph may make such consequential additions, omissions and amendments in paragraph 8(3) below as the Secretary of State considers are appropriate in consequence of any changes made by virtue of this paragraph in paragraph 2 above.

Note: For incremental periods after April 6, 2005 the words in para.1 above "period of enhancement" will be read as "period of deferment" and the definition of period of enhancement in para.(2) is repealed. Also the fraction of 1/7 in para.(3) will be read as 1/5. See Pensions Act 1995 Sch.4 para.6.

[⁵ Lump sum where pensioner's entitlement is deferred

3A.—(1) This paragraph applies where—   **1.548**
    (a) a person's entitlement to a Category A or Category B retirement pension is deferred, and
    (b) the person has made (or is treated as having made) an election under paragraph A1(1)
        (b) in relation to the period of deferment.
(2) The person is entitled to an amount calculated in accordance with paragraph 3B (a "lump sum").

Calculation of lump sum

3B.—(1) The lump sum is the accrued amount for the last accrual period beginning during   **1.549**
the period of deferment.
(2) In this paragraph—

"accrued amount" means the amount calculated in accordance with sub-paragraph (3);
"accrual period" means any period of seven days beginning with a prescribed day of the week, where that day falls within the period of deferment.

(3) The accrued amount for an accrual period for a person is—

$$(A + P) \times 52 \frac{\sqrt{(1 + R)}}{100}$$

where—
A is the accrued amount for the previous accrual period (or, in the case of the first accrual period beginning during the period of deferment, zero);
P is the amount of the Category A or Category B retirement pension to which the person would have been entitled for the accrual period if his entitlement had not been deferred;
R is—
    (a) a percentage rate two per cent. higher than the Bank of England base rate, or
    (b) if regulations so provide, such higher rate as may be prescribed.
(4) For the purposes of sub-paragraph (3), any change in the Bank of England base rate is to be treated as taking effect—
    (a) at the beginning of the accrual period immediately following the accrual period during which the change took effect, or
    (b) if regulations so provide, at such other time as may be prescribed.
(5) For the purposes of the calculation of the lump sum, the amount of Category A or Category B retirement pension to which the person would have been entitled for an accrual period—
    (a) includes any increase under section 47(1) and any increase under paragraph 4 of this Schedule, but
    (b) does not include—
        (i) any increase under section 83A or 85 or [⁶ paragraphs 5 to 6A] of this Schedule,
        (ii) any graduated retirement benefit, or
        (iii) in prescribed circumstances, such other amount of Category A or Category B retirement pension as may be prescribed.
(6) The reference in sub-paragraph (5)(a) to any increase under subsection (1) of section 47 shall be taken as a reference to any increase that would take place under that subsection if subsection (2) of that section and section 46(5) of the Pensions Act were disregarded.]

Choice between increase of pension and lump sum where pensioner's deceased spouse [⁶ or civil partner] has deferred entitlement

1.550 **3C.**—(1) Subject to paragraph 8, this paragraph applies where—

(a) [⁶ widow, widower or surviving civil partner] ("W") is entitled to a Category A or Category B retirement pension,

(b) W was married to [⁶ or was the civil partner of] the other party to the marriage [⁶ or civil partnership] ("S") when S died,

(c) S's entitlement to a Category A or Category B retirement pension was deferred when S died, and

(d) S's entitlement had been deferred throughout the period of 12 months ending with the day before S's death.

(2) We shall within the prescribed period elect in the prescribed manner either—

(a) that paragraph 4 (entitlement to increase of pension) is to apply in relation to S's period of deferment, or

(b) that paragraph 7A (entitlement to lump sum) is to apply in relation to S's period of deferment.

(3) If no election under sub-paragraph (2) is made within the period prescribed under that sub-paragraph, W is to be treated as having made an election under sub-paragraph (2)(b).

(4) Regulations—

(a) may enable a person who has made an election under sub-paragraph (2) (including one that the person is treated by sub-paragraph (3) as having made) to change the election within a prescribed period and in a prescribed manner, if prescribed conditions are satisfied, and

(b) if they enable a person to make an election under sub-paragraph (2)(b) in respect of a period of deferment after receiving any increase of pension under paragraph 4 by reference to that period, may for the purpose of avoiding duplication of payment—

(i) enable an amount determined in accordance with the regulations to be recovered from the person in a prescribed manner and within a prescribed period, or

(ii) provide for an amount determined in accordance with the regulations to be treated as having been paid on account of the amount to which the person is entitled under paragraph 7A.

(5) The making of an election under sub-paragraph (2)(b) does not affect the application of [⁶ paragraphs 5 to 6A] (which relate to an increase in pension where the pensioner's deceased spouse [⁶ or civil partner] had deferred an entitlement to a guaranteed minimum pension).]

Increase of pension where pensioner's deceased spouse [⁶ or civil partner] has deferred entitlement

1.551 **4.**[⁵ (1) Subject to paragraph 8, this paragraph applies where a [⁶ widow, widower or surviving civil partner] ("W") is entitled to a Category A or Category B retirement pension and was married to [⁶ or was the civil partner of] the other party to the marriage [⁶ or civil partnership] ("S") when S died and one of the following conditions is met—

(a) S was entitled to a Category A or Category B retirement pension with an increase under this Schedule,

(b) W is a [⁶ widow, widower or surviving civil partner] to whom paragraph 3C applies and has made an election under paragraph 3C(2)(a), or

(c) paragraph 3C would apply to W but for the fact that the condition in sub-paragraph (1)(d) of that paragraph is not met.

(1A) Subject to sub-paragraph (3), the rate of W's pension shall be increased—

(a) in a case falling within sub-paragraph (1)(a), by an amount equal to the increase to which S was entitled under this Schedule, apart from [⁶ paragraphs 5 to 6A] [⁹ [¹¹ . . .]],

(b) in a case falling within sub-paragraph (1)(b), by an amount equal to the increase to which S would have been entitled under this Schedule, apart from [⁶ paragraphs 5 to 6A] [⁹ [¹¹ . . .]], if the period of deferment had ended immediately before S's death and S had then made an election under paragraph A1(1)(a), or

(c) in a case falling within sub-paragraph (1)(c), by an amount equal to the increase to which S would have been entitled under this Schedule, apart from [⁶ paragraphs 5 to 6A] [¹¹ ...], if the period of deferment had ended immediately before S's death.]

(2) [² . . .]

(3) If a married person dies after [¹² 5ᵗʰ October 2002] [⁶ or civil partner dies on or after 5 December, 2005] the rate of the retirement pension for that person's [⁶ widow, widower or surviving civil partner] shall be increased by an amount equivalent to the sum of—

(a) the increase in the basic pension to which the deceased spouse [⁶ or civil partner] was entitled; and

(b) one-half of the increase in the additional pension.

(4) In any case where—

(a) there is a period between the death of the former spouse [⁶ or civil partner] and the date on which the surviving spouse [⁶ or civil partner] becomes entitled to a Category A or Category B retirement pension, and

(b) one or more orders have come into force under section 150 of the Administration act during that period,

the amount of the increase to which the surviving spouse [⁶ or civil partner] is entitled under this paragraph shall be determined as if the order or orders had come into force before the beginning of that period.

(5) This paragraph does not apply in any case where the deceased spouse died before 6th April, 1979 and the widow or widower attained pensionable age before that date.

[³ 5.—(1) Where—

(a) a [⁶ widow, widower or civil partner] (call that person 'W') is entitled to a Category A or Category B retirement pension and was married to [⁶ or was the civil partner of] the other party to the marriage [⁶ or civil partnership] (call that person 'S') when S died, and

(b) S either—

    (i) was entitled to a guaranteed minimum pension with an increase under section 15(1) of the Pensions Act, or

    (ii) would have been so entitled if S had retired on the date of S's death,

the rate of W's pension shall be increased by the following amount.

(2) The amount is—

[¹⁰ (a) where W is a woman—

    (i) whose deceased spouse was a man; or

    (ii) who falls within paragraph 7(3) below,

an amount equal to the sum of the amounts set out in paragraph 5A(2) or (3) below (as the case may be),],

(b) where W is a [¹⁰ man whose deceased spouse was a woman], an amount equal to the sum of the amounts set out in paragraph 6(2), (3) or (4) below (as the case may be).

[⁶ , and

[¹⁰ (c) where W is—

    (i) a woman who does not fall within paragraph 7(3) below and whose deceased spouse was a woman;

    (ii) a man whose deceased spouse was a man; or

    (iii) a surviving civil partner,

an amount equal to the sum of the amounts set out in paragraph (6A)(2) below.]

5A.—[¹⁰ (1) This paragraph applies where W (referred to in paragraph 5 above) is a woman—

(a) whose deceased spouse was a man; or

(b) who falls within paragraph 7(3) below.]

(2) Where the [¹⁰ spouse] dies before [¹² 6ᵗʰ October 2002], the amounts referred to in paragraph 5(2)(a) above are the following—

(a) an amount equal to one-half of the increase mentioned in paragraph 5(1)(b) above,

(b) [⁹ *repealed*]

(c) an amount equal to any increase to which the [¹⁰ spouse] had been entitled under paragraph 5 above.

(3) Where [¹³ the apouse] dies after [¹² 6ᵗʰ October 2002], the amounts referred to in paragraph 5(2)(a) above are the following—

(a) [⁹ repealed]

(b) one-half of any increase to which [¹³ the apouse] had been entitled under paragraph 5 above.

6.—(1) This paragraph applies where W (referred to in paragraph 5 above) is a [¹⁰ man whose deceased spouse was a woman]

(2) Where the wife dies before 6th April, 1989, the amounts referred to in paragraph 5(2)(b) above are the following—

(a) an amount equal to the increase mentioned in paragraph 5(1)(b) above,

(b) [⁹ repealed]

(c) an amount equal to any increase to which the wife had been entitled under paragraph 5 above.

(3) Where the wife dies after 5th April, 1989 but before [¹² 6ᵗʰ October 2002], the amounts referred to in paragraph 5(2) above are the following—

1.552

(a) the increase mentioned in paragraph 5(1)(b) above, so far as attributable to employment before 6th April, 1988,

(b) one-half of that increase, so far as attributable to employment after 5th April, 1988,

(c) [⁹ repealed]

(d) any increase to which the wife had been entitled under paragraph 5 above.

(4) Where the wife dies after [¹² 6ᵗʰ October 2002], the amounts referred to in paragraph 5(2)(b) above are the following—

(a) one-half of the increase mentioned in paragraph 5(1)(b) above, so far as attributable to employment before 6th April, 1988,

(b) [⁹ repealed]

(c) one-half of any increase to which the wife had been entitled under paragraph 5 above].

1.553 [⁶ **6A.**—[¹⁰ (1) This paragraph applies where W (referred to in paragraph 5 above) is—

(a) a woman who does not fall within paragraph 7(3) below and whose deceased spouse was a woman;

(b) a man whose deceased spouse was a man; or

(c) a surviving civil partner.]

(2) The amounts referred to in paragraph 5(2)(c) above are the following—

(a) one-half of the increase mentioned in paragraph 5(1)(b) above, so far as attributable to employment before 6th April 1988,

(b) [⁹ repealed]

(c) one-half of any increase to which the deceased [¹⁰ spouse or] civil partner had been entitled under paragraph 5 above.]

7.—(1) [⁹ *repealed*]

(2) Where an amount is required to be calculated in accordance with the provisions of [⁶ paragraphs 5, 5A, 6 or 6A] or sub-paragraph (1) above—

(a) the amount so calculated shall be rounded to the nearest penny, taking any 1/2p as nearest to the next whole penny above; and

(b) where the amount so calculated would, apart from this sub-paragraph, be a sum less than 1/2p, that amount shall be taken to be zero, notwithstanding any other provision of this Act, the Pensions Act or the Administration Act.

[¹⁰ (3) For the purposes of paragraphs 5, 5A and 6A above, a woman falls within this sub-paragraph if—

(a) she was married to another woman who, at the time of her death, was a woman by virtue of a full gender recognition certificate having been issued under the Gender Recognition Act 2004; and

(b) that marriage subsisted before the time when that certificate was issued.].

1.554 [¹¹ **7ZA.**–(1) This paragraph modifies paragraphs 5A to 6A in cases where—

(a) W became entitled to a Category A or Category B retirement pension before 6 April 2012, and

(b) S died before 6 April 2012.

("W" and "S" have the same meaning as in paragraph 5.)

(2) Paragraph 5A applies as if—

(a) in sub-paragraph (2), after paragraph (a), there were inserted—
"(b) the appropriate amount; and";

(b) in sub-paragraph (3), after "following—", there were inserted—
"(a) one half of the appropriate amount; and".

(3) Paragraph 6 applies as if—

(a) in sub-paragraph (2), after paragraph (a), there were inserted—
"(b) the appropriate amount; and";

(b) in sub-paragraph (3), after paragraph (b), there were inserted—
"(c) the appropriate amount reduced by the amount of any increases under section 109 of the Pensions Act; and";

(c) in sub-paragraph (4), after paragraph (a), there were inserted—
"(b) one half of the appropriate amount; and".

(4) Paragraph 6A applies as if in sub-paragraph (2), after paragraph (a), there were inserted—
"(b) one half of the appropriate amount; and".

(5) In paragraphs 5A to 6A as modified by this paragraph, the "appropriate amount" means the greater of—

(a) the amount by which the deceased person's Category A or Category B retirement pension had been increased under section 150(1)(e) of the Administration Act; or

(b) the amount by which his or her Category A or Category B retirement pension would have been so increased had he or she died immediately before the surviving spouse or civil partner became entitled to a Category A or Category B retirement pension.

(6) In sub-paragraph (1)(a) the reference to becoming entitled to a pension before 6 April 2012 includes a reference to becoming entitled on or after that day to the payment of a pension in respect of a period before that day.]

[⁵ Entitlement to lump sum where pensioner's deceased spouse [⁶ or civil partner] has deferred entitlement

7A.—(1) This paragraph applies where a person to whom paragraph 3C applies ("W") has made (or is treated as having made) an election under paragraph 3C(2)(b).   **1.555**

(2) W is entitled to an amount calculated in accordance with paragraph 7B (a "widowed person's [⁶ or surviving civil partner's] lump sum").

Calculation of widowed person's [⁶ or surviving civil partner's] lump sum

7B.—(1) The widowed person's [⁶ or surviving civil partner's] lump sum is the accrued amount for the last accrual period beginning during the period which—   **1.556**
    (a) began at the beginning of S's period of deferment, and
    (b) ended on the day before S's death.

(2) In this paragraph—

"S" means the other party to the marriage; [⁶ or civil partnership]
"accrued amount" means the amount calculated in accordance with sub-paragraph (3);
"accrual period" means any period of seven days beginning with a prescribed day of the week, where that day falls within S's period of deferment.

(3) The accrued amount for an accrual period for W is—

$$\frac{(A + P) \times 52 \sqrt{(1 + R)}}{100}$$

where—
A is the accrued amount for the previous accrual period (or, in the case of the first accrual period beginning during the period mentioned in sub-paragraph (1), zero);
    P is—
    (a) the basic pension, and
    (b) half of the additional pension, to which S would have been entitled for the accrual period if his entitlement had not been deferred during the period mentioned in sub-paragraph (1);
    R is—
    (a) a percentage rate two per cent. higher than the Bank of England base rate, or
    (b) if regulations so provide, such higher rate as may be prescribed.
(4) For the purposes of sub-paragraph (3), any change in the Bank of England base rate is to be treated as taking effect—
    (a) at the beginning of the accrual period immediately following the accrual period during which the change took effect, or
    (b) if regulations so provide, at such other time as may be prescribed.
(5) For the purposes of the calculation of the widowed person's lump sum, the amount of Category A or Category B retirement pension to which S would have been entitled for an accrual period—
    (a) includes any increase under section 47(1) and any increase under paragraph 4 of this Schedule, but
    (b) does not include—
        (i) any increase under section 83A or 85 or [⁶ paragraphs 5 to 6A] of this Schedule [⁹ [¹¹ . . .]],
        (ii) any graduated retirement benefit, or
        (iii) in prescribed circumstances, such other amount of Category A or Category B retirement pension as may be prescribed.
(6) The reference in sub-paragraph (5)(a) to any increase under subsection (1) of section 47 shall be taken as a reference to any increase that would take place under that subsection if subsection (2) of that section and section 46(5) of the Pensions Act were disregarded.
(7) In any case where—
    (a) there is a period between the death of S and the date on which W becomes entitled to a Category A or Category B retirement pension, and

(b)   one or more orders have come into force under section 150 of the Administration Act during that period,

the amount of the lump sum shall be increased in accordance with that order or those orders.]

[⁵ Supplementary

1.557   **7C.**—(1) Any lump sum calculated under paragraph 3B or 7B must be rounded to the nearest penny, taking any 1/2p as nearest to the next whole penny above.

(2) In prescribing a percentage rate for the purposes of paragraphs 3B and 7B, the Secretary of State must have regard to—

(a)   the national economic situation, and

(b)   any other matters which he considers relevant.]

[⁵ Married Couples [⁶ and civil partners]]

1.558   [² **8.**—(1) [² . . .]

(2) [⁸ . . .]]

[² (3) [⁸ . . .]

[⁵(4) The conditions in paragraph 3C(1)(c) and 4(1)(a) are not satisfied by a Category B retirement pension to which S was or would have been entitled by virtue of W's contributions.

(5) Where the Category A retirement pension to which S was or would have been entitled includes an increase under section 51A(2) attributable to W's contributions, the increase or lump sum to which W is entitled under paragraph 4(1A) or 7A(2) is to be calculated as if there had been no increase under that section.

(6) In sub-paragraphs (4) and (5), "W" and "S" have the same meaning as in paragraph 3C, 4 or 7A, as the case requires.]

Uprating

1.559   **9.**—The sums which are the increases in the rates of retirement pension under this Schedule are subject to alteration by order made by the Secretary of State under section 150 of the Administration Act.

AMENDMENTS

1. Tax Credits Act 2002 Sch.6 (April 6, 2003).

2. Pensions Act 1995 Sch.4 (July 19, 1995) and Sch.7 (April 6, 2005).

3. Social Security (Incapacity for Work) Act 1994 Sch.1 para.40 (April 13, 1995).

4. Pensions Schemes Act 1993 Sch.8 (Feb. 7, 1994).

5. Pensions Act 2004 Sch.11 (April 6, 2005).

6. Civil Partnership (Pensions and Benefit Payments) (Consequential Provisions) Order 2005 (SI 2005/2053) (December 5, 2005).

7. Pensions Act 2007 Sch.1 para.19 (July 26, 2007).

8. Pensions Act 2007 Sch.7 (September 26, 2007 and April 6, 2010).

9. Pensions Act 2011 s.2(5) and (6) and Sch.2 (April 6, 2012).

10. Marriage and Civil Partnership (Scotland) Act 2014 and Civil Partnership Act 2004 (Consequential Provisions and Modifications) Order 2014 (SI 2014/3229) Sch.4 para.2 (December 14, 2014)

11. Pensions Act 2014 Sch.12 para. 94 (April 6, 2016).

12. Child Support, Pensions and Social Security Act 2000 s.39, which provides that the amendments have retrospective effect.

13. SI 2014/3168, in relation to England and Wales (December 10, 2014); SI 2014/3229, in relation to Scotland (December 16, 2014).

GENERAL NOTE

1.560   Under para.4(1) above a man reaching pensionable age before April 6, 2010 is also required to have been over pensionable age when his wife (S) died. (See Pensions Act 1995 Sch.4 para.21 (14) and (16).)

In relation to any incremental period and accrual period beginning before April 6, 2010 references in para.2 (5)(b), 3B (5)(b) and 7B (5)(b) to section 83A of the principal Act are to be taken as references to s.83 or 84 of that Act—see Sch.11 of Pensions Act 2004.

The changes made by s.2 of the Pensions Act 2011 to this schedule do not apply if W became entitled to either a Category A or B retirement pension before those changes came into force and S died before that day. See s.2(7) and (8) of that Act.

The sums which are lump sums to which surviving spouses or civil partners will become entitled under para.7A of this Schedule on becoming entitled to a Category A or Category B retirement pension were increased by 2.4 per cent with effect from April 8, 2019: see Social Security Benefits Up-rating Order 2019 (SI 2019/480) art.4(4).

In *KH v Secretary of State for Work and Pensions* [2014] UKUT 138 (AAC) Judge Wikeley refused permission to appeal to a claimant because there was no arguable error of law in the decision by the First-tier Tribunal in refusing a claim about deferral put forward by a claimant. The Upper Tribunal reported the decision because the claimant had argued his case on the specific wording of the Departmental leaflet *Your Guide to State Pension deferral (SPD1)*. The leaflet was wrong and did not accurately reflect the law, which the First-tier Tribunal had rightly applied.

[¹ SCHEDULE 5A

PENSION INCREASE OR LUMP SUM WHERE ENTITLEMENT TO SHARED ADDITIONAL PENSION
IS DEFERRED

Choice between pension increase and lump sum where entitlement to shared additional pension is deferred

1.—(1) Where a person's entitlement to a shared additional pension is deferred and the period of deferment is at least 12 months, the person shall, on claiming his pension or within a prescribed period after claiming it, elect in the prescribed manner either—

    (a) that paragraph 2 (entitlement to increase of pension) is to apply in relation to the period of deferment, or

    (b) that paragraph 4 (entitlement to lump sum) is to apply in relation to the period of deferment.

(2) If no election under sub-paragraph (1) is made within the period prescribed under that sub-paragraph, the person is to be treated as having made an election under sub-paragraph (1)(b).

(3) Regulations—

    (a) may enable a person who has made an election under sub-paragraph (1) (including one that the person is treated by sub-paragraph (2) as having made) to change the election within a prescribed period and in a prescribed manner, if prescribed conditions are satisfied, and

    (b) if they enable a person to make an election under sub-paragraph (1)(b) in respect of a period of deferment after receiving any increase of pension under paragraph 2 by reference to that period, may for the purpose of avoiding duplication of payment—

        (i) enable an amount determined in accordance with the regulations to be recovered from the person in a prescribed manner and within a prescribed period, or

        (ii) provide for an amount determined in accordance with the regulations to be treated as having been paid on account of the amount to which the person is entitled under paragraph 4.

Increase of pension where entitlement deferred

2.—(1) This paragraph applies where a person's entitlement to a shared additional pension is deferred and either—

    (a) the period of deferment is less than 12 months, or

    (b) the person has made an election under paragraph 1(1)(a) in relation to the period of deferment.

(2) The rate of the person's shared additional pension shall be increased by an amount equal to the aggregate of the increments to which he is entitled under paragraph 3, but only if that amount is enough to increase the rate of the pension by at least 1 per cent.

1.561

1.562

Calculation of increment

1.563   **3.**—(1) A person is entitled to an increment under this paragraph for each complete incremental period in his period of deferment.

(2) The amount of the increment for an incremental period shall be 1/5th per cent. of the weekly rate of the shared additional pension to which the person would have been entitled for the period if his entitlement had not been deferred.

(3) Amounts under sub-paragraph (2) shall be rounded to the nearest penny, taking any 1/2p as nearest to the next whole penny.

(4) Where an amount under sub-paragraph (2) would, apart from this sub-paragraph, be a sum less than 1/2p, the amount shall be taken to be zero, notwithstanding any other provision of this Act, the Pensions Act or the Administration Act.

(5) In this paragraph "incremental period" means any period of six days which are treated by regulations as days of increment for the purposes of this paragraph in relation to the person and pension in question.

(6) Where one or more orders have come into force under section 150 of the Administration Act during the period of deferment, the rate for any incremental period shall be determined as if the order or orders had come into force before the beginning of the period of deferment.

(7) The sums which are the increases in the rates of shared additional pension under this paragraph are subject to alteration by order made by the Secretary of State under section 150 of the Administration Act.

GENERAL NOTE

1.564   The sums which are increases in the rates of retirement pensions under this Schedule are to be increased by 4 per cent with effect from April 8, 2019. (See Social Security Benefits Up-rating Order 2019 (SI 2019/480) art.4(4)).

Lump sum where entitlement to shared additional pension is deferred

1.565   **4.**—(1) This paragraph applies where—
  (a) a person's entitlement to a shared additional pension is deferred, and
  (b) the person has made (or is treated as having made) an election under paragraph 1(1)
      (b) in relation to the period of deferment.

(2) The person is entitled to an amount calculated in accordance with paragraph 5 (a "lump sum").

Calculation of lump sum

1.566   **5.**—(1) The lump sum is the accrued amount for the last accrual period beginning during the period of deferment.

(2) In this paragraph—

'accrued amount' means the amount calculated in accordance with sub-paragraph (3);
'accrual period' means any period of seven days beginning with a prescribed day of the week, where that day falls within the period of deferment.

(3) The accrued amount for an accrual period for a person is—

$$\frac{(A + P) \times 52 \sqrt{(1 + R)}}{100}$$

where—
A is the accrued amount for the previous accrual period (or, in the case of the first accrual period beginning during the period of deferment, zero);
P is the amount of the shared additional pension to which the person would have been entitled for the accrual period if his entitlement had not been deferred;
R is—
  (a) a percentage rate two per cent. higher than the Bank of England base rate, or
  (b) if a higher rate is prescribed for the purposes of paragraphs 3B and 7B of Schedule 5, that higher rate.

(4) For the purposes of sub-paragraph (3), any change in the Bank of England base rate is to be treated as taking effect—

    (a) at the beginning of the accrual period immediately following the accrual period during which the change took effect, or

    (b) if regulations so provide, at such other time as may be prescribed.

(5) For the purpose of the calculation of the lump sum, the amount of the shared additional pension to which the person would have been entitled for an accrual period does not include, in prescribed circumstances, such amount as may be prescribed.

(6) The lump sum must be rounded to the nearest penny, taking any 1/2p as nearest to the next whole penny.]

AMENDMENT

1. Pensions Act 2004 Sch.11 (April 6, 2005).

GENERAL NOTE

The sums which, under paragraph 2 of this Schedule are increases in the rates   **1.567** of shared additional pensions, were increased, with effect from April 8, 2019, by 2.4 per cent: see art.4(5) of the Social Security Benefits Up-rating Order 2019 (SI 2019/480).

SCHEDULE 6

ASSESSMENT OF EXTENT OF DISABLEMENT

General provisions as to method of assessment

1.—For the purposes of [¹ section 103] above and Part II of Schedule 7 to this Act, the   **1.568** extent of disablement shall be assessed, by reference to the disabilities incurred by the claimant as a result of the relevant loss of faculty in accordance with the following general principles—

    (a) except as provided in paragraphs (b) to (d) below, the disabilities to be taken into account shall be all disabilities so incurred (whether or not involving loss of earning power or additional expense) to which the claimant may be expected, having regard to his physical and mental condition at the date of the assessment, to be subject during the period taken into account by the assessment as compared with a person of the same age and sex whose physical and mental condition is normal;

    (b) [¹ . . .] regulations may make provision as to the extent (if any) to which any disabilities are to be taken into account where they are disabilities which, though resulting from the relevant loss of faculty, also result, or without the relevant accident might have been expected to result, from a cause other than the relevant accident;

    (c) the assessment shall be made without reference to the particular circumstances of the claimant other than age, sex, and physical and mental condition;

    (d) the disabilities resulting from such loss of faculty as may be prescribed shall be taken as amounting to 100 per cent. disablement and other disabilities shall be assessed accordingly.

2.—Provisions may be made by regulations for further defining the principles on which the extent of disablement is to be assessed and such regulations may in particular direct that a prescribed loss of faculty shall be treated as resulting in a prescribed degree of disablement; and, in connection with any such direction, nothing in paragraph 1(c) above prevents the making of different provision, in the case of loss of faculty in or affecting hand or arm, for right-handed and for left-handed persons.

3.—Regulations under paragraph 1(d) or 2 above may include provision—

    (a) for adjusting or reviewing an assessment made before the date of the coming into force of those regulations;

    (b) for any resulting alteration of that assessment to have effect as from that date; so however that no assessment shall be reduced by virtue of this paragraph.

1.569   **4.**— [¹ . . .]
            5.— [¹ . . .]

Disablement benefit

1.570   **6.**—(1) Subject to sub-paragraphs (2) and (3) below, the period to be taken into account by an assessment for the purposes of section 103 above and Part II of Schedule 7 to this Act of the extent of a claimant's disablement shall be the period (beginning not earlier than the end of the period of 90 days referred to in section 103(6) above and in paragraph 9(3) of that Schedule and limited by reference either to the claimant's life or to a definite date) during which the claimant has suffered and may be expected to continue to suffer from the relevant loss of faculty.

(2) If on any assessment the condition of the claimant is not such, having regard to the possibility of changes in that condition (whether predictable or not), as to allow of a final assessment being made up to the end of the period provided by sub-paragraph (1) above, then, subject to sub-paragraph (3) below—

(a) a provisional assessment shall be made, taking into account such shorter period only as seems reasonable having regard to his condition and that possibility; and

(b) on the next assessment the period to be taken into account shall begin with the end of the period taken into account by the provisional assessment.

(3) Where the assessed extent of a claimant's disablement amounts to less than 14 per cent., then, subject to sub-paragraphs (4) and (5) below, that assessment shall be a final assessment and the period to be taken into account by it shall not end before the earliest date on which it seems likely that the extent of the disablement will be less than 1 per cent.

(4) Sub-paragraph (3) above does not apply in any case where it seems likely that—

(a) the assessed extent of the disablement will be aggregated with the assessed extent of any present disablement, and

(b) that aggregate will amount to 14 per cent. or more.

(5) Where the extent of the claimant's disablement is assessed at different percentages for different parts of the period taken into account by the assessment, then—

(a) sub-paragraph (3) above does not apply in relation to the assessment unless the per-centage assessed for the latest part of that period is less than 14 per cent., and

(b) in any such case that sub-paragraph shall apply only in relation to that part of that period (and subject to sub-paragraph (4) above).

7.—An assessment for the purposes of section 103 above and Part II of Schedule 7 to this Act shall—

(a) state the degree of disablement in the form of a percentage;

(b) specify the period taken into account by the assessment; and

(c) where that period is limited by reference to a definite date, specify whether the assess-ment is provisional or final;

but the percentage and the period shall not be specified more particularly than is necessary for the purpose of determining in accordance with section 103 above and Parts II and IV of Schedule 7 to this Act the claimant's rights as to disablement pension or gratuity and reduced earnings allowance (whether or not a claim has been made).

Special provision as to entitlement to constant attendance allowance, etc.

1.571   **8.**—(1) For the purpose of determining whether a person is entitled—

(a) to an increase of a disablement pension under section 104 above; or

(b) to a corresponding increase of any other benefit by virtue of paragraph 6(4)(b) or 7(2) (b) of Schedule 8 to this Act,

regulations may provide for the extent of the person's disablement resulting from the relevant injury or disease to be determined in such manner as may be provided for by the regulations by reference to all disabilities to which that person is subject which result either from the relevant injury or disease or from any other injury or disease in respect of which there fall to be made to the person payments of any of the descriptions listed in sub-paragraph (2) below.

(2) Those payments are—

(a) payments by way of disablement pension;

(b) payments by way of benefit under paragraph 4 or 7(1) of Schedule 8 to this Act; or

(c) payments in such circumstances as may be prescribed by way of such other benefit as may be prescribed (being benefit in connection with any hostilities or with service as a member of Her Majesty's forces or of such other organisation as may be specified in the regulations).

AMENDMENT

1. Welfare Reform and Pensions Act 1999 Sch.13(IV) para.1 (April 6, 2001).

DERIVATION

SSA 1975 Sch.8.   1.572

GENERAL NOTE

Regulation 11 of the Social Security (General Benefit) Regulations 1982 is   1.573
treated (by s.2(2) of the SSCPA 1992) as having been made under this Schedule to
further define the principles on which the extent of disablement is to be assessed.

In the case of some prescribed diseases, special provision is made by the
Prescribed Diseases Regulations and this Schedule and reg.11 of the General
Benefit Regulations must be read as subject to that.

Paragraph 1
Sub-paras (a) and (c) make it plain that disablement is to be assessed by com-   1.574
paring the claimant with a person of the same age and sex whose physical and
mental condition is normal *without* taking into account loss of earning power, additional expense or other circumstances peculiar to the claimant (e.g. the distance
from home to public transport or other facilities) other than, of course, age, sex
and physical and mental condition. This cannot be too strongly emphasised. As
Commissioner Fellner rightly noted in a deafness case, *CI/5092/2002*

> "It must not be forgotten that the comparison under Schedule 6 is simply
> with another person of the same age and sex, and that individual hobbies and
> preferences are not to be taken into account. Thus, this claimant's complaints of
> loss of pleasure in particular kinds of music and in birdsong, and having to have
> the TV volume high, are relevant only in so far as other men of his age might be
> able to have, or not to be burdened with, these things. His being a radio ham, as
> he told the tribunal, would not be relevant" (para.17).

The one exception is allowed by sub-para.(b) which permits the taking into
account of disabilities which are due not only to the relevant accident or disease but
also to another cause (see reg.11(2)–(4) of the General Benefit Regulations).

Sub-para.(d) enables regulations to prescribe disabilities amounting to 100 per
cent. Other disabilities must be assessed accordingly (see reg.11(7) of, and Sch.2
to, the General Benefit Regulations). In *R(I) 30/61*, it was made clear that "a man
entitled to an assessment of 100 per cent is not necessarily totally disabled, and that
any scale of values which a member of an assessing body has in the back of his mind
should take account of that fact".

While there are certain prescribed degrees of disablement in respect of certain
injuries in Sch.2 to the General Benefit Regulations (e.g. loss of the sight in one eye
[30 per cent]), these can be departed from, whether by way of increase or decrease,
as may be reasonable in the case if that prescribed degree of disablement does not
provide a reasonable assessment of the extent of disablement resulting from the
relevant loss of faculty (reg.11(6) of the General Benefit Regulations).

Coming to a decision, within those parameters, on the appropriate percentage
assessment of disablement flowing from the relevant loss of faculty is a difficult
matter of judgment, the matter of guidance on which has been considered in many
Commissioners' decisions (e.g. *CI/499/2000, CI/1802/2001, CI/2553/2001, CI/3758
and 3759/2003*). It has most recently been considered by a Tribunal of Commissioners
in *R(I) 2/06*. In most respects, since it found no relevant error of law in the approach
and decision of the tribunals appealed from, the comments are ultimately *obiter*.

That Tribunal of Commissioners, dealt specifically with two appeal tribunal decisions awarding 7 per cent and 4 per cent respectively in respect of claimants suffering from PD A11 (Vibration White Finger) as a result of their work with percussive

tools as coal miners. While making it clear that it was not possible to produce a template for assessment decisions, the Tribunal hoped that its comments would assist advisers, decision-makers, and tribunals by identifying the correct approach to such decisions and indicating matters which should be taken into account, matters which should not be taken into account, and matters which need not be taken into account (para.78). The scheme leaves considerable discretion to decision-makers and tribunals. (*ibid.*). Commissioners and courts can only interfere if the decision appealed exhibits an error of law (on which see: paras 28-31, citing *R(A)1/72* and *R. (Iran)* v *Secretary of State for the Home Department* [2005] EWCA Civ 982, paras 9–10 per Brooke L.J.; and Vol III of this series). The Tribunal of Commissioners rightly stressed that the matter of assessment of the percentage of functional disablement in any given case is essentially a factual and medical assessment for the tribunal hearing and seeing the evidence in the case to make. A disputed judgement of degree on a question of fact is not an error of law in the sense set out in those cases. It is not for an appellate body whose jurisdiction is limited to points of law to offer or impose its substituted view (para.31). That said, however,

"Commissioners have always regarded it as part of their function to give guidance where needed for the assistance of tribunals and departmental decision makers on the relevant principles of law to be applied in this specialised jurisdiction: this is an area where certainty and consistency of approach and an orderly development of the law are of particular importance given the complex nature of the legislation and the very large number of individual cases potentially involved. However it is a function to be exercised cautiously, particularly in an instance such as the present where the questions of assessment of an individual's percentage level of functional disablement are not primarily matters of legal interpretation at all, but of factual judgment - including judgment on medical matters - entrusted by the legislation to the specialist tribunals best qualified to decide them. There is a danger in misinterpreting the observations of individual Commissioners on the facts of such cases as laying down additional rules of law where only helpful guidance on the fact-finding process was intended. There was some evidence of that in the way the notices of appeal before us were formulated. What matters is not whether express reference is made to some such guidance, but whether the substance of the tribunal's decision, and its statement of the factors taken into account in reaching it, demonstrates any error of law" (para. 68).

Following *R(I) 2/06(T)*, Judge Wikeley held in *AJ v SSWP (II)* [2012] UKUT 209 (AAC) that the simple fact that the claimant's own doctors disagreed with the first-tier tribunal's assessment of disablement did not mean that the tribunal had erred in law (paras 17–19).

1.575   One species of error of law, of course, is a failure of an appeal tribunal to give adequate reasons for its decision. Thus in *CI/499/2000*, Commissioner Jacobs held erroneous in law a tribunal assessment of disablement because it focused purely on impaired manual dexterity resulting from the claimant's laceration to his finger. It should also have considered any mental effect, the effect of pain preventing or hindering the performance of an activity, and disfigurement (a scar had been left). The Tribunal should have made clear why it did not believe the claimant to be as disabled as he claimed. Nor had it properly explained its assessment of 8 per cent. Such explanation is required and an assessment could be explained in several ways. A Tribunal could give a general indication of why it made an assessment at a particular level (e.g. the effects were intermittent). It might properly explain its assessment by reference to the prescribed degrees of disablement in Sch.2 to the General Benefit Regulations. It might explain the significance of its clinical findings in terms of function (e.g. findings on the movement of joints might be explained in terms of how much useful grip was retained by the claimant). On this matter of giving adequate reasons, the Tribunal of Commissioners expressly approved, in para.45 of its decision, Deputy Commissioner Warren's statements in *CI/1802/2001* on what was required of tribunals assessing the degree of disablement. The Deputy Commissioner there stated:

> "7. Vibration white finger is not one of those conditions for which there is a pre-scribed degree of disablement in Schedule 2 of the General Benefit Regulations. Those Regulations therefore state only that the tribunal 'may have such regard as may be appropriate to the prescribed degrees of disablement' when making its assessment. This indicates the very broad discretion which individual tribu-nals have in this type of case. In many cases it is simply not possible for a tribu-nal to give precise reasons for the conclusion which it has reached.
>
> 8. In my judgment, however, as a minimum, the claimant and the Secretary of State are entitled to know the factual basis upon which the assessment has been made; in other words what disabilities were taken into account by the tri-bunal in concluding that a particular percentage disablement was appropriate.
>
> 9. This can often be simply expressed. In many cases it will be enough to say that the evidence given by the claimant about the effect of a particular accident or disease on his or her daily life has been accepted. In some cases, where the claimant's evidence is for some reason found to be unreliable, it may be that the tribunal will state that it felt able to accept only those disabilities which in its expert opinion were likely to flow from problems disclosed on clinical examination. Other cases may need more detail. But if it is not possible to discern the material on which the assessment is based, then the tribunal's statement of reasons is likely to be inadequate."

Commissioners had, of course, proffered guidance for tribunals approaching the task of assessment of the degree of disablement. Both Deputy Commissioner Warren and Commissioner Jacobs in their decisions referred with caveats to the role of Sch.2 of the General Benefit Regulations (and see also approval of such cross-referral in *R(I) 5/95*. The Tribunal of Commissioners had taken on board at their oral hearing a debate on whether the degrees of disablement there prescribed for hand and finger conditions could offer assistance to tribunals dealing with disa-blement from vibration white finger (VWF). It considered that the assistance to be derived from them to be "relatively small" (para.72). The Schedule might well inform to an extent an appropriate percentage for a particular VWF case but was of "very limited value in assessing percentages for such conditions" (para.73). In three decisions (*CI/2553/2001, CI/3758 and 3759/2003*), Commissioner Williams had drawn the attention of tribunals to judicial guidelines on assessing damages in civil personal injury claims in tort, but had stressed the need to approach this with caution. As the Tribunal of Commissioners saw it, Commissioner Williams has stressed that he drew nothing from the bands of damages set out in those guide-lines. Rather, as the Tribunal of Commissioners put it, he "merely directed the tribunal to take into account certain specific criteria referred to in those guidelines, namely the length and severity of the claimant's attacks and symptoms, the extent and/or severity and/or rapidity of deterioration of his condition, and his age and prognosis" (para.57). To that degree, the guidelines may provide a useful list of entirely unexceptional matters for a tribunal to take into account in its assessment of functional disablement (*ibid.*). Those guidelines were drawn up for an entirely different purpose (see Diplock L.J., as he then was, in *R. v Medical Appeal Tribunal Ex p Cable* reported as an Appendix to *R(I) 11/66*, quoted in full in para.75 of the Tribunal of Commissioners' decision). His caution there against cross-referencing across schemes would extend to proposed comparison with any other system, such as the Criminal Injuries Compensation Scheme (para.75). Both Commissioner Jacobs in *CI/499/2000* and Commissioner Williams in *CI/2553/2001* offered guidance on the proper role of Departmental guidance such as the MAF (Medical Assessment Framework) used by examining doctors for disablement benefit and severe disablement allowance. Both had counseled extreme caution in referring to this "rough guide". The Tribunal of Commissioners made no

1.576

specific comment on the MAF other than noting with approval that Dr Reed, the doctor giving evidence on behalf of the Secretary of State, had stressed the emphasis given to all medical staff that nothing in MAF (the current version of which needed review) was to fetter their own individual judgment on a particular case (para.77). The Tribunal of Commissioners confirmed that it was no part of a tribunal's function to apply, or even necessarily to take into account, such internal guidance which, while properly aiming at clarity and consistency of approach, sets out merely the view of one of the parties to an appeal (the Government) on what was required by the law and by good practice. Such guidance was in no way binding on tribunals. A tribunal wanting to take such guidance into account had to bear all those caveats and cautions in mind (*ibid.*).

Paragraph 2

1.577 Regulation 11 of the General Benefit Regulations is made under this paragraph. There is no specific provision for compensating for the loss of the "dominant hand" but, even in a case where the injury is one specified in Sch.2 to the Regulations, reg.11(6) permits "such increase or reduction in [the prescribed] degree of disablement as may be reasonable in the circumstances in the case".

Paragraph 6

1.578 This looks back as well as forward: the period of assessment is to be that during which the claimant has suffered and may be expected to continue to suffer from the relevant loss of faculty resulting in disablement of at least one per cent.

As regards looking back, where a prescribed disease was only prescribed after the claimant had begun (due to his work) to suffer from it, however, it is not necessary to specify more particularly the period other than to say that it began at a date before prescription and then to assess the degree of disablement from the date of prescription. In *JR v SSWP (II)* [2011] UKUT 450 (AAC), Judge Ward, drawing on observations (albeit not made following argument on the point) of an experienced Commissioner in *CI/3521/1999*, preferred this construction of the legislation because a claimant cannot have any right to disablement benefit or REA before the date of prescription (see especially paras 33–35).

As regards looking to the future, if the prognosis is uncertain and the assessment is at least 14 per cent a provisional assessment should be made so that the extent of the claimant's disability is reassessed at the end of the period of the provisional assessment. A final assessment which is for a definite period rather than "life" implies *either* that the claimant will be suffering from no loss of faculty *or* the resulting disablement will be less than 1 per cent from the end of the period of assessment *or* that any disablement from which the claimant may be expected to be suffering at the end of the period of assessment would have been present even if the relevant accident had not occurred. If the claimant is still disabled at the end of the period, he or she may apply for revision under s.9 of the SSA 1998. There is no reason why the claimant's disablement should not be assessed at different percentages for different parts of the period; nor why those parts should be lengthy. In *R(I) 30/61*, the medical appeal tribunal assessed disablement from January 11 to March 25, 1960, at 30 per cent; March 26 to June 24, 1960, at 100 per cent; June 25 to July 24, 1960, at 40 per cent; and from June 25, 1960 to January 24, 1961, at 30 per cent. That was a provisional assessment and reflected the fact that the claimant had been in hospital from March to June and was then recuperating. Although an appeal was allowed on the ground of inadequate reasons, the tribunal's general approach was not criticised and the Commissioner said,

"the disabilities resulting from the relevant loss of faculty must be related to the period covered by the assessment, and . . . the assessing body must not be misled by the fact that a very serious disability is expected not to last long. The answer to that situation is a high assessment for a short period."

Since disablement benefit is calculated on a weekly basis, it might be slightly more convenient for decision-makers if short periods were calculated in weeks rather than months if the evidence permits it.

Sub-paras (3)–(5) normally prevent a provisional assessment if the assessment, at least for the last part of the period, is less than 14 per cent. If the extent of the claimant's disablement resulting from the relevant loss of faculty is likely to become less over time, the adjudicating medical authority is then bound to determine a date from which the claimant's extent of disablement may be expected to be less than 1 per cent. If the extent of disablement is expected to become greater but the adjudicating medical authority cannot tell when and so is unable to include an assessment of at least 14 per cent within the period of assessment, a life assessment should be made and the burden rests upon the claimant to make an application for revision under s.9 of the SSA 1998 when the extent of disablement does become at least 14 per cent. An exception is made by sub-para.(4) if the assessment of the extent of disablement may be aggregated with another assessment and the aggregate may amount to 14 per cent or more. In such a case, a provisional assessment may be made if the prognosis is uncertain.

1.579

Regulation 20(3) of the Prescribed Diseases Regulations provides that the minimum period of assessment in a case of byssinosis shall be one year. Reg.29 provides that the initial assessment in a case of occupational deafness shall always be provisional and for a period of five years and that all subsequent assessments shall be for a period of at least five years.

Paragraph 6

Where a claim is made in respect of diffuse mesothelioma, see reg.20(4) of the Prescribed Diseases Regulations.

1.580

Paragraph 7

An assessment shall not specify the percentage or period more particularly than is necessary for the purpose of determining entitlement to industrial injuries benefits. This means that, where the assessment is under 14 per cent but not under 1 per cent, it is not necessary for the adjudicating medical authority to go into greater detail unless either the assessment may be aggregated with another and the aggregate might be more than 14 per cent or else the claimant is suffering from pneumoconiosis, byssinosis or diffuse mesothelioma in which case it matters whether the assessment is greater than 10 per cent or not for the purpose of determining the amount of disablement benefit payable (reg.20 of the Prescribed Diseases Regulations).

1.581

Paragraph 8

See reg.20 of the General Benefit Regulations.

1.582

SCHEDULE 7

INDUSTRIAL INJURIES BENEFITS

PART I

UNEMPLOYABILITY SUPPLEMENT

Availability

1.—This Part of this Schedule applies only in relation to persons who were beneficiaries in receipt of unemployability supplement under section 58 of the 1975 Act immediately before 6th April 1987.

1.583

Rate and duration

1.584   2.—(1) The weekly rate of a disablement pension shall, if as the result of the relevant loss of faculty the beneficiary is incapable of work and likely to remain so permanently, be increased by the amount specified in Schedule 4, Part V, paragraph 5.

(2) An increase of pension under this paragraph is referred to in this Act as an "unemployability supplement".

(3) For the purposes of this paragraph a person may be treated as being incapable of work and likely to remain so permanently, notwithstanding that the loss of faculty is not such as to prevent him being capable of work, if it is likely to prevent his earnings in a year exceeding a prescribed amount not less than £104.

(4) An unemployability supplement shall be payable for such period as may be determined at the time it is granted, but may be renewed from time to time.

Increase of unemployability supplement

1.585   3.—(1) Subject to the following provisions of this paragraph, if on the qualifying date the beneficiary was—

(a) a man under the age of 60, or

(b) a woman under the age of 55,

the weekly rate of unemployability supplement shall be increased by the appropriate amount specified in Schedule 4, Part V, paragraph 6.

(2) Where for any period the beneficiary is entitled to a Category A or Category B retirement pension [¹ . . .] and the weekly rate of the pension includes an additional pension such as is mentioned in section 44(3)(b) above, for that period the relevant amount shall be deducted from the amount that would otherwise be the increase under this paragraph and the beneficiary shall be entitled to an increase only if there is a balance after that deduction and, if there is such a balance, only to an amount equal to it.

(3) In this paragraph "the relevant amount" means an amount equal to the additional pension reduced by the amount of any reduction in the weekly rate of the retirement pension [¹ . . .] made by virtue of [² section 46] [¹⁰ or 46A] of the Pensions Act.

[¹² (3A) In sub-paragraphs (2) and (3) above references to additional pension do not include any amount of additional pension attributable to units of additional pension.

(3B) For units of additional pension, see section 14A.]

(4) In this paragraph references to an additional pension are references to that pension after any increase under section 52(3) above but without any increase under paragraphs 1 and 2 of Schedule 5 to this Act.

(5) In this paragraph "the qualifying date" means, subject to sub-paragraphs (6) and (7) below, the beginning of the first week for which the beneficiary qualified for unemployability supplement.

(6) If the incapacity for work in respect of which unemployability supplement is payable forms part of a period of interruption of employment which has continued from a date earlier than the date fixed under sub-paragraph (5) above, the qualifying date means the first day in that period which is a day of incapacity for work, or such earlier day as may be prescribed.

(7) Subject to sub-paragraph (6) above, if there have been two or more periods for which the beneficiary was entitled to unemployability supplement, the qualifying date shall be, in relation to unemployability supplement for a day in any one of those periods, the beginning of the first week of that period.

(8) for the purposes of sub-paragraph (7) above—

(a) a break of more than 8 weeks in entitlement to unemployability supplement means that the periods before and after the break are two different periods; and

(b) a break of 8 weeks or less is to be disregarded.

(9) The Secretary of State may by regulations provide that sub-paragraph (8) above shall have effect as if for the references to 8 weeks there were substituted references to a larger number of weeks specified in the regulations.

(10) In this paragraph "period of interruption of employment" has the same meaning as [³ a jobseeking period and any period linked to such a period has for the purposes of the Jobseekers Act 1995].

(11) The provisions of this paragraph are subject to [² section 46(6) and (7) (entitlement to guaranteed minimum pensions and increases of unemployability supplement).]

Increase for beneficiary's dependent children [⁸ and qualifying young persons]

1.586   4.—(1) Subject to the provisions of this paragraph and paragraph 5 below, the weekly rate of a disablement pension where the beneficiary is entitled to an unemployability supplement shall be increased for any period during which the beneficiary is entitled to child benefit in respect of [⁸ one or more children or qualifying young persons].

(2) The amount of the increase shall be as specified in Schedule 4, Part V, paragraph 7.

(3) In any case where—

[⁷(a) a beneficiary is one of two persons who are—
    (i) spouses or civil partners residing together,
    [¹¹(ii) two people who are not married to, or civil partners of, each other but are living together as a married couple, and]

(b) the other person had earnings in any week,

the beneficiary's right to payment of increases for the following week under this paragraph shall be determined in accordance with sub-paragraph (4) below.

(4) No such increase shall be payable—

(a) in respect of the first child [⁸ or qualifying young person] where the earnings were [⁹ £215] or more; and

(b) in respect of a further child [⁸ or qualifying young person] for each complete [⁴ £28] by which the earnings exceeded [⁹ £215].

(5) The Secretary of State may by order substitute larger amounts for the amounts for the time being specified in sub-paragraph (4) above.

(6) In this paragraph "week" means such period of 7 days as may be prescribed by regulations made for the purposes of this paragraph.

Additional provisions as to increase under paragraph 4

5.—(1) An increase under paragraph 4 above of any amount in respect of a particular child [⁸ or qualifying young person] shall for any period be payable only if during that period one or other of the following conditions is satisfied with respect to the child [⁸ or qualifying young person]   **1.587**

(a) the beneficiary would be treated for the purposes of Part IX of this Act as having the child [⁸ or qualifying young person] living with him; or

(b) the requisite contributions are being made to the cost of providing for the child [⁸ or qualifying young person].

(2) The condition specified in paragraph (b) of sub-paragraph (1) above is to be treated as satisfied if, and only if—

(a) such contributions are being made at a weekly rate not less than the amount referred to in that sub-paragraph—
    (i) by the beneficiary, or
    (ii) where the beneficiary is one of two spouses [⁷ or civil partners] residing together, by them together; and

(b) except in prescribed cases, the contributions are over and above those required for the purposes of satisfying section 143(1)(b) above.

Increase for adult dependants

6.—(1) The weekly rate of a disablement pension where the beneficiary is entitled to an unemployability supplement shall be increased under this paragraph for any period during which—   **1.588**

(a) the beneficiary is—
    (i) residing with his spouse [⁷ or civil partner], or
    (ii) contributing to the maintenance of his spouse [⁷ or civil partner] at the requisite rate; or

(b) a person—
    (i) who is neither the spouse [⁷ or civil partner] of the beneficiary nor a child [⁸ or qualifying young person], and
    (ii) in relation to whom such further conditions as may be prescribed are fulfilled,

has the care of [⁸ one or more children or qualifying young persons] in respect of whom the beneficiary is entitled to child benefit.

(2) The amount of the increase under this paragraph shall be that specified in Schedule 4, Part V, paragraph 8 and the requisite rate for the purposes of sub-paragraph (1)(a) above is a weekly rate not less than that amount.

(3) Regulations may provide that, for any period during which—

(a) the beneficiary is contributing to the maintenance of his or her spouse [⁷ or civil partner] at the requisite rate, and

(b) the weekly earnings of the spouse [⁷ or civil partner] exceed such amount as may be prescribed

there shall be no increase of benefit under this paragraph.

(4) Regulations may provide that, for any period during which the beneficiary is residing with his or her spouse [⁷ or civil partner] and the spouse [⁷ or civil partner] has earnings—

    (a) the increase of benefit under this paragraph shall be subject to a reduction in respect of the spouse's [⁷ or civil partner's] earnings; or

    (b) there shall be no increase of benefit under this paragraph.

(5) Regulations may, in a case within sub-paragraph (1)(b) above in which the person there referred to is residing with the beneficiary and fulfils such further conditions as may be prescribed, authorise an increase of benefit under this paragraph, but subject, taking account of the earnings of the person residing with the beneficiary, other than such of that person's earnings from employment by the beneficiary as may be prescribed, to provisions comparable to those that may be made by virtue of sub-paragraph (4) above.

(6) Regulations under this paragraph may, in connection with any reduction or extinguishment of an increase of benefit in respect of earnings, prescribe the method of calculating or estimating the earnings.

(7) A beneficiary shall not be entitled to an increase of benefit under this paragraph in respect of more than one person for the same period.

Earnings to include occupational and personal pensions for purposes of disablement pension

1.589   7.—(1) Except as may be prescribed, any reference to earnings in paragraph 4 or 6 above includes a reference to payments by way of occupational or personal pension.

(2) For the purposes of those paragraphs, the Secretary of State may by regulations provide, in relation to cases where payments by way of occupational or personal pension are made otherwise than weekly, that any necessary apportionment of the payments shall be made in such manner and on such basis as may be prescribed.

Dependency increases: continuation of awards in cases of fluctuating earnings

1.590   8.—(1) Where a beneficiary—

    (a) has been awarded an increase of benefit under paragraph 4 or 6 above, but

    (b) ceases to be entitled to the increase by reason only that the weekly earnings of some other person ("the relevant earner") exceed the amount of the increase or, as the case may be, some specified amount,

then, if and so long as the beneficiary would have continued to be entitled to the increase, disregarding any such excess of earnings, the award shall continue in force but the increase shall not be payable for any week if the earnings relevant to that week exceed the amount of the increase or, as the case may be, the specified amount.

(2) In this paragraph the earnings which are relevant to any week are those earnings of the relevant earner which, apart from this paragraph, would be taken into account in determining whether the beneficiary is entitled to the increase in question for that week.

PART II

DISABLEMENT GRATUITY

1.591   9.—(1) An employed earner shall be entitled to a disablement gratuity, if—

    (a) he made a claim for disablement benefit before 1st October, 1986;

    (b) he suffered as the result of the relevant accident from loss of physical or mental faculty such that the extent of the resulting disablement assessed in accordance with Schedule 6 to this Act amounts to not less than 1 per cent.; and

    (c) the extent of the disablement is assessed for the period taken into account as amounting to less than 20 per cent.

(2) A disablement gratuity shall be—

    (a) of an amount fixed, in accordance with the length of the period and the degree of the disablement, by a prescribed scale, but not in any case exceeding the amount specified in Schedule 4, Part V, paragraph 9; and

    (b) payable, if and in such cases as regulations so provide, by instalments.

(3) A person shall not be entitled to disablement gratuity until after the expiry of the period of 90 days (disregarding Sundays) beginning with the day of the relevant accident.

Part III

Increase of Disablement Pension During Hospital Treatment

10.—(1) This Part of this Schedule has effect in relation to a period during which a person   **1.592** is receiving medical treatment as an in-patient in a hospital or similar institution and which—
  (a) commenced before 6th April 1987; or
  (b) commenced after that date but within a period of 28 days from the end of the period during which he last received an increase of benefit under section 62 of the 1975 Act or this paragraph in respect of such treatment for the relevant injury or loss of faculty.

(2) Where a person is awarded disablement benefit, but the extent of his disablement is assessed for the period taken into account by the assessment at less than 100 per cent., it shall be treated as assessed at 100 per cent. for any part of that period, whether before or after the making of the assessment or the award of benefit, during which he receives, as an in-patient in a hospital or similar institution, medical treatment for the relevant injury or loss of faculty.

(3) Where the extent of the disablement is assessed for that period at less than 20 per cent., sub-paragraph (2) above shall not affect the assessment; but in the case of a disablement pension payable by virtue of this paragraph to a person awarded a disablement gratuity wholly or partly in respect of the same period, the weekly rate of the pension (after allowing for any increase under Part V of this Act) shall be reduced by the amount prescribed as being the weekly value of his gratuity.

Part IV

Reduced Earnings Allowance

11.—(1) Subject to the provisions of this paragraph, an employed earner shall be entitled to   **1.593** reduced earnings allowance if—
  (a) he is entitled to a disablement pension or would be so entitled if that pension were payable where disablement is assessed at not less than 1 per cent.; and
  (b) as a result of the relevant loss of faculty, he is either—
    (i) incapable, and likely to remain permanently incapable, of following his regular occupation; and
    (ii) incapable of following employment of an equivalent standard which is suitable in his case,

or is, and has at all times since the end of the period of 90 days referred to in section 103(6) above been, incapable of following that occupation or any such employment; but a person shall not be entitled to reduced earnings allowance to the extent that the relevant loss of faculty results from an accident happening on or after 1st October 1990 (the day on which section 3 of the Social Security Act 1990 came into force) [⁵ and a person shall not be entitled to reduced earnings allowance—
    (i) in relation to a disease prescribed on or after 10th October 1994 under section 108(2) above; or
    (ii) in relation to a disease prescribed before 10th October 1994 whose prescription is extended on or after that date under section 108(2) above but only in so far as the prescription has been so extended].

(2) A person—
  (a) who immediately before that date is entitled to reduced earnings allowance in consequence of the relevant accident; but
  (b) who subsequently ceases to be entitled to that allowance for one or more days,
shall not again be entitled to reduced earnings allowance in consequence of that accident; but this sub-paragraph does not prevent the making at any time of a claim for, or an award of, reduced earnings allowance in consequence of that accident for a period which commences not later than the day after that on which the claimant was last entitled to that allowance in consequence of that accident.

(3) For the purposes of sub-paragraph (2) above—
  (a) a person who, apart from section 103(6) above, would have been entitled to reduced earnings allowance immediately before 1st October 1990 shall be treated as entitled to that allowance on any day (including a Sunday) on which he would have been entitled to it apart from that provision;
  (b) regulations may prescribe other circumstances in which a person is to be treated as

entitled, or as having been entitled, to reduced earnings allowance on any prescribed day.

(4) The Secretary of State may by regulations provide that in prescribed circumstances employed earner's employment in which a claimant was engaged when the relevant accident took place but which was not his regular occupation is to be treated as if it had been his regular occupation.

(5) In sub-paragraph (1) above—

    (a) references to a person's regular occupation are to be taken as not including any subsidiary occupation, except to the extent that they fall to be treated as including such an occupation by virtue of regulations under sub-paragraph (4) above; and

    (b) employment of an equivalent standard is to be taken as not including employment other than employed earner's employment;

and in assessing the standard of remuneration in any employment, including a person's regular occupation, regard is to be had to his reasonable prospect of advancement.

(6) For the purposes of this Part of this Schedule a person's regular occupation is to be treated as extending to and including employment in the capacities to which the persons in that occupation (or a class or description of them to which he belonged at the time of the relevant accident) are in the normal course advanced, and to which, if he had continued to follow that occupation without having suffered the relevant loss of faculty, he would have had at least the normal prospects of advancement; and so long as he is, as a result of the relevant loss of faculty, deprived in whole or in part of those prospects, he is to be treated as incapable of following that occupation.

(7) Regulations may for the purposes of this Part of this Schedule provide that a person is not to be treated as capable of following an occupation or employment merely because of his working thereat during a period of trial or for purposes of rehabilitation or training or in other prescribed circumstances.

(8) Reduced earnings allowance shall be awarded—

    (a) for such period as may be determined at the time of the award; and

    (b) if at the end of that period the beneficiary submits a fresh claim for the allowance, for such further period, commencing as mentioned in sub-paragraph (2) above, as may be determined.

(9) The award may not be for a period longer than the period to be taken into account under paragraph 4 or 6 of Schedule 6 to this Act.

(10) Reduced earnings allowance shall be payable at a rate determined by reference to the beneficiary's probable standard of remuneration during the period for which it is granted in any employed earner's employments which are suitable in his case and which he is likely to be capable of following as compared with that in the relevant occupation, but in no case at a rate higher than 40 per cent of the maximum rate of a disablement pension or at a rate such that the aggregate of disablement pension (not including increases in disablement pension under any provision of this Act) and reduced earnings allowance awarded to the beneficiary exceeds 140 per cent. of the maximum rate of a disablement pension.

(11) Sub-paragraph (10) above shall have effect in the case of a person who retired from regular employment before 6th April 1987 with the substitution for "140 per cent." of "100 per cent.".

(12) In sub-paragraph (10) above "the relevant occupation" means—

    (a) in relation to a person who is entitled to reduced earnings allowance by virtue of regulations under sub-paragraph (4) above, the occupation in which he was engaged when the relevant accident took place; and

    (b) in relation to any other person who is entitled to reduced earnings allowance, his regular occupation within the meaning of sub-paragraph (1) above.

[6 (12A) The reference in sub-paragraph (11) above to a person who has retired from regular employment includes a reference—

    (a) to a person who under subsection (3) of section 27 of the 1975 Act was treated for the purposes of that Act as having retired from regular employment; and

    (b) to a person who under subsection (5) of that section was deemed for those purposes to have retired from it.]

(13) On any award except the first the probable standard of his remuneration shall be determined in such manner as may be prescribed; and, without prejudice to the generality of this sub-paragraph, regulations may provide in prescribed circumstances for the probable standard of remuneration to be determined by reference—

    (a) to the standard determined at the time of the last previous award of reduced earnings allowance; and

(b) to scales or indices of earnings in a particular industry or description of industries or any other data relating to such earnings.

(14) In this paragraph "maximum rate of a disablement pension" means the rate specified in the first entry in column (2) of Schedule 4, Part V, paragraph 1 and does not include increases in disablement pension under any provision of this Act.

Supplementary

12.—(1) A person who on 10th April 1988 or 9th April 1989 satisfies the conditions—   **1.594**
  (a) that he has attained pensionable age;
  (b) that he has retired from regular employment; and
  (c) that he is entitled to reduced earnings allowance,
shall be entitled to that allowance for life.

(2) In the case of any beneficiary who is entitled to reduced earnings allowance by virtue of sub-paragraph (1) above, the allowance shall be payable, subject to any enactment contained in Part V or VI of this Act or in the Administration Act and to any regulations made under any such enactment, at the weekly rate at which it was payable to the beneficiary on the relevant date or would have been payable to him on that date but for any such enactment or regulations.

(3) For the purpose of determining under sub-paragraph (2) above the weekly rate of reduced earnings allowance payable in the case of a qualifying beneficiary, it shall be assumed that the weekly rate at which the allowance was payable to him on the relevant date was—
  (a) £25.84, where that date is 10th April 1988, or
  (b) £26.96, where that date is 9th April 1989.

(4) In sub-paragraph (3) above "qualifying beneficiary" means a person entitled to reduced earnings allowance by virtue of sub-paragraph (1) above who—
  (a) did not attain pensionable age before 6th April 1987, or
  (b) did not retire from regular employment before that date,
and who, on the relevant date, was entitled to the allowance at a rate which was restricted under paragraph 11(10) above by reference to 40 per cent. of the maximum rate of disablement pension.

(5) For a beneficiary who is entitled to reduced earnings allowance by virtue of satisfying the conditions in sub-paragraph (1) above on 10th April 1988 the relevant date is that date.

(6) For a beneficiary who is entitled to it by virtue only of satisfying those conditions on 9th April 1989 the relevant date is that date.

[[6] (7) The reference in sub-paragraph (1) above to a person who has retired from regular employment includes a reference—
  (a) to a person who under subsection (3) of section 27 of the 1975 Act was treated for the purposes of that Act as having retired from regular employment; and
  (b) to a person who under subsection (5) of that section was deemed for those purposes to have retired from it.]

PART V

RETIREMENT ALLOWANCE

13.—(1) Subject to the provisions of this Part of this Schedule, a person who—   **1.595**
  (a) has attained pensionable age; and
  (b) gives up regular employment on or after 10th April 1989; and
  (c) was entitled to reduced earnings allowance (by virtue either of one award or of a number of awards) on the day immediately before he gave up such employment,
shall cease to be entitled to reduced earnings allowance as from the day on which he gives up regular employment.

(2) If the day before a person ceases under sub-paragraph (1) above to be entitled to reduced earnings allowance he is entitled to the allowance (by virtue either of one award or of a number of awards) at a weekly rate or aggregate weekly rate of not less than £2.00, he shall be entitled to a benefit, to be known as "retirement allowance".

(3) Retirement allowance shall be payable to him (subject to any enactment contained in Part V or VI of this Act or in the Administration Act and to any regulations made under any such enactment) for life.

(4) Subject to sub-paragraph (6) below, the weekly rate of a beneficiary's retirement allowance shall be—

(a) 25 per cent of the weekly rate at which he was last entitled to reduced earnings allowance; or

(b) 10 per cent of the maximum rate of a disablement pension, whichever is the less.

(5) For the purpose of determining under sub-paragraph (4) above the weekly rate of retirement allowance in the case of a beneficiary who—

(a) retires or is deemed to have retired on 10th April 1989, and

(b) on 9th April 1989 was entitled to reduced earnings allowance at a rate which was restricted under paragraph 11(10) above by reference to 40 per cent. of the maximum rate of disablement pension,

it shall be assumed that the weekly rate of reduced earnings allowance to which he was entitled on 9th April 1989 was £26.96.

(6) If the weekly rate of the beneficiary's retirement allowance—

(a) would not be a whole number of pence; and

(b) would exceed the whole number of pence next below it by ½p or more,

the beneficiary shall be entitled to retirement allowance at a rate equal to the next higher whole number of pence.

(7) The sums falling to be calculated under sub-paragraph (4) above are subject to alteration by orders made by the Secretary of State under section 150 of the Administration Act.

(8) Regulations may—

(a) make provision with respect to the meaning of "regular employment" for the purposes of this paragraph; and

(b) prescribe circumstances in which, and periods for which, a person is or is not to be regarded for those purposes as having given up such employment.

(9) Regulations under sub-paragraph (8) above may, in particular—

(a) provide for a person to be regarded—

(i) as having given up regular employment, notwithstanding that he is or intends to be an earner; or

(ii) as not having given up regular employment, notwithstanding that he has or may have one or more days of interruption of employment; and

(b) prescribe circumstances in which a person is or is not to be regarded as having given up regular employment by reference to—

(i) the level or frequency of his earnings during a prescribed period; or

(ii) the number of hours for which he works during a prescribed period calculated in a prescribed manner.

[³ (10) "Day of interruption of employment" means a day which forms part of—

(a) a jobseeking period (as defined by the Jobseekers Act 1995), or

(b) a linked period (as defined by that Act).]

(11) In this paragraph "maximum rate of a disablement pension" means the rate specified in the first entry in column (2) of Schedule 4, Part V, paragraph 1 and does not include increases in disablement pension under any provision of this Act.

GENERAL NOTE

1.596   The sums falling to be calculated under para.13(4) above are to be increased by 2.7 per cent with effect from April 9, 2014. (See Social Security Benefits Up-rating Order 2014 (SI 2014/516) art.4(2) and art.6(8)).

PART VI

INDUSTRIAL DEATH BENEFIT

Introductory

1.597   **Paras 14.–21.** *Omitted. With effect from December 5, 2012, s.67 of the Welfare Reform Act 2012 amended para.14 so that no claim for industrial death benefit can be made on or after that date. Since claims had already been restricted to deaths occurring before April 10, 1988 it is unlikely that any new claims will be forthcoming (none have been made for many years), but any that do will instead be dealt with under the bereavement benefit legislation.*

AMENDMENTS

1. Social Security (Incapacity for Work) Act 1994 Sch.1 para.41 (April 13, 1995).
2. Pensions Schemes Act 1993 Sch.8 para.43 (February 7, 1994).

3. Jobseekers Act 1995 Sch.2 para.36 (October 14, 1994).

4. Social Security (Industrial Injuries) (Dependency) (Permitted Earnings Limits) Order 2012 (SI 2012/823) art.2 (April 11, 2012).

5. Social Security (Industrial Injuries) (Prescribed Diseases) Regulations 1985 reg.14A (October 10, 1994).

6. Social Security (Consequential Provisions) Act 1992 Sch.4 paras.10 and 11 (transitorily).

7. Civil Partnership Act 2004 s.254 and Sch.24 Pt 3, para.52 (December 5, 2005).

8. Child Benefit Act 2005 ss.1 and 2, Sch.1 para.16 (April 10, 2006).

9. Social Security (Industrial Injuries) (Dependency) (Permitted Earnings Limits) Order 2012 (SI 2012/823) art.2 (April 11, 2012).

10. Pensions Act 2008 Sch.4 para.13 (January 3, 2012).

11. Marriage (Same Sex Couples) Act 2013 (Consequential and Contrary Provisions and Scotland) Order 2014 art.2, Sch.1 para.22 (March 13, 2014). (England and Wales only) and Marriage and Civil Partnership (Scotland) Act 2014 and Civil Partnership Act 2004 (Consequential Provisions and Modifications) Order 2014 (SI 2014/3229) art.5(3) Sch.4 para.2(1) and (20) (December 16, 2014) (Scotland only).

12. Pensions Act 2014 (Consequential Amendments) (Units of Additional Pension) Order 2014 (SI 2016/3213) art.3 (October 12, 2015).

DERIVATIONS

SSA 1975 ss.57–59B, 62, 64–64A and 84A; SS (No. 2)A, s.3(4); SSA 1986 s.39 and Sch.3; SSA 1988 s.2.

1.598

GENERAL NOTE

This Schedule preserves for certain claimants entitlement to industrial injuries benefits that have been abolished. Pt I preserves unemployability supplement, which was an increase of disablement pension for those incapable of work owing to an industrial accident or prescribed disease, but only for those who were entitled to it immediately before April 6, 1987. Pt II preserves disablement gratuities, which were lump sums paid instead of disablement pension for those whose disablement was assessed at between 1 per cent and 19 per cent. It applies where the claim was made before October 1, 1986 and still has relevance where there has been a series of provisional assessments since then. Pt III preserves hospital treatment allowance for those who have been more or less continuously entitled to it since April 6, 1987. Parts IV and V preserve reduced earnings allowance and retirement allowance for those whose earning capacity has been reduced by an industrial accident occurring before, or an industrial disease the onset of which was before, October 1, 1990 (see *CI/3178/2003*).

1.599

No entitlement to REA (and therefore also retirement allowance) can arise in respect of a disease prescribed on or after October 10, 1994, nor in respect of the extension aspect of a disease prescribed prior to that date, but extended on or after October 10, 1994. Those who were entitled to reduced earnings allowance before April 10, 1989 and had retired before that date, remain entitled to the allowance for life at a frozen rate. Otherwise, people who have reached pensionable age are no longer entitled to reduced earnings allowance and become entitled to retirement allowance instead, unless they remain in regular employment for at least 10 hours a week (see the Social Security (Industrial Injuries) (Regular Employment) Regulations 1990 (SI 1990/256) as amended and *R(I) 2/99* in which the tortuous history of this legislation is examined).

As Commissioner Howell put it in *CI/5138/2002*,

"a person must *either* have a contract of service whose terms include the minimum 10-hour average requirement in (a), *or* be actually undertaking work, e.g. on his or her own account as a self-employed person or as a casual employee, which when one looks at the amount and duration of work actually done meets the alternative 10-hour average condition in (b). If there is any break, however short, in the continuity of meeting those conditions, then the person concerned is regarded for good as having given up regular employment from the start of the first week in which the conditions are no longer met, and can never thereafter regain the right to reduced earnings allowance" (para.7).

Whether activities carried on by the claimant amount to "gainful employment" is a matter of fact and degree for the tribunal seeing and hearing the evidence to determine (*ibid*, para.12). Pt VI, which is omitted, provides for industrial death benefit in relation to deaths before April 11, 1988.

Sch. Pt IV: Reduced Earnings Allowance

1.600   *(1) Reduced Earnings Allowance: its creation and slow demise*
         The precursor of this Part (SSA 1975 s.59A) was inserted by SSA 1986 Sch.3, para.5(1) with effect from October 1, 1986, and was further amended with effect from October 1, 1990, so as to provide for the gradual phasing out of the benefit, as is explained below.
         Reduced Earnings Allowance (REA) replaced the misnamed Special Hardship Allowance and is a benefit in its own right, rather than a mere supplement to disablement benefit. The benefits remain linked and a claimant cannot be entitled to REA without making a claim to disablement benefit (*Whalley* v *Secretary of State for Work and Pensions* [2001] EWCA Civ 166, reported as *R(I) 2/03*, disapproving Commissioner Williams on this point in *CI 6207/1999*). The conditions of entitlement are, however, similar to those that applied to Special Hardship Allowance, so that decisions on the meaning of the same statutory phrases in the context of that allowance remain authoritative. REA can continue in payment after retirement, but only for those entitled to it at retirement, who retired on or before April 9, 1989. For those retiring after that date, and entitled to REA immediately before retirement, retirement allowance (see Pt V, below) is available as a replacement for REA during retirement, and is payable for life.
         In *Chief Adjudication Officer* v *Maguire* (reported as *R(I) 3/99*), the Court of Appeal held that it is still possible to claim special hardship allowance which was the predecessor of reduced earnings allowance. However, the Secretary of State does not issue claim forms for special hardship allowance and so must be persuaded to accept some other document as a claim although it is arguable that the fact that he does not issue proper claim forms may limit the extent to which he can properly decide not to accept other documents as valid claims.
         The October 1990 changes implemented the Government's policy of preventing arising new entitlements to reduced earnings allowance, while preserving existing entitlements until they otherwise cease, so that ensuing phased reductions in expenditure on this benefit (estimated £1m in 1990–91, £15m in 1991–82 and £40m in 1992–93—see *Hansard*, HC Vol.165, col.630, *per* the Secretary of State for Social Security) could be deployed to help finance a package of new benefits to improve the position of disabled people as a whole during the 1990s. It was considered that payment of reduced earnings allowance was in many cases unnecessarily duplicative, since many non-working recipients of it also received invalidity benefit.
         Note that in general, references to the date of an accident are to be construed, in the case of prescribed diseases, as references to the date of onset of the disease (see ss.108 and 109, Prescribed Diseases Regs, regs.11 and 12; (*CI/3178/2003*).
         The wording of para.11(1) ("but a person shall not be entitled . . . from an accident happening on or after the appointed day") prevents arising any new entitlement, or the enhancement through increased incapacity of an existing entitlement, in respect of a loss of faculty resulting from an accident which happens on or after October 1, 1990 (that being the date s.3 of the SSA 1990 came into force.) In *JR* v *Secretary of State for Work and Pensions (II)* [2013] UKUT 317 (AAC), Judge Mesher considered the effect of the October 1994 amendment to para.11(1):

"and a person shall not be entitled to reduced earnings allowance—

...

     (ii) in relation to a disease prescribed before 10th October 1994 whose prescription is extended on or after that date under section 108(2) above but only in so far as the prescription has been so extended]."

He held that since the

"prescription process under section 108 can only be regarded as covering the definition of both diseases and occupational groups. [there was] nothing in the fact that the reference in paragraph 11(1) of Schedule 7 is to section 108(2) to suggest that extension of the prescription is limited to the definition of occupational groups covered. ... the identification of those groups of employed earners for whom a disease ought to be treated as a risk of their occupation is directed just as much (if not more so in the light of paragraph (b)) at the identification and definition of the disease concerned as at the identification of the appropriate occupational groups" (para. 20)

A decision by a tribunal determining the date of onset for a PD, whether given in respect of disablement benefit or REA, as the case may be, binds a later tribunal considering the issue for either benefit. Where there was a refusal by a tribunal of a claim for disablement benefit on the ground that the claimant did not have PD A11 at the date of the decision, a later decision-maker, faced with a new claim for that benefit or for REA, cannot specify a date of onset for the disease which is prior to the refusal of the first claim. See also *CI/2531/2001*, para.15:

1.601

"if a person makes a claim or successive claims for disablement benefit (and, by the same token, reduced earnings allowance, which depend on establishing the same loss of faculty) in respect of occupational deafness, the 'date of onset' can never be earlier than that of the *first* such claim which results in the actual payment of benefit; and the date so determined is also, by regulation 6(1), to be treated as the date of onset for the purposes of each subsequent claim" (*per* Commissioner Howell).

See further *CI/4249/2003*, another decision of Commissioner Howell. But note that two Commissioners take the view that *Whalley* is not wholly applicable in respect of decisions made under the DMA regime post SSA 1998. Commissioner Rowland in *R(I) 2/04* considered the remarks in *Whalley* to have been *obiter*. Moreover, the reasoning applied on the basis of the decision-making processes prior to the SSA 1998, so that the demise of the earlier provisions on finality of an MAT's decision, means that the binding nature of a decision on a date of onset of a PD for disablement benefit purposes flows from the terms of Prescribed Diseases Regs, reg.6(para.14), a view endorsed by Commissioner Howell in *R(I) 5/04* (paras 16–18). See further the commentary to that regulation, below.

As modified from October 10, 1994, para. 11(1) also precludes entitlement to REA in respect of a disease prescribed on or after that date, and prevents entitlement to the allowance in respect of the extension aspect of a disease prescribed prior to that date, but extended on or after October 10, 1994 (see reg.3 of the Social Security (Industrial Injuries) (Prescribed Diseases) Amendment Regulations 1994 (SI 1994/2343), inserting Social Security (Industrial Injuries) (Prescribed Diseases) Regulations 1985 (SI 1985/967), reg.14A).

Sub-paras (2) and (3) set out the circumstances in which entitlement to reduced earnings allowance is protected. In effect entitlement is here a wider than normal notion since the provisions protect both those who were beneficiaries immediately before October 1, 1990, and those whose accident or onset of a prescribed industrial disease occurred before that date and who would have been beneficiaries but for the fact that the 90-day waiting period set by s.103(6) had not expired. Moreover, regulations can extend the categories of persons entitled (sub-para.(3)(b)). A single day's gap in entitlement on or after October 1, 1990, brings the preserved entitlement to an end; to remain, preserved entitlement must exist on and be continuous after October 1, 1990. Entitlement, of course, depends on the making of a valid claim (SSAA 1992, s.1). So, no doubt to prevent loss of title for example because a renewal claim is not made on the day following the lapse of the previous award, and to cater for late claims and the consequence of revision or appeal of a decision, sub-para.(2) specifically provides, to allay any doubts, that its preclusive rule does not prevent the making at any time of a claim for, or an award of, reduced earnings allowance in consequence of an accident which occurred before October 1, 1990, for a period providing complete continuity with the previous period of entitlement in respect of that accident.

On the application of para.(2) to seasonal workers who lose entitlement to REA during their off-season because there is then no reduction in earning power, see *CI/4940/01* applying *R(I) 56/53*.

1.602 *(2) Reduced Earnings Allowance: conditions of entitlement*

For those not precluded from REA by the provisions noted above, the key conditions of entitlement are set out in para.11.

The structure of the paragraph is as follows:

Sub-para.(1) Conditions of entitlement—basic concepts of "the relevant loss of faculty", "regular occupation", "suitable employment of an equivalent standard", "incapacity".

Sub-para.(4) Regular occupation—deeming regulations.

Sub-para.(5) Regular occupation; equivalent standard; standard of remuneration—partial definitions.

Sub-para.(6) Regular occupation—effect of prospects of advancement.

Sub-para.(7) Incapacity—trial period and rehabilitative work.

Sub-para.(8) Length of award—general.

Sub-para.(9) Length of award—limitation to period of assessment.

Sub-paras (10), (11) Amount of award—method of calculation.

Sub-para.(12) Relevant occupation—definition.

1.603 In *CI/4478/1999* (reported as part of *R(I)2/02*), Commissioner Rowland held that where someone had a cumulative loss of earnings due to a number of industrial accidents *each of which made him incapable of following a different "regular occupation"*, he can have only one award of REA, subject to the statutory maximum, in respect of all the accidents. In *Hagan v Secretary of State for Social Security* (neutral citation EWCA Civ 1452—reported as part of *R(I) 2/02*), the Court of Appeal on July 30, 2001 set this aside as erroneous in law. The Court of Appeal accepted the Secretary of State's argument, summarised as follows:

"(1) there can be multiple claims for awards of REA in circumstances where there are successive industrial injuries each of which causes a change from the previous regular occupation; (2) on each claim the maximum amount of REA payable is 40 per cent of the maximum disablement pension; but (3) this 40 per cent limit applies only to each claim separately and if there are multiple claims then the maximum amount payable is not 40 per cent but the 140 per cent referred to in the last part of paragraph 11(10).

The Secretary of State put before the court the following example. In 1986 a mining foreman suffers an injury in the mine and loses his hearing such that he can no longer be a foreman and has to be 'demoted' to a miner. The assessment of disability by reason of the loss of hearing is 20 per cent and the reduction in earnings is significantly in excess of 40 per cent of the disablement pension. On a claim for REA and disablement pension immediately after this accident he would have been awarded 20 per cent of the maximum disablement pension as disablement pension, and 40 per cent of the maximum disablement pension as REA. Two years later he lost the use of an arm by reason of an explosion in the mine, as a result of which he could no longer work down the mine and had to be further 'demoted' to a 'winchman'. His assessment of disability in relation to this accident (loss of use of arm) is 30 per cent, leading to an aggregated disablement pension award under section 103(2) of 50 per cent. His loss of earnings is again substantially in excess of 40 per cent of the maximum disablement pension and so on the basis of his second accident and the second change of regular occupation, he would again be entitled to 40 per cent of REA. The cumulative effect is 80 per cent of the maximum disablement pension by way of REA and 50 per cent by way of disability pension. This is less than the maximum in the final part of para.11(10) and therefore total benefit amounting to 130 per cent of the maximum amount of disablement pension is payable by reason of the two accidents under the separate benefits.

On the analysis of the Social Security Commissioner on the same facts, the miner would be entitled to 50 per cent disablement pension because of the aggregated effect of the injuries pursuant to section 103(2) but would only be entitled to make one REA claim giving rise to a maximum entitlement of 40 per cent of REA and thus an overall total of 90 per cent of the maximum disability pension. That example illustrates why it is that I said at the beginning of this judgment that the Secretary of State is in the relatively unusual position of arguing for a more generous interpretation of the law.' (paras 28–30).

In *CI/1052/2001*, Commissioner Rowland distinguished *Hagan*, which　　　　　　1.604

> "was concerned with a case where the claimant claimed to have lost earnings due to becoming incapable of following one occupation as a result of one accident and then to have lost further earnings due to becoming incapable of following another regular occupation as a result of another accident. In the present case, it is the Secretary of State's case that the claimant's regular occupation at the onset of his vibration white finger was the same as his regular occupation at the time of his 1985 accident" (para.7).

In the situation before him in the present case, citing *R(I) 2/56*, the Commissioner considered that

> "only one award of reduced earnings allowance, which might equally well have been made in respect of either the 1985 accident or the vibration white finger, may be made. As an award had already been made at the maximum rate in respect of the 1985 accident, the tribunal's decision in respect of the vibration white finger was not erroneous in point of law" (para.9).

Sub-paragraph (1)(a): For entitlement to disablement pension see s.103 and notes,　　1.605
above. The allowance may be paid where the assessment of disablement is at least 1 per cent, and one of the other two conditions in sub-para.1(b), below, is satisfied. Note that the allowance is still linked with disablement pension—the claimant must actually be entitled to disablement pension, or entitled but for the level of assessment. The allowance will not, therefore, be payable until the 15-week waiting period (see s.103(6), above) has elapsed.

Sub-paragraph (1)(b): The claimant must show that he is (as a result of the relevant　　1.606
loss of faculty) incapable of following his regular occupation or suitable employment of an equivalent standard. In addition, he must show *either* that he is likely to remain permanently incapable of following his regular occupation (the "permanent" condition), *or* that he has been incapable of following his regular occupation or employment of an equivalent standard at all times since the end of the 15 week waiting period (the "continuous" condition). Incapacity for the regular occupation must be caused by the relevant loss of faculty. Thus, the claim for REA failed in *IE v SSWP (II)* [2011] UKUT 383 (AAC) where the claimant's incapacity for his regular occupation instead resulted solely from degenerative disease and not in any material degree from loss of faculty due to his industrial accident.

In *CI/3379/2002*, Commissioner Howell reminded us that

"[as] was held by the Commissioner in reported decision *R(I) 7/53* . . ., the question of whether a claimant is likely to remain permanently incapable of following his regular occupation for the purposes of reduced earnings allowance is one to be assessed by the tribunal, on the probabilities of the case, and having regard to the evidence before them. As the Commissioner says in paragraph 10, the burden of proving that he is likely to remain permanently incapable rests on the claimant; or as I would for my part prefer to put it in an inquisitorial jurisdiction, the tribunal must be affirmatively satisfied on the evidence before them that he *is* so incapable, on one test or the other, before they can hold him entitled to the benefit (para.14).

While PD A11 (Vibration white finger) is degenerative and will not improve once contracted, no rule of law can be deduced from *R(I) 2/81, CI 15803/1996* or AOG, para.85738 to the effect that a tribunal must necessarily assume, regardless of the full evidence, that a claimant suffering from vibration white finger cannot continue with his regular occupation. This may be so in many cases, and be a sensible medical and administrative assumption. But a tribunal must consider the matter in the light of all the evidence. Future injury and risk are relevant factors to consider, but no more than that. Nor can the claimant rely on statements in the AOG (now DMG) as creating a legitimate expectation, since neither Guide is binding on tribunals. Commissioner Williams so held in *CI/3038/2000*.

See also *SSWP v RD (II)* [2018] UKUT 481 (AAC), where Judge Rowland held that *R(I) 2/81* could not simply be read to mean that a person suffering from occupational deafness cannot continue with his regular employment, regardless of the evidence and facts. Judge Rowland also accepted that the claimant's return to his regular occupation demonstrated that he was capable of following that occupation; moreover, this will normally preclude entitlement to REA on the basis of satisfying the 'continuous' conditions. However, Judge Rowland further held that different considerations apply if REA is claimed in respect of a period *after* the claimant has given up their regular occupation, with reliance being placed on the 'permanent' conditions (applying *R(I) 15/74*).

1.607   *Regular occupation:* The claimant's regular occupation is to be determined as a matter of fact taking into account the provisions of sub-paras (4), (5) and (6) and decided cases. Sub-para.(4) gives the Secretary of State power to make "deeming" regulations (see the note to the sub-para., below).

The normal case of the claimant who has worked in one job for a number of years presents no problem nor, probably, does the case of the claimant who changes jobs very frequently for it will be easy to regard him as "acquiring" a regular occupation very quickly—and in this context, regular occupation means a *type* of job not limited by reference to a particular area or a particular employer (*R. v Deputy I.I. Commissioner Ex p. Humphreys* [1966] 2 W.L.R. 63). But what of claimants with a new job, more than one job, in training for a job, or with prospects of promotion from the job they were doing at the time of the accident?

The normal approach seems to be to consider that the job which caused the loss of earning capacity should be regarded as the regular occupation (*R(I) 5/52*) (even if it was a new job) unless there is evidence that the claimant did not so regard it, or he had been in it an exceptionally short time (*R(I) 18/60*), or he had been in a previous job for a long period (*R(I) 22/52, R(I) 65/54*).

1.608   *Sub-paragraph (5):* excludes subsidiary occupations from consideration but that does not prevent the decision-maker or tribunal from finding that more than one job makes up the claimant's regular occupation if neither, or none, of them can be said to be truly subsidiary to the other(s). If the claimant does more than one job for the same employer, then it is probably right to regard them together as his regular occupation unless one or more of them is abnormal and irregular (*R(I) 42/52, R(I) 24/55* and *R(I) 10/65*): but such claims are not always successful (*R(I) 58/54* and *R(I) 13/62*). Where the jobs are done for different employers the question is the same—can one (or more) of the jobs be regarded as subsidiary to the other(s)?—but the claimant may have more difficulty in establishing that his regular occupation consists of the totality of the jobs *(R(I) 33/58* and *R(I) 2/70).* There is no easy test emerging from the decisions as to what will constitute subsidiary as against regular occupation, although in settling this question of fact, the number of employers, the relative remuneration in each job, and the amount of time spent on them will be significant factors.

The difficulty of ascertaining the regular occupation of a claimant in training is eased by the provision of sub-para.(7) (below) if it is reasonably clear what job the training is directed towards. Otherwise, the decision-maker or tribunal will have to speculate about future job prospects and then use the subsection (as in *R(I) 6/75),* or categorise training as the regular occupation (as in *R(I) 4/60)* with the likely disadvantages for the claimant of a low standard of remuneration in the regular occupation when it comes to determining title to benefit and, ultimately, the amount of the award.

Sub-paragraph (6): extends the ambit of regular occupation to jobs to which the claimant would have been promoted but for the loss of faculty, although the wording has been interpreted to mean that promotions must be almost automatic rather than selective. In *R(I) 8/67,* the claimant contended that, as a result of contracting a prescribed disease, he had been prevented from progressing from shipwright grade B to grade A. The Commissioner formulated the appropriate questions thus:

    1.609

(1) In general, are persons in the claimant's position normally promoted or advanced to a higher grade or level?

(2) Would the claimant himself have had the normal prospects of advancement if he had continued in his regular occupation without loss of faculty?

(3) Was the claimant deprived in part or in whole of those prospects by the industrial injury?

R(I) 8/73 placed the emphasis in those questions on the word "normal". The Commissioner said:

"I doubt whether (the subsection) will, as a rule, assist a claimant unless the occupation which he follows is a broad-based one in which some degree of advancement is regarded as almost automatic. Where the predominant factor in a claimant's occupation or profession is that of selectivity the claimant will rarely, I think, be able successfully to invoke [the subsection]." (See also *R(I) 8/80.*)

A sideways move to a better paid job in the same basic grade was not, in *R(I) 12/81,* evidence of prospects of advancement. In determining that the new job, which the claimant actually did before ill-health forced him to abandon it, did not constitute a job of a higher grade or level, the Commissioner found that the skill and training involved was largely the same as in the former job (the regular occupation) and that the enhanced pay was merely to compensate for other unattractive features of the new job.

Employment of an equivalent standard . . . suitable in his case: Reduced earnings allowance compensates the claimant for loss of earning capacity, so that it is logical to require him to show not only that he cannot do his regular job, but also that he cannot do another suitable job which will bring him just as much money.

    1.610

The word "standard" appears here and in sub-para.(10), below, where it has a slightly different meaning. Here, "employment of an equivalent standard" is determined by considering the normal earnings in a job of which the claimant is capable with the normal earnings in the claimant's regular occupation. If the earnings in the alternative job are at least equal to those in the regular occupation, the alternative job is of an equivalent standard:

"[T]he comparison of the standard of remuneration afforded by the two employments, the regular employment and the prospective new employment, is one which in this subsection is unaffected by any consideration personal to the beneficiary and has to be treated objectively. The standard of remuneration in each case must, I think, be taken to be the standard of remuneration which an employee of normal efficiency and industriousness, where efficiency and industriousness are relevant considerations, will be likely to earn working in that employment for such number of hours in a week or other period which can be regarded as normal for persons employed in that employment, having regard to the conditions of the employment and the circumstances of the trade or industry in the appropriate geographical area under consideration." (*R. v N.I. Commissioner Ex p. Mellors* [1971] 2 W.L.R. 593. See also *R(I) 1/72, R(I) 1/76*.)

A payment designed to cover expenses is not remuneration for the purposes of deciding whether one employment is of an equivalent standard to another (*R(I) 1/54*). So in *CO v SSWP (II)* [2011] UKUT 105 (AAC), Judge Rowland held that a £175.03 pw non-taxable subsistence payment for living in digs near a construction site and away from home had to be ignored since the evidence showed that the allowance was paid only where expense was incurred and was only made when the claimant worked away from home. This meant that his remuneration was below that of his regular employment so that the job being done was not of an equivalent standard to that employment. Judge Rowland also distinguished *R(I) 24/59*: there a "subsistence allowance" counted as remuneration because on the facts of the case it was properly seen as a "perquisite annexed to his wages", since it was paid regardless of whether the employee worked away from home or not.

An element of subjectivity is introduced into the test by the requirement that employment of equivalent standard should be suitable for the claimant. Once it can be shown that jobs which the claimant can do (for the test of incapacity, see next paragraph) pay as much or more than his regular occupation, the claim will fail unless the alternative job is unsuitable. The department will normally produce a list of jobs for the tribunal which are said to be suitable (see the comments of the Commissioner in *R(S) 7/85*) and each must be examined in the light of all evidence. "Suitability refers to such matters as education, experience or training and has to be judged by reference to the claimant's past industrial history" (*R(I) 22/61*). Employments which are so exceptional that they ought not to be considered as proper comparisons may be excluded (*R(I) 6/77*, employment in sheltered work offered by Remploy Ltd—see also *R(I) 42/52, R(I) 73/52, R(I) 7/58*). In *R(I) 1/74* the Commissioner pointed up an important distinction between unsuitability and incapacity—unsuitability may result from *any* of the claimant's personal characteristics (see also *R(I) 29/52*).

1.611   *Incapable:* See also the discussion of incapacity for work in relation to sickness and invalidity benefit in the annotation to SSCBA 1992, s.57 as in force prior to April 13, 1995 (the introduction of incapacity benefit), which can be found in Bonner, Hooker and White, *Non-Means Tested Benefits: Legislation 1994*, pp.187–194. Just as with those benefits, so for reduced earnings allowance it is relevant to look beyond the claimant's state of health (important though that is) to his age, education and other personal factors.

The statutory rubric requires that the claimant demonstrates that, as a result of the relevant loss of faculty, he is incapable of following his regular occupation or suitable employment of an equivalent standard. "Regular occupation", it will be recalled, means a *type* of job not limited by reference to a particular area or a particular employer (*R. v Deputy I.I. Commissioner Ex p. Humphreys* [1966] 2 W.L.R. 63). This matter of incapacity in respect of his regular occupation or of suitable employment of an equivalent standard, is more complicated when the claimant has returned to work after the accident, and even more so if he has returned to his regular occupation. Returning to his regular occupation is, of course, good evidence that he is indeed capable of it. But such a claimant may, in some cases, be able to derive assistance from regulations which leave out of account periods of rehabilitative work (see annotation to sub-para.(7), below). Assistance in such a case may also be derived from a range of Commissioner's decisions which require that one ascertain the degree to which he is actually capable of fulfilling the normal requirements of the type of job in issue, and the basis on which he has been employed to do that job. In *CI/443/50(KL)* *(reported)*, a Tribunal of Commissioners laid down the relevant broad test and illustrated its application:

> "If a person cannot obtain employment in his regular field of labour because (as a result of the relevant loss of faculty) he is unable to fulfil all the ordinary requirements of employers in that field of labour, he is incapable of following his regular occupation . . .
>
> The matter may be illustrated thus. If a person obtains employment in his old job only through charity or because he has an exceptional employer, he should be regarded as incapable of following his regular occupation. On the other hand if a person is able to do his old job except that as a result of the relevant loss of faculty he cannot work overtime, he should not be regarded as incapable of following his regular occupation, unless as a result of this inability he cannot comply with the ordinary requirements of employers in his regular field of labour" (paras 11, 12).

In that particular case a tool-room fitter, temporarily unable to do overtime was held capable of following his regular occupation. But ultimately the precise application of this broad test depends on the facts of the instant case with decided cases illustrating matters constituting some of the relevant factors, rather than invariably being decisive considerations (*CI/1589/1998*, paras 14, 19). It is important also to recall that in pre-1987 cases Commissioners were able to reconsider all the issues (factual or legal) arising in the case and, since Commissioner's decisions are only binding in so far as they decide points of law, "it is necessary to disentangle statements of law from the Commissioner's analysis of the facts and the application of the law to those facts" (*ibid.*, para.12). Finally, note carefully that it is not a matter of whether the claimant is doing the same job as before, nor is the test one of what is acceptable to the claimant's employer, but rather is to be related to the normal requirements of "employers in that field of labour" (*ibid.*, para.19; and see *R(I) 10/59*, para.13). So, if the claimant has to be helped by workmates (*R(I) 29/52*, *R(I) 39/52*), or if he cannot meet the normal requirements of that type of job (*R(I) 39/55*), or if he has to pay other workers to carry out some of his duties (*R(I) 5/58*), or if the employer retains him only out of sympathy (*CI/445/50(KL) (reported)*), these will all be relevant factors in deciding in the context of the case as a whole whether he is incapable of performing his regular occupation. In the five cases just mentioned, the claimants were held incapable of their regular occupation. But it does depend on the particular circumstances and on the reference point of "the ordinary requirements of employers in his regular field of labour". So, in *CI 446/50(KL) (reported)*, while the claimant farm-worker was unable to do piecework, he did remain capable of a wide range of farm work and so was held capable of his regular occupation (see para.6). Application of the test is particularly difficult where the claimant has returned to the same occupation as before the accident but, as a result of the loss of faculty, "follows it more slowly, or for fewer hours, or less productively, or omits some parts of the occupation he used to perform" (*CI 443/50(KL) (reported)*, para.9). If the hours he can work are substantially reduced by comparison with the period prior to the loss of faculty, this may point to his being incapable of following his regular occupation. A reduction from five days to three and a half had that effect in *CI/444/50(KL) (reported)* (although there was also some element of having to have others do some lifting and carrying, that the claimant had previously managed herself), as did a drop from 44 hours to 31 hours in *R(I) 6/66*. A reduction in output or speed must be to such a degree as to prevent the claimant satisfying the ordinary requirements of employers in his regular field of labour (*CI/447/50(KL)*, *CI/448/50(KL) (both reported)*). Jobs involving piecework pose obvious difficulties here. In *R(I) 4/77*, the Commissioner warned against applying the language of the test in *CI/443/50(KL) (reported)* as if it were a statute and of the danger of isolating statements of law from the factual context of the case in which they were laid down and applied (a point re-emphasised in *CI/1589/1998*). The Commissioner in *R(I) 4/77* saw the claimant's remuneration as an important factor. He referred to the significance of remuneration in determining whether employment was of an equivalent standard and held that in determining incapacity in the case of a pieceworker it was proper to ask whether as a result of the relevant loss of faculty the claimant can attain the same level of remuneration in his regular occupation as he did before that loss of faculty.

1.612   *As a result of the relevant loss of faculty:* The incapacity must be caused by the loss of faculty. Causation is a matter of fact for the Secretary of State or tribunal. See note to s.94(1), above, on causation.

1.613   *Sub-paragraph (4):* Refer to note on regular occupation above. The regulation made under this section is reg.2 of the Social Security (Industrial Injuries and Diseases) Miscellaneous Provisions Regulations 1986 (SI 1986/1561).

1.614   *Sub-paragraph (5):* This subsection is discussed in the notes on sub-para.(1), above.

1.615   *Sub-paragraph (6):* See note on "regular occupation" in sub-para.(1), above.

1.616   *Sub-paragraph (7):* The regulations referred to are the General Benefit Regulations, reg.17.

1.617   *Sub-paragraph (9):* The period referred to in the section is the period for which disablement is assessed in accordance with the provisions of the Act.

1.618   *Sub-paragraphs (10) and (11):* The phrase "standard of remuneration" used in sub-para.(1), above, to determine entitlement to the allowance is also used in this subsection to determine the amount of the award, but it bears a different meaning. In quantifying the award, the right approach is to determine the normal earnings of the claimant in the occupation which he is capable of following without any regard to the number of hours worked, the rate paid, or the working conditions in the new job. It is a crude comparison between the money the claimant would have got in his old job, and the money he gets in his new job (see the *Mellors* case, above, and *R(I) 6/68*, *R(I) 1/72*).

The amount of the allowance is eventually determined by the difference between the two figures, subject to the 40 per cent maximum. It is important to note that the 140 per cent figure in this subsection is modified to 100 per cent in respect of persons who retired from regular employment before April 6, 1987 (sub-para.(11)). Note that it is possible to show entitlement to the allowance by meeting the conditions in sub-para.(1), but discover that the amount is nil on applying the test in this subsection.

The "relevant occupation" for the purposes of comparison is defined in sub-para.(12).

1.619   *Sub-paragraph (13):* The difficulties of calculating the probable standard of remuneration in individual cases, often many years after the accident, have been alleviated by the provisions of this subsection. The regulations referred to are the Social Security (Industrial Injuries) (Reduced Earnings Allowance and Transitional) Regulations 1987, below. This section and the regulations apply to any award of the allowance except the first subject to specific situations covered by the regulations. See further the notes to the regulations.

1.620   *Sub-paragraph (14):* The predecessor of this sub-paragraph was inserted by SSA 1988, s.16(1), with effect from March 15, 1988.

(3) Reduced Earnings Allowance: the rate for those retired persons entitled to it

1.621   *Paragraph 12(1)* preserves entitlement to REA for those who are of pensionable age and have retired from regular employment either on April 10, 1988, or on April 9, 1989. Although entitlement is preserved for life, the rate of REA is frozen: see sub-paras (2)–(6).

Sch.7, Pt V: Retirement Allowance

It was the intention of the Government that the new benefit which replaced Special Hardship Allowance (Reduced Earnings Allowance) should only subsist during the working life of the claimant up to pensionable age. A further new benefit was introduced to compensate, in retirement, the claimant who, as a result of an industrial accident or disease, may find that an earnings-related pension has been diminished by reduced earnings during his working life. This new benefit, retirement allowance, was created by the Social Security Act 1988 and introduced by way of an insertion of a new section (s.59B) into the Social Security Act 1975.

1.622

Sub-paragraph (1): terminates entitlement to reduced earnings allowance on retirement on or after attainment of pensionable age. It ceases from the day on which regular employment is given up. It also precludes a person being entitled to REA for a period falling after the attainment of pensionable age and the giving up of regular employment in circumstances in which that person had another award of REA prior to those dates (*TA v SSWP (II)* [2014] UKUT 127 (AAC), paras 70-79). In *TA*, however, Judge Wright declined to decide whether (as the Secretary of State accepted) REA can still be awarded *for the first time* on a backdated claim made after the claimant has given up regular employment and reached pensionable age with such award continuing, in effect, for life (para.63), a strange situation given that post retirement and giving up employment it is difficult to see how a remuneration comparison can meaningfully be made (paras 64-70).

1.623

The words "gives up regular employment" are not used in an unusual sense. They are to be construed in their natural and ordinary meaning, so that they did not catch the particular claimant who was dismissed from his job at a newsagents shop (*R(I) 2/93*, paras 20 and 21). This does not mean, however, that all dismissals fall outwith the phrase. Citing instances where a dismissed claimant has nevertheless been held to have voluntarily left his employment for disqualification purposes under SSCBA 1992, s.28(1)(a) (*R(U) 16/52, R(U) 2/74*) (see now Jobseekers Act, s.19), the Commissioner in *R(I) 2/93* said:

"A claimant may act in such a way as to force his employer to dismiss him and it will be a question of fact in each case whether or not the claimant had by his conduct evinced an intention to give up regular employment (para.13)."

In any event, to be caught by sub-para.(1), the claimant must have given up regular employment *on or after April 10, 1989*, so that those in receipt of REA when they gave up such employment before that date, are not thereby disentitled to it by virtue of para.13 of Sch.7 (see *R(I) 3/93, CI/11015/1995* and decision *CI/209/1991*).

Note, however, that with effect from March 24, 1996, regulations dictate a broader approach to "gives up regular employment" than that taken in *R(I) 2/93*. With effect from that date, reg.3 of the Social Security (Industrial Injuries) (Regular Employment) Regulations 1990 (inserted by reg.6(3) of the Social Security (Industrial Injuries and Diseases) (Miscellaneous Amendment) Regulations 1996 (SI 1996/425) provides that a person who has attained pensionable age must be regarded as having given up regular employment at the start of the first week in which *he is not in regular employment* after the later of the week during which the regulation came into force or the week in which he attained pensionable age. But this does not apply if the person is entitled to REA for life by virtue of para.12(1), above. It is submitted that the "week during which this regulation comes into force" (reg.3(a)) must be the week including March 24, 1996, the date the amendment took effect, and not that including April 1, 1990, the date set out in reg.1(1) of the 1990 Regs, which merely sets out the date the original set of regulations, not including reg.3, came into operation. Had the intention been to make the reg.3, retrospective, one would have expected clear words to that effect.

"gives up regular employment": the effect of the new reg.3.

1.624   *R(I) 2/99* is very useful in charting the bumpy and twisting path of attempts to make entitlement to REA cease on retirement, and the decisions reported there make clear that reg.3 is *intra vires* the rule-making power in SSCBA 1992, Sch.7, para.13(8).

In *Hepple v CAO* (Case C–196/98, judgment of May 23, 2000 reported as *R(I) 2/00*), the ECJ held that the discriminatory cut-off conditions introduced by the UK from 1986 onwards for REA claimants over state pension age were not invalid under the Equal Treatment Directive 79/7 as they were within the permitted exclusion in Art.7 for the determination of state pension age and "the possible consequences for other benefits". The court rejected the Advocate-General's opinion. It rejected the argument that Art.7 did not permit Member States to introduce fresh heads of discrimination in non-pension benefits by linking them to the pension age long after the Directive itself was in full effect. The court held that since "the principal aim of the legislative amendments . . . was to discontinue payment of REA . . . to persons no longer of working age by imposing conditions based on the statutory retirement age", then "maintenance of the rules at issue . . . is objectively necessary to preserve . . . coherence" between REA and the state pension. In consequence, the discrimination was held "objectively and necessarily linked to the difference between the retirement age for men and that for women". It was, therefore, permitted by Art.7.

The end result is that reg.3 has now been conclusively upheld as valid in both UK national and EU law. Decisions are now being given in the numerous REA appeals stayed pending the ECJ's judgment.

A person cannot be in employment under a contract which has ceased to exist, and is thus to be treated as having given up regular employment on its cessation—on the harsh operation of the rule in the case of seasonal and casual workers, see *SSWP v NH (II)* [2010] UKUT 84 (AAC)

1.625   *Sub-paragraph (2):* transfers a claimant to retirement allowance if, on the day before he ceases to be entitled to reduced earnings allowance under subs.(1), he was entitled to reduced earnings allowance at a weekly rate of not less than £2. There is some potential difficulty in the subsection since the use of the word "entitled" might suggest that the decision-maker or tribunal could investigate entitlement even if there had been no claim. However, the qualifying words in brackets, "by virtue either of one award or of a number of awards", suggest that the benefit must actually have been awarded at the relevant time. However many awards of REA the claimant was receiving, there can only be entitlement to one award of retirement allowance (*TA v SSWP (II)* [2010] UKUT 101 (AAC)).

1.626   *Sub-paragraph (3)–(7):* stipulate that entitlement to retirement allowance is for life, and fix the rate at which benefit will be paid. Consistent with the freezing of reduced earnings allowance for those retired people over pensionable age in receipt of that benefit (see para.12 noted above), retirement allowance will be paid at a rate fixed by reference to the date of retirement. Note, however, that the sums falling to be calculated under sub-para.(4) are subject to alteration by up-rating orders (sub-para. (7)).

The whole of s.59B was amended and subss.(7) and (8) added by SSA 1989 to take account of the abolition of the earnings rules and the substitution of the text of "giving up regular employment" for the text of retirement or deemed retirement.

The meaning of "regular employment" for the purposes of the section is defined by the Social Security (Industrial Injuries) (Regular Employment) Regulations 1990 (SI 1990/256) which are included in the regulations on individual injuries set out at the end of the volume.

1.627   *Sub-paragraph (10):* Note the link to "jobseeking period" and "linked period" as defined in the Jobseekers Act 1995. These terms are in fact given real definition in JSA Regs1996, regs47–49. See *Vol.II: Income Support, Jobseeker's Allowance, State Pension Credit and the Social Fund.*

Schedule 8. *Repealed by Welfare Reform Act 2012, s. 64 (December 5, 2012).*   **1.628**

Schedules 9–11: *Omitted. See Vol. IV: Tax Credits and HMRC-administered Social Security Benefits.*   **1.629**

SCHEDULE 12

RELATIONSHIP OF STATUTORY SICK PAY WITH BENEFITS AND OTHER PAYMENTS, ETC.

The general principle

1.—Any day which—   **1.630**
   (a) is a day of incapacity for work in relation to any contract of service; and
   (b) falls within a period of entitlement (whether or not it is also a qualifying day),
        shall not be treated for the purposes of this Act as a day of incapacity for work for the
        purposes of determining whether a period is [¹] [² a period of incapacity for work for
        the purposes of incapacity benefit.]

Contractual remuneration

2.—(1) Subject to sub-paragraphs (2) and (3) below, any entitlement to statutory sick pay   **1.631**
shall not affect any right of any employee in relation to remuneration under any contract of
service ("contractual remuneration").
   (2) Subject to sub-paragraph (3) below—
   (a) any contractual remuneration paid to any employee by an employer of his in respect of
        a day of incapacity for work shall go towards discharging any liability for that employer
        to pay statutory sick pay to that employee in respect of that day; and
   (b) any statutory sick pay paid by an employer to an employee of his in respect of a day of
        incapacity for work shall go towards discharging any liability of that employer to pay
        contractual remuneration to that employee in respect of that day.
   (3) Regulations may make provision as to payments which are, and those which are not, to
be treated as contractual remuneration for the purposes of sub-paragraph (1) or (2) above.

[² Incapacity benefit

3.—(1) This paragraph and paragraph 4 below have effect to exclude, where a period of   **1.632**
entitlement as between an employee and an employer of his comes to an end, the provisions
by virtue of which short-term incapacity benefit is not paid for the first three days.
   (2) If the first day immediately following the day on which the period of entitlement came
to an end—
   (a) is a day of incapacity for work in relation to that employee, and
   (b) is not a day in relation to which paragraph 1 above applies by reason of any entitle-
        ment as between the employee and another employer,
that day shall, except in prescribed cases, be or form part of a period of incapacity for work
notwithstanding section 30C(1)(b) above (by virtue of which a period of incapacity for work
must be at least 4 days long).
   (3) Where each of the first two consecutive days, or the first three consecutive days, following
the day on which the period of entitlement came to an end is a day to which paragraphs (a) and (b)
of sub-paragraph (2) above apply, that sub-paragraph has effect in relation to the second day or,
as the case may be, in relation to the second and third days, as it has effect in relation to the first.
   4.—(1) Where a period of entitlement as between an employee and an employer of his
comes to an end, section 30A(3) above (exclusion of benefit for first 3 days of period) does not
apply in relation to any day which—
   (a) is or forms part of a period of incapacity for work (whether by virtue of paragraph 3
        above or otherwise), and
   (b) falls within the period of 57 days immediately following the day on which the period
        of entitlement came to an end.
   (2) Where sub-paragraph (1) above applies in relation to a day, section 30A(3) above does
not apply in relation to any later day in the same period of incapacity for work.]

[² Incapacity benefit for widows and widowers

1.633   5.—Paragraph 1 above does not apply for the purpose of determining whether the conditions specified in section 40(3) or (4) or section 41(2) or (3) above are satisfied.]

Unemployability supplement

1.634   6.—Paragraph 1 above does not apply in relation to paragraph 3 of Schedule 7 to this Act and accordingly the references in paragraph 3 of that Schedule to a period of interruption of employment shall be construed as if the provisions re-enacted in this Part of this Act had not been enacted.

AMENDMENTS

1. Jobseekers Act 1995 Sch.3 para.1. (October 7, 1996).
2. Social Security (Incapacity for Work) Act 1994 Sch.1 para.44 (April 13, 1995).

DERIVATION

1.635   SSHBA 1982 Sch.2.

GENERAL NOTE

Paragraph 1
1.636   No day of incapacity (whether or not a qualifying day) within a period of entitlement can count as part of a period of interruption of employment. Thus such a day cannot give entitlement to, say, incapacity benefit.

Paragraphs 3 and 4
1.637   These assist certain persons not caught by para.1, who have days of incapacity subsequent to the end of a period of entitlement, to qualify for State benefits by not applying the normal rules on period of interruption of employment and waiting days. See also with respect to para.3., reg.12 of the SSP (Gen.) Regulations.

SCHEDULE 13

RELATIONSHIP OF STATUTORY MATERNITY PAY WITH BENEFITS AND
OTHER PAYMENTS, ETC.

The general principle
1.638   [¹ 1.—Except as may be prescribed, a day which falls within the maternity pay period shall not be treated as a day of incapacity for work for the purposes of determining, for this Act, whether it forms part of a period of incapacity for work for the purposes of incapacity benefit.]

[² Incapacity benefit
1.639   2.—(1) Regulations may provide that in prescribed circumstances a day which falls within the maternity pay period shall be treated as a day of incapacity for work for the purpose of determining entitlement to the higher rate of short-term incapacity benefit or to long-term incapacity benefit.
   (2) Regulations may provide that an amount equal to a woman's statutory maternity pay for a period shall be deducted from any such benefit in respect of the same period and a woman shall be entitled to such benefit only if there is a balance after the deduction and, if there is such a balance, at a weekly rate equal to it.]

Contractual remuneration
1.640   3.—(1) Subject to sub-paragraphs (2) and (3) below, any entitlement to statutory maternity pay shall not affect any right of a woman in relation to remuneration under any contract of service ("contractual remuneration").

310

(2) Subject to sub-paragraph (3) below—
  (a) any contractual remuneration paid to a woman by an employer of hers in respect of a week in the maternity pay period shall go towards discharging any liability of that employer to pay statutory maternity pay to her in respect of that week; and
  (b) any statutory maternity pay paid by an employer to a woman who is an employee of his in respect of a week in the maternity pay period shall go towards discharging any liability of that employer to pay contractual remuneration to her in respect of that week.
  [³ (2A) In sub-paragraph (2) "week" means a period of seven days beginning with the day of the week on which the maternity pay period begins.]
  (3) Regulations may make provision as to payments which are, and those which are not, to be treated as contractual remuneration for the purposes of sub-paragraphs (1) and (2) above.

AMENDMENTS

  1. Jobseekers Act 1995 Sch.2 para.37 (October 7, 1996).
  2. Social Security (Incapacity for Work) Act 1994 Sch.1 para.45 (April 13, 1995).
  3. Work and Families Act 2006 Sch.1 para.23 (October 1, 2006).

Social Security (Consequential Provisions) Act 1992

(1992 C.6)

For the text and commentary on this Act, see Vol I of the 2015/16 edition of this series.　　**1.641**

Pensions Schemes Act 1993

(1993 C.48)

SECTIONS REPRODUCED

PART III

CERTIFICATION OF PENSION SCHEMES AND EFFECTS ON MEMBERS' STATE SCHEME RIGHTS AND DUTIES

Preliminary

CHAPTER II

REDUCTION IN STATE SCHEME CONTRIBUTIONS AND SOCIAL SECURITY BENEFITS FOR MEMBERS OF CERTIFIED SCHEMES

SECTION

46. Effect of entitlement to guaranteed minimum pensions on payment of social security benefits.　　**1.642**
47. Further provisions concerning entitlement to guaranteed minimum pensions for the purposes of section 46.
48. Reduced benefits where minimum payments or minimum contributions paid.

GENERAL NOTE

1.643
The main scope of Part III of the Pensions Schemes Act 1993 was to provide the legislative authority for the introduction of the state second pension or additional pension in place of its predecessor SERPS or the state earnings related pension scheme.

The Pensions Act 2014 abolished all aspects of the state second pension with effect from April 6, 2016 for anyone reaching state pensionable age on or after that date. Until that date employees could join occupational schemes that provided them with second pensions in place of the state second pension. They would normally be required to pay pension contributions for the second pension but in exchange could be entitled to pay reduced rates of Class 1 National Insurance contributions if the pension scheme was registered for contracted-out employment.

April 6, 2016 is the second stage of abolition of the state second pension. From that date there is no status of contracted-out employment and no reduced rate of Class 1 contributions. The first stage, which took place with effect from April 6, 2012, was the abolition of contracted-out status for defined contribution schemes and the availability of reduced rates for such schemes. From April 6, 2016 those reaching state pensionable age can claim only the single rate state pension. Any occupational pensions are for arrangement between employers and employees and do not involve the National Insurance contribution or state pension systems.

To give effect to this, the Pensions Act 2014 abolishes contracted-out status for salary-related schemes and repeals the relevant provisions in the Pension Schemes Act 1993—see s.24 of, and Sch.13 to, that Act. These came into effect on April 6, 2016: s.56 of that Act.

However, the Pensions Act 2014 (Savings) Order 2015 (SI 2015/1502) keeps some of those provisions in effect for the purpose of ensuring continuity of entitlement to those already drawing pensions under such schemes. Both the scope of that Order and most of the remaining provisions of the 1993 Act are beyond the scope of this work. A few sections remain in force and of relevance to those who have reached state pensionable age before April 6, 2016 and also have entitlements to a second pension. These sections are set out in this volume. However, the lengthy explanation and analysis of these sections is now only of relevance to such transitional cases. It has therefore been edited down for the purposes of this volume. Anyone wishing to read a fuller analysis is referred to the 2015/16 edition of this volume (or its annual predecessors).

Effect of entitlement to guaranteed minimum pensions on payment of social security benefits

1.644
46.—(1) Where for any period a person is entitled both—
(a) to a Category A or Category B retirement pension, a widowed mother's allowance [¹, a widowed parent's allowance] [² or a widow's pension] under the Social Security Contributions and Benefits Act 1992; and
(b) to one or more guaranteed minimum pensions
the weekly rate of the benefit mentioned in paragraph (a) shall for that period be reduced by an amount equal—
[³ (i) to that part of its additional pension which is attributable to earnings factors for any tax years ending before the principal appointed day], or
(ii) to the weekly rate of the pension mentioned in paragraph (b) (or, if there is more than one such pension, their aggregate weekly rates), whichever is the less.
(2) [² ...]
[² (3) Where for any period—
(a) a person is entitled to one or more guaranteed minimum pensions; and

312

(b) he is also entitled to long-term incapacity benefit under section 30A of the Social Security Contributions and Benefits Act 1992,

for that period an amount equal to the weekly rate or aggregate weekly rates of the guaranteed minimum pension or pensions shall be deducted from any increase payable under regulations under section 30B(7) of that Act and he shall be entitled to such an increase only if there is a balance after the deduction and, if there is such a balance, at a weekly rate equal to it.]

(4) Where for any period—

(a) a person is entitled to one or more guaranteed minimum pensions;

(b) he is also entitled to a Category A retirement pension under section 44 of the Social Security Contributions and Benefits Act 1992; and

(c) the weekly rate of his pension includes an additional pension such as is mentioned in section 44(3)(b) of that Act,

for that period section 47 of that Act shall have effect as if the following subsection were substituted for subsection (3)—

"(3) In subsection (2) above 'the relevant amount' means an amount equal to the aggregate of—

(a) the additional pension; and

(b) the weekly rate or aggregate weekly rates of the guaranteed minimum pension or pensions,

reduced by the amount of any reduction in the weekly rate of the Category A retirement pension made by virtue of section 46(1) of the Pension Schemes Act 1993.".

(5) Where for any period—

(a) a person is entitled to one or more guaranteed minimum pensions;

(b) he is also entitled to a Category A retirement pension under section 44 of the Social Security Contributions and Benefits Act 1992; and

(c) the weekly rate of his Category A retirement pension does not include an additional pension such as is mentioned in subsection (3) (b) of that section,

for that period the relevant amount shall be deducted from the amount that would otherwise be the increase under section 47(1) of that Act and the pensioner shall be entitled to an increase under that section only if there is a balance remaining after that deduction and, if there is such a balance, of an amount equal to it.

(6) Where for any period—

(a) a person is entitled to one or more guaranteed minimum pensions;

(b) he is also entitled—

(i) [² . . .]

(ii) to a Category A retirement pension under section 44 of that Act; or

(iii) to a Category B retirement pension under [⁴ section [⁵ . . .] [¹, 48B or 48BB] of that Act; and

(c) the weekly rate of the pension includes an additional pension such as is mentioned in section 44(3)(b) of that Act,

for that period paragraph 3 of Schedule 7 to that Act shall have effect as if the following sub-paragraph were substituted for sub-paragraph (3)—

"(3) In this paragraph 'the relevant amount' means an amount equal to the aggregate of—

    (a) the additional pension; and

    (b) the weekly rate or aggregate weekly rates of the guaranteed minimum pension or pensions,

reduced by the amount of any reduction in the weekly rate of the pension made by virtue of section 46(1) of the Pension Schemes Act 1993.".

(7) Where for any period—

    (a) a person is entitled to one or more guaranteed minimum pensions;

    (b) he is also entitled to any of the pensions under the Social Security Contributions and Benefits Act 1992 mentioned in subsection (6) (b); and

    (c) the weekly rate of the pension does not include an additional pension such as is mentioned in section 44(3)(b) of that Act,

for that period the relevant amount shall be deducted from the amount that would otherwise be the increase under paragraph 3 of Schedule 7 to that Act and the beneficiary shall be entitled to an increase only if there is a balance after that deduction and, if there is a balance, only to an amount equal to it.

(8) In this section "the relevant amount" means an amount equal to the weekly rate or aggregate weekly rates of the guaranteed minimum pension or pensions—

    (a) [^{2} . . .]

    (b) in the case of subsection (5), reduced by the amount of any reduction in the weekly rate of the Category A retirement pension made by virtue of subsection (1);

and references in this section to the weekly rate of a guaranteed minimum pension are references to that rate without any increase under section 15(1).

    (9) [^{2} . . .]

[^{6} (10) In this section a reference to "additional pension" does not include any amount of additional pension attributable to units of additional pension.

(11) For units of additional pension, see section 14A of the Social Security Contributions and Benefits Act 1992.]

AMENDMENTS AND REPEALS

    1. Welfare Reform and Pensions Act 1999 s.70 (April 9, 2001).

    2. Social Security (Incapacity for Work) Act 1994 Sch.1 (April 13, 1995).

    3. Pensions Act 1995 Sch.5 para.44, (April 6, 1997).

    4. Pensions Act 1995 Sch.4 para.22 (July 19, 1995).

    5. Pensions Act 2014 Sch.12 para.71.

    6. Pensions Act (Consequential Amendments)(Units of Additional Pension) Order 2014 (SI 2014/3213) art.4 (October 12, 2015).

GENERAL NOTE

1.645   This section provides the mechanism to offset any claim for the former state second pension or SERPS by reference to any entitlement to pensions payable under contracted-out schemes (for which the pensioner will have paid reduced Class 1 contributions). As noted in the general note to the Act, contracted-out schemes all closed with effect from April 6, 2016 so this problem no longer arises in respect of those reaching state pensionable age on or after April 6, 2016 save in transitional cases. Readers are referred to previous editions of this work for a detailed discussion of the section.

Further provisions concerning entitlement to guaranteed minimum pensions for the purposes of section 46

47.—(1) The reference in section 46(1) to a person entitled to a guaranteed minimum pension shall be construed as including a reference to a person so entitled by virtue of being the widower [¹¹, surviving same sex spouse] [⁷ or surviving civil partner] of an earner [⁵ in any case where he is entitled to a benefit other than a widowed parent's allowance] [¹ . . .] only if—

[⁵ (a) he is also entitled to a Category B retirement pension by virtue of the earner's contributions (or would be so entitled but for section 43(1) of the Social Security Contributions and Benefits Act 1992); or]

(b) he is also entitled to a Category A retirement pension by virtue of [⁵ section 41(5)] of [⁵ that Act].

(2) For the purposes of [⁹ [¹² section 46]] a person shall be treated as entitled to any guaranteed minimum pension to which he would have been entitled—

(a) if its commencement had not been postponed, as mentioned in section 13(4); or

(b) if there had not been made a transfer payment or transfer under regulations made by virtue of section 20 as a result of which—

(i) he is no longer entitled to guaranteed minimum pensions under the scheme by which the transfer payment or transfer was made, and

(ii) he has not become entitled to guaranteed minimum pensions under the scheme to which the transfer payment or transfer was made.

(3) Where—

(a) guaranteed minimum pensions provided for a member or the member's [⁷ widow, widower or surviving civil partner] under a contracted-out scheme have been wholly or partly secured as mentioned in subsection (3) of section 19; and

(b) either—

(i) the transaction wholly or partly securing them was carried out before 1st January 1986 and discharged the trustees or managers of the scheme as mentioned in subsection (1) of that section; or

(ii) it was carried out on or after that date without any of the requirements specified in subsection (5)(a) to (c) of that section being satisfied in relation to it and the scheme has been wound up; and

(c) any company with which any relevant policy of insurance or annuity contract was taken out or entered into is unable to meet the liabilities under policies issued or securities given by it; and

(d) the combined proceeds of—

(i) any relevant policies and annuity contracts, and

(ii) any cash sums paid or alternative arrangements made under the [⁴ Financial Services Compensation Scheme],

the member and the member's [⁷ widow, widower or surviving civil partner] shall be treated for the purposes of [⁹[¹² section 46]] as only entitled to such part (if any) of the member's or, as the case may be, the member's [⁷widow's, widower's or surviving partner's] guaranteed minimum pension as is provided by the proceeds mentioned in paragraph (d).

(4) A policy or annuity is relevant for the purposes of subsection (3) if

1.646

taking it out or entering into it constituted the transaction to which section 19 applies.

(5) For the purposes of [⁹[¹² section 46]] a person shall be treated as entitled to any guaranteed minimum pension to which he would have been entitled—

  (a) if a lump sum had not been paid instead of that pension under provisions included in a scheme by virtue of section 21(1); or

  (b) if that pension had not been forfeited under provisions included in a scheme by virtue of section 21(2).

[² (6) For the purposes of [⁹[¹² section 46]], a person shall be treated as entitled to any guaranteed minimum pension to which he would have been entitled but for any reduction under section 15A.]

[³ (7) For the purposes of [⁹[¹² section 46]], a person shall be treated as entitled to any guaranteed minimum pension to which he would have been entitled but for any order under section 32A of the Insolvency Act 1986 (recovery of excessive pension contributions) or under [¹³ s.101 of the Bankruptcy (Scotland) Act 2016].]

[⁶ (8) For the purposes of [⁹[¹² section 46]], a person shall be treated as entitled to a guaranteed minimum pension to which he would have been entitled but for the fact that the trustees or managers were discharged from their liability to provide that pension on the Board of the Pension Protection Fund assuming responsibility for the scheme.]

[⁸(9) For the purposes of [⁹[¹² section 46]], a person shall be treated as entitled to a guaranteed minimum pension to which, in the opinion of the Commissioners for Her Majesty's Revenue and Customs, he would have been entitled but for the amendment of a scheme so that it no longer contains the guaranteed minimum pension rules.

(10) Where the earner's accrued rights have been transferred after the amendment of the scheme, in making the calculation under subsection (9) the Commissioners shall assume the application of section 16(1) after the transfer.

(11) In making the calculation under subsection (9) the Commissioners shall ignore any effect of the scheme being wound up.]

AMENDMENTS

1. Social Security (Incapacity for Work Act) 1994 Sch.1 para.57 and Sch.2 (April 13, 1995).

2. Welfare Reform and Pensions Act 1999 s.32(4) (December 1, 2000).

3. Welfare Reform and Pensions Act 1999 s.18 and Sch.2 para.6 (April 6, 2002).

4. Financial Services and Markets Act 2000 (Consequential Amendments and Repeals) Order 2001 (SI 2001/3649) reg.120 (December 1, 2001).

5. State Pension Credit Act 2002 s.18 (March 19, 2002).

6. Pensions Act 2004 s.165(3) (April 6, 2006).

7. Civil Partnership (Contracted-out Occupational and Appropriate Personal Pension Schemes) (Surviving Civil Partners) Order 2005 (SI 2005/2050) Sch.1 para.14 (December 5, 2005).

8. Pensions Act 2007 s.14(5), (April 6, 2009).

9. Pensions Act 2008 Sch.4 para.17 (January 3, 2012).

10. Marriage (Same Sex Couples) Act 2013 Sch.4 Pt.5 para.24. (March 13, 2014).

11. Civil Partnership Act 2004 (Consequential Provisions and Modifications) Order 2014 (SI 2014/3229) Sch.5 para.11 (December 12, 2014).

12. Pensions Act 2014 Sch.12 para.72 (April 6, 2016).

13. The Bankruptcy (Scotland) Act 2016 (Consequential Provisions and Modifications) Order 2016 (SI 2016/1034) Sch.1 para.11 (November 30, 2016).

Reduced benefits where minimum payment or minimum contributions paid

48.—(1) Subject to subsection (3), this subsection applies where for any period—

(a) minimum payments have been made in respect of an earner to an occupational pension scheme which is a money purchase contracted-out scheme in relation to the earner's employment, or

(b) minimum contributions have been paid in respect of an earner under section 43.

1.647

(2) Where subsection (1) applies then, for the purposes of [⁴ sections 46 and 46A]—

(a) the earner shall be treated, as from the date on which he reaches pensionable age, as entitled to a guaranteed minimum pension at a prescribed weekly rate arising from that period in that employment;

(b) [² . . .], and

(c) in prescribed circumstances [² . . .] any [³ widow, widower or surviving civil partner] or the earner shall be treated as entitled to a guaranteed minimum pension at a prescribed weekly rate arising from that period;

and where subsection (1)(b) applies paragraphs (a) to (c) of this subsection apply also for the purposes of [¹ section] 47(2) of the Social Security Contributions and Benefits Act 1992] and paragraph 3(2) of Schedule 7 to that Act, but with the omission from paragraph (a) of the words "in that employment".

(3) Where the earner is a married woman or widow, subsection (1) shall not have effect by virtue of paragraph (a) of that subsection in relation to any period during which there is operative an election that her liability in respect of primary Class 1 contributions shall be a liability to contribute at a reduced rate.

(4) The power to prescribe a rate conferred by subsection (2)(a) includes power to prescribe a nil rate.

AMENDMENTS AND REPEALS

1. Social Security (Incapacity for Work) Act 1994 Sch.1 (April 13, 1995).
2. Pensions Act 1995 s.140(2) (April 6, 1996).
3. Civil Partnership (Contracted-out Occupational and Appropriate Personal Pension Schemes) (Surviving Civil Partners) Order 2005 (SI 2005/2050) Sch.1, para.14 (December 5, 2005).
4. Pensions Act 2008 Sch.4 para.18 (January 3, 2012).

GENERAL NOTE

Section 48 ceases to have effect for minimum payments and minimum contributions from April 6, 1997 (Pensions Act 1995 s.140(3)).

1.648

In *Secretary of State for Work and Pensions v MH* [2014] UKUT 113 (AAC) Judge Jacobs found himself unable to read modifications to the pensionable age of women made by subsequent legislation into section 48 of the Pension Schemes Act 1993. He records that the Department for Work and Pensions accepted that this was an error in drafting the legislation but he was unable to interpret the provision to remove the error. Nor, as a judge of the Upper Tribunal, was he able to consider any incompatibility with human rights legislation.

Note, however, that in the subsequent case of *SSWP v GS (WB)* [2015] UKUT

33 (AAC), the Secretary of State argued that no such concession by the DWP had been made in *MH*. In *GS* Judge Mark held, contrary to the finding in *MH*, that for the purposes of the calculations under s.46 up to the date the claimant qualified for the state pension, then "the Secretary of State ought to have determined how much, if any, of the Respondent's GMP was attributable to payments before 6 April 1997 which fell within section 48 of the 1993 Act, and to have excluded that part of the pension in calculating how much should be deducted from the additional element of the widow's pension" (at para.(16i)). Permission to appeal to the Court of Appeal was granted in *GS* but the case was subsequently settled between the parties (*Swan v SSWP* C3/2016/0431).

[¹ Effect of reduced contributions and rebates on social security benefits

1.649

48A.—(1) [⁴ In relation to—

(a) any tax week falling before the first abolition date where the amount of a Class 1 contribution attributable to section 8(1)(a) of the Social Security Contributions and Benefits Act 1992 in respect of the earnings paid to or for the benefit of an earner in that week was reduced under section 42A of this Act (as it then had effect),

(b) any tax week falling before the second abolition date where the amount of a Class 1 contribution attributable to section 8(1)(a) of the Social Security Contributions and Benefits Act 1992 in respect of the earnings paid to or for the benefit of an earner in that week was reduced under section 41 of this Act (as it then had effect), or

(c) any tax week falling before the first abolition date where an amount was paid under section 45(1) of this Act (as it then had effect) in respect of the earnings paid to or for the benefit of an earner,]

section 44(6) of the Social Security Contributions and Benefits Act 1992 (earnings factors for additional pension) shall have effect, except in prescribed circumstances, as if no [² such] primary Class 1 contributions had been paid or treated as paid upon those earnings for that week and section 45A of that Act did not apply (where it would, apart from this subsection, apply).

(2) Where the whole or part of a contributions equivalent premium has been paid or treated as paid in respect of the earner, the Secretary of State may make a determination reducing or eliminating the application of subsection (1).

(3) Subsection (1) is subject to regulations under paragraph 5(3A) to (3E) of Schedule 2.

(4) Regulations may, so far as is required for the purpose of providing entitlement to additional pension (such as is mentioned in section 44(3)(b) of the Social Security Contributions and Benefits Act 1992) but to the extent only that the amount of additional pension is attributable to provision made by regulations under section 45(5) of that Act, disapply subsection (1).

(5) In relation to earners where, by virtue of subsection (1), section 44(6) of the Social Security Contributions and Benefits Act 1992 has effect, in any tax year, as mentioned in that subsection in relation to some but not all of their earnings, regulations may modify the application of section 44(5) of that Act.]

AMENDMENTS

1. Pensions Act 1995 s.140(1) (April 6, 1997).
2. National Insurance Act 2002 Sch.1 para.39 (April 6, 2003).

3. Pensions Act 2007 Sch.4 para.23 (September 26, 2007).
4. Pensions Act 2014 Sch.13 para.31 (April 6, 2016).

[¹ **Women, married women and widows**

49. [*repealed*]   1.650

<small>AMENDMENTS</small>

1. Pensions Act 2014 s.24 Sch.13 para.32 (April 6, 2016).

Social Security (Incapacity for Work) Act 1994

(1994 C.18)

For the text of and commentary to relevant sections of this Act, see the 2011/12   1.651
edition of this Volume.

Pensions Act 1995

(1995 C.26)

<small>SECTIONS REPRODUCED</small>

<small>PART II</small>

<small>STATE PENSIONS</small>

126. Equalisation of pensionable age and of entitlement to certain benefits.   1.652
127. [*Repealed*].
128. Additional pension: calculation of surpluses.

<small>SCHEDULES</small>

Schedule 4—Equalisation.
Part I—Pensionable ages for men and women.
Part II—Entitlement to certain pension and other benefits. Part III—Consequential
amendments.

<small>PART II</small>

<small>STATE PENSIONS</small>

Equalisation of pension age and of entitlement to certain benefits   1.653
  [¹ and increase in pensionable age]

126.—Schedule 4 to this Act, of which—
  (a) Part I has effect to equalise pensionable age for men and women [¹ [²
      and then to increase it.]],
  (b) Part II makes provision for bringing equality for men and women to
      certain pension and other benefits, and

(c) Part III makes consequential amendments of enactments,
shall have effect.

AMENDMENT

1. Pensions Act 2007 Sch.3 paras 1 and 2 (September 26, 2007).
2. Pensions Act 2011 Sch.1 (January 3, 2012).

Enhancement of additional pension, etc., where family credit or disability working allowance paid

1.654   **127.**—[¹ . . .]

AMENDMENT

1. Tax Credits Act 2002 Sch.6 para.1 (April 6, 2003).

Additional Pension: calculation of surplus

1.655   **128.**—(1) and (2) omitted.

(3) Section 148 of the Social Security Administration Act 1992 (revaluation of earnings factors) shall have effect in relation to surpluses in a person's earnings factors under section 44(5A) of the Social Security Contributions and Benefits Act 1992 [¹ for the purposes of section 45(1) and (2)(a) and (b) of that Act] as it has effect in relation to earnings factors.

(4) Subject to subsections (5) [², (5A)] and (6) below, this section has effect in relation to a person ("the pensioner") who attains pensionable age after 5th April, 2000.

(5) Where the pensioner is a woman, this section has effect in the case of additional pension falling to be calculated under sections 44 and 45 of the Social Security Contributions and Benefits Act 1992 by virtue of section 39 of that Act (widowed mother's allowance and widow's pension), including Category B retirement pension payable under section 48B(4), if her husband—

(a) dies after 5th April, 2000, and

(b) has not attained pensionable age on or before that date.

[² (5A) This section has effect in the case of additional pension falling to be calculated under sections 44 and 45 of the Social Security Contributions and Benefits Act 1992 by virtue of section 39C(1) of that Act (widowed parent's allowance), including Category B retirement pension payable under section 48BB(2), if the pensioner's spouse—

(a) dies after 5th April, 2000; and

(b) has not attained pensionable age on or before that date.]

(6) This section has effect where additional pension falls to be calculated under sections 44 and 45 of the Social Security Contributions and Benefits Act 1992 as applied by section [³ . . .] [², 48B(2) or 48BB(5)] of that Act (other Category B retirement pension) if—

(a) the pensioner attains pensionable age after 5th April, 2000, and

(b) the pensioner's spouse has not attained pensionable age on or before that date.

AMENDMENTS

1. Child Support, Pensions and Social Security Act 2000 s.33 (January 25, 2001).
2. Welfare Reform and Pensions Act 1999 s.70 (April 9, 2001).
3. Pensions Act 2014 Sch.12 para.72 (April 6, 2016).

SCHEDULE 4

[³ EQUALISATION OF AND INCREASE IN PENSIONABLE AGE FOR MEN AND WOMEN]

PART I

PENSIONABLE AGES FOR MEN AND WOMEN

1.—The following rules apply for the purposes of the enactments relating to social security, that is, the following Acts and the instruments made, or having effect as if made, under them: the Social Security Contributions and Benefits Act 1992, the Social Security Administration Act 1992 [¹ the Pension Schemes Act 1993][⁵, the State Pension Credit Act 2002][⁹, Part 1 of the Welfare Reform Act 2007 and the Pensions Act 2014.]

1.656

Rules

(1) A man [³ born before [⁴ December 6, 1953]] attains pensionable age when he attains the age of 65 years.

(2) A woman born before 6th April 1950 attains pensionable age when she attains the age of 60.

(3) A woman born on any day in a period mentioned in column 1 of [³ table 1] attains pensionable age at the commencement of the day shown against that period in column 2.

[³ (4) [⁴*omitted*].]

1.657

[² TABLE 1]

(1) *Period within which woman's birthday falls*	(2) *Day pensionable age attained*
6th April 1950 to 5th May 1950	6th May 2010
6th May 1950 to 5th June 1950	6th July 2010
6th June 1950 to 5th July 1950	6th September 2010
6th July 1950 to 5th August 1950	6th November 2010
6th August 1950 to 5th September 1950	6th January 2011
6th September 1950 to 5th October 1950	6th March 2011
6th October 1950 to 5th November 1950	6th May 2011
6th November 1950 to 5th December 1950	6th July 2011
6th December 1950 to 5th January 1951	6th September 2011
6th January 1951 to 5th February 1951	6th November 2011
6th February 1951 to 5th March 1951	6th January 2012
6th March 1951 to 5th April 1951	6th March 2012
6th April 1951 to 5th May 1951	6th May 2012
6th May 1951 to 5th June 1951	6th July 2012
6th June 1951 to 5th July 1951	6th September 2012
6th July 1951 to 5th August 1951	6th November 2012
6th August 1951 to 5th September 1951	6th January 2013
6th September 1951 to 5th October 1951	6th March 2013
6th October 1951 to 5th November 1951	6th May 2013
6th November 1951 to 5th December 1951	6th July 2013
6th December 1951 to 5th January 1952	6th September 2013
6th January 1952 to 5th February 1952	6th November 2013
6th February 1952 to 5th March 1952	6th January 2014
6th March 1952 to 5th April 1952	6th March 2014
6th April 1952 to 5th May 1952	6th May 2014
6th May 1952 to 5th June 1952	6th July 2014
6th June 1952 to 5th July 1952	6th September 2014
6th July 1952 to 5th August 1952	6th November 2014
6th August 1952 to 5th September 1952	6th January 2015
6th September 1952 to 5th October 1952	6th March 2015
6th October 1952 to 5th November 1952	6th May 2015

1.658

[² TABLE 1]

(1) *Period within which woman's birthday falls*	(2) *Day pensionable age attained*
6th November 1952 to 5th December 1952	6th July 2015
6th December 1952 to 5th January 1953	6th September 2015
6th January 1953 to 5th February 1953	6th November 2015
6th February 1953 to 5th March 1953	6th January 2016
6th March 1953 to 5th April 1953	6th March 2016
[6th April 1953 to 5th May 1953	6th July 2016
6th May 1953 to 5th June 1953	6th November 2016
6th June 1953 to 5th July 1953	6th March 2017
6th July 1953 to 5th August 1953	6th July 2017
6th August 1953 to 5th September 1953	6th November 2017
6th September 1953 to 5th October 1953	6th March 2018
6th October 1953 to 5th November 1953	6th July 2018
6th November 1953 to 5th December 1953	6th November 2018]

[² (5) A person born on any day in a period mentioned in column 1 of table 2 attains pensionable age at the commencement of the day shown against that period in column 2.

1.659

[¹⁰TABLE 2

(1) *Period within which birthday falls*	(2) *Day pensionable age attained*
6th December 1953 to 5th January 1954	6th March 2019
6th January 1954 to 5th February 1954	6th May 2019
6th February 1954 to 5th March 1954	6th July 2019
6th March 1954 to 5th April 1954	6th September 2019
6th April 1954 to 5th May 1954	6th November 2019
6th May 1954 to 5th June 1954	6th January 2020
6th June 1954 to 5th July 1954	6th March 2020
6th July 1954 to 5th August 1954	6th May 2020
6th August 1954 to 5th September 1954	6th July 2020
6th September 1954 to 5th October 1954	6th September 2020]

(6) A person born after 5th October 1954 but before [⁵ 6th April 1960] attains pensionable age when the person attains the age of 66.

[⁵ (7) A person born on any day in a period mentioned in column 1 of table 3 attains pensionable age when the person attains the age shown against that period in column 2.

1.660

TABLE 3

(1) *Period within which birthday falls*	(2) *Day pensionable age attained*
6th April 1960 to 5th May 1960	66 years and 1 month
6th May 1960 to 5th June 1960	66 years and 2 months
6th June 1960 to 5th July 1960	66 years and 3 months
6th July 1960 to 5th August 1960	66 years and 4 months
6th August 1960 to 5th September 1960	66 years and 5 months
6th September 1960 to 5th October 1960	66 years and 6 months
6th October 1960 to 5th November 1960	66 years and 7 months
6th November 1960 to 5th December 1960	66 years and 8 months
6th December 1960 to 5th January 1961	66 years and 9 months

TABLE 3   **1.660**

(1) *Period within which birthday falls*	(2) *Day pensionable age attained*
6th January 1961 to 5th February 1961	66 years and 10 months
6th February 1961 to 5th March 1961	66 years and 11 months

(7A) For the purposes of table 3—
   (a) a person born on 31st July 1960 is to be taken to attain the age of 66 years and 4
      months at the commencement of 30th November 2026;
   (b) a person born on 31st December 1960 is to be taken to attain the age of 66 years and
      9 months at the commencement of 30th September 2027;
   (c) a person born on 31st January 1961 is to be taken to attain the age of 66 years and 10
      months at the commencement of 30th November 2027.

(8) A person born after [⁷ 5th March 1961] but before 6th April 1977 attains pensionable
age when the person attains the age of 67.

(9) A person born on any day in a period mentioned in column 1 of table 4 attains pensionable age at the commencement of the day shown against that period in column 2.

TABLE 4   **1.661**

(1) *Period within which birthday falls*	(2) *Day pensionable age attained*
6th April 1977 to 5th May 1977	6th May 2044
6th May 1977 to 5th June 1977	6th July 2044
6th June 1977 to 5th July 1977	6th September 2044
6th July 1977 to 5th August 1977	6th November 2044
6th August 1977 to 5th September 1977	6th January 2045
6th September 1977 to 5th October 1977	6th March 2045
6th October 1977 to 5th November 1977	6th May 2045
6th November 1977 to 5th December 1977	6th July 2045
6th December 1977 to 5th January 1978	6th September 2045
6th January 1978 to 5th February 1978	6th November 2045
6th February 1978 to 5th March 1978	6th January 2046
6th March 1978 to 5th April 1978	6th March 2046

(10) A person born after 5th April 1978 attains pensionable age when the person attains
the age of 68.]

PART II

ENTITLEMENT TO CERTAIN PENSIONS AND OTHER BENEFITS

Pension increases for dependent spouses

2.— [⁴ . . .]   **1.662**

Category B retirement pensions

3.—(1) *Omitted.*   **1.663**
(2) [¹⁰ . . .]
(3) [¹⁰ . . .]

Home responsibilities protection

4.—(1) In paragraph 5 of Schedule 3 to the Social Security Contributions and Benefits Act   **1.664**
1992 (contribution conditions for entitlement to retirement pension), in sub-paragraph (7)(a)

(condition that contributor must have paid or been credited with contributions of the relevant class for not less than the requisite number of years modified in the case of those precluded from regular employment by responsibilities at home), "(or at least 20 of them, if that is less than half)" is omitted.

(2) This paragraph shall have effect in relation to any person attaining pensionable age on or after 6th April 2010.

5.—*Omitted.*

Increments

1.665

6.—(1) In section 54(1) of the Social Security Contributions and Benefits Act 1992 (election to defer right to pension), in paragraph (a), the words from "but" to "70" are omitted.

(2) In Schedule 5 to that Act—

(a) in paragraph 2(2), the definition of "period of enhancement" (and the preceding "and") are omitted, and

(b) for "period of enhancement" (in every other place in paragraphs 2 and 3 where it appears) there is substituted "period of deferment".

(3) In paragraph 2(3) of that Schedule, for "1/7th per cent." there is substituted "1/5th per cent."

(4) In paragraph 8 of that Schedule, sub-paragraphs (1) and (2) are omitted.

[²(5) The preceding sub-paragraphs shall come into force as follows—

(a) sub-paragraphs (1) and (4) shall come into force on 6th April 2005;

(b) sub-paragraphs (2) and (3) shall have effect in relation to incremental periods (within the meaning of Schedule 5 to the Social Security Contributions and Benefits Act 1992 (c. 4)) beginning on or after that date.]

Graduated retirement benefit

1.666

7.—*Omitted.*

Christmas bonus for pensioners

1.667

8.—*Omitted.*

PART III

CONSEQUENTIAL AMENDMENTS

Category B retirement pensions

1.668

21.—(1)–(13) *Omitted.*

(14) Paragraph 4(1) of that Schedule (as inserted by sub-paragraph (13) above) shall have effect where W is a man who attains pensionable age before 6th April, 2010 as if paragraph (a) also required him to have been over pensionable age when S died.

(15) *Omitted.*

(16) Paragraph 5(1) of that Schedule (inserted by sub-paragraph (15) above) shall have effect, where W is a man who attained pensionable age before 6th April, 2010, as if paragraph (a) also required him to have been over pensionable age when S died.

(17) and (18) *Omitted.*

AMENDMENTS

1. State Pension Credit Act 2002 s.14 Sch.2 Pt.3 para.39 (October 6, 2003).
2. Pensions Act 2004 s.297 (April 6, 2005).
3. Pensions Act 2007 Sch.3 para.3 (September 26, 2007).
4. Pensions Act 2007 Sch.7 Pt 2 (September 26, 2007).
5. Welfare Reform Act 2007 s.28(1) Sch.3 para.13 (October 27, 2008).
6. Pensions Act 2011 s.1 (subs.2–6) (January 3, 2012).
7. Pensions Act 2014 s.26 (July 14, 2014).

8. Pensions Act 2014 s.23 Sch.12 Pt.1 para.30 (April 6, 2016).
9. Pensions Act 2014 Sch.12 para.73 (April 6, 2016).
10. Pensions Act 2011 s.1 (January 3, 2012).

GENERAL NOTE

Reference to that Schedule in para.21 above is a reference to Sch.5 of the SSCBA   **1.669**
1992.

Welfare Reform and Pensions Act 1999

(1999 C.30)

SECTIONS REPRODUCED

PART IV

PENSION SHARING

CHAPTER II

SHARING OF STATE SCHEME RIGHTS

47. Shareable state scheme rights.   **1.670**
48. Activation of benefit sharing.
49. Creation of state scheme pension debits and credits: transferor in old state pension system or pension sharing activated before 6 April 2016.
49A. Creation of debits and credits: transferor in new state pension system and sharing activated on or after 6 April 2016.
50. Effect of state scheme pension debits and credits.
51. Interpretation of Chapter II.

CHAPTER II

SHARING OF STATE SCHEME RIGHTS

Shareable State Scheme rights

47.—(1) Pension sharing is available under this Chapter in relation to a   **1.671**
person's shareable state scheme rights.

[¹ (1A) For the purposes of this Chapter, a person's shareable state scheme rights are—

   (a) the person's shareable old state scheme rights;
   (b) the person's shareable new state scheme rights.]

(2) For the purposes of this Chapter, a person's shareable [¹ old] state scheme rights are—

   (a) his entitlement, or prospective entitlement, to a Category A retirement pension by virtue of section 44(3)(b) of the Contributions and Benefits Act ([² . . .] additional pension), and

325

Welfare Reform and Pensions Act 1999

(b) his entitlement, or prospective entitlement, to a pension under section 55A [¹ or 55AA] of that Act (shared additional pension).

[¹ (3) For the purposes of this Chapter, a person's shareable new state scheme rights are the person's entitlement, or prospective entitlement, to the excess amount in a state pension under section 4 of the Pensions Act 2014.

(4) "The excess amount", in relation to a state pension under section 4 of the Pensions Act 2014, means any amount by which the rate of the pension exceeds the full rate of the state pension (see section 3 of that Act).

(5) In determining the rate of a state pension under section 4 of the Pensions Act 2014 for the purposes of this Chapter, ignore Schedule 6 to that Act (reduced rate elections: effect on rate of section 4 pension).]

AMENDMENTS

1. Pensions Act 2014 Sch.11 para.10 (April 6, 2016).
2. Pensions Act 2014 Sch.15 para. 14 (October 12, 2015).

Activation of Benefits and Sharing

1.672   **48.**—(1) [² Section 49 or 49A applies where any of the following has taken effect in relation to a person's shareable state scheme rights]—

(a) a pension sharing order under the Matrimonial Causes Act 1973,
[¹ (aa) a pensions sharing order under Schedule 5 to the Civil Partnership Act 2004,]
(b) [³ . . .]
(c) [³ . . .]
(d) an order under Part III of the Matrimonial and Family Proceedings Act 1984 (financial relief in England and Wales in relation to overseas divorce etc.) corresponding to such an order as is mentioned in paragraph (a),
[⁴ (da) an order under Schedule 7 to the 2004 Act (financial relief in England and Wales after overseas dissolution etc of a civil partnership) corresponding to such an order as is mentioned in paragraph (aa),]
(e) a pension sharing order under the Family Law (Scotland) Act 1985,
(f) provision which corresponds to the provision which may be made by such an order and which—
   (i) is contained in a qualifying agreement between the parties to a marriage [⁴ or between persons who are civil partners of each other],
   (ii) is in such form as the Secretary of State may prescribe by regulations, and
   (iii) takes effect on the grant, in relation to the marriage, of decree of divorce under the Divorce (Scotland) Act 1976 or of declarator of nullity [⁴ or (as the case may be) on the grant, in relation to the civil partnership, of decree of dissolution or of declarator of nullity],
(g) an order under Part IV of the Matrimonial and Family Proceedings Act 1984 (financial relief in Scotland in relation to overseas divorce etc.) [⁴ [or under Schedule 11 to the 2004 Act (financial provision in Scotland after overseas proceedings)]] corresponding to such an order as is mentioned in paragraph (e),

326

(h) a pension sharing order under [⁴ the Matrimonial Causes (Northern Ireland) Order 1978 (SI 1978/1045 (NI 15)),], and

(i) an order under Part IV of the Matrimonial and Family Proceedings (Northern Ireland) Order 1989 (financial relief in Northern Ireland in relation to overseas divorce etc.) corresponding to such an order as is mentioned in paragraph (h).

[⁴ (j) a pension sharing order under Schedule 15 to the 2004 Act, and

(k) an order under Schedule 17 to the 2004 Act (financial relief in Northern Ireland after overseas dissolution etc of a civil partnership) corresponding to such an order as is mentioned in paragraph (j)].

(2) [³ . . .]

(3) [³ . . .]

(4) [³ . . .]

(5) [³ . . .]

(6) For the purposes of this section, an order or provision falling within subsection (1)(e), (f) or (g) shall be deemed never to have taken effect if the Secretary of State does not receive before the end of the period of 2 months beginning with the relevant date—

(a) copies of the relevant [¹ . . .] documents, and

(b) such information relating to the transferor and transferee as the Secretary of State may prescribe by regulations under section 34(1)(b)(ii).

(7) The relevant date for the purposes of subsection (6) is—

(a) in the case of an order or provision falling within subsection (1)(e) or (f), the date of the extract of the decree or declarator responsible for the divorce [⁴, dissolution] or annulment to which the order or provision relates, and

(b) in the cases of an order falling within subsection (1)(g), the date of disposal of the application under section 28 of the Matrimonial and Family Proceedings Act 1984 [⁴ or, where the order is under Schedule 11 to the 2004 Act, the date of disposal of the application under paragraph 2 of that Schedule].

(8) The reference in subsection (6)(a) to the relevant [¹ . . .] documents is—

(a) in the case of an order falling within subsection (1)(e) or (g), to copies of the order and the order, decree or declarator responsible for the divorce or annulment to which it relates, and

(b) in the case of provision falling within subsection (1)(f), to—

(i) copies of the provision and the order, decree or declarator responsible for the divorce [⁴, dissolution] or annulment to which it relates, and

(ii) documentary evidence that the agreement containing the provision is one to which subsection (3)(a) applies.

(9) [⁵ The Court of Session or the sheriff] may, on the application of any person having an interest, make an order—

(a) extending the period of two months referred to in subsection (6), and

(b) if that period has already expired, providing that, if the Secretary of State receives the documents and information concerned before the end of the period specified in the order, subsection (6) is to be treated as never having applied.

1. Civil Partnership Act 2004 Sch.24 (December 5, 2005).
2. Pensions Act 2014 Sch.11 para.11 (April 6, 2016).
3. Children and Families Act 2014 s.18(3) (May 13, 2014).
4. Civil Partnership Act 2004 Sch.27 (December 5, 2005).
5. Pensions Act 2008 s.128 (26 January, 2009).

Creation of State Scheme pension debits and credits [²: transferor in old state pension system or pension sharing activated before 6 April 2016]

1.673

49.—[² (A1) This section applies if—

(a) the transferor is in the old state pension system, or

(b) the transferor is in the new state pension system but the transfer day was before 6 April 2016.

(1) Where this section applies because of a relevant order or provision—

(a) the transferor is subject, for the purposes of the relevant state pension legislation, to a debit of the appropriate amount, and

(b) the transferee is entitled, for the purposes of the relevant state pension legislation, to a credit of that amount.]

(2) Where the relevant order or provision specifies a percentage value to be transferred, the appropriate amount for the purposes of subsection (1) is the specified percentage of the cash equivalent on the transfer day of the transferor's shareable [² old] state scheme rights immediately before that day.

(3) Where the relevant order or provision specifies an amount to be transferred, the appropriate amount for the purposes of subsection (1) is the lesser of—

(a) the specified amount, and

(b) the cash equivalent on the transfer day of the transferor's [² shareable old] state scheme rights immediately before that day.

[¹ (4) The Secretary of State may by regulations make provision about the calculation and verification of cash equivalents for the purposes of this section.

(4A) The power conferred by subsection (4) above includes power to provide–

(a) for calculation or verification in such manner as may be approved by or on behalf of the Government Actuary, and

(b) for things done under the regulations to be required to be done in accordance with guidance from time to time prepared by a person prescribed by the regulations.]

(5) In determining prospective entitlement to a Category A retirement pension for the purposes of this section, only tax years before that in which the transfer day falls shall be taken into account.

[² (5A) The fact that a person who reaches pensionable age on or after 6 April 2016 is not entitled to a pension of the kind mentioned in section 47(2)(a) or (b) does not affect the calculation under this section of the appropriate amount by reference to the transferor's prospective entitlement, immediately before the transfer day, to a pension of that kind.]

(6) In this section—

"relevant order or provision" means the order or provision by virtue of which this section applies;

[² "the relevant state pension legislation"—
(a) in relation to a transferor or transferee in the old state pension system, means Part 2 of the Contributions and Benefits Act, and
(b) in relation to a transferor or transferee in the new state pension system, means Part 1 of the Pensions Act 2014.]
"transfer day" means the day on which the relevant order or provision takes effect;
"transferor" means the person to whose rights the relevant order or provision relates;
"transferee" means the person for whose benefit the relevant order or provision is made.

AMENDMENTS

1. Child Support, Pensions and Social Security Act 2000 s.41(1) (September 29, 2000).
2. Pensions Act 2014 Sch.11 para.12 (April 6, 2016).

[¹ Creation of debits and credits: transferor in new state pension system and sharing activated on or after 6 April 2016

49A.–(1) This section applies if—   1.674
(a) the transferor is in the new state pension system, and
(b) the transfer day is 6 April 2016 or any later date.
(2) Where this section applies because of a relevant order or provision—
(a) the transferor is subject, for the purposes of section 14 of the Pensions Act 2014, to a debit of the shared weekly amount, and
(b) the transferee is entitled, for the purposes of the relevant state pension legislation, to a credit of the shared weekly amount.
(3) The shared weekly amount is the specified percentage of the excess amount of the transferor's state pension under section 4 of the Pensions Act 2014 as at the transfer day.
(4) For the purposes of calculating the shared weekly amount—
(a) a transferor who is under pensionable age on the transfer day is to be treated as having reached pensionable age and to have become entitled to the state pension under section 4 of the Pensions Act 2014 on the transfer day;
(b) a transferor who has reached pensionable age on the transfer day but who has not yet become entitled to the state pension under section 4 of the Pensions Act 2014 is to be treated as having become entitled to the pension on that day.
(5) In this section—
"the excess amount" has the meaning given by section 47(4);
"relevant order or provision" means the order or provision by virtue of which this section applies (see section 48);
"the relevant state pension legislation"—
(a) in relation to a transferee in the old state pension system, means Part 2 of the Contributions and Benefits Act, and
(b) in relation to a transferee in the new state pension system, means Part 1 of the Pensions Act 2014;
"specified percentage" means the percentage specified in the relevant order or provision for the purposes of subsection (3);
"transfer day" means the day on which the relevant order or provision takes effect;

"transferor" means the person to whose rights the relevant order or provision relates;

"transferee" means the person for whose benefit the relevant order or
provision is made.]"

AMENDMENTS

1. Pensions Act 2014 Sch.11 para.13 (April 6, 2016).

Interpretation of Chapter II

1.675

51.—(1) In this chapter—
[¹ "shareable state scheme rights", and related expressions, have the
meaning given by section 47;]
[¹ (2) For the purposes of this Chapter—
(a) a person is in the old state pension system if the person reached
pensionable age before 6 April 2016 (or would have done so if the
person had lived until pensionable age), and
(b) a person is in the new state pension system if the person reached
pensionable age on or after 6 April 2016 (or will do so if the person
lives until pensionable age).]

AMENDMENTS

1. Pensions Act 2014 Sch.11 para.14 (April 6, 2016).

Gender Recognition Act 2004

(2004 C.7)

ARRANGEMENT OF SECTIONS

1.676
    13.   Social security benefits and pensions.
    25.   Interpretation

SCHEDULES

1.676   Schedules 1–4—*Omitted.*
1.676   Schedule 5—Benefits and pensions.
1.676   Schedule 6—*Omitted.*

COMMENCEMENT

Certain formalities provisions entered into force on Royal Assent, but the
whole Act entered into force on April 4, 2005: The Gender Recognition Act 2004
(Commencement) Order 2005 (SI 2005/54).

GENERAL NOTE

1.677

This Act makes provision, for the first time, for recognition of a change of gender
identity for a transsexual. It follows judgments of the European Court of Human
Rights against the United Kingdom finding violations of Convention rights in
Goodwin v United Kingdom (App. 28957/95), Judgment of July 11, 2002, (2002) 35

E.H.R.R. 18, and *I v United Kingdom* (App. 25680/94), Judgment of July 11, 2002, (2003) 36 E.H.R.R. 53.

The scheme introduced by the Act is essentially a system of recognition of gender identity through the issue of a gender recognition certificate. The qualifying conditions for such a certificate are that the applicant (1) has or has had gender dysphoria; (2) has lived in the acquired gender for at least two years; and (3) intends to continue to live in the acquired gender until death. There is no requirement that an applicant has undergone gender reassignment surgery. Provision is made for recognition of a change of gender identity under the law of another country.

Provision is made for two types of certificate: an interim certificate and a full certificate. Unmarried applicants can only receive full certificates, whereas prior to the coming into force of the Marriage (Same Sex Couples) Act 2013 married applicants could only receive interim certificates. Matrimonial law was amended so that the issue of an interim certificate constitutes a ground for a marriage to be declared a nullity provided that proceedings are begun within six months of issue of the certificate. A court declaring a marriage a nullity under this ground must also issue a full gender recognition certificate. Since the 2013 Act came into force, the Gender Recognition Panel is obliged to issue a full certificate to a married applicant if the appliciant's spouse consents.

In *C-451/16 MB v SSWP* the requirement (in a pre-2013 Act case) for a person claiming retirement pension in their acquired gender who was married to have had that marriage annulled was held by the CJEU to constitute unlawful direct discrimination contrary to Council Directive 79/7/EEC.

The effect of the full certificate is to be found in s.9 which provides that a person's gender becomes for all purposes the acquired gender, although it does not affect things done or events occurring before the certificate is issued. This general principle is made subject to the express provisions of this Act and any other enactment. It is destined to become known as the "section 9 principle".

1.678

A challenge to the DWP's policies for retention and processing of historic gender data on the grounds inter alia that they contravened ss.9 and 22 of the Act failed in *R(C) v SSWP* [2017] UKSC 72.

The Act contains a range of provisions seeking to work out the practical implications of the issue of a gender recognition certificate. Section 13 and Sch.5 concern social security benefits and pensions. These provisions are concerned only with old age and survivors benefits. The operation of the provisions of the section 9 principle will apply in relation to applications for any social security benefit not covered in this part of the Act, and that should be the starting point for any determination of an application for such benefit by the holder of a full gender recognition certificate.

The UK Government conducted a review of the Act during 2018 and at the time of writing (April 2019) the Government's response is awaited.

Social security benefits and pensions

13. Schedule 5 (entitlement to benefits and pensions) has effect.

1.679

GENERAL NOTE

The provisions of the Schedule constitute a set of free-standing rules rather than amendments to the Contributions and Benefits Act (and its counterparts elsewhere in the United Kingdom). They apply where a person holds a full gender recognition certificate. Perhaps unsurprisingly where the change of gender identity is from female to male, the rules applicable to men apply. These are, of course, generally less favourable in the field of old age and survivors benefits because of the age discrimination still operative in this area of social security. However, where the change of identity is from male to female, the position is less straightforward. Provision is made for entitlement to a retirement pension at age 60, but generally in relation to entitlement to benefits based on a spouse's national insurance contributions, there is no automatic passport to these.

1.680

Commissioners have decided that provisions of the Gender Recognition Act 2004 are not compatible with the prohibition of discrimination in art.4(1) of Directive 79/7/EEC. Note, in particular, *CIB/2248/2006* and the decisions of a Tribunal of Commissioners in *R(P) 1/09* and *R(P) 2/09*. These, and other cases, are discussed in more detail in the annotations to art.4 of Directive 79/7/EEC in Vol.III.

Note also *Timbrell v SSWP* [2010] EWCA Civ 701, which concerned entitlement to a retirement pension by a male-to-female transsexual under the legal regime applicable *prior to* the entry into force of the Gender Recognition Act. This case is also discussed in the annotations to art.4 of Directive 79/7 in Vol.III.

SP v SSWP (RP) [2013] UKUT 156 considers the effect of the *Timbrell* judgment on R(P) 1/09 and R(P) 2/09. It finds that claims for backdated payments of retirement pension will only be possible where, as in the *Timbrell* case, there is an earlier claim upon which no decision has been made. In the absence of such a claim, the most that can be done is payment of arrears of deferred pension from April 27, 2006 (the date of the *Richards* judgment). The decision contains a useful summary of *R(P)1/09, R(P)2/09* and the *Timbrell* judgment.

SSWP v HY and LO (RP) [2017] UKUT 303 (AAC) concerned a claim by two male-to-female persons that precluding their being able to receive retirement pensions in respect of periods before they acquired gender recognition certificates constituted discrimination in breach of art.4 of Directive 79/7/EEC. The first claimant underwent gender reassignment surgery in 1986, but did not obtain a gender recognition certificate until February 2015. This had been prompted by refusal to award a retirement pension from July 2014 when she reached pensionable age for a woman. The second claimant underwent gender reassignment surgery in 1988. She obtained a gender recognition certificate in February 2014 by which time she was already aged 65. She claimed a retirement pension from May 2008 when she had reached the age of 60. Judge Rowland reviews both the relevant legislative and case law history. He concludes that the circumstances of the two claimants were distinguishable from those which had arisen in the *Richards* and *Timbrell* cases. Those cases had been concerned with entitlements in respect of periods in the absence of a national scheme for recognition of a changed gender identity. In the instant cases, there had been delay in obtaining a gender recognition certificate after the scheme in the Gender Recognition Act 2004 had come into force. On the facts, both claimants could have sought gender recognition certificates in a timely manner to enable claims to be successful from the relevant pensionable ages for a woman. The claimants argued that there was nonetheless unfavourable treatment when they compared themselves to persons who had been registered as women from birth. Judge Rowland concluded that the Directive did not require the United Kingdom to establish a scheme which permitted the retrospective award of gender recognition certificates, and the United Kingdom had chosen to make them prospective only. There was accordingly no discrimination which fell foul of the prohibition in art.4 of Directive 79/7/EEC. Any difference in treatment could be objectively justified.

In *C-451/16 MB v SSWP* the requirement (in a pre-2013 Act case) for a person claiming retirement pension in their acquired gender who was married to have had that marriage annulled was held by the CJEU to constitute unlawful direct discrimination contrary to Council Directive 79/7/EEC.

Interpretation

1.681   **25.** In this Act—

"the acquired gender" is to be construed in accordance with s.1(2),

"approved country or territory" has the meaning given by s.2(4),

"the appointed day" means the day appointed by order under s.26,

[² . . .]

"enactment" includes an enactment contained in an Act of the Scottish Parliament or in any Northern Ireland legislation, "full gender recognition certificate" and "interim gender recognition certificate" mean the certificates issued as such under [¹ section 4, 5 or 5A] and "gender recognition certificate" means either of those sorts of certificate,

"gender dysphoria" means the disorder variously referred to as gender dysphoria, gender identity disorder and transsexualism,

"Gender Recognition Panel" (and "Panel") is to be construed in accordance with Schedule 1,

[³ "protected civil partnership" means a civil partnership under the law of England and Wales'

"protected marriage" means—

(a) a marriage under the law of England and Wales, or

(b) a marriage under the law of a country or territory outside the United Kingdom,]

[² "registered psychologist" means a person registered in the part of the register maintained under the [⁴ Health and Social Work Professions Order 2001] which relates to practitioner psychologists,]

[³ "statutory declaration of consent" has the meaning given by section 3(6B)(a),]

"subordinate legislation" means an Order in Council, an order, rules, regulations, a scheme, a warrant, bye-laws or any other instrument made under an enactment, and

"UK birth register entry" has the meaning given by s.10(2).

AMENDMENTS

1. Civil Partnership Act 2004 Pt 7 s.250(7) (December 5, 2005).

2. Health Care and Associated Professions (Miscellaneous Amendments and Practitioner Psychologists) Order 2009 (SI 2009/1182) Sch.5(1) para.8 (July 1, 2009).

3. The Marriage (Same Sex Couples) Act 2013 Sch.5(1) para.14 (December 10, 2014); insertion has effect as subject to transitional and transitory provision: SI 2014/3169.

4. Health and Social Care Act 2012 s.213(8) (August 1, 2012).

SCHEDULE 5

BENEFITS AND PENSIONS

PART I

INTRODUCTORY

1. This Schedule applies where a full gender recognition certificate is issued to a person.   **1.682**

PART II

STATE BENEFITS

Introductory

2.—(1) In this Part of this Schedule "the 1992 Act" means—   **1.683**
  (a) in England and Wales and Scotland, the Social Security Contributions and Benefits Act 1992 (c. 4), and
  (b) in Northern Ireland, the Social Security Contributions and Benefits (Northern Ireland) Act 1992 (c. 7).
(2) In this Part of this Schedule "the Administration Act" means—

(a) in England and Wales and Scotland, the Social Security Administration Act 1992 (c. 5), and

(b) in Northern Ireland, the Social Security Administration (Northern Ireland) Act 1992 (c. 8).

(3) Expressions used in this Part of this Schedule and in Part 2 of the 1992 Act have the same meaning in this Part of this Schedule as in Part 2 of the 1992 Act.

Widowed mother's allowance

1.684   3.—(1) If (immediately before the certificate is issued) the person is, or but for section 1 of the Administration Act would be, entitled to a widowed mother's allowance under section 37 of the 1992 Act (allowance for woman whose husband died before 9th April 2001)—

(a) the person is not entitled to that allowance afterwards, but

(b) (instead) subsections (2) to (5) of section 39A of the 1992 Act (widowed parent's allowance) apply in relation to the person.

(2) If (immediately before the certificate is issued) the person is (actually) entitled to a widowed mother's allowance, the entitlement to widowed parent's allowance conferred by sub-paragraph (1) is not subject to section 1 of the Administration Act.

GENERAL NOTE

1.685   This paragraph applies in the case of a female to male transsexual. If, immediately prior to the issue of the certificate, the person was (or would be but for having made a claim) entitled to widowed mother's allowance, entitlement to that benefit ceases on issue of the certificate, but the man becomes entitled to claim a widowed parent's allowance under the specified provisions of the Contributions and Benefits Act. If, however, widowed mother's allowance has been claimed and awarded, then the benefit converts to widowed parent's allowance without the need for a claim.

Widow's pension

1.686   4. If (immediately before the certificate is issued) the person is entitled to a widow's pension under section 38 of the 1992 Act (pension for woman whose husband died before 9th April 2001), the person is not entitled to that pension afterwards.

GENERAL NOTE

1.687   This paragraph applies in the case of a female to male transsexual. Since there is no equivalent pension under the bereavement benefits scheme (a widower's pension), the entitlement to the widow's pension ceases on issue of the certificate.

Widowed parent's allowance

1.688   5. If (immediately before the certificate is issued) the person is, or but for section 1 of the Administration Act would be, entitled to a widowed parent's allowance by virtue of subsection (1)(b) of section 39A of the 1992 Act (allowance for man whose wife died before 9th April 2001), subsections (2) to (5) of that section continue to apply in relation to the person afterwards.

GENERAL NOTE

1.689   Widowed parent's allowance is predominantly a gender neutral benefit, and the provision here is simply for entitlement to widowed parent's allowance to continue where a man has claimed in respect of a bereavement before April 2001. However, women in receipt of widowed mother's allowance have the potential right to move on to widow's pension, but no provision is made for transfer in a relevant case from widowed parent's allowance to widowed mother's allowance.

Long-term incapacity benefit etc.

1.690   6. If (immediately before the certificate is issued) the person is entitled to incapacity benefit, or a Category A retirement pension, under—

(a) section 40 of the 1992 Act (long-term incapacity benefit etc. for woman whose husband died before 9th April 2001), or

(b) section 41 of the 1992 Act (long-term incapacity benefit etc. for man whose wife died before that date),

the person is not so entitled afterwards.

GENERAL NOTE

The effect of these provisions is at first surprising. Sections 40 and 41 make provision respectively for widow and widowers which enabled a person incapable of work at the time of the bereavement to claim incapacity benefit even though the contribution conditions were not satisfied. On reaching pensionable age, the incapacity benefit would convert into a Category A retirement pension if the person was not otherwise entitled to retirement pension. For both male to female, and female to male, transsexuals, the entitlement to incapacity benefit on this basis ceases. This would appear to be because the principle adopted throughout the Schedule would seem to be to treat all those holding a gender recognition certificate as if they had been bereaved *after* April 2001. Sections 40 and 41 apply only where the person was bereaved before April 2001.

1.691

[¹ Pension under Part 1 of the Pensions Act 2014

6A.–(1) Any question—

(a) whether the person is entitled to a state pension under Part 1 of the Pensions Act 2014 for any period after the certificate is issued, and

(b) (if so) the rate at which the person is so entitled for the period,

is to be decided as if the person's gender were the acquired gender.

(2) Accordingly, if (immediately before the certificate is issued) the person—

(a) is a woman entitled to a state pension under Part 1 of the Pensions Act 2014, but

(b) has not attained the age of 65,

the person ceases to be so entitled when it is issued.

(3) And, conversely, if (immediately before the certificate is issued) the person—

(a) is a man who has attained the age at which a woman of the same age attains pensionable age, but

(b) has not attained the age of 65, the person is to be treated for the purposes of Part 1 of the Pensions Act 2014 as attaining pensionable age when it is issued.

(4) But sub-paragraph (1) does not apply if and to the extent that the decision of any question to which it refers is affected by the payment or crediting of contributions, or the crediting of earnings, in respect of a period ending before the certificate is issued.

(5) If the person's acquired gender is the male gender, sections 11 and 12 of, and Schedules 6 and 7 to, the Pensions Act 2014 (effect of reduced rate elections) apply in relation to the person as they apply in relation to a woman (but only once the person has reached pensionable age for a man).

(6) Paragraph 10 makes provision about deferment of state pensions under Part 1 of the Pensions Act 2014.]

Paragraph 6B omitted

1.692

Category A retirement pension

7.—(1) Any question—

(a) whether the person is entitled to a Category A retirement pension (under section 44 of the 1992 Act) for any period after the certificate is issued, and

(b) (if so) the rate at which the person is so entitled for the period,

is to be decided as if the person's gender had always been the acquired gender [² (but this is subject to sub-paragraph (3))].

(2) Accordingly, if (immediately before the certificate is issued) the person—

(a) is a woman entitled to a Category A retirement pension, but

(b) has not attained the age of 65,

the person ceases to be so entitled when it is issued.

(3) And, conversely, if (immediately before the certificate is issued) the person—

(a) is a man who has attained the age at which a woman of the same age attains pensionable age, but

(b) has not attained the age of 65,

1.693

the person is to be treated for the purposes of section 44 of the 1992 Act as attaining pensionable age when it is issued.

(4) But sub-paragraph (1) does not apply if and to the extent that the decision of any question to which it refers is affected by—

    (a) the payment or crediting of contributions, or the crediting of earnings, in respect of a period ending before the certificate is issued, or

    (b) preclusion from regular employment by responsibilities at home for such a period.

(5) Paragraph 10 makes provision about deferment of Category A retirement pensions.

GENERAL NOTE

1.694   The general principle in sub-paragraph (1) is an exception to the section 9 principle, because for these purposes the person's acquired gender is treated as though it has always been the person's gender. So a female to male transsexual who changes gender between the ages of 60 and 65 ceases to be entitled to any Category A retirement pension awarded, whereas a male to female transsexual who changes gender between the ages of 60 and 65 is treated for the purposes of determining entitlement to a Category A retirement pension as though she attained pensionable age on the date of issue of the certificate, but not before. There is no retrospectivity of entitlement.

Note that, although art.7(1) provides that any question of entitlement, and, if so, the rate of entitlement, is to be decided as if the person's acquired gender had always been their gender, this is subject to an exception in para.(4) that covers the payment and crediting of contributions, and the treatment of earnings that have been made before the change of gender. In *CP/98/2007*, the claimant was over 65 at the time she changed her gender from male to female. The decision maker decided that the contributions she had made between the ages of 60 and 65, when she was a man, should not be included in calculating her additional state pension, but the Commissioner allowed her appeal on the basis of the exception provided in para.(4).

Category B retirement pension etc.

1.695   8.—(1) Any question whether the person is entitled to—

    (a) a Category B retirement pension (under [³ section 48A, 48B, 48BB or 51] of the 1992 Act), or

    (b) an increase in a Category A retirement pension under section 51A or 52 of the 1992 Act (increase in Category A retirement pension by reference to amount of Category B retirement pension),

for any period after the certificate is issued is (in accordance with section 9(1)) to be decided as if the person's gender were the acquired gender (but subject to sub-paragraph (4)).

(2) Accordingly, if (immediately before the certificate is issued) the person is a woman entitled to—

    (a) a Category B retirement pension, or

    (b) an increase in a Category A retirement pension under section 51A or 52 of the 1992 Act,

the person may cease to be so entitled when it is issued.

(3) And, conversely, if (immediately before the certificate is issued) the person—

    (a) is a man who has attained the age at which a woman of the same age attains pensionable age, but

    (b) has not attained the age of 65,

the person is to be treated for the purposes of [³ sections 48A, 48AA, 48B and 48BB] of the 1992 Act as attaining pensionable age when it is issued.

(4) But a person who is a man (immediately before the certificate is issued) is not entitled to a Category B retirement pension under section 48B of the 1992 Act for any period after it is issued if the person—

    (a) attains (or has attained) the age of 65 before 6th April 2010, and

    (b) would not have been entitled to a Category B retirement pension under section 51 of the 1992 Act for that period if still a man.

(5) Paragraph 10 makes provision about deferment of Category B retirement pensions.

GENERAL NOTE

These rather complex provisions reflect the four different routes to entitlement   **1.696**
to a Category B retirement pension coupled with the change which came into effect
in 2010 under which men began to acquire entitlement to Category B retirement
pension. The general principle adopted in relation to acquisition of entitlement to
a Category B retirement pension is that any question of entitlement after the issue
of a gender recognition certificate is to be determined by applying the rules applicable to persons of the acquired gender. That means that if the acquired gender is
that of a woman, the rules applicable to women are applied to the claimant, and, if
the acquired gender is that of a man, the rules applicable to men are applied to the
claimant. In both cases no concessions to the change of gender identity are made.
The exception is sub-paragraph (4) which limits the ability of a male to female transsexual acquiring entitlement under s.48B of the Contributions and Benefits Act.

Shared additional pension

9.—(1) Any question—   **1.697**
    (a) whether the person is entitled to a shared additional pension (under section 55A [⁴ or
        55AA] of the 1992 Act) for any period after the certificate is issued, and
    (b) (if so) the rate at which the person is so entitled for the period,
is to be decided on the basis of the person attaining pensionable age on the same date as
someone of the acquired gender (and the same age).
  (2) Accordingly, if (immediately before the certificate is issued) the person—
    (a) is a woman entitled to a shared additional pension, but
    (b) has not attained the age of 65,
the person ceases to be so entitled when it is issued.
  (3) And, conversely, if (immediately before the certificate is issued) the person—
    (a) is a man who has attained the age at which a woman of the same age attains pension-
        able age, but
    (b) has not attained the age of 65,
the person is to be treated for the purposes of section 55A [⁴ or 55AA] of the 1992 Act as
attaining pensionable age when it is issued.
  (4) Paragraph 10 makes provision about deferment of shared additional pensions.

Deferment of pensions

10.—(1) The person's entitlement to—   **1.698**
[⁵ (za) a state pension under Part 1 of the Pensions Act 2014,]
    (a) a Category A retirement pension,
    (b) a Category B retirement pension, or
    (c) a shared additional pension,
is not to be taken to have been deferred for any period ending before the certificate is issued
unless the condition in sub-paragraph (2) is satisfied.
  (2) The condition is that the entitlement both—
    (a) was actually deferred during the period, and
    (b) would have been capable of being so deferred had the person's gender been the
        acquired gender.

GENERAL NOTE

The principle applied here is that there can be no notional deferment of pension   **1.699**
on recognition of a change of gender identity.

Category C retirement pension for widows

11. [⁶ . . .]   **1.700**

GENERAL NOTE

It would be surprising if this provision proves problematic in operation, since it   **1.701**
relates (a) to persons who attained pensionable age before July 5, 1948, and (b) to

the wives and widows of such persons. A change of gender identity from woman to man results in the loss of the entitlement.

Graduated retirement benefit: Great Britain

1.702   12.—(1) The provision that may be made by regulations under paragraph 15 of Schedule 3 to the Social Security (Consequential Provisions) Act 1992 (c. 6) (power to retain provisions repealed by Social Security Act 1973 (c. 38), with or without modification, for transitional purposes) includes provision modifying the preserved graduated retirement benefit provisions in consequence of this Act.

(2) "The preserved graduated retirement benefit provisions" are the provisions of the National Insurance Act 1965 (c. 51) relating to graduated retirement benefit continued in force, with or without modification, by regulations having effect as if made under that paragraph.

Graduated retirement benefit: Northern Ireland

1.703   13.—(1) The provision that may be made by regulations under paragraph 15 of Schedule 3 to the Social Security (Consequential Provisions) (Northern Ireland) Act 1992 (c. 9) (corresponding power for Northern Ireland) includes provision modifying the Northern Ireland preserved graduated retirement benefit provisions in consequence of this Act.

(2) "The Northern Ireland preserved graduated retirement benefit provisions" are the provisions of the National Insurance Act (Northern Ireland) 1966 (c. 6 (N.I.)) relating to graduated retirement benefit continued in force, with or without modification, by regulations having effect as if made under that paragraph.

PART 3

OCCUPATIONAL PENSION SCHEMES

GENERAL NOTE

1.704   The Schedule does not make any rules about occupational pension schemes, but it does have to deal with the provisions guaranteeing those in receipt of occupational pensions the guaranteed minimum pension, and preserved equivalent pension benefits.

Guaranteed minimum pensions etc.: Great Britain

1.705   14.—(1) In this paragraph "the 1993 Act" means the Pension Schemes Act 1993 (c. 48); and expressions used in this paragraph and in that Act have the same meaning in this paragraph as in that Act.

(2) The fact that the person's gender has become the acquired gender does not affect the operation of section 14 of the 1993 Act (guaranteed minimum) in relation to the person, except to the extent that its operation depends on section 16 of the 1993 Act (revaluation); and sub-paragraphs (3) and (5) have effect subject to that.

(3) If (immediately before the certificate is issued) the person is a woman who is entitled to a guaranteed minimum pension but has not attained the age of 65—

    (a) the person is for the purposes of section 13 of the 1993 Act and the guaranteed minimum pension provisions to be treated after it is issued as not having attained pensionable age (so that the entitlement ceases) but as attaining pensionable age on subsequently attaining the age of 65, and

    (b) in a case where the person's guaranteed minimum pension has commenced before the certificate is issued, it is to be treated for the purposes of Chapter 3 of Part 4 of the 1993 Act (anti-franking) as if it had not.

(4) But sub-paragraph (3)(a) does not—

    (a) affect any pension previously paid to the person, or

    (b) prevent section 15 of the 1993 Act (increase of guaranteed minimum where commencement of guaranteed minimum pension postponed) operating to increase the person's guaranteed minimum by reason of a postponement of the commencement of the person's guaranteed minimum pension for a period ending before the certificate is issued.

(5) If (immediately before the certificate is issued) the person is a man who—

    (a) has attained the age of 60, but

    (b) has not attained the age of 65,

the person is to be treated for the purposes of section 13 of the 1993 Act and the guaranteed minimum pension provisions as attaining pensionable age when it is issued.

(6) If at that time the person has attained the age of 65, the fact that the person's gender has become the acquired gender does not affect the person's pensionable age for those purposes.

(7) The fact that the person's gender has become the acquired gender does not affect any guaranteed minimum pension to which the person is entitled as a widow or widower immediately before the certificate is issued (except in consequence of the operation of the previous provisions of this Schedule).

(8) If a transaction to which section 19 of the 1993 Act applies which is carried out before the certificate is issued discharges a liability to provide a guaranteed minimum pension for or in respect of the person, it continues to do so afterwards.

(9) "The guaranteed minimum pension provision" means so much of the 1993 Act (apart from section 13) and of any other enactment as relates to guaranteed minimum pensions.

Guaranteed minimum pensions etc.: Northern Ireland

15.—(1) In this paragraph "the 1993 Act" means the Pension Schemes (Northern Ireland) Act 1993 (c. 49); and expressions used in this paragraph and in that Act have the same meaning in this paragraph as in that Act.

(2) The fact that the person's gender has become the acquired gender does not affect the operation of section 10 of the 1993 Act (guaranteed minimum) in relation to the person, except to the extent that its operation depends on section 12 of the 1993 Act (revaluation); and sub-paragraphs (3) and (5) have effect subject to that.

(3) If (immediately before the certificate is issued) the person is a woman who is entitled to a guaranteed minimum pension but has not attained the age of 65—

    (a) the person is for the purposes of section 9 of the 1993 Act and the guaranteed minimum pension provisions to be treated after it is issued as not having attained pensionable age (so that the entitlement ceases) but as attaining pensionable age on subsequently attaining the age of 65, and

    (b) in a case where the person's guaranteed minimum pension has commenced before the certificate is issued, it is to be treated for the purposes of Chapter 3 of Part 4 of the 1993 Act (anti-franking) as if it had not.

(4) But sub-paragraph (3)(a) does not—

    (a) affect any pension previously paid to the person, or

    (b) prevent section 11 of the 1993 Act (increase of guaranteed minimum where commencement of guaranteed minimum pension postponed) operating to increase the person's guaranteed minimum by reason of a postponement of the commencement of the person's guaranteed minimum pension for a period ending before the certificate is issued.

(5) If (immediately before the certificate is issued) the person is a man who—

    (a) has attained the age of 60, but

    (b) has not attained the age of 65,

the person is to be treated for the purposes of section 9 of the 1993 Act and the guaranteed minimum pension provisions as attaining pensionable age when it is issued.

(6) If at that time the person has attained the age of 65, the fact that the person's gender has become the acquired gender does not affect the person's pensionable age for those purposes.

(7) The fact that the person's gender has become the acquired gender does not affect any guaranteed minimum pension to which the person is entitled as a widow or widower immediately before the certificate is issued (except in consequence of the operation of the previous provisions of this Schedule).

(8) If a transaction to which section 15 of the 1993 Act applies which is carried out before the certificate is issued discharges a liability to provide a guaranteed minimum pension for or in respect of the person, it continues to do so afterwards.

(9) "The guaranteed minimum pension provision" means so much of the 1993 Act (apart from section 9) and of any other enactment as relates to guaranteed minimum pensions.

Equivalent pension benefits: Great Britain

16.—(1) The provision that may be made by regulations under paragraph 15 of Schedule 3 to the Social Security (Consequential Provisions) Act 1992 (c. 6) (power to retain provisions repealed by Social Security Act 1973 (c. 38), with or without modification, for transitional purposes) includes provision modifying the preserved equivalent pension benefits provisions in consequence of this Act.

1.706

1.707

(2) "The preserved equivalent pension benefits provisions" are the provisions of the National Insurance Act 1965 (c. 51) relating to equivalent pension benefits continued in force, with or without modification, by regulations having effect as if made under that paragraph.

Equivalent pension benefits: Northern Ireland

1.708   17.—(1) The provision that may be made by regulations under paragraph 15 of Schedule 3 to the Social Security (Consequential Provisions) (Northern Ireland) Act 1992 (c. 9) (corresponding power for Northern Ireland) includes provision modifying the Northern Ireland preserved equivalent pension benefits provisions in consequence of this Act.

(2) "The Northern Ireland preserved equivalent pension benefits provisions" are the provisions of the National Insurance Act (Northern Ireland) 1966 (c. 6 (N.I.)) relating to equivalent pension benefits continued in force, with or without modification, by regulations having effect as if made under that paragraph.

AMENDMENTS

1. Added by Pensions Act 2014 Sch.12(1) para.48(2) (April 6, 2016).
2. Pensions Act 2014 Sch.12(1) para.48(3) (April 6, 2016).
3. Pensions Act 2014 Sch.12(2) para.76 (April 6, 2016).
4. Pensions Act 2014 Sch.11 para.16 (April 6, 2016).
5. Pensions Act 2014 Sch.12(1) para.48(4) (April 6, 2016).
6. Pensions Act 2014 Sch.12(2) para.83 (April 6, 2016).

Welfare Reform Act 2007

(2007 c.5)

ARRANGEMENT OF SECTIONS

PART 1

EMPLOYMENT AND SUPPORT ALLOWANCE

Entitlement

1.   Employment and support allowance   **1.709**
1A.   Duration of contributory allowance
1B.   Further entitlement after time-limiting
2.   Amount of contributory allowance
3.   Deductions from contributory allowance: supplementary
4.   Amount of income-related allowance
5.   Advance award of income-related allowance
6.   Amount payable where claimant entitled to both forms of allowance
7.   Exclusion of payments below prescribed minimum

Assessments relating to entitlement

8.   Limited capability for work
9.   Limited capability for work-related activity
10.   Report

Conditionality

11.   Work-focused health-related assessments
12.   Work-focused interviews
13.   Work-related activity
14.   Action plans in connection with work-focused interviews
15.   Directions about work-related activity
15A. Persons dependent on drugs etc.
16.   Contracting out
16A. Hardship payments

Miscellaneous

17.   Income and capital: general
18.   Disqualification
19.   Pilot schemes
20.   Relationship with statutory payments
21.   Deemed entitlement for other purposes
22.   Supplementary provisions
23.   Recovery of sums in respect of maintenance

General

24.   Interpretation of Part 1
25.   Regulations and orders

26.   Parliamentary control
27.   Financial provisions relating to Part 1
28.   Consequential amendments relating to Part 1
29.   Transition relating to Part 1
30–63. *Omitted*

PART 5

General

64.   Northern Ireland
65.   General interpretation
66.   Financial provisions: general
67.   Repeals
68.   Transition
69.   Extent
70.   Commencement
71.   Short title

SCHEDULES

Schedule 1—Employment and support allowance: additional conditions
    Part 1
    Contributory allowance
    Part 2
    Income-related allowance
Schedule 1A—Persons dependent on drugs etc.
Schedule 2—Employment and support allowance: supplementary provisions
Schedule 3—Consequential amendments relating to Part 1
Schedule 4—Transition relating to Part 1
Schedule 5—*Omitted*
Schedule 6—*Omitted*
Schedule 7—*Omitted*
Schedule 8—Repeals

An Act to make provision about social security; to amend the Vaccine Damage Payments Act 1979; and for connected purposes.

[3rd May 2007]

PART 1

EMPLOYMENT AND SUPPORT ALLOWANCE

Entitlement

Employment and support allowance

1.710   **1.**—(1) An allowance, to be known as an employment and support allowance, shall be payable in accordance with the provisions of this Part.

(2) Subject to the provisions of this Part, a claimant is entitled to an employment and support allowance if he satisfies the basic conditions and either—

(a) the first and the second conditions set out in Part 1 of Schedule 1 (conditions relating to national insurance) or the third condition set out in that Part of that Schedule (condition relating to youth), or

(b) the conditions set out in Part 2 of that Schedule (conditions relating to financial position).

(3) The basic conditions are that the claimant—

(a) has limited capability for work,

[⁴ (aa) has accepted a claimant commitment]

(b) is at least 16 years old,

(c) has not reached pensionable age,

(d) is in Great Britain,

(e) is not entitled to income support, and

(f) is not entitled to a jobseeker's allowance (and is not a member of a couple who are entitled to a joint-claim jobseeker's allowance).

[¹(3A) After the coming into force of this subsection no claim may be made for an employment and support allowance by virtue of the third condition set out in Part 1 of Schedule 1 (youth).]

(4) For the purposes of this Part, a person has limited capability for work if—

(a) his capability for work is limited by his physical or mental condition, and

(b) the limitation is such that it is not reasonable to require him to work.

(5) An employment and support allowance is payable in respect of a week.

(6) In subsection (3)—

"joint-claim jobseeker's allowance" means a jobseeker's allowance entitlement to which arises by virtue of section 1(2B) of the Jobseekers Act 1995 (c. 18);

"pensionable age" has the meaning given by the rules in paragraph 1 of Schedule 4 to the Pensions Act 1995 (c. 26).

[³(6A) In subsection (3)(f), in relation to a contributory allowance, the reference to a couple entitled to a joint-claim jobseeker's allowance does not include a couple so entitled by virtue of regulations under paragraph 8A of Schedule 1 to the Jobseekers Act 1995.]

(7) In this Part—

"contributory allowance" means an employment and support allowance entitlement to which is based on subsection (2)(a) [² (and see section 1B(2))];

"income-related allowance" means an employment and support allowance entitlement to which is based on subsection (2)(b).]

AMENDMENTS

1. Welfare Reform Act 2012 s.53 (May 1, 2012).
2. Welfare Reform Act 2012 s.52(2) (May 1, 2012).
3. Welfare Reform Act 2012 s.50(1) (May 8, 2012).
4. Welfare Reform Act 2012 s.54(2) (April 29, 2013 and various dates).

MODIFICATIONS

Section 1(2) is modified by Sch.1 para.2 of the Employment and Support Allowance (Transitional Provisions, Housing Benefit and Council Tax Benefit) (Existing Awards) (No.2) Regulations 2010 (SI 2010/1907) (as amended) for the purposes specified in reg.6(1).

Section 1(2) is modified by Sch.2 para.2(a) of the Employment and Support Allowance (Transitional Provisions, Housing Benefit and Council Tax Benefit)

(Existing Awards) (No. 2) Regulations 2010 (SI 2010/1907) (as amended) for the purposes specified in reg.16(1).

Section 1(7) is modified by Sch.2 para.2(b) of the Employment and Support Allowance (Transitional Provisions, Housing Benefit and Council Tax Benefit) (Existing Awards) (No.2) Regulations 2010 (SI 2010/1907) (as amended) for the purposes specified in reg.16(1).

For details of the modifications, see the text of those Regulations, below.

DEFINITIONS

> "contributory allowance"—see subs.(7).
> "income-related allowance"—see subs.(7).
> "joint-claim jobseeker's allowance"—see subs.(6).
> "pensionable age"—see subs.(6).

GENERAL NOTE

Subsection (1)

1.711   This establishes Employment and Support Allowance (ESA), which is payable in accordance with the terms set out in the remainder of Part I of the Act, a framework clothed with the detail afforded by several sets of regulations:

- *Employment and Support Allowance Regulations 2008 (SI 2008/794) (ESA Regulations) (as amended)*
  Like the JSA and IS Regs which in many respects they emulate, these set out the key detailed rules on ESA.

- *Employment and Support Allowance (Transitional Provisions) Regulations 2008 (SI 2008/795) (as amended)*
  These deal with the transition to ESA (key rules for "existing customers" of the IB/IS/SDA incapacity benefits' regime).

- *Employment and Support Allowance (Consequential Provisions) Regulations 2008 (SI 2008/1082)*
  These effect amendments to Housing and Council Tax benefits and are not reproduced.

- *Employment and Support Allowance (Consequential Provisions) (No. 2) Regulations 2008 (SI 2008/1554)*
  These effect a variety of changes to legislation covered in *Social Security Legislation.*

- *Employment and Support Allowance (Consequential Provisions) (No. 3) Regulations 2008 (SI 2008/1879)*
  These effect a variety of changes to tax credits and child benefit.

A brief overview of ESA and its purpose may be useful to place the detailed rules and commentary in context.

State support towards the income replacement needs of those incapable of work has been the province of incapacity benefit (IB), income support (IS), or a mixture of both, since the non-contributory incapacity benefit, Severe Disablement Allowance (SDA), was closed to new claimants from April 6, 2001. From October 27, 2008 (the "appointed day", "commencement") both were closed to new claimants who claim benefit on the basis of a health condition or disability which so affects their ability to work that it is not reasonable to expect them to do so. From then, any such claim was treated as one for Employment and Support Allowance (ESA), claimed to be less complex and easier to claim. "Existing customers" (those already in receipt of those benefits, or whose claim for a new spell of incapacity links back to a period of incapacity for work prior to commencement) were able to retain entitlement to them after the appointed day, but lost it once the relevant period of incapacity for work came to an end without linking to another which started prior to commencement. All new claimants (and those "existing customers" unable to link in that way) had to look for income replacement to the new ESA. Thus yet another client group has been removed from IS, leaving it very much as a residual benefit, ultimately to be abolished and replaced by universal credit. Indeed, now that universal credit has been rolled out nationwide, in most cases it is no longer possible to get income-related ESA on a new claim.

Like JSA, ESA is a single benefit with two forms: contributory ESA (CESA) and income-related ESA (IRESA). A claimant may be entitled to one or the other or, in some cases, both. See further *LH v SSWP (ESA)* [2014] UKUT 480 (AAC); [2015] AACR 14, where Judge Rowland confirmed that employment and support allowance is a single benefit with two routes to qualification and that it is not necessary to make separate claims for each of the contributory allowance and the income-related allowance (para. 12); see also *DS v SSWP* [2018] UKUT 270 (AAC). On the standard claim form a claimant has the opportunity to indicate which of the types s/he seeks (both types or one or the other), something which has advantages both for the claimant (no need to disclose details of financial position if seeking only CESA) and for the Secretary of State (no need to check contribution records where someone seeks only IRESA). However, as Judge Rowland stated

> "despite the language usually used, an indication that one or other of the allowances is not "claimed" amounts to a waiver of the need for the Secretary of State to consider entitlement to that element of employment and support allowance, rather than amounting to a true failure to claim it. The legislation does not actually contemplate there being a claim for only one element of the allowance" (para.13).

Where someone has initially sought only one form and later wishes to seek the other form as well, the matter should be raised not through a new claim but through an application for supersession under SSA 1998 s.10 or through revision under SSA 1998 s.9 or a subsequent appeal under SSA 1998 s.12 (para.15).

ESA, payable in respect of a week, is a benefit to provide support to those clearly unable to work, through a "support component" paid in addition to their basic allowance, and to require those capable of work-related activity to engage in it in return (at least for claims made before April 3, 2017) for a "work-related activity component" on top of their basic allowance, the hope being that they will eventually return to the labour force. ESA is a benefit with similarities to JSA (even CESA can be reduced on account of certain other income), but initially had no time limit on either its contributory or income related forms, save that entitlement ceased on reaching pensionable age (s.1(3)(c)). For those not in the support group, CESA has from May 1, 2012 been time-limited to 365 days (counting days of entitlement before, on and after that date) (see: ss.1A and 1B; the Employment and Support Allowance (Duration of Contributory Allowance) (Consequential Amendments) Regulations 2012 (SI 2012/913); the Employment and Support Allowance (Amendment of Linking Rules) Regulations 2012 (SI 2012/919)).

ESA is accessible by persons with an employer (after SSP is exhausted) (s.20(1)), the self-employed, and those without employment.

Eligibility for CESA depends, like that for IB, on fulfilment of contribution conditions showing a recent connection with the world of work. But, as with IB after the abolition of SDA for new claimants, persons incapacitated in youth (before 20 or in some cases 25) can have access to this ostensibly contributory form without meeting the contribution conditions. This route was barred to new claimants claiming on or after May 1, 2012 (see subs.(3A)). Otherwise, claimants who do not meet those conditions will have to seek IRESA. Depending on their precise financial circumstances, and the intricacies of the income related "balance sheet", in terms of capital and income (including income from capital), those entitled to the CESA may also receive IRESA as a top-up.

The conditions of entitlement common to the basic allowance aspect of both forms of ESA are that the claimant is at least 16; has not reached pensionable age; is in Great Britain; is not entitled to IS; is not entitled to JSA in his own right or

1.712

1.713

as part of a joint-claim couple; and has limited capability for work (see subs.(3)). The matter of capacity is either assessed by a work-related capability assessment (a functional test similar to the IB personal capability assessment or all work test), involving a medical examination, or, is deemed to exist for a much reduced set of "exempt" groups. Generally, three "waiting days" of non-entitlement have to be served (s.22, Sch.2 para.4; ESA Regs reg.144). During the (generally 13-week) assessment period, only basic allowance ESA is payable. Additional components (support or work-related activity) depend on the claimant being assessed or treated as having limited capability for work/work-related activity respectively (albeit not for (broadly speaking) new claims made on or after April 3, 2017). The personal allowance aspect of ESA basic allowance (a lower rate for those under 25) is based on the personal allowances in JSA (single person, lone parent or couple), but those able to qualify for IRESA can also access applicable premiums. After the assessment period ends (when the claimant has been assessed or treated as having limited capacity for work), claimants become eligible for one (but not both) of two additional components: the *support* component; or the *work-related activity* component. However, the work-related activity component is not payable on (broadly speaking) new claims made on or after April 3, 2017. To be eligible for the *support* component, claimants must have limited capability for work-related activity (capacity for that must be limited by their physical or mental condition to such an extent that it is not reasonable to require them to undertake such activity). If they do not have limited capacity for work-related activity (i.e. capability for work-related activity is not limited by physical or mental condition or, if it is, the limitations are not such as to render it unreasonable to undertake such activity), they will be eligible for the work-related activity component on top of the basic allowance (at least for claims made before April 3, 2017), provided they meet prescribed conditions on work-related activity. Should they not do so, they can be sanctioned by progressive reduction (ultimately removal) of the amount of that component to which they would otherwise be entitled.

As with IB/IS, claimants entitled to ESA can be disqualified from it where their conduct conduces to their incapacity (e.g. because of misconduct in bringing it about or in refusing treatment which would alleviate it) or their failure to adhere to prescribed rules of behaviour (s.18; ESA Regs regs 157, 159). "Persons in hardship" cannot be disqualified but receive a reduced rate of personal allowance (ESA Regs reg.158, Sch.5, para.14). Absences from Great Britain (other than certain temporary absences) preclude entitlement to ESA (s.18(4), Sch.2 paras 5, 6, 8; ESA Regs regs 151–155). Imprisonment or detention in legal custody each disqualify from CESA and, if longer than six weeks, results in the person being treated as not having limited capability for work, thus impacting on ability to link spells of limited capability for work (s.18(4); ESA Regs reg.159 and Sch.5 para.3).

ESA is part of a broader governmental strategy to assist people with a health condition or disability. Government is convinced that benefit dependency, particularly strong in respect of benefits for incapacity, is a major element in hardship and deprivation, and that work is the route out of poverty. The measures set out in its 2006 Green Paper (Cm 6730) were intended to increase the numbers who are able to remain in work when they fall sick or become disabled; to raise the numbers moving from benefits into employment; and better to meet the needs of those requiring extra help and support because of a health condition. Unlike IB (rather caricatured by a Government determined like its predecessors to reduce the cost to the public purse of supporting the once favourably-treated group—those incapable of work), ESA does not automatically assume incapacity for work merely because someone has a significant health condition or disability. It was built on experience with the pilots of the Pathways to Work project which was rolled out nationally in April 2008. It was claimed that this initiative had significantly increased the IB claimants being helped into work, and that "these pilots have demonstrated that, with the right help and support, many people on incapacity benefits can move back into work, reinforcing the view that labelling people on incapacity benefits as 'incapable of work' is wrong and damaging". Government considered that no lesser approach than ESA would provide the necessary cultural shift, from a benefits package based on "incapacity for work" to one founded firmly on what a person can do.

Government expects that ESA will have a significant and wide-ranging positive impact on disabled people and people with health conditions who are out of work. ESA is a benefit designed to help these people overcome barriers, and where appropriate move into work and improve their lives. The Work Capability Assessment (WCA) seeks to relate more accurately to modern context than the 12-year-old IB/IS system, and to focus more on what people can do, rather on what they are unable to do. The conditionality regime for those with limited capability for work seeks to engage customers placed in the work-related activity group. It affords them access to employment and condition management programmes. But ESA recognises the needs of those in the Support Group; their entitlement to the support component is not conditional on work-related activity but they can engage, if they wish, with those programmes. ESA seeks better to reflect the aspirations of disabled people, and improve the "customer experience" of individuals on the benefit.

1.714

ESA in outline was broadly welcomed as to its purpose of, and potential for, helping disabled people fulfil their aspiration to work, by spokespersons across all parties, and as a potential route out of poverty by groups representing the disabled. But concerns (becoming stronger as more detail emerged) were nonetheless expressed about a range of aspects: conditionality (sanctions welcomed and seen as vital by some to "persuade" the reluctant to engage with help and knowledge, seen as problematic or unnecessary by others); the impact on persons with a variety of conditions (mental health problems, cancer sufferers, Asperger's syndrome), particularly fluctuating ones, and on the terminally ill; which groups would be exempt from the WCA; what would be the categories of permitted work so vital to building confidence that someone could return to work; the nature of the law-making process leaving too much to secondary legislation or ministerial fiat; adding to the complexity of the benefits system with a supposed single benefit involving six rates; the nature and interrelationship of two capability assessments with different criteria; and, crucially, the other side of the coin—the provisions deal with the attitude of the disabled to work but leave untouched the attitude of employers to the disabled would-be worker.

Note that for the purpose of making "conversion decisions" under the "Migration Regulations" from November 1, 2010, subs.(2) is to be read as if there were substituted the text set out in Sch.1 para.2 of those Regulations: see the Employment and Support Allowance (Transitional Provisions, Housing Benefit and Council Tax Benefit) (Existing Awards) (No. 2) Regulations 2010 (SI 2010/1907). After a conversion decision has been made, subs.(2) is to be read as modified by reg.16(1) and Sch.2 para.(2)(a) to those Regulations.

From October 1, 2010, after a conversion decision has been made under the "Migration Regulations", subs.(7) is to read as if there were substituted the text contained in Sch.2 para.(2)(b) to those Regulations.

Since ESA was introduced in October 2008, there have been a series of amendments to the secondary legislation governing the descriptors that apply for the purposes of the WCA. These changes are discussed below in the commentary to Sch.2 and Sch.3 to the Employment and Support Allowance Regulations 2008 (SI 2008/794). There have also been two major changes since the 2007 Act to the framework in the primary legislation. The first has been the gradual introduction of universal credit under the Welfare Reform Act 2012, which increasingly is replacing income-related ESA in affected areas. The second has been the abolition of the work-related activity component in ESA for (broadly speaking) claims made on or after April 3, 2017.

The National Audit Office report *Investigation into errors in Employment and Support Allowance* (March 2018) examined DWP errors in converting people's existing IB claims into ESA awards where claimants were only awarded contribution-based ESA despite being entitled to income-related ESA. It is estimated some 70,000 people had not been paid the full amount of ESA that they were entitled to (on average underpayments were £5,000). The Public Accounts Committee is holding an inquiry into the DWP's handling of these errors.

Subsections (2), (3A), (7)

1.715   As with JSA, read together these envisage two ways of gaining title to ESA: the "contributory route" to the "contributory allowance" (CESA); and the "income-related" route to "income-related allowance" (IRESA). They provide that entitlement to CESA is grounded on satisfaction of the "basic conditions" in subs.(3) plus *either* (a) satisfaction of the national insurance contribution conditions (Sch.1 Pt 1) *or* (b) that the claimant is someone incapacitated in youth (Sch.1 Pt 1). But no new claims for CESA on the grounds of youth (see subs.(2)(a) and Pt 1 of Sch.1) may be made on or after May 1, 2012 (subs.(3A). Those claimants who would have been entitled on those grounds will instead have to meet the usual National Insurance contribution conditions for a claim for CESA. Entitlement to IRESA is grounded on satisfaction of the basic conditions in subs.(3) plus those relating to financial position (Sch.1 Pt 2).

Subsection (3)

1.716   This stipulates the "basic conditions" which must be satisfied whether the claimant claims CESA, IRESA or both. The claimant must

- *be at least 16*
  this is the current school-leaving age and so this lower limit is apt for a benefit that is an earnings replacement one;

- *be under pensionable age*
  "pensionable age" is here defined according to the rules in Pensions Act 2004, Sch.4, para.1 (see subs.(6)). It thus links to the sliding scale of pensionable ages found there as the pensions system moves steadily towards equal pension ages for men and women;

- *be in Great Britain*
  absences from Great Britain (other than certain temporary absences) preclude entitlement to ESA. See further s.18(4), Sch.2 paras 5, 6, 8; ESA Regs regs 151–155. Essentially this is a presence rather than a residence test. However, note that ESA Regs regs 69–70 and Sch.5, apply to IRESA much the same rules on residence as apply in IS and IBJSA;

- *not be entitled to IS under SSCBA 1992, s.124*
  this establishes the mutual exclusivity of ESA and IS;

- *not be entitled to JSA whether in his/her own right or as part of a joint-claim couple*
  this establishes the mutual exclusivity of ESA and JSA. Entitlement to JSA as a joint-claim couple arises under Jobseekers Act 1995 s.1(2B);

- *have limited capability for work*
  the basic test for this is set out in subs.(4): claimants will have limited capability for work where their capability for work is limited by their physical or mental condition and that limitation is such that it is not reasonable to require them to work. ESA Regs 2008 reg.19(1) elaborates that this is to be determined on the basis of a limited capability for work assessment (hereinafter WCAt), one element in the three-element Work Capability Assessment which has been developed out of a review of the Personal Capability Assessment (PCA) in the IB/IS/SDA incapacity benefits' regime. The WCAt is

  "an assessment of the extent to which a claimant who has some specific disease or bodily or mental disablement is capable of performing the activities prescribed in Schedule 2 [to the ESA Regs] or is incapable by reason of such disease or bodily or mental disablement of performing those activities" (ESA Regs reg.19(2)).

  This is familiar stuff to anyone who has worked with the PCA or its predecessor, the "all work" test. The claimant is to be matched, in the light of all the evidence, by the decision-maker or tribunal against a reformulated range of activities and descriptors, and an appropriate "score" awarded. The threshold "score" for entitlement remains 15 points, but as regards its computation, there are both "old" and "new" elements". See further the commentary to s.8 and to ESA Regs Pt 5 (regs 19–33) and Sch.2.

The further basic condition of having accepted a claimant commitment (subpara.(2)(aa)), inserted by s.54(2) of the WRA 2012, initially applied only to new-style ESA in universal credit areas. It is due to be implemented more widely as from the summer of 2017, including for new claims for old-style ESA, starting with live service areas where the claimant does not satisfy the universal credit gateway conditions.

Subsection (4)
This sets out the basic definition of "limited capability for work". See commentary to subs.(3), s.8 and to ESA Regs Pt 5 (regs 19–33) and Sch.2.   1.717

Subsection (5)
Emulating JSA, ESA is a weekly benefit, one paid in respect of a week. For cases   1.718
of part-week entitlement see s.22, Sch.2 para.3 and ESA Regs Pt 14 (regs 165–169).

Subsection (6)
This defines, by reference to other legislation, "joint-claim jobseeker's allowance"   1.719
and "pensionable age".

Subsection (6A)
This provides that subs.(3)(f), excluding single claimants and joint-claim couples   1.720
entitled to JSA, does not exclude from CESA a joint-claim couple entitled to JSA by virtue of regulations made under Jobseekers Act 1995 Sch.1 para.8A. The regulations are JSA Regs 1996 regs 3D and 3E. For these JSA provisions, see Vol.II in this series.
Note that Welfare Reform Act 2012 s.50(2) gives this subs.(6A) retrospective effect where to do so would benefit a claimant. It provides:
"(2) In a case where—
(a) an award of an employment and support allowance is made to a person in respect of any period of time before the coming into force of subsection (1), and
(b) the person was not entitled to an employment and support allowance in relation to that period but would have been had subsection (1) been in force in relation to that period,
subsection (1) shall be regarded as having been in force in relation to that period."

Subsection (7)
Another definition provision. See commentary to subss.(2), (7), above.   1.721

[¹ Duration of contributory allowance

1A.—(1) The period for which a person is entitled to a contributory   1.722
allowance by virtue of the first and second conditions set out in Part 1 of Schedule 1 shall not exceed, in the aggregate, the relevant maximum number of days in any period for which his entitlement is established by reference (under the second condition set out in Part 1 of Schedule 1) to the same two tax years.
(2) In subsection (1) the "relevant maximum number of days" is—
(a) 365 days, or
(b) if the Secretary of State by order specifies a greater number of days, that number of days.
(3) The fact that a person's entitlement to a contributory allowance has

ceased as a result of subsection (1) does not prevent his being entitled to a further such allowance if—

> (a) he satisfies the first and second conditions set out in Part 1 of Schedule 1, and
> (b) the two tax years by reference to which he satisfies the second condition include at least one year which is later than the second of the two years by reference to which (under the second condition) his previous entitlement was established.

(4) The period for which a person is entitled to a contributory allowance by virtue of the third condition set out in Part 1 of Schedule 1 (youth) shall not exceed—

> (a) 365 days, or
> (b) if the Secretary of State by order specifies a greater number of days, that number of days.

(5) In calculating for the purposes of subsection (1) or (4) the length of the period for which a person is entitled to a contributory allowance, the following are not to be counted—

> (a) days in which the person is a member of the support group,
> (b) days not falling within paragraph (a) in respect of which the person is entitled to the support component referred to in section 2(1)(b), and
> (c) days in the assessment phase, where the days immediately following that phase fall within paragraph (a) or (b).

(6) In calculating for the purposes of subsection (1) or (4) the length of the period for which a person is entitled to a contributory allowance, days occurring before the coming into force of this section are to be counted (as well as those occurring afterwards).]

AMENDMENT

1. Welfare Reform Act 2012 s.51 (May 1, 2012).

DEFINITIONS

"contributory allowance" — see s.1(7), above, and s.1B(2), below.
"relevant maximum number of days" — see subs.(2).

GENERAL NOTE

1.723   As noted in the annotation to WRA 2007 s.1, this has the effect that for *those not in the support group* CESA—whether obtained by the contributory route (subs.(2)) or as a person incapacitated in youth (subs.(4))—is from May 1, 2012 time-limited to 365 days (counting days of entitlement before, on and after that date), even if the period of limited capability for work exceeds this period. Termination on this ground is appealable, and in any such appeal termination can be contested on the basis that the claimant at the point of termination, although not regarded by the Secretary of State as being in the support group, ought to have been because the claimant at that point in fact had limited capability for work-related activity (or was to be treated as such) (*MC and JH v SSWP (ESA)* [2014] UKUT 125 (AAC)). Note that the Secretary of State can by order increase the time-limit (subss.(2)(b) and (4)(b)). To requalify for a further period of entitlement to CESA the conditions in subs.(3) must be met with the second contribution condition being met in at least one tax year later than the second of the two tax years by reference to which (under the second contribution condition) his previous period of entitlement to CESA had been based.

Since someone may move from the support group to the work-related activity group and back again, calculating when the maximum period of entitlement to CESA is reached can be more complicated than simply counting 365 days of entitlement. Hence, the days stipulated in subs.(5) do not count in calculating the maximum period of entitlement.

[¹ Further entitlement after time-limiting

1B.—(1) Where a person's entitlement to a contributory allowance has ceased as a result of section 1A(1) or (4) but—

   (a) the person has not at any subsequent time ceased to have (or to be treated as having) limited capability for work,

   (b) the person satisfies the basic conditions, and

   (c) the person has (or is treated as having) limited capability for work-related activity,

the claimant is entitled to an employment and support allowance by virtue of this section.

(2) An employment and support allowance entitlement to which is based on this section is to be regarded as a contributory allowance for the purposes of this Part.]

1.724

AMENDMENT

1. Welfare Reform Act 2012 s.51 (May 1, 2012).

DEFINITIONS

"basic conditions"—see s.1(3), above.
"contributory allowance"—see s.1(7), above, and subs.(2).

GENERAL NOTE

This has the effect that where a person's contributory ESA ceased under s.1A as a result of time limiting, but their health condition has deteriorated so that they are later placed in the support group, they will be able to re-qualify for an award of CESA (see subs.(2) which ranks it as such) if the three conditions in subs.(1) are satisfied:

1.725

- the person has not ceased to have (or be treated as having) limited capability for work;

- the person satisfies the basic conditions (see WRA 2007 s.1(3)); and

- the person has (or is treated as having) limited capability for work-related activity.

Entitlement to the award only subsists for as long as the person has (or is treated as having) limited capability for work-related activity (and so falls into the support group). If a subsequent work capability assessment places the recipient in the work related activity group, then entitlement to an award arising by virtue of this section ceases.

Amount of contributory allowance

2.—(1) In the case of a contributory allowance, the amount payable in respect of a claimant shall be calculated by—

   (a) taking such amount as may be prescribed;

   (b) if in his case the conditions of entitlement to the support component [¹ . . .] are satisfied, adding the amount of that component; and

   (c) making prescribed deductions in respect of any payments to which section 3 applies.

(2) The conditions of entitlement to the support component are—

   (a) that the assessment phase has ended;

1.726

(b) that the claimant has limited capability for work-related activity; and

(c) that such other conditions as may be prescribed are satisfied.

(3) [¹ . . .]

(4) Regulations may—

(a) prescribe circumstances in which paragraph (a) of subsection (2) [¹ . . .] is not to apply;

(b) prescribe circumstances in which entitlement under subsection (2) [¹ . . .] is to be backdated;

(c) make provision about the amount of the component under subsection (2) [¹ . . .].

(5) For the purposes of this Part, a person has limited capability for work-related activity if—

(a) his capability for work-related activity is limited by his physical or mental condition; and

(b) the limitation is such that it is not reasonable to require him to undertake such activity.

AMENDMENT

1. Welfare Reform and Work Act 2016 s.15(2) (April 3, 2017).

MODIFICATION

Section 2(2), (3) are modified by Sch.1 para.3 of the Employment and Support Allowance (Transitional Provisions, Housing Benefit and Council Tax Benefit) (Existing Awards) (No. 2) Regulations 2010 (SI 2010/1907) (as amended) for the purposes specified in reg.6(1).

Section 2(2), (3) are modified by Sch.2 para.3 of the Employment and Support Allowance (Transitional Provisions, Housing Benefit and Council Tax Benefit) (Existing Awards) (No. 2) Regulations 2010 (SI 2010/1907) (as amended) for the purposes specified in reg.16(1).

For details of the modification(s), see the text of those Regulations, below.

DEFINITIONS

"assessment phase"—see s.24(2), (3).
"claimant"—see s.24(1).
"contributory allowance"—see s.1(6).
"limited capability for work-related activity"—see subs.(5).
"prescribed"—see s.24(1).
"regulations"—see s.24(1).
"work-related activity"—see ss.24(1), 13(7), below.

GENERAL NOTE

1.727   This section deals with the calculation of amount of contributory allowance (CESA) (see s.1(6)) to which a particular claimant can be entitled, both during the "assessment phase" and after it has ended (subss.(1)–(3)). It provides rule-making powers to modify some of the conditions, to set amounts and to enable backdating of entitlement (subs.(4)). Finally it defines when someone has "limited capability for work-related activity" (subs.(5)).

Subsection (1)

1.728   This sets out the elements making up CESA and the basic arithmetic for determining the amount of CESA to which the claimant is entitled. The basic arithmetic during the "assessment phase" is prescribed amount (age-related) minus any s.3 deductions. After the "assessment phase", it changes to single prescribed amount plus appropriate component (support or, at least for claims predating April 3, 2017, work related activity) minus any s.3 deductions. Since entitlement varies as between the period of the "assessment phase" and after it has ended, it is useful to begin with analysis of that concept.

The "assessment phase" starts on the first day of the period for which the claimant is entitled to ESA (the day after service of the three waiting days of non-entitlement (see s.22, Sch.2 para.2, and ESA Regs reg.144)). It ends on whichever is the later of either 13 weeks from that first day of entitlement or the date of determination of limited capability for work (either of actual limited capability or of "deemed" limited capability (treated as having limited capability) (see s.24(2), ESA Regs reg.4). The ESA scheme deals with intermittent incapacity through "linking" rules. These impact on identification of the end of the "assessment phase". Under ESA Regs reg.145, periods of limited capability for work "link" and are treated as one single period (to which further ones may be added if the linking rules are met). Typically periods not separated by more than 12 weeks' "link" in this way (see ESA Regs reg.145(1)), but for "work or training beneficiaries" (see ESA Regs reg.148), the separation period rises to a maximum 104 weeks (see ESA Regs reg.145(2)). Where the assessment phase had not ended in the first such period, it ends at the appropriate point (the later of 13 weeks or the date of the limited capability of work determination) in the linked period(s). There can only be one assessment period in any single period of limited capability for work. So where another spell of such limited capability arises and is forged into one with an earlier period by the appropriate linking rules (12 or 104 weeks), and the "assessment phase" had ended in the earlier period, the claimant's entitlement in this second (or subsequent "spell") will be to prescribed amount plus appropriate component minus any s.3 deductions (s.2(4)(a); ESA Regs reg.7(1)(b)). If the linking rules do not operate so as to forge the two spells into one, the second "spell" constitutes a new period of incapacity, in respect of which the three "waiting days" will again have to be served and a new "assessment phase" will begin again on the first day of entitlement after service of those waiting days and end according to the rules considered above.

Note finally that appealing against a determination that the claimant does not have limited capability for work extends the "assessment phase" until the appeal is determined by an appeal tribunal (s.24(2)(b); ESA Regs, regs 6, 7(2)).

The first element of CESA is the prescribed amount of "basic allowance". Although this is not a term used in the Act or the Regulations, its use is standard in the literature, policy and explanatory documents on ESA, and accordingly is also deployed here. It is normally the only element of CESA to which a claimant (other than one terminally ill) can be entitled during the "assessment phase". During that phase, the amount of CESA (subject to any s.3 deductions) to which the claimant can be entitled varies according to age. If under 25, a lower weekly rate is prescribed. The rates are equivalent to those in CBJSA.

During the assessment phase (whether ending after 13 weeks or a later date of determination of limited capability for work), it will have been determined whether the claimant has limited capability for work (actual limited capability) or should be treated as having it (deemed limited capability). It will also have been determined whether the claimant has limited capability for work related activity or should be treated as having it. If the claimant does have (or is treated as having) such limited capacity, this grounds entitlement to "support component", subject to other conditions set out in regulations, but generally only once the assessment phase has ended (subs.(2)) (see below for an exception in respect of the terminally ill). For claims before April 3, 2017, if the claimant does not have (or is treated as not having) such limited capacity, entitlement (subject to conditionality (see commentary to ss.11–16)) can only be to the work-related activity component (see subs.(3)). For claims made on or after April 3, 2017, the only additional element available is the support component, following the abolition of the work-related activity component. So the basic picture after the assessment period is prescribed amount plus appropriate component minus any s.3 deductions.

Once the assessment phase is ended there is a single prescribed weekly amount, regardless of age (see ESA Regs reg.67(2), Sch.4, para.1(1)(b)). To this will be added, as appropriate, either the support component (see para.(b); ESA Regs reg.67(3), Sch.4 Pt 4, para.13) or, at least for claims predating April 3, 2017, the lower value work-related activity component (see para.(b); ESA Regs reg.67(3), Sch.4, Pt 4, para.12). The amount of CESA actually payable, however, is subject to reduction in accordance with s.3.

For those who are "terminally ill" (subs.(4)(a); ESA Regs regs 2(1), 7(1)(a)), entitlement to the components (support or work-related activity) is not conditioned on the assessment phase having ended. So throughout their period of limited capability for work, entitlement will be to CESA composed of basic allowance plus appropriate component minus any s.3 deductions.

Subsection (2)

1.729   This sets out the conditions of entitlement to the support component in ESA. Entitlement can generally only arise after the assessment phase has ended. An exception to this is in the case of the terminally ill (subs.(4)(a); ESA Regs reg.7(1)(a)). The claimant must be assessed as having, or be treated by regulations as having, limited capability for work-related activity. Entitlement also depends on other prescribed conditions (i.e. ones set out in regulations).

Subsection (3)

1.730   This sub-section previously stipulated the conditions of entitlement to the work-related activity component of ESA. Entitlement generally only arose after the assessment phase had ended (subs.(3)(a)). An exception to this was in the case of the terminally ill (subs.(4)(a); ESA Regs reg.7(1)(a)). The claimant must also have been assessed as not having, or be treated by regulations as not having, limited capability for work-related activity (subs.(3)(b)). Entitlement also depended on other prescribed conditions (i.e. ones set out in regulations; subs.(3)(c))).

However, subs.(3) was repealed by s.15(2) of the Welfare Reform and Work Act 2016 with effect from April 3, 2017 (see reg.3(a) of the Pensions Act 2014 (Commencement No. 9) and the Welfare Reform and Work Act 2016 (Commencement No. 4) Regulations 2017 (SI 2017/111)). This implemented an announcement first made in the Summer 2015 Budget, namely that the work-related activity component paid to those in the work-related activity group would be abolished for new ESA claims as from April 3, 2017. A parallel amendment was made to the legislation governing universal credit. The policy justification for the change was said to be the need to remove the financial incentives in the benefits system that could otherwise discourage claimants from taking steps back into work. The practical effect of the reform was a cut of £29.05 a week (at 2017/18 rates), so aligning the rate of ESA for this group with the rate of benefit paid to JSA claimants. This was anticipated to save £450 million a year by 2020/21 (Budget 2016 estimate).

In broad terms, the abolition of the work-related activity component applies only to new claims as from April 3, 2017. Those claimants already in receipt of that component will continue to receive it, providing they remain on ESA. The transitional rules are in Sch.2 to the Employment and Support Allowance and Universal Credit (Miscellaneous Amendments and Transitional and Savings Provisions) Regulations 2017 (SI 2017/207). These cover the following circumstances:

- where an ESA claim was made before April 3, 2017 and that claim results in an award after that date;

- where an ESA claim was made on or after April 3, 2017 but the claimant had previously been entitled to ESA and their period of limited capability for work started before April 3, 2017 with a linking period of less than 12 weeks;

- where an existing incapacity benefit claimant who, as part of the conversion process to ESA, is subsequently found to have limited capability for work after April 3, 2017;

- where an ESA claim was made on or after April 3, 2017 but ESA is deemed payable from before April 3, 2017;

- where an ESA claim was made on or after April 3, 2017 but the claimant's assessment phase is deemed to have started before April 3, 2017;

- where a claimant (who was previously entitled to ESA as part of a claim made before April 3, 2017) having been in receipt of a maternity allowance makes a new claim for ESA within 12 weeks of the date that their maternity allowance ended (and where their maternity allowance terminated their award to contributory ESA).

Applying Subsections (2) or (3) after a break in entitlement

It is submitted that the approach of Judge Mesher in *SSWP v PT (ESA)* [2011] UKUT 317 (AAC) to breaks of entitlement are equally applicable as regards the component of the allowance returned to after a comparable break in entitlement. See further commentary to WRA 2007 s.4, below.   1.731

Subsection (5)

This defines "limited capability for work-related activity". Whether the claimant has it or not is crucial for identifying which component of ESA (support or work related activity) is applicable in the case. A claimant has it where his capability for work-related activity is limited by his physical or mental condition such that it is not reasonable to require him to undertake such activity. "Work-related activity" is defined as activity which makes it more likely that the person whose capability is being tested will obtain or remain in work or be able to do so (ss.24(1), 13(7)).   1.732

Deductions from contributory allowance: supplementary

3.—(1) This section applies to payments of the following kinds which are payable to the claimant—   1.733
   (a) pension payments,
   (b) PPF periodic payments, and
   (c) payments of a prescribed description made to a person who is a member of, or has been appointed to, a prescribed body carrying out public or local functions.
(2) Regulations may—
   (a) disapply section 2(1)(c), so far as relating to pension payments or PPF periodic payments, in relation to persons of a prescribed description;
   (b) provide for pension payments or PPF periodic payments of a prescribed description to be treated for the purposes of that provision as not being payments to which this section applies;
   (c) provide for sums of a prescribed description to be treated for the purposes of this section as payable to persons as pension payments or PPF periodic payments (including, in particular, sums in relation to which there is a deferred right of receipt);
   (d) make provision for the method of determining how payments to which this section applies are, for the purposes of section 2, to be related to periods for which a person is entitled to a contributory allowance.

(3) In this section—
"pension payment" means—
    (a) a periodical payment made in relation to a person under a personal pension scheme or, in connection with the coming to an end of an employment of his, under an occupational pension scheme or a public service pension scheme,
    (b) a payment of a prescribed description made under an insurance policy providing benefits in connection with physical or mental illness or disability, and
    (c) such other payments as may be prescribed;
"PPF periodic payment" means—
    (a) any periodic compensation payment made in relation to a person, payable under the pension compensation provisions as specified in section 162(2) of the Pensions Act 2004 (c.35) or Article 146(2) of the Pensions (Northern Ireland) Order 2005 (S.I. 2005/255) (NI 1) (the pension compensation provisions), and
    (b) any periodic payment made in relation to a person, payable under section 166 of the Pensions Act 2004 or Article 150 of the Pensions (Northern Ireland) Order 2005 (duty to pay scheme benefits unpaid at assessment date etc.).
(4) For the purposes of subsection (3), "occupational pension scheme", "personal pension scheme" and "public service pension scheme" each have the meaning given by section 1 of the Pension Schemes Act 1993 (c.48), except that "personal pension scheme" includes—
    (a) an annuity contract or trust scheme approved under section 620 or 621 of the Income and Corporation Taxes Act 1988 (c. 1), and
    (b) a substituted contract within the meaning of section 622(3) of that Act,
which is treated as having become a registered pension scheme by virtue of paragraph 1(1)(f) of Schedule 36 to the Finance Act 2004 (c.12).

DEFINITIONS

    "claimant"—see s.24(1), below.
    "occupational pension scheme"—see subs.(4).
    "pension payment"—see subs.(3).
    "personal pension scheme"—see subs.(4).
    "PPF periodic payment"—see subs.(3).
    "prescribed"—see s.24(1), below.
    "public service pension scheme"—see subs.(4).
    "regulations"—see s.24(1), below.

GENERAL NOTE

1.734   Under s.2, the amount of CESA to which the claimant is otherwise entitled will normally (see subs.(2)(a) of this section) be reduced as set out in regulations (ESA Regs regs 72–79) by the payments set out in this section which are payable to the claimant. This section and ESA Regs, regs 72–79 thus bring into ESA the concept of abatement of contributory benefit familiar from unemployment benefit (see SSCBA 1992 s.30 and USI Regs 23–28 in the 1995 edition of Bonner, Hooker and White, *Non-Means Tested Benefits: the Legislation*), jobseeker's allowance (see JSA 1995 s.21, Sch.1 para.7; JSA Regs regs 80, 81 in Vol.II) and incapacity benefit (see SSCBA 1992 ss.30DD [pension and PPF periodic payments] and 30E [councillor's allowance]; IB Regs regs 20–26 in Vol.I). While not making them fully income-related benefits along the lines of income support, income-related jobseeker's allowance or tax credits, such abatement of ESA nonetheless continues the practice of bringing into a contributory benefit an element of means testing. In interpreting this section and its associated regulations, cross-reference to case law under those JSA and IB schemes will be appropriate insofar as the definitions are identical or analogous.

Subsection (1)

This stipulates that this section covers pension payments (para.(a)—defined in subss.(3), (4)), PPF periodic payments (para.(b)—defined in subs.(3)) and "payments of a prescribed description made to a person who is a member of, or has been appointed to, a prescribed body carrying out public or local functions" (para. (c)). For the rules on taking pension payments and PPF payments into account, see ESA Regs reg.74. Currently, under para.(c), ESA Regs reg.73 prescribes only "councillor's allowance" in respect of those councils referred to in the definition of "councillor in ESA Regs reg.2(1). For the rules on taking "councillor's allowance" into account, see ESA Regs reg.76.

On "payable to", see *R(IB) 1/04* and *R(IB) 1/05*.

1.735

Subsection (2)

Under para.(b), see ESA Regs reg.75.
Under para.(d), see ESA Regs 77–79.

1.736

Subsection (3)

Under para.(b) of the definition of pension payment, see ESA Regs reg.72 whereby "pension payment" includes a "permanent health insurance payment" as defined in that reg.

1.737

Amount of income-related allowance

4.—(1) In the case of an income-related allowance, the amount payable in respect of a claimant shall be—

1.738

(a) if he has no income, the applicable amount;

(b) if he has an income, the amount by which the applicable amount exceeds his income.

(2) Subject to subsection (3), the applicable amount for the purposes of subsection (1) shall be calculated by—

(a) taking such amount, or the aggregate of such amounts, as may be prescribed, and

(b) if in the claimant's case the conditions of entitlement to the support component [¹ . . .] are satisfied, adding the amount of that component.

(3) Regulations may provide that, in prescribed cases, the applicable amount for the purposes of subsection (1) shall be nil.

(4) The conditions of entitlement to the support component are—

(a) that the assessment phase has ended,

(b) that the claimant has limited capability for work-related activity, and

(c) that such other conditions as may be prescribed are satisfied.

(5) [¹ . . .]

(6) Regulations may—

(a) prescribe circumstances in which paragraph (a) of subsection (4) [¹ . . .] is not to apply;

(b) prescribe circumstances in which entitlement under subsection (4) [¹ . . .] is to be backdated;

(c) make provision about the amount of the component under subsection (4) [¹ . . .].

AMENDMENT

1. Welfare Reform and Work Act 2016 s.15(3) (April 3, 2017).

MODIFICATION

Section 4 is modified by Sch.1, para.4 of the Employment and Support Allowance (Transitional Provisions, Housing Benefit and Council Tax Benefit) (Existing Awards) (No. 2) Regulations 2010 (SI 2010/1907) (as amended) for the purposes specified in reg.6(1) and by Sch.2 para.4 of those Regulations for the purposes specified in reg.16(1). For details of the modification, see the text of those Regulations below.

DEFINITIONS

"assessment phase"—s.24(2)
"income-related allowance"—ss.24(1) and 1(7).
"limited capability for work-related activity"—ss.24(1) and 2(5).
"prescribed"—s.24(1).
"regulations"—*ibid*.

GENERAL NOTE

1.739   This section is similar in effect to ss.124(4) and 135(1)–(2) of the Contributions and Benefits Act and ss.3(1)(a) and (4) of the Jobseekers Act. Applicable amounts (including the work-related activity component and the support component) are prescribed by regs 67–70 of, and Schs 4 and 5 to, the ESA Regulations. Income (including tariff income from capital) is governed by s.17 and Pt 10 of, and Schs 7, 8 and 9 to, the ESA Regs.

Subsections (4) and (5)

1.740   On the repeal of subs. (5) with effect from April 3, 2017, see the annotation to the former s.2(3) above (see further s.15(3) of the Welfare Reform and Work Act 2016 and reg.3(a) of the Pensions Act 2014 (Commencement No. 9) and the Welfare Reform and Work Act 2016 (Commencement No. 4) Regulations 2017 (SI 2017/111)).

The requirement that the claimant should have (or should not have) limited capability for work-related activity in s.4(4)(b) (and, before it was repealed, s.4(5)(b)) was considered by the Upper Tribunal in *SSWP v PT (ESA)* [2011] UKUT 317 (AAC); [2012] AACR 17. In that case, the claimant had been entitled to ESA with the work-related activity component but his entitlement ended when he resumed full-time work. However, his job ended after nine days. He reclaimed ESA and was awarded benefit at the basic rate (i.e. *without* the work-related activity component). The Secretary of State submitted that the component could not be paid until there had been a fresh work capability assessment because, although s.4(5)(a) was disapplied by ESA Regs, reg.7(1)(b) (made under the powers conferred by s.4(6)(a)), the claimant did not satisfy s.4(5)(b): the condition of not having limited capability for work-related activity could only be satisfied after the question of whether or not the claimant had such limited capability had been freshly determined in an assessment for that purpose. Rejecting that submission, Upper Tribunal Judge Mesher stated (at para.15):

"15. I do not accept the submissions for the Secretary of State. I go back to the plain words of section 4(4)(b) and (5)(b) of the 2007 Act. Looked at in isolation the natural and obvious meaning is that together the two provisions exhaust all possibilities in relation to limited capability for work-related activity. Providing that paragraph (a) on the ending of the assessment phase is satisfied or does not apply, either a claimant is so limited, in which case section 4(4)(b) applies, or is not, in which case section 4(5)(b) applies. ... If someone in the circumstances of the claimant here cannot be said to have limited capability for work-related activity because there has not yet been an assessment, so as not to fall within section 4(4)(b), then the person falls within section 4(5)(b). The person does not have limited capability for work-related activity because it has not yet been determined that the person does have such limited capability."

Advance award of income-related allowance

5.—(1) This section applies to claims for an employment and support allowance by a person who— 1.741

(a) would be entitled to an income-related allowance, but for the fact that he does not satisfy the condition in paragraph 6(1)(a) of Schedule 1,

(b) would satisfy that condition if he were entitled to the component mentioned in section 4(4) or (5), and

(c) is not entitled to a contributory allowance.

(2) In relation to claims to which this section applies, section 5(1) of the Administration Act (regulations about claims for benefit) shall have effect as if—

(a) in paragraph (d) (power to permit an award on a claim for benefit for a future period to be made subject to the condition that the claimant satisfies the requirements for entitlement when the benefit becomes payable under the award), there were inserted at the end "and to such other conditions as may be prescribed", and

(b) in paragraph (e) (power to provide for such an award to be revised or superseded under the Social Security Act 1998 (c. 14) if any of those requirements are found not to have been satisfied), for "any of those requirements" there were substituted "any of the conditions to which the award is made subject".

(3) Regulations may, in relation to claims to which this section applies, make provision enabling an award to be made on terms such that the time at which benefit becomes payable under the award is later than the start of the period for which the award is made.

MODIFICATION

Section 5 is modified by Sch.1 para.5 of the Employment and Support Allowance (Transitional Provisions, Housing Benefit and Council Tax Benefit) (Existing Awards) (No.2) Regulations 2010 (SI 2010/1907) (as amended) for the purposes specified in reg.6(1). For details of the modification, see the text of those Regulations below.

DEFINITIONS

"Administration Act"—s.65.
"contributory allowance"—ss.24(1) and 1(7).
"income-related allowance"—*ibid.*

General Note

1.742   The support component and, at least for claims predating April 3, 2017, work-related activity component (see s.4(4) and (5) above) are only paid after the end of the assessment phase. During that phase, there will be some claimants who are not entitled to income-related ESA because their income exceeds their applicable amount, who would be so entitled if their applicable amount included the support component or work-related activity component. This section allows an advance award to be made in such a case. See also reg.146 of the ESA Regulations.

Amount payable where claimant entitled to both forms of allowance

1.743   **6.**—(1) This section applies where a claimant is entitled to both a contributory allowance and an income-related allowance.

(2) If the claimant has no income, the amount payable by way of an employment and support allowance shall be the greater of—

(a) his personal rate, and

(b) the applicable amount.

(3) If the claimant has an income, the amount payable by way of an employment and support allowance shall be the greater of—

(a) his personal rate, and

(b) the amount by which the applicable amount exceeds his income.

(4) Where the amount payable to the claimant by way of an employment and support allowance does not exceed his personal rate, the allowance shall be treated as attributable to the claimant's entitlement to a contributory allowance.

(5) Where the amount payable to the claimant by way of an employment and support allowance exceeds his personal rate, the allowance shall be taken to consist of two elements, namely—

(a) an amount equal to his personal rate, and

(b) an amount equal to the excess.

(6) The element mentioned in subsection (5)(a) shall be treated as attributable to the claimant's entitlement to a contributory allowance.

(7) The element mentioned in subsection (5)(b) shall be treated as attributable to the claimant's entitlement to an income-related allowance.

(8) In this section—

"applicable amount" means the amount which, in the claimant's case, is the applicable amount for the purposes of section 4(1);

"personal rate" means the amount calculated in accordance with section 2(1).

Definitions

"applicable amount"—see subs.(8), s.4(1).
"claimant"—see s.24(1).
"contributory allowance"—see s.1(7).
"income-related allowance"—see s.1(7).
"personal rate"—see subs.(8), s.2(1).

General Note

1.744   This is similar to Jobseekers Act 1995 s.4(6)–(12), where, as with ESA, JSA has both a contributory element and an income related element. Like those provisions, this section deals with situations where a claimant is entitled to both a contributory allowance (CESA) and an income-related allowance (IRESA).

Here, the amount calculated under s.2(1) (amount of CESA) is referred to as the "personal rate". The applicable amount for IRESA is made up of an amount in respect of the claimant and any partner, plus applicable premiums plus eligible housing costs (see s.4(1); ESA Regs reg.67(1)). If the claimant has no income and the personal rate is higher than the applicable amount (the amount for the purposes of IRESA), the claimant receives the personal rate (the CESA amount). If the claimant has no income and the applicable amount exceeds the personal rate, he will receive the personal rate, topped up with an additional amount of IRESA equal to the excess. If the person has an income, the amount payable will be the greater of the personal allowance and the amount by which his applicable amount exceeds his income.

Exclusion of payments below prescribed minimum

7.—Except in such circumstances as regulations may provide, an employment and support allowance shall not be payable where the amount otherwise payable would be less than a prescribed minimum.   1.745

DEFINITIONS

"prescribed"—see s.24(1).
"regulations"—see s.24(1).

GENERAL NOTE

ESA is not payable where it falls below the minimum amount prescribed in regulations. This amount is set at 10p in the Claims and Payments Regs 1987 reg.26C(6), inserted with effect from October 27, 2008 by reg.21 of the ESA (Consequential Provisions) (No.2) Regs 2008 (SI 2008/1554). Compare JSA Regs reg.87A.   1.746

Assessments relating to entitlement

Limited capability for work

8.—(1) For the purposes of this Part, whether a person's capability for work is limited by his physical or mental condition and, if it is, whether the limitation is such that it is not reasonable to require him to work shall be determined in accordance with regulations.   1.747

(2) Regulations under subsection (1) shall—

(a) provide for determination on the basis of an assessment of the person concerned;

(b) define the assessment by reference to the extent to which a person who has some specific disease or bodily or mental disablement is capable or incapable of performing such activities as may be prescribed;

(c) make provision as to the manner of carrying out the assessment.

(3) Regulations under subsection (1) may, in particular, make provision—

(a) as to the information or evidence required for the purpose of determining the matters mentioned in that subsection;

(b) as to the manner in which that information or evidence is to be provided;

(c) for a person in relation to whom it falls to be determined whether he has limited capability for work to be called to attend for such medical examination as the regulations may require.

(4) Regulations under subsection (1) may include provision—

(a) for a person to be treated as not having limited capability for work if he fails without good cause—

    (i) to provide information or evidence which he is required under such regulations to provide,

    (ii) to provide information or evidence in the manner in which he is required under such regulations to provide it, or

    (iii) to attend for, or submit himself to, a medical examination for which he is called under such regulations to attend;

(b) as to matters which are, or are not, to be taken into account in determining for the purposes of any provision made by virtue of paragraph (a) whether a person has good cause for any act or omission;

(c) as to circumstances in which a person is, or is not, to be regarded for the purposes of any such provision as having good cause for any act or omission.

(5) Regulations may provide that, in prescribed circumstances, a person in relation to whom it falls to be determined whether he has limited capability for work, shall, if prescribed conditions are met, be treated as having limited capability for work until such time as—

(a) it has been determined whether he has limited capability for work, or

(b) he falls in accordance with regulations under this section to be treated as not having limited capability for work.

(6) The prescribed conditions referred to in subsection (5) may include the condition that it has not previously been determined, within such period as may be prescribed, that the person in question does not have, or is to be treated as not having, limited capability for work.

DEFINITIONS

    "limited capability for work"—see s.1(4).
    "medical examination"—
    "prescribed"—see s.24(1).
    "regulations"—see s.24(1).

GENERAL NOTE

Subsections (1), (2)

1.748   A key condition of entitlement to ESA is that the claimant has limited capability for work, namely that his capability for work is limited by his physical or mental condition such that it is not reasonable to require him to work (s.1(3)(a), (4)). This section provides that whether this is so is to be determined in accordance with regulations made under subss.(2)–(6) of this section. The regulations are Pt 5 of the ESA Regs, regs 19–33. These embody the first element in the new three-part Work Capability Assessment, governing entitlement to ESA, an analogue of the Personal Capability Assessment (PCA) in the previous incapacity benefits' regime (Incapacity Benefit/Income Support/Severe Disablement Allowance). But while there are many similarities with the PCA there are some significant differences as regards activities/descriptors, those exempt from the test and the system of scoring. The approach taken here, however, is that where terminology and basic issues are the same as with the PCA, the extensive case law interpreting and applying the PCA will carry over into the interpretation and application of comparable provisions and the resolution of comparable issues with this first element of the WCA, referred to for convenience as the WCAt to distinguish it from the other two elements of the

---

WCA which only come into play if, applying the WCAt, the claimant is found not to have limited capability for work. These other two elements are the work-related activity assessment (WRAAt) (more stringent than the WCAt) (see s.9) and the work-focused health related assessment (WFHRAt) (see s.11). The former determines whether or not a claimant has limited capability for work-related activity. If he does, he will be placed in the support group as eligible for the support component and will not have to undergo the WFHRAt. If he does not have limited capability for work-related activity, he will be placed in the work-related activity group, eligible for work-related activity component, subject to the conditionality regime (see ss.11–16), including (until its suspension from July 19, 2010 and its demise on June 1, 2011) having normally to undergo the WFHRAt (see s.11), participate in work-related interviews (see s.12) and (eventually) work-related activity (see s.13).

Note that payment of the separate work-related activity component has not been available for new claims to ESA since April 3, 2017 (subject to transitional provisions): see the annotation to the former s.2(3) above (and see further section 15(2) and (3) of the Welfare Reform and Work Act 2016 and regulation 3(a) of the Pensions Act 2014 (Commencement No. 9) and the Welfare Reform and Work Act 2016 (Commencement No. 4) Regulations 2017 (SI 2017/111)).

Subsections (3), (4)

Note that whether the claimant has good cause for failure to comply with the information-gathering and examination aspects of that assessment is to some extent structured by regulations in that ESA Regs, reg.24 provides an non-exhaustive list of matters to be taken into account in determining that good cause issue. No regulations have yet been made under para.(4)(c) to determine what does, or does not, rank as good cause.

1.749

Limited capability for work-related activity

9.—(1) For the purposes of this Part, whether a person's capability for work-related activity is limited by his physical or mental condition and, if it is, whether the limitation is such that it is not reasonable to require him to undertake such activity shall be determined in accordance with regulations.

1.750

(2) Regulations under subsection (1) shall—

(a) provide for determination on the basis of an assessment of the person concerned;

(b) define the assessment by reference to such matters as the regulations may provide;

(c) make provision as to the manner of carrying out the assessment.

(3) Regulations under subsection (1) may, in particular, make provision—

(a) as to the information or evidence required for the purpose of determining the matters mentioned in that subsection;

(b) as to the manner in which that information or evidence is to be provided;

(c) for a person in relation to whom it falls to be determined whether he has limited capability for work-related activity to be called to attend for such medical examination as the regulations may require.

(4) Regulations under subsection (1) may include provision—

(a) for a person to be treated as not having limited capability for work-related activity if he fails without good cause—

(i) to provide information or evidence which he is required under such regulations to provide,

(ii) to provide information or evidence in the manner in which he is required under such regulations to provide it, or

>   (iii) to attend for, or submit himself to, a medical examination for
>   which he is called under such regulations to attend;
>   (b) as to matters which are, or are not, to be taken into account in deter-
>   mining for the purposes of any provision made by virtue of paragraph
>   (a) whether a person has good cause for any act or omission;
>   (c) as to circumstances in which a person is, or is not, to be regarded for
>   the purposes of any such provision as having good cause for any act
>   or omission.

DEFINITIONS

>   "regulations"—see s.24(1).
>   "work-related activity"—see ss.24(1), 13(7).

GENERAL NOTE

Subsections (1), (2)

1.751   Whether an ESA claimant is entitled to the more generous support component or, at least for claims predating April 3, 2017, the less generous work-related activity component in addition to his basic allowance turns on whether he does (support component) or does not (work-related activity component) have limited capability for work-related activity (s.2(2), (3)). He has "limited capability for work-related activity" where his capability for such activity is limited by his physical or mental condition such that it is not reasonable to require him to undertake it (s.2(5)). "Work-related activity" is activity which makes it more likely that he will obtain or remain in work or be able to do so (ss.24(1), 13(7)). This section provides that whether or not he has such limited capability is to be determined in accordance with regulations under subss.(2), (4) of this section. The regulations in question are ESA Regs, Pt 6, regs 34–39. These flesh out the second element in the new three element Work Capability Assessment: the work related activity assessment (WRAAt).

Subsections (3), (4)

1.752   Note that whether the claimant has good cause for failure to comply with the information-gathering and examination aspects of that assessment is to some extent structured by regulations in that ESA Regs, reg.39 provides an non-exhaustive list of matters to be taken into account in determining that good cause issue. No regulations have yet been made under para.(4)(c) to determine what does, or does not, rank as good cause.

Report

1.753   **10.**—The Secretary of State shall lay before Parliament an independent report on the operation of the assessments under sections 8 and 9 annually for the first five years after those sections come into force.

GENERAL NOTE

1.754   The new capability assessments in respect of work and work related activity were controversial. So this section provides—but only for the first five years after commencement—for independent annual review of their operation, a report on which must be laid before Parliament by the Secretary of State.

Conditionality

Work-focused health-related assessments

1.755   [*omitted*]

This section has been omitted because work-focused health related assessments 1.756
were suspended for a period of two years from July 19, 2010 pending reconsideration of its purpose and delivery. Following that review and from June 1, 2011 the
ESA Regs governing it (regs 47–49, 51–53) were revoked (see Employment and
Support Allowance (Work-Related Activity) Regulations 2011 (SI 2011/1349),
reg.11).

Work-focused interviews

12.—(1) Regulations may make provision for or in connection with 1.757
imposing on a person who is—
  (a) entitled to an employment and support allowance, and
  (b) not a member of the support group [¹or a lone parent of a child
    under the age of one],
a requirement to take part in one or more work-focused interviews as a
condition of continuing to be entitled to the full amount payable to him in
respect of the allowance apart from the regulations.
  (2) Regulations under this section may, in particular, make provision—
  (a) prescribing circumstances in which such a person is subject to a
    requirement to take part in one or more work-focused interviews;
  (b) for notifying such a person of any such requirement;
  (c) prescribing the work-focused interviews in which a person who is
    subject to such a requirement is required to take part;
  (d) for determining, in relation to work-focused interviews under the
    regulations, when and how the interview is to be conducted and, if it
    is to be conducted face to face, where it is to take place;
  (e) for notifying persons who are required under the regulations to take
    part in a work-focused interview of what is determined in respect of
    the matters mentioned in paragraph (d);
  (f) prescribing circumstances in which a person who is a party to a
    work-focused interview under the regulations is to be regarded as
    having, or not having, taken part in it;
  (g) for securing that the appropriate consequence follows if a person
    who is required under the regulations to take part in a work-focused
    interview—
      (i) fails to take part in the interview, and
      (ii) does not, within a prescribed period, show that he had good
        cause for that failure;
  (h) prescribing matters which are, or are not, to be taken into account
    in determining whether a person had good cause for any failure to
    comply with the regulations;
  (i) prescribing circumstances in which a person is, or is not, to be
    regarded as having good cause for any such failure.
  (3) For the purposes of subsection (2)(g), the appropriate consequence
of a failure falling within that provision is that the amount payable to the
person in question in respect of an employment and support allowance is
reduced in accordance with regulations.
  (4) Regulations under subsection (3) may, in particular, make provision
for determining—
  (a) the amount by which an allowance is to be reduced,
  (b) when the reduction is to start, and
  (c) how long it is to continue,

and may include provision prescribing circumstances in which the amount of the reduction is to be nil.

(5) Regulations under this section shall include provision for a requirement to take part in one or more work-focused interviews to cease to have effect if the person subject to the requirement becomes a member of the support group.

(6) Regulations under this section may include provision—

(a) that in such circumstances as the regulations may prescribe a requirement to take part in a work-focused interview that would otherwise apply to a person by virtue of such regulations is not to apply, or is to be treated as not having applied;

(b) that in such circumstances as the regulations may prescribe such a requirement is not to apply until a prescribed time;

(c) that in such circumstances as the regulations may prescribe matters mentioned in subsection (2)(d) may be redetermined.

(7) In this section, "work-focused interview" means an interview by the Secretary of State conducted for such purposes connected with getting the person interviewed into work, or keeping him in work, as may be prescribed.

AMENDMENT

1. Welfare Reform Act 2009 s.3(3) (October 31, 2011).

DEFINITIONS

"appropriate consequence"—see subs.(3).
"entitled"—see s.24(1).
"prescribed"—see s.24(1).
"regulations"—see s.24(1).
"support group"—see s.24(4).
"work-focused interview"—see subs.(7).

GENERAL NOTE

1.758   This section covers those claimants, entitled to ESA, who do not have limited capability for work-related activity and who are thus entitled not to the support component (they are not part of the "support group" (see s.24(4)). Those only with limited capability for work but not limited capability for work-related activity must comply with certain conditions—the regime is one of "conditionality" (stipulating required behaviour and using sanctions to regulate and change behaviour). One of these conditions is participation in one or more work-focused interviews conducted either by Jobcentre Plus or (as envisaged by s.16) one of the contractors in the private or voluntary sectors (PVS).

A "work-focused interview" is one conducted for such purposes connected with keeping the interviewee in work or getting him into work, as may be set out in regulations (subs.(7)).

This section enables the making of regulations to impose the requirement of participation in such an interview and to exempt persons from it, whether totally or delaying its application for a particular period (subss.(1), (5), (6)); to deal with the process of carrying out such an interview, and with the consequences of not participating in one without good cause (subs.(2)). Subsection (3) stipulates that a reduction in the amount of ESA otherwise payable is the appropriate consequence, and that subsection and subs.(4) enable the making of regulations determining the amount and period of the reduction and the circumstances in which the reduction is to be nil. Subsection (5) enables regulations to provide that the requirement shall cease to have effect if the person becomes a member of the support group, that is, if it is determined that he has, or is to be treated as having, limited capability for work-related activity.

The relevant regulations are the ESA Regs, Pt 8 (Conditionality) Ch.2 (work-focused interviews), regs 54–62. Despite the width of the rule-making power (which would appear to authorise reduction in the amount of ESA payable) the sanction originally (at least until December 2012) operated only by reduction of the work-related activity component of ESA, rather than on the whole allowance. It would appear that this has always been the policy intention, but, if so, it would have been better in terms of compliance with Convention Rights so to confine the rule-making power (see JHRC, *Second Report of Session 2006–07*, HL 34/HC 263 (2006–07), para.3.18). That recommendation has been given added force by subsequent developments. In December 2012 the sanctions regime was amended so the reduction in benefit applied to the whole of the basic amount or personal allowance for a single claimant (but did not operate on the work-related activity component). However, the abolition of the work-related activity component for (broadly speaking) new claims since April 3, 2017 means that if a new claimant in the work-related activity group is sanctioned they would lose the entirety of their standard ESA benefit.

Note that whether the claimant has good cause for failure to participate in a work-focused health-related interview is to some extent structured by regulations in that ESA Regs, reg.61(3) provides a non-exhaustive list of matters which may be taken into account by decision-maker or appeal tribunal in determining that good cause issue. No regulations have yet been made under para.(2)(i) to determine what does, or does not, rank as good cause.

Work-related activity

13.—(1) Regulations may make provision for or in connection with imposing on a person who is subject to a requirement imposed under section 12(1) a requirement to undertake work-related activity in accordance with regulations as a condition of continuing to be entitled to the full amount payable to him in respect of an employment and support allowance apart from the regulations.   1.759

(2) Regulations under this section may, in particular, make provision—

(a) prescribing circumstances in which such a person is subject to a requirement to undertake work-related activity in accordance with regulations;

(b) for notifying such a person of any such requirement;

(c) prescribing the time or times at which a person who is subject to such a requirement is required to undertake work-related activity and the amount of work-related activity he is required at any time to undertake;

(d) prescribing circumstances in which a person who is subject to such a requirement is, or is not, to be regarded as undertaking work-related activity;

(e) for securing that the appropriate consequence follows if a person who is subject to such a requirement—
  (i) fails to comply with the regulations, and
  (ii) does not, within a prescribed period, show that he had good cause for that failure;

(f) prescribing the evidence which a person who is subject to such a requirement needs to provide in order to show that he has complied with the regulations;

(g) prescribing matters which are, or are not, to be taken into account in determining whether a person has complied with the regulations;

(h) prescribing matters which are, or are not, to be taken into account in determining whether a person had good cause for any failure to comply with the regulations;

(i) prescribing circumstances in which a person is, or is not, to be regarded as having good cause for any such failure.

(3) For the purposes of subsection (2)(e), the appropriate consequence of a failure falling within that provision is that the amount payable to the person in question in respect of an employment and support allowance is to be reduced in accordance with regulations.

(4) Regulations under subsection (3) may, in particular, make provision for determining—

(a) the amount by which an allowance is to be reduced,

(b) when the reduction is to start, and

(c) how long it is to continue,

and may include provision prescribing circumstances in which the amount of the reduction is to be nil.

(5) Regulations under this section shall include provision for a requirement to undertake work-related activity in accordance with regulations to cease to have effect if the person subject to the requirement becomes a member of the support group.

(6) Regulations under this section may include provision that in such circumstances as the regulations may provide a person's obligation under the regulations to undertake work-related activity at a particular time is not to apply, or is to be treated as not having applied.

(7) In this Part, "work-related activity", in relation to a person, means activity which makes it more likely that the person will obtain or remain in work or be able to do so.

[¹(8) The reference to activity in subsection (7) includes work experience or a work placement.]

AMENDMENT

1. Welfare Reform Act 2012 s.55 (December, 2012).

DEFINITIONS

"appropriate consequence"—see subs.(3).
"regulations"—see s.24(1).
"support group"—see s.24(4).
"work-related activity"—see subss.(7), (8).

GENERAL NOTE

1.760   This section applies only to those subject to a requirement to participate in a work-focused interview ("a requirement imposed under s.12(1)"). It thus covers those claimants, entitled to ESA, who do not have limited capability for work-related activity and who are thus entitled not to the support component (they are not part of the "support group" (see s.24(4)), who have not been exempted from the requirement or had it delayed. Those only with limited capability for work but not limited capability for work-related activity must comply with certain conditions in order to retain entitlement—the regime is one of "conditionality" (stipulating required behaviour and using sanctions to regulate and change behaviour). The first envisaged condition was participation in a work-focused health related assessment", but that was suspended from July 19, 2010 and the ESA Regs dealing with it revoked from June 1, 2011 (s.11). The second is participation in a work-focused interview (s.12). This section enables the imposition on those subject to the second of a third condition: a requirement to undertake work-related activity. That is to undertake activity which makes it more likely that the person to be subjected to the condition will obtain or remain in work or be able to do so (ss.24(1), 13(7), (8)).

This section enables the making of regulations to impose the requirement to undertake such activity and to exempt persons from it, whether totally or delaying its application for a particular period (subss.(1), (5), (6)); to deal with the process of imposition of the requirement, and with the consequences of not undertaking it without good cause (subs.(2)). Subsection (3) stipulates that a reduction in the amount of ESA otherwise payable is the appropriate consequence, and that subsection and subs.(4) enable the making of regulations determining the amount and period of the reduction and the circumstances in which the reduction is to be nil. Subsection (5) enables regulations to provide that the requirement shall cease to have effect if the person becomes a member of the support group, that is, if it is determined that he has, or is to be treated as having, limited capability for work-related activity.

No such regulations have ever been made, but regulations laid in May 2011 and operative from June 1, 2011 enable the Secretary of State to require ESA claimants in the work-related activity group to undertake work-related activity. They do not apply to lone parents with a child under five or to ESA claimants also receiving carer's allowance or carer's premium. See the Employment and Support Allowance (Work-Related Activity) Regulations 2011 (SI 2011/1349). Activities envisaged are work tasters; programmes to manage health in work; job search assistance; and programmes to assist in stabilising the individual's life (*Explanatory Notes to the Welfare Reform Act 2007*, paras 86–91). Information presented to the Commons by the DWP when the Welfare Reform Bill was being considered there indicated that claimants would be asked to participate in a minimum amount of work-related activity (e.g. one activity) in a given time period (e.g. four weeks), and in between each period they would in their work-focused interview review what they had done and discuss what they would like to do in the next period (DWP, *Welfare Reform Bill: Draft Regulations and Supporting Material*, January 2007). That same material stressed that no-one would be forced to undertake a particular activity; the requirement is to participate in some work-related activity. Perhaps an appropriate analogy may be with the proper approach to the question in JSA of whether a claimant is actively seeking work (see commentary to Jobseekers Act 1995 ss.7, 9; and to JSA Regs regs 18. Note also the power to direct that specific activity will not count a work-related activity for a particular person (s.15).

Despite the width of the rule-making power (which would appear to authorise reduction in the amount of ESA payable) it was originally envisaged that, as with that applicable to the other elements in respect of work-related activity "conditionality' (see ss.11, 12, above), the sanction would operate only by reduction of the work-related activity component of ESA, rather than on the whole allowance. It would appear that this has always been the policy intention, but, if so, it would have been better so to confine the rule-making power (see JHRC, *Second Report of Session 2006–07*, HL 34/HC 263 (2006–07), para.3.18). That recommendation has been given added force by subsequent developments. In December 2012 the sanctions regime was amended so the reduction in benefit applied to the whole of the basic amount or personal allowance for a single claimant (but did not operate on the work-related activity component). However, the abolition of the work-related activity component for (broadly speaking) new claims since April 3, 2017 means that if a new claimant in the work-related activity group is sanctioned they would lose the entirety of their standard ESA benefit.

Action plans in connection with work-focused interviews

14.—(1) The Secretary of State shall in prescribed circumstances provide a person subject to a requirement imposed under section 12(1) with a

1.761

document prepared for such purposes as may be prescribed (in this section referred to as an action plan).

(2) Regulations may make provision about—

(a) the form of action plans;

(b) the content of action plans;

(c) the review and updating of action plans.

(3) Regulations under this section may, in particular, make provision for action plans which are provided to a person who is subject under section 13 to a requirement to undertake work-related activity to contain particulars of activity which, if undertaken, would enable the requirement to be met.

(4) Regulations may make provision for reconsideration of an action plan at the request of the person to whom the plan is provided and may, in particular, make provision about—

(a) the circumstances in which reconsideration may be requested;

(b) the period within which any reconsideration must take place;

(c) the matters to which regard must be had when deciding on reconsideration whether the plan should be changed;

(d) notification of the decision on reconsideration;

(e) the giving of directions for the purpose of giving effect to the decision on reconsideration.

DEFINITIONS

"action plan"—see subs.(1).
"prescribed"—see s.24(1).
"regulations"—see s.24(1).
"work-related activity"—see ss.24(1), 13(7).

GENERAL NOTE

1.762   Part of the "work-related activity" process requires the drawing up of written "action plans" as part of the work-related interview process, envisaging that these will be reviewed and amended as conditions change. This section imposes that requirement and authorises regulations to give it effect. The regulation is the ESA Regs, reg.58. An action plan records the interview; any work-related activity the claimant is willing to undertake; and any other information considered appropriate by the Secretary of State. The plan will doubtless influence the shape of future interviews and be relevant to the question of whether the claimant is undertaking work-related activity and whether he should be sanctioned by reduction or eventually removal of work-related activity component in accordance with ESA Regs regs 63, 64. It may be tempting to draw analogies with the jobseeker's agreement in JSA, but the plan is just that: a plan drawn up by officialdom and agreement to it is not as yet directly a condition of entitlement to ESA.

Directions about work-related activity

1.763   **15.**—[¹(1) In prescribed circumstances, the Secretary of State may by direction given to a person subject to a requirement imposed under section 13(1) provide that the activity specified in the direction is—

(a) to be the only activity which, in the person's case, is to be regarded as being work-related activity; or

(b) to be regarded, in the person's case, as not being work-related activity.

(1A) But a direction under subsection (1) may not specify medical or surgical treatment as the only activity which, in any person's case, is to be regarded as being work-related activity.

(2) A direction under subsection (1) given to any person—

(a) must be reasonable, having regard to the person's circumstances;

(b) must be given to the person by being included in an action plan provided to the person under section 14; and

(c) may be varied or revoked by a subsequent direction under subsection (1).]

(3) Where a direction under subsection (1) varies or revokes a previous direction, it may provide for the variation or revocation to have effect from a time before the giving of the direction.

AMENDMENT

1. Welfare Reform Act 2009 s.10 (February 10, 2010).

DEFINITIONS

"prescribed"—see s.24(1).
"work-related activity"—see ss.24(1), 13(7).

GENERAL NOTE

For ESA claims made before April 3, 2017, engagement in work-related activity   1.764
is a condition of entitlement to work-related activity component for most of the claimants who are not in the support group. Failure to engage in such activity can be sanctioned by reduction or removal of work-related activity component, leaving such a claimant reliant solely on basic allowance ESA. This section enables a written direction to be given to a claimant with the effect that the activity specified in the direction will in his case be treated as not being work-related activity. The DWP envisages that this power will only be used in limited circumstances "where a given activity was wholly inappropriate for the claimant" (DWP, *Welfare Reform Bill: Draft Regulations and Supporting Material*, January 2007). Since engagement in work-related activity will not be an operative part of "conditionality" until resources permit (probably not before 2011 (see commentary to s.13), the regulations envisaged by subs.(1), setting out the circumstances, in which a direction can be given, have not yet been made

[¹ Persons dependent on drugs etc.

Persons dependent on drugs etc.

15A. [² *Repealed.*]]   1.765

AMENDMENT

1. Welfare Reform Act 2009 s.11 and, Sch.3 para.6 (November 12, 2009).
2. Welfare Reform Act 2012 ss.60(2), 150(2)(b) (May 8, 2012).

Contracting out

16.—(1) The following functions of the Secretary of State may be exer-   1.766
cised by, or by employees of, such person (if any) as the Secretary of State may authorise for the purpose, namely—

(a) conducting interviews under section 12;

(b) providing documents under section 14;

(c) giving, varying or revoking directions under section 15;

[¹ (d) . . .]

[¹ (e) . . .]

[¹ (f) . . .]

(2) Regulations may provide for any of the following functions of the Secretary of State to be exercisable by, or by employees of, such person (if any) as the Secretary of State may authorise for the purpose—

    (a) any function under regulations under any of sections 11 to 15 [¹ . . .], except the making of a decision to which subsection (3) applies (an "excluded decision");

    (b) the function under section 9(1) of the Social Security Act 1998 (c. 14) (revision of decisions), so far as relating to decisions, except excluded decisions, that relate to any matter arising under such regulations;

    (c) the function under section 10(1) of that Act (superseding of decisions), so far as relating to decisions, except excluded decisions, of the Secretary of State that relate to any matter arising under such regulations;

    (d) any function under Chapter 2 of Part 1 of that Act (social security decisions), except section 25(2) and (3) (decisions involving issues that arise on appeal in other cases), which relates to the exercise of any of the functions falling within paragraphs (a) to (c).

(3) This subsection applies to the following decisions—

    (a) a decision about whether a person has failed to comply with a requirement imposed by regulations under section 11, 12 or 13 [¹ . . .];

    (b) a decision about whether a person had good cause for failure to comply with such a requirement;

    (c) a decision about reduction of an employment and support allowance in consequence of failure to comply with such a requirement.

(4) Regulations under subsection (2) may provide that a function to which that subsection applies may be exercised—

    (a) either wholly or to such extent as the regulations may provide,

    (b) either generally or in such cases or areas as the regulations may provide, and

    (c) either unconditionally or subject to the fulfilment of such conditions as the regulations may provide.

(5) An authorisation given by virtue of subsection (1), or by virtue of regulations under subsection (2), may authorise the exercise of the function concerned—

    (a) either wholly or to such extent as may be specified in the authorisation,

    (b) either generally or in such cases or areas as may be so specified, and

    (c) either unconditionally or subject to the fulfilment of such conditions as may be so specified.

(6) In the case of an authorisation given by virtue of regulations under subsection (2), subsection (5) is subject to the provisions of the regulations.

(7) An authorisation given by virtue of subsection (1), or by virtue of regulations under subsection (2)—

    (a) may specify its duration,

    (b) may be revoked at any time by the Secretary of State, and

    (c) shall not prevent the Secretary of State or any other person from exercising the function to which the authorisation relates.

(8) Where a person is authorised to exercise any function by virtue of subsection (1), or by virtue of regulations under subsection (2), anything done or omitted to be done by or in relation to him (or an employee of his)

in, or in connection with, the exercise or purported exercise of the function shall be treated for all purposes as done or omitted to be done by or in relation to the Secretary of State.

(9) Subsection (8) shall not apply—

(a) for the purposes of so much of any contract made between the authorised person and the Secretary of State as relates to the exercise of the function, or

(b) for the purposes of any criminal proceedings brought in respect of anything done or omitted to be done by the authorised person (or an employee of his).

(10) Any decision which a person authorised to exercise any function by virtue of subsection (1), or by virtue of regulations under subsection (2), makes in exercise of the function shall have effect as a decision of the Secretary of State under section 8 of the Social Security Act1998.

(11) Where—

(a) a person is authorised to exercise any function by virtue of subsection (1), or by virtue of regulations under subsection (2), and

(b) the authorisation is revoked at a time when a relevant contract is subsisting,

the authorised person shall be entitled to treat the relevant contract as repudiated by the Secretary of State (and not as frustrated by reason of the revocation).

(12) In subsection (11), the reference to a relevant contract is to so much of any contract made between the authorised person and the Secretary of State as relates to the exercise of the function.

(13) In this section, references to functions of the Secretary of State under—

(a) an enactment contained in, or in regulations under, this Part, or

(b) an enactment contained in Chapter 2 of Part 1 of the Social Security Act 1998,

include a reference to any function which the Secretary of State has by virtue of the application in relation to that enactment of section 8(1)(c) of that Act (decisions under certain enactments to be made by the Secretary of State).

AMENDMENT

1. Welfare Reform Act 2012 ss.147, 150(2)(b), Sch.14 Pt 6 (May 8, 2012).

DEFINITIONS

"regulations"—see s.24(1).

GENERAL NOTE

This section authorises, to such a degree as is specified in regulations and/or an authorisation (subss.(5), (6)), the contracting out of certain functions vested in the Secretary of State (DWP/JobCentre Plus decision-makers and Personal Advisers) in respect of the conditionality aspect of membership to the work-related activity group, and of a wide (but not unlimited) range of decisions related to the exercise of those functions.   1.767

Those functions are conducting work-focused interviews under s.12; providing documents under s.14 (action plans in connection with work-focused interviews); and giving, varying or revoking directions under s.15 (subs.(1)). The functions can be exercised by the contractor ("such person as the Secretary of State may authorise for the purpose") or by employees of the contractor (subs.(1)). Anything done (or omitted to be done) by them must be treated as if done (or omitted to be done) by the Secretary of State (subss.(8), (9)). Their decisions in respect of the authorised functions are to be given effect as ones of the Secretary of State under s.8 SSA 1998 (subs.(10). Revocation of the authorisation may be treated as a repudiation of the contract by the Secretary of State and not as a matter of frustration of the contract (subss.(11, (12)).

In addition, subs.(2) enables the making of regulations authorising a number of other functions to be so exercisable by the contractor or the contractor's employees. The regulations can authorise the exercise of any functions under ss.11–15, above (subs.(2)(a)), other than "excluded decisions" which are enumerated in subs.(3). Put shortly, this prevents authorising contractors or their employees to make decisions in respect of the sanctioning aspect of "conditionality" as regards entitlement to the work-related activity component, although information and material from them will perforce feed into and inform decisions on these matters made by DWP/ JobCentre Plus decision-makers. Thus subs.(3) provides that regulations cannot enable the making by contractors or their employees of decisions on whether the claimant has failed to comply with requirements, set out in regulations, on work-focused health-related assessments (s.11), work-focused interviews (s.12) or work-related activity (s.13) (para.(a)). Regulations cannot authorise them to make decisions on whether the claimant had good cause for any failure to comply with such a requirement (para.(b)), or on whether failure to comply must be sanctioned by reduction or removal of the amount of work-related activity component to which the claimant would otherwise be entitled (para.(c)). But, save so far as they relate to excluded decisions, regulations can authorise contractors or their employees to exercise powers of revision and supersession under ss.9 and 10, respectively, of the Social Security Act 1998, in respect of any functions under ss.11–15 (subs.(2)(b), (c)). Subsection (2)(d) enables regulations to authorise them also to exercise, in respect of those functions, any function under Ch.2 of Pt I of that 1998 Act, other than ones under ss.25(2) and (3) of it (decisions involving issues that arise on appeal in other cases).

The ESA regime envisages that helping claimants return to work or to the labour market need not solely be the task of the DWP or Jobcentre Plus, important as their role is. Contractors in the private and voluntary sector (PVS) have specialist knowledge and innovative approaches which, properly harnessed and deployed, may well ensure the best possible support for claimants in the work-related activity group. As with the Provider Led Pathways aspect of the Pathways to Work project on which the ESA approach was built, JobCentre Plus will conduct the first work-focused interview. It will be recalled that a "work-focused interview" is one conducted for such purposes connected with keeping the interviewee in work or getting him into work, as may be set out in regulations (s.12(7)). A secondary purpose will be to provide information on benefit and service entitlement. This renders it appropriate that it be done by JobCentre Plus. But a principal reason for its staff doing so is that at that stage, very early in a claim, eligibility for ESA will not have been determined by the medical test. Although interviews after the claimant's first work-focused interview may well be carried out by PVS providers, JobCentre Plus will during the lifetime of the claim exercise functions relating to entitlement to benefit, sanctioning decisions and processing of benefit payments.

[¹ **Hardship payments**

1.768   **16A.**—(1) Regulations may make provision for the making of payments ("hardship payments") by way of an employment and support allowance to a person where—

   (a) the amount otherwise payable to the person in respect of an employment and support allowance is reduced by virtue of regulations under section 11(3), 12(3) or 13(3), and

374

(b) the person is or will be in hardship.

(2)   Regulations under this section may in particular make provision as to—

(a) circumstances in which a person is to be treated as being or not being in hardship;

(b) matters to be taken into account in determining whether a person is or will be in hardship;

(c) requirements or conditions to be met by a person in order to receive hardship payments;

(d) the amount or rate of hardship payments;

(e) the period for which hardship payments may be made.]

AMENDMENT

1. Welfare Reform Act 2012 s.56 (November 26, 2012).

GENERAL NOTE

Regulations 64A–64D of the ESA Regulations (see below) were made under the powers conferred by this section.

Miscellaneous

Income and capital: general

17.—(1) In relation to a claim for an employment and support allowance, the income and capital of a person shall be calculated or estimated in such manner as may be prescribed.   1.769

(2) A person's income in respect of a week shall be calculated in accordance with prescribed rules, which may provide for the calculation to be made by reference to an average over a period (which need not include the week concerned).

(3) Circumstances may be prescribed in which—

(a) a person is to be treated as possessing capital or income which he does not possess;

(b) capital or income which a person does possess is to be disregarded;

(c) income is to be treated as capital;

(d) capital is to be treated as income.

(4) Regulations may provide that a person's capital shall be deemed for the purposes of this Part to yield him an income at a prescribed rate.

DEFINITIONS

"prescribed"—see s.24(1).
"regulations"—*ibid.*
"week"—*ibid.*

GENERAL NOTE

This section is very similar to s.136(3)–(5) of the Contributions and Benefits Act   1.770
and s.12 of the old style Jobseekers Act 1995 (see *Vol.II: Income Support, Jobseekers Allowance, State Pension Credit and the Social Fund*).

It enables the Secretary of State to introduce detailed regulations governing the treatment of income and capital for the purposes of old style ESA. See Pt 10 of and Schs 7, 8 and 9 to the ESA Regulations 2008.

See also para.6(2) of Sch.1 which contains the "aggregation rule" for the purposes of income-related ESA, i.e., that where the claimant is a member of a couple, his partner's income and capital counts as that of the claimant (except in prescribed circumstances).

Disqualification

1.771

18.—(1) Regulations may provide for a person to be disqualified for receiving an employment and support allowance, or treated for such purposes as the regulations may provide as not having limited capability for work, if—

(a) he has become someone who has limited capability for work through his own misconduct,

(b) he remains someone who has limited capability for work through his failure without good cause to follow medical advice, or

(c) he fails without good cause to observe any prescribed rules of behaviour.

(2) Regulations under subsection (1) shall provide for any such disqualification, or treatment, to be for such period not exceeding 6 weeks as may be determined in accordance with Chapter 2 of Part 1 of the Social Security Act 1998 (c. 14).

(3) Regulations may prescribe for the purposes of subsection (1)—

(a) matters which are, or are not, to be taken into account in determining whether a person has good cause for any act or omission;

(b) circumstances in which a person is, or is not, to be regarded as having good cause for any act or omission.

(4) Except where regulations otherwise provide, a person shall be disqualified for receiving a contributory allowance for any period during which he is—

(a) absent from Great Britain, or

(b) undergoing imprisonment or detention in legal custody.

DEFINITIONS

"contributory allowance"—see s.1(7).
"limited capability for work"—see s.1(4).
"prescribed"—see s.24(1).
"regulations"—see s.24(1).
"week"—see s.24(1).

GENERAL NOTE

Subsections (1)–(3)

1.772

Like previous incapacity benefits' regimes (compare SSCBA 1992 s.171E and IW (General) Regs reg.18), ESA embodies disqualification from benefit, or treating someone as not having limited capability for work, for a period not exceeding six weeks as sanctions in respect of conduct which conduces to a person's limited capability for work either by bringing it about through misconduct (subs.(1)(a)) or by remaining someone with limited capacity by failing without good cause to follow medical advice (subs.(1)(b)) or by failing without good cause to adhere to prescribed rules of behaviour (subs.(1)(c)). These subsections provide rule-making power for the regime of disqualification. The relevant regulations are the ESA Regs regs 157–158. Note the protection from disqualification for a "person in hardship" (regs 157(3)(a), 158) and someone disqualified from receiving ESA because of regulations made pursuant to s.7 of the Social Security Fraud Act 2001 (reg.157(3) (b); for that section and the consequent Social Security (Loss of Benefit) Regs 2001, see Vol.III).

Although subs.(3) enables regs to be made dealing with aspects of the "good cause" issue (matters to take into or leave out of account; things which do or do not rank as "good cause"), no such regs have yet been made. "Good cause" thus remains a matter for the decision-maker or tribunal, circumscribed by case law on analogous provisions.

Subsection (4)

This mandates for the ESA regime disqualification from CESA in respect 1.773 of periods of absence from GB or of imprisonment or detention in legal custody. Exceptions from disqualification can be afforded by regs : see ESA Regs regs 151–155 (temporary absence from GB), 160, 161 (imprisonment or detention in legal custody). Compare, with respect to incapacity benefit, SSCBA 1992 s.113.

Pilot schemes

19.—(1) Any regulations to which this subsection applies may be made 1.774 so as to have effect for a specified period not exceeding [¹36 months].

(2) Subject to subsection (3), subsection (1) applies to—

(a) regulations which are made under any provision of this Part, other than sections 3, 8 and 9;

(b) regulations which are made under the Administration Act, so far as they relate to an employment and support allowance.

(3) Subsection (1) only applies to regulations if they are made with a view to ascertaining whether their provisions will or will be likely to—

(a) encourage persons to obtain or remain in work, or

(b) make it more likely that persons will obtain or remain in work or be able to do so.

(4) Regulations which, by virtue of subsection (1), are to have effect for a limited period are referred to in this section as a "pilot scheme".

(5) A pilot scheme may provide that its provisions are to apply only in relation to—

(a) one or more specified areas;

(b) one or more specified classes of person;

(c) persons selected—

(i) by reference to prescribed criteria, or

(ii) on a sampling basis.

(6) A pilot scheme may make consequential or transitional provision with respect to the cessation of the scheme on the expiry of the specified period.

(7) A pilot scheme may be replaced by a further pilot scheme making the same or similar provision.

AMENDMENT

1. Welfare Reform Act 2009 s.28(2) (November 12, 2009).

DEFINITIONS

"Administration Act"—see. s.65.
"prescribed"—see. s.24(1).
"regulations"—*ibid.*

1.775   This is similar to s.29 of the old style Jobseekers Act 1995 (see Vol.II in this series). From November 12, 2009 the initial period for which a pilot scheme can run has been extended to three years; in addition such a scheme can be repeated (see subs.(7)). Any regulations under Pt 1 of the Act or associated rules under the SSAA 1992 may be piloted, other than regulations concerning deductions from contributory ESA (s.3), limited capability for work (s.8) and limited capability for work-related activity (s.9). Regulations made under this section are subject to the affirmative resolution procedure (s.26(1)(c)).

The power under s.29 of the old style Jobseekers Act 1995 has been used on a fairly regular basis to test in particular changes to "conditionality" and it seems likely that this will also be the case for ESA.

Relationship with statutory payments

1.776   **20.**—(1) A person is not entitled to an employment and support allowance in respect of a day if, for the purposes of statutory sick pay, that day—

(a) is a day of incapacity for work in relation to a contract of service, and

(b) falls within a period of entitlement (whether or not it is a qualifying day).

(2) Except as regulations may provide, a woman who is entitled to statutory maternity pay is not entitled to a contributory allowance in respect of a day that falls within the maternity pay period.

(3) Regulations may provide that—

(a) an amount equal to a woman's statutory maternity pay for a period shall be deducted from a contributory allowance in respect of the same period,

(b) a woman shall only be entitled to a contributory allowance if there is a balance after the deduction, and

(c) if there is such a balance, a woman shall be entitled to a contributory allowance at a weekly rate equal to it.

(4) Except as regulations may provide, a person who is entitled to statutory adoption pay is not entitled to a contributory allowance in respect of a day that falls within the adoption pay period.

(5) Regulations may provide that—

(a) an amount equal to a person's statutory adoption pay for a period shall be deducted from a contributory allowance in respect of the same period,

(b) a person shall only be entitled to a contributory allowance if there is a balance after the deduction, and

(c) if there is such a balance, a person shall be entitled to a contributory allowance at a weekly rate equal to it.

(6) Except as regulations may provide, a person who is entitled to additional statutory paternity pay is not entitled to a contributory allowance in respect of a day that falls within the additional paternity pay period.

(7) Regulations may provide that—

(a) an amount equal to a person's additional statutory paternity pay for a period shall be deducted from a contributory allowance in respect of the same period,

(b) a person shall only be entitled to a contributory allowance if there is a balance after the deduction, and

(c) if there is such a balance, a person shall be entitled to a contributory allowance at a weekly rate equal to it.

(8) In this section—

"the additional paternity pay period" has the meaning given in section 171ZEE(2) of the Contributions and Benefits Act;

"the adoption pay period" has the meaning given in section 171ZN(2) of that Act;

"the maternity pay period" has the meaning given in section 165(1) of that Act.

DEFINITIONS

"the additional paternity pay period"—see subs.(8).
"the adoption pay period"—see subs.(8).
"Contributions and Benefits Act"—see s.65.
"contributory allowance"—see s.1(7).
"entitled"—see s.24(1).
"the maternity pay period"—see subs.(8).

GENERAL NOTE

This deals with the relationship between ESA and certain other "employer paid" statutory payments, the overall responsibility for them lying with HMRC. The payments covered by this section are statutory sick pay (SSP), statutory maternity pay (SMP), statutory adoption pay (SAP) and additional statutory paternity pay (ASPP). They are dealt with in *Vol.IV: Tax Credits and HMRC-administered Social Security Benefits.* The relationships are not all of a piece. ESA cannot be paid in respect of days for which there is SSP entitlement (subs.(1)). As regards SMP, SAP and ASPP, the interrelationship only concerns CESA. The general rule is that CESA cannot be payable at the same time as any of these other payments, but exceptions can be made by regulations (subss.(2)–(7)). The relevant regs are the ESA Regs, regs 80 (SMP), 81 (SAP) and 82 (ASPP). Where they operate to enable ESA to be paid, however, the amount of CESA payable is reduced by the amount of the relevant statutory payment, and only any balance of CESA remaining is payable.

1.777

Deemed entitlement for other purposes

21.—Regulations may provide for a person who would be entitled to an employment and support allowance but for the operation of any provision of, or made under, this Part, the Administration Act or Chapter 2 of Part 1 of the Social Security Act 1998 (c. 14) (social security decisions and appeals) to be treated as if entitled to the allowance for the purposes of any rights or obligations (whether his own or another's) which depend on his entitlement, other than the right to payment of it.

1.778

DEFINITIONS

"Administration Act"—see s.65.
"regulations"—see s.24(1).

GENERAL NOTE

This section is identical to SSCBA 1992 s.113(3). It enables regs to be made enabling someone to be treated as still entitled to ESA, though not to payment of it, even though provisions of or made under this Part of the WRA, the AA 1992 or SSA 1998, Pt I Ch.2 operate to disentitle him. The person will only be treated as entitled in this way to enable him or someone else to retain rights and obligations under social security law more generally.

1.779

Supplementary provisions

1.780   **22.**—Schedule 2 (which contains further provisions in relation to an employment and support allowance) has effect.

GENERAL NOTE

1.781   This provides the basis for giving effect to the detailed provisions on ESA set out in Sch.2. These concern rule making in respect of: treating someone as having or not having limited capability for work/work-related activity (as the case may be), waiting days, linking periods, payments of benefit for less than a week, presence in GB, entitlement to CESA by persons not in GB, retained entitlement to IRESA after someone has left GB, modifying entitlement to CESA in respect of employment on ships, vessels, aircraft or hovercraft, the effect of work, treating ESA as "benefit", attribution of reductions where someone is entitled both to CESA and IRESA, ESA information to be treated as social security information, the making of advance claims, and modifying provisions in respect of ESA as regards Members of Her majesty's forces.

Recovery of sums in respect of maintenance

1.782   **23.**—(1) Regulations may make provision for the court to have power to make a recovery order against any person where an award of income-related allowance has been made to that person's spouse or civil partner.

(2) The reference in subsection (1) to a recovery order is to an order requiring the person against whom it is made to make payments to the Secretary of State or to such other person or persons as the court may determine.

(3) Regulations under subsection (1) may include—

(a) provision as to the matters to which the court is, or is not, to have regard in determining any application under the regulations;

(b) provision as to the enforcement of orders under the regulations;

(c) provision for the transfer by the Secretary of State of the right to receive payments under, and to exercise rights in relation to, orders under the regulations.

(4) In this section, "the court" means—

(a) in relation to England and Wales, a magistrates' court;

(b) in relation to Scotland, the sheriff.

DEFINITIONS

"income-related allowance"— see s.1(7).
"regulations"— see s.24(1).

GENERAL NOTE

1.783   This is similar to the powers in relation to income-based JSA in s.23 of the Jobseekers Act (see Vol.II in this series). For the powers in relation to income support and universal credit, see s.106 of the Administration Act (to be found in Vol.III in this series).

General

Interpretation of Part 1

24.—(1) In this Part— 1.784

"claimant" means a person who has claimed an employment and support allowance;

"contributory allowance" has the meaning given by section 1(7);

"employment" and "employed" have the meanings prescribed for the purposes of this Part;

"entitled", in relation to an employment and support allowance, is to be construed in accordance with—

(a) the provisions of this Act,

(b) section 1 of the Administration Act (entitlement dependent on making of claim), and

(c) section 27 of the Social Security Act 1998 (c. 14) (restrictions on entitlement in certain cases of error);

"income-related allowance" has the meaning given by section 1(7);

"income support" means income support under section 124 of the Contributions and Benefits Act;

"limited capability for work" shall be construed in accordance with section 1(4);

"limited capability for work-related activity" shall be construed in accordance with section 2(5);

"period of limited capability for work" has the meaning prescribed for the purposes of this Part;

"prescribed" means specified in, or determined in accordance with, regulations;

"regulations" means regulations made by the Secretary of State;

"week" means a period of 7 days beginning with a Sunday or such other period of 7 days as may be prescribed;

"work-related activity" has the meaning given by section 13(7).

(2) For the purposes of this Part, the assessment phase, in relation to a claimant, is the period—

(a) beginning, subject to subsection (3), with the first day of the period for which he is entitled to an employment and support allowance, and

(b) ending with such day as may be prescribed.

(3) Regulations may prescribe circumstances in which the assessment phase is to begin with such day as may be prescribed.

[¹(3A) For the purposes of this Part, a person is a lone parent if the person—

(a) is not a member of a couple (within the meaning given by section 137(1) of the Contributions and Benefits Act), and

(b) is responsible for, and a member of the same household as, a person under the age of 16.

(3B) For the purposes of subsection (3A)(b) regulations may make provision—

(a) as to circumstances in which one person is to be treated as responsible or not responsible for another;

(b) as to circumstances in which persons are to be treated as being or not being members of the same household.]

(4) For the purposes of this Part, a person is a member of the support group if he is a person in respect of whom it is determined that he has, or is to be treated as having, limited capability for work-related activity.

AMENDMENT

1. Welfare Reform Act 2009 s.3(5) (October 6, 2011 (regulation-making purposes) and October 31, 2011 (all other purposes)).

DEFINITIONS

"Administration Act"—see s.65.
"Contributions and Benefits Act"—see s.65.

GENERAL NOTE

1.785   This defines, sometimes by referring the reader to other provisions or leaving the meaning to be set out in regulations, a number of key terms in respect of ESA. Note in particular that the "assessment phase", during which there can generally only be entitlement to basic allowance ESA, is generally to begin on the first such day of entitlement and to end in accordance with regulations (subss.(2), (3)). See on this ESA Regs regs (4)–(7). Note also that membership of the support group, and thus eligibility for the more generous "support component" in addition to basic allowance ESA, is dependent on a determination that the person has, or is to be treated as having, limited capability for work-related activity (subs.(4)).

General

Regulations [² and orders]

1.786   **25.**—(1) Any power under this Part to make regulations [² or an order] shall be exercisable by statutory instrument.
(2) Any such power may be exercised—
(a) in relation to all cases to which it extends,
(b) in relation to those cases subject to specified exceptions, or
(c) in relation to any specified cases or classes of case.
(3) Any such power may be exercised so as to make, as respects the cases in relation to which it is exercised—
(a) the full provision to which the power extends or any less provision (whether by way of exception or otherwise);
(b) the same provision for all cases in relation to which it is exercised, or different provision for different cases or different classes of case or different provision as respects the same case or class of case for different purposes of this Part;
(c) any such provision either unconditionally or subject to any specified condition.
(4) Where any such power is expressed to be exercisable for alternative purposes, it may be exercised in relation to the same case for all or any of those purposes.
(5) Any such power includes power—
(a) to make such incidental, supplementary, consequential or transitional provision or savings as appear to the Secretary of State to be expedient;

(b) to provide for a person to exercise a discretion in dealing with any matter.

(6) Without prejudice to the generality of the provisions of this section, regulations under any of sections 11 to 15 [¹ ³ . . .] may make provision which applies only in relation to an area or areas specified in the regulations.

(7) The fact that a power to make regulations is conferred by this Part is not to be taken to prejudice the extent of any other power to make regulations so conferred.

AMENDMENT

1. Welfare Reform Act 2009 s.11 and Sch.3 para.8(3) (November 12, 2009).
2. Welfare Reform Act 2012 s.51(2) (March 20, 2012 (regulation-making purposes); May 1, 2012 (all other purposes)).
3. Welfare Reform Act 2012 s.147 and Sch.14 Pt 6 para.1 (May 8, 2012).

GENERAL NOTE

This section is similar to s.175 of the Contributions and Benefits Act and s.36 of the Jobseekers Act. 1.787

Parliamentary control

26.—(1) None of the following regulations shall be made unless a draft 1.788
of the statutory instrument containing them has been laid before, and approved by a resolution of, each House of Parliament—
   (a) regulations under section 2(2)(c) or (3)(c) or 4(4)(c) or (5)(c);
[⁴ (aa) the first regulations under section 11D(2)(d) or 11J;]
   (b) the first regulations under section 13;
   (c) regulations which by virtue of section 19(1) are to have effect for a limited period.
[¹ ³ . . .]
   (2) A statutory instrument that—
   (a) contains regulations made under this Part, and
   (b) is not subject to a requirement that a draft of the instrument be laid before, and approved by a resolution of, each House of Parliament,
shall be subject to annulment in pursuance of a resolution of either House of Parliament.
   [² (3) A statutory instrument containing an order under section 1A shall be subject to annulment in pursuance of a resolution of either House of Parliament.]

AMENDMENT

1. Welfare Reform Act 2009 s.11 and Sch.3 para.8(4) (November 12, 2009).
2. Welfare Reform Act 2012 s.51(3) (March 20, 2012 (regulation-making purposes); May 1, 2012 (all other purposes)).
3. Welfare Reform Act 2012 s.147 and Sch.14 Pt 6 para.1 (May 8, 2012).
4. Welfare Reform Act 2012 s.57(6) (February 25, 2013).

GENERAL NOTE

This section is similar to s.176 of the Contributions and Benefits Act and s.37 of the Jobseekers Act. 1.789

Financial provisions relating to Part 1

1.790   **27.**—(1) There shall be paid out of the National Insurance Fund so much of any sums payable by way of employment and support allowance as is attributable to entitlement to a contributory allowance.

(2) There shall be paid out of money provided by Parliament—

(a) so much of any sums payable by way of employment and support allowance as is attributable to entitlement to an income-related allowance, and

(b) any administrative expenses of the Secretary of State or the Commissioners for Her Majesty's Revenue and Customs in carrying this Part into effect.

(3) The Secretary of State shall pay into the National Insurance Fund sums estimated by him to be equivalent in amount to sums recovered by him in connection with payments of contributory allowance.

(4) The Secretary of State shall pay into the Consolidated Fund sums estimated by him to be equivalent in amount to sums recovered by him in connection with payments made by way of income-related allowance.

DEFINITIONS

"contributory allowance"—ss.24(1) and 1(7).
"income-related allowance"—*ibid.*

GENERAL NOTE

1.791   This section is similar to s.163 of the Administration Act, s.38 of the Jobseekers Act and s.20 of the State Pension Credit Act.

Consequential amendments relating to Part 1

1.792   **28.**—(1) Schedule 3 (which makes amendments consequential on this Part) has effect.

(2) Regulations may make provision consequential on this Part amending, repealing or revoking any provision of—

(a) an Act passed on or before the last day of the Session in which this Act is passed, or

(b) an instrument made under an Act before the passing of this Act.

(3) In subsection (2), "Act" includes an Act of the Scottish Parliament.

DEFINITIONS

"Act"—see subs.(3).
"regulations"—see s.24(1).

GENERAL NOTE

Subsection (1)
1.793   This gives effect to a range of consequential amendments of other Acts of Parliament set out in Sch.3 incorporated elsewhere in this book.

Subsection (2)
1.794   This enables the making of consequential regulations amending Acts (including ones of the Scottish Parliament) passed on or before the last day of the 2006–07 Westminster parliamentary session (the one in which the WRA 2007 was passed) (para.(a), subs.(3)). It also enables consequential regulations to amend subordinate legislation, already made before the passing of the WRA 2007, under Acts (including those of the Scottish Parliament) (para.(b), subs.(3)).

Transition relating to Part 1

29.—Schedule 4 (which makes provision with respect to transition in relation to this Part) has effect.

1.795

GENERAL NOTE

This gives effect to Sch.4, reproduced in full with provisions not yet in force set out in italics. That Schedule embodies rule-making powers for pre- and post-commencement claims, awarding ESA in respect of a pre-commencement period, converting existing awards of IB/IS/SDA to ESA, the post-commencement up-rating of IB/SDA, and a general power to provide for transitional matters with respect to ESA. The regulations so made are the Employment and Support Allowance (Transitional Provisions) Regulations 2008 (SI 2008/795) and the Employment and Support Allowance (Transitional Provisions, Housing Benefit and Council Tax Benefit) (Existing Awards) (No.2) Regulations 2010 (SI 2010/1907).

1.796

Sections 30–63 Omitted

PART 5

GENERAL

Northern Ireland

64.—(1) This section applies to an Order in Council under paragraph 1(1) of the Schedule to the Northern Ireland Act 2000 (c. 1) (legislation for Northern Ireland during suspension of devolved government) which contains a statement that it is made only for purposes corresponding to those of this Act.

(2) Such an Order—

(a) is not subject to paragraph 2 of that Schedule (affirmative resolution of both Houses of Parliament), but

(b) is subject to annulment in pursuance of a resolution of either House of Parliament.

1.797

GENERAL NOTE

Part I of the WRA 2007 dealing with ESA applies only to Great Britain (England, Wales and Scotland). This is true of the social security system generally. But comparable provision in respect of social security for Northern Ireland is always made by Order in Council under its devolution Act. This section deals with parliamentary scrutiny and control over such an Order. It provides that any such Order, stated to be made only for purposes corresponding to those of the WRA 2007, is to be subject to annulment by either House of Parliament rather than to the affirmative resolution procedure that would otherwise be applicable.

1.798

General interpretation

65.—In this Act—

"Administration Act" means the Social Security Administration Act 1992 (c. 5);

"Contributions and Benefits Act" means the Social Security Contributions and Benefits Act 1992 (c. 4).

1.799

Financial provisions: general

66.—(1) There shall be paid out of money provided by Parliament—

1.800

(a) any expenditure incurred by the Secretary of State in consequence of Parts 2 to 4 of this Act, and

(b) any increase attributable to this Act in the sums payable out of money so provided under any other enactment.

(2) There shall be paid into the Consolidated Fund any increase attributable to this Act in the sums payable into that Fund under any other enactment.

Repeals

1.801   **67.**—The enactments specified in Schedule 8 are hereby repealed to the extent specified.

Section 68 omitted

Extent

1.802   **69.**—(1) Subject to the following provisions, this Act extends to England and Wales and Scotland only.

(2) The following provisions extend to England and Wales only—

(a) sections 42(1) to (10) and 43, and

(b) paragraphs 6, 11(2) and 16 of Schedule 3.

(3) Paragraphs 1, 2, 4, 11(3), 14 and 22 of Schedule 3 extend to Scotland only.

(4) The following provisions also extend to Northern Ireland—

(a) sections 33(7), 49, 56, 57, 61, 64, 65, 68, this section and sections 70 and 71,

(b) paragraph 15 of Schedule 2, and sections 22 and 24 to 26 so far as relating thereto,

(c) paragraphs 5, 10(1) and (28), 17(1) and (2), 19, 23(1) to (3) and (6) to (8) and 24 of Schedule 3, and section 28 so far as relating thereto,

(d) paragraph 1 of Schedule 7, and section 63 so far as relating thereto, and

(e) Schedule 8, so far as relating to the Vaccine Damage Payments Act 1979 (c. 17), the Income and Corporation Taxes Act 1988 (c. 1), the Disability (Grants) Act 1993 (c. 14), section 2 of the Social Security Act 1998 (c. 14) and the Income Tax (Earnings and Pensions) Act 2003 (c. 1), and section 67 so far as relating thereto.

(5) The following provisions extend to Northern Ireland only—

(a) section 45, and

(b) Schedule 8, so far as relating to the Social Security Administration (Northern Ireland) Act 1992 (c. 8), and section 67 so far as relating thereto.

(6) The following provisions also extend to the Isle of Man—

(a) sections 56 and 57, section 68, this section and sections 70 and 71,

(b) paragraph 1 of Schedule 7, and section 63 so far as relating thereto, and

(c) Schedule 8, so far as relating to the Vaccine Damage Payments Act 1979, and section 67 so far as relating thereto.

GENERAL NOTE

Only subs.(1) concerns ESA. It means that the ESA scheme under Pt I of the Act   **1.802A**
applies only to England, Wales and Scotland. Comparable provision can be made
for Northern Ireland through Order in Council under the devolution legislation
(s.64). The devolution arrangements and the complicated political background
in Northern Ireland may, however, mean that relevant legislation may have to be
enacted by the Northern Ireland Assembly.

Commencement

70.—(1) The following provisions shall come into force at the end   **1.803**
of the period of 2 months beginning with the day on which this Act is
passed—
  (a) sections 41(2) and (3), 44, 45, 54, 55, 59, 61(1)(b) and (2) to (6)
      and 62,
  (b) paragraphs 1 to 4, 10, 11 and 14 of Schedule 5, and section 40 so far
      as relating thereto,
  (c) paragraphs 2(1) and (3), 3 and 4 of Schedule 7, and section 63 so far
      as relating thereto, and
  (d) Schedule 8, so far as relating to—
      (i) section 3(5) of the Pneumoconiosis etc. (Workers'
          Compensation) Act 1979 (c. 41),
      (ii) section 140(1A) of the Contributions and Benefits Act,
      (iii) sections 71(5), 71ZA(2), 134(8)(a) and 168(3)(d) of the
          Administration Act,
      (iv) section 69(5) of the Social Security Administration (Northern
          Ireland) Act 1992,
      (v) Schedule 13 to the Local Government etc. (Scotland) Act
          1994 (c. 39), (vi) section 38(7)(a) of, and paragraph 81(2) of
          Schedule 7 to, the Social Security Act 1998 (c. 14), and
      (vii) paragraph 65 of Schedule 24 to the Civil Partnership Act 2004
          (c. 33), and section 67 so far as relating thereto.
  (2) The remaining provisions of this Act, except—
  (a) this section,
  (b) sections 64, 65, 66, 68, 69 and 71, and
  (c) paragraph 8 of Schedule 5, and section 40 so far as relating
      thereto,
shall come into force on such day as the Secretary of State may by
order made by statutory instrument appoint, and different days may be so
appointed for different purposes.

GENERAL NOTE

The key operative date for the ESA regime is October 27, 2008.   **1.804**

Short title

71.—This Act may be cited as the Welfare Reform Act 2007.   **1.805**

SCHEDULES

SCHEDULE 1   **Section 1**

PART 1

CONTRIBUTORY ALLOWANCE

Conditions relating to national insurance

1.806
    1.—(1) The first condition is that—
      (a) the claimant has actually paid Class 1 or Class 2 contributions in respect of one of the last [²two] complete tax years ("the base tax year") before the beginning of the relevant benefit year,
      (b) those contributions must have been paid before the relevant benefit week, and
      [²(c) the claimant's earnings determined in accordance with sub-paragraph (2) must be not less than the base tax year's lower earnings limit multiplied by 26.]
    [²(2) The earnings referred to in sub-paragraph (1)(c) are the aggregate of—
      (a) the claimant's relevant earnings for the base tax year upon which primary Class 1 contributions have been paid or treated as paid, and
      (b) the claimant's earnings factors derived from Class 2 contributions.
    (3) Regulations may make provision for the purposes of sub-paragraph (2)(a) for determining the claimant's relevant earnings for the base tax year.
    (3A) Regulations under sub-paragraph (3) may, in particular, make provision—
      (a) for making that determination by reference to the amount of a person's earnings for periods comprised in the base tax year;
      (b) for determining the amount of a person's earnings for any such period by—
        (i) first determining the amount of the earnings for the period in accordance with regulations made for the purposes of section 3(2) of the Contributions and Benefits Act, and
        (ii) then disregarding so much of the amount found in accordance with sub-paragraph (i) as exceeded the base tax year's lower earnings limit (or the prescribed equivalent).]
    (4) Regulations may—
      (a) provide for the condition set out in sub-paragraph (1) to be taken to be satisfied in the case of [³persons—
        (i) who] have been entitled to any prescribed description of benefit during any prescribed period or at any prescribed time [³or
        (ii) who satisfy other prescribed conditions]
      (b) with a view to securing any relaxation of the requirements of that condition in relation to persons who have been [³entitled as mentioned in paragraph (a)(i)], provide for that condition to apply in relation to them subject to prescribed modifications.
    (5) In sub-paragraph (4), "benefit" means—
    [⁴(za) universal credit,]
      (a) any benefit within the meaning of section 122(1) of the Contributions and Benefits Act,
      (b) any benefit under Parts 7 to 12 of that Act,
      (c) credits under regulations under section 22(5) of that Act,
    [¹(ca) credits under section 23A of that Act,]
      (d) a contributory allowance, and
      (e) working tax credit.
    2.—(1) The second condition is that—
      (a) the claimant has in respect of the last two complete tax years before the beginning of the relevant benefit year either paid or been credited with Class 1 or Class 2 contributions or been credited with earnings, and
      (b) the earnings factor derived as mentioned in sub-paragraph (2) must be not less in each of those years than the year's lower earnings limit multiplied by 50.
    (2) The earnings factor referred to in sub-paragraph (1)(b) is the aggregate of the claimant's earnings factors derived—

(a) from so much of his earnings as did not exceed the upper earnings limit for the year and upon which primary Class 1 contributions have been paid or treated as paid or from earnings credited, and

(b) from Class 2 contributions.

(3) Where primary Class 1 contributions have been paid or treated as paid on any part of a person's earnings, sub-paragraph (2)(a) shall have effect as if such contributions had been paid or treated as paid on so much of the earnings as did not exceed the upper earnings limit for the year.

3.—(1) For the purposes of paragraphs 1 and 2—

(a) "benefit year" means a period which is a benefit year for the purposes of Part 2 of the Contributions and Benefits Act or such other period as may be prescribed for the purposes of this Part of this Schedule;

(b) "Class 1 contributions", "Class 2 contributions" and "primary Class 1 contributions" have the same meaning as in the Contributions and Benefits Act (see section 1 of that Act);

(c) "earnings" shall be construed in accordance with sections 3, 4 and 112 of that Act;

(d) "earnings factor" shall be construed in accordance with sections 22 and 23 of that Act;

(e) "lower earnings limit" and "upper earnings limit" shall be construed in accordance with section 5 of that Act and references to the lower or upper earnings limit of a tax year are to whatever is (or was) the limit in force for that year under that section;

(f) "relevant benefit year" is the benefit year which includes the beginning of the period of limited capability for work which includes the relevant benefit week;

(g) "tax year" means the 12 months beginning with 6th April in any year.

(2) Regulations may provide for sub-paragraph (1)(f) to have effect in prescribed circumstances with prescribed modifications in the case of—

(a) a person who has previously ceased to be entitled to a contributory allowance;

(b) a person who has made a claim for an employment and support allowance in connection with which he failed to satisfy one or both of the conditions in paragraphs 1 and 2.

Condition relating to youth

4.—(1) The third condition is that—

(a) the claimant was under 20 or, in prescribed cases, 25 when the relevant period of limited capability for work began,

(b) he is not receiving full-time education,

(c) he satisfies such conditions as may be prescribed with respect to residence or presence in Great Britain (or both), and

(d) there has been a day in the relevant period of limited capability for work—

(i) which was a day on which he was aged at least 16, and

(ii) which was preceded by a period of 196 consecutive days throughout which he had limited capability for work.

(2) In sub-paragraph (1), "relevant period of limited capability for work" means the period of limited capability for work which includes the relevant benefit week.

(3) Regulations may prescribe circumstances in which sub-paragraph (1)(a) does not apply in the case of a person who has previously ceased to be entitled to an employment and support allowance to which he was entitled by virtue of satisfying the condition set out in sub-paragraph (1).

(4) Regulations may make provision about when, for the purposes of sub-paragraph (1)(b), a person is, or is not, to be treated as receiving full-time education.

[⁵Exemption

4A. Regulations may prescribe circumstances in which a person may be entitled to employment and support allowance without having accepted a claimant commitment.]

"Relevant benefit week"

5.—In this Part of this Schedule, "relevant benefit week" means the week in relation to which the question of entitlement to an employment and support allowance is being considered.

AMENDMENTS

1. Pensions Act 2007 Sch.1 para.11 (September 27, 2007).
2. Welfare Reform Act 2009 s.13 (November 1, 2010).
3. Welfare Reform Act 2009 s.13(5) (November 29, 2011).

4. Welfare Reform Act 2012 s.31 and Sch.2 para.65 (April 29, 2013).
5. Welfare Reform Act 2012 s.54(6) (February 25, 2013).

MODIFICATION

Schedule 1 is modified by Sch.1, para.6(a) of the Employment and Support Allowance (Transitional Provisions, Housing Benefit and Council Tax Benefit) (Existing Awards) (No. 2) Regulations 2010 (SI 2010/1907) (as amended) for the purposes specified in reg.6(1). For details of the modification, see the text of those Regulations, below. For the purpose of making "conversion decisions", Sch.1 is thus to be read as if paras 1–5 were omitted.

DEFINITIONS

"the base tax year"—see para.1(1)(a).
"benefit"—see para.1(5).
"benefit year"—see para.3(1)(a).
"Class 1 contributions"—see para.3(1)(b).
"Class 2 contributions"—see para.3(1)(b).
"Contributions and Benefits Act"—see s.65.
"earnings"—see para.3(1)(c).
"earnings factor"—see para.3(1)(d).
"entitled"—see s.24(1).
"limited capability for work"—see s.1(4).
"lower earnings limit"—see para.3(1)(e).
"primary Class 1 contributions"—see para.3(1)(b).
"regulations"—see s.24(1).
"relevant benefit week"—see para.5.
"relevant benefit year"—see para.3(1)(f).
"relevant period of limited capability for work"—see para.4(2).
"tax year"—see para.3(1)(g).
"upper earnings limit"—see para.3(1)(e).
"week"—see s.24(1).

GENERAL NOTE

Paragraphs (1)–(3)

1.807
CESA is principally a contributory or national insurance benefit. Entitlement to it generally requires the claimant to have an adequate contribution record. He must satisfy the first and second conditions set out in paras 1 and 2 (s.1(2)(a)), with respect to which paras 3 and 5 provide key definitions. Paragraph 3 also enables modifications to be effected by Regs. This annotation should be read in the light of those parts of the commentary to SSCBA 1992 Sch.3 dealing with "Contributions matters: a division of responsibility" and "an outline of the contributory system: payments, credits and the earnings generated(the amount of earnings added to the contribution record)".

The changes effected from November 1, 2010 by s.13 of the Welfare Reform Act 2009 significantly tighten the contribution conditions for CESA by requiring a more recent and stronger connection with the world of work than was previously the case, whether under ESA or IB. The changes do so in that the first condition can from then only be satisfied in one of the last *two* (rather than three) tax years (April 6–April 5) complete before the start of the relevant benefit year (early January) (as with JSA); and by raising the requisite level of earnings in the tax year relied on to 26 (rather than 25) times that year's lower earnings limit. Moreover, the conditions now only count earnings at that lower earnings limit (ignoring earnings in excess of it) so that new claimants will have to have worked for at least 26 weeks in one of the last two tax years. Prior to these amendments, when the level was 25 times the LEL and the scheme looked also to earnings between the lower and upper earnings limits, a high-earner could qualify on less than four weeks' work in the tax year and someone at the national minimum wage could qualify in about 12 weeks.

The national insurance conditions: Unless he is a person incapacitated in youth (before   **1.808**
20 or sometimes 25) (see s.1(2)(a)) a claimant must satisfy both of the contribution
conditions elaborated in paras 1 and 2. The first (para.1) can be met only by *paid* contributions of the relevant class (primary Class 1 or Class 2) reaching the requisite level
in a specific tax year. The second can be satisfied by *paid and/or credited* contributions
in both of two specific tax years. Like those applicable to IB since April 2001, the conditions thus require a more recent connection with the world of work in terms of paid
contributions than had previously been the case, whether with incapacity benefit or its
predecessors, sickness and invalidity benefit. However, the rigour of the first condition
is relaxed in certain situations (paras 1(4), 3(2), ESA Regs Pt IA, reg.8).

In order to appreciate the requirements of paras 1 and 2, and the terms and operation of the contribution conditions, take first, as an illustrative example, the position
of someone claiming CESA for the very first time in August 2018 (that is, with no
link back to any previous period of incapacity for work) and never having claimed or
received any other benefit. He must meet *both of the two contribution conditions* set out
in paras 1 and 2. The first step is to identify the relevant benefit year, the one which
includes the first day of the period of limited capability for work of which his claim is
part (para.3(1)(f)). This identification of the relevant benefit year is the real substantive matter for the Secretary of State or the tribunal to focus on, since that determines
the tax years in which the requisite record must be fulfilled. His first day of claim in
the relevant benefit week (para.5) in August 2018 falls in benefit year 2018/2019 (the
relevant benefit year: defined to refer to SSCBA 1992 s.21(6) and any modifying regulations made for the purposes of this Part of this Schedule (see para.3(1)(a))). The tax
years in *one of which* the first contribution condition (sub-para.(2)) must be fulfilled
are the last two tax years (April 6–April 5) (para.3(1)(g)) complete before the start of
the relevant benefit year (early January 2018). The tax years to which to have regard
are thus 2015/2016 and 2016/2017. The contribution record in tax year 2018/2019
cannot be taken into account because it was not complete at the start of the relevant benefit year (early January 2018). The first contribution condition (para.1(1))
can only be met with paid contributions of the relevant class—Class 1 (employed
earners) or Class 2 (self-employed earners)—reaching the requisite level (26 times
the lower earnings limit (LEL) for Class 1 contributions purposes) for the tax year in
question—remember that each Class 2 contribution generates earnings equal to the
LEL pertinent to the tax/contribution year in question, while the amount of earnings
on which Class 1 contributions are paid generates the earnings for an employed earner
claimant. Note here that the November 2010 changes now only count earnings at that
lower earnings limit (ignoring earnings in excess of it) so that new claimants will have
to have worked for at least 26 weeks in one of the last two tax years.

The second contribution condition (para.1(2)) requires examination of the last
two tax years complete before the start of the relevant benefit year (early January
2018), that is 2015/2016 and 2016/2017. The claimant's contribution record in
each of those tax/contribution years must attain 50 times the lower earnings limit for
the year. But the condition can be met through paid and/or credited contributions
(a Class 1 credit can be received, for example, for each week of unemployment; see
further Social Security (Credits) Regulations 1975).

Note that para.1(4) enables regulations to provide for the first condition to be
taken to be satisfied by certain benefit recipients and provide for it to apply in modified form. The relevant "relaxation" regulation is ESA Regs reg.8 and is the subject
of commentary there. Note also that para.3(2) enables regulations to relax the rules
on relevant benefit year. The product is ESA Regs reg.13.

Various groups will have difficulty meeting the contribution conditions:

   (a) *those who have never been employed:* The requirement in the first contribu-
        tion condition for payment of contributions effectively excludes those who,
        whether through unemployment, incapacity or disability, have been unable
        to build a contribution record in terms of paid contributions.

(b) *some of the long-term unemployed:* (last employed in a tax year earlier than the first of the three on which the first contribution condition focuses).

(c) *very low-paid, probably part-time, employees:* those whose weekly or monthly earnings fall below the lower earnings limit for the whole or main part of the relevant tax years will not satisfy the contribution conditions since there is no liability or ability to pay Class 1 contributions where earnings fall below that limit, and, because they are in work, no Class 1 credits are generated from unemployment.

(d) *certain married women and widows paying reduced rate contributions:* these do not generate any earnings factor (and so do not count) for ESA purposes (para.3(d); SSCBA 1992 s.22(4)).

Paragraph 4

1.809   Severe Disablement Allowance (SDA) was introduced in 1984 to cater for those who were incapacitated below the age of 20, or, if incapacitated later, were also assessed as 80 per cent disabled (see SSCBA 1992 ss.68, 69). SDA was abolished on April 6, 2001 for new claims, but non-contributory access was afforded to IB for persons incapacitated in youth (before 20 or sometimes 25). This paragraph affords the same facility in respect of CESA. Those incapacitated, even through severe disability, later in life, will have to look to IRESA, with its disability premiums, to underwrite their incapacity for work. They may well also be eligible for various components of disability living allowance. That is not an income replacement benefit, but is rather one designed to provide for the extra costs that disability, as opposed to incapacity for work, brings with it.

1.810   *Non-contributory access to CESA: Condition relating to youth:* This is the third condition referred to in s.1(2)(a). The provisions are similar to those brought into IB (SSCBA 1992 30A(1)(b), (2A); IB Regulations 14–19) when the non-contributory incapacity benefit SDA was closed to new claimants from April 6, 2001. There is an immediate key difference, however, in that under the IB scheme the "person incapacitated in youth" route only opened if the person did not satisfy the contribution conditions (SSCBA 1992 s.30A(1)(b)), whereas with CESA there is no such pre-condition (WRA 2007 s.1(2)(a)).

To succeed by this "youth" route, all of a number of conditions must be fulfilled: (1) the claimant must be under 20 (or in some cases defined in regs, under 25) when the period of limited capability for work began (sub-para.(1)(a)); (2) he must not be receiving full-time education (sub-para.(1)(b)); (3) he must meet prescribed conditions with respect to residence and/or presence in GB (sub-para.(1)(c); ESA Regs reg.11); and (4) in his period of limited capacity for work there must be a day on which he was at least 16 which was preceded by a period of 196 days throughout which he had limited capability for work (sub-para.(1)(d)).

The age condition in sub-para.(1)(a) is disapplied by ESA Regs reg.10 in respect of certain claimants previously entitled to ESA as a person incapacitated in youth whose previous entitlement ended solely with a view to him taking up employment or training.

Note that regs can specify when someone is or is not to be treated as receiving full-time education (sub-para.(4)). The regulation in question is ESA Regs reg.12.

This route was barred to new claimants claiming on or after May 1, 2012 (see: Welfare Reform Act 2012 s.53, inserting a new subs.(3A) into s.1 of this Act).

PART 2

INCOME RELATED ALLOWANCE

1.811   **6.**—(1) The conditions are that the claimant–

(a) has an income which does not exceed the applicable amount or has no income;

(b) does not have capital which, or a prescribed part of which, exceeds the prescribed amount;

(c) is not entitled to state pension credit;

(d) is not a member of a couple the other member of which is entitled to an income-related allowance, state pension credit, income support or an income-based jobseeker's allowance;

(e) is not engaged in remunerative work;

    (f) is not a member of a couple the other member of which is engaged in remunerative work;

    (g) is not receiving education.

(2) Where the claimant is a member of a couple, the income and capital of the other member of the couple shall, except in prescribed circumstances, be treated for the purpose of this paragraph as income and capital of the claimant.

(3) Regulations may prescribe circumstances in which, for the purposes of sub-paragraph (1)(e) and (f)—

    (a) a person who is not engaged in remunerative work is to be treated as engaged in remunerative work; or

    (b) a person who is engaged in remunerative work is to be treated as not engaged in remunerative work

(4) Regulations may—

    (a) make provision about when, for the purposes of sub-paragraph (1)(g), a person is, or is not, to be treated as receiving education;

    (b) prescribe circumstances in which sub-paragraph (1)(g) does not apply.

(5) In this paragraph—

"applicable amount" means the amount which, in the claimant's case, is the applicable amount for the purposes of section 4(1);

[² [¹ "couple" means-

    (a) two people who are married to, or civil partners of, each other and are members of the same household; or

    (b) two people who are not married to, or civil partners of, each other but are living together as a married couple otherwise than in prescribed circumstances;]]

"education" has such meaning as may be prescribed;

"income-based jobseeker's allowance" has the same meaning as in the Jobseekers Act 1995(c.18);

"remunerative work" has such meaning as may be prescribed.

(6) [² [¹ . . .]]

(7) Regulations may make provision for the preceding provisions of this paragraph to have effect with prescribed modifications in a case where—

    (a) the claimant is a husband or wife by virtue of a marriage entered into under a law which permits polygamy,

    (b) either party to the marriage has for the time being any spouse additional to the other party, and

    (c) the claimant, the other party to the marriage and the additional spouse are members of the same household.

(8) Regulations may make provision for the purposes of this paragraph as to circumstances in which people are to be treated as being or not being members of the same household.

AMENDMENTS

1. Marriage (Same Sex Couples) Act 2013 (Consequential and Contrary Provisions and Scotland) Order 2014 (SI 2014/560) art.2 and Sch.1, para.32 (March 13, 2014). The amendment extends to England and Wales only (see SI 2014/560 art.6(1)).

2. Marriage and Civil Partnership (Scotland) Act 2014 and Civil Partnership Act 2004 (Consequential Provisions and Modifications) Order 2014 (SI 2014/3229) art.29 and Sch.5, para. 17 (December 16, 2014). The amendment only relates to Scotland (see SI 2014/3229 art.3(4)) but is in the same terms as the amendment made in relation to England and Wales by SI 2014/560 (see above).

MODIFICATIONS

Paragraph 6 is modified by Sch.1, para.6(b) of the Employment and Support Allowance (Transitional Provisions, Housing Benefit and Council Tax Benefit) (Existing Awards) (No. 2) Regulations 2010 (SI 2010/1907) (as amended) for the purposes specified in reg.6(1) of the 2010 Regulations and by Sch.2, para.4A for the purposes specified in reg.16(1) of those Regulations. For details of the modifications, see the text of those Regulations in Pt IX. The modifications are further modified in those cases in relation to which universal credit has come into force—see the General Note to the 2010 Regulations.

DEFINITIONS

"civil partner"—see Interpretation Act 1978 Sch.1
"education"—see ESA Regulations 2008 reg.14.
"prescribed"—see s.24(1).
"regulations"—*ibid.*
"remunerative work"—see ESA Regulations 2008 regs 2(1), 41 and 42.

GENERAL NOTE

Sub-paragraph (1)

1.812   This sets out the extra conditions for entitlement to income-related ESA that are additional to the basic conditions of entitlement for ESA in s.1(3). All of the conditions in sub-para.(1) must be satisfied for there to be entitlement to income-related ESA.

Under head (a) the claimant's income (which includes the income of any partner (sub-para.(2)) must not exceed the applicable amount (effectively the figure set for the claimant's, or the claimant's and any partner's, requirements under s.4).

Head (b) contains the capital test. The capital limit for income-related ESA is the same as for income support and income-based JSA, i.e., £16,000 (see reg.110 of the ESA Regulations 2008). See further the note to s.134(1) SSCBA in Vol II in this series. For capital that is disregarded for the purposes of income-related ESA see Sch.9 to the ESA Regulations 2008.

Entitlement to state pension credit excludes entitlement to income-related ESA (head (c)). If a claimant has reached the qualifying age for state pension credit (between April 2010 and November 2018 this will increase by stages to 65 in line with the increase in pensionable age for a woman from April 2010) but has not reached pensionable age (currently 65 for a man and from April 2010 increasing by stages from 60 to 65 in November 2018 for a woman), it will normally be advantageous to claim state pension credit rather than income-related ESA. Note that the equalisation of the state pension age for men and women was previously to have been completed by April 5, 2020 but the timetable for this in the Pensions Act 1995 is being accelerated with effect from April 2016 so that the women's state pension age will now be 65 by November 2018; in addition, the increase in state pension age to 66 for both men and women has been brought forward—it will start to rise from 65 in December 2018 to reach 66 by October 2020 (see s.1 of the Pensions Act 2011). Between 2026 and 2028 it will rise to 67 (see s.26 of the Pensions Act 2014).

A claimant who is a member of a couple (defined in sub-para.(5)) will also not qualify for income-related ESA if the partner is entitled to state pension credit, income support, income-based JSA or income-related ESA (head (d)). The definition of "couple" in sub-para.(5) was amended (and sub-para.(6) was omitted) with effect from March 13, 2014 in England and Wales, and December 16, 2014 in Scotland, as a consequence of the Marriage (Same Sex Couples) Act 2013 and the Marriage and Civil Partnership (Scotland) Act 2014 respectively.

Under heads (e) and (f) if either the claimant or any partner is in remunerative work there is no entitlement to income-related ESA. However note that the meaning of "remunerative work" is not the same for the claimant as it is for the partner. Regulation 41 of the ESA Regulations 2008 sets out the test for the claimant; the test for the partner is in reg.42 of those Regulations. See the notes to regs 41 and 42, and note also regs 40 and 43–45.

In addition the claimant will be excluded from entitlement to income-related ESA if he is receiving education (head (g)). See further regs 14–18 of the ESA Regulations 2008 (made under sub-para.(4)) and the notes to those regulations. See in particular reg.18 which provides that head (g) does not apply if the claimant is entitled to disability living allowance ("DLA"), personal independence payment ("PIP") or armed forces independence payment (see reg.2(1) for the definition of "armed forces independence payment").

Note that head (g) does not apply in the case of claimants who had an existing award of income support by virtue of reg.13(2)(b) or (bb) (persons in relevant education who are ill or disabled) of, or paras 10 or 12 (disabled or deaf students) of Sch.1B to, the Income Support Regulations (see the 2015/16 edition of Vol.II in this series for these provisions) and who have been transferred to ESA as a result of a conversion decision under the Employment and Support Allowance (Transitional Provisions, Housing Benefit and Council Tax Benefit) (Existing Awards) (No. 2) Regulations 2010 (SI 2010/1907) (as amended) (see Pt IX for these Regulations). The modifications to s.1(2) of the Act made by Sch.1, para.2 and Sch.2, para.2 of the 2010 Regulations mean that such claimants will be able to get ESA while in education even if they do not get DLA, PIP or armed forces independence payment.

Sub-paragraph (2)

This provides that the general rule for income-related ESA is that where the claimant is a member of a couple (defined in sub-para.(5)) both the claimant's and his partner's income and capital are aggregated together and treated as the claimant's.

1.813

[¹ SCHEDULE 1A   Section 15A

PERSONS DEPENDENT ON DRUGS ETC.

[² *Repealed.*]]

1.814

AMENDMENTS

1. Welfare Reform Act 2009 s.11 and Sch.3 para.7 (November 12, 2009).
2. Welfare Reform Act 2012 ss.60(2), 150(2)(b) (May 8, 2012).

SCHEDULE 2

EMPLOYMENT AND SUPPORT ALLOWANCE: SUPPLEMENTARY PROVISIONS

Limited capability for work

1.—Regulations may make provision—
   (a) for a person to be treated in prescribed circumstances as having, or as not having, limited capability for work;
   (b) for the question of whether a person has limited capability for work to be determined notwithstanding that he is for the time being treated by virtue of regulations under sub-paragraph (a) as having limited capability for work;
   (c) for the question of whether a person has limited capability for work to be determined afresh in prescribed circumstances.

1.815

Waiting days

2.—Except in prescribed circumstances, a person is not entitled to an employment and support allowance in respect of a prescribed number of days at the beginning of a period of limited capability for work.

1.816

Periods of less than a week

3.—Regulations may make provision in relation to—
   (a) entitlement to an employment and support allowance, or
   (b) the amount payable by way of such an allowance,
in respect of any period of less than a week.

1.817

Linking periods

4.—(1) Regulations may provide for circumstances in which a period of limited capability for work which is separated from another period of limited capability for work by not more than a prescribed length of time is to be treated for the purposes of this Part as a continuation of the earlier period.
   (2) Regulations may provide, in relation to periods which are linked by virtue of regulations

1.818

under sub-paragraph (1), that a condition which was satisfied in relation to the earlier period is to be treated for the purposes of this Part as satisfied in relation to the later period.

[² **4A** Regulations may prescribe circumstances in which a person may be entitled to employment and support allowance without having accepted a claimant commitment.]

Presence in Great Britain

1.819   **5.**—Regulations may make provision for the purposes of this Part as to the circumstances in which a person is to be treated as being, or not being, in Great Britain.

Contributory allowance: entitlement in case of absence from Great Britain

1.820   **6.**—Regulations may provide that in prescribed circumstances a claimant who is not in Great Britain may nevertheless be entitled to a contributory allowance.

Contributory allowance: modification in relation to employment on ships etc.

1.821   **7.**—(1) Regulations may modify any provision of this Part, so far as relating to a contributory allowance, in its application to any person who is, has been, or is to be—
  (a) employed on board any ship, vessel, hovercraft or aircraft,
  (b) outside Great Britain at any prescribed time or in any prescribed circumstances, or
  (c) in prescribed employment in connection with continental shelf operations.
(2) Regulations under this paragraph may, in particular, provide—
  (a) for any provision of this Part to apply even though it would not otherwise apply;
  (b) for any such provision not to apply even though it would otherwise apply;
  (c) for the taking of evidence, in a country or territory outside Great Britain, by a consular official or other prescribed person;
  (d) for enabling the whole, or any part, of a contributory allowance to be paid to such of the claimant's dependants as may be prescribed.
(3) In this paragraph, "continental shelf operations" has the same meaning as in section 120 of the Contributions and Benefits Act.

Income-related allowance: entitlement in case of absence from Great Britain

1.822   **8.**—(1) Regulations may provide that in prescribed circumstances a claimant who is entitled to an income-related allowance immediately before ceasing to be in Great Britain continues to be entitled to such an allowance after ceasing to be in Great Britain.
(2) Regulations may modify any provision of this Part, so far as relating to an income-related allowance, in its application to a person who is entitled to such an allowance by virtue of regulations under sub-paragraph (1).
(3) Regulations under sub-paragraph (2) may, in particular, provide—
  (a) for any provision of this Part to apply even though it would not otherwise apply;
  (b) for any such provision not to apply even though it would otherwise apply.

Limited capability for work-related activity

1.823   **9.**—Regulations may make provision—
  (a) for a person to be treated in prescribed circumstances as having, or as not having, limited capability for work-related activity;
  (b) for the question of whether a person has limited capability for work-related activity to be determined notwithstanding that he is for the time being treated by virtue of regulations under sub-paragraph (a) as having limited capability for work-related activity;
  (c) for the question of whether a person has limited capability for work-related activity to be determined afresh in prescribed circumstances.

Effect of work

1.824   **10.**—Regulations may prescribe circumstances in which a person is to be treated as not entitled to an employment and support allowance because of his doing work.

Treatment of allowance as "benefit"

1.825   **11.**—Regulations may provide for—
  (a) an employment and support allowance,
  (b) a contributory allowance, or
  (c) an income-related allowance,

to be treated, for prescribed purposes of the Contributions and Benefits Act, as a benefit, or a benefit of a prescribed description.

Attribution of reductions in cases where allowance taken to consist of two elements

12.—Where an employment and support allowance is taken by virtue of section 6(5) to consist of two elements, any reduction in the amount payable in respect of the allowance which falls to be made by virtue of—
  (a) section 11,
  (b) section 12,
  (c) section 13,
 [¹(ca) Schedule 1A,]
  (d) section 2AA of the Administration Act (full entitlement to certain benefits conditional on work-focused interview for partner),
shall be treated as reducing such of those elements by such amount as may be prescribed.

1.826

Treatment of information supplied as information relating to social security

13.—Information supplied in pursuance of regulations under any of sections 8, 9 and 11 to 13 [¹, or under any paragraph of Schedule 1A other than paragraph 8,] shall be taken for all purposes to be information relating to social security.

1.827

Advance claims

14.—This Part shall have effect with prescribed modifications in relation to cases where a claim to an employment and support allowance is by virtue of regulations under section 5(1)(c) of the Administration Act (advance claims) made, or treated as if made, for a period wholly or partly after the date on which it is made.

1.828

Members of the forces

15.—(1) Regulations may modify—
  (a) any provision of this Part, or
  (b) any corresponding provision made for Northern Ireland,
in its application to persons who are or have been members of Her Majesty's forces.
  (2) For the purposes of this paragraph, Her Majesty's forces shall be taken to consist of prescribed establishments and organisations in which persons serve under the control of the Defence Council.

1.829

AMENDMENTS

1. Welfare Reform Act 2009 s.11 and Sch.3 para.8(5) (November 12, 2009).
2. Welfare Reform Act 2012 s.54(1) and (6) (February 25, 2013).

DEFINITIONS

"Administration Act"—see s.65.
"continental shelf operations"—see para.7(3).
"Contributions and Benefits Act"—see s.65.
"contributory allowance"—see s.1(7).
"employed"—see s.24(1).
"employment"—see s.24(1).
"entitled"—see s.24(1).
"Her Majesty's forces"—see para.15(2).
"income-related allowance"—see s.1(7).
"limited capability for work-related activity"—see s.2(5).
"period of limited capability for work"—see s.24(1).
"prescribed"—see s.24(1).
"regulations"—see s.24(1).
"week"—see s.24(1).
"work-related activity"—see ss.24(1), 13(7).

GENERAL NOTE

Paragraph 2 (waiting days)
  See ESA Regs reg.144. The general rule, as with previous contributory incapacity benefit regimes, is that there is no entitlement to ESA in respect of a number of

1.830

"waiting days" at the beginning of a period of limited capability for work. The general rule has a number of exceptions set out in reg.144(2). In addition, the general rule is, of course, affected by the "linking rules" (on which see reg.145) in a case of intermittent incapacity where those rules fuse into one ostensibly separate spells of limited capability for work: the "waiting days" only have to be served once in a period of limited capability for work. Regulation 144 originally set the number of these days of non-entitlement ("waiting days") at three. From October 27, 2014 that was increased to seven with respect to a new claim in respect of a waiting period starting on or after that date.

Paragraph 3 (periods of less than a week)

1.831   Like JSA, ESA is a weekly benefit, paid in respect of a week of limited capability for work. It is paid fortnightly in arrears, and the day of the week on which payment is to be made is determined by reference to the last two digits of the claimant's national insurance number (Claims and Payments Regs, reg.26C (see updating material with respect to Vol.III). This para of Sch.2 enables regs to make provision for payment in respect of periods of less than a week: see ESA Regs, regs 165–169.

Paragraph 4 (linking periods)

1.832   See ESA Regs, reg.145. The linking rules are crucial for those suffering from intermittent incapacity. They impact, to the claimant's benefit, as regards "waiting days"; those days of non-entitlement (see para.(2) and ESA Regs reg.144) only have to be served once in any period of limited capability for work. They are also relevant to determining the relevant benefit year and hence the appropriate tax years to which to have regard with respect to the application of the national insurance contribution conditions (see further the commentary to Sch.1 Pt 1 paras 1–3).

The linking rule works on the basis that two ostensibly separate spells of limited capability for work will be fused into one where the separation period between the spells is not more than 12 weeks. This fusing does not, however, mean that days in the separation period thereby become ones of limited capability for work (*Chief Adjudication Officer v Astle* (Court of Appeal, judgment of March 17, 1999, available on LEXIS and noted in [1999] 6 J.S.S.L. 203). See further for more detail the commentary to SSCBA 1992, s.30C(1)(c) (the "linking" rule)). A period of limited capability for work can only be formed of days of actual limited capability for work and/or ones which the legislative scheme treats as ones of limited capability for work.

Note that the Employment and Support Allowance (Amendment of Linking Rules) Regulations 2012 (SI 2012/919) regs 5 and 6 heavily amended the linking rules and a variety of other rules in the ESA Regs and the Migration Regs with effect from May 1, 2012.

Paragraph 5 (presence in Great Britain)

1.833   Entitlement to ESA generally requires presence in Great Britain (s.1(3)(d)). This paragraph enables regulations to treat someone, whatever the actual reality in terms of presence or absence, as being or not being in Great Britain. See ESA Regs reg.11 (condition relating to youth—residence or presence).

Paragraph 6 (entitlement to CESA when absent from Great Britain)

1.834   Entitlement to CESA generally requires presence in Great Britain (s.1(3)(d)). This para. enables regulations to give entitlement where the claimant is not in Great Britain. See ESA Regs regs 151–155, dealing with periods of temporary absence. Note also that CESA is an exportable benefit for purposes of EC law.

Paragraph 7 (Modification of CESA for those employed on ships etc)

1.835   This enables regulations to modify the rules on entitlement to CESA as regards those who are, have been or are to be, employed on any ship, vessel, hovercraft or aircraft; outside Great Britain; or in prescribed employment in connection with continental shelf operations. See the various amendments made with effect from October 27, 2008 by the Employment and Support Allowance (Consequential Provisions) (No.2) Regulations 2008 (SI 2008/1554), regs 65 and 67, respectively to the Social Security (Airmen's Benefits) Regulations 1975 (SI 1975/494), Social Security (Mariners' Benefits) Regulations 1975 (SI 1975/529).

Paragraph (8) (retaining entitlement to IRESA when absent from Great Britain)
See ESA Regs regs 151–155.   1.836

Paragraph 10 (effect of work)
Unsurprisingly, in a benefits regime founded on limited capability for work, the   1.837
general rule in respect of ESA is that the doing of any work negatives limited capability: see ESA Regs, reg.40, precluding entitlement to ESA in any week in which
a claimant does work. But like the previous incapacity benefit regime, the general
preclusive rule is modified to permit engagement in a range of work without loss
of benefit. This recognizes that work can assist recovery or help the claimant into
thinking about work and a possibility to return to work, or merely not wanting to
exclude the sick and disabled from participation in civic office or a range of voluntary or charitable work. Under ESA, unlike its predecessor regime, the rules more
fully protect through more generous earnings disregards those only in receipt of the
income related form of the benefit as well as those receiving its contributory form.
See ESA Regs regs 41–46.

Paragraph 12 (attribution of deductions from ESA)
A claimant may be entitled to CESA to IRESA or to both. Where someone is   1.838
entitled to both IRESA and CESA, this para enables the making of regulations to
provide for which component or components is or are to be reduced because of
provisions enabling reduction set out in the specified provisions dealing with ESA
conditionality (ss.11–13) or where, under SSAA 1992 s.2AA, entitlement depends
on the claimant's partner complying with conditions in respect of work-focused
interviews. See ESA Regs reg.63. See also, in Vol.III, with respect to SSAA 1992
s.2AA, the Social Security (Jobcentre Plus Interviews for Partners) Regs 2003 (SI
2003/1886), reg.11, as amended with effect from October 27, 2008, by reg.71 of the
Employment and Support Allowance (Consequential Provisions) (No.2) Regs 2008
(SI 2008/1554).

Paragraph 14 (Advance claims)
See ESA Regs reg.66.   1.839

Paragraph 15 (members of Her Majesty's forces)
This enables regulations to modify the rules on entitlement to ESA in respect   1.840
of persons who are or have been members of those forces. See ESA Regs regs 155
and Sch.1. See also the Social Security (Benefit) (Members of the Forces) Regs
1975 (SI 1975/493) as amended with effect from October 27, 2008 by reg.66 of the
Employment and Support Allowance (Consequential Provisions) (No.2) Regs 2008
(SI 2008/1554).

SCHEDULE 3   **Section 28**

CONSEQUENTIAL AMENDMENTS RELATING TO PART 1

Insofar as the provisions in this Schedule amend legislation contained   1.841
in the main volumes, these amendments have been taken into account in
preparing the legislative text.

SCHEDULE 4

Section 29

TRANSITION RELATING TO PART 1

General power to provide for transition relating to Part 1

1.842   **1.**—(1) Regulations may make such provision as the Secretary of State considers necessary or expedient—

    (a) in connection with the coming into force of any provision of, or repeal relating to, this Part, or

    (b) otherwise for the purposes of, or in connection with, the transition to employment and support allowance.

(2) The following provisions of this Schedule are not to be taken as prejudicing the generality of sub-paragraph (1).

Pre-commencement claims

1.843   **2.**—Regulations may—

    (a) make provision for a claim for incapacity benefit, income support or severe disablement allowance which is made before the appointed day to be treated wholly or partly as a claim for an employment and support allowance;

    (b) make provision for the purpose of enabling claims for an employment and support allowance to be made before the appointed day for a period beginning on or after that day.

Post-commencement claims

1.844   **3.**—Regulations may—

    (a) make provision excluding the making of a claim for incapacity benefit or severe disablement allowance on or after the appointed day;

    (b) make provision for a claim for incapacity benefit, income support or severe disablement allowance which is made on or after the appointed day to be treated in prescribed circumstances as a claim for an employment and support allowance;

    (c) make provision for a claim for an employment and support allowance to be treated wholly or partly as a claim for incapacity benefit, income support or severe disablement allowance;

    (d) make provision excluding the making of a claim for an employment and support allowance by a person who is entitled to an existing award.

Award of employment and support allowance for pre-commencement period

1.845   **4.**—*Regulations may—*

    (a) make provision for an employment and support allowance of such a kind as the regulations may provide to be awarded in prescribed circumstances for a period before the appointed day;

    (b) make provision with respect to conditions of entitlement in relation to an award under sub-paragraph (a) and the amount payable by way of an allowance under such an award.

Matching of awards of employment and support allowance

1.846   **5.**—*(1) For the purposes of this paragraph, an award of an employment and support allowance is one that falls to be made on matching terms if—*

    (a) it is made in pursuance of a claim by a person who was previously entitled to an existing award, and

    (b) had it continued to be possible to make an award of incapacity benefit, income support on grounds of incapacity for work, or severe disablement allowance, the award which would have been made to him ("the hypothetical award") would have been made on the basis of the linking of periods of incapacity for work.

(2) Regulations may—

    (a) make provision for the purpose of securing that an award of an employment and support allowance that falls to be made on matching terms is made on terms which match in whole or part the hypothetical award;

    (b) make provision for the modification of matched awards for the purpose of securing that the person with the award is put in the position he would have been had he been made the hypothetical award which was then the subject of conversion under paragraph 7.

(3) In sub-paragraph (2)(b), the reference to matched awards is to awards of an employment and support allowance that have been the subject of matching in pursuance of regulations under sub-paragraph (2)(a).

6.—*(1) For the purposes of this paragraph an award of an employment and support allowance is one which falls to be made on matching terms if—*

    (a) it is made in pursuance of a claim by a person who was previously entitled to an existing award,

    (b) had he continued to be entitled to that award, it would have been the subject of conversion under paragraph 7 before the date of his claim for an employment and support allowance, and

    (c) had it continued to be possible to make an award of incapacity benefit, income support on grounds of incapacity for work, or severe disablement allowance, the award which would have been made to him would have been made on the basis of the linking of periods of incapacity for work.

(2) Regulations may make provision for the purpose of securing that an award of an employment and support allowance that falls to be made on matching terms is made on terms which match in whole or part the award that would have resulted from conversion under paragraph 7 had entitlement to the existing award continued.

1.847

Treatment of existing awards

7.—(1) Regulations may—

    (a) make provision for converting existing awards into awards of an employment and support allowance, and with respect to the terms of conversion;

    (b) make provision for the termination of existing awards in prescribed circumstances.

(2) Regulations under sub-paragraph (1)(a) may, in particular—

    (a) make provision for conversion of an existing award—

        (i) on application, in accordance with the regulations, by the person entitled to the award, or

        (ii) without application;

    (b) make provision about the conditions to be satisfied in relation to an application for conversion;

    (c) make provision about the timing of conversion;

    (d) provide for an existing award to have effect after conversion as an award of an employment and support allowance—

        (i) of such a kind,

        (ii) for such period,

        (iii) of such an amount, and

        (iv) subject to such conditions,

        as the regulations may provide;

    (e) make provision for determining in connection with conversion of an existing award whether a person has limited capability for work-related activity.

    [¹(f) make provision modifying the application of section 1A in relation to awards of an employment and support allowance to persons previously entitled to existing awards.]

(3) Regulations under sub-paragraph (1)(a) may, in relation to existing awards which have been the subject of conversion under this paragraph, include provision about revision under section 9 of the Social Security Act 1998 (c. 14), or supersession under section 10 of that Act in respect of the period before conversion.

1.848

Transitional allowances

8.—(1) Regulations may—

    (a) make provision for a person's continuing entitlement to an employment and support allowance awarded by virtue of regulations under paragraph 7 (a "transitional allowance") to be determined by reference to such provision as may be made by the regulations;

    (b) make provision for the review of an award of a transitional allowance;

    (c) make provision for the termination of an award of a transitional allowance;

    (d) make provision for this Part, or any other enactment relating to social security, to have effect with prescribed modifications in relation to a person with a transitional allowance;

    (e) make provision for the purpose of enabling a transitional allowance to be revised under section 9 of the Social Security Act 1998 (c. 14) or superseded under section 10 of that Act.

(2) In this paragraph "enactment" includes an enactment contained in subordinate legislation (within the meaning of the Interpretation Act 1978 (c. 30)).

1.849

1.850   **9.**—*(1) Regulations may prescribe circumstances in which a person who is entitled to a transitional allowance immediately before reaching pensionable age is to be treated as having satisfied the condition in paragraph 5(2) of Schedule 3 to the Contributions and Benefits Act (first contribution condition for entitlement to state pension).*

(2) In this paragraph, "pensionable age" has the meaning given by the rules in paragraph 1 of Schedule 4 to the Pensions Act 1995 (c. 26).

Post-commencement up-rating of incapacity benefit and severe disablement allowance

1.851   **10.**—Regulations may provide for section 150 of the Administration Act (annual up-rating of benefits), so far as relating to—

(a) incapacity benefit under section 30A of the Contributions and Benefits Act, or

(b) severe disablement allowance,

to have effect with prescribed modifications in relation to tax years beginning on or after the appointed day.

Interpretation

1.852   **11.**—In this Schedule—

"appointed day" means the day appointed for the coming into force of section 1;

"existing award" means—

(a) an award of incapacity benefit,

(b) an award of severe disablement allowance, and

(c) an award of income support made to a person to whom regulation 6(4)(a) or 13(2)(b) or (bb) of, or paragraph 7(a) or (b), 10, 12 or 13 of Schedule 1B to, the Income Support (General) Regulations 1987 (S.I. 1987/1967) (persons incapable of work or disabled) applies;

"incapacity benefit" (except in paragraph 10(a)) means—

(a) incapacity benefit under section 30A, 40 or 41 of the Contributions and Benefits Act,

(b) long-term incapacity benefit under regulation 11(4) of the Social Security (Incapacity Benefit) (Transitional) Regulations 1995 (S.I. 1995/310) (former sickness benefit), and

(c) invalidity benefit which has effect by virtue of regulation 17(1) of those regulations as if it were long-term incapacity benefit;

"severe disablement allowance" means severe disablement allowance under section 68 of that Act (as it has effect by virtue of article 4 of the Welfare Reform and Pensions Act 1999 (Commencement No. 9, and Transitional and Savings Provisions) Order 2000 (S.I. 2000/2958) (C. 89));

"transitional allowance" has the meaning given by paragraph 8(1)(a).

AMENDMENT

1. Welfare Reform Act 2012 s.51(4) (March 20, 2012).

DEFINITIONS

"Administration Act"—see s.65.

"appointed day"—see para.11.

"Contributions and Benefits Act"—see s.65.

"enactment"—see para.8(2).

"existing award"—see para.11.

"the hypothetical award"—see para.5(1)(b).

"incapacity benefit" (except in paragraph 10(a))—see para.11.

"income support"—see s.24(1).

"limited capability for work-related activity"—see s.2(5).

"pensionable age"—see para.9(2).

"prescribed"—see s.24(1).

"regulations"—see s.24(1).

"severe disablement allowance"—see para.11.

"transitional allowance"—see paras 11, 8(1)(a).

"work-related activity"—see ss.24(1), 13(7).

GENERAL NOTE

1.853   Provisions in italics were not yet in force as at April 8, 2019.

Paragraphs 1–3

See further the Employment and Support Allowance (Transitional Provisions) Regs 2008, regs 1–4 of which entered into force on July 27, 2008.

1.854

Paragraphs 7–8

See the Employment and Support Allowance (Transitional Provisions, Housing Benefit and Council Tax Benefit) (Existing Awards) (No. 2) Regulations 2010 (SI 2010/1907), the key provisions of which came into force on October 1, 2010. Put shortly, these Regulations provide for the migration to ESA of most of those people with current awards of benefit on incapacity grounds (IB, SDA and IS on the grounds of incapacity). The Regulations make appropriate transitional provision, where appropriate, for those whose awards qualify for conversion. The Explanatory Note for the No. 2 Regulations (SI 2010/1907) identifies the policy intent, timetable for and effects of, the migration process:

1.855

> "The policy intent is, with few exceptions, for existing incapacity benefits customers to go through the migration process between October 2010 and the end of March 2014. This will determine if they qualify for Employment and Support Allowance and will eventually enable the other incapacity benefit schemes to be wholly wound down.
>
> Migration to the Employment and Support Allowance regime, (to which the Government committed in the December 2008 White Paper), will align and simplify the benefit system, by ensuring that, over time, all customers with a health condition or disability in similar circumstances will be treated equally, receiving support to get into to work and the same level of financial help.
>
> Some current incapacity benefits customers will be found fit for work and disallowed benefit on grounds of incapacity. They may claim Jobseeker's Allowance or remain on Income Support if they qualify on grounds other than incapacity" (paras 7.2–7.4 (footnotes omitted)).

The exceptions mentioned include those who reach state pension age during migration and those over pension age in receipt of SDA. The migration of existing "national insurance credits only" claimants will take place when the main migration has been completed.

ESA rates are different from those of the benefits it replaced. The governmental commitment was that transferees would not suffer a cash reduction at the point of change. The Regulations envisage the following situations:

- Where someone receives more from their existing benefit than the amount they would otherwise receive by way of ESA, this level will be frozen on a mark-time basis; and they will receive a 'transitional addition' that will make their ESA up to the level of their old benefit entitlement until the earlier of either the ESA rate catching up or April 5, 2020.

- Where someone's existing award is the same amount as the amount of ESA receivable, the transferee will get ESA at the same rate from the effective date of migration.

- Where someone receives less on their existing benefit than the amount they would receive by way of ESA, they will receive the appropriate ESA rate on migration.

Child Maintenance and Other Payments Act 2008

(2008 c.6)

ARRANGEMENT OF SECTIONS

PART 4

LUMP SUM PAYMENTS: MESOTHELIOMA ETC.

Mesothelioma lump sum payments

1.856   46. Lump sum payments
        47. Conditions of entitlement
        48. Determination of claims
        49. Reconsideration
        50. Appeal to appeal tribunal
        51. *[repealed]*
        52. Minors and people who lack capacity
        53. Regulations: Part 4

Recovery of mesothelioma and other lump sum payments

54. Amendment of Social Security (Recovery of Benefits Act 1997 *[omitted]*

GENERAL NOTE

1.857   Part 4 of the Child Maintenance and Other Payments Act 2008 establishes a new no-fault compensation scheme for victims of mesothelioma, an asbestos-related cancer that is invariably fatal. Known as the 2008 Diffuse Mesothelioma Scheme, the new arrangements are modelled on, but also extend the scope of, the provisions of the Pneumoconiosis etc. (Workers' Compensation) Act 1979 (on which see *Ballantine v Newalls Insulation Co Ltd* [2001] ICR 25). Most mesothelioma victims are middle-aged or elderly men who were employed in industries where heavy exposure to asbestos dust was commonplace until better controls were gradually introduced from the 1970s onwards. There are currently about 2,000 mesothelioma deaths in Great Britain each year, a figure which is expected to rise to about 2,400 a year by 2013, before the total begins to fall away to an expected annual toll of 500 in 2050. Mesothelioma, unlike asbestosis and asbestos-related lung cancer, can be caused by relatively low levels of exposure and so can also occur outside the workplace (see generally N.J. Wikeley, *Compensation for Industrial Disease*, (Aldershot: Dartmouth Publishing Group, 1993)).

Before these reforms, mesothelioma sufferers had three main routes to claiming compensation: (1) a civil claim for damages against their former employer; (2) where no such potential defendant remained in existence, a claim under the Pneumoconiosis etc. (Workers' Compensation) Act 1979; and (3) a claim for industrial disablement benefit on the basis of having a prescribed disease (subject to the recovery rules under the Social Security (Recovery of Benefits) Act 1997). However, three groups of mesothelioma victims found it difficult or impossible to bring a claim under any of these arrangements (see further N.J. Wikeley, "The New Mesothelioma Compensation Scheme" (2009) 16 J.S.S.L. 30, on the background to the 2008 Scheme).

The first group were self-employed workers, who by definition had no employer to sue for damages in tort. As they were not "employed earners", they also did not qualify for industrial disablement benefit (or under the 1979 Act). Self-employment has always been common in the construction industry, one of the occupations in which exposure levels to asbestos dust were at their highest in the four decades or so after the Second World War, leaving large numbers of victims with no effective means of redress.

The second category comprised para-occupational mesothelioma victims (or cases of "household exposure"), e.g. family members who were exposed to asbestos dust at home because of close contact with an asbestos worker's overalls, such as by shaking and washing overalls. Household victims may in theory have a claim in tort, but in many cases the difficulties of establishing the requisite date of knowledge on the employer's part for the purposes of establishing a duty of care will be fatal (see e.g. *Maguire v Harland and Wolff plc* [2005] EWCA Civ 1). Family members who contract mesothelioma indirectly through household exposure are not themselves "employed earners", and so have no claim under the industrial disablement scheme or the 1979 Act.

1.858

The third (and probably smallest) group comprises environmental cases, where victims have been exposed to asbestos dust in the vicinity of their home. In extreme cases they may be able to recover in tort (see e.g. *Margereson and Hancock v J. W. Roberts Ltd* [1996] EWCA Civ 1316) but again they have no claim under the industrial disablement scheme or 1979 Act because of the absence of a personal occupational link.

The new scheme under Part 4 is designed to provide early assistance to all such mesothelioma victims, irrespective of their previous employment status. The Government anticipates that up to 600 mesothelioma victims who previously received no state support will receive an average payment of £6,000 during the first year of the scheme's operation. The scheme is to be funded from recoveries from subsequent compensation payments made by defendants and insurers. The Government anticipates that payments will be brought up to the levels under the 1979 Act by the third year of the new scheme, as compensation recoveries begin to accrue. The Child Maintenance and Other Payments Act 2008 (Commencement) Order 2008 (SI 2008/1476 (C.67)) brought Part 4 into force with effect from October 1, 2008.

PART 4

LUMP SUM PAYMENTS: MESOTHELIOMA ETC.

Mesothelioma lump sum payments

Lump sum payments

46.—(1) A claim for a payment under this Part may be made by—

    (a) a person with diffuse mesothelioma, or

    (b) a dependant of a person who, immediately before death, had diffuse mesothelioma.

1.859

(2) The Secretary of State must make the payment to the claimant if satisfied that the conditions of entitlement in section 47 are fulfilled.

(3) Regulations—

    (a) may prescribe the amount of any payment;

    (b) may prescribe different amounts for different cases or classes of cases or for different circumstances.

(4) In this Part—

"dependant" has the meaning given by section 3 of the Pneumoconiosis etc. (Workers' Compensation) Act 1979 (c. 41) ("the 1979 Act");

"diffuse mesothelioma" has the same meaning as in the 1979 Act.

(5) Where, because of section 3(1)(b) or (d) of the 1979 Act (children, siblings etc.), a payment may be claimed by two or more persons, the payment is to be made to one of them or divided between some or all of them as the Secretary of State thinks fit.

DEFINITIONS

"dependant"—subs.(4).
"diffuse mesothelioma"—*ibid.*

GENERAL NOTE

1.860   This section provides for the Secretary of State to make lump sum payments to persons with diffuse mesothelioma, or to their dependants, if the person in question has died (subs.(1); if the payment is to a dependent minor, see s.52). Indeed, if the criteria set out in s.47 are satisfied the Secretary of State *must* make such a lump sum payment (subs.(2)). Regulations may prescribe the amounts in question, which may be different for different cases or classes of cases and circumstances (subs. (3); see further reg.5 and the Schedule to the Mesothelioma Lump Sum Payments (Conditions and Amounts) Regulations 2008 (SI 2008/1963). These regulations, like the Pneumoconiosis etc. (Workers' Compensation) Act 1979, set payments at different levels by age and according to whether they are made to a sufferer or a dependant. The terms "dependant" and "diffuse mesothelioma" both carry the same meaning as in the 1979 Act (subs.(4); note that the definition of "dependant" in the 1979 Act was amended and updated by s.59 of the Welfare Reform Act 2007). If there are two or more dependants eligible to claim, the payment may be apportioned (or not) according to the discretion of the Secretary of State (subs.(5)).

Conditions of entitlement

1.861   **47.**—(1) In the case of a person who has diffuse mesothelioma, the conditions of entitlement are—
> (a) that no payment within subsection (3) has been made in consequence of the disease;
> (b) that the person is not eligible for any payment in consequence of the disease that is of a description prescribed by regulations;
> (c) that such requirement, if any, as may be prescribed by regulations as to the person's connection with the United Kingdom is satisfied.

(2) In the case of a dependant of a person who, immediately before death, had diffuse mesothelioma, the conditions of entitlement are—
> (a) that no payment within subsection (3) has been made in consequence of the disease to that or another dependant or to the deceased or the deceased's personal representatives;
> (b) that the dependant is not, and the deceased was not, eligible for any payment in consequence of the disease that is of a description prescribed by regulations;
> (c) that such requirement, if any, as may be prescribed by regulations as to the deceased's connection with the United Kingdom is satisfied.

(3) The payments referred to in subsections (1)(a) and (2)(a) are—
> (a) a payment under this Part or under corresponding provision made for Northern Ireland;
> (b) a payment under the 1979 Act or under corresponding provision made for Northern Ireland;
> [¹ (ba) a payment under the Diffuse Mesothelioma Payment Scheme (for the scheme, see the Mesothelioma Act 2014);]

(c) an extra-statutory payment;

(d) damages or a payment in settlement of a claim for damages;

(e) a payment of a description prescribed by regulations.

(4) A payment is to be disregarded for the purposes of subsection (1)(a) or (2)(a) if it has been, or is liable to be, repaid—

(a) under section 49 of this Act or under corresponding provision made for Northern Ireland;

(b) under section 5 of the 1979 Act or under corresponding provision made for Northern Ireland;

(c) under the terms of an extra-statutory payment;

(d) in circumstances prescribed for the purposes of this section by regulations.

(5) In this section "extra-statutory payment" has the meaning given by section 1A(5)(d) of the Social Security (Recovery of Benefits) Act 1997.

AMENDMENT

1. Mesothelioma Act 2014 Sch.2 para.2 (March 31, 2014).

DEFINITIONS

"extra-statutory payment"—subs.(5).

GENERAL NOTE

This section sets out the conditions of entitlement for a lump sum payment. The relevant conditions for a mesothelioma sufferer are in subs.(1) and for a dependant of a mesothelioma sufferer in subs.(2). In both instances there are three criteria, each of which must be met.   1.862

First, there must have been no payment already in consequence of the disease, as defined by subs.(3) (and subject to the disregards in subs.(4)). Such payments include a payment of damages or settlement of a claim for damages, as well as payments under this Part, payments under the 1979 Act, extra-statutory payments and payments of a prescribed nature. The definition of "extra-statutory payment" is the same as for recoupment purposes, namely one made where a claim has been rejected under the 1979 Act (subs.(5) and see s.54, inserting a new s.1A(5) into the Social Security (Recovery of Benefits) Act 1997). The category of prescribed payments includes payments by government departments (including the Ministry of Defence) and payments by various public sector and other employers which are exempt from employers' liability compulsory insurance (see Employers' Liability (Compulsory Insurance) Regulations 1998 (SI 1998/2573) Sch.2, paras 1-13 and see the Mesothelioma Lump Sum Payments (Conditions and Amounts) Regulations 2008 (SI 2008/1963) reg.2(1)). Note that where a lump sum payment is made under s.46 and there is a later award of damages or settlement in a civil case, the Secretary of State may recoup part or all of the cost of the earlier payment from that figure (see s.54 and the new s.1A of the Social Security (Recovery of Benefits) Act 1997).

Second, there must be no eligibility for any payment of a description as prescribed by regulations. This category includes payments under the Ministry of Defence's War Pensions Scheme or Armed Forces Compensation Scheme: see the Mesothelioma Lump Sum Payments (Conditions and Amounts) Regulations 2008 (SI 2008/1963) reg.2(2).

Third, the mesothelioma victim must have satisfied the prescribed "connection with the United Kingdom" test. The Government's concern is to protect the scheme against (the probably fairly remote) risk of "benefit tourism" by persons who contracted mesothelioma while living abroad and who then travel to the United Kingdom to take advantage of the compensation arrangements. See further the Mesothelioma Lump Sum Payments (Conditions and Amounts) Regulations 2008 (SI 2008/1963) reg.4.   1.863

In this context it should be noted that there is no freestanding express statutory requirement that the victim contracted mesothelioma *as a result of* asbestos exposure. In practice, of course, asbestos is the only known cause of mesothelioma. However, a minority of victims have no known exposure to asbestos (this may be because they were in fact exposed, but there is no record of such exposure, or because there are indeed some instances of cryptogenic mesothelioma unrelated to asbestos exposure). The statute simply requires that the person has "diffuse mesothelioma", as defined by s.10(2) of the 1979 Act (see s.46(4)), which in turn refers to the social security definition for the purposes of the industrial injuries scheme. Regulation 1(2) of the Social Security (Industrial Injuries) (Prescribed Diseases) Regulations 1985 (SI 1985/967) defines "diffuse mesothelioma" as the disease numbered P.D. D3 in the Schedule to those Regulations. This refers (under the column headed "Prescribed disease or injury") to "primary neoplasm of the mesothelium of the pleura or of the pericardium or of the peritoneum". It is arguable that this is the limit of the definition, and that it does not include the occupational test in the next column of the Schedule, which refers specifically to asbestos exposure. If that is right, it is arguable that the terms of reg.4 of the Mesothelioma Lump Sum Payments (Conditions and Amounts) Regulations 2008 may be ultra vires, as that provision requires that the person concerned "was in the United Kingdom at a time when and place where" that person "*was exposed to asbestos*" (emphasis added).

Determination of claims

1.864   **48.**—(1) A claim under section 46 must be made in the manner and within the period prescribed by regulations.

(2) Regulations may prescribe different periods for different cases or classes of cases or for different circumstances.

(3) Regulations may in particular provide that no claim may be made in cases where the prescribed period expired before the commencement of section 46 (or would have done but for any discretion to extend it).

(4) The Secretary of State may, before determining any claim under section 46, appoint a person to inquire into any question arising on the claim, or any matters arising in connection with it, and to report on the question, or on those matters, to the Secretary of State.

GENERAL NOTE

Subsections (1) and (2)

1.865   This section deals with the determination of claims made under s.46. Claims must be made in the prescribed manner and within time limits: see further the Mesothelioma Lump Sum Payments (Claims and Reconsiderations) Regulations 2008 (SI 2008/1595) regs 2 and 3. The general time limit for claims is 12 months from the diagnosis of mesothelioma (or, in the case of a dependant, 12 months from the death of the person with mesothelioma), as under s.4(1) of the Pneumoconiosis etc. (Workers' Compensation) Act 1979. As under the 1979 Act, this time limit is subject to extension for good cause.

Subsection (3)

1.866   There is an initial absolute time limit on backdating of 12 months prior to the regulations coming into force, to avoid the possibility of claims by dependants going back as far as 1948: see Mesothelioma Lump Sum Payments (Claims and Reconsiderations) Regulations 2008 (SI 2008/1595) reg.3(1).

This provision is modelled on the now repealed s.17(4) of the Social Security   **1.867** Administration Act 1992, although that referred to an appointment to a person "to hold an inquiry" rather than merely "to inquire" (see also to similar effect s.4(2) of the Pneumoconiosis etc. (Workers' Compensation) Act 1979).

Reconsideration

49.—(1) Subject to subsection (2), the Secretary of State—   **1.868**
  (a) may reconsider a determination that a payment should not be made under this Part, on the ground that there has been a material change of circumstances since the determination was made; and
  (b) may reconsider a determination either that a payment should or that a payment should not be made under this Part, on the ground that the determination was made in ignorance of, or was based on a mistake as to, a material fact.
(2) Regulations must prescribe the manner in which and [¹ may prescribe the period within which—
  (a) an application may be made to the Secretary of State for reconsideration of a determination; or
  (b) the Secretary of State may institute such a reconsideration without an application.
(3) Section 48(4) applies in relation to any reconsideration of a determination under this section as it applies in relation to the determination of a claim.
(4) Subsection (5) applies if—
  (a) whether fraudulently or otherwise, any person misrepresents or fails to disclose any material fact, and
  (b) in consequence of the misrepresentation or failure, a payment is made under this Part.
(5) The person to whom the payment was made is liable to repay the amount of that payment to the Secretary of State unless that person can show that the misrepresentation or failure occurred without that person's connivance or consent.
(6) Except as provided by subsection (5), no payment under this Part is recoverable by virtue of a reconsideration of a determination under this section.
(7) Any sums repaid to the Secretary of State by virtue of subsection (5) are to be paid into the Consolidated Fund.

AMENDMENT

1. Welfare Reform Act 2012 s.102(6) and Sch.11 paras 15 &16 (February 25, 2013).

GENERAL NOTE

This section makes provision for the Secretary of State to carry out a reconsideration of a determination made under s.48.   **1.869**

Subsection (1)
Reconsiderations are possible where there has been a material change in circumstances or the original determination was made in ignorance of or based on a mistake as to a material fact (subs.(1)). These grounds have been borrowed from   **1.870**

the social security jurisdiction. This section also broadly follows the model of s.5 of the Pneumoconiosis etc. (Workers' Compensation) Act 1979.

Subsections (2) and (3)

1.871   See the Mesothelioma Lump Sum Payments (Claims and Reconsiderations) Regulations 2008 (SI 2008/1595) regs 4 and 5. The Secretary of State has the same power as when dealing with an initial determination to appoint a person to inquire into matters arising (see s.48(4)).

Subsections (4) and (5)

1.872   The Secretary of State may recover payments under the scheme where they have been caused by misrepresentation or failure to disclose; again, these concepts are borrowed from social security law—see Social Security Administration Act 1992 s.71. However the potential defence under subs.(5) that the misrepresentation or failure to disclose "occurred without that person's connivance or consent" does not appear in social security law (except in the context of s.5(4) of the Vaccine Damages Act 1979).

Appeal to [¹ First-tier Tribunal]

1.873   **50.**—(1) A person who has made a claim under section 46 may appeal against a determination made by the Secretary of State—

  (a) on the claim, or

  (b) on reconsideration under section 49 of a determination made on the claim.

  [² (1A) Regulations may provide that, in such cases or circumstances as may be prescribed, a person may appeal against a determination made on a claim only if the Secretary of State has decided whether to reconsider the determination under section 49.

  (1B) The regulations may in particular provide that that condition is met only where—

  (a) the decision of the Secretary of State was on an application,

  (b) the Secretary of State considered issues of a specified description, or

  (c) the decision of the Secretary of State satisfied any other condition specified in the regulations.]

  (2) Subject to regulations under subsection (4)(c), the Secretary of State must refer any appeal to [¹ the First-tier Tribunal].

  (3) On an appeal the tribunal may substitute for the determination concerned any determination which could have been made in accordance with this Part.

  (4) Regulations may make provision—

  (a) as to the manner in which, and the time within which, an appeal may be made;

  (b) [¹. . .];

  (c) for the purpose of enabling an appeal under subsection (1)(a) [² (or, where in accordance with regulations under subsection (1A) there is no right of appeal, any purported appeal)] to be treated as an application for reconsideration under section 49 of the determination made on the claim.

AMENDMENTS

1. Transfer of Tribunal Functions Order 2008 (SI 2008/2833) art.6, Sch.3 para.226 (November 3, 2008).

2. Welfare Reform Act 2012 s.102(6) and Sch.11 paras 15 &17(1)-(3) (February 25, 2013).

GENERAL NOTE

A person making a claim under s.46 has a right of appeal to the First-tier Tribunal   **1.874**
against the Secretary of State's determination on the claim under s.48 or reconsideration under s.49. There is a further right of appeal (on a point of law and with permission) from the First-tier Tribunal to the Upper Tribunal (Tribunals, Courts and Enforcement Act 2007 s.11).

Note that the right of appeal is under the 2008 Act; there is no right of appeal to a tribunal in respect of decisions made under the 1979 Act, although there is a reconsideration process under that legislation.

Appeal to Social Security Commissioner

51.—[¹. . .]   **1.875**

AMENDMENT

1. Transfer of Tribunal Functions Order 2008 (SI 2008/2833) art.6, Sch.3 para.227 (November 3, 2008).

GENERAL NOTE

As originally enacted, there was a further right of appeal from the decision of   **1.876**
an appeal tribunal (now the First-tier Tribunal) under s.50 to the Social Security Commissioner. The jurisdiction of the Commissioner has now been assumed by the Upper Tribunal under the Tribunals, Courts and Enforcement Act 2007. The bringing into force of s.11 of that Act, which provides for a right of appeal, subject to permission being granted, from the First-tier Tribunal to the Upper Tribunal on a point of law swiftly made s.51 redundant.

Minors and people who lack capacity

52.—(1) This section applies where a payment under this Part falls to be   **1.877**
made to—
- (a) a person aged under 18, or
- (b) a person who lacks capacity within the meaning of the Mental Capacity Act 2005 (or, in Scotland, who is incapable within the meaning of the Adults with Incapacity (Scotland) Act 2000 (asp 4)) in relation to financial matters.

(2) Subject to section 46(5) the payment is to be made for that person's benefit by paying it to such trustees as the Secretary of State may appoint.

(3) The trustees are to hold the payment on such trusts or, in Scotland, for such purposes and on such conditions as the Secretary of State may declare.

GENERAL NOTE

This section makes special provision for cases in which a payment is due to be   **1.878**
made to a child or to a person who lacks capacity; in such cases payments are to be made to trustees. This provision is similar to s.6 of the Pneumoconiosis etc. (Workers' Compensation) Act 1979.

Regulations: Part 4

53.—(1) A reference in this Part to regulations is a reference to regula-   **1.879**
tions made by the Secretary of State.

(2) The power to make regulations under this Part—

(a) is exercisable by statutory instrument;

(b) includes power to make such incidental, supplementary or transitional provision as the Secretary of State thinks fit;

(c) may be exercised so as to provide for a person to exercise a discretion in dealing with any matter.

[¹ (2A) The power to make regulations under section 50(1A) may be exercised—

(a) in relation to all cases to which it extends, in relation to those cases but subject to specified exceptions or in relation to any specified cases or classes of case;

(b) so as to make, as respects the cases in relation to which it is exercised—

(i) the full provision to which it extends or any lesser provision (whether by way of exception or otherwise);

(ii) the same provision for all cases, different provision for different cases or classes of case or different provision as respects the same case or class of case but for different purposes of this Act;

(iii) provision which is either unconditional or is subject to any specified condition.]

(3) No regulations may be made under section 46 [¹or 50(1A)] unless a draft of the statutory instrument containing the regulations has been laid before, and approved by a resolution of, each House of Parliament.

(4) No regulations may be made under any provision of section 47 if they are the first regulations to be made under that section, unless a draft of the statutory instrument containing the regulations has been laid before, and approved by a resolution of, each House of Parliament.

(5) A statutory instrument that—

(a) contains regulations under this Part, and

(b) is not subject to a requirement that a draft of the instrument be laid before, and approved by a resolution of, each House of Parliament,

shall be subject to annulment in pursuance of a resolution of either House of Parliament.

AMENDMENT

1. Welfare Reform Act 2012, s.102(6) and Sch.11 paras.15 &18(1)-(3) (February 25, 2013).

GENERAL NOTE

1.880   Regulations made under s.46 which make provision for lump sum payments in respect of mesothelioma are subject to the affirmative procedure (subs.(3)); all other regulations under this Part are subject to the negative procedure (subs.(4)).

Recovery of mesothelioma and other lump sum payments

Amendment of Social Security (Recovery of Benefits) Act 1997

1.881   54—(*omitted:* see Vol.III).

This section inserts a new s.1A into the Social Security (Recovery of Benefits)   **1.882**
Act 1997. The 1997 Act applies wherever a person makes a payment "to or in
respect of any other person in consequence of any accident, injury or disease suffered by the other" and where as a result certain prescribed benefits have been (or
are likely) to be paid to or for the other person during the relevant period. The new
s.1A allows the Secretary of State to make regulations providing for the recovery
of lump sum payments in analogous circumstances: see further the Social Security
(Recovery of Benefits) (Lump Sum Payments) Regulations 2008 (SI 2008/1596).
These regulations establish a freestanding compensation recovery scheme to recoup
lump sum mesothelioma payments under Part 4 of the present Act as well as those
under the Pneumoconiosis etc. (Workers' Compensation) Act 1979 and certain
extra-statutory payments. The intention is to recover such payments from any civil
compensation award paid to the person in respect of the same disease (or diseases)
for which the lump sum payment was made. The underlying principle is that a person
should not be compensated twice for the same loss.

Welfare Reform Act 2009

(2009 C.24)

SECTIONS REPRODUCED

PART 1

SOCIAL SECURITY

"Work for your benefit" schemes etc.

8.   Parliamentary procedure: regulations imposing work-related activity   **1.883**
       requirements on lone parents of children under 7

Jobseeker's allowance and employment and support allowance: drugs

11.   Claimants dependent on drugs etc.

Contributory jobseeker's allowance and employment and support allowance

13.   Conditions for contributory employment and support allowance

Abolition of adult dependency increases

15.   Maternity allowance and carer's allowance

Miscellaneous

37.   Minor amendments

PART 5

GENERAL

57. Consequential amendments of subordinate legislation
59. Financial provisions
60. Extent
61. Commencement
62. Short title
Sch.3 *Claimants Dependent on Drugs etc. (repealed)*

An Act to amend the law relating to social security; to make provision enabling disabled people to be given greater control over the way in which certain public services are provided for them; to amend the law relating to child support; to make provision about the registration of births; and for connected purposes. [12th November 2009]

Parliamentary procedure: regulations imposing work-related activity requirements on lone parents of children under 7

1.884   **8.** [¹ *Repealed.*]

AMENDMENT

1. Welfare Reform Act 2012 Sch.14(5) para.1 (April 29, 2013).

Jobseeker's allowance and employment and support allowance: drugs

Claimants dependent on drugs etc.

1.885   **11.** [¹ *Repealed.*]

AMENDMENT

1. Welfare Reform Act 2012 ss.60(3), 150(2)(b) (May 8, 2012).

Contributory jobseeker's allowance and employment and support allowance

Conditions for contributory employment and support allowance

1.886   **13.**—(1) Paragraph 1 of Schedule 1 to the Welfare Reform Act 2007 (c. 5) (employment and support allowance: conditions relating to national insurance) is amended as follows.

(2)–(5) *amendments made by these subsections have been embodied in the current text of Sch.1 to the WRA 2007*

GENERAL NOTE

1.887   The changes effected from November 1, 2010 by this section and the regulations made under it, significantly tighten the contribution conditions for CESA by requiring a more recent and stronger connection with the world of work. It does so in that the first condition can from then only be satisfied in one of the last *two* (rather than three) tax years (April 6–April 5) complete before the start of the relevant benefit year (early January) (as with JSA); and by raising the requisite level of earnings in the tax year relied on to 26 (rather than 25) times that year's lower earnings limit. Moreover, since the conditions now only count earnings at that lower earnings limit (ignoring earnings in excess of it) new claimants will have to have worked for at least 26 weeks in one of the last two tax years (in effect each week's work at or above the LEL generates in essence one "contribution" (a virtual equivalent of the old regime of NI stamps) towards the target of 26 contributions, and has redolence with the earliest years of the National Insurance scheme operative from 1913 which worked on "flat-rate" contributions. Prior to these amendments, when the level was 25 times the LEL and the scheme looked also to earnings between the lower and upper earnings limits, a high-earner could qualify on less than four weeks work in the tax year and someone at the national minimum wage could qualify in about 12 weeks. The relevant regulations made under subss.(3) and (3A) are the Social Security (Contribution Conditions for Jobseeker's Allowance and Employment and Support Allowance) Regulations 2010 (SI 2010/2446), and amendments effected by them have been taken into account in producing the current text of the ESA Regulations.

Abolition of adult dependency increases

Maternity allowance and carer's allowance

15.—(1) The following provisions of the Social Security Contributions and Benefits Act 1992 (c. 4) ("the Benefits Act") are omitted on 6 April 2010—
   (a) section 82 (maternity allowance: increase for adult dependants); and
   (b) section 90 (carer's allowance: increase for adult dependants).

1.888

(2) Nothing in subsection (1) or Part 2 of Schedule 7 applies in relation to—
   (a) the amount of a maternity allowance payable for a maternity allowance period (within the meaning of section 35(2) of the Benefits Act) which begins before 6 April 2010 but ends on or after that date, or
   (b) the amount of a carer's allowance payable to a qualifying person at any time on or after 6 April 2010 but before the appropriate date.

(3) In subsection (2)(b)—
"a qualifying person" means a person who—
   (a) has, before 6 April 2010, made a claim for an increase in a carer's allowance under section 90 of the Benefits Act; and
   (b) immediately before that date is either entitled to the increase claimed or a beneficiary to whom section 92 of the Benefits Act applies in respect of that increase (continuation of awards where fluctuating earnings);
"the appropriate date" means whichever is the earlier of—
   (a) 6 April 2020; and
   (b) the date when the qualifying person ceases to be either entitled to that increase or a beneficiary to whom section 92 of the Benefits Act applies in respect of that increase.

Miscellaneous

37. Minor amendments

1.889   (1) Sections 80 and 81 of the Benefits Act (which continue to have effect in certain cases despite their repeal by the Tax Credits Act 2002 (c.21)) are to have effect as if the references in those sections to a child or children included references to a qualifying young person or persons.

(2) "Qualifying young person" has the same meaning as in Part 9 of the Benefits Act.

(3)—*amendments made by this subsection have been taken into account in Vol. III*

(4) Despite the provision made by the Welfare Reform Act 2007 (Commencement No. 6 and Consequential Provisions) Order 2008 (S.I. 2008/ 787), paragraph 9(7) and (8) of Schedule 3 to the Welfare Reform Act 2007 (c.5) (which amend sections 88 and 89 of the Benefits Act) are deemed not to be in force by virtue of the provision made by that order at any time after the passing of this Act.

(5) In this section "the Benefits Act" means the Social Security Contributions and Benefits Act 1992 (c.4).

PART 5

GENERAL

Consequential amendments of subordinate legislation

1.890   **57.**—(1) The Secretary of State may by regulations made by statutory instrument make such provision amending or revoking any instrument made under any other Act before the passing of this Act as appears to the Secretary of State to be appropriate in consequence of any provision of this Act, other than a provision contained in Part 2.

(2) Regulations under this section may include—

(a) transitional provisions or savings, and

(b) provision conferring a discretion on any person.

(3) A statutory instrument containing regulations under this section is subject to annulment in pursuance of a resolution of either House of Parliament.

Repeals and revocations

1.891   **58.**—(1) Schedule 7 contains repeals and revocations.

(2) *Lists repeals and revocations in Pt 2 of that Schedule (made in consequence of s.15(1)) which have effect on April 6, 2010. They have been incorporated in the text of the legislation in the appropriate Volume in this series*

(3) The repeal in that Part of paragraph 9 of Part 4 of Schedule 4 to the Social Security Contributions and Benefits Act 1992 is not to be taken as affecting the operation of article 3 of the Tax Credits Act 2002 (Commencement No. 3 and Transitional Provisions and Savings) Order 2003 (S.I. 2003/ 938) (savings in relation to the abolition of child dependency increases).

Financial provisions

59.—(1) There is to be paid out of money provided by Parliament—   1.892
  (a) any expenditure incurred in consequence of this Act by a Minister of the Crown, a government department or the Registrar General for England and Wales, and
  (b) any increase attributable to this Act in the sums payable under any other Act out of money so provided.

(2) There is to be paid into the Consolidated Fund any increase attributable to this Act in the sums payable into that Fund under any other Act.

Extent

60.—(1) The following provisions of this Act extend to England and   1.893
Wales, Scotland and Northern Ireland—
  section 24 and Schedule 4 (loss of benefit provisions);
  section 36 (power to rename council tax benefit); and
  this section and sections 61 and 62.

(2) Section 56 and Schedule 6 (birth registration) extend to England and Wales only.

(3) Subject to subsection (4), the other provisions of this Act extend to England and Wales and Scotland only.

(4) Any amendment, repeal or revocation made by this Act has the same extent as the enactment to which it relates.

(5) Subsection (4) is subject to paragraph 20(2) of Schedule 6.

Commencement

61.—(1) The following provisions of this Act come into force on the day   1.894
on which this Act is passed—
  sections 1 and 2;
  section 8;
  section 11;
  section 23;
  sections 27 and 28;
  section 37;
  section 57;
  sections 59 and 60;
  this section;
  section 62; and
  Schedule 3.

(2) The following provisions of this Act come into force at the end of the period of 2 months beginning with the day on which this Act is passed—
  section 15;
  section 34;
  Part 2;
  section 58(2) and (3); and
  Part 2 of Schedule 7 so far as relating to the repeals and revocation mentioned in section 58(2).

(3) The other provisions of this Act come into force on such day as the Secretary of State may by order made by statutory instrument appoint.

(4) An order under subsection (3) may—

(a) appoint different days for different purposes and in relation to different areas;

(b) make such provision as the Secretary of State considers necessary or expedient for transitory, transitional or saving purposes in connection with the coming into force of any provision falling within that subsection.

(5) Before making an order under subsection (3) in relation to any provision of Part 1 of Schedule 6 (birth registration), the Secretary of State must consult the Registrar General for England and Wales.

Short title

1.895 **62.**—This Act may be cited as the Welfare Reform Act 2009

SCHEDULE 3

CLAIMANTS DEPENDENT ON DRUGS ETC.

1.896 [¹ *Repealed.*]

REPEALS

1. Welfare Reform Act 2012 ss.60(3), 150(2)(b) (May 8, 2012).

Welfare Reform Act 2012

(2012 C. 5)

SECTIONS REPRODUCED

PART 3

OTHER BENEFIT CHANGES

Industrial Injuries

1.897 64.   Injuries arising before 5 July 1948
66.   Trainees

PART 4

PERSONAL INDEPENDENCE PAYMENT

Personal independence payment

77.   Personal independence payment   1.898
78.   Daily living component
79.   Mobility component
80.   Ability to carry out daily living activities or mobility activities
81.   Required period condition: further provision

Entitlement and payability: further provision

82.   Terminal illness   1.899
83.   Persons of pensionable age
84.   No entitlement to daily living component where UK is not competent state
85.   Care home residents
86.   Hospital in-patients
87.   Prisoners and detainees

Supplementary

88.   Claims, awards and information   1.900
89.   Report to Parliament

General

90.   Abolition of disability living allowance   1.901
91.   Amendments
92.   Power to make supplementary and consequential provision
93.   Transitional
94.   Regulations
95.   Interpretation of Part 4

PART 3

OTHER BENEFIT CHANGES

Industrial Injuries

Injuries arising before 5 July 1948

64.—(1) and (2): *amendments made by these subsections have been taken into*   1.902
account in updating the legislative text in this Volume.
   (3) The Secretary of State may make regulations—
   (a) for, and in relation to, the payment of industrial injuries benefit to persons to whom, before the commencement of this section, compensation or benefits were payable under section 111 of, and Schedule 8 to, the Social Security Contributions and Benefits Act 1992;

(b) for claims for the payment of such compensation or benefit to be treated as claims for industrial injuries benefit.

(4) In subsection (3) "industrial injuries benefit" has the meaning given by section 122(1) of the Social Security Contributions and Benefits Act 1992.

(5) Regulations under this section are to be made by statutory instrument.

(6) A statutory instrument containing regulations under this section is subject to annulment in pursuance of a resolution of either House of Parliament.

GENERAL NOTE

1.903   This entered into force on October 30, 2012 for the purpose of making regulations and for all other purposes (the amendments effected by subss.(1) and (2)) on December 5, 2012.

From July 1948 until December 5, 2012 there was separate provision for State compensation to be paid for accidents and diseases at work occurring before July 5, 1948 through the "pre-1948 schemes: the Workmen's Compensation (Supplementation) Scheme 1982 and the Pneumoconiosis Byssinosis and Miscellaneous Diseases Benefit Scheme 1983. These two schemes are known collectively as the "pre-1948 schemes". This section repeals the legislation that maintains the existence of two separate schemes for providing State compensation for work injuries occurring before 1948.

This means that on or after December 5, 2012 all claims for State "no-fault" compensation for work injuries will be dealt with as claims under the main Industrial Injuries Disablement Benefit (IIDB) scheme regardless of when the disease or accident occurred. The Industrial Injuries Benefit (Injuries arising before July 5, 1948) Regulations 2012 (SI 2012/2743) (as amended) give further effect to this so that all claims for industrial injured will be made, decided and appealed in the same way regardless of the date of the accident or onset of the prescribed disease.

Trainees

1.904   **66.**—(1) *This inserted the new s.95A into SSCBA 1992 with effect from October 31, 2013.*

(2) *Omitted.*

(3) The Secretary of State may make regulations—

(a) for, and in relation to, the payment of industrial injuries benefit to persons to whom, before the commencement of this section, payments were payable under section 11(3) of the Employment and Training Act 1973;

(b) for claims for such payments to be treated as claims for industrial injuries benefit.

(4) In subsection (3) "industrial injuries benefit" has the meaning given by section 122(1) of the Social Security Contributions and Benefits Act 1992.

(5) Regulations under this section are to be made by statutory instrument.

(6) A statutory instrument containing regulations under this section is subject to annulment in pursuance of a resolution of either House of Parliament.

PART 4

PERSONAL INDEPENDENCE PAYMENT

Personal independence payment

Personal independence payment

77.—(1) An allowance known as personal independence payment is payable in accordance with this Part.

(2) A person's entitlement to personal independence payment may be an entitlement to—

(a) the daily living component (see section 78);

(b) the mobility component (see section 79); or

(c) both those components.

(3) A person is not entitled to personal independence payment unless the person meets prescribed conditions relating to residence and presence in Great Britain.

GENERAL NOTE

Personal independence payments replace Disability Living Allowance for claimants of working age. Like DLA this benefit is a non-contributory benefit for persons who are so disabled, mentally or physically, as to require assistance to lead a normal life or so disabled as not to be able to walk properly or to walk without guidance and support. Like DLA, it too, is composed of two components, a living component and a mobility component. PIP will not be payable to claimants under 16. Nor will it be payable to claimants over 65, or, in the case of women, those who are over pensionable age as defined in Sch.4 of the Pensions Act 1995 (as amended). DLA will continue as the disability benefit for those claimants aged less than 16. Attendance Allowance will be available for new claimants aged over 65. Those who are in receipt of PIP when they reach the age of 65 (or pensionable age as referred to above) will be able to continue in receipt of PIP so long as they continue otherwise to qualify.

A person may be entitled to PIP whether they are in or out of work; the qualifying condition is that they are so disabled in some respect that they require assistance to the requisite extent to enable them to live a normal life. Similarly a claimant for PIP may be in receipt of other benefits. Most commonly that will be Employment and Support Allowance which is awarded following an assessment of disability in relation to the claimant's ability to work. The test to be applied in relation to PIP is not the same as that for ESA, but where a claimant has claimed for both, the evidence used in relation to one may be relevant to the other. Similarly, a claimant for PIP may be in receipt of Carer's Allowance – the fact that they are able to care for another is relevant only in respect of the fact finding to be undertaken by a tribunal in determining whether the evidence before them, of the claimant's disability, is consistent with the care that he is providing, in just the same way that the evidence of disability must be consistent with the work done by a claimant who is in work. See *PB v SSWP (PIP)* [2017] UKUT 493 (AAC).

PIP was introduced for new claims during 2013. Claimants who are of working age and in receipt of DLA are being transferred to PIP by stages from 2013.

PIP is intended to achieve broadly the same or a similar coverage of disability as that provided by DLA though some of the standards to be applied may be stricter. In a few cases a claim may succeed for PIP when it would fail for DLA. The chief difference will be in the way that an assessment of that disability is made and in the fact that almost all awards are intended to be for a fixed period and subject to review, rather than an award for life as was usual for DLA. Some of the words and

1.905

1.906

phrases used to define entitlement to PIP are the same or similar to those used for DLA. To that extent, decisions that have been made in relation to DLA may be relevant to PIP.

1.907   In *BTC v SSWP* [2015] UKUT 155 (AAC) the tribunals hearing appeals in relation to claims for PIP are advised that some of the procedural principles that have developed in relation to claims for DLA are likely to be applicable also to PIP appeals. For example in the instant case the tribunal had reduced the claimant's entitlement in a case where she had appealed for an increase in the award. The argument adopted by the FTT had not been raised by the respondent at all. Judge Bano, in the UT, makes the point that such a course of action should be taken with caution and possibly only after an adjournment to enable the parties to prepare fully for that argument. In this case the tribunal had proceeded after warning that her appeal might result in a loss of benefit, but the claimant had declined to withdraw. Another principle that is likely to be adopted in PIP cases is that which has been applied to renewal claims (or even fresh claims that follow a recent award) in which the tribunal is minded to reduce or to remove entitlement to benefit. In those cases it has been held that the tribunal has a duty to make clear the reasons why that has been the result of the appeal. (See *R(M)* 1/96 and cases following it including most recently *AB v SSWP* [2015] UKUT 89 (AAC)). This situation may be expected to arise more frequently in relation to PIP awards because, although DWP have now accepted that some awards should be made for an indefinite period, most will still be of limited duration. And note *BB v SSWP (PIP)* [2017] UKUT 506 (AAC), where the tribunal had failed to explain its reasons for a reduced award on a renewal claim.

     The correct approach to be followed in such cases where the claimant may be in receipt of, or at least claiming, both parts of PIP is considered again in *ET v SSWP (PIP)* [2017] UKUT 478 (AAC). Judge Wright suggests, following that earlier case law and *Hooper v SSWP* [2007] EWCA Civ 495 in the Court of Appeal, that the correct approach is to determine first, if an issue is raised on the appeal; if it is, then the tribunal must give its attention to it, but if it is not raised the tribunal may still consider it, but in doing so must act consciously and judicially and must give adequate warning and explanation to the claimant of their reasons for doing so. On a related matter Judge Hemingway has pointed out in *KKL v SSWP (PIP)* [2018] UKUT 17 (AAC) that where a concession is made by a claimant that matter no longer remains as an issue in the appeal, but, for that reason where the concession is made by an unrepresented claimant the tribunal must take care to ensure that the claimant does so having properly understood the consequences of their action.

     In *KM v SSWP (PIP)* [2018] UKUT 296 (AAC) Judge Rowland adopted a novel approach to the problem that arises where the claimant has appealed to the UT on a decision where they have been successful in claiming one component of PIP and is appealing only against refusal of the other. If the judge in the UT upholds that appeal, but directs that there should be a rehearing of the matter before a fresh tribunal, the claimant may lose their income from the part to which they are entitled pending the outcome of the whole appeal. He observes that the ability of DWP to make payment on account of benefit is more limited in relation to PIP. In this case he agreed, unusually, to set aside only that part of the decision which he found to be wrong in law and return that part to an FTT to, in effect, complete the decision. Note, however, that he does warn that this course will be appropriate only in certain cases because it does risk decisions as to entitlement being made at different times and possibly on inconsistent views of the facts.

Subsection (3)

1.908   Conditions as to residence and presence are prescribed in Pt 4 of the Social Security (Personal Independence Payments) Regulations 2013.

Daily living component

1.909   **78.**—(1) A person is entitled to the daily living component at the standard rate if—

(a) the person's ability to carry out daily living activities is limited by the person's physical or mental condition; and

(b) the person meets the required period condition.

(2) A person is entitled to the daily living component at the enhanced rate if—

(a) the person's ability to carry out daily living activities is severely limited by the person's physical or mental condition; and

(b) the person meets the required period condition.

(3) In this section, in relation to the daily living component—

(a) "the standard rate" means such weekly rate as may be prescribed;

(b) "the enhanced rate" means such weekly rate as may be prescribed.

(4) In this Part "daily living activities" means such activities as may be prescribed for the purposes of this section.

(5) See sections 80 and 81 for provision about determining—

(a) whether the requirements of subsection (1)(a) or (2)(a) above are met;

(b) whether a person meets "the required period condition" for the purposes of subsection (1)(b) or (2)(b) above.

(6) This section is subject to the provisions of this Part, or regulations under it, relating to entitlement to the daily living component (see in particular sections 82 (persons who are terminally ill) and 83 (persons of pensionable age)).

GENERAL NOTE

The daily living component will be paid at one of two rates; at a standard rate if **1.910** the claimant's ability to accomplish daily living activities is limited to the requisite extent and at an enhanced rate if their ability to do so is limited severely. Daily living activities are defined by regulation—see the Personal Independence Payment Regulations 2013 Sch.1, part. 2.

The claimant must be disabled "physically or mentally". These words have been the subject of decisions in relation to DLA—see *R(DLA)3/06.*There it was decided that it was not necessary for the claimant to have a diagnosis of a specific disease or medical condition, but only to show that his limited ability had some cause that was either physical or mental. Physical, in this context, will mean anything connected with the claimant's body including experiencing sensation such as pain or dizziness, while mental, includes any mental health condition or intellectual or cognitive impairment. But the cause must be some "condition" and that will mean something more than just a defect of character or irresponsible behaviour. The line that has been drawn in relation to DLA for claims based on alcoholism is between those where the claimant can be said to be able to desist in his behaviour and those where he is compelled by an addiction that he cannot reasonably be expected to control. (Though even where alcoholism is an addiction, care should be taken in examining how much of the time the claimant is so affected as to need assistance etc.).

The extent to which the claimant is limited in doing those activities will be measured by their ability to achieve the tasks listed in the PIP Regulations. This will be assessed from the information provided by the claimant (see reg.8 of the PIP Regs) and, where the claimant is called upon to attend what is referred to in the regulations as a consultation, (see reg.9 of the PIP Regs) by the results observed in that consultation.

For the purposes of administering PIP the decision makers will be known as Case Managers (CM). The consultation will be undertaken with a Health Professional (HP) engaged by one of the companies that will work under a contract made with DWP.

Each of the activities prescribed in Pt 2 of the schedule to the PIP Regs has a range of descriptors. Each descriptor has a point score and the points for each activity are aggregated to measure the claimant's degree of disability. A "score" of eight points qualifies the claimant for PIP at the standard rate and a total of 12 for the enhanced rate.

Subsection (1)(b)

1.911
"the required period condition" is defined by reg.12 of the PIP Regs made in accordance with s.81 below.

Mobility component

1.912
79.—(1) A person is entitled to the mobility component at the standard rate if—

(a) the person is of or over the age prescribed for the purposes of this subsection;

(b) the person's ability to carry out mobility activities is limited by the person's physical or mental condition; and

(c) the person meets the required period condition.

(2) A person is entitled to the mobility component at the enhanced rate if—

(a) the person is of or over the age prescribed for the purposes of this subsection;

(b) the person's ability to carry out mobility activities is severely limited by the person's physical or mental condition; and

(c) the person meets the required period condition.

(3) In this section, in relation to the mobility component—

(a) "the standard rate" means such weekly rate as may be prescribed;

(b) "the enhanced rate" means such weekly rate as may be prescribed.

(4) In this Part "mobility activities" means such activities as may be prescribed for the purposes of this section.

(5) See sections 80 and 81 for provision about determining—

(a) whether the requirements of subsections (1)(b) or (2)(b) above are met;

(b) whether a person meets "the required period condition" for the purposes of subsections (1)(c) or (2)(c) above.

(6) This section is subject to the provisions of this Part, or regulations under it, relating to entitlement to the mobility component (see in particular sections 82 and 83).

(7) Regulations may provide that a person is not entitled to the mobility component for a period (even though the requirements in subsections (1) or (2) are met) in prescribed circumstances where the person's condition is such that during all or most of the period the person is unlikely to benefit from enhanced mobility.

GENERAL NOTE

1.913
The mobility component will be paid at one of two rates; at the standard rate if a person's mobility activity is limited to the requisite extent and at an enhanced rate if it is limited severely. Mobility activities are defined by regulation—see Personal Independence Payment Regulations 2013 Sch.1 Pt 3.

The extent to which the claimant is limited in doing those activities will be measured by their ability to achieve the tasks listed there and this will be assessed by the CM from the information provided by the claimant—see reg.8 of the PIP Regs). Where the claimant is called upon to attend what is referred to in the regulations as a consultation (see reg.9 of the PIP Regs) by the results observed in that consultation.

Each of the activities prescribed in Pt 3 of the schedule to the PIP Regs has a range of descriptors. Each descriptor has a point score and the points for each activity are aggregated to measure the claimant's degree of disability. A score of eight points qualifies the claimant for the mobility component at the standard rate and a total of 12 for the enhanced rate.

The claimant's limitation must be by reason of their "mental or physical condition"—(see the note to s.78 above for the meaning of this phrase). The mobility component of DLA is limited in most cases to the claimant's physical disability. For PIP a mental disability will suffice so long as the claimant satisfies the assessment procedure; so an agoraphobic should now qualify at the standard rate. (See Sch.1 Activity 1 Descriptor e).

Subsection (1) (a)

PIP is presently limited to claimants of 16 years and over. This provision seems to have been included in anticipation of extending PIP, eventually, to include children. **1.914**

Subsection (1)(c)

"the required period condition" is defined by reg.12 of the PIP Regs made in accordance with s.81 below. **1.915**

Subsection (7)

Regulations may be made to provide that entitlement could be withheld where a claimant is unlikely to benefit from enhanced mobility during all or most of the period. (cf. reg.12(8) of the Disability Living Allowance Regulations). **1.916**

Ability to carry out daily living activities or mobility activities

80.—(1) For the purposes of this Part, the following questions are to be determined in accordance with regulations— **1.917**
  (a) whether a person's ability to carry out daily living activities is limited by the person's physical or mental condition;
  (b) whether a person's ability to carry out daily living activities is severely limited by the person's physical or mental condition;
  (c) whether a person's ability to carry out mobility activities is limited by the person's physical or mental condition;
  (d) whether a person's ability to carry out mobility activities is severely limited by the person's physical or mental condition.
  (2) Regulations must make provision for determining, for the purposes of each of sections 78(1) and (2) and 79(1) and (2), whether a person meets "the required period condition" (see further section 81).
  (3) Regulations under this section—
  (a) must provide for the questions mentioned in subsections (1) and (2) to be determined, except in prescribed circumstances, on the basis of an assessment (or repeated assessments) of the person;
  (b) must provide for the way in which an assessment is to be carried out;
  (c) may make provision about matters which are, or are not, to be taken into account in assessing a person.
  (4) The regulations may, in particular, make provision—
  (a) about the information or evidence required for the purpose of determining the questions mentioned in subsections (1) and (2);
  (b) about the way in which that information or evidence is to be provided;
  (c) requiring a person to participate in such a consultation, with a person approved by the Secretary of State, as may be determined

under the regulations (and to attend for the consultation at a place, date and time determined under the regulations).

(5) The regulations may include provision—

(a) for a negative determination to be treated as made if a person fails without a good reason to comply with a requirement imposed under subsection (4);

(b) about what does or does not constitute a good reason for such a failure;

(c) about matters which are, or are not, to be taken into account in determining whether a person has a good reason for such a failure.

(6) In subsection (5)(a) a "negative determination" means a determination that a person does not meet the requirements of—

(a) section 78(1)(a) and (b) or (2)(a) and (b) (daily living component);

(b) section 79(1)(a) to (c) or (2)(a) to (c) (mobility component).

GENERAL NOTE

1.918   Regulations made under this section are the Personal Independence Payment Regulations 2013 (SI 2013/377).

Required period condition: further provision

1.919   **81.**—(1) Regulations under section 80(2) must provide for the question of whether a person meets "the required period condition" for the purposes of section 78(1) or (2) or 79(1) or (2) to be determined by reference to—

(a) whether, as respects every time in the previous three months, it is likely that if the relevant ability had been assessed at that time that ability would have been determined to be limited or (as the case may be) severely limited by the person's physical or mental condition; and

(b) whether, as respects every time in the next nine months, it is likely that if the relevant ability were to be assessed at that time that ability would be determined to be limited or (as the case may be) severely limited by the person's physical or mental condition.

(2) In subsection (1) "the relevant ability" means—

(a) in relation to section 78(1) or (2), the person's ability to carry out daily living activities;

(b) in relation to section 79(1) or (2), the person's ability to carry out mobility activities.

(3) In subsection (1)—

(a) "assessed" means assessed in accordance with regulations under section 80;

(b) "the previous 3 months" means the three months ending with the prescribed date;

(c) "the next 9 months" means the nine months beginning with the day after that date.

(4) Regulations under section 80(2) may provide that in prescribed cases the question of whether a person meets "the required period condition" for the purposes of sections 78(1) or (2) or 79(1) or (2)—

(a) is not to be determined in accordance with the provision made by virtue of subsections (1) to (3) above;

(b) is to be determined in accordance with provision made in relation to those cases by the regulations.

GENERAL NOTE

Regulations made under this section are regs 12 and 13 of the Personal   **1.920**
Independence Payment Regulations 2013 (SI 2013/377).

To qualify for either component under these regulations the claimant must be able to show that he would have fulfilled the requirements of an assessment (at which ever rate of benefit is appropriate) for the whole of a past period of three months and that he may be expected to continue to satisfy that requirement for a further nine months.

Entitlement and payability: further provision

Terminal illness

82.—(1) This section applies to a person who—   **1.921**
(a) is terminally ill; and
(b) has made a claim for personal independence payment expressly on the ground of terminal illness.

(2) A person to whom this section applies is entitled to the daily living component at the enhanced rate (and accordingly section 78(1) and (2) do not apply to such a person).

(3) Section 79(1)(c) and (2)(c) (required period condition for mobility component) do not apply to a person to whom this section applies.

(4) For the purposes of this section a person is "terminally ill" at any time if at that time the person suffers from a progressive disease and the person's death in consequence of that disease can reasonably be expected within six months.

(5) For the purposes of this section, where—
(a) a person purports to make a claim for personal independence payment on behalf of another, and
(b) the claim is made expressly on the ground that the person on whose behalf it purports to be made is terminally ill,
that person is to be regarded as making the claim despite its being made without that person's knowledge or authority.

(6) In subsection (2) "the enhanced rate" has the meaning given by section 78(3).

GENERAL NOTE

A claimant will qualify automatically for the daily living component of PIP, at   **1.922**
the enhanced rate, if their claim is made expressly on the ground that they are suffering from a terminal illness. A person is terminally ill if they are suffering from a progressive disease and their death from that disease can be reasonably expected within six months.

A claim for benefit on the ground that the claimant is terminally ill is made by a special, fast-track procedure. Whether or not a claimant is terminally ill will be determined by the CM, but only after the claim and the information received, has been referred to the HP for a report. This report should be returned to the CM within 48 hours.

Guidance issued to the HP requires that they must find, on the balance of probabilities, that it is "more likely than not" that the claimant will die within six months. This seems a more stringent test than that which has applied in relation to DLA where the same words are used. For DLA it seems that a claim would succeed so long as death within six months was not unlikely. A reasonable expectation (which is what the section requires) should not necessarily require a finding of probability. Where medical opinion is that the claimant's death within six months "is quite possible, though they might live longer", it seems correct, as a matter of ordinary language to say that their death within six months "can reasonably be expected". Decisions on this matter are likely to turn on the way in which the question has been put to the claimant's consultant and by any further inquiry made by the HP.

It is not necessary for such a claimant to fulfil a qualifying period so that their claim, if successful, is paid from the time that it is made.

Although it remains necessary for a claimant to show that they are present and habitually resident in Great Britain it will not be necessary for them to show that they have been present for a period amounting to 104 weeks out of the preceding three years. (See regs 16 and 21 of the Personal Independence Regulations 2013 (SI 2013/377)).

A terminally ill claimant does not qualify automatically for the mobility component; they must satisfy the assessment criteria in the usual way, but, if successful, they will be exempted from the need to fulfil a qualifying period for that component too.

A claim on the ground of terminal illness can be made by another person without the consent, or even the knowledge, of the person on whose behalf it is made—see subs.(5) above.

Persons of pensionable age

1.923   **83.**—(1) A person is not entitled to the daily living component or the mobility component for any period after the person reaches the relevant age.

(2) In subsection (1) "the relevant age" means—

(a) pensionable age (within the meaning given by the rules in paragraph 1 of Schedule 4 to the Pensions Act 1995); or

(b) if higher, 65.

(3) Subsection (1) is subject to such exceptions as may be provided by regulations.

GENERAL NOTE

1.924   Entitlement to PIP by virtue of a new claim will generally cease when a claimant reaches the age of 65. However, until the end of 2018 a woman will continue to reach the "relevant age" when they reach pensionable age. Pensionable age for women is advanced progressively in accordance with the provisions of Sch.4 of the Pensions Act 1995, but will reach 65 by the end of 2018.

Claimants who have an existing award of either or both components of PIP when they reach the relevant age will continue to be entitled in accordance with regs 25–27 of the Personal Independence Payment Regulations (SI 2013/377).

No entitlement to daily living component where UK is not competent state

1.925   **84.**—(1) A person to whom a relevant EU Regulation applies is not entitled to the daily living component for a period unless during that period the United Kingdom is competent for payment of sickness benefits in cash to the person for the purposes of Chapter 1 of Title III of the Regulation in question.

(2) Each of the following is a "relevant EU Regulation" for the purposes of this section—

(a) Council Regulation (EC) No.1408/71 of 14 June 1971[1, as amended from time to time,] on the application of social security schemes to employed persons, to self-employed persons and to members of their families moving within the Community;

(b) Regulation (EC) No.883/2004 of the European Parliament and of the Council of 29 April 2004 [¹, as amended from time to time,] on the coordination of social security systems.

AMENDMENTS

1. Social Security (Updating of EU References) (Amendment) Regulations (SI 2018/1084) reg. 3 (November 15, 2018).

Care home residents

85.—(1) Regulations may provide that no amount in respect of personal independence payment which is attributable to entitlement to the daily living component is payable in respect of a person for a period when the person meets the condition in subsection (2).

(2) The condition is that the person is a resident of a care home in circumstances in which any of the costs of any qualifying services provided for the person are borne out of public or local funds by virtue of a specified enactment.

(3) In this section "care home" means an establishment that provides accommodation together with nursing or personal care.

(4) The following are "qualifying services" for the purposes of subsection (2)—

(a) accommodation;

(b) board;

(c) personal care;

(d) such other services as may be prescribed.

(5) The reference in subsection (2) to a "specified enactment" is to an enactment which is specified for the purposes of that subsection by regulations or is of a description so specified.

(6) The power to specify an enactment for the purposes of subsection (2) includes power to specify it only in relation to its application for a particular purpose.

(7) In this section "enactment" includes an enactment comprised in an Act of the Scottish Parliament or in an instrument made under such an Act.

GENERAL NOTE

The regulations made under this section are regs 28, 30 and 32 of the Personal Independence Payment Regulations 2013 (SI 2013/377).

Hospital in-patients

86.—(1) Regulations may provide as mentioned in either or both of the following paragraphs—

(a) that no amount in respect of personal independence payment which is attributable to entitlement to the daily living component is payable in respect of a person for a period when the person meets the condition in subsection (2);

(b) that no amount in respect of personal independence payment which is attributable to entitlement to the mobility component is payable in respect of a person for a period when the person meets the condition in subsection (2).

1.926

1.927

1.928

429

(2) The condition is that the person is undergoing medical or other treatment as an in-patient at a hospital or similar institution in circumstances in which any of the costs of the treatment, accommodation and any related services provided for the person are borne out of public funds.

(3) For the purposes of subsection (2) the question of whether any of the costs of medical or other treatment, accommodation and related services provided for a person are borne out of public funds is to be determined in accordance with the regulations.

GENERAL NOTE

1.929   The regulations made under this section are regs 29, 30 and 32 of the Personal Independence Payment Regulations 2013 (SI 2013/377). This section (and regulation 29 made under it) were held not to discriminate unjustifiably by the withholding of the mobility component so as to be in breach of art.14 of the European Convention on Human Rights (and hence of the Human Rights Act 1998) in *MH v SSWP (PIP)* [2017] UKUT 424 (AAC; [2018] AACR 15. The claimant was resident in a Neurodisability centre which, it was agreed, was similar to a publicly funded hospital. Judge Lane held that neither disabled claimants living at home, nor those living in a care home, were sufficiently similar to constitute valid comparators for the claimant, but, even if the latter group were to be considered as comparators, she also held that the difference in treatment under this section and regulation 29 would be justified on the ground that payment of the mobility component of PIP would amount to double provision from public funds.

Prisoners and detainees

1.930   **87.**—Except to the extent that regulations provide otherwise, no amount in respect of personal independence payment is payable in respect of a person for a period during which the person is undergoing imprisonment or detention in legal custody.

GENERAL NOTE

1.931   The regulations made under this section are regs 31 and 32 of the Personal Independence Payments Regulations 2013 (SI 2013/377).

Under these regulations a claimant who is in receipt of PIP at the time he enters prison will remain entitled for the first 28 days of that imprisonment.

Supplementary

Claims, awards and information

1.932   **88.**—(1) A person is not entitled to personal independence payment for any period before the date on which a claim for it is made or treated as made by that person or on that person's behalf.

(2) An award of personal independence payment is to be for a fixed term except where the person making the award considers that a fixed term award would be inappropriate.

(3) In deciding whether a fixed term award would be inappropriate, that person must have regard to guidance issued by the Secretary of State.

(4) Information supplied under this Part is to be taken for all purposes to be information relating to social security.

PIP, like DLA, is not payable in respect of any period before a claim for it is made, though the period of three months before the date of claim can count as the qualifying period.

Subsection (2) provides that payment of benefit is to be for a fixed term unless the DM considers that a fixed term is inappropriate. In *RS v SSWP* [2016] UKUT 85 (AAC) Judge Mitchell decided that this decision by a DM is appealable. The claimant, who had been in receipt of DLA, considered that his condition had worsened and informed the DWP of a change of circumstances. He was invited to apply for PIP under the transitional provisions. That claim succeeded and he was awarded benefit at a rate that was higher than his previous entitlement—in fact at the highest possible rate. But his DLA award had been indefinite and new award was for a fixed term of three years. The claimant appealed against the decision to award only for a fixed term (the appeal was also against the date at which his increased entitlement commenced, but that part of the decision was upheld). The FTT had struck out his appeal against the length of his award, but Judge Mitchell held that the decision to make that award and the exercise of the discretion in subs.(2) which requires the DM to consider whether the fixed term award might be "inappropriate" were appealable and that reasons should be produced to the FTT to justify that decision. The judge observed that the permanence or otherwise of the claimant's condition and the relative ease with which an application for review could be taken were factors to which the FTT might have regard. He observed also that the FTT should have regard to the guidance provided for under subs.(3), but with the caveat that it was only guidance and not the law.

This decision was affirmed by Judge Hemingway in *GT v SSWP (PIP)* [2019] UKUT 30 (AAC). The judge thought that more emphasis need be given to the possibility that an appeal might be made solely on the basis that an award had been made for a fixed term. The DWP has since modified their practice and accepted that on-going awards may be more appropriate in some cases.

Report to Parliament

89.—[*omitted*]

General

Abolition of disability living allowance

90.—Sections 71 to 76 of the Social Security Contributions and Benefits Act 1992 (Disability Living Allowance) are repealed.

This provision is not yet in force and, presumably, will not be brought into force until all claims to DLA are replaced by this or another benefit.

Amendments

91.—[*omitted*].

Power to make supplementary and consequential provision

92.—(1) Regulations may make such consequential, supplementary or incidental provision in relation to any provision of this Part as the Secretary of State considers appropriate.

1.933

1.934

1.935

1.936

1.937

1.938

431

(2) Regulations under this section may—

(a) amend, repeal or revoke any primary or secondary legislation passed or made before the day on which this Act is passed, or

(b) amend or repeal any provision of an Act passed on or after that day but in the same session of Parliament.

(3) In this section—

(a) "primary legislation" means an Act or Act of the Scottish Parliament;

(b) "secondary legislation" means any instrument made under primary legislation.

Transitional

1.939   **93.**—(1) Regulations may make such provision as the Secretary of State considers necessary or expedient in connection with the coming into force of any provision of this Part.

(2) Schedule 10 (transitional provision for introduction of personal independence payment) has effect.

GENERAL NOTE

1.940   The regulations made under this section and in accordance with Sch.10, are the Personal Independence Payment (Transitional Provisions) Regulations 2013 (SI 2013/387).

Regulations

1.941   **94.**—(1) Regulations under this Part are to be made by the Secretary of State.

(2) A power to make regulations under this Part may be exercised—

(a) so as to make different provision for different cases or purposes;

(b) in relation to all or only some of the cases or purposes for which it may be exercised.

(3) Such a power includes—

(a) power to make incidental, supplementary, consequential or transitional provision or savings;

(b) power to provide for a person to exercise a discretion in dealing with any matter.

(4) The power under subsection (2)(a) includes, in particular, power to make different provision for persons of different ages.

(5) Regulations under this Part are to be made by statutory instrument.

(6) A statutory instrument containing (whether alone or with other provision) any of the following—

(a) the first regulations under sections 78(4) or 79(4);

(b) the first regulations under section 80;

(c) the first regulations under that section containing provision about assessment of persons under the age of 16,

may not be made unless a draft of the instrument has been laid before, and approved by a resolution of, each House of Parliament.

(7) Any other statutory instrument containing regulations under this Part is subject to annulment in pursuance of a resolution of either House of Parliament.

GENERAL NOTE

The regulations made under this section are the Social Security (Personal Independence Payment) Regulations (SI 2013/377).

1.942

Interpretation of Part 4

95.—In this Part—

1.943

"daily living activities" has the meaning given by section 78(4);

"daily living component" means the daily living component of personal independence payment;

"mobility activities" has the meaning given by section 79(4);

"mobility component" means the mobility component of personal independence payment;

"prescribed" means prescribed by regulations.

Mesothelioma Act 2014

(2014 C.1)

ARRANGEMENT OF SECTIONS

Diffuse Mesothelioma Payment Scheme

1.944

1. Power to establish the scheme

Eligibility

2. Eligible people with diffuse mesothelioma
3. Eligible dependants

Payments and procedure

4. Payments
5. Applications and procedure
6. Reviews and appeals

Scheme administration

7. Scheme administration
8. Unauthorised disclosure of information: offence [*omitted*]
9. Unauthorised disclosure of information: penalties etc. [*omitted*]

Recovery of payments etc.

10. Power of scheme administrator to help people bring proceedings
11. Recovery of benefits etc from payments and recovery of payments

Relationship with other legislation

12.   Exclusion of payments under other legislation

Levy on insurers

13.   *The levy [omitted]*
14.   *Collecting information for purposes of levy [omitted]*

Insurance disputes

15.   *Technical Committee to decide certain insurance disputes [omitted]*
16.   *Challenging decisions of the Technical Committee [omitted]*

General

17.   *Regulations under this Act [omitted]*
18.   Defined terms used in more than one section of this Act
19.   Commencement
20.   Extent
21.   Short title

Schedule 1   *Recovery of benefits etc from payments and recovery of payments [omitted]*
Schedule 2   *Exclusion of payments under other legislation [omitted]*

An Act to establish a Diffuse Mesothelioma Payment Scheme and make related provision; and to make provision about the resolution of certain insurance disputes.

[30th January 2014]

GENERAL NOTE

1.945   The Mesothelioma Act 2014 paves the way for the Diffuse Mesothelioma Payment Scheme 2014, which is the third statutory scheme to provide a degree of compensation for victims of the asbestos-related cancer mesothelioma, outside the normal arrangements for personal injuries claims in the law of torts. The 2014 Act thus follows in the footsteps of the Pneumoconiosis etc. (Workers' Compensation) Act 1979 and, more recently, the Diffuse Mesothelioma Scheme 2008, established by the Child Maintenance and Other Payments Act 2008.

The Mesothelioma Act 2014 is essentially a State-driven but privately-funded measure which seeks to correct a significant market failure in the employers' liability (EL) insurance industry. It establishes a limited scheme of last resort to pay eligible applicants in mesothelioma cases who are unable either to find their employer or to trace their employer's EL insurer. Most employers carrying on business in Great Britain have been required, since January 1, 1972, to insure their liability to their employees for bodily injury or disease sustained in the course of their employment, as a result of the Employers' Liability (Compulsory Insurance) Act 1969, although EL insurance was also widespread, if not actually compulsory, before the 1969 Act. For many years now, proving that their employer acted in breach of their duty of care in negligence has been the least of the difficulties facing employees who have contracted mesothelioma. Thus, in practice, establishing liability is usually relatively straightforward for those who were exposed to asbestos in the workplace and who bring a civil claim. However, mesothelioma has a long latency period (typically 30-40 years) and by the time the worker is diagnosed with the disease, many years later, the relevant insurance records may have already been lost or destroyed. Thus a victim may be unable actually to recover compensation because no solvent employer remains to be sued, and the employee's solicitors may be unable to trace any insurer who was providing EL insurance cover to their employer at the material time. All this happens at a time that the victim is, literally, living on borrowed time—the average life expectancy from date of diagnosis is in the order of 9–12 months.

In February 2010, under the then Labour government, the DWP published a consultation document, seeking stakeholders' views on proposals for improving the process for tracing employment and insurance records and for providing access to compensation (DWP, *Accessing Compensation—Supporting people who need to trace Employers' Liability Insurance*). The Coalition Government's response to the consultation exercise was eventually published in July 2012 (DWP, *Accessing Compensation - Supporting people who need to trace Employers' Liability Insurance: Government response to consultation*). In that response the Government announced (p.8):

> "we propose setting up a support scheme for those people with mesothelioma who were exposed to asbestos through their employer's negligence and who remain unable to trace a liable insurer or employer.
>
> The proposed scheme will be funded by a levy on insurers currently writing EL policies. Payments from the scheme will be at a level set such that the overall amount received by the claimant will be somewhere between that offered by state benefits and average payouts from civil action. This will ensure that those who are able to trace an insurer remain incentivised to do so in order to claim full compensation."

The Mesothelioma Bill, which emerged from this consultation process, was introduced in the House of Lords on May 9, 2013 and received the Royal Assent on January 30, 2014. It is a UK-wide measure (s.20(1)). The long title declares that its purpose is "to establish a Diffuse Mesothelioma Payment Scheme and make related provision; and to make provision about the resolution of certain insurance disputes". The Act itself is essentially an enabling measure, which provides no hard-edged detail about the 2014 Scheme (see s.1(1)). However, the Act makes provision for both mandatory and optional elements in such a scheme (see s.1(2)). The mandatory elements of the scheme include both the right to request a review of a decision taken under the scheme (s.6(1)(a)) and a right of appeal to the First-tier Tribunal against a decision taken on a review (s.6(3)). Sections 2 and 3 of the Act set out the core eligibility criteria for the two categories of claimants, namely "eligible people with diffuse mesothelioma" and "eligible dependants" respectively. The remaining provisions of the Act deal with payments and procedure (ss.4-6), scheme administration (ss.7-9), recovery of payments (ss.10 and 11), relationship with other legislation (s.12), the levy on insurers (ss.13 and 14) and insurance disputes (ss.15 and 16), along with various general provisions (ss.17-21). Further and more detailed provision for the new scheme is contained in the Diffuse Mesothelioma Payment Scheme Regulations 2014 (SI 2014/916). For details of the levy imposed on EL insurers, see now the Diffuse Mesothelioma Payment Scheme (Levy) Regulations 2014 (SI 2014/2904).

1.946

It should be noted that the Mesothelioma Act 2014, unlike the 1979 and 2008 Acts, does *not* establish a no-fault scheme. Thus it is a condition of entitlement that "a relevant employer has negligently or in breach of statutory duty caused or permitted the person to be exposed to asbestos" (s.2(1)(a)). Similarly, the scheme administrator must "in considering an application, apply the normal civil standard of proof (the balance of probability) when deciding all matters of fact which require evidence to establish them" (Diffuse Mesothelioma Payment Scheme Regulations 2014, reg.5(3)(a)). The fact that the new scheme is to be paid for by a levy on existing EL insurers means that it is necessarily a compromise measure. Three aspects of the scheme proved to be particularly controversial during the debates in Parliament.

The first was the "cut-off", namely the fact that the new scheme is only available to those victims who were first diagnosed *after* July 25, 2012 (s.2(1)(b); this was the date of the publication of the Government response, whereas many argued that the relevant date should have been the issue of the original consultation document in 2010). The second concerned the levels of compensation, which were originally set at a ceiling representing 80 per cent of average civil compensation awards (but were subsequently increased to 100 per cent of such an average; see further the commentary to the Diffuse Mesothelioma Payment Scheme Regulations 2014 reg.19). The third was the decision to focus this scheme of last resort on mesothelioma, so excluding other asbestos-related cancers (notably asbestos-related lung cancer), let alone other long-tail occupational diseases where there are similar problems in locating a former employer and/or their EL insurer. For further analysis, see N. Wikeley, "Diffuse Mesothelioma Payment Scheme 2014" (2014) 21 J.S.S.L. 61–78.

Diffuse Mesothelioma Payment Scheme

Power to establish the scheme

1.947   **1.**—(1) The Secretary of State may by regulations establish a scheme called the Diffuse Mesothelioma Payment Scheme for making payments to—
> (a) eligible people with diffuse mesothelioma, and
> (b) eligible dependants of those who have died with diffuse mesothelioma.

(2) Later sections of this Act set out things that must be included in the scheme and some of the things that may be included.

Eligibility

Eligible people with diffuse mesothelioma

1.948   **2.**—(1) A person diagnosed with diffuse mesothelioma is eligible for a payment under the scheme if—
> (a) a relevant employer has negligently or in breach of statutory duty caused or permitted the person to be exposed to asbestos,
> (b) the person was first diagnosed with the disease on or after 25 July 2012,
> (c) the person has not brought an action for damages in respect of the disease against the relevant employer or any insurer with whom the employer maintained employers' liability insurance at the time of the person's exposure to asbestos,
> (d) the person is unable to bring an action for damages in respect of the disease against any employer of the person or any insurer with whom such an employer maintained employers' liability insurance (because they cannot be found or no longer exist or for any other reason), and
> (e) the person has not received damages or a specified payment in respect of the disease and is not eligible to receive a specified payment.

(2) In this section—
"first diagnosed" has the meaning to be given to it by the scheme;
"relevant employer" means an employer who, at the time of the person's exposure to asbestos—

(a) was required by the compulsory insurance legislation to maintain insurance covering any liability arising because of the exposure to asbestos, or

(b) would have been required by the compulsory insurance legislation to maintain insurance covering any liability arising because of the exposure to asbestos if the legislation had been in force at that time; "specified payment" has the meaning to be given to it by the scheme.

Eligible dependants

3.—(1) A dependant of a person who has died with diffuse mesothelioma is eligible for a payment under the scheme if —   1.949

(a) the person with the disease was eligible for a payment under the scheme (see section 2) but did not make an application in accordance with the scheme,

(b) no one has brought an action for damages in respect of the disease under the fatal accidents legislation, or on behalf of the estate of the person with the disease, against the relevant employer or any insurer with whom the employer maintained employers' liability insurance at the time of that person's exposure to asbestos,

(c) no one is able to bring an action for damages in respect of the disease under the fatal accidents legislation, or on behalf of the estate of the person with the disease, against any employer of that person or any insurer with whom such an employer maintained employers' liability insurance (because they cannot be found or no longer exist or for any other reason), and

(d) no one has received damages or a specified payment in respect of the disease or is eligible to receive a specified payment.

(2) Where a person who has died with diffuse mesothelioma is first diagnosed with the disease following his or her death and would have been eligible for a payment under the scheme if the diagnosis had been made immediately before the death, assume for the purposes of subsection (1)(a) that the person was eligible for a payment under the scheme.

(3) A person ceases to be an eligible dependant if the person gives notice in accordance with the scheme that he or she does not want a payment (and this may increase a payment for other dependants - see section 4(2)(b)).

(4) Where a person with diffuse mesothelioma died on or after 25 July 2012 but before this Act came into force, assume for the purposes of subsections (1)(a) and (2) that this Act has been in force since immediately before the death.

(5) In this section—

"first diagnosed" has the meaning to be given to it by the scheme;

"specified payment" has the meaning to be given to it by the scheme.

General note

Note that HMRC may disclose information held by them to a person who applies   1.950 for a payment under the Diffuse Mesothelioma Payment Scheme, on the basis that he or she is eligible for such a payment under s.3, for use in connection with the application (Deregulation Act 2015 s.85(1)(c)). Further note that in addition, and with effect from July 31, 2017, s.77 of the Digital Economy Act 2017 enables HMRC to share the name and address of an employer and associated reference numbers with the Employer Liability Tracing Office (ELTO) for the purpose of assisting with such claims. ELTO is a non-profit making company that maintains a database of insurance policies to enable employees to trace former or current employers and their insurers in order to obtain compensation for workplace injuries. It is anticipated that access to this information will help to improve the quality of the ELTO databases.

Payments and procedure

Payments

1.951   **4.**—(1) The amount of a payment under the scheme is to be determined in accordance with the scheme.

(2) The scheme—

(a) may provide for the amount of the payment to depend on the age of the person with diffuse mesothelioma, and

(b) must ensure that where there are two or more eligible dependants, the amount for each of them is the amount for a single eligible dependant divided by the number of eligible dependants in the case in question.

(3) The scheme may—

(a) make provision for payments to be made subject to conditions (including conditions as to how a payment may be used), and

(b) in particular, give the scheme administrator power to decide when to impose conditions or what conditions to impose.

(4) The scheme may make provision for payments to be repaid (in whole or in part) in specified circumstances.

(5) An amount that falls to be repaid under subsection (4) is recoverable by the scheme administrator as a debt.

(6) The scheme must provide that where an eligible person has made an application in accordance with the scheme and has died before the payment is made, the payment must be made to his or her personal representatives.

Applications and procedure

1.952   **5.**—(1) The scheme may deal with the procedure for the making and deciding of applications and, in particular, may—

(a) impose time limits for making an application or taking other steps;

(b) enable the scheme administrator to require a person to produce documents;

(c) make other provision about evidence.

(2) The scheme may enable a court to order a person to comply with a requirement to produce documents.

Reviews and appeals

1.953   **6.**—(1) The scheme—

(a) must give an applicant the right to request a review of a decision taken under the scheme, and

(b) may require or allow reviews in other circumstances.

(2) The scheme may contain provision about initiating and deciding reviews (including provision imposing time limits).

(3) The scheme must confer a right of appeal to the First-tier Tribunal against a decision taken on a review.

(4) In a case where a person makes an application and then dies, the reference in subsection (1)(a) to an applicant is to be read as a reference to his or her personal representatives.

Scheme administration

Scheme administration

7.—(1) The Secretary of State may—   1.954
(a) administer the scheme, or
(b) make arrangements for a body to administer the scheme.
(2) Arrangements under subsection (1)(b)—
(a) may include provision for payments by the Secretary of State;
(b) may allow the body to arrange for someone else to administer the scheme or any part of the scheme on behalf of the body;
(c) may include provision about bringing the arrangements to an end.
(3) Arrangements under subsection (1)(b) may be made with—
(a) a company formed by the Secretary of State under the Companies Act 2006 for that purpose,
(b) a body corporate established by the Secretary of State by regulations under this paragraph for that purpose, or
(c) any other body.
(4) A body administering the scheme in accordance with arrangements under subsection (1)(b) is not to be regarded as exercising functions of the Secretary of State or as acting on behalf of the Secretary of State.
(5) The Secretary of State may by regulations make transitional provision for when there is a change in the scheme administrator (including provision modifying the application of any enactment).
(6) For the purposes of this Act, a reference to administering the scheme includes carrying out any functions conferred by or under any enactment on the scheme administrator.

Sections 8 and 9 omitted.   1.955

Recovery of payments etc

Power of scheme administrator to help people bring proceedings

10.—(1) Where a payment is made under the scheme, the scheme   1.956
administrator may help a person to bring relevant proceedings (for example by conducting proceedings or by giving advice or financial help).
(2) "Relevant proceedings" means—
(a) proceedings by the person with diffuse mesothelioma against—
   (i) an employer for the negligence or breach of statutory duty mentioned in section 2(1)(a), or
   (ii) an insurer with whom the employer maintained insurance covering that liability,
(b) proceedings by any other person against the employer or insurer for damages under the fatal accidents legislation in respect of the death of the person with diffuse mesothelioma, or
(c) any appeal arising out of proceedings within paragraph (a) or (b).
(3) In subsection (2) a reference to a person includes a reference to his or her personal representatives.
(4) The scheme may include provision about the scheme administrator's functions under this section, including provision as to the circumstances in which the scheme administrator may help a person to bring proceedings.
(5) The Secretary of State may by regulations amend subsection (2) to

include other proceedings (which may be proceedings against someone other than an employer or insurer).

Recovery of benefits etc from payments and recovery of payments

1.957   **11.**—Schedule 1 contains amendments to other legislation. Broadly—

Part 1 allows benefits and other sums to be recovered from scheme payments,

Part 2 allows scheme payments to be recovered from compensation, and

Part 3 contains related amendments to do with information sharing.

Relationship with other legislation

Exclusion of payments under other legislation

1.958   **12.**—Schedule 2 contains amendments to other legislation to ensure that where an application is made under the scheme a person does not receive certain other payments.

1.959   *Sections 13–17 omitted.*

Defined terms used in more than one section of this Act

1.960   **18.**—(1) In this Act—

"application" means an application for a payment under the scheme;

"active insurer" has the meaning given by section 13;

"the compulsory insurance legislation" means—

(a) the Employers' Liability (Compulsory Insurance) Act 1969, or

(b) the Employer's Liability (Defective Equipment and Compulsory Insurance) (Northern Ireland) Order 1972 (S.I. 1972/963 (N.I. 6));

"damages" includes a payment in settlement of a claim for damages;

"dependant", in relation to a person who has died with diffuse mesothelioma, has the meaning given by section 3(1) of the Pneumoconiosis etc (Workers' Compensation) Act 1979 (reading the reference to the Secretary of State as a reference to the scheme administrator);

"employers' liability insurance", in relation to an employer and a particular time, means insurance that the employer—

(a) was required by the compulsory insurance legislation to maintain at that time, or

(b) would have been required by the compulsory insurance legislation to maintain if that legislation had been in force at that time;

"the fatal accidents legislation" means—

(a) the Fatal Accidents Act 1976,

(b) the Fatal Accidents (Northern Ireland) Order 1977 (S.I. 1977/1251 (N.I. 18)), or

(c) section 4 of the Damages (Scotland) Act 2011;

"levy" means a levy under section 13;

"relevant employer" has the meaning given by section 2;

"the scheme" means the Diffuse Mesothelioma Payment Scheme;

"scheme administrator" means the person for the time being administering the scheme (see section 7);

"the Technical Committee" means a committee established in accordance with arrangements under section 15.

(2) In determining for the purposes of this Act whether an employer

would have been required to maintain insurance if the compulsory insurance legislation had been in force at any given time, assume that any exemption that has at any time applied under the following provisions applied at the time in question—

(a) section 3(1)(a) to (c) of the Employers' Liability (Compulsory Insurance) Act 1969, and

(b) Article 7(a) to (c) of the Employer's Liability (Defective Equipment and Compulsory Insurance) (Northern Ireland) Order 1972.

(3) The scheme may specify circumstances in which a person is, or is not, to be treated as able to bring an action for the purposes of section 2(1)(d) or 3(1)(c).

Commencement

19.—(1) This Act comes into force on such day or days as the Secretary of State may by order appoint, subject as follows. 1.961

(2) This section and sections 20 and 21 come into force on the day on which this Act is passed.

(3) The Secretary of State may by order make transitional, transitory or saving provision in connection with the coming into force of any provision of this Act.

(4) An order under subsection (1) may appoint different days for different purposes.

(5) An order under this section is to be made by statutory instrument.

Extent

20.—(1) This Act extends to— 1.962

(a) England and Wales,

(b) Scotland, and

(c) Northern Ireland.

(2) Any amendment or repeal made by this Act has the same extent as the enactment to which it relates.

Short title

21.—This Act may be cited as the Mesothelioma Act 2014. 1.963

Pensions Act 2014

(2014 C.19)

ARRANGEMENT OF SECTIONS

PART 1

STATE PENSION

Introduction

1 State pension 1.964

State pension at the full or reduced rate

2 Entitlement to state pension at full or reduced rate
3 Full and reduced rates of state pension

State pension at the transitional rate

4 Entitlement to state pension at transitional rate
5 Transitional rate of state pension
6 Recalculation and backdating of transitional rate in special cases

Transitional entitlement based on contributions of others

7 Survivor's pension based on inheritance of additional old state pension
8 Choice of lump sum or survivor's pension under section 9 in certain cases
9 Survivor's pension based on inheritance of deferred old state pension
10 Inheritance of graduated retirement benefit

Transition: women who have had a reduced rate election

11 Reduced rate elections: effect on section 4 pensions
12 Reduced rate elections: pension for women with no section 4 pension

Transition: pension sharing on divorce etc

13 Shared state pension on divorce etc
14 Pension sharing: reduction in the sharer's section 4 pension
15 Pension sharing: amendments

Postponing or suspending state pension

16 Pensioner's option to suspend state pension
17 Effect of pensioner postponing or suspending state pension
18 Section 17 supplementary: calculating weeks, overseas residents, etc

Prisoners and overseas residents

19 Prisoners
20 Overseas residents

Definitions

21 "Old state pension"
22 General definitions etc

Consequential and other amendments

23 Amendments
24 Abolition of contracting-out for salary related schemes etc

PART 2

OPTION TO BOOST OLD RETIREMENT PENSIONS

25 Option to boost old retirement pensions

PART 3

PENSIONABLE AGE

26 Increase in pensionable age to 67
27 Periodic review of rules about pensionable age
...

PART 5

BEREAVEMENT SUPPORT PAYMENT

30 Bereavement support payment
31 Bereavement support payment: contribution condition and amendments
32 Bereavement support payment: prisoners

PART 7

FINAL PROVISIONS

53 Power to make consequential amendments etc
54 Regulations and orders
55 Extent
56 Commencement
57 Short title

SCHEDULES

Schedule 1 — Transitional rate of state pension: calculating the amount
    Part 1 — Introduction
    Part 2 — Amount for pre-commencement qualifying years
    Part 3 — Amount for post-commencement qualifying years
Schedule 2 — Transitional rate of state pension: up-rating
Schedule 3 — Survivor's pension under section 7: inherited amount
Schedule 4 — Survivor's pension under section 7: up-rating
Schedule 5 — Survivor's pension under section 9: inherited deferral amount
Schedule 6 — Reduced rate elections: effect on rate of section 4 pension
Schedule 7 — Reduced rate elections: basic amount of state pension under
section 12
Schedule 8 — Pension sharing: appropriate weekly rate under section 13
Schedule 9 — Pension sharing: up-rating state pension under section 13
Schedule 10 — Pension sharing: appropriate weekly reduction under
section 14
Schedule 11 — Pension sharing: amendments

Schedule 12 — State pension: amendments
  Part 1 — Amendments to do with new state pension system
  Part 2 — Amendments to do with old state pension system
  Part 3 — Amendments to do with state pension credit
  Part 4 — Other amendments to do with Part 1
Schedules 13 to 20 omitted

PART 1

STATE PENSION

Introduction

State pension

1.965   **1.-** (1) This Part creates a benefit called state pension.

(2) A person who reaches pensionable age before 6 April 2016 is not entitled to benefits under this Part (but may be entitled to similar benefits under Part 2 of the Contributions and Benefits Act).

GENERAL NOTE

1.966   Part 1 of the Pensions Act 2014 and the associated Schedules (1 to 14) entered fully into effect on April 6, 2016: Pensions Act 2014, s.56(4). Subject to transitional provisions noted below, the Act abolishes the pension that used to be called state retirement pension and replaces it with the "state pension". In the consultative and explanatory literature issued before the Act it was described as a "single tier pension", but the Act has gone for the simplest name. In doing so it removes from the statute book most continuing mentions of the old title of "state retirement pension" or "retirement pension". Pensions payable under legislation in effect before April 6, 2016 are labelled "old state pensions".

The provisions strip away much of the potential complication of the old state pensions save for transitional cases. While, as with all pension law, it will be many years before all transitional provisions have expired, it is important to note that in principle anyone reaching state pensionable age on or after April 6, 2016 is now covered **exclusively** by the state pension and has no claim under the previous law.

State pensionable age for men as at April 6, 2016 is the 65th birthday and therefore applied to all men born on or after April 6, 1951. State pensionable age for women is increasing under the terms of the Pension Act 2011. Under that Act any woman born   on or before April 5, 1953 reached state pensionable age on March 6, 2016. Those born on or after April 6, 1953 reach state pensionable age on July 6, 2016.

The Government consulted widely on the new pension and issued several papers detailing the proposals, as well as the Bill and the usual explanatory notes. These documents are all accessible on the GOV.UK website. The key policy paper was issued under the title *The single-tier pension: a simple foundation for saving* in January 2013. A formal White Paper was issued as CM 8528. These are included, together with a useful executive summary, on the website.

State pension at the full or reduced rate

Entitlement to state pension at full or reduced rate

2.- (1) A person is entitled to a state pension payable at the full rate if—   1.967
(a) the person has reached pensionable age, and
(b) the person has 35 or more qualifying years.
(2) A person is entitled to a state pension payable at the reduced rate if—
(a) the person has reached pensionable age, and
(b) the person has at leat the minimum number of qualifying years but fewer than 35 qualifying years.
(3) The minimum number of qualifying years for a state pension payable at the reduced rate is to be specified in regulations and may not be more than 10.
(4) In this Part "qualifying year" means a tax year, during a person's working life, in which the person's earnings factor (or the sum of the person's earnings factors) is equal to or greater than the qualifying earnings factor for the year.
(5) For earnings factors, see sections 22 and 23 of the Contributions and Benefits Act.
(6) For transitional cases in which a person may be entitled to a different state pension (instead of a state pension under this section), see sections 4 and 12.
(7) There are provisions elsewhere that affect a person's entitlement to a state pension under this section or the rate at which it is payable.

GENERAL NOTE

This section sets the two key rules for the new state pension. To receive a full   1.968
pension the pensioner must have completed 35 years during each of which adequate levels of National Insurance contribution are paid or credited. This is the same rule for both women and men, and is a reduction on a requirement based on the traditional full working life (from 16 to 65 for men) required for many years under the National Insurance Acts.

This emphasises that the state pension remains a contributory pension and that anyone claiming a pension must satisfy the contribution conditions. As with state retirement pension, the issues about payment of contributions and a claimant's contribution record are matters for decision by the National Insurance Contributions Office of Her Majesty's Revenue and Customs (HMRC) with any appeals going to the First-tier Tribunal Tax Chamber and so are beyond the scope of this work.

In the jargon of the policy documents, to obtain a full pension the pensioner must have a "foundation amount" equal to 35 years. To obtain any pension, the pensioner must have a foundation amount that meets the requirements of s.2(3). The minimum number of years for s.2(3) is set at 10 by reg.13 of the State Pension Regulations 2015 (below).

The policy documents identify four groups of pensioners for whom provision must be made. The first group is those whose records show that they have completed the necessary contribution requirements to have obtained a full foundation amount.

The three other groups are: those who have not reached the full 35 year level and/ or have been in contracted-out employment for part of that period; those whose contribution records (in particular those before April 6, 2016) exceed the total; and those with an inadequate record (or none at all) so that they are outside the Act.

The section also flags up ss.4 and 12 which provide for the second and third groups of pensioners. Those with no state pension entitlement may have entitlement to state pension credit, and are not otherwise considered in this Act.

Full and reduced rates of state pension

1.969   **3.-** (1) The full rate of the state pension is the weekly rate for the time being specified in regulations.

(2) The reduced rate of the state pension for a person is the following proportion of the full rate—

$$1/35 \times \text{the person's number of qualifying years}$$

(3) Once the full rate has been specified, the power to make regulations under subsection (1) may not be re-exercised so as to reduce the rate.

GENERAL NOTE

1.970   The full rate of state pension is set by reg.1A of the State Pension Regulations 2015, see para.6.169.

State pension at the transitional rate

Entitlement to state pension at transitional rate

1.971   **4.-** (1) A person is entitled to a state pension payable at the transitional rate if—

(a) the person has reached pensionable age,

(b) the person has at least the minimum number of qualifying years, and

(c) the person has at least one pre-commencement qualifying year.

(2) The minimum number of qualifying years for a state pension payable at the transitional rate is to be specified in regulations and may not be more than 10.

(3) A person entitled to a state pension payable at the transitional rate is not entitled to a state pension under section 2.

(4) In this Part—

"post-commencement qualifying year" means a qualifying year beginning on or after 6 April 2016;

"pre-commencement qualifying year" means—

(a) a qualifying year beginning on or after 6 April 1978 and ending before 6 April 2016, or

(b) a reckonable year that would have been treated under regulation 13(1) of the Social Security (Widow's Benefit, Retirement Pensions and Other Benefits) (Transitional) Regulations 1979 as a qualifying year for the purposes of determining the person's entitlement to an old state pension that is a Category A retirement pension.

(5) A reckonable year mentioned in paragraph (b) of the definition of "precommencement qualifying year" counts towards the minimum number of qualifying years required by subsection (1)(b) (even though it does not come within the definition of "qualifying year" for the purposes of this Part).

(6) For earnings factors, see sections 22 and 23 of the Contributions and Benefits Act.

(7) There are provisions elsewhere that affect a person's entitlement to a state pension under this section or the rate at which it is payable.

GENERAL NOTE

1.972   This section together with s.5 and Sch.1 provide for the main group of those entitled to a transitional award under the new state pension scheme rather than receiving the state pension without more. These are those who, on reaching state pensionable age on or after April 6, 2016, have not received the full foundation amount of 35 contribution years but have received more than the minimum amount. That amount, set under the terms of subs.(2) above is 10 years, the same lower limit a for s.2. See reg.13 of the State Pension Regulations 2015 (below).

The detailed calculations to be made to find out the foundation amount for these claimants are set out in Sch.1. The most important aspect of that schedule is that it requires HMRC to calculate both the "new" and the "old" levels of contribution payment or credit, and to base the calculation entitlement on which ever of the two is the larger. See steps 1, 2 and 3 of the calculation in Part 2 of Sch.1. As noted above, that remains within the remit of HMRC so is not part of the formal determination of a pension by DWP.

Transitional rate of state pension

5.- (1) The transitional rate of the state pension for a person is a weekly rate equal to—   1.973

    (a) the sum of the amounts calculated under Schedule 1 for the person's pre-commencement and post-commencement qualifying years capped at the full rate of the state pension on the day on which the person reaches pensionable age, or

    (b) if higher, the amount for the person's pre-commencement qualifying years alone.

(2) The transitional rate of the state pension for a person is to be increased from time to time in accordance with the applicable paragraph of Schedule 2.

(3) Section 6 requires the transitional rate of the state pension for a person to be recalculated in certain circumstances.

(4) There are special rules about the transitional rate for certain women: see section 11 (reduced rate elections).

Recalculation and backdating of transitional rate in special cases

6.- (1) This section modifies the transitional rate of the state pension for a person if, after the person has reached pensionable age, a determination is made under section 48A(2) of the Pension Schemes Act 1993 (contracting-out: reinstatement in state scheme following payment of contributions equivalent premium).   1.974

(2) The person's transitional rate is to be recalculated (taking the determination into account under paragraph 3(8) of Schedule 1).

(3) The recalculated rate has effect as from the day on which the person reached pensionable age (and the other provisions of this Part apply accordingly).

Transitional entitlement based on contributions of others

Survivor's pension based on inheritance of additional old state pension

7.- (1) A person is entitled to a state pension under this section if—   1.975

    (a) the person has reached pensionable age,

    (b) the person's spouse died while they were married or the person's civil partner died while they were civil partners of each other, and

(c) the person is entitled to an inherited amount under Schedule 3.

(2) A state pension under this section is payable at a weekly rate equal to the inherited amount.

(3) The rate of the state pension for a person under this section is to be increased from time to time in accordance with the applicable paragraph of Schedule 4.

(4) Regulations may provide that if at any time the sum of the relevant state pensions for a person exceeds an amount provided for by regulations, the rate of any state pension payable to the person under this section is to be reduced by the amount of the excess.

(5) The "sum of the relevant state pensions" for a person is the sum of—

(a) the rate of any state pension payable to the person under this section (ignoring any reduction under subsection (4)), and

(b) the rate of any state pension payable to the person under section 2, 4 or 12.

(6) In subsections (4) and (5) a reference to the rate of a person's state pension is to the rate—

(a) taking into account any reduction under section 14 (in the case of a state pension under section 4), but

(b) ignoring any increase under section 17.

(7) There are provisions elsewhere that affect a person's entitlement to a state pension under this section or the rate at which it is payable.

GENERAL NOTE

1.976   This section, together with ss.8 and 9 and Schs.3 to 5 deal with the transitional provisions dealing with pensioners seeking to claim in whole or part on the basis of the contributions paid by a spouse or partner during their joint lives. These measures are necessary because there are no derived or inherited rights to a new state pension under s.2 and amendments have removed any entitlement for anyone to rely on the National Insurance contributions of any other person with effect from April 6, 2016. This effectively stops any new rights to a Category B (or Category AB) pension, to use the old language. However, the transitional right to have the benefit of past contributions taken into account includes, through these provisions, the right to continue to rely on derived and inherited contributions made before April 6, 2016.

Choice of lump sum or survivor's pension under section 9 in certain cases

1.977   **8.-** (1) A person is entitled to a choice under this section if—

(a) the person has reached pensionable age,

(b) the person's spouse died while they were married or the person's civil partner died while they were civil partners of each other,

(c) the spouse or civil partner's entitlement to an old state pension was deferred at the time of death and throughout the period of 12 months ending with the day before the death,

(d) either:

   (i) the person was under pensionable age when the spouse or civil partner died and did not marry or form a civil partnership after the death and before reaching pensionable age, or

   (ii) the person was over pensionable age when the spouse or civil partner died, and

(e) the person would, on reaching pensionable age or on the death of the spouse or civil partner, have been entitled to an old state pension if in the relevant provisions of the Contributions and Benefits Act:

    (i) the words "before 6 April 2016" were omitted, and

    (ii) any reference to a bereavement allowance included a reference to bereavement support payment under section 30 of this Act.

(2) The person may choose—

(a) to be paid a lump sum under this section, or

(b) to be paid a state pension under section 9.

(3) Regulations are to set out the manner in which, and the period within which, that choice is to be made.

(4) A person who chooses to be paid a lump sum under this section, or who fails to choose within that period, is entitled to a "widowed person's or surviving civil partner's lump sum" calculated under paragraph 7B of Schedule 5 to the Contributions and Benefits Act.

(5) In that paragraph as it applies for the purposes of this section—

(a) read the references to "W" as references to the person,

(b) read sub-paragraph (5) as if it required increases under paragraph 4 of the Schedule to be excluded, and

(c) read the reference in sub-paragraph (7)(a) to the date on which W becomes entitled to a Category A or Category B retirement pension as a reference to the date on which the person becomes entitled to make a choice under this section.

(6) There are provisions elsewhere that affect a person's entitlement to a lump sum under this section.

(7) Regulations may allow a person, in specified circumstances—

(a) to alter his or her choice under this section;

(b) to make a late choice.

(8) Regulations under subsection (7) may, for the purpose of avoiding the duplication of payment—

(a) enable recovery of an amount paid to the person, or

(b) reduce the amount of a lump sum to be paid to the person.

(9) For the purposes of this section—

(a) "deferred" has the meaning given by section 55(3) of the Contributions and Benefits Act,

(b) "the relevant provisions" of the Contributions and Benefits Act are—

        section 44(1)(a);

        section 48(1);

        section 48A(1) and (3);

        section 48B(1), (1A), (4) and (4A);

        section 48BB(1) and (3), and

(c) in determining whether a person would have been entitled to an old state pension as mentioned in subsection (1)(e) ignore any requirement to make a claim.

Survivor's pension based on inheritance of deferred old state pension

9.- (1) A person is entitled to a state pension under this section if—   1.978

(a) the person has reached pensionable age,

(b) the person's spouse died while they were married or the person's civil partner died while they were civil partners of each other,

(c) either:
   (i) the person was under pensionable age when the spouse or civil partner died and did not marry or form a civil partnership after the death and before reaching pensionable age, or
   (ii) the person was over pensionable age when the spouse or civil partner died,
(d) the person is entitled to an inherited deferral amount under Schedule 5, and
(e) in the case of a person entitled to a choice under section 8, the person has chosen to be paid a state pension under this section.

(2) A state pension under this section is payable at a weekly rate equal to the inherited deferral amount.

(3) But if at any time an order under section 151A of the Administration Act comes into force, the rate of the person's state pension under this section is increased (at that time) by the percentage specified in the order.

(4) A person may be entitled to more than one state pension under this section.

(5) There are provisions elsewhere that affect a person's entitlement to a state pension under this section or the rate at which it is payable.

GENERAL NOTE

1.979   The amounts which, under this section are survivor's pensions based on inheritance of deferred old state pension, were increased by 2.4 per cent with effect from April 8, 2019: see art.6(4) of the Social Security Benefits Up-rating Order 2019 (SI 2019/480). For the meaning of "old state pension", see s.21.

Inheritance of graduated retirement benefit

1.980   **10.- (1)** Regulations may make provision corresponding or similar to any provision of sections 7 to 9 and Schedules 3 to 5 for the purpose of conferring benefits on a person whose dead spouse or civil partner paid graduated contributions as an insured person.

(2) The regulations may—
(a) include provision corresponding or similar to any provision that may be made by regulations under section 7 or 8;
(b) amend or otherwise modify this Act or any other enactment (whenever passed or made).

(3) In this section "graduated contributions" and "insured person" have the meanings given by section 36(8) of the National Insurance Act 1965.

GENERAL NOTE

1.981   For the provisions giving effect to this section see regs.15-20 of the State Pension Regulations 2015 below. Together the provisions protect a transitional claim drawing on contributions made under the former graduated retirement benefit scheme.

Transition: women who have had a reduced rate election

Reduced rate elections: effect on section 4 pensions

1.982   **11.- (1)** Section 4(1)(b) (minimum number of qualifying years for state pension at the transitional rate) does not apply to a woman if a reduced rate election was in force in respect of her at the beginning of the relevant 35-year period.

(2) Schedule 6 modifies the rules about the transitional rate of the state pension for a woman if a reduced rate election was in force in respect of her at the beginning of the relevant 35-year period.

(3) In this section—

"reduced rate election" means an election made, or treated as having been made, under regulations under section 19(4) of the Contributions and Benefits Act;

"relevant 35-year period" means the 35-year period ending with the tax year before the one in which the woman reached pensionable age.

GENERAL NOTE

This section, together with s.12 and Schs. 6 and 7, deal with transitional cases involving another of the major changes made by the Pensions Act 2014, namely the abolition of the right of a woman to pay National Insurance contributions at a reduced rate. At the same time, provisions are required to prevent a woman who paid only the reduced rate contributions from being treated as if those reduced rate contributions had not been paid.

1.983

These provisions contain the necessary provisions to adjust the foundation amount or alternative contribution record of anyone within this group of pensioners to ensure that pension is not overpaid.

Reduced rate elections: pension for women with no section 4 pension

12.- (1) A woman is entitled to a state pension under this section if—

1.984

(a) she has reached pensionable age,

(b) a reduced rate election was in force in respect of her at the beginning of the relevant 35-year period,

(c) she does not have any pre-commencement qualifying years, and

(d) she is entitled to a basic amount under Schedule 7.

(2) A state pension under this section is payable at a weekly rate equal to the basic amount.

(3) But if at any time the full rate of the state pension is increased, the rate of the woman's state pension under this section is increased (at that time) by the same percentage as the increase in the full rate.

(4) In subsection (3) the reference to the rate of the woman's state pension is to the

rate ignoring any increase under section 17.

(5) A woman is not entitled to a state pension under this section and section 2 at the same time: she is only entitled to the one with the higher rate.

(6) There are provisions elsewhere that affect a woman's entitlement to a state pension under this section or the rate at which it is payable.

(7) In this section—

"reduced rate election" means an election made, or treated as having been made, under regulations under section 19(4) of the Contributions and Benefits Act;

"relevant 35-year period" means the 35-year period ending with the tax year before the one in which the woman reached pensionable age.

Shared state pension on divorce etc

1.985   **13.-** (1) A person is entitled to a state pension under this section if—

(a) the person has reached pensionable age, and

(b) the person is entitled to a state scheme pension credit.

(2) A state pension under this section is payable at the appropriate weekly rate set out in Schedule 8.

(3) The rate of the state pension for a person under this section is to be increased from time to time in accordance with the applicable paragraph of Schedule 9.

(4) A person may be entitled to more than one state pension under this section.

(5) There are provisions elsewhere that affect a person's entitlement to a state pension under this section or the rate at which it is payable.

(6) In this Part—

"state scheme pension credit" means—

(a) a new state scheme pension credit, or

(b) an old state scheme pension credit;

"new state scheme pension credit" means a credit under section 49A(2)
   (b) of the Welfare Reform and Pensions Act 1999;

"old state scheme pension credit" means a credit under section 49(1)(b)
   of that Act.

GENERAL NOTE

1.986   This section, together with s.14 and Schs.8 to 10 deal with the need to continue the shareable state scheme rights created under the Welfare Reform and Pensions Act 1999 (see above in this volume). Section 15 incorporates Sch.11 which sets out amendments to that Act and related provisions. These are included in the relevant provisions above.

Pension sharing: reduction in the sharer's section 4 pension

1.987   **14.-** (1) The rate of a person's state pension under section 4 is reduced under this section if the person is subject to a state scheme pension debit.

(2) The amount by which the rate is reduced is the amount of the appropriate weekly reduction set out in Schedule 10.

(3) A person's state pension may be reduced more than once under this section.

(4) In this Part—

"state scheme pension debit" means—

(a) a new state scheme pension debit, or

(b) an old state scheme pension debit.

"new state scheme pension debit" means a debit under section 49A(2)(a)
   of the Welfare Reform and Pensions Act 1999;

"old state scheme pension debit" means a debit under section 49(1)(a)
   of that Act.

Pension sharing: amendments

1.988   **15.-** Schedule 11 contains amendments to do with pension sharing.

Postponing or suspending state pension

Pensioner's option to suspend state pension

16.- (1) A person who has become entitled to a state pension under this   **1.989**
Part may opt to suspend his or her entitlement in accordance with regulations.

(2) A person is not entitled to any state pension under this Part for the
period for which the person has opted to suspend his or her entitlement.

(3) For other effects of a person exercising the option, see section 17.

(4) A person may not opt to suspend his or her entitlement to a state
pension under this Part on more than one occasion.

(5) Regulations may specify other circumstances in which a person may
not opt to suspend his or her entitlement to a state pension under this Part.

(6) Regulations may allow a person who has opted to suspend his or her
entitlement to a state pension under this Part to cancel the exercise of that
option (in whole or in part) in relation to a past period.

GENERAL NOTE

This section, with ss.17 and 18 deal with what is usually called deferral of a state   **1.990**
pension. It continues the right of someone reaching state pension age to defer her
or his pension until a later date. Detailed provisions to give effect to this right are
contained in regs.4 to 12A of the State Pension Regulations 2015 below.

Effect of pensioner postponing or suspending state pension

17.- (1) If a person's entitlement to a state pension under this Part has   **1.991**
been deferred for a period, the weekly rate of the person's state pension is
increased by an amount equal to the sum of the increments to which the
person is entitled.

(2) But the weekly rate is not to be increased under subsection (1) if the
increase would be less than 1% of the persons weekly rate ignoring that
subsection.

(3) A person is entitled to one increment for each whole week in the period
during which the person's entitlement to a state pension was deferred.

(4) The amount of an increment is equal to a specified percentage of the
weekly rate of the state pension to which the person would have been entitled immediately before the end of that period if the person's entitlement
had not been deferred.

(5) In subsection (4) "specified" means specified in regulations.

(6) The amount of an increase under this section is itself to be increased
from time to time in accordance with any order made under section 150 of
the Administration Act (annual up-rating of benefits).

(7) For the purposes of this section and section 18 a person's entitlement
to a state pension under this Part is deferred for a period if the person has
opted under section 16 to suspend his or her entitlement for that period.

(8) For the purposes of this section and section 18 a person's entitlement
to a state pension under this Part is also deferred for a period if the person
is not entitled to it for that period by reason only of—

(a) not satisfying the conditions in section 1 of the Administration Act
(entitlement dependent on claim etc), or

(b) subsection (9) below.

(9) A person is not entitled to a state pension under this Part for any period during which his or her entitlement to any other state pension under this Part is deferred.

GENERAL NOTE

1.992   The sums which are increases under this section in the rates of state pensions under Part 1 of the Act were increased by 2.4 per cent with effect from April 8, 2019: see art.6(3) of the Social Security Benefits Up-rating Order 2019 (SI 2019/480).

Section 17 supplementary: calculating weeks, overseas residents, etc

1.993   **18.-** (1) Regulations may—
(a) provide for circumstances in which a part of a week is to be treated for the purposes of section 17(3) as a whole week, and
(b) provide for circumstances in which a day does not count in determining a number of whole weeks for the purposes of section 17(3) (for example if the person is receiving other benefits).

(2) Regulations may modify section 17(4) in cases where, at any time in the period during which a person's entitlement to a state pension is deferred, the rate for the person would have changed otherwise than because of an up-rating increase.

(3) Regulations may modify section 17(4) in relation to a person who has been an overseas resident during any part of the period for which the person's entitlement to a state pension has been deferred.

(4) In subsection (3) "overseas resident" means a person who is not ordinarily resident in Great Britain or any other territory specified in the regulations.

(5) Regulations may amend the percentage specified in section 17(2).

Prisoners and overseas residents

Prisoners

1.994   **19.-** (1) Regulations may provide that a person is not to be paid a state pension under this Part for any period during which the person is a prisoner.

(2) "Prisoner" means a person (in Great Britain or elsewhere) who is—
(a) imprisoned or detained in legal custody, or
(b) unlawfully at large.

(3) In the case of a person remanded in custody for an offence, regulations under subsection (1) may be made so as to apply only if a sentence of a specified description is later imposed on the person for the offence.

GENERAL NOTE

1.995   There was some lack of clarity in previous law about the extent to which the fact that someone was or should have been a prisoner affected entitlement to a state pension. This section, read with regs.2 and 3 of the State Pension Regulations 2015 (below) seeks to remove any ambiguity and to prevent pension awards to those who are in custody either here or elsewhere with a few clearly defined limits.

Overseas residents

20.- (1) Regulations may provide that an overseas resident who is entitled to a state pension under this Part is not entitled to up-rating increases.

(2) In this section "overseas resident" means a person who is not ordinarily resident in Great Britain or any territory specified in the regulations.

(3) Regulations under this section do not affect the rate of an overseas resident's state pension for any period during which he or she is in Great Britain or a territory specified in the regulations (but once the overseas resident ceases to be in Great Britain or a specified territory the rate reverts to what it would have been had he or she not been in Great Britain or a specified territory).

(4) Regulations under this section do not affect the rate of a person's state pension once the person stops being an overseas resident.

1.996

GENERAL NOTE

Regulations to give effect to this section are in regs.21 to 23 of the State Pension Regulations 2015 below.

1.997

Definitions

"Old state pension"

21.- (1) In this Part "old state pension" means a Category A retirement pension or a Category B retirement pension.

(2) A reference in this Part to the rate of an old state pension (however expressed) does not include—

(a) graduated retirement benefit under the National Insurance Act 1965, or

(b) any increase in the rate because of Schedule 5 to the Contributions and Benefits Act (deferral increases).

1.998

General definitions etc

22.- (1) In this Part—

"the Administration Act" means the Social Security Administration Act 1992;

"Category A retirement pension" means a Category A retirement pension under Part 2 of the Contributions and Benefits Act;

"Category B retirement pension" means a Category B retirement pension under Part 2 of the Contributions and Benefits Act;

"the Contributions and Benefits Act" means the Social Security Contributions and Benefits Act 1992;

"enactment" includes an enactment contained in subordinate legislation within the meaning of the Interpretation Act 1978;

"full rate" means the rate mentioned in section 3(1);

"old state pension" has the meaning given by section 21 (and references to the rate of an old state pension are to be read in accordance with that section);

"pensionable age" has the meaning given by section 122(1) of the Contributions and Benefits Act; and a person is "over" pensionable age if the person has reached that age (and is otherwise "under" that age);

1.999

"post-commencement qualifying year" has the meaning given by section 4(4);

"pre-commencement qualifying year" is to be read in accordance with section 4(4) and (5);

"qualifying earnings factor" has "qualifying earnings factor" has the meaning given by section 122(1) of the Contributions and Benefits Act;

"qualifying year" has the meaning given by section 2(4);

"reduced rate" means the rate mentioned in section 3(2);

"regulations" means regulations made by the Secretary of State;

"state scheme pension credit", and related expressions, have the meaning given by section 13;

"state scheme pension debit", and related expressions, have the meaning given by section 14;

"tax year" has the meaning given by section 122(1) of the Contributions and Benefits Act;

"transitional rate" means the rate mentioned in section 5;

"up-rating increase", in relation to a state pension under this Part, means—

(a) an increase in the rate of the state pension because of an increase in the amount specified in regulations under section 3(1),[1 ...]

(b) an increase in the rate of the state pension because of section 9(3), 12(3) or 17(6) or Schedule 2, 4 or 9; [1 or

(c) an increase in the rate of the state pension because of regulations under section 10 which make provision corresponding or similar to section 9(3) or Schedule 4;]

"working life" has the meaning given by section 122(1) of the Contributions and Benefits Act.

(2) For the purposes of any other provision of this Part two people are to be treated as if they are not married to each other in relation to times when either of them is married to a third person.

Consequential and other amendments

Amendments

1.1000 **23.-** In Schedule 12—
Part 1 contains amendments to do with state pensions under this Part;
Part 2 contains key amendments to do with the old state pension system;
Part 3 contains amendments to do with state pension credit;
Part 4 contains other amendments to do with this Part.

Abolition of contracting-out for salary related schemes etc

1.1001 **24.-** (1) Schedule 13 contains amendments to abolish contracting-out for salary related schemes.

(2) An employer may amend an occupational pension scheme in relation to some or all of its members to take account of increases in the employer's national insurance contributions in respect of some or all of the members to whom the amendments apply because of the repeal of section 41 of the Pension Schemes Act 1993 (by Schedule 13 to this Act).

(3) The power may be used to make amendments that will apply in rela-

tion to future members and correspond to the amendments being made in relation to current members.

(4) The power may not be used—

(a) to make amendments that apply to a member who is a protected person in relation to a scheme, or

(b) to amend a public service pension scheme or a scheme of a description specified in regulations under this paragraph.

(5) Regulations must define what is meant by a protected person in relation to a scheme for the purposes of subsection (4)(a).

(6) Schedule 14 contains more detail about the power.

(7) In this section and Schedule 14—

"current member", in relation to a scheme, means a person who is a member of the scheme at the time that the power is used (and "future member" is to be read accordingly);

"employer", in relation to a scheme, means the employer of persons in the description of employment to which the scheme relates;

"member" has the meaning given by section 124(1) of the Pensions Act 1995;

"national insurance contributions", in relation to an employer, means secondary Class 1 national insurance contributions payable by the employer;

"occupational pension scheme" has the meaning given by section 1 of the Pension Schemes Act 1993;

"public service pension scheme" has the meaning given by that section.

(8) Subsections (2) to (7) and Schedule 14 are repealed at the end of the period of 5 years beginning with 6 April 2016.

(9) The Secretary of State may by order amend subsection (8) to extend the period for the time being mentioned there.

PART 2

OPTION TO BOOST OLD RETIREMENT PENSIONS

Option to boost old retirement pensions

25.- In Schedule 15—   1.1002

Part 1 contains amendments to allow certain people to pay additional contributions to boost their retirement pensions;

Part 2 contains amendments to allow corresponding legislation to be put in place for Northern Ireland.

PART 3

PENSIONABLE AGE

Increase in pensionable age to 67

26.   *This amends Sch.4 to the Pensions Act 1995, and the amendments are*   1.1003
set out there.

Periodic review of rules about pensionable age

1.1004   27.- (1) The Secretary of State must from time to time—

(a) review whether the rules about pensionable age are appropriate, having regard to life expectancy and other factors that the Secretary of State considers relevant, and

(b) prepare and publish a report on the outcome of the review.

(2) The first report must be published before 7 May 2017.

(3) Each subsequent report must be published before the end of the period of 6 years beginning with the day on which the previous report was published.

(4) For the purposes of each review, the Secretary of State must require the Government Actuary or Deputy Government Actuary to prepare a report for the Secretary of State on—

(a) whether the rules about pensionable age mean that, on average, a person who reaches pensionable age within a specified period can be expected to spend a specified proportion of his or her adult life in retirement, and

(b) if not, ways in which the rules might be changed with a view to achieving that result.

(5) The Secretary of State must, for the purposes of a review, appoint a person or persons to prepare a report for the Secretary of State on other specified factors relevant to the review.

(6) The Secretary of State must lay before Parliament any report prepared under this section.

(7) For the purposes of subsection (4)—

(a) a person's adult life is the part of the person's life after he or she reaches the specified age;

(b) the proportion of a person's adult life spent in retirement is the proportion of his or her adult life spent after reaching pensionable age.

(8) In this section—

"pensionable age" has the meaning given by the rules in paragraph 1 of Schedule 4 to the Pensions Act 1995 (and "the rules about pensionable age" means those rules);

"specified" means specified by the Secretary of State.

PART 5

BEREAVEMENT SUPPORT PAYMENT

Bereavement support payment

1.1005   30- (1) A person is entitled to a benefit called bereavement support payment if—

(a) the person's spouse or civil partner dies,

(b) the person is under pensionable age when the spouse or civil partner dies,

(c) the person is ordinarily resident in Great Britain, or a specified territory, when the spouse or civil partner dies, and

(d) the contribution condition is met (see section 31).

(2) The Secretary of State must by regulations specify—

(a) the rate of the benefit, and

(b) the period for which it is payable.

(3) The regulations may specify different rates for different periods.

(4) In the case of a person who is pregnant or entitled to child benefit in specified circumstances, the regulations may—

(a) specify a higher rate;

(b) provide for the allowance to be payable for a longer period.

(5) A person is not entitled to bereavement support payment for periods after the person has reached pensionable age.

(6) A person is not entitled to bereavement support payment if the death occurred before this section came fully into force.

(7) In this section—

"pensionable age" has the meaning given by the rules in paragraph 1 of Schedule 4 to the Pensions Act 1995;

"specified territory" means a territory specified in regulations made by the Secretary of State.

Bereavement support payment: contribution condition and amendments

31- (1) For the purposes of section 30(1)(d) the contribution condition is that, for at least one tax year during the deceased's working life— 1.1006

(a) he or she actually paid Class 1 or Class 2 national insurance contributions, and

(b) those contributions give rise to an earnings factor (or total earnings factors) equal to or greater than 25 times the lower earnings limit for the tax year.

(2) For earnings factors, see sections 22 and 23 of the Social Security Contributions and Benefits Act 1992.

(3) For the purposes of section 30(1)(d) the contribution condition is to be treated as met if the deceased was an employed earner and died as a result of—

(a) a personal injury of the kind mentioned in section 94(1) of the Social Security Contributions and Benefits Act 1992, or

(b) a disease or personal injury of the kind mentioned in section 108(1) of that Act.

(4) In this section the following expressions have the meaning given by section 122(1) of the Social Security Contributions and Benefits Act 1992—

"employed earner",

"lower earnings limit",

"tax year", and

"working life".

(5) Schedule 16 contains amendments to do with bereavement support payment.

Bereavement support payment: prisoners

32- (1) The Secretary of State may by regulations provide that a person is not to be paid bereavement support payment for any period during which the person is a prisoner. 1.1007

(2) "Prisoner" means a person (in Great Britain or elsewhere) who is—

(a) imprisoned or detained in legal custody, or

(b) unlawfully at large.

(3) In the case of a person remanded in custody for an offence, regula-

tions under subsection (1) may be made so as to apply only if a sentence of a specified description is later imposed on the person for the offence.

GENERAL NOTE

1.1008   Bereavement support payment is payable to the spouse or civil partner of a person who dies after April 6, 2017. It replaces all of the bereavement payments under earlier legislation. When introduced to Parliament it was described as a modern benefit appropriate to our society in the 21st century. This led some campaigners to hope that it might dispense with the requirement that the claimant be in a marriage or civil partnership with the deceased, but a committee recommendation to this effect was rejected by the government on the grounds of cost and the difficulty in determining at what point a relationship might be regarded as so secure that a sufficient state of dependency would be shown to exist. It was also pointed out that such an examination of the relationship would be intrusive at an emotional time and further, that it would open the possibility of conflicting claims from a spouse and a cohabiting partner.

Bereavement support payments are a contributory benefit the requirement for which is defined in s.31. As with the benefits that it replaces both Class 1 and Class 2 contributions will qualify and the extent of the contribution required is the "lighter" test that demonstrates involvement in the labour force at some time in the deceased's working life; there are special provisions in respect of a person who dies in an industrial accident or as a result of an industrial disease.

In other respects the essential requirements of a claim are similar to those of the benefits that preceded bereavement support payment. The claimant must be under pensionable age at the time their spouse or civil partner dies, and they must be within the UK or a specified territory defined by regulations. It remains necessary to prove a valid marriage or civil partnership and to prove the fact of death, and the rule of forfeiture will apply. But in respect of this benefit there is no disqualification if a claimant remarries, or lives with another person as if in a marriage or civil partnership. This will be so even if the claimant is living with another partner at the time of the death so long as their marriage or civil partnership to the deceased is still subsisting.

Bereavement support payment, like bereavement benefits and widow's benefits before them, depends upon proof of a valid marriage (including same sex marriage) or civil partnership subsisting at the time of the spouse's death. Although neither the Marriage (Same Sex Couples) Act 2013, nor this Act contains a definition of "spouse" (upon which entitlement to these benefits depend) it is clear that the intent of the former act is to treat same-sex marriage as if it were a marriage between persons of the opposite sex: see Marriage (Same Sex Couples) Act 2013 s.11.

It is now possible for a valid marriage to be contracted with a transsexual where that person holds a full gender recognition certificate in accordance with the Gender Recognition Act 2004: see s.9 of that Act.

The essential requirements to qualify for these benefits are that there should have been a valid subsisting marriage or civil partnership and that the spouse or civil partner has died. Without any marriage or civil partnership at all, or even a belief that there had been a marriage (see below), there can be no claim for bereavement benefits. See *Shackell v United Kingdom* (ECHR) April 27, 2000, unreported (Application No. 45851/99), where the court rejected a claim for widowed mother's allowance by the mother of two children whose father, her partner, had died.

1.1009   In *R(G) 1/04* a claim to bereavement benefits was made by a woman following the death of her long term partner. Her claim was made firstly on the ground that there should be a marriage presumed after long term cohabitation or, alternatively, that the words of ss.36 to 38 should be construed in the light of the Human Rights Act to extend to such a common law marriage. The Commissioner rejected both arguments. There could be no room for presumption of marriage where the parties had expressly decided against marrying. Nor was it necessary to construe the Benefits Act in accordance with the Human Rights Act because the decision refusing benefit, and now under appeal, was made before that Act came into force. Even if it had been necessary to so construe the Benefits Act it would be impossible to read those words in any way other than to require there to have been a valid marriage. Finally, it would not have been open to the Commissioner to make a declaration of incompatibility and in any case the *Shackell* case showed that there was no discrimination in the different treatment of married and unmarried couples.

A further attempt to claim bereavement benefits by the survivor of a long standing common law marriage has been rejected by Judge Levenson in *ES v SSWP (MA)* [2010] UKUT 200 (AAC). An argument was made that earlier cases had turned, directly or indirectly, upon the meaning given to the words "marriage" and "husband" which had been the terminology used in relation to the benefits existing previously only for widows. Bereavement benefits, on the other hand, were available for a "spouse" whose partner had died and earlier cases had not focused on the change in terminology. Judge Leveneson held that the word "spouse" still required a valid marriage subsisting at the time of the partner's death. He also held that as a matter of human rights law, the difference in treatment, although discriminatory, was justified as a proportionate measure protecting a valid preference for the institution of marriage in our society.

But the matter has been considered again in a case coming from Northern Ireland. The claimant had lived with the deceased for a period of 23 years and she had 4 children by him for which she was still responsible. The claim was for both a bereavement payment and for widowed parent's allowance. In the High Court Treacy J. held that the claim for a bereavement payment failed because an argument based on comparability could not succeed when the claimant had chosen not to marry. He regarded the contract of marriage as a public declaration that gave notice of the status that the parties were choosing to adopt; where they chose not to adopt that status their position could not be truly comparable. But the claim for widowed parent's allowance succeeded in the High Court on the ground that refusal of the benefit would be in breach of the claimant's human rights under the ECHR and the HRA 1998 because her obligation to support her children rested upon her as a parent, regardless of whether she were married or not. The basis of that decision has been upheld by the Supreme Court in *McLaughlin, Re Judicial Review (Northern Ireland)* [2018] UKSC 48. The court held, by a majority, that s.39A of the Contributions and Benefits Act is incompatible with art.14 read with art.8 of the ECHR insofar as it precluded entitlement to widowed parent's allowance by the surviving partner of the deceased.

The decision does not necessarily establish the claimant's entitlement to the benefit, because the effect of a declaration of incompatibility is just that – it remains for the DWP to determine what they will do in relation to the claim. Although at the time of writing this note the response of DWP is still not known, it seems reasonably clear that some claimants, at least, should become entitled to widowed parent's allowance. Lady Hale, in the leading judgment, observed that the case would be strongest in respect of children of whom both members of the couple are a parent, as was the case here. The decision makes clear that the other old-style bereavement benefits (except conceivably widowed mother's allowance) are not affected by this decision. In a separate judgment Lord Mance (with whom the rest of the majority agree) finds that *Shackell* should not be followed because it made no distinction between benefits intended for support of children of the couple, and other benefits. It was notable that in all other European countries (except Malta) the benefit was paid as a benefit of the child, and not as a benefit of the surviving spouse. In Malta the benefit is paid to the surviving parent, but without regard to the legitimacy of the child. The court makes no reference to the new Bereavement Support Payment. It is arguable that payment of the enhanced rate of that benefit (which includes an element of child support) only to a surviving spouse and not to a cohabitee who has responsibility for children, might equally be incompatible with the ECHR, but (depending on the response that the DWP now makes) that may require further litigation. An application for judicial review of this benefit has been made.

Meanwhile, similar claims to that in *Re McLaughlin* have been coming forward. In at least one case there is the added complication that the claimant believed herself to have been validly married by a Muslim (Nikah) ceremony. Her claim for WPA had been refused and an application for leave to appeal to the UT also refused, but that was at a time prior to the SC decision in *Re McLaughlin*. An application for judicial review of the UT refusal has been allowed by the High Court, following the Secretary of State's withdrawal of an application to be an interested party. It seems therefore, that DWP is likely to accept at least some of these claims when amending legislation is prepared.

Proof of a valid marriage

1.1010   As to whether a marriage is valid the matter is determined by the general law including those rules of law concerning the recognition of foreign marriages and divorces. A marriage celebrated in England and Wales must satisfy the formalities of the law as to notice and ceremony, civil or religious, and is usually proved by production of a copy of the marriage certificate. If the certificate is not available, other evidence of the ceremony coupled with subsequent cohabitation will raise a presumption that there was a valid marriage. That presumption can be rebutted by evidence that the marriage was invalid, but it will probably require proof beyond reasonable doubt that it was invalid *(R(G) 2/70)*. It should be noted that in this instance the presumption of marriage is supported by the evidence of cohabitation but only when there is also evidence that the appropriate ceremony took place. In *R(G) 2/70* the parties went through what was apparently a bogus ceremony (though it was thought by the claimant to be genuine) followed by many years of cohabitation. It was held that no marriage could be presumed. This case must now be viewed as doubtful. Although it was distinguished by the Court of Appeal in *Adjudication Officer v Bath* reported as *R(G) 1/00* Lord Justice Evans, giving the leading judgment, says that the basis of the argument used in *R(G) 2/70* is not correct. The decision in *R(G) 1/00* would suggest that the presumption should have also availed the claimant in the earlier case. In *R(G) 1/00* the partners were "married" in a religious ceremony in a Sikh Temple in West London (1956). They lived together thereafter for 37 years, bringing up a family, until the "husband" died in 1994. The Sikh Temple was not at that time a registered building for marriages under the Marriage Act 1949. (It was so registered in 1983 but such registration is not retrospective.)

There was no evidence, and it was not suggested by the claimant, that there had been any other civil ceremony of marriage at a Registry Office. It appears that the claimant believed herself to have been validly married in the religious ceremony and made her claim to widow's benefits accordingly.

The AO rejected that claim on the basis that no marriage, valid in accordance with the Marriage Act 1949, had been shown. That decision was upheld by the SSAT, with an expression of sympathy for the claimant's situation. The Commissioner allowed an appeal after recourse to the presumption outlined above as stated in *Halsbury's Laws of England*, paras 992 and 993 (4th edn, Vol.22).

The second of these paragraphs is headed "Presumption from cohabitation after Ceremony" and would appear to be the more appropriate. That paragraph makes clear, however, that the presumption is only that all essentials of the ceremony will be presumed valid *unless the contrary is proved*. Here, it would seem the evidence rebutted the validity of the ceremony because the Temple was not a registered building. However, the footnotes in *Halsbury* include the case of *Re Shephard, George v Thyer* (1904) in which the presumption was applied although the only ceremony alleged was a marriage in France that was agreed to be invalid. The Commissioner took the view that he could follow this case as an earlier High Court precedent. In doing so he rejects the conclusion of the Commissioner in *R(G) 2/70* who had himself refused to follow *Re Shephard*. In any case, Commissioner Goodman suggests that *R(G) 2/70* might be distinguished on the narrow ground that the ceremony relied upon there had been in a bogus Registry Office (although believed to be genuine by the claimant), whereas the ceremony in this case had been in a genuine religious Temple.

The Commissioner also found the claim to be supportable under the first paragraph cited. This paragraph is headed "Presumption from Cohabitation without Ceremony". This presumption should apply after long cohabitation even in the absence of evidence of a marriage ceremony. The Commissioner's reasoning here seems to be that someone who has gone through what they believed to be a valid ceremony should not be worse off than someone who believed themselves to be married without any ceremony at all.

The Commissioner seems to have created a marriage very similar to the Scottish marriage "by habit and repute". There is, however, this difference. In Scotland, marriage can be presumed by long cohabitation with a willingness (and ability) to marry. In the English case it would seem to be necessary to prove a *belief* that the parties were married. That is just as well for otherwise we would have invented a true common law marriage that depended only on the parties long monogamous cohabitation.

The Court of Appeal's decision confirms the reasoning of the Commissioner, though they did also doubt whether the evidence available was sufficient to prove that the Sikh Temple was not a registered building in 1956. The sympathy of the judges was apparent for the widow of a man who had duly paid his income tax and national insurance contributions throughout his working life only for her to be told, when it was already too late, that she had never been married at all, but the key to their reasoning seems to be that nothing in the Marriage Act 1949 invalidates such a marriage unless the parties "knowingly and wilfully" intermarry without compliance with that Act. There was no evidence in this case that the parties were acting otherwise than in the honest belief that their marriage was validly celebrated, and in the absence of any statutory disqualification they were entitled to the benefit of the presumption outlined above.

The case of *Akhter v Khan and the Attorney General* [2018] EWFC 54 has raised the question of whether religious ceremonies in this country other than those in the Church of England should be regarded as creating a marriage recognised for any purpose by the law. In this case it was an Islamic marriage ceremony (a Nikah) in which both parties regarded it as being the first step in formalising their relationship and intended to be followed by a civil ceremony in accordance with English law. Although the parties lived together for 18 years and had 4 children together, the civil ceremony never took place. The "wife" contended that she had constantly pressed her partner to complete the process, but that he had refused to do so. These proceedings were brought seeking divorce and consequent orders for matrimonial relief. Williams J. concluded that, on these facts, there had been a marriage that was void under the Matrimonial Causes Act 1973 and in respect of which the wife was entitled to a decree of nullity. That decree could give access to further orders for matrimonial relief. The judge was referred to a long line of cases that established that where, as here, the purported marriage ceremony did not comply with the Marriage Act 1949 it could not be regarded as a valid marriage nor was it to be regarded as a void marriage for the purposes of matrimonial relief. In this case however, Williams J. has recourse to arguments based on the provisions of the ECHR and the HRA 1998. He finds that reading the Matrimonial Causes Act 1973 and the Marriage Act in accordance with the Convention principles leads him to the view that a religious ceremony such as this should be accepted as giving rise to a marriage that is void, but which is capable giving to orders for matrimonial relief. This decision does not however give any right to claim a Bereavement Support Payment. On the contrary, the marriage was found to be void. It was not a valid marriage at all; its status as a void marriage has effect only to support the action under the Matrimonial Causes Act.

This matter has now been visited again by Judge Wikeley in the case of *NA v SSWP (BB)* [2019] UKUT 144 (AAC). In this case the parties had gone through a ceremony of marriage in Pakistan. This marriage was void under English law because at the time the husband was domiciled in the UK and was already married to another who was alive and living in the UK. (It may have been that the parties believed that their marriage in Pakistan was monogamous because the husband had pronounced a talaq divorce in the UK, but that talaq was ineffective). After the couple returned to the UK the husband obtained a divorce from his first wife, and thereafter their marriage was in fact monogamous. Following the husband's death, the claimant made a claim for bereavement benefits for herself and for a child of the marriage. In a previous case (*SSWP v MN (BB)* [2018] UKUT 68 (AAC) referred to in the notes below) Judge Wikeley had held that, in similar circumstances, the claim should fail because the marriage, though monogamous at the time of death, had never been a valid marriage at all because the husband, being domiciled at the time in the UK and already married, lacked the capacity to marry. In that case, however, no argument had been considered in relation to the claimant's position under the ECHR and the HRA. Now, in the light of those arguments, and of the position taken by the SC in the case of *Re McLaughlin*, Judge Wikeley has found that reg.2 of the Polygamous Marriages Regulations 1975 should be read in such a way as to make the claimant eligible for both a bereavement payment and a widowed parent's allowance in accordance with the legislation then in force.

1.1011 Until 2006 it was possible as well, in Scotland, to prove a marriage "by cohabitation with habit and repute". This rule has been abolished with effect from May 4, 2006. (Family Law (Scotland) Act 2006 s.3). That abolition is, however, prospective only; couples whose living arrangements began before that date may still be able to take advantage of the rule—see s.3(2) of the act. Furthermore, in the special case of widow or a widower whose marriage was celebrated outside the United Kingdom and has subsequently been discovered to have been invalid, the rule may still be applied even if the cohabitation with habit and repute began after May 2006. But this will only apply where the surviving party became aware of the invalidity of the marriage after the spouse's death—see s.3 (3) and s.3 (4).

In its modern form, proof of marriage by cohabitation with habit and repute, required that the parties prove that they were free to marry, that they were, or had been, cohabiting in Scotland as husband and wife (there appears to have been no suggestion that this might extend to civil partnerships) and that they had done so for a sufficient period of time- generally this meant a long time. More problematically, they must have been reputed to be husband and wife; this meant not merely that they lived as if they were married to each other, but that people generally believed that they were so married. Given modern attitudes to cohabitation it seems unlikely that the rule would have had much scope for application. For more detailed information about this form of marriage see earlier editions of this book.

Foreign marriages, and divorces, raise difficult and often obscure points of law that may depend upon proof of foreign law. It is impossible to deal fully with these points in this note. Tribunals which require assistance on matters of foreign law should identify the party raising the issue that required proof of foreign law and require that party to obtain suitable evidence. Note that the foreign law as found by a Commissioner is a finding of fact. When the Commissioner applies that law it does not thereby become a part of the social security law being used by the Commissioner. This means that a subsequent tribunal is not bound to accept the same conclusion as to the foreign law as has been accepted in a previous Commissioner's decision. In the absence of a contrary expert opinion a tribunal will doubtless accept the view adopted in an earlier decision when that is provided to them, but where there is conflicting expert evidence available, the tribunal must consider all of the evidence and choose that which is most persuasive to them.

This was the course adopted in *R(G) 2/00*. The issue there was the validity of a foreign marriage which itself depended upon the recognition of the previous divorce of one of the parties. The divorce was by talaq in Bangladesh in 1973. Earlier Commissioners' decisions had accepted that a talaq divorce would be recognised only when the formalities had included its notification to the Chairman of the Union Council. In the present case, new expert evidence was given to the effect that, at the time when Bangladesh was only very recently created as a state, there was no such official. In any case, further evidence suggested that more recently talaq divorces were accepted in Bangladesh as valid without notification and might therefore be recognised in English law also. In this case, the Commissioner upheld the decision of a tribunal which had accepted the validity of the divorce and subsequent marriage (and therefore awarded a widow's pension) notwithstanding the contrary conclusion in earlier cases. Other cases involving foreign law include *R(G) 4/93* (marriage celebrated in Bangladesh) and *R(G) 1/94* (talaq divorce). Note that a talaq divorce, even if valid by the law of domicile of the parties, cannot be effective if it is proclaimed in this country. This is because s.16 of the Domicile and Matrimonial Proceedings Act 1973, provides that no proceedings in this country shall be regarded as validly dissolving marriage unless those proceedings are instituted in a court of law.

The capacity of a person to marry is determined by that person's domicile (see below) at the time of the marriage, but the formalities of a marriage (sometimes referred to as the formal validity of that marriage) are determined by the law of the place that the marriage takes place (often referred to as the *lex loci celebrationus*). Thus, an Englishman can effect a valid marriage in Las Vegas, or on the beach in the Bahamas, provided that the ceremony is in accordance with the law of that place. Further complications arise, however, where the place that the marriage occurs is unclear. That was the problem in *SB v SSWP* [2014] UKUT 495 (AAC), [2015] AACR 15. The claimant was the widow of a man originally from Pakistan. She married him in Pakistan and had had three children by him. Her claim for bereavement benefits had been refused because there was evidence that the deceased had been married already at the time of the claimant's marriage and there was no evidence that that marriage had been dissolved, or that his first wife had predeceased him. The factual background was confused, but by the time the case came before the Upper Tribunal it had become clear that the earlier marriage had been conducted by telephone at a time that the deceased was in the UK and the putative wife was in Pakistan. The question was, therefore, by what law the ceremony of marriage should be governed when the parties were in different places; or to put it another way—what is the place of a marriage transacted on the telephone? The decision of Judge West in the UT is unequivocal—to be valid the marriage must be valid by the laws of both places. As a telephone marriage is not valid in the UK it followed that the first marriage of the deceased had been void and that the claimant's marriage was, therefore, good and her claim succeeded. This appears to be the first time that the validity of a telephonic marriage has been determined in English law. The decision of Judge West was in accordance with the revised opinion expressed on behalf of the Secretary of State and represented the considered views of other departments of state (e.g. the Border Agency) to whom these are matters of great concern.

Even proving the existence of a marriage that is claimed to have been celebrated in a foreign country may be difficult where there is, or was at the time, little formality in connection with the ceremony and no reliable records of marriages are maintained The difficulties associated with proof of some marriages have been demonstrated in *CP/4062/2004* and again in *CP/891/2008*. In both these cases the parties had been married in Yemen from where no formal record of the marriage was available. Both parties to the marriage made statements about the celebration of the marriage and the wife, who had remained at all times in Yemen, was interviewed there through an interpreter. Some of the information that was given about the marriage appeared to be contradictory. For that reason, and others, the claim for a Category B pension was refused. The interest in both of these cases lies in the approach taken by Commissioner Jacobs, and adopted in the later case by Deputy Commissioner Wikeley, to the absence of reliable documentary evidence of the marriage. In both cases the DM and the appeal tribunal had relied upon that absence, at least in part, as the reason for their decision that no marriage had been shown to exist. The commissioners find this to be a wrong approach. In the words of Commissioner Jacobs the absence of contemporary documentary evidence

1.1012

"is a neutral factor. The decision maker and the tribunal have to decide if the claimant is genuine or dishonest. It is wrong to approach that task by taking the lack of contemporaneous evidence as a factor against the claimant. To do so would be to assume what has to be decided."

This point has been reiterated in *AR v SSWP* [2012] UKUT 467 (AAC). There the question was whether it could be proved that the claimant's late husband had been divorced from his first wife at the time of his marriage to the claimant. Both marriages and the alleged divorce had taken place in the Yemen where there was no official record kept. In the UT, Judge Wikeley, was able to allow the appeal and substitute his own decision largely because a retirement pension, awarded on the basis of her husband's contribution record, had already been in payment to the claimant for more than 13 years. Payment was stopped when the department received a claim from another woman in the Yemen also claiming to be a widow of the deceased husband. This was his first wife whom the claimant said had been divorced before her own marriage. The FTT had approached the question on the basis that the claimant would have to prove the validity of that divorce in order to succeed in her claim. Judge Wikeley points out that this was an error of law. As the pension was already in payment the onus of proof rested with the department to prove that her husband had not been divorced so that the claimant's marriage was polygamous—as to which see below. On the evidence before him the judge was able to find that they had not done so.

Further consideration of the way in which evidence as to the existence of a marriage should be approached has been given in *SA v SSWP* [2013] 436 (AAC). The claim for bereavement benefits had been rejected for various reasons, but by the time the matter came before Judge Wikeley in the UT it was settled that the issue concerned a possible earlier marriage of the deceased to a wife who had remained in Bangladesh and by whom he had claimed, some years earlier, to have had four children. Evidence of this claim (and therefore the marriage) was contained in a statutory declaration that the deceased had made to the tax authority in this country. In the FTT the claim for bereavement benefit made by the woman now claiming to have been his wife was refused. They found that a claimed talaq divorce from his alleged first wife was invalid because by the time of the divorce he was already domiciled in the UK (see below) and consequently his marriage to the claimant was bigamous and invalid. But the question remained-was he ever in fact married in Bangladesh? The FTT held that the evidence provided by the statutory declaration was decisive; they said that there would need to be "the strongest possible evidence" to rebut the conclusion that the deceased had been married. Judge Wikeley found this to be an error of law. (The representative of the SSWP had supported that view). The judge found that while a statutory declaration is more "than a statement written down" so as to reflect the formality and solemnity with which it is made, it still needs to be examined within the context of all the other evidence presented with it. In this case there was a considerable amount of contrary evidence. In particular the claimant's representative had suggested that the deceased's declaration had probably been made untruthfully to gain some advantage in relation to his tax coding. The judge found that on the totality of the evidence before him it was probable that the deceased had not been married in Bangladesh and he adds an appendix that refers to some research of his own that would give credence to the explanation offered by the representative.

Polygamous marriages raise special problems of their own. As the law stands, a marriage which is actually polygamous will not be recognised as a valid marriage at all—even when only one wife is in this country. However, where the marriage is only potentially polygamous or was previously polygamous, but is no longer so, it will be treated as a valid marriage for any period in which it is in fact monogamous (See reg.2 of the Social Security and Family Allowances (Polygamous Marriages) Regulations 1975 (SI 1975/561)). But the marriage must be valid according to the foreign law in question, and a person domiciled in England at the time cannot contract a valid polygamous marriage. See s.11(d) of the Matrimonial Causes Act 1973. There have been several recent Commissioners' decisions on this point. All of them involve parties from the Indian subcontinent who have married there, then come to live in the UK (or at least the husband has) and then returned to India for a period during which the husband has contracted a second marriage. This second marriage is valid by the law of, say, Bangladesh, but will not be valid in English law if the husband at the time of that marriage had acquired a domicile of choice in the UK. If he was then domiciled in the UK the second marriage is void and his first marriage remains legally monogamous. In the event of his death the first wife may then claim a widow's pension whether she is resident in the UK or not (*R(G) 1/95*).

Note the importance of identifying the time at which the domicile of the parties, or one of them, must be determined. See the decision of Judge Wikeley in *SB v SSWP* [2010] UKUT 219 (AAC) where the critical point was the domicile of the husband at the time of his marriage to the claimant. If he were then domiciled in England that marriage was polygamous and so invalid, but if he were then domiciled in Bangladesh, it was a valid polygamous marriage by the law of that country and his other wife having predeceased him, the claimant was now his only surviving widow, and entitled to the benefit.

1.1013

The capacity of a person to marry (or divorce) is determined by that person's domicile at that time. Domicile is a technical status and often poses a complex question of law. In *R(G) 1/93*, the Commissioner relied upon the principle set out in the standard work, Dicey and Morris, *Conflict of Laws*. He puts it as follows:

"Under English law every person receives a domicile of origin at birth and, throughout his life, cannot ever be without a domicile and, further, at any one time, can only have one domicile. However, a person can acquire a domicile of choice by residing in a country, other than that of his domicile of origin, with the intention of staying there either permanently or indefinitely. All surrounding circumstances must be taken into account when determining whether a person has acquired a domicile of choice, including his motive for taking up residence initially and whether or not that residence was precarious. A person may abandon a domicile of choice only if he both ceases to reside and ceases to intend to reside there; it is not, for example, necessary to show a positive intention not to return, it suffices to prove an absence of intention to continue to reside. When a person abandons a domicile of choice he either acquires a new domicile of choice or his domicile of origin revives."

In the present case the Commissioner substituted his own decision for that of the tribunal. He found that the husband had a domicile of origin in what is now Bangladesh; had acquired a domicile of choice by many years of residence in the UK, but that he had abandoned that domicile of choice when he returned to Bangladesh for a period of two years and tried to set up business there. It was at that time that he married a second wife. Subsequently, he returned to England and to his first wife who had remained here all along. At the time of his death in England he may well have re-acquired his domicile of choice here but that was not important. What mattered was his domicile at the time of the second marriage. Since that was in Bangladesh the marriage was valid and since both wives survived him they were both polygamous marriages. Neither wife could therefore claim a widow's pension.

The importance of determining the deceased's domicile at the time of marriage has been reiterated in another case before Judge Wikeley in *SSWP v MN (BB)* [2018] UKUT 68 (AAC). In his case the first wife had predeceased her husband, but there were insufficient facts found by the FTT from which to determine his domicile at the time of his second marriage; if at that time he had already acquired a domicile of choice in England and Wales his marriage to the claimant was invalid under the Matrimonial Causes Act 1973 which meant that she was not married to him at all and hence could not be a surviving spouse for the purposes of a claim for Bereavement Benefit.

Even where no issue of domicile arises it will still be necessary for the claimant to show that her marriage was in fact monogamous at the time of her husband's death. Where the marriage has been polygamous at some earlier time that may require proof either that all other wives have predeceased their husband or that the earlier marriage has been dissolved by a valid decree of divorce as well as proof that the claimant's own marriage was valid. All of these issues arose in *CG/1822/1998*.

Deputy Commissioner Gamble gave extensive instructions to the legally qualified member of the tribunal, to whom the decision was returned, which other tribunals may find of assistance.

1.1014   The complications of qualifying for a widow's benefit and the difficulties that can arise in determining the validity of the claimant's foreign marriage when that in turn depends upon a foreign divorce, are graphically illustrated in *CP/3108/2004*.

The divorce and marriage had taken place in Pakistan in 1961 so this required consideration of no fewer than three recognition statutes, and two versions of the common law. Perhaps the most interesting feature of this case is, however, that the claimant was the second widow to claim a pension on the basis of marriage to the same husband; both claims have gone before a Commissioner and both have been successful! There are, therefore, conflicting decisions as to the validity of the same divorce. Commissioner Edward Jacobs points out that at the moment there is no way effectively to avoid the possibility of this happening. He suggests that there should be a power for the Secretary of State to refer decisions to be considered together by a Tribunal or by a Commissioner. An appeal to the Court of Appeal might be expected, but the decision in respect of the first widow is now probably out of time.

The effect of the Human Rights Act on the treatment of polygamous marriages has been considered by a Tribunal of Commissioners considering appeals in three cases. (*R(P)2/06*).

1.1015   In all of them both marriages had taken place in Bangladesh and all the partners had been domiciled there at the time of those marriages. Both marriages would therefore be regarded by English Law as valid marriages for most purposes. However, it was accepted that for widow's benefits the Court Appeal had decided in *(Fuljuan) Bibi v CAO* [1998] 1 F.L.R. 375 that where a man was survived by two polygamously married wives neither of them could qualify as his "widow" for the purpose of claiming benefits. The question was, therefore, whether this treatment amounted to an improper interpretation of the legislation in the light of the Human Rights Act. It was conceded, at least before the commissioners, that the claim engaged their rights under Art.8 (right to family life) and it was argued that disqualifying a polygamous wife was unlawful discrimination under Art.14. All of the tribunal held that it was not. A majority (Chief Commissioner Hickinbottom and Commissioner Howell) held that to treat a person who was polygamously married at the relevant time, differently from one who was monogamously (even if potentially polygamously) married, was not discrimination within any of the grounds of Art.14. In their view it was a difference of treatment based upon a factual difference that was rational and in accordance with the accepted norms of our society, and therefore, not discrimination.

Perhaps more convincingly, Commissioner Levenson held that it was discrimination on the grounds of "status", but that it was justified and proportional for the same reasons.

A marriage lasts until it is dissolved by a decree of divorce or of annulment. In either case the marriage persists until the decree absolute is granted. Foreign divorces raise the same problems as foreign marriages. Recognition is provided for under s.46 of the Family Law Act 1986. Foreign divorces will be recognised where they are valid by the law of the country in which they are obtained and if, at that time, either party to the marriage was habitually resident in that country, or was domiciled there, or was a national of that country. Where a marriage is void, for example, because it is bigamous, it has no legal effect whatsoever, and no benefits can be claimed on the basis of it. Where, however, a marriage is annulled for a reason that makes it only voidable, for example because of non-consummation, it is now clear that the marriage is to be regarded as valid and subsisting up to the date of annulment (see Nullity of Marriage Act 1975 s.5 and *R(G) 1/85*).

Proof of death

1.1016   The death of the claimant's spouse is usually proved by production of the death certificate. Difficulties can arise, however, where no certificate is issued because the spouse has simply disappeared. Since October 1, 2014 it has been possible in England and Wales to apply to the High Court for a declaration of presumption of death. (The same has been possible in Scotland since 1977). The application may be made where the court is satisfied that a person has died, or where that cannot be established that they have not been known to be alive for a period of at least 7 years. Any person may make the application, but the person who is missing must have been domiciled in this country or to have been resident here for at least one year when they were last known to be alive and where the applicant is the spouse or civil partner of the missing person they too, must be either domiciled in this country or to have been resident here for a year at the date the application is made. Where the application is made by a person who is not a spouse, civil partner or a close relative the court must refuse to make the declaration if they consider that the application does not have a sufficient interest in that decision. Where the court is satisfied that the person has died the declaration will include a finding as to the date and time of death; where that is uncertain it will be at the end of the period after which the court is satisfied that they have died. Where the court cannot be satisfied that the person is dead, but is satisfied that they have been missing and not known to have been alive for at least seven years, the finding will be that they have died at the end of the seven years after they were last known to have been alive. Although this jurisdiction applies only to the High Court the act does not abolish the power of any other court or tribunal to make a decision based upon the common law presumption of death. Thus it appears possible for social security tribunals to continue to consider an application for bereavement benefits on that basis. In doing so it appears to have been accepted that the decision can be based on either a finding that the missing person has died (where on the evidence it is appropriate to do so) or, on the basis that death can be presumed because the person has been missing and not known to have been alive for at least seven years. (See the High Court decision in *Chard v Chard* [1956] P. 259) That this is the correct approach seems to be confirmed by s.16 of the Presumption of Death Act because that section requires any other court or tribunal making such a determination to include the requirements of s.2 as to date and time of death. Note, however, that the Act does not require that a spouse or civil partner who is seeking that finding before a tribunal to be domiciled or resident in this country, so it would appear to be possible still for a widow living overseas to make a claim based on that presumption.

Special provision is now made in ss.3 and 4 of the Administration Act for late claims to be made in respect of a death which is only recently discovered or presumed so that such spouses can claim back-payment of benefit in respect of a period of more than the usual one year. Note, however, that in the case of a widow who had only just discovered the fact of her husband's death, though that may have occurred several years earlier, the effect of s.3 is only to permit a claim for back-payment of benefit for up to 24 months at most (see *CG/75/96*).

There is one situation in which a spouse will forfeit all their rights to bereavement benefit though it is not mentioned in the legislation at all. This is where the claimant has been guilty of the homicide of the spouse (see *R. v Chief N.I. Commissioner Ex p. Connor* [1981] 1 Q.B. 758). The rule is one of public policy, based upon the principle that no one should profit by their own wrongdoing and applies generally to all interests deriving from the death of the deceased.

At common law the consequence of the forfeiture rule was that the spouse lost the pension rights entirely, but since the introduction of the Forfeiture Act 1982, it has been possible for a Commissioner (now a judge of the Upper Tribunal) to modify the effect of the rule. Under the Forfeiture Act 1982, the question whether a spouse's right to any benefit is to be forfeited must be determined at first instance by the UT. The matter can no longer come before an appeal tribunal though where the UT has determined that the right to benefit is not to be forfeited, any other issues as to entitlement should be determined by a decision-maker in the usual way, unless the claimant has consented to the UT deciding the matter (*R(G) 3/84*).

Not all homicides will result in forfeiture. Even before 1982 the courts had   1.1017 developed some exceptions to the rule, e.g. in motor manslaughter cases and, later, in cases of diminished responsibility where the level of culpability was non-existent. Now, however, the Court of Appeal has suggested (in *Dunbar v Plant* [1997] 4 All E.R. 289) that the better approach is to regard the forfeiture rule as applicable to all homicides and to leave any relief against the rule to be achieved using the Forfeiture Act. In *Dunbar v Plant* the rule was applied to the property rights of the survivor of a suicide pact, though the majority of that court thought that she should then be relieved from any forfeiture at all, so that she took both the title to joint property by survivorship, and the proceeds of an insurance policy on the life of her partner. In that case also the Court of Appeal settles a point previously the subject of dispute; it is now clear that the Forfeiture Act permits the court (the UT) to remove the effect of forfeiture entirely where it is appropriate to do so.

In *CFP/2688/2004* (to be reported as *R(FP) 1/05*) Commissioner Rowland confirms that the effect of *Dunbar v Plant* is that the forfeiture rule should normally apply in all cases where the UT is satisfied that the claimant is guilty of manslaughter. That applies even where the claimant may have been acquitted of manslaughter in the Crown Court, as in *Gray v Barr* [1971] 2 Q.B. 554.

Commissioner Rowland does leave open the possibility, however, that the UT could find a conviction of manslaughter on the ground of diminished responsibility to be inappropriate, and conclude that the claimant should be regarded instead, as not guilty of homicide by reason of insanity. This could happen, for example, where the claimant has pleaded guilty to manslaughter on the ground of diminished responsibility and a hospital order has been imposed, rather than to have stood trial and pleaded not guilty to murder by reason of insanity. In such a case, if the UT finds that a claimant should have been found not guilty by reason of insanity, the rule of forfeiture would not apply at all. It is likely, however, that it will be more usual for the forfeiture rule to be applied and the UT then grant full, or partial, relief against that forfeiture. In the present case no relief was allowed because the sum involved was only 47p per week and the commissioner felt its loss reflected the role of the claimant in causing the death of his wife.

1.1018   The Act, however, does not permit any relief where the party claiming has committed murder. A spouse convicted of murder, therefore, must lose all bereavement benefits—see *R(G) 1/90*. In *R(FG) 1/04* the claimant had been convicted of soliciting her husband's murder (an offence under the Offences Against the Person Act, 1861). She claimed a widow's pension after her release from prison. The Commissioner held that the forfeiture rule applied to her claim because she had "unlawfully counselled" her husband's death within s.1(2) of the Forfeiture Act 1982, but that it was not caught by s.5 of that Act which proscribed any relief where the claimant was convicted of murder. This meant that it was open to the Commissioner to modify the effect of forfeiture. On the facts of this case however, he held that no modification was appropriate because she had been closely and directly involved in the murder. Where the spouse has been convicted only of manslaughter the matter will depend upon all the circumstances of the case, in particular upon the degree of culpability inherent in the act (compare *R(G) 1/83 and R(G) 3/84*) and upon whether the killing was the result of provocation—see *R(G) 1/98* where the Commissioner restored benefits from the date of his decision, some seven years after the death, and limited, to 50 per cent, the widow's future entitlement to a Category B pension. *BC v SSWP* [2014] UKUT 237 (AAC) is a further example of the claimant's being relieved entirely of the effect of the forfeiture rule. The claimant had been convicted of the manslaughter of her husband after pleading guilty at trial. The death resulted from a drunken brawl after many years in a violent marriage. The trial judge imposed only a 3 year period of probation as her sentence. The Upper Tribunal Judge took account of the leniency of the sentence in deciding that the relief against forfeiture should be given in full- thus the claimant was able to rely upon her deceased husband's contribution record in now making a claim for retirement pension. Although the claimant had delayed making her claim for many years (and the rules against back-dating a claim would apply) the relief was granted, with effect from the date of her conviction, so that she was able to take advantage of the enhancement by deferment that had occurred. In *CFG 4622/03* the claimant had been convicted of manslaughter of his wife on his own admission (the jury having been directed to find him not guilty of murder because of his wife's provocation). The Commissioner, taking account of the comments made by the judge in passing sentence, applied the rule of forfeiture to the bereavement payment, but relieved him of forfeiture in all other respects so that he was entitled to Widowed Parent's Allowance in respect of 2 children for whom he was responsible, and for any potential pension entitlement that he might have as a result of his wife's contributions.

Note that it is not necessary that the spouse should have been convicted of the homicide; it is enough that they have committed it. Accordingly, when bereavement benefits have been paid between the death and the conviction (or more usually apprehension) there will be an overpayment that is almost certainly recoverable. Note as well, that although forfeiture is mandatory following a conviction for murder, there is no principle under which there must necessarily be relief when the claimant is convicted of manslaughter. In *R(G) 1/91* the claimant's conviction of murder was quashed, because some evidence was admitted that was technically hearsay, but a sentence of life imprisonment was imposed and the Commissioner held that there should be no relief of the forfeiture rule.

Part 7

Final provisions

Power to make consequential amendments etc

53.- (1) The Secretary of State or the Treasury may by order make consequential, incidental or supplementary provision in connection with any provision made by this Act.   **1.1019**

(2) An order under this section may amend, repeal, revoke or otherwise modify any enactment (whenever passed or made).

(3) "Enactment" includes an enactment contained in subordinate legislation within the meaning of the Interpretation Act 1978.

Regulations and orders

54.- (1) Regulations and orders under this Act are to be made by statutory instrument.   **1.1020**

(2) A statutory instrument containing (whether alone or with other provisions)—

(a) regulations under section 3, 17, 18(3) or (5), 19, 20, 30, 32 or 34,

(b) the first regulations under section 10,

(c) an order under section 53 that amends or repeals a provision of an Act,

(d) regulations under Schedule 17,

(e) regulations under paragraph 2 of Schedule 18 or regulations under paragraph 7 of that Schedule that amend a provision of an Act, or

(f) the first regulations under paragraph 1 or 3 of that Schedule, may not be made unless a draft of the instrument has been laid before and approved by a resolution of each House of Parliament.

(3) Any other statutory instrument containing regulations or an order under this Act is subject to annulment in pursuance of a resolution of either House of Parliament.

(4) Subsection (3) does not apply to a statutory instrument containing an order under section 56(1), (6) or (8) only.

(5) A power to make regulations or an order under this Act may be used—

(a) to make different provision for different purposes;

(b) in relation to all or only some of the purposes for which it may be used.

(6) Regulations or orders under this Act may include incidental, supplementary, consequential, transitional, transitory or saving provision.

Extent

1.1021   **55.-** (1) This Act extends to England and Wales and Scotland only, subject to the

following provisions of this section.

(2) Any amendment or repeal made by this Act has the same extent as the enactment to which it relates.

(3) This Part extends also to Northern Ireland.

Commencement

1.1022   **56.-** (1) This Act comes into force on such day or days as the Secretary of State may by order appoint, subject as follows.

(2) The following come into force on the day on which this Act is passed—

(a) section 29;

(b) section 51;

(c) this Part.

(3) The following come into force at the end of the period of 2 months beginning with the day on which this Act is passed—

(a) Part 3;

(b) sections 34 and 35;

(c) section 41;

(d) sections 47 and 48;

(e) paragraph 30(2) of Schedule 13.

(4) Part 1 comes into force on 6 April 2016, so far as not brought into force earlier by an order under subsection (1).

(5) The Secretary of State may by order—

(a) amend subsection (4) so as to replace the reference to 6 April 2016 with a later date, and

(b) make corresponding amendments in Part 1 or any enactment amended by it.

(6) Section 52 comes into force on such day or days as the Treasury may by order appoint.

(7) An order under subsection (1) or (6) may appoint different days for different purposes.

(8) The Secretary of State may by order make transitional, transitory or saving provision in connection with the coming into force of any provision of this Act.

GENERAL NOTE

1.1023   All the provisions relevant to the new state pension came into effect on or before April 6, 2016 (the earlier introduction of some provisions being to allow regulations to be made). The power in subs. (5) was not used. That being so, this volume does not include the various commencement regulations under which provisions were introduced before April 6, 2016. If reference need to be made to a particular date, then this can be seen most conveniently in the schedule to the last of the eight commencement orders used to introduce the provisions of the Act. See Pensions Act

(Commencement No.8) Order 2016 (SI 2016/203) made on February 22, 2016, where the other commencement orders are also detailed.

Short title

57.- This Act may be cited as the Pensions Act 2014.   1.1024

SCHEDULE 1

TRANSITIONAL RATE OF STATE PENSION: CALCULATING THE AMOUNT

PART 1

INTRODUCTION

1 (1) This Schedule sets out how to calculate the amounts used to work out the transitional   1.1025
rate of a person's state pension.

(2) Part 2 of the Schedule sets out how to calculate the amount for a person's pre-commencement qualifying years.

(3) Part 3 of the Schedule sets out how to calculate the amount for a person's post-commencement qualifying years (if any).

PART 2

AMOUNT FOR PRE-COMMENCEMENT QUALIFYING YEARS

How to calculate the amount for pre-commencement qualifying years

2 A person's amount for pre-commencement qualifying years is calculated as follows.   1.1026

Step 1 - calculate the person's pension under the old system

Calculate the weekly rate based on the old state pension and graduated retirement benefit (see paragraph 3 for more about this).

Step 2 - calculate a pension based on the new system

Calculate the weekly rate based on the new state pension (see paragraph 4 for more about this).

Step 3 - take whichever rate is higher (the foundation amount)

Take whichever of the rates found under Steps 1 and 2 is higher.

Step 4 - revalue to date when the person reached pensionable age

Revalue the amount of that rate in accordance with paragraph 6.

The amount for the person's pre-commencement qualifying years is the amount as revalued under Step 4.

Step 1: calculation of the person's pension under the old system

3 (1) For the purposes of Step 1 of the calculation in paragraph 2, the weekly rate   1.1027
based on the old state pension and graduated retirement benefit is

    (a) the rate of any Category A retirement pension and graduated retirement benefit to which the person would have been entitled if the person had reached pensionable age on 6 April 2016, or

    (b) the rate of any graduated retirement benefit to which the person would have been entitled under section 36(7) of the National Insurance Act 1965 (persons not entitled to retirement pension) if the person had reached pensionable age on that date.

(2) The following rules apply for the purposes of calculating that rate.

(3) Calculate the rate that would have had effect on 6 April 2016 (but see subparagraph (6)).

(4) Ignore—

    (a) the amendments made by paragraphs 53 and 55 of Schedule 12 (which limit Category A retirement pensions and graduated retirement benefit to people who reach pensionable age before 6 April 2016);

    (b) any requirement to make a claim;

    (c) any provision suspending payment of, or disqualifying a person from receiving, any amount;

    (d) section 45B of the Contributions and Benefits Act (reduction of additional pension because of pension sharing);

473

(e) section 37 of the National Insurance Act 1965 (graduated retirement benefit for widows etc).

(5) Read the reference in section 45(4)(b) of the Contributions and Benefits Act (additional pension) to a person's working life as a reference to the period—

(a) beginning with the tax year in which the person reached 16, and

(b) ending with the tax year before the one in which the person actually reached pensionable age.

(6) If an order under section 150 or 150A of the Administration Act (up-rating) is made before 6 April 2016 and it provides for an increase to come into force after that date, it is to be treated for the purposes of calculating the rate under this paragraph as having already come into force.

(7) Where regulations under section 22(5ZA) of the Contributions and Benefits Act have the effect that a person is credited, on or after 6 April 2016, with earnings or contributions for a tax year starting before that date, the earnings or contributions are to be treated for the purposes of calculating the rate under this paragraph as having been credited before 6 April 2016.

(8) A determination under section 48A(2) of the Pension Schemes Act 1993 (contracting-out: reinstatement in state scheme following payment of contributions equivalent premium) made on or after 6 April 2016 is to be treated for the purposes of calculating the rate under this paragraph as having been made before 6 April 2016.

Step 2: calculation of a pension based on the new system

1.1028
4 (1) For the purposes of Step 2 of the calculation in paragraph 2, the weekly rate based on the new state pension is as follows.

(2) If the person has 35 or more pre-commencement qualifying years, the rate is equal to—

(a) the full rate of the state pension on 6 April 2016, less

(b) any amount to reflect contracting out under the old system (see paragraph 5).

(3) If the person has fewer than 35 pre-commencement qualifying years, the rate is equal to—

(a) the appropriate proportion of the full rate of the state pension on 6 April 2016, less

(b) any amount to reflect contracting out under the old system (see paragraph 5).

(4) The "appropriate proportion", in relation to a person, is—

5 (1) In paragraph 4(2) and (3) references to an "amount to reflect contracting out under the old system" are to an amount equal to any difference between—

(a) the amount of any additional pension included in the Category A retirement pension calculated for the purposes of Step 1 of the calculation in paragraph 2, and

(b) the amount of any additional pension that would have been included if—

(i) sections 46 and 48A of the Pension Schemes Act 1993 were ignored, and

(ii) for the purposes of calculating the amounts referred to in section 45(2)(c) and (d) of the Contributions and Benefits Act any earnings paid to or for the benefit of the person in respect of contracted-out employment were treated as if they were not in respect of contracted-out employment.

(2) "Contracted-out employment" means employment qualifying a person for a pension provided by a salary related contracted-out scheme, a money purchase contracted-out scheme or an appropriate personal pension scheme (and expressions used in this definition have the same meaning as in the Pension Schemes Act 1993).

Step 4: revaluation

1.1029
6 (1) This paragraph determines how the amount mentioned in Step 4 of the calculation in paragraph 2 is to be revalued for the purposes of that Step.

(2) If the amount is equal to or less than the full rate of the state pension on 6 April 2016, the amount is to be revalued in accordance with increases in the full rate of the state pension (see sub-paragraph (4)).

(3) If the amount is greater than the full rate of the state pension on 6 April 2016—

(a) so much of the amount as is equal to the full rate of the state pension on 6 April 2016 is to be revalued in accordance with increases in the full rate of the state pension (see sub-paragraph (4)), and

(b) so much of the amount as exceeds the full rate of the state pension on that date is to be revalued in accordance with increases in the general level of prices (see sub-paragraph (5)).

(4) For the purposes of sub-paragraphs (2) and (3)(a), an amount is revalued in accordance with increases in the full rate of the state pension by increasing it by the same percentage as any increase in the full rate of the state pension in the period—

(a) beginning with 6 April 2016, and

(b) ending with the day on which the person reached pensionable age.

(5) For the purposes of sub-paragraph (3)(b), an amount is revalued in accordance with increases in the general level of prices by adding—

(a) the amount, and

(b) the amount multiplied by the revaluing percentage specified in the last order under section 148AC(3) of the Administration Act to come into force before the person reached pensionable age.

PART 3

AMOUNT FOR POST-COMMENCEMENT QUALIFYING YEARS

7 (1) A person's amount for post-commencement qualifying years (if any) is calculated as **1.1030** follows.

(2) If the person has 35 or more post-commencement qualifying years, the amount is equal to the full rate of the state pension on the day on which the person reached pensionable age.

(3) If the person has fewer than 35 post-commencement qualifying years, the amount is equal to the following proportion of the full rate of the state pension on the day on which the person reached pensionable age—

1/35 x number of person's post commencement qualifying years

GENERAL NOTE

Paragraph 4

In *FE v Secretary of State for Work & Pensions* (RP) [2019] UKUT 61 (AAC) Upper **1.1031** Tribunal Judge Wikeley held that (a) pre-March 2001 periods of Australian residency were to be taken into account for the purposes of Step 1, but (b) to be ignored for the purposes of Step 2. The reason for (a) is that, until March 2001, a Reciprocal Social Security Agreement between the UK and Australia had effect and the recognition of Australian periods of residency provided for by the Agreement are preserved in relation to the benefits mentioned in s.299 of the Pensions Act 2004, which includes retirement pension. Step 1 is concerned with how a claimant's retirement pension (as opposed to the new state pension) would have been calculated. The reason for (b) is that the effect of the former Reciprocal Agreement has not been preserved by s.299 for the purposes of the new state pension. Accordingly, periods of Australian residency cannot be relied upon in calculating entitlement to the new state pension and Step 2 operates by reference to the entitlement rules for the new state pension.

SCHEDULE 2   **Section 5**

TRANSITIONAL RATE OF STATE PENSION: UP-RATING

1 This Schedule sets out how to up-rate the transitional rate of a person's state pension. **1.1032**

2 In this Schedule a reference to the transitional rate of a person's state pension is to the rate—

(a) taking into account any reduction under section 14, but

(b) ignoring any increase under section 17.

3 (1) The transitional rate of a person's state pension is to be increased under this paragraph if it is equal to or less than the full rate.

(2) If at any time the full rate of the state pension is increased, the person's transitional rate is increased (at that time) by the same percentage as the increase in the full rate.

4 (1) The transitional rate of a person's state pension is to be increased under this paragraph if it exceeds the full rate.

(2) If at any time the full rate of the state pension is increased, the person's transitional rate is increased (at that time) by the same amount as the amount by which the full rate is increased.

(3) If at any time an order under section 151A of the Administration Act comes into force, the person's transitional rate is increased (at that time) by an amount equal to the appropriate percentage of the excess.

(4) In sub-paragraph (3)—

"the appropriate percentage" means the percentage specified in the order, and

"the excess" means the amount by which the transitional rate exceeded the full rate immediately before the order came into force.

GENERAL NOTE

1.1033   The sums which, under paragraph 4(3), are the amounts of state pensions under Part 1 of the Pensions Act at the transitional rate which exceed the full rate were increased by 2.4 per cent with effect from April 8, 2019: see art.6(4) of the Social Security Benefits Up-rating Order 2019 (SI 2019/480).

SCHEDULE 3   **Section 7**

SURVIVOR'S PENSION UNDER SECTION 7: INHERITED AMOUNT

Introduction

1.1034   1 This Schedule—
  (a) sets out the circumstances in which a person (the "pensioner") is entitled to an inherited amount for the purpose of section 7, and
  (b) determines that amount.

Dead spouse or civil partner in old state pension system etc

1.1035   2 (1) A pensioner whose spouse or civil partner has died is entitled to an inherited amount under this paragraph if—
  (a) the marriage took place or the civil partnership was formed before 6 April 2016,
  (b) the spouse or civil partner died before 6 April 2016,
  (c) the pensioner was under pensionable age when the spouse or civil partner died, and
  (d) the pensioner would, on reaching pensionable age, have been entitled to a Category B retirement pension under section 48B(4) or (4A) or 48BB of the Contributions and Benefits Act if the words "before 6 April 2016" were omitted.
(2) The inherited amount is equal to the weekly rate at which that Category B retirement pension would have been payable on the day on which the pensioner reached pensionable age if any element of the rate attributable to the basic pension were ignored.
    3 (1) A pensioner whose spouse or civil partner has died is entitled to an inherited amount under this paragraph if—
  (a) the marriage took place or the civil partnership was formed before 6 April 2016,
  (b) the spouse or civil partner reached pensionable age before 6 April 2016 but died on or after that date,
  (c) the pensioner was under pensionable age when the spouse or civil partner died, and
  (d) the pensioner would, on reaching pensionable age, have been entitled to a Category B retirement pension under section 48BB of the Contributions and Benefits Act if in subsection (3) of that section:
      (i) the words "before 6 April 2016" were omitted, and
      (ii) the reference to a bereavement allowance were a reference to bereavement support payment under section 30 of this Act.
(2) The inherited amount is equal to the weekly rate at which that Category B retirement pension would have been payable on the day on which the pensioner reached pensionable age if section 48BB(8) and (9) of the Contributions and Benefits Act were ignored.
    4 (1) A pensioner whose spouse or civil partner has died is entitled to an inherited amount under this paragraph if—
  (a) the marriage took place or the civil partnership was formed before 6 April 2016,
  (b) the spouse or civil partner reached pensionable age before 6 April 2016 but died on or after that date,
  (c) the pensioner was over pensionable age when the spouse or civil partner died, and
  (d) the pensioner would, when the spouse or civil partner died, have been entitled to a Category B retirement pension under section 48B(1) or (1A) of the Contributions and Benefits Act if the words "before 6 April 2016" were omitted.
(2) The inherited amount is equal to the weekly rate at which that Category B retirement pension would have been payable on the day on which the spouse or civil partner died if any element of the rate attributable to the basic pension were ignored.

Dead spouse or civil partner in new state pension system

1.1036   5 (1) A pensioner whose spouse or civil partner has died is entitled to an inherited amount under this paragraph if—

(a the marriage took place or the civil partnership was formed before 6 April 2016,

(b) the pensioner was over pensionable age when the spouse or civil partner died,

(c) the spouse or civil partner was, immediately before his or her death, entitled to a state pension payable at the transitional rate, and

(d) that transitional rate exceeded the full rate of the state pension.

(2) The inherited amount is half of the amount by which the transitional rate of the state pension for the spouse or civil partner exceeded the full rate of the state pension immediately before the death.

6 (1) A pensioner whose spouse or civil partner has died is entitled to an inherited amount under this paragraph if—

(a) the marriage took place or the civil partnership was formed before 6 April 2016,

(b) the pensioner was under pensionable age when the spouse or civil partner died,

(c) the spouse or civil partner was, immediately before his or her death, entitled to a state pension payable at the transitional rate,

(d) that transitional rate exceeded the full rate of the state pension, and

(e) the pensioner did not marry or form a civil partnership after the death and before reaching pensionable age.

(2) The inherited amount is half of the amount by which the transitional rate of the state pension for the spouse or civil partner would have exceeded the full rate of the state pension if he or she had been alive on the day on which the pensioner reached pensionable age.

7 (1) A pensioner whose spouse or civil partner has died is entitled to an inherited amount under this paragraph if—

(a) the marriage took place or the civil partnership was formed before 6 April 2016,

(b) the pensioner was over pensionable age when the spouse or civil partner died,

(c) the spouse or civil partner was under pensionable age when he or she died but would have been entitled to a state pension payable at the transitional rate if he or she had reached pensionable age on the day of the death, and

(d) that transitional rate would have exceeded the full rate of the state pension.

(2) The inherited amount is half of the amount by which the transitional rate of the state pension for the spouse or civil partner would have exceeded the full rate of the state pension if he or she had reached pensionable age on the day of the death.

8 (1) A pensioner whose spouse or civil partner has died is entitled to an inherited amount under this paragraph if—

(a) the marriage took place or the civil partnership was formed before 6 April 2016,

(b) the pensioner was under pensionable age when the spouse or civil partner died,

(c) the spouse or civil partner died on or after 6 April 2016,

(d) the spouse or civil partner was under pensionable age when he or she died,

(e) the spouse or civil partner would have been entitled to a state pension payable at the transitional rate if he or she had reached pensionable age on the same day as the pensioner,

(f) that transitional rate would have exceeded the full rate of the state pension, and

(g) the pensioner did not marry or form a civil partnership after the death and before reaching pensionable age.

(2) The inherited amount is half of the amount by which the transitional rate of the state pension for the spouse or civil partner would have exceeded the full rate of the state pension if he or she had reached pensionable age on the same day as the pensioner.

Supplementary

9 When determining entitlement to, or calculating, an inherited amount under this Schedule based on entitlement to an old state pension or a state pension under this Part of this Act ignore—   **1.1037**

(a) any requirement to make a claim for that pension;

(b) any provision suspending payment of, or disqualifying a person from receiving, any amount of that pension.

Schedule 4   **Section 7**

Survivor's pension under section 7: up-rating

Introduction

1 This Schedule sets out how to up-rate the rate of a person's state pension under section 7.   **1.1038**

2 In this Schedule a reference to the rate of a person's state pension is to the rate—

(a) ignoring any reduction under section 7(4) (in the case of a state pension under section 7),

(b) taking into account any reduction under section 14 (in the case of a state pension under section 4), and

(c) ignoring any increase under section 17.

3 In this Schedule a reference to "the amount of any state pension that has priority" means the rate of any state pension to which the person is entitled under section 2, 4 or 12.

Rate of section 7 pension, when added to any priority pension, is less than the full rate

1.1039   4 (1) The rate of the person's state pension under section 7 is to be increased under this paragraph if, when added to the amount of any state pension that has priority, it is equal to or less than the full rate of the state pension.

(2) If at any time the full rate is increased, the rate of the person's state pension under section 7 is increased (at that time) by the same percentage as the increase in the full rate.

Rate of section 7 pension, when added to any priority pension, straddles the full rate

1.1040   5 (1) The rate of the person's state pension under section 7 is to be increased under this paragraph if—

(a) the amount of any state pension that has priority is less than the full rate of the state pension, but

(b) the rate of the state pension under section 7, when added to the amount of any state pension that has priority, exceeds the full rate.

(2) If at any time the full rate of the state pension is increased, the rate of the person's state pension under section 7 is increased (at that time) by an amount equal to the appropriate percentage of the shortfall immediately before that time.

(3) If at any time an order under section 151A of the Administration Act comes into force, the rate of the person's state pension under section 7 is increased (at that time) by an amount equal to the appropriate percentage of the excess immediately before the order comes into force.

(4) In this paragraph—

"the appropriate percentage"—

(a) in sub-paragraph (2), means the percentage by which the full rate is increased;

(b) in sub-paragraph (3), means the percentage specified in the order;

"the excess" means the amount by which the rate of the state pension under section 7, when added to the amount of any state pension that has priority, exceeds the full rate;

"the shortfall" means the amount by which the amount of any state pension that has priority is less than the full rate.

Priority pension alone is equal to or higher than the full rate

1.1041   6 (1) The rate of the person's state pension under section 7 is to be increased under this paragraph if the amount of any state pension that has priority is equal to or higher than the full rate of the state pension.

(2) If at any time an order under section 151A of the Administration Act comes into force, the rate of the person's state pension under section 7 is increased (at that time) by the percentage specified in the order.

GENERAL NOTE

1.1042   The amounts which, under paras 5(3) and 6, are the amounts of survivor's pensions which either alone or in combination with one or more other pensions under Part 1 of the Act exceed the full rate, were increased by 2.4 per cent with effect from April 8, 2019: see art.6(4) of the Social Security Benefits Up-rating Order 2019 (SI 2019/480).

SCHEDULE 5   **Section 9**

SURVIVOR'S PENSION UNDER SECTION 9: INHERITED DEFERRAL AMOUNT

Introduction

1.1043   1 This Schedule—

(a) sets out the circumstances in which a person (the "pensioner") is entitled to an inherited deferral amount for the purpose of section 9, and

(b) determines that amount.

Dead spouse or civil partner entitled to old state pension with deferral increase

2 (1) A pensioner whose spouse or civil partner has died is entitled to an inherited deferral amount under this paragraph if— **1.1044**

(a) the spouse or civil partner was entitled to an old state pension with an increase under paragraph 1 or 2A of Schedule 5 to the Contributions and Benefits Act, and

(b) the pensioner would, on reaching pensionable age or on the death of the spouse or civil partner, have been entitled to an old state pension if in the relevant provisions of the Contributions and Benefits Act:

　　(i) the words "before 6 April 2016" were omitted, and

　　(ii) any reference to a bereavement allowance included a reference to bereavement support payment under section 30 of this Act.

(2) The inherited deferral amount is equal to the amount by which the weekly rate of the old state pension for the pensioner would have been increased under paragraph 4 of Schedule 5 to the Contributions and Benefits Act on the day on which the pensioner became entitled to the inherited deferral amount.

(3) For the purposes of calculating the amount of that increase, paragraph 4(1A) of Schedule 5 to the Contributions and Benefits Act has effect as if after the words "apart from" (in each place) there were inserted "this paragraph and".

Dead spouse or civil partner's entitlement to old state pension deferred at time of death

3 (1) A pensioner whose spouse or civil partner has died is entitled to an inherited deferral amount under this paragraph if— **1.1045**

(a) the spouse or civil partner's entitlement to an old state pension was deferred when he or she died, and

(b) the pensioner would, on reaching pensionable age or on the death of the spouse or civil partner, have been entitled to an old state pension if in the relevant provisions of the Contributions and Benefits Act:

(i) the words "before 6 April 2016" were omitted, and

(ii) any reference to a bereavement allowance included a reference to bereavement support payment under section 30 of this Act.

(2) The inherited deferral amount is equal to the amount by which the weekly rate of the old state pension for the pensioner would have been increased under paragraph 4 of Schedule 5 to the Contributions and Benefits Act on the day on which the pensioner became entitled to the inherited deferral amount.

(3) For the purposes of calculating the amount of that increase—

(a) a pensioner who is not entitled to a choice under section 8 is to be treated as having met the condition in paragraph 4(1)(c) of Schedule 5 to the Contributions and Benefits Act,

(b) a pensioner who has chosen under section 8 to be paid a state pension under section 9 is to be treated as having met the condition in paragraph 4(1)(b) of Schedule 5 to the Contributions and Benefits Act, and

(c) paragraph 4(1A) of Schedule 5 to the Contributions and Benefits Act has effect as if after the words "apart from" (in each place) there were inserted "this paragraph and".

(4) In this paragraph "deferred" has the meaning given by section 55(3) of the Contributions and Benefits Act.

"The relevant provisions" of the Contributions and Benefits Act

4 For the purposes of this Schedule "the relevant provisions" of the Contributions and Benefits Act are those mentioned in section 8(9)(b). **1.1046**

Supplementary

5 When determining entitlement to, or calculating, an inherited deferral amount under this Schedule based on entitlement to an old state pension ignore— **1.1047**

(a) any requirement to make a claim for that pension;

(b) any provision suspending payment of, or disqualifying a person from receiving, any amount of that pension.

Pensions Act 2014

SCHEDULE 6   **Section 11**

REDUCED RATE ELECTIONS: EFFECT ON RATE OF SECTION 4 PENSION

Introduction

1.1048   1 This Schedule modifies the rules about the transitional rate of the state pension for a woman if a reduced rate election was in force in respect of her at the beginning of the relevant 35-year period (and expressions used in this paragraph have the same meaning as in section 11).

Increased transitional rate for woman married to person over pensionable age etc

1.1049   2 (1) This paragraph applies to the woman if on reaching pensionable age—
    (a) she is married to a person who has reached pensionable age, or
    (b) she is in a civil partnership with a person who has reached that age.
(2) The transitional rate of the state pension for the woman is—
    (a) the rate determined for her under section 5, or
    (b) if higher, a weekly rate equal to the modified amount for her precommencement qualifying years alone.
(3) The modified amount for the woman's pre-commencement qualifying years alone is the amount that would be calculated under Schedule 1 for her precommencement qualifying years alone if the basic pension in any Category A retirement pension calculated for her for the purposes of paragraph 3 of that Schedule were equal to the basic Category B amount.
(4) "The basic Category B amount" is the amount specified in paragraph 5 of Part 1 of Schedule 4 to the Contributions and Benefits Act on 6 April 2016.
(5) To find out what happens if the marriage or civil partnership comes to an end, see paragraph 4.

Increased transitional rate for widows or divorcees etc

1.1050   3 (1) This paragraph applies to the woman if on reaching pensionable age she is not married or in a civil partnership but she has been married or in a civil partnership before.
(2) The transitional rate of the state pension for the woman is—
    (a) the rate determined for her under section 5, or
    (b) if higher, a weekly rate equal to the modified amount for her precommencement qualifying years alone.
(3) The modified amount for the woman's pre-commencement qualifying years alone is the amount that would be calculated under Schedule 1 for her precommencement qualifying years alone if the basic pension in any Category A retirement pension calculated for her for the purposes of paragraph 3 of that Schedule were equal to the full amount of the basic pension.
(4) "The full amount of the basic pension" is the amount of the basic pension specified in section 44(4) of the Contributions and Benefits Act on 6 April 2016.

Recalculation of transitional rate where circumstances change

1.1051   4 If the woman is married or in a civil partnership on reaching pensionable age but the marriage or civil partnership comes to an end (because of the death of her spouse or civil partner or otherwise)—
    (a) her transitional rate is to be recalculated applying paragraph 3(2), and
    (b) Schedule 2 (up-rating) applies as if the recalculated rate had been the woman's transitional rate on the day on which she reached pensionable age.
5 (1) If neither of paragraphs 2 and 3 apply to the woman but she subsequently comes within paragraph (a) or (b) of paragraph 2(1)—
    (a) her transitional rate is to be recalculated applying paragraph 2(2), and
    (b) Schedule 2 (up-rating) applies as if the recalculated rate had been the woman's transitional rate on the day on which she reached pensionable age.
(2) But the woman's rate is not to be recalculated under sub-paragraph (1) if it has already been recalculated under paragraph 4.
6 Nothing in paragraph 4 or 5 affects—
    (a) the amount of state pension to which a woman is entitled for periods before that paragraph applies to her, or

480

(b) the amount of any increase under section 17 in a case where the period for which the woman's state pension is deferred has ended before that paragraph applies to her.

SCHEDULE 7 **Section 12**

REDUCED RATE ELECTIONS: BASIC AMOUNT OF STATE PENSION UNDER SECTION 12

1 This Schedule— 1.1052
  (a) sets out the circumstances in which a woman is entitled to a basic amount for the purpose of section 12, and
  (b) determines that basic amount.
2 (1) A woman is entitled to a basic amount under this paragraph if she has reached pensionable age and—
  (a) she is married to a person who has reached pensionable age, or
  (b) she is in a civil partnership with a person who has reached that age.
(2) The basic amount is the amount specified in paragraph 5 of Part 1 of Schedule 4 to the Contributions and Benefits Act on the day on which the woman became entitled under this paragraph.
3 (1) A woman is entitled to a basic amount under this paragraph if—
  (a) on reaching pensionable age she is not married or in a civil partnership but she has been married or in a civil partnership before, or
  (b) on reaching pensionable age she was married or in a civil partnership and the marriage or civil partnership has come to an end (because of the death of her spouse or civil partner or otherwise).
(2) The basic amount is the amount of the basic pension specified in section 44(4) of the Contributions and Benefits Act on the day on which the woman became entitled under this paragraph.
4 A woman who is entitled to a basic amount under paragraph 3 is not entitled to a basic amount under paragraph 2.

SCHEDULE 8 **Section 13**

PENSION SHARING: APPROPRIATE WEEKLY RATE UNDER SECTION 13

Introduction

1 This Schedule sets out the appropriate weekly rate of a person's state pension under 1.1053
section 13.

Appropriate weekly rate for pensioner with old state scheme pension credit

2 (1) This paragraph sets out the appropriate weekly rate if the person is entitled to a state 1.1054
pension under section 13 because of an old state scheme pension credit.
(2) If the person became entitled to the old state scheme pension credit in or after the final relevant year, the appropriate weekly rate is a weekly rate equal to the person's notional rate.
(3) If the person became entitled to the old state scheme pension credit before the final relevant year, the appropriate weekly rate is a weekly rate equal to the person's notional rate multiplied by the appropriate revaluation percentage.
(4) For the purposes of sub-paragraphs (2) and (3), a person's "notional rate" is the weekly rate of a notional pension under section 13 the cash equivalent of which would, on the valuation day, have been equal to the amount of the old state scheme pension credit.
(5) For the purposes of sub-paragraph (4) assume that the notional pension becomes payable on the later of—
  (a) the day on which the person reaches pensionable age, and
  (b) the valuation day.
(6) The "appropriate revaluation percentage" is the percentage specified, in relation to earnings factors for the tax year in which the person became entitled to the old state scheme pension credit, by the last order under section 148 of the Administration Act to come into force before the end of the final relevant year.
(7) In this paragraph—
"final relevant year" means the tax year immediately before that in which the person reaches pensionable age;

"valuation day" means the day on which the person became entitled to the old state scheme pension credit.

Appropriate weekly rate for pensioner with new state scheme pension credit

1.1055   3 (1) This paragraph sets out the appropriate weekly rate if the person is entitled to a state pension under section 13 because of a new state scheme pension credit.

(2) If the person was over pensionable age when he or she became entitled to the new state scheme pension credit, the appropriate weekly rate is a weekly rate equal to the amount of the credit.

(3) If the person was under pensionable age when he or she became entitled to the new state scheme pension credit, the appropriate weekly rate is a weekly rate equal to the amount of the credit multiplied by the appropriate revaluation percentage.

(4) The "appropriate revaluation percentage" is the percentage specified, in relation to the tax year in which the person became entitled to the new state scheme pension credit, by the last order under section 148AD of the Administration Act to come into force before the person reached pensionable age.

Supplementary

1.1056   4 (1) Regulations may make provision about the calculation and verification of notional rates under paragraph 2.

(2) The regulations may, in particular, provide—
  (a) for calculation or verification in such manner as may be approved by or on behalf of the Government Actuary, or
  (b) for things done under the regulations to be required to be done in accordance with guidance from time to time prepared by a person specified in the regulations.

SCHEDULE 9   **Section 13**

PENSION SHARING: UP-RATING STATE PENSION UNDER SECTION 13

Introduction

1.1057   1 This Schedule sets out how to up-rate the rate of a person's state pension under section 13.

2 In this Schedule a reference to the rate of a person's state pension is to the rate—
  (a) ignoring any reduction under section 7(4) (in the case of a state pension under section 7),
  (b) taking into account any reduction under section 14 (in the case of a state pension under section 4), and
  (c) ignoring any increase under section 17.

3 (1) In this Schedule "the total amount of any state pension that has priority", in relation to a person's state pension under section 13, means the sum of—
  (a) the rate of any state pension to which the person is entitled under section 2, 4 or 12,
  (b) the rate of any state pension to which the person is entitled under section 7, [¹ ...
  (ba) the rate of any state pension to which the person is entitled under regulations made under section 10 which make provision corresponding or similar to section 7 and Schedules 3 and 4, and]
  (c) the rate of any earlier state pension to which the person is entitled under section 13 (see sub-paragraph (2)).

(2) Where a person is entitled to two or more state pensions under section 13 because he or she has become entitled to two or more state scheme pension credits, a pension arising because of an earlier credit is an "earlier" state pension for the purposes of sub-paragraph (1)(c).

Rate of section 13 pension, when added to any priority pension, is less than the full rate

1.1058   4 (1) The rate of the person's state pension under section 13 is to be increased under this paragraph if, when added to the total amount of any state pension that has priority, it is equal to or less than the full rate of the state pension.

(2) If at any time the full rate is increased, the rate of the person's state pension under section 13 is increased (at that time) by the same percentage as the increase in the full rate.

Rate of section 13 pension, when added to any priority pension, straddles the full rate

5 (1) The rate of the person's state pension under section 13 is to be increased under this paragraph if—

(a) the total amount of any state pension that has priority is less than the full rate of the state pension, but

(b) the rate of the state pension under section 13, when added to the total amount of any state pension that has priority, exceeds the full rate.

(2) If at any time the full rate of the state pension is increased, the rate of the person's state pension under section 13 is increased (at that time) by an amount equal to the appropriate percentage of the shortfall immediately before that time.

(3) If at any time an order under section 151A of the Administration Act comes into force, the rate of the person's state pension under section 13 is increased (at that time) by an amount equal to the appropriate percentage of the excess immediately before the order comes into force.

(4) In this paragraph—

"the appropriate percentage"—

(a) in sub-paragraph (2), means the percentage by which the full rate is increased;

(b) in sub-paragraph (3), means the percentage specified in the order;

"the excess" means the amount by which the rate of the state pension under section 13, when added to the total amount of any state pension that has priority, exceeds the full rate;

"the shortfall" means the amount by which the total amount of any state pension that has priority is less than the full rate.

1.1059

Priority pension alone is equal to or higher than the full rate

6 (1) The rate of the person's state pension under section 13 is to be increased under this paragraph if the total amount of any state pension that has priority is equal to or higher than the full rate of the state pension.

(2) If at any time an order under section 151A of the Administration Act comes into force, the rate of the person's state pension under section 13 is increased (at that time) by the percentage specified in the order.

1.1060

AMENDMENT

1. State Pension and Occupational Pension Schemes (Miscellaneous Amendments) Regulations 2016 (SI 2016/169) reg.5 (April 6, 2016).

GENERAL NOTE

The amounts which, under paras 5(3) and 6, are the amounts of shared state pensions under Part 1 of the Act which either alone or in combination with one or more other pensions under Part 1 exceed the full rate, were increased by 2.4 per cent with effect from April 8, 2019: see art.6(4) of the Social Security Benefits Up-rating Order 2019 (SI 2019/480).

1.1061

SCHEDULE 10   **Section 14**

PENSION SHARING: APPROPRIATE WEEKLY REDUCTION UNDER SECTION 14

Introduction

1 This Schedule sets out the appropriate weekly reduction in the rate of a person's state pension for the purposes of section 14.

1.1062

Appropriate weekly reduction for person subject to old state scheme pension debit

2 (1) This paragraph sets out the appropriate weekly reduction if the person is subject to an old state scheme pension debit.

(2) If the person became subject to the old state scheme pension debit in or after the final relevant year, the appropriate weekly reduction is an amount equal to the person's notional rate.

(3) If the person became subject to the old state scheme pension debit before the final

1.1063

relevant year, the appropriate weekly reduction is an amount equal to the person's notional rate multiplied by the appropriate revaluation percentage.

(4) For the purposes of sub-paragraphs (2) and (3), a person's "notional rate" is the weekly rate of a notional pension under section 4 the cash equivalent of which would, on the valuation day, have been equal to the amount of the old state scheme pension debit.

(5) For the purposes of sub-paragraph (4) assume that the notional pension becomes payable on the later of—

(a) the day on which the person reaches pensionable age, and

(b) the valuation day.

(6) The "appropriate revaluation percentage" is the percentage specified, in relation to earnings factors for the tax year in which the person became subject to the old state scheme pension debit, by the last order under section 148 of the Administration Act to come into force before the end of the final relevant year.

(7) In this paragraph—

"final relevant year" means the tax year immediately before that in which the person reaches pensionable age;

"valuation day" means the day on which the person became subject to the old state scheme pension debit.

Appropriate weekly reduction for person subject to new state scheme pension debit

1.1064

3 (1) This paragraph sets out the appropriate weekly reduction if the person is subject to a new state scheme pension debit.

(2) If the person was over pensionable age when he or she became subject to the new state scheme pension debit, the appropriate weekly reduction is an amount equal to the amount of the debit.

(3) If the person was under pensionable age when he or she became subject to the new state scheme pension debit, the appropriate weekly reduction is an amount equal to the amount of the debit multiplied by the appropriate revaluation percentage.

(4) The "appropriate revaluation percentage" is the percentage specified, in relation to the tax year in which the person became subject to the new state scheme pension debit, by the last order under section 148AD of the Administration Act to come into force before the person reached pensionable age.

Supplementary

1.1065

4 (1) Regulations may make provision about the calculation and verification of notional rates under paragraph 2.

(2) The regulations may, in particular, provide—

(a) for calculation or verification in such manner as may be approved by or on behalf of the Government Actuary, or

(b) for things done under the regulations to be required to be done in accordance with guidance from time to time prepared by a person specified in the regulations.

SCHEDULE 11 **Section 15**

PENSION SHARING: AMENDMENTS

1.1066

The amendments relevant to this volume are included in the appropriate provisions above.

SCHEDULE 12 **Section 23**

STATE PENSION: AMENDMENTS

1.1067

The amendments relevant to this volume are included in the appropriate provisions above.

SCHEDULE 13 **Section 24**

ABOLITION OF CONTRACTING-OUT FOR SALARY RELATED SCHEMES

1.1068

The amendments relevant to this volume are included in the appropriate provisions above.

SCHEDULE 14   **Section 24**

POWER TO AMEND SCHEMES TO REFLECT ABOLITION OF CONTRACTING-OUT

Not included in this work as the provisions relate only to former salary related contracted-out pension   **1.1069**
schemes now closed by the provisions in Schedule 13.

SCHEDULE 15   **Section 25**

OPTION TO BOOST OLD RETIREMENT PENSIONS

Not included in this volume. See the note to s. 25 of the Act above.   **1.1070**

Welfare Reform and Work Act 2016

(2016 C. 7)

SECTIONS REPRODUCED

15. Employment and support allowance: work-related activity compo-   **1.1071**
nent

An Act to make provision about reports on progress towards full employment and the apprenticeships target; to make provision about reports on the effect of certain support for troubled families; to make provision about life chances; to make provision about the benefit cap; to make provision about social security and tax credits; to make provision for loans for mortgage interest and other liabilities; and to make provision about social housing rents.

[16th March 2016]

Employment and support allowance: work-related activity component

15.—(1) Part 1 of the Welfare Reform Act 2007 (employment and support allowance) is amended as follows.

(2) In section 2 (amount of contributory allowance)—

(a) in subsection (1)(b), omit "or the work-related activity component";
(b) omit subsection (3);
(c) in subsection (4), in each of paragraphs (a), (b) and (c), omit "or (3)".

(3) In section 4 (amount of income-related allowance) (so far as it remains in force)—

(a) in subsection (2)(b), omit "or the work-related activity component";
(b) omit subsection (5);
(c) in subsection (6), in each of paragraphs (a), (b) and (c), omit "or (5)".

(4) The Secretary of State may by regulations make such transitional or transitory provision or savings as the Secretary of State considers necessary

or expedient in connection with the coming into force of subsections (1) to (3).

(5) Regulations under subsection (4) may in particular make provision about including a work-related activity component in an award of employment and support allowance that is converted under paragraph 7 of Schedule 4 to the Welfare Reform Act 2007 from an award of incapacity benefit, severe disablement allowance or income support after the coming into force of subsections (1) to (3).

(6) Regulations under this section must be made by statutory instrument.

(7) A statutory instrument containing regulations under this section is subject to annulment in pursuance of a resolution of either House of Parliament.

GENERAL NOTE

1.1072   For discussion of the significant effects of the important amendments made by subs.(2) and (3), see the commentary to ss.2 and 4 of the WRA 2007 above.

REGULATIONS

Preliminary Note: change of name from Department of Social Security to Department for Work and Pensions

1.1073   The Secretaries of State for Education and Skills and for Work and Pensions Order 2002 (SI 2002/1397) make provision for the change of name from the Department of Social Security to Department for Work and Pensions. Article 9(5) provides:

> "(5) Subject to article 12 [which makes specific amendments], any enactment or instrument passed or made before the coming into force of this Order shall have effect, so far as may be necessary for the purposes of or in consequence of the entrusting to the Secretary of State for Work and Pensions of the social security functions, as if any reference to the Secretary of State for Social Security, to the Department of Social Security or to an officer of the Secretary of State for Social Security (including any reference which is to be construed as such a reference) were a reference to the Secretary of State for Work and Pensions, to the Department for Work and Pensions or, as the case may be, to an officer of the Secretary of State for Work and Pensions."

PART II

CONTRIBUTION CREDITS AND HOME RESPONSIBILITIES PROTECTION

The Social Security (Credits) Regulations 1975

(SI 1975/556) (*as amended*)

ARRANGEMENT OF REGULATIONS

		2.1
1.	Citation and commencement.	
2.	Interpretation.	
3.	General provisions relating to the crediting of contributions and earnings.	
4.	Starting credits for the purposes of a retirement pension, a widowed mother's allowance, a widowed parent's allowance and a widow's pension.	
5.	*Revoked.*	
6.	*Revoked.*	
7.	Credits for approved training.	
7A.	Credits for carer's allowance.	
7B.	Credits for disability element of working tax credit.	
7C.	Credits for working tax credit.	
8.	Credits on termination of full-time education, training or apprenticeship.	
8A.	Credits for unemployment.	
8B.	Credits for incapacity for work.	
8C.	Credits on termination of bereavement benefits.	
8D.	Credits for the purposes of entitlement to incapacity benefit following official error	
8E.	Credits for the purposes of entitlement to retirement pension following official error	
8F.	Credits for the purposes of entitlement to contribution-based jobseeker's allowance following official error	
8G.	Credits for person entitled to universal credit	
9.	*Revoked.*	
9A.	Credits for persons approaching pensionable age.	
9B.	Credits for jury service.	
9C.	Credits for adoption pay period, shared parental pay period, additional paternity pay period and maternity pay period.	
9D.	Credits for certain periods of imprisonment or detention in legal custody.	
9E.	Credits for certain spouses and civil partners of members of Her Majesty's forces	
9F.	Credits for persons providing care for a child under the age of 12	
10.	*Revoked.*	

The Secretary of State for Social Services in exercise of the powers conferred upon her by section 13(4) of the Social Security Act 1975 and section 2(1) of, and paragraph 3 of Schedule 3 to, the Social Security (Consequential Provisions) Act 1975 and of all other powers enabling her in that behalf, without having referred any proposals on the matter to the National Insurance Advisory Committee since it appears to her that by reason of urgency it is inexpedient to do so, hereby makes the following regulations:

Citation and commencement

1.—These regulations may be cited as the Social Security (Credits) 2.2
Regulations 1975 and shall come into operation on 6th April 1975.

Interpretation

2.—(1) In these regulations, unless the context otherwise requires,— 2.3
"the Act" means the Social Security Act 1975;

[11"the 2012 Act" means the Welfare Reform Act 2012;]
[12 "benefit"—
(a) includes—
    (i) a contribution-based jobseeker's allowance;
    (ii) a contributory employment and support allowance;
(b) does not include—
    (i) an income-based jobseeker's allowance;
    (ii) an income-related employment and support allowance;
    (iii) a state pension under Part 1 of the Pensions Act 2014;]
[2 [13 . . .];
[13 . . .]
[1 . . .]
[11"contribution-based jobseeker's allowance" means an allowance under the Jobseekers Act 1995 as amended by the provisions of Part 1 of Schedule 14 to the 2012 Act that remove references to an income-based allowance, and a contribution-based allowance under the Jobseekers Act 1995 as that Act has effect apart from those provisions;]
[11"contributory employment and support allowance" means an allowance under Part 1 of the Welfare Reform Act as amended by the provisions of Schedule 3, and Part 1 of Schedule 14, to the 2012 Act that remove references to an income-related allowance, and a contributory allowance under Part 1 of the Welfare Reform Act as that Part has effect apart from those provisions;]
[3 "the Contributions and Benefits Act" means the Social Security Contributions and Benefits Act 1992;]
"credits" and "a credit" shall be construed in accordance with regulation 3;
[4 . . .];
[1 . . .];
[1 "income-based jobseeker's allowance" has the same meaning as in the Jobseekers Act 1995;
"jobseeker's allowance" means an allowance payable under Part I of the Jobseekers Act 1995;]
[10 "income-related employment and support allowance" means an income-related allowance under Part 1 of the Welfare Reform Act (employment and support allowance);
[1 . . .];
[9 "reckonable year" means a year for which the relevant earnings factor of the contributor concerned was sufficient to satisfy—
    (a) in relation to short-term incapacity benefit, widowed mother's allowance, [widowed parent's allowance, [13 . . .]] widow's pension or Category A or Category B retirement pension, paragraph (b) of the second contribution condition specified in relation to that benefit in Schedule 3 to the Contributions and Benefits Act; [10 . . .]
    (b) in relation to contribution-based jobseeker's allowance, the additional condition specified in section 2(3) of the Jobseekers Act 1995;][10 or
    (c) in relation to a contributory employment and support allowance, the condition specified in paragraph 2(1) of Schedule 1 to the Welfare Reform Act (conditions relating to national insurance);]

"relevant benefit year" [¹ has the same meaning as it has—
- (a) in relation to short-term incapacity benefit, in paragraph 2(6)
- (b) of Schedule 3 to the Contributions and Benefits Act; and
- (b) in relation to contribution-based jobseeker's allowance, the additional condition specified in section 2(4)(b) of the Jobseekers Act 1995;]

"relevant earnings factor" [⁵ in relation to any benefit, means—
- (a) [¹ if the benefit is a contribution-based jobseeker's allowance or if the contributions relevant to the benefit under section 21 of the Contributions and Benefits Act] are Class 1 contributions, the earnings factor derived from earnings [⁶ in respect of which] primary Class 1 contributions have been paid or treated as paid, or credited earnings;
- (b) if the contributions relevant to that benefit under that section are Class 1 and Class 2 contributions, the earnings factor or the aggregate of the earnings factors derived from—
  - (i) earnings [⁶ in respect of] which primary Class 1 contributions have been paid or treated as paid, or credited earnings, and
  - (ii) Class 2 contributions;
- (c) if the contributions relevant to that benefit under [6 that section] are Class 1, Class 2 and Class 3 contributions, the earnings factor or the aggregate of the earnings factors derived from—
  - (i) earnings [⁶ in respect of which] primary contributions have been paid or treated as paid, or credited earnings,
  - (ii) Class 2 contributions, and
  - (iii) Class 3 contributions paid or credited];

[⁷ "relevant past year" means the last complete year before the beginning of the relevant benefit year;]

[¹¹"universal credit" means universal credit under Part 1 of the 2012 Act;]

[¹⁰ "the Welfare Reform Act" means the Welfare Reform Act 2007;

[² "widowed parent's allowance" means an allowance referred to in section 39A of the Contributions and Benefits Act;]

[⁴ "working tax credit" means a working tax credit under section 10 of the Tax Credits Act 2002];

[⁸ "year" means tax year;]

and other expressions have the same meanings as in the Act.

(2) The rules for the construction of Acts of Parliament contained in the Interpretation Act 1889 shall apply for the purposes of the interpretation of these regulations as they apply for the purposes of the interpretation of an Act of Parliament.

(3) Unless the context otherwise requires, any reference in these regulations—
- (a) to a numbered section is a reference to the section of the Act bearing that number;
- (b) to a numbered regulation is a reference to the regulation bearing that number in these regulations, and any reference in a regulation to a numbered paragraph is a reference to the paragraph of that regulation bearing that number;
- (c) to any provision made by or contained in any enactment or instrument shall be construed as a reference to that provision as amended

or extended by any enactment or instrument and as including a reference to any provision which it re-enacts or replaces or which may re-enact or replace it with or without modification.

(4) Nothing in these regulations shall be construed as entitling any person to be credited with contributions for the purposes of any benefit for a day, period or event occurring before 6th April 1975.

AMENDMENTS

1. Social Security (Credits and Contributions) (Jobseeker's Allowance Consequential and Miscellaneous Amendments) Regulations 1996 (SI 1996/2367) reg.2(2) (October 7, 1996).

2. Social Security (Benefits for Widows and Widowers) (Consequential Amendments) Regulations 2000 (SI 2000/1483) reg.3(2).

3. Social Security (Incapacity Benefit) (Consequential and Transitional Amendments and Savings) Regulations 1995 (SI 1995/829) reg.6(2) (April 13, 1995).

4. Social Security (Working Tax Credit and Child Tax Credit) (Consequential Amendments) Regulations 2003 (SI 2003/455) reg.6 and Sch.4 para.1 (April 7, 2003).

5. Social Security (Credits) Amendment Regulations 1987 (SI 1987/414) reg.2 (April 6, 1987).

6. Social Security (Contributions and Credits) (Miscellaneous Amendments) Regulations 1999 (SI 1999/568) reg.20(a) (April 6, 1999).

7. Social Security (Credits) Amendment (No. 4) Regulations 1988 (SI 1988/1545) reg.2(2) (October 2, 1988).

8. Social Security (Credits) Amendment (No. 2) Regulations 1988 (SI 1988/1230) reg.2(2) (October 2, 1988).

9. Social Security (Miscellaneous Amendments) (No.3) Regulations 2007 (SI 2007/1749) reg.8(2) (July 16, 2007).

10. Employment and Support Allowance (Consequential Provisions) (No.2) Regulations 2008 (SI 2008/1554) reg.48(2) (October 27, 2008).

11. Universal Credit (Consequential, Supplementary, Incidental and Miscellaneous Provisions) Regulations 2013 (SI 2013/630) reg.70(1), (2) (April 29, 2013).

12. Pensions Act 2014 (Consequential, Supplementary and Incidental Amendments) Order 2015 (SI 2015/1985) art.2 (April 6, 2016)

13. Pensions Act 2014 (Consequential, Supplementary and Incidental Amendments) Order 2017 (SI 2017/422) art.4(2) (April 6, 2017).

General provisions relating to the crediting of contributions [¹ and earnings]

2.4   **3.**—[²(1) Any contributions or earnings credited in accordance with these Regulations shall be only for the purpose of enabling the person concerned to satisfy—

[⁴(aa) in relation to short-term incapacity benefit, the second contribution condition specified in paragraph 2(3) of Schedule 3 (contribution conditions for entitlement to benefit) to the Contributions and Benefits Act;

(ab) in relation to—

    (i) widowed mother's allowance;

    (ii) widowed parent's allowance;

    (iii) [⁵ . . .]

    (iv) widow's pension,

the second contribution condition specified in paragraph 5(3) of Schedule 3 to the Contributions and Benefits Act;

(ac) in relation to a Category A or Category B retirement pension—
    (i) in the case of a retirement pension to which paragraph 5 of Schedule 3 to the Contributions and Benefits Act applies, the second contribution condition specified in paragraph 5(3); and
    (ii) otherwise, the contribution condition specified in paragraph 5A(2) of Schedule 3 to that Act;]
(b) in relation to contribution-based jobseeker's allowance, the condition specified in section 2(1)(b) of the Jobseekers Act 1995; [³or
(c) in relation to a contributory employment and support allowance, the condition specified in paragraph 2(1) of Schedule 1 to the Welfare Reform Act,]

and accordingly, where under any of the provisions of these Regulations a person would, but for this paragraph, be entitled to be credited with any contributions or earnings for a year, or in respect of any week in a year, he shall be so entitled for the purposes of any benefit only if and to no greater extent than that by which his relevant earnings factor for that year falls short of the level required to make that year a reckonable year.]

(2) Where under these regulations a person is entitled for the purposes of any benefit to—
    (a) be credited [¹ with earnings] for a year, he is to be credited with such amount of [¹earnings] as may be required to bring his relevant earnings factor to the level required to make that year a reckonable year
    (b) [¹ ...];

(3) Where under these regulations a person is entitled to be credited [¹with earnings] or a contribution in respect of a week which is partly in one tax year and partly in another, he shall be entitled to [¹ be credited with those earnings or that contribution] for the tax year in which that week began and not for the following year.

AMENDMENTS

1. Social Security (Credits) Amendment Regulations 1987 (SI 1987/414) reg.3 (April 6, 1987).
2. Social Security (Credits and Contributions) (Jobseeker's Allowance Consequential and Miscellaneous Amendments) Regulations 1996 (SI 1996/2367) reg.2(3) (October 7, 1996).
3. Employment and Support Allowance (Consequential Provisions) (No. 2) Regulations 2008 (SI 2008/1554) reg.48(3) (October 27, 2008).
4. Social Security (State Pension and National Insurance Credits) Regulations 2009 (SI 2009/2206) reg.29 (April 6, 2010).
5. Pensions Act 2014 (Consequential, Supplementary and Incidental Amendments) Order 2017 (SI 2017/422) art.4(3) (April 6, 2017).

DEFINITIONS

"benefit"—see reg.2(1).
"reckonable year"—see reg.2(1).
"relevant earnings factor"—see reg.2(1).
"tax year"—see SSCBA 1992 s.122(1).
"year": see reg.2(1).

GENERAL NOTE

This provides that credits can only be awarded under these regulations to enable   2.5
the person to satisfy the second contribution condition for particular benefits (paras (1) and (2) read with reg.2(1)):

- short-term incapacity benefit (SSCBA 1992 s.30A);

- widowed mother's allowance (SSCBA 1992 s.37);

- widowed parent's allowance (SSCBA 1992 s.39A);

- widow's pension (SSCBA 1992 s.38);

- Category A or B retirement pension (SSCBA 1992 ss.43–54);

- contribution-based jobseeker's allowance (Jobseekers Act 1995 s.2—see *Vol. II: Income Support, Jobseeker's Allowance, State Pension Credit and the Social Fund*).

- contributory employment and support allowance

Moreover, they can only be awarded to the extent necessary to make up the short-fall between the actual record in paid contributions in the relevant tax year and the level needed to satisfy the particular second condition (50 times the lower earnings limit for Class 1 contributions liability purposes in that year—52 times for retirement pension), that is, to make that year a "reckonable year" (para.(2)).

Paragraph (3) deals with the situation where the week in which someone is entitled to be credited spans two tax years, and provides that the tax year to be credited is the one in which the week began.

The role and importance of reg.3 is generally overlooked. It is, however, crucial in determining whether "credits" (crediting earnings and earnings factors to a claimant's contribution account) for which the claimant is eligible under other provisions of these regulations can actually be awarded in respect of the specified benefits. It is as if it had to be read as an integral part of each of those other regulations. It is, moreover, a provision that causes particular problems in respect on its interaction with the provision on credits for unemployment in reg.8A. Commissioner Williams sets out the law on crediting contributions in *CIB/1602/2006*:

"Provision is made to allow credited earnings under section 22(5) of the 1992 Act. This provides, as relevant to this appeal:
'Regulations may provide for crediting—

(a) for 1987–88 or any subsequent year, earnings . . .
for the purpose of bringing a person's earnings factor for that tax year to a figure which will enable him to satisfy contribution conditions of entitlement to . . . any prescribed description of benefit . . .'"

This applies to D's claim for incapacity benefit. It makes clear that credited earnings can only apply when the individual has not paid enough actual contributions for the year. This, equally clearly, can only be decided after the end of the tax year, which occurs in April each calendar year. (For employed earners this will be in practice after the time limit in the following May or June when all employers are required to make a return of total contributions collected for their employees during the year ending in April. See Sch.4 para.22 to the Social Security (Contributions) Regulations 2001 (SI 2001 No 1004)).

The regulations allowing credited earnings for periods of unemployment are regulations 3 (general provisions relating to the crediting of contributions and earnings) and 8A (credits for unemployment) of the Social Security (Credits) Regulations 1975 ("the Credits Regulations") (SI 1975 No 556). These are complicated and much amended regulations. Little attention has been paid for years past to the structure of the Credits Regulations and the way that they are empowered by, and link to, section 22(5) of the 1992 Act and its predecessors back to section 13 of the Social Security Act 1975. The Regulations follow the usual pattern of stating the commencement provisions in regulation 1 and definitions in regulation 2. Regulation 3 then lays down general provisions relating to the crediting of contributions and earnings. Regulations 4 to 9D follow with provisions for specific forms of credit or credited earnings in specific situations. It is abundantly clear from this that, reflecting the authority granted in section 22(5), regulation 3 is to be applied in each case along with the specific regulation. That has not happened here. As

Commissioner Rowland commented in CIB 3327 2004, regulation 3 is rarely mentioned in connection with the award of credited earnings. It is not the subject, so far as I can see, of any comment in the *DMG*. Nor has it been mentioned in this appeal.

The Credits Regulations have been amended many times since first being written. The most important of the amendments—only partially executed—take account of the abolition of contribution credits on 6 04 1987. From that date (the start of the tax year 1987–88) the previous system of awarding weekly credits was abolished. It was replaced by a system of crediting earnings and earnings factors to a claimant only when necessary at the end of a tax year. Commissioner Rowland explores these concepts in CIB 3327 2004, and I do not repeat that. The difficulties in cases such as this are because the fundamental change in the nature of contribution "credits" does not appear yet to have been absorbed into the relevant administrative processes for identifying and awarding credited earnings. That failure is in part hidden because of a failure fully to amend the Credits Regulations themselves to reflect the changes made in 1987" (paras 24–26).

The problem this generates with claims for credits for unemployment were then considered by Commissioner Williams (and a solution found). The matter is considered in the update to the commentary to reg.8A, below. For further consideration of some of the difficulties arising where records have been destroyed as part of normal administrative processes and for the text of the regulations on unemployment credits covering 1977-89, see Commissioner Williams' decision in *CP/1792/2007*.

Starting credits for the purposes of a retirement pension, a widowed mother's allowance, a widowed parent's allowance [⁴ . . .] and a widow's pension

4.—(1) [³ Subject to paragraph (1A),] for the purposes of entitlement to a Category A or a Category B retirement pension, a widowed mother's allowance [¹, a widowed parent's allowance [⁴ . . .]] or a widow's pension [² by virtue of a person's earnings or contributions], he shall be credited with such number of Class 3 contributions as may be required to bring his relevant earnings factor in respect of the tax year in which he attained the age of 16 and for each of the two following tax years to the level required to make those years reckonable years; so however, subject to paragraph (2), no contribution shall be credited under this regulation in respect of any tax year commencing before 6th April 1975.

[³(1A) For the purposes of entitlement to a Category A or a Category B retirement pension, no contribution shall be credited under this regulation—

(a) in respect of any tax year commencing on or after 6th April 2010;
(b) in respect of any other tax year, where an application under regulation 9 (application for allocation of national insurance number) of the Social Security (Crediting and Treatment of Contributions, and National Insurance Numbers) Regulations 2001 is made on or after 6th April 2010.]

(2) Where a person was in Great Britain on 6th April 1975 and had attained the age of 16 but was not an insured person under the National Insurance Act 1965, he shall be credited with contributions under paragraph (1) in respect of the tax year commencing on 6th April 1974.

2.6

AMENDMENTS

1. Social Security (Benefits for Widows and Widowers) (Consequential Amendments) Regulations 2000 (SI 2000/1483) reg.3(4).

2. Social Security (Credits) Amendment (No. 4) Regulations 1988 (SI 1988/1545) reg.2(5) (October 2, 1988).

3. National Insurance Contributions Credits (Miscellaneous Amendments) Regulations 2011 (SI 2011/709) reg.2 (April 5, 2011).

4. Pensions Act 2014 (Consequential, Supplementary and Incidental Amendments) Order 2017 (SI 2017/422) art.4(4) (April 6, 2017).

DEFINITIONS

"reckonable year"—see reg.2(1).
"relevant earnings factor"—see reg.2(1).
"tax year"—see SSCBA 1992 s.122(1).

GENERAL NOTE

2.7   As with all of the Regulations making claimants eligible for the award of credits, this must be read with reg.3 (*CIB/1602/2006*; *CIB/3327/2004*). One can only have them insofar as they are necessary to bring one's record up to the level required for satisfying the second contribution condition for the relevant benefit (see para.(1), reg.3 and reg.2(1) ("reckonable year")).

This applies only for the purposes of a retirement pension, a widowed mother's allowance, a widowed parent's allowance, a bereavement allowance and a widow's pension. It awards someone sufficient Class 3 credits to bring his contribution record in a particular tax year up to the requisite level for the second contribution condition (to make the year a "reckonable year"). The tax years in question are the one in which he reached 16 and the two tax years following that year. No credits are awardable prior to April 6, 1975, save that tax year 1974–75 can be credited as respects someone 16 or over, who was in Great Britain on that date but was not an insured person under the National Insurance Act 1965.

As regards Category A or B pensions, note that para.(1A) precludes contribution credits ("starting credits") for any tax year later than 2009/10 or in respect of any tax year where applications for a national insurance number are made after April 6, 2010. The governmental view was that the reduction in the number of qualifying years needed for a full basic State Pension to 30 years, effected in April 2010, meant that few people who have spent most of their working lives in the UK will need starting credits for this purpose.

Starting credits for the purposes of unemployment benefit, sickness benefit and maternity allowance

2.8   **5.**—[¹ . . .]

REVOCATION

1. Social Security (Credits) Amendment (No. 2) Regulations 1988 (SI 1988/1230) reg.3(1).

Starting credits for the purposes of a maternity grant

2.9   **6.**—[¹ . . .]

REVOCATION

1. Social Security (Credits) Amendment Regulations 1988 (SI 1988/516), reg.3(1).

Credits for approved training

2.10   **7.**—(1) For the purposes of entitlement to any benefit [¹ by virtue of a person's earnings or contributions] he shall, subject to [⁵ paragraphs (2) to (4)], be entitled to [² be credited with earnings equal to the lower earnings limit then in force], in respect of each week in any part of which he was undergoing (otherwise than in pursuance of his employment as an employed earner) a course of [³ . . .] training approved by the Secretary of State for the purposes of this regulation.

[³ (2) Paragraph (1) shall apply to a person only if—

(a) the course is—
  (i) a course of full-time training; or
  (ii) a course of training which he attends for not less than 15 hours in the week in question and he is a disabled person within the meaning of the Disabled Persons (Employment) Act 1944; or
  (iii) a course of training introductory to a course to which paragraph (i) or (ii) above applies; and

(b) when the course began it was not intended to continue for more than 12 months or, if he was a disabled person within the meaning of the Disabled Persons (Employment) Act 1944 and the training was provided under the Employment and Training Act 1973 [⁴ or the Enterprise and New Towns (Scotland) Act 1990], for such longer period as is reasonable in the circumstances of his case; and

(c) he had attained the age of 18 before the beginning of the tax year in which the week in question began.]

(3) Paragraph (1) shall not apply to a woman in respect of any week in any part of which she was a married woman in respect of whom an election made by her under regulations made under section 3(2) of the Social Security Pensions Act 1975 had effect.

[⁵(4) Paragraph (1) shall not apply to a person in respect of any week in any part of which that person was entitled to universal credit.]

AMENDMENTS

1. Social Security (Credits) Amendment (No. 4) Regulations 1988 (SI 1988/1545) reg.2(5) (October 2, 1988).

2. Social Security (Credits) Amendment Regulations 1987 (SI 1987/414) reg.5 (April 6, 1987).

3. Social Security (Credits) Amendment (No. 3) Regulations 1988 (SI 1988/1439) reg.2 (September 4, 1988).

4. Enterprise (Scotland) Consequential Amendments Order 1991 (SI 1991/387) art.3(a) (April 1, 1991).

5. Universal Credit (Consequential, Supplementary, Incidental and Miscellaneous Provisions) Regulations 2013 (SI 2013/630) reg.70(1), (3) (April 29, 2013).

DEFINITIONS

"benefit"—see reg.2(1).
"employed earner"—see SSCBA 1992 s.2(1)(a).
"lower earnings limit"—see SSCBA 1992 s.122(1).
"tax year"—see SSCBA 1992 s.122(1).

GENERAL NOTE

As with all of the Regulations making claimants eligible for the award of credits, this must be read with reg.3 (*CIB/1602/2006; CIB/3327/2004*). One can only have them insofar as they are necessary to bring one's record up to the level required for satisfying the second contribution condition for the relevant benefit (see para.(1), reg.3 and reg.2(1) ("reckonable year")). 2.11

It enables credits to be awarded to a person for each week in which he was undergoing an approved course of training, otherwise than in pursuance of his employed earner's employment. Approved means approved by the Secretary of State for the purposes of this regulation. The conditions in para.(2) must be met. The course must be full time or, where someone is disabled within the meaning of the Disabled Persons (Employment) Act 1944, one attended for at least 15 hours in the week for which the credit is sought, or it must be a course of training introductory to such a course (para.(2)(a). In addition the person must have been 18 before the beginning of the tax year containing the week sought to be credited (para.(2)(c)). Furthermore, when commenced the course must not have been intended to last more than 12 months, or, where the person is disabled within the meaning of that 1944 Act and the training was provided under specified legislation, for such longer period as is reasonable in his case (para.(2)(b)).

A woman cannot gain a credit under this provision in respect of any week in any part of which as a married woman a certificate of election to pay contributions at reduced rate applied to her (para.(3)). Nor can a person obtain a credit under this provision in respect of a week in any part of which that person was entitled to universal credit (para.(4)).

[¹ Credits for [² carer's allowance]

2.12   **7A.**—(1) For the purposes of entitlement to any benefit [³ by virtue of a person's earnings or contributions] he shall, subject to paragraph (2), be entitled to [⁴ be credited with earnings equal to the lower earnings limit then in force], in respect of each week for any part of which [² a carer's allowance] is paid to him, [⁵ or would be paid to him but for a restriction under section [⁸ 6B or] 7 of the Social Security Fraud Act 2001 (loss of benefit provisions)] or in the case of [⁷ widow, widower or surviving civil partner] would have been so payable but for the provisions of the Social Security (Overlapping Benefits) Regulations 1975, as amended by the Social Security (Invalid Care Allowance) Regulations 1976, requiring adjustment of [² a carer's allowance] against widow's benefit, [⁹ widowed parent's allowance] or benefit by virtue of section 39(4) corresponding to a widowed mother's allowance or a widow's pension.

(2) Paragraph (1) shall not apply—

(a) to a person in respect of any week where he is entitled to [⁴ be credited with earnings] under [⁶ regulation 8A or 8B] in respect of the same week; or

(b) to a woman in respect of any week in any part of which she was a married woman in respect of whom an election made by her under regulations made under section 3(2) of the Social Security Pensions Act 1975 had effect.]

AMENDMENTS

1. Social Security (Invalid Care Allowance) Regulations 1976 (SI 1976/409) reg.19 (April 12, 1976).

2. Social Security Amendment (Carer's Allowance) Regulations 2002 (SI 2002/2497) reg.3 and Sch.2 (April 1, 2003).

3. Social Security (Credits) Amendment (No. 4) Regulations 1988 (SI 1988/1545) reg.2(5) (October 2, 1988).

4. Social Security (Credits) Amendment Regulations 1987 (SI 1987/414) reg.6 (April 6, 1987).

5. Social Security (Loss of Benefit) (Consequential Amendments) Regulations (SI 2002/490) reg.3(a) (April 1, 2002).

6. Social Security (Credits and Contributions) (Jobseeker's Allowance Conseq

uential and Miscellaneous Amendments) Regulations 1996 (SI 1996/2367) reg.2 (October 7, 1996).

7. Civil Partnership (Pensions, Social Security and Child Support) (Consequential, etc. Provisions) Order 2005 (SI 2005/2877) art.2(3) and Sch.3, para.4(2) (December 5, 2005).

8. Social Security (Loss of Benefit) Amendment Regulations 2010 (SI 2010/1160) reg.13 (April 1, 2010).

9. Pensions Act 2014 (Consequential, Supplementary and Incidental Amendments) Order 2017 (SI 2017/422) art.4(5) (April 6, 2017).

DEFINITIONS

"benefit"—see reg.2(1).
"lower earnings limit"—see SSCBA 1992 s.122(1).

GENERAL NOTE

As with all of the Regulations making claimants eligible for the award of credits, **2.13** this must be read with reg.3 (*CIB/1602/2006*; *CIB/3327/2004*). One can only have them insofar as they are necessary to bring one's record up to the level required for satisfying the second contribution condition for the relevant benefit (see para.(1), reg.3 and reg.2(1) ("reckonable year")).

It enables a credit equal to that tax year's lower earnings limit to be awarded for each week in respect of part of which someone has a carer's allowance paid to him; or where it would have been paid to him but for the loss of benefit provision in the Social Security Fraud Act 2001 s.7; or where, as a widow or widower it is not because of the adjustment provisions in the Overlapping Benefit Regulations. In *CG/2902/2003*, Deputy Commissioner Mark considered when it could be said that invalid care allowance (now care allowance) was "paid" to someone for the purposes of this regulation. He concluded that it is not "paid" in the required sense:

"where it has been decided subsequent to payment that the claimant was not entitled to such an allowance for that period. Accordingly, the secretary of state was correct not to award credits in respect of that period and the tribunal was correct to dismiss the claimant's appeal" (para.22).

He expressed no view as to the effect on an existing award of credits where the award of invalid care allowance is revised or superseded.

Note that a woman cannot gain a credit under this provision in respect of any week in any part of which as a married woman a certificate of election to pay contributions at reduced rate applied to her (para.(2)(b)). Nor can a credit be awarded under this provision if a credit entitlement for the week arises under reg.8A (unemployment) or 8B (incapacity for work) (para.(2)(a)).

[¹ Credits for [² disability element of working tax credit]

7B.—(1) For the purposes of entitlement to any benefit by virtue of a **2.14** person's earnings or contributions he shall, subject to paragraphs (2) and (3), be credited with earnings equal to the lower earnings limit then in force in respect of each week for any part of which [² the disability element or the severe disability element of working tax credit as specified in regulation 20(1) (b) and (f) of the Working Tax Credit (Entitlement and Maximum Rate) Regulations 2002 is included in an award of working tax credit which] is paid to him.

(2) Paragraph (1) shall apply to a person only if he is—

(a) an employed earner; [⁴ . . .]

[⁴ (b) a self-employed earner whose profits for the year are below the small profits threshold specified in section 11(4) of the Contributions and Benefits Act, who would otherwise be liable to pay a Class 2 contribution; or

(c) excepted from liability to pay a Class 2 contribution by virtue of regulation 43 of the Social Security (Contributions) Regulations 2001.]

(3) Paragraph (1) shall not apply—

(a) to a person in respect of any week where he is entitled to be credited with earnings under [³ regulation 8A or 8B] in respect of the same week; or

(b) to a woman in respect of any week in any part of which she was a married woman in respect of whom an election made by her under regulations made under section 3(2) of the Social Security Pension Act 1975 had effect.]

AMENDMENTS

1. Social Security (Credits) Amendment Regulations 1991 (SI 1991/2772) reg.3 (April 6, 1992).

2. Social Security (Working Tax Credit and Child Tax Credit) (Consequential Amendments) Regulations 2003 (SI 2003/455) reg.6 and Sch.4 para.1 (April 7, 2003).

3. Social Security (Credits and Contributions) (Jobseeker's Allowance Conseq uential and Miscellaneous Amendments) Regulations 1996 (SI 1996/2367) reg.2 (October 7, 1996).

4. Social Security (Credits, and Crediting and Treatment of Contributions) (Consequential and Miscellaneous Amendments) Regulations 2016 (SI 2016/1145) reg.3(2) (January 1, 2017).

DEFINITIONS

"employed earner"—see SSCBA 1992 s.2(1)(a).
"lower earnings limit"—see SSCBA 1992 s.122(1).
"self-employed earner"—see SSCBA 1992 s.2(1)(b).
"working tax credit"—see reg.2(1).

GENERAL NOTE

2.15   As with all of the Regulations making claimants eligible for the award of credits, this must be read with reg.3 (*CIB/1602/2006*; *CIB/3327/2004*). One can only have them insofar as they are necessary to bring one's record up to the level required for satisfying the second contribution condition for the relevant benefit (see para.(1), reg.3 and reg.2(1) ("reckonable year")).

It enables a credit equal to that tax year's lower earnings limit to be awarded for each week in respect of part of which someone has a working tax credit inclusive of the disability or severe disability element paid to him (para.(1)). He must either be an employed earner, or a self-employed earner exempt from paying Class 2 contributions because of the "small earnings" exception (para.(2)). Note that a woman cannot gain a credit under this provision in respect of any week in any part of which as a married woman a certificate of election to pay contributions at reduced rate applied to her (para.(3)(b)). Nor can a credit be awarded under this provision if a credit entitlement for the week arises under reg.8A (unemployment) or 8B (incapacity for work) (para. (3)(a)).

[¹ Credits for [² working tax credit]

2.16   **7C.**—(1) [² Subject to regulation 7B], for the purposes of entitlement to a Category A or a Category B retirement pension, a widowed mother's allow-

ance, a widowed parent's allowance [⁷. . .] or a widow's pension by virtue
of a person's earnings or contributions, where [² working tax credit] is paid
for any week in respect of—
(a) an employed earner; [⁶. . .]
[⁶ (b) a self-employed earner—
    (i) whose profits for the year are below the small profits threshold
        specified in section 11(4) of the Contributions and Benefits
        Act, who would otherwise be liable to pay a Class 2 contribu-
        tion; or
    (ii) who is excepted from liability to pay a Class 2 contribution by
        virtue of regulation 43 of the Social Security (Contributions)
        Regulations 2001,]
that person shall, subject to paragraphs (4) and (5), be credited with earnings equal to the lower earnings limit then in force in respect of that week.

(2) The reference in paragraph (1) to the person in respect of whom
[² working tax credit] is paid—
(a) where it is paid to one of [⁵ a couple], is a reference to the member
    of that couple specified in paragraph (3); and
(b) in any other case, is a reference to the person to whom it is paid.

(3) the member of [⁵ a couple] specified for the purposes of paragraph (2)
(a) is—
(a) where only one member is assessed for the purposes of the award of
    [² working tax credit] as having income consisting of earnings, that
    member; or
(b) [². . .]
(c) where the earnings of each member are assessed [². . .], the member
    to whom the [² working tax credit] is paid.

(4) Paragraph (1) shall not apply—
(a) to a person in respect of any week he is entitled to be credited
    with earnings under regulation 8A or 8B in respect of the same
    week; or
(b) to a woman in respect of any week in any part of which she is a
    married woman in respect of whom an election made by her under
    regulations made under section 19(4) of the Contributions and
    Benefits Act has effect.

(5) [². . .].

(6) In this regulation [⁵ couple has] the same meaning as in Part VII of
the Contributions and Benefits Act.]

AMENDMENTS

1. Social Security (Credits) Amendment Regulations 1995 (SI 1995/2558) reg.2
(November 1, 1995).
2. Social Security (Working Tax Credit and Child Tax Credit) (Consequential
Amendments) Regulations 2003 (SI 2003/455) reg.6 and Sch.4 para.1 (April 7,
2003).
3. Social Security (Credits and Contributions) (Jobseeker's Allowance
Consequential and Miscellaneous Amendments) Regulations 1996 (SI 1996/2367)
reg.2 (October 7, 1996).
4. Social Security (Benefits for Widows and Widowers) (Consequential
Amendments) Regulations 2000 (SI 2000/1483) reg.3(6).
5. Civil Partnership (Pensions, Social Security and Child Support) (Consequential,
etc. Provisions) Order 2005 (SI 2005/2877) art.2(3) and Sch.3 para.4(3) (December
5, 2005).

6. Social Security (Credits, and Crediting and Treatment of Contributions) (Consequential and Miscellaneous Amendments) Regulations 2016 (SI 2016/1145) reg.3(3) (January 1, 2017).

7. Pensions Act 2014 (Consequential, Supplementary and Incidental Amendments) Order 2017 (SI 2017/422) art.4(6) (April 6, 2017).

DEFINITIONS

"employed earner"—see SSCBA 1992 s.2(1)(a).
"married couple"—see para.(6); SSCBA 1992 s.137(1).
"pensionable age"—see SSCBA 1992 s.122(1).
"self-employed earner"—see SSCBA 1992 s.2(1)(b).
"unmarried couple"—see para.(6); SSCBA 1992 s.137(1).
"working families' tax credit"—see reg.2(1); SSCBA 1992 s.128.

GENERAL NOTE

2.17   As with all of the Regulations making claimants eligible for the award of credits, this must be read with reg.3 (*CIB/1602/2006*; *CIB/3327/2004*). One can only have them insofar as they are necessary to bring one's record up to the level required for satisfying the second contribution condition for the relevant benefit (see para.(1), reg.3 and reg.2(1) ("reckonable year")).

It covers an employed earner, or a self-employed earner exempt from paying Class 2 contributions because of the "small earnings" exception, to whom working tax credit is paid for any week, and enables a credit equal to that tax year's lower earnings limit to be awarded for each such week. Where the person is one of a married or unmarried couple, note the rules in para.(3) stipulating who gets the award of the credit: the sole assessed earner; or, where both are assessed, the partner to whom working tax credit is paid.

The credit is only awardable to those attaining or due to attain pensionable age after April 5, 1999 and only with respect to weeks falling wholly or partly in tax year 1995–96 or subsequent tax years (para.(5)).

Note that a woman cannot gain a credit under this provision in respect of any week in any part of which as a married woman a certificate of election to pay contributions at reduced rate applied to her (para.(4)(b)). Nor can a credit be awarded under this provision if a credit entitlement for the week arises under reg.8A (unemployment) or 8B (incapacity for work) (para.(4)(a)).

Credits on termination of full-time education, training or apprenticeship

2.18   8.—[¹ (1) For the purposes of his entitlement to [² a contribution based jobseeker's allowance] [³ short-term incapacity benefit or a contributory employment and support allowance] a person shall be entitled to be credited with earnings equal to the lower earnings limit then in force for either one of the last two complete years before the beginning of the relevant benefit year if—

(a) during any part of that year he was—
   (i) undergoing a course of full-time education; or
   (ii) undergoing—
      (a) a course of training which was full-time and which was arranged under section 2(1) of the Employment and Training Act 1973 or [⁴ section 2(3) of the Enterprise and New Towns (Scotland) Act 1990]; or
      (b) any other full-time course the sole or main purpose of which was the acquisition of occupational or vocational skills; or

502

        (c) if he is a disabled person within the meaning of the Disabled Persons (Employment) Act 1944 a part-time course attended for at least 15 hours a week which, if it was full-time, would fall within either of heads (a) or (b) above; or

    (iii) an apprentice; and

  (b) the other year is, in his case, a reckonable year; and

  (c) that course or, as the case may be, his apprenticeship has terminated.]

(2) Paragraph (1) shall not apply—

    (a) where the course of education or training or the apprenticeship commenced after the person had attained the age of 21;

    (b) to a woman in respect of any tax year immediately before the end of which she was a married woman and an election made by her under regulations made [5 under section 3(2) of the Social Security Pensions Act 1975] had effect[6;

    (c) to a person in respect of any tax year before that in which he attains the age of 18.]

AMENDMENTS

1. Social Security (Credits) Amendment Regulations 1989 (SI 1989/1627) reg.3 (October 1, 1989).

2. Social Security (Credits and Contributions) (Jobseeker's Allowance Consequential and Miscellaneous Amendments) Regulations 1996 (SI 1996/2367) reg.2(5).

3. Employment and Support Allowance (Consequential Provisions) (No. 2) Regulations 2008 (SI 2008/1554) reg.48(4) (October 27, 2008).

4. Enterprise (Scotland) Consequential Amendments Order 1991 (SI 1991/387) art.3 (April 1, 1991).

5. Social Security (Credits) Amendment and (Earnings Factor) Transitional Regulations 1978 (SI 1978/409) reg.2(2) (April 6, 1978).

6. Social Security (Credits) Amendment (No. 2) Regulations 1988 (SI 1988/1230) reg.2(3) (October 2, 1988).

DEFINITIONS

    "lower earnings limit"—see SSCBA 1992 s.122(1).
    "relevant benefit year"—see reg.2(1).
    "tax year"—see SSCBA 1992 s.122(1).
    "year"—see reg.2(1).

GENERAL NOTE

As with all of the Regulations making claimants eligible for the award of credits, **2.19** this must be read with reg.3 (*CIB/1602/2006; CIB/3327/2004*). One can only have them insofar as they are necessary to bring one's record up to the level required for satisfying the second contribution condition for the relevant benefit (see para.(1), reg.3 and reg.2(1) ("reckonable year")).

This applies only for purposes of entitlement to contribution-based jobseeker's allowance (CBJSA), short-term incapacity benefit (STIB) or a contributory employment and support allowance (CESA). For both these benefits, the second contribution condition requires that the contribution record in terms of paid and/or credited contributions reaches the requisite level (50 times the tax year's lower earnings limit) in respect of *each* of the last two tax years complete before the beginning of the relevant benefit year (the year in which there falls the first day of the jobseeking period or linked period [CBJSA: see Jobseekers Act 1995, s.2(1)(b)] or period of incapacity for work [STIB: see SSCBA 1992, Sch.3, para.2] or period of limited capability for work [CESA, see WRA 2007,

Sch.1, para.2] of which the claim for benefit is part). It enables credits to be awarded, where in one of those tax years the second condition is met (it is a "reckonable year"), in order to make the record in the other tax year up to the requisite level (to make it also a "reckonable year"). The provision applies where during any part of the relevant benefit year, he was an apprentice, or was someone undergoing a course of full-time education, or a course of full-time training under specified legislation, or a full-time course the sole or main purpose of which was the acquisition of occupational or vocational skills (para.(1)(a)). Where he is disabled within the meaning of the Disabled Persons (Employment) Act 1944, it suffices that such a course was part-time (attended for at least 15 hours a week) (para.(1)(a)(ii)(c)). The final condition for the award of the credit is that the apprenticeship or course must have terminated (para.(1)(c)).

No award can be made where the apprenticeship or course commenced after the person attained the age of 21 (para.(2)(a)) or in respect of any tax year prior to that in which he became 18 (para.(2)(c)). Note finally that a woman cannot gain a credit under this provision in respect of any tax year immediately before the end of which she was a married woman and a certificate of election to pay contributions at reduced rate had effect in relation to her (para.(2)(b)).

2.20 **[¹Credits for unemployment**

8A.—(1) For the purposes of entitlement to any benefit by virtue of a person's earnings or contributions, he shall be entitled to be credited with earnings equal to the lower earnings limit then in force, in respect of each week to which this regulation applies.

(2) Subject to paragraph (5) this regulation applies to a week which, in relation to the person concerned, is—

(a) a week for the whole of which he was paid a jobseeker's allowance; or

[¹¹(b) a week for the whole of which the person in relation to old style JSA—

    (i) satisfied or was treated as having satisfied the conditions set out in paragraphs (a), (c) and (e) to (h) of section 1(2) of the Jobseekers Act 1995 (conditions for entitlement to a jobseeker's allowance); and

    (ii) satisfied the further condition specified in paragraph (3) below; or

(ba) a week for the whole of which the person in relation to new style JSA—

    (i) satisfied or was treated as having satisfied the conditions set out in paragraphs (e) to (h) of section 1(2) of the Jobseekers Act 1995 (conditions for entitlement to a jobseeker's allowance);

    (ii) satisfied or was treated as having satisfied the work-related requirements under section 6D and 6E of the Jobseekers Act 1995 (work search and work availability requirements); and

    (iii) satisfied the further condition specified in paragraph (3) below; or]

(c) a week which would have been a week described in sub-paragraph (b) [¹¹or (ba)] but for the fact that he was incapable of work [⁵or had limited capability for work] for part of it, or

[³(d) a week in respect of which he would have been paid a jobseeker's allowance but for a restriction imposed pursuant to [⁶ . . .] [²section [⁷6B,] 7, 8 or 9 of the Social Security Fraud Act 2001 (loss of benefit provisions)]].

(3) The further condition referred to in paragraph (2)(b) [¹¹and (ba)] is that the person concerned—
  (a) furnished to the Secretary of State notice in writing of the grounds on which he claims to be entitled to be credited with earnings—
      (i) on the first day of the period for which he claims to be so entitled in which the week in question fell; or
      (ii) within such further time as may be reasonable in the circumstances of the case; and
  (b) has provided any evidence required by the Secretary of State that the conditions referred to in paragraph (2)(b) [¹¹or the conditions and requirements in paragraph (2)(ba)] are satisfied.
(4) [¹⁰*Omitted.*]
(5) This regulation shall not apply to—
  (a) a week in respect of which the person concerned was not entitled to a jobseeker's allowance (or would not have been if he had claimed it) because of section 14 of the Jobseekers Act 1995 (trade disputes); or
  (b) a week in respect of which, in relation to the person concerned, there was in force a direction under section 16 of that Act (which relates to persons who have reached the age of 16 but not the age of 18 and who are in severe hard ship); or
[¹¹(c) a week in respect of which, in relation to the person concerned—
      (i) an old style JSA was reduced in accordance with section 19 or 19A, or regulations made under section 19B, of the Jobseekers Act 1995; or
      (ii) a new style JSA was reduced in accordance with section 6J or 6K of the Jobseekers Act 1995; or]
  (d) a week in respect of which a jobseeker's allowance was payable to the person concerned only by virtue of regulation 141 of the Jobseeker's Allowance Regulations 1996 (circumstances in which an income-based jobseeker's allowance is payable to a person in hard ship); or
[⁴(dd) a week in respect of which a joint-claim jobseeker's allowance was payable in respect of a joint-claim couple of which the person is a member only by virtue of regulation 146C of the Jobseeker's Allowance Regulations 1996 (circumstances in which a joint –claim jobseeker's allowance is payable where a joint-claim couple is a couple in hard ship);
[¹¹(de) a week where paragraph (2)(b), (ba) or (c) apply and the person concerned was entitled to universal credit for any part of that week; or]
  (e) where the person concerned is a married woman, a week in respect of any part of which an election made by her under regulations made under section 19(4) of the Contributions and Benefits Act had effect.]
[¹¹(6) In this regulation—
"new style JSA" means a jobseeker's allowance under the Jobseekers Act 1995 as amended by the provisions of Part 1 of Schedule 14 to the 2012 Act that remove references to an income-based allowance;
"old style JSA" means a jobseeker's allowance under the Jobseekers Act 1995 as it has effect apart from the amendments made by Part 1 of Schedule 14 to the 2012 Act that remove references to an income-based allowance.]

AMENDMENTS

1. Social Security (Credits and Contributions) (Jobseeker's Allowance Consequential and Miscellaneous Amendments) Regulations 1996 (SI 1996/2367) reg.2(6) (October 7, 1996).

2. Social Security (Loss of Benefit) (Consequential Amendments) Regulations 2002 (SI 2002/490) reg.3 (April 1, 2002).

3. Social Security (Breach of Community Order) (Consequential Amendments) Regulations 2001 (SI 2001/1711) reg.2(5) (October 15, 2001).

4. Social Security Amendment (Joint Claims) Regulations 2001 (SI 2001/518) reg.3 (March 19, 2001).

5. Employment and Support Allowance (Consequential Provisions) (No. 2) Regulations 2008 (SI 2008/1554) reg.48(5) (October 27, 2008).

6. Welfare Reform Act 2009 (Section 26) (Consequential Amendments) Regulations 2010 (SI 2010/424) reg.2 (April 2, 2010).

7. Social Security (Loss of Benefit) Amendment Regulations 2010 (SI 2010/1160) reg.13 (April 1, 2010).

8. Jobseeker's Allowance (Sanctions for Failure to Attend) Regulations 2010 (SI 2010/509) reg.4(5) (April 6, 2010).

9. Jobseeker's Allowance (Sanctions) (Amendment) Regulations 2012 (SI 2012/2568) reg.9 (October 22, 2012).

10. Social Security (Miscellaneous Amendments)(No.3) Regulations 2013 (SI 2013/2536) reg.3 (October 29, 2013).

11. Universal Credit (Consequential, Supplementary, Incidental and Miscellaneous Provisions) Regulations 2013 (SI 2013/630) reg.70(1), (4) (April 29, 2013).

DEFINITIONS

"benefit"—see reg.2(1).
"jobseeker's allowance"—see reg.2(1).
"lower earnings limit"—see SSCBA 1992 s.122(1).

GENERAL NOTE

2.21   As with all of the Regulations making claimants eligible for the award of credits, this must be read with reg.3 (*CIB/1602/2006; CIB/3327/2004*). One can only have them insofar as they are necessary to bring one's record up to the level required for satisfying the second contribution condition for the relevant benefit (see para.(1), reg.3 and reg.2(1) ("reckonable year")).

It enables a credit equal to that tax year's lower earnings limit to be awarded for each week in respect of which one of the situations in para.(1) pertains.

The position is that it cannot be known whether a claimant is entitled to claim credits (credited with earnings) until some time after the end of the tax year for which the claim for them is made. The difficulties that can be caused by this complex interaction of Credits Regulations with those applicable to Jobseeker's Allowance, in a context in which there appear to be decision-making problems as a result of responsibilities divided between the DWP and HMRC, are explored in *CIB/1602/2006*.

Regulation 8A(3)(a)(i) stipulates that to be eligible for unemployment credits, in respect of a period of non-payment of JSA under para.(2)(b), a person must give notice in writing of the grounds on which he claims to be entitled to be credited with earnings

"(i) on the first day of the period for which he claims to be entitled in which the week in question fell; or (ii) within such further time as may be reasonable in the circumstances of the case".

2.22   In reality it is the second (fallback) option which will have to apply. This means that in a case such as that in *CIB/1602/2006*, where the claimant on a claim for incapacity benefit was arguing that he should have been awarded credits for a period of unemployment several years earlier in which he was not entitled to payment of JSA, that

> "the Secretary of State can do no more than require that a claimant makes a claim in writing, setting out the grounds for it, within a reasonable time of becoming entitled. That is a question of fact. It will take into account the guidance given to a claimant (all of which is set out above, unless something is added orally).
>
> Noting the guidance and correspondence put in evidence to the tribunal in this appeal, I have little difficulty in finding on the facts that D's correspondence with the Jobcentre and with the Member of Parliament and the Minister did raise the matter adequately in writing and within a reasonable time" (paras 33, 34).

The decision on whether earnings should be credited is not a HMRC decision, but one for the Secretary of State and appealable to the appeals tribunal, the Commissioner and the courts. In *CIB/1602/2006*, it was whether reg.8A(2)(b) applied in the claimant's case. The claimant needed two weeks' credited earnings to bring his record to the requisite level (50 times the lower earnings limit), having already been credited with 48 times that limit. Here, the Commissioner found from the correspondence that a decision had been made to refuse to credit the claimant with earnings for the period at issue because during the time at issue he was out of the United Kingdom. The Commissioner found that, although on holiday, he had satisfied the availability condition because he had informed the Jobcentre of his holiday with his children (and could thus have returned on request with the 48 hour notice period allowed). In terms of actively seeking work he could also take advantage of the "deemed actively seeking work" for two weeks of properly notified holiday (Jobseeker's Regulations 1996, reg.19(1)(p)). Absence from Great Britain precludes entitlement to JSA. But it does not as such preclude entitlement to unemployment credits for the period of absence, since reg.8A(2)(b) while linking back to specifically enumerated conditions in Jobseekers Act 1995, s.1(2), does not include the "present in Great Britain" condition. Accordingly, Commissioner Williams concluded that the claimant met the second contribution condition for entitlement to incapacity benefit.

No credit, however, can be awarded as regards a week in respect of which one of the situations in para.(5) exists.

[¹ Credits for incapacity for work [⁴ or limited capability for work]

8B.—(1) [² For] the purposes of entitlement to any benefit by virtue of a person's earnings or contributions, he shall be entitled to be credited with earnings equal to the lower earnings limit then in force, in respect of each week to which this regulation applies.

2.23

(2) Subject to paragraphs [⁷ (2A),] (3) and (4) this regulation applies to—
[⁵(a) a week in which, in relation to the person concerned, each of the days—
  (i) was a day of incapacity for work under section 30C of the Contributions and Benefits Act (incapacity benefit: days and periods of incapacity for work); or
  (ii) would have been such a day had the person concerned claimed short-term incapacity benefit or maternity allowance within the prescribed time; or
  (iii) was a day of incapacity for work for the purposes of statutory sick pay under section 151 of the Contributions and Benefits Act and fell within a period of entitlement under section 153 of that Act; or
  (iv) was a day of limited capability for work for the purposes of Part 1 of the Welfare Reform Act (limited capability for work) or

would have been such a day had the person concerned been entitled to an employment and support allowance by virtue of section 1(2)(a) of the Welfare Reform Act; or

[⁶(iva) would have been a day of limited capability for work for the purposes of Part 1 of the Welfare Reform Act (limited capability for work) where the person concerned would have been entitled to an employment and support allowance but for the application of section 1A of that Act; or]

(v) would have been a day of limited capability for work for the purposes of Part 1 of the Welfare Reform Act (limited capability for work) had that person claimed an employment and support allowance or maternity allowance within the prescribed time;]

[⁵(aa) . . .];

[³(b) a week for any part of which an unemployability supplement or allowance was payable by virtue of—

(i) Schedule 7 to the Contributions and Benefits Act;

[⁵ (ii) Article 12 of the Naval, Military and Air Forces Etc. (Disablement and Death) Service Pensions Order 2006;] or

(iii) Article 18 of the Personal Injuries (Civilians) Scheme 1983.]

[⁷(2A) This regulation shall not apply to a week where—

(a) under paragraph (2)(a)(i) the person concerned was not entitled to incapacity benefit, severe disablement allowance or maternity allowance;

(b) paragraph (2)(a)(ii), (iva) or (v) apply; or

(c) under paragraph (2)(a)(iv) the person concerned was not entitled to an employment and support allowance by virtue of section 1(2)(a) of the Welfare Reform Act,

and the person concerned was entitled to universal credit for any part of that week.

(3) Where the person concerned is a married woman, this regulation shall not apply to a week in respect of any part of which an election made by her under regulations made under section 19(4) of the Contributions and Benefits Act had effect.

(4) A day shall not be a day to which paragraph (2)(a) applies unless the person concerned has—

(a) before the end of the benefit year immediately following the year in which that day fell; or

(b) within such further time as may be reasonable in the circumstances of the case,

furnished to the Secretary of State notice in writing of the grounds on which he claims to be entitled to be credited with earnings.]

AMENDMENTS

1. Social Security (Credits and Contributions) (Jobseeker's Allowance Consequential and Miscellaneous Amendments) Regulations 1996 (SI 1996/2367) reg.2(6) (October 7, 1996).

2. Social Security (Incapacity Benefit) Miscellaneous Amendments Regulations 2000 (SI 2000/3120) reg.4(b) (April 6, 2001).

3. Social Security (Miscellaneous Amendments) (No.3) Regulations 2007 (SI 2007/1749) reg.8(3) (July 16, 2007).

4. Employment and Support Allowance (Consequential Provisions) (No.2) Regulations 2008 (SI 2008/1554) reg.48(6) (October 27, 2008).

5. Social Security (Credits)(Amendment) Regulations 2010 (SI 2010/385) reg.2(2) (April 6, 2010).

6. Employment and Support Allowance (Duration of Contributory Allowance) (Consequential Amendments) Regulations 2012 (SI 2012/913) reg.2 (May 1, 2012).

7. Universal Credit (Consequential, Supplementary, Incidental and Miscellaneous Provisions) Regulations 2013 (SI 2013/630) reg.70(1), (5) (April 29, 2013).

DEFINITIONS

"benefit"—see reg.2(1).
"benefit year"—see SSCBA 1992 s.21(6).
"lower earnings limit"—see SSCBA 1992 s.122(1).
"year"—see reg.2(1).

GENERAL NOTE

As with all of the Regulations making claimants eligible for the award of credits, **2.24**
this must be read with reg.3 (*CIB/1602/2006*; *CIB/3327/2004*). One can only have them insofar as they are necessary to bring one's record up to the level required for satisfying the second contribution condition for the relevant benefit (see para.(1), reg.3 and reg.2(1) ("reckonable year")).

It enables a credit equal to that tax year's lower earnings limit to be awarded for each week in respect of which one of the following situations pertains (para.(1)):

- each of its days was one of incapacity for work under SSCBA 1992 s.30C (or would have been had s/he claimed in time for short-term incapacity benefit or maternity allowance or been entitled to incapacity benefit under s.30A)—provided that the written notification and statement of grounds conditions in para.(4) are met (para.(2)(a)(i), (ii));

- each of its days was one of incapacity for work within a period of entitlement for SSP purposes (SSCBA 1992 ss.151 and 153)—provided that the written notification and statement of grounds conditions in para.(4) are met (para.2(a)(iii));

- each of its days was one of limited capability for work for the purposes of Pt I of the WRA 2007 or would have been had s/he claimed in time for ESA or maternity allowance or had been entitled to ESA under WRA 2007 s.1(2)(a)—provided that the written notification and statement of grounds conditions in para.(4) are met (para.(2)(a) (iv), (v));

- each of its days was one of continuing limited capability for work where entitlement to CESA has ceased only because the time-limit (currently 365 days for those not in the support group) set by the WRA 2007 s.1A has been reached.

- unemployability supplement was payable for part of it (see SSCBA 1992 Sch.7 Pt I) (para.(2)(b)).

Commissioner Mesher considered this phrase in *CIB/2445/2006* when concluding that the appeal tribunal was within its permitted area of judgment when concluding that what would have been a reasonable time for claiming credits for any of the years 1989/90 to 2000/01 had expired by the time the claimant claimed them on May 13, 2005 (para.27). As the Commissioner pointed out, the test in reg.8B(4) is not one of "good cause" for a late claim but

"the more general test of what is a reasonable time in the circumstances for a claim to be made. Therefore . . . the length of the time after the period for which credits are claimed is a factor, along with all the other circumstances. When entitlement to credits rests on proof of incapacity for work, the assessment of the evidence and the making of a proper decision becomes more difficult the further away from the period in question one gets. As a general proposition it can be accepted that the longer the gap from the tax year in question the more compelling the other circumstances must be for it to be concluded that the time for claiming, outside the following benefit year, is reasonable" (para.29).

Even with respect to the most recent tax years in respect of which credits were claimed (2000/01), the range of communications indicating a shortfall in his contributions record were such that the tribunal was entitled to conclude that the time for claiming credits was, by May 2005, no longer reasonable.

Note that a woman cannot gain a credit under this provision in respect of any week in any part of which as a married woman a certificate of election to pay contributions at reduced rate applied to her (para.(3)). Nor can one be given where any of the situations in para.(2A) exists, involving entitlement to universal credit.

Credits on termination of bereavement benefits

2.25   [¹ **8C.**—(1) This regulation applies for the purpose only of enabling a person who previously received a bereavement benefit ("the recipient") to satisfy, as the case may be, the condition referred to in—

    (a) paragraph 2(3)(b) of Schedule 3 to the Contributions and Benefits Act in relation to short-term incapacity benefit; [³ . . .]

    (b) section 2(1)(b) of the Jobseekers Act 1995 in relation to contribution-based jobseeker's allowance. [;³ or

    (c) paragraph 2(1) of Schedule 1 to the Welfare Reform Act in relation to a contributory employment and support allowance.]

[¹(2) For every year up to and including that in which the recipient ceased to be entitled to a bereavement benefit otherwise than by reason of remarriage [², forming a civil partnership], or living together with [⁴another person as a married couple], the recipient shall be credited with such earnings as may be required to enable the condition referred to above to be satisfied.]

[⁵ (3) In this regulation, "bereavement benefit" means—

    (a) a bereavement payment referred to in section 36 of the Contributions and Benefits Act as in force immediately before it was repealed by paragraph 8 of Schedule 16 to the Pensions Act 2014;

    (b) a bereavement allowance referred to in section 39B of the Contributions and Benefits Act as in force immediately before it was repealed by paragraph 13 of Schedule 16 to the Pensions Act 2014; and

    (c) widowed parent's allowance.]

REVOCATION AND AMENDMENTS

1. Social Security (Benefits for Widows and Widowers) (Consequential Amendments) Regulations 2000 (SI 2000/1483) reg.3(7) (April 9, 2001).

2. Civil Partnership (Pensions, Social Security and Child Support) (Consequential, etc. Provisions) Order 2005 (SI 2005/2877) art.2(3) and Sch.3 para.4(4) (December 5, 2005).

3. Employment and Support Allowance (Consequential Provisions) (No. 2) Regulations 2008 (SI 2008/1554) reg.48(7) (October 27, 2008).

4. Marriage (Same Sex Couples) Act 2013 and Marriage and Civil Partnership (Scotland) Act 2014 (Consequential Provisions) Order 2014 (SI 2014/3061) art.2 and Sch.1 para,4(1), (2) (December 10, 2014 (England and Wales) and December 16, 2014 (Scotland) (see art.1).

5. Pensions Act 2014 (Consequential, Supplementary and Incidental Amendments) Order 2017 (SI 2017/422) art.4(7) (April 6, 2017).

DEFINITIONS

"bereavement benefit"—para.(3); SSCBA 1992 s.20(1)(ea).
"the recipient"—para.(1).

GENERAL NOTE

As with all of the Regulations making claimants eligible for the award of credits, **2.26**
this must be read with reg.3 (*CIB/1602/2006*; *CIB/3327/2004*). One can only have
them insofar as they are necessary to bring one's record up to the level required for
satisfying the second contribution condition for the relevant benefit (see para.(1),
reg.3 and reg.2(1) ("reckonable year")).

Regulation 8C applies only in respect of awarding sufficient credits to satisfy
the second contribution condition for contribution-based jobseeker's allowance
[CBJSA], short-term incapacity benefit [STIB] or contributory employment and
support allowance [ESA]. For these benefits, the second contribution condition
requires that the contribution record in terms of paid and/or credited contributions
reaches the requisite level (50 times the tax year's lower earnings limit) in respect
of *each* of the last two tax years complete before the beginning of the relevant
benefit year (the year in which there falls the first day of the jobseeking period or
linked period [CBJSA: see Jobseekers Act 1995 s.2(1)(b); *Vol.II: Income Support,
Jobseeker's Allowance, State Pension Credit and the Social Fund*], period of incapacity
for work [STIB: see SSCBA 1992 Sch.3, para.2] or period of limited capability
for work [CESA, see WRA 2007 Sch.1, para.2] of which the claim for benefit is
part). It enables the award of sufficient credits to someone who previously received
a "bereavement benefit". Those credits can be awarded for every tax year up to
and including the one in which the person ceased to be entitled to the bereavement
benefit, provided that entitlement was not lost by reason of remarriage or cohabitation as husband and wife with someone of the opposite sex. "Bereavement benefit"
has the same meaning as in SSCBA 1992 s.20(1)(ea), above (reg.2(1)).

[1 Credits for the purposes of entitlement to incapacity benefit fol-
lowing official error

8D.—(1) This regulation applies for the purpose only of enabling a **2.27**
person who was previously entitled to incapacity benefit to satisfy the condition referred to in paragraph 2(3)(a) of Schedule 3 to the Contributions
and Benefits Act in respect of a subsequent claim for incapacity benefit
where his period of incapacity for work is, together with a previous period
of incapacity for work, to be treated as one period of incapacity for work
under section 30C of that Act.

(2) Where—

(a) a person was previously entitled to incapacity benefit;

(b) the award of incapacity benefit was as a result of satisfying the condition referred to in paragraph (1) by virtue of being credited with
earnings for incapacity for work or approved training in the tax years
from 1993–94 to 2007–08;

(c) some or all of those credits were credited by virtue of official error
derived from the failure to transpose correctly information relating to
those credits from the Department for Work and Pensions' Pension
Strategy Computer System to Her Majesty's Revenue and Customs'
computer system (NIRS2) or from related clerical procedures;

(d) that person makes a further claim for incapacity benefit; and

(e) his period of incapacity for work is, together with the period of
incapacity for work to which his previous entitlement referred to in

sub-paragraph (a) related, to be treated as one period of incapacity for work under section 30C of the Contributions and Benefits Act, that person shall be credited with such earnings as may be required to enable the condition referred to in paragraph (1) to be satisfied.

(3) In this regulation and in regulations 8E and 8F, "official error" means an error made by—

    (a) an officer of the Department for Work and Pensions or an officer of Revenue and Customs acting as such which no person outside the Department or Her Majesty's Revenue and Customs caused or to which no person outside the Department for Work and Pensions or Her Majesty's Revenue and Customs materially contributed; or

    (b) a person employed by a service provider and to which no person who was not so employed materially contributed,

but excludes any error of law which is shown to have been an error by virtue of a subsequent decision of a Commissioner or the court.

(4) In paragraph (3)—

"Commissioner" means the Chief Social Security Commissioner or any other Social Security Commissioner and includes a tribunal of three or more Commissioners constituted under section 16(7) of the Social Security Act 1998;

"service provider" means a person providing services to the Secretary of State for Work and Pensions or to Her Majesty's Revenue and Customs.]

AMENDMENT

1. Social Security (National Insurance Credits) Amendment Regulations 2007 (SI 2007/2582) reg.2 (October 1, 2007).

Credits for the purposes of entitlement to retirement pension following official error

2.28   **8E.** —(1) This regulation applies for the purpose only of enabling the condition referred to in paragraph 5(3)(a) of Schedule 3 to the Contributions and Benefits Act to be satisfied in respect of a claim for retirement pension made by a person ("the claimant")—

    (a) who would attain pensionable age no later than 31st May 2008;

    (b) not falling within sub-paragraph (a) but based on the satisfaction of that condition by another person—

        (i) who would attain, or would have attained, pensionable age no later than 31st May 2008; or

        (ii) in respect of whose death the claimant received a bereavement benefit.

(2) Where—

    (a) a person claims retirement pension;

    (b) the satisfaction of the condition referred to in paragraph (1) would be based on earnings credited for incapacity for work or approved training in the tax years from 1993–94 to 2007–08; and

    (c) some or all of those credits were credited by virtue of official error derived from the failure to transpose correctly information relating to those credits from the Department for Work and Pensions' Pension Strategy Computer System to Her Majesty's Revenue and Customs' computer system (NIRS2) or from related clerical procedures,

those earnings shall be credited.

(3) In this regulation, "bereavement benefit" means a bereavement allowance [² referred to in section 39B of the Contributions and Benefits Act as in force immediately before it was repealed by paragraph 13 of Schedule 16 to the Pensions Act 2014], a widowed mother's allowance, a widowed parent's allowance or a widow's pension.

AMENDMENTS

1. Social Security (National Insurance Credits) Amendment Regulations 2007 (SI 2007/2582) reg.2 (October 1, 2007).
2. Pensions Act 2014 (Consequential, Supplementary and Incidental Amendments) Order 2017 (SI 2017/422) art.4(8) (April 6, 2017).

[¹ Credits for the purposes of entitlement to contribution-based job-seeker's allowance following official error

8F.—(1) This regulation applies for the purpose only of enabling a person to satisfy the condition referred to in section 2(1)(b) of the Jobseekers Act 1995.

2.29

(2) Where—

(a) a person claims a jobseeker's allowance;
(b) the satisfaction of the condition referred to in paragraph (1) would be based on earnings credited for incapacity for work or approved training in the tax years from 1993–94 to 2007–08; and
(c) some or all of those credits were credited by virtue of official error derived from the failure to transpose correctly information relating to those credits from the Department for Work and Pensions' Pension Strategy Computer System to Her Majesty's Revenue and Customs' computer system (NIRS2) or from related clerical procedures,

that person shall be credited with those earnings.]

AMENDMENT

1. Social Security (National Insurance Credits) Amendment Regulations 2007 (SI 2007/2582) reg.2 (October 1, 2007).

[¹ Credits for persons entitled to universal credit

8G.—(1) For the purposes of entitlement to a benefit to which this regulation applies, a person shall be credited with a Class 3 contribution in respect of a week if that person is entitled to universal credit under Part 1 of the Welfare Reform Act 2012 for any part of that week.

2.30

(2) This regulation applies to—

(a) a Category A retirement pension;
(b) a Category B retirement pension;
(c) a widowed parent's allowance;
(d) [² . . .]

AMENDMENTS

1. Universal Credit (Consequential, Supplementary, Incidental and Miscellaneous Provisions) Regulations 2013 (SI 2013/630) reg.70(1), (6) (April 29, 2013).
2. Pensions Act 2014 (Consequential, Supplementary and Incidental Amendments) Order 2017 (SI 2017/422) art.4(9) (April 6, 2017).

Crediting of earnings for the purposes of entitlement to short-term incapacity benefit—further conditions

2.31   **9.**—[¹ . . .]

REVOCATION

1. Social Security (Incapacity Benefit) Miscellaneous Amendments Regulations 2000 (SI 2000/3120) reg.4(c) (April 16, 2001).

[¹ Credits for persons approaching pensionable age

2.32   **9A.**—(1) For the purposes of entitlement to any benefit by virtue of a person's earnings or contributions [³ a person to whom this regulation applies] shall, subject to the following paragraphs, be credited with such earnings as may be required to bring his relevant earnings factor in respect of a tax year to which this regulation applies to the level required to make that year a reckonable year.

[³ (1A) This regulation applies to a man born before 6th October 1954 but who has not attained the age of 65.]

[³ (2) This regulation shall apply to—

(a) the tax year in which a man attains the age which is pensionable age in the case of a woman born on the same day as that man; and

(b) to any succeeding tax year,

but not including the tax year in which he attains the age of 65 or any subsequent tax year.]

(3) Paragraph (1) shall apply, in the case of a self-employed earner, only if he is—

(a) liable to pay a Class 2 contribution in respect of any week in a tax year to which this regulation applies; or

(b) excepted from liability to pay Class 2 contributions in respect of any week in a tax year to which this regulation applies by virtue of his earnings being less than, or being treated by regulations as less than, the amount specified in section 11(4) of the Social Security Contributions and Benefits Act 1992 (exception from liability for Class 2 contributions on account of small earnings),

so that he shall be credited with earnings equal to the lower earnings limit then in force in respect of each week for which he is not so liable.

(4) [² . . .]

(5) Where in any tax year to which this regulation applies a person is absent from Great Britain for more than 182 days, he shall not by virtue of this regulation be credited with any earnings or contributions in that tax year.]

AMENDMENTS

1. Social Security (Credits) Amendment Regulations 1994 (SI 1994/1837) reg.3 (August 8, 1994).

2. Social Security (Credits and Contributions) (Jobseeker's Allowance Consequential and Miscellaneous Amendments) Regulations 1996 (SI 1996/2367) reg.2(8) (October 7, 1996).

3. Social Security (State Pension and National Insurance Credits) Regulations 2009 (SI 2009/2206) reg.30 (April 6, 2010).

DEFINITIONS

"benefit"—see reg.2(1).
"pensionable age"—see SSCBA 1992 s.122(1).
"reckonable year"—see reg.2(1).
"relevant earnings factor"—see reg.2(1).
"self-employed earner"—see SSCBA 1992 s.2(1)(b).
"tax year"—see SSCBA 1992 s.122(1).
"year"—see reg.2(1).

GENERAL NOTE

As with all of the Regulations making claimants eligible for the award of credits, 2.33
this must be read with reg.3 (*CIB/1602/2006; CIB/3327/2004*). One can only have
them insofar as they are necessary to bring one's record up to the level required for
satisfying the second contribution condition for the relevant benefit (see para.(1),
reg.3 and reg.2(1) ("reckonable year")).

It is applicable only to the tax year in which the person attained 60 and to each of
the four succeeding tax years (para.(2)). It enables the award of sufficient credits to
give the requisite record for the purposes of the second contribution condition (to
make that year a "reckonable year") (para.(1)). As respects a self-employed earner,
it can only do so if he is exempt from paying Class 2 contributions because of the
"small earnings" exception (para.(3)). It cannot do so in respect of any tax year to
which this regulation applies, if in that year the person is absent from Great Britain
for more than 182 days (para.(4)).

[¹ Credits for jury service

9B.—(1) Subject to paragraphs (2) and (3), for the purposes of entitle- 2.34
ment to any benefit [² by virtue of a person's earnings or contributions] he
shall be entitled to be credited with earnings equal to the lower earnings
limit then in force, in respect of each week for any part of which he attended
at Court for jury service.

(2) A person shall be entitled to be credited with earnings in respect of a
week by virtue of the provisions of this regulation only if—

(a) his earnings in respect of that week from any employment of his as
an employed earner are below the lower earnings limit then in force;
and

(b) he furnished to the Secretary of State notice in writing of his claim
to be entitled to be credited with earnings and did so before the end
of the benefit year immediately following the tax year in which that
week or part of that week fell or within such further time as may be
reasonable in the circumstances of his case.

(3) Paragraph (1) shall not apply—

(a) to a woman in respect of any week in any part of which she was a
married woman in respect of whom an election made by her under
Regulations made under section 3(2) of the Social Security Pensions
Act 1975 had effect; or

(b) in respect of any week falling wholly or partly within a year commencing before 6th April 1988[³, or

(c) to a person in respect of any week in any part of which he is a self-
employed earner.]]

AMENDMENTS

1. Social Security (Credits) Amendment Regulations 1988 (SI 1988/516)
reg.2(3) (April 6, 1988).

2. Social Security (Credits) Amendment (No. 4) Regulations 1988 (SI 1988/1545) reg.2(5) (October 2, 1988).
3. Social Security (Credits) Amendment Regulations 1994 (SI 1994/1837) reg.4.

DEFINITIONS

"benefit"—see reg.2(1).
"benefit year"—see SSCBA 1992 s.21(6).
"employed earner"—see SSCBA 1992 s.2(1)(a).
"lower earnings limit"—see SSCBA 1992 s.122(1).
"self-employed earner"—see SSCBA 1992 s.2(1)(b).
"tax year"—see SSCBA 1992 s.122(1).

GENERAL NOTE

2.35   As with all of the Regulations making claimants eligible for the award of credits, this must be read with reg.3 (*CIB/1602/2006; CIB/3327/2004*). One can only have them insofar as they are necessary to bring one's record up to the level required for satisfying the second contribution condition for the relevant benefit (see para.(1), reg.3 and reg.2(1) ("reckonable year")).

It enables the award of a credit equal to the lower earnings limit for the tax year in question only to an employed earner as regards a week for any part of which he attended at Court for jury service, provided that his earnings in respect of that week from his employment fall below the then applicable lower earnings limit. He must claim in time and in writing (para.(2)(b)).

No award is possible in respect of a week falling wholly or partly in a tax year before April 6, 1988 (para.(3)(b)). Nor can one be made to someone in any week in part of which he is a self-employed earner (thus ruling out the person who in that week is both employed and self-employed, or who changes from one category to another during that week) (para.(3)(c)).

Note, finally, that a woman cannot gain a credit under this provision in respect of any week in any part of which as a married woman a certificate of election to pay contributions at reduced rate applied to her (para.(3)).

[²Credits for adoption pay period, [³ shared parental pay period,] additional paternity pay period and maternity pay period]

2.36   [¹9C.—(1) For the purposes of entitlement to any benefit by virtue of—
   (a) in the case of a person referred to in paragraph (2)(a) or (aa), that person's earnings or contributions;
   (b) in the case of a woman referred to in paragraph (2)(b), her earnings or contributions, [³; or]
   [³ (c) the shared parental pay period in respect of which statutory shared parental pay is paid to a person.]
that person or that woman, as the case may be, shall be entitled to be credited with earnings equal to the lower earnings limit then in force in respect of each week to which this regulation applies.

(2) Subject to paragraphs (3) and (4), this regulation applies to each week during—
   (a) the adoption pay period in respect of which statutory adoption pay was paid to a person; or
   [²(aa) the additional paternity pay period in respect of which additional statutory paternity pay was paid to a person; or]
   (b) the maternity pay period in respect of which statutory maternity pay was paid to a woman.

(3) A person or woman referred to above shall be entitled to be credited with earnings in respect of a week by virtue of this regulation only if he or she—

  (a) furnished to the Secretary of State notice in writing of his or her claim to be entitled to be credited with earnings; and

  (b) did so—

    (i) before the end of the benefit year immediately following the tax year in which that week began, or

    (ii) within such further time as may be reasonable in the circumstances of his or her case.

(4) This regulation shall not apply to a woman in respect of any week in any part of which she was a married woman in respect of whom an election made by her under regulations made under section 19(4) of the Contributions and Benefits Act had effect.

(5) In this regulation

  (a) "adoption pay period", [²"additional paternity pay period",] "maternity pay period", "statutory adoption pay", [²"additional statutory paternity pay"] and "statutory maternity pay" have the same meaning as in the Contributions and Benefits Act.]

  [(b) "statutory shared parental pay" means statutory shared parental pay payable in accordance with Part 12ZC of that Act and "shared parental pay period" means the weeks in respect of which statutory shared parental pay is payable to a person under section 171ZY(2) of that Act.]

AMENDMENTS

1. Social Security (Credits) Amendment Regulations 2003 (SI 2003/521) reg.2(3) (April 6, 2003).
2. Social Security (Credits) (Amendment) Regulations 2012 (SI 2012/766) reg.2 (April 5, 2012).
3. Shared Parental Leave and Statutory Shared Parental Pay (Consequential Amendments to Subordinate Legislation) Order 2014 (SI 2014/3255) art.2 (April 5, 2015).

DEFINITIONS

"additional paternity pay period"—para.(5); SSCBA 1992 s.171ZEE(2);
"additional statutory paternity pay"—para.(5); SSCBA 1992 ss.171ZEA(1), 171ZEB(1);
"adoption pay period"—para.(5); SSCBA 1992 ss.171ZN(2), 171ZS(1).
"benefit"—see reg.2(1).
"benefit year"—see SSCBA 1992 s.21(6).
"lower earnings limit"—see SSCBA 1992 s.122(1).
"maternity pay period"—see para.(5); SSCBA 1992 s.165(1).
"statutory adoption pay"—see para.(5); SSCBA 1992 s.171ZL(1).
"statutory maternity pay"—see para.(5); SSCBA 1992 s.164(1).
"tax year"—see SSCBA 1992 s.122(1).

GENERAL NOTE

As with all of the Regulations making claimants eligible for the award of credits,   **2.37** this must be read with reg.3 (*CIB/1602/2006; CIB/3327/2004*). One can only have them insofar as they are necessary to bring one's record up to the level required for satisfying the second contribution condition for the relevant benefit (see para.(1), reg.3 and reg.2(1) ("reckonable year")).

It enables the award of a credit equal to the lower earnings limit for the tax year in question in respect of each week (for a woman) a maternity pay period, (for a man) an additional paternity pay period or (for any person) an adoption pay period in respect of which, as the case may be, statutory maternity pay, additional statutory paternity pay or statutory adoption pay was paid to the person. This regulation does not apply to a woman who has elected to pay contributions at a reduced rate (para.(4)).

[¹ **Credits for certain periods of imprisonment or detention in legal custody**

2.38   **9D.**—(1) Subject to paragraphs (2) and (4), for the purposes of entitlement to any benefit by virtue of a person's earnings or contributions, where—

   (a) a person is imprisoned or otherwise detained in legal custody by reason of his conviction of an offence or convictions in respect of two or more offences;

   (b) that conviction or, as the case may be, each of those convictions is subsequently quashed by the Crown Court, the Court of Appeal or the High Court of Justiciary; and

   (c) he is released from that imprisonment or detention, whether prior, or pursuant, to the quashing of that conviction or, as the case may be, each of those convictions,

that person shall, if he has made an application in writing to the Secretary of State for the purpose, be entitled to be credited with earnings or, in the case of any year earlier than 1987–88, contributions, in accordance with paragraph (3).

(2) Paragraph (1) shall not apply in respect of any period during which the person was also imprisoned or otherwise detained in legal custody for reasons unconnected with the conviction or convictions referred to in that paragraph.

(3) The earnings or, as the case may be, the contributions referred to in paragraph (1) are, in respect of any week in any part of which the person was—

   (a) detained in legal custody—

      (i) prior to the conviction or convictions referred to in that paragraph, but,

      (ii) for the purposes of any proceedings in relation to any offence referred to in sub-paragraph (a) of that paragraph; or

   (b) imprisoned or otherwise detained in legal custody by reason of that conviction or those convictions,

those necessary for the purpose of bringing his earnings factor, for the year in which such a week falls, to the level required to make that year a reckonable year.

(4) Subject to paragraph (5), paragraph (1) shall not apply to a woman in respect of any week referred to in paragraph (3) in any part of which she was a married woman in respect of whom an election made by her under regulations made under section 19(4) of the Contributions and Benefits Act had effect.

(5) Paragraph (4) shall not apply to any woman—

   (a) who was imprisoned or otherwise detained in legal custody as referred to in paragraph (3) for a continuous period which included 2 complete years; and

   (b) whose election ceased to have effect in accordance with regulation 101(1)(c) of the Social Security (Contributions) Regulations 1979 (which provides for an election to cease to have effect at the end of 2 consecutive years which began on or after 6th April 1978 during which the woman is not liable for primary Class 1 or Class 2 contributions).

(6) An application referred to in paragraph (1) may be transmitted by electronic means.]

AMENDMENT

1. Social Security (Credits and Incapacity Benefit) Amendment Regulations 2001 (SI 2001/573) reg.2.

DEFINITIONS

"benefit"—see reg.2(1).
"reckonable year"—see reg.2(1).
"year"—see reg.2(1).

GENERAL NOTE

As with all of the Regulations making claimants eligible for the award of credits, this must be read with reg.3 (*CIB/1602/2006; CIB/3327/2004*). One can only have them insofar as they are necessary to bring one's record up to the level required for satisfying the second contribution condition for the relevant benefit (see para.(1), reg.3 and reg.2(1) ("reckonable year")).

2.39

It enables the award of a credit equal to the relevant lower earnings limit for each week for part of which the person was imprisoned or detained in legal custody because of a conviction of an offence, where the conviction that alone grounded that imprisonment or detention (whether prior to or *post* conviction) is quashed by a specified court. Credits can be so awarded to meet the amount by which the record for the tax year containing the weeks of imprisonment or detention falls short of the requisite level for the second condition for the benefit in question (paras (1)–(3)). The person must claim in time and in the proper manner, which can include e-mail (paras (1), (6)).

Note, finally, that a woman cannot gain a credit under this provision in respect of any week in any part of which as a married woman a certificate of election to pay contributions at reduced rate applied to her, unless the relevant period of imprisonment included two complete tax years so that the election ceased to have effect under Social Security (Contributions) Regulations 1979, reg.101(1)(c) (paras (4), (5)). See now Social Security (Contributions) Regulations 2001 (SI 2001/1004), reg.128(1)(c).

[¹Credits for certain spouses and civil partners of members of Her Majesty's forces

9E.—(1) For the purposes of entitlement to any benefit by virtue of a person's earnings or contributions, that person shall, subject to the following paragraphs, be entitled to be credited with earnings equal to the lower earnings limit then in force, in respect of each week to which paragraph (2) applies.

2.40

(2) This paragraph applies to each week for any part of which the person is—

(a) the spouse or civil partner of a member of Her Majesty's forces or treated as such by the Secretary of State for the purposes of occupying accommodation, and

(b) accompanying the member of Her Majesty's forces on an assignment outside the United Kingdom or treated as such by the Secretary of State.

(3) A person referred to in paragraph (2) shall be entitled to be credited

with earnings in respect of a week by virtue of this regulation only if that person has made an application to the Secretary of State for the purpose.

(4) An application under paragraph (3) must—

(a) be properly completed and on a form approved by the Secretary of State, or in such manner as the Secretary of State accepts as sufficient in the particular circumstances, and

(b) include—

    (i) a statement confirming that the conditions referred to in paragraph (2) are met and signed by or on behalf of the Defence Council or a person authorised by them, and

    (ii) such other information as the Secretary of State may require.

(5) An application under paragraph (3) is to be made—

(a) once the end date of the assignment referred to in paragraph (2) has been confirmed, or

(b) at such earlier time as the Secretary of State is prepared to accept in the particular circumstances of the case.

(6) An application made in accordance with paragraph (5)(a) must be made before the end of the tax year immediately following the tax year in which the assignment referred to in paragraph (2) ended, or within such further time as may be reasonable in the circumstances of the case.

(7) Where the Secretary of State accepts an application in accordance with paragraph (5)(b), this regulation entitles the person referred to in paragraph (2) to be credited with earnings in respect of any week subsequent to that application only if that person has made a further application to the Secretary of State in accordance with paragraphs (3) to (6).

(8) This regulation shall not apply—

(a) to a person in respect of any week where the person is entitled to be credited with earnings under regulation 7A, 8A or 8B in respect of the same week;

(b) to a woman in respect of any week in any part of which she was a married woman in respect of whom an election made by her under regulations made under section 19(4) of the Contributions and Benefits Act had effect; or

(c) in respect of any week commencing before 6th April 2010.]

AMENDMENT

1. Inserted by Social Security (Credits) (Amendment) Regulations 2010 (SI 2010/385) reg.2(3) (April 6, 2010).

DEFINITIONS

"benefit"—see reg.2(1).
"reckonable year"—see reg.2(1).
"year"—see reg.2(1).

GENERAL NOTE

2.41   As with all of the Regulations making claimants eligible for the award of credits, this must be read with reg.3 (*CIB/1602/2006; CIB/3327/2004*). One can only have them insofar as they are necessary to bring one's record up to the level required for satisfying the second contribution condition for the relevant benefit (see para.(1), reg.3 and reg.2(1) ("reckonable year")). From April 6, 2010, this regulation provides for a credit of earnings equal to the relevant lower earnings limit to the accompanying spouse or civil partner of a member of Her Majesty's forces who is on an assignment outside the United Kingdom. It cannot apply in respect of any week prior to April 6, 2010 (para.(8)(c)), and will not apply where the person is entitled to be credited for the same week under regs 7A, 8A or 8B (para.8(a)). Nor can it provide credits where the married woman concerned has made a reduced rate contributions election (para. (8)(b)).

[¹Credits for persons providing care for a child under the age of 12

9F.—(1) Subject to paragraphs (2), (5) and (6), the contributor con-   2.42
cerned in the case of a benefit listed in paragraph (3) shall be credited with
a Class 3 contribution for each week ("the relevant week") falling after 6th
April 2011 during which that contributor satisfied the conditions in paragraph (4).

(2) Contributions shall only be credited in so far as is necessary to enable
the contributor concerned to satisfy—

   (a) in relation to a Category A or Category B retirement pension, the
        contribution condition specified in paragraph 5A(2) of Schedule 3
        to the Contributions and Benefits Act;

   (b) in relation to a widowed parent's allowance [³. . .], the second con-
        tribution condition specified in paragraph 5(3) of Schedule 3 to the
        Contributions and Benefits Act.

(3) This regulation applies to the following benefits—

   (a) a Category A retirement pension in a case where the contributor
        concerned attains pensionable age on or after 6th April 2012;

   (b) a Category B retirement pension payable by virtue of section 48A of
        the Contributions and Benefits Act in a case where the contributor
        concerned attains pensionable age on or after that date;

   (c) a Category B retirement pension payable by virtue of section 48B of
        that Act in a case where the contributor concerned dies on or after
        that date without having attained pensionable age before that date;

   (d) a widowed parent's allowance payable in a case where the contribu-
        tor concerned dies on or after that date;

   (e) [³. . .].

(4) The conditions are that in the relevant week the contributor
concerned—

   (a) provided care in respect of a child under the age of 12;

   (b) is, in relation to that child, a person specified in the Schedule (other
        than a person who is a relevant carer for the purposes of section 23A
        of the Contributions and Benefits Act); and

   (c) was ordinarily resident in Great Britain.

(5) Only one contributor may be credited with Class 3 contributions
under this Regulation in respect of any relevant week.

(6) The contributor concerned shall not be credited with Class 3 contributions by virtue of paragraph (1) unless—

   (a) a person other than that contributor satisfies the conditions in para-
        graph (7); and

   (b) an application to the Secretary of State to be so credited is made in
        accordance with paragraph (8).

(7) The conditions are that—

   (a) child benefit was awarded to that other person in relation to the child
        for whom, and in respect of the week in which, child care was pro-
        vided by the contributor concerned; and

(b) the aggregate of that other person's earnings factors, [² other than where those earnings factors are derived from Class 3 contributions credited by virtue of section 23A(2) and (3)(a) of the Contributions and Benefits Act (crediting of contributions for a person awarded child benefit in respect of a child under 12)], exceed the qualifying earnings factor for the year in which the relevant week falls.

(8) An application under paragraph (6)(b) must—

(a) include the name and date of birth of the child cared for;

(b) where requested by the Secretary of State or the Commissioners for Her Majesty's Revenue and Customs, include a declaration by the person awarded child benefit in respect of that child that the conditions in paragraph (4) are satisfied;

(c) specify the relevant week or weeks in which the child was cared for; and

(d) be received after the end of the tax year in which a week, which is the subject of the application, falls.

(9) In this regulation, "the contributor concerned" has the meaning given in section 21(5)(a) of the Contributions and Benefits Act.]

AMENDMENTS

1. National Insurance Contributions Credits (Miscellaneous Amendments) Regulations 2011 (SI 2011/709) reg.2(3) (April 5, 2011).

2. Social Security (Credits) (Amendment) (No. 2) Regulations 2012 (SI 2012/2680) reg.2 (December 1, 2012).

3. Pensions Act 2014 (Consequential, Supplementary and Incidental Amendments) Order 2017 (SI 2017/422) art.4(10) (April 6, 2017).

GENERAL NOTE

2.43   This new regulation provides for the award of Class 3 National Insurance contribution credits, for a tax year commencing on or after April 6, 2011, in respect of a claim for a basic state pension or bereavement benefits for specified adults who provide care for children under 12. The specified adults are listed in the new Sch. to these Regulations. The provision reflects concern over the position of grandparents and other adult relatives undertaking familial child care to enable the child's parent(s) to work.

Transitional provisions

2.44   **10.**—[¹ . . .].

REVOCATION

1. Social Security (Credits) Amendment Regulations 1987 (SI 1987/414) reg.10 (April 6, 1987).

[¹SCHEDULE

Persons who may qualify as carers for a child under the age of 12

2.45   **1.**—(1) Parent.

(2) Grandparent.

(3) Great-grandparent.

(4) Great-great-grandparent.

(5) Sibling.

(6) Parent's sibling.

(7) Spouse or former spouse of any of the persons listed in sub-paragraphs (1) to (6).

(8) Civil partner or former civil partner of any of the persons listed in sub-paragraphs (1) to (6).

(9) Partner or former partner of any of the persons listed in sub-paragraphs (1) to (8).

(10) Son or daughter of persons listed in sub-paragraphs (5) to (9).

(11) In respect of the son or daughter of a person listed in sub-paragraph (6), that person's—

(a)   spouse or former spouse;

(b)   civil partner or former civil partner; or

(c)   partner or former partner.

2. For the purposes of paragraph 1(5) and (6), a sibling includes a sibling of the half blood, a step sibling and an adopted sibling.

3. For the purposes of paragraph 1(9) and (11)(c), a partner is the other member of a couple consisting of [¹two people who are not married to or civil partners of each other but are living together as a married couple].   2.46

AMENDMENT

1. Marriage (Same Sex Couples) Act 2013 and Marriage and Civil Partnership (Scotland) Act 2014 (Consequential Provisions) Order 2014 (SI 2014/3061) art.2 and Sch.1 para.4(1), (3) (December 10, 2014 (England and Wales) and December 16, 2014 (Scotland) (see art.1)).

The Social Security Pensions (Home Responsibilities) Regulations 1994

(SI 1994/704) (AS AMENDED)

ARRANGEMENT OF REGULATIONS

1.	Citation, commencement and interpretation.	2.47
2.	Preclusion from regular employment for the purpose of paragraph 5(7)(b) of Schedule 3 to the Act.	
3.	*Omitted.*	
Schedule. *Omitted.*		

The Secretary of State for Social Security, in exercise of the powers conferred on him by sections 21(3) and 175(1) to (5) of, and paragraph 5(7)(b) of Schedule 3 to, the Social Security Contributions and Benefits Act 1992 and of all other powers enabling him in that behalf, after agreement by the Social Security Advisory Committee that proposals to make these Regulations should not be referred to it, hereby makes the following Regulations:

Citation, commencement and interpretation

1.—(1) These Regulations may be cited as the Social Security Pensions (Home Responsibilities) Regulations 1994, and shall come into force on 6th April 1994.   2.48

(2) In these Regulations, unless the context otherwise requires—

"the Act" means the Social Security Contributions and Benefits Act 1992;

"child benefit" means child benefit within the meaning of section 141 of the Act;

[¹ "foster parent" means a person approved as—

(a)   a foster parent in accordance with the provisions of Part IV of the

Fostering Services Regulations 2002 (approval of foster parents); or

(b) a foster carer in accordance with the provisions of Part II of the Fostering of Children (Scotland) Regulations 1996(approval of foster carers);]

[² "the General Regulations" means the Child Benefit (General) Regulations 2003;]

"Personal Injuries Scheme", "Pneumoconiosis and Byssinosis Benefit Scheme", "Service Pensions Instrument" and "1914–1918 War Injuries Scheme" have the same meaning as assigned to them in regulation 2 of the Social Security (Overlapping Benefits) Regulations 1979;

"year" means tax year.

AMENDMENTS

1. Social Security Pensions (Home Responsibilities) Amendment Regulations 2003 (SI 2003/1767) reg.2(2) (September 1, 2003).
2. Social Security Pensions (Home Responsibilities) (Amendment) Regulations 2005 (SI 2005/48) reg.2(2) (February 9, 2005).

DEFINITION

"tax year"—see SSCBA 1992, s.122(1).

Preclusion from regular employment for the purpose of paragraph 5(7)(b) of Schedule 3 to the Act

2.49   **2.**—(1) For the purpose of paragraph 5(7)(b) of Schedule 3 to the Act a person shall, subject to paragraph (5) below, be taken to be precluded from regular employment by responsibilities at home in any year—

(a) throughout which he satisfies any of the conditions specified in paragraph (2) below;

(b) throughout which he satisfies the conditions specified in paragraph (3) below; or

(c) in which he satisfies, for part of the year, any of the conditions specified in paragraph (2) below and for the remainder of the year, the condition specified in paragraph (3)(a) below.

(2) The conditions specified in this paragraph are—

(a) that child benefit awarded to him was payable in respect of a child under the age of 16;

[⁶ (aa) that child benefit awarded to his partner was payable in respect of a child under the age of 16;]

(b) that—

  (i) [⁶ he is a person to whom paragraphs 4 to 6 of Schedule 1B to the Income Support (General) Regulations 1987 apply, and]

  (ii) income support is payable to him;

[³ (c) that he was a foster parent] [⁶ throughout the year 2003–2004 or any subsequent year].

(3) The conditions specified in this paragraph are—

(a) that he was regularly engaged, for at least 35 hours per week, in caring for a person in respect of whom there was payable any of the benefits specified in paragraph (4) below;

(b) that those benefits were payable to that person for at least 48 weeks in that year.

(4) The benefits referred to in paragraph (3) above are an attendance allowance under section 64 of the Act, the care component of disability living allowance at the highest or middle rate prescribed in accordance with section 72 of the Act, a constant attendance allowance under any Service Pensions Instrument, Personal Injuries Scheme or 1914–1918 War Injuries Scheme, an increase of disablement pension under section 104 of the Act in respect of constant attendance and any benefit corresponding to such an increase under a Pneumoconiosis and Byssinosis Benefit Scheme or under Regulations under paragraph 7(2) of Schedule 8 to the Act.

[¹ (4A) For the purposes of paragraph (2)(a) above, where—

(a) child benefit first becomes payable to a person in respect of a child on the first Monday in a year; and

(b) child benefit would, but for the provisions of section 147(2) of the Act, have been payable to that person in respect of that child for the part of that year falling before that Monday,

that person shall be treated as if he were entitled to child benefit and, accordingly, as if child benefit were payable to him for that part of that year.]

[⁵ (4B) For the purposes of paragraph (2)(a) above, in respect of the year 2004–2005 or any subsequent year, where—

(a) a notice is given under regulation 15(1) of the General Regulations (modification of priority between persons entitled to child benefit) by the person who is entitled to child benefit;

(b) that notice becomes effective in relation to any week falling in the first three months of a year;

(c) as a result of that notice, child benefit becomes payable to another person ("the new payee") in priority to anyone else;

(d) for each week of that year prior to that notice becoming effective, child benefit would, but for the provisions of regulation 15(2)(b) of those Regulations, have been payable to the new payee; and

(e) no other notice under regulation 15(1) of those Regulations was given in respect of the same child which became effective during any week referred to in sub-paragraph (d);

the new payee shall be treated as if he were entitled to child benefit and, accordingly, as if child benefit were payable to him for each week of the year prior to the notice becoming effective.]

[⁶ (4C) In paragraph (2)(aa), "partner" means the person with whom he was both residing and sharing responsibility for the child throughout that year.]

(5) Except where paragraph (6) below applies, paragraph (1) above shall not apply in relation to any year—

(a) if the person in question is a woman who has made or is treated as having made an election in accordance with regulations having effect under section 19(4) of the Act and that election had effect at the beginning of that year; or

[⁶ (aza) in the case of a person who satisfies the condition in paragraph (2) (aa) above—

(i) such information is not furnished as the Secretary of State may from time to time require which is relevant to the question of whether in that year he was precluded from regular employment by responsibilities at home within the meaning of these Regulations;

(ii) he attained pensionable age on or before 5th April 2008 or, in relation to a claim for a bereavement benefit in respect of his death, he died on or before that date; or

    (iii) the aggregate of his partner's earnings factors—

        (aa) in respect of any year preceding 2002–2003;

        (bb) in respect of the year 2002–2003 or any subsequent year, where those earnings factors are derived from so much of his earnings as do not exceed the upper earnings limit and upon which primary Class 1 contributions have been paid or treated as paid,

is less than the qualifying earnings factor for the year in question.]

[⁴(aa) in the case of a person who satisfies the condition in paragraph (2)(c) above in respect of the year 2003–04 or any subsequent year, if he does not furnish such information as the Secretary of State may from time to time require which is relevant to the question of whether in that year he was precluded from regular employment by responsibilities at home within the meaning of these Regulations; or]

[²(b) in the case of a person who satisfies the conditions in paragraph (3) above in respect of any year preceding 2002–2003, if he does not furnish such information as the Secretary of State may from time to time require which is relevant to the question of whether in that year he was precluded from regular employment by responsibilities at home within the meaning of these Regulations; or

  (c) in the case of a person who satisfies the conditions in paragraph (3) above in respect of the year 2002–2003 or any subsequent year, if he does not, within the period of three years immediately following the end of that year, furnish such information as the Secretary of State may from time to time require which is relevant to the question of whether, in that year, he was precluded from regular employment by responsibilities at home within the meaning of these Regulations.]

(6) This paragraph applies to a woman who throughout the period beginning on 6th April 1975 and ending on 5th April 1980—

  (a) had no earnings in respect of which primary Class 1 contributions were payable; and

  (b) was not at any time a self-employed earner.

AMENDMENTS

1. Social Security Pensions (Home Responsibilities) (Amendment) Regulations 2001 (SI 2001/1265) reg.2 (April 6, 2002).

2. Additional Pension and Social Security Pensions (Home Responsibilities) (Amendment) Regulations 2001 (SI 2001/1323) reg.7 (April 6, 2002).

3. Social Security Pensions (Home Responsibilities) Amendment Regulations 2003 (SI 2003/1767) reg.2(3) (September 1, 2003).

4. Social Security Pensions (Home Responsibilities) Amendment Regulations 2003 (SI 2003/1767) reg.2(4) (September 1, 2003).

5. Social Security Pensions (Home Responsibilities) (Amendment) Regulations 2005 (SI 2005/48) reg.2(3) (February 9, 2005).

6. Social Security Pensions (Home Responsibilities) Amendment Regulations 2008 (SI 2008/498) reg.2 (April 6, 2008).

DEFINITIONS

"child benefit"—see reg.1(2); SSCBA 1992 s.141.
"the General Regulations"—see reg.1(2).
"year"—see reg.1(2).

GENERAL NOTE

This deals with home responsibilities protection, which provides help in satisfying   **2.50**
the second contribution condition for the range of long-term benefits in SSCBA
1992, Sch.3 para.5:

- widowed mother's allowance (SSCBA 1992 s.37);

- widowed parent's allowance (SSCBA 1992 s.39A);

- widow's pension (SSCBA 1992 s.38);

- Category A or B retirement pension (SSCBA 1992 ss.43–54).

It helps by stipulating when a year is one of home responsibilities protection. Such
years are then deducted from the number of years in which the person would otherwise have to satisfy the contribution conditions, but the reduction effected can only
halve the requisite number of years or reduce them to 20 whichever is the lower
(SSCBA 1992, Sch.3, para.5(a)).

Note that home responsibilities protection was abolished on 6 April 2010 and
replaced with national insurance credits for certain parents and carers.

A tax year is one of home responsibilities protection in the following situations:

- throughout it the person received child benefit for a child under 16 (paras (1)
  (a), (2)(a), (4A)) (see *CG/173/2002*) and note the aid afforded by para.(4B) in
  satisfying the "throughout" element; but see further, below, the note on *SF
  v SSWP and HMRC (HRP)* [2013] UKUT 175 (AAC) with respect to the
  position of a UK national, exercising free movement rights under EU law,
  who had received the equivalent of child benefit in another Member State.

- throughout it the person received income support as someone looking after a
  disabled person (paras (1)(a), (2)(b));

- throughout it the person was an approved foster parent (this applies in
  respect of the year 2003–04 and any subsequent year);

- for 48 weeks of the tax year the person spent 35 hours a week looking after
  someone receiving attendance allowance, constant attendance allowance
  under the industrial injuries or war pensions schemes, or the higher or
  middle rate components of disability living allowance (paras (1)(b), (3),
  (4));

- a tax year which is a mix of such periods (para.(1)(c)).

A person must claim in time and in the proper manner (para.5(aa)(b), (c)).

In *SF v SSWP and HMRC (HRP)* [2013] UKUT 175 (AAC), Judge Wikeley
considered the position as regards HRP of a woman who had received one year of
child benefit and HRP in the UK before moving to Belgium where she received
several years of the Belgian equivalent of child benefit, *allocation familiales*. He held
that, as regards HRP, HMRC makes decisions as an agent of the Secretary of State
so that its decisions on HRP are decisions on social security benefits and properly
within the jurisdiction of the First-tier Tribunal (Social Entitlement Chamber)
(paras 9, 10). He also decided that art.21 TFEU and reg.1408/71 required the
Secretary of State, for the purposes of awarding a UK state retirement pension, to
take account of the claimant's child-raising period in Belgium as if that period had
been completed in the UK and her pre-existing award of child benefit had continued without interruption, thus treating her periods of receipt of *allocations familiales*
as if they were periods of receipt of UK child benefit. This was because the "receipt
of child benefit" requirement for HRP, linked as it was to the presence or residence
in the UK test as regards child benefit, acts as a restriction on the right of free movement in the EU which is not objectively justified (paras 28–52). From May 1, 2010,
reg.1408/71 was replaced by reg.883/2004. While art.5 thereof corresponds to the

claimant's position, it could not aid her in these proceedings since it entered into force after the date of the HMRC decision on HRP (paras 53–57).

See further *FH v HMRC and SSWP (HRP)* [2015] UKUT 672 (AAC), emphasising that years which are qualifying years in any event cannot qualify for HRP. See also *JM v SSWP and HMRC* [2018] UKUT 2 (AAC), where the claimant and her husband had lived in the Netherlands from 1982 to 1984 and received Dutch family benefits. The claimant qualified for a UK state pension in 2002, at age 60, and a Dutch state pension, based on the 2-year child-raising period, in 2007, when she was aged 65. Judge Wikeley held that neither EU nor domestic law required the claimant to receive HRP for the 1982-84 period, which would effectively amount to double recovery given the receipt of the Dutch pension (even though it was paid later).

Although home responsibilities protection can be claimed by both sexes, substantially more women than men are covered by it. Although it affords less help when compared to an equivalent period of unemployment for which credits are awarded, deputy Commissioner Gamble held in *CP/4017/2006* that this differentiation did not constitute indirect discrimination contrary to art.14 ECHR. *McAuslane v Secretary of State for Work and Pensions*, the appeal against this decision, is pending before the Court of Appeal, but has been removed from the list pending resolution of a costs issue.

Note finally that a woman with an election to pay reduced rate contributions, which was in effect at the beginning of the tax year, cannot have that year treated as one of home responsibilities protection, unless throughout the period April 6, 1975 to April 5, 1980, she is not a self-employed earner and had no earnings in respect of which primary Class 1 contributions were payable (paras (5)(a), (6)).

REVOCATIONS

3.—*Omitted* as not relevant.
Schedule. *Omitted* as not relevant.

The Social Security (Benefit) (Married Women and Widows Special Provisions) Regulations 1974

(SI 1974/2010) (*AS AMENDED*)

REGULATION REPRODUCED

2.51   3. Modifications, in relation to widows, of provisions with respect to short term incapacity benefit, employment and support allowance, maternity allowance and Category A retirement pension

Modifications, in relation to widows, of provisions with respect to [¹short-term incapacity benefit] [³ ...][²employment and support allowance], maternity allowance, and Category A retirement pension

2.52   **3.**—(1) Subject to the following provisions of this regulation, where, otherwise than by reason of remarriage or cohabitation with a man as his wife, a woman ceases to be entitled either to a widow's allowance or to a widowed mother's allowance—

(a) she shall be deemed to have satisfied the first contribution condition for [¹ . . .] [¹ short-term incapacity benefit] or [¹ . . .] maternity allowance [¹ . . .] referred to in paragraph 1 [¹ or] 3 [¹ . . .], as the case may be, of Schedule 3 to the Act [² or, in relation to [³ ...] employment and support allowance, she shall be deemed to have satisfied the first condition referred to in paragraph 1(1) of Schedule 1 to the Welfare Reform Act;

(b) for the purpose only of enabling her to satisfy the second contribution condition for unemployment and [¹short-term incapacity benefit] or maternity allowance referred to in paragraph 1 or 3, as the case may be, of Schedule 3 to the Act, [² or, in relation to [³ ...] employment and support allowance, she shall be deemed to have satisfied the second condition referred to in paragraph 2(1) of Schedule 1 to the Welfare Reform Act], there shall be credited to her such Class 1 contributions (if any) for every year up to and including that in which she ceased to be entitled as aforesaid as are required to enable her to satisfy that condition; and

(c) [¹ . . .]

(2)–(10) *omitted as not relevant and/or revoked.*

<small>AMENDMENTS</small>

1. Social Security (Incapacity Benefit) (Consequential and Transitional Amendments and Savings) Regulations 1995 (SI 1995/829) reg.2(a) (April 13, 1995).

2. Employment and Support Allowance (Consequential Provisions) (No. 2) Regulations 2008 (SI 2008/1554) reg.64(3) (October 27, 2008).

3. Universal Credit (Consequential, Supplementary, Incidental and Miscellaneous Provisions) Regulations 2013 (SI 2013/630) reg.20(1), (3) (April 29, 2013).

<small>GENERAL NOTE</small>

Taken together with Social Security (Credits) Regulations 1975, reg.8C, above, the effect of para.(1)(a) appears effectively to waive altogether the contributions conditions for short-term incapacity benefit or employment and support allowance for certain widows. 2.53

The Social Security (Crediting and Treatment of Contributions, and National Insurance Numbers) Regulations 2001

<small>(SI 2001/769) (AS AMENDED)</small>

<small>REGULATIONS REPRODUCED</small>

1. Citation, commencement and interpretation. 2.54
2. Appropriation of Class 3 contributions.
3. Crediting of Class 3 contributions.
4. Treatment for the purpose of any contributory benefit of late paid contributions.
5. Treatment for the purpose of any contributory benefit of late paid primary Class 1 contributions where there was no consent, connivance or negligence by the primary contributor.

5A.   Treatment for the purpose of any contributory benefit of duly paid primary Class 1 contributions in respect of retrospective earnings

6.   Treatment for the purpose of any contributory benefit of contributions under the Act paid late through ignorance or error.

6A.   Treatment for the purposes of any contributory benefit of certain Class 3 contributions

6B.   Treatment for the purposes of any contributory benefit of certain Class 2 or Class 3 contributions

6C.   Treatment of Class 3 contributions paid under section 13A of the Act

7.   Treatment for the purpose of any contributory benefit of contributions paid under certain provisions relating to the payment and collection of contributions

7A.   Treatment for the purpose of a contribution-based jobseeker's allowance or a contributory employment and support allowance of Class 2 contributions paid in accordance with the Act

9.   Application for allocation of national insurance number

10.-12. *Omitted*

Schedule. *Omitted.*

The Secretary of State for Social Security, with the concurrence of the Inland Revenue in so far as required, in exercise of powers conferred by sections 13(3), 22(5), 122(1) and 175(1) to (4) of, and paragraphs 8(1)(d) and (1A) and 10 of Schedule 1 to, the Social Security Contributions and Benefits Act 1992 and sections 182C and 189(1) and (3) to (6) of the Social Security Administration Act 1992 and of all other powers enabling him in that behalf and for the purpose only of consolidating other regulations hereby revoked, hereby makes the following Regulations:

Citation, commencement and interpretation

2.55   **1.**—(1) These Regulations may be cited as the Social Security (Crediting and Treatment of Contributions, and National Insurance Numbers) Regulations 2001 and shall come into force on 6th April 2001.

(2) In these Regulations, including this regulation—

"the Act" means the Social Security Contributions and Benefits Act 1992;

"the Contributions Regulations" means the Social Security (Contributions) Regulations [⁵ 2001];

"contribution week" means a period of seven days beginning with midnight between Saturday and Sunday;

[⁴"contribution-based jobseeker's allowance" means an allowance under the Jobseekers Act 1995 as amended by the provisions of Part 1 of Schedule 14 to the Welfare Reform Act 2012 that remove references to an income-based allowance, and a contribution-based allowance under the Jobseekers Act 1995 as that Act has effect apart from those provisions;]

"contributory benefit" includes a contribution-based jobseeker's allowance but not an income-based jobseeker's allowance; [² and includes a contributory employment and support allowance but not an income-related employment and support allowance]

[⁴"contributory employment and support allowance" means an allowance under Part 1 of the Welfare Reform Act as amended by the provisions of Schedule 3, and Part 1 of Schedule 14, to the Welfare Reform Act 2012 that remove references to an income-related allowance, and a contributory allowance under Part 1 of the Welfare Reform Act as that Part has effect apart from those provisions;]

[⁵ "due date" (subject to regulation 4(11)) means, in relation to—

(a) any Class 1 contribution, the date by which payment falls to be made;

(b) any Class 2 contribution which a person is liable or entitled to pay, the 31st January following the end of the year in respect of which it is payable;

(c) any Class 3 contribution, the date 42 days after the end of the year in respect of which it is paid;]

"earnings factor" has the meaning assigned to it in section 21(5)(c) of the Act;

[⁴"income-based jobseeker's allowance" has the same meaning as in the Jobseekers Act 1995;]

[² "income-related employment and support allowance" means an income-related allowance under Part 1 of the Welfare Reform Act (employment and support allowance);]

"relevant benefit year" has the meaning assigned to it in—

(a) section 2(4)(b) of the Jobseekers Act 1995, in relation to a contribution-based jobseeker's allowance;

(b) paragraph 2(6)(b) of Schedule 3 to the Act (contribution conditions for entitlement to short-term incapacity benefit), in relation to short-term incapacity benefit;

[² (c) paragraph 3(1)(f) of Schedule 1 to the Welfare Reform Act (conditions relating to national insurance), in relation to a contributory employment and support allowance.]

"relevant time", in relation to short-term incapacity benefit, has the meaning assigned to it in paragraph 2(6)(a) of Schedule 3 to the Act;

[² "the Welfare Reform Act" means the Welfare Reform Act 2007;]

"year" means tax year.

[¹ (3) In these Regulations, "official error" means an error made by—

(a) an officer of the Department for Work and Pensions or an officer of Revenue and Customs acting as such which no person outside the Department or Her Majesty's Revenue and Customs caused or to which no person outside the Department or Her Majesty's Revenue and Customs materially contributed; or

(b) a person employed by a service provider and to which no person who was not so employed materially contributed,

but excludes any error of law which is shown to have been an error by virtue of a subsequent decision of [³ the Upper Tribunal] or the court.

(4) [³. . .]

"service provider" means a person providing services to the Secretary of State for Work and Pensions or to Her Majesty's Revenue and Customs.]

AMENDMENTS

1. Social Security (National Insurance Credits) Amendment Regulations 2007 (SI 2007/2582) reg.3 (October 1, 2007).

2. Employment and Support Allowance (Consequential Provisions) (No. 2) Regulations 2008 (SI 2008/1554) reg.49(2) (October 27, 2008).

3. Tribunals, Courts and Enforcement Act 2007 (Transitional and Consequential Provisions) Order 2008 (SI 2008/2683) art.6(1) and Sch.1 para.147 (November 3, 2008).

4. Universal Credit (Consequential, Supplementary, Incidental and Miscellaneous Provisions) Regulations 2013 (SI 2013/630) reg.71 (April 29, 2013).

5. Social Security (Credits, and Crediting and Treatment of Contributions) (Consequential and Miscellaneous Amendments) Regulations 2016 (SOI 2016/1145) reg. 5(2) (January 1, 2017).

Appropriation of Class 3 contributions

2.56   **2.**—Any person paying Class 3 contributions in one year may appropriate such contributions to the earnings factor of another year if such contributions are payable in respect of that other year or, in the absence of any such appropriation, the Inland Revenue may, with the consent of the contributor, make such appropriation.

Crediting of Class 3 contributions

2.57   **3.**—Where, for any year, a contributor's earnings factor derived from—
   (a) earnings upon which primary Class 1 contributions have been paid or treated as paid;
   (b) credited earnings;
   (c) Class 2 or Class 3 contributions paid by or credited to him; or
   (d) any or all of such earnings and contributions,
falls short of a figure which is 52 times that year's lower earnings limit for Class 1 contributions by an amount which is equal to, or less than, half that year's lower earnings limit, that contributor shall be credited with a Class 3 contribution for that year.

Treatment for the purpose of any contributory benefit of late paid contributions

2.58   **4.**—(1) Subject to the provisions of regulations 5 [¹ to 6C] below and regulation [⁶ 61] of the Contributions Regulations (voluntary Class 2 contributions not paid within permitted period), for the purpose of entitlement to any contributory benefit, [⁵ paragraphs (1B)] to (9) below shall apply to contributions ("relevant contributions")—
   (a) paid after the due date; or
   (b) treated as paid after the due date under regulation 7(2) below.
[² (1A) Any relevant contribution which is paid—
   (a) by virtue of an official error; and
   (b) more than six years after the end of the year in which the contributor was first advised of that error,
shall be treated as not paid.]
[⁵(1B) Where contributions are paid in accordance with regulation 63A of the Social Security (Contributions) Regulations 2001 (collection of unpaid Class 2 contributions through PAYE code), any relevant contributions are to be treated as paid on 5th April of the tax year in which they are paid.]
   (2) Subject to the provisions of paragraph (4) below, any relevant contribution other than one referred to in paragraph (3) below–
   (a) if paid [⁶ after the end of the second year]—
      (i) [⁶ . . .] following the year in which liability for that contribution arises, [⁶ or]

[⁶ (ii) following the year in respect of which a person is entitled, but
not liable, to pay the contribution,]
    shall be treated as not paid;
(b) if paid before the end of the said second year, shall, subject to paragraphs (7) and (8) below, be treated as paid on the date on which
payment of the contribution is made.

(3) Subject to the provisions of paragraph (4) below, any relevant Class 2
contribution payable in respect of a contribution week after 5th April 1983
or any relevant Class 3 contribution payable in respect of a year after 5th
April 1982 [⁶ after the end of the sixth year]—
  (a) if paid—
      (i) [⁶ . . .] following the year in which liability for that contribution
arises, [⁶ or]
    [⁶ (ii) following the year in respect of which a person is entitled, but
not liable, to pay the contribution,]
    shall be treated as not paid;
  (b) if paid before the end of the said sixth year, shall, subject to paragraphs (7) [⁶ or] (8) below, be treated as paid on the date on which
payment of the contribution is made.

(4) A Class 3 contribution payable by a person to whom regulation [⁶
48(3)(b)(ii) or (iii)] of the Contributions Regulations (which specify the
conditions to be complied with before a person may pay a Class 3 contribution) applies in respect of a year which includes a period of education,
apprenticeship, training, imprisonment or detention in legal custody such
as is specified in that regulation—
  (a) if paid after the end of the sixth year specified in that regulation, shall
be treated as not paid;
  (b) if paid before the end of the said sixth year shall, subject to the provisions of paragraphs (7) and (8) below, be treated as paid on the date
on which payment of the contribution is made.

(5) Notwithstanding the provisions of paragraph (4) above, for the
purpose of entitlement to any contributory benefit, where—
  (a) a Class 3 contribution other than one referred to in sub-paragraph
(b) below which is payable in respect of a year specified in that sub-
paragraph, is paid after—
    (i) the due date, and
    (ii) the end of the second year following the year preceding that in
which occurred the relevant time or, as the case may be, the
relevant event,
    that contribution shall be treated as not paid;
  (b) in respect of a year after 5th April 1982, a Class 3 contribution which
is payable in respect of a year specified in paragraph (4) above, is
paid after—
    (i) the due date, and
    (ii) the end of the sixth year following the year preceding that in
which occurred the relevant time or, as the case may be, the
relevant event,
    that contribution shall be treated as not paid.

(6) For the purposes of paragraph (5) above, "relevant event" means the
date on which the person concerned attained pensionable age or, as the
case may be, died under that age.

(7) Notwithstanding the provisions of paragraphs (2), (3) and (4) above,

in determining whether the relevant contribution conditions are satisfied in whole or in part for the purpose of entitlement to any contributory benefit, any relevant contribution which is paid within the time specified in paragraph (2)(b), (3)(b) or, as the case may be, (4)(b) above shall be treated—

    (a) for the purpose of entitlement in respect of any period before the date on which the payment of the contribution is made, as not paid; and

    (b) subject to the provisions of paragraph (8) below, for the purpose of entitlement in respect of any other period, as paid on the date on which the payment of the contribution is made.

[⁵(7A) In determining whether the relevant contribution conditions are satisfied in whole or in part for the purpose of entitlement to any contributory benefit, any relevant contribution which is treated as paid on the date specified in paragraph (1B) shall be treated—

    (a) for the purpose of entitlement in respect of any period before the date on which payment of the contribution is treated as paid, as not paid; and

    (b) subject to the provisions of paragraph (8) below, for the purpose of entitlement in respect of any other period, as paid on the date specified in paragraph (1B).]

[⁶ (8) For the purpose of determining whether the second contribution condition for entitlement to a contribution-based jobseeker's allowance or a contributory employment and support allowance is satisfied in whole or in part a relevant contribution is to be treated—

    (a) if a Class 1 contribution paid before the beginning of the relevant benefit year, as paid on the due date;

    (b) if, subject to paragraph (2)(a), a Class 1 contribution paid after the end of the benefit year immediately preceding the relevant benefit year or, subject to paragraph (3)(a), a Class 2 contribution—

        (i) as not paid in relation to the benefit claimed in respect of any day before the expiry of a period of 42 days (including Sundays) commencing with the date on which the payment of that contribution is made; and

        (ii) as paid at the expiry of that period in relation to entitlement to such benefit in respect of any other period.]

(9) For the purposes of paragraph (8) above, "second contribution condition" in relation to—

    (a) a contribution-based jobseeker's allowance is a reference to the condition specified in section 2(1)(b) of the Jobseekers Act 1995;

    (b) short-term incapacity benefit is a reference to the condition specified in paragraph 2(3) of Schedule 3 to the Act;

[⁴ (c) a contributory employment and support allowance is a reference to the condition specified in paragraph 2(1) of Schedule 1 to the Welfare Reform Act.]

(10) This regulation shall not apply to Class 4 contributions.

[³ (11) Where an amount is retrospectively treated as earnings ("retrospective earnings") by regulations made by virtue of section 4B(2) of the Act, the "due date" for earnings-related contributions in respect of those earnings is the date given by paragraph 11A of Schedule 4 to the Social Security (Contributions) Regulations 2001, for the purposes of this regulation and regulations 5 and 5A.]

AMENDMENTS

1. Social Security (Additional Class 3 National Insurance Contributions) Amendment Regulations 2009 (SI 2009/659) reg.3(2) (April 6, 2009).
2. Social Security (National Insurance Credits) Amendment Regulations 2007 (SI 2007/2582) reg.4(3)(b) (October 1, 2007).
3. Social Security, Occupational Pension Schemes and Statutory Payments (Consequential Provisions) Regulations 2007 (SI 2007/1154) reg.2(2) (April 6, 2007).
4. Employment and Support Allowance (Consequential Provisions) (No.2) Regulations 2008 (SI 2008/1554) reg.49(3) (October 27, 2008).
5. Social Security (Crediting and Treatment of Contributions, and National Insurance Numbers) (Amendment) Regulations 2013 (SI 2013/3165) reg. 2 (April 6, 2014).
6. Social Security (Credits, and Crediting and Treatment of Contributions) (Consequential and Miscellaneous Amendments) Regulations 2016 (SOI 2016/1145) reg. 5(3) (January 1, 2017).

Treatment for the purpose of any contributory benefit of late paid primary Class 1 contributions where there was no consent, connivance or negligence by the primary contributor

5.—(1) This regulation applies where a primary Class 1 contribution which   2.59
is payable on a primary contributor's behalf by a secondary contributor—
(a) is paid after the due date; or
(b) in relation to any claim for—
    (i) a contribution-based jobseeker's allowance, is not paid before the beginning of the relevant benefit year,
    (ii) short-term incapacity benefit, is not paid before the relevant time,[2 or
    (iii) a contributory employment and support allowance, is not paid before the beginning of the relevant benefit year,]
and the delay in making payment is shown to the satisfaction of [1an officer of] the Inland Revenue not to have been with the consent or connivance of, or attributable to any negligence on the part of, the primary contributor.
(2) Where paragraph (1) above applies, the primary Class 1 contribution shall be treated—
(a) for the purpose of the first contribution condition of entitlement to a contribution-based jobseeker's allowance [2, short-term incapacity benefit or a contributory employment and support allowance], as paid on the day on which payment is made of the earnings in respect of which the contribution is payable; and
(b) for any other purpose relating to entitlement to any contributory benefit, as paid on the due date.
(3) For the purposes of this regulation—
(a) "first contribution condition" in relation to—
    (i) a contribution-based jobseeker's allowance is a reference to the condition specified in section 2(1)(a) of the Jobseekers Act 1995,
    (ii) short-term incapacity benefit is a reference to the condition specified in paragraph 2(2) of Schedule 3 to the Act;
    [2 "(iii) a contributory employment and support allowance is a reference to the condition specified in paragraph 1(1) of Schedule 1 to the Welfare Reform Act;]
(b) "primary contributor" means the person liable to pay a primary

Class 1 contribution in accordance with section 6(4)(a) of the Act (liability for Class 1 contributions);

(c) "secondary contributor" means the person who, in respect of earnings from employed earner's employment, is liable to pay a secondary Class 1 contribution in accordance with section 6(4)(b) of the Act.

AMENDMENTS

1. Social Security, Occupational Pension Schemes and Statutory Payments (Consequential Provisions) Regulations 2007 (SI 2007/1154) reg.2(2) (April 6, 2007).
2. Employment and Support Allowance (Consequential Provisions) (No.2) Regulations 2008 (SI 2008/1554) reg.49(4) (October 27, 2008).

[¹ Treatment for the purpose of any contributory benefit of duly paid primary Class 1 contributions in respect of retrospective earnings

2.60   **5A.**—Where a primary Class 1 contribution payable in respect of retrospective earnings is paid by the due date, it shall be treated—

(a) for the purposes of the first contribution condition of entitlement to a contribution-based jobseeker's allowance [², short-term incapacity benefit or a contributory employment and support allowance], as paid on the day on which payment is made of the retrospective earnings in respect of which the contribution is payable; and

(b) for any other purpose relating to entitlement to any contributory benefit, as paid on the due date.]

AMENDMENTS

1. Social Security, Occupational Pension Schemes and Statutory Payments (Consequential Provisions) Regulations 2007 (SI 2007/1154) reg.2(2) (April 6, 2007).
2. Employment and Support Allowance (Consequential Provisions) (No.2) Regulations 2008 (SI 2008/1554) reg.49(5) (October 27, 2008).

Treatment for the purpose of any contributory benefit of contributions under the Act paid late through ignorance or error

2.61   **6.**—(1) In the case of a contribution paid by or in respect of a person after the due date, where—

(a) the contribution is paid after the time when it would, under regulation 4 or 5 above, have been treated as paid for the purpose of entitlement to contributory benefit; and

(b) it is shown to the satisfaction of [¹ an officer of] the Inland Revenue that the failure to pay the contribution before that time is attributable to ignorance or error on the part of that person or the person making the payment and that that ignorance or error was not due to any failure on the part of such person to exercise due care and diligence,

[¹ an officer of the Inland Revenue may direct], for the purposes of those regulations, the contribution shall be treated as paid on such earlier day as [¹ the officer considers] appropriate in the circumstances, and those regulations shall have effect subject to any such direction.

(2) This regulation shall not apply to a Class 4 contribution.

[¹ Treatment for the purposes of any contributory benefit of certain Class 3 contributions

6A.—(1) For the purposes of entitlement to any contributory benefit, this regulation applies in the case of a Class 3 contribution paid after the due date— 2.62

(a) which would otherwise under regulation 4—
  (i) have been treated as paid on a day other than on the day on which it was actually paid; or
  (ii) have been treated as not paid; and
(b) which is paid in respect of a year after 5th April 1996 but before 6th April 2002.

(2) A contribution referred to in paragraph (1), where it is paid on or before 5th April 2009 by or in respect of a person who attains pensionable age on or after 6th April 2008, shall be treated as paid on the day on which it is paid.

(3) A contribution referred to in paragraph (1), where it is paid on or before 5th April 2009 by or in respect of a person who attains pensionable age on or after 24th October 2004 but before 6th April 2008, shall be treated as paid on—

(a) the day on which it is paid; or
(b) the date on which the person attained pensionable age,
whichever is the earlier.

(4) A contribution referred to in paragraph (1), where it is paid on or before 5th April 2010 by or in respect of a person who attains pensionable age on or after 6th April 1998 but before 24th October 2004, shall be treated as paid on—

(a) 1st October 1998; or
(b) the date on which the person attained pensionable age,
whichever is the later.]

AMENDMENT

1. Social Security (Crediting and Treatment of Contributions, and National Insurance Numbers) Amendment Regulations 2004 (SI 2004/1361) reg.2(b) (May 17, 2004).

[¹ Treatment for the purpose of any contributory benefit of certain Class 2 or Class 3 contributions

6B.—For the purpose of entitlement to any contributory benefit, a Class 2 or a Class 3 contribution paid after the due date— 2.63

(a) which would otherwise under regulation 4 (apart from paragraph (1A) of that regulation)—
  (i) have been treated as paid on a day other than the day on which it was actually paid; or
  (ii) have been treated as not paid; and
(b) which was paid after the due date by virtue of an official error,
shall be treated as paid on the day on which it is paid.]

AMENDMENT

1. Social Security (National Insurance Credits) Amendment Regulations 2007 (SI 2007/2582) reg.4(4) (October 1, 2007).

[¹Treatment of Class 3 contributions paid under section 13A of the Act

2.64

6C.—(1) This regulation applies to a Class 3 contribution paid by an eligible person under section 13A (right to pay additional Class 3 contributions in certain cases) of the Act.

(2) A contribution paid after 5th April 2009 but before 6th April 2011 shall be treated as paid on—

(a) the day on which it is paid; or

(b) the date on which the person attained pensionable age,

whichever is the earlier.

(3) A contribution paid after 5th April 2011 shall be treated as paid on the day on which it is paid.]

AMENDMENT

1. Social Security (Additional Class 3 National Insurance Contributions) Amendment Regulations 2009 (SI 2009/659) reg.3(3) (April 6, 2009).

[¹ Treatment for the purpose of any contributory benefit of contributions paid under certain provisions relating to the payment and collection of contributions]

2.65

7.—[¹ (1) Subject to the provisions of paragraph (2), for the purpose of entitlement to any contributory benefit except a contribution-based jobseeker's allowance or a contributory employment and support allowance, where—

(a) a person pays a Class 2 contribution under section 11(2) or (6) of the Act, or a Class 3 contribution in accordance with regulation 89, 89A, 90 or 148C of the Contributions Regulations (provisions relating to the method of, and time for, payment of Class 2 and Class 3 contributions etc.); and

(b) the due date for payment of that contribution is a date after the relevant day,

that contribution is treated as paid by the relevant day.]

(2) Where, in respect of any part of a late notification period, a person pays a Class 2 contribution which he is liable [¹ or entitled] to pay, that contribution shall be treated as paid after the due date, whether or not it was paid by the due date.

(3) For the purposes of this regulation—

(a) "late notification period" means the period beginning with the day a person liable [¹ or entitled] to pay a Class 2 contribution was first required to notify the Inland Revenue in accordance with the provisions of regulation [¹ 87, 87A or 87AA] of the Contributions Regulations (notification of commencement or cessation of payment of Class 2 or Class 3 contributions) and ending on the [¹ day on] which he gives that notification;

(b) "relevant day" means the first day in respect of which a person would have been entitled to receive the contributory benefit in question if any contribution condition relevant to that benefit had already been satisfied.

(c) [¹ . . .]

AMENDMENT

1. Social Security (Credits, and Crediting and Treatment of Contributions) (Consequential and Miscellaneous Amendments) Regulations 2016 (SOI 2016/1145) reg. 5(4) (January 1, 2017).

[¹ Treatment for the purpose of a contribution-based jobseeker's allowance or a contributory employment and support allowance of Class 2 contributions paid in accordance with the Act

7A.—(1) For the purpose of entitlement to a contribution-based job-seeker's allowance or a contributory employment and support allowance, a Class 2 contribution is to be treated as paid as set out in paragraph (2) if the contribution is paid— **2.65A**

(a) in relation to—
   (i) a contribution-based jobseeker's allowance, on or after the first day of the week for which the jobseeker's allowance is claimed; or
   (ii) a contributory employment and support allowance, on or after the first day of the relevant benefit week; and
(b) by the due date.

(2) The contribution is treated as paid—
(a) in relation to a contribution-based jobseeker's allowance, before the week for which the jobseeker's allowance is claimed; or
(b) in relation to a contributory employment and support allowance, before the relevant benefit week.

(3) "Relevant benefit week" has the meaning given in paragraph 5 of Schedule 1 to the Welfare Reform Act.]

AMENDMENT

1. Social Security (Credits, and Crediting and Treatment of Contributions) (Consequential and Miscellaneous Amendments) Regulations 2016 (SOI 2016/1145) reg. 5(5) (January 1, 2017).

Treatment for the purpose of any contributory benefit of contributions paid under an arrangement

8. For the purposes of regulations 4 to [¹ 7A] above and regulation [¹ 61] of the Contributions Regulations (voluntary Class 2 contributions not paid within permitted period)— **2.66**

(a) where a contribution is paid under an arrangement to which regulations [¹ 68 and 84] or, as the case may be, regulation [¹ 90] of the Contributions Regulations (other methods of collection and recovery of earnings-related contributions; special provisions relating to primary Class 1 contributions and arrangements approved by the Inland Revenue for method of, and time for, payment of Class 2 and Class 3 contributions respectively) apply, the date by which, but for the said regulations 4 to [¹ 7A] and [¹ 61], the contribution would have fallen due to be paid shall, in relation to that contribution, be the due date;
(b) any payment made of, or as on account of, a contribution in accordance with any such arrangement shall, on and after the due date, be treated as a contribution paid on the due date.

AMENDMENT

1. Social Security (Credits, and Crediting and Treatment of Contributions) (Consequential and Miscellaneous Amendments) Regulations 2016 (SOI 2016/1145) reg. 5(6) (January 1, 2017).

Application for allocation of national insurance number

2.67

9.—(1) Subject to the provisions of [⁴ paragraphs (2) and (2A)] below, every person, who is over the age of 16 and satisfies the conditions specified in regulation 87 or 119 of the Contributions Regulations(conditions of domicile or residence and conditions as to residence or presence in Great Britain respectively), shall, unless he has already been allocated a national insurance number under the Act, the Social Security Act 1975 or the National Insurance Act 1965, apply either to the Secretary of State or to [the Commissioners for Her Majesty's Revenue and Customs] for the allocation of a national insurance number and shall make such application at such time and in such manner as the Secretary of State shall direct.

[¹ (1A) An application under paragraph (1) shall be accompanied by a document of a description specified [³ in Schedule 1].]

(2) As respects any person who is neither an employed earner nor a self-employed earner the provisions of paragraph (1) above shall not apply unless and until that person wishes to pay a Class 3 or 3A contribution.

[⁴ (2A) The provisions of paragraph (1) shall not apply to a person in respect of whom the Secretary of State or the Commissioners for Her Majesty's Revenue and Customs are notified that a biometric immigration document is to be issued pursuant to regulation 13 [⁵ or 13A] of the Immigration (Biometric Registration) Regulations 2008.]

(3) The Secretary of State may authorise arrangements for the allocation of a national insurance number to any person during the 12 months before that person reaches the age of 16, and in particular may direct that a person who will attain the age of 16 within 12 months after such direction shall apply for the allocation of a national insurance number before attaining the age of 16, and any such person shall accordingly comply with such direction.

[² (4) Where a person–

(a) qualifies for a loan made in accordance with regulations made under section 22 of the Teaching and Higher Education Act 1998 (new arrangements For giving financial support to students) or sections 73 to 74(1) of the Education (Scotland) Act 1980 in connection with an academic year beginning on or after 1st September 2007; and

(b) has been required as a condition of entitlement to payment of the loan to provide his national insurance number, he shall, unless he has already been allocated a national insurance number, apply to the Secretary of State or the Commissioners for Her Majesty's Revenue and Customs for one to be allocated to him, and the Secretary of State or, as the case may be, the Commissioners may direct how the application is to be made.]

AMENDMENTS

1. Social Security (National Insurance Numbers) Amendment Regulations 2006 (SI 2006/2897) reg.2(a) (December 11, 2006).

2. Social Security (National Insurance Numbers) Amendment Regulations 2006 (SI 2006/2897) reg.2(b) (March 1, 2007).

3. Social Security (National Insurance Numbers) Amendment Regulations 2008 (SI 2008/223) reg.2(2) (February 29, 2008).

4. Social Security (Miscellaneous Amendments) Regulations 2015 (SI 2015/67) reg.5 (February 23, 2015).

5. Social Security (Crediting and Treatment of Contributions, and National Insurance Numbers) (Amendment) Regulations 2015 (SI 2015/1828) reg.2 (November 30, 2015).

Regs 10 to 12 and Schedule are omitted as within responsibility of HMRC and not the Secretary of State or beyond the scope of this work.

2.68

The Social Security (Contributions Credits for Parents and Carers) Regulations 2010

(SI 2010/19)

ARRANGEMENT OF REGULATIONS

PART 1

GENERAL PROVISIONS

1.   Citation and commencement
2.   Interpretation
3.   Transitional provision

2.69

PART 2

MEANING OF "FOSTER PARENT" AND "ENGAGED IN CARING"

4.   Meaning of "foster parent"
5.   Meaning of "engaged in caring"
6.   Limit on the period in respect of partners of persons awarded child benefit
7.   Additional period in respect of entitlement to carer's allowance and relevant benefits
8.   Disqualification due to residence or imprisonment

PART 3

APPLICATIONS

9.   Applications: foster parents and partners of persons awarded child benefit
10.   Applications: carers for 20 or more hours per week
11.   Provision of information: carers for 20 or more hours per week
12.   Time limit for applications

The Secretary of State makes the following Regulations in exercise of the powers conferred by section 23A(3)(c), (4) and (9) and section 175(1), (4) and (5) of the Social Security Contributions and Benefits Act 1992.

A draft of this instrument was laid before and approved by a resolution of each House of Parliament in accordance with section 176(1)(aa) of that Act.

The Social Security Advisory Committee has agreed that proposals in respect of these Regulations should not be referred to it.

PART 1

GENERAL PROVISIONS

Citation and commencement

2.70   **1.**—These Regulations may be cited as the Social Security (Contributions Credits for Parents and Carers) Regulations 2010 and shall come into force on 6th April 2010.

GENERAL NOTE

2.71   SSCBA 1992 s.23A introduces weekly National Insurance credits (which replace Home Responsibilities Protection for periods of caring from April 6, 2010) for parents (including foster-parents) and carers in respect of their caring activities.

Although the task of awarding these credits in cases despendent on the award of child benefit has been transferred to HMRC, their administration is done on behalf of the Secretary of State and appeals lie to the First-tier Tribunal (Social Entitlement Chamber) and the Upper Tribunal (Administrative Appeals Chamber) rather than to the tax commissioners (see the National Insurance Contribution Credits (Transfer of Functions) Order 2009 (SI 2009/1377)). These regulations govern the award of these parents and carers credits. Generally, application for credits has to be made to HMRC (regs 9, 12: where the person is a carer because of the award of child benefit) or the Secretary of State (regs 10–12: persons engaged in caring because of the award of a relevant benefit), and generally before the end of the tax year in which the week(s) of engagement in caring fall (reg.12).

Section 23A applies to the benefits listed in subs.(1) where the determining event (attainment of pensionable age or death) occurs on or after April 6, 2010. The benefits are: Category A retirement pension; Category B retirement pension (under s.48A or 48B; widowed parent's allowance; and bereavement allowance. In respect of such benefits, the contributor concerned (see subs.(9) and s.21(5)(a)) is to be credited with a Class 3 contribution for each week falling after April 6, 2010 in respect of which the contributor was a "relevant carer". Subsection (3) stipulates that someone is a "relevant carer" in respect of a week) if he is awarded child benefit for any part of that week in respect of a child under the age of 12, or is a foster parent for any part of that week, or is in that week engaged in caring, within the meaning given by these regulations.

Interpretation

2.72   **2.**—(1) In these Regulations—

"partner" means the person with whom another person—

(a) resides; and

(b) shares responsibility for a child under the age of 12;

"relevant benefit" means—

(a) attendance allowance in accordance with section 64 (entitlement);

(b) the care component of disability living allowance in accordance with

section 72 (the care component), at the middle or highest rate prescribed in accordance with subsection (3) of that section;

(c) an increase in the rate of disablement pension in accordance with
section 104 (increase where constant attendance needed);

(d) any benefit by virtue of—

   (i) the Pneumoconiosis, Byssinosis and Miscellaneous Diseases
Benefit Scheme 1983; or

   (ii) regulations made under paragraph 7(2) in Part 2 (regulations
providing for benefit) of Schedule 8 (industrial injuries and
diseases (old cases)),

which is payable as if the injury or disease were one in respect of which
a disablement pension were for the time being payable in respect of an
assessment of 100 per cent.;

(e) a constant attendance allowance payable by virtue of—

   (i) article 8 (constant attendance allowance) of the Naval, Military
and Air Forces etc. (Disablement and Death) Service Pensions
Order 2006; or

   (ii) article 14 (constant attendance allowance) of the Personal
Injuries (Civilians) Scheme 1983.

[¹(f) the daily living component of personal independence payment in
accordance with section 78 of the Welfare Reform Act 2012;

[²(g) armed forces independence payment in accordance with the Armed
Forces and Reserve Forces (Compensation Scheme) Order 2011.]

(2) In these Regulations, a reference to a section or Schedule by number
alone is a reference to the section or Schedule so numbered in the Social
Security Contributions and Benefits Act 1992.

AMENDMENTS

1. Personal Independence Payment (Supplementary Provisions and Consequential
Amendments) Regulations 2013 (SI 2013/388) reg.8 and Sch. para.46 (April 8,
2013).

2. Armed Forces and Reserve Forces Compensation Scheme (Consequential
Provisions: Subordinate Legislation) Order 2013 art.7, Sch. para.44 (April 8, 2013).

Transitional provision

3.—For the period of 12 weeks from the date on which these Regulations   2.73
come into force, regulation 7(1)(a) has effect as if the reference in regulation 7(1) to 12 weeks were a reference to the number of complete weeks
since these Regulations came into force.

PART 2

MEANING OF "FOSTER PARENT" AND "ENGAGED IN CARING"

Meaning of "foster parent"

4.—(1) For the purposes of subsection (3)(b) of section 23A (contribu-   2.74
tions credits for relevant parents and carers), a foster parent is a person
approved as—

(a) a foster parent in accordance with Part 4 (approval of foster parents) of the Fostering Services Regulations 2002; [¹ . . .

(aa) a kinship carer in accordance with Part 5 (kinship care) of the Looked After Children (Scotland) Regulations 2009;]

(b) a foster carer in accordance with Part 7 (fostering) of the Looked After Children (Scotland) Regulations 2009. [¹; or

(c) a foster parent in accordance with Part 2 (approvals and placements) of the Foster Placement (Children) Regulations (Northern Ireland) 1996.]

(2) Paragraph (1) is subject to regulation 8.

AMENDMENT

1. National Insurance Contributions Credits (Miscellaneous Amendments) Regulations 2011 (SI 2011/709) reg.3 (April 5, 2011).

GENERAL NOTE

2.75   This regulation—subject to reg.8, below—defines "foster parent" for the purposes of SSCBA 1992 s.23(3)(b) by reference to the definitions in the stipulated legislation. Regulation 8 provides that a foster-parent ceases to be such when not ordinarily resident in Great Britain or when undergoing a period of imprisonment or detention in legal custody.

Meaning of "engaged in caring"

2.76   5.—(1) For the purposes of subsection (3)(c) of section 23A, a person is engaged in caring in a week—

(a) if that person is the partner of a person who is awarded child benefit for any part of that week in respect of a child under the age of 12;

(b) if that person is caring for another person or persons for a total of 20 or more hours in that week and—

(i) that other person is, or each of the persons cared for are, entitled to a relevant benefit for that week; or

(ii) the Secretary of State considers that level of care to be appropriate;

(c) if that person is one to whom any of paragraphs 4 to 6 (persons caring for another person) of Schedule 1B (prescribed categories of person) to the Income Support (General) Regulations 1987 applies.

(2) Paragraph (1) is subject to regulations 6 to 8.

DEFINITIONS

"partner"—see reg.2(1).
"relevant benefit"—see reg.2(1).

GENERAL NOTE

2.77   Paragraph (1) of this regulation sets out when, for the purposes of s.23A(3)(c), a person is "engaged in caring". The three alternatives set out in para.(1) are, however, all subject to regs 6–8, below (para.(2))

Limit on the period in respect of partners of persons awarded child benefit

2.78   6.—(1) Regulation 5(1)(a) does not apply to any week which falls within a tax year in respect of which the person awarded child benefit satisfies the following condition.

(2) The condition is that that person's earnings factor for the purposes of section 45 (additional pension in a Category A retirement pension) does not exceed the qualifying earnings factor for that year.

(3) In calculating a person's earnings factor for the purposes of paragraph (2), no account is to be taken of any earnings factor derived from contributions credited by virtue of that person being a relevant carer due to an award of child benefit.

GENERAL NOTE

Regulation 5(1)(a) specifies that someone is engaged in caring in any week where they are the partner of a person awarded for any part of that week child benefit in respect of a child under 12. This regulation provides that this shall not be the case in any week in a tax year where the person awarded child benefit has an earnings factor less than that year's qualifying earnings factor for purposes of the additional pension in Category A retirement pension. In calculating that earnings factor no account is to be taken of contributions credited by virtue of that person being a relevant carer because of a child benefit award. 2.79

Additional period in respect of entitlement to carer's allowance and relevant benefits

7.—(1) A person is engaged in caring for a period of 12 weeks— 2.80
  (a) prior to the date on which that person becomes entitled to carer's allowance by virtue of subsection (1) of section 70 (carer's allowance);
  (b) subject to paragraph (2), following the end of the week in which that person ceases to be entitled to carer's allowance by virtue of that subsection;
  (c) following the end of a week in which regulation 5(1)(b) ceases to be satisfied.

(2) For the purposes of paragraph (1)(b), a person is not engaged in caring in a week in respect of which that person is entitled, under regulations made under subsection (5) of section 22 (earnings factors), to be credited with contributions by virtue of being entitled to an allowance under section 70.

Disqualification due to residence or imprisonment

8.—A person is not a foster parent or engaged in caring for the purposes of section 23A during any period in respect of which that person is— 2.81
  (a) not ordinarily resident in Great Britain; or
  (b) undergoing imprisonment or detention in legal custody.

GENERAL NOTE

On "undergoing imprisonment or detention in legal custody" see the commentary to SSCBA 1992 s.113(1)(b) and WRA 2009 s.18(4)(b). 2.82

PART 3

APPLICATIONS

Applications: foster parents and partners of persons awarded child benefit

9.—A person shall not be entitled to be credited with Class 3 contributions under— 2.83

(a) subsection (3)(b) (foster parent) of section 23A; or
(b) subsection (3)(c) (person engaged in caring) of section 23A by virtue of regulation 5(1)(a),

unless an application to be so credited is received by the Commissioners for Her Majesty's Revenue and Customs.

Applications: carers for 20 or more hours per week

2.84 **10.**—(1) A person shall not be entitled to be credited with Class 3 contributions under subsection (3)(c) of section 23A by virtue of regulation 5(1)(b) unless an application to be so credited is received by the Secretary of State.

(2) Paragraph (1) does not apply where that person—
(a) [¹ . . .]
(b) is a married woman who is not entitled to be credited with contributions under paragraph (1) of regulation 7A (credits for carer's allowance) of the Social Security (Credits) Regulations 1975 by virtue of paragraph (2)(b) (reduced contribution rate election under regulations under section 19(4)) of that regulation.

Provision of information: carers for 20 or more hours per week

2.85 **11.**—(1) With respect to an application to which regulation 10(1) applies, the application must include—
(a) a declaration by the applicant that the applicant cares for a person or persons for 20 or more hours per week;
(b) the name and, where known, the national insurance number of each person cared for;
(c) where applicable, which relevant benefit each person cared for is entitled to; and
(d) where requested by the Secretary of State, a declaration signed by an appropriate person as to the level of care which is required for each person cared for.

(2) For the purposes of paragraph (1)(d), an appropriate person is a person who is—
(a) involved in the health care or social care of the person cared for; and
(b) considered by the Secretary of State as appropriate to make a declaration as to the level of care required.

Time limit for applications

2.86 **12.**—An application under regulation 9 or 10 must be received—
(a) before the end of the tax year following the tax year in which a week, which is the subject of the application, falls; or
(b) within such further time as the Secretary of State or the Commissioners for Her Majesty's Revenue and Customs, as the case may be, consider reasonable in the circumstances.

AMENDMENT

1. Social Security (Credits) (Amendment) Regulations 2010 (SI 2010/385) reg.3 (April 6, 2010).

PART III

REGULATIONS COMMON TO SEVERAL BENEFITS

The Social Security Benefit (Computation of Earnings) Regulations 1996

(SI 1996/2745) (*as amended*)

ARRANGEMENT OF REGULATIONS

PART I

GENERAL

1.	Citation and commencement.	3.1
2.	Interpretation.	
3.	Calculation of earnings.	
4.	Notional earnings.	
5.	Rounding of fractions.	

PART II

EMPLOYED EARNERS

6.   Calculation of earnings of employed earners.
7.   Date on which earnings are treated as paid.
8.   Calculation of weekly amount of earnings.
9.   Earnings of employed earners.
10.   Calculation of net earnings of employed earners.

PART III

SELF-EMPLOYED EARNERS

11.   Calculation of earnings of self-employed earners.
12.   Earnings of self-employed earners.
13.   Calculation of net profit of self-employed earners.
14.   Deduction of tax and contributions for self-employed earners.

PART IV

TRANSITIONAL PROVISIONS, CONSEQUENTIAL AMENDMENTS AND REVOCATIONS

15.–18. *Omitted.*

SCHEDULES

Schedule 1—Sums to be disregarded in the calculation of earnings.
Schedule 2—Child care charges to be deducted in the calculation of earnings.
Schedule 3—Care charges to be deducted in the calculation of earnings for entitlement to carer's allowance.
Schedule 4—*Omitted*.

The Secretary of State for Social Security, in exercise of the powers conferred by sections 3(2) and (3), 80(7), 89, 112, 119 and 175(1), (3) and (4) of, and paragraph 4(6) of Schedule 7 to, the Social Security Contributions and Benefits Act 1992, sections 5(1)(n) and (r), 71(7), 189(4) and (5) and 191 of the Social Security Administration Act 1992 and of all other powers enabling him in that behalf, after agreement by the Social Security Advisory Committee that the proposals to make these Regulations should not be referred to it hereby makes the following Regulations:

PART I

GENERAL

Citation and commencement

3.2   **1.**—These Regulations may be cited as the Social Security Benefit (Computation of Earnings) Regulations 1996 and shall come into force on 25th November 1996.

GENERAL NOTE

3.3   These regulations replace the Computation of Earnings Regulations 1978 (SI 1978/1698). They contain in a more detailed manner the rules for determining earnings and include provision for determining notional earnings.

Interpretation

3.4   **2.**—(1) In these Regulations, unless the context otherwise requires—
[¹ . . .]
[⁶ "basic rate" means the rate of income tax of that name in pursuance of section 6(2) of the Income Tax Act 2007;]
"benefit week" means—
   (a) any period of 7 days corresponding to the week in respect of which the relevant social security benefit is due to be paid, and, where appropriate in respect of payments due to be paid before that week,
   (b) the period of 7 days ending on the day before the first day of the first such week following the date of claim or any one of the consecutive periods of seven days prior to that period;
"board and lodging accommodation" means—
   (a) accommodation provided to a person or, if he is a member of a family, to him or any other member of his family, for a charge which is inclusive of the provision of that accommodation and at least some cooked or prepared meals which both are cooked or prepared (by a person other than the person to whom the accommodation is provided or a member of his family) and are consumed in that accommodation or associated premises; or

(b) accommodation provided to a person in a hotel, guest house, lodging house or some similar establishment,

except accommodation provided by a close relative of his or of any other member of his family, or other than on a commercial basis;

"claim" means a claim for a benefit, pension or allowance under Parts II to V of the Contributions and Benefits Act;

"claimant" means a person claiming a benefit, pension or allowance under Parts II to V of the Contributions and Benefits Act and includes a claimant's spouse or partner and any adult in respect of whom a claim for an increase in benefit is made under Part IV of that Act;

[4 "clinical commissioning group" means a body established under section 14D of the National Health Service Act 2006;]

"close relative" means a parent, parent-in-law, son, son-in-law, daughter, daughter-in-law, step-parent, step-son, step-daughter, brother, sister, [3 or if any of the preceding persons is one member of a couple, the other member of that couple;]

"the Contributions and Benefits Act" means the Social Security Contributions and Benefits Act 1992;

[5 "couple" means

(a) two people who are married to, or civil partners of, each other and are members of the same household; or

(b) two people who are not married to, or civil partners of, each other but are living together as a married couple;]

"Crown property" means property held by Her Majesty in right of the Crown or by a government department or which is held in trust for Her Majesty for the purposes of a government department, except (in the case of an interest held by Her Majesty in right of the Crown) where the interest is under the management of the Crown Estate Commissioners;

"date of claim" means the date on which the claimant makes, or is treated as making, a claim for a benefit, pension or allowance for the purposes of regulation 6 of the Social Security (Claims and Payments) Regulations 1987;

"dwelling occupied as the home" means the dwelling together with any garage, garden and outbuildings, normally occupied by the claimant as his home including any premises not so occupied which it is impracticable or unreasonable to sell separately, in particular, in Scotland, any croft land on which the dwelling is situated;

"earnings" has the meaning prescribed in regulation 9 or, as the case may be, 12, and for the purposes only of sections 80, 82 to 86A and 89 of, and paragraphs 4, 6 and 7 of Schedule 7 to, the Contributions and Benefits Act includes payments by way of occupational or personal pension within the meaning of section 122 of the Contributions and Benefits Act (interpretation);

"employed earner" means a person who is in gainful employment in Great Britain under a contract of service, or in an office (including elective office) with emoluments chargeable to income tax under Schedule E and includes—

(a) a person in any employment which would be such employment if it were in Great Britain, and

(b) a person in any such employment which, in accordance with the provisions of the Contributions and Benefits Act and of any regulations made thereunder, is to be disregarded in relation to liability for contributions;

"employment" includes any trade, business, profession, office or vocation;

"invalid carriage or other vehicle" means a vehicle propelled by petrol engine or by electric power supplied for use on the road and to be controlled by the occupant;

"lone parent" means a person who has no partner and who is responsible for, and a member of the same household as, a child within the meaning of section 142 of the Contributions and Benefits Act (meaning of "child");

[⁶. . .]

[². . .];

"net earnings" means such earnings as are calculated in accordance with regulation 10(4);

"net profit" means such profit as is calculated in accordance with regulation 13(4);

"occupational pension scheme" has the same meaning as in section 1 of the Pension Schemes Act 1993;

"partner" means where a claimant—

(a) is a member of a [³. . .] couple, the other member of that couple;

(b) is married polygamously to two or more members of his household, any such member;

"payment" includes a part of a payment;

"pay period" means the period in respect of which a claimant is, or expects to be, normally paid by his employer, being a week, a fortnight, four weeks, a month or other shorter or longer period as the case may be;

"personal pension scheme" has the same meaning as in section 1 of the Pension Schemes Act 1993 and, in the case of a self-employed earner, includes a scheme approved by the Inland Revenue under Chapter IV of Part XIV of the Income and Corporation Taxes Act 1988;

"polygamous marriage" means any marriage during the subsistence of which a party to it is married to more than one person and the ceremony of marriage took place under the law of a country which permits polygamy;

"relevant earnings limit" means the amount of a claimant's earnings in excess of which the benefit, supplement, allowance, pension or increase in question is not payable;

"retirement annuity contract" means a contract or trust scheme approved under Chapter III of Part XIV of the Income and Corporation Taxes Act 1988;

[⁶ "Scottish basic rate" means the rate of income tax of that name calculated in accordance with section 6A of the Income Tax Act 2007;]

[⁶ "Scottish taxpayer" has the same meaning as in Chapter 2 of Part 4A of the Scotland Act 1998;]

"self-employed earner" means a person who is in gainful employment in Great Britain otherwise than as an employed earner and includes—

(a) a person in any employment which would be such employment if it were in Great Britain, and

(b) a person in any such employment which, in accordance with the provisions of the Contributions and Benefits Act and of any regulations made thereunder, is to be disregarded in relation to liability for contributions;

"voluntary organisation" means a body, other than a public or local authority, the activities of which are carried on otherwise than for profit;

"week" means a period of 7 days and for the purposes of section 80 of, and paragraph 4(6) of Schedule 7 to, the Contributions and Benefits Act, a period of 7 days being the relevant benefit week;

"year of assessment" has the meaning prescribed in section 832(1) of the Income and Corporation Taxes Act 1988.

(2) In these Regulations, unless the context otherwise requires, a reference—

(a) to a numbered regulation or Schedule is to the regulation in or Schedule to these Regulations bearing that number;

(b) in a regulation or Schedule to a numbered paragraph is to the paragraph in that regulation or Schedule bearing that number;

(c) in a paragraph to a lettered or numbered sub-paragraph is to the sub-paragraph in that paragraph bearing that letter or number.

AMENDMENTS

1. The Social Security Act 1998 (Commencement No. 9 and Savings and Consequential and Transitional Provisions) Order 1999 (SI 1999/2422) Sch.13 para.2 (September 6, 1999).

2. The Social Security Benefit (Computation of Earnings) (Amendment) Regulations 2002 (SI 2002/2823) reg.2 (April 1, 2003).

3. The Civil Partnership Act 2004 (Tax Credits, etc.) (Consequential Amendments) Order 2005 (SI 2005/2919) (December 5, 2005).

4. The National Treatment Agency (Abolition) and the Health and Social Care Act 2012 (Consequential, Transitional and Savings Provisions) Order 2013 (SI 2013/235) art.11 and para.32(2) of Pt 1 of Sch.2 (April 1, 2013).

5. The Marriage (Same Sex Couples) Act 2013 (Consequential Provisions) Order 2014 (SI 2014/107) reg.20 (March 13, 2014).

6. The Social Security Benefit (Computation of Earnings) (Amendment) Regulations 2016 (SI 2016/267) reg.2 (April 6, 2016).

GENERAL NOTE

With effect from December 5, 2005, art.3 of the Civil Partnership Act 2004 (Relationships Arising Through Civil Partnership) Order 2005 (SI 2005/3137) applies the provisions of s.246 of the Civil Partnership Act 2004 to the definition of "close relative" in reg.2(1). For the text of s.246, see para.1.638 in Vol.III.

For a decision which is of significance in drawing the dividing line between employer earners and self-employed earners, which arose in the context of computing the earnings of a GCSE examiner, see *CG/4139/2006.* The Commissioner concludes his decision with the words:

"12. . . . . I also hope that the Secretary of State takes steps to ensure that the guidance given to officers dealing with carer's allowance and other benefits to which the Computation of Earnings Regulations are relevant takes account of the deeming in regulation 2(3) and paragraph 6 of Schedule 1 to the Categorisation of Earners Regulations."

With effect from December 16, 2014, art.29 and Sch.6 para.14 of the Marriage and Civil Partnership (Scotland) Act 2014 and Civil Partnership Act 2004 (Consequential Provisions and Modifications Order 2001 (SI 2014/3229) amended the definition of "couple" by substituting a definition in the same terms as the existing definition. However, the existing definition applied only to England and Wales; the new definition applies to England, Wales, Scotland and Northern Ireland.

3.5

Calculation of earnings

3.6   **3.**—(1) For the purposes of Parts II to V (other than those of Schedule 8) of the Contributions and Benefits Act (a) and of any regulations made thereunder which relate to benefit under those Parts of that Act or regulations, the earnings of a claimant shall be calculated by determining in accordance with these Regulations the weekly amount of his earnings.

(2) The amount of a claimant's earnings for any period shall be the whole of those earnings (including any earnings which he is treated as possessing under regulation 4 (notional earnings)) except in so far as regulations 10 and 13 provide that certain sums shall be disregarded or deducted as appropriate.

General Note

3.7   The calculation of earnings is to be carried out in accordance with the rules contained in the Regulations. The whole of earnings after making the deductions and allowing the disregards provided for by the Regulations is to be taken into account. The provisions for estimating earnings are replaced by the notional earnings rules set out in reg.4. The rules apply to all benefits listed in Pts II to V of the Contributions and Benefits Act: incapacity benefit, sickness and invalidity benefits (so far as still relevant), maternity benefits, bereavement benefits, retirement pensions, child's special allowance, attendance allowance, disability living allowance, guardian's allowance, and increases for dependants, as well as benefits for industrial injuries.

Some of the broad areas of discretion previously available under the former Regulations are replaced by regulation-based rules for determining earnings.

In *Secretary of State for Work and Pensions v Doyle* [2006] EWCA Civ 466, reported as *R(IB) 1/06*, the Court of Appeal ruled that these regulations apply to the computation of earnings for the purposes of entitlement to incapacity benefit where a person is working "on the advice of a doctor". The essential grounding of entitlement of incapacity benefit in Pt II of the Act was sufficient for reg.3 to apply even though Pt XIIA lays down the detailed scheme.

Notional earnings

3.8   **4.**—(1) Where a claimant's earnings are not ascertainable at the date [¹ on which a decision falls to be made by the Secretary of State under Chapter II of Part I of the Social Security Act 1998 or regulations made thereunder the claimant shall be treated] as possessing such earnings as is reasonable in the circumstances of the case having regard to the number of hours worked and the earnings paid for comparable employment in the area.

(2) [² . . .]

(3) Where a claimant is treated as possessing any earnings under paragraph (1) [² . . .] these Regulations shall apply for the purposes of calculating the amount of those earnings as if a payment had actually been made and as if they were actual earnings which he does possess except that paragraph (4) of regulation 10 (calculation of net earnings of employed earners) shall not apply and his net earnings shall be calculated by taking into account the earnings which he is treated as possessing, less—

   (a) an amount in respect of income tax equivalent to an amount calculated by applying to those earnings the [⁵ basic rate, or in the case of a Scottish taxpayer, the Scottish basic rate,] of tax in the year of assessment less only the [⁵ personal reliefs to which the claimant is entitled under Chapters 2, 3 and 3A of Part 3 of the Income Tax Act 2007 as are] appropriate to his circumstances; but, if the period over which those earnings are to be taken into account is less than a year, the earnings to which the [⁵ basic rate, or the Scottish basic rate,] of tax is to be applied and the amount of the personal [⁵ reliefs] deductible under this paragraph shall be calculated on a pro rata basis;

(b) where the weekly amount of those earnings equals or exceeds the lower earnings limit, an amount representing primary Class 1 contributions under the Contributions and Benefits Act, calculated by applying to those earnings the initial and main primary percentages in accordance with section 8(1)(a) and (b) of that Act; and

(c) one half of any sum payable by the claimant in respect of a pay period by way of a contribution towards an occupational or personal pension scheme.

AMENDMENTS

1. The Social Security Act 1998 (Commencement No. 11 and Transitional Provisions) Order 1999 (SI 1999/2860) Sch.15, para.3(a) (October 18, 1999).
2. The Social Security Benefit (Computation of Earnings) (Amendment) Regulations 2016 (SI 2016/267) reg.2(3) (April 6, 2016).

GENERAL NOTE

The provisions on notional earnings are new in relation to the benefits covered by these regulations.   3.9

Earnings not ascertainable (paragraph (1))

The first question for the decision-maker will be to determine whether the earnings (which may be from employment or self-employment) are ascertainable. That is not the same as saying that they have not yet been ascertained. Whether the earnings are ascertainable will be for the judgment of the decision-maker. In these cases, the claimant is treated as possessing such earnings as he or she might reasonably be paid for comparable employment in the area. It is not clear who has the burden of proof. But the decision-maker is likely to be in a better position than the claimant to present the evidence needed to form the conclusions required by the regulation. Furthermore, in many cases the earnings will serve to disentitle the person from a benefit, and there is an argument that in those cases the burden should be on the decision-maker. In practice the burden is likely to be "neutral" in that both parties can be expected to come to the decision-maker with as much information as possible from which a conclusion can be drawn.   3.10

Though the terms used in para.(1) apply to both employment and self-employment, the remainder of the regulation requires that the calculation of notional earnings should be made on the basis that the person is a notional employed earner. This is presumably because there are no valid comparators in the case of self-employment. So a self-employed painter whose earnings are not ascertainable will be treated as possessing the earnings paid for comparable employment as a painter.

Paragraph (3)

Paragraph (3) provides the mechanism for determining notional earnings, which will need to be added to any actual earnings.   3.11

Rounding of fractions

5.—Where any calculation under these Regulations results in a fraction of a penny that fraction shall, if it would be to the claimant's advantage, be treated as a penny, otherwise it shall be disregarded.   3.12

PART II

EMPLOYED EARNERS

GENERAL NOTE

3.13   Regulations 6 to 10 are replete with difficulty. In *DC v SSWP* [2008] UKUT 23 (AAC) the Judge said:

"... I have been trying to understand the operation of regulations 6 to 9 of the Social Security (Computation of Earnings) Regulations 1996. In the end, I have decided that was too ambitious a task. The way that those provisions operate is not entirely clear and they would benefit from being reconsidered, if not redrafted" (para.1).

It is perhaps trite to say that the purpose of the regulations is to identify what counts as earnings, to attribute earnings to particular weeks, and to provide a means for converting them to weekly amounts. The starting point is perhaps reg.9 which defines what constitute earnings of employed earners, and reg.10 which concerns net earnings. Regulation 6 provides the means for calculating the earnings of employed earners in terms of weeks. Regulation 7 treats earnings as paid on a particular date which means that the weeks to which they are attributable can be determined. Finally reg.8 provides the methods of converting earnings to weekly amounts. Particular difficulties seem to arise in relation to certain payments when employment comes to an end. The Commissioner in *CG/4172/2001* and the Judge in *DC v SSWP* [2008] UKUT 23 (AAC) both accepted that such payments are attributable to a future period, since the money received is available for future expenditure. But the judge in the latter case also concluded:

"... the regulations do not necessarily produce an income that is in any way tied to the reality of the period for which payments are made or over which they are likely to be spent" (para.29).

The appeal against the Judge's decision has been dismissed in *Cotton v SSWP*, [2009] EWCA Civ 1333, [2010] AACR 17, where Goldring L.J. said:

"30. As it seems to me (as Mr. Forsdick submitted) the function of the 1996 Regulations is firstly to identify what counts as earnings. Regulation 9 does that. Secondly, they attribute those earnings to a particular week or weeks. Regulation 7 determines the date on which the earnings are treated as paid. Regulation 6 determines the period over which they are to be attributed. Thirdly, regulation 8 converts the earnings into weekly amounts in order to determine whether the earnings threshold (laid down in regulation 8(1) of the 1976 Regulations) has been exceeded.
31. The range of possible earnings in regulation 9 is wide. Many different kinds of periodic earnings are encompassed. Some may be paid at regular intervals. Some may be one off (as in the present case). The regulations have to provide a workable means of assessing and attributing this wide range of periodic earnings to the many different circumstances which can arise as simply as possible.
32. An assessment of the beginning of the period is straightforward. The same cannot be said of the assessment of the end. To ascertain that would in many cases be difficult or impossible. That is why, as I conclude, a deeming provision was necessary. It results in a scheme which imposes a general rule under which all regulation 9 earnings payable in respect of a period are treated as payable for a period starting with the first day of the benefit week in which they are paid and ending on the day before the next payment of ordinary earnings (the next pay day). That deemed end date is not tied to the actual length of the period in respect of which any particular payment was made."

Calculation of earnings of employed earners

6.—(1) Earnings derived from employment as an employed earner shall   **3.14**
be calculated or estimated over a period determined in accordance with the
following paragraphs and at a weekly amount determined in accordance
with regulation 8 (calculation of weekly amount of earnings).

(2) Subject to paragraphs (3) and (5) to (8), the period over which a
payment is to be taken into account—

  (a) in a case where it is payable in respect of a period, shall be a period
equal to a benefit week or such number of benefit weeks as comprise
the period commencing on the date on which earnings are treated as
paid under regulation 7 (date on which earnings are treated as paid)
and ending on the day before the date on which earnings of the
same kind (excluding earnings of the kind mentioned at regulation
9(1)(a) to (j)) and from the same source would, or would if the
employment was continuing, next be treated as paid under that regulation;

  (b) in any other case, shall be a period equal to such number of weeks
as is equal to the number (less any fraction of a whole number)
calculated in accordance with the formula—

$$\frac{P}{Q + R}$$

where—

P is the net earnings;

Q is the amount of the relevant earnings limit plus one penny;
and

R is the total of the sums which would fall to be disregarded or
deducted as appropriate under regulation 10(2) or (3) (calculation
of net earnings of employed earners),

and that period shall begin on the date on which the payment is treated as
paid under regulation 7 (date on which earnings are treated as paid).

(3) Where earnings not of the same kind are derived from the same
source and the periods in respect of which those earnings would, but for
this paragraph, fall to be taken into account overlap, wholly or partly, those
earnings shall be taken into account over a period—

  (a) equal to the aggregate length of those periods, and

  (b) beginning with the earliest date on which any part of those earnings would otherwise be treated as paid under regulation 7 (date on
which earnings are treated as paid).

(4) In a case to which paragraph (3) applies, earnings under regulation 9
(earnings of employed earners) shall be taken into account in the following
order of priority—

  (a) earnings normally derived from the employment;

  (b) any payment to which paragraph (1)(b) or (c) of that regulation
applies;

  (c) any payment to which paragraph (1)(i) of that regulation applies;

  (d) any payment to which paragraph (1)(d) of that regulation applies.

(5) Where earnings to which regulation 9(1)(b) to (d) (earnings of
employed earners) applies are paid in respect of part of a day, those earnings shall be taken into account over a period equal to a week.

(6) Where earnings to which regulations 9(1)(i)(i) (earnings of employed earners) applies are paid in respect of or on the termination of any employment which is not part-time employment, the period over which they are to be taken into account shall be—

(a) a period equal to such number of weeks as is equal to the number (less any fraction of a whole number) obtained by dividing the net earnings by the maximum weekly amount which, on the date on which the payment of earnings is made, is specified in section 227(1) of the Employment Rights Act 1996; or

(b) a period equal to the length of the specified period,

whichever is the shorter, and that period shall begin on the date on which the payment is treated as paid under regulation 7 (date on which earnings are treated as paid).

(7) Any earnings to which regulation 9(1)(i)(ii) applies which are paid in respect of or on the termination of part-time employment, shall be taken into account over a period equal to one week.

(8) In this regulation—

"part-time employment" means—

(a) subject to the provisions of sub-paragraphs (b) to (d) of this definition, employment in which a person is engaged, or, where his hours of work fluctuate, he is engaged on average, for less than 16 hours a week being work for which payment is made or which is done in expectation of payment;

(b) subject to sub-paragraph (c) of this definition, the number of hours for which a person is engaged in work shall be determined—

(i) where no recognisable cycle has been established in respect of a person's work, by reference to the number of hours or, where those hours are likely to fluctuate, the average of the hours, which he is expected to work in a week;

(ii) where the number of hours for which he is engaged fluctuate, by reference to the average of hours worked over—

(aa) if there is a recognisable cycle of work, the period of one complete cycle (including, where the cycle involves periods in which the person does not work, those periods but disregarding any other absences);

(bb) in any other case, the period of five weeks immediately before the date of claim or the date [¹on which a revision or supersession of a decision falls to be made], or such other length of time as may, in the particular case, enable the person's average hours of work to be determined more accurately;

(c) where for the purpose of sub-paragraph (b)(ii)(aa) of this definition, a person's recognisable cycle of work at a school, other educational establishment or other place of employment is one year and includes periods of school holidays or similar vacations during which he does not work, those periods and any other periods not forming part of such holidays or vacations during which he is not required to work shall be disregarded in establishing the average hours for which he is engaged in work;

(d) for the purposes of sub-paragraphs (a) and (b) of this definition, in determining the number of hours for which a person is engaged in work, that number shall include any time allowed to that person by his employer for a meal or for refreshment, but only where that person is, or expects to be, paid earnings in respect of that time;

"specified period" means a period equal to—

(a) a week or such number of weeks (less any fraction of a whole number) as comprise the period of notice which is applicable to a person, or would have been applicable if it had not been waived; less

(b) any part of that period during which the person has continued to work in the employment in question or in respect of which he has received a payment to which regulation 9(1)(c) applies,

and for the purposes of this definition "period of notice" means the period of notice of termination of employment to which a person is entitled by statute or by contract, whichever is the longer, or, if he is not entitled to such notice, the period of notice which is customary in the employment in question.

AMENDMENT

1. The Social Security Act 1998 (Commencement No.9 and Savings and Consequental and Transitional Provisions) Order 1999 (SI 1999/2422) Sch.13 para.4 (September 6, 1999).

GENERAL NOTE

There are similarities between provisions of this regulation and reg.29 of the   3.15
Income Support (General) Regulations 1987 and references to the annotations in *Vol.II: Income Support, Jobseeker's Allowance, State Pension Credit and the Social Fund.*

Earnings are always related to a week or number of weeks. Those paid weekly or fortnightly (or other multiples of weeks) are likely to be easiest to deal with. In other cases (for example, monthly paid employees) the formula set out in the regulation will need to be applied.

Special rules apply to termination payments, which frequently causes difficulty, particularly where claimants have not fully appreciated their impact on benefit claims.

Paragraph (2)

In *CG/4172/2001,* the appellant received two final payments in respect of the   3.16
termination of his employment on July 3, 2000. One was paid on June 25, 2000 representing his last full month's salary from his employment. Regulations 6(2)(a) and 7(b) could readily be applied to this payment. The second was paid on July 25, 2000 a consisted of a payment of £278.35 gross in respect of salary for the final working weeks and £1,031.13 gross representing 14 days accrued holiday pay up to his termination date in respect of holiday which had not been taken. The application of the same regulations enabled the salary payment to be taken into account: the start date was July 24, 2000 (the first day of the benefit week in which it was due to be paid) and the end date was August 20, 2000 (the day before the first day of the benefit week in which the next salary payment would have been made if the employment continued): para.9.

The holiday pay was much more problematic. Regulation 6(2)(a) only applies if the holiday pay was payable "in respect of a period". If it was not, then reg.6(2)(b) applied. The Commissioner concludes (following earlier decisions) that it was paid "in respect of a period". The Commissioner also concludes that the holiday pay was due on the termination of the employment. This should be interpreted in accordance with its ordinary meaning: the employment terminated on July 3, 2000 and so this was the start date for attributing this period. Determining the end date was considerably less straightforward. Regulation 6(2)(a) could not easily be applied to payments such as holiday pay. Regulation 6(2)(a) refers to "earnings of the same kind"; and reg.9 lists types of payments which are included within the concept of "earnings". This includes "holiday pay". The Commissioner concludes that the only sensible meaning of the words in reg.9 is that holiday pay and ordinary earnings both constitute earnings of the same kind.

That conclusion, according to the Commissioner, left a problem with the interpretation of paragraphs (3) and (4) of regulation 6: see para.14 of the decision. The Commissioner felt compelled to conclude that the words "earnings of the same kind" have a different meaning in reg.6(2)(a) from that in reg.6(3) and (4). As a result the end date for the holiday pay was July 23, 2000. But the effect of the overlapping provisions in paragraphs (3) and (4) is that holiday pay (as having a lower order of priority is deemed to run for the period of three weeks from July 24, 2000. So the final conclusion was as follows:

- First salary payment attributable to June 19 to July 23, 2000,

- Second salary payment attributable to July 24, to August 20, 2000,

- Holiday pay attributable to July 24 to August 13, 2000.

3.17   The judge in *DC v SSWP* [2008] UKUT 23 (AAC) has followed the Commissioner's decision. In doing so, the judge observes:

44. Left entirely to my own devices, I would have been tempted to decide that, within the meaning of regulation 6(2), accrued holiday pay was not paid in respect of a period. That would mean that regulation 6(2)(b) would apply.

45. I have not taken that course for three reasons. First, in *Chief Benefit Officer v Cunningham* [1985] ICR 660, Waller LJ (at page 665) said that one day accrued holiday pay was paid for a period. Second, neither party argued that regulation 6(2)(b) applied. Third, regulation 6(2)(b) operates to attribute a payment to the maximum number of weeks over which the claimant can be excluded from benefit. Mr Richards argued that the claimant had an entitlement under section 70 to a carer's allowance and that a provision that deprived him of it should be interpreted restrictively. I do not accept that argument. Section 70 does not confer an entitlement. It sets out the basic conditions and provides for more detailed provisions to be made by regulations. Regulation 6 is one of those regulations. However, given that the provision does operate harshly on claimant and the Secretary of State has not argued that it applies, I do not consider it appropriate to apply regulation 6(2)(b).

In dismissing the appeal against this decision in *Cotton v SSWP*, [2009] EWCA Civ 1333, [2010] AACR 17, Goldring L.J., giving the lead judgment, had this to say on the interpretation of reg.6:

"38. While it may be unfortunate that the words "*earnings not of the same kind*" may bear a different meaning for the purposes of regulation 6(3) than "*earnings of the same kind*" in regulation 6(2)(a), the context in which the words are used in each regulation is somewhat different. The words in parenthesis in regulation 6(2)(a) are absent in regulation 6(3). Moreover, the words as used in regulation 6(2)(a) are performing an essentially different function from those in regulation 6(3) (taken in conjunction with regulation 6(4)).

39. While any statutory scheme should be understood as a whole, this cannot lead to the immutable rule that the same words used in the same legislation necessarily have the same meaning.

40. In short, in spite of the opacity of the language, I have come to the view that this is a deeming provision which seeks to make relatively simple the assessment of the end date when a periodic payment is made which does not consist of ordinary pay."

Wilson L.J. also dismissed the appeal but for reasons different from those of Goldring L.J. and Laws L.J.

Date on which earnings are treated as paid

7.—Earnings to which regulation 6 (calculation of earnings of employed   3.18
earners) or 11(2) (calculation of earnings of self-employed earners) applies
shall be treated as paid—
- (a)   (i) in the case of a payment in respect of an adult dependant of an increase of maternity allowance payable under section 82(2) of the Contributions and Benefits Act or an increase of [¹ carer's allowance] payable under paragraph 7 of Schedule 2 to the Social Security Benefit (Dependency) Regulations 1977; or
-     (ii) in the case of a payment in respect of an adult dependant who is not residing with the claimant of an increase of Category A or Category C retirement pension payable under section 83(2) (b) or 84(1) and 84(2)(b) of the Contributions and Benefits Act or a disablement pension where the claimant is entitled to an unemployability supplement payable under paragraph 6(1)(a)(ii) of Schedule 7 to the Contributions and Benefits Act,

    on the first day of the benefit week following the benefit week in which the payment is due to be paid;
- (b) in any other case, on the first day of the benefit week in which the payment is due to be paid.

AMENDMENT

1. The Social Security Benefit (Computation of Earnings) (Amendment) Regulations 2002 (SI 2002/2823) reg.2 (April 1, 2003).

Calculation of weekly amount of earnings

8.—(1) For the purposes of regulation 6 (calculation of earnings of   3.19
employed earners), subject to paragraphs (2) to (4), where the period in
respect of which a payment is made—
- (a) does not exceed a week, the weekly amount shall be the amount of that payment;
- (b) exceeds a week, the weekly amount shall be determined—
  - (i) in a case where that period is a month, by multiplying the amount of that payment by 12 and dividing the product by 52;
  - (ii) in a case where that period is three months, by multiplying the amount of the payment by 4 and dividing the product by 52;
  - (iii) in a case where that period is a year, by dividing the amount of the payment by 52;
  - (iv) in any other case, by multiplying the amount of the payment by 7 and dividing the product by the number equal to the number of days in the period in respect of which it is made.

(2) Where a payment of earnings from a particular source is or has been paid regularly and that payment falls to be taken into account in the same benefit week as a payment of the same kind and from the same source, the amount of those earnings to be taken into account in any one benefit week shall not exceed the weekly amount determined under paragraph (1)(a) or (b), as the case may be, of the payment which under regulation 7 (date on which earnings are treated as paid) is treated as paid first.

(3) Where the amount of the claimant's net earnings fluctuates and has changed more than once, or a claimant's regular pattern of work is such that he does not work every week, the application of the foregoing paragraphs may be modified so that the weekly amount of his earnings is determined by reference to his average weekly earnings—

(a) if there is a recognisable cycle of work, over the period of one complete cycle (including, where the cycle involves periods in which the claimant does no work, those periods but disregarding any other absences);

(b) if any other case, over a period of five weeks or such other period as may, in the particular case, enable the claimant's average weekly earnings to be determined more accurately.

(4) Where any payment of earnings is taken into account under paragraph (7) of regulation 6 (calculation of earnings of employed earners), over the period specified in that paragraph, the amount to be taken into account shall be equal to the amount of the payment.

GENERAL NOTE

3.20   *CG/4941/2003* concerned an overpayment of invalid care allowance (now carer's allowance) which had arisen when fluctuations in the claimant's earnings took her out of entitlement to the benefit for certain weeks. The Commissioner provides useful guidance on the interpretation of reg.8 in the decision:

18. Thus in simple terms, for a person both working and paid on a regular weekly basis, say on Fridays, the earnings for each benefit week starting on Monday will be the amount of the payment he or she receives on the Friday of the same week, and the normal rule is that if those earnings are over the weekly limit in force on the last day of that week, he or she will be "gainfully employed" for ICA purposes throughout the next benefit week starting on the following Monday. For a person paid on a regular monthly basis on the last working day of each calendar month, as this claimant was from 1 July 2001 onwards, the monthly earnings are treated as paid on the Monday of the benefit week that contains the actual monthly pay day, and that payment is treated as giving the claimant "earnings" for each of the (four or five) benefit weeks starting with that one and ending with the one before the week that will contain the next regular monthly pay day; the weekly amount of the earnings in each of those weeks being taken as the most recent monthly payment multiplied by 12 and divided by 52. For persons such as the claimant having fluctuating earnings (but, as is agreed, no recognisable "cycle" of work and non-work to bring into play the separate provision in regulation 8(3)(a) for such cases) the weekly or monthly payments received *may* instead be averaged under regulation 8(3)(b), so as to substitute a different weekly figure for the "earnings" attributable to the claimant, though still over the period of benefit weeks which each actual payment of earnings is treated as having to cover for the purposes of regulations 6 and 7.

19. As the very helpful and detailed written submission of Mr Cahill on behalf of the Secretary of State points out, regulation 8(3)(b) gives the Secretary of State a discretion to be applied rationally on a case by case basis, but is limited in its purpose to the use of a five-week or other period in place of the actual weekly, monthly or other calculation under regulation 8(1) to **"enable the claimant's average weekly earnings to be determined more accurately"**; and this is less clear that it might be since strictly the *accuracy* of an average is simply a matter of doing the arithmetic correctly, irrespective of the periods you happen to select for the calculation. Regulation 8(3) must I think be taken as intended less literally (or mathematically), to mean that the Secretary of State is to have the power of substituting an alternative

averaging calculation to produce a standardised weekly figure for the week or month, etc., identified in regulation 8(1) as the one in respect of which a given payment is actually made *where he is satisfied this would more accurately reflect the true rate of the claimant's weekly earnings* current at the period for which a week by week figure for those earnings has to be identified, in order to determine some question of entitlement: such as the one here, of whether or at what point the claimant had crossed the line of having weekly earnings over the limit to make her count as "gainfully employed" for invalid care allowance purposes in each day of the following benefit week.

20. It has to be borne in mind that the overriding purpose of the exercise, in the context of a weekly benefit such as invalid care allowance which is there to provide assistance with current weekly living expenses for people without sufficient weekly earnings of their own, is the relatively short term one of producing a working week by week figure so as to know as quickly as possible whether benefit is payable or not. Mr Cahill is I think right in saying that the application of regulation 8(3) in this context may often have to be more a matter of judgment than of science, and there may be no necessarily "right" answer: it has to be a matter of dealing reasonably with the evidence of actual earnings for the current payment periods as disclosed (or as it should be disclosed) by the claimant to the Secretary of State week by week or month by month. It cannot in my judgment be said that the existence of the discretionary power in regulation 8(3)(b) requires the Secretary of State in a case such as this to "wait and see" over a very extended period, and then juggle and aggregate a whole succession of payments that were each in fact made in respect of specific weekly and monthly periods either side of a significant change in the rate of working and earning, so as to treat them as in effect equivalent to one lumped-together payment for work spread evenly throughout. There are no grounds on which it could be described as "more accurate" to ignore a step-change in the rate of working and earning such as shown here in the late summer of 2001, and pretend that the claimant's work and earnings had carried on at one uniform rate all year.

CG/0607/2008 concerned the calculation of earnings in relation to the earnings limit for entitlement to a carer's allowance. This lengthy decision contains much useful comment and guidance on such cases, which seem to be a problematic area (perhaps because there is no taper—if a person's earnings are one penny over the limit, then entitlement to the carer's allowance ceases completely). The context was one in which an informal employment contract was intended to provide the appellant with earnings at, but not above, the earnings limit for entitlement to a carer's allowance. The appeal turned on the proper calculation of the appellant's weekly earnings. The Commissioner counsels care in looking at the definition provision in the regulations, and goes on to comment: **3.21**

36. The Regulations have the primary purpose of identifying the weekly amount of a claimant's earnings. They provide answers to the questions necessary for the conversion of actual earnings of an employee into weekly amounts of earnings by which to test those earnings against the earnings limit. They are the same essential questions that must be asked in any exercise of assessing earnings for the application of any social security or tax rate or limit. There must be defined periods with defined start and end dates and defined rules for attributing actual earnings to those periods. The key questions are:

(1) Are earnings included when received, or when entitlement arises, or on some other basis?
(2) When are specific earnings received or earned?
(3) How are specific earnings linked to specific periods of assessment or benefit?

The use of deeming provisions in the Regulations means that the answers provided to those questions for carer's allowance purposes are not findings of fact about what happened, but are questions of law about how the deeming provisions in the Regulations are to be applied to those facts.

CG/0607/2008 has been considered and distinguished in *KJ v SSWP (CA)* [2011] AACR 8. The case concerned a full-time employee who reduced his hours in order to be able to care for his sick mother and to enable him to claim carer's allowance. For the month of March 2008, the employee was paid the pro-rata equivalent of his full-time salary for two days and the reduced amount for the remaining days in the month, but he also received a tax rebate. The question which arose was how this monthly pay should be used for the purpose of determining his earnings in relation to his claim for carer's allowance. The Upper Tribunal Judge concluded that this was not a case in which earnings fluctuated such that the more flexible provisions in reg.8(3) applied; that paragraph contemplated a situation in which the amount "has changed more than once". There was no basis for separating out the March salary into two payments: one attributable to the first two days of the month and so attributable to only one week. The "normal" calculation in converting the monthly pay into weekly earnings applied.

Earnings of employed earners

3.22   **9.**—(1) Subject to paragraphs (2) and (3), "earnings", in the case of employment as an employed earner, means any remuneration or profit derived from that employment and includes—

(a) any bonus or commission;

(b) any payment in lieu of remuneration except any periodic sum paid to a claimant on account of the termination of his employment by reason of redundancy;

(c) any payment in lieu of notice;

(d) any holiday pay except any payable more than four weeks after the termination or interruption of employment;

(e) any payment by way of a retainer;

(f) any payment made by the claimant's employer in respect of expenses not wholly, exclusively and necessarily incurred in the performance of the duties of the employment, including any payment made by the claimant's employer in respect of—

　(i) travelling expenses incurred by the claimant between his home and place of employment;

　(ii) expenses incurred by the claimant under arrangements made for the care of a member of his family owing to the claimant's absence from home;

(g) any award of compensation made under section 112(4) or 117(3)(a) of the Employment Rights Act 1996 (remedies and compensation);

(h) any such sum as is referred to in section 112(3) of the Contributions and Benefits Act (certain sums to be earnings for social security purposes);

(i) where—

　(i) a payment of compensation is made in respect of employment which is not part-time employment and that payment is not less than the maximum weekly amount, the amount of the compensation less the deductible remainder, where that is applicable;

　(ii) a payment of compensation is made in respect of employment which is part-time employment, the amount of the compensation;

[¹ (j) any remuneration paid by or on behalf of an employer to the claimant in respect of a period throughout which the claimant is—

    (i) on maternity leave;

    (ii) on paternity leave;

    (iii) on adoption leave; or

    (iv) absent from work because he is ill.]

(2) For the purposes of paragraph (1)(i)(i) the "deductible remainder"—

(a) applies in cases where dividing the amount of the compensation by the maximum weekly amount produces a whole number plus a fraction; and

(b) is equal to the difference between—

    (i) the amount of the compensation; and

    (ii) the product of the maximum weekly amount multiplied by the whole number.

[²(3)"Earnings" shall not include any payment in respect of expenses—

(a) wholly, exclusively and necessarily incurred in the performance of the duties of the employment; or

(b) arising out of the [⁴ claimant participating as a service user].

[⁴ (3A) The reference in paragraph (3)(b) to a claimant participating as a service user is to—

(a) a person who is being consulted by or on behalf of—

    (i) a body which has a statutory duty to provide services in the field of health, social care or social housing; or

    (ii) a body which conducts research or undertakes monitoring for the purpose of planning or improving such services,

    in their capacity as a user, potential user, carer of a user or person otherwise affected by the provision of those services;

(b) a person who is being consulted by or on behalf of—

    (i) the Secretary of State in relation to any of his functions in the field of social security or child support or under section 2 of the Employment and Training Act 1973; or

    (ii a body which conducts research or undertakes monitoring for the purpose of planning or improving such functions,

    in their capacity as a person affected or potentially affected by the exercise of those functions or the carer of such a person; or

    (c) the carer of a person consulted under sub-paragraphs (a) or (b).]

(4) In this regulation—

[¹ "adoption leave" means a period of absence from work on ordinary or additional adoption leave under section 75A or 75B of the Employment Rights Act 1996;]

"compensation" means any payment made in respect of or on the termination of employment in a case where a person has not received or received only part of a payment in lieu of notice due or which would have been due to him had he not waived his right to receive it, other than—

(a) any payment specified in paragraph (1)(a) to (h);

(b) any payment specified in paragraph (3);

(c) any redundancy payment within the meaning of section 135 of the Employment Rights Act 1996;

(d) any refund of contributions to which that person was entitled under an occupational pension scheme;

   (e) any compensation payable by virtue of section 173 or section 178(3)
       or (4) of the Education Reform Act 1988;

[² "enactment" includes an enactment comprised in, or an instrument
   made under, an Act of the Scottish Parliament;]

[¹ "maternity leave" means a period during which a woman is absent from
   work because she is pregnant or has given birth to a child, and at the
   end of which she has a right to return to work either under the terms of
   her contract of employment or under Part 8 of the Employment Rights
   Act 1996;]

"maximum weekly amount" means the maximum weekly amount which,
   on the date on which the payment of compensation is made, is specified in section 227(1) of the Employment Rights Act 1996;

"part-time employment" has the same meaning as in regulation 6(8)
   (calculation of earnings of employed earners);

[¹ "paternity leave" means a period of absence from work on leave under
   section 80A or 80B of the Employment Rights Act 1996.]

[² "public authority" includes any person certain of whose functions are
   functions of a public nature;]

[² [⁴ ...]]

AMENDMENTS

1. The Social Security Benefit (Computation of Earnings) (Amendment)
Regulations 2002 (SI 2002/2823) reg.2 (April 1, 2003).
2. The Social Security Benefit (Computation of Earnings) (Amendment)
Regulations 2009 (SI 2009/2678) reg.2 (October 26, 2009).
3. The Housing and Regeneration Act 2008 (Consequential Provisions) (No. 2)
Order 2010 (SI 2010/671) art.4 and Sch.1 (April 1, 2010).
4. The Social Security Benefit (Computation of Earnings) (Amendment)
Regulations 2015 (SI 2015/784) reg.2 (July 1, 2015).

GENERAL NOTE

3.23   This regulation mirrors reg.35 of the Income Support (General) Regulations
1987 and reference to the annotations in *Social Security Legislation: Vol.II* is advised
since a number of the provisions of reg.35 have been the subject of consideration
by the Commissioners.
   The claimant in *CP/3017/2004* had made an advance claim for an increase of his
retirement pension in respect of his wife. She had earnings and the decision maker
had determined that these were in excess of the specified figure with the result
that the claimant had no entitlement to the increase. The appeal tribunal confirmed the decision, but the Commissioner found that they had erred in law and
substituted his own decision awarding the increase. The claimant's wife worked
as a sales promoter of a variety of goods in supermarkets. She made the planning
arrangements for promotional visits to the supermarkets from home and attended
at supermarkets in the region to ensure the successful operation of the promotion.
She received expenses relating to travel (including travel from home), maintenance
of her car and car parking. The Commissioner concluded that, in the particular
circumstances of this case, the expenses were to be excluded from the calculation
of the earnings of the claimant's wife under reg.9(3), which trumped the provisions
in reg.9(1)(f)(i).
   CG/0645/2008 raised, among other things, the question of the proper computation of a person's weekly earnings in relation to the earnings limit for entitlement to
a carer's allowance. The tribunal made its decision without reference to the regulations, which are described as "a comprehensive code" (para.54). The facts were

complex since the appellant argued that part of what she received was on behalf of a third party. The Deputy Commissioner says:

> 57. In my view there is a common thread running through the definitions in section 3 of SSCBA 1992 and the 1996 Regulations. That is, however expansively one defines "earnings", the earnings in question must still be the earnings of the individual in question. Thus "any remuneration or profit derived from employment" must mean derived from the claimant's employment, not from someone else's employment.

The Deputy Commissioner agrees that what are to be taken into account are payments actually received, not entitlement which has not resulted in payments, that is, payments actually received for service rendered under that person's own contract of employment.

SSWP v KM [2009] UKUT 85 (AAC) is a further appeal from the First-tier Tribunal following the remission of the appeal for a re-hearing in *CG/0645/2008*. The appeal had again to be remitted since the tribunal had not found all the facts necessary to determine all the issues identified in the earlier decision. The Upper Tribunal Judge strongly criticises the Secretary of State for failing to comply with a direction on the earlier appeal that the Secretary of State should be represented in a case with the complexity of issues presented by this appeal.

Calculation of net earnings of employed earners

10.—(1) For the purposes of regulations 3 (calculation of earnings) and 6 (calculation of earnings of employed earners) the earnings of a claimant derived from employment as an employed earner to be taken into account shall, subject to paragraphs (2) and (3), be his net earnings.

3.24

(2) Except in a case to which paragraph (3) applies, there shall be disregarded or deducted as appropriate from a claimant's net earnings—

(a) any sum, where applicable, specified in Schedule 1; and
(b) any relevant child care charges to which Schedule 2 applies up to a maximum deduction in respect of any claimant of £60 per week.

(3) In the case of entitlement to [¹ carer's allowance] under section 70 of the Contributions and Benefits Act there shall be disregarded or deducted as appropriate from a claimant's net earnings—

(a) any sum, where applicable, specified in Schedule 1; and
(b) any care charges to which Schedule 3 applies up to a maximum deduction, in respect of such care charges incurred by any claimant, of 50% of his net earnings less those sums, if any, specified in Schedule 1 which are disregarded.

(4) For the purposes of paragraph (1) net earnings shall be calculated by taking into account the gross earnings of the claimant from that employment less—

(a) any amount deducted from those earnings by way of—
   (i) income tax;
   (ii) primary Class 1 contributions under the Contributions and Benefits Act; and
(b) one half of any sum paid by the claimant in respect of a pay period by way of a contribution towards an occupation or personal pension scheme.

AMENDMENT

1. The Social Security Benefit (Computation of Earnings) (Amendment) Regulations 2002 (SI 2002/2823) reg.2 (April 1, 2003).

The Social Security Benefit (Computation of Earnings) Regulations 1996

GENERAL NOTE

3.25   This regulation follows, with modification, reg.36 of the Income Support (General) Regulations 1987. Child care costs are to be disregarded if Sch.2 applies provided they do not exceed £60 per week. Where entitlement to carer's allowance (formerly invalid care allowance) is the relevant benefit, care charges are to be disregarded if Sch.3 applies provided they do not exceed the maximum calculated in accordance with reg.10(3)(b).

Paragraph (3)

3.26   In *CG/4024/2001* the Commissioner had to consider whether the cost of the rental for a careline telephone link constituted a "care charge" under reg.10(3). The claimant paid a small rental for the telephone line, which allowed her daughter (who suffered from epilepsy) to press a button held on a cord around her neck. This sounded a warning with the monitoring station and established a telephone link; the claimant could then attend to provide care, or arrange for someone else to do so. Both the tribunal and the Commissioner decided that the cost of the rental was not a care charge. The Commissioner says,

> "16. It is not necessary for me to define the word 'care'. It is sufficient to say that in the context it is not appropriate to cover the link. The natural interpretation of the arrangement is that the monitoring arrangement exists to allow someone to be called who can care for the claimant's daughter. It does not itself provide that care. Nor does the person who monitors alarms at the station.

> 17. The tribunal came to the correct conclusion and the only one that was open to it as a reasonable tribunal familiar with the use of language. I direct the tribunal at the rehearing that the cost of the line rental is not deductible."

PART III

SELF-EMPLOYED EARNERS

Calculation of earnings of self-employed earners

3.27   **11.**—(1) Except where paragraph (2) applies, where a claimant's earnings consist of earnings from employment as a self-employed earner the weekly amount of his earnings shall be determined by reference to his average weekly earnings from that employment
  (a) over a period of one year; or
  (b) where the claimant has recently become engaged in that employment or there has been a change which is likely to affect the normal pattern of business, over such other period as may, in any particular case, enable the weekly amount of his earnings to be determined more accurately.

(2) Where the claimant's earnings consist of [¹ any items to which paragraph (2A) applies] those earnings shall be taken into account over a period equal to such number of weeks as is equal to the number (less any fraction of the whole number) calculated in accordance with the formula—

$$\frac{S}{T + U}$$

where—
S is the earnings
T is the relevant earnings limit plus one penny; and

U is the total of the sums which would fall to be disregarded or deducted as appropriate under regulation 13(2) or (3) (calculation of net profit of self-employed earners).

[¹ (2A) This paragraph applies to—

(a) royalties or other sums paid as a consideration for the use of, or the right to use, any copyright, design, patent or trade mark; or

(b) any payment in respect of any—

    (i) book registered under the Public Lending Right Scheme 1982, or

    (ii) work made under any international public lending right scheme that is analogous to the Public Lending Rights Scheme 1982,

where the claimant is the first owner of the copyright, design, patent or trade mark, or any original contributor to the book or work concerned.]

(3) The period mentioned in paragraph (2) shall begin on the date on which the payment is treated as paid under regulation 7 (date on which earnings are treated as paid).

AMENDMENT

1. The Social Security Benefit (Computation of Earnings) (Amendment) Regulations 2009 (SI 2009/2678) reg.2 (October 26, 2009).

Earnings of self-employed earners

12.—(1) [¹ . . .] "Earnings", in the case of employment as a self-employed earner, means the gross receipts of the employment and shall include any allowance paid under section 2 of the Employment and Training Act 1973 or section 2 of the Enterprise and New Towns (Scotland) Act 1990 to the claimant for the purpose of assisting him in carrying on his business.

[¹ . . .]

3.28

AMENDMENT

1. The Social Security Benefit (Computation of Earnings) (Amendment) Regulations 2007 (SI 2007/2613) (October 1, 2007).

Calculation of net profit of self-employed earners

13.—(1) For the purposes of regulations 3 (calculation of earnings) and 11 (calculation of earnings of self-employed earners), the earnings of a claimant to be taken into account shall be—

(a) in the case of a self-employed earner who is engaged in employment on his own account, the net profit derived from that employment;

(b) in the case of a self-employed earner whose employment is carried on in partnership or is that of a share fisherman his share of the net profit derived from that employment less—

    (i) an amount in respect of income tax and of social security contributions payable under the Contributions and Benefits Act calculated in accordance with regulation 14 (deduction of tax and contributions for self-employed earners); and

    (ii) one half of any premium paid in the period that is relevant under regulation 11 in respect of a retirement annuity contract or a personal pension scheme;

(c) in paragraph (b) "share fisherman" means any person who—

    (i) is ordinarily employed in the fishing industry otherwise than under

3.29

a contract of service, as a master or member of the crew of any
fishing boat manned by more than one person, and is remuner-
ated in respect of that employment in whole or in part by a share
of profits or gross earnings of the fishing boat; or

(ii) has ordinarily been so employed, but who by reason of age
or infirmity permanently ceases to be so employed and becomes
ordinarily engaged in employment ashore in Great Britain,
otherwise than under a contract of service, making or mending
any gear appurtenant to a fishing boat or performing other
services ancillary to or in connection with that boat and is remu-
nerated in respect of that employment in whole or in part by a
share of the profits or gross earnings of that boat and has not
ceased to be ordinarily engaged in such employment.

(2) Except in a case to which paragraph (3) applies, there shall be disregarded or deducted as appropriate from a claimant's net profit—

(a) any sum, where applicable, specified in Schedule 1; and
(b) any relevant child care charges to which Schedule 2 applies up to
a maximum deduction in respect of any claimant of £60 per week.

(3) In the case of entitlement to [¹ carer's allowance] under section 70 of
the Contributions and Benefits Act there shall be disregarded or deducted
as appropriate from a claimant's net profit—

(a) any sum where applicable, specified in Schedule 1; and
(b) any care charges to which Schedule 3 applies up to a maximum
deduction, in respect of such care charges incurred by any claimant,
of 50% of his net profit less those sums, if any, specified in Schedule
1 which are disregarded.

(4) For the purposes of paragraph (1)(a), the net profit of the employment shall, except where paragraph (10) applies, be calculated by taking into
account the earnings of the employment over the period determined under
regulation 11 (calculation of earnings of self-employed earners) less—

(a) subject to paragraphs (6) to (8), any expenses wholly and exclusively
defrayed in that period for the purposes of that employment;
(b) an amount in respect of—
(i) income tax; and
(ii) social security contributions payable under the Contributions
and Benefits Act, calculated in accordance with regulation 14
(deduction of tax and contributions for self-employed earners);
and
(c) one half of any premium paid in the period that is relevant under
regulation 11 in respect of a retirement annuity contract or a personal pension scheme.

(5) For the purposes of paragraph (1)(b), the net profit of the employment shall be calculated by taking into account the earnings of the employment over the period determined under regulation 11 less, subject to
paragraphs (6) to (8), any expenses wholly and exclusively defrayed in that
period for the purposes of that employment.

(6) Subject to paragraph (7), no deduction shall be made under paragraph (4)(a) or (5) in respect of—

(a) any capital expenditure;
(b) the depreciation of any capital asset;
(c) any sum employed or intended to be employed in the setting up or
expansion of the employment;

(d) any loss incurred before the beginning of the period determined under regulation 11 (calculation of earnings of self-employed earners);

(e) the repayment of capital on any loan taken out for the purposes of the employment;

(f) any expenses incurred in providing business entertainment.

[⁴ (g) where the claimant provides accommodation to another person in the dwelling the claimant occupies as his home, any expenses defrayed by the claimant in providing the accommodation to that person (including any defrayed in providing board as well as lodging).]

(7) A deduction shall be made under paragraph (4)(a) or (5) in respect of the repayment of capital on any loan used for—

(a) the replacement in the course of business of equipment or machinery; and

(b) the repair of an existing business asset except to the extent that any sum is payable under an insurance policy for its repair.

(8) [² A deduction shall not be made] in respect of any expenses under paragraph (4)(a) or (5) where [³ the Secretary of State] is not satisfied that the expense has been defrayed or, having regard to the nature of the expense and its amount, that it has been reasonably incurred.

(9) For the avoidance of doubt—

(a) a deduction shall not be made under paragraph (4)(a) or (5) in respect of any sum unless it has been expended for the purposes of the business;

(b) a deduction shall be made thereunder in respect of—

(i) the excess of any VAT paid over VAT received in the period determined under regulation 11 (calculation of earnings of self-employed earners);

(ii) any income expended in the repair of an existing asset except to the extent that any sum is payable under an insurance policy for its repair;

(iii) any payment of interest on a loan taken out for the purposes of the employment.

(10) Where a claimant is engaged in employment as a child minder the net profit of the employment shall be one-third of the earnings of that employment, less—

(a) an amount in respect of—

(i) income tax;

(ii) social security contributions payable under the Contributions and Benefits Act, calculated in accordance with regulation 14 (deduction of tax and contributions for self-employed earners); and

(b) one half of any premium paid in respect of a retirement annuity contract or a personal pension scheme.

(11) Notwithstanding regulation 11 (calculation of earnings of self-employed earners) and the foregoing paragraphs, [³ the Secretary of State] may assess any item of a claimant's earnings or expenditure over a period other than that determined under regulation 11 as may, in the particular case, enable the weekly amount of that item of earnings or expenditure to be determined more accurately.

(12) For the avoidance of doubt where a claimant is engaged in employment as a self-employed earner and he is engaged in one or more other employments as a self-employed or employed earner any loss incurred in

any one of his employments shall not be offset against his earnings in any other of his employments.

AMENDMENTS

1. The Social Security Benefit (Computation of Earnings) (Amendment) Regulations 2002 (SI 2002/2823) reg.2 (April 1, 2003).
2. The Social Security Act 1998 (Commencement No.9 and Savings and Consequential and Transitional Provisions) Order 1999 (SI 1999/2422) Sch.13 para.5 (September 6, 1999).
3. The Social Security Act 1998 (Commencement No.9 and Savings and Consequential and Transitional Provisions) Order 1999 (SI 1999/2422) Sch.13 para.1 (September 6, 1999).
4. The Social Security Benefit (Computation of Earnings) (Amendment) Regulations 2007 (SI 2007/2613) (October 1, 2007).

GENERAL NOTE

3.30   This regulation largely mirrors reg.38 of the Income Support (General) Regulations 1987. See annotations to that provision in *Social Security Legislation, Vol.II*.

SSWP v SK [2014] UKUT 12 (AAC) considers the significance of the use of the word 'defrayed' in reg.13(5) and concludes, after a review of the authorities, that a reduction in the value of stock at the end of the accounting period compared with the beginning of the accounting period cannot be taken into account in determining weekly earnings from self employment.

In *Secretary of State v Doyle*, reported as *R(IB) 1/06*, the Court of Appeal ruled that the Computations of Earnings Regulations apply for the purpose of the calculation of entitlement to entitlement to incapacity benefit. *R(IB)3/07* is the Commissioner's consideration of the application of the Computation of Earnings Regulations to the circumstances of the case on remission of the appeal for consideration by the Commissioner. The decision also includes as appendices the earlier decision and the decision of the Court of Appeal.

The Commissioner had to consider whether the deduction provided for in reg.13(2) and para.3 to Sch.1 for a fixed-rate deduction to be made from earnings from board and lodging accommodation is in addition to the disregard provided for in reg.13(4)(a). The Commissioner concluded that the regulations did provide for both to be applied to a claimant's case (though in the particular circumstances presented by the claimant that was not necessary to bring him within the earnings limit for incapacity benefit).

Note the effect of the amendment to reg.13(6) by the addition of a new sub-paragraph (f). The explanatory memorandum to the amending regulations says:

"A Social Security Commissioner recently decided that due to way the regulations were drafted, when the accommodation is provided in the customer's home, the formula disregard is to be applied twice, together with a further disregard of any other allowable business expenses. This provides for the provision of 3 separate disregards. The amended regulations will ensure that only one disregard of £20 and then 50% of the balance will be applied to any income from boarders, and restore the original policy intent."

Deduction of tax and contributions for self-employed earners

3.31   **14.**—(1) The amount to be deducted in respect of income tax under regulation 13(1)(b)(i), (4)(b)(i) or (10)(a)(i) (calculation of net profit of self-employed earners) shall be calculated on the basis of the amount of chargeable income and as if that income were assessable to income tax at the [³ basic rate, or in the case of a Scottish taxpayer, the Scottish basic rate, of tax less only the personal reliefs to which the claimant is entitled under Chapters 2, 3 and 3A of Part 3 of the Income Tax Act 2007 as are] appropriate to his circumstances; but, if the period determined under regulation 11 (calculation of earnings of self-employed earners) is less than a year, the earnings to which the [³ basic rate, or the Scottish basic rate,] of tax is to be applied and the amount of the personal [³ reliefs] deductible under this paragraph shall be calculated on a pro rata basis.

(2) The amount to be deducted in respect of social security contributions under regulation 13(1)(b)(i), (4)(b)(ii) or (10)(a)(ii) shall be the total of—

(a) the amount of Class 2 contributions payable under section [² 11(2)] or, as the case may be, [² 11(8)] of the Contributions and Benefits Act at the rate applicable at the date [¹ on which a decision is made by the Secretary of State under Chapter II of Part I of the Social Security Act 1998 or regulations made thereunder] except where the claimant's chargeable income is less than the amount specified in section 11(4) of that Act [² small profits threshold] for the tax year in which that date falls; but if the assessment period is less than a year, the amount specified for that year shall be reduced pro rata; and

(b) the amount of Class 4 contributions (if any) which would be payable under section 15 of that Act (Class 4 contributions recoverable under the Income Tax Acts) at the percentage rate applicable at the date [¹ on which a decision is made by the Secretary of State under Chapter II of Part I of the Social Security Act 1998 or regulations made thereunder] on so much of the chargeable income as exceeds the lower limit but does not exceed the upper limit of profits and gains applicable for the tax year in which that date falls; but if the assessment period is less than a year, those limits shall be reduced pro rata.

(3) In this regulation "chargeable income" means—

(a) except where sub-paragraph (b) applies, the earnings derived from the employment less any expenses deducted under paragraph (4)(a) or, as the case may be, (5) of regulation 13;

(b) in the case of employment as a child minder, one-third of the earnings of that employment.

AMENDMENTS

1. The Social Security Act 1998 (Commencement No.9 and Savings and Consequential and Transitional Provisions) Order 1999 (SI 1999/2422) Sch.13 para.6 (September 6, 1999).

2. The Social Security (Miscellaneous Amendments No. 2) Regulations 2015 (SI 2015/478) reg.30 (April 6, 2015).

3. The Social Security Benefit (Computation of Earnings) (Amendment) Regulations 2016 (SI 2016/267) reg.2(4) (April 6, 2016).

PART IV

TRANSITIONAL PROVISIONS, CONSEQUENTIAL AMENDMENTS AND
REVOCATIONS

3.32   *Regulations 15–18 omitted.*

SCHEDULE 1   **Regulations 10(2) and 13(2)**

SUMS TO BE DISREGARDED IN THE CALCULATION OF EARNINGS

3.33   **1.**—Any payment made to the claimant by a person who normally resides with the claimant, which is a contribution towards that person's living and accommodation costs, except where that person is residing with the claimant in circumstances to which paragraph 2 or 3 refers.

2.—Where the claimant occupies a dwelling as his home and the dwelling is also occupied by another person and there is a contractual liability to make payments to the claimant in respect of the occupation of the dwelling by that person or a member of his family—

[³ (a) where the aggregate of any payments made in respect of any one week in respect of the occupation of that dwelling by that person or a member of his family, or by that person and a member of his family, is less than £20, the whole of that amount; or

(b) where the aggregate of any such payments is £20 or more per week, £20.]

3.—Where the claimant occupies a dwelling as his home and he provides in that dwelling board and lodging accommodation, an amount, in respect of each person for whom such accommodation is provided for the whole or any part of a week, equal to—

(a) where the aggregate of any payments made in respect of any one week in respect of such accommodation provided to such person does not exceed £20.00, 100% of such payments; or

(b) where the aggregate of any such payments exceeds £20.00, £20.00 and 50% of the excess over £20.00.

4.—Except in the case of a claimant who is absent from Great Britain and not disqualified for receiving any benefit, pension, allowance or supplement, by virtue of the Social Security Benefit (Persons Abroad) Regulations 1975—

(a) any earnings derived from employment which are payable in a country outside the United Kingdom for such period during which there is a prohibition against the transfer to the United Kingdom of those earnings;

(b) where a payment of earnings is made in a currency other than sterling, any banking charge or commission payable in converting that payment into sterling.

5.—Any earnings which are due to be paid before the date of claim and which would otherwise fall to be taken into account in the same benefit week as a payment of the same kind and from the same source.

6.—Any payment made by a local authority to the claimant with whom a person is accommodated by virtue of arrangements made under section 23(2)(a) of the Children Act 1989 (provision of accommodation and maintenance for a child whom they are looking after) [⁸ , section 81 of the Social Services and Well-being (Wales) Act 2014, or] section 21 of the Social Work (Scotland) Act 1968 or by a voluntary organisation under section 59(1)(a) of the 1989 Act (provision of accommodation by voluntary organisations) or by a care authority under regulation 9 of the Boarding-out and Fostering of Children (Scotland) Regulations 1985 (provision of accommodation and maintenance for children in care).

7.—Any payment made by a health authority, [⁶ a clinical commissioning group, the National Health Service Commissioning Board, a local authority or a voluntary organization] to the claimant in respect of a person who is not normally a member of the claimant's household but is temporarily in his care.

8.—In respect of regulation 16 of the Social Security (General Benefit) Regulations 1982 any earnings not earned during the period of the award.

9.—Any bounty paid at intervals of at least one year and derived from employments as—

[⁷ (a) a part-time fire-fighter employed by a fire and rescue authority under the Fire and Rescue Services Act 2004 or by the Scottish Fire and Rescue Service established under section 1A of the Fire (Scotland) Act 2005;]

[⁷ (aa) ...]

[⁷ (ab) ...]

(b) an auxiliary coastguard in respect of coastal rescue activities;

574

(c) a person engaged part-time in the manning or launching of a lifeboat;

(d) a member of any territorial or reserve force prescribed in Part I of Schedule 3 to the Social Security (Contributions) Regulations 1979.

10.—Any amount by way of refund of income tax deducted from profits or emoluments chargeable to income tax under Schedule D or E.

11.—In the case of employment as an employed earner, any advance of earnings or any loan made by the claimant's employer.

[² **12.**—(1) Any earnings, other than items to which sub-paragraph (2) applies, paid or due to be paid from the claimant's employment as an employed earner which ended before the day in respect of which the claimant first satisfies the conditions for entitlement to the benefit, pension or allowance to which the claim relates.

(2) This sub-paragraph applies to—

(a) any payment by way of occupational or personal pension; and

(b) except in a case where the claimant's employment terminated by reason of retirement at a time when he had attained pensionable age (within the meaning given by rules in paragraph 1 of Schedule 4 to the Pensions Act 1995)—

    (i) any payment or remuneration of the nature described in regulation 9(1)(e) or (j), and

    (ii) any award or sum of the nature described in regulation 9(1)(g) or (h) (including any payment made following the settlement of a complaint to an employment tribunal or of court proceedings).

(3) Sub-paragraph (1) is subject to the following provisions.

(4) Sub-paragraph (1) does not apply in relation to a claim for, or an award of, incapacity benefit (within the meaning given by paragraph 11 of Schedule 4 to the Welfare Reform Act 2007) or severe disablement allowance (also within the meaning given by that paragraph).

(5) Sub-paragraph (1) applies in relation to a claim for an increase in benefit under Part IV of the Contributions and Benefits Act (increases in respect of dependants) only in a case where—

(a) the spouse or partner or other adult in respect of whom that claim is made was in employment as an employed earner, but

(b) that employment ended before the day referred to in sub-paragraph (1).]

AMENDMENTS

1. The Fire and Rescue Services Act 2004 (Consequential Amendments) (England) Order 2004 (SI 2004/3168) art.39 (December 30, 2004) (in relation to England only). The Fire and Rescue Services Act 2004 (Consequential Amendments) (Wales) Order 2005 (SI 2005/2929) (October 25, 2005) (in relation to Wales only).

2. The Social Security Benefit (Computation of Earnings) (Amendment) Regulations 2007 (SI 2007/2613) (October 1, 2007).

3. The Social Security Benefit (Computation of Earnings) (Amendment) Regulations 2007 (SI 2007/2613) (April 7, 2008).

4. The Fire (Scotland) Act 2005 (Consequential Provisions and Modifications) Order 2005 (SI 2005/2060) art.3 (August 2, 2005)

5. The Police and Fire Reform (Scotland) Act 2012 (Consequential Provisions and Modifications) Order 2013 (SI 2013/602) Sch.2 para.75 (April 1, 2013).

6. The National Treatment Agency (Abolition) and the Health and Social Care Act 2012 (Consequential, Transitional and Savings Provisions) Order 2013 (SI 2013/235) art.11 and para.32(3) of Pt 1 of Sch.2 (April 1, 2013).

7. The Social Security (Miscellaneous Amendments) (No. 3) Regulations 2013 (SI 2013/2536) reg.7 (October 29, 2013).

8. The Social Security Benefit (Computation of Earnings) (Amendment) Regulations 2016 (SI 2016/267) reg.2(5) (April 6, 2016).

GENERAL NOTE

Pt I of Sch.3 to the Social Security (Contributions) Regulations 1979 (SI 1979/591, as amended) reads: **3.34**

"*Prescribed establishments and organisations for purposes of section 128(3) of the Act*

1. Any of the regular navy, military or air forces of the Crown.

2. Retired and Emergency Lists of Officers of the Royal Navy.

3. Royal Naval Reserves (including Women's Royal Naval Reserve and Queen Alexandra's Royal Naval Nursing Service Reserve).

4. Royal Marines Reserve.

5. Army Reserves (including Regular Army Reserve of Officers, Regular Reserves, Long Term Reserve and Army Pensioners).

6. Territorial and Army Volunteer Reserve.

7. Royal Air Force Reserves (including Royal Air Force Reserve of Officers, Women's Royal Air Force Reserve of Officers, Royal Air Force Volunteer Reserve, Women's Royal Air Force Volunteer Reserve, Class E Reserve of Airmen, Princess Mary's Royal Air Force Nursing Service Reserve, Officers on the Retired List of the Royal Air Force and Royal Air Force Pensioners).

8. Royal Auxiliary Air Force (including Women's Royal Auxiliary Air Force).

9. The Royal Irish Regiment, to the extent that its members are not members of any force falling within paragraph 1 of this Part of this Schedule."

In *CG/1752/2006*, the Commissioner considered the proper interpretation of the word "temporarily" in para.7. Following *CIS/17020/1996* (which was about a paragraph in the same terms in the Income Support General Regulations), the Commissioner concluded that "an arrangement which is not permanent is not necessarily temporary." In defining the term "temporarily" as meaning "not permanent", the tribunal had erred in law.

SCHEDULE 2   **Regulations 10(2) and 13(2)**

CHILD CARE CHARGES TO BE DEDUCTED IN THE CALCULATION OF EARNINGS

3.35

1.—This Schedule applies where a claimant is incurring relevant child care charges and—

    (a) is a lone parent;

    (b) is a member of a couple both of whom are engaged in employment; or

    (c) is a member of a couple where one member is engaged in employment and the other member is incapacitated.

2.—In this Schedule—

"relevant child care charges" means the charges paid by the claimant for care provided for any child of the claimant's family who is under the age of 11 years, other than charges paid in respect of the child's compulsory education or charges paid by a claimant to a partner or by a partner to a claimant in respect of any child for whom either or any of them is responsible in accordance with section 143 of the Contributions and Benefits Act (circumstances in which a person is to be treated as responsible or not responsible for another), where the care is provided—

    (a) by persons registered under section 71 of the Children Act 1989 (registration of child minders and persons providing day care for young children); or

    (b) for children aged 8 and over but under 11, out of school hours, by a school on school premises or by a local authority; or

    (c) by a child care scheme operating on Crown property where registration under section 71 of the Children Act 1989 is not required; or

    (d) in schools or establishments which are exempted from registration under section 71 of the Children Act 1989 by virtue of section 71(16) of, and paragraph 3 or 4 of Schedule 9 to, that Act,

    [¹ or

    (e) by persons registered under Part XA of the Children Act 1989; or

    (f) in schools or establishments which are exempted from registration under Part XA of the Children Act 1989 by virtue of paragraph 1 of Schedule 9A to that Act; or

    [³ (g) by—

        (i) persons registered under section 59(1) of the Public Services Reform (Scotland) Act 2010; or

        (ii) local authorities registered under section 83(1) of that Act,

        where the care provided is child minding or day care of children within the meaning of that Act,]

and shall be calculated on a weekly basis in accordance with paragraphs 4 to 7;

"school term-time" means the school term-time applicable to the child for whom care is provided.

3.—The age of a child referred to in paragraph 2 shall be determined by reference to the age of the child at the date on which the benefit week began.

4.—Subject to paragraphs 5 to 7, relevant child care charges shall be calculated in accordance with the formula—

$$\frac{X + Y}{52}$$

where—

X is the average weekly charge paid for child care in the most recent 4 complete weeks which fall in school term-time in respect of the child or children concerned, multiplied by 39; and

Y is the average weekly charge paid for child care in the most recent 2 complete weeks which fall out of school term-time in respect of that child or those children, multiplied by 13.

5.—Subject to paragraph 6, where child care charges are being incurred in respect of a child who does not yet attend school, the relevant child care charges shall mean the average weekly charge paid for care provided in respect of that child in the most recent 4 complete weeks.

6.—Where in any case the charges in respect of child care are paid monthly, the average weekly charge for the purposes of paragraph 4 shall be established—

    (a) where the charges are for a fixed monthly amount, by multiplying that amount by 12 and dividing the product by 52;

    (b) where the charges are for variable monthly amounts, by aggregating the charges for the previous 12 months and dividing the total by 52.

7.—In a case where there is no information or insufficient information for establishing the average weekly charge paid for child care in accordance with paragraphs 4 to 6, the average weekly charge for care shall be estimated by reference to information provided by the child minder or person providing the care or, if such information is not available, by reference to information provided by the claimant.

8.—For the purposes of paragraph 1(c) the other member of a couple is incapacitated where—

    (a) [5 . . .] housing benefit is payable under Part VII of the Contributions and Benefits Act to the other member or his partner and the applicable amount of the person entitled to the benefit includes—

        (i) a disability premium; or

        [2 (ii) a higher pensioner premium by virtue of the satisfaction of—

            [5 (aa) . . .]

            (bb) in the case of housing benefit, paragraph 11(2)(b) of Schedule 3 to the Housing Benefit Regulations 2006;

on account of the other member's incapacity or [5 . . .] regulation 28(1)C of the Housing Benefit Regulations 2006 (treatment of child care charges) applies in that person's case;]

    (b) there is payable in respect of him one or more of the following pensions [4, payments] or allowances—

        (i) long-term incapacity benefit under section 30A, 40 or 41 of the Contributions and Benefits Act;

        (ii) attendance allowance under section 64 of that Act;

        (iii) severe disablement allowance under section 68 of that Act;

        (iv) disability living allowance under section 71 of that Act;

        (v) an increase of disablement pension under section 104 of that Act;

        (vi) a pension increase under a war pension scheme or an industrial injuries scheme which is analogous to an allowance or increase of disablement pension under head (ii), (iv) or (v) above;

    [4 (vii) personal independence payment under Part 4 of the Welfare Reform Act 2012;]

    [6 (viii) armed forces independence payment under the Armed Forces and Reserve Forces (Compensation Scheme) Order 2011]

    (c) a pension [4, payment] or allowance to which head (ii), (iv), (v) [4, (vi) or (vii)] of sub-paragraph (b) refers, was payable on account of his incapacity but has ceased to be payable—

        [4 (i)] in consequence of his becoming a patient (other than a person who is serving a sentence imposed by a court in a prison or youth custody institution) who is regarded as receiving free in-patient treatment within the meaning of the Social Security (Hospital In-Patients) Regulations 1975; [4 or]

        [4 (ii) in accordance with regulations made [under] section 86(1) (hospital in-patients) of the Welfare Reform Act 2012;]

(d) sub-paragraph (b) or (c) would apply to him if the legislative provisions referred to in those sub-paragraphs were provisions under any corresponding enactment having effect in Northern Ireland; or

(e) he has an invalid carriage or other vehicle provided to him by the Secretary of State under section 5(2)(a) of, and Schedule 2 to, the National Health Service Act 1977 or under section 46 of the National Health Service (Scotland) Act 1978 or provided by the Department of Health and Social Services for Northern Ireland under article 30(1) of the Health and Personal Social Services (Northern Ireland) Order 1972.

AMENDMENTS

1. The Social Security Benefit (Computation of Earnings) (Child Care Charges) Regulations 2002 (SI 2002/842) (April 1, 2002).

2. The Housing Benefit and Council Tax Benefit (Consequential Provisions) Regulations 2006 (SI 2006/217) (March 6, 2006).

3. Public Services Reform (Scotland) Act 2010 (Consequential Modifications of Enactments) Order 2011 (SI 2011/2581) Sch.2 para.23 (October 28, 2011).

4. The Personal Independence Payments (Supplementary Provisions and Consequential Amendments) Regulations 2013 (SI 2013/388) reg.8 and Sch. para.17 (April 8, 2013).

5. The Council Tax Benefit Abolition (Consequential Provision) Regulations 2013 (SI 2013/458) reg.3 (April 1, 2013).

6. The Armed Forces and Reserve Forces Compensation Scheme (Consequential Provisions: Subordinate Legislation) Order 2013 (SI 2013/591) reg.7 and Sch. para.12 (April 8, 2013).

SCHEDULE 3   **Regulations 10(3) and 13(3)**

CARE CHARGES TO BE DEDUCTED IN THE CALCULATION OF EARNINGS FOR ENTITLEMENT TO
[¹ CARER'S ALLOWANCE]

3.36   **1.**— This Schedule applies where a claimant is—

(a) entitled to [¹ carer's allowance] under section 70 of the Contributions and Benefits Act; and

(b) incurring relevant care charges.

2.—In this Schedule—

"close relative" means a parent, son, daughter, brother, sister or partner;

"relevant care charges" means the charges paid by the claimant for care which is provided by a person, who is not a close relative of either the severely disabled person or the claimant, for—

(a) the severely disabled person; or

(b) any child aged under 16 on the date on which the benefit week begins in respect of whom the claimant or his partner is entitled to child benefit under section 141 of the Contributions and Benefits Act because the claimant is unable to care for any of those persons because he is carrying out duties in connection with his employment;

"severely disabled person" means the severely disabled person in respect of whom entitlement to *invalid care allowance* arises.

AMENDMENT

1. The Social Security Benefit (Computation of Earnings) (Amendment) Regulations 2002 (SI 2002/2823) reg.2 (April 1, 2003).

GENERAL NOTE

3.37   The italicised words must now be taken as referring to carer's allowance.

3.38   *Schedule 4 omitted.*

The Social Security Benefit (Dependency) Regulations 1977

(SI 1977/343) (AS AMENDED)

ARRANGEMENT OF REGULATIONS

PART I

GENERAL

1.   Citation, commencement and interpretation.   3.39
2.   Provisions as to maintenance for the purposes of increase of benefit in respect of dependants.
3.   Allocation of contributions for spouse or civil partner.
4.   Deeming benefit under the Act abated under [section 74(3) of the Social Security Contributions and Benefits Act 1992] to be a contribution for the maintenance of children or adult dependants.
4A. Circumstances in which a person who is not entitled to child benefit is to be treated as if he were so entitled.
4B. Circumstances in which a person entitled to child benefit is to be treated as if he were not so entitled.

PART II

CHILD DEPENDANTS

5.   Contribution towards cost of providing for child.
6.   *Revoked.*
7.   *Revoked.*

PART III

ADULT DEPENDANTS

8.   Earnings rules for increases for adult dependants.
9.   *Revoked.*
9A. Apportionment of payments by way of occupational or personal pension made otherwise than weekly.
10. Increase of benefit for person having care of child or qualifying young person.
11. Contribution to maintenance of adult dependant.

PART IV

MISCELLANEOUS

12. Prescribed circumstances for purposes of section 90 of the Social Security Contributions and Benefits Act.
13. *Revoked.*
14. *Revoked.*

PART V

TRANSITIONAL PROVISIONS AND REVOCATIONS

15.   Preservation of entitlement to benefit in payment before April 4, 1977 for a child dependant.

15A. *Revoked.*

16.   *Omitted.*

SCHEDULE

Schedule 2—Prescribed Circumstances for Increase of a Carer's Allowance.

The Secretary of State for Social Services, in exercise of the powers conferred upon him by sections 33(2), 44, 46, 47, 49, 66 and 84 of, and Schedule 20 to, the Social Security Act 1975, as amended in the case of the said sections 44, 46 and 66 and Schedule 20 by section 21(1) of, and Schedule 4 to, the Child Benefit Act 1975 and section 20(1) of the Child Benefit Act 1975 and all other powers enabling him in that behalf, hereby makes the following regulations for the purpose only of consolidating regulations hereby revoked:

PART I

GENERAL

Citation, commencement and interpretation

3.40   **1.**—(1) These regulations may be cited as the Social Security Benefit (Dependency) Regulations 1977 and shall come into operation on April 4, 1977, immediately after the coming into operation of the Social Security (Child Benefit Consequential) Regulations 1977.

(2) In these regulations, unless the context otherwise requires—

"the Act" means the Social Security Act 1975;

"the Child Benefit Act" means the Child Benefit Act 1975;

[¹ "the Contributions and Benefits Act" means the Social Security Contributions and Benefits Act 1992];

[² "the determining authority" means, as the case may require, the Secretary of State, [⁷ the First-tier Tribunal or the Upper Tribunal]];

"entitled to child benefit" includes treated as so entitled;

"parent" has the meaning assigned to it by section 24(3) of the Child Benefit Act;

"the standard rate of increase" means the amount specified in Part IV or Part V of Schedule 4 to the Act as the amount of an increase for an adult dependant of the benefit in question,

and other expressions have the same meanings as in the Act.

[³ (3) Regulations 2(2) and (3), 4 and 5(1) shall, with any necessary modifications, apply to [⁴ carer's allowance] as they apply to retirement pension.]

[⁵ (3A) Nothing in these Regulations applies for the purposes of incapacity benefit under section 30A of the Contributions and Benefits Act.]

(4) Unless the context otherwise requires, any reference in these regulations to—

(a) a numbered section is to the section of the Act bearing that number;

(b) a numbered regulation is a reference to the regulation bearing that number in these regulations and any reference in a regulation to a numbered paragraph is a reference to the paragraph of that regulation bearing that number;

(c) any provision made by or contained in any enactment or instrument shall be construed as a reference to that provision as amended or extended by any enactment or instrument and as including a reference to any provision which may re-enact or replace it, with or without modification.

(5) The rules for the construction of Acts of Parliament contained in the Interpretation Act 1889 shall apply in relation to this instrument and in relation to any revocation effected by it as if this instrument, the regulations revoked by it and any regulations revoked by the regulations so revoked were Acts of Parliament, and as if each revocation were a repeal.

AMENDMENTS

1. The Social Security Benefit (Dependency) Amendment Regulations 1992 (SI 1992/3041) reg.2 (December 5, 1992).

2. The Social Security Act 1998 (Commencement No. 12 and Consequential and Transitional Provisions) Order 1999 (SI 1999/3178) Sch.2 (November 29, 1999).

3. The Social Security (Incapacity—Increases for Dependants) Regulations 1994 (SI 1994/2945) reg.15(2)(a) (April 13, 1995).

4. The Social Security Amendment (Carer's Allowance) Regulations 2002 (SI 2002/2497) reg.3 and Sch.2 (April 1, 2003).

5. The Social Security (Incapacity—Increases for Dependants) Regulations 1994 (SI 1994/2945) reg.15(2)(b) (April 13, 1995).

6. The Social Security Act 1998 (Commencement No. 9 and Savings and Consequential and Transitional Provisions) Order 1999 (SI 1992/2422), Sch.2, and The Social Security Act 1998 (Commencment No. 11 and Transitional Provisions) Order 1999 (SI 1999/2860) Sch.2 (October 18, 1999).

7. The Tribunals, Courts and Enforcement Act 2007 (Transitional and Consequential Provisions) Order 2008 (SI 2008/2683) reg.7 (November 3, 2008).

GENERAL NOTE

Interpretation Act 1889
By s.25(2) of the Interpretation Act 1978, this reference is to be treated as a reference to the 1978 Act.

3.41

Provisions as to maintenance for the purposes of increase of benefit in respect of dependants

2.—(1) Subject to paragraph (2), a beneficiary shall not for the purposes of the Act be deemed to be wholly or mainly maintaining another person unless the beneficiary—

3.42

(a) when [^{1}...] incapable of work, or, as the case may be, [^{2}entitled to a Category A or Category B retirement pension], contributes towards the maintenance of that person an amount not less than the amount of increase of benefit received in respect of that person; and

(b) when in employment, or not incapable of work, or, as the case may be, not so [^{2}entitled] (except in a case where the dependency did not arise until after that time) contributed more than half of the actual cost of maintenance of that person.

(2) In a case where—

(a) a person is partly maintained by each of 2 or more other persons each of whom could be entitled to an increase of benefit under the Act in respect of that person if he were wholly or mainly maintaining that person, and

(b) the contributions made by those other persons towards the maintenance of that person amount in the aggregate to sums which, if they were contributed by one of them, would be sufficient to satisfy the foregoing requirements of this regulation,

that person shall for the purposes of the Act be deemed to be wholly or mainly maintained by that one of the said other persons who—

(i) makes the larger or largest contributions to the maintenance of that person, or

(ii) in a case where no person makes the larger or largest contributions as aforesaid, is the elder or eldest of the said other persons, or

(iii) in any case, is a person designated in that behalf by a notice in writing signed by a majority of the said other persons and addressed to the Secretary of State,

so long as that one of the said other persons continues to be entitled to benefit under the Act and to satisfy the condition contained in paragraph (1)(a) of this regulation.

(3) A notice and the designation contained therein given under the foregoing paragraph may be revoked at any time by a fresh notice signed by a majority of such persons and another one of their number may be designated.

AMENDMENTS

1. The Social and Child Support (Jobseeker's Allowance) (Consequential Amendments) Regulations 1996 (SI 1996/1345) reg.12(2) (October 7, 1996).

2. The Social Security (Abolition of Earnings Rule) (Consequential) Regulations 1989 (SI 1989/1642) reg.4 (October 1, 1989).

DEFINITIONS

"the Act"—para.(1).
"beneficiary"—SSCBA 1992 s.122.

GENERAL NOTE

3.43   The primary rule in reg.2(1) requires two conditions to be satisfied:

(1) when incapable of work, the claimant must contribute to the maintenance of the other person an amount equal to or exceeding the amount of the increase of benefit, *and*

(2) when not incapable of work, the claimant must contribute towards the maintenance of the other person an amount exceeding half the *actual* cost of maintaining that other person.

The test under (1) is largely mathematical, but the test under (2) requires a judgment as to what amounts to the actual cost of maintaining a person. It is also arguable that maintenance may be in kind. There are certainly some old Commissioner's decisions which regard payment in kind of items the cost of which would normally be expenditure on day to day living as payment of maintenance: *R(I) 10/51*. Examples would be provision of food, clothes or coal. The principle may also be applicable to the transfer of property to a spouse: *R(U) 3/66*; or even to the transfer of a business share: *R(I) 37/54*.

The secondary rule in para.(2) deals with those rare cases where a dependant is being maintained by more than one person and establishes the order of priority between them in relation to entitlement to an increase of benefit. Note that the preferred beneficiary must also satisfy the condition in para.(1)(a). This is consistent with the principle that increases of benefit are not a means of benefiting the claimant, but to help meet the cost of supporting dependants.

The Family Fund Test

Where a number of people live in the same household, it will often be difficult to determine who supports whom and to what extent. An elaborate test known as the "family fund test" or "method" has been devised over many decades as a means of determining the actual cost of maintaining dependants in such cases and so of determining the amount of contribution required to qualify for an increase of benefit. The applicability of the test was re-affirmed by Tribunals of Commissioners in *R(I) 1/57*, *R(I) 20/60*, and *CS/130/1987*, a starred decision of a Tribunal of Commissioners. In *R(I) 20/60* the Tribunal of Commissioners confirmed that the family fund basis of calculation should be adopted unless it can be shown that it would produce a result which is clearly at variance with the evidence as to the family circumstances. More recently in *R(S) 12/83* the test has been approved and guidance given as to its application. The Commissioner said, "[T]he method should be applied where the maintainer and the person maintained are living in the same household unless there are wholly exceptional circumstances." (para.6). The Commissioner went on to spell out the test as it applies to a claimant. This may be summarised as follows:

3.44

(1) The members of the household are identified.

(2) The weekly income of the household (including its source) is calculated. Income here includes earnings, social security payments including supplementary benefit and family income supplement (now income support and working families' tax credit), and maintenance payments. From these will be deducted reasonable expenses, such as tax and national insurance contributions. The crucial date for determination is the period immediately prior to the incident which gives rise to the claim for an increase for a dependant (for example, immediately before the claimant became incapable of work or unemployed): *CS/130/1987*.

(3) The net weekly income is the family fund which is assumed to be the aggregate cost of maintaining the whole household. Each member of the household aged 14 or over counts as one unit and each member aged 13 or less counts as one-half a unit. The total number of units in the household enables the "unit cost" of each member of the household to be calculated by sharing the family fund in proportion to the units in the household. In *R(S) 7/89*, para.12, the Commissioners note that the time may now be ripe to reconsider the allocation of units and half units "to take account of social conditions at the end of the twentieth century." This point is repeated in *CS/299/1988*.

(4) The net earnings of each member of the household are treated as contributed to the family fund by that member of the household. Occupational pensions are treated as contributed by the member entitled to them (*CS/58/49*) and contributory benefits are regarded as provided by the person on whose national insurance contributions they are paid. Supplementary benefit (and presumably now income support) is *not* attributed to its recipient: *R(S) 7/89(T)* approving para.21 of *R(I) 1/57(T)* and disapproving para.7 of *R(S) 2/85*. It would seem to follow that family income supplement (and now working families' tax credit) is not treated as attributed to its recipient.

(5) Child benefit is not treated as earmarked for the child or children in respect of whom it is paid (see below), though the Commissioner leaves open the question of whether it is contributed by "outsiders" or by the member of the family to whom it is actually paid. The Commissioner's preference in *R(S) 12/83* appears to be that child benefit is contributed by "outsiders". The rationale for the view that child benefit is not earmarked for the child in respect of whom it is payable is that in practice child benefit simply augments the family fund rather than provides resources solely for the child.

(6) The contributions to the family fund are then divided into three groups: (a) those derived from the claimant: (b) those derived from other members of the household; and (c) those derived from "outsiders". The claimant's contribution is first used up against his or her own unit cost. Only if the contribution exceeds the unit cost will there be any surplus available which can be used to contribute to the cost of maintaining others. The same principle is applied to other members of the household. The result is that each member of the household ends up with a surplus or a deficit.

(7) Contributions from outsiders are classified into those which are earmarked for particular members of the household and those which are not. Earmarked contributions are set on one side for the moment, but other contributions are applied rateably to reduce any deficits of members of the household.

(8) Earmarked contributions to the family fund by "outsiders" (for example, additions for dependants, payments of maintenance for children) are applied to reduce any deficit of the member of the household for whom they are earmarked.

(9) Where the amount of a claimant's surplus applied rateably towards meeting the deficits of members of the household amounts to more than one-half of the net unit cost of any member, the claimant is wholly or mainly maintaining that person. If it is less, the claimant is not.

3.45 An example based on figures as at January 1988 for the facts of *R(S) 12/83* will help unravel this complex provision. Suppose a household consists of an unmarried couple, M and W. There are four children, all aged under 11. M is the father of one of them, but not of the other three. Immediately before he becomes incapable of work M's net earnings are £65.00 per week. The family also receives child benefit of £29.00 and FIS of £35.70. The total net income per week is £129.70.

The family consists of four units. M and W are each one unit and each child is one-half unit. The unit cost of M and W is therefore £32.43 (£129.70 divided by four) and of each of the children is £16.21 (£129.70 divided by eight).

The only contributor to the family's income other than outsiders is M who contributes his net wages less his own unit costs: £32.57 (£65.00 less £32.43). M has a surplus of £32.57. By contrast W and each of the children have deficits of £32.43 and £16.21 respectively because they have no income of their own to contribute.

Child benefit and FIS, as contributions from "outsiders" to the family fund, are applied rateably to reduce the deficits of W and the children. So £21.57 is deducted from W's deficit leaving a deficit of £10.86 and £10.79 is deducted from the deficits of each child leaving each with a deficit of £5.42.

It is now the time to consider how M's surplus of £32.57 is to be distributed in order to determine whether he is wholly or mainly maintaining W and the children. In order to be wholly or mainly maintaining them M must contribute more than half of their unit costs out of his surplus. So M must contribute £16.21 to W's maintenance and £8.10 to the maintenance of each child in order to qualify as wholly or mainly maintaining them. Since the remaining deficits are less than these sums, M cannot be said to be wholly or mainly maintaining them. To put it another way M's contribution would need to be £48.61 before he would be deemed on the application of the family fund test to contribute sufficient to meet the test. His contribution is his surplus of £32.57.

In *CS/229/1988* the Commissioner held, distinguishing the treatment of constant attendance allowance in *R(I) 1/57*, that attendance allowance for a child is not to be taken as a contribution to the family fund by either the child or the child's mother as the person with legal entitlement. The Commissioner says that the attendance allowance must be "disregarded altogether".

CU/108/1993 provides a helpful example of the application of the family fund test to modern day circumstances. It clarifies one or two points. Child benefit should be treated as a contribution by the recipient, that is, the parent who receives it (para.5). Maintenance paid for a child should always be earmarked for the child in respect of whom it is paid (para.6). School fees are treated no differently than other payments for the maintenance of the child (para.7). Absence of a child at boarding school does not affect the unit costs for that child (para.8). Loans are disregarded (para.9). Gifts can be distinguished from payments in kind, such as the regular supply of coal to a miner, and should be disregarded (para.9).

Allocation of contributions for [¹ . . .] [² . . .] [¹⁰ spouse or civil partner.]

3.—(1) Subject to the provisions of this regulation, any sum or sums paid by a person by way of contribution towards either or both of the following, that is to say the maintenance of his [¹ spouse] [¹⁰ or civil partner] and the cost of providing for one or more children to which this regulation refers, shall be treated for the purposes of section 31(c)(i), [² . . .], [³ . . .], [⁴ 44(3)(a),] 45(2)(b), [⁴ 45A(2)(b), [⁵ . . .]] 65(1), 66(1)(a), or [⁶ 70(2)] (conditions as to maintenance) as such contributions of such respective amounts equal in the aggregate to the said sum or sums, in respect of such of the persons hereinafter mentioned, that is to say, his [⁷ spouse] [¹⁰ or civil partner] or any child or children to which this regulation refers, as may be determined by the determining authority so as to secure as large a payment as possible by way of benefit in respect of dependants.

3.46

(2) A sum paid by way of contribution towards the maintenance of a [⁸ spouse] [¹⁰ or civil partner] shall not be treated by virtue of this regulation as a sum paid by way of contribution towards the cost of providing for a child or children, and a sum paid by way of contribution towards the cost of providing for a child or children shall not be so treated as a sum paid by way of contribution towards the maintenance of a [⁸ spouse], [¹⁰ or civil partner] unless in either case the [⁸ spouse] [¹⁰ or civil partner] is entitled to child benefit in respect of the child or children.

(3) Except for the purposes of [section 56(1)(c) of the Social Security Contributions and Benefits Act 1992] (child's special allowance), the children to whom this regulation refers are any children in respect of whom, in the period for which the sum in question is paid by the person, that person is entitled to child benefit or could have been so entitled by virtue of regulations had he contributed to the cost of providing for the child at a sufficient weekly rate.

(4) For the purposes of [section 56(1)(c)]—

(a) the children to whom this regulation refers are any such children to whom [section 56(1)(b)] applies;

(b) a determination made under paragraph (1) in order to ascertain the weekly rate at which the husband had before his death been contributing to the cost of providing for a child may be [⁹ superseded] from time to time by the [⁹ Secretary of State] so often as may be necessary to secure as large a payment as possible by way of the child's special allowance, so however that no such [⁹ supersession] shall affect entitlement in respect of any period before the date of the [⁹ supersession]; and

(c) the condition in paragraph (2) shall be deemed to be satisfied if it would have been satisfied but for the fact that the child was not then in Great Britain.

[¹ (5) In the heading to this regulation and in paragraphs (1) and (2) the word "spouse" includes both husband and wife except in relation to maintenance contributions for the purposes of [sections 82(1)(b), 82(3), of the Social Security Contributions and Benefits Act 1992] where it means wife only, and in relation to maintenance contributions for the purposes of [sections 83(2)(b) and 84(2)(b) of the Social Security Contributions and Benefits Act 1992] where it means husband only].

AMENDMENTS

1. The Social Security Benefit (Dependency) Amendment Regulations 1983 (SI 1983/1001) reg.2(2) and (3) (November 21, 1983).
2. The Social Security (Working Tax Credit and Child Tax Credit) (Consequential Amendments) (No.2) Regulations 2003 (SI 2003/937) reg.2 (April 6, 2003).
3. The Social Security and Child Support (Jobseeker's Allowance) (Consequential Amendments) Regulations 1996 (SI 1996/1345) reg.12(3)(a) (October 7, 1996).
4. The Social Security Benefit (Dependency) Amendment (No. 2) Regulations 1985 (SI 1985/1305) reg.2(2) (September 16, 1985).
5. The Social Security (Incapacity—Increases for Dependants) Regulations 1994 (SI 1994/2945) reg.15(3)(a) (April 13, 1995).
6. The Social Security Benefit (Dependency, Claims and Payments and Hospital In-Patients) Amendment Regulations 1984 (SI 1984/1699) reg.3(a) (November 28, 1984).
7. The Social Security Benefit (Dependency) Amendment (No. 2) Regulations 1985 (SI 1985/1305), reg.2(3) (September 16, 1985) and The Social Security and Child Support (Jobseeker's Allowance) (Consequential Amendments) Regulations 1996 (SI 1996/1345) reg.12(3)(b) (October 7, 1996).
8. The Social Security Benefit (Dependency) Amendment Regulations 1983 (SI 1983/1001) reg.2(3) and (4) (November 21, 1983).
9. The Social Security Act 1998 (Commencement No. 12 and Consequential and Transitional Provisions) Order 1999 (SI 1999/3178) Sch.2 (November 29, 1999).
10. Civil Partnership (Pensions, Social Security and Child Support) (Consequential, etc. Provisions) Order 2005 (SI 2005/2877) (December 5, 2005).

GENERAL NOTE

3.47   This regulation contains a principle of allocation which is designed to assist claimants. Regardless of the designation of payments by the payer, maintenance payments are to be apportioned by determining authorities in such a way as to entitle the claimant to the largest payment by way of an increase of benefit. The approach to be taken is to aggregate all maintenance payments and to allocate as the first slice the prescribed amount of maintenance for an adult dependant, as the second slice the prescribed amount for the maintenance of a child, and so on, although there can be no unapportioned residue. There is no possibility of carrying forward any surplus unless, of course, the payment is intended to cover more than one week: *R(S) 3/74*.

[¹ Deeming benefit under the Act abated under [section 74(3) of the Social Security Contributions and Benefits Act 1992] to be a contribution for the maintenance of children or adult dependants]

4.—Where for any period a person (in this regulation referred to as A) is entitled to, or to an increase in the amount of, any benefit prescribed pursuant to [section 74(3)(a) of the Social Security Contributions and Benefits Act 1992] (prevention of duplication of payments) in respect of another person (in this regulation referred to as B) and the amount of, or of the increase in, any such benefit is abated under [section 74(3) of the Social Security Contributions and Benefits Act 1992] then in determining for the purpose of the Act whether A is wholly or mainly maintaining or is contributing at any weekly rate to the maintenance of, or is or has been contributing at any weekly rate to the cost of providing for, B, the amount by which such benefit for any week has been so abated shall be deemed to be a contribution of that amount for that week made by A for the maintenance of B.]

3.48

AMENDMENT

1. The Social Security Benefit (Dependency) Amendment Regulations 1988 (SI 1988/554) reg.2 (April 11, 1988).

GENERAL NOTE

Most payments of most social security benefits, training allowances and social security benefits paid by other Member States of the European Union are prescribed under s.74 of the Administration Act. Section 74(3) provides that where a prescribed benefit, such as child benefit, can be claimed by a person (called A) on the basis of making contributions to the maintenance of another person (called B), then if income support has been paid to B because the contribution was not in fact made, the additional benefit paid to B as a consequence may be deducted from the prescribed benefit paid to A. This regulation contains a corresponding rule to the effect that such deductions count as contributions made by A to the maintenance of B if an issue arises as to whether A is wholly or mainly maintaining B.

3.49

Secretary of State for Work and Pensions v Adams [2003] EWCA Civ 796, Judgment of June 18, 2003, reported as *R(G) 1/03* concerned the question of whether the decision to resume payment of invalid care allowance (now carer's allowance) following the application of reg.4 was a supersession decision under s.10 SSA 1998 or a decision under s.8 SSA 1998 either on a claim for a benefit or under or by virtue of a relevant enactment.

The claimant had for a number of years being caring for his severely disabled partner and had become entitled to an invalid care allowance. He subsequently became entitled to, and in receipt of, an incapacity benefit which overlapped with his invalid care allowance. In accordance with reg.4 the contributory benefit (incapacity benefit) was deducted from the non-contributory benefit (invalid care allowance). The result was that invalid care allowance ceased to be payable. The claimant's incapacity benefit subsequently terminated and the effect was to revive his entitlement to an invalid care allowance. The Court of Appeal concludes that the decision to resume payments is a decision under s.8. The court describes reg.4 as an "accounting provision designed to ensure that parallel payments do not result in excessive payment." (para.20). Were the decision allocated to s.10 the claimant would be deprived of the possibility of backdating the decision.

Circumstances in which a person who is not entitled to child benefit is to be treated as if he were so entitled

3.50   **4A.**—(1) For the purposes of [section 77 of the Social Security Contributions and Benefits Act 1992] (guardian's allowance) or [sections [¹ . . .] 82(4), 85(2) and 90 of the Social Security Contributions and Benefits Act 1992] (increase of benefit in respect of dependent children, and [² . . .] persons having care of dependent children) a person shall be treated as if he were entitled to child benefit in respect of a child for any period throughout which—

(a) child benefit has been awarded to a parent of that child with whom that child is living and with whom that person is residing and either—

(i) the child is being wholly or mainly maintained by that person; or

(ii) that person is also a parent of the child; or

(b) he, or his spouse [⁶ or civil partner] with whom he is residing, would have been entitled to child benefit in respect of that child had the child been born at the end of the week immediately preceding the week in which birth occurred.

(2) [² . . .]

(3) For the purpose of determining whether a person is entitled to a guardian's allowance under [section 77], where in respect of a child that allowance is payable to a person for a continuous period of 7 days and would have been payable to that person for the immediately preceding 7 days had he been entitled to child benefit in respect of that child for an earlier week, he shall be treated as if he were entitled to child benefit in respect of that child for that earlier week.

(4) If for any period a person who is in Great Britain could have been entitled to receive payment of an amount by way of a benefit or allowance or an increase of a benefit or an allowance under the Act in respect of a child or [⁴ . . .] person who has the care of a child but for the fact that in pursuance of any agreement with the government of a country outside the United Kingdom he, or his [⁵ spouse] [⁶ or civil partner] who is residing with him, is entitled in respect of the child in question to the family benefits of that country and is not entitled to child benefit, he shall for the purposes of entitlement to the said payment be treated as if he were entitled to child benefit for the period in question.

(5) The expression "earlier week" in paragraph (3) means the week immediately preceding the first week for which the person referred to in that paragraph was entitled to child benefit in respect of the child referred to in that paragraph.

(6) For the purposes of paragraph (1) the word "week" has the meaning assigned to it by [section 147(1) of the Social Security Contributions and Benefits Act 1992]; and for the purposes of paragraphs (1) and (2) a child shall not be regarded as living with a person unless he can be so regarded for the purposes of [section 143 of the Social Security Contributions and Benefits Act 1992] (meaning of "person responsible for child") of the said Act.

AMENDMENTS

Regulation 4A was inserted by The Social Security Benefit (Dependency) Amendment Regulations 1980 (SI 1980/585) reg.2 (June 2, 1980).

1. The Social Security (Working Tax Credit and Child Tax Credit) (Consequential Amendments) (No. 2) Regulations 2003 (SI 2003/937) reg.2 (April 6, 2003).

2. The Social Security Benefit (Dependency) Amendment Regulations 1989 (SI 1989/523) reg.2 (April 11, 1989).

3. The Social Security Benefit (Dependency) Amendment Regulations 1984 (SI 1984/1698) reg.2(13) (November 26, 1984) subject to savings contained in SI 1984/1698 reg.3.

4. The Social Security Benefit (Dependency) Amendment Regulations 1984 (SI 1984/1968) reg.2(3) (November 26, 1984).

5. The Social Security Benefit (Dependency) Amendment Regulations 1984 (SI 1984/1968) reg.2(3) (November 26, 1984).

6. Civil Partnership (Pensions, Social Security and Child Support) (Consequential, etc. Provisions) Order 2005 (SI 2005/2877) (December 5, 2005).

GENERAL NOTE

This is a deeming rule. If the conditions are satisfied, a person is to be treated as if he or she is entitled to child benefit even though not in fact entitled to the benefit. **3.51**

On "residing together" see the Persons Residing Together Regulations.

The family fund test will be important in determining whether the child is being wholly or mainly maintained under para.(1)(a)(i). See *R(S) 12/83* and notes to reg.2.

[¹ Circumstances in which a person entitled to child benefit is to be treated as if he were not so entitled

4B.—(1) For the purposes of— **3.52**

(a) section 56 (child's special allowance);

(b) section 77 (guardian's allowance);

(c) [² . . .];

(d) section 82(4) (short-term benefits—increase for adult dependants);

(e) [² . . .];

(f) section 90 (increase in benefits for beneficiaries under sections 68 and 70), of the Contributions and Benefits Act, and

(g) paragraphs 4(1) (unemployability supplement: increase for beneficiary's dependent children) and 6(1) (unemployability supplement: increase for dependent adults) of Schedule 7 to,

that Act, a person who is entitled to child benefit in respect of a child shall be treated as if he were not so entitled for the periods referred to in paragraph (2) below.

(2) The periods referred to in paragraph (1) above are—

(a) any period throughout which—

(i) the person referred to in that paragraph, not being a parent of the child, does not fall to be treated as responsible for the child under section 143(1)(a) of the Contributions and Benefits Act, and

(ii) a parent of that child falls to be treated as responsible for the child under the said section 143(1)(a); or

(b) any period throughout which—

(i) that person, not being a parent of that child, falls to be treated as responsible for the child under section 143(1)(a) of the Contributions and Benefits Act, and

589

    (ii) a parent of that child also falls to be treated as responsible for the child under the said section 143(1)(a); or

(c) any day following that day on which that child died.

(3) Sub-paragraph (b) of paragraph (2) shall not apply in the case of a person who is wholly or mainly maintaining the child referred to in that sub-paragraph.

(4) For the purposes of—

    (a) section 37(1) (entitlement to a widowed mother's allowance);

    (b) section 39A(2) (entitlement to a widowed parent's allowance);

    (c) section 56(1)(b);

    (d) section 77(1);

    (e) section 80;

    (f) section 82(4);

    (g) section 85(2);

    (h) section 90;

of the Contributions and Benefits Act, and

    (i) paragraphs 4(1), 6(1) and 18(1)(a)(ii) of Schedule 7 (industrial death benefit: child of deceased's family) to,

that Act, a person who is entitled to child benefit in respect of a child shall be treated as if he were not so entitled for any period for which that benefit is not payable by virtue of any of the provisions referred to in paragraph (5) below.

(5) The provisions referred to in paragraph (4) above are—

    (a) regulation 7 (circumstances in which a person who has ceased to receive full-time education is to continue to be treated as a child);

    (b) regulation 7A (exclusion from benefit of children aged 16 but under the age of 19 who are receiving advanced education);

    (c) regulation 7B (child receiving training under the youth training scheme); or

    (d) regulation 7C (child receiving income support),

of the Child Benefit (General) Regulations 1976 or any provision contained in regulations made under section 144(1) of the Contributions and Benefits Act in so far as those regulations provide that child benefit is not to be payable by virtue of section 142(1)(b) of that Act and regulations made thereunder.]

AMENDMENTS

1. The Social Security (Benefits for Widows and Widowers) (Consequential Amendments) Regulations 2000 reg.5 (SI 2000/1483) (April 9, 2001).

2. The Social Security (Working Tax Credit and Child Tax Credit) (Consequential Amendments) (No. 2) Regulations 2003 (SI 2003/937) reg.2 (April 6, 2003).

GENERAL NOTE

3.53   This regulation contains a corresponding deeming rule to that contained in reg.4A. It deems a person entitled to child benefit not to be so entitled if the conditions of the regulation are satisfied.

PART II

CHILD DEPENDANTS

Contributions towards cost of providing for child

5.—(1) Where, apart from [section 81(1) and (2) of the Social Security   3.54
Contributions and Benefits Act 1992], a person is entitled to receive, in
respect of a particular child, payment under the Act of an amount by way
of a child's special allowance ([section 56]), or a guardian's allowance
([section 77]) or of an increase under any of the provisions of [section 80
of the Social Security Contributions and Benefits Act 1992] of any benefit,
or payment of an increase or allowance of any amount under section 64
or section 70, for any period, and neither of the conditions set out in the
following paragraphs is satisfied, that person shall nevertheless for the purposes of the said [section 81(1) or (2) of the Social Security Contributions
and Benefits Act 1992] be deemed as respects that period to be making the
contributions so required at a weekly rate not less than that required by the
said section [81(1) or (2)] if—
   (a) he gives an undertaking in writing to make such contributions; and
   (b) on receiving the amount of the allowance or increase in question, he
       in fact makes such contributions.
   (2) The conditions referred to in paragraph (1) are—
   (a) the person would be treated for the purposes of [Part IX of the Social
       Security Contributions and Benefits Act 1992] as having the child
       living with him; or
   (b) contributions are being made to the cost of providing for the child at
       a rate equal to the amount of the relevant increase of benefit.
   (3) Where, in respect of any period, the person referred to in this regulation fails to make the contributions which he has undertaken to make in
accordance with the first paragraph of this regulation, the decision awarding the increase or allowance in question for that period in respect of the
child shall be revised.
   (4) [¹ . . .]
   [² (5) Except in a case to which regulation 15 (preservation of entitlement to benefit in payment before April 4, 1977 for a child dependant) or
regulation 13A of the Social Security Benefit (Persons Abroad) Regulations
1975, as amended (modification of the Act in relation to title to benefit for
beneficiary's child dependants) applies, paragraph (b) of [section 81(3) of
the Social Security Contributions and Benefits Act 1992] (contributions
mentioned in those paragraphs to be over and above those required for the
purposes of [section 143(1)(b) of the Social Security Contributions and
Benefits Act 1992]) shall not apply in a case where neither the beneficiary
nor his spouse [³ or, as the case may be, his civil partner] (or if he has a
spouse [³ or civil partner] and his spouse [³ or civil partner] is residing with
him) is in fact entitled to child benefit in respect of the child in question.]

AMENDMENTS

   1. The Social Security Benefit (Miscellaneous Amendments) Regulations 1978
(SI 1978/433) reg.7 (April 3, 1978).

2. The Social Security Benefit (Dependency) Amendment Regulations 1977 (SI 1977/620) reg.2 (April 4, 1977).

3. The Civil Partnership (Pensions, Social Security and Child Support) (Consequential, etc. Provisions) Order 2005 (SI 2005/2877) (December 5, 2005).

GENERAL NOTE

3.55   This useful regulation allows a claimant who fails to satisfy the requirements of para.(2) to give an undertaking in writing to make contributions for the maintenance of a child of an amount equal to the benefit or increase of benefit in order to qualify for one of the benefits mentioned in the regulation. Failure to make the promised payments results in revision of entitlement (para.(3)). Care must be taken that the claimant increases the payments to the level of any benefit increases: *R(S) 3/74.* The undertaking cannot operate retrospectively for more than a week; *R(U) 3/78,* but a later undertaking may be regarded as merely confirming an earlier undertaking even though there has been a break in the payments made under the earlier undertaking: *R(U) 6/79.*

3.56   *Regulation 6 revoked by The Social Security (Computation of Earnings) Regulations 1996 (SI 1996/2745), Sch.4 (November 25, 1996).*

3.57   *Regulation 7 revoked by The Social Security Benefit (Dependency) Amendment Regulations 1980 (SI 1980/585), reg.3 (June 2, 1980).*

PART III

ADULT DEPENDANTS

Earnings rules for increases for adult dependants

3.58   **8.**—(1) This paragraph applies in cases where an increase of benefit is claimed [¹ . . .] in respect of a spouse who is residing with the beneficiary and the increase is claimed under any of the following provisions of the Contributions and Benefits Act—

(a) section 83(2) (increase of Category A or Category C retirement pension in respect of a wife); [⁴ or]

(b) section 84(1) (increase of Category A retirement pension in respect of a husband); [⁴ . . .]

(c) [⁴ . . .]

[⁴ (1A)This paragraph applies in cases where an increase of benefit is claimed in respect of a spouse or a civil partner who, in either case, is residing with the beneficiary and the increase is claimed under paragraph 6(1)(a)(i) of Schedule 7 to the Contributions and Benefits Act (increase of disablement pension in respect of a spouse or civil partner where beneficiary entitled to unemployability supplement).]

(2) Where paragraph (1) [⁴ or (1A)] applies, there shall be no increase of benefit for any period during which the beneficiary is residing with his spouse [⁴ or civil partner] and his spouse [⁴ or civil partner] has earnings if the earnings of the spouse [⁴ or civil partner] in the week in that period which falls immediately before the week in which the beneficiary is entitled to benefit under any provision specified in paragraph (1) exceed [² the amount for the time being

specified in regulation 79(1)C of the Jobseeker's Allowance regulations 1996 (age related amount for a claimant who has attained the age of 25).]

(3) Where the person referred to in section 85(2) of the Contributions and Benefits Act ("the dependant") is residing with the pensioner, the weekly rate of a pension to which section 85 of that Act applies shall be increased by the amount specified in relation to that pension in column 3 of Part IV of Schedule 4 to that Act but there shall be no increase of pension for any period—

(a) during which the pensioner is residing with the dependant; and

(b) the dependant has earnings,

if the earnings of the dependant in the week in that period which falls immediately before the week in which the pensioner is entitled to the pension exceed [² the amount as for the time being specified in regulation 79(1)(c) of the Jobseeker's Allowance Regulations 1996 (age related amount for a claimant who has attained the age of 25).]

(4) Where the person referred to in paragraph 6(1)(b) of Schedule 7 to the Contributions and Benefits Act ("the dependant") is residing with the beneficiary, the weekly rate of the disablement pension to which that paragraph applies shall be increased by the amount referred to in paragraph 8 of Part V of Schedule 4 to that Act but there shall be no increase of disablement pension for any period—

(a) during which the beneficiary is residing with the dependant; and

(b) the dependant has earnings,

if the earnings of the dependant in the week in that period which falls immediately before the week in which the beneficiary is entitled to a disablement pension [² exceed the amount as for the time being specified in regulation 79(1)(c) of the Jobseeker's Allowance Regulations 1996 (age related amount for a claimant who has attained the age of 25).]

(5) In determining the earnings of a dependant for the purposes of paragraphs (3) and (4), no account shall be taken of any earnings of that person from employment by the pensioner or the beneficiary as the case may be in caring for a child or children in respect of whom the pensioner or the beneficiary is entitled to child benefit.

(6) Where an increase of benefit is claimed in respect of a spouse [⁴ or civil partner] who is not residing with the beneficiary and the increase is claimed under paragraph 6(1)(a)(ii) of Schedule 7 to the Contributions and Benefits Act there shall be no increase of benefit for any period during which the beneficiary is contributing to the maintenance of the spouse at a rate less than the standard rate of the increase and the weekly earnings of the spouse [⁴ or civil partner] exceed that rate.

(7) In this regulation—

(a) "week" means—

(i) in relation to Category A or Category C retirement pension the period of 7 days beginning with the day on which in accordance with the provisions of regulation 22 of and paragraph 5 of Schedule 6 to the Social Security (Claims and Payments) Regulations 1987(a) is the day for payment of the retirement pension in question; and

(ii) in relation to any other benefit [³ any period of 7 days corresponding to the week in respect of which the relevant social security benefit is due to be paid or ending on the day before the first day of the first such week following the date of claim]; and

(b) any reference to earnings includes a reference to payments by way of occupational or personal pension.

AMENDMENTS

This regulation was substituted by the Social Security (Dependency) Amendment Regulations 1992 (SI 1992/3041) reg.3 (December 5, 1992).

1. The Social Security (Incapacity—Increases for Dependants) Regulations 1994 (SI 1992/2945) reg.15(4) (April 13, 1995).

2. The Social Security and Child Support (Jobseeker's Allowance) (Consequential Amendments) Regulations 1996 (SI 1996/1345) reg.12(4) (October 7, 1996).

3. The Social Security (Computation of Earnings) Regulations 1996 (SI 1996/2745) reg.17(a) (November 25, 1996).

4. The Civil Partnership (Pensions, Social Security and Child Support) (Consequential, etc. Provisions) Order 2005 (SI 2005/2877) (December 5, 2005).

GENERAL NOTE

3.59   On "having the care of a child" see annotations to s.82 of the C & BA 1992. The revised text of reg.8 set out above was inserted with effect from December 5, 1992, by the Social Security Benefit (Dependency) Amendment Regulations 1992 (SI 1992/3041). There is an important transitional provision in reg.4 of the Amendment Regulations preserving entitlement under the earlier text for those in receipt of an increase of benefit on December 4, 1992.

Two relevant unreported decisions on reg.8(6) as previously enacted are *CP/068/1989* (printed as Appendix to *R(P) 3/93*) and *R(P) 3/93*. The latter decision holds that increases of invalidity benefit and of retirement pension are different increases even though the amounts at the material time were the same. So a claimant moving from increase of invalidity benefit to increase of retirement pension on attaining the age of 70 lost the protection of reg.8(6).

In *CP/3017/2004* the Commissioner said,

"6. Before going on to mention the legislative provisions that set out rules for calculating earnings for the purposes of benefits including retirement pension, there is one oddity arising from regulation 8(2) of the Dependency Regulations to be examined. Regulation 8(2) lays down a test to be applied week by week for each week of payment of retirement pension (see the definition in regulation 8(7)(a)), which test depends on the spouse's earnings in the previous week. The application of a week by week test seems to be reinforced by section 92 of the Social Security Contributions and Benefits Act 1992, which applies where an award of an increase has been made and causes the award to continue in force even though entitlement is interrupted by a week or weeks in which the spouse's earnings exceed the limit. In the present case, the first week of payment of retirement pension to the claimant would have been that beginning on Monday 31 May 2004. It might be said that at the date of the decision in question there could have been absolutely no evidence of what the wife's earnings would be in the week commencing Monday 24 May 2004 or in any subsequent week. How therefore could a decision be given disallowing an increase?

7. The main answer stems from regulation 15(1) of the Claims and Payments Regulations and the decision of the Tribunal of Commissioners in *CDLA/2751/2003* and others, about advance renewal claims for disability living allowance (DLA). It was held there that the legislative power to make an award of DLA in advance of the start date of the period of the award carried with it the power to disallow the claim in advance. The same must also apply to regulation 15(1), so that there is a power to disallow a claim for an increase of retirement pension for a wife up to four months before a claimant might become entitled to the pension. Then, in accordance with section 8(2) of the Social Security Act 1998 as explained by the Tribunal of Commissioners, in making such a decision

the Secretary of State would be prohibited from taking into account any changes of circumstances anticipated to occur after the date of the decision. Equally, on appeal, an appeal tribunal would be prohibited from taking into account any actual changes of circumstances after that date (Social Security Act 1998, section 12(8)(b)). The Tribunal of Commissioners seems to have thought that if there was change of circumstances in favour of a claimant between the date of the decision and the date from which the disallowance of the claim took effect, there could be a supersession on the ground of relevant change of circumstances (Social Security and Child Support (Decisions and Appeals) Regulations 1999, regulation 6(2)(a)(i)). However, there is a problem with that view because regulation 6(2)(a)(i), as amended with effect from 5 May 2003, allows supersession only where there has been a relevant change of circumstances since the decision to be superseded "had effect". That seems to rule out a supersession for a change occurring between the date of an advance decision and its effective date. A claimant would thus be restricted to making a fresh claim, on the basis of the changed circumstances, from some date after the effective date of the disallowing decision.
8. In paragraph 24 of *CDLA/2751/2003* and others, the Tribunal of Commissioners did suggest that, in some cases where there was likely to be a significant change of circumstances before the start date of the period covered by a claim, it might well be good practice to defer making a decision until it was known whether that change had actually materialised. It seems to me that the present case is one where that course should have been taken. It was plain from the evidence provided that the claimant's wife's earnings fluctuated a great deal from one pay period to another. And the nature of the case is different from that of a person suffering some potentially disabling or incapacitating condition, where in most cases there can be a sensible prediction about how the condition might progress in the future. It was simply unknown on 3 March 2004 what the claimant's wife's earnings might be in the week prior to 31 May 2004. Quite apart from the doubts that I explain below about the averaging process carried out by the officer, it would have been better to have waited until close to 28 May 2004 and then considered the current evidence about the wife's earnings. I do not think that there would have been any difficulty in making an advance decision on the claimant's own retirement pension entitlement, but deferring the decision on the increase. However, that did not happen. A decision disallowing the increase was made on 3 March 2004 and I must deal with the consequences."

In para.21 of his decision, the Commissioner concluded,   **3.60**

"21. If I adopt the same method as the officer who made the decision of 3 March 2004 and take an average of the seven payslips, counting only the taxable pay, the result is £32.59 per week. With the addition of the weekly amount of the wife's occupational pension, the total earnings are well below the limit in regulation 8(2) of the Dependency Regulations. I have doubts about the use of averaging under regulation 8(3) of the Computation of Earnings Regulations. That provision allows averaging over a recognisable cycle of work or some other period that will allow average weekly earnings to be identified more accurately. But, for the reasons given in paragraph 6 above, the Dependency Regulations may properly work on the amount of actual earnings received week by week (with payments received at other intervals spread according to the rules in regulation 8(1) and (2) of the Computation of Earnings Regulations). If so, the use of an average figure might not be appropriate at all. But I do not have to decide the issue. I have already shown that the result of averaging under regulation 8(3) is in favour of the claimant. If I do not apply regulation 8(3), the circumstances as at 3 March 2004 were that, for six of the payments in evidence, the weekly equivalent of the earnings received was below the limit, usually well below. It was only in respect of the payment received on 14 December 2003 that the weekly equivalent (£98) was over the limit. There might well have been unusual circumstances in the run-up to Christmas. Looking at that evidence, and not knowing what earnings had been received immediately before 3 March 2004, I have no difficulty in concluding that the level of the wife's earnings to be taken into account in respect of the period from 28 May 2004 onwards is below the limit in regulation 8(2) of the Dependency Regulations. Thus, on either approach, the claimant's appeal succeeds and he is to be awarded the increase of retirement pension."

There has been no reg.9 since September 16, 1985 when the former regs 8 and 9 were replaced by a revised reg.8.

Apportionment of payments by way of occupational [¹ or personal] pension made otherwise than weekly

3.61   **9A.**—[² For the purposes of section 89(1) of, and paragraph 7(1) of Schedule 7 to, the Contributions and Benefits Act, where payment by way of occupational or personal pension, or for the purposes of section 89(1A) of that Act by way of PPF periodic payment,] is for any period made otherwise than weekly, the amount of any such payment for any week in that period shall be determined—

(a) where payment is made for a year, by dividing the total by 52;

(b) where payment is made for three months, by dividing the total by 13;

(c) where payment is made for a month, by multiplying the total by 12 and dividing the result by 52;

(d) where payment is made for two or more months, otherwise than for a year or for three months, by dividing the total by the number of months, multiplying the result by 12 and dividing the result of that multiplication by 52; or

(e) in any other case, by dividing the amount of the payment by the number of days in the period for which it is made and multiplying the result by 7.

AMENDMENTS

Regulation 9A was inserted by The Social Security Benefit (Dependency) Amendment Regulations 1989 (SI 1989/523) reg.5 (April 11, 1989).

1. The Social Security (Miscellaneous Provisions) Amendment Regulations 1992 (SI 1992/247) reg.4(2) (March 9, 1992). This amendment is superseded by the amendment listed below.

2. The Social Security (PPF Payments and FAS Payments) (Consequential Amendments) Regulations 2006 (SI 2006/1069) reg.2 (May 5, 2006).

Increase of benefit for [¹ . . .] person having care of child [¹⁴ or qualifying young person]

3.62   **10.**—(1) Subject to the provisions of [section 82 of the Social Security Contributions and Benefits Act 1992] (increase [² . . .] of a maternity allowance), [section 85 of the Social Security Contributions and Benefits Act 1992] (increase of a Category A or Category C retirement pension [³ . . .]), or section 66 (increase [² . . .] of a disablement pension where the beneficiary is entitled to an unemployability supplement), this regulation shall apply for the purpose of determining whether a beneficiary is entitled to an increase of benefit under [section 82(3) and 85(2) of the Social Security Contributions and Benefits Act 1992] in respect of a [⁴ . . .] person who has the care of a child or children [^{14} or a qualifying young person or persons] in respect of whom the beneficiary is entitled to child benefit.

(2) A beneficiary shall not be entitled to an increase under the said [section 82(3) and 85(2)] unless the [^{4} . . .] person referred to in those sections—

    (a) has the care of such a child [^{14} or qualifying young person] as is referred to in those sections [^{5} . . .]; and

    (b) either—

        (i) is residing with the beneficiary, or

        (ii) is employed by him in an employment in respect of which the weekly expenses incurred by the beneficiary are not less than the standard rate of increase and was so employed by him before he became [^{6} . . .] incapable of work or [^{7} entitled to a Category A or Category B retirement pension], as the case may be, subject to the qualification that the condition of employment before that event shall not apply in a case where the necessity for [^{8} the] employment first arose thereafter; or

        (iii) is a person to whose maintenance the beneficiary is contributing at a weekly rate not less than the standard rate of increase; and

    (c) subject to paragraph (3), is not absent from Great Britain; and

    (d) is not undergoing imprisonment or detention in legal custody; and

[^{9} (e) either—

        (i) has no earnings or has earnings but they do not exceed the standard rate of increase (there being disregarded for this purpose any earnings derived from employment by the beneficiary in caring for a child or children [^{14} or a qualifying young person or persons] in respect of whom the beneficiary is entitled to child benefit), or

        (ii) is employed by the beneficiary in caring for such child or children [^{14} or a qualifying young person or persons] and is not residing with him;]

    (f) [^{10} . . .]

(3) In the case of [^{11} . . .] any pension to which this regulation applies, the condition referred to in sub-paragraph (c) of paragraph (2) shall not apply as respects any period during which the said [^{11} . . .] person is residing with the beneficiary outside Great Britain and for which by virtue of the provisions of any regulations made under section 82(5) (disqualification) or 131 (persons outside Great Britain) the beneficiary is not disqualified for receiving that benefit.

    (4) [^{12} . . .].

    (5) [^{13} . . .].

AMENDMENTS

1. The Social Security Benefit (Dependency) Amendment Regulations 1984 (SI 1984/1698) reg.10 (November 26, 1984).

2. The Social Security and Child Support (Jobseeker's Allowance) (Consequential Amendments) Regulations 1996 (SI 1996/1345) reg.12(7)(a) (October 7, 1996).

3. The Social Security (Incapacity—Increases for Dependants) Regulations 1994 (SI 1994/2945) reg.15(5)(a) (April 13, 1995).

4. The Social Security (Abolition of Injury Benefit) (Consequential) Regulations 1983 (SI 1983/186) reg.7(3) (April 6, 1983).

5. The Social Security Benefit (Dependency, Claims and Payments and

Hospital In-Patients) Amendments Regulations 1984 (SI 1984/1699) reg.3(b) (November 26, 1984).

6. The Social Security and Child Support (Jobseeker's Allowance) (Consequential Amendments) Regulations 1996 (SI 1996/1345) reg.12(7)(b) (October 7, 1996).

7. The Social Security (Abolition of Earnings Rule) (Consequential) Regulations 1989 (SI 1989/1642) reg.4 (October 1, 1989).

8. The Social Security Benefit (Dependency) Amendment Regulations 1984 (SI 1984/1698) reg.2(6) (November 26, 1984).

9. The Social Security Benefit (Dependency) Amendment Regulations 1989 (SI 1989/523) reg.6 (April 11, 1989).

10. The Social Security Benefit (Dependency) Amendment Regulations 1989 (SI 1989/523) reg.7 (April 11, 1989).

11. The Social Security Benefit (Dependency) Amendment Regulations 1984 (SI 1984/1698) reg.2(9) (November 26, 1984).

12. The Social Security Benefit (Dependency) Amendment Regulations 1985 (SI 1985/1190) reg.5 (September 16, 1985).

13. The Social Security Benefit (Dependency) Amendment Regulations 1984 (SI 1984/1698) reg.8 (January 1, 1979).

14. The Social Security (Provisions relating to Qualifying Young Persons) (Amendment) Regulations 2006 (SI 2006/692) (April 10, 2006).

GENERAL NOTE

3.63   On "residing together," see the Persons Residing Together Regulations.
On "having the care of a child," see annotations to s.82 of the SSCBA 1992.

Contribution to maintenance of adult dependant

3.64   **11.**—(1) Subject to paragraphs (2) and (3), for the purposes of [section 82(1) and (3), 83(2), 84 of the Social Security Contributions and Benefits Act 1992] (increase of a Category A or Category C retirement pension or benefit to which section 66 applies in respect of a spouse) or of regulation 10(2)(b)(iii) (increase of a Category A or Category C retirement pension or benefit to which section 66 applies in respect of a person having the care of a child [or qualifying young person])—

(a) a beneficiary shall not be deemed to satisfy the requirement contained in the said sections or the said regulation that he is contributing to the maintenance of the spouse or the person having the care of a child [or qualifying young person], as the case may be, at a weekly rate of not less than the standard rate of increase unless when in employment, or not incapable of work, or not entitled to a Category A or Category B retirement pension, as the case may be (except in a case where the dependency did not arise until later), he contributed to that spouse's or person's maintenance at a weekly rate of not less than the standard rate of increase;

(b) in a case where an increase of benefit is, apart from the said requirement, payable at a weekly rate less than the standard rate of increase, a beneficiary shall, subject to sub-paragraph (a) above, be deemed to satisfy the said requirement if he is contributing to the maintenance of the spouse or person having the care of a child [or qualifying young person], as the case may be, at a weekly rate of not less than that of the increase.

[(1A) Subject to paragraphs (2) and (3), for the purposes of section 82 of, and paragraph 6(1)(a)(i) of Schedule 7 to, the Contributions and Benefits Act (increase of maternity allowance and increase of disablement pension where beneficiary entitled to unemployability supplement) a beneficiary shall not be deemed to satisfy the requirement contained in those provisions (that he is contributing to the maintenance of his civil partner at a weekly rate of not less than the standard rate of increase) unless when in employment, or not incapable of work, or not entitled to a Category A or a Category B retirement pension, as the case may be (except in a case where the dependency did not arise until later), he contributed to his civil partner's maintenance at a weekly rate not less than the standard rate of increase.]

(2) Where, within one month of having been entitled to an increase of unemployment benefit under [section 82(1) of the Social Security Contributions and Benefits Act 1992] or under [section 82(3)(c) of the Social Security Contributions and Benefits Act 1992] by virtue of having satisfied the requirement in head (iii) of sub-paragraph (b) of regulation 10(2) (but no other requirement in that sub-paragraph), or of having been entitled to an increase of short-term incapacity benefit by virtue of having satisfied the requirements of regulation 9(1)(b) or (3) (b) of the Social Security (Incapacity Benefit—Increases for Dependents) Regulations 1994, a person becomes entitled to a benefit which attracts a standard rate of increase higher than that of the benefit to which he had been entitled, he shall be deemed to satisfy the condition in paragraph (1) (a) if he satisfies it in relation to the benefit to which he had been entitled; and in this paragraph "entitled" includes deemed to have been entitled.

(2A) Where, within one month of having been entitled to an increase of unemployment benefit under [section 82(3)(a) of the Social Security Contributions and Benefits Act 1992] by virtue of contributing to the maintenance of her husband at a weekly rate not less than the standard rate of the increase, or of having been entitled to an increase of shortterm incapacity benefit by virtue of having satisfied the requirements of regulation 9(1)(b) or (3)(b) of the Social Security (Incapacity Benefit—Increases for Dependents) Regulations 1994, a woman becomes entitled to a benefit which attracts a standard rate of increase higher than that of the benefit to which she had been entitled, she shall be deemed to satisfy the condition in paragraph (1)(a) if she satisfies it in relation to the benefit to which she had been entitled, and in this paragraph "entitled" includes deemed to have been entitled.

(3) For the purposes of paragraphs (2) and (2A) a person shall be deemed to have been entitled to an increase of unemployment benefit at a lower standard rate of increase if (assuming satisfaction of the relevant contribution conditions) he would have been so entitled but for the provisions of [section 82(1)(b) of the Social Security Contributions and Benefits Act 1992] or, as the case may be, regulation 10(2)(e) or the condition of [section 82(3)(a) of the Social Security Contributions and Benefits Act 1992] that her husband is not engaged in any one or more employments from which his weekly earnings exceed the standard rate of increase.

(4) Where a person is entitled to an addition to a contribution-based jobseeker's allowance under regulation 9(4) of the Jobseeker's Allowance (Transitional Provisions) Regulations 1995 by virtue of having satisfied the requirements for an increase of unemployment benefit referred to in paragraphs (2), (2A) or (3), he shall be treated for the purposes of those paragraphs as if he had been entitled to an increase of unemployment benefit.

AMENDMENTS

There have been multiple small amendments to the text of reg.11, none of which appear to be time sensitive. Accordingly the text of the regulation is printed above without multiple annotations.

Paragraph (1) has been amended by:

> The Social Security Benefit (Dependency) Amendment Regulations 1983 (SI 1983/1001); The Social Security Benefit (Dependency) Amendment Regulations 1984 (SI 1984/1698);

> The Social Security (Abolition of Earnings Rule) (Consequential) Regulations 1989 (SI 1989/1642);

> The Social Security (Incapacity—Increases for Dependants) Regulations 1994 (SI 1994/2945); and

> The Social Security and Child Support (Jobseeker's Allowance) (Consequential Amendments) Regulations 1996 (SI 1996/1345).

> Paragraph (1A) was inserted by the Civil Partnership (Pensions, Social Security and Child Support) (Consequential, etc. Provisions) Order 2005 (SI 2005/2877) (December 5, 2005).

> The Social Security (Provisions relating to Qualifying Young Persons) (Amendment) Regulations 2006 (SI 2006/692) (April 10, 2006).

Paragraph (2) has been amended by:

> The Social Security Benefit (Amendment) Regulations 1987 (SI 1987/355);

> The Social Security (Incapacity—Increases for Dependants) Regulations 1994 (SI 1994/2945).

Paragraph (2A) was inserted by The Social Security Benefit (Amendment) Regulations 1987 (SI 1987/355) and has been amended by The Social Security (Incapacity—Increases for Dependants) Regulations 1994 (SI 1994/2945).

Paragraph (3) has been amended by The Social Security (Incapacity—Increases for Dependants) Regulations 1994 (SI 1994/2945).

Paragraph (4) was added by The Social Security and Child Support (Jobseeker's Allowance) (Consequential Amendments) Regulations 1996 (SI 1996/1345).

GENERAL NOTE

3.65   On "having the care of a child," see annotations to s.82 of the SSCBA 1992.

PART IV

MISCELLANEOUS

Prescribed circumstances for the purposes of section 90 of the Social Security Contributions and Benefits Act

3.66   **12.**—(1) The provisions of Part IV of the Contributions and Benefits Act (increases for dependants) and of the Social Security (Incapacity Benefit—Increases for Dependants) Regulations 1994 shall apply in relation to increases of severe disablement allowance for child or adult dependants under section 90 of the Contributions and Benefits Act as they apply to increases of long-term incapacity benefit for child or adult dependants.

(2) For the purposes of increases of [¹ carer's allowance] for child or adult dependants under section 90 of the Contributions and Benefits Act, the prescribed circumstances in which a beneficiary is entitled to such an increase shall be as set out in Schedule 2 to these Regulations.

AMENDMENTS

Regulation 12 substituted by The Social Security (Incapacity—Increases for Dependants) Regulations 1994 (SI 1994/2945) reg.15(7) (April 13, 1995).
1. The Social Security Amendment (Carer's Allowance) Regulations 2002 (SI 2002/2497) reg.3 and Sch.2 (April 1, 2003).

Regulation 13 revoked by The Social Security and Child Support (Jobseeker's Allowance) (Consequential Amendments) Regulations 1996 (SI 1996/1345) from October 7, 1996.   **3.67**

Regulation 14 ceased to have effect from October 5, 1986.   **3.68**

PART V

TRANSITIONAL PROVISION AND REVOCATIONS

Preservation of entitlement to benefit in payment before 4th April, 1977 for a child dependant

15.—Where—   **3.69**
  (a) immediately before 4th April, 1977 a person is absent from Great Britain other than temporarily; and
  (b) as respects a period before and including 3rd April, 1977 he satisfies the conditions then in force for, and is entitled to receive, payment of an amount by way of a benefit or allowance or an increase of a benefit or an allowance under the Act in respect of a child who is ordinarily resident in Great Britain; and
  (c) would cease, as from 4th April, 1977, to be entitled to that payment by reason of the fact that he does not satisfy one of the conditions for receiving such a payment, namely, that he is entitled to child benefit in respect of that child,
that person shall, for any period beginning not earlier than 4th April, 1977 during which he would, or could had he made an appropriate claim, be entitled to child benefit in respect of that child were he not absent from Great Britain, be treated as so entitled while he continues to satisfy all other conditions applicable to such a payment (including making contributions to the cost of providing for that child over and above those that would have been required for the purpose of satisfying subsection (1)(b) of section 3 of the Child Benefit Act) unless subsequent to 4th April, 1977 he becomes ordinarily resident in Great Britain.

Regulation 15A revoked by The Social Security Benefit (Dependency) Amendment Regulations 1984 (SI 1984/1698) as from November 26, 1984.   **3.70**

Regulation 16 omitted.   **3.71**

PRESCRIBED CIRCUMSTANCES FOR INCREASE OF [⁴ A CARER'S ALLOWANCE]

PART I

Increase of [⁴ carer's allowance] for child dependants

3.72   **1.**—For the purposes of increases of [⁴ carer's allowance] for child dependants under [section 90 of the Contributions and Benefits Act 1992], the prescribed circumstances in which a beneficiary is entitled to such an increase for any period shall be as set out in the following paragraphs.

2.—The week rate of [⁴ a carer's allowance] for any period for which the beneficiary is entitled to child benefit in respect of a child or children shall be increased in respect of that child, or each respectively of those children, by the appropriate amount specified in relation to that allowance in column (2) of Part IV of Schedule 4 to the Act.

[² **2A.**—Where—

[⁶ (a) a beneficiary is a member of a couple; and]

(b) the other [⁶ member of a couple] has earnings in any week,

the beneficiary's right to payment of increases for the following week under paragraph 2 above shall be determined in accordance with paragraph 2B below.

2B.—No such increase shall be payable—

(a) in respect of the first child where the earnings were [¹² £240] or more; and

(b) in respect of a further child for each complete [¹⁰ £32] by which the earnings exceeded [¹² £240].

[² **2BB.**—The provisions of paragraphs 2A and 2B above shall not apply so as to affect entitlement to an increase of [⁴ carer's allowance] in respect of a child in any case where the beneficiary—

(a) was entitled to receive such an increase immediately before 26th November, 1984; and

(b) throughout the period from and including that date to the date of coming into operation of this paragraph was, or but for the operation of those paragraphs would have been, continuously so entitled,

until such time as he would otherwise first cease to be so entitled.]

[² **2C.**—In this Part of this Schedule—

[⁶ . . .]

[¹¹ "couple" means—

(a) two people who are married to, or civil partners of, each other and are members of the same household; or

(b) two people who are not married to, or civil partners of, each other but are living together as a married couple;]

[³ "week" means any period of 7 days corresponding to the week in respect of which the relevant social security benefit is due to be paid or ending on the day before the first day of the first such week following the date of claim.]]

3.—Where a person is entitled to receive payment of an amount by way of an increase of [⁴ a carer's allowance] under paragraph 2 above, that increase shall not be payable unless one of the following conditions is satisfied—

(a) that the beneficiary would be treated for the purposes of [Part IX of the Contributions and Benefits Act 1992] as having the child living with him; or

(b) that the requisite contributions are being made to the cost of providing for the child.

4.—The condition specified in paragraph 3(b) above is to be treated as satisfied if, but only if—

(a) such contributions are being made at a weekly rate not less than the amount referred to in paragraph 2 above—

(i) by the beneficiary, or

(ii) where the beneficiary is one of two spouses [⁶ or civil partners] residing together, by them together; and

(b) the contributions are over and above those required for the purposes of satisfying [section 143(1)(b) of the Social Security Contributions and Benefits Act 1992].

5.—Any sum or sums paid by a person by way of contribution towards the cost of providing for two or more children being children in respect of whom, in the period for which the sum in question is paid by the person, he is entitled to child benefit shall be treated as such contributions, of such respective amounts equal in the aggregate to the said sum or sums, in respect of those children so as to secure as large a payment as possible by way of [¹ carer's allowance] in respect of them.

Part II

Increase of [⁴ carer's allowance] for adult dependants

6.—For the purposes of increases of [⁴ carer's allowance] for adult dependants under [⁹ section 90 of the Social Security Contributions and Benefits Act], the prescribed circumstances in which a beneficiary is entitled to such an increase for any period shall be as set out in paragraph 7 below.

3.73

7.—The weekly rate of an [⁴ carer's allowance] shall be increased by the amount specified in relation to that allowance in column (3) of Part IV of Schedule 4 to [⁹ the Contributions and Benefits Act] for any period during which the beneficiary is residing with—

    (a) a spouse [⁶ or civil partner] whose weekly earnings do not exceed that amount; or

    (b) some person (not being a child [⁷ or qualifying young person]) who—

        (i) has the care of a child or children [⁷ or a qualifying young person or persons] in respect of whom the beneficiary is entitled to child benefit;

       (ii) is not undergoing imprisonment or detention in legal custody;

      (iii) if he has earnings, does not have weekly earnings exceeding that amount and for this purpose there shall be disregarded any weekly earnings derived from employment by the beneficiary in caring for a child or children [⁷ or a qualifying young person or persons] in respect of whom the beneficiary is entitled to child benefit;

      (iv) is not absent from Great Britain, except for any period during which the person is residing with the beneficiary outside Great Britain and for which the beneficiary is entitled to an [⁴ carer's allowance].

8.—A person who is entitled to an increase of [⁴ a carer's allowance] under paragraph 7(a) above shall not be entitled to an increase of that benefit under paragraph 7(b) above. [⁸ or PPF periodical payment.]

9.—(1) Subject to sub-paragraph (2) below in this Schedule any reference to earnings includes a reference to payments by way of occupational or personal pension.

(2) Sub-paragraph (1) above shall not apply so as to affect entitlement to an increase of [⁴ carer's allowance] in respect of a child or adult dependant in any case where the beneficiary—

    (a) was entitled to receive such an increase immediately before this paragraph came into operation; and

    (b) but for the operation of sub-paragraph (1) above would continue to be so entitled, until such time as he would first otherwise cease to be so entitled.

AMENDMENTS

1. The Social Security Benefit (Dependency, Claims and Payments and Hospital In-Patients) Amendment Regulations 1984 (SI 1984/1699) reg.3 (November 26, 1984).

2. The Social Security Benefit (Dependency) Amendment Regulations 1987 (SI 1987/355) reg.5 (April 6, 1987).

3. The Social Security Benefit (Computation of Earnings) Regulations 1996 (SI 1996/2745) reg.17 (November 26, 1996).

4. The Social Security Amendment (Carer's Allowance) Regulations 2002 (SI 2002/2497) reg.3 (April 1, 2003).

5. The Social Security Benefits Up-rating Regulations 2013 (SI 2013/599) reg.4 (April 8, 2013).

6. The Civil Partnership (Pensions, Social Security and Child Support) (Consequential, etc. Provisions) Order 2005 (SI 2005/2877) (December 5, 2005).

7. The Social Security (Provisions relating to Qualifying Young Persons) (Amendment) Regulations 2006 (SI 2006/692) (April 10, 2006).

8. The Social Security (PPF Payments and FAS Payments) (Consequential Amendments) Regulations 2006 (SI 2006/1069) (May 5, 2006).

9. The Social Security (Miscellaneous Amendments) (No. 3) Regulations 2011 (SI 2011/2425) reg.5 (October 31, 2011).

10. The Social Security Benefits Up-rating Regulations 2019 (SI 2019/552) reg.5 (April 8, 2019).

11. The Marriage and Civil Partnership Act (Scotland) Act 2014 and Civil Partnership Act 2004 (Consequential Provisions and Modifications) Order 2014 (SI 2014/3229) art.29 and Sch.6 para.2 (December 16, 2014).

12. The Social Security Benefits Up-rating Regulations 2019 (SI 2019/552) reg.5 (April 8, 2019).

The Social Security (Hospital In-Patients) Regulations 2005

(SI 2005/3360) (*AS AMENDED*)

ARRANGEMENT OF REGULATIONS

3.74
1. Citation and commencement.
2. Hospital in-patients entitled to an increase in benefit for a dependant.
3. *Omitted—amends General Benefit Regulations.*
4. *Omitted—amends the Income Support General Regulations.*
5. *Omitted—amends the Housing Benefit General Regulations and the Council Tax Benefit General Regulations.*
6. *Omitted—amends the Jobseeker's Allowance Regulations.*
7. *Omitted—amends the Social Fund Winter Fuel Payment Regulations.*
8. *Omitted—amends the State Pension Credit Regulations.*
9. Revocation of the Social Security (Hospital In-Patients) Regulations 1975 and other regulations.

SCHEDULE

Omitted—revocations

The Secretary of State for Work and Pensions makes the following regulations in exercise of the powers conferred upon him by sections 113(1)(b), 123(1)(a), (d) and (e), 124(5), 130(4), 131(10), 135(1), 136(3), 137(1), 138(2) and (4) and 175(1), (3) and (4) of the Social Security Contributions and Benefits Act 1992, sections 5(1)(p), 73(1)(b) and 189(1), (4) and (5) of the Social Security Administration Act 1992, sections 4(5) and 36(1), (2) and (4)(a) of the Jobseekers Act 1995 and sections 2(3), (6) and (9), 3(8), 17(1) and 19(1) of the State Pension Credit Act 2002.

The Social Security Advisory Committee has agreed that the proposals to make these Regulations should not be referred to it.

GENERAL NOTE

3.75   Very broadly, these regulations mark the end of the era of what has come to be known as "hospital downrating" under which benefits are reduced following lengthy periods in hospital. But some aspects of the abolished system are retained.

A challenge relating to the exclusion from benefits of prisoners transferred to mental hospital under these regulations as being in breach of Article 14 of the European Convention when read with Article 1 of Protocol No. 1 has failed with one exception: see *R. (on the application of M)* v *Secretary of State for Work and Pensions*, [2009] EWHC 454 (Admin). The excepted class is a small group (there were 45 such persons in detention when the case was decided) of what are described as "technical lifers", namely those, although sentenced to life imprisonment, are treated by the Secretary of State after transfer to hospital as though they had been made the subject of a hospital order under s.37 of the Mental Health Act 1983 and to a restriction order under s.41 of that Act. The trial judge said that:

> "The reality is that the 45 technical lifers are the unintended victims of a policy that had different objects in its sight. The technical lifer cannot be returned to

prison and is treated for all other purposes as if he was subject to a section 37
order with a section 41 restriction. The arguments advanced by the Secretary of
State in support of the policy barely touched this group of patient." (para.40)

Citation and commencement

1. These Regulations may be cited as the Social Security (Hospital   3.76
In-Patients) Regulations 2005 and shall come into force for the purposes of—
  (a) this regulation and regulations 2, 5, 7 and 8, on 10th April 2006,
  (b) regulation 3—
        (i) in so far as it relates to a particular beneficiary other than a
            beneficiary in receipt of incapacity benefit or severe disable-
            ment allowance, on 10th April 2006 if it is his day for payment
            or, if not, on his day for payment next following 10th April
            2006 ("day for payment" has the same meaning as in regulation
            22(3) of, and Schedule 6 to, the Social Security (Claims and
            Payments) Regulations 1987),
       (ii) in so far as it relates to a particular beneficiary in receipt of inca-
            pacity benefit or severe disablement allowance, on 10th April
            2006,
  (c) regulation 4, in so far as it relates to a particular beneficiary, on the
      first day of the first benefit week to commence for that beneficiary on
      or after 10th April 2006 ("benefit week" has the same meaning as in
      the Income Support (General) Regulations 1987),
  (d) regulation 6, in so far as it relates to a particular beneficiary, on the
      first day of the first benefit week to commence for that beneficiary on
      or after 10th April 2006 ("benefit week" has the same meaning as in
      the Jobseeker's Allowance Regulations 1996), and
  (e) regulation 9—
        (i) in so far as it relates to a beneficiary specified in paragraphs
            (b) to (d), on the dates specified in those paragraphs for that
            beneficiary, and
       (ii) otherwise, on 10th April 2006.

Hospital in-patients entitled to an increase in benefit for a dependant

2.—(1) Paragraphs (2) and (3) apply where a beneficiary is entitled to   3.77
an increase in benefit for an adult or child dependant under Part IV of the
Social Security Contributions and Benefits Act 1992.
  (2) Where the beneficiary has received free in-patient treatment for a
period of not less than 52 weeks, the increase shall not be payable unless the
beneficiary applies to the Secretary of State to pay the increase on behalf of
the beneficiary to—
  (a) the dependant, or
  (b) some other person who is approved by the Secretary of State and
      who satisfies the Secretary of State that he will apply the increase for
      the benefit of the dependant.
  (3) Where both the beneficiary and the dependant are in-patients and
each has received free inpatient treatment for a period of not less than 52
weeks, the increase shall not be payable unless the beneficiary applies to the
Secretary of State to pay the increase on behalf of the beneficiary to—
  (a) the dependant, or

(b) some other person who is approved by the Secretary of State and who satisfies the Secretary of State that he will apply the increase for the benefit of a child [¹ of the beneficiary.]

(4) For the purposes of this regulation, a person shall be regarded as receiving or having received free in-patient treatment for any period for which he is or has been maintained free of charge while undergoing medical or other treatment as an in-patient—

(a) in a hospital or similar institution under the National Health Service Act 1977, the National Health Service (Scotland) Act 1978 or the National Health Service and Community Care Act 1990, or

(b) in a hospital or similar institution maintained or administered by the Defence Council,

and such a person shall for the purposes of sub-paragraph (a) be regarded as being maintained free of charge in a hospital or similar institution unless his accommodation and services are provided under section 65 of the National Health Service Act 1977, section 57 of the National Health Service (Scotland) Act 1978 or paragraph 14 of Schedule 2 to the National Health Service and Community Care Act 1990.

(5) For the purposes of paragraph (4), a period during which a person is regarded as receiving or having received free in-patient treatment shall be deemed to begin on the day after the day on which he enters a hospital or similar institution referred to in that paragraph and to end on the day on which he leaves such a hospital or similar institution.

(6) For the purposes of this regulation—

(a) where an increase in a person's benefit is payable in respect of an adult or child dependant the increase shall be treated as a separate benefit, and

(b) where a beneficiary's spouse or civil partner ("dependant") is temporarily absent from Great Britain for the purpose of being treated for incapacity which commenced before he left Great Britain the absence shall be disregarded for the purpose of determining whether the beneficiary is residing with the dependant and is entitled to an increase in benefit for him.

AMENDMENT

1. The Social Security (Miscellaneous Amendments) Regulations 2006 (SI 2006/588) (March 10, 2006).

GENERAL NOTE

3.78   Provision is made for continued payment of an increase in benefit for a dependant after 52 weeks on application to the Secretary of State. This is the only remaining free-standing provision on payments in relation to hospital in-patients. All other aspects of payments are incorporated into the specific benefit rules by the amendments made by regs 3 to 8 of these Regulations. Note that there are no linking rules in relation to these provisions. The regulation is drafted such that the only reading possible is that the beneficiary must have been in hospital for a continuous period of at least 52 weeks. Separate periods in hospital cannot be linked to form the 52 week qualifying period.

The question of whether a person is in a "hospital or similar institution" is nowadays determined not so much by the inherent nature of the accommodation but by whether the person's assessed needs for care is such that the National Health Service is under a duty to fund the accommodation free of charge. In the less straightforward cases, tribunals will need to take evidence and consider who is actually funding the accommodation. *R(DLA) 2/06* is instructive of the complexities which can arise.

Revocation of the Social Security (Hospital In-Patients) Regulations 1975 and other regulations

9.—(1) The Social Security (Hospital In-Patients) Regulations 1975 shall be revoked.

(2) The provisions in the subordinate legislation set out in the Schedule shall be revoked.

3.79

The Social Security (Overlapping Benefits) Regulations 1979

(SI 1979/597) *(as amended)*

ARRANGEMENT OF REGULATIONS

1. Citation and commencement.
2. Interpretation.
3. *Revoked.*
4. Adjustment of personal benefit under Parts II and II of the Contributions and Benefits Act where other personal benefit under those Parts or graduated retirement benefit is payable.
5. Special provisions for earnings-related supplements and earnings-related addition to widow's allowance.
6. Adjustments of personal benefit under Chapters I and II of Part II of the Act by reference to industrial injuries benefits and benefits not under the Act, and adjustments of industrial injuries benefits.
7. Adjustment of dependency benefit in respect of a child where other dependency benefit is payable for that child.
8. Child benefit.
9. Adjustment of dependency benefit in respect of an adult dependant where other dependency benefit is payable.
10. Adjustment of dependency benefit where certain personal benefit is payable.
11. Dependency benefit under the Act not to be payable if a training allowance is payable.
12. Special provision relating to the adjustment of severe disablement allowance and carer's allowance.
13. Increases in respect of more than one dependant to be treated as separate dependency benefits.
14. Provisions for adjusting benefit for part of a week.
15. Priority between persons entitled to increase of benefit.
16. Persons to be treated as entitled to benefit for certain purposes.
17. Prevention of double adjustments.
18. *Omitted.*

3.80

SCHEDULES

Schedule 1—Personal benefits which are required to be adjusted by reference to benefits not under Chapters I and II of Part II of the Act.
Schedule 2—*Omitted.*

The Secretary of State for Social Services, in exercise of powers conferred by sections 83(1) and 85 of the Social Security Act 1975 and of all other powers enabling him in that behalf hereby makes the following regulations which only consolidate the regulations herein revoked and which accordingly by virtue of paragraph 20 of Schedule 15 to the Social Security Act 1975, are not subject to the requirement of section 139(1) of that Act for prior reference to the National Insurance Advisory Committee:

Citation and commencement

3.81   **1.**—These regulations may be cited as the Social Security (Overlapping Benefits) Regulations 1979 and shall come into operation on 29th June, 1979.

Interpretation

3.82   **2.**—(1) In these regulations, unless the context otherwise requires—
[15 "the 2012 Act" means the Welfare Reform Act 2012;]
"the Act" means the Social Security Act 1975;
[16 "armed forces independence payment" means a payment under Article 24A of the Armed Forces and Reserve Forces (Compensation Scheme) Order 2011;]
[1 "the Contributions and Benefits Act" means the Social Security Contributions and Benefits Act 1992];
"the Pensions Act" means the Social Security Pensions Act 1975;
"benefit under Chapters I and II of Part II of the Act" includes benefit treated as included in Chapter I of Part II of the Act by virtue of section 66(2)(b) of the Pensions Act;
[20 . . .]
"the Child Benefit Act" means the Child Benefit Act 1975;
"child benefit" means benefit under Part I of the Child Benefit Act;
[17 "contribution-based jobseeker's allowance" means an allowance under the Jobseekers Act as amended by the provisions of Part 1 of Schedule 14 to the 2012 Act that remove references to an income-based allowance, and a contribution-based allowance under the Jobseekers Act as that Act has effect apart from those provisions;]
[3 "contributory benefit" means any benefit payable under Part II of the Contributions and Benefits Act, [12 a contribution-based jobseeker's allowance and a contributory employment and support allowance];
[17 "contributory employment and support allowance" means an allowance under Part 1 of the Welfare Reform Act as amended by the provisions of Schedule 3, and Part 1 of Schedule 14, to the 2012 Act that remove references to an income-related allowance, and a contributory allowance under Part 1 of the Welfare Reform Act as that Part has effect apart from those provisions;]
[15 "the daily living component of personal independence payment" means a payment in accordance with section 78 of the 2012 Act;]
[16 "the enhanced rate" in relation to the daily living component of personal independence payment means the rate prescribed in regulation 24(1)(b) of the Social Security (Personal Independence Payment) Regulations 2013;]
"death benefit" means any benefit, pension or allowance which, apart from these regulations, is payable (whether under the Act or otherwise) in respect of the death of any person;

"the deceased" means, in relation to any death benefit, the person in respect of whose death that benefit, apart from these regulations, is payable;

"dependency benefit" means that benefit, pension or allowance which, apart from these regulations, is payable (whether under the Act or otherwise) to a person in respect of another person who is a child or an adult dependant, it includes child's special allowance and any personal benefit by way of pension payable to a child under any Personal Injuries Scheme, Service Pensions Instrument or 1914–1918 War Injuries Scheme but does not include benefit under section 73 of the Act (allowances to a woman who has care of children of person who died as a result of an industrial accident) [4 or child tax credit under the Tax Credits Act 2002];

"disablement pension" includes a disablement payment on a pension basis and retired pay or pension in respect of any disablement, wound, injury or disease;

[17 "income-based jobseeker's allowance" means an income-based allowance under the Jobseekers Act;

"income-related employment and support allowance" means an income-related allowance under Part 1 of the Welfare Reform Act;]

[5 "the Jobseekers Act" means the Jobseekers Act 1995];

"personal benefit" means any benefit, pension or allowance [11 , except a shared additional pension] [6 (whether under the Act or otherwise)] which is not a dependency benefit [17 or universal credit under Part 1 of the Welfare Reform Act] [6 and includes [12 a contributory employment and support allowance but not an income-related employment and support allowance and includes] a contribution-based jobseeker's allowance but not an income-based jobseeker's allowance] and which [6 apart from these regulations,] is payable to any person;

[15 "personal independence payment" means personal independence payment under Part 4 of the 2012 Act;]

"Personal Injuries Scheme" means any scheme made under the Personal Injuries (Emergency Provisions) Act 1939 or under the Pensions (Navy, Army, Air Force and Mercantile Marine) Act 1939;

"Pneumoconiosis and Byssinosis Benefit Scheme" means any scheme made under section 5 of the Industrial Injuries and Diseases (Old Cases) Act 1975;

[7 "Service Pensions Instrument" means any instrument described in sub-paragraphs (a) or (b) below in so far, but only in so far, as the pensions or other benefits provided by that instrument are not calculated or determined by reference to length of service, namely:—

(a) any instrument made in exercise of powers—
   (i) referred to in section 12(1) of the Social Security (Miscellaneous Provisions) Act 1977 (pensions or other benefits for disablement or death due to service in the armed forces of the Crown); or
   (ii) under section 1 of the Polish Resettlement Act 1947 (pensions and other benefits for disablement or death due to service in certain Polish forces); or

(b) any instrument under which a pension or other benefit may be paid to a person (not being a member of the armed forces of the Crown) out of public funds in respect of death or disablement,

wound, injury, or disease due to service in any nursing service or
other auxiliary service of any of the armed forces of the Crown,
or in any other organisation established under the control of the
Defence Council or formerly established under the control of the
Admiralty, the Army Council or the Air Council.]

[¹¹ "shared additional pension" means a shared additional pension under
section 55A [¹⁹ or 55AA] of the Contributions and Benefits Act;]

"training allowance" means an allowance (whether by way of
periodical grants or otherwise) payable out of public funds by
a Government department or by or on behalf of [⁸ Scottish
Enterprise, Highlands and Islands Enterprise] [¹⁴ ...] [¹³ [¹⁹ the
Secretary of State]] [¹⁰ , the National Assembly of Wales] or the
Secretary of State to a person for his maintenance, or in respect of
any dependant of his, for the period, or part of the period, during
which he is following a course of training or instruction provided by
that department in relation to him or so provided by or on behalf
of [⁸ Scottish Enterprise, Highlands and Islands Enterprise] [¹⁰ , the
National Assembly for Wales] or the Secretary of State; but it does
not include—

(a) an allowance paid by any Government department to or in respect
of a person by reason of the fact that he is following a course of
full-time education or is in training as a teacher; or

(b) a payment made by or on behalf of [⁸ Scottish Enterprise,
Highlands and Islands Enterprise] or the Secretary of State to
any person by way of training premium or training bonus in
consequence of that person's use of facilities for training provided in pursuance of arrangements made under section 2 of
the Employment and Training Act 1973 or [⁸ section 8 of the
Enterprise and New Towns (Scotland) Act 1990.]

"treatment allowance" means an allowance payable under a Personal
Injuries Scheme, Service Pensions Instrument or 1914–1918 War
Injuries Scheme only to a person undergoing a course of medical, surgical or rehabilitative treatment in consequence of a disablement in
respect of which a pension may be or has been paid, or an allowance
payable to any such person pending the determination of the question
whether he is entitled to receive such a pension;

"unemployment supplement" includes an increase on account of unemployability under—

(a) any Pneumoconiosis and Byssinosis Benefit Scheme; and

(b) any Personal Injuries Scheme, Service Pensions Instrument or
1914–1918 War Injuries Scheme;

"war pension death benefit" means a death benefit by way of pension
or allowance under any Personal Injuries Scheme, Service Pensions
Instrument or 1914–1918 War Injuries Scheme, but does not include
a rent allowance or a grant payable by reason of the beneficiary being
in receipt of a pension and being a specific age which is not less than 65
or a pension or an allowance calculated by reference to the necessities
of the beneficiary;

[¹² "the Welfare Reform Act" means the Welfare Reform Act 2007].

[¹⁹ "widowed mother's allowance" means an allowance referred to in
section 37 of the Contributions and Benefits Act (widowed mother's
allowance);]

[² "widowed parent's allowance" means an allowance referred to in section 39A of the Contributions and Benefits Act;]

[¹⁹ "widow's pension" means a pension referred to in section 38 of the Contributions and Benefits Act (widow's pension);]

"1914–1918 War Injuries Scheme" means any scheme made under the Injuries in War (Compensation) Act 1914 or under the Injuries in War Compensation Act 1914 (Session 2) or any Government scheme for compensation in respect of persons injured in any merchant ship or fishing vessel as the result of hostilities during the 1914–1918 War.

(2) For the purposes of these regulations, unless otherwise specified, [⁹ additional pension] payable by virtue of the Act or the Pensions Act shall be deemed to include any increase so far as attributable to any additional pension or to any increase by virtue of section 126A of the Act or paragraph 4A of Schedule 1 to the Pensions Act or to any increase of graduated retirement benefit and shall be treated as a separate personal benefit included in Chapter I of Part II of the Act.

AMENDMENTS

1. The Social Security (Overlapping Benefits) Amendment (No. 2) Regulations 1992 (SI 1992/3194) reg.2 (January 13, 1993).

2. The Social Security (Benefits for Widows and Widowers) (Consequential Amendments) Regulations 2000 (SI 2000/1483) reg.6 (April 9, 2001).

3. The Social Security and Child Support (Jobseeker's Allowance) (Consequential Amendments) Regulations 1996 (SI 1996/1345) reg.22(2)(a) (October 7, 1996).

4. The Social Security (Working Tax Credit and Child Tax Credit) (Consequential Amendments) (No. 2) Regulations 2003 (SI 2003/937) reg.2 (April 6, 2003).

5. The Social Security and Child Support (Jobseeker's Allowance) (Consequential Amendments) Regulations 1996 (SI 1996/1345) reg.22(2)(b) (October 7, 1996).

6. The Social Security and Child Support (Jobseeker's Allowance) (Consequential Amendments) Reglations 1996 (SI 1996/1345) reg.22(2)(c) (October 7, 1996).

7. The Social Security (Overlapping Benefits) Amendments Regulations 1980 (SI 1980/1927) reg.2(b) (January 5, 1981).

8. The Enterprise (Scotland) Consequential Amendments Order 1991 (SI 1991/387) reg.2(1) (April 4, 1991).

9. Social Security Act 1986 s.18(1) (April 6, 1987).

10. The Social Security, Child Support and Tax Credits (Miscellaneous Amendments) Regulations 2005 (SI 2005/337) reg.11 (March 18, 2005).

11. The Social Security (Shared Additional Pension) (Miscellaneous Amendments) Regulations 2005 (SI 2005/1551) (July 6, 2005).

12. The Employment and Support Allowance (Consequential Provisions) (No. 2) Regulations 2008 (SI 2008/1554) reg.51 (October 27, 2008).

13. The Apprenticeship, Skills, Children and Learning Act 2009 (Consequential Amendments to Subordinate Legislation) (England) Order 2010 (SI 2010/1941) reg.2 (September 1, 2010).

14. The Young People's Learning Agency Abolition (Consequential Amendments to Subordinate Legislation) (England) Order 2012 (SI 2012/956) reg.2 (May 1, 2012).

15. The Personal Independence Payments (Supplementary Provisions and Consequential Amendments) Regulations 2013 (SI 2013/388) reg.8 and Sch. para.10 (April 8, 2013).

16. The Armed Forces and Reserve Forces Compensation Scheme (Consequential Provisions: Subordinate Legislation) Order 2013 (SI 2013/591) reg.7 and Sch. para.3 (April 8, 2013).

17. The Universal Credit (Consequential Supplementary, Incidental and Miscellaneous Provisions) Regulations 2013 (SI 2013/630) reg.25 (April 29, 2013).

18. Deregulation Act 2015 (Consequential Amendments) Order 2015 (SI 2015/971) art.2 and Sch.3 para.1 (May 26, 2015).

19. The Pensions Act 2014 (Consequential, Supplementary and Incidental Amendments) Order 2015 (SI 2015/1985) art.4(2) (April 6, 2016).

20. Pensions Act 2014 (Consequential, Supplementary and Incidental Amendments) Order 2017 (SI 2017/422) art.6 (April 6, 2017).

3.83 *Regulation 3 revoked by The Social Security (Incapacity Benefit) Consequential and Transitional Amendments and Savings) Regulations 1995 (SI 1995/829), reg.14(2) (April 13, 1995) subject to the savings set out below.*

TRANSITIONAL PROTECTION

3.84   Regulation 3 is revoked with effect from April 13, 1995, but reg.14(9) of the Social Security (Incapacity Benefit)(Consequential and Transitional Amendments and Savings) Regulations 1995 (SI 1995/829) provides as follows:

"(9) Where before the appointed day regulation 3 of the Overlapping Benefits Regulations (special provisions for widow's benefit and invalidity pension) applied to a widow; and

(a) on or after that day she remains entitled to either a widowed mother's allowance or a widow's pension; and

(b) she is either a transitional case for the purposes of Part IV of the Social Security (Incapacity Benefit) (Transitional) Regulations 1995 or, has an award of long-term incapacity benefit by virtue of regulation 19 or 20 of the Social Security (Incapacity Benefit) (Transitional) Regulations 1995; and

(c) she is under pensionable age,

regulation 3 of the Overlapping Benefits Regulations shall continue to apply to her as if the revocation made by paragraph (2) above had not been made subject to the modification made in paragraph (10) below."

3.85   Regulation 14(10) of the Social Security (Incapacity Benefit)(Consequential and Transitional Amendments and Savings) Regulations 1995 (SI 1995/829) modifes revoked reg.3 so that it reads as follows in its application to those covered by the saving in Regulation 14(9) above.

"**3.**—(1) This regulation applies where, apart from these regulations, there is payable for the same period to a person under pensionable age both—

(a) a long-term incapacity benefit; and

(b) a widowed mother's allowance or widow's pension (hereafter referred to in this regulation as "the widow's benefit").

(2) The total amount payable in respect of these benefits under this regulation shall be—

(a) an amount equal to either the basic rate of long-term incapacity benefit referred to in regulation 18(1)(a) of the Social Security (Incapacity Benefit) (Transitional) Regulations 1995 paid in a transitional case or an award of widow's basic pension calculated by reference to section 44(1) of the Contributions and Benefits Act or an amount equal to the greater of them; and

(b) the sum of the incapacity benefit payable at the additional rate in accordance with regulation 18(1)(b) of the Social Security (Incapacity Benefit) (Transitional) Regulations 1995 and widow's pension determined in accordance with section 44(3) of the Contributions and Benefits Act.

(3) Subject to paragraph (4)—

(a) where the beneficiary has made application, before the payment is made, that the total amount should be treated as being made up of the rate of the long-term incapacity benefit, any balance being the widow's benefit, it shall be so treated;

(b) in any other case, that amount shall be treated as being made up of the rate of the widow's benefit, any balance being the long-term incapacity benefit.

(4) For the purposes of the remainder of these regulations (other than regulation 6(5)), which shall apply after adjustment has been made under this regulation, the total amount payable under this regulation shall be treated as a single long-term benefit payable on a weekly basis."

Adjustment of personal benefit under Parts II and III of the Contributions and Benefits Act where other personal benefit under those Parts or graduated retirement benefit is payable

4.—[1 (1) Subject to paragraphs (2), (3) and (4) and regulation 12, an adjustment shall be made in accordance with paragraph (5) where either—

(a) two or more personal benefits (whether of the same or a different description) are, or but for this regulation would be, payable under Parts II and III of the Contributions and Benefits Act (which relate to benefits other than industrial injuries benefits) [9 Part 1 of the Welfare Reform Act] [10 , Part 1 of the Pensions Act 2014] [2 or under the Jobseekers Act] for any period; or

(b) graduated retirement benefit is payable under sections 36 and 37 of the National Insurance Act 1965 together with one or more personal benefits (whether of the same or a different description) which are, or but for this regulation would be, payable under Parts II and III of the Contributions and Benefits Act for any period].

3.86

(2) Paragraph (1) shall not require the adjustment of, or by reference to—

(a) a death grant;

(b) a maternity grant;

(c) any other sum paid otherwise than in respect of a period;

(d) an earnings-related supplement or earnings-related addition to any benefit (except as provided by regulation 5 and in the case of [3 severe disablement allowance] or [8carer's allowance]);

(e) an attendance allowance;

(f) [4 additional pension] or graduated retirement benefit (except as provided by paragraph (4) [10 and (4A)]);

(g) [5disability living allowance]

[6 (2A) Paragraph (1) shall not require an adjustment of widow's pension reduced in accordance with section 39(4) of the Contributions and Benefits Act only by reference to long-term incapacity benefit in accordance with section 40(5)(b) of that Act].

(3) Paragraph (1) shall require an adjustment of age addition only by reference to another age addition.

(4) [10 Except where paragraph (4A) applies,] where there are payable two or more personal benefits to which this regulation applies with which [4 additional pension] or graduated retirement benefit is payable as part of the rate of benefit or as an increase of benefit, or, in a case where the person entitled to receive the benefits is over pensionable age and one or

more of the benefits includes either additional pension or graduated retirement benefit while another of the benefits is payable at the rate referred to in [section 31(6) or 33(4) of the Social Security Contributions and Benefits Act 1992], then the following provisions shall apply—

    (a) for the purposes of adjustment falling to be made under paragraph (5) that [⁴ additional pension] or graduated retirement benefit shall be treated as part of the personal benefit with which it is so payable;

    (b) the provisions of sub-paragraph (a) shall apply before any further adjustment under these regulations; and

    (c) for the purpose of any such further adjustment, the beneficiary shall be treated as having a single long-term benefit inclusive of whichever before adjustment under sub-paragraph (a) is the highest of the following amounts—

        (i) the highest additional pension payable, or

        (ii) the highest graduated retirement benefit payable, or

        (iii) the highest total of additional pension and graduated retirement benefit payable together as part of the rate of and as an increase of any of those personal benefits.

[¹⁰ (4A) Where the person is entitled to additional pension, a state pension under Part 1 of the Pensions Act 2014 and either widow's pension or widowed mother's allowance, paragraph (1) shall require adjustment of additional pension.]

(5) Where an adjustment falls to be made in accordance with this paragraph and—

    (a) one of the benefits is a contributory benefit and one is a noncontributory benefit, the non-contributory benefit shall be adjusted by deducting from it the amount of the contributory benefit and only the balance, if any, shall be payable;

    (b) sub-paragraph (a) above does not apply, if one of the benefits is payable on a weekly basis—

        (i) where the beneficiary has made application, before the payment is made, to have the benefit payable on a weekly basis adjusted, it shall be adjusted by deducting from it the amount of the other benefit and only the balance of it, if any, shall be payable,

        (ii) in any other case, the benefit not payable on a weekly basis shall be adjusted by deducting from it the amount of the other benefit and only the balance of it, if any, shall be payable;

    (c) sub-paragraphs (a) and (b) above do not apply, the amount payable in respect of the benefits in question shall be an amount equal to that which would but for this provision be payable in respect of—

        (i) one of them, if they would have been payable at the same rate, or

        (ii) the higher or highest of them, if they would have been payable at different rates,

so however that in a case where more than 2 benefits would be payable then the total amount payable shall not exceed the amount which would be ascertained under sub-paragraph (c).

[⁷ (6) For the purposes of this regulation—

"additional pension" means a pension payable with a personal benefit under Part II of the Contribution and Benefits Act or an additional rate; and "additional rate" means an additional amount equal to the rate paid or payable as an additional pension with invalidity benefit immediately before 13 April 1995 which is payable after that date pursuant to regulation 18 of the Social Security (Incapacity Benefit) (Transitional) Regulations 1995.]

AMENDMENTS

1. The Social Security (Overlapping Benefits) Amendment (No. 2) Regulations 1992 (SI 1992/3194) reg.3(2) (January 13, 1993).
2. The Social Security and Child Support (Jobseeker's Allowance) (Consequential Amendments) Regulations 1996 (SI 1996/1345) reg.22(3) (October 7, 1996).
3. The Social Security (Severe Disablement Allowance) Reglations 1984 (SI 1984/1303) reg.11 (November 29, 1984).
4. Social Security Act 1986 s.18(1) (April 6, 1987).
5. The Disability Living Allowance and Disability Working Allowance (Consequential Provisions) Regulations 1991 (SI 1991/2742) reg.5(2) (April 6, 1992).
6. The Social Security (Incapacity Benefit) Consequential and Transitional Amendments and Savings) Regulations 1995 (SI 1995/829) reg.14(3) (April 13, 1995).
7. The Social Security (Incapacity for Work and Miscellaneous Amendments) Regulations 1996 (SI 1996/3207) reg.4 (January 6, 1997).
8. The Social Security (Carer's Allowance) Regulations 2002 (SI 2002/2497) Sch.2 (April 1, 2003).
9. The Employment and Support Allowance (Consequential Provisions) (No. 2) Regulations 2008 (SI 2008/1554) reg.51 (October 27, 2008).
10. The Pensions Act 2014 (Consequential, Supplementary and Incidental Amendments) Order 2015 (SI 2015/1985) art.4(3) (April 6, 2016).

DEFINITIONS

"benefit under Chapters I and II of Part II of the Act"—reg.2.
"personal benefit"—reg.2.

GENERAL NOTE

This complex regulation states in para.(5) the basic general rules on overlapping benefits (though no adjustment is needed for any of the benefits specified in para. (2)). **3.87**

Unless reg.3 applies, only the highest of the following benefits is payable: carer's allowance, invalidity pension, maternity allowance, non contributory widow's benefit, retirement pension, severe disablement allowance, sickness benefit, unemployment benefit, widowed mother's allowance, widow's pension, employment and support allowance and jobseeker's allowance.

There are a number of points to note in relation to additions to benefits. An age addition only overlaps with another age addition (para.(3)). Paragraph (4) contains special rules where additional pensions under SERPS or graduated retirement pension is payable.

Special provision for earnings-related supplements and earnings-related addition to widow's allowance

5.—(1) Where two or more earnings-related supplements to any benefits under the Act would apart from this regulation be payable for the same **3.88**

period, for the purposes of regulation 4(1) each such supplement shall be treated as part of the benefit it supplements.

(2) Where an earnings-related addition to widow's allowance would apart from this regulation be payable for the same period as any other benefit under the Act which is calculated whether wholly or in part by reference to the contributions of a husband who has died, that other benefit shall be adjusted by deducting from it the amount of the earnings-related addition, provided that where the widow is also entitled for the same period to graduated retirement benefit or [¹ additional pension], or both of them, by virtue of her own contributions and the contributions of the husband who has died, the graduated retirement benefit or [¹ additional pension] to be adjusted shall be only that part which is payable by virtue of the contributions of the husband who has died.

(3) Paragraph (1) shall not apply where apart from this regulation a widow's allowance would be payable for the same period as 2 or more other benefits under the Act; in such a case the earnings-related supplement to any of those other benefits shall be adjusted so that only the higher or highest of them is payable.

(4) For the purposes of paragraph (2), [¹ additional pension] or graduated retirement benefit, where it is, or but for this regulation would be, payable as part of the rate of or as an increase of another personal benefit, shall be treated as part of the personal benefit with which it is so payable.

AMENDMENT

1. Social Security Act 1986 s.18(1) (April 6, 1987).

Adjustments of personal benefit under Chapters I and II of Part II of the Act by reference to industrial injuries benefits and benefits not under the Act, and adjustments of industrial injuries benefits

3.89   **6.**—(1) Subject to paragraph (5) and regulation 12, where a personal benefit which is specified in column (1) of Schedule 1 to these regulations ("the column (1) benefit") is, or but for this regulation would be payable to a person for the same period as a personal benefit which is specified in the corresponding paragraph of column (2) of that Schedule ("the column (2) benefit") the column (1) benefit shall be adjusted by deducting from it the amount of the column (2) benefit and, subject to any further adjustment under regulation 4, only the balance, if any, shall be payable.

(2) Any reference in paragraph (1), or in Schedule 1 to these regulations, to a benefit, other than a training allowance, does not include an earnings-related supplement or earnings-related addition to it.

[⁶ (3) Paragraph (1) and Schedule 1 have effect in relation to—
(a) the following allowances and payments—
    (i) an attendance allowance;
    (ii) the care component of disability living allowance; and
    (iii) the daily living component of personal independence payment; [⁷ . . .]
    [⁷ (iv) armed forces independence payment up to the value of the daily living component of personal independence payment at the enhanced rate; and]

(b) any benefit by reference to which an allowance or payment under paragraph (a) above is to be adjusted;

as requiring adjustment where both that allowance or payment and the benefit are payable in respect of the same person (whether or not one or both of them are payable to that person).]

(4) Paragraph (1) and Schedule 1 to these regulations shall not require the adjustment of, or by reference to, [² additional pension] or graduated retirement benefit.

(5) Where—

(a) the column (2) benefit is industrial death benefit or war pension death benefit in either case payable to the beneficiary as the surviving spouse [⁵ or civil partner], and

(b) the column (1) benefit is Category A retirement pension [³ . . .] which

   (i) [⁴ . . .]

   (ii) has a [² basic pension] by virtue of the beneficiary's own contributions (but not by virtue of those of a former spouse [⁵ or civil partner]) which consists of either the rate specified in [section 44(3)(a) and (4) of the Social Security Contributions and Benefits Act 1992] or some percentage of that rate prescribed by regulations made under [section 60(1) of the Social Security Contributions and Benefits Act 1992],

the adjustment under paragraph (1) shall not reduce that Column (1) benefit to less than the appropriate rate in sub-paragraph (b)(ii), together with, if any, increments payable under paragraph 2 of [Schedule 5 of the Social Security Contributions and Benefits Act 1992] and increase under [section 47(1) of the Social Security Contributions and Benefits Act 1992].

AMENDMENTS

1. The Disability Living Allowance and Disability Working Allowance (Consequential Provisions) Regulations 1991 (SI 1991/2742) reg.5(3) (April 6, 1992).

2. Social Security Act 1986 s.18(1) (April 6, 1987).

3. The Social Security (Incapacity Benefit) (Consequential and Transitional Amendments and Savings) Regulations 1995 (SI 1995/829) reg.14(4)(a) (April 13, 1995).

4. The Social Security (Incapacity Benefit) Consequential and Transitional Amendments and Savings) Regulations 1995 (SI 1995/829) reg.14(4)(b) (April 13, 1995).

5. The Civil Partnership (Pensions, Social Security and Child Support) (Consequential, etc. Provisions) Order 2005 (SI 2005/2877) (December 5, 2005).

6. The Personal Independence Payments (Supplementary Provisions and Consequential Amendments) Regulations 2013 (SI 2013/388) reg.8 and Sch. para.10(3) (April 8, 2013).

7. The Armed Forces and Reserve Forces Compensation Scheme (Consequential Provisions: Subordinate Legislation) Order 2013 (SI 2013/591) reg.7 and Sch. para.3 (April 8, 2013).

GENERAL NOTE

Regulation 14(4) of the Social Security (Incapacity Benefit) (Consequential and Transitional Amendments and Savings) Regulations 1995 (SI 1995/829) amends this regulation with effect from April 13, 1995 by revoking the reference to invalidity benefit in para.(5)(b) and omitting para.(5)(b)(i), but reg.14(11) contains a saving provision as follows:

3.90

"(11) Notwithstanding the amendment made by paragraph (4) above, where in a transitional case long-term incapacity benefit falls to be adjusted by reference to a benefit within column (2) of Schedule 1 to the Overlapping Benefits Regulations, that benefit shall be adjusted on or after the appointed day as if the words 'or invalidity benefit' had not been omitted from regulation 6 of those Regulations."

Adjustment of dependency benefit in respect of a child where other dependency benefit is payable for that child

3.91

7.—(1) Subject to regulation 12, where dependency benefit under the Act is payable, or but for this regulation would be payable, to any person in respect of a child and any other dependency benefit specified in paragraph (2) is payable to that or any other person in respect of that child for the same period, an adjustment shall be made in accordance with regulation 4(5) so however that where one of the dependency benefits is death benefit under [paras. 18 and 19 of Schedule 7 to the Social Security Contributions and Benefits Act 1992] by way of an allowance, or is a guardian's allowance under [section 77 of the Social Security Contributions and Benefits Act 1992] (the other dependency benefit not being benefit under either the said [section 77 or paragraphs 18 and 19 to Schedule 7 of the Social Security Contributions and Benefits Act 1992]) the adjustment shall be made in accordance with paragraph (4) of this regulation.

(2) Subject to paragraph (3), the other dependency benefit referred to in paragraph (1) is any dependency benefit under—

(a) the Act;

(b) any Personal Injuries Scheme, Service Pensions Instrument or 1914–1918 War Injuries Scheme;

(c) any Pneumoconiosis and Byssinosis Benefit Scheme;

(d) any scheme, being a benefit by way of training allowance.

(3) Sub-paragraph (b) of paragraph (2) does not include an allowance payable or the purpose of the child's education and for the purposes of that sub-paragraph—

(a) any personal benefit by way of a pension payable to a child shall be treated as a dependency benefit payable to another person in respect of that child;

(b) any dependency benefit payable as part of a disablement pension shall be disregarded unless it is payable as an increase of an unemployability supplement.

(4) Where one of the dependency benefits is death benefit under section 70 by way of an allowance or is a guardian's allowance, except in a case to which paragraph (5) applies, the other dependency benefit shall be adjusted by deducting from it the amount of that death benefit or, as the case may be, guardian's allowance, and only the balance, if any, shall be payable.

(5) Where a death benefit by way of an allowance under section 70 or a guardian's allowance is payable to a person in respect of a child and any other dependency benefit specified in sub-paragraph (b) or (d) of paragraph (2) is payable to that or any other person in respect of that child for the same period, the death benefit or, as the case may be, the guardian's allowance shall be adjusted by deducting from it the other benefit and only the balance, if any, shall be payable.

Child benefit

8.—(1) Subject to the following provisions of this regulation, where any   3.92
benefit, or increase of a benefit, under the Act is payable to a beneficiary,
the weekly rate of that benefit or increase shall not be adjusted by reference
to child benefit.

(2) Where child benefit is payable to a beneficiary at the rate for the
time being specified in regulation 2(1)(a)(ii) of the Child Benefit and
Social Security (Fixing and Adjustment of Rates) Regulations 1976 (in
this regulation referred to as the "Child Benefit Rates Regulations")
(weekly rate for only, elder or eldest child of a lone parent) and for the
same period, in respect of the same child, any benefit or increase in
benefit under the Contributions and Benefits Act [¹ except where that
benefit is guardian's allowance payable to any person under section 77
of that Act,] the weekly rate of that benefit or increase thereof shall be
reduced by—

    (a) [² . . .];
    (b) [² . . .] an amount equal to the amount, less [³ £3.65], by which the
        rate specified in regulation 2(1)(a)(ii) of the Child Benefit Rates
        Regulations exceeds the rate specified in regulation 2(1)(b) of those
        Regulations.

(3) Subject to paragraph (6) of this regulation, where child benefit is
payable to a beneficiary at the rate for the time being specified in regulation 2(1)(a)(i) of the Child Benefit Rates Regulations (weekly rate for only,
elder or eldest child) and for the same period, in respect of the same child,
any benefit or increase in benefit under the Contributions and Benefits Act
[¹ except where that benefit is guardian's allowance payable to any person
under section 77 of that Act,] the weekly rate of that benefit or the increase
thereof shall be reduced by an amount equal to the amount, less [³ £3.65],
by which the rate specified in regulation 2(1)(a)(i) of the Child Benefit
Rates Regulations exceeds the rate specified in regulation 2(1)(b) of those
Regulations.

(4) [¹ . . .]
(5) [¹ . . .]
(6) Where the weekly rate of any benefit or increase of benefit under the
Act or the weekly rate of child benefit or both are increased in consequence
of an order under section 63(2) of the Social Security Act 1986 and as a
result the amount by which the benefit being adjusted under paragraph
(3) changes, the weekly rate of benefit or increase shall not be reduced by
the increased amount until the date on which the change in that benefit or
increase of benefit has effect.

    (7) [¹ . . .]]

AMENDMENTS

Regulation 8 was substituted by The Social Security (Overlapping Benefits)
Amendment Regulations 1991 (SI 1991/547) reg.2 (April 8, 1991). Paragraphs
(2) and (3) were substituted by The Child Benefit, Child Support and
Social Security (Miscellaneous Amendments) Regulations 1996 (SI 1996/1803)
reg.47(a) (April 7, 1997), and para.(6) was substituted by The Social Security
(Overlapping Benefits) Amendment Regulations 1992 (SI 1992/589) reg.2(c)
(April 6, 1992).

1. The Child Benefit, Child Support and Social Security (Miscellaneous
Amendments) Regulations 1996 (SI 1996/1803) reg.47(b) (April 7, 1997).

2. The Social Security (Overlapping Benefits) Amendment Regulations 2003 (SI 2003/136) reg.2 (April 7, 2003).

3. The Social Security (Miscellaneous Amendments) Regulations 2004, SI 2004/565 reg.8, (April 12, 2004).

Adjustment of dependency benefit in respect of an adult dependant where other dependency benefit is payable

3.93   **9.**—(1) Subject to paragraph (3) and regulation 12, where for any period any dependency benefit under the Act is, or but for this regulation would be, payable to any person in respect of an adult dependant and any other dependency benefit specified in paragraph (2) is payable for that period to—

(a) that person in respect of that or any other adult dependant; or

(b) any other person in respect of that dependant,

an adjustment shall be made in accordance with regulation 4(5).

(2) The other dependency benefit referred to in paragraph (1) is any dependency benefit under—

(a) the Act;

(b) any Personal Injuries Scheme, Service Pensions Instrument or 1914–1918 War Injuries Scheme;

(c) any Pneumoconiosis and Byssinosis Benefit Scheme;

(d) any scheme being a benefit by way of training allowance.

(3) Paragraph (1) shall not require an adjustment to be made where one of the dependency benefits in question is an increase of benefit under [section 82(4) or 85(2) of the Social Security Contributions and Benefits Act 1992] in respect of a person who is employed by the beneficiary but is not residing with him and the other such benefit is payable to a person other than the beneficiary [¹ or to a person entitled to an increase of incapacity benefit under regulation 9(1)(d) of the Social Security (Incapacity Benefit—Increases for Dependants) Regulations 1994 who satisfies the requirements of paragraph (3)(a) of that regulation.]

(4) For the purposes of paragraph (2)(b) any dependency benefit which is payable with a disablement pension shall be disregarded unless it is payable as an increase of an unemployability supplement.

AMENDMENT

1. The Social Security (Incapacity Benefit) (Consequential and Transitional Amendments and Savings) Regulations 1995 (SI 1995/829) reg.14(5) (April 14, 1995).

Adjustment of dependency benefit where certain personal benefit is payable

3.94   **10.**—(1) Subject to the following provisions of this regulation, where a dependency benefit under the Act is payable for the same period as one or more of the following personal benefits is, or but for the provisions of these regulations would be, payable to the dependant—

(a) a personal benefit under Chapter I or II of Part II of the Act (other than a benefit specified in regulation 4(2)(a)(b)(c)(e) or (g));

(b) an unemployability supplement;

(c) [¹ . . .];

(d) industrial death benefit;

(e) war pension death benefit;

   (f) a training allowance,

[² (g) a temporary allowance under the provisions of section 1 of the Job Release Act 1977];

[³ (h) a weekly allowance pursuant to arrangements made by the Manpower Services Commission under section 2 of the Employment and Training Act 1973 or section 2 of the Enterprise and New Towns (Scotland) Act 1990 for the purpose of the Enterprise Allowance Scheme];

[⁴ (i) graduated retirement benefit];

[⁵ (j) a contribution-based jobseeker's allowance].

[⁸ (k) a contributory employment and support allowance;]

the dependency benefit shall be adjusted in accordance with paragraph (2).

   (2) Where the weekly rate of the personal benefit (or, if more than one, the aggregate weekly rate payable after any adjustment made by virtue of regulations 4(1) or 6(1)—

   (a) is equal to or exceeds the weekly rate of the dependency benefit, the dependency benefit shall not be paid;

   (b) in any other case, the weekly rate of the dependency benefit payable shall be adjusted, if necessary, so that it does not exceed the difference between the weekly rate of the personal benefit and that of the unadjusted dependency benefit.

   (3) Paragraph (1) does not apply to an increase of benefit under [section 82(4) or 85(2) of the Social Security Contributions and Benefits Act 1992] in respect of a person who is employed by, but is not residing with, the beneficiary [⁶ or to a person entitled to an increase of incapacity benefit under regulation 9(1)(d) of the Social Security (Incapacity Benefit—Increases for Dependants) Regulations 1994 who satisfies the requirements of paragraph (3)(a) of that regulation.]

   (4) Where the personal benefit to which paragraph (1) applies is sickness benefit [⁷ but not incapacity benefit] payable to a married woman which falls to be adjusted by virtue of regulations under [section 73(1)(b) of the Social Security Administration Act 1992] (hospital in-patients) and the dependency benefit would be payable to her husband, the rate of sickness benefit to be taken into account for the purposes of paragraph (1) shall be the rate after it has been so adjusted.

Amendments

   1. The Social Security (Abolition of Injury Benefit) (Consequential) Regulations 1983 (SI 1983/186) reg.10(2) (April 6, 1983).

   2. The Social Security (Overlapping Benefits) Amendment Regulations 1980 (SI 1980/1927) reg.2 (January 5, 1981).

   3. The Social Security (Overlapping Benefits) Amendment Regulations 1982 (SI 1982/1173) reg.2 (September 14, 1982).

   4. The Social Security (Overlapping Benefits) Amendment (No. 2) Regulations 1992 (SI 1992/3194) reg.4 (January 13, 1993).

   5. The Social Security and Child Support (Jobseeker's Allowance) (Consequential Amendments) Regulations 1996 (SI 1996/1345) reg.22(4) (October 7, 1996).

   6. The Social Security (Incapacity Benefit) (Consequential and Transitional Amendments and Savings) Regulations 1995 (SI 1995/829) reg.14(6)(a) (April 13, 1995).

   7. The Social Security (Incapacity Benefit) (Consequential and Transitional Amendments and Savings) Regulations 1995 (SI 1995/829) reg.14(6)(b) (April 13, 1995).

8. The Employment and Support Allowance (Consequential Provisions) (No. 2) Regulations 2008 (SI 2008/1554) reg.51 (October 27, 2008).

GENERAL NOTE

3.95   In *Jones v Chief Adjudication Officer* [1990] I.R.L.R. 533, *R(G) 2/91*, the Court of Appeal held that reg.10 is not discriminatory on grounds of sex contrary to Art.4 of EEC Directive 79/7 on the Progressive Implementation of the Principle of Equal Treatment of Men and Women in Matters of Social Security.

The facts arising in *R(S) 5/94* were that the claimant received an increase of invalidity benefit in respect of his wife. She had retired and received a pension consisting of three components: the basic pension, an additional pension, and a graduated retirement pension. The question was the extent to which the pension benefits received by the wife should be taken into account as overlapping with the increase of invalidity benefit. No one doubted that reg.10 applied, nor that the basic component of the retirement pension was a personal benefit to be taken into account. The argument concerned the graduated retirement pension and the additional pension. The Commissioner held, first, that the graduated retirement pension was not to be taken into account. This had been established in *Pearse v Chief Adjudication Officer and Secretary of State for Social Security*, CA (Civ Div), Judgment of June 12, 1992, *The Times*, June 18, 1992. The additional pension and the basic pension are aggregated for the purposes of the application of reg.10 and the total must be deducted from the increase of invalidity benefit.

Dependency benefit under the Act not to be payable if a training allowance is payable

3.96   **11.**—Dependency benefit under the Act shall not be payable to any person for any period in respect of which any personal benefit by way of training allowance is payable to him so however that this regulation shall not apply where such personal benefit has itself been adjusted by reference to any benefit under the Act.

Special provision relating to the adjustment of [1 severe disablement allowance] and [2 carer's allowance]

3.97   **12.**—In any case where personal benefit or dependency benefit by way of a severe disablement allowance or [2 a carer's allowance] would, in accordance with the provision of regulations 4, 6, 7 or 9, fall to be adjusted by reference to any other personal benefit (other than [3 additional pension] or graduated retirement benefit) or dependency benefit, it shall be reduced by the amount which is, or but for these regulations would be, payable by way of that other benefit both as personal benefit and as dependency benefit, so however that the amount payable by way of a [1 severe disablement allowance] or [2 a carer's allowance] and that other benefit shall in no case be less than the sum of the amounts which, but for any adjustment, would have been payable by way of a [1 severe disablement allowance] or [2 a carer's allowance] as personal benefit and dependency benefit.

AMENDMENTS

1. The Social Security (Severe Disablement Allowance) Regulations 1984 (SI 1984/1303) reg.11 (November 29, 1984).
2. The Social Security Amendment (Carer's Allowance) Regulations 2002 (SI 2002/2497) reg.3 and Sch.2 (April 1, 2003).
3. Social Security Act 1986 s.18(1) (April 6, 1987).

Increases in respect of more than one dependant to be treated as separate dependency benefits

13.—For the purposes of these regulations, where dependency benefit by way of an increase is payable in respect of more than one person (whether a child or adult dependant), each such increase shall be treated as a separate dependency benefit.

3.98

Provisions for adjusting benefit for part of a week

[² **14.**—(1) Where an adjustment falls to be made under these regulations for part of a week, benefit (whether under the Contributions and Benefits Act or otherwise) shall be deemed to be payable at a rate equal to one-seventh of the appropriate weekly rate for each day of the week in respect of any such benefit.]

3.99

(2) [¹ . . .]

(3) In paragraph (1) "appropriate weekly rate" means the weekly rate at which the benefit in question would be payable but for these regulations.

AMENDMENTS

1. The Social Security and Child Support (Jobseeker's Allowance) (Consequential Amendments) Regulations 1996 (SI 1996/1345) reg.14(2) (October 7, 1996).

2. The Statutory Maternity Pay, Social Security (Maternity Allowance) and Social Security (Overlapping Benefits) (Amendment) Regulations 2006 (SI 2006/2379) (October 1, 2006).

Priority between persons entitled to increase of benefit

15.—(1) Subject to paragraphs (5) and (6), the following provisions shall apply for the purpose of determining priority as between two persons entitled to an increase of benefit under the Act in respect of a third person.

3.100

(2) Where, but for the provisions of this paragraph, a man and his wife would both be entitled to an increase of retirement pension (being an increase of Category A or Category C retirement pension in his case and a Category B or Category C retirement pension in hers) in respect of the same child or children, that man shall, and his wife shall not, be entitled to the increase; and he shall be treated as so entitled for the purposes of this paragraph during any period for which he would be entitled but for the operation of any provision of the Act, with the exception of [section 113(1)(b) of the Social Security Contributions and Benefits Act 1992] (disqualification while undergoing imprisonment or detention), disqualifying him for the receipt of benefit.

(3) Subject to paragraphs (2), (5) and (6), where, but for the provisions of this paragraph, more than one person would be entitled to an increase of benefit in respect of the same child for the same period—

(a) in a case where one of those persons has been awarded child benefit in respect of the child for that period, that one of them shall be entitled to the said increase;

(b) in the case where sub-paragraph (a) does not apply but where one of those persons is entitled otherwise than by virtue of regulations made under Schedule 20 to the Act to child benefit in respect of the child for that period, that one of them shall be entitled to the said increase;

  (c) in a case where neither sub-paragraph (a) nor sub-paragraph (b) applies but where the child is living with one and no other of those persons for that period, that one of them with whom the child is living shall be entitled to the said increase;

  (d) in a case where none of the preceding sub-paragraphs applies but where one of those persons is a parent of the child, that one of them shall be entitled to the said increase.

(4) Subject to paragraphs (5) and (6), where, but for the provisions of this paragraph, more than one person would be entitled to an increase of benefit in respect of an adult dependant for the same period—

  (a) in a case where one of those persons is the spouse [¹ or civil partner] of the adult dependant that one of them shall be entitled to the said increase;

  (b) in a case where sub-paragraph (a) above does not apply that one of them with whom the adult dependant is residing shall be entitled to the said increase.

(5) Nothing in paragraphs (3) and (4) shall prevent a written notice signed by one or, as the case may be, a majority of the said persons designating another of them as the person to be entitled to the increase, being sent to the Secretary of State; so however that such notice shall not be effective to confer entitlement to an increase in respect of any period for which such increase has already been paid to someone other than the person so designated.

(6) Nothing in paragraphs (3) and (4) shall prevent a person who, in accordance with any of those paragraphs, is not entitled to an increase from being paid an amount equivalent to the amount, if any, by which the increase which would otherwise have been paid to such person exceeds the increase payable to the person entitled by virtue of any of the said paragraphs.

AMENDMENT

  1. The Civil Partnership (Pensions, Social Security and Child Support) (Consequential, etc. Provisions) Order 2005 (SI 2005/2877) (December 5, 2005).

Persons to be treated as entitled to benefit for certain purposes

3.101   **16.** Any person who would be entitled to any benefit under the Act [², Part 1 of the Welfare Reform Act] [³ , under Part 4 of the 2012 Act] [⁴ or under the Jobseekers Act, or entitled to armed forces independence payment] but for these regulations shall be treated as if he were entitled thereto for the purpose of any rights or obligations under the Act and the regulations made under it [² , Part 1 of the Welfare Reform Act and regulations made under it] [⁴ or under the Jobseekers Act and regulations made under it, or entitled to armed forces independence payment] [³ , Part 4 of the 2012 Act and regulations made under it] (whether of himself or some other person) which depend on his being so entitled, other than for the purposes of the right to payment of that benefit.

AMENDMENTS

  1. The Social Security and Child Support (Jobseeker's Allowance) (Consequential Amendments) Regulations 1996 (SI 1996/1345) reg.22(6)(a) and (b) (October 7, 1996).
  2. The Employment and Support Allowance (Consequential Provisions) (No. 2) Regulations 2008 (SI 2008/1554) reg.51 (October 27, 2008).
  3. The Personal Independence Payments (Supplementary Provisions and

Consequential Amendments) Regulations 2013 (SI 2013/388) reg.8 and Sch. para.10(4) (April 8, 2013).

4. The Armed Forces and Reserve Forces Compensation Scheme (Consequential Provisions: Subordinate Legislation) Order 2013 (SI 2013/591) reg.7 and Sch. para.3 (April 8, 2013).

Prevention of double adjustments

17.—No adjustment shall be made under regulations 6 to 10 to any benefit under the Act [¹ . . .] [² the Jobseekers Act [³ , Part 1 of the Welfare Reform Act or Part 4 of the 2012 Act]] by reference to any other benefit, whether under the Act [¹ . . .] [² the Jobseekers Act or Part 1 of the Welfare Reform Act] or otherwise, where the latter benefit has itself been adjusted by reference to the former benefit.

3.102

AMENDMENTS

1. The Social Security and Child Support (Jobseeker's Allowance) (Consequential Amendments) Regulations 1996 (SI 1996/1345) reg.22(7) (October 7, 1996).
2. The Employment and Support Allowance (Consequential Provisions) (No. 2) Regulations 2008 (SI 2008/1554) reg.51 (October 27, 2008).
3. The Personal Independence Payments (Supplementary Provisions and Consequential Amendments) Regulations 2013 (SI 2013/388) reg.8 and Sch. para.10(5) (April 8, 2013).

Regulation 18 omitted.

3.103

SCHEDULE 1   **Regulation 6**

PERSONAL BENEFITS WHICH ARE REQUIRED TO BE ADJUSTED BY REFERENCE TO BENEFITS NOT UNDER CHAPTERS I AND II OF PART II OF THE ACT

3.104

Column (1) Personal benefit	Column (2) Other personal benefit by reference to which the benefit in column (1) is to be adjusted
1. A contribution-based jobseeker's allowance or short-term incapacity benefit.	1. Unemployability supplement and training allowance.
2. Maternity allowance.	2. Training allowance.
3. Widow's benefit, [[¹ . . .] widowed parent's allowance] and benefit by virtue of [section 78(9) of the Contributions and Benefits Act] corresponding to widowed mother's allowance or widow's pension.	3. Unemployability supplement, industrial death benefit or war pension death benefit in either case payable to a woman as widow of the deceased and (except where the benefit in column (1) is widow's allowance) training allowance.
4. Retirement pension of any category (except any age addition) or incapacity benefit, severe disablement allowance, contributory employment and support allowance or carer's allowance.	4. Unemployability supplement, industrial death benefit or war pension death benefit in either case payable to that person as the surviving spouse or civil partner, and training allowance.
4A. State pension under Part 1 of the Pensions Act 2014	4A. Unemployability supplement and training allowance.
5. Attendance allowance, the care component of disability living allowance, the daily living component of personal independence payment or armed forces independence payment up to the value of the daily living component of personal independence payment at the enhanced rate;	5. Any benefit based on need for attendance under section 61 or under any Pneumoconiosis and Byssinosis Benefit Scheme, Personal Injuries Scheme, Service Pensions Instruments or 1914–1918 War Injuries Scheme.

Column (1) Personal benefit	Column (2) Other personal benefit by reference to which the benefit in column (1) is to be adjusted
5a. Personal independence payment, attendance allowance or disability living allowance.	5a. Armed forces independence payment
6. Invalidity allowance or an increase in the rate of incapacity benefit in accordance with regulation 10(1) of the Social Security (Incapacity Benefit) Regulation 1994.	6. An increase under section 59(1) of an unemployability supplement and an additional allowance payable only to a beneficiary who is entitled to an unemployability supplement under any Personal Injuries Scheme, Service Pensions Instrument or 1914–1918 War Injuries Scheme.
7. [. . .]	7. [. . .]
8. Unemployability supplement.	8. Any other unemployability supplement.
9. Increase of disablement pension during hospital treatment.	9. Treatment allowance.

AMENDMENTS

For the sake of clarity of the text of the Schedule, it is reproduced without indication of the amendments up to April 2019. The Schedule has been amended by:

The Social Security (Abolition of Injury Benefit) (Consequential) Regulations 1983 (SI 1983/186) (April, 1983).

The Social Security (Severe Disablement Allowance) Regulations 1984 (SI 1984/1303) (November 29, 1984).

The Disability Living Allowance and Disability Working Allowance (Consequential Provisions) Regulations 1991 (SI 1991/2742) (April 6, 1992).

The Social Security (Incapacity Benefit) (Consequential and Transitional Amendments and Savings) Regulations 1995 (SI 1995/829) (April 13, 1995). The Social Security and Child Support (Jobseeker's Allowance) (Consequential Amendments) Regulations 1996 (SI 1996/1345) (October 7, 1996).

The Social Security (Benefits for Widows and Widowers) (Consequential Amendments) Regulations 2000 (SI 2000/1483), reg.6 (April 9, 2001).

Social Security Amendment (Carer's Allowance) Regulations 2002/2497 reg.3 and Sch.2 (April 1, 2003).

The Civil Partnership (Pensions, Social Security and Child Support) (Consequential, etc. Provisions) Order 2005 (SI 2005/2877) (December 5, 2005).

The Employment and Support Allowance (Consequential Provisions) (No. 2) Regulations 2008 (SI 2008/1554), reg.51 (October 27, 2008).

The Personal Independence Payment (Supplementary Provisions and Consequential Amendments) Regulations 2013 (SI 2013/388), reg.8 and Sch. para.10(6) (April 8, 2013).

The Armed Forces and Reserve Forces Compensation Scheme (Consequential Provisions: Subordinate Legislation) Order 2013 (SI 2013/591), reg.7 and Sch. para.3 (April 8, 2013).

The Pensions Act 2014 (Consequential, Supplementary and Incidental Amendments) Order 2015 (SI 2015/1985) art.4(4) (April 6, 2016).

The Pensions Act 2014 (Consequential, Supplementary and Incidental Amendments) Order 2017 (SI 2017/422) art.6 (April 6, 2017).

3.105   *Schedule 2 omitted.*

The Social Security Benefit (Persons Abroad) Regulations 1975

(SI 1975/563) (as amended)

ARRANGEMENT OF REGULATIONS

1.   Citation, commencement and interpretation.   3.106
2.   Modification of the Act in relation to incapacity benefit, severe disablement allowance, unemployability supplement and maternity allowance.
3.   *Revoked.*
4.   Modification of the Act in relation to widow's benefit, bereavement-benefit, child's special allowance, guardian's allowance and retirement pension.
5.   Application of disqualification in respect of up-rating of benefits.
5A.   Rate of guaranteed minimum pension for the purposes of section 29 of the Pensions Act.
6.   Modification of right to elect to be treated as not having retired.
7.   *Revoked.*
8.   Modification of the Act in relation to age addition.
9.   Modification of the Act in relation to title to disablement benefit and industrial death benefit.
10.   Modification of the Act in relation to attendance allowance.
10A. *Revoked.*
10B. Modification of the Act in relation to carer's allowance.
10C. Modification of Parts II and III of the Act in relation to accidents happening or prescribed diseases contracted outside Great Britain.
11.   Modification of the Act in relation to employment on the Continental Shelf.
12.   Modification of the Act in relation to the Channel Islands.
13.   Modification of the Act in relation to a dependant.
13A. Modification of the Act in relation to title to benefit for beneficiary's child dependants.
13B. *Revoked.*
14.   Administrative arrangements about payments of benefits.
15.   *Omitted.*
Schedule. Up-rating in respect of certain awards made between 1st September 1985 and 7th August 1991.

The Secretary of State for Social Services, in exercise of powers conferred upon her by sections 21(3), 30(3), 32(5), 114(1), 131 and 132 of the Social Security Act 1975 and of all other powers enabling her in that behalf, without having referred any proposals on the matter to the National Insurance Advisory Committee or the Industrial Injuries Advisory Council since it appears to her that by reasons of urgency it is inexpedient to do so, hereby makes the following regulations:

Citation, commencement and interpretation

1.—(1) These regulations may be cited as the Social Security Benefit   3.107
(Persons Abroad) Regulations 1975 and shall come into operation on April 6, 1975.

(2) In these regulations, unless the context otherwise requires—
"the Act" means the Social Security Act 1975;

[¹² . . .]

[³ "child benefit" means benefit under Part I of the Child Benefit Act;]

[⁴ "the Child Benefit Act" means the Child Benefit Act 1975];

[⁵ "the Contributions and Benefits Act" means the Social Security Contributions and Benefits Act 1992];

"the Contributions Regulations" means the Social Security (Contributions) Regulations [³ 1979];

[³ "entitled to child benefit" includes treated as so entitled;]

"the former Death Grant Regulations" means the National Insurance (Death Grant) Regulations 1973;

"the former Principal Act" means the National Insurance Act 1965;

"the former Widow's Benefit and Retirement Pensions Regulations" means the National Insurance (Widow's Benefit and Retirement Pensions) Regulations 1972;

[⁶ "guaranteed minimum pension" has the meaning given to it in section 26(2) of the Social Security Pensions Act 1975 as construed in accordance with section 9 of the Social Security Act 1986];

[¹⁰ . . .]

"the Industrial Injuries Employment Regulations" means the Social Security (Employed Earners' Employments for Industrial Injuries Purposes) Regulations 1975;

[¹¹ "jobseeker's allowance" means an allowance under the Jobseekers Act 1995 as amended by the provisions of Part 1 of Schedule 14 to the Welfare Reform Act 2012 that remove references to an income-based allowance, and a contribution-based allowance under the Jobseekers Act 1995 as that Act has effect apart from those provisions;]

["the other party" in the case of a person who has been married or been in a civil partnership more than once, refers to the person by virtue of whose contributions that person is entitled to the benefit in question;]

"the Overlapping Benefits Regulations" means the National Insurance (Overlapping Benefit) Regulations 1975;

"the former Old Persons' Pensions Regulations" means the National Insurance (Old Persons' Pensions) Regulations 1970;

"retired" means retired from regular employment;

[⁷ "serving member of the forces" has the meaning given to it in regulation 1(2) of the Contributions Regulations];"

[⁹ "shared additional pension" means a shared additional pension under section 55A or the Contributions and Benefits Act;]

"the Special Provisions Regulations" means the Social Security (Benefit) (Married Women and Widows Special Provisions) Regulations 1974;

"the Widow's Benefit and Retirement Pensions Regulations" means the Social Security (Widow's Benefit and Retirement Pensions) Regulations 1974;

"widow's benefit" and "widow's pension" include benefit under section 39(4) of the Act corresponding to a widow's pension or a widowed mother's allowance;

[¹ "widowed parent's allowance" means an allowance referred to in section 39A of the Social Security Contributions and Benefits Act 1992;]

and other expressions have the same meanings as in the Act.

(3) Any reference in these regulations to any provision made by or contained in any enactment or instrument shall, except in so far as the context

otherwise requires, be construed as a reference to that provision as amended or extended by any enactment or instrument, and as including a reference to any provision which it re-enacts or replaces, or which may re-enact or replace it, with or without modification.

(4) The rules for the construction of Acts of Parliament contained in the Interpretation Act 1889 shall apply for the purposes of the interpretation of these regulations as they apply for the purposes of the interpretation of an Act of Parliament.

AMENDMENTS

1. The Welfare Reform and Pensions (Persons Abroad: Benefits for Widows and Widowers) (Consequential Amendments) Regulations 2000 (SI 2000/2876) reg.2 (April 9, 2001).
2. The Welfare Reform and Pensions (Persons Abroad: Benefits for Widows and Widowers) (Consequential Amendments) Regulations 2001 (SI 2001/2618) reg.2(2) (August 20, 2001).
3. The Social Security (Child Benefit) (Consequential) Regulations 1977 (SI 1977/342) reg.13(2) (April 4, 1977).
4. The Social Security (Child Benefit) (Consequential) Regulations 1977 (SI 1977/342) reg.13(2) (April 4, 1977).
5. The Social Security (Maternity Grant) Amendment Regulations 1981 (SI 1981/1157) reg.3(2) (April 1, 1982).
6. The Social Security Benefit (Persons Abroad) Amendment (No. 2) Regulations 1990 (SI 1990/621) reg.2(2) (April 6, 1990).
7. The Social Security Benefit (Persons Abroad) Amendment Regulations 1990 (SI 1990/40) reg.2(2) (February 8, 1990).
8. The Social Security (Miscellaneous Provisions) Amendment (No. 2) Regulations 1992 (SI 1992/2595) reg.9 (November 16, 1992).
9. The Social Security (Shared Additional pension (Miscellaneous Amendments) Regulation 2005 (SI 2005/1551) (July 6, 2005).
10. The Social Security Benefit (Persons Abroad) (Amendment) Regulations 2010 (SI 2010/788) reg.3 (April 6, 2010).
11. The Universal Credit (Consequential Supplementary, Incidental and Miscellaneous Provisions) Regulations 2013 (SI 2013/630) reg.23(2) (April 29, 2013).
12. The Pensions Act 2014 (Consequential, Supplementary and Incidental Amendments) Order 2017 (SI 2017/422) art.5 (April 6, 2017).

GENERAL NOTE

Interpretation Act 1889
By s.25(2) of the Interpretation Act 1978, the reference to the Interpretation Act 1889 is to be treated as a reference to the 1978 Act.   **3.108**

Regulation 1(2) refers to the definition of "serving member of the forces" in the Social Security (Contributions) Regulations 1979 (SI 1979/591). There the item is defined as follows:

> "'serving member of the forces' means a person (not being a person mentioned in Part II of Schedule 3 to these regulations) who, being over the age of 16, is a member of any establishment or organisation in Part I of Schedule 3 to these regulations (being a member who gives full pay service) but does not include any such person while absent on desertion."

Part I of Sch.3 of these Regulations is reproduced in the annotations to reg.3 of the Computation of Earnings Regulations.

Part II of Sch.3 reads as follows:

"By virtue of regulation 113 of these regulations, Her Majesty's forces shall not be taken to consist of any of the establishments or organisations specified in Part I of this Schedule by virtue only of the employment in such establishment of the following persons—

(a) any person who is serving as a member of any naval force of Her Majesty's forces and who (not having been an insured person under the former principal Act or, as the case may be, the National Insurance Act (Northern Ireland) 1966 and not being a contributor under the Act) locally entered that force at an overseas base;

(b) any person who is serving as a member of any military force of Her Majesty's forces and who entered that force, or was recruited for that force outside the United Kingdom, and the depot of whose unit is situated outside the United Kingdom;

(c) any person who is serving as a member of any air force of Her Majesty's forces and who entered that force, or was recruited for that force, outside the United Kingdom, and is liable under the terms of his engagement to serve only in a specified part of the world outside the United Kingdom."

Modification of the Act in relation to [¹ incapacity benefit], severe disablement allowance, unemployability supplement and maternity allowance

3.109   **2.**—(1) [² Except as provided by paragraph (1A) or (1B) below, a] [person shall not be disqualified for receiving [² any benefit in respect of incapacity]] by reason of being temporarily absent from Great Britain for any day [³ falling within the first 26 weeks beginning with the day following the day on which he left Great Britain] if—

[⁴ (a) the Secretary of State has certified that it is consistent with the proper administration of the Act that, subject to the satisfaction of one of the conditions in sub-paragraphs (b), (bb) and (c) below, the disqualification under [section 113(1)(a) of the Social Security Contributions and Benefits Act 1992] should not apply, and]

(b) the absence is for the specific purpose of being treated for incapacity which commenced before he left Great Britain, or

[⁵ (bb) in the case of incapacity benefit, the incapacity for work is the result of a personal injury of a kind mentioned in [section 94(1) of the Social Security Contributions and Benefits Act 1992], and the absence is for the specific purpose of receiving treatment which is appropriate to that injury, or]

[⁶ (c) on the day on which the absence began he was, and had for the past 6 months continuously been, incapable of work and on the day for which benefit is claimed he has remained continuously so incapable since the absence began]

(d) [⁷ . . .]

[⁸ (1A) Subject to paragraph (1B), a person who is in receipt of attendance allowance [¹⁴ , disability living allowance [¹⁵ , armed forces independence payment under the Armed Forces and Reserve Forces (Compensation Scheme) Order 2011] or personal independence payment under Part 4 of the Welfare Reform Act 2012] shall not by reason of being temporarily absent from Great Britain be disqualified for receiving any benefit in respect of incapacity if—

(a) the absence is for the specific purpose of being treated for incapacity which commenced before he left Great Britain; or

(b) in the case of [² incapacity benefit] the incapacity for work is the result of a personal injury of a kind mentioned in section 94(1) of the Social Security Contributions and Benefits Act 1992 and the absence is for the specific purpose of receiving treatment which is appropriate to that injury; or

(c) on the day on which the absence began he was, and had for the past 6 months continuously been, incapable of work and on the day for which benefit is claimed he has remained continuously so incapable since the absence began.

(1B) A person who is a member of the family of a serving member of the forces and temporarily absent from Great Britain by reason only of the fact that he is living with that member shall not by reason of being temporarily absent be disqualified—

(a) for receiving any benefit in respect of incapacity except severe disablement allowance if—

(i) the absence is for the specific purpose of being treated for incapacity which began before he left Great Britain, or

(ii) in the case of [¹ incapacity benefit] the incapacity for work is the result of a personal injury of the kind mentioned in section 94(1) of the Social Security Contributions and Benefits Act 1992 and the absence is for the specific purpose of receiving treatment which is appropriate to that injury, or

(iii) on the day on which the absence began he was, and had for the past 6 months continuously been, incapable of work and on the day for which benefit is claimed he has remained continuously so incapable since the absence began; or

(b) for the receipt of severe disablement allowance.]

(2) [⁹ . . .]

(3) [¹⁰ . . .]

(4) [¹⁰ . . .]

[¹¹ (5) In this regulation—

(a) "benefit in respect of incapacity" means [¹ incapacity benefit], severe disablement allowance, an unemployability supplement or a maternity allowance;

(b) "member of the family of a serving member of the forces" means the spouse, [¹³ civil partner,] son, daughter, step-son, step-daughter, father, father-in-law, step-father, mother, mother-in-law or step-mother of such a member; and

(c) "week" means any period of seven days.]

AMENDMENTS

1. The Social Security (Incapacity Benefit) (Consequential and Transitional Amendments and Savings) Regulations 1995 (SI 1995/829) reg.7 (April 13, 1995).

2. The Social Security Benefit (Persons Abroad) Amendment Regulations 1994 (SI 1994/268) reg.2(2)(a) (March 8, 1994).

3. The Social Security Benefit (Persons Abroad) Amendment Regulations 1994 (SI 1994/268) reg.2(2)(c) (March 8, 1994).

4. The Social Security (Persons Abroad) Amendment Regulations 1977 (SI 1977/1679) reg.2(2) (November 14, 1977); The Social Security (Abolition of Injury Benefit) (Consequential) Regulations 1983 (SI 1983/186) reg.5(2) (April

6, 1983); The Social Security Benefit (Persons Abroad) Amendment Regulations 1990 (SI 1990/40) reg.2(3)(a)(ii) (February 8, 1990); and The Social Security Benefit (Persons Abroad) Amendment Regulations 1994 (and SI 1994/268) reg.2(2)(d) (March 8, 1994).

5. The Social Security (Abolition of Injury Benefit) (Consequential) Regulatins 1983 (SI 1983/186) reg.5(2) (April 4, 1983); The Social Security Benefit (Persons Abroad) Amendment (No.2) Regulations 1986 (SI 1986/1545) reg.2 (October 1, 1986); and The Social Security (Incapacity Benefit) (Consequential and Transitional Amendments and Savings) Regulations 1995 (SI 1995/829) reg.7(b) (April 13, 1995).

6. The Social Security Benefit (Persons Abroad) Amendment Regulations 1990 (SI 1990/40) reg.2(3)(b) (February 8, 1990); and The Social Security Benefit (Persons Abroad) Amendment Regulations 1994 (SI 1994/268) reg.2(2)(e) (March 8, 1994).

7. The Social Security Benefit (Persons Abroad) Amendment Regulations 1994 (SI 1994/268) reg.2(2)(e) (March 8, 1994).

8. Reg. 2(1A) and (1B) inserted by The Social Security Benefit (Persons Abroad) Amendment Regulations 1994 (SI 1994/268) reg.2(3) (March 8, 1994).

9. The Social Security Benefit (Persons Abroad) Amendment Regulations 1977 (SI 1977/1679) reg.2(4) (November 14, 1977).

10. The Social Security (Incapacity Benefit) (Consequential and Transitional Amendment and Savings) Regulations 1995 (SI 1995/829) reg 7(e) (April 13, 1995).

11. The Social Security Benefit (Persons Abroad) Amendment Regulations 1994 (SI 1994/268) reg.2(4) (March 8, 1994).

12. The Social Security (Severe Disablement Allowance) Regulations 1984 (SI 1984/1303) reg.16 (November 28, 1984).

13. The Civil Partnership (Pensions, Social Security and Child Support) (Consequential, etc. Provisions) Order 2005 (SI 2005/2877) (December 5, 2005).

14. The Personal Independence Payments (Supplementary Provisions and Consequential Amendments) Regulations 2013 (SI 2013/388) reg.8 and Sch. para.8 (April 8, 2013).

15. The Armed Forces and Reserve Forces Compensation Scheme (Consequential Provisions: Subordinate Legislation) Order 2013 (SI 2013/591) reg.7 and Sch. para.1 (April 8, 2013).

DEFINITIONS

"the Act"—reg.1.
"the former Principal Act"—reg.1.
"Great Britain"—by art.1 of the Union with Scotland Act 1706, this means England, Scotland and Wales.

GENERAL NOTE

3.110   This regulation applies to the specified benefits for incapacity. Three conditions must be satisfied for the disqualification in s.113 of the Contributions and Benefits Act to be avoided for the first 26 weeks:

(a) The absence from Great Britain must be temporary.

(b) The Secretary of State must certify that it is consistent with the proper administration of the Act that the disqualification should not apply.

(c) The claimant must establish that either

    (i) the absence is for the specific purpose of being treated for incapacity that existed before he or she left Great Britain; or

    (ii) in the case of incapacity benefit, the incapacity is the result of an industrial injury and the absence is for the specific purpose of receiving treatment appropriate to that injury; or

    (iii) on the day the absence began, the claimant was, and had for six months continuously been, incapable of work and the claimant has been continuously incapable of work since leaving Great Britain.

Paragraph (1A) exempts from the limitation to 26 weeks of the continuation of benefit those in receipt of attendance allowance or disability living allowance who meet the three conditions set out in that paragraph.

Paragraph (1B) makes a similar exemption for someone who is a member of the family of a serving member of the forces temporarily absent from Great Britain as a consequence of that status who meets the conditions set out in the paragraph.

Civil Partnership Act 2004

With effect from December 5, 2005, art.3 of the Civil Partnership Act 2004 (Relations Arising Through Civil Partnership) Order 2005 (SI 2005/3137) applies the provisions of s.246 of the Civil Partnership Act 2004 to the definition of "member of the family of a serving member of the forces" in reg.2(5)(b). Section 246 of the Civil Partnership Act 2004 is reproduced at para.1.638 of Vol.III.

3.111

Temporary absence

What amounts to temporary absence is not defined and so is a matter for the exercise of judgment by the adjudicating authorities, though considerable guidance is now available from Commissioners' decisions. In *R(S) 1/85*, Commissioner Edwards-Jones offered the following guidance:

3.112

> "There is, in my judgment, no universal period by reference to which the issue as to an absence being, or not being, temporary falls to be determined: the particular circumstances of the case are crucial." (para.19).
> "The phrase 'temporarily absent from Great Britain' . . . is to be construed as to give rise to the position that whilst demonstration that an absence is 'permanent' will preclude it counting as 'temporary,' demonstration that it is not necessarily 'permanent' does not of itself establish that it is 'temporary.' In particular, an absence may though intended as 'temporary' at its outset cease to count as such if by force of circumstances no certain time (and I do not by a 'certain time' mean necessarily a precise date or hour, but something broader) can be set as to when it will terminate. It is not a 'temporary' absence if it is indefinite." (para.20).

Relevant factors will be all the surrounding circumstances (including in the case of determination by tribunals events subsequent to the adjudication officer's decision: *R(S) 10/83*), which include the claimant's intentions though these will not be decisive: *R(S) 10/83*. As a general rule absences of more than 12 months are not temporary unless there are exceptional circumstances: *R(U) 16/62*. Serious doubts were cast in *R(S) 1/85* on the correctness of *R(S) 9/55* in which it was held that absence of three years and nine months undergoing treatment for tuberculosis in Switzerland was temporary, but the Commissioner in *R(S) 9/55* regarded the case in any event as restricted to its own rather special facts and notes that absences of more than a year will not normally be temporary.

In *CS/207/1990* the claimant suffered from multiple sclerosis and had been resident in Malta for almost seven years because the climate provided relief for his symptoms. He had, nevertheless, expressed a wish to return to Great Britain if and when his health improved sufficiently. Commissioner Johnson upheld the decision of the tribunal that the claimant could not be regarded as temporarily absent from Great Britain.

The Court of Appeal has considered the meaning of the word "temporarily" in this Regulation in *Chief Adjudication Officer v Belmer and Ahmed*, CA, March 16, 1994, *Guardian*, April 18, 1994 reported as *R(S) 1/96*. Neill L.J. giving judgment said that it was wrong to construe "temporarily" as being synonymous with "not permanent". Though it would be exceptional to show that an absence lasting for some years remained temporary, the proper approach was to consider whether the absence could be considered as temporary in the light of all the circumstances. The quality of the absence could change with the passage of time.

What began as a temporary absence could change to one of permanent absence. Equally the fact that there was no fixed return date could not be taken as showing that the absence was necessarily not temporary. The claimant's expressed intention would be relevant but not decisive, so there is an element of objectivity in the determination.

CDLA/2089/2004 concerned the interpretation of differently worded reg.2(2)(d) and (e) of the Disability Living Allowance Regulations on temporary absence from Great Britain, but the point the Commissioner makes may well have relevance when the provisions of this regulation are considered. The Commissioner rules that the continuation of benefit payment is based on two facts: first, that the absence from Great Britain must be for a temporary purpose, and secondly, that the absence has not lasted for more than 26 weeks. The period of 26 weeks does not define the word "temporary"; it merely limits to a maximum of 26 weeks the period during which benefit can remain in payment if the absence is temporary (provided that any other conditions set out in the regulations are satisfied).

Secretary of State's certificate

3.113   The certificate condition was introduced in 1975 to limit some of the problems inherent in the test. The regulation introducing it was held to be ultra vires by a Commissioner in *CS/5/76* and the regulation was replaced in 1977 in its current form. This formulation has been held to be lawful: *R(S) 8/83*.

Paragraph (1)(b) and (bb)

3.114   In *R(S) 2/86* a Tribunal of Commissioners reviewed the effect of para.(1)(b) in the light of a sizeable case law and in a majority decision explained that the requirements of para.(1)(b) were threefold:

(1) the claimant must show that immediately prior to the departure from Great Britain, he or she was incapacitated for work by reason of some specific disease or bodily or mental disablement (so pregnancy will not suffice: *R(S) 1/75*); and

(2) the going abroad is for the purpose of having treatment for the condition; and

(3) the condition giving rise to the incapacity abroad is capable of being identified with the condition giving rise to the incapacity subsisting at the date of departure abroad.

The majority specifically left open the question whether or not the incapacity for work arising during absence abroad must have continued unbroken between the start of the absence abroad and the day or days for which the claim is made. Their view was, however, that the period of incapacity need not be continuous. Commissioner Penny, the dissenting Commissioner, doubted the correctness of this view.

In *R(S) 2/86* a number of earlier decisions were qualified. In particular the presumption suggested in *R(S) 6/61* that the specific purpose of going abroad is for treatment where treatment for an incapacity is received abroad was rejected. Statements in *R(S) 1/75* were qualified by making it clear that it remained to be settled to what extent absence abroad could be for the specific purpose of receiving treatment where the initial absence was for some other reason, for example, where a person suffering an incapacity goes abroad for a holiday but subsequently extends the period abroad in order to receive treatment for the incapacity.

Treatment means "some activity by someone other than the claimant": *R(S) 10/51*. So trips abroad for convalescence, for a change of environment or for relaxation will not qualify: *R(S) 1/69, R. v National Insurance Commissioner Ex p. McMenemey* (Appendix to *R(S) 2/69*), *R(S) 4/80* and *R(S) 6/81*. Whether treatment involves some specific medical supervision or care is uncertain: *R(S) 2/51* and *R(S) 10/51* seem to assume that it does not, while *R(S) 16/51, R(S) 5/61, R(S) 10/62* and *R(S) 2/69* seem to assume that it does. Indeed it seems that being under a doctor's professional care may not be conclusive particularly if the incapacity is mental illness: *R(S) 5/61*, though treatment here may include non-medical treatment: *R(S) 1/65*.

Some Commissioners' decisions on absence for the specific purpose of receiving   3.115
treatment under paras (1)(b) and (bb) have stressed that specific medical supervision is required to bring a claimant within the ambit of the provisions.

In *CS/061/1992* Commissioner Morcom adds to the list of such authorities by concluding that treatment by a herbalist in Sri Lanka who "derived his occupation partly by family tradition and partly by experience . . . does not represent the qualified skill or service required to justify the decision that the claimant's absence from Great Britain was for the specific purpose of being treated for his incapacity." (para.5). The more modern authorities requiring specific medical supervision now considerably outnumber the earlier authorities which seem to suggest that treatment need not involve such a regime.

So decision-makers are left with a confusing body of authority on the meaning of treatment from which it is difficult to draw any clear guidance. In such circumstances, tribunals should take great care to make findings of facts as to the precise nature of the incapacity and the treatment proposed for it, including findings as to the personnel who will administer it. Once this has been done, whether it constitutes "treatment" within para.(1)(b) is essentially a matter for the judgment of the tribunal in the light of all the circumstances of the case.

R(S) 1/90 is an important decision of a Tribunal of Commissioners. It contains a   3.116
comprehensive review of the requirements of reg.2(1)(b) and (bb) on the intention of the claimant in going abroad. The nub of the decision is to be found in paras 29–30:

> "**29.** If we were required to approach the problem afresh, we would without hesitation take the view that for paragraph (b) to apply the purpose or intention to be treated (or to receive treatment under paragragh (bb)) must have been formed before the claimant's departure from Great Britain. There is great force in the observations of the Tribunal of Commissioners in *R(S) 2/86* at paragraph 12 . . . and we agree with them that 'it is a necessary and basic requirement for success in invoking regulation 2(1)(b)' that the claimant, in addition to the other requirements 'went abroad for the purpose of having treatment.'
>
> **30.** In our view, the decisions which favour the claimant in the present case— namely, that a claimant will avoid disqualification if, while abroad, he obtains or receives treatment although he had no such purpose or intention at the time of departure—are an over-liberal and erroneous interpretation of paragraph (b). The decisions to which we have referred span a period of 40 years. Overseas travelling facilities have in that period of time been radically changed and a re-appraisal of those earlier decisions is overdue. It falls to this tribunal to make that re-appraisal. We accept the strict construction adopted by the Tribunal of Commissioners in *R(S) 2/86* at paragraph 12, and have reached the decision set out in paragraph 29 above."

The effect of this decision is that the interpretation of the regulation in the following cases is no longer good law: *CS/317/1949(KL)*, *CSS/71/1949*, *R(S) 6/61*, *CS/01/1971*, *R(S) 1/75* and *R(S) 1/77*.

CIB/1956/2001 concerned a claimant who suffered from, among other ailments, eczema of both hands and feet. He had retired from work as a labourer on medical grounds. He received sickness benefit, followed by invalidity benefit which converted to incapacity benefit on its introduction. The principal point in the appeal concerned his absence in India for what was described by the claimant as a holiday but during which he consulted a hakim about his eczema. It was accepted that *R(S) 6/61* remained good authority for the proposition that the claimant's absence abroad must be for the specific purpose of being treated, but need not be for the sole purpose of being treated. The Commissioner goes further and indicates that medical treatment need not be the main purpose of the trip abroad, although an intention to secure treatment must have been in mind before the absence started. Just because a person has treatment abroad, it should not, however, be assumed that this was in mind before the trip began. In this case, there was enough evidence to meet that requirement. The Commissioner says,

> "I have no doubt that the trip was also a holiday and, like the tribunal, I incline to the view that that was the main purpose of the journey. I therefore do not find it surprising that the claimant referred to it as a holiday. However, I accept that the claimant's eczema, which was one cause of his retirement and was obviously defeating Western medical science, was so irritating for the claimant that finding a cure for it added to his desire to go to India, even though he had no high hopes of success. That, in my view, is enough to make "being treated" in India a "specific purpose" of the absence." (para.8).

Paragraph (1)(c)

3.117   This condition is designed to assist the long-term incapacitated. For this group the absence, though temporary, need not be for the specific purpose of receiving treatment.

In *CS/143/1993* the claimant had been awarded sickness benefit followed by invalidity benefit from January 3, 1989 to September 20, 1990. There was then a break in the payment of invalidity benefit until July 8, 1991, because she had been on an employment training course and received an allowance from the Secretary of State. In August 1991 she went on an extended holiday to Australia returning to Great Britain in February 1992. A question arose as to her continued entitlement to invalidity benefit when outside Great Britain. The claimant sought to rely on the provisions of reg.2(1)(c) to sustain her claim to receive the benefit while abroad. The adjudication officer argued that she could not establish the necessary six months' incapacity for work because reg.7(1)(f) of the USI Regulations provides that a day is not to be *treated* as a day of incapacity for work if on that day a person is attending a training course provided by or on behalf of the Secretary of State.

Commissioner Heggs concludes that the adjudication officer's case is misconceived and that provisions included in one set of regulations are not, without clear indication that they are intended to be, to be incorporated into other sets of regulations. The test in reg.2(1)(c) is a *factual* test contained in regulations made for a different purpose than the USI Regulations.

The 1994 amendments

3.118   The Persons Abroad Amendment Regulations 1994 (SI 1994/268) make changes to this regulation with effect from March 8, 1994 which, subject to exceptions, restricts the availability of benefits to a 26 week period.

There is a transitional provision in reg.3 of the amending regulations preserving entitlement to those who already had it in the following terms:

> "**3.**—(1) In this regulation "the former regulation 2" means regulation 2 of the principal Regulations as in force immediately before these Regulations came into force.
>
> (2) Where immediately before the coming into force of these Regulations, a person was absent from Great Britain but by virtue of the former regulation 2 was not disqualified for receiving any benefit, allowance or supplement referred to in paragraph (1) of the former regulation 2, that person shall continue not to be disqualified in respect of any day, if he—
>
> > (a) has been continuously absent from Great Britain since these Regulations came into force; and
> >
> > (b) would, had the former regulation 2 been in force on that day, have satisfied the provisions of that regulation in respect of that benefit, allowance or supplement."

Regulation 3 revoked by The Social Security Benefit (Persons Abroad)   **3.119**
Amendment Regulations 1990 (SI 1990/40), reg.3 (February 8, 1990).

Modification of the Act in relation to widow's benefit, [¹² widowed parent's allowance]] child's special allowance, guardian's allowance and retirement pension

4.—(1) Subject to the provisions of this regulation and of regulation   **3.120**
5 below, a person shall not be disqualified for receiving widow's benefit,
[¹² widowed parent's allowance]] child's special allowance, a guardian's
allowance [², a retirement pension of any category [⁹, a shared additional
pension] or graduated retirement benefit] by reason of being absent from
Great Britain.

(2) In the case of a widow's allowance paragraph (1) above shall apply
only where either—

(a) the woman or her late husband was in Great Britain at the time of his
death; or

(b) the contribution conditions for widowed mother's allowance and
widow's pension set out in paragraph 5 of Schedule 3 to [¹¹ the
Contributions and Benefits Act] or in regulation [³ 6 of the Social
Security (Widow's Benefit and Retirement Pensions) Regulations
1979] are satisfied in relation to the woman.

[³ (2A) In the case of a widow's payment, paragraph (1) above shall apply
only where—

(a) the woman or her late husband was in Great Britain at the time of his
death; or

(b) sub-paragraph (a) above does not apply but the woman returned to
Great Britain within 4 weeks of her husband's death; or

(c) the contribution conditions for widowed mother's allowance and
widow's pension set out in paragraph 5 of Schedule 3 to [¹¹ the
Contributions and Benefits Act] or in regulation 6 of the Social
Security (Widow's Benefit and Retirement Pensions) Regulations
1979 are satisfied in relation to the woman.]

(2B)[¹² . . .]

[⁵ (3) In the case of a Category A retirement pension the [⁶ basic pension]
of which falls to be increased under the provisions of [¹¹ section 51A(2) or
52(2) of the Contributions and Benefits Act (special provision for married
people and for surviving spouses)], the amount of the increase shall not
exceed the sum which would be required to raise the [⁶ basic pension] of
that Category A retirement pension to the sum specified in [¹¹ section 44(4)
of the Contributions and Benefits Act] (rate of [⁶ basic pension] of Category
A retirement pension) or the weekly rate of Category B retirement pension
specified in [¹¹ paragraph 5 of Part 1 of Schedule 4 to the Contributions and
Benefits Act], as the case may be, current at—

[⁷ (a) the date on which the person whose pension falls to be increased first
became entitled to that pension; or]

(b) the date on which that person was last ordinarily resident in Great
Britain; whichever is the later.

(4) Where, in the case of Category A retirement pension the [⁶ additional
pension] of which falls to be increased under the provisions of [¹¹ section
52(3) of the Contributions and Benefits Act], the surviving spouse [¹⁰ or
surviving civil partner] whose pension falls to be so increased, being over

pensionable age at the date of the death of the former spouse [¹⁰ or former civil partner], is not ordinarily resident in Great Britain, the amount of the increase shall not exceed the sum which would be required to raise the additional pension of that Category A retirement pension to the maximum prescribed by [¹¹ regulation 3 of the Social Security (Maximum Additional Pension) Regulations 2010] which would have been appropriate had the former spouse [¹⁰ or former civil partner] died on—

    (a) the date on which the surviving spouse was last ordinarily resident in Great Britain; or

    (b) April 1979; whichever is the later.

AMENDMENTS

1. The Welfare Reform and Pensions (Persons Abroad: Benefits for Widows and Widowers) (Consequential Amendments) Regulations 2000 (SI 2000/2876) reg.2 (April 9, 2001).

2. The Social Security Benefit (Persons Abroad) Amendment Regulations 1992 (SI 1992/1700) reg.2 (August 5, 1992).

3. The Social Security Benefit (Persons Abroad) Amendment Regulations 1988 (SI 1988/435) reg.2 (April 11, 1988).

4. The Welfare Reform and Pensions (Persons Abroad: Benefits for Widows and Widowers) (Consequential Amendments) Regulations 2001 (SI 2001/2618) reg.2(3) (August 20, 2001).

5. The Social Security Benefit (Persons Abroad) Amendment (No.2) Regulations 1979 (SI 1979/1432) reg.2(b) (November 10, 1979).

6. Social Security Act 1986 s.18(1) (April 6, 1987).

7. The Social Security (Abolition of Earnings Rule) (Consequential) Regulations 1989 (SI 1989/1642) reg.4(3) (October 1, 1989).

8. The Social Security Benefit (Persons Abroad) Amendment (No. 2) Regulations 1979 (SI 1979/1432) reg.2(a) (November 10, 1979).

9. The Social Security (Shared Additional pension (Miscellaneous Amendments) Regulation 2005 (SI 2005/1551) (July 6, 2005).

10. The Civil Partnership (Pensions, Social Security and Child Support) (Consequential, etc. Provisions) Order 2005 (SI 2005/2877) (December 5, 2005).

11. The Social Security Benefit (Persons Abroad) (Amendment) Regulations 2010 (SI 2010/788) reg.4 (April 6, 2010).

12. The Pensions Act 2014 (Consequential, Supplementary and Incidental Amendments) Order 2017 (SI 2017/422) art.5 (April 6, 2017).

GENERAL NOTE

3.121   The broad effect of this regulation taken together with regs 5 and 6 is that for the specified benefits, absence abroad is not a disqualifying condition. The reason is that the benefits are contributory, are not related to capacity to work and so require less supervision. Up-rating of benefit applies automatically only to those "ordinarily resident" in Great Britain (see notes to reg.5). A claimant cannot defer retirement if not ordinarily resident in Great Britain (reg.6).

In the case of widow's benefit, the woman or her late husband must additionally have been in Great Britain at the date of his death and the specified contribution conditions have to be met.

Application of disqualification in respect of up-rating of benefits

3.122   5.—(1) Where regulations made in consequence of an order under [¹⁹ section 150 (annual up-rating of benefits) or 150A (annual uprating of basic pension etc and standard minimum guarantee) of the Social Security

Administration Act 1992] provide for the application of this regulation to any additional benefit becoming payable by virtue of that order, the following provisions of this regulation shall, subject to regulation 12 below and the provisions of those regulations, have effect in relation to the entitlement to that benefit of persons absent from Great Britain.

(2) In this regulation [² and in regulation 5A]—

(a) references to additional benefit of any description are to be construed as referring to additional benefit of that description which is, or but for this regulation would be, payable by virtue (either directly or indirectly) of the said order; and

(b) "the appointed date" means the date appointed for the coming into force of the said order.

(3) [³ Subject to paragraph (8) and the Schedule below,] where a person is not ordinarily resident in Great Britain immediately before the appointed date the provisions of these regulations (except this regulation) shall not, unless and until he becomes ordinarily resident in Great Britain, affect his disqualification while he is absent from Great Britain for receiving—

(a) in the case of a [¹⁹ person] who immediately before the appointed date was a [¹⁹ married person or civil partner] and [⁴ was not entitled to a Category B retirement pension], any additional Category B retirement pension, if immediately before that date [¹⁹ the other party to the marriage or civil partnership] [⁴ was entitled to a Category A retirement pension] and was not ordinarily resident in Great Britain;

[⁵ (aa) in the case of a married person or civil partner], any additional Category B retirement pension if immediately before the appointed day [¹⁹ the other party to the marriage or civil partnership] was entitled to a Category A retirement pension and was not ordinarily resident in Great Britain (whether or not [19 they were married to each other or were partners of the other] immediately before that date);]

[⁶ (b) in the case of a person who immediately before the appointed date is [¹⁸ a widow, a widower or a surviving civil partner], any additional Category B retirement pensions, if the former spouse [¹⁸ or former civil partner] had died before the appointed day.]

[¹⁹ (ba) in the case of a married person or civil partner entitled to a Category B retirement pension under section 48A of the Contributions and Benefits Act (Category B retirement pension for a married person or a civil partner), other than a case that falls within sub-paragraphs (a) to (b), any additional Category B retirement pension where immediately before the appointed date that person's spouse or civil partner was not ordinarily resident in Great Britain;]

[⁷ (c) in any other case, any additional retirement pension of any category [¹⁷, any additional shared additional pension] or any additional graduated retirement benefit, if that person had become entitled to a retirement pension [¹⁷, a shared additional pension] or to graduated retirement benefit before the appointed date;]

(d) any additional widow's benefit [⁸ or [²⁰ widowed parent's allowance] if the deceased spouse] [¹⁸ or deceased civil partner] [⁹ had become entitled to a Category A retirement pension or had] die before the appointed date;

(e) any additional child's special allowance if her former husband had died before the appointed date;

[¹⁰ (f) any additional guardian's allowance in respect of a child if he were entitled to that allowance in respect of that child before the appointed date.]

(4) [¹¹ . . .]

(5) The provisions of these regulations shall not affect the disqualification while absent from Great Britain of a widow who—

    (a) is not ordinarily resident in Great Britain immediately before the appointed date, and was entitled to widow's benefit immediately before attaining pensionable age, or would, but for any provision of the Act disqualifying her for the receipt of such benefit, have been so entitled; and

    (b) is or becomes entitled to a Category A retirement pension the right to which is determined by taking into account under [¹² regulation 8 of the Social Security (Widow's Benefit and Retirement Pensions) Regulations 1979] her husband's contributions;

for receiving any additional Category A retirement pension the right to which is so determined unless and until she becomes ordinarily resident in Great Britain if—

    (i) before the appointed date her husband [¹³ was entitled to a Category A retirement pension] and was not ordinarily resident in Great Britain; or

    (ii) he died before the appointed date.

[¹⁴ (6) Subject to paragraph (8) and the Schedule below, the provisions of these regulations shall not affect the disqualification while absent from Great Britain of a person referred to in regulation 8 of the Social Security (Widow's Benefit and Retirement Pensions) Regulations 1979, being any such person other than a widow, who—

    (a) is not ordinarily resident in Great Britain immediately before the appointed date; and

    (b) is or becomes entitled to a Category A retirement pension the right to which is determined by taking into account under regulation 8 of the Social Security (Widow's Benefit and Retirement Pensions) Regulations 1979 the contribution of that person's former spouse [¹⁸ or former civil partner];

for receiving any additional Category A retirement pension the right to which is so determined unless and until that person becomes ordinarily resident in Great Britain if—

    (i) before the appointed date the former spouse [¹⁸ or former civil partner] was entitled to a Category A retirement pension and was not ordinarily resident in Great Britain; or

    (ii) the former spouse [¹⁸ or former civil partner] died before the appointed date.]

[¹⁵ (7) Paragraph (3)(c) of this regulations shall not apply to a person in relation to a Category B retirement pension if that person's spouse [¹⁸ or civil partner] was not entitled to a Category A retirement pension before the appointed date and either that person and that person's spouse [¹⁸ or civil partner]—

    (i) were husband and wife [¹⁸ or were civil partners] immediately before that date; or

    (ii) became husband and wife [¹⁸ or formed a civil partnership] on or after that date.]

[¹⁵ (8) The Schedule below shall have effect in relation to disqualifications for receiving additional benefit in the circumstances specified in that

Schedule (being certain cases in which a person was awarded a widow's benefit or a retirement pension or a higher rate of retirement pension between 1st September 1985 and 7th August 1991).]

AMENDMENTS

1. The Social Security Benefit (Persons Abroad) Amendment Regulations 1988 (SI 1988/435) reg.3 (April 11, 1988).
2. The Social Security Benefit (Persons Abroad) Amendment (No. 2) Regulations 1990 (SI 1990/621) reg.2(3) (April 6, 1990).
3. The Social Security Benefit (Persons Abroad) Amendment (No. 2) Regulations 1994 (SI 1994/1832) reg.2(2) (August 6, 1994).
4. The Social Security (Abolition of Earnings Rule) (Consequential) Regulations 1989 (SI 1989/1642) reg.8(3)(a)(i) (October 1, 1989).
5. The Social Security Benefit (Persons Abroad) Amendment (No. 2) Regulations 1994 (SI 1994/1832) reg.2(3) (August 6, 1994).
6. The Social Security Benefit (Persons Abroad) Amendment (No. 2) Regulations 1979 (SI 1979/1432) reg.3(3) (November 11, 1979).
7. The Social Security (Abolition of Earnings Rule) (Consequential) Regulations 1989 (SI 1989/1642) reg.8(3)(a)(ii) (October 1, 1989); and The Social Security Benefit (Persons Abroad) Amendment Regulations 1992 (SI 1992/1700) reg.3 (August 5, 1992).
8. The Welfare Reform and Pensions (Persons Abroad: Benefits for Widows and Widowers) (Consequential Amendments) Regulations 2000 (SI 2000/2876) reg.2 (April 9, 2001).
9. The Social Security (Abolition of Earnings Rule) (Consequential) Regulations 1989 (SI 1989/1642) reg.8(3)(a)(iii) (October 1, 1989).
10. The Social Security (Child Benefit) (Consequential) Regulations 1977 (SI 1977/342) reg.13(3) (April 4, 1977).
11. The Social Security (Child Benefit) (Consequential) Regulations 1977 (SI 1977/342) reg.13(3)(b) (April 4, 1977).
12. The Social Security Benefit (Person Abroad) Amendment (No. 2) Regulations 1979 (SI 1979/1432) reg.3(4) (November 10, 1979).
13. The Social Security (Abolition of Earnings Rule) (Consequential) Regulations 1989 (SI 1989/1642) reg.3(5) (October 1, 1989).
14. The Social Security Benefit (Person Abroad) Amendment (No. 2) Regulations 1979 (SI 1979/1432) reg.3(5) (November 10, 1979); The Social Security (Abolition of Earnings Rule) (Consequential) Regulations 1989 (SI 1989/1642) reg.8(3)(c) (October 1, 1989); and The Social Security Benefit (Persons Abroad) Amendment (No. 2) Regulations 1994 (SI 1994/1832) reg.2(2) (August 6, 1994).
15. The Social Security Benefit (Persons Abroad) Amendment (No. 2) Regulations 1979 (SI 1979/1432) reg.3(6) (November 10, 1979); and The Social Security (Abolition of Earnings Rule) (Consequential) Regulations 1989 (SI 1989/1642) reg.8(3)(d) (October 1, 1989).
16. The Social Security Benefit (Persons Abroad) Amendment (No. 2) Regulations 1994 (SI 1994/1832) reg.2(4) (August 6, 1994).
17. The Social Security (Shared Additional pension (Miscellaneous Amendments) Regulation 2005 (SI 2005/1551) (July 6, 2005).
18. The Civil Partnership (Pensions, Social Security and Child Support) (Consequential, etc. Provisions) Order 2005 (SI 2005/2877) (December 5, 2005).
19. The Social Security Benefit (Persons Abroad) (Amendment) Regulations 2010 (SI 2010/788) reg.5 (April 6, 2010).
20. The Pensions Act 2014 (Consequential, Supplementary and Incidental Amendments) Order 2017 (SI 2017/422) art.5 (April 6, 2017).

GENERAL NOTE

3.123   See annotations to reg.4.

"ordinarily resident"

3.124   These words are used rather less frequently in the social security regulations than simple "residence" and must mean something different from "resident". Guidance as to the meaning of ordinary residence was given in *R(P) 1/78*. It imports more than residence (on which see guidance in *R(P)2/67*). In *R(P) 1/78* the Commissioner said "ordinary residence . . . connotes residence in a place with some degree of continuity and apart from accidental and temporary absences." He went on to say that the words are used with the intention of "seeking to exclude from entitlement to an increase persons . . . who live mostly abroad, and come to reside here intermittently without the intention of settling indefinitely." Such persons cannot be said to be ordinarily resident here. Such an approach is consistent with the general law. In *R. v London Borough of Barnet Ex p. Shah* [1983] 2 W.L.R. 16, the House of Lords considered the meaning of ordinary residence as used in regulations made under the Education Act 1962. In the absence of a statutory definition the words are to be given their natural and ordinary meaning. The House of Lords unanimously concluded that ordinary residence referred to a person's "abode in a particular place or country which he has adopted voluntarily and for settled purposes as part of the regular order of his life for the time being, whether of short or long duration." This could not apply to residence which was unlawful, for example because it was in breach of immigration laws. The reasoning of the House of Lords was adopted by the Commissioner in *R(M) 1/85*.

The authorities were reviewed by Newey LJ in *Arthur v HMRC* [2017] EWCA Civ 1756, who helpfully summarised the relevant legal principles as follows:

"16. Guidance on the meaning of "ordinarily resident" can be found in three decisions of the House of Lords: *Levene v Inland Revenue Commissioners* [1928] AC 217, *Inland Revenue Commissioners v Lysaght* [1928] AC 234 and *R (Shah) v Barnet LBC* [1983] 2 AC 309. Those cases provide authority for the following propositions:

i) The expression "ordinary residence" "connotes residence in a place with some degree of continuity and apart from accidental or temporary absences" (*Levene*, at 225, per Viscount Cave LC);

ii) "[T]he converse to 'ordinarily' is 'extraordinarily' and ... part of the regular order of a man's life, adopted voluntarily and for settled purposes, is not 'extraordinary'" (*Lysaght*, at 243, per Viscount Sumner). Consistently with this, "ordinarily resident" "refers to a man's abode in a particular place or country which he has adopted voluntarily and for settled purposes as part of the regular order of his life for the time being, whether of short or long duration" (*Shah*, at 343, per Lord Scarman);

iii) "Ordinary residence" differs little from "residence" (*Levene*, at 222, per Viscount Cave LC). "Ordinarily resident" means "no more than that the residence is not casual and uncertain but that the person held to reside does so in the ordinary course of his life" (*Lysaght*, at 248, per Lord Buckmaster);

iv) A person can be resident in a place even though "from time to time he leaves it for the purpose of business or pleasure" and, conversely, "a person who has his home abroad and visits the United Kingdom from time to time for temporary purposes without setting up an establishment in this country is not considered to be resident here" (*Levene*, at 222-223, per Viscount Cave LC);

v) A person can also be resident in a place even though he would prefer to be elsewhere. In *Lysaght*, Lord Buckmaster said (at 248):

"A man might well be compelled to reside here completely against his will; the exigencies of business often forbid the choice of residence, and though a man may make his home elsewhere and stay in this country only because business compels him, yet none the less, if the periods for which and the conditions under which he stays are such that they may be regarded as constituting residence, as in my opinion they were in this case, it is open to the Commissioners to find that in fact he does so reside";

vi) A person may reside in more than one place (*Levene*, at 223, per Viscount Cave LC);

vii) "Ordinary residence" is not synonymous with "domicile" or "permanent home" (*Shah*, at 342-343 and 345, per Lord Scarman);

viii) "Immigration status" "may or may not be a guide to a person's intention in establishing a residence in this country" (*Shah*, 348, per Lord Scarman); and

ix) "There are two, and no more than two, respects in which the mind of the 'propositus' is important in determining ordinary residence": "[t]he residence must be voluntarily adopted" and "there must be a degree of settled purpose", which could potentially be "a specific limited purpose" (*Shah*, at 344 and 348, per Lord Scarman). Lord Scarman explained in *Shah* (at 344):

"The purpose may be one; or there may be several. It may be specific or general. All that the law requires is that there is a settled purpose. This is not to say that the 'propositus' intends to stay where he is indefinitely; indeed his purpose, while settled, may be for a limited period. Education, business or profession, employment, health, family, or merely love of the place spring to mind as common reasons for a choice of regular abode. and there may well be many others. All that is necessary is that the purpose of living where one does has a sufficient degree of continuity to be properly described as settled.'"

CP/3638/2006 was a complex case which concerned the question of the up-rating of a wife's benefit following the death of her husband. The claim in issue was initially by a wife, but later by a widow (the appellant). Her husband had become entitled to a Category A retirement pension in March 1976. When he emigrated to Canada the amount of that pension ceased to be up-rated; it was frozen at the November 1975 rate. In September 2001 the appellant married him. She then became entitled to a Category B retirement pension based upon his contributions. That pension was fixed at the November 1975 rate rather than the higher September 2001 rate. The husband died in May 2002 and the appellant's claim was converted to one on widowhood. The Commissioner ruled that there had been a change of status, the effect of which was that the restriction on up-rating applied only from the new award which should be made at the rate effective at the time of that award.

The decision has been reversed on appeal as *SSWP v Yates* [2009] EWCA Civ 479. Carnwath L.J., delivering the judgment of the Court reversed the Commissioner essentially on the application of the policy behind the restriction on up-rating. He says:

"37. I have not found this an easy question to resolve. I see the force of the Commissioner's interpretation, on a strict reading of the wording of the regulation. However, it makes no sense in practical terms. The general statutory policy (under section 113) is to deprive those absent from the country from any entitlement to such benefits, but to restore it only to the extent that Regulations provided. It is hard to see any reason for restoring the benefit for husbands at rates frozen by reference to the time when they left the country, while allowing a more generous rate for their wives, whose entitlement is equally dependent on their husbands' contributions. There is therefore a strong incentive to read any ambiguity in the Regulations so as to accord with the evident policy intention."

AY v SSWP (RP) [2011] UKUT 324 (AAC) is the decision of the Upper Tribunal on the remission of the case to the Upper Tribunal following the judgment of the Court of Appeal in *SSWP v Yates* [2009] EWCA Civ 479. The Judge addresses two remaining issues: (1) whether reg.5 is ultra vires; and (2) whether there has been discrimination in breach of the European Convention on Human Rights.

On the first issue, the judge finds that reg.5 is not ultra vires, though it is poorly drafted. On the second issue, the judge finds, on a concession by the Secretary of State, that there has been a breach of art.14 ECHR when read with art.1 of Protocol 1. The judge also concludes that the situation falls within the ambit of art.8 ECHR, but that the outcome would be exactly the same. For further discussion of the human rights point, see Part IV of Volume III.

[¹ Rate of guaranteed minimum pension for the purposes of section 29 of the Pensions Act

3.125   **5A.**—Where a person is absent from Great Britain and disqualified for receiving additional Category A or Category B retirement pension, additional widowed mother's allowance [², [³ . . .] widowed parent's allowance] or additional widow's pension then—

>   (a) the rate of guaranteed minimum pension shall for the purposes only of section 29(1) of the Pensions Act be determined in his case as if any Order under section 37A of the Pensions Act which came into force while he was disqualified had instead come into force on the first day on which he ceased to be disqualified, and
>
>   (b) so long as the person is disqualified, section 37A(7) shall apply to him as if the reference to section 29(1) were omitted.]

AMENDMENTS

1. The Social Security Benefit (Persons Abroad) Amendment (No. 2) Regulations 1990 (SI 1990/621) reg.2(4) (April 6, 1990).

2. The Welfare Reform and Pensions (Persons Abroad: Benefits for Widows and Widowers) (Consequential Amendments) Regulations 2000 (SI 2000/2876) reg.2 (April 9, 2001).

3. The Pensions Act 2014 (Consequential, Supplementary and Incidental Amendments) Order 2017 (SI 2017/422) art.5 (April 6, 2017).

Modification of right to elect to be treated as not having retired

3.126   **6.**—Notwithstanding the provisions of regulation 2 of the Widow's Benefit and Retirement Pensions Regulations [¹ . . .] a person who is not ordinarily resident in Great Britain shall not be entitled to elect that that regulation shall apply in his case.

AMENDMENT

1. The Social Security (Abolition of Earnings Rule) (Consequential) Regulations 1989 (SI 1989/1642) reg.8(4) (October 1, 1989).

GENERAL NOTE

3.127   See annotations to reg.4.

3.128   *Regulation 7 revoked by The Social Security Benefit (Persons Abroad) Amendment Regulations 1990 (SI 1990/40) reg.3 (February 8, 1990).*

Modification of the Act in relation to age addition

8.—(1) A person shall not be disqualified for receiving age addition by reason of being absent from Great Britain if—

   (a) he is ordinarily resident in Great Britain; or

   (b) he was ordinarily resident in Great Britain and was entitled to age addition before he ceased to be ordinarily so resident; or

   (c) in the case of a person who ceased to be ordinarily resident in Great Britain before September 20, 1971, he is entitled to a retirement pension of any category and, by virtue of an Order in Council made under section 143 of the Act or under section 105 of the former Principal Act, he is not disqualified for receiving that pension at a higher rate than was applicable in his case when he was last ordinarily resident in Great Britain; or

   (d) in the case of a person who ceased to be ordinarily resident in Great Britain on or after September 20, 1971, he is entitled to a retirement pension of any category, and had he ceased to be ordinarily resident in Great Britain before that date, by virtue of an Order in Council made under section 143 of the Act or under section 105 of the former Principal Act, he would not have been disqualified for receiving that pension at a higher rate after that date than before it.

(2) Where a person is entitled to a retirement pension of any category at a rate which is calculated by reference to any period completed by that person in some territory outside Great Britain, any age addition to which he may be entitled shall be calculated as if it were an increase in that pension.

3.129

GENERAL NOTE

On the meaning of "ordinarily resident" see annotations to reg.5.

3.130

Modification of the Act in relation to title to [¹ . . .] disablement benefit and industrial death benefit

9.—(1) [² . . .]

   (2) [³ . . .]

   (3) A person shall not be disqualified for receiving [⁴ disablement benefit (other than any increase thereof under sections 58, 59, 61, 62, 63 or 66 of the Act)] by reason of being absent from Great Britain.

   (4) A person shall not be disqualified for receiving an increase of disablement pension in respect of the need for constant attendance under section 61, or under regulations made under section 159(3), or in respect of exceptionally severe disablement under section 63, of the Act, by reason of being temporarily absent from Great Britain during the period of 6 months from the date on which such absence commences or during such longer period as the Secretary of State may, having regard to the purpose of the absence and any other factors which appear to him to be relevant, allow.

   (5) A person shall not be disqualified for receiving [⁵ reduced earnings allowance under section 59A of the Act,] by reason of being temporarily absent from Great Britain during the period of 3 months from the date on which such absence commences or during such longer period as the Secretary of State may, having regard to the purpose of the absence and

3.131

any other factors which appear to him to be relevant, allow, so however that—

(a) such absence or any part thereof is not for the purpose of or in connection with any employment, trade or business;

(b) a claim as a result of which a decision is given awarding such allowance in respect of such period of absence or part thereof was made before the commencement of such absence; and

(c) the period taken into account by the award of such allowance to that person either includes the day of commencement of such absence or follows a period so taken into account which includes that day without there being a break in entitlement by that person to such increase from that day.

(6) A person shall not be disqualified for receiving industrial death benefit by reason of being absent from Great Britain.

[⁶ (7) A person shall not be disqualified for receiving retirement allowance under paragraph 13 of Schedule 7 to the Contributions and Benefits Act by reason of being absent from Great Britain.]

AMENDMENTS

1. The Social Security (Abolition of Injury Benefit) (Consequential) Regulations 1983 (SI 1983/186) reg.5(3) (April 6, 1983).
2. The Social Security (Abolition of Injury Benefit) (Consequential) Regulations 1983 (SI 1983/186) reg.5(4) (April 6, 1983).
3. The Social Security (Persons Abroad) Amendment Regulations 1977 (SI 1977/1679) reg.2(4) (November 14, 1977).
4. The Social Security (Industrial Injuries and Diseases) (Miscellaneous Provisions) Regulations 1986 (SI 1986/1561) reg.4(a) (October 1, 1986).
5. The Social Security (Industrial Injuries and Diseases) (Miscellaneous Provisions) Regulations 1986 (SI 1986/1561) reg.4(b) (October 1, 1986).
6. The Social Security (Miscellaenous Provisions) Amendment (No.2) Regulations 1992 (SI 1992/2595) reg.10 (November 16, 1992).

Modification of the Act in relation to attendance allowance

3.132   **10.**—A person shall not be disqualified for receiving attendance allowance [¹ or disability living allowance] by reason of being absent from Great Britain.

AMENDMENT

1. The Disability Living Allowance and Disability Working Allowance (Consequential Provisions) Regulations 1991 (SI 1991/2742) reg.2(2) (April 6, 1992).

3.133   *Regulation 10A revoked by The Disability Living Allowance and Disability Working Allowance (Consequential Provisions) Regulations 1991 (SI 1991/2742) reg.2(3) (April 6, 1992).*

Modification of the Act in relation to [² carer's allowance]

3.134   [¹ **10B.**—A person shall not be disqualified for receiving [² a carer's allowance] by reason of being absent from Great Britain.]

AMENDMENTS

1. The Social Security (Invalid Care Allowance) Regulations 1976 (SI 1976/409) reg.20 (April 12, 1976).

2. The Social Security Amendment (Carer's Allowance) Regulations 2002 (SI 2002/2497) reg.3 and Sch.2 (April 1, 2003).

Modification of Parts II and III of the Act in relation to accidents happening or prescribed diseases contracted outside Great Britain

10C.—(1) In this regulation—   3.135

"prescribed area" means an area over which Norway or any member State (other than the United Kingdom) exercises sovereign rights for the purpose of exploring the seabed and subsoil and exploiting their natural resources, being an area outside the territorial seas of Norway or such member State;

"prescribed disease" means a disease or injury prescribed for the purposes of Chapter V of Part II of the Act; and

"prescribed employment" means employment in a prescribed area in connection with the exploration of the seabed and subsoil and the exploitation of the natural resources of that area, or prescribed employment as defined in regulation 11 of these regulations (modification of the Act in relation to the United Kingdom continental shelf).

(2) Where on or after 30th November 1964 a person sustains or has sustained an accident or contracts or has contracted a prescribed disease while outside Great Britain, for the purposes of Chapter IV or V of Part II of the Act (benefit for industrial injuries and diseases) [section 94(5) of the Social Security Contributions and Benefits Act 1992] or regulation 14 of the Social Security (Industrial Injuries) (Prescribed Diseases) Regulations 1975 shall not operate to make benefit not payable in respect of that accident or prescribed disease if that person—

  (a) in connection with prescribed employment has sustained the accident or contracted the prescribed disease in a prescribed area, or while travelling between one prescribed area and another, or while travelling between a designated area (as defined in regulation 11 of these regulations) and a prescribed area, or while travelling between Norway or a member State (including the United Kingdom) and a prescribed area; or

  (b) has sustained the accident or contracted the prescribed disease while in the territory of a member State (other than the United Kingdom).

[¹ (2A) Where a person sustains an accident or contracts a prescribed disease while outside Great Britain in circumstances to which paragraph (2)(a) applies and the employment of that person would, but for the employment being outside of Great Britain, have been employed earner's employment, that employment shall for the purposes of Chapter IV or V of Part II of the Act (benefit for industrial injuries and diseases) be treated as employed earner's employment if:—

  (a) that person is ordinarily resident in Great Britain and immediately before the commencement of the employment was resident therein, and

  (b) the employer of that person has a place of business in Great Britain.]

(3) Where, before the date on which this regulation comes into operation, a decision has been given disallowing a claim for industrial injuries benefit in respect of an accident sustained or a prescribed disease contracted on or after 30th November 1964, then notwithstanding the provisions of section 107(6)(b) of the Act (decision that an accident not an industrial accident not reviewable) that decision may be reviewed by an insurance officer under

[section 25(1)(b) of the Social Security Administration Act 1992] (review on ground of relevant change of circumstances) if he is satisfied that had paragraphs (1) and (2) of this regulation been in force when that decision was given those paragraphs would have applied, but a decision on review under this paragraph shall not make industrial injuries benefit payable for any period before the date on which this regulation comes into operation.

(4) Paragraph (3) of this regulation shall apply to a decision refusing a declaration that an accident was an industrial accident as it applies to a decision disallowing a claim for industrial injuries benefit.

[² (5) Where on or after October 1, 1986 a person to whom this paragraph applies sustains an accident arising out of, and in the course of, his employment, or contracts a prescribed disease due to the nature of his employment, such employment shall for the purposes of Chapters IV and V of Part II of the Act (benefit for industrial injuries and diseases) be treated as employed earner's employment notwithstanding that he is employed outside Great Britain, and any benefit which would be payable under those chapters but for the provisions of [section 94(5) of the Social Security Contributions and Benefits Act 1992] and regulation 14 of the Social Security (Industrial Injuries) (Prescribed Diseases) Regulations 1985 shall be payable from the date of his return to Great Britain notwithstanding that the accident happened or the disease was contracted while he was outside it.

(6) Paragraph (5) applies to any person in respect of whom Class 1 contributions are payable by virtue of regulation 120 of the Social Security (Contributions) Regulations 1979 or who is paying Class 2 (volunteer development workers) contributions under Case G of those regulations.]

AMENDMENTS

1. The Social Security Benefit (Persons Abroad) Amendment Regulations 1979 (SI 1982/388) reg.2 (April 14, 1982).
2. Paragraphs (5) and (6) added by the Social Security Benefit (Persons Abroad) Amendment (No. 2) Regulations 1986 (SI 1986/1545) reg.3 (October 1, 1986).
3. The Social Security Benefit (Persons Abroad) Amendment Regulations 1979 (SI 1979/463) reg.2 (April 17, 1979).

Modification of the Act in relation to employment on the Continental Shelf

3.136   **11.**—(1) In this regulation—
"the Continental Shelf Act" means the Continental Shelf Act 1964;
"designated area" means any area which may from time to time be designated by Order in Council under the Continental Shelf Act as an area within which the rights of the United Kingdom with respect to the seabed and subsoil and their natural resources may be exercised;
"prescribed disease" means a disease or injury prescribed for the purposes of [sections 108–110 of the Social Security Contributions and Benefits Act 1992]; and
[¹ "prescribed employment" means any employment (whether under a contract of service or not) in any designated area or prescribed area, being employment in connection with any activity mentioned in section 23(2) of the Oil and Gas (Enterprise) Act 1982 in any designated area or in any prescribed area]; and
[¹ "prescribed area" means any area over which Norway or any member State (other than the United Kingdom) exercises sovereign rights for the

purpose of exploring the seabed and subsoil and exploiting their natural resources, being an area outside the territorial seas of Norway or such member State, or any other area which is from time to time specified under section 22(5) of the Oil and Gas (Enterprise) Act 1982.]

[³ (1A) Where a claimant would be entitled to a [⁵ . . .] jobseeker's allowance but for section 1(2)(i) of the Jobseekers Act 1995 (conditions of entitlement to a jobseeker's allowance: requirement to be in Great Britain), he shall be entitled to a [⁵ . . .] jobseeker's allowance notwithstanding his absence from Great Britain if—

(a) the absence from Great Britain is due to his being or having been in prescribed employment in a designated area; or

(b) subject to paragraph (2B), he is, in connection with prescribed employment—

   (i) in a prescribed area; or

   (ii) travelling between one prescribed area and another; or

   (iii) travelling between a designated area and a prescribed area; or

   (iv) travelling between Norway or a Member State (including the United Kingdom) and a prescribed area.]

(2) Where benefit under Part II of the Act would, but for the provisions of [section 113(1)(a) of the Social Security Contributions and Benefits Act 1992] (absence from Great Britain), be payable to a person in a designated area, that benefit shall be payable notwithstanding the absence of that person from Great Britain, if the absence is due to his being or having been in prescribed employment in [¹ a designated area].

[³ (2A) Subject to paragraph (2B) where benefit under Part II of the Act would be payable to a person were that person in Great Britain, that person shall not be disqualified for receiving such benefit by reason only of the fact that he is, in connection with prescribed employment:—

(a) in a prescribed area; or

(b) travelling between one prescribed area and another; or

(c) travelling between a designated area and a prescribed area; or

(d) travelling between Norway or a member State (including the United Kingdom) and a prescribed area.

(2B) Paragraphs (1A) and (2A) shall not apply where, under the legislation administered by Norway or any member State (other than the United Kingdom) benefit is payable in respect of a person for the same contingency and for the same period for which benefit is claimed under the Act.]

(3) Where benefit under Chapter IV or V of Part II of the Act would, but for the provisions of [section 94(5) of the Social Security Contributions and Benefits Act 1992], be payable to a person in respect of an accident arising out of and in the course of, or a prescribed disease due to the nature of, any employment by virtue of which any person is treated as an employed earner under paragraph 7 of Part I of Schedule 1 to the Industrial Injuries Employments Regulations, that benefit shall be payable notwithstanding that the accident happens or the disease is contracted while such person is outside Great Britain, if at the time that the accident happens or the disease is contracted the person is either in a designated area or travelling from one designated area to another or from or to Great Britain to or from a designated area.

(4) The provisions of the Act and of the regulations and orders made thereunder[³, and the Jobseekers Act 1995 and regulations made thereunder] shall, so far as they are not inconsistent with the provisions of this regulation, apply in relation to persons in prescribed employment with this

modification, that where such a person is, on account of his being outside Great Britain by reason of his employment, being prescribed employment, unable to perform any act required to be done either forthwith or on the happening of a certain event or within a specified time, he shall be deemed to have complied with that requirement if he performs the act as soon as is reasonably practicable, although after the happening of the event or the expiration of the specified time.

AMENDMENTS

1. The Social Security and Statutory Sick Pay (Oil snd Gas (Enterprise) Act 1982 (Consequential) Regulations (SI 1982/1738) reg.2 (December 31, 1982).
2. Paras (2A) and (2B) added by The Social Security and Statutory Sick Pay (Oil and Gas (Enterprise) Act 1982) (Consequential) Regulations 1982 (SI 1982/1738), reg.2 (December 31, 1982). Word added to para.(2B) by The Jobseeker's Allowance Regulations 1996 (SI 1996/207) reg.165(3) (October 7, 1996).
3. The Jobseeker's Allowance Regulations 1996 (SI 1996/207) reg.165(4) (October 7, 1996).
4. The Jobseeker's Allowance Regulations 1996 (SI 1996/207) reg 165(2) (October 7, 1996).
5. The Universal Credit (Consequential Supplementary, Incidental and Miscellaneous Provisions) Regulations 2013 (SI 2013/630) reg.23(3) (April 29, 2013).

Modification of the Act in relation to the Channel Islands

3.137   **12.**—(1) Notwithstanding any provisions of the Act or of these regulations a person shall not—
(a) be disqualified for receiving any benefit under the Act by reason of absence from Great Britain [¹ . . .];
(b) be disentitled to a maternity grant in respect of a confinement outside Great Britain; or
(c) be disqualified for receiving a death grant in respect of a death occurring outside Great Britain,
if that person is, or, as the case may be, that confinement or that death occurred, in a part of the Channel Islands which is not subject to an order made under section 143 of the Act or section 105 of the former Principal Act.
(2) A person who—
(a)
    (i) is in any part of the Channel Islands which is not the subject of an order made under section 143 of the Act or section 84 of the National Insurance (Industrial Injuries) Act 1965, or
    (ii) is going from (or to) Great Britain to (or from) such a part of the Channel Islands; and who
(b) suffers an industrial accident in the course of his employment (being employed earner's employment by virtue of regulation 94 of the Contributions Regulations),
shall, subject to the provisions of [section 95 of the Social Security Contributions and Benefits Act 1992], be treated as if the employment were employed earner's employment for the purposes of industrial injuries and as if the accident occurred in Great Britain.

AMENDMENT

1. The Social Security and Child Support (Jobseeker's Allowance) (Consequential Amendments) Regulations 1996 (SI 1996/1345) reg.15(2) (October 7, 1996).

Modification of the Act in relation to a dependant

13.—A husband or wife [¹ or civil partner] shall not be disqualified **3.138** for receiving any increase (where payable) of benefit in respect of his or her spouse [¹ or civil partner] by reason of the spouse's [¹ or civil partner's] being absent from Great Britain provided that the spouse [¹ or civil partner] is resident with [¹ the husband, wife or civil partner], as the case may be.

AMENDMENT

1. The Civil Partnership (Pensions, Social Security and Child Support) (Consequential, etc. Provisions) Order 2005 (SI 2005/2877) (December 5, 2005).

GENERAL NOTE

See annotations to reg.2 of the Persons Residing Together Regulations. **3.139**

[Modification of the Act in relation to title to benefit for beneficiary's child dependants

13A.—(1) By reason only of the fact that he is not entitled to child benefit **3.140** in respect of a child, a person shall not be disentitled from receiving a benefit or an allowance or an increase of a benefit or an allowance under the Act in respect of a child (hereafter in this regulation referred to as "child dependency benefit") in respect of that child for any period during which he and the child are, or the child is, absent from Great Britain in a country in circumstances in which he would, in pursuance of any agreement with the government of a country outside the United Kingdom, be entitled to receive child dependency benefit in respect of the child were he entitled to child benefit in respect of the child if—

(a) he would, or could, had he made an appropriate claim, have been entitled to child benefit in respect of the child had all the requirements of [section 146(2) and (3) of the Social Security Contributions and Benefits Act 1992] (requirements as to presence in Great Britain) been satisfied; and

(b) in a case where he would not be treated for the purposes of [Part IX of the Social Security Contributions and Benefits Act 1992] as having the child living with him, he is contributing to the cost of providing for the child, in addition to any contribution he may be required to make under the Act, at a weekly rate not less than that of the child benefit which would be payable to him in respect of the child were child benefit so payable to him; and

(c) no other person is entitled to child benefit in respect of the child.

(2) For any period during which a person who is absent from Great Britain would satisfy the requirements of paragraph (1) in relation to a child but for the fact that that child is present in Great Britain that child shall, for the purposes of that paragraph, be treated as being present in the country in which that person is.

(3) By reason only of the fact that he is not entitled to child benefit in respect of a child, a person shall not be disentitled from receiving child dependency benefit in respect of that child for any period during which he or the child is, or both of them are, absent from Great Britain in circumstances in which, otherwise than in pursuance of such an agreement as is

651

referred to in paragraph (1) or of regulations made under section 142 of the Act (co-ordination with Northern Ireland) were he entitled to child benefit in respect of the child he would be entitled to receive child dependency benefit in respect of the child if—

(a) he would, or could had he made an appropriate claim, have been entitled to child benefit in respect of the child had all the requirements of [section 146(2) and (3) of the Social Security Contributions and Benefits Act 1992] (requirements as to presence in Great Britain) been satisfied; and

(b) in a case where he would not be treated for the purposes of [Part IX of the Social Security Contributions and Benefits Act 1992] as having the child living with him, he is contributing to the cost of providing for the child, in addition to any contribution he may be required to make under the Act, at a weekly rate not less than that of the child benefit which would be payable to him in respect of the child were child benefit so payable to him; and

(c) he establishes that any absence from Great Britain of himself or the child was, when it began, intended to be temporary and has throughout continued to be temporary; and

(d) no other person is entitled to child benefit in respect of the child.

(4) For the purpose of paragraph (1), such a person or child as is there referred to may be treated as being absent from Great Britain notwithstanding that he has not previously been present in Great Britain; and for the purposes of paragraph (3), a child born during the absence from Great Britain of his mother shall, if she was pregnant of that child at a time when she was present in Great Britain, be treated as having been present in Great Britain on the date on which his mother was last present in Great Britain before the child was born.

(5) Where a person—

(a) immediately before returning to Great Britain was entitled to receive child dependency benefit in respect of a child; and

(b) would on his return to Great Britain have continued to be entitled to receive child dependency benefit in respect of that child were he entitled to child benefit in respect of the child,

he shall not be disentitled from receiving child dependency benefit in respect of the child by reason only of the fact that he is not entitled to child benefit in respect of the child if—

(i) he would, or could had he made an appropriate claim, have been entitled to child benefit in respect of the child had all the requirements of [section 146(2) and (3) of the Social Security Contributions and Benefits Act 1992] (requirements as to presence in Great Britain) been satisfied; and

(ii) in a case where he would not be treated for the purposes of [Part IX of the Social Security Contributions and Benefits Act 1992] as having the child living with him, he is contributing to the cost of providing for the child, in addition to any contribution he may be required to make under the Act, at a weekly rate not less than that of the child benefit which would be payable to him in respect of the child were child benefit so payable to him; and

(iii) no other person is entitled to child benefit in respect of the child.

(6) Where a person who was absent from Great Britain immediately before April 4, 1977, (the date on which child benefit first becomes payable) or a subsequent date on which the rate or any of the rates of child benefit is or are increased—

(a) is entitled to receive child dependency benefit in respect of a child for a continuous period beginning before and continuing after that date; and

(b) no other person is entitled to child benefit in respect of that child for that period,

any provision made pursuant to section 17(1) or (4) of the Child Benefit Act whereby, having regard to the introduction of child benefit or to an increase in the rate or any of the rates of child benefit, the weekly rate of child dependency benefit payable in respect of that child would be subject to a reduction shall not have effect so as (by reason only of that reduction) to reduce the total weekly rate of benefit (including benefit (if any) which is not child dependency benefit payable in respect of that child) payable to that person below the total weekly rate of such benefit payable to him immediately before that date.]

AMENDMENT

1. The Social Security (Child Benefit) (Consequential) Regulations 1977 (SI 1977/342) reg.13(5) (April 4, 1977).

GENERAL NOTE

The effect of this regulation is that if the claimant's child dependant is abroad,   **3.141** the claimant remains entitled to an increase for the child if the claimant is entitled to child benefit for the child. See Child Benefit (Residence and Persons Abroad) Regulations 1976.

If the claimant is not entitled to child benefit but would be if in Great Britain, the claimant will receive the increase if there is no one else entitled to child benefit for the child.

Regulation 13B revoked by The Social Security and Child Support (Jobseeker's   **3.142** *Allowance) (Consequential Amendments) Regulations 1996 (SI 1996/1345), Sch. (October 7, 1996).*

Administrative arrangements about payment of benefits

14.—Where the right to benefit arises by virtue of these regulations   **3.143** the benefit shall be payable subject to the furnishing of such information and evidence as the Secretary of State may from time to time require; and the Secretary of State shall make arrangements as to the time and manner of payment which shall have effect in place of the provisions as to time and manner of payment which would have been applicable by virtue of other regulations made under the Act [1], or in connection with jobseeker's allowance,] if the person concerned had not been absent from Great Britain.

AMENDMENT

1. The Social Security and Child Support (Jobseeker's Allowance) (Consequential Amendments) Regulations 1996 (SI 1996/1345) reg.15(3) (October 7, 1996).

Regulation 15 omitted.   **3.144**

UP-RATING IN RESPECT OF CERTAIN AWARDS MADE BETWEEN 1ST SEPTEMBER 1985 AND 7TH AUGUST 1991

3.145   **1.**—A person referred to in a case set out in column (1) shall not be disqualified by reason of being absent from Great Britain for receiving any additional widow's benefit or retirement pension which became payable by virtue of an up-rating order which came into force on or before the date referred to in column (3) if—

    (a) the award referred to in column (1) was made during the period specified in column (2); and

    (b) immediately before 6th August 1994 that person was being paid a widow's benefit or a retirement pension (as the case may be) at the rate current at the date referred to in column (3).

(1) Case	(2) Period in which award was made	(3) Date after which disqualification to take effect
1. A woman who was awarded a widow's benefit	after 30th May 1988 but not later than 19th February 1990	the date on which she became entitled to a widow's benefit
2. A woman who had been receiving a Category B retirement pension and was awarded that pension at a higher rate after her husband's death	after 13th September 1988 but not later than 6th August 1991	the date of her husband's death
3. A woman who was first awarded a Category B retirement pension on the death of her husband after she attained the age of 60	after 31st January 1990 but not later than 6th August 1991	the date on which she became entitled to a Category B retirement pension
4. A man who had been receiving a Category A retirement pension and was awarded a Category B retirement pension after his wife's death	after 16th November 1986 but not later than 6th August 1991	the date on which he became entitled to a Category B retirement pension
5. A woman who had been receiving a Category B retirement pension and was awarded a Category A retirement pension	after 1st September 1985 but not later than 6th August 1991	the date on which she became entitled to a Category A retirement pension
6. A person who was awarded a Category A retirement pension determined by taking into account the contributions of his or her former spouse under regulation 8 of the Social Security (Widow's Benefit and Retirement Pensions) Regulations 1979	after 16th November 1986 but not later than 6th August 1991	the date on which that person first became entitled to a Category A retirement pension

    2.—In paragraph 1 "up-rating order" means an order which was made under section 124 of the Act or section 63 of the Social Security Act 1986.]

AMENDMENT

    1. Schedule added by The Social Security Benefit (Persons Abroad) Amendment (No. 2) Regulations 1994 (SI 1994/1832) reg.3 (August 6, 1994).

The Social Security Benefit (Persons Residing Together) Regulations 1977

(SI 1977/956) (as amended)

ARRANGEMENT OF REGULATIONS

1. Citation, commencement and interpretation.
2. Circumstances in which a person is to be treated as residing or not residing with another person or in which persons are to be treated as residing or not residing together.
3. *Omitted.*

3.146

The Secretary of State for Social Services, in exercise of the powers conferred upon him by section 22(1) of the Social Security (Miscellaneous Provisions) Act 1977 and of all other powers enabling him in that behalf hereby makes the following regulations:

Citation, commencement and interpretation

1.—(1) These regulations may be cited as the Social Security Benefit (Persons Residing Together) Regulations 1977 and shall come into operation on June 27, 1977.

(2) In these regulations "the Act" means the Social Security Act 1975 and other expressions have the same meanings as in the Act.

(3) Any reference in these regulations to any provision made or contained in any enactment or instrument shall be construed as a reference to that provision as amended or extended by any enactment or instrument and as including a reference to any provision which may re-enact or replace it, with or without modification.

(4) The rules for the construction of Acts of Parliament contained in the Interpretation Act 1889 shall apply in relation to this instrument and in relation to any revocation effected by it as if this instrument, the regulations revoked by it and any regulations revoked by the regulations so revoked were Acts of Parliament, and as if each revocation were a repeal.

3.147

GENERAL NOTE

Interpretation Act 1889
By s.25(2) of the Interpretation Act 1978, this reference is to be treated as a reference to the 1978 Act.

3.148

Circumstances in which a person is to be treated as residing or not residing with another person or in which persons are to be treated as residing or not residing together

2.—(1) As respects any requirement of the Act, or contained in any provision made for the purposes thereof, any question as to whether—

(a) a person is or was residing with another person; or

(b) persons are residing together,

shall be determined in accordance with the following provisions of this regulation.

3.149

(2) In relation to—

(a) an increase in respect of an adult dependant under section 44 [⁴ (short-term benefits: increase for adult dependants)], 45 (increase of Category A or Category C retirement pension [³ ...]), 49 (increase of [² severe disablement allowance] or invalid care allowance) or 66 (increase [¹ ...] of a disablement pension where the beneficiary is entitled to unemployability supplement) [³ or section 86A of the Social Security Contributions and Benefits Act 1992 (incapacity benefit: increases for adult dependants)]; or

(b) an adjustment of benefit under section 85(1)(b) (hospital in-patients)

two spouses [⁵ or civil partners] shall not be treated as having ceased to reside together by reason only of the fact that either of them is, or they both are, undergoing medical or other treatment as an in-patient in a hospital or similar institution, whether such absence is temporary or not.

(3) In the case of a woman who has been widowed, she shall not be treated as having ceased to reside together with a child or person under the age of 19 by reason of any absence the one from theh other which is not likely to be permanent.

(4) Subject to the foregoing provisions of this regulation, two persons shall not be treated as having ceased to reside together by reason of any temporary absence the one from the other.

AMENDMENTS

1. The Social Security (Abolition of Injury Benefit) (Consequential) Regulations 1983 (SI 1983/186) reg.8 (April 6, 1983).

2. The Social Security (Severe Disablement Allowance) Regulations 1984 (SI 1984/1303) reg.11 (November 29, 1984).

3. The Social Security (Incapacity Benefit) (Consequential and Transitional Amendments and Savings) Regulations 1995 (SI 1995/829) reg.10 (April 13, 1995)

4. The Social Security and Child Support (Jobseeker's Allowance) (Consequential Amendments) Regulations 1996 (SI 1996/1345) reg.16 (October 7, 1996).

5. The Civil Partnership (Pensions, Social Security and Child Support) (Consequential, etc. Provisions) Order 2005 (SI 2005/2877) (December 5, 2005).

DEFINITIONS

"the Act"—reg.1.
"medical treatment"—CB & A 1992 s.122.

GENERAL NOTE

3.150   Compare reg.11 of the Child Benefit (General) Regulations. As in those regulations, "residing with" does not mean the same as "living with": *R(I) 10/51; R(U) 11/62* and *R(F) 2/79*. It is somewhat broader requiring only an element of continuity and permanence, which is to be assessed in the light of all the relevant circumstances of particular cases.

The general rule is that only permanent separation of two people constitutes not residing together. But the regulation sets out two specific rules.

First, if it is the sole cause of the absence of a spouse, periods by one or both spouses as in-patients in a hospital or similar institution are to be treated as periods residing together whether or not the absence is likely to be permanent. This presumably covers situations such as where a spouse is admitted to hospital for terminal care. Difficulties have arisen as to when a patient is an "inpatient". The approach consistently adopted has been that the patient must be "housed overnight" at the hospital or similar institution: *CS/65/49, R(S) 8/51* and *R(I) 14/56.*

Secondly, a widow and her child are treated as residing together if their absence from one another can be regarded as temporary, but they are to be treated as residing apart if their absence from one another is likely to be permanent. This appears to add little to the general rule and may owe its origins to particular difficulties over widow's benefit where persons under 19 are away from home for the purposes of full-time education and training. Such persons are presumed to be residing with the widow unless the absence can be said to be permanent.

It is clear that what constitutes a permanent residing together or parting will be a matter of judgment for adjudication officers, tribunals and Commissioners in the light of all the facts of particular cases.

3.151

The facts of *CSS/18/88* illustrate the importance of determining each case on its own facts and of avoiding an *a priori* approach to cases. In that case a couple had been married for over 40 years. In April 1978 the wife went to Canada to visit relatives. During that visit her brother-in-law was seriously injured in a road traffic accident. The wife remained in Canada to provide care for him. He subsequently died, but the wife's sister was diagnosed as suffering from cancer and the wife again remained in Canada to nurse her. Meanwhile the husband had sought permission to emigrate to Canada. This was obtained, but his own ill health prevented his travelling. The couple remained in touch and the wife returned to Scotland for visits home. This situation lasted until 1987, when the issue of the husband's receipt of an increase of benefit for his wife came before a tribunal.

The tribunal concluded that the absence of the wife in Canada could not be regarded as temporary. The Commissioner disagreed, though he noted the unusual circumstances of the case. The couple had not ceased to reside together permanently. The tribunal had erred by focusing on the nature of the absence *from the United Kingdom*, rather than by focusing on whether they were temporarily absent *from one another.* Provided the husband and wife are residing together, the absence of one spouse abroad is not a disqualifying factor (see reg.13 of the Persons Abroad Regulations).

In *R(P) 1/90* Commissioner Skinner advised:

3.152

"Whether or not there is a temporary absence is a question of fact for the tribunal, but the Commissioners have evolved a series of tests over the years which assists the members in dealing with such question. In the earlier cases the purpose of the absence of the husband was considered to be of great importance, but in the later decisions more importance was attached to the duration of the absence. In *C(P)84/50* it was said that a period of absence which has lasted for more than a year, and of which there is no reasonable prospect of its coming to an end, cannot be spoken of as 'temporary.' If a man left home, and if it was ascertained after more than a year had elapsed that there was still no prospect of his return, he would not be said to be temporarily absent. In *R(P)7/53* it was held that this was the established test for deciding whether absence had ceased to be temporary. It was pointed out that it was not a hard and fast rule, for there may be cases where it can be said long before the year is up the absence is not going to be temporary. It was pointed out that the reasonable prospect [sic] of return are not limited to the prospects within any particular period. In my judgment while the duration of the absence must be part of the test to be applied by the tribunal, the purpose of the absence and the intention of the parties are also of relevance. Indeed that is recognised in *R(P)7/53* where the absence [of] more than a year was only fatal to the claimant where there was no reasonable prospect of the absence coming to an end. I do not think it is practicable to lay down any hard and fast rules by which the question can be determined, but the intention of the claimant, the purpose of the absence and its duration are all relevant." (para.8).

In *CS/202/1991*, the Deputy Commissioner adopted the conclusion in *R(P) 1/90* that reg.2(4) modifies reg.13 of the Persons Abroad Regulations, but suggests that the approach to the determination of the temporary nature of any absence in that reported decision may be too stringent in the light of the decision in *Ex p. Akbar* (1992) 4 Admin. L.R. 602 (see annotations to reg.2 of the Persons Abroad Regulations).

3.153   *Regulation 3 omitted.*

The Social Security and Family Allowances (Polygamous Marriages) Regulations 1975

(SI 1975/561) *(as amended)*

3.154
1.   Citation, commencement and interpretation.
2.   General rule as to consequences of a polygamous marriage for the purpose of the Social Security Act and the Family Allowances Act.
3.   Special rules for retirement pension for women.

The Secretary of State for Social Services, in exercise of powers conferred upon her under section 162(b) of the Social Security Act 1975 and section 12(2) of the Family Allowance Act 1965, as substituted by paragraph 18 of Schedule 2 to the Social Security (Consequential Provisions) Act 1975, hereby makes the following regulations:

Citation, commencement and interpretation

3.155   **1.**—(1) These regulations may be cited as the Social Security and Family Allowances (Polygamous Marriages) Regulations 1975 and shall come into operation on 6th April 1975.

(2) In these regulations, unless the context otherwise requires—
"the Social Security Act" means the [¹ Social Security Contributions and Benefits Act 1992]
[² "the Family Allowances Act" means the Family Allowances Act 1965;]
"polygamous marriage" means a marriage celebrated under a law which, as it applies to the particular ceremony and to the parties thereto, permits polygamy;
"monogamous marriage" means a marriage celebrated under a law which does not permit polygamy, and "in fact monogamous" is to be construed in accordance with regulation 2(2) below;
and other expressions shall, as appropriate, have the same meanings as in the Social Security Act and the Family Allowances Act.

(3) Any reference in these regulations to any provision made by or contained in any enactment or instrument shall, except in so far as the context otherwise requires, be construed as a reference to that provision as amended or extended by any enactment or instrument and as including a reference to any provision which it re-enacts or replaces, or which may re-enact or replace it, with or without modification.

(4) The rules for the construction of Acts of Parliament contained in the Interpretation Act 1889 shall apply for the purposes of the interpretation of

these regulations as they apply for the purposes of the interpretation of an Act of Parliament.

General rule as to the consequences of a polygamous marriage for the purpose of the Social Security Act and the Family Allowances Act

2.—(1) Subject to the following provisions of these regulations, a polyg-   3.156
amous marriage shall, for the purpose of the Social Security Act [² and the Family Allowances Act] and any enactment construed as one with those Acts, be treated as having the same consequences as a monogamous marriage for any day, but only for any day, throughout which the polygamous marriage is in fact monogamous.

(2) In this and the next following regulation—

(a) a polygamous marriage is referred to as being in fact monogamous when neither party to it has any spouse additional to the other; and

(b) the day on which a polygamous marriage is contracted, or on which it terminates for any reason, shall be treated as a day throughout which that marriage was in fact monogamous if at all times on that day after it was contracted, or as the case may be, before it terminated, it was in fact monogamous.

GENERAL NOTE

In *CG/2611/2003* the Commissioner was determining an appeal in relation to a   3.157
claim for widow's benefit in respect of a man who married three times. It seems that that the husband, a Bangladeshi, entered into his first marriage in Bangladesh in the early 1960s. In 1968 he married the claimant in Bangladesh in accordance with Muslim law. Some time in the 1970s the husband took a third wife in Bangladesh. At the time of the husband's death, there was some uncertainty about the status of the first marriage, but the second and third marriages were still subsisting. The second wife claimed widow's benefit. The Secretary of State's argument was that the claim to the widow's benefit must be disallowed because the husband had contracted polygamous marriages, at least two of which subsisted at his death, and the claimant was not the husband's only wife at the date he died. Under the Polygamous Marriages Regulations, the claim could only succeed if, at the material time, the marriage was, in fact, monogamous.

The tribunal had concluded that at the time of marriage to the claimant, the husband was domiciled in the United Kingdom. The Commissioner casts doubt on the correctness of that conclusion but refers the matter back to a fresh tribunal for determination. Were it to be correct, then the marriage contracted with the claimant would have been void by the law of the law of the husband's domicile.

The decision highlights the need for the most careful (and consistent) findings of fact in these complex cases. Subject to what is said below in this note, the place of domicile of the husband at the dates of each of the marriages he contracts will be of fundamental importance in determining the validity of those marriages and consequently the application of the Polygamous Marriages Regulations to any claim for benefit.

SSWP v MN (BB) [2018] UKUT 68 (AAC) demonstrates that the question of the husband's domicile–and hence whether or not he is legally able to enter into a polygamous marriage at all–logically comes before consideration of reg.2. As Judge Wikeley put it, the regulation

"does not have the effect of converting a void marriage into a valid one simply by virtue of the parties being in practice monogamously married immediately prior to one party's death. Instead, it means that a valid polygamous marriage can be treated as "a monogamous marriage for any day … throughout which the polygamous marriage is in fact monogamous".

However, existing lines of authority must now be read in the light of the successful challenge on human rights grounds in *NA v SSWP (BB)* [2019] UKUT 144 (AAC).

The claimant had entered into a marriage under Islamic law with Mr A in 2008. At that time, while the claimant was domiciled in Pakistan, Mr A was domiciled in the United Kingdom. Mr A had previously married a Ms B at a time when both he and Ms B were domiciled in Pakistan. The marriage to Ms B was valid under the law of England and Wales. Mr A became domiciled in the UK with the consequence that when in 2001 he pronounced a *talaq* in respect of his marriage with Ms B, it was invalid to terminate that marriage under English law. Consequently, when in 2008 the claimant and Mr A married in Pakistan, their marriage was polygamous and, because of Mr A's domicile at the time, void under English law. Mr A's marriage to Ms B was only terminated under English law by decree absolute in 2009. Ms B died in 2011. The claimant moved to the UK in 2010, had a child with Mr A in 2012 but in 2016 Mr A died. At no point did Mr A live with both the claimant and Ms B.

Judge Wikeley upheld the claimant's appeal against the FtT's decision refusing her claim for bereavement payment and widowed parent's allowance on human rights grounds (see vol III for further discussion of that aspect), so the question of remedy arose.

The judge, referring to the definitions in regs 1(2) and 2, observed:

"104. These interlocking definitions can arguably be read in either of two ways. The conventional or orthodox reading is that the definition of a "polygamous marriage" in regulation 1(2) is only referring to a polygamous marriage which is recognised as being valid by the law of England and Wales. It excludes a polygamous marriage which is void under our domestic law owing to section 11(d) of the MCA 1973. So, it involves reading into the definition the words in italics:

""polygamous marriage" means a *valid* marriage *recognised according to the law of England and Wales and* celebrated under a law which, as it applies to the particular ceremony and to the parties thereto, permits polygamy;".

105. There is, however, a second possible reading. The definition refers to a "polygamous marriage" as meaning "a marriage celebrated under a law (etc)…"; in the present case, the Appellant's marriage to Mr A was indeed in its own terms a marriage celebrated "under a law which, as it applies to the particular ceremony and to the parties thereto, permits polygamy". There has been no suggestion that there were any irregularities in the form of the marriage ceremony conducted in Pakistan. The law of that jurisdiction, as it applied to both (a) the particular ceremony and (b) the parties, plainly permits polygamy. On that basis the Appellant's marriage to Mr A fell within the scope of the statutory definition of "polygamous marriage" in regulation 1(2) of the 1975 Regulations.

106. That then takes us to regulation 2(1) and the general rule. Such a polygamous marriage "shall … be treated as having the same consequences as a monogamous marriage for any day, but only for any day, throughout which the polygamous marriage is in fact monogamous." This provision does not in terms require that the polygamous marriage only achieves parity with a monogamous marriage if it was *actually* monogamous *throughout,* i.e. from the date it was contracted to the date (if relevant) that it ended. Rather, it is to have the same consequences "for any day, but only for any day" that it was in fact monogamous. The Appellant's marriage was necessarily monogamous at least from the date of Mr A's English divorce from Ms B in 2009.

107. The expression "in fact monogamous" is then defined by regulation 2(2). The requirement in regulation 2(2)(a) is not limited in point of time to the

precise date on which the marriage was contracted. From the relevant date of Ms B's divorce in 2009 "neither party to it has any spouse additional to the other" and so was "in fact monogamous". However, the further requirement in regulation 2(2)(b) might be read as requiring monogamy throughout the marriage, i.e. from the date of the marriage to the date of termination. There is, however, an alternative reading. The regulation refers to being "in fact monogamous", which can be read in contradistinction to being "in law monogamous". As previously noted, Mr A and Ms B separated in 2001. When Mr A married the Appellant in 2008, he was in the eyes of the law of England and Wales still married to Ms B so the relationship with the Appellant could not be "in law monogamous". His marriage to the Appellant, however, was "in fact monogamous" as in fact he only ever lived with one spouse.

108. Ms Leventhal seeks to resist a reading down of regulations 1 and 2 of the 1975 Regulations on the basis that it is inconsistent with the definition of "spouse" as understood in the terms of section 11(d) of the MCA 1973. However, the meaning of "spouse" is not central to the interpretation and application of the 1975 Regulations. Rather, the focus of the exercise is the expression "polygamous marriage" and how that should be read in a Convention-compliant manner. I conclude, for the purposes of the Appellant's entitlement to a bereavement payment, that the 1975 Regulations can be read down under section 3 of the Human Rights Act 1998 so as to be Convention-compliant."

Special rules for retirement pension for women

3.—(1) Subject to the provisions of paragraphs (2) and (3) of this regulation, where on or after the date on which she attained pensionable age a woman was a married woman by virtue of a polygamous marriage and either—   3.158

(a) throughout a day, falling on or after the date on which both she and her spouse have attained pensionable age [³ and in respect of which neither of them has an entitlement to a Category A or Category B retirement pension which is deferred,] that marriage was in fact monogamous, or

(b) throughout the day on which her spouse died that marriage was in fact monogamous,

that marriage, whether or not it has at all times been or continues to be in fact monogamous, shall, for the purposes of determining her right to and the rate of a retirement pension of any category under the Social Security Act be treated as having the same consequences as a monogamous marriage from and including the date on which she attained pensionable age or, if the marriage was contracted after that date, from and including the date of the marriage.

(2) Paragraph (1) of this regulation shall not operate so as to entitle a woman to a retirement pension for any period before the first such day as is referred to in sub-paragraph (a) of that paragraph or, in a case where that sub-paragraph does not apply, the day referred to in sub-paragraph (b) of that paragraph.

(3) Where the marriage of a woman is a polygamous marriage which was contracted—

(a) before she attained pensionable age and—

    (i) was not in fact monogamous when she attained that age, but

    (ii) became in fact monogamous on a date after she attained that age; or

(b) on or after the day on which she attained pensionable age and—

    (i) was not in fact monogamous when it was contracted, but

(ii) became in fact monogamous on a date after it was contracted; that marriage shall be treated as having the same consequences as a monogamous marriage for the purposes of section 29(10) of the Social Security Act (increase of Category B retirement pension in certain circumstances) only with effect from the date referred to in sub-paragraph (a)(ii) or, as the case may be, sub-paragraph (b)(ii) of this paragraph.

(4) In a case where section 28(3) of and Schedule 7 to the Social Security Act (retirement pension for widows who were widowed before attaining pensionable age) or regulation 4 of the Social Security (Benefit) (Married Women and Widows Special Provisions) Regulations 1974 (retirement pension for women whose marriages have been dissolved) applies to a woman and the relevant marriage for the purposes of that section and Schedule or that regulation was a polygamous marriage and throughout the day on which either—

(a) her marriage was dissolved, or

(b) her spouse died,

that marriage was in fact monogamous, that polygamous marriage shall, for those purposes, notwithstanding that it has not at all times been in fact monogamous, be treated as having the same consequences as if it had been a monogamous marriage.

(5) Where a woman is a married woman by virtue of a polygamous marriage which is in fact monogamous on the date from which she becomes entitled to a Category D retirement pension under section 39(1)(c) of the Social Security Act (retirement pensions for persons over age 80), that marriage, notwithstanding that it ceases to be in fact monogamous, shall, for the purpose of determining the rate of her Category D retirement pension, be treated as having the same consequences as a monogamous marriage.

AMENDMENTS

1. Substituted by Social Security (Consequential Provisions) Act 1992 s.2(4).

2. This provision (or reference) has lapsed with the repeal of the Family Allowances Act.

3. Words substituted by the Social Security (Abolition of Earnings Rule) (Consequential) Regulations 1989 (SI 1989/1642) (October 1, 1989).

PART IV

DISABILITY BENEFITS

The Social Security (Attendance Allowance) Regulations 1991

(SI 1991/2740) (*as amended*)

ARRANGEMENT OF REGULATIONS

		4.1
1.	Citation, commencement and interpretation.	
1A.	Disapplication of section 1(A) of the Administration Act.	
2.	Conditions as to residence and presence in Great Britain.	
2A.	Persons residing in Great Britain to whom a relevant EU Regulation applies	
2B.	Persons residing in an EEA state other than the United Kingdom or in Switzerland to whom a relevant EU Regulation applies	
2C.	Refugees	
3.	Extension of qualifying period.	
4.	Allowance payable before the date of claim in renewal cases.	
5.	Renal dialysis.	
6.	Hospitalisation.	
7.	Persons in certain accommodation other than hospitals.	
7A.	Persons to whom regulations 7 and 8 apply with modifications.	
8.	Exemption from regulations 6 and 7.	
8A.	Adjustment of allowance where medical expenses are paid from public funds under war pensions instruments.	
8B.	Exemption from regulation 8A.	
8BA.	Prescribed circumstances for entitlement.	
8C.	*Revoked.*	
8D.	*Revoked.*	
8E.	*Revoked.*	
9.	*Omitted.*	

SCHEDULE

Schedule—Persons to whom regulations 7 and 8 apply with modifications.

The Secretary of State for Social Security, in exercise of the powers conferred upon him by sections 35(1), (2)(b), (2A), (4A) and (6), 85(1)(b) and 166(2) and (3) of, and Schedule 20 to, the Social Security Act 1975 and of all other powers enabling him in that behalf, by this instrument, which contains regulations which relate to matters which, in accordance with section 140 of that Act, have been referred to the Attendance Allowance Board, hereby makes the following Regulations:

Citation, commencement and interpretation

1.—(1) These Regulations may be cited as the Social Security (Attendance   4.2
Allowance) Regulations 1991 and shall come into force on 6th April 1992.
  (2) In these Regulations—
"the Act" means the Social Security Act 1975;
"the NHS Act of 1978" means the National Health Service (Scotland) Act 1978;
[¹ "the NHS Act of 2006" means the National Health Service Act 2006 and "the NHS (Wales) Act of 2006" means the National Health Service (Wales) Act 2006];
"terminally ill" shall be construed in accordance with section 35(2C) of the Act.
  (3) Unless the context otherwise requires, any reference in these Regu-

lations to a numbered regulation is a reference to the regulation bearing that number in these Regulations and any reference in a regulation to a numbered paragraph is a reference to the paragraph of that regulation bearing that number.

AMENDMENTS

1. Social Security (Attendance Allowance, Disability living Allowance and Carer's Allowance) (Amendment) Regulations 2013 (SI 2013/389) reg.3 (April 8, 2013).

[¹ Disapplication of section 1(1A) of the Administration Act

4.3   **1A.**—Section 1(1A) of the Administration Act (requirement to state national insurance number) shall not apply to any claim for attendance allowance made or treated as made before 9th February, 1998.]

AMENDMENT

1. Social Security (National Insurance Information: Exemption) Regulations 1997 (SI 1997/2676) (December 1, 1997).

Conditions as to residence and presence in Great Britain

4.4   **2.**—(1) Subject to the following provisions of this regulation [⁵ and regulations [⁶2A, 2B and 2C]], the prescribed conditions for the purposes of section 35(1) of the Act as to residence and presence in Great Britain in relation to any person on any day shall be that—

(a) on that day—
    (i) he is [⁵habitually] resident in [⁵the United Kingdom, the Republic of Ireland, the Isle of Man or the Channel Islands], and
[¹ (ib) he is not a person subject to immigration control within the meaning of section 115(9) of the Immigration and Asylum Act 1999 or section 115 of that Act does not apply to him for the purposes of entitlement to attendance allowance by virtue of regulation 2 of the Social Security (Immigration and Asylum) Consequential Amendments Regulations 2000,
    (ii) he is present in Great Britain, and
    (iii) he has been present in Great Britain for a period of, or for periods amounting in the aggregate to, not less than [⁵104] weeks in the [⁵ 156] weeks immediately preceding that day;
(b) [⁴ . . .]
[² (1A)—[¹ *Omitted*]].

(2) For the purposes of paragraph (1)(a)(ii) and (iii), notwithstanding that on any day a person is absent from Great Britain, he shall be treated as though he were present in Great Britain if his absence is by reason only of the fact that on that day—

(a) he is abroad in his capacity as—
    (i) a serving member of the forces,
    (ii) an airman or mariner within the meaning of regulations [⁵111 and 115] respectively of the Social Security (Contributions) Regulations [⁵2001], and for the purpose of this provision, the expression "serving members of the forces" has the same meaning as in regulation 1(2) of the Regulations of [⁵2001]; or
(b) he is in employment prescribed for the purposes of section 132 of the Act in connection with continental shelf operations; or

(c) he is living with a person mentioned in sub-paragraph (a)(i) and is the spouse, [³ civil partner,] son, daughter, step-son, step-daughter, father, father-in-law, step-father, mother, mother-in-law or step-mother of that person; or

[⁵ (d) he is temporarily absent from Great Britain and that absence has not lasted for a continuous period exceeding 13 weeks.]

(e) [⁵ *omitted*]

(3) Where a person is terminally ill and makes a claim for attendance allowance expressly on the ground that he is such a person, paragraph (1) shall apply to him as if head (iii) of sub-paragraph (a) was omitted.

[⁵ (3A) A person shall be treated as habitually resident in Great Britain for the purpose of paragraph (1)(a)(i) where—

(a) he is resident outside Great Britain in his capacity as a serving member of the forces and for this purpose "serving member of the forces" has the meaning given in regulation 1(2) of the Social Security (Contributions) Regulations 2001; or

(b) he is living with a person mentioned in para.(a) and is the spouse, civil partner, son, daughter, step-son, step-daughter, father, father-in-law, step-father, mother, mother-in-law or step-mother of that person.";

[⁵ (3B) Where a person is temporarily absent from Great Britain, he is treated as present in Great Britain for the purposes of paragraph (1)(a)(ii) and (iii) for the first 26 weeks of that absence, where—

(a) this absence is solely in connection with arrangements made for the medical treatment of him for a disease or bodily or mental disablement which commenced before he left Great Britain; and

(b) the arrangements referred to in sub-paragraph (a) relate to medical treatment–

  (i) outside Great Britain,

  (ii) during the period whilst he is temporarily absent from Great Britain, and

  (iii) by, or under the supervision of, a person appropriately qualified to carry out that treatment, and

"medical treatment" means medical, surgical or rehabilitative treatment (including any course or diet or regimen), and references to a person receiving or submitting to medical treatment are to be construed accordingly.";

[⁵ (3C) For the purpose of paragraph (2)(d) and (3B) a person is "temporarily absent" if, at the beginning of the period of absence, that absence is unlikely to exceed 52 weeks.]

(4) [⁴. . .]

AMENDMENTS

1. Social Security (Immigration and Asylum) Consequential Amendments Regulations 2000 (SI 2000/636), reg.10 (April 3, 2000).

2. Social Security (Persons From Abroad) Miscellaneous Amendments Regulations 1996 (SI 1996/30) reg.2 (February 5, 1996), subject to a saving under reg.12(3).

3. Civil Partnership Act 2004, Sch.24 (December 5, 2005).

4. Social Security (Miscellaneous Amendments) (No.4) Regulations 2006 (SI 2006/2378) reg.7 (October 1, 2006).

5. Social Security (Attendance Allowance, Disability Living Allowance and Carer's Allowance) (Amendment) Regulations 2013 (SI 2013/389) reg.3 (April 8, 2013).

6. Social Security (Miscellaneous Amendment No.4) Regulations (SI 2017/1015) reg.6(2) (November 16, 2017).

GENERAL NOTE

4.5   Section 35(1) of the 1975 Act has now been replaced by s.64(1) of the Social Security Contributions and Benefits Act 1992.

Until April 8, 2013 a claimant need only have shown that they were "ordinarily resident" and there is a saving for existing claims made on that basis. Neither "ordinary" nor "habitual" residence is defined in the statute or regulations. Ordinary residence has usually been taken to mean that you have a settled intention to live in the country (technically now the "common travel area") as your home, but, not necessarily, permanently. Habitual residence, which is intended to be a more stringent test, requires as well that that the claimant has been in the country already for an extended period. How long, will depend upon the circumstances of the claimant; a former resident returning from a period abroad may satisfy this test almost immediately, while a new immigrant may be required to demonstrate a considerable period of residence. The meaning of "habitual residence" has been the subject of extensive case law in relation to claims for means-tested benefits where it has applied for some time. Readers are referred to the notes to relevant sections of Vol.II of this Work. In *MM and SI v SSWP (DLA)* [2016] UKUT 149 (AAC) Judge Markus QC has held that reg.2 (1)(a)(iii) (the past presence test or PPT) must be disapplied in respect of claims made on behalf of applicants who were family members of persons granted refugee status in the UK. She held that the PPT was indirectly discriminatory and could not be justified (when compared to the treatment of UK nationals) under art.28 of the EU Directive 2004/8 3/EC (which gives protection to refugees) and which she held had direct effect in the UK. For the same reason she held that PPT was in breach of the claimant's rights under art.14 of the ECHR. At the time the claims were made, the applicants satisfied the other conditions of reg.2 which meant that their claims should proceed accordingly. This was a decision on a claim for DLA but the ruling applies equally to attendance allowance.

For questions that involve persons either coming from or going to another country that is a part of the European Union reference should be made to the relevant sections of Vol.III of this Work.

Subsection (2)(e) which provided for a person to be absent with a certificate issued by the Secretary of State has been abolished with effect from April 8, 2013, but there is a saving provision for those persons who were abroad on that basis at that time—see reg.5 of SI 2013/389.

[¹ Persons residing in Great Britain to whom a relevant EU Regulation applies

4.6   **2A.**—(1) Regulation 2(1)(a)(iii) shall not apply where on any day—

(a) the person is habitually resident in Great Britain;

(b) a relevant EU Regulation applies; and

(c) the person can demonstrate a genuine and sufficient link to the United Kingdom social security system.

(2) For the purposes of paragraph (1)(b) and regulation 2B, "relevant EU Regulation" has the meaning given by section 84(2) of the Welfare Reform Act 2012.]

AMENDMENT

1. Social Security (Attendance Allowance, Disability living Allowance and Carer's Allowance) (Amendment) Regulations 2013 (SI 2013/389) reg.3 (April 8, 2013).

GENERAL NOTE

The relevant regulations referred to are (EC) No.1408/71 and (EC) No.883/2004.   **4.7**
For detailed discussion see Vol.III of this Work.

The operation of this subsection has been considered by the CA in *Kavanagh and Mohamed v SSWP* [2019] EWCA Civ 272. Both cases had been before Judge Jacobs in the UT where, while it was accepted that each claimant was now habitually resident in the UK, he held that neither was able to establish that they had a genuine and sufficient link to the UK. Judge Jacobs took the view that their reason for coming to the UK could not contribute to establishing that link. The CA have held that the reason for coming here could be relevant. In the case of *MM* the claimant was a 65 year old German national who was claiming AA. She had come to the UK because she needed the care and support of her daughter who was resident here. The CA held that this reason, together with her actual presence here, was enough to establish that link. In the UT Judge Jacobs had observed that the requirement in subs. (2A)(c) that the link be to the UK social security system was unlawful; the CA proceeded on the basis that that was correct and therefore the last three words of that paragraph are to be ignored.

[¹Persons residing in an EEA state other than the United Kingdom or in Switzerland to whom a relevant EU Regulation applies

2B.—Regulation 2(1)(a)(i) to (iii) shall not apply where on any day—   **4.8**
(a) the person is habitually resident in—
  (i) an EEA state other than the United Kingdom; or
  (ii) Switzerland;
(b) a relevant EU Regulation applies; and
(c) the person can demonstrate a genuine and sufficient link to the United Kingdom social security system.]

AMENDMENTS

1. Social Security (Attendance Allowance, Disability Living Allowance and Carer's Allowance) (Amendment) Regulations 2013 (SI 2013/389) reg.3 (April 8, 2013).

[¹ Refugees

2C.—(1) Regulation 2(1)(a)(iii) shall not apply where the person has—   **4.9**
(a) been granted refugee status or humanitarian protection under the immigration rules; or
(b) leave to enter or remain in the United Kingdom as the dependant of a person granted refugee status or humanitarian protection under the immigration rules.
(2) For the purposes of this regulation "immigration rules" means the rules laid before Parliament under section 3(2) of the Immigration Act 1971.]

AMENDMENTS

1. Social Security (Miscellaneous Amendment No.4) Regulations 2017 (SI 2017/1015) reg.6(3) (November 16, 2017).

Extension of qualifying period

3.—The period prescribed for the purposes of section 35(2)(b) of the   **4.10**
Act (claimant to satisfy one or both of the conditions in section 35(1) of the Act for 6 months immediately preceeding the date from which attendance allowance is to be awarded) shall be 2 years.

4.11   Section 35(2)(b) of the 1975 Act has now been replaced by s.65(1)(b) of the Social Security Contributions and Benefits Act 1992.

Allowance payable before the date of claim in renewal cases

4.12   **4.**—*Revoked by Social Security (Miscellaneous Amendments) (No. 2) Regulations 1997 (SI 1997/793) reg.19(b) with effect from September 1, 1997.*

GENERAL NOTE

4.13   This regulation had allowed a renewal claim made within six months of the date of termination of an earlier award to be backdated to that date.

Renal dialysis

4.14   **5.**—(1) Subject to paragraph (3), a person who suffers from renal failure and who is undergoing the treatment specified in paragraph (2) shall be deemed to satisfy the conditions—

(a) in section 35(1)(a) of the Act (severe physical and mental disability) if he undergoes renal dialysis by day;

(b) in section 35(1)(b) of the Act if he undergoes renal dialysis by night;

(c) in either paragraph (a) or paragraph (b) of section 35(1) of the Act, but not both, if he undergoes renal dialysis by day and by night.

(2) The treatment referred to in paragraph (1) is the undergoing of renal dialysis—

(a) two or more times a week; and

(b) which either—

(i) is of a type which normally requires the attendance of or supervision by another person during the period of dialysis, or

(ii) which, because of the particular circumstances of his case, in fact requires another person, during the period of dialysis, to attend in connection with the bodily functions of the person undergoing renal dialysis or to supervise that person in order that he avoids substantial danger to himself.

(3) Except as provided in paragraph (4), paragraph (1) does not apply to a person undergoing the treatment specified in paragraph (2) where the treatment—

(a) is provided under [¹ the NHS Act of 1978, the NHS Act of 2006 or the NHS (Wales) Act of 2006];

(b) is in a hospital or similar institution;

(c) is out-patient treatment; and

(d) takes place with the assistance or supervision of any member of staff of the hospital or similar institution.

(4) Paragraph (3) does not apply for the purposes of determining whether a person is to be taken to satisfy either of the conditions specified in paragraph (1) during the period of 6 months referred to in section 35(2)(b) of the 1975 Act (qualifying period for attendance allowance).

AMENDMENTS

1. Social Security (Attendance Allowance, Disability living Allowance and Carer's Allowance) (Amendment) Regulations 2013 (SI 2013/389) reg.3 (April 8, 2013).

GENERAL NOTE

Under this regulation, a person undergoing renal dialysis at least twice a week   4.15
may be deemed to satisfy *either* the day *or* the night attendance condition, but not both.
Some degree of attention or supervision must be required. This regulation is in slightly
different terms from regs 5B and 5C of the Social Security (Attendance Allowance)
(No. 2) Regulations 1975 which governed entitlement before April 6, 1992.

Paragraph (1)
The conditions previously to be found in s.35(1)(a) and (b) of the 1975 Act are   4.16
now to be found in s.64(2) and (3) of the Social Security Contributions and Benefits
Act 1992.

Paragraph (2)(b)
The dialysis must be *either* of a type which *normally* requires the attendance of   4.17
or supervision by another person (in which case the actual purpose of the attention or supervision is irrelevant) *or* the dialysis must *in the particular case* require
the attention or supervision of the claimant (for the purpose specified in para.(2)(b)(ii)).

Paragraph (3)
This excludes from the scope of the regulation claimants whose treatment satisfies   4.18
all four conditions in sub-paras (a)–(d). It is not entirely clear what assistance or supervision actually falls within sub-para.(d) but presumably it is the attention or supervision falling within para.(2)(b) so that only assistance and supervision *during the period
of dialysis* is relevant and not any assistance at the beginning or end of the treatment. By
virtue of para.(4), para.(3) does not apply in respect of the six-month qualifying period
for attendance allowance. This means that a person previously excluded under para.
(3) can qualify for attendance allowance under this reg.as soon as one of the excluding conditions of para.(3) ceases to be satisfied. S.35(2)(b) of the 1975 Act has been
replaced by s.65(1)(b) of the Social Security Contributions and Benefits Act 1992.

Hospitalisation

6.—[¹ (1) Subject to regulation 8, it shall be a condition for the receipt of   4.19
an attendance allowance for any period in respect of any person that during
that period he is not maintained free of charge while undergoing medical or
other treatment as an in-patient—
- (a) in a hospital or similar institution under [⁴ the NHS Act of 1978, the
NHS Act of 2006 or the NHS (Wales) Act of 2006]; or
- (b) in a hospital or similar institution maintained or administered by the
Defence Council.]

(2) For the purposes of [¹ paragraph (1)(a)], a person shall only be regarded
as not being maintained free of charge in a hospital or similar institution for any
period where his accommodation and services are provided under
[⁴ (a) section 57 of, and paragraph 14 of Schedule 7A to, the NHS Act of
1978;
- (b) section 13 of, and paragraph 15 of Schedule 2 to, the NHS Act of
2006;
- (c) section 28 of, and paragraph 11 of Schedule 6 to, the NHS Act of
2006;
- (d) section 44(6) of, and paragraph 19(1) of Schedule 4 to, the NHS Act
of 2006;
- (e) section 11 of, and paragraph 15 of Schedule 2 to, the NHS (Wales)
Act of 2006;
- (f) section 18 of, and paragraph 19(1) of Schedule 3 to, the NHS
(Wales) Act of 2006; or

(g) section 22 of, and paragraph 11 of Schedule 5 to, the NHS (Wales) Act of 2006.]

[² (2A) For the purpose of paragraph (1), a period during which a person is maintained free of charge while undergoing medical or other treatment as an in-patient shall be deemed to begin on the day after the day on which he enters a hospital or similar institution referred to in that paragraph and to end on the day [³ before the day] on which he leaves such a hospital or similar institution.]

(3)[¹ . . .].

AMENDMENTS

1. Social Security (Disability Living Allowance and Attendance Allowance) (Amendment) Regulation 1992 (SI 1992/2869) reg.2 (December 15, 1992).

2. Social Security (Hospital In-Patients, Attendance Allowance and Disability Living Allowance) (Amendment) Regulations 1999 (SI 1999/1326) (June 7, 1999).

3. Social Security (Attendance Allowance and Disability Living Allowance) (Amendment) Regulations 2000, (SI 2000/1401) reg.2 (June 19, 2000).

4. Social Security (Attendance Allowance, Disability Living Allowance and Carer's Allowance) (Amendment) Regulations 2013 (SI 2013/389) reg.3 (April 8, 2013).

GENERAL NOTE

4.20   By virtue of reg.8, this regulation applies only after a person has been in hospital (or in accommodation to which reg.7 applies) for 28 days although periods separated by intervals not exceeding 28 days may be linked.

If a person is receiving treatment as an in-patient in one of the hospitals or institutions specified in para.(1), he or she is deemed to be being maintained free of charge unless a private patient (in which case para.(2) will apply). Although the wording of this regulation is different from that considered in *R(S) 4/84*, the overall conclusion reached by the Commissioner appears to be relevant here. The claimant was able to attend college during the day but received treatment from the hospital at night. The Commissioner held that she was not receiving free in-patient treatment because "any period" and "period" must relate to a period of not less than one day.

In *CDLA/11099/95*, the Commissioner decided that the equivalent provision in reg.8 of the Social Security (Disability Living Allowance) Regulations 1991 applied so as to make it a condition of entitlement to benefit only for "complete calendar (i.e. midnight-to-midnight) days throughout which the claimant is not undergoing medical or other treatment as an in-patient" but that the state of affairs existing at the beginning of a day was presumed to continue until the end. However, in *CSS/617/97*, where the claimant of severe disablement allowance went home from hospital from a Friday morning to a Monday evening, the Commissioner construed reg.2(2) of the Social Security (Hospital In-Patients) Regulations 1975 so as to find the claimant entitled to the full rate of benefit for the Friday as well as the Saturday to Monday. The explanation for the different approaches may lie in the slightly different form of the statutory provisions under consideration, in which case the approach taken in *CDLA/11099/95* must be preferred in attendance allowance cases.

In *Chief Adjudication Officer v White (R(IS) 18/94)*, a health authority had made arrangements for patients in a hospital to be moved to a nursing home. It was held by the Court of Appeal that they were receiving treatment in hospital or similar institution under the National Health Service Act 1977. In *CDLA/7980/95*, the claimant was discharged from hospital and the tribunal found that she had gone to live in a house where she was one of six tenants who were all cared for by health authority staff. The tribunal found that the house was not a "hospital or similar institution". The adjudication officer appealed but the Commissioner held that the tribunal had not erred in law in reaching the conclusion they did. He distinguished *White* on the basis that it had not been disputed in that case that the nursing home was an institution. He also rejected submissions that the tribunal ought to have investigated the arrangements further, observing that the adjudication officer had failed to challenge the evidence before the tribunal. The Chief Adjudication Officer was given leave to appeal by the Commissioner but he did not lodge the appeal within time and was refused an extension by the Court of Appeal.

[¹ Persons in care homes

7.—(1) Subject to regulation 8, a person shall not be paid any amount in respect of an attendance allowance for any period where throughout that period he is a resident in a care home in circumstances where any of the costs of any qualifying services provided for him are borne out of public or local funds under a specified enactment.

    4.21

(2) The specified enactments for the purposes of paragraph (1) are—
(a)
    (i) Part III of the National Assistance Act 1948
    (ii) [² sections 59 and 59A] of the Social Work (Scotland) Act 1968,
    (iii) the Mental Health (Care and Treatment) (Scotland) Act 2003,
    (iv) the Community Care and Health (Scotland) Act 2002,
    (v) the Mental Health Act 1983,
    [³ (vi) section 57 of the Health and Social Care Act 2001,]
    [⁴ (vii) Part 1 of the Care Act 2014 (care and support),]
    [⁵ (viii) Part 4 of the Social Services and Well-being (Wales) Act 2014 (meeting needs), or]
(b) any other enactment relating to persons under disability.

(3) In this regulation, and in regulation 8, references to the costs of any qualifying services shall not include the cost of—
(a) domiciliary services, including personal care, provided in respect of a person in a private dwelling; or
(b) improvements made to, or furniture or equipment provided for, a private dwelling on account of the needs of a person under disability; or
(c) improvements made to, or furniture or equipment provided for, a care home in respect of which a grant or payment has been made out of public or local funds except where the grant or payment is of a regular or repeated nature; or
(d) social and recreational activities provided outside the care home in respect of which grants or payments are made out of public or local funds; or
(e) the purchase or running of a motor vehicle to be used in connection with any qualifying service provided in a care home in respect of which grants or payments are made out of public or local funds; or
(f) [² omitted]

(4) For the purposes of paragraph (1), a period during which a person is a resident in a care home in the circumstances set out in that paragraph shall, subject to paragraphs (5) and (6), be deemed—
(a) to begin on the day after the day on which he enters a care home, and
(b) to end on the day before the day on which he leaves a care home.

(5) Where a person enters a care home from a hospital or similar institution in circumstances in which paragraph (1) of regulation 6 applies, the period during which he is a resident in the care home shall be deemed to begin on the day he enters that care home.

(6) Where a person leaves a care home and enters a hospital or similar institution in circumstances in which paragraph (1) of regulation 6 applies,

the period during which he is a resident in the care home shall be deemed to end on the day he leaves that care home.]

AMENDMENTS

1. Attendance Allowance and Disability Living Allowance (Amendment) Regulations 2007 (SI 2007/2875) (October 29, 2007).
2. Social Security (Attendance Allowance, Disability Living Allowance and Carer's Allowance) (Amendment) Regulations 2013 (SI 2013/389) reg.3 (April 8, 2013).
3. Community Care, Services for Carers and Children's Services (Direct Payments) (England) (Amendment) Regulations (SI 2013/2270) reg.5 (November 1, 2013).
4. Care Act 2014 (Consequential Amendments) (Secondary Legislation) Order 2015 (SI 2015/643) art.6 (April 1, 2015).
5. Social Services and Well-being (Wales) Act 2014 and the Regulation and Inspection of Social Care (Wales) Act 2016 (Consequential Amendments) Order 2017 (SI 2017/901) art.3 (November 3, 2017).

GENERAL NOTE

4.22   There is a transitional and saving provision in reg.4 of the Amendment regulations to the effect that this amendment shall not prevent any day before the coming into force of the amended regulations from counting towards the first 28 day period specified in reg.8.

This is a new version of reg.7, but the commentary that follows remains relevant.

By virtue of reg.8, this regulation applies only after a person has been in the relevant accommodation or in hospital for 28 days although periods separated by intervals not exceeding 28 days may be linked.

The former paragraph (c), now repealed, also provided for disqualification where the cost of accommodation could have been met from public funds even if it was not. Now the regulation applies only where the cost is being met. A question may still arise where costs are being met temporarily while a claimant waits to release funds from which they can meet the costs themselves, by the sale of their former home. In such cases it is usual for the claimant to undertake to reimburse the local authority when their own funds become available.

The effect of the decision in *CAO v Creighton* [2000] N.I. 222 for Northern Ireland, and its adoption in England and Wales in *R(A) 1/02* is that such arrangements do not involve the local authority in meeting the cost of accommodation because the claimant does meet and always has met that cost by virtue of the agreement to reimburse any sums advanced. It follows that the claimant then does have the resources to provide his own accommodation, and the local authority has no power to provide for his accommodation under Pt III—reg.7 does not therefore apply. The position is more doubtful in Scotland. In *CSA/469/2005* (and in *CSA/164/2004* which preceded it), the Commissioner holds that the cost of accommodation in a private nursing home that is met by a payment made to the claimant for personal care allowances under the Community Care and Health (Scotland) Act 2002 is a payment that disqualifies the claimant from entitlement to Attendance Allowance under reg.7. This is so even though the same payment made to a claimant who was living in their own home would not disqualify them. The Commissioner finds that to be the inevitable outcome of legislation that has been enacted only for Scotland and without any amendment to the legislation for Attendance Allowance.

The matters of entitlement to Attendance Allowance and the recovery of nursing home costs by a local authority have been considered again by Judge Mesher in *MP v SSWP* [2010] UKUT 231 (AAC). In this case, when the local authority began to meet the nursing home fees under Pt III of the 1948 act they determined to recover them, eventually, from the claimant and created a charge against the interest that the claimant had in her former home. They were unable to register that charge because the title to the home was shared with the claimant's daughter and at that time the daughter (who held a power of attorney for the claimant), and other members of the family, refused to agree to repayment of the fees, or to registration of the charge. Judge Mesher concluded that agreement to repay was not a necessary part of recovery of the fees because the local authority could create an enforceable charge against the property without their agreement and that charge would be enforceable whether registered or not. This meant that following the *Creighton* case the claimant was still meeting her accommodation costs and should, therefore, have been entitled to the allowance. The case was referred back for further possible findings of fact. The case is useful also for the judge's reference to other legislation that is relevant in this area.

The question of repayment of fees has been considered further in *Secretary of State for Work and Pensions v JL* [2011] UKUT 293 [2012] AACR 14. This was a decision by a three-judge panel of the Appeal Chamber. The case was on DLA but the provisions are the same for AA. The primary point in contention was whether it was necessary for there to have been a prior agreement for the repayment of the nursing home fees. The panel concluded that there is no necessity for a prior agreement. This is in accordance with both *Creighton* and the subsequent case of *R(A) 1/02*. The judges note also that the DMG may be misleading in this regard. But further, this decision considers the effect of several amendments to the regulations, the difference between entitlement to DLA and payability of DLA and whether the effect of the amendment to reg.7 in 2007 should have retrospective effect so as to deprive the claimant of benefit while he was residing in a nursing home. The tribunal held that it did not.

The treatment of a claimant for whom the cost of accommodation is being met by a Local Authority on a temporary basis and subject to repayment by the claimant, was also considered in *CDLA/5106/2001*. In this case the cost of the accommodation was met initially by the Local Authority, but first a contribution was required, and then an obligation to repay in full under s.22 of the 1948 Act. By the time of the hearing, full repayment had been made. Commissioner Turnbull, nevertheless, held that she was disqualified from receiving benefit because her accommodation was provided in accordance with reg.7(1)(a) and the claimant was not exempted by reg.8(6)(b) until she ceased to be entitled to Income Support because she was not, until then, meeting the whole of the cost of accommodation from her own resources. Although the Commissioner makes no reference to *R(A) 1/02*, his decision accords with that case because there, too, the claimant was disqualified for part of the period in question because she was then in receipt of Income Support. It does not appear that in either case an argument was made that the claimant's entitlement to Income Support should be regarded as a part of her own resources.

This has all been carried a stage further by the decision in *CA/3800/2006*. There the claimant had been in receipt of benefit because she was funding the care home fees from her own resources. Eventually, it became necessary to sell her former home and the proceeds were invested to continue that funding. The investments failed and for a time the claimant became dependant upon the local authority for continued payment of fees. The claimant's daughter, acting under a power of attorney, complained to the Financial Services Ombudsman about the investment advice given to her mother and that complaint was upheld, resulting in a compensation payment to her mother. The claimant resumed payment of fees herself and the local authority required repayment of the fees which they had advanced. The question before the Commissioner was whether the claimant should now be entitled to benefit for the period covered by the local authority. The Commissioner held that she was. The decision taken to cancel her benefit when the local authority first assumed responsibility for payment, should have been a decision to suspend payment rather than a decision to supercede. That it was not, was an official error – that being so, the appeal tribunal should have substituted its own decision to suspend and that would mean the claimant would have remained "entitled" to benefit throughout the period, though not entitled to payment during the period of suspension.

This reasoning has now been applied by Judge Mesher in *SSWP v DA* [2009]

UKUT 214 (AAC). The case involved the more usual instance of a claimant whose nursing home fees were paid by the local authority for an interim period while the house that had been her home was sold. The difficulties that are presented by the current provisions for revising and for superseding decisions (provisions that have come into existence since the decision in *Creighton* and the other decisions following it) were explained, but effectively overcome by finding that the superseding decision should have been to the effect that the claimant became entitled to benefit (under reg.8(6) below), though payment was suspended, from the time that the arrangements for repayment to the local authority were made known to the department.

Persons to whom regulations 7 and 8 apply with modifications

4.23   **7A.**—[¹ . . .]

REPEAL

1. Social Security Amendment (Residential Care and Nursing Homes) Regulations 2001 (SI 2001/3767) reg.3 (April 8, 2002).

Exemption from regulations 6 and 7

4.24   **8.**—[¹ (1) Regulation 6, or as the case may be, regulation 7, shall not, [² subject to the following provisions of this regulation], apply to a person in respect of the first 28 days of any period during which he—
  (a) is undergoing medical or other treatment in a hospital or other institution in any of the circumstances mentioned in regulation 6; or
  (b) would, but for this regulation, be prevented from receiving an attendance allowance by reason of regulation 7(1).]
  (2) For the purposes of paragraph (1)—
  (a) two or more distinct periods separated by an interval not exceeding 28 days, or by two or more such intervals, shall be treated as a continuous period equal in duration to the total of such distinct periods and ending on the last day of the later or last such period;
  (b) any period or periods to which either regulation 6 or regulation 7 refers shall be taken into account and aggregated with any period to which the other of them refers.
  (3) Where, on the day a person's entitlement to an attendance allowance commences, he is in accommodation in the circumstances mentioned in regulation 6 or regulation 7, paragraph (1) shall not apply to him for any period of consecutive days, beginning with that day, on which he remains in that accommodation.
  [² (4) Regulation 6 or, as the case may be, regulation 7 shall not apply [³ [⁴ . . .] in the case of a person who is residing in a hospice and is terminally ill where the Secretary of State has been informed that he is terminally ill—
  (a) on a claim for attendance allowance,
  (b) on an application for a [⁵ revision under section 9 of the Social Security Act 1998 or supersession under section 10 of that Act] of an award of attendance allowance, or
  (c) in writing in connection with an award of, or a claim for, or an application for a [⁵ revision under section 9 of the Social Security Act 1998 or supersession under section 10 of that Act] of an award of, attendance allowance.
  (5) In paragraph (4) "hospice" means a hospital or other institution [⁴ whose primary function is to provide palliative care for persons resident there who are suffering from a progressive disease in its final stages] other than—

(a) [⁷ *omitted*]
(b) a health service hospital (within the meaning of section 108(1) of the NHS Act of 1978) in Scotland;
[⁷(ba) a health service hospital (within the meaning of section 275 of the NHS Act of 2006) in England;
(bb) a hospital in Wales vested in—
    (i) an NHS Trust;
    (ii) a Local Health Board; or
    (iii) the Welsh Ministers, for the purpose of functions under the NHS (Wales) Act of 2006;]
(c) a hospital maintained or administered by the Defence Council; or
(d) an institution similar to a hospital mentioned in any of the preceding sub-paragraphs of this paragraph.
[⁶ (6) Regulation 7 shall not apply in any particular case for any period during which the whole costs of all of the qualifying services are met—
(a) out of the resources of the person for whom the qualifying services are provided, or partly out of his own resources and partly with assistance from another person or a charity, or
(b) on his behalf by another person or a charity.]
[⁷ (6A) For the purpose of paragraph (5)(bb)—
(a) "NHS Trust" means a body established under section 18 of the NHS (Wales) Act of 2006; and
(b) "Local Health Board" means a body established under section 11 of the NHS (Wales) Act of 2006.]
(7)[³ [⁴ . . .]]

AMENDMENTS

1. Social Security (Attendance Allowance) Amendment Regulations 1992 (SI 1992/703) reg.5 (April 6, 1992).
2. Social Security Benefits (Amendments Consequential Upon the Introduction of Community Care) Regulations 1992 (SI 1992/3147) reg.8 (April 1, 1993 with saving).
3. Social Security (Attendance Allowance and Disability Living Allowance) (Amendment) Regulations 2000, (2000/1401) reg.2(4) (June 19, 2000).
4. Social Security Benefits (Miscellaneous Amendments) Regulations 1993 (SI 1993/518) reg.2(3) (April 1, 1993).
5. Social Security Act 1998 (Commencement No.11, and savings and consequential and Transitional Provisions) Order 1999 (SI 1999/2860) Sch.8 (October 18, 1999).
6. Attendance Allowance and Disability Living Allowance (Amendment) Regulations 2007 (SI 2007/2875) (October 29, 2007).
7. Social Security (Attendance Allowance, Disability Living Allowance and Carer's Allowance) (Amendment) Regulations 2013 (SI 2013/389) reg.3 (April 8, 2013).

GENERAL NOTE

See notes above to reg.7. 4.25

[¹ Adjustment of allowance where medical expenses are paid from public funds under war pensions instruments

8A.—(1) In this regulation— 4.26
"article 25B" means article 25B of the Personal Injuries (Civilians) Scheme 1983 (medical expenses) and includes that article as applied by article 48B of that Scheme; "article [²21]" means article [²21] of the

Naval, Military and Air Forces etc. (Disablement and Death) Service Pensions Order [²2006] (medical expenses);
and in this regulation and regulation 8B "relevant accommodation" means accommodation provided as a necessary ancillary to nursing care where the medical expenses involved are wholly borne by the Secretary of State pursuant to article 25B or article [² 21].

(2) This regulation applies where a person is provided with relevant accommodation.

(3) Subject to regulation 8B, where this regulation applies and there are payable in respect of a person both a payment under either article 25B or article 26 and an attendance allowance, the allowance shall be adjusted by deducting from it the amount of the payment under article 25B or article [² 21], as the case may be, and only the balance shall be payable.]

AMENDMENTS

1. Social Security (Attendance Allowance and Disability Living Allowance) (Amendment) Regulations 1994 (SI 1994/1779) reg.2(4) (August 1, 1994).
2. Social Security (Attendance Allowance, Disability Living Allowance and Carer's Allowance) (Amendment) Regulations 2013 (SI 2013/389) reg.3 (April 8, 2013).

[¹ Exemption from regulation 8A

4.27   **8B.**—(1) Regulation 8A shall not, subject to the following provisions of this regulation, apply to a person in respect of the first 28 days of any period during which the amount of any attendance allowance would be liable to be adjusted by virtue of regulation 8A(3).

(2) For the purposes of paragraph (1) two or more distinct periods separated by an interval not exceeding 28 days, or by two or more such intervals, shall be treated as a continuous period equal in duration to the aggregate of such distinct periods and ending on the last day of the later or last such period.

(3) For the purposes of this paragraph a day is a relevant day in relation to a person if it fell not earlier than 28 days before the first day on which he was provided with relevant accommodation; and either—

(a) was a day when he was undergoing medical treatment in a hospital or similar institution in any of the circumstances mentioned in regulation 6; or

(b) was a day when he was, or would but for regulation 8 have been, prevented from receiving an attendance allowance by virtue of regulation 7(1);

and where there is in relation to a person a relevant day, paragraph (1) shall have effect as if for "28 days" there were substituted such lesser number of days as is produced by subtracting from 28 the number of relevant days in his case.]

AMENDMENT

1. Social Security (Attendance Allowance and Disability Living Allowance) (Amendment) Regulations 1994 (SI 1994/1779) reg.2(4) (August 1, 1994).

[¹ Prescribed circumstances for entitlement

4.28   **8BA.**—For the purposes of section 64(4) of the Social Security Contributions and Benefits Act 1992 (prescribed circumstances in which a person is to be taken to satisfy or not to satisfy the conditions mentioned in section 64(2) and (3) of that Act), a person shall not be taken to satisfy

(2)(a) (day attention) or (3)(a) (night attention) unless the attention the severely disabled person requires from another person is required to be given in the physical presence of the severely disabled person.]

AMENDMENT

1. Social Security (Attendance Allowance and Disability Living Allowance) (Amendment) (No. 2) Regulations 2000 (2000/1401) reg.2 (September 25, 2000).

Regulations 8C, 8D and 8E have been revoked by Social Security Act 1998 **4.29**
(Commencement No.11, and Savings and Consequential and Transitional Provisions) Order 1999 (SI 1999/2860) Sch.8, with effect from October 18, 1999.

Regulation 9 omitted.

[¹ SCHEDULE   **Regulation 7A(1)**

[¹ . . .]   **4.30**

REPEAL

1. Social Security Amendment (Residential Care and Nursing Homes) Regulations 2001 (SI 2001/3767) reg.3 (April 8, 2002).

The Social Security (Disability Living Allowance) Regulations 1991

(SI 1991/2890) *(as amended)*

ARRANGEMENT OF REGULATIONS

PART I

INTRODUCTION

1.   Citation, commencement and interpretation.   **4.31**

PART II

GENERAL

1A.   Disapplication of section 1(1A) of the Administration Act.
2.   Conditions as to residence and presence in Great Britain.
2A.   Persons residing in Great Britain to whom a relevant EU Regulation applies
2B.   Persons residing in an EEA state other than the United Kingdom or in Switzerland to whom a relevant EU Regulation applies
2C.   Refugees
3.   Age 65 or over.
4.   Rate of benefit.
5.   *Repealed.*
5A.   *Repealed.*
5B.   *Repealed.*
5C.   *Repealed.*

PART III

CARE COMPONENT

6.   Qualifying period for care component after an interval.
7.   Renal Dialysis.
8.   Hospitalisation.
9.   Persons in certain accommodation other than hospitals.
9A.   *Repealed.*
10.   Exemption from regulations 8 and 9.
10A. Adjustment of allowance where medical expenses are paid from public funds under war pensions instruments.
10B. Exemption from regulation 10A.
10C. Prescribed circumstance for entitlement to the care component.

PART IV

MOBILITY COMPONENT

11.   Qualifying period for mobility component after an interval.
12.   Entitlement to the mobility component.
12A. Hospitalisation in mobility component cases.
12B. Exemption from regulation 12A.
12C. Adjustment of benefit to certain persons exempted from regulation 12A.
13.   Invalid Vehicle Scheme.

SCHEDULES

Schedule 1.—Persons aged 65 and over.
Schedule 2.—Invalid Vehicle Scheme.
Schedule 3.—*Repealed.*

Whereas a draft of this instrument was laid before Parliament in accordance with section 12(1) of the Disability Living Allowance and Disability Working Allowance Act 1991 and approved by resolution of each House of Parliament; now therefore the Secretary of State for Social Security, in exercise of the powers conferred by sections 37ZA(6), 37ZB(2), (3), (7) and (8), 37ZC, 37ZD, 37ZE(2), 85(1), 114(1) and 166(2) to (3A) of and Schedule 20 to the Social Security Act 1975, section 13 of the Social Security (Miscellaneous Provisions) Act 1977 and section 5(1) of the Disability Living Allowance and Disability Working Allowance Act 1991, and of all other powers enabling him in that behalf, by this instrument, which contains only regulations made consequential upon section 1 of the Disability Living Allowance and Disability Working Allowance Act 1991, hereby makes the following Regulations:

PART I

INTRODUCTION

Citation, commencement and interpretation

4.32   **1.**—(1) These Regulations may be cited as the Social Security (Disability Living Allowance) Regulations 1991 and shall come into force on 6th April 1992.

(2) In these Regulations—

[¹ "the Act" means the Social Security Contributions and Benefits Act 1992;

"the Administration Act" means the Social Security Administration Act 1992];

[² "the 1998 Act" means the Social Security Act 1998]

[⁴ *omitted*];

"the NHS Act of 1978" means the National Health Service (Scotland) Act 1978;

[⁴ "the NHS Act of 2006" means the National Health Service Act 2006; and "the NHS (Wales) Act of 2006" means the National Health Service (Wales) Act 2006;]

[⁴ *omitted*];

[² "adjudicating authority" means, as the case may require, the Secretary of State, [³ the First-tier Tribunal or the Upper Tribunal];]

"care component" means the care component of a disability living allowance;

"mobility component" means the mobility component of a disability living allowance;

"terminally ill" shall be construed in accordance with [¹ section 66(2) of the Act].

(3) Unless the context otherwise requires, any reference in these Regulations to a numbered regulation or Schedule is a reference to the regulation or Schedule bearing that number in these Regulations and any reference in a regulation or Schedule to a numbered paragraph is a reference to the paragraph of that regulation or Schedule bearing that number.

[⁴(4) With effect from 6th December 2018, any reference in these Regulations to—

(a) "age 65 or over", "the age of 65 years", "the age of 65", "65" and "age 65 and over" shall be construed as a reference to "pensionable age";

(b) "aged 65 or over" and "aged 65 and over" shall be construed as a reference to "of pensionable age"; and

(c) "his 65ᵗʰ birthday" shall be construed as a reference to "the day on which he attained pensionable age".

(5) For the purpose of paragraph (4), "pensionable age" has the meaning given by the rules in paragraph 1 of Schedule 4 to the Pensions Act 1995.]

AMENDMENTS

1. Social Security (Disability Living Allowance) (Amendment) Regulations 1993 (SI 1993/1939) reg.2(2) (August 26, 1993).

2. Social Security Act 1998 (Commencement No.11 and Savings and Consequential and Transitional Provisions) Order 1999 (SI 1999/2860) (October 18, 1999).

3. Tribunals, Courts and Enforcement Act 2007 Sch.1 (November 3, 2008).

4. Social Security (Attendance Allowance, Disability Living Allowance and Carer's Allowance) (Amendment) Regulations 2013 (SI 2013/389) reg.4 (April 8, 2013).

PART II

GENERAL

[¹ Disapplication of section 1(1A) of the Administration Act

4.33   **1A.**—Section 1(1A) of the Administration Act (requirement to state national insurance number) shall not apply—
    (a) to a person under the age of 16;
    (b) to any claim for disability living allowance made or treated as made before 9th February, 1998.]

AMENDMENT

1. Social Security (National Insurance Information: Exemption) Regulations (SI 1997/2676) (December 1, 1997).

Conditions as to residence and presence in Great Britain

4.34   **2.**—(1) Subject to the following provisions of this regulation [⁶ and regulations [⁷ 2A, 2B and 2C]], the prescribed conditions for the purposes of [¹ section 71](6) of the Act as to residence and presence in Great Britain in relation to any person on any day shall be that—
    (a) on that day—
        (i) he is [⁶ habitually] resident in [⁶ the United Kingdom, the Republic of Ireland, the Isle of Man or the Channel Islands]; and
    [² (ib) he is not a person subject to immigration control within the meaning of section 115(9) of the Immigration and Asylum Act 1999 or section 115 of that Act does not apply to him for the purposes of entitlement to disability living allowance by virtue of regulation 2 of the Social Security (Immigration and Asylum) Consequential Amendments Regulations 2000, and]
        (ii) he is present in Great Britain; and
        (iii) he has been present in Great Britain for a period of, or for periods amounting in the aggregate to, not less than [⁶ 104] weeks in the [⁶ 156] weeks immediately preceding that day;
    (b) [⁵ . . .]
    (1A) [² *omitted*]]
    (2) For the purposes of paragraph (1)(a)(ii) and (iii), notwithstanding that on any day a person is absent from Great Britain, he shall be treated as though he was present in Great Britain if his absence is by reason only of the fact that on that day—
    (a) he is abroad in his capacity as—
        (i) a serving member of the forces,
        (ii) an airman or mariner within the meaning of regulations [⁶ 111 and 115] respectively of the Social Security (Contributions) Regulations [⁶ 2001], and for the purpose of this provision, the expression "serving members of the forces" has the same meaning as in regulation 1(2) of the Regulations of [⁶ 2001]; or
    (b) he is in employment prescribed for the purposes of [¹ section 120] of the Act in connection with continental shelf operations; or
    (c) he is living with a person mentioned in sub-paragraph (a)(i) and is

the spouse, [⁴ civil partner] son, daughter, step-son, step-daughter, father, father-in-law, step-father, mother, mother-in-law or step-mother of that person; or

[⁶ (d) he is temporarily absent from Great Britain and that absence has not lasted for a continuous period exceeding 13 weeks.]

(e) [⁶ *omitted*]

(3) [⁵ . . .]

[⁶ (3A) A person shall be treated as habitually resident in Great Britain for the purpose of paragraph (1)(a)(i) where—

(a) he is resident outside Great Britain in his capacity as a serving member of the forces and for this purpose "serving member of the forces" has the meaning given in regulation 1(2) of the Social Security (Contributions) Regulations 2001; or

(b) he is living with a person mentioned in paragraph (a) and is the spouse, civil partner, son, daughter, step-son, step-daughter, father, father-in-law, step-father, mother, mother-in-law or step-mother of that person.

[⁶ (3B) Where a person is temporarily absent from Great Britain, he is treated as present in Great Britain for the purposes of paragraph (1)(a)(ii) and (iii) for the first 26 weeks of that absence, where—

(a) this absence is solely in connection with arrangements made for the medical treatment of him for a disease or bodily or mental disablement which commenced before he left Great Britain; and

(b) the arrangements referred to in sub-paragraph (a) relate to medical treatment—

    (i) outside Great Britain,

    (ii) during the period whilst he is temporarily absent from Great Britain, and

    (iii) by, or under the supervision of, a person appropriately qualified to carry out that treatment, and

"medical treatment" means medical, surgical or rehabilitative treatment (including any course or diet or regimen), and references to a person receiving or submitting to medical treatment are to be construed accordingly.

[⁶ (3C) For the purpose of paragraph (2)(d) and (3B) a person is "temporarily absent" if, at the beginning of the period of absence, that absence is unlikely to exceed 52 weeks.]

(4) Where a person is terminally ill and—

(a) makes a claim for disability allowance; or

(b) an application is made for a [³ revision under section 9 of the 1998 Act or supersession under section 10 of that Act] of his award of disability living allowance, expressly on the ground that he is such a person, paragraph (1) shall apply to him as if head (iii) of sub-paragraph (a) was omitted.

(5) Paragraph (1) shall apply in the case of a child under the age of 6 months as if in head (iii) of sub-paragraph (a) for the reference to [⁶ 104] weeks there was substituted a reference to 13 weeks.

(6) Where in any particular case a child has by virtue of paragraph (5), entitlement to the care component immediately before the day he attains the age of 6 months, then until the child attains the age of 12 months, head (iii) of sub-paragraph (a) of paragraph (1) shall continue to apply in his case as if for the reference to [⁶ 104] weeks there was substituted a reference to 13 weeks.

[⁶ (7) Paragraph (1) shall apply in the case of a child who is over the age of six months but who has not exceeded the age of 36 months as if in head (iii) of sub-paragraph (a) for the reference to 104 weeks there was substituted a reference to 26 weeks.]

AMENDMENTS

1. Social Security (Disability Living Allowance) (Amendment) Regulations 1993 (SI 1993/1939) reg.2 (August 26, 1993).
2. Social Security (Immigration and Asylum) Consequential Amendments Regulations 2000 (SI 2000/636) reg.11 (April 3, 2000).
3. Social Security Act 1998 (Commencement No. 11, and savings and consequential and Transitional Provisions) Order 1999 (SI 1999/2860) Sch.7 (October 18, 1999).
4. Civil Partnership (Pensions, Social Security and Child Support) (Consequential, etc. Provisions) Order 2005 (SI 2005/2877) (December 5, 2005).
5. Social Security (Miscellaneous Amendments) (No.4) Regulations 2006 (SI 2006/2378) reg.8 (October 1, 2006).
6. Social Security (Attendance Allowance, Disability Living Allowance and Carer's Allowance) (Amendment) Regulations 2013 (SI 2013/389) reg.4 (April 8, 2013).
7. Social Security (Miscellaneous Amendment No.4) Regulations 2017 (SI 2017/1015) reg.6(2) (November 16, 2017).

GENERAL NOTE

4.35   Regulation 2 has been amended since 1996 to require the claimant to be without any restriction on their permission to be in the UK. That restriction was subject to a saving in respect of claimants already entitled to benefit at the time it came into force. A series of decisions culminating in an appeal to the House of Lords has established that the saving is effective only in respect of an award in force at February 5, 1996, and not for a renewal of that award. Where the award was for life it remains effective until reviewed. This decision has now been reported as *R(DLA) 7/01.*

In *MS v SSWP (DLA)* [2016] UKUT 42 (AAC) the claimant was a child born in Israel to an Israeli father. He had been brought to the UK by his mother, who was a UK citizen, on a six month visitor visa and by the time of the application for DLA was an over-stayer. Judge Hemingway applied the view expressed (obiter) by Lord Scarman in *R. v London Borough Council Ex parte Shah* [1983] 2 W.L.R. 16, that the child could not be ordinarily resident in the UK because he was not lawfully present in the UK, even though his mother was.

Until April 8, 2013 a claimant need only have shown that they were "ordinarily resident" and there is a saving for existing claims made on that basis. Neither "ordinary" nor "habitual" residence is defined in the statute or regulations. Ordinary residence has usually been taken to mean that you have a settled intention to live in the country (technically now the "common travel area") as your home, but, not necessarily, permanently. Habitual residence, which is intended to be a more stringent test, requires as well that that the claimant has been in the country already for an extended period. How long, will depend upon the circumstances of the claimant; a former resident returning from a period abroad may satisfy this test almost immediately, while a new immigrant may be required to demonstrate a considerable period of residence. The meaning of "habitual residence" has been the subject of extensive case law in relation to claims for means-tested benefits where it has applied for some time. Readers are referred to the notes to relevant sections of Vol.II of this Work.

In *MM and SI v SSWP (DLA)* [2016] UKUT 149 (AAC); [2016] AACR 38 Judge Markus QC has held that regulation 2(1)(a)(iii) (the past presence test or PPT) must be disapplied in respect of claims made on behalf of applicants who were family members of persons granted refugee status in the UK. She held that the PPT was indirectly discriminatory and could not be justified (when compared to the treatment of UK nationals) under art.28 of the EU Directive 2004/83/EC (which gives protection to refugees) and which she held had direct effect in the UK. For the same reason she held that PPT was in breach of the claimant's rights under art.14 of the ECHR. At the time the claims were made the applicants satisfied the other conditions of regulation 2 which meant that their claims should proceed accordingly.

In *FM v SSWP (DLA)* [2017] UKUT 380 (AAC) Judge Jacobs has held that the past presence test when applied in the case of a child is not discriminatory so as to be a breach of the claimant's rights under the European Convention on Human Rights and the Human Rights Act 1998. The judge doubted that the claimant's residence before coming to this country could be regarded as a status, but that in any case the difference in treatment between a child who had been resident in this country, and the claimant, was justified. He held also that no breach had been shown of the public sector equality duty under the Equality Act 2010 and that the action of the Department was in accordance with the United Nations Convention on the Rights of the Child 1989.

For questions that involve persons either coming from or going to another country that is a part of the European Union reference should be made to the relevant sections of Vol.III of this Work.

Subsection (2)(e) which provided for a person to be absent with a certificate issued by the Secretary of State has been abolished with effect from April 8, 2013, but there is a saving provision for those persons who were abroad on that basis at that time—see reg.5 of SI 2013/389.

[[1]Persons residing in Great Britain to whom a relevant EU Regulation applies

2A.—(1) Regulation 2(1)(a)(iii) shall not apply where on any day—   4.36
  (a) the person is habitually resident in Great Britain;
  (b) a relevant EU Regulation applies; and
  (c) the person can demonstrate a genuine and sufficient link to the United Kingdom social security system.

(2) For the purpose of paragraph (1)(b) and regulation 2B, "relevant EU Regulation" has the meaning given by section 84(2) of the Welfare Reform Act 2012.]

AMENDMENT

1. Social Security (Attendance Allowance, Disability living Allowance and Carer's Allowance) (Amendment) Regulations 2013 (SI 2013/389) reg.4 (April 8, 2013).

GENERAL NOTE

The relevant regulations referred to are (EC) No.1408/71 and (EC) No.883/2004.   4.37
For detailed discussion see Vol.III of this Work.

The operation of this provision was considered by Judge Wright in *PB v SSWP (DLA)* [2016] UKUT 280 (AAC). In this case the applicant was a disabled child of 13 years who was brought by his mother from the Czech Republic to live with his sister in this country. The sister had by this time been living in Great Britain for at least five years, was in full time employment, and had been awarded both Child Tax Credits and Working Tax Credits in respect of the applicant. The FTT had rejected his appeal against refusal of a claim for DLA on the ground that he did not satisfy the past presence test under reg.2 above. His appeal was allowed on the ground that he was a person to whom reg.2A applied. It was accepted that he was now habitually resident in the UK and that EU Regulation 883/2004 applied to him. It was not necessary that he should fall within the definition of a "family member" under that regulation; all that was required was that he show a "genuine and sufficient link" to the UK social security system and that he could do, as he was now living with, and being cared for by, his sister who had a record of at least five years' employment in this country.

The operation of this subsection has been considered by the CA in *Kavanagh and Mohamed v SSWP* [2019] EWCA Civ 272. Both cases had been before Judge Jacobs in the UT where, while it was accepted that each claimant was now habitually resident in the UK, he held that neither was able to establish that they had a genuine and sufficient link to the UK. Judge Jacobs took the view that their reason for coming to the UK could not contribute to establishing that link. The CA, however, held that the reason for coming here could be relevant. In the case of *BK* the claimant was a child for whom a claim of DLA had been made by his mother. The mother was a UK national who had lived most of her life in Ireland, but had come to the UK to escape domestic violence and receive the support that she needed with the claimant and two other children from her mother, grandmother and brothers, all of whom were resident here. The CA held that this reason, together with her actual presence here, was enough to establish that link. In the UT Judge Jacobs had observed that the requirement in subs. (2A)(c) that the link be to the UK social security system was unlawful; the CA proceeded on the basis that that was correct and therefore the last three words of that paragraph are to be ignored.

[¹Persons residing in an EEA state other than the United Kingdom or in Switzerland to whom a relevant EU Regulation applies

4.38

2B.—Regulation 2(1)(a)(i) to (iii) shall not apply in relation to the care component where on any day—
- (a) the person is habitually resident in—
    - (i) an EEA state other than the United Kingdom; or
    - (ii) Switzerland;
- (b) a relevant EU Regulation applies; and
- (c) the person can demonstrate a genuine and sufficient link to the UK social security system.]

AMENDMENTS

1. Social Security (Attendance Allowance, Disability living Allowance and Carer's Allowance) (Amendment) Regulations 2013 (SI 2013/389) reg.4 (April 8, 2013).

[¹ Refugees

4.39

2C.—(1) Regulation 2(1)(a)(iii) shall not apply where the person has—
- (a) been granted refugee status or humanitarian protection under the immigration rules; or
- (b) leave to enter or remain in the United Kingdom as the dependant of a person granted refugee status or humanitarian protection under the immigration rules.

(2) For the purposes of this regulation "immigration rules" means the rules laid before Parliament under section 3(2) of the Immigration Act 1971.]

AMENDMENTS

1. Social Security (Miscellaneous Amendment No.4) Regulations 2017 (SI 2017/1015) reg.7(3) (November 16, 2017).

Age 65 or over

4.40

3.—(1) A person shall not be precluded from entitlement to either component of disability living allowance by reason only that he has attained the age of 65 years [¹ if he is a person to whom paragraphs (2) and (3) apply].

(2) Paragraph (3) applies to a person who—

(a) made a claim for disability living allowance before he attained the age of 65, which was not determined before he attained that age, and

(b) did not at the time he made the claim have an award of disability living allowance for a period ending on or after the day he attained the age of 65.

(3) In determining the claim of a person to whom this paragraph applies, where the person otherwise satisfies the conditions of entitlement to either or both components of disability living allowance for a period commencing before his 65th birthday (other than the requirements of [² section 72](2) (a), or, as the case may be, [² section 73](9)(a) of the Act (3 months qualifying period)), the determination shall be made without regard to the fact that he is aged 65 or over at the time the claim is determined.

[³(3A) A person shall not be precluded from entitlement to the care component of disability living allowance by reason only that he has attained the age of 65 years if the claim is treated as made on 18th October 2007 in accordance with regulation 6(35) of the Social Security (Claims and Payments) Regulations 1987 (date of claim).]

(4) Schedule 1, which makes further provision for persons aged 65 or over shall have effect.

AMENDMENTS

1. Social Security (Disability Living Allowance) Amendments Regulations 1997 (SI 1997/349) reg.2 (October 6, 1997).

2. Social Security (Disability Living Allowance) (Amendment) Regulations 1993 (SI 1993/1939) reg.2 (August 26, 1993).

3. Social Security (Disability Living Allowance, Attendance and Carer's Allowance) (Miscellaneous Amendments) Regulations 2011 (SI 2011/2426) reg.4 (October 31, 2011).

GENERAL NOTE

Paragraph (1)

Section 75(1) of the Social Security Contributions and Benefits Act 1992 has the effect that normally a person cannot be entitled to disability living allowance after he or she has attained the age of 65 unless awarded it before that age. Before its amendment, this paragraph enabled a person who would have satisfied the conditions of entitlement continuously since the age of 65 to qualify provided he or she made a claim before reaching the age of 66. The amendment means that it is now necessary for the claimant to have made a claim before reaching the age of 65. An earlier unsuccessful claim is irrelevant (*R(M) 4/86*). Where a claim has been determined in the claimant's favour before his or her 65th birthday, para.(4) and Sch.1 apply and make provision for reviews and renewal claims. Where a claim has not been determined before the claimant's 65th birthday, paras (2) and (3) apply. Those who are too old to be entitled to disability living allowance but who would otherwise qualify for the highest or middle rate of the care component will be entitled to attendance allowance instead, subject to satisfying the longer six-month qualifying condition. **4.41**

Paragraphs (2) and (3)

Section 75(1) of the 1992 Act specifically provides that a claimant cannot be entitled to disability living allowance unless the *award* has been made before his or her 65th birthday. These paragraphs make provision for a person whose *claim* was made before the 65th birthday and who is not making an advance claim to follow an existing **4.42** award ending on or after that birthday. In such a case, provided that the conditions of entitlement are satisfied for a period commencing before the claimant's 65th birthday, entitlement is to be determined without regard to the fact that he or she is aged 65 or over at the time of the determination. Note that it is not necessary for the three-month qualifying condition to be satisfied before the claimant reaches the age of 65. Thus a person who becomes seriously disabled, say, a month before his or her birthday, can become entitled to disability living allowance two months after the birthday.

Paragraph (3A)

4.43   This amendment preserves the entitlement of claimants over 65 who have moved to live in another part of the European Economic Area or to Switzerland. This is achieved by the effect of reg.6(35) of the Claims and Payments regulations which gives effect to the judgment of the European Court of Justice in case C-299/05, *Commission of the European Communities v European Parliament and European Union*.

Paragraph 4

4.44   See the notes to Sch.1 which deals with the determination of reviews and renewal claims after a person's 65th birthday and with the position of former beneficiaries under the invalid vehicle scheme.

Rate of benefit

4.45   **4.**—(1) The three weekly rates of the care component are—
   (a) the highest rate, payable in accordance with [¹ section 72](4)(a) of the Act, [²£87.65];
   (b) the middle rate, payable in accordance with [¹section 72](4)(b) of the Act, [²£58.70];
   (c) the lowest rate, payable in accordance with [¹ section 72](4)(c) of the Act, [²£23.20].
   (2) The two weekly rates of the mobility component are—
   (a) the higher rate, payable in accordance with [¹ section 73] (11)(a) of the Act, [²£61.20]; and
   (b) the lower rate, payable in accordance with [¹ section 73] (11)(b) of the Act, [²£23.20].

Amendments

1. Social Security (Disability Living Allowance) (Amendment) Regulations 1993 (SI 1993/1939) reg.2 (August 26, 1993).
2. Social Security Benefits Up-rating Order 2019 (SI 2019/480) art.15 (April 8, 2019).

Late claim by a person previously entitled

4.46   **5.**—[¹ . . .]
   5A.—[² . . .]
   5B.—[² . . .]
   5C.—[² . . .]

Repeals

1. Repealed by Social Security (Miscellaneous Amendments) (No. 2) Regulations 1997 (SI 1997/793) reg.19 (September 1, 1997).
2. Repealed by Social Security Act 1998 Sch.7 (October 18, 1999).

PART III

CARE COMPONENT

Qualifying period for care component after an interval

6.—(1) The period prescribed for the purposes of [¹ section 72] (2)(a)(ii)   4.47
of the Act is a period of 3 months ending on the day on which the person was
last entitled to the care component or to attendance allowance where that day
falls not more than 2 years before the date on which entitlement to the care
component would begin, or would have begun but for any regulations made
under [¹ section 5(1)(k) of the Administration Act] (which enables regulations
to provide for the day on which entitlement to benefit is to begin or end).

(2) Except in a case to which paragraph (3) applies, this regulation shall
apply to a person to whom paragraph 3 or 7 of Schedule 1 refers as if for
the reference to 3 months there was substituted a reference to 6 months.

(3) Paragraph (1) and not paragraph (2), shall apply to those persons
referred to in paragraph (2) who, on the day before they attained the age of
65, had already completed the period of three months referred to in paragraph (1).

(4) For the purposes of paragraph (3), the modification made in
Schedule 1—

(a) in paragraph 3 (2) and 7(2), to [¹ section 72] (2)(a) of the Act, and

(b) in paragraph 5 (2), to [¹ section 73] (9)(a) of the Act,

shall be treated as not having been made.

AMENDMENT

1. Social Security (Disability Living Allowance) (Amendment) Regulations 1993
(SI 1993/1939), reg.2 (August 26, 1993).

GENERAL NOTE

The general effect of this provision is that the three-month qualifying period (six   4.48
months for people aged 65 or over) for the care component is deemed to be satisfied
if the new claim is within two years of a previous period of entitlement to the care
component (or attendance allowance) at the relevant rate.

Renal Dialysis

7.—(1) A person who suffers from renal failure and falls within the pro-   4.49
visions in paragraph (2) shall be taken to satisfy—

(a) where he undergoes renal dialysis by day, the conditions in paragraph (b) of subsection (1) of [¹ section 72] of the Act (severe physical or mental disability);

(b) where he undergoes renal dialysis by night, the conditions in paragraph (c) of that subsection; or

(c) where he undergoes renal dialysis by day and by night, the conditions
in either paragraph (b) or paragraph (c) of subsection (1), but not
both.

(2) Subject to paragraph (3), a person falls within this paragraph—

(a) if—

(i) he undergoes renal dialysis two or more times a week; and

(ii) the renal dialysis he undergoes is of a type which normally requires the attendance or supervision of another person during the period of the dialysis; or

    (iii) because of the particular circumstances of his case he in fact requires another person, during the period of the dialysis, to attend in connection with his bodily functions or to supervise him in order to avoid substantial danger to himself; and

  (b) if, where he undergoes dialysis as an out-patient in a hospital or similar institution, being treatment provided under [² the NHS Act of 1978, the NHS Act of 2006 or the NHS (Wales) Act of 2006], no member of the staff of the hospital or institution assists with or supervises the dialysis.

[¹ (3) Paragraph (2)(b) does not apply for the purpose of determining whether a person is to be taken to satisfy any of the conditions mentioned, in paragraph (1) during the periods mentioned in section 72(2)(a)(i) and (b)(i) of the Act.]

(4) Except to the extent that provision is made in paragraph (2)(b), a person who undergoes treatment by way of renal dialysis as an outpatient in a hospital or similar institution, being treatment provided under [² the NHS Act of 1978, the NHS Act of 2006 or the NHS (Wales) Act of 2006], shall not be taken solely by reason of the fact that he undergoes such dialysis, as satisfying any of the conditions mentioned in subsection (1)(a) to (c) of [¹ section 72] of the Act.

AMENDMENT

1. Social Security (Disability Living Allowance) (Amendment) Regulations 1993 (SI 1993/1939) reg.2 (August 26, 1993).

2. Social Security (Attendance Allowance, Disability Living Allowance and Carer's Allowance) (Amendment) Regulations 2013 (SI 2013/389) reg.4 (April 8, 2013).

GENERAL NOTE

4.50   Under this regulation, a person undergoing renal dialysis at least twice a week may be deemed to satisfy *either* the "day" *or* the "night" attendance conditions of s.72(1)(b) and (c) of the Social Security Contributions and Benefits Act 1992, but not both. Some degree of attention or supervision must be required. This regulation is in slightly different terms from reg.5 of the Social Security (Attendance Allowance) Regulations 1991.

Paragraph (2)(a)

4.51   The dialysis must be *either* of a type which *normally* requires the attendance of or supervision by another person (in which case the actual purpose of the attention or supervision is irrelevant) *or* the dialysis must *in the particular case* require the attention or supervision of the claimant (for the purpose specified in para.(2)(a)(iii)).

Paragraphs (2)(b), (3) and (4).

4.52   Under paras (2)(b) and (4), a person receiving treatment under the National Health Service cannot qualify for the care component under this regulation if he or she receives assistance or supervision during the dialysis from a member of staff of the hospital or other relevant institution, although there is nothing in para.(4) to prevent the need for any such assistance or supervision from being taken into account when considering whether the ordinary "day" or "night" conditions are satisfied. Para.(3) has the effect that, where a person has been undergoing dialysis falling within para.(2)(a) but para.(2)(b) was not satisfied because, say, supervision was provided in a National Health Service hospital, he or she can qualify under this regulation as soon as that supervision ceases, as long as he or she had been undergoing the dialysis for the usual three-month qualifying period. Presumably para.(3) applies equally to the six-month qualifying period substituted under para.3 of Sch.1 for claimants aged 65 or over.

[⁵ Hospitalisation of persons aged 18 or over]

8.—[¹ (1) Subject to [⁵ paragraph (2B) and] regulation 10, it shall be a   4.53
condition for the receipt of a disability living allowance which is attributable to entitlement to the care component for any period in respect of any
person that during that period he is not maintained free of charge while
undergoing medical or other treatment as an in-patient—
  (a) in a hospital or similar institution under [⁴ the NHS Act of 1978, the
       NHS Act of 2006 or the NHS (Wales) Act of 2006]; or
  (b) in a hospital or other similar institution maintained or administered
       by the Defence Council.]
  (2) For the purposes of [¹ paragraph (1)(a)] a person shall only be regarded
as not being maintained free of charge in a hospital or similar institution during
any period when his accommodation and services are provided under[—]
[⁴ (a) section 57 of, and paragraph 14 of Schedule 7A to, the NHS Act of
       1978;
  (b) section 13 of, and paragraph 15 of Schedule 2 to, the NHS Act of
       2006;
  (c) section 28 of, and paragraph 11 of Schedule 6 to, the NHS Act of
       2006;
  (d) section 44(6) of, and paragraph 19(1) of Schedule 4 to, the NHS Act
       of 2006;
  (e) section 11 of, and paragraph 15 of Schedule 2 to, the NHS (Wales)
       Act of 2006;
  (f) section 18 of, and paragraph 19(1) of Schedule 3 to, the NHS
       (Wales) Act of 2006; or
  (g) section 22 of, and paragraph 11 of Schedule 5 to, the NHS (Wales)
       Act of 2006.]
  [² (2A) For the purposes of paragraph (1), a period during which a person
is maintained free of charge while undergoing medical or other treatment
as an in-patient shall be deemed to begin on the day after the day on which
he enters a hospital or similar institution referred to in that paragraph and
to end on the day [³ before the day] on which he leaves such a hospital or
similar institution].
  [⁵(2B) This regulation does not apply to a person who was under the age
of 18 on the day on which he entered the hospital or other similar institution
referred to in paragraph (1) to begin his current period as an in-patient.]
  (3) [¹ . . .].

AMENDMENTS

  1. Social Security (Disability Living Allowance and Attendance Allowance)
(Amendment) Regulations 1992 (SI 1992/2869) reg.4 (December 15, 1992).
  2. Social Security (Hospital In-Patients, Attendance Allowance and Disability
Living Allowance) (Amendment) Regulations 1999 (SI 1999/1326) (June 7, 1999).
  3. Social Security (Attendance Allowance and Disability Living Allowance)
(Amendment) Regulations 2000, (SI 2000/1401) reg.3 (June 19, 2000).
  4. Social Security (Attendance Allowance, Disability Living Allowance and
Carer's Allowance) (Amendment) Regulations 2013 (SI 2013/389) reg.4 (April 8,
2013).

5. Social Security (Disability Living Allowance and Personal Independence Payment) (Amendment) Regulations 2016 (SI 2016/556) regulation 2 (June 29, 2016).

GENERAL NOTE

4.54   Note that this regulation has been amended in response to the decision of the Supreme Court in *Cameron Mathieson v SSWP* [2015] UKSC 47. That decision concerned a claim made on behalf of an infant claimant. The SC held that the previous version of this regulation breached the claimant's rights under the Human Rights Act 1998 and under the European Convention on Human Rights. Accordingly this regulation now applies only to claimants who are aged 18 years or over.

See the annotations to reg.6 of the Social Security (Attendance Allowance) Regulations 1991 which is in identical terms.

Note that, by virtue of reg.10, a person may remain entitled to the care component for up to 28 days in hospital but that separate periods in hospital or such accommodation are aggregated unless they are more than 28 days apart.

This regulation disqualifies a claimant who is being treated in a publicly financed hospital. In decision *CDLA/11099/1995* the Commissioner had to decide if it applied to a patient who spent each night in such a hospital but was at home through the day. He held that it did; because the claimant spent a part of each day in a publicly funded hospital he could not qualify for benefit on any day.

Note that a similar issue has arisen in relation to reg.2(2) of the Hospital In-Patients Regulation 1975, where there has been a conflict in Commissioners' decisions. This decision is in accordance with the more recent of those decisions.

In decision *CSDLA/1282/01* the Commissioner holds that a claimant is being maintained free of charge in hospital notwithstanding that the claimant may continue to receive care and support from their family. In this case the claimant was fed and bathed, etc. by her family because she refused to allow nursing staff to provide those services.

In *CDLA/7980/95* the Commissioner had to decide if this provision could cover the case of a claimant formerly accomodated in a hospital, but now living in a privately rented house with full-time care provided by the local Health Service Trust, under the Care in the Community policy. He held that it did not. A privately rented home which the claimant shared with six others, and in which they paid not only the rent, but also for their own food, etc. did not become either a "hospital" or a "similar institution" simply because they were cared for there at public expense. Equally, the Commissioner could have found that while they were living there they were not "maintained free of charge" because they were paying their own rent and other outgoings—presumably being maintained includes the provision of housing, food, etc. as well as care.

It should be noted that there may be some overlap between this regulation and reg.9 because in *CAO v White* (reported as *R(IS) 18/94*) (referred to in *CDLA/7980/95*) it was held that a registered nursing home (which could fall within reg.9) also fell within the description of a "hospital or similar institution" for the purposes of the Hospital In-Patients Regulations 1975 which uses the same expression.

The complex issue of whether care has been provided for in a "hospital or similar institution" so as to be disqualified from benefit under this regulation, or whether instead it was provided under arrangements made by the local authority so as to be disqualified under reg.9, has been examined by a Tribunal of Commissioners in *R(DLA) 2/06*. Put thus, it might seem to matter little to the claimant under which regulation the claim for care must fail, but for claimants entitled also to a mobility component which is covered by transitional protection, and for claimants who are able to claim Income Support, the distinction will be significant because there is no equivalent to reg.9 disqualification for those other benefits. Indeed, in this case it was also argued that neither reg.8 or reg.9 should apply, though then any resulting benefit entitlement would be paid to the local authority for them to pay to the nursing home as had been happening in these cases.

The cases involved claimants who were formerly patients in a mental hospital and who, under the changes made in the early 1990's, were moved into private nursing homes where they still continued to receive the high level of care and nursing services consistent with their condition. No formal assessment of their needs was made, but it was clear from the charges levied for each of them that the service provided was for far more than accommodation with incidental nursing care. The Commissioners concluded therefore that the nursing home fell within the description of an institution similar to a hospital and the disqualification applied. (See *CAO v White R(1S) 18/94*)

The real protagonists in this case were the local health authority and the DWP. This was because, if the claimants' needs really were those of a hospital patient, then the health authority was liable to supply those needs under the National Health Service Act 1997. But under the ill constructed and poorly evidenced arrangements that the health authority and the local authority had tried to make in this case, they purported to make the claimants into self funding residents of the care homes so that all their benefit entitlements would be available as a contribution to their fees, the balance of which was then made up by the health authority, though paid through the local authority.   **4.55**

The argument put forward by the DWP was that either they were still in a "hospital" and therefore caught by reg.8, or they were being accommodated by the local authority under Pt III of the National Assistance Act and then caught by reg.9. Either way the DWP should not have been paying to the extent of the care component of DLA. In deciding that the arrangements necessary for these claimants amounted to hospital care the commissioners were also saying that the claimants could not be accommodated under Pt III because that power does not extend to accommodating persons who need full hospital care—the whole of such costs, therefore, should have been met by the health authority. The net effect was that some patients (those not qualifying for IS) had been charged considerable sums for which they should not have been liable. None of this was in issue before the Commissioners and was relevant only as being a necessary step in reaching the decisions that they did, but the Commissioners conclude by referring to the ill standards of public administration that this revealed.

The further complications involved in administering this provision (and regs 8 and 12A) are demonstrated in *SSWP v TR (DLA)* [2013] UKUT 622 (AAC). The claimant was accommodated in a home for which the health authority and the local authority had agreed to share the costs on a 50/50 basis. The claimant was subjected to a statutory charge which he paid to the local authority. In the home, 31 per cent of the staff were qualified nurses, there was as well a "physio team", and the home was registered to provide care with nursing and rehabilitation services. The question to be determined was whether the claimant, in these circumstances, was being "maintained free of charge while undergoing medical or other treatment as an in-patient in a hospital or similar institution". The judge in the UT, Judge Fordham, found that he was not. He would have found that the home was a "hospital or similar institution" and he would have found too, that the claimant was "receiving medical treatment as an in-patient" there, but he did not find that the claimant was being "maintained free of charge" in the home. This was not because the claimant was paying a contribution towards his costs- that would have been the effect of giving this phrase its natural and ordinary meaning, but the phrase has a restricted meaning in reg.8(2) (and in reg.12A(2)). The effect of that definition is that a claimant can only be said to be not being maintained in the hospital free of charge if they are there entirely as a private patient; thus for someone in the claimant's position although he was being charged a contribution, he could still be regarded as being there "free of charge"! The judge's decision turns upon what is meant by being "maintained" and the interpretation given to that word in the earlier cases of *R (DLA) 2/06* and *CDLA/509/2009* which followed it. Those cases establish that a claimant is to be regarded as maintained in the hospital or other institution only as long as the health authority has a duty to do so under the relevant National Health Service Act. Correspondingly he cannot be maintained by the local authority while that is so, and he can be maintained by the local authority only when they have a duty to so under Pt III of the National Assistance Act 1948.

In this case it appeared that the local authority took the view that they were obliged to maintain under Pt III and it followed that the health authority were not, therefore "maintaining" him.

This meant that the claimant was entitled to be paid DLA under both reg.8 and reg.12A. But he was not entitled to payment of the care component of DLA because under reg.9 (see below) at least some part of the cost of his accommodation and care was met from public funds.

This a complex area of law that seems to be encumbered by provisions derived from past practices and badly in need of updating.

4.56   The meanings of the phrases, "medical or other treatment" and "hospital or similar institution", have been considered at length by Judge Turnbull in *AS v SSWP* [2010] UKUT 482 (AAC). The claimant was living in a private care home that specialised in providing accommodation for autistic people. None of the staff in the home was medically qualified, but the whole of the cost was paid by the health authority. While he had been living at home the claimant had been in receipt of care component of DLA at the highest rate and of mobility component at the higher rate. When he moved to the care home both components were stopped (the care component under reg.8 and the mobility component under reg.12A (see below)) on the basis that he was now "maintained free of charge while undergoing medical or other treatment as an in-patient . . . in a hospital or similar institution". His parents appealed on the basis that, though he might not be entitled to the care component, he should still be receiving the mobility component, as would be the case if his disqualification were made under reg.9 (see below), where disqualification applies only to the care component. However, on closer examination the judge pointed out that reg.9 could not apply in this case, as the fees were being paid by the health authority; reg.9 applies only where fees are being met by a local authority. Thus, unless the care home could be classed as a "hospital or similar institution" the claimant would be entitled to both components despite the fact that all of his living expenses (though arguably not his mobility) were being met from public funds. The judge referred to the case of *Minister of Health v House for Incurables at Leamington Spa* [1954] 1 Ch. 530 (CA), a case arising from the creation of the National Health Service, as well as two cases where the same phrases occur in relation to other benefits; *CAO v White R(IS) 18/94* and *Botchett v CAO R(IS) 10/96*. He felt that these cases, together with the interrelated meaning of "medical or other treatment" compelled him to conclude that the care home could not be a hospital or similar institution unless the care that was provided there was delivered by medically qualified staff. In the cases referred to above all of the institutions had qualified nurses on the staff. While he stops short of holding that it is essential to have a nursing staff he does suggest that there should at least be persons who could be described as health-care professionals who are regularly providing services on the premises to those accommodated there. This decision has now been upheld by the Court of Appeal and reported as *Secretary of State for Work and Pensions v Slavin* [2011] EWCA Civ 1515. [2012] AACR 30 The court rejected an argument put on behalf of the Secretary of State that regs 8 (care component) and 12A (mobility component) should be read so as to achieve a broad policy objective of avoiding the payment of benefit for needs that were provided from public funds in some other way. The court denied that any such broad policy objective could be read into those regulations. The court also confirmed that, although nursing practice may have moved on considerably since the time of the *Leamington* decision, the test of whether the claimant was in receipt of "medical or other treatment" should remain that of whether such services were provided by medically qualified staff, which meant at least a nursing qualification or training. Furthermore, they confirmed that such treatment must take place in the institution where the claimant was accommodated. The court did not decide whether the place of accommodation could be regarded as a "hospital or similar institution" in which the claimant received "medical or other treatment" if the treatment were provided by professionally qualified persons at that place, but not by persons employed by the institution. This question was left open because the case had been referred to the court on the basis that the information necessary for a determination of that question had not been obtained from the parties. A further decision may therefore be necessary to determine this point, but such arrangements would presumably have to go beyond the treatment that might normally be available to a patient in their own home.

This case concerned only the claimant's entitlement to the mobility component (It appears that the decision in respect of the care component had not been appealed at the First-tier Tribunal in the mistaken belief that entitlement was removed under reg.9), but the court accepts that the interpretation they apply in relation to reg.12A must apply equally to reg.8.

The meaning of the phrases "undergoing medical or other treatment as an in-patient" and "in a hospital or similar institution" has been considered again by Judge Turnbull in *JP v SSWP* [2013] UKUT 524 (AAC). There the claimant was a young man who suffered from a serious form of epilepsy. Until 2007 he had lived at home with his parents, but then it had been necessary to move him from his home to a place run by a charity that provided accommodation and specialist services for persons with conditions of that kind. The premises extended over a campus like arrangement that included accommodation units, medical and other services and a GP surgery. The claimant lived in an accommodation unit that was staffed only by non-medically qualified persons, but the charity had engaged a number of other medically qualified staff including nurses, a doctor (other than the GP), psychologists and consultants who came to the campus to provide their services. On behalf of the claimant it was argued that where he lived was staffed only by care staff and that the medical services that he received were no more than would have been available from a local hospital etc had he been living still at his parents' home. Judge Turnbull, however, decided that the charity's premises should be regarded as a collective unit that, although clearly not a hospital, could fall within the description of a "similar institution". Furthermore, in his view, the treatment that the claimant received on the premises (though not that from the GP surgery) constituted "medical or other treatment as an in patient". Consequently the appeal against refusal of both the living component (under reg.8) and the mobility component (under reg.12A) was dismissed.

[¹ Persons in care homes

9.—(1) Except in the cases specified in paragraphs (3) to (5), and subject to regulation 10, a person shall not be paid any amount in respect of a disability living allowance which is attributable to entitlement to the care component for any period where throughout that period he is a resident in a care home in circumstances where any of the costs of any qualifying services provided for him are borne out of public or local funds under a specified enactment.

4.57

(2) The specified enactments for the purposes of paragraph (1) are—

(a)

(i) Part III of the National Assistance Act 1948,

   (ii) [³ sections 59 and 59A] of the Social Work (Scotland) Act 1968,

   (iii) the Mental Health (Care and Treatment) (Scotland) Act 2003,

   (iv) the Community Care and Health (Scotland) Act 2002,

   (v) the Mental Health Act 1983;

[⁴ (vi) section 57 of the Health and Social Care Act 2001,]
[⁵ (vii) Part 1 of the Care Act 2014 (care and support),]
[⁶ (viii) Part 4 of the Social Services and Well-being (Wales) Act 2014 (meeting needs), or]
  (b) any other enactment relating to persons under disability or to young persons or to education or training.
  (3) Paragraph (2)(b) shall not apply in circumstances where any of the costs of the qualifying services provided for him are borne wholly or partly out of public or local funds by virtue of—
  (a) section 485 of the Education Act 1996, section 14 of the Education Act 2002 or section 73 of the Education (Scotland) Act 1980 (which relate to grants in aid of educational services);
  (b) [³ *omitted*] sections 49 or 73 of the Education (Scotland) Act 1980 (which relate respectively to the power of education authorities to assist persons to take advantage of educational facilities and the powers of the Secretary of State to make grants to education authorities and others);
  (c) section 65 of the Further and Higher Education Act 1992 or sections 4 or 11 of the Further and Higher Education (Scotland) Act 2005 (which relate respectively to the funding of further education and the administration of funds);
  (d) [³ *omitted*]
  (e) section 22 of the Teaching and Higher Education Act 1998.
  (4) Subject to paragraph (5), paragraphs (1) and (2) shall not apply in the case of a child [⁶ . . .]—
  (a) [⁶ who] has not attained the age of 16 and is being looked after by a local authority; or
  (b) [⁶ who] has not attained the age of 18 and to whom—
      (i) section 17(10)(b) of the Children Act 1989 or section 93(4)(a) (ii) of the Children (Scotland) Act 1995 (impairment of health and development) applies because his health is likely to be significantly impaired, or further impaired, without the provision of services for him, or
      (ii) section 17(10)(c) of the Children Act 1989 (disability) or section 93(4)(a)(iii) of the Children (Scotland) Act 1995 (disability) applies; or
      [⁶ (ba) to whom section 37, 38 or 42 of the Social Services and Wellbeing (Wales) Act 2014 applies; or]
  (c) who is accommodated outside the United Kingdom and the costs of any qualifying services are borne wholly or partly by a local authority pursuant to their powers under section 320 of the Education Act 1996 or section 25 of the Education (Additional Support for Learning) (Scotland) Act 2004.
  (5) Sub-paragraphs [⁶ (a) (b) and (ba)] of paragraph (4) shall only apply during any period which the local authority looking after the child place him in a private dwelling with a family, or a relative of his, or some other suitable person.
  (6) In this regulation and in regulation 10, references to the costs of any qualifying services shall not include the cost of—
  (a) domiciliary services, including personal care, provided in respect of a person in a private dwelling; or
  (b) improvements made to, or furniture or equipment provided for, a

private dwelling on account of the needs of a person under disability; or

(c) improvements made to, or furniture or equipment provided for, a care home in respect of which a grant or payment has been made out of public or local funds except where the grant or payment is of a regular or repeated nature; or

(d) social and recreational activities provided outside the care home in respect of which grants or payments are made out of public or local funds; or

(e) the purchase or running of a motor vehicle to be used in connection with any qualifying service provided in a care home in respect of which grants or payments are made out of public or local funds; or

(f) [³ *omitted*]

(7) For the purposes of paragraph (1), a period during which a person is a resident in a care home in the circumstances set out in that paragraph shall, subject to paragraphs (8) and (9), be deemed—

(a) to begin on the day after the day on which he enters a care home, and

(b) to end on the day before the day on which he leaves a care home.

(8) Where a person enters a care home from a hospital or similar institution in circumstances in which paragraph (1) of regulation 6 applies, the period during which he is a resident in the care home shall be deemed to begin on the day he enters that care home.

(9) Where a person leaves a care home and enters a hospital or similar institution in circumstances in which paragraph (1) of regulation 6 applies, the period during which he is a resident in the care home shall be deemed to end on the day he leaves that care home.]

AMENDMENTS

1. Attendance Allowance and Disability Living Allowance (Amendment) Regulations 2007 (SI 2007/2875) (October 29, 2007).

2. Local Education Authorities (Integration of Functions) (Local and Subordinate Legislation) Order 2010 (SI 2010/1172) art.4 and Sch.3 (May 5, 2010).

3. Social Security (Attendance Allowance, Disability Living Allowance and Carer's Allowance) (Amendment) Regulations 2013 (SI 2013/389) reg.4 (April 8, 2013).

4. Community Care, Services for Carers and Children's Services (Direct Payments) (England) (Amendment) Regulations (SI 2013/2270) reg.6 (November 1, 2013).

5. Care Act 2014 (Consequential Amendments) (Secondary Legislation) Order 2015 (SI 2015/643) art.7 (April 1, 2015).

6. Social Services and Well-being (Wales) Act 2014 and the Regulation and Inspection of Social Care (Wales) Act 2016 (Consequential Amendments) Order 2017 (SI 2017/901) art.4 (November 3, 2017).

GENERAL NOTE

There is a transitional and saving provision in reg.4 of the Amendment regulations to the effect that this amendment shall not prevent any day before the coming into force of the amended regulation from counting towards the 28 day and 84 day periods specified in reg.10. 4.58

Paragraphs (1) and (3)–(6) are in identical terms to reg.7(1)–(5) of the Social Security (Attendance Allowance) Regs 1991. For further annotations, see those Regulations. Note in particular the development of the law with regard to claimants who have moved from their own home into a publicly-funded nursing home and where the claimant subsequently repays the public body for the costs incurred. The decision of a panel of three judges in *Secretary of State for Work and Pensions v JL* [2011] UKUT 293; [2012] AACR 14 has made clear that there is no need for a prior agreement with the local authority for the fees to be paid. The decision also explores the distinction between entitlement to benefit and payability of benefit and the difference between revision, supersession and suspension of benefit. For further comment see the annotation to reg.7 of Attendance Allowance Regulations. Whether or not a claimant is being accommodated in a "hospital or similar institution" has been examined in *R(DLA)2/06*. For comment on that decision see the notes to reg.8, above.

Note that, by virtue of reg.10, a person may remain entitled to the care component for up to 28 days in accommodation covered by reg.9 or in a hospital, but that separate periods in such accommodation or hospital are aggregated unless they are more than 28 days apart.

4.59   Paragraphs (3) to (5) make provisions that enable certain children to qualify for the care component even though they might otherwise fall within the provisions of paras (1) and (2).

This regulation has been considered in the UT in *ML v SSWP (DLA)* [2016] UKUT 323 (AAC); [2017] AACR 2. The appellant argued that the disqualification provided for here should not apply in the case of his 21-year-old disabled son who had been accommodated in a care home, because the care provided was so inadequate that he had found it necessary to remove his son from that home. The period in question was that while the son was so accommodated there. Judge Markus QC held that the quality of the care provided was not determinative of whether the regulation applied. That was because the regulation made under s.72 of the SSCBA 1992 applied while the claimant was accommodated in a "care home", defined there as "an establishment that provides accommodation together with nursing or personal care". Although evidence had been accepted on the claimant's behalf that his parents were attending to his needs for 90 hours per week, the judge was satisfied that during the rest of the time the home must been providing attention of that kind. She held further that it was inconceivable that the DWP and the tribunal system could have been expected to assess the quality of care provided in order to determine whether the disqualification should apply when there was a special statutory procedure provided under the Health and Social Care Act 2008 by registration with the Care Quality Commission to make that very assessment. More significantly perhaps, the judge also held that regulation 9 is not discriminatory under art.14 of the ECHR. The appellant had argued that, following *Cameron Mathieson v SSWP* [2015] UKSC 47 in the SC, the same reasoning should apply to the claimant and to reg.9 in this case. Judge Markus considered whether the claimant's residence and needs might amount to a "status" so as to come within art.14, but found it unnecessary to reach a conclusion because she felt it was clear that, in this case, any difference in treatment between a person in a care home with those needs, and that of a person who was not so accommodated, was justified.

In *CDLA/1465/98*, the claimant was living in accommodation rented from a county council. The tribunal found that the accommodation was not provided under Pt III of the National Assistance Act 1948. The adjudication officer appealed on the ground that the county council had had no power to enter into the arrangements with the claimant save under Pt III of the 1948 Act. The appeal was dismissed because the Commissioner was not satisfied that the county council could not have acted as they did outside Pt III of the 1948 Act and he was not satisfied that the tribunal had erred in law in their approach, given the way the adjudication officer had argued the case before them. However, he suggested that the claimant's evidence as to the extent to which he could live without assistance called into question the award of the highest rate of the care component, although that was not a matter within the jurisdiction of the tribunal (which was a social security appeal tribunal and not a disability appeal tribunal). In *CA/2985/97*, it was held that provisions identical to reg.9(1)(b) and (c) had ceased to have any effect in England and Wales following amendments made to the National Assistance Act 1948 by the National Health Service and Community Care Act 1990.

In *R(DLA) 6/04* the claimant was accommodated on week days in residential accommodation run by the local authority. This accommodation was provided under the Mental Health Act 1983. The Commissioner holds that the situation is covered by sub-para.(b) of reg.9(1). The Mental Health Act 1983 is not mentioned specifically in sub-para.(a), nor is it listed in the DM guidance, but s.117 of that Act requires the local authority in exercise of its social services function to provide after- care for persons who are under supervision. The question to be answered therefore was whether persons released from hospital, but still receiving after-care under supervision, are persons under a disability within the meaning of reg.9. The Commissioner had no doubt that they were.

[¹ Persons to whom regulations 9 and 10 apply with modifications

9A.—[¹ . . .]   4.60

REPEAL

1. Social Security Amendment (Residential Care and Nursing Homes) Regulations 2001 (SI 2001/3767) reg.4 (April 8, 2002).

Exemption from regulation 8 and 9

10.—(1) Regulation 8, or as the case may be, regulation 9, shall not,   4.61
[¹ subject to the following provisions of this regulation], apply to a person for the first 28 days of any period throughout which he is someone to whom paragraph (4) applies.

(2) [¹² . . .]

(3) Where on the day the person's entitlement to the care component commenced, he is a person to whom paragraph (4) refers, then paragraph (1) [¹² . . .] shall not apply to him for any period of consecutive days, beginning with that day, in which he continues to be a person to whom paragraph (4) refers.

(4) This paragraph refers to a person who—

(a) is undergoing medical or other treatment in a hospital or other institution in any of the circumstances mentioned in regulation 8; or

[² (b) would, but for this regulation, be prevented from receiving the care component of a disability working allowance by reason of regulation 9.]

(5) For the purposes of [¹² paragraph (1)]—

(a) 2 or more distinct periods separated by an interval not exceeding 28 days, or by 2 or more such intervals shall be treated as a continuous period equal in duration to the total of such distinct periods and ending on the last day of the later or last such period;

(b) any period or periods to which regulations 8(1) or 9(1) refers shall be taken into account and aggregated with any period to which the other of them refers.

[¹ (6) Regulation 8 or as the case may be regulation 9 shall not apply [³ . . .] in the case of a person who is residing in a hospice and is terminally ill where the Secretary of State has been informed that he is terminally ill—

(a) on a claim for the care component,

(b) on an application for a [⁴revision under section 9 of the 1998 Act or supersession under section 10 of that Act] of an award of disability living allowance, or

(c) in writing in connection withan award of, or a claim for, or an application for a [⁴ revision under section 9 of the 1998 Act or supersession under section 10 of that Act] of an award of, disability living allowance.

(7) In paragraph (6) "hospice" means a hospital or other institution [⁵ whose primary function is to provide palliative care for persons resident there who are suffering from a progressive disease in its final stages] other than—

(a) [¹¹ *omitted*]

(b) a health service hospital (within the meaning of section 108(1) of the NHS Act of 1978) in Scotland;

[¹¹ (ba) a health service hospital (within the meaning of section 275 of the NHS Act of 2006) in England;

(bb) a hospital in Wales vested in—

    (i) an NHS Trust;

    (ii) a Local Health Board; or

    (iii) the Welsh Ministers, for the purpose of functions under the NHS (Wales) Act of 2006;]

(c) a hospital maintained or administered by the Defence Council; or

(d) an institution similar to a hospital mentioned in any of the preceding sub-paragraphs of this paragraph.

[¹⁰ (8) Regulation 9 shall not apply in any particular case for any period during which the whole costs of all of the qualifying services are met—

(a) out of the resources of the person for whom the qualifying services are provided, or partly out of his own resources and partly with the assistance from another person or a charity, or

(b) on his behalf by another person or a charity.]

[¹¹ (8A) For the purpose of paragraph (7)(bb)—

(a) "NHS Trust" means a body established under section 18 of the NHS (Wales) Act of 2006; and

(b) "Local Health Board" means a body established under section 11 of the NHS (Wales) Act of 2006.]

[⁵ (9) ³ . . .]

AMENDMENTS

1. Social Security Benefits (Amendments Consequential Upon the Introduction of Community Care) Regulations 1992 (SI 1992/3147) reg.7 (April 1, 1993).

2. Social Security (Disability Living Allowance) Amendment Regulations 1992 (SI 1992/633) (April 6, 1992).

3. Social Security (Attendance Allowance) (Amendment) Regulations 2000 (SI 2000/1401) reg.3 (June 19, 2000).

4. Social Security Act 1998 (Commencement No. 11, and Savings and Consequential and Transitional Provisions) Order 1999 (SI 1999/2860) Sch.7 (October 18, 1999).

5. Social Security Benefits (Miscellaneous Amendments) Regulations 1993 (SI 1993/518) reg.3(3) (April 1, 1993).

6. State Pension Credit (Consequential, Transitional and Miscellaneous Provisions) Regulations 2002 (SI 2002/3019) reg.28 (April 1, 2003).

7. Social Security and Child Support (Jobseeker's Allowance) (Consequential Amendments) Regulations 1996 (SI 1996/1345) reg. 17 (October 7, 1996).

8. Social Security (Attendance Allowance and Disability Living Allowance) (Amendment) Regulations 2002, (SI 2002/208) reg.3 (March 1, 2002).

9. Social Security (Attendance Allowance and Disability Allowance) (Amendment) Regulations 2003 (SI 2003/2259) reg.3 (October 6, 2003).

10. Attendance Allowance and Disability Living Allowance (Amendment) Regulations 2007 (SI 2007/2875) (October 29, 2007).

11. Social Security (Attendance Allowance, Disability Living Allowance and Carer's Allowance) (Amendment) Regulations 2013 (SI 2013/389) reg.4 (April 8, 2013).

12. Social Security (Disability Living Allowance and Personal Independence Payment) (Amendment) Regulations 2016 (SI 2016/556) reg.2 (June 29, 2016).

GENERAL NOTE

A person may remain entitled to the care component for up to 28 days or, in the case of a child, 84 days (see subs.(2)) in a hospital covered by reg.8 or accommodation covered by reg.9. However, separate periods in such a hospital or such accommodation are aggregated unless they are more than 28 days apart. Furthermore, under para.(3), a person cannot first qualify for the care component while in hospital or the relevant accommodation.

In *CM (by appointee Mr CM) v SSWP (DLA)* [2013] 27 (AAC) the claimant was a child aged three who had to enter hospital for a protracted period. While he was there his parents continued to provide care and attention 24 hours of the day by one of them staying in accommodation provided at the hospital by a charity. In doing so they continued to incur considerable expenses in living costs and in travelling costs. They appealed against a decision to suspend his payment of DLA, under reg.(10)(2), after 84 days, on the ground that to do so was a breach of his human rights. Judge Ward held, reluctantly, that it was not.

Although *CM* subsequently died in hospital, these proceedings were continued by his father on his behalf. In the Supreme Court (*CM (dec'd) by his father CM* [2015] UKSC 47; [2015] AACR 19) his argument succeeded. The court held that the child's need for care and attention from his parents was at least as great while in hospital as it had been when at home and that, as there was no requirement in primary legislation for entitlement to the benefit to be withdrawn, it followed that to do so had been unlawful. The court declined, however, to hold that reg.10 in its application to children should be regarded as invalid—in their view there might be cases where the exercise of a discretion to withdraw benefit might not breach a claimant's human rights and that it should be left to the Secretary of State to see whether, with appropriate adjustment, reg.10(2) might still be applied.

[¹ Adjustment of allowance where medical expenses are paid from public funds under war pensions instruments

10A.—(1) In this regulation—

"article 25B" means article 25B of the Personal Injuries (Civilians) Scheme 1983 (medical expenses) and includes that article as applied by article 48B of that Scheme;

"article [²21]" means article [²21] of the Naval, Military and Air Forces etc. (Disablement and Death) Service Pensions Order [² 2006] (medical expenses);

and in this regulation and regulation 10B "relevant accommodation" means accommodation provided as a necessary ancillary to nursing care where the medical expenses involved are wholly borne by the Secretary of State pursuant to article 25B or article [² 21].

(2) This regulation applies where a person is provided with relevant accommodation.

(3) Subject to regulation 10B where this regulation applies and there are payable in respect of a person both a payment under article 25B or article [² 21] and a disability living allowance which is attributable to the care

4.62

4.63

component, the allowance, in so far as it is so attributable, shall be adjusted by deducting from it the amount of the payment under article 25B or article [² 21], as the case may be, and only the balance shall be payable.]

AMENDMENTS

1. Social Security (Attendance Allowance and Disability Living Allowance) (Amendment) Regulations 1994 (SI 1994/1779) reg.3(4) (August 1, 1994).
2. Social Security (Attendance Allowance, Disability Living Allowance and Carer's Allowance) (Amendment) Regulations 2013 (SI 2013/389) reg.4 (April 8, 2013).

[¹ Exemption from regulation 10A

4.64   **10B.**—(1) Regulation 10A shall not, subject to the following provisions of this regulation, apply to a person in respect of the first 28 days of any period during which the amount of any disability living allowance attributable to the care component would be liable to be adjusted by virtue of regulation 10A(3).

(2) For the purposes of paragraph (1) two or more distinct periods separated by an interval not exceeding 28 days, or by two or more such intervals, shall be treated as a continuous period equal in duration to the aggregate of such distinct periods and ending on the last day of the later or last such period.

(3) For the purposes of this paragraph a day is a relevant day in relation to a person if it fell not earlier than 28 days before the first day on which he was provided with relevant accommodation; and either—

(a) was a day when he was undergoing medical treatment in a hospital or similar institution in any of the circumstances mentioned in regulation 8; or

(b) was a day when he was, or would but for regulation 10 have been, prevented from receiving a disability living allowance attributable to the care component by virtue of regulation 9(1);

and where there is in relation to a person a relevant day, paragraph (1) shall have effect as if for "28 days" there were substituted such lesser number of days as is produced by subtracting from 28 the number of relevant days in his case.]

AMENDMENT

1. Social Security (Attendance Allowance and Disability Living Allowance) (Amendment) Regulations 1994 (SI 1994/1779) reg.3(4) (August 1, 1994).

[¹ Prescribed circumstance for entitlement to the care component

4.65   **10C.**—For the purposes of section 72(7) of the Act (prescribed circumstances in which a person is to be taken to satisfy or not to satisfy the conditions mentioned in section 72(1)(a) to (c) of that Act), a person shall not be taken to satisfy subsection (1)(a)(i) or (b)(i) (day attention) or (c)(i) (night attention) unless the attention the severely disabled person requires from another person is required to be given in the physical presence of the severely disabled person].

AMENDMENT

1. Social Security (Attendance Allowance and Disability Living Allowance) (Amendment) (No.2) Regulations 2000 (SI 2000/2313) reg.3 (September 25, 2000).

GENERAL NOTE

An interesting point on the effect of this regulation was made in *CDLA/4333/2004*.   **4.66**
The claimant suffered from depression and required support and attention during
the day. Some of this was provided by regular telephone calls from her mother.
The mother was herself in poor health and unable to visit her daughter. Clearly
the telephone calls could not themselves count as attention because of reg.10C,
but it was argued that they were evidence of the claimant's need for attention, that
would have been provided by a visit, were the mother able to do so. In this particular case the argument failed because the tribunal appeared to have taken account
of the telephone calls as if they were "attention", presumably having overlooked
reg.10C. But could this situation breathe new life into the concept that attention
must be "required"? Would the claimant need to show that her needs were not sufficiently met, or not as effectively met, by the telephone calls in order to succeed?
If the mother did in fact visit in person it would be a harsh decision that held such
visits were not necessary and that a telephone call would do, but where, as here, the
attention is given by telephone, and if it suffices, it may be reasonable to argue that
attendance in person is not required.

There is an interesting example of the application of this argument shown in *HP
v SSWP* [2013] UKUT 248 (AAC). There the claimant was suffering from depressive mental illness. Although she was living on her own she was able to function to a
reasonable extent in managing her own daily care, but only if she received frequent
attention in the form of encouragement and reminders from members of her family.
At first this was provided chiefly by her sister who did that in person, but her sister
moved to live in the USA. Thereafter, the attention was provided by means of a
visual telephonic communication system ("Skype"). Evidence was given by the
claimant that, without that support, she would not be able to function normally at
all. Unfortunately, the FTT that heard her appeal against a refusal of benefit did
not refer to this evidence at all; nor did they refer to reg.10C. They simply found
that the claimant was self caring and therefore refused the appeal. In the UT Judge
Fordham QC found that the decision was deficient in providing reasons for reaching
the conclusion that they did. He holds that the only question is whether the claimant
needs (requires) such attention and that evidence of attention given in the manner
above can be evidence of such need. The reasons given by the FTT did not explain
whether they rejected that evidence as untrue, or as irrelevant, or whether they had
failed to notice it at all. Judge Fordham suggests, as an example of where telephonic
assistance might succeed in showing such need, the case of a carer who formerly
assisted in person, but who is prevented, by breaking their leg, from attending in
person. He suggests that evidence of telephonic assistance will always be of limited
weight and that it is likely to succeed only where the non-presence is involuntary,
the claimant and the assistant would unhesitatingly say that actual presence would
be preferable and that the telephone assistance is, at best, "fragile or not wholly successful". It remains the case then, that if the telephoned assistance is reliable and
is sufficient for the claimant to achieve a reasonably normal level of daily activity
it will not have been shown that anything more (i.e. actual assistance in person) is
required. The case was returned to a new FTT for rehearing.

PART IV

MOBILITY COMPONENT

Qualifying period for mobility component after an interval

11.—The period prescribed for the purposes of [¹ section 73](9)(a)(ii)   **4.67**
of the Act is a period of 3 months ending on the day which the person was

last entitled to the mobility component or to mobility allowance, where that day falls not more than 2 years before the date on which entitlement to the mobility component would begin or would have begun but for any regulations made under [¹ section 5(1)(k) of the Administration Act] (which enables regulations to provide for the day on which entitlement to benefit is to begin or end).

AMENDMENT

1. Social Security (Disability Living Allowance) (Amendment) Regulations 1993 (SI 1993/1939) reg.2 (August 26, 1993).

GENERAL NOTE

4.68   The general effect of this provision is that the three-month qualifying period for the mobility component is deemed to be satisfied if the new claim is within two years of a previous period of entitlement to the mobility component (or mobility allowance) at the relevant rate.

Entitlement to the mobility component

4.69   **12.**—(1) A person is to be taken to satisfy the conditions mentioned in [¹ section 73](1)(a) of the Act (unable or virtually unable to walk) only in the following circumstances—

(a) his physical condition as a whole is such that, without having regard to circumstances peculiar to that person as to the place of residence or as to place of, or nature of, employment—

    (i) he is unable to walk; or

    (ii) his ability to walk out of doors is so limited, as regards the distance over which or the speed at which or the length of time for which or the manner in which he can make progress on foot without severe discomfort, that he is virtually unable to walk; or

    (iii) the exertion required to walk would constitute a danger to his life or would be likely to lead to a serious deterioration in his health; or

(b) he has both legs amputated at levels which are either through or above the ankle, or he has one leg so amputated and is without the other leg, or is without both legs to the same extent as if it, or they, had been so amputated.

[⁴(1A) (a) For the purposes of section 73(1AB)(a) of the Act (mobility component for the severely visually impaired) a person is to be taken to satisfy the condition that he has a severe visual impairment if—

    (i) he has visual acuity, with appropriate corrective lenses if necessary, of less than 3/60; or

    (ii) he has visual acuity of 3/60 or more, but less than 6/60, with appropriate corrective lenses if necessary, a complete loss of peripheral visual field and a central visual field of no more than 10° in total.

(b) For the purposes of section 73(1AB)(b), the conditions are that he has been certified as severely sight impaired or blind by a consultant ophthalmologist.

(c) In this paragraph—

    (i) references to visual acuity are to be read as references to the combined visual acuity of both eyes in cases where a person has both eyes;

(ii) references to measurements of visual acuity are references to visual acuity measured on the Snellen Scale;

(iii) references to visual field are to be read as references to the combined visual field of both eyes in cases where a person has both eyes.]

(2) For the purposes of [[1] section 73](2)(a) of the Act (mobility component for the blind and deaf) a person is to be taken to satisfy—

(a) the condition that he is blind only where the degree of disablement resulting from the loss of vision amounts to 100 per cent; and

(b) the condition that he is deaf only where the degree of disablement resulting from loss of hearing [[2] when using any artificial aid which he habitually uses or which is suitable in his case] amounts to not less than 80 per cent on a scale where 100 per cent represents absolute deafness.

(3) For the purposes of [[1] section 73](2)(b) of the Act, the conditions are that by reason of the combined effects of the person's blindness and deafness, he is unable, without the assistance of another person, to walk to any intended or required destination while out of doors.

(4) Except in a case to which paragraph (1)(b) applies, a person is to be taken not to satisfy the conditions mentioned in [[1] section 73](1)(a) of the Act if he—

(a) is not unable or virtually unable to walk with a prosthesis or artificial aid which he habitually wears or uses, or

(b) would not be unable or virtually unable to walk if he wore or used a prosthesis or an artificial aid which is suitable in his case.

(5) A person falls within subsection (3)(a) of [[1] section 73] of the Act (severely mentally impaired) if he suffers from a state of arrested development or incomplete physical development of the brain, which results in severe impairment of intelligence and social functioning.

(6) A person falls within subsection (3)(b) of [[1] section 73] of the Act (severe behavioural problems) if he exhibits disruptive behaviour which—

(a) is extreme,

(b) regularly requires another person to intervene and physically restrain him in order to prevent him causing physical injury to himself or another, or damage to property, and

(c) is so unpredictable that he requires another person to be present and watching over him whenever he is awake.

[[3] (7) For the purposes of section 73(1)(d) of the Act, a person who is able to walk is to be taken not to satisfy the condition of being so severely disabled physically or mentally that he cannot take advantage of the faculty out of doors without guidance or supervision from another person most of the time if he does not take advantage of the faculty in such circumstances because of fear or anxiety.

(8) Paragraph (7) shall not apply where the fear or anxiety is:

(a) a symptom of a mental disability; and

(b) so severe as to prevent the person from taking advantage of the faculty in such circumstances.]

AMENDMENTS

1. Social Security (Disability Living Allowance) (Amendment) Regulations 1993 (SI 1993/1939) reg.2 (August 26, 1993).

2. Social Security (Attendance Allowance and Disability Living Allowance) (Amendment) Regulations 1994 (SI 1994/1779) reg.3(5)(August 1, 1994).

3. Social Security (Disability Living Allowance) (Amendment) Regulations 2002 (SI 2002/648) reg.2 (April 8, 2002).

4. Social Security (Disability Living Allowance) (Amendment) Regulations 2010 (SI 2010/1651) reg.2 (November 15, 2010 and April 11, 2011).

GENERAL NOTE

Sub-paragraph (1)(a)

4.70 This re-enacts reg.3(1)(a) of the Mobility Allowance Regulations 1975 and some of the words and phrases used have been considered by the Commissioners.

"physical disablement" "physical condition"

4.71 It seems fairly clear that the use of the word "physical" is intended to be limiting so that the scope of s.73(1)(a) of the Social Security Contributions and Benefits Act 1992 does not extend to those suffering from purely psychiatric conditions although such people may qualify under s.73(1)(c) or (d).

In *KS v SSWP (DLA)* [2013] UKUT 390 (AAC) it was argued that the limitation of the higher rate of the mobility component mainly to conditions having a physical cause was overruled by the provisions of the Equality Act 2010 as being discriminatory on the grounds of mental disablement. The argument failed because the terms of that act specify that nothing is unlawful if that action is required by the terms of legislation (see Sch.22 para.(1) of that Act).

Whether or not a person is suffering from "physical" disablement is regarded as primarily a medical question although, in principle, the process of reasoning used by a disability appeal tribunal to reach the conclusion is challengeable on the ground that it is erroneous in point of law. In a fairly uncontroversial case, a medical appeal tribunal did not err in law in holding that, because agoraphobia was not a physical condition, the claimant could not succeed (*R(M) 1/80*). More famously, in *R(M) 2/78*, a Commissioner held that a medical appeal tribunal had not erred in law in deciding that a child (Robert) suffering from Down's syndrome was suffering from a physical condition. The tribunal had said:

> "We agree that the boy is suffering from mongolism, a condition which is due to faulty genetic inheritance and can therefore be classified as a physical disorder. We accept the evidence that while he walks for some yards he is liable to run, stop, lie down and refuse to go further; this reaction which severely impairs mobility is directly due to the physical condition of mongolism".

In refusing leave to appeal, the Chairman added:

> "The submission of the Secretary of State seeks to separate the claimant's mental state from the physical condition to which that mental state is directly due. This cannot be accepted because the mental state is the direct consequence of the physical malformation of a particular chromosome (No. 21)."

The Chief Commissioner said:

> "I think it is plain that the medical appeal tribunal regarded Robert's physical condition as a whole as being a disabling condition, preventing him from doing the particular action of walking. The weight to be attached to physical and mental disablement in cases where both factors may be present is for the medical authorities to decide, and the answer to the question whether the one or the other is, or both are responsible for an inability or virtual inability to walk is for their decision as a medical question. I do not consider that the medical appeal tribunal misapprehended what physical disablement means, or that it can be said that they were wrong in law in concluding from their findings that it was physical disablement which was responsible for his virtual inability to walk."

He stressed that not all Down's cases would have the same result, although it is not entirely clear whether that was because he thought that different conclusions might be reached as to whether the condition was a physical one or whether it was because not all people suffering from Down's syndrome are disabled to the same extent. The Mobility Allowance Regulations 1975 were amended in 1979 following *R(M) 2/78* but, in *R(M) 1/83*, a Tribunal of Commissioners held that the amendments did not affect the reasoning of the Commissioner in *R(M) 2/78*. *R(M) 3/86* concerned a child who had suffered brain damage at birth leading to severe mental subnormality. While capable of the physical movements of walking, his behaviour while doing so was erratic and unpredictable. In setting aside the decision of a medical appeal tribunal who had disregarded the behavioural problems, the Tribunal of Commissioners held that *R(M) 2/78* is still good law despite what was said in *Lees v Secretary of State for Social Services* (see below) and that behavioural problems arising out of a physical disability were relevant. It should be noted that in *Harrison v Secretary of State for Social Services*, reported as an appendix to *R(M) 1/88*, Lloyd L.J. suggested that *R(M) 2/78* should be regarded with caution in the light of *Lees*, but it is not clear which part of the Commissioner's decision he had in mind.

Furthermore it is not sufficient that the claimant shows that he is unable to walk out of doors because of a physical condition. It is necessary to go further and show the inability to be the result of the physical act of walking. In *Hewitt v Chief Adjudication Officer*, and *Diment v Chief Adjudication Officer* reported as *R(DLA) 6/99* the Court of Appeal held that claimants who suffered from severe porphyria, a condition of the skin that meant they could spend very little time out of doors, were not entitled to mobility component. The Court said the claimants could walk physically and that their inability to walk out of doors had nothing to do with the physical process of walking. In *CDLA/1639/2006* the claimant gave evidence that he suffered from severe attacks of migraine that caused pain, dizziness, and lack of vision. At such times—at least 80 hours a week—he could do nothing more than sit down or lie down. A tribunal, by a majority allowed his appeal, but the Commissioner held that in doing so their decision demonstrated an error of law. They had failed to examine sufficiently the way in which his headaches affected his ability to walk. The loss of vision, he said, is not relevant to a claim for higher rate mobility component because that relates only to the direction of walking and not to the ability to walk itself. Pain, too, would not count as that had nothing to do with the physical process of walking though it might clearly make the claimant disinclined to walk outside. Dizziness, or loss of balance, however, was relevant because it affects the manner of walking or even the ability to walk at all. The appeal was allowed and returned to a new tribunal to consider the extent of the element of dizziness and its effect. As well, they were asked to consider whether the claimant should qualify for mobility at the lower rate, on the basis of his need for supervision in case of a sudden onset of a migraine attack.

In *R(M) 1/88*, the claimant had injured his back in an accident in 1979. He was awarded mobility allowance up to 1983 but, on a renewal claim, a medical appeal tribunal held that his inability to walk was not due to a physical cause but was hysterical in origin. In the course of his decision, the Commissioner said: **4.72**

"It may be that in the last analysis all mental disablement may be ascribed to physical causes. But, if so, it is obvious that the Act on drawing the distinction between physical and mental disablement did not mean this last analysis to be resorted to."

He held that the question what was and what was not a physical inability to walk was a medical question for the tribunal to determine but he added:

"This does not mean that in every case of hysteria the medical authorities are bound to hold that a claimant's hysteria is not a manifestation of his physical condition as a whole; but it does mean that if they do so find it will be impossible to disturb their decision on the ground that they ought to have found it to be a manifestation of the claimant's physical condition."

An appeal to the Court of Appeal was dismissed (*Harrison v Secretary of State for Social Services*, reported as an appendix to *R(M) 1/88*). The Court effectively adopted the Commissioner's reasoning. Stocker L.J. said: "Hysteria is not itself a physical condition, since physical and hysterical conditions are often used in contrasting terms, and in my view correctly so." The Commissioner points out, however, that where hysteria is itself a consequence of a physical condition, it is open to a Tribunal or medical board, as a matter of medical opinion, to find that where hysteria is caused by a physical condition, for example due to pain owing to some spinal condition, the inability to walk may itself be caused by that same physical condition. He drew attention, without apparent criticism, to the fact that the claimant has since been awarded mobility allowance on a further claim.

This question has now been considered, at length, by a Tribunal of Commissioners in *R(DLA) 4/06*. Were it not for the Court of Appeal's decision in *Harrison* the Tribunal would have accepted that the phrases "physical disability" (in s.73) and "physical condition as a whole" (in reg.12) should be interpreted to include any claimant whose condition manifested an inability to walk out of doors in the form of physical symptoms of a medical condition, whether that medical condition was physical or mental. (The Tribunal refer to these physical symptoms as being those of a medical condition though they do, as well, affirm the decision reached in *R(DLA) 3/06* so that perhaps their emphasis should have been rather on whether the claimants inability to walk was manifested by physical symptoms whether the cause of those symptoms was physical or mental.) Thus, on the view the Tribunal would prefer to have taken, the agoraphobic would still fail, but a claimant whose psychosomatic condition made it difficult or painful to walk would succeed, effectively adopting the views expressed in cases such as *CDLA/3323/2003*. However, the Tribunal held that they were bound by the decision in *Harrison*. This meant that they affirmed the view that in order to succeed, the claimant must show that his inability to walk outside has some physical cause. Pain, dizziness and fatigue that are purely psychosomatic or mental, are therefore not sufficient to qualify for the higher rate of mobility component, and cases such as *CSDLA/265/97*, *CDLA/948/2000* and *CDLA/3323/2003* should, therefore, no longer be followed.

4.73　　But the Tribunal goes on to consider in some detail the difficulties and problems that decision makers will face in determining what is a physical cause. It is accepted that once it is shown that a disability involving some mental element has either a physical origin (e.g. brain damage), or a physical consequence (e.g. muscle wasting from lack of use when a claimant is depressed), that this will suffice to support the claim. The test of causation they suggest, should be one of "material contribution", so that once it is shown that the claimant's inability to walk derives to an extent that is more than trivial, from some physical factor he should succeed even though his disability is caused in part by psychological factors. A majority of the Tribunal held because of the use of the present tense in both s.73 and reg.12 that it was necessary for the physical factor to be still a current operating cause of the claimant's condition. A psychosomatic condition that derived from a past physical cause that is now corrected, would not suffice.

In applying all this to the facts of the two cases that were before them the Tribunal obtained much assistance from expert evidence given on behalf of the Department of Work and Pensions Corporate Medical group. This evidence is reproduced at para.108 of the decision and again, in relation particularly to back pain, at para.145, and for dizziness, at para.162. On the basis of this evidence the Tribunal allowed both appeals and returned the cases for a new Tribunal to consider whether there was any physical element (that was more than minimal) in the cause of the claimant's disability.

In both cases the Tribunal observes "that it may well be that in the past Tribunals have been too ready to conclude that the fact that no specific and precisely identified organic cause for [the particular disability] has been found means that there is not in fact a physical cause".

4.74　　Finally the Tribunal was careful to point out that the cases before them involved only back pain, and dizziness. They say that conditions such as autism, Down's Syndrome, learning disabilities, and the extent to which mental disorders such as depression may be the result of genetics or chemical changes in the brain, and therefore also a physical condition was not before them and they refrain from expressing an opinion on these matters. However, to the extent that some of these matters have already been the subject of Commissioner's decisions it is not suggested that they are anything other than still good law. A view which has been confirmed, at least in regard to Down's Syndrome, by the directions given by Judge Levenson in *SC v SSWP (DLA)* [2010] UKUT 76 (AAC). In *CDLA/1525/2008* Judge May has considered the case of a claimant suffering from anorexia nervosa. In his view the claimant could qualify (though the case was returned to another tribunal) because her condition manifested clear physical disablement that affected her ability to walk. It was not necessary, in his view, to consider how those physical conditions might have been caused.

The question of whether a claimant could qualify for mobility component, at the higher rate, on the basis of being "virtually unable to walk" under reg. 12(1)(a)(ii) when, because of Alzheimer's disease, she could not progress effectively on her own was considered in *CSDLA/399/2005*. The Commissioner concludes that no error of law had been shown in the decision of a tribunal that had dismissed the claimant's appeal against a refusal of benefit, but she does so on the ground that the appellant had failed at the original hearing to make out a sufficient factual basis for her claim. On the question of whether an Alzheimer's patient could be said to be suffering from a "physical disability", the Commissioner adopted the view expressed in *CDLA/156/1994* which was in favour of such a conclusion, but felt that the claimant may still need to produce evidence in the form of medical opinion to support that view – the time had not yet come, she thought, when a tribunal could take judicial notice of the aetiology of the condition. In the present case the report of the doctor had described the claimant's condition as "100% mental due to Alzheimer's disease" and while this statement could have contained some ambiguity it did mean that there was no evidence before the tribunal to suggest a physical disability.

CDLA/3420/2005 is an example of the application of this to a claimant suffering from Marfan's disease. The risk of aortic aneurysm, which that condition causes, by the exertion of walking had caused anxiety and depression in the claimant. That, combined with his physical condition, made him reluctant to walk. His case was referred to a fresh tribunal for reconsideration on the basis that the physical contribution may have been more than minimal.

Diagnoses of chronic fatigue syndrome raise difficult questions. In *CSDLA/ 265/97*, the Commissioner said that, if the claimant's muscle pains and other physical problems were not mental, illusory or imaginary, they could be regarded as physical disabilities.

> "The need to determine anything more, such as whether they are in turn caused by a physical condition, such as a virus, a lesion or a malfunction, may matter little for the purposes of section 73 of the Act."

In *CDLA/5183/97*, another case involving chronic fatigue syndrome, the Deputy Commissioner said:

> "This is a controversial and sensitive issue. Accordingly, it is important to be clear about how the Commissioner and tribunals approach this question when it arises. It is not for the Commissioner to rule on whether or not chronic fatigue syndrome has a physical cause. It is not a question of law. Nor is it for the DAT to have some kind of general rule or policy on this matter. What the DAT must do in each individual case, is to examine the evidence before it and reach a conclusion on whether the walking difficulties which an individual appellant experiences arise from 'physical disablement', in order to satisfy the statute; and the individual appellant's 'physical condition as a whole' in order to satisfy the regulation. This evaluation of the evidence is a question of fact for the DAT. See *R(M) 2/78*."

In that case, the Deputy Commissioner found that the tribunal had not erred in law and had reached a decision they were entitled to reach on the evidence before them.

"In particular, they have regarded the advice of the DLAAB not as binding on them in any way but simply as a factor to be taken into account."

Further support for the acceptance of chronic fatigue syndrome as the basis of a claim is found in *CDLA/4486/2000*. That case accepts that the condition may not have a clinical explanation but emphasises that it is the effect of the conditions on the claimant's physical ability that matters, not the cause. Note also the discussion of psychosomatic disability in the notes following s.72 above.

"without having regard to circumstances peculiar to that person as to place of residence or as to place of, or nature of, employment"

4.75   Note that it is simply the claimant's physical condition which is relevant. The distance to his or her local shops is not relevant although it is often helpful for a tribunal to know whether, and if so how, a claimant manages to get to the local shops and then, having ascertained how far that is, to consider ability to walk in the light of that evidence.

"unable to walk"

4.76   In *R(M) 3/78*, the Commissioner said:

"The word 'walk' is an ordinary English word in common usage and, in the context of regulation 3 [now reg.12(1) of these regulations]], means to move by means of a person's legs and feet or a combination of them."

In *R(M) 1/83*, no definition was attempted but the Tribunal of Commissioners said:

"We consider that a person who can walk at all ought not to be regarded as unable to walk, though he may well be regarded as virtually unable to walk. This does not of course preclude the medical authorities from finding that a claimant's method of moving about does not amount to walking at all."

In the course of the litigation in *Lees* (see below) O'Connor L.J., in the Court of Appeal, said:

"A person is unable to walk if he cannot use his legs for walking, so a person who is bedridden, a person who is a paraplegic and indeed a person who has a leg amputated is unable to walk. The last category can be enabled to walk by artificial aids such as a false limb or crutches and for that reason we find regulation 3(2) [now regulation 12(4)] applies" (see the appendix to *R(M) 1/84*).

In *R(M) 2/89*, it was made clear that a person with only one foot cannot "walk" in the absence of an artificial limb. Where a person uses crutches, it is necessary to consider the way in which they are used. Unless they are used so that the claimant can walk, as opposed to simply swinging through the crutches, the claimant will satisfy the condition of reg.12(1)(a)(i) even if the distance he or she can travel is such that reg.12(1)(a)(ii) would not be satisfied.

The case of *R(M) 2/89* was approved by the court of appeal in *Sandhu v Secretary of State for Work and Pensions* [2010] EWCA Civ 962. They also approved of the reasoning in *CDLA/97/2001*, which, like *Sandhu*, was a case of a claimant with two legs, but only one of which could be used to bear any weight. In *CDLA/97/2001* the claim succeeded because the commissioner accepted that a person who could carry his weight only upon one leg could not be said to be walking, any more than might a person who had only one leg and this was so even though the claimant might make progress with crutches by moving alternate legs. The test was whether the claimant did, or could, rest any weight upon alternate legs. In the *Sandhu* case the court declined an invitation to attempt any further or better definition of walking, though the matter was remitted to another tribunal for further findings of fact.

"virtually unable to walk"

4.77   In *R(M) 1/91* the Commissioner said that "the base point is total inability to walk, which is extended [by reg.12(1)(a)(ii)] to take in people who can technically walk but only to an insignificant extent". There is clearly some scope for disagreement as to what is meant by "virtually" or "insignificant".

It is to be noted that the virtual inability to walk must be a virtual inability to do so "out of doors". A First-tier tribunal may observe the claimant walking indoors and may infer from that that the claimant is not virtually unable to walk out of doors although they should indicate that they have addressed their minds to the different conditions pertaining out of doors. In *R(M) 1/91*, the Commissioner held that the test envisaged walking on the kind of pavement or road which one would normally expect to find in the course of walking out of doors, any unusual hazards peculiar to the claimant's situation being ignored. He also pointed out that some degree of incline must be contemplated but that the question is not whether the claimant is unable or virtually unable to *climb* and any inability to surmount hills or mountains is irrelevant.

The tribunal should have regard to whether what they observe is generally true of the claimant's walking ability and the claimant should be given the opportunity to comment on the inferences that the tribunal intend to draw.

In *R(DLA) 4/02* the Commissioner held that notes made after covert observation of the claimant's walking ability, and a videotape of her walking, were admissible as evidence before a tribunal. None of this evidence, all of which related to the claimant's behaviour in a public place, could be regarded as having been obtained in breach of her human rights, and all of it was admissible without breach of her right to a fair trial.

The assessment of evidence generally on Disability Living Allowance claims, but in particular in relation to walking ability has been considered by Judge Jacobs in *DC* v *SSWP* [2009] UKUT 45 (AAC). He reminds First-tier Tribunals that their assessment of the evidence must be not only rational but also reasoned and that those reasons must be clearly expressed. In relation to the "walking test" he says specifically:

> "22. In order to apply that test, the tribunal has to make findings of fact on the relevant factors. That involves analysing the evidence as a whole to the extent that it can properly be subjected to analysis. The findings of fact can be made with no greater precision than the law requires and the evidence allows. If that means that the findings cannot be expressed in terms of metres per minute or any other precise terms, so be it. All that is necessary is that the findings should be sufficient to support the tribunal's decision whether or not the claimant is virtually unable to walk. It is my view that the findings may have to be expressed more generally than is the current practice of the First-tier Tribunal and that the Upper Tribunal should accept that this is all that is attainable, given the nature of the test and the evidence available to the tribunal. This is not an excuse for poor quality analysis and fact-finding. It is, in fact, more demanding, because it does not allow tribunals to rely on illusory precision to find differences of opinion where they do not exist on a more rigorous analysis of the substance of the evidence."

A good example of a tribunal leaping too readily to a conclusion that the claimant was not virtually unable to walk can be found in *JT v SSWP (DLA)* [2013] UKUT 221 (AAC). There, evidence had been given that the claimant had recently been on holiday to Greece and that in doing so he had been able to walk to and from the aircraft at the airports on either end of his journeys. The FTT accepted this as showing that he was not "virtually unable to walk". The UT allowed an appeal on several grounds. First, the holiday in Greece was at a time after the decision against which he had appealed was made and no reason was given to show that, as evidence, it could be related to the earlier time (though to do so may not have been difficult). Secondly, no attempt had been made to examine the distance over which, the time in which, or the manner in which the claimant had accomplished this walk. Thirdly, it was likely that most, if not all, of the airport walking was done indoors—no attention had been given to the possible differences that might relate to walking out of doors. It is easy to see why the FTT might have been tempted to seize on what looked like clear evidence of walking ability, but it remains essential that the evidence is tested rationally and careful reasons given for the conclusions that are drawn.

Evidence provided by the claimant, as well as that of medical advisers, will be crucial in determining the claimant's ability to walk. But even this evidence must be considered carefully by tribunals to ascertain its reliability. In *CDLA/2423/2007* the claimant was a child whose mother said that on a "good day" her daughter could walk as far as 3 miles in 30 to 40 minutes. This was accepted by the tribunal as clear evidence that she was not "virtually unable to walk". But as the Commissioner pointed out this would suggest a walking speed of between 4.5 and 6 miles per hour; a speed that even a fit adult would find difficult, if not impossible, to achieve.

distance, speed and time

4.78   The distance a person can walk is important but it should not be considered without reference to the other relevant factors of speed, length of time and manner of walking. In *R(M) 1/78*, it was held that a medical appeal tribunal had erred in law in holding that a claimant was virtually unable to walk when she could walk a mile. However, whether the distance a person can walk means that he or she is virtually unable to walk is generally regarded as a matter of judgment for a tribunal and Commissioners have shown no inclination to interfere. Thus, medical appeal tribunals have not been held to have erred *in law* in holding that claimants were not virtually unable to walk where their walking ability has been very limited. In *CM/39/84*, the claimant could manage 100 yards at 2 mph and, in *CM/47/86*, the claimant could manage only 50 yards. On the other hand, in *R(M) 5/86*, it seems to have been accepted that a claimant who could walk only 50 yards should qualify. Apart from speed, a tribunal should probably consider how long it takes a person to recover after walking a short distance. A claimant who can walk a substantial distance provided that he or she stands still for a couple of minutes every hundred yards has a greater ability to walk than a person who has to rest for an hour after walking a hundred yards. In *CDLA/805/94* the Commissioner suggested that this factor should be taken into account when considering "the length of time for which" the claimant could walk. He pointed out that, as speed is a function of time and distance, consideration of the length of time for which the claimant can walk must involve consideration of something beyond the mere time it necessarily takes the claimant to walk the distance he can manage at the speed he can manage.

In *CDLA/717/98*, the Commissioner considered *CM 145/88* in which a Commissioner said that an ability to walk 90 yards in five minutes was "arguably" tantamount to being "virtually unable to walk". In the later case, the tribunal had found that the claimant was able to cover 100 yards in five to six minutes, including stops, and concluded that the claimant was not "virtually unable to walk". The Commissioner held that

> "it is not for a Commissioner to attempt to lay down a precise formula for determining whether or not a claimant is unable to walk when the legislation does not do so. The legislation allows adjudication officers and tribunals a margin of appreciation."

He declined to interfere with the tribunal's decision, although he said that a tribunal that had reached the opposite conclusion on those facts would also have been entitled to do so. Guidance was also given in *CDLA/608/94*:

> "It is impossible to lay down *a priori* rules for such questions as the distance a person must be found to walk without severe discomfort before he ceases to count as 'virtually unable' to walk, since so much depends on the circumstances and physical state of each particular claimant. However, it has been said that what 'virtually unable to walk' means is a question of law (*R(M) 1/78* para.11), and some general guidance can be gleaned from the reported decisions. In the absence of any special indications from the other three factors, if a claimant is unable to cover more than 25 or 30 yards without suffering severe discomfort, his ability to walk is not 'appreciable' or 'significant'; while if the distance is

more than 80 or 100 yards, he is unlikely to count as 'virtually unable to walk' as those words have generally been interpreted in section 73 and regulation 12. In the difficult ground in between, I for my part find helpful the approach of the Commissioner in case *CM 78/89* at para.13, where he said that mobility allowance (as it then was) was never designed to—and does not—embrace those who can walk 60 or 70 yards without severe discomfort. In such a case, therefore, there would have to be some other factor such as extreme slowness or difficulty because of the manner of moving forward on foot before a claimant would count as 'virtually unable'."

The importance of not considering the distance a claimant can walk in isolation from other factors was again emphasised in *CDLA/1389/97* at para.31 but the Commissioner also said, at para.35, that a tribunal did not necessarily err in not referring to all four factors mentioned in reg.12(1)(a)(ii). It depended whether the other factors arose as issues in the circumstances of the case. This issue has been considered again by the Commissioner Rowland in *CDLA/4388/1999*. There a tribunal had held that the claimant was not entitled when the evidence showed that he could walk, with a limp for 50 metres in about 4 minutes. The Commissioner emphasised that the question of whether this should be regarded as being "virtually unable to walk" was a question of fact to be determined by the tribunal and that unless it was a decision that no tribunal, properly directed on the points of law, could have reached, it was unassailable on appeal. At the same time he expressly disagreed with the statement of another Commissioner in *CSDLA/252/94*, that someone who could limp slowly for 50 yards could not "as a matter of law" be virtually unable to walk. In either case the question is one of fact for a tribunal and whichever way they decide could, *in law*, be correct. In the instant case, however, the appeal was allowed and returned for a re-hearing before a different tribunal because the tribunal had not considered what the claimant's condition and walking ability would be after going 50 metres. Would he need to rest? And if so for how long and in what way before he could go further? In *CDLA 2195/2008* Judge Williams was given evidence of the newly introduced guidelines on walking speed that will be used by DM and by medical examiners to assess walking ability. But he reiterated the importance of treating the test as one of overall impression of the claimant's walking ability:

> "Before leaving this topic, I endorse the more general submission by the Secretary of State on this appeal. Whether or not someone is virtually unable to walk is essentially a question of fact that must take into account all the matters referred to in the legislation. In one sense "speed" is central to this because regard must be had to "the distance over which or the speed at which or the length of time for which. . ." the claimant makes progress on foot (regulation 12 of the Social Security (Disability Living Allowance) Regulations 1991). And, of course, speed is distance covered divided by time taken. But those who are virtually unable to walk often do not walk at a consistent speed. It is therefore the whole way in which progress on foot takes place before or with discomfort that must, in fact, be determined. There are no easy ways of turning that into an arithmetical calculation."

the manner in which

Consideration of the manner of walking involves consideration of behaviour while walking as well as the steadiness of the claimant's gait. However, a need for supervision or attendance while walking is not, of itself, relevant under this regulation; it is, of course, relevant under s.73(1)(d). In *R(M) 1/78*, it was not material that the claimant was always accompanied because she suffered from fits. Thus a person who suffers from fits only occasionally is unlikely to qualify on that ground alone but, in *CM/125/1983*, a Commissioner held that the fact that a claimant was liable to suffer from three fits in half a mile might lead to the conclusion that the quality of walking was so poor as to amount to a virtual inability to walk. Similarly, a "propensity to

4.79

trip . . . would have to be extremely marked before it became relevant to the manner of a claimant's walking" (*CM/364/92*).

4.80   While in *R(M) 1/83* it was pointed out that the need for attendance and supervision was met through the social security system by entitlement to attendance allowance (see now the care component of disability living allowance and also the lower rate of the mobility component), the Tribunal of Commissioners did consider that the need for such assistance was a facet of the manner in which a person can make progress on foot and was to be taken into account by the medical authorities in conjunction with any other matters in determining whether the person concerned was virtually unable to walk. They said:

> "The main question in each case will be whether the child is so incapable inasmuch as his ability to walk out of doors is so limited as regards the manner in which he is able to make progress on foot, since behavioural limitations on a person's walking generally affect the manner of walking. It is possible also that speed of walking from place to place may enter into it. It will clearly be relevant that tantrums or refusals to walk are of frequent occurrence or not. We accept the submission made to us that the reference in reg.3(1)(b) [now reg.12(1)(a)(ii)] to the making of progress on foot means that it is proper to take account of the fact that a major purpose of walking is to get to a designated place. It follows that if a person can be caused to move himself to a designated place only with the benefit of guidance and supervision and possibly after much cajoling *the point may be reached at which he may be found to be virtually unable to walk*. There may be other factors such as blindness and deafness . . . to be taken into account in addition."

That passage needs to be treated with some caution in the light of the decision of the House of Lords in *Lees v Secretary of State for Social Services* (reported as an appendix to *R(M) 1/84*) but it is not inconsistent with it. Christine Lees was blind and suffered from hydrocephalus with symptoms including some impairment of balance and marked impairment of capacity for spatial orientation. She needed an intelligent adult as a "pilot". Lord Scarman rejected the argument that she was virtually unable to walk because the legislation points to consideration of the physical ability to get about on foot. In effect, he said that her position was no different from that of any other blind person who would need a guide of some sort. He also said that some Commissioners' decisions cited to the House and which differ must be regarded as erroneous in law. But it is not clear from his speech which decisions he had in mind or to what extent they are erroneous.

As already noted, in *Harrison*, Lloyd L.J. suggested that *R(M) 2/78* must be treated with caution but in *R(M) 3/86* a Tribunal of Commissioners said that it was correctly stating the law in that a claimant's behavioural problems, including a failure on occasion to exercise his walking powers (stemming from a physical disability) were necessarily relevant. "What is relevant is whether or not they suffer from temporary paralysis (as far as walking is concerned) and, if so, to what extent." In *CM/186/1985*, the Commissioner, relying on *R(M) 3/86*, drew a distinction between, on one hand, a child who suffered from

> "temperamental refusal episodes, these episodes occurring at distances varying between 20 and several hundred yards and on occasion [made] progress impossible by sitting down"

as a result of his physical condition (autism) and, on the other hand, the hypothetical "case of a child who is open to coaxing". Thus once it is established that, due to physical disablement, a person cannot be persuaded to walk in a desired direction, that person may be regarded as virtually unable to walk and so be entitled to the higher rate of the mobility component of disability living allowance and not just to the lower rate under s.73(1)(d) of the Social Security Contributions and Benefits Act 1992.

The distinction that was drawn by the Tribunal of Commissioners in *R(M) 3/86* between a claimant (in most cases of this sort, a child) who *could* not walk and a claimant who *would* not walk was based upon the simple question of whether such a person could be made to move by coaxing or by bribery. The Commissioners' conclusion was that if the child could be persuaded to move, it followed that the disablement was a matter of volition and could not then be the result of his physical condition.

A series of subsequent cases have questioned this conclusion. They are sum-   **4.81**
marised, and the counter-argument put most powerfully, in *CDLA/4565/2003* by Deputy Commissioner McGavin. There a child suffered from Williams syndrome, a rare condition that caused both learning difficulties and behavioural problems as well as some physical symptoms. But like some claimants suffering from Down's Syndrome, autism and brain damage, though she could walk in a physical sense, she might then sit or lie down, and might become aggressive if her wishes were thwarted.

The Commissioner points out that in the case of claimants such as these, to describe their behaviour as simply that of a naughty child (as the can't walk/won't walk test would seem to compel him to do) flies in the face of all the medical evidence provided and of the combined experience of the claimants' carers. As the Commissioner in *CM/98/1989* (a case concerning the claim of an 18-year-old man with brain damage) put the matter:

> "If . . . the relevant behavioural problems have nothing to do with physical damage what do they derive from? In the case of this 18-year-old are the tribunal suggesting that his behaviour was that of a naughty child who just would not walk when required? And, if they were, is not the fact that a brain damaged 18-year-old behaves like a child something to do with the brain damage?"

In the present case the Commissioner suggests that a tribunal should not conclude that a claimant who can be persuaded to move must be regarded as capable of walking, but instead should look at the medical evidence from which they might conclude that the refusal to walk was still a consequence of the malfunctioning of the brain, rather than simply wilful naughtiness. If so, then a refusal to walk that was frequent, sustained and not easily overcome could still constitute an inability to walk. The can't walk/won't walk distinction has been considered again by Commissioner Jacobs in *CDLA/3839/2007*. The Commissioner concludes that the distinction apparently drawn in *R(M) 3/86* between a deliberate election not to walk and physical disablement; is no such thing. In his view (and that of others he cites), this was simply a disposal of the facts as presented in that particular case, and did not lay down any principle of law to be applied in others. In this case, the claimant was a child suffering from autism (a physical condition) who generally required two adults holding him firmly when taken on any public route to avoid the danger that would be caused to himself and others by his running off uncontrollably. The case was returned to a tribunal for them to consider, and give clear reasons, as to whether, on the evidence presented, the claimant should be regarded as virtually unable to walk.

R(M) 2/81 concerned a blind person who could get around perfectly well with a guide dog until some scaffolding fell on his head and caused a physical injury. The medical appeal tribunal found:

> "The claimant's legs are capable of making the movements required in the activity of walking but he is blind and has a physical disablement in his balance mechanism and sense of direction which makes it impossible for him to control the direction in which he wishes to move . . . With human guidance he can be steered and can with much help progress in a straight line in a desired direction."

In *R(M) 3/86* it was held that that case did not survive *Lees* but it is interesting that the Court of Appeal in *Lees* would have distinguished it on the facts. O'Connor L.J. said:

> "I repeat it is a medical question as to whether physical disablement including a disturbance of directional mechanism, if the doctors decide that that is a physical disablement, renders a person unable to walk or virtually unable to walk."

The House of Lords suggested that they were not disagreeing with the Court of Appeal at all. The extent to which assistance can be of use would appear to be relevant but some of the sweeping *dicta* in *R(M) 2/81* clearly go.

The distance over which, the speed at which, the length of time for which and the manner in which the claimants can make progress are all relevant. However, the need to make findings on each of the factors only applies where the factors are all in issue (*CDLA/8462/95*). Whether a tribunal errs in law in failing to deal with some factors depends very much on the evidence in the particular case.

without severe discomfort

4.82   Any ability to make progress on foot must, to be relevant, be without severe discomfort. In *R(M) 1/81*, it was held that a tribunal must ignore any walking which can be managed only with severe discomfort. The most obvious form of discomfort to be suffered by a claimant is pain. The assessment of pain is a frequent and difficult issue before tribunals. Guidance on a proper approach to the issue of pain has been given by Commissioner Jacobs in *CDLA/0902/2004*.

In *Cassinelli v Secretary of State for Social Services (R(M) 2/92)*, the Court of Appeal held that a medical appeal tribunal had erred in law when holding that a person was not virtually unable to walk because the exertion of walking did not cause "severe pain or distress". Glidewell L.J. said that that phrase seemed,

> "to be drawing a distinction between the factor of pain, of which discomfort is a lesser concomitant, and the factor of distress which may arise for other reasons than pain; distress may result of course from pain or discomfort, but may also result from breathlessness, which is another matter to which the tribunal referred."

He rejected the argument put on behalf of the Secretary of State that the tribunal had, inferentially at least, applied the right test and answered the right question. It is difficult to follow the logic of the decision but it is clear that tribunals depart from the statutory language at their peril.

Note that the test to be applied is of "severe discomfort" not pain, or severe pain, and the evidence relied upon must be as to that test; or, at least explain the relationship with that test. In *CDLA/3292/2007* the Commissioner allowed the appeal of a claimant whose claim had been denied by a tribunal that relied, in part, on the evidence of her GP that she could walk only 50–100 yards "without being in severe pain". While this might have been consistent with the rest of the evidence relied upon, it could not be said that it was necessarily so, and the tribunal had failed to advert to the difference stated between "severe pain" and "severe discomfort".

In *CDLA/1389/97*, the Commissioner considered the relationship between pain and discomfort and he warned, at para.41, that a tribunal failing to use the statutory term "severe discomfort" was at risk of being held to have applied the wrong test. He suggested that there might be an escalating scale of severity from pain through severe discomfort to severe pain but it was unnecessary for him to decide the point. This issue was considered in greater detail in *R(DLA) 4/98* where the Commissioner said:

> "The fact that someone suffers pain as a result of walking, or walks 'in pain', does not automatically mean that he or she is walking with severe discomfort. The pain may be mild, moderate or severe, short-lived or chronic. The tribunal must decide for itself whether there is severe discomfort considering all the evidence, and perhaps taking into account other factors causing discomfort in addition to the pain."

In *R(DLA) 4/03* Commissioner Parker gave further consideration to the relationship between walking ability and severe discomfort. The appellant had appealed against refusal of benefit arguing that his walking ability should be assessed only up to the point when he began to experience severe discomfort. In *CSDLA/ 678/99* a Commissioner had said that severe discomfort—

"may onset and then be relieved by rest so that a further distance can be walked before further onset. In such a case the test stops at the first onset."

Commissioner Parker rejects this view as making an unwarranted gloss upon the statutory definition. "Without severe discomfort" is not the same, she argues, as before the onset of severe discomfort. To apply the test in that way would be to devalue the test of overall walking ability contained in the distance-time-speed formula provided by the regulation. The phrase "without discomfort" means that the claimant is not to be assessed with the inclusion of any progress that he makes only while suffering that discomfort, but so long as the rest time taken to avoid or relieve discomfort is included in the overall time taken for a journey then the con sequent calculation of speed will reflect the degree of disablement he suffers. A person who can progress with short, and infrequent periods of rest will probably be able to walk for this purpose; someone who requires frequent or prolonged stops probably will not. The judgment of distance, time and speed is then a matter of fact for the tribunal.

The possibility of reducing the level of discomfort by taking medication may be   **4.83**
taken into account, provided the tribunal explains why taking the medication would be "a reasonable, safe and appropriate thing to do" (*CDLA/3925/97*).

Pain that is suffered after walking, as well as while walking, yet still as a result of walking, should also be taken into account in deciding whether the claimant cannot walk without severe discomfort (*CDLA/3896/2006*).

In *R(DLA) 4/04*, Commissioner Bano held that a claimant who suffered pain all of the time, and whose pain was not made worse by attempting to walk, could still qualify if it was the pain that made it impossible or difficult for the claimant to walk.

Discomfort may take forms other than pain. Breathlessness may result in severe discomfort and other conditions have also been accepted. But the severe discomfort must be some thing that is caused by the act of walking. In *Diment v Chief Adjudication Officer* and *Hewitt v Chief Adjudication Officer* reported as *R(DLA) 6/99*, the claimants suffered from porphyria, a condition that meant they could not expose their skin to the sun, but otherwise were capable of normal perambulation.

In *CDLA/1361/99*, the evidence was that, when walking a very short distance, the claimant suffered pain and then lost control of her bowels. The Commissioner held that the claimant was virtually unable to walk. He said:

> "The discomfort in this case comprises not only the pain but also the physical sensation of having soiled oneself in the ways described in the papers (which would certainly be discomfort in the ordinary sense of the word, though possibly not 'severe'), the embarrassment of knowing that one has soiled oneself (which would again cause discomfort), and the distress caused. Looking at all these elements together they are in my view of such a magnitude in this case that I conclude that walking to any extent causes the claimant severe discomfort after the walking, if not during it (and often both)."

Further support for the view that acute diarrhoea might contribute to severe discomfort so as to qualify the claimant for the higher award of benefit can be found in *MMF v Secretary of State for Work and Pensions* [2012] UKUT 312 (AAC). There, the claimant was an eight-year-old girl who suffered from ulcerative colitis, Judge Lane took the view that her consequent chronic diarrhoea could contribute to her condition as a whole so as to make her virtually unable to walk. The case was remitted for rehearing.

In *CDLA/313/2005* the claimant, who was a teenage girl, was disabled in one leg and as a result, was likely to fall. This could be avoided with the use of a walking stick but the claimant said she was too embarrassed to use the stick. It was argued that her embarrassment was a form of discomfort under reg.12(1)(a)(ii) and that she should be regarded as unable or virtually unable to walk within the meaning prescribed. Commissioner May rejects this argument. Her discomfort, he says, must be of a kind that was part of her "physical condition as a whole" (reg.12(1)(a)), and could not, therefore, include her embarrassment. In doing so he disapproves of the reasoning adopted by the Commissioner in *CDLA/1361/1999* though there it could be suggested that the embarrassment had more to do with physical condition of the claimant than just embarrassment at the use of a device.

4.84   An attempt to extend the reasoning of *R(DLA) 1/04* to the case of a blind man suffering from depression was made in *CDLA/3898/2006*. The claimant's depression was said to derive from his blindness and that it caused the claimant to suffer anxiety to the point of severe discomfort so that he was virtually unable to walk outside. He would thus qualify for the higher rate of benefit. This claim was refused and his appeal was rejected by Commissioner Mesher. The Commissioner held that the appeal must fail because the appeal tribunal had found, as a fact, that the claimant did not suffer discomfort from anxiety so long as he had guidance and support from someone to accompany him. The claimant argued that this finding was unjustified because his anxiety would continue unless the particular person he had for company was someone with whom he had a particular relationship of trust, and in whom he could then be confident. But no evidence of this was before the appeal tribunal, and the Commissioner held, therefore, that there could be no error of law in the conclusion they had reached. But the Commissioner comments more generally upon the argument that had been put to him. It is important, he says, in a field such as this, which is so complex as to be sometimes almost unjusticiable, (in the sense that it may appear difficult to distinguish clearly and consistently between those cases which succeed and those which fail) that one should return to the basics as explained in *Lees*, and having done so he says:

> "I doubt in the light of *Lees*, and of the decision of the Tribunal of Commissioners in *R (M)3/86*, whether 'mere' mental distress, turmoil or anxiety (as opposed to physical manifestations like breathlessness, palpitations, dizziness, chest pain or nausea) can amount to severe discomfort even where a physical disorder contributes to the effect to more than a minimal extent. There would also, if such things could count, be difficulty in distinguishing a perfectly rational heightening of caution, vigilance and concentration which presumably could not be regarded as severe discomfort on any basis."

exertion and danger to life or serious risk to health
4.85   In *R(M) 3/78*, the claimant needed oxygen to be available in case of a drop attack (which might also have occurred while she was asleep). The Commissioner held that what is now reg.12(1)(a)(iii)

> "does not extend to conditions or symptoms which might intervene during the course of walking without there being any connection or relationship to or with walking or being precipitated by the exertion of walking."

Although the word "exertion" might suggest the sort of condition associated with pulmonary and cardiac deficiency there are several decisions that have extended it to include any sufficient deterioration in health effected by the act of walking. Thus, in *CDLA/5494/1997*, Commissioner Levenson accepted that a claimant who had been warned that to continue walking would endanger the spine could succeed, and in *CDLA/2973/1999* Commissioner Fellner has held that a claimant whose diabetes had led to neuropathy in his legs and feet could qualify because walking was likely to lead to ulceration of the claimant's feet and a consequent risk of amputation. The meaning of this phrase has been further considered in *CDLA/3941/2005*. The Commissioner allowed an appeal by a claimant who suffered from cartilage damage and arthritis in her knee. The effect of walking for extensive distances, which she had to do in taking her children to and from school, was said to be likely to result in more frequent arthroscopies (wash-out of the knee joint) and eventually would hasten the need for a knee replacement. This, the Commissioner thought should satisfy the test in reg.(12)(1)(a)(iii). He gave his own decision that she was entitled to benefit. The decision in *CDLA/3941/2005* has been disagreed with by Judge Turnbull in *IP v SSWP* [2013] UKUT 235 (AAC). This is an important decision because it suggests a much more restricted interpretation of the subparagraph. In the earlier case Mr Commissioner Angus had suggested that the test to be applied was whether, without endangering life or health, the claimant could walk a distance that would be normal for a healthy person of her age. Judge Turnbull rejects this construction because it might be far too generous. It could result in claimants succeeding when they could walk far beyond, and in a far better manner, than claimants who failed the test under subparagraph (ii). It would mean that a claimant who could point to a serious endangerment to health would succeed, when someone whose walking was limited by pain would not, even though the former might walk much better. In his view this could not have been the intention that the legislation sought to express. This is to adopt a fairly extreme instance of purposive interpretation, but it may well be right.

Judge Turnbull points out that the subparagraphs in reg.12 (1) are made (under s.73(5) of the C&B Act) to define the circumstances specified in s.73(1)(a) of that act-*viz* "unable to walk or virtually unable to do so". Subpara.(i) simply repeats the phrase unable to walk; subparas. (ii) and (iii) should therefore both be seen as expanding the meaning of "virtually unable to do so". This construction would mean that both of those subparagraphs were conditioned by the claimant being rendered virtually unable to walk by reason of his disability. In the present case the claimant could walk for 10 or 12 minutes at a slow pace, even on a bad day, before her heart condition caused her to rest as a result of breathlessness. In the judge's view she was certainly not "virtually unable to walk" and her appeal failed. Judge Turnbull also thought the result of adopting this construction would necessarily mean that the claimant in the case above should have failed—if she could walk 3 miles, even at risk to her knees, she was not virtually unable to walk. But need this be so. If the idea of virtual ability to walk were to include an element of what it was reasonable for the claimant to do, (as earlier cases under this subparagraph have done), rather than a standard of what a person in good health might do, then it could be argued that the 3 miles a day that would have to be walked by the claimant in *CDLA/3941/2005* to get her children to and from school was a justifiable target, whereas more than a 10 minute walk by a middle aged woman was not. But this seems to take decision makers and tribunals into difficult territory and an area of social judgment best avoided.

The deterioration in health need not be permanent or last for any great length of time (*CM/23/1985*) but it must be serious. In *CM/158/94*, the tribunal had found that, although exertion left the claimant exhausted, "it did not result in a serious deterioration in his health since, having rested, he would improve." The Commissioner dismissed the claimant's appeal and suggested that a serious deterioration in a claimant's health would only be shown where:

"(a) there was a worsening of his condition from which he never recovered, or
(b) there was a worsening from which he only recovered after a significant period of time, e.g. 12 months, or
(c) there was a worsening from which recovery could only be effected by some form of medical intervention."

Sub-paragraph (1)(b)

Double amputees may qualify under this provision even if they have recovered sufficiently to have artificial limbs fitted and are no longer either unable to walk or virtually unable to walk.   **4.86**

Paragraph (1A)

Regulation 12(1A) has been held to be ultra vires by Judge Sir Crispin Agnew in *YR v SSWP* [2014] UKUT 80 (AAC). This was a case in which the claimant, who was   **4.87** registered blind, suffered from retinitis pigmontosa. This meant that her eyesight was significantly better indoors with ambient light, but virtually non-existent when she was in either reduced light or in bright light, as she would be when out of doors. The test stated in reg.12(1A) is solely by reference to the Snellen test—a test by reading letters from a board conducted under ambient lighting indoors. This meant that she could not satisfy the requirement to qualify for the higher rate of the mobility component. In the FTT it had been held that the claimant could succeed on the basis that the tribunal found her degree of disability out of doors, was equal to that of a person who failed the Snellen test when indoors. In the Upper Tribunal Sir Crispin Agnew held that the invention of an equivalent test by the tribunal below went beyond any power of legitimate interpretation of the regulations and therefore allowed the Secretary of State's appeal. But he went on from there to hold that the regulation was discriminatory in the sense of the *Thlimmenos* type of discrimination (see *Thlimmenos v Greece* (2001) 31 EHRR 411). This applies when a rule fails to treat differently persons whose situations are significantly different (yet remain similarly affected by a disability).

A similar case of visual disability had been considered by Judge Bano in *SSWP v MS (DLA)* [2013] UKUT 267 (AAC). There (as here) it was held that the claim must fail because the only test provided under reg.12(1A) was by the Snellen test and no other measurement of the claimant's visual ability could be applied. It does not appear that in that case the discrimination argument had been advanced. In this case counsel for the Secretary of State argued that even if the test were discriminatory, it was indirectly discriminatory and could be justified on the ground that the policy that the regulation sought to achieve was to apply a "bright line" test that would be simple and effective in determining entitlement.

Judge Sir Crispin Agnew rejects that argument; for entitlement to a benefit that was aimed at providing for people to get about independently out of doors, the failure to set a different test for those whose visual acuity was significantly worse when out of doors, was not justified, even allowing for an appropriate "margin of appreciation". But that did not mean that the claimant succeeded. The judge held that although the regulation was ultra vires it was not for that reason a nullity. This meant that the regulation remains in force as the only means by which entitlement to this part of the benefit can be achieved. Indeed, had the judge found that the regulation was a nullity, it would have served the claimant no better, for that would mean that neither she, nor any other visually impaired claimants (even those who would succeed under the Snellen test), could be entitled.

The case was appealed by the Secretary of State to the Court of Session under the title of *SSWP v Robertson* [2015] CSIH 82. It appears that the Secretary of State took the view that the regulation could not be relied upon unless the judge's finding was reversed. However, the Court of Session decided that the appeal was incompetent as the finding of ultra vires had not formed a part of the decision. Although the representative of the Secretary of State had indicated to the court that the DWP would feel bound by the judge's decision, it is understood now that they have decided to continue to apply the regulation without amendment (this is confirmed in DMG 18/15). This may be, in part at least, because it would appear that in such a case a successful claim might be made for Personal Independence Payment—see Descriptor (f) of Activity 1 of Mobility Activities.

The validity of this regulation has been considered again in *JA-K v SSWP (DLA)* [2017] UKUT 420 (AAC). In this case the issue arose not from the method of determining what amounted to severe visual impairment, but from the fact that under s.75 of the Contributions and Benefits Act it could not be awarded to a claimant who was over the age of 65 years at the time the claim was made. The claimant was undoubtedly visually impaired to the requisite extent, but by the time the regulations were made that enabled the higher rate of the mobility component to become available by this route, in 2011, the claimant was already aged 71. She argued that to deny the benefit to her when it was available to a claimant aged less than 65, was a clear case of age discrimination. Judge Wright considered first whether the regulation might be considered to be invalid as being in breach of the public sector equality duty under the Equality Act 2010. He concluded that it could not be because the regulation was made in June 2010, but the Equality Act only came into force in April 2011. The same applied, he thought, to the decisions taken by the SSWP in not superseding the claimant's award of the mobility component to include the higher rate. As well, he pointed out that the discrimination, if there were any, resulted from s.75 of the Contributions and Benefits Act, not from reg.12(1A), and the UT was not competent to make any declaration in respect of an Act of Parliament. More importantly, however, Judge Wright considered the issue of whether the UT is competent to make a decision as to the validity of regulations in relation to the Equality Act 2010. This is a matter on which UT judges have given differing views though in some cases the matter was not put in dispute before them. Judge Wright's view was that, in consequence of s.113 of that Act, the UT was not competent to make a determination of invalidity except in the exercise of its jurisdiction in judicial review; to do that would require the claimant to commence proceedings in the High Court from where the matter might be referred to the UT. The judge would also have held that the SSWP did have due regard to the equality duty when making the regulation. The judge considered, too, an argument based on the Human Rights Act 1998. He rejected that argument also in following *NT v SSWP (DLA)* [2009] UKUT 37 (AAC) (also reported as *R(DLA)* 1/09)—see discussion in note following s.75 of the C&BA 1992.

For the purposes of determining entitlement to benefit under this provision an optometrist or an orthoptist who is registered with their appropriate professional Council is a healthcare professional for the purposes of s.39 of the Social Security Act 1998.

The meaning of the phrase "with appropriate corrective lenses" has been considered in *NC v SSWP (DLA)* [2012] UKUT 384 (AAC). There, the claimant's eyesight would qualify automatically for the benefit without her contact lenses, but not if she wore the lenses. (The claimant was unable to wear glasses.) She said that her eyes had become intolerant to wearing contact lenses and that she could use them for only a limited amount of time each week. The judge held that lenses that could be worn only with severe discomfort could not be regarded as "appropriate" for the claimant and remitted the case for rehearing.

Paragraph (2)

There is no indication given as to how the degree of disablement is to be assessed. However, Sch.2 to the Social Security (General Benefit) Regulations 1982 provides that 100 per cent disablement is appropriate for "loss of sight to such an extent as to render the claimant unable to perform any work for which eyesight is essential". Schedule 3 to the Social Security (Industrial Injuries) (Prescribed Diseases) Regulations 1985 sets out a test for establishing an assessment of 80 per cent for occupational deafness. In *R(DLA)* 3/95 the Commissioner said that these tests should be used for the purposes of reg.12(2). When the 1982 Regulations are being applied in industrial accident cases, an assessment of 100 per cent for loss of vision is regarded as appropriate where the vision is found to be less than 6/60, using both eyes whilst glasses are used; or where finger counting is not possible beyond one foot. Before *R(DLA)* 3/95 was decided, an assessment of 80 per cent for deafness was regarded as appropriate where the claimant was unable to hear a shout beyond one metre using both ears (with aids). This was tested by shouting an instruction or question from just beyond one metre behind the claimant. *CDLA/7090/1999* rejects the use of that test. It emphasises the need for controlled testing and suggests that this should be in an outdoor environment.

The test for blindness under para.(2) has been examined extensively by Judge Wright in *GB v SSWP (DLA)* [2016] UKUT 566 (AAC). The judge examines parliamentary material going back as far as 1917, in the form of a white paper preparatory to the Blind Persons Act 1920, from which the wording in para.(2)(a) would seem to have been inherited. He concludes that the "degree of disablement

4.88

resulting from the loss of vision [amounting] to 100%" is correctly determined in accordance with the approach adopted in *R)DLA) 3/95,* by reference to the claimant's ability to perform work for which eyesight is essential, and not by reference to any numerical score on an eye test. The score on an eye test can be only evidence from which the claimant's working ability might be inferred, but it is not determinative of the result. This demonstrates the difference that there must be between the test in regulation 12(1A)(a), where the test is determined by a numerical score, and under regulation 12(2)(a) which concerns a person who is both blind and deaf. The task of a decision maker and hence a tribunal should be to infer the claimant's ability to undertake tasks that might be involved in paid employment or work for a profit. In this case the FTT had attempted to do that, but they erred in relying on the claimant's manual dexterity and ability to undertake tasks in an educational or social environment drawing inferences from that rather than considering his ability in a work place environment where speed, reliability and possibly a degree of adaptability would be required.

Paragraph (3)

4.89   Note that it is only an inability to walk in the right direction due to the *combined* effects of blindness and deafness which can be relevant.

Paragraph (4)

4.90   An ability to wear an artificial prosthesis or to use an artificial aid (such as a pair of crutches) must be taken into account and the claimant's ability to get about must usually be assessed on the basis that a prosthesis or aid is used. However, if the claimant does not in fact habitually wear or use such a prosthesis or aid, it is necessary to consider whether one would be suitable for him or her (*R(M) 2/89*). If a prosthesis is habitually, or could be, worn but any walking is, or would be, achieved only with severe discomfort, such ability to walk would not fall within para.(1)(a)(ii) anyway. But a prosthesis might not be suitable even if the discomfort were not severe. It is arguable that a prosthesis or aid cannot be "suitable" until it is actually available to the claimant. Reg.12(4) cannot be read as requiring a person to undergo surgery to improve his or her medical condition (*R(M) 1/95*).

In *MH v SSWP* [2009] UKUT 94 (AAC) the claimant was a woman who habitually used a shopping trolley to support her whenever she walked outside. This was not only when going to the shops and doing the shopping, but also when she was out for any other reason, for instance walking with her grandchildren. Judge Lane upheld the decision of a First-tier Tribunal that had refused benefit on the ground that she was not unable to walk when she was using an artificial aid. The judge confirms that the word "artificial" has no technical meaning in the regulation; if the claimant chooses to use a shopping trolley as her form of walking aid there is no reason why the ordinary meaning of the words "artificial aid" should not include that trolley. Alternatively, she said, it was clear that the claimant was able to make progress on foot with some form of support and if the shopping trolley were not to be regarded as being within the meaning of the regulation, then para.(b) would apply on the basis that she could be expected to walk with the aid of a wheeled walking frame.

Paragraph (5)

4.91   Only those suffering from a state of arrested development or incomplete physical development of the brain can qualify under those provisions. The significance of this construction has been pointed out by Judge Levenson in the context of a Down's Syndrome child in *SC v SSWP* [2010] UKUT 76 (AAC). The First-tier Tribunal had refused to find that the child suffered from "arrested or incomplete development of the mind", but the judge points out that this ellipsis of the words in the section may diminish the correct meaning of the full phrase. He says:

"28. The meaning of severely mentally impaired is found in regulation 12(5), which is set out above. The First-tier Tribunal found that there was no evidence of "arrested or incomplete development of the brain". However, this is a common but mistaken paraphrase of regulation 12(5), which refers to "arrested development" or "incomplete physical development of the brain". There are two aspects to this error. One is that a distinction is drawn between arrested development generally (not limited to the brain, although there must still be a physical cause) and incomplete physical development of the brain. The other is that "arrested development" does not mean arrested *physical* development (otherwise the regulation would say so, as it says "incomplete *physical* development"). Thus, regulation 12(5) can apply to a person who has arrested emotional or functional development which has a physical cause even if that cause is not related to the development of the brain."

If someone becomes disabled as a result of an injury after the brain has reached full development, he or she will probably have to rely on para.(1)(a) instead. In *R(DLA) 2/96*, the Commissioner, having heard expert medical evidence, held that sufferers from Alzheimer's disease do not satisfy the condition mentioned in reg.12(5). He found that the disease resulted in a deterioration of a developed brain rather than an arrest of development, rejecting the idea that the brain develops throughout life which, he pointed out, would render otiose the restriction implied by reg.12(5). In that case, the expert evidence suggested that the brain had reached maturity by the time a person was aged 30. In *CDLA/393/94*, the claimant was in her early 20s when she became ill and it was held to be arguable that her brain had not fully developed and that she suffered from a state of arrested development or incomplete physical development. The burden of proof rested on the claimant. In *R(DLA) 3/98*, the Commissioner heard evidence in respect of a claimant suffering from schizophrenia and concluded that she suffered from arrested development of the brain but that that did not result in severe impairment of intelligence in her case.

In *NMcM v SSWP (DLA)* [2014] UKUT 312 (AAC) Judge Wikeley has decided two important points about para. (5). First, the so called "age 30 cut off" rule in *R (DLA) 2/96* is disapproved and secondly the novel construction of the paragraph that had been suggested by Judge Levenson in *SC v SSWP* [2010] UKUT 76 referred to at the beginning of this note is also disapproved. As to the first, Judge Wikeley finds that the basis upon which the rule was adopted, namely the state of medical knowledge then held about the development of the brain, was no longer sustainable. In the light of more recent medical research, and especially the benefits of MRI imaging, it was no longer possible to assert that the brain could be regarded as fully developed by that age. Judge Wikeley had before him a report agreed by both the parties, which showed that in one sense the brain continues to develop at least into the third decade of life and possibly in some persons into their forties. In another sense, the brain continues to develop when acquiring new skills that can be reflected in physical changes in the brain, throughout life. The present case, which involved a claimant who had suffered brain damage in a road accident at the age of 32, had been rejected on that ground without further consideration at the FTT. The case has now been referred back for further matters to be considered. First among them will be the question of whether the claimant can be said to be suffering from a state of arrested development or incomplete development of the brain. In doing so they will follow the other part of the Judge's decision which is that each of these phrases is to be read as referring to "the brain". Thus, what must be found is "arrested development of the brain" or, alternatively, "incomplete physical development of the brain". It might be thought that this would present a difficulty, given that the claimant's problems were palpably caused by what we would popularly refer to as "brain damage", but, as the judge points out, the test here is not one of causation; it is, at this stage, just one of medical fact and given the way in which the terms above are now used to describe the medical situation, he thought it possible that the FTT might find accordingly.

A further claim in respect of a woman suffering from schizophrenia has been considered in *DM v SSWP (DLA)* [2015] UKUT 87 (AAC). In this case the claimant had first been diagnosed as suffering from the condition at age 21. The FTT was held to have made an error of law in accepting without further enquiry the opinion of the claimant's medical consultant that she was not suffering from any arrested development or incomplete physical development of the brain. The FTT had made this finding of fact based only on the opinion expressed in the consultant's letter and for which he gave no supporting reasons. It appeared to have been made, in part at least, on the basis that there had been no brain scan ever made of the patient. The case was returned to a fresh tribunal to enquire further as to evidence on this point. The claimant, on whom the burden of proof will lie may find difficulty in doing so. A brain scan will not necessarily form a part of any treatment plan for her condition. Without that being so the cost of an MRI scan is likely to be prohibitive. In the earlier case of *NMcM v SSWP* (above) the department had been able to provide a detailed report on recent medical researches that had been agreed by both parties; without a similar intervention it is likely that the strict conditions imposed by *para.(5)* will again defeat the claim. However Judge Wikeley has pointed out in his judgement that this is one instance where the rules of entitlement to Personal Independence Payment may be more generous than for the mobility component. (See descriptor (f) of the Mobility Activities in Sch.1 of those regulations). This decision also considers whether *para.(5)* might be discriminatory and in breach of the claimant's human rights. In the judge's view this was unlikely to be so, but that a decision on this point was unnecessary to dispose of the present appeal.

In *CDLA/1678/97*, the Commissioner heard expert evidence in a case where the claimant suffered from autism. He concluded that autism arises out of a state of arrested or incomplete development of the brain but he was not satisfied that the claimant's intelligence was severely impaired. The expert evidence was to the effect that only those with an I.Q. of 55 or below were regarded as having *severely* impaired intelligence and that fewer than 10 per cent of those suffering from autism fell within that category. The Commissioner found, on the basis of medical reports and other evdence, that the particular claimant before him was not one of those 10 per cent. In *M (a child) v Chief Adjudication Officer* reported as *R (DLA) 1/00*, the Court of Appeal has held that an intelligence test should not be regarded as a definitive measure of whether a child has a severe impairment of intelligence. In that case the child, who was autistic, had an intelligence quotient well above the quotient of 55 that had been suggested by the medical experts as consistent with a rating of severe impairment. The Court of Appeal held that an intelligence test result is a useful starting point but should not be conclusive. They suggest a full assessment of intelligence should include factors such as "insight and sagacity". It is worth noting that subs.(5) includes the words "social functioning" as well as "intelligence". Although they are linked by the word "and" which suggests that they should be read as cumulative rather than as alternatives, it may be possible to argue that social functioning should be regarded as lending colour in the interpretation of intelligence to support the wider view. This seems to be the position taken in *CD v SSWP (DLA)* [2013] UKUT 68 where the appeal was allowed by Judge Bano because the FTT had failed to take sufficient account of the claimant's lack of awareness of danger. The claimant in this case was another autistic child. The judge held that the FTT had made an error of law also by comparing the behaviour of the claimant with that of a child of similar age who was not disabled. It seems likely that in doing so the FTT were importing the requirements of s.73 (4A), but that subsection applies only to a claim made under s.73 (1)(d); the claim in the present case was made under s.73 (3).It is possible, however, that such comparison might be relevant to assessing the claimant's social functioning.

The approach that treats intelligence and social functioning as parts of a combined test of the claimant's ability to function in "real life situations" has been approved in *MP v SSWP (DLA)* [2014] UKUT 426 (AAC). Judge G. Knowles QC, directed the FTT to whom the case was returned that they should regard *R (DLA) 1/00* as "authority for the proposition that evidence about a person's insight and sagacity can satisfy both the test of severe impairment of intelligence **and** severe impairment of social functioning required by regulation 12(5)."

This case was another involving a child (four years old) with autistic spectrum disorder. An appeal was allowed largely because insufficient regard had been given to the communication difficulties that the child was experiencing. As the judge put it,

"The emphasis in *R (DLA) 1/00* [. . .] on *"the ability to function in real life situations"* or *"useful intelligence"* invites active consideration of a person's language difficulties when considering their social functioning for the purposes of regulation 12(5)."

The judge directed also that when rehearing the case regard must be had to the child's ability to function in less structured situations rather than just his abilities within the home and at school. Furthermore, he thought it necessary that account should be taken of the child's ability to function in relation to strangers and not just those who were familiar to him. He rejected the suggestion made on behalf of the Secretary of State that it would be difficult to assess a child's ability to interact with strangers because many young children are shy with strangers. To do so, he thought, would be to introduce a comparison with a child of that age who was not disabled; a test he points out that is applied specifically only in para.4A. However, it is likely that some reference to the generality of youthful shyness is inevitable because it will still be necessary for there to be a finding that the child's condition has resulted in "impairment".

Regulation 12(5) was considered in *CDLA/5153/97* where the claimant suffered from attention deficit hyperactivity disorder. The Commissioner had detailed medical evidence before him as to the causes of the condition and he was not satisfied that, in the present state of medical knowledge, it was possible to attribute the claimant's condition to "a state of arrested development or incomplete physical development of the brain" as is required to satisfy the condition of reg.12(5). Such a finding by a Commissioner on a question of fact is not binding on tribunals and the Commissioner himself acknowledged that different evidence might become available.

"It may become possible to make such an attribution for ADHD in the future, with the advances in scanning techniques and genetic knowledge for which Professor Barkley hopes: but it is not so now."

Nonetheless, the decision provides helpful guidance and unless a claimant has technically detailed evidence in support of his or her case, tribunals are likely to adopt the Commissioner's finding.

Paragraph (6)

Physical restraint must be *regularly* required and the behaviour must be *disruptive*   **4.92**
and *unpredictable*. Indeed, since "extreme" conditions "disruptive behaviour", it is probably right to say that the behaviour must be extremely disruptive. A person who satisfies the conditions of sub-paras (b) and (c) but who does not exhibit extremely disruptive behaviour may qualify for the mobility component at the lower rate (under s.73(1)(d) of the 1992 Act).

Regulation 12(6) was examined in *CDLA/2054/98*. The Deputy Commissioner held that in applying sub-para.(a), it was the claimant's behaviour when taking advantage of the faculty of mobility that had to be considered. But this view has been rejected in the reported decision *R(DLA) 7/02*, by Commissioner (as he then was) Turnbull. He accepted that the rational for this benefit was the claimant's mobility, but in his view the words of the regulation are too plain—the claimant must satisfy the condition in para.(c) "whenever he is awake", and thus must include his behaviour both indoors and outside. This has been followed in a string of decisions (see *CDLA 2470/2006, CSDLA 202/2007, CDLA 2167/2010*) and now in *SSWP v MG (DLA)* [2012] UKUT 429 (AAC) by Judge Wikeley. That much about reg.12 (6) can be regarded as established.

Judge Wikeley goes on in this judgment to give guidance on several of the other points that arise in applying para.(6). These points are reproduced here as a useful source of guidance to tribunals dealing with such cases. The case concerned a claim for higher rate mobility made on behalf of an autistic child. (In the UT the claimant was represented by Mr. Stagg and the secretary of state by Mr. Heath).

"What does 'extreme' signify in the context of regulation 12(6)(a)?

4.93

22. Mr Deputy Commissioner Bano described the word 'extreme' as 'an ordinary English word, connoting behaviour which is wholly out of the ordinary' (CDLA/2054/1998 at paragraph 7a). Although the rest of that passage, which concerned the 'indoors/out of doors' point has been disapproved in R(DLA) 7/02, I am not sure that this definition of 'extreme' can be usefully improved upon very much. However, as Mr Commissioner Rowland observed in CDLA/2470/2006, reading the sub-conditions cumulatively, 'extreme' behaviour is 'of a type that regularly requires a substantial degree of intervention and physical restraint' (at paragraph 13). In other words, the behaviour must be extremely disruptive. Furthermore, the disruptive behaviour must result from the severe mental impairment: 'insofar as such problems are primarily a manifestation of a claimant's age rather than of such mental impairment, they are irrelevant to entitlement' (CSDLA/202/2007 at paragraph 11). This is ultimately a question of fact for the tribunal, involving 'a large element of judgment' (CDLA/2167/2010 at paragraph 8).

What does 'regularly' mean in the context of regulation 12(6)(b)?

23. The claimant' extreme behaviour need not occur constantly, continuously or all the time. That would be to set the threshold for eligibility too high. Rather, it must be such that it 'regularly requires another person to intervene and physically restrain him in order to prevent him causing physical injury to himself or another, or damage to property'. The word 'regularly' is a protean one, so taking its meaning from its context. The Commissioner in CDLA/2470/2006 commented that 'such a degree of intervention and restraint is likely to be required on a significant proportion of occasions when the claimant walks moderate distances outdoors'. I agree with that observation as far as it goes.

24. I do not agree with Mr Stagg's further submission that this means that regularity under regulation 12(6)(b) can be met by such incidents occurring just outdoors. Such an analysis seems to me to be inconsistent with R(DLA) 7/02. Rather, that sort of intervention to deal with extreme disruptive behaviour will also need to be required sufficiently often indoors as well such that, taken overall, one can say that it is required 'regularly' or 'in the ordinary course of events' (see CDLA/2054/1998 at paragraph 7d). When the claimant is outdoors, the need for intervention in the proximity of traffic is the obvious example. The indoors intervention may take any number of different forms: in *MMcG v Department for Social Development (DLA)* the claimant had to be stopped from jumping off the top step of the household stairs. Other examples—and they are no more than that—might be the need for physical restraint to stop the claimant trying to put his fingers in electrical sockets or to stop him damaging internal doors, walls or household furniture when frustrated. As Mr Deputy Commissioner (now Judge) Warren noted in CDLA/17611/1996, the requirements of regulation 12(6) 'fall to be answered in respect of the claimant's condition generally and not with any special emphasis on behaviour when walking out of doors' (at paragraph 11). However, I also agree with Judge Mark's helpful formulation that 'interventions may be regular if they are fre-

quent in one context but infrequent, or even rare, in another context provided that looked at overall there is a regular requirement to intervene and physically restrain the claimant' (*Secretary of State for Work and Pensions v DM (DLA)* [2010] UKUT 318 (AAC) at paragraph 9).

What does 'physically restrain' signify in the context of regulation 12(6)(b)?
25. The 'regularity' requirement under regulation 12(6)(b) is for 'another person to intervene and physically restrain' the claimant. In CDLA/2470/2006 Mr Commissioner Rowland qualified that expression by the comment 'i.e. something much more than merely taking the person by the arm'. I note that the facts of that case concerned a young man with Down's Syndrome who was aged 16 at the date of the tribunal hearing. However, more recently Judge Mesher expressed the view that the Commissioner in CDLA/2470/2006 was not intending 'to lay down any hard and fast rule of general application' (CDLA/2167/2010 at paragraph 15). Judge Mesher found that on the facts of that case the tribunal was entitled to conclude that 'what was needed was a very firm grip to stop U from rushing off towards whatever caught his attention and that that constituted physical restraint to prevent injury' (also at paragraph 15). In CDLA/2617/2010 the boy U was aged 11 at the date of the FTT hearing.

26. I agree with Mr Stagg's further submission that the nature of the intervention and physical restraint required to satisfy regulation 12(6)(c) will be fact- and context-specific. Obviously a strapping 16-year-old may require a considerably higher level of physical restraint than a slight 5-year-old. A firm grip on the arm of such a 5-year-old may well be sufficient to avert danger, whereas it may have no effect at all on a 16-year-old who may have the strength of an adult. I therefore agree with Judge Mesher in CDLA/2617/2010 that Mr Commissioner Rowland should not be read as imposing some categorical rule by way of the illustration given on the facts of that case.

What does 'watching over' mean in the context of regulation 12(6)(c)?
27. The new tribunal should bear in mind the guidance in the leading case of R(DLA) 9/02. As Mr Commissioner (now Judge) May noted there, the test is 'specifically restrictive' and the carer must be both 'present' and 'watching over': 'It does not seem to me these conditions can be fulfilled when the claimant's bedroom door is closed and he is on one side of it and the carer on the other' (at paragraph 12). Both Mr Heath and Mr Stagg agreed, as I do, that this proposition is subject to a *de minimis* rider, so that for example 'very short intervals without watching over' e.g. for a carer's 'comfort break' (but not, for example, a leisurely cup of tea and a prolonged respite break in the garden whilst the claimant is inside) can be ignored for this purpose (see CDLA/2714/2009 at paragraph 10, cited in *JH v Secretary of State for Work and Pensions (DLA)* [2010] UKUT 456 (AAC) at paragraph 11).

28. Since the oral hearing of this appeal, Judge Mark has issued his decision in *AH v Secretary of State for Work and Pensions (DLA)* [2012] UKUT 387 (AAC). Judge Mark held that 'requires' in regulation 12(6)(c) means 'reasonably requires' (at paragraph 16). That seems to be uncontroversial. Judge Mark also expressed the view that if the carer is present close enough to hear what the claimant is doing and so to intervene if necessary, and is either looking in with sufficient regularity or (conceivably) observing the claimant on CCTV, then the fact that the claimant's bedroom door is shut does not inevitably mean that the carer is not present and watching over the claimant whenever he is awake (at paragraphs 14 and 19). This is at the very least a significant gloss on the Commissioner's ruling in R(DLA) 9/02, although Judge Mark sought support from the observations in CDLA/2167/2010 (at paragraph 13). I considered whether to seek further submissions from both representatives on this issue in the light of the newly available decision. I decided not to, given that the question was not central to this appeal and the case has gone on long enough already.

29. I simply make the following observation. It seems to me that there is some force in Judge Mark's qualification. Obviously the statutory language must take its ordinary meaning from its context, in the absence of any indication to the contrary. 'Watching' means observing, being on the lookout, keeping someone or something in sight, or keeping vigil. However, 'watching over' may carry a slightly different nuance in meaning, of exercising protective care over someone or something. After all, regulation 12(6)(b) does say 'watching over' and not 'looking at'. It is arguable that the Commissioner in R(DLA) 9/02 may have elided the meanings of 'watching over' and 'watching' (see e.g. at paragraph 12). That is not to say that the meaning of 'watching over' can be stretched like a piece of elastic, not least as it is coupled with the restrictive requirement that the carer be 'present'. That, of course, is ultimately a question of fact for the first instance tribunal.

What is the significance of a 'structured environment' in the context of regulation 12(6) (c)?

30. As noted at paragraph 18 above, the submissions of Mr Heath and Mr Stagg were principally concerned with the significance of the claimant's behaviour within a 'structured environment' for the purpose of the regulation 12(6) conditions. Both advocates recognised that there appeared to be a divergence of opinion in the case law on this issue.

31. Mr Heath's argument was that if the claimant was subject to a 'structured environment', whether e.g. at home or at school, such that he did not become extremely disruptive, then by definition regulation 12(6) was not satisfied. He relied in particular on the following passage of Mr Commissioner Turnbull's reported decision in R(DLA) 2/07:

'14. The first finding of importance for this purpose was that 'he is not disruptive at school, where it is structured and safe.' That finding clearly came from the evidence given by the claimant's mother to that effect before the Tribunal (p.166 of the case papers). The claimant's mother has since confirmed its correctness (see p.195: 'He is well behaved at school due to the extreme structure and teacher/children ratio').

4.94

15. Now it is no doubt the case that while the claimant is at school there is always an adult 'watching over' him. It may be (although this is unclear) that it is the presence and active interest of a teacher which results in the claimant not being disruptive at school—i.e. that he would become disruptive if left alone there or if left unsupervised with other children. But that is in my judgment not sufficient to satisfy Reg. 12(6)(c). Limb (c) of Reg. 12(6) is in my judgment only satisfied if the constant presence of an adult is necessary in order to intervene and deal with the claimant *if and when he starts actually to become disruptive*. Giving a fair reading to Reg. 12(6)(c) in the context of Reg. 12(6) as a whole, I think the clear meaning is that the 'watching over' must be necessary in order that the person watching (or, I suppose, someone who can be summoned immediately by the person watching) can intervene when the claimant actually does become disruptive. If the structured regime of the school is of itself sufficient to prevent the claimant becoming disruptive, Reg. 12(6)(c) is in my judgment not satisfied. I reach that conclusion for three main reasons. First, that is simply how the provision strikes me. Secondly, the presence of limb (b), referring to physical restraint, before limb (c), leads naturally to the meaning that the presence must be necessary in order actually to deal with unpredictable disruptive behaviour, and not merely (by presence short of physical restraint) to avoid it. Thirdly, Reg. 12(6) can only apply if the claimant does in fact regularly require physical restraint. That means that if a particular claimant were, by supervision short of physical restraint, prevented from ever being disruptive, or from being disruptive on a regular basis, Reg. 12(6) would plainly not be satisfied.

16. The same consequence in my judgment flows from the Tribunal's findings that at home he only becomes disruptive if his mother leaves the room, or her attention is diverted away from him, or he does not get his own way. (The correctness of that finding has in my view again since been confirmed by the long letter from the claimant's mother at pages 195 to 197 of the case papers). Reg.12(6)(c), again read in the context of Reg.12(6) as a whole, requires that the claimant's disruptive behaviour is so unpredictable that another person is required to be present at all times *in order to deal with the claimant should he become disruptive*. It is not sufficient that the presence and active interest of the claimant's mother at home is sufficient to prevent disruptive behaviour occurring at all.'

32. Mr Stagg, in contrast, relied on Judge Levenson's unreported decision in *LM v Secretary of State for Work and Pensions* [2008] UKUT 24 (AAC) (also known as CDLA/2955/2006). Referring to Mr Commissioner Turnbull's discussion, in paragraph 15 of R(DLA) 7/02, of regulation 12(6)(c), Judge Levenson stated as follows (at paragraph 10):

'. . . The Commissioner held that it is not enough if the presence of an adult prevents the claimant from becoming disruptive. In my opinion this is to confuse 12(6)(b) and 12(6)(c). The point about (c) is the unpredictability, not the intervention. If there is no actual requirement to intervene then (b) is not satisfied. Thus, if a claimant is sometimes in an environment that is so well controlled that intervention is unnecessary, but at other times is in an environment where intervention is regularly required, it is still possible for the claimant to fall within section 73(3).'

33. In *Secretary of State for Work and Pensions v DM (DLA)* [2010] UKUT 318 (AAC) Judge Mark then sought to square that circle by both following paragraph 15 of R(DLA) 7/02 and recognising Judge Levenson's point in *LM v Secretary of State for Work and Pensions* that one must not confuse the requirements of regulation 12(6)(b) with those of regulation 12(6)(c). Judge Mark concluded as follows (at paragraph 10):

'10. If, however, the structured environment is such that there is no real risk of unpredictable violence or not such a risk as to make it reasonable for somebody to be present and watching over him whenever he is awake, then he cannot be said to need another person to be present and watching over him because of his unpredictable disruptive behaviour. If, in practice, he is regularly left alone in his room for lengthy periods while awake, or is not watched over at school because of his unpredictable disruptive behaviour, then that would suggest that his behaviour is not unpredictable, or at least is not unpredictable to such an extent as to require another person to be present and watching over him whenever he is awake.'

34. In *JH v Secretary of State for Work and Pensions (DLA)* [2010] UKUT 456 (AAC) Judge May QC nailed his colours firmly to the mast of R(DLA) 2/07 in preference to *LM v Secretary of State for Work and Pensions* (at paragraph 14). Similarly, in CDLA/1498/2011 Judge Turnbull, remitting an appeal for re-hearing, directed the new tribunal in the following uncompromising terms (at paragraph 10):

'10. I refer the new tribunal to what I said in paras. 15 and 16 of R(DLA) 7/02. I held that reg. 12(6)(c) is only satisfied if the constant presence of an adult is necessary in order to intervene and deal with the claimant if and when he actually starts to become disruptive, and therefore that if the structured regime of the school is of itself sufficient to prevent the claimant becoming disruptive, reg. 12(6)(c) is not satisfied. In so far as Judge Levenson departed from that in CDLA/2955/2008, I direct the new tribunal not to follow Judge Levenson's decision.'

35. However, Judge Levenson's observations in *LM v Secretary of State for Work and Pensions* received support from Judge Mesher in CDLA/2167/2010 at paragraph 13:

'. . . Although the report confirmed that U had dangerous tendencies or behaviour problems, the problems were stated mainly in terms of wandering off indoors or outdoors and eating inappropriate items, leading to a need for supervision. It was arguable that in that environment U did not require the quality of close watching over necessary to satisfy regulation 12(6)(c). That is so even if (as I tend to think is right) the approach of paragraph 10 of decision CDLA/2955/2008 (Mr Commissioner Levenson) is preferred to that in paragraph 15 of R(DLA) 7/02 (Mr Commissioner Turnbull) that if 'the structured regime of the school is of itself sufficient to prevent the claimant becoming disruptive, [regulation 12(6)(c)] is in my judgment not satisfied'. Judge Levenson's view was that that was to confuse the conditions in sub-paragraphs (b) and (c), which should be kept separate, as seems also to have been the view of Judge Mark in *Secretary of State for Work and Pensions v DM (DLA)* [2010] UKUT 318 (AAC).'

36. In sum, the case law undoubtedly reveals a divergence of views. Despite Judge Mark's valiant effort in *Secretary of State for Work and Pensions v DM (DLA)* I am not sure those authorities can be satisfactorily reconciled. This is demonstrated by the fact that in CDLA/1498/2011 (at paragraph 10) Judge Turnbull regarded Judge Mark as having adopted the same approach to regulation 12(6)(c) as he had done in R(DLA) 7/02, while in CDLA/2167/2010 Judge Mesher found support in Judge Mark's decision for the view expressed by Judge Levenson in *LM v Secretary of State for Work and Pensions*. Certainly in his recent decision in *AH v Secretary of State for Work and Pensions (DLA)* Judge Mark regarded himself as following Judge Levenson's approach (at paragraph 9).

37. Which view should the new First-tier Tribunal prefer? The principles governing precedent in the former Commissioners' jurisdiction were laid down in R(I) 12/75 (at paragraphs 19-21) and have been adapted for the new tribunal regime in *Dorset Healthcare NHS Foundation Trust v MH* [2009] UKUT 4 (AAC) (at paragraphs 36 & 37). As a general rule a First-tier Tribunal should follow a reported decision of the Upper Tribunal (or previously of the Commissioners) in preference to an unreported decision, if only because a reported decision is one that necessarily commands the general assent of the majority of relevant judges. However, that presumption does not apply if the reported decision has been carefully considered in a later unreported decision but not followed (see R 1/00 (FC)).

38. For myself I prefer what I understand to be the approach of Judges Levenson, Mesher and Mark. In my view an undue focus on labels such as 'structured regimes' or 'structured environments' runs the risk of losing sight of the plain statutory language. It also obscures the need for the tribunal's careful fact-finding. In practice there is a diverse range of 'structured environments' in both mainstream and special needs schools. What the tribunal must do in applying regulation 12(6)(c) is to start by establishing the predictability or otherwise of the extreme disruptive behaviour. At one extreme, is it solely triggered by readily identifiable factors (e.g. traffic, sudden noise or being denied access to a particular activity)? If so, it may be predictable. Or, at the other extreme, is the behaviour typically random, such that, as it was put in CDLA/2470/2006, the carers are 'in a permanent state of apprehension as to

what he will do whenever he is out of sight' (at paragraph 11). If so, it may be unpredictable. This will then require consideration of both what happens and what is reasonably required on a regular basis, and whether that amounts to requiring 'another person to be present and watching over him whenever he is awake.' Thus the nature, degree and intensity of the supervision involved all need to be examined.

39. It may be significant that on the facts of R(DLA) 7/02 the child in question attended a specialist autistic unit attached to a mainstream school. It may well be that on those facts it was always going to be difficult to meet the necessary statutory criteria. However, for the most severely disabled and vulnerable young people in some special needs schools, I would not agree with the observation in R(DLA) 7/02 that regulation 12(6)(c) is not satisfied if 'the structured regime of the school is of itself sufficient to prevent the claimant becoming disruptive' (at paragraph 15). It all depends on the nature of the type of supervision that is reasonably required."

It is clear that the question of "structured environment" will continue to give trouble to DM and to tribunals until some resolution might be made by a three judge court, but it should be arguable that if it is the very presence of a teacher or other authority figure, there, ready to intervene when necessary, that creates that structured environment then the claimant would seem to succeed in satisfying para. (6). Where the presence of another (e.g. a parent) placates the claimant without the potential for intervention then he would not.

The operation of paras (5) and (6) of this regulation and therefore also of s.73(3) of the Act has been considered again by Judge Gray in *EC (by SC) v SSWP (DLA)* [2017] UKUT 391 (AAC). The judge held that the FTT had erred in their application of para.(6)(b) because they said that the claimant should be shown to require restraint "for the majority of the time". Judge Gray said that this was not in keeping with the interpretation of Judge Wikeley in *SSWP v MG (DLA)* [2012] UKUT 429 (AAC), where he had held that "regularly" should be interpreted more generally to mean on a significant number of occasions. The judge also observed that the FTT appeared to have treated the evidence of a medical consultant as relevant to the matter of impairment of intelligence and the evidence of the claimant's teacher as relevant to social functioning. She refers to other cases (cited in the notes to this regulation) as showing that all of the evidence was relevant to both these criteria. Judge Gray found that, on the written evidence that was before her, she was able to decide the case in the claimant's favour.

Paragraphs (7) and (8) (fear and anxiety)
These paras have been inserted despite the opposition of the Social Security Advisory Committee. Their purpose is to negative the effect of certain words used, in passing, in the decision of the Tribunal of Commissioners *R(DLA) 4/01*.

4.95

That decision was chiefly concerned with the question of whether attention or supervision which qualified the claimant for care component could equally qualify him for lower rate mobility component when it consisted of supervision of outdoor walking.

The Tribunal of Commissioners held that it could, but in doing so remarked also that when a claimant had some disability (e.g. prelingual deafness) which inhibited his ability to go out alone through fear of getting lost and being unable to seek assistance, that this "fear and anxiety" should provide the causal link between that physical disability and his inability to take advantage of outdoor mobility. In his statement to Parliament the Secretary of State explains that the purpose of this amendment is to prevent that phrase from being used too widely to extend to anyone with a disability who then expresses a fear of going out alone because of that disability. Regrettably the Secretary of State did not respond to the request of SSAC for specific examples to be given to illustrate the intended operation and limits of these new paragraphs. While it is understandable that the department might wish to stem the possible flood of claims from, say, those suffering from a heart condition who might be afraid to walk out alone, it could be argued that fear and anxiety about onset of a heart condition is no less limiting than fear and anxiety of becoming lost for the prelingually deaf; and if not the deaf then what of the blind. It is generally accepted that the lower rate of mobility component was introduced to provide some benefit to claimants such as *Mallinson* who could not undertake routes unfamiliar to them because of blindness. Yet what was Mr. Mallinson's inability to walk unfamiliar routes based upon other than a fear that, if he did so, he might injure himself? To carry the effect of this amendment so far would be absurd, and the Secretary of State's statement to Parliament says clearly that there is no dispute with the conclusion reached in *R(DLA) 4/01* which did accord entitlement to three prelingually deaf claimants.

4.96   Paragraph (8) also provides a saving for those whose fear and anxiety is a symptom of mental disability and is so severe as to prevent the person from walking alone. The statement recognises that there will be difficulty in defining a line at which fear and anxiety become a severe mental disability. It seems likely that a clear medical diagnosis will be necessary.

The operation of these paragraphs has been considered in *R(DLA) 3/04* where the claimant was unable to walk outside for any distance unless she was accompanied by a member of her family who could, by giving her reassurance and encouragement, prevent her from having panic attacks. These attacks were a symptom of a severe state of anxiety and depression from which she was suffering. Commissioner Rowland allowed her appeal, finding that although her inability to walk outside clearly arose from fear and anxiety it was equally clear that, in her case, that anxiety was a symptom of her mental illness. The wording of para.(8) did not require that the mental disability should be some illness other than the anxiety itself.

These paragraphs were also considered in *CSDLA/430/2004*. There, the claimant suffered from asthma and also a chronic anxiety state that made him reluctant to walk outside alone for fear of suffering an asthma attack. Commissioner Parker, in allowing an appeal, points out that in this case there are really two separate questions to be answered. The first, (referring to para.(8)) is whether the anxiety attack was a symptom of mental illness and whether it was so severe as to prevent him walking unaccompanied. The second, and wholly separate question, (in accordance with s.73(1)(d)) was whether real asthma attacks did occur that disabled him, so as to make it necessary for him to be accompanied for the purpose of supervision for most of the time.

The decision in *SSWP v DC (DLA)* [2011] UKUT (AAC) 235 does provide an example of where these provisions have been applied. There the claimant suffered from urinary incontinence. He said that he was embarrassed by incidents that occurred when he was out so that he required his wife always to accompany him and to assist him. The judge rejected his appeal because his need for assistance arose only from "fear and anxiety" on his part.

[¹ Hospitalisation [⁵ of persons aged 18 or over] in mobility component cases

4.97   **12A.**—(1) Subject to [⁵ paragraph (3) and] regulation 12B (exemption), it shall be a condition for the receipt of a disability living allowance which is attributable to entitlement to the mobility component for any period in respect of any person that during that period he is not maintained free of charge while undergoing medical or other treatment as an in-patient—

(a) in a hospital or similar institution under [⁴ the NHS Act of 1978, the NHS Act of 2006 or the NHS (Wales) Act of 2006]; or

(b) in a hospital or other similar institution maintained or administered by the Defence Council.

(2) For the purposes of paragraph (1)(a) a person shall only be regarded

as not being maintained free of charge in a hospital or similar institution during any period when his accommodation and services are provided under[—]

[⁴ (a) section 57 of, and paragraph 14 of Schedule 7A to, the NHS Act of 1978;

(b) section 13 of, and paragraph 15 of Schedule 2 to, the NHS Act of 2006;

(c) section 28 of, and paragraph 11 of Schedule 6 to, the NHS Act of 2006;

(d) section 44(6) of, and paragraph 19(1) of Schedule 4 to, the NHS Act of 2006;

(e) section 11 of, and paragraph 15 of Schedule 2 to, the NHS (Wales) Act of 2006;

(f) section 18 of, and paragraph 19(1) of Schedule 3 to, the NHS (Wales) Act of 2006; or

(g) section 22 of, and paragraph 11 of Schedule 5 to, the NHS (Wales) Act of 2006.]

[² (2A) For the purposes of paragraph (1), a period during which a person is maintained free of charge while undergoing medical or other treatment as an in-patient shall be deemed to begin on the day after the day on which he enters a hospital or similar institution referred to in that paragraph and to end on the day [³ before the day] on which he leaves such a hospital or similar institution.]

[⁵ (3) This regulation does not apply to a person who was under the age of 18 on the day on which he entered the hospital or other similar institution referred to in paragraph (1) to begin his current period as an in-patient.]

AMENDMENTS

1. Social Security (Disability Living Allowance and Claims and Payments) Amendment Regulations 1996 (SI 1996/1436) reg.2 (July 31, 1996).

2. Social Security (Hospital In-Patients, Attendance Allowance and Disability Living Allowance) (Amendment) Regulations 1999 (SI 1999/1326) (June 7, 1999).

3. Social Security (Attendance Allowance and Disability Living Allowance) (Amendment) Regulations 2000, (SI 2000/1401) reg.3 (June 19, 2000).

4. Social Security (Attendance Allowance, Disability Living Allowance and Carer's Allowance) (Amendment) Regulations 2013 (SI 2013/389) reg.4 (April 8, 2013).

5. Social Security (Disability Living Allowance and Personal Independence Payment) (Amendment) Regulations 2016 (SI 2016/556) reg. 2 (June 29, 2016).

GENERAL NOTE

Until this regulation was introduced in 1996, the mobility component of disability living allowance, like mobility allowance before it, was payable however long the claimant was in hospital. It was only if a claimant ceased to be able to benefit at all from enhanced facilities for locomotion (see s.73(8) of the Social Security Contributions and Benefits Act 1992) that he might lose entitlement. Regs 12B and 12C set out a large number of exemptions and adjustments to the basic rule.

An argument that this regulation was ultra vires was rejected in *R. v Secretary of State for Social Security Ex p. Perry and Ex p. McGillivray* (CA, June 30, 1998). In *CDLA/1338/02* a further attack based on the argument that the regulation was contrary to the Human Rights Act 1998 was also rejected. The Commissioner held that he would not regard the right to a non-contributory benefit as a "possession" to be

4.98

protected by Art.1. Neither did he think that the withdrawal of the benefit for those in a publicly funded hospital could be regarded as discriminatory under Art.14 because decisions based upon the source of funding could not be regarded as unjustified or irrational.

The phrase "medical or other treatment as an in-patient ... in a hospital or similar institution" is used also in reg.8. Decisions relating to the meaning of those words are discussed in the notes following that regulation.

[¹ Exemption from regulation 12A

4.99

12B.—(1) Subject to paragraph (2), regulation 12A shall not apply to a person—

(a) for the first 28 days; [⁶ . . .]

(b) [⁶ . . .]

of any period throughout which he is a person to whom paragraph (10) applies.

(2) Where, on the day on which a person's entitlement to the mobility component commences, he is a person to whom paragraph (10) applies, paragraph (1) shall not apply to him for any period of consecutive days, beginning with that day, in which he continues to be a person to whom paragraph (10) applies.

(3) For the purposes of paragraphs [⁵ (1), (4), (7), (8) and (8A)], two or more distinct periods separated by an interval not exceeding 28 days, or by two or more such intervals, shall be treated as a continuous period equal in duration to the total of such distinct periods and ending on the last day of the later such period.

(4) Subject to paragraph (5) and regulation 12C, where—

(a) immediately before 31st July 1996, a person has, for a continuous period of not less than 365 days, been a person to whom paragraph (10) applies and in receipt of the mobility component and on 31st July 1996 is a person to whom that paragraph applies; or

(b) on a day not more than 28 days prior to 31st July 1996, a person has, for a continuous period of not less than 365 days, been a person to whom paragraph (10) applies and in receipt of the mobility component, and on or after 31st July 1996 and not more than 28 days after the last day of the previous distinct period during which that paragraph applies, becomes a person to whom that paragraph again applies,

regulation 12A shall not apply until such time as paragraph (10) first ceases to apply to him for more than 28 consecutive days.

(5) Paragraph (4) shall not apply where on 31st July 1996 a person is detained under Part II or III of the Mental Health Act 1983 or [⁴ Part 5, 6 or 7 or section 136 of the Mental Health (Care and Treatment) (Scotland) Act 2003 or section 52D or 52M of the Criminal Procedure (Scotland) Act 1995].

(6) Where, on a day after 31st July 1996, a person—

(a) becomes detained under Part II or III of the Mental Health Act 1983 or [⁴ Part 5, 6 or 7 or section 136 of the Mental Health (Care and Treatment) (Scotland) Act 2003 or section 52D or 52M of the Criminal Procedure (Scotland) Act 1995].; or

(b) ceases to be entitled to the mobility component,

paragraph (4) shall cease to be applicable to that person and shall not again become applicable to him.]

[⁵ (7) Subject to regulation 12C, where on 8th April 2013, paragraph (10) applies to a person and a Motability agreement entered into by or on behalf of that person is in force, regulation 12A shall, for the period following that referred to in paragraph (1)(a) [⁶ . . .], continue not to apply to that person for the period that terminates in accordance with paragraph (8).]

[⁵ (8) The period referred to in paragraph (7) terminates—
(a) on the first day after 8th April 2013 on which paragraph (10) first ceases to apply to the person for more than 28 consecutive days;
(b) in accordance with paragraph (8A); or
(c) on 8th April 2016; whichever is the earliest.]

[⁵ (8A) The period referred to in paragraph (8)(b) terminates—
(a) in the case of the hire of a vehicle—
   (i) where the vehicle is returned to the owner before the expiration of the current term of hire, on the date that the vehicle is returned to the owner;
   (ii) where the vehicle is returned to the owner at the expiration of the current term of hire, on expiry of the current term of hire;
   (iii) where the vehicle is retained with the owner's consent by or on behalf of the person after the expiration of the current term of hire, on expiry of the current term of hire;
   (iv) where the vehicle is retained otherwise than with the owner's consent by or on behalf of the person after the expiration of the current term of hire, on expiry of the current term of hire; or
   (v) where the vehicle is retained otherwise than with the owner's consent by or on behalf of the person after the date of an early termination of the current term of hire, on the date of that early termination; and
(b) in the case of a hire-purchase agreement—
   (i) on the purchase of the vehicle;
   (ii) where the vehicle is returned to the owner under the terms of the agreement before the completion of the purchase, on the date that the vehicle is returned to the owner; or
   (iii) where the vehicle is repossessed by the owner under the terms of the agreement before the completion of the purchase, on the date of repossession.]

[⁵ (8B) In paragraph (8A)(a) the "current term of hire" means the last term of hire that was agreed on or before 8th April 2013 but does not include any extension of that last term of hire after 8th April 2013.]

(9) [⁵ *omitted*]

[² (9A) Regulation 12A shall not apply in the case of a person who is residing in a hospice and is terminally ill where the Secretary has been informed that he is terminally ill—
(a) on a claim for disability living allowance;
(b) on an application for a [³ revision under section 9 of the 1998 Act or supersession under section 10 of that Act] of an award of disability living allowance; or
(c) in writing in connection with an award of, or a claim for, or an application for [³ revision under section 9 of the 1998 Act or supersession under section 10 of that Act] of an award of, disability living allowance.]

(10) This paragraph refers to a person who is undergoing medical or other treatment in a hospital or other institution in any of the circumstances referred to in regulation 12A.

(11) For the purposes of paragraph (4), receipt of mobility allowance prior to 6th April 1992 shall be treated as receipt of the mobility component.

(12) In this regulation—

[² (za) "hospice" has the same meaning as that given in paragraph (7) of regulation 10;]

(a) "motability agreement" means an agreement such as is referred to in regulation 44(1) of the Social Security (Claims and Payments) Regulations 1987 (payment of disability living allowance on behalf of a beneficiary in settlement of liability for payments under an agreement for the hire or hire-purchase of a vehicle);

(b) "Motability" means the company, set up under that name as a charity and originally incorporated under the Companies Act 1985 and subsequently incorporated by Royal Charter.]

AMENDMENTS

1. Social Security (Disability Living Allowance and Claims, and Payments) Amendment Regulations 1996 (SI 1996/1436) reg.2 (July 31, 1996).

2. Social Security (Disability Living Allowance) Amendment Regulations 1996 (SI 1996/1767) reg.2 (July 31, 1996).

3. Social Security Act 1998 (Commencement No. 11, and Savings and Consequential and Transitional Provisions) Order 1999 (SI 1999/2860) Sch.7 (October 18, 1999).

4. Mental Health (Care and Treatment) (Scotland) Act 2003 (Consequential Provisions) Order 2005 (SI 2005/2078) Sch.2, para.13 (October 5, 2005).

5. Social Security (Attendance Allowance, Disability Living Allowance and Carer's Allowance) (Amendment) Regulations 2013 (SI 2013/389) reg.4 (April 8, 2013).

6. Social Security (Disability Living Allowance and Personal Independence Payment) (Amendment) Regulations 2016 (SI 2016/556) reg. 2 (June 29, 2016).

[¹ Adjustment of benefit to certain persons exempted from regulation 12A

4.100   **12C.**—(1) Subject to paragraph (3), where a person is a person to whom regulation 12B(4) applies and the mobility component would otherwise be payable at the higher rate prescribed by regulation 4(2)(a), the benefit shall be adjusted so that it is payable at the lower rate prescribed by regulation 4(2)(b).

(2) Subject to paragraph (3), where regulation 12B(7) applies, the benefit shall be adjusted so that it is payable at a rate equal to the weekly amount payable under the relevant agreement for the period referred to in that regulation.

(3) Where paragraphs (4) and (7) of regulation 12B both apply, the benefit shall be adjusted so that it is payable either at the lower rate prescribed by regulation 4(2)(b) or at a rate equal to the weekly amount payable under the relevant agreement referred to in regulation 12B(7), whichever is the greater.]

1. Social Security (Disability Living Allowance and Claims and Payments) Amendment Regulations 1996 (SI 1996/1436) reg.2 (July 31, 1996).

Invalid Vehicle Scheme

13.—Schedule 2, which relates to the entitlement to mobility component of certain persons eligible for invalid carriages shall have effect.   4.101

SCHEDULES

SCHEDULE 1   **Regulation 3(4)**

PERSONS AGED 65 AND OVER

[¹ Revision or Supersession] of an award made before person attained 65
  1.—(1) This paragraph applies where—   4.102
   (a) a person is aged 65 or over;
   (b) the person has an award of disability living allowance made before he attained the age of 65;
   (c) an application [¹ is made in accordance with section 9 of the 1998 Act or section 10 of that Act for that award to be revised or superseded.]
   (d) an adjudicating authority is satisfied that the decision awarding disability living allowance ought to be [¹ revised or superseded].
  (2) Where paragraph (1) applies, the person to whom the award relates shall not, subject to paragraph (3), be precluded from entitlement to either component of disability living allowance solely by reason of the fact that he is aged 65 or over when the [¹ revision or supersession] is made.
  (3) Where the adjudicating authority determining the application is satisfied that the decision ought to be [¹ superseded] on the ground that there has been a relevant change of circumstances since the decision was given, paragraph (2) shall apply only where the relevant change of circumstances occurred before the person attained the age of 65.

[¹ Revision or Superssesion of an award other than a review to which paragraph 1 refers
  2.—References in the following paragraphs of this Schedule to a [¹ revision or supersession] of an award refer only to those [¹revisions or supersessions] where the awards which are being [¹ revised or superseded] were made—   4.103
   (a) on or after the date the person to whom the award relates attained the age of 65; or
   (b) before the person to whom the award relates attained the age of 65 where the award is [¹ superseded] by reference to a change in the person's circumstances which occurred on or after the day he attained the age of 65.

Age 65 and over and entitled to the care component
  3.—(1) This paragraph applies where a person on or after attaining the age of 65—   4.104
   (a) is entitled to the care component and an adjudicating authority is satisfied that the decision awarding it ought to be [¹ revised under section 9 of the 1998 Act or superseded under section 10 of that Act]; or
   (b) makes a renewal claim for disability living allowance.
  (2) Where a person was entitled on the previous award or on the award [¹ being revised or superseded] to the care component payable—
   (a) at the lowest rate, that person shall not be precluded, solely by reason of the fact that he is aged 65 or over, from entitlement to the care component; or
   (b) at the middle or highest rate, that person shall not be precluded, solely by reason of the fact that he has attained the age of 65, from entitlement to the care component payable at the middle or highest rate,
but in determining that person's entitlement, [² section 72] of the Act shall have effect as if in paragraph (a) of subsection (2) of that section for the reference to 3 months there was substituted a reference to 6 months and paragraph (b) of that subsection was omitted.

(3) In this paragraph, a renewal claim is a claim made for a disability living allowance where the person making the claim had—

    (a) within the period of 12 months immediately preceding the date the claim was made, been entitled under an earlier award to the care component or to attendance allowance (referred to in this paragraph as "the previous award"); and

    (b) attained the age of 65 before that entitlement ended.

Invalid Vehicle Scheme

4.105
    4.—(1) Where—

    (a) a certificate issued in respect of a person under section 13(1) of the Social Security (Miscellaneous Provisions) Act 1977 is in force, or

    (b) an invalid carriage or other vehicle is or was on or after January 1, 1976 made available to a person by the Secretary of State under [³ section 46(1) of the NHS Act of 1978 or paragraph 9 of Schedule 1 to the NHS Act of 2006 or paragraph 9 of Schedule 1 to the NHS (Wales) Act of 2006], being a carriage or other vehicle which is—

        (i) propelled by a petrol engine or an electric motor;

        (ii) provided for use on a public road; and

        (iii) controlled by the occupant,

that person shall not be precluded from entitlement to mobility component payable at the higher rate specified in regulation 4(2)(a), or a care component payable at the highest or middle rate specified in regulation 4(1)(a) or (b) by reason only that he has attained the age of 65.

(2) In determining a person's entitlement where paragraph (1) applies, [² section 72] of the Act shall have effect as if in paragraph (a) of subsection (2) of that section for the reference to 3 months there was substituted a reference to 6 months and paragraph (b) of that subsection was omitted.

Age 65 or over and entitled to mobility component

4.106
    5.—(1) This paragraph applies where a person on or after attaining the age of 65 is entitled to the mobility component payable at the higher rate specified in regulation 4(2)(a), and—

    (a) an adjudicating authority is satisfied that the decision giving effect to that entitlement ought to be [¹ revised under section 9 of the 1998 Act or superseded under section 10 of that Act], or

    (b) the person makes a renewal claim for disability living allowance.

(2) A person to whom this paragraph applies shall not be precluded, solely by reason of the fact that he has attained the age of 65, from entitlement to the mobility component by virtue of having satisfied or being likely to satisfy one or other of the conditions mentioned in subsection (1)(a), (b) or (c) of [² section 73] of the Act.

(3) In this paragraph and paragraph 6 and 7 a renewal claim is a claim made for a disability living allowance where the person making the claim had—

    (a) within the period of 12 months immediately preceding the date the claim was made been entitled under an earlier award to the mobility component (referred to in these paragraphs as "the previous award"); and

    (b) attained the age of 65 before that entitlement ended.

Aged 65 or over and award of lower rate mobility component

4.107
    6.—(1) This paragraph applies where a person on or after attaining the age of 65 is entitled to the mobility component payable at the lower rate specified in regulation 4(2) and—

    (a) an adjudicating authority is satisfied that the decision giving effect to that entitlement ought to be [¹ revised under section 9 of the 1998 Act or superseded under section 10 of that Act], or

    (b) the person makes a renewal claim for disability living allowance.

(2) A person to whom this paragraph applies shall not be precluded, solely by reason of the fact that he has attained the age of 65, from entitlement to the mobility component, but in determining the person's entitlement to that component [² section 73](11) of the Act shall have effect in his case as if paragraph (a), and the words "in any other case" in paragraph (b), were omitted.

Award of care component where person entitled to mobility component

4.108
    7.—(1) This paragraph applies where a person on or after attaining the age of 65 is entitled to the mobility component and—

    (a) an adjudicating authority is satisfied that the decision giving effect to that entitlement ought to be [¹ revised under section 9 of the 1998 Act or superseded under section 10 of that Act], or

(b) the person makes a renewal claim for disability living allowance.

(2) A person to whom this paragraph applies shall not be precluded solely by reason of the fact that he has attained the age of 65 from entitlement under [² section 72](1) of the Act by virtue of having satisfied either the conditions mentioned in subsection (1)(b) or in subsection (1)(c), or in both those subsections, but in determining a person's entitlement, [² section 72] of the Act shall have effect as if in paragraph (a) of subsection (2) of that section, for the reference to 3 months there was substituted a reference to 6 months and paragraph (b) of that subsection were omitted.

AMENDMENTS

1. Social Security Act 1998 (Commencement No.11, and Savings and Consequential and Transitional Provisions) Order 1999 (SI 1999/2860) Sch.7 (October 18, 1999).

2. Social Security (Disability Living Allowance) (Amendment) Regulations 1993 (SI 1993/1939) reg.2(2) (August 26, 1993).

3. Social Security (Attendance Allowance, Disability Living Allowance and Carer's Allowance) (Amendment) Regulations 2013 (SI 2013/389) reg.4 (April 8, 2013).

GENERAL NOTE

Paragraph 1

This is concerned with reviews (now revisions or supersessions) of awards which partly cover a period before the claimant's 65th birthday and partly cover a later period. On a review, entitlement in respect of the latter period is to be determined as though the claimant was under the age of 65 unless the review is on the ground of a change of circumstances which occurred on or after the claimant's 65th birthday (in which case see *para.2*). See *CSDLA/388/2000* noted after s.75 above.

4.109

The operation of para.1 of Sch.1. Is considered in some detail in *CDLA/301/05*. The claimant had been in receipt of the middle rate of DLA since before she attained the age of 65. Nine years later, and now over that age, she responded to a routine enquiry form sent out by the Secretary of State in consequence of which it was decided that her award should be superseded on the ground that it had been made under a mistake of fact; namely that she had not ever needed any care at night. The claimant appealed against this decision, but added, as well, that in the event of that appeal failing she should be entitled to, at least, the lowest rate of DLA. At her present age the claimant could not, of course, succeed on the basis of a new claim. She could succeed only if the provisions of para.1 covered her case. (The rest of that schedule being appropriate only to cases where the award that was being reviewed had been made after the age of 65.) Paragraph 1 presented two difficulties. First, the opening words of para.(1)(c), "an application is made" seem to limit the operation of the paragraph to cases where the claimant has made an application for review, and in this case the claimant had not done so. Commissioner Mesher rejected the suggestion that the enquiry form should be treated as an application. He held instead, that the words above could not be read as limiting the paragraph in the way suggested. He did this after referring to the history of the legislation, which, prior to its amendment in 1999, would not have been so limited. The amendments that were then made were expressed to be only for giving effect to the new terminology introduced by the 1998 Act, and, therefore, he reasoned, could not have been intended to make a substantive change to the claimant's rights.

The second difficulty arose because there was some doubt as to whether this claimant's need for assistance in preparing a meal (which had been accepted by the appeal tribunal) had existed before she reached the age of 65, or had developed only later.

The Secretary of State, and the appeal tribunal contended that it was only in the former case that an award could now be made under para.1. Commissioner Mesher disagreed. In his view all the elements of para.1(1) were satisfied, and para.1(3) also was satisfied, because the change of circumstances on which the review was based, was the mistake of fact made on the original application before she reached the age of 65. This left para.1(2) to operate simply as it stated i.e. that her claim should not be precluded on the ground only that she was now over the age of 65. The whole case was returned to a new tribunal for reconsideration.

Paragraph 2

4.110   This is concerned with revisions or supersessions of awards relating solely to a period no earlier than the claimant's 65th birthday or to an award beginning before that birthday but reviewed on the ground of a change of circumstances which occurred on or after that birthday. In such cases, paras 3–7 have the effect that the conditions of entitlement may be different from those applying to younger claimants and are the same as those governing certain renewal claims made at or after the age of 65.

Paragraph 3

4.111   On a revision or supersession (within para.2) or a renewal claim (within sub-para.(3)), a person of or over 65 can continue to be entitled to the care component at the same rate as before or at a higher rate. A person who was previously entitled to the highest rate but no longer satisfies both the "day" and "night" conditions can also become entitled at the middle rate. However, a person previously entitled to either the highest or the middle rate and who no longer satisfies either of the "day" or "night" conditions cannot become entitled to the component at the lowest rate and so will cease to be entitled to any care component. Furthermore, the qualifying period required of those hoping for entitlement to the component at a higher rate than before, is six months rather than three months as it would be for younger claimants. The overall effect of this paragraph is to make the conditions for entitlement to the care component the same as those for entitlement to attendance allowance under s.64 of the Social Security Contributions and Benefits Act 1992 which is the benefit which a person would be required to claim if the claim were an entirely fresh one or a repeat claim too late to be included as a renewal claim within sub-para.(3).

Paragraph 4

4.112   Former vehicle scheme beneficiaries who have attained the age of 65 are eligible for the middle or highest rates of the care component or the higher rate of the mobility component. The three-month qualifying period is increased to six months in respect of the care component but is removed altogether in the case of the mobility component. This effectively re-creates the position as it was before disability living allowance replaced attendance allowance and mobility allowance on April 6, 1992. Under s.74(1) of the Social Security Contributions and Benefits Act 1992, a person issued with a certificate under Sch.2 to these Regulations is deemed to satisfy the conditions for the mobility component at the higher rate.

Paragraph 5

4.113   On a revision or supersession (within para.2) or a renewal claim (within sub-para. (3)), a person of or over 65 previously entitled to the higher rate of the mobility component can continue to be entitled to the higher rate even if the ground of entitlement is different. However, if he or she no longer satisfies one of the conditions for entitlement to the higher rate, he or she cannot qualify for the lower rate instead. See *CDLA/754/2000* noted after s.75 above.

Paragraph 6

4.114   On a revision or supersession (within para.2) or a renewal claim (within para.5(3)), a person of or over 65 previously entitled to the lower rate of the mobility component can still be awarded the lower rate but cannot qualify for the higher rate. However, if he or she does not qualify for the lower rate on the usual ground (by satisfying the condition of s.73(1)(d) of the Social Security Contributions and Benefits Act 1992), the claimant may qualify for the lower rate by satisfying one of the conditions of s.73(1) (a), (b) or (c) which are usually the grounds for qualifying for the higher rate.

The operation of para.6 of this Schedule has been considered in *DB v SSWP (DLA)* [2016] UKUT 205 (AAC). The claimant had qualified for the care component at the middle rate and for the mobility component at the lower rate before he reached his 65th birthday. On two subsequent occasions after he had reached that age, the awards of benefit were reviewed, but the award for mobility component remained the same. The claimant had applied again for an increase in the mobility component arguing that the original award had been made under a mistake of fact because he was, even when the original award was made, unable or virtually unable to walk. The FTT had approached the case as if it were to be determined under para.1 of this Schedule. They dismissed the appeal on the ground that they were not satisfied that the claimant's condition then could be shown to have been such as to qualify. In the UT Judge Gray explains that this was in error; para.1 of the Schedule applies only to the revision or supersession of an award made before the claimant's 65th birthday. In this case two further awards had been made after that date and the present application was for supersession of the later of those awards. In this case para.1 did not apply; only para.6 could do so, and under para.6(2) an award, on whatever grounds he qualified, could only ever be made at the lower rate.

Paragraph 7

On a revision or supersession (within para.2) or a renewal claim (within para.5(3)), a person of or over 65 previously entitled to the mobility component can be awarded the care component at the higher or middle rates but the qualifying period for the care component is six months rather than the usual three months for younger claimants. Effectively, the conditions are then the same as for attendance allowance which is what a claimant of that age would claim if he or she were not entitled to the mobility component.

4.115

SCHEDULE 2 **Regulation 13**

INVALID VEHICLE SCHEME

Interpretation

1.— In this Schedule, unless the context otherwise requires,—
"the 1977 Act" means the Social Security (Miscellaneous Provisions) Act 1977;
"vehicle scheme beneficiary" means any person of a class specified in section 13(3)(a), (c) or (d) of the 1977 Act or any person of the class specified in section 13(3)(b) of the 1977 Act whose application was approved on or after 1st January 1976 and, where an invalid carriage or other vehicle was provided or as the case may be applied for, is a person of any such class in respect of whom the invalid carriage or other vehicle provided or applied for was a vehicle—
  (a) propelled by a petrol engine or by an electric motor,
  (b) supplied for use on a public road, and
  (c) to be controlled by the occupant;
"certificate" means a certificate issued in accordance with paragraph 3.

4.116

Prescribed periods for purposes of section 13(3)(c) of the 1977 Act

2.—For the purposes of section 13(3)(c) of the 1977 Act—
  (a) the prescribed period before 1 January 1976 shall be that commencing with 31st January 1970 and ending with 31st December 1975; and
  (b) the prescribed period after 1st January 1976 shall be that commencing with 2nd January 1976 and ending with 31st March 1978.

4.117

Issue of certificates

4.118   **3.**—(1) The Secretary of State shall issue a certificate in the form approved by him in respect of any person—

(a) who has made an application for a certificate in the form approved by the Secretary of State; and

(b) whom the Secretary of State considers satisfies the conditions specified in subparagraph (2).

(2) The conditions specified in this sub-paragraph are that—

(a) the person is a vehicle scheme beneficiary; and

(b) his physical condition has not improved to such an extent that he no longer satisfies the conditions which it was necessary for him to satisfy in order to become a vehicle scheme beneficiary.

Duration and cancellation of certificates

4.119   **4.**—(1) Subject to sub-paragraph (2) the period during which a certificate is in force shall commence on the day specified in the certificate as being the date on which it comes into force and shall continue for the life of the person concerned.

(2) If in any case the Secretary of State determines that the condition specified in paragraph 3(2)(b) is not satisfied, the certificate shall cease to be in force from the date of such non-satisfaction as determined by the Secretary of State (or such later date as appears to the Secretary of State to be reasonable in the circumstances).

Application of these Regulations in relation to vehicle scheme beneficiaries

4.120   **5.**—In relation to a person in respect of whom a certificate is in force these Regulations shall have effect as though regulation 2(1)(a)(iii) were omitted.

GENERAL NOTE

4.121   These provisions replace the Mobility Allowance (Vehicle Scheme Beneficiaries) Regulations 1977 (SI 1977/1229). A person issued with a certificate under this Schedule is deemed, by s.74(1) of the Social Security Contributions and Benefits Act 1992, to satisfy the condition of s.73(1)(a) so that he or she can qualify for the mobility component at the higher rate. He or she is also deemed to have satisfied that condition during the three-month qualifying period. Paragraph 1 of Sch.1 to these Regulations entitles such a person to the mobility component notwithstanding that he or she has attained the age of 65. Note that, under reg.7 of the 1977 Regulations, a person could be entitled to mobility allowance for a period *before* the date of claim for the allowance as long as it was after the certificate came into force. No equivalent provision appears in respect of the mobility component of disability living allowance.

[¹ SCHEDULE 3   **Regulation 9A(1)**

4.122   PERSONS TO WHOM REGULATIONS 9 AND 10 APPLY WITH MODIFICATIONS

[¹ . . .]

REPEAL

1. Social Security Amendment (Residential Care and Nursing Homes) Regulations 2001 (SI 2001/3767) reg.4 (April 8, 2002).

The Social Security (Invalid Care Allowance) Regulations 1976

(SI 1976/409) *(as amended)*

ARRANGEMENT OF REGULATIONS

PART I

GENERAL

1.   Citation and commencement.   4.123
2.   Interpretation.
2A.   Disapplication of section 1(1A) of the Administration Act.

PART II

MISCELLANEOUS PROVISIONS RELATING TO INVALID CARE ALLOWANCE

3.   Prescribed payments out of public funds which constitute the persons in respect of whom they are payable as severely disabled persons.
4.   Circumstances in which persons are or are not to be treated as engaged or regularly and substantially engaged in caring for severely disabled persons.
5.   Circumstances in which persons are to be regarded as receiving full-time education.
6.   Severely disabled persons prescribed for the purposes of section 70(1)(c) of the Contributions and Benefits Act.
7.   Manner of electing the person entitled to [a carer's allowance] in respect of a severely disabled person where, but for section 70(7) of the Contributions and Benefits Act, more than one person would be entitled to [a carer's allowance] in respect of that severely disabled person.
8.   Circumstances in which a person is or is not to be treated as gainfully employed.
9.   Conditions relating to residence and presence in Great Britain.
9A.   Persons residing in Great Britain to whom a relevant EU Regulation applies
9B.   Persons residing in an EEA state other than the United Kingdom or in Switzerland to whom a relevant EU Regulation applies
9C.   Refugees
10.   *Revoked.*
10A.   Women aged 65 before 28th October 1994.
11.   *Revoked.*
11A.   Men aged 65 before 28th October 1994.
12–13. *Revoked.*
14.   Application of the Social Security (General Benefit) Regulations 1982 to [carer's allowance].
15–20. *Omitted.*
21.   *Revoked.*
Schedule 1. Provisions of the Social Security (General Benefit) Regulations 1982 applied to [¹ carer's allowance].

The Secretary of State for Social Services, in exercise of the powers conferred upon her by sections 13(4), 37, 40(2), 49, 79(1), 80, 81(1), (2) and (6), 82(1),

(5) and (6), 84(1) and (2), 85(1), 86(5) and 119(3) of the Social Security Act 1975, section 36(7) of the National Insurance Act 1965, as continued in force by regulation 2(2) of the Social Security (Graduated Retirement Benefit) Regulations 1975, and of all other powers enabling her in that behalf, and after reference to the National Insurance Advisory Committee, hereby makes the following regulations:

GENERAL NOTE

4.124   Until 2003 what is now known as Carer's Allowance under s.70 of the Contributions and Benefits Act 1992, was known as Invalid Care Allowance. Despite all references to that benefit being then changed the title of these regulations (and the heading to s.70) have remained unchanged. (See Regulatory Reform (Carer's Allowance) Order (SI 2002/1457) art.2 (April 1, 2003).

PART I

GENERAL

Citation and commencement

4.125   **1.**—These regulations may be cited as the Social Security (Invalid Care Allowance) Regulations 1976 and shall come into operation on 12th April 1976.

Interpretation

4.126   **2.**—[¹ (1) In these Regulations, "the Contributions and Benefits Act" means the Social Security Contributions and Benefits Act 1992].

(2) Any reference in these regulations to any provision made by or contained in any enactment or instrument shall, except in so far as the context otherwise requires, be construed as a reference to that provision as amended or extended by any enactment or instrument and as including a reference to any provision whichmay re-enact or replace it, withor without modification.

(3) The rules for the construction of Acts of Parliament contained in the Interpretation Act 1889 shall apply for the purposes of the interpretation of these regulations as they apply for the purposes of the interpretation of an Act of Parliament.

AMENDMENT

1. Social Security (Invalid Care Allowance) Amendment Regulations 1996 (SI 1996/2744) reg.2 (November 25, 1996).

[¹ Disapplication of section 1(1A) of the Administration Act

4.127   **2A.**—Section 1(1A) of the Administration Act (requirement to state national insurance number) shall not apply—
(a) [² *omitted*];
(b) to any claim for [³ carer's allowance] made or treated as made before 9th February, 1998;
(c) to an adult dependant in respect of whom a claim for an increase of [³ carer's allowance] is made or treated as made before 5th October, 1998.]

[⁴ (d) to an adult dependant who—
    (i) is a person in respect of whom a claim for an increase of carer's allowance is made;
    (ii) is subject to immigration control within the meaning of section 115(9)(a) of the Immigration and Asylum Act 1999; and
    (iii) has not previously been allocated a national insurance number.]

AMENDMENTS

1. Social Security (National Insurance Information: Exemption) Regulations (SI 1997/2676) (December 1, 1997).
2. Social Security (Working Tax Credit and Child Tax Credit) (Consequential Amendments) (No. 2) Regulations 2003 (SI 2003/937) reg.2 (April 6, 2003).
3. Social Security Amendment (Carer's Allowance) Regulations 2002 (SI 2002/2497) reg.3 (April 1, 2003).
4. Social Security (National Insurance Number Information: Exemption) Regulations 2009 (SI 2009/471) reg.2 (April 6, 2009).

PART II

MISCELLANEOUS PROVISIONS RELATING TO INVALID CARE ALLOWANCE

Prescribed payments out of public funds which constitute the persons in respect of whom they are payable as severely disabled persons

3.—(1) For the purposes of [¹ Section 70 of the Contributions and Benefits Act] [² carer's allowance] the prescribed payments out of public funds which constitute the persons in respect of whom they are payable as severely disabled persons are—
    (a) a payment under [¹ section 104 of the Contributions and Benefits Act] (increase of disablement pension where constant attendance needed);
    (b) a payment suchas is referred to in section 7(3)(b) of the Industrial Injuries and Diseases (Old Cases) Act 1975 (increase of an allowance under that Act where the person in respect of whom that allowance is payable requires constant attendance as a result of his disablement);
    (c) a payment under regulation 44 of the Social Security (Industrial Injuries) (Benefit) Regulations 1975 in respect of the need of constant attendance;
    (d) a payment by way of an allowance in respect of constant attendance on account of disablement for which a person is in receipt of a war disablement pension,
being a payment the weekly rate of which is not less than the amount specified in [¹ paragraph 7(a) of Part V of Schedule 4 to the Contributions and Benefits Act].
(2) For the purposes of paragraph (1)(d) of this regulation "war disablement pension" means—
    (a) retired pay, pension or allowance granted in respect of disablement under powers conferred by or under the Ministry of Pensions Act 1916, the Air Force (Constitution) Act 1917, the Personal Injuries (Emergency Provisions) Act 1939, the Pensions (Navy, Army, Air Force and Mercantile Marine) Act 1939, the Polish Resettlement Act

4.128

1947, the Home Guard Act 1951 or the Ulster Defence Regiment Act 1969,

(b) any retired pay or pension to which section 365(1) of the Income and Corporation Taxes Act 1970 applies, not being retired pay, pension or allowance to which sub-paragraph (a) of this paragraphapplies; or

(c) any payment which the Secretary of State has certified can be accepted as being analogous to any suchretired pay, pension or allowance as is referred to in sub-paragraph (a) or (b) of this paragraph.

AMENDMENTS

1. Social Security (Invalid Care Allowance) Amendment Regulations 1996 (SI 1996/2744) reg.2 (November 25, 1996).

2. Social Security Amendment (Carer's Allowance) Regulations 2002 (SI 2002/2497) reg.3 (April 1, 2003).

Circumstances in which persons are or are not to be treated as engaged or regularly and substantially engaged in caring for severely disabled persons

4.129

4.—(1) [¹ Subject to paragraph (1A) of this regulation,] a person shall be treated as engaged and as regularly and substantially engaged in caring, for a severely disabled person on every day in a week if, and shall not be treated as engaged or regularly and substantially engaged in caring for a severely disabled person on any day in a week unless, as at that week he is, or is likely to be, engaged and regularly engaged for at least 35 hours a week in caring for that severely disabled person.

[¹ (1A) A person who is caring for two or more severely disabled persons in a week shall be treated as engaged and regularly and substantially engaged in caring for a severely disabled person only where he is engaged and regularly engaged for at least 35 hours in that week in caring for any one severely disabled person, considered without reference to any other severely disabled person for whom he is caring.]

(2) A week in respect of which a person fails to satisfy the requirements of paragraph (1) of this regulation shall be treated as a week in respect of which that person satisfies those requirements if he establishes—

(a) that he has only temporarily ceased to satisfy them; and

(b) that (disregarding the provisions of this sub-paragraph) he has satisfied them for at least 14 weeks in the period of 26 weeks ending with that week and would have satisfied them for at least 22 weeks in that period but for the fact that either he or the severely disabled person for whom he has been caring was undergoing medical or other treatment as an inpatient in a hospital or similar institution.

AMENDMENT

1. Social Security (Invalid Care Allowance) Amendment (No.2) Regulations 1993 (SI 1993/1851) reg.2 (August 17, 1993).

GENERAL NOTE

Paragraph (1)

4.130

A person is entitled to benefit in respect of "any day" on which he is caring, etc. for his patient (see s.70(1) SSCBA 1992). This regulation, however, has the effect of shifting the entitlement to the basis of a week by providing that every day in the week will qualify where the 35-hour test is satisfied, and that no day in the week will qualify where it is not (except under para.(2) below). This is much more administratively convenient.

The decision in *R(G) 3/91* confirms that the hours must be counted in respect of each week and cannot be averaged over a period of weeks to satisfy the 35 hour rule.

Note that for Carer's Allowance a week is defined in s.122 as a period from Sunday to Saturday—this may affect a claimant who cares only on alternate week-ends.

A person qualifies for benefit where "he is, or is likely to be, engaged and regularly engaged" in caring for a patient for at least 35 hours per week. There are several difficulties in this phrase but none of them seem to have caused problems. It may be easy to determine that a person "is engaged . . . in caring," but it is not clear what is meant by "is likely to be . . . engaged". The words are probably intended to be prospective so that the benefit can be awarded for a forward period, but they might extend to cover an unexpected temporary absence by the claimant. If the absence is short and no more in total than four weeks in six months the matter would be covered by para.(2) below, but if those weeks have already been consumed or allocated to a "holiday" period, there may be an argument for saying that an unexpected absence due to, say, illness, continues to satisfy para.(1) as being a week in which the claimant had been "likely to be" caring.

Nor does the definition tell us anything about what is meant by "regularly engaged". It is probably sufficient if the care arrangement is intended to be for a reasonable period. It might preclude, for example, someone who is on unpaid holiday from his job, or a student in his vacation.

The activities of the claimant that can be regarded as caring and consequently can satisfy the 35-hour test of caring are considered in two unreported Commissioners' decisions: *CG/012/1991* and *CG/006/1990*. See the discussion of these decisions at s.70 of the Act.

Paragraph (1A)

This amendment reverses (from August 1993) the effect of an unreported Commissioners' decision that permitted a claimant to aggregate the hours spent in looking after more than one patient to satisfy the total of 35 hours per week. In that case the claimant was the mother of two severely disabled sons neither of whom could stay at home for a full week, but the claimant could look after each of them separately, for part of the week—in some weeks their combined time at home amounted to more than 35 hours per week. This paragraph now precludes such an arrangement. The only scheme now possible would involve each son staying at home for 35 hours (if that were possible) in alternate weeks. A system of care every other week, if consistent, should still be regarded as "regular".

4.131

Paragraph (2)

A break in the provision of care is disregarded so long as the break is temporary and so long as it has lasted, or a series of breaks has totalled, no more than four weeks in the past 26 weeks (or 12 weeks in the past 26 if the patient or the claimant has spent at least eight of those weeks in hospital for treatment). In effect the claimant can enjoy a break or "holiday" from his caring of up to four weeks in every six months. Benefit will continue to be payable for the weeks of holiday, but if the claimant continues to receive the benefit himself, it cannot be paid as well to any person who provides substitute care during that period. (See s.70(7) of the Act.)

4.132

The decision in *Secretary of State for Work and Pensions v Pridding,* [2002] EWCA Civ 306, CA, reported as *R(G) 1/02* limits the effect of this regulation. It does not extend entitlement where the person cared for, has entered hospital beyond the four week period for which that person will be entitled to their own benefits.

Circumstances in which persons are to be regarded as receiving full-time education

4.133   [¹ **5.**—(1) For the purposes of [² section 70(3) of the Contributions and Benefits Act] a person shall be treated as receiving full-time education for any period during which he attends a course of education at a university, college, school or other educational establishment for twenty-one hours or more a week.

(2) In calculating the hours of attendance under paragraph (1) of this regulation—

(a) there shall be included the time spent receiving instruction or tuition, undertaking supervised study, examination or practical work or taking part in any exercise, experiment or project for which provision is made in the curriculum of the course; and

(b) there shall be excluded any time occupied by meal breaks or spent on unsupervised study, whether undertaken on or off the premises of the educational establishment.

(3) In determining the duration of a period of full-time education under paragraph (1) of this regulation, a person who has started on a course of education shall be treated as attending it for the usual number of hours per week throughout any vacation or any temporary interruption of his attendance until the end of the course or such earlier date as he abandons it or is dismissed from it.]

AMENDMENTS

1. Social Security (Invalid Care Allowance) Amendment Regulations 1992 (SI 1992/470).

2. Social Security (Invalid Care Allowance) Amendment Regulations 1996 (SI 1996/2744) reg.2 (November 25, 1996).

GENERAL NOTE

4.134   The meaning of "full-time education" has been thoroughly explored by the Court of Appeal in *Secretary of State for Work and Pensions v Deane* [2010] EWCA Civ 699, (AAC), [2010] AACR 42. The court began by holding that the definition of full-time education in reg.5 is not an exhaustive one. This approach had been suggested by Judge Mesher, but was one not open to him, he felt, by reason of earlier precedents in the Court of Appeal. In this case however, the court held that they were not bound by those earlier decisions—that of *Wright-Turner* (CA of NI) [2002] CARC 3567, because the point appeared to have been conceded and in any case did not then form a part of the narrower basis of that decision, and that of *Flemming v Secretary of State for Work and Pensions* [2002] EWCA Civ 641, because, even if it had been accepted, it did not form a part of the decision. The court in the present case contrasted the wording of regs 4 and 8, in both of which the regulation expressly defines what is, and what is not, to be regarded as a part of that definition, with the wording of reg.5 which refers only to what is to be regarded as "full-time education". What this means is that the definition of full-time education by reference to attending a course for 21 or more hours per week is only a partial definition; there may be also be courses of a lesser period which are full-time education. This would have been enough to dispose of the case, because in the view of all the judges who have been involved in these cases, a normal three-year undergraduate degree course (which is what the claimant had been enrolled on) should be full-time education for the purposes of a claim to Carer's Allowance. However, they went on to hold, as well, that the proper approach to the assessment of hours of attendance was by reference to the expectation of the educational establishment rather than the actual hours worked by the student.

This should resolve most difficulties in relation to university courses, though the court did accept that there may still be difficult cases in relation to colleges and in cases where exemptions from course requirements have been made.

The case of an atypical student who had been granted exemption from parts of the course was considered in *CG/3189/2004*. There the case was referred to a fresh tribunal for re-consideration of the information provided by the university (and perhaps provided again more exactly for that particular student).

The *Deane* case has already been applied in *SSWP v PW* [2011] UKUT 3 (AAC). There the claimant was a 17-year-old carer who was taking a course provided as a preparation for employment. She attended classes for 18 hours per week, which was confirmed by the course provider upon enquiry by the DWP, but the provider also asserted that the course was a full-time course. Judge Ward held that the First-tier Tribunal were perfectly entitled to find on the basis of the evidence before them that the course was a part-time course; the assertion of the provider was not conclusive (and *Deane*'s case did not suggest that it should be), but must be considered as a part of all the evidence before the tribunal. In this case the provider also asserted that the course included periods of placement in work. On the evidence it appeared unlikely that the placements were properly to be regarded as a part of the course, but even if they had been, they would not have increased the attendance hours beyond 21 taking the time spent on placements as spread across the whole period of the course. Nor should the course, taken as a whole, be regarded as full-time applying the reasoning in *Deane* that a course might be full-time under s.70 without reference to the partial definition in reg.5. This was a very different case from that of a normal undergraduate course at a university (as in *Deane*) where a tribunal might properly take judicial notice that a claimant was on a full-time course.

The same judge considered such a case in *SSWP v ZC* [2011] UKUT 2 (AAC); [2011] AACR 28. The claimant had completed studies for a BTEC qualification and then commenced a degree course in a related field. She argued that because of her prior courses and the grades that she had obtained in them, she could undertake the degree course by devoting fewer hours to study than the university said that it would require. The First-tier Tribunal had allowed her appeal against refusal of benefit by applying the test in reg.5. They accepted her evidence that she needed to study only 20 hours per week to pass the course. Judge Ward allowed an appeal. Applying what, by this time, had become the correct approach in *Deane*, he concluded that in this case the description given by the university of what they regarded as a full-time course must also lead to that conclusion under the words of s.70(3). The judgment is notable also for the examination of the way in which reg.5 should be applied although, in reaching his decision, the judge does so under s.70.

In *SM v SSWP (CA)* [2016] UKUT 406 (AAC) Judge Mitchell had to decide if a student who had entered upon a course of study, but then had a one year deferral of the course by agreement with the university that she was attending, should be regarded as undertaking a "temporary interruption" of the course within the meaning of para.(3) of this regulation. The year of deferral was taken in order to care for her disabled son. Before the UT the Department's representative accepted that the year of deferral was not within the meaning of the phrase "temporary interruption" as used here and the Judge agreed. In doing so he refers to an equivalent provision (though worded differently) in the rules relating to means tested benefits where the Court of Appeal had held that a student on an intercalated year would qualify for benefit. Treating this deferred year in a similar way was possible if the word "temporary" was given the colloquial meaning of relatively short, rather than the more literal meaning of not permanent. On that basis a break in the course of a whole year was not temporary.

4.135

Severely disabled persons prescribed for the purposes of [² section 70(1)(c) of the Contributions and Benefits Act]

4.136

[¹ **6.**—For the purposes of [² section 70(1)(c) of the Contributions and Benefits Act] (condition of entitlement to [³ a carer's allowance] that the severely disabled person is either such relative of the person caring for him as may be prescribed or a person of any such other description as may be prescribed) where a severely disabled person is being cared for by another person, that disabled person shall be a prescribed person for the purposes of that section, whether he is related to the person caring for him or not.]

AMENDMENTS

1. Social Security (Invalid Care Allowance) Amendment Regulations 1981 (SI 1981/655).
2. Social Security (Invalid Care Allowance) Amendment Regulations 1996 (SI 1996/2744) reg.2 (November 25, 1996).
3. Social Security Amendment (Carer's Allowance) Regulations 2002 (SI 2002/2497) reg.3 (April 1, 2003).

Manner of electing the person entitled to [¹ a carer's allowance] in respect of a severely disabled person where, but for [² section 70(7) of the Contributions and Benefits Act], more than one person would be entitled to [¹ a carer's allowance] in respect of that severely disabled person

4.137

7.—(1) For the purposes of the provision in [² section 70(7) of the Contributions and Benefits Act] which provides that where, apart from that section, two or more persons would [³ have a relevant entitlement for the same day] in respect of the same severely disabled person one of them only [³ shall have that entitlement], being such one of them as they may jointly elect in the prescribed manner, an election shall be made by giving the Secretary of State a notice in writing signed by the persons who but for the said provision would [³ have a relevant entitlement] in respect of the same severely disabled person specifying one of them as the person [³ to have that entitlement].

(2) An election under paragraph (1) of this regulation shall not be effective to confer [³ a relevant entitlement] either for the day on which the election is made or for any earlier day if such day is one for which [³ a carer's allowance or the care element of universal credit] has been paid in respect of the severely disabled person in question and has not been repaid or recovered.

[³ (3) In paragraph (2) "the carer element of universal credit" means an amount included in an award of universal credit in respect of the fact that a person has regular and substantial caring responsibilities for a severely disabled person.]

AMENDMENTS

1. Social Security Amendment (Carer's Allowance) Regulations 2002 (SI 2002/2497) reg.3 (April 1, 2003).
2. Social Security (Invalid Care Allowance) Amendment Regulations 1996 (SI 1996/2744), reg.2 (November 25, 1996).
3. Universal Credit and Miscellaneous Amendment Regulations (SI 2015/1754) reg.12 (November 5, 2015).

Circumstances in which a person is or is not to be treated as gainfully employed

8.—(1) For the purposes of [³ section 70(1)(b) of the Contributions and Benefits Act] (condition of a person being entitled to [² a carer's allowance] for any day that he is not gainfully employed) a person shall not be treated as gainfully employed on any day in a week unless his earnings in the immediately preceding week have exceeded [⁴ [⁵ £123]] and, subject to paragraph (2) of this regulation, shall be treated as gainfully employed on every day in a week if his earnings in the immediately preceding week have exceeded [⁵ £123].

4.138

(2) There shall be disregarded for the purposes of paragraph (1) above a person's earnings—

(a) for any week which under paragraph (2) of regulation 4 of these regulations is treated as a week in which that person satisfies the requirements of paragraph (1) of that regulation;

(b) [³ . . .]

(c) [¹ . . .]

(3) *Revoked.*

AMENDMENTS

1. Social Security (Invalid Care Allowance) Amendment Regulations 1996 (SI 1996/2744) reg.2 (November 25, 1996 with saving under reg.3).

2. Social Security Amendment (Carer's Allowance) Regulations 2002 (SI 2002/2497) reg.3 (April 1, 2003).

3. Social Security (Invalid Care Allowance) Amendment Regulations 1995 (SI 1995/2935) reg.2 (December 12, 1995 with saving under reg.3).

4. Social Security (Invalid Care Allowance) (Amendment) Regulations 2018 (SI 2018/280) reg.2 (April 9, 2018).

5. Social Security Benefits Up-rating Regulations 2019 (SI 2019/552) reg.4 (April 8, 2019).

GENERAL NOTE

Paragraph (1)

Earnings include remuneration or profit from either employment or self-employment. See s.3 of the Act and definition of "employment" in s.122.

4.139

For the method of calculating earnings see Computation of Earnings Regulations.

In *CG/734/2003*, and again in *CG/4018/2005* it has been confirmed that those regulations do properly apply to the calculation of earnings for the purpose of the benefit, despite the doubts that had been expressed earlier in *CG/6329/1997*, on which see the 2005 edition of this work.

Note the observations of the Commissioner in *CG/607/2008*. Whereas most social security benefits (and most taxes) provide for a taper in respect of earnings that exceed an earnings limit, there is no such thing for Carer's Allowance; earnings that are a penny over the limit result in the total loss of benefit. In this case the claimant had taken part-time work for a charity working with the disabled. She was employed for 10 hours per week at an hourly rate calculated so that her earnings would exactly match the earnings limit currently in force. Such a carefully constructed and informed work plan should not have resulted in difficulties, but a complication arose from the fact that although the wages had been expressed to be a weekly sum, for the convenience of the employer, they were, in fact, paid monthly. Because the regulations define benefit weeks for Carer's Allowance as being each week beginning on a Monday, and because some calendar months contain five Mondays rather than four, this meant that in those months her earnings, if spread over a calendar month,

4.140

exceeded the weekly earnings limit. As this was discovered only after five years it meant that the claimant was faced with a substantial claim for overpayment. The complexity of the Computation of Earnings Regulations resulted in four different decisions, and four different overpayment claims, by the DM, together with a different calculation by the appeal tribunal (which had allowed her appeal) and yet another by her representative before the commissioner. The Commissioner came to the rescue of all of them. He suggested going back to basics. This meant examining the definitions of the concepts that are used in the regulations. From this it emerged that earnings should be the sums payable under the claimant's contract of employment. Although the contract was oral, it was clear both from the parties' intentions, and from their consistent pattern of behaviour over almost all of the five years, that her wages were to be earned weekly even though they may have been paid monthly. This meant that the correct attribution of earnings was on a weekly basis, not monthly. There were a few weeks early in the arrangement when the claimant had worked extra hours and therefore had exceeded the earnings limit, but for the most part she had remained within that limit and, therefore, her overpayment was minimal.

Another example of the all-or-nothing character of Carer's Allowance is *SJ v SSWP* [2009] UKUT 37 (AAC); *R(G) 1/09* where Judge Bano had to consider the effect of PAYE income tax liability on the claimant's earnings. The claimant was not liable to pay tax on her earnings, which were just above the earnings limit for the allowance, but, had she been in receipt of the allowance, she would then have been liable for income tax and that liability, if collected through PAYE, would have reduced her earnings to below the earnings limit, and she would then have been entitled to the allowance. This looks like a classic "Catch 22". But the refusal of benefit was correct. It is clear that Carer's Allowance is a taxable benefit (see Table A of the Income Tax (Earnings and Pensions) Act 1992) and it is also clear that the tax could, and normally would, be collected through the PAYE system, but to qualify for benefit, in the first place, the claimant must have earnings below the earnings limit, and that must be determined before the benefit is paid, not afterwards.

Paragraph (2)

4.141   This exempts from the earnings limit any week in which the claimant is on "holiday" from his patient. Para.(b) which exempted an employee absent from work with the consent of his employer was revoked with effect from December 12, 1995. Para.(c) which exempted earnings from the week preceding the first week of claim was revoked with effect from November 25, 1996. In bothcases there is a saving provision in respect of continuous claims commencing before those dates.

Conditions relating to residence and presence in Great Britain

4.142   **9.**—(1) Subject to the following provisions of this regulation[⁹ and regulations [¹⁰ 9A, 9B and 9C]], the prescribed conditions for the purposes of [¹ section 70(4) of the Contributions and Benefits Act] (person not to be entitled to [² a carer's allowance] unless he satisfies prescribed conditions as to residence or presence in Great Britain) in relation to any person in respect of any day shall be—

(a) that he is [⁹ habitually] resident in [⁹ the United Kingdom, the Republic of Ireland, the Isle of Man or the Channel Islands]; and

[³ (ia) he is not a person subject to immigration control within the meaning of section 115(9) of the Immigration and Asylum Act 1999 or section 115 of that Act does not apply to him for the purposes of entitlement to [² a carer's allowance] by virtue of regulation 2 of the Social Security (Immigration and Asylum) Consequential Amendments Regulations 2000, and]

(b) that he is present in Great Britain; and
(c) that he has been present in Great Britain for a period of, or periods amounting in the aggregate to, not less than [⁹ 104] weeks in the [⁹ 156 weeks] immediately preceding that day.

[⁴ (1A) [³ *omitted*]]

(2) For the purposes of paragraph (1)(b) and (c) of this regulation, a person who is absent from Great Britain on any day shall be treated as being present in Great Britain—

(a) if his absence is, and when it began was, for a temporary purpose and has not lasted for a continuous period exceeding 4 weeks; or

[⁹ (b) if his absence is temporary and for the specific purpose of caring for the severely disabled person who is also absent from Great Britain and where any of the following is payable in respect of that disabled person for that day—

   (i) attendance allowance;
   (ii) the care component of disability living allowance at the highest or middle rate prescribed in accordance with section 72(3) of the Contributions and Benefits Act;
   (iii) the daily living component of personal independence payment at the standard or enhanced rate prescribed in accordance with section 78(3) of the Welfare Reform Act 2012; or
   (iv) a payment specified in regulation 3(1) of these Regulations.]

[⁹ (3) Notwithstanding that on any day a person is absent from Great Britain, he shall be treated as though he were—

(a) habitually resident and present in Great Britain for the purposes of paragraphs (1)(a) to (c) if—

   (i) his absence is by reason only of the fact that on that day he is abroad in his capacity as a serving member of the forces and for this purpose "serving member of the forces" has the meaning given in regulation 1(2) of the Social Security (Contributions) Regulations 2001 ("the 2001 Regulations"); or
   (ii) he is living with a person mentioned in sub-paragraph (a)(i) and is the spouse, civil partner, son, daughter, step-son, step-daughter, father, father-in-law, step-father, mother, mother-in-law or step-mother of that person; and

(b) present in Great Britain for the purposes of paragraph (1)(b) and (c) if his absence is by reason only of the fact that on that day he is—

   (i) abroad in his capacity as an airman within the meaning of regulation 111 of the 2001 Regulations or a mariner within the meaning of regulation 115 of those Regulations; or
   (ii) in prescribed employment in connection with continental shelf operations within the meaning of regulation 114(1) of those Regulations.]

(a) he is abroad in his capacity as—

   (i) a serving member of the forces within the meaning of the definition of "serving member of the forces" in regulation 1(2) of the Social Security (Contributions) Regulations 1975, as amended, or
   (ii) an airman or mariner within the meaning of regulation 72 and regulation 77 respectively of those Regulations; or

(b) he is in prescribed employment in connection with continental shelf operations within the meaning of regulation 76 of those Regulations; or

(c) he is living with a person mentioned in sub-paragraph (a)(i) and is the spouse, [⁷ civil partner] son, daughter, father, father-in-law, mother or mother-in-law of that person.]

AMENDMENTS

1. Social Security (Invalid Care Allowance) Amendment Regulations 1996 (SI 1996/2744) reg.2 (November 25, 1996).

2. Social Security Amendment (Carer's Allowance) Regulations 2002 (SI 2002/2497) reg.4 (April 1, 2003).

3. Social Security (Miscellaneous Amendments) Regulations 1998 (SI 1998/563) reg.18(1) (April 6, 1998).

4. Social Security (Persons From Abroad) Miscellaneous Amendments Regulations 1996 (SI 1996/30) reg.9 (February 5, 1996, subject to a saving under reg.12(3)).

5. Disability Living Allowance and Disability Working Allowance Regulations 1991 (SI 1991/2742) reg.3 (April 6, 1992).

6. Social Security (Child Benefit Consequential) Regulations 1977 (SI 1977/342) reg.18 (April 4, 1977).

7. Civil Partnership (Pensions, Social Security and Child Support) (Consequential, etc. Provisions) Order 2005 (SI 2005/2877) (December 5, 2005).

8. Personal Independence Payment (Supplementary and Consequential Amendments) Regulations 2013 (SI 2013/388) Sch.1 para.9 (April 8, 2013).

9. Social Security (Attendance Allowance, Disability living Allowance and Carer's Allowance) (Amendment) Regulations 2013 (SI 2013/389) reg.2 (April 8, 2013).

10. Social Security (Miscellaneous amendment No.4) Regulations 2017 (SI 2017/1015) reg.2(3) (November 16, 2017).

GENERAL NOTE

4.143   Until April 8, 2013 a claimant need only have shown that they were "ordinarily resident" and there is a saving for existing claims made on that basis. Neither "ordinary" nor "habitual" residence is defined in the statute or regulations. Ordinary residence has usually been taken to mean that you have a settled intention to live in the country (technically now the "common travel area") as your home, but, not necessarily, permanently. Habitual residence, which is intended to be a more stringent test, requires as well that that the claimant has been in the country already for an extended period. How long, will depend upon the circumstances of the claimant; a former resident returning from a period abroad may satisfy this test almost immediately, while a new immigrant may be required to demonstrate a considerable period of residence. The meaning of "habitual residence" has been the subject of extensive case law in relation to claims for means-tested benefits where it has applied for some time. Readers are referred to the notes to relevant sections of Vol. II of this Work.

In *MM and SI v SSWP (DLA)* [2016] UKUT 149 (AAC) Judge Markus QC has held that reg.2(1)(a)(iii) of the DLA regulations, the equivalent of reg.9(1)(c) of these regulations (the past presence test or PPT) must be disapplied in respect of claims made on behalf of applicants who were family members of persons granted refugee status in the UK. She held that the PPT was indirectly discriminatory and could not be justified (when compared to the treatment of UK nationals) under art.28 of the EU Directive 2004/8 3/EC (which gives protection to refugees) and which she held had direct effect in the UK. For the same reason she held that PPT was in breach of the claimant's rights under art.14 of the ECHR. At the time the claims were made the applicants satisfied the other conditions of reg.2 which meant that their claims should proceed accordingly. That was a decision in respect of a claim to DLA but the ruling will apply equally to a claim for carer's allowance.

For questions that involve persons either coming from or going to another country that is a part of the European Union (or to Switzerland) reference should be made to the relevant sections of Vol.III of this Work.

Paragraph (2)

A person is regarded as being still present in Great Britain for up to four weeks of temporary absence, or for longer periods if he is abroad caring for his patient who continues to receive the attendance benefit. The four-week period ties in with the period for a break in caring under reg.4 above. 4.144

Paragraph (3)

A person is also regarded as present in Great Britain if his absence is for one of the specified reasons, though if the absence is for more than four weeks it would be necessary for the claimant to continue caring for his patient. 4.145

[¹Persons residing in Great Britain to whom a relevant EU Regulation applies

9A.—(1) Regulation 9(1)(c) shall not apply where on any day— 4.146
(a) the person is habitually resident in Great Britain;
(b) a relevant EU Regulation applies; and
(c) the person can demonstrate a genuine and sufficient link to the United Kingdom social security system.
(2) For the purposes of paragraph (1)(b) and regulation 9B, "relevant EU Regulation" has the meaning given by section 84(2) of the Welfare Reform Act 2012.]

AMENDMENT

1. Social Security (Attendance Allowance, Disability living Allowance and Carer's Allowance) (Amendment) Regulations 2013 (SI 2013/389) reg.2 (April 8, 2013).

GENERAL NOTE

The relevant regulations referred to are (EC) No.1408/71 and (EC) No.883/2004. For detailed discussion see Vol.III of this Work. 4.147

[¹Persons residing in an EEA state other than the United Kingdom or in Switzerland to whom a relevant EU Regulation applies

9B.—Regulation 9(1)(a) to (c) shall not apply where on any day— 4.148
(a) the person is habitually resident in—
  (i) an EEA state other than the United Kingdom; or
  (ii) Switzerland;
(b) a relevant EU Regulation applies; and
(c) the person can demonstrate a genuine and sufficient link to the UK social security system]

AMENDMENT

1. Social Security (Attendance Allowance, Disability living Allowance and Carer's Allowance) (Amendment) Regulations 2013 (SI 2013/389) reg.2 (April 8, 2013).

GENERAL NOTE

The relevant regulations referred to are (EC) No.1408/71 and (EC) No.883/2004. For detailed discussion see Vol.III of this Work. The aggregation of periods of residence in another EU country has been considered by Judge Jacobs in *BK v* 4.149

SSWP and SSWP v MM [2016] UKUT 547 (AAC). Relying on the case of *Stewart v SSWP* (C-503/09) the Judge held that mere residence in this country was not sufficient to aggregate that time with time spent in another EU country, but neither was it necessary to show a link with this country's social security system. This decision may be subject to appeal. For further detail see Vol.III of this work.

[¹ Refugees

4.150   **9C.**—(1) Regulation 9(1)(c) shall not apply where the person has—

(a) been granted refugee status or humanitarian protection under the immigration rules; or

(b) leave to enter or remain in the United Kingdom as the dependant of a person granted refugee status or humanitarian protection under the immigration rules.

(2) For the purposes of this regulation "immigration rules" means the rules laid before Parliament under section 3(2) of the Immigration Act 1971.]

AMENDMENT

1. Social Security (Miscellaneous Amendments No.4) Regulations 2017 (SI 2017/1015) reg.2(3) (November 16, 2017).

Circumstances in which a person over [¹ the age of 65] is to be treated as having been entitled to invalid care allowance immediately before attaining that age

4.151   **10.**—[¹ *Revoked.*]

AMENDMENT

1. Social Security Amendment (Carer's Allowance) Regulations 2002 (SI 2002/2497) reg.3 (October 28, 2002).

[¹Women aged 65 before 28th October 1994

4.152   **10A.**—A woman shall be entitled to [² a carer's allowance] if—

(a) she attained the age of 65 before 28th October 1994;

(b) immediately before attaining the age of 65 she would have satisfied the requirements for entitlement to [² a carer's allowance], whether or not she made a claim, but for the condition, which applied prior to 28th October 1994, in section 70(5) of the Contributions and Benefits Act (exclusion of persons who had attained pensionable age and had not been entitled to that allowance immediately before attaining that age); and

(c) she satisfies the requirements for entitlement to [² a carer's allowance] apart from the conditions in section 70(1)(a) and (b) [³ . . .] of the Contributions and Benefits Act.]

AMENDMENTS

1. Social Security (Severe Disablement Allowance and Invalid Care Allowance) Amendment Regulations 1994 (SI 1994/2556) reg.5 (October 28, 1994).

2. Social Security Amendment (Carer's Allowance) Regulations 2002 (SI 2002/2497) reg.3 (April 1, 2003).

3. Social Security Amendment (Carer's Allowance) Regulations 2002 (SI 2002/2497) reg.3 (October 28, 2002).

Invalid care allowance for persons over [¹the age of 65]

11.—[*Revoked.*]

4.153

AMENDMENT

1. Social Security Amendment (Carer's Allowance) Regulations 2002 (SI 2002/2497) reg.3 (October 28, 2002).

[¹Men aged 65 before 28th October 1994

11A.—A man who—

4.154

(a) attained the age of 65 before 28th October 1994; and

(b) was entitled to [² a carer's allowance] immediately before he attained that age,

shall be entitled to that allowance notwithstanding that, after he attained that age, he was not caring for a severely disabled person or no longer satisfied the requirements of section 70(1)(a) or (b) of the Contributions and Benefits Act, if he satisfies the other requirements for entitlement to that allowance.]

AMENDMENTS

1. Social Security (Severe Disablement Allowance and Invalid Care Allowance) Amendment Regulations 1994 (SI 1994/2556), reg.5 (October 28, 1994).

2. Social Security Amendment (Carer's Allowance) Regulations 2002 (SI 2002/2497) reg.3 (April 1, 2003).

Regulations 12 and 13 revoked.

4.155

Application of the Social Security (General Benefit) Regulations 1982 to [¹ carer's allowance]

14.—The provisions of the Social Security (General Benefit) Regulations 1982, specified in column (1) of Schedule 1 to these regulations, the subject matter of which is described in column (2) of that Sch., shall, with any necessary modifications, apply to [¹ carer's allowance] as they apply to incapacity benefit.

4.156

AMENDMENT

1. Social Security Amendment (Carer's Allowance) Regulations 2002 (SI 2002/2497) reg.3 (April 1, 2003).

Regulations 15–20 omitted.

4.157

Regulation 21 revoked.

4.158

SCHEDULE 1   **Regulation 14**

PROVISIONS OF THE SOCIAL SECURITY (GENERAL BENEFIT) REGULATIONS 1982 APPLIED TO [¹ CARER'S ALLOWANCE]

4.159

Regulation applied (1)	Subject matter (2)
2	Exceptions from disqualification for imprisonment, etc.
3	Suspension of payment of benefit during imprisonment, etc.
4	Interim payments by way of benefit under the Act
9	Payment of benefit and suspension of payments pending a decision on appeals or references, arrears and repayments.

AMENDMENT

1. Social Security Amendment (Carer's Allowance) Regulations 2002 (SI 2002/2497) reg.3 (April 1, 2003).

The Social Security (Severe Disablement Allowance) Regulations 1984

(SI 1984/1303) *(as amended)*

4.160   For text of, and commentary on, these Regulations, see the 2005 edition of this volume.

The Social Security (Personal Independence Payment) Regulations 2013

(SI 2013/377) *(as amended)*

PART 1

GENERAL

4.161   1.   Citation and commencement
         2.   Interpretation

PART 2

PERSONAL INDEPENDENCE PAYMENT ASSESSMENT

4.162   3.   Daily living activities and mobility activities
         4.   Assessment of ability to carry out activities
         5.   Scoring for daily living activities
         6.   Scoring for mobility activities
         7.   Scoring: further provision
         8.   Information or evidence required for determining limited or severely limited ability to carry out activities
         9.   Claimant may be called for a consultation to determine whether the claimant has limited or severely limited ability to carry out activities
        10.   Matters to be taken into account in determining good reason in relation to regulations 8 and 9
        11.   Re-determination of ability to carry out activities

PART 3

REQUIRED PERIOD CONDITION

4.163   12.   Required period condition: daily living component
        13.   Required period condition: mobility component
        14.   The prescribed date
        15.   The prescribed date: claims for personal independence payment after an interval

PART 4

Residence and presence conditions

16. Conditions relating to residence and presence in Great Britain   **4.164**
17. Absence from Great Britain
18. Absence from Great Britain to receive medical treatment
19. Absence from Great Britain in special cases
20. Serving members of Her Majesty's forces and their family members—
       further provision
21. Terminal illness
22. Persons residing in Great Britain to whom a relevant EU Regulation applies
23. Persons residing in an EEA state other than the United Kingdom or in
       Switzerland to whom a relevant EU Regulation applies
23A. Refugees

PART 5

RATE OF PERSONAL INDEPENDENCE PAYMENT

24. Rate of personal independence payment   **4.165**

PART 6

PROVISIONS RELATING TO AGE

25. Exceptions to section 83 where entitlement exists or claim made before rel-   **4.166**
       evant age
26. Claim for personal independence payment after an interval and after reach-
       ing the relevant age
27. Revision and supersession of an award after the person has reached the rel-
       evant age

PART 7

PAYABILITY WHEN PERSON IS RESIDING IN CERTAIN ACCOMMODATION OR IS
DETAINED IN CUSTODY

28. Care home residents   **4.167**
29. Hospital in-patients
30. Payability exceptions: care homes and hospitals
31. Prisoners and detainees
32. Periods of residence

4.168   Schedule 1

Personal independence payment assessment

Schedule 2

Members of her majesty's forces: excluded persons

The Secretary of State for Work and Pensions, in exercise of the powers conferred by sections 77(3), 78(3) and (4), 79(3) and (4), 80(1), (2), (3), (4) and (5)(a) and (c), 81(1), (3)(b) and (4), 83(3), 85(1), (5) and (6), 86(1) and (3), 87, 92(1) and 94(1), (2), (3)(a) and (4) of the Welfare Reform Act 2012, makes the following Regulations.

A draft of this instrument has been laid before, and approved by a resolution of, each House of Parliament pursuant to section 94(6) of that Act.

These Regulations are made under the provisions of that Act and are made before the end of a period of six months beginning with the coming into force of those provisions.

Part 1

General

Citation and commencement

4.169   **1.**—(1) These Regulations may be cited as the Social Security (Personal Independence Payment) Regulations 2013.

(2) These Regulations come into force in relation to a particular case on the day on which Part 4 of the Act comes into force in relation to that case.

Interpretation

4.170   **2.** In these Regulations —

"the 1998 Act" means the Social Security Act 1998

"the Act" means the Welfare Reform Act 2012;

"aid or appliance"—

(a) means any device which improves, provides or replaces C's impaired physical or mental function; and

(b) includes a prosthesis;

"assessment" means the assessment referred to in regulation 4;

"C" means a person who has made a claim for or, as the case may be, is entitled to personal independence payment;

"component" means the daily living component or, as the case may be, the mobility component of personal independence payment;

"descriptor" means a descriptor in column 2 of the tables in Parts 2 and 3 of Schedule 1;

"disability living allowance" means disability living allowance under section 71 of the Social Security Contributions and Benefits Act 1992;

"medical treatment" means medical, surgical or rehabilitative treatment (including any course or diet or other regimen), and references to a person receiving or submitting to medical treatment are to be construed accordingly;

"prescribed date" means the date prescribed by regulation 14 or 15;

"previous award" means an award of either or both components to which C has ceased to be entitled;

"revised" means revised under section 9 of the 1998 Act, and "revision" is to be construed accordingly;

"superseded" means superseded under section 10 of the 1998 Act, and "supersession" is to be construed accordingly; and

terms defined for the purposes of a provision of Part 4 of the Act have the same meaning in these Regulations.

GENERAL NOTE

"Aids and appliances" are defined as any device that improves, provides or replaces the claimant's impaired function and goes on to add "including a prosthesis". In *MR v SSWP (PIP)* [2017] UKUT 86 (AAC) Judge Gray has considered how this definition might relate to devices that have been implanted in the claimant's body. The claimant had a retinal implant in one eye. The question was whether this should be regarded as an aid or appliance for the purpose of his PIP assessment. In the event the judge found it unnecessary to decide that question, but offers some advice nevertheless. She accepts that this, and any other implanted device, would seem to fulfil the literal interpretation of the definition in regulation 2. But to do that would mean, as the argument put forward on behalf of the DWP showed, that someone with a pacemaker or an artificial heart valve would score points on every daily living Activity and qualify for benefit because, in doing any Activity he would do so using an aid or appliance, yet would have no apparent functional disability at all. Judge Gray thought that this absurdity would justify her in examining the legislative preparatory material in accordance with the rule in *Pepper v Hart.* Doing so revealed that the legislative intent had been to benefit those with the greatest functional disablement and that meant that an implant that effected what was almost total (or in the case of eyesight, sufficient) and permanent restoration of the claimant's function should not be regarded as an aid, etc. This did leave the question of whether an implanted device should be regarded as a prosthesis. Again, a literal interpretation might well include any such device. The judge thought that the reference to prosthesis should be confined to replacement limbs and had been included in an excess of caution to ensure that amputees were covered. The result seems to be that permanently implanted devices such as artificial joints, heart valves, stents and retinas will not be an aid or appliance, though detachable ones may be. Hearing aids are accepted as aids (spectacles are specifically excluded) though Judge Gray leaves open the matter of cochlear implants. What then of removable false teeth? Perhaps they should be regarded as being of no evidence of disability in accordance with the approach applied in the *CW* case discussed below.

The use of a dosette box as being an aid in managing medication has been accepted in *AK v SSWP (CSPIP)* [2016] UKUT 256 (AAC) and a commode has been accepted in *KW v SSWP (PIP)* [2017] UKUT 54 (AAC), where its use was made necessary because the claimant had difficulty climbing the stairs to the lavatory. In *YW v SSWP (PIP)* [2017] UKUT 42 (AAC) Judge Wikeley suggests, though not as part of the decision, that light weight pans are not an aid or appliance when used by the claimant in the kitchen. This is despite the fact that they are given as an example of an aid etc in the *PIP Assessment Guide.* The judge justified his view first, by reference to the status of the *Guide* as advice within the DWP and not determinative of the law and, secondly, by reference to the test suggested by Judge Jacobs in the case of *CW* discussed below – in effect, if light weight pans are in such common everyday use by non-disabled people then they are not indicative of any disability.

In *KR v SSWP* [2015] UKUT 547 (AAC) Judge Rowley considered the meaning of "aid or appliance" in relation to the mobility component. The FTT had found that the claimant could move a distance of at least 50 metres and they upheld

4.171

a decision to award the claimant four points for the mobility component under Descriptor 2b. Before the UT, the claimant's representative contended that in order to achieve that distance the claimant would require to take a puff on an inhaler and argued that this qualified him under Descriptor 2c: "can ... move unaided ... no more than 50 metres". The question, therefore, (that had not been before the FTT) was whether the inhaler should be regarded as an aid or appliance. Superficially, it certainly appears to satisfy that definition as a "device which improves ... [a claimant's] physical ... function", but Judge Rowley rejects that conclusion. A distinction must be made, she says, between an aid that assists the claimant's function and a device that delivers medication that assists that function. So, as was conceded by the claimant's representative, the teaspoon that delivers a liquid analgesic could not be regarded as a device that aided the claimant's function and neither, in this case, could the inhaler. This is consistent with the advice given to the HCP in the *PIP Assessment Guide* where it is suggested (in relation to Activity 3 of the daily living component) that "needles, glucose meters and inhalers are not aids" whereas "pill boxes, dosette boxes, blister packs, and alarms" that help to manage medication apparently are. No explanation is given for this distinction, though elsewhere an inhaler is described as being "medication" while a nebuliser is "therapy". The need for an aid or appliance to relate to the activity in question has been affirmed in *RB v SSWP (PIP)* [2016] UKUT 556 (AAC). Judge Jacobs refers to his earlier decision in *CW v SSWP* (discussed below) in which he had said

> "*Aid or appliance* is defined by reference to whether it improves, provides or replaces the claimant's impaired *function*, which for convenience I describe as assisting in overcoming the consequences of a function being impaired. Putting all that together, an aid must help to overcome consequences of a function being impaired that is involved in carrying out an activity and is limited by the claimant's condition. To satisfy an aid or appliance descriptor, the claimant must need an aid to assist in respect of a function involved in the activity that is impaired."

In the present case, the question was whether a nebuliser (which the claimant could manage himself) might be regarded as an aid in relation to Activity 3 (b) (i)– to be able to manage medication. As in the previous case, the nebuliser was the means of delivering the medication; it was an aid to his breathing, but that was not the activity in question. It was agreed that someone who uses an inhaler to ease his breathing was not using an aid (see *KR v SSWP (PIP)* [2015] UKUT 547 (AAC)), but the judge leaves open the question whether, in an appropriate case, the nebuliser might be an aid because it delivered medication in the form of a fine mist that would assist a claimant when the inhaler would not. That might mean the claimant needed help in "managing" his medication, but on the facts of this case that question did not arise. While it is possible to see that this might apply to an *extra* device that is used by someone who lacks the dexterity to manage his own medication, e.g. when using a syringe, it is less easy to see why the means of delivering the medication should become a device just because the form in which the medication is delivered is different.

Several other decisions noted in connection with both the daily living Activities and mobility Activities (see below) have accepted various devices as aids or appliances, some of which might be used by a non-disabled person. These have included a chair to assist in dressing, a stool when cooking and a lever arm tap in the kitchen. It has been pointed out that the criterion is not whether other people might equally choose to use that device, but whether a disabled claimant finds it necessary to do so and whether then, it improves his physical function.

But doubt has been thrown on this principle in a series of cases that have addressed the question of the circumstances in which ordinary items of household furniture and equipment might be regarded as an aid or appliance when used in a particular way to assist a claimant achieve a task that might otherwise be beyond them. In the first, *NA v SSWP (PIP)* [2015] UKUT 572 (AAC), Judge Mark had suggested that it mattered not that the item in question might equally be used by an able person; he thought the question was whether the claimant was unable to accomplish the task without that item. However, a more restrictive approach has emerged. In *CW v SSWP (PIP)* [2016] UKUT 197 (AAC) Judge Jacobs held that the claimant's use of her bed to sit on, whilst she put her jeans on and when she took them off, was not the use of an aid in connection with the activity of dressing and undressing. As he puts it:

> "The question is this: would this 'aid' usually or normally be used by someone without any limitation in carrying out this particular aspect of the activity? If it would, the 'aid' is not assisting to overcome the consequences of an impaired function that is involved in the activity and its descriptors."

In effect the judge is saying that because sitting on a bed (or chair) is a practice so commonly adopted by non-disabled people the need to do so, even if required all the time, does not indicate a disability; i.e. the claimant is not disabled in relation to that element of dressing and undressing. This reasoning is approved by Judge Markus QC in *AP v SSWP (PIP)* [2016] UKUT 501 (AAC). This was another case involving the use of a bed to assist in dressing by sitting while putting garments on the lower body. As was pointed out in this case, the reasoning in *CW v SSWP* calls in question whether the use of a number of other household items might similarly now be in doubt. The representative of the Secretary of State indicated that use of lever arm taps that had been accepted as an aid in *GB v SSWP (PIP)* [2015] UKUT 546 (and was suggested in the original version of the *PIP Assessment Guide*) was now thought to be wrong. The *Guide* has now been rewritten (Part 2 para.2.1.21) to suggest that where a device might be used in the same way by a non-disabled person it is "unlikely to be considered an aid or appliance". The same reasoning has been adopted in *JM v SSWP (PIP)* [2016] UKUT 542 (AAC) where it was said that a claimant who could manage only slip-on shoes is not to be regarded as using an aid or appliance in dressing. But the question should remain - is the use of the device by this person, in the way that they use it, evidence of a disability?

The reasoning adopted by Judge Jacobs in *CW v SSWP (PIP)* [2016] UKUT 197 (AAC) has been applied too in *DR v SSWP (PIP)* [2018] UKUT 209 (AAC). There, the claimant had been awarded 2 points by the FTT for needing a "perching stool" to use while preparing a meal (Descriptor 1b). On appeal Judge Lane found that this was an error. On the facts before her she found that the claimant had no greater need to sit while preparing food and cooking a meal than might any person without a disability. Consequently, she said, applying the reasoning of the *CW* case, his need to sit from time to time was no evidence of a need to use an aid or appliance; it was, in effect, no evidence of any disability. Note that much the same result will be achieved if emphasis is placed on the claimant having to show that they *need* to use the aid or appliance to achieve a particular task; it would not be sufficient to show merely that the claimant chooses to use that device, or that their house happens to be equipped in a certain way. What is necessary is to show that without the aid their disability prevents them from performing that Descriptor.

There is a danger that, in focussing on the normality of behaviour in using devices, the point of the PIP Activities and Descriptors may be lost. The point of these Descriptors is to serve as a measure of the claimant's disablement by reference to a number of ordinary daily living actions, but if the test were worded instead as "Can the claimant stand on one leg for more than 3 seconds without support" the actions of other people in putting on their trousers would be irrelevant. Similarly, a test that said "Can the claimant turn on and off a standard bathroom tap" would serve as a measure of his manual strength and dexterity with relevance to a whole host of daily living actions and then reference to lever arm taps as an aid or appliance can be seen as a distraction from the real purpose of these tests. Similarly whether or not a person can tie a bow in their shoe laces is not just about their ability to dress – it is indicative of the extent to which a person afflicted with arthritic hands will require help in other ways. Perhaps the "trouser test", as treated in *CW* above, does produce the right result because the ability to stand on one leg has little relevance in assessing a claimant's abilities to undertake daily living activities, but the use of other devices may have such relevance.

PART 2

PERSONAL INDEPENDENCE PAYMENT ASSESSMENT

Daily living activities and mobility activities

4.172 **3.**—(1) For the purposes of section 78(4) of the Act and these Regulations, daily living activities are the activities set out in column 1 of the table in Part 2 of Schedule 1.

(2) For the purposes of section 79(4) of the Act and these Regulations, mobility activities are the activities set out in column 1 of the table in Part 3 of Schedule 1.

GENERAL NOTE

4.173 PIP is a benefit that is aimed at broadly the same target group of claimants (of working age) as DLA. The chief difference between the benefits is the method of identifying those who will qualify for benefit. DLA was administered largely on the basis of self declared information about the help that a claimant required to cope with day to day living and mobility supported, where necessary, by evidence from the claimant's health professional advisers. PIP, by contrast, approaches the matter by asking what the claimant can do for themselves. This will be based on the claimant's own response (on a questionnaire), but introduces, as well, an assessment report to be made by an independent Health Professional (HP) engaged to make a detailed report on the basis of the activities and descriptors prescribed in the schedule below. The Health Professional (HP) is equivalent to the Health Care Professional (HCP) that is engaged in Employment and Support Allowance decisions. Because the members of tribunals and UT judges have grown familiar with that terminology the abbreviation HCP will be used also in these notes.

Guidance is given to the HCP in conducting these assessments in the *PIP Assessment Guide* (sometimes referred to as PIPAG) that is available on the DWP website. The *Guide* has been referred by many UT judges in their decisions though always with the warning that the views expressed there are those of the Secretary of State and are not necessarily determinative of the law.

This method of assessment is not dissimilar to that adopted in relation to Employment Support Allowance (ESA). (Though there, unfitness is measured on a descending scale of descriptors; for PIP there is an ascending scale of disability). Advice given by the DWP says that the results of an assessment for ESA will not be used for the purposes of deciding a claim for PIP and *vice versa*. (Though, where there is a claim for PIP on the basis of terminal illness, information contained in the ESA record will be used). In administering claims for PIP the DWP has directed that those taking decisions should be referred to as Case Managers (CM). However, because tribunal members and UT judges are familiar with the more usual nomenclature of Decision Maker (DM) we will use that terminology in these notes.

To the extent that PIP and DLA have a similar objective it is not surprising that some of the same words and phrases are common to both benefits. Where that is the case it will be not unreasonable to suppose that the same meaning should be given to those words as they have been given for the purposes of DLA.

Details of the procedure that will be followed in administering PIP can be found on the DWP website. The process to be followed in dealing with a claim for PIP is explained there in some detail. In *HB v SSWP* [2015] UKUT 346 (AAC) it appears that a further stage may be involved in, at least, some cases. The claimant had been seen at a face-to-face interview by an HCP as a part of the normal process of assessment. She was scored at nine points for the daily living component and would have succeeded on her claim for benefit. But it then appears that, before a decision on her claim was made, the assessment was referred to another HCP for review. That assessment, conducted only as a desk assessment, reduced the score on three descriptors and in consequence the claim failed. The claimant's appeal to an FTT was refused. In the UT, Judge Wikeley allowed the appeal because the FTT had failed to explain why they had accepted the score recorded on review, rather than that made at the face-to-face interview. No explanation seems to have been offered to either tribunal for the desk reassessment. It may be that it was a part of the "reworking" procedure that is provided as a part of the Quality Audit procedure, but if that were the case some explanation ought to have been forthcoming. The FTT should have involved its inquisitorial role to elicit that information and its reasons might then have been able to satisfy both the claimant and the UT.

The correct procedure to be followed by the FTT in a case of supersession has been explained by Judge Jacobs in *P v SSWP (PIP)* [2019] UKUT 82 (AAC). The tribunal had decided that a reassessment by the HCP in which it was found that the claimant was not entitled to the benefit was a ground for supersession. The judge holds that this was an error of law; the correct sequence, he says, is for the tribunal first to assess the evidence, then to make findings of fact, and on the basis of those findings decide whether there was a ground for supersession, before finally deciding what the claimant's entitlement should be. In this case neither the DM nor the FTT had made findings of fact as to the claimant's condition; they had simply referred to the conclusion that had been reached by the HCP.

In *LS v SSWP* [2019] UKUT 3 (AAC) Judge Bano affirms that new medical evidence can always be a ground for supersession provided that the FTT explains why they have decided to depart from the earlier award. In doing that to accord with what Judge Jacobs said in the case above they will have necessarily made new findings of fact. Judge Bano has also pointed out that an FTT is not limited in their supersession decision to an award of benefit for the same period as that which they are superseding. In this case the new decision removed entitlement to the mobility component from the date of supersession, but awarded benefit to the care component for a further period which the judge said, if the original award had been for a period that had already expired, could be for a new period beyond the end of that award.

The decision of Judge Wikeley in *SF v SSWP (PIP)* [2016] UKUT 481 (AAC) reaffirms that the principle that was established in relation to claims for DLA and AA that, where a previous award of benefit was revised to the detriment of the claimant, clear reasons should be given by a tribunal to explain that revision – see e.g. *R(M)1/96* and *R(A)2/83*. This case applies the same principle where an award of personal independence payment has been superseded. The claimant had received 16 points awarded by the DM upon his initial application for PIP. The award was made for a period of three years (some of which was paid in arrears), but 12 months after the award was made the claimant was invited to complete a new PIP form in what was a planned review of his claim. Following a second examination by an HCP, the claimant scored zero points and his award was withdrawn forthwith. The claimant's appeal was refused, but the FTT made no reference to the earlier award, no reference to the basis upon which that award had been made, and hence no explanation of why they were now upholding such a dramatically different conclusion. Judge Wikeley reiterates the point that simply in the interests of justice such an outcome must demand an explanation.

The case makes another point about the application of the Universal Credit, Personal Independence Payment, Jobseeker's Allowance and Employment Support Allowance (Decisions and Appeals) Regulations 2013 in cases of supersession. Under those regulations supersession might arise either on a change of circumstances— (under reg.23) or upon receipt of a further medical evidence—usually a further report from a HCP—(under reg.26). Where reg.23 is used the tribunal is required to identify the ground on which supersession takes place and also the date from which it is to have effect, or will adopt the default date under s.10(5) of the Social Security Act 1998 (i.e. the date on which the decision is made). Where reg.26 is in issue the grounds will be self-evident and the effective date will be the default date under s.10.

For that reason the representative for the Secretary of State accepted that the regulations should be considered by a tribunal in that order; in other words, reg.23 should be considered first and reg.26 should be a last resort. Judge Wikeley explains that there is a very good reason why this should be so because the supersession following a review might equally have the effect of increasing the claimant's award and adopting this sequence will ensure that he has the advantage of that award being back-dated to the change of circumstances where it is appropriate to do so. This view was not shared by Judge Mesher in the subsequent case of *DS v SSWP (PIP)* [2016] UKUT 538 (AAC); [2017] AACR 19. In a case raising essentially the same points as *SF,* Judge Mesher found no need to adopt the sequential approach to the application of regs 23 and 26; in his view it was open to the DM to adopt either of these provisions and to choose an effective date that reflected the evidence upon which the supersession was made.

Where the DM chose to act upon a fresh report of a HCP or other medical evidence, but chose not to explore the question of whether the claimant should have been aware of his condition so as to put him under an obligation to report a change in his circumstances, that was a course that was open to him and a tribunal that heard an appeal against that decision would be under no obligation to consider whether or not reg.23 should have been applied first. If, however, evidence before the FTT (possibly not available to the DM) raised the possibility that an earlier date was relevant, there was no reason for the FTT not to follow that course under s.12(8)(a) of the Social Security Act 1998. The need for a decision of supersession has been further considered in a series of cases *DS v SSWP (PIP)* [2016] UKUT 538 (AAC), *KB v SSWP (PIP)* [2016] UKUT 537 (AAC), *PM v SSWP (PIP)* [2017] UKUT 37 (AAC) and *TH v SSWP (PIP)* [2017] UKUT 231 (AAC) in the last of which Judge Wikeley confirms his acceptance of the approach that had been adopted by Judge Mesher above in this note.

On the related question of whether, in case like this where the claimant has been in receipt of benefit that is now withdrawn, the report of the HCP that had previously been relied upon should be made available in evidence, Judge Mesher refers to the decision in *FN v SSWP (ESA)* [2015] UKUT 670 (AAC) now reported as [2016] AACR 24. He suggests, by analogy to that decision, that there is no rule of law that requires a tribunal to enquire as to the evidence in the previous claim, but where there is such relevant evidence of which the tribunal is aware the issue should be pursued. In this case the claimant had put the earlier medical condition in issue by asserting that his condition now was the same, or possibly worse, than before and, in the judge's view, that required the FTT to decide if an earlier medical report was relevant, and if it was not, to explain why not, and what they made of the contention that he was now as bad, or possibly worse. Finally, Judge Mesher agrees with the decision of Judge Wikeley in *SF* that the principle applied in *R(M) 1/96,* requiring an FTT to explain the reason for the difference in result, should apply in PIP cases like this. The circumstances in which it might be relevant for an FTT to call for medical evidence that could be available from an earlier award of DLA or of ESA has been considered in a number of cases—see *AP v SSWP (PIP)* [2016] UKUT 416 (AAC), *MA v SSWP (PIP)* [2017] UKUT 351 (AAC) and *GD v SSWP (PIP)* [2017] UKUT 415 (AAC). For a discussion of these cases see the notes following reg.8 of these regulations. The most frequent occasion on which it may be relevant for a tribunal to consider the medical evidence and the basis of an earlier award of benefit is likely to be when a claimant is transitioned from an award of DLA to a claim for PIP. When subsequently there is an appeal against the PIP decision the DWP has argued that evidence from the DLA award is not relevant and need not to be produced on that appeal because it is not an award of the same benefit and the qualifying conditions are not the same for both benefits. This argument is rejected by Judge Ward in *YM v SSWP (PIP)* [2018] UKUT 16 (AAC). Applying the reasoning of Judge Howell in the *R(M) 1/96* he suggests that where the conditions on which a previous benefit has been awarded are reasonably capable of being material to the subsequent benefit the principle established in that case should be applied so as to offer the claimant an explanation for what would otherwise appear to be an inconsistency. The giving of adequate reasons for the appeal decision requires no less. And note too, that where the claim for PIP has been preceded by an earlier award of PIP the tribunal is not necessarily relieved of the need to enquire as to the relevance of earlier medical evidence and the basis of that earlier award merely because the present claim is presented as a new claim, rather than a supersession of the old one–see *BB v SSWP (PIP)* [2017] UKUT 506 (AAC).

The circumstances in which an FTT is obliged to consider evidence that may have been relevant to an earlier claim for benefit, usually on entitlement to DLA, when they are considering an appeal for PIP have been reviewed by Judge Markus QC in two cases heard together, *CH and KN v SSWP (PIP)* [2018] UKUT 330 (AAC). These were both cases arising on the transfer of former DLA claimants to PIP, but similar issues can arise where the claimant seeks to involve as evidence on the claim for PIP evidence from earlier or contemporaneous claims for ESA, and even from claims for industrial injuries benefit. Judge Markus found that she was required to answer two questions. First, in what circumstances should an FTT obtain evidence of an earlier award of DLA, and secondly, when will the FTT be required to give reasons that explain a difference that arises when the claimant's award of PIP is less beneficial than their previous award of DLA.

In answering the first question the Judge offers detailed advice on when the evidence from the earlier claim will be relevant followed by advice on the circumstances in which an FTT should call for evidence from an earlier claim. This advice can be found in paragraphs 45 to 66 of her judgment. (Judge Markus had been given details of the improved procedures that should now be followed by DWP so that the evidence should already be before the FTT on transfer cases, such as these, if the claimant has requested it.)

In answering the second question Judge Markus supports the remarks that had been made by Judge Ward in *YM v SSWP (PIP)* [2018] UKUT 16 (AAC). She says that she supports Judge Ward's approach in saying that there is no rule of law that requires a difference of outcome to be explained and that it is for the tribunal to determine in the circumstances of a particular case whether there is such an apparent inconsistency that reasons for it, are called for.

On the facts of these two cases she found that, in the first case, the Secretary of State had failed to include medical evidence in the file, even though it had been requested (at the FTT the claimant had not complained of its absence), but Judge Markus thought the evidence before the FTT was so complete, and given that the DLA evidence would have been 12 years old, that there was no error of law in failing to adjourn for that evidence. Nor in those circumstances was there any need for the FTT to explain the reasons for the difference between the claimant's awards. The reason that he did not succeed on the PIP claim was clear, though she does suggest that a brief single sentence to explain why the FTT had preferred the evidence on the current claim might have been desirable. In the second case the judge found that there was sufficient overlap between what was probably the basis of the DLA claim and hence the evidence on which that was based, and the current evidence of panic attacks suffered by the claimant and affecting her ability to go out alone, that the FTT had made an error of law in failing to call for the DLA evidence. The case was remitted for reconsideration by a new tribunal.

In *AW v SSWP (PIP)* [2018] UKUT 76 (AAC) Judge Wright has considered another case where the evidence on which an award of DLA had been made was not available to the FTT. In that case, however, he felt able on the basis of what could be inferred from the claimant's condition (which counsel for the Secretary of State agreed was unlikely to have changed) to decide the case himself and award the mobility component at the standard rate.

Two further cases deal with these issues. Both are decisions of Judge May QC. In the first, *AR v SSWP (PIP)* [2018] UKUT 313 (AAC) the judge decided that even applying what was said by Judge Ward in the *YM* case that the appeal failed because, as Judge Ward had expressed it in the *YM* case, the evidence from the one claim would need to be "reasonably capable of being material" to the other. In this case the claimant suffered from epilepsy, but the FTT found no evidence that he was at risk of a seizure when he was out. Judge May thought that the DLA claim must have been based on him being "unable or virtually unable to walk" for it to have awarded at the higher rate and could have no relevance to his PIP claim. Again, in *SM v SSWP (PIP)* [2018] UKUT 314 (AAC) Judge May observes that the requirement to explain the award of PIP when it differs from an earlier award of DLA as set out by Judge Ward in *YM v SSWP (PIP)* [2018] UKUT 16 (AAC) was obiter, but, in any case, he finds that the principle should not apply in this appeal because the reasons for which the earlier benefit were awarded (unable or virtually unable to walk) were not relevant to the criteria that the FTT had applied in the present case. The claimant, who suffered from arthritis, was found to satisfy Descriptor 2(d) of the Mobility Activities. It does not appear that she disputed this conclusion; her appeal was based on the fact that she had an abdominal stoma which made it impossible, she said, to use public transport. There was no evidence to suggest that she could walk only 20 metres so as to satisfy Descriptor 2(e) and qualify for the higher rate of mobility.

A different aspect of this matter is considered by Judge Wikeley in *FJ v SSWP (PIP)* [2019] UKUT 27 (AAC). This case concerned not the evidence that might be provided by reports from claims for other benefits, but evidence of the claimant's earlier record in relation to this benefit. A claim for PIP had been refused and the claimant had appealed, but after her appeal to the FTT had been refused she made a fresh claim for PIP because she thought that might produce results more quickly than by making a further appeal to the UT. Her representative, in correspondence to the DWP, referred to evidence from the earlier proceedings but the DWP declined to make any refence on the ground that this was a new claim. The claimant appealed again to the FTT and then to the UT. Judge Wikeley took the view that in order to satisfy Rule 24 of the Tribunal Procedure Rules the DWP should have provided a copy of documents relating to the earlier claim.

Further guidance on the procedure to be followed when a claimant has appealed against only one component of a PIP award has been given in *MW v SSWP (PIP)* [2016] UKUT 540 (AAC). Provided that the tribunal is satisfied that the claimant has understood that both components of an award are "at risk" in the appeal, there is no need for an adjournment to be offered. This is certainly the case where the claimant is represented at the hearing because the tribunal is entitled to assume that the representative is competent; it may be otherwise where there is no representative. On the question of whether an adjournment should be considered where the claimant is appealing against only one component of a combined award see also the more considered approach adopted by Judge Markus QC in *GA v SSWP (PIP)* [2017] UKUT 416 (AAC), although there the appeal was allowed because the FTT did not seem to have appreciated that they were making a supersession and had not given the ground upon which the supersession was made.

In *JC v SSWP (PIP)* [2016] UKUT 533 (AAC) representatives were reminded of the dangers of submitting a complete medical record where some of the record had not been read. In this case the very long record (350 pages) included material that was confidential and highly sensitive.

Assessment of ability to carry out activities

4.174   **4.**—(1) For the purposes of section 77(2) and section 78 or 79, as the case may be, of the Act, whether C has limited or severely limited ability to carry out daily living or mobility activities, as a result of C's physical or mental condition, is to be determined on the basis of an assessment.

(2) C's ability to carry out an activity is to be assessed—

(a) on the basis of C's ability whilst wearing or using any aid or appliance which C normally wears or uses; or

(b) as if C were wearing or using any aid or appliance which C could reasonably be expected to wear or use.

[¹(2A) Where C's ability to carry out an activity is assessed, C is to be assessed as satisfying a descriptor only if C can do so—

(a) safely;

(b) to an acceptable standard;

(c) repeatedly; and

(d) within a reasonable time period.

(3) Where C has been assessed as having severely limited ability to carry out activities, C is not to be treated as also having limited ability in relation to the same activities.

[¹(4) In this regulation—

(a) "safely" means in a manner unlikely to cause harm to C or to another person, either during or after completion of the activity;

(b) "repeatedly" means as often as the activity being assessed is reasonably required to be completed; and

(c) "reasonable time period" means no more than twice as long as the maximum period that a person without a physical or mental condition which limits that person's ability to carry out the activity in question would normally take to complete that activity.]

AMENDMENTS

1. Social Security (Personal Independence Payment) (Amendment) Regulations 2013 (SI 2013/455) reg.2 (April 8, 2013).

DEFINITIONS

"aid or appliance"—see reg.2.   4.175

GENERAL NOTE

A more detailed discussion of how the assessment procedure should be carried out can be found in the notes following Pts 1 and 2 of the Schedule to these regulations.   4.176

Note that the Personal Independence Payment Regulations 2013 were amended with effect from March 16, 2017 by the Personal Independence Payment (Amendment) Regulations 2017 (SI 2017/194). In *RF v SSWP* [2017] EWHC 3375 (Admin); [2018] AACR 13 Mostyn J. held that para. 2(4) of the amending regulations (SI 2017/194) was in breach of Art.14 of the ECHR and that it was *ultra vires* the regulation making power in Part 4 of the Welfare Reform Act 2012 under which it purported to have been made. The DWP have accepted that that decision is correct. This means that the amendment effected by that part of the regulation is of no effect and the text of original version in Part 3 of Schedule 1 (Mobility Activity, Planning and following journeys) is restored. The law stated in this work is as at April 9, 2018 which means that it is the amended version, apart from Part 3 of Schedule 1, that appears here; for full original version of the regulations the reader is referred to the 2016/17 edition of this work.

These amendments were made in consequence of two decisions in the UT. The first, *SSWP v LB (PIP)* [2016] UKUT 530 (AAC) concerned the definitions of therapy and of managing therapy, managing medication and of monitoring a health condition, together with amendments to Activity 3 in Part 2 of Schedule 1. These amendments remain in force, but because these changes are substantive rather than procedural they affect decisions that were made only after the date that they came into effect (March 16, 2017). This is confirmed in *RS-G v SSWP (PIP)* [2017] UKUT 152 (AAC). This means that for appeals that are brought now, to the FTT or the UT, in respect of decisions made before March 16, 2017, the law to be applied (at least in the FTT) will that in the *LB* decision above.

The second, a decision of a three judge panel, *MH v SSWP (PIP)* [2016] UKUT 531 (AAC); [2018] AACR 12 concerned the application of Activity 1 in Part 3 of the Schedule; it is that part of the amending regulation that has been found to be of no effect and an appeal against the *MH* decision has been withdrawn. This means that all decisions coming before an FTT or the UT now, should be decided in accordance with that decision.

An assessment will be made taking into account the claimant's ability when wearing or using any aid or appliance that he normally wears or, where he does not wear or use such aid etc., taking account of any aid etc. that he could reasonably be expected to wear or use. Whether someone can reasonably be expected to use such a device may depend upon many factors—e.g. whether the claimant already possesses that device, or, where he does not the cost and availability of the item, whether persons suffering from the same condition as the claimant commonly use that item, whether they are commonly advised by health professionals to do so and other factors such as the size and the storage facilities that that might be necessary for the claimant.

An "aid or appliance" is defined in reg.2 above. It will include any device that improves the claimant's ability to accomplish any activity including, most obviously, a wheelchair. Previously this note has suggested that a wheelchair might have to be excluded from the definition of an appliance in order to make sense of Descriptors in Activity 2 relating to the mobility component. However, the better view may be that a wheelchair is an appliance, and a more complex interpretation needs to be given to those Descriptors—see the note to Descriptor f.

The correct approach to be adopted by an FTT in making an assessment of the claimant's ability to perform the tasks required in the Activities and Descriptors is explained in two respects in the decision of Judge Gray in *PM v SSWP (PIP)* [2017] UKUT 154 (AAC). The FTT had concluded that the claimant should not score certain points because they felt (no doubt with the advantage of advice from the medical member of the tribunal) that with an appropriate adjustment of her pain relief medication that she would be able to achieve the tasks required satisfactorily. The Judge said that, while it was the role of the tribunal to be inquisitorial, an assumption about the claimants' treatment should be made only with extreme caution; in this case such an assumption was certainly inappropriate because the claimant's notes stated that a variation of the medication had been tried, but was unsuitable for the claimant. The second point was made in relation to the claim for a mobility component, but the general point is applicable across both components. The FTT had concluded that the claimant should be able to walk up to 50 metres as often as was "reasonably required". To the extent that this seemed to suggest an objective standard that might be set by the tribunal, the Judge thought it to be wrong. While the claimant would not be able to set herself an "extreme regime" of walking so as to generate a higher score, the test should focus more upon what the claimant might wish to do and especially how often she might want to do so. The test, she says, drawing on the words of Lord Slynn of Hadley in *Secretary of State v Fairey* (R(A) 2/98) (a case that involved a claim for Attendance Allowance) should be a comparison with a "normal life," and that should include an element that reflects the life-style of the claimant.

The claimant can be said to accomplish one of the tasks set in the activities prescribed only if he can do so "safely". This is defined in subs.(4) to mean that harm to himself or another person is "unlikely" This is a narrower definition of safety than is commonly used. Safety is usually defined in terms of risk and risk is taken to include the degree of harm that may be caused, as well as the likelihood of that harm happening. The definition above would not regard something as unsafe, even though it might be fatal, if it were unlikely to happen.

This was the meaning adopted, reluctantly, by the judge in *CE v SSWP (PIP)* [2015] UKUT 643 (AAC) and followed in several other cases. But there has now been a contrary conclusion reached by a panel of three judges in *RJ and others v SSWP (PIP)* [2017] UKUT 105 (AAC); [2017] AACR 32. These cases all concerned claimants whose disability put them at considerable risk if a certain event were to occur, but that event occurred only infrequently; they included claimants who suffered from epilepsy and others who were deaf. All these claimants needed to be accompanied or supervised in carrying out certain of the PIP Activities, but the need for intervention from another person at any particular time was "unlikely". The panel decision relies on two earlier decisions in other contexts, one in the House of Lords in *In re H (Minors) (Sexual Abuse): (Standards of Proof)* [1996] AC 563 and the other *Wallis v Bristol Water plc* [2010] PTSR 1986. In the first it was necessary for the local authority to be able to show that harm to a child was "likely" to occur – the court held that this did not require it to be shown that harm was more probable than not; it was sufficient if there was a real likelihood that harm might occur. Similarly, in the second case the water authority was required to show that an improper method of attaching fittings to the water system made it "likely" that contamination would be caused. Again, it was sufficient to show a real possibility of the harm occurring because, were it to do so, the damage could be catastrophic – as that court put it "a possibility that cannot sensibly be ignored having regard to the nature and gravity of the feared harm". Applying this reasoning to the word "unlikely" that is used here means that the claimant cannot be found to accomplish a PIP Activity safely if the risk involved is one that cannot sensibly be ignored. The UT in this case also drew support from the consultation material that was produced when the PIP scheme was developed. From that it became clear that those designing the scheme had intended risk to be treated in the same way as had been done with DLA; there the degree of harm as well as the likelihood of harm was accounted for. See *Moran v Secretary of State for Social Services (The Times March 14, 1987, CA)* where the Court said:

> "the relative frequency or infrequency of the attacks is immaterial so long as the risk of 'substantial' danger is not so remote a possibility that it ought reasonably to be disregarded."

Note too, that this meaning of safely means that there is no longer any need to make any distinction between the word as used in regulation 4(2A) and the definition of "supervision" (presence of another person required to ensure C's safety) in Sch.1.

In *SH v SSWP (PIP)* [2018] UKUT 251 (AAC) Judge Hemingway has made some observations about the functioning of the test for a claimant being able to accomplish an activity safely. The claimant was a profoundly deaf young woman. She had been fitted with cochlear implants that gave a good degree of hearing when she was wearing the external part of the appliance, but those had to be removed when she was bathing or taking a shower. It was argued that she could not bathe or shower safely without some supervision because, in the event of a fire or other catastrophe, she would not be able to hear any alarm or other warning sound. Her circumstances were the same as those of one of the claimants in the *RJ* case. In that case the three-judge tribunal had observed: "On our analysis of regulation 4 and 'supervision', these facts would indicate that she needed supervision to bathe". It seemed that, initially, counsel for the present claimant had argued before the UT that this meant that her client was entitled to succeed in respect of Activity 4b (need for supervision when washing and bathing) but subsequently accepted that a determination on the facts of the case was still required. Judge Hemingway agreed with that position and noted that even in the *RJ* case itself the matter had been remitted to a new tribunal for determination. In the present case he thought that the FTT had applied the correct test in relation to the risk apparent and that their conclusion rejecting the claim was one that they were entitled to reach, except in one respect; in deciding that the claimant could bathe safely without the need for supervision they had suggested that she could reduce the risk of harm occurring by limiting the time spent in the bath or in a shower. This, he decided they were not entitled to do. He refers to *EG v SSWP (PIP)* [2017] UKUT 101 (AAC) in which it was held that the claimant should be assessed in accordance with what they would choose to do and not circumscribe their activities. Doubtless there are limits to a claimant's choice of behaviour but this accords with the approach taken in *Secretary of State v Fairey* [1997] 1 W.L.R. 799 for DLA.

Note too, that the harm risked must be to a person; a risk of damage to property, even if significant, will not suffice; though then the claimant could hardly be said to accomplish the task "to an acceptable standard"—see para.(2A)(b). The harm may be either to the claimant or to another person. This was the point relied upon by the appellant in *JT v SSWP (PIP)* [2018] UKUT 101 (AAC). The claimant suffered from uncontrolled epilepsy; he had about two grand mal fits each week and several petit mal fits. It was argued that this made it too dangerous for him to prepare a meal because of the risk that he might injure himself either when using a knife or when handling hot items. Furthermore, when having a grand mal fit he thrashed about in a manner that might endanger anyone who was there to assist him. For this reason, it was argued, he could not prepare and cook a meal safely at all. Judge Hemingway allowed an appeal on the ground that the FTT had failed to give adequate reasons for their decision refusing benefit. The case was remitted for rehearing and see too, below, the meaning of supervision as might apply to these facts.

Whether the claimant can do something "repeatedly" is only likely to become an issue where the activity requires some degree of exertion- most obviously, perhaps, in relation to mobility (moving). This will bring into question the claimant's need for rest periods as to both frequency and duration and will then link with whether the claimant can be said to be achieving movement to "an acceptable standard".

CE v SSWP (PIP) [2015] UKUT 643 (AAC) also explores new ground in relation to the meaning of the word "repeatedly" in para.(4)(b). The judge in the UT returned the case for rehearing before a new tribunal and gave some guidance for that tribunal. The evidence before the FTT suggested that the claimant's inability to cope with some daily living activities arose from the fact that after an epileptic episode she needed to sleep until late in the morning and even then, when she awoke, she was lethargic and felt dizzy, sick, weak and tired so that she was unable to do very much at all until late morning or midday. The appeal by the Secretary of State had been allowed on the ground that the FTT had failed to explain sufficiently, why they were awarding some of the points that they did. In offering guidance to the new tribunal the judge suggests that they should take a comprehensive account of the times that the claimant was so affected and then, having referred to reg.4(2A), should consider whether the claimant could do those things repeatedly, as defined there, and to a satisfactory standard. As he put it:

> "It seems to me it makes no sense to say a person is able to perform an activity as often as reasonably required if they cannot do so for a part of the day in which they would otherwise reasonably wish or need to do so."

The judge refers also to his own decision in *TR v SSWP (PIP)* [2015] UKUT 626 (AAC); [2016] AACR 23 in which he had adopted the advice given in the *PIP Assessment Guide* that if a descriptor was satisfied for any part of a day (after allowing for the *de minimis* rule) it should be regarded as applying on that day. It seems that he is suggesting that a claimant, whose daily routine was so affected that they could not conform to normal hours for meals, work etc., could be regarded as satisfying some of the Descriptors. The difficulty with this may be to apply that approach to the words of the Descriptors. There is nothing in Descriptor 1, for example, that relates to the time at which the claimant should be capable of preparing a meal, and the reference in para.(2A)(d) to a reasonable time period is only to the speed with which the claimant can accomplish a task – see the definition in para.(4)(c).

It would be odd to describe a claimant who took their breakfast at midday as being unable to prepare a meal though note, it would not mean that every person who lies abed until late, could make a claim because for any claim to succeed it would have to be the result of that claimant's mental or physical disability and, even then, not a matter of choice on their part. It is clear that a person with this claimant's degree of disability has a life that is seriously affected by their disability, but unless they can be seen to need supervision for their own safety and that of others, it is difficult to see how their claim can succeed.

The effect on the score of a claimant who takes an unreasonable time (defined in this regulation as more than twice as long as an able-bodied person) to complete daily living activities is demonstrated in recent decision of Judge Gray in *GP v SSWP (PIP)* [2016] UKUT 444 (AAC). The claimant was a young man who suffered considerably from Obsessive Compulsive Disorder (OCD). On his claim for PIP the DM had allowed four points for daily living activities – two points for each of Activities 1 and 6. The FTT to whom he had appealed allowed a further eight points under Activity 4 (washing and bathing). The evidence before the FTT was that because of his OCD it took the claimant more than twice as long as is normal for him to eat, wash and dress. They allowed the extra points on the ground that this meant that the claimant could not effectively wash or bathe at all, and was therefore entitled to the maximum points allowable under that activity; they did not alter the points already awarded at all. The Secretary of State appealed on the ground that it was inconsistent, and therefore revealed some error of law, for the FTT to award eight points in relation to Activity 6 while retaining only two points for each of the other activities. Judge Gray held that there was no error of law; there was no compulsion for the FTT to reconsider the points awarded if the claimant had already reached the maximum score required. It was reasonable for the FTT to adopt this practice as a time saving measure in what was usually a busy schedule, though she did observe that where a tribunal does this, it may be as well to add a note to the effect that that is their reason for doing so, to avoid confusion and misunderstanding as in the present case.

What this case does highlight, however, is the inappropriate conclusions to which the fact-finders may be forced as a consequence of the operation of reg.4(2A). In this case, having found that the claimant would take more than twice as long as another person to wash and bathe, the tribunal were required to conclude that he could not wash etc at all — but descriptor 6(g) reads that the claimant "cannot wash at all and needs another person to wash their entire body". It is unlikely that such a measure could ever be adopted with an OCD young man. Further, if the FTT had tried to carry through their reasoning in relation to eating a meal they would have to find that he could not convey food to his mouth and required another person to feed him–another unlikely scenario.

A solution to this conundrum is suggested by the decision of Judge Ovey in *AB v SSWP (PIP)* [2017] UKUT 217 (AAC). This was a case in which the claimant's evidence suggested that he suffered distress when he tried to engage socially with others (Activity 9). Judge Ovey suggests that the requirements of reg.4(2A) should apply only to those Descriptors which test what the claimant can do, and are not applicable to those descriptors that describe what the claimant cannot do. In her view the structure of PIP Activities ranges from a Descriptor at one end that specifies a claimant who can accomplish the activity described without any need for assistance at all, to another at the other extreme where the claimant cannot accomplish that activity at all. By way of illustration she refers to Activity 6—dressing and undressing; that ranges from "can dress and undress unaided'" to "cannot dress or undress at all". It makes sense to test, in accordance with reg.4(2A), whether a claimant can dress (with or without aid) to a satisfactory extent, safely and in a reasonable time, but it does not, she says, make sense to ask whether someone who cannot dress at all does so satisfactorily, safely and timeously.

The inference is that reg.4(2A) was not intended to apply to the "cannot-do" descriptors. Regulation 4(2A) was a late addition to the regulations (as can be seen from the numbering) and in this, as well as other respects, the regulations as a whole, and the Descriptors in particular, have evolved somewhat piecemeal. For those Activities that are worded in the appropriate way this may provide a solution. Some Activities are worded in terms of the claimant's needs (e.g. Activity 3—Managing therapy etc) where the same problem may not arise, but for those in which the cannot-do at all Descriptor is used and is then conditioned by a further phrase, as in the case of Activity 4—washing and bathing, where the descriptor is "cannot wash at all and needs another to wash their entire body", there remains the difficulty of having to ignore the final element.

The effect of a slow walking pace has been considered in *KL v SSWP (PIP)* [2016] UKUT 545 (AAC). There the claimant walked slowly, but did not exceed the time limit prescribed in para.(4)(c). The UT judge held that it was not relevant then to consider the slowness of pace again in relation to whether the claimant could accomplish the Activity to an "an acceptable standard" under para.(2A)(b).

Scoring for daily living activities

4.177   5.—(1) The score C obtains in relation to daily living activities is determined by adding together the number of points (if any) awarded for each activity listed in column 1 of the table in Part 2 of Schedule 1 ("the daily living activities table").

(2) For the purpose of paragraph (1), the number of points awarded to C for each activity listed in column 1 of the daily living activities table is the number shown in column 3 of the table against whichever of the descriptors set out in column 2 of the table for the activity applies to C under regulation 7.

(3) Where C has undergone an assessment, C has—

(a) limited ability to carry out daily living activities where C obtains a score of at least eight points in relation to daily living activities; and

(b) severely limited ability to carry out daily living activities where C obtains a score of at least 12 points in relation to daily living activities.

GENERAL NOTE

4.178   For the daily living component there are 10 activities each of which contains a number of descriptors.

Note that the claimant scores the points for only one descriptor (the higher or highest where he satisfies more than one) in each activity; the aggregate of the scores from all activities is then the measure of the claimant's disability.

In *GP v SSWP (PIP)* [2016] UKUT 444 (AAC) the claimant had been awarded the maximum number of points required to qualify for benefit at the higher rate without the FFT having considered all of the possible Activities on which she might have scored some points. She appealed to the UT on the ground that she should have been assessed on all the Activities. The Judge rejected that appeal; cutting short the hearing at the point where the claimant had nothing further to gain was a legitimate strategy to save the tribunal's time, though he did add that it might be useful to record that reason in the decision.

Scoring for mobility activities

4.179   6.—(1) The score C obtains in relation to mobility activities is determined by adding together the number of points (if any) awarded for each activity listed in column 1 of the table in Part 3 of Schedule 1 ("the mobility activities table").

(2) For the purpose of paragraph (1), the number of points awarded to C for each activity listed in column 1 of the mobility activities table is the

number shown in column 3 of the table against whichever of the descriptors set out in column 2 of the table for the activity applies to C under regulation 7.

(3) Where C has undergone an assessment, C has—

(a) limited ability to carry out mobility activities where C obtains a score of at least eight points in relation to mobility activities; and

(b) severely limited ability to carry out mobility activities where C obtains a score of at least 12 points in relation to mobility activities.

GENERAL NOTE

For the mobility component there are two activities each of which contains a number of descriptors.

4.180

Note that the claimant scores the points for only one descriptor (the higher or highest where he satisfies more than one) in each activity; the aggregate of the scores from all activities is then the measure of the claimant's disability

An application by way of judicial review for a declaration that the Personal Independence Payments Regulations were invalid failed in *R (Sumpter) v SSWP* [2015] EWCA Civ 1033. The applicant had argued that the consultation process that preceded the making of the regulations was unfair and therefore unlawful. In particular he argued that the threshold at which a claimant might be awarded the enhanced rate of benefit in respect of their ability to move about had been changed at a late stage of the process. The early versions of the proposed criteria had appeared to adopt the standard that had been accepted, in practice, in relation to claims for DLA as an ability to move unaided no more than 50 metres, whereas the standard adopted in the draft regulations became effectively no more than 20 metres. The Secretary of State had then undertaken a further period of consultation relating specifically to that point. In the High Court Hickinbottom J. had held that, whatever might have been said about the fairness of the initial consultation, this later extension of consultation made the process, as a whole, fair: *R. (Sumpter) v Secretary of State for Work and Pensions* [2014] EWHC 2434 (Admin). The Court of Appeal upheld that decision.

Scoring: further provision

7.—(1) The descriptor which applies to C in relation to each activity in the tables referred to in regulations 5 and 6 is—

4.181

(a) where one descriptor is satisfied on over 50% of the days of the required period, that descriptor;

(b) where two or more descriptors are each satisfied on over 50% of the days of the required period, the descriptor which scores the higher or highest number of points; and

(c) where no descriptor is satisfied on over 50% of the days of the required period but two or more descriptors (other than a descriptor which scores 0 points) are satisfied for periods which, when added together, amount to over 50% of the days of the required period—

(i) the descriptor which is satisfied for the greater or greatest proportion of days of the required period; or,

(ii) where both or all descriptors are satisfied for the same proportion, the descriptor which scores the higher or highest number of points.

(2) For the purposes of paragraph (1), a descriptor is satisfied on a day in the required period if it is likely that, if C had been assessed on that day, C would have satisfied that descriptor.

(3) In paragraphs (1) and (2), "required period" means —

   (a) in the case where entitlement to personal independence payment falls to be determined, the period of 3 months ending with the prescribed date together with–

      (i) in relation to a claim after an interval for the purpose of regulation 15, the period of 9 months beginning with the date on which that claim is made;

     (ii) in relation to any other claim, the period of 9 months beginning with the day after the prescribed date.

   (b) in the case where personal independence payment has been awarded to C—

      (i) during the period of 3 months following a determination of entitlement under a claim for the purpose of regulation 15, the period of 3 months ending with the prescribed date together with, for each day of the award, the period of 9 months beginning with the day after that date;

     (ii) in any other case, for each day of the award, the period of 3 months ending with that date together with the period of 9 months beginning with the day after that date.

DEFINITIONS

4.182   "prescribed date"—see reg.14 or 15
           "required period"—see para.(3)

GENERAL NOTE

4.183   The required period over which the claimant is assessed is a period of three months that must precede the claim together with a period of nine months that follows. This means that a claimant will ordinarily have to satisfy a descriptor on a majority of the days over a year long period. This does not mean, of course, that the claimant must attempt to undertake the task every other day (e.g. make budgetary decisions), but only that, were he to do so, he would satisfy that Descriptor. Where the activity is measured by hours spent on it in a week (e.g. managing therapy) he might also undertake that Activity on fewer than half the days in a year.

The view expressed above has been confirmed in *DO v SSWP (PIP)* [2017] UKUT 115 (AAC). The claimant there was a cancer patient who, following surgery was incapacitated to a considerable extent but who had made a significant recovery after about six months following the surgery. In the FTT it was found that the claimant scored more than the qualifying points in a period that was more than 50% of the weeks in the required period as defined by regulation 7. But when reference is also made to the required period as defined in regulation 12, it was clear that he could not satisfy the prospective period in regulation 12(1)(b) because he would not have a qualifying score if he were "assessed at every time" in that period as that regulation requires. The question was which "required period" was determinative. Judge Mitchell has held that priority must be given to regulation 12. To do otherwise would mean that regulation 12 was otiose and it was clear that the legislative intention in the WRA was to require the claimant to qualify throughout the 12 month period. Another decision on the effect of regulation 7 and regulation 12 and the required period condition is in *AH v SSWP (PIP)* [2016] UKUT 541 (AAC). In this case Judge Jacobs affirms the rule that a tribunal must judge the case on the information available to it down to the date of the decision that is appealed against. A prospective claim under regulation 33 of the Claims and Payment Regulations can be made only if the tribunal can infer that, using the information available at the date of the decision appealed against, the claimant can be expected to satisfy conditions within the next three months.

Note that, where the claimant is undertaking an Activity that takes place overnight (e.g. renal dialysis or therapeutic feeding) provided some part of the process for which points are scored takes place before midnight and another afterwards, the claimant will satisfy the Descriptor on each of two days–see *SSWP v KS (PIP)* [2018] UKUT 102 (AAC). Judge Mesher held that a claimant who required assistance with a therapeutic source on three nights each week both in the evening when setting it up and again next morning when taking down, satisfied the 50% rule because she required that assistance on six days each week.

The decision of the three judge panel in *RJ v SSWP (PIP)* [2017] UKUT 105 (AAC); [2017] AACR 32 regarding the meaning of the word "safely" in regulation 4 has also resolved the question that had arisen with regard to the relationship between that definition and regulation 7. The UT in that case decides that there can be a need for supervision to ensure that the claimant accomplishes an Activity safely, even though an intervention is required much less frequently than every other day – it is the supervision that is required, perhaps on a daily basis, and not the intervention. The decision in *RJ v SSWP (PIP)* [2017] UKUT 105 (AAC); [2017] AACR 32 has been applied by Judge Mesher in *SSWP v NH (PIP)* [2017] UKUT 258 (AAC). There the claimant wore continence pads every day, though a leakage into them occurred, on average, only two days in the week. The judge held that such precautionary use was reasonably necessary every day and therefore the appropriate descriptor was satisfied on more than 50 percent of the days each week.

Where the claimant's condition varies the process defined by Regulation 7 must be followed to the exclusion of any more general approach that was previously used in relation to DLA. See *JC v SSWP* [2015] UKUT 144 where the appeal was allowed because the FTT had substituted their own assessment in relation to Daily Living Activities by adopting the approach suggested in *Moyna v SSWP* [2003] UKHL44. In this case the UT made clear that for PIP claims the tribunal must follow the 50% rules prescribed by reg.7.

The problem that arises when a claimant's ability to perform a task varies at different times within a single day has been dealt with in a decision of Judge Hemingway, *TR v SSWP* [2015] UKUT 626 AAC; [2016] AACR 23. The claimant there had restricted eyesight such that she had difficulty in seeing in low light conditions. She had been provided with what she described as her "special lamp" to assist her in reading and she used that also when preparing meals, though her husband still needed to assist her by checking things such as whether the gas was alight, or whether things were boiling on the stove. Her restricted eyesight also limited her ability to go out at night and she would use a taxi if she needed to go to unfamiliar places. Her claim had been refused and an appeal to the FTT failed. The FTT apparently took the view that if she could perform these tasks satisfactorily "the majority of the time" her claim would fail. This may have been an application by the tribunal of the approach that has applied in claims for DLA, or, it may have been that the tribunal thought they should be applying the 50% rule applicable to the case of daily variation as required by reg.7. In the UT counsel for the Secretary of State helpfully referred the judge to the Government's response to consultation on these regulations. There, it was clearly stated that if a Descriptor applied at any time within a period of 24 hours it should be regarded as applying on that day. Furthermore she referred also to the DWP Guidance to the HCP assessors which contained the same criterion in two associated paragraphs to accomplish a task "repeatedly" meaning as often as reasonably required. If it were reasonable for the claimant to go out at night, for example, she should be able to do that without adopting special measures to do so. But the judge approved also two limitations suggested by counsel for the Secretary of State on this approach. First, that the inability to perform a task should be the direct result of the claimant's disability; so that, for example, where the claimant chose not to go out at night for some other reason, that day would not count, and secondly, that any inability to perform a task would be subject to a *de minimis* rule. If, therefore, the claimant's inability could properly be described as fleeting, or even just brief, this would not qualify. In particular this might cover the case of a claimant whose inability arose only until he had taken his usual medication; if the medication acted quickly and enabled the claimant then to manage tasks such as washing and dressing, they would not qualify, whereas, if the medication took so long to be effective as to mean there was an unacceptable delay in the claimant's daily business, that would qualify as an inability to perform that Descriptor.

The provisions of this regulation will provide guidance in some cases where the claimant's condition fluctuates between "good days" and "bad days".

The case of *AK v SSWP (PIP)* [2015] UKUT 620 AAC poses another question in applying reg.7. The claimant suffered from two independent medical conditions each of which affected his living abilities on certain days of the week. One was chronic obstructive pulmonary disease (COPD) and the other was rheumatoid arthritis. Neither disease was causatively linked to the other, but neither were they mutually exclusive- in other words on some days the claimant might be inhibited by one or other of these diseases, on some days it might be by both, and on yet others he might not be inhibited at all by either. The evidence accepted by the FTT supported a finding that the claimant was affected by COPD on average for three days per week and by arthritis for two or three days of the week. Each of these conditions affected his ability to perform various descriptors in four of the daily living activities and one of the mobility activities. The tribunal in this case appears to have assumed that the medical conditions both occurred simultaneously so that the claimant failed the 50% test (required by reg.7) on each descriptor. But would the claimant have failed the 50% rule if the medical conditions did not occur simultaneously? The FTT had made no findings that related each medical condition to the separate descriptors and the case was remitted to a fresh tribunal for that to be done.

Assuming that each medical condition, or both together, might affect the claimant's ability to perform each of the relevant descriptors it would still then be necessary to determine on how many days he was so affected. One way to do this would be for the claimant to have kept a diary of his medical conditions and how they affected him each day, but that had not been done in this case and might not be done in other cases coming before tribunals. More likely, the claimant will report, as here, an estimate of the days in each week that they are affected. Evidence on a weekly basis does not accord with the "required period" as defined in reg.7(3) which refers to the period of three months before (and the nine months after) the date of claim, but it seems likely that tribunals (and others involved in this decision making) will extrapolate from the estimates that claimants can make on a weekly basis, because that is the timescale on which most claimants will think. This point was not referred to in the present case.

Assuming that the tribunal is faced with the situation, as here, where the only information available is that on some days the claimant may be affected by only one of two conditions and on other days by both conditions together, it will be necessary for the tribunal to calculate the probability that they would be affected by one, or other, or by both. This may seem a daunting task, but the method of calculating probability was supplied in this case by the Secretary of State. Using that method, the probability that the claimant might be incapacitated by one or other or both of his conditions was, in the case of rheumatism on three days of the week and COPD also on three days, a probability of 4.7 days, and if rheumatism occurred on only two days of the week and COPD on three days a probability of 4.1 days. This assumes that the each medical condition dealt with separately would affect the claimant's ability on the relevant descriptor to the same extent and both together would do the same. In that case, then the claimant would have satisfied that descriptor on more than 50% of the days in that week. If only one of the medical conditions affected a particular descriptor while the other did not (though it might have affected a lesser descriptor) then the calculation becomes much more complicated and the outcome will depend upon the extent to which each condition affects the claimant's ability in relation to each descriptor and his ability when both conditions occur simultaneously, and as well, as in this case, upon whether the rheumatism affects him on two or on three days of a week! What this does emphasise is the importance of detailed fact finding in relation to each condition, each activity and each descriptor by the FTT.

Judge Ward, in this case, has attached the Secretary of State's method of calculating probabilities as a schedule to his decision. Tribunals that are called upon to perform this exercise can read it there. That calculation produced the number of days on which the claimant was affected by one or other or both of his medical conditions. Readers of this note may find the process easier to understand if they focus, instead, on the number of days in the week that the claimant might be expected to be free of any disabling condition. If we assume that the claimant suffers from condition A on three days of the week, and from an unconnected condition B also for three days of the week, then, the chances of him being free of condition A within the week are 4/7 of the week. His chance then of not having condition B *either* in that week, are only 4/7 of those days on which he does not have A. Represented mathematically this is $4/7 \times 4/7 = 16/49$ of a week, or $16/49 \times 7 = 2.3$. The claimant would be expected to have 2.3 days in a week on which he suffered no disability and, therefore 4.7 days on which he did.

One further point should be noted. In order to satisfy the 50% rule prescribed in reg.7 the probability (expectation value) shown by this calculation will have to be greater than 3.5—reg. 7 requires "over 50% of the days", but what if the result is more than three though less than 3.5. Can the claimant then argue that by applying the "any part of a day" rule exemplified above, he should then have the days' of disablement rounded up to four? The answer is—No. To do that would amount to "double counting" because the part-day rule will have already been employed in identifying the days on which the claimant is affected by each of his conditions. The calculation of the probabilities is then purely an exercise in statistics.

The assessment report made by the HCP will contain advice on the claimant's abilities over both the past three months (the qualifying period) and the likely ability over the next nine months (the prospective period). Most awards of benefit will be made for a fixed period (seldom more than three years—see s.88 (2) WRA 2012 above and the notes that follow it), but the assessment report will also contain advice as to how long the claimant should be left before a review is made of his ability even within that period. In some cases this will be to a claimant's advantage as he will then be picked up automatically when a condition has worsened; in others benefit will be reduced or will end when his condition has improved. Where the claimant's condition is expected to improve within the nine month period (e.g. he is scheduled for corrective surgery in the near future) the claimant will not qualify for benefit, but DWP guidance suggests that he may still be scheduled for review in case the surgery is postponed or unsuccessful.

Information or evidence required for determining limited or severely limited ability to carry out activities

8.—(1) The Secretary of State may require C to provide any information or evidence required to determine whether C has limited ability or severely limited ability to carry out daily living activities or mobility activities.   4.184

(2) Where information or evidence is requested under paragraph (1), C must provide the information or evidence to the Secretary of State within one month from the date of the request being made or within such longer period as the Secretary of State may consider reasonable in the circumstances of the particular case.

(3) Where C fails without good reason to comply with the request referred to in paragraph (1), a negative determination in relation to the component to which the failure related must be made.

GENERAL NOTE

The procedure to be followed on a claim for PIP is described in detail on the DWP website. In brief it is envisaged that most PIP claims will commence with a   4.185

telephone call or by an online application. For claimants who do not have access to the DWP website, or to a telephone, or who are uncomfortable using one, a paper route is available. When a claim has been received it should contain sufficient information for the DM to decide if the "lay" conditions of entitlement are satisfied. These are the conditions as to residence and presence — see regs 16-23 below.

Provided those are satisfied the DM will issue a claimant questionnaire to gather information about the claimant's condition. The claimant will be invited at the same time to provide any supporting information and details of his health care professional and others who may be able to help determine his condition. The DM refers the file to the HCP provider. The HCP can then decide whether further evidence is necessary, (which may be obtained by telephone), whether he can then (or with any further evidence obtained) make a report on the basis of the "paperwork" (in fact an e-file) that is available to him, or whether there should be a face-to-face interview with the claimant. In most cases there will be an interview with the claimant. This assessment interview can be at the provider's premises, some other location or, if necessary, in the claimant's home. In claims based upon terminal illness there is a special fast-track procedure that will not involve a face-to-face interview.

The question of whether medical reports and evidence that supported a previous award of DLA should be available to a tribunal when the claimant has appealed following transition from DLA to PIP has been considered in several cases. In *GD v SSWP (PIP)* [2017] UKUT 415 (AAC) it emerged that in all transition cases when the claimant is first interviewed by an officer of the DWP on the PIP claim, the claimant will always be asked if they wish evidence that was used for the DLA award to be considered in relation to their claim for PIP. This question does not appear on the PIP claim form. The SSWP also confirmed that where that information has been asked for by the claimant and used in making a decision it should subsequently appear as part of that claimant's file and be available on an appeal. Judge Markus QC returned the case for a rehearing, but in the light of this information and the fact that although the criteria for DLA and for PIP are different it was, in this case, likely that the information that had supported the award of DLA would have been relevant in assessing the report of the HCP, the judge directed that the SSWP provide that evidence to the new FTT if it were available. (She had also been provided with information from the DWP as to how long such evidence was retained in certain circumstances; that information appears in the judgment).

The information that claimants who are to be transitioned are asked this question will probably come as a surprise to a number of judges who have decided similar cases in the past. In *AP v SSWP (PIP)* [2016] UKUT 416 (AAC) Judge Hemingway decided just such a case. There, the representative of the SSWP had accepted that there was a duty to provide a copy of all documents in the DM's possession that were relevant to the claim, but argued that because the criteria for DLA and for PIP were different and because any medical evidence or other report would necessarily relate to a different time, that such evidence would rarely be required. Judge Hemingway decided this case on the basis that the FTT had erred in law in failing to give sufficient weight to medical evidence with which they had been provided, but he gave as his opinion, as well, that in a case like this, where the claimant had alleged that there was copious evidence relating to the DLA award, that the SSWP should provide at least a list of that evidence, and that the FTT should consider asking for that evidence to be produced where, as here, there was a marked disparity in the decision that had been reached on the award of DLA and that for PIP. He suggests that it might be so too, where there was reason to think that the HCP report might be unreliable; given the frequency with which that is said to be the case by PIP claimants this might turn out to be quite frequent. Judge Hemingway noted that a different conclusion had been reached in *DC v SSWP (PIP)* [2016] UKUT 117 (AAC) but there the DLA evidence related to the claimant's condition eight years before, as well as to the differing criteria. The same point is made by Judge Gray in *MA v SSWP (PIP)* [2017] UKUT 351 (AAC). She directs that the new FTT to whom the case was remitted should be provided with both the relevant DLA award evidence and also evidence from an ESA examination.

It appears that the directions now given to DM preparing cases for appeal to a tribunal may be different from those that applied in earlier cases. That emerges from the information that is contained in the decision of Judge Markus QC in *CH and KN v SSWP (PIP)* [2018] UKUT 330 (AAC). That case, and others, is discussed in the General Note following reg.4 above. Members of FTT will find the guidance offered by Judge Markus and the information provided by the Secretary of State regarding the current process used in transfer cases very helpful.

Claimant may be called for a consultation to determine whether the claimant has limited or severely limited ability to carry out activities

9.—(1) Where it falls to be determined whether C has limited ability or severely limited ability to carry out daily living activities or mobility activities, C may be required to do either or both of the following —   4.186

(a) attend for and participate in a consultation in person;

(b) participate in a consultation by telephone.

(2) Subject to paragraph (3), where C fails without good reason to attend for or participate in a consultation referred to in paragraph (1), a negative determination must be made.

(3) Paragraph (2) does not apply unless —

(a) written notice of the date, time and, where applicable, place for, the consultation is sent to C at least 7 days in advance; or

(b) C agrees, whether in writing or otherwise, to accept a shorter period of notice of those matters.

(4) In paragraph (3), reference to written notice includes notice sent by electronic communication where C has agreed to accept correspondence in that way and "electronic communication" has the meaning given in section 15(1) of the Electronic Communications Act 2000.

(5) In this regulation, a reference to consultation is to a consultation with a person approved by the Secretary of State.

GENERAL NOTE

See notes to reg.8 above. Where the consultation is by telephone a written record   4.187
of the conversation must be made and must be read back to the claimant. Where there is a face-to-face consultation the claimant may be permitted to record the interview, but only an aural recording, only on certain equipment and only if that then permits him to provide a full and accurate copy of the recording immediately the interview ends.

Two cases have been decided on the operation of this regulation. The regulation calls for a claimant to co-operate by attending for assessment with a HCP or by taking part in a telephone conversation to assist in determining their claim. Where a claimant fails to do so, without good reason, para.(2) provides that a "negative determination must be made". Matters to be taken into account in determining "good reason" are defined in reg.10; they include the claimant's state of health and the nature of any disability.

In the first case, *SY v SSWP (PIP)* [2017] UKUT 363 (AAC) Judge Wikeley allowed the claimant's appeal against a decision that she had failed without good reason to attend or participate in a consultation to which she had been called in accordance with reg.9. This case reveals the problems that can arise in consequence of confusion about the roles of the DWP and of the provider of the independent assessment (in this case ATOS). The claimant, who had several mental health conditions, had made telephone calls to both the DWP and to ATOS. Before the UT the representative of the SSWP accepted that, as a result of these calls, the claimant had been told, and reasonably believed, that she was not required to attend for an assessment provided that she filed further medical evidence, which she had done. Indeed, before the UT a letter was produced that had been sent by ATOS clearly stating that she should not attend as the appointment was cancelled; this letter was not before the FTT. In the light of this, as well as other evidence, the judge was able to allow the appeal and directed that the claim be allowed to proceed for decision by the DM on the evidence that was available to him. What this case does highlight is the lack of any evidence provided to the FTT in support of the negative determination. The papers before the FTT and the UT simply recited that the claimant had failed to attend on four occasions when appointments had been made for her; no evidence was available in the form of appointment letters, other correspondence, records of telephone calls or otherwise, in support of these allegations. Judge Wikeley thought that, at the very least, such information should be provided. Judge Wikeley has dealt with this issue again, twice in respect of the same claimant, the second appeal being *TC v SSWP (No.2) (PIP)* [2018] UKUT 286 (AAC). On both occasions he emphasises the importance of FTT examining thoroughly the evidence on which the decision to reach a negative determination has been made. Yet another consideration of the complications that have arisen from confusion in the DWP and in the FTT are illustrated by another decision of Judge Wikeley in *AI v SSWP (PIP)* [2019] UKUT 103 (AAC). In this case the claimant had failed both to return a medical enquiry form under reg. 8, and to attend an assessment under reg.9. An appeal made originally against the reg. 8 decision but subsequently treated as an appeal against the striking out of his claim after he had eventually attended an assessment and been awarded 0 points was allowed by Judge Wikeley because it did not appear that at any time the DM had taken a decision to refuse benefit!

The second case, a decision of Judge Mesher in *OM v SSWP (PIP)* [2017] UKUT 458 (AAC), has the added complication that the claimant had an appointee in respect of his dealings with the DWP. The construction of reg.9 does not sit comfortably with that situation. In this case too, the judge was able to allow the appeal and reinstate the claim. But here, the decision to discontinue the PIP claim had meant also the termination of the claimant's DLA claim, so that claim was also reinstated. This case again illustrates the confusion that arises from communication being between the appointee (this time with assistance also from a representative some of the time) and both DWP and the healthcare assessment provider (ATOS). The appointee had requested that the claimant be seen at a home visit; at some stage this was approved by the DWP, but was refused by ATOS on the ground of past incidents of aggression by the claimant. Judge Mesher allowed the appeal, ultimately, on the ground that the FTT had not taken a broad enough view of the factors to be considered in relation to the rejection of the element of good reason in reaching a decision of negative determination. Reg.10 "includes" the two reasons given above, but in the judge's view (applying an approach similar to that which has applied to jobseeker's allowance and formerly to unemployment benefit) regard should be had also to the suitability for that claimant of the arrangements that had been made for assessment. As well, he thought that the claimant should be entitled to include in his reasons the likelihood of that assessment producing any evidence that was not to be obtained already from his medical reports and possibly from evidence on his DLA award if that were relevant. The judge suggests also that where the FTT gave as the crux of their decision that the claimant had, in the end, made a conscious choice not to attend the appointment, they had failed to deal sufficiently, or at any rate failed to record their reasons for not doing so, with the fact that the claimant had an appointee whose very existence suggests that the DWP accepted that he was not capable of organising his own affairs when dealing with a claim. He observed also that the language they had used in this part of their decision—that the claimant had not shown that he was "incapable" of attending and that he was not "prevented" from attending, might indicate that they were applying a higher standard than the words of the regulation—having "good reason" not to attend. Judge

Mesher outlines a number of other concerns raised by this appeal without reaching final conclusions on them. These included the following:

(1) That reg.9 was validly made under s.80 of the Welfare Reform Act 2012.

(2) That in accordance with the regime disclosed in *GD v SSWP (PIP)* [2017] UKUT 415 (AAC) for a claimant to be offered the opportunity that his DLA award evidence be included for consideration, it was reasonable to infer that, in a case such as this, the claimant would be very likely to have done so even though no mention of that was made in the case file.

(3) Although reg.9 did not specify who should require the claimant to attend for assessment he inferred that this must be a decision for the DM, as too, would be the decision whether a telephone conversation might suffice. This raised a question as to whether that decision might be open to appeal to the tribunal, but Judge Mesher found it unnecessary to decide that point because it could be adequately subsumed in the issue of good reason as he had interpreted it. (In the UT, counsel for the Secretary of State had conceded that the FTT had erred in not considering whether a telephone consultation might have sufficed in this case, though whether as an appeal against the decision in choosing a face-to-face assessment, or as a factor in the good reason issue, was not clear).

(4) Assuming that the DM has correctly decided that an assessment appointment is necessary, can the decision and subsequent arrangements be left to another (i.e. the healthcare assessment provider) to be completed to fulfil the requirements of reg.9? The judge thought it could, though he thought that it should then be necessary for that body to provide evidence to support the allegation that appointments had been made etc. He thought that at least a standard letter with evidence that it had been used in this case would be necessary.

(5) The judge points out that the provision relating to appointees in the Claims and Payments Regulations (reg.57(5)) applies only to things required to be done in respect of those regulations and not of other regulations. This raised the question of whether in relation to the PIP regulations requests addressed to the appointee could impose the duty to attend on the claimant and a consequent negative determination. He recognised that this might be the only effective way to communicate that requirement to a claimant, but the difficulty in applying the regulations remained unless an argument based on the principle of agency were used instead.

(6) The judge thought that even if the assessment arrangements could correctly be delegated to the healthcare assessment provider it was still competent for the DWP to remain involved in the arrangements. It might for example be appropriate for the DM to withdraw the case from the assessment process at this stage, but it was more difficult to determine how DWP involvement might impinge on other aspects of the arrangements—e.g. whether a home visit was appropriate.

(7) By not attending an appointment he accepted that the claimant would be "failing" to attend, but left open how that concept might be nuanced by a claimant's late arrival, or choice to leave early when the venue was running late, especially given the consequences of a negative determination. Most of these points, he felt, would be better dealt with as a part of the good reason issue.

(8) In judging good reason where there is an appointee there is a further question as to whose personal circumstances are to be taken account of—obviously those of the claimant are relevant, but what about those of the appointee? Does the claimant have good reason not to attend if his appointee is not available—must the possibility of another substitute be considered? Judge Mesher leaves these issues open.

Matters to be taken into account in determining good reason in relation to regulations 8 and 9

10. The matters to be taken into account in determining whether C has good reason under regulation 8(3) or 9(2) include— 4.188

(a) C's state of health at the relevant time; and

(b) the nature of any disability that C has.

GENERAL NOTE

4.189   Where the claimant fails to return a questionnaire within one month, (see reg.8 above) or if he fails to attend an interview, or to respond to a telephone consultation the DM may make a negative determination (refuse the claim) after having due regard to the matters above i.e. the claimant's state of health and their disabling condition—e.g. a claimant suffering from depression so as not to be able to manage his affairs effectively.

The claimant will have the right to appeal against that determination, but in most cases it will be as well to commence a new claim unless there has been a long delay before the appeal is commenced.

Re-determination of ability to carry out activities

4.190   **11.** Where it has been determined that C has limited ability or severely limited ability to carry out either or both daily living activities or mobility activities, the Secretary of State may, for any reason and at any time, determine afresh in accordance with regulation 4 whether C continues to have such limited ability or severely limited ability.

GENERAL NOTE

4.191   This regulation appears to mean that PIP, unlike DLA can be reviewed and superseded by the Secretary of State at any time and for any reason; there would be no need to identify a change of circumstances as has been necessary in respect of other benefits. However, there may be reason to question that conclusion. The literal interpretation that the regulation invites seems to be inconsistent with the provisions made in the relevant Decisions and Appeals regulations (Universal Credit, Personal Independence Payment, Jobseeker's Allowance and Employment Support Allowance (Decisions and Appeals) Regulations 2013 (SI 2013/381). In which case it may be more correct to interpret this regulation merely as authorising a reassessment, in accordance with reg.4, of the claimant's capability at any time, though it would still remain necessary to show that there is a ground for revision or supersession in accordance with the Decisions and Appeals regulations. This, more limited interpretation, of the regulation has been adopted by Judge Mesher in *KB v SSWP (PIP)* [2016] UKUT 537 (AAC). He concludes, though only provisionally because in the event it was not necessary for him to decide the point, that regulation 11 only creates the opportunity for the Secretary of State to re-determine the issue of the claimant's abilities in relation to the prescribed activities and that it remains necessary thereafter for the normal decision process of supersession to be followed under the Decisions and Appeals Regulations. That this interpretation of the regulation is correct is now affirmed in a series of UT decisions— see *DS v SSWP (PIP)* [2016] UKUT 538 (AAC), *KB v SSWP (PIP)* [2016] UKUT 537 (AAC), *PM v SSWP (PIP)* [2017] UKUT 37 (AAC) and *TH v SSWP (PIP)* [2017] UKUT 231 (AAC). A full analysis of the provisions and the procedure to be followed is provided in the decision of Judge Wright in the *PM* case.

PART 3

REQUIRED PERIOD CONDITION

Required period condition: daily living component

4.192   **12.**—(1) C meets the required period condition for the purposes of section 78(1) of the Act (daily living component at standard rate) where—

    (a) if C had been assessed at every time in the period of 3 months ending with the prescribed date, it is likely that the Secretary of State would have determined at that time that C had limited ability to carry out daily living activities; and

(b) if C were to be assessed at every time in the period of 9 months beginning with the day after the prescribed date, it is likely that the Secretary of State would determine at that time that C had limited ability to carry out daily living activities.

(2) C meets the required period condition for the purposes of section 78(2) of the Act (daily living component at enhanced rate) where—

(a) if C had been assessed at every time in the period of 3 months ending with the prescribed date, it is likely that the Secretary of State would have determined at that time that C had severely limited ability to carry out daily living activities; and

(b) if C were to be assessed at every time in the period of 9 months beginning with the day after the prescribed date, it is likely that the Secretary of State would determine at that time that C had severely limited ability to carry out daily living activities.

GENERAL NOTE

See above the notes to reg.7.   4.193

Required period condition: mobility component

13.—(1) C meets the required period condition for the purposes of   4.194
section 79(1) of the Act (mobility component at standard rate) where —

(a) if C had been assessed at every time in the period of 3 months ending with the prescribed date, it is likely that the Secretary of State would have determined at that time that C had limited ability to carry out mobility activities; and

(b) if C were to be assessed at every time in the period of 9 months beginning with the day after the prescribed date, it is likely that the Secretary of State would determine at that time that C had limited ability to carry out mobility activities.

(2) C meets the required period condition for the purposes of section 79(2) of the Act (mobility component at enhanced rate) where—

(a) if C had been assessed at every time in the period of 3 months ending with the prescribed date, it is likely that the Secretary of State would have determined at that time that C had severely limited ability to carry out mobility activities; and

(b) if C were to be assessed at every time in the period of 9 months beginning with the day after the prescribed date, it is likely that the Secretary of State would determine at that time that C had severely limited ability to carry out mobility activities.

GENERAL NOTE

See above the notes to reg.7.   4.195

The prescribed date

14. Except where paragraph (2) or (3) of regulation 15 applies, the pre-   4.196
scribed date is—

(a) where C has made a claim for personal independence payment which has not been determined, the date of that claim or, if later, the earliest date in relation to which, if C had been assessed in relation to C's ability to carry out daily living activities or, as the case may be, mobility activities, at every time in the previous 3 months, it is likely that the Secretary of State would have determined at that time that C had limited ability or, as the case may be, severely limited ability to carry out those activities; and

(b) where C has an award of either or both components, each day of that award.

GENERAL NOTE

4.197   This means that the prescribed date (the date at which both the qualifying period and, a day later, the prospective period will run) will normally be the date of claim. But it may be a later date where the DM can determine that although the claimant would not have satisfied the assessment requirements at that date he has done so at some later time.

Where the claimant has an existing award of benefit para.(b) means that he must always be able to show that his condition can be expected to continue for the next nine months. This may create some difficulty where the claimant reports that he is expecting, within that period, to receive surgery or treatment that will greatly alleviate his condition.

This situation arose in *BM v SSWP (PIP)* [2017] UKUT 486 (AAC). The claimant had a recurring condition that was alleviated by periodic injections of cortisone, but the effect of those injections wore off and there was then a delay before he could get another injection. The claimant was in receipt of the Daily Living component and had claimed previously, unsuccessfully for the Mobility component. He notified the DWP of a deterioration in his condition and completed a new claim form. This claim was to be treated as a supersession of his existing award. The question that then arose was, what was to be treated as the relevant time period (both the past and the prospective period) for the purposes of s.81 of the Welfare Reform Act 2012. That was to be determined in accordance with para. (b) above, but Judge Bano decided that the words "each day of that award" did not mean every day of the award; to do that he thought would make nonsense of the provision because it would mean that the period would be elongated to the full term of the award. The words must mean instead any day of the award that was chosen by the FTT as the prescribed date—in this case the day on which the claimant had reported his deterioration. This Judge Bano held was correct, though he allowed the appeal on another ground.

The prescribed date: claims for personal independence payment after an interval

4.198   **15.**—(1) Paragraphs (2) and (3) apply where—

(a) C makes a claim for personal independence payment ("the new claim");

(b) C had a previous award which ended not more than 2 years before the date on which the new claim is made;

(c) the previous award referred to in sub-paragraph (b) consisted of the same component as the one to which C is entitled (or would be entitled if C met the required period condition) under the new claim; and

(d) the Secretary of State determines that the entitlement under the new claim results from—

(i) substantially the same physical or mental condition or conditions for which the previous award was made; or

(ii) a new physical or mental condition which developed as a result of a condition for which the previous award was made.

(2) In relation to determination of entitlement under the new claim—

(a) the prescribed date for the purposes of regulations 12(1)(a) and (2)(a) and 13(1)(a) and (2)(a) is the date on which the previous award ended; and

(b) regulations 12(1)(b) and (2)(b) and 13(1)(b) and (2)(b) have effect in relation to the new claim as if, for the words "the prescribed date" there were substituted "the date on which the new claim for personal independence payment is made".

(3) Where C is awarded either or both components under the new claim, in relation to continued entitlement to that component or, as the case may be, those components, for the period of 3 months following the date of the new claim—

(a) the prescribed date for the purposes of regulations 12(1)(a) and (2) (a) and 13(1)(a) and (2)(a) is the date on which the previous award ended; and

(b) regulations 12(1)(b) and (2)(b) and 13(1)(b) and (2)(b) have effect in relation to that award as if, for the words "the prescribed date" there were substituted "each day of the award".

(4) This regulation is subject to regulation 26.

GENERAL NOTE

This regulation assists claimants who have a condition that fluctuates in the sense   **4.199**
that they may experience protracted periods of remission and then a further onset of the condition. Provided that the episodes of disability occur at intervals not greater than two years the claimant can re-qualify for benefit immediately (no qualifying period) so long as the award will be for the same component of PIP and so long as the new disability results from the same disabling condition, or another condition that is derived from the earlier one.

PART 4

RESIDENCE AND PRESENCE CONDITIONS

Conditions relating to residence and presence in Great Britain

16. Subject to the following provisions of this Part, the prescribed con-   **4.200**
ditions for the purposes of section 77(3) of the Act as to residence and presence in Great Britain are that on any day for which C claims personal independence payment C—

(a) is present in Great Britain;

(b) has been present in Great Britain for a period of, or periods amounting in aggregate to, not less than 104 weeks out of the 156 weeks immediately preceding that day;

(c) is habitually resident in the United Kingdom, the Republic of Ireland, the Isle of Man or the Channel Islands; and

(d) is a person—

(i) who is not subject to immigration control within the meaning of section 115(9) of the Immigration and Asylum Act 1999; or

(ii) to whom, by virtue of regulation 2 of the Social Security (Immigration and Asylum) Consequential Amendments Regulations 2000, section 115 of that Act does not apply for the purpose of personal independence payment.

GENERAL NOTE

4.201   A claimant must show that he is both present in Great Britain and habitually resident in what is commonly referred to as the common travel area (UK, Republic of Ireland, Channel Islands and the Isle of Man).

Presence is simply a matter of being physically present and is subject to exceptions in regs 17, 18 and 19 below.

Habitual residence is more complicated. It is not defined in any statutory form, but it has been the subject of extensive case-law, mainly in relation to means-tested benefits. (Details and discussion of these cases may be found in the notes to the relevant sections of Vol.II of this Work).

In brief, habitual residence requires that you have a settled intention to live in this country as your home, but not necessarily to live here permanently. As well, it requires that that the claimant has been in the country already for an extended period. How long he must have been here, will depend upon the circumstances of the claimant; a former resident returning from a period abroad may satisfy this test almost immediately, while a new immigrant may be required to demonstrate a considerable period of residence.

In *MM and SI v SSWP (DLA)* [2016] UKUT 149 (AAC) Judge Markus QC has held that reg.2(1)(a)(iii) of the DLA regulations, the equivalent of reg.16(b) of these regulations (the past presence test or PPT) must be disapplied in respect of claims made on behalf of applicants who were family members of persons granted refugee status in the UK. She held that the PPT was indirectly discriminatory and could not be justified (when compared to the treatment of UK nationals) under art.28 of the EU Directive 2004/8 3/EC (which gives protection to refugees) and which she held had direct effect in the UK. For the same reason she held that PPT was in breach of the claimant's rights under art.14 of the ECHR. At the time the claims were made, the applicants satisfied the other conditions of reg.2 which meant that their claims should proceed accordingly. That decision was in respect of a claim for DLA, but the ruling applies equally to a claim for personal independence payment.

Absence from Great Britain

4.202   **17.**—(1) Where C is temporarily absent from Great Britain, C is treated as present in Great Britain for the purposes of regulation 16(a) and (b) for the first 13 weeks of absence.

(2) C is temporarily absent if, at the beginning of the period of absence, C's absence is unlikely to exceed 52 weeks.

Absence from Great Britain to receive medical treatment

4.203   **18.**—(1) Where C is temporarily absent from Great Britain, C is treated as present in Great Britain for the purposes of regulation 16(a) and (b) for the first 26 weeks of that absence, where—

(a) C's absence is solely in connection with arrangements made for the medical treatment of C for a disease or bodily or mental disablement which commenced before C left Great Britain; and

(b) the arrangements referred to in paragraph (1)(a) relate to medical treatment—

   (i) outside Great Britain;

   (ii) during the period whilst C is temporarily absent from Great Britain; and

   (iii) by, or under the supervision of, a person appropriately qualified to carry out that treatment.

(2) In this regulation, "temporarily absent" has the same meaning as in regulation 17(2).

"medical treatment" – see reg.2

Absence from Great Britain in special cases

19.—(1) Where C is absent from Great Britain, C is treated as present in   4.204
Great Britain for the purposes of regulation 16(a) and (b), where—
 (a) C is abroad in the capacity of—
  (i) a member of Her Majesty's forces;
  (ii) an aircraft worker; or
  (iii) a mariner; or
 (b) C is in employment prescribed for the purposes of section 120
   (employment at sea (continental shelf operations)) of the Social
   Security Contributions and Benefits Act 1992 in connection with
   continental shelf operations; or
 (c) C is living with a person mentioned in paragraph (a)(i) and is the
   spouse, civil partner, son, daughter, step-son, step-daughter, father,
   father-in-law, step-father, mother, mother-in-law or step-mother of
   that person.
(2) In this regulation and in regulation 20, "a member of Her Majesty's
forces" means a member of "the regular forces" or "the reserve forces" as
defined in section 374 of the Armed Forces Act 2006, other than a person
who is specified in Schedule 2, who is—
 (a) over the age of 16; and
 (b) not absent on desertion.
(3) In this regulation—
"aircraft worker" means a person who is employed under a contract of
service either as a pilot, commander, navigator or other member of the crew
of any aircraft, or in any other capacity on board any aircraft where—
 (a) the employment in that other capacity is for the purposes of the aircraft or its crew or of any passengers or cargo or mail carried on that
   aircraft; and
 (b) the contract is entered into in the United Kingdom with a view to its
   performance (in whole or in part) while the aircraft is in flight, but
   does not include a person who is in employment as a member of Her
   Majesty's forces;
"mariner" means a person who is in employment under a contract of
service either as a master or member of the crew of any ship or vessel, or in
any other capacity on board any ship or vessel where—
 (a) the employment in that other capacity is for the purposes of that ship
   or vessel or the crew or any passengers or cargo or mail carried by the
   ship or vessel; and
 (b) the contract is entered into in the United Kingdom with a view to
   its performance (in whole or in part) while the ship or vessel is on
   voyage, but does not include a person who is in employment as a
   member of Her Majesty's forces.

Serving members of Her Majesty's forces and their family members—further provision

20. C is treated as habitually resident in Great Britain for the purposes of   4.205
regulation 16(c) where—

(a) C is resident outside Great Britain in the capacity of a member of Her Majesty's forces; or

(b) C is living with a person mentioned in paragraph (a) and is the spouse, civil partner, son, daughter, step-son, step-daughter, father, father-in-law, step-father, mother, mother-in-law or step-mother of that person.

Terminal illness

4.206   **21.** Where C is terminally ill and makes a claim for personal independence payment expressly on that ground, regulation 16 applies as if paragraph (b) were omitted.

GENERAL NOTE

4.207   The claimant must still be present in Great Britain (or treated as present—see regs 17, 18 and 19 above) but if the claim is made on the basis of terminal illness it will not be necessary to show that they have been in the country for two out of the past three years.

The claimant must still be habitually resident in the common travel area and not subject to immigration control etc.

Persons residing in Great Britain to whom a relevant EU Regulation applies

4.208   **22.** Regulation 16(b) does not apply in relation to a claim for personal independence payment where on any day—

(a) C is habitually resident in Great Britain;

(b) a relevant EU Regulation applies; and

(c) C can demonstrate a genuine and sufficient link to the United Kingdom social security system.

GENERAL NOTE

4.209   The relevant EU regulations are those specified in s.84 of the WRA 2012.

If the claimant is an EU national he will still need to be present in Great Britain though not necessarily for 104 weeks out of the past 156 weeks. He will also need to be habitually resident in Great Britain and to demonstrate a sufficient link to the UK social security system.

The aggregation of periods of residence in another EU country has been considered by Judge Jacobs in *BK v SSWP and SSWP v MM* [2016] UKUT 547 (AAC). Relying on the case of *Stewart v SSWP* (C-503/09), the Judge held that mere residence in this country was not sufficient to aggregate that time with time spent in another EU country, but neither was it necessary to show a link with this country's social security system. This decision may be subject to appeal. The matter has been considered again in *Kavanagh v SSWP* CDLA/373/2016. This case is being appealed to the court of appeal. For further detail see Vol.III of this work.

Persons residing in an EEA state other than the United Kingdom or in Switzerland to whom a relevant EU Regulation applies

4.210   **23.** Regulation 16(a) to (c) does not apply in relation to entitlement to the daily living component of personal independence payment where on any day—

(a) C is habitually resident in—

(i) an EEA state other than the United Kingdom; or

(ii) Switzerland;

(b) a relevant EU Regulation applies; and
(c) C can demonstrate a genuine and sufficient link to the United Kingdom social security system.

GENERAL NOTE

The relevant EU regulations are those specified in s.84 of the WRA 2012.   4.211
A claimant who satisfies those regulations and is living abroad will be entitled to PIP (daily living component) if they are habitually resident in an EEA country not being the UK or Switzerland, and if they can demonstrate a sufficient link to the UK social security system. In *SSWP v LT* [2012] UKUT 282 (AAC) it was held, in relation to a claim for DLA (care component), that the claimant had a sufficient connection to the social security system when she had a past record of contributions and an expectation of Retirement Pension in the future.
This decision, and therefore that of the UT, has been upheld by the answers provided by the EUECJ. (See *SSWP v Tolley* [2017] EUECJ C-430/15). They confirm that the care component is a "sickness benefit" and that the claimant's past contribution record made her an "employed person" and therefore within the protection of the regulation. This case is concerned with the old Regulation 1408/71 but it is likely that the same result would follow under the current Regulation 883/04.

[¹ Refugees

23A.—(1) Regulation 16(b) does not apply in relation to a claim for personal   4.212
independence payment where C has—
  (a) been granted refugee status or humanitarian protection under the immigration rules; or
  (b) leave to enter or remain in the United Kingdom as the dependant of a person granted refugee status or humanitarian protection under the immigration rules.
(2) For the purposes of this regulation "immigration rules" means the rules laid before Parliament under section 3(2) of the Immigration Act 1971.]

AMENDMENT

1. Social Security (Miscellaneous Amendments No.4) Regulations 2017 (SI 2017/1015) reg.14 (November 16, 2017).

PART 5

RATE OF PERSONAL INDEPENDENCE PAYMENT

Rate of personal independence payment

24.—(1) The prescribed weekly rates of the daily living component for   4.213
the purposes of section 78(3) of the Act are—
  (a) the standard rate, [¹ £58.70]; and
  (b) the enhanced rate, [¹ £87.65].
(2) The prescribed weekly rates of the mobility component for the purposes of section 79(3) of the Act are—
  (a) the standard rate, [¹ £23.20]; and
  (b) the enhanced rate, [¹ £61.20].

AMENDMENT

1. Social Security Benefits Up-rating Order 2019 (SI 2019/480) art.16 (April 8, 2019).

PART 6

PROVISIONS RELATING TO AGE

Exceptions to section 83 where entitlement exists or claim made before relevant age

4.214   **25.** Section 83(1) of the Act (persons of pensionable age) does not apply where C has reached the relevant age if C—
(a) was entitled to an award of either or both components on the day preceding the day on which C reached the relevant age; or
(b) made a claim for personal independence payment before reaching the relevant age and that claim was not determined before C reached that age but an award of either or both components would be made in respect of C but for section 83(1) of the Act.

GENERAL NOTE

4.215   No new claim for PIP can normally be made beyond the "relevant age"—currently this means the age of 65.

Persons who have an award of PIP at the time they reach the relevant age will be able to continue entitlement to PIP so long as they continue to satisfy the other conditions of entitlement. Given that by 2017 all awards of DLA for persons of working age should have been converted to PIP it does mean that DLA for the elderly will disappear eventually.

Persons who have made a claim for PIP before reaching the relevant age will also be entitled to continue that entitlement if their claim is successful.

Claim for personal independence payment after an interval and after reaching the relevant age

4.216   **26.**—(1) Where C has reached the relevant age and makes a new claim in the circumstances set out in regulation 15 the following exceptions apply.
(2) The exceptions referred to in paragraph (1) are—
(a) section 83(1) of the Act (persons of pensionable age) does not apply;
(b) the reference to "2 years" in regulation 15(1)(b) is to be read as "1 year";
(c) where C is assessed as having severely limited ability to carry out mobility activities for the purposes of the new claim—
(i) C is entitled to the enhanced rate of the mobility component only if C was entitled to that rate of that component under the previous award; and
(ii) where C is not entitled to the enhanced rate of that component because of paragraph (i), C is entitled to the standard rate of that component provided that C was entitled to that rate of that component under the previous award; and
(d) where C is assessed as having limited ability to carry out mobility activities for the purposes of the new claim, C is entitled to the standard rate of the mobility component only if C was entitled to that component, at either rate, under the previous award.

General Note

A person who is over pensionable age may make a new claim for either component   4.217
of PIP, subject to the same conditions that apply under reg.15, but only if the previous
award referred to there ended no more than one year before the new claim is made.
Where the new claim is in respect of a mobility component further restrictions apply.
The award can only be for the enhanced rate where that rate was in payment in the
previous claim; otherwise the award must be at the standard rate whatever the claimant's condition is now. (And the claimant must have been in receipt of the mobility
component, presumably at that rate, in the previous award in order to satisfy reg.15).
Where the claimant's condition now would justify only an award at the standard rate
they can qualify for that rate if they were entitled to either rate in the previous award.

Revision and supersession of an award after the person has reached the relevant age

27.—(1) Subject to paragraph (2), section 83(1) of the Act (persons of   4.218
pensionable age) does not apply where—
  (a) C has reached the relevant age and is entitled to an award ("the origi-
      nal award") of either or both components pursuant to an exception
      in regulation 25 or 26; and
  (b) that award falls to be revised or superseded.
  (2) Where the original award includes an award of the mobility component and is superseded for a relevant change of circumstance which
occurred after C reached the relevant age, the restrictions in paragraph (3)
apply in relation to the supersession.
  (3) The restrictions referred to in paragraph (2) are—
  (a) where the original mobility component award is for the standard rate
      then, regardless of whether the award would otherwise have been for
      the enhanced rate, the Secretary of State—
      (i) may only make an award for the standard rate of that compo-
          nent; and
      (ii) may only make such an award where entitlement results from
           substantially the same condition or conditions for which the
           mobility component in the original award was made.
  (b) where the original mobility component award is for the enhanced
      rate, the Secretary of State may only award that rate of that compo-
      nent where entitlement results from substantially the same condition
      or conditions for which the mobility award was made.
  (4) Where the original award does not include an award of the mobility
component but C had a previous award of that component, for the purpose
of this regulation entitlement under that previous award is to be treated as
if it were under the original award provided that the entitlement under the
previous award ceased no more than 1 year prior to the date on which the
supersession takes or would take effect.

General Note

Where a claimant is over retirement age and an existing award (referred to in   4.219
this regulation as the "original award") of either component of PIP is to be revised
or superseded there are further restrictions that apply in relation to the mobility
component. If the revision and supersession is on the ground of a change of circumstances then, where the existing award is for the standard rate the new award can
only be at that rate regardless of the claimant's condition now. Where the existing
award is for the enhanced rate the new award can only be at that rate if the current

condition results from substantially the same conditions as did the existing award. Where the existing award does not contain the mobility component it is possible for a person over retirement age, exceptionally, to renew a previous award (i.e. an award that was previous to the award that is to be reviewed), at either rate, but only if the claimant had an entitlement to that rate in the previous award and that award ended no more than one year before the new revision and supersession will take effect.

PART 7

PAYABILITY WHEN PERSON IS RESIDING IN CERTAIN ACCOMMODATION OR IS DETAINED IN CUSTODY

Care home residents

4.220   **28.**—(1) Subject to paragraph (3) and regulation 30, no amount of personal independence payment which is attributable to the daily living component is payable in respect of C for any period during which C meets the condition in section 85(2) of the Act (care home residents: costs of qualifying services borne out of public or local funds).

(2) For the purpose of section 85(2) of the Act the specified enactments are—

   (a) Part 3 of the National Assistance Act 1948 (Local Authority Services);
   (b) Sections 59 and 59A of the Social Work (Scotland) Act 1968 (provision of residential and other establishments by local authorities and maximum period for repayment of sums borrowed for such provision and grants in respect of secure accommodation for children respectively);
   (c) the Mental Health Act 1983
   (d) the Community Care and Health (Scotland) Act 2002);
   (e) the Mental Health (Care and Treatment) (Scotland) Act 2003;
[¹ (ee) section 57 of the Health and Social Care Act 2001;]
[² (eea) Part 1 of the Care Act 2014 (care and support);]
[³ (eeb) Part 4 of the Social Services and Well-being (Wales) Act 2014 (meeting needs), or]
   (f) any other enactment relating to persons under a disability or to young persons or to education or training except—
      (i) section 485 of the Education Act 1996 (grants in aid of educational services or research);
      (ii) section 14 of the Education Act 2002 (power of Secretary of State or National Assembly for Wales to give financial assistance for purposes related to education or children etc.);
      (iii) section 49 of the Education (Scotland) Act 1980 (power of education authorities to assist persons to take advantage of educational facilities) or section 73 of that Act (power of Scottish Ministers to make grants to education authorities and others);
      (iv) section 65 of the Further and Higher Education Act 1992 (administration of funds by councils);
      (v) section 4 of the Further and Higher Education (Scotland) Act 2005 (general duty of Scottish Ministers to provide support for funding of higher education) or section 11 of that Act (administration of funds); and

(vi) section 22 of the Teaching and Higher Education Act 1998 (new arrangements for giving financial support to students).

(3) Subject to paragraph (4), paragraph (1) does not apply in the case of C, where C is a person—

(a) who has not reached the age of 18 and to whom—

    (i) section 17(10)(b) of the Children Act 1989 (provision of services for children in need: impaired health and development) or section 93(4)(a)(ii) of the Children (Scotland) Act 1995 (interpretation: children in need of care and attention due to impaired health and development) applies because C's health is likely to be significantly impaired, or further impaired, without the provision of services for C; or

    (ii) section 17(10)(c) of the Children Act 1989 (provision of services for children in need: disability) or section 93(4)(a)(iii) of the Children (Scotland) Act 1995 (interpretation: children in need of care and attention due to disability) applies; or

    [³ (aa) to whom section 37, 38 or 42 of the Social Services and Well-being (Wales) Act 2014 applies; or]

(b) who is accommodated outside the United Kingdom if the costs of any qualifying services are borne wholly or partly by a local authority pursuant to their powers under section 320 of the Education Act 1996 (provision outside England and Wales for certain children) or section 25 of the Education (Additional Support for Learning) (Scotland) Act 2004 (attendance at establishments outwith the United Kingdom).

(4) [³ Paragraphs (3)(a) and (aa) only apply] during any period in which the local authority looking after C places C in a private dwelling with a family, or with a relative of C, or with some other suitable person.

AMENDMENTS

1. Community Care, Services for Carers and Children's Services (Direct Payments) (England) (Amendment) Regulations (SI 2013/2270) reg.7 (November 1, 2013).

2. Care Act 2014 (Consequential Amendments) (Secondary Legislation) Order 2015 (SI 2015/643) art.40 (April 1, 2015).

3. Social Services and Well-being (Wales) Act 2014 and the Regulation and Inspection of Social Care (Wales) Act 2016 (Consequential Amendments) Order 2017 (SI 2017/901) art.16 (November 3, 2017).

GENERAL NOTE

This regulation will have the same effect as reg.7 of the Attendance Allowance Regulations and reg.9 of the Disability Living Allowance Regulations. It removes payability only in respect of the daily living component. Because it is payability, not entitlement, that is removed a claimant will be able to resume payment of the benefit immediately on leaving the care home and does not need to re-qualify for benefit The meaning of such expressions as "borne out of public or local funds" should be the same as those words as used in those regulations. The treatment accorded to arrangements under which claimants, or their representatives, agree to refund fees paid by a local authority when, for example, the claimant's home has been sold, should apply here too. For discussion of cases detailing these points see the notes following those regulations elsewhere in this book.

4.221

[¹ Hospital in-patients aged 18 or over]

4.222   **29.**—(1) Subject to [¹ paragraph (3) and] regulation 30, no amount of personal independence payment which is attributable to either component is payable in respect of C for any period during which C meets the condition in section 86(2) of the Act (in-patient treatment: costs of treatment, accommodation and related services borne out of public funds).

(2) For the purposes of section 86(3) of the Act, the costs of treatment, accommodation or any related services are borne out of public funds if C is undergoing medical or other treatment as an in-patient in—

    (a) a hospital or similar institution under—

        (i) the National Health Service Act 2006;

        (ii) the National Health Service (Wales) Act 2006; or

        (iii) the National Health Service (Scotland) Act 1978; or

    (b) a hospital or similar institution maintained or administered by the Defence Council.

[¹ (3) This regulation does not apply if C was under the age of 18 on the day on which C entered the hospital or similar institution referred to in section 86(2) of the Act to begin C's current period as an in-patient.]

AMENDMENT

1. Social Security (Disability Living Allowance and Personal Independence Payment) (Amendment) Regulations 2016 (SI 2016/556) reg.3 (June 29, 2016).

GENERAL NOTE

4.223   This regulation will have the same effect as reg.6 of the Attendance Allowance Regulations and reg.8 of the Disability Living Allowance Regulations. It removes Payability in respect of both components. Because it is payability, not entitlement, that is removed a claimant will be able to resume payment of the benefit immediately on leaving the hospital and does not need to re-qualify for benefit.

The meaning of terms such as "medical or other treatment as an in-patient in a hospital or other institution" should be the same as those words as used in those other regulations. In particular the meaning of "medical treatment" and "hospital" has been considered in a number of cases that are discussed in the notes that follow those regulations elsewhere in this book.

This regulation has been amended to accord with the decision of the Supreme Court in *Cameron Mathieson v SSWP* [2015] UKSC 47. That decision held that the previous version of this regulation breached the child claimant's rights under the Human Rights Act 1998 and under the European Convention on Human Rights.

An attempt to show that suspension of benefit under this regulation was unlawfully discriminatory as being in breach of the claimant's rights under art.14 of the ECHR failed in *MH v SSWP (PIP)* [2017] UKUT 424 (AAC); [2018] AACR 15. The claimant was permanently resident in accommodation similar to a hospital and maintained out of public funds. Judge Lane held that his status as a hospital in-patient was not analogous to a similarly disabled person living at home and was only weakly analogous to a patient living in a care home (for whom only the daily living component would be removed under reg.28 above). But even if the latter case were sufficiently comparable, the judge found that the difference in treatment by withholding the mobility component as well was justified.

Payability exceptions: care homes and hospitals

4.224   **30.**—(1) Subject to the following paragraphs, regulation 28(1) or, as the case may be, regulation 29(1) does not apply to C in respect of the first 28 days of any period during which C is someone to whom that regulation applies.

(2) Where, on the day on which C's entitlement to personal independence payment commences, C meets the condition in section 85(2) of the Act (care home residents: costs of qualifying services borne out of public or local funds) or section 86(2) of the Act (in-patient treatment: costs of treatment, accommodation and related services borne out of public funds), paragraph (1) does not apply to C in respect of any period of consecutive days, beginning with that day, on which C continues to satisfy that condition.

(3) Regulation 28 or, as the case may be, regulation 29 does not apply where C is residing in a hospice and is terminally ill, and the Secretary of State has been informed that C is terminally ill—

(a) on a claim for personal independence payment;

(b) on an application for a revision or a supersession of an award of personal independence payment; or

(c) in writing in connection with an award of, or a claim for, or an application for a revision or a supersession of an award of, personal independence payment.

(4) In paragraph (3), "hospice" means a hospital or other institution whose primary function is to provide palliative care for persons resident there who are suffering from a progressive disease in its final stages, other than—

(a) a health service hospital in England (within the meaning of section 275 of the National Health Service Act 2006);

(b) a hospital in Wales vested in—

    (i) an NHS trust;

    (ii) a Local Health Board; or

    (iii) the Welsh Ministers,

for the purpose of functions under the National Health Service (Wales) Act 2006;

(c) a health service hospital in Scotland (within the meaning of section 108(1) of the National Health Service (Scotland) Act 1978);

(d) a hospital maintained by the Defence Council; or

(e) an institution similar to a hospital mentioned in any of the preceding sub-paragraphs of this paragraph.

(5) Regulation 28(1) does not apply to a case where, during any period the total cost of the qualifying services are met—

(a) out of the resources of the person for whom the qualifying services are provided, or partly out of that person's own resources and partly with assistance from another person or a charity; or

(b) on that person's behalf by another person or a charity.

(6) In this regulation—

"NHS trust" means a body established under section 18 of the National Health Service (Wales) Act 2006; and

"Local Health Board" means a body established under section 11 of that Act.

(7) In the application of these Regulations to Scotland, "charity" is to be construed as if these Regulations were an enactment to which section 7 of the Charities Act 2011 (application in relation to Scotland) applied.

GENERAL NOTE

4.225   The disqualifications under regs 28 and 29 do not apply for the first 28 days that the claimant is in the care home or the hospital, but when the claimant is in such accommodation already, when the award of benefit commences, the disqualification will still apply. Nor does disqualification apply if the claimant is in a hospice and is terminally ill. For the meaning of "hospice" see above para.(4) and for the meaning of "terminally ill" see s.82 of the WRA 2012. The disqualification does not apply where (even if the claimant is in an NHS hospital) all of the "qualifying services" are paid for privately or by a charity. For the meaning of "qualifying services" see s.85(4) of the WRA 2012.

Prisoners and detainees

4.226   **31.**—(1) Subject to paragraph (2), section 87 of the Act (prisoners and detainees) does not apply in respect of the first 28 days of any period during which C is a person to whom that section would otherwise apply.

(2) Where, on the day on which C's entitlement to personal independence payment commences, C is a person to whom that section applies, paragraph (1) does not apply to C in respect of any period of consecutive days, beginning with that day, on which C continues to be a person to whom that section applies.

(3) Section 87 of the Act does not apply to C in respect of any period after the conclusion of criminal proceedings as a result of which C is detained in a hospital or similar institution in Great Britain as a person suffering from mental disorder unless C satisfies either of the conditions set out in paragraph (4).

(4) The conditions referred to in paragraph (3) are—

(a) C is—

(i) detained under section 45A of the Mental Health Act 1983 (power of higher courts to direct hospital admission) or section 47 of that Act (removal to hospital of persons serving sentences of imprisonment, etc); and

(ii) being detained on or before the day which the Secretary of State has certified to be C's release date within the meaning of section 50(3) of that Act; or

(b) C is being detained under—

(i) section 59A of the Criminal Procedure (Scotland) Act 1995 (hospital direction); or

(ii) section 136 of the Mental Health (Care and Treatment) (Scotland) Act 2003 (transfer of prisoners for treatment of mental disorder).

(5) For the purposes of this regulation—

(a) "hospital or similar institution" means any place (not being a prison, a detention centre, a young offenders institution or remand centre and not being at or in any such place) in which persons suffering from mental disorder are or may be received for care or treatment;

(b) criminal proceedings against any person are deemed to be concluded upon that person being found insane in those proceedings with the effect that that person cannot be tried or the trial of that person cannot proceed.

(6) Section 87 of the Act does not apply to C where—

(a) C is undergoing imprisonment or detention in legal custody outside Great Britain; and

(b) in similar circumstances in Great Britain, C would have been excepted from the application of that section by virtue of the operation of any provision of this regulation.

GENERAL NOTE

The disqualification of prisoners and detainees does not apply for the first 28 days of imprisonment. This is a more generous rule than that applies to AA and DLA where disqualification is immediate. In another sense, however, this regulation is less generous because there seems to be no provision for benefit to be only suspended while the prisoner is on remand and does not subsequently receive a sentence of imprisonment. (See Social Security (General Benefit) Regulations 1982 reg.2).

4.227

Disqualification ends when the prisoner is released from detention. It ends, under this regulation, also when a prisoner continues to be detained on the grounds of mental disorder after his sentence is completed. In that case, however, the claimant may then be disqualified under s.85 (care homes) or s.86 (hospitals) of the WRA 2012.

Periods of residence

32.—(1) In these Regulations, a "period of residence" is a period during which C—

4.228

(a) meets the condition in section 85(2) of the Act (care home residents);
(b) meets the condition in section 86(2) of the Act (hospital in-patients); or
(c) is a person who is undergoing imprisonment or detention in legal custody.

(2) Subject to paragraph (3), for the purposes of section 87 of the Act and regulations 28 and 29, a period of residence—

(a) begins on the day after the day on which C enters a care home, hospital or similar institution or commences a period of imprisonment or detention in legal custody; and
(b) ends on the day before the day on which C leaves a care home, hospital or similar institution or on which a period of imprisonment or detention in legal custody ends.

(3) Where, immediately following a period of residence for the purpose of sub-paragraph (a), (b) or (c) of paragraph (1), C commences another period of residence for the purpose of any of those sub-paragraphs, the earlier period of residence is deemed to end on the day on which C leaves the care home, hospital or similar institution or, as the case may be, on which the period of imprisonment or detention ends.

(4) Subject to paragraph (5), for the purposes of regulations 30(1) and 31(1),—

(a) two or more distinct periods of residence separated by an interval not exceeding 28 days, or by two or more such intervals, are to be treated as a continuous period equal in duration to the total duration of such distinct periods and ending on the last day of the later or last such period; and
(b) any period or periods to which those regulations refer are to be taken into account and aggregated with any other period referred to in those regulations.

(5) Paragraph (4) is, where the periods referred to in sub-paragraph (a) of that paragraph are both or all periods to which section 87 applies, to have effect as if—

   (a) the words "subject to paragraph (5)" and "regulation 30(1) and" were omitted;

   (b) the reference to "28 days" in sub-paragraph (a) of that paragraph read "one year"; and

   (c) the references to "those regulations" in sub-paragraph (b) read "that regulation" and the reference to "refer" read "refers".

GENERAL NOTE

4.229   This regulation provides for the linking together of two or more periods spent in one or more of the accommodations referred to in regs 28, 29 and 31. Thus, where a claimant has spent time in a care home, a hospital, or undergoing imprisonment or detention, two or more such periods will be linked together to form a single period when they are separated by no more than 28 days—and the claimant will not enjoy another period of entitlement under reg.30(1) or reg.31(1). Where, however, both (or several) periods were ones of imprisonment or detention, those periods are linked if they occur within one year of each other.

SCHEDULE 1

PERSONAL INDEPENDENCE PAYMENT ASSESSMENT

PART 1

INTERPRETATION

4.230   1. In this Schedule—

"aided" means with—

   (a) the use of an aid or appliance; or

   (b) supervision, prompting or assistance;

"assistance" means physical intervention by another person and does not include speech;

"assistance dog" means a dog trained to guide or assist a person with a sensory impairment;

"basic verbal information" means information in C's native language conveyed verbally in a simple sentence;

"basic written information" means signs, symbols and dates written or printed standard size text in C's native language;

"bathe" includes get into or out of an unadapted bath or shower;

"communication support" means support from a person trained or experienced in communicating with people with specific communication needs, including interpreting verbal information into a non-verbal form and vice versa;

"complex budgeting decisions" means decisions involving—

   (a) calculating household and personal budgets;

   (b) managing and paying bills; and

   (c) planning future purchases;

"complex verbal information" means information in C's native language conveyed verbally in either more than one sentence or one complicated sentence;

"complex written information" means more than one sentence of written or printed standard size text in C's native language;

"cook" means heat food at or above waist height;

"dress and undress" includes put on and take off socks and shoes;

"engage socially" means—

(a) interact with others in a contextually and socially appropriate manner;

(b) understand body language; and

(c) establish relationships;

"manage incontinence" means manage involuntary evacuation of the bowel or bladder, including use a collecting device or self-catheterisation, and clean oneself afterwards;

"manage medication [¹ ...]" means take medication [¹ ...], where a failure to do so is likely to result in a deterioration in C's health;

[¹ "manage therapy" means undertake therapy, where a failure to do so is likely to result in a deterioration in C's health;]

"medication" means medication to be taken at home which is prescribed or recommended by a registered—

(a) doctor;

(b) nurse; or

(c) pharmacist;

[¹ "monitor a health condition"] means—

(a) detect significant changes in C's health condition which are likely to lead to a deterioration in C's health; and

(b) take action advised by a—

    (i) registered doctor;

    (ii) registered nurse; or

    (iii) health professional who is regulated by the Health Professions Council,

    without which C's health is likely to deteriorate;

"orientation aid" means a specialist aid designed to assist disabled people to follow a route safely;

"prepare", in the context of food, means make food ready for cooking or eating;

"prompting" means reminding, encouraging or explaining by another person;

"psychological distress" means distress related to an enduring mental health condition or an intellectual or cognitive impairment;

"read" includes read signs, symbols and words but does not include read Braille;

"simple budgeting decisions" means decisions involving—

(a) calculating the cost of goods; and

(b) calculating change required after a purchase;

"simple meal" means a cooked one-course meal for one using fresh ingredients;

"social support" means support from a person trained or experienced in assisting people to engage in social situations;

"stand" means stand upright with at least one biological foot on the ground;

"supervision" means the continuous presence of another person for the purpose of ensuring C's safety;

"take nutrition" means—

(a) cut food into pieces, convey food and drink to one's mouth and chew and swallow food or drink; or

(b) take nutrition by using a therapeutic source;

"therapeutic source" means parenteral or enteral tube feeding, using a rate-limiting device such as a delivery system or feed pump;

"therapy" means therapy to be undertaken at home which is prescribed or recommended by a—

(a) registered—

(i) doctor;

(ii) nurse; or

(iii) pharmacist; or

(b) health professional regulated by the Health Professions Council;

[¹ but does not include taking or applying, or otherwise receiving or administering, medication (whether orally, topically or by any other means), or any action which, in C's case, falls within the definition of "monitor a health condition;]

"toilet needs" means—

(a) getting on and off an unadapted toilet;

(b) evacuating the bladder and bowel; and

(c) cleaning oneself afterwards; and

"unaided" means without—

(a) the use of an aid or appliance; or

(b) supervision, prompting or assistance.

GENERAL NOTE

4.231   Part 1 of this Schedule, together with regulation 2 above, provides the definitions of words used in the assessment of a claim for PIP. Some of these definitions have been changed with effect from March 16, 2017. This book is up to date with effect as at April 10, 2017. Hence only the amended version of the regulations appears here. In so far as it may be necessary for tribunals to have access to the earlier version of the Schedule they should have recourse to an earlier version of this work. This may be necessary because these amendments were made to reverse the effect of the UT decision in *SSWP v LB (PIP)* [2016] UKUT 530 (AAC). The Secretary of State has withdrawn the appeal against the decision in *SSWP v LB (PIP)* [2016] UKUT 530 (AAC). This means that appeals to a FTT, or to the UT, from decisions made on the original version of these regulations should be determined in accordance with that decision. At the same time two appeals on the same matters that were to have been heard before a three-judge panel of the UT were also withdrawn. In *KM v SSWP (PIP)* [2018] UKUT 296 (AAC) Judge Rowland has given helpful guidance to tribunals applying the original version of the Schedule in accordance with the decision of Judge Mesher in *SSWP v LB (PIP)* [2016] UKUT 530 (AAC).

PART 2

DAILY LIVING ACTIVITIES

Column 1 *Activity*	Column 2 *Descriptors*	Column 3 *Points*
1. Preparing food.	a. Can prepare and cook a simple meal unaided.	0
	b. Needs to use an aid or appliance to be able to either prepare or cook a simple meal.	2
	c. Cannot cook a simple meal using a conventional cooker but is able to do so using a microwave.	2
	d. Needs prompting to be able to either prepare or cook a simple meal.	2
	e. Needs supervision or assistance to either prepare or cook a simple meal.	4
	f. Cannot prepare and cook food.	8
2. Taking nutrition.	a. Can take nutrition unaided.	0
	b. Needs—	2
	(i) to use an aid or appliance to be able to take nutrition; or	
	(ii) supervision to be able to take nutrition; or	
	(iii) assistance to be able to cut up food.	
	c. Needs a therapeutic source to be able to take nutrition.	2
	d. Needs prompting to be able to take nutrition.	4
	e. Needs assistance to be able to manage a therapeutic source to take nutrition.	6
	f. Cannot convey food and drink to their mouth and needs another person to do so.	10
3. Managing therapy or monitoring a health condition.	a. Either—	0
	(i) does not receive medication or therapy or need to monitor a health condition; or	
	(ii) can manage medication or therapy or monitor a health condition unaided.	
	b. Needs [¹ any one or more of the following]—	1
	(i) to use an aid or appliance to be able to manage medication; [¹ . . .]	
	(ii) supervision, prompting or assistance to be able to manage medication [¹ . . .].	
	[¹ (iii) supervision, prompting or assistance to be able to monitor a health condition.]	

4.232

803

Column 1 Activity	Column 2 Descriptors	Column 3 Points
	c. Needs supervision, prompting or assistance to be able to manage therapy that takes no more than 3.5 hours a week.	2
	d. Needs supervision, prompting or assistance to be able to manage therapy that takes more than 3.5 but no more than 7 hours a week.	4
	e. Needs supervision, prompting or assistance to be able to manage therapy that takes more than 7 but no more than 14 hours a week.	6
	f. Needs supervision, prompting or assistance to be able to manage therapy that takes more than 14 hours a week.	8
4. Washing and bathing.	a. Can wash and bathe unaided.	0
	b. Needs to use an aid or appliance to be able to wash or bathe.	2
	c. Needs supervision or prompting to be able to wash or bathe.	2
	d. Needs assistance to be able to wash either their hair or body below the waist.	2
	e. Needs assistance to be able to get in or out of a bath or shower.	3
	f. Needs assistance to be able to wash their body between the shoulders and waist.	4
	g. Cannot wash and bathe at all and needs another person to wash their entire body.	8
5. Managing toilet needs or incontinence.	a. Can manage toilet needs or incontinence unaided.	0
	b. Needs to use an aid or appliance to be able to manage toilet needs or incontinence.	2
	c. Needs supervision or prompting to be able to manage toilet needs.	2
	d. Needs assistance to be able to manage toilet needs.	4
	e. Needs assistance to be able to manage incontinence of either bladder or bowel.	6
	f. Needs assistance to be able to manage incontinence of both bladder and bowel.	8
6. Dressing and undressing.	a. Can dress and undress unaided.	0
	b. Needs to use an aid or appliance to be able to dress or undress.	2
	c. Needs either—	2

Column 1 *Activity*	Column 2 *Descriptors*	Column 3 *Points*
	(i) prompting to be able to dress, undress or determine appropriate circumstances for remaining clothed; or	
	(ii) prompting or assistance to be able to select appropriate clothing.	
	d. Needs assistance to be able to dress or undress their lower body.	2
	e. Needs assistance to be able to dress or undress their upper body.	4
	f. Cannot dress or undress at all.	8
7. Communicating verbally.	a. Can express and understand verbal information unaided.	0
	b. Needs to use an aid or appliance to be able to speak or hear.	2
	c. Needs communication support to be able to express or understand complex verbal information.	4
	d. Needs communication support to be able to express or understand basic verbal information.	8
	e. Cannot express or understand verbal information at all even with communication support.	12
8. Reading and understanding signs, symbols and words.	a. Can read and understand basic and complex written information either unaided or using spectacles or contact lenses.	0
	b. Needs to use an aid or appliance, other than spectacles or contact lenses, to be able to read or understand either basic or complex written information.	2
	c. Needs prompting to be able to read or understand complex written information.	2
	d. Needs prompting to be able to read or understand basic written information.	4
	e. Cannot read or understand signs, symbols or words at all.	8
9. Engaging with other people face to face.	a. Can engage with other people unaided.	0
	b. Needs prompting to be able to engage with other people.	2
	c. Needs social support to be able to engage with other people.	4
	d. Cannot engage with other people due to such engagement causing either—	8
	(i) overwhelming psychological distress to the claimant; or	

Column 1 *Activity*	Column 2 *Descriptors*	Column 3 *Points*
	(ii) the claimant to exhibit behaviour which would result in a substantial risk of harm to the claimant or another person.	
10. Making budgeting decisions.	a. Can manage complex budgeting decisions unaided.	0
	b. Needs prompting or assistance to be able to make complex budgeting decisions.	2
	c. Needs prompting or assistance to be able to make simple budgeting decisions.	4
	d. Cannot make any budgeting decisions at all.	6

PART 3

MOBILITY ACTIVITIES

4.233

Column 1 *Activity*	Column 2 *Descriptors*	Column 3 *Points*
1. Planning and following journeys.	a. Can plan and follow the route of a journey unaided.	0
	b. Needs prompting to be able to undertake any journey to avoid overwhelming psychological distress to the claimant.	4
	c. Cannot plan the route of a journey.	8
	d. Cannot follow the route of an unfamiliar journey without another person, assistance dog or orientation aid.	10
	e. Cannot undertake any journey because it would cause overwhelming psychological distress to the claimant.	10
	f. Cannot follow the route of a familiar journey without another person, an assistance dog or an orientation aid.	12
2. Moving around.	a. Can stand and then move more than 200 metres, either aided or unaided.	0
	b. Can stand and then move more than 50 metres but no more than 200 metres, either aided or unaided	4
	c. Can stand and then move unaided more than 20 metres but no more than 50 metres.	8
	d. Can stand and then move using an aid or appliance more than 20 metres but no more than 50 metres.	10
	e. Can stand and then move more than 1 metre but no more than 20 metres, either aided or unaided.	12
	f. Cannot, either aided or unaided, – (i) stand; or (ii) move more than 1 metre.	12

(SI 2013/377 Sch.1) (as amended)

AMENDMENTS

1. Social Security (Personal Independence Payment) (Amendment) Regulations 2017 (SI 2017/194) reg.2 (March 16, 2017).

GENERAL NOTE

This Schedule was amended with effect from March 16, 2017 by the Social Security (Personal Independence Payment) (Amendment) Regulations 2017 (SI 2017/194). But in December 2017, Mostyn J. held, in *RF v SSWP* [2017] EWHC 3375 [2018] AACR 13, that para.2(4) of those regulation was *ultra vires* the rule making power in Part 4 of the Welfare Reform Act 2012. That decision was then accepted as correct by the DWP. This meant that amendments made in that paragraph to Activity 1 of the Mobility Activities were of no effect and never had been of any effect. The text of the Descriptors c, d and f in Activity 1 of Part 3 of the Schedule has accordingly been restored to its original wording in this volume; otherwise the text shown in this volume is the text as amended by those regulations. However, for some time it will be necessary for advisers and for tribunals to have access to the text of the schedule as it was before these amendments. That is because in determining appeals from decisions of a DM made before that date, the law to be applied will be the law as it was before that date. (See the observations of Judge Gray on this point in *PM v SSWP (PIP)* [2017] UKUT 154 (AAC)). These amendments were made to reverse the effect of two decisions of the Upper Tribunal.

4.234

In the first, *SSWP v LB (PIP)* [2016] UKUT 530 (AAC), Judge Mesher had resolved what he found to be an incongruous result under the original wording, by distinguishing between those cases where the claimant required help with either taking medication or monitoring a health condition, and those where they required help with both. The amended regulation makes clear that each of these actions, and that of managing therapy, are separate and distinct functions; the definitions in Part 1 of the schedule have been amended accordingly. In *KM v SSWP (PIP)* [2018] UKUT 296 (AAC) Judge Rowland has given helpful guidance to tribunals applying the original version of the Schedule in accordance with the decision of Judge Mesher in *SSWP v LB (PIP)* [2016] UKUT 530 (AAC).

The second case was a decision of a three judge tribunal in *MH and others v SSWP (PIP)* [2016] UKUT 531 (AAC); [2018] AACR 12 regarding the first Activity for the mobility component. That decision held that in appropriate circumstances an "overwhelming psychological distress" might be relevant not merely to those descriptors where it is mentioned specifically, but that it might apply also to the other descriptors and in particular to Descriptors (d) and (f). The UT held that it could. However, since the amendment to the regulations was held to be void (see *RF v SSWP* noted above) the original wording of the Descriptors in Mobility Activity 1 has been restored and the DWP has withdrawn its appeal in the *MH* case. This means that the law as explained in that case should now be followed.

This Schedule contains the criteria by which an assessment for PIP will be measured. This is the crux of the difference between this benefit and AA and DLA. Whereas the qualification for those benefits focused on the care and attention that the claimant needs, this test focuses on the things that the claimant can, and cannot, do for themselves. But broadly speaking both tests are aimed at the same target- to identify those who need help, to the requisite extent, to cope with the demands of living a normal everyday life. Although it is expected that qualification for PIP might involve a more rigorous standard, some of these new criteria will accept conditions that were not provided for before.

The tables in Pts 2 and 3 of the schedule each contain a list of "Activities" and of "Descriptors".

Part 2 relates to the Daily Living Component and Pt 3 relates to the Mobility Component.

Each Activity covers some aspect of normal everyday living, or of mobility and each is then divided into a number of Descriptors. The Descriptors pose a series of criteria by which the ability, and thus the disability, of the claimant is measured. Each set of Descriptors begins with a benchmarking criterion (for which the score is zero), that sets the standard for an able person. The subsequent Descriptors describe an ascending scale of disablement.

These criteria, most of which can be thought of as tasks, are designed to measure both physical and mental disability. Any lack of ability to accomplish the task set by a Descriptor must derive from some physical or mental cause; a mere lack of skill, knowledge or training will not suffice unless that has itself some origin in a physical or mental deficiency—see *R(DLA) 3/06* where there was said to be a need to "unbundle" the functional deficiency that the claimant exhibited, in order to see if it might have some physical or mental cause. It is not necessary that the physical or mental cause is a specific disease or condition for which there is a medical diagnosis, but only to show that the limited ability has some cause that was either physical or mental. Physical, in this context, will mean anything connected with the claimant's bodily function including experiencing sensation such as pain, breathlessness or dizziness, while mental, includes any mental health condition or intellectual or cognitive impairment. This approach is confirmed by Judge Gray in *MR v SSWP (PIP)* [2017] UKUT 86 (AAC).

4.235　　That this will include a psychosomatic condition is confirmed in *NK v SSWP* [2016] UKUT 146 (AAC). The claimant suffered a mental health condition that included experiencing pain for which no physical cause could be found. In the UT Judge Rowley confirmed the decision of the FTT refusing her claim for the mobility component (the evidence showed that she could walk more than 200 metres without difficulty), but she confirmed that the origin of any pain experienced was irrelevant; the question was whether the claimant did experience pain whatever might be its origin.

But the cause must be some "condition" and that will mean something more than just a defect of character or irresponsible behaviour. The line that has been drawn in relation to DLA for claims based on alcoholism, is between those where the claimant can be said to be able to desist in his behaviour and those where he is compelled by an addiction that he cannot reasonably be expected to control. (Though even where alcoholism is an addiction, care should be taken in examining how much of the time the claimant is so affected as to need assistance etc.).

More recent cases relevant to this question are *JG v SSWP* [2013] UKUT 37 (AAC) and *SD v SSWP* [2016] UKUT 100 (AAC); [2016] AACR 35 both cases of a claim for ESA, but where the principles applicable in DLA and now, presumably, PIP may be assumed to be the same. These cases explain the relevance of evidence given by reference to the Diagnostic and Statistical Manual of Mental Disorders of the American Psychiatric Association, DSM-IV and DSM-5. Both cases are more fully discussed in the notes that follow the relevant sections relating to ESA elsewhere in this volume.

The approach to alcohol dependency in relation to benefits that was adopted in the ESA cases was that which had been developed for DLA in *R(DLA) 6/06*. That same approach has now been applied to PIP by Judge Hemingway in *SD v SSWP (PIP)* [2017] UKUT 310 (AAC). The judge affirms that alcohol dependency may be a mental condition for the purposes of this benefit and that an FTT must, therefore, assess and record the extent to which the claimant's ability to achieve the various Activities is affected by their condition. In this case, although the tribunal appeared to accept that the claimant's alcoholism was a mental condition, they failed to make any findings regarding the extent to which that affected his abilities. The judge points out that the degree to which a claimant's ability is affected will vary greatly and will require careful fact finding by the tribunal and that the extent to which they are affected may differ throughout the day, so that the time at which the claimant is required to perform any particular activity will also be relevant.

Note that in applying the schedules only one Descriptor (the one with the higher or highest points) will count in relation to each Activity; the sum of the points for each Activity is then the claimant's score.

Note too, that where a claimant is able to achieve the task required of a Descriptor on some days, but not on others, then reg.7 prescribes the basis on which those Descriptors will be scored.

In relation to each component of PIP a score of eight points will entitle the claimant to benefit at the standard rate; a score of 12 points will entitle him to the enhanced rate. (See regs 5 and 6 above).

Note that where the claimant is assessed as being entitled to the enhanced rate he cannot at the same time be entitled to the standard rate of that same component—(see reg.4(3)).

Although all but one of the Activities will qualify a claimant, at the standard rate at least, if he is disabled to the greatest extent measured in that Activity, for most claimants it is likely that a qualifying score will be compiled from the aggregate points scored in more than one Activity in respect of each component.

To the extent that most Activities and Descriptors involve similar demands to those that have featured in claims for AA or DLA, it is reasonable to expect that some of the decisions that have been reached in relation to those benefits will be relied upon as giving guidance in relation to decisions for PIP. In other respects we may find that the new benefit is taken as an opportunity for a fresh start. The notes that follow are an attempt to draw some of that earlier experience to bear and also to note where it may be of less relevance.

There are a number of terms that occur frequently throughout the tables of Descriptors that are defined in Pt 1 of the Schedule. Those used most often are:

"*aided*" means either with the use of an "aid or appliance" or with "supervision, prompting or assistance".

An "aid or appliance" is defined, not in the schedule, but in reg.2, as any device which improves, provides or replaces the claimant's impaired physical or mental function including a prosthesis. The device need not be something that is designed exclusively for use by a person who is disabled; it may include any device that is used more commonly, but assists the claimant in a particular way. Examples will include an electric tin opener and a slow cooker, as well as a microwave that is mentioned specifically in the Descriptors.

The meaning of "aid or appliance" has been considered by Judge Mark in *NA v SSWP (PIP)* [2015] UKUT 572 (AAC). There, the claimant had been found to require the use of a perching stool when preparing a meal and of a chair when taking a shower or bath, but the FTT had not allowed any points in relation to Activity 6, dressing and undressing. The claimant had said that she could dress and undress by sitting on a chair; the FTT evidently took the view that using a chair when dressing and undressing was not the use of an aid or appliance. Judge Mark held that it could be and the fact that a chair might have some other primary purpose, did not mean that it could not be a "device which improves" the claimant's physical function in accordance with the definition of an aid in reg.2. The fact that able people might also use a chair in that manner was not the point; the question to be answered was whether the claimant could dress safely etc and in accordance with reg.4(2A) without using such a chair.

4.236

However, a different conclusion on similar facts has been reached by Judge Jacobs in *CW v SSWP* [2016] UKUT 197 (AAC); [2016] AACR 44. There the claimant said that she had to sit on her bed in order to dress herself. The judge held that a bed, which might equally be used by a non-disabled person should not, in these circumstances be regarded as an aid to dressing. While he begins by agreeing with the decision of Judge Mark that an ordinary object may become an aid to a disabled person if that person cannot accomplish the task without it, he goes on to say that the need for assistance must relate to the particular function in question- what might be necessary as an aid in washing and toileting will not necessarily be an aid in dressing. The use of the aid must then be related to the function:

"The question is this: would this 'aid' usually or normally be used by someone without any limitation in carrying out this particular aspect of the activity? If it would, the 'aid' is not assisting to overcome the consequences of an impaired function that is involved in the activity and its descriptors".

On this basis he concludes that while the claimant needed to sit whilst she took her jeans on and off it was just as normal for able persons to do the same— in effect the claimant was not disabled in respect of the function of dressing and undressing because that is commonly the way that dressing etc is done. Note that the use of a perching stool as an aid when preparing food in Activity 1 has been questioned in the decision of Judge Lane in *DR v SSWP (PIP)* [2018] UKUT 209 (AAC). The decision does not deny that a stool might be an aid in some appropriate cases, but it does affect how often that will be so. Judge Lane adopts the reasoning used by Judge Jacobs in *CW v SSWP (PIP)* [2016] UKUT 197 (AAC). She found that on the facts of this case the claimant had not shown that he needed to sit more often than might be the case for any other person and hence he did not need the stool as an aid in relation to that activity.

In December 2015 the DWP issued a discussion paper entitled *Personal Independence Payment: aids and appliances descriptors*. This resulted in a proposal that certain of the point scores in the daily living Activities should be reduced, but that proposal was subsequently withdrawn.

An appliance will include, most obviously, a wheelchair. However, in relation to the mobility component the claimant's ability to move (activity 2) must be regarded as his ability to do so without the use of a wheelchair; otherwise very few claimants would succeed on that activity in a claim for the mobility component. This is accepted by the DWP in the *PIP Assessment Guide*, though there it is explained on the basis that Descriptor requires the claimant to be unable to stand and then move. In the case of a claimant who can stand, but who cannot then move even one metre, there will need to be another justification. See the notes that follow Activity 2 of the mobility component. Note that a wheelchair may be taken account of as an appliance in relation to other Activities such as the ability to cook and to wash and use a shower.

Note that under reg.4(2), where the claimant normally wears or uses an aid or appliance, he is to be assessed with that aid or appliance. Furthermore, even if the claimant does not wear or use such an aid or appliance, but he could reasonably be expected to do so, he will be assessed as if he were wearing or using the aid or appliance. See the note to reg.4 for discussion of the factors to be taken into account in making such a determination.

"*unaided*" obviously carries the converse meaning to "aided". It means that the claimant can achieve that task without any aid, appliance, assistance, prompting or supervision. If the claimant requires even just one of these forms of help he is not accomplishing the task "unaided", though whether he can then score on any subsequent Descriptor will depend upon whether that form of help is prescribed by that Descriptor.

4.237 "*assistance*" requires physical intervention and is not satisfied by mere speech. The meaning of assistance has been explored by Judge Jacobs in *SSWP v GM (PIP)* [2017] UKUT 268 (AAC). He points out that the definition in Part I of the schedule is exhaustive—it means "physical intervention by another person". In his view this requires that the person giving assistance is inserting their help into something that is being done by the claimant, and not merely doing the whole of a task for the claimant. In this case the claimant suffered from depression and did not cook himself any meals; instead he lived on snacks. The only time that he ate a whole meal was when his neighbour cooked one for him. In *AI v SSWP (PIP)* [2016] UKUT 322 (AAC) Judge Mesher had suggested that at some future time it might be necessary to decide whether the doing of an entire task for the claimant could amount to assistance- Judge Jacobs decides that it does not. While it is clear that preparing and cooking a whole meal cannot be assistance in relation to Activity 1, there remains the possibility that the Activity might be regarded as a single task, in which case help given in respect of just one part of that task might amount to intervention and hence assistance (e.g. if someone does all the knife work and then hands over to the claimant to complete the meal). This conclusion is supported in the decision of Judge Hemingway in *CP v SSWP (PIP)* [2018] UKUT 5 (AAC).

There, the claimant suffered from narcolepsy and cataplexy. At various times while she was preparing and cooking a meal it might be necessary for another person to intervene to prevent the claimant injuring herself or burning the meal. The judge suggested (though as an obiter comment) that such intervention in taking over a part of the process could amount to assistance in relation to Activity 1.

In *JT v SSWP (PIP)* [2018] UKUT 101 (AAC) it is suggested that there may be two sorts of assistance – assistance that supplements the claimant's deficiency by helping him to do something that he is already engaged upon or possibly intervening to prevent harm to the claimant as he is doing a task, and precautionary assistance that would avoid the risk of harm to the claimant by taking over some part of the task for him. The claimant suffered from uncontrolled epilepsy; he had about two grand mal fits each week and several petit mal fits. It was argued that this made it too dangerous for him to prepare a meal because of the risk that he might injure himself either when using a knife or when handling hot items. Furthermore, when having a grand mal fit he thrashed about in a manner that might endanger anyone who was there to assist him. Judge Hemingway suggests that while assistance only of the first sort might mean that the claimant could not cook a meal at all without endangering either himself or the assistant, assistance that was precautionary by taking over the dangerous parts of the process might mean that the claimant was capable of preparing and cooking a meal with assistance. He does concede that if the parts taken over amounted to almost all of the task it could mean that the claimant could not do that task at all.

"*prompting*" means reminding, encouraging or explaining by another person. This does not require the actual presence of the person who is prompting as some of the other definitions do; this means that a telephone call, made for that purpose, should be sufficient to be prompting (cf. reg.10C of the DLA Regulations which was made specifically to prevent a telephone call sufficing for the purposes of DLA). Whether written reminders, left for the claimant, could suffice is doubtful— "prompting" might be thought to convey a sense of immediacy that would be missing in a written note.

In *GG v SSWP (PIP)* [2016] UKUT 194 (AAC) Judge Hemingway considers the circumstances in which the claimant might demonstrate a need for prompting. He begins by accepting that what he had said in the earlier case of *CPIP/1534/2015* was correct—i.e. that a need is not demonstrated merely because the claimant does in fact get prompted, and nor is it shown that there is no need if the claimant is not prompted. The problem in this case was that the claimant, an alcoholic, did motivate himself satisfactorily on those occasions when he had a specific impetus to act, such as an appointment to keep. The evidence given on his behalf showed, however, that when such impetus was lacking he might need prompting to carry out a number of the daily living activities such as washing and dressing as well as preparing food. The FTT had taken the view that he did not need prompting on the majority of days because when there was some impetus to act he was capable of doing so. Judge Hemingway took the view that this was not determinative of the matter. He says:

"That seems to me to be too simplistic an approach. The mere fact that a claimant might be sufficiently motivated to perform a task when there is specific or unusual impetus to do so does not, of itself, inform as to the overall position and the generality of the situation. So it is not appropriate to limit the scope of the enquiry to such days. True an ability to perform a task without prompting when there is particular pressure to do so might be indicative of a claimant simply exercising a choice not to perform such a task on impetus absent days but that will not necessarily follow. What has to be undertaken is a more general and all-encompassing consideration. So, there needs to be an assessment, in such cases, of why it is that, on days when a claimant does not perform certain tasks, he/she does not do so. If it is because, without any specific impetus, he/she is not motivated to do so as a result of health difficulties and that such days exist for more than 50% of the time in the relevant assessment period, then absent other

811

pertinent considerations, the relevant descriptor or descriptors will apply. That was not this tribunal's approach and I conclude that, in consequence, it did err in law. Of course, though, and obviously, mere indolence will not lead to a genuine need for prompting being established."

This has been confirmed by Judge Markus QC in *PM v SSWP (PIP)* [2017] UKUT 502 (AAC) in giving advice to a tribunal to whom the case was remitted. The claimant suffered from depression; he was the father of two children who stayed with him three and four nights each week alternatively. When his children were with him the claimant was motivated to care for himself properly, but when they were absent he would not dress or wash etc. The judge observes that prompting requires some active steps by another person – mere passive presence would not be enough. In her view though, the presence of the children and what they did with the claimant might have amounted to prompting even if they were not consciously doing so. But the matter did not end there because, in her view, an alternative approach could be that the presence of the children demonstrated that the claimant had a need for prompting even if he did not receive prompting when he needed it. If the need arose on a majority of the days so as to satisfy reg.7 then the prompting descriptor might be satisfied. But it will still be necessary to show that prompting is necessary because the claimant's inability results from his disability - in this case his depression. In *EH v Department for Communities (PIP)* [2018] NI Comm 55 the claimant suffered from depression. He admitted that he had never learned to cook and now that he lived apart from his family he ate only sandwiches and takeaway meals. He said he did not know how to turn a cooker on and did not use the kettle. On appeal it had been contended that this meant that he required prompting to prepare a meal. The Commissioner found that the FTT had been correct in concluding that the claimant was capable of cooking a meal; his failure to do so was the result of a cultural or behavioural choice when he had lived as part of a family and his meals were prepared by his mother and then by his wife. Because he had never learned to cook, there was no evidence before the FTT of a connection between his mental health and his ability to cook.

4.238   *"supervision"* means the continuous presence of another person, there to ensure the safety of the claimant. Whether presence will require actual line-of-sight presence will need to be established. A line of cases decided in relation to reg.12(6)(c) of the DLA Regulations suggests that it might not—see for example *AH v SSWP* [2012] UKUT 387 (AAC). It is possible that the type of "presence" required, might vary with the function that is being supervised.

The meaning of supervision has been considered by Judge Wright in *LB v SSWP (PIP)* [2017] UKUT 436 (AAC). The claimant usually cooked a meal at school in a group of eight students who were watched over by two teachers. The FTT had found that this did not amount to "supervision'", apparently because this was not a one-to-one relationship. Judge Wright held that there was no reason to limit the words in Part 1 of the Schedule in this way; those words required only the continuous presence of another person for the purpose of ensuring the claimant's safety. In his view that could be achieved by someone watching over a group of others.

Note that "supervision" must relate to the safety of the claimant. This is more restricted than the definition of "safely" in reg.4 which requires that the claimant accomplish tasks without endangering himself or other people. It would seem that if supervision is required to ensure the safety of others then, without it, the claimant could not be said to accomplish the activity "safely" (e.g. Activity 9, engaging with other people). Though where the presence of another person can be avoided this argument may not apply—see the decision of Judge Gray in *SC v SSWP (PIP)* [2017] 317 (AAC) discussed below. Again, if supervision is required to prevent the claimant causing damage to property, it could be argued that, without it, the claimant cannot accomplish a task "to an acceptable standard"—see reg.4(2A)(b), but there may be some difficulty in identifying the Activity to which the claimant's behaviour can be related.

Other forms of supervision may only amount to "prompting" and, as these terms often occur in separate Descriptors, the difference may be critical.

Note that since the decision in *RJ v SSWP (PIP)* [2017] UKUT 105 (AAC); [2017] AACR 32 relating to the meaning of "safely" in reg.4(2A), it is no longer necessary to distinguish between the need for supervision of the claimant in order to ensure his safety and the test of whether he can perform a task safely – cf. the decision of Judge Bano in *SB v SSWP (PIP)* [2016] UKUT 219 (AAC).

Other terms also defined in Pt 1 are referred to in the discussion of each of the Activities and the Descriptors below.

The Daily Living Component—Activities and Descriptors

Activity 1—Preparing food

Like the so called "cooking test" for DLA it is safe to assume that a claimant's inability to cook must be attributed to a disability of some kind. It will not be sufficient that the claimant is unable to prepare and cook a simple meal because of a lack of experience, or training, or even of the inclination to cook. (See *R v SS for Social Security Ex p. Armstrong* (1996) 8, Admin. LR. 626 CA). This activity is a measure of the claimant's personal ability and not the circumstances in which they are required to perform it. This has been affirmed in *SC v SSWP (PIP)* [2017] UKUT 317 (AAC). There, Judge Gray had to consider the case of a claimant who, it was said, could not prepare a meal because of the presence of her son who suffered from ADHD and was autistic. She said that it was dangerous for her to cook while he was in the kitchen and that he required constant attention. The judge allowed an appeal, but returned the case to a fresh tribunal with a direction that the test to be applied was of the claimant's physical and mental ability to cook without regard to the presence or otherwise of her son.

"prepare"," cook" and "simple meal" are all defined in Pt 1 of the schedule above.

"prepare" means making food ready to cook or to eat and will include the opening of packages peeling and cutting with knives and probably the ability to check the age and condition of the raw materials.

"cook" means to heat food at or above waist height- so the ability to bend and to use an oven, will not be required. This has been confirmed in *RH v SSWP (PIP)* [2015] UKUT 281 (AAC) where an appeal by the Secretary of State was allowed, when the FTT had awarded two points under this Descriptor because the claimant could not bend down to use the oven. It appears that the FTT had overlooked the definition of "cook" in art.1 of the Schedule, meaning to heat food at or above waist height. Given that most claimants' "conventional cooker" will provide only a low level oven this means that cooking a meal may have to be accomplished without the use of an oven. The judge does anticipate problems in identifying what is meant by a conventional cooker (compare with DLA where the term used was a traditional cooker). In practice this is likely to be taken as the cooker that is currently available to the claimant. If that cooker is for some reason unusable by them (e.g. the claimant is allergic to gas, or has a phobia about the use of gas) the only issue that could arise would be whether it was reasonable to expect the claimant to replace that cooker with another one—possibly a microwave.

"waist height" in this context presumably means the claimant's own waist height so that, where the claimant is disabled by a condition that causes him to be abnormally short, he will still be able to cook by the use of a "Baby Belling" type cooker and this is likely to come within the term "conventional cooker" used in Descriptor c. (cf. *CDLA/4351/2006*).

"simple meal" means a meal of one course sufficient for one person- so just for the claimant himself. This means that it should be unnecessary to handle large quantities and heavy utensils. (cf. *CDLA/2267/95*).

The simple meal must be a "cooked" meal—a diet of salads will not suffice and

4.239

it must be prepared from "fresh" ingredients. By fresh it may be taken to mean raw ingredients, so that reheating ready cooked meals will not suffice, and being able to "prepare" the ingredients will exclude frozen and other pot-ready ingredients and note the decision in *AI v SSWP* [2015] UKUT 176 (AAC) (a DLA decision) where it was held that a "cooked main meal" should not take account of ethnic or religious dietary differences. The definition of a "simple meal" makes no reference to this point and cooking a meal "to an acceptable standard" must be essentially an objective test, yet it might seem reasonable to take some account of ethnic and religious differences if they could be shown to be relevant.

Two recent cases relate to the question of cultural or other special dietary requirements. In the first, *ZI v SSWP (PIP)* [2016] UKUT 572 (AAC); [2018] AACR 1 Judge Levenson has followed the line adopted in the DLA decision in holding that a simple meal must be the same for all claimants. The case concerned a claimant who ate an Asian diet that was prepared for him by his wife. The FTT had concluded that, with the aid of a perching-stool he would be able to cook for himself a meal that included the items of an Asian diet if that were required, but the claimant was given leave to appeal. It was argued that the FTT had given insufficient attention to the difficulty that he might have in cooking chapattis. The judge held that it could not have been the intention of Parliament, in making these regulations, that people from different cultural, religious or ethnic backgrounds with the same level of disability, would have a different entitlement to benefit on the basis of their community affiliation.

The second, *SSWP v KJ (PIP)* [2017] UKUT 358 (AAC) was an appeal by the Secretary of State against a decision awarding benefit to a 16 year old boy following his transition from DLA to PIP. The claimant was diabetic. It appears that his mother prepared meals for him, but it was argued that he would need supervision when cooking for himself to ensure that he got quantities and ingredients correct and that, left to himself, he would not eat the "right" sort of food. Judge Wright held that, although the need for a special diet arose from his medical condition, there had been no evidence that showed that the claimant could not prepare a simple meal for himself in the manner required by the descriptors and he allowed the appeal. The case does illustrate the different criteria that apply as between DLA and PIP. A DLA claim could have succeeded when the boy was under 16 because the issue would be how much care and attention he required from his mother; the issue now was simply how much could he do for himself.

In *SSWP v DT (PIP)* [2017] UKUT 272 (AAC) Judge Hemingway has considered the extent to which a claimant's inability to read or to tell the time might affect his ability to prepare a simple meal. The FTT had awarded this claimant, who was dyslexic, 4 points under descriptor 1(e) on the ground that he needed his wife's assistance to read recipes, instructions on packages and to set a timer or to tell the time. Without that help they had accepted that he would not be able to cook a meal to a satisfactory standard. The Secretary of State argued that none of these actions were necessary to satisfy this Activity because cooking a simple meal could be achieved "as a sensory and instinctive act"—in other words that it is unnecessary to read a recipe and that a person can tell when food is cooked by looking at it and testing it with a fork. Judge Hemingway took neither view. In his view the effect of an inability to read and tell the time may vary according to the limitations that it imposes on the particular individual; in such case the tribunal will be required to make careful and detailed findings of fact as to the effect on the claimant. In this case the FTT had made no such findings. The case was returned for rehearing.

Further complexity in applying the Descriptors in this Activity is revealed in *AI v SSWP (PIP)* [2016] UKUT 322 (AAC). There, Judge Mesher has considered the case of a claimant, who had a degree of mental disability and whose evidence, accepted by the HCP and it seems by the FTT, was that he could not prepare a meal himself; all that he ever did was to buy ready prepared meals that he heated in a microwave. The DM had awarded him two points under para.(1)(c) — apparently accepting that he could not cook a simple meal using a conventional oven, but was able to do so using a microwave. The FTT had for an unexplained reason awarded two points but under para.1(b) — needs an aid or appliance to be able to prepare or cook a simple meal. Judge Mesher points out that there is an important difference between para.1(c) and the other paragraphs in the Activity; while all the others refer to both preparing and cooking this paragraph refers only to an ability to cook. That seems to raise the possibility, he suggests, that a claimant might fail to satisfy para.1(c) if he could take fresh ingredients that had been prepared by another person and cook them himself in a microwave oven. However, this does not seem problematical because in that case the enquiry should proceed to consider why the claimant cannot prepare the meal himself. If his mental condition means that he is, at best, able to do so only with prompting he will score two points under para.1(d), while if his physical condition requires that he use aids and appliances then he will again score two points under para.1(b). (It may be that the FTT thought that he should score under para.1(b) treating the use of the microwave as an "aid or appliance". Judge Mesher held that would not be appropriate given the definition of aid or appliance in regulation 2 — "any device that improves . . . the claimant's impaired . . . function." It could hardly be said that the microwave does that.) The Judge upheld the appeal on the ground that the FTT had not gone on to consider whether either of the other (higher) scoring descriptors might have applied to the claimant and he returned the case to a fresh FTT for rehearing.

A similar conclusion has been reached by Judge Hemingway in *GG v SSWP (PIP)* [2016] UKUT 194 (AAC). There, the claimant, an alcoholic, who was said to be lacking in motivation, was found by the FTT to be able to cook himself a meal by putting a ready-prepared meal in a microwave — he could cook, they said, when he was hungry enough. Judge Hemingway points out that in relation to prompting (Descriptor 1(d)) it was necessary that the claimant both prepare a meal from fresh ingredients and cook it. Even to cook a simple meal in a microwave requires that the meal is prepared from fresh ingredients, so to heat a ready prepared meal in a microwave would not satisfy Descriptor 1(c) if that meal has been bought from a shop. Judge Hemingway does not consider the possibility of a meal prepared for the claimant by someone else which he then cooks, as suggested by Judge Mesher. Given that even a shop-bought ready meal will have been prepared by someone, at some time, from fresh ingredients, this idea must also require some sort of more personal service to the claimant if it is to have any effect at all.

Decisions under the DLA test have envisaged an ability to achieve a reasonably varied and healthy diet. The DWP guidance to HCP says that menu planning to achieve a varied and healthy diet is not a part of this descriptor which is confined to the simple practical test of preparing and cooking a meal. It might be argued that being limited to a very restricted range of dishes was not to achieve the Descriptor to "an acceptable standard" (see reg.4), and in cases of severe depression and where the claimant has limited intellectual capacity, this could be important; in other cases a very limited diet might be more the result of a want of inclination than the result of a disability.

4.240

The use of a microwave oven is now expressly provided for in Descriptor c, but it should be noted that what is allowed for is the ability to cook fresh food in that oven and not simply reheating food that has been prepared by others. This has been confirmed in *LC v SSWP (PIP)* [2016] UKUT 150 (AAC). There, an appeal was allowed because the claimant, who had been injured in a motor accident, had lost the use of one arm and hand. The FTT had rejected her appeal because she was able to heat meals in a microwave. Judge Gray, in allowing an appeal, pointed out that they must have overlooked the fact that she was required as well to be able to prepare the meal from fresh ingredients and that the FTT must be assumed to have treated her as capable by cooking ready prepared meals.

As with DLA it is safe to assume that the claimant will be expected to use the appliances that he possesses though not to use ones that he does not possess; the claimant could hardly be said to be able to cook a meal using a microwave (for descriptor c.) if he does not possess a microwave. Although reg.4(2)(b) requires a claimant to be assessed as if using an appliance that he could reasonably be expected to use, in some cases it will not be reasonable to expect the claimant to acquire a microwave oven- though, query, he might well be expected to possess a conventional cooker and the usual utensils.

For the factors that might be taken into account in determining what the claimant might reasonably be expected to possess and what to acquire see the notes to reg.4 above.

For the purpose of Descriptor b. an aid or appliance will include tools that are ergonomically designed to assist people whose ability to grip is reduced, as well as devices that are commonly used by people who are not disabled, but without which the claimant would not be able to achieve a particular task—an electric tin opener and a slow cooker are items that have featured in relation to claims for DLA.

The use of a chair or stool (a so-called perching stool) in the kitchen to assist a claimant whose condition restricted the amount of time for which they could stand, has long been accepted in relation to claims for DLA—so too then, for PIP, it has been accepted in *EG v SSWP (PIP)* [2015] UKUT 275 (AAC) and was referred to specifically in the original version of the *PIP Assessment Guide*. The current version suggests that where a device is in common use by persons who are not disabled the item is unlikely to be regarded as an "aid or appliance." The *EG* case went further because Judge Wright accepts, though without the benefit of full argument, that the same might be said of a walking stick, if that were used by the claimant to improve their steadiness in the kitchen. This might be especially so (with regard to reg.4(2A)) where, without a stick, the claimant would be in danger of falling. Note that the use of a perching stool as an aid when preparing food in Activity 1 has been questioned in the decision of Judge Lane in *DR v SSWP (PIP)* [2018] UKUT 209 (AAC). The decision does not deny that a stool might be an aid in some appropriate cases, but it does affect how often that will be so. Judge Lane adopts the reasoning used by Judge Jacobs in *CW v SSWP (PIP)* [2016] UKUT 197 (AAC). She found that on the facts of this case the claimant had not shown that he needed to sit more often than might be the case of any person without a disability and hence he did not need the stool as an aid in that activity. Given that she observes that most food preparation and cooking can be accomplished with relatively little time spent standing, and that most people sit at frequent stages while cooking, it seems that the need to use a stool as an appliance might seldom be shown.

It has been held, in *GB v SSWP (PIP)* [2015] UKUT 546 (AAC), that a lever-arm type tap fitted in the claimant's kitchen was an aid or appliance used in preparing food. The judge held that cooking and preparing food were separate processes, but the use of such a tap in connection with the preparation of food alone would suffice to for the purpose of this Descriptor. This point might be unimportant in this case as one could hardly cook certain foods without adding water, but there will be other devices whose use applies only in preparation and not in cooking. The FTT had rejected this part of the claim though it is not clear whether that was because they found that the tap could not be an aid or appliance, or whether they thought that this claimant did not need the aid. The case was returned for rehearing on this and other points. It might be noted, as did the judge, that use of lever type taps is specified as an aid or appliance in the *PIP Assessment Guide*. Presumably if the claimant needs such taps in the kitchen he could equally be shown to have a similar need in the bathroom. And see the discussion of these and other points in the notes to reg.2 above.

In *AM v SSWP* [2015] UKUT 215 (AAC) Judge Mark dealt with a case concerning a claimant who suffered from Asperger's Syndrome and from OCD (obsessive compulsive disorder). When following a recipe those conditions compelled him to cook each ingredient separately with the effect that any meal he prepared became inedible. The FTT had awarded him four points under Descriptor 1e on the ground that he needed someone to assist him in cooking the meal. The Secretary of State had appealed against this finding on the ground that only an award under

Descriptor 1d would be appropriate, because what seemed to be called for was prompting, rather than assistance. Judge Mark said the FTT had failed to explain the reason for preferring the higher score, but in the event this error did not matter because the claim succeeded on other grounds.

The vexed question of variable conditions that affect a claimant on some days more than others is likely still to cause difficulty. Regulation 4(2A) requires that the claimant's ability should be assessed so that he satisfies a descriptor only if he can achieve that action "repeatedly". In relation to complex daily tasks like meal preparation, however, more regard is likely to be given to reg.7 where standards are set by reference to the number of days in which a Descriptor can be achieved over the required period.

Regulation 4(2A) also requires that a Descriptor is fulfilled "safely". This may benefit a claimant who can prepare a meal only at some risk to himself—cf. *R(DLA)1/97* in which a haemophiliac was regarded as capable of cooking and *CDLA/1471/2004* in which a self-harmer was not- in either case it might be argued that the claimant satisfies descriptor e. which refers to needing supervision to prepare a meal. Note the points made in relation to preparing and cooking a meal safely and the effect of assistance or supervision in *JT v SSWP (PIP)* [2018] UKUT 101 (AAC) discussed above.

It is usual for a disabled person to take considerably longer over preparing food because of their disability. Regulation 4(2A) also requires that a Descriptor is satisfied within "a reasonable time period". This is further defined in reg.4(2A)(4)(c). being no more than twice as long as would be taken by an able-bodied person.

See the case of *GP v SSWP (PIP)* [2016] UKUT 444 (AAC) discussed in the notes to reg.4 above where the claimant was a young man who suffered from OCD and for whom preparing and eating a meal took more than twice as long. The FTT was able to find that he should then be treated as being unable to prepare a meal at all.

Activity 2—Taking nutrition

"take nutrition" is defined as cutting up food, conveying food to the mouth, chewing and swallowing food and drink, or taking nutrition by means of a therapeutic source—see below.

"aid or appliance" in this context it will obviously include specially shaped cutlery, plates and cups.

In *DF v SSWP (CSPIP)* [2017] UKUT 160 (AAC) Judge May QC has held that plastic cutlery cannot be an aid or appliance for the purpose of this Activity. The claimant was a young man whose OCD caused him distress when he had to use objects with reflective surfaces. He could eat his meals, but only when he used plastic cutlery because the reflections in steel or silver cutlery upset him. The Judge refused to accept that plastic cutlery could be an aid or appliance. He says that merely to make the item of a different material does not mean that it becomes a "device" within the definition in regulation 2. Nor does he think that being made of plastic can be said to "improve, provide or replace C's impaired physical or mental condition" as the rest of that definition requires; the fact that it "obviates the claimant's asserted anxiety in using metal cutlery" is, in his view, incidental. But, could it not be argued that, by being made of plastic, the cutlery does improve C's physical (and mental) function in cutting up and eating food, because he would not be able to do so with metal cutlery?

"Therapeutic source" is defined as being feeding through a tube that is either enteral (i.e. into the gastric system) or parenteral (i.e. intravenously) and that uses a rate limiting device and pump. In *SSWP v KS (PIP)* [2018] UKUT 102 (AAC) Judge Mesher was able to award 6 points under Descriptor e on the basis that the claimant needed assistance to set up and take down the therapeutic equipment (a feeding line) each time that she used it overnight. This was on the basis of facts found by the FTT that the strict standards of hygiene and sterile equipment necessitated that help. (Rather confusingly the FTT appeared also to have held that she

4.241

did not need help in managing the procedure, but it seems that there, they may have been referring to the process throughout the night rather than the set up and taking down of the equipment). Before the UT it had been argued that because the process was followed on only 3 nights of the week that the claimant did not satisfy the 50% rule under reg.7, but Judge Mesher points out that the process being over-night meant that the claimant did need the assistance in respect of two days on each occasion the equipment was used and hence needed assistance on 6 days each week.

In *SA v SSWP (PIP)* [2015] UKUT 512 (AAC) Judge Mark has considered the case of a woman who had a loss of appetite and lacked motivation to either prepare food or to eat it. She stayed with her daughter four days of the week where she could share the meal cooked by her daughter, though still then only with encouragement; the rest of the week she lived on soup and coffee and sometimes a sandwich. The FTT had found that although she lacked motivation to prepare food, that when it was provided for her, she could take food without assistance and refused to award any points. The UT reinstated the four points that had been awarded by the HCP. The judge observed that no attention had been given by the tribunal to the number of days on which the claimant needed assistance, and that the FTT appeared to have confused her lack of motivation to prepare food with her reluctance to eat. On the evidence found by the FTT it required encouragement from her daughter to do so even on the days when a meal had been prepared for her. As this was more than 50 per cent of the days in a week that alone was sufficient to qualify under Descriptor 2b, but the judge seems to suggest also, that the diet followed on the other three days, of soup and coffee etc, was not to be regarded as a satisfactory diet. "Nutrition" is not defined in the regulation, but this suggests that there might be some minimal level of food value necessary to constitute nutrition.

The suggestion that taking nutrition might involve eating a satisfactory diet in the sense that it was healthy and nutritious has been rejected by Judge Wright in two cases that were brought before him together — *MM and BJ v SSWP (PIP)* [2016] UKUT 490 (AAC); [2017] AACR 17. In the first, the claimant had reported that although she could feed herself, she sometimes felt sick or bloated and could eat only cereal or soup. In the second the claimant was depressed and diabetic and reported that he could manage to make himself only a sandwich. In both cases it had been argued that the claimants should score points under this activity on the ground that they needed either supervision or prompting to be able to take nutri-tion and that without that help, their diet could not be said to satisfy regulation 4(2A) because they would not be taking nutrition to an acceptable standard. Judge Wright rejects that argument. The flaw in it, he points out, is the activity of taking nutrition is defined in Part 1 of Sch.1 to mean (so far as applies in these appeals) to "cut food to pieces, convey food to one's mouth and chew and swallow food or drink". It is that process, and only that process, which must be accomplished to an acceptable standard so the quality of that which is ingested is not relevant to the questions that must be answered. The Judge concedes that where a claimant can, for reasons arising from their physical or mental condition, consume only a liquid diet it might be said that they were not capable of taking nutrition as defined; alternatively he says, a person's diet might be so eccentric that it did not amount to taking food at all, but that would be a truly extreme case. He accepts the decision of Judge Mark in *AI v SSWP (PIP)* [2016] UKUT 512 (AAC) would be correct if it is understood to be decided on the ground that the claimant needed to be prompted to eat, even when meals had been prepared for her by her daughter; the further com-ments regarding her diet at other times, he suggests, should be regarded as *obiter*. Judge Wright declined to refer to the *PIP Assessment Guide* or to the Government's response to consultation; he did not see how either source could be justified in rela-tion the question of interpretation that was before him. In fact neither source would have helped the argument of the claimants.

The problem of whether neglecting to eat or even a reluctance to eat so as to require prompting by another person can satisfy Descriptor 2d has been referred to by Judge Hemingway in *JW v SSWP (PIP)* [2018] UKUT 169 (AAC). The claimant was autistic. He was currently studying at university for a degree in Game Design. The evidence given to the FTT suggested that he became so engrossed in his work that he would neglect to eat or drink for long periods unless he was prompted by another person to do so. The FTT did not award points in this respect, but they did so on the basis that he had said that he ate when he was hungry and they observed that he appeared well nourished. They concluded that he did not need prompting to take nutrition. Judge Hemingway, however, thought that the FTT had also accepted that sometimes the claimant might neglect to eat for so long as to become weak with hunger, and that sometimes he was distracted from eating even when the pains of hunger might tell him to do so. He felt that no clear finding had been made on that matter and returned the case on that, and other grounds, for reconsideration by a fresh tribunal. In doing so he does remark that if the meaning of this Activity is to be confined by the strict definition as suggested in the *MM* and *BJ* cases, it may be difficult to see how neglect or disinclination to eat can lead to a need for prompting to take nutrition since that involves only the process of getting food to the mouth, chewing and swallowing it. But he did accept that those earlier cases were concerned with the quality of the food taken and did not involve the issue when the claimant might fail to eat at all.

The need for a person to receive assistance in feeding themselves should involve the cultural requirements of the claimant. In *CA/137/1984* (approved in *R(DLA)3/06*) a claim for DLA was rejected for a Muslim child whose disabled right hand prevented him eating in a manner consistent with the family's religious beliefs. (In Islam all eating must be done with the right hand because the left is used for toileting purposes). This case has been difficult to reconcile with other decisions where emphasis has been on enabling the claimant to lead a normal life, and in relation to PIP the guidance given by DWP to HCP has referred in general (though not in this specific example) to taking account of cultural requirements.

Activity 3 – Managing therapy or monitoring a health condition

This Activity is one of those affected by the *Personal Independence Payment Amendment Regulations* 2017 which came into effect on March 16, 2017. Those regulations have amended the definitions, in Part 1 of the schedule, that are to be used in applying this Activity. In doing so they have reversed the effect of Judge Mesher's decision in *SSWP v LB (PIP)* [2016] UKUT 530 (AAC). The Secretary of State has withdrawn the appeal against that decision so any appeal to an FTT, or to the UT, where the original decision was made prior to March 16, 2017 should be determined in accordance with that decision. In that decision Judge Mesher has tried to make sense of what was an ill drafted and confusing set of Descriptors. In his view they could best be made sense of, and justice be done, if Descriptor 3.b.(ii) were read as applying only when the claimant need help either with medication, or to manage a health condition; if the claimant needed help in both respects, then they should be treated instead (and assuming that it was possible to do so) as needing help with therapy under one or other of paras c–f as appropriate. He did so because, in his opinion the Activity should not be read as meaning that a claimant (as in the current case) who needed help in both monitoring her condition and managing medication, several times each day, and for significant periods of time, would only ever score one point, while someone who needed help with therapy could score between two and eight points depending upon the time involved. For a more detailed discussion of this decision see the notes to p.793 in Part II of the Supplement to this work for 2016/17.

The new definitions in Part I of the Schedule make clear that each concept of managing medication and monitoring a health condition is separate and that therapy cannot include the taking of medication (however that might be administered) nor any part of monitoring a health condition. The result is that someone who needs to use an aid or appliance to manage medication, or needs help (in any of the ways prescribed- supervision, prompting or assistance), or needs help with

4.242

monitoring a health condition, cannot ever score more than one point even if they need that assistance in more than one, or even in all three, ways. Only the claimant who needs help with therapy, as now defined to exclude medication and monitoring, will score more points.

"Manage medication" means take medication where not doing so is likely to result in a deterioration in the claimant's health. The meaning of "manage medication" might appear to be narrow. This point has emerged in *EH v Department for Communities (PIP)* [2018] NI Com 55, a decision of the Commissioner in Northern Ireland. The Commissioner observed that the definition in Part 1 of the Schedule applied only to a "failure" to take medication "so as to result in a deterioration in the claimant's health". He thought that this might mean that where a claimant requires supervision so as to prevent them overdosing, the definition would not apply. Even if the phrase "deterioration in C's health" could be read, broadly, to include an attempted suicide, the words "failure to [take]" would be difficult to apply to an overdose. Only if "take medication" could be read as meaning, implicitly, taking it correctly, could taking an excess be regarded as a failure to take.

"medication" means something (a medication) taken at home on the prescription or the recommendation of a registered doctor, nurse or pharmacist. Presumably the word medication itself will require that the substance has some curative or therapeutic effect, but it should include pain relief and may extend to health foods and other remedies, so long as they are taken on the recommendation of the registered person described.

"Manage therapy" is now defined as undertaking therapy where failure to do so is likely to result in a deterioration in the claimant's health. Provided that "health" is given a broad interpretation so as to include comfort, it can be assumed that the decision in *RH v SSWP (PIP)* [2015] UKUT 281 (AAC) will still be followed. There, the claimant used a TENS machine every day to relieve his pain and required help in the morning to attach the machine and in the evening to remove it. The machine would probably not have had any therapeutive effect on the condition from which he was suffering so as to avoid any deterioration in his health, but it is probably fair to say that the relief of pain made him more comfortable and in that sense his health was made better.

4.243   It is a pity that the opportunity was not taken in these amending regulations to resolve the ambiguity that is inherent in the words of Descriptors c–f as discussed in both the *RH* case and in *HH v SSWP (PIP)* [2015] UKUT 558. The issue in both cases was whether the time referred to in those Descriptors was the time taken for the assistance, or the time taken for the therapy. In both cases the Judge took the view that it was the former. As this regulation has been amended and no reference made to that interpretation it could be argued that this amounts to parliamentary affirmation of that interpretation. It is also the position taken in the *PIP Assessment Guide*.

Therapy has now been defined to make clear that it does not include the administration of medication however that might be done. This means that the application of emollient cream, as in *PC v SSWP (PIP)* [2015] UKUT 622 (AAC) cannot be therapy, and nor can the use of an epipen, as in *IM v SSWP (PIP)* [2015] UKUT 680 (AAC). But difficulties remain in distinguishing between medication and therapy because apart from requiring that medication or therapy must be prescribed or at least recommended by a health professional the definition does not help in determining what else each word might mean. The meaning of each word is otherwise left to the tribunal, no doubt with the help of a dictionary and the advice of the medical member.

The meaning to be given to the word "therapy" and the distinction between that and other forms of care and support that might be given to a claimant has arisen in several cases. To begin with the judges are agreed that the word "therapy", in the absence of any more helpful statutory definition, must be given its ordinary dictionary meaning which is "the medical treatment of disease; curative medical or psychiatric treatment" (Oxford English Dictionary). In the first of these cases, *DC v SSWP (PIP)* [2016] UKUT 11 (AAC), Judge Jacobs decides that therapy must involve something more than keeping an eye on the claimant and giving support to general living activities. Nor, he suggests would providing employment for the claimant amount to therapy; it might be described as being therapeutic for him but would not be therapy in this sense. In *KM v SSWP (PIP)* [2018] UKUT 296 (AAC) Judge Rowland agrees with that conclusion though on the case before him he returned the matter to a fresh tribunal to take evidence as to the forms of support that the family provided. In *AH v SSWP (PIP)* [2016] UKUT 276 (AAC) the emphasis was on the need for therapy to have occurred on the advice of a health care professional and "at home". In that case, the encouragement of friends to give up smoking and the attendance at keep-fit classes in a gym, failed for one or both of those reasons. The judge found also that, even if the action had been taken on the advice of her GP, it would not be therapy unless there was a direct correlation to a disease or condition for which it was curative treatment. In *KM*, Judge Rowland adds a gloss to this by saying that he thought the requirement that the activity be "at home" was intended to exclude things done at a hospital or other specialist venues as had been the case in *AH*, rather than to confine activity to being in the house. In other words, support that was given by family members on the advice of a medical professional that took place out of doors, such as walking for exercise in the park might also qualify if it could be shown to be a part of a curative treatment programme.

In *KM v SSWP (PIP)* [2018] UKUT 296 (AAC) Judge Rowland also gives useful advice in relation to the way that attention given to the claimant in relation to more than one PIP Activity and hence, therefore, suggest the possibility of double counting, must be approached. He summarises the effect of these and other cases as follows:

"20. The overall effect of the case law as it applies for the purposes of this case is therefore that a need for "prompting . . . to be able to manage therapy" must be a need for something more than, or different from, ordinary interactions within a household and also more than, or different from, a need for supervision, prompting or assistance such as would score points either under descriptor 3(b)(ii) as construed in LB or under any of the other daily living or mobility activities.

21. Subject to that qualification, it seems to me that, insofar as engaging with other people may be therapeutic for a claimant and is in a form recommended by a relevant health professional, engagement by those other people with the claimant may amount to prompting the claimant to undertake therapy for the purposes of descriptors 3(c) to 3(f)"

A wide meaning to the terms "manage therapy" and within that "health" has been suggested by Judge Hemingway in *MM v SSWP (PIP)* [2018] UKUT 193 (AAC). The claimant was a young person who was profoundly deaf. She had been fitted with cochlear implants that improved her ability to hear, but on the advice of her audiologist she undertook exercises, with which her mother assisted, to train her brain so as to take full advantage of the implants. It was contended that this assistance should score under Activity 3 c or d depending on the time taken each week. The judge did not make a conclusive decision on the point because he had not had full argument on it; he did reject a suggestion put on behalf of the Secretary of State that the mother's help amounted to no more than encouragement to give up a bad habit or to take up a good pastime, but the question of whether training the brain could be therapy to avoid a deterioration in health was not argued. Judge Hemingway thought that it possibly could be. He refers to *RH v SSWP (PIP)* [2015] UKUT 281 (AAC) where the UT judge had accepted that a TENS machine that relieved the claimant's pain could be regarded as therapy because it improved his health in the sense of making him more comfortable and hence its absence might be regarded as a deterioration in health. In the present case the judge thought it was arguable that the exercises might amount to therapy (they were advised by a health professional) if they facilitated her ability to hear and that, without them, her hearing would be reduced by more than a minimal degree.

The meaning of "therapy" has been touched on by Judge Perez in *PM v SSWP (PIP)* [2018] UKUT 138 (AAC). There the claimant, who suffered extensively from arthritis had been advised by her consultant to apply a compression bandage to her lower leg daily. She said that doing so caused her pain and that she was slow in doing it. It was not suggested that the bandage was medicated. The UT judge found that there were sufficient findings of fact in the case file to be able to award 2 points under Descriptor c - needs assistance to manage therapy that takes no more than 3.5 hours a week.

The importance of understanding the use of each term is brought out by the facts of *MF v SSWP (PIP)* [2015] UKUT 554 (AAC); [2016] AACR 20. The claimant suffered from a condition that necessitated daily use of a dilator to maintain the function of her urethra. She used this device herself for about an hour each day at home in the evening. Clearly the dilator was an "aid" and its use would seem to constitute managing therapy rather than medication. The claimant could not, therefore, manage her therapy "unaided" because she needed to use an appliance, but neither subparagraph of Descriptor 3b seems applicable because subpara.(i) refers only to managing medication, while subpara.(ii) relates only to supervision, prompting or assistance, and in this case the claimant managed the therapy for herself. Nor could she satisfy any of the remaining descriptors because none of them refers to the use of an aid. This meant that the claimant was forced to argue that she needed supervision, prompting or assistance to manage her therapy, which would have scored four points under Descriptor 3c. The judge appears to have accepted (perhaps just for the sake of argument) the claimant's argument that the prescribing and recommendation by her doctor and advice from a nurse, could amount to the necessary supervision, prompting or assistance, but of these, supervision and assistance are defined art.1 of the schedule so as to require the presence of the person supervising or assisting which did not appear to be the case here, and neither did it appear that the claimant required any prompting. It appears, therefore, that the only way this claimant could have scored even one point, would be if her use of the dilator could be regarded as "managing medication" with use of an aid. While it is now clear that therapy cannot include giving medication or monitoring of health, the difference between medication and therapy is still not entirely clear; hence it might be possible to argue that the converse could still apply – therapy (in this case by oneself with an appliance) might also be a form of medication and therefore score under para.3.b.(i), but only so as to gain one point.

4.244   The distinction between medication and therapy may also be important in relation to the various forms in which medication is delivered to the claimant. While an inhaler (or rather the medicine that it contains) and insulin needles are a medication they can usually be handled by the claimant themselves and therefore score no points under Descriptor 3.a.(ii). (It will be otherwise where, for example the claimant has a needle phobia, and needs another person to administer the injection – he will score 1 point under 3.b.(ii)). A question also remains as to whether certain forms of treatment are medication. Clearly physiotherapy is not, but is the delivery of oxygen to the lungs of a person who suffers from COPD medication, or is it therapy? If it is the latter then the claimant could qualify under paras c–f – but then only if he requires help with the equipment and then to score points only in respect of the time for which the assistance is necessary. The same question might be asked if the claimant requires help with a nebuliser; the *PIP Assessment Guide* says that the use of nebuliser is therapy. If these claimants need no help they could score points then only if the equipment can be regarded as an "aid or appliance" and so score 1 point under para b.(i). Cases of *KR* and *RB* discussed below leave open the question of whether equipment such as this could be a device and hence an aid for this purpose. Because the meaning of therapy is unclear it is not uncommon for a claim to be made for points to be scored under this Activity at the same time as points are claimed in respect of the same disability under another Activity. While it is common place for a disability to affect a claimant's ability in several different ways and hence score points under more than one Activity (see *MF v SSWP (PIP)* [2015] UKUT 554 (AAC); [2016] AARC 20) and *PE v SSWP (PIP)* [2015] UKUT 309 (AAC)) what is in question is whether points can be scored more than once in respect of the same action by the claimant. See, for example *AS v SSWP (PIP)* [2017] UKUT 104 (AAC); [2017] AACR 31 where Judge Bano (applying a principle first stated by Judge Gamble in *CSPIP/386/2015*) held that the claimant who needed help with using a catheter could not score under both this Activity and under Activity 5 for toilet needs. The principle to be applied was that where words are used in a statute that refer specifically to the matter in question they displace any more general reference that might otherwise be thought to apply. On that basis, to allow the claimant to score in more than one Activity would be double counting by allowing them to score points for exactly the same limitation. This principle has been applied again by Judge Mesher in *SSWP v KS (PIP)* [2018] UKUT 102 (AAC) where he accepted that the claimant could not score for both this Activity (Managing therapy) and Activity 2 (Taking nutrition) when it was the same process of using her therapeutic resource that was the basis of the claim. Judge Mesher points out that the *AS* decision should now be regarded as having the general agreement of judges in the Administrative Appeals Chamber of the Upper Tribunal because it is now reported there, but he does mention that it may be considered again by a three-judge panel and also suggests that it could be confined to the instance of assistance being required, rather than of prompting or supervision.

An aid or appliance can be something as simple as a tablet organiser box (referred to in the *PIP Assessment Guide* as a dosette box) – see decision of Judge May QC in *AK v SSWP (CSPIP)* [2016] UKUT 256 (AAC). Certainly if the box is used to help a claimant who otherwise could not be relied upon to get their medication correct it would seem to comply with this definition, though, if the use of the box is to avoid a risk to the claimant's safety, then "supervision" might be equally appropriate. Where, however the box is prepared by a person who will not be present (as in the case of a dispenser prepared by the pharmacy or by a person who visits) the box will have to be an "aid or appliance"—in this case it would make no difference as the descriptors have the same score. It now seems reasonably clear that an inhaler is not an aid when used to deliver medication – see *KR v SSWP (PIP)* [2015] UKUT 547 (AAC). This was a case on mobility component where the claimant had argued that he needed the inhaler as an aid to move more than 50 metres, but the principle should be the same for this Activity. The UT held that the inhaler was a means by which the medicine was delivered (cf. a teaspoon for a linctus) and not an aid to improving his physical function – that was done by the medicine not the inhaler. The same has been held in the case of a nebuliser in *RB v SSWP (PIP)* [2016] UKUT 556 (AAC) though there the judge left open the possibility that a nebuliser might be an aid in delivering medication when an inhaler was insufficient for that patient – see the discussion of this case in the Notes to regulation 2.

"Monitor a health condition" means that the claimant needs someone to detect significant changes in the claimant's health that may lead to a likely deterioration, to be followed by taking action to avoid that deterioration— the action having been advised by a registered doctor, nurse or health professional who is regulated by a Health Professions Council. Presumably this includes action advised in advance of the event as well as advice that is sought immediately and could be as simple as calling an ambulance. See for an example of monitoring health the case of *IM v SSWP (PIP)* [2015] UKUT 680 (AAC) referred to above and also *DC v SSWP (PIP)* [2016] UKUT 11 (AAC) where the claimant was a schizophrenic who lived in sheltered accommodation. He was required to attend at the nurse's room each day to ensure that he took his medication, but otherwise took care of himself. It was held that he could score, at most, two points on the basis that he might need prompting to take his medication though Descriptor 3 b(ii) seems equally appropriate.

"therapy" means treatment (therapy) to be undertaken at home and which is prescribed or recommended by a registered doctor, nurse, pharmacist or other health professional who is regulated by a Health Professions Council. Under the amendment to this definition, referred to above, it is made clear that therapy cannot include the taking of medication in any way, nor any action that can constitute monitoring of a health condition. Therapy will include renal dialysis and physiotherapy, especially for claimants such as those with cystic fibrosis. Note that PIP will be available for renal dialysis only when the claimant dialyses at home whereas AA and DLA could be available in a hospital if no help was given by hospital staff. Whether the claimant will be entitled to benefit on the basis of this activity alone will depend upon the time for which therapy is needed each week. In the case of renal dialysis, the time will be that for which the claimant needs assistance, supervision etc not the time spent dialysing—see *HH v SSWP (PIP)* [2015] UKUT 558 (AAC) discussed above.

Activity 4—Washing and bathing

4.245   A claimant will score points if he is unable either to wash or to bathe unaided.

"Wash" is not defined but will probably involve the use of water—using "wet-wipes" alone should not suffice, but sponging down will.

"bathe" includes the process of getting into and out of an unadapted bath or shower.

There are many devices designed to make it safer to get into and out of a bath or shower; most of which should be classed as an "aid or appliance". A single grab-handle that might be just as likely to be used by an able person would not be an aid for this purpose (See *CW v SSWP (PIP)* [2016] UKUT 197 (AAC)) discussed above in Note to regulation 2 but any extra handles that are necessary for the claimant to use in bathing or showering probably will be. Lever arm taps that were accepted as an aid in *GB v SSWP (PIP)* [2015] UKUT 546 (AAC) and were suggested in the original version of the *PIP Assessment Guide* have been doubted in the *CW* case. The *Guide* now suggests that items that are in common use by non-disabled persons are unlikely to be accepted as aids. (See discussion of these cases in Note to regulation 2 above). The use of a chair in the shower was accepted in *NA v SSWP (PIP)* [2015] UKUT 572 (AAC).

The meaning of Descriptor e has been examined by Judge Rowley in *SP v SSWP (PIP)* [2016] UKUT 190 (AAC); [2016] AACR 43. The claimant had moved into a house where there was a walk-in bath left by a previous occupier. He said on his claim form that he would require assistance to get in or out of an unadapted bath, but it appears to be accepted that he could use the walk-in bath unaided. The judge had to decide two points. First, whether Descriptor e prescribed a test that was disjunctive or whether it was conjunctive. In other words would it suffice for a claimant to show that he could not climb in and out of a bath unaided, even though he might be able to use a shower, or must he show that he was capable of using neither the bath, nor the shower, without assistance? The judge found the word "or" was disjunctive and therefore the former test applied. (For especially clear explanation of this distinction see paras.11–16 of this judgment). Secondly, she had to decide if the "bath or shower" referred to in Descriptor e was an unadapted bath etc or whether it might suffice if the claimant could use the walk-in bath with which he was provided. The judge had little difficulty in accepting that Descriptor e must be taken to refer to an unadapted bath- that was the meaning given to the word "bathe" as defined in Part 1 of the Schedule and as used elsewhere in this activity. The word bathe does not appear in Descriptor e, but that is the consequence of the history of this provision. In this case it appears that the FTT had taken the claimant's ability to use his walk-in bath as determinative and the case was returned for rehearing.

A decision of Judge Mitchell in *MB v SSWP (PIP)* [2018] UKUT 139 (AAC) has considered the meaning of Descriptor f in this Activity. The claimant had said that she could not wash the upper part of her back satisfactorily and therefore needed assistance to do so. The FTT had found that most people are unable to reach the upper spinal region of their body and that therefore the claimant's inability to do so could not score points under this descriptor. The Judge finds that this was an error of law. He says that doubtless the tribunal was correct in their assumption about the ability of most people, but that such people are able to wash their back to a satisfactory extent by the use of a sponge or other appliance. The question that they should have considered was whether the claimant was unable to do that in a similar way so as to achieve a similar result without requiring the assistance of another. The claimant had raised a separate point about her ability to dry her back. Although neither the definitions of wash or bathe nor the words of Activity 4 refer to drying oneself, the judge was able to conclude that in this case (and probably in almost all others) the two activities are so closely related in functional terms that an ability to do the one will inevitably include an ability to do the other.

Note that in *SH v SSWP (PIP)* [2018] UKUT 251 (AAC) Judge Hemingway has made the point that just because the claimant may have to remove cochlear implants when washing and bathing does not mean that they must always qualify to have a need for supervision. That was the same situation in *RJ and others v SSWP (PIP)* [2017] UKUT 105 (AAC); [2017] AACR 32 where the judges had suggested that supervision might be necessary to ensure the safety of the claimant when her implants were removed. In the present case Judge Hemingway suggests that so long as the question of safety is considered correctly in accordance with the meaning of safety in reg.4, and on the evidence before them, an FTT might still conclude that the claimant does not require supervision while bathing. But note that the judge rejects an argument made on behalf of the Secretary of State that the claimant could be expected to minimise risk by reducing the time that she took to shower.

Activity 5—Managing toilet needs or incontinence

"toilet needs" include getting on and off an unadapted toilet, evacuating the bowel or bladder and cleaning oneself afterwards.   **4.246**

Extra handles and support bars in the toilet area will constitute an "aid or appliance" in this context. The use of grab handles and support bars to assist when using the toilet (and elsewhere in the bathroom) has been accepted in *FK v SSWP (PIP)* [2017] UKUT 375 (AAC). There, the point was made that such handles and bars are not mentioned in the list of items suggested to be aids and that a claimant is invited to consider when answering the relevant question on the PIP claim form. The judge suggests that might lead a claimant to answer "no" to that question, but he confirms that the handles are an aid or appliance when used to access the toilet. Note that it must be shown that it is necessary for the claimant to use those handles and that they are not there merely as a matter of convenience (see above in relation to Activity 4—Washing and bathing).

Different toilet arrangements that arise from cultural differences should be taken into account.

"managing incontinence" involves dealing with involuntary evacuation of the bowel or bladder and includes doing so with the use of devices such as colostomy bags and a catheter. In previous versions of the note to this Activity it was suggested that this definition meant using such devices would mean that the claimant could manage toilet needs unaided and would therefore score no points. Two cases in the UT have shown that to be wrong.

In the first of these, *JM v SSWP (PIP)* [2016] UKUT 296 (AAC), the claimant was given a stoma following surgery for a bowel cancer that meant the use of colostomy bags to manage incontinence. In the FTT the two points that he had been awarded under this Activity by the DM were removed. In the UT however, attention was given to the inconsistency that then arises between Descriptor 5(a) where the claimant might be regarded as managing incontinence unaided, and Descriptor 5(b) where he might be regarded as needing to use an aid or appliance to manage incontinence. A colostomy bag would certainly fall within the definition of an "aid or appliance" in reg.2 as a "device that improves, provides or replaces C's impaired physical function". It would be only if that definition should be read to exclude a colostomy bag because of the reference to a collecting device in the subsequent definition of "managing incontinence" found in Part 1 of the schedule that the claimant could be deprived of the two points awarded under 5(b). In the UT Judge Lane found that the ambiguity appearing in these descriptors, coupled with what she saw as the absurdity that might then to be said to arise if a claimant such as this scored no points when someone using something as simple as a dosette box did, would justify her in having recourse to the legislative preparatory materials under the principles in *Pepper v Hart* [1992] UKHL 3. From these it was clear that a colostomy bag (referred to there as a stoma bag) was intended to be treated as an aid or appliance.

Following this case a similar conclusion has been reached in respect of incontinence pads – see *BS v SSWP (PIP)* [2016] UKUT 456 (AAC). The precautionary use of incontinence pads on a daily basis, even though they were soiled only infrequently, has been held to satisfy the 50 percent rule required by reg.7: see *SSWP v NH (PIP)* [2017] UKUT 258 (AAC). Further it is important to note that what is in issue is whether the claimant has a need for incontinence pads - whether they actually use them or not—see *KO v SSWP (PIP)* [2018] UKUT 78 (AAC). In this case there was evidence that the claimant wet the bed at night (frequency not specified); it was unclear from the FTT decision whether they had found that the claimant did not wear incontinence pads during the day or whether she wore them neither by day nor by night. The case was remitted with a reminder that the test was that of need rather than of actual use. Catheters are not mentioned in the preparatory material, but by a parity of reasoning it would seem right to say that any catheter used (whether by self-insertion or fitted more permanently) is equally an aid or appliance used in accordance with Descriptor 5(b). That much seems to have been accepted by the UT judge in *AS v SSWP (PIP)* [2017] UKUT 104 (AAC); [2017] AACR 31. There the claimant was a woman who had to use a catheter several times a day to empty her bladder; she claimed that she was unable to catheterise herself and needed help from her partner to do so. The FTT hearing her appeal had granted two points on the ground that she was using an aid or appliance to manage toilet needs, but did not accept that she needed help for which she would have scored four points. An appeal was allowed because Judge Bano, in the UT, thought that the FTT had failed to deal adequately with the evidence that was before them. It appears, however that the claimant alleged that she should also score points under Activity 3 by needing assistance to manage therapy. Judge Bano held that it should not be so. Where, as here, an action is dealt with specifically under one Activity it should not be considered again under a more general Activity. Although it will be common for a claimant's disability to affect more than one daily living Activity (as has been accepted in several cases (see *MF v SSWP (PIP)* [2016] AARC 20, [2015] UKUT 554 (AAC) and *PE v SSWP (PIP)* [2015] UKUT 309 (AAC)) it is an accepted principle of statutory construction that the specific should displace the general (see an expression of this principle by Judge Gamble in *CSPIP/386/2015*). And note too that in this case it is not just the claimant's form of disability that affects more than one Activity, but precisely the same action that is being offered as the reason to score in both Activities.

In the case of *GP v SSWP (PIP)* [2015] UKUT 498 (AAC) Judge Hemingway has dealt with the question whether a difficulty in dressing and undressing could count for both Activity 6 and for this activity when it was necessary for the claimant to remove and replace clothing when using the toilet. He held that it does not, but not because, as argued by the representative of the Secretary of State, that to do so would amount to "double counting"—he observes that the same disability will frequently entitle a claimant to score under more than one activity. The reason why dressing and undressing does not count here, is because of the way that "toilet needs" and "managing incontinence" are defined in Part 1 of this schedule. Each is defined in such a way that the process of undressing and dressing does not form part of that activity- hence no points can be scored in respect of difficulty in doing so.

The decision in *GW v SSWP* [2015] UKUT 570 (AAC) also explains the meaning of "toilet needs" as defined in Part1 of the schedule. There, getting on and off the toilet, evacuating bowels and bladder, and cleaning oneself afterwards, are all linked by the conjunction "and". In the FTT it was held that this meant that a claimant must be unable to accomplish all three parts of this definition before they could qualify for two points under Descriptor 5b. In the UT Judge Rowley held that this was wrong. In this context, she said, the word was used disjunctively and hence an inability to accomplish any one of these parts would qualify. In this case the claimant was an obese man. He had been allowed points under both Activity 4 (Washing and bathing) and under Activity 6 (Dressing and undressing) because he needed to use an aid to assist in those functions. In the toilet he needed to use a shower head or brush to clean himself and so was awarded two points under this descriptor also.

The decision in *MF v SSWP (PIP)* [2015] UKUT 554 (AAC); [2016] AACR 20 deals with a possible relationship between this activity and Activity 3 (Managing therapy etc). The claimant in that case needed to use a dilator on a daily basis in order to maintain the use of her urethra—if she did not do so she would need to undergo surgery to reopen the urethra and permit her to evacuate her bladder. It did not appear from the evidence recorded that she used the dilator when actually using the toilet, but her claim seems to have been based on the argument that she needed to use an aid (the dilator) to manage her toilet needs—Descriptor 5b. The FTT had rejected her claim on the basis that they did not see a sufficiently direct connection between the use of the dilator and the use of the toilet, but they seem also to have taken the view that because the claimant's use of the dilator was pertinent in relation to Activity 3, it could not be considered, as well, in relation to Activity 5. Judge Williams allowed an appeal and returned the case for consideration by a fresh tribunal. In doing so he deals first with this point about overlap between the activities. As he puts it, simply because a particular disability is relevant in relation to one activity is no reason why it should not apply also to another- there will be numerous cases where upper body disabilities or mental disabilities affect several activities. What was not clear, and was why the judge returned the case to another tribunal, was whether the claimant did, at the relevant time, have to use a catheter to empty her bladder, or to use incontinence pads, both of which would be aids or appliances that she used to manage toiletry needs. But the real question in this case is, if the dilator is used only as device that will subsequently facilitate the passing of urine, as and when that may be necessary, can it be said to be used to manage toiletry needs? There must be some point at which the management of a condition relates to the medical treatment of the claimant, rather than to the management of their toiletry needs otherwise the surgery that the claimant had undergone, on at least two occasions, would be "assistance" in managing her toiletry needs. It was only the daily repetition of the dilation procedure that might seem to make it a part of her toileting management.

Managing incontinence, as defined in Pt 1, also involves "cleaning oneself" afterwards, but cleaning oneself does not include washing soiled clothes or bedding. (cf. *Cockburn R(DLA) 2/98* where the immediate cleaning of the bedding was regarded as sufficiently close to a bodily function to qualify for DLA, though not doing the laundry next day). Someone who needs help only in dealing with the aftermath will not qualify.

Activity 6—Dressing and undressing

"dress and undress" includes both putting on and taking off socks and shoes.   4.247
But note that it is not necessary that a claimant has difficulty in both dressing and undressing; difficulty with either function will suffice. Also, if the claimant needs to use a device to put on socks though not his shoes, that will suffice. For both of these points see *JM v SSWP (PIP)* [2016] UKUT 542 (AAC). In that case it was also held that a claimant who could manage slip-on shoes, though not shoes with laces, could not score points for this Activity. This was a decision of Judge Rowley

applying the same reasoning as had been done in the case of *CW* and others discussed below.

Dressing and undressing unaided will require that the claimant can manage all buttons, zips and other fasteners and it will require that the claimant is able to dress in garments that are appropriate to themselves in a cultural sense, as well as being able to choose clothes that are appropriate to the weather conditions and to the event, or the circumstances, in which they are to be worn. The reference here to clothes that are appropriate in a cultural sense was based originally on the inclusion of that element in the first version of the *PIP Assessment Guide* for DM. Those words have now been removed from the Guide. Nevertheless it remains the role of the tribunal to reach a decision on the basis of the claimant's ability to dress and undress in clothing that is appropriate for them. There seems no reason why this should not take account of what is culturally appropriate clothing. What might be doubted is whether dressing in such clothing, when the claimant is accustomed to doing so, should be any more difficult than any other mode of dress. Presumably if dressing in this way takes longer, the time taken is to be compared with time that would be taken to dress that way by a non-disabled person.

Note that the descriptors for PIP make no distinction between activities by day and by night. This will be of most relevance in relation to dressing, undressing, washing and bathing and undertaking toilet needs. In *DP v SSWP (PIP)* [2017] UKUT 156 (AAC) Judge Hemingway has held that a claimant may be said to require help in dressing if, because of mental or physical disability, he might select items of clothing that are malodorous or are unhygienic. In *ML v SSWP (PIP)* [2017] UKUT 171 (AAC) Judge Hemingway has considered the case of a claimant whose medical condition caused her to hesitate and prolong the process of dressing. The FTT had accepted that her condition might extend the time that she took to dress—they said that "she was able to make a decision eventually", but they made no finding as to how long the delay might be and in particular did not refer to reg.4(4) and the definition there of what might be a reasonable time. For that reason the case was returned to a new tribunal, but in doing so the judge affirms that hesitation in choosing clothes, even on the basis of the appearance presented, could be reason to satisfy Activity 6, provided always that the claimant's difficulty in doing so could be attributed to their physical or mental condition.

In *NA v SSWP (PIP)* [2015] UKUT 572 (AAC) Judge Mark held that the claimant's use of a chair, or a bed, to dress and undress could satisfy Descriptor 6b. It mattered not that able people might similarly use a chair or bed to dress or to help put on their shoes; what mattered was whether the claimant was *unable* to do those things without that aid to assist them.

However, a different conclusion on similar facts has now been reached by Judge Jacobs in *CW v SSWP* [2016] UKUT 197 (AAC); [2016] AACR 44. There the claimant said that she had to sit on her bed in order to dress herself. The judge held that a bed, which might equally be used by a non-disabled person should not, in these circumstances be regarded as an aid to dressing. While he begins by agreeing with the decision of Judge Mark that an ordinary object may become an aid to a disabled person if that person cannot accomplish the task without it, he goes on to say that the need for assistance must relate to the particular function in question-what might be necessary as an aid in washing and toileting will not necessarily be an aid in dressing. The use of the aid must then be related to the function:

"The question is this: would this 'aid' usually or normally be used by someone without any limitation in carrying out this particular aspect of the activity? If it would, the 'aid' is not assisting to overcome the consequences of an impaired function that is involved in the activity and its descriptors".

On this basis he concludes that while the claimant needed to sit whilst she took her jeans on and off it was just as normal for able persons to do the same— in effect the claimant was not disabled in respect of the function of dressing and undressing because that is commonly the way that dressing etc is done. The decision of Judge Jacobs in *CW v SSWP (PIP)* [2016] UKUT 197 (AAC) has been followed by Judge Markus QC in *AP v SSWP (PIP)* [2016] UKUT 501 (AAC). She supports the reasoning in that decision and adds to it herself in the following way:

> "The activities in Schedule 1 to the Regulations can be performed in a variety of ways. Dressing and undressing is no exception. A person who has little or no choice as to the manner in which they can carry out an activity but who can do it nonetheless, is not limited in doing so. I respectfully agree with Judge Jacobs' reasoning at paragraph 31 and 32 of CW. Otherwise a claimant who can eat sitting down but needs an aid or assistance to eat standing up would qualify for points under activity 2, and a claimant who can sit in a bath but needs an aid or assistance to lie down in it would qualify for points under activity 4. Once that is understood, it can be seen that what is usual or normal is both a relevant and a necessary consideration. It provides the limits for what a claimant can be expected to do and not to do (see Judge Jacobs' example at paragraph 30 of his decision) in order to undertake an activity."

And see the discussion of these cases in the note that follows regulation 2 above.

The meaning of "dressing" has been explored by Judge Jacobs in *PE v SSWP (PIP)* [2015] UKUT 309 (AAC); [2016] AACR 10. The claimant had failed in her claim because although in her claim pack she had stated that she needed help when dressing, when before the FTT, she said that she managed to dress by wearing "easy to wear" clothing. The judge allowed her appeal on the basis that the test in Activity 6 was based upon an abstract test of normal clothing which the representative of the Secretary of State appears to have accepted means "clothing which is appropriate to the general norms of society at large." In this case she argued the FTT had clearly found that the claimant's "easy to wear" clothing was appropriate. The judge returned the case for rehearing. In his view, just as a claimant could not elevate their degree of disability by insisting on wearing clothes that were particularly difficult to manage, so too, they would not be required to reduce their disability by wearing only loose fitting and elasticated clothes. The judge suggested that the new tribunal should focus first upon the ways in which the claimant's disability affected her ability to dress - bending, reaching, and twisting, together with any degree of pain associated with the process. They should also consider the effect that reg.4(2A) might have in assessing her ability to do so to an acceptable standard and within a reasonable time.

In this case it does not appear that the judge had been referred to the *PIP Assessment Guide* as has been done in other cases. Although the *Guide* is not determinative of meaning in the regulations it has been accepted as helpful in interpreting them. The judge might have found helpful the first paragraph relating to Activity 6 which reads as follows:

> "This activity assesses a claimant's ability to put on and take off [. . .] un-adapted clothing that is suitable for the situation. This may include the need for fastenings, such as zips or buttons and considers the ability to put on/take off socks and shoes."

In *LC v SSWP (PIP)* [2016] UKUT 150 (AAC) the point was also made that the claimant who had lost the use of one arm and her hand in a motor accident would not be able to manage buttons, zips and most other fasteners. Judge Gray observed that this would make it difficult for the claimant to put on most outer garments without assistance from another person. For much of the time a coat would be required when out of doors and this would be relevant to the 50% rule under reg.7.

Activity 7—Communicating verbally

4.248   This Activity is entitled communicating verbally. Taken literally that could mean both spoken and written communication, but it appears that the use of the term verbal occurs because this Activity was originally combined with that in Activity 8 – written communication. It is now clear that this Activity is concerned only with making and receiving oral/aural communication. This is established in the decision of Judge Gray in *EG v SSWP (PIP)* [2017] UKUT 101 (AAC). In that case it became clear that the DWP does not now use the claimant's ability to lip-read as a way to receive oral information, although there are several reported decision in which lip-reading has been taken account of in the past. Judge Gray could find no basis upon which she could read that limitation into the PIP legislation, but accepted, at least for the purposes of this case, that it was a concession properly made on the basis of a pragmatic approach to the matter under regulation 4 – in other words lip-reading might be thought to be so ineffective and unreliable that it should not be regarded as a way of receiving information to an acceptable standard.

Judge Gray has referred again to the matter of lip-reading in *CC v SSWP (PIP)* [2017] UKUT 429 (AAC). The same concession was made by counsel representing the Secretary of State and although no general direction has been issued to judges in the Social Entitlement Chamber as the judge had requested, she was advised that guidance to this effect has been issued to decision makers, and that this should ensure a common treatment across all claimants. Judge Gray observes that DM guidance is not binding on tribunals, but suggests that, were a tribunal to reject that advice, they would need to explain their reasons with some particularity.

The matter of whether lip-reading should be taken account of in assessing a claimant's ability to communicate has been considered again in *MM v SSWP (PIP)* [2018] UKUT 193 (AAC) and also in *SB v SSWP (PIP)* [2018] UKUT 122 (AAC). In both cases the UT has held that for an FTT to take lip-reading into account amounts to an error of law so long as the Secretary of State continues to direct DMs that it is not an acceptable means of communication. In *P v SSWP (PIP)* [2018] UKUT 376 (AAC) Judge Mitchell has put this matter beyond any doubt (at least so far as the FTT is concerned) by holding that lip-reading is not a means of communicating verbally. He holds that this is not because of any concession by the Secretary of State but because that is the correct interpretation of the law having regard to reg.4(2A) that would require communication to an acceptable standard.

Confining Article 7 to oral/aural communication also means that use of telephones and other devices to send and receive text messages plays no part in Activity 7. Judge Gray takes the view that this Activity requires that the claimant can both speak and hear; thus someone who can speak, but not hear and uses a hearing aid, or, someone who can hear, but not speak and uses a text-to-speech machine, is in each case communicating only with the use of an aid or appliance and will score 2 points under Descriptor b. This case concerned a young person who suffered from a serious hearing loss from an early age. She had learned to speak and had some benefit from hearing aids, but had difficulty in using a telephone and sought out quiet places to in which she could communicate more easily. A major point made in this case is the need for a tribunal to assess the claimant's ability in the range of environments that might be regard as normal for that claimant. The claimant should not be judged in a quiet environment if she chooses to go there only because her disability. This means that the tribunal must try to distinguish between what the claimant does as a matter of her genuine preference and what she does because of her disability. (cf. *PE v SSWP (PIP)* [2015] 309 (AAC) where the issue was claimant's choice of clothes).

"Basic verbal information" means information in the claimant's native language. It is "basic if it is in just one simple sentence.

"Complex verbal information" is more than one sentence or, just one complex sentence- again in the claimant's native language.

In *GJ v SSWP (PIP)* [2016] UKUT 8 (AAC) Judge Hemingway has underlined the need for tribunals to make clear in their reasons that they have taken account of the meaning of "complex" communications as defined in Part 1 of the schedule. Although it might have been inferred, at least in relation to written communication where the claimant had been found to have difficulty in dealing with correspondence from the DWP and in completing his PIP claim form, that he did have difficulty with complex information in the requisite sense, the judge held that the FTT should have made specific reference to that matter.

This case is important also in dealing with the relationship between Activity 7 and Activity 9. The claimant was a schizophrenic who needed support in relation to both activities. But the judge accepts that the sort of support that is necessary in relation to Activity 9—help in dealing with other people in a face to face situation will not be sufficient to satisfy Activity 7 as well. There the difficulty experienced by the claimant must be such as to make him unable to communicate as distinct from just relate socially to others. He explains this as follows:

"I accept that anxiety caused by mental health difficulties can potentially lead to the scoring of points under activity 7 such that the activity and its associated descriptors are not simply concerned with physical or sensory impairments to communication. I also accept though, as highlighted in the government response, that there is a distinction to be drawn between the sorts of tasks the two different activities, and the associated descriptors, are seeking to test. In this context there is a difference between communication and engagement. If a claimant has difficulty in speaking as a result of anxiety, or perhaps some other mental health problem, it must be asked what it is that causes that difficulty. Is it a fear of social engagement? Or is it something simply connected to the activity of communicating verbally? It could, of course, be both but, equally, it could be one or the other. So, it seems to me an anxious claimant who, for example, is not able to communicate with strangers or persons who are not well known to him or is not able to do so when in the company of a large number of people but is able to verbally express himself or herself and understand communication with a person with whom they are familiar and comfortable would, in all probability, score points under activity 9 but not under activity 7. That is because, in such a case, it is likely to be the engagement with others which is triggering the difficulty. So, such a claimant would not be able to score points under both activity 9 and activity 7 as a consequence of an anxiety problem impacting upon the ability to engage with other people. However, if a claimant was so anxious that not only was he impaired with respect to engaging with others but was also impaired with respect to the function of communicating verbally, perhaps a most unlikely eventuality, he might score under both activities."

In this case the claimant would probably show that he could satisfy Activity 9 more easily than he could Activity 7. The converse was probably the case in *HB v SSWP (PIP)* [2016] UKUT 160 (AAC). There the claimant was a girl who was bilaterally deaf though she could lip-read and used hearing aids. Judge Rowley agreed with the view expressed in the case above and returned the case to an FTT for further facts to be found relating to the claimant's need for social support.

"communication support" is help given by a person with training or experience in assisting people with specific communication needs. Superficially this could cover any communication need, but limiting the test to the claimant's native language will have the effect of eliminating the foreign language interpreter. The most obvious cases of a person giving communication support will be a signer for the deaf. Note that communication support (which satisfies Descriptor c.) must be given by a person, so that a claimant who uses a computer generated voice will be using an aid or appliance to communicate and will satisfy only Descriptor b.

In *TC v SSWP (PIP)* [2016] UKUT 550 (AAC) Judge Rowley has held that communication support should be treated in the same way as is social support in

4.249

relation to Activity 9. That means that it is not only persons who have been trained to provide support to persons in general who qualify, but also persons, such as friends and family, who have experience in supporting that claimant.

It is interesting to note that, at a time when the use of a hearing aid, at least among the elderly, has become almost commonplace; it will still count as the use of an appliance in order to communicate and therefore, satisfy Descriptor b. (cf. the wearing of spectacles below).

Activity 8—Reading and understanding signs, symbols and words

4.250   The definitions of basic and complex written information approach the difference in a similar manner to that for verbal information in Activity 7.

"basic written information" is signs symbols or dates in standard size text written in the claimant's native language.

"complex written information" is more than one sentence written in standard size text in the claimant's native language. By implication then, basic information is limited to one sentence.

"read" means the ability to understand signs, symbols and words in the claimant's native language and in standard size text. To "read" does not include Braille, so a person who is visually impaired so as not to be able to read standard size text will score under Descriptor d. (four points). In order to score under Descriptor e (eight points) the claimant would need to show that he cannot read signs, symbols or words at all, and the shift from "written information" (i.e. standard size text) in the preceding Descriptors, to any words seems to be deliberate. Note that the shift to the use of "words" and the use of that word in the definition of "read" in contrast to "signs and symbols" may mean that a claimant who can understand numbers and other symbols, might succeed under this Activity if he cannot understand words though he may still understand symbols. The importance of examining the claimant's ability to read all kinds of information has been emphasised by Judge Lane in *SSWP v SH (PIP)* [2017] UKUT 301 (AAC). There the FTT had focused on her ability to read official letters, and her tendency to have difficulty when she got upset, rather than the whole range of any possible literature and signage. The judge said that they had erred too, in relying on the oral evidence given to them at the hearing, when there was other and contradictory evidence in the tribunal file.

Two cases have been decided that show that illiteracy is not relevant to this Activity unless it can be shown to derive from the claimant's mental or physical condition – see *SSWP v IV (PIP)* [2016] UKUT 420 (AAC) which was a case on the mobility component and *KP v SSWP (PIP)* [2017] UKUT 30 (AAC). In both cases the illiteracy was from a failure to learn to read rather than any demonstrated relevant condition.

The descriptors for written communication make no reference to communication support. This means that someone who is blind so as to require the services of a reader will qualify under Descriptor e.

The benchmark of normality in this case includes the use of spectacles or contact lenses- Descriptor a. A person who chooses to use a magnifying glass rather than spectacles, will also be treated as meeting Descriptor a. so long as it is possible (and reasonable) to expect him to so—see reg.4(2)(b) above. Where it is not, the use of a magnifier will mean that the claimant is using an aid or appliance.

Activity 9—Engaging with other people face to face

4.251   "engage socially" means to interact with people in an appropriate manner both a contextually and socially and it will require the claimant to understand body language and to be able to establish relationships. It is important to note that the function required here of the claimant is to engage socially. Although those words do not appear directly in the Activity it has been accepted that they are to be imported from the definitions in Part 1 of the schedule. This means that it is the claimant's ability to meet and engage with others in a social context that is to be tested. Evidence that the claimant engaged effectively with the HCP, or that he could attend for hospital appointments, or take part in work related group sessions does not meet the point – see *SF v SSWP (PIP)* [2016] UKUT 543 (AAC). In *HA v SSWP (PIP)* [2018] UKUT 56 (AAC) Judge Rowley has emphasised the need for a tribunal in considering this Activity to examine the claimant's ability to satisfy all three parts of engaging socially—i.e. to interact in a contextually and socially appropriate manner, to understand body language and to establish relationships. In this case the claimant had profound difficulty in relating to adults and the judge directed that being able to engage only with other young people or with others who were already known to him would not suffice. The requirement that the claimant must be able to engage "face to face" also precluded a finding that he could engage with others by sending texts on his telephone.

"social support" means help from a person who is trained or experienced in assisting people to engage in social situations. It is not clear whether "social" in this context is intended to be confined to what might be described as non-business relationships or whether it might extend to all inter-personal contacts. As the descriptors refer only to "engaging with other people" and that must be in a contextually appropriate (as well as a socially appropriate) manner it is suggested that the wider meaning should be preferred. In *AM v SSWP (PIP)* [2017] UKUT 7 (AAC) Judge Jacobs has held that engaging face to face means engaging one to one or within a small group and does not necessarily require the ability to cope with a crowd.

The application of this Activity in the case of a claimant whose sight is severely restricted is examined by Judge Sutherland Williams in *DV v SSWP (PIP)* [2017] UKUT 244 (AAC); [2017] AACR 38. The judge reviewed several helpful passages drawn from earlier cases. The case was returned to fresh tribunal who would be required to make findings, in particular of the extent to which the claimant could read the body language of those with whom he was interacting, and of the extent to which prompting or support would assist him in that situation. The judge emphasised also, that the test was of the claimant's ability to interact generally one to one, or in a small group and in social situations. Inferences that the FTT had drawn from the claimant's interaction with them in the hearing room were either of limited relevance, or, if they were to be relied upon as the reason for their decision, they should have been put to the claimant as a part of the hearing.

A decision of Judge Mark *PR v SSWP (PIP)* [2015] UKUT 584 (ACC) has clarified two points in applying this descriptor. First, the definition in para.1 of this Schedule of "social support" as support from a person "trained or experienced in assisting people to engage in social situations" might reasonably have been thought to include only those people who have had training or experience in handling this situation for people in general, but this case establishes that it will suffice if the person assisting does so in light of experience only of that particular claimant. This means that assistance from family members and friends will qualify as social support. This was pointed out by the representative of the Secretary of State as having been explained in the Government's response to consultation on the assessment guide and is now contained in the *Guide* itself. In this case it appears that the family and friends had not in fact supplied any social support—indeed, as the judge put it, they showed a singular lack of empathy with her. It seems that doubt has been expressed as to whether the decision of Judge Mark does then settle that point. For that reason the matter has been decided again in *SL v SSWP (PIP)* [2016] UKUT 147 (AAC) and should now be regarded as settled.

The second point made by Judge Mark is that for social support to be given, does not require that the assistant is there at the time of engaging face to face; the support may be given by counselling beforehand, but without which, the claimant would be unable to engage with other people. Indeed, the *PIP Assessment Guide* goes even further—it points out that the claimant may not have support at all—what is required is that the claimant *needs* social support and that may be the case even when none has been provided.

The meaning of "social support" in Descriptor c and in particular the difference between that and "prompting" in Descriptor b is examined by Judge Agnew in *MMcK v SSWP (PIP)* [2016] UKUT 191 (AAC); [2017] AACR 38 (CS only). Prompting, he points out, can be provided by anyone, but social support must be by someone trained or experienced, even as a friend or family, in filling that role. It must be ascertained whether the claimant *needs* more than just prompting, not just whether he is accustomed to getting support and he affirms that support can be given in advance of the occasion when the claimant interacts with others and without the person giving support having to be there. This decision was appealed to the Court of Session in Scotland and is reported as *SSWP v MMcK* [2017] CSIH 57. The court upheld that part of the decision which held that prompting need not be contemporaneous with the social interaction, though they do say that there must be some "temporal or causal link" between the prompting or encouragement and the event at which it is to be effective, so that, especially where that encouragement has taken the form of psychological counselling, there will come a time that it becomes just a part of the past history of the claimant's condition and is no longer effective as an act of encouragement. But they do not accept that "prompting" in Descriptor b. is to be totally separated from "social support" in Descriptor c. Before this decision there had been a number of other decisions in which the judges had emphasised that support required something that had a qualitative difference from that which was prompting. (See for example *CPIP/1861/2015, CSPIP/203/2015* and *CSPIP/210/2015*). Why else, it was said, would the points in Descriptor c. amount to double the score in b. The test, it was suggested, was to remove all the help that could properly be regarded as prompting and encouraging to see what remained – only if there were something more that was done would that be seen as support. The Court of Session did not accept this view. In their opinion there could be an overlap between what was prompting and what was support. The critical difference, they say, is that social support can be given only by those who are trained or experienced in that role and they confirm too, that support can be given by friends and family on the basis that they are experienced in supporting that claimant—they need not be otherwise trained or experienced. (See *SL v SSWP (PIP)* [2016] UKUT 147 (AAC)). But there does need to be some difference between what might be just prompting to make it into social support; the difference, they suggest, is that the help given, must be made effective or its effectiveness increased because it is given by that person. In other words the help given is effective either because of the training and experience of that person in a professional sense, or because of the training and experience of that person as a result of their relationship with the claimant.

While this case was proceeding in the Scottish courts the matter had been considered again in England in *AH v SSWP (PIP)* [2016] UKUT 276 (AAC). There, Judge Humphrey rejected the argument put by the claimant that the only difference between prompting and support lay in the training or experience of the person giving that help; in her view there must be a qualitative difference in the help given in order to justify the difference in points scored under each Descriptor. This case has now been appealed to the Court of Appeal in *Hickey v Secretary of State for Work and Pensions* [2018] EWCA Civ 851. Leave to appeal had been granted on only one rather narrow point subsequently abandoned, but leave was given by the court to amend the grounds to cover first, the qualitative difference point, secondly the contemporaneity point, and thirdly (a new point) that the FTT had not considered the claimant's ability to form relationships. As well, the appellant argued that the Court of Appeal was bound to follow the decision reached in the Court of Session being a court of equal standing in a common jurisdiction following *Young v Bristol Aeroplane Co. Ltd.* [1944] K.B. 718 (CA) though that was an earlier decision of the same court. Regrettably, the Court of Appeal had decided none of these questions. (In part, this was because the court was aware that an application for leave to appeal to the Supreme Court has been made in the *MMcK* case). Because of the conclusion that they were about to reach on the grounds presented, the court found it unnecessary to express any view on the precedent point. On the grounds of appeal before them they decided that even if they were to apply the law as stated in *SSWP v MMcK* the appellant would lose her appeal on each of the grounds on the basis of the facts that had been found by the FTT. What the court does say seems to accept that there may be an overlap between actions that are "prompting" and those that are "social support", but then observes that support must be something different from prompting because Descriptor c. does not say simply "prompting by a person trained etc". Again, it is doubted that encouragement that merely increases the effectiveness of the prompting (as had been suggested by Lord Glennie in the *MMcK* case) could be sufficient. On the contemporaneity point it is accepted that prompting or encouragement immediately before an event might have a sufficiently direct causal effect, but suggests that that should be a relatively rare event.

In *SSWP v AM (PIP)* [2015] UKUT 215 (AAC) Judge Mark has upheld the decision of an FTT that awarded benefit to a claimant who suffered from both Asperger's Syndrome and from OCD (obsessive compulsive disorder). The judge held that while they may have failed to give sufficient reasons for one part of their decision (see Activity 1, above) this would make no difference to the outcome of the case. In upholding the decision in respect of Activity 9, an award of 8 points under Descriptor d, the judge found no mistake. He did, though, point up some difficulties with the wording of this activity. First, although Part 1 of this Schedule contains a definition of "engage socially" that expression does not appear in this activity or, indeed, anywhere else in the Schedule. But that definition does serve to identify the factors that might be involved in measuring a claimant's ability to engage effectively. More problematically, there may be difficulty in reconciling the requirements under reg.4(2A) for the claimant to engage with other people safely and to an acceptable standard, and for the need in Descriptor d for the claimant to do so without overwhelming psychological distress or causing a substantial risk of harm. If the evidence shows that the claimant cannot (on at least 50% of the days in the relevant period) engage safely and to a satisfactory extent is it necessary to find, as well, that the same behaviour shows the necessary overwhelming distress and risk to safety? In the view of Judge Mark it was sufficient for the tribunal to have found, on the evidence that was before them, that the claimant could not engage socially safely and to an acceptable extent; it was not necessary for them then to make a separate finding that this was because of overwhelming psychological distress or the risk of substantial harm. Perhaps the best explanation is that the same evidence fulfilled both requirements. And see below the further decision of Judge Jacobs in *RC v SSWP (PIP)* [2017] UKUT 352 (AAC)

In *HJ v SSWP (PIP)* [2016] UKUT 487 (AAC) Judge Markus QC has considered the requirements that must be shown for a claimant to be engaging with other people to a satisfactory extent. She accepts, as had Judge Mark in *AM v SSWP (PIP)* [2015] UKUT 215 (AAC), that although the words "engage socially" do not appear in the descriptors for this activity, the definition that is given for them in Part 1 of the Schedule should be used as a guide to what engaging face to face might involve. In this case the claimant, who was an alcoholic and suffered from depression, had said that she visited one or other of three pubs each day. The FTT had dismissed the appeal against refusal of her claim taking the view that this was inconsistent with any claimed inability to engage with others. The claimant had said that at the pub she stood at the bar alone and moved away if anyone tried to talk with her. She also gave evidence of self-harming when under stress. Judge Markus thought that this, and other evidence, had been overlooked by the FTT so as to be an error of law or, at any rate, they had failed to give sufficient reasons to explain why they had done so. The judge thought it may have been possible that the claimant's behaviour at the pub and her other dealings with people, did not evince an interaction that was "in a contextually and socially appropriate manner", and that the evidence showed that she might not be able to "establish relationships with others". The case was returned to a fresh tribunal.

A decision of Judge Jacobs in *RC v SSWP (PIP)* [2017] UKUT 352 (AAC) has considered further the meaning of engaging socially and in particular what might be required to "establish relationships". The claimant suffered from a mental health

4.252

condition which caused him to have thoughts of a homosexual nature whenever he came into contact with other men. He found this extremely distressing and said that he wished he could kill himself. The FTT had awarded 2 points for Descriptor 9(b) on the basis that, with prompting (though their reasons would suggest that they should have awarded 4 points under 9(c)), he could engage with other men (he had no difficulty in respect of women) to the extent of making a reciprocal exchange. Judge Jacobs held that this was not sufficient to constitute establishing a relationship. As he points out a brief conversation about the weather with a stranger, would be a reciprocal exchange, but we would not, as a matter of ordinary language, call that establishing a relationship. The judge returned the case to a new tribunal without attempting to prescribe what would be necessary to establish a relationship. He considered that it would be impossible to list the essential characteristics of a relationship in all circumstances—he doubted, for example, that he would have been able to anticipate the facts of this case if he had tried to list the situations that such a list might be required to encompass. This means that these words, as ordinary words of the English language, should be interpreted by a new tribunal (as the finders of the facts) relying upon their own experience and common sense.

One further point that arises from this case is the relationship between a claimant's ability to achieve an Activity to an acceptable standard, in accordance with reg.4(2A)(b), and the need to show, in Activity 9(d)(i), overwhelming psychological distress. In *SSWP v AM (PIP)* [2015] UKUT 215 (AAC) Judge Mark held that where the claimant had been unable to engage socially in a manner that was safe and to an acceptable standard, that it was not necessary to find, as well, that he would suffer overwhelming distress. In this case Judge Jacobs does not refer to the earlier case and his disposition of the case suggests that he did expect the new tribunal to make a finding about the level of distress that the claimant might suffer. Yet, he also suggests that neither prompting nor support might be sufficient to enable the claimant to engage socially to a satisfactory standard in accordance with reg.4(2A). It therefore seems open to a new tribunal, following the *AM* case, to find in the claimant's favour without needing to find overwhelming distress. The trouble with this conclusion is that the Descriptor 9(d)(i) is satisfied only when such a finding has been made. This creates the same conundrum that emerges from cases such as *GP v SSWP (PIP)* [2016] UKUT 444 (AAC) where the FTT was forced to conclude that the claimant could not wash himself at all (because he took more than twice as long as a normal person would to do so) when the descriptor to be satisfied read "cannot wash and bathe at all and needs another person to wash their entire body". While that might have been physically possible (though unlikely) in that case, it is difficult to see how Descriptor 9(d)(i) can be said to be satisfied at all unless the overwhelming distress is shown.

But an alternative and perhaps more viable approach to this conundrum is suggested by Judge Ovey in *AB v SSWP (PIP)* [2017] UKUT 217 (AAC). This was another case where the claimant's evidence suggested that he suffered distress when he tried to engage socially with others. Judge Ovey suggests that the requirements of reg.4(2A) should apply only to those descriptors which test what the claimant *can* do, and are not applicable to those descriptors that describe what the claimant *cannot* do. In her view the structure of PIP Activities ranges from a descriptor at one end that specifies a claimant who can accomplish the activity described without any need for assistance at all, to another at the other extreme where the claimant cannot accomplish that activity at all. By way of illustration she refers to Activity 6—dressing and undressing; that ranges from "can dress and undress unaided" to "cannot dress or undress at all". It makes sense applying reg.4(2A) to test whether a claimant can dress (with or without aid) to a satisfactory extent, safely and in a reasonable time, but it does not, she says, make sense to ask whether someone who cannot dress at all does so satisfactorily, safely and timeously.

The inference is that reg.4(2A) was not intended to apply to the "cannot-do" descriptors. Regulation 4(2A) was a late addition to the regulations (as can be seen from the numbering) and in this, as well as other respects, the regulations as a whole, and the descriptors in particular, have evolved somewhat piecemeal. The advantage of this approach in relation to Activity 9 is that the tribunal can sensibly decide if the claimant can engage with others with or without prompting or support, to a satisfactory extent and do so safely, but, if it is shown that he cannot do that, then the sole question is whether, when he tries to engage, he suffers either overwhelming psychological distress or becomes a danger to himself or others.

The decision of Judge Gray in *EG v SSWP (PIP)* [2017] UKUT 101 (AAC) discussed in the Note to Activity 7 above, has also made extensive and helpful observations in relation to this Activity and to the relationship between both Activities. She emphasises that the help (prompting, supervision or assistance) that might be given to the claimant will need to be different in respect of each Activity. Help given in respect of verbal communication cannot also be the basis of a score for social support in engaging with other people. This is a further example of a disability that is dealt with specifically in one Activity not being acceptable as the basis of a score in another, more general Activity – see *AS v SSWP (PIP)* [2017] UKUT 104 (AAC); [2017] AACR 31 discussed in Note to Activity 5 above. In her view also "social support" requires something more than "prompting". There is a qualitative difference between what is required of social support and prompting and in her view social support requires the presence of the person giving that support, though she agrees with Judge Parker in *CSPIP/203/2015* that this will not require constant vigilance. Again in *PM v SSWP (PIP)* [2017] UKUT 154 (AAC) Judge Gray has dealt with the nature of the face-to-face event that this Activity involves. It is not sufficient that the claimant should be competent in dealing with friends and other persons that she knows, or those with whom there is a specific objective such as a health professional. The definition of "interact socially" informs this Activity and seems to envisage the ability to interact with others so as to *establish* relationships. 4.253

"psychological distress" means distress that relates to an "enduring mental health condition or to an intellectual or cognitive impairment".

Psychological distress could have a physical trigger as in the case of the person who has episodes of incontinence, but to satisfy this Descriptor that would need to link with a mental health condition or impairment. A person who suffers acute embarrassment as a result of episodes of incontinence will qualify only under Activity 5, if at all.

Activity 10—Making budgeting decisions

This is the only Activity in which no Descriptor will give a qualifying score on its own and any score must, therefore be combined with a score from another Activity. 4.254

"simple budgeting decisions" are those relating to calculating the cost of goods and the change required after making a purchase. Presumably, the touchstone for this Activity would be if the claimant could be relied upon to go shopping on their own.

"complex budgeting decisions" will require the claimant to be able to calculate household and personal budgets as well as managing the payment of bills and planning for future purchases. Again, it will usually be fairly obvious when someone needs another to take over the management of their affairs, though that must be in consequence of the claimant's mental or physical condition; irresponsible indebtedness is not unknown among those who are not disabled!

The distinction between the ability to make complex budgeting decisions and simple ones is explored in *CPIP/3015/2015*. The claimant had a number of disabling conditions including alcohol dependency. The judge, by way of illustration, suggests that an alcoholic who had no control over his addiction might be compelled to spend every penny on drink so as to be incapable of planning and undertaking complex budgeting decisions, but be quite capable of the simple decisions involved in purchasing items and accounting for the change. In *RB v SSWP (PIP)* [2016] UKUT 393 (AAC) Judge White accepted that the claimant's physical condition as well as his mental condition could be relevant in relation to this activity. The claimant had argued that the pain he suffered from osteoarthritis interfered with his ability to make complex budgeting decisions – he said that he had to leave all such matters for his wife to deal with. The judge accepted that while this might be so he thought that it could arise only in extreme conditions and that was not shown in this case. It should be noted too that all the descriptors for this activity involve the claimant's ability to make "decisions", so a physical disability that affects only the claimant's ability to undertake the physical part of a transaction such as to go shopping, or to handle money, or write a cheque will not qualify under this activity. (See for example in *CPIP/0184/2016*).

The decision in *CPIP/1650/2015* carries this a step further. Judge Markus QC accepted the argument of the Secretary of State that the focus of this activity is upon the cognitive process of decision making rather than the claimant's inability to obtain the information necessary to make that decision. Thus a person who is blind and not able to read braille, but has full cognitive ability, would score no points because, given the information, they would be able to make budgeting decisions. This argument was put to Judge Mesher in *SSWP v LB (PIP)* [2016] UKUT 530 (AAC), discussed above in relation to Activity 3. The claimant suffered from diabetes and depression and was dyslexic. She had been allowed two points under this activity by the HCP on the ground that because of her dyslexia she needed prompting or assistance to be able to take complex budgeting decisions. This had not been the subject of her appeal to the FTT, but in the UT counsel for the Secretary of State put the argument as above, that this was not help with the cognitive process of decision making, but with the gathering of information to begin that process. He found support for this in the definition of "assistance" (in Part 1 of the schedule) because that does not include assistance given by speech, and assistance would seem the most apt way to describe the help given to a person who is dyslexic (or blind) when a bill or other information is read to them. (Note though, that "prompting" as defined includes explaining to the claimant, which might be equally apt). Counsel argued, too that an inability to read that was the result of some physical or mental condition was covered by Activity 8 (Reading and understanding signs symbols and words) and to allow points under this activity as well, would be providing a double benefit. This argument is unconvincing; many activities will involve the claimant scoring twice, or even multiple times, as a result of the same physical or mental condition – a person who suffers badly from arthritis in their arms and hands, for example, might score for difficulty in dressing, as well as washing and cooking and other activities. The counter argument put by counsel for the claimant focused chiefly on the words of the descriptors – "needs prompting or assistance *to be able to make budgeting decisions*"; this, he thought, should include help in obtaining the information necessary to make decisions. Judge Mesher did not find it necessary or appropriate for him to reach a decision on these arguments because his decision on other activities gave the claimant sufficient points to be awarded benefit at the enhanced rate and hence a decision on this activity would serve no useful purpose, but he thought that an arguable case could be put that deserved a decision where the facts were fully explored and after argument had been heard.

The need to be able to make budgeting decisions, even complex ones, has been accepted as a proper Activity in respect of a claimant who was 16 or 17 years old by Judge Hemingway in *DP v SSWP (PIP)* [2017] UKUT 156 (AAC). In that case he also suggests that where the claimant, because of his condition (he was considering the suggestion of someone suffering from ADHD), is able to make a complex budgeting decision about the need to prioritise certain expenses, but then goes out and spends his money impulsively on something else, he might yet satisfy this Activity because his behaviour would be about "decisions involving . . . paying bills" within the definition in Part 1 of the Schedule.

The Mobility Component—Activities and Descriptors

4.255   The test of mobility has been reduced to just two activities—planning a journey and moving about.

Activity 1—Planning and following journeys

The mobility component for PIP is not restricted to a physical disability. Section   **4.256**
79 of WRA 2012 refers specifically to a person's "physical or mental condition".
In *NK v SSWP (PIP)* [2016] UKUT 146 (AAC) Judge Rowley affirmed that this
could include a claimant whose psychosomatic condition caused her to believe that
she was unable to walk even though there was no physical reason that prevented
her from doing so. The sole question was whether that belief, or the pain she
experienced was real to the claimant; though on the evidence available in this case
the judge was able to find that the claimant was able to move satisfactorily and the
appeal was dismissed. This means that PIP (unlike DLA) will be available to an agoraphobic person. Whether they will qualify under Descriptor b or under Descriptor
e will depend upon whether they can be persuaded to go out with prompting, or
whether they will not go out at all without overwhelming psychological distress.

"psychological distress" must relate to the claimant's mental health condition
or an intellectual or cognitive impairment. This means that the claimant who is
inhibited from going out just because of a fear of being embarrassed by an episode
of incontinence would not succeed unless their distress was linked to such a health
condition. (cf. *SSWP v DC* [2011] UKUT 235 (AAC) where the claim failed
because the claimant's reluctance to go out arose just from fear and anxiety).

Following a journey in this context means being able to follow a route. The route
may have been prepared in advance (planned) by the claimant or by someone else,
but the benchmark for this activity requires that the claimant must be able to both
plan and to follow a route. If the claimant can follow, though not plan, a route he
will score under Descriptor c. If the claimant can plan a route, but is then unable
to follow that route without some level of assistance or encouragement he will score
under which ever of the descriptors is appropriate for that assistance etc.

The difference of opinion that had arisen between judges of the UT in the
application of this Activity has been resolved by a decision of a three judge panel
in *MH v SSWP (PIP)* [2016] UKUT 531 (AAC); [2018] AACR 12. The disagreement revealed in the previous decisions turned upon the meaning to be given to
Descriptors d and f of this Activity. In two decisions (*DA v SSWP (PIP)* [2015]
UKUT 344 (AAC) and *HL v SSWP (PIP)* [2015] UKUT 694 (AAC)) the judges
took the view that the words "follow the route" meant only an ability to navigate a
route, while in another (*RC v SSWP (PIP)* [2015] UKUT 386 (AAC)) the judge
thought that the words should include the case of a claimant who was prevented
from following the route by a fear of, or an inability to interact with, other people
along the route if, for example, it became necessary to ask for alternative or better
directions. Such a claimant might then be able to follow the route if he were accompanied by another person as required in Descriptors d and f. The second view would
mean that both of these Descriptors were available to a claimant who could not
undertake a journey because of overwhelming psychological distress and in particular a person who suffered from agoraphobia might qualify for the higher rate (12
points) under Descriptor f and not the lower rate (10 points) under Descriptor e.
The three judge panel decided in favour of that second view- though they restricted
their conclusion to claimants for whom they thought the psychological distress
would be truly exceptional. The Personal Independence Payment (Amendment)
Regulations 2017 (SI 2017/194) were made, in part, to reverse the effect of this
decision, but para.4(2) of reg.2 of those regulations that effected the change was
held (in *RF v SSWP* [2017] EWHC 3375; [2018] AACR 13) to have been made
ultra vires the regulation-making power in Part 4 of the Welfare Reform Act 2014
and hence to be of no effect. The text of Descriptors in Activity 1 of Part 3 of the
schedule has been restored to its original form in this volume. The appeal that had
been lodged by the DWP against the decision in *MH* has also been withdrawn and
hence decisions on this Activity should now be decided in accordance with the decision of the three-judge panel.

Several issues arising from the application of psychological distress and anxiety under the Descriptors to Activity 1 have been considered in *AA v SSWP (PIP)* [2018] UKUT 339 (AAC). The claimant suffered from paranoid schizophrenia. He had periods of low mood, lacked motivation and suffered high levels of anxiety. His evidence, which was accepted by the FTT, was that he would usually need encouragement to venture out of doors at all; that he could sometimes accomplish familiar journeys on his own, but that he would never go somewhere unfamiliar without someone to accompany him. Evidence was given that when he did go out alone he wore earphones and looked at the ground. Even when accompanied he might wear the earphones—his companion was there to provide what he described as "moral support" rather than to tell him where to go. The FTT allowed him 4 points under Descriptor 1b. Judge Hemingway, in the UT, observed that this meant that they accepted that he did need at least encouraging to avoid overwhelming psychological distress in order to leave his home. But they did not think that he qualified under Descriptor 1d or 1f. (It seems that they did not consider 1e because it was clear that he could undertake journeys so long as he had a companion). Judge Hemingway thought that they had probably refused his claim under 1d or 1f because they thought that his companion should need to provide some more positive intervention, that was more than just passive presence, to satisfy those Descriptors.

Judge Hemingway thought that two questions arose—does the companion have to play an active role when he accompanies the claimant; and can a claim succeed under Descriptor 1f if the claimant can undertake some familiar journeys but not others. As to the first Judge Hemingway decided that active intervention was not necessary; with this the representative of the Secretary of State agreed and as the judge demonstrated this was in accordance with the reasoning of the UT in the *MH* case. As to the second, the representative of the Secretary of State had observed that the wording of both 1d and 1f is "a" journey rather than "any" journey; therefore she said it should suffice that the claimant was sometimes unable to accomplish that journey without support. The judge held that thereafter the matter would be governed by reg.7—does the situation apply on more than 50% of the days on which it might arise. This was a helpful conclusion for the claimant in this case but the judge anticipated a further argument that could arise from this distinction between "a" journey and "any" journey. He thought that in applying the same reasoning to Descriptors 1b and 1e that the claimant might fail if they were able to make a journey occasionally because the wording suggests that they would need to be incapable of "any" journey. He suggests that he would reject that argument; the use of the word "any" in that context means, he suggests, simply there is no distinction between familiar and unfamiliar journeys. He then goes on to consider the case of a claimant who can make some familiar journeys on most, but not on all days, and other familiar journeys on some but not most days! This is not a case for the application of reg.7 because it is not a matter of the days so much as the various journeys. Judge Hemingway says that the answer is to approach the question as a broad assessment of the claimant's ability to tackle familiar routes in general.

When the amending regulations were before Parliament they met with considerable criticism on the ground that they refuted the principle stated in the enabling act (s.79 WRA 2012) that PIP would be available equally to claimants whose disability was mental as to those that were physical. The DWP was challenged to produce examples where Descriptors c, d and f might still be satisfied by claimants whose disability was mental in origin. The DWP responded in a House of Commons Briefing Paper Number 7911 (April 13, 2017) entitled *Changes to the Personal Independence Payment eligibility criteria* by giving the following four examples (although these examples are no longer necessary to serve the original purpose for which they were produced they may be useful to tribunals and advisers to illustrate further cases where there should be no difficulty in satisfying the terms of these Descriptors):

A person (person A) with a cognitive impairment who cannot, due to their impairment, work out where to go, follow directions or deal with unexpected changes in their journey, even when the journey is familiar, would score 12 points under descriptor f in mobility activity 1 ("planning and following journeys"), and hence be entitled to the enhanced rate of the mobility component. Examples of such conditions could include dementia, or a learning disability such as Down's Syndrome. (Some people covered by this example may experience psychological distress as well, and may also meet descriptor b, requiring "prompting" – i.e. reminding, encouraging or explaining – from another person in order to be able to undertake a journey. They will still receive 12 points under Descriptor f and be entitled to the enhanced rate.)

A person (person B) with a developmental disorder could qualify on a similar basis to person A if the disorder affects their ability to work out where to go, follow directions or deal with unexpected changes in their journey. If their disorder results in them having difficulty assessing and responding to risks, or in impulsivity, then they could also score 12 points under Descriptor f on the basis that they need to be accompanied for their own safety. Examples of developmental disorders which could have these effects include Autistic Spectrum Disorder and Attention Deficit Hyperactivity Disorder (ADHD).

A person (person C) who suffers psychosomatic pain could qualify for the   **4.257** enhanced rate through satisfying Descriptors e or f in mobility activity 2 ("moving around"). The case of *NK v SSWP (PIP)* [2016] UKUT 146 (AAC) concerned a claimant who suffered significant pain when moving around, but the pain resulted from a mental condition rather than any physical impairment. The Upper Tribunal found that the claimant could score points towards an award of the mobility component under mobility activity 2, even though her pain did not have a physical cause.

A person (person D) who has chronic fatigue syndrome (CFS) and experiences symptoms including significant fatigue following physical exertion, muscular and joint pain and balance problems, together with psychological difficulties which manifest as depression and panic attacks, could qualify for the enhanced rate under mobility activity 2, or by scoring points on a combination of mobility activity 1 (4 points under Descriptor b, for requiring prompting to avoid psychological distress when undertaking any journey) and mobility activity 2 (eight points under descriptor c, for being able to stand and then move unaided more than 20m but no more than 50m). As explained above, Chronic Fatigue Symptom (CFS), also known as myalgic encephalomyelitis (ME), has complex causes which are still not well understood, but which may involve both physical and psychological factors. Note that where the claim is based upon an argument that the claimant needs to be accompanied when undertaking a journey, it is necessary to demonstrate, with evidence in support, that without that company the claimant would be at risk of harm in some way. See the decision of Judge May QC in *AR v SSWP (PIP)* [2018] UKUT 313 (AAC). The claimant suffered from epilepsy, but there was no evidence that he was prone to having a seizure when he was out.

An "assistance dog" is a dog that has been trained to guide or assist a person with sensory perception.

The obvious example is a guide-dog for the blind, but it could include a hearing-dog if the claimant is deaf and needs to be warned of a danger of which others would be alerted by sound.

An "orientation aid" is a specialist aid designed to enable a disabled person to follow a route safely so that should include a long cane or white stick that is used to give the claimant information to locate objects, kerbs etc. It will include too, any echolocation device that provides similar information to the claimant, though it is presumably not a "device" if the claimant uses his own tongue to emit clicks. It is doubtful if a white stick that is used only to inform other people that the claimant is visually impaired could be regarded as an orientation aid.

In *RB v SSWP (PIP)* [2016] UKUT 304 (AAC) Judge Rowley has considered the question whether a satellite navigation device (a SatNav) could be considered to be an orientation aid so as to qualify a claimant for points under Descriptors 1d and 1f of this activity. She held that it did not. The same conclusion had been reached by Judge May QC in *CSPIP/229/2015* and the reason, in both cases, was the same; an orientation aid is defined in Part 1 of the schedule to mean "a specialist aid designed to assist disabled people to follow a route safely". The device in each of these cases was a standard SatNav and although the equipment in this later case was a built-in version, that would not mean that it had been designed specifically to aid disabled people. The consequence would seem to be that a person who is blind and uses an ordinary walking stick, rather than a white stick or an extending stick, to guide himself would not satisfy this descriptor either. This reasoning also throws doubt on the use of an eye patch that was in question in *SSWP v SS (PIP)* [2015] UKUT 240 (AAC) The claimant needed to wear a patch over one eye because without it he suffered from dazzling that disorientated him. It would seem that the eye patch, as used there, would still be an aid, though not an orientation aid. While it might be said that an eyepatch was designed to assist disabled people, it would not normally be thought to have been designed to assist them to follow a route safely. The claimant in that case would then not satisfy descriptor 1a for zero points (because he could not follow a route *unaided*), but it is difficult to see which of the Descriptors that follow could be applied to him. The same point might have been made in the current case, but it would still be necessary to show that the claimant was unable to follow a route without the use of her SatNav and that the inability arose from some mental or physical condition; such inability had been accepted in the earlier case. The same conclusion regarding the use of a SatNav has been reached by Judge Humphrey in *SSWP v NF (PIP)* [2017] UKUT 480 (AAC). There the claimant suffered from memory problems as a result of a stroke. Although she was able to drive, she was unable to remember a route for any journey, even a very simple one with which she had been familiar, and consequently she needed to use her SatNav to make any journey at all. The judge allowed the Secretary of State's appeal following the cases above because the SatNav had not been designed for use as a specialist aid for disabled people, but in this case the claimant might have succeeded in scoring 8 points under Descriptor 1c if it could be shown that she was incapable of planning the route of a journey.

In *SSWP v IV (PIP)* [2016] UKUT 420 (AAC) Judge Jacobs has decided two important points about Activity 1. First, that the journey to be undertaken and the route to be followed is not necessarily a local one. The *PIP Assessment Guide* directs the DM to consider only a local journey in respect of both a familiar route and an unfamiliar one. Nowhere in the legislation to be applied does this limitation appear. In this case, the FTT which had allowed the claimant's appeal, had asked the claimant if he could find his way to London – a considerable distance away. Judge Jacobs accepted that the destination was irrelevant; what mattered was the claimant's ability to follow the route wherever that was leading to. The FTT were entitled to test that ability by posing a variety of journeys including one that might be intimidating to many people. In this case the FTT had in fact also discussed with the claimant his ability to follow several other more local routes. Secondly, and more importantly, the judge emphasises that any inability to satisfy a Descriptor must be as a result of the claimant's mental or physical condition. In this case the claimant, who suffered also some physical disabilities, was illiterate. It was for that reason that the FTT were satisfied that he could not undertake an unfamiliar journey on his own. But the claimant's illiteracy was not shown on the evidence to be the result of any mental or physical condition. It appeared that his illiteracy was because he had failed to learn, rather than because he was incapable of learning; the FTT had already rejected his claim in respect of Activity 8 (reading and understanding signs symbols and words) for the daily living component, and their finding in relation to mobility was inconsistent with that.

Activity 2—Moving around

4.258   In discussing this activity it should be noted first of all, that the general prerequisite in reg.4 that an assessment of the claimant's capability must be made using or wearing any aid or appliance that he normally uses, or which he can reasonably be expected to use, must be suspended because some of the descriptors in this activity specify the claimant's ability when unaided. In *KL v SSWP (PIP)* [2015] UKUT 612 (AAC) Judge Mitchell accepts that the well-recognised principle of statutory interpretation to the effect that a specific provision in a piece of legislation overrides the more general expression in that same legislation means, in this instance, that the assessment of the claimant must be made when unaided if that is what is specified.

Although there is no definition of "move" in the regulations it must be taken to mean that the claimant must progress by the movement of his own limbs or, where appropriate, by the aid of a prosthesis, a crutch or a stick. Any of these things can be regarded as an "aid or appliance" Query whether a wheelchair should be regarded as an appliance? If it is, that might lead to difficulty in applying Descriptor f of this activity. The guidance given by DWP to the HCP explains this by saying that the requirement for most of these Descriptors is that the claimant must be able to "stand" and then "move" which means that the moving must be whilst he is still standing. In broad terms moving will equate with the popular notion of walking even though the walking may be with the use of sticks, walking frames or crutches. Note that for PIP making forward progress even with two crutches will still be "moving". (cf. for DLA where progressing by "swinging through" was not regarded as walking).

The prerequisite to any degree of movement in these Descriptors is for the claimant to be able to stand. "stand" is defined as being able to stand upright with at least one biological foot on the ground; so a double lower-limb amputee, even an Olympic champion, will qualify under Descriptor f.

In *DT v SSWP (PIP)* [2016] UKUT 240 (AAC) Judge Rowley has considered the nature of the terrain over which the ability to move around must be judged. She accepts the concession made by the representative for the Secretary of State that the surface must be of a type that is commonly experienced by pedestrians when walking out of doors. This meant a reasonably flat pavement taking into account the usual rise and fall that one might normally encounter, including the need to negotiate kerbs, but not necessarily involving steps and slopes. In this case the claimant, who had a back problem, reported difficulty in stepping on and off the kerb; the FTT had not addressed that matter and the case was returned to a fresh tribunal.

Provided that the claimant can stand, then the extent of ability to move depends upon both the distance over which the claimant can move and whether there is a need for "aid", which in most cases will include either an appliance or some form of assistance, encouragement or supervision.

A single lower-limb amputee who is able to use a prosthesis and can stand and then move, even if he uses an aid to do so, may find that he does not qualify at all.

Descriptor a. The benchmark of normality, in this instance, is being able to stand and move more than 200 metres, even if that is possible only with the use of an aid or with assistance etc. If the claimant can do this, he scores no points.

Descriptor b. is satisfied if the claimant can move at least 50 metres, but no more than 200 metres, even if he can do that only by using an aid or with assistance, encouragement or supervision etc.

Descriptor c. (which marks the point at which a claimant could qualify, on movement grounds alone, for the standard rate) is satisfied if the claimant can move more than 20 metres but no more than 50 metres without using an appliance or having assistance etc. If, to go further, he needs to use an aid, appliance or have supervision, prompting (which itself means reminding, encouraging or explaining) or assistance, then he will qualify at the standard rate.

There are now two conflicting decisions on the interpretation of Descriptor c. This is important because that descriptor awards eight points—sufficient to qualify the claimant at the standard rate for the mobility component. The application of Activity 2 was always going to be difficult. Reading Descriptor c. literally, a person who could move more than 20 but no more than 50 metres unaided, satisfies that descriptor and that could be said to be the case even if, with an aid or appliance, they could then progress a further 1000 metres! That was the meaning accepted originally in the commentary to this descriptor, but is now questioned because if this descriptor is given its literal meaning it then makes nonsense of Descriptor a. That descriptor says a claimant who can move more than 200 metres *aided or unaided* scores nothing. It is not, of course unusual for a claimant to satisfy more than one of the descriptors in any particular activity and if he does reg.7 prescribes that he should take the higher or highest score. But in this instance it could be argued that the claimant who could move unaided up to 50 metres and thereafter required the use of a stick would be treated more favourably than someone who needed to use his stick from the outset. This was the argument accepted by Judge Hemingway in *JP v SSWP (PIP)* [2015] UKUT 529 (AAC) As the representative of the Secretary of State had put it to him, a claimant who could walk, more than 200 metres, but only with the aid of a stick or other appliance used for the *whole* of that journey, would be treated less favourably that one who could walk up to 50 metres unaided and could then carry on indefinitely with the aid of a stick—arguably the former person was the more disabled and therefore more deserving. He suggests that, reading Descriptor c. in the context of all the other descriptors, it must be read as applying only to a person who can move up to 50 metres without an aid, but then can move no further at all even if aided. (The difference between c.—(eight points) and d.—(10 points) then depends upon whether the claimant can do that unaided or only with an aid).

This interpretation of Descriptor c. has been rejected in *KL v SSWP (PIP)* [2015] UKUT 612 AAC by Judge Mitchell. In this case the claimant had a condition of her ankle which required her to use a crutch or walking stick. With that aid she could walk more than 200 metres. It does not appear from the evidence whether, without an aid she could move at all. The FTT to whom she had appealed rejected that appeal applying the words of Descriptor a: "can stand and move more than 200 metres aided or unaided". They did not consider her ability to move unaided and hence did not refer to Descriptor c. Judge Mitchell finds that it was an error of law not to do so and referred the case back for rehearing. The argument made in the case above, *JP v SSWP*, was not put to the judge in this case, but he refers to it on the basis that it might well be put before the new FTT on rehearing. In his view the logic, or lack of it, in the construction of this activity and the descriptors provided there, was not a sufficient reason to depart from what he found to be the clear literal meaning of Descriptor c.

The conflict between the decision in *JP v SSWP (PIP)* [2015] UKUT 529 (AAC) and that in *KL v SSWP (PIP)* [2015] UKUT 612 (AAC) is addressed again by Judge Markus QC in *AP v SSWP (PIP)* [2016] UKUT 501 (AAC). Her decision is in agreement with that of Judge Hemingway in the former case. This decision is reached after full argument based on the submissions of both parties and should before an FTT, for that reason, be regarded as settling the matter unless and until there has been an appeal to the Court of Appeal or a contrary decision of a three-judge panel.

4.259   *Descriptor d.* will be satisfied if the claimant needs to use an aid or appliance to move a distance between 20 and 50 metres. This level of disability scores 10 points, but unless the claimant also has problems in planning a journey, he will have no further points to aggregate and will therefore qualify only for the standard rate of benefit.

Descriptor e. is satisfied if the claimant can stand and move at least 1 metre but no more than 20 metres even with an aid or with assistance etc.

Descriptor f. requires that the claimant can either not stand, or cannot move more than one metre, in either case even with aid or assistance etc.

Although both descriptors e. and f. carry the same score of 12 points (and hence qualify the claimant for the component at the enhanced rate) Descriptor f. has probably been included because it best describes the extreme case of a claimant who needs to use a wheelchair to be able to move, effectively, at all.

A claimant's ability to walk may fluctuate over a period of time and even on a day to day basis. Such cases will need to satisfy the 50% rule in reg.7 and the appropriate Descriptor to be applied will be determined in accordance with that regulation, but there is no reason why, in applying that regulation, account should not be taken of days on which the claimant is so afflicted as to not be able to walk at all. In *BM v SSWP (PIP)* [2017] UKUT 486 (AAC) Judge Bano considered the case of a claimant whose condition was such that on seven to ten days each month he was bedridden. The judge held that to ignore these days in the overall assessment of how limited the claimant's ability to walk was, and on how many days it was so limited, was an error of law.

In these descriptors there is no explicit criterion that relates to time and speed, but reg.4(2A) does require that he must be able to accomplish the task "within a reasonable time". A reasonable time is defined in reg.4(2A) as being, no more than twice the time that would be taken by an able-bodied person.

Regulation 4(2A) also requires that the claimant can perform a task "repeatedly". This is defined in that regulation as being as often as it might reasonably be expected to be completed. This will introduce consideration of the claimant's condition when he completes a journey and the recovery time that would be needed, if it were reasonable to expect the journey to be done again. So a claimant who could walk more than, say, 200 metres to the shops, but would need then to rest for an hour before he could return, would not have satisfied Descriptor a.

In applying any of these Descriptors due account will need to be taken of pain, breathlessness and other forms of discomfort such as dizziness, vertigo, etc. Where the exertion involved in completing the task might endanger the claimant's health the Descriptor will not be satisfied unless such harm would be "unlikely"—see reg.4(4). But this must now be read in the sense decided in *RJ v SSWP (PIP)* UKUT [2017] UKUT 105 (AAC); [2017] AACR 32 so that the Descriptor will be satisfied when there is a real risk of harm such that it would not be sensible to ignore – see above in the note that follows reg.4.

The number and extent of any rests that the claimant might need to take will also be relevant to the question of whether the claimant can complete the Descriptor "to an acceptable standard".

Given the precise distances that have been prescribed and the wording of most descriptors as "stand and then move" it might be argued that the test should envisage a single unbroken progress to the requisite distance. But that approach has been rejected in two UT decisions; the preferred view in both decisions is that stops and pauses should be taken account of as a part of the overall assessment of a claimant's ability to move when regard is had to the criteria specified in reg. 4(2A). In particular the need to accomplish the distance repeatedly and within a reasonable time, but regard might be had also to achieving movement "to an acceptable standard". A person who could achieve the distance only by taking long rests would be unlikely to satisfy the definition of a reasonable time period in that regulation (no more than twice as long as an able bodied person), but it may still be possible for a claimant to succeed if they can accomplish the distance only with a great deal of effort or with a great deal of pain; such a person might not be said to carry out the activity to an acceptable standard. This was the view taken by Judge Parker in *TF v SSWP (PIP)* [2015] UKUT 661 (AAC) and that decision was followed by Judge Hemingway in *KN v SSWP* [2016] UKUT 261 (AAC). In the latter case the judge thought it was unclear if the FTT had taken account of the claimant's need to "stop" and to "pause" (though if they had done so, would have made no difference to the decision), but he did allow the appeal because the tribunal had not then gone on to consider, specifically, the time that the claimant needed to cover the distance.

In *PS v SSWP (PIP)* [2016] UKUT 326 (AAC) Judge Markus QC refers again to the matter of pain suffered by a claimant while walking and the effect that might have on the application of regulation 4(2A) – ability to achieve the activity to an acceptable standard. In this case the claimant suffered from spinal stenosis and his evidence was that he could walk a distance of about 50 yards but always in considerable pain and that, at that point, the pain was such that he was forced to stop. In the view of Judge Markus the FTT had failed to give proper consideration to this part of the evidence and the case was returned to a fresh tribunal. In *PM v SSWP (PIP)* [2017] UKUT 154 (AAC) Judge Gray has added further to the consideration of what walking might reasonably be required under regulation 4 by emphasising that the test should reflect the claimant's choice as to how far and how often she might wish to do so at least to the extent that she wishes to lead a normal life. The judge refers to the test adopted in the House of Lords in *Secretary of State v Fairey* *(R(A)2/98)*. When a claimant walks slowly but can nevertheless achieve the distance prescribed in less than twice the time required by an able person (so that the test relating to speed in regulation 4(4) is satisfied) the question can then arise whether that slowness might still be taken into account in determining whether the claimant can walk "to an acceptable standard". In *KL v SSWP (PIP)* [2017] UKUT 545 (AAC) Judge Hemingway has held that it should not. In his view, because slowness is specifically provided for by the test in regulation 4(4)(c) it would result in inconsistency if it were to be taken account of elsewhere as well. But he does say that this conclusion is limited to the context of speed in relation to the walking test.

SCHEDULE 2

MEMBERS OF HER MAJESTY'S FORCES: EXCLUDED PERSONS

4.260   1. The following persons are not members of Her Majesty's forces for the purpose of these Regulations —
   (a) subject to paragraph (2), any person who is serving as a member of any naval force of Her Majesty's forces and who locally entered that force at a naval base outside the UK;
   (b) any person who is serving as a member of any military force of Her Majesty's forces and who entered that force, or was recruited for that force, outside the UK, and the depot of whose unit is situated outside the UK;
   (c) any person who is serving as a member of any air force of Her Majesty's forces and who entered that force, or was recruited for that force, outside the UK, and is liable under the terms of engagement to serve only in a specified part of the world outside the UK.
   2. Paragraph (1)(a) does not include any person who—
   (a) has previously been an insured person under Part 1 of the National Insurance Act 1965; or
   (b) is paying or has previously paid one or more of the following classes of contributions under the Social Security Act 1975 or the Social Security Contributions and Benefits Act 1992—
      (i) primary Class 1;
      (ii) Class 2; or
      (iii) Class 3.

The Personal Independence Payment (Transitional Provisions) Regulations 2013

(SI 2013/387)

ARRANGEMENT OF REGULATIONS

4.261   1.   Citation, commencement and interpretation
        2.   (1) In these Regulations—"the Act" means the Welfare Reform Act 2012.
        3.   Invitations to persons entitled to disability living allowance to claim personal independence payment.

4. Claims by persons entitled to disability living allowance for personal independence payment other than by invitation.
5. Persons under 16 not entitled to claim personal independence payment.
6. Persons in the course of claiming disability living allowance not entitled to claim personal independence payment.
7. Form of notification inviting a person to claim personal independence payment.
8. Making a claim for personal independence payment following notification.
9. Suspension of disability living allowance where no claim for personal independence payment made.
10. Further opportunity to claim personal independence payment.
11. Termination of entitlement to disability living allowance following failure to claim personal independence payment.
12. Defective claims by voluntary transfer claimants.
13. Failure to provide information etc.
14. Express intention not to claim personal independence payment.
15. Withdrawal of claim for personal independence payment.
16. Death before or after making claim for personal independence payment.
17. Procedure following and consequences of determination of claim for personal independence payment.
18. Extension of certain fixed term period awards of disability living allowance for persons reaching 16.
19. General power to extend fixed term period awards of disability living allowance.
20. Notifications of change of circumstances.
21. Extinguishment of rights of appeal, etc. under disability living allowance regime.
22. Extinguishment of right to claim disability living allowance.
23. Assessment of claim: transfer claimants to be taken to meet part of required period condition.
24. Assessment of claim: date by reference to which assessment is to be made.
25. Treatment of persons in hospital or care home during transfer to personal independence payment.
26. Temporary absence from Great Britain when transfer claimant becomes entitled to personal independence payment.
27. Persons aged 65 and over to be entitled to personal independence payment in certain circumstances.
28. Persons unable to act: claims for personal independence payment.
29. Persons unable to act: transfer to personal independence payment.
30. Application of these Regulations to certain persons becoming entitled to disability living allowance while claiming personal independence payment.
31. Disabled people: badges for motor vehicles.

The Secretary of State, in exercise of the powers conferred by sections 93 and 94 of, and Schedule 10 to, the Welfare Reform Act 2012, makes the following regulations.

These Regulations are made under the provisions of that Act and are made before the end of a period of six months beginning with the coming into force of those provisions of that Act.

Citation, commencement and interpretation

1. These Regulations may be cited as the Personal Independence Payment (Transitional Provisions) Regulations 2013 and come into force on 8th April 2013.   4.262

2.—(1) In these Regulations—

"the Act" means the Welfare Reform Act 2012;

"the 1987 Regulations" means the Social Security (Claims and Payments) Regulations 1987;

"the 1991 Regulations" means the Social Security (Disability Living Allowance) Regulations 1991;

"the 1992 Act" means the Social Security Contributions and Benefits Act 1992;

"the 1998 Act" means the Social Security Act 1998;

"the 1999 Regulations" means the Social Security and Child Support (Decisions and Appeals) Regulations 1999;

"the Claims and Payments Regulations" means the Universal Credit, Personal Independence Payment, Jobseeker's Allowance and Employment and Support Allowance (Claims and Payments) Regulations 2013;

"the PIP Regulations" means the Social Security (Personal Independence Payment) Regulations 2013;

"the Decisions and Appeals Regulations" means the Universal Credit, Personal Independence Payment, Jobseeker's Allowance and Employment and Support Allowance (Decisions and Appeals) Regulations 2013;

"appropriate office" has the meaning given by regulation 2 (interpretation) of the Claims and Payments Regulations;

"assessment determination" means the determination, under regulation 4 (assessment of ability to carry out activities) of the PIP Regulations, of a claim for personal independence payment made by a transfer claimant;

"change of circumstances" means a change of circumstances which a person might reasonably have been expected to know might affect the continuance of that person's entitlement to disability living allowance (by ending entitlement to one component or both components or resulting in entitlement to one or both components being at a different rate);

"component", in relation to disability living allowance, means one of the components of disability living allowance referred to in section 71 (disability living allowance) of the 1992 Act;

"disability living allowance" means the benefit known by that name that is provided for in sections 71 to 76 of the 1992 Act;

"DLA entitled person" means a person aged 16 or over who is entitled to either component or both components of disability living allowance;

"electronic communication" has the meaning given by subsection (1) of section 15 (general interpretation) of the Electronic Communications Act 2000;

[2 "exempt person" means a DLA entitled person in respect of whom, by virtue of regulation 8(2B) or 12A(3) of the 1991 Regulations (person under the age of 18 on the day of entry into hospital), a disability living allowance is payable even though they are maintained free of charge while undergoing medical or other treatment as an in-patient in a hospital or other similar institution;]

"notified person" means a DLA entitled person who has been sent a notification by the Secretary of State under regulation 3(1);

"pay day", in relation to disability living allowance, means—

(a) in the case of a payment of disability living allowance in respect of a period to which paragraph (2) of regulation 25 of the 1987 Regulations applies, the day on which the payment is made in accordance with paragraph (1) of that regulation;

(b) in the case of any other payment of disability living allowance, the day on which the allowance is payable in accordance with paragraph 1 of Schedule 6 (days for payment of long term benefits) to the 1987 Regulations.

[¹ "relevant date" means the date, specified by the Secretary of State in relation to any category of DLA entitled person, from which the Secretary of State is satisfied that satisfactory arrangements will be in place to assess the entitlement of persons in that category to personal independence payment;]

"transfer claimant" means a person who is either—

(a) a notified person who has claimed personal independence payment in response to a notification sent by the Secretary of State under regulation 3(1), or

(b) a voluntary transfer claimant;

"voluntary transfer claimant" means a DLA entitled person who has claimed personal independence payment under regulation 4.

(2) For the purpose of these Regulations, except regulations 8, 12 and 16—

(a) a claim for personal independence payment is made—

(i) in the case of a claim made in writing other than by means of an electronic communication, on the day on which a form, authorised by the Secretary of State for the purpose, containing all the information requested in the form is delivered to or received at the appropriate office,

(ii) in the case of a claim made in writing by means of an electronic communication made in accordance with the provisions set out in Part 1 of Schedule 2 (use of electronic communications) to the Claims and Payments Regulations, on the day on which an electronic communication containing all the information requested by the Secretary of State in the form referred to in paragraph (i), or completing that information, is received at the appropriate office, and

(iii) in the case of a claim made by telephone, on the day on which a telephone call takes place during which all the information requested by the Secretary of State in the form referred to in paragraph (i) is supplied or which results in all that information having been supplied; and

(b) references to the making of a claim do not include the making of a defective claim.

(3) The Claims and Payments Regulations, the PIP Regulations and the Decisions and Appeals Regulations apply to the claims for personal independence payment referred to in these Regulations except where—

(a) these Regulations provide otherwise, or

(b) the application of those Regulations would be inconsistent with the application of these Regulations.

[¹(4) As soon as practicable after specifying a relevant date in relation to any category of DLA entitled person, the Secretary of State must publish, in such manner as the Secretary of State considers appropriate, information sufficient to enable any DLA entitled person to ascertain the relevant date, if any, which applies in their case.]

AMENDMENTS

1. Personal Independence Payment (Transitional Provisions) (Amendment) (No.2) Regulations 2013 (2013/2698) reg.2(2) (October 25, 2013).

2. Social Security (Disability Living Allowance and Personal Independence Payment) (Amendment) Regulations 2016 (SI 2016/556) reg.4(2) (June 29, 2016).

Invitations to persons entitled to disability living allowance to claim personal independence payment

4.263   3.—(1) At any time after [¹ 27th October 2013], the Secretary of State may by written notification invite a DLA entitled person to make a claim for personal independence payment.

(2) The Secretary of State must not send a notification under paragraph (1) to any person who, on 8th April 2013, was 65 or over.

(3) [²Subject to paragraphs [³ (3A), (4) and (4A)],] The Secretary of State must send a notification under paragraph (1) to a DLA entitled person who reaches 16 after [¹ 27th October 2013] as soon as reasonably practicable after the person reaches that age.

[²(3A) Paragraph (3) does not apply unless—

(a) the Secretary of State has specified a relevant date which applies in the case of the DLA entitled person, and

(b) that person reaches 16 on or after that relevant date.]

(4) Paragraph (3) does not apply to a DLA entitled person whose entitlement, on the day that the person reaches 16, is on the basis that the person is terminally ill within the meaning given by subsection (2) of section 66 (attendance allowance for the terminally ill) of the 1992 Act.

[³ (4A) If the DLA entitled person referred to in paragraph (3) is an exempt person, the Secretary of State must not send the notification required by paragraph (3) until the DLA entitled person ceases to be an exempt person.]

(5) [²Subject to [³ paragraph (5A) and (5B)]]] where, after [¹ 27th October 2013], a DLA entitled person who has neither—

(a) been sent a notification under paragraph (1), nor

(b) made a claim for personal independence payment under regulation 4, notifies the Secretary of State of a change of circumstances other than a change to which paragraph (6) applies, the Secretary of State must, as soon as reasonably practicable, send the person a notification under paragraph (1).

([²(5A) Paragraph (5) does not apply unless—

(a) the Secretary of State has specified a relevant date which applies in the case of the DLA entitled person, and

(b) that person notifies the Secretary of State of the change of circumstances on or after that relevant date.]

[³ (5B) If the DLA entitled person referred to in paragraph (5) is an exempt person, the Secretary of State must not send the notification required by paragraph (5) until the DLA entitled person ceases to be an exempt person.]

(6) This paragraph applies to a change of circumstances where the change notified is that the DLA entitled person is to become or has become absent, whether temporarily or permanently, from Great Britain.

AMENDMENTS

1. Personal Independence Payment (Transitional Provisions) (Amendment) Regulations 2013 (SI 2013/2231) reg.2(2) (October 6, 2013).
2. Personal Independence Payment (Transitional Provisions) (Amendment) Regulations 2013 (SI 2013/2689) reg.2(3) (October 25, 2013).
3. Social Security (Disability Living Allowance and Personal Independence Payment) (Amendment) Regulations 2016 (SI 2016/556) reg.4(3) (June 29, 2016).

DEFINITIONS

"change of circumstances"—see reg. 2(1).   4.264
"DLA entitled person"—see reg. 2(1).

GENERAL NOTE

In *DC v SSWP (PIP)* [2016] UKUT 117 (AAC) the claimant contacted the   4.265
DWP to enquire about transition from his current award of DLA. The DWP treated this contact as if it were notice of a change of circumstances and sent him a claim form for PIP which he duly completed. That claim for PIP failed entirely and his DLA entitlement terminated. The claimant appealed. He argued first, that his original communication to the DWP was not in fact notice of a change of circumstances (that would have triggered an obligation on the part of the Secretary of State to send a claim form), but was merely an enquiry as to his position in the future when transition to PIP might occur. His communication was not in fact available to the FTT that heard his appeal, but Judge Mitchell in the UT found that that did not matter because, in any case, the Secretary of State had a more general power under reg.3(1) to invite a claim from a DLA entitled person at any time. Once the process was begun the claimant was effectively on a conveyer-belt towards the determination of a PIP claim. (The case was in fact returned for rehearing but that was because the FTT appeared to have misunderstood the evidence that was before them).

An attempt to have these regulations declared invalid was unsuccessful in *TW v SSWP (PIP)* [2017] UKUT 25 (AAC). The claimant had been entitled to DLA and on mandatory transfer to PIP she was awarded a greater amount of benefit – she was a PIP "winner". But under these regulations by reg.17 her award of PIP was delayed for 28 days and her entitlement to DLA continued at the lower rate. She argued that this discriminated against her as a PIP transfer claimant because a payment of PIP to a new claimant would have been made from the date of claim. She argued that this meant the regulations were in breach of her art.14 rights under the ECHR and should be disapplied. A three judge panel of the UT rejected her argument. The delay applied equally to those claimants who were PIP "losers" and was a part of a necessarily complex scheme to provide for a fair and efficient system to transfer claimants. That being so the delay was, they said, objectively justified.

This case and the reasoning used has been upheld by the Court of Appeal in *Worley v SSWP* [2019] EWCA Civ 15.

Claims by persons entitled to disability living allowance for personal independence payment other than by invitation

[¹4. A DLA entitled person who has not been sent a notification under   4.266
regulation 3(1) may not make a claim for personal independence payment unless—
(a) they were aged under 65 on 8th April 2013,
(b) the Secretary of State has specified a relevant date which applies in their case, and
(c) they make the claim on or after that relevant date.]

AMENDMENTS

1. Personal Independence Payment (Transitional Provisions) (Amendment) Regulations 2013 (SI 2013/2689) reg.2(3) (October 25, 2013).

GENERAL NOTE

4.267   For the period from October 6, 2013 until October 25, 2013 reg.4 in its original form was amended in reg.4(2) to read as the date October 28, 2013.

DEFINITIONS

4.268   "DLA" entitled person"—see reg.2(1).
"disability living allowance"—see reg.2(1).

Persons under 16 not entitled to claim personal independence payment

4.269   **5.**—(1) No claim for personal independence payment may be made by a person who has not reached 16.

(2) Paragraph (1) applies whether or not a person is entitled to disability living allowance.

GENERAL NOTE

4.270   In the case of a child who has an appointee in in respect of their claim to DLA the DWP has a process that they follow when the claimant approaches the age of 16. A letter sent to the claimant enquires as to whether they will still require an appointee for the purposes of a claim to PIP. If they reply to the effect that they will, then an appointment is made, by the Secretary of State, under the powers that she has in reg. 28 to appoint for persons unable to act. In *P v SSWP (PIP)* [2018] UKUT 359 (AAC) there was no evidence before the FTT of such a process having been followed but the judge held that the tribunal (had they been aware of the deficiency) would be entitled to assume (applying the presumption of regularity) that the correct procedure had been followed in the absence of any evidence to the contrary.

Persons in the course of claiming disability living allowance not entitled to claim personal independence payment

4.271   **6.**—(1) This regulation applies to a person who is not entitled to disability living allowance if—

(a) the person claimed disability living allowance before [¹28ᵗʰ October 2013], and

(b) that claim remains under consideration on that date.

(2) A person to whom this regulation applies may not claim personal independence payment while the person's claim for disability living allowance remains under consideration.

(3) For the purpose of this regulation a person's claim for disability living allowance remains under consideration only if it has not—

(a) been decided by the Secretary of State under section 8 (decisions by the Secretary of State) of the Social Security Act 1998,

(b) been withdrawn in accordance with paragraph (2) of regulation 5 (amendment and withdrawal of claim) of the 1987 Regulations, or

(c) otherwise ceased to be under consideration before being decided by the Secretary of State as mentioned in subparagraph (a).

AMENDMENT

1. Personal Independence Payment (Transitional Provisions) (Amendment) Regulations 2013 (SI 2013/2231) reg.2(4) (October 6, 2013).

DEFINITIONS

"disability living allowance"—see reg.2(1).
"the 1987 Regulations—see reg. 2(1).

Form of notification inviting a person to claim personal independence payment

7. A notification to a DLA entitled person under regulation 3(1) inviting the person to claim personal independence payment must—

(a) explain that the person's entitlement to disability living allowance will end if the person does not claim personal independence payment,

(b) state the date of the last day of the period within which the person should claim personal independence payment, that period being one of 28 days starting with the day that is the stated date of notification,

(c) tell the person how to claim personal independence payment,

and may contain such additional guidance and information as the Secretary of State considers appropriate.

4.272

DEFINITIONS

"disability living allowance"—see reg.2(1).
"DLA entitled person"—see reg.2(1).

4.273

Making a claim for personal independence payment following notification

8.—(1) In this regulation and regulation 9 "the claim period" means the period of 28 days referred to in regulation 7(b).

(2) For the purposes of this regulation a claim, whether or not it is defective as mentioned in paragraph (3) or (4) of regulation 11 (making a claim for personal independence payment) of the Claims and Payments Regulations, must be made in accordance with and by a means set out in paragraph (1)(a), (b) or (c) of that regulation.

(3) Such a claim is made—

(a) in the case of a claim made in writing, other than by means of an electronic communication, on a form authorised by the Secretary of State, on the day on which it is delivered to or received at the appropriate office,

(b) in the case of a claim in writing made by means of an electronic communication in accordance with the provisions set out in Part 2 of Schedule 2 to the Claims and Payments Regulations, on the day on which it is received at the appropriate office, and

(c) in the case of a claim made by telephone, on the day on which the telephone call takes place.

(4) Neither paragraph (6) of regulation 11 of the Claims and Payments Regulations nor paragraph (2) of regulation 12 (date of claim for personal independence payment) of those Regulations shall apply in relation to a claim made by a notified person but—

(a) in a case where the claim is defective as mentioned in paragraph (3)

4.274

or (4) of the said regulation 11, the Secretary of State must extend the claim period by a period of 28 days, or such longer period as the Secretary of State thinks fit, starting with the day following the last day of the claim period, and

(b) in any other case the Secretary of State may extend the claim period by such further period as the Secretary of State thinks fit.

(5) The duty in paragraph (4)(a) and power in paragraph (4)(b) to extend the claim period may be exercised before the claim period would otherwise have expired or after it has expired.

(6) The Secretary of State may further extend a claim period extended under paragraph (4) either before the extended period would have expired or after it has expired.

(7) Where the claim period has been extended under paragraph (4), the Secretary of State must treat the claim as properly made if a claim is made—

(a) before the end of the period by which the claim period was extended or further extended, and

(b) in accordance with any instructions of the Secretary of State as to the way in which the claim is to be completed.

DEFINITIONS

4.275   "the Claims and Payments Regulations"—see reg.2(1).
"appropriate office"—see reg.2(1).
"electronic communication"—see reg.2(1).

Suspension of disability living allowance where no claim for personal independence payment made

4.276   9.—(1) Where a notified person makes no claim for personal independence payment before the end of the claim period or, where applicable, that period as extended under regulation 8(4) or (6), the person's entitlement to disability living allowance shall be suspended.

(2) The suspension shall take effect on the first pay day after the last day of the claim period or, where applicable, of that period as extended or further extended.

DEFINITIONS

4.277   "notified person"—see reg.2(1).
"disability living allowance"—see reg.2(1).

Further opportunity to claim personal independence payment

4.278   10.—(1) The Secretary of State must send any notified person in relation to whom regulation 9 takes effect a notice in writing informing the person—

(a) that the person's entitlement to disability living allowance will be or has been suspended,

(b) of the day on which the suspension takes or took effect, and

(c) that the person's entitlement to disability living allowance will be terminated unless the person makes a claim for personal independence payment before the end of the period of 28 days beginning with the day on which the suspension takes or took effect.

(2) The Secretary of State must send a notice under paragraph (1) before, on or as soon as practicable after, the day on which the suspension takes effect in accordance with regulation 9(2).

(3) Where a notice is sent to a notified person under paragraph (1), and the person makes a claim for personal independence payment before the end of the period specified in paragraph (1)(c), the person's entitlement to disability living allowance shall be reinstated as if the suspension of the entitlement had never taken effect.

<small>DEFINITIONS</small>

"notified person"—see reg.2(1).   4.279
"disability living allowance"—see reg.2(1).

Termination of entitlement to disability living allowance following failure to claim personal independence payment

11.—(1) Where a notice is sent to a notified person under paragraph   4.280
10(1) and the person makes no claim for personal independence payment before the end of the period specified in regulation 10(1)(c), the person's entitlement to disability living allowance shall terminate with effect from the day on which the suspension of the person's entitlement took effect in accordance with regulation 9(2).

(2) The Secretary of State must send any person in relation to whom paragraph (1) takes effect a notice in writing—

(a) informing the person that the person's entitlement to disability living allowance has terminated and of the date on which the termination took effect, and

(b) explaining that it is no longer possible for the person's entitlement to disability living allowance to be reinstated but that it remains open to the person to claim personal independence payment.

<small>DEFINITIONS</small>

"notified person"—see reg.2(1).   4.281
"disability living allowance"—see reg.2(1).

Defective claims by voluntary transfer claimants

12.—(1) This regulation applies in relation to a claim for personal inde-   4.282
pendence payment by a voluntary transfer claimant if—

(a) the claim was defective as mentioned in paragraphs (3) or (4) of regulation 11 of the Claims and Payments Regulations, and

(b) no claim completed in accordance with the instructions of the Secretary of State is received within the period of one month or longer which applies under paragraph (6) of that regulation.

(2) Where this regulation applies—

(a) regulation 9(1) shall apply to the voluntary transfer claimant as if the claimant were a notified person who has failed to claim before the end of the claim period, and

(b) for the purpose of that regulation the claim period for the voluntary transfer claimant shall be treated as ending on the last day of the period of one month or longer referred to in paragraph (6) of regulation 11 of the Claims and Payments Regulations, and regulations 9(2), 10 and 11 shall apply as if the voluntary transfer claimant were a notified person.

4.283   "voluntary transfer claimant"—see reg.2(1).

Failure to provide information etc.

4.284   **13.**—(1) Where, in relation to a claim for personal independence payment made by a transfer claimant—

(a) a negative determination is made in relation to both components under regulation 8 (information or evidence required for determining limited or severely limited ability to carry out activities) of the PIP Regulations or paragraph (2) of regulation 9 (claimant may be called for consultation to determine whether the claimant has limited or severely limited ability to carry out activities) of the PIP Regulations, or

(b) there is a determination by the Secretary of State that the transfer claimant has—

    (i) unreasonably failed to comply with a requirement imposed on the claimant by the Secretary of State under regulation 35 (attendance in person) of the Claims and Payments Regulations, or

    (ii) failed to comply with a requirement imposed on the claimant by the Secretary of State under regulation 37 (evidence and information in connection with a claim) of the Claims and Payments Regulations,

the transfer claimant's entitlement to disability living allowance shall terminate with effect from the last day of the period of 14 days starting with the first pay day after the day on which the determination is made.

(2) Where—

(a) for any reason an assessment determination is made on a claim by a transfer claimant in respect of which there has been a determination referred to in paragraph (1)(a) or (b) (for example, because the determination is revised by the Secretary of State under section 9 of the 1998 Act or there is a successful appeal in respect of the determination under section 12 of that Act), and

(b) personal independence payment is awarded to the transfer claimant,

the transfer claimant shall be entitled to personal independence payment in accordance with regulation 17(2)(b).

4.285   "transfer claimant"—see reg.2(1).
         "the PIP Regulations—see reg.2(1).
         "the Claims and Payments Regulations—see reg.2(1).
         "disability living allowance"—see reg.2(1).
         "assessment determination"—see reg.2(1).

Express intention not to claim personal independence payment

4.286   **14.**—(1) This regulation applies where a DLA entitled person who has not made a claim for personal independence payment informs the Secretary of State, whether in writing or by telephone, that the person does not intend to claim personal independence payment.

(2) Where this regulation applies the person's entitlement to disability

living allowance shall terminate with effect from the last day of the period of 14 days starting with the first pay day after the day on which the Secretary of State decides that the person has informed the Secretary of State as mentioned in paragraph (1).

(3) Paragraph (2) does not apply unless the Secretary of State is satisfied that the person was told, before the person informed the Secretary of State of the person's intention not to claim personal independence payment, that the person's entitlement to disability living allowance would terminate if the person expressed that intention.

<small>DEFINITIONS</small>

"DLA entitled person"—see reg.2(1).　　　　　　　　　　　　　　　4.287
"disability living allowance"—see reg.2(1).

Withdrawal of claim for personal independence payment

15. Where a claim for personal independence payment is withdrawn by a　4.288
transfer claimant under regulation 31 (withdrawal of claim) of the Claims and Payments Regulations before an assessment determination is made in relation to it, the claimant's entitlement to disability living allowance shall terminate with effect from the last day of the period of 14 days starting with the first pay day after the day on which the Secretary of State decides that the transfer claimant has withdrawn the claim.

<small>DEFINITIONS</small>

"transfer claimant"—see reg.2(1).　　　　　　　　　　　　　　　4.289
"the Claims and Payments Regulations"—see reg.2(1).
"assessment determination"—see reg. 2(1).
"disability living allowance"—see reg. 2(1).

Death before or after making claim for personal independence payment

16.—(1) Where a notified person dies before making a claim for per-　4.290
sonal independence payment the law relating to the person's entitlement to disability living allowance shall apply as if the notification had never been sent.

(2) Where a transfer claimant dies—

(a) before any assessment determination is made in relation to the claim, or

(b) where an assessment determination is made in relation to the claim, before the day on which the claimant becomes entitled to personal independence payment in accordance with regulation 17(2), the claim shall be treated as if it had never been made and, if the transfer claimant is a notified person, as if no notification under regulation 3(1) had been sent.

<small>DEFINITIONS</small>

"notified person"—see reg.2(1).　　　　　　　　　　　　　　　4.291
"disability living allowance"—see reg.2(1).
"transfer claimant"—see reg.2(1).
"assessment determination"—see reg.2(1).

Procedure following and consequences of determination of claim for personal independence payment

4.292   17.—(1) Upon an assessment determination being made on a claim by a transfer claimant—

(a) the Secretary of State must, as soon as practicable, send the claimant written notification of the outcome of the determination, and

[¹ (b) except where paragraph (2) of regulation 13 applies to the claimant, the claimant's entitlement to disability living allowance shall terminate—

(i) where paragraph (1B) applies, on the earlier of—

(aa) the last day of the payment period during which the assessment determination is made, or

(bb) the first Tuesday after the making of the assessment determination;

(ii) in any other case, on the last day of the period of 28 days starting with the first pay day after the making of the assessment determination.]

[¹ (1A) In paragraph (1), "payment period" means a period in respect of which disability living allowance is paid to the claimant in accordance with regulation 22 of the 1987 Regulations.

(1B) This paragraph applies if—

(a) the transfer claimant is terminally ill for the purposes of section 82 of the Act,

(b) the outcome of an assessment determination in respect of that claimant is an award of personal independence payment, and

(c) the total weekly rate of personal independence payment payable by virtue of that award is greater than the total weekly rate of disability living allowance payable by virtue of that claimant's existing award of disability living allowance.]

(2) Where the outcome of an assessment determination is an award in respect of either or both components of personal independence payment, the claimant's entitlement to personal independence payment starts with effect from the day immediately following—

[¹ (a) the day on which the claimant's entitlement to disability living allowance terminates in accordance with paragraph (1)(b) of this regulation,]

(b) where paragraph (2) of regulation 13 applies to the claimant, the day [¹ ...] on which the claimant's entitlement to disability living allowance terminated under regulation 13(1).

(3) The notification referred to in paragraph (1) must state—

(a) except where paragraph (2) of regulation 13 applies to the claimant, the day on which the claimant's entitlement to disability living allowance will terminate in accordance with paragraph (1)(b), and

(b) if personal independence payment is awarded, the day on which the claimant's entitlement to personal independence payment starts in accordance with paragraph (2).

(4) This paragraph applies to a person—

(a) whose claim for disability living allowance was refused,

(b) who claimed personal independence payment after that refusal, and

(c) who, as a result of the determination of legal proceedings initiated

858

under the 1998 Act in relation to that refusal, becomes entitled, after the assessment determination, to disability living allowance.

(5) The entitlement of a person to whom paragraph (4) applies to disability living allowance shall terminate—

(a) where personal independence payment is awarded, on the day before that on which the person becomes entitled to personal independence payment, and

(b) where personal independence payment is not awarded, on the last day of the period of 28 days starting with the first pay day after the making of the assessment determination.

DEFINITIONS

"assessment determination"—see reg.2(1).   4.293
"transfer claimant"—see reg.2(1).
"disability living allowance"—see reg.2(1).
"the 1998 Act"—see reg.2(1).

AMENDMENT

1. The Personal Independence Payment (Transitional Provisions) (Amendment) Regulations 2016 (SI 2016/189) reg.2 (April 4, 2016).

Extension of certain fixed term period awards of disability living allowance for persons reaching 16

18.—(1) Where there is an award of disability living allowance to a DLA   4.294
entitled person and—

(a) the award is of—
  (i) both components and the award in respect of either or both is for a fixed term period, or
  (ii) one component only and for a fixed term period,
(b) the person reaches 16 after [¹27th October 2013], and
(c) the fixed term period expires in the period starting with the day before the person reaches 16 and ending with the day before the person reaches 16 years and six months, the fixed term period shall be extended.

(2) A fixed term period extended under paragraph (1) shall expire on the day before the person reaches 17 or, where these Regulations have the effect that the person's entitlement to disability living allowance terminates on an earlier day, on that day.

AMENDMENT

1. Personal Independence Payment (Transitional Provisions) (Amendment) Regulations (SI 2013/2231) reg.2(5) (October 6, 2013).

DEFINITIONS

"disability living allowance"—see reg.2(1).
"components"—see reg.2(1).

General power to extend fixed term period awards of disability living allowance

19.—(1) Where there is an award of disability living allowance to a DLA   4.295
entitled person and—

(a) the award is of—
  (i) both components and the award in respect of either or both is for a fixed term period, or
  (ii) one component only and for a fixed term period, and
(b) the Secretary of State considers that the fixed term period may expire [¹ while the DLA entitled person is an exempt person to whom a notification cannot be sent by virtue of regulation 3(4A) or (5B), or] before an assessment determination can be made, the Secretary of State may extend the period by such further period as the Secretary of State considers appropriate.

(2) The Secretary of State may extend a fixed term period under paragraph (1)—
(a) regardless of whether the person has yet made a claim for personal independence payment,
(b) where the fixed term period has already been extended under regulation 18, and
(c) on more than one occasion.

(3) A fixed term period extended under paragraph (1) shall expire—
(a) on the last day of the period by which the Secretary of State extended or last extended it, or
(b) where these Regulations have the effect that the person's entitlement to disability living allowance terminates on an earlier day, on that day.

AMENDMENTS

1. Social Security (Disability Living Allowance and Personal Independence Payment) (Amendment) Regulations 2016 (SI 2016/556) reg.4(4) (June 29, 2016).

DEFINITIONS

4.296   "disability living allowance"—see reg.2(1).
"DLA entitled person"—see reg.2(1).
"components"—see reg.2(1).
"assessment determination"—see reg.2(1).

Notifications of change of circumstances

4.297   **20.**—(1) This regulation applies where—
(a) a person notifies the Secretary of State of a change of circumstances, and
(b) paragraph (3), (4) or (5) applies.

(2) If this regulation applies—
(a) the notification shall not be regarded as relating to disability living allowance and accordingly neither section 10 (decisions superseding earlier decisions) nor any other provision of the 1998 Act shall apply, and
(b) the notification to the Secretary of State must be treated in all respects as if it were a notification under paragraph (4) of regulation 38 (evidence and information in connection with an award) of the Claims and Payments regulations of a change of circumstances which the person might reasonably be expected to know might affect the continuance of entitlement to personal independence payment.

(3) This paragraph applies where a notified person notifies the Secretary of State of a change of circumstances before the person makes a claim for personal independence payment.

(4) This paragraph applies where a transfer claimant notifies the Secretary of State of a change of circumstances.

(5) This paragraph applies where a DLA entitled person notifies the Secretary of State of a change of circumstances and, as a result, the Secretary of State is required by regulation 3(5) to send a notification under regulation 3(1) inviting the person to claim personal independence payment.

(6) Paragraphs (3) and (4) do not apply where the change of circumstances notified is that the notified person or the transfer claimant, as the case may be, is to become or has become absent, whether temporarily or permanently, from Great Britain.

DEFINITIONS

"change of circumstances"—see reg.2(1).   4.298
"disability living allowance"—see reg.2(1).
"the 1998 Act"—see reg.2(1).
"the Claims and Payments Regulations"—see reg.2(1).
"notified person"—see reg.2(1).
"transfer claimant"—see reg.2(1).
"DLA entitled person"—see reg.2(1).

Extinguishment of rights of appeal etc. under disability living allowance regime

21. No suspension of a person's entitlement to disability living allowance   4.299
that takes place by virtue of the application of these Regulations is to be
regarded as a decision of the Secretary of State to which section 8 (decisions
by the Secretary of State) or 10 (decisions superseding earlier decisions) of
the 1998 Act applies, and accordingly—
  (a) no revision by the Secretary of State may take place in relation to the
      suspension under section 9 (revision of decisions) of that Act, and
  (b) no right of appeal in respect of the suspension is to be available to the
      person under section 12 (appeal to appeal tribunal) of that Act.

DEFINITIONS

"disability living allowance"—see reg.2(1).   4.300
"the 1998 Act"—see reg.2(1).

Extinguishment of right to claim disability living allowance

22.—(1) No person may claim disability living allowance who is—   4.301
  (a) entitled to personal independence payment, or
  (b) entitled to claim personal independence payment.

(2) Paragraph (1) does not apply to a person whose award of disability living allowance is of—
  (a) both components and the award in respect of either or both is for a
      fixed term period, or
  (b) one component only and the award is for a fixed term period,
if, [¹[²*omitted*]], the person has been notified by the Secretary of State that, because the fixed term period is due to come to an end, the person needs to claim disability living allowance again, or to apply for a supersession of the award, if the person wishes to continue to be entitled to disability living allowance in respect of the component or components subject to the fixed term period.

4.302   "disability living allowance"—see reg.2(1).
"component"—see reg.2(1).

AMENDMENTS

1. Personal Independence Payment (Transitional Provisions) (Amendment) Regulations 2013 (SI 2013/2231 reg.2(6) (October 6, 2013).
2. Personal Independence Payments (Transitional Provisions) (Amendment) (No.2) Regulation 2013 (SI 2013/2689) reg.2(5) (October 25, 2013).

GENERAL NOTE

4.303   For the period between October 6, 2013 and October 25, 2013 this regulation was amended to read "before 28th October 2013".

Assessment of claim: transfer claimants to be taken to meet part of required period condition

4.304   **23.**—(1) In applying the required period condition under Part 3 (required period condition) of the PIP Regulations to a claim by a transfer claimant or by a person to whom paragraph (2) or (3) applies, the claimant shall be regarded as meeting such of the conditions contained in the following provisions of Part 3 (which relate to a claimant's abilities in the past) as are relevant to the claim regardless of whether those conditions have been met—

(a) in regulation 12 (required period condition: daily living component), paragraph (1)(a) or (2)(a),

(b) in regulation 13 (required period condition: mobility component), paragraph (1)(a) or (2)(a).

(2) This paragraph applies to a person claiming personal independence payment who—

(a) had not reached 65 on 8th April 2013,

(b) was not entitled to disability living allowance on the day the claim was made but was so entitled on the day falling twenty four months before that day or at any time between those days, and

(c) is not a person to whom paragraph (3) applies.

(3) This paragraph applies to a person claiming personal independence payment who—

(a) was aged 65 or over on the day the claim was made, and

(b) was not entitled to disability living allowance on that day but was so entitled on the day falling 12 months before that day or at any time between those days.

DEFINITIONS

4.305   "the PIP Regulations"—see reg.2(1).
"transfer claimant"—see reg.2(1).
"disability living allowance"—see reg.2(1).

GENERAL NOTE

4.306   This regulation provides that in the case of a transfer claimant (defined in reg.2 of these regulations as a person who is transferring from an award of DLA to one of PIP) the 3 month past period condition required by reg.12 of the PIP regulations should be deemed to have been satisfied. The complication that arose in *EB v SSWP (PIP)* [2017] UKUT 311 (AAC) was that one of the possible disabling conditions that the claimant suffered from at the time his PIP claim came to be determined may have not existed then for 3 months (it arose from prostate surgery and the FTT had not determined the exact date of the surgery) and neither did it form any part of the basis on which the claimant had been awarded DLA—(that much was clear because his DLA award had been only for the mobility component). The claimant argued that on the literal interpretation of reg.23 he should be deemed to have satisfied the past period condition, but Judge Farbey QC held that a proper interpretation of this regulation confined its meaning to those conditions that existed at the time of the DLA award and on which that award was based. The judge does this on the basis that transitional legislation is intended to facilitate transfer from one regime to another, but not to authorise innovation. (See the HL in *Britnell v Secretary of State for Social Security* [1991] 1 W.L.R. 198). But an appeal was allowed on the basis that the FTT should have gone on to consider the claim under reg.33 of the Claims and Payments Regulations which allows for an advance award for conditions arising in the 3 months period after the DM decision. As the claimant had been scored 6 points in respect of other daily living Activities this meant that he might have succeeded on a claim for the daily living component under PIP when regard was had to Activity 5—Managing toilet needs or incontinence. The case was returned for rehearing.

Assessment of claim: date by reference to which assessment is to be made

24. In applying the required period condition under Part 3 of the PIP Regulations to a claim by a transfer claimant the "prescribed date" referred to in—

    (a) paragraphs (1) and (2) of regulation 12 of those Regulations, and

    (b) paragraphs (1) and (2) of regulation 13 of those Regulations,

is the date on which the claim is made.

    4.307

DEFINITIONS

"the PIP Regulations"—see reg.2(1).
"transfer claimant"—see reg.2(1).

    4.308

Treatment of persons in hospital or care home during transfer to personal independence payment

25.—(1) This regulation applies to a transfer claimant awarded personal independence payment if, on the day on which the claimant's entitlement to disability living allowance terminates in accordance with regulations 13(1) or 17(1)(b), the claimant is a person who—

    (a) fails to meet the condition in paragraph (1) of regulation 8 (hospitalisation) of the 1991 Regulations but is nevertheless entitled to payment of the care component by reason of the application of regulation 10 (exemption from regulations 8 and 9) of the 1991 Regulations,

    (b) fails to meet the condition in paragraph (1) of regulation 12A (hospitalisation in mobility component cases) of the 1991 Regulations but is nevertheless entitled to payment of the mobility component by reason of the application of regulation 12B of the 1991 Regulations (exemption from regulation 12A), or

    (c) fails to meet both of the conditions referred to in subparagraphs (a) and (b) but is nevertheless entitled to payment of both components by reason of the application of regulations 10 and 12B of the 1991 Regulations,

and, on the day on which the claimant's entitlement to personal independence

    4.309

payment starts in accordance with regulation 17(2), the claimant meets the condition in subsection (2) of section 86 (hospital in-patients) of the Act.

(2) This regulation also applies to a transfer claimant awarded personal independence payment if—

(a) on the day on which the claimant's entitlement to disability living allowance terminates in accordance with regulations 13(1) or 17(1)(b), the claimant is a person—

   (i) to whom the care component of disability living allowance is not payable under paragraph (1) of regulation 9 (persons in care homes) of the 1991 Regulations, but

   (ii) who is nevertheless entitled to payment of that component by reason of the application of regulation 10 of the 1991 Regulations, and

(b) on the day on which the claimant's entitlement to personal independence payment starts in accordance with regulation 17(2), the claimant meets the condition in subsection (2) of section 85 (care home residents) of the Act.

(3) Where this regulation applies to a transfer claimant—

(a) the day on which the claimant's entitlement to personal independence payment starts in accordance with regulation 17(2) shall be treated as being the first day of the period referred to in paragraph (1) of regulation 30 (payability exceptions: care homes and hospitals) of the PIP Regulations, and

(b) paragraph (2) of regulation 30 of the PIP Regulations shall not apply to the claimant in respect of either that day or any consecutive period of days starting with that day during which the claimant meets the condition in section 85(2) of the Act (care home residents: costs of qualifying services borne out of public or local funds) or section 86(2) of the Act (in-patient treatment: costs of treatment, accommodation and related services borne out of public funds).

DEFINITIONS

4.310   "transfer claimant"—see reg.2(1).
"disability living allowance"—see reg.2(1).
"the 1991 Regulations"—see reg.2(1).
"the Act"—see reg.2(1).
"the PIP Regulations"—see reg.2(1).

Temporary absence from Great Britain when transfer claimant becomes entitled to personal independence payment

4.311   **26.**—(1) This paragraph applies to a transfer claimant awarded personal independence payment if, on the day that the claimant's entitlement to disability living allowance terminates in accordance with regulations 13(1) or 17(1)(b), the claimant would otherwise be temporarily absent from Great Britain but is treated as present in Great Britain by virtue of—

(a) paragraph (2)(d) of regulation 2 (conditions as to residence and presence in Great Britain) of the 1991 Regulations), because the first 13 weeks of absence referred to in that regulation have not expired, or

(b) paragraph (3B) of regulation 2 of the 1991 Regulations, because the first 26 weeks of absence referred to in that regulation have not expired.

(2) In applying regulation 17 (absence from Great Britain) of the PIP Regulations to a transfer claimant to whom paragraph (1)(a) applies, the period—

(a) starting with the first day on which the claimant was treated as present in Great Britain by virtue of regulation 2(2)(d) of the 1991 Regulations, and

(b) ending with the day on which the claimant's entitlement to disability living allowance terminates in accordance with regulations 13(1) or 17(1)(b) shall be counted towards the 13 weeks of absence referred to in regulation 17 of the PIP Regulations.

(3) In applying regulation 18 (absence from Great Britain to receive medical treatment) of the PIP Regulations to a transfer claimant to whom paragraph (1)(b) applies the period—

(a) starting with the first day of absence for the purpose of regulation (3B) of the 1991 Regulations, and

(b) ending with the day on which the claimant's entitlement to disability living allowance terminates in accordance with regulation 13(1) or 17(1)(b) shall be counted towards the 26 weeks of absence referred to in regulation 18 of the PIP Regulations.

DEFINITIONS

"transfer claimant"—see reg.2(1).   4.312
"disability living allowance"—see reg.2(1).
"the 1991 Regulations"—see reg.2(1).
"the PIP Regulations"—see reg.2(1).

Persons aged 65 and over to be entitled to personal independence payment in certain circumstances

27.—(1) Section 83(1) (persons of pensionable age) of the Act does not   4.313
apply to a person to whom this regulation applies.

(2) This regulation applies to a person who—

(a) had not reached 65 on 8th April 2013,

(b) is a DLA entitled person, and

(c) claims personal independence payment—

(i) in response to a notification sent to the person by the Secretary of State under regulation 3(1), or

(ii) under regulation 4.

(3) This regulation also applies to a person who—

(a) had not reached 65 on 8th April 2013,

(b) claims personal independence payment, and

(c) is not entitled to disability living allowance on the day the claim is made but was so entitled on the day falling 12 months before that day or at any time between those days.

DEFINITIONS

"DLA entitled person"—see reg.2(1).   4.314
"disability living allowance"—see reg.2(1).

Persons unable to act: claims for personal independence payment

28.—(1) This regulation applies where, immediately before any claim   4.315
for personal independence payment is made by or on behalf of a person

entitled to disability living allowance, there is a person ("the appointed person")—

(a) appointed by the Secretary of State in accordance with paragraph (1) of regulation 33 (persons unable to act) of the 1987 Regulations, or

(b) treated, by virtue of paragraph (1A) of the said regulation 33, as being a person appointed by the Secretary of State in accordance with paragraph (1) of that regulation, to exercise rights on behalf of the person entitled to disability living allowance and receive and deal with any sums payable to that person.

(2) Where this regulation applies the appointed person shall be regarded as acting on behalf of the person entitled to disability living allowance for the purposes of the making and pursuit of a claim for personal independence payment under these Regulations and, where applicable, the Claims and Payments Regulations.

DEFINITIONS

4.316   "disability living allowance"—see reg.2(1).
"the 1987 Regulations"—see reg.2(1).
"the Claims and Payments Regulations"—see reg.2(1).

Persons unable to act: transfer to personal independence payment

4.317   **29.**—(1) This regulation applies if a transfer claimant is awarded personal independence payment and, on the day that the person's entitlement to disability living allowance terminates in accordance with regulations 13(1) or 17(1)(b), there is a person ("the appointed person") who, under paragraph (2) of regulation 28, is to be regarded as acting on behalf of the claimant for the purposes set out in that paragraph.

(2) Where this regulation applies then, with effect from the first day on which the transfer claimant is entitled to personal independence payment in accordance with regulation 17(2), the appointed person shall be treated as being a person appointed by the Secretary of State in accordance with regulation 57(1) (persons unable to act) of the Claims and Payments Regulations to exercise rights on behalf of the transfer claimant and receive and deal with any sums payable to the transfer claimant.

DEFINITIONS

4.318   "transfer claimant"—see reg.2(1).
"disability living allowance"—see reg.2(1).
"the Claims and Payments Regulations"—see reg.2(1).

Application of these Regulations to certain persons becoming entitled to disability living allowance while claiming personal independence payment

4.319   **30.**—(1) If paragraph (2) applies to a person then, with effect from the date of the determination referred to in subparagraph (c) of paragraph (2), the regulations referred to in paragraphs (3), (4), (5) and (6) shall apply in relation to that person in accordance with the provisions of those paragraphs.

(2) This paragraph applies to a person—

(a) whose claim for disability living allowance was refused,

(b) who claimed personal independence payment after that refusal, and

(c) who, as a result of the determination of legal proceedings initiated

866

under the 1998 Act in relation to that refusal, becomes entitled, before the assessment determination, to disability living allowance.

(3) Regulations 13, 15, 16(2), 17(1) to (3), 20(1), (2), (4) and (6) (so far as it applies to paragraph (4) of regulation 20), 23(1) (in its application to transfer claimants), 24, 25, and 26 shall apply to the person as if the person were a transfer claimant.

(4) Regulations 18 and 19 shall apply to the person as if the person were a DLA entitled person.

(5) Where a person to whom paragraph (2) applies also satisfies the condition in regulation 27(2)(a), regulation 27 shall be treated as applying to the person as if the person satisfied all the conditions in regulation 27(2).

(6) Regulation 29 shall apply to the person as if the person were a transfer claimant if, on the day that the person's entitlement to disability living allowance terminates in accordance with regulation 13(1) or 17(1)(b), there is a person ("the appointed person")—

(a) appointed by the Secretary of State in accordance with paragraph (1) of regulation 33 of the 1987 Regulations, or

(b) treated by virtue of paragraph (1A) of the said regulation 33 as being a person appointed by the Secretary of State in accordance with paragraph (1) of that regulation, to exercise rights on behalf of the person entitled to disability living allowance and receive and deal with any sums payable to that person.

DEFINITIONS

"disability living allowance"—see reg.2(1).   4.320
"the 1998 Act"—see reg.2(1).
"assessment determination"—see reg.2(1).
"transfer claimant"—see reg.2(1).
"DLA entitled person"—see reg.2(1).
"the 1987 Regulations"—see reg.2(1).

Disabled people: badges for motor vehicles

31.—(1) In this regulation, "the 2000 Regulations" means the Disabled   4.321
Persons (Badges for Motor Vehicles) (England) Regulations 2000.

(2) Where a person satisfies paragraph (3)—

(a) the person shall be treated as being a disabled person for the purpose of regulation 7 of the 2000 Regulations, and

(b) regulation 9(1)(c) of the 2000 Regulations shall not apply to the person, until the expiration of the period for which the disabled person's badge referred to in paragraph (3)(b)(i) was issued.

(3) A person satisfies this paragraph if—

(a) the entitlement of the person to disability living allowance terminates in accordance with these Regulations,

(b) on the last day on which the person is entitled to disability living allowance the person—

   (i) is a holder of a disabled person's badge in accordance with the 2000 Regulations, and

   (ii) is a disabled person for the purposes of the 2000 Regulations by virtue of satisfying regulation 4(1)(a) and (2)(a) of the 2000 Regulations,

(c) with effect from the following day the person is no longer a disabled person for the purposes of the 2000 Regulations because the person does not satisfy regulation 4(1)(a) and (2)(g) of the 2000 Regulations, and

(d) the period for which the badge mentioned above in sub-paragraph (b) was issued has not yet expired.

DEFINITIONS

4.322   "disability living allowance"—see reg.2(1).

PART V

MATERNITY BENEFITS

The Social Security (Maternity Allowance) Regulations 1987

(SI 1987/416) (*as amended*)

ARRANGEMENT OF REGULATIONS

1.   Citation, commencement and interpretation.   5.1
1A.   Disapplication of section 1(1A) of the Administration Act.
2.   Disqualification for the receipt of a maternity allowance.
3.   Modification of the maternity allowance period.
4.   *Omitted.*

The Secretary of State for Social Services, in exercise of the powers conferred by section 22(3) of, and Schedule 20 to, the Social Security Act 1975 and sections 84(1) and 89(1) of the Social Security Act 1986, and of all other powers enabling him in that behalf, by this instrument, which is made before the end of the period of 12 months from the commencement of the enactments under which it is made, makes the following Regulations:

Citation, commencement and interpretation

1.—(1) These regulations may be cited as the Social Security (Maternity   5.2
Allowance) Regulations 1987 and shall come into operation on 6th April 1987.
(2) In these regulations—
"the Act" means the Social Security Act 1975;
"the 1986 Act" means the Social Security Act 1986.
[[1]"the 1992 Act" means the Social Security Contributions and Benefits
    Act 1992.]
(3) Unless the context otherwise requires, any reference in any of these
regulations—
  (a) to a numbered paragraph is a reference to the paragraph bearing that
      number in that regulation; and
  (b) in these regulations to a Schedule is to the Schedule to these regula-
      tions.

AMENDMENT

1. Social Security (Maternity Allowance) (Miscellaneous Amendments) Regulations 2014 (SI 2014/884) reg.2 (May 18, 2014).

[1 Disapplication of section 1(1A) of the Administration Act

[[2] **1A.** Section 1(1A) of the Social Security Administration Act 1992   5.3
(requirement to state a national insurance number) shall not apply to an adult dependant who—
  (a) is a person in respect of whom a claim for an increase of maternity
      allowance is made;
  (b) is subject to immigration control within the meaning of section
      115(9)(a) of the Immigration and Asylum Act 1999; and
  (c) has not previously been allocated a national insurance number.]

AMENDMENTS

1. Social Security (National Insurance Information: Exemption) Regulations (SI 1997/2676) (December 1, 1997).

2. Social Security (National Insurance Number Information: Exemption) Regulations 2009 (SI 2009/471) reg.4 (April 6, 2009).

Disqualification for the receipt of a maternity allowance

5.4   [¹**2.** (1) A woman shall be disqualified for receiving a maternity allowance under section 35 of the 1992 Act if during the maternity allowance period she does any work in employment as an employed or self-employed earner, for more than 10 days, whether consecutive or not, falling within that period.

(2) The disqualification referred to in paragraph (1) shall be for such part of the maternity allowance period as may, in the opinion of the Secretary of State, be reasonable in the circumstances, provided that the disqualification shall, in any event, be for at least the number of days on which she so worked in excess of 10 days.

(3) A woman shall be disqualified for receiving a maternity allowance under section 35B of the 1992 Act if during the maternity allowance period—

    (a) she works with S (as defined in subsection (1)(b) of that section); or

    (b) she does any work in employment as an employed or self-employed earner.

(4) The disqualification referred to in paragraph (3) shall be for such part of the maternity allowance period as may, in the opinion of the Secretary of State, be reasonable in the circumstances and in any event shall be for at least the number of days she so worked.

(5) [² *omitted*]

(6) [² *omitted*]

(7) A woman shall be disqualified for receiving maternity allowance under section 35 or 35B of the 1992 Act if at any time before she is confined she fails without good cause to attend for or to submit herself to any medical examination for which she was given at least 3 days notice in writing by or on behalf of the Secretary of State.

(8) The disqualification referred to in paragraph (7) shall be for such part of the maternity allowance period (being a part beginning not earlier than the day on which the failure occurs) as may, in the opinion of the Secretary of State, be reasonable in the circumstances, except that in the event of her being confined after such failure the woman shall not by reason of such failure be so disqualified for the day on which the confinement occurs or any day thereafter.]

AMENDMENT

1. Social Security (Maternity Allowance) (Miscellaneous Amendments) Regulations 2014 (SI2014/884) reg.2 (May 18, 2014).

2. Social Security (Miscellaneous Amendments) Regulations 2015 (SI 2015/67) reg.3 (February 23, 2015).

Modification of the maternity allowance period

5.5   **3.**—(1) [Section 35(2)] of the Social Security Contributions and Benefits Act 1992] (which relates to the maternity allowance period) shall be modified in accordance with [⁵paragraph (2A)].

(2) [³omitted].

[¹ (2A) In relation to a woman who—

    (a) is not entitled to maternity allowance at the 11th week before the expected week of confinement; and

    (b) subsequently becomes entitled to maternity allowance before being confined; and

(c) has stopped work

the maternity allowance period shall be a period of [⁴39 weeks commencing no earlier than the day she becomes entitled to maternity allowance and no later than the day following the day on which she is confined]]

[⁵(2B) The provisions of section 35B of the 1992 Act which relate to the maternity allowance period shall, in relation to a woman who–

(a) is not entitled to maternity allowance at the 11th week before the expected week of confinement;

(b) subsequently becomes entitled to maternity allowance before being confined; and

(c) has ceased to work with S,

be modified in accordance with paragraph (2C).

(2C) The maternity allowance period shall be a period of 14 weeks commencing—

(a) on the day after she ceases work, or, if later, the day she becomes entitled to maternity allowance; and

(b) no later than the day following the day on which she is confined.]

(3)–(6) [³omitted].

AMENDMENTS

1. Social Security Maternity Benefits and Statutory Sick Pay (Amendment) Regulations 1994 (SI 1994/1367) reg.3 (where the expected week of confinement begins after October 16, 1994).

2. Social Security (Miscellaneous Amendments) (No. 2) Regulations 1997 (SI 1997/793) reg.18 (April 7, 1997).

3. Social Security, Statutory Maternity Pay and Statutory Sick Pay (Miscellaneous Amendment) Regulations 2002 (SI 2002/2690) Reg.15 (November 24, 2002).

4. Statutory Maternity Pay, Social Security (Maternity Allowance) and Social Security (Overlapping Benefits) (Amendment) Regulations 2006 (SI 2006/2379) reg.4(3)(October 1, 2006).

5. Social Security (Maternity Allowance) (Miscellaneous Amendments) Regulations 2014 (SI 2014/884) reg.2 (May 18, 2014).

The Social Security (Maternity Allowance) (Work Abroad) Regulations 1987

(SI 1987/417) (*as amended*)

ARRANGEMENT OF REGULATIONS

1.   Citation and commencement.

2.   Special provision for certain persons who have been employed abroad.

5.6

The Secretary of State for Social Services, in exercise of the powers conferred by section 131 of and Schedule 20 to the Social Security Act 1975 and of all other powers enabling him in that behalf, after agreement by the Social Security Advisory Committee that proposals to make these Regulations should not be referred to it, hereby makes the following Regulations:

Citation and commencement

5.7   **1.**—(1) These regulations may be cited as the Social Security (Maternity Allowance) (Work Abroad) Regulations 1987 and shall come into force on 6th April 1987.

(2) In these regulations—

"the Act" means the Social Security Act 1975;

"the Contributions Regulations" means the Social Security (Contributions) Regulations 1979.

Special provision for certain persons who have been employed abroad

5.8   **2.**—(1) This regulation applies, subject to paragraph (5), for the purpose of determining entitlement to a maternity allowance in respect of a woman who—

(a) has been absent from Great Britain;

(b) has returned to Great Britain; and

(c) throughout the whole period of her absence was ordinarily resident in Great Britain.

(2) [¹ Where a woman has paid, or is treated as having actually paid, Class 1 contributions under the Act either]

(a) to the full extent of her liability under regulation 120 of the Contributions Regulations; or

(b) in respect of the first 52 weeks of her employment abroad by virtue of either—

(i) an Order in Council made under section 143 of the Act (reciprocity with countries outside the United Kingdom); or

(ii) Council Regulation No. 1408/71 EEC [³, as amended from time to time,] (application of social security schemes to employed persons and their families moving within the Community), [³ or Regulation (EC) No. 833/2004 of the European Parliament and of Council of 29 April 2004, as amended from time to time, on the coordination of social security systems]

and the employment by reference to which the liability arose continued throughout the first 52 weeks after the commencement of that liability, she shall be treated for any week in which she was in fact engaged in gainful employment as having been engaged in employment as an employed earner [¹ and for any such week, and for any weeks following the period of that liability and before the date of her return to Great Britain so far as those weeks are relevant to her claim for a maternity allowance, as having received an amount of specified payments for the purposes of section 35A(4) of the Social Security Contributions and Benefits Act 1992 equal to the lower earnings limit in force on the last day of that week.]

(3) Where—

(a) a woman would have been liable to pay Class 1 contributions under regulation 120 of the Contributions Regulations but for the provisions of an Order in Council made under section 143 of the Act,

(b) in relation to her case the Order does not provide for periods of insurance, employment or residence in the other country to which the Order relates to be taken into account in determining title to benefit, and

(c) the employment by reference to which she would have been liable under that regulation continued throughout the first 52 weeks,

she shall be treated for any week during her absence in which she was in fact engaged in gainful employment as having been engaged in employment as an employed earner [¹ and for each week of her absence as having received an amount of specified payments for the purposes of section 35A(4) of the Social Security Contributions and Benefits Act 1992 equal to the lower earnings limit in force on the last day of the week].

(4) Where—

(a) a woman would have been liable to pay Class 1 contributions under regulation 120 of the Contributions Regulations but for the provisions of either an Order in Council made under section 143 or Council Regulation No. 1408/71/EEC [³, as amended from time to time, or Regulation EC No. 883/2004 of the European Parliament and of the Council of 29 April 2004, as amended from time to time];

(b) the employment by reference to which she would have been liable under regulation 120 continued throughout the first 52 weeks from the time that the liability would have commenced; and

(c) the Order of the Council Regulations [³ or Regulation of the European Parliament and of the Council], as the case may be, provides for aggregation of periods of insurance, employment or residence only if an insurance period has been completed since her return to Great Britain, and an insurance period has not been so completed,

any period of insurance, or employment in the other country to which that Order of Council Regulations [³ or Regulation of the European Parliament and of the Council], as the case may be, relates which falls in the [²66 weeks immediately preceding] the expected week of confinement shall be treated as a period in respect of which she was engaged in employment as employed earner [¹ and in eachweek of which she received an amount of specified payments for the purposes of section 35A(4) of the Social Security Contributions and Benefits Act 1992 equal to the lower earnings limit in force on the last day of that week.]

(5) Paragraphs (2) (except in a case to which paragraph (2)(a) applies), (3) and (4) shall not apply in relation to a claim for maternity allowance for any day in respect of which the woman concerned is entitled to a corresponding benefit under the social security scheme of the country in which she was employed.

(6) Where a woman satisfies the requirements of paragraph (3)(a) or (4)(a) but the employment did not continue for 52 weeks, she shall be treated in respect of those weeks in which her employment did continue as having been engaged in employment as an employed earner [¹ and as having received an amount of specified payments for the purposes of section 35A(4) of the Social Security Contributions and Benefits Act 1992 equal to the lower limit in force on the last day of each of those weeks].

AMENDMENTS

1. Social Security (Maternity Allowance) (Work Abroad) (Amendment) Regulations 2000 (2000/691) reg.2 (April 2, 2000).

2. Social Security Maternity Benefits and Statutory Sick Pay (Amendment) Regulations 1994 (SI 1994/1367) reg.8 (where the expected week of confinement begins after October 16, 1994).

3. Social Security (Uprating of EU References) (Amendment) Regulations (SI 2018/1084) reg.4 and Sch. para. 4 (November 15, 2018).

The Social Security (Maternity Allowance) (Earnings) Regulations 2000

(SI 2000/688) *(as amended)*

ARRANGEMENT OF REGULATIONS

5.9
1. Citation, commencement and interpretation.
2. Specified payments for employed earners.
3. Specified payments for self-employed earners.
4. Aggregation of specified payments.
5. The specified period.
6. Determination of average weekly amount of specified payments.

The Secretary of State for Social Security, in exercise of powers conferred by sections 35A(4), (5) and (6)(c), 122(1) and 175(1) to (4) of the Social Security Contributions and Benefits Act 1992 and of all other powers enabling him in that behalf by this instrument, which is made before the end of the period of six months beginning with the coming into force of the enactments under which it is made, hereby makes the following Regulations:

Citation, commencement and interpretation

5.10 **1.**—(1) These regulations may be cited as the Social Security (Maternity Allowance) (Earnings) Regulations 2000 and shall come into force on April 2, 2000.

(2) In these Regulations—

[¹ *omitted*]

"the Contributions Regulations" means the [² Social Security (Contributions) Regulations 2001]

"the Contributions and Benefits Act" means the Social Security Contributions and Benefits Act 1992;

"test period" means the period of 66 weeks specified in section 35(1)(b) of the Contributions and Benefits Act.

AMENDMENT

1. Social Security (Maternity Allowance) (Earnings) (Amendment) Regulations 2015 (SI 2015/342) reg.2 (April 6, 2015).

Specified payments for employed earners

5.11 **2.**—(1) Subject to paragraph (2), for the purposes of section 35A(4)(a) of the Contributions and Benefits Act, the payments specified for a woman who is an employed earner in any week falling within the test period shall be all payments made to her or for her benefit as an employed earner including—

[² (za) any amount retrospectively treated as earnings by regulations made by virtue of section 4B(2) of the Contributions and Benefits Act];

(a) any sum payable in respect of arrears of pay in pursuance of an order for reinstatement under section 114 or re-engagement under section 115 of the Employment Rights Act 1996 (orders for reinstatement and re-engagement);

(b) any sum payable by way of pay in pursuance of an order made under section 129 of the Employment Rights Act 1996 (procedure on hearing of application and making of order) for the continuation of a contract of employment;

(c) any sum payable by way of remuneration in pursuance of a protective award under section 189 of the Trade Union and Labour Relations (Consolidation) Act 1992 (complaint and protective award);

(d) any sum payable by way of statutory sick pay, including sums payable in accordance with regulations made under section 151(6) of the Contributions and Benefits Act (employers' liability);

(e) any sum payable by way of statutory maternity pay, including sums payable in accordance with regulations made under section 164(9) (b) of the Contributions and Benefits Act.

[¹(f) any sum payable by way of statutory paternity pay, including any sums payable in accordance with regulations made under section 171ZD(3) of the Contributions and Benefits Act;

(g) any sum payable by way of statutory adoption pay, including any sums payable in accordance with regulations made under section 171ZM(3) of the Contributions and Benefits Act,]

[³ (h) any sum payable by way of statutory shared parental pay, including any sums payable in accordance with regulations made under section 171ZX(3) of the Contributions and Benefits Act.]

(2) The payments specified shall not include any sum excluded from the computation of a person's earnings under regulation [²25, 27 or 123 of Schedule 3 to] the Contributions Regulations (payments to be disregarded).

AMENDMENTS

1. Social Security, Statutory Maternity Pay and Statutory Sick Pay (Miscellaneous Amendments) Regulations (SI 2002/2690) reg.16 (December 8, 2002).

2. Social Security, Occupational Pensions Schemes and Statutory Payments (Consequential Provisions) Regulations 2007 (SI 2007/1154) reg.3 (April 6, 2007).

3. Shared Parental Leave and Statutory Shared Parental Pay (Consequential Amendments to Subordinate Legislation) Order 2014 (SI 2014/3255) art.8 (December 31, 2014).

Specified payments for self-employed earners

3.—For the purposes of section 35A(4)(b) of the Contributions and Benefits Act, where a woman is a self-employed earner in any week falling within the test period, the payments treated as made to her or for her benefit shall be—   5.12

(a) a payment equal to [¹ an amount 90 per cent of which is equal to the weekly rate prescribed under section 66(1)(b) of the Contributions and Benefits Act that is in force] on the last day of that week where she has paid a Class 2 contribution [² . . .]

(b) a payment equal to the maternity allowance threshold in force on the last day of that week, [² if she could have paid but has not paid such a contribution] in respect of that week

AMENDMENT

1. Social Security, Statutory Maternity Pay and Statutory Sick Pay Regulations 2002 (SI 2002/2690) reg.17 (November 24, 2002).
2. Social Security (Maternity Allowance) (Earnings) (Amendment) Regulations 2015 (SI 2015/342) reg.2 (April 6, 2015).

Aggregation of specified payments

5.13   **4.**—(1) In a case [¹. . .] where a woman, either in the same week or in different weeks falling within the test period, is engaged in two or more employments (whether, in each case, as an employed earner or a self-employed earner), any payments which are made, or treated in accordance with these Regulations as made to her or for her benefit shall be aggregated for the purpose of determining the average weekly amount of specified payments applicable in her case.

(2) In a case to which regulation 5(2) applies, any payments which are made or treated in accordance with these Regulations as made, to her or for her benefit shall not be aggregated for the purpose of determining the average weekly amount of specified payments applicable in her case.

AMENDMENT

1. Social Security, Statutory Maternity Pay and Statutory Sick Pay Regulations 2002 (SI 2002/2690) reg.17 (November 24, 2002).

[¹ The specified period

5.14   **5.**—(1) Subject to paragraph (2) below, for the purposes of section 35A(4) and (5) of the Contributions and Benefits Act, the specified period shall be the test period.

(2) Where a woman is treated by virtue of regulation 3(a) above as having received payments for at least 13 weeks (whether consecutive or not) falling within the test period, the first 13 weeks shall be the specified period.]

AMENDMENT

1. Social Security (Maternity Allowance) (Earnings) (Amendment) Regulations 2003 (SI 2003/659) reg.2 (April 6, 2003).

Determination of average weekly amount of specified payments

5.15   **6.**—[¹ (1) For the purposes of section 35A(4) of the Contributions and Benefits Act a woman's average weekly amount of specified payments shall, subject to paragraph (2), be determined by dividing by 13 the payments made, or treated in accordance with these Regulations as made, to her or for her benefit—

(a) in the case of a woman to whom paragraph (2) of regulation 5 applies, in the 13 weeks referred to in that paragraph;

(b) in any other case, in the 13 weeks (whether consecutive or not) falling within the specified period in which such payments are greatest.]

(2) In any case where a woman receives a back-dated pay increase after the end of the period specified in regulation 5 above which includes a sum in respect of any week falling within that period, her average weekly amount

of specified payments shall be determined as if such sum had been paid in that week.

AMENDMENT

1. Social Security (Maternity Allowance) (Earnings) (Amendment) Regulations 2003 (SI 2003/659) reg.3 (April 6, 2003).

The Maternity Allowance (Curtailment) Regulations 2014

(SI 2014/3053)

ARRANGEMENTS OF REGULATIONS

1. Citation and commencement
2. Interpretation
3. Curtailment of maternity allowance period (statutory shared parental pay: P)
4. Curtailment of maternity allowance period (shared parental leave: P)
5. Maternity allowance period curtailment notification
6. Revocation (maternity allowance period curtailment notification)

This instrument contains only regulations made by virtue of, or consequential upon, section 120(1) and (2) of the Children and Families Act 2014 and is made before the end of the period of 6 months beginning with the coming into force of that enactment.   5.16

The Secretary of State for Work and Pensions, in exercise of the powers conferred by sections 35(3A), (3B), (3C) and (3D) and 175(1), (3), (4) and (5) of the Social Security Contributions and Benefits Act 1992, makes the following Regulations:

Citation and commencement

1. These Regulations may be cited as the Maternity Allowance   5.17
(Curtailment) Regulations 2014 and come into force on 1st December 2014.

Interpretation

2. In these Regulations—   5.18
"the 1992 Act" means the Social Security Contributions and Benefits Act 1992;
"the 1996 Act" means the Employment Rights Act 1996;
"C" means the child in respect of whom an entitlement to—
(a) shared parental leave arises under section 75E (entitlement to shared parental leave: birth) of the 1996 Act; or
(b) statutory shared parental pay arises under section 171ZU (entitlement: birth) of the 1992 Act;
"M" means the mother (or expectant mother) of C;
"maternity allowance period curtailment date" means, subject to regulation 5(5), the date specified in a maternity allowance period curtailment notification;
"maternity allowance period curtailment notification" means a notification given in accordance with regulation 5 and regulation 6(4);

"P" means the father of C, or the person who is married to, or the civil partner or the partner of, M;

"partner" in relation to M, means a person (whether of a different sex or the same sex) who lives with M and C in an enduring family relationship but is not M's child, parent, grandchild, grandparent, sibling, aunt, uncle, niece or nephew;

"SPL Regulations" means the Shared Parental Leave Regulations 2014;

"ShPP Regulations" means the Statutory Shared Parental Pay (General) Regulations 2014.

Curtailment of maternity allowance period (statutory shared parental pay: P)

5.19   **3.** M's maternity allowance period shall end on the maternity allowance period curtailment date if—

(a) M gives a maternity allowance period curtailment notification (unless the notification is revoked under regulation 6);

(b) P satisfies the condition in sub-paragraph (a) of regulation 5(2) (entitlement of father or partner to statutory shared parental pay (birth)) of the ShPP Regulations; and

(c) M satisfies the conditions in sub-paragraphs (b) and (c) of regulation 5(3) of the ShPP Regulations.

Curtailment of maternity allowance period (shared parental leave: P)

5.20   **4.** M's maternity allowance period shall end on the maternity allowance period curtailment date if—

(a) M gives a maternity allowance period curtailment notification (unless the notification is revoked under regulation 6);

(b) P satisfies the condition in sub-paragraph (a) of regulation 5(2) (father's or partner's entitlement to shared parental leave) of the SPL Regulations; and

(c) M satisfies the conditions in sub-paragraphs (a) and (c) of regulation 5(3) of the SPL Regulations.

Maternity allowance period curtailment notification

5.21   **5.**—(1) A maternity allowance period curtailment notification must—

(a) be given to the Secretary of State; and

(b) specify the date on which M wants her maternity allowance period to end.

(2) The date specified in accordance with paragraph (1)(b) must be—

(a) the last day of a week;

(b) if M has the right to maternity leave under section 71 (ordinary maternity leave) of the 1996 Act, at least one day after the end of the compulsory maternity leave period or, if M does not have that right, at least two weeks after the end of the pregnancy;

(c) at least eight weeks after the date on which M gives the maternity allowance period curtailment notification; and

(d) at least one week before the last day of M's maternity allowance period.

(3) Where the Secretary of State considers it appropriate the eight week period set out in paragraph (2)(c) may be reduced in any particular case.

(4) In paragraph (2)(b) "the end of the compulsory maternity leave period" means whichever is the later of—

    (a) the last day of the compulsory maternity leave period provided for in regulations under section 72(2) (compulsory maternity leave) of the 1996 Act; or

    (b) where section 205 of the Public Health Act 1936 (women not to be employed in factories or workshops within four weeks after birth of a child) applies to M's employment, the last day of the period in which an occupier of a factory is prohibited from knowingly allowing M to be employed in that factory.

(5) Where M—

    (a) returns to work before giving a notification under paragraph (1); and

    (b) subsequently gives such a notification;

the "maternity allowance period curtailment date" shall be the last day of the week in which that notification is submitted (irrespective of the date given in that notification under paragraph (1)).

(6) For the purposes of paragraphs (2)(a) and (5), "week" has the meaning given in section 165(8) of the 1992 Act (the maternity pay period).

(7) For the purposes of paragraph (5)(a), a woman is treated as returning to work where maternity allowance is not payable to her in accordance with regulation 2(1) of the Social Security (Maternity Allowance) Regulations 1987 (disqualification for the receipt of a maternity allowance).

Revocation (maternity allowance period curtailment notification)

6.—(1) Subject to paragraph (2), M may revoke a maternity allowance period curtailment notification before the maternity allowance period curtailment date if—   5.22

    (a) M provided the maternity allowance period curtailment notification before the birth of C; or

    (b) P dies.

(2) Revocation is effective under paragraph (1) where M gives a notification ("a revocation notification") to the Secretary of State that—

    (a) if given under paragraph (1)(a), is given within six weeks of the date of C's birth;

    (b) if given under paragraph (1)(b), is given within a reasonable period from the date of P's death.

(3) A revocation notification must—

    (a) state that M revokes the maternity allowance period curtailment notification; and

    (b) if given under paragraph (1)(b), state the date of P's death.

(4) M may not give a maternity allowance period curtailment notification in respect of the same maternity allowance period subsequent to giving a revocation notification unless the revocation was made in accordance with paragraph (1)(a).

PART VI

PENSIONS, SURVIVORS' BENEFITS AND GRADUATED RETIREMENT BENEFIT

The Social Security (Deferral of Retirement Pensions) Regulations 2005

(SI 2005/453) (*as amended*)

ARRANGEMENT OF REGULATIONS

1.   Citation, commencement and interpretation.   6.1
2.   Beginning of accrual period.
3.   Amount of retirement pension not included in the calculation of the lump
      sum.
4.   *Omitted.*

The Secretary of State for Work and Pensions, in exercise of the powers conferred upon him by sections 54(1), 122(1) and 175(3) of, and paragraphs 2(2), 3(1), 3B(2) and (5)(b)(iii) and 7B(2) and (5)(b)(iii) of Schedule 5 to, the Social Security Contributions and Benefits Act 1992, and of all other powers enabling him in that behalf, after agreement by the Social Security Advisory Committee that proposals in respect of regulation 4 should not be referred to it, the remainder of this Instrument containing only regulations made under provisions introduced by section 297 of, and Schedule 11 to, the Pensions Act 2004 and being made before the end of the period of 6 months beginning with the coming into force of those provisions, hereby makes the following Regulations:

Citation, commencement and interpretation

1.—(1) These Regulations may be cited as the Social Security (Deferral   6.2
of Retirement Pensions) Regulations 2005 and shall come into force on 6th April 2005.
(2) In these Regulations—
"the Act" means the Social Security Contributions and Benefits Act 1992;
"retirement pension" means a Category A or Category B retirement pension.
[¹ "shared additional pension" means a shared pension under section 55A [² or 55AA] of the Act.]

AMENDMENTS

1. Shared Additional Pensions (Miscellaneous Amendments) Regulations 2005 (SI 2005/1551) (July 6, 2005).
2. The Pensions Act 2014 (Consequential, Supplementary and Incidental Amendments) Order 2015 (SI 2015/1985) art.26 (April 6, 2016).

GENERAL NOTE

Following the reforms introduced from April 6, 2016 by the Pensions Act 2014   6.3
these regulations only apply directly to periods before that date. For the provisions that apply from that date see Part 3 of the State Pension Regulations 2015 below.

Beginning of accrual period

[¹**2.**—(1) This regulation applies for the purposes of paragraphs 3B and   6.4
7B of Schedule 5 and paragraph 5 of Schedule 5A to the Act (calculation of lump sum).

(2) In the case of a retirement pension or shared additional pension to which regulation 22 (long term benefits) of the Social Security (Claims and Payments) Regulations 1987 ("the 1987 Regulations") applies, the accrual period shall begin with the day of the week on which benefit would have been payable had entitlement not been deferred.

(3) In the case of a retirement pension to which regulation 22C (retirement pension for persons reaching pensionable age on or after 6th April 2010) of the 1987 Regulations applies, the accrual period shall begin with the first day of the benefit week in relation to which benefit would have been payable had entitlement not been deferred.

(4) In this regulation, "benefit week" has the same meaning as in regulation 22D (payment of retirement pension at a daily rate) of the 1987 Regulations.]

AMENDMENT

1. Social Security (Deferral of Retirement Pensions) (Amendment) Regulations 2011 (SI 2011/786) reg.2 (April 5, 2011).

Amount of retirement pension not included in the calculation of the lump sum

6.5   **3.**—(1) For the purposes of the calculation of the lump sum under paragraphs 3B and 7B of Schedule 5 to the Act, the amount of retirement pension to which the person ("the deferrer") would have been entitled for the accrual period if his entitlement had not been deferred shall not include any such pension where, for the entire accrual period—

    (a) the deferrer has received any of the following benefits—
        (i) any benefit under Parts II and III of the Act other than child's special allowance, attendance allowance, disability living allowance [¹, a shared additional pension] and guardian's allowance;
        (ii) any severe disablement allowance under sections 68 and 69 of the Act as in force before 6th April 2001;
        (iii) any unemployability supplement within the extended meaning in regulation 2(1) of the Social Security (Overlapping Benefits) Regulations 1979 and including benefit corresponding to an unemployability supplement by virtue of regulations under paragraph 7(2) of Schedule 8 to the Act;
    [³(iv) state pension credit under section 1 of the State Pension Credit Act 2002]
    [³(aa) in the case of a deferrer who was a member of a couple, the other member of the couple was in receipt of—
        (i) income support under section 124 of the Act;
        (ii) income-based jobseeker's allowance under section 1 of the State Pension Credit Act 2002; or
        (iii) state pension credit under section 1 of the State Pension Credit Act 2002;
        (iv) income-related employment and support allowance under section 1 of the Welfare Reform Act 2007;]
        [⁴ or
        (v) universal credit under Part 1 of the Welfare Reform Act 2012;]
    (b) an increase of any of the benefits specified in sub-paragraph (a) is being paid to a married man in respect of his wife where the wife is a

deferrer whose period of deferment began before 6th April 2005 and who would have been entitled to a Category B retirement pension or to an increase under section 51A(2) of the Act;

(c) an increase of any of the benefits specified in sub-paragraph (a) is being paid to any person in respect of a deferrer whose period of deferment began on or after 6th April 2005 except where that deferrer is neither married to [² or in a civil partnership with,], nor residing with, that person;

(d) the deferrer would have been disqualified for receiving retirement pension by reason of imprisonment or detention in legal custody.

[¹ (1A) For the purposes of the calculation of the lump sum under paragraph 5 of Schedule 5A to the Act, the amount of a shared additional pension to which a person ("the deferrer") would have been entitled for the accrual period if his entitlement had not been deferred shall not include any such pension where, for the entire accrual period, the deferrer would have been disqualified for receiving shared additional pension by reason of imprisonment or detention in legal custody.]

(2) Where any of the benefits referred to in paragraph (1)(a) [³ or (aa)] or an increase referred to in paragraph (1)(b) or (c) has been received for part only of an accrual period, the amount of retirement pension not included by paragraph (1) shall be reduced by 1/7th for each day of the accrual period in respect of which the benefit or increase has not been received.

(3) Where the deferrer would have been disqualified for receiving retirement pension as specified in paragraph (1)(d) [¹ or a shared additional pension as specified in paragraph (1A)] for part only of an accrual period, the amount of retirement pension not included by paragraph (1) [¹ or a shared additional pension not included by paragraph (1A)] shall be reduced by 1/7th for each day of the accrual period for which he would not have been so disqualified.

(4) Subject to paragraph (5), where—

(a) a person has, in respect of any day in an accrual period, received one or more of the benefits referred to in paragraph (1)(a) [³ or (aa)] or increases referred to in paragraph (1)(b) and (c) or both;

(b) the determining authority has determined that in respect of that day, he was not entitled to the benefit or increase; and

(c) the whole of the benefit or increase in respect of that day has been repaid or, as the case may be, recovered on or before the relevant date,

that day shall be treated as a day in respect of which he did not receive that benefit or increase or both.

(5) Where the benefit or increase in respect of a day to which paragraph (4)(a) and (b) applies is repaid or, as the case may be, recovered on or after the relevant date, that day shall only be treated as a day in respect of which that person did not receive that benefit or increase once the benefit or increase has been repaid in respect of all the days to which those sub-paragraphs relate and which fall within the period of deferment.

[³[⁴(5A) In paragraph (1), couple has the meaning—

(a) in relation to universal credit, given by section 39 of the Welfare Reform Act 2012; and

(b) in relation to the other benefits referred to in paragraph (1)(a) or (aa), given by section 137(1) of the Act.]]

(6) In paragraph (4), "the determining authority" means as the case may require, the Secretary of State, an appeal tribunal constituted under

Chapter I of Part I of the Social Security Act 1998 or a Commissioner, or a tribunal consisting of three or more such Commissioners constituted in accordance with section 16(7) of that Act.

(7) In paragraphs (4) and (5), "relevant date" means—

(a) the last day of the period of deferment; or

(b) where entitlement to a lump sum arises under paragraph 7A of Schedule 5 to the Act, the date of S's death.

(8) Any amount of retirement pension [[1] or a shared additional pension] not included in the calculation of the lump sum in accordance with this regulation must be rounded to the nearest penny, taking any 1/2 p as nearest to the next whole penny above.

AMENDMENTS

1. Shared Additional Pension (Miscellaneous Amendments) Regulations 2005 (SI 2005/1551) (July 6, 2005).

2. Civil Partnership (Consequential Amendments) Regulations 2005 (SI 2005/2878) (December 6, 2005).

3. Social Security (Deferral of Retirement Pensions) Regulations 2011 (SI 2011/634) reg.3 (April 6, 2011).

4. Universal Credit (Consequential, Supplementary, Incidental and Miscellaneous Provisions) Regulations 2013 (SI 2013/630) reg.34 (April 29, 2013).

GENERAL NOTE

6.6 The amendment effected by the Deferral of Retirement Pensions Regulations, 2011 will apply only in relation to an accrual period, or part of a period, falling on or after April 6, 2011.

Amendment of the Social Security (Widow's Benefit and Retirement Pensions) Regulations 1979

6.7 **4.**—*Taken into account in the text of those regulations.*

The Social Security (Deferral of Retirement Pensions, Shared Additional Pension and Graduated Retirement Benefit) (Miscellaneous Provisions) Regulations 2005

(SI 2005/2677)

ARRANGEMENT OF REGULATIONS

PART 1

GENERAL

6.8 1.   Citation, commencement and interpretation.

PART 2

DEFERRAL OF RETIREMENT PENSIONS AND SHARED ADDITIONAL PENSION

2.   Interpretation.
3.   Timing of election.
4.   Manner of making election.

5.   Change of election.
6.   Amendment of the Social Security (Retirement Pensions etc.) (Transitional Provisions) Regulations 2005.

PART 1

GENERAL

Citation, commencement and interpretation

1. —(1) These Regulations may be cited as the Social Security (Deferral of Retirement Pensions, Shared Additional Pension and Graduated Retirement Benefit) (Miscellaneous Provisions) Regulations 2005 and shall come into force on 6th April 2006.   **6.9**

(2) In these Regulations—
"the Claims and Payments Regulations" means the Social Security (Claims and Payments) Regulations 1987;
"the Housing Benefit Regulations" means the Housing Benefit (General) Regulations 1987.

PART 2

DEFERRAL OF RETIREMENT PENSIONS AND SHARED ADDITIONAL PENSION

Interpretation

2.—(1) In this Part—   **6.10**
"elector" means the person who may make an election under paragraph A1(1) or 3C(2) of Schedule 5 or paragraph 1(1) of Schedule 5A;
"retirement pension" means a Category A or a Category B retirement pension.

(2) In this Part, references to Schedules 5 and 5A are to those Schedules to the Social Security Contributions and Benefits Act 1992.

Timing of election

3.—(1) The period for making an election under—   **6.11**
(a) paragraph A1(1) of Schedule 5 (choice between increase of pension and lump sum where pensioner's entitlement is deferred); and
(b) paragraph 1(1) of Schedule 5A (choice between pension increase and lump sum where entitlement to shared additional pension is deferred),
is, subject to paragraph (4), three months starting on the date shown on the notice issued by the Secretary of State following the claim for retirement pension or shared additional pension, confirming that the elector is required to make that election.

(2) The period for making an election under paragraph 3C(2) of Schedule 5 (choice between increase of pension and lump sum where pensioner's deceased spouse or civil partner has deferred entitlement) is, subject to paragraph (4), three months starting on the date shown on the notice issued by the Secretary of State following W's claim for retirement pension or, if later, the date of S's death, confirming that the elector is required to make that election.

(3) Where more than one notice has been issued by the Secretary of State

in accordance with paragraph (1) or (2), the periods prescribed in those paragraphs shall only commence from the date shown on the latest such notice.

(4) The periods specified in paragraphs (1) and (2) may be extended by the Secretary of State if he considers it reasonable to do so in any particular case.

(5) Nothing in this regulation shall prevent the making of an election on or after claiming retirement pension or, as the case may be, shared additional pension but before the issue of the notice referred to in paragraph (1) or (2).

Manner of making election

6.12   **4.**—An election under paragraph A1(1) or 3C(2) of Schedule 5 or under paragraph 1(1) of Schedule 5A may be made—
   (a) in writing to an office specified by the Secretary of State for accepting such elections; or
   (b) except where the Secretary of State directs in any particular case that the election must be made in accordance with paragraph (a), by telephone call to the telephone number specified by the Secretary of State.

Change of election

6.13   **5.**—(1) Subject to paragraphs (2) and (6), this regulation applies in the case of an election which—
   (a) has been made under paragraph A1(1) or 3C(2) of Schedule 5 or under paragraph 1(1) of Schedule 5A; or
   (b) has been treated as made under paragraph A1(2) or 3C(3) of Schedule 5 or under paragraph 1(2) of Schedule 5A.

(2) This regulation does not apply in the case of an election which is—
   (a) made, or treated as made, by an elector who has subsequently died; or
   (b) treated as having been made by virtue of [¹ regulation 30(5E) or (5G)] of the Claims and Payments Regulations.

(3) An election specified in paragraph (1) may be changed by way of application made no later than the last day of the period specified in paragraph (4).

(4) The period specified for the purposes of paragraph (3) is, subject to paragraph (5), three months starting on the date shown on the written notification issued by the Secretary of State to the elector, confirming the election which the elector has made or is treated as having made.

(5) The period specified in paragraph (4) may be extended by the Secretary of State if he considers it reasonable to do so in any particular case.

(6) An election specified in paragraph (1) may not be changed where—
   (a) there has been a previous change of election under this regulation in respect of the same period of deferment;
   (b) the application is to change the election to one under paragraph A1(1)(a) or 3C(2)(a) of Schedule 5 or paragraph 1(1)(a) of Schedule 5A and any amount paid to him by way of, or on account of, a lump sum pursuant to Schedule 5 or 5A, has not been repaid in full to the Secretary of State within the period specified in paragraph (4) or, as the case may be, (5); or
   (c) the application is to change the election to one under paragraph A1(1)(b) or 3C(2)(b) of Schedule 5 or paragraph 1(1)(b) of Schedule 5A and the amount actually paid by way of an increase of retirement pension or shared additional pension, or actually paid on

890

account of such an increase, would exceed the amount to which the elector would be entitled by way of a lump sum.

(7) For the purposes of paragraph (6)(b), repayment in full of the amount paid by way of, or on account of, a lump sum shall only be treated as having occurred if repaid to the Secretary of State in the currency in which that amount was originally paid.

(8) Where the application is to change the election to one under paragraph A1(1)(b) or 3C(2)(b) of Schedule 5 or paragraph 1(1)(b) of Schedule 5A and paragraph (6)(c) does not apply, any amount paid by way of an increase of retirement pension or shared additional pension, or on account of such an increase, in respect of the period of deferment for which the election was originally made, shall be treated as having been paid on account of the lump sum to which the elector is entitled under paragraph 3A or 7A of Schedule 5 or, as the case may be, paragraph 4 of Schedule 5A.

(9) An application under paragraph (3) to change an election may be made—

(a) in writing to an office specified by the Secretary of State for accepting such applications; or

(b) except where the Secretary of State directs in any particular case that the application must be made in accordance with sub-paragraph (a), by telephone call to the telephone number specified by the Secretary of State.

Amendment of the Social Security (Retirement Pensions etc.) (Transitional Provisions) Regulations 2005

6.—Regulation 2(6)(a) of the Social Security (Retirement Pensions etc.) 6.14
(Transitional Provisions) Regulations 2005 (modification of Schedule 5) is omitted.

AMENDMENT

1. Social Security (Deferral of Retirement Pensions etc) Regulations 2006 (SI 2006/516) reg.4 (April 6, 2006).

The Social Security (Graduated Retirement Benefit) (No. 2) Regulations 1978

(SI 1978/393) *(as amended)*

ARRANGEMENT OF REGULATIONS

1. Citation, commencement and interpretation. 6.15
2. Application of sections 150 and 155 of the Social Security Administration Act 1992.
3. Continuation in force of sections 36, 37 and 118(1) of the 1965 Act.
4. Modification of regulations concerning graduated retirement benefit.
5. *Omitted.*
Sch. 1
Sch. 2
Sch. 3

The Secretary of State for Social Services, in exercise of the powers conferred on him by section 2(1) of and paragraphs 3, 7 and 9 of Schedule 3 to the Social Security (Consequential Provisions) Act 1975 and section 24(1) of the Social Security Pensions Act 1975, and of all other powers enabling him in that behalf, hereby makes the following regulations, which only make provision consequential on the passing of the last-mentioned Act and accordingly by virtue of section 61(1)(e) of that Act are exempt from the requirements of section 139(1) of the Social Security Act 1975 (duty to consult National Insurance Advisory Committee about proposed regulations):

GENERAL NOTE

6.16   Responsibility for decisions made in respect of Graduated Retirement Pension, even those relating to contributions and the record of the claimant's contributions, remains that of the Department of Work and Pensions. This is because no transfer of function in this respect was made when other aspects of the administration of contributions was transferred to Her Majesty's Revenue. The consequence is that all such decisions made in relation to GRP entitlement that depend upon contribution questions, must either be made by officers of Department of Work and Pensions, or, if made by HMRC, must be made by them as agents of that department. The result is that all such decisions are appealable only to the Social Entitlement Chamber of the First-tier Tribunal rather than the Tax Chamber. See First-tier Tribunal and Upper Tribunal (Chambers) Order (SI 2008/2684), art.4.

Citation, commencement and interpretation

6.17   **1.**—(1) These regulations may be cited as the Social Security (Graduated Retirement Benefit) (No.2) Regulations 1978.

(2) This regulation and regulation 2 below shall come into operation on 6th April 1978.

(3) The remainder of these regulations shall, for the purpose only of determining, before 6th April 1979, claims for, or questions arising as to, benefit for any period after 5th April 1979, come into operation on 6th December 1978.

(4) Except as mentioned in paragraphs (2) and (3) above, these regulations shall come into operation on 6th April 1979.

(5) In these regulations—

"the Act" means the Social Security Act 1975;

"the Pensions Act" means the Social Security Pensions Act 1975;

"the 1965 Act" means the National Insurance Act 1965;

"the 1975 regulations" means the Social Security (Graduated Retirement Benefit) Regulations 1975, as amended;

"the 1978 regulations" means the Social Security (Graduated Retirement Benefit) Regulations 1978;

and other expressions have the same meanings as in the Act.

(6) Any reference in these regulations to any provision made by or contained in any enactment or instrument shall, except in so far as the context otherwise requires, be construed as a reference to that provision as amended or extended by any enactment or instrument and as including a reference to any provision which it re-enacts or replaces, or which may re-enact or replace it, with or without modification.

(7) The rules for the construction of Acts of Parliament contained in the Interpretation Act 1889 shall apply in relation to this instrument and in relation to the revocations effected by it as if this instrument and the regulations revoked by it were Acts of Parliament and as if the revocations were repeals.

[² Application of sections 150 and 155 of the Social Security Administration Act 1992

6.18   **2.**—The provisions of sections 150 and 155 of the Social Security Administration Act 1992, (annual up-rating of benefits and effect of alteration of rates of benefit) shall apply to—

(a) the amount of graduated retirement benefit payable for each unit of graduated contributions;

(b) increases of such benefit under the provisions of Schedule 2 to these Regulations; and

(c) any addition under section 37(1) of the 1965 Act (addition to weekly rate of retirement pension for [¹ widows, widowers and surviving civil partners]) to the amount of such benefit.

as if that amount, those increases and that addition were included in the sums mentioned in section 150(1) and (3) and graduated retirement benefit were a benefit referred to in section 155(2).]

AMENDMENT

1. Social Security (Retirement Pensions and Graduated Retirement Benefit) (Widowers and Civil Partnership) Regulations 2005 (SI 2005/3078) (April 6, 2006).

Continuation in force of sections 36, 37 and 118(1) of the 1965 Act

3.—(1) The provisions of this regulation shall have effect for the purpose   6.19
of securing continuity between the Act and the 1965 Act in the case of persons who had, immediately before 6th April 1975, rights or prospective rights to or expectations of graduated retirement benefit under sections 36 and 37 of the 1965 Act, by preserving those rights and temporarily retaining the effect of those sections for transitional purposes.

(2) Paragraph (3) below shall have effect so that notwithstanding their repeal by the Social Security Act 1973 those sections shall, for the purpose aforesaid, continue in force subject to the making in them of the modifications required—

(a) to bring them into conformity with the provisions of the Act and the Pensions Act and to enable them to have effect as if contained in the scheme of social security benefits established by those Acts;

(b) to replace section 36(4) of the 1965 Act (increase of graduated retirement benefit in cases of deferred retirement) with provisions corresponding to those of paragraphs 1 to 3 of Schedule 1 to the Pensions Act;

(c) to extend section 37 of the 1965 Act (increase of woman's retirement pension by reference to her late husband's graduated retirement benefit) to men and their late wives. [¹; [² ...]

(d) to extend section 37 of the 1965 Act (increase of women's retirement pension by reference to her late husband's graduated retirement benefit) to civil partners and surviving civil partners.] [²and

(e) to extend section 37 of the 1965 Act to men and their late husbands, and women and their late wives.]

(3) On and after 6th April 1979 those sections shall continue in force in the modified form in which they are set out in Schedule 1 to these regulations, but not so as to save the National Insurance (Graduated Retirement Benefit and Consequential Provisions) Regulations 1961, so far as deemed to have been made under those sections, from being invalidated by the repeal; and section 118(1) of the 1965 Act (short title) shall also continue in force.

AMENDMENTS

1. Social Security (Retirement Pensions and Graduated Retirement Benefit) (Widowers and Civil Partnership) Regulations 2005 (SI 2005/3078) (April 6, 2006).
2. Social Security (Graduated Retirement Benefit) (Marriage Same Sex Couples) Regulations 2014 (SI 2014/76) reg.3 (March 13, 2014). See also the Marriage

and Civil Partnership (Scotland) Act 2014 and Civil Partnership Act 2004 (Consequential Provisions and Modifications) Order 2014 (SI 2014/3229) Sch.6 art.3 (December 12, 2014).

Modification of regulations concerning graduated retirement benefit

6.20   **4.**—The provisions of regulations 2 and 3 of the 1978 regulations (which were made under sections 36 and 37 of the 1965 Act) shall continue in force in the modified form set out in Schedule 3 to these regulations; and paragraphs (1) (so far as it relates to citation), (2) and (3) (interpretation) of regulation 1 of the 1978 regulations shall also continue in force.

Revocations

6.21   **5.**—*Omitted.*

SCHEDULES

SCHEDULE 1   **Regulation 3(3)**

SECTIONS 36 AND 37 OF THE NATIONAL INSURANCE ACT 1965 AS CONTINUED IN FORCE BY THESE REGULATIONS

Graduated retirement benefit

6.22   **36.**—(1) Subject to the provisions of the Act, graduated retirement benefit shall be payable to any person who is over pensionable age and who [¹ is entitled to a retirement pension], and shall be an increase in the weekly rate of his retirement pension equal to [¹² 14.16] pence for each unit, ascertained in accordance with subsections (2) and (3) of this section, of the graduated contributions properly paid by him as an insured person, the result being rounded to the nearest whole penny, taking 1/2p as nearest to the next whole penny above.

(2) For the purpose of graduated retirement benefit [⁹a unit of graduated contributions shall be £7.50.]

(3) Where a person's graduated contributions calculated at the said rate do not make an exact number of units any incomplete fraction of a unit shall, if it is one-half or more, be treated as a complete unit.

[⁷(4) Where a person's entitlement to graduated retirement benefit is deferred—

    (a) Schedule 2 to the Social Security (Graduated Retirement Benefit) (No.2) Regulations 1978; and

    (b) Schedule 1 to the 2005 Regulations,

shall have effect and both those Schedules shall be construed and have effect as if they were part of this subsection.

(4A) For the purposes of subsection (4), a person's entitlement to graduated retirement benefit is deferred—

    (a) where he would be entitled to a Category A or Category B retirement pension but for the fact that his entitlement is deferred within the meaning in section 55(3) of the Social Security Contributions and Benefits Act 1992, if and so long as his entitlement to such a pension is deferred;

    (b) where he is treated under subsection (7) as receiving a Category A or a Category B retirement pension at a nominal weekly rate, if and so long as he does not become entitled to graduated retirement benefit by reason only of not satisfying the conditions in section 1 of the Social Security Administration Act 1992 (entitlement to benefit dependent on claim),

and in relation to graduated retirement benefit, "period of deferment" shall be construed accordingly.]

(5) For the purposes of subsection (4) of this section, the Secretary of State may by regulations provide for treating all or any of the graduated contributions paid by a person in the tax year in which he attained pensionable age as having been paid before, or as having been paid after, the day on which he attained that age, whether or not the contribution in question was so paid.

(7) A person who has attained pensionable age and [¹has claimed], but is not entitled to a retirement pension [²(except a person who is not so entitled because of an election under section 54(1) of the Social Security Contributions and Benefits Act 1992 or because he has

withdrawn his claim)], shall be treated for the purposes of the foregoing provisions of this section as receiving a retirement pension at a nominal weekly rate:

Provided that—

(a) this subsection shall not confer any right to graduated retirement benefit on a person who would be entitled to a retirement pension but for some provision of the Act or of regulations disqualifying him for receipt of it; and

(b) regulations may provide that any right by virtue of this subsection to benefit at less than a specified weekly rate shall be satisfied either altogether or for a specified period by the making of a single payment of the prescribed amount.

(8) In this section and in section 37 below—

"graduated contributions" means graduated contributions under the National Insurance Act 1965 or the National Insurance Act 1959;

"insured person" means insured person under the National Insurance Act 1965 or the National Insurance Act 1946;

"retirement pension" means retirement pension of any category;

"the Act" means the Social Security Act 1975;

[7 "the 2005 Regulations" means the Social Security (Graduated Retirement Benefit) Regulations 2005;]

and any reference in section 37 below to "section 36 of this Act" or to any of its subsections is a reference to that section or subsection as it is here set out.

(9) This section and section 37 below and the Act shall be construed and have effect as if this section and section 37 below were included in Chapter I of Part II of that Act (contributory benefits); and references to that Chapter, that Part or that Act in any other enactment or in any instrument shall be construed accordingly:

Provided that nothing in this subsection shall affect the construction of any reference to section 36 or 37 of this Act or of that Act or to any of the subsections of those sections; and any increase in the weekly rate of a person's retirement pension, to the extent that it is attributable to subsection (4) of this section, shall be left out of account in determining the weekly rate of that pension for the purposes of [3 section 30B(3) of the Social Security Contributions and Benefits Act 1992 regulations 11(1) and 18(7) of the Social Security (Incapacity Benefit) (Transitional Regulations 1995] and [4 regulation 10(6) of the Jobseeker's Allowance (Transitional Provisions) Regulations 1996] (rates of incapacity benefit and jobseeker's allowance in transitional cases for persons over pensionable age)].

(10) [5 . . .]

37.—(1) Subject to the provisions of this section [7 and to Schedule 1 to the 2005 Regulations]—

[10, where a person, having paid graduated contributions as an insured person, dies leaving a widow, widower [11 surviving same sex spouse] or surviving civil partner and the survivor—

(a) has attained pensionable age at the time of the death; or

(b) remains that person's widow, widower [11 surviving same sex spouse] or surviving civil partner (as the case may be) when attaining pensionable age,] [8 ; or

(c) where a person, having paid graduated contributions as an insured person, dies on or after 5th December 2005 leaving a surviving civil partner, and they have both attained pensionable age at the time of his or her death,] [11 ; or

(d) where a man, having paid graduated contributions as an insured person, dies leaving a widower, and they have both attained pensionable age at the time of his death; or

(e) where a woman, having paid graduated contributions as an insured person, dies leaving a widow, and they have both attained pensionable age at the time of her death,]

then section 36 of this Act shall apply as if the increase in the weekly rate of the retirement pension of the [8 widow, widower [11 surviving same sex spouse] or surviving civil partner], as the case may be, provided for by subsection (1) thereof were the amount there specified by reference to his or her graduated contributions with the addition of one-half of the weekly rate of the graduated retirement benefit of his or her former spouse [8 or civil partner] (any amount including 1/2p being rounded to the next whole penny above) [10 . . .]

(2) For the purposes of subsection (1) of this section, the weekly rate of the deceased spouse's [8 or civil partner's] graduated retirement benefit shall (whether or not he or she was receiving or entitled to receive any such benefit) be taken to have been the weekly rate appropriate to the amount of graduated contributions paid by him or her (determined as if any orders which have come into force under section 124 of the Act (increases in rates of benefit) since the date of the deceased spouse's [8 or civil partner's] death had come into force before that date), excluding any addition under section 37(1) of this Act, but including any addition under section 36(4), thereof (and for the purpose of calculating the addition under section 36(4) taking into account any addition under section 37(1)); and where at his or her death he or she had attained pensionable age but had [1 not] become entitled to graduated retirement

benefit, that addition shall be computed as if he or she had [¹ . . .] become entitled to graduated retirement benefit immediately before his or her death.

(3) A person's right to graduated retirement benefit by virtue of this section shall be brought into account under section 36(4) of this Act in determining the graduated retirement benefit payable to him or her under the said section 36:

Provided that, if the termination of the marriage [⁸ or civil partnership] by death occurred after he or she attained pensionable age, he or she shall for the purposes of this subsection be treated as not having attained pensionable age until the date of that termination.

(4) A person's right to graduated retirement benefit by virtue of this section in respect of a spouse he or she marries [⁸ or as the case may be, a civil partner he or she forms a civil partnership with] after attaining pensionable age shall be subject to such additional conditions as may be prescribed; and except as may be provided by regulations a person more than once married [⁸ or who has formed a civil partnership more than once or who has been both married and a civil partner] shall not be entitled for the same period to any graduated retirement benefit by virtue of this section in respect of more than one of his or her spouses [⁸ or civil partners].

(5) Regulations may provide that where a woman is entitled to graduated retirement benefit and to a widowed mother's allowance the graduated retirement benefit shall be an increase in the weekly rate of that allowance; and where the benefit is such an increase, section 36(7) of this Act shall not apply.

GENERAL NOTE

6.23   The amendments made to ss.36(1) and 37(1) above by the Social Security (State Pension and National Insurance Credits) Regulations 2009 (SI 2009/2206), which have effect from April 6, 2010, do not apply in the case of a woman who attained pensionable age before that date or, in the case of a deceased person in accordance with s.37, where that person is a woman who would have reached pensionable age before that date. Nor does the amendment in s.37(1) apply where the survivor attained pensionable age before that date and it is immaterial in that case when the deceased person died. (See reg.3(2) and reg.4(4) of those regulations). For the text of the original sections applicable in those cases please see earlier editions of this book.

SCHEDULE 2   **Regulation 3(3)**

PROVISIONS REPLACING SECTION 36(4) OF THE NATIONAL INSURANCE ACT 1965

6.24   1.—Where a person [¹defers his entitlement to a Category A or Category B retirement pensions] after attaining pensionable age, or has made an election by virtue of section 30(3) of the Act and has not revoked it, then for the purpose of calculating the graduated retirement benefit payable to him from the date of his retirement—

(a) there shall be added to the amount of the graduated contributions properly paid by him as an insured person one-half of the aggregate graduated retirement benefit which would have been payable to him for any period before 6th April 1979 (disregarding the effect of any order made under section 124 of the Act) if he had retired from regular employment on attaining pensionable age and had received that benefit for the whole of the period without any interruption or abatement:

Provided that, in computing the addition to be made in accordance with this paragraph in the case of a person who has made an election by virtue of section 30(3) of the Act (re-entry into regular employment) or the corresponding provisions of any earlier Act, no account shall be taken of any period between 6th April 1975 and 5th April 1979 (both dates inclusive) which falls between the date of that election and the date of his previous [¹entitlement]; and

[⁷omitted]

GENERAL NOTE

6.25   This version of Schedule 2 is applicable to periods of deferment ending before April 6, 2005 and to incremental periods beginning after that date. For earlier periods see the text of this Schedule as it was in SI 1978/393 and in earlier editions of this book.

The sums which are the increases of graduated retirement benefit under Schedule 2 were increased by 2.4 per cent with effect from April 8, 2019: see art.12(2) of the Social Security Benefits Up-rating Order 2019 (SI 2019/480).

SCHEDULE 3   **Regulation 4**

REGULATIONS 2 AND 3 OF THE 1978 REGULATIONS AS MODIFIED BY THESE REGULATIONS

Graduated retirement benefit when retirement is deferred

2.—For the purposes of paragraph 1(a) of Schedule 2 to the Social Security (Graduated Retirement Benefit) (No. 2) Regulations 1978 (provision, where a person attains pensionable age before 6th April 1979 but does not retire from regular employment until after 5th April 1979, for calculating the graduated retirement benefit payable to him from the date of his retirement) all the graduated contributions paid by a person in the income tax year in which he attained pensionable age shall be treated as having been paid before the day on which he attained that age:　**6.26**

Provided that where, in any case, the aggregate amount of the graduated contributions paid by him in that year exceeded the aggregate amount of graduated contributions which would have been payable by him in that part of the year which ended with the income tax week, in which he attained pensionable age if, in each income tax week beginning in that part of the year, a graduated contribution as for an employment which was not a non-participating employment had been payable by him in respect of a weekly payment of remuneration made in that week at a level equal to the upper limit on the amount of weekly pay then taken into account under section 4(1)(c) of the 1965 Act as amended, the excess shall be treated as having been paid after the day on which he attained that age.

Graduated retirement benefit for persons who have been married more than once

3.—For the purposes of section 37 of the 1965 Act (special provisions as to graduated retirement benefit for widows and widowers) a person who has been married more than once [⁸ or has formed more than one civil partnership or who has been both married and a civil partner] and who is entitled to graduated retirement benefit for any period by virtue of the provisions of that section in respect of a second or subsequent spouse [⁸ or civil partner] shall not be precluded from entitlement to graduated retirement benefit for that period by virtue of that section in respect of a former spouse [⁸ or civil partner], but shall be so entitled to the extent only that it is payable to him or her by the application of section 36(4) of the 1965 Act in respect of any period before the death of the first-mentioned spouse [⁸ or civil partner].　**6.27**

AMENDMENTS

1. Social Security (Abolition of Earnings Rule) Regulations 1989 (SI 1989/1642) reg.5 (October 1, 1989).

2. Social Security (Graduated Retirement Benefit) Amendment Regulations 1995 (SI 1995/2606) reg.2 (November 1, 2005).

3. Social Security and Child Support (Jobseeker's Allowance) (Consequential Amendments) Regulations 1996 (SI 1996/1345) reg.18 (July 10, 1996).

4. Social Security (Miscellaneous Amendments) Regulations 1997 (SI 1997/454) reg.5 (March 21, 1997).

5. Social Security Act 1998 (Commencement No.9, and Savings and Consequential and Transitional Provisions) Order 1999 (SI 1999/2422) (September 6, 1999).

6. Social Security Benefits Up-rating Order 2015 (SI 015/457) art.8 (April 8, 2015).

7. Social Security (Graduated Retirement Benefit) Regulations 2005 (SI 2005/454) reg.2 and reg.3 (April 6, 2005).

8. Social Security (Retirement Pensions and Graduated Benefit) (Widowers and Civil Partnership) Regulations 2005 (SI 2005/3078) (April 6, 2006).

9. Social Security (State Pension and National Insurance Credits) Regulations 2009 (SI 2009/2206) reg.3 (April 6, 2010).

10. Social Security (State Pension and National Insurance Credits) Regulations 2009 (SI 2009/2206) reg.4 (April 6, 2010).

11. Social Security (Graduated Retirement Benefit) (Married Same Sex Couples) Regulations 2014 (SI 2014/76) reg.2, (March 13, 2014).

12. The Social Security Benefits Up-rating Order 2019 (SI 2019/480) art.12(1) (April 8, 2019).

GENERAL NOTE

6.28   Regulation 3 of the Graduated Retirement Benefit Regulations 2005 makes further changes to Sch.2 of these regulations but only in respect of periods of deferment ending after April 6, 2005. Regulation 5 of the same regulations makes provision for transitional cases, being those cases where the period of deferment begins before April 6, 2005 but ends after that date.

The Additional Pension and Social Security Pensions (Home Responsibilities) (Amendment) Regulations 2001

(SI 2001/1323) (*as amended*)

ARRANGEMENT OF REGULATIONS

6.29   1. Citation, commencement and interpretation.
2. Calculation of additional pension where contributions equivalent premium paid or treated as paid.
3. Calculation of additional pension: earnings partly from employment with contracted-out scheme membership.
4. Calculation of additional pension: earnings partly from employment with scheme membership.
5. Calculation of additional pension: other cases of mixed forms of contracted-out employment.
5A. Earnings factor credits eligibility for pensioners to whom employment and support allowance was payable.
6. Preclusion from regular employment.
7. *Omitted.*

The Secretary of State for Social Security, in exercise of powers conferred by sections 44A(2)(c)(ii), 122(1) and 175(1) and (5) of, and paragraph 5(7A) of Schedule 3 to and paragraph 9 of Schedule 4A to, the Social Security Contributions and Benefits Act 1992 and of all other powers enabling him in that behalf, by this instrument, which contains only regulations made before the end of the period of 6 months beginning with the coming into force of sections 30(3) and 40 of, and Schedule 4 to, the Child Support, Pensions and Social Security Act 2000 makes the following Regulations:

Citation, commencement and interpretation

6.30   1.—(1) These Regulations may be cited as the Additional Pension and Social Security Pensions (Home Responsibilities) (Amendment) Regulations 2001 and shall come into force on 6th April 2002.
(2) In these Regulations—
[1"the 2007 Act" means the Welfare Reform Act 2007;]
"the Administration Act" means the Social Security Administration Act 1992;
[4 "appropriate personal pension scheme" means an appropriate scheme within the meaning of section 7B(6) (meaning of "contracted-out scheme" etc) of the Pension Schemes Act 1993;]
"appropriate table" means—

(a) in the case of a person attaining pensionable age after the end of the year 2002–2003 but before 6th April 2009, Table 5 of paragraph 7(3) of Schedule 4A to the Contributions and Benefits Act,

(b) in the case of a person attaining pensionable age on or after 6th April 2009, Table 6 of paragraph 7(4) of that Schedule;

"the Contributions and Benefits Act" means the Social Security Contributions and Benefits Act 1992;

"the 1994 Regulations" means the Social Security Pensions (Home Responsibilities) Regulations 1994;

"contracted-out employment" means [¹subject to regulation 3(5),] employed earner's employment qualifying a person for a pension provided by a salary related contracted-out scheme or a money purchase contracted-out scheme or an appropriate personal pension scheme, as the case may be;

[⁴ "contributions equivalent premium" has the meaning given in section 181(1) (general interpretation) of the Pension Schemes Act 1993;]

[⁴ "money purchase contracted-out scheme" has the meaning given in section 7B(5) of the Pension Schemes Act 1993;]

[⁴ "salary related contracted-out scheme" has the meaning given in section 7B(4) of the Pension Schemes Act 1993;]

"contributions equivalent premium" means the premium referred to in section 55(2) of the Pension Schemes Act 1993;

"non-contracted-out employment" means employed earner's employment which is not contracted-out employment;

"year" means a tax year.

Calculation of additional pension where contributions equivalent premium paid or treated as paid

2. Where a contributions equivalent premium—   6.31

(a) is paid in accordance with the provisions of sections 55 to 61 of the Pension Schemes Act 1993 (which deal with the payment of a contributions equivalent premium in respect of specified periods of contracted-out employment) and regulations made thereunder; or

(b) is treated as having been paid in accordance with the provisions of paragraph 5(3) to (3E) of Schedule 2 to that Act (which provide for a contributions equivalent premium to be treated as paid in respect of contracted-out employment in certain circumstances) and regulations made thereunder,

the amount referred to in [¹section 45(2)(c) or (d) of the Contributions and Benefits Act] (which provides for the calculation of the amount of additional pension in a Category A retirement pension in relation to the 2002–2003 tax year and subsequent tax years) is to be calculated in accordance with Parts I and II of [¹Schedule 4A to the Contributions and Benefits Act or, as the case may be, Parts 1 and 2 of Schedule 4B to that Act] (additional pension) as if the employment in respect of which a premium is paid, or treated as paid, had not been contracted-out employment.

Calculation of additional pension: earnings partly from employment with contracted-out scheme membership

3.—(1) This regulation applies in relation to any year where earnings are   6.32
paid to or for the benefit of an earner—

(a) partly in respect of non-contracted-out employment; and

(b) partly in respect of employment qualifying him for a pension provided by a salary related contracted-out scheme or a money purchase contracted-out scheme, or both.

(2) For any year in relation to which this regulation applies, the amount referred to in paragraph 1(1)(a) of Schedule 4A [¹or, as the case may be, in paragraph 1(1) of Schedule 4B] to the Contributions and Benefits Act shall be amount C where—

(a) amount C is equal to amount A minus amount B; and

(b) amounts A and B are calculated in accordance with the following paragraphs.

(3) Amount A is to be calculated in accordance with paragraph 5 of Schedule 4A [¹or, as the case may be, in paragraphs 8 and 9 of Schedule 4B] to the Contributions and Benefits Act.

(4) Amount B is to be calculated as follows:—

(a) find the earnings factor derived from the aggregate of the amounts of weekly earnings paid in that year in respect of the employment referred to in paragraph (1)(b) above;

(b) deduct from that earnings factor an amount equal to the weekly lower earnings limit for the year multiplied by the number of tax weeks in which earnings were paid in respect of weeks of that employment;

(c) multiply the amount found under sub-paragraph (b) above in accordance with the last order under section 148 of the Administration Act to come into force before the end of the final relevant year;

(d) multiply the amount found under sub-paragraph (c) above by the percentage specified in paragraph 6(3) of Schedule 4A [¹or, as the case may be, in paragraph 10(1)(c) of Schedule 4B] to the Contributions and Benefits Act which is applicable in the case of the earner.

[¹(5) In so far as paragraphs (1) to (4) apply in respect of the calculation of additional pension under Schedule 4B to the Contributions and Benefits Act, the definition of "contracted-out employment" has effect as if the words from "or a money purchase contracted-out scheme" to the end were omitted.]

Calculation of additional pension: earnings partly from employment with scheme membership

6.33   **4.**—(1) This regulation applies in relation to any year where earnings are paid to or for the benefit of an earner—

(a) partly in respect of non-contracted-out employment; and

(b) partly in respect of employment qualifying him for a pension provided by an appropriate personal pension scheme.

(2) For any year in relation to which this regulation applies, the amount referred to in paragraph 1(1)(a) of Schedule 4A [¹or, as the case may be, in paragraph 1(1) of Schedule 4B] to the Contributions and Benefits Act shall be amount C where—

(a) amount C is equal to amount A minus amount B; and

(b) amounts A and B are calculated in accordance with the following paragraphs.

(3) Amount A is to be calculated in accordance with paragraph 5 of Schedule 4A to the Contributions and Benefits Act.

(4) Amount B is to be calculated as follows:—

(a) find the earnings factor derived from the aggregate of the amounts of weekly earnings paid in that year in respect of employment qualifying the earner for a pension provided by an appropriate personal pension scheme;

(b) deduct from that earnings factor an amount equal to the qualifying earnings factor for that year;

(c) calculate the part of the amount found under sub-paragraph (b) above falling into each of the bands specified in the appropriate table;

(d) multiply the amount of each such part in accordance with the last order under section 148 of the Administration Act to come into force before the end of the final relevant year;

(e) multiply each amount found under sub-paragraph (d) above by such percentage specified in the appropriate table in relation to the appropriate band as is applicable in the case of the earner;

(f) add together the amounts calculated under sub-paragraph (e) above.

Calculation of additional pension: other cases of mixed forms of contracted-out employment

5.—(1) This regulation applies in relation to any year where earnings are paid to or for the benefit of an earner— 6.34

(a) partly in respect of—
  (i) employment qualifying him for a pension provided by a salary related contracted-out scheme or a money purchase contracted-out scheme, or both, and
  (ii) employment qualifying him for a pension provided by an appropriate personal pension scheme; or

(b) partly in respect of—
  (i) non-contracted-out employment,
  (ii) employment qualifying him for a pension provided by a salary related contracted-out scheme or a money purchase contracted-out scheme, or both, and
  (iii) employment qualifying him for a pension provided by an appropriate personal pension scheme.

(2) For any year in relation to which this regulation applies, the amount referred to in paragraph 1(1)(a) of Schedule 4A to the Contributions and Benefits Act shall be amount C where—

(a) amount C is equal to amount A minus amount B; and

(b) amounts A and B are calculated in accordance with the following paragraphs.

(3) Amount A is to be determined in accordance with paragraph 5 of Schedule 4A to the Contributions and Benefits Act.

(4) Amount B is the sum of amount D and amount E and—

(a) amount D is to be found as follows:—
  (i) find the earnings factor derived from the aggregate of the amounts of weekly earnings paid in that year in respect of the employment referred to in paragraph (1)(a)(i) or, as the case may be, (1)(b)(ii) above,
  (ii) deduct from that earnings factor an amount equal to the weekly lower earnings limit for the year multiplied by the number of tax weeks in which earnings were paid in respect of that employment,
  (iii) multiply the amount found under head (ii) above in accordance

with the last order under section 148 of the Administration Act to come into force before the end of the final relevant year,

    (iv) multiply the amount found under head (iii) above by the percentage specified in paragraph 6(3) of Schedule 4A to the Contributions and Benefits Act which is applicable in the case of the earner;

  (b) amount E is to be found as follows:—

    (i) find the earnings factor derived from the aggregate of the amounts of weekly earnings paid in the year in which this regulation applies in respect of the employment referred to in paragraph (1)(a)(ii) or, as the case may be, (1)(b)(iii) above,

    (ii) add to that earnings factor an amount equal to the weekly lower earnings limit for the year multiplied by the number of tax weeks in which earnings were paid in respect of the employment referred to in paragraph (1)(a)(i) or, as the case may be, (1)(b)(ii) above,

    (iii) deduct from the amount found under head (ii) above an amount equal to the qualifying earnings factor for that year,

    (iv) calculate the part of the amount found under head (iii) above falling into each of the bands specified in the appropriate table,

    (v) multiply the amount of each such part in accordance with the last order under section 148 of the Administration Act to come into force before the end of the final relevant year,

    (vi) multiply each amount found under head (v) above by such percentage specified in the appropriate table in relation to the appropriate band as is applicable in the case of the earner;

    (vii) add together the amounts calculated under head (vi) above.

[¹Earnings factor credits eligibility for pensioners to whom employment and support allowance was payable

6.35   **5A.**—(1) For the purposes of subsection (3) of section 44C (earnings factor credits) of the Contributions and Benefits Act(**9**), a pensioner is eligible for earnings factor enhancement in respect of a week if that pensioner satisfies one or more of the conditions in paragraph (2) and was—

  (a) a person to whom employment and support allowance was payable for any part of that week;

  (b) a person to whom that allowance would have been payable but for the fact that that person did not satisfy the contribution condition in paragraph 1 or paragraph 2 of Schedule 1 to the 2007 Act; or

  (c) a person to whom that allowance would have been payable but for the fact that under regulations the amount was reduced to nil because of—

    (i) receipt of other benefits; or

    (ii) receipt of payments from an occupational pension scheme or personal pension scheme.

  (2) The conditions are—

  (a) immediately prior to that week, employment and support allowance was payable or would have been payable for—

    (i) a continuous period of 52 weeks; or

    (ii) a period of 52 weeks treated as continuous by virtue of regulations made under paragraph 4 of Schedule 2 to the 2007 Act;

(b) that allowance included or would have included the support component under section 2(2) of the 2007 Act; or

(c) immediately prior to that week, in the case of—

    (i) a man born in the period beginning with 6th April 1946 and ending with 5th April 1947; or

    (ii) a woman born in the period beginning with 6th October 1950 and ending with 5th April 1951,

that allowance was payable or would have been payable for a continuous period of 13 weeks immediately following a period throughout which statutory sick pay was payable.

(3) In this regulation [³ and regulation 5C], "employment and support allowance" means an employment and support allowance under Part 1 (employment and support allowance) of the 2007 Act.]

[² Earnings factor credits eligibility for certain persons entitled to universal credit

5B.—(1) For the purposes of subsection (3) of section 44C (earnings factor credits) of the   **6.36**

Contributions and Benefits Act, a pensioner is eligible for earnings factor enhancement in respect of a week if that pensioner was a person entitled to an award of universal credit under Part 1 of the Welfare Reform Act 2012 in respect of any part of that week which includes—

(a) if the person satisfies the condition in paragraph (2), an amount under regulation 27(1)(a) of the Universal Credit Regulations 2013 in respect of the fact that the person has limited capability for work;

(b) an amount under regulation 27(1)(b) of those Regulations in respect of the fact that the person has limited capability for work and work-related activity; or

(c) an amount under regulation 29(1) of those Regulations where the person has regular and substantial caring responsibilities for a severely disabled person, or would include any of those amounts but for regulation 27(4) or 29(4) of those Regulations.

(2) The condition referred to in paragraph (1)(a) is that for each of the 52 weeks immediately prior to that week—

(a) the person was entitled to universal credit inrespect of the fact that the person had limited capability for work or would have included an amount in respect of the fact that the person had limited capability for work but for regulation 27(4) or 29(4) of the Universal Credit Regulations 2013; or

(b) employment and support allowance under Part 1 (employment and support allowance) of the Welfare Reform Act 2007 ("the 2007 Act")—

    (i) was payable to the person;

    (ii) would have been payable to the person but for the fact that the person did not satisfy the contribution condition in paragraph 1 or paragraph 2 of Schedule 1 to the 2007 Act;

    (iii) would have been payable to the person but for the fact that the person had been entitled to it for the relevant maximum number of days under section 1A of the 2007 Act; or

    (iv) would have been payable to the person but for the fact that under regulations the amount was reduced to nil because of—

(aa) receipt of other benefits; or

(bb) receipt of payments from an occupational pension scheme or personal pension scheme.

(3) Paragraph (2)(b) of this regulation is satisfied in respect of a week which falls between periods which are linked by virtue of regulations under paragraph 4 (linking periods) of Schedule 2 to the 2007 Act.].

[³ Earnings factor credit eligibility for pensioners to whom section 1A of the 2007 Act applied

6.37 **5C.**—(1) For the purposes of section 44C(3) (earnings factor credits) of the Contributions and Benefits Act, a pensioner is eligible for earnings factor enhancement in respect of a week to which paragraph (2) applies.

(2) This paragraph applies to a week in which, in relation to the pensioner concerned, each of the days would have been—

(a) a day of limited capability for work; or

(b) a day on which that pensioner would have been treated as having limited capability for work,

for the purposes of Part 1 of the 2007 Act (limited capability for work) where that pensioner would have been entitled to an employment and support allowance but for the application of section 1A of the 2007 Act.]

Preclusion from regular employment

6.38 **6.**—The condition referred to in section 44A(2)(c)(ii) of the Contributions and Benefits Act (which relates to the condition to be satisfied for a person to be taken to be precluded from regular employment by responsibilities at home throughout a year for the purposes of paragraph 5(7)(b) of Schedule 3 to that Act) is that specified in regulation 2(2)(b) or (3) of the 1994 Regulations (which refer respectively to a person to whom income support is payable and a person regularly engaged in caring for at least 35 hours a week for someone in receipt of certain benefits).

AMENDMENTS

1. Social Security (State Pensions and National Insurance Credits) Regulations 2009 (SI 2009/2206) regs 23–27 (April 6, 2010).

2. Universal Credit (Consequential, Supplementary, Incidental and Miscellaneous Amendments) Regulations 2013 (SI 2013/630 (April 29, 2013).

3. Social Security (Miscellaneous Amendments) Regulations 2014 (SI 2014/591) reg.2 (April 28, 2014).

4. Pensions Act 2014 (Abolition of Contracting-out for Salary Related Pension Schemes) (Consequential Amendments and Savings) Order 2016 (SI 2016/200) art.19 (April 6, 2016).

The Social Security (Graduated Retirement Benefit) Regulations 2005

(SI 2005/454)

ARRANGEMENT OF REGULATIONS

6.39 1.   Citation, commencement, effect and interpretation.
2.   Amendment of the 1965 Act.

3.   Amendment of Schedule 2 to the Social Security (Graduated Retirement Benefit) (No.2) Regulations 1978 and saving.
4.   Schedule 1.
5.   Modification of Schedule 1 in transitional cases.
Schedule 1: Further Provisions Replacing Section 36(4) of the National Insurance Act 1965: increases of graduated retirement benefit and lump sum.
Schedule 2: Modification of Schedule 1.

The Secretary of State for Work and Pensions, in exercise of the powers conferred upon him by sections 62(1)(a) and (c) and 175(3) and (4) of the Social Security Contributions and Benefits Act 1992, and of all other powers enabling him in that behalf, after agreement by the Social Security Advisory Committee that proposals in respect of regulations 3 and 4, and paragraphs 2, 3, 7, 13, 14 and 18 of Schedule 1 in so far as they apply to regulation 4, should not be referred to it, the remainder of this Instrument containing only regulations made under provisions introduced by section 297 of, and Schedule 11 to, the Pensions Act 2004 and being made before the end of the period of 6 months beginning with the coming into force of those provisions, hereby makes the following Regulations:

Citation, commencement, effect and interpretation

1.—(1) These Regulations may be cited as the Social Security (Graduated Retirement Benefit) Regulations 2005 and shall come into force on 6th April 2005.   6.40

(2) Regulation 4 and paragraphs [¹4(2) and (3) and 14(2) and (3)] of Schedule 1 in so far as they apply to that regulation, shall not have effect in relation to incremental periods beginning before 6th April 2005.

(3) In these Regulations—
"the 1965 Act" means the National Insurance Act 1965;
"the Administration Act" means the Social Security Administration Act 1992;
"the Benefits Act" means the Social Security Contributions and Benefits Act 1992 and references to Schedule 5 are to Schedule 5 to that Act;
"incremental period" shall have the meaning ascribed to it in paragraph 4(6) of Schedule 1.

Amendment of the 1965 Act

2.—*Omitted as taken into account in the text of the Act set out in the Social Security (Graduated Retirement Benefit) (No.2) Regulations 1978.*   6.41

Amendment of Schedule 2 to the Social Security (Graduated Retirement Benefit) (No.2) Regulations 1978 and saving

3.—(1) Subject to paragraph (2), in Schedule 2 to the Social Security (Graduated Retirement Benefit) (No.2) Regulations 1978—   6.42
    (a) the word "and" at the end of paragraph 1(a) and paragraph 1(b); and
    (b) paragraphs 2 to 4,
shall be omitted.

(2) Schedule 2 to those Regulations shall have effect as if the amendments made by paragraph (1) had not been made in the case of—
    (a) periods of deferment (as defined by section 36(4A) of the 1965 Act) ending before 6th April 2005; and
    (b) incremental periods beginning before that date.

Schedule 1

6.43   **4.**—Schedule 1 to these Regulations (which makes further provision replacing section 36(4) of the 1965 Act) shall have effect.

Modification of Schedule 1 in transitional cases

6.44   **5.**—Schedule 1 shall be modified by Schedule 2 in relation to transitional cases and in this regulation, a "transitional case" means a case where a person's entitlement to graduated retirement benefit is deferred and the period of deferment begins before 6th April 2005 and continues on or after that day.

SCHEDULE 1   **Regulation 4**

FURTHER PROVISIONS REPLACING SECTION 36(4) OF THE NATIONAL INSURANCE ACT 1965:
INCREASES OF GRADUATED RETIREMENT BENEFIT AND LUMP SUMS

PART 1

INCREASE AND LUMP SUM WHERE ENTITLEMENT TO RETIREMENT PENSION
IS DEFERRED

Scope

6.45   **1.**—This Part applies only in respect of a person who is deferring entitlement to graduated retirement benefit by virtue of section 36(4A)(a) of the 1965 Act.

Increase or lump sum where pensioner's entitlement is deferred

6.46   **2.**—(1) Where a person's entitlement to a Category A or Category B retirement pension is deferred and that person elects, [² . . .]—

(a) that paragraph 1 of Schedule 5 (increase of pension) is to apply in relation to the period of deferment, paragraph 3 of this Schedule shall also apply in relation to that period;

(b) that paragraph 3A of Schedule 5 (lump sum) is to apply in relation to the period of deferment, paragraph 5 of this Schedule shall also apply in relation to that period.

(2) The reference to an election in sub-paragraph (1) includes an election a person is treated as having made under paragraph A1(2) of Schedule 5.

Increase where pensioner's entitlement is deferred

6.47   **3.**—(1) This paragraph applies where—

(a) entitlement to a Category A or Category B retirement pension is deferred and the period of deferment is less than 12 months; or

(b) paragraph 2(1)(a) applies.

(2) The rate of the person's graduated retirement benefit shall be increased by an amount equal to the aggregate of the increments to which he is entitled under paragraph 4 but only if that amount is enough to increase the rate of the benefit by at least 1 per cent.

Calculation of increment

6.48   **4.**—(1) A person is entitled to an increment under this paragraph for each complete incremental period in his period of deferment.

(2) The amount of the increment for an incremental period shall be 1/5th per cent. of the weekly rate of the graduated retirement benefit to which the person would have been entitled for the period if his entitlement to a Category A or Category B retirement pension had not been deferred.

(3) For the purposes of sub-paragraph (2), the weekly rate of graduated retirement benefit shall be taken to include any increase in the weekly rate of that benefit and the amount of the increment in respect of such an increase shall be 1/5th per cent. of its weekly rate for each incremental period in the period of deferment beginning on the day the increase occurred.

(4) Amounts under sub-paragraphs (2) and (3) shall be rounded to the nearest penny, taking any 1/2p as nearest to the next whole penny.

(5) Where an amount under sub-paragraph (2) or (3) would, apart from this sub-paragraph, be a sum less than 1/2p, the amount shall be taken to be zero, notwithstanding any provision of the Benefits Act, the Administration Act or the Pension Schemes Act 1993.

(6) In this paragraph, "incremental period" means any period of six days which are treated by the Social Security (Widow's Benefit and Retirement Pensions) Regulations 1979 as days of increment for the purposes of paragraph 2 of Schedule 5 in relation to the person and pension in question.

(7) Where one or more orders have come into force under section 150 of the Administration Act during the period of deferment, the rate for any incremental period shall be determined as if the order or orders had come into force before the beginning of the period of deferment.

Lump sum where pensioner's entitlement is deferred

5.—(1) This paragraph applies where paragraph 2(1)(b) applies.   **6.49**

(2) The person is entitled to an amount calculated in accordance with paragraph 6 (a "lump sum").

Calculation of lump sum

6.—(1) The lump sum is the accrued amount for the last accrual period beginning during   **6.50** the period of deferment.

(2) In this paragraph—

"accrued amount" means the amount calculated in accordance with sub-paragraph (3);

"accrual period" means any period of seven days beginning with the day of the week on which Category A or Category B retirement pension would have been payable to a person in accordance with regulation 22(3) of, and paragraph 5 of Schedule 6 to, the Social Security (Claims and Payments) Regulations 1987 [⁵ or in accordance with regulation 22C(3) or (4) of those Regulations], if his entitlement to a retirement pension had not been deferred, where that day falls within the period of deferment.

(3) The accrued amount for an accrual period for a person is—

$$(A + P) \times \sqrt[52]{(1 + R/100)}$$

where—

A is the accrued amount for the previous accrual period (or, in the case of the first accrual period beginning during the period of deferment, zero);

P is, subject to sub-paragraph (5), the amount of graduated retirement benefit to which the person would have been entitled for the accrual period if his entitlement to a Category A or Category B retirement pension had not been deferred;

R is—

(a) a percentage rate two per cent. higher than the Bank of England base rate; or

(b) if a higher rate is prescribed for the purposes of paragraphs 3B and 7B of Schedule 5, that higher rate.

(4) For the purposes of sub-paragraph (3), any change in the Bank of England base rate is to be treated as taking effect—

(a) at the beginning of the accrual period immediately following the accrual period during which the change took effect; or

(b) if regulations under paragraph 3B(4) of Schedule 5 so provide, at such other time as may be prescribed in those Regulations.

(5) Regulation 3 of the Social Security (Deferral of Retirement Pensions) Regulations 2005 shall have effect for the purposes of this paragraph in like manner to graduated retirement benefit as it does to retirement pension in the calculation of the lump sum under paragraph 3B of Schedule 5.

Increase or lump sum where pensioner's deceased spouse [² or civil partner] has deferred entitlement

7.—(1) This paragraph applies where—   **6.51**

(a) a [² widow, widower or surviving civil partner] ("W") is entitled to a Category A or Category B retirement pension;

(b) W was married to [² or in a civil partnership with] the other party to the marriage [² or civil partnership] ("S") when S died;

(c) S's entitlement to a Category A or Category B retirement pension was deferred when S died; and

(d) S's entitlement had been deferred throughout the period of 12 months ending with the day before S's death.

(2) Where W elects—

    (a) that paragraph 4 of Schedule 5 (increase of pension) is to apply in relation to the period of deferment, paragraph 8 of this Schedule shall also apply in relation to that period;

    (b) that paragraph 7A of Schedule 5 (lump sum) is to apply in relation to the period of deferment, paragraph 9 of this Schedule shall also apply in relation to that period.

(3) The reference to an election in sub-paragraph (2) includes an election W is treated as having made under paragraph 3C(3) of Schedule 5.

Increase where pensioner's deceased spouse [² or civil partner] has deferred entitlement

6.52   **8.**—(1) This paragraph applies where a [² widow, widower or surviving civil partner] is entitled to a Category A or Category B retirement pension, was married to [² or in a civil partnership with] the other party to the marriage [² or civil partnership] when S died and one of the following conditions is met—

    (a) S was entitled to graduated retirement benefit with an increase under this Schedule;

    (b) paragraph 7(2)(a) applies; or

    (c) paragraph 7 would apply to W but for the fact that the condition in sub-paragraph (1) (d) of that paragraph is not met.

(2) The increase in the weekly rate of W's graduated retirement benefit shall, in a case to which sub-paragraph (1) applies, be determined in accordance with section 37 of the 1965 Act as continued in force by virtue of regulations made under Schedule 3 to the Social Security (Consequential Provisions) Act 1975 or under Schedule 3 to the Social Security (Consequential Provisions) Act 1992.

Entitlement to lump sum where pensioner's deceased spouse [² or civil partner] has deferred entitlement

6.53   **9.**—(1) This paragraph applies where paragraph 7(2)(b) applies.

(2) W is entitled to an amount calculated in accordance with paragraph 10 (a "widowed person's [² or surviving civil partner's] lump sum").

Calculation of widowed person's [² or surviving civil partner's] lump sum

6.54   **10.**—(1) The widowed person's [² or surviving civil partner's] lump sum is the accrued amount for the last accrual period beginning during the period which—

    (a) began at the beginning of S's period of deferment; and

    (b) ended on the day before S's death.

(2) In this paragraph—

"S" means the other party to the marriage [² or civil partnership];

"accrued amount" means the amount calculated in accordance with sub-paragraph (3);

"accrual period" means any period of seven days beginning with the day of the week on which Category A or Category B retirement pension would have been payable to S in accordance with regulation 22(3) of, and paragraph 5 of Schedule 6 to, the Social Security (Claims and Payments) Regulations 1987 [⁵ or in accordance with regulation 22C(3) or (4) of those Regulations], if his entitlement to a retirement pension had not been deferred, where that day falls within S's period of deferment.

(3) The accrued amount for an accrual period for W is—

$$(A + P) \times {}^{52}\!\sqrt{(1 + R/100)}$$

where—

A is the accrued amount for the previous accrual period (or, in the case of the first accrual period beginning during the period mentioned in sub-paragraph (1), zero);

P is, subject to sub-paragraph (5), one-half of the graduated retirement benefit to which S would have been entitled for the accrual period if his entitlement had not been deferred during the period mentioned in sub-paragraph (1);

R is—

    (a) a percentage rate two per cent. higher than the Bank of England base rate; or

    (b) if a higher rate is prescribed for the purposes of paragraphs 3B and 7B of Schedule 5, that higher rate.

(4) For the purposes of sub-paragraph (3), any change in the Bank of England base rate is to be treated as taking effect—

(a) at the beginning of the accrual period immediately following the accrual period during which the change took effect; or

(b) if regulations under paragraph 7B(4) of Schedule 5 so provide, at such other time as may be prescribed.

(5) Regulation 3 of the Social Security (Deferral of Retirement Pensions) Regulations 2005 shall have effect for the purposes of this paragraph in like manner to graduated retirement benefit as it does to retirement pension in the calculation of the lump sum under paragraph 7B of Schedule 5.

(6) In any case where—

(a) there is a period between the death of S and the date on which W becomes entitled to a Category A or Category B retirement pension; and

(b) one or more orders have come into force under section 150 of the Administration Act during that period,

the amount of the lump sum shall be increased in accordance with that order or those orders.

PART 2

INCREASE OR LUMP SUM WHERE PERSON IS TREATED AS RECEIVING RETIREMENT PENSION AT A NOMINAL WEEKLY RATE

Scope

11.—This Part applies only in respect of a person who is deferring entitlement to graduated retirement benefit by virtue of section 36(4A)(b) of the 1965 Act.

6.55

Choice between increase and lump sum

12.—(1) Where the period of deferment is at least 12 months, a person shall, on becoming entitled to graduated retirement benefit, elect that—

6.56

(a) paragraph 13; or

(b) paragraph 15, is to apply in respect of that period.

[² (2) The election referred to in sub-paragraph (1) shall be made—

(a) on the date on which he claims graduated retirement benefit; or

(b) within the period after claiming graduated retirement benefit prescribed in paragraph 20B,

and in the manner prescribed in paragraph 20C.]

(3) If no election under sub-paragraph (1) is made within the period referred to in sub-paragraph (2)(b), the person is to be treated as having made an election under sub-paragraph (1)(b).

(4) A person who has made an election under sub-paragraph (1) (including one that the person is treated by sub-paragraph (3) as having made) may change the election in the circumstances [², manner and within the period prescribed, in paragraph 20D].

Increase

13.—(1) This paragraph applies where—

6.57

(a) the period of deferment is less than 12 months; or

(b) the person has made an election under paragraph 12(1)(a) in respect of the period of deferment.

(2) The rate of the person's graduated retirement benefit shall be increased by an amount equal to the aggregate of the increments to which he is entitled under paragraph 14 but only if that amount is enough to increase the rate of the benefit by at least one per cent.

Calculation of increment

14.—(1) A person is entitled to an increment under this paragraph for each complete incremental period in the period of deferment.

6.58

(2) The amount of the increment for an incremental period shall be 1/5th per cent. of the weekly rate of the graduated retirement benefit to which the person would have been entitled for the period if his entitlement to graduated retirement benefit had not been deferred.

(3) For the purposes of sub-paragraph (2), the weekly rate of graduated retirement benefit shall be taken to include any increase in the weekly rate of that benefit and the amount of the increment in respect of such an increase shall be 1/5th per cent. of its weekly rate for each incremental period in the period of deferment beginning on the day the increase occurred.

(4) Amounts under sub-paragraphs (2) and (3) shall be rounded to the nearest penny, taking any 1/2p as nearest to the next whole penny.

(5) Where an amount under sub-paragraph (2) or (3) would, apart from this sub-paragraph,

be a sum less than 1/2p, the amount shall be taken to be zero, notwithstanding any provision of the Benefits Act, the Administration Act or the Pension Schemes Act 1993.

(6) Where one or more orders have come into force under section 150 of the Administration Act during the period of deferment, the rate for any incremental period shall be determined as if the order or orders had come into force before the beginning of the period of deferment.

Lump sum

6.59   **15.**—(1) This paragraph applies where paragraph 12(1)(b) applies.

(2) The person is entitled to an amount calculated in accordance with paragraph 16 (a "lump sum").

Calculation of lump sum

6.60   **16.**—(1) The lump sum is the accrued amount for the last accrual period beginning during the period of deferment.

(2) In this paragraph—

"accrued amount" means the amount calculated in accordance with sub-paragraph (3);

"accrual period" means any period of seven days beginning with the day of the week on which Category A or Category B retirement pension would have been payable to a person in accordance with regulation 22(3) of, and paragraph 5 of Schedule 6 to, the Social Security (Claims and Payments) Regulations 1987 [5 or in accordance with regulation 22C(3) or (4) of those Regulations], if he had been entitled to it, where that day falls within the period of deferment.

(3) The accrued amount for an accrual period for a person is—

$$(A + P) \times {}^{52}\sqrt{(1 + R/100)}$$

where—

A is the accrued amount for the previous accrual period (or, in the case of the first accrual period beginning during the period of deferment, zero);

P is, subject to sub-paragraph (5), the amount of graduated retirement benefit to which the person would have been entitled for the accrual period if he had been entitled to it;

R is—

(a) a percentage rate two per cent. higher than the Bank of England base rate; or

(b) if a higher rate is prescribed for the purposes of paragraphs 3B and 7B of Schedule 5, that higher rate.

(4) For the purposes of sub-paragraph (3), any change in the Bank of England base rate is to be treated as taking effect—

(a) at the beginning of the accrual period immediately following the accrual period during which the change took effect; or

(b) if regulations under paragraph 3B(4) of Schedule 5 so provide, at such other time as may be prescribed in those Regulations.

(5) Regulation 3 of the Social Security (Deferral of Retirement Pensions) Regulations 2005 shall have effect for the purposes of this paragraph in like manner to graduated retirement benefit as it does to retirement pension in the calculation of the lump sum under paragraph 3B of Schedule 5.

Choice between increase and lump sum where person's deceased spouse [3 or civil partner] has deferred entitlement to graduated retirement benefit

6.61   **17.**—(1) This paragraph applies where—

(a) a [3 widow, widower or surviving civil partner] ("W") is entitled to a Category A or Category B retirement pension;

(b) W was married to [3 or in a civil partnership with] the other party to the marriage [3 or civil partnership] ("S") when S died;

(c) S's entitlement to graduated retirement benefit was deferred when S died; and

(d) S's entitlement had been deferred throughout the period of 12 months ending with the day before S's death.

(2) W shall elect either that—

(a) paragraph 18; or

(b) paragraph 19,

is to apply in respect of S's period of deferment.

[² (3) The election referred to in sub-paragraph (2) shall be made within the period prescribed in paragraph 20B and in the manner prescribed in paragraph 20C.]

(4) If no election under sub-paragraph (2) is made within the period referred to in sub-paragraph [² (3)], the person is to be treated as having made an election under subparagraph (2)(b).

[² (5) A person who has made an election under sub-paragraph (2) (including one that the person is treated by sub-paragraph (4) as having made) may change the election in the circumstances, manner and within the period prescribed in paragraph 20D.]

Increase where person's deceased spouse [³ or civil partner] has deferred entitlement to graduated retirement benefit

18.—(1) This paragraph applies where a [³ widow, widower or surviving civil partner] is entitled to graduated retirement benefit, was married to [³ or in a civil partnership with] the other party to the marriage [³or civil partnership] when S died and one of the following conditions is met— **6.62**

  (a) S was entitled to graduated retirement benefit with an increase under this Schedule;
  (b) W is a widow or widower to whom paragraph 17 applies and has made an election under paragraph 17(2)(a); or
  (c) paragraph 17 would apply to W but for the fact that the condition in sub-paragraph (1)(d) of that paragraph is not met.

(2) The increase in the weekly rate of W's graduated retirement benefit shall, in a case to which sub-paragraph (1) applies, be determined in accordance with section 37 of the 1965 Act as continued in force by virtue of regulations made under Schedule 3 to the Social Security (Consequential Provisions) Act 1975 or under Schedule 3 to the Social Security (Consequential Provisions) Act 1992.

Entitlement to lump sum where person's deceased spouse [³ or civil partner] has deferred entitlement to graduated retirement benefit

19.—(1) This paragraph applies where paragraph 17(2)(b) applies. **6.63**

(2) W is entitled to an amount calculated in accordance with paragraph 20 (a "widowed person's [³ or surviving civil partner's] lump sum").

Calculation of widowed person's [³ or surviving civil partner's] lump sum

20.—(1) The widowed person's lump sum is the accrued amount for last accrual period beginning during the period which— **6.64**

  (a) began at the beginning of S's period of deferment; and
  (b) ended on the day before S's death.

(2) In this paragraph—

"S" means the other party to the marriage [³ or civil partnership];
"accrued amount" means the amount calculated in accordance with sub-paragraph (3);
"accrual period" means any period of seven days beginning with the day of the week on which Category A or Category B retirement pension would have been payable to S in accordance with regulation 22(3) of, and paragraph 5 of Schedule 6 to, the Social Security (Claims and Payments) Regulations 1987 [⁵ or in accordance with regulation 22C(3) or (4) of those Regulations], if he had been entitled to it, where that day falls within S's period of deferment.

(3) The accrued amount for an accrual period for W is—

$$(A + P) \times \sqrt[52]{(1 + R/100)}$$

where—
A is the accrued amount for the previous accrual period (or, in the case of the first accrual period beginning during the period mentioned in sub-paragraph (1), zero);
P is, subject to sub-paragraph (5), one-half of the graduated retirement benefit to which S would have been entitled for the accrual period if he had been entitled to it during the period mentioned in sub-paragraph (1);
R is—

  (a) a percentage rate two per cent. higher than the Bank of England base rate; or
  (b) if a higher rate is prescribed for the purposes of paragraphs 3B and 7B of Schedule 5, that higher rate.

(4) For the purposes of sub-paragraph (3), any change in the Bank of England base rate is to be treated as taking effect—

(a) at the beginning of the accrual period immediately following the accrual period during which the change took effect; or

(b) if regulations under paragraph 7B(4) of Schedule 5 so provide, at such other time as may be prescribed.

(5) Regulation 3 of the Social Security (Deferral of Retirement Pensions) Regulations 2005 shall have effect for the purposes of this paragraph in like manner to graduated retirement benefit as it does to retirement pension in the calculation of the lump sum under paragraph 7B of Schedule 5.

(6) In any case where—

(a) there is a period between the death of S and the date on which W becomes entitled to graduated retirement benefit; and

(b) one or more orders have come into force under section 150 of the Administration Act during that period,

the amount of the lump sum shall be increased in accordance with that order or those orders.

[³ Transitional provision relating to widower's entitlement to increase of graduated retirement benefit or lump sum

6.65
20ZA.—In the case of a widower who attains pensionable age before 6th April 2010, paragraphs 17 to 19 shall not apply unless he was over pensionable age when his wife died.

Transitional provision relating to civil partner's entitlement to increase of graduated retirement benefit or lump sum

6.66
20ZB.—In the case of a civil partner who attains pensionable age before 6th April 2010, paragraphs 17 to 19 shall not apply unless he or she was over pensionable age when his or her civil partner died.]

[² PART 2A

ELECTIONS UNDER PART 2

Scope and interpretation

6.67
20A.—(1) This Part applies in respect of elections which a person makes or is treated as having made under Part 2.

(2) In this Part, "elector" means the person who may make an election under paragraph 12(1) or 17(2).

Timing of election

6.68
20B.—(1) The period for making an election under paragraph 12(1) is, subject to sub-paragraph (4), three months starting on the date shown on the notice issued by the Secretary of State following the claim for graduated retirement benefit, confirming that the elector is required to make that election.

(2) The period for making an election under paragraph 17(2) is, subject to sub-paragraph (4), three months starting on the date shown on the notice issued by the Secretary of State following W's claim for a Category A or Category B retirement pension or, if later, the date of S's death, confirming that the elector is required to make that election.

(3) Where more than one notice has been issued by the Secretary of State in accordance with sub-paragraph (1) or (2), the periods prescribed in those sub-paragraphs shall only commence from the date shown on the latest such notice.

(4) The periods specified in sub-paragraphs (1) and (2) may be extended by the Secretary of State if he considers it reasonable to do so in any particular case.

(5) Nothing in this paragraph shall prevent the making of an election on or after claiming graduated retirement benefit or, as the case may be, Category A or Category B retirement pension, but before the issue of the notice referred to in sub-paragraph (1) or (2).

Manner of making election

6.69
20C.—An election under paragraph 12(1) or 17(2) may be made—

(a) in writing to an office specified by the Secretary of State for accepting such elections; or

(b) except where the Secretary of State directs in any particular case that the election must be made in accordance with sub-paragraph (a), by telephone call to the telephone number specified by the Secretary of State.

Change of election

6.70
20D.—(1) Subject to sub-paragraphs (2) and (6), this paragraph applies in the case of an election which—

   (a) has been made under paragraph 12(1) or 17(2); or

   (b) has been treated as made under paragraph 12(3) or 17(4).

  (2) This paragraph does not apply in the case of an election which is—

   (a) made, or treated as made, by an elector who has subsequently died; or

   (b) treated as having been made by virtue of regulation [⁴ 30(5E) or (5G)] of the Social Security (Claims and Payments) Regulations 1987.

  (3) An election specified in sub-paragraph (1) may be changed by way of application made no later than the last day of the period specified in sub-paragraph (4).

  (4) The period specified for the purposes of sub-paragraph (3) is, subject to sub-paragraph (5), three months after the date shown on the written notification issued by the Secretary of State to the elector, confirming the election which the elector has made or is treated as having made.

  (5) The period specified in sub-paragraph (4) may be extended by the Secretary of State if he considers it reasonable to do so in any particular case.

  (6) An election specified in sub-paragraph (1) may not be changed where—

   (a) there has been a previous change of election under this paragraph in respect of the same period of deferment;

   (b) the application is to change the election to one under paragraph 12(1)(a) or 17(2)(a) and any amount paid to him by way of, or on account of, a lump sum pursuant to paragraph 15 or 19, has not been repaid in full to the Secretary of State within the period specified in sub-paragraph (4) or, as the case may be, (5); or

   (c) the application is to change the election to one under paragraph 12(1)(b) or 17(2)(b) and the amount actually paid by way of an increase of graduated retirement benefit, or actually paid on account of such an increase, would exceed the amount to which the elector would be entitled by way of a lump sum.

  (7) For the purposes of sub-paragraph (6)(b), repayment in full of the amount paid by way of, or on account of, a lump sum shall only be treated as having occurred if repaid to the Secretary of State in the currency in which that amount was originally paid.

  (8) Where the application is to change the election to one under paragraph 12(1)(b) or 17(2)(b) and sub-paragraph (6)(c) does not apply, any amount paid by way of an increase of graduated retirement benefit, or on account of such an increase, in respect of the period of deferment for which the election was originally made, shall be treated as having been paid on account of the lump sum to which the elector is entitled under paragraph 15 or 19.

  (9) An application under sub-paragraph (3) to change an election may be made—

   (a) in writing to an office specified by the Secretary of State for accepting such applications; or

   (b) except where the Secretary of State directs in any particular case that the application must be made in accordance with paragraph (a), by telephone call to the telephone number specified by the Secretary of State].

PART 3

SUPPLEMENTARY

Supplementary

  21.—Any lump sum calculated under paragraph 6, 10, 16 or 20 must be rounded to the nearest penny, taking any 1/2p as nearest to the next whole penny above.   6.71

GENERAL NOTE

  The sums which are lump sums to which surviving spouses or civil partners will become entitled under Sch.1 were increased by 2.4 per cent with effect from April 8, 2019: see art.12(3) of the Social Security Benefits Up-rating Order 2019 (SI 2019/480).   6.72

SCHEDULE 2   **Regulation 5**

MODIFICATION OF SCHEDULE 1

  1.—In paragraph 2(1), for paragraph (b) there shall be substituted the following paragraph—   6.73

"(b) that paragraph 1 of Schedule 5 is to apply in relation to so much of the period of deferment which falls before the first day of the first accrual period (as defined by paragraph 3B(2) of that Schedule) beginning on or after 6th April 2005 ('the first part') and that paragraph 3A of that Schedule is to apply in relation to the remainder of the period of deferment ('the second part'), paragraph 3 of this Schedule shall apply in relation to the first part and paragraph 5 of this Schedule shall apply in relation to the second part.".

2.—In paragraph 3(2), for the words from "that amount" to the end of the sub-paragraph, there shall be substituted—

"—

(a) there are at least 7 incremental periods in the period of deferment;
(b) there are at least 5 incremental periods in the period of deferment and the amount of the increment for at least one of those periods is calculated in accordance with paragraph 4(2); or
(c) paragraph 2(1)(b) applies and there is at least one incremental period before the first day of the first accrual period.".

3.—At the end of paragraph 6(1), there shall be added the words "or, if greater, the amount equal to the total amount of graduated retirement benefit which would have been payable to the person during the period of 12 months ending with the last day of the period of deferment if his entitlement had not been deferred".

4.—In paragraph 7—
(a) at the end of sub-paragraph (1)(d), there shall be added the words "and throughout the period of 12 months falling after 5th April 2005";
(b) for sub-paragraph (2)(b) there shall be substituted the following sub-paragraph—

"(b) that paragraph 4 of Schedule 5 is to apply in relation to so much of S's period of deferment which falls before the first day of the first accrual period (as defined by paragraph 7B(2) of that Schedule) beginning on or after 6th April 2005 ('the first part') and that paragraph 7A of that Schedule is to apply in relation to the remainder of the period of deferment ('the second part'), paragraph 8 of this Schedule shall apply in relation to the first part and paragraph 9 of this Schedule shall apply in relation to the second part.".

5.—[² *Omitted*].

6.—In paragraph 12(1)—
(a) after the words "12 months" there shall be inserted the words "and at least 12 months of that period falls after 5th April 2005";
(b) for sub-paragraph (b), there shall be substituted the following sub-paragraph—

"(b) that paragraph 13 is to apply in relation to so much of the period of deferment which falls before the first day of the first accrual period (as defined in paragraph 16(2)) for the purposes of paragraph 15 and that paragraph 14 is to apply in relation to the remainder of the period of deferment.".

7.—In paragraph 13(2), for the words from "that amount" to the end of the sub-paragraph, there shall be substituted—

"—

(a) there are at least 7 incremental periods in the period of deferment;
(b) there are at least 5 incremental periods in the period of deferment and the amount of the increment for at least one of those periods is calculated in accordance with paragraph 14(2); or
(c) the person has made (or is treated as having made) an election under paragraph 12(1)(b) and there is at least one incremental period before the first day of the first accrual period.".

8.—At the end of paragraph 16(1), there shall be added the words "or, if greater, the amount equal to the total amount of graduated retirement benefit to which the person would have been entitled for the period of 12 months ending with the last day of the period of deferment if his entitlement had not been deferred".

9.—In paragraph 17—
(a) at the end of sub-paragraph (1)(d), there shall be added the words "and throughout the period of 12 months falling after 5th April 2005";
(b) for sub-paragraph (2)(b), there shall be substituted the following paragraph—

"(b) that paragraph 18 is to apply in relation to so much of S's period of deferment which falls before the first day of the first accrual period (as defined in paragraph 20(2)) for the purposes of paragraph 19 and that paragraph 19 is to apply in relation to the remainder of that period of deferment.".

10.—[² *Omitted*].

AMENDMENTS

1. Social Security (Graduated Retirement Benefit)(Amendment) Regulations 2005 (SI 2005/846) reg.2 (April 5, 2005)

2. Social Security (Deferral of Retirement Pensions, Shared Additional Pensions and Graduated Retirement Benefit) (Miscellaneous Provisions) Regulations 2005 (SI 2005/2677) (April 6, 2006).

3. Social Security (Retirement Pensions and Graduated Retirement Benefits) (Widowers and Civil Partnership) Regulations 2005 (SI 2005/3078) (April 6, 2006).

4. Social Security (Deferral of Pensions etc) Regulations 2006 (SI 2006/516) (April 6, 2006).

5. Occupational Pension Schemes and Social Security (Schemes that were Contracted-out and Graduated Retirement Benefit) (Miscellaneous Amendments) Regulations 2017 (SI 2017/354) reg.3 (April 6, 2017).

The Social Security (Maximum Additional Pension) Regulations 2010

(SI 2010/426) *(as amended)*

ARRANGEMENT OF REGULATIONS

1.   Citation and Commencement   6.74
2.   Interpretation.
3.   Prescribed maximum additional pension.
3A. Prescribed maximum additional pension for survivors who become entitled on or after 6th April 2016.

The Secretary of State for Work and Pensions makes the following Regulations in exercise of the powers conferred by sections 52(3), 122(1), 175(1) of the Social Security Contributions and Benefits Act 1992.

The Social Security Advisory Committee has agreed that proposals in respect of these Regulations should not be referred to it.

Citation and commencement

1.—These Regulations may be cited as the Social Security (Maximum   6.75
Additional Pension) Regulations 2010 and shall come into force on 6th April 2010.

GENERAL NOTE

Following the reforms introduced from April 6, 2016 by the Pensions Act   6.76
2014, these regulations only apply directly to periods before that date, save for the new reg.3A. For the provisions that apply from that date see the State Pension Regulations 2015 below.

Interpretation

2.—(1) In these Regulations—   6.77
"applicable limit" has the meaning given by section 44(7)(c);

[¹ "relevant day" means the day on which the survivor would, but for section 43 (persons entitled to more than one retirement pension), have become entitled to both—

(a) a Category A retirement pension; and

(b) a Category B retirement pension by virtue of the contributions of a spouse or civil partner who has died,

or would have become so entitled if the survivor's entitlement to a Category A or Category B retirement pension had not been deferred;]

"relevant year" has the meaning given by section 44(7)(a);

"survivor" means surviving spouse or surviving civil partner.

(2) In these Regulations a reference to a section by number alone is a reference to the section so numbered in the Social Security Contributions and Benefits Act 1992.

AMENDMENT

1. Pensions Act (Consequential, Supplementary and Incidental Amendments) Order 2015 (SI 2015/1985) art.33 (April 6, 2016).

Prescribed maximum additional pension

6.78
3.—[¹ (A1) This regulation applies to a survivor whose relevant day is before 6th April 2016.]

(1) For the purposes of section 52(3) (increase of additional pension in the Category A retirement pension for surviving spouses) the maximum additional pension shall be the amount of additional pension to which a person is entitled where that person—

(a) has reached pensionable age on [¹ the survivor's relevant day]; and

(b) in respect of each relevant year has an earnings factor specified in paragraph (3).

(2) [¹ ...]

(3) For the purposes of paragraph (1)(b), the specified earnings factor is an earnings factor which—

(a) is equal to 53 times that year's applicable limit, before any increase under section 148 of the Social Security Administration Act 1992 (revaluation of earnings factors); and

(b) is derived from earnings on which primary Class 1 contributions were paid.

AMENDMENT

1. Pensions Act (Consequential, Supplementary and Incidental Amendments) Order 2015 (SI 2015/1985) art.33 (April 6, 2016).

6.79
[¹ Prescribed maximum additional pension for survivors who become entitled on or after 6th April 2016

3A.—(1) This regulation applies to a survivor whose relevant day is on or after 6th April 2016.

(2) For the purposes of section 52(3), the maximum additional pension shall be [² £176.41.]

AMENDMENTS

1. Pensions Act (Consequential, Supplementary and Incidental Amendments) Order 2015 (SI 2015/1985) art.33 (April 6, 2016).

2. Social Security Benefits Up-rating Order 2019 (SI 2019/480) art.14 (April 8, 2019).

The Social Security (Retirement Pensions etc.) (Transitional Provisions) Regulations 2005

(SI 2005/469) (as amended)

ARRANGEMENT OF REGULATIONS

1.	Citation, commencement and interpretation.	6.80
2.	Modification of Schedule 5 to the Act.	
3.	Modification of Schedule 5A to the Act.	

The Secretary of State for Work and Pensions, in exercise of the powers conferred upon him by paragraph 27 of Schedule 11 to the Pensions Act 2004 and of all other powers enabling him in that behalf, hereby makes the following Regulations:

Citation, commencement and interpretation

1.—(1) These Regulations may be cited as the Social Security (Retirement   6.81
Pensions etc.) (Transitional Provisions) Regulations 2005 and shall come into force on 6th April 2005.

(2) In these Regulations—

"the Act" means the Social Security Contributions and Benefits Act 1992;

"period of deferment" shall be construed in accordance with section 55(3) or, as the case may be, section 55C(3), of the Act;

"transitional case" means a case where a person's entitlement to retirement pension or shared additional pension is deferred and the period of deferment begins before 6th April 2005 and continues on or after that day.

GENERAL NOTE

Following the reforms introduced from April 6, 2016 by the Pensions Act 2014   6.82
these regulations only apply directly to periods before that date. For the provisions that apply from that date see the State Pension Regulations 2015 below.

Modification of Schedule 5 to the Act

2.—(1) Schedule 5 to the Act (pension increase or lump sum where entit-   6.83
lement to retirement pension is deferred) shall be modified in relation to transitional cases in accordance with the following paragraphs.

(2) In paragraph A1(1) (choice between increase of pension and lump sum where pensioner's entitlement is deferred)—

(a) after the words "12 months" there shall be inserted the words "and at least 12 months of that period fall after 5th April 2005";

(b) for paragraph (b) there shall be substituted the following paragraph—

"(b) that paragraph 1 is to apply in relation to so much of the period of deferment as falls before the first day of the first accrual period (as defined by paragraph 3B(2)) beginning on or after 6th April 2005 and that paragraph 3A

917

(entitlement to lump sum) is to apply in relation to the remainder of the period of deferment.".

(3) In paragraph 1(2) (increase of pension where pensioner's entitlement is deferred), for the words from "that amount" to the end of the sub-paragraph, there shall be substituted—

"(a) there are at least 7 incremental periods in the period of deferment;

(b) there are at least 5 incremental periods in the period of deferment and the amount of the increment for at least one of those periods is calculated in accordance with paragraph 2(3) as in force in relation to incremental periods beginning on or after 6th April 2005; or

(c) the person has made (or is treated as having made) an election under paragraph A1(1)(b) and there is at least one incremental period before the first day of the first accrual period (as defined by paragraph 3B(2)) beginning on or after 6th April 2005.".

(4) In paragraph 3B (calculation of lump sum)—

(a) at the end of sub-paragraph (1), there shall be added the words "or, if greater, the amount equal to the total amount of Category A or Category B retirement pension [² (excluding any increase under section 83, 84 or 85)] which would have been payable to the person during the period of 12 months ending with the last day of the period of deferment if his entitlement had not been deferred";

(b) in the definition of "accrual period" in sub-paragraph (2), for the words "a prescribed day of the week", there shall be substituted the words "the day of the week on which the person's retirement pension would have been payable had his entitlement not been deferred";

(5) In paragraph 3C (choice between increase of pension and lump sum where pensioner's deceased spouse has deferred entitlement)—

(a) at the end of paragraph (1)(d), there shall be added the words "and throughout the period of 12 months beginning with 6th April 2005";

(b) for paragraph (2)(b) there shall be substituted the following paragraph—

"(b) that paragraph 4 is to apply in relation to so much of S's period of deferment as falls before the first day of the first accrual period (as defined by paragraph 7B(2)) beginning on or after 6th April 2005 and that paragraph 7A (entitlement to lump sum) is to apply in relation to the remainder of that period of deferment.".

(6) In paragraph 7B (calculation of lump sum)—

(a) [¹ *omitted*];

(b) in the definition of "accrual period" in sub-paragraph (2), for the words "a prescribed day of the week", there shall be substituted the words "the day of the week on which S's retirement pension would have been payable had his entitlement not been deferred".

AMENDMENTS

1. Social Security (Deferral of Retirement Pensions, Shared Additional Pensions and Graduated Retirement Benefit) (Miscellaneous Provisions) Regulations 2005 (SI 2005/2677) (April 6, 2006).

2. Social Security (Deferral of Retirement Pensions etc.) Regulations 2006 (SI 2006/516) (April 6, 2006)

Modification of Schedule 5A to the Act

3.—(1) Schedule 5A to the Act (pension increase or lump sum where entitlement to shared additional pension is deferred) shall be modified in relation to transitional cases in accordance with the following paragraphs.

(2) In paragraph 1(1) (choice between increase of pension and lump sum where pensioner's entitlement is deferred)—

(a) after the words "12 months" there shall be inserted the words "and at least 12 months of that period fall after 5th April 2005";

(b) for paragraph (b) there shall be substituted the following paragraph—

"(b) that paragraph 2 is to apply in relation to so much of the period of deferment as falls before the first day of the first accrual period (as defined by paragraph 5(2)) beginning on or after 6th April 2005 and that paragraph 4 (entitlement to lump sum) is to apply in relation to the remainder of the period of deferment.".

(3) In paragraph 2(2) (increase of pension where pensioner's entitlement is deferred), for the words from "that amount" to the end of the sub-paragraph, there shall be substituted—

"(a) there are at least 7 incremental periods in the period of deferment;

(b) there are at least 5 incremental periods in the period of deferment and the amount of the increment for at least one of those periods is calculated in accordance with paragraph 3(2); or

(c) the person has made (or is treated as having made) an election under paragraph 1(1)(b) and there is at least one incremental period before the first day of the first accrual period (as defined by paragraph 5(2)) beginning on or after 6th April 2005."

(4) In paragraph 5 (calculation of lump sum)—

(a) at the end of sub-paragraph (1), there shall be added the words "or, if greater, the amount equal to the total amount of shared additional pension which would have been payable to the person during the period of 12 months ending with the last day of the period of deferment if his entitlement had not been deferred";

(b) in the definition of "accrual period" in sub-paragraph (2), for the words "a prescribed day of the week", there shall be substituted the words "the day of the week on which the person's shared additional pension would have been payable had his entitlement not been deferred".

Social Security (Widow's Benefit and Retirement Pensions) Regulations 1979

(SI 1979/642) *(as amended)*

ARRANGEMENT OF REGULATIONS

1. Citation, commencement and interpretation.
1A. Disapplication of section 1(1A) of the Administration Act for the purposes of retirement pension.
2. Election to be treated as not having retired.
3. Provisions applying after election.

6.84

6.85

3A. Calculating periods of incapacity for work for welfare to work beneficiaries entitled to an increase of long-term incapacity benefit.
4. Days to be treated as days of increment.
5. Modification of paragraph 2(1) to (3) of Schedule 1 to the Pensions Act.
6. Rate of benefit where the second contribution condition in paragraph 5 of Schedule 3 to the Social Security Contributions and Benefits Act 1992 is not satisfied
6A. Proportion of retirement pension where the contribution condition in paragraph 5A of Schedule 3 to the Social Security Contributions and Benefits Act 1992 is not satisfied
6B. Regulations 6A and 6B: supplemental
7. Category B retirement pension for certain widows by virtue of husband's contributions.
7A. Category B retirement pension for surviving spouses and surviving civil partners by virtue of deceased spouse's or deceased civil partner's contributions
8. Substitution of former spouse's or former civil partner's contribution record to give entitlement to a Category A retirement pension.
9. Conditions of entitlement to a Category C retirement pension.
10. Conditions for entitlement to a Category D retirement pension.
11. Category C retirement pension for widows of men over pensionable age on 5th July, 1948.
12. Category C retirement pension for certain women whose marriage has been terminated otherwise than by death.
13. Benefit corresponding to a widow's pension for widows of men over pensionable age on 5th July, 1948.
14. Benefit corresponding to a widowed mother's allowance for widows of men over pensionable age on 5th July, 1948.
15. Restriction on benefit under regulations 13 and 14 in certain cases.
16. Provision in relation to entitlement to child benefit for the purposes of a widowed mother's allowance.
16ZA. Provision in relation to entitlement to child benefit for the purposes of a widowed parent's allowance.
16A. Disapplication of section 1(1A) of the Administration Act for the purposes of widowed mother's allowance.
17. Provisions relating to age addition for persons not in receipt of a retirement pension.
18. *Omitted.*

The Secretary of State for Social Services, in exercise of the powers conferred upon him by sections 29(5), 30(3), 33, 39(1) and (4), 40(2), 85(1) and 162 of, and Schedule 20 to, the Social Security Act 1975, section 20 of, and paragraphs 2(2)(a) and 3 of Schedule 1 to, the Social Security Pensions Act 1975 and of all other powers enabling him in that behalf, hereby makes the following regulations which only consolidate the regulations herein revoked and which accordingly, by virtue of paragraph 20 of Schedule 15 to the Social Security Act 1975, are not subject to the requirement of section 139(1) of that Act for prior reference to the National Insurance Advisory Committee:

Citation, commencement and interpretation

6.86   1.—(1) These regulations may be cited as the Social Security (Widow's Benefit and Retirement Pensions) Regulations 1979 and shall come into operation on 10th July 1979.

(2) In these regulations, unless the context otherwise requires—

"the Act" means Social Security Act 1975

[¹ "bereavement allowance" means an allowance awarded in accordance with section 39B of the Social Security Contributions and Benefits Act 1992 [¹¹ (as in force immediately before it was repealed by paragraph 13 of Schedule 16 to the Pensions Act 2014)];]

[² "civil partner" in relation to any person who has been in a civil partnership more than once means the last civil partner;]

[⁹ . . .]

"husband", "wife" or "spouse" in relation to any person who has been married more than once means the last husband, last wife or last spouse respectively;

"a period of at least 10 years" means a period of, or periods amounting in the aggregate to, at least 3,652 days;

[⁵ . . .]

[⁹ . . .]

[³ "the determining authority" means, as the case may require, the Secretary of State, [⁸ the First tier Tribunal or the Upper Tribunal]]

"section 9(2), 9(3) or 10(2) increase" means an increase under section 9(2), 9(3) or 10(2), respectively, of the Act of a person's Category A retirement pension attributable to his spouse's contributions;

"Service Pensions Instrument" means a provision and only a provision of any Royal Warrant, Order in Council or other instrument (not being a 1914–18 War Injuries Scheme) under which a disablement pension (not including a pension calculated or determined by reference to length of service) may be paid out of public funds in respect of any disablement, wound, injury or disease due to service in the naval, military or air force of the Crown or in any nursing service or other auxiliary service of any of the said forces or in the Home Guard or in any other organisation established under the control of the Defence Council or formerly established under the control of the Admiralty, the Army Council, or the Air Council;

[⁶ "shared additional pension" means a shared additional pension under Section 55A [¹⁰ or 55AA] of the Social Security Contributions and Benefit Act 1992;]

"1914–18 War Injuries Scheme" means any scheme made under the Injuries in War (Compensation) Act 1914 or under the Injuries in War Compensation Act 1914 (Session 2) or any Government scheme for compensation in respect of persons injured in any merchant ship or fishing vessel as the result of hostilities during the 1914–18 war;

"unemployability supplement" has the extended meaning assigned to it in regulation 2 of the Social Security (Overlapping Benefits) Regulations 1979 and further includes benefit corresponding to an unemployability supplement by virtue of regulations under section 159(3) (a) of the Act;

[¹² widowed mother's allowance" means an allowance referred to in section 37 of the Social Security Contributions and Benefits Act 1992 (widowed mother's allowance: deaths before 9 April 2001).]

[¹ "widowed parent's allowance" means an allowance referred to in section 39A of the Social Security Contributions and Benefits Act 1992;]

"year" means tax year.

(3) For the purposes of these regulations a person who has obtained a decree absolute of presumption of death and dissolution of marriage under the Matrimonial Causes Act 1973 shall, notwithstanding that the

spouse whose death has been presumed is dead, be treated as a person whose marriage has been terminated otherwise than by the death of his spouse unless the date of his death is established to the satisfaction of the determining authority, and, in relation to a person who is so treated, the marriage in question shall be treated as having been terminated on the date of the decree absolute.

[⁴ (3A) For the purposes of regulation 8 of these Regulations, where, before the coming into force of the Nullity of Marriages Act 1971 a decree of nullity was granted in relation to a person on the ground that the marriage was voidable, that person shall be treated as a person whose marriage has been terminated by divorce from the date on which that decree was made absolute.]

(4) For the purposes of regulations 11(1)(d), 12(3) and 13(2) a person shall be deemed to be, or to have been, entitled to a pension or benefit if he would have been entitled had he made a claim for it.

AMENDMENTS

1. Social Security (Benefits for Widows and Widowers) (Consequential Amendments) Regulation 2000 (SI 2000/1483) reg.8 (April 9, 2001).

2. Social Security (Abolition of Earnings Rule) (Consequential) Regulations 1989 (SI 1989/1642), reg.11 (October 1, 1989).

3. Social Security Act 1998 (Commencement No. 9, and Savings and Consequential and Transitional Provisions) Order 1999 (SI 1999/2422) (September 6, 1999).

4. Social Security (Widows' Benefit and Retirement Pensions) Amendment Regulations 1995 (SI 1995/74) reg.1 (February 10, 1995).

5. Social Security (Deferral of Retirement Pensions) Regulations 2005 (SI 2005/453) reg.4 (April 6, 2005).

6. Shared Additional Pensions (Miscellaneous Amendments) regulations 2005 (SI 2005/1551) (July 6, 2005).

7. Civil Partnership (consequential amendments) Regulations 2005 (SI 2005/2878) (December 5, 2005).

8. Tribunals, Courts and Enforcement Act 2007 Sch.1 (November 3, 2008).

9. Social Security (State Pensions and National Insurance Credits) Regulations 2009 (SI 2009/2206) reg.6 (April 6, 2010).

10. The Pensions Act 2014 (Consequential, Supplementary and Incidental Amendments) Order 2015 (SI 2015/1985) art.5 (April 6, 2016).

11. The Pensions Act 2014 (Consequential, Supplementary and Incidental Amendments) Order 2017 (SI 2017/422) art.7 (April 6, 2017).

12. Social Security (Miscellaneous Amendments) Regulations 2017 (SI 2017/1015) reg.3(2) (December 6, 2018).

GENERAL NOTE

6.87   Following the reforms introduced from April 6, 2016 by the Pensions Act 2014 these regulations only apply directly to retirement pensions in or for periods before that date. For the provisions that apply from that date see the State Pension Regulations 2015 below.

Note that the amendment effected by the Social Security (State Pensions and National Insurance Credits) Regulations 2009 (SI 2009/2206) above, does not apply where the person concerned reached pensionable age before April 6, 2010. For the text applicable in such cases please see earlier editions of this book.

[¹ Disapplication of section 1(1A) of the Administration Act for the purposes of retirement pension

1A.—Section 1(1A) of the Administration Act (requirement to state national insurance number) shall not apply— 6.88

    (a) [² *omitted*];

    (b) to an adult dependant in respect of whom a claim for an increase of retirement pension is made or treated as made before 5th October, 1998.]

  [³(c) to an adult dependant who—

      (i) is a person in respect of whom a claim for an increase of retirement pension is made;

      (ii) is subject to immigration control within the meaning of section 115(9)(a) of the Immigration and Asylum Act 1999; and

      (iii) has not previously been allocated a national insurance number.]

AMENDMENTS

1. Social Security (National Insurance Information: Exemption) Regulations (SI 1997/2676) (December 1, 1997).

2. Social Security (Working Tax Credit and Child Tax Credit) (Consequential Amendments) (No. 2) Regulations 2003 (SI 2003/937) reg.2 (April 6, 2003).

3. Social Security (National Insurance Number Information: Exemption) Regulations 2009, (SI 2009/471) reg.3 (April 6, 2009).

Election to be treated as not having retired

2.—(1) Subject to the provisions of these regulations, where any person (other than one mentioned in paragraph (2))— 6.89

    (a) has become entitled to either a Category A or a Category B retirement pension [³ or a shared additional pension] [² . . .]; and

    (b) elects that this regulation shall apply in his case,

the Act shall have effect as if that person had not become entitled as aforesaid.

  [⁴(2) Paragraph (1) shall not apply to a person who has previously made such an election.]

  [²(3) Notice of election for the purposes of this regulation may be given by telephone call to the telephone number specified by the Secretary of State unless the Secretary of State directs in any particular case that the notice [⁴ . . .] must be given in writing.

  (4) Subject to [⁴paragraph (6)], an election shall take effect—

    (a) on the date on which it is given; or

    (b) on such other date specified by the person making the election, being no earlier than the date on which it is given and no later than 28 days after the date on which it is given.]

  (5) [⁴. . .]

  (6) Where a woman entitled to a Category B retirement pension under section 29(4) of the Act has, on or after 6th April 1979, made an election and has not revoked it, then, for the purpose only of determining her right to increments under paragraph 2 of Schedule 1 to the Pensions Act, her election shall be treated as if it took effect from 6th April, 1979 or, if later, the date of the death of her husband by virtue of whose contributions she is so entitled.

AMENDMENTS

1. Social Security Miscellaneous Provisions Regulations 1989 (SI 1989/893) reg.4 (May 28, 1989).

2. Social Security (Deferral of Retirement Pensions) Regulations 2005 (SI 2005/453) reg.4 (April 6, 2005).

3. Shared Additional Pensions (Miscellaneous Amendments) Regulations 2005 (SI 2005/1551) (July 6, 2005).

4. Social Security (State Pensions and National Insurance Credits) Regulations 2009 (SI 2009/2206) reg.7 (April 6, 2010).

GENERAL NOTE

Paragraph (5)

6.90   For the circumstances in which it is suggested that a wife's consent might be unreasonably withheld, see note to s.55 of the Act.

Provisions applying after election

6.91   **3.**—Where an election has been made in accordance with regulation 2—

(a) subject to the provisions of regulations made under section 82(2)(a) of the Act (adjustment to prevent payments for periods of less than a week or at different rates for different parts of a week), no Category A or B retirement pension [² or a shared additional pension] shall be payable to a person [³ . . .] for any period on or after the date of his election and before he subsequently [¹ becomes entitled to a Category A or Category B retirement pension] [² or a shared additional pension] or dies; and

(b) where the person who has made the election is a woman who became entitled to a Category B retirement pension in accordance with section 29(4) of the Act and she revokes her election, she shall cease to be treated as if she had not become entitled to such a retirement pension; [³ . . .]

(c) [³ . . .]

AMENDMENTS

1. Social Security (Abolition of Earnings Rule) (Consequential) Regulations 1989 (SI 1989/1642) reg.3 (October 1, 1989).

2. Shared Additional Pensions (Miscellaneous Amendments) Regulations 2005 (SI 2005/1551) (July 6, 2005).

3. Social Security (State Pensions and National Insurance Credits) Regulations 2009 (SI 2009/2206) reg.8 (April 6, 2010).

Calculating periods of incapacity for work for welfare to work beneficiaries entitled to an increase of long-term incapacity benefit

6.92   [¹ **3A.**—Section 47(1) of the Social Security Contributions and Benefits Act 1992 (increase of Category A retirement pension for long-term incapacity) shall have effect, in any case where a person is treated in accordance with regulation 13A of the Social Security (Incapacity for Work) (General) Regulations 1995 as a welfare to work beneficiary, as if for the reference to 8 weeks there were substituted a reference to [²104] weeks.]

AMENDMENTS

1. Social Security (Welfare to Work) Regulations 1998 (SI 1998/2231), reg.7 (October 5, 1998).
2. Social Security (Miscellaneous Amendment) (No.4) Regulations 2006 (SI 2006/2378), reg.2 (October 9, 2006).

Days to be treated as days of increment

4.—(1) For the purposes of paragraph 2 of Schedule 1 to the Pensions   **6.93**
Act a day shall be treated as a day of increment in relation to any person if it is a day in that person's [¹ period of [⁵deferment]] other than a Sunday, in respect of which—

[¹ (a) if that person had not deferred his entitlement to a Category A or Category B retirement pension, [⁹ . . .] that person would have been entitled to such a pension (and would not have been disqualified for receiving it by reason of imprisonment or detention in legal custody); and]

(b) that person had not received any of the following benefits:—

    (i) any benefit under Chapters I and II of Part II of the Act other than child's special allowance, attendance allowance, [² disability living allowance] and guardian's allowance; or

    [⁸ (ii) graduated retirement benefit where that person's period of deferment ended on or before 5th April 2006; or

    (iii) an unemployability supplement;] [¹⁰ or]

    [¹⁰(iv) state pension credit under section 1 of the State Pension Credit Act 2002; and]

(c) in the case of a married woman who would have been entitled to a Category B retirement pension or a section 10(2) increase [⁵and whose period of deferment began before 6ᵗʰ April 2005], her husband had not received an increase of any of the benefits mentioned in paragraph (1)(b) in respect of her.

[⁵ and

(d) in the case of a person who would have been entitled to a Category A or Category B retirement pension ("the deferrer") and whose period of deferment begins on or after 6th April 2005—

    (i) no other person has received an increase of any of the benefits mentioned in sub-paragraph (b) in respect of the deferrer; or

    (ii) another person has received such an increase in respect of the deferrer and the deferrer is neither married to, [⁷ or in a civil partnership with,] nor residing with, that other person.]

[¹⁰ and

(e) in the case of a person who was a member of a couple, the other member of the couple was not in receipt of—

    (i) income support under section 124 of the Social Security Contributions and Benefits Act 1992;

    (ii) income-based jobseeker's allowance under section 1 of the Jobseeker's Act 1995;

    (iii) state pension credit under section 1 of the State Pension Credit Act 2002; or

    (iv) income-related employment and support allowance under section 1 of the Welfare Reform Act 2007.]

[¹¹ or

(v) universal credit under Part 1 of the Welfare Reform Act 2012;]

(2) Subject to the following paragraph, for the purposes of this regulation, where in respect of any day—

(a) a person has received one or more of the benefits mentioned in paragraph (1)(b) or (c), and

(b) either—

(i) the determining authority, has determined that in respect of that day he was not entitled to that benefit; or

(ii) by virtue of the provisions of the Employment Protection (Recoupment of Unemployment Benefit and Supplementary Benefit) Regulations 1977 the Secretary of State has recovered from that person's employer sums on account of [⁴[¹. . .] jobseeker's allowance] received by that person in respect of that day; and

(c) the whole of the benefit or sum on account of benefit in respect of that day has been repaid or, as the case may be, recovered before the relevant date,

that day shall be treated as a day in respect of which he did not receive that benefit; and in this paragraph "relevant date" means—

(i) where a person's entitlement to increments under paragraph 2 of Schedule 1 to the Pensions Act is in question, the end of his [¹ period of [⁵deferment;]] or

(ii) where a person's entitlement to increments under paragraph 4 or 4A of that Schedule in relation to the [¹deferred entitlement] of a deceased spouse is in question, the date of the death of that spouse.

(3) Where the benefit or sum on account of benefit in respect of a day to which paragraph (2)(a) and (b) applies is repaid or, as the case may be, recovered on or after the said relevant date, that day shall not be treated as a day in respect of which that person did not receive that benefit until the benefit has been repaid or, as the case may be, sums on account of the benefit have been recovered in respect of all the days to which those sub-paragraphs relate and which fall within the period to which this regulation applies.

[⁶ (4) For the purpose of paragraph 3 of Schedule 5A to the Social Security Contributions and Benefits Act 1992 a day shall be treated as a day of increment in relation to any person if it is a day in that person's period of deferment, other than a Sunday, in respect of which if that person had not deferred his entitlement to a shared additional pension he would have been entitled to it (and would not have been disqualified from receiving it by reason of imprisonment or detention in legal custody).]

[¹⁰ [¹¹(5) In this regulation—

(a) in paragraph (1), "couple" has the meaning—

(i) apart from in relation to universal credit, given by section 137(1) of the Social Security Contributions and Benefits Act 1992 (interpretation of Part VII and supplementary provisions);

(ii) in relation to universal credit, given by section 39 of the Welfare Reform Act 2012 (couples);

(b) in paragraph (2), "jobseeker's allowance" means an allowance under the Jobseekers Act 1995 as amended by the provisions of Part 1 of Schedule 14 to the Welfare Reform Act 2012 that remove references to an income-based allowance, and a contribution-based allowance under the Jobseekers Act 1995 as that Act has effect apart from those provisions; and

(c) "universal credit" means universal credit under Part 1 of the Welfare Reform Act 2012.]]

AMENDMENTS

1. Social Security (Abolition of Earnings Rule) (Consequential) Regulations 1989 (SI 1989/1642) reg.11 (October 1, 1989).

2. Social Security Disability Living Allowance and Disability Working Allowance (Consequential Provisions) Regulations 1991 (SI 1991/2742) reg.6 (April 6, 1992).

3. Social Security (Widows' Benefit and Retirement Pensions) (Amendment) Regulations 1992 (SI 1992/1692) reg.2 (August 5, 1992).

4. Social Security and Child Support (Jobseeker's Allowance) (Consequential Amendments) Regulations 1996 (SI 1996/1345) reg.26 (October 7, 1996).

5. Social Security (Deferral of Retirement Pensions) Regulations 2005 (SI 2005/453) reg.4 (April 6, 2005).

6. Shared Additional Pensions (Miscellaneous Amendments) Regulations 2005 (SI 2005/1551) (July 6, 2005).

7. Civil Partnership (Consequential Amendments) Regulations (SI 2005/2878) (December 5, 2005).

8. Social Security (Deferral of Retirement Pensions etc) Regulations 2006 (SI 2006/516) (April 6, 2006).

9. Social Security (State Pensions and National Insurance Credits) Regulations 2009 (SI 2009/2206) reg.9 (April 6, 2010).

10. Social Security (Deferral of Retirement Pensions) Regulations 2011 (SI 2011/634) reg.2 (April 6, 2011).

11. Universal Credit (Consequential, Incidental, Supplementary, Incidental and Miscellaneous Provisions) Regulations 2013 (SI 2013/630) reg.26 (April 29, 2013).

GENERAL NOTE

Regulation 4(1)(a) is difficult to follow but an unreported Commissioner's deci- **6.94** sion (*CP/037/1991*) confirms that the increment accrues in respect of a married woman and her Category B pension only if both that pension and her husband's Category A pension have been deferred. In this case the husband had reached retirement age and had deferred his pension for four years. He then retired some eight months before his wife reached the age of 60 and claimed her Category B pension. In such a case the husband has an increment to his Category A pension because entitlement to that has been deferred, but his wife has no increment because her entitlement was not deferred.

Sub-paragraph (1)
Regulation 4(1)(b)(ii) has been amended to include graduated retirement **6.95** pension with effect from August 5, 1992. This amendment is the response to the case of *Chief Adjudication Officer and Sec. of State v Pearse (R(P) 2/93)*. Mr Pearse had deferred his retirement and accrued increments to his Category A retirement pension. Mrs Pearse had, however, been refused increments to her Category B pension because she had during the deferred period been in receipt of Graduated Retirement Pension. The Department argued that GRP was covered by sub-para.(i) of reg.4(1)(b). The Commissioner, and the Court of Appeal, held that it was not. (Regulations deeming GRP to be a benefit under Pt II of the Act applied only for the purpose of continuity.) Mrs Pearse was therefore entitled to receive the increments to her Category B pension. The Department has now closed the door on this argument by amending sub-para.(ii) specifically to include GRP. But the amendment applies only from August 5, 1992. Married

women whose husbands deferred their retirement for a period before that date and who were refused increments for the same reasons as Mrs Pearse will be entitled to arrears of their pension. Also married women who opted not to take the GRP so as to be allowed to accrue increments should now receive a payment of arrears for the GRP.

Sub-paragraph (1) has been further amended by the Deferral of Retirement Pensions Regulations 2011, to disqualify a claimant who is in receipt of that benefit or other income-related benefits, during the relevant period, but this amendment affects only a period after April 6, 2011.

Modification of paragraph 2(1) to (3) of Schedule 1 to the Pensions Act

6.96   **5.**—(1) This regulation applies to a person referred to in paragraph 1 of Schedule 1 to the Pensions Act during whose [²period of [³ deferment]] there has been an increase, other than an increase made by an order under [¹ section 63 of the Social Security Act 1986] in the rate of the Category A or Category B retirement pension to which he would have been entitled if his [² entitlement to the pension had commenced on the day on which he attained pensionable age.]

(2) In relation to a person to whom this regulation applies, paragraph 2(1) to (3) of the said Schedule 1 shall have effect with the additions, omissions and amendments prescribed below.

(3) In paragraph 2(1) for the words after "incremental period" there shall be substituted—

"(a) in his [² period of [³ deferment]] and

(b) in each period beginning with the day on which an increase in the weekly rate of his pension took place and ending with the day before [² his entitlement arose]".

(4) After paragraph 2(2)(b) there shall be added—
"and

(c) 'weekly rate of his pension' means the weekly rate of the Category A or Category B retirement pension to which that person would have been entitled on attaining pensionable age; and

(d) 'increase' means an increase in the weekly rate of his pension other than an increase made by such an order as is mentioned in sub-paragraph (5) below".

(5) In paragraph 2(3) for the words after "incremental period" there shall be substituted—

"(a) in the case of an incremental period specified in paragraph 2(1)(a) above, shall be [³ 1/5th per cent.] of the weekly rate of his pension immediately after he attained pensionable age; and

(b) in the case of an incremental period specified in paragraph 2(1)(b) above, shall be [³ 1/5th per cent.] of that increase".

AMENDMENTS

1. Social Security (Widow's Benefits and Retirement Pensions) Amendment Regulations 1987 (SI 1987/1854) reg.2 (April 11, 1988).

2. Social Security (Abolition of Earnings Rule) (Consequential) Regulations 1989 (SI 1989/1642) reg.11 (October 1, 1989).

3. Social Security (Deferral of Retirement Pensions) Regulations 2005 (SI 2005/453) reg.4 (April 6, 2005).

[⁵Rate of benefit where the second contribution condition in paragraph 5 of Schedule 3 to the Social Security Contributions and Benefits Act 1992 is not satisfied]

[² **6.**—(1) Subject to paragraph (2) of this regulation, where the second   6.97
contribution condition specified in paragraph 5(3) of Schedule 3 to the Act
is not satisfied a person shall be entitled to—

    (a) widowed mother's allowance;

[¹(aa) widowed parent's allowance;

  (ab) [⁶ .. .];]

    (b) widow's pension;

    (c) Category A retirement pension; or

    (d) Category B retirement pension,

provided the percentage of the number of qualifying years in the working
life of that person calculated in accordance with paragraph (3B) of this regulation is 25 per cent. or more.

(2) Where a person to whom paragraph (1) alone would otherwise apply
is not entitled to benefit under that paragraph because the percentage of the
number of qualifying years in his working life, calculated in accordance with
paragraph (3B) of this regulation, is less than 25 per cent., but there are one
or more surpluses in that person's earnings factors for the relevant years,
that person shall be entitled to—

    (a) widowed mother's allowance;

[¹(aa) widowed parent's allowance;]

    (b) widow's pension;

    (c) Category A retirement pension; or

    (d) Category B retirement pension

consisting only of the additional pension in that benefit.

(3) Where a person is entitled to benefit under paragraph (1) of this regulation, the benefit payable shall be—

    (a) the basic pension in that benefit at a reduced rate calculated in
accordance with paragraph (3B) of this regulation as a percentage of
the higher of the sums specified in section 6(1)(a) of the Pensions Act;
and

    (b) any additional pension arising from one or more surpluses in the
pensioner's earnings factors for the relevant years; and

    (c) any increase of benefit to which he may be entitled under sections
41, 45, 45A and 46 of the Act—

        (i) in respect of an adult dependant calculated in accordance with
paragraph (3B) of this regulation as a percentage of the appropriate increase specified in Part IV of Schedule 4 to the Act;

      (ii) [² *omitted*].

(3A) Where a person is entitled to benefit under paragraph (2) of this
regulation, the benefit payable shall be only the additional pension in that
benefit.

(3B) [⁵The] percentage referred to in paragraphs (1), (2), (3)(a) and (3)
(c)(i) of this regulation shall be ascertained by taking the number of qualifying years in the working life of the contributor concerned, expressing that
number as a percentage of the requisite number of years specified for that
working life in paragraph 5(4) of Schedule 3 to the Act and rounding up that
percentage to the next whole number.]

    (4) [⁵ *omitted*]

(5) Where a person is entitled by virtue of this regulation to a Category A retirement pension and also to a section 9(2), 9(3) or 10(2) increase, an uprating order shall have the effect of increasing—
  (a) the [⁴ basic pension] in that pension
        (i) where there is a section 10(2) increase, in proportion to the increase under that order of the [³ higher of the sums] specified in section 6(1)(a) of the Pensions Act 10(2) and
       (ii) where there is a section [53(2)] increase, in proportion to the increase under that order of the sum specified in paragraph 9 of Part I of Schedule 4 to the Act;
  (b) the [⁴ additional pension] where there is a section 9(2) increase, by the percentage specified in that order for an increase of the sums [³ which are the additional pensions in the rates of long-term benefits.]
    [⁵(6) For the purposes of this regulation, "qualifying year" means a year for which a person's earnings factor is sufficient to satisfy paragraph 5(3)(b) of Schedule 3 to the Social Security Contributions and Benefits Act 1992 and includes a year which is treated as such a year by virtue of regulation 8(4).]

AMENDMENTS

1. Social Security (Benefits for Widows and Widowers) (Consequential Amendments) Regulations 2000 (SI 2000/1483) reg.7 (April 9, 2001).
2. Social Security (Working Tax Credit and Child Tax Credit) (Consequential Amendments) (No. 2) Regulations 2003 (SI 2003/937) reg.2 (April 6, 2003).
3. Social Security (Widows' Benefits and Retirement Pensions) Amendment Regulations 1990 (SI 1990/2642) reg.2 (January 29, 1991).
4. Social Security Act 1986 s.18 (April 6, 1987).
5. Social Security (State Pensions and National Insurance Credits) Regulations 2009 (SI 2009/2206) regs 10 and 11 (April 6, 2010).
6. The Pensions Act 2014 (Consequential, Supplementary and Incidental Amendments) Order 2017 (SI 2017/422) art.7 (April 6, 2017).

GENERAL NOTE

6.98   Note that the amendments made by the Social Security (State Pensions and National Insurance Credits) Regulations 2009 (SI 2009/2206) above, do not apply where the contributor concerned attained pensionable age, or died, before April 6, 2010. For the text applicable in such cases please see earlier editions of this book.

[¹**Proportion of retirement pension where the contribution condition in paragraph 5A of Schedule 3 to the Social Security Contributions and Benefits Act 1992 is not satisfied**

6.99   **6A.**—(1) This regulation applies where the contribution condition in paragraph 5A of Schedule 3 (contribution conditions for entitlement to benefit) to the Social Security Contributions and Benefits Act 1992 ("the 1992 Act") is not satisfied in relation to a benefit to which that paragraph applies.
    (2) The amount of such a benefit to which a person is nevertheless entitled shall be—
  (a) 1/30th of the weekly rate of basic pension in that benefit for each year in the contributor's working life in relation to which the require-

ments of paragraph 5A(2)(a) and (b) of Schedule 3 to the 1992 Act are satisfied; and

(b) any additional pension in that benefit arising from one or more surpluses in the contributor's earnings factors for the relevant years.

(3) For the purposes of paragraph (2)(a), satisfaction of the requirements of paragraph 5A(2)(a) and (b) of Schedule 3 to the 1992 Act in relation to a year includes satisfaction of those requirements by virtue of regulation 8.

(4) Paragraph (5) of regulation 6 applies to entitlement to a Category A retirement pension by virtue of this regulation as it does to such entitlement by virtue of that regulation.

Regulations 6 and 6A: supplemental

6B.—In regulations 6 and 6A, "basic pension" includes the weekly rate   **6.100** of Category B retirement pension specified in paragraph 5 of Part 1 (contributory periodical benefits) of Schedule 4 (rates of benefit, etc) to the Social Security Contributions and Benefits Act 1992.]

AMENDMENT

1. These regulations were inserted by the Social Security (State Pensions and National Insurance Credits) Regulations 2009 (SI 2009/2206) reg.12 (April 6, 2010).

Category B retirement pension for certain widows by virtue of husband's contributions

7.—For the purposes of a woman's entitlement to a Category B retire-   **6.101** ment pension under section 29(5) of the Act, she shall be treated as being entitled to a widow's pension if she would have been so entitled but for any one or more of the following circumstances:

(a) her failure to make, or delay in making, a claim for that widow's pension;

(b) her entitlement to a widowed mother's allowance;

(c) the operation of section 82 of the Act (disqualification and suspension) or section 85 of the Act (overlapping benefits and hospital in-patients) or any regulations made under either of those sections, except for the operation of section 82(5)(a) of the Act (absence from Great Britain);

(d) the operation of any provision of the Act or any regulations made under the Act disqualifying her for the receipt of that widow's pension for any period, except for the operation of the said section 82(5)(a);

(e) her having attained [¹ pensionable age];

(f) her remarriage after 4th April 1971,

[¹ (g) her having ceased to be entitled to a widowed mother's allowance at a time when she had reached the age of 65 but was under pensionable age,]

and for the purposes of section 29(7)(c) of the Act the weekly rate of the widow's pension shall be the weekly rate to which she would have been entitled but for any one or more of the said circumstances.

AMENDMENTS

1. Social Security (Miscellaneous Amendments No.4) Regulations 2017 (SI 2017/1015) reg.3(3) (December 6, 2018).

[¹ **Category B retirement pension for surviving spouses [² and surviving civil partners] by virtue of deceased spouse's [² or deceased civil partner's] contributions**

6.102   **7A.**—(1) For the purposes of entitlement of any person ("the pensioner") to a Category B retirement pension under section 48BB of the Social Security Contributions and Benefits Act 1992 (Category B retirement pension: entitlement by reference to benefit under section 39A or 39B) ("the 1992 Act"), the pensioner shall be treated as being entitled to a widowed parent's allowance or a bereavement allowance as the case may be, if he would have been so entitled but for any one or more of the circumstances specified in paragraph (2) below.

(2) The circumstances referred to in paragraph (1) above are—

(a) the pensioner's failure to make, or his delay in making, a claim for that widowed parent's allowance or bereavement allowance;

(b) the operation of section 113 of the 1992 Act (disqualification and suspension) or section 73 of the Social Security Administration Act 1992 (overlapping benefits) or any regulations made under either of those sections, except for the operation of section 113(1)(a) of the 1992 Act (absence from Great Britain);

(c) the operation of any provision of the 1992 Act or any regulations made under the 1992 Act, disqualifying the pensioner from receipt of that widowed parent's allowance or bereavement allowance for any period except for the operation of the said section 113(1)(a);

(d) the pensioner's having attained pensionable age;

(e) the pensioner's having remarried [² or formed a civil partnership].

(3) Where this regulation applies the weekly rate of a Category B pension shall—

(a) in the case of a pensioner treated as being entitled to widowed parent's allowance immediately before attaining pensionable age in consequence of the death of his or her spouse [² or civil partner], be that specified in section 48BB(2) of the 1992 Act;

(b) in the case of a pensioner treated as being entitled to—

(i) widowed parent's allowance at any time when over the age of 45 but not immediately before attaining pensionable age, or

(ii) bereavement allowance at any time prior to obtaining pensionable age,

be that specified in section 48BB(5) and (6) of the 1992 Act as the case may be.]

AMENDMENTS

1. Social Security (Benefits for Widows and Widowers) (Consequential Amendments) Regulations 2000 (SI 2000/1483) reg.7 (April 9, 2001).

2. Civil Partnership (Pensions, Social Security and Child Support) (Consequential, etc. Provisions) Regulations 2005 (SI 2005/2877) art.10(2) (December 5, 2005).

[¹ **Notional entitlement to Category B retirement pension for new State Pension purposes**

7B.—(1) This regulation applies for the purposes of determining whether, in accordance with paragraph 3(1)(d) of Schedule 3 to the Pensions Act 2014 (survivor's pension inherited amount: dead spouse or civil partner in old state pension scheme)(5), a person ("the pensioner") would have been entitled to a Category B retirement pension.

(2) The pensioner shall be treated as being entitled to bereavement support payment if the pensioner would have been so entitled but for one or both of the circumstances specified in paragraph (3).

(3) The circumstances referred to in paragraph (2) are—

(a) the pensioner's failure to make, or the pensioner's delay in making, a claim for that bereavement support payment;

(b) the operation of section 32 of the Pensions Act 2014 (bereavement support payment: prisoners) or any regulations made under that section.]

AMENDMENTS

1. The Pensions Act 2014 (Consequential, Supplementary and Incidental Amendments) Order 2017 (SI 2017/422) art.7 (April 6, 2017).

Substitution of former spouse's [³ or former civil partner's] contribution record to give entitlement to a Category A retirement pension

8.—(1) This regulation applies to—   6.103

(a) any person whose last marriage terminated before he attained pensionable age and who did not remarry [³ or, as the case may be, form a civil partnership] before that date;

[³ (aa) any person whose last civil partnership terminated before he attained pensionable age and who did not form a subsequent civil partnership or, as the case may be, marry before that date;]

[¹ (b) any man or woman widowed on or after attaining pensionable age [³ or whose civil partner died on or after the man or woman had attained that age], his or her former spouse [³ or former civil partner], as the case may be, being under pensionable age when she or he died; and]

(c) any person [⁴other than one to whom regulation 8A applies,] whose last marriage [³ or last civil partnership] terminated on or after the date on which he attained pensionable age otherwise than by the death of his spouse [³ or, as the case may be, his civil partner],

and any such person shall be referred to in this regulation as "the beneficiary".

(2) Where the beneficiary does not, in respect of the year in which his marriage [³ or civil partner] terminated or any previous year, with his own contributions satisfy the contribution conditions for a Category A retirement pension specified in paragraph 5 of Schedule 3 [⁴to the Social Security Contributions and Benefits Act 1992 ("the 1992 Act") or the contribution condition for such a pension specified in paragraph 5A of that Schedule to that Act], then, for the purpose of enabling him to satisfy those conditions, the contributions of his former spouse [³ or former civil partner] may, if it is advantageous to him, be treated to the extent specified in paragraphs (3) to (6) as though they were his own.

[⁴ (3) The beneficiary shall be treated as satisfying the first contribution condition specified in paragraph 5 of Schedule 3 to the 1992 Act if his former spouse or former civil partner—

(a) had satisfied that condition; or

(b) would have satisfied that condition had paragraph 5A of Schedule 3 not been applicable,

as respects any year of his working life up to (inclusive) the year in which the marriage or civil partnership terminated.]

[5 (3A) The beneficiary shall be treated as satisfying the first contribution condition specified in paragraph 5 of Schedule 3 to the 1992 Act if his former spouse or former civil partner would have satisfied that condition had Part 1 of the Pensions Act 2014 not been applicable, as respects any year of his working life up to the year ending on 5th April 2016 (inclusive).]

(4) The beneficiary shall be treated as satisfying the second contribution condition [4specified in paragraph 5 of Schedule 3 to the 1992 Act or the contribution condition specified in paragraph 5A of that Schedule to that Act] as respects the number of years arrived at under paragraph 2 or 3 of Schedule 1 to these regulations, whichever is the more beneficial to him.

(5) Where a person is entitled for any period to any [2 basic pension] in his Category A retirement pension by virtue of this regulation and regulation 6 [4or 6A], he shall not be entitled for that period to a section 9(2) increase.

(6) [4*omitted*].

AMENDMENTS

1. Social Security (Benefits for Widows and Widowers) (Consequential Amendments) Regulations 2000 (SI 2000/1483) reg.7 (April 9, 2001).
2. Social Security Act 1986 s.18 (April 6, 1987).
3. Civil Partnership (Pensions, Social Security and Child Support) (Consequential etc. Provisions) Regulations 2005 (SI 2005/2877) (December 5, 2005).
4. Social Security (State Pensions and National Insurance Credits) Regulations 2009 (SI 2009/2206) reg.13 (April 6, 2010).
5. Pensions Act (Consequential, Supplementary and Incidental Amendments) Order 2015 (SI 2015/1985) art.5 (April 6, 2016).

GENERAL NOTE

6.104   For the meaning of marriage, see the notes following s.39c of the Act.
A marriage terminated by divorce or by a decree of nullity is terminated from the date of decree absolute. A marriage terminated by a decree of presumption of death and dissolution of marriage is treated as terminated otherwise than by death, and is treated as terminated from the date of the decree absolute unless the Secretary of State or the determining authority is satisfied as to the date of the death, in which case it is presumably also treated as terminated by death (see reg.1(3) above).
The omission of reg.8(6) above does not apply where the person concerned attained pensionable age before April 6, 2010. For the text to be applied in such cases please see earlier editions of this book.

6.105   [1*8A.*—(1) This regulation applies to a person—
(a) whose marriage or civil partnership terminated otherwise than by the death of that person's spouse or civil partner;
(b) whose marriage or civil partnership terminated after—
(i) that person; and
(ii) that person's former spouse or former civil partner, attained pensionable age;
(c) who attained pensionable age on or after 6th April 2010;

(d) whose former spouse or former civil partner attained pensionable age on or after 6th April 2010; and

[² (e) whose former spouse or former civil partner—

    (i) satisfied the contribution condition specified in paragraph 5A(2) of Schedule 3 (contribution conditions for entitlement to benefit) to the Social Security Contributions and Benefits Act 1992 ("the 1992 Act"); or

    (ii) would have satisfied the contribution condition specified in paragraph 5A(2) of Schedule 3 to the 1992 Act in respect of contributions paid before 6th April 2016 had Part 1 of the Pensions Act 2014 not been applicable.]

(2) Where a person to whom this regulation applies does not satisfy the contribution condition specified in paragraph 5A(2) of Schedule 3 to the 1992 Act, that person shall be treated as having satisfied that condition by virtue of the contributions of the former spouse or civil partner.]

AMENDMENTS

1. This regulation has been inserted by the Social Security (State Pensions and National Insurance Credits) Regulations 2009 (SI 2009/2206) reg.14 (April 6, 2010).

2. Pensions Act (Consequential, Supplementary and Incidental Amendments) Order 2015 (SI 2015/1985) art.5 (April 6, 2016).

Conditions for entitlement to a Category C retirement pension

9.—The conditions for entitlement to a Category C retirement pension shall be that the person concerned—　　　　　　　　　　　　　　　　　6.106

(a) was resident in Great Britain for a period of at least 10 years between 5th July 1948 and 1st November 1970, inclusive of both dates; and

(b) was ordinarily resident in Great Britain on 2nd November 1970 or on the date of his claim for that pension.

GENERAL NOTE

Category C pensions were abolished by the Pensions Act 2014 with respect to any 　6.107
prior from April 6, 2016. The amendment to reg.11 below converts the entitlements that continue into a specific rate of state pension rather than a category.

For the meaning of "resident" and "ordinarily resident", see the notes to Persons Abroad Regulations.

Conditions for entitlement to a Category D retirement pension

10.—The conditions for entitlement to a Category D retirement pension shall be that the person concerned—　　　　　　　　　　　　　　　　　　6.108

[¹(a) was resident in Great Britain for a period of at least 10 years in any continuous period of 20 years which included the day before that on which he attained the age of 80 or any day thereafter; and]

(b) was ordinarily resident in Great Britain either—

    (i) on the day he attained the age of 80; or

    (ii) if he was not so ordinarily resident on that day and the date of his claim for the pension was later than that day, on the date of his claim, so however that where a person satisfies this condition under this head he shall be deemed to have satisfied it on the date that he became so ordinarily resident.

AMENDMENT

1. Social Security (Widows' Benefit and Retirement Pensions) Amendment Regulations 1984 (SI 1984/1704) reg.2 (November 26, 1984).

GENERAL NOTE

6.109   For the meaning of "resident" and "ordinarily resident", see the notes to Persons Abroad Regulations.

Category C retirement pension for widows of men over pensionable age on 5th July, 1948

6.110   **11.**—(1) Subject to the provisions of these regulations, a widow whose husband was over pensionable age on 5th July 1948 shall be entitled to a Category C retirement pension at a rate ascertained in accordance with paragraph (3) if—

(a) she is over pensionable age; and

(b) [¹ . . .]

(c) she was over the age of [² 45] either—

  (i) when her husband died; or

  (ii) if she was entitled under regulation 14 to benefit corresponding to a widowed mother's allowance, when she ceased to be so entitled; and either

(d) her husband was at any time entitled to a Category C retirement pension or a retirement pension under section 1(1)(a) of the National Insurance Act 1970; or

(e) her husband died before 2nd November 1970 and—

  (i) she was resident in Great Britain for a period of at least 10 years between 5th July 1948 and 1st November 1970, inclusive of both dates; and

  (ii) she was ordinarily resident in Great Britain on 2nd November 1970 or on the date of her claim for a Category C retirement pension; and

  (iii) he was ordinarily resident in Great Britain on the date of his death.

(2) A pension payable under paragraph (1) shall commence on 6th April 1975 or the date on which the requirements of sub-paragraphs (a) to (c) and either (d) or (e) of that paragraph are satisfied in relation to the beneficiary, whichever is the later, and shall be payable for life.

(3) The pension under paragraph (1) shall be at the [³ weekly rate of [⁴£77.45]] so however that—

(a) in the case of a widow who was under the age of [² 55] either when her husband died, or, if she was entitled under regulation 14 to benefit corresponding to a widowed mother's allowance, when she ceased to be so entitled, the rate of such pension shall be reduced as if the provisions of section 26(2) of the Act applied to it;

(b) [¹ . . .].

AMENDMENTS

1. Social Security (Abolition of Earnings Rule) (Consequential) Regulations 1989 (SI 1989/1642) reg.11 (October 1, 1989).

2. Social Security (Widows' Benefit and Retirement Pensions) Amendment Regulations 1987 (SI 1987/1854) reg.2 (April 11, 1988).

3. Pensions Act (Consequential, Supplementary and Incidental Amendments) Order 2015 (SI 2015/1985) art.5 (April 6, 2016).

4. Social Security Benefits Up-rating Order 2019 (SI 2019/480) art.13 (April 8, 2019).

GENERAL NOTE

For the meaning of "resident" and "ordinarily resident", see the notes to Persons Abroad Regulations.   6.111

For the purpose of para.(1)(d) a person is entitled to the benefit if he would have been entitled had he made a claim for it. (See reg.1(4).)

Category C pensions were abolished by the Pensions Act 2014 with respect to any prior from April 6, 2016. The amendment to reg.11(3) converts the entitlements that continue into a specific rate of state pension rather than a category.

Category C retirement pension for certain women whose marriage has been terminated otherwise than by death

12.—(1) Subject to the provisions of these regulations, a woman whose marriage to a husband who was over pensionable age on 5th July 1948 was terminated otherwise than by his death shall be entitled to a Category C retirement pension at the higher rate specified in relation to such a pension in Part III of Schedule 4 to the Act if—   6.112

(a) she had attained pensionable age before the date of the termination of the marriage; and

(b) [¹ . . .]

(c) the conditions set out in paragraph (2) or (3), as the case may be, are satisfied.

(2) The conditions applicable in the case of a woman whose marriage was terminated before 2nd November 1970 shall be—

(a) that she was resident in Great Britain for a period of at least 10 years between 5th July 1948, and 1st November 1970, inclusive of both dates; and

(b) that she was ordinarily resident in Great Britain on 2nd November 1970, or on the date of her claim for a Category C retirement pension; and

(c) that her husband was ordinarily resident in Great Britain on the date of the termination of the marriage; and

(d) that she did not remarry between the date of that termination and 2nd November 1970.

(3) The conditions applicable in the case of a woman whose marriage was terminated on or after 2nd November 1970 shall be that her husband was entitled to a Category C retirement pension or a retirement pension under section 1(1)(a) of the National Insurance Act 1970.

(4) A pension payable under paragraph (1) shall commence on 6th April 1975 or the date on which the requirements of sub-paragraphs (a) to (c) of that paragraph are satisfied in relation to the beneficiary, whichever is the later, and shall be payable for life.

AMENDMENT

1. Social Security (Abolition of Earnings Rule) (Consequential) Regulations 1989 (SI 1989/1642) reg.11 (October 1, 1989).

6.113   For the meaning of "resident" and "ordinarily resident", see the notes to Persons Abroad Regulations.

For the purposes of para.(3) a person is entitled to the benefit if he would have been entitled had he made a claim for it. (See reg.1(4).)

Benefit corresponding to a widow's pension for widows of men over pensionable age on 5th July 1948

6.114   **13.**—(1) Subject to the provisions of these regulations, a widow whose husband was over pensionable age on 5th July 1948 shall be entitled to benefit corresponding to a widow's pension at a rate ascertained in accordance with paragraph (3) if—

(a) she was over the age of [¹ 45] but under the age of 65 either—
   (i) when her husband died; or
   (ii) if she was entitled under regulation 14 to benefit corresponding to a widowed mother's allowance, when she ceased to be so entitled; and
(b) the requirements of sub-paragraph (d) or (e) of regulation 11(1) are satisfied in her case.

(2) The period for which benefit is payable under paragraph (1) shall be any period commencing on the date on which the requirements of sub-paragraph (d) or (e) of regulation 11(1) are first satisfied in the case of the widow, and during which she is under the age of 65 and for which she is not entitled under regulation 14 to benefit corresponding to a widowed mother's allowance; so however that the benefit shall not be payable for any period after the widow's remarriage or for any period during which she and a man to whom she is not married are living together as husband and wife.

(3) The benefit under paragraph (1) shall be at the higher rate specified in relation to a Category C retirement pension in Part III of Schedule 4 to the Act; so however that in the case of a widow who was under the age of [¹ 55] either when her husband died, or, if she was entitled under regulation 14 to benefit corresponding to a widowed mother's allowance, when she ceased to be so entitled, the rate of such benefit shall be reduced as if the provisions of section 26(2) of the Act applied to it.

AMENDMENT

1. Social Security (Widows' Benefit and Retirement Pensions) Amendment Regulations 1987 (SI 1987/1854) reg.2 (April 11, 1988).

GENERAL NOTE

6.115   For the purposes of para.(2) a person is entitled to the benefit if he would have been entitled had he made a claim for it. (See reg.1(4).)

Benefit corresponding to a widowed mother's allowance for widows of men over pensionable age on 5th July 1948

6.116   **14.**—(1) Subject to the provisions of these regulations, a widow whose husband was over pensionable age on 5th July 1948 shall be entitled to benefit corresponding to a widowed mother's allowance, which shall be at the higher rate specified in relation to a Category C retirement pension in Part III of Schedule 4 to the Act, for any period commencing on the date on which the requirements of sub-paragraph (d) or (e) of regulation 11(1) are first satisfied in her case and during which she would have been entitled to a widowed mother's allowance under section 25 of the Act had her husband satisfied the contribution conditions set out in paragraph 5 of Schedule 3 to the Act; so however that the benefit shall not be payable for any period after the widow's remarriage or for any period during which she and a man to whom she is not married are living together as husband and wife.

(2) The provisions of section 41(4) of the Act (which related to increases of widowed mother's allowance in respect of children) shall apply to benefit payable under this regulation as they apply to an allowance payable under section 25(1)(A) of the Act.

Restriction on benefit under regulations 13 and 14 in certain cases

15.—(1) In the case of a widow of a member of a police force or of a special constable who, as such a widow, is in receipt of a pension under regulations from time to time in force made under—
  (a) the Police Pensions Act 1976;
  (b) section 34 of the Police Act 1964;
  (c) section 26 of the Police (Scotland) Act 1967,
benefit under regulation 13 or 14 corresponding to a widow's pension or a widowed mother's allowance shall not be payable in respect of any week during which she is receiving an increase of the said pension under either—
    (i) the provisions of regulation 12 or 15 of the Police Pensions Regulations 1971, or of any corresponding regulations from time to time in force and made as mentioned in sub-paragraph (a); or
    (ii) those provisions as applied by regulations from time to time in force and made as mentioned in sub-paragraph (b) or (c).

(2) For the purposes of paragraph (1), any reference in that paragraph to an enactment or regulation shall include a reference to any corresponding Northern Ireland legislation, or, as the case may be, any order or regulation having effect by virtue of such legislation, being in each case passed or made for purposes similar to the purposes of the enactment or regulation specified in that paragraph.

Provision in relation to entitlement to child benefit for the purposes of a widowed mother's allowance

16.—(1) For the sole purpose of determining whether a woman who has been widowed satisfies the requirements of section 25(1)(a) of the Act (entitlement to a widowed mother's allowance)—
[¹(a) [² any person under the age of 20 residing with the widow shall be deemed to be] within section 25(2) of the Act if—
    (i) the requirements of section 25(2)(a) are satisfied in his case and child benefit would have been payable in respect of him had he not been absent from Great Britain and had a claim for it been made in the manner prescribed under section 6 of the Child Benefit Act 1975, or
    (ii) the requirements of section 25(2)(b) or (c) would have been satisfied, and child benefit would have been payable in respect of him continuously since the date of death of the late husband, had he not been absent from Great Britain and had a claim for child

6.117

6.118

benefit been made in respect of him in the manner prescribed under section 6 of the Child Benefit Act 1975 and]

(b) a widow shall be treated as entitled to child benefit in respect of any person deemed, in accordance with sub-paragraph (a), to be [2 . . .] within the said section 25(2).

(2) In determining whether a woman who has been more than once married and who was not residing with her late husband immediately before his death is entitled to a widowed mother's allowance under section 25 of the Act, her late husband shall, for the purposes of section 25(2)(b) of the Act, be treated as having been entitled to child benefit in respect of any child [2 or qualifying young person] in respect of whom—

(a) a previous husband of that woman by a marriage which ended with that husband's death was, immediately before his death, entitled or treated as entitled to child benefit; and

(b) that woman was entitled or treated as entitled to child benefit immediately before the death of her late husband.

(3) For the purposes of paragraph (2)(a) or (b), if the death there referred to occurred before 4th April 1977 the previous husband or, as the case may be, the woman, shall be treated as entitled to child benefit in respect of the child [2 or qualifying young person] in question if he or she satisfied the relevant requirement in section 25(2)(c) of the Act as originally enacted.

AMENDMENTS

1. Social Security (Widows' Benefit and Retirement Pensions) Amendment Regulations 1987 (SI 1987/1854) reg.2 (April 11 1988).

2. Social Security (Provisions Relating to Qualifying Young Persons) (Amendment) Regulations 2006 (SI 2006/692) reg.3(2) (April 10, 2006).

GENERAL NOTE

6.119   Regulation 16(1)(a) has been amended as from April 11, 1988 to make it clear that children under 19 living with the widow will be the basis for an award of widowed mother's allowance only so long as child benefit is payable in respect of them—in other words, so long as they remain in full-time education, or are deemed so to remain. The original drafting of this regulation, under which a widow qualified by virtue of any child living with her and under the age of 19, appears to have been accidental, but nevertheless a saving provision in favour of such widows who qualify for widowed mother's allowance before April 11, 1988 was contained in the Widow's Benefit and Retirement Pension Amendment Regs 1987. For text of the earlier version of this reg., see earlier editions of this work.

[1 Provision in relation to entitlement to child benefit for the purposes of a widowed parent's allowance

6.120   **16ZA.**—(1) For the purpose only of determining whether a man or a woman who has been widowed ("the surviving spouse") [2 or where civil partner has died ("surviving civil partner")] satisfies the requirements of subsection (2)(a) of section 39A of the Social Security Contributions and Benefits Act 1992 ("the 1992 Act")—

(a) a person shall be treated for the purposes of subsection (3)(b) or (c) of that section as having been entitled to child benefit in respect of a child [3 or qualifying young person] where that person would have been so entitled had—

   (i) that child [³ or qualifying young person] not been absent from Great Britain, and

   (ii) a claim for child benefit been made in respect of the child [³ or qualifying young person] in the manner prescribed under section 13 of the Social Security Administration Act 1992; and

(b) the surviving spouse [² or surviving civil partner] shall be treated, for the purposes of subsection (2)(a) of section 39A, as entitled to child benefit in respect of the child [³ or qualifying young person] who, by virtue of sub-paragraph (a) above, falls within subsection (3) of that section.

(2) In determining whether a surviving spouse [² or surviving civil partner] who has been more than once married [² has formed more than one civil partnership, or who has been both married and formed a civil partnership] and who was not residing with the deceased spouse [" or, as the case may be, the deceased civil partner] immediately before his or her death is entitled to a widowed parent's allowance under section 39A of the 1992 Act, the deceased spouse [" or deceased civil partner] shall, for the purposes of subsection (3)(b) of that section, be treated as having been entitled to child benefit in respect of any child [³ or qualifying young person] in respect of whom—

(a) a previous spouse [² or civil partner] of that surviving spouse [² or civil partner] by a marriage [² or, as the case may be, by the formation at a civil partnership] which ended with that previous spouse's [² or previous civil partner's] death was, immediately before his or her death, entitled or treated as entitled to child benefit; and

(b) that surviving spouse [² or civil partner] was entitled or treated as entitled to child benefit immediately before the death of the deceased spouse [² or civil partner].]

AMENDMENTS

1. Social Security (Widow's Benefits and Retirement Pensions) Amendment Regulations 2001 (SI 2001/1235) (April 9, 2001).
2. Civil Partnership (Pensions Social Security and Child Support) (Consequential etc. Provisions) order 2005 (SI 2005/2877) (December 5, 2005).
3. Social Security (Provisions relating to Qualifying Young Persons) (Amendment) Regulations (SI 2006/692) reg.3(3) (April 10, 2006).

[¹ Disapplication of section 1(1A) of the Administration Act for the purposes of widowed mother's allowance

16A.—Section 1(1A) of the Administration Act (requirement to state national insurance number) shall not apply to a child [³ or qualifying young person] in respect of whom an increase of widowed mother's allowance [² or widowed parent's allowance] is claimed.]

    6.121

AMENDMENTS

1. Social Security (National Insurance Information: Exemption) Regulations (SI 1997/2676) (December 1, 1997).
2. Social Security (Widow's Benefit and Retirement Pensions) Amendment Regulations 2001 (SI 2001/1235) (April 9, 2001).
3. Social Security (Provisions relating to Qualifying Young Persons) Regulations (SI 2006/692) reg.3(4) (April 10, 2006).

Provisions relating to age addition for persons not in receipt of a retirement pension

6.122   17.—(1) For the purposes of section 40(2) of the Act (age addition for persons over the age of 80 who are not entitled to a retirement pension but are in receipt of certain other payments) the prescribed enactments and instruments shall be—

    (a) Chapter IV or V of Part II of the Act;

    (b) any scheme made under section 5 of the Industrial Injuries and Diseases (Old Cases) Act 1975;

    (c) any Service Pensions Instrument;

    (d) any scheme made under the Personal Injuries (Emergency Provisions) Act 1939 or under the Pensions (Navy, Army, Air Force and Mercantile Marine) Act 1939;

    (e) any 1914–18 War Injuries Scheme;

    (f) section [36] of the Act (severe disablement allowance);

    (g) section [37] of the Act ([1] carer's allowance]).

[2] (h) sections 36 and 37 of the National Insurance Act 1965 as continued in force by the Social Security (Graduated Retirement Benefit) (No. 2) Regulations 1978.]

    (2) The following shall [2] subject to paragraph (3)] be additional conditions of entitlement to age addition under section 40(2) of the Act—

    (a) that the person concerned is in receipt of a payment under an enactment or instrument specified in paragraph (1), by reference to which the amount of a retirement pension would, if it were otherwise payable to him, be extinguished by virtue of any regulations made under section 85(1)(a) of the Act (overlapping benefits); and

    (b) that had he made a claim for it, he would have been entitled to a retirement pension of any category by virtue of any provision of the Act or any regulations made under it.

    [2] (3) Paragraph (2) shall not apply to a person who is in receipt of a payment under the enactment specified in paragraph (1)(h)].

AMENDMENTS

    1. Social Security Amendment (Carer's Allowance) Regulations 2002 (SI 2002/2497) reg.3 (April 1, 2003).

    2. Social Security (Widows' Benefit and Retirement Pensions) Amendment Regulations 1993 (SI 1993/1242) reg.2 (June 7, 1993).

6.123   *Regulation 18 omitted.*

SCHEDULE 1

6.124   **Method of treating former spouse's [1] or former civil partner's] contributions as those of the beneficiary so as to entitle him to a Category A retirement pension**

    1. In this Schedule—

    (a) A is the number of former souse's or [1] former civil partner's] qualifying years up to (exclusive) the year in which the marriage [1or, as the case may be the former civil partnership] terminated [3 but where Part 1 of the Pensions Act 2014 applies to the former spouse or former civil partner, A is the number of his qualifying years up to the year ending on 5th April 2016 (inclusive)];

    (b) B is the number of years in the former spouse's [1 or former civil partner's] working life up to (exclusive) the year in which the marriage [1 or, as the case may be the former civil partnership] terminated. [2; and

(c) "qualifying year" means a year for which the former spouse's or former civil partner's earnings factor is sufficient to satisfy—
    (i) paragraph 5(3)(b); or
    (ii) paragraph 5A(2)(b),
of Schedule 3 to the Social Security Contributions and Benefits Act 1992 and does not include a year which is treated as such a year by virtue of regulation 8(4).]

2. The number of years arrived at under this paragraph is that which is obtained by—
    (a) taking the number of years in the beneficiary's working life between (inclusive) the first year in that working life and (inclusive) the year in which the marriage [¹ or former civil partnership] terminated, multiplying it by A/B and rounding up the result to the next whole number; and
    (b) adding to that number of years the number of the beneficiary's qualifying years falling after the year in which the marriage [¹ or former civil partnership] terminated.

3. The number of years arrived at under this paragraph is that which is obtained by—
    (a) taking the number of years in the beneficiary's working life between (inclusive) the year in which the marriage took place [¹ or the civil partnership was formed] and (inclusive) the year [¹ in which the marriage or civil partnership terminated], multiplying it by A/B and rounding up the result to the next whole number; and
    (b) adding to that number of years the number of the beneficiary's qualifying years falling—
        (i) before the year in which the marriage took place [¹ or the civil partnership was formed] and
        (ii) after that in which the marriage [¹ or civil partnership] terminated.

AMENDMENTS

1. Civil Partnership (Pensions Social Security and Child Support) (Consequential etc. Provisions) order 2005 (SI 2005/2877) (December 5, 2005).

2. Social Security (State Pensions and National Insurance Credits) Regulations 2009 (SI 2009/2206) reg.15 (April 6, 2010).

3. Pensions Act (Consequential, Supplementary and Incidental Amendments) Order 2015 (SI 2015/1985) art.5 (April 6, 2016).

GENERAL NOTE

Note that the inclusion of sub-para.(c) does not apply so as to include in the definition of "qualifying year" any years credited by virtue of s.23A(5) of the Social Security Contributions and Benefits Act 1992 where the marriage or civil partnership terminated before April 6, 2010.

6.125

The Social Security (Widow's Benefit, Retirement Pensions and Other Benefits) (Transitional) Regulations 1979

(SI 1979/643) *(as amended)*

The Secretary of State for Social Services, in exercise of the powers conferred upon him by section 2 of, and paragraphs 3, 4, 5, 7 and 9 of Schedule 3 to, the Social Security (Consequential Provisions) Act 1975 and section 63 of the Social Security Pensions Act 1975 and of all other powers enabling him in that behalf, hereby makes the following regulations which only consolidate other regulations herein revoked and which, accordingly, by virtue of paragraph 20 of Schedule 15 to the Social Security Act 1975, are not subject to the requirement of section 139(1) of that Act for prior reference to the National Insurance Advisory Committee.

6.126

ARRANGEMENT OF REGULATIONS

6.127
1. Citation and commencement
2. Interpretation
3. Modifications of pensions legislation in its application to pre-1975 beneficiaries and pre-1975 contributors
4. Benefit in respect of events or for periods commencing before 6th April 1975
5. Provision of alternative rights to benefit
6. Modifications relating to the first contribution condition for widowed mother's allowance, widow's pension and Category A and B retirement pension
7. Modifications relating to the second contribution condition for widowed mother's allowance, widow's pension and Category A and B retirement pension and to the contribution conditions for category A and B retirement pension for those attaining pensionable age on or after 6th April 2010
8. Modifications relating to the contribution condition for child's special allowance
9. Modifications in respect of claims and questions relating to persons who attained pensionable age before 6th April 1975 but who retire thereafter
10. Modifications relating to increases of retirement pension for deferred retirement
11. Modifications in respect of increases of retirement pension relating to persons who attained pensionable age before 6th April 1979 but who retire thereafter
12. Provision relating to increase of retirement pension where pensioner's deceased spouse or deceased civil partner had deferred retirement
12A. Provision relating to increase of a woman's Category A or B retirement pension on termination of marriage
13. Provision relating to treatment of reckonable years
14. Provision relating to Category B retirement pension for widowers
15. Provision relating to widow's election to be treated as not having retired
16. Provision relating to increase under Schedule 1 to the Pensions Act of married woman's Category B retirement pension
16A. Disapplication of section 1(1A) of the Administration Act for the purposes of widowed mother's allowance
17. Alternative benefit rights in place of widow's basic pension
18. Alternative benefit rights in place of contributory old age pension
19. Provision relating to widow's pension for certain widows incapable of self-support by reason of an infirmity

SCHEDULES

SCHEDULE 1—ALTERNATIVE RIGHTS TO BENEFIT

Citation and commencement

6.128   **1.**—These regulations may be cited as the Social Security (Widow's Benefit, Retirement Pensions and Other Benefits) (Transitional) Regulations 1979 and shall come into operation on 10th July 1979.

GENERAL NOTE

Those provisions in these regulations that apply to entitlement to a state pension   **6.129**
must now be read subject to the Pensions Act 2014 and State Pension Regulations
2015. These abolish Category B pensions with effect from April 6, 2016 and replace
all relevant provisions about entitlement to a state pension with new provisions from
that date. However, they protect transitional cases where a person's entitlement has
arisen under this law and many of these provisions continue in effect subject to the
new scheme.

Interpretation

2.—(1) In these regulations, unless the context otherwise requires:—   **6.130**
[¹" the 1992 Act" means the Social Security Contributions and Benefits
   Act 1992;]
"the Act" means the Social Security Act 1975;
"the former principal Act" means the National Insurance Act 1965;
"the Pensions Act" means the Social Security Pensions Act 1975;
"contribution week" means a period of 7 days beginning with midnight
   between Sunday and Monday;
"the Contributory Pensions Acts" means the Widows', Orphans' and
   Old Age Contributory Pensions Acts 1936 to 1941;
"pre-1975 beneficiary" means—
(a) a person to or in respect of whom benefit under the former principal
   Act (including such benefit, pension or allowance as is mentioned in
   paragraph 17(2)(b) of Schedule 11 to that Act is, or but for a disqualification or forfeiture would be, payable immediately before 6th
   April 1975; and
(b) a person who immediately before that date had a prospective right
   to, or expectation of, such benefit;
" pre-1975 contribution" means a contribution of any class paid under
   the former principal Act in respect of a week before the contributor
   concerned attained pensionable age and also means—
(a) in relation to widowed mother's allowance, widow's pension, child's
   special allowance and a Category B retirement pension to which a
   woman is entitled by virtue of section 29(5) of the Act, a contribution
   paid under the Contributory Pensions Acts by a pre-1948 contributor
   in respect of a period between the date of the contributor's last entry
   into insurance under those Acts and 5th July 1948 and paid for purposes which included widows' and orphans' pensions purposes; and
(b) in relation to a Category A retirement pension or a Category B retirement pension, other than such a pension as is referred to in the preceding sub-paragraph, a contribution paid under the Contributory
   Pensions Acts by a pre-1948 contributory in respect of a period
   between the date of his last entry into insurance under those Acts and
   5th July 1948 and paid for purposes which included old age pensions
   purposes;
"pre-1975 contributor" means a person who was insured under the
   former principal Act;
"pre-1948 contributor" means a person who, within the prescribed
   time referred to in paragraph 17(1)(a) of Schedule 11 to the former
   principal Act, was, or was deemed to be, or was treated as insured
   under the Contributory Pensions Acts;
"reckonable year" for the purposes of the contribution conditions for any

benefit means a tax year before 6th April 1978 in which the contributor concerned paid or was credited with contributions of a relevant class and the earnings factor derived from those contributions amounted to not less than that year's lower earnings limit multiplied by 50; " year" means tax year.

(2) Any reference in these regulations to a pre-1975 beneficiary who is entitled to benefit under the former principal Act shall include a person who but for any disqualification or forfeiture would be entitled to such benefit; and where, on or after 6th April 1975, a person is, by virtue of these regulations, entitled to benefit under the Act or the Pensions Act, such entitlement shall be subject to any disqualification or forfeiture and subject to any reduction in the rate of benefit payable to which that person's entitlement to benefit under the former principal Act would have been subject if that Act had continued on or after 6th April 1975.

(3) For the purposes of these regulations a person who has obtained a decree absolute of presumption of death and dissolution of marriage under the Matrimonial Causes Act 1973 shall, notwithstanding that the spouse whose death has been presumed is dead, be treated as a person whose marriage has been terminated otherwise than by the death of his spouse unless the date of his death is established to the satisfaction of the Secretary of State, a Commissioner [² or an appeal tribunal constituted under Chapter I of Part I of the Social Security Act 1998], whichever is appropriate; and, in relation to a person who is so treated, the marriage in question shall be treated as having been terminated on the date of the decree absolute.

AMENDMENTS

1. Social Security (Widow's Benefit, Retirement Pensions and other Benefits) (Transitional) Amendment Regulations 1981 (SI 1981/1627) regs 2, 3 (December 14, 1981).
2. Social Security Act 1998 (Commencement No. 9, and Savings and Consequential and Transitional Provisions) Order (SI 1999/2422) Sch.4 para.2 (September 6, 1999).

Modifications of [⁷the Act and the Pensions Act in their] application to pre-1975 beneficiaries and pre-1975 contributors

6.131   **3.**—In relation to pre-1975 beneficiaries and pre-1975 contributors the provisions of [¹the Act, the Pensions Act and the 1992 Act] and the orders and regulations for the time being in force thereunder shall have effect subject to the modifications made by these regulations.

AMENDMENTS

1. Social Security (State Pension and National Insurance Credits) Regulations 2009 (SI 2009/2206) regs 16–22 (April 6, 2010).

Benefit in respect of events or for periods commencing before 6th April 1975

6.132   **4.**—Where, on or after 6th April 1975, a person claims, in respect of an event falling or for a period commencing before 6th April 1975, benefit under the former principal Act of a description specified in Column (1) of Schedule 1to these regulations, the claim shall, subject to the provisions of regulation 5, be determined as respects such event or for such period as if the provisions of the former principal Act and the enactments specified in the third column of Schedule 1 to the Social Security (Consequential Provisions) Act 1975 covering entitlement to such benefit had continued in force in place of the provisions of the Act and the Pensions Act covering entitlement to benefit of a corresponding description.

Provision of alternative rights to benefit

5.—(1) Subject to regulation 2(2) where, immediately before 6th April 1975, a pre-1975 beneficiary was entitled to benefit under the former principal Act of a description specified in Column (1) of Schedule 1 to these regulations or to any increase of such benefit for a child or adult dependant, he shall as from that date be entitled, without any claim being made therefore, or award being made thereof, to benefit under the Act or the Pensions Act of a description set out in Column (2) of that Schedule opposite the said benefit under the former principal Act specified in Column (1) as if such benefit had been claimed and awarded under the Act or the Pensions Act, and to any increase of such benefit for a child or adult dependant to which he may be entitled under or by virtue of those Acts.   6.133

(2) Where, immediately before 6th April 1975, a woman was entitled to a widow's pension under the former principal Act by virtue of regulation 13 of the National Insurance (Widow's Benefit and Retirement Pensions) Regulations 1972 as being incapable of self-support by reason of an infirmity, she shall, subject to regulation 2(2), be entitled as from 6th April 1975 to a widow's pension under the Act for any period for which she would have been entitled to such a pension under the former principal Act if the said regulation 13 and the provisions referred to in that regulation had continued in force.

Modifications relating to the first contribution condition for widowed mother's allowance, widow's pension and Category A and B retirement pension

6.—(1) The first contribution condition for a widowed mother's allowance, a widow's pension or a Category A or Category B retirement pension specified in paragraph 5(2) of Schedule 3 to the Act shall be deemed to be satisfied in any case where the contributor concerned is, or was, a pre-1975 contributor who had paid not less than 50 pre-1975 contributions.   6.134

(2) The said contribution condition for a Category A retirement pension shall be deemed to be satisfied in the case of a woman who attains pensionable age on or after 6th April 1975 if—

(a) she was a widow who was entitled to a widow's allowance or a widowed mother's allowance under the former principal Act at any time before 6th April 1975 and has not re-married before attaining pensionable age; or

(b) her marriage was terminated before 6th April 1975 otherwise than by the death of her husband and she has not re-married before attaining pensionable age and her husband had paid not less than 50 pre-1975 contributions before the termination of the marriage.

Modifications relating to the second contribution condition for widowed mother's allowance, widow's pension and Category A and B retirement pension [²and to the contribution condition for Category A and B retirement pension for those attaining pensionable age on or after 6ᵗʰ April 2010]

6.135   7.—(1) The following provisions of this regulation shall, except where expressly provided otherwise, have effect [²for the purposes of—

(a) the second contribution condition for a widowed mother's allowance, a widow's pension or a Category A or Category B retirement pension specified in paragraph 5(3) of Schedule 3 to the 1992 Act; and

(b) the contribution condition for a Category A or Category B retirement pension specified in paragraph 5A(2) of that Schedule.]

(2) Subject to paragraph (3), where the contributor concerned is, or was, a pre-1975 contributor he shall, in respect of that part of his working life falling before 6th April 1975, have the number of reckonable years obtained by taking the total number of contributions of any class paid by or credited to him, in accordance with the provisions of the former principal Act or regulations made thereunder, for each week in the said part of his working life or credited to him by any provision of these regulations and dividing it by 50 and, if the resultant quotient is not a whole number, by rounding it up to the nearest whole number;

provided that the number of reckonable years so obtained shall not exceed the number of years of a person's working life falling before 6th April 1975.

(3) For the purposes of a Category B retirement pension under section 29(2)or (3) of the Act where the contributor concerned was a pre-1975 contributor who attained pensionable age before 6th April 1975, the second contribution condition shall be deemed to be satisfied to the same extent as it was satisfied in relation to that contributor for the purposes of his Category A retirement pension; so however that this paragraph shall not apply where that contributor died on or after that date.

(4) A contribution as payable by a non-employed person under the former principal Act shall be credited to a pre-1975 contributor—

(a) if he was a pre-1948 contributor, for each contribution week during the period from 6th April 1936, or if later, 6th April of the year in which he last entered into insurance under the Contributory Pensions Acts, to 4th July 1948; or

(b) if he was not a pre-1948 contributor but was insured under the former principal Act and—

(i) he was over the age of 16 on 5th July 1948, for each contribution week in the period from 6th April 1948 to 4th July 1948; or

(ii) he attained the age of 16 on or after 5th July 1948, for each contribution week in the period from 6th April of the year in which he attained the age of 16 up to the contribution week immediately before that in which he reached the upper limit of compulsory school age or, if later, the contribution week immediately before that in which he attained the age of 16;

provided that a contribution credited to a pre-1975 contributor under this paragraph for any contribution week specified therein shall be treated as credited in place of any contribution under the Contributory Pensions Acts or a contribution of any class under the former principal Act that may have been paid by, or otherwise credited to, that contributor in respect of such a week.

(5) In any case where the contributor concerned attained the age of 16 before 6th April 1975 and is not a pre-1975 contributor, a contribution as payable by a non-employed person under the former principal Act shall be credited to him—

(a) if he attained the age of 16 before 5th July 1948, for each contribution week in the period from 6th April 1948 to 4th July 1948;

(b) if he attained the age of 16 on or after 5th July 1948, for each contribution week from 6th April of the year in which he attained the age of 16 up to the contribution week immediately before that in which he attained that age;

provided that the maximum number of weeks for which a contribution may be credited to any person by virtue of the provisions of this paragraph shall be 50.

(6) For the purposes of paragraphs (4) and (5), if the period for which contributions are to be credited does not commence with midnight between Sunday and Monday, the days from the beginning of such period up to the first such midnight shall be treated as constituting a contribution week and if the period for which contributions are to be credited does not cease with midnight between Sunday and Monday, the days from the last such midnight to the end of such period shall be disregarded.

(7) Subject to paragraph (8), the working life of a person who attained the age of 16 before 5th July 1948 shall—

(a) if he was a pre-1948 contributor, be the period between 6th April 1936 or, if later, 6th April of the year in which he last entered into insurance under the Contributory Pensions Acts, and the end of the year immediately before that in which he attains pensionable age or dies under that age; or

(b) if he was not a pre-1948 contributor, be the period between 6th April 1948 and the end of the year immediately before that in which he attains pensionable age or dies under that age.

(8) Where the contributor concerned has died on or after 6th April 1975 and he was—

(a) a pre-1948 contributor whose last date of entry into insurance under the Contributory Pensions Acts was before 30th September 1946 and who at that date of entry was within 5 years of pensionable age; or

(b) a pre-1948 contributor whose last date of entry into insurance under the Contributory Pensions Acts was on or after 30th September 1946 and who at that date of entry was within 10 years of pensionable age; or

(c) a person who was not a pre-1948 contributor and who was, immediately before 5th July 1948, within 10 years of pensionable age,

his working life shall be—

(d) where the contributor concerned is a person to whom paragraph (a) or (b) applies, the period from 6th April of the year in which he last entered into insurance under the Contributory Pensions Acts to 5th April immediately before the date on which he completed—

    (i) where paragraph (a) applies, the said period of 5 years; (ii) where paragraph (b) applies, the said period of 10 years;

(e) where the contributor concerned is a person to whom paragraph (c)
applies, the period from 6th April 1948 to 5th April 1958,

and the provisions of paragraph (2) shall apply as if any employer's contribution paid in respect of any person to whom this paragraph applies for any period after such person reached pensionable age were a contribution paid by that person.

(9) If a pre-1948 contributor's last dates of entry into insurance under the Contributory Pensions Acts were different dates for widows' and orphans' pensions purposes and old age pensions purposes, his date of entry into insurance under those Acts for the purposes of the second contribution condition for a widowed mother's allowance, a widow's pension or a Category B retirement pension for a widow by virtue of her husband's contributions shall be his last date of entry into insurance for widows' and orphans' pensions purposes, and for the purpose of the said contribution condition for a Category A retirement pension shall be his last date of entry into insurance for old age pensions purposes.

(10) In the case of a person (hereinafter called " the beneficiary") whose former spouse [³ or former civil partner]:- was a pre-1975 contributor and who has the contributions of his said spouse [³ or former civil partner] treated, by virtue of regulation 8 of, and Schedule 1 to, the Social Security (Widow's Benefit and Retirement Pensions) Regulations 1979 as if they were contributions of his own so as to entitle him to a Category A retirement pension—

(a) the number of any qualifying years before 6th April 1975 which, by
virtue of regulations 7(2) and 13 , were or could have been obtained
by his former spouse [³ or former civil partner]:- and which may
be taken into account towards the beneficiary's said entitlement,
shall be ascertained by reference to the number of contributions of
any class paid by or credited to his former spouse [³ or former civil
partner]:- [¹in respect of] the period of the former spouse's [³ or
former civil partner's] working life between (inclusive) the first year
of his working life and (exclusive) the year in which the marriage
terminated or the year 1975/76, whichever is the earlier, [³ (or, in the
case of a civil partnership, the year 1975/76)] and shall not exceed
the number of years in that period; and

(b) the number of any qualifying years before 6th April 1975 which, by
virtue of regulations 7(2) and 13, are obtained by the beneficiary by
virtue of paragraph 2(b)or, as the case may be, paragraph 3(b)of the
said Schedule and which may be taken into account towards his said
entitlement shall be ascertained by reference to the number of contributions of any class paid by or credited to him during the period
or periods specified in the said paragraphs which fell before 6th April
1975 and shall not exceed the number of years in that period or in
each of those periods, as the case may be;

(c) where the beneficiary is a woman, if her husband died on or after 5th
July 1948 and immediately before that date he was insured under the
Contributory Pensions Acts for purposes which included widows'
and orphans' pensions purposes, the working life of her said husband
may, if it would be more favourable to her, be treated as the period
between 6th April 1936 or, if later, 6th April of the year in which he
last entered into insurance for widows' and orphans' pensions purposes and the end of the year immediately before that in which he
attained pensionable age or died under that age.

AMENDMENTS

1. Social Security (Widow's Benefit, Retirement Pensions and other Benefits) (Transitional) Amendment Regulations 1981 (SI 1981/1627) regs 2, 3 (December 14, 1981).
2. Social Security (State Pension and National Insurance Credits) Regulations 2009 (SI 2009/2206) regs 16–22 (April 6, 2010).
3. Marriage (Same Sex Couples) Act 2013 and Marriage and Civil Partnership (Scotland) Act 2014 (Consequential Provisions) Order 2014 (SI 2014/3061) art.2 and Sch.1 (December 10, 2014 and in respect of Scotland December 16, 2014).

Modifications relating to the contribution condition for child's special allowance

8.—The contribution condition for a child's special allowance specified in paragraph 6(1) of Schedule 3 to the Act shall be deemed to be satisfied in any case where the contributor concerned is, or was, a pre-1975 contributor who attained pensionable age or died under that age on or after 6th April 1975 and had paid not less than 50 pre-1975 contributions.   6.136

Modifications in respect of claims and questions relating to persons who attained pensionable age before 6th April 1975 but who retire thereafter

9.—Where a person who, having attained pensionable age before 6th April 1975, retires on or after that date or, having made an election before that date under section 35 of the former principal Act, retires on or after that date—   6.137

(a) any question under the former principal Act relating to that person's entitlement to a retirement pension determined in advance of a claim before 6th April 1975 shall be treated, for the purpose of facilitating the determination of a subsequent claim to a Category A or a Category B retirement pension, as a question determined under the Act in relation to that person's entitlement to such a pension; and

(b) subject to regulation 4, any claim for, or question relating to, that person's entitlement to a retirement pension that has not been determined before 6th April 1975 shall be for determination as a claim for, or a question under the Act relating to that person's entitlement to, a Category A or, as the case may be, a Category B retirement pension.

Modifications relating to increases of retirement pension for deferred retirement

10.—(1) In this regulation and in regulations 11 and 12—   6.138
" a pre-1975 increment" means an increase of retirement pension under section 31(1) or 34(1) of the former principal Act;
" a post-1975 increment" means an increase of a Category A or B retirement pension which accrued under section 28(4), 28(5) or 29(10) of the Act between 6th April 1975 and 5th April 1979 (both dates inclusive);
and the pre-1975 beneficiaries to whom the said regulations relate are those who, immediately before 6th April 1975, were, or but for any disqualification or forfeiture would be, entitled to, or who have prospective rights to, or expectation of, a pre-1975 increment.

(2) The weekly rate of a Category A or B retirement pension payable to a pre-1975 beneficiary to whom this regulation relates shall, in addition to any post-1975 increments that fall to be made, be increased by the amount of any pre-1975 increments to which, immediately before 6th April 1975 he was, or but for any disqualification or forfeiture would have been, entitled or to which he had a prospective right or expectation, together with increases (if any) of the said amount calculated in accordance with the provisions of section 124 of the Act and section 23(3) of the Pensions Act.

(3) The weekly rate of a Category B retirement pension payable to the widow of a pre-1975 beneficiary to whom this regulation applies, whom she married on or after 6th April 1975 shall, in addition to any post-1975 increments that fall to be made, be increased by one half of the amount of any pre-1975 increments by which the Category A retirement pension of her husband would, if were still alive, be increased for him by the provisions of paragraph (2).

(4) Where a pre-1975 beneficiary to whom this regulation relates has, immediately before 6th April 1979, entitlement, or a prospective right, to at least one pre-1975 increment, paragraph 1 of Schedule 1 to the Pensions Act shall apply to his case as if—

(a) the words " " but only if that amount is enough to increase the rate of the pension by at least 1 per cent" " were omitted from that paragraph, and

(b) any contribution as an employed or self-employed person, paid by him under the former principal Act in respect of any period after he attained pensionable age and not taken into account for a pre-1975 or a post-1975 increment, were treated as an incremental period for the purposes of Schedule 1 to the Pensions Act.

(5) Where a pre-1975 beneficiary to whom this regulation relates is a woman who has attained pensionable age but has not yet attained the age of 65, any Category B retirement pension payable to her by virtue of regulation 18 for any day before the day on which she attains the age of 65 or retires before attaining that age shall be disregarded for the purposes of regulation 4 of the Social Security (Widow's Benefit and Retirement Pensions) Regulations 1979.

Modifications in respect of increases of retirement pension relating to persons who attained pensionable age before 6th April 1979 but who retire thereafter

6.139

11.—(1) The following provisions of this regulation relate to a person who, having attained pensionable age before 6th April 1979, retires from regular employment on or after that date or, having made an election before that date under section 30(3) of the Act or section 35 of the former principal Act, retires on or after that date.

(2) Where a person, before 6th April 1979, satisfied the condition in section 28(4) of the Act that the number of days of increment was at least 48, paragraph 1 of Schedule 1 to the Pensions Act shall apply to his case as if the words " but only if that amount is enough to increase the rate of the pension by at least 1 per cent" were omitted from that paragraph.

(3) Where a person, before 6th April 1979, did not satisfy the condition in section 28(4) of the Act that the number of days of increment was at least 48, then, subject to the condition specified in paragraph 1 of

Schedule 1 to the Pensions Act (that an increase under that paragraph is payable only if its amount would increase the retirement pension by at least 1 per cent)—

(a) that person's retirement pension shall be increased by 1/8th per cent of its rate for each period of six days of increment which fell before 6th April 1979, and

(b) any such day of increment which does not form part of a period as aforesaid shall be treated as a day of increment for the purposes of Schedule 1 to the Pensions Act.

(4) For the sole purpose of determining whether the condition specified in paragraph 1 of Schedule 1 to the Pensions Act (referred to in paragraph (3) above) has been satisfied by a married woman whose husband's days of increment before 6th April 1979 amounted to less than 48, her entitlement to an increase of a Category B retirement pension in respect of the period before 6th April 1979 shall be calculated on the basis of an increase of 1/8th per cent for each incremental period which fell within the period beginning with the day on which her husband attained pensionable age, she attained pensionable age or they were married, whichever is the latest, and ending on 5th April 1979.

Provision relating to increase of retirement pension where pensioner's deceased spouse [²or deceased civil partner] had deferred retirement

12.—For the purpose of calculating entitlement to an increase of retirement pension under paragraph 4 of Schedule 1 to the Pensions Act (increase of Category A or Category B retirement pension by amount to which deceased spouse [²or deceased civil partner] was entitled) in the case of a person whose spouse dies on or after 6th April 1979 [² or whose civil partner dies on or after 5th December 2005] , or, in the case of a widow, who attains pensionable age on or after [²6th April 1979] , any pre-1975 increment or post-1975 increment to which the deceased spouse [²or deceased civil partner] was entitled or [¹would at his death have been entitled if his entitlement had not been deferred] shall be treated as an increase to which he was entitled under the said Schedule.

6.140

AMENDMENTS

1. Social Security (Abolition of Earnings Rule) (Consequential) Regulations (SI 1989/1642) reg.12(4) (October 1, 1989).

2. Social Security (State Pension and National Insurance Credits) Regulations 2009 (SI 2009/2206) regs 16–22 (April 6, 2010).

[¹ Provision relating to increase of a woman's Category A or B retirement pension on termination of marriage

12A.—In the case of a woman—

(a) who before 6th April 1979 was or, if both she and her husband had retired immediately before that date, would have been entitled under section 29(10)(a) of the Act (increase of a woman's Category B retirement pension where her husband deferred his retirement) to an increase of the weekly rate of her Category B retirement pension, and

(b) whose marriage has terminated on or after 6th April 1979,

the weekly rate of her Category B retirement pension or, where by virtue

6.141

of section 9 or section 20 of the Pensions Act she has become entitled to a Category A retirement pension, the weekly rate of her Category A retirement pension shall be increased, with effect from the date on which this regulation comes into operation or of the said termination or, in the case of a Category A retirement pension, her retirement, whichever is the latest, by the amount by which her Category B retirement pension was, or would have been, increased under the said section 29(10)(a) together with any increase of that amount by virtue of section 124 of the Act (increase of rates of benefit).]

AMENDMENT

1. Social Security (Widow's Benefit, Retirement Pensions and other Benefits) (Transitional) Amendment Regulations 1981 (SI 1981/1627), reg 3, (December 14, 1981).

Provision relating to treatment of reckonable years

6.142   **13.**—(1) For the purposes of [¹paragraph 5(2)(b) and (3)(b) and paragraph 5A(2)(b) of Schedule 3 to the 1992 Act] and Schedule 1 to the Social Security (Widow's Benefit and Retirement Pensions) Regulations 1979 any reckonable year or years shall be treated as a qualifying year or years.

(2) In this regulation " qualifying year" means a year in which a person's earnings factor is sufficient for satisfaction of paragraph (b) of the second contribution condition specified in paragraph 5(3) of Schedule 3 [¹to the 1992 Act or paragraph (b) of the contribution condition specified in paragraph 5A(2) of that Schedule.]

AMENDMENT

1. Social Security (State Pension and National Insurance Credits) Regulations 2009 (SI 2009/2206) regs 16–22 (April 6, 2010).

Provision relating to Category B retirement pension for widowers

6.143   **14.**—The condition in section 8(1)(c) of the Pensions Act (that the deceased wife satisfied the contribution conditions in paragraph 5 of Schedule 3 to the Act) shall not be satisfied by virtue of any contributions of a woman's former husband which were treated as her own by virtue of section 28(3) of, and Schedule 7 to, the Act or regulation 4(1) of, and the Schedule to, the Social Security (Benefit) (Married Women and Widows Special Provisions) Regulations 1974 as in force immediately before 6th April 1979.

Provision relating to widow's election to be treated as not having retired

6.144   **15.**—Where a woman who became entitled to a Category B retirement pension under section 29(4) of the Act before 6th April 1979, has, on or after that date, made an election under section 30(3) of the Act and has not revoked it then, for the purpose only of determining her right to increments under Schedule 1to the Pensions Act, her election shall be treated as if it took effect from 6th April 1975 or, if later, the date of the death of her husband by virtue of whose contributions she is so entitled.

Provision relating to increase under Schedule 1 to the Pensions Act of married woman's Category B retirement pension

16.—In relation to a woman who—
6.145

(a) attained pensionable age before 6th April 1979, and

(b) is married to a man who attained pensionable age before 6th April 1979, and

(c) on or after 6th April 1979 is entitled to a Category B retirement pension under section 29(2) or 29(3) of the Act,

regulation 4(1)(b)(i) of the Social Security (Widow's Benefit and Retirement Pensions) Regulations 1979 (days of deferred retirement not to be treated as days of increment when certain benefits have been received) shall not apply by reason only of the fact that the woman has received graduated retirement benefit by virtue of her having paid graduated contributions as an insured person.

[¹Disapplication of section 1(1A) of the Administration Act for the purposes of widowed mother's allowance

16A.—Section 1(1A) of the Administration Act (requirement to state
6.146
national insurance number) shall not apply to a child in respect of whom an increase of widowed mother's allowance is claimed.]

AMENDMENT

1. Social Security (National Insurance Number Information: Exemption) Regulations 1997 (SI 1997/2676) reg.15(3) (December 1, 1997).

Alternative benefit rights in place of widow's basic pension

17.—(1) Subject to regulation 2(2) where, immediately before 6th April
6.147
1975, a pre-1975 beneficiary was entitled to a widow's basic pension under the former principal Act, she shall be entitled, as from that date and until she either attains pensionable age and [¹ is entitled to a Category A or Category B retirement pension], to a widow's pension under the Act as through she had been 40 years of age at her husband's death.

(2) A person entitled to a widow's pension by virtue of this regulation shall be treated as having not been so entitled immediately before attaining pensionable age for the purposes of any regulations under the Act disqualifying a widow, not ordinarily resident in Great Britain, for receiving a retirement pension at a rate higher than the rate of widow's pension to which she was entitled immediately before attaining pensionable age.

AMENDMENT

1. Social Security (Abolition of Earnings Rule) (Consequential) Regulations (SI 1989/1642) reg.12(4) (October 1, 1989).

Alternative benefit rights in place of contributory old age pension

18.—(1) Subject to regulation 2(2)where, immediately before 6th April
6.148
1975, a pre-1975 beneficiary was entitled to a contributory old age pension under the former principal Act, such beneficiary shall, as from that date, be entitled—

(a) if entitled to a contributory old age pension by virtue of his or her own insurance, to a Category A retirement pension;

(b) if she is a woman who was entitled to a contributory old age pension by virtue of her husband's insurance, to a Category B retirement pension;

and, in either case, the rate of retirement pension to which any such person becomes entitled on 6th April 1975 shall, subject to the provisions of *regulation 5*, be at the same rate as the contributory old age pension to which that person was entitled immediately before that date.

(2) [¹. . .]

AMENDMENT

1. Social Security (Abolition of Earnings Rule) (Consequential) Regulations (SI 1989/1642) reg.12(4) (October 1, 1989).

Provision relating to widow's pension for certain widows incapable of self-support by reason of an infirmity

6.149

19.—(1) Where before 7th January 1957 a widow ceased to be entitled to a widow's benefit under the former principal Act and when she so ceased she was incapable of self-support by reason of an infirmity, she shall for any subsequent period during which she is under the age of 65 and is incapable of self-support by reason of that infirmity have the same right (if any) to a widow's pension in respect of the marriage in respect of which she was entitled to the widow's benefit as if she was over the age of 50 when her husband died.

(2) [¹ [². . .]

AMENDMENTS

1. Social Security (Widow's Benefit, Retirement Pensions and other Benefits) (Transitional) Amendment Regulations 1981 (SI 1981/1627) regs 2, 3 (December 14, 1981).
2. Social Security Act 1998 (Commencement No. 9, and Savings and Consequential and Transitional Provisions) Order (SI 1999/2422) Sch.4 para.2 (September 6, 1999).

Revocations

6.150

20.—*Omitted.*

SCHEDULE 1

ALTERNATIVE RIGHTS TO BENEFIT

6.151

Column (1)	Column (2)
Benefits under the former principal Act	**Benefits under the Act or the Pensions Act**
widowed mother's allowance	widowed mother's allowance
widow's pension	widow's pension
retirement pension by virtue of own insurance	Category A retirement pension
retirement pension by virtue of husband's insurance whilst husband alive	Category B retirement pension at the rate specified in paragraph 9 of Part I of Schedule 4 to the Act

Column (1)	Column (2)
Benefits under the former principal Act	**Benefits under the Act or the Pensions Act**
retirement pension by virtue of husband's insurance and husband no longer alive	Category B retirement pension at the rate specified in section 6(1)(a) of the Pensions Act for the [¹basic pension of a Category A retirement] pension
retirement pension for, or in respect of, person over pensionable age on 5th July 1948	Category C retirement pension at rate determined in accordance with section 39(2) of the Act
retirement pension for person over 80 years of age	Category D retirement pension
age addition	age addition
invalidity increase of retirement pension	invalidity increase of Category A retirement pension
widow's basic pension	widow's pension as provided for by regulation 17
contributory old age pension	Category A or B retirement pension as provided for by *regulation 18*
child's special allowance	child's special allowance
death grant	death grant
widow's pension by virtue of section 1(1) of the National Insurance Act 1970	benefit by virtue of section 39(4) of the Act corresponding to a widow's pension
widowed mother's allowance by virtue of the said section 1(1)	benefit by virtue of the said section 39(4) corresponding to a widowed mother's allowance

AMENDMENT

1. Social Security Act 1986 s.18(1) (April 6, 1987).

The Rate of Bereavement Benefits Regulations 2010

(SI 2010/2818)

ARRANGEMENT OF REGULATIONS

1. Citation and commencement
2. Rate of widowed mother's allowance and widow's pension
3. Rate of widowed parent's allowance and bereavement allowance

6.152

The Secretary of State makes the following Regulations in exercise of the powers conferred by sections 39(2A), 39C(1A), 122(1) and 175(1) of the Social Security Contributions and Benefits Act 1992.

The Social Security Advisory Committee has agreed that proposals in respect of these Regulations should not be referred to it.

Citation and commencement

6.153   **1.** These Regulations may be cited as the Rate of Bereavement Benefits Regulations 2010 and shall come into force on 1st January 2011.

Rate of widowed mother's allowance and widow's pension

6.154   **2.** The amount prescribed for the purposes of subsection (2A) of section 39 (rate of widowed mother's allowance and widow's pension) of the Social Security Contributions and Benefits Act 1992 is [² £117.10].

Rate of widowed parent's allowance and bereavement allowance

6.155   **3.** The amount prescribed for the purposes of subsection (1A) of section 39C (rate of widowed parent's allowance [¹ . . .]) of the Social Security Contributions and Benefits Act 1992 is [² £117.10].

AMENDMENTS

1. Pensions Act 2014 (Consequential, Supplementary and Incidental Amendments) Order (SI 2017/422) art.38 (April 6, 2017). There are saving provisions in arts 2 and 3 of this Order in respect of persons who would have been entitled to the benefits had a claim been made before that date.
2. Social Security Benefits Up-rating Order 2018 (SI 2018/281) art.19 (April 9, 2018).

The Marriage and Civil Partnership (Scotland) Act 2014 and Civil Partnership Act 2004 (Consequential Provisions and Modifications) Order 2014

(SI 2014/3229)

The Secretary of State makes the following Order in exercise of the powers conferred by sections 104, 112(1) and 113(2) to (5) and (7) of the Scotland Act 1998 and section 259(1) of the Civil Partnership Act 2004. In accordance with paragraphs 1, 2 and 3 of Schedule 7 to the Scotland Act 1998 and section 259(8) of the Civil Partnership Act 2004, a draft of this Order has been laid before and approved by a resolution of each House of Parliament.

PART 1

INTRODUCTION

Citation and commencement

6.156   **1.**—(1) This Order may be cited as the Marriage and Civil Partnership (Scotland) Act 2014 and Civil Partnership Act 2004 (Consequential Provisions and Modifications) Order 2014.

(2) This Order comes into force on 16th December 2014.

Interpretation

2.- In this Order—   6.157
"the 1977 Act" means the Marriage (Scotland) Act 1977;
"the 1992 Act" means the Social Security Contributions and Benefits
    Act 1992;
"the 2004 Act" means the Gender Recognition Act 2004;
"the 2006 Act" means the Armed Forces Act 2006;
"the 2013 Act" means the Marriage (Same Sex Couples) Act 2013;
"the 2014 Act" means the Marriage and Civil Partnership (Scotland)
    Act 2014.

Extent

3.—(1) Articles 1 to 3, 7, 29, paragraph 15(7) and paragraph 16 of   6.158
Schedule 5 extend to England and Wales, Scotland and Northern Ireland.

(2) Articles 12 to 28, paragraph 2(7) of Schedule 4 and paragraphs
15(1), (2), (3), (4) and 19 of Schedule 5 extend to England and Wales and
Scotland only.

(3) Paragraph 15(6) of Schedule 5 extends to England and Wales only.

(4) Articles 4, 5, 8 to 11, and Schedule 1, Schedule 2, Schedule 3,
Schedule 4 (except as specified in paragraph (2) of this article), Schedule
5 (except as specified in paragraphs (1), (2) and (3) of this article) and
Schedule 6 extend to Scotland only.

(5) Article 6 extends to Northern Ireland only.

PART 2

CONSEQUENTIAL PROVISIONS

Omitted   6.159

PART 3

SCOTTISH SAME SEX MARRIAGE IN NORTHERN IRELAND

Omitted   6.160

PART 4

STATE PENSIONS

Articles 8, 9, 10 and 12 of this Order were revoked with effect from   6.161
April 6, 2016 by Pensions Act (Consequential, Supplementary and Incidental
Amendments) Order 2015 (SI 2015/1985) art. 44.

Adult dependency increases

6.162   **11.**—(1) In a case where a full gender recognition certificate is issued to a person under the 2004 Act—

> (a) section 83 of the 1992 Act (pension increase (wife)) does not cease to apply by virtue of the change of gender; and
>
> (b) in the continued application of section 83 in such a case, references to a pension payable to a man, or references to his wife, are to be construed accordingly.

(2) In a case where a full gender recognition certificate is issued to a person under the 2004 Act—

> (a) section 84 of the 1992 Act (pension increase (husband)) does not cease to apply by virtue of the change of gender; and
>
> (b) in the continued application of section 84 in such a case, references to a pension payable to a woman, or references to her husband, are to be construed accordingly.

SCHEDULE 5

CONSEQUENTIAL MODIFICATIONS TO PRIMARY LEGISLATION

6.163   *The relevant legislation is amended elsewhere in the volume*

The Pensions Act 2014 (Commencement No.4) Order 2015

(SI 2015/134)

The Secretary of State for Work and Pensions makes the following Order in exercise of the powers conferred by section 56(1), (4) and (7) of the Pensions Act 2014.

Citation

6.164   **1.-** This Order may be cited as the Pensions Act 2014 (Commencement No.4) Order 2015.

Commencement of provisions

2.—(1) 5th February 2015 is the day appointed for the coming into force of the provisions of the Pensions Act 2014 listed in paragraph (4) for the purposes of making regulations.

(2) 23rd February 2015 is the day appointed for the coming into force of section 24(2) to (9) of, and Schedule 14 to, the Pensions Act 2014.

(3) 1st October 2015 is the day appointed for the coming into force of section 36 of the Pensions Act 2014.

(4) The provisions of the Pensions Act 2014 mentioned in paragraph (1) are—

> (a) section 2(3);
> (b) section 4(2);
> (c) section 8(3), (7) and (8);
> (d) section 16(1) and (6);

(e) section 17(4) and (5);
(f) section 18(1);
(g) section 19(1) and (3);
(h) section 22(1);
(i) paragraph 4 of Schedule 8 and section 13(2) in so far as it relates to that paragraph;
(j) paragraph 4 of Schedule 10 and section 14(2) in so far as it relates to that paragraph; and
(k) paragraph 11 of Schedule 11 and section 15 in so far as it relates to that paragraph.

GENERAL NOTE

This is the fourth Commencement Order made under the Pensions Act 2014. **6.165** This Order brings into force provisions relating to the new state pension for people reaching pensionable age on or after 6th April 2016 (see Part 1 of that Act)and provisions relating to occupational pension schemes on short service benefits and on the abolition of contracting-out for salary related schemes. Article 2(1) and (4) brings provisions into force to enable the State Pensions Regulations 2015 (SI 2015/119) to be made. Those Regulations set out some of the detailed rules relating to the new state pension, in particular relating to prisoners, deferral of state pension, the minimum number of qualifying years and pension sharing on divorce or dissolution of a civil partnership. The provisions are brought into force on 5th February 2015 for the purposes of enabling the Regulations to be made. (Section 56(4) of the Pensions Act 2014 brings the provisions into force on 6th April 2016 for all other purposes – that is the date the new state pension is introduced.)

Earlier commencement orders

The earlier commencement orders (bringing in provisions not relevant to **6.166** the current year save for regulation powers) are SI 2014/1965 with effect from September 11, 2014 and SI 2014/2377 with effect from October 1, 2014.

The State Pension Regulations 2015

(SI 2015/173)

ARRANGEMENT OF REGULATIONS

PART 1

GENERAL

1. Citation, commencement, application and interpretation **6.167**

PART 1A

1A. Full rate of State Pension

PART 2

PRISONERS

2.   Prisoners who are not to be paid state pension
3.   Paying state pension to persons who are remanded in custody

PART 3

DEFERRAL OF STATE PENSION

4.   When a choice of lump sum or survivor's pension may be made
5.   How a choice of lump sum or survivor's pension may be made
6.   Changing a choice of lump sum or survivor's pension
7.   How entitlement to a state pension may be suspended
8.   Date from which a suspension of a state pension begins
9.   Cancelling a suspension of a state pension
10.   Percentage for the weekly rate of increases resulting from deferral of state pension
11.   Days which are not included in determining the period of deferral
12.   Part weeks treated as whole weeks in determining the amount of entitlement during deferral

PART 4

MINIMUM QUALIFYING PERIOD

13.   Minimum number of qualifying years

PART 5

AMENDMENTS TO OTHER LEGISLATION

14.   Sharing of state pension scheme rights

PART 6

GRADUATED RETIREMENT BENEFIT

15.   Survivor's state pension based on inheritance of graduated retirement benefit
16.   Survivor's state pension under regulation 15: inherited amount
17.   Survivor's state pension under regulation 15: up-rating
18.   Choice of lump sum or state pension based on inheritance of deferred graduated retirement benefit
19.   Survivor's lump sum based on inheritance of deferred graduated retirement benefit
20.   Survivor's state pension based on inheritance of deferred graduated retirement benefit

PART 7

OVERSEAS RESIDENTS

21. Entitlement to state pension for overseas residents
22. Modification of the amount of an increment for an overseas resident
23. Modification of the amount of an increment where regulations 12A and 22 both apply

PART 8

NATIONAL INSURANCE CREDITS

CHAPTER 1

GENERAL

24. Interpretation
25. General provisions relating to the crediting of earnings or contributions

CHAPTER 2

Crediting earnings or contributions in respect of a pre-commencement qualifying year

26. Credits under the 1975 Regulations
27. Credits for parents and carers
28. Credits for spouses and civil partners of members of Her Majesty's forces

CHAPTER 3

Crediting earnings or contributions in respect of a qualifying year or a post-commencement qualifying year

29. Credits under the 1975 Regulations
30. Credits for persons in receipt of working tax credit
31. Credits for persons entitled to universal credit
32. Credits for persons approaching pensionable age
33. Credits for spouses and civil partners of members of Her Majesty's forces
34. Credits in respect of an award of child benefit
35. Credits for persons providing care for a child under the age of 12
36. Credits for being a foster parent
37. Credits for persons engaged in caring
38. Credits for an additional period in respect of entitlement to carer's allowance and relevant benefits
39. Time limit for making an application under regulation 34(1)(b), 35, 36 or 37

SCHEDULE

Amendments to other legislation – sharing of state pension rights

The Secretary of State for Work and Pensions makes the following Regulations in exercise of the powers conferred by sections 55A(6) and 175(4) of the Social Security Contributions and Benefits Act 1992), sections 23(1)(a), (b)(ii) and (c)(i) and (2), 48(1)(f)(ii) and 49(4) and (4A) of the Welfare Reform and Pensions Act 1999) and sections 2(3), 4(2), 8(3), (7) and (8), 16(1) and (6), 17(4) and (5), 18(1), 19(1) and (3), 22(1) and 54(5) and (6) of, and paragraph 4 of Schedule 8 and paragraph 4 of Schedule 10 to, the Pensions Act 2014).

The Social Security Advisory Committee has agreed that the proposals in respect of Part 5 of these Regulations should not be referred to it).

The remainder of these Regulations have not been referred to the Social Security Advisory Committee because they are made before the end of the period of six months beginning with the coming into force of the provisions of the Pensions Act 2014 under which they are made).

In accordance with section 83(11) of the Welfare Reform and Pensions Act 1999, due to the exercise of powers to make regulations under Part 4 of that Act, the Secretary of State has consulted such persons as he considers appropriate about Part 5 of these Regulations).

A draft of these Regulations has been laid before Parliament in accordance with section 54(2)(a) of the Pensions Act 2014 and approved by a resolution of each House of Parliament.

PART 1

GENERAL

Citation, commencement, application and interpretation

6.168   **1.**—(1) These Regulations may be cited as the State Pension Regulations 2015.

(2) These Regulations come into force on 6th April 2016.

(3) These Regulations (except Part 5) do not apply to a person who reaches pensionable age before 6th April 2016.

[¹ (4) In these Regulations—

"the 1965 Act" means the National Insurance Act 1965;

"the 2014 Act" means the Pensions Act 2014;

"deferral period" means the period during which a person's entitlement to a state

pension under Part 1 of the 2014 Act is deferred;

"graduated retirement benefit" means any benefit under section 36 (graduated retirement benefit) or 37 (special provisions as to graduated retirement benefit for widows) of the 1965 Act.]

(5) For the purposes of these Regulations (except this paragraph), two people are to be treated as if they are not married to each other in relation to times when either of them is married to a third person.

AMENDMENT

1. State Pension Regulations 2015 (SI 2015/173) reg.2 (April 6, 2016).

[¹ PART 1A

FULL RATE OF STATE PENSION

Full rate of state pension

1A. The full rate of the state pension for the purposes of section 3(1) of   **6.169**
the 2014 Act (full rate of state pension) is [² £168.60 per week.]

AMENDMENTS

1. State Pension (Amendment) Regulations 2016 (SI 2016/227) reg.2 (April 6, 2016).
2. Social Security Benefits Up-rating Order 2019 (SI 2019/480) art.6(2) (April 8, 2019).

PART 2

PRISONERS

Prisoners who are not to be paid state pension

2.—(1) Subject to regulation 3, a person is not to be paid a state pension   **6.170**
under Part 1 of the 2014 Act (state pension) for any period during which
the person is a prisoner who is mentioned in paragraph (2).

(2) Except where paragraph (3) applies, a person is a prisoner for the
purposes of paragraph (1) where the person is—
  (a) a prisoner in Great Britain or elsewhere who is imprisoned or
      detained in legal custody in connection with, or as a result of, crimi-
      nal proceedings;
  (b) a prisoner in Great Britain or elsewhere who is unlawfully at large;
  (c) a prisoner in Great Britain who is being detained—
      (i) under section 47 of the Mental Health Act 1983 (removal to
          hospital of persons serving sentences of imprisonment etc); and
      (ii) on or before the day which the Secretary of State certifies to be
          the person's release date (if any) within the meaning in section
          50(3) of that Act;
  (d) a prisoner in Great Britain who is being detained under section 136
      of the Mental Health (Care and Treatment) (Scotland) Act 2003
      (transfer of prisoners for treatment of mental disorder).

(3) Where a person outside Great Britain is a prisoner within paragraph
(2)(a) or (b) and, in similar circumstances in Great Britain, the person
would not have been a prisoner, the person is not a prisoner within paragraph (2)(a) or (b).

Paying state pension to persons who are remanded in custody

3.—(1) Where a person is remanded in custody for an offence, regulation   **6.171**
2(1) does not apply unless a sentence described in paragraph (2) is later
imposed on the person for the offence.

(2) Subject to paragraph (3), the described sentences for the purposes of
paragraph (1) are—

(a) a sentence of imprisonment or detention in legal custody as a result of criminal proceedings;

(b) a sentence of detention where the provisions mentioned in regulation 2(2)(c)(i) or (d) apply;

(c) a suspended sentence within the meaning in section 189 of the Criminal Justice Act 2003 (suspended sentences of imprisonment).

(3) A sentence described in paragraph (2)(a) which is imposed outside Great Britain is not a described sentence for the purposes of paragraph (1) if, in similar circumstances in Great Britain, a sentence described in paragraph (2)(a) would not have been imposed.

PART 3

DEFERRAL OF STATE PENSION

When a choice of lump sum or survivor's pension may be made

6.172

4.—(1) Where a person falls within section 8(1) of the 2014 Act (choice of lump sum or survivor's pension under section 9 in certain cases), paragraphs (2) and (3) set out the period within which that person is to make any choice under section 8(2) of that Act to be paid—

(a) a lump sum under section 8 of that Act; or

(b) a state pension under section 9 of that Act (survivor's pension based on inheritance of deferred old state pension).

(2) Where the Secretary of State has issued a notice which confirms that the person may make the choice, the period is three months starting on the date in that notice (or, where there is more than one notice which confirms that the person may make that choice, the date in the most recent such notice).

(3) Where the person makes the choice before the Secretary of State has issued any such notice, the period—

(a) starts on the later of the date—

(i) the person claims a state pension; or

(ii) the person's spouse or civil partner died; and

(b) ends on the date the person makes the choice.

(4) A person may make a late choice after the period set out in this regulation in circumstances where—

(a) the Secretary of State considers it is reasonable in any particular case; and

(b) any amount paid by way of (or on account of) a lump sum under section 8(4) of the 2014 Act has been repaid to the Secretary of State—

(i) in full; and

(ii) in the currency in which that amount was originally paid.

(5) The amount of any lump sum to be paid to the person under section 8(4) is reduced to nil where the person makes a late choice under paragraph (4) to be paid a state pension under section 9 of the 2014 Act.

How a choice of lump sum or survivor's pension may be made

6.173

5.—(1) Where a person falls within section 8(1) of the 2014 Act, this regulation sets out the manner in which that person is to make any choice under section 8(2) of that Act to be paid—

(a) a lump sum under section 8 of that Act; or

(b) a state pension under section 9 of that Act.

(2) The manner is—

(a) in writing to an office which is specified to the person in writing by the Secretary of State as accepting any such choice; or

(b) by telephone to a telephone number which is specified to the person in writing by the Secretary of State as accepting any such choice.

(3) The person must use the manner set out in paragraph (2)(a) where the Secretary of State directs in any particular case that that manner must be used.

Changing a choice of lump sum or survivor's pension

6.—(1) Any choice under section 8(2) of the 2014 Act to be paid—   6.174

(a) a lump sum under section 8 of that Act; or

(b) a state pension under section 9 of that Act,

may be altered in the circumstances specified in paragraph (2).

(2) The circumstances referred to in paragraph (1) are—

(a) the person who made the choice has not subsequently died;

(b) an application is made to alter the choice;

(c) the application is made within—

(i) the period of three months starting on the date in the notification issued by the Secretary of State which confirms the choice that has been made; or

(ii) such longer period as the Secretary of State considers reasonable in any particular case;

(d) the application is made in the manner set out in—

(i) regulation 5(2)(a), where the Secretary of State directs in any particular case that the manner in regulation 5(2)(a) must be used; or

(ii) regulation 5(2)(a) or (b), in all other cases;

(e) where the application is to alter the choice so that it becomes a choice to be paid a state pension under section 9 of the 2014 Act, any amount paid by way of (or on account of) a lump sum under section 8 of the 2014 Act has been repaid to the Secretary of State—

(i) in full;

(ii) within the period mentioned in sub-paragraph (c); and

(iii) in the currency in which that amount was originally paid;

(f) where the application is to alter the choice so that it becomes a choice to be paid a lump sum under section 8 of the 2014 Act, any amount paid by way of (or on account of) a state pension under section 9 of the 2014 Act would be less than the amount which would be paid as a lump sum under section 8 of the 2014 Act;

(g) no previous alteration has been made under this regulation in respect of the same deferral mentioned in section 8(1)(c) of the 2014 Act; and

(h) the choice has not been treated as made under regulation 30(5G) [¹ or (5H)] of the Social Security (Claims and Payments) Regulations 1987 (payments on death).

(3) Where the circumstance in paragraph (2)(f) applies, any amount paid by way of (or on account of) a state pension under section 9 of the 2014 Act in respect of the deferral mentioned in section 8(1)(c) of the 2014 Act for

which the choice was originally made is to be treated as having been paid on account of the lump sum to be paid under section 8 of the 2014 Act.

AMENDMENT

1. Pensions Act (Consequential, Supplementary and Incidental Amendments) Order 2015 (SI 2015/1985) art.45 (April 6, 2016).

How entitlement to a state pension may be suspended

6.175 **7.**—(1) A person who has become entitled to a state pension under Part 1 of the 2014 Act may opt to suspend their entitlement if they give notice to the Secretary of State.

(2) The manner in which the notice must be given is—

(a) in writing to an office which is specified to the person in writing by the Secretary of State as accepting any such notice; or

(b) by telephone to a telephone number which is specified to the person in writing by the Secretary of State as accepting any such notice.

(3) But the person must use the manner set out in paragraph (2)(a) where the Secretary of State directs in any particular case that that manner must be used.

Date from which a suspension of a state pension begins

6.176 **8.**—(1) Where a person exercises their option to suspend their entitlement to a state pension under Part 1 of the 2014 Act, the suspension takes effect from the date set out in this regulation.

(2) The date is any date which the person specifies that is—

(a) not before the date on which the option was exercised; and

(b) not after 28 days starting with the date on which the option was exercised.

(3) Where the person does not specify a date in accordance with paragraph (2), the date is the date on which the option was exercised.

Cancelling a suspension of a state pension

6.177 **9.**—(1) Where a person has opted to suspend their entitlement to a state pension under Part 1 of the 2014 Act, the person may cancel the exercise of that option in relation to the whole of, or part of, a past period referred to in paragraph (3).

(2) The person cancels the suspension by making a claim for their state pension whilst their state pension is suspended.

(3) The past period mentioned in paragraph (1) is any period of up to 12 months before the date on which the person cancels the suspension.

Percentage for the weekly rate of increases resulting from deferral of state pension

6.178 **10.** For the purposes of section 17(4) of the 2014 Act (effect of pensioner postponing or suspending state pension), the specified percentage is one-ninth of 1%.

Days which are not included in determining the period of deferral

6.179 **11.**—(1) In the circumstances set out in paragraph (2), a day does not count in determining a number of whole weeks for the purposes of section 17(3) of the 2014 Act.

(2) The circumstances mentioned in paragraph (1) are where the day is—

(a) a day on which the person whose entitlement to a state pension under Part 1 of the 2014 Act is deferred has received any of the following benefits—

  (i) state pension credit under section 1 of the State Pension Credit Act 2002 (entitlement to state pension credit);

  (ii) income support under section 124 of the Contributions and Benefits Act (income support);

  (iii) an income-related employment and support allowance (which means an income-related allowance under Part 1 of the Welfare Reform Act 2007 (employment and support allowance);

  (iv) an income-based jobseeker's allowance within the meaning in section 1(4) of the Jobseekers Act 1995 (the jobseeker's allowance);

  (v) universal credit under Part 1 of the Welfare Reform Act 2012 (universal credit);

  (vi) a carer's allowance under section 70 of the Contributions and Benefits Act (carer's allowance);

  (vii) an unemployability supplement within the meaning in regulation 2(1) of the Social Security (Overlapping Benefits) Regulations 1979 (interpretation);

  (viii) severe disablement allowance under section 68 of the Contributions and Benefits Act (entitlement and rate of severe disablement allowance);

  (ix) a widow's pension under section 39 of the Contributions and Benefits Act (rate of widowed mother's allowance and widow's pension);

  (x) a widowed mother's allowance under section 37 of the Contributions and Benefits Act (widowed mother's allowance);

  (xi) incapacity benefit under section 30A of the Contributions and Benefits Act (incapacity benefit: entitlement);

(b) a day on which a person—

  (i) has received an increase of any of the benefits mentioned in sub-paragraph (a) in respect of the person whose entitlement to a state pension under Part 1 of the 2014 Act is deferred; and

  (ii) is married to, in a civil partnership with or residing with the person whose entitlement to a state pension under Part 1 of the 2014 Act is deferred; or

(c) a day on which the person whose entitlement to a state pension under Part 1 of the 2014 Act is deferred would not, if their entitlement was not deferred, be paid that state pension because they were a prisoner (see section 19 of the 2014 Act (prisoners) and regulations 2 and 3).

Part weeks treated as whole weeks in determining the amount of entitlement during deferral

12.—(1) In the circumstances set out in paragraph (2), a part of a week is   6.180
to be treated as a whole week for the purposes of section 17(3) of the 2014 Act.

(2) The circumstances mentioned in paragraph (1) are where there is a part of a week in the total period during which the person's entitlement to

a state pension was deferred, after any days have been discounted under regulation 11.

[¹ Modification of the amount of an increment for other cases during deferral

6.181   **12A.**—(1) Subject to regulation 23, this regulation applies in cases where, at any time in the deferral period, the weekly rate of the person's state pension, had the person's entitlement not been deferred, would have changed otherwise than because of an up-rating increase ("a non-uprating change").

(2) Section 17(4) of the 2014 Act (amount of an increment for pensioner postponing or suspending state pension) is modified to provide that the amount of an increment for each modification period is equal to a percentage specified in regulations of the weekly rate of the state pension to which the person, if their entitlement had not been deferred, would have been entitled immediately before the end of the modification period.

(3) The first modification period begins at the start of the deferral period and ends immediately before the date of the first or only non-uprating change.

(4) Further modification periods begin on the date of the most recent or only non-uprating change and end—

(a) immediately before the end of the deferral period, where there is no subsequent non-uprating change; or

(b) immediately before the date of the subsequent non-uprating change, where there is a subsequent non-uprating change.]

AMENDMENT

1. State Pension and Occupational Pension Schemes (Miscellaneous Amendments) Regulations 2016 (SI 2016/199) reg.3 (April 6, 2016).

PART 4

MINIMUM QUALIFYING PERIOD

Minimum number of qualifying years

6.182   **13.**—(1) For the purposes of section 2(3) of the 2014 Act (entitlement to state pension at full or reduced rate), the minimum number of qualifying years(**a**) for a state pension payable at the reduced rate is ten.

(2) For the purposes of section 4(2) of the 2014 Act (entitlement to a state pension at transitional rate), the minimum number of qualifying years for a state pension payable at the transitional rate is ten.

PART 5

AMENDMENTS TO OTHER LEGISLATION

Sharing of state pension scheme rights

6.183   **14.** The Schedule to these Regulations (which makes amendments relating to the sharing of state pension rights) has effect.

[¹ PART 6

GRADUATED RETIREMENT BENEFIT

Survivor's state pension based on inheritance of graduated retirement benefit

15.—(1) A person whose dead spouse or civil partner paid graduated contributions as an insured person is entitled to a state pension in accordance with this regulation.

(2) Such a person is entitled to a state pension if—

(a) that person has reached pensionable age;

(b) that person's spouse died while they were married or that person's civil partner died while they were civil partners of each other;

(c) the marriage took place, or the civil partnership was formed, before 6th April 2016; and

(d) that person is entitled to an inherited amount under regulation 16(1), (2) or (3).

(3) A state pension under this regulation is payable at a weekly rate equal to the inherited amount determined in accordance with regulation 16(4) to (6).

(4) The rate of the state pension for a person under this regulation is to be increased from time to time in accordance with regulation 17.]

6.184

AMENDMENT

1. State Pension and Occupational Pension Schemes (Miscellaneous Amendments) Regulations 2016 (SI 2016/199) reg.4 (April 6, 2016).

[¹ Survivor's state pension under regulation 15: inherited amount

16.—(1) For the purposes of regulation 15(2)(d), a person is entitled to an inherited amount if—

(a) their spouse or civil partner died before 6th April 2016;

(b) they were under pensionable age when their spouse or civil partner died; and

(c) they have not married or formed a civil partnership after the death and before the time they reach pensionable age.

(2) For the purposes of regulation 15(2)(d), a person is entitled to an inherited amount if—

(a) their spouse or civil partner reached pensionable age before 6th April 2016 but died on or after 6th April 2016;

(b) they were under pensionable age when their spouse or civil partner died; and

(c) they have not married or formed a civil partnership after the death and before the time they reach pensionable age.

(3) For the purposes of regulation 15(2)(d), a person is entitled to an inherited amount if—

(a) their spouse or civil partner reached pensionable age before 6th April 2016 but died on or after 6th April 2016; and

(b) they were over pensionable age when their spouse or civil partner died.

(4) The inherited amount is half of the weekly rate of the deceased spouse's or civil partner's graduated retirement benefit, determined in

6.185

accordance with paragraph (5), on the date referred to in paragraph (6) (whether or not the deceased was receiving, or entitled to receive, any such benefit).

(5) The determination for the purposes of paragraph (4) is carried out by—

    (a) taking the weekly rate of graduated retirement benefit appropriate to the amount of graduated contributions paid by the deceased;

    (b) determining that weekly rate as if any provisions in orders under section 150 of the Administration Act (annual up-rating of benefits) (**a**) which—

        (i) increase that weekly rate; and

        (ii) have come into force since the date of the deceased's death, had come into force before that date; and

    (c) excluding any addition under—

        (i) section 36(4) of the 1965 Act; or

        (ii) section 37(1) of that Act.

(6) The date mentioned in paragraph (4) is—

    (a) where the person falls within paragraph (1) or (2), the date on which the person reaches pensionable age; or

    (b) where the person falls within paragraph (3), the date on which the person's spouse or civil partner died.]

AMENDMENT

1. State Pension and Occupational Pension Schemes (Miscellaneous Amendments) Regulations 2016 (SI 2016/199) reg.4 (April 6, 2016).

[¹ Survivor's state pension under regulation 15: up-rating

6.186   **17.**—(1) The rate of a person's state pension under regulation 15 is to be increased as follows.

(2) In this regulation, a reference to the rate of a person's state pension is to the rate—

    (a) without any reduction under Regulations made under section 7(4) (survivor's pension based on inheritance of additional old state pension) of the 2014 Act (in the case of a state pension under section 7 of the 2014 Act);

    (b) taking into account any reduction under section 14 (pension sharing: reduction in the sharer's section 4 pension) of the 2014 Act (in the case of a state pension under section 4 of the 2014 Act); and

    (c) without any increase under section 17 of the 2014 Act.

(3) The rate of the person's state pension is increased in accordance with paragraph (4) where—

    (a) that rate, when added to the sum of the rate of any state pension to which the person is entitled under section 7 and section 2, 4 or 12 of the 2014 Act (entitlement to state pension at various rates), is equal to or less than the full rate of the state pension; and

    (b) the full rate of the state pension is increased at any time.

(4) Where paragraph (3) applies—

    (a) the rate of the person's state pension is increased by the same percentage as the increase in the full rate; and

    (b) that increase of the person's state pension is to be made at the same time as the increase in the full rate.

(5) The rate of the person's state pension is increased in accordance with either or both of paragraphs (6) and (7) where—

    (a) both—

        (i) that rate, when added to the sum of the rate of any state pension to which the person is entitled under section 7 and section 2, 4 or 12 of the 2014 Act, exceeds the full rate of the state pension; and

        (ii) the sum of the rate of any state pension to which the person is entitled under section 7 and section 2, 4 or 12 of the 2014 Act is less than the full rate of the state pension; and

    (b) either or both of the following occurs at any time—

        (i) the full rate of the state pension is increased;

        (ii) an uprating order comes into force.

(6) Where paragraph (5)(a) and (b)(i) applies, the rate of the person's state pension is increased—

    (a) by an amount equal to the appropriate percentage of the shortfall immediately before the full rate of the state pension is increased ("the appropriate percentage" means the percentage by which the full rate is increased); and

    (b) at the same time as paragraph (5)(b)(i) applies.

(7) Where paragraph (5)(a) and (b)(ii) applies, the rate of the person's state pension is increased—

    (a) by an amount equal to the appropriate percentage of the excess immediately before the uprating order mentioned in paragraph (5) (b)(ii) comes into force ("the appropriate percentage" means the percentage specified in that uprating order); and

    (b) at the same time as that uprating order comes into force.

(8) The rate of the person's state pension is increased in accordance with paragraph (9) where—

    (a) the sum of the rate of any state pension to which the person is entitled under section 7 and section 2, 4 or 12 of the 2014 Act is equal to or higher than the full rate of the state pension; and

    (b) an uprating order comes into force at any time.

(9) Where paragraph (8) applies—

    (a) the rate of the person's state pension is increased by the percentage specified in the uprating order mentioned in paragraph (8)(b); and

    (b) that increase of the person's state pension is to be made at the same time as that uprating order comes into force.

(10) In this regulation—

"the excess" means the amount by which the rate of the state pension, when added to the sum of the rate of any state pension to which the person is entitled under section 7 and section 2, 4 or 12 of the 2014 Act, exceeds the full rate;

"the shortfall" means the amount by which the sum of the rate of any state pension to which the person is entitled under section 7 and section 2, 4 or 12 of the 2014 Act, is less than the full rate;

"uprating order" means an order under section 151A of the Administration Act (uprating of transitional state pensions under the 2014 Act).]

AMENDMENT

1. State Pension and Occupational Pension Schemes (Miscellaneous Amendments) Regulations 2016 (SI 2016/199) reg.4 (April 6, 2016).

[¹ Choice of lump sum or state pension based on inheritance of deferred graduated retirement benefit

6.187   **18.**—(1) Subject to paragraph (8), a person is entitled to a choice under this regulation if—

(a) that person has reached pensionable age;

(b) that person's spouse died while they were married or that person's civil partner died while they were civil partners of each other;

(c) the spouse's or civil partner's entitlement to graduated retirement benefit was deferred at the time of death and throughout the period of 12 months ending with the day before the death; and

(d) either—

(i) that person was under pensionable age when the spouse or civil partner died and did not marry or form a civil partnership between the date of death and the date that person reached pensionable age; or

(ii) that person was over pensionable age when the spouse or civil partner died.

(2) The person may choose to be paid—

(a) a lump sum under regulation 19; or

(b) a state pension under regulation 20.

(3) The manner in which that choice is to be made is the manner set out in regulation 5(2) and (3).

(4) The period within which that choice is to be made is the period set out in regulation 4(2) and (3) and a person may make a late choice after that period where—

(a) the Secretary of State considers it is reasonable in any particular case; and

(b) any amount paid by way of (or on account of) a lump sum under regulation 19 has been repaid to the Secretary of State—

(i) in full; and

(ii) in the currency in which that amount was originally paid.

(5) Where the person fails to make a choice within the period set out in regulation 4(2) and (3), they are to be paid a lump sum under regulation 19.

(6) The amount of any lump sum to be paid to the person under regulation 19 is reduced to nil where the person makes a late choice under paragraph (4) to be paid a state pension under regulation 20.

(7) A choice under this regulation may be altered in the circumstances specified in regulation 6(2), and for that purpose—

(a) regulation 6(3) applies where the circumstance in regulation 6(2)(f) applies;

(b) any references in regulation 6(2) and (3) to section 8 of the 2014 Act are to be read as references to regulation 19; and

(c) any references in regulation 6(2) and (3) to section 9 of the 2014 Act are to be read as references to regulation 20.

(8) A person is not entitled to a choice under this regulation if they are entitled to a choice under section 8(2) of the 2014 Act.

(9) Where paragraph (1) applies to a person and that person makes a choice under—

    (a) section 8(2)(a) of the 2014 Act, they are to be paid a lump sum under regulation 19 (subject to paragraph (10));

    (b) section 8(2)(b) of the 2014 Act, they are to be paid a state pension under regulation 20 (subject to paragraph (10)).

(10) Where paragraph (1) applies to a person and that person alters a choice under regulation 6—

    (a) they are to be paid a lump sum under regulation 19 where their new choice is to be paid a lump sum under section 8 of the 2014 Act;

    (b) they are to be paid a state pension under regulation 20 where their new choice is to be paid a state pension under section 9 of the 2014 Act.

(11) Where paragraph (1) applies to a person and that person fails to make a choice under section 8(2) of the 2014 Act, they are to be paid a lump sum under regulation 19.]

AMENDMENT

1. State Pension and Occupational Pension Schemes (Miscellaneous Amendments) Regulations 2016 (SI 2016/199) reg.4 (April 6, 2016).

[¹ Survivor's lump sum based on inheritance of deferred graduated retirement benefit

19.—(1) Where a person is to be paid a lump sum by virtue of regulation 18, they are entitled to a lump sum calculated in accordance with paragraph 10 or, where appropriate, paragraph 20 of Schedule 1 to the Social Security (Graduated Retirement Benefit) Regulations 2005.

(2) In paragraphs 10(6) and 20(6) of Schedule 1 to those Regulations as they apply for the purposes of this regulation, the references to the date on which the person becomes entitled to a Category A or Category B retirement pension or to graduated retirement benefit are to be read as a reference to the date on which the person becomes entitled to make a choice under regulation 18.]

6.188

AMENDMENT

1. State Pension and Occupational Pension Schemes (Miscellaneous Amendments) Regulations 2016 (SI 2016/199) reg.4 (April 6, 2016).

[¹ Survivor's state pension based on inheritance of deferred graduated retirement benefit

20.—(1) A person is entitled to a state pension under this regulation if—

    (a) that person has reached pensionable age;

    (b) that person's spouse died while they were married or that person's civil partner died while they were civil partners of each other;

    (c) either—

        (i) that person was under pensionable age when the spouse or civil partner died and did not marry or form a civil partnership between the date of death and the date that person reached pensionable age; or

        (ii) that person was over pensionable age when the spouse or civil partner died;

    (d) either—

6.189

   (i) that person's spouse or civil partner was entitled to an increase in graduated retirement benefit; or

   (ii) that person's spouse's or civil partner's entitlement to graduated retirement benefit was deferred when the spouse or civil partner died;

  (e) in the case of a person entitled to a choice under regulation 18, that person has chosen to be paid a state pension under this regulation; and

  (f) in the case of a person who is not entitled to a choice under regulation 18 because regulation 18(8) applies to them, that person is to be paid a state pension under this regulation by virtue of regulation 18(9)(b) or (10)(b).

(2) Subject to paragraph (3), a state pension under this regulation is payable at a weekly rate equal to half of the weekly rate of—v

  (a) the deceased spouse's or civil partner's increase in graduated retirement benefit; or

  (b) where the deceased spouse's or civil partner's entitlement to graduated retirement benefit was deferred when they died, the increase in graduated retirement benefit, determined in accordance with paragraph (4), that would have been payable if the deferral had ended immediately before their death.

(3) For the purposes of paragraph (2), if at any time an order under section 151A of the Administration Act comes into force, the rate of the person's state pension under this regulation is increased (at that time) by the percentage specified in the order.

(4) For the purposes of paragraph (2), the increase is to be determined as if—

  (a) any provisions in orders under section 150 of the Administration Act which—

   (i) increase the weekly rate of the graduated retirement benefit; and

   (ii) have come into force between the date of the deceased's death and the date on which the person reaches pensionable age, had come into force before the date of death; and

  (b) the weekly rate of the deceased spouse's or civil partner's increase did not include any addition under section 37(1) of the 1965 Act.

(5) In this regulation, "increase in graduated retirement benefit" means an increase determined in accordance with section 36(4) of the 1965 Act.]

AMENDMENT

1. State Pension and Occupational Pension Schemes (Miscellaneous Amendments) Regulations 2016 (SI 2016/199) reg.4 (April 6, 2016).

PART 7

OVERSEAS RESIDENTS

Entitlement to state pension for overseas residents

6.190   **21.**—(1) An overseas resident who is entitled to a state pension under Part 1 of the 2014 Act is not entitled to up-rating increases in accordance with this regulation.

(2) This regulation—

(a) applies in relation to an up-rating increase if Regulations are made—

    (i) in consequence of an order under section 150A (annual up-rating) or 151A of the Administration Act or in consequence of any other legislation; and

    (ii) which provide that this regulation applies to that up-rating increase; and

(b) is subject to the Regulations made as mentioned in sub-paragraph (a).

(3) Paragraph (4) applies in a case where—

(a) a person's entitlement to a state pension under Part 1 of the 2014 Act has been deferred for a period; and

(b) when the deferral period ends, that person is—

    (i) entitled to a state pension under Part 1 of the 2014 Act; and

    (ii) an overseas resident.

(4) Where this paragraph applies, the person mentioned in paragraph (3) is not entitled to any up-rating increases—

(a) in respect of the deferral period if—

    (i) the person was an overseas resident at the time of that increase; and

    (ii) the person continued to be an overseas resident until the deferral period ended; and

(b) after the deferral period ended if the person is an overseas resident at the time of that increase.

(5) In all other cases, a person is not entitled to up-rating increases where, immediately before the up-rating increase comes into force, they were—

(a) entitled to a state pension under Part 1 of the 2014 Act; and

(b) an overseas resident.

(6) For the purposes of sections 18(4) and 20(2) and (3) of the 2014 Act, the territory specified is any part of the Channel Islands which is not subject to an Order made under section 179 of the Administration Act.]

AMENDMENT

1. State Pension and Occupational Pension Schemes (Miscellaneous Amendments) Regulations 2016 (SI 2016/199) reg.4 (April 6, 2016).

GENERAL NOTE

Regulation 3 of the Social Security Up-rating Regulations 2019 (SI 2019/552) applies regulation 21 to any up-rating increase as defined in s.22(1) of the Pensions Act 2014.   **6.191**

Modification of the amount of an increment for an overseas resident

22.—(1) Subject to regulation 23, this regulation applies in cases where, during any part of the deferral period, a person has been an overseas resident.   **6.192**

(2) For any part of the deferral period during which the person was an overseas resident and was not in Great Britain or a territory specified in regulation 21(6), section 17(4) of the 2014 Act is modified to provide that the amount of an increment is equal to a percentage specified in regulations of the weekly rate of the state pension to which the person would have been entitled immediately before the start of that part of the deferral period if the person's entitlement had not been deferred.

(3) For any part of the deferral period during which the person was not an overseas resident, section 17(4) of the 2014 Act is modified to provide that the amount of an increment is equal to a specified percentage of the weekly rate of the state pension to which the person would have been entitled immediately before the end of that part of the deferral period if the person's entitlement had not been deferred.]

AMENDMENT

1. State Pension and Occupational Pension Schemes (Miscellaneous Amendments) Regulations 2016 (SI 2016/199) reg.4 (April 6, 2016).

Modification of the amount of an increment where regulations 12A and 22 both apply

6.193   **23.**—(1) This regulation applies in a case where section 17(4) of the 2014 Act falls to be modified under both regulations 12A and 22 at the same time.

(2) Section 17(4) of the 2014 Act is modified to provide that the amount of an increment is determined as set out in the following paragraphs.

(3) The amount of the increment is first determined in accordance with the modifications set out in regulation 22.

(4) The amount of the increment is then determined in accordance with the modifications set out in regulation 12A as if the reference in regulation 12A(2) to the weekly rate of the state pension were a reference to the weekly rate referred to in—

(a) regulation 22(2), for any part of the deferral period during which the person was an overseas resident and was not in Great Britain or a territory specified in regulation 21(6); and

(b) regulation 22(3), for any part of the deferral period during which the person was not an overseas resident.

(5) Any increase or decrease of the increment as determined in accordance with paragraph (4) is then added to, or subtracted from, the amount of the increment as determined in accordance with paragraph (3).]

AMENDMENT

1. State Pension and Occupational Pension Schemes (Miscellaneous Amendments) Regulations 2016 (SI 2016/199) reg.4 (April 6, 2016).

[¹ PART 8

NATIONAL INSURANCE CREDITS

CHAPTER 1

GENERAL

Interpretation

6.194   **24.**—(1) In this Part—

"the 1975 Regulations" means the Social Security (Credits) Regulations 1975;

"the 1992 Act" means the Social Security Contributions and Benefits
    Act 1992;
"the 2012 Act" means the Welfare Reform Act 2012;
"post-commencement qualifying year" and "pre-commencement quali-
    fying year" have the same meaning as in section 4(4) of the 2014 Act;
"qualifying year" has the same meaning as in section 2(4) of the 2014
    Act;
"working tax credit" means a working tax credit under section 10 of the
    Tax Credits Act 2002;
"year" means a tax year.

(2) Nothing in Chapter 3 is to be construed as entitling any person to
be credited with earnings or contributions for any day or in respect of any
event occurring before 6th April 2016.

General provisions relating to the crediting of earnings or contributions

25.—(1) For the purposes of Part 1 of the 2014 Act—   6.195
  (a) Chapter 2 makes provision for crediting earnings or contributions in
      respect of a pre-commencement qualifying year;
  (b) Chapter 3 makes provision for crediting earnings or contributions in
      respect of a qualifying year or a post-commencement qualifying year.

(2) Where under this Part a person would, but for this paragraph, be
entitled to be credited with any earnings or contributions for a year, or in
respect of any week in a year, that person is only to be credited to the extent
necessary to make that year a qualifying year.

(3) Where under this Part a person is entitled to be credited with earnings
or a contribution in respect of a week that falls partly in one tax year and
partly in another, that week is to be treated as falling in the year in which it
begins and not in the following year.

GENERAL NOTE

Part 6 of the Regulations is in effect a partial code for dealing with all contribu-   6.196
tions credits entitlement issues in connection with pension claims arising on or after
April 6, 2016. Note that Chapter 2 deals with years before that date, while Chapter
3 deals with years after that date. Both Chapter 2 (reg.26) and Chapter 3 (reg.29)
keep in being provisions of the Social Security (Credits) Regulations 1975 (above in
this volume). But they do not do so in entirety, with some of the regulations being
rewritten by these provisions while others are accepted without change.

CHAPTER 2

Crediting earnings or contributions in respect of a pre-commencement qualifying
year

Credits under the 1975 Regulations

26. A person is to be credited with the earnings or contributions to which   6.197
the person would have been entitled under the 1975 Regulations for the
purposes of entitlement to a Category A retirement pension had—
  (a) the amendment made by paragraph 55 of Schedule 12 to the 2014
      Act (which limits Category A retirement pensions to people who

reach pensionable age before 6th April 2016) not come into force, and

(b) the person attained pensionable age on 6th April 2016.

Credits for parents and carers

6.198   **27.** A person is to be credited with a Class 3 contribution to which the person would have been entitled under section 23A of the 1992 Act (contributions credits for relevant parents and carers), or regulations made under that section, for the purposes of entitlement to a Category A retirement pension had—

(a) the amendment made by paragraph 55 of Schedule 12 to the 2014 Act (which limits Category A retirement pensions to people who reach pensionable age before 6th April 2016) not come into force, and

(b) the person attained pensionable age on 6th April 2016.

Credits for spouses and civil partners of members of Her Majesty's forces

6.199   **28.**—(1) Subject to paragraph (5), a person who satisfies the conditions in paragraph (2) for any part of a week to which this regulation applies is to be credited with a Class 3 contribution in respect of that week.

(2) The conditions are that the person—

(a) is a spouse or civil partner of a member of Her Majesty's forces, or is treated as such by the Secretary of State for the purposes of occupying accommodation, and

(b) is accompanying the member of Her Majesty's forces on an assignment outside the United Kingdom, or is treated as such by the Secretary of State.

(3) This regulation applies to a week which falls within a year beginning on or after 6th April 1975 and ending before 6th April 2016 for which the earnings factors of the member of Her Majesty's forces exceed the qualifying earnings factor.

(4) Paragraph (1) does not apply to—

(a) a person in respect of a week in which the person is entitled to be credited with earnings under—

(i) regulation 7A (credits for carer's allowance),

(ii) regulation 8A (credits for unemployment),

(iii) regulation 8B (credits for incapacity for work or limited capability for work), or

(iv) regulation 9E (credits for certain spouses and civil partners of members of Her Majesty's forces), of the 1975 Regulations; or

(b) a woman in respect of a week in any part of which an election made by her under regulations under section 19(4) of the 1992 Act (reduced rate election for married women) is in force.

(5) A person is not entitled to be credited with a Class 3 contribution under paragraph (1) unless an application to be so credited is received by the Secretary of State in accordance with paragraph (6).

(6) An application under paragraph (5) may only be made in respect of a past period and must—

(a) be on a form approved by the Secretary of State, or made in such manner as the Secretary of State accepts as sufficient in the circumstances, and

(b) include such information as may be specified by the Secretary of State or the Commissioners for Her Majesty's Revenue and Customs.

CHAPTER 3

Crediting earnings or contributions in respect of a qualifying year or a post-commencement qualifying year

Credits under the 1975 Regulations

29.—(1) Where a person is credited with earnings or contributions under the provisions of the 1975 Regulations specified in paragraph (2), the person is also to be credited with those earnings or contributions for the purposes of Part 1 of the 2014 Act.

6.200

(2) The provisions specified are—
(a) regulation 7 (credits for approved training);
(b) regulation 7A (credits for carer's allowance);
(c) regulation 7B (credits for disability element of working tax credit);
(d) regulation 8A (credits for unemployment);
(e) regulation 8B (credits for incapacity for work or limited capability for work);
(f) regulation 9B (credits for jury service);
(g) regulation 9C (credits for maternity pay etc.);
(h) regulation 9D (credits for certain periods of imprisonment or detention in legal custody);
(i) regulation 9E (credits for certain spouses and civil partners of members of Her Majesty's forces).

Credits for persons in receipt of working tax credit

30.—(1) Where working tax credit is paid to a person in respect of a week in which the person is—

6.201

(a) an employed earner,
(b) a self-employed earner whose profits for the year are below the small profits threshold specified by section 11(4) of the 1992 Act, who would otherwise be liable to pay a Class 2 contribution, or
(c) excepted from liability to pay a Class 2 contribution by virtue of regulation 43 of the Social Security (Contributions) Regulations 2001, the person is to be credited with earnings equal to the lower earnings limit then in force in respect of that week.

(2) Where working tax credit is paid in respect of a couple, the reference in paragraph (1) to the person in respect of whom working tax credit is paid is a reference to —
(a) where only one member of the couple is assessed for the purposes of the award of working tax credit as having income consisting of earnings, that member, or
(b) where the earnings of each member are assessed, the member of the couple to whom working tax credit is paid.

(3) Paragraph (1) does not apply to—

(a) a person in respect of a week in which the person is entitled to be credited with earnings under—
  (i) regulation 7B (credits for disability element of working tax credit),
  (ii) regulation 8A (credits for unemployment), or
  (iii) regulation 8B (credits for incapacity for work or limited capability for work), of the 1975 Regulations; or
(b) a woman in respect of a week in any part of which an election made by her under regulations under section 19(4) of the 1992 Act (reduced rate election for married women) is in force.

(4) In this regulation, "couple" has the same meaning as in section 3(5A) of the Tax Credits Act 2002.

Credits for persons entitled to universal credit

6.202   **31.** A person is to be credited with a Class 3 contribution in respect of a week for any part of which the person is entitled to universal credit under Part 1 of the 2012 Act.

Credits for persons approaching pensionable age

6.203   **32.**—(1) Subject to paragraph (4), a man born before 6th October 1953 is to be credited with earnings equal to the lower earnings limit then in force in respect of a week to which paragraph (2) applies.

(2) This paragraph applies to a week which falls within—
(a) the year in which the man attains the age which is pensionable age in the case of a woman born on the same day, and
(b) a subsequent year prior to that in which he attains the age of 65.

(3) Paragraph (2) does not apply to a week which falls within a year during which the man is absent from Great Britain for more than 182 days.

(4) Paragraph (1) applies to a man who is a self-employed earner only if he—
(a) would be liable to pay a Class 2 contribution but for the fact that his profits for the year are below the small profits threshold specified by section 11(4) of the 1992 Act, or
(b) is excepted from liability to pay a Class 2 contribution by virtue of regulation 43 of the Social Security (Contributions) Regulations 2001 in respect of any week in a year to which this regulation applies.

Credits for spouses and civil partners of members of Her Majesty's forces

6.204   **33.**—(1) Subject to paragraph (5), a person who satisfies the conditions in paragraph (2) for any part of a week to which this regulation applies is to be credited with a Class 3 contribution in respect of that week.

(2) The conditions are that the person—
(a) is a spouse or civil partner of a member of Her Majesty's forces, or is treated as such by the Secretary of State for the purposes of occupying accommodation, and
(b) is accompanying the member of Her Majesty's forces on an assignment outside the United Kingdom, or is treated as such by the Secretary of State.

(3) This regulation applies to a week which falls within a year beginning

982

on or after 6th April 2016 for which the earnings factors of the member of Her Majesty's forces exceed the qualifying earnings factor.

(4) Paragraph (1) does not apply to—

(a) a person in respect of a week in which the person is entitled to be credited with earnings under—

   (i) regulation 7A (credits for carer's allowance),

   (ii) regulation 8A (credits for unemployment),

   (iii) regulation 8B (credits for incapacity for work or limited capability for work), or

   (iv) regulation 9E (credits for certain spouses and civil partners of members of Her Majesty's forces), of the 1975 Regulations; or

(b) a woman in respect of a week in any part of which an election made by her under regulations under section 19(4) of the 1992 Act (reduced rate election for married women) is in force.

(5) A person is not entitled to be credited with a Class 3 contribution under paragraph (1) unless an application to be so credited is received by the Secretary of State in accordance with paragraph (6).

(6) An application under paragraph (5) may only be made in respect of a past period and must—

(a) be on a form approved by the Secretary of State, or made in such manner as the Secretary of State accepts as sufficient in the circumstances, and

(b) include such information as may be specified by the Secretary of State or the Commissioners for Her Majesty's Revenue and Customs.

Credits in respect of an award of child benefit

34.—(1) A person is entitled to be credited with a Class 3 contribution in respect of a week in which the person is—   6.205

(a) awarded child benefit for any part of that week in respect of a child under the age of 12, or

(b) in the circumstances specified by paragraph (2) and subject to paragraph (3), the partner of a person to whom child benefit is awarded.

(2) The circumstances are that the partner—

(a) resides with the person to whom child benefit is awarded,

(b) shares responsibility for the child in respect of whom child benefit is awarded with that person,

(c) is ordinarily resident in Great Britain,

(d) is not undergoing imprisonment or detention in legal custody, and7

(e) makes an application to the Commissioners for Her Majesty's Revenue and Customs to be so credited in accordance with regulation 39.

(3) Paragraph (1)(b) only applies in respect of a week that falls within a year for which the earnings factors of the person to whom child benefit is awarded exceed the qualifying earnings factor.

(4) In calculating the earnings factors for the purpose of paragraph (3), no account is to be taken of any earnings factors derived from contributions credited by virtue of that person being awarded child benefit.

Credits for persons providing care for a child under the age of 12

6.206   35.—(1) Subject to paragraphs (3) and (4), a person is to be credited with a Class 3 contribution in respect of a week ("the relevant week") in which the conditions in paragraph (2) are satisfied.

(2) The conditions are that in the relevant week the person—

(a) provided care in respect of a child under the age of 12,

(b) is, in relation to that child, a person specified in paragraph (6), and

(c) was ordinarily resident in Great Britain.

[¹ (3) The person ('A') referred to in paragraph (1) is not entitled to be credited with a Class 3 contribution unless—

(a) child benefit was awarded to another person ('B') in respect of—

(i) the child, or each child, for whom A provided care, and

(ii) the week in which A provided that care,

(b) B's earnings factors, other than those derived from a Class 3 contribution credit awarded under regulation 34, exceed the qualifying earnings factor for the year in which the relevant week falls, and

(c) A makes an application to the Secretary of State to be so credited in accordance with paragraph (5) and regulation 39.

(4) Where the requirements relating to the provision of care by A in paragraph (3)(a)(i) can be satisfied by more than one person in respect of a week in which B was awarded child benefit—

(a) those persons shall elect, with the agreement of B, which of them is to be credited with a Class 3 contribution credit (and then only the elected person is to be so credited), or

(b) the Secretary of State is to exercise his discretion to determine which of those persons is to be credited with that contribution, in default of the agreement referred to in sub-paragraph (a).]

(5) An application under paragraph [¹ (3)(c)] must—

(a) include the name and date of birth of the child [¹, or each child,] cared for,

(b) where requested by the Secretary of State or the Commissioners for Her Majesty's Revenue and Customs, include a declaration by B that the conditions in paragraph (2) are satisfied, and

(c) specify the relevant week or weeks in which the child [¹, or each child,] was cared for.

(6) The person specified in paragraph (2)(b) is—

(a) a non-resident parent;

(b) a grandparent;

(c) a great-grandparent;

(d) a great-great-grandparent;

(e) a sibling;

(f) a parent's sibling;

(g) a spouse or former spouse of any persons listed in sub-paragraphs (a) to (f);

(h) a civil partner or former civil partner of any persons listed in sub-paragraphs (a) to (f);

(i) a partner or former partner of any persons listed in sub-paragraphs (a) to (h);

(j) a son or daughter of any persons listed in sub-paragraphs (e) to (i);

(k) in respect of a son or daughter of a person listed in sub-paragraph (f), that person's—

   (i) spouse or former spouse,
   (ii) civil partner or former civil partner, or
   (iii) partner or former partner.

(7) For the purposes of paragraph (6)(e) and (f), a sibling includes a sibling of the half blood, a step sibling and an adopted sibling.

(8) For the purposes of paragraph (6)(i) and (k)(iii), a partner is a person who is the other member of a couple who are not married to, or civil partners of, each other but are living together as a married couple.

AMENDMENT

1. Social Security (Miscellaneous Amendments) Regulations 2017 (SI 2017/1015), reg.17 (November 16 2017).

Credits for being a foster parent

36.—(1) Subject to paragraph (3), a person is to be credited with a Class 3 contribution in respect of a week in which the person is a foster parent and is—   **6.207**
   (a) ordinarily resident in Great Britain, and
   (b) not undergoing imprisonment or detention in legal custody.

(2) For the purposes of this regulation, a foster parent is a person approved as—
   (a) a foster parent in accordance with Part 5 (approval of foster parents) of the Fostering Services (England) Regulations 2011,
   (b) a kinship carer in accordance with Part 5 (kinship care) of the Looked After Children (Scotland) Regulations 2009,
   (c) a foster carer in accordance with Part 7 (fostering) of those Regulations, or
   (d) a foster parent in accordance with Part 2 (approvals and placements) of the Foster Placement (Children) Regulations (Northern Ireland) 1996.

(3) A person is not entitled to be credited with a Class 3 contribution under paragraph (1) unless an application to be so credited is received by the Commissioners for Her Majesty's Revenue and Customs in accordance with regulation 39.

Credits for persons engaged in caring

37.—(1) Subject to paragraph (5), a person is to be credited with a Class 3 contribution in respect of a week in which the person is engaged in caring.   **6.208**

(2) A person is engaged in caring in a week if the person is—
   (a) caring for another person or persons for a total of 20 or more hours in that week and—
      (i) that other person is, or each of the persons cared for are, entitled to a relevant benefit for that week, or
      (ii) the Secretary of State considers that level of care to be appropriate; or
   (b) a person to whom one or more of paragraphs 4 to 6 (persons caring for another person) of Schedule 1B (prescribed categories of person) to the Income Support (General) Regulations 1987 applies.

(3) A person is not engaged in caring for the purposes of this regulation during any period in respect of which the person is—

(a) not ordinarily resident in Great Britain, or
(b) undergoing imprisonment or detention in legal custody.
(4) For the purposes of paragraph (2)(a)(i), "relevant benefit" means—
(a) attendance allowance in accordance with section 64 of the 1992 Act;
(b) the care component of disability living allowance in accordance with `section 72 of the 1992 Act, at the middle or highest rate prescribed in accordance with subsection (3) of that section;
(c) an increase in the rate of disablement pension in accordance with section 104 of the 1992 Act;
(d) any benefit which is payable as if an injury or disease were one in respect of which a disablement pension would for the time being be payable in respect of an assessment of 100 per cent., by virtue of—
   (i) the Pneumoconiosis, Byssinosis and Miscellaneous Diseases Benefit Scheme 1983; or
   (ii) regulations made under section 64(3) of the 2012 Act (injuries arising before 5 July 1948);
(e) a constant attendance allowance payable by virtue of—
   (i) article 8 (constant attendance allowance) of the Naval, Military and Air Forces etc. (Disablement and Death) Service Pensions Order 2006; or
   (ii) article 14 (constant attendance allowance) of the Personal Injuries (Civilians) Scheme 1983;
(f) the daily living component of personal independence payment in accordance with section 78 of the 2012 Act;
(g) armed forces independence payment in accordance with the Armed Forces and Reserve Forces (Compensation Scheme) Order 2011.
(5) Except in a case to which paragraph (8) applies, a person is not entitled to be credited with a Class 3 contribution under paragraph (2)(a) unless an application to be so credited is received by the Secretary of State in accordance with paragraph (6) and regulation 39.
(6) An application under paragraph (5) must include—
(a) a declaration by the applicant that the applicant cares for a person or persons for 20 or more hours in a week,
(b) the name and, where known, the national insurance number of each person cared for,
(c) where applicable, which relevant benefit each person cared for is entitled to, and
(d) where requested by the Secretary of State, a declaration signed by an appropriate person as to the level of care which is required for each person cared for.
(7) For the purposes of paragraph (6)(d), an appropriate person is a person who is—
(a) involved in the health care or social care of the person cared for, and
(b) considered by the Secretary of State as appropriate to make a declaration as to the level of care required.
(8) This paragraph applies in the case of a woman in respect of a week in any part of which an election made by her under regulations under section 19(4) of the 1992 Act (reduced rate election for married women) is in force.

Credits for an additional period in respect of entitlement to carer's allowance and relevant benefits

38.—(1) A person is to be credited with a Class 3 contribution for a period of 12 weeks—

    (a) prior to the date on which that person becomes entitled to carer's allowance by virtue of subsection (1) of section 70 of the 1992 Act;

    (b) subject to paragraph (2), following the end of the week in which that person ceases to be entitled to carer's allowance by virtue of that subsection;

    (c) following the end of a week in which regulation 37(2)(a) ceases to be satisfied.

(2) A person is not entitled to be credited with a Class 3 contribution under paragraph (1)(b) in a week in respect of which that person is entitled under regulation 7A of the 1975 Regulations to be credited with contributions by virtue of being entitled to an allowance under section 70 of the 1992 Act.

6.209

Time limit for making an application under regulation 34(1)(b), 35, 36 or 37

39. An application must be received—

    (a) where the application is under regulation 34(1)(b), 36 or 37—

        (i) before the end of the year following that in which a week, which is the subject of the application, falls, or

        (ii) within such further time as the Secretary of State or the Commissioners for Her Majesty's Revenue and Customs, as the case may be, consider reasonable in the circumstances, or

    (b) where the application is under regulation 35, after the end of the year in which a week, which is the subject of the application, falls.]

6.210

AMENDMENT

1. State Pension (Amendment) (No 2) Regulations 2016 (SI 2016/240) reg.2 (April 6, 2016).

SCHEDULE   **Regulation 14**

Omitted as not within the scope of the volume.   6.211

The Pensions Act 2014 (Pension Sharing on Divorce etc.) (Transitional Provision) Order 2016

(SI 2016/39)

The Secretary of State for Work and Pensions makes the following Order in exercise of the power conferred by section 56(8) of the Pensions Act 2014.

Citation, commencement and interpretation

6.212   **1.**—(1) This Order may be cited as the Pensions Act 2014 (Pension Sharing on Divorce etc.) (Transitional Provision) Order 2016 and shall come into force on 6th April 2016.

(2) For the purposes of this Order—

(a) a petition or application is issued on the date entered on the petition or application form by a member of the court staff;

(b) an initial writ or summons is presented on the date entered on the initial writ or summons by a member of the court staff.

Transitional provision in connection with the coming into force of amendments to pension sharing on divorce etc.

6.213   **2.**—(1) This Order applies in a case where section 49A of the Welfare Reform and Pensions Act 1999 (creation of debits and credits: transferor in new state pension system and sharing activated on or after 6 April 2016) would otherwise apply and either—

(a) in England and Wales—

    (i) the petition for divorce or nullity of a marriage was issued before 6th April 2016;

    (ii) the application for dissolution or annulment of a civil partnership was issued before 6th April 2016; or

    (iii) in the case of the application for financial relief after overseas divorce or nullity of a marriage or overseas dissolution or annulment of a civil partnership, the application for permission of the court for financial relief was issued before 6th April 2016; or

(b) in Scotland—

    (i) the initial writ or summons in the proceedings for divorce or nullity of a marriage or for dissolution or annulment of a civil partnership was presented before 6th April 2016;

    (ii) the initial writ or summons in the application for an order for financial provision after overseas divorce or nullity of a marriage or overseas dissolution or annulment of a civil partnership was presented before 6th April 2016; or

    (iii) the qualifying agreement, referred to in section 48(1)(f)(i) of the Welfare Reform and Pensions Act 1999 (activation of benefit sharing), was executed by the parties before 6th April 2016.

(2) In a case where this Order applies—

(a) section 49 of the Welfare Reform and Pensions Act 1999 (creation of state scheme pension debits and credits: transferor in old state pension system or pension sharing activated before 6 April 2016) applies;

(b) section 49A of that Act does not apply; and

(c) the relevant order or provision is to be treated as taking effect on 5th April 2016.

The Pensions Act 2014 (Transitional and Transitory Provisions) Order 2016

(SI 2016/408)

The Secretary of State for Work and Pensions makes the following Order in exercise of the power conferred by section 56(8) of the Pensions Act 2014.

Citation, commencement and cessation

1.—(1) This Order may be cited as the Pensions Act 2014 (Transitional and Transitory Provisions) Order 2016.

(2) This Order comes into force on 6th April 2016.

(3) Article 2 of this Order ceases to have effect on the day on which section 30 of the Pensions Act 2014 (bereavement support payment) comes fully into force.

6.214

GENERAL NOTE

These regulations deal with problems arising because the reforms to the bereavement payments under the Pensions Act 2014 do not come into force at the same time as the reforms to the state pension, the intention being to start them in 2017.

6.215

Transitory provision

2. Section 36(1)(a) of the Social Security Contributions and Benefits Act 1992 (bereavement payment) is to be read as if after "under section 44 below" the words "or a state pension under Part 1 of the Pensions Act 2014" appear.

6.216

Transitional provisions

3.—(1) This article applies to a case in which the spouse or civil partner mentioned in paragraph 3(1) of Schedule 3 to the Pensions Act 2014 (survivor's pension: inherited amount where dead spouse or civil partner was in the old state pension system) died—

(a) on or after 6th April 2016; but

(b) before the day on which section 30 of the Pensions Act 2014 comes fully into force.

(2) In a case to which this article applies—

(a) paragraph 3(1)(d) of Schedule 3 to the Pensions Act 2014 is to be read as if it provides—

"(d) the pensioner would, on reaching pensionable age, have been entitled to a Category B retirement pension under section 48BB of the Contributions and Benefits Act if in subsections (1) and (3) of that section the words "before 6 April 2016" were omitted."; and

(b) paragraph 3(2) of that Schedule is to be read as if it provides—

"(2) The inherited amount is equal to the weekly rate at which that Category B retirement pension would have been payable on the day on which the pensioner reached pensionable age if any element of the rate attributable to the basic pension were ignored.".

6.217

The Bereavement Support Payment Regulations 2017

(2017/410)

The Secretary of State for Work and Pensions makes the following Regulations in exercise of the powers conferred by sections 30(1)(c), (2), (3), (4)(a) and (7), 32(1) and (3) and 54(5) and (6) of the Pensions Act 2014.

These Regulations have not been referred to the Social Security Advisory Committee because they are made before the end of the period of six months beginning with the coming into force of the provisions of the Pensions Act 2014 under which they are made.

A draft of these Regulations has been laid before Parliament in accordance with section 54(2)(a) of the Pensions Act 2014 and approved by a resolution of each House of Parliament.

Citation and commencement

6.218   **1.**—(1) These Regulations may be cited as the Bereavement Support Payment Regulations 2017.

(2) These Regulations come into force on the day on which section 30 of the Pensions Act 2014 (bereavement support payment) comes into force for all purposes.

Period for which bereavement support payment is payable

6.219   **2.**—(1) The period for which bereavement support payment is payable is as follows.

(2) The period starts—

(a) on the date the person's spouse or civil partner died, where the person claims the payment three months or less after that date; or

(b) at the beginning of the period of three months preceding the date the person claims the payment, where the person claims the payment—

(i) more than three months after the date the person's spouse or civil partner died; and

(ii) no more than three months after the date the period finishes under paragraph (3).

(3) The period finishes at the end of the period of 18 months beginning with the day after the date the person's spouse or civil partner died.

GENERAL NOTE

6.220   Bereavement Support payments will be made for a maximum of 18 monthly payments. This was extended from the original period proposed of 12 months to avoid the last of the payments coinciding with the anniversary of the death on which the payment is based. The payment period begins on the date of the death where the claim is made within three months of the death; where the claim is made more than three months after the death, the payment period begins three months before the date of claim, but it ends 18 months after the day following the date of death. This means that a claim made later than the three months period of grace allowed will be foreshortened; a claim made 20 months after the date of the death will run for only one month.

Rate of bereavement support payment

3.—(1) The higher rate of bereavement support payment is £350 for each monthly recurrence of the day of the month on which the person's spouse or civil partner died during the period for which bereavement support payment is payable (see regulation 2).

(2) Where the person claims bereavement support payment 12 months or less after the date their spouse or civil partner died, the higher rate of bereavement support payment is £3,500 for the first month of the period for which bereavement support payment is payable.

(3) Any higher rate mentioned in paragraph (2) is in addition to any higher rate mentioned in paragraph (1).

(4) The standard rate of bereavement support payment is £100 for each monthly recurrence of the day of the month on which the person's spouse or civil partner died during the period for which bereavement support payment is payable.

(5) Where the person claims bereavement support payment 12 months or less after the date their spouse or civil partner died, the standard rate of bereavement support payment is £2,500 for the first month of the period for which bereavement support payment is payable.

(6) Any standard rate mentioned in paragraph (5) is in addition to any standard rate mentioned in paragraph (4).

(7) Where a person's spouse or civil partner died on the 31st day of a month, the monthly recurrence of the day of death is to be treated for the purposes of paragraphs (1) and (4) as falling on the last day of the month.

(8) Where a person's spouse or civil partner died on the 29th or 30th day of a month, the monthly recurrence of the day of death in February is to be treated for those purposes as falling on the last day of February.

6.221

GENERAL NOTE

Bereavement Support payments will be made at two rates and in each case will consist of two components. Payments will be made at a higher rate for a claimant who has responsibility for children (as defined in regulation 4 below) and at the standard rate for those without children. In each case the first monthly payment will be enhanced by a lump sum payment again at different rates. Note that, because the lump sum is an enhancement of the monthly payment rather than a separate payment, this means that where the claimant has lost entitlement to a payment altogether, by delaying more than 20 months after the day following the date of death, entitlement to the lump sum will be lost as well. The Social Security Benefits Up-rating Order 2018 (SI 2018/281) has provided, in art.20, that these rates of bereavement support payment will remain unchanged.

6.222

Persons entitled to the higher rate of bereavement support payment

4.—(1) A person falling within any of paragraphs (2) to (4) is entitled to the higher rate of bereavement support payment under regulation 3(1) to (3).

(2) A person who was pregnant when their spouse or civil partner died.

(3) A person who was entitled to child benefit under section 141 of the Social Security Contributions and Benefits Act 1992 (child benefit) when their spouse or civil partner died.

(4) A person who, after their spouse or civil partner died, becomes entitled to child benefit under section 141 of that Act for a child or qualifying

6.223

young person who was residing with the person or their deceased spouse or civil partner immediately before the spouse or civil partner died.

(5) Paragraph (4) applies to a person whether or not they later cease to be entitled to child benefit for that child or qualifying young person.

(6) In this regulation, "child" and "qualifying young person" have the same meaning as in section 142 of the Social Security Contributions and Benefits Act 1992 (definitions of "child" and "qualifying young person").

Persons entitled to the standard rate of bereavement support payment

6.224   **5.** A person is entitled to the standard rate of bereavement support payment under regulation 3(4) to (6) if they are not entitled to the higher rate of bereavement support payment.

Prisoners who are not to be paid bereavement support payment

6.225   **6.**—(1) Subject to regulation 7, a person is not to be paid bereavement support payment for any period during which the person is a prisoner.

(2) Except where paragraph (3) applies, a person is a prisoner for the purposes of paragraph (1) where the person is—

(a) a prisoner in Great Britain or elsewhere who is imprisoned or detained in legal custody in connection with, or as a result of, criminal proceedings;

(b) a prisoner in Great Britain or elsewhere who is unlawfully at large;

(c) a prisoner in Great Britain who is being detained—

   (i) under section 47 of the Mental Health Act 1983 (removal to hospital of persons serving sentences of imprisonment, etc); and

   (ii) on or before the day which the Secretary of State certifies to be the person's release date (if any) within the meaning in section 50(3) of that Act (further provisions as to prisoners under sentence);

(d) a prisoner in Great Britain who is being detained under section 136 of the Mental Health (Care and Treatment) (Scotland) Act 2003 (transfer of prisoners for treatment of mental disorder).

(3) Where a person outside Great Britain is a prisoner within paragraph (2)(a) or (b) and, in similar circumstances in Great Britain, the person would not have been a prisoner, the person is not a prisoner within paragraph (2)(a) or (b).

Paying bereavement support payment to persons who are remanded in custody

6.226   **7.**—(1) Where a person is remanded in custody for an offence, regulation 6(1) does not apply unless a sentence described in paragraph (2) is later imposed on the person for the offence.

(2) Subject to paragraph (3), the sentences described for the purposes of paragraph (1) are—

(a) a sentence of imprisonment or detention in legal custody as a result of criminal proceedings;

(b) a sentence of detention where the provisions mentioned in regulation 6(2)(c)(i) or (d) apply;

(c) a suspended sentence within the meaning in section 189 of the Criminal Justice Act 2003 (suspended sentences of imprisonment).

(3) A sentence described in paragraph (2)(a) which is imposed outside Great Britain is not a sentence described for the purposes of paragraph (1) if, in similar circumstances in Great Britain, a sentence described in paragraph (2)(a) would not have been imposed.

Territory in which a person may be entitled to bereavement support payment

8. For the purposes of section 30(1)(c) of the Pensions Act 2014   6.227 (bereavement support payment), the territory specified is any part of the Channel Islands which is not subject to an Order made under section 179 of the Social Security Administration Act 1992 (reciprocal agreements with countries outside the United Kingdom).

PART VII

UNEMPLOYMENT, SICKNESS AND INVALIDITY BENEFIT

For the text of the few remaining Unemployment, Sickness and Invalidity Benefit Regulations (SI 1983/1598 as amended) see the 2005 edition of this volume.

PART VIII

INCAPACITY BENEFIT AND INCAPACITY FOR WORK

For the text and commentary to the Regulations on this subjects, see the 2010/11 edition of this Volume. These regulations have had to be omitted from this edition in order to accommodate the Regulations governing migration from IB to ESA and crucial legislative changes to the ESA LCWA and LCWRA.

PART IX

"OLD STYLE" EMPLOYMENT AND SUPPORT ALLOWANCE

The Employment and Support Allowance Regulations 2008

(SI 2008/794) (*as amended*)

PART 1

GENERAL

1.   Citation, commencement and application   **9.1**
2.   Interpretation
3.   Rounding of fractions

PART 2

THE ASSESSMENT PHASE

4.   The end of the assessment phase
5.   The assessment phase—previous claimants
6.   The assessment phase—claimants appealing against a decision
7.   Circumstances where the condition that the assessment phase has ended before entitlement to the support component arises does not apply

PART 3

CONDITIONS OF ENTITLEMENT—CONTRIBUTORY ALLOWANCE

8.   Relaxation of the first contribution condition
9.   Condition relating to youth—claimants aged 20 or over but under 25
10.   Condition relating to youth—previous claimants
11.   Condition relating to youth—residence or presence
12.   Condition relating to youth—full-time education
13.   Modification of the relevant benefit year

PART 4

CONDITIONS OF ENTITLEMENT—INCOME-RELATED ALLOWANCE

14.   Meaning of education
15.   Claimants to be treated as receiving education
16.   Claimants not to be treated as receiving education
17.   Courses of study
18.   Circumstances in which the condition that the claimant is not receiving education does not apply

PART 5

LIMITED CAPABILITY FOR WORK

19.   Determination of limited capability for work
20.   Certain claimants to be treated as having limited capability for work
21.   Information required for determining capability for work
22.   Failure to provide information in relation to limited capability for work
23.   Claimant may be called for a medical examination to determine whether the claimant has limited capability for work
24.   Matters to be taken into account in determining good cause in relation to regulations 22 or 23
25.   Hospital patients
26.   Claimants receiving certain regular treatment
27.   Claimant to be treated as having limited capability for work throughout a day
28.   Night workers
29.   Exceptional circumstances
30.   Conditions for treating a claimant as having limited capability for work until a determination about limited capability for work has been made
31.   Claimant who claims jobseeker's allowance to be treated as not having limited capability for work
32.   Certain claimants to be treated as not having limited capability for work
32A. Claimants to be treated as not having limited capability for work at the end of the period covered by medical evidence
33.   Additional circumstances where claimants are to be treated as having limited capability for work

PART 6

LIMITED CAPABILITY FOR WORK-RELATED ACTIVITY

34.   Determination of limited capability for work-related activity
35.   Certain claimants to be treated as having limited capability for work-related activity
35A. Relevant linked cases – limited capability for work-related activity
36.   Information required for determining capability for work-related activity
37.   Failure to provide information in relation to work-related activity
38.   Claimant may be called for a medical examination to determine whether the claimant has limited capability for work-related activity
39.   Matters to be taken into account in determining good cause in relation to regulations 37 or 38

PART 7

EFFECT OF WORK ON ENTITLEMENT TO AN EMPLOYMENT AND SUPPORT ALLOWANCE

40.   A claimant who works to be treated as not entitled to an employment and support allowance

41.   Meaning of "remunerative work" for the purposes of paragraph 6(1)(e) of Schedule 1 to the Act
42.   Meaning of "remunerative work" for the purposes of paragraph 6(1)(f) of Schedule 1 to the Act
43.   Circumstances under which partners of claimants entitled to an income-related allowance are not to be treated as engaged in remunerative work
44.   Claimants who are treated as not entitled to any allowance at all by reason of regulation 40(1) are to be treated as not having limited capability for work
45.   Exempt work
46.   Effect of work on entitlement to contributory allowance where claimant is receiving certain regular treatment

PART 8

CONDITIONALITY

CHAPTER 1

WORK-FOCUSED HEALTH-RELATED ASSESSMENT

47.   Requirement to take part in a work-focused health-related assessment
48.   Work-focused health-related assessment
49.   Notification of assessment
50.   Determination of the place of the work-focused health-related assessment
51.   Taking part in a work-focused health-related assessment
52.   Deferral of requirement to take part in a work-focused health-related assessment
53.   Failure to take part in a work-focused health-related assessment

CHAPTER 2

WORK-FOCUSED INTERVIEWS

54.   Requirement to take part in a work-focused interview
55.   Work-focused interview
56.   Notification of interview
57.   Taking part in a work-focused interview
58.   Action plan *(revoked)*
59.   Deferral of requirement to take part in a work-focused interview
60.   Requirement to take part in a work-focused interview not to apply
61.   Failure to take part in a work-focused interview
62.   Contracting out certain functions relating to work-focused interviews

CHAPTER 3

REDUCTION OF EMPLOYMENT AND SUPPORT ALLOWANCE

63.   Reduction of employment and support allowance
64.   Cessation of reduction

64A.   Hardship payments
64B.   Circumstances in which a claimant is to be treated as being in hardship
64C.   Matters to be taken into account in determining hardship
64D.   The amount of a hardship payment

CHAPTER 4

NOTIFICATION

65.   Notification under this Part

CHAPTER 5

MODIFICATION OF THE ACT IN RELATION TO CLAIMS TO WHICH SECTION 5(1)(C) OF THE ADMINISTRATION ACT APPLIES

66.   Modifications of the Act

PART 9

AMOUNTS OF ALLOWANCE

CHAPTER 1

PRESCRIBED AMOUNTS

67.   Prescribed amounts
68.   Polygamous marriages
69.   Special cases
70.   Special cases: supplemental—persons from abroad
71.   Definition of non-dependant

CHAPTER 2

DEDUCTIONS FROM THE CONTRIBUTORY ALLOWANCE

72.   Permanent health insurance
73.   Councillor's allowance
74.   Deductions for pension payment and PPF payment
75.   Payments treated as not being payments to which section 3 applies
76.   Deductions for councillor's allowance
77.   Date from which payments are to be taken into account
78.   Date from which a change in the rate of the payment takes effect
79.   Calculation of payment made other than weekly

Chapter 3

Statutory Payments

80.   Effect of statutory maternity pay on a contributory allowance
81.   Effect of statutory adoption pay on a contributory allowance
82.   Effect of additional statutory shared parental pay on a contributory allowance *(revoked)*
82A.   Effect of statutory shared parental pay on a contributory allowance

Part 10

Income and Capital

Chapter 1

General

83.   Calculation of income and capital of members of claimant's family and of a polygamous marriage
84.   Income of participants in the self-employment route
85.   Liable relative payments
86.   Child support
87.   Calculation of income and capital of students
88.   Calculation of income which consists of earnings of participants in exempt work
89.   Calculation of income where pension payments, PPF periodic payments or councillor's allowance payable

Chapter 2

Income

90.   Calculation of income
91.   Calculation of earnings derived from employed earner's employment and income other than earnings
92.   Calculation of earnings of self-employed earners
93.   Date on which income is treated as paid
94.   Calculation of weekly amount of income

Chapter 3

Employed Earners

95.   Earnings of employed earners
96.   Calculation of net earnings of employed earners

CHAPTER 4

SELF-EMPLOYED EARNERS

97.   Earnings of self-employed earners
98.   Calculation of net profit of self-employed earners
99.   Deduction of tax and contributions for self-employed earners

CHAPTER 5

PARTICIPANTS IN THE SELF-EMPLOYMENT ROUTE

100.   Interpretation
101.   Treatment of gross receipts of participants in the self-employment route
102.   Calculation of income of participants in the self-employment route
103.   Deduction in respect of tax for participants in the self-employment route

CHAPTER 6

OTHER INCOME

104.   Calculation of income other than earnings
105.   Capital treated as income
106.   Notional income—deprivation and income on application
107.   Notional income—income due to be paid or income paid to or in respect of
         a third party
108.   Notional income—other income
109.   Notional income—calculation and interpretation

CHAPTER 7

CAPITAL

110.   Capital limit
111.   Calculation of capital
112.   Income treated as capital
113.   Calculation of capital in the United Kingdom
114.   Calculation of capital outside the United Kingdom
115.   Notional capital
116.   Diminishing notional capital rule
117.   Capital jointly held
118.   Calculation of tariff income from capital

CHAPTER 8

LIABLE RELATIVES

119.   Interpretation
120.   Treatment of liable relative payments
121.   Disregard of payments treated as not relevant income
122.   Period over which periodical payments are to be taken into account
123.   Period over which payments other than periodical payments are to be taken
        into account
124.   Calculation of the weekly amount of a liable relative payment
125.   Date on which a liable relative payment is to be treated as paid
126.   Liable relative payments to be treated as capital *(revoked)*

CHAPTER 9

CHILD SUPPORT

127.   Treatment of child support maintenance *(revoked)*
128.   Calculation of the weekly amount of payments of child support maintenance
        (revoked)
129.   Date on which child support maintenance is to be treated as paid *(revoked)*
130.   Disregard of payments treated as not relevant income *(revoked)*

CHAPTER 10

STUDENTS

131.   Interpretation
132.   Calculation of grant income
133.   Calculation of covenant income where a contribution is assessed
134.   Calculation of covenant income where no grant income or no contribution
        is assessed
135.   Relationships with amounts to be disregarded under Schedule 8
136.   Other amounts to be disregarded
137.   Treatment of student loans
138.   Treatment of payments from access funds
139.   Treatment of fee loans
139A. Treatment of special support loans
140.   Disregard of contribution
141.   Further disregard of student's income
142.   Income treated as capital
143.   Disregard of changes occurring during summer vacation

PART 11

SUPPLEMENTARY PROVISIONS

CHAPTER 1

MISCELLANEOUS

144.   Waiting days
145.   Linking rules
146.   Advance awards
147.   Recovery orders
147A. Claimants appealing a decision

CHAPTER 2

WORK OR TRAINING BENEFICIARIES

148.   Work or training beneficiaries *(revoked)*
149.   Linking rules—limited capability for work *(revoked)*
150.   Linking rules—limited capability for work-related activity *(revoked)*

CHAPTER 3

TEMPORARY ABSENCE FROM GREAT BRITAIN

151.   Absence from Great Britain
152.   Short absence
153.   Absence to receive medical treatment
154.   Absence in order to receive NHS treatment
155.   Absence of member of family of member of Her Majesty's forces

CHAPTER 4

MEMBERSHIP OF HOUSEHOLD

156.   Circumstances in which a person is to be treated as being or not being a member of the household

PART 12

DISQUALIFICATION

157.   Disqualification for misconduct etc.
158.   Meaning of "person in hardship"
159.   Treating a claimant as not having limited capability for work

160. Exceptions from disqualification for imprisonment
161. Suspension of payment of a contributory allowance during imprisonment

PART 13

URGENT CASES

162. Urgent cases
163. Applicable amounts in urgent cases
164. Assessment of income and capital in urgent cases

PART 14

PERIODS OF LESS THAN A WEEK

165. Entitlement for less than a week—amount of an employment and support
     allowance payable
166. Relevant week
167. Modification in the calculation of income
168. Reduction in certain cases
169. Payment of a contributory allowance for days of certain regular treatment

SCHEDULE 1   9.2

HER MAJESTY'S FORCES

PART 1

PRESCRIBED ESTABLISHMENTS AND ORGANISATIONS

PART 2

ESTABLISHMENTS AND ORGANISATIONS OF WHICH HER MAJESTY'S FORCES
DO NOT CONSIST

SCHEDULE 2

ASSESSMENT OF WHETHER A CLAIMANT HAS LIMITED CAPABILITY FOR WORK

PART 1

PHYSICAL DISABILITIES

PART 2

MENTAL, COGNITIVE AND INTELLECTUAL FUNCTION ASSESSMENT

SCHEDULE 3

ASSESSMENT OF WHETHER A CLAIMANT HAS LIMITED CAPABILITY FOR WORK-
RELATED ACTIVITY

The Employment and Support Allowance Regulations 2008

SCHEDULE 4

AMOUNTS

PART 1

PRESCRIBED AMOUNTS

PART 2

PREMIUMS

PART 3

WEEKLY AMOUNT OF PREMIUMS SPECIFIED IN PART 2

PART 4

THE COMPONENTS

SCHEDULE 5

SPECIAL CASES

PART 1

AMOUNTS PRESCRIBED FOR THE PURPOSES OF SECTION 4(2) OF THE ACT

PART 2

AMOUNTS PRESCRIBED FOR THE PURPOSES OF SECTIONS 2(1) AND 4(2) OF THE ACT

SCHEDULE 6

HOUSING COSTS

SCHEDULE 7

SUMS TO BE DISREGARDED IN THE CALCULATION OF EARNINGS

SCHEDULE 8

SCHEDULE 9

Capital to be Disregarded

The Secretary of State for Work and Pensions, in exercise of the powers conferred by sections 2(1)(a) and (c), (4)(a) and (c), 3(1)(c), (2)(b) and (d) and (3)(1), 4(2)(a), (3), (6)(a) and (c), 5(2) and (3), 8(1) to (3), (4)(a) and (b), (5) and (6), 9(1) to (3) and (4)(a) and (b), 11(1), (2) (a) to (g), (3) to (5), (6)(a) and (7)(c), 12(1), (2)(a) to (h), (3) to (7), 14(1) and (2)(a) and (b), 16(2)(a) and (4), 17, 18(1), (2) and (4), 20(2) to (7), 22(2), 23(1) and (3), 24(1)(3), (2) (b) and (3), 25(1) to (5) and 26(2) of, and paragraphs 1(4), 3(2), 4(1)(a) and (c), (3) and (4) and 6(1)(b), (2) to (5)(4), (7) and (8) of Schedule 1 to, and paragraphs 1 to 7, 8(1), 9, 10, 12 and 14 of Schedule 2 to, the Welfare Reform Act 2007, section 5(1) of the Social Security Administration Act 1992 and section 21(1)(a) of the Social Security Act 1998(7) makes the following Regulations, which are made by virtue of, or consequential on, the provisions of the Welfare Reform Act 2007 and which are made before the end of a period of 6 months beginning with the coming into force of those provisions:

PART 1

General

[¹ Citation, commencement and application]

1. These Regulations may be cited as the Employment and Support Allowance Regulations 2008 and shall come into force—

    (a) subject to paragraphs (b) and (c), on 27th October 2008;

    (b) in relation to regulation 128(6)(a) and paragraph 15(2) of Schedule 6, so far as it applies to a maintenance calculation, in relation to a particular case, on the day on which paragraph 11(20)(d) of Schedule 3 to the 2000 Act comes into force for the purposes of that type of case;

    (c) [² . . .]

[¹ (2) These Regulations do not apply to a particular case on any day on which section 33(1)(b) of the 2012 Act (abolition of income-related employment and support allowance) is in force and applies in relation to that case.]

9.3

Amendments

    1. Universal Credit (Consequential, Supplementary, Incidental and Miscellaneous Provisions) Regulations 2013 (SI 2013/630) reg.37(1) and (2) (April 29, 2013).

    2. Shared Parental Leave and Statutory Shared Parental Pay (Consequential Amendments to Subordinate Legislation) Order 2014 art.20(2) (April 5, 2014).

Interpretation

2.—(1) In these Regulations—

[²³ "the 2012 Act" means the Welfare Reform Act 2012;]

9.4

"Abbeyfield Home" means an establishment run by the Abbeyfield Society including any body corporate or incorporate which is affiliated to that Society;

"the Act" means the Welfare Reform Act 2007;

[¹² ...]

"adoption leave" means a period of absence from work on ordinary or additional adoption leave under section 75A or 75B of the Employment Rights Act 1996;

"aircraft worker" means a person who is, or has been, employed under a contract of service either as a pilot, commander, navigator or other member of the crew of any aircraft, or in any other capacity on board any aircraft where—

  (a) the employment in that other capacity is for the purposes of the aircraft or its crew or of any passengers or cargo or mail carried on that aircraft; and

  (b) the contract is entered into in the United Kingdom with a view to its performance (in whole or in part) while the aircraft is in flight, but does not include a person who is in employment as a member of Her Majesty's forces;

[⁴⁰ "approved blood scheme" means a scheme established or approved by the Secretary of State, or trust established with funds provided by the Secretary of State, for the purpose of providing compensation in respect of a person having been infected from contaminated blood products;]

"Armed Forces and Reserve Forces Compensation Scheme" means the scheme established under section 1(2) of the Armed Forces (Pensions and Compensation) Act 2004;

[²⁴ "armed forces independence payment" means armed forces independence payment under the Armed Forces and Reserve Forces (Compensation Scheme) Order 2011;]

"attendance allowance" means—

  (a) an attendance allowance under section 64 of the Contributions and Benefits Act;

  (b) an increase of disablement pension under section 104 or 105 of that Act;

  (c) [²⁶ ...]

  (d) [²⁶ ...]

  (e) a payment by virtue of article 14, 15, 16, 43 or 44 of the Personal Injuries (Civilians) Scheme 1983 or any analogous payment;

  (f) any payment based on the need for attendance which is paid as an addition to a war disablement pension;

[¹ "basic rate" has the same meaning as in the Income Tax Act 2007 (see section 989 of that Act);]

"benefit Acts" means the Contributions and Benefits Act, Jobseekers Act [³⁵, Part 1 of the Act and the Pensions Act 2014];

"benefit week" means a period of 7 days ending on such day as the Secretary of State may direct but for the purposes of calculating any payment of income "benefit week" means the period of 7 days ending on the day before the first day of the first benefit week following the date of claim or the last day on which an employment and support allowance is paid if it is in payment for less than a week;

"board and lodging" means—

    (a) accommodation provided to a person or, if the person is a member of a family, to that person or any other member of that person's family, for a charge which is inclusive of the provision of that accommodation and at least some cooked or prepared meals which both are cooked or prepared (by a person other than the person to whom the accommodation is provided or a member of that person's family) and are consumed in that accommodation or associated premises; or

    (b) accommodation provided to a person in a hotel, guest house, lodging house or some similar establishment, except accommodation provided by a close relative of the person or any other member of the person's family, or other than on a commercial basis;

"care home" in England [42 ...] has the meaning assigned to it by section 3 of the Care Standards Act 2000, [42 in Wales means a care home service within the meaning of Part 1 of the Regulation and Inspection of Social Care (Wales) Act 2016 which is provided wholly or mainly to persons aged 18 or over] and in Scotland means a care home service within the meaning assigned to it by [16 paragraph 2 of schedule 12 to the Public Services Reform (Scotland) Act 2010];

"carer's allowance" means an allowance under section 70 of the Contributions and Benefits Act;

"child" means a person under the age of 16;

[14 "the Caxton Foundation" means the charitable trust of that name established on 28th March 2011 out of funds provided by the Secretary of State for the benefit of certain persons suffering from hepatitis C and other persons eligible for payment in accordance with its provisions;]

"child tax credit" means a child tax credit under section 8 of the Tax Credits Act;

"close relative" means a parent, parent-in-law, son, son-in-law, daughter, daughter-in-law, step-parent, step-son, step-daughter, brother, sister, or if any of the preceding persons is one member of a couple, the other member of that couple;

"college of further education" means a college of further education within the meaning of Part 1 of the Further and Higher Education (Scotland) Act 1992;

"concessionary payment" means a payment made under arrangements made by the Secretary of State with the consent of the Treasury which is charged [3 ...] to a Departmental Expenditure Vote to which payments of benefit or tax credits under the benefit Acts or the Tax Credits Act are charged;

"confinement" has the meaning given to it by section 171(1) of the Contributions and Benefits Act;

[25 "contribution-based jobseeker's allowance" means an allowance under the Jobseekers Act as amended by the provisions of Part 1 of Schedule 14 to the 2012 Act that remove references to an income-based allowance, and a contribution-based allowance under the Jobseekers Act as that Act has effect apart from those provisions;]

"co-ownership scheme" means a scheme under which a dwelling is let by a housing association and the tenant, or the tenant's personal representative, will, under the terms of the tenancy agreement or of the agreement under which the tenant became a member of the association, be entitled, on that tenant ceasing to be a member and subject to any condition stated in either agreement, to a sum calculated by reference directly or indirectly to the value of the dwelling and "co-ownership agreement" will be construed accordingly;

"councillor" means—

(a) in relation to England and Wales, a member of a London borough council, a county council, [26 a county borough council,] a district council, a parish or community council, the Common Council of the City of London or the Council of the Isles of Scilly; and

(b) in relation to Scotland, a member of a council constituted under section 2 of the Local Government etc. (Scotland) Act 1994;

"councillor's allowance" means—

(a) in England [26 ...], an allowance under or by virtue of—

(i) section 173 or 177 of the Local Government Act 1972; or

(ii) a scheme made by virtue of section 18 of the Local Government and Housing Act 1989, other than such an allowance as is mentioned in section 173(4) of the Local Government Act 1972; or

(b) in Scotland, an allowance or remuneration under or by virtue of—

(i) a scheme made by virtue of section 18 of the Local Government and Housing Act 1989; or

(ii) [26 section 11] of the Local Governance (Scotland) Act 2004; [26 or

(c) in Wales, an allowance under or by virtue of a scheme made by virtue of section 18 of the Local Government and Housing Act 1989 other than such an allowance as is mentioned in section 173(4) of the Local Government Act 1972;]

[27 29 "couple" means—

(a) two people who are married to, or civil partners of, each other and are members of the same household; or

(b) two people who are not married to, or civil partners of, each other but are living together as a married couple;]

"Crown tenant" means a person who occupies a dwelling under a tenancy or licence where the interest of the landlord belongs to Her Majesty in right of the Crown or to a government department or is held in trust for Her Majesty for the purposes of a government department, except (in the case of an interest belonging to Her Majesty in right of the Crown) where the interest is under the management of the Crown Estate Commissioners;

[23 "daily living component" means the daily living component of personal independence payment under section 78 of the 2012 Act;]

"dependent child" means any child or qualifying young person who is treated as the responsibility of the claimant or the claimant's partner, where that child or young person is a member of the claimant's household;

"descriptor" means, in relation to an activity specified in column (1) of Schedule 2, a descriptor in column (2) of that Schedule which describes a person's ability to perform that activity;

"disability living allowance" means a disability living allowance under section 71 of the Contributions and Benefits Act;

"doctor" means a registered medical practitioner, or in the case of a medical practitioner practising outside the United Kingdom of whom the Secretary of State may request a medical opinion, a person registered or recognised as such in the country in which the person undertakes medical practice;

"dwelling" means any residential accommodation, whether or not consisting of the whole or part of a building and whether or not comprising separate and self-contained premises;

"dwelling occupied as the home" means the dwelling together with any garage, garden and outbuildings, normally occupied by the claimant as the claimant's home including any premises not so occupied which it is impracticable or unreasonable to sell separately, in particular, in Scotland, any croft land on which the dwelling is situated;

"Eileen Trust" means the charitable trust of that name established on 29th March 1993 out of funds provided by the Secretary of State for the benefit of persons eligible for payment in accordance with its provisions;

"employed earner" is to be construed in accordance with section 2(1)(a) of the Contributions and Benefits Act;

"employment" includes any trade, business, profession, office or vocation and "employed" has a corresponding meaning;

[13 "the Employment, Skills and Enterprise Scheme" means a scheme within section 17A (schemes for assisting persons to obtain employment: "work for your benefit" schemes etc.) of the Jobseekers Act 1995, known by that name and provided pursuant to arrangements made by the Secretary of State that is designed to assist claimants to obtain employment or self-employment, and which may include for any individual work-related activity (including work experience or job search);]

"employment zone" means an area within Great Britain designated for the purposes of section 60 of the Welfare Reform and Pensions Act 1999 and an "employment zone programme" means a programme established for such an area or areas designed to assist claimants for a jobseeker's allowance to obtain sustainable employment;

[5 "enactment" includes an enactment comprised in, or in an instrument made under, an Act of the Scottish Parliament [26 or the National Assembly for Wales];]

"failure determination" has the meaning given by regulation 63(1);

"family" means—

    (a) a couple;

    (b) a couple and a member of the same household for whom one of them is or both are responsible and who is a child or a young person;

    (c) a person who is not a member of a couple and a member of the same household for whom that person is responsible and who is a child or a young person;

"first contribution condition" means the condition set out in paragraph 1(1) of Schedule 1 to the Act;

[11 "First-tier Tribunal" has the meaning given by section 3(1) of the Tribunals, Courts and Enforcement Act 2007;]

[33 "first year of training" means a period of one year beginning with a person's first day of training.]

"full-time student" has the meaning prescribed in regulation 131 (students: interpretation);

"the Fund" means monies made available from time to time by the

Secretary of State for the benefit of persons eligible for payment in accordance with the provisions of a scheme established by the Secretary of State on 24th April 1992 or, in Scotland, on 10th April 1992;

"guaranteed income payment" means a payment made under article 14(1)(b) or 21(1)(a) of the Armed Forces and Reserve Forces (Compensation Scheme) Order 2005;

[20 "hardship payment" means an income-related employment and support allowance payable at a reduced rate in accordance with the provisions of regulation 64D;]

"health care professional" means—

(a) a registered medical practitioner;

(b) a registered nurse; or

(c) an occupational therapist or physiotherapist registered with a regulatory body established by an Order in Council under section 60 of the Health Act 1999;

"Health Service Act" means the National Health Service Act 2006;

"Health Service (Wales) Act" means the National Health Service (Wales) Act 2006;

"housing association" has the meaning given to it by section 1(1) of the Housing Associations Act 1985;

"housing benefit expenditure" means expenditure in respect of which housing benefit is payable as specified in regulation 12(1) of the Housing Benefit Regulations 2006 but does not include any such expenditure in respect of which an additional amount is applicable under regulation 67(1)(c) or 68(1)(d)(housing costs);

"Immigration and Asylum Act" means the Immigration and Asylum Act 1999;

"income-related benefits" means the benefits listed in section 123(1) of the Contributions and Benefits Act;

"Income Support Regulations" means the Income Support (General) Regulations 1987;

[9 "independent hospital"—

(a) in England, means a hospital as defined by section 275 of the National Health Service Act 2006 that is not a health service hospital as defined by that section;

(b) in Wales, has the meaning assigned to it by section 2 of the Care Standards Act 2000; and

[16 (c) in Scotland, means an independent health care service as defined in section 10F(1)(a) and (b) of the National Health Service (Scotland) Act 1978;]]

[1 ...]

"the Independent Living Fund (2006)" means the Trust of that name established by a deed dated 10th April 2006 and made between the Secretary of State for Work and Pensions of the one part and Margaret Rosemary Cooper, Michael Beresford Boyall and Marie Theresa Martin of the other part;

[1 ...]

"Jobseekers Act" means the Jobseekers Act 1995;

"Jobseeker's Allowance Regulations" means the Jobseeker's Allowance Regulations 1996;

"last day of the course" means the last day of the final academic term of the course in which the student is enrolled;

"limited capability for work assessment" means the assessment of whether a person has limited capability for work as set out in regulation 19(2) and in Schedule 2;

[²² "local welfare provision" means occasional financial or other assistance given by a local authority, the Scottish Ministers or the Welsh Ministers, or a person authorised to exercise any function of, or provide a service to, them, to or in respect of individuals for the purpose of—

(a) meeting, or helping to meet, an immediate short term need—
  (i) arising out of an exceptional event, or exceptional circumstances; and
  (ii) that requires to be met in order to avoid a risk to the well-being of an individual; or
(b) enabling individuals to establish or maintain a settled home, where those individuals have been or, without the assistance, might otherwise be—
  (i) in prison, hospital, a residential care establishment or other institution; or
  (ii) homeless or otherwise living an unsettled way of life;]

"London Bombings Relief Charitable Fund" means the company limited by guarantee (number 5505072) and registered charity of that name established on 11th July 2005 for the purpose of (amongst other things) relieving sickness, disability or financial need of victims (including families or dependants of victims) of the terrorist attacks carried out in London on 7th July 2005;

[³⁹ "the London Emergencies Trust" means the company of that name (number 09928465) incorporated on 23rd December 2015 and the registered charity of that name (number 1172307) established on 28th March 2017;]

[¹⁵ ...]

"long tenancy" means a tenancy granted for a term of years certain exceeding twenty one years, whether or not the tenancy is, or may become, terminable before the end of that term by notice given by or to the tenant or by re-entry, forfeiture (or, in Scotland, irritancy) or otherwise and includes a lease for a term fixed by law under a grant with a covenant or obligation for perpetual renewal unless it is a lease by sub-demise from one which is not a long tenancy;

"Macfarlane (Special Payments) Trust" means the trust of that name, established on 29th January 1990 partly out of funds provided by the Secretary of State, for the benefit of certain persons suffering from haemophilia;

"Macfarlane (Special Payments) (No. 2) Trust" means the trust of that name, established on 3rd May 1991 partly out of funds provided by the Secretary of State, for the benefit of certain persons suffering from haemophilia and other beneficiaries;

"Macfarlane Trust" means the charitable trust, established partly out of funds provided by the Secretary of State to the Haemophilia Society, for the relief of poverty or distress among those suffering from haemophilia;

"main phase employment and support allowance" means an employment and support allowance where the calculation of the amount payable in respect of the claimant includes a component under section 2(1)(b) or 4(2)(b) of the Act [³⁸ or where the claimant is a member of the work-related activity group];

[¹³ "the Mandatory Work Activity Scheme" means a scheme within section 17A of the Jobseekers Act 1995, known by that name and provided pursuant to arrangements made by the Secretary of State that is designed to provide work or work-related activity for up to 30 hours per week over a period of four consecutive weeks with a view to assisting claimants to improve their prospects of obtaining employment;]

"mariner" means a person who is or has been in employment under a contract of service either as a master or member of the crew of any ship or vessel, or in any other capacity on board any ship or vessel where—

    (a) the employment in that other capacity is for the purposes of that ship or vessel or her crew or any passengers or cargo or mails carried by the ship or vessel; and

    (b) the contract is entered into in the United Kingdom with a view to its performance (in whole or in part) while the ship or vessel is on her voyage; but does not include a person who is in employment as a member of Her Majesty's forces;

[²⁸ . . .]

"medical evidence" [¹¹, except in regulation 32A,] means—

    (a) evidence from a health care professional approved by the Secretary of State; and

    (b) evidence (if any) from any health care professional or a hospital or similar institution, or such part of such evidence as constitutes the most reliable evidence available in the circumstances;

"Medical Evidence Regulations" means the Social Security (Medical Evidence) Regulations 1976;

[⁸ . . .]

"medical treatment" means medical, surgical or rehabilitative treatment (including any course or diet or other regimen), and references to a person receiving or submitting to medical treatment are to be construed accordingly;

"member of Her Majesty's forces" means a person, other than one mentioned in Part 2 of Schedule 1 who is—

    (a) over 16 years of age; and

    (b) a member of an establishment or organisation specified in Part 1 of that Schedule who gives full pay service, but does not include any such person while absent on desertion;

[³⁸ "member of the work-related activity group" means a claimant who has or is treated as having limited capability for work under Part 5 of these Regulations other than by virtue of regulation 30 of these Regulations;]

[⁷ "MFET Limited" means the company limited by guarantee (number 7121661) of that name, established for the purpose in particular of making payments in accordance with arrangements made with the Secretary of State to persons who have acquired HIV as a result of treatment by the NHS with blood or blood products;]

"mobility supplement" means any supplement under article 20 of the Naval, Military and Air Forces Etc. (Disablement and Death) Service Pensions Order 2006 including such a supplement by virtue of any other scheme or order or under article 25A of the Personal Injuries (Civilians) Scheme 1983;

[[11] "National Minimum Wage" means the rate of the national minimum wage specified in regulation 11 of the National Minimum Wage Regulations 1999 (rate of the national minimum wage);]

"net earnings" means such earnings as are calculated in accordance with regulation 96;

"net profit" means such profit as is calculated in accordance with regulation 98;

"New Deal options" means the employment programmes specified in regulation 75(1)(a)(ii) of the Jobseeker's Allowance Regulations and the training scheme specified in regulation 75(1)(b)(ii) of those Regulations;

[[25] "new style ESA" means an allowance under Part 1 of the Act as amended by the provisions of Schedule 3, and Part 1 of Schedule 14, to the 2012 Act that remove references to an income-related allowance;]

"non-dependant" has the meaning prescribed in regulation 71;

"non-dependant deduction" means a deduction that is to be made under regulation 67(1)(c) (prescribed amounts) and paragraph 19 of Schedule 6 (housing costs);

"occupational pension" means any pension or other periodical payment under an occupational pension scheme but does not include any discretionary payment out of a fund established for relieving hardship in particular cases;

"occupational pension scheme" has the meaning given by section 1 of the Pension Schemes Act 1993;

"ordinary clothing or footwear" means clothing or footwear for normal daily use, but does not include school uniforms, or clothing or footwear used solely for sporting activities;

"partner" means where a claimant—

    (a) is a member of a couple, the other member of that couple;

    (b) is a husband or wife by virtue of a polygamous marriage, the other party to the marriage or any spouse additional to either party to the marriage;

"passenger" means any person carried on a ship except—

    (a) a person employed or engaged in any capacity on board the ship on the business of the ship; or

    (b) a person on board the ship either in pursuance of the obligation to carry shipwrecked, distressed or other persons, or by reason of any circumstance that neither the master nor the owner nor the charterer (if any) could have prevented or forestalled;

[[17] "paternity leave" means a period of absence from work on [[31] ...] paternity leave by virtue of section 80A or 80B of the Employment Rights Act 1996 [[31] ...];]

"payment" includes a part of a payment;

"pay period" means the period in respect of which a claimant is, or expects to be, normally paid by the claimant's employer, being a week, a fortnight, four weeks, a month or other shorter or longer period as the case may be;

"pension fund holder" means in relation to a personal pension scheme or an occupational pension scheme, the trustees, managers or scheme administrators, as the case may be, of the scheme concerned;

"pensionable age" has the meaning given by the rules in paragraph 1 of Schedule 4 to the Pensions Act 1995;

"period of limited capability for work" means [⁸ except in paragraph (5), a period throughout which a person has, or is treated as having, limited capability for work, and does not include a period which is outside the prescribed time for claiming as specified in regulation 19 of the Social Security (Claims and Payments) Regulations 1987];

"period of study" means the period beginning with the date on which a person starts attending or undertaking a course of study and ending with the last day of the course or such earlier date (if any) as that person finally abandons it or is dismissed from it;

[²³ "personal independence payment" means personal independence payment under Part 4 of the 2012 Act;]

"personal pension scheme" means—

    (a) a personal pension scheme as defined by section 1 of the Pension Schemes Act 1993;

    (b) an annuity contract or trust scheme approved under section 620 or 621 of the Income and Corporation Taxes Act 1988 or a substituted contract within the meaning of section 622(3) of that Act which is treated as having become a registered pension scheme by virtue of paragraph 1(1)(f) of Schedule 36 to the Finance Act 2004;

    (c) a personal pension scheme approved under Chapter 4 of Part 14 of the Income and Corporation Taxes Act 1988 which is treated as having become a registered pension scheme by virtue of paragraph 1(1)(g) of Schedule 36 to the Finance Act 2004;

"policy of life insurance" means any instrument by which the payment of money is assured on death (except death by accident only) or the happening of any contingency dependent on human life, or any instrument evidencing a contract which is subject to payment of premiums for a term dependent on human life;

"polygamous marriage" means any marriage entered into under a law which permits polygamy where—

    (a) either party has for the time being any spouse additional to the other party; and

    (b) the claimant, the other party to the marriage and the additional spouse are members of the same household;

[⁵ "public authority" includes any person certain of whose functions are functions of a public nature;

"the qualifying age for state pension credit" means—

    (a) in the case of a woman, pensionable age, and

    (b) in the case of a man, the age which is pensionable age in the case of a woman born on the same day as the man;]

"qualifying person" means a person in respect of whom payment has been made from the Fund, the Eileen Trust, [⁷ MFET Limited] the Skipton Fund [¹⁴, the Caxton Foundation] [³⁷, the Scottish Infected Blood Support Scheme] [⁴⁰, an approved blood scheme] [³⁹, the London Emergencies Trust, the We Love Manchester Emergency Fund] or the London Bombings Relief Charitable Fund;

"qualifying remunerative work" has the meaning given by Part 1 of the Tax Credits Act;

"qualifying young person" has the meaning given by section 142 of the Contributions and Benefits Act (child and qualifying young person);

"relative" means close relative, grand-parent, grand-child, uncle, aunt, nephew or niece;

[[14] ...]

"relevant enactment" means the Army Act 1955, the Air Force Act 1955, the Naval Discipline Act 1957, the Matrimonial Proceedings Children Act 1958, the Social Work (Scotland) Act 1968, the Family Law Reform Act 1969, the Children and Young Persons Act 1969, the Matrimonial Causes Act 1973, the Domestic Proceedings and Magistrates' Courts Act 1978, the Adoption (Scotland) Act 1978, the Family Law Act 1986, the Children Act 1989 and the Adoption and Children Act 2002;

[[14] [[26] ...]]

"remunerative work" has the meaning prescribed in regulations 41 and 42 except in relation to Schedules 6 and 7;

[[36] "Scottish basic rate" means the rate of income tax of that name calculated in accordance with section 6A of the Income Tax Act 2007;

[[37] "Scottish Infected Blood Support Scheme" means the scheme of that name administered by the Common Services Agency (constituted by section 10 of the National Health Service (Scotland) Act 1978);]

"Scottish taxpayer" has the same meaning as in Chapter 2 of Part 4A of the Scotland Act 1998;]

"second contribution condition" means the condition set out in paragraph 2(1) of Schedule 1 to the Act;

"self-employed earner" is to be construed in accordance with section 2(1)(b) of the Contributions and Benefits Act;

"self-employment route" means assistance in pursuing self-employed earner's employment whilst participating in—

    (a) an employment zone programme; or

    (b) a programme provided or other arrangements made under section 2 of the Employment and Training Act 1973 (functions of the Secretary of State) or section 2 of the Enterprise and New Towns (Scotland) Act 1990 (functions in relation to training for employment etc.);

[[5] [[26] ...[[21]]]]]

[[30] "shared parental leave" means leave under section 75E or 75G of the Employment Rights Act 1996;]

"single claimant" means a claimant who neither has a partner nor is a lone parent [[15] or a person who has no partner and who is responsible for and a member of the same household as a young person];

"Skipton Fund" means the ex-gratia payment scheme administered by the Skipton Fund Limited, incorporated on 25th March 2004, for the benefit of certain persons suffering from hepatitis C and other persons eligible for payment in accordance with the scheme's provisions;

"sports award" means an award made by one of the Sports Councils named in section 23(2) of the National Lottery etc. Act 1993 out of sums allocated to it for distribution under that section;

[[1] ...]

[[1] "state pension credit" means a state pension credit under the State Pension Credit Act 2002;]

"subsistence allowance" means an allowance which an employment zone contractor has agreed to pay to a person who is participating in an employment zone programme;

"the Tax Credits Act" means the Tax Credits Act 2002;

"terminally ill", in relation to a claimant, means the claimant is suffering from a progressive disease and death in consequence of that disease can reasonably be expected within 6 months;

[[41] "traineeship" means a course which—

  (a) is funded (in whole or in part) by, or under arrangements made by, the—

    (i) Secretary of State under section 14 of the Education Act 2002, or

    (ii) Chief Executive of Education and Skills Funding;

  (b) lasts for no more than 6 months;

  (c) includes training to help prepare the participant for work and a work experience placement, and

  (d) is open to persons who on the first day of the course have reached the age of 16 but not the age of 25;]

"training" means—

  (a) training in pursuance of arrangements made under section 2(1) of the Employment and Training Act 1973 or section 2(3) of the Enterprise and New Towns (Scotland) Act 1990; or

  (b) any training received on a course which a person attends for 16 hours or more a week, the primary purpose of which is the teaching of occupational or vocational skills;

"training allowance" means an allowance, (whether by way of periodical grants or otherwise) payable—

  (a) out of public funds by a Government department or by or on behalf of the Secretary of State for Work and Pensions, [[4] Skills Development Scotland] or Highlands and Islands Enterprise, the [[19] ...], [[10] [[34] ...]] or the Welsh Ministers;

  (b) to a person for that person's maintenance or in respect of a member of that person's family; and

  (c) for the period, or part of the period, during which the person is following a course of training or instruction provided by, or in pursuance of arrangements made with, that department or approved by that department in relation to that person or so provided or approved by or on behalf of the Secretary of State for Work and Pensions, [[4] Skills Development Scotland] or Highlands and Islands Enterprise, or the Welsh Ministers, but does not include an allowance paid by any Government department to or in respect of a person by reason of the fact that that person is following a course of full-time education, other than under arrangements made under section 2 of the Employment and Training Act 1973 or section 2 of the Enterprise and New Towns (Scotland) Act 1990, or is training as a teacher;

[[25] "universal credit" means universal credit under Part 1 of the 2012 Act;]

"voluntary organisation" means a body, other than a public or local authority, the activities of which are carried on otherwise than for profit;

"war disablement pension" means [[3] retired pay or pension or allowance payable] in respect of disablement under an instrument specified in section 639(2) of the Income Tax (Earnings and Pensions) Act 2003;

"war widow's pension" [[3] means any pension or allowance] payable to a woman as a widow under an instrument specified in section 639(2) of the Income Tax (Earnings and Pensions) Act 2003 in respect of the death or disablement of any person;

"war widower's pension" [³ means any pension or allowance] payable to a man as a widower or to a surviving civil partner under an instrument specified in section 639(2) of the Income Tax (Earnings and Pensions) Act 2003 in respect of the death or disablement of any person;

"water charges" means—

    (a) as respects England and Wales, any water and sewerage charges under Chapter 1 of Part 5 of the Water Industry Act 1991;

    (b) as respects Scotland, any water and sewerage charges under Part 2 of the Local Government etc. (Scotland) Act 1994, in so far as such charges are in respect of the dwelling which a person occupies as the home;

[³⁹ "the We Love Manchester Emergency Fund" means the registered charity of that name (number 1173260) established on 30th May 2017;]

"week" means a period of 7 days except in relation to regulation 26;

[¹⁸ . . .]

"working day" means any day except for a Saturday, Sunday, Christmas Day, Good Friday or bank holiday under the Banking and Financial Dealings Act 1971 in England, Wales or Scotland;

"working tax credit" means a working tax credit under section 10 of the Tax Credits Act;

"young person" is a person who, except where section 6 of the Children (Leaving Care) Act 2000 (exclusion from benefits) applies, falls within the definition of qualifying young person in section 142 of the Contributions and Benefits Act (child and qualifying young person).

(2) In [² . . .] paragraph 15(2) of Schedule 6 (housing costs—linking rule)—

"child support maintenance" means such periodical payments as are referred to in section 3(6) of the Child Support Act 1991 and includes any payments made by the Secretary of State in lieu of such payments;

"the 1991 Act" means the Child Support Act 1991;

"the 2000 Act" means the Child Support, Pensions and Social Security Act 2000;

"maintenance assessment" has the same meaning as in the 1991 Act by virtue of section 54 of that Act as it has effect apart from the 2000 Act;

"maintenance calculation" has the same meaning as in the 1991 Act by virtue of section 54 of that Act as amended by the 2000 Act.

(3) Any reference to the claimant's family is to be construed as if it included in relation to a polygamous marriage a reference to any partner and any child or young person who is a member of the claimant's household.

(4) For the purposes of paragraph 5 of Schedule 1 to the Act, "week" means a period of 7 days.

[⁸ (5) For the purposes of paragraph 4 of Schedule 1 to the Act (condition relating to youth) "period of limited capability for work" means a period throughout which a person has, or is treated as having, limited capability for work.]

[¹⁵ (6) Subject to paragraph (7), for the purposes of section 24(3A)(b) of the Act, a lone parent is to be treated as responsible for, and a member of the same household as, a person under the age of 16 only where the circumstances set out in regulation 156 apply.

(7) For the purposes of sections 12 and 13 of the Act, and regulations made under those sections, a lone parent is to be treated as responsible for, and a member of the same household as a child only where the lone parent would be treated as responsible for and a member of the same household as such a child under regulations 15 and 16 of the Income Support (General) Regulations 1987, if references in those Regulations to income support were to employment and support allowance.]

[²⁶ (8) References in these Regulations to a person or claimant participating as a service user are to—

    (a) a person who is being consulted by or on behalf of—

        (i) a body which has a statutory duty to provide services in the field of health, social care or social housing; or

       (ii) a body which conducts research or undertakes monitoring for the purpose of planning or improving such services, in their capacity as a user, potential user, carer of a user or person otherwise affected by the provision of those services; or

[³² (ab) a person who is being consulted by or on behalf of—

        (i) the Secretary of State in relation to any of the Secretary of State's functions in the field of social security or child support or under section 2 of the Employment and Training Act 1973; or

       (ii) a body which conducts research or undertakes monitoring for the purpose of planning or improving such functions,

      in their capacity as a person affected or potentially affected by the exercise of those functions or the carer of such a person;]

    (b) the carer of a person consulted under [³² sub-paragraphs (a) or (ab)].]

AMENDMENTS

1. Employment and Support Allowance (Miscellaneous Amendments) Regulations 2008 (SI 2008/2428) reg.3 (October 27, 2008).

2. Employment and Support Allowance (Miscellaneous Amendments) Regulations 2008 (SI 2008/2428) reg.20(1) (October 27, 2008).

3. Social Security (Miscellaneous Amendments) (No.7) Regulations 2008 (SI 2008/3157) reg.11(2) (January 5, 2009).

4. Social Security (Miscellaneous Amendments) Regulations 2009 (SI 2009/583) reg.10(2) (April 6, 2009).

5. Social Security (Miscellaneous Amendments) (No.4) Regulations 2009 (SI 2009/2655) reg.11(1) and (2) (October 26, 2009).

6. Housing and Regeneration Act 2008 (Consequential Provisions) (No.2) Order 2010 (SI 671/2010) reg.4 and Sch.1 para.70 (April 1, 2010).

7. Social Security (Miscellaneous Amendments) (No.2) Regulations 2010 (SI 2010/641) reg.12(2) (April 6, 2010).

8. Social Security (Miscellaneous Amendments) (No.3) Regulations 2010 (SI 2010/840) reg.9(1) and (2) (June 29, 2010).

9. Health and Social Care Act 2008 (Miscellaneous Consequential Amendments) Order 2010 (SI 2010/1881) regs 2 and 25 (September 1, 2010).

10. Apprenticeships, Skills, Children and Learning Act 2009 (Consequential Amendments to Subordinate Legislation) (England) Order 2010 (SI 2010/1941) regs 28(1) and (2) (September 1, 2010).

11. Social Security (Miscellaneous Amendments) Regulations 2011 (SI 2011/674) reg.16(2) (April 11, 2011).

12. Employment and Support Allowance (Work-Related Activity) Regulations 2011 (SI 2011/1349) reg.10 (June 1, 2011).

13. Social Security (Miscellaneous Amendments) (No.2) Regulations 2011 (SI 2011/1707) reg.4(2)(b) and (3) (August 5, 2011).

14. Social Security (Miscellaneous Amendments) (No.3) Regulations 2011 (SI 2011/2425) reg.23(2) (October 30, 2011).

15. Social Security (Work-focused Interviews for Lone Parents and Partners) (Amendment) Regulations 2011 (SI 2011/2428) reg.5(2) (October 30, 2011).

16. Public Services Reform (Scotland) Act 2010 (Consequential Modifications of Enactments) Order 2011 (SI 2011/2581) art.2 and Sch.2 para.58 (October 28, 2011).

17. Social Security (Miscellaneous Amendments) Regulations 2012 (SI 2012/757) reg.6 (April 1, 2012).

18. Employment and Support Allowance (Amendment of Linking Rules) Regulations 2012 (SI 2012/919), reg.5(2) (May 1, 2012).

19. Young People's Learning Agency Abolition (Consequential Amendments to Subordinate Legislation) (England) Order 2012 (SI 2012/956) reg.22(1) and (2) (May 1, 2012). (The fact that the amended text does not make grammatical sense, reflects the wording of the amending instrument and is not an editorial error).

20. Employment and Support Allowance (Sanctions) (Amendment) Regulations 2012 (SI 2012/2756) reg.2 (December 3, 2012).

21. National Treatment Agency (Abolition) and the Health and Social Care Act 2012 (Consequential, Transitional and Saving Provisions) Order 2013 (SI 2013/235) art.9 and Sch.1 para.116(1) and (2) (April 1, 2013).

22. Social Security (Miscellaneous Amendments) Regulations 2013 (SI 2013/443) reg.9(1) and (2) (April 2, 2013).

23. Personal Independence Payment (Supplementary Provisions and Consequential Amendments) Regulations 2013 (SI 2013/388) reg.8 and Sch. para.40(1) and (2) (April 8, 2013).

24. Armed Forces and Reserve Forces Compensation Scheme (Consequential Provisions: Subordinate Legislation) Order 2013 (SI 2013/591) art.7 and Sch. para.37(1) and (2) (April 8, 2013).

25. Universal Credit (Consequential, Supplementary, Incidental and Miscellaneous Provisions) Regulations 2013 (SI 2013/630) reg.37(1) and (3) (April 29, 2013).

26. Social Security (Miscellaneous Amendments) (No.3) Regulations 2013 (SI 2013/2536) reg.13(1)-(3) (October 29, 2013).

27. Marriage (Same Sex Couples) Act 2013 (Consequential Provisions) Order 2014 (SI 2014/107) reg.2 and Sch.1, para.45 (March 13, 2014). The amendment extends to England and Wales only (see SI 2014/107, art.1(4)).

28. Social Security (Maternity Allowance) (Miscellaneous Amendments) Regulations 2014 (SI 2014/884) reg.5(2) (May 18, 2014).

29. Marriage and Civil Partnership (Scotland) Act 2014 and Civil Partnership Act 2004 (Consequential Provisions and Modifications) Order 2014 (SI 2014/3229) art.29 and Sch.6, para.32 (December 16, 2014). The amendment relates only to Scotland (see SI 2014/3229, art.3(4)) but is in the same terms as the amendment made in relation to England and Wales by SI 2014/107 (see note 27 above).

30. Shared Parental Leave and Statutory Shared Parental Pay (Consequential Amendments to Subordinate Legislation) Order 2014 art.20(3)(c) (December 31, 2014).

31. Shared Parental Leave and Statutory Shared Parental Pay (Consequential Amendments to Subordinate Legislation) Order 2014 art.20(3)(a) and (b) (April 5, 2015).

32. Social Security (Miscellaneous Amendments) Regulations 2015 (SI 2015/67) reg.2(1)(f) and (2) (February 23, 2015).

33. Social Security (Members of the Reserve Forces) (Amendment) Regulations 2015 (SI 2014/389) reg.4(2) (April 6, 2015).

34. Deregulation Act 2015 (Consequential Amendments) Order 2015 (SI 2015/971) art.2 and Sch.3, para.14(1) and (2) (May 26, 2015).

35. Pensions Act 2014 (Consequential, Supplementary and Incidental Amendments) Order 2015 (SI 2015/1985) art.31(1) and (2) (April 6, 2016).

36. Social Security (Scottish Rate of Income Tax etc.) (Amendment) Regulations 2016 (SI 2016/233) reg.6(1) and (2) (April 6, 2016).

37. Social Security (Scottish Infected Blood Support Scheme) Regulations 2017 (SI 2017/329) reg.8(1) and (2) (April 3, 2017).

38. Employment and Support Allowance (Miscellaneous Amendments and Transitional and Savings Provision) Regulations 2017 (SI 2017/581) reg.7(1) and (2) (June 23, 2017, subject to the transitional and savings provision in reg.10).

39. Social Security (Emergency Funds) (Amendment) Regulations 2017 (SI 2017/689) reg.8(1) and (2) (June 19, 2017).

40. Social Security (Infected Blood and Thalidomide) Regulations 2017 (SI 2017/870) reg.8(1) and (2) (October 23, 2017).

41. Social Security (Qualifying Young Persons Participating in Relevant Training Schemes) (Amendment) Regulations 2017 (SI 2017/987) reg.3(1) and (2) (November 6, 2017).

42. Social Security and Child Support (Regulation and Inspection of Social Care (Wales) Act 2016) (Consequential Provision) Regulations 2018 (SI 2018/228) reg.11(1) and (2) (April 2, 2018).

GENERAL NOTE

9.5   Most of these definitions are either self-explanatory, or references to definitions in other regulations or are similar to those in reg.2(1) of the IS Regs and reg.1(2) of the JSA Regs. See the notes to those Regulations in Vol.II of this series. The following merit comment

"aircraft worker": The definition is used in reg.11 (Condition relating to youth—residence or presence). By para.4 of Sch.1 to the Welfare Reform Act, those under 20 (or in prescribed cases 25) may, if they satisfy certain conditions (set out in reg.11), be entitled to contributory ESA even though they do not satisfy the second contribution condition. For the purposes of reg.11, the claimant is treated as being resident and present in Great Britain while absent "abroad in the capacity of being an aircraft worker or mariner". The definition covers all those employed on an aircraft while in flight under a contract that was entered into in the UK, other than members of the armed forces.

"confinement": The definition in s.171 of the Contributions and Benefits Act reads as follows:

"confinement" means—

    (a) labour resulting in the issue of a living child, or

    (b) labour after 24 weeks of pregnancy resulting in the issue of a child whether alive or dead,

    and "confined" shall be construed accordingly; and where a woman's labour begun on one day results in the issue of a child on another day she shall be taken to be confined on the day of the issue of the child or, if labour results in the issue of twins or a greater number of children, she shall be taken to be confined on the day of the issue of the last of them;"

"dependent child": This definition (which does not appear in the IS Regulations or the JSA Regs) refers to any child or qualifying young person who a member of the claimant's household and is treated as the responsibility of the claimant or the claimant's partner (i.e., under reg.156(10)).

"mariner": See the commentary on "aircraft worker" above. The definition is similar except that the reference to "aircraft" is to "ship or vessel".

"member of Her Majesty's forces": Members of the armed forces and their families

are, in certain circumstances, treated as being in Great Britain while abroad. The definition is supplemented by Sch.1 below.

"National Minimum Wage" is defined as the rate of the national minimum wage specified in regulation 11 of the National Minimum Wage Regulations 1999. However, those Regulations were revoked and replaced by the National Minimum Wage Regulations 2015. In those circumstances, the reference in the definition to the 1999 Regulations is to be taken to be to the 2015 Regulations (Interpretation Act 1978 ss.17 and 23). Since reg.11 of the 1999 Regulations originally specified the single hourly rate of the national minimum wage, the equivalent must presumably be taken as being reg.4 of the current form of the 2015 Regulations. Regulation 4 now specifies the single hourly rate (i.e. the rate applicable to workers aged at least 25) and reg.4A specifies lower rates for workers of younger ages, so that for old style ESA purposes the over-25 rate is to be used regardless of the age of the person concerned.

[¹ Disapplication of section 1(1A) of the Social Security Administration Act 1992

2A. Section 1(1A) of the Social Security Administration Act 1992   9.6
(requirement to state a national insurance number) shall not apply to a person who—
- (a) is a person in respect of whom a claim for employment and support allowance is made;
- (b) is subject to immigration control within the meaning of section 115(9)(a) of the Immigration and Asylum Act;
- (c) does not satisfy the basic conditions of entitlement to employment and support allowance for the purposes of section 1(3) of the Act; and
- (d) has not previously been allocated a national insurance number.]

AMENDMENT

1. Social Security (National Insurance Number Information: Exemption) Regulations 2009 (SI 2009/471) reg.13 (April 6, 2009).

GENERAL NOTE

See the commentary to reg.2A(c) of the Income Support Regulations.   9.7

Rounding of fractions

3. For the purposes of these Regulations—   9.8
- (a) where any calculation under these Regulations results in a fraction of a penny that fraction is, if it would be to the claimant's advantage, to be treated as a penny, otherwise it must be disregarded;
- (b) where an employment and support allowance is awarded for a period which is not a complete benefit week and the applicable amount in respect of the period results in an amount which includes a fraction of a penny that fraction is to be treated as a penny.

GENERAL NOTE

Fractions are always rounded in the claimant's favour.   9.9

PART 2

THE ASSESSMENT PHASE

MODIFICATION

9.10   Note that for the purpose of making "conversion decisions" under the "Migration Regulations" from October 1, 2010, Pt 2 (the assessment phase) does not apply. See reg.6(1) and Sch.1 para.8 to those Regulations: the Employment and Support Allowance (Transitional Provisions, Housing Benefit and Council Tax Benefit) (Existing Awards) (No. 2) Regulations 2010 (SI 2010/1907) (as amended), below.

The end of the assessment phase

9.11   **4.**—(1) Subject to [²paragraphs (2) and (3)] and [¹regulation 5], the assessment phase in relation to a claimant ends on the last day of [³ the relevant period].

[²(2) Where paragraph (3) applies, the assessment phase is to end when it is determined whether the claimant has limited capability for work.

(3) This paragraph applies where, at the end of [³ the relevant period]—

(a) the claimant has not been assessed in accordance with a limited capability for work assessment; and

(b) the claimant has not been treated as having limited capability for work in accordance with regulations 20, 25, 26, 29 or 33(2) (persons to be treated as having limited capability for work).]

[³(4) In this regulation, "the relevant period" means the period of 13 weeks beginning with—

(a) the first day of the assessment phase as determined under section 24(2)(a) of the Act; or

(b) where that day immediately follows an extended period of sickness, the first day of the extended period of sickness.

(5) In paragraph (4), "extended period of sickness" means a period in which the claimant was—

(a) entitled to a jobseeker's allowance; and

(b) treated as capable of work or as not having limited capability for work under regulation 55ZA of the Jobseeker's Allowance Regulations 1996 or regulation 46A of the Jobseeker's Allowance Regulations 2013 (extended period of sickness).]

AMENDMENTS

1. Social Security (Miscellaneous Amendments) (No.3) Regulations 2010 (SI 2010/840) reg.9(3) (June 28, 2010).

2. Social Security (Miscellaneous Amendments) (No.3) Regulations 2013 (SI 2013/2536) reg.13(4) (October 29, 2013).

3. Jobseeker's Allowance (Extended Period of Sickness) Amendment Regulations 2015 (SI 2015/339) reg.4 (March 30, 2015).

DEFINITIONS

"the assessment phase"—see WRA 2007 s.24(2).
"claimant"—see WRA 2007 s.24(1).
"extended period of sickness"—see para.(5).
"limited capability for work"—see WRA 2007 s.1(4).
"limited capability for work assessment"—see reg.2(1).
"the relevant period"—see para.(4).
"week"—see reg.2(1).

GENERAL NOTE

During an initial "assessment phase", generally (reg.7, below, affords exceptions)   9.12
a claimant can only be entitled to "basic allowance" ESA; entitlement to the appropriate additional component (support or work-related) only arises after the end of
that phase (WRA 2007 s.2(2), (3)). The assessment phase ends on the last day of
the "relevant period" (para.(1)). That period is one of 13 weeks beginning either
with the first day of the assessment phase determined by WRA 2007 s.24(2)(a) or
if that day followed an extended period of sickness in which the claimant remained
entitled to JSA under the specified regulations, with the first day of that extended
period of sickness (paras(4), (5)). Section 24(2)(a) of the WRA 2007 stipulates that
the "assessment phase" begins on the first day of entitlement to ESA, i.e. the first
day of limited capability for work after service of the "waiting days" (these are days
of non-entitlement: see WRA 2007 Sch.2, para.2 and reg.144). This regulation in
contrast sets out when the "assessment phase" ends. It ends after 13 weeks, unless
at that time it still has not been determined whether the claimant has, or is to be
treated under the regulations enumerated in para.(3) as having, limited capability
for work. In that case the "assessment phase" lasts longer than the 13-week period
and ends when the limited capability for work determination is made, that is, when
it is decided whether or not the person has, or is to be treated as having, limited
capability for work.

In short, the assessment phase ends after the later of 13 weeks or the decision on whether the claimant has (or is to be treated as having) limited capability for work. Where, however, the claimant appeals a decision embodying an
adverse determination on limited capability for work, the assessment phase ends
only when the appeal is determined by an appeal tribunal (see regs 5(4) and
147A).

In *SSWP v NC (ESA)* [2013] UKUT 477 (AAC), Judge Bano held that, despite
poor wording, the effect of the then reg.4(2) (now reg.4(2), (3)) was that "subject to
exceptions in cases involving appeals, the assessment phase lasts until the end of the
three month period, or until a determination that a claimant has (or is to be treated
as having) limited capability for work, whichever is the later" (para.9). In *SSWP v
RM* [2014] UKUT 42 (AAC), Judge Jacobs agreed with Judge Bano both as to the
result of a proper reading of reg.4 and that reg.4(2) as worded before the October
2013 amendments was poorly worded, but considered that it could be rendered
coherent by inserting "by" at the beginning of the then para.(2)(a). Fortunately, the
October 2013 amendment makes things much clearer and with the same effect as
in these two decsions.

The assessment phase—previous claimants

5.—(1) Where the circumstances in paragraph (2) apply in relation to a   9.13
claimant the assessment phase —
   (a) begins on the first day of the period for which the claimant was previ-
       ously entitled to an employment and support allowance; and
   (b) subject to [³ paragraphs (3), (3A) and (4)], ends on the day when the
       sum of the period for which the claimant was previously entitled to
       an employment and support allowance and the period for which the
       claimant is currently entitled to such an allowance is 13 weeks.
   [⁴(1A) For the purposes of paragraph (1), any period when the claimant
was—
   (a) entitled to a jobseeker's allowance; and
   (b) treated as capable of work or as not having limited capability for work
       under regulation 55ZA of the Jobseeker's Allowance Regulations
       1996 or regulation 46A of the Jobseeker's Allowance Regulations
       2013,

is to be treated as a period when the claimant was previously entitled to an employment and support allowance.]

(2) The circumstances are that—

(a) (i) the claimant's current period of limited capability for work is to be treated as a continuation of an earlier period of limited capability for work under regulation 145(1) [².. .];

    (ii) the claimant was entitled to an employment and support allowance in the earlier period of limited capability for work;

   (iii) the assessment phase had not ended in the previous period for which the claimant was entitled to an employment and support allowance; and

   (iv) the period for which the claimant was previously entitled was no more than 13 weeks; or

[²(b) (i) the claimant's current period of limited capability for work is to be treated as a continuation of an earlier period of limited capability for work under regulation 145(1),

    (ii) the claimant was entitled to an employment and support allowance in the earlier period of limited capability for work,

   (iii) the previous period of limited capability for work was terminated by virtue of a determination that the claimant did not have limited capability for work,

   (iv) the period for which the claimant was previously entitled was no more than 13 weeks, and

    (v) a determination is made in relation to the current period of limited capability for work that the claimant has or is treated as having limited capability for work, other than under regulation 30; or

(c) (i) the claimant's current period of limited capability for work is to be treated as a continuation of an earlier period of limited capability for work under regulation 145(1),

    (ii) the claimant was entitled to an employment and support allowance in the earlier period of limited capability for work,

   (iii) in relation to the previous award of an employment and support allowance, a determination was made that the claimant had limited capability for work or was treated as having limited capability for work, other than under regulation 30, and

   (iv) the period for which the claimant was previously entitled was no more than 13 weeks.]

[³(3) Where paragraph (3A) applies, the assessment phase is to end when it is determined whether the claimant has limited capability for work.

(3A) This paragraph applies where on the day referred to in paragraph (1)(b)—

(a) the claimant has not been assessed in accordance with a limited capability for work assessment; and

(b) the claimant has not been treated as having limited capability for work in accordance with regulations 20, 25, 26, 29 or 33(2) (persons to be treated as having limited capability for work).]

[¹(4) Where a person has made and is pursuing an appeal against a decision of the Secretary of State that embodies a determination that the claimant does not have limited capability for work—

(a) [³ paragraphs (3) and (3A) do] not apply; and

(b) paragraph (1) does not apply to any period of limited capability for work to which regulation 147A(2) applies until a determination of limited capability for work has been made following the determination of the appeal by the First-tier Tribunal.]

AMENDMENTS

1. Social Security (Miscellaneous Amendments) (No.3) Regulations 2010 (SI 2010/840) reg.9(4) (June 28, 2010).
2. Employment and Support Allowance (Amendment of Linking Rules) Regulations 2012 (SI 2012/919) reg.5(3) (May 1, 2012).
3. Social Security (Miscellaneous Amendments) (No.3) Regulations 2013 (SI 2013/2536) reg.13(5) (October 29, 2013).
4. Jobseeker's Allowance (Extended Period of Sickness) Amendment Regulations 2015 (SI 2015/339) reg.4 (March 30, 2015).

DEFINITIONS

"the assessment phase"—see WRA 2007 s.24(2).
"claimant"—see WRA 2007 s.24(1).
"entitled"—see WRA 2007 s.24(1).
"limited capability for work"—see WRA 2007 s.1(4).
"limited capability for work assessment"—see reg.2(1).
"week"—see reg.2(1).

GENERAL NOTE

This regulation deals with determining the end of the "assessment phase" in cases of intermittent limited capability for work (where spells of limited capability for work are interspersed with spells in which capability for work is not limited), where the ostensibly separate spells of limited capability are fused into one by the operation of the "linking rule" in reg.145. As noted in the commentary to that regulation, this will happen where the two spells are not separated by more than 12 weeks. Until May 1, 2012, in some cases the permissible separation period could have been as long as 104 weeks, but that date saw the abolition of the 104 week linking rule for work or training beneficiaries, that abolition itself being the result of time-limiting entitlement to CESA for those not in the support group to 365 days (see WRA 2007 s.1A, above). A period in which a claimant remained entitled to JSA during an extended period of sickness under the specified JSA Regs counts as a period of previous entitlement to ESA (paras (1), (1A)). The effect of reg.5 is that the weeks of entitlement to ESA in each period thus linked are added together and the assessment phase ends when their sum reaches 13, unless no limited capability for work determination (see commentary to reg.4) has by then been made, in which case, as with continuous periods of limited capability for work under reg.4, it ends when that determination has been made. In short, the assessment phase ends after the later of 13 weeks (in two or more linked spells of limited capability) or the decision on whether the claimant has (or is to be treated as having) limited capability for work. Where, however, the claimant appeals a decision embodying an adverse determination on limited capability for work, the assessment phase ends only when the appeal is determined by an appeal tribunal (see reg.147A).

9.14

The assessment phase—claimants appealing against a decision

[¹**6.** *Omitted.*]

9.15

AMENDMENT

1. Social Security (Miscellaneous Amendments) (No.3) Regulations 2010 (SI 2010/840) reg.9(5) (June 28, 2010).

Circumstances where the condition that the assessment phase has ended before entitlement to the support component [⁶...] arises does not apply

9.16   7.—(1) Subject to paragraph (2), [⁶ sections 2(2)(a) and 4(4)(a)] of the Act do not apply where—

    (a) a claimant is terminally ill and has either—

        (i) made a claim expressly on the ground of being terminally ill; or

        (ii) made an application for supersession or revision in accordance with the Social Security and Child Support (Decisions and Appeals) Regulations 1999 which contains an express statement that the claimant is terminally ill; [¹ ...]

    (b) [⁴ the case is a relevant linked case;]

    [¹(c) (i) the claimant's entitlement to an employment and support allowance commences within 12 weeks of the claimant's entitlement to income support coming to an end;

        (ii) in relation to that entitlement to income support, immediately before it ended the claimant's applicable amount included the disability premium by virtue of satisfying the conditions in paragraphs 11 and 12 of Schedule 2 to the Income Support Regulations; and

        (iii) that entitlement to income support ended solely by virtue of the coming into force, in relation to the claimant, of the Social Security (Lone Parents and Miscellaneous Amendments) Regulations] [⁵2012] [³; or

    (d) a claimant is entitled to an employment and support allowance by virtue of section 1B of the Act (further entitlement after time-limiting).]

    [⁴(1A) For the purposes of paragraph (1)(b) a relevant linked case is a case mentioned in paragraph (1B) where a period of limited capability for work is to be treated as a continuation of an earlier period of limited capability for work under regulation 145(1).

    (1B) Paragraph (1A) applies to the following cases—

    (a) case 1 is where—

        (i) the claimant was entitled to an employment and support allowance (including entitlement to a component under sections [⁶ 2(2) or 4(4)] of the Act [⁷ or the claimant was a member of the work-related activity group]) in the earlier period of limited capability for work, and

        (ii) the previous period for which the claimant was entitled to an employment and support allowance was terminated other than by virtue of a determination that the claimant did not have limited capability for work;

    (b) case 2 is where—

        (i) the claimant was entitled to an employment and support allowance in the earlier period of limited capability for work,

        (ii) the previous period for which the claimant was entitled to an employment and support allowance was 13 weeks or longer,

        (iii) the previous period for which the claimant was entitled to an employment and support allowance was terminated by virtue of a determination that the claimant did not have, or was treated as not having, limited capability for work, and

        (iv) it is determined in relation to the current period of limited

capability for work that the claimant has limited capability for
work or is treated as having limited capability for work, other
than under regulation 30;

(c) case 3 is where—
  (i) the claimant was entitled to an employment and support allowance in the earlier period of limited capability for work,
  (ii) the previous period for which the claimant was entitled to an
  employment and support allowance was 13 weeks or longer,
  (iii) the previous period for which the claimant was entitled to an
  employment and support allowance was terminated before
  it could be determined whether the claimant had limited
  capability for work or was treated as having limited capability
  for work, other than under regulation 30, and
  (iv) it is determined in relation to the current period of limited capability for work that the claimant has limited capability for work
  or is treated as having limited capability for work, other than
  under regulation 30; and

(d) case 4 is where—
  (i) the claimant was entitled to an employment and support allowance (including entitlement to a component under sections [⁶
  2(2) or 4(4)] of the Act [⁷ or the claimant was a member of the
  work-related activity group]) in the earlier period of limited
  capability for work,
  (ii) the previous period for which the claimant was entitled to an
  employment and support allowance was terminated because it was
  determined that the claimant did not have limited capability for
  work or was treated as not having limited capability for work, and
  (iii) it is determined in relation to the current period of limited capability for work that the claimant has limited capability for work
  or is treated as having limited capability for work, other than
  under regulation 30.]

(2) Paragraph (1)(b) does not apply to [²any period of limited capability
for work to which regulation 147A(2) applies until the determination of
limited capability for work has been made following the determination of
the appeal by the First-tier Tribunal].

AMENDMENTS

1. Social Security (Lone Parents and Miscellaneous Amendments) Regulations
2008 (SI 2008/3051) reg.12(2) (November 24, 2008).

2. Social Security (Miscellaneous Amendments) (No.3) Regulations 2010 (SI
2010/840) reg.9(6) (June 28, 2010).

3. Employment and Support Allowance (Duration of Contributory Allowance)
(Consequential Amendments) Regulations 2012 (SI 2012/913) reg.9(2) (May 1, 2012).

4. Employment and Support Allowance (Amendment of Linking Rules)
Regulations 2012 (SI 2012/919) reg.5(4) (May 1, 2012 immediately after amendment 3, above—see reg.1(2)).

5. Social Security (Lone Parents and Miscellaneous Amendments) Regulations
2012 (SI 2012/874) reg.6 (May 21, 2012).

6. Employment and Support Allowance and Universal Credit (Miscellaneous
Amendments and Transitional and Savings Provisions) Regulations 2017 (SI
2017/204) reg.2(2) (April 3, 2017).

7. Employment and Support Allowance (Miscellaneous Amendments and
Transitional and Savings Provision) Regulations 2017 (SI 2017/581) reg.7(3) (June
23, 2017).

DEFINITIONS

> "claimant"—see WRA 2007 s.24(1).
> "entitled"—see WRA 2007 s.24(1).
> "limited capability for work"—see WRA 2007 s.1(4).
> "period of limited capability for work"—see reg.2(1).
> "relevant linked case"—see paras (1)(b), (1A), (1B).
> "terminally ill"—see reg.2(1).
> "the assessment phase"—see WRA 2007 s.24(2).

GENERAL NOTE

9.17   WRA 2007 ss.2 and 4 provide that until the "assessment phase" ends there can be no entitlement other than to basic allowance ESA; entitlement to the support component normally cannot arise until the assessment phase has ended (on which see WRA 2007 s.24(2) and ESA Regs regs 4–6). This regulation provides that the general rule precluding entitlement does not apply in four situations. First of all it does not apply to someone terminally ill who has claimed ESA expressly on that basis or has sought supersession or revision expressly stating that he is terminally ill (para.(1)(a)). Note that someone is terminally ill where he is suffering from a progressive disease and death as a consequence of it can reasonably be expected within six months (reg.2(1)). The second situation where the general preclusive rule is disapplied is where the claimant's entitlement to ESA arises within 12 weeks of entitlement to IS which had included the disability premium, ending solely because of the entry into force in relation to him of the Social Security (Lone Parents and Miscellaneous Amendments) Regulations 2012 (para.(1)(c)). The third situation of disapplication of the general preclusive rule is where the claimant is entitled to ESA because of the further entitlement after time-limiting provisions in WRA 2007 s.1B (para.(1)(d)).

The fourth situation in which the general preclusive rule is disapplied is where the claimant's position falls within one of the four cases each constituting "a relevant linked case" (paras (1)(b), (1A), (1B)). A "relevant linked case" is one of those in para.(1B) in which a period of limited capability for work is to be treated as a continuation of an earlier one under reg.145(1) (the 12 week rule) (paras (1)(b), (1A)). Case 1 covers the situation in which the previous entitlement to ESA was one in which there was entitlement to the support component and that entitlement to ESA ended other than by virtue of it being determined that the claimant did not have limited capability for work (para.(1B)(a)). Case 2 embraces the situation in which the previous period of entitlement to ESA lasted 13 weeks or more, was ended because of a determination that the claimant did not have, or was treated as not having, limited capability for work and in the current period of ESA entitlement it has been decided that the claimant has limited capability for work or is to be treated as having it other than through reg.30 (treating someone as having limited capability for work pending an actual determination) (para.(1B)(b)). Case 3 covers the situation in which the previous period of ESA entitlement lasted 13 weeks or more but was ended before a determination of actual or deemed limited capability for work had been made (other than under reg.30), and in the current period of ESA entitlement it has been decided that the claimant has limited capability for work or is to be treated as having it other than through reg.30 (treating someone as having limited capability for work pending an actual determination) (para.(1B)(c)). Case 4 embraces the situation where the claimants previous period of entitlement to ESA included a component, was ended because it was decided the claimant did not have limited capability for work or was to be treated as not having it, and in the current period of ESA entitlement it has been decided that the claimant has limited capability for work or is to be treated as having it other than through reg.30 (para.(1B)(d)).

PART 3

CONDITIONS OF ENTITLEMENT—CONTRIBUTORY ALLOWANCE

[¹Conditions relating to national insurance and relevant earnings

7A.—(1) A claimant's relevant earnings for the purposes of paragraph   9.18
1(2)(a) of Schedule 1 to the Act (employment and support allowance: conditions relating to national insurance) are the total amount of the claimant's
earnings at the lower earnings limit for the base tax year.

(2) For the purposes of paragraph (1), earnings which exceed the lower
earnings limit are to be disregarded.]

AMENDMENT

1. Social Security (Contribution Conditions for Jobseeker's Allowance and
Employment and Support Allowance) Regulations 2010 (SI 2010/2446) reg.3(1)
(November 1, 2010).

GENERAL NOTE

As noted in the General Note to Sch.1, para.1 to the Welfare Reform Act 2007,   9.19
the changes effected by s.13 of the Welfare Reform Act 2009 and this regulation
made in consequence significantly tighten the contribution conditions for CESA.
Together they mean that the requisite level of "relevant earnings" in the tax year
relied on for the first contribution condition is now 26 times that year's lower earnings limit, rather than 25. This new regulation defines "relevant earnings" to cover
only earnings at that lower earnings limit, so that new claimants will have to have
worked for at least 26 weeks in one of the last two tax years (April 6–April 5)
complete before the start of the benefit year (beginning in early January) which
includes the first day of claim in the relevant period of limited capability for work.

Relaxation of the first contribution condition

8.—(1) A claimant who satisfies any of the conditions in paragraph (2) is   9.20
to be taken to satisfy the first contribution condition if—
  (a) the claimant paid Class 1 or Class 2 contributions before the relevant
     benefit week in respect of any one tax year; and
[¹(b) the claimant has—
     (i) earnings at the lower earnings limit in that tax year on which
        primary Class 1 contributions have been paid or treated as paid
        which in total, and disregarding any earnings which exceed the
        lower earnings limit for that year, are not less than that limit
        multiplied by 26; or
     (ii) earnings factors in that tax year derived from Class 2 contribu-
        tions multiplied by 26.]
(2) The conditions referred to in paragraph (1) are that the claimant—
  (a) was entitled to a carer's allowance in the last complete tax year
     immediately preceding the relevant benefit year;
  (b) had been engaged in qualifying remunerative work for a period of
     more than 2 years immediately before the first day of the period
     of limited capability for work and who was entitled to working tax
     credit where the disability element or the severe disability element
     of working tax credit specified in regulation 20(1) (b) or (f) of the
     Working Tax Credit (Entitlement and Maximum Rate) Regulations
     2002 was included in the award;

    (c) in respect of any week in any tax year preceding the relevant benefit year—

        (i) is entitled to be credited with earnings or contributions in accordance with regulation 9D of the Social Security (Credits) Regulations 1975 (credits for certain periods of imprisonment or detention in legal custody); or

       (ii) would have been so entitled had an application to the Secretary of State been made for the purpose of that regulation; [³or]

[²(ca) in respect of any week in the last complete tax year preceding the relevant benefit year, is entitled to be credited with earnings in accordance with regulation 9E of the Social Security (Credits) Regulations 1975 (credits for certain spouses and civil partners of members of Her Majesty's forces); [³. . .

    (d) *revoked*].

AMENDMENT

1. Social Security (Miscellaneous Amendments) (No.3) Regulations 2011 (SI 2011/2425) reg.23(3) (October 31, 2011).

2. Social Security (Contribution Conditions for Jobseeker's Allowance and Employment and Support Allowance) Regulations 2011 (SI 2011/2862) reg.3 (January 1, 2012).

3. Social Security (Miscellaneous Amendments) Regulations 2012 (SI 2012/757), reg.20(2) (May 1, 2012).

DEFINITIONS

"benefit week"—see reg.2(1).
"carer's allowance"—see reg.2(1).
"claimant"—see WRA 2007 s.24(1).
"Class 1 contributions"—see WRA 2007 s.1, Sch.1 Pt 1 para.3(1)(b).
"Class 2 contributions—see WRA 2007 s.1, Sch.1 Pt 1 para.3(1)(b).
"contributory allowance"—see WRA 2007 s.1(7).
"earnings"—see WRA 2007 s.1, Sch.1 Pt 1 para.3(1)(c).
"earnings factor"—see WRA 2007 s.1, Sch.1 Pt 1 para.3(1)(d).
"first contribution condition"—see reg.2(1); WRA 2007 Sch.1 para.1(1).
"lower earnings limit"—see WRA 2007 s.1, Sch.1 Pt 1 para.3(1)(e).
"period of limited capability for work,"—see reg.2(1).
"primary Class 1 contributions"—see WRA 2007 s.1, Sch.1 Pt 1 para.3(1)(b).
"qualifying remunerative work"—see reg.2(1).
"relevant benefit year"—see WRA 2007 s.1, Sch.1 Pt 1 para.3(1)(f).
"tax year"—see WRA 2007 s.1, Sch.1 Pt 1 para.3(1)(g).
"week"—see reg.2(1).

GENERAL NOTE

9.21   The national insurance contribution conditions, affording the sole route into CESA for anyone not incapacitated in youth, are found in WRA 2007 s.1(2)(a) and Sch.1, Pt 1, paras 1–3. They are the same as those governing access to IB from April 6, 2001 (SSCBA 1992 s.30A and Sch.3, para.2). The conditions were tightened from then so as to require a recent connection with the world of paid employment. Prior to that date the first contribution condition (then, as now, only able to be met by paid contributions) governing access to IB could be met by a sufficient record of paid contributions in any tax year prior to the claim. As now, IB contribution condition one had from April 6 2001 to be met in one of the last three tax years (April 6–April 5) complete before the start of the benefit year (early January–early January) in which falls the first day of the period of incapacity for work (now limited capability for work) of which the claim is part. This reg. affords some relief for some of the people disadvantaged by that rule. It is comparable to (but not wholly coterminous with) the relaxation in IB Regs, Pt 1A, reg.2B.

Regulation 8 affords the claimants covered by it the concession that the first contribution condition can be met in any year rather than one of the two (previously three) tax years complete before the start of the benefit year which includes the first day of claim in the relevant period of limited capability for work. The amendment to para.(1)(b) reflecting the tightening of contribution conditions, achieves parity in terms of the requisite level of "earnings" on which Class 1 contributions have been paid, or the earnings factor from Class 2 contributions made (each weekly one generating an earnings factor equivalent to that year's LEL), or a combination of the two, at 26 times the lower earnings limit for the tax year relied on. Moreover, here as in the main rules on contributions, from that date in respect of paid Class 1 contributions, only earnings at that lower earnings limit count, so that claimants will have had to have worked for at least 26 weeks in the relevant tax year. Prior to the amendment, the level of earnings was 25 times the lower earnings limit and in respect of paid Class 1 contributions all earnings between the lower and upper earnings limit on which Class 1 contributions had been paid counted, so that, in effect, claimants were subject to the first contribution condition as it stood before the April 2001 changes to IB.

The amendment to para.(1)(b) was originally effective from November 1, 2010. With effect from October 31, 2011, however, it was substituted in exactly the same terms because the initial amending provision had not been validly made since it had not, as the law required, been referred to the Social Security Advisory Committee. The Department:

"recognises that, in applying the defective provision, some claimants may have been deprived of a valid entitlement to ESA and that, as a consequence, there needs to be an exercise to identify those concerned and to award them benefit as appropriate. The Department is currently considering the most appropriate way to achieve this" (para.7.48 of the Explanatory Memorandum to SI 2011/2425).

Regulation 28 of the Social Security (Miscellaneous Amendments) (No.3) Regulations 2011 (SI 2011/2425) revoked the defective amending regulation.

The rules are relaxed in the following situations: **9.22**

(i) where the claimant was, in the last complete tax year immediately preceding the relevant benefit year in which occurred the first day of limited capability for work, entitled to carer's allowance (para.2(a))(in express terms (but not effect) this is narrower than IB reg.2B(2)(a) which also explicitly covered someone who would have been entitled to one but for the provisions of reg.4 of the Overlapping Benefit Regs (he was receiving another higher value benefit), but this is because that regulation merely precluding benefit being payable, rather than affecting entitlement, the explicit reference was in law otiose);

(ii) where the claimant was engaged in qualifying remunerative work for a period of more than two years immediately before the first day of limited capability for work and throughout that period was in receipt of working tax credit which included in the award the disability or severe disability element (para.(2)(b));

(iii) certain convicted prisoners whose conviction is overturned whose contribution record is credited in respect of their period of imprisonment under Social Security (Credits) Regulations 1975, reg.9D or would be if they applied to the Secretary of State (para.(2)(c));

(iv) spouses and civil partners, returning from accompanying a member of Her Majesty's forces on a posting abroad, provided they have been awarded a NI credit under reg.9E of the Social Security (Credits) Regulations 1975 in respect of at least one week during the last complete tax year prior to their claim to benefit from the change effected by this regulation (para.(2) (ca)).

Condition relating to youth—claimants aged 20 or over but under 25

9.23   **9.**—(1) For the purposes of paragraph 4(1)(a) of Schedule 1 to the Act, a claimant who satisfies the conditions specified in paragraph (2) falls within a prescribed case.

(2) The conditions are that the claimant—

(a) registered on a course of—

    (i) full-time advanced or secondary education; or

    (ii) training,

at least 3 months before attaining the age of 20; and

(b) not more than one academic term immediately after registration attended one or more such courses in respect of a period referred to in paragraph (3).

(3) The period mentioned in sub-paragraph (2)(b) is a period which—

(a) began on or before a day at least 3 months before the day the claimant attained the age of 20; and

(b) ended no earlier than the beginning of the last two complete tax years before the relevant benefit year which would have applied if the claimant was entitled to an employment and support allowance having satisfied the first contribution condition and the second contribution condition.

(4) For the purposes of this regulation a claimant is to be treated as attending a course on any day on which the course is interrupted by an illness or domestic emergency.

(5) In this regulation—

"advanced education" means education for the purposes of—

(a) a course in preparation for a degree, a diploma of higher education, a higher national diploma, a higher national diploma of the Business and [² Technology] Education Council or the Scottish Qualifications Authority, or a teaching qualification; or

(b) any other course which is of a standard above ordinary national diploma, a diploma of the Business and [² Technology] Education Council or a higher or advanced higher national certificate of the Scottish Qualifications Authority or a general certificate of education (advanced level);

"full-time" includes part-time where the person's disability prevents attendance at a full-time course;

"secondary education" means a course of education below a course of advanced education—

(a) by attendance at an establishment recognised by the Secretary of State as being, or as comparable to, a university, college or school; or

(b) elsewhere where the Secretary of State is satisfied that the education is equivalent to that given in an establishment recognised as being, or as comparable to, a university, college or school.

[¹(6) A claimant is to be treated as not having limited capability for work on a day which is not, for the purposes of paragraph 4(1)(d)(ii) of Schedule 1 to the Act (period of 196 consecutive days preceding the relevant period of limited capability for work), part of any consecutive days of limited capability for work.]

Amendments

1. Employment and Support Allowance (Miscellaneous Amendments) Regulations 2008 (SI 2008/2428) reg.4 (October 27, 2008).

2. Social Security (Miscellaneous Amendments) (No.3) Regulations 2013 (SI 2013/2536) reg.13(6) (October 29, 2013).

DEFINITIONS

"advanced education"—see para.(5).
"claimant"—see WRA 2007 s.24(1).
"first contribution condition"—see reg.2(1); WRA 2007 Sch.1, para.1(1).
"full-time"—see para.(5).
"relevant benefit year"—see WRA 2007 s.1, Sch.1, Pt 1, para.3(1)(f).
"secondary education"—see para.(5).
"second contribution condition"—see reg.2(1); WRA 2007 Sch.1, para.2(1).
"tax year"—see WRA 2007 s.1, Sch.1, Pt 1, para.3(1)(g).
"training"—see reg.2(1).

GENERAL NOTE

Meeting the national insurance contributions conditions affords only one route to CESA (WRA 2007 s.1(2)(a) and Sch.1, Pt 1, paras 1–3; reg.8). The second route (condition relating to youth) is covered by WRA 2007 s.1(2)(a), Sch.1, Pt 1, para.4 (the key provision), this regulation and regs 10–12. This regulation stipulates when there can be access to CESA through the "youth" route for those 20 or over but under 25; it sets out the conditions in which their case is a "prescribed" one for purposes of WRA 2007 Sch.1, Pt 1, para.4(1)(a) (para.(1)). The comparable IB provision is IB Regs, reg.15. It is here assumed that case law on that almost identically worded provision will carry over into interpretation of this ESA provision.   **9.24**

Someone over 20 but under 25 can qualify for the "youth" route where, at least three months before reaching 20, he registered on a course of full time education or of training (see below), provided that not more than one academic term immediately after his registration, he attended one or more such courses in respect of a specified period (para.(2)). Note that he is treated as attending on any day on which the course or training is interrupted by an illness or domestic emergency (para.4). The specified period is set out in para.(3): a period beginning on or before a day three months before his twentieth birthday (para.(3)(a)) and ending on a day not earlier than the beginning of the last two complete tax years before the benefit year which would have governed a claim for CESA by the national insurance route. The terms "advanced education" and "secondary education" are defined in para.(5) in an interlocking way, so that "secondary education" is a level below that of "advanced education" and it requires attendance at a educational establishment recognised by the Secretary of State as, or as comparable, to a university, college or school, or elsewhere so long as the Secretary of State is satisfied that the education afforded there is equivalent to that in such an establishment. Note that while both "advanced education" and "secondary education" require a "full-time" course, para.(5) stipulates that "full-time" covers also "part-time" where the claimant's disability is such as to preclude him attending a full-time course.

The reference in the IB provision was to "vocational or work-based training". This regulation refers to "training", defined in reg.2(1) as (a) training in pursuance of arrangements made under s.2(1) of the Employment and Training Act 1973 or s.2(3) of the Enterprise and New Towns (Scotland) Act 1990; or (b) any training received on a course which a person attends for 16 hours or more a week, the primary purpose of which is the teaching of occupational or vocational skills. In respect of the IB provision, whether the claimant was registered on a "full-time" course or on a course of "vocational or work-based training" was considered by Commissioner Jacobs in *CIB/1410/2005*. Her course was described as part-time by the College in question (not conclusive in itself) and she was required to attend College one day a week and undertake eight to ten hours of private study. She had also to arrange and undertake 60 hours of work experience over the period of the course. Commissioner Jacobs held that the tribunal was entitled to disregard the work experience, since it was essential to, but not part of, the course, and to regard the course as part-time. Moreover, she could not in such circumstances be regarded as registered on a course of vocational or work-based training.

Condition relating to youth—previous claimants

9.25   **10.**—(1) Paragraph 4(1)(a) of Schedule 1 to the Act does not apply to a claimant—

(a) who has previously ceased to be entitled to an employment and support allowance, entitlement for which was as a result of satisfying the condition set out in sub-paragraph (1) of that paragraph;

(b) whose previous entitlement had not been ended by a decision which embodied a determination (other than a determination in the circumstances applicable to a claimant under paragraph (2)(a)) that the claimant did not have limited capability for work;

(c) in relation to whom regulation 145 (linking rules) does not apply;

(d) aged 20 or over, or, where regulation 9 would otherwise apply to the person, aged 25 or over; and

(e) to whom paragraph (2) applies.

(2) This paragraph applies to a claimant—

(a) whose previous entitlement to an employment and support allowance ended solely with a view to that person taking up employment or training;

(b) whose earnings factor from an employment or series of employments pursued in the period from the end of the previous entitlement to the beginning of the period of limited capability for work, was below the lower earnings limit multiplied by 25 in any of the last three complete tax years before the beginning of the relevant benefit year; and

(c) who—

(i) in respect of the last two complete tax years before the beginning of the relevant benefit year has either paid or been credited with earnings equivalent in each of those years to the year's lower earnings limit multiplied by 50, of which at least one, in the last tax year, was in respect of the disability element or severe disability element of working tax credit; or

(ii) makes a claim for an employment and support allowance within a period of 12 weeks after the day on which the last such employment pursued in accordance with sub-paragraph (b) ceased.

DEFINITIONS

"claimant"—see WRA 2007 s.24(1).
"earnings factor"—see WRA 2007 s.1, Sch.1 Pt 1 para.3(1)(d).
"employment"—see reg.2(1).
"limited capability for work"—see WRA 2007 s.1(4).
"lower earnings limit"—see WRA 2007 s.1, Sch.1 Pt 1 para.3(1)(e).
"period of limited capability for work"—see reg.2(1).
"relevant benefit year"—see WRA 2007 s.1, Sch.1 Pt 1 para.3(1)(f).
"tax year"—see WRA 2007 s.1, Sch.1 Pt 1 para.3(1)(g).
"training"—see reg.2(1).
"week"—see reg.2(1).
"working tax credit"—see reg.2(1).

GENERAL NOTE

Made pursuant to WRA 2007 Sch.1 Pt 1 para.4(3), this regulation, comparable   **9.26**
to IB Regulations, reg.18, prescribes circumstances in which someone previously
entitled to CESA under the youth route, can again be entitled even though the
age condition in WRA 2007 Sch.1 Pt 1 para.4(1)(a) is not met. It deals with the
situation where someone has been entitled to incapacity benefit as a person incapacitated in youth, ceases to be entitled to it other than on the basis of being found
not to have limited capability for work, and claims again in a new period of limited
capability for work (not being helped by the variety of linking rules in the ESA
scheme (reg.145), but is over age (20 or 25 as the case may be) when he makes
that new claim. He can again become entitled in certain cases where his previous
entitlement was terminated solely with a view to him taking up employment or
training which proved to be very low paid or very intermittent. The rule will not
operate where entitlement ended because of a determination that he did not have
limited capability for work (para.(1)(c)). The regulation covers the person whose
entitlement terminated solely with a view to him taking up an employment or training (see definition of "training" in reg.2(1)) (para.(2)(a)). He can qualify by way
of the "youth" route (albeit over-age) if his earnings factor from the employment
or series of employments pursued since the termination of his previous entitlement was below a specified level in *any* of the three complete tax years relevant for
qualification by way of the national insurance contributions route (see WRA 2007
s.1(2)(a), Sch.1, paras (1)–(3)). The specified level is less than 25 times the lower
earnings level set for Class 1 contributions purposes in the tax year in question.
However, he can only be eligible if in addition, he is either: (a) claiming by way
of the youth route within 12 weeks of his last such employment (para.(2)(c)(ii));
or (b) in each of the last two complete tax years (identified as above) he has paid
or been credited with earnings to the level of 50 times the year's lower earnings
limit for Class 1 contributions purposes, and at least one of those contributions or
creditings was, in the last such year, in respect of the disability or severe disability
element of working tax credit (para.(2)(c)(i)).

Condition relating to youth—residence or presence

11.—(1) The prescribed conditions for the purposes of paragraph 4(1)   **9.27**
(c) of Schedule 1 to the Act as to residence or presence in Great Britain are
that the claimant—
   (a) is ordinarily resident in Great Britain;
   (b) is not a person subject to immigration control within the meaning of
       section 115(9) of the Immigration and Asylum Act or is a person to
       whom paragraph (3) applies;
   (c) is present in Great Britain; and
   (d) has been present in Great Britain for a period of, or for periods
       amounting in aggregate to, not less than 26 weeks in the 52 weeks
       immediately preceding the relevant benefit week.
   (2) For the purposes of paragraph (1), a claimant is to be treated as being
resident and present in Great Britain where the claimant is absent from
Great Britain by reason only of being—
   (a) the spouse, civil partner, son, daughter, father, father-in-law, mother
       or mother-in-law of, and living with, a member of Her Majesty's
       forces who is abroad in that capacity;
   (b) in employment prescribed for the purposes of paragraph 7(1)(c) of
       Schedule 2 to the Act in connection with continental shelf opera-
       tions; or
   (c) abroad in the capacity of being an aircraft worker or mariner.
   (3) This paragraph applies where a person is—

(a) a member of a family of a national of an European Economic Area state;

(b) a person who is lawfully working in Great Britain and is a national of a State with which the Community has concluded an agreement under Article 310 of the Treaty of Amsterdam amending the Treaty on European Union, the Treaties establishing the European Communities and certain related Acts providing, in the field of social security, for the equal treatment of workers who are nationals of the signatory State and their families;

(c) a person who is a member of a family of, and living with, a person specified in sub-paragraph (b); or

(d) a person who has been given leave to enter, or remain in, the United Kingdom by the Secretary of State upon an undertaking by another person or persons pursuant to the immigration rules within the meaning of the Immigration Act 1971 to be responsible for that person's maintenance and accommodation.

(4) A person is to be treated as having satisfied the residence or presence conditions in paragraph (1) throughout a period of limited capability for work where those conditions are satisfied on the first day of that period of limited capability for work.

DEFINITIONS

"aircraft worker"—see reg.2(1).
"benefit week"—see reg.2(1).
"claimant"—see WRA 2007 s.24(1).
"continental shelf operations"—see WRA 2007 s.22, Sch.2 para.7(3).
"employment"—see reg.2(1).
"family"—see reg.2(1).
"Immigration and Asylum Act"—see reg.2(1).
"member of Her Majesty's forces"—see reg.2(1).
"mariner"—see reg.2(1).
"period of limited capability for work"—see reg.2(1).
"prescribed"—see WRA 2007 s.24(1).
"week"—see reg.2(1).

GENERAL NOTE

9.28   WRA 2007 Sch.1, para.4(1)(c) requires that to gain non-contributory access to incapacity benefit as a person incapacitated in youth, a claimant must on the relevant day satisfy the prescribed conditions as to residence or presence in Great Britain. This regulation sets out those prescribed conditions. They are such as to require both residence and presence. Residence is "ordinary residence" rather than simple residence (para.(1)(a)). There is no requirement of "habitual residence". "Presence" (para.(1)(c)) means "physically present". The requirements are that the claimant must on the first day of claim in the period of incapacity for work (see para.(4)) be both ordinarily resident and present in Great Britain. (On "ordinarily resident", see further the commentary to Persons Abroad Regs, reg.5.) He must also have been present in Great Britain for a period or aggregate periods of at least 26 weeks in the immediately preceding 52 weeks (para.(1)(d)). In addition he must not be subject to immigration control within the meaning of Immigration and Asylum Act 1999 s.115(9) (set out in *Vol.II: Income Support, Jobseeker's Allowance, State Pension Credit and the Social Fund* and see the provisions noted in the commentary thereto) or (if prima facie he is) he must be someone protected by para.(3). That paragraph protects the same groups as are covered in Pt II of the Schedule to the Social Security (Immigration and Asylum) Consequential Amendments Regulations 2000, set out in *Vol. II: Income Support, Jobseeker's Allowance, State Pension Credit and the Social Fund.*

Absence from Great Britain would negate presence. Paragraph (2) enables certain actual absences to be treated, legally speaking, as if the person was present or resident in Great Britain. It protects aircraft workers and mariners within the meaning of reg.2(1). It protects also those in employment prescribed for the purposes of SSCBA 1992, s.120 in connection with continental shelf operations. It also protects someone abroad as the spouse, son, daughter, father, mother, father-in-law, mother-in-law of and living with a member of the forces abroad.

Condition relating to youth—full-time education

12.—(1) For the purposes of paragraph 4(4) of Schedule 1 to the Act, a claimant is to be treated as receiving full-time education for any period during which the claimant—

    (a) is at least 16 years old but under the age of 19; and

    (b) attends a course of education for 21 hours or more a week.

(2) For the purposes of paragraph (1)(b), in calculating the number of hours a week during which a claimant attends a course, no account is to be taken of any instruction or tuition which is not suitable for persons of the same age who do not have a disability.

(3) In determining the duration of a period of full-time education under paragraph (1) any temporary interruption of that education may be disregarded.

(4) A claimant who is 19 years of age or over is not to be treated for the purposes of paragraph 4(1)(b) of Schedule 1 to the Act as receiving full-time education.

9.29

DEFINITIONS

    "claimant"—see WRA 2007 s.24(1).
    "week"—see reg.2(1).

GENERAL NOTE

WRA 2007 Sch.1 para.4(41)(b) precludes someone from ranking as a person incapacitated in youth (thus denying non-contributory access to incapacity benefit) where on the day of claimed incapacity he is receiving full-time education. This regulation, pursuant to para.4(4) of that Schedule, sets out what is, and what is not, to be regarded as full-time education. Someone who is 19 or over cannot be so precluded even though he is in fact undergoing a full-time education (para.(4)). Preclusive "full-time education" covers a person aged 16–18 inclusive for any period in which he attends a course of education for 21 or more hours a week (para.(1)). In determining the length of any such preclusive period, a decision-maker may disregard any temporary interruption of that education (para.(3)). This, it is submitted, is ambiguous, leaving it unclear whether such periods are to be counted as part of the preclusive period or ones that are to be left out. The DMG offers no assistance in resolving the ambiguity. As regards the 21 hours aspect, no account is to be taken in calculating those hours of any instruction or tuition unsuitable for a person of the same age as the claimant but who is not suffering from a physical or mental disability (para.(2)). In other words, one ignores special classes for the disabled.

9.30

[¹Modification of the relevant benefit year

13.—(1) Where paragraph (2) applies, sub-paragraph (1)(f) of paragraph 3 of Schedule 1 to the Act has effect as if "relevant benefit year" is any

9.31

benefit year which includes all or part of the period of limited capability for work which includes the relevant benefit week.

(2) This paragraph applies where a claimant has made a claim to employment and support allowance but does not satisfy—

(a) the first contribution condition;

(b) the second contribution condition; or

(c) both contribution conditions,

but would satisfy those conditions if the modified definition of "relevant benefit year" provided in paragraph (1) applied.]

AMENDMENT

1. Social Security (Miscellaneous Amendments) (No.3) Regulations 2010 (SI 2010/840) reg.9(7) (June 28, 2010).

DEFINITIONS

"claimant"—see WRA 2007 s.24(1).
"first contribution condition"—see reg.2(1); WRA 2007 s.1, Sch.1, para.1(1).
"period of limited capability for work"—see reg.2(1).
"relevant benefit year"—see para.(1).
"second contribution condition"—see reg.2(1); WRA 2007 s.1, Sch.1, para.2(1).

GENERAL NOTE

9.32   This operates where a claimant fails to satisfy one or both of the standard contribution conditions for ESA. As noted in the commentary to WRA 2007 Sch.1 paras 1–3, the key to determining the tax years to which to have regard is determined by identifying the benefit year in which there falls the first day of the period of limited capability for work. The effect of the linking rules (where one period is fused with an earlier one) may mean that the benefit year in question is not the current one in which the most recent claim falls. The previous version of reg.13 allowed for the modification of the normal rules around establishing the benefit year and relevant tax years for the purpose of meeting the contributory requirements of ESA. This was to help those who fail the contribution conditions when first making a claim, who may have paid significant contributions immediately before falling ill, and so would be able to re-claim and be successful in a later benefit year. But it only did so if there was a break in the period of limited capability for work, by providing that the linking rules in reg.145 were to be disregarded. This was not likely often to occur. The substituted version removes the requirement for a break in the period of limited capability for work, and allows decision-makers and tribunals to look to any benefit year in which there occurs all or part of the period of limited capability for work of which the relevant week of claim is part.

PART 4

CONDITIONS OF ENTITLEMENT—INCOME-RELATED ALLOWANCE

Meaning of education

9.33   **14.**—(1) Subject to regulations 15 and 16, for the purposes of paragraph 6 of Schedule 1 to the Act, "education" means a course of study to which paragraph (2) applies which is being undertaken at an educational establishment.

(2) This paragraph applies to a course of study which is—

(a) a full-time course which is not funded in whole or in part by—

[¹ (i) the [³ Secretary of State under section 14 of the Education Act

2002] [⁵ or section 100 of the Apprenticeships, Skills, Children and Learning Act 2009];

(ia) [⁵ . . .];]

(ii) the Welsh Ministers; or

(iii) the Scottish Ministers at a college of further education;

(b) a full-time course of higher education which is funded in whole or in part by the Scottish Ministers;

(c) funded in whole or in part by the [¹[³ Secretary of State under section 14 of the Education Act 2002], [⁵ or section 100 of the Apprenticeships, Skills, Children and Learning Act 2009]] or by the Welsh Ministers if it involves more than 16 guided learning hours per week for the student in question, according to the number of guided learning hours per week for that student set out—

[¹ (i) in the case of a course funded by the [³ Secretary of State [⁵ . . .]], in the student's learning agreement signed on behalf of the establishment which is funded by [⁵ the Secretary of State] for the delivery of that course;]

(ii) in the case of a course funded by the Welsh Ministers, in a document signed on behalf of the establishment which is funded by those Ministers for the delivery of that course;

(d) not a course of higher education and which is funded in whole or in part by the Scottish Ministers at a college of further education and involves—

(i) more than 16 hours per week of classroom-based or workshop-based programmed learning under the direct guidance of teaching staff according to the number of hours set out in a document signed on behalf of the college; or

(ii) 16 hours or less per week of classroom-based or workshop-based programmed learning under the direct guidance of teaching staff and it involves additional hours using structured learning packages supported by the teaching staff where the combined total of hours exceeds 21 per week according to the number of hours set out in a document signed on behalf of the college; or

(e) a sandwich course within the meaning prescribed in regulation 2(9) of the Education (Student Support) Regulations 2007, regulation 4(2) of the Education (Student Loans) (Scotland) Regulations 2007 or regulation 2(8) of the Education (Student Support) Regulations (Northern Ireland) 2007.

[² (2A) Paragraph (2) does not apply to any course of study which the claimant is required to attend for the purpose of meeting a requirement to undertake work-related activity.]

[⁶ (2B) Paragraph (2) does not apply to a traineeship.]

(3) In this regulation "higher education" means higher education within the meaning of Part 2 of the Further and Higher Education (Scotland) Act 1992.

AMENDMENTS

1. Apprenticeships, Skills, Children and Learning Act 2009 (Consequential Amendments to Subordinate Legislation) (England) Order 2010 (SI 2010/1941), reg.28(3) (September 1, 2010).

2. Social Security (Miscellaneous Amendments) Regulations 2012 (SI 2012/757) reg.20(3) (April 1, 2012).

3. Young People's Learning Agency Abolition (Consequential Amendments to Subordinate Legislation) (England) Order 2012 (SI 2012/956), art.22(3)(a) (May 1, 2012).

4. Young People's Learning Agency Abolition (Consequential Amendments to Subordinate Legislation) (England) Order 2012 (SI 2012/956), art.22(3)(b) (May 1, 2012).

5. Deregulation Act 2015 (Consequential Amendments) Order 2015 (SI 2015/971), art.2 and Sch.3 para.14(3) (May 26, 2015).

6. Social Security (Qualifying Young Persons Participating in Relevant Training Schemes) (Amendment) Regulations 2017 (SI 2017/987) reg.3(3) (November 6, 2017).

GENERAL NOTE

9.34   It is a condition of entitlement to income-related ESA that a claimant is not receiving education (see para.6(1)(g) of Sch.1 to the Welfare Reform Act 2007). But see reg.18 below which exempts claimants who are entitled to disability living allowance ("DLA"), personal independence payment ("PIP") or armed forces independence payment (see reg.2(1) for the definition of "armed forces independence payment") from this requirement.

Note that para.6(1)(g) of Sch.1 does not apply in the case of claimants who had an existing award of income support by virtue of reg.13(2)(b) or (bb) (persons in relevant education who are ill or disabled) of, or paras 10 or 12 (disabled or deaf students) of Sch.1B to, the Income Support Regulations (see the 2015/16 edition of Vol.II in this series for these provisions) and who have been transferred to ESA as a result of a conversion decision under the Employment and Support Allowance (Transitional Provisions, Housing Benefit and Council Tax Benefit) (Existing Awards) (No.2) Regulations 2010 (SI 2010/1907) (as amended) (see p.1329 for these Regulations). The modifications to s.1(2) of the 2007 Act made by Sch.1, para.2 and Sch.2, para.2 of the 2010 Regulations mean that such claimants will be able to get ESA 1329 while in education even if they do not get DLA, PIP or armed forces independence payment.

"Education" for these purposes means a course of study that comes within para. (2) that is being undertaken at an educational establishment. Paragraph (2) is in the same terms as the definitions of "full-time course of study" and "sandwich course" in reg.131(1) (which in turn reproduces the definitions of these terms in reg.61(1) of the Income Support Regulations; see also the definitions of "full-time student" and "sandwich course" in reg.1(3) of the JSA Regulations 1996). Regulation 17 provides when a person will count as undertaking a course of study. It is in the same terms as reg.131(2)–(4) (which in turn reproduces the provisions in reg.61(2)–(4) of the Income Support Regulations and reg.1(3A)–(3C) of the JSA Regulations 1996). The combined effect of regs 14 and 17 is to exclude full-time students from income-related ESA (except those who are entitled to DLA, PIP or armed forces independence payment: see reg.18 and the note to that regulation). But note that in the case of a person aged under 19 this will only apply if he is attending a course of advanced education (reg.16).

Paragraph (2A), inserted with effect from April 1, 2012, confirms that a claimant will not be treated as receiving education in relation to any course of study that he is required to attend as part of his work-related activity.

In addition, a "qualifying young person", unless he is entitled to DLA, PIP or armed forces independence payment, is to be treated as receiving education (see reg.15).

See also *RVS v SSWP (ESA)* [2019] UKUT 102 (AAC), discussed in the note to reg.17 below.

Claimants to be treated as receiving education

15. [¹ (1)] Subject to regulation 18 [¹ and paragraph (2)], a qualifying   9.35
young person is to be treated as receiving education for the purposes of
paragraph 6(1)(g) of Schedule 1 to the Act.

[¹ (2) A qualifying young person is not to be treated as receiving education if they are participating in a traineeship.]

AMENDMENTS

1. Social Security (Qualifying Young Persons Participating in Relevant Training
Schemes) (Amendment) Regulations 2017 (SI 2017/987) reg.3(4) (November 6,
2017).

DEFINITION

"qualifying young person"—reg.2(1), s.142 SSCBA.

GENERAL NOTE

A qualifying young person (other than one who is entitled to disability living   9.36
allowance ("DLA"), personal independence payment ("PIP") or armed forces independence payment (see reg.2(1) for the definition of "armed forces independence
payment"): see reg.18) is to be treated as receiving education and so is excluded
from income-related ESA. A "qualifying young person" (as defined in s.142 of
the Contributions and Benefits Act) is a person who is 16 or over but who has not
attained a prescribed age and who satisfies prescribed conditions.

The substance of the definition of "qualifying young person" is in reg.3 of the
Child Benefit Regulations 2006 (see Vol.IV in this series). It applies to a person who
is (i) under 20; *and* (ii) undertaking a course of full-time, non-advanced education,
which is not provided by virtue of his employment or any office held by him, but
which is provided at a school or college, or elsewhere as approved by the Revenue
(in the latter case he must have been receiving the approved education before he
was 16); *or* (iii) undertaking approved training that is not provided by means of a
contract of employment. "Approved training" covers various training programmes
under "arrangements made by the Government" (see the definition of both these
terms in reg.1(3) of the 2006 Regulations). "Full-time education" (also defined in
reg.1(3)) requires contact hours of at least 12 a week during term-time. Note that a
person aged 19 can only be a qualifying young person if he began, or was enrolled
on, or had been accepted to undertake, the full-time, non-advanced education or
approved training before he was 19 (although a person who was on such a course/
training and has been accepted or enrolled to undertake another such course/train-
ing is also included).

Claimants not to be treated as receiving education

16. Where a claimant is under 19 but not a qualifying young person, that   9.37
claimant is not to be treated as receiving education where the course of
study is not—
  (a) a course leading to a postgraduate degree or comparable qualifica-
      tion, a first degree or comparable qualification, a diploma of higher
      education or a higher national diploma; or
  (b) any other course which is of a standard above advanced GNVQ or
      equivalent, including a course which is of a standard above a general
      certificate of education (advanced level) or above a Scottish national
      qualification (higher or advanced higher).

"qualifying young person"—see reg.2(1), s.142 SSCBA.

GENERAL NOTE

9.38   The effect of this regulation is that if the claimant is aged less than 19 and is not a qualifying young person (see the note to reg.15), he will not count as receiving education unless he is undertaking a course of advanced education (see the definition of "course of advanced education" in reg.131(1) which is in the same terms as paras (a) and (b), and which in turn reproduces the definition of "course of advanced education" in reg.61(1) of the Income Support Regulations and reg.1(3) of the JSA Regulations 1996). See further the note to reg.14.

Courses of study

9.39   **17.**—(1) For the purposes of the definition of "education" in regulation 14, a person is to be regarded as undertaking a course of study—

(a) subject to paragraph (2), in the case of a person undertaking a part of a modular course that would be a course of study for the purposes of these Regulations, for the period beginning on the day on which that part of the course starts and ending—

   (i) on the last day on which the person is registered with the educational establishment as attending or undertaking that part as a full-time course of study; or

   (ii) on such earlier date (if any) as the person finally abandons the course or is dismissed from it;

(b) in any other case, throughout the period beginning on the date on which the person starts undertaking the course and ending on the last day of the course or on such earlier date (if any) as the person finally abandons it or is dismissed from it.

(2) For the purpose of sub-paragraph (a) of paragraph (1), the period referred to in that sub-paragraph includes—

(a) where a person has failed examinations or has failed to successfully complete a module relating to a period when the person was attending or undertaking a part of the course as a course of study, any period in respect of which the person attends or undertakes the course for the purpose of retaking those examinations or that module;

(b) any period of vacation within the period specified in that paragraph or immediately following that period except where the person has registered with the educational establishment to attend or undertake the final module in the course and the vacation immediately follows the last day on which the person is required to attend or undertake the course.

(3) In paragraph (1), "modular course" means a course of study which consists of two or more modules, the successful completion of a specified number of which is required before a person is considered by the educational establishment to have completed the course.

GENERAL NOTE

9.40   Regulation 14 defines "education" as a course of study undertaken at an educational establishment while reg.17 sets out when a person is to be regarded as undertaking a course of study. In *RVS v SSWP (ESA)* [2019] UKUT 102 (AAC) the claimant was enrolled on a modular University course, of which he had completed two years. He then "intermitted" (suspended) his studies for the final 2017/18 academic year for reasons of ill-health. His claim for ESA in November 2017 was refused on the basis that he was receiving education and so not entitled (WRA 2007, s.1(2)(b) and Sch.1 para. 6(1)(g)). The FTT dismissed his appeal. Allowing his appeal to the Upper Tribunal, Judge Poynter held the FTT had erred by applying the standard test for non-modular courses (see reg.17(1)(b)) rather than investigating the facts to see if the claimant had the benefit of the potentially more favourable rules for modular courses in reg.17(1)(a). Remaking the decision to the effect that the claimant was not receiving education, and so was not excluded from entitlement to ESA, the judge held that (a) each year of study amounted to a "part" of a modular course and (b) the claimant had completed his second year successfully and never embarked on the next "part" of that course, namely the third and final year. Accordingly, when the claimant applied for ESA, having intermitted, he was not undertaking part of a modular course as the previous part had ended on the last day of his second year of study (see reg.17(1)(a)(i)).

Circumstances in which the condition that the claimant is not receiving education does not apply

18. Paragraph 6(1)(g) of Schedule 1 to the Act does not apply where the claimant is entitled to a disability living allowance [² , armed forces independence payment] [¹ or personal independence payment].   9.41

AMENDMENTS

1. Personal Independence Payment (Supplementary Provisions and Consequential Amendments) Regulations 2013 (SI 2013/388) reg.8 and Sch., Pt II, para.40(3) (April 8, 2013).
2. Armed Forces and Reserve Forces Compensation Scheme (Consequential Provisions: Subordinate Legislation) Order 2013 (SI 2013/591) art.7 and Sch. para.37(3) (April 8, 2013).

DEFINITIONS

"armed forces independence payment"—see reg.2(1).
"disability living allowance"—*ibid.*
"personal independence payment"—*ibid.*

GENERAL NOTE

Paragraph 6(1)(g) of Sch.1 to the Welfare Reform Act 2007 provides that it is a condition of entitlement to income-related ESA that the claimant is not receiving education—this effectively excludes full-time students and qualifying young persons from income-related ESA: see regs 14–17. However the effect of reg.18 is that such claimants will not be excluded if they are entitled to disability living allowance ("DLA") (either component at any rate), personal independence payment ("PIP") (either component at either rate) or armed forces independence payment.   9.42

See also reg.33(2) which treats a claimant who is receiving education but who is entitled to DLA, PIP or armed forces independence payment as having limited capability for work for the purposes of income-related ESA. But this does not apply in the case of a qualifying young person (reg.33(2)(a)). A qualifying young person who is entitled to DLA, PIP or armed forces independence payment and who claims income-related ESA will have to satisfy the limited capability for work test (as will any claimant who counts as receiving education who claims contributory ESA, even though he is entitled to DLA, PIP or armed forces independence payment).

See *MW v SSWP (ESA)* [2018] UKUT 304 (AAC), confirming that although there is a general entitlement condition that a claimant "is not receiving education" (see Welfare Reform Act 2007, Sch.1, para. 6(1)(g)) this regulation disapplies that requirement to a claimant entitled to PIP, DLA or armed forces independence payment. Moreover, reg.33(2) provides that, for the purposes of income-related ESA, a claimant is to be treated as having limited capability for work where they are (a) not a qualifying young person, (b) receiving education and (c) not subject to Sch.1, para.6(1)(g) in accordance with reg.18.

Note that para.6(1)(g) of Sch.1 does not apply in the case of claimants who had an existing award of income support by virtue of reg.13(2)(b) or (bb) (persons in relevant education who are ill or disabled) of, or paras 10 or 12 (disabled or deaf students) of Sch.1B to, the Income Support Regulations (see the 2015/16 edition of Vol.II in this series for these provisions) and who have been transferred to ESA as a result of a conversion decision under the Employment and Support Allowance (Transitional Provisions, Housing Benefit and Council Tax Benefit) (Existing Awards) (No. 2) Regulations 2010 (SI 2010/1907) (as amended) (see p.1329 for these Regulations). The modifications to s.1(2) of the 2007 Act made by Sch.1, para.2 and Sch.2, para.2 of the 2010 Regulations mean that such claimants will be able to get ESA while in education even if they do not get DLA, PIP or armed forces independence payment.

PART 5

LIMITED CAPABILITY FOR WORK

Determination of limited capability for work

9.43   19.—(1) For the purposes of Part 1 of the Act, whether a claimant's capability for work is limited by the claimant's physical or mental condition and, if it is, whether the limitation is such that it is not reasonable to require the claimant to work is to be determined on the basis of a limited capability for work assessment of the claimant in accordance with this Part.

(2) The limited capability for work assessment is an assessment of the extent to which a claimant who has some specific disease or bodily or mental disablement is capable of performing the activities prescribed in Schedule 2 or is incapable by reason of such disease or bodily or mental disablement of performing those activities.

(3) Subject to paragraph (6), for the purposes of Part 1 of the Act a claimant has limited capability for work if, by adding the points listed in column (3) of Schedule 2 against [² each descriptor] listed in that Schedule [² which applies in the claimant's case], the claimant obtains a total score of at least—

   (a) 15 points whether singly or by a combination of descriptors specified in Part 1 of that Schedule;
   (b) 15 points whether singly or by a combination of descriptors specified in Part 2 of that Schedule; or
   (c) 15 points by a combination of descriptors specified in Parts 1 and 2 of that Schedule.

[¹(4) In assessing the extent of a claimant's capability to perform any activity listed in Part 1 of Schedule 2, the claimant is to be assessed as if—

   (a) fitted with or wearing any prosthesis with which the claimant is normally fitted or normally wears; or, as the case may be,
   (b) wearing or using any aid or appliance which is normally, or could reasonably be expected to be, worn or used.

(5) In assessing the extent of a claimant's capability to perform any activity listed in Schedule 2, it is a condition that the claimant's incapability to perform the activity arises—

(a) in respect of any descriptor listed in Part 1 of Schedule 2, from a specific bodily disease or disablement;

(b) in respect of any descriptor listed in Part 2 of Schedule 2, from a specific mental illness or disablement; or

(c) in respect of any descriptor or descriptors listed in—

(i) Part 1 of Schedule 2, as a direct result of treatment provided by a registered medical practitioner for a specific physical disease or disablement; [² or]

(ii) Part 2 of Schedule 2, as a direct result of treatment provided by a registered medical practitioner for a specific mental illness or disablement.]

(6) Where more than one descriptor specified for an activity [² applies] to a claimant, only the descriptor with the highest score in respect of each activity which applies is to be counted.

(7) Where a claimant—

(a) has been determined to have limited capability for work; or

(b) is to be treated as having limited capability for work under regulations 20, 25, 26, 29 or 33(2),

the Secretary of State may, if paragraph (8) applies, determine afresh whether the claimant has or is to be treated as having limited capability for work.

(8) This paragraph applies where—

(a) the Secretary of State wishes to determine whether there has been a relevant change of circumstances in relation to the claimant's physical or mental condition;

(b) the Secretary of State wishes to determine whether the previous determination of limited capability for work or that the claimant is to be treated as having limited capability for work, was made in ignorance of, or was based on a mistake as to, some material fact; or

(c) at least 3 months have passed since the date on which the claimant was determined to have limited capability for work or to be treated as having limited capability for work.

AMENDMENTS

1. Employment and Support Allowance (Amendment) Regulations 2012 (SI 2012/3096) reg.3(2) (January 28, 2013, subject to application, transitional and savings provisions in reg.2 of this amending instrument, below, para.9.554).

2. Social Security (Miscellaneous Amendments) (No. 3) Regulations 2013 (SI 2013/2536) reg.13(7) (October 29, 2013).

DEFINITIONS

"claimant"—see WRA 2007 s.24(1).
"descriptor"—see reg.2(1).
"limited capability for work"—see WRA 2007 s.1(4).
"limited capability for work assessment"—see para.(2).

GENERAL NOTE

Entitlement to ESA requires that the claimant has limited capability for work (WRA 2007, s.1(3)(a)). Whether his capability for work is limited by his physical or mental condition such that it is not reasonable to require him to work is to be   **9.44** determined in accordance with regulations (WRA 2007 s.8(1)). This regulation, setting out how "actual" limited capability to work is to be determined through the limited capability for work assessment is the product. The remainder of this Part (regs 20–33), deal with situations in which someone, whatever the reality, is to be treated as having limited capability for work, and also with aspects of the decision-making process.

Paragraph (1)

9.45 ESA is a benefit designed to help people with a limiting health condition overcome barriers, and where appropriate move into work and improve their lives. The Work Capability Assessment (WCA) seeks more accurately to relate to modern context than the IB/IS system, and to focus more on what people can do, rather on what they are unable to do. The matter of whether the claimant's capability for work is limited by his physical or mental condition, and, if so, whether the limitation is to such an extent that it is not reasonable to require him to work, is to be decided on the basis of the "limited capability for work assessment" (WCAt or LCWA). This is the first element in a new three-part "work capability assessment" (WCA), developed out of the review of the IB "personal capability assessment" (PCA), which governs entitlement to the basic allowance and the additional components of ESA. The new WCA underpinning ESA was devised by the DWP's Health Work and Wellbeing Directorate with input from two technical working groups, one focusing on mental health and learning difficulties, the other on physical function and conditions (hereinafter "review group"). The review group consisted of medical and other relevant experts. It examined how the IB Personal Capability Assessment (PCA) (characterized by them as "the best assessment of its type in the world" could nonetheless be improved and updated so as to reflect the many changes since its inception:

> "in the prevalence of disabling conditions; in advances in medical science resulting in the availability of new and more effective medical interventions; and in the workplace environment. The Disability Discrimination Act, introduced after the PCA had been developed, has influenced the ability of employers to make reasonable adjustments to accommodate people with long term disabilities. It has also raised the expectations of disabled people that adjustments should be made to enable them to work."

The three-element WCA is not merely an incapacity-based tool for determining entitlement to ESA. That remains true of its first element the subject of this regulation. However, its second element is rather a more positive assessment considering ability to benefit from work-related activity with a view to promoting capacity for work. The assessment has two aspects: an assessment of limited capability to work (WCAt) and an assessment of limited capacity to engage in work-related activity (WRAAt). Both assessments will generally be conducted at the same time. The WCAt is a more rigorous test than the PCA and far fewer groups are exempted from it.

Paragraphs (2) and (5)

9.46 This defines the "limited capability for work assessment" (WCAt). Like the IB "personal capability assessment" (PCA) and its predecessor, the "all work" test, the ESA WCAt is an assessment of the extent to which someone with a specific disease or bodily or mental disablement is (despite that) capable of performing the activities set out in Sch.2 or is because of it incapable of performing them. Since the test is thus so similar to that in IB (see Incapacity for Work Regs, reg.24 and Sch.), the position taken here is that case authorities (whether Commissioner or court) on the PCA will also apply to the WCAt. As with the IB PCA, the tasks involved in applying the WCAt are twofold:

1. ascertaining from all the evidence in the case which descriptors apply (paras (2), (5) and Sch.2);
2. computing the scores (paras (3), (6)).

The terms of para.(2) require the incapacity to perform the Sch.2 activities to arise by reason of "some specific disease or bodily or mental disablement". This is further stressed in paras (5)(a) and (b), the latter of which specifically also brings in "mental illness", while para.(5)(c) in effect adds that the rubric will also cover incapability as a direct result of treatment provided by a registered medical practitioner for such a disease, illness or disablement. Para.(5) was introduced with effect from January 28, 2013 and was not explicitly subject to the transitional protection afforded by reg.2 of the amending instrument to claimants who had completed an ESA questionnaire issued to them based on the pre-January 28, 2013 versions of Schs 2 and 3; that reg on its face appeared only to give protection in respect of the changes to the Schs themselves, effected by reg.5 of the amending instrument, whereas the para.(5) amendment was effected by reg.3 (see, below, para.9.554). In *FR v SSWP (ESA)* [2015] UKUT 175 (AAC), however, Judge Ward accepted the Secretary of State's submission that the tribunal had erred in law in applying the para.(5) "split" to this claimant who had completed such a questionnaire. Judge Ward interpreted the Secretary of State's concession "as being that the requirement for the provisions of Schedule 2 "to continue to apply. . .*as they had effect* immediately before the commencement date" [Judge Ward's emphasis] is sufficient [in a case such as this] to maintain the pre-2013 position of no physical/mental split as part of how Schedule 2 "had effect"" (para.2). This "specific disease or bodily or mental disablement" phraseology was found in the sickness/invalidity benefits statutory test and in both the "own occupation" test and the IB PCA, so decisions on this phraseology from those regimes will still be authoritative here. In *VT v SSWP (ESA)* [2016] UKUT 241 (AAC) Judge Ward subsequently rejected an attempt by the Secretary of State to resile from the concession made in *FR v SSWP (ESA)*.

"Specific" means "of a kind identified by medical science" (*CS/57/82*, noted in [1983] J.S.W.L. 306). "Specific" is designed to keep out conditions that may in some ordinary sense be said to be mental illness or disablement but which are not (as yet) recognised, or accounted for, as physical or mental conditions by medical science" (*JG v SSWP (ESA)* [2013] UKUT 37 (AAC); [2013] AACR 23 (a decision of a three judge panel of Upper Tribunal Judges, para.38, citing to similar effect (*R(IB)2/98*, para.7). A "specific mental illness" is a mental disease and also falls within the term "mental disablement" (*JG*, paras 36, 37). "Disease" has been described as "a departure from health capable of identification by its signs and symptoms, an abnormality of some sort", and sickness falls within the definition (*CS/221/49*, para.3; *CS/7/82*, noted in [1983] J.S.W.L. 306). "Disablement"—which may be bodily or mental—constitutes a state of deprivation or incapacitation of ability measured against the abilities of a normal person (*CS/7/82, ibid.*).

In most cases there will be little problem, given the medical evidence, as to whether the claimant's condition amounts to disease or disablement; disagreement will generally centre on whether it prevents him carrying out the activities in Sch.2. However, a number of areas can be identified where difficult lines may have to be drawn on whether or not the condition comes within the rubric "disease or . . . disablement" at all. Pregnancy alone does not, but a disease or disablement associated with, but going beyond the normal incidents of, pregnancy does, as in *CS/221/49* where the certified incapacity, "sickness of pregnancy", was suffered throughout the day. See also *R(S) 4/93*. But note now that certain pregnant women are to be treated as incapable of work (see reg.20(e)). Alcoholism can come within the rubric, but in some circumstances might bring about a period of disqualification from benefit (see reg.157). Whether certain conditions constitute a disease of the mind or a mental disablement can be problematical in that the line between a recognisable mental illness or disablement, on the one hand, and states of malingering or being workshy on the other, can be fine and uncertain. The difficulty is to decide from the available evidence whether the claimant is genuinely ill or disabled and thereby incapacitated for work in the sense understood above, or whether his is a voluntary attitude of work shyness where he could but will not work. The problem will be compounded where the outward symptoms of these alternative states are the same. What will be crucial will be the terms in which the medical (psychiatric) evidence is cast, and the inevitable value judgments about whether a particular claimant's attitudes to doing work are voluntary or involuntary. Perhaps here the appellate authorities' jurisdiction to seek further medical (in this case psychiatric) reports at public expense could prove valuable. In *R(S) 6/59*, the Commissioner considered a particular case of Munchausen's syndrome, under which condition a person repeatedly presents himself for treatment to a hospital or series of hospitals recounting symptoms of a particular disease or disability from which he is not in fact suffering, which the Commissioner there described as a strange condition in the nature of malingering. The Commissioner in that case was not satisfied on the evidence that the claimant believed the symptoms actually to exist, and felt unable to regard the condition as a psychosis, which would have come within the statutory rubric. The claim for benefit failed, the Commissioner stating as an additional ground for the decision his view that the syndrome in any event did not affect that particular claimant's capacity to work since he had driven from hospital to hospital in his lorry. In effect, the condition was treated as a defect of character. In *CS/1/81* (noted in [1982] J.S.W.L. 48), the dispute initially centred on whether the claimant, suffering from what the RMO (now a DWP MS doctor) and his own doctor described as an anxiety state, was as a result incapable of work. The consultant psychiatrist to whom the claimant was referred considered him an inadequate personality by reason of his total self-indulgence and extreme degree of sheltering behind psychiatric symptoms to avoid responsibility. His condition resulted from a dismal personality structure rather than illness. Accordingly the Commissioner held that he was incapable of work but not by reason of disease or disablement, so the claim failed. Mesher (now Commissioner Mesher) suggests in [1982] J.S.W.L. 48 that the Commissioner there gave inadequate consideration to whether the defect (clearly on the evidence not an illness) could nevertheless be a mental disablement. In contrast, *CS 7/82* (noted in [1983] J.S.W.L. 306) dealt with a situation in which the claimant was said to have a severe personality disorder but not to be mentally ill. "Personality disorder" is a term sometimes used as a euphemism for workshy. The Commissioner held that its use in the particular case conveyed a notion of disability of mind sufficient to bring the claimant within the statutory rubric. It is submitted that one should avoid using euphemisms which may confuse; the loser in the case is entitled to know why he has lost. If he is thought workshy, that should be stated and reasons given for that conclusion. Sheltering behind euphemisms may also cloud the steps in reasoning which go towards good adjudication and decision-making.

In *DMcK v SSWP (ESA)* [2014] UKUT 45 (AAC), having allowed the appeal on other grounds, Judge Wikeley went on to consider the fact that the tribunal had found that the appellant had exhibited "illness behaviour" so that it did not find credible the level of her claimed physical disabilities. Judge Wikeley gave some guidance for the new tribunal to which the case was remitted. He thought it unclear whether the tribunal's rejection of the claimant's appeal "was indeed a recognition that she was displaying genuine but abnormal responses or whether it was a polite way of suggesting that she was malingering" (para.18). Citing para.43(ii) of the panel of three Upper Tribunal Judges in *JG*, below, an adjournment would have enabled the claimant to deal with a new point not taken by the Secretary of State, namely whether she had a recognized disease or disablement. On "illness behaviour" itself, Judge Wikeley referred the new tribunal to two unreported cases, one from the industrial injuries area, the other on incapacity benefit. In *CSI/1180/2001*, Commissioner (now Judge) Parker observed

> "The new tribunal, if it considers that there is an insufficient organic basis for all of the claimant's problems, must decide if he is consciously exaggerating or if he is

genuine and his complaints form part of an abnormal illness behaviour linked to his accident. In the latter situation, it can form part of the relevant loss of faculty. The courts have long recognised there can be compensation for an unconscious reaction to physical injury sustained, provided the latter remains a material cause of the former" (para.8).

In *CIB/4841/2002*, Commissioner (now Judge) Jacobs gave this guidance:

"10. The Secretary of State's medical advice, which I accept, is in summary this. Abnormal illness behaviour is one of a number of terms used to describe symptoms which are caused by the influence of psychological makeup and social environment on the perception of the disabling effects of a medical condition. This phenomenon is reflected by more modern approaches to treatment, which address the psychosocial as well as the medical factors. The symptoms are subjective in the sense that they depend on an experience of pain or fatigue. In order to distinguish between claimants who genuinely experience a particular disability from those who merely claim to do so, it is helpful to consider the history of their daily activity and unobtrusive observations. This can identify consistency or inconsistency.
11. In this case, the examining doctor detected resistance on examination and exaggeration of response to the testing of the reflexes. The claimant was also observed to walk normally and to be able to stand erect, albeit briefly. The claimant's performance on examination and the observations recorded by the doctor are not consistent with a genuine experience of illness behaviour. This was confirmed by the tribunal, who observed the claimant to walk differently at the beginning and end of the hearing. All of this was in conflict with the Surgeon's evidence, which accepted that the claimant was genuinely experiencing the symptoms he exhibited. In view of the actual observations of the examining doctor and the tribunal, the Surgeon's opinion could obviously not be accepted."

What has to be established, to what standard of proof, and by what evidence, is analysed well by Commissioner Jacobs in *CIB/26/2004*. There must be established, on the civil standard of balance of probabilities, that the claimant has a recognised medical condition (paras 18, 25, citing *R2/99 (IB)*, para.8; *CSDLA/552/2001*, para.27; and *CDLA/944/2001*, paras 9 and 10). A medical diagnosis is useful evidence, but is not decisive in that an appeal tribunal, giving appropriate reasons, can refuse to accept it. The cogency of a diagnosis varies according to a number of factors: the nature of the condition (some being easier to diagnose than others); how well qualified in the relevant area of medicine the doctor is who makes the diagnosis; the range of information and material on which the diagnosis is based; and the degree of certainty with which it is made (e.g. is the diagnosis "firm", or qualified as "working", "presumptive" or "provisional") (para.22). If there is general consensus among medical authorities as to the existence of a particular condition, a tribunal (even one containing a medical member) will normally err in law if, being sceptical, it denies its existence (para.21, citing a Northern Ireland Tribunal of Commissioners in *C38/03–04 (DLA)*, para.20(3)). If a medical diagnosis is not necessarily decisive, nor is the lack of one necessarily fatal; in appropriate circumstances a tribunal can make a diagnosis without medical evidence (para.19). While agreeing to some extent with Commissioner Brown's view (*R 2/99 (IB)*, para.11) that a tribunal should be cautious of making a diagnosis of mental disease or disablement in the absence of supportive medical evidence, Commissioner Jacobs qualified that by noting that at the time of that decision there was no medical member on the tribunal—it merely then had advice from an assessor—that change in composition rendering it easier now for a tribunal to make a diagnosis on the evidence available (para.20).

9.47

In *AD v SSWP (ESA)* [2011] UKUT 307 (AAC), Judge Levenson considered a case where the First-tier tribunal had upheld a decision that the claimant did not have limited capability for work on the basis that the claimant's abuse of alcohol and drugs were "a lifestyle choice" rather than coming about because of a specific physical or mental illness or disability. He held that it had erred in law. Alcohol or drug dependence, whether for DLA, incapacity benefit or ESA, constitutes a "mental condition". That was decided as regards DLA by a tribunal of Commissioners in *R (DLA) 6/06 (T)* and correctly applied to incapacity benefit by Commissioner Jacobs in *CIB/1296/2007*. Judge Levenson thought mistaken Judge May's decision in *RA v SSWP (ESA)* [2010] UKUT 301 (AAC) to disapprove Commissioner Jacob's decision on incapacity benefit and to seek there to confine *R (DLA) 6/06(T)* to the effects of the wording in ss.72 and 73 of the SSCBA 1992. In *RA*, Judge May stated that a "mental condition" is not necessarily the same as "specific disease or bodily or mental disablement" (para.13), but had already held that the claimant could not succeed under Activity 11 of the original ESA Regs, Sch.2 because that required a link to a *physical* disease or disablement.

In *JG v SSWP (ESA)* [2013] UKUT 37 (AAC); [2013] AACR 23 a three judge panel of Upper Tribunal Judges held that Parliament clearly intended that alcohol dependency falls within the phrase "specific disease or bodily or mental disablement". Were that not so, WRA 2007 s.15A and Sch.1A would have nothing to bite on. WRA 2007 s.18 and ESA Regs reg.157 on disqualification indicate that self-induced or self-inflicted physical or mental conditions can still amount to a "specific disease or bodily or mental disablement" (paras 18–20). Moreover, the three judge panel held that the summary of the expert evidence on alcohol dependence in *R(DLA)6/06*, itself a decision of a tribunal of Commissioners, "can and should be adopted by decision makers and tribunals in ESA cases as representing the currently accepted and mainstream medical view in respect of alcohol dependence" (para.47). That expert evidence is summarised in paras 16–19 of *R(DLA)6/)06* and set out in para.44 of *JG v SSWP (ESA)*. The three judge panel thus disapproved Judge May's rejection of this approach in *RA v SSWP (ESA)*, above, and saw nothing wrong with Judge Jacobs's direction in *CIB/1296/2007* that alcohol dependence was a mental condition rather than a physical one. See further, on drug dependency, *SD v SSWP (ESA)* [2016] UKUT 100 (AAC); [2016] AACR 35, discussed in the ESA commentary.

The current version of para.(5) entered into force on January 28, 2013, subject to application, transitional and savings provisions in reg.2 of the amending instrument (see, below, para.9.554). It brings in the requirement—familiar from the IB regime—that Pt 1 of Sch.2 must be linked to incapability arising from a specific bodily disease or disablement or as a direct result of treatment provided by a registered medical practitioner for such a disease or disablement. Similarly it introduces the requirement that Pt 2 of Sch.2 must be linked to incapability arising from a specific mental illness or disablement or as a direct result of treatment provided by a registered medical practitioner for such an illness or disablement. Commenting on the new wording, Judge Rowland in *MC v SSWP (ESA)* [2015] UKUT 646 (AAC) has observed as follows:

> "the correct approach, best giving effect to the purpose behind the legislation – is that the claimant's "specific mental illness or disablement" had to be an *effective* cause of her inability to go out unaccompanied. That is not the same as being the root cause or the primary cause. In my judgement, where a specific mental illness or disablement would not by itself have been sufficiently serious to enable a claimant to satisfy a descriptor, it is enough for the purposes of regulation 19(5)(b) that it has made the difference between the claimant being able to satisfy a descriptor and not being able to do so even though there may have been another, perhaps more important, cause" (at para.9).

Under the previous wording of the paragraph (still applicable to some cases after January 28, 2013—see reg.2 of the amending instrument, below, para.9.554), there was no such link (*JG v SSWP (ESA)* [2013] UKUT 37 (AAC); [2013] AACR 23 (a decision of a three judge panel of Upper Tribunal Judges, disapproving Judge May's decision in *RA v SSWP*, above, which should not be followed on this issue); *KP v*

SSWP (ESA) [2011] UKUT 216 (AAC); *KN v SSWP (ESA)* [2011] UKUT 229 (AAC); *RM v SSWP (ESA)* [2011] UKUT 454 (AAC); *AH v SSWP (ESA)* [2011] UKUT 333 (AAC)).

See also *NC v SSWP (ESA)* [2016] UKUT 401 (AAC) (Judge Gray) for confirmation that the term 'mental illness or disablement' in reg.19(5)(b) as amended "encompasses not merely mental ill-health in the form of conditions such as depression or schizophrenia but mental disablement of all kinds, for example learning difficulties and cognitive deficiency whether that be by reason of age or acquired brain injury" (at para.13).

Paragraph (4)

The current version of para.(4) entered into force on January 28, 2013, subject to application, transitional and savings provisions in reg.2 of the amending instrument (see, below, para.9.554). In *RP v SSWP* (ESA) [2011] UKUT 449 (AAC), Judge Levenson had thought the approach now embodied in sub-para.(b) was implicit in the previous wording. In addition, however, he thought that there had to be some "explanation of how the aid or appliance could help the particular claimant . . . . The degree of detail is a matter for the tribunal on the facts of each particular case, but in my view, in the absence of actual use or prescription, there does need to be some explanation" (para.16). See also *TM v SSWP (ESA)* [2018] UKUT 9 (AAC), where Judge Wikeley accepted a concession by the Secretary of State that reg.19(4) limits consideration of aids and appliances to the *physical health* descriptors in Part 1 of Sch.2. and so in the context of activity 15 (getting about) the FTT should not have considered the claimant's ability to navigate by a mobile phone app. **9.48**

Paragraphs (3) and (6)

Computing the scores: Achievement of a particular score is required before the claimant can be found to have limited capability for work. Under ESA, the scoring system is simpler. The score attained must be at least 15 points whether from Sch.2, Pt 1 alone (physical disabilities), Pt 2 alone (mental, cognitive and intellectual function assessment), or from a combination of the descriptors in both parts. In each case, where more than one descriptor for an activity applies, only the highest scoring one counts (para.(6)). Following the approach to the IB PCA, it is submitted that there are no implied limits on simply adding together the highest scores from each activity (*R(IB) 3/98*). **9.49**

Paragraphs (7), (8)

These make clear that the matters of whether someone actually has limited capability for work, or whether he is to be treated as having it under regs 20, 25, 26, 29 or 33(2), are ones that can be revisited where one or more of the situations in para. (8) arise: **9.50**

  a desire to determine whether there has been a relevant change of circumstances in relation to the claimant's health condition (is he getting better or worse?) (sub-para.(a);

- a wish to determine whether the prior determination of actual or deemed limited capability was made in ignorance of, or was based on a mistake as to, a material fact (sub-para.(b);

- at least three months have elapsed since the previous decision on actual or deemed limited capability (sub-para.(c)).

Certain claimants to be treated as having limited capability for work

20.—[²(1)] A claimant is to be treated as having limited capability for work if— **9.51**

(a) the claimant is terminally ill;
(b) the claimant is—
    (i) receiving treatment for cancer by way of chemotherapy or radiotherapy;
    (ii) likely to receive such treatment within six months after the date of the determination of capability for work; or
    (iii) recovering from such treatment,
and the Secretary of State is satisfied that the claimant should be treated as having limited capability for work];
(c) the claimant is—
    (i) excluded or abstains from work [2...] pursuant to a request or notice in writing lawfully made [2or given] under an enactment; or
    (ii) otherwise prevented from working pursuant to an enactment, by reason of it being known or reasonably suspected that the claimant is infected or contaminated by, or has been in contact with a case of, a relevant infection or contamination;
(d) in the case of a pregnant woman, there is a serious risk of damage to her health or to the health of her unborn child if she does not refrain from work;
(e) in the case of a pregnant woman, she—
    (i) is within the maternity allowance period [2(which has the meaning it has in section 35(2) of the Contributions and Benefits Act)]; and
    (ii) is entitled to a maternity allowance under section 35(1) of the Contributions and Benefits Act;
(f) in the case of a pregnant woman whose expected or actual date of confinement has been certified in accordance with the Medical Evidence Regulations, on any day in the period—
    (i) beginning with the first date of the 6th week before the expected week of her confinement or the actual date of her confinement, whichever is earlier; and
    (ii) ending on the 14th day after the actual date of her confinement,
if she would have no entitlement to a maternity allowance or statutory maternity pay were she to make a claim in respect of that period.
(g) [2the claimant meets] [1any of the descriptors at paragraph 15 or 16 of Schedule 3] [2in accordance with regulation 34(2), (3) and (6) where applicable].
[2(2) In this regulation, "relevant infection or contamination" means—
(a) in England and Wales—
    (i) any incidence or spread of infection or contamination, within the meaning of section 45A(3) of the Public Health (Control of Disease) Act 1984 in respect of which regulations are made under Part 2A of that Act (public health protection) for the purpose of preventing, protecting against, controlling or providing a public health response to, such incidence or spread; or
    (ii) tuberculosis or any infectious disease to which regulation 9 of the Public Health (Aircraft) Regulations 1979 (powers in respect of persons leaving aircraft) applies or to which regulation 10 of the Public Health (Ships) Regulations 1979 (powers in respect of certain persons on ships) applies; and
(b) in Scotland, any—

(i) infectious disease within the meaning of section 1(5) of the Public Health etc (Scotland) Act 2008, or exposure to an organism causing that disease; or

(ii) contamination within the meaning of section 1(5) of that Act, or exposure to a contaminant,

to which sections 56 to 58 of that Act (compensation) apply.]

AMENDMENTS

1. Employment and Support Allowance (Limited Capability for Work and Limited Capability for Work-Related Activity) (Amendment) Regulations 2011 (SI 2011/228) reg.3(2) (March 28, 2011).

2. Social Security (Miscellaneous Amendments) (No. 3) Regulations 2013 (SI 2013/2536) reg.13(8) (October 29, 2013).

DEFINITIONS

"claimant"—see WRA 2007 s.24(1).
"confinement"—see reg.2(1).
"Contributions and Benefits Act"—see WRA 2007 s.65.
"limited capability for work"—see WRA 2007 s.1(4).
"maternity allowance period"—see reg.2(1).
"Medical Evidence Regulations"—see reg.2(1).
"relevant infection or contamination"—see reg.2(1).
"terminally ill"—see reg.2(1).
"week"—see reg.2(1).

GENERAL NOTE

This regulation—the parent power for which is WRA 2007 s.22 and Sch.2, para.9—sets out the situations in which a claimant is to be treated as having limited capability for work. This is important because such claimants will be exempt from the WCA and its information gathering processes (see reg.21). Those exempt are: 9.52

- the terminally ill (para.(1)(a))—"suffering from a progressive disease and death in consequence of that disease can reasonably be expected within 6 months" (reg.2(1));

- provided that the Secretary of State is satisfied that the claimant should be treated as having limited capability for work (note the discretion), the claimant is receiving treatment for cancer by way of chemotherapy or radiotherapy; likely to receive such treatment within six months from the date of the determination of capability for work; or recovering from such treatment (para.(1)(b));

- those excluded or prevented from working by reason of it being known or reasonably suspected that the claimant is infected or contaminated by, or has been in contact with a case of, a relevant infection or contamination covered by a variety of public health enactments) (paras (1)(c), (2));

- pregnant women where there is a serious risk of damage to their or their unborn child's health if they do not refrain from work (para.(1)(d));

- pregnant women at a certain stage in pregnancy (paras (1)(e), (f)). Paragraph (1)(e) covers the pregnant woman during the maternity allowance period (see reg.2(1) and SSCBA 1992, s.35(2)) entitled to a maternity allowance under SSCBA 1992, s.35. Para.(1)(f) in contrast deals with the pregnant woman whose expected or actual date of confinement has been duly certified in accordance with the Medical Evidence Regulations. It covers her during a period beginning with the earlier of the actual date of confinement or the first day of the sixth week before the expected week of confinement and ending on the 14th day after the actual date of confinement. But it does so only where she would not be entitled to maternity allowance or SMP if she were to claim in respect of that period.

- in accordance with reg.34(2), (3) and (6), where applicable, those to whom there applies any of the descriptors in para.15 or 16 of Sch.2 operable from that date (para.(1)(g)).

Paragraph (1)(b): "recovering" from treatment for cancer by way of chemotherapy or radiotherapy

9.53 In *W Da-C v SSWP (ESA)* [2015] UKUT 158 (AAC), Judge Markus considered that, since "recovering" was not defined in the legislation, it had to bear its ordinary meaning. She had no doubt

> "that, when used in a health context, "recovering" refers to a process of getting better. It may not result in a person's condition reverting to the way it was before the treatment in question, but it denotes a process of some improvement or, at the very least, hoped-for improvement. Thus the Shorter Oxford English Dictionary defines the word, in so far as it relates to health, as "restoration or return to health from sickness". At some stage a person will cease to recover. This may occur when they are completely better. Or it may occur when they have reached a point when no further recovery will take place" (para.12).

Looking at the wider legislative context confirmed her view that this was "the only sensible way" in which the term could be understood; other ESA Regulations (e.g. regs 25, 26) suggested a period of recovery was time-limited. Moreover, interpreting para.(1)(b) to be without limit of time would jar with the underlying policy with respect to ESA that it should not simply be assumed that someone with a significant health condition or disability must be incapable of work.

The case concerned recovery from radiotherapy. Judge Markus accepted the Secretary of State's argument that

> "the normal recovery period following the immediate side effects of radiotherapy is up to six months and that the evidence in this case indicates that after six months the appellant had [completely] recovered from the short term effects of radiotherapy . . . [so] that where the long-term effects of radiotherapy are chronic it cannot be said that the appellant is recovering. The treatment has caused a separate health condition from which she has not recovered" (para.10).

In essence in this case, since there was no prospect of recovery, the claimant could not be said to be "recovering" (para.16).

Information required for determining capability for work

9.54 **21.**—(1) Subject to paragraphs (2) and (3), the information or evidence required to determine whether a claimant has limited capability for work is—

(a) evidence of limited capability for work in accordance with the Medical Evidence Regulations (which prescribe the form of doctor's statement or other evidence required in each case);

(b) any information relating to a claimant's capability to perform the activities referred to in Schedule 2 as may be requested in the form of a questionnaire; and

(c) any such additional information as may be requested.

(2) Where the Secretary of State is satisfied that there is sufficient information to determine whether a claimant has limited capability for work without the information specified in paragraph (1)(b), that information [¹ must] not be required for the purposes of making the determination.

(3) Paragraph (1) does not apply in relation to a determination whether a claimant is to be treated as having limited capability for work under any of regulations 20 (certain claimants to be treated as having limited capability for work), 25 (hospital in-patients), 26 (claimants receiving certain regular treatment) and 33(2) (additional circumstances in which a claimant is to be treated as having limited capability for work).

AMENDMENT

1. Social Security (Miscellaneous Amendments) (No.3) Regulations 2013 (SI 2013/2536) reg.13(9) (October 29, 2013).

DEFINITIONS

"claimant"—see WRA 2007 s.24(1).
"doctor"—see reg.2(1).
"limited capability for work"—see WRA 2007 s.1(4).
"Medical Evidence Regulations"—see reg.2(1).

GENERAL NOTE

This regulation deals with the information required for determining whether someone has limited capability for work. It is designed to give the decision-maker sufficient information to decide that matter for himself (the minority of cases), or whether to seek advice from a health care professional on the basis of the papers in respect of that decision, or to refer the claimant for a face to face WCAt, including a medical examination (see reg.23). **9.55**

Unless para.(3) operates, the claimant will have to supply: (i) evidence of his incapacity for work in accordance with the Medical Evidence Regs (para.(1)(a)); and (ii) such additional information relating to the relevant test as the Secretary of State asks for (para.(1)(c)). Furthermore, he must generally complete and return the appropriate questionnaire (para.(1)(b)), unless para.(3) operates or the Secretary of State decides that completion of the questionnaire is not necessary because without it he has sufficient information to determine whether the claimant does or does not have limited capability for work (para.(2)). Note that where the claimant is requested by the Secretary of State to complete and return the questionnaire, failure to do so can result in his being treated as capable of work (and thus not entitled to ESA) (reg.22).

The impact on claimants with mental health problems (MHP) of the information collecting and assessment process originally administered by Atos Healthcare, the medical services provider for the DWP (although Atos was subsequently replaced by MAXIMUS Health and Human Services Ltd from March 2015 was the subject of challenge by way of the Upper Tribunal's judicial review jurisdiction, as constituting disability discrimination under the Equality Act 2010. The decision of a three judge tribunal in favour of the applicants in *MM & DM* v *SSWP* [2013] UKUT 259 was appealed to the Court of Appeal by the Secretary of State.

On December 4, 2013, that Court rejected the appeal as to several matters and upheld it as to another in *Secretary of State for Work and Pensions* v *The Queen on the application of MM and DM (as respondents) and MIND, the National Autistic Society, Rethink Mental Illness and the Equality and Human Rights Commission (as interveners)* [2013] EWCA Civ 1565; [2016] AACR 11. The Court held that the Upper Tribunal was correct in holding that it had jurisdiction to deal with the matter of discrimination contrary to the Equality Act 2010 by way of judicial review, and that the applicants and the interveners had the requisite standing to maintain the application for judicial review. The Court also found that the Upper Tribunal's declaration that the information and examination process caused substantial disadvantage to claimants with mental health problems (and was thus discriminatory) was not erroneous in law nor, in the light of the evidence, was it perverse or irrational. However, the Court held that the Upper Tribunal had misunderstood the scope of its powers and should not have directed the Secretary of State to carry out an investigation or assessment within a specified time to see how the "Evidence Seeking Recommendation" (see below) could be implemented. Rather it was for the applicants to advance a reasonable adjustment proposal, leaving "the Secretary of State to adduce such evidence and advance such arguments as he thinks appropriate in order to discharge the burden now falling on him" of showing that such adjustment cannot reasonably be made (para.83).

The "Evidence Seeking Recommendation" was a less rigorous one than the proposal that in every case involving a mental health patient the decision-maker should always be required to seek further medical evidence (FME) before a decision was reached thus in many cases obviating the need for the ESA50 questionnaire and/ or the face to face interview, both of which substantially disadvantaged mental health patients. The Upper Tribunal had rejected that as unduly onerous. Instead, the "Evidence Seeking Recommendation", seen by the Upper Tribunal as a prima facie "reasonable adjustment", proposes that "the decision-maker should at least be required to consider obtaining FME in the case of MHP claimants and if FME was not sought, should explain why it was thought to be unnecessary" (para.2).

It should be noted that the need for this change was also supported as part of the independent review undertaken by Professor Harrington (see para.40 of his third report, cited in para.21 of the Court of Appeal judgment).

The judicial review challenge then returned to the Upper Tribunal for a renewed hearing on remedies (*R (MM and DM) v SSWP* [2015] UKUT 107 (AAC); [2016] AACR 11). The three judge panel disallowed the applications, holding that it was clear from the Court of Appeal's decision that ss.20 and 21 of the Equality Act created a two stage approach to determining whether an individual applicant could establish discrimination, namely: (i) has there been a failure to comply with a duty to make reasonable adjustments; and (ii) has the individual applicant shown a failure to comply with that duty in relation him or her. At the second stage, the individual applicant has to show that he or she was put at such a disadvantage by the failure to comply with the duty to make reasonable adjustments (paragraphs 49 and 51). The Upper Tribunal ruled that the individual applicants could not show that the alleged failure of the Secretary of State to comply with his anticipatory duty by making the adjustments said to be reasonable had caused (or indeed was causing or would cause) them any substantial disadvantage or had, was or would subject them to any detriment that caused them an unreasonably adverse experience. This was fatal to the applicants' claims for judicial review (para.58). Thus, despite proceeding on the assumption that the Secretary of State had failed to establish that the adjustments suggested by the applicants were not reasonable, the applicants had failed to establish that there had been an individual breach, and so discrimination, as required by s.21(2) of the Equality Act 2010 (paragraphs 60 to 62, 78 and 90).

Following the Upper Tribunal decision, the Secretary of State subsequently issued new guidance in the form of Memo DMG 13/17 about the circumstances in which further medical evidence (FME) for assessing limited capability for work should be obtained. This circular states that additional medical evidence should be gathered at the scrutiny (or "filework") stage "where the HCP considers that further information would be helpful to the assessing HCP and Decision Maker. This is FME to inform the assessment." It adds that "there MUST be a reasonable expectation that the FME would assist the assessing HCP and subsequently the Decision Maker."

Failure to provide information in relation to limited capability for work

9.56   **22.**—(1) Where a claimant fails without good cause to comply with the request referred to in regulation 21(1)(b), that claimant is, subject to paragraph (2), to be treated as not having limited capability for work.

(2) Paragraph (1) does not apply unless—

(a) [²(a) the claimant was sent a further request at least three weeks after the date of the first request;]

(b) [². . .] at least [¹1 week has] passed since the further request was sent.

AMENDMENT

1. Social Security (Miscellaneous Amendments) (No.3) Regulations 2011 (SI 2011/2425) reg.23(5), (6) (October 31, 2011).
2. Social Security (Miscellaneous Amendments) (No.3) Regulations 2013 (SI 2013/2536) reg.13(10) (October 29, 2013).

DEFINITIONS

"claimant"—see WRA 2007 s.24(1).
"limited capability for work"—see WRA 2007 s.1(4).
"week"—see reg.2(1)

GENERAL NOTE

If a claimant fails without good cause (on which more, below) to comply with the requirement to complete and return a limited capability for work questionnaire, he must be treated as not having limited capability for work, that is, as having no entitlement to ESA. This can only happen, however, if a further request for information was sent at least three weeks after the first and at least one week has gone by since the second request was sent. Commissioners' decisions on IB establish that as regards calculating a period before the end of which something cannot be done (e.g. "at least six weeks have passed"—para.(2)(a)), one must ignore the day from which the period runs as well as the day on which it expires (per Commissioner Jacobs in *R(IB) 1/00*). "Week" here means any period of seven days (reg.2(1)). But note that the para refers, like the IB provision, to a request being "sent" rather than "received" (as stressed by Commissioner Rowland in *CIB/3512/1998*). Non-receipt has, however, an important bearing on "good cause". "Good cause" is not exhaustively defined in legislation, although reg.24 non-exhaustively prescribes certain matters which must be taken into account in determining the issue. Some guidance may be found in authorities on the corresponding area in unemployment benefit (see USI Regs regs 7(1)(i), (j)—see pp.720–21 of Bonner, Hooker and White, *Non Means Tested Benefits: The Legislation* (1996)), the matter of relief from disqualification from sickness and invalidity benefit under the now revoked USI Regs reg.17 (see pp.737–740 of the 1994 edition of *Non Means Tested Benefits, The Legislation*), and that from disqualification/being treated as incapable under Incapacity for Work Regs reg.18 or, in time, reg.157 of these ESA Regs.

9.57

Determining when a request/reminder was "sent"

9.58

In *CT v SSWP (ESA)* [2013] UKUT 414 (AAC), Judge Mark (following his decision in *CIB/4012/2004*) stressed the need for very careful appraisal of the evidence to determine exactly when requests and reminders were sent and their exact nature. However, it appears that elsewhere in this decision Judge Mark arguably set the bar too high for the Secretary of State and those acting on his behalf. Three other Upper Tribunal decisions have adopted a rather more pragmatic approach to the evidential requirements imposed on the Secretary of State. In *AL v SSWP (ESA)* [2011] UKUT 512 (AAC), Judge May QC held that a tribunal was entitled to make a finding that an appointment letter had been sent on the basis of a computer generated letter history log. In particular, he accepted (at para.27) the Secretary of State's submission that the fact that the word "triggered" was used in the log did not mean it was uncertain whether that letter was actually posted. Similarly, in *SH v SSWP (ESA)* [2014] UKUT 574 (AAC), Judge Ward expressed the view that "printouts of the type in issue are capable of providing evidence from which a tribunal may draw inferences that a document was 'sent'. It is then for the tribunal of fact to decide what weight to put on it" (at para.36).

Both those decisions were approved and followed by Judge Wright in *DW v SSWP (ESA)* [2016] UKUT 179 (AAC), a decision which contains a useful review of the authorities.

Claimant may be called for a medical examination to determine whether the claimant has limited capability for work

9.59   **23.**—(1) Where it falls to be determined whether a claimant has limited capability for work, that claimant may be called by or on behalf of a health care professional approved by the Secretary of State to attend for a medical examination.

(2) Subject to paragraph (3), where a claimant fails without good cause to attend for or to submit to an examination [¹mentioned] in paragraph (1), the claimant is to be treated as not having limited capability for work.

[¹(3) Paragraph (2) does not apply unless—

(a) written notice of the date, time and place for the examination was sent to the claimant at least seven days in advance; or

(b) that claimant agreed to accept a shorter period of notice whether given in writing or otherwise.]

1. Social Security (Miscellaneous Amendments) (No.3) Regulations 2013 (SI 2013/2536) reg.13(11) (October 29, 2013).

DEFINITIONS

"claimant"—see WRA 2007 s.24(1).
"health care professional"—see reg.2(1).
"limited capability for work"—see WRA 2007 s.1(4).

GENERAL NOTE

9.60   This regulation enables the DWP to have a claimant medically examined by a DWP Medical Service (DWPMS) health service professional (technically any health service professional approved by the Secretary of State) when a question arises as to the claimant's capability for work. Failure without good cause to attend for or submit to such an examination, of which he was given proper written notice (see para.(3)), will result in the claimant being treated as not having limited capability for work and not entitled to ESA.

An appeal against a decision under reg. 23 is heard by a judge sitting alone: *CH v SSWP (ESA)* [2017] UKUT 6 (AAC). See also the annotation to regulation 21, above, on the judicial review challenge under the Equality Act 2010 with regard to the system of medical examinations and its impact on those with mental health problems.

The notion of "good cause" (see also reg.24) will necessarily be fact and context-specific, as reinforced by Judge Church in *SA v SSWP (ESA)* [2019] UKUT 118 (AAC). There the claimant, who had epilepsy, had a seizure on the day of his appointment and did not attend. The DWP argued that, having also missed previous appointments due to seizures, the claimant should have anticipated the possibility that he might have a seizure on the day and should therefore have requested a home visit. Judge Church held that the FTT's findings that the claimant did not act reasonably when he failed to ask in advance for a home visit, and that his state of health at the relevant time did not amount to good cause for his failure to attend, fell outside the range of reasonable decisions open to it on the facts.

Note that proper written notice means written notice of the date, time and place of the examination, sent to him at least seven days beforehand, unless the person agreed to accept a shorter period of notice, whether given in writing or otherwise. On determining whether and when a written notice was sent, see the commentary to reg.22, above. Interpreted by analogy with the approach to another time period issue in *R(IB)2/00*, para.(3) requires at least seven days' clear notice so that neither the day of sending nor that of receipt count in determining that period (*CIB/2576/2007*, para.6). The notice may be given by or on behalf of the approved (generally DWPMS) health care professional concerned (para.(1)). The notice must, however, be written. So, where an appointment had been made over the telephone by leaving a message with the claimant's sister, which the claimant asserted was not passed on, he could not properly be treated as capable of work for not having attended without good cause, since the regulation's clear requisite of written notice had not been satisfied (see *CIB/969/97*). In *R(IB) 1/01*, Commissioner Rowland considered that where, when a claimant stated that he would not be able to attend a medical examination, the Department in consequence said they would cancel it, the claimant cannot be held not to have attended it. If, however, a claimant makes it clear that he or she will not be medically examined, then that arguably constitutes failure to "submit to" an examination. Going to the medical examination but refusing to be examined, constitutes attendance but also a failure to submit. In *CIB/849/2001*, Commissioner Turnbull stated:

> "The purpose of the medical examination was of course to enable the adjudication officer, with the benefit of the doctor's report, to determine whether the Claimant passed the all work test. The condition which the Claimant wished to impose on his submitting to an examination—i.e. that the doctor's report should not be passed to any layman, including an adjudication officer—rendered an examination useless for the purpose for which it was required. I have no doubt that, by imposing such a condition, the Claimant was failing to submit himself to a medical examination within the meaning of reg.8(2) [by analogy ESA Regs, reg.23(2)]. A person 'fails' to submit himself to an examination not only if he absolutely refuses to be examined, but also if he seeks to impose as a condition of being examined a term which would render the examination useless for the purpose for which it is required" (para.11).

The importance of careful fact-finding in such cases is demonstrated by *PH v SSWP (ESA)* [2016] UKUT 119 (AAC). In that case the claimant (Mr H) attended the examination centre and entered the examination room with the HCP, who asked him to sign an audio-recording agreement. Mr H could not take in its contents so signed the form but added "unread". The HCP informed him this was not acceptable, but added he could take the agreement away to read and another examination would be arranged for another date. On the day Mr H could not agree a new date as he did not have his diary with him. After having remonstrated with staff at the reception desk, security guards were called and he then left the centre. A tribunal dismissed his appeal against the Secretary of State's decision that he had "failed to participate" without good cause in a medical examination. As Judge Mitchell notes, reg.23 does not use the concept of "participating". Rather, it deals with failing to (a) "attend for" or (b) "submit to" a medical examination: "To put it in more everyday terms, (a) refers to a person who fails to turn up for an examination of which s/he has been duly notified and (b) refers to a person who fails to co-operate with the examination process so as to thwart its purpose" (at para.22). On the undisputed facts of the case, Mr H had plainly attended for a medical examination but the examination itself had never started, so he could not have failed to "submit to" such an examination:

> "32. On this case's undisputed facts, Mr H's medical examination did not begin. The evidence cannot support a contrary finding. The planned medical examination was abandoned or cancelled once it became clear to the healthcare professional that Mr H would not, on the day, complete the audio-recording form in the way the centre's management thought he should. If Mr H's refusal was in the circumstances unreasonable, in the light of the examination's purpose, he could properly be said to have failed to submit to the examination. However, it was

not viewed as unreasonable by the assessment staff as is shown, in my view, by the staff informing Mr H that another examination could be arranged. For that reason, I conclude that Mr H's conduct before the planned examination was cancelled was not unreasonable. And what happened afterwards is not relevant to the question whether he failed to submit to the medical examination."

The decision in *PH v SSWP (ESA)* may be usefully contrasted with that in *JW v SSWP (ESA)* [2016] UKUT 207 (AAC), where the assessment interview did actually commence, only to be abandoned when the claimant began cross-examining the HCP about her qualifications and insisted on recording the interview on his mobile phone. Judge Hemingway held "that if a claimant seeks to impose an unreasonable condition and, absent that unreasonable condition's fulfilment, withholds consent to the examination taking place, then he does not submit to the examination" (at para.13). However, in that case the tribunal's failure to find sufficient facts resulted in the decision being set aside and the appeal remitted for rehearing. See also *JW v SSWP (ESA)* [2016] UKUT 208 (AAC), where the claimant had sought to insist on e.g. knowing the details of the HCP's experience as a nurse, the history of her nursing career and the qualifications she had over and above the fact that she was a qualified general nurse. Judge Hemingway upheld the tribunal's decision that the appellant had failed without good cause to submit to a medical examination:

"38. It seems to me that, given my acceptance that, as a matter of law, a person can fail to submit by imposing unreasonable conditions and given the tribunal's findings it was clearly open to it to conclude that the additional information he was seeking, as a condition of allowing the examination to proceed, was being unreasonably required and did amount to a failure to submit. He already knew he was to be examined by a person whose name he was aware of and he knew that she was qualified as a registered general nurse. He also knew that she was authorised to carry out the examination for the purpose for which it was required. That ought to have been sufficient to reassure him as to any genuine concerns he might have had. It was open to the tribunal to conclude his insistence on more than that, even absent the intimidating behaviour it found him guilty of, amounted to a failure to submit."

Judge Hemingway's decision in *JW v SSWP (ESA)* [2016] UKUT 208 (AAC) was followed by Judge Mitchell in *RO v SSWP (ESA)* [2016] UKUT 402 (AAC), in which the claimant insisted on proof that the HCP (who was not wearing a name badge) was a registered nurse. The claimant (Mr O) was offered access to the relevant website but declined that offer in the absence of photographic evidence and left the examination centre. The First-tier Tribunal decided he did not have good cause for failing to participate in the medical examination. Judge Mitchell, having referred to the terms of the statutory provisions defining who is qualified to be a HCP, ruled that "a claimant is entitled to make a reasonable request for proof that a purported healthcare professional is in fact a health care professional" (at para.17), not least because a medical examination is an invasion of privacy (at para.22). However, the claimant's appeal failed on the facts. *RO v SSWP (ESA)* was followed by Judge Gray in *CH v SSWP (ESA)* [2017] UKUT 6 (AAC), where she expressed the view (obiter on the facts) that "it is for the Secretary of State to decide on the type of health care professional who will conduct the examination, and for a claimant to refuse to submit to the examination on the basis that the healthcare professional chosen was not a doctor, or to insist as a precondition of attendance that it must be a doctor conducting the examination, would amount to a failure to attend" (para.22).

The nature and extent of the medical examination to which the claimant must submit is a matter for the examining health care professional rather than the claimant, tribunal or Commissioner, "fundamentally a medical matter and for the judgment of the clinician in each individual case" (*C1/07–08(IB)*, para.12). The health care professional's demands of the claimant must, however, fall within the bounds of a "medical examination" and there remains the issue of whether a claimant has good cause for refusing to submit to the examination (*C1/07–08(IB)*, para.15).

A health care professional can insist on the presence of a suitable chaperone (e.g. a DWP employee bound by confidentiality not to broadcast details to the world at large), and unreasonable refusal to allow such a chaperone to be present constitutes refusing to submit to the examination (*CIB/2645/99*; *CIB/2011/2001*, para.15). Claimants cannot expect their medical details to be kept from those who must determine their claims; those who insist on strict medical confidentiality can do so, but only at the cost of foregoing their rights to benefit or credits (*CIB/2011/2001*, para.15). In *CIB/1381/2003*, Deputy Commissioner Wikeley declined, after reviewing a range of authority on analogous provisions in child support and jobseeker's allowance, to determine whether "sent" meant "despatched" or "delivered", since a failure to attend because of not receiving the notice could in any event constitute "good cause" as the tribunal had held. In *CSIB/721/2004*, however, Commissioner Parker was of the view that where the claimant proved that the notification duly despatched (a matter for the Secretary of State to establish) had not in fact been received by him, in the ordinary course of post or at all, then it had not been "sent" within the meaning of para.(3), thus precluding treating the claimant as capable of work for "failure to attend or submit to examination" so that the issue of "good cause" never arose. She there took account of a Secretary of State concession on the point noted in *CIB/4512/2002* (not on the Commissioners' website), to which the Secretary of State's representative referred her. But in contrast note that Commissioner Rowland in *CIB/3512/1998*, dealing with an analogous Incapacity for Work Reg., stressed that it said "sent" rather than "received", albeit that non-receipt would be a matter as regards "good cause".

The Northern Ireland decision *C11/03–04(IB)* is a useful reminder of the need to ascertain the precise facts and be careful in applying to them the concept of "good cause". The case concerned a common "defence", where the claimant alleged he had never received a particular letter sent by the Department, a typical case of conflict of evidence. Deputy Commissioner Powell thought that sometimes it is right to reject such allegations in a robust manner, for example, where the excuse extends to a number of letters, or is coupled with suspicious circumstances, or if the non-receipt of mail is selective so that only certain letters are not received. The case before him, however, concerned a rather different situation—the uncontradicted evidence of the claimant, who did not attend the appeal hearing, of the non-receipt of a single letter in plausible circumstances, namely, a communal delivery of mail to particular premises and the possibility that another went through it before the claimant had a chance to do so. The Commissioner could not see how an effective challenge could be mounted to the claim and that, in these circumstances, the claimant had established good cause. The Secretary of State bears the burden of proof in establishing that the requirements of para.(3) have been met, a precondition for being able to find the claimant capable of work for non-attendance etc. **9.61**

In *CIB/4012/2004*, deputy Commissioner Mark, considering the cases noted above, found that the burden had not been discharged. Computer records showing that a letter had been issued were not sufficient evidence of it being "sent" on the facts of that case. However, in other respects it appears that Judge Mark arguably set the bar too high for the Secretary of State and those acting on his behalf. Three other Upper Tribunal decisions have adopted a rather more pragmatic approach to the evidential requirements imposed on the Secretary of State. See further *AL v SSWP (ESA)* [2011] UKUT 512 (AAC), *SH v SSWP (ESA)* [2014] UKUT 574 (AAC) and *DW v SSWP (ESA)* [2016] UKUT 179 (AAC)—the last a decision which contains a useful review of the authorities—all discussed in the commentary to reg.22 above.

The effect of a finding of lack of good cause precludes benefit until a new claim is submitted and a new period of incapacity for work begins (para.6 of the decision). It may also prevent the claimant being treated under reg.30 as incapable of work pending a limited capability for work assessment. However, if the claimant is found to have limited capability for work in that assessment, benefit can be backdated to the beginning of the period covered by the new claim or application. See also on this aspect *R(IB)2/01* and para.8 of *CIB/3512/1998*. On "good cause", see the commentary to reg.22 and note the non-exhaustive prescription in reg.24 of matters which must be taken into account in determining good cause. If it was unreasonable of the Secretary of State to arrange a medical examination, the claimant can argue that he had good cause for refusing to submit to it (*CIB/2645/99*; *CIB/2011/2001*, para.16). But since, as Commissioner Rowland stressed, "the integrity of the system depends upon their being appropriate tests in place" (*CIB/2011/2001*, para.16), establishing unreasonableness is unlikely to be easy.

Matters to be taken into account in determining good cause in relation to regulations 22 or 23

9.62   **24.** The matters to be taken into account in determining whether a claimant has good cause under regulations 22 (failure to provide information in relation to limited capability for work) or 23 (failure to attend a medical examination to determine limited capability for work) include—

(a) whether the claimant was outside Great Britain at the relevant time;

(b) the claimant's state of health at the relevant time; and

(c) the nature of any disability the claimant has.

DEFINITION

"claimant"—see WRA 2007 s.24(1).

GENERAL NOTE

9.63   This regulation, made pursuant to WRA 2007 s.8(4), stipulates that in determining whether someone had good cause for failing to provide information (under reg.22) or for failing to attend for or submit to a medical examination (under reg.23) decision-makers and appellate bodies must take into account (i) whether the person was outside Great Britain at the relevant time, (ii) his state of health at the relevant time, and (iii) the nature of his disability. This list is not, however, exhaustive (the regulation says "shall include"). On "good cause", see further the commentary to regs 22 and 23.

[¹Hospital patients

9.64   **25.**—(1) A claimant is to be treated as having limited capability for work on any day on which that claimant is undergoing medical or other treatment as a patient in a hospital or similar institution, or on any day which is a day of recovery from that treatment.

(2) The circumstances in which a claimant is to be regarded as undergoing treatment falling within paragraph (1) include where the claimant is attending a residential programme of rehabilitation for the treatment of drug or alcohol addiction.

(3) For the purposes of this regulation, a claimant is to be regarded as undergoing treatment as a patient in a hospital or similar institution only if that claimant has been advised by a health care professional to stay in a hospital or similar institution for a period of 24 hours or longer.

(4) For the purposes of this regulation, "day of recovery" means a day on which a claimant is recovering from treatment as a patient in a hospital or similar institution and the Secretary of State is satisfied that the claimant should be treated as having limited capability for work on that day.]

AMENDMENT

1. Employment and Support Allowance (Amendment) Regulations 2012 (SI 2012/3096), reg.3(4) (January 28, 2013, subject to application, transitional and savings provisions in reg.2 of this amending instrument, below, para.9.554).

DEFINITIONS

"claimant"—see WRA 2007 s.24(1).
"day of recovery"—see para.(4).
"limited capability for work"—see WRA 2007 s.1(4).
"medical treatment"—see reg.2(1).

GENERAL NOTE

Paragraphs (1), (3)
This regulation stipulates that those undergoing medical or other treatment as a   9.65
patient in a hospital or other institution, must be treated as having limited capability
for work on any day on which they are undergoing that treatment, or on any day of
recovery from that treatment.

The notion of "undergoing treatment as a patient in a hospital or similar institution" was initially not defined at all and was the subject of criticism and guidance by Judge Williams in *CJ v SSWP (ESA)* [2012] UKUT 201 (AAC) which still has application to those cases still subject, after the amended version of reg.25 inserted from January 28, 2013, to the previously worded reg.25.

The current wording was subject to analysis by Judge Mitchell in *SJ v SSWP (ESA)* [2015] UKUT 180 (AAC). He regarded himself as bound in several respects by the Court of Appeal decision in *Secretary of State for Work and Pensions* v *Slavin* [2012] AACR 30, interpreting similar terms in the DLA Regs 1991 reg.9, the appeal from Judge Turnbull's decision in *AS v SSWP (DLA)* [2010] UKUT 482 (AAC) (see, above, para.4.53) (hereinafter "*Slavin*").

Judge Mitchell considered that the regulation has to be "read as a whole". Para.(1) read with para.(3) sets out four elements all of which must be fulfilled for a day to be treated as one of limited capability for work:

"(a) the claimant must be undergoing medical or other treatment; and

(b) the treatment must be as a patient; and

(c) the treatment must be in a hospital or similar institution; and

(d) the claimant must have been advised by a health care professional to stay in the hospital or other institution for a period of 24 hours or longer" (para.15).

If any element is absent, the claim based on para.(1) must fail. Therefore, a tribunal can reject an argument founded on para.(1) "simply by reference to the non-satisfaction of any one element" (para.16).

"Hospital or similar institution": this is not defined in the ESA Regs, but features in a number of social security legislative contexts and its meaning has been elucidated by case law on them and is to be applied to the term in this regulation (para.52). Essentially, a hospital is any institution for the reception and treatment of persons suffering from illness, with "illness" being defined as including mental illness and any injury or disability requiring medical or dental treatment or nursing (para.38).

"Medical or other treatment": "medical treatment" is defined in reg.2(1), above, as

"medical, surgical or rehabilitative treatment (including any course or diet or other regimen), and references to a person receiving or submitting to medical treatment are to be construed accordingly".

Judge Mitchell considered that *Slavin* (binding on him) held that "medical or other treatment is confined to medical treatment, dental treatment or nursing care" (para.42). He also approved Judge Turnbull's view in para.88 of *AS*, noting that nothing in the Court of Appeal's decision in *Slavin* upholding that of Judge Turnbull in *AS* indicated disapproval of it. Judge Turnbull accepted counsel's view that "nursing" and "treatment" could not be confined to "care and skill exercised by doctors and nurses", but had to extend to that administered by other health care professionals (e.g. physiotherapy or occupational therapy) (paras 46-48, 60). Para.(2) of reg.25 (see further, below) stipulates that treatment falling within para.(1) includes attendance at "a residential programme of rehabilitation for the treatment of drug or alcohol addiction".

Accordingly, Judge Mitchell upheld the tribunal's decision that the refuge in which the claimant was staying as a victim of domestic violence did not fall within para.(1) because she was not undergoing medical or other treatment there. Nor had she been advised by a health care professional to stay in the refuge for a period of at least 24 hours so that the condition in para.(3) was not met. Judge Mitchell considered that his decision did not mean that all refuges would fall outside reg.25; labels "are of no intrinsic significance. . . What matters is whether the facts of a particular case come within regulation 25" (para.67), but stated, by way of general guidance, that he "would not be surprised if most refuge placements have characteristics matching, in material respects, [this claimant's] so that their residents fall outside regulation 25(1)" (para.68).

Paragraphs (1), (4)

9.66   The regulation protects not only those "undergoing medical or other treatment as a patient in a hospital or other institution" but also their days of "recovery from that treatment". "Day of recovery" is defined in para.(4). Note the discretion given to the Secretary of State—the day on which the former in-patient is recovering from that treatment will only count if the Secretary of State is satisfied that the claimant should on that day be treated as having limited capability for work. In *SI v SSWP (ESA)* [2013] UKUT 453 (AAC), Judge Mark was not satisfied

> "that the tribunal did properly consider the question whether the claimant was still recovering from the treatment. It does not follow just because the wound had scarred over and he had restricted movement back in his joint that he was fully recovered. The remaining limitations could in part still be due to the fact that he had not fully recovered. There does not appear to have been any investigation of the extent of his limitation previously or the nature of the operation or of his prognosis or the reasons for his continuing therapies and consultations or of the expected period within which recovery from the operation was to be expected" (para.10).

This lapse did not assist the claimant because the tribunal on the facts was entitled to conclude that there was no good ground for treating him as incapable of work.

Paragraphs (1), (2)

9.67   Attendance at a residential programme of rehabilitation for the treatment of drug or alcohol addiction counts as undergoing "treatment falling within paragraph (1)". This statutory stipulation is exhaustive and does not permit extension by analogy so as to cover other rehabilitation programmes (*SJ v SSWP (ESA)* [2015] UKUT 180 (AAC), paras 65, 66).

Regulation 21(1) (information gathering requirements) does not apply to a determination under this regulation (see reg.21(3)).

Claimants receiving certain regular treatment

9.68   **26.**—(1) Subject to paragraph (2), a claimant receiving—
  (a) regular weekly treatment by way of haemodialysis for chronic renal failure;

(b) treatment by way of plasmapheresis [².. .]; or
(c) regular weekly treatment by way of total parenteral nutrition for gross impairment of enteric function,
is to be treated as having limited capability for work during any week in which that claimant is engaged in [³receiving] that treatment or has a day of recovery from that treatment.

[¹(2) A claimant who receives the treatment referred to in paragraph (1) is only to be treated as having limited capability for work from the first week of treatment in which the claimant undergoes no fewer than—
(a) two days of treatment;
(b) two days of recovery from any of the forms of treatment listed in paragraph 1(a) to (c); or
(c) one day of treatment and one day of recovery from that treatment, but the days of treatment or recovery from that treatment or both need not be consecutive.]

(3) For the purpose of this regulation "day of recovery" means a day on which a claimant is recovering from any of the forms of treatment listed in paragraph (1)(a) to (c) and the Secretary of State is satisfied that the claimant should be treated as having limited capability for work on that day.

AMENDMENTS

1. Employment and Support Allowance (Miscellaneous Amendments) Regulations 2008 (SI 2008/2428) reg.5(1) (October 27, 2008).
2. Employment and Support Allowance (Amendment) Regulations 2012 (SI 2012/3096) reg.3(5) (January 28, 2013, subject to application, transitional and savings provisions in reg.2 of this amending instrument, below, para.9.554).
3. Social Security (Miscellaneous Amendments) (No.3) Regulations 2013 (SI 2013/2536) reg.13(12) (October 29, 2013).

DEFINITIONS

"claimant"—see WRA 2007 s.24(1).
"day of recovery"—see para.(3).
"limited capability for work"—see WRA 2007 s.1(4).
"week"—see WRA 2007 s.24(1); reg.2(1).

GENERAL NOTE

Someone undergoing certain treatments is treated as having limited capability **9.69** for work on during any week in which he is engaged in that treatment or has a day of recovery from that treatment (para.(1)). The treatments concerned are: regular weekly treatment by way of haemodialysis for chronic renal failure (para.(1)(a)); treatment by way of plasmapheresis (para.(1)(b); or regular weekly treatment by way of total parenteral nutrition for gross impairment of enteric function (para.(1)(c)). "Day of recovery" is defined in para.(3) as one on which the claimant is recovering from any of the forms of treatment so long as the Secretary of State (note the discretion) is satisfied that the claimant should be treated as having limited capability for work on that day. Paragraph (2) deals with the first week of any such treatment. During that week, the claimant can only be treated as having limited capability for work if in that week he undergoes no fewer than two days of treatment, or two days of recovery from such treatment or one day of treatment and one day of recovery. The days of treatment or recovery from it need not be consecutive.

Regulation 21(1) (information gathering requirements) does not apply to a determination under this regulation (see reg.21(3)).

Claimant to be treated as having limited capability for work throughout a day

9.70   **27.** A claimant who at the commencement of any day has, or thereafter develops, limited capability for work as determined in accordance with the limited capability for work assessment is to be treated as having limited capability for work throughout that day.

DEFINITIONS

"claimant"—see WRA 2007 s.24(1).
"limited capability for work"—see WRA 2007 s.1(4).
"limited capability for work assessment"—see reg.2(1).

GENERAL NOTE

9.71   The situation encompassed here in which someone is to be treated as having limited capability for work, confers no exemption from the information gathering processes for the limited capability for work assessment (reg.21(3)).

The effect of this regulation is that those with limited capability for work at the start of a day or who thereafter develop it on that day are to be treated as having limited capability for work throughout that day. In *CIB/6244/1997*, Commissioner Jacobs considered the application of the IB regulation to intermittent and variable conditions. He considered that the provision must be read in the light that, under the all work test/PCA and its descriptors, one cannot confine consideration merely to a particular time on a particular day—otherwise a claimant could always satisfy the "cannot" descriptors and the "sometimes" ones (not in any event in the ESA limited capability for work assessment activities and descriptors) would never apply. The "cannot" and "sometimes" descriptors inevitably require a focus over a period and not at a specific moment in time. Thus he thought that Incapacity for Work Regs, reg.15 "does not operate to ensure that a claimant with a variable condition that incapacitates him for a part of each day must be considered as incapable throughout the whole of every day" (para.23).However, it will "apply where there is a sudden onset of or recovery from an incapacitating condition, including an intermittent incapacitating condition or the incapacitating intermittent features of a condition" (*ibid.* and see also *CIB/15482/1996*, paras 7–9). In *CIB/243/1998*. Deputy Commissioner Mark considered that a claimant who suffered an asthma attack for part of a day had to be treated as incapable of work throughout that day under this regulation, provided that the effect of the attack when ongoing was such that he would score at least 15 points for more than a minimal period on that day. In *CIB/399/2003*, Commissioner Mesher very firmly rejected that approach of Deputy Commissioner Mark in *CIB/243/1998* and preferred the approach taken by Commissioner Jacobs in *CIB/6244/1997* and by Deputy Commissioner Ramsay in *CIB/15482/1996*, thus establishing a strong line of authority against Deputy Commissioner Mark's view of the application of Incapacity for Work Regs, reg.15. Commissioner Mesher thought the rejected approach to be inconsistent with the concept of "reasonable regularity" applicable to the "cannot" descriptors and out of tune with the tenor of *R(IB)2/99(T)* (on which see further the commentary to Sch.2).

Night workers

9.72   **28.**—(1) Where a claimant works for a continuous period which extends over midnight into the following day, that claimant is to be treated as having limited capability for work on the day on which the lesser part of that period falls if that claimant had limited capability for work for the remainder of that day.

(2) Where, in relation to a period referred to in paragraph (1), the number of hours worked before and after midnight is equal—

(a) if the days in question fall at the beginning of a period of limited capability for work, the claimant is to be treated as having limited capability on the second day; and
(b) if the days in question fall at the end of a period of limited capability for work, the claimant is to be treated as having limited capability for work on the first day.

DEFINITIONS

"claimant"—see WRA 2007 s.24(1).
"limited capability for work"—see WRA 2007 s.1(4).
"period of limited capability for work"—see reg.2(1).

GENERAL NOTE

Although unlike IB, ESA is a weekly rather than a daily benefit, there is still need to **9.73** be able to attribute limited capability for work to a particular day, where the person doing nightwork has a shift spanning midnight and thus covering two days. The ESA scheme in some circumstances permits awards for periods of less than a week (the amount payable being determined under regs 165–169) (e.g. the period at the start or end of a claim; persons receiving certain regular treatments). Although the ESA scheme neither in Act or Regs defines "day", the general rule for benefit purposes has been that a day is the period midnight to midnight, and performance of work on a day will generally preclude the week in which it is done ranking as one of entitlement to ESA (see reg.40(1)). But there are exceptions to that preclusive rule (regs 40(4), 46) where the preclusion is only to affect the day(s) actually worked. There is thus a need to attribute a nightshift spanning two days to one day or the other. Otherwise, the application of the rules to nightworkers whose shifts span midnight could cause hardship since they would, without this regulation, be regarded as working on two days and thus be treated less favourably than their day worker counterparts whose shift of exactly the same length (period of work) would be attributed to one day. Equally, even though the nightworker suffered the same degree of limited capability for work on one of those days, the day could not count as one of limited capability for work This regulation attempts some easing of the position of nightworkers in this regard.

Paragraph (1) provides that where someone works for a continuous period beginning one day and spanning midnight into the following day, the day on which there falls the lesser part of the period worked will be treated as one of limited capability for work if the claimant has limited capability for work for the rest of that day. To put it another way, the day with the longer period worked is to be treated for the purpose of the exceptions to the preclusive rules noted above as the day of work. Paragraph (2) deals with the situation in which the hours worked each side of midnight are equal. If the two days in question fall at the beginning of a period of limited capability for work, the second day is to be treated as one of incapacity and the first as the one of work. If the two days fall at the end of a period of incapacity for work, the first day is the one to be regarded as a day of limited capability for work and the second as the one of work.

Exceptional circumstances

29.—(1) A claimant who does not have limited capability for work as **9.74** determined in accordance with the limited capability for work assessment is to be treated as having limited capability for work if paragraph (2) applies to the claimant.

(2) [¹ Subject to paragraph (3)] this paragraph applies if—
(a) the claimant is suffering from a life threatening disease in relation to which—

>   (i) there is medical evidence that the disease is uncontrollable, or
>   uncontrolled, by a recognised therapeutic procedure; and
>   (ii) in the case of a disease that is uncontrolled, there is a reason-
>   able cause for it not to be controlled by a recognised therapeutic
>   procedure; or
> (b) the claimant suffers from some specific disease or bodily or mental dis-
>   ablement and, by reasons of such disease or disablement, there would
>   be a substantial risk to the mental or physical health of any person if the
>   claimant were found not to have limited capability for work.

[¹(3) Paragraph (2)(b) does not apply where the risk could be reduced by a significant amount by—

> (a) reasonable adjustments being made in the claimant's workplace; or
> (b) the claimant taking medication to manage the claimant's condition
>   where such medication has been prescribed for the claimant by a
>   registered medical practitioner treating the claimant.]

[²(4) In this regulation "medical evidence" means—

> (a) evidence from a health care professional approved by the Secretary
>   of State; and
> (b) evidence (if any) from any health care professional or a hospital or
>   similar Institution,

or such part of such evidence as constitutes the most reliable evidence available in the circumstances.]

AMENDMENTS

1. Employment and Support Allowance (Amendment) Regulations 2012 (SI 2012/3096) reg.3(6) (January 28, 2013, subject to application, transitional and savings provisions in reg.2 of this amending instrument, below, para.9.554).
2. Social Security (Miscellaneous Amendments) (No.3) Regulations 2013 (SI 2013/2536) reg.13(13) (October 29, 2013).

DEFINITIONS

> "claimant"—see WRA 2007 s.24(1).
> "limited capability for work"—see WRA 2007 s.1(4).
> "limited capability for work assessment"—see reg.2(1).
> "medical evidence"—see para.(4).

GENERAL NOTE

Paragraph (1): background and role

9.75   Like reg.27 in the IB scheme, this regulation reflects the fact that functional assessment systems like the IB PCA or the ESA LCWA would not properly measure the incapacitating effect of certain conditions, and so would "fail" some people who properly ought to be regarded as being incapable of work (IB) or having limited capability for work (ESA). Headed "exceptional circumstances", the regulation can only come into play where the claimant has been found *not* to have limited capability for work under reg.19 and Sch.2; where s/he has attained an insufficient score (less than 15 points) applying those descriptors.

The regulation envisages two classes of case in which someone assessed as not having limited capability for work can nonetheless be treated as having it.

Paragraph (2)(a): claimant suffering from a life threatening disease uncontrolled or
uncontrollable by a recognised therapeutic procedure

9.76   The first class of case is where the claimant suffers from a life threatening disease (the IB requirement that it be "severe" is not continued into ESA) which *medical evidence establishes* is uncontrollable by a recognized therapeutic procedure or (but only with reasonable cause) is uncontrolled by such a procedure.

Dealing with the substantially similarly worded IB provision in *CIB/4506/01*, Commissioner Howell stated that here:

"the question is only whether the nature of [the claimant's] condition is such that it is capable of being controlled by medical science, or not. Consequently the tribunal were right in taking account not only of the inhalers and adrenaline injector she is able to use for herself, but also the hospital treatment which unhappily she finds also has to be used on occasions as a means of bringing the condition under control. On the tribunal's findings the claimant's condition is thus controllable in the relevant sense, and their reasons are clearly and adequately given" (para.10).

The tribunal had not erred in law.

What level of "control" does the provision envisage? In *CIB/155/2004*, Commissioner Jacobs thought it inappropriate to deploy as a test whether the level of control would suffice to allow the claimant to work; since that test would always be satisfied. Rather, he thought that IB reg.27 [ESA reg.29] comes into play where a claimant is capable of work but has a condition that makes it inappropriate that he be expected to work. Since, as regards para.(2)(a) what makes that inappropriate is the fact that the condition is a threat to the claimant's life, the threshold for control should be whether the control is sufficient to remove the threat to the claimant's life. In the case at hand, while the evidence disclosed that the claimant's diabetes was poorly controlled, it was nonetheless sufficiently controlled that para.(2)(a) was inapplicable. While there were longer-term complications to which the Consultant referred, they were not yet present, and not currently threatening the claimant's life.

"Reasonable cause for it not to be controlled by a recognised therapeutic procedure":   **9.77** even where a tribunal with the assistance of its medical member considers that a procedure would be of benefit, a claimant had reasonable cause for not taking advantage of it where two cardiologists had advised him not to do so and it had not been offered to him (*KR v SSWP (ESA)* [2013] UKUT 637 (AAC), para.6).

There must be "medical evidence" that the disease is uncontrollable or uncontrolled. The term "medical evidence" embraces (i) evidence from a health care professional approved by the Secretary of State, (ii) evidence (if any) from any other health care professional, hospital or similar institution, or such part of evidence in (i) or (ii) as constitutes the most reliable evidence available in the circumstances (para.(4)). "Health care professional" covers a registered medical practitioner, a registered nurse or an occupational therapist or physiotherapist registered with a regulatory body established by an Order in Council under section 60 of the Health Act 1999 (reg.2(1)). In a Northern Ireland decision *C5/00–01(IB)* Commissioner Brown stressed that the evidence "must relate to the claimant himself, it is not constituted by extracts from medical textbooks unless the doctor relates them to the claimant" (para.16). The medical evidence must have been issued before the Secretary of State's decision in the case. In *GC v SSWP (ESA)* [2013] UKUT 271 (AAC), the claimant sought to rely on medical evidence issued after the Secretary of State had made his decision, on the evidence then before him, that the claimant's disease (bladder cancer) was controlled. Judge Jacobs considered reg.29 in the context of SSA 1998 s.12(8)(b) (an appeal tribunal shall not take into account any circumstances not obtaining at the time when the decision appealed against was made). He held that this was not the same situation as that in *R(DLA) 2 & 3/01* where later evidence could properly be adduced to show the circumstances prevailing at the date of decision:

"Regulation 29([2])(a)(i) is different. It does not refer to the claimant having a disease that is uncontrolled or uncontrollable. It refers to the need for *medical evidence* that that is so. In applying section 12(8)(b), the relevant circumstance is the existence of the evidence of the state of the claimant's condition. In Mr C's case, the evidence that his cancer had returned and required surgery did not exist until after the Secretary of State made the decision under appeal. In such a case, it makes no sense to say that later evidence shows that there was evidence at the time of the decision. Such talk is entirely inconsistent with the requirements of [regulation 29(2)(a)] as it renders the requirement for contemporaneous evidence redundant" (para.12).

Paragraph (2)(b), (3): "by reasons of [the claimant's health condition or disability]
    there would be a substantial risk to the mental or physical health of any person if the
    claimant were found not to have limited capability for work"

9.78   The second class of case in which someone not assessed as having limited capability for work can nonetheless be treated as having it, concerns a claimant, suffering from some specific disease or bodily or mental disablement, and by reasons of such there would be substantial risk to the mental or physical health of any person if the claimant were found not to have limited capability for work. The scheme thus carries into ESA something the Department had tried unsuccessfully to remove as regards IB in 1997.

With effect from January 28, 2013, para.(2) was made "subject to paragraph (3)", so that the "substantial risk" provision in para.(2)(b) does not apply if the risk could be reduced by a "significant amount" by reasonable adjustments being made in the claimant's workplace or by the claimant taking medication prescribed by a registered medical practitioner treating the patient (para.(3)). "Significant amount" unfortunately is not defined but, given the protective purpose of para. (2)(b) should preferably be interpreted as one reducing the risk to a level describable as less than "substantial". The *Explanatory Memorandum* to the amending instrument refers to the risk being "greatly reduced" (See para.7.14) (*http:// www. legislation.gov.uk/uksi/2012/3096/pdfs/uksiem_20123096_en.pdf*). In contrast the two examples given in para.7.15 of Memo *DMG 1/13* to the *Decision Makers Guide* (*http://www.dwp.gov.uk/docs/m-1-13.pdf*) rather confusingly refer respectively to "the risk to his health could be alleviated" and "the risk could be substantially reduced". It is to be expected that the proper interpretation will be a matter appealed to the Upper Tribunal in due course.

Note that the old wording of para.(2) will still apply to some cases after January 28, 2013 (see reg.2 of the amending instrument, below, para.9.554).

On "specific disease or bodily or mental disablement", see the commentary to reg.19.

9.79   *The "substantial risk" must arise "by reasons of" a specific disease or bodily or mental disablement:* In *DR v SSWP (ESA)* [2014] UKUT 188 (AAC); [2014] AACR 38, Judge May held erroneous in law a tribunal decision that the claimant satisfied reg.29 because it had not made the necessary connection between the risk and the disease or disablement (see para.3). Alcohol misuse in itself is not such a disablement. To rank as disablement the misuse of alcohol must rank as "alcohol dependency" in terms of the "constellation of markers" found in quotations from *R(DLA) 6/06* in the Three-Judge Panel's decision in *JG v SSWP (ESA)* [2013] UKUT 37 (AAC); [2013] AACR 23 (see paras 5-7, 10 of *DR*). Para.45 of the panel decision sets out the constellation of markers as follows:

"A maladaptive pattern of substance use, leading to clinically significant impairment or distress, as manifested by three (or more) of the following, occurring at any time in the same 12-month period

(1) tolerance, as defined by either of the following:
    (a) a need for markedly increased amounts of the substance to achieve intoxication or desire effect

(b) markedly diminished effect with continued use of the same amount of the substance

(2) withdrawal, as manifested by either of the following:

(a) the characteristic withdrawal syndrome for the substance . . .
(b) the same (or a closely related) substance is taken to relieve or avoid withdrawal symptoms

(3) the substance is often taken in larger amounts or over a longer period than was intended

(4) there is a persistent desire or unsuccessful efforts to cut down or control substance use

(5) a great deal of time is spent in activities necessary to obtain the substance (e.g. visiting multiple doctors or driving long distances), use the substance (eg chain-smoking), or recover from its effects

(6) important social, occupational, or recreational activities are given up or reduced because of substance use

(7) the substance use is continued despite knowledge of having a persistent or recurrent physical or psychological problem that is likely to have been caused or exacerbated by the substance (e.g. current cocaine use despite recognition of cocaine-induced depression, or continued drinking despite recognition that an ulcer was made worse by alcohol consumption)."

These various factors were adopted from those listed in the category of Substance Dependence contained in the Diagnostic and Statistical Manual of Mental Disorders of the American Psychiatric Association (DSM IV). In *SD v SSWP (ESA)* [2016] UKUT 100 (AAC); [2016] AACR 35, in which the claimant used street heroin (an opoid), Judge Knowles QC held that the factors pointing towards alcohol dependence as set out in *JG v SSWP (ESA)* (above) also have application in the case of drug dependency: **9.80**

"31. I note that the factors listed in the category of Substance Dependence in DSM-IV are not alcohol specific [see (vii) above for example] and thus, as a matter of logic, they must apply to other substances such as heroin and cocaine. I find that the constellation of markers set out in paragraph 45 is therefore equally applicable to drug dependence (such as that probably seen in this particular case)."

Judge Knowles QC observed that DSM-IV has now been superseded by DSM-5, in which substance-related/addictive disorders are divided into two categories, namely substance use disorders (including opioid use disorder) and substance induced disorders. Judge Knowles QC concluded as follows:

"37. The diagnostic criteria for opioid use disorder (heroin being an opioid) are as follows:

"*a problematic pattern of opioid use leading to clinically significant impairment or distress as manifested by at least two of the following occurring within a 12 month period:*

i) *opioids are often taken in larger amounts or over a longer period than was intended;*
ii) *a persistent desire or unsuccessful attempts to cut down or control opiate use;*
iii) *a great deal of time is spent in activities necessary to obtain the opioid, use the opioid or recover from its effects;*
iv) *craving or a strong desire to use opioids;*
v) *recurrent opioid use resulting in a failure to fulfil major role obligations at work, school or home;*
vi) *continued opioid use despite having persistent or recurrent social or interpersonal problems caused or exacerbated by the use of opioids;*

   vii) important social, occupational or recreational activities are given up or their engagement is reduced because of opioid use;

  viii) recurrent opioid use in situations in which it is physically hazardous;

    ix) continued opioid use despite knowledge of having a persistent or recurrent physical of psychological problem that is likely to have been caused or exacerbated by the substance;

    x) tolerance as defined by either a need for markedly increased amounts of opioids to achieve intoxication/desired effect or a markedly diminished effect with continued use of the same amount of opioid;

   xi) and withdrawal as manifested by either the characteristic opioid withdrawal syndrome or opioids (or a closely related substance) being taken to relieve or avoid withdrawal symptoms."

38. Severity is specified as follows: mild substance use disorder is the presence of 2-3 of the above symptoms; moderate is the presence of 4-5 symptoms; and severe is the presence of six or more symptoms.

39. The category of opioid induced disorders includes opioid intoxication, opioid withdrawal; opioid induced anxiety disorder and opioid induced depressive disorder.

40. *JG* concluded that a diagnosis of alcohol dependence or alcohol dependency syndrome plainly brought that condition within regulation 19(5) of the Regulations [paragraph 48]. The position now is rather more complex given the adjustments made by DSM-5 to the category of substance related disorders.

41. I have come to the conclusion that a diagnosis of mild substance abuse disorder in accordance with DSM-5 would not bring that condition within regulation 19(5) or 29(2)(b) of the Regulations. I consider that, in order to fall within the ambit of the relevant regulations, the substance abuse disorder must fall within either the moderate or severe categories. My reasons for so concluding are as follows.

42. A DSM-IV diagnosis of alcohol dependency required three or more symptoms from the list occurring at any time in the same 12 month period. It is clear that all of the factors listed in DSM-IV are incorporated into the factors for substance abuse disorder listed in paragraph 37. The presence of three or more factors in a twelve month period from the DSM-5 list would establish a diagnosis of mild substance use disorder. However a DSM-5 diagnosis of substance use disorder equivalent to DSM-IV substance dependency requires, in my view, the presence of, at least 4-5 symptoms from the eleven listed, thus bringing it within the moderately severe category of substance use disorder. This is because the distinction between abuse and dependence In DSM-IV was based on the concept of substance abuse as a mild or early phase and substance dependence as the more severe manifestation."

9.81   *"Substantial risk to the mental or physical health of any person"*: "Substantial" does not only refer to the likelihood of the risk occurring: "a risk may be 'substantial' if the harm would be serious, even though it was unlikely to occur and, conversely, may not be 'substantial' if the harm would be insignificant, even though the likelihood of some such harm is great. Paragraph (b) must be viewed in the light of the other paragraphs of regulation 27 [now ESA Regs reg.29] and the general scheme of the Regulations" (*CIB/3519/2002*, para.7). Commissioner Fellner accepted this as "probably right" in *CIB/2767/2004*, but added that:

> "invocation of the other paragraphs of regulation 27 as guides to interpretation suggests that the interpretation should be rather narrow. . . . the other paragraphs refer to more or less factual medical questions—presence of life-threatening or severe uncontrolled or uncontrollable disease, need for an identified major medical procedure within a short time" (para.6).

In *MW v SSWP (ESA)* [2012] UKUT 31 (AAC) Judge Parker was of the opinion that the question of "substantial risk" is an objective one and, as regards physical health, one to which the claimant's personal belief system and subjective views are not likely to be pertinent. In contrast, the position may well be different as regards mental health:

> "while the determination of the point is still an objective one, what are the subjective beliefs of a claimant must form part of the background to the question whether, looked at objectively, she might suffer a significant deterioration in mental health, faced with the thought that, in work, she could not follow out her preferred therapeutic regime. The tribunal erred in concentrating only on a reaction mentally to the distressing news of a cancer diagnosis or on whether the state of her cancer was at the relevant date physically harmful. It ought also to have applied an objective test in consideration of the question whether, in all her circumstances, the prospect of having to give up her daily time-consuming regime which she believed was the right and only way to combat her cancer, could constitute the necessary substantial risk" (para.3).

In relation to which employment contexts must the "substantial risk to health" be **9.82** *evaluated?* Charlton *and its application:* Whether "substantial risk to health" had to be evaluated against specific employments or in the abstract generated a number of conflicting Commissioners' decisions on IFW Regs, reg.27(b), but its meaning and the approach to take to its application was resolved by the Court of Appeal in *Charlton v Secretary of State for Work and Pensions* [2009] EWCA Civ 42 (the appeal from the decision of Commissioner Williams in *CIB/143/2007*) in judgments that make it clear that they apply also to the same terms in the relevant ESA Regulations.

Regulation 29(2)((b) requires (as noted above) a decision firstly that a person suffers as a consequence of some specific disease or bodily or mental disablement which does not of itself cause such functional limitation as to justify a total score warranting a finding of limited capability for work; it can only come into play where it has been found that the claimant does not have limited capability for work under the LCWA. It requires, secondly, a decision on whether because of the disease or disablement there would be a substantial risk to the mental or physical health of *any person* if the claimant were found capable of work (*Charlton*, para.30). The risk to be assessed must arise as a consequence of work the claimant would be found capable of undertaking, but for reg.29 (*Charlton*, para.33). Paragraph 2(b) might be satisfied

> "where the very finding of capability might create a substantial risk to a claimant's health or that of others, for example when a claimant suffering from anxiety or depression might suffer a significant deterioration on being told that the benefit claimed was being refused. Apart from that, probably rare, situation, the determination must be made in the context of the journey to or from work or in the workplace itself" (*Charlton*, para.34).

Although the regulation is headed "exceptional circumstances" and the wording of para.(2)(b) refers to the the health of "any person", in *HR v SSWP (ESA)* [2013] UKUT 55 (AAC), Judge Wikeley rightly pointed out that its coverage is in law determined by the words used in the body of the regulation. It cannot cover any circumstance describable as "exceptional". There was no evidence before the tribunal to enable it to conclude that the claimant being found capable of work posed any substantial risk to her. She did have an adult daughter recently diagnosed with terminal cancer, but again there was no evidence to show that the claimant being found capable of work would put the daughter's health at substantial risk. Indeed the claimant's regular visits to her daughter of about two hours a day were maintainable if having to claim JSA or being in full or part-time work. He thought the tribunal entitled to proceed and not adjourn to seek more evidence on that. ESA was not designed to cover a difficult case such as this. The more appropriate benefits might be DLA for the daughter and carer's allowance for the mother.

On one view the "proper approach" to para.(2)(b)—accepted as such in *CF v SSWP (ESA)* [2012] UKUT 29 (AAC) (Judge Parker); *SP v SSWP (ESA)* [2014]

UKUT 522 (AAC) (Judge Parker); *SD v SSWP (ESA)* [2014] UKUT 240 (AAC) (Judge Mark); *GS v SSWP (ESA)* [2014] UKUT 16 (AAC) (Judge Mark)—is to start with the statement of Judge Mark in *IJ v SSWP (IB)* [2010] UKUT 408 (AAC):

> "the test is not limited to whether there would be a substantial risk to the claimant from any work he may undertake. *The test is as to the risk as a result of being found capable of work.* If he was found capable of work, he would lose his incapacity benefit, and would very possibly need to seek work and apply for jobseeker's allowance. That would involve his attending interviews, and going through all the other steps that would be needed to obtain and keep jobseeker's allowance. In the present economic climate, a claimant who is 62 years old with mental health problems, and who has not worked since the early 1990's is unlikely to find work quickly and would very possibly never find it. His GP's assessment that it is inconceivable that he would ever be able to earn his living may be right. The tribunal would then have to determine how this change from his being in receipt of incapacity benefit would affect the claimant's mental health, looking not at some work he may do, but at the effect on his mental health of fruitless and repeated interviews and the possibly hopeless pursuit of jobs until he reached retirement age. These factors were not considered by the tribunal, and indeed they did not elicit the information necessary to enable them to be considered, such as whether he had in fact applied for jobseeker's allowance and if not, how he was coping or would cope" (para.10, emphasis supplied by commentator).

Such cases will be rare (*Charlton*, para.34; *MB v SSWP (ESA)* [2012] UKUT 228 (AAC), para.14 (Judge Jacobs)), so that in most cases the key task is to identify the nature of the relevant work and workplace and to consider the nature of the risk to the health of the claimant or another person in the context of that work, that workplace, and the journey to and from it.

9.83   The passage from Judge Mark's decision in *IJ v SSWP (IB)* [2010] UKUT 408 (AAC) (at para.10) cited immediately above was approved by Judge White in *NS v SSWP (ESA)* [2014] UKUT 115 (AAC); [2014] AACR 33, with the observation that reg.29(2)(b) "is not just about whether there is any work or type of work which a claimant can do without substantial risk to the mental or physical health of any person. It is about whether a substantial risk would arise from a claimant's being found not to have limited capability for work" (para.45). The same passage in *IJ v SSWP (IB)* was criticised by Judge Lane in *MW v SSWP (ESA)* [2015] UKUT 665 (AAC); however, Judge Lane's decision makes no reference to the previous reported decision of *NS v SSWP (ESA)*, which would appear to settle the point that e.g. conditionality issues *may* be relevant to the regulation 29 assessment. See further *JT v SSWP (ESA)* [2018] UKUT 124 (AAC).

Be that as it may, the Court in *Charlton* held that the correct approach to identifying the nature of the relevant work and workplace for the claimant was that identified with respect to IFW Regs, reg.27(b) in paras 17-18 of Deputy Commissioner Paines' decision in *CIB/360/2007*. It rejected the view that decision-makers and tribunals had to speculate as to the type of job which would have been set out for purposes of a JSA claim in a hypothetical Jobseeker's Agreement. Rather (reading Personal Capability Assessment as LCWA):

> "The decision-maker must assess the range or type of work which a claimant is capable of performing sufficiently to assess the risk to health either to himself or to others.
>
> Sufficient information may be elicited by reference to the claimant's completion of the initial questionnaire, questioning during his medical examination, or by any evidence he may choose to give on an appeal to the Tribunal. The process to be adopted by the decision-maker or Tribunal is to be regarded as inquisitorial and not adversarial. It is a process described by Diplock J. in *R. v Medical Appeal Tribunal (North Midland Region ex-parte Hubble)* 1958 2 QB 228 at 240

as a fact gathering exercise in which there is no formal burden of proof on either side. There should be no difficulty provided the decision-maker or Tribunal recall that the essential question is whether there is an adequate range of work which the claimant could undertake without creating a substantial risk to himself or to others. This conclusion is consistent with the practical application of these regulations. Any interpretation must bear in mind that the regulations are designed to provide a fair and effective system for assessing entitlement to incapacity benefit and to allied benefits when a claimant has passed the Personal Capability Assessment. It would not be possible to achieve the aim of those regulations were the decision-maker to be required to make findings of the particularity for which the claimant contends. The decision-maker, it must be recalled, will be provided only with the report of the doctor based upon the doctor's interview with the claimant and the claimant's completion of the questionnaire. It is quite impossible for the decision-maker to identify actual positions of employment or the nature of the duties and location of any job which the claimant might undertake, not least because the decision-maker may often be based in Belfast, or elsewhere, and can have no possible means of discovering employment circumstances throughout the country. The conclusion which requires no more than that the decision-maker or Tribunal assess the range of work of which the claimant is capable for the purposes of assessing risk to health has the merit of achieving the objective of the regulations" (*Charlton*, paras 45-47).

The Court upheld Commissioner Williams' finding that Mr Charlton was capable of performing the kind of work:— **9.84**

". . . to which a person with no physical limitations, no qualifications, no skills and no experience might be directed ([section] 48) and that he could undertake straightforward and unstructured, unskilled work."

There is undoubtedly a tension between the approach of Judge Mark in *IJ v SSWP (IB)* and that of Judge Lane in *MW v SSWP (ESA)*, as recognised by Judge Bano in *JT v SSWP (ESA)* [2018] UKUT 124 (AAC). In the circumstances of that case, Judge Bano did not find it necessary to resolve that tension, although the tenor of his decision is more in keeping with the approach in *IJ v SSWP (IB)*. Thus Judge Bano held that "in the case of claimants with fragile mental health the possible effects on a claimant of any compulsion to perform a particular type of work may have to be taken into account when considering regulation 29(2)(b)." Furthermore, the inquiry necessary under reg.29(2)(b):

"can only be sensibly undertaken if full account is taken of risks to a particular claimant resulting from any compulsion to undertake the work because of an element of 'conditionality' in the relevant benefits regime. Regulation 29(2)(b) is intended to protect third parties as well as claimants, and there is no indication in the legislation that any matter which is relevant to an assessment of the risks resulting from a claimant carrying out a particular type of work should not be taken into account."

Should a tribunal consider whether a claimant could work from home? It is submitted that the better view is that it should *not* do so, save perhaps in one rare case. In *SM v SSMP (ESA)* [2014] UKUT 241 (AAC), Judge Wikeley held that a tribunal erred in law by looking at work from home That approach is supported by references in *Charlton* to travelling to and from a workplace and by the amendment to the regulation about taking account of an employer's reasonable adjustments to the workplace. Although working from home is more common that in the past it is entirely dependent on an employer's discretion and to take it into account would deprive the regulation of any real purpose for large number of cases and defeat the legislative purpose of protecting exceptionally vulnerable people, especially those with mental health problems (paras 7–11). He cited in support of his interpretation the tenor of Judge Ward's decision in *PD v SSWP (ESA)* [2014] UKUT 148. Judge

Wikeley noted that Judge Ward there

> "identified the central issue in that appeal as being the impact of regulation 29 "on persons who by reason of mental ill-health have an impaired ability to get to places, such as a hypothetical workplace" (at paragraph 1). If claimants could not avail themselves of regulation 29 simply because they could get a home-working job, then the whole premise of Judge Ward's analysis was flawed. I do not accept that it was" (para.11).

It should be noted, however, that later in *PD*, Judge Ward seemed to indicate that a tribunal *could* look at the viability and suitability of work from home before looking at ability to travel to a workplace. Judge Ward stated

> "The tribunal may wish to explore types of work which the person could do from home. Even if the traditional fields for such activity have declined, information technology must bring with it a number of such opportunities for some people. But if such work is not appropriate to the particular claimant, the tribunal will have to conduct the assessment of risk, which is the primary purpose of regulation 29, as best it can in relation to the sort of range of work mandated by *Charlton*, outside the home. If someone has been found to be unable to do something, I find it hard to see how it might be possible to hold that there would be no substantial risk to their health on an assumption that they were effectively made to do that which had been found to be impossible for them (i.e. go to work unaccompanied), though I do not intend to lay that down as a proposition of law. Far more likely is it that what is required is an evaluation of their circumstances when making the hypothetical journey, in particular in relation to being accompanied, in order to see whether the conditions could be satisfied which would alleviate or avoid the risk to health" (para.16).

Agreeing that Judge Wikeley was correct on the facts of *SM*, in *CL v SSWP (ESA)* [2015] UKUT 375 (AAC), Judge Jacobs declined to find in *SM* an absolute prohibition on considering home working under this regulation, stating that it was possible, albeit rare, "that the only type of work for which the claimant is suitable might be in an industry where home working is possible, even encouraged" (para.12).

9.85 *Where the claimant has an existing job to go back to but is as yet unable to do so, the relevance of that job to the reg.29(2) question lies solely in the reasons why the claimant cannot return to that job. In AJ v SSWP (ESA) [2013] UKUT 279 (AAC), Judge Wright stated:*

> "For example, and these are no more than examples, if the appellant was not then doing the job because the police had in place a temporary cleaner whose contract still had a month to run and they did not want to have the appellant back at the same time, that may have little or nothing relevant to say about risk in terms of the appellant carrying out such a job. On the other hand, if the police had made its own assessment and found that the appellant needed until, say, the end of August 2010 before she could safely work as a cleaner then that would have been very relevant to regulation 29(2)(b) risk assessment. That may then have ruled out dexterous manual work as relevant work and would have needed the tribunal to look elsewhere for work the appellant was suited both as a matter of training and aptitude" (para.13).

Regulation 29(2)(b) looks to risk and not to more remote matters such as the ultimate or longer-term benefit to the claimant. What is at issue is not the claimant's positive attitude to work but rather whether there is a substantial risk to health if he were found not to have limited capability for work; if that risk exists it is not altered by the claimant's attitude to it (*JW v SSWP* (ESA) [2011] UKUT 416 (AAC), para.12). Similarly, whether work would be good for the claimant is not the correct test (*CH v SSMP) (ESA)* [2014] UKUT 11 (AAC)).

In terms of timescale, the claimant being found not to have limited capability for work occurs when the Secretary of State makes his decision and tribunals must look at the risk as at that date. But that decision has to look to the future, at what will be the effect of the finding given that *Charlton* widened the scope of the enquiry to take account of how the claimant would function in work (*CH v SSWP (ESA)* [2014] UKUT 11 (AAC), paras11-13). As Judge Mark put it in *GS v SSWP (ESA)* [2014] UKUT 16 (AAC):

"the job of the tribunal was to assess . . ., as at the date of the decision, the risk to the claimant's health of her being found not to have limited capability for work. As pointed out repeatedly, this does not prevent tribunals from having regard to evidence coming into existence after the date of the decision, or of events after the decision under appeal, so long as it is relevant to the prognosis at that date. Thus in *R(DLA) 3/01* the actual rate of recovery of a claimant from a health problem was held to be relevant to the question whether as at the date of the decision the claimant was likely to satisfy the relevant conditions for benefit for 6 months after the date of the decision. So too, in the present case, the tribunal needed to assess whether there was a deterioration in the claimant's health following the decision, the extent of the deterioration, and the extent to which it was as a result of her being found not to have limited capability for work. This includes the stress from an appeal, successful or otherwise, the stress of dealing with the Jobcentre and possible interviews, the prospects of employment, and the ways in which it is said that the claimant's mental health can be kept stabilised bearing in mind, if the evidence is accepted, that it appears to have deteriorated even without seeking or obtaining work and without both the pressures of work and the additional pressures on daily life if she did spend part of it working" (paras 16, 17).

However, the breadth of this passage has been criticised by Judge Lane in *MW v SSWP (ESA)* [2015] UKUT 665 (AAC) as being inconsistent with Court of Appeal authority in *Charlton v Secretary of State for Work and Pensions* [2009] EWCA Civ 42; see further above.

In *MB v SSWP (ESA)* [2012] UKUT 228 (AAC), Judge Jacobs was concerned with the case of a claimant (Mr B) addicted to drugs and taking part in a drug recovery programme. The argument was made that since wages from work which were higher than benefit income would enable him to buy more drugs than when on benefit, this would increase the risk to his health and so reg.29(2)(b) should apply. Judge Jacobs identified the issue as: what connection does there have to be between the risk and being found capable of work? Must the risk arise from the work itself or is it enough that it arises from some consequence (in this case increased income) that follows from the work but is unrelated to the nature of the work? Applying *Charlton*, he accepted the Secretary of State's argument (see para.10) that the provision did not embrace the claimant's argument. As Judge Jacobs saw it, *Charlton*

"decided that the trigger for the risk had to be found in the work the claimant would be undertaking. It had to arise from: (i) the decision that the claimant had capability for work; (ii) the work that the claimant might do; or (iii) travelling to and from work. (i) will be rare.

The argument for Mr B is that the wages he would receive for the work would put more money in his pocket than he would spend on drugs. That is not a risk that arises from the work. The work is merely the circumstance that gives rise to it. It would not arise if his wages were so low that he would have been better off on benefit. Nor would it arise if the street price for the drugs increased in line with his income so that he could not afford any more drugs than previously. In other words, the risk arises from the comparative value of Mr B's benefit and the wages he might receive relative to the price of drugs" (paras 14, 15).

Where travelling to work unaccompanied is the potential risk, a question arises as to whether **9.86** *third party assistance can be considered as alleviating it.* In *PD v SSWP (ESA)* [2014] UKUT 148 (AAC), Judge Ward considered that the risk with respect to travelling to work arising from physical elements was likely to be rare; the traveller contemplated by the Court of Appeal in *Charlton* was "the person whose mental health problems cause difficulties with the journey to work" (para.15). Judge Ward's starting point was that where there was appropriate evidence third party help could be taken into account, that line of argument was open to the Secretary of State (paras 23, 26):

> "There will be cases, for instance where a partner is not working, there is no one else at home who uses the car and where the evidence shows a pattern of the partner driving the claimant to wherever s/he wants or needs to go, that it may be open to a tribunal to infer that such help would similarly be available to get a claimant to the *Charlton*-mandated hypothetical workplace. If a scheme such as Access to Work were available on a sufficiently reliable basis, it is hard to see why it should not be taken into account. Such are ultimately conclusions of fact and not matters on which I need say more, except to observe that this may be, par excellence, a field in which tribunals can look to the principles of *Kerr v Department for Social Development* [2004] UKHL 23; [2004] 1 WLR 1372" (para.26).

Judge Ward also stated that

> "What is difficult in relation to transport is yet harder in relating to accompaniment within the workplace. Such a setup would be highly unusual, even if only to help with the first few days. I did not hear argument on whether that, unlike the provision of transport, could constitute a reasonable adjustment for Equality Act purposes" (para.27).

Judge Hemingway in *HT v SSWP (ESA)* [2018] UKUT 174 (AAC) has agreed with Judge Ward in *PD v SSWP (ESA)* [2014] UKUT 148 (AAC) that the risk within reg.29 with respect to travelling to work is likely to be "rare (though not impossible)" in the context of "physical health difficulties in circumstances where those same difficulties do not lead to the risk arising in the workplace itself" (at para.19). Likewise, "the prospect of third party assistance on the journey will be a potentially relevant consideration though the availability of such cannot simply, without evidence, be assumed. Where the arguments as to risk relate to falling the use of such as walking sticks and walking frames will need to be considered."

Where someone satisfies descriptor 15(c) in Sch.2 (needs assistance to get to an unfamiliar place), third party assistance might be a possibility of avoiding the risk to health for an initial period until the journey to and from the workplace became familiar (*EJ v SSWP (ESA)* [2014] UKUT 551 (AAC) paras 19, 21 (Judge Wikeley)). But practicalities need to be looked at (*SS v SSWP (ESA)* [2015] UKUT 101 (AAC), para.5 (Judge Rowland)). In another context, the three-judge panel in *JC v SSWP (ESA)* [2014] UKUT 352 (AAC); [2015] AACR 12, did not consider that a person could properly be regarded "as able to engage in social contact if she or he can do so only if accompanied by someone, *at least without further explanation as to how it is envisaged that that might be realistic in the workplace*" (para.45, emphasis supplied by commentator).

It should also be noted that in stark contrast in *MT v SSWP (ESA)* [2013] UKUT 545 (AAC), in the context of reg.35(2), Judge Gray firmly rejected looking at capacity to perform activities with third party assistance, observing:

> "I do need to deal however with the observation of the FTT in its statement of reasons that the appellant could take another person with her to any work-related activities. It may be that the Secretary of State would be facilitative in any matter which helped a claimant engage so as to improve their ultimate prospects of retaining work. I do not know. Whether or not that is so, is not relevant. As a matter of law any work-related activity which could only be accomplished because of the presence of another person must be looked upon as not being an activity that the claimant can carry out. *The issue under regulation 35 (2) (b) as to whether there would be a substantial risk to the mental or physical health of any*

person if the claimant were found not to have limited capability for work-related activity cannot be assessed as if the claimant under consideration had somebody else by their side. There will be claimants who have a need for the personal reassurance of another person, but who do not have anybody available to perform that role. Even if they did, it would not be reasonable for such an assessment to be made on the basis of reliance on another's goodwill. Legal tests cannot depend upon that. Where an appellant who is found to have limited capability for work-related activities wishes to engage voluntarily, it may be that they choose to do so with the help of another person, and it may (or may not, I do not know) be possible for them to do so, but the capacity to engage only with that assistance cannot be part of the test of capability" (para.34, emphasis added by commentator).

In *PD*, Judge Ward agreed with the italicised passage insofar as it meant "without consideration as to whether the third party's presence would be made out in fact" (para.21), but otherwise distinguished the passage as focussing on the claimant's capability to perform activities (agreeing that there third party assistance should be ignored) rather than the different question of what risks would ensue (where, with respect to travelling, at least, third party assistance available in fact might obviate the risk). See also *SP v SSWP (ESA)* [2014] UKUT 522 (AAC), where Judge Parker did not categorically reject as inadmissible the Secretary of State's submission that the claimant could be accompanied (at least initially) to some interviews, but instead concluded that "this would not address some of the potential stress to which Judge Mark referred [in *IJ v SSWP (IB)* [2010] UKUT 408 (AAC)" (para.7).

As the foregoing discussion makes clear Charlton *must be applied in the light of all the available evidence.* In *LD v SSWP (ESA)* [2014] UKUT 131 (AAC), Judge Ward held that retirement on health grounds 17 years earlier could be of probative value and ongoing relevance since it had involved an assessment by experts that at that time the claimant was permanently incapable of doing a particular type of job and other evidence before the tribunal had indicated a deterioration rather than an improvement in the claimant's condition since that time. In *GS v SSWP (ESA)* [2014] UKUT 16 (AAC), Judge Mark held:

9.87

"It was the duty of the decision maker in relation to the present appeal, under rule 24(4)(b) of the Tribunal Procedure (First-tier Tribunal) (SEC) Rules 2008, to provide with the response to the appeal copies of all documents relevant to the case in the decision maker's possession. It was also the duty of the Secretary of State, under rule 2(4) of the same Rules, to help the tribunal to deal with the case fairly and justly. Under one head or the other, if not both, the tribunal ought to have been provided with copies of the evidence before the previous tribunal which had heard the appeal only 7 months before the new decision now under appeal. It is a duty which the new tribunal [to which he remitted the case] ought to have enforced" (para.5).

The effect of failure to follow the steps required by Charlton: Generally failing to follow the steps approved in *Charlton* will mean that the tribunal errs in law as in *JW v SSWP* (ESA) [2011] UKUT 416 (AAC). In *SSWP v Cattrell* [2011] EWCA Civ 572; [2011] AACR 35, however, the Court of Appeal held that while tribunals should normally identify the range of work that a claimant might be capable of, in this particular case because the first-tier tribunal had accepted evidence that there was no prospect of this claimant finding any suitably safe work, adopting the approach in *Charlton* and speculating about a range of possible work was not appropriate. But so doing was not here an error of law and the decision that this claimant was entitled to IB on the basis of "substantial risk" (there IFW Regs, reg.27(b), the equivalent of ESA Regs, reg.29(2)(b)) should stand. In contrast, in *RB v SSWP (ESA)* [2012] UKUT 431 (AAC), the tribunal merely stated that there was no evidence to suggest that reg.29 applied. Judge Ward held that it had erred in law in not identifying in its reasons that it had considered the range of work the claimant might be expected to do; given his knee problem and work background the answer was not self-evident (paras 4–7).

9.88   *A question which has troubled tribunals at both levels is whether reg.29(2)(b) must always be considered where the claimant has failed to achieve a sufficient score on the LCWA?* It need not be considered as a matter of routine, but whether it should be considered in any particular case depends on all the circumstances of that case (*PC v SSWP (ESA)* [2014] UKUT 1 (AAC); *SP v SSWP (ESA)* [2014] UKUT 10 (AAC); *DB v SSWP (ESA)* [2014] UKUT 41 (AAC); *NS v SSWP (ESA)* [2014] UKUT 115 (AAC); [2014] AACR 33). If a competent representative chooses not to raise it, then, absent unusual circumstances, a tribunal need not consider it. However, the more narrowly focused the descriptors in the LCWA become, the more likely it is that reg.29(2)(b) will be put in issue (*RB v SSWP (ESA)* [2012] UKUT 431 (AAC), para.7; *NS v SSWP (ESA)* [2014] UKUT 115 (AAC); [2014] AACR 33, para.50). It is likely particularly to be relevant where mental health issues are involved. In *NS v SSWP (ESA)* [2014] UKUT 115 (AAC); [2014] AACR 33, Judge White proffered the following useful guidance to tribunals:

"There will be some cases in which a tribunal need say nothing about regulation 29(2)(b). I give one clear example. Where a claimant is represented, claims only problems with physical functions, is found to score no points under Part 1 of Schedule 2 to the Employment and Support Allowance Regulations 2008, and where the representative does not put regulation 29(2)(b) in issue, a tribunal can safely leave out any mention of regulation 29(2)(b). However, in such a case a wise tribunal would seek confirmation from the representative that no issue is raised under regulation 29(2)(b) if they were to find that no points are scored under the Part 1 descriptors.

There will be some cases in which a tribunal must address regulation 29(2)(b). Clearly, if it is put in issue by a claimant, it must be fully and properly addressed. This will not require repetition of the findings of fact made in respect of the descriptors in Schedule 2, but that will be the obvious starting point for the explanation of why regulation 29(2)(b) does or does not apply.

In cases in which the descriptors relating to mental, cognitive and intellectual functions are in issue, it is more likely that regulation 29(2)(b) will be relevant. After all, in cases which come before the tribunal, more often than not the claimant's GP has issued a certificate that the claimant is incapable of work (though I accept that the GP may not be making that judgment against the Schedule 2 assessment). If the GP has submitted a letter in support of the claimant's appeal, that will often indicate why the GP considers that the claimant is incapable of work" (paras 47–49).

That guidance was followed by Judge Gray in *KB v SSWP (ESA)* [2014] UKUT 303 (AAC).

Although reg.29(2)(b) can only come into play where the person has failed to achieve a sufficient score in the LCWA, the question of which descriptors a claimant satisfies is relevant to the application of the paragraph because one is determining the matter taking due account of the claimant's disabilities (*CF v SSWP (ESA)* [2012] UKUT 29 (AAC), paras 14, 15). Indeed, a claimant's satisfaction of descriptor 15(b) (9 points) must inevitably raise the question of the applicability of reg.29 since that means that the claimant has been found to be "unable to get to a particular place with which the claimant is familiar, without being accompanied by another person", thus raising issues about substantial risk to the claimant's health in terms of the journey to work (*SS v SSWP (ESA)* [2015] UKUT 101 (AAC), para.4 (Judge Rowland)).

While a Med 3 issued by the claimant's GP is not conclusive on the issue under reg.29(2), the implications of the certificate must be addressed and facts found to the extent possible (*SP v SSWP (ESA)* [2014] UKUT 278 (AAC), para.16). In *RU v SSWP (ESA)* [2014] UKUT 77 (AAC), Judge Ward held that:

"if the claimant's GP was advising his or her patient to refrain from work for 6 months by a Med 3 issued more or less contemporaneously with the decision under appeal, it was incumbent on the tribunal to consider the implications of that. The work capability assessment is an artificial construct, which looks at certain activities only, and there is no necessary correlation between a doctor's views as to what the patient can manage and the outcome of the WCA applied to that person, or vice versa. Regulation 29 has the function of a safety valve addressing that lack of correlation, protecting claimants (and others) from the effect of determinations which in the circumstances set out in that regulation would otherwise result in substantial risk to health" (para.6).

In addition, the existence of a recent DLA award on the ground of day supervision is likely to be material evidence and required to be addressed (*NA (by ST) v SSWP (ESA)* [2012] UKUT 428 (AAC), para.3).

The standard of tribunal decision-making and giving of reasons as the applicability or otherwise of reg. 29(2)(b) has caused concern among Upper Tribunal Judges. If a tribunal chooses to address the provision, whether at the request of the claimant, representative or of its own volition, "it must do so properly . . . and an inadequate analysis" will not suffice (*EJ v SSWP (ESA)* [2014] UKUT 551 (AAC), para.18). Its findings on reg.29(2)(b) must be consistent with those it has made on the application of the Sch.2 descriptors (*CC v SSWP (ESA)* [2015] UKUT 62 (AAC), para.22; *SS v SSWP (ESA)* [2015] UKUT 101 (AAC), para.4). In *NS v SSWP (ESA)* [2014] UKUT 115 (AAC); [2014] AACR 33, Judge White proffered the following useful guidance to tribunals:

9.89

"I do not consider that the level of detail required for proper reasons on the application of regulation 29(2)(b) is high. The more obvious it is that regulation 29(2)(b) does not apply, the easier it should be to give reasons why that is so.

What is frequently missing from brief statements that regulation 29(2)(b) does not apply is the addition of a statement as to why it does not apply. This is exemplified by the statement in the appeal before me, where the tribunal said:

Regulation 29 does not apply as the Tribunal was not satisfied that there was a substantial risk to the appellant or to any person if he were not found to have limited capability for work.

What is needed is for that sentence to end in a comma and to be followed by the word "because" and then a phrase or two explaining why regulation 29(2) (b) does not apply. After all, if the tribunal has done a proper job in considering regulation 29(2)(b) they must have considered why the regulation did not apply. Otherwise, this is a mere formulaic response to the issue. A tribunal which embarks upon a consideration of regulation 29(2)(b) must do a proper job of considering it" (paras 50–53).

For a further example of a case in which the Upper Tribunal followed the same approach, namely that the more obvious it is that reg.29 does not apply, the easier it is to say why that is so, see *JH(S) v Secretary of State for Work and Pensions (ESA)* [2015] UKUT 567 (AAC). The following observation was made by Judge Hemingway in *RK v Secretary of State for Work and Pensions (ESA)* [2015] UKUT 549 (AAC), allowing an appeal on the reg.29 point:

"16. I would just wish to add one brief final comment. It seems to me that a consideration of the type or range of work a claimant might reasonably be expected to undertake is something which is often (though by no means always) missed by a tribunal. Often that will not be fatal. Indeed, as was made clear in *NS*, cited above, it will sometimes not be fatal even if regulation 29 is not referred to at all. However, there will be cases, as here, and it seems to me they are not infrequent, where there are indications that the range might be limited for various reasons, perhaps a lack of experience of or aptitude for certain categories of work, perhaps a difficulty with written or spoken English, perhaps an established physical or mental disablement, perhaps something else, such that a proper consideration of this aspect is needed. Of course, the test does not require anything like the sort of detailed analysis which might be involved in, say, testing the degree of risk to health by reference to specific jobs or job descriptions. A short assessment, perhaps only a couple of sentences or so, will often be enough. A tribunal will often already have some background information in the documents before it and will be able to ask questions about the sorts of matters referred to above if an oral hearing is held. Where competent representatives are involved it may well assist a tribunal if any written submission lodged in advance of a hearing can specify whether and on what basis regulation 29 is relied upon and can deal with, if thought to be relevant, the question of the range or type of work."

Merely reiterating the statutory test in negative form will not suffice. As Judge Bano rightly stressed in *PH v SSWP (ESA)* [2014] UKUT 502 (AAC)

"[t]he difficult issues which may arise under regulation 29 will often require detailed findings of fact to be made by the tribunal, rather than mantra-like recitations of the terms of the legislation and unparticularised references to adjustments in the workplace" (para.5).

In *MF v SSWP (ESA)* [2014] UKUT 523 (AAC), Judge Mark allowed the appeal stating that

". . .The tribunal does not indicate what occupation or range of occupations it had in mind. More seriously it totally failed to deal with the points actually made in the written submissions. It was dealing with a claimant who had not worked for 20 years, whose appearance was described by the disability analyst as unkempt, and whose behaviour was described as restless with reduced facial expression, and whom it had found was prone to episodes of depression when he may lack the motivation to do things.
   The tribunal needed to address how he would have coped not just with an interview and with some unspecified job when not having a depressive episode, but with all the matters identified by the claimant's representative in his written submissions and then determine whether there was a substantial risk to his mental or physical health (or that of anybody else) if he were found not to have limited capability for work. There have also been raised, at least before me, issues as to the extent to which the claimant can use public transport or travel at busy times and the tribunal may need to consider this both in connection with any requirements imposed in connection with jobseeker's allowance and in connection with any employment he may obtain. In failing to identify the correct issues and to make appropriate reasoned findings, the tribunal was in error of law. Its decision must be set aside and the matter remitted for rehearing by a new tribunal" (paras 7–8).

Similarly, Judge Wikeley in *CC v SSWP (ESA)* [2015] UKUT 62 (AAC) held erroneous in law a tribunal decision which inadequately explained why reg.29(2)(b) failed to apply. It had awarded the claimant 9 points under descriptor 8(c): "unable to navigate around unfamiliar surroundings, without being accompanied by another person, due to sensory impairment". The tribunal's finding that the claimant could "get about safely and see right in front of him at a short distance" was not, without further explanation, consistent with its decision on that descriptor (para.22).

Ultimately the adequacy of reasons required is going to be context-specific. For example, in *DB v SSWP (ESA)* [2016] UKUT 493 (AAC) Judge Gray, in dismissing the claimant's appeal, observed as follows:

"21. Regulation 29 whilst relevant at the outset of the appeal, really ceased to be so in view of the findings of the tribunal that the somewhat extreme difficulties the appellant put forward as being caused by her continuing chronic pain were not made out. The tribunal . . . simply did not accept that she would have either the problems that she said she had, or, indeed, any problems at all under the descriptors. In those factual circumstances there could be no question of substantial risk. It would not have been inappropriate for the tribunal, having made its findings, to have decided not to formally consider regulation 29, or, to put it perhaps more accurately, to consider it only in order to confirm that it was not, or was not any longer, an applicable consideration in the light of those findings. In any event read as a whole the explanation satisfied the test set out by the Court of Appeal in *Charlton.*"

In *DB v Secretary of State for Work and Pensions (ESA)* [2017] UKUT 251 (AAC) Judge Bano gave the following guidance on the application of reg.29:

"9. It is clear from the judgment of the Court of Appeal in *Charlton* that the question of whether regulation 29 applies to a claimant is fact-specific and that a tribunal's findings in relation to the Regulation must therefore be based specifically on a claimant's individual circumstances. That is not to say that the reasons for a tribunal's decision on whether regulation 29 applies to a claimant need necessarily be long or elaborate, and in many cases the tribunal's findings in relation to matters such as the nature and extent of a claimant's disablement will also provide a basis for their conclusions in relation to regulation 29. However, in carrying out the risk assessment required by the Regulation, it is in my view necessary that it should be reasonably apparent from the reasons, read as a whole, that the individual circumstances of the particular claimant have been fully and properly taken into account when deciding whether the Regulation applies."

The (in)applicability of the Equality Act 2010: the Equality Act 2010 has been mentioned and subject to varying degrees of consideration in a number of Upper Tribunal decisions in a number of contexts. But its specific applicability in the context of reg.29(2)(b) was most fully argued before Judge Wright in *JS v SSWP (ESA)* [2014] UKUT 428; [2015] AACR 12, a case in which an oral hearing was held, and the matter analysed in a judgment running to 78 paragraphs. His conclusion was that

"the assessment of risk under regulation 29(2)(b) of the ESA Regs does not require or involve the decision maker (be that the Secretary of State's delegate or the First-tier Tribunal) in making an assessment as to whether employers would owe a duty under the Equality Act 2010 to make reasonable adjustments in respect of the individual claimant whose case falls for decision, and in my judgment the tribunal therefore erred in law in relying on the Equality Act 2010 to that effect" (para.5).

It is submitted that his conclusion that the Equality Act 2010 is not applicable is the correct approach to the matter, for the reasons he gave (summarised below). His decision has been reported, and is accepted as the correct approach by the Secretary of State; in *SB v SSWP (ESA)* [2015] UKUT 88 (AAC), Judge Ward accepted as "properly made" the concession by the Secretary of State in the appeal. The Secretary of State considered that in *JS*

"Judge Wright held that:

- it is not sufficient for the First-tier Tribunal (FtT) to assume that because the Equality Act 2010 will require an employer not to discriminate against and make reasonable adjustments in the work place to accommodate a disabled person, there will be no risk arising from the person being found fit for work;

- the assessment of risk under regulation 29(2)(b) of the ESA Regs 2008 however does <u>not</u> require or involve the SSWP or FtT in making an assessment as to whether employers would owe a duty under the Equality Act to make reasonable adjustments in respect of the individual claimant (specifically disagreeing with Judge Mark in *JB v SSWP (ESA)* [2013] UKUT 518 AAC.)"

The Secretary of State conceded that in practical terms, this meant "that in assessing [any] reg.29 risk, SSWP [and the First-tier Tribunal] must make a claimant specific risk assessment". While this includes the matter of what steps could reasonably and realistically be taken on the facts of the specific case to avoid substantial risk (a requirement now statutorily set by reg.29(3)(a)), it does not require evidence of what a potential employer would or might do by way of reasonable adjustments in compliance with any Equality Act duties the employer might be subject to.

Judge Wright supported his conclusion with a number of lines of reasoning which he saw as "incremental" (para.46).

He argued, firstly, that the Equality Act 2010 and employment and support allowance schemes have different statutory aims and materially different statutory contents. That the ESA Regs are not to be divorced from the real world (see *AS* and *SI*, above) points to the 2010 Act having potential relevance to the ESA Regs. But, as regards "statutory intendment", against that must be set the plain fact that the ESA Regs (and their predecessors for IB) have never on their face made any express link to the Equality Act 2010 or its predecessor, the Disability Discrimination Act 1995. Indeed, even where as now, para.(3)(a) requires consideration in applying para.(2)(b) to be given to "reasonable adjustments being made in the claimant's workplace" no link was made, pointing to para.(2)(b) "being intended to embody a test separate to the tests under the Equality Act 2010" (para.48). In addition, the ESA scheme applies to persons not in employment and unable to work, whereas the duties under the Equality Act 2010 apply only to employees or applicants for employment who have made known to the employer their disability. Moreover key elements for assessing disability are different, and noticeably different, under the two schemes (paras 53, 54).

Secondly, the Equality Act 2010 test sits uneasily with *Charlton*. That case eschewed an "actual employment" test which is essentially the test embodied in that Act (para.51). *Charlton* embraces the impact in respect of travelling to work; the 2010 Act does not (para.55). In addition, *Charlton* took account of the test under para (2)(b) "having to be applied practically". Requiring a decision-maker to consider whether "the claimant would be likely to be owed a duty by an employer or employers to make reasonable adjustments under the statutory machinery contained within the Equality Act 2010" would be likely to render impracticable "a timeous decision" (para. 58).

Thirdly, the First-tier Tribunal is ill-equipped to make proper assessments under the Equality Act 2010, which matters are vested in the specialist employment tribunal. While the First-tier tribunal is also specialist in its sphere of operation, "on its face it is not concerned with assessing whether an employer will in fact owe a duty to make reasonable adjustments in respect of an individual disabled person" (para.57).

Finally, *recourse to the Equality Act 2010 is simply unnecessary*. The matter of applying the para.(2)(b) test in the light of reasonable adjustments which might be made in the envisaged range of workplaces is now explicit in para.(3)(a), but has also always been inherent in the risk assessment required by para.(2)(b),as interpreted in *Charlton*; as Judge Wright put it the wording is:

"wide enough and flexible enough to encompass reasonable steps that realistically on the evidence may be taken by, or in respect of, the [specific individual] claimant, including by prospective employers. But that does not require an assessment to be made of employers' duties under the Equality Act 2010" (para.61).

There must first be analysis of the range and types of work which as a matter of training or aptitude the claimant is suited to do "and which his or her disabilities do not render him [or her] incapable of performing". There must then be assessed the risk the individual's disease(s) or disablement(s) would, on the balance of probabilities, give rise to

"if the claimant was travelling to and from, and working in, employments he or she was otherwise suited to do. Part of that risk assessment will involve consideration of the steps that, on the evidence and having regard to the individual claimant's health conditions and other circumstances, could reasonably and realistically be taken to avoid any substantial risk to health" (para.62).

SB v SSWP (ESA) [2015] UKUT 88 (AAC) has been considered and followed in *SP v SSWP (ESA)* [2018] UKUT 205 (AAC), where the claimant had a latex allergy and appealed a refusal to award ESA on the basis of reg.29(2)(b). The tribunal dismissed her appeal, noting the duty of an employer to make adjustments under the Equality Act 2010, the claimant's responsibility to also consider making adjustments at work to minimise risk, and the claimant's failure to check for latex the chair she sat on at the tribunal hearing. Judge Poole QC held that the tribunal had made adequate findings of fact to support its conclusion under reg.29(2)(b). These included identifying the gravity of risk to health from the potential effects of allergic reactions to latex, the likelihood of the risk occurring, and risk mitigation measures (such as the claimant's use of medication and her experience in monitoring the environment around her to check for latex).

Paragraph (3)(a): reasonable adjustments in the claimant's workplace
See *SP v SSWP (ESA)* [2018] UKUT 205 (AAC), where the claimant had a   **9.90** latex allergy and had appealed a refusal to award ESA on the basis of reg.29(2)(b) (discussed above). Judge Poole QC held as follows (at para.11):

"The wording of regulation 29(3)(a) refers to reasonable adjustments in the claimant's workplace, without confining its application to adjustments made only by an employer. It is normal in the workplace to expect both employer and employee to play their parts in keeping the working environment as risk free as practicable. In my view both employer and employee can be expected to take reasonable measures. Accordingly, measures that a claimant may reasonably take to reduce risk are relevant either under the reasonable adjustment wording in regulation 29(3)(a), or even if that was wrong to the general consideration of whether a risk is substantial under regulation 29(2)(b)."

Conditions for treating a claimant as having limited capability for work until a determination about limited capability for work has been made

30.—(1) A claimant is, if the conditions set out in paragraph (2) are met,   **9.91** to be treated as having limited capability for work until such time as it is determined—

    (a) whether or not the claimant has limited capability for work;

    (b) whether or not the claimant is to be treated as having limited capability for work otherwise than in accordance with this regulation; or

    (c) whether the claimant falls to be treated as not having limited capability for work in accordance with regulation 22 (failure to provide information in relation to limited capability for work) or 23 (failure to attend a medical examination to determine limited capability for work).

    (2) The conditions are—

    (a) that the claimant provides evidence of limited capability for work in accordance with the Medical Evidence Regulations; and

[³(b) in relation to the claimant's entitlement to any benefit, allowance or advantage which is dependent on the claimant having limited capability for work, it has not been determined—

    (i) in the last determination preceding the date of claim for an employment and support allowance, that the claimant does not have limited capability for work; or

    (ii) within the 6 months preceding the date of claim for an employment and support allowance, that the claimant is to be treated as not having limited capability for work under regulation 22 or 23,

unless paragraph (4) applies;]

  (c) [²*omitted*].

[³(3) Paragraph 2(b) does not apply where a claimant has made and is pursuing an appeal against a relevant decision of the Secretary of State, and that appeal has not yet been determined by the First-tier Tribunal.]

[²(4) This paragraph applies where—

  (a) the claimant is suffering from some specific disease or bodily or mental disablement from which the claimant was not suffering at the time of that determination;

  (b) a disease or bodily or mental disablement from which the claimant was suffering at the time of that determination has significantly worsened; or

  (c) in the case of a claimant who was treated as not having limited capability for work under regulation 22 (failure to provide information), the claimant has since provided the information requested under that regulation.]

[³(5) In this regulation a "relevant decision" means—

  (a) a decision that embodies the first determination by the Secretary of State that the claimant does not have limited capability for work; or

  (b) a decision that embodies the first determination by the Secretary of State that the claimant does not have limited capability for work since a previous determination by the Secretary of State or appellate authority that the claimant does have limited capability for work.

(6) In this regulation, "appellate authority" means the First-tier Tribunal, the Upper Tribunal, the Court of Appeal, the Court of Session, or the Supreme Court.]

AMENDMENTS

1. Social Security (Miscellaneous Amendments) Regulations 2011 (SI 2011/674) reg.16(3) (April 11, 2011).

2. Social Security (Miscellaneous Amendments) (No.3) Regulations 2013 (SI 2013/2536) reg.13(14) (October 29, 2013).

3. Employment and Support Allowance (Repeat Assessments and Pending Appeal Awards) (Amendment) Regulations 2015 (SI 2015/437) reg.3 (March 30, 2015).

MODIFICATION

Regulation 30 is modified by Sch.1 para.10 of the Employment and Support Allowance (Transitional Provisions, Housing Benefit and Council Tax Benefit) (Existing Awards) (No.2) Regulations 2010 (SI 2010/1907) (as amended) for the purposes specified in reg.6(1). For details of the modification, see the text of those Regulations, below.

DEFINITIONS

"appellate authority"—see para.(6).
"claimant"—see WRA 2007 s.24(1).
"limited capability for work"—see WRA 2007 s.1(4).
"Medical Evidence Regulations"—see reg.2(1).
"relevant decision"—see para.(5).

GENERAL NOTE

This regulation deals with the position of claimants for ESA pending a decision   9.92
on eligibility. As amended with effect from March 30, 2015, it applies (a) where the
claimant makes, or is treated as making a claim for ESA on or after that date, and
(b) where, in respect of such a claim, the claimant makes and pursues an appeal
against a Secretary of State's decision that s/he does not have limited capability for
work (see reg.2 of the amending Regs). Claims made before March 30, 2015 and
appeals in respect of them are instead regulated by the previous version of this regulation (for which see the 2014/15 edition of this book and the detailed analysis by
Judge Wright in *EI v SSWP (ESA)* [2016] UKUT 397 (AAC))).

The March 2015 amendments were made to rectify an unintended consequence
of the previous version of this regulation whereby someone whose entitlement had
ended because of a finding that s/he did not have limited work could make a repeat
claim after six months and gain a further period of entitlement to ESA pending a
decision on eligibility even where the claimant could provide no evidence to suggest
that their condition had significantly worsened or that they had a new health condition to be considered. One unwanted effect was that even where a First-tier Tribunal
had upheld a fit for work decision, if the appeal process had taken longer than six
months, a claimant could immediately make a repeat claim for ESA on the basis of
exactly the same condition, and would be entitled to receive ESA at the assessment
phase rate (the same rate as JSA) pending a new LCWA. The cycle between ESA
claim, LCWA and disallowance would begin again.

As amended, the regulation provides that on a "repeat claim" for ESA (see below)
the claimant will *not* be treated as having limited capability for work (and thus ESA
entitlement at assessment rate pending determination of the claim) unless they can
demonstrate either a significant deterioration in their health condition or that a new
health condition has developed.

Paragraphs (1), (2)
If the conditions in para.(2) are met, this treats the claimant as having limited capa-   9.93
bility for work (thus grounding eligibility for ESA) until:

(a) the matter of actual capability is determined in accordance with the work
     capability assessment (LCWA) under reg.19 and Sch.2;

(b) it is decided whether some other "treated as having limited capability for
     work" regulation applies (e.g. person receiving certain regular treatment); or

(c) a decision is made that, as a sanction for non-compliance with information
     gathering or medical examination aspects of the assessment process under
     regs 22 and 23, he is to be treated as not having limited capability for work
     and thus disentitled to ESA (para.(1)).

Since the regulation only applies until the claimant has been "assessed", it
cannot apply where the claimant is immediately assessed (*CIB/1959/1997 and
CIB/2198/1997*, paras 28, 29).

Clearer analysis is afforded if one distinguishes between "a new claim" and a
"repeat claim".

The position in respect of a "new claim": by "new claim" is envisaged the situation
where there has never been a "determination" that the claimant does not have, or

cannot be treated as having, limited capability for work. For example, this is the first ever claim for ESA. In such a case this regulation applies to treat the claimant as having that limited capability, provided that the claimant continues to provide a doctor's statement in accordance with the Medical Evidence Regs (paras (1), (2) (a)). "Determination" here is not confined to one on ESA eligibility but encompasses one on entitlement to any benefit, allowance or advantage dependent on the claimant having limited capability for work (para.(2)(b)).

9.94   *The position in respect of a "repeat claim":*   by "repeat claim is here envisaged a situation in which there has been a previous "determination" that the claimant does not have limited capability for work, or was treated as not having such limited capability because of non-compliance with the medical examination aspect of assessment. On such a claim, the claimant can only be treated as having limited capability for work under this regulation in two situations (paras (2)(b), (4)(a), (b)):-

   (i)   if suffering from some specific disease or bodily or mental disablement from which he was not suffering at the time of that "determination" (a "new health condition"); or

   (ii)   there has been significant worsening of the disease or bodily or mental disablement suffered at the time of that "determination".

Similarly, if within the six months prior to the ESA claim, there has been a determination that the claimant is to be treated as not having limited capability for work under reg.22 (in effect one thereby applying a sanction for non-compliance with information gathering aspect of the assessment process), the claimant can nonetheless be treated as having limited capability for work (i) if s/he has since provided the information requested (paras (2)(b), (4)); or (ii) if they have a "new health condition" or their existing condition has significantly worsened. In addition, the claimant treated as not having limited capability for work under reg. 22 who reclaims more than six months after that determination can again be treated as having limited capability for work pending assessment (para.(2)(b)(ii)).

The words "significantly worsened", as regards the claimant's condition, must be related to the limited capability for work assessment (LCWA), so that it will only have significantly worsened if it has done so to an extent that it is fair to assume the claimant would satisfy that test of limited capability for work if he were subjected to it (see *EI v SSWP (ESA)* [2016] UKUT 397 (AAC) at paragraphs 34-42). If there is actual evidence that he would fail to satisfy that test, the Secretary of State can proceed on the basis that the condition has not significantly worsened (*CIB/1959/1977* and *CIB/2198/1997*, para.30). See further *EI v SSWP (ESA)* [2016] UKUT 397 (AAC) at paras 34–42 (but query whether this applies in relation to the period from the date of the repeat claim to the date of the assessment). That decision is also noteworthy because of the detailed but obiter consideration of whether there should be a right of appeal regarding whether a person's consideration has "significantly worsened" (see at paras 43–59). For the approach of decision-makers, see *Memo DMG 10/15*, paras 24–28.

On "specific disease or bodily or mental disablement", see commentary to reg.19.

Those making a "repeat claim" who do not satisfy these conditions will not be treated as having limited capability for work pending assessment, and will thus not be entitled to ESA. Instead, if they wish to obtain a benefit they would have to resort to JSA (paid at the same rate as the assessment rate in ESA) and be subject to the JSA conditionality regime. The Government was not prepared to accept the SSAC's recommendation that, in such cases, claimants "should be offered back to work support on a voluntary basis but exempted from conditionality beyond attendance at a work-focused interview". The Government took the view that the recently introduced "extended period of sickness" changes and the flexibility of availability and actively seeking work rules afforded sufficient protection.

Paragraph (3): Continued entitlement to ESA pending appeal

This para, when read with paras (2) and (4), has the effect that the supply of medical **9.95** certificates will ground continued ESA entitlement pending an appeal against a "relevant decision", as defined in para.(5). This covers only appeals against the first ever decision that the claimant does not have limited capability for work, either in the context of a decision on a wholly new claim or on an ongoing claim where previous determinations (whether by the Secretary of State or an appellate authority) had found limited capability for work. In such cases, no claim is required (see Claims and Payments Regs 1987, reg.3(1)(l)) and ESA Regs. 2008, reg.147A applies.

Where, however, one is dealing with a "repeat claim", the position is different. By "repeat claim is here envisaged a situation in which there *has been* a previous "determination" that the claimant does not have limited capability for work, or was treated as not having such limited capability. Where the claimant appeals in such a case, para. (3) does not operate to disapply para. (2)(b) since this appeal is not one against a "relevant decision", and the condition for continued entitlement in para.(2) cannot be met. For the approach of decision-makers, see *Memo DMG 10/15*, paras 31–35. The intention of this as the DWP explained in the *Explanatory Memorandum* to the amending Regs, is

"to align ESA with what happens for all other social security benefits where if a claimant is found not to be entitled, no benefit is paid whilst awaiting the outcome of the appeal. We believe this is reasonable because in their previous claim, the claimant will have had the opportunity to appeal to a tribunal if they disagreed with the decision. Claimants will instead be signposted to JSA as it is the appropriate benefit for someone who has been found fit for work. JSA provides claimants with personalised support to return to work taking into account their health condition or disability. It is acknowledged that not all ESA claimants will be eligible for JSA because they may not meet the conditions of entitlement" (para.7.5).

Claimant who claims jobseeker's allowance to be treated as not having limited capability for work

31. [¹ *Revoked.*]   **9.96**

Certain claimants to be treated as not having limited capability for work

32. [¹(1)] A claimant [²who is or has been a member of Her Majesty's **9.97** Forces] is to be treated as not having limited capability for work on any day which is recorded by the Secretary of State [⁴. . .] as a day of sickness absence from duty.

[³(2) A claimant is to be treated as not having limited capability for work on any day on which the claimant attends a training course in respect of which the claimant is paid a training allowance or premium pursuant to arrangements made under section 2 of the Employment and Training Act 1973 or section 2(3) of the Enterprise and New Towns (Scotland) Act 1990.

(3) Paragraph (2) is not to apply—

(a) for the purposes of any claim to employment and support allowance for a period commencing after the claimant ceased attending the training course in question; or

(b) where any training allowance or premium paid to the claimant is paid for the sole purpose of travelling or meal expenses incurred or to be incurred under the arrangement made under section 2 of the Employment and Training Act 1973 or section 2(3) of the Enterprise and New Towns (Scotland) Act 1990.]

AMENDMENTS

1. Employment and Support Allowance (Miscellaneous Amendments) Regulations 2008 (SI 2008/2428) reg.5(2)(a) (October 27, 2008).
2. Employment and Support Allowance (Miscellaneous Amendments) Regulations 2008 (SI 2008/2428) reg.5(2)(b) (October 27, 2008).
3. Employment and Support Allowance (Miscellaneous Amendments) Regulations 2008 (SI 2008/2428) reg.5(2)(c) (October 27, 2008).
4. Social Security (Miscellaneous Amendments) (No.3) Regulations 2013 (SI 2013/2536) reg.13(15) (October 29, 2013).

DEFINITIONS

"claimant"—see WRA 2007 s.24(1).
"limited capability for work"—see WRA 2007 s.1(4).

GENERAL NOTE

Paragraph (1)

9.98   This draws a boundary between ESA and the sickness payment scheme operated by the Ministry of Defence. Days recorded by the Secretary of State as ones of sickness absence from duty are to be treated for ESA purposes as ones on which the person concerned does not have limited capability for work.

[¹Claimants to be treated as not having limited capability for work at the end of the period covered by medical evidence

9.99   **32A.** [²(1)] Where the Secretary of State is satisfied that it is appropriate in the circumstances of the case [³ . . .] a claimant may be treated as not having limited capability for work if—
(a) the claimant has supplied medical evidence [² . . .];
(b) the period for which medical evidence was supplied has ended;
(c) the Secretary of State has requested further medical evidence; and
(d) the claimant has not, before whichever is the later of either the end of the period of 6 weeks beginning with the date of the Secretary of State's request or the end of 6 weeks beginning with the day after the end of the period for which medical evidence was supplied—
(i) supplied further medical evidence, or
(ii) otherwise made contact with the Secretary of State to indicate that they wish to have the question of limited capability for work determined.]

[²(2) In this regulation "medical evidence" means evidence provided under regulation 2 or 5 of the Medical Evidence Regulations.]

AMENDMENTS

1. Social Security (Miscellaneous Amendments) (No. 3) Regulations 2010 (SI 2010/840) reg.9(9) (June 28, 2010).
2. Social Security (Miscellaneous Amendments) Regulations 2011 (SI 2011/674) reg.16(4) (April 11, 2011).

3. Social Security (Miscellaneous Amendments) (No.3) Regulations 2013 (SI 2013/2536) reg.13(16) (October 29, 2013).

Additional circumstances where claimants are to be treated as having limited capability for work

33.—(1) For the purposes of paragraph 4(1)(d)(ii) of Schedule 1 to the Act, a claimant is to be treated as having limited capability for work on any day in respect of which that claimant is entitled to statutory sick pay.

(2) For the purposes of an income-related allowance, a claimant is to be treated as having limited capability for work where—

(a) that claimant is not a qualifying young person;

(b) that claimant is receiving education; and

(c) paragraph 6(1)(g) of Schedule 1 to the Act does not apply in accordance with regulation 18.

9.100

DEFINITIONS

"claimant"—see WRA 2007 s.24(1).
"income-related allowance"—see WRA 2007 s.1(7).
"limited capability for work"—see WRA 2007 s.1(4).
"qualifying young person"—see reg.2(1).

GENERAL NOTE

Paragraph (1)
Like WRA 2007, s.20(1), this regulation deals with the relationship between ESA and employer paid statutory sick pay (SSP). Days of entitlement to SSP cannot rank as ones of entitlement to ESA. However, para.(1) of this regulation stipulates that such days are to be treated as ones of limited capability for work for the purposes of computing the 196 consecutive days of limited capability for work essential if someone is to qualify through the "condition relating to youth route" to CESA (WRA 2007, Sch.1, para.4(1)(d)(ii)). Being so treated confers no exemption from the information gathering requirements in reg.21 (see para.(3) of that regulation).

9.101

Paragraph (2)
This deals only with IRESA. It treats certain disabled students as having limited capability for work. It covers someone receiving education (sub-para.(b)) but not debarred from IRESA on account of that because he is receiving PIP, DLA or armed forces independence payment (sub-para.(c) [WRA 2007, Sch.1, para.6(1)(g) disapplied by reg.18]). If this person is not a qualifying young person, he is to be treated as having limited capability for work. A qualifying young person bears the same meaning as in SSCBA 1992, s.142 (see reg.2(1)): someone aged 16–19 inclusive undergoing a full-time course of non-advanced education or approved training which commenced before he attained 19 (see Child Benefit Regs, reg.3). See also *MW v SSWP (ESA)* [2018] UKUT 304 (AAC), confirming that although there is a general entitlement condition that a claimant "is not receiving education" (see Welfare Reform Act 2007, Sch.1, para. 6(1)(g) this is disapplied to a claimant entitled to PIP, DLA or armed forces independence payment by virtue of reg.18.

Being treated as having limited capability for work in this way confers exemption from the information gathering requirements in reg.21 (see para.(3) of that regulation).

9.102

PART 6

LIMITED CAPABILITY FOR WORK-RELATED ACTIVITY

Determination of limited capability for work-related activity

9.103   **34.**—(1) For the purposes of Part 1 of the Act, where, by reason of a claimant's physical or mental condition, at least one of the descriptors set out in Schedule 3 applies to the claimant, the [² claimant has limited] capability for work-related activity [² . . .] and the limitation [² must] be such that it is not reasonable to require that claimant to undertake such activity.

(2) A descriptor applies to a claimant if that descriptor applies to the claimant for the majority of the time or, as the case may be, on the majority of the occasions on which the claimant undertakes or attempts to undertake the activity described by that descriptor.

[¹(3) In determining whether a descriptor applies to the claimant, the claimant is to be assessed as if—

(a) the claimant were fitted with or wearing any prosthesis with which the claimant is normally fitted or normally wears; or, as the case may be,

(b) wearing or using any aid or appliance which is normally, or could reasonably be expected to be, worn or used.]

(3A) [² *Omitted.*]

(4) Where a determination has been made about whether a claimant—

(a) has limited capability for work-related activity;

(b) is to be treated as having limited capability for work-related activity; or

(c) is to be treated as not having limited capability for work-related activity,

the Secretary of State may, if paragraph (5) applies, determine afresh whether the claimant has or is to be treated as having limited capability for work-related activity.

(5) This paragraph applies where—

(a) the Secretary of State wishes to determine whether there has been a relevant change of circumstances in relation to the claimant's physical or mental condition;

(b) the Secretary of State wishes to determine whether the previous determination about limited capability for work-related activity or about treating the claimant as having or as not having limited capability for work-related activity, was made in ignorance of, or was based on a mistake as to, some material fact; or

(c) at least 3 months have passed since the date of the previous determination about limited capability for work-related activity or about treating the claimant as having or as not having limited capability for work-related activity.

[²(6) In assessing the extent of a claimant's capability to perform any activity listed in Schedule 3, it is a condition that the claimant's incapability to perform the action arises—

(a) in respect of descriptors 1 to 8, 15(a), 15(b), 16(a) and 16(b)—

(i) from a specific bodily disease or disablement; or

(ii) as a direct result of treatment provided by a registered medical practitioner for a specific physical disease or disablement; or

(b) in respect of descriptors 9 to 14, 15(c), 15(d), 16(c) and 16(d)—

(i) from a specific mental illness or disablement; or

(ii) as a direct result of treatment provided by a registered medical practitioner for a specific mental illness or disablement.]

AMENDMENTS

1. Employment and Support Allowance (Amendment) Regulations 2012 (SI 2012/3096) reg.4(2) (January 28, 2013, subject to application, transitional and savings provisions in reg.2 of this amending instrument, below, para.9.554).

2. Social Security (Miscellaneous Amendments) (No.3) Regulations 2013 (SI 2013/2536) reg.13(17) (October 29, 2013).

DEFINITIONS

"the Act"—see reg.2(1).
"claimant"—see WRA 2007 s.24(1).
"descriptor"—see reg.2(1).
"limited capability for work-related activity"—see WRA 2007 s.2(5).
"work-related activity"—see WRA 2007 ss.24(1), 13(7).

GENERAL NOTE

Establishing limited capability for work is the central condition governing entitlement to ESA. Establishing limited capacity for work related activity is, in contrast, the core condition of entitlement to support component, the more generous of the two components (support or work-related activity) only one of which can be added to ESA basic allowance. This regulation, read with WRA 2007, s.9 and Sch.3 to these Regs, sets out how limited capacity for work related activity is assessed and determined.

9.104

The assumption behind ESA is that the vast majority of claimants, if given the right support, are in fact capable of some work. Government anticipated that only some 10 per cent of claimants (those with more severe health conditions) will be entitled to the support allowance and so not be subject to work-related activity conditionality requirements (DWP, *Employment and Support Allowance Regulations 2008: Equality Impact Assessment* in *Explanatory Memorandum to Employment and Support Allowance Regulations 2008 (SI 2008/794)* and the *Employment and Support Allowance (Transitional Provisions) Regulations 2008 (SI 2008/795)*, p.19). Recent statistics indicate, however, that some 27 per cent of new claimants are put into the support group (DWP Press Release, April 24, 2012: see *http://www.dwp.gov.uk/newsroom/press-releases/2012/apr-2012/dwp042-12.shtml*). Entry to this protected support group depends on it being established—generally through a work-related activity assessment (WRAAt) of a more stringent nature than the WCAt—that the claimant has limited capacity for work related activity. The WRAAt is the second element in the new Work Capability Assessment (WCA) which will eventually replace the IB PCA. Establishing limited capability for work related activity is based on someone demonstrating that they have a severe level of functional limitation. This is established when by reason of the claimant's physical or mental condition, at least one of the ranges of descriptors in Sch.3 applies to the claimant (WRA 2007, s.9; para.(1)).

There is no scoring system (it is a matter of the descriptor being applicable that counts) and the criteria are deliberately more stringent than in the WCAt:

"The levels of functional limitation used in the descriptors for determining limited capability for work-related activity are greater because we intend to place in the support group only the minority of customers who are so severely impaired that it would not be reasonable to require them to undertake work-related activity . . . People with less severe functional limitations across a range of descriptors might score highly and be inappropriately included in the support group when they might benefit from work-related activity. . . . A number of case studies were provided in the background information, which hon. Members will find helpful [see DWP, *Welfare Reform Bill: Draft Regulations and Supporting Material* (January 2007), pp.13–17]. Under the revised PCA, someone with a moderate learning disability would score 50 points. They would be significantly above the 15-point threshold, but we clearly would not wish to put even someone with 50 points into the support group automatically, because we are determined to ensure that the new system does not write off people with learning disabilities. The technical groups considered all the options. A crude points-based system would have unintended consequences." (*Hansard*, Standing Committee A, October 19, 2006 (afternoon), col.120 (Mr Jim Murphy MP, Minister for Employment and Welfare Reform)).

Paragraph (2)

9.105   Paragraph (2) makes clear (as indeed does the expected transposition to the WRAAt of central elements in existing case law on approaching the PCA) that a descriptor applies to a claimant if it applies to him for the majority of the time or, as the case may be, on the majority of the occasions on which he undertakes or attempts to undertake the relevant activity. Moreover, as is the case with the IB PCA and the ESA WCAt, in matching claimant to descriptor, the claimant is to be assessed as if fitted with or wearing any prosthesis with which the claimant is normally fitted or normally wears; or wearing or using any aid or appliance which is normally, or could reasonably be expected to be, worn or used (para.(3), and see commentary to reg.19(4)). The interrelationship of para.(2) with descriptors in Sch.3 deploying differing wording on periodicity ("at least once a week" [activity/ descriptor 8], "always" [activity/descriptor 13], "on a daily basis" [activity/descriptor 14],) has been explored in a number of cases.

In *KB* v *SSWP (ESA)* [2013] UKUT 152 (AAC), Judge Parker considered the relationship between this wording (the requisite of "always") and the stipulation in reg.34(2) that "a descriptor applies to a claimant if that descriptor applies to the claimant for the majority of the time or, as the case may be, on the majority of the occasions on which the claimant undertakes or attempts to undertake the activity described by that descriptor". Having looked at definitions of "always" in the Concise Oxford Dictionary, Judge Parker concluded that neither this activity and descriptor, nor its counterpart in Activity 16 of Sch.2 set out an "all or nothing test". Rather "always" here "means 'repeatedly' or 'persistent' or 'often':

> "A 'majority' may be constituted by events which happen only on 50.1 per cent of the possible occasions, but a greater frequency is required by the use of the word 'always'. It is a question of degree, but a fact finding tribunal is eminently suited to applying these subtle nuances of difference in a common sense way. It suffices to say in the present case, that because a claimant attends one tribunal hearing, and his GP accepts that he comes to the surgery very occasionally, does not necessarily entail the conclusion, as the tribunal clearly considered that it did, that it 'cannot be said that engagement in social contact is always precluded'" (para.14).

Judge Fordham took much the same approach in *CH* v *SSWP (ESA)* [2013] UKUT 207 (AAC) (para.8).

In *LM* v *SSWP (ESA)* [2013] UKUT 552 (AAC) (see update to p. 1076), however, Judge Mark agreed that "always" meant repeatedly or "persistent" but considered it did not mean "often" or "for the majority of the time".

In *WT* v *SSWP (ESA)* [2013] UKUT 556 (AAC), Judge Ward was more definitive than Judge Parker on the relationship between reg.34(2) and activity/descriptor 14, stating that "the terminology of the descriptor in question excludes the application of regulation 34 (2), in that it cannot apply to qualify the meaning of the words "on a daily basis" to mean "the majority of the time" or, "on the majority of occasions that the claimant undertakes or tries to undertake the activity", which would in logic lead to satisfaction of the test if it was satisfied on more than half of the days or attempts. That would drive a coach and horses through the descriptor, rendering the inclusion of any reference to the word "daily" pointless. That cannot be what was intended. Regulation 34(2) does not apply to a schedule 3 descriptor where the "majority of the time" approach would be inconsistent with the actual wording of the descriptor" (para.36).

Judge Parker's decision was appealed to the Court of Session. In *SSWP v Brade* [2014] CSIH 39 XA81/13 (May 1, 2014); [2014] AACR 29, the Court held that the wording cannot have been intended to mean "always" in the sense of the claimant never, at any time, whatever the circumstances, being able to engage in "social contact " (para. 35). Instead, the provision required a purposive construction:

"descriptor 13 must apply if a claimant suffers from a mental disorder which has the consequence that, for the majority of the time, he cannot engage in social contact. That construction properly embraces regulation 34(1), 34(2) and the terms of descriptor 13 and accords with their evident intention. Such a person is not likely to have labour market potential and, moreover, if, for the majority of the time, that person cannot engage in social contact, requiring participation in the work focused interview would be not only unreasonable but pointless. Further, that construction avoids the fact finder being necessarily driven to the absurd conclusion that descriptor 13 is not satisfied if, for instance, on a single occasion, a claimant has given instructions to a representative for the purposes of a tribunal hearing. The question of whether or not a person is wholly precluded from engagement in social contact for the majority of the time is one of fact having regard to the statutory provisions as understood by the guidance we have sought to provide. That question is not answered by the application of any precise mathematical approach but by the fact finding tribunal having regard to the evidence in the particular case of the effects of the claimant's condition in a realistic way whilst bearing in mind the purpose of the legisation" (para.37).

Activities in Sch.3

There are now 16 activities in Sch.3: mobilising unaided; transferring from one seated position to another; reaching; picking up and moving or transferring; manual dexterity; making self understood; understanding communication; absence or loss of control leading to extensive evacuation of the bowel and/or voiding of the bladder; learning tasks; awareness of hazard; initiating and completing personal action; coping with change; coping with social engagement; appropriateness of behaviour; conveying food or drink to the mouth; chewing or swallowing food or drink. The terms of the descriptors are also more stringent than in the WCAt, to avoid removing too many people from the group which affords incentive to engage in work-related activity and thus denying them the opportunity to take steps to make real their fundamental right to work. Thus, as regards walking, the single descriptor can only be met where a claimant cannot "mobilise" more than 50 metres on level ground without stopping to avoid significant discomfort or exhaustion (or cannot "repeatedly mobilise 50 metres...(etc)"). Most, with counterparts in the WCAt, are couched in terms equivalent to the more difficult of their 15 point descriptors. With effect from January 28, 2013, in deciding which descriptor applies, incapability must arise in respect of descriptors 1 to 8, 15(a), 15(b), 16(a) and 16 (b), from a specific bodily disease or disablement or as a direct result of treatment provided by a registered medical practitioner for such a disease or disablement (para.(3A) (a), (c)(i)). Similarly, as regards descriptors 9 to 14, 15(c), 15(d), 16(c) and 16 (d), incapability must arise from a specific mental illness or disablement; or as a direct result of treatment provided by a registered medical practitioner for such an illness or disablement (para.(3A)(b), (c)(i)). Note that for some cases after January 28, 2013, for a six month period, the previous version of reg.34 can be applicable (see reg.2 of the amending instrument, below, para.9.554).

Those meeting the WRAAt test will be placed in the support group and receive support component without having to satisfy work-related activity conditions, although they can voluntarily participate in those programmes. Their position can be reviewed periodically or where there has been a change of circumstances in the claimant's physical or mental condition or it is thought that a previous determina-

9.106

tion was made in ignorance of or a mistake as to some material fact (paras (4), (5)) The threshold for membership of the support group is high; CPAG consider that "many claimants in receipt of the middle and higher rates of Disability Living Allowance (DLA) may not meet the eligibility criteria". Those who fail to establish limited capability for work-related activity will instead be in the work-related activity group, which has stringent conditions attached in terms of appropriate behaviour (participation in work focussed health related assessments, work focused interviews and, eventually, specified work-related activity (see regs 47–60), involving the private and voluntary sector as well as JobCentre Plus).

Certain claimants to be treated as having limited capability for work-related activity

9.107   **35.**—(1) A claimant is to be treated as having limited capability for work-related activity if—

(a) the claimant is terminally ill;

[¹(b) the claimant is—

(i) receiving treatment for cancer by way of chemotherapy or radiotherapy;

(ii) likely to receive such treatment within six months after the date of the determination of capability for work-related activity; or

(iii) recovering from such treatment,

and the Secretary of State is satisfied that the claimant should be treated as having limited capability for work-related activity; or]

(c) in the case of a woman, she is pregnant and there is a serious risk of damage to her health or to the health of her unborn child if she does not refrain from work-related activity.

(2) A claimant who does not have limited capability for work-related activity as determined in accordance with regulation 34(1) is to be treated as having limited capability for work-related activity if—

(a) the claimant suffers from some specific disease or bodily or mental disablement; and

(b) by reasons of such disease or disablement, there would be a substantial risk to the mental or physical health of any person if the claimant were found not to have limited capability for work-related activity.

AMENDMENT

1. Employment and Support Allowance (Amendment) Regulations 2012 (SI 2012/3096) reg.4(3) (January 28, 2013, subject to application, transitional and savings provisions in reg.2 of this amending instrument, below, para.9.554).

DEFINITIONS

"claimant"—see WRA 2007 s.24(1).
"limited capability for work-related activity"—see WRA 2007 s.2(5).
"terminally ill"—see reg.2(1).
"work-related activity"—see WRA 2007 ss.24(1), 13(7).

GENERAL NOTE

Paragraph (1)

9.108   This has affinities with reg.20 (treating someone as having limited capability for work). Regulation 35 (1) treats someone as having limited capability for work-related activity but the range of groups so treated is much narrower. The terminally ill (para.(1)(a)) and those undergoing or (as amended from March 28, 2011) likely to undergo within six months, or recovering from chemotherapy (para.(1)(b)) are so treated, as is a pregnant woman where there is a serious risk of damage to her health or that of her unborn child if she does not refrain from work-related activity (para. (1)(c). Unlike reg.20 there is no protection for other pregnant women or for those receiving hospital treatment or certain regular treatments such as dialysis.

Paragraph (2)

This is a partial equivalent of the "exceptional circumstances" provision (reg.29) applicable to the limited capability for work question, considered above. *A claimant who does not pass the LCWRA* can nonetheless be treated as having the requisite limited capability for work-related activity grounding membership of the support group where, by reasons of the specific disease or bodily or mental disablement from which s/he suffers, "there would be a substantial risk to the mental or physical health of any person if the claimant were found not to have limited capability for work-related activity". Given the structure of the ESA legislative scheme, it is axiomatic that reg.35(2) can only come into play where the claimant has been found to have limited capability for work (either under the LCWA scoring 15 or more in terms of Sch.2 descriptors or through the operation of reg.29) and has also failed to satisfy any of the Sch.3 descriptors, thus being found not to have limited capability for work-related activity (*LH v SSWP (ESA)* [2015] UKUT 154 (AAC)). In such a case, reg.35(2) becomes that claimant's last hope of being placed in the support group by being treated as having limited capability for work-related activity. On "specific disease or bodily or mental disablement", see commentary to reg.19(2). **9.109**

For an extreme example of reg.35(2) being found to apply, see *JL v SSWP (ESA)* [2018] UKUT 346 (AAC). The claimant had previously been placed in the support group. The evidence of two ESA medical assessments and the claimant's own GP showed that the claimant's blood pressure was indisputably high and uncontrolled. Moreover, the DWP's own guidance to decision-makers (Memo DMG 17/15, paragraph 25(3)) gives the example of a claimant with hypertension which is uncontrolled despite medication as an instance of "immediate substantial risk" in the context of reg.35(2). The FTT's decision (upholding the conclusion that reg.35(2) did not apply, despite the HCP terminating the assessment and advising the claimant to attend A&E forthwith) was set aside for inadequate reasoning and the decision re-made.

On "substantial risk to the mental or physical health of any person if the claimant were found not to have limited capability for work-related activity", see the commentary to reg.29, but note that there is in reg.35(2) no statutory counterpart to the modification effected by reg.29(3) (medication and reasonable adjustments to the claimant's workplace). As with reg. 29(2)(b), the key case is *Charlton v Secretary of State for Work and Pensions* [2009] EWCA Civ. 42.

The application of Charlton *to reg.35(2)*: in *AH v SSWP (ESA)* [2013] UKUT 118 (AAC); [2013] AACR 32 Judge Jacobs considered how (if at all) the approach in *Charlton* on the predecessor of reg.29 should be applied to the differently worded context of reg.35 dealing as it does not with "work" but "work-related activity". He thought the Court of Appeal's conclusion on reg.29(2)(b) equally applicable to reg.35(2) so that the paragraph applies both to the effect of work-related activity and not just to the effect of being found capable of it; so that it applies (i) not only to the immediate effects of the decision on capability, but (ii) to the consequences of having to undertake work-related activity and (iii) to having to travel to and from it. Translating the Court's language on the range of work to be contemplated to fit this analogous context of "work-related activity" means that the **9.110**

"decision-maker must assess the range or type of work-related activity which a claimant is capable of performing and might be expected to undertake sufficiently to assess the risk to health either to himself or to others" (para.26).

The Secretary of State ought in such cases to provide some evidence of the range of "work- related activity" in contemplation. The tribunal should then assess that in light of evidence on the claimant's conditions and limitations for it. It would need to be able to consider, for example, what type of adjustments might be reasonable in the claimant's case, and what type of support the Advisor might provide (para.32). *KB v SSWP (ESA)* [2013] UKUT 152 (AAC) also took this approach to the applicability of *Charlton* reasoning to para.(2):

> "it is necessary, under regulation 35, to make the evaluation of substantial risk, not just an exercise limited to the ability to cope with the work related interview at the Job Centre, but also "in the context of the journey to or from" such an interview. This point has particular relevance to a claimant arguing under activity 13 of Schedule 3. The tribunal therefore went wrong in applying too narrow a statutory test, saying only "he should be able to cope with a work related interview at the Jobcentre" (para.18).

In *MN v SSWP (ESA)* [2013] UKUT 262 (AAC); [2014] AACR 6, Judge Wright endorsed Judge Jacobs's point in *AH* on the Secretary of State and evidence, but added two slight caveats. First, it might be enough in most cases to give a general indication of what is involved in work-related activity. Secondly, where the claimant's grounds of appeal specifically raise reg.35(2), r.24(2)(e) of the Tribunal Procedure Rules mandates the Secretary of State to say whether he opposed the appellant's case on reg.35(2) and state "any grounds for such opposition which are not set out in documents which are before the Tribunal" (paras 16, 17).

In *ML v SSWP (ESA)* [2013] UKUT 174 (AAC); [2013] AACR 33, a follow-up decision to *AH*, Judge Jacobs stressed the need for the Secretary of State to go beyond general formulaic statements to make effective the statutory right of appeal by providing the necessary information to enable claimants to participate in the appeal and the tribunal to make a decision" (para.15). He also considered the relationship between regs 29 and 35. He accepted that a paragraph in the DWP, Medical Services Handbook for ESA was merely guidance but also incorrect in stating that someone found to be "at substantial risk for work" would be extremely unlikely to be found not to be at "substantial risk for work-related activity". Instead Judge Jacobs stated that it all depends on the precise circumstances of each case:

> "Regulations 29 and 35 use similar wording, but they do so for different purposes. The claimant's condition is a constant for both provisions. But the activities to which the provisions apply differ. The former is concerned with the risk of work; the latter is concerned with the risk of work-related activity. There is no reason why the former should automatically be determinative of the latter. This will depend on: (i) the nature of the claimant's condition; (ii) its effects; and (iii) the nature of the work-related activity. It may be that the condition will give rise to the same risk whether the claimant undertakes work or work-related activity. Or it may give rise to different risks. Or it may give rise to risk in respect of one but not the other" (para.14).

9.111   *What evidence of work-related activity must be provided by the Secretary of State and what can a tribunal do where no such evidence is supplied?*   How to deal with the practical difficulties posed for tribunals by the decisions in *AH*, *MN* and *ML* produced divergent views from Upper Tribunal judges (see *AK v SSWP (ESA)* [2013] UKUT 435 (AAC); *MT v SSWP (ESA)* [2013] UKUT 545 (AAC); *DH v SSWP (ESA)* [2013] UKUT (ESA) 573 (AAC); *HS v SSWP (ESA)* [2013] UKUT 591 (AAC); *AP v SSWP (ESA)* [2014] UKUT 35 (AAC); *AP v SSWP (ESA)* [2013] UKUT 553 (AAC); *PF v SSWP (ESA)* [2013] UKUT 634 (AAC); and *NA v SSWP (ESA)* [2014] UKUT 305 (AAC)). Those difficulties relate to avoiding the need for adjournments clogging up the adjudication system in a context in which the decision appealed against will have been made *before* the claimant has had an initial consultation with an adviser on appropriate work-related activity and in which there is generally no representative of the Secretary of State present at First-tier tribunals to be questioned as to what activity might be appropriate. In *NA*, Judge Gray depre-cated the Secretary of State's failure to provide sufficient information to the tribunal; had the "action plan" seen by Judge Gray on appeal, and which predated the hearing before the First-tier tribunal, been made available to that tribunal the further appeal to the Upper Tribunal might well have been avoided (presumably because that tri-bunal would then have applied the regulation in the claimant's favour).

Fortunately, this divisive issue has now been dealt with authoritatively by a panel of three Upper Tribunal judges. In *IM v SSWP (ESA)* [2014] UKUT 412 (AAC); [2015] AACR 10, the panel dealt with the question of "the amount of detail the regulation 35(2) decision-makers should have of the possible results of the work-focused interview" to which those found not to be incapable of work-related activity will be subject.

The panel considered that the problem with decision-making on reg.35(2) arises because at the stage the decision maker (Secretary of State or First-tier tribunal) has to decide the matter of "substantial risk" exactly what will be required of this particular claimant at any such work-focused interview is unknown, a matter of conjecture, and the decision-maker must perforce engage in a degree of "crystal ball gazing" (para.75), with "substantial risk" bearing the commonly agreed meaning of a risk "that cannot sensibly be ignored having regard to the nature and gravity of the feared harm in the particular case" (para.65).

Having considered the range of case law on the provision noted above, the panel rightly held that a purposive approach, reflecting practicalities apparent in *Charlton*, must be taken to the regulation (para.83). In the view of the panel,

> "the absence of any system for ensuring that relevant information obtained, and findings made, in the course of carrying out a work capability assessment and applying regulation 35(2) and the reasoning behind the decision made on regu-lation 35(2) are made available to a person considering whether a requirement to engage in work-related activity should be imposed on the claimant effectively destroys the Secretary of State's argument that only generalised information about some types of work-related activity need be taken into account by the regulation 35(2) decision-maker when considering the possible consequences of a particular claimant being found not to have limited capability for work-related activity. The purpose underlying regulation 35(2) requires that those applying it make predictions about the consequences to the particular claimant of him being found not to have limited capability for work-related activity. In a few cases, the risks of an inappropriate requirement to engage in work-related activity being imposed will be too great to be ignored" (para.101).

Given the present system of administering the legislation, the First-tier tribunal needs to know

> "not only what the least demanding types of work-related activity are but also what the most demanding types are in the area where the claimant lives.
> . . . .
> [O]n an appeal in which regulation 35(2) is in issue, [the Secretary of State] cannot be expected to anticipate exactly what work-related activity a particular claimant would in fact be required to do. This is axiomatic.
> But what the Secretary of State can and should provide is evidence of the types of work-related activity available in each area [Wolverhampton in this claimant's case] and by reference thereto what the particular claimant may be required to undertake and those which he considers it would be reasonable for the provider to require the claimant to undertake. The First-tier Tribunal would then be in a position to assess the relevant risks.
> [T]he types of work-related activity available may vary from provider to provider,

but it should not be beyond the wit of the Department and providers to produce and maintain a list, perhaps for each of the regions into which the First-tier Tribunal is organised, of what is available in each area within the region. The relevant information could then be included in submissions in individual cases. The First-tier Tribunal would be able to assess the evidential force of such a submission.
. . .
Being unable to carry out an activity does not necessarily imply that there will be a substantial risk to anyone's health if the claimant is required to engage in the activity. Nor does the risk of being sanctioned. Therefore, it may be fairly obvious in most cases that the claimant does not have any realistic argument under regulation 35 and indeed, if made aware of the issues, the claimant may often accept that that is so. But where there turns out to be a serious argument in relation to regulation 35, the provision of the basic information about the more demanding types of work-related activity would enable the First-tier Tribunal to make the necessary predictions by reference to possible outcomes for the particular claimant" (paras.104-107, 110).

The panel considered that where the Secretary of State has accepted that the claimant has limited capability for work, the Secretary of State will be able to aid the tribunal with a more focused submission on why, given the claimant's disablement, reg. 35(2) does not apply. It noted that in some cases (see e.g. *CMcC v SSWP (ESA)* [2014] UKUT 176 (AAC); [2015] AACR 9) the work-focused interview will have taken place before the tribunal hears the appeal and its outcome and basis should be provided to it where possible, thereby reducing the element of prediction required, but always remembering that, because of SSA 1998 s.12(8)(b) any such evidence "should only be taken into account so far as it is relevant to the position at the time of the decision of the Secretary of State" (para.113).
The panel held that merely identifying that there is some work-related activity that a claimant could do is insufficient to ground a finding

"that there would not be risk to someone's health if the claimant were found not to have limited capability for work-related activity. That is because it does not wholly answer the statutory question" (para.116).

In *CL v SSWP (ESA)* [2015] UKUT 375 (AAC), Judge Jacobs considered it permissible to take into account work-related activity that the claimant could carry out at home (para.17).

9.112   *But what if the Secretary of State fails to provide the required evidence?* In such a case, the panel considered that the First-tier Tribunal has a number of options as to how to proceed. It can use its own knowledge, if it is confident that it is up-to-date and complete as to the more demanding types of work-related activity. It may instead adjourn to obtain that evidence or decide that it can properly determine the case one way or the other without it. The right approach depends on the circumstances and, in particular, on how vulnerable the claimant is (para. 118).
Interestingly, the panel also made clear that there were ways in which the reg.35(2) risk could be greatly reduced or even eliminated by a change of practice in the way in which the scheme is administered (paras 98-100). But, unless and until the scheme of decision-making and the legislation is changed the approach in *IM* must be followed (see *EH v SSWP (ESA)* [2014] UKUT 473 (AAC); *KW v SSWP (ESA)* [2015] UKUT 131 (AAC); *GB v SSWP (ESA)* [2015] UKUT 200 (AAC)). Problems of decision-making are likely to be exacerbated where the claimant is unlikely to be able to engage in social contact with the provider so as explain their difficulties (*IM, GB*).

9.113   Thus the decision of the three-judge panel in *IM* highlighted:

"that, because the results of work capability assessments are not routinely passed to providers who determine what work-related activity a claimant should be required to do, there may a risk of a provider requiring a person with, say, mental health problems to perform unsuitable work-related activity, due to the provider's ignorance of the those problems or their extent. This difficulty is liable to be exacerbated if, as in both *IM* and the present case, the claimant is, or is likely to be, unable to engage in social contact with the provider and so explain her difficulties herself" (see also *GB v SSWP (ESA)* [2015] UKUT 200 (AAC), *per* Judge Rowland).

This point was further emphasised by Judge Gray in *XT v SSWP (ESA)* [2015] UKUT 581 (AAC). There the First-tier Tribunal had decided that the appellant could undertake all likely work-related activities with the exception of work placements and work experience (because of her fragile mental health). The tribunal found she did not qualify for the support group, working on the assumption that its reservations would be communicated to the relevant provider of work-related activity. That assumption was misplaced in the light of *IM v SSWP (ESA)*. Judge Gray accordingly held the tribunal's decision to be in error of law; she went ahead to re-make the decision in the appellant's favour, explaining why there was a substantial risk within the terms of reg.35(2).

For another helpful example of a case in which the Upper Tribunal allowed the claimant's appeal and re-made the decision under reg.35, finding and explaining its reasoning as to why the claimant qualified on mental health grounds for the support group, see *SL v SSWP (ESA)* [2016] UKUT 170 (AAC). In that case Judge Sutherland Williams also approved of the DWP's guidance since *IM* (Memo ADM 7/16), which encourages decision makers to make better and more informed decisions in relation to reg.35 and LCRWA:

"80. I might go further. If the Secretary of State can provide a tribunal with the types of work-related activity available in each area after the DM's decision is made, then it does not appear to me to be overly onerous on the DWP to provide HCP's with similar information before the decision is made, assuming that is not happening already. The HCP should then be able to provide a more reasoned statement in relation to regulation 35(2) in appropriate cases; and in turn the decision-maker could make a more informed decision in terms of predicative risk or otherwise, without that function being essentially passed onto the FTT."

The DWP's guidance since *IM* (both in its original format in Memo DMG 17/15 and its subsequent form in Memo ADM 7/16) was critiqued in more detail in *KC and MC v SSWP (ESA)* [2017] UKUT 94 (AAC). Judge Wright expressed the opinion that the DWP guidance for the most part accurately reflected the ruling in *IM*, subject to two notable exceptions.

The first was the erroneous suggestion in Memo DMG 17/15 that *IM* does not require a list of the most and least demanding types of work-related activity to be produced in appeals against whether a claimant even has limited capability for work (see paragraphs 87-90).

The second was in relation to para.36 of Memo DMG 17/15, which stated that tribunals should be provided with "examples of the most and last demanding WRA which it is considered the claimant *could* undertake" (emphasis added) rather than the whole list. Judge Wright took the view that "might be required to" was a better form of words than "could", which elided the two-stage approach required by *IM*. The first stage was to compile a list of work related activities in a given area, identifying the most and least demanding activities. The second stage was to explain the range of such activities that the particular appellant was capable of doing and might have been expected to undertake (see paragraphs 111-114).

The decision in *KC and MC v SSWP (ESA)* is also significant for the light it sheds on the DWP's provision of work-related activity through the so-called 'Jobcentre Plus Offer', a process which remarkably had not been properly disclosed to, and clarified before, the three-judge panel in *IM*. It transpired that the key distinction was between work-related activity delivered via an external work programme provider and such activity organised internally through the Jobcentre Plus Offer. Between June 2011 and April 2013, if the claimant's reassessment was scheduled for more than 6 months, then the Jobcentre Plus Offer applied. In April 2013 the prognosis criterion for the Jobcentre Plus Offer to apply increased to 12 months. The detailed arrangements under this internal form of provision are explained in Judge Wright's decision (at para.48), which also noted that the Jobcentre Plus Offer applied to all contributory ESA claimants living elsewhere in the EU (see para.95). The 'information gap' identified by the three-judge panel in *IM* still existed, at least until September 2016 (para.102). Judge Wright criticised the fact that the Jobcentre Plus Offer appeared to be unknown to large parts of the DWP responsible for applying regulation 35(2) (para.103). The judge also criticised the deficiencies in external work provider lists (paragraphs 104-110) relating to regulation 35(2).

Proper application of reg.35(2) requires "a determination to be made as to *the extent to which* a person has met Schedule 2 [the LCWA] at the date of the decision under appeal as that informs the factors to be take into account in assessing the regulation 35(2) risk" (*KW v SSWP (ESA)* [2015] UKUT 131 (AAC), para.8 (Judge Wright), emphasis in the original).

The burgeoning case law on this regulation covers five more issues, dealt with in turn, below.

9.114   *Issue 1: how does reg.35(2) apply if the claimant could never work again or if there is no work-related activity that could reasonably be required of him?* Here Judge Mark and Judge Jacobs take diametrically opposed positions, the former arguing that in such circumstances the provision can have no application, the latter arguing that it can and must in order to protect the most vulnerable by affording them an opportunity to be placed in the support group in circumstances in which their condition has not met the tailored specifics of ESA Regs 2008, Sch. 3. It is submitted that Judge Jacobs' approach is the better one in that promotes the purpose behind reg.35(2) and thus sits better with the purposive approach taken to the provision by the panel in *IM*, above.

Both judges rightly see the position as involving consideration of the WRA 2007, the ESA Regs 2008 and the Employment and Support Allowance (Work-Related Activity) Regulations 2011 (SI 2011/1349) ("the W-RA Regs"). Both note the definition of "work-related activity" in WRA 2007, s.13(7): "activity which makes it more likely that the person will obtain or remain in work or be able to do so". Although s.13(8) was not in force at the date of the decisions concerned, both judges noted its stipulation that such activity "includes work experience or a work placement". Similarly both took on board, reg. 3 of the W-RA Regs (see para.9.590) giving the Secretary of State discretion on whether or not to require a person in the work-related activity group actually to undertake any such activity, and providing that any such requirement imposed "must be reasonable in the view of the Secretary of State, having regard to the person's circumstances", and may not require him/her to undergo medical treatment or to apply for a job or undertake work, whether as an employee or otherwise.

In *JS v SSWP (ESA)* [2013] UKUT 635 (AAC), followed by him in *RV v SSWP (ESA)* [2014] UKUT 56 (AAC), Judge Mark held that the initial work-focused interview cannot constitute work-related activity since work-related activities can only be required once it has taken place (para.16). Moreover, the work-focused health assessment was also separate from such activity being an assessment, dealt with separately, and not meeting the s.13(7) definition, above (para.16). Given that definition, he considered "that if a person is patently not going to be able to obtain work at any stage, it is difficult to see how they could be required to carry out work-related activities" (para.15). Accordingly in his judgment, in this case reg.35(2) could not assist this claimant:

"On the basis of the tribunal's finding as to his health problems, there would seem to be no real possibility of his resuming work and it is difficult to see how any interview could come within the definition of work-focused interview in section 12(7) of the 2007 Act since, due to his ill health, there would seem to be no prospect of his getting into work. For the same reason, there would not seem to be any work-related activity that the claimant could be required to do, in that, because of his health problems, there would be no activity which would make it even arguably more likely that he would be able to obtain work.

It follows that, on the basis of the tribunal's findings of fact, there are no work-focused interviews or work-related activities that the Secretary of State could lawfully require the claimant to attend or undertake and that, in the absence of any other issue, there is no risk to his health as a result of not being found to have limited capability for work-related activity. Accordingly he does not fall within regulation 35(2)." (paras 27–28).

Judge Mark reiterated this in *GS v SSWP (ESA)* [2014] UKUT 16 (AAC), para.26.

In marked contrast, in *NS v SSWP (ESA)* [2014] UKUT 149 (AAC), Judge Jacobs rejected this way of looking at reg.35(2). Nor, in that case, did the Secretary of State support Judge Mark's analysis. There, Ms Wilkinson, appearing for the Secretary of State, argued that his analysis could not be right because it would remove from the most vulnerable claimants "who will not work again and for whom any WRA [work-related activity] will pose a substantial risk to their health" their final chance of being placed in the support group, final, of course, because reg.35(2) can only be applied where the claimant was not regarded as having limited capability for work-related activity, applying reg.34(1) and Sch.3 (para.23). Her suggested approach, based on s.13(7) requiring only that the activity make it "more likely" that the claimant will be able to obtain work and the chance that circumstances might change (e.g. "through a new form of treatment or medication"), was not accepted by Judge Jacobs as enough to cover the claimant who would clearly never work again. The approach, he thought, required a tribunal to make contradictory findings and, viewed as a statement that there was *at present* no work the claimant could do, left unresolved the question of whether reg.35(2) applied for the time being (para.24). The provision had to be applied effectively, whether before or after consideration had been given to the sort of work-related activity appropriate for a claimant (para.25). For him, it was critical to see reg.35(2) as being a *hypothesis* requiring the identification of "the possible consequences of a particular postulate (the *if* bit)" (para.26). The flaw in Judge Mark's analysis was to ignore the postulate. Judge Jacobs explained further:

"If a possible consequence would be a substantial risk to health, the provision is satisfied and the claimant qualifies for the support group. As I have already said, the postulate cannot be read literally. The tribunal does not simply have to postulate the claimant being found not to have limited capability for work-related activity. It also has to postulate the claimant actually undertaking such activity.

It does not have to identify that activity with precision. That is a separate stage that will only be reached if the tribunal decides that the claimant does not qualify for the support group. If and when that stage is reached, it is a matter for the Secretary of State, not the tribunal. The tribunal's task is preliminary to and necessarily more speculative and more general than the actual application of regulation 3 of the 2011 Regulations. The tribunal has to apply the hypothesis embodied in regulation 35(2). In doing so, it cannot deny the postulate. That, with respect to Judge Mark, is what he did. He denied that the postulate (the *if* bit) could ever apply in certain circumstances. But that is the very foundation of the provision. It is what the tribunal is required to accept. It cannot reject the basis of the hypothesis that forms the structure of regulation 35(2).

In doing so, the tribunal has to limit itself to applying regulation 35(2) and avoid trespassing into the Secretary of State's decision-making under regulation 3 of the 2011 Regulations. . . . The way to remain properly within the tribunal's jurisdiction lies in the level of generality at which the tribunal has to consider work-related activity. Ms Wilkinson accepted that my decision in *AH* was correct.

What the tribunal has to do is to identify in a general way 'the range and type of work-related activity which a claimant is capable of performing and might be expected to undertake' (to quote *AH*); and it must do so regardless of whether the Secretary of State would actually require the claimant to undertake any activity and regardless of whether any such activity would have any effect on the claimant's ability to 'obtain or remain in work' (to quote section 13(7))" (paras 26-28).

Judge Jacobs, in effect, requires the tribunal to ignore what might be done under reg.3 of the W-RA Regs. Judge Ward calls this a "thought experiment" and in *KB v SSWP (ESA)* [2015] UKUT 179 (AAC) applied it to require to be ignored in the application of reg. 35(2) the fact that this claimant, a carer entitled to carer's allowance, could not lawfully under the W-RA Regs be required to undertake work-related activity. This approach chimes well with the answer given by the three-judge panel in *IM* to the question in Issue 2, which must now be examined

9.115   *Issue 2: given that reg. 3 of the Employment and Support Allowance (Work-Related Activity) Regulations 2011 (SI 2011/1349) ("the W-RA Regs") stipulates that the work-related activity required must be "reasonable ..., having regard to the person's circumstances", does this mean that the condition in reg.35(2) cannot be met?* In *IM v SSWP (ESA)* [2014] UKUT 412 (AAC); [2015] AACR 10), the panel of three Upper Tribunal judges answered this in the negative since an affirmative answer would undermine the purpose of the provision. In so deciding they endorsed the decisions on this point given by Judge Jacobs in *NS v SSWP (ESA)* [2014] UKUT 149 (AAC) (paras 30, 34) and Judge Bano in *CMcC v SSWP (ESA)* [2014] UKUT 176 (AAC); [2015] AACR 9. As Judge Bano put it (in a passage endorsed by Judge Jacobs as consonant with his own view in *NS*):

> "If regulation 35(2) is to have any real meaning, it is not open to a tribunal to find that work-related activity does not present a risk of harm to a claimant on the basis that the claimant will not actually be required to undertake *any* meaningful activity if it turns out to be harmful. I therefore consider that the action of the employment adviser of effectively bringing the claimant's action plan to an end out of concern for her health was evidence which the tribunal should have taken into account when evaluating the risk of harm to the claimant if she were not found to have limited capability for work-related activity" (para.12).

Judge Gray's decision in *YA and SA v SSWP (ESA)* [2017] UKUT 80 (AAC) is authority for two propositions in this context. First, the duty under s.26(6) of the Equality Act 2010 to make reasonable adjustments added nothing to the duty under regulation 3 of the W-RA Regs that the WRA activity is reasonable (paragraphs 49-53). Second, subject to safeguards, the WRA requirements made between the date of the decision under appeal and the FTT hearing may be considered. In particular, tribunals cannot simply assume that a claimant will not be required to undertake any more onerous types of WRA than those already stipulated (paragraphs 39-48).

Issue 3: the "substantial risk" must arise "by reasons of" a specific disease or bodily or mental disablement: in *DR v SSWP (ESA)* [2014] UKUT 188 (AAC); [2014] AACR 38, Judge May held erroneous in law a tribunal decision that the claimant satisfied reg.29 because it had not made the necessary connection between the risk and the disease or disablement (see para.3). He considered the same principle applied to reg.35 (para.10). Alcohol misuse in itself is not such a disablement. To rank as disablement the misuse of alcohol must rank as "alcohol dependency" in terms of the "constellation of markers" found in quotations from *R(DLA)* 6/06 in the Three-Judge Panel's decision in *JG v SSWP (ESA)* [2013] UKUT 37 (AAC); [2013] AACR 23 (see paras 5-7, 10 of *DR*). See further, commentary to reg.29(2)(b), above.

Issue 4: can the availability of third party assistance be taken into account? In *MT v*   **9.116**
SSWP (ESA) [2013] UKUT 545 (AAC), in the context of reg.35(2) Judge Gray
firmly rejected looking at capacity to perform activities with third party assistance,
observing:

> "I do need to deal however with the observation of the FTT in its statement
> of reasons that the appellant could take another person with her to any work-
> related activities. It may be that the Secretary of State would be facilitative in
> any matter which helped a claimant engage so as to improve their ultimate pros-
> pects of retaining work. I do not know. Whether or not that is so, is not relevant.
> As a matter of law any work-related activity which could only be accomplished
> because of the presence of another person must be looked upon as not being
> an activity that the claimant can carry out. *The issue under regulation 35 (2) (b)*
> *as to whether there would be a substantial risk to the mental or physical health of any*
> *person if the claimant were found not to have limited capability for work-related activity*
> *cannot be assessed as if the claimant under consideration had somebody else by their side.*
> There will be claimants who have a need for the personal reassurance of another
> person, but who do not have anybody available to perform that role. Even if they
> did, it would not be reasonable for such an assessment to be made on the basis
> of reliance on another's goodwill. Legal tests cannot depend upon that. Where an
> appellant who is found to have limited capability for work-related activities wishes
> to engage voluntarily, it may be that they choose to do so with the help of another
> person, and it may (or may not, I do not know) be possible for them to do so,
> but the capacity to engage only with that assistance cannot be part of the test of
> capability" (para.34, emphasis added by commentator).

In *PD v SSWP (ESA)* [2014] UKUT 148 (AAC), in the context of the similarly
worded reg. 29(2)(b), Judge Ward agreed with the italicised passage insofar as it
meant "without consideration as to whether the third party's presence would be
made out in fact" (para.21), but otherwise distinguished the passage as focussing
on the claimant's capability to perform activities (agreeing that there third party
assistance should be ignored) rather than the different question of what risks would
ensue (where, with respect to travelling, at least, third party assistance available in
fact might obviate the risk). See further commentary to reg.29(2)(b), above, substituting for "in the workplace" the different context of "the places where work-related
activities might be performed".

Insofar as there is a difference of view between the two decisions in *MT v SSWP*
(ESA) [2013] UKUT 545 (AAC) and *PD v SSWP (ESA)* [2016] UKUT 148
(AAC), Judge Hemingway in *MP v SSWP (ESA)* [2016] UKUT 502 (AAC)
expressed a preference for the latter approach, noting that he could not:

> "see any reason why a third party's assistance ought not to be taken into account,
> in principle, when assessing whether or not the risk envisaged by the regulation
> would arise. There is nothing within the legislation which suggests that third
> party assistance cannot be relevant. The language of the test focuses upon risk.
> It would be artificial to approach the question of risk in a vacuum and without
> having regard to the prevailing circumstances. Such circumstances might include
> the availability of assistance" (at para.22).

See also *KN v SSWP (ESA)* [2016] UKUT 521 (AAC). In addition, Judge Gray
in *YA and SA v SSWP (ESA)* [2017] UKUT 80 (AAC) accepted that third-party
assistance may be considered, but "the circumstances need to be closely investigated and assessed prior to a finding that such assistance is reasonably available"
(para.54). Thus "what should not be assumed is regular and open ended input from
another person" (para.58).

In *NN-K v Secretary of State for Work and Pensions (ESA)* [2015] UKUT 385   **9.117**
(AAC) Judge Jacobs reminded tribunals that, as a result of the decision in *IM v*

Secretary of State for Work and Pensions [2014] UKUT 412 (AAC), a tribunal applying reg.35 must have regard to the type of work-related activity that the claimant
might be expected to undertake in her area; in doing so, the tribunal must consider
whether the activity would "be reasonable ... having regard to the person's circumstances" (reg.3(4)(a)). In that context the compatibility of any such activity with a
claimant's existing education course would be one of those circumstances (para.9).
However:

> "10. But such factors are only relevant in so far as they relate to the existence
> of a substantial risk to health. The tribunal should ignore any factor that is not
> relevant to that. If the tribunal does not have, and is not to be treated as having,
> limited capability for work-related activity, any issues such as the reasonable-
> ness of the activity would arise subsequently. In particular, the issue might arise
> whether to give a direction on work-related activity or whether she had good
> cause for not undertaking it or whether to reduce her benefit for failing to comply
> with the direction."

Issue 5: how does reg.35(2) operate if the claimant lives outside the UK? In *BB v
Secretary of State for Work and Pensions (ESA)* [2015] UKUT 545 (AAC) the claimant lived in Spain and later in the Republic of Ireland. Following a conversion decision, he was found to qualify for ESA without the support component. A tribunal
dismissed his appeal, finding that reg.35(2) was not satisfied. On appeal to the
Upper Tribunal, the Secretary of State's representative confirmed that there were
no arrangements in place to provide work-related activities in countries outside the
UK and argued that the reg. 35(2) test has to be applied on a hypothetical basis,
namely "what could happen if a claimant were required to undertake work-related
activity, not what would happen" (para.14(b)). Judge Mitchell allowed the claimant's appeal, as he had not had "a fair opportunity to put forward a case in relation
to regulation 35(2) because he was unaware of the type of work-related activity by
reference to which regulation 35(2) would be applied" (para.20). The Secretary of
State's representative further argued that "Where the claimant lives outside the UK
and elects to have a paper hearing (as in this case) the hearing is almost always going
to take place in Newcastle. However if the claimant chooses to attend in person they
can choose a venue suitable to them. Thus, in such cases the relevant WRA evidence
will be from the Newcastle area, or the area in which the tribunal was that the claimant attended" (para.17). Remitting the appeal to a new tribunal, Judge Mitchell
observed as follows:

> "22. I acknowledge the conceptual difficulties raised by the application of
> regulation 35(2), given the existing authorities, in foreign cases such as this. The
> Secretary of State's proposed solution has the benefit of levelling, to an extent,
> the playing field. It reduces the chances of different reg. 35(2) outcomes solely
> by reason of a person's country of residence. If an appellant does not object, the
> First-tier Tribunal ought to adopt the course suggested by the Secretary of State.
> If the appellant does object, the Tribunal will need to decide for itself how to
> proceed taking into account the reasons for the objection and any submissions of
> the Secretary of State" (para.22).

[¹Relevant linked cases—limited capability for work-related activity

9.118   **35A.**—A claimant is to be treated as having limited capability for work-
related activity where–
  (a) they fall within case 1, as defined in regulation 7(1B)(a); and
  (b) in respect of the earlier period of limited capability for work referred
        to in regulation 7(1B)(a)(i), they had been entitled to a support com-
        ponent under sections 2(2) or 4(4) of the Act.]

AMENDMENT

1. Employment and Support Allowance (Amendment of Linking Rules) Regulations 2012 (SI 2012/919) reg.5(5) (May 1, 2012).

Information required for determining capability for work-related activity

36.—(1) Subject to paragraph (2), the information or evidence required to determine whether a claimant has limited capability for work-related activity is—

(a) any information relating to the descriptors set out in Schedule 3 as may be requested in the form of a questionnaire; and

(b) any such additional information as may be requested.

(2) Where the Secretary of State is satisfied that there is sufficient information to determine whether a claimant has limited capability for work-related activity without the information specified in paragraph (1)(a), that information [¹must] not be required for the purposes of making the determination.

9.119

AMENDMENT

1. Social Security (Miscellaneous Amendments) (No.3) Regulations 2013 (SI 2013/2536) reg.13(18) (October 29, 2013).

DEFINITIONS

"claimant"—see WRA 2007 s.24(1).
"limited capability for work-related activity"—see WRA 2007 s.2(5).
"work-related activity"—see WRA 2007 ss.24(1), 13(7).

GENERAL NOTE

This regulation deals with the information required for determining whether someone has limited capability for work-related activity. It is designed to give the decision-maker sufficient information to decide that matter for himself (the minority of cases), or whether to seek advice from a health care professional on the basis of the papers in respect of that decision, or to refer the claimant for a face to face WRAAt, including a medical examination (see reg.38).

9.120

Unless para.(2) operates, the claimant will have to supply (i) any information relating to the descriptors set out in Sch.3 as may be requested in the form of a questionnaire (para.(1)(a)), and (ii) such additional information relating to the relevant test as the Secretary of State asks for (para.(1)(b)). He must generally complete and return the appropriate questionnaire (para.(1)(a)), unless the Secretary of State decides that completion of the questionnaire is not necessary because without it he has sufficient information to determine whether the claimant does or does not have limited capability for work-related activity (para.(2)). Note that where the claimant is requested by the Secretary of State to complete and return the questionnaire, failure to do so can result in his being treated as not having limited capability for work-related activity (and thus not entitled to support component) (reg.37).

Failure to provide information in relation to work-related activity

37.—(1) Where a claimant fails without good cause to comply with the request referred to in regulation 36(1)(a), the claimant is, subject to paragraph (2), to be treated as not having limited capability for work-related activity.

(2) Paragraph (1) does not apply unless—

(a) at least [¹4] weeks have passed since the claimant was sent the first request for the information; and

(b) [².. .] at least [¹1 week has] passed since the further request was sent.

9.121

AMENDMENTS

1. Social Security (Miscellaneous Amendments) (No. 3) Regulations 2011 (SI 2011/2425) reg.23(5), (6) (October 31, 2011).
2. Social Security (Miscellaneous Amendments) (No.3) Regulations 2013 (SI 2013/2536) reg.13(19) (October 29, 2013).

DEFINITIONS

"claimant"—see WRA 2007 s.24(1).
"limited capability for work-related activity"—see WRA 2007 s.2(5).
"week"—see reg.2(1).
"work-related activity"—see WRA 2007 ss.24(1), 13(7).

GENERAL NOTE

9.122   If a claimant fails without good cause (on which more, below) to comply with the requirement in reg.36(1)(a) to complete and return a limited capability for work-related activity questionnaire, he must be treated as not having limited capability for work-related activity, that is, as having no entitlement to support component. This can only happen, however, if a further request for information was sent at least three weeks after the first and at least one week has gone by since the second request was sent.

On applicable IB case law on calculating periods and on the matter of good cause, see further the commentary to the analogous reg.22, applicable in respect of similar processes with respect to determination of limited capability for work questions.

Claimant may be called for a medical examination to determine whether the claimant has limited capability for work-related activity

9.123   **38.**—(1) Where it falls to be determined whether a claimant has limited capability for work-related activity, that claimant may be called by or on behalf of a health care professional approved by the Secretary of State to attend for a medical examination.

(2) Subject to paragraph (3), where a claimant fails without good cause to attend for or to submit to an examination [¹mentioned] in paragraph (1), the claimant is to be treated as not having limited capability for work-related activity.

[¹(3) Paragraph (2) does not apply unless—
   (a) written notice of the date, time and place for the examination was sent to the claimant at least seven days in advance; or
   (b) the claimant agreed to accept a shorter period of notice whether given in writing or otherwise.]

AMENDMENT

1. Social Security (Miscellaneous Amendments) (No.3) Regulations 2013 (SI 2013/2536) reg.13(20) (October 29, 2013).

DEFINITIONS

"claimant"—see WRA 2007 s.24(1).
"health care professional"—see reg.2(1).
"limited capability for work-related activity"—see WRA 2007 s.2(5).
"work-related activity"—see WRA 2007 ss.24(1), 13(7).

GENERAL NOTE

9.124   This regulation enables the DWP to have a claimant medically examined by a DWP Medical Service (DWPMS) health service professional (technically any health service professional approved by the Secretary of State) when a question arises as to the claimant's capability for work-related activity. Failure without good cause to attend for or submit to such an examination, of which he was given proper written notice (see para.(3)), will result in the claimant being treated as not having limited capability for work-related activity and thus be excluded from the support group.

This regulation is a direct analogue of reg.23 with respect to medical examination as regards the matter of limited capability for work. The points, including the application of relevant IB case law, made in the commentary to reg.23 are equally applicable here.

Matters to be taken into account in determining good cause in relation to regulations 37 or 38

39. The matters to be taken into account in determining whether a claim-   9.125
ant has good cause under regulations 37 (failure to provide information in relation to work-related activity) or 38 (failure to attend a medical examination to determine limited capability for work-related activity) include—
  (a) whether the claimant was outside Great Britain at the relevant time;
  (b) the claimant's state of health at the relevant time; and
  (c) the nature of any disability the claimant has.

DEFINITION

  "claimant"—see WRA 2007 s.24(1).

GENERAL NOTE

This regulation, made pursuant to WRA 2007 s.9(4), stipulates that in determin-   9.126
ing whether someone had good cause for failing to provide information (under reg.37) or for failing to attend for or submit to a medical examination (under reg.38) decision-makers and appellate bodies must take into account: (i) whether the person was outside Great Britain at the relevant time; (ii) his state of health at the relevant time; and (iii) the nature of his disability. This list is not, however, exhaustive (the regulation says "shall include"). On "good cause", see further the commentary to regs 22 and 23.

PART 7

EFFECT OF WORK ON ENTITLEMENT TO AN EMPLOYMENT AND SUPPORT
ALLOWANCE

A claimant who works to be treated as not entitled to an employment and support allowance

40.—(1) Subject to the following paragraphs, a claimant is to be treated   9.127
as not entitled to an employment and support allowance in any week in which that claimant does work.
  (2) Paragraph (1) does not apply to—
  (a) work as a councillor;
  (b) duties undertaken on either one full day or two half-days a week
      as—
      (i) a member of the Disability Living Allowance Advisory Board; or
    [²(ii) a member of the First-tier Tribunal where the member is eligi-
          ble for appointment to be such a member in accordance with
          article 2(3) of the Qualifications for Appointment of Members
          to the First-tier Tribunal and Upper Tribunal Order 2008.]

    (c) domestic tasks carried out in the claimant's own home or the care of a relative;

    (d) duties undertaken in caring for another person who is accommodated with the claimant by virtue of arrangements made under any of the provisions referred to in paragraphs [⁴28, 29 or 29A] of Schedule 8 (sums to be disregarded in the calculation of income other than earnings) [³or] where the claimant is in receipt of any payment specified in those paragraphs;

[⁴ (da) duties undertaken in caring for another person who is provided with continuing care by a local authority by virtue of arrangements made under section 26A of the Children (Scotland) Act 1995 and is in receipt of a payment made under that section of that Act;]

    (e) any activity the claimant undertakes during an emergency to protect another person or to prevent serious damage to property or livestock; or

    (f) any of the categories of work set out in regulation 45 (exempt work).

(3) This regulation is subject to regulation 46 (effect of work on entitlement to contributory allowance where claimant is receiving certain regular treatment).

(4) A claimant who does work to which this regulation applies in a week which is—

    (a) the week in which the claimant first becomes entitled to a benefit, allowance or advantage on account of the claimant's limited capability for work in any period; or

    (b) the last week in any period in which the claimant has limited capability for work or is treated as having limited capability for work,

is to be treated as not entitled to an employment and support allowance by virtue of paragraph (1) only on the actual day or days in that week on which the claimant does that work.

(5) Regulation 145 (linking rules) does not apply for the purposes of calculating the beginning or end of any period of limited capability for work under paragraph (4).

(6) The day or days in a week on which a night worker works, for the purposes of [¹paragraph (4)] above, are to be calculated by reference to regulation 28 (night workers).

(7) In this regulation—

"week" means a week in respect of which a claimant is entitled to an employment and support allowance;

"work" means any work which a claimant does, whether or not that claimant undertakes it in expectation of payment;

"work as a councillor" is to be taken to include any work which a claimant undertakes as a member of any of the bodies referred to in section 177(1) of the Local Government Act 1972 or sub-sections 49(1) or 49(1A) of the Local Government (Scotland) Act 1973, of which the claimant is a member by reason of being a councillor.

AMENDMENTS

1. Employment and Support Allowance (Miscellaneous Amendments) Regulations 2008 (SI 2008/2428) reg.6(1) (October 27, 2008).

2. Tribunals, Courts and Enforcement Act 2007 (Transitional and Consequential Provisions) Order 2008 (SI 2008/2683) art.6(1), Sch1 para.342 (November 3, 2008).

3. Social Security (Miscellaneous Amendments) (No.3) Regulations 2013 (SI 2013/2536) reg.13(20) (October 29, 2013).

4. Social Security and Child Support (Care Payments and Tenant Incentive Scheme) (Amendment) Regulations 2017 (SI 2017/995) regs.7(2) and 13(2) (November 7, 2017).

DEFINITIONS

"claimant"—see WRA 2007 s.24(1).
"entitled"—see WRA 2007 s.24(1).
"relative"—see reg.2(1).
"week"—see para.(7) and reg.2(1).
"work"—see para.(7).
"work as a councillor"—see para.(7).

GENERAL NOTE

This regulation needs to be read in conjunction with regs 44–46.   **9.128**

To find in any incapacity regime a general rule that working (whether or not for payment) negatives incapacity for work is unsurprising since, in principle, it is a strong indication of ability to work. This regulation contains just such a rule, precluding entitlement to ESA in any week in which a claimant does work. Moreover, in that period of non-entitlement, he or she will be treated as not having limited capability for work, unless the work done only negatives entitlement to IRESA (reg.44). That can happen in that work done in a week when someone, entitled to CESA, is receiving or recovering from certain regular treatments, does not negative title to CESA, but can to IRESA (regs 46 (to which para.(3) makes this regulation subject) and 44(3)). But like the incapacity benefit regime, the general preclusive rule is modified to permit engagement in a range of work without loss of benefit ("subject to the following paragraphs", one of which para.(2)(f) links this regulation to reg.45 and the concept of "exempt work"). These modifications recognize that work can assist recovery or help the claimant into thinking about work and a possibility to return to work, or merely not wanting to exclude the sick and disabled from participation in civic office or a range of voluntary or charitable work.

Although, unlike its IB comparator (Incapacity for Work Regs, reg.16) the point is no longer explicit, it is submitted that the regulation can operate despite the fact that, applying the limited capability for work assessment (WCAt), the person in fact has limited capability for work, or is someone treated as having such limited capability by virtue of other regs.

Paragraph (1) sets out the general preclusive rule: a person must be treated as capable of work on each day of any week during which he does work. "Work" for the purposes of the regulation is defined in para.(7) as any work done whether or not undertaken in expectation of payment. "Week" is a period of seven days beginning with Sunday (para.(7)).

Note, however, that this ostensibly very wide general preclusive rule is subject to the partial relief afforded by para.(4) and by reg.46 (see para.(3)) and the complete relief afforded by para.(2). Execution of some de minimis tasks can also be ignored as not constituting "work". Discussion is divided accordingly.

Partial relief

Paras (4), (5): Together these afford some relief from the general preclusive rule   **9.129**
set out in para.(1). Paragraph (4) contains an obviously necessary one, it covers the worker who initially falls sick part way through his working week and/or the period in which he is incapable of work finishes part way through a week in the course of which he returns to work. Here, the preclusive effect of the regulation is confined to ruling out only the days actually worked in that or those weeks.

Note that the linking rules in reg.145 do not apply for determining when, for the purposes of this relieving rule, a period of limited capability for work begins and ends (para.(5)). In effect, each "spell" of limited capability for work" is treated separately, thus helping those whose limited capability for work is intermittent and removing a disincentive to trying work for a while.

Para. (3): This regulation is "subject to regulation 46". That provides that those treated under reg.26 as having limited capability for work on days when receiving or recovering from certain regular treatments (e.g. chemotherapy), who work on other days of the week in which they receive or are recovering from such treatment such treatment, will not have their entitlement to CESA affected by doing that work. For the impact of such work on entitlement to IRESA, see the exclusionary "remunerative work" rules (WRA 2007 Sch.1, para.6(1)(e); reg.41) and, in terms of the IRESA "balance sheet", the impact of earnings on entitlement.

Complete relief

9.130 *Para. (2)* prevents the general preclusive rule in para.(1) applying to:
(i) any of the categories of work in reg.45 (para.(2)(f));
(ii) work as a councillor (see para.(7) for its breadth and see reg.88 for the abating effect on CESA of amounts of councillor's allowance over a specified weekly amount) (para.(2)(a);
The scheme, as before, seeks to encourage sick and disabled people to participate in civic office by enabling them to receive CESA reduced or abated by the amount by which their councillor's allowance applicable to that week exceeds a specified amount.
(iii) care of a relative or domestic tasks carried out in his own home (para.(2)(c);
(iv) work as a foster parent or other specified carer in respect of someone accommodated in one's home or where the claimant is in receipt of any payment specified in Sch.8, paras. 28, 29;
(v) limited duties (one full day or two half days per week) as a member of a the DLA Advisory Board or as First-tier Tribunal member with a disability qualification (para.(2)(b)) (i.e. someone other than a registered medical practitioner, who is experienced in dealing with the physical or mental needs of disabled persons because they work with disabled persons in a professional or voluntary capacity, or are themselves disabled (see art.2(3) of the Qualifications for Appointment of Members to the First-tier Tribunal and Upper Tribunal Order 2008 (SI 2008/2692));
(vi) any activity undertaken during an emergency solely to protect another person or to prevent serious damage to property or livestock (para.(2)(e)).
This exemption is essential to protect the benefit position of the rescuer; of the good neighbour who looks after his/her neighbour's children when she is rushed to hospital; of the person who helps round up livestock which have strayed into a busy road; or of the good neighbour who helps fight a fire until the emergency services arrive; or the husband on ESA who is compelled to drive to rush his pregnant wife in labour to hospital because the ambulance has not arrived. These can be but speculative examples.

"Emergency" is not defined. However, note it is not qualified by terms such as "severe" or "serious" or "great", so it ought not to be construed too narrowly. By way of comparison, in the industrial injuries context, case law dealing with "in the course of employment" has brought within that phrase persons responding to emergency. There "emergency" was construed broadly to encompass a wide range of unexpected occurrences (see commentary to SSCBA 1992, s.100). A broad approach ought to be taken, similarly, to the notion of "any activity to protect another person".

Applying the de minimis principle to ignore trivial or negligible amounts of work

9.131 It is submitted that this long-standing principle, which has applied to previous inpacity for work regimes, is equally applicable to ESA and that previous case law applies here.

CIB/5298/1997 supports the view (then found in AOG, paras 18782 and 18783) that the de minimis principle applies to enable trivial or negligible amounts of work to be ignored (paras 5–12), recognising as a practical proposition something seen as a theoretical one in *CIB/14656/96*. Deputy Commissioner Wikeley's decision in *CIB/6777/1999* contains a thorough review of the authorities on this matter. He notes that the rule here can apply irrespective of whether the work might in any event be treated as exempt under Incapacity for Work Regs reg.17 (and thus ESA Regs regs 40, 45). Whether work done is trivial or negligible is a matter of fact and degree. Like Commissioner Williams in *CIB/5298/1997*, who had approved guidance in the AOG, the Deputy Commissioner supported as illustrative but not exhaustive, relevant factors, those set out in DMG para.13867:

> "whether work on a day is negligible depends on its proportion to the normal working hours, the type of work and the effort required in relation to normal working duties."

Stressing the role of incapacity benefit as "an earnings replacement . . . benefit for those with the appropriate contributions record who cannot work in the labour market" he (rightly in the opinion of this commentator) disagreed with Commissioner Williams in *CIB/5298/1997* who took the view that the amount of remuneration earned was always wholly irrelevant since para.(6) states that work is "work" whether or not undertaken in expectation of payment. That means, of course, that the lack of remuneration or of the expectation of it is irrelevant. The key question is really what the tasks performed tell one about the person's capacity for work. But, in contrast to the irrelevance of lack of remuneration, this author, like the Deputy Commissioner, believes that the amount of remuneration received for a relatively small degree of work-like activity, when contrasted with the weekly rate of incapacity benefit (and now ESA), surely *is* a relevant factor in deciding whether work done should be disregarded as trivial or negligible—it brings into play the "anti-abuse" element of the rules here, which arguably takes one into the realm of when the public (including other recipients of benefit) might view as inappropriate receipt of incapacity benefit or ESA by someone with what looks like a source of income from "employment", albeit only in that one week. Is that not one purpose behind the earnings limits on exempt work in Incapacity for Work Regs, reg.17 (ESA Regs reg.45)? However, that Incapacity for Work Regs reg.16 (ESA Regs reg.40) stipulates particular worthy tasks as ones to be disregarded seems to cast doubt on the Deputy Commissioner's view that the identity of the person for whom the task is performed may be a material factor in applying the de minimis rule.

CIB/3507/2002 affords another illustration of work being disregarded as de minimis. The work in question was described by the Commissioner as follows: **9.132**

> "On 28th November 2001, DW Windows wrote a letter in which they said: 'In July of this year we approached [the claimant] to see if he would like to do a couple of hours each week at [DW Windows] doing various light duties. i.e. Making coffees, emptying bins etc and occasionally driving a vehicle to transport [Mr S. E.] the Manager who holds no driving license. There is no dispute about what DW Windows say. Nor is there any dispute about the fact that the claimant was paid £3.85 per hour and that he worked between one and three hours per week. A schedule of his weekly hours and earnings between the beginning of July and the first week of October 2001 has been produced by DW Windows. He never worked for more than three hours and consequently never earned more than £11.55, in any one week. The period covered is one of 14 weeks. During three of those weeks he worked for 1 hour only. He worked for two hours for five of those weeks and for three hours for the remaining six weeks. The average is a little above two hours per week'" (paras 6, 7).

In marked contrast, in *CIB/4684/2003*, Commissioner Jacobs found the work done by the claimant was not so minimal that it could be disregarded. He did so, however, for a different reason to the tribunal which had so found on the basis that the claimant's contribution to the earnings from the post office was significant when compared to his wife's. Instead Commissioner Jacobs approached the matter thus:

> "For 8 hours a week, spread over 2 mornings, the claimant manned the post office. He was not there merely to summon his wife if a customer arrived. He was there to serve any customer who wanted any of the services offered by the office. Covering the office in those circumstances amounted to work, even if there were no customers at all. He was in exactly the same position as a stallholder on a market who had no customers. Surely that stallholder would be working, even if no one bought from, or even visited, the stall? How the claimant spent his time when he was not actually serving customers is irrelevant. It would be just as irrelevant whether a market stallholder at a market spent the time trying to entice customers to the stall or merely sat reading a book" (paras 10, 11).

PART 7

EFFECT OF WORK ON ENTITLEMENT TO AN EMPLOYMENT AND SUPPORT ALLOWANCE

Meaning of "remunerative work" for the purposes of paragraph 6(1)(e) of Schedule 1 to the Act

9.133   **41.**—(1) For the purposes of paragraph 6(1)(e) of Schedule 1 to the Act (conditions of entitlement to an income-related allowance), "remunerative work" means any work which a claimant does for which payment is made or which is done in expectation of payment, other than work listed in paragraph (2) of regulation 40.

(2) Subject to paragraph (3), a claimant who was, or who was being treated as—

(a) engaged in remunerative work; and

(b) in respect of that work earnings to which regulation 95(1)(b) and (d) applies are paid, is to be treated as being engaged in remunerative work for the period for which those earnings are taken into account in accordance with Part 10 of these Regulations.

(3) Paragraph (2) does not apply to earnings disregarded under paragraph 1 of Schedule 7 (sums to be disregarded in the calculation of earnings).

DEFINITIONS

"claimant"—Welfare Reform Act 2007 s.24(1).
"earnings"—regs 95 and 97.

GENERAL NOTE

9.134   Under para.6 of Sch.1 to the Welfare Reform Act, it is a condition of entitlement to income-related ESA that (among other things) the claimant is not engaged in remunerative work (para.6(1)(e)) and that, where the claimant is a member of a couple, neither is the other member of the couple (para.6(1)(f)). The meaning of the phrase "remunerative work" differs according to whether it is the claimant or her/his partner that is being considered. Regulation 41 sets out the test for the claimant and reg.42 (below), the test for the partner.

ESA is a benefit for those with limited capability for work and the general principle is that a claimant who does any work will normally not be entitled to ESA for that week (see reg.40 above). That is subject to the exceptions set out in reg.40(2). Paragraph (1) defines remunerative work as any work other than that specified in reg.40(2) with the additional requirement that it should be work "for which payment is made or which is done in expectation of payment". It is difficult to see what purpose this serves. The reg.41(1) definition is narrower than the reg.40 definition and therefore anyone falling within reg.41(1) will already have been disentitled by reg.40.

Perhaps more importantly, some claimants who are not actually working (and are not therefore disentitled by reg.40) are nevertheless *treated as* being in remunerative work (and therefore not entitled to income-related ESA) under powers conferred by para.6(3) of Sch.1 to the Act. Paragraphs (2) and (3) provide that where a claimant's employment is interrupted or comes to an end and he or she receives payment in lieu of remuneration (other than a redundancy payment) or holiday pay (unless it is payable more than four weeks after the termination or interruption of employment) then, except where those earnings are disregarded under para.1 of Sch.7, s/he is treated as engaged in remunerative work for the period during which those earnings are taken into account under Pt 10.

Meaning of "remunerative work" for the purposes of paragraph 6(1) (f) of Schedule 1 to the Act

42.—(1) For the purposes of paragraph 6(1)(f) of Schedule 1 to the Act, (conditions of entitlement to an income-related allowance where a claimant must not be a member of a couple the other member of which is engaged in remunerative work), "remunerative work" means work in which the claimant's partner is engaged or, where the partner's hours of work fluctuate, the partner is engaged on average, for not less than 24 hours a week, being work for which payment is made or which is done in expectation of payment.

(2) In calculating the number of hours for which a claimant's partner is engaged in work so as to determine whether that partner is engaged in remunerative work, the number of hours are to be determined in accordance with paragraphs (8) and (9) of regulation 45 and those paragraphs are to be read as though they referred to the claimant's partner.

(3) The claimant's partner is to be treated as engaged in remunerative work during any period for which that partner is absent from work referred to in paragraph (1) if the absence is either without good cause or by reason of a recognised, customary or other holiday.

(4) Subject to paragraph (5), a claimant's partner who was, or who was being treated as—

(a) engaged in remunerative work; and

(b) in respect of that work earnings to which regulation 95(1)(b) and (d) applies are paid, is to be treated as being engaged in remunerative work for the period for which those earnings are taken into account in accordance with Part 10 of these Regulations.

(5) Paragraph (4) does not apply to earnings disregarded under paragraph 1 of Schedule 7 (sums to be disregarded in the calculation of earnings).

(6) For the purposes of this regulation, in determining the number of hours in which a claimant's partner is engaged or treated as engaged in remunerative work, no account is to be taken of any hours in which the claimant's partner is engaged in an employment or a scheme to which regulation 43(1) or (2) (claimants' partners not treated as engaged in remunerative work) applies.

9.135

DEFINITIONS

"claimant"—Welfare Reform Act 2007 s.24(1).
"couple"—reg.2(1).
"earnings"—regs 95 and 97.
"partner"—reg.2(1).

GENERAL NOTE

9.136   In contrast to the position for ESA claimants, it is not a condition of entitlement that their partners should also have limited capability for work. Regulation 42 therefore defines "remunerative work" for the claimant's partner in terms that are similar to reg.5 of the IS Regulations and reg.51 of the JSA Regulations.

Circumstances under which partners of claimants entitled to an income-related allowance are not to be treated as engaged in remunerative work

9.137   **43.**—(1) A claimant's partner is not to be treated as engaged in remunerative work in so far as—

(a) the partner is engaged in child minding in the partner's home;

(b) the partner is engaged by a charity or voluntary organisation, or is a volunteer, where the only payment received by the partner or due to be paid to the partner, is a payment which is to be disregarded under regulation 104(2) (calculation of income other than earnings) and paragraph 2 of Schedule 8 (sums to be disregarded in the calculation of income other than earnings);

(c) the partner is engaged on a scheme for which a training allowance is being paid;

(d) the partner is receiving assistance under the self-employment route;

(e) the partner is engaged in employment as any one of the following—

[³ (i) a part-time fire-fighter employed by a fire and rescue authority under the Fire and Rescue Services Act 2004 or by the Scottish Fire and Rescue Service established under section 1A of the Fire (Scotland) Act 2005;]

(ii) [³ ...]

(iii) [³ ...[²]]

(iv) an auxiliary coastguard in respect of coast rescue activities;

(v) a person engaged part-time in the manning or launching of a life boat;

(vi) a member of any [⁵ ...] reserve force prescribed in Part 1 of Schedule 6 to the Social Security (Contributions) Regulations 2001; or

(f) the partner is undertaking work as a councillor;

(g) the partner is engaged in caring for a person who is accommodated with the partner by virtue of arrangements made under any of the provisions referred to in paragraphs 28 or 29 of Schedule 8 (sums to be disregarded in the calculation of income other than earnings) and the partner is in receipt of any payment specified in those paragraphs;

(h) the partner is engaged in an activity in respect of which—

(i) a sports award has been made, or is to be made, to the partner; and

(ii) no other payment is made or is expected to be made to the partner.

(2) A claimant's partner is not to be treated as engaged in remunerative work, where the partner is—

(a) [¹ . . .]

(b) subject to regulation 42(4) (partners treated as engaged in remunerative work), a person who would otherwise have satisfied section 126(1) of the Contributions and Benefits Act (trade disputes) or in respect of whom section 124(1) of that Act (conditions of entitlement to income support) would otherwise have had effect as modified by section 127(b) of that Act (effect of return to work);

(c) a person who would otherwise satisfy the conditions set out in paragraph 4 of Schedule 1B to the Income Support Regulations;

(d) [¹ . . .]

(3) The claimant's partner is not to be treated as engaged in remunerative work on any day on which that partner is on maternity leave, paternity leave [⁴ , shared parental leave] or adoption leave or is absent from work because the partner is ill.

(4) In this regulation—

"work as a councillor" has the same meaning as in regulation 40;

"volunteer" means a person who is engaged in voluntary work otherwise than for a relative, where the only payment received or due to be paid to the person by virtue of being so engaged is in respect of any expenses reasonably incurred by the person in connection with that work.

AMENDMENTS

1. Social Security (Miscellaneous Amendments) (No.5) Regulations 2009 (SI 2009/3228) reg.4(1)(c) (January 25, 2010).

2. Police and Fire Reform (Scotland) Act 2012 (Consequential Provisions and Modifications) Order 2013 (SI 2013/602) art.26 and Sch.2 Pt 3 para.91 (April 1, 2013).

3. Social Security (Miscellaneous Amendments) (No.3) Regulations 2013 (SI 2013/2536) reg.13(1) and (22) (October 29, 2013).

4. Shared Parental Leave and Statutory Shared Parental Pay (Consequential Amendments to Subordinate Legislation) Order 2014 art.20(4) (December 31, 2014).

5. Social Security (Members of the Reserve Forces) (Amendment) Regulations 2015 (SI 2014/389) reg.4(5) (April 6, 2015).

DEFINITIONS

"Abbeyfield Home"—reg.2(1).
"adoption leave"—*ibid.*
"claimant"—WRA Act 2007 s.24(1).
"Contributions and Benefits Act"—WRA 2007 s.65.
"councillor"—reg.2(1).
"employment"—*ibid.*
"Income Support Regulations"—*ibid.*
"independent hospital"—*ibid.*
"maternity leave" "—*ibid.*
"partner"—*ibid.*
"remunerative work"—regs 2(1), 41 and 42.
"self-employment route"—reg.2(1).
"sports award"—*ibid.*
"training allowance"—*ibid.*
"work as a councillor"—reg.40.

9.138   This regulation is similar to reg.6 of the IS Regs and reg.52 of the JSA Regs.

The revocation of paras (2)(a) and (d) with effect from January 25, 2010 is subject to a savings provision for those entitled to ESA in respect of January 24, 2010: see regs 4(3), (6) and (7) of SI 2009/3228 in Vol.II.

Claimants who are treated as not entitled to any allowance at all by reason of regulation 40(1) are to be treated as not having limited capability for work

9.139   **44.**—(1) Where a claimant is treated as not entitled to an employment and support allowance by reason of regulation 40(1), subject to paragraph (2), the claimant is to be treated as not having limited capability for work.

(2) Paragraph (1) does not apply where the claimant remains entitled to a contributory allowance, but is not entitled to an income-related allowance by reason of regulation 40(1).

(3) Paragraph (1) applies even if—

(a) it has been determined that the claimant has or is to be treated as having, under any of regulations 20 (certain claimants to be treated as having limited capability for work), 25 (hospital in-patients), 26 (claimants undergoing certain regular treatment) or 29 (exceptional circumstances), limited capability for work; or

(b) the claimant meets the conditions set out in regulation 30(2) for being treated as having limited capability for work until a determination is made in accordance with the limited capability for work assessment.

DEFINITION

"claimant"

GENERAL NOTE

9.140   Regulation 40(1) precludes entitlement to ESA in any week in which a claimant does work. In the light of that, this regulation provides, moreover, that in that period of non-entitlement, he or she will be treated as not having limited capability for work (para.(1), unless the work done only negatives entitlement to IRESA (para. (2)). Such a situation can arise where reg.46 applies in that work done in a week when someone, entitled to CESA, is receiving or recovering from certain regular treatments, does not negative title to CESA, but can to IRESA. Paragraph (3) makes clear that the regulation can operate despite the fact that, applying the limited capability for work assessment (WCAt), the person in fact has limited capability for work incapable of work, or is someone treated as having such limited capability by virtue of certain other regs: 20 (certain claimants to be treated as having limited capability for work); 25 (hospital in-patients); 26 (claimants undergoing certain regular treatment); or 29 (exceptional circumstances). This suggests that this rule on treating the person as not having limited capability for work will not operate in other cases where regs treat someone (whatever the reality) as having limited capability for work: regs 30 (treated as having limited capability pending assessment) and 33(2) (certain disabled students). In those cases there will be no entitlement to ESA where the person is caught by reg.40, but the days might still rank as ones of limited capability for work.

Exempt work

9.141   **45.**—(1) The categories of work referred to in regulation 40(2)(f) are set out in the following paragraphs.

(2) Work for which the earnings in any week do not exceed £20.00.

(3) Work for which the earnings in any week do not exceed [¹16 x National Minimum Wage, subject to paragraph (9A),] and which—

(a) is part of the claimant's treatment programme and is done under medical supervision while the claimant is an in-patient, or is regularly attending as an out-patient, of a hospital or similar institution; or

(b) is supervised by a person employed by a public or local authority or [²a] voluntary organisation [²or community interest company] engaged in the provision or procurement of work for persons who have disabilities.

(4) Work which is done for less than 16 hours a week, for which earnings in any week do not exceed [¹16 x National Minimum Wage, subject to paragraph (9A)] [⁴ . . .].

(4A) [⁴ . . .]

(5) Work done in the course of receiving assistance in pursuing self-employed earner's employment whilst participating in a programme provided or other arrangements made under section 2 of the Employment and Training Act 1973 (functions of the Secretary of State) or section 2 of the Enterprise and New Towns (Scotland) Act 1990(functions in relation to training for employment etc.).

(6) Work done where the claimant receives no payment of earnings and where the claimant—

(a) is engaged by a charity or voluntary organisation; or

(b) is a volunteer,

where the Secretary of State is satisfied in any of those cases that it is reasonable for the claimant to provide the service free of charge.

(7) Work done in the course of participating in a work placement approved in writing by the Secretary of State before the placement starts.

(8) The number of hours for which a claimant is engaged in work is to be determined—

(a) where no recognisable cycle has been established in respect of a claimant's work, by reference to the number of hours or, where those hours are likely to fluctuate, the average of the hours, which the claimant is expected to work in a week;

(b) where the number of hours for which the claimant is engaged fluctuate, by reference to the average of hours worked over—

(i) if there is a recognisable cycle of work, the period of one complete cycle (including, where the cycle involves periods in which the claimant does no work, those periods but disregarding any other absences);

(ii) in any other case, the period of five weeks immediately before the date of claim or the date on which a superseding decision is made under section 10 (decisions superseding earlier decisions) of the Social Security Act 1998, or such other length of time as may, in the particular case, enable the claimant's average hours of work to be determined more accurately.

(9) For the purposes of determining the number of hours for which a claimant is engaged in work, that number is to include any time allowed to that claimant by the claimant's employer for a meal or for refreshment, but only where that claimant is, or expects to be, paid earnings in respect of that time.

[¹(9A) Where the amount determined by the calculation in paragraphs (3) and (4) would, but for this paragraph, include an amount of—

(a) less than 50p, that amount shall be rounded up to the nearest 50p; or

(b) less than £1 but more than 50p, that amount shall be rounded up to the nearest £1.]

(10) In this regulation—

[⁴ . . .]

[⁴ . . .]

"supervised work" means work done in accordance with paragraph (3) (a) or (b);

"volunteer" has the same meaning it has in regulation 43;

"work placement" means practical work experience with an employer, which is neither paid nor undertaken in expectation of payment.

AMENDMENTS

1. Social Security (Miscellaneous Amendments) Regulations 2011 (SI 2011/674) reg.16(5) (April 11, 2011).

2. Social Security (Miscellaneous Amendments) (No.3) Regulations 2010 (SI 2010/840) reg.9(10) (June 28, 2010).

3. Social Security (Miscellaneous Amendments) (No.3) Regulation 2013 (SI 2013/2536), reg.13(1) and (23) (October 29,2013).

4. Employment and Support Allowance (Exempt Work & Hardship Amounts) (Amendment) Regulations 2017 (SI 2017/205) reg.3 (April 3, 2017).

DEFINITIONS

"the Act"—see reg.2(1).

"claimant"—see WRA 2007 s.24(1).

"Contributions and Benefits Act"—see WRA 2007 s.65.

"employment"—see reg.2(1).

"relevant benefit"—see para.(10).

"self-employed earner"—see reg.2(1).

"specified work"—see paras (10), (4).

"supervised work"—see paras (10), (3) (a) or (b).

"voluntary organisation"—see reg.2(1).

"volunteer"—see para.(10) and reg.43(4).

"week"—see reg.2(1).

"work placement"—see para.(10).

GENERAL NOTE

9.142   This regulation needs to be read in conjunction with reg.40(1) which precludes entitlement to ESA in any week in which a claimant does work. "Work" for the purposes of that regulation is defined in reg.40(7) as any work done whether or not undertaken in expectation of payment. "Week" is a period of seven days beginning with Sunday (reg.40(7)). This regulation in contrast defines a variety of work which ranking as "exempt work" does not pursuant to reg.40(2)(f) preclude entitlement to ESA under the general preclusive rule in reg.40(1).

The regulation is part of the welfare to work strategy, of encouraging people to try out work, the better to enable a return to work.

The current categories of exempt work

9.143   Some embody an earnings limit, others both an earnings and hours limit. The matters of determining the hours of engagement and assessing earnings are examined further below, after considering the seven categories of exempt work:

(1) *Work for which the earnings in any week do not exceed £20 (para.(2)):* there is no hours limit as such here, but it is anticipated that in practice the effect

of the minimum wage laws will mean that DWP staff will expect a claimant in this category to be working less than 5 hours a week. Its prime role is the encouragement of social contact.

(2) *Unpaid work for a charity or voluntary organization (para. (6) (a)):* Work done where the claimant is engaged by a charity or voluntary organization is exempt where he receives no payment of earnings and the Secretary of State is satisfied that it is reasonable for him to provide the service free of charge. "Charity" is not defined in the ESA Regs, so must bear the meaning it does in charity law. "Voluntary organization" means a body, other than a public or local authority, the activities of which are carried on otherwise than for profit (reg.2(1)).

(3) *Work done as a volunteer (paras (6) (b), (10)):* Voluntary work other than that covered by para.(6)(1)(a) is thus also protected where the claimant receives no payment of earnings and the Secretary of State is satisfied that it is reasonable for him to provide the service free of charge. "Volunteer" is defined in para.(10) by reference to reg.43(4) to embrace a person who is engaged in voluntary work otherwise than for a relative, where the only payment received by him or due to be paid to him by virtue of being so engaged is in respect of any expenses reasonably incurred by him in connection with that work. "Relative" is widely defined: it means a close relative, grand-parent, grand-child, uncle, aunt, nephew or niece (reg.2(1)). "Close relative" covers a parent, parent-in-law, son, son-in-law, daughter, daughter-in-law, step-parent, step-son, step-daughter, brother, sister, or the spouse of any of these persons, or if that person is one of an unmarried couple, the other member of that couple (reg.2(1)). There are no hours or earnings limits.

(3) *Supervised work (paras (3), (10)):* there are two categories here. First, work done with the supervision of bodies providing or finding work for disabled people (para.(3)(a)). The bodies in question are a public or local author-ity or a voluntary organisation (that is, a body, other than a public or local authority, whose activities are carried on otherwise than for profit (reg.2(1)). The second category covers work while a patient of a hospital or similar institution under medical supervision as part of a treatment programme. The patient must be an in-patient or a regularly attending out-patient (para. (3)(b)). Whichever of the two categories, the earnings from the work must not exceed 16 x National Minimum Wage a week (see further para.(9A)). On "hospital or similar institution", some guidance is given in DMG, paras 18031–18033, 24018–24023. But this is not binding on tribunals or courts.

(4) *Work done in the course of receiving assistance in pursuing self-employed earner's employment whilst participating in certain programmes or arrangements (para. (5)):* this makes it easier for people receiving ESA to attempt self employ-ment. Test Trading allows people to try out 'self employment' for a period of up to 26 weeks. Its introduction prevents participants being regarded as in work with the possibility of a loss of benefit should earnings exceed the permitted work limits.

(5) *Work done by those having, or treated as having, limited capability for work-related activity (para. (4) (b)):* those in the support group (receiving or eligible for support component) can work for an unlimited period providing it is for less than 16 hours a week (see further, below) and the earnings do not exceed 16 x National Minimum Wage a week (see further para.(9A)). This provides a new category of permitted work for people who face the greatest barriers to full-time employment.

(6) *Permitted ("Specified") work for an initial period of up to 52 weeks (paras (4) (a), (10)):* The work done must be for less than 16 hours a week (see further, below) and the earnings in any week must not exceed 16 x National Minimum Wage (see further, para.(9A)). To qualify for this permitted work period, the person must: (i) have not previously done specified work (i.e. work protected by this particular head (para.(10)); or (ii) since the beginning of the last period of specified work, he must have ceased to be entitled to a "relevant" benefit

(see para.(10)) for a continuous period of more than twelve weeks; or (iii) at least 52 weeks have elapsed since he last did specified work.

(7) *approved, unpaid work placements (paras (7), (10)):* "Work placement" is practical work experience with an employer, which is neither paid nor taken on in expectation of payment (para.(10)). The work placement must have been approved by the Secretary of State in writing prior to its commencement.

In determining the number of hours of engagement in work (paras (8), (9)) an averaging approach applies, varying according to whether there is or is not a recognizable cycle and whether the claimant's hours fluctuate (para.(8)). The hours of engagement include time the employer allows for meals or refreshment where the claimant is, or expects to be, paid earnings in respect of that time (para.(9)).

The earnings limit—Computation of Earnings Regs not applicable here

9.144   Unlike the position with IB, ESA is not within the sphere of the SSCBA 1992 and so the Computation of Earnings Regs cannot apply. Calculation of earnings is to be done under the rules in the ESA Regs.

Effect of work on entitlement to contributory allowance where claimant is receiving certain regular treatment

9.145   **46.** Where a claimant who is entitled to a contributory allowance and is treated as having limited capability for work by virtue of regulation 26 works on any day during a week when the claimant is, in accordance with regulation 26, receiving certain regular treatment or recovering from that treatment, that work is to have no effect on the claimant's entitlement to the contributory allowance.

DEFINITIONS

"claimant"—see WRA 2007 s.24(1).
"contributory allowance"—see WRA 2007 s.1(7).
"entitled"—see WRA 2007 s.24(1).
"limited capability for work"—see WRA 2007 s.24(1).
"week"—see reg.2(1), WRA 2007 s.24(1).

GENERAL NOTE

9.146   This (affording an exception to the preclusive rule on work in reg.40(1)) provides that those treated under reg.26 as having limited capability for work on days when receiving or recovering from certain regular treatments (e.g. chemotherapy), who work on other days of the week in which they receive or are recovering from such treatment such treatment, will not have their entitlement to CESA affected by doing that work. For the impact of such work on entitlement to IRESA, see the exclusionary "remunerative work" rules (WRA 2007, Sch.1 para.6(1)(e); reg.41) and, in terms of the IRESA "balance sheet", the impact of earnings on entitlement.

PART 8

CONDITIONALITY

CHAPTER 1

WORK-FOCUSED HEALTH-RELATED ASSESSMENT

Regs 47–53

9.147   Note that on June 24, 2010, in a letter to the JCP customer representative group, the DWP announced the suspension of the work-focused health related assessment for a period of two years from July 19, 2010. It noted that ongoing external evaluation had shown mixed results for the assessment. Its two-year suspension affords an opportunity for DWP reconsideration of the assessment's purpose and delivery, as well as freeing up capacity to deal with the demands of re-assessing existing incapacity benefits customers as part of the process of migration to ESA or—for those who fail the limited capability for work assessment—denial of ESA, cancellation of the existing award of an incapacity benefit and effective transfer either to JSA or (if qualifying in another category than "incapable of work") to IS. See further the Migration Regulations: the Employment and Support Allowance (Transitional Provisions, Housing Benefit and Council Tax Benefit) (Existing Awards) (No. 2) Regulations 2010 (SI 2010/1907) (as amended). Note further that from June 1, 2011 the Regs governing the work-focused health related assessment (regs 47–49, 51–53, below) were revoked (see Employment and Support Allowance (Work-Related Activity) Regulations 2011 (SI 2011/1349) reg.11).

CHAPTER 2

WORK-FOCUSED INTERVIEWS

Requirement to take part in a work-focused interview

54.—(1) The Secretary of State may require a claimant who satisfies the requirements in paragraph (2) to take part in one or more work-focused interviews as a condition of continuing to be entitled to the full amount of employment and support allowance payable to the claimant.

9.148

(2) The requirements referred to in paragraph (1) are that the claimant—
  (a) is either—
    (i) entitled to an employment and support allowance; or
    (ii) a person in respect of whom the Secretary of State has made an award under regulation 146(1);
  (b) is not a member of the support group;
  (c) has not reached the age at which a woman of the same age as the claimant would attain pensionable age; [¹ ...]
  (d) is not only entitled to a contributory allowance payable at a nil rate [¹; and
  (e) is not a lone parent who is responsible for and a member of the same household as a child under one.]

(3) Any requirement to take part in a work-focused interview ceases to have effect if the claimant ceases to satisfy the requirements in paragraph (2).

AMENDMENT

1. Social Security (Work-focused Interviews for Lone Parents and Partners) (Amendment) Regulations 2011 (SI 2011/2428) reg.5(3) (October 31, 2011).

DEFINITIONS

  "claimant"—see WRA 2007 s.24(1).
  "contributory allowance"—see WRA 2007 ss.24(1), 1(7).
  "member of the support group"—see WRA 2007 s.24(4).
  "pensionable age"—see reg.2(1).
  "work-focused interview"—see WRA 2007 s.12(7).

GENERAL NOTE

9.149   This regulation, read with WRA 2007 s.11 and regs 48–53, deals with the second aspect of "conditionality", the requirements imposed on most of those who fall outside the support group as not having limited capability for work-related activity. The policy is that ESA brings rights, responsibilities and opportunities to people with health conditions and disabilities by asking them to engage with Jobcentre Plus (and contracted providers in the private and voluntary sectors [PVS]) to work towards fulfilling their ambitions. The key to this is seen in the incorporation in membership of work-related activity group of ESA of an element of conditionality modelled on those applied in the Pathways to Work programme. This has a number of elements: (i) participation in a work-focused health related assessment (WFHRAt) (WRA 2007 s.11; regs 47–53); (ii) participation in a work-focused interview; and (iii) as resources permit (and not before 2011), undertaking work-related activity that increases the likelihood of getting a job (e.g. work trials). This regulation stipulates that as a condition of receiving the full amount of ESA, a claimant may be required to participate in one or more work-focused interviews, the second element of taking part in work-related activity (para.(1)). This requirement may, however, only be imposed on a claimant not in the support group, awarded ESA or an advance award of it under reg.146, who, whether male or female, has not reached the female pensionable age by reference to his/her date of birth, who is not merely entitled to CESA at a nil rate (e.g. because of abatement under WRA 2007 ss.2, 3) (para.(2), reg.2(1) and link to Pensions Act 1995, Sch.4, para.1) and who is not a lone parent with responsibility for a child under one in the same household. Should such a requirement have been imposed when those conditions were met, it will cease to have effect when the claimant no longer satisfies one or more of them (e.g. becomes a member of the support group because the health condition and it limiting effects have worsened, or has reached the exempting age, or whose ESA entitlement drops to CESA at a nil rate) (para.(3)).

Although WRA 2007 s.16 and reg.63 enable contracting out so as to bring expertise from the private and voluntary sectors (PVS) into the process of assisting claimants to prepare for and enhance their prospects of starting or returning to work, it is envisaged, however, that the first work-focused interview will always be with someone from Jobcentre Plus and will be held around the eighth week of the assessment period.

Note that failure, without good cause, to participate in a work-focused interview (regs 55, 57, 58, 61) is sanctioned initially by halving the amount of work-related activity component and eventually by reducing it to nil (reg.63), the reduction to cease after compliance has been induced or the requirement to participate has ceased to have effect under para.(3) (reg.64).

Work-focused interview

9.150   **55.** The purposes of a work-focused interview are any or all of the following—

(a) assessing the claimant's prospects for remaining in or obtaining work;

(b) assisting or encouraging the claimant to remain in or obtain work;

(c) identifying activities that the claimant may undertake that will make remaining in or obtaining work more likely;

(d) identifying training, educational or rehabilitation opportunities for the claimant which may make it more likely that the claimant will remain in or obtain work or be able to do so;

(e) identifying current or future work opportunities, including self-employment opportunities, for the claimant, that are relevant to the claimant's needs and abilities.

DEFINITIONS

"claimant"—see WRA 2007 s.24(1).
"training"—see reg.2(1).
"work-focused interview"—see WRA 2007 s.12(7).

GENERAL NOTE

Pursuant to WRA 2007, s.12(7) this regulation prescribes the purposes of a work-focused interview as any or all of those listed in paras (a)–(e). **9.151**

Notification of interview

56.—(1) The Secretary of State must notify the claimant of the require- **9.152**
ment to ['take part in] the work-focused interview including details of the
date, time and ['if required to attend in person, the] place of the interview.

(2) A work-focused interview may take place at a claimant's home if it
is determined that requiring the claimant to attend elsewhere would cause
undue inconvenience to, or endanger the health of, the claimant.

(3) The notification referred to in paragraph (1) may be in writing or otherwise.

AMENDMENT

1. Employment and Support Allowance (Work-Related Activity) Regulations
2011 (SI 2011/1349) reg.12 (June 1, 2011).

DEFINITIONS

"claimant"—see WRA 2007 s.24(1).
"work-focused interview"—see WRA 2007 s.12(7).

GENERAL NOTE

The Secretary of State must give proper notification to the claimant that he is **9.153**
required to take part in the work-focused interview. This must include details of its
date, time and (if required to attend in person) place (para.(1)). The notification
need not be in writing (para.(2)). This is in marked contrast to other provisions
imposing requirements with respect to the three elements of the work capability
assessment (WCA) (see regs 22–24, 36–38, 49). So is the absence of any stipulation as to due period of notice. As to place, none is specified (a consequence of
ability to contract-out the interviews—reg.62). But the interview can take place at
the claimant's home if it is decided that requirement to attend elsewhere would
endanger his health or simply cause undue convenience.

Taking part in a work-focused interview

57.—(1) A claimant is regarded as having taken part in a work-focused **9.154**
interview if the claimant—
  (a) ['if required to attend in person,] attends for the interview at the
    place and at the date and time notified in accordance with regulation
    56;
  ['(aa) if not required to attend in person, is available and responds at the
    date and time notified in accordance with regulation 56 to any contact
    made at that time for the purpose of carrying out the interview;]
  (b) provides information, if requested by the Secretary of State, about
    any or all of the matters set out in paragraph (2);
  (c) participates in discussions to the extent the Secretary of State consid-
    ers necessary, about any or all of the matters set out in paragraph (3);

(d) [¹ . . .].

(2) The matters referred to in paragraph (1)(b) are—

(a) the claimant's educational qualifications and vocational training;

(b) the claimant's work history;

(c) the claimant's aspirations for future work;

(d) the claimant's skills that are relevant to work;

(e) the claimant's work-related abilities;

(f) the claimant's caring or childcare responsibilities; and

(g) any paid or unpaid work that the claimant is undertaking.

(3) The matters referred to in paragraph (1)(c) are—

(a) any activity the claimant is willing to undertake which may make obtaining or remaining in work more likely;

(b) any such activity that the claimant may have previously undertaken;

(c) any progress the claimant may have made towards remaining in or obtaining work;

(d) any work-focused health-related assessment the claimant may have taken part in; and

(e) the claimant's opinion as to the extent to which the ability to remain in or obtain work is restricted by the claimant's physical or mental condition.

AMENDMENT

1. Employment and Support Allowance (Work-Related Activity) Regulations 2011 (SI 2011/1349) reg.13 (June 1, 2011).

DEFINITIONS

"claimant"—see WRA 2007 s.24(1).
"work-focused health-related assessment"—see WRA 2007 s.11(7).
"work-focused interview"—see WRA 2007 s.12(7).

GENERAL NOTE

9.155   Failure, without good cause, to take part in a work-focused interview (regs 55, 57, 58, 61) is sanctioned initially by halving the amount of work-related activity component and eventually by reducing it to nil (reg.63), the reduction to cease after compliance has been induced or the requirement to participate has ceased to have effect under para.(3) (reg.64).

This regulation sets out when a claimant is to be regarded as having taken part: attendance at the proper place, date and time (para.(1)(a)) or, if not required to attend in person, is available and responds at the notified date and time to any contact made for the purpose of the interview (para.(1)(aa)); provision of the requisite information required by the Secretary of State (paras (1)(b), (2)); participation to such an extent as the Secretary of State considers necessary in discussion about the key matters stipulated in para.(3); and assisting the Secretary of State (in reality someone in Jobcentre Plus or a contractor or employee of a contractor) in drawing up an "action plan" as defined in reg.58.

Action plan

9.156   **58.**—*Revoked by Employment and Support Allowance (Work-Related Activity) Regulations 2011 (SI 2011/1349) reg.14 (June 1, 2011).*

Deferral of requirement to take part in a work-focused interview

59.—(1) A requirement to take part in a work-focused interview may be deferred or treated as having been deferred if at the time the work-focused interview is to take place, or was due to take place, such an interview would not at that time be or have been—

(a) of assistance to the claimant; or

(b) appropriate in the circumstances.

(2) A decision under paragraph (1) may be made at any time after the requirement to take part in the work-focused interview is imposed, including after the time that the work-focused interview was due to take place or took place.

(3) Where a requirement to take part in a work-focused interview is deferred, or treated as having been deferred, then the time that the work-focused interview is to take place must be re-determined.

9.157

DEFINITIONS

"claimant"—see WRA 2007 s.24(1).
"work-focused interview"—see WRA 2007 s.12(7).

GENERAL NOTE

This regulation enables deferral of a work-focused interview (or treating it as deferred) if holding it would not assist the claimant or otherwise be inappropriate (para.(1)). The decision on deferral can be made at any time after the requirement to take part was imposed on the claimant, whether before or after it was due to take place (para.(2)). If deferred, the matter of when such an interview is to take place has to be re-determined (para.(3)).

9.158

Requirement to take part in a work-focused interview not to apply

60. The Secretary of State may determine that a requirement on a claimant to take part in a work-focused interview is not to apply, or is to be treated as not having applied, if that interview would not be, or would not have been, of assistance because the claimant is or was likely to be starting or returning to work.

9.159

DEFINITIONS

"claimant"—see WRA 2007 s.24(1).
"work-focused interview"—see WRA 2007 s.12(7).

GENERAL NOTE

This enables lifting of the requirement to take part in a work-focused interview, whether before or after it was due to take place, where it would not be (or be likely to have been of assistance) because the claimant is or was likely to be starting or returning to work.

9.160

Failure to take part in a work-focused interview

61.—(1) A claimant who is required to take part in a work-focused interview but fails to do so must show good cause for that failure within 5 working days of the date on which the Secretary of State gives notification of that failure.

(2) The Secretary of State must determine whether a claimant who is required to take part in a work-focused interview has failed to do so and, if

9.161

so, whether the claimant has shown good cause for that failure in accordance with paragraph (1).

[¹(3) *Revoked in respect of failures on or after December 3, 2012. For text of provision prior to that date see the previous edition of this Volume.*]

DEFINITIONS

"claimant"—see WRA 2007 s.24(1).
"relative"—see reg.2(1).
"work-focused interview"—see WRA 2007 s.12(7).

GENERAL NOTE

9.162   Failure, without good cause, to participate in a work-focused interview (regs 55, 57, 58) is sanctioned initially by halving the amount of work-related activity component and eventually by reducing it to nil (reg.63), the reduction to cease after compliance has been induced or the requirement to participate has ceased to have effect under para.(3) (reg.64).

Contracting out certain functions relating to work-focused interviews

9.163   **62.**—(1) Any function of the Secretary of State specified in paragraph (2) may be exercised by, or by employees of, such person (if any) as may be authorised by the Secretary of State.

(2) The functions are any function under—

(a) regulation 54(1) (requirement to take part in a work-focused interview);

(b) regulation 56(1) and (2) (notification requirement);

(c) regulation 57(1)(b) and (c) (taking part in a work-focused interview);

(d) [¹. . .];

(e) regulation 59(1) and (3) (deferral of requirement to take part in a work-focused interview);

(f) regulation 60 (requirement to take part in a work-focused interview not to apply).

AMENDMENT

1. Employment and Support Allowance (Work-Related Activity) Regulations 2011 (SI 2011/1349) reg.15 (June 1, 2011).

GENERAL NOTE

9.164   Pursuant to WRA 2007 s.16, which enables contracting-out, this regulation sets out in para.(2) functions of the Secretary of State under these regulations which can be exercise by an authorised contractor or the employees of such a contractor. The idea is to bring expertise from the private and voluntary sectors (PVS) into the process of assisting claimants to prepare for and enhance their prospects of starting or returning to work. It is envisaged, however, that the first work-focused interview will always be with someone from Jobcentre Plus and will be held around the eighth week of the assessment period. Note that sanctioning decisions (regs 63, 64) are not-contracted out, although clearly information provided by contractors will inform those decisions.

CHAPTER 3

REDUCTION OF EMPLOYMENT AND SUPPORT ALLOWANCE

Reduction of employment and support allowance

63.—[¹(1) Where the Secretary of State has determined— 9.165
 (a) that a claimant who was required to take part in a work-focused interview has failed to do so and has failed to show good cause for that failure in accordance with regulation 61; or
 (b) that a claimant who was required to undertake work-related activity has failed to do so and has failed to show good cause for that failure in accordance with regulation 8 of the Employment and Support Allowance (Work-Related Activity) Regulations 2011,
("a failure determination") the amount of the employment and support allowance payable to the claimant is to be reduced in accordance with this regulation.]

[²(2) Subject to paragraph (3), the amount of the reduction in relation to each failure determination is 100% of the prescribed amount for a single claimant as set out in paragraph (1)(a) of Part 1 of Schedule 4.]

(3) In any benefit week, the amount of an employment and support allowance payable to a claimant is not, by virtue of this regulation, to be reduced—
 (a) below 10 pence;
 (b) in relation to more than—
  (i) one failure determination relating to work-related activity; and
  (ii) one failure determination relating to a work-focused interview; and
 (c) by more than 100% of the [² prescribed amount for a single claimant as set out in paragraph 1(a) of Part 1] of Schedule 4 in any circumstances.

(4) Where a claimant is entitled to both a contributory allowance and an income-related allowance, any reduction in the claimant's allowance must first be applied to the part of that allowance treated as attributable to the claimant's contributory allowance and only if there is any amount outstanding is it to be applied to the part of that allowance treated as attributable to the claimant's income-related allowance.

(5) For the purposes of determining the amount of any income-related allowance payable, a claimant is to be treated as receiving the amount of any contributory allowance [³including new style ESA] which would have been payable but for any reduction made in accordance with this regulation [³or section 11J of the Act respectively].

[² (6) Subject to paragraph (10), the reduction is to have effect for—
 (a) one week for each seven day period during which the claimant fails to meet a compliance condition; and
 (b) a further fixed period determined in accordance with paragraph (7).
[⁴ (7) The fixed period that applies in the circumstances described in the first column of the following table is set out in the second column.

Circumstances applicable to claimant's case	Fixed period
Where there has been no previous failure by the claimant that falls within paragraph (8)	1 week
Where there have been one or more previous failures by the claimant that fall within paragraph (8) and the date of the most recent previous failure is not within 52 weeks beginning with the date of the current failure	1 week
Where there have been one or more previous failures by the claimant that fall within paragraph (8) and the date of the most recent previous failure is within 52 weeks, but not within 2 weeks, beginning with the date of the current failure and the period of reduction applicable to the most recent previous failure is or, but for paragraph (3), would have been—	
(a) 1 week	2 weeks
(b) 2 weeks	4 weeks
(c) 4 weeks	4 weeks
Where there have been one or more previous failures by the claimant that fall within paragraph (8) and the date of the most recent previous failure is within 2 weeks beginning with the date of the current failure and the period of reduction applicable to the most recent previous failure is or, but for paragraph (3), would have been—	
(a) 1 week	1 week
(b) 2 weeks	2 weeks
(c) 4 weeks	4 weeks.]

(8) A previous failure falls within this paragraph if—
(a) it relates to a failure for which a reduction was imposed under this regulation, or would have been but for paragraph (3); [⁴ . . .]
(b) that failure occurred on or after 3rd December 2012; [⁴ . . .]
(c) [⁴ . . .].

(9) This paragraph applies where the claimant meets a compliance condition before the end of the period of one week after the date of the failure to which the failure determination relates.

(10) Where paragraph (9) applies, the claimant's employment and support allowance is reduced only for the fixed period set out in paragraph (7) applicable to the claimant.

(11) In this regulation—
"compliance condition" means—
(a) where the failure by the claimant relates to a requirement to take part in a work-focused interview, either—
  (i) taking part in a work-focused interview, or
  (ii) making an agreement with the Secretary of State to take part in a work-focused interview at an agreed date;
(b) where the failure by the claimant relates to a requirement to undertake work-related activity, either—
  (i) undertaking the activity specified in the action plan, or
  (ii) where so notified by the Secretary of State, undertaking an alternative activity, or
  (iii) making an agreement with the Secretary of State to undertake the activity referred to in sub-paragraph (i) or (ii) at an agreed date;
"current failure" means a failure which may lead to a reduction under

this regulation in relation to which the Secretary of State has not yet determined whether the amount of the employment and support allowance payable to the claimant is to be reduced in accordance with this regulation.]

AMENDMENTS

1. Employment and Support Allowance (Work-Related Activity) Regulations 2011 (SI 2011/1349) reg.17 (June 1, 2011).
2. Employment and Support Allowance (Sanctions) (Amendment) Regulations 2012 (SI 2012/2756) reg.4 (December 3, 2012).
3. Universal Credit (Consequential, Supplementary, Incidental and Miscellaneous Provisions) Regulations 2013 (SI 2013/630) reg.37(1), (4) (April 29, 2013).
4. Social Security (Jobseeker's Allowance, Employment and Support Allowance and Universal Credit) (Amendment) Regulations 2016 (SI 2016/678) regulation 4 (July 25, 2016).

DEFINITIONS

"the Act"—see reg.2(1).
"claimant"—see WRA 2007 s.24(1).
"compliance condition"—see para.(11).
"contributory allowance"—see WRA 2007 ss.24(1), 1(7).
"current failure"—see para.(11).
"failure determination"—see para.(1).
"income-related allowance"—see WRA 2007 ss.24(1), 1(7).
"new style ESA"—see reg.2(1).
"work-focused health- related assessment"—see WRA 2007 s.11(7).
"work-focused interview"—see WRA 2007 s.12(7).

GENERAL NOTE

In accordance with WRA 2007 ss.12(3), 13(3), this regulation provides the sanction for failure without good cause to take part in a work-focused interview or work-related activity. The sanction, put simply, is a reduction in the amount of ESA to which the person would otherwise be entitled (para.(1)). On the face of the Act and the first paragraph of this regulation, that could be a reduction of ESA as a whole, even to nil. The legal reality—effected by the words "in accordance with the provisions of this regulation" in para.(1) and by paras (2) and (3)—is that the reduction in any benefit week is set at 100 per cent of the prescribed amount for a single claimant (see para.1(a), Pt 1, Sch.4), whatever the number of failures and whether relating to work-related interview or work-related activity or both, and cannot exceed that in any circumstances (para.(3)). Nor can this sanction of reduction take the claimant's entitlement in any benefit week below 10 pence (para.(3).

9.166

The current version of para.(2), requiring the sanction to be by way of a reduction amounting to the standard or basic rate for ESA, has been in force since December 3, 2012. Before that date the sanctions regime operated solely on the work-related activity component). That component was not subject to reduction after December 2012. However, the abolition by s.15 of the Welfare Reform and Work Act 2016 of the work-related activity component for (broadly speaking) new claims since April 3, 2017 means that if a new claimant in the work-related activity group is sanctioned they would presumably now lose the entirety of their standard rate of ESA.

The period of reduction is one week for each seven day period in which the claimant fails to meet a "compliance condition" (see para.(11)) *plus* a fixed period, varying according to whether the failure is a first, second or third or subsequent failure (paras (6), (7). However, where the claimant meets a compliance condition within a week of the failure at issue, only the fixed period of reduction is to apply (paras (9), (10)). As regards the appropriate fixed period, looking at the current failure in the context of the previous 52 weeks, the period for which reduction is to be effected is set at one week for a first failure, two weeks for a second failure and four weeks for a third or subsequent failure (paras (7), (8)). A previous failure cannot be one occurring before December 3, 2012 (para. (8)).

Paragraphs (4) and (5) deal with the situation where the claimant's ESA is composed both of CESA and IRESA (a common situation). Reduction is to be effected first against the amount attributable to CESA and only if after that there is a balance of reduction still to be applied, against IRESA (para.(4)). However, even where CESA is thus reduced, for the purposes of deciding on the amount of IRESA when drawing up the IRESA "balance sheet" of "needs" and "resources", the claimant is to be treated as if he were receiving the full amount of CESA to which he would otherwise be entitled but for reduction in accordance with this regulation, and not the reduced amount of CESA left after the reduction demanded by this regulation has been effected (para.(5)).

Paragraph (7)

9.167   The purpose of the 2016 amendment, according to the accompanying Explanatory memorandum, was "to clarify the length of a sanction to be imposed on a claimant. In each case, the existing provisions do not meet the policy intention in a number of certain circumstances concerning multiple sanctions and this instrument rectifies that anomaly" (para.2.1). The policy intention was that in order to prevent anyone incurring lengthy penalties over a short period, a failure which occurs within two weeks of the most recent previous failure should incur a sanction of the same length as the sanction imposed for that previous failure, rather than the length of the sanction increasing. In addition, any sanction imposed for a failure more than 12 months before the failure currently under consideration should not increase the duration of the next sanction. However, DWP identified that the previous form of the regulation did not fully support this policy in specific, limited circumstances namely when a claimant has three or more sanctionable failures and either each occurred within 14 days of the next (and there are more than 14 days between the first and third) or the last two occurred within 14 days of each other (and there are more than 365 days between the first and third). The amendments were designed to ensure that in all cases, where a failure has occurred within 14 days of a previous one, the length of the subsequent sanction is for the same duration as the previous sanction so as to fully reflect the policy intention.

Regulation 64, below, sets out the circumstances in which a reduction imposed for a failure determination under this regulation is to cease.

Cessation of reduction

9.168   **64.**—[¹(1) Any reduction imposed as a result of a failure determination which resulted from a failure to undertake work-related activity in accordance with the Employment and Support Allowance (Work-Related Activity) Regulations 2011 ceases to have effect if—

(a) [²*omitted*]

(b) the claimant subsequently ceases to be subject to a requirement to undertake work-related activity; or

(c) the Secretary of State decides it is no longer appropriate to require the person to undertake work-related activity at that time.

(1A) The Secretary of State must notify the person in writing—

(a) [²*omitted*]

(b) of any decision under paragraph (1)(c).]

(2) Any reduction imposed as a result of a failure determination which

resulted from a failure to take part in a work-focused interview ceases to have effect if—

    (a) [²*omitted*]

    (b) the claimant subsequently ceases to meet the requirements set out in regulation 54(2).

AMENDMENTS

    1. Employment and Support Allowance (Work-Related Activity) Regulations 2011 (SI 2011/1349) reg.18 (June 1, 2011).

    2. Employment and Support Allowance (Sanctions) (Amendment) Regulations 2012 (SI 2012/2756) reg.5 (December 3, 2012).

DEFINITIONS

    "claimant"—see WRA 2007 s.24(1).   9.169

    "failure determination"—see reg.63(1).

    "work-focused interview"—see WRA 2007 s.12(7).

GENERAL NOTE

    Any reduction in ESA effected in respect of a failure determination under reg.63   9.170
ceases to have effect in the circumstances set out in this regulation.

    As regards failure determinations in respect of work-related activity, the sanction ceases once the claimant is no longer subject to a requirement to undertake such activity (para.(1)(b)) or where the Secretary of State decides that his undertaking work-related activity is no longer appropriate at that time and notifies him of that in writing (paras (1)(c), (1A)).

    As regards failure determinations in respect of work-focused interviews, the reduction ceases where the claimant no longer meets the requirements set by reg.54(2) (e.g. becomes a member of the support group) (para.(2)(b)).

[¹ Hardship payments

    64A.—The Secretary of State must make a hardship payment to a claim-   9.171
ant only where—

    (a) the Secretary of State is satisfied that the claimant is or will be in hardship unless a hardship payment is made;

    (b) the claimant's employment and support allowance has been reduced in accordance with regulation 63;

    (c) the claimant meets the conditions of entitlement to an income-related employment and support allowance;

    (d) the claimant completes and submits an application—

        (i) approved for the purpose by the Secretary of State, or in such other form as the Secretary of State accepts as sufficient, and

        (ii) in such manner as the Secretary of State determines; and

    (e) the claimant provides such information or evidence as the Secretary of State may require, in such manner as the Secretary of State determines.]

AMENDMENT

    1. Employment and Support Allowance (Sanctions) (Amendment) Regulations 2012 (SI 2012/2756) reg.6 (December 3, 2012).

[¹ **Circumstances in which a claimant is to be treated as being in hardship**

9.172
64B. A claimant is to be treated as being in hardship if the claimant's partner, or a child or qualifying young person for whom the claimant or the claimant's partner is responsible, is or will be in hardship unless a hardship payment is made.]

AMENDMENT

1. Employment and Support Allowance (Sanctions) (Amendment) Regulations 2012 (SI 2012/2756) reg.6 (December 3, 2012).

[¹ **Matters to be taken into account in determining hardship**

9.173
64C.—(1) The Secretary of State must take the following matters into account in determining hardship—

   (a) whether the claimant's partner or a person in the claimant's family satisfies the requirements for a disability premium specified in paragraphs 6 and 7 of Schedule 4, or an element of child tax credit in respect of a child or young person who is disabled or severely disabled within the meaning of regulation 8 of the Child Tax Credit Regulations 2002;

   (b) the resources which are likely to be available to the household without a hardship payment, including resources from persons who are not members of the household, but excluding any payment referred to in paragraph (2);

   (c) the difference between the resources referred to in sub-paragraph (b) and the amount of the hardship payment that the claimant would receive;

   (d) whether there is substantial risk that the household will not have access to essential items (including food, clothing, heating and accommodation), or will have access to such essential items at considerably reduced levels, without a hardship payment; and

   (e) the length of time that the factors set out in sub-paragraphs (b) to (d) are likely to continue.

   (2)   The payments to be excluded from the resources referred to in paragraph (1)(b) are payments made under paragraph 7(1) or (2) of Schedule 8 (sums to be disregarded in the calculation of income other than earnings: child tax credit and child benefit) to the claimant or the claimant's partner in respect of a child or young person who is a member of the claimant's household or family.]

AMENDMENT

1. Employment and Support Allowance (Sanctions) (Amendment) Regulations 2012 (SI 2012/2756) reg.6 (December 3, 2012).

[¹ **The amount of a hardship payment**

9.174
64D.—(1) A hardship payment is 60% of the prescribed amount for a single claimant as set out in paragraph (1)(a) of Part 1 of Schedule 4.

   (2) A payment calculated in accordance with paragraph (1) shall, if it is not a multiple of 5p, be rounded to the nearest such multiple or, if it is a multiple of 2.5p but not of 5p, to the next lower multiple of 5p.]

AMENDMENT

1. Employment and Support Allowance (Sanctions) (Amendment) Regulations 2012 (SI 2012/2756) reg.6 (December 3, 2012).

CHAPTER 4

NOTIFICATION

Notification under this Part

65.—(1) Where written notification is to be given in accordance with this Part, such notification may be sent by post.   9.175

(2) Any notification sent by post is to be taken to have been received on the second working day after posting.

GENERAL NOTE

This deals with notifications in respect of the conditionality elements in Pt 8 of these regulations. It stipulates that where written notifications are thereby required or envisaged (see regs 49(2),56(3)) they may be sent by post (para.(1)). If so the rule is that such notification is to be taken to have been received on the second working day after posting. (para.(2)).   9.176

CHAPTER 5

MODIFICATION OF THE ACT IN RELATION TO CLAIMS TO WHICH
SECTION 5(1)(C) OF THE ADMINISTRATION ACT APPLIES

Modifications of the Act

66.—(1) Where a person has made a claim for an employment and support allowance to which section 5(1)(c) of the Administration Act applies, the Act applies with the following modifications.   9.177

(2) Section 11(1) of the Act applies—

(a) as if for sub-paragraph (a) there were substituted—

"(a) either—

    (i) entitled to an employment and support allowance; or

    (ii) a person who has made a claim for an employment and support allowance to which regulations under section 5(1)(c) of the Administration Act apply; and"; and

(b) as if for "continuing to be" there were substituted "being".

(3) Section 12(1) of the Act applies—

(a) as if for sub-paragraph (a) there were substituted—

    "(a) either—

        (i) entitled to an employment and support allowance; or

        (ii) a person who has made a claim to which section 5 applies; and"; and

(b) as if for "continuing to be" there were substituted "being".

DEFINITIONS

"the Act"—see reg.2(1).
"Administration Act"—see WRA 2007 s.65.

The Employment and Support Allowance Regulations 2008

GENERAL NOTE

9.178 This regulation alters the terms of WRA 2007 ss.11(1) ("work-focused health-related assessment") and 12(1) ("work-focused interview") where a person has made a claim for ESA which falls to be governed by the AA 1992 s.5(1)(c) (a claim made, or treated as made, for a period wholly or partly after the date on which it is made). In such cases, s.11(1) is to read (modifications in square brackets):

"(1) Regulations may make provision for or in connection with imposing on a person who is—
[(a) either—
    (i) entitled to an employment and support allowance; or
    (ii) a person who has made a claim for an employment and support allowance to which regulations under section 5(1)(c) of the Administration Act apply; and]
  (b) not a member of the support group,
a requirement to take part in one or more work-focused health-related assessments as a condition of [being] entitled to the full amount payable to him in respect of the allowance apart from the regulations."

Similarly, s.12(1) is to read (modifications in square brackets):

"(1) Regulations may make provision for or in connection with imposing on a person who is—
[(a) either—
    (i) entitled to an employment and support allowance; or
    (ii) a person who has made a claim to which section 5 applies; and]
  (b) not a member of the support group,
a requirement to take part in one or more work-focused interviews as a condition of [being] entitled to the full amount payable to him in respect of the allowance apart from the regulations."

PART 9

AMOUNTS OF ALLOWANCE

CHAPTER 1

PRESCRIBED AMOUNTS

Prescribed amounts

9.179 67.—(1) Subject to regulations 68, 69 [¹ . . .] (amounts in other cases, special cases [¹ . . .]), the amounts prescribed for the purposes of the calculation of the amount of an income related allowance under section 4(2)(a) of the Act in relation to a claimant are such of the following amounts as may apply in the claimant's case—
  (a) an amount in respect of the claimant or, if the claimant is a member of a couple, an amount in respect of both of them determined in accordance with paragraph 1(1), (2) or (3) of Schedule 4 (amounts) as the case may be;
  (b) the amount of any premiums which may be applicable to the claimant determined in accordance with Parts 2 and 3 of that Schedule (premiums);
  (c) any amounts determined in accordance with Schedule 6 (housing

1142

costs) which may be applicable to the claimant in respect of [³ housing costs as prescribed] in that Schedule.

(2) Subject to regulation 69 (special cases) the amount prescribed for the purposes of the calculation of the amount of a claimant's contributory allowance under section 2(1)(a) of the Act is the amount determined in accordance with paragraph 1(1) of Schedule 4 as may apply in the claimant's case.

(3) Subject to regulation 69, the amount of the [² ...] support component [² is] prescribed in Part 4 of Schedule 4.

AMENDMENTS

1. Social Security (Miscellaneous Amendments) (No. 5) Regulations 2009 (SI 2009/3228) reg.3(4)(a) (January 25, 2010).

2. Employment and Support Allowance and Universal Credit (Miscellaneous Amendments and Transitional and Savings Provisions) Regulations 2017 (SI 2017/204) reg.2(1) and (3) (April 3, 2017).

3. Loans for Mortgage Interest Regulations 2017 (SI 2017/725) reg.18 and Sch.5, para.1(a) (April 6, 2018).

MODIFICATION

Regulation 67 is modified by Sch.2, para.12 of the Employment and Support Allowance (Transitional Provisions, Housing Benefit and Council Tax Benefit) (Existing Awards) (No. 2) Regulations 2010 (SI 2010/1907) (as amended) for the purposes specified in reg.16(1). For details of the modification, see the text of those Regulations below.

DEFINITIONS

"claimant"—see WRA 2007 s.24(1).
"contributory allowance"—see WRA 2007 s.1(7).
"couple"—see reg.2(1).
"income related allowance"—see WRA 2007 s.1(7).

GENERAL NOTE

Paragraph (1)
This regulation is similar to reg.17 of the IS Regulations and reg.83 of the JSA   **9.180**
Regulations. The applicable amounts are set out in Sch.4 below.

In the same manner as IS and JSA, this read with Sch.4 paras 1(1) (single claimant, age related), (2) (lone parent, age-related) or (3) (couple, age related) as appropriate, specifies the amounts applicable in respect of a claimant as regards IRESA: an amount for him and any partner (para.(1)(a)); applicable premiums (para.(1)(b), Sch.4 Pts 2 and 3); and applicable housing costs (para.(1)(c), Sch.6). This is, however, subject to regs 68 (amounts in other cases polygamous marriages), 69 (special cases) and 163 (urgent cases).

Paragraph (2)
This sets the prescribed amount (basic allowance) of CESA (WRA 2007 s.2(1)   **9.181**
(a)) by reference to Sch.4 para.1(1). There are two rates, a higher one for those aged 25 or over, or who have been awarded the support component, and a lower one for those aged under 25 (Sch.4, para.1(1)). As the support component is only awarded from the end of the assessment phase, all claimants aged under 25 receive the lower rate during that phase. Until April 3, 2015 all claimants, irrespective of age, received the higher rate once the assessment phase was over. Claimants to whom any of the circumstances in paragraphs 2 to 7 of Sch. 2 to the Employment and Support Allowance and Universal Credit (Miscellaneous Amendments and Transitional

and Savings Provisions) Regulations 2017 (SI 2017/204) (see below) have transitional protection from the change. It appears that this aspect of the April 3, 2017 changes was unintended. Regulation 7 of the Employment and Support Allowance (Miscellaneous Amendments and Transitional and Savings Provision) Regulations 2017 (SI 2017/581) reinstates the former law with effect from June 23, 2017.

For those terminally ill covered by reg.7(1)(a) the higher rate component is available from the start of the claim on the basis of terminal illness or the date of an application for revision or suppression on that basis.

The prescription of the amount is, however, subject to reg.69 (special cases). Note also that, whatever the amount of CESA thus set, it is, under WRA 2007 ss.2(1)(c) and 3, subject to reduction in respect of a variety of payments: pension payments (including permanent health insurance payments) (s.3(1)(a), (3); regs 72, 74 and 75); PPF periodic payments (s.3(1)(b), (3); reg.74); and prescribed payments to members of prescribed bodies carrying out public or local functions (currently limited to councillor's allowance and the bodies in the definition of councillor in reg.2(1)) (s.2(1)(c); regs 73, 76). The amount of CESA is also to be reduced by the amount of statutory maternity pay (s.2(2), (3); reg.80), statutory adoption pay (s.2(4), (5); reg.81) or additional statutory paternity pay (s.2(6), (7)); reg.82) to which the claimant is entitled during his period of limited capability for work.

Paragraph (3)

9.182   Subject to reg.69 (special cases), read with Sch.4, para.4, this specifies the amount of the support component. The former work-related activity component was abolished with effect from April 3, 2017, except for those claimants to whom any of the circumstances in paragraphs 2 to 7 of Sch.2 to SI 2017/204 apply: see below.

Polygamous marriages

9.183   **68.**—(1) Subject to regulation 69 [¹ . . .] (special cases [¹ . . .]), where a claimant is a husband or wife by virtue of a polygamous marriage the amounts prescribed for the purposes of the calculation of the amount of an income-related allowance under section 4(2)(a) of the Act are such of the following amounts as may apply in the claimant's case—

(a) an amount in respect of the claimant and the other party to the marriage determined in accordance with paragraph 1(3) of Schedule 4;

(b) an amount equal to the difference between the amounts specified in paragraph 1(3)(a) (couple where both aged 18 and over) and 1(1)(b) (single claimant aged 25 and over) of Schedule 4 in respect of each spouse additional to the marriage;

(c) the amount of any premiums which are applicable to the claimant determined in accordance with Parts 2 and 3 of that Schedule (premiums);

(d) any amounts determined in accordance with Schedule 6 (housing costs) which may be applicable to the claimant in respect of [² housing costs as prescribed] in that Schedule.

(2) In the case of a partner who is aged less than 18, the amount which applies in respect of that partner is nil unless—

(a) that partner is treated as responsible for a child; or

(b) that partner is a person who—

(i) had that partner not been a member of a polygamous marriage would have qualified for an income-related allowance; or

(ii) satisfies the requirements of section 3(1)(f)(iii) of the Jobseekers Act (prescribed circumstances for persons aged 16 but less than 18); or

(iii) is the subject of a direction under section 16 of that Act (persons under 18: severe hardship).

AMENDMENTS

1. Social Security (Miscellaneous Amendments) (No.5) Regulations 2009 (SI 2009/3228) reg.3(4)(b) (January 25, 2010).
2. Loans for Mortgage Interest Regulations 2017 (SI 2017/725) reg.18 and Sch.5, para.1(b) (April 6, 2018).

MODIFICATION

Regulation 68 is modified by Sch.2, para.13 of the Employment and Support Allowance (Transitional Provisions, Housing Benefit and Council Tax Benefit) (Existing Awards) (No.2) Regulations 2010 (SI 2010/1907) (as amended) for the purposes specified in reg.16(1). For details of the modification, see the text of those Regulations below.

DEFINITIONS

"the Act"—reg.2(1).
"claimant"—WRA 2007 s.24(1).
"couple"—reg.2(1).
"income-related allowance"—WRA 2007 s.24(1) and 1(7).
"Jobseekers Act"—reg.2(1).
"partner"—*ibid.*
"polygamous marriage"—*ibid.*
"single claimant"—*ibid.*

GENERAL NOTE

This regulation is similar to reg.18 of the IS Regulations and reg.84 of the JSA Regulations.

9.184

Special cases

69.—(1) In the case of a claimant to whom any paragraph in column (1) of Schedule 5 applies (amounts in special cases), the amount in respect of the claimant is to be the amount in the corresponding paragraph in column (2) of that Schedule.

9.185

(2) In Schedule 5—

"partner of a person subject to immigration control" means a person—

(a) who is not subject to immigration control within the meaning of section 115(9) of the Immigration and Asylum Act; or

(b) to whom section 115 of that Act does not apply by virtue of regulation 2 of the Social Security (Immigration and Asylum) Consequential Amendments Regulations 2000; and

(c) who is a member of a couple and the member's partner is subject to immigration control within the meaning of section 115(9) of that Act and section 115 of that Act applies to the partner for the purposes of exclusion from entitlement to an income-related allowance;

"patient" means a person (other than a prisoner) who is regarded as receiving free in-patient treatment within the meaning of regulation 2(4) and (5) of the Social Security (Hospital In- Patients) Regulations 2005;

"person from abroad" has the meaning given in regulation 70;

"person in hardship" means a person who satisfies regulation 158 but only for a period not exceeding 6 weeks;

"prisoner" means a person who—

(a) is detained in custody pending trial or sentence on conviction or under a sentence imposed by a court; or

(b) is on temporary release in accordance with the provisions of the Prison Act 1952 or the Prisons (Scotland) Act 1989, other than a person who is detained in hospital under the provisions of the Mental Health Act 1983 or, in Scotland, under the provisions of the Mental Health (Care and Treatment) (Scotland) Act 2003 or the Criminal Procedure (Scotland) Act 1995.

[² (3) In Schedule 5 "person serving a sentence of imprisonment detained in hospital" means a person ("P") who satisfies either of the following conditions.

(4) The first condition is that—

(a) P is being detained under section 45A or 47 of the Mental Health Act 1983 (power of higher courts to direct hospital admission; removal to hospital of persons serving sentences of imprisonment etc.); and

(b) in any case where there is in relation to P a release date within the meaning of section 50(3) of that Act, P is being detained on or before the day which the Secretary of State certifies to be that release date.

(5) The second condition is that P is being detained under—

(a) section 59A of the Criminal Procedure (Scotland) Act 1995 (hospital direction); or

(b) section 136 of the Mental Health (Care and Treatment) (Scotland) Act 2003 (transfer of prisoners for treatment of mental disorder).]

AMENDMENTS

1. Social Security (Miscellaneous Amendments) (No.5) Regulations 2009 (SI 2009/3228) reg.3(4)(b) (January 25, 2010).

2. Social Security (Persons Serving a Sentence of Imprisonment Detained in Hospital) Regulations 2010 reg.5(2) (March 25, 2010).

DEFINITIONS

"claimant"—WRA 2007 s.24(1).
"couple"—reg.2(1).
"Immigration and Asylum Act"—*ibid.*
"income-related allowance"—WRA 2007 s.24(1) and 1(7).
"partner"—reg.2(1).

GENERAL NOTE

9.186   This regulation is similar to reg.21 of the IS Regulations and reg.85 of the JSA Regulations. Applicable amounts in special cases are prescribed by Sch.5 below.

Special cases: supplemental—persons from abroad

9.187   **70.**—(1) "Person from abroad" means, subject to the following provisions of this regulation, a claimant who is not habitually resident in the United Kingdom, the Channel Islands, the Isle of Man or the Republic of Ireland.

(2) A claimant must not be treated as habitually resident in the United Kingdom, the Channel Islands, the Isle of Man or the Republic of Ireland unless the claimant has a right to reside in (as the case may be) the United Kingdom, the Channel Islands, the Isle of Man or the Republic of Ireland other than a right to reside which falls within paragraph (3).

(3) A right to reside falls within this paragraph if it is one which exists by virtue of, or in accordance with, one or more of the following—

 (a) regulation 13 of the Immigration (European Economic Area) Regulations 2006;

 (b) regulation 14 of those Regulations, but only in a case where the right exists under that regulation because the claimant is—

     (i) a jobseeker for the purpose of the definition of "qualified person" in regulation 6(1) of those Regulations; or

     (ii) a family member (within the meaning of regulation 7 of those Regulations) of such a jobseeker;

 [4 (bb) regulation 15A(1) of those Regulations, but only in a case where the right exists under that regulation because the claimant satisfies the criteria in regulation 15A(4A) of those Regulations;]

 (c) Article 6 of Council Directive No. 2004/38/EC; [4 ...]

 (d) [3 Article 45 of the treaty on the Functioning of the European Union] (in a case where the claimant is a person seeking work in the United Kingdom, the Channel Islands, the Isle of Man or the Republic of Ireland) [4 ; or

 (e) Article 20 of the Treaty on the Functioning of the European Union (in a case where the right to reside arises because a British citizen would otherwise be deprived of the genuine enjoyment of the substance of their rights as a European Union citizen).]

(4) A claimant is not a person from abroad if the claimant is—

[7 (za) a qualified person for the purposes of regulation 6 of the Immigration (European Economic Area) Regulations 2006 as a worker or a self-employed person;

 (zb) a family member of a person referred to in sub-paragraph (za) within the meaning of regulation 7(1)(a), (b) or (c) of those Regulations;

 (zc) a person who has a right to reside permanently in the United Kingdom by virtue of regulation 15(1)(c), (d) or (e) of those Regulations;]

 (g) a refugee within the definition in Article 1 of the Convention relating to the Status of Refugees done at Geneva on 28th July 1951, as extended by Article 1(2) of the Protocol relating to the Status of Refugees done at New York on 31st January 1967;

 [6 (h) a person who has been granted leave or who is deemed to have been granted leave outside the rules made under section 3(2) of the Immigration Act 1971 where that leave is—

     (i) discretionary leave to enter or remain in the United Kingdom;

     (ii) leave to remain under the Destitution Domestic Violence concession; or

     (iii) leave deemed to have been granted by virtue of regulation 3 of the Displaced Persons (Temporary Protection) Regulations 2005;]

 (i) a person who has humanitarian protection granted under those rules; [6 or]

 (j) a person who is not a person subject to immigration control within the meaning of section 115(9) of the Immigration and Asylum Act and who is in the United Kingdom as a result of deportation, expulsion or other removal by compulsion of law from another country to the United Kingdom; [1 ...]

 (k) [6 ...]

 (l) [1 [6 ...]]

AMENDMENT

1. Social Security (Habitual Residence) (Amendment) Regulations 2009 (SI 2009/362) reg.9 (March 18, 2009).
2. Social Security (Miscellaneous Amendments) (No. 3) Regulations 2011 (SI 2011/2425) reg.23(1) and (7) (October 31, 2011).
3. Treaty of Lisbon (Changes in Terminology or Numbering) Order 2012 (SI 2012/1809) art.3(1) and Sch.1 Pt.2 (August 1, 2012).
4. Social Security (Habitual Residence) (Amendment) Regulations 2012 (SI 2012/2587) reg.2 (November 8, 2012).
5. Social Security (Croatia) Amendment Regulations 2013 (SI 2013/1474) reg.7 (July 1, 2013).
6. Social Security (Miscellaneous Amendments) (No.3) Regulations 2013 (SI 2013/2536) reg.13(1) and (24) (October 29, 2013).
7. Social Security (Habitual Residence) (Amendment) Regulations 2014 (SI 2014/902) reg.7 (May 31, 2014).

MODIFICATION

Regulation 70 is modified by Sch.1, para.10A of the Employment and Support Allowance (Transitional Provisions, Housing Benefit and Council Tax Benefit) (Existing Awards) (No.2) Regulations 2010 (SI 2010/1907) as amended for the purposes specified in reg.6(1) of those Regulations. For the details of the modification, see the text of those Regulations, below.

DEFINITION

"Immigration and Asylum Act"—reg.2(1).

GENERAL NOTE

9.188   See the commentary to the Immigration (European Economic Area) Regulations 2016 in Vol.V.

Definition of non-dependant

9.189   **71.**—(1) In these Regulations, "non-dependant" means any person, except someone to whom paragraph (2), (3) or (4) applies, who normally resides with a claimant or with whom a claimant normally resides.

(2) This paragraph applies to—

(a) any member of the claimant's family;

(b) a child or young person who is living with the claimant but who is not a member of the claimant's household;

(c) a person who lives with the claimant in order to care for the claimant or for the claimant's partner and who is engaged for that purpose by a charitable or voluntary organisation which makes a charge to the claimant or the claimant's partner for the care provided by that person;

(d) the partner of a person to whom sub-paragraph (c) applies.

(3) This paragraph applies to a person, other than a close relative of the claimant or the claimant's partner—

(a) who is liable to make payments on a commercial basis to the claimant or the claimant's partner in respect of the person's occupation of the claimant's dwelling;

(b) to whom the claimant or the claimant's partner is liable to make payments on a commercial basis in respect of the claimant's occupation of that person's dwelling;

(c) who is a member of the household of a person to whom sub-para-graph (a) or (b) applies.

(4) Subject to paragraph (5), this paragraph applies to—

(a) a person who jointly occupies the claimant's dwelling and who is either—

    (i) a co-owner of that dwelling with the claimant or the claimant's partner (whether or not there are other co-owners); or

    (ii) jointly liable with the claimant or the claimant's partner to make payments to a landlord in respect of the person's occupation of that dwelling;

(b) a partner of a person to whom sub-paragraph (a) applies.

(5) Where a person is a close relative of the claimant or the claimant's partner, paragraph (4) applies to that person only if the claimant's, or the claimant's partner's, co-ownership, or joint liability to make payments to a landlord in respect of occupation of the dwelling arose either before 11th April 1988 or, if later, on or before the date on which the claimant or the claimant's partner first occupied the dwelling in question.

(6) For the purposes of this regulation a person resides with another only if they share any accommodation except a bathroom, a lavatory or a communal area but not if each person is separately liable to make payments in respect of occupation of the dwelling to the landlord.

(7) In this regulation "communal area" means any area (other than rooms) of common access (including halls and passageways) and rooms of common use in sheltered accommodation.

DEFINITIONS

"child"—reg.2(1).
"claimant"—WRA s.24(1).
"close relative"—*ibid.*
"family"—reg.2(1) and (3).
"partner"—reg.2(1).
"voluntary organisation"—*ibid.*
"young person"—*ibid.*

GENERAL NOTE

See the notes to reg.3 of the IS Regs.   9.190

CHAPTER 2

DEDUCTIONS FROM THE CONTRIBUTORY ALLOWANCE

Permanent health insurance

72.—(1) For the purposes of sections 2(1)(c) and 3 of the Act (deduc-   9.191
tions from contributory allowance) pension payment is to include a permanent health insurance payment.

(2) In this regulation "permanent health insurance payment" means any periodical payment arranged by an employer under an insurance policy providing benefits in connection with physical or mental illness or disability, in relation to a former employee on the termination of that person's employment.

"pension payment"—see WRA 2007 s.3(3).
"permanent health insurance payment"—see para.(2).

GENERAL NOTE

9.192 WRA 2007 ss.2(1)(c) and 3(1)(a) stipulate that deductions are to be made from CESA in respect of pension payments. "Pension payments" are defined in s.3(3) in terms enabling expansion by regulations (category (c) in the definition). This regulation does just that specifying "permanent health insurance payment", defined in para.(2), as included in the term "pension payment". Note, however, that reg.75(f) means that any such payment in respect of which the employee had contributed more than 50% to the premium will be treated as not counting for reduction purposes.

[¹Financial Assistance Scheme

9.193 **72A.**—(1) For the purposes of sections 2(1)(c) and 3 of the Act (deductions from contributory allowance) pension payment is to include a Financial Assistance Scheme payment.

(2) In this regulation "Financial Assistance Scheme payment" means a payment made under the Financial Assistance Scheme Regulations 2005.]

AMENDMENTS

1. Employment and Support Allowance (Miscellaneous Amendments) Regulations 2008 (SI 2008/2428) reg.7(1) (October 27, 2008).

DEFINITIONS

"Financial Assistance Scheme payment"—see para.(2).
"pension payment"—see WRA 2007 s.3(3).

GENERAL NOTE

9.194 WRA 2007, ss.2(1)(c) and 3(1)(a) stipulate that deductions are to be made from CESA in respect of pension payments. "Pension payments" are defined in s.3(3) in terms enabling expansion by regulations (category (c) in the definition). This regulation does just that by specifying a "Financial Assistance Scheme payment" (defined in para.(2)) as a pension payment.

Councillor's allowance

9.195 **73.** For the purposes of section 3(1)(c) of the Act—
(a) a councillor's allowance is a payment of a prescribed description; and
(b) the prescribed bodies carrying out public or local functions are those councils referred to in the definition of "councillor".

DEFINITIONS

"councillor"—see reg.2(1).
"councillor's allowance"—see reg.2(1).

GENERAL NOTE

9.196 Whatever the amount of CESA set by regs 67(2) (usual cases) or 69 (special cases), it is, under WRA 2007, ss.2(1)(c) and 3, subject to reduction in respect of a variety of payments: including prescribed payments to members of prescribed bodies carrying out public or local functions. This regulation defines councillor's allowance as a prescribed payment and stipulates that "prescribed bodies carrying out public or local functions" are those bodies in the definition of councillor in reg.2(1). On the reductive effect of councillor's allowance see reg.76.

Deductions for pension payment and PPF payment

74.—(1) Where—   9.197
(a) [¹a claimant] is entitled to a contributory allowance in respect of any period of a week or part of a week;
(b) there is—
   (i) a pension payment;
   (ii) a PPF periodic payment; or
   (iii) any combination of the payments specified in paragraphs (i) and (ii),
   payable to that person in respect of that period (or a period which forms part of that period or includes that period or part of it); and
(c) the amount of the payment, or payments when taken together, exceeds—
   (i) if the period in question is a week, £85.00; or
   (ii) if that period is not a week, such proportion of the amount mentioned in paragraph (i) as falls to be calculated in accordance with regulation 94(1) or (6) (calculation of weekly amount of income),
   the amount of that allowance is to be reduced by an amount equal to 50% of the excess.

(2) For the purposes of this Chapter "payment" means a payment or payments, as the case may be, referred to in paragraph (1)(b).

AMENDMENTS

1. Employment and Support Allowance (Miscellaneous Amendments) Regulations 2008 (SI 2008/2428) reg.7(2) (October 27, 2008).

DEFINITIONS

   "claimant"—see WRA 2007 s.24(1).
   "payment"—see para.(2).
   "pension payment"—see WRA 2007 s.3(3); regs 73, 73A.
   "PPF periodic payment"—see WRA 2007 s.3(3).

GENERAL NOTE

WRA 2007 ss.2(1)(c) and 3(1)(a) stipulate that deductions are to be made from   9.198
CESA in respect of "pension payments" and "PPF periodic payments". This regulation provides that where one or more of these is payable to a claimant in respect of a week in respect of which he is entitled to CESA, then where the amount (or combined amount) of that payment (those payments) exceeds £85, the amount of CESA otherwise due is to be reduced by half of the excess over £85. Where the period of CESA entitlement is less than a week, 50% of the excess over an appropriate proportion of the amount of £85 as determined under regs 94(1) or (6) (calculation of amount of income) is instead to be deducted.

Payments treated as not being payments to which section 3 applies

75. The following payments are to be treated as not being payments to   9.199
which section 3 applies—
   (a) any pension payment made to a claimant as a beneficiary on the death of a member of any pension scheme;
   (b) any PPF periodic payment made to a claimant as a beneficiary on the death of a person entitled to such a payment;

(c) where a pension scheme is in deficit or has insufficient resources to meet the full pension payment, the extent of the shortfall;
(d) any pension payment made under an instrument specified in section 639(2) of the Income Tax (Earnings and Pensions) Act 2003;
(e) any guaranteed income payment;
(f) any permanent health insurance payment in respect of which the employee had contributed to the premium to the extent of more than 50%.

MODIFICATION

Regulation 75 is modified by Sch.1, para.11 of the Employment and Support Allowance (Transitional Provisions, Housing Benefit and Council Tax Benefit) (Existing Awards) (No.2) Regulations 2010 (SI 2010/1907) (as amended) for the purposes specified in reg.16(1). For details of the modification, see the text of those Regulations, below.

DEFINITIONS

"claimant"—see WRA 2007 s.24(1).
"guaranteed income payment"—see reg.2(1).
"pension payment"—see WRA 2007 s.3(3); regs 73, 73A.
"permanent health insurance payment"—see reg.72(2).
"PPF periodic payment"—see WRA 2007 s.3(3).

GENERAL NOTE

9.200   WRA 2007 ss.2(1)(c) and 3(1)(a) stipulate that deductions are to be made from CESA in respect of "pension payments" and "PPF periodic payments". This regulation provides that the payments listed in it which would otherwise so rank are not to be treated as payments to which s.3 applies, and so are not to be deducted from CESA.

Deductions for councillor's allowance

9.201   76.—(1) Where the net amount of councillor's allowance to which a claimant is entitled in respect of any week exceeds [¹16 x National Minimum Wage, subject to paragraph (3)], an amount equal to the excess is to be deducted from the amount of a contributory allowance to which that [²claimant] is entitled in respect of that week, and only the balance remaining (if any) is to be payable.

(2) In paragraph (1) "net amount", in relation to any councillor's allowance to which a claimant is entitled, means the aggregate amount of the councillor's allowance or allowances, or remuneration to which that claimant is entitled for the week in question, reduced by the amount of any payment in respect of expenses wholly, exclusively and necessarily incurred by that claimant, in that week, in the performance of the duties of a councillor.

[¹(3) Where the amount determined by the calculation in paragraph (1) would, but for this paragraph, include an amount of—
(i) less than 50p, that amount shall be rounded up to the nearest 50p; or
(ii) less than £1 but more than 50p, that amount shall be rounded up to the nearest £1.]

AMENDMENTS

1. Social Security (Miscellaneous Amendments) Regulations 2011 (SI 2011/674) reg.16(6) (April 11, 2011).
2. Social Security (Miscellaneous Amendments) (No.3) Regulations 2013 (SI 2013/2536) reg.13(25) (October 29, 2013).

DEFINITIONS

"contributory allowance"—see WRA 2007 s.1(7).
"councillor's allowance"—see reg.2(1).
"net amount"—see para.(2).

GENERAL NOTE

This regulation provides that where the net amount of councillor's allowance or remuneration to which the claimant is entitled in any week exceed 16 × National Minimum Wage (rounded as per para.(3)), the amount of the excess must be deducted from the amount of CESA to which he would otherwise be entitled in respect of that week. The reduction can be to nil. Only the balance of CESA remaining (if any) is to be payable. On para.(2) (determination of net amount), compare SSCBA 1992 s.30E(3). That is in similar terms apart from not specifying as para.(2) of this regulation does that the expenses must be *"wholly, exclusively and necessarily* incurred by that claimant, in that week, in *the performance of the duties* of a councillor". The IB provision specified that the expenses must have been incurred in that week in connection with his membership of the [relevant council(s)]. Subject to that, however, existing IVB and IB case law on "net amount" is relevant.

9.202

Unlike the position with computation of earnings under the Computation of Earnings Regs, no concept of averaging across the year is to be applied. In *CS 7934/95*, Commissioner Rice decided:

"that the expenses incurred in any week by the claimant for the performance of her duties as a local authority councillor (whether for clothes, telephone rental, telephone calls, subscriptions, travel, or whatever it might be) shall for the purposes of calculating her entitlement to invalidity benefit [pursuant to SSCBA 1992, s.58(4), the similarly worded precursor of para.(3) of this section, defining 'net amount'], be deducted from the allowance or allowances to which she is entitled in respect of that week" (para.1).

It is immaterial that the benefits of expenses incurred in that week (e.g. the purchase of a dress to be worn more than once for official functions) are enjoyed in future weeks (para.9). In *CIB 2858, 2859* and *2864/2001*, Commissioner Jacobs supported as correct the approach taken by Commissioner Rice in *CS 7934/95*. He disagreed with Commissioner Williams in *R(IB) 3/01*. He accepted that s.30E should be interpreted as a whole. The phrase "in connection with" membership of the council set a limit of reasonableness on the expenditure. An expense is incurred when the liability to discharge it arises (a matter on which he agreed with Commissioner Williams), but it is not incurred in the week in which the item is used (a matter of disagreement with Commissioner Williams). In Commissioner Jacobs's view the result is that s.30E has to be applied week by week, either in each week or retrospectively over a past period. The change of wording to the stricter "in the performance of the duties of a councillor" (the stricter tax approach noted by Commissioner Williams in *R(IB) 3/01*, para.22) may well affirm that approach. An expense is incurred in the week in which the liability arises and can only be used to reduce the reduction in incapacity benefit for that week. Income tax and national insurance deductions do not rank as "expenses in connection with a claimant's membership of a council" and cannot be deducted from the gross councillor's allowances for purposes of incapacity benefit (*R(IB) 3/01*). It is difficult to see that the alteration to "in the performance of his duties as a councillor" alters the status of income tax and NI deductions in this respect.

Date from which payments are to be taken into account

77. Where regulations 74(1) and 76(1) apply, deductions must have effect, calculated where appropriate in accordance with regulation 94(1) or

9.203

(6), from the first day of the benefit week in which the payment or councillor's allowance is paid to a claimant who is entitled to a contributory allowance in that week.

DEFINITIONS

> "benefit week"—see reg.2(1).
> "claimant"—see WRA 2007 s.24(1).
> "contributory allowance"—see WRA 2007 s.1(7).
> "councillor's allowance"—see reg.2(1).
> "payment—see reg.74(2).

GENERAL NOTE

9.204   Deductions for pension payments, PPF periodic payments and councillor's allowance, calculated where appropriate under reg.94(1) or (6) (calculation of weekly amount of income) are to have effect from the first day of the benefit week in which they are paid to a claimant entitled to CESA in that week.

Date from which a change in the rate of the payment takes effect

9.205   **78.** Where a payment or councillor's allowance is already being made to a claimant and the rate of that payment or that allowance changes, the deduction at the new rate must take effect, calculated where appropriate in accordance with regulation 94(1) or (6), from the first day of the benefit week in which the new rate of the payment or councillor's allowance is paid.

DEFINITIONS

> "benefit week"—see reg.2(1).
> "claimant"—see WRA 2007 s.24(1).
> "contributory allowance"—see WRA 2007 s.1(7).
> "councillor's allowance"—see reg.2(1).
> "payment—see reg.74(2).

GENERAL NOTE

9.206   Changes in the rate of pension payments, PPF periodic payments and councillor's allowance affect the amount to be deducted from CESA. The deduction at the new rate, calculated where appropriate under reg.94(1) or (6) (calculation of weekly amount of income), is to have effect from the first day of the benefit week in which the new rate of payment or councillor's allowance is paid to a claimant entitled to CESA in that week.

Calculation of payment made other than weekly

9.207   **79.**—(1) Where the period in respect of which a payment or councillor's allowance is paid is otherwise than weekly, an amount calculated or estimated in accordance with regulation 94(1) or (6) is to be regarded as the weekly amount of that payment or allowance.

(2) In determining the weekly payment, where two or more payments are payable to a claimant, each payment is to be calculated separately in accordance with regulation 94(1) or (6) before aggregating the sum of those payments for the purposes of the reduction of a contributory allowance in accordance with regulation 74.

DEFINITIONS

> "benefit week"—see reg.2(1).
> "claimant"—see WRA 2007 s.24(1).

"contributory allowance"—see WRA 2007 s.1(7).
"councillor's allowance"—see reg.2(1).
"payment—see reg.74(2).

GENERAL NOTE

This provides for the case where pension payments, PPF periodic payments and councillor's allowance are paid otherwise than weekly. The amount to be deducted is to be calculated or estimated, taking each payment or allowance separately, in accordance with reg.94(1) or (6) to ascertain an appropriate weekly equivalent for the pension payment, the PPF periodic payment and the councillor's allowance (para.(1)) For the purposes of the deduction rule in reg.74, the weekly equivalents for each pension payment or PPF payment are then to be aggregated (para.(2)).

9.208

CHAPTER 3

STATUTORY PAYMENTS

Effect of statutory maternity pay on a contributory allowance

80.—(1) This regulation applies where—

9.209

(a) a woman is entitled to statutory maternity pay and, on the day immediately preceding the first day in the maternity pay period—
   (i) is in a period of limited capability for work; and
   (ii) satisfies the conditions of entitlement to a contributory allowance in accordance with section 1(2)(a) of the Act; and

(b) on any day during the maternity pay period—
   (i) she is in a period of limited capability for work; and
   (ii) that day is not a day where she is treated as not having limited capability for work.

(2) Where this regulation applies, notwithstanding section 20(2) of the Act, a woman who is entitled to statutory maternity pay is to be entitled to a contributory allowance in respect of any day that falls within the maternity pay period.

(3) Where by virtue of paragraph (2) a woman is entitled to a contributory allowance for any week (including part of a week), the total amount of such benefit payable to her for that week is to be reduced by an amount equivalent to any statutory maternity pay to which she is entitled in accordance with Part 12 of the Contributions and Benefits Act for the same week (or equivalent part of a week where entitlement to a contributory allowance is for part of a week) and only the balance, if any, of the contributory allowance is to be payable to her.

DEFINITIONS

"the Act"—see reg.2(1).
"contributory allowance"—see WRA 2007 s.1(7).
"Contributions and Benefits Act"—see WRA 2007 s.65.
"maternity pay period"—see WRA 2007 s.20(8); SSCBA 1992 s.165(1).
"week"—see reg.2(1).

GENERAL NOTE

In essence this provides that, where a woman's ongoing entitlement to CESA and statutory maternity pay (SMP) overlap, then during the period they coincide,

9.210

despite WRA 2007, s.20(2), entitlement to CESA is preserved, but the amount payable in respect of the week or part week, as appropriate, is to be reduced (even to nil) by the amount of SMP for that week or part week—only the balance (if any) of CESA is payable.

Effect of statutory adoption pay on a contributory allowance

9.211   **81.**—(1) This regulation applies where—
  (a) a claimant is entitled to statutory adoption pay and, on the day immediately preceding the first day in the adoption pay period—
      (i) is in a period of limited capability for work; and
      (ii) satisfies the conditions of entitlement to a contributory allowance in accordance with section 1(2)(a) of the Act; and
  (b) on any day during the adoption pay period—
      (i) that claimant is in a period of limited capability for work; and
      (ii) that day is not a day where that claimant is treated as not having limited capability for work.

(2) Where this regulation applies, notwithstanding section 20(4) of the Act, a claimant who is entitled to statutory adoption pay is to be entitled to a contributory allowance in respect of any day that falls within the adoption pay period.

(3) Where by virtue of paragraph (2) a claimant is entitled to a contributory allowance for any week (including part of a week), the total amount of such benefit payable to that claimant for that week is to be reduced by an amount equivalent to any statutory adoption pay to which that claimant is entitled in accordance with Part 12ZB of the Contributions and Benefits Act for the same week (or equivalent part of a week where entitlement to a contributory allowance is for part of a week) and only the balance, if any, of the contributory allowance is to be payable to that claimant.

DEFINITIONS

  "the Act"—see reg.2(1).
  "adoption pay period"—see WRA 2007 s.20(8).
  "claimant"—see WRA 2007 s.24(1).
  "Contributions and Benefits Act"—see WRA 2007 s.65.
  "contributory allowance"—see WRA 2007 s.1(7).
  "week"—see reg.2(1).

GENERAL NOTE

9.212   In essence this provides that, where a claimant's ongoing entitlement to CESA and statutory adoption pay (SAP) overlap, then during the period they coincide, despite WRA 2007 s.20(2), entitlement to CESA is preserved, but the amount payable in respect of the week or part week, as appropriate, is to be reduced (even to nil) by the amount of SAP for that week or part week—only the balance (if any) of CESA is payable.

Effect of additional statutory paternity pay on an employment and support allowance

9.213   **82.** — [¹. . .].

REVOCATION

  1. Shared Parental Leave and Statutory Shared Parental Pay (Consequential Amendments to Subordinate Legislation) Order 2014 (SI 2014/3255) art.20 (1), (5) (April 5, 2015).

[¹Effect of statutory shared parental pay on a contributory allowance

82A.—(1) This regulation applies where—   9.214
(a) a claimant is entitled to statutory shared parental pay and, on the day immediately preceding the first day in the shared parental pay period—
    (i) is in a period of limited capability for work; and
    (ii) satisfies the conditions for a contributory allowance in accordance with section 1(2)(a) of the Act; and
(b) on any day during the statutory shared parental pay period—
    (i) that claimant is in a period of limited capability for work; and
    (ii) that day is not a day where that claimant is treated as not having limited capability for work.

(2) Where this regulation applies, notwithstanding section 20(6) of the Act, a claimant who is entitled to statutory shared parental pay is to be entitled to a contributory allowance in respect of any day that falls within the shared parental pay period.

(3) Where by virtue of paragraph (2) a person is entitled to a contributory allowance for any week (including part of a week), the total amount of such benefit payable to that claimant for that week is to be reduced by an amount equivalent to any statutory shared parental pay to which that claimant is entitled in accordance with Part 12ZC of the Contributions and Benefits Act for the same week (or equivalent part of a week where entitlement to a contributory allowance is for part of a week) and only the balance, if any, of the contributory allowance is to be payable to that claimant.

(4) In this regulation "statutory shared parental pay period" means the weeks in respect of which statutory shared parental pay is payable to a person under section 171ZY(2) of the Social Security Contributions and Benefits Act 1992.]

AMENDMENT

1. Shared Parental Leave and Statutory Shared Parental Pay (Consequential Amendments to Subordinate Legislation) Order 2014 (SI 2014/3255) art.20 (1), (6) (December 31, 2014).

DEFINITIONS

    "the Act"—see reg.2(1).
    "claimant"—see WRA 2007 s.24(1).
    "contributory allowance"—see WRA 2007 s.1(7).
    "Contributions and Benefits Act"—see WRA 2007 s.65.
    "statutory shared parental pay period"—see para.(4).
    "week"—see reg.2(1).

GENERAL NOTE

    In essence this provides that, where a claimant's ongoing entitlement to CESA   9.215
and statutory shared parental pay (SSPP) overlap, then during the period they coincide, despite WRA 2007, s.20(6), entitlement to CESA is preserved, but the amount payable in respect of the week or part week, as appropriate, is to be reduced (even to nil) by the amount of SSPP for that week or part week—only the balance (if any) of CESA is payable.

PART 10

INCOME AND CAPITAL

CHAPTER 1

GENERAL

Calculation of income and capital of members of claimant's family and of a polygamous marriage

9.216

83.—(1) Subject to paragraph (4), the income and capital of a claimant's partner which by virtue of paragraph 6(2) of Schedule 1 to the Act is to be treated as income and capital of the claimant, is to be calculated in accordance with the following provisions of this Part in like manner as for the claimant; and any reference to the "claimant" is, except where the context otherwise requires, to be construed, for the purposes of this Part, as if it were a reference to the claimant's partner.

(2) Subject to the following provisions of this Part, the income paid to, or in respect of, and capital of, a child or young person who is a member of the claimant's family is not to be treated as the income or capital of the claimant.

(3) Subject to paragraph (5), where a claimant or the partner of a claimant is married polygamously to two or more members of the claimant's household—

(a) the claimant is to be treated as possessing capital and income belonging to each such member; and

(b) the income and capital of that member is to be calculated in accordance with the following provisions of this Part in like manner as for the claimant.

(4) Where at least one member of a couple is aged less than 18 and the applicable amount of the couple falls to be determined under paragraph 1(3)(e), (f), (g), (h) or (i) of Schedule 4 (amounts), the income of the claimant's partner is not to be treated as the income of the claimant to the extent that—

(a) in the case of a couple where both members are aged less than 18, the amount specified in paragraph 1(3)(c) of that Schedule exceeds the amount specified in paragraph 1(3)(i) of that Schedule; and

(b) in the case of a couple where only one member is aged less than 18, the amount specified in paragraph 1(3)(a) of that Schedule exceeds the amount which is specified in paragraph 1(3)(h) of that Schedule.

(5) Where a member of a polygamous marriage is a partner aged less than 18 and the amount which applies in respect of that partner under regulation 68(2) (polygamous marriages) is nil, the claimant is not to be treated as possessing the income of that partner to the extent that an amount in respect of that partner would have been included in the applicable amount if the partner had fallen within the circumstances set out in regulation 68(2)(a) or (b).

DEFINITIONS

"child"—see reg.2(1).
"family"—*ibid.*
"partner"—*ibid.*
"polygamous marriage"—*ibid.*
"young person"—*ibid.*; s.142 SSCBA.

GENERAL NOTE

This regulation contains the basic rule on aggregation of resources of the claimant **9.217**
and any partner for the purposes of income-related ESA. It is similar to reg.23 of the
Income Support Regulations/reg.88 of the JSA Regulations 1996.

The rules governing income and capital for the purposes of income-related old
style ESA are very similar to those applying to income support and income-based
old style JSA. Where there are differences between the income support and the
income-based JSA provisions ESA generally follows the income support model.
The reader should therefore refer to the notes to the corresponding income support
provision in Vol.II of this series for further explanation of the provisions in this Part.

Income of participants in the self-employment route

84. Chapters 2, 3, 4, 6, 8 and 9 of this Part and regulations 132 to 137, **9.218**
142 and 143 do not apply to any income which is to be calculated in accordance with Chapter 5 of this Part (participants in the self-employment route).

DEFINITION

"self-employment route"—see reg.2(1).

GENERAL NOTE

This is similar to reg.23A of the Income Support Regulations/reg.88A of the JSA **9.219**
Regulations 1996.

[¹ [³ . . .]] Liable relative payments

85. Regulations 91 to 109, 111 to 117 and Chapter 10 of this Part do not **9.220**
apply to any payment which is to be calculated in accordance with Chapter
8 of this Part ([²[⁴ . . .] liable relative payments]).

AMENDMENTS

1. Employment and Support Allowance (Miscellaneous Amendments)
Regulations 2008 (SI 2008/2428) reg.20(2)(a) (October 27, 2008).
2. Employment and Support Allowance (Miscellaneous Amendments)
Regulations 2008 (SI 2008/2428) reg.20(3) (October 27, 2008).
3. Social Security (Miscellaneous Amendments) (No.4) Regulations 2009 (SI
2009/2655) reg.11(4) (April 12, 2010).
4. Social Security (Miscellaneous Amendments) (No.4) Regulations 2009 (SI
2009/2655) reg.11(5) (April 12, 2010).

GENERAL NOTE

This is similar to reg.25 of the Income Support Regulations/reg.89 of the JSA **9.221**
Regulations 1996.

Child support

86. [¹ . . .] **9.222**

AMENDMENT

1. Employment and Support Allowance (Miscellaneous Amendments)
Regulations 2008 (SI 2008/2428) reg.20(4)(a) (October 27, 2008).

Calculation of income and capital of students

9.223   **87.** The provisions of Chapters 2 to 7 of this Part (income and capital) are to have effect in relation to students and their partners subject to the modifications set out in Chapter 10 of this Part (students).

DEFINITION

"partner"—see reg.2(1).

GENERAL NOTE

9.224   This is similar to reg.26 of the Income Support Regulations/reg.91 of the JSA Regulations 1996.

Calculation of income which consists of earnings of participants in exempt work

9.225   **88.** Notwithstanding the other provisions of this Part, regulations 91(2), 92 to 99 and 108(3) and (4) and Schedule 7 (sums to be disregarded in the calculation of earnings) are to apply to any income which consists of earnings which is to be calculated for the purposes of regulations 45(2) to (4) (exempt work—earnings limits).

GENERAL NOTE

9.226   The general rule is that a claimant who does any work in a week will not normally be entitled to old style ESA for that week (see reg.40(1)), but this does not apply to exempt work (see reg.40(2)(f)). See reg.45 for the rules for exempt work; in the case of work referred to in reg.45(2)-(4) this is subject to earnings limits. Regulation 88 is necessary because the exempt work provisions are relevant to both contributory and income-related ESA.

It provides that the following regulations apply for the purposes of calculating a claimant's earnings under the exempt work provisions in reg.45(2)-(4): reg.91(2) (period over which a payment is taken into account); reg.92 (calculation of earnings of self-employed earners); reg.93 (date on which income is treated as paid); reg.94 (calculation of weekly amount of income); reg.95 (earnings of employed earners); reg.96 (calculation of net earnings of employed earners); reg.97 (earnings of self-employed earners); reg.98 (calculation of net profit of self-employed earners); reg.99 (deduction of tax and contributions for self-employed earners); reg.108(3) and (4) (notional earnings) and Sch.7 (sums to be disregarded in the calculation of earnings). The broad effect is that earnings from exempt work (for both contributory and income-related ESA) will be assessed in the same way as earnings generally are for income-related ESA.

Note that if the claimant is doing exempt work, any earnings that do not exceed the relevant weekly limit under reg.45(2), (3) or (4) are disregarded (see para.5 of Sch.7). The limit is £20 or, in some circumstances, 16 x the national minimum wage hourly rate, subject to rounding up to the nearest 50p or £1 (thus, currently, from April 2019, £131.50 per week: see the note to the out-dated definition of "National Minimum Wage" in reg.2(1)). In addition, if the claimant's earnings from the exempt work are less than the relevant limit, the remainder of the disregard (up to a maximum of £20, can be applied to a partner's earnings (see paras 6 and 7 of Sch.7). If the claimant is undertaking exempt work and also has earnings from work as a member of the Disability Living Allowance Advisory Board or as a disability member of a tribunal, the £20 disregard of such earnings under para.7 of Sch.7 only applies to the extent that the claimant's earnings from exempt work are less than the relevant limit. Note that the Disability Living Allowance Advisory Board was abolished on February 7, 2013 by the Public Bodies (Abolition of the Disability Living Allowance Advisory Board) Order 2013, arts 1(2) and (3).

Calculation of income where pension payments, PPF periodic payments or councillor's allowance payable

89. Notwithstanding the other provisions of this Part, regulation 94(1) and (6) is to apply for the purposes of calculating the amount of any pension payments, PPF periodic payments or councillor's allowance to which Chapter 2 of Part 9 (deductions from the contributory allowance) applies.

9.227

DEFINITIONS

"councillor"—see reg.2(1).
"councillor's allowance"—*ibid.*
"pension payments"—see WRA 2007 s.3(3); regs 72 and 72A.
"PPF periodic payment"—see WRA 2007 s.3(3).

GENERAL NOTE

Contributory ESA may be reduced if a claimant receives certain pension payments, PPF periodic payments or councillor's allowances (see regs 72 to 79). This regulation provides that paras (1) and (6) of reg.94 (calculation of weekly amount of income) are to apply for the purposes of calculating such payments.

9.228

CHAPTER 2

INCOME

Calculation of income

90.—(1) For the purposes of paragraph 6(1) of Schedule 1 to the Act (conditions of entitlement to an income-related allowance), the income of a claimant is to be calculated on a weekly basis—

(a) by determining in accordance with this Part, other than Chapter 7, the weekly amount of the claimant's income; and

(b) by adding to that amount the weekly income calculated under regulation 118 (calculation of tariff income from capital).

(2) For the purposes of paragraph (1) "income" includes capital treated as income under regulation 105 (capital treated as income) and income which a claimant is treated as possessing under regulations 106 to 109 (notional income).

(3) For the purposes of paragraph 10 of Schedule 2 to the Act (effect of work), the income which consists of earnings of a claimant is to be calculated on a weekly basis by determining the weekly amount of those earnings in accordance with regulations 91(2), 92 to 99 and 108(3) and (4) and Schedule 7.

(4) For the purposes of paragraph (3), "income which consists of earnings" includes income which a claimant is treated as possessing under regulation 108(3) and (4).

(5) For the purposes of pension payments, PPF periodic payments and a councillor's allowance to which section 3 of the Act applies, the income other than earnings of a claimant is to be calculated on a weekly basis by determining in accordance with regulation 94(1), (2), (5) and (6) the weekly amount of the pension payments, PPF periodic payment or a councillor's allowance paid to the claimant.

9.229

DEFINITIONS

"claimant"—see reg.83(1).
"councillor"—see reg.2(1).
"councillor's allowance"—*ibid.*
"pension payments"—see WRA 2007 s.3(3); regs 72 and 72A.
"PPF periodic payment"—see WRA 2007 s.3(3).

GENERAL NOTE

9.230   Paragraphs (1) and (2) are similar to reg.28 of the Income Support Regulations/reg.93 of the JSA Regulations 1996. They confirm that all income resources, including resources specifically treated as earnings or income, are to be taken into account for the purposes of calculating entitlement to income-related ESA.

Paragraphs (3) to (4)
9.231   Paragraph 10 of Sch.2 to the Welfare Reform Act 2007 provides for regulations to treat a person as not entitled to ESA because of undertaking work. See regs 40–46 which implement this for old style ESA. Under reg.45 certain categories of work are exempt; in the case of work referred to in reg.45(2)–(4) this is subject to earnings limits. Paragraph (3) provides that for the purpose of calculating a claimant's weekly earnings in these circumstances the following regulations apply: reg.91(2) (period over which a payment is taken into account); reg.92 (calculation of earnings of self-employed earners); reg.93 (date on which income is treated as paid); reg.94 (calculation of weekly amount of income); reg.95 (earnings of employed earners); reg.96 (calculation of net earnings of employed earners); reg.97 (earnings of self-employed earners); reg.98 (calculation of net profit of self-employed earners); reg.99 (deduction of tax and contributions for self-employed earners); reg.108(3) and (4) (notional earnings) and Sch.7 (sums to be disregarded in the calculation of earnings). See also reg.88 which makes similar provision. Paragraph (4) specifically provides that such earnings include notional earnings.

Paragraph (5)
9.232   Section 3 of the WRA 2007 (together with s.2(1)(c)) provides for deductions to be made from claimants' contributory ESA if they receive certain pension payments, PPF periodic payments or councillor's allowances. See regs 72 to 79. Paragraph (5) provides that paras (1), (2), (5) and (6) of reg.94 (calculation of weekly amount of income) apply for the purposes of calculating the weekly amount of such payments. See also reg.89 which makes similar, but not identical, provision, since it only brings reg.94(1) and (6) into play for the purpose of calculating the amount of such payments (the reason for this difference is not clear).

Calculation of earnings derived from employed earner's employment and income other than earnings

9.233   **91.**—(1) Earnings derived from employment as an employed earner and income which does not consist of earnings are to be taken into account over a period determined in accordance with the following provisions of this regulation and at a weekly amount determined in accordance with regulation 94 (calculation of weekly amount of income).

(2) Subject to the following provisions of this regulation, the period over which a payment is to be taken into account is to be—

(a) where the payment is monthly, a period equal to the number of weeks from the date on which the payment is treated as paid to the date immediately before the date on which the next monthly payment would have been so treated as paid whether or not the next monthly payment is actually paid;

(b) where the payment is in respect of a period which is not monthly, a period equal to the length of the period for which payment is made;

(c) in any other case, a period equal to such number of weeks as is equal to the number obtained (and any fraction is to be treated as a corresponding fraction of a week) by dividing—

    (i) the net earnings; or

    (ii) in the case of income which does not consist of earnings, the amount of that income less any amount paid by way of tax on that income which is disregarded under paragraph 1 of Schedule 8 (income other than earnings to be disregarded),

by the amount of an [¹ employment and support] allowance which would be payable had the payment not been made plus an amount equal to the total of the sums which would fall to be disregarded from that payment under Schedule 7 (earnings to be disregarded) or, as the case may be, any paragraph of Schedule 8 other than paragraph 1 of that Schedule, as is appropriate in the claimant's case,

and that period is to begin on the date on which the payment is treated as paid under regulation 93 (date on which income is treated as paid).

(3) The period over which a Career Development Loan, which is paid pursuant to section 2 of the Employment and Training Act 1973, is to be taken into account is the period of education and training intended to be supported by that loan.

(4) Where grant income as defined in Chapter 10 of this Part has been paid to a claimant who ceases to be a full-time student before the end of the period in respect of which that income is payable and, as a consequence, the whole or part of that income falls to be repaid by that claimant, that income is to be taken into account over the period beginning on the date on which that income is treated as paid under regulation 93 (date on which income is treated as paid) and ending—

(a) on the date on which repayment is made in full;

(b) where the grant is paid in instalments, on the day before the next instalment would have been paid had the claimant remained a full-time student; or

(c) on the last date of the academic term or vacation during which that claimant ceased to be a full-time student,

whichever is the earlier.

[² [³ (4A)(a) This paragraph applies where earnings are derived by a claimant as a member of a reserve force prescribed in Part 1 of Schedule 6 to the Contributions Regulations—

    (i) in respect of a period of annual continuous training for a maximum of 15 days in any calendar year; or

    (ii) in respect of training in the claimant's first year of training as a member of a reserve force for a maximum of 43 days in that year.

(b) Earnings, whether paid to the claimant alone or together with other earnings derived from the same source, are to be taken into account—

    (i) in the case of a period of training which lasts for the number of days listed in column 1 of the table in sub-paragraph (c), over a period of time which is equal to the number of days set out in the corresponding row in column 2 of that table; or

  (ii) in any other case, over a period which is equal to the duration of the training period.

  (c) This is the table referred to in sub-paragraph (b)(i)—

Column 1 Period of training in days	Column 2 Period of time over which earnings are to be taken into account in days
8 to 10	7
15 to 17	14
22 to 24	21
29 to 31	28
36 to 38	35
43	42]

(4B) The period over which earnings to which paragraph (4A) applies are to be taken into account shall begin on the date on which the payment is treated as paid under regulation 93.]

  (5) Where, but for this paragraph—

  (a) earnings not of the same kind are derived from the same source; and

  (b) the periods in respect of which those earnings would fall to be taken into account overlap, wholly or partly,

those earnings are to be taken into account over a period equal to the aggregate length of those periods and that period is to begin with the earliest date on which any part of those earnings would otherwise be treated as paid under regulation 93.

  (6) In a case to which paragraph (5) applies, earnings under regulation 95 (earnings of employed earners) are to be taken into account in the following order of priority—

  (a) earnings normally derived from the employment;

  (b) any payment to which paragraph (1)(b) or (c) of that regulation applies;

  (c) any payment to which paragraph (1)(j) of that regulation applies;

  (d) any payment to which paragraph (1)(d) of that regulation applies.

  (7) Where earnings to which regulation 95(1)(b) to (d) applies are paid in respect of part of a day, those earnings are to be taken into account over a period equal to a day.

  (8) Any earnings to which regulation 95(1)(j) applies which are paid in respect of, or on the termination of, part-time employment, are to be taken into account over a period equal to one week.

  (9) In this regulation "part-time employment" means, if the claimant were entitled to income support, employment in which the claimant is not to be treated as engaged in remunerative work under regulation 5 or 6(1) and (4) of the Income Support Regulations (persons treated, or not treated, as engaged in remunerative work);

  (10) For the purposes of this regulation the claimant's earnings and income which does not consist of earnings are to be calculated in accordance with Chapters 3 and 6 respectively of this Part.

AMENDMENTS

  1. Social Security (Miscellaneous Amendments) Regulations 2009 (SI 2009/583), reg.10(3) (April 6, 2009).

2. Social Security (Miscellaneous Amendments) (No.2) Regulations 2012 (SI 2012/2575) reg.5(2) (November 5, 2012).
3. Social Security (Members of the Reserve Forces) (Amendment) Regulations 2015 (SI 2015/389) reg. 4(3) (April 6, 2015).

DEFINITIONS

"claimant"—see reg.83(1).
"employed earner"—see reg.2(1).
"first year of training"—*ibid.*
"full-time student"—*ibid.*
"grant income"—see reg.131(1).

GENERAL NOTE

This is similar to reg.29 of the Income Support Regulations/reg.94(1) to (5) **9.234** and (10) of the JSA Regulations 1996. Paragraphs (6) to (9) of reg.94 of the JSA Regulations 1996 contain different provisions defining the length of the period for which a "compensation payment" is to be taken into account.

In relation to earnings to which paras (4A) and (4B) apply (earnings from training as a member of a reserve force), see the disregard in para.11A of Sch.7. This ignores such earnings to the extent that they would have the effect of reducing entitlement to income-related ESA to less than 10p per week.

Although the current form of para.(4A) refers to earnings "derived by a claimant", it seems likely that it is intended to primarily refer to the claimant's partner's earnings as a member of a reserve force, not the claimant's (for obvious reasons). The previous form of para.(4A) referred to such earnings that were "derived by a claimant's partner".

Calculation of earnings of self-employed earners

92.—(1) Except where paragraph (2) applies, where a claimant's income **9.235** consists of earnings from employment as a self-employed earner the weekly amount of the claimant's earnings is to be determined by reference to the claimant's average weekly earnings from that employment—
(a) over a period of one year; or
(b) where the claimant has recently become engaged in that employment or there has been a change which is likely to affect the normal pattern of business, over such other period as may, in any particular case, enable the weekly amount of the claimant's earnings to be determined more accurately.
[¹(2)(a) Where the claimant's earnings consist of any items to which this paragraph applies those earnings shall be taken into account over a period equal to such number of weeks as is equal to the number obtained (and any fraction shall be treated as a corresponding fraction of a week) by dividing the earnings by the amount of employment and support allowance which would be payable had the payment not been made plus an amount equal to the total of the sums which would fall to be disregarded from the payment under Schedule 7 (earnings to be disregarded) as is appropriate in the claimant's case;
(b) This paragraph applies to—
(i) royalties or other sums paid as a consideration for the use of, or the right to use, any copyright, design, patent or trade mark; or
(ii) any payment in respect of any book registered under the Public Lending Right Scheme 1982 or work made under any inter-

national public lending right scheme that is analogous to the
Public Lending Right Scheme 1982,
where the claimant is the first owner of the copyright, design, patent or
trademark, or an original contributor to the book or work concerned.]
(3) For the purposes of this regulation the claimant's earnings are to be
calculated in accordance with Chapter 4 of this Part.

AMENDMENT

1. Social Security (Miscellaneous Amendments) Regulations 2009 (SI 2009/583)
reg.10(3) (April 6, 2009).

DEFINITIONS

"claimant"—see reg.83(1).
"self-employed earner"—see reg.2(1).

GENERAL NOTE

9.236   This is similar to reg.30 of the Income Support Regulations/reg.95 of the JSA
Regulations 1996.

Date on which income is treated as paid

9.237   **93.**—(1) Except where paragraph (2) [² . . .] applies, a payment of income
to which regulation 91 (calculation of earnings derived from employed
earner's employment and income other than earnings) applies is to be
treated as paid—
(a) in the case of a payment which is due to be paid before the first
benefit week pursuant to the claim, on the date on which it is due to
be paid;
(b) in any other case, on the first day of the benefit week in which it is
due to be paid or the first succeeding benefit week in which it is practicable to take it into account.
(2) Employment and support allowance, income support, jobseeker's
allowance, maternity allowance, short-term or long-term incapacity benefit,
[³ severe disablement allowance or universal credit] is to be treated as paid
on [³ on any day] in respect of which it is payable.
(3) [² . . .]
[¹ (4) [² . . .]]

AMENDMENTS

1. Social Security (Miscellaneous Amendments) Regulations 2009 (SI 2009/583)
reg.10(5) (April 6, 2009).
2. Social Security (Miscellaneous Amendments) Regulations 2011 (SI 2011/674)
reg.16(7) (April 11, 2011).
3. Universal Credit (Consequential, Supplementary, Incidental and Miscellaneous
Provisions) Regulations 2013 (SI 2013/630) reg.37(5) (April 29, 2013).

DEFINITIONS

"benefit week"—see reg.2(1).
"universal credit"—*ibid.*

GENERAL NOTE

9.238   This is similar to reg.31 of the Income Support Regulations/reg.96 of the JSA
Regulations 1996.

Calculation of weekly amount of income

94.—(1) For the purposes of regulation 91 (calculation of earnings 9.239 derived from employed earner's employment and income other than earnings) and Chapter 2 of Part 9 (deductions from contributory allowance), subject to paragraphs (2) to (8), where the period in respect of which a payment is made—

(a) does not exceed a week, the weekly amount is to be the amount of that payment;

(b) exceeds a week, the weekly amount is to be determined—

(i) in a case where that period is a month, by multiplying the amount of the payment by 12 and dividing the product by 52;

(ii) in a case where that period is 3 months, by multiplying the amount of the payment by 4 and dividing the product by 52;

[² (iii) in a case where that period is a year and the payment is an award of working tax credit, by dividing the payment by the number of days in the year and multiplying the result by 7;

(iiia) in a case where that period is a year and the payment is income other than an award of working tax credit, by dividing the amount of the payment by 52;]

(iv) in any other case by multiplying the amount of the payment by 7 and dividing the product by the number equal to the number of days in the period in respect of which it is made.

(2) Where a payment for a period not exceeding a week is treated under regulation 93(1)(a) (date on which income is treated as paid) as paid before the first benefit week and a part is to be taken into account for some days only in that week (the relevant days), the amount to be taken into account for the relevant days is to be calculated by multiplying the amount of the payment by the number equal to the number of relevant days and dividing the product by the number of days in the period in respect of which it is made.

(3) Where a payment is in respect of a period equal to or in excess of a week and a part thereof is to be taken into account for some days only in a benefit week (the relevant days), the amount to be taken into account for the relevant days is, except where paragraph (4) applies, to be calculated by multiplying the amount of the payment by the number equal to the number of relevant days and dividing the product by the number of days in the period in respect of which it is made.

(4) In the case of a payment of—

(a) maternity allowance, short-term or long-term incapacity benefit or severe disablement allowance, the amount to be taken into account for the relevant days is to be the amount of benefit payable in respect of those days;

(b) an employment and support allowance, income support or a job-seeker's allowance, the amount to be taken into account for the relevant days is to be calculated by multiplying the weekly amount of the benefit by the number of relevant days and dividing the product by 7.

(5) Except in the case of a payment which it has not been practicable to treat under regulation 93(1)(b) (date on which income is treated as paid) as paid on the first day of the benefit week in which it is due to be paid, where a payment of income from a particular source is or has been paid regularly

and that payment falls to be taken into account in the same benefit week as a payment of the same kind and from the same source, the amount of that income to be taken into account in any one benefit week is not to exceed the weekly amount determined under paragraph (1)(a) or (b) of the payment which under regulation 93(1)(b) is treated as paid first.

(6) Where the amount of the claimant's income fluctuates and has changed more than once, or a claimant's regular pattern of work is such that the claimant does not work every week, the foregoing paragraphs may be modified so that the weekly amount of the claimant's income is determined by reference to the claimant's average weekly income—

    (a) if there is a recognisable cycle of work, over the period of one complete cycle (including, where the cycle involves periods in which the claimant does no work, those periods but disregarding any other absences);

    (b) in any other case, over a period of 5 weeks or such other period as may, in the particular case, enable the claimant's average weekly income to be determined more accurately.

(7) Where income is taken into account under paragraph (4) of regulation 91 over the period specified in that paragraph, the amount of that income to be taken into account in respect of any week in that period is to be an amount equal to the amount of that income which would have been taken into account under regulation 132 (calculation of grant income) had the person to whom that income was paid not ceased to be a full-time student.

(8) Where any payment of earnings is taken into account under [¹paragraph (8)] of regulation 91 (calculation of earnings derived from employed earner's employment and income other than earnings), over the period specified in that paragraph, the amount to be taken into account is to be equal to the amount of the payment.

AMENDMENTS

1. Employment and Support Allowance (Miscellaneous Amendments) Regulations 2008 (SI 2008/2428) reg.8(1) (October 27, 2008).

2. Social Security (Miscellaneous Amendments) Regulations 2009 (SI 2009/583) reg.10(6) (April 6, 2009).

DEFINITIONS

    "benefit week"—see reg.2(1).
    "claimant"—see reg.83(1).
    "full-time student"—see reg.2(1).

GENERAL NOTE

9.240   This is similar to reg.32 of the Income Support Regulations/reg.97 of the JSA Regulations 1996 (except that there is no equivalent of para.(8) in reg.97 as the JSA rules for the treatment of compensation payments made on the termination of part-time employment are different (see the note to reg.94(6)–(9) of the JSA Regs 1996 in Vol.II of this series)).

CHAPTER 3

EMPLOYED EARNERS

Earnings of employed earners

95.—(1) Subject to [¹paragraphs (2) and (3)], "earnings" means, in the   9.241
case of employment as an employed earner, any remuneration or profit
derived from that employment and includes—

  (a) any bonus or commission;
  (b) any payment in lieu of remuneration except any periodic sum paid to
       a claimant on account of the termination of the claimant's employ-
       ment by reason of redundancy;
  (c) any payment in lieu of notice;
  (d) any holiday pay except any payable more than 4 weeks after the ter-
       mination or interruption of employment;
  (e) any payment by way of a retainer;
  (f) any payment made by the claimant's employer in respect of expenses
       not wholly, exclusively and necessarily incurred in the performance
       of the duties of the employment, including any payment made by the
       claimant's employer in respect of—
       (i) travelling expenses incurred by the claimant between the claim-
            ant's home and place of employment;
       (ii) expenses incurred by the claimant under arrangements made
            for the care of a member of the claimant's family owing to the
            claimant's absence from home;
  (g) any award of compensation made under section 112(4) or 117(3)
       (a) of the Employment Rights Act 1996 (the remedies: orders and
       compensation, enforcement of order and compensation);
  (h) any payment or remuneration made under [⁴section] 28, 34, 64, 68
       [⁴or] 70 of the Employment Rights Act 1996 (right to guarantee
       payments, remuneration on suspension on medical or maternity
       grounds, complaints to employment tribunals);
  (i) any such sum as is referred to in section 112(3) of the Contributions and
       Benefits Act (certain sums to be earnings for social security purposes);
  (j) where a payment of compensation is made in respect of employment
       which is part-time employment, the amount of the compensation;
  (k) the amount of any payment by way of a non-cash voucher which
       has been taken into account in the computation of a person's earn-
       ings in accordance with Part 5 of Schedule 3 to the Social Security
       (Contributions) Regulations 2001.

  (2) "Earnings" are not to include—
  (a) subject to paragraph (3), any payment in kind;
  (b) any remuneration paid by or on behalf of an employer to the claim-
       ant in respect of a period throughout which the claimant is on mater-
       nity leave, paternity leave [⁵, shared parental leave] or adoption leave
       or is absent from work because the claimant is ill;
  (c) any payment in respect of expenses wholly, exclusively and necessarily
       incurred in the performance of the duties of the employment;
  (d) any occupational pension;
  (e) any lump sum payment made under the Iron and Steel Re-adaptation
       Benefits Scheme.

[² (f) any payment in respect of expenses arising out of the [³ claimant participating as a service user].]

(3) Paragraph (2)(a) is not to apply in respect of any non-cash voucher referred to in paragraph (1)(k).

(4) In this regulation—

"compensation" means any payment made in respect of, or on the termination of, employment in a case where a claimant has not received or received only part of a payment in lieu of notice due or which would have been due to the claimant had that claimant not waived the right to receive it, other than—

(a) any payment specified in paragraph (1)(a) to (i);

(b) any payment specified in paragraph (2)(a) to [³ (f)];

(c) any redundancy payment within the meaning of section 135(1) of the Employment Rights Act 1996;

(d) any refund of contributions to which that person was entitled under an occupational pension scheme; and

(e) any compensation payable by virtue of section 173 of the Education Reform Act 1988;

"part-time employment" means, if the claimant were entitled to income support, employment in which the claimant is not to be treated as engaged in remunerative work under regulation 5 or 6(1) and (4) of the Income Support Regulations (persons treated, or not treated, as engaged in remunerative work).

AMENDMENTS

1. Employment and Support Allowance (Miscellaneous Amendments) Regulations 2008 (SI 2008/2428) reg.8(2) (October 27, 2008).

2. Social Security (Miscellaneous Amendments) (No. 4) Regulations 2009 (SI 2009/2655) reg.11(6) (October 26, 2009).

3. Social Security (Miscellaneous Amendments) (No.3) Regulations 2013 (SI 2013/2536) reg.13(26) (October 29, 2013).

4. Social Security (Miscellaneous Amendments) Regulations 2014 (SI 2014/591) reg.10(2) (April 28, 2014).

5. Shared Parental Leave and Statutory Shared Parental Pay (Consequential Amendments to Subordinate Legislation) Order 2014 (SI 2014/3255) art.20(7) (December 31, 2014).

DEFINITIONS

"adoption leave"—see reg.2(1).
"claimant"—see reg.83(1).
"claimant participating as a service user"—see reg. 2(8).
"employed earner"—see reg.2(1).
"family"—*ibid.*
"occupational pension"—*ibid.*
"shared parental leave"—*ibid.*

GENERAL NOTE

9.242   The equivalent income support and old-style JSA are regs 35 and 98 respectively. This regulation adopts the model of reg.35 of the Income Support Regulations rather than reg.98 of the JSA Regulations 1996. For the differences between reg.98 and this regulation (and reg.35 of the Income Support Regulations), see the notes to reg.98 of the JSA Regulations 1996 in Vol.II of this series. Note also that unlike the equivalent provisions in reg.35 and reg.98, para.(1)(d) (which relates to holiday pay) does not contain any special rule relating to trade disputes.

Calculation of net earnings of employed earners

96.—(1) For the purposes of regulation 91 (calculation of earnings derived   9.243
from employed earner's employment and income other than earnings) the
earnings of a claimant derived from employment as an employed earner to be
taken into account, subject to paragraph (2), are the claimant's net earnings.

(2) There is to be disregarded from a claimant's net earnings, any sum,
where applicable, specified in paragraphs 1 to 12 of Schedule 7 (sums to be
disregarded in the calculation of earnings).

(3) For the purposes of paragraph (1) net earnings are to be calculated
by taking into account the gross earnings of the claimant from that employment less—

(a) any amount deducted from those earnings by way of—
   (i) income tax;
   (ii) primary Class 1 contributions under section 6(1)(a) of the
        Contributions and Benefits Act;
(b) one-half of any sum paid by the claimant in respect of a pay period by
    way of a contribution towards an occupational or personal pension
    scheme.

DEFINITIONS

"claimant"—see reg.83(1).
"Contributions and Benefits Act"—see WRA 2007 s.65.
"employed earner"—see reg.2(1).
"occupational pension scheme"—*ibid.*
"pay period"—*ibid.*
"personal pension scheme"—*ibid.*

GENERAL NOTE

This is similar to reg.36 of the Income Support Regulations/reg.99 of the JSA   9.244
Regulations 1996.

CHAPTER 4

SELF-EMPLOYED EARNERS

Earnings of self-employed earners

97.—(1) Subject to paragraph (2), "earnings", in the case of employ-   9.245
ment as a self-employed earner, means the gross receipts of the employment and include any allowance paid under section 2 of the Employment
and Training Act 1973 or section 2 of the Enterprise and New Towns
(Scotland) Act 1990 to the claimant for the purpose of assisting the claimant in carrying on the claimant's business.

(2) "Earnings" do not include—

(a) where a claimant is involved in providing board and lodging accom-
    modation for which a charge is payable, any payment by way of such
    a charge;
(b) any payment to which paragraph [¹28, 29 or 29A] of Schedule 8 refers
    (payments in respect of a person accommodated with the claimant
    under an arrangement made by a local authority or voluntary organi-
    sation[¹, payments] made to the claimant by a health authority, local
    authority or voluntary organisation in respect of persons temporarily

in the claimant's care) [¹and any payments made to a claimant under section 73(1)(b) of the Children and Young People (Scotland) Act 2014 (kinship care allowance)];

[² (ba) any payment made in accordance with section 26A of the Children (Scotland) Act 1995 (duty to provide continuing care)—
  (i) to a claimant; or
  (ii) where paragraph (3) applies, to another person ("A") which A passes on to the claimant;]
  (c) any sports award.
[² (3) This paragraph applies only where A—
  (a) was formerly in the claimant' s care;
  (b) is aged 16 or over; and
  (c) continues to live with the claimant.]

AMENDMENTS

1. Social Security and Child Support (Care Payments and Tenant Incentive Scheme) (Amendment) Regulations 2017 (SI 2017/995) reg.7(3) (November 7, 2017).

2. Social Security and Child Support (Care Payments and Tenant Incentive Scheme) (Amendment) Regulations 2017 (SI 2017/995) reg.13(3) (November 7, 2017).

DEFINITIONS

"board and lodging"—see reg.2(1).
"claimant"—see reg.83(1).
"self-employed earner"—see reg.2(1).
"sports award"—*ibid.*
"voluntary organisation"—*ibid.*

GENERAL NOTE

9.246   This is similar to reg.37 of the Income Support Regulations/reg.100 of the JSA Regulations. See the notes to reg.37 for the effect of the 2017 amendments and payments under s.73 of the Children and Young People (Scotland) Act 2014.

Calculation of net profit of self-employed earners

9.247   **98.**—(1) For the purposes of regulation 92 (calculation of earnings of self-employed earners), the earnings of a claimant to be taken into account are to be—
  (a) in the case of a self-employed earner who is engaged in employment on that self-employed earner's own account, the net profit derived from that employment;
  (b) in the case of a self-employed earner whose employment is carried on in partnership or is that of a share fisherman within the meaning of the Social Security (Mariners' Benefits) Regulations 1975, that self-employed earner's share of the net profit derived from that employment less—
    (i) an amount in respect of income tax and of National Insurance contributions payable under the Contributions and Benefits Act calculated in accordance with regulation 99 (deduction of tax and contributions for self-employed earners); and
    (ii) one half of any premium paid in the period that is relevant

under regulation 92 (calculation of earnings of self-employed earners) in respect of a personal pension scheme.

(2) There is to be disregarded from a claimant's net profit any sum, where applicable, specified in paragraphs 1 to 11 of Schedule 7.

(3) For the purposes of paragraph (1)(a) the net profit of the employment, except where paragraph (9) applies, is to be calculated by taking into account the earnings of the employment over the period determined under regulation 92 less—

(a) subject to paragraphs (5) to (7), any expenses wholly and exclusively defrayed in that period for the purposes of that employment;

(b) an amount in respect of—
  (i) income tax; and
  (ii) National Insurance contributions payable under the Contributions and Benefits Act,
  calculated in accordance with regulation 99 (deduction of tax and contributions for self-employed earners); and

(c) one half of any premium paid in the period that is relevant under regulation 92 in respect of a personal pension scheme.

(4) For the purposes of paragraph (1)(b), the net profit of the employment is to be calculated by taking into account the earnings of the employment over the period determined under regulation 92 less, subject to paragraphs (5) to (7), any expenses wholly and exclusively defrayed in that period for the purpose of that employment.

(5) Subject to paragraph (6), a deduction is not to be made under paragraph (3)(a) or (4) in respect of—

(a) any capital expenditure;

(b) the depreciation of any capital asset;

(c) any sum employed or intended to be employed in the setting up or expansion of the employment;

(d) any loss incurred before the beginning of the period determined under regulation 92 (calculation of earnings of self-employed earners);

(e) the repayment of capital on any loan taken out for the purposes of the employment;

(f) any expenses incurred in providing business entertainment.

(6) A deduction is to be made under paragraph (3)(a) or (4) in respect of the repayment of capital on any loan used for—

(a) the replacement in the course of business of equipment or machinery; and

(b) the repair of an existing business asset except to the extent that any sum is payable under an insurance policy for its repair.

(7) The Secretary of State will refuse to make a deduction in respect of any expenses under paragraph (3)(a) or (4) where the Secretary of State is not satisfied that the expense has been defrayed or, having regard to the nature of the expense and its amount, that it has been reasonably incurred.

(8) For the avoidance of doubt—

(a) a deduction is not to be made under paragraph (3)(a) or (4) in respect of any sum unless it has been expended for the purposes of the business;

(b) a deduction is to be made thereunder in respect of—
  (i) the excess of any VAT paid over VAT received in the period determined under regulation 92;
  (ii) any income expended in the repair of an existing asset except to

the extent that any sum is payable under an insurance policy for its repair;

(iii) any payment of interest on a loan taken out for the purposes of the employment.

(9) Where a claimant is engaged in employment as a child minder the net profit of the employment is to be one-third of the earnings of that employment, less—

(a) an amount in respect of—

(i) income tax; and

(ii) National Insurance contributions payable under the Contributions and Benefits Act,

calculated in accordance with regulation 99 (deduction of tax and contributions for self-employed earners); and

(b) one half of any premium paid in respect of a personal pension scheme.

(10) Notwithstanding regulation 92 (calculation of earnings of self-employed earners) and the foregoing paragraphs, the Secretary of State may assess any item of a claimant's income or expenditure over a period other than that determined under regulation 92 as may, in the particular case, enable the weekly amount of that item of income or expenditure to be determined more accurately.

(11) For the avoidance of doubt where a claimant is engaged in employment as a self-employed earner and that claimant is also engaged in one or more other employments as a self-employed or employed earner any loss incurred in any one of the claimant's employments is not to be offset against the claimant's earnings in any other of the claimant's employments.

DEFINITIONS

"claimant"—see reg.83(1).
"Contributions and Benefits Act"—see WRA 2007 s.65.
"employment"—see reg.2(1).
"personal pension scheme"—*ibid.*
"self-employed earner"—*ibid.*

GENERAL NOTE

9.248   This is similar to reg.38 of the Income Support Regulations/reg.101 of the JSA Regulations 1996 (except that there is no equivalent of reg.101(3) of the JSA Regulations which is concerned with calculating the amount of any earnings to be deducted from old style contribution-based JSA).

Deduction of tax and contributions for self-employed earners

9.249   **99.**—(1) Subject to paragraph (2), the amount to be deducted in respect of income tax under regulation 98(1)(b)(i), (3)(b)(i) or (9)(a)(i) (calculation of net profit of self-employed earners) is to be calculated on the basis of the amount of chargeable income and as if that income were assessable to income tax at the [¹ . . .] [³ basic rate, or in the case of a Scottish taxpayer, the Scottish basic rate, of tax less only the personal reliefs to which the claimant is entitled under Chapters 2, 3 and 3A of Part 3 of the Income Tax Act 2007 as are appropriate to the claimant's circumstances].

(2) If the period determined under regulation 92 is less than a year the earnings to which the [¹basic rate] [³, or the Scottish basic rate,] of tax is to

be applied and the amount of the personal reliefs deductible under [³ paragraph (1) are] to be calculated on a pro rata basis.

(3) The amount to be deducted in respect of National Insurance contributions under regulation 98(1)(b)(i), (3)(b)(ii) or (9)(a)(ii) is to be the total of—

(a) the amount of Class 2 contributions payable under section [² 11(2)] or, as the case may be, [² 11(8)] of the Contributions and Benefits Act at the rate applicable at the date of claim except where the claimant's chargeable income is less than the amount specified in section 11(4) of that Act ([² small profits threshold]) for the tax year in which the date of claim falls; but if the assessment period is less than a year, the amount specified for that tax year is to be reduced pro rata; and

(b) the amount of Class 4 contributions (if any) which would be payable under section 15 of that Act (Class 4 contributions recoverable under the Income Tax Acts) at the percentage rate applicable at the date of claim on so much of the chargeable income as exceeds the lower limit but does not exceed the upper limit of profits and gains applicable for the tax year in which the date of claim falls; but if the assessment period is less than a year, those limits are to be reduced pro rata.

(4) In this regulation "chargeable income" means—

(a) except where sub-paragraph (b) applies, the earnings derived from the employment less any expenses deducted under paragraph (3)(a) or, as the case may be, (4) of regulation 98;

(b) in the case of employment as a child minder, one-third of the earnings of that employment.

AMENDMENTS

1. Employment and Support Allowance (Miscellaneous Amendments) Regulations 2008 (SI 2008/2428) reg.8(3) (October 27, 2008).

2. Social Security (Miscellaneous Amendments No. 2) Regulations 2015 (SI 2015/478) reg.35 (April 6, 2015)

3. Social Security (Scottish Rate of Income Tax etc.) (Amendment) Regulations 2016 (SI 2016/233) reg.6(3) (April 6, 2016).

DEFINITIONS

"claimant"—see reg.83(1).
"Contributions and Benefits Act"—see WRA 2007 s.65.
"Scottish basic rate" – see reg.2(1).
"Scottish taxpayer" – *ibid.*

GENERAL NOTE

This is similar to reg.39 of the Income Support Regulations/reg.102 of the JSA Regulations 1996.

9.250

CHAPTER 5

PARTICIPANTS IN THE SELF-EMPLOYMENT ROUTE

Interpretation

9.251   **100.** In this Chapter "special account" means, where a claimant was carrying on a commercial activity in respect of which assistance is received under the self-employment route, the account into which the gross receipts from that activity were payable during the period in respect of which such assistance was received.

DEFINITIONS

> "claimant"—see reg.83(1).
> "self-employment route"—see reg.2(1).

GENERAL NOTE

9.252   This is similar to reg.39A of the Income Support Regulations/reg.102A of the JSA Regulations 1996.

Treatment of gross receipts of participants in the self-employment route

9.253   **101.** The gross receipts of a commercial activity carried on by a claimant in respect of which assistance is received under the self-employment route, are to be taken into account in accordance with the following provisions of this Chapter.

DEFINITIONS

> "claimant"—see reg.83(1).
> "self-employment route"—see reg.2(1).

GENERAL NOTE

9.254   This is similar to reg.39B of the Income Support Regulations/reg.102B of the JSA Regulations 1996.

Calculation of income of participants in the self-employment route

9.255   **102.**—(1) The income of a claimant who has received assistance under the self-employment route is to be calculated by taking into account the whole of the monies in the special account at the end of the last day on which such assistance was received and deducting from those monies—

(a) an amount in respect of income tax calculated in accordance with regulation 103 (deduction in respect of tax for participants in the self-employment route); and

(b) any sum to which paragraph (4) refers.

(2) Income calculated pursuant to paragraph (1) is to be apportioned equally over a period which starts on the date the income is treated as paid under paragraph (3) and is equal in length to the period beginning with the day on which assistance was first received under the self-employment route and ending on the last day on which such assistance was received.

1176

(3) Income calculated pursuant to paragraph (1) is to be treated as paid —

(a) in the case where it is due to be paid before the first benefit week in respect of which the participant or the participant's partner first claims an income-related allowance following the last day on which assistance was received under the self-employment route, on the day in the week in which it is due to be paid which corresponds to the first day of the benefit week;

(b) in any other case, on the first day of the benefit week in which it is due to be paid.

(4) This paragraph refers, where applicable in each benefit week in respect of which income calculated pursuant to paragraph (1) is taken into account pursuant to paragraphs (2) and (3), to the sums which would have been disregarded under paragraph 7(1) of Schedule 7 had the income been earnings.

DEFINITIONS

"benefit week"—see reg.2(1).
"claimant"—see reg. 83(1).
"self-employment route"—see reg.2(1).

GENERAL NOTE

This is similar to reg.39C of the Income Support Regulations/reg.102C of the JSA Regulations 1996.

9.256

Deduction in respect of tax for participants in the self-employment route

103.—(1) The amount to be deducted in respect of income tax under regulation 102(1)(a) (calculation of income of participants in the self-employment route) in respect of the period determined under regulation 102(2) is to be calculated as if—

9.257

(a) the chargeable income is the only income chargeable to tax;

[²(b) the personal reliefs applicable to the person receiving assistance under the self-employment route under Chapters 2, 3 and 3A of Part 3 of the Income Tax Act 2007 are allowable against that income;] and

(c) the rate at which the chargeable income less the [² personal reliefs] is assessable to income tax is the [¹ . . .] basic rate [², or in the case of a Scottish taxpayer, the Scottish basic rate,] of tax.

(2) For the purpose of paragraph (1), the [² basic rate, or the Scottish basic rate, of tax to be applied and the amount of personal reliefs deductible are], where the period determined under regulation 102(2) is less than a year, to be calculated on a pro rata basis.

(3) In this regulation, "chargeable income" means the monies in the special account at the end of the last day upon which assistance was received under the self-employment route.

AMENDMENTS

1. Employment and Support Allowance (Miscellaneous Amendments) Regulations 2008 (SI 2008/2428) reg.8(4) (October 27, 2008).

2. Social Security (Scottish Rate of Income Tax etc.) (Amendment) Regulations 2016 (SI 2016/233) reg.6(4) (April 6, 2016).

DEFINITIONS

"self-employment route"—see reg.2(1).
"Scottish basic rate"—*ibid.*
"Scottish taxpayer"—*ibid.*

GENERAL NOTE

9.258   This is similar to reg.39D of the Income Support Regulations/reg.102D of the JSA Regulations 1996.

CHAPTER 6

OTHER INCOME

Calculation of income other than earnings

9.259   **104.**—(1) For the purposes of regulation 91 (calculation of earnings derived from employed earner's employment and income other than earnings) [² [³ . . .]] the income of a claimant which does not consist of earnings to be taken into account will, subject to paragraphs (2) to (7), be the claimant's gross income and any capital treated as income under regulation 105 (capital treated as income).

(2) There is to be disregarded from the calculation of a claimant's gross income under paragraph (1), any sum, where applicable, specified in Schedule 8.

(3) Where the payment of any benefit under the benefit Acts is subject to any deduction by way of recovery the amount to be taken into account under paragraph (1) is to be the gross amount payable.

(4) [¹Paragraphs (5) and (5A) apply] where—

(a)   a relevant payment has been made to a claimant in an academic year; and

(b)   that claimant abandons, or is dismissed from, that claimant's course of study before the payment to the claimant of the final instalment of the relevant payment.

(5) [¹Where a relevant payment is made quarterly, the] amount of a relevant payment to be taken into account for the assessment period for the purposes of paragraph (1) in respect of a claimant to whom paragraph (4) applies, is to be calculated by applying the formula—

$$\frac{A - (B \times C)}{D}$$

where—

A = the total amount of the relevant payment which that claimant would have received had that claimant remained a student until the last day of the academic term in which the person abandoned, or was dismissed from, the course, less any deduction under regulation 137(6) (treatment of student loans);

B = the number of benefit weeks from the benefit week immediately following that which includes the first day of that academic year to the benefit week immediately before that which includes the day on which the claimant abandoned, or was dismissed from, that claimant's course;

C = the weekly amount of the relevant payment, before the application of the £10 disregard, which would have been taken into account as income under regulation 137(3) had the claimant not abandoned or been dismissed from, the course and, in the case of a claimant who was not entitled to an income-related allowance immediately before that claimant abandoned or was dismissed from the course, had that claimant, at that time, been entitled to an income-related allowance;

D = the number of benefit weeks in the assessment period.

[[1](5A) Where a relevant payment is made by two or more instalments in a quarter, the amount of a relevant payment to be taken into account for the assessment period for the purposes of paragraph (1) in respect of a person to whom paragraph (4) applies, shall be calculated by applying the formula in paragraph (5) but as if—

A = the total amount of relevant payments which that person received, or would have received, from the first day of the academic year to the day the person abandoned the course, or was dismissed from it, less any deduction under regulation 137(6).]

(6) [[1]In this regulation]—

"academic year" and "student loan" have the same meanings as for the purposes of Chapter 10 of this Part;

[[1]"assessment period" means—

(a) in a case where a relevant payment is made quarterly, the period beginning with the benefit week which includes the day on which the claimant abandoned, or was dismissed from, the course and ending with the benefit week which includes the last day of the last quarter for which an instalment of the relevant payment was payable to that claimant;

(b) in a case where the relevant payment is made by two or more instalments in a quarter, the period beginning with the benefit week which includes the day on which the claimant abandoned, or was dismissed from, the course and ending with the benefit week which includes—

  (i) the day immediately before the day on which the next instalment of the relevant payment would have been due had the payments continued; or

  (ii) the last day of the last quarter for which an instalment of the relevant payment was payable to that claimant,

  whichever of those dates is earlier;]

"quarter" for the purposes of the definition of "assessment period" in relation to an academic year means a period in that year—

(a) beginning on 1st January and ending on 31st March;

(b) beginning on 1st April and ending on 30th June;

(c) beginning on 1st July and ending on 31st August; or

(d) beginning on 1st September and ending on 31st December;

"relevant payment" means either a student loan or an amount intended for the maintenance of dependants referred to in regulation 132(6) (calculation of grant income) or both.

(7) In the case of income to which regulation 91(4) (calculation of income of former students) applies, the amount of income to be taken into account for the purposes of paragraph (1) is to be the amount of that income calculated in accordance with regulation 94(7) (calculation of weekly amount of income) and on the basis that none of that income has been repaid.

(8) Subject to paragraph (9), for the avoidance of doubt there is to be included as income to be taken into account under paragraph (1)—

(a) any payment to which regulation 95(2) or 97(2) (payments not earnings) applies; or

(b) in the case of a claimant who is receiving support provided under section 95 or 98 of the Immigration and Asylum Act including support provided by virtue of regulations made under Schedule 9 to that Act, the amount of such support provided in respect of essential living needs of the claimant and the claimant's partner (if any) as is specified in regulations made under paragraph 3 of Schedule 8 to that Act.

(9) In the case of a claimant who is the partner of a person subject to immigration control and whose partner is receiving support provided under section 95 or 98 of the Immigration and Asylum Act including support provided by virtue of regulations made under Schedule 9 to that Act, there is not to be included as income to be taken into account under paragraph (1) the amount of support provided in respect of essential living needs of the partner of the claimant and the claimant's dependants (if any) as is specified in regulations made under paragraph 3 of Schedule 8 to the Immigration and Asylum Act.

[⁴ (10) Where a claimant is a member of a couple and the claimant's partner is receiving a contributory allowance, and that benefit has been reduced under regulation 63 or section 11J of the Act, the amount of the benefit to be taken into account is the amount as if it had not been so reduced.

(11) Where a claimant is a husband or wife by virtue of a polygamous marriage and the other party to the marriage or any spouse additional to the marriage is receiving a contributory allowance, and that benefit has been reduced under regulation 63 or section 11J of the Act, the amount of the benefit to be taken into account is the amount as if it had not been so reduced.]

AMENDMENTS

1. Social Security (Students and Miscellaneous Amendments) Regulations 2008 (SI 2008/1599) reg.7(2) (October 27, 2008).

2. Social Security (Miscellaneous Amendments) (No. 4) Regulations 2009 (SI 2009/2655) reg.11(7) (October 26, 2009).

3. Social Security (Miscellaneous Amendments) Regulations 2011 (SI 2011/674) reg.16(8) (April 11, 2011).

4. Social Security (Miscellaneous Amendments) (No.3) Regulations 2013 (SI 2013/2536) reg.13(27) (October 29, 2013).

DEFINITIONS

"academic year"—see reg.131(1).
"benefit week"—see reg.2(1).
"claimant"— see reg.83(1).
"full-time student"—see reg.2(1).
"student loan"—see reg.131(1).

GENERAL NOTE

9.260   This is similar to reg.40 of the Income Support Regulations/reg.103 of the JSA Regulations 1996 (except that there is no equivalent to para.(9) in reg.103 of the JSA Regulations).

Capital treated as income

105.—(1) Capital which is payable by instalments which are outstanding   **9.261**
on—
- (a) the first day in respect of which an income-related allowance is payable or the date of the determination of the claim, whichever is earlier; or
- (b) in the case of a supersession, the date of that supersession,

is to be treated as income if the aggregate of the instalments outstanding and the amount of the claimant's capital otherwise calculated in accordance with Chapter 7 of this Part exceeds £16,000.

(2) Any payment received under an annuity is to be treated as income.

(3) Any earnings to the extent that they are not a payment of income are to be treated as income.

(4) Any Career Development Loan paid pursuant to section 2 of the Employment and Training Act 1973 is to be treated as income.

(5) Where an agreement or court order provides that payments are to be made to the claimant in consequence of any personal injury to the claimant and that such payments are to be made, wholly or in part, by way of periodical payments, any such periodical payments received by the claimant (but not a payment which is treated as capital by virtue of this Part), are to be treated as income.

DEFINITION

"claimant"—see reg.83(1).

GENERAL NOTE

This is similar to reg.104 of the JSA Regulations 1996/reg.41 of the Income   **9.262**
Support Regulations (except that there is no equivalent to reg.41(4) (repayment of PAYE tax in trade dispute cases)).

Notional income—deprivation and income on application

106.—(1) A claimant is to be treated as possessing income of which the   **9.263**
claimant has deprived himself or herself for the purpose of securing entitlement to an employment and support allowance or increasing the amount of that allowance, or for the purpose of securing entitlement to, or increasing the amount of, income support or a jobseeker's allowance.

(2) Except in the case of—
- (a) a discretionary trust;
- (b) a trust derived from a payment made in consequence of a personal injury;
- (c) an employment and support allowance;
- (d) a jobseeker's allowance;
- (e) working tax credit;
- (f) child tax credit;
- (g) a personal pension scheme, occupational pension scheme or a payment made by the Board of the Pension Protection Fund where the claimant [² has not attained the qualifying age for state pension credit];
- [¹(ga) any sum to which paragraph (9) applies;]
- [³(gb) any sum to which regulation 137(4A) (treatment of student loans) applies;]
- (h) any sum to which paragraph 43(2)(a) of Schedule 9 (capital to be

1181

disregarded) applies which is administered in the way referred to in paragraph 43(1)(a) of that Schedule;

(i) any sum to which paragraph 44(a) of Schedule 9 refers; or

(j) rehabilitation allowance made under section 2 of the Employment and Training Act 1973,

income which would become available to the claimant upon application being made but which has not been acquired by the claimant is to be treated as possessed by the claimant but only from the date on which it could be expected to be acquired were an application made.

(3) A claimant who has attained the [² qualifying age for state pension credit] is to be treated as possessing—

(a) the amount of any income from an occupational pension scheme, a personal pension scheme or the Board of the Pension Protection Fund—

(i) for which no claim has been made; and

(ii) to which the claimant might expect to be entitled if a claim for it were made;

(b) income from an occupational pension scheme which the claimant elected to defer,

but only from the date on which it could be expected to be acquired were an application for it to be made.

(4) This paragraph applies where a claimant [² who has attained the qualifying age for state pension credit]—

(a) is entitled to money purchase benefits under an occupational pension scheme or a personal pension scheme;

(b) fails to purchase an annuity with the funds available in that scheme; and

(c) either—

(i) defers in whole or in part the payment of any income which would have been payable to the claimant by that claimant's pension fund holder; or

(ii) fails to take any necessary action to secure that the whole of any income which would be payable to the person by that claimant's pension fund holder upon the person applying for it, is so paid; or

(iii) income withdrawal is not available to the claimant under that scheme.

(5) Where paragraph (4) applies, the amount of any income foregone is to be treated as possessed by that claimant, but only from the date on which it could be expected to be acquired were an application for it to be made.

(6) The amount of any income foregone in a case where paragraph (4) (c)(i) or (ii) applies is to be the [⁵ rate of the annuity which may have been purchased with the fund] and is to be determined by the Secretary of State who will take account of information provided by the pension fund holder in accordance with regulation 7(5) of the Social Security (Claims and Payments) Regulations 1987.

(7) The amount of any income foregone in a case where paragraph (4) (c)(iii) applies is to be the income that the claimant could have received without purchasing an annuity had the funds held under the relevant occupational or personal pension scheme been held under a scheme where income withdrawal was available and is to be determined in the manner specified in paragraph (6).

(8) In paragraph (4), "money purchase benefits" has the meaning it has in section 181 of the Pension Schemes Act 1993.

[¹(9) Paragraphs (1) and (2) do not apply in respect of any amount of income other than earnings, or earnings derived from employment as an employed earner, arising out of the [⁴ claimant participating as a service user].]

AMENDMENTS

1. Social Security (Miscellaneous Amendments) (No. 4) Regulations 2009 (SI 2009/2655) reg.11(8) (October 26, 2009).
2. Social Security (Miscellaneous Amendments) (No. 2) Regulations 2010 (SI 2010/641) reg.12(4) (April 6, 2010).
3. Social Security (Miscellaneous Amendments) (No. 5) Regulations 2010 (SI 2010/2429) reg.11(2) (November 1, 2010).
4. Social Security (Miscellaneous Amendments) (No. 3) Regulations 2013 (SI 2013/2536) reg.13(28) (October 29, 2013).
5. Social Security (Miscellaneous Amendments No.4) Regulations 2017 (SI 2017/1015) reg.13 (November 16, 2017).

DEFINITIONS

"claimant"—see reg.83(1).
"claimant participating as a service user"—see reg.2(8).
"occupational pension scheme"—see reg.2(1).
"payment"—*ibid.*
"pension fund holder"—*ibid.*
"personal pension scheme"—*ibid.*
"the qualifying age for state pension credit"—*ibid.*

GENERAL NOTE

This is similar to reg.42(1)–(2CA) and (8ZA) of the Income Support Regulations reg.105(1)–(5A) and (15A) of the JSA Regulations 1996.

9.264

Note that under para.(1) persons who have deprived themselves of income will be caught by this rule if the purpose of the deprivation was to secure entitlement to or increase the amount of ESA *or income support or JSA*. This avoids the question that might otherwise have arisen on a claimant transferring from income support (or JSA) to ESA whether a deprivation which had only been for the purposes of income support (or JSA) could be caught by para.(1). The provision has not yet been extended to cover universal credit.

On para.(2)(gb) (which has no equivalent in the Income Support or JSA Regulations), see the note to reg.137.

Notional income—income due to be paid or income paid to or in respect of a third party

107.—(1) Except in the case of a discretionary trust, or a trust derived from a payment made in consequence of a personal injury, any income which is due to be paid to the claimant but—

9.265

(a) has not been paid to the claimant;
(b) is not a payment prescribed in regulation 8 or 9 of the Social Security (Payments on Account, Overpayment and Recovery) Regulations 1988 (duplication and prescribed payments or maintenance payments) and not made on or before the date prescribed in relation to it,

is, except for any amount to which paragraph (2) applies, to be treated as possessed by the claimant.

(2) This paragraph applies to—

(a) an amount which is due to be paid to the claimant under an occupational pension scheme but which is not paid because the trustees or managers of the scheme have suspended or ceased payments due to an insufficiency of resources;

(b) any amount by which a payment made to the claimant from an occupational pension scheme falls short of the payment to which the claimant was due under the scheme where the shortfall arises because the trustees or managers of the scheme have insufficient resources available to them to meet in full the scheme's liabilities; or

(c) any earnings which are due to an employed earner on the termination of that employed earner's employment by reason of redundancy but which have not been paid to that employed earner.

(3) Any payment of income, other than a payment of income specified in paragraph (5), made to a third party in respect of a single claimant or the claimant's partner (but not a member of the third party's family) is to be treated—

(a) in a case where that payment is derived from—
    (i) a payment of any benefit under the benefit Acts;
    (ii) a payment from the Armed Forces and Reserve Forces Compensation Scheme;
    (iii) a war disablement pension, war widow's pension or war widower's pension; or
    (iv) a pension payable to a person as a widow, widower or surviving civil partner under any power of Her Majesty otherwise than under an enactment to make provision about pensions for or in respect of persons who have been disabled or have died in consequence of service as members of the armed forces of the Crown,
    as possessed by that single claimant, if it is paid to the claimant or by the claimant's partner, if it is paid to the claimant's partner;

(b) in a case where that payment is a payment of an occupational pension, a pension or other periodical payment made under a personal pension scheme or a payment made by the Board of the Pension Protection Fund, as possessed by that single claimant or, as the case may be, by the claimant's partner;

(c) in any other case, as possessed by that single claimant or the claimant's partner to the extent that it is used for the food, ordinary clothing or footwear, household fuel, rent for which housing benefit is payable, or any housing costs to the extent that they are met under regulations 67(1)(c) or 68(1)(d) (housing costs), of that single claimant or, as the case may be, of the claimant's partner, or is used for any council tax or water charges for which that claimant or that partner is liable,

but, except where sub-paragraph (a) applies, this paragraph does not apply to any payment in kind to the third party.

(4) Any payment of income, other than a payment of income specified in paragraph (5), made to a single claimant or the claimant's partner in respect of a third party (but not in respect of another member of the claimant's family) is to be treated as possessed by that single claimant or, as the case may be, the claimant's partner, to the extent that it is kept or used by that claimant or used by or on behalf of the claimant's partner but, except where paragraph (3)(a) applies, this paragraph does not apply to any payment in kind to the third party.

(5) Paragraphs (3) and (4) do not apply in respect of a payment of income made—

(a) under [⁴or by] the Macfarlane Trust, the Macfarlane (Special

Payments) Trust, the Macfarlane (Special Payments) (No. 2) Trust, the Fund, the Eileen Trust[³, MFET Limited] [⁶, the Skipton Fund, the Caxton Foundation] [⁹, the Scottish Infected Blood Support Scheme] [¹¹, an approved blood scheme][¹⁰, the London Emergencies Trust, the We Love Manchester Emergency Fund] or [¹the Independent Living Fund (2006)];

  (b) pursuant to section 19(1)(a) of the Coal Industry Act 1994 (concessionary coal); or

  (c) pursuant to section 2 of the Employment and Training Act 1973 in respect of a person's participation—

    (i) in an employment programme specified in regulation 75(1)(a) (ii) of the Jobseeker's Allowance Regulations;

    (ii) in a training scheme specified in regulation 75(1)(b)(ii) of those Regulations;

    (iii) in the Intensive Activity Period specified in regulation 75(1)(a) (iv) of those Regulations;

    (iv) in a qualifying course within the meaning specified in regulation 17A(7) of those Regulations; or

[⁵ (ca) in respect of a person's participation in [⁷ a scheme prescribed in regulation 3 of the Jobseeker's Allowance (Schemes for Assisting Persons to Obtain Employment) Regulations 2013] or the Mandatory Work Activity Scheme; or]

  (d) under an occupational pension scheme, in respect of a pension or other periodical payment made under a personal pension scheme or a payment made by the Board of the Pension Protection Fund where—

    (i) a bankruptcy order has been made in respect of the person in respect of whom the payment has been made or, in Scotland, the estate of that person is subject to sequestration or a judicial factor has been appointed on that person's estate under section 41 of the Solicitors (Scotland) Act 1980;

    (ii) the payment is made to the trustee in bankruptcy or any other person acting on behalf of the creditors; and

    (iii) the person referred to in paragraph (i) and that person's partner (if any) does not possess, or is not treated as possessing, any other income apart from that payment.

(6) Where the claimant resides in a care home, an Abbeyfield Home or an independent hospital, or is temporarily absent from such a home or hospital, any payment made by a person other than the claimant or a member of the claimant's family in respect of some or all of the cost of maintaining the claimant or the claimant's partner in that home or hospital is to be treated as possessed by the claimant or the claimant's partner.

(7) In paragraph (2)(a) and (b) "resources" has the same meaning as in section 181(1) of the Pension Schemes Act 1993.

[² (8) Paragraphs (1), (3) and (4) do not apply in respect of any amount of income other than earnings, or earnings derived from employment as an employed earner, arising out of the [⁸ claimant participating as a service user].]

AMENDMENTS

1. Employment and Support Allowance (Miscellaneous Amendments) Regulations 2008 (SI 2008/2428) reg.8(5) (October 27, 2008).

2. Social Security (Miscellaneous Amendments) (No. 4) Regulations 2009 (SI 2009/2655) reg.11(9) (October 26, 2009).

3. Social Security (Miscellaneous Amendments) (No. 2) Regulations 2010 (SI 2010/641) reg.12(3)(b) (April 6, 2010).

4. Social Security (Miscellaneous Amendments) (No. 2) Regulations 2010 (SI 2010/641) reg.12(5)(a) (April 6, 2010).

5. Social Security (Miscellaneous Amendments) (No. 2) Regulations 2011 (SI 2011/1707) reg.4(4)(b) and (5) (August 5, 2011).

6. Social Security (Miscellaneous Amendments) (No. 3) Regulations 2011 (SI 2011/2425) reg.23(8) (October 31, 2011).

7. Jobseeker's Allowance (Schemes for Assisting Persons to Obtain Employment) Regulations 2013 reg.15(b) (February 12, 2013).

8. Social Security (Miscellaneous Amendments) (No. 3) Regulations 2013 (SI 2013/2536) reg.13(29) (October 29, 2013).

9. Social Security (Scottish Infected Blood Support Scheme) Regulations 2017 (SI 2017/329) reg.8(3)(a) (April 3, 2017).

10. Social Security (Emergency Funds) (Amendment) Regulations 2017 (SI 2017/689) reg.8(3)(a) (June 19, 2017).

11. Social Security (Infected Blood and Thalidomide Regulations 2017 (SI 2017/870) reg.8(3)(a) (October 23, 2017).

DEFINITIONS

"Abbeyfield Home"—see reg.2(1).
"approved blood scheme"—*ibid.*
"Armed Forces and Reserve Forces Compensation Scheme"—*ibid.*
"benefit Acts"—*ibid.*
"care home"—*ibid.*
"Caxton Foundation"—*ibid.*
"claimant"—see reg.83(1).
"claimant participating as a service user"—see reg.2(8).
"Eileen Trust"—see reg.2(1).
"family"—*ibid.*
"the Fund"—*ibid.*
"independent hospital"—*ibid.*
"the Independent Living Fund (2006)"—*ibid.*
"the London Emergencies Trust"—*ibid.*
"Macfarlane (Special Payments) Trust"—*ibid.*
"Macfarlane (Special Payments) (No. 2) Trust"—*ibid.*
"Macfarlane Trust"—*ibid.*
"MFET Limited"—*ibid.*
"occupational pension"—*ibid.*
"occupational pension scheme"—*ibid.*
"ordinary clothing and footwear"—*ibid.*
"partner"—*ibid.*
"payment"—*ibid.*
"personal pension"—*ibid.*
"personal pension scheme"—*ibid.*
"Scottish Infected Blood Support Scheme"—*ibid.*
"single claimant"—*ibid.*
"Skipton Fund"—*ibid.*
"war disablement pension"—*ibid.*
"war widow's pension"—*ibid.*
"war widower's pension"—*ibid.*
"water charges"—*ibid.*
"the We Love Manchester Emergency Fund"—*ibid.*

GENERAL NOTE

This is similar to reg.42(3)–(4A), (8A) and (8ZA) of the Income Support   9.266
Regulations/reg.105(6)–(11) and (15A), together with the definition of "resources"
in reg.105(16), of the JSA Regulations 1996 (except that paras (3) and (4) do not
contain any special provisions relating to trade disputes).

Notional income—other income

108.—(1) Where a claimant's earnings are not ascertainable at the time   9.267
of the determination of the claim or of any revision or supersession the
Secretary of State will treat the claimant as possessing such earnings as is
reasonable in the circumstances of the case having regard to the number
of hours worked and the earnings paid for comparable employment in the
area.

(2) Where the amount of a subsistence allowance paid to a claimant
in a benefit week is less than the amount of income-based jobseeker's
allowance that claimant would have received in that benefit week had it
been payable to the claimant, less 50p, the claimant is to be treated as
possessing the amount which is equal to the amount of income-based
jobseeker's allowance which the claimant would have received in that
week, less 50p.

(3) Subject to paragraph (4), where—

(a) a claimant performs a service for another person; and

(b) that person makes no payment of earnings or pays less than that paid
for a comparable employment in the area,

the Secretary of State is to treat the claimant as possessing such earnings
(if any) as is reasonable for that employment unless the claimant satisfies
the Secretary of State that the means of that person are insufficient for the
person to pay, or to pay more, for the service.

(4) Paragraph (3) will not apply—

(a) to a claimant who is engaged by a charitable or voluntary organisation or who is a volunteer if the Secretary of State is satisfied in any
of those cases that it is reasonable for the claimant to provide the
service free of charge;

(b) in a case where the service is performed in connection with—

   (i) the claimant's participation in an employment or training
programme in accordance with regulation 19(1)(q) of the
Jobseeker's Allowance Regulations, other than where the service
is performed in connection with the claimant's participation in
the Intensive Activity Period specified in regulation 75(1)(a)(iv)
of those Regulations; or

   (ii) the claimant's or the claimant's partner's participation in an
employment or training programme as defined in regulation
19(3) of those Regulations for which a training allowance is not
payable or, where such an allowance is payable, it is payable for
the sole purpose of reimbursement of travelling or meal expenses
to the claimant or the claimant's partner participating in that
programme;

(c) to a claimant who is engaged in work experience whilst participating
in—

   (i) the New Deal for Lone Parents; or

   (ii) a scheme which has been approved by the Secretary of State as
supporting the objectives of the New Deal for Lone Parents; or

(d) to a claimant who is participating in a work placement approved in writing by the Secretary of State before the placement starts;

(e) in sub-paragraph (d) "work placement" means practical work experience with an employer, which is neither paid nor undertaken in expectation of payment.

[¹ (5) Paragraphs (1) and (3) do not apply in respect of any amount of income other than earnings, or earnings derived from employment as an employed earner, arising out of the [² claimant participating as a service user].]

AMENDMENTS

1. Social Security (Miscellaneous Amendments) (No. 4) Regulations 2009 (SI 2009/2655) reg.11(10) (October 26, 2009).
2. Social Security (Miscellaneous Amendments) (No. 3) Regulations 2013 (SI 2013/2536) reg.13(30) (October 29, 2013).

DEFINITIONS

"benefit week"—see reg.2(1).
"claimant"—see reg.83(1).
"claimant participating as a service user"—see reg. 2(8).
"partner"—see reg.2(1).
"payment"—*ibid*.
"subsistence allowance"—*ibid*.
"voluntary organisation"—*ibid*.

GENERAL NOTE

9.268   This is similar to reg.42(5)–(6AA) and (8ZA) of the Income Support Regulations/reg.105(11A)–(13A) and (15A), together with the definition of "work placement" in reg.105(16), of the JSA Regulations 1996. There are some differences in reg.105 of the JSA Regulations (e.g. there is no equivalent to para.(4)(c) which relates to lone parents).

Notional income—calculation and interpretation

9.269   **109.**—(1) Where a claimant is treated as possessing any income under regulation 106 or 107 the foregoing provisions of this Part are to apply for the purposes of calculating the amount of that income as if a payment had actually been made and as if it were actual income which the claimant does possess.

(2) Where a claimant is treated as possessing any earnings under regulation 108(1) or (3) the foregoing provisions of this Part are to apply for the purposes of calculating the amount of those earnings as if a payment had actually been made and as if they were actual earnings which the claimant does possess except that paragraph (3) of regulation 96 (calculation of net earnings of employed earners) does not apply and the claimant's net earnings are to be calculated by taking into account the earnings which the claimant is treated as possessing, less—

(a) where the period over which those earnings are to be taken into account is a year or more, an amount in respect of income tax equivalent to an amount calculated by applying to those earnings the [¹ . . .] [² basic rate, or in the case of a Scottish taxpayer, the Scottish basic rate, of tax in the year of assessment less only personal reliefs to which the claimant is entitled under Chapters 2, 3 and 3A of Part 3 of the Income Tax Act 2007 as are appropriate to the claimant's circumstances];

(b) where [² . . .] the period over which those earnings are to be taken into account is less than a year, the earnings to which the [¹basic rate] [², or the Scottish basic rate,] of tax is to be applied and the amount of the [²personal reliefs deductible under this paragraph are] to be calculated on a pro rata basis;

(c) where the weekly amount of those earnings equals or exceeds the lower earnings limit, an amount representing primary Class 1 contributions under section 6(1)(a) of the Contributions and Benefits Act, calculated by applying to those earnings the initial and main primary percentages in accordance with section 8(1)(a) and (b) of that Act; and

(d) one-half of any sum payable by the claimant in respect of a pay period by way of a contribution towards an occupational or personal pension scheme.

AMENDMENTS

1. Employment and Support Allowance (Miscellaneous Amendments) Regulations 2008 (SI 2008/2428) reg.8(6) (October 27, 2008).

2. Social Security (Scottish Rate of Income Tax etc.) (Amendment) Regulations 2016 (SI 2016/233) reg.6(5) (April 6, 2016).

DEFINITIONS

"claimant"—see reg.83(1).
"employed earner"—see reg.2(1).
"pay period"—*ibid.*
"payment"—*ibid.*
"Scottish basic rate" – *ibid.*
"Scottish taxpayer" – *ibid.*

GENERAL NOTE

This is similar to reg.42(7)–(8) of the Income Support Regulations/reg.105(14)–(15) of the JSA Regulations 1996.   9.270

CHAPTER 7

CAPITAL

Capital limit

110. For the purposes of paragraph 6(1)(b) of Schedule 1 to the Act as it applies to an income-related allowance (no entitlement to benefit if capital exceeds prescribed amount), the prescribed amount is £16,000.   9.271

DEFINITION

"the Act"—see reg.2(1).

GENERAL NOTE

This contains a similar provision to that in reg.45 of the Income Support Regulations/reg.107 of the JSA Regulations 1996.   9.272

Calculation of capital

9.273
111.—(1) For the purposes of [¹sections 1(2)] and 4 of, and Part 2 of Schedule 1 to, the Act as it applies to an income-related allowance, the capital of a claimant to be taken into account is, subject to paragraph (2), to be the whole of the claimant's capital calculated in accordance with this Part and any income treated as capital under regulation 112 (income treated as capital).

(2) There is to be disregarded from the calculation of a claimant's capital under paragraph (1) any capital, where applicable, specified in Schedule 9.

AMENDMENT

1. Employment and Support Allowance (Miscellaneous Amendments) Regulations 2008 (SI 2008/2428) reg.8(7) (October 27, 2008).

DEFINITIONS

"the Act"—see reg. 2(1).
"claimant"—see reg.83(1).

GENERAL NOTE

9.274
This is similar to reg.46 of the Income Support Regulations/reg.108 of the JSA Regulations 1996. See e.g. *RB v SSWP (ESA)* [2016] UKUT 384 (AAC).

Income treated as capital

9.275
112.—(1) Any bounty derived from employment to which regulation 43(1)(e) and paragraph 12 of Schedule 7 apply and paid at intervals of at least one year is to be treated as capital.

(2) Any amount by way of a refund of income tax paid in respect of, or deducted from, profits or income chargeable to tax under the provisions in Part 2 of the Income Tax (Trading and Other Income) Act 2005 or Part 2 of the Income Tax (Earnings and Pensions) Act 2003 is to be treated as capital.

(3) Any holiday pay which is not earnings under regulation 95(1)(d) (earnings of employed earners) is to be treated as capital.

(4) Except any income derived from capital disregarded under paragraph 1, 2, 4 to 8, 10, 16, 43 or 44 of Schedule 9, any income derived from capital is to be treated as capital but only from the date it is normally due to be credited to the claimant's account.

(5) In the case of employment as an employed earner, any advance of earnings or any loan made by the claimant's employer is to be treated as capital.

(6) Any payment under section 30 of the Prison Act 1952 (payments for discharged prisoners) or allowance under section 17 of the Prisons (Scotland) Act 1989 (allowances to prisoners on discharge) is to be treated as capital.

(7) Any charitable or voluntary payment which is not made or not due to be made at regular intervals, other than one to which paragraph (8) applies, is to be treated as capital.

(8) This paragraph applies to a payment which is made under [³or by] the Macfarlane Trust, the Macfarlane (Special Payments) Trust, the Macfarlane (Special Payments) (No. 2) Trust, the Fund, the Eileen Trust [² , MFET Limited][⁴ , the Skipton Fund, the Caxton Foundation][⁵, the Scottish Infected Blood Support Scheme][⁷, an approved blood scheme]

[⁶, the London Emergencies Trust, the We Love Manchester Emergency Fund] or [¹the Independent Living Fund (2006)].

(9) Any arrears of subsistence allowance which are paid to a claimant as a lump sum are to be treated as capital.

AMENDMENTS

1. Employment and Support Allowance (Miscellaneous Amendments) Regulations 2008 (SI 2008/2428) reg.8(5) (October 27, 2008).

2. Social Security (Miscellaneous Amendments) (No.2) Regulations 2010 (SI 2010/641) reg.12(3)(c) (April 6, 2010).

3. Social Security (Miscellaneous Amendments) (No.2) Regulations 2010 (SI 2010/641) reg.12(5)(b) (April 6, 2010).

4. Social Security (Miscellaneous Amendments) (No.3) Regulations 2011 (SI 2011/2425) reg.23(8) (October 31, 2011).

5. Social Security (Scottish Infected Blood Support Scheme) Regulations 2017 (SI 2017/329) reg.8(3)(b) (April 3, 2017).

6. Social Security (Emergency Funds) (Amendment) Regulations 2017 (SI 2017/689) reg.8(3)(b) (June 19, 2017).

7. Social Security (Infected Blood and Thalidomide Regulations 2017 (SI 2017/870) reg.8(3)(b) (October 23, 2017).

DEFINITIONS

"approved blood scheme"—see reg.2(1).
"Caxton Foundation"—*ibid*.
"claimant"—see reg.83(1).
"Eileen Trust"—see reg.2(1).
"employed earner"—*ibid*.
"the Fund"—*ibid*.
"the Independent Living Fund (2006)"—*ibid*.
"the London Emergencies Trust"—*ibid*.
"Macfarlane (Special Payments) Trust"—*ibid*.
"Macfarlane (Special Payments) (No. 2) Trust"—*ibid*.
"Macfarlane Trust"—*ibid*.
"MFET Limited"—*ibid*.
"Scottish Infected Blood Support Scheme"—*ibid*.
"Skipton Fund"—*ibid*.
"subsistence allowance"—*ibid*.
"the We Love Manchester Emergency Fund"—*ibid*.

GENERAL NOTE

This is similar to reg.48 of the Income Support Regulations/reg.110 of the JSA Regulations 1996 (except that it does not contain any special provisions relating to trade disputes).

9.276

Calculation of capital in the United Kingdom

113. Capital which a claimant possesses in the United Kingdom is to be calculated at its current market or surrender value less—

    (a) where there would be expenses attributable to sale, 10%; and

    (b) the amount of any incumbrance secured on it.

9.277

DEFINITION

"claimant"—see reg.83(1).

9.278   This is similar to reg.49 of the Income Support Regulations/reg.111 of the JSA Regulations.

Calculation of capital outside the United Kingdom

9.279   **114.** Capital which a claimant possesses in a country outside the United Kingdom is to be calculated—

    (a) in a case in which there is no prohibition in that country against the transfer to the United Kingdom of an amount equal to its current market or surrender value in that country, at that value;

    (b) in a case where there is such a prohibition, at the price which it would realise if sold in the United Kingdom to a willing buyer,

less, where there would be expenses attributable to sale, 10% and the amount of any incumbrance secured on it.

DEFINITION

    "claimant"—see reg.83(1).

GENERAL NOTE

9.280   This is similar to reg.50 of the Income Support Regulations/reg.112 of the JSA Regulations 1996.

Notional capital

9.281   **115.**—(1) A claimant is to be treated as possessing capital of which the claimant has deprived himself or herself for the purpose of securing entitlement to an employment and support allowance or increasing the amount of that allowance, or for the purpose of securing entitlement to, or increasing the amount of, income support or a jobseeker's allowance except—

    (a) where that capital is derived from a payment made in consequence of any personal injury and is placed on trust for the benefit of the claimant;

    (b) to the extent that the capital which the claimant is treated as possessing is reduced in accordance with regulation 116 (diminishing notional capital rule);

    (c) any sum to which paragraph 43(2)(a) of Schedule 9 (capital to be disregarded) applies which is administered in the way referred to in paragraph 43(1)(a); or

    (d) any sum to which paragraph 44(a) of Schedule 9 refers.

(2) Except in the case of—

    (a) a discretionary trust;

    (b) a trust derived from a payment made in consequence of a personal injury;

    (c) any loan which would be obtainable only if secured against capital disregarded under Schedule 9;

    (d) a personal pension scheme;

    (e) an occupational pension scheme or a payment made by the Board of the Pension Protection Fund where the claimant [⁴ has not attained the qualifying age for state pension credit]; or

    (f) any sum to which paragraph 43(2)(a) of Schedule 9 (capital to be disregarded) applies which is administered in a way referred to in paragraph 43(1)(a); or

(g) any sum to which paragraph 44(a) of Schedule 9 refers,
any capital which would become available to the claimant upon application
being made but which has not been acquired by the claimant is to be treated
as possessed by the claimant but only from the date on which it could be
expected to be acquired were an application made.

(3) Any payment of capital, other than a payment of capital specified in paragraph (5), made to a third party in respect of a single claimant or the claimant's
partner (but not a member of the third party's family) is to be treated—

(a) in a case where that payment is derived from—
   (i) a payment of any benefit under the benefit Acts;
   (ii) a payment from the Armed Forces and Reserve Forces
      Compensation Scheme;
   (iii) a war disablement pension, war widow's pension or war wid-
      ower's pension; or
   (iv) a pension payable to a person as a widow, widower or surviving civil
      partner under any power of Her Majesty otherwise than under an
      enactment to make provision about pensions for or in respect of
      persons who have been disabled or who have died in consequence
      of service as members of the armed forces of the Crown,
   as possessed by that single claimant, if it is paid to that claimant, or
   by the claimant's partner, if it is paid to that partner;
(b) in a case where that payment is a payment of an occupational
   pension, a pension or other periodical payment made under a
   personal pension scheme or a payment made by the Board of the
   Pension Protection Fund, as possessed by that single claimant or, as
   the case may be, by the claimant's partner;
(c) in any other case, as possessed by that single claimant or the claimant's
   partner to the extent that it is used for the food, ordinary clothing or
   footwear, household fuel, rent for which housing benefit is payable
   or any housing costs to the extent that they are met under regulation
   67(1)(c) and 68(1)(d) (housing costs) of that single claimant or, as
   the case may be, of the claimant's partner, or is used for any council
   tax or water charges for which that claimant or partner is liable.

(4) Any payment of capital, other than a payment of capital specified in
paragraph (5) made to a single claimant or the claimant's partner in respect
of a third party (but not in respect of another member of the claimant's
family) is to be treated as possessed by that single claimant or, as the case
may be, the claimant's partner, to the extent that it is kept or used by that
claimant or used by or on behalf of the claimant's partner.

(5) Paragraphs (3) and (4) will not apply in respect of a payment of
capital made—

(a) under [³or by] the Macfarlane Trust, the Macfarlane (Special
   Payments) Trust, the Macfarlane (Special Payments) (No. 2) Trust,
   the Fund, the Eileen Trust [², MFET Limited][¹, the Independent
   Living Fund (2006)], the Skipton Fund[⁶, the Caxton Foundation]
   [⁸, the Scottish Infected Blood Support Scheme][¹⁰, an approved
   blood scheme][⁹, the London Emergencies Trust, the We Love
   Manchester Emergency Fund] or the London Bombings Relief
   Charitable Fund;
(b) pursuant to section 2 of the Employment and Training Act 1973 in
   respect of a claimant's participation—
   (i) in an employment programme specified in regulation 75(1)(a)

(ii) of the Jobseeker's Allowance Regulations;
  (ii) in a training scheme specified in regulation 75(1)(b)(ii) of those Regulations; or
  (iii) in the Intensive Activity Period specified in regulation 75(1)(a)(iv) of those Regulations; or
  (iv) in a qualifying course within the meaning specified in regulation 17A(7) of those Regulations;
[⁵ (ba) in respect of a person's participation in [⁷ a scheme prescribed in regulation 3 of the Jobseeker's Allowance (Schemes for Assisting Persons to Obtain Employment) Regulations 2013] or the Mandatory Work Activity Scheme;]
  (c) under an occupational pension scheme, in respect of a pension or other periodical payment made under a personal pension scheme or a payment made by the Board of the Pension Protection Fund where—
    (i) a bankruptcy order has been made in respect of the person in respect of whom the payment has been made or, in Scotland, the estate of that person is subject to sequestration or a judicial factor has been appointed on that person's estate under section 41 of the Solicitors (Scotland) Act 1980;
    (ii) the payment is made to the trustee in bankruptcy or any other person acting on behalf of the creditors; and
    (iii) the person referred to in paragraph (i) and that person's partner (if any) does not possess, or is not treated as possessing, any other income apart from that payment.

(6) Where a claimant stands in relation to a company in a position analogous to that of a sole owner or partner in the business of that company, the claimant is to be treated as if that claimant were such sole owner or partner and in such a case—
  (a) the value of the claimant's holding in that company, notwithstanding regulation 111 (calculation of capital), is to be disregarded; and
  (b) the claimant will, subject to paragraph (7), be treated as possessing an amount of capital equal to the value or, as the case may be, the claimant's share of the value of the capital of that company and the foregoing provisions of this Chapter are to apply for the purposes of calculating that amount as if it were actual capital which the claimant does possess.

(7) For so long as the claimant undertakes activities in the course of the business of the company, the amount which the claimant is treated as possessing under paragraph (6) is to be disregarded.

(8) Where a claimant is treated as possessing capital under any of paragraphs (1) to (6), the foregoing provisions of this Chapter are to apply for the purposes of calculating its amount as if it were actual capital which the claimant does possess.

(9) For the avoidance of doubt a claimant is to be treated as possessing capital under paragraph (1) only if the capital of which the claimant has deprived himself or herself is actual capital.

AMENDMENTS

1. Employment and Support Allowance (Miscellaneous Amendments) Regulations 2008 (SI 2008/2428) reg.8(8) (October 27, 2008).
2. Social Security (Miscellaneous Amendments) (No. 2) Regulations 2010 (SI 2010/641) reg.12(3)(d) (April 6, 2010).

3. Social Security (Miscellaneous Amendments) (No. 2) Regulations 2010 (SI 2010/641) reg.12(5)(c) (April 6, 2010).

4. Social Security (Miscellaneous Amendments) (No. 2) Regulations 2010 (SI 2010/641) reg.12(6) (April 6, 2010).

5. Social Security (Miscellaneous Amendments) (No. 2) Regulations 2011 (SI 2011/1707) reg.4(6)(b) and (7) (August 5, 2011).

6. Social Security (Miscellaneous Amendments) (No. 3) Regulations 2011 (SI 2011/2425) reg.23(9) (October 31, 2011).

7. Jobseeker's Allowance (Schemes for Assisting Persons to Obtain Employment) Regulations 2013 (SI 2013/276) reg.15(b) (February 12, 2013).

8. Social Security (Scottish Infected Blood Support Scheme) Regulations 2017 (SI 2017/329) reg.8(3)(c) (April 3, 2017).

9. Social Security (Emergency Funds) (Amendment) Regulations 2017 (SI 2017/689) reg.8(3)(c) (June 19, 2017).

10. Social Security (Infected Blood and Thalidomide Regulations 2017 (SI 2017/870) reg.8(3)(c) (October 23, 2017).

DEFINITIONS

"approved blood scheme"—see reg.2(1).
"Armed Forces and Reserve Forces Compensation Scheme"—*ibid.*
"benefit Acts"—*ibid.*
"Caxton Foundation"—*ibid.*
"claimant"—see reg.83(1).
"Eileen Trust"—see reg.2(1).
"family"—*ibid.*
"the Fund"—*ibid.*
"the Independent Living Fund (2006)"—*ibid.*
"London Bombings Relief Charitable Fund"—*ibid.*
"the London Emergencies Trust"—*ibid.*
"Macfarlane (Special Payments) Trust"—*ibid.*
"Macfarlane (Special Payments) (No. 2) Trust"—*ibid.*
"Macfarlane Trust"—*ibid.*
"MFET Limited"—*ibid.*
"occupational pension"—*ibid.*
"occupational pension scheme"—*ibid.*
"ordinary clothing and footwear"—*ibid.*
"partner"—*ibid.*
"payment"—*ibid.*
"personal pension scheme"—*ibid.*
"the qualifying age for state pension credit"—*ibid.*
"Scottish Infected Blood Support Scheme"—*ibid.*
"single claimant"—*ibid.*
"Skipton Fund"—*ibid.*
"war disablement pension"—*ibid.*
"war widow's pension"—*ibid.*
"war widower's pension"—*ibid.*
"water charges"—*ibid.*
"the We Love Manchester Emergency Fund"—*ibid.*

GENERAL NOTE

This is similar to reg.51 of the Income Support Regulations /reg.113 of the JSA Regulations 1996. See e.g. *RB v SSWP (ESA)* [2016] UKUT 384 (AAC).   **9.282**

Note that under para.(1) persons who have deprived themselves of capital will be caught by this rule if the purpose of the deprivation was to secure entitlement to or increase the amount of ESA *or income support or JSA*. This avoids the question that might otherwise have arisen on a claimant transferring from income support (or JSA) to ESA whether a deprivation which had only been for the purposes of income support (or JSA) could be caught by para.(1). The provision has not yet been extended to cover universal credit.

Diminishing notional capital rule

9.283   **116.**—(1) Where a claimant is treated as possessing capital under regulation 115(1) (notional capital), the amount which the claimant is treated as possessing—

(a) in the case of a week that is subsequent to—

    (i) the relevant week in respect of which the conditions set out in paragraph (2) are satisfied; or

    (ii) a week which follows that relevant week and which satisfies those conditions,

is to be reduced by an amount determined under paragraph (2);

(b) in the case of a week in respect of which paragraph (1)(a) does not apply but where—

    (i) that week is a week subsequent to the relevant week; and

    (ii) that relevant week is a week in which the condition in paragraph (3) is satisfied,

is to be reduced by the amount determined under paragraph (3).

(2) This paragraph applies to a benefit week or part-week where the claimant satisfies the conditions that—

(a) the claimant is in receipt of an income-related allowance; and

(b) but for regulation 115(1), the claimant would have received an additional amount of an income-related allowance in that benefit week or, as the case may be, that part-week,

and in such a case, the amount of the reduction for the purposes of paragraph (1)(a) is to be equal to that additional amount.

(3) Subject to paragraph (4), for the purposes of paragraph (1)(b) the condition is that the claimant would have been entitled to an income-related allowance in the relevant week, but for regulation 115(1), and in such a case the amount of the reduction is to be equal to the aggregate of—

(a) the amount of an income-related allowance to which the claimant would have been entitled in the relevant week but for regulation 115(1); and for the purposes of this sub-paragraph if the relevant week is a part-week that amount is to be determined by dividing the amount of an income-related allowance to which the claimant would have been so entitled by the number equal to the number of days in the part-week and multiplying the quotient by 7;

(b) the amount of housing benefit (if any) equal to the difference between the claimant's maximum housing benefit and the amount (if any) of housing benefit which the claimant is awarded in respect of the benefit week, within the meaning of regulation 2(1) of the Housing Benefit Regulations 2006 (interpretation), which includes the last day of the relevant week;

(c) the amount of council tax benefit (if any) equal to the difference between the claimant's maximum council tax benefit and the amount (if any) of council tax benefit which the claimant is awarded in respect of the benefit week which includes the last day of the relevant week, and for this purpose "benefit week" [¹ means a period of 7 consecutive days beginning on a Monday and ending on a Sunday].

(4) The amount determined under paragraph (3) is to be re-determined

under that paragraph if the claimant makes a further claim for an income-related allowance and the conditions in paragraph (5) are satisfied, and in such a case—

(a) sub-paragraphs (a) to (c) of paragraph (3) will apply as if for the words "relevant week" there were substituted the words "relevant subsequent week"; and

(b) subject to paragraph (6), the amount as re-determined is to have effect from the first week following the relevant subsequent week in question.

(5) The conditions are that—

(a) a further claim is made 26 or more weeks after—

(i) the date on which the claimant made a claim for an income-related allowance in respect of which the claimant was first treated as possessing the capital in question under regulation 115(1);

(ii) in a case where there has been at least one re-determination in accordance with paragraph (4), the date on which the claimant last made a claim for an income-related allowance which resulted in the weekly amount being re-determined; or

(iii) the date on which the claimant last ceased to be in receipt of an income-related allowance;

whichever last occurred; and

(b) the claimant would have been entitled to an income-related allowance but for regulation 115(1).

(6) The amount as re-determined pursuant to paragraph (4) is not to have effect if it is less than the amount which applied in that case immediately before the re-determination and in such a case the higher amount is to continue to have effect.

(7) For the purposes of this regulation—

"part-week" means a period to which Part 14 (periods of less than a week) applies;

"relevant week" means the benefit week or part-week in which the capital in question of which the claimant has deprived himself or herself within the meaning of regulation 115(1)—

(a) was first taken into account for the purpose of determining the claimant's entitlement to an income-related allowance, a jobseeker's allowance or income support; or

(b) was taken into account on a subsequent occasion for the purpose of determining or re-determining the claimant's entitlement to an income-related allowance, a jobseeker's allowance or income support on that subsequent occasion and that determination or re-determination resulted in the claimant's beginning to receive, or ceasing to receive, an income-related allowance, a jobseeker's allowance or income support;

and where more than one benefit week or part-week is identified by reference to paragraphs (a) and (b) of this definition the later or latest such benefit week or, as the case may be, the later or latest such part-week;

"relevant subsequent week" means the benefit week or part-week which includes the day on which the further claim or, if more than one further claim has been made, the last such claim was made.

AMENDMENT

1. Council Tax Benefit Abolition (Consequential Provision) Regulations 2013 (SI 2013/458) reg.4 and Sch.2 para.8 (April 1, 2013).

DEFINITIONS

"benefit week"—see reg.2(1).
"claimant"—see reg.83(1).
"week"—see reg.2(1).

GENERAL NOTE

9.284   This is similar to reg.51A of the Income Support Regulations/reg.114 of the JSA Regulations 1996.

Capital jointly held

9.285   **117.** Except where a claimant possesses capital which is disregarded under regulation 115(6) (notional capital), where a claimant and one or more persons are beneficially entitled in possession to any capital asset they are to be treated as if each of them were entitled in possession to the whole beneficial interest therein in an equal share and the foregoing provisions of this Chapter are to apply for the purposes of calculating the amount of capital which the claimant is treated as possessing as if it were actual capital which the claimant does possess.

DEFINITION

"claimant"—see reg.83(1).

GENERAL NOTE

9.286   This is similar to reg.52 of the Income Support Regulations/reg.115 of the JSA Regulations 1996.

Calculation of tariff income from capital

9.287   **118.**—(1) Except where the circumstances prescribed in paragraph (3) apply to the claimant, where the claimant's capital calculated in accordance with this Part exceeds £6,000 it is to be treated as equivalent to a weekly income of £1 for each complete £250 in excess of £6,000 but not exceeding £16,000.

(2) Where the circumstances prescribed in paragraph (3) apply to the claimant and that claimant's capital calculated in accordance with this Part exceeds £10,000, it is to be treated as equivalent to a weekly income of £1 for each complete £250 in excess of £10,000 but not exceeding £16,000.

(3) For the purposes of paragraph (2) the prescribed circumstances are that the claimant lives permanently in—

(a) a care home or an independent hospital;

(b) an Abbeyfield Home; or

(c) accommodation provided under section 3 of, and Part 2 of the Schedule to, the Polish Resettlement Act 1947 (provision of accommodation in camps) where the claimant requires personal care by reason of old age, disablement, past or present dependence on alcohol or drugs, past or present mental disorder or a terminal illness and the care is provided in the home.

(4) For the purposes of paragraph (3), a claimant is to be treated as living

permanently in such home, hospital or accommodation where the claimant is absent—

    (a) from a home, hospital or accommodation referred to in sub-paragraph (a) or (b) of paragraph (3)—

        (i) in the case of a claimant over pensionable age, for a period not exceeding 52 weeks; and

        (ii) in any other case, for a period not exceeding 13 weeks;

    (b) from accommodation referred to in sub-paragraph (c) of paragraph (3), where the claimant, with the agreement of the manager of the accommodation, intends to return to the accommodation in due course.

(5) Notwithstanding paragraphs (1) and (2), where any part of the excess is not a complete £250 that part is to be treated as equivalent to a weekly income of £1.

(6) For the purposes of paragraphs (1) and (2), capital includes any income treated as capital under [¹regulation 112 (income treated as capital)].

AMENDMENT

1. Employment and Support Allowance (Miscellaneous Amendments) Regulations 2008 (SI 2008/2428) reg.20(6) (October 27, 2008).

DEFINITIONS

"Abbeyfield Home"—see reg.2(1).
"care home"—*ibid.*
"claimant"—see reg.83(1).
"independent hospital"—see reg.2(1).

GENERAL NOTE

This is similar to reg.53 of the Income Support Regulations/reg.116 of the JSA   **9.288**
Regulations 1996. It is not entirely clear why para.(4)(a) contains a separate rule for a claimant over pensionable age (reg.53(1C)(a) of the Income Support Regulations does the same but not reg.116 of the JSA Regulations), since claimants over pensionable age are not entitled to ESA (or income support or indeed JSA).

CHAPTER 8

[¹ [² . . .] LIABLE RELATIVE PAYMENTS]

AMENDMENTS

1. Employment and Support Allowance (Miscellaneous Amendments) Regulations 2008 (SI 2008/2428) reg.20(5) (October 27, 2008).
2. Social Security (Miscellaneous Amendments) (No.4) Regulations 2009 (SI 2009/2655) reg.11(5) (April 12, 2010).

Interpretation

119. In this Chapter—   **9.289**
[¹ [² . . .]]
"claimant" includes a young claimant;
[¹"claimant's family" shall be construed in accordance with section 137 of the Contributions and Benefits Act (interpretation of part 7 and supplementary provisions);

"housing costs" means those costs which may be met under paragraph 1(2) of Schedule 6;]

"liable relative" means—

(a) a spouse, former spouse, civil partner or former civil partner of a claimant or of a member of the claimant's family;

(b) a parent of a child or young person who is a member of the claimant's family or of a young claimant;

(c) a person who has not been adjudged to be the father of a child or young person who is a member of the claimant's family or of a young claimant where that person is contributing towards the maintenance of that child, young person or young claimant and by reason of that contribution the claimant may reasonably be treated as the father of that child, young person or young claimant;

(d) a person liable to maintain another person by virtue of section 78(6)(c) of the Administration Act (liability to maintain) where the latter is the claimant or a member of the claimant's family,

and, in this definition, a reference to a child's, young person's or young claimant's parent includes any person in relation to whom the child, young person or young claimant was treated as a child or a member of the family;

[¹"ordinary clothing and footwear" means clothing and footwear for normal daily use but does not include school uniforms;]

"payment" means a periodical payment or any other payment made by or derived from a liable relative [¹ . . .] but it does not include any payment—

(a) arising from a disposition of property made in contemplation of, or as a consequence of—

(i) an agreement to separate;

(ii) any proceedings for judicial separation, divorce or nullity of marriage; or

(iii) any proceedings for separation, dissolution or nullity in relation to a civil partnership;

(b) made after the death of the liable relative;

(c) made by way of a gift but not in aggregate or otherwise exceeding £250 in the period of 52 weeks beginning with the date on which the payment, or if there is more than one such payment the first payment, is made; and, in the case of a claimant who continues to be in receipt of an income-related allowance at the end of the period of 52 weeks, this provision is to continue to apply thereafter with the modification that any subsequent period of 52 weeks is to begin with the first day of the benefit week in which the first payment is made after the end of the previous period of 52 weeks;

[¹(d) made to a third party, or in respect of a third party, unless the payment is—

(i) in relation to the claimant or the claimant's [² partner or is made or derived from a person falling within sub-paragraph (d) of the definition of liable relative]; and

(ii) [³ . . .] in respect of food, ordinary clothing or footwear, fuel, [³ rent for which housing benefit is payable, housing costs to the extent that they are met under regulation

67(1)(c) or 68(1)(d) (housing costs),] council tax or water charges;]
(e) in kind;
(f) to, or in respect of, a child or young person who is to be treated as not being a member of the claimant's household under regulation 156 (circumstances in which a person is to be treated as being or not being a member of the same household);
(g) which is not a periodical payment, to the extent that any amount of that payment—
  (i) has already been taken into account under this Part by virtue of a previous claim or determination;
  (ii) has been recovered under section 74 of the Administration Act (income support and other payments) or is currently being recovered; or
  (iii) at the time the determination is made, has been used by the claimant except where the claimant has deprived himself or herself of that amount for the purpose of securing entitlement to an income-related allowance or increasing the amount of that allowance;
[² (h) to which paragraph 60 of Schedule 8 (sums to be disregarded in the calculation of income other than earnings) applies.]
"periodical payment" means—
  (a) a payment which is made or is due to be made at regular intervals [¹ . . .];
  (b) in a case where the liable relative has established a pattern of making payments at regular intervals, any such payment;
  (c) any payment [¹ [² . . .] that does not exceed] the amount of an income-related allowance payable had that payment not been made;
  (d) any payment representing a commutation of payments to which paragraph (a) or (b) of this definition applies whether made in arrears or in advance,
but does not include a payment due to be made before the first benefit week pursuant to the claim which is not so made;
"young claimant" means a person aged 16 or over but under 20 who makes a claim for an income-related allowance.

AMENDMENTS

1. Employment and Support Allowance (Miscellaneous Amendments) Regulations 2008 (SI 2008/2428) reg.20(7) (October 27, 2008).
2. Social Security (Miscellaneous Amendments) (No. 4) Regulations 2009 (SI 2009/2655) reg.11(11) (April 12, 2010).
3. Social Security (Miscellaneous Amendments) Regulations 2013 (SI 2013/443) reg.9(3) (April 2, 2013).

DEFINITIONS

"benefit week"—see reg.2(1).
"child"—*ibid.*
"claimant"—see reg.83(1).
"family"—see reg.2(1).
"young person"—*ibid.*

9.290   This is similar to reg.54 of the Income Support Regulations/reg.117 of the JSA Regulations 1996.

The amendments made to Ch.8 with effect from April 12, 2010 were as a consequence of the introduction of a total income disregard of child maintenance from that date, replacing the previous partial disregard (see the form of para.60 of Sch.8 introduced on April 12, 2010). Any lump sum payments of child maintenance will presumably count as capital. Note that child maintenance under the child support legislation is now identified in para.60 of Sch.8, and is therefore excluded from the meaning of "payment" for the purposes of Ch.8 (para.(h) of the definition above). Chapter 8 therefore once again only deals with liable relative payments.

Treatment of [¹ [² . . .]] liable relative payments

9.291   **120.** Subject to regulation 121 (disregard of payments treated as not relevant income) [³ . . .] a payment—
(a) to the extent that it is not a payment of income, is to be treated as income;
(b) is to be taken into account in accordance with the following provisions of this Chapter.

AMENDMENTS

1. Employment and Support Allowance (Miscellaneous Amendments) Regulations 2008 (SI 2008/2428) reg.20(2)(b) (October 27, 2008).
2. Social Security (Miscellaneous Amendments) (No. 4) Regulations 2009 (SI 2009/2655) reg.11(4) (April 12, 2010).
3. Social Security (Miscellaneous Amendments) (No. 4) Regulations 2009 (SI 2009/2655) reg.11(12) (April 12, 2010).

DEFINITION

"payment"—*ibid.*

GENERAL NOTE

9.292   This is similar to reg.55 of the Income Support Regulations/reg.118 of the JSA Regulations 1996.

Disregard of payments treated as not relevant income

9.293   **121.** Where the Secretary of State treats any payment as not being relevant income for the purposes of section 74A of the Administration Act (payment of benefit where maintenance payments collected by Secretary of State), that payment is to be disregarded in calculating a claimant's income.

DEFINITIONS

"payment"—see reg.119.
"relevant income"—see reg.2(c), Social Security Benefits (Maintenance Payments and Consequential Amendments) Regulations 1996 (SI 1996/940).

GENERAL NOTE

9.294   This is similar to reg.55A of the Income Support Regulations/reg.119 of the JSA Regulations 1996.

For reg.2(c) of the Social Security Benefits (Maintenance Payments and Consequential Amendments) Regulations 1996 see Vol.II of this series.

Period over which periodical payments are to be taken into account

9.295   **122.**—(1) The period over which a periodical payment is to be taken into account is to be—

(a) in a case where the payment is made at regular intervals, a period equal to the length of that interval;

(b) in a case where the payment is due to be made at regular intervals but is not so made, such number of weeks as is equal to the number (and any fraction is to be treated as a corresponding fraction of a week) obtained by dividing the amount of that payment by the weekly amount of that periodical payment as calculated in accordance with regulation 124(4) (calculation of the weekly amount of a liable relative payment);

(c) in any other case, a period equal to a week.

(2) The period under paragraph (1) is to begin on the date on which the payment is treated as paid under regulation 125 (date on which a liable relative payment is to be treated as paid).

DEFINITION

"periodical payment"—see reg.119.

GENERAL NOTE

This is similar to reg.56 of the Income Support Regulations/reg.120 of the JSA Regulations 1996.

9.296

[¹ Period over which payments other than periodical payments are to be taken into account

123.—(1) The period over which a payment other than a periodical payment (a "non-periodical payment") is to be taken into account shall be determined as follows.

9.297

(2) Except in a case where paragraph (4) applies, the number of weeks over which a non-periodical payment is to be taken into account shall be equal to the number obtained by dividing that payment by the amount referred to in paragraph (3).

(3) The amount is the aggregate of £2 and—

(a) the amount of employment and support allowance that would be payable had no payment been made [² . . .].

(4) This paragraph applies in a case where a liable relative makes a periodical payment and a non-periodical payment concurrently and the weekly amount of the periodical payment (as calculated in accordance with regulation 124) is less than B.

(5) In a case where paragraph (4) applies, the non-periodical payment shall, subject to paragraphs (6) and (7), be taken into account over a period of the number of weeks equal to the number obtained by applying the formula—

$$\frac{A}{B-C}$$

(6) If the liable relative ceases to make periodical payments, the balance (if any) of the non-periodical payment shall be taken into account over the number of weeks equal to the number obtained by dividing that balance by the amount referred to in paragraph (3).

(7) If the amount of any subsequent periodical payment varies, the balance (if any) of the non-periodical payment shall be taken into account over a period of the number of weeks equal to the number obtained by applying the formula—

$$\frac{D}{B-E}$$

(8) The period under paragraph (2) or (4) shall begin on the date on which the payment is treated as paid under regulation 125 (date on which a liable relative payment is to be treated as paid) and the period under paragraph (6) or (7) shall begin on the first day of the benefit week in which the cessation or variation of the periodical payment occurred.

(9) Any fraction which arises by applying a calculation or formula referred to in this regulation shall be treated as a corresponding fraction of a week.

(10) In paragraphs (4) to (7)—

A = the amount of the non-periodical payment;

B = the aggregate of £2 and the amount of employment and support allowance that would be payable had the periodical payment not been made [² . . .];

C = the weekly amount of the periodical payment;

D = the balance (if any) of the non-periodical payment.

E = the weekly amount of any subsequent periodical payment.]

AMENDMENTS

1. Employment and Support Allowance (Miscellaneous Amendments) Regulations 2008 (SI 2008/2428) reg.20(9) (October 27, 2008).

2. Social Security (Miscellaneous Amendments) (No. 4) Regulations 2009 (SI 2009/2655) reg.11(13) (April 12, 2010).

DEFINITIONS

"liable relative"—see reg.119.
"payment"—*ibid.*
"periodical payment"—*ibid.*

GENERAL NOTE

9.298   This is similar to reg.57 of the Income Support Regulations/reg.121 of the JSA Regulations 1996.

Calculation of the weekly amount of a [¹ [² . . .]] liable relative payment

9.299   **124.**—(1) Where a periodical payment is made or is due to be made at intervals of one week, the weekly amount is to be the amount of that payment.

(2) Where a periodical payment is made or is due to be made at intervals greater than one week and those intervals are monthly, the weekly amount is to be determined by multiplying the amount of the payment by 12 and dividing the product by 52.

(3) Where a periodical payment is made or is due to be made at intervals and those intervals are neither weekly nor monthly, the weekly amount is to be determined by dividing that payment by the number equal to the number of weeks (including any part of a week) in that interval.

(4) Where a payment is made and that payment represents a commutation of periodical payments whether in arrears or in advance, the weekly amount is to be the weekly amount of the individual periodical payments so commuted as calculated under paragraphs (1) to (3) as is appropriate.

(5) The weekly amount of a payment to which regulation 123 (period over which payments other than periodical payments are to be taken into account) applies, is to be equal to the amount of the divisor used in calculating the period over which the payment or, as the case may be, the balance is to be taken into account.

AMENDMENTS

1. Employment and Support Allowance (Miscellaneous Amendments) Regulations 2008 (SI 2008/2428) reg.20(2)(c) (October 27, 2008).
2. Social Security (Miscellaneous Amendments) (No. 4) Regulations 2009 (SI 2009/2655) reg.11(4) (April 12, 2010).

DEFINITIONS

"payment"—see reg. 119
"periodical payment"—*ibid.*

GENERAL NOTE

This is similar to reg.58 of the Income Support Regulations/reg.122 of the JSA Regulations 1996.

9.300

Date on which a [¹ [² . . .]] liable relative payment is to be treated as paid

125.—(1) A periodical payment is to be treated as paid—

9.301

(a) in the case of a payment which is due to be made before the first benefit week pursuant to the claim, on the day in the week in which it is due to be paid which corresponds to the first day of the benefit week;

(b) in any other case, on the first day of the benefit week in which it is due to be paid unless, having regard to the manner in which an income-related allowance is due to be paid in the particular case, it would be more practicable to treat it as paid on the first day of a subsequent benefit week.

(2) Subject to paragraph (3), any other payment is to be treated as paid—

(a) in the case of a payment which is made before the first benefit week pursuant to the claim, on the day in the week in which it is paid which corresponds to the first day of the benefit week;

(b) in any other case, on the first day of the benefit week in which it is paid unless, having regard to the manner in which an income-related allowance is due to be paid in the particular case, it would be more practicable to treat it as paid on the first day of a subsequent benefit week.

(3) Any other payment paid on a date which falls within the period in respect of which a previous payment is taken into account, not being a periodical payment, is to be treated as paid on the first day following the end of that period.

AMENDMENTS

1. Employment and Support Allowance (Miscellaneous Amendments) Regulations 2008 (SI 2008/2428) reg.20(2)(d) (October 27, 2008).
2. Social Security (Miscellaneous Amendments) (No. 4) Regulations 2009 (SI 2009/2655) reg.11(4) (April 12, 2010).

DEFINITIONS

"benefit week"—see reg.2(1).
"payment"—see reg. 119
"periodical payment"—*ibid*.

GENERAL NOTE

9.302   This is similar to reg.59 of the Income Support Regulations/reg.123 of the JSA Regulations 1996.

Liable relative payments to be treated as capital

9.303   **126.** [¹ . . .]

AMENDMENT

1. Employment and Support Allowance (Miscellaneous Amendments) Regulations 2008 (SI 2008/2428) reg.20(4)(b) (October 27, 2008).

CHAPTER 9

CHILD SUPPORT

Treatment of child support maintenance

9.304   **127.** [¹ . . .]

AMENDMENT

1. Employment and Support Allowance (Miscellaneous Amendments) Regulations 2008 (SI 2008/2428) reg.20(4)(c) (October 27, 2008).

Calculation of the weekly amount of payments of child support maintenance

9.305   **128.** [¹ . . .]

AMENDMENT

1. Employment and Support Allowance (Miscellaneous Amendments) Regulations 2008 (SI 2008/2428) reg.20(4)(c) (October 27, 2008).

Date on which child support maintenance is to be treated as paid

9.306   **129.** [¹ . . .]

AMENDMENT

1. Employment and Support Allowance (Miscellaneous Amendments) Regulations 2008 (SI 2008/2428) reg.20(4)(c) (October 27, 2008).

Disregard of payments treated as not relevant income

9.307   **130.** [¹ . . .]

AMENDMENT

1. Employment and Support Allowance (Miscellaneous Amendments) Regulations 2008 (SI 2008/2428) reg.20(4)(c) (October 27, 2008).

CHAPTER 10

STUDENTS

Interpretation

131.—(1) In this Chapter—   9.308
"academic year" means the period of twelve months beginning on 1st
January, 1st April, 1st July or 1st September according to whether the
course in question begins in the winter, the spring, the summer or the
autumn respectively but if students are required to begin attending the
course during August or September and to continue attending through
the autumn, the academic year of the course is to be considered to
begin in the autumn rather than the summer;
"access funds" means—
(a) grants made under section [³ 68] of the Further and Higher
    Education Act 1992 [³ . . .] for the purpose of providing funds on a
    discretionary basis to be paid to students;
(b) grants made under sections 73(a) and (c) and 74(1) of the Education
    (Scotland) Act 1980;
(c) grants made under Article 30 of the Education and Libraries
    (Northern Ireland) Order 1993, or grants, loans or other payments
    made under Article 5 of the Further Education (Northern Ireland)
    Order 1997 in each case being grants, or grants, loans or other pay-
    ments as the case may be, made for the purpose of assisting students
    in financial difficulties;
(d) discretionary payments, known as "learner support funds", which
    are made available to students in further education by institutions
    out of funds provided by the [⁵ [⁷ Secretary of State under section 14
    of the Education Act 2002] or [⁸ . . .] under sections 100 and 101 of
    [⁷ the Apprenticeships, Skills, Children and Learning Act 2009]]; or
(e) Financial Contingency Funds made available by the Welsh Ministers;
"college of further education" means, in Scotland, an educational estab-
    lishment by which further education is provided;
[² "contribution" means—
(a) any contribution in respect of the income of a student or any person
    which the Secretary of State, the Scottish Ministers or an education
    authority takes into account in ascertaining the amount of a stu-
    dent's grant or student loan; or
(b) any sums, which in determining the amount of a student's allowance
    or bursary in Scotland under the Education (Scotland) Act 1980, the
    Scottish Ministers or education authority takes into account being
    sums which the Scottish Ministers or education authority consider
    that it is reasonable for the following persons to contribute towards
    the holder's expenses—
    (i) the holder of the allowance or bursary;
    (ii) the holder's parents;
    (iii) the holder's parent's spouse, civil partner or a person ordinarily
        living with the holder's parent as if he or she were the spouse or
        civil partner of that parent; or
    (iv) the holder's spouse or civil partner;]

"course of advanced education" means—

(a) a course leading to a postgraduate degree or comparable qualification, a first degree or comparable qualification, a diploma of higher education or a higher national diploma; or

(b) any other course which is of a standard above advanced GNVQ, or equivalent, including a course which is of a standard above a general certificate of education (advanced level), a Scottish national qualification (higher or advanced higher);

"covenant income" means the income payable to a student under a Deed of Covenant by a person whose income is, or is likely to be, taken into account in assessing the student's grant or award;

"education authority" means a government department, [⁴a local authority as defined in section 579 of the Education Act 1996 (interpretation)], an education authority as defined in section 123 of the Local Government (Scotland) Act 1973, an education and library board established under Article 3 of the Education and Libraries (Northern Ireland) Order 1986, any body which is a research council for the purposes of the Science and Technology Act 1965 or any analogous government department, authority, board or body, of the Channel Islands, Isle of Man or any other country outside Great Britain;

"full-time course of advanced education" means a course of advanced education which is—

(a) a full-time course of study which is not funded in whole or in part by the [⁵ [⁷ Secretary of State under section 14 of the Education Act 2002][⁸ or under section 100 of the Apprenticeships, Skills, Children and Learning Act 2009]] or by the Welsh Ministers or a full-time course of study which is not funded in whole or in part by the Scottish Ministers at a college of further education or a full-time course of study which is a course of higher education and is funded in whole or in part by the Scottish Ministers;

(b) a course of study which is funded in whole or in part by the [⁵ [⁷ Secretary of State under section 14 of the Education Act 2002][⁸ or under section 100 of the Apprenticeships, Skills, Children and Learning Act 2009]] or by the Welsh Ministers if it involves more than 16 guided learning hours per week for the student in question, according to the number of guided learning hours per week for that student set out—

[⁵ (i) in the case of a course funded by the [⁷ Secretary of State [¹⁰. . .]], in the student's learning agreement signed on behalf of the establishment which is funded by [⁸ the Secretary of State] for the delivery of that course; or]

(ii) in the case of a course funded by the Welsh Ministers, in a document signed on behalf of the establishment which is funded by that Council for the delivery of that course; or

(c) a course of study (not being higher education) which is funded in whole or in part by the Scottish Ministers at a college of further education if it involves—

(i) more than 16 hours per week of classroom-based or workshop-based programmed learning under the direct guidance of teaching staff according to the number of hours set out in a document signed on behalf of the college; or

(ii) 16 hours or less per week of classroom-based or workshop-based programmed learning under the direct guidance of teaching staff and it involves additional hours using structured learning packages supported by the teaching staff where the combined total of hours exceeds 21 per week, according to the number of hours set out in a document signed on behalf of the college;

"full-time course of study" means a full-time course of study which—

(a) is not funded in whole or in part by the [⁵ [⁷ Secretary of State under section 14 of the Education Act 2002][⁸ or section 100 of the Apprenticeships, Skills, Children and Learning Act 2009]] or by the Welsh Ministers or a full-time course of study which is not funded in whole or in part by the Scottish Ministers at a college of further education or a full-time course of study which is a course of higher education and is funded in whole or in part by the Scottish Ministers;

(b) a course of study which is funded in whole or in part by the [⁵ [⁷ Secretary of State under section 14 of the Education Act 2002][⁸ or section 100 of the Apprenticeships, Skills, Children and Learning Act 2009]] or by the Welsh Ministers if it involves more than 16 guided learning hours per week for the student in question, according to the number of guided learning hours per week for that student set out—

[⁵ (i) in the case of a course funded by the [⁷ Secretary of State [⁸ . . .], in the student's learning agreement signed on behalf of the establishment which is funded by [⁸ the Secretary of State] for the delivery of that course; or]

(ii) in the case of a course funded by the Welsh Ministers, in a document signed on behalf of the establishment which is funded by that Council for the delivery of that course; or

(c) is not higher education and is funded in whole or in part by the Scottish Ministers at a college of further education if it involves—

(i) more than 16 hours per week of classroom-based or workshop-based programmed learning under the direct guidance of teaching staff according to the number of hours set out in a document signed on behalf of the college; or

(ii) 16 hours or less per week of classroom-based or workshop-based programmed learning under the direct guidance of teaching staff and it involves additional hours using structured learning packages supported by the teaching staff where the combined total of hours exceeds 21 per week, according to the number of hours set out in a document signed on behalf of the college;

"full-time student" means a person who is not a qualifying young person or child within the meaning of section 142 of the Contributions and Benefits Act (child and qualifying young person) and who is—

(a) aged less than 19 and is attending or undertaking a full-time course of advanced education;

(b) aged 19 or over but under pensionable age and is attending or undertaking a full-time course of study at an educational establishment; or

(c) on a sandwich course;

"grant" (except in the definition of "access funds") means any kind of educational grant or award and includes any scholarship, studentship, exhibition, allowance or bursary but does not include a payment from access funds or any payment to which paragraph 13 of Schedule 8 or paragraph 52 of Schedule 9 applies;

"grant income" means—

(a) any income by way of a grant;

(b) in the case of a student other than one to whom paragraph (c) refers, any contribution which has been assessed whether or not it has been paid;

(c) in the case of a student who is a lone parent [⁶ , is a person who has no partner and who is responsible for and a member of the same household as a young person] or is a person to whom Part 4 applies, any contribution which has been assessed and which has been paid,

and any such contribution which is paid by way of a covenant is to be treated as part of the student's grant income;

"higher education" means higher education within the meaning of Part 2 of the Further and Higher Education (Scotland) Act 1992;

"last day of the course" means the date on which the last day of the final academic term falls in respect of the course in which the student is enrolled;

"period of study" means—

(a) in the case of a course of study for one year or less, the period beginning with the start of the course and ending with the last day of the course;

(b) in the case of a course of study for more than one year, in the first or, as the case may be, any subsequent year of the course, other than the final year of the course, the period beginning with the start of the course or, as the case may be, that year's start and ending with either—

(i) the day before the start of the next year of the course in a case where the student's grant or loan is assessed at a rate appropriate to the student's studying throughout the year or, if the claimant does not have a grant or loan, where a loan would have been assessed at such a rate had the claimant had one; or

(ii) in any other case the day before the start of the normal summer vacation appropriate to the student's course;

(c) in the final year of a course of study of more than one year, the period beginning with that year's start and ending with the last day of the course;

"periods of experience" means periods of work experience which form part of a sandwich course;

[⁹ "postgraduate master's degree loan" means a loan which a student is eligible to receive under the Education (Postgraduate Master's Degree Loans) Regulations 2016;]

"sandwich course" has the meaning prescribed in regulation 2(9) of the Education (Student Support) Regulations 2007, regulation 4(2) of the Education (Student Loans) (Scotland) Regulations 2007 or regulation 2(8) of the Education (Student Support) Regulations (Northern Ireland) 2007;

"standard maintenance grant" means—

(a) except where paragraph (b) or (c) applies, in the case of a student attending or undertaking a course of study at the University of

London or an establishment within the area comprising the City of London and the Metropolitan Police District, the amount specified for the time being in paragraph 2(2)(a) of Schedule 2 to the Education (Mandatory Awards) Regulations 2003 ("the 2003 Regulations") for such a student;

(b) except where paragraph (c) applies, in the case of a student residing at the student's parent's home, the amount specified in paragraph 3(2) of Schedule 2 to the 2003 Regulations;

(c) in the case of a student receiving an allowance or bursary under the Education (Scotland) Act 1980, the amount of money specified for the relevant year appropriate for the student set out in the Student Support in Scotland Guide issued by the Student Awards Agency for Scotland, or its nearest equivalent in the case of a bursary provided by a college of further education or a local education authority;

(d) in any other case, the amount specified in paragraph 2(2) of Schedule 2 to the 2003 Regulations other than in paragraph (a) or (b) of that paragraph;

"student" means a person, other than a person in receipt of a training allowance, who is attending or undertaking a course of study at an educational establishment;

"student loan" means a loan towards a student's maintenance pursuant to any regulations made under section 22 of the Teaching and Higher Education Act 1998, sections [¹73(f)], 73B and 74 of the Education (Scotland) Act 1980 or article 3 of the Education (Student Support) (Northern Ireland) Order 1998 and is to include, in Scotland, amounts paid under regulation 4(1)(c) of the Students' Allowances (Scotland) Regulations 2007.

(2) For the purposes of the definition of "full-time student" in paragraph (1), a person is to be regarded as attending or, as the case may be, undertaking a full-time course of study, a full-time course of advanced education or as being on a sandwich course—

(a) subject to paragraph (3), in the case of a person attending or undertaking a part of a modular course which would be a full-time course of study for the purposes of this Part, for the period beginning on the day on which that part of the course starts and ending—

(i) on the last day on which the claimant is registered with the educational establishment as attending or undertaking that part as a full-time course of study; or

(ii) on such earlier date (if any) as the claimant finally abandons the course or is dismissed from it;

(b) in any other case, throughout the period beginning on the date on which the claimant starts attending or undertaking the course and ending on the last day of the course or on such earlier date (if any) as the claimant finally abandons it or is dismissed from it.

(3) For the purpose of sub-paragraph (a) of paragraph (2), the period referred to in that sub-paragraph is to include—

(a) where a person has failed examinations or has failed to successfully complete a module relating to a period when the claimant was attending or undertaking a part of the course as a full-time course of study, any period in respect of which the claimant attends or undertakes the course for the purpose of retaking those examinations or that module;

(b) any period of vacation within the period specified in that paragraph or immediately following that period except where the person has registered with the educational establishment to attend or undertake the final module in the course and the vacation immediately follows the last day on which the claimant is required to attend or undertake the course.

(4) In paragraph (2), "modular course" means a course of study which consists of two or more modules, the successful completion of a specified number of which is required before a person is considered by the educational establishment to have completed the course.

AMENDMENTS

1. Employment and Support Allowance (Miscellaneous Amendments) Regulations 2008 (SI 2008/2428) reg.8(9) (October 27, 2008).

2. Social Security (Miscellaneous Amendments) Regulations 2009 (SI 2009/583) reg.10(7) (April 6, 2009).

3. Social Security (Miscellaneous Amendments) (No. 4) Regulations 2009 (SI 2009/2655) reg.11(14) (October 26, 2009).

4. Local Education Authorities and Children's Services Authorities (Integration of Functions) (Local and Subordinate Legislation) Order 2010 (SI 2010/1172) art.5 and Sch.3, para.81 (May 5, 2010).

5. Apprenticeships, Skills, Children and Learning Act 2009 (Consequential Amendments to Subordinate Legislation) (England) Order 2010 (SI 2010/1941) reg.28(4) (September 1, 2010).

6. Social Security (Work-focused Interviews for Lone Parents and Partners) (Amendment) Regulations 2011 (SI 2011/2428) reg.5(4) (October 31, 2011).

7. Young People's Learning Agency Abolition (Consequential Amendments to Subordinate Legislation) (England) Order 2012 (SI 2012/956) art.22(4) (May 1, 2012).

8. Deregulation Act 2015 (Consequential Amendments) Order 2015 (SI 2015/971) art.2 and Sch.3 para.14(4) (May 26, 2015).

9. Social Security (Treatment of Postgraduate Master's Degree Loans and Special Support Loans) (Amendment) Regulations 2016 (SI 2016/743) reg.5(2) (August 4, 2016).

DEFINITIONS

"training allowance"—see reg.2(1).
"young person"—*ibid.*

GENERAL NOTE

9.309   This is similar to reg.61 of the Income Support Regulations. Under old style JSA the definitions applying to full-time students are in a slightly different form. See reg.130 of the JSA Regulations 1996 for some of the definitions but the main ones are to be found in reg.1(3) and (3A)–(3E) of those Regulations (see further the note to reg.130 of the JSA Regulations 1996 in Vol.II of this series).

Note that in the definition of "grant income" the cases where a contribution will only be included if it is actually paid are a lone parent, a single person who is responsible for and a member of the same household as a young person or a person "to whom Part 4 applies". Since Part 4 concerns who is or is not to be treated as receiving education for the purposes of para.6(1)(g) of Sch.1 to the Welfare Reform Act 2007 it is not clear what this reference means. If the aim is to mirror the income support definition of "grant income", the reference is presumably only intended to be to reg.18 in Part 4 (which provides that students who are entitled to a disability living allowance, personal independence payment or armed forces independence payment are not to be treated as receiving education for the purposes of para.6(1)(g) and so can qualify for income-related ESA). In this connection note that the equivalent provision for the treatment of student loans (see reg.137(5)(a)(ii)) only includes a student who is entitled to income-related ESA by virtue of reg.18.

See the note to reg.61 of the Income Support (General) Regulations 1987 in Vol. II of this series for the operation of the new definition of "postgraduate master's degree loan".

Calculation of grant income

132.—(1) The amount of student's grant income to be taken into account, subject to paragraphs (2) and (3), is to be the whole of the student's grant income.

(2) There is to be disregarded from the amount of a student's grant income any payment—

  (a) intended to meet tuition fees or examination fees;

  (b) intended to meet additional expenditure incurred by a disabled student in respect of that student's attendance on a course;

  (c) intended to meet additional expenditure connected with term time residential study away from the student's educational establishment;

  (d) on account of the student maintaining a home at a place other than that at which the student resides while attending the course but only to the extent that the student's rent is not met by housing benefit;

  (e) on account of any other person but only if that person is residing outside of the United Kingdom and there is no applicable amount in respect of that person;

  (f) intended to meet the cost of books and equipment;

  (g) intended to meet travel expenses incurred as a result of the student's attendance on the course;

  (h) intended for the maintenance of a child dependant;

  (i) intended for the child care costs of a child dependant;

  [¹(j) of higher education bursary for care leavers made under Part III of the Children Act 1989 [⁵ or under Part 6 of the Social Services and Well-being (Wales) Act 2014].]

(3) Where a student does not have a student loan [⁴ or a postgraduate master's degree loan] and is not treated as possessing [⁴ a student loan or a postgraduate master's degree loan], there is to be excluded from the student's grant income—

  (a) the sum of [²£303] per academic year in respect of travel costs; and

  (b) the sum of [³£390] per academic year towards the costs of books and equipment,

whether or not any such costs are incurred.

(4) Subject to paragraph (6), a student's grant income except any amount intended for the maintenance of adult dependants under Part 3 of Schedule 2 to the Education (Mandatory Awards) Regulations 2003 is to be apportioned—

  (a) subject to paragraph (7), in a case where it is attributable to the period of study, equally between the weeks in the period beginning with the benefit week, the first day of which coincides with, or immediately follows, the first day of the period of study and ending with the benefit week, the last day of which coincides with, or immediately precedes, the last day of the period of study;

  (b) in any other case, equally between the weeks in the period beginning

9.310

with the benefit week, the first day of which coincides with, or immediately follows, the first day of the period for which it is payable and ending with the benefit week, the last day of which coincides with, or immediately precedes, the last day of the period for which it is payable.

(5) Any grant in respect of an adult dependant paid under section 63(6) of the Health Services and Public Health Act 1968 (grants in respect of the provision of instruction to officers of hospital authorities) and any amount intended for the maintenance of an adult dependant under the provisions referred to in paragraph (4) is to be apportioned equally over a period of 52 weeks or, if there are 53 benefit weeks (including part-weeks) in the year, 53 weeks.

(6) In a case where a student is in receipt of a student loan or where that student could have acquired a student loan by taking reasonable steps but had not done so, any amount intended for the maintenance of an adult dependant under provisions other than those referred to in paragraph (4) is to be apportioned over the same period as the student's loan is apportioned or, as the case may be, would have been apportioned.

(7) In the case of a student on a sandwich course, any periods of experience within the period of study is to be excluded and the student's grant income is to be apportioned equally between the weeks in the period beginning with the benefit week, the first day of which immediately follows the last day of the period of experience and ending with the benefit week, the last day of which coincides with, or immediately precedes, the last day of the period of study.

AMENDMENTS

1. Social Security (Miscellaneous Amendments) Regulations 2009 (SI 2009/583) reg.10(8) (April 6, 2009).

2. Social Security (Students and Miscellaneous Amendments) Regulations 2009 (SI 2009/1575) reg.2(2) and (4)(e) (September 1, 2009 (or if the student's period of study begins between August 1 and August 31, 2009, the first day of the period).

3. Social Security (Students and Miscellaneous Amendments) Regulations 2009 (SI 2009/1575) reg.2(3) and (4)(e) (September 1, 2009 (or if the student's period of study begins between August 1 and August 31, 2009, the first day of the period)).

4. Social Security (Treatment of Postgraduate Master's Degree Loans and Special Support Loans) (Amendment) Regulations 2016 (SI 2016/743) reg.5(3) (August 4, 2016).

5. Social Services and Well-being (Wales) Act 2014 and the Regulation and Inspection of Social Care (Wales) Act 2016 (Consequential Amendments) Order 2017 (SI 2017/901) art.13(2) (November 3, 2017).

DEFINITIONS

"benefit week"—see reg.2(1).
"grant"—see reg.131(1).
"grant income"—*ibid.*
"period of study"—*ibid.*
"periods of experience"—*ibid.*
"postgraduate master's degree loan"—*ibid.*
"sandwich course"—*ibid.*
"student"—*ibid.*
"student loan"—*ibid.*

GENERAL NOTE

This is similar to reg.62 of the Income Support Regulations/reg.131 of the JSA   9.311
Regulations 1996. See the note to reg.62 in Vol.II of this series for the effect of the
new rule on "postgraduate master's degree loans".

Calculation of covenant income where a contribution is assessed

133.—(1) Where a student is in receipt of income by way of a grant   9.312
during a period of study and a contribution has been assessed, the amount
of the student's covenant income to be taken into account for that period
and any summer vacation immediately following is to be the whole amount
of the student's covenant income less, subject to paragraph (3), the amount
of the contribution.

(2) The weekly amount of the student's covenant income is to be determined—

  (a) by dividing the amount of income which falls to be taken into
      account under paragraph (1) by 52 or, if there are 53 benefit weeks
      (including part-weeks) in the year, 53; and
  (b) by disregarding from the resulting amount, £5.

(3) For the purposes of paragraph (1), the contribution is to be treated
as increased by the amount, if any, by which the amount excluded under
regulation 132(2)(g) (calculation of grant income) falls short of the
amount for the time being specified in paragraph 7(2) of Schedule 2 to the
Education (Mandatory Awards) Regulations 2003 (travel expenditure).

DEFINITIONS

  "benefit week"—see reg.2(1).
  "contribution"—see reg.131(1).
  "covenant income"—*ibid.*
  "grant"—*ibid.*
  "grant income"—*ibid.*
  "period of study"—*ibid.*
  "student"—*ibid.*

GENERAL NOTE

This is similar to reg.63 of the Income Support Regulations/reg.132 of the JSA   9.313
Regulations 1996.

Calculation of covenant income where no grant income or no con-tribution is assessed

134.—(1) Where a student is not in receipt of income by way of a grant   9.314
the amount of the student's covenant income is to be calculated as follows—

  (a) any sums intended for any expenditure specified in regulation 132(2)
      (a) to (e), necessary as a result of the student's attendance on the
      course, are to be disregarded;
  (b) any covenant income, up to the amount of the standard mainte-
      nance grant, which is not so disregarded is to be apportioned equally
      between the weeks of the period of study and there is to be disre-
      garded from the covenant income to be so apportioned the amount
      which would have been disregarded under regulation 132(2)(f) and
      (g) and (3) had the student been in receipt of the standard mainte-
      nance grant;

(c) the balance, if any, is to be divided by 52 or, if there are 53 benefit weeks (including part-weeks) in the year, 53 and treated as weekly income of which £5 is to be disregarded.

(2) Where a student is in receipt of income by way of a grant and no contribution has been assessed, the amount of the student's covenant income is to be calculated in accordance with paragraph (1), except that—

(a) the value of the standard maintenance grant is to be abated by the amount of the student's grant income less an amount equal to the amount of any sums disregarded under regulation 132(2)(a) to (e); and

(b) the amount to be disregarded under paragraph (1)(b) is to be abated by an amount equal to the amount of any sums disregarded under regulation 132(2)(f) and (g) and (3).

DEFINITIONS

"benefit week"—see reg.2(1).
"contribution"—see reg.131(1).
"covenant income"—*ibid.*
"grant"—*ibid.*
"grant income"—*ibid.*
"period of study"—*ibid.*
"student"—*ibid.*

GENERAL NOTE

9.315   This is similar to reg.64 of the Income Support Regulations/reg.133 of the JSA Regulations 1996.

Relationships with amounts to be disregarded under Schedule 8

9.316   **135.** No part of a student's covenant income or grant income is to be disregarded under paragraph 16 of Schedule 8 (charitable and voluntary payments).

DEFINITIONS

"covenant income"—see reg.131(1).
"grant income"—*ibid.*
"student"—*ibid.*

GENERAL NOTE

9.317   This is similar to reg.65 of the Income Support Regulations/reg.134 of the JSA Regulations.

Other amounts to be disregarded

9.318   **136.**—(1) For the purposes of ascertaining income other than grant income, covenant income and loans treated as income in accordance with regulation 137 (treatment of student loans), any amounts intended for any expenditure specified in regulation 132(2) (calculation of grant income) necessary as a result of the student's attendance on the course is to be disregarded but only if, and to the extent that, the necessary expenditure exceeds or is likely to exceed the amount of the sums disregarded under regulation 132(2) and (3), 133(3) (calculation of covenant income where a contribution is assessed), 134(1)(a) or (b) (calculation of covenant income where no grant income or no contribution is assessed) and 137(6) on like expenditure.

(2) Where a claim is made in respect of any period in the normal summer vacation and any income is payable under a Deed of Covenant which commences or takes effect after the first day of that vacation, that income is to be disregarded.

DEFINITIONS

"covenant income"—see reg.131(1).
"grant income"—*ibid.*

GENERAL NOTE

This is similar to reg.66 of the Income Support Regulations/reg.135 of the JSA Regulations 1996.

9.319

Treatment of student loans [⁴ and postgraduate master's degree loans]

137.—(1) [⁴ A student loan and a postgraduate master's degree loan are to be treated as income unless the loan] is a specified loan or award in which case it is to be disregarded.

9.320

(2) For the purposes of paragraph (1), a "specified loan or award" means—

  (a) in relation to England, a loan made by the Higher Education Funding Council for England under section 65 of the Further and Higher Education Act 1992;

  (b) in relation to Wales, a loan made by the Higher Education Funding Council for Wales under section 65 of the Further and Higher Education Act 1992;

  (c) in relation to Scotland, a loan made by an educational institution from funds it has received under the Education (Access Funds) (Scotland) Regulations 1990;

  (d) in relation to Northern Ireland, an award made by the Department for Employment and Learning under article 51 of the Education and Libraries (Northern Ireland) Order 1986.

(3) In calculating the weekly amount of the loan to be taken in account as income—

  (a) in respect of a course that is of a single academic year's duration or less, a loan which is payable in respect of that period is to be apportioned equally between the weeks in the period beginning with—

    (i) except in a case where paragraph (ii) applies, the benefit week, the first day of which coincides with, or immediately follows, the first day of the single academic year;

    (ii) where the student is required to start attending the course in August or where the course is less than an academic year's duration, the benefit week, the first day of which coincides with, or immediately follows, the first day of the course,

  and ending with the benefit week, the last day of which coincides with, or immediately precedes, the last day of the course;

  (b) in respect of an academic year of a course which starts other than on 1st September, a loan which is payable in respect of that academic year is to be apportioned equally between the weeks in the period beginning with the benefit week, the first day of which coincides with, or immediately follows, the first day of that academic year and ending with the benefit week, the last day of which coincides with, or immediately precedes, the last day of that academic year but excluding any benefit weeks falling entirely within the quarter during which, in the opinion of the Secretary of State, the longest of any vacation is taken;

(c) for the purposes of sub-paragraph (b), "quarter" is to have the same meaning as for the purposes of regulation 104(6) (calculation of income other than earnings);

(d) in respect of the final academic year of a course (not being a course of a single year's duration), a loan which is payable in respect of that final academic year is to be apportioned equally between the weeks in the period beginning with—

    (i) except in a case where paragraph (ii) applies, the benefit week, the first day of which coincides with, or immediately follows, the first day of that academic year;

    (ii) where the final academic year starts on 1st September, the benefit week, the first day of which coincides with, or immediately follows, the earlier of 1st September or the first day of the autumn term,

and ending with the benefit week, the last day of which coincides with, or immediately precedes, the last day of the course;

(e) in any other case, the loan is to be apportioned equally between the weeks in the period beginning with the earlier of—

    (i) the first day of the first benefit week in September; or

    (ii) the benefit week, the first day of which coincides with, or immediately follows, the first day of the autumn term,

and ending with the benefit week, the last day of which coincides with, or immediately precedes, the last day of June,

and, in all cases, from the weekly amount so apportioned there is to be disregarded £10.

(4) A student is to be treated as possessing a student loan [⁴ or a postgraduate master's degree loan] in respect of an academic year where—

(a) a student loan [⁴ or a postgraduate master's degree loan] has been made to that student in respect of that year; or

(b) [³ subject to paragraph (4A)] the student could acquire [⁴ a student loan or a postgraduate master's degree loan] in respect of that year by taking reasonable steps to do so.

[³ (4A) A student is not to be treated as possessing any part of a student loan [⁴ or a postgraduate master's degree loan] which has not been paid to that student in respect of an academic year where the educational institution at which the student was attending a course has confirmed in writing that the student has suspended attendance at the course due to a health condition or disability that renders the student incapable of continuing that course.]

(5) Where a student is treated as possessing a student loan under paragraph (4), the amount of the student loan to be taken into account as income is to be, subject to paragraph (6)—

(a) in the case of a student to whom a student loan is made in respect of an academic year, a sum equal to the maximum student loan the student is able to acquire in respect of that year by taking reasonable steps to do so and either—

    (i) in the case of a student other than one to whom paragraph (ii) refers, any contribution whether or not it has been paid to that student; or

    (ii) in the case of a student who is entitled to an income-related allowance by virtue of being a student to whom regulation 18 (circumstances in which the condition that the claimant is not receiving education does not apply) applies;

(b) in the case of a student to whom a student loan is not made in respect of an academic year, the maximum student loan that would be made to the student if—

    (i) the student took all reasonable steps to obtain the maximum student loan that student is able to acquire in respect of that year; and

    (ii) no deduction in that loan was made by virtue of the application of a means test.

[⁴ (5A) Where a student is treated as possessing a postgraduate master's degree loan under paragraph (4) in respect of an academic year, the amount of that loan to be taken into account as income shall be, subject to paragraph (6), a sum equal to 30 per cent. of the maximum postgraduate master's degree loan the student is able to acquire in respect of that academic year by taking reasonable steps to do so.]

(6) There is to be deducted from the amount of income taken into account under paragraph (5) [⁴ or (5A)]—

(a) the sum of [¹£303] per academic year in respect of travel costs; and

(b) the sum of [²£390] per academic year towards the costs of books and equipment,

whether or not any such costs are incurred.

AMENDMENTS

1. Social Security (Students and Miscellaneous Amendments) Regulations 2009 (SI 2009/1575) reg.2(2) and (4)(e) (September 1, 2009 (or if the student's period of study begins between August 1 and August 31, 2009, the first day of the period)).

2. Social Security (Students and Miscellaneous Amendments) Regulations 2009 (SI 2009/1575) reg.2(3) and (4)(e) (September 1, 2009 (or if the student's period of study begins between August 1 and August 31, 2009, the first day of the period)).

3. Social Security (Miscellaneous Amendments) (No.5) Regulations 2010 (SI 2010/2429) reg.11(3) (November 1, 2010).

4. Social Security (Treatment of Postgraduate Master's Degree Loans and Special Support Loans) (Amendment) Regulations 2016 (SI 2016/743) reg.5(4) (August 4, 2016).

DEFINITIONS

"academic year"—see reg.131(1).
"benefit week"—see reg.2(1).
"last day of the course"—see reg.131(1).
"postgraduate master's degree loan"—*ibid.*
"student"—*ibid.*
"student loan"—*ibid.*

GENERAL NOTE

Except in relation to the disregard of a "specified loan or award" (see paras (1)   **9.321** and (2)), this is similar to reg.136 of the JSA Regulations 1996/reg.66A of the Income Support Regulations. See the notes to reg.66A in Vol.II of this series, in particular for the effect of the new provisions on "postgraduate mater's degree loans". Note however that the rules as to when the amount of the student loan will not include an assessed contribution if it has not been paid differ for each benefit: in the case of income-related ESA it applies if the student is entitled to disability living allowance, personal independence payment or armed forces independence payment (regs 137(5)(a)(ii) and 18); for income-based JSA it applies if the claimant qualifies for the disability premium; and in the case of income support it applies to disabled students and lone parents/lone foster parents.

Under para.(1) a "specified loan or award" (defined in para.(2)) is disregarded. Regulation 66A(1) of the Income Support Regulations and reg.136(1) of the JSA Regulations 1996 used to provide that a "hardship loan" (defined in para. (1A) of both sets of Regulations) was disregarded. However the words "unless it is a hardship loan in which case it shall be disregarded" were omitted from reg.66A(1)/reg.136(1), and regs 66A(1A) and 136(1A) were also omitted, with effect from November 17, 2008 by regs 2(10) and 4(9) respectively of the Social Security (Miscellaneous Amendments) (No. 6) Regulations 2008 (SI 2008/2767). According to the Explanatory Memorandum which accompanied these amending regulations these amendments were being made because hardship loans had not been payable since May 2004. It is not known why similar provision for a disregard of a "specified loan or award" has not been made in the Income Support/JSA Regulations.

The effect of para.(4A), inserted with effect from November 1, 2010, is that a student whose university/college has confirmed in writing that he "has suspended attendance at the course due to a health condition or disability that renders [him] incapable of continuing that course" will not be treated as possessing any part of a student loan or a postgraduate master's degree loan that has not been paid to him. Nor will it count as notional income (see reg.106(2)(gb)). If the loan or any part of it has already been paid to him, it will count as income (see paras (1) and (4)(a)). No amendments equivalent to para.(4A) and reg.106(2)(gb) have been made to the Income Support/JSA Regulations 1996, presumably because the appropriate benefit for such a student to claim is old style ESA.

Treatment of payments from access funds

9.322   **138.**—(1) This regulation applies to payments from access funds that are not payments to which regulation 142(2) or (3) (income treated as capital) applies.

(2) A payment from access funds, other than a payment to which paragraph (3) applies, is to be disregarded as income.

(3) Subject to paragraph (4) and paragraph 39 of Schedule 8, any payments from access funds which are intended and used for food, ordinary clothing or footwear, household fuel, rent for which housing benefit is payable or any housing costs to the extent that they are met under regulation 67(1)(c) or 68(1)(d) (housing costs), of a single claimant or, as the case may be, of the claimant's partner, and any payments from access funds which are used for any council tax or water charges for which that claimant or partner is liable is to be disregarded as income to the extent of £20 per week.

(4) Where a payment from access funds is made—
 (a) on or after 1st September or the first day of the course, whichever first occurs, but before receipt of any student loan in respect of that year and that payment is intended for the purpose of bridging the period until receipt of the student loan; or
 (b) before the first day of the course to a person in anticipation of that person becoming a student,
that payment is to be disregarded as income.

DEFINITIONS

 "access funds"—see reg.131(1).
 "claimant"—see reg.83(1).
 "ordinary clothing or footwear"—see reg.2(1).
 "payment"—*ibid.*

"single claimant"—*ibid.*
"student"—see reg.131(1).
"student loan"—*ibid.*

GENERAL NOTE

This is similar to reg.66B of the Income Support Regulations/reg.136A of the JSA   9.323
Regulations 1996.

Treatment of fee loans

139. A loan for fees, known as a fee loan or a fee contribution loan, made   9.324
pursuant to regulations made under Article 3 of the Education (Student
Support) (Northern Ireland) Order 1998, section 22 of the Teaching and
Higher Education Act 1998 or section 73(f) of the Education (Scotland)
Act 1980, is to be disregarded as income.

GENERAL NOTE

This is similar to reg.66C of the Income Support Regulations/reg.136B of the JSA   9.325
Regulations 1996.

[¹ Treatment of special support loans

139A. A special support loan within the meaning of regulation 68 of
the Education (Student Support) Regulations 2011 is to be disregarded as
income.]

AMENDMENT

1. Social Security (Treatment of Postgraduate Master's Degree Loans and Special
Support Loans) (Amendment) Regulations 2016 (SI 2016/743) reg.5(5) (August
4, 2016).

GENERAL NOTE

See the note to reg.66D of the Income Support Regulations in Vol.II of this series.

Disregard of contribution

140. Where the claimant or the claimant's partner is a student and, for the   9.326
purposes of assessing a contribution to the student's grant or student loan,
the other partner's income has been taken into account, an amount equal
to that contribution is to be disregarded for the purposes of assessing that
other partner's income.

DEFINITIONS

"claimant"—see reg.83(1).
"contribution"—see reg.131(1).
"grant"—*ibid.*
"partner"—see reg.2(1).
"student"—see reg.131(1).
"student loan"—*ibid.*

GENERAL NOTE

This is similar to reg.67 of the Income Support Regulations/reg.137 of the JSA   9.327
Regulations 1996.

Further disregard of student's income

9.328   **141.** Where any part of a student's income has already been taken into account for the purposes of assessing that student's entitlement to a grant [¹, student loan or postgraduate master's degree loan], the amount taken into account is to be disregarded in assessing that student's income.

AMENDMENT

1. Social Security (Treatment of Postgraduate Master's Degree Loans and Special Support Loans) (Amendment) Regulations 2016 (SI 2016/743) reg.5(6) (August 4, 2016).

DEFINITIONS

"grant"—see reg.131(1).
"postgraduate master's degree loan"—*ibid.*
"student"—*ibid.*
"student loan"—*ibid.*

GENERAL NOTE

9.329   This is similar to reg.67A of the Income Support Regulations/reg.137A of the JSA Regulations 1996.

Income treated as capital

9.330   **142.**—(1) Any amount by way of a refund of tax deducted from a student's income is to be treated as capital.

(2) An amount paid from access funds as a single lump sum is to be treated as capital.

(3) An amount paid from access funds as a single lump sum which is intended and used for an item other than food, ordinary clothing or footwear, household fuel, rent for which housing benefit is payable or any housing costs to the extent that they are met under regulation 67(1)(c) or 68(1)(d), of a single claimant or, as the case may be, of the claimant's partner, or which is used for an item other than any council tax or water charges for which that claimant or partner is liable is to be disregarded as capital but only for a period of 52 weeks from the date of the payment.

DEFINITIONS

"access funds"—see reg.131(1).
"claimant"—see reg.83(1).
"ordinary clothing or footwear"—see reg.2(1).
"payment"—*ibid.*
"single claimant"—*ibid.*
"student"—see reg.131(1).

GENERAL NOTE

9.331   This is similar to reg.68 of the Income Support Regulations/reg.138 of the JSA Regulations 1996.

Disregard of changes occurring during summer vacation

9.332   **143.** In calculating a student's income there is to be disregarded any change in the standard maintenance grant occurring in the recognised summer vacation appropriate to the student's course, if that vacation does not form part of the student's period of study, from the date on which the change occurred up to the end of that vacation.

DEFINITIONS

"period of study"—see reg.131(1).
"standard maintenance grant"—*ibid.*
"student"—*ibid.*

GENERAL NOTE

This is similar to reg.69 of the Income Support Regulations/reg.139 of the JSA Regulations 1996.

9.333

PART 11

SUPPLEMENTARY PROVISIONS

CHAPTER 1

MISCELLANEOUS

Waiting days

144.—(1) A claimant is not entitled to an employment and support allowance in respect of [³ 7] days at the beginning of a period of limited capability for work.

9.334

(2) Paragraph (1) does not apply where—

(a) the claimant's entitlement to an employment and support allowance commences within 12 weeks of the claimant's entitlement to income support, state pension credit, a jobseeker's allowance, a carer's allowance [¹, statutory sick pay or a maternity allowance] coming to an end;

(b) the claimant is terminally ill and has—
   (i) made a claim expressly on the ground of being terminally ill; or
   (ii) made an application for supersession or revision in accordance with the Social Security and Child Support (Decisions and Appeals) Regulations 1999 which contains an express statement of being terminally ill; or

(c) the claimant has been discharged from being a member of Her Majesty's forces and 3 or more days immediately before that discharge were days of sickness absence from duty, which are recorded by the Secretary of State for Defence [¹, or

(d) the claimant is the other member of a couple to whom regulation 4I(2) of the Social Security (Claims and Payments) Regulations 1987 applies and the former claimant was not entitled to an employment and support allowance in respect of [³ 7] days at the beginning of the period of limited capability for work which relates to the former claimant's entitlement.

[²; or

(e) the claimant is entitled to an employment and support allowance by virtue of section 1B of the Act (further entitlement after time-limiting).]

AMENDMENTS

1. Employment and Support Allowance (Miscellaneous Amendments) Regulations 2008 (SI 2008/2428) reg.9(1) (October 27, 2008).
2. Employment and Support Allowance (Duration of Contributory Allowance) (Consequential Amendments) Regulations 2012 (SI 2012/913) reg.9(2) (May 1, 2012).
3. Social Security (Jobseeker's Allowance and Employment and Support Allowance) (Waiting Days) Amendment Regulations 2014 (SI 2014/2309), reg.2(2) (October 27, 2014).

MODIFICATION

Regulation 144 is disapplied by Sch.1, para.14 of the Employment and Support Allowance (Transitional Provisions, Housing Benefit and Council Tax Benefit) (Existing Awards) (No.2) Regulations 2010 (SI 2010/1907) (as amended) for the purposes specified in reg.6(1). For details of the modification, see the text of those Regulations on p. 1329. The modification is further modified in those cases in relation to which universal credit has come into force—see the General Note to the 2010 Regulations.

DEFINITIONS

"claimant"—see WRA 2007, s.24(1).
"a member of Her Majesty's forces"—see reg.2(1).
"terminally ill"—see reg.2(1).

GENERAL NOTE

9.335   WRA 2007, s.22 and Sch.2 para.2 provide that "except in prescribed circumstances" a claimant cannot be entitled to ESA for a prescribed number of days at the beginning of a period of limited capability for work. This regulation originally set the number of these days of non-entitlement ("waiting days") at three. From October 27, 2014 that was increased to seven with respect to a new claim in respect of a waiting period starting on or after that date; regulation 4 of the amending instrument ensures that the changes made to reg. 144 do not apply where a waiting period began before that date.

It further provides in para.(2) for the exceptions to that general rule:

- where entitlement to ESA begins within 12 weeks of entitlement to IS, SPC, JSA, carer's allowance or SSP coming to an end (sub-para.(a));

- terminally ill claimants (including those seeking revision or supersession on the basis of being terminally ill) (sub-para.(b));

- discharge from Her Majesty's forces where three or more days of recorded sickness absence from duty preceded it (sub-para.(c));

- the claimant is the other member of a couple to whom reg.4I of the Claims and Payments Regs applies (change of claimant during a period of limited capability for work) and the previous claimant had already served the waiting days (sub-para.(d));

- where for someone not in the support group entitlement to CESA ended because of the time limit set by WRA 2007 s.1A (currently 365 days), but further entitlement arises under s.IB of that Act because subsequent deterioration in health now places that person in the support group (sub-para.(e)).

In addition, the general rule is, of course, affected by the "linking rule" (on which see reg.145) in a case of intermittent incapacity where that rule fuses into one ostensibly separate spells of limited capability for work: the "waiting days" only have to be served once in a period of limited capability for work.

Linking rules

145.—(1) Any period of limited capability for work which is separated   9.336
from another such period by not more than 12 weeks is to be treated as a
continuation of the earlier period.

[¹ (2)–(5) *Revoked.*]

AMENDMENT

1. Employment and Support Allowance (Amendment of Linking Rules)
Regulations 2012 (SI 2012/919), reg.5(6) (May 1, 2012).

DEFINITIONS

"child tax credit"—see reg.2(1).
"claimant"—see WRA 2007 s.24(1).
"qualifying remunerative work"—see reg.2(1).
"relevant tax credit conditions"—see para.(4).
"training"—see reg.2(1).
"week"—see reg.2(1).
"work or training beneficiary"—see reg.148.
"working tax credit"—see reg.2(1).

GENERAL NOTE

Linking rules are crucial for those suffering from intermittent incapacity. They   9.337
impact, to the claimant's benefit, as regards "waiting days"; those days of non-
entitlement (see para.(2) and ESA Regs, reg.144) only have to be served once in
any period of limited capability for work. They are also relevant to determining the
relevant benefit year and hence the appropriate tax years to which to have regard
with respect to the application of the national insurance contribution conditions
(see further the commentary to Sch.1 Pt 1 paras 1–3).

There is now only one linking rule: two ostensibly separate spells of limited capability for work will be fused into one where the separation period between the spells
is not more than 12 weeks (para.(1)). This fusing does not, however, mean that days
in the separation period thereby become ones of limited capability for work (*Chief
Adjudication Officer v Astle* (Court of Appeal, judgment of March 17, 1999, available
on LEXIS and noted in [1999] 6 J.S.S.L. 203). See further for more detail the
commentary to SSCBA 1992, s.30C(1)(c) (the "linking" rule)). A period of limited
capability for work can only be formed of days of actual limited capability for work
and/or ones which the legislative scheme treats as ones of limited capability for work.

Advance awards

146.—(1) Where section 5 of the Act (advance award of income-related   9.338
allowance) applies to a claim and the claimant satisfies the conditions in
paragraph (3)—
  (a) the claim is to be treated as if made for a period from the relevant
      day; and
  (b) the Secretary of State may award an employment and support allow-
      ance from the relevant day.
(2) In this regulation the "relevant day" is the day after the end of a period
of 13 weeks beginning on the first day on which the claimant would be entitled to an income-related allowance if the claimant satisfied the condition in
paragraph 6(1)(a) of Schedule 1 to the Act. (3) The conditions are that—
  (a) the Secretary of State is of the opinion that unless there is a change
      of circumstances the claimant will satisfy the conditions set out in

section 1(3)(b) to (f) of, and Part 2 of Schedule 1 to, the Act when an income-related allowance becomes payable under the award; and

(b) the claimant is treated as having limited capability for work under regulation 20, 25, 26, [¹ 30] or 33(2) (conditions for treating a person as having limited capability for work) for the period before an income-related allowance becomes payable under the award.

(4) Where an award is made under paragraph (1)—

(a) the award for an employment and support allowance will become payable on the date on which the claimant would have been entitled to a main phase employment and support allowance if the claimant had satisfied the condition in paragraph 6(1)(a) of Schedule 1 to the Act before the relevant day;

(b) sections 4(4)(a) and 4(5)(a) of the Act do not apply to that award.

AMENDMENT

1. Employment and Support Allowance (Miscellaneous Amendments) Regulations 2008 (SI 2008/2428) reg.9(2) (October 27, 2008).

DEFINITION

"claimant"—Welfare Reform Act 2007, s.24(1).
"income-related allowance"—Welfare Reform Act 2007, s.24(1) and 1(7).
"main phase employment and support allowance"—reg.2(1).

GENERAL NOTE

9.339   See the General Note to s.5 of the Welfare Reform Act 2007.

Recovery orders

9.340   **147.**—(1) Where an award of income-related allowance has been made to a claimant, the Secretary of State may apply to the court for a recovery order against the claimant's partner.

(2) On making a recovery order the court may order the partner to pay such amount at such intervals as it considers appropriate, having regard to all the circumstances of the partner and, in particular, the partner's income.

(3) Except in Scotland, a recovery order is to be treated for all purposes as if it were a maintenance order within the meaning of section 150(1) of the Magistrates Courts Act 1980.

(4) Where a recovery order requires the partner to make payments to the Secretary of State, the Secretary of State may, by giving notice in writing to the court which made the order, the liable person and the claimant, transfer to the claimant the right to receive payments under the order and to exercise the relevant rights in relation to the order.

(5) In paragraph 4, "the relevant rights" means, in relation to a recovery order, the right to bring any proceedings, take any steps or do any other thing under or in relation to the order.

DEFINITIONS

"partner"—see reg.2(1).
"payment"—*ibid.*

GENERAL NOTE

See s.23 of the Welfare Reform Act 2007 and the note to that section.   **9.341**
This regulation is similar to reg.169 of the JSA Regulations 1996.

[¹ Claimants appealing a decision

147A.—[⁴ (1) This regulation applies where a claimant has made and is   **9.342**
pursuing an appeal against a relevant decision of the Secretary of State as
defined in regulation 30.]

(2) Subject to paragraph (3), where this regulation applies, a determination
of limited capability for work by the Secretary of State under regulation 19
shall not be made until the appeal is determined by the First-tier Tribunal.

(3) Paragraph (2) does not apply where either—

(a) the claimant suffers from some specific disease or bodily or mental
disablement from which the claimant was not suffering when entitlement began; or

(b) a disease or bodily or mental disablement from which the claimant
was suffering at that date has significantly worsened.

(4) Where this regulation applies and the Secretary of State makes a
determination—

(a) in a case to which paragraph (3) applies (including where the determination is not the first such determination) that the claimant does
not have or, by virtue of regulation 22 or 23, is to be treated as not
having limited capability for work; or

(b) subsequent to a determination that the claimant is to be treated as
having limited capability for work by virtue of a provision of these
Regulations other than regulation 30, that the claimant is no longer
to be so treated,

this regulation and regulation 30 apply as if that determination had not
been made.

(5) Where this regulation applies and—

(a) the claimant is entitled to an employment and support allowance
by virtue of being treated as having limited capability for work in
accordance with regulation 30;

(b) neither of the circumstances in paragraph (3) applies, or, subsequent
to the application of either of those circumstances, the claimant has
been determined not to have limited capability for work; and

(c) the claimant's appeal is dismissed, withdrawn [² , struck out or has
been discontinued in accordance with the provisions of regulation
33(10) of the Social Security and Child Support (Decisions and
Appeals) Regulations 1999 (notice of appeal),]

the claimant is to be treated as not having limited capability for work [² with
effect from the day specified in paragraph (5A).]

[² (5A) The day specified for the purposes of paragraph (5) is the first day
of the benefit week following the date on which the Secretary of State [³ ...]

(a) receives the First-tier Tribunal's notification that the appeal is dismissed, withdrawn or struck out, [³ ...]

(b) [³ ...]]

(6) Where a claimant's appeal is successful, subject to paragraph (7), any
finding of fact or other determination embodied in or necessary to the decision of the First-tier Tribunal or on which the First-tier Tribunal's decision
is based shall be conclusive for the purposes of the decision of the Secretary

of State, in relation to an award made in a case to which this regulation applies, as to whether the claimant has limited capability for work or limited capability for work-related activity.

(7) Paragraph (6) does not apply where, due to a change of circumstances after entitlement to which this regulation applies began, the Secretary of State is satisfied that it is no longer appropriate to rely on such finding or determination.]

MODIFICATION

Regulation 147A is modified by Sch.2 para.15 of the Employment and Support Allowance (Transitional Provisions, Housing Benefit and Council Tax Benefit) (Existing Awards) (No. 2) Regulations 2010 (SI 2010/1907) (as amended) for the purposes specified in reg.16(1) of those Regulations. For details of the modifications, see the text of those Regulations on p. 1329. The modification is further modified in those cases and in relation to which universal credit has come into force—see the General Note to the 2010 Regulations.

AMENDMENTS

1. Social Security (Miscellaneous Amendments) (No. 3) Regulations 2010 (SI 2010/840) reg.9(15) (June 28, 2010).

2. Social Security (Miscellaneous Amendments) (No. 3) Regulations 2011 (SI 2011/2425) reg.23(10) and (11) (October 31, 2011).

3. Social Security, Child Support, Vaccine Damage and Other Payments (Decisions and Appeals) (Amendment) Regulations 2013 (SI 2013/2380) reg.7(2) (October 28, 2013).

4. Employment and Support Allowance (Repeat Assessments and Pending Appeal Awards) (Amendment) Regulations 2015 (SI 2015/437) reg. 3(3) (March 30, 2015).

DEFINITION

"relevant decision"—see reg. 30(5).

GENERAL NOTE

9.343   Before June 28, 2010, reg.6 provided that where a claimant appealed against a decision that he did not have limited capability for work the assessment phase did not end until the appeal was determined by a tribunal. In addition, reg.3(j) of the Claims and Payments Regulations 1987 (see Vol.III in this series) provided that a claim was not required where a claimant had made and was pursuing an appeal against a decision that he did not have limited capability for work. Thus the effect of reg.3(j) was that a further award of ESA could be made when a claimant appealed, without the claimant having to make a claim, thereby allowing the claimant to continue to receive ESA (paid at the basic rate) pending the tribunal's decision on his appeal ("the pending appeal award"). This was, however, subject to the production of medical evidence, which was necessary so that the claimant could be treated as having limited capability for work under reg.30. The "six months rule" in reg.30(2)(b) was disapplied by reg.30(3) where the claimant's appeal against a decision that he did not have limited capability for work had not yet been determined by a tribunal (note, however, that where the appeal is against a decision that the claimant does not have limited capability for work in respect of a claim for ESA made on or after March 30, 2015, reg.30(3) now only applies where the claimant is appealing against a "relevant decision"—see the amendments to reg.30 made on March 30, 2015 and see below).

This procedure, however, raised a number of issues, for example, whether this prevented retrospective payment of the relevant component in the case of a successful appeal. This is because under s.2(2)(a) and (3)(a) and s.4(4)(a) and (5)(a) of the

Welfare Reform Act 2007, one of the conditions of entitlement to the work-related activity/support component is that the assessment period has ended. It seems that in practice the DWP was paying the appropriate component from the beginning of the 14th week after the claimant's entitlement to ESA began if the appeal succeeded under the authority of ss.2(4)(b) and 4(6)(b) (see the advice given in paras 44647 to 44650 of Vol.8 of the *Decision Makers Guide*).

Another issue was the grounds for bringing the pending appeal award to an end, once the tribunal had made its decision on the appeal. In *CG v SSWP (ESA)* [2011] UKUT 384 (AAC) Judge Turnbull stated that he had "found considerable difficulty in trying to work out the effect of the legislation". The claimant in that case had appealed on June 3, 2009 against a decision made on May 26, 2009 that she did not have limited capability for work. A tribunal dismissed her appeal on February 1, 2010. As Judge Turnbull pointed out, this meant from February 1, 2010 reg.30(3) no longer applied. The consequence was that the claimant was no longer exempt from the condition in reg.30(2)(b) that it had not been determined in the six months preceding the date of claim that she did not have limited capability for work.

Judge Turnbull then went on to decide that in relation to a pending appeal award "date of claim" in reg.30(2)(b) should probably be read as referring to the date of the appeal against the decision that the claimant did not have limited capability for work (in this case June 3, 2009). In his view, it could not have been the intention that reg.30(2)(b) would never become applicable because there was no "date of claim" in relation to pending award appeals. He continued:

"9. ... The effect of the view which I prefer, therefore, is from 1 February 2010 the condition in reg. 30(2)(b) became applicable, and was not satisfied because it had, within 6 months before 3 June 2009 (the date of appeal – and therefore in my view the date of claim for this purpose) been determined that the Claimant did not have limited capability for work. The position was in my judgment therefore probably that from 1 February 2010 the Secretary of State was entitled to supersede and remove the Claimant's award of ESA from that date on the simple ground that the Claimant no longer fulfilled the conditions for being treated as not [*sic*] having limited capability for work.

10. ... Although the Secretary of State could have made a decision terminating entitlement simply by reason of the fact that the appeal had been dismissed on 1 February, I do not think that there was anything to stop the Secretary of State making a decision as to [...] whether the Claimant actually had limited capability for work. Further, the terms of reg. 21(1)(b) and (c), and reg. 21(2), would appear to have entitled the Secretary of State to make such a determination without requiring the claimant to fill in a further ESA 50 questionnaire, or submit to a further medical examination."

In this case the Secretary of State had in fact made a determination on actual limited capability for work when deciding to terminate the pending appeal award.

It will be noted that Judge Turnbull took the view that the Secretary of State was entitled to end the claimant's award of ESA from February 1, 2010 simply on the ground that the claimant no longer fulfilled the conditions for being treated as having limited capability for work. The Secretary of State, however, had submitted that the effect of reg.30(1)(a) was that the claimant continued to be entitled to be treated as having limited capability for work until it had been determined whether or not she actually had limited capability for work (this was the approach taken in DMG Memo 7/10, paras 23 and 24). Judge Turnbull, however, doubted whether this was right because in his view the intention must have been that a pending appeal award could be superseded by reason of the fact that the appeal had been decided. But in *TW v SSWP* [2012] UKUT 152 (AAC) (another pre-June 28, 2010 appeal) Judge Jupp accepted that when terminating a pending appeal award it was necessary for the decision-maker to decide on the claimant's actual capability for work at the date of that decision.

Furthermore, case law on the operation of the comparable IB regulation (reg.28 of the Social Security (Incapacity for Work) (General) Regulations 1995 (SI 1995/311), see the 2010/11 edition of this Volume) held that where a claimant could not be treated as incapable of work because of a determination on incapacity within the previous six months, it was necessary to go on to determine whether the claimant was actually incapable of work (see *CIB/1031/2000, CIB/3106/2003* and *R(IB)8/04*). Judge Turnbull, however, did not refer to any of these decisions.

Introduction of reg.147A

9.344   With effect from June 28, 2010, however, reg.6 was revoked and replaced by reg.147A. Regulation 3(j) of the Claims and Payments Regulations was also amended from the same date. As amended, it provided that a claim for ESA was not required where the claimant's appeal "relates to a decision to terminate or not to award a benefit *for which a claim was made*" (emphasis added). In other words, reg.3(j) did not apply where the appeal related to a decision where a claim was not made because it was not required (under reg.3(j)). Without this amendment it would seem possible for ESA to have remained in payment indefinitely on the basis of continuous appeals, supported by a medical certificate, each time a pending appeal award came to an end.

Paragraph (1)

9.345   Up to March 30, 2015 reg.147A applied where a claimant had made and was pursuing an appeal against a decision that he did not have limited capability for work. The new form of reg.147A(1), however, only applies where the claimant has made and is pursuing an appeal against a "relevant decision of the Secretary of State as defined in regulation 30". Note that the new form only applies where the decision under appeal was in respect of a claim made, or treated as made, on or after March 30, 2015 (see reg.2 of the ESA (Repeat Assessment and Pending Appeal Awards) (Amendment) Regulations 2015 (SI 2015/437)).

A "relevant decision" is a decision that *first* determines that the claimant does not have limited capability for work, or *first* determines this after a previous decision (by the Secretary of State or on appeal) that the claimant does have limited capability for work (see reg.30(5)).

Thus reg.147A (and the other provisions discussed below) will no longer apply to appeals against repeat claims for ESA where the claim is made at any time on or after March 30, 2015, *unless* the claimant is suffering from a new condition or there has been a significant worsening of an existing condition (see reg.30(2)(b) and (4)).

What if there has been a previous decision that the claimant did not have limited capability for work but it is accepted that his condition has significantly worsened, or that he has a new condition, and so he is treated as having limited capability for work under reg.30, but he then fails the work capability assessment and appeals that decision? Although the position is not entirely clear, it is suggested that that decision *is* a "relevant decision" within the meaning of reg.30(5) because it is the first determination in relation to this new condition or significantly worsened condition. This does not, however, appear to be the view of the DWP (see example 4 at the end of DMG Memo 10/15).

The effect of the claimant appealing was that he could be awarded ESA without making a claim (reg.3(j) of the Claims and Payments Regulations). Note, however, that reg.3(j) was also amended on March 30, 2015. Where the appeal is against a decision that the claimant does not have limited capability for work in respect of a claim for ESA made on or after March 30, 2015, reg.3(j) only applies where the claimant is appealing against a "relevant decision". In other cases, the claimant will have to make a new claim for ESA.

In addition, the claimant could be treated as having limited capability for work until the appeal was determined—see reg.30(3) which disapplied the "six months rule" in reg.30(2)(b) where the claimant's appeal against a decision that he did not have limited capability for work had not yet been determined by a tribunal. However, reg.30(2)(b) and (3) were also amended on March 30, 2015. The effect is that reg.30(3) now only applies where the claimant is appealing against a "relevant decision".

These provisions therefore allow a new award to be made and basic rate ESA to be paid pending the determination of the appeal, *provided that* the claimant submits medical evidence in accordance with reg. 30(2)(a) so that he can be treated as having limited capability for work under reg.30(1) (and provided that he continues to satisfy the other conditions of entitlement to ESA), but in respect of claims for ESA made on or after March 30, 2015 this only applies where the claimant is appealing against a "relevant decision". According to para.37 of DMG Memo 33/10 the new award will normally begin on the day after the last day of entitlement under the award that is the subject of the appeal or the day the medical evidence begins, if later.

Note *AR v SSWP (ESA)* [2013] UKUT 358 (AAC) in which the claimant had misrepresented a material fact on her original claim form. The fact that no new claim was required meant that the Secretary of State was entitled to rely on the information provided in the original claim form when making the pending appeal award and so the misrepresentation on the original claim form remained an effective cause of the overpayment in relation to the pending appeal award.

Paragraphs (2) and (4)

The effect of para.(2) is that the Secretary of State will not make a determination of limited capability for work in relation to the pending appeal award until the appeal is decided by a tribunal.

Paragraph (2) does not apply, however, if the claimant's condition significantly worsens or he develops a new condition. This exception is necessary because without it the Secretary of State would not be able to decide that the claimant has limited capability for work on the basis of the new/worsened condition pending the determination of the appeal. Note, however, that in the case of a new/worsened condition, if the Secretary of State determines that the claimant does not have, or is to be treated under reg.22 (failure to return the limited capability for work questionnaire) or reg.23 (failure to attend a medical examination) as not having, limited capability for work, reg.147A and reg.30 will apply (para.(4)(a)). Regulation 147A and reg.30 will also apply if, having determined that the claimant is to be treated as having limited capability for work (*other* than under reg.30), the Secretary of State subsequently determines that he is no longer to be so treated (para.(4)(b)).

Note that para.(2) only applies until the appeal is determined by the First-tier Tribunal. Therefore it will not apply while a claimant pursues an appeal to the Upper Tribunal.

Paragraph (5)

If the claimant's appeal (in relation to his original/earlier claim) is then dismissed, withdrawn or struck out, the claimant will be treated as not having limited capability for work from the first day of the benefit week following the date on which the Secretary of State was notified by the First-tier Tribunal of its decision (paras (5)(c) and (5A)(a)). From October 31, 2011 this also applied if, before the appeal was submitted to the First-tier Tribunal, the claimant (or an authorised representative) notified the Secretary of State in writing that he did not wish the appeal to continue. In this case the claimant was treated as not having limited capability for work from the first day of the benefit week following the date on which the Secretary of State discontinued action on the appeal (paras (5)(c) and (5A)(b)). However, para.(5A)(b) was omitted with effect from October 28, 2013. This was due to the revocation of reg.33 of the Decisions and Appeals Regulations 1999 (SI 1999/991) with effect from October 28, 2013. This is because of the extension of "mandatory reconsideration" and "direct lodgement" of appeals to, inter alia, social security benefits that was introduced on October 28, 2013. See further the note to r.22 of the Tribunal

9.346

9.347

Procedure (First-tier Tribunal) (Social Entitlement Chamber) Rules 2008 (SI 2008/2685) in Vol. III of this series. It is not clear why a similar amendment has not been made to para.(5)(c).

The purpose of this provision is to provide a mechanism for bringing the decision awarding ESA pending the determination of the appeal to an end. Such a mechanism is needed because the tribunal will of course only have dealt with the question of whether the claimant had limited capability for work/work-related activity at the date of the decision under appeal to it; the tribunal's decision has no direct effect on the decision awarding ESA pending the determination of the appeal.

However, para.(5) will not apply if the claimant's condition has significantly worsened or he has developed a new condition (unless in such a case the Secretary of State has subsequently decided that the claimant does not have limited capability for work).

The claimant will of course have a right of appeal against a decision under para. (5) in the normal way.

What issues does a tribunal have to consider in relation to such an appeal? Paragraphs (5) and (5A) provide for a decision to be made that the claimant is to be treated as not having limited capability for work from the start of the benefit week following notification of the First-tier Tribunal's decision. (Until October 28, 2013 this provision also applied where the Secretary of State had discontinued action on an appeal under reg.33(10) of the Decisions and Appeals Regulations 1999.) The effect of such a decision is that the claimant will not be entitled to ESA.

However, in order for a decision to be made under paras (5) and (5A) all of the conditions in para.(5) have to be met. This includes the condition in para.(5)(b) that neither of the circumstances in para.(3) apply (or if either of them has applied, it has since been determined that the claimant does not have limited capability for work). The circumstances in para.(3) are that the claimant is suffering from a new disease or bodily or mental disablement or that a disease or bodily or mental disablement has significantly worsened. It is suggested that, in order to decide this, the work capability assessment ("WCA") has to be applied because if the claimant satisfies the WCA at the date of the decision under paras (5) and (5A) there will, by definition, have been a significant worsening by the date of that decision and so a circumstance in para.(3) *will* apply. See *CIB/1959/1997* and *CIB/2198/1997* referred to in the note to reg.30 which held that "significantly worsened", as regards the claimant's condition, must be related to what is now the WCA (and what was then the personal capability assessment), so that it will only have significantly worsened if it has done so to an extent that the claimant would satisfy what is now the WCA if he were subjected to it (although note *SK v SSWP* [2009] UKUT 121 (AAC) which doubted that the question of significant worsening required that a judgment be made as to whether the claimant might satisfy what was then the personal capability assessment (see para.8)). In this connection note also reg.21(1)(b) and (c) and (2) under which the Secretary of State can determine limited capability for work without requiring a claimant to complete an ESA 50 or submit to a medical examination. If the Secretary of State can so act, so can the tribunal. If the tribunal does decide that at the date of the decision under paras (5) and (5A) the claimant satisfied the WCA, the conditions for treating the claimant as not having limited capability for work under paras (5) and (5A) will not be met. In addition, as the tribunal has decided that the claimant has satisfied the WCA, the relevant component will be immediately payable, as the conditions in ss.2(2) and (3) or 4(4) and (5) of the Welfare Reform Act 2007 will inevitably be met as the assessment phase will have ended long ago (see also *SSWP v PT (ESA)* [2011] UKUT 317 (AAC); [2012] AACR 17).

But what if new evidence, which establishes that the claimant in fact satisfied the WCA at the time of the original disallowance and which was not before the tribunal which confirmed that disallowance, is presented to a tribunal hearing an appeal against a decision made under paras (5) and (5A)? In this situation the claimant's condition may not have significantly worsened or he may not have developed a new condition and so neither of the circumstances in para.(3) may apply. Is the effect of para.(5) that the claimant has to be treated as not having limited capability for work or can the tribunal consider the question of whether the claimant actually has limited capability for work/work-related activity at the date of the decision terminating the pending appeal award. See, by way of analogy, *CIB/1031/2000, CIB/3106/2003* and *R(IB)8/04* which held that where a tribunal found that a claimant could not be treated as being incapable of work under reg.28 of the Incapacity for Work Regulations (the comparable IB provision to reg.30), the tribunal should go on to consider whether the claimant had actual incapacity for work.

It could be argued that because para.(5) treats a person as *not* having limited capability for work (emphasis added) that the analogy does not apply and that a new claim for ESA is required. However, it is also arguable that all that para.(5) does is to undo the deeming of limited capability for work in reg.30 (see the other condition for the application of para.(5) that the claimant is entitled to ESA by virtue of reg.30 (para.(5)(a)) and that actual limited capability for work can (and should) be considered. Moreover, if a tribunal is not able to consider whether the claimant did have actual limited capability for work/work-related activity at the date of the decision terminating the pending appeal award, this could cause substantial unfairness in some situations. The claimant may well have not made a new claim for ESA, thinking that the whole matter would be resolved when the tribunal heard his appeal against the decision terminating his pending appeal award. Depending on the length of time before the appeal against the termination of the pending appeal award is heard, this could cause injustice if the claimant only becomes aware of the fact that he needs to make a new claim at that tribunal hearing. Paragraph (5) is a deeming provision and arguably should not be applied to require a claimant to be treated as not having limited capability for work where the evidence is clearly to the contrary and shows that the claimant has actual limited capability for work/work-related activities. It could be argued that reg.22 (failure to return the ESA 50) and reg.23 (failure to attend a medical examination) also treat a claimant as not having limited capability for work and yet it has not been suggested that the question of whether the claimant has actual limited capability for work needs to be considered when these regulations are applied. Regulations 22 and 23 are, however, penalty provisions for non-cooperation and it is suggested therefore merit a different approach.

Unfortunately the operation of reg.147A has led to considerable confusion in some cases. It is often not clear when a claimant appeals following the termination of his pending appeal award whether he wishes to appeal against that decision or against the tribunal's original/earlier decision (or both). This will require clarification with the claimant at an early stage. In addition, appeal submissions from the Department frequently do not make clear that this is an appeal against a decision terminating a pending appeal award, thus causing confusion for both the appellant and the tribunal.

Note also that the Department found it necessary (at the end of June 2012) to issue further guidance on the operation of reg.147A following requests from decision makers (see DMG Memo 26/12).

Paragraphs (6) and (7)

If the claimant's appeal (against the original/earlier decision) is successful, subject 9.348 to any change of circumstances that has occurred since the claimant was awarded ESA pending the determination of his appeal, any finding of fact or determination by the tribunal will be conclusive for the purposes of the Secretary of State's decision in relation to the pending appeal award as to whether the claimant has limited capability for work/work-related activity (paras (6) and (7)). Note reg.3(5E) of the Decisions and Appeals Regulations 1999 (see Vol.III in this series) which allows revision of the pending appeal award if the appeal is successful. This is necessary so that the relevant component can be paid since the claimant will only have been paid ESA at the basic rate until the appeal was determined.

The result should therefore be that the claimant will be paid arrears of ESA, including the relevant component, from the beginning of the 14th week of his entitlement to ESA. It seems, however, that the DWP was not doing this where the claimant had claimed and been awarded JSA while the appeal was pending. This was apparently because of reg.31. Regulation 31 provided that a claimant who had claimed JSA and had a reasonable prospect of obtaining employment was to be treated as not having limited capability for work for the period of the JSA claim, even though it had been determined that he had (or was to be treated under regs 20, 25. 26 or 29 as having) limited capability for work. The DWP stated that reg.31 would be revoked and indeed this has happened (see reg.25(1) of the Employment and Support Allowance (Transitional Provisions, Housing Benefit and Council Tax Benefit) (Existing Awards) (No. 2) Regulations 2010 (SI 2010/1907) which revokes reg.31 with effect from October 1, 2010). For an argument as to why full payment of arrears of ESA was possible even before the revocation of reg.31 (based on reg.3(5A) of the Decisions and Appeals Regulations) see CPAG's *Welfare Rights Bulletin 218.*

See *NC v SSWP (ESA)* [2015] UKUT 147 (AAC) (in particular para. 42) as to the operation of paras (6) and (7) in circumstances where the claimant had limited capability for work as at the date of the decision under appeal but on the facts she ceased to do so two weeks later.

Note the modified form of reg.147A (and reg.30) which apply where the claimant is appealing against a conversion decision under the Employment and Support Allowance (Transitional Provisions, Housing Benefit and Council Tax Benefit) (Existing Awards) (No. 2) Regulations 2010 (SI 2010/1907) (as amended) which determined he did not have limited capability for work. See also the modified form of reg.3(j) of the Claims and Payments Regulations which applies in the case of appeals against conversion decisions. The effect is that a claimant who appeals against a conversion decision will be paid basic rate ESA from the date of his appeal.

The main difference under the modified form of reg.147A is that if the claimant's appeal is successful, his entitlement under reg.147A terminates at the start of the benefit week following the date on which the Secretary of State receives notification of the tribunal's decision (see the modified para.(6)). The claimant will be entitled to ESA (with the relevant component) under the conversion decision.

Chapter 2

Work or Training Beneficiaries

9.349   *Regulations 148, 149, and 150 were revoked with effect from May 1, 2012 by reg.5(7) of the Employment and Support Allowance (Amendment of Linking Rules) Regulations 2012 (SI 2012/919).*

Chapter 3

Temporary Absence From Great Britain

Absence from Great Britain

9.350   **151.**—(1) A claimant who is entitled to an employment and support allowance is to continue to be so entitled during a period of temporary absence from Great Britain only in accordance with this Chapter.

(2) A claimant who continues to be entitled to a contributory allowance during a period of temporary absence will not be disqualified for receiving that allowance during that period under section 18(4) of the Act.

DEFINITIONS

"claimant"—Welfare Reform Act 2007 s.24(1).
"contributory allowance"—Welfare Reform Act 2007 s.24(1) and 1(7).

GENERAL NOTE

Under s.1(3) of the Welfare Reform Act, it is a condition of entitlement to ESA **9.351** that the claimant should be "in Great Britain". However, para.5 of Sch.2 to that Act empowers the Secretary of State to "make provision . . . as to the circumstances in which a person is to be treated as being, or not being, in Great Britain".

In addition, those entitled to a contributory allowance are disqualified under s.18(4)(a) while they are absent from Great Britain "except where regulations otherwise provide". Paragraph 6 of Sch.2 to the Act provides that "regulations may provide that in prescribed circumstances a claimant who is not in Great Britain may nevertheless be entitled to a contributory allowance".

The regulations in this Chapter are made under those powers

Short absence

152. A claimant is to continue to be entitled to an employment and **9.352** support allowance during the first 4 weeks of a temporary absence from Great Britain if—
(a) the period of absence is unlikely to exceed 52 weeks; and
(b) while absent from Great Britain, the claimant continues to satisfy the other conditions of entitlement to that employment and support allowance.

GENERAL NOTE

See the commentary to reg.4(1) and (2) of the IS Regs. **9.353**

Absence to receive medical treatment

153.—(1) A claimant is to continue to be entitled to an employment and **9.354** support allowance during the first 26 weeks of a temporary absence from Great Britain if—
(a) the period of absence is unlikely to exceed 52 weeks;
(b) while absent from Great Britain, the claimant continues to satisfy the other conditions of entitlement to that employment and support allowance;
(c) the claimant is absent from Great Britain solely—
   (i) in connection with arrangements made for the treatment of the claimant for a disease or bodily or mental disablement directly related to the claimant's limited capability for work which commenced before leaving Great Britain; or
   (ii) because the claimant is accompanying a dependent child in connection with arrangements made for the treatment of that child for a disease or bodily or mental disablement;
(d) those arrangements relate to treatment—
   (i) outside Great Britain;

> (ii) during the period whilst the claimant is temporarily absent from Great Britain; and
>
> (iii) by, or under the supervision of, a person appropriately qualified to carry out that treatment; and
>
> (e) [¹ . . .]

(2) In paragraph (1)(d)(iii), "appropriately qualified" means qualified to provide medical treatment, physiotherapy or a form of treatment which is similar to, or related to, either of those forms of treatment.

AMENDMENT

1. Social Security (Miscellaneous Amendments) (No.4) Regulations 2009 (SI 2009/2655) reg.11(1) and (15) (October 26, 2009).

GENERAL NOTE

9.355   Where the temporary absence is in connection with receiving medical treatment for a condition related to the claimant's limited capacity for work, or because the claimant is accompanying a dependent child who is receiving medical treatment, ESA remains payable for the first 26 weeks of absence, as long as the total length of the absence is unlikely to exceed 52 weeks. From October 26, 2009, there is no longer any requirement to obtain the Secretary of State's permission before departure. Where the medical treatment abroad is paid for by the NHS, see reg.154 below.

Absence in order to receive NHS treatment

9.356   **154.** A claimant is to continue to be entitled to an employment and support allowance during any period of temporary absence from Great Britain if—

(a) while absent from Great Britain, the claimant continues to satisfy the other conditions of entitlement to that employment and support allowance;

(b) that period of temporary absence is for the purpose of the claimant receiving treatment at a hospital or other institution outside Great Britain where the treatment is being provided—

> (i) under section 6(2) of the Health Service Act (Performance of functions outside England) or section 6(2) of the Health Service (Wales) Act (Performance of functions outside Wales);
>
> (ii) pursuant to arrangements made under section 12(1) of the Health Service Act (Secretary of State's arrangements with other bodies), section 10(1) of the Health Service (Wales) Act (Welsh Ministers' arrangements with other bodies), paragraph 18 of Schedule 4 to the Health Service Act (Joint exercise of functions) or paragraph 18 of Schedule 3 to the Health Service (Wales) Act (Joint exercise of functions); or
>
> (iii) under any equivalent provision in Scotland or pursuant to arrangements made under such provision; [¹ . . .]

AMENDMENT

1. Social Security (Miscellaneous Amendments) (No. 3) Regulations 2010 (SI 2010/840) reg.9(1) and (16) (June 29, 2010).

GENERAL NOTE

9.357   See the commentary to reg.4(3A) of the IS Regs.

Absence of member of family of member of Her Majesty's forces

155.—(1) A claimant is to continue to be entitled to an employment and support allowance during any period of temporary absence from Great Britain if—

(a) the claimant is a member of the family of a member of Her Majesty's forces and temporarily absent from Great Britain by reason only of the fact that the claimant is living with that member; [¹ . . .]

(2) In this regulation "member of the family of a member of Her Majesty's forces" means the spouse, civil partner, son, daughter, step-son, step-daughter, father, father-in-law, step-father, mother, mother-in-law or step-mother of such a member.

AMENDMENT

1. Social Security (Miscellaneous Amendments) (No.3) Regulations 2010 (SI 2010/840) reg.9(1) and (17) (June 29, 2010).

CHAPTER 4

MEMBERSHIP OF HOUSEHOLD

Circumstances in which a person is to be treated as being or not being a member of the household

156.—(1) Subject to the following provisions of this regulation—

(a) the claimant and the claimant's partner; and

(b) where the claimant or the claimant's partner is responsible for a child or young person, that child or young person and any child of that child or young person,

are to be treated as being members of the same household.

(2) Paragraph (1) applies even where any of them is temporarily living away from the other members of the family.

(3) Paragraph (1) does not apply to a person who is living away from the other members of the family where—

(a) that person does not intend to resume living with the other members of the family; or

(b) that person's absence from the other members of the family is likely to exceed 52 weeks, unless there are exceptional circumstances (for example where the person is in hospital or otherwise has no control over the length of absence), and the absence is unlikely to be substantially more than 52 weeks.

(4) Paragraph (1) does not apply in respect of any member of a couple or of a polygamous marriage where—

(a) one, both or all of them are patients detained in a hospital provided under section 4 of the Health Service Act (high security psychiatric services), section 4 of the Health Service (Wales) Act (high security psychiatric services) or section 102 of the National Health Service (Scotland) Act 1978 (state hospitals);

(b) one, both or all of them are—

(i) detained in custody pending trial or sentence upon conviction or under a sentence imposed by a court; or

(ii) on temporary release in accordance with the provisions of the Prison Act 1952 or the Prisons (Scotland) Act 1989;

9.358

9.359

    (c) the claimant is abroad and does not satisfy the conditions of Chapter 4 of this Part (temporary absence from Great Britain); or

    (d) any one of them is permanently residing in a care home, an Abbeyfield Home or an independent hospital.

(5) A child or young person is not to be treated as a member of the claimant's household where that child or young person is—

    (a) placed with the claimant or the claimant's partner by a local authority under [⁴ section 22C(2)] of the Children Act 1989 or by a voluntary organisation under section 59(1)(a) of that Act;

[³(aa) placed with the claimant or the claimant's partner by a local authority under section 81(2) of the Social Services and Well-being (Wales) Act 2014;]

    (b) placed with the claimant or the claimant's partner prior to adoption;

    (c) in accordance with a relevant enactment, boarded out with the claimant or the claimant's partner, whether or not with a view to adoption; or

    (d) placed for adoption with the claimant or the claimant's partner pursuant to a decision under the [¹ Adoption and Children Act 2002] or the Adoption Agencies (Scotland) Regulations 1996.

(6) Subject to paragraphs (7) and (8), paragraph (1) does not apply to a child or young person who is not living with the claimant and who—

    (a) in a case which does not fall within sub-paragraph (b), has been continuously absent from Great Britain for a period of more than four weeks commencing—

        (i) where that child or young person went abroad before the date of the claim for an employment and support allowance, on the date of that claim;

        (ii) in any other case, on the day which immediately follows the day on which that child or young person went abroad;

    (b) where regulation 153 (absence to receive medical treatment) applies, has been continuously absent from Great Britain for a period of more than 26 weeks, that period commencing—

        (i) where that child or young person went abroad before the date of the claim for an employment and support allowance, on the date of that claim;

        (ii) in any other case, on the day which immediately follows the day on which that child or young person went abroad;

    (c) has been an in-patient or in accommodation for a continuous period of more than 12 weeks commencing—

        (i) where that child or young person became an in-patient or, as the case may be, entered that accommodation, before the date of the claim for an employment and support allowance, with that date; or

        (ii) in any other case, with the date on which that child or young person became an inpatient or entered that accommodation, and, in either case, has not been in regular contact with either the claimant or any member of the claimant's household;

    (d) is being looked after by, or in the care of, a local authority under a relevant enactment;

    (e) has been placed with a person other than the claimant prior to adoption;

(f) has been boarded out under a relevant enactment with a person other than the claimant prior to adoption;

(g) has been placed for adoption pursuant to a decision under the [¹ Adoption and Children Act 2002] or the Adoption Agencies (Scotland) Regulations 1996; or

(h) is detained in custody pending trial or sentence upon conviction or under a sentence imposed by a court.

(7) Sub-paragraphs (a)(i), (b)(i) and (c)(i) of paragraph (6) do not apply in a case where immediately before the date of claim for an employment and support allowance the claimant was entitled to an income-based job-seeker's allowance or income support.

(8) A child or young person to whom any of the circumstances mentioned in sub-paragraphs (d) or (h) of paragraph (6) applies is to be treated as being a member of the claimant's household only for that part of any benefit week where that child or young person lives with the claimant.

(9) In this regulation—

"accommodation" means accommodation provided by a local authority in a home owned or managed by that local authority—

(a) under sections 21 to 24 of the National Assistance Act 1948 (provision of accommodation);

[² (aa) under Part 1 of the Care Act 2014 (care and support);]

(b) in Scotland, under section 13B or 59 of the Social Work (Scotland) Act 1968 (provision of residential or other establishment; [³ . . .]

[³ (ba) in Wales, under section 35 or 36 of the Social Services and Well-being (Wales) Act 2014; or]

(c) under section 25 of the Mental Health (Care and Treatment) (Scotland) Act 2003 (care and support services etc.), where the accommodation is provided for a person whose stay in that accommodation has become other than temporary; and

"voluntary organisation" has the meaning assigned to it in the Children Act 1989, or in Scotland, by section 94 of the Social Work (Scotland) Act 1968.

(10) For the purposes of these Regulations a person is responsible for a child or young person if that child or young person usually lives with that person.

AMENDMENTS

1. Employment and Support Allowance (Miscellaneous Amendments) Regulations 2008 (SI 2008/2428) reg.9(3) (October 27, 2008).

2. Care Act 2014 (Consequential Amendments) (Secondary Legislation) Order 2015 (SI 2015/643) art.2 and Sch. para.29(1) and (2) (April 1, 2015).

3. Social Services and Well-being (Wales) Act 2014 and the Regulation and Inspection of Social Care (Wales) Act 2016 (Consequential Amendments) Order 2017 (SI 2017/901) art.13(1) and (3) (November 3, 2017).

4. Social Services and Well-being (Wales) Act 2014 and the Regulation and Inspection of Social Care (Wales) Act 2016 (Consequential Amendments) Order 2017 (SI 2017/901) art.27(1) and (2) (November 3, 2017).

DEFINITIONS

"Abbeyfield Home"—reg.2(1).
"child"—*ibid.*

"claimant"—WRA 2007, s.24(1).
"family"—reg.2(1) and (3).
"income-based jobseeker's allowance"—*ibid.*
"income support"—*ibid.*
"independent hospital"—*ibid.*
"partner"—*ibid.*
"polygamous marriage"—*ibid.*
"relevant enactment"—*ibid.*
"young person"—*ibid.*

GENERAL NOTE

9.360   See the commentary to reg.16 of the IS Regs. Note however that the ESA has no equivalent of reg.15 of the IS Regs. Under para.(10) whether or not a person is responsible for a child or young person for the purpose of ESA depends upon whether the "child or young person usually lives with that person" rather than, for IS, who receives child benefit.

PART 12

DISQUALIFICATION

Disqualification for misconduct etc.

9.361   **157.**—(1) Subject to paragraph (3), paragraph (2) applies where a claimant—

(a) has limited capability for work through the claimant's own misconduct, except in a case where the limited capability is due to pregnancy or a sexually transmitted disease; or

(b) fails without good cause to attend for or submit to medical or other treatment (excluding vaccination, inoculation or major surgery) recommended by a doctor with whom, or a hospital or similar institution with which, the claimant is undergoing medical treatment, which would be likely to remove the limitation on the claimant's capability for work;

(c) fails without good cause to refrain from behaviour calculated to retard the claimant's recovery; or

(d) is, without good cause, absent from the claimant's place of residence without leaving word with the Secretary of State where the claimant may be found.

(2) A claimant referred to in paragraph (1) is to be disqualified for receiving an employment and support allowance for such period not exceeding 6 weeks as the Secretary of State may determine.

(3) Paragraph (1) does not apply where the claimant—

(a) is disqualified for receiving an employment and support allowance by virtue of regulations made under section [¹6B or] 7 of the Social Security Fraud Act 2001; or

(b) is a person in hardship.

AMENDMENT

1. Social Security (Loss of Benefit) (Amendment) Regulations 2010 (SI 2010/1160) reg.12(2) (April 1, 2010).

DEFINITIONS

"claimant"—see WRA 2007 s.24(1).
"doctor"—see reg.2(1).
"medical treatment"—see reg.2(1).
"person in hardship"—see reg.158.
"week"—see reg.2(1).

GENERAL NOTE

Disqualification here represents an attempt to deny ESA to those whose   9.362
behaviour has in some way brought about their limited capability for work, or has
worsened it, or where the claimant has behaved inappropriately in some other
way.

This regulation provides that (subject to the two exceptions in para.(3)),
someone who falls within one of the several "heads" of disqualification examined
below must be disqualified for receiving ESA. As under the sickness and invalidity
benefits regime (on which see USI Regs reg.17, revoked from April 13, 1993—
pp.737–40 of Bonner, Hooker and White, *Non-Means Tested Benefit: The Legislation*
(1994)), and the incapacity benefit system, the maximum period imposable is six
weeks. No minimum is specified (unlike disqualification in JSA where one week is
specified—Jobseekers Act 1995 s.19(3)). Although, like JSA, ESA is in principle a
weekly benefit, payment for less than a week is possible, so arguably the minimum
should still be one day (the minimum unit for benefit purposes). While there have
been some changes of wording from that in USI Regs reg.17, governing sickness
and invalidity benefits disqualifications and from Incapacity for Work (General)
Regulations 1995 reg.18, in so far as the wording remains the same as that incapacity benefit provision, case authorities on that regime and its predecessors remain
authoritative. Some of the "heads" are subject to a "good cause" saving. The rule-
making power to further define or restrict "good cause" has not been exercised in
this context (WRA 2007 s.18(3)).

If one or more of the "heads" apply, there must be some disqualification: the discretion afforded by the regulation goes only to the length of the period (maximum
six weeks). As with exercising the equivalent discretion for jobseeker's allowance
purposes, the determining authorities must act judicially and consider each case in
the light of its circumstances and give reasons for their choice of period (see *R(U)
8/74(T)*; *R(S) 1/87*; *CS/002/1990*, para.6). The same rules on considering and
recording decisions on the matter would apply (*R(U) 4/87*). Some of the factors
relevant in exercising the discretion in that context may equally be relevant here.
The burden lies on the decision maker to show that the claimant falls clearly and
squarely within the head of disqualification (*R(S) 7/83*). Where "good cause" is
the issue, it falls to the claimant to establish that he had it (*R(S) 9/51*). *R(S) 1/87*
made it abundantly clear that in the same case the same facts could put in issue
more than one of the heads of disqualification in USI Regs reg.17(1). There the
heads at issue were paras 17(1)(b) and (1)(d)(ii). The poorly completed record of
the SSAT's decision did not make clear on which head they rested disqualification.
This was an error of law, a breach of the duty to record reasons for the decision
and the material facts on which it is based. Presumably as well as complying with
this duty, a tribunal should also comply with *R(U) 2/71* where the case involves
the Secretary of State relying on a head of disqualification not set out in the
appeal papers or the tribunal relying on a different ground to that relied on by the
Secretary of State.

Paragraph (1)(a)

This penalises certain behaviour by the claimant. Disqualification must be   9.363
imposed if his incapacity is due to his own misconduct, but two instances where
incapacity may have arisen in consequence of what might otherwise be treated
as sexual misconduct are expressly stated not to ground disqualification: (a)

where the incapacity is due to a sexually transmitted disease; and (b) the case of pregnancy.

Misconduct has not been exhaustively defined. Presumably, by analogy with its use in the unemployment benefit and jobseeker's allowance contexts, it denotes conduct which is blameworthy, reprehensible and wrong. It is unclear in this context, whether merely reckless or negligent conduct will suffice. *R(S)2/53* has been thought to import a requirement of wilfulness, but this may be to read too much into a particular example of misconduct. In that case the Commissioner considered alcoholism, and upheld disqualification. Drinking to such an extent to endanger health raises a prima facie inference of misconduct which can only be rebutted if the claimant proves that the alcoholism was involuntary, the result of disease or disablement which destroyed his willpower, so that he was *unable* to refrain from excessive drinking. The particular evidence in that case of an anxiety state was insufficient to rebut the presumption. Whether in the current medical and social climate the provision could apply to incapacity through heavy smoking remains to be seen. The paragraph could have unfortunate implications for some AIDS victims such as intravenous drug users who become infected nonsexually.

Paragraph (1)(b)

9.364   This seems designed to deal with a specific aspect of behaviour which may contribute to further limited capability for work or hinder recovery. Disqualification must be imposed where the claimant fails to attend for or submit to medical or other treatment. The medical or other treatment must be recommended by a doctor with whom, or a hospital or similar institution with which, he is undergoing medical treatment and be such as would be likely to render him capable of work. This formulation may reverse *R(S) 3/57*, depending on the scope of "other treatment". There the blind claimant gave up a vocational training course when she became pregnant and refused to resume it thereafter; under USI Regs reg.17(1)(c) she had not refused treatment for her disablement since the course could have no effect on her blindness (para.6; *cf. R2/60SB*). Failure to attend for or submit to certain medical or other treatment is explicitly exempt from the sanction, namely failure to attend for or submit to vaccination or inoculation of any kind or to major surgery.

Establishing "good cause" for non-compliance precludes disqualification. In *R(S) 9/51* the claimant did so. Her non-attendance was founded on her own firm conviction that her religious beliefs (Christian Scientist) required her not to. It would not have been enough merely to establish membership of a sect whose religious rules forbade submission to treatment or examination.

Paragraph (1)(c)

9.365   Disqualification here penalises a claimant who fails to refrain from behaviour calculated to retard his recovery. "Calculated to retard his recovery" does not import an intention on his part to do so; the test is an objective one: was his behaviour likely to do so. Thus in *R(S) 21/52* the Commissioner upheld disqualification of the claimant, suffering from influenza bronchitis who was taken ill after undertaking a 60-mile drive when so suffering. However in *R(S) 3/57* (above para.(1)(b)) the course was irrelevant to recovery from blindness, so leaving and refusing to resume the course could not ground disqualification. Establishing good cause for the failure precludes disqualification. Mere ignorance of the rules is not good cause (*R(S) 21/52*).

Paragraph (1)(d)

9.366   This requires the claimant not to be absent from his place of residence without leaving word as to where he can be found. It is designed to penalise those who deliberately seek to avoid the Department's visiting officers who may call as part of the Department's claims control mechanisms. It will only be invoked where visits have already proved ineffective, and as a matter of law the absence must have occurred during the currency of a claim. The rule cannot apply unless the claimant has a residence; it is not to be interpreted as imposing a requirement to have one *(R(S) 7/83)*, so claimants of no fixed abode cannot be caught by it. *R(S) 1/87* requires findings be made as to place of residence, any absence in the relevant period, and on whether the claimant had failed to leave word where he could be found. If those findings showed the claimant's absence from his residence without leaving word as to his whereabouts, it would then fall to the claimant to establish good cause for so acting (see para.12). A claimant's genuine difficulty in leaving word where he might be found was held to constitute good cause in *R(S) 6/55*. There the claimant lived with relatives who were out at work on the three occasions that the visiting officer called. The claimant was out in the park or at the cinema on those occasions, and there was no one with whom he could leave a message. His doctor had advised him to get out as much as possible. Mere ignorance of the rules is not good cause *(R(S) 21/52)*.

Exceptions (paragraph (3))

Someone disqualified under the specified fraud provision cannot be disqualified under this regulation (sub-para.(b)). Nor can someone who qualifies as a "person in hardship" as defined in reg.158 (sub-para.(b)).   9.367

Meaning of "person in hardship"

158.—(1) A claimant is a "person in hardship" if the claimant—   9.368
(a) has informed the Secretary of State of the circumstances on which the claimant relies to establish that fact; and
(b) falls within paragraph (2), (3) or (5).
(2) A claimant falls within this paragraph if—
(a) she is pregnant;
(b) a member of the claimant's family is pregnant;
(c) the claimant is a single claimant aged less than 18; or
(d) the claimant is a member of a couple and both members are aged less than 18.
(3) Subject to paragraph (4), the claimant falls within this paragraph if the claimant or the claimant's partner—
(a) is responsible for a child or young person who is a member of the claimant's household;
(b) has been awarded an attendance allowance [², the care component [³ , armed forces independence payment] or the daily living component];
(c) has claimed either attendance [², disability living allowance [³, armed forces independence payment] or personal independence payment] and the claim has not been determined;
(d) devotes a considerable portion of each week to caring for another person who—
   (i) has been awarded an attendance allowance [², the care component [³ , armed forces independence payment] or the daily living component]; or
   (ii) has claimed either attendance allowance [², disability living allowance [³, armed forces independence payment] or personal independence payment] and the claim has not been determined; or
(e) [¹ has attained the qualifying age for state pension credit].

(4) A claimant to whom paragraph (3)(c) or (3)(d)(ii) applies is a person in hardship only for 26 weeks from the date of the claim unless the claimant is a person in hardship under another provision of this regulation.

(5) The claimant falls within this paragraph where the Secretary of State is satisfied, having regard to all the circumstances and, in particular, the matters set out in paragraph (6), that unless an employment and support allowance is paid, the claimant, or a member of the claimant's family, will suffer hardship.

(6) The matters referred to in paragraph (5) are—

(a) the resources which are likely to be available to the claimant and the claimant's family and the length of time for which they might be available; and

(b) whether there is a substantial risk that essential items, including food, clothing and heating, will cease to be available to the claimant or a member of the claimant's family, or will be available at considerably reduced levels and the length of time for which this might be so.

(7) In this regulation "care component" means the care component of disability living allowance at the highest or middle rate prescribed under section 72(3) of the Contributions and Benefits Act.

AMENDMENTS

1. Social Security (Equalisation of State Pension Age) Regulations 2009 (SI 2009/1488) reg.43 (April 6, 2010).

2. Personal Independence Payment (Supplementary Provisions and Consequential Amendments) Regulations 2013 (SI 2013/388) reg.8 and Sch. para.40(1) and (4) (April 8, 2013).

3. Armed Forces and Reserve Forces Compensation Scheme (Consequential Provisions: Subordinate Legislation) Order 2013 (SI 2013/591) art.7 and Sch. para.37(1) and (4) (April 8, 2013).

DEFINITIONS

"attendance allowance"—see reg.2(1).
"care component"—see para.(7).
"claimant"—see WRA 2007 s.24(1).
"Contributions and Benefits Act"—see WRA 2006 s.65.
"disability living allowance"—see reg.2(1).
"family"—see reg.2(1).
"person in hardship"—see para.(1).

GENERAL NOTE

9.369   The effect of this regulation is similar to reg.140 of the JSA Regulations.

Paragraph (1)

9.370   A person in hardship cannot be disqualified from receiving ESA under reg.157 (see para.(3)(b) of that regulation). This paragraph defines someone as a "person in hardship" who notifies the Secretary of State of the circumstances relied on to establish this, so long as he satisfies the conditions set in paras (2), (3) or (5).

Paragraph (2)

9.371   This covers a claimant who is pregnant; a claimant where a family member is pregnant; the claimant is single and under 18; and the claimant who is a member of a couple and both the claimant and partner are under 18.

Paragraphs (3), (4)

This covers someone aged 60 or over; someone responsible for a child or young 9.372
person who is a member of his household someone who has been awarded attendance allowance (note the wider coverage of that term in reg.2(1)) or the care component (middle or higher rate) of disability living allowance (see para.(7)); and a
carer who devotes a considerable portion of a week to caring for another who has
been awarded attendance allowance (again note the wider coverage of that term in
reg.2(1)) or the care component of DLA at middle of higher rate (see para.(7)). The
paragraph also brings in, but only for 26 weeks unless the claimant also qualifies
under another head, someone who has claimed attendance allowance (again note
the wider coverage of that term in reg.2(1)) or middle or higher rate care component
of DLA (see para.(7)), but the claim remains undetermined, or the carer devoting a
substantial portion of the week to caring for someone in that position (paras (3)(c),
(d)(ii), (4)).

Paragraphs (5), (6)

These cover the claimant where the Secretary of State is satisfied that unless ESA 9.373
is paid, the claimant or a member of his family will suffer hardship. In considering
whether that is the case, he must have regard to all the circumstances, particularly
those set out in para.(6).

Treating a claimant as not having limited capability for work

159.—(1) Subject to paragraph (2), the claimant is to be treated as not 9.374
having limited capability for work if the claimant is disqualified for receiving
a contributory allowance during a period of imprisonment or detention in
legal custody if that disqualification is for more than 6 weeks.

(2) Where the claimant is entitled to an amount under paragraph 3 of
Schedule 5 (special cases: prisoners) during a period of imprisonment
or detention in legal custody, the claimant is to be treated as not having
limited capability for work from the day after the day on which entitlement
ended.

DEFINITIONS

"claimant"—see WRA 2007 s.24(1).
"contributory allowance"—see WRA 2007 s.1(7).

GENERAL NOTE

Those disqualified for contributory ESA under s.18(4) of the Welfare Reform Act 9.375
for more than six weeks because they are imprisoned or detained in custody are
treated by para.(1) as not having limited capability for work.

Under reg.69 and para.3(b) of Sch.5, a person may be entitled to income-related
ESA at a reduced rate while detained in custody pending trial or pending sentence
following conviction. In those circumstances, the person is treated by para.(2) as not
having limited capability for work from the day after that entitlement ends.

Exceptions from disqualification for imprisonment

160.—(1) Notwithstanding section 18(4)(b) of the Act, a claimant is not 9.376
disqualified for receiving a contributory allowance for any period during
which that claimant is undergoing imprisonment or detention in legal
custody—
    (a) in connection with a charge brought or intended to be brought
        against the claimant in criminal proceedings;
    (b) pursuant to any sentence; or

(c) pursuant to any order for detention,
made by a court in such proceedings, unless paragraph (2) applies.

(2) This paragraph applies where—

(a) a penalty is imposed on the claimant at the conclusion of the proceedings referred to in paragraph (1); or

(b) in the case of default of payment of a sum adjudged to be paid on conviction a penalty is imposed in respect of such default.

(3) Notwithstanding section 18(4)(b) of the Act, a claimant [² "C"] is not to be disqualified for receiving a contributory allowance, for any period during which C is undergoing detention in legal custody after the conclusion of criminal proceedings if it is a period during which [³ C is detained in a hospital or similar institution in Great Britain as a person suffering from mental disorder unless C satisfies either of the following conditions.

(4) The first condition is that—

(a) C is being detained under section 45A or 47 of the Mental Health Act 1983 (power of higher courts to direct hospital admission; removal to hospital of persons serving sentences of imprisonment etc.); and

(b) in any case where there is in relation to C a release date within the meaning of section 50(3) of that Act, C is being detained on or before the day which the Secretary of State certifies to be that release date.

(4A) The second condition is that C is being detained under—

(a) section 59A of the Criminal Procedure (Scotland) Act 1995 (hospital direction); or

(b) section 136 of the Mental Health (Care and Treatment) (Scotland) Act 2003 (transfer of prisoners for treatment of mental disorder).]

(5) For the purposes of this regulation—

(a) "court" means any court in the United Kingdom, the Channel Islands or the Isle of Man or in any place to which the Colonial Prisoners Removal Act 1884 applies or any naval court-martial, army court-martial or air force court-martial within the meaning of the Courts-Martial (Appeals) Act 1968 or the Courts-Martial Appeal Court;

(b) "hospital or similar institution" means any place (not being a prison, a young offender institution, a secure training centre, secure accommodation in a children's home [³, a place at which a secure accommodation service within the meaning of Part 1 of the Regulation and Inspection of Social Care (Wales) Act 2016 is being provided] or a remand centre, and not being at or in any such place) in which persons suffering from mental disorder are or may be received for care or treatment;

(c) "penalty" means a sentence of imprisonment or detention under section 90 or 91 of the Powers of Criminal Courts (Sentencing) Act 2000, a detention and training order under section 100 of that Act, a sentence of detention for public protection under section 226 of the Criminal Justice Act 2003 or an extended sentence under section 228 of that Act or, in Scotland, under section 205, 207 or 208 of the Criminal Procedure (Scotland) Act 1995;

(d) in relation to a person who is liable to be detained in Great Britain as a result of any order made under the Colonial Prisoners Removal Act 1884, references to a prison must be construed as including references to a prison within the meaning of that Act;

(e) criminal proceedings against any person must be deemed to be concluded upon that person being found insane in those proceedings so that the person cannot be tried or that person's trial cannot proceed.

(6) Where a claimant outside Great Britain is undergoing imprisonment or detention in legal custody and, in similar circumstances in Great Britain, the claimant would, by virtue of this regulation, not have been disqualified for receiving a contributory allowance, the claimant is not disqualified for receiving that allowance by reason only of the imprisonment or detention.

AMENDMENTS

1. Employment and Support Allowance (Miscellaneous Amendments) Regulations 2008 (SI 2008/2428) reg.10 (October 27, 2008).
2. Social Security (Persons Serving a Sentence of Imprisonment Detained in Hospital) Regulations 2010 (SI 2010/442) reg.5(3) (March 25, 2010).
3. Social Security and Child Support (Regulation and Inspection of Social Care (Wales) Act 2016) (Consequential Provision) Regulations 2018 (SI 2018/228) reg.11(1) and (3) (April 2, 2018).

DEFINITIONS

"claimant"—see WRA 2007 s.24(1).
"court"—see para.(5)(a).
"hospital or similar institution"—see para.(5)(b).
"penalty"—see para.(5)(c).
"prison"—see para.(5)(d).

GENERAL NOTE

Under s.18(4) of the WRA 2007, a claimant is disqualified for contributory ESA   **9.377** while "undergoing imprisonment or detention in legal custody". This regulation establishes exceptions to that rule. Under paras (1) and (2), there is no disqualification while the claimant is in custody pending trial or sentence unless a penalty is imposed. Payment of contributory ESA is suspended under reg.161 below during the period when it is not known whether a penalty will eventually be imposed. By para.(6), the same rule is applied to claimants imprisoned outside Great Britain. Under para.(3), there is no disqualification where the claimant is compulsorily detained in hospital following the conclusion of criminal proceedings unless a prison sentence is imposed and the claimant is subsequently transferred to hospital under the specified legislation.

Suspension of payment of a contributory allowance during imprisonment

161.—(1) Subject to the following provisions of this regulation, the   **9.378** payment of a contributory allowance to any claimant—
 (a) which is excepted from the operation of section 18(4)(b) of the Act by virtue of the provisions of regulation 160[¹ (1)], (3) or (6); or
 (b) which is payable otherwise than in respect of a period during which the claimant is undergoing imprisonment or detention in legal custody,
is suspended while that claimant is undergoing imprisonment or detention in legal custody.
 (2) A contributory allowance is not to be suspended while the claim-

ant is liable to be detained in a hospital or similar institution, as defined in regulation 160(5), during a period for which in the claimant's case, the allowance is or would be excepted from the operation of section 18(4)(b) by virtue of the provisions of regulation 160(3).

(3) Where, by virtue of this regulation, payment of a contributory allowance is suspended for any period, the period of suspension is not to be taken into account in calculating any period under the provisions of regulation 38 of the Social Security (Claims and Payments) Regulations 1987 (extinguishment of right to sums payable by way of benefit which are not obtained within the prescribed time).

AMENDMENT

1. Social Security (Miscellaneous Amendments) (No.3) Regulations 2011 (SI 2011/2425) reg.23(13) (October 30, 2011).

DEFINITIONS

"claimant"—see WRA 2007 s.24(1).
"contributory allowance"—see WRA 2007 s.1(7).
"hospital or similar institution"—see reg.160(5).

GENERAL NOTE

9.379   See the commentary to reg.160.

PART 13

URGENT CASES

GENERAL NOTE

9.380   Part 13 (regs 162–164), which provided for 'urgent cases" payments of ESA to certain claimants who were treated as possessing notional income under reg.107, was revoked the Social Security (Miscellaneous Amendments) (No.5) Regulations 2009 (SI 2009/3228) reg.2 with effect from January 25, 2010.

The revocation was subject to two savings. The first covered any person to whom reg.162(2) applied (i.e. who was treated as possessing notional income) on January 24, 2010. The second covered any person who, on the same date, fell within para.1 of Pt 1 of the Schedule to the Social Security (Immigration and Asylum) Regulations 2000 (SI 2000/636). That paragraph relates to some persons subject to immigration control with limited leave to enter or remain in the UK and whose remittances from abroad had been disrupted. The second saving is necessary because such a person may not be affected by reg.107 on January 24, 2010, but might subsequently become so during the same period of limited leave. It applies for a period, or the aggregate of any periods, of 42 days within the period of limited leave or until the claimant ceases to fall within para.1 of Pt 1 of the Schedule to SI 2000/636. See regs 2(2)–(4) of SI 2009/3229 in Vol.II.

For the abolition of urgent cases payments generally, see the commentary to Pt VI of the Income Support Regulations in Vol.II.

PART 14

PERIODS OF LESS THAN A WEEK

Entitlement for less than a week—amount of an employment and support allowance payable

165.—(1) This regulation applies where the claimant is entitled to an   9.381
employment and support allowance for a part-week and is subject to the
following provisions of this Part.

(2) The amount payable by way of an income-related allowance in respect
of that part-week is to be calculated by applying the formula—

(a) where the claimant has no income—

$$\frac{(N \times A)}{7}$$

or

(b) where the claimant has an income—

$$\frac{N \times (A - 1)}{7} - B$$

where—

A is the claimant's weekly applicable amount in the relevant week;

B is the amount of any employment and support allowance, jobseeker's
allowance, income support, maternity allowance, incapacity benefit or
severe disablement allowance payable to the claimant or the claimant's
partner in respect of any day in the part-week;

I is the claimant's weekly income in the relevant week; and

N is the number of days in the part week.

(3) The amount payable by way of a contributory allowance in respect of
a part-week is to be calculated by applying the formula—

$$\frac{(N \times X) - Y}{7}$$

where—

X is the amount calculated in accordance with section 2(1) of the Act;

Y is the amount of any widow's benefit, widowed parent's allowance,
[¹ bereavement support payment under section 30 of the Pensions Act
2014], training allowance, carer's allowance and any increase in disablement pension payable in accordance with Part 1 of Schedule 7 to the
Contributions and Benefits Act (Unemployability Supplement) payable
in respect of any day in the part-week;

N is the number of days in the part-week.

(4) In this Part—

"part-week" means an entitlement to an employment and support allowance in respect of any period of less than a week;

"relevant week" means the period of 7 days determined in accordance
with regulation 166.

AMENDMENT

1. Pensions Act 2014 (Consequential, Supplementary and Incidental Amendments) Order 2017 (SI 2017/422), art.31(2) (April 6, 2017).

GENERAL NOTE

9.382   This regulation is similar to reg.150 of the JSA Regs.

Relevant week

9.383   **166.**—(1) Where a part-week—

(a) is the whole period for which an employment and support allowance is payable, or occurs at the beginning of an award, the relevant week is the period of 7 days ending on the last day of that part-week; or

(b) occurs at the end of an award, the relevant week is the period of 7 days beginning on the first day of the part-week.

(2) Where a claimant has an award of an employment and support allowance and that claimant's benefit week changes, for the purpose of calculating the amounts of an employment and support allowance payable for the part-week beginning on the day after the last complete benefit week before the change and ending immediately before the change, the relevant week is the period of 7 days beginning on the day after the last complete benefit week.

DEFINITIONS

"benefit week"—reg.2(1).
"claimant"—WRA 2007 s.24(1).
"part-week"—reg.165(4).
"relevant week"—*ibid*.

GENERAL NOTE

9.384   This regulation is similar to reg.152 of the JSA Regs.

Modification in the calculation of income

9.385   **167.** For the purposes of regulation 165 (entitlement for less than a week—amount of an employment and support allowance payable), a claimant's income and, in determining the amount payable by way of an income-related allowance, the income of any person which the claimant is treated as possessing under regulations made under section 17(3) of the Act, regulation 68 (polygamous marriages) or regulation 83 (calculation of income and capital of members of claimant's family and of a polygamous marriage), is to be calculated in accordance with Parts 10 (income and capital) and 13 (urgent cases) subject to the following changes—

(a) any income which is due to be paid in the relevant week is to be treated as paid on the first day of that week;

(b) in determining the amount payable by way of an income-related allowance, any jobseeker's allowance, employment and support allowance, income support [¹ , universal credit] maternity allowance, incapacity benefit or severe disablement allowance payable in the relevant week but not in respect of any day in the part-week is to be disregarded;

(c) the amount referred to as B in regulation 165(2) is to be disregarded;

(d) in determining the amount payable by way of a contributory allowance, any widow's benefit, training allowance, widowed parent's allowance, [² bereavement support payment under section 30 of the Pensions Act 2014], carer's allowance and any increase in disablement pension payable in accordance with Part 1 of Schedule 7 to the Contributions and Benefits Act (unemployability supplement) which is payable in the relevant week but not in respect of any day in the part-week is to be disregarded;

(e) where the part-week occurs at the end of the claim—
  (i) any income; or
  (ii) any change in the amount of income of the same kind, which is first payable within the relevant week but not on any day in the part-week is to be disregarded;

(f) where only part of the weekly balance of income is taken into account in the relevant week, the balance is to be disregarded.

AMENDMENTS

1. Universal Credit (Consequential, Supplementary, Incidental and Miscellaneous Provisions) Regulations 2013 (SI 2013/630) reg.37(1) and (6) (April 29, 2013).
2. Pensions Act 2014 (Consequential, Supplementary and Incidental Amendments) Order 2017 (SI 2017/422) art.31(3) (April 6, 2017).

GENERAL NOTE

This regulation is similar to reg.153 of the JSA Regs.   9.386

[¹ Reduction in certain cases

168.—(1) Where a disqualification is to be made in accordance with   9.387
regulation 157 in respect of a part-week, the amount referred to in paragraph (2) is to be payable by way of an employment and support allowance in respect of that part-week.

(2) The amount mentioned in paragraph (1) is—

(a) one seventh of the employment and support allowance which would have been paid for the part-week if—
  (i) there was no disqualification under regulation 157; and
  (ii) it was not a part-week; multiplied by

(b) the number of days in the part-week in respect of which no disqualification is to be made in accordance with regulation 157.]

AMENDMENT

1. Social Security (Miscellaneous Amendments) (No.3) Regulations 2013 (SI 2013/2536) reg.13(1) and (31) (October 29, 2013).

GENERAL NOTE

This regulation is similar to reg.154 of the JSA Regs.   9.388

Payment of a contributory allowance for days of certain regular treatment

169.—(1) Where a claimant is entitled to a contributory allowance as a   9.389
result of being treated as having limited capability for work in accordance with regulation 26 the amount payable is to be equal to one seventh of the

amount of the contributory allowance which would be payable in respect of a week in accordance with section 2(1) of the Act multiplied by N.

(2) In paragraph (1), N is the number of days in that week on which the claimant was receiving treatment referred to in regulation 26 or recovering from that treatment, but does not include any day during which the claimant does work.

SCHEDULE 1   **Regulation 2(2)**

HER MAJESTY'S FORCES

PART 1

PRESCRIBED ESTABLISHMENTS AND ORGANISATIONS

9.390

1. Any of the regular naval, military or air forces of the Crown.
2. Royal Fleet Reserve.
3. Royal Navy Reserve.
4. Royal Marines Reserve.
5. Army Reserve.
6. Territorial Army.
7. Royal Air Force Reserve.
8. Royal Auxiliary Air Force.
9. The Royal Irish Regiment, to the extent that its members are not members of any force falling within paragraph 1.

PART 2

ESTABLISHMENTS AND ORGANISATIONS OF WHICH HER MAJESTY'S FORCES DO NOT CONSIST

10. Her Majesty's forces are not to be taken to consist of any of the establishments or organisations specified in Part 1 of this Schedule by virtue only of the employment in such establishment or organisation of the following persons—

(a) any person who is serving as a member of any naval force of Her Majesty's forces and who (not having been an insured person under the National Insurance Act 1965 and not having been a contributor under the Social Security Act 1975 or not being a contributor under the Contributions and Benefits Act) locally entered that force at an overseas base;

(b) any person who is serving as a member of any military force of Her Majesty's forces and who entered that force, or was recruited for that force outside the United Kingdom, and the depot of whose unit is situated outside the United Kingdom;

(c) any person who is serving as a member of any air force of Her Majesty's forces and who entered that force, or was recruited for that force, outside the United Kingdom, and is liable under the terms of engagement to serve only in a specified part of the world outside the United Kingdom.

GENERAL NOTE

9.391   See the commentary to the definition of "member of Her Majesty's forces" in reg.2(1).

IMPORTANT PRELIMINARY NOTE ABOUT SCHEDULES 2 (LIMTED CAPABILITY FOR WORK ASSESSMENT) AND 3 (LIMITED CAPABILITY FOR WORK-RELATED ACTIVITY ASSESSMENT)

9.392   Completely new Schedules were substituted on March 28, 2011 by the Employment and Support Allowance (Limited Capability for Work and Limited Capability for Work-Related Activity) (Amendment) Regulations 2011 (SI

2011/228) reg.4. Regulation 2 of those regulations sets out the cases to which the new Schedules apply. It provides:

"Application

2.—(1) These Regulations apply to:—
  (a) a person who makes a claim for an employment and support allowance on or after 28 March 2011 (including a claim in respect of any period before that date);
  (b) subject to paragraphs (2) and (3), a person who made a claim for an employment and support allowance before 28 March 2011 in respect of whom a determination is made on or after that date as to whether that person has or is to be treated as having limited capability for work under Part 5 of the ESA Regulations or as to whether that person has or is to be treated as having limited capability for work-related activity under Part 6 of those Regulations;
  (c) subject to paragraphs (2) and (3), a person who is entitled to an employment and support allowance immediately before 28 March 2011 in respect of whom, on or after that date–
     (i) the Secretary of State determines afresh under regulation 19(7) of the ESA Regulations whether the person has or is to be treated as having limited capability for work;
     (ii) the Secretary of State determines afresh under regulation 34(4) of the ESA Regulations whether the person has or is to be treated as having limited capability for work-related activity; and
  (d) subject to paragraphs (2) and (3), a notified person as defined by regulation 4 of the Reassessment Regulations in respect of whom a determination is made on or after 28 March 2011 as to whether that person has or is to be treated as having limited capability for work under Part 5 of the ESA Regulations or as to whether that person has or is to be treated as having limited capability for work-related activity under Part 6 of the ESA Regulations.

(2) Where, before 28 March 2011, a questionnaire relating to the previous version of Schedule 2 to the ESA Regulations was issued to a person in accordance with regulation 21(1)(b) of those Regulations (information required for determining capability for work), regulation 4(1) does not apply to that person for the purposes of making a determination as to limited capability for work under Part 5 of the ESA Regulations;

(3) Where, before 28 March 2011, a questionnaire relating to the previous version of Schedule 3 to the ESA Regulations was issued to a person in accordance with regulation 36(1)(a) of those Regulations (information required for determining capability for work-related activity) regulation 4(2) does not apply to that person for the purposes of making a determination as to limited capability for work-related activity under Part 6 of the ESA Regulations.

(4) In this regulation "the previous version of Schedule 2 to the ESA Regulations" and "the previous version of Schedule 3 to the ESA Regulations" mean those Schedules as they have effect immediately before the date on which these Regulations come into force.

(5) The provisions of paragraphs (2) to (4) do not apply to any determination made on or after 28 September 2011."

The text and commentary immediately following this Note is that operative from March 28, 2011, as amended from January 28, 2013.

[¹SCHEDULE 2 **Regulation 19(2) and (3)**

Assessment of Whether a Claimant has Limited Capability for Work

Part 1

Physical disabilities

(1) Activity	(2) Descriptors		(3) Points
1. [²Mobilising unaided by another person with or without a walking stick, manual wheelchair or other aid if such aid is normally, or could reasonably be, worn or used.]	1 (a)	Cannot [³unaided by another person] either:	15
	(i)	mobilise more than 50 metres on level ground without stopping in order to avoid significant discomfort or exhaustion; or	
	(ii)	repeatedly mobilise 50 metres within a reasonable timescale because of significant discomfort or exhaustion.	
	(b)	Cannot [³unaided by another person] mount or descend two steps [³...] even with the support of a handrail.	9
	(c)	Cannot [³unaided by another person] either	9
	(i)	mobilise more than 100 metres on level ground without stopping in order to avoid significant discomfort or exhaustion; or	
	(ii)	repeatedly mobilise 100 metres within a reasonable timescale because of significant discomfort or exhaustion.	
	(d)	Cannot [³unaided by another person] either:	6
	(i)	mobilise more than 200 metres on level ground without stopping in order to avoid significant discomfort or exhaustion; or	
	(ii)	repeatedly mobilise 200 metres within a reasonable timescale because of significant discomfort or exhaustion.	
	(e)	None of the above [³applies].	0
2. Standing and sitting.	2 (a)	Cannot move between one seated position and another seated position located next to one another without receiving physical assistance from another person.	15
	(b)	Cannot, for the majority of the time, remain at a work station, either:	9
	(i)	standing unassisted by another person (even if free to move around); or	
	(ii)	sitting (even in an adjustable chair) [²; or	
	(iii)	a combination of (i) and (ii),] for more than 30 minutes, before needing to move away in order to avoid significant discomfort or exhaustion.	

(1) Activity	(2) Descriptors	(3) Points
	(c) Cannot, for the majority of the time, remain at a work station, either:	6
	(i) standing unassisted by another person (even if free to move around); or	
	(ii) sitting (even in an adjustable chair) [²; or	
	(iii) a combination of (i) and (ii),] for more than an hour before needing to move away in order to avoid significant discomfort or exhaustion.	
	(d) None of the above apply	0
3. Reaching.	3 (a) Cannot raise either arm as if to put something in the top pocket of a coat or jacket.	15
	(b) Cannot raise either arm to top of head as if to put on a hat.	9
	(c) Cannot raise either arm above head height as if to reach for something.	6
	(d) None of the above apply.	0
4. Picking up and moving or transferring by the use of the upper body and arms.	(a) Cannot pick up and move a 0.5 litre carton full of liquid.	15
	(b) Cannot pick up and move a one litre carton full of liquid.	9
	(c) Cannot transfer a light but bulky object such as an empty cardboard box.	6
	(d) None of the above apply.	0
5. Manual dexterity.	5. [³(a) Cannot press a button (such as a telephone keypad) with either hand or cannot turn the pages of a book with either hand.]	15
	(b) Cannot pick up a £1 coin or equivalent with either hand.	15
	(c) Cannot use a pen or pencil to make a meaningful mark [³ with either hand].	9
	(d) Cannot [² single-handedly] use a suitable keyboard or mouse.	9
	(e) None of the above [³ applies].	0
[² 6. Making self understood through speaking, writing, typing, or other means which are normally, or could reasonably be, used, unaided by another person.]	6 (a) Cannot convey a simple message, such as the presence of a hazard.	15
	(b) Has significant difficulty conveying a simple message to strangers.	15
	(c) Has some difficulty conveying a simple message to strangers.	6
	(d) None of the above apply.	0
[² 7. Understanding communication by— (i) verbal means (such as hearing or lip reading) alone,	7. (a) Cannot understand a simple message [³,such as the location of a fire escape,] due to sensory impairment [³…].	15

(1) *Activity*	(2) *Descriptors*	(3) *Points*
[(ii) non-verbal means (such as reading 16 point print or Braille) alone, or (iii) a combination of (i) and (ii), using any aid that is normally, or could reasonably be, used, unaided by another person.]	(b) Has significant difficulty understanding a simple message from a stranger due to sensory impairment.	15
	(c) Has some difficulty understanding a simple message from a stranger due to sensory impairment.	6
	(d) None of the above [³ applies].	0
[² 8. Navigation and maintaining safety, using a guide dog or other aid if either or both are normally, or could reasonably be, used.]	8 (a) Unable to navigate around familiar surroundings, without being accompanied by another person, due to sensory impairment.	15
	(b) Cannot safely complete a potentially hazardous task such as crossing the road, without being accompanied by another person, due to sensory impairment.	15
	(c) Unable to navigate around unfamiliar surroundings, without being accompanied by another person, due to sensory impairment.	9
	(d) None of the above apply.	0
[² 9. Absence or loss of control whilst conscious leading to extensive evacuation of the bowel and/or bladder, other than enuresis (bed-wetting), despite the wearing or use of any aids or adaptations which are normally, or could reasonably be, worn or used.]	9 (a) At least once a month experiences: (i) loss of control leading to extensive evacuation of the bowel and/or voiding of the bladder; or (ii) substantial leakage of the contents of a collecting device sufficient to require cleaning and a change in clothing.	15
	(b) [² The majority of the time is at risk] of loss of control leading to extensive evacuation of the bowel and/or voiding of the bladder, sufficient to require cleaning and a change in clothing, if not able to reach a toilet quickly.	6
	(c) [³ Neither of the above applies.]	0
10. Consciousness during waking moments.	10 (a) At least once a week, has an involuntary episode of lost or altered consciousness resulting in significantly disrupted awareness or concentration.	15
	(b) At least once a month, has an involuntary episode of lost or altered consciousness resulting in significantly disrupted awareness or concentration.	6
	(c) None of the above apply.	0

PART 2

MENTAL, COGNITIVE AND INTELLECTUAL FUNCTION ASSESSMENT

(1) *Activity*	(2) *Descriptors*	(3) *Points*
11. Learning tasks.	11 (a) Cannot learn how to complete a simple task, such as setting an alarm clock.	15
	(b) Cannot learn anything beyond a simple task, such as setting an alarm clock.	9
	(c) Cannot learn anything beyond a moderately complex task, such as the steps involved in operating a washing machine to clean clothes.	6
	(d) None of the above apply.	0
12. Awareness of everyday hazards (such as boiling water or sharp objects).	12.(a) Reduced awareness of everyday hazards leads to a significant risk of: (i) injury to self or others; or (ii) damage to property or possessions such that [⁴the claimant requires] supervision for the majority of the time to maintain safety.	15
	(b) Reduced awareness of everyday hazards leads to a significant risk of (i) injury to self or others; or (ii) damage to property or possessions such that [⁴the claimant frequently requires] supervision to maintain safety	9
	(c) Reduced awareness of everyday hazards leads to a significant risk of: (i) injury to self or others; or (ii) damage to property or possessions such that [⁴the claimant occasionally requires] supervision to maintain safety.	6
	(d) None of the above apply.	0
13. Initiating and completing personal action (which means planning, organisation, problem solving, prioritising or switching tasks).	13 (a) Cannot, due to impaired mental function, reliably initiate or complete at least 2 sequential personal actions.	15
	(b) Cannot, due to impaired mental function, reliably initiate or complete at least 2 [⁴ sequential] personal actions for the majority of the time.	9
	(c) Frequently cannot, due to impaired mental function, reliably initiate or complete at least 2 [⁴ sequential] personal actions.	6
	(d) None of the above [⁴ applies].	0
14. Coping with change.	14 (a) Cannot cope with any change to the extent that day to day life cannot be managed.	15
	(b) Cannot cope with minor planned change (such as a pre-arranged change to the routine time scheduled for a lunch break), to the extent that overall day to day life is made significantly more difficult.	9

(1) Activity	(2) Descriptors	(3) Points
	(c) Cannot cope with minor unplanned change (such as the timing of an appointment on the day it is due to occur), to the extent that overall, day to day life is made significantly more difficult.	6
	(d) None of the above apply.	0
15. Getting about.	15 [²(a) Cannot get to any place outside the claimant's home with which the claimant is familiar.]	15
	(b) Is unable to get to a specified place with which the claimant is familiar, without being accompanied by another person.	9
	(c) Is unable to get to a specified place with which the claimant is unfamiliar without being accompanied by another person.	6
	(d) None of the above apply.	0
16. Coping with social engagement due to cognitive impairment or mental disorder.	16 (a) Engagement in social contact is always precluded due to difficulty relating to others or significant distress experienced by the [⁴ claimant].	15
	(b) Engagement in social contact with someone unfamiliar to the claimant is always precluded due to difficulty relating to others or significant distress experienced by the [⁴ claimant].	9
	(c) Engagement in social contact with someone unfamiliar to the claimant is not possible for the majority of the time due to difficulty relating to others or significant distress experienced by the [⁴ claimant].	6
	(d) None of the above [⁴ applies].	0
17. Appropriateness of behaviour with other people, due to cognitive impairment or mental disorder.	17 (a) Has, on a daily basis, uncontrollable episodes of aggressive or disinhibited behaviour that would be unreasonable in any workplace.	15
	(b) Frequently has uncontrollable episodes of aggressive or disinhibited behaviour that would be unreasonable in any workplace.	15
	(c) Occasionally has uncontrollable episodes of aggressive or disinhibited behaviour that would be unreasonable in any workplace.	9
	(d) None of the above apply.	0.]

AMENDMENTS

1. Employment and Support Allowance (Limited Capability for Work and Limited Capability for Work-Related Activity) (Amendment) Regulations 2011 (SI 2011/228) reg.4(1) (March 28, 2011).
2. Employment and Support Allowance (Amendment) Regulations 2012 (SI 2012/3096) reg.5(2) (January 28, 2013, subject to application, transitional and savings provisions in reg. 2 of this amending instrument, below, para.9.601).

3. Social Security (Miscellaneous Amendments) (No.3) Regulations 2013 (SI 2013/2536) reg.13(32) (October 29, 2013).

4. Social Security (Miscellaneous Amendments) (No.3) Regulations 2013 (SI 2013/2536) reg.13(33) (October 29, 2013).

DEFINITION

"claimant"—see WRA 2007 s.24(1).

GENERAL NOTE

I. A Note on the Background to the WCA and the new Schs 2 and 3 inserted on March 28, 2011

In 1995, a new test for incapacity for work was introduced: the "all work test". In 2000 this was renamed the personal capability assessment (PCA). This, like the "all work" test, lay at the heart of the reform effected by the Social Security (Incapacity for Work) Act 1994. According to Government, the results of two large scale evaluation studies to assess the validity and reliability of this essentially medical and functional test indicated:

> "that [it provided] a more effective means of assessing incapacity, which [would] help ensure that benefit is targeted on those people who are incapable of work, because of their medical condition" (DSS/Benefits Agency, *The medical assessment for incapacity benefit* (HMSO, 1994), p.35).

9.394

The "personal capability assessment" was one which—like the WCA—ignored the other personal/environmental factors governing access to employment by people with disabilities (R. Berthoud, "The 'medical' assessment of incapacity: a case study of the (lack of) influence of research on policy" [1995] 2 J.S.S.L. 61, at pp.70, 75). It did not measure people against the requirements of specific jobs (the "personal capability assessment" contained no definition of work for none was required given its nature). Its exclusionary effect would, it was thought by Berthoud, largely deny benefit to persons who probably were capable of work (*ibid.* at p.82). However, it was thought possible that some, who would have failed the previously applicable informal and more holistic test, might qualify as incapable on the AWT/PCA, while some, who failed the AWT/PCA, might well in fact be incapable of work.

The "personal capability assessment" was an assessment of the extent of the claimant's incapacity, by reason of some specific disease or bodily or mental disablement which he has, to perform the activities prescribed in the Schedule [to the IFW Regulations], entitled "disabilities which may make a person incapable of work" (IFW Regulations reg.24).

The new Work Capability Assessment (WCA) underpinning ESA followed similar lines, but embodied important changes to reflect the demands of the modern workplace, the development and availability of adaptive technology, and the legal obligations on employers to make reasonable adjustments better to accommodate those people with long term disabilities. In consequence, the 15 physical activities in the AWT/PCA were reduced to 11, in order to better reflect the activities that an employer might reasonably expect of his workforce. More radically, the mental health provisions in the IFW Regulations were thought not to be the most relevant to activities requisite for remaining in or returning to work. Consequently, the four activities dealing with mental functions in the AWT/PCA were increased to the ten activities in the original WCA with respect to mental, cognitive and intellectual function, reflecting a desire to deal better with the problems of a client group which made up some 41 per cent of the IB caseload.

The difficulties of applying the AWT/PCA are evident in a burgeoning case law. The difficulties of devising a test which accurately ascertains capability for work or for work-related activity are emphasized by ongoing review and the frequent amendments that are the subject of this commentary. Less than three years after its introduction, the WCA was thoroughly revised with new Schs 2 and 3 operating from March 28, 2011 for all new claims after that date, and for most determinations

and assessments made after that date. The development of the WCA from the AWT/
PCA and its recent revision are examined in some depth here on the basis that this
will aid the task of decision-makers and tribunals, who must interpret and apply
the wording of the activities and descriptors to the varied circumstances of individual cases, by casting light on the changes and their purpose. It is, of course, for
decision-makers and tribunals to decide what the wording chosen to achieve those
purposes actually means. Setting out the antecedents of the current provisions also
highlights the continued application to similar or identical wording of pertinent case
law authorities both on the AWT/PCA and the previous version of the WCA itself,
which can be found in para.9.365 of the 2012/13 edition of this volume as updated
by the 2012/13 Supplement.

The original WCA was devised by the DWP's Health Work and Wellbeing Directorate
with input from two technical working groups, one focusing on mental health and
learning difficulties, the other on physical function and conditions (hereinafter "review
group"). The review group consisted of medical and other relevant experts. It examined
how the incapacity benefits regime's Personal Capability Assessment (PCA) could be
improved and updated so as to reflect the many changes since its inception:

> "in the prevalence of disabling conditions; in advances in medical science result-
> ing in the availability of new and more effective medical interventions; and in the
> workplace environment. The Disability Discrimination Act, introduced after the
> PCA had been developed, has influenced the ability of employers to make reason-
> able adjustments to accommodate people with long term disabilities. It has also
> raised the expectations of disabled people that adjustments should be made to
> enable them to work."

The work of the review group fed into the drafting of the regulations on the WCA.
After that first element had been developed work continued on the second and third
elements of the WCA, although nothing has been published on this. Government
anticipated that the WCA would "fail" some 60,000 claimants a year who would have
"passed" the PCA (DWP, *Impact Assessment of the Employment and Support Allowance
Regulations 2008—Public sector Impact Only* in *Explanatory Memorandum to Employment
and Support Allowance Regulations 2008 (SI 2008/794) and the Employment and Support
Allowance (Transitional Provisions) Regulations 2008 (SI 2008/795)*, p.9). Statistics
from 2012 suggested that some 54 per cent of new claimants were found capable of
work (DWP Press Release, April 24, 2012: see *http://www.dwp.gov.uk/newsroom/press-
releases/2012/apr-2012/dwp042-12.shtml*), exceeding the DWP's expectations of 38 per
cent (DWP, Explanatory Memorandum to the SSAC on the Amending Regulations:
App 1a: Revising the WCA – assessment of impact, para.9). Figures published by the
DWP in January 2014, however, indicated that 61% of new claimants with a completed
claim were found to have limited capability of work. But the WCA is not merely an
incapacity-based tool for determining entitlement to ESA. That remains true of its first
element, but its second element is rather a more positive assessment considering ability
to benefit from work-related activity with a view to promoting capacity for work. The
first element is an assessment of limited capability to work (hereinafter the LCWA)
(the subject of this Schedule). The second element is an assessment of limited capacity
to engage in work-related activity (hereinafter LCWRA) (the subject of Sch.3). Both
assessments will generally be conducted at the same time by the same health care professional. Those found not to have limited capacity for work-related activity (expected
to be some 90 per cent of new claimants) were originally required to undergo the third
element of the WCA: a work-focused health related assessment (WFHRAt).

In many cases, it was envisaged all three elements of the new WCA would be
covered in a single appointment with a health care professional working for Atos
Origin Medical Services (MS), the company which originally contracted with the
DWP to deliver these assessments. However, the WFHRAt was suspended for a two-
year period beginning July 19, 2010; ongoing external evaluation of it had shown
mixed results, and the suspension affords an opportunity for the DWP to reconsider
the assessment's purpose and delivery and frees up capacity to deal with the "migra-

tion" of existing incapacity benefits customers to ESA or a more appropriate benefit (typically JSA). The regs dealing with it were revoked from June 1, 2011.

Schedule 2 deals with the LCWA and establishing limited capability for work: the core element of entitlement to ESA. The vast majority of claimants for ESA will be subject to this first element of the new WCA through a face to face assessment with a trained healthcare professional testing the claimant against the activities and descriptors in the Schedule, in the light of the material in the claimant's questionnaire, any evidence from the GP and the professional's examination. Assessment will take place much earlier than in an equivalent claim for IB.

The Government's view remains that the overwhelming majority of customers are capable of some work, given the right support. The approach is designed to treat people in line with their capabilities, instead of making assumptions based on their condition. Hence, because the ESA tests are designed to assess which claimants can benefit from the help towards work afforded by work-related activity, to "write off" from the chance of work as few people as possible, very few groups are exempt from the LCWA: the terminally ill; those receiving treatment by way of intravenous, intraperitoneal or intrathecal chemotherapy; such of those recovering from such treatment as the Secretary of State is satisfied should be treated as having limited capability for work; (from March 28, 2011) those likely to receive such treatment in the next six months; those excluded or prevented from working as a carrier, or having been in contact with a case of relevant disease (food poisoning, infectious or notifiable diseases covered by a variety of public health enactments); pregnant women at a certain stage in pregnancy or where there is a serious risk of damage to their or their unborn child's health if they do not refrain from work (reg.20); and (from March 28, 2011) those who would be found to have limited capability for work-related activity under any of the descriptors in paras 15 and 16 of the revised Sch.3. Hospital inpatients (reg.25) and persons undergoing or recovering from certain regular treatments (e.g. plasmapheresis, radio therapy, dialysis, parenteral nutrition) for at least two days a week (reg.26) are also treated as having limited capability for work. All such persons are exempt from the information gathering requirements with respect to the LCWA (reg.21(3)).

Decision-makers have discretion in respect of all claimants on whether it is necessary in their case to complete the questionnaire or require more information than is provided by the claimant's doctor under the Medical Evidence Regs (reg.21(2)). Whether someone is required to undergo a medical examination is also a matter of decision-maker discretion (reg.23). Typically, most claimants will have to both complete the questionnaire (form ESA50) and undergo medical examination, usually at a medical examination centre, but sometimes in the claimant's home. Failure to do so, without good cause, is as usual sanctioned by treating the person as not having limited capability for work, thus denying benefit (regs 22–24). The Work Capability Assessment is a face-to-face meeting, lasting between 75 and 90 minutes, depending on whether just two or (originally) all three elements of the WCA are carried out. It explores how the claimant's illness or disability affects their ability to work and carry out day-to-day activity Each part of the assessment will be carried out by specially trained healthcare professionals (whether doctor or nurse) approved by the Secretary of State to assess these matters and report to the decision-maker, generally in the form of a computer-generated report.

The WRA 2007 stipulates merely that whether a person's capability for work is limited by his physical or mental condition and, if so, whether the limitation is such that it is not reasonable to require him to work is to be determined in accordance with regulations. ESA Regs, reg.19(1) elaborates that this is to be determined on the basis of a limited capability for work assessment (LCWA), that is by:

> "an assessment of the extent to which a claimant who has some specific disease or bodily or mental disablement is capable of performing the activities prescribed in Schedule 2 or is incapable by reason of such disease or bodily or mental disablement of performing those activities" (reg.19(2)).

This is familiar stuff for those who have worked with the AWT/PCA. The claimant is to be matched, in the light of all the evidence, by the decision-maker or tribunal against a reformulated range of activities and descriptors, and an appropriate "score" awarded. The threshold "score" for entitlement under the WCA remains 15 points, but as regards its computation, there are both "old" and "new" elements.

It is stressed that incapability to perform an activity must arise from a specific bodily disease or disablement, a specific mental illness or disablement, or as a direct result of treatment provided by a registered medical practitioner, for such a disease, illness or disablement (reg.19(5)). The extent of capability to perform a physical activity has, as with IB, to be assessed as if the claimant is wearing any prosthesis with which he is fitted or wearing or using any aid or appliance which is normally worn or used. In computing the score, where more than one descriptor in respect of a particular activity applies, only the highest is counted towards the total "score" (reg.19(4)). Otherwise one simply adds up the total of the particular scores in respect of each activity, whether physical or mental, to see if the threshold of 15 points is reached. If it is, or is exceeded, the claimant has established limited capability for work, grounding entitlement to the basic allowance in ESA. The matter may be determined afresh where the Secretary of State wishes to ascertain: (i) whether there has been a relevant change of circumstances in relation to the claimant's physical or mental condition; (ii) whether the previous decision was made in ignorance of, or was based on a mistake as to, some material fact; or at least three months have passed since the last decision (reg.19(7), (8)).

If the threshold score is not attained, limited capability for work has not been established, there can be no entitlement to ESA and the unsuccessful claimant (subject to retention of ESA pending appeal) will have to look for income maintenance, typically to JSA or, more rarely, IS.

9.395   *The radical revision of Schs 2 and 3, effective March 28, 2011:* Given the careful preparatory work in devising the WCA, which came into being on October 27, 2008, it might be thought surprising that it was thought necessary to wholly replace Schs 2 and 3 with effect from March 28, 2011, especially as the precise wording of the original ESA Regs had further been honed even before they had entered into force. In fact, the process of review began very early in the operative life of the WCA, with a DWP-led review being announced in the December 2008 White Paper, *Raising Expectations* (Cm.7506). It was thought important that the WCA continued to "provide an up-to-date accurate assessment of a person's functional capability for work and work related activity" (Secretary of State's Statement in accordance with s.174(2) of the SSAA 1992). Led by officials in the DWP, the review began in March 2009, a mere six months after the introduction of ESA. The review, however, also involved representatives of stakeholder groups and employers, experts from the fields of physical, mental and occupational health, and a member of the Social Security Advisory Committee attending in her personal capacity. This Departmental-led review (hereinafter *"Review"*) reported in October 2009 and its report can be found online at *http://www.dwp.gov.uk/docs/work-capability-assessment-review.pdf*.

Representations were made by disability groups that some of the recommendations from that the *Review* did not adequately address their concerns. Consequently, the Secretary of State asked the Chief Medical Adviser (CMA) to undertake a further technical review, part of which involved work with representatives of those specialist disability groups which had been part of the group conducting the internal *Review*. This CMA honing with stakeholders (hereinafter *"CMA"*) was published in March 2010 and can be found online as an addendum to the *Review* at *http://www. dwp.gov.uk/docs/work-capability-assessment-review.pdf*. This technical review, led by the CMA and taking into account the work done by the *Review* group, saw work undertaken by medical experts within the DWP "with the aim of ensuring that the recommendations of the internal review would lead to a revised WCA which would more accurately and fairly assess an individual's capability for work and thus their entitlement to benefits" (*CMA*, p.3). That technical review proposed a number of changes to the proposals of the internal review and those changes were accepted by the Secretary of State and embodied in the amending Regulations which inserted the new Schedules now under consideration. The draft amending Regulations were also the subject of consideration and report by the SSAC. Its unsupportive

Report and recommendations as regards the new Schedules was considered by the Secretary of State. The SSAC Report, material submitted to it by the DWP explaining the draft Regulations, and the Secretary of State's reasons for rejecting the SSAC recommendations (hereinafter "*SSAC Report*") can be found online at *http://www. official-documents.gov.uk/document/other/9780108509698/9780108509698.pdf).*

This DWP-led review and subsequent CMA honing was distinct from the independent annual review envisaged by the WRA 2007 s.10. The first of those five statutory reviews was undertaken by Professor Michael Harrington and published in November 2010.

The DWP-led *Review* saw ESA as an "active benefit", a temporary benefit for the majority of claimants, providing support and encouragement to assist the journey of an individual from an ESA claimant into the workplace. The policy behind ESA is premised on a large body of research evidence (described by Harrington as "incontrovertible") which shows both that work is generally good for physical and mental health and well-being and also the converse—that there is a strong association between worklessness and ill-health, with prolonged time away from work rendering recovery and return to work progressively less likely. The *Review* considered that the WCA was generally working well: 9.396

> "There was broad consensus amongst the experts that the WCA was performing according to design. The descriptors used in the WCA were indeed reliably identifying individuals according to capability" (*Review*, para.4.1, p.16).

Despite involvement of stakeholders in that process it is clear that this view not altogether shared by them. The SSAC commented:

> "We recognise that any assessment of benefit entitlement that necessarily involves testing and scoring an individual's functional capabilities is going to be both potentially challenging and controversial. As many of our respondents have pointed out, the assessment process, and the experience of the benefit claimant, can be stressful and frustrating. We have also noted the concern expressed by respondents about the Department's conclusions with regard to the internal review of the WCA, and the manner in which they have been presented with regard to the current proposals. It appears to us that there is a disagreement of substance between the Department and the external stakeholders who participated in the review as to whether the WCA in its present form could be said to be working satisfactorily" (*SSAC Report*, para.6.2).

In particular, the SSAC thought that the view that the WCA was not working well was supported by the high rate of success on appeal (some 40 per cent of appeals are upheld) (*SSAC Report*, para.4.10). Harrington also found that the WCA:

> "is not working as well as it should. There are clear and consistent criticisms of the whole system and much negativity surrounding the process. There is strong evidence that the system can be impersonal and mechanistic, that the process lacks transparency and that a lack of communication between the various parties involved contributes to poor decision making and a high rate of appeals".

He did not, however, consider the system as "broken or beyond repair", and proposed a substantial series of recommendations to improve its effectiveness—all of which have been accepted by the Government—which would have a positive impact on the WCA process "making it fairer and more effective, changing perceptions so the WCA is seen as a positive first step towards work, and reducing the rate on appeals". He noted that more subjective conditions such as mental health and fluctuating conditions were difficult to assess so that "some of the descriptors used in the assessment may not adequately measure or reflect the full impact of such conditions on the individual's capability for work". He recommended for the second WRA 2007 s.10 review further work on the descriptors, particularly in assessing fluctuating conditions and, possibly, generalised pain. Harrington established a review group (composed of Mind, Mencap and the National Autistic Society to look in detail at the mental, intellectual and cognitive descriptors, to make recommendations to him about any refinements to the descriptors as a basis for his consideration of recommendations to be made to Ministers early in 2011. Like Harrington, the judicial review decision of the Upper Tribunal (AAC) in *MM & DM v SSWP* [2013] UKUT 259; [2016] AACR 11 also called for amendment of the testing procedures in mental health cases so as to increase the gathering of further medical evidence. See further the annotation to reg. 21, above, on the judicial review challenge under the Equality Act 2010 with respect to aspects of the decision-making process. The January 2013 changes do not respond to these pressures, however, but are rather the governmental response to a number of Upper Tribunal decisions seen as thwarting the policy intention behind the statutory provisions.

9.397   The substantial redrawing of Schs 2 and 3 effective from March 28, 2011 was designed to fulfil a number of aims or objectives:

- Removing unnecessary complexities and overlaps in order to simplify the descriptors, to remove inappropriate double counting and to ensure ease of administration and greater transparency for the claimant.

- Expanding the support group in relation to certain mental function and communication problems.

- Improving the assessment of fluctuating conditions by ensuring that the effects of exhaustion and discomfort are recognised.

- Taking greater account of the effects of adaptations and aids in improving an individual's function so as more accurately to identify those lacking the capability to work rather than simply assuming lack of capability merely because of a particular functional impairment.

It was expected that the changes to the LCWA would increase by some five per cent the number of new claims not eligible for ESA, but that the revisions to the LCWRA would slightly increase the percentage of successful claims allocated to the support group *(Review,* para.5.2). The DWP-led review group tested the proposed new activities and descriptors through a detailed analysis of ESA cases. That analysis:

"revealed that in the vast majority of cases experts thought that the new descriptors would result in appropriate changes in the entitlement decision. The descriptors were thought to be functioning as anticipated and providing a more concise and clearer assessment. The re-focusing of the physical function areas better reflect the activities most applicable to the workplace. The mental function descriptors were found to be clearer and consequently minimised double scoring in addition to providing improved clarity.

The small number of cases that members felt would be inappropriately assessed resulted in further minor refinements of the descriptors" *(Review,* para.5.4).

The *Review* considered that while the existing WCA was working well, the wholesale revision effected would represent "a more robust and accurate evaluation of limited capability for work", because it was founded on recent experience with ESA, simplifying the LCWA, reflecting reasonable adaptation of the disabled to their disability and, because of the Disability Discrimination Act (now the Equality Act 2010), of the reasonable adjustment of workplaces and further consideration of the necessary functions of the modern workplace *(Review,* para.5.5).

The SSAC, in contrast was less sanguine, both about the original WCA and the proposed revisions to it. It saw the WCA as rigid and unnecessarily prescriptive, encouraging a focus on the claimant's specific condition or disability covered by the descriptors, rather than looking at their capability for work, and adaptation to their disability, holistically. A functional assessment cannot easily measure the significance of the many factors which in reality determine capability for work. It regarded the result of the WCA as essentially an expression of the judgment and opinion of the assessor, albeit something based on professional knowledge, training, experience and observation. It considered that some of the streamlining in the proposed new Schedules had removed some of the assessment's necessary subtleties without enhancing its relevance to the real world. It thought that theoretical work capability had not enabled significant numbers to move into work and called for a cost-benefit analysis of the end-to-end process of assessing an ESA claimant where in reality what was determined was not "benefit or work" but rather which out-of-work benefit (ESA or JSA) was the more appropriate. It reported:

"a widespread perception that, overall, rather than simplifying, streamlining and refining the test, these amendments will make it harder in practice for claimants to demonstrate that they have limited capacity for work or work related activity" (*SSAC Report*, para.4.3).

While it welcomed some of the changes (e.g. the extension of the "deemed" limited capability for work categories), the SSAC recommended that the DWP not proceed with the revisions to the Schs until these had been considered in the light of Harrington and the experience of the trial of the migration of IB claimants to ESA (*SSAC Report*, para.7.3).

In February 2011, having considered Harrington, the Secretary of State declined to do so. The amending Regulations were a carefully-crafted package following a thorough, holistic DWP-led review and CMA honing. The WCA would remain subject to ongoing review, but the Government must retain freedom to implement changes when it considers them necessary to improve the assessment without always awaiting the outcome of the next stage of the review process. (*SSAC Report*, Secretary of State's Response, para.24). The DWP Explanatory Memorandum to the SSAC on the amending Regulations indicated that it was expected that the changes to the mental, cognitive and intellectual function descriptors would have a minimal impact on the disallowance rate (para.4.6), but that overall the changes both to physical and mental descriptors would increase by five per cent the number of claimants being found capable of work (para.4.9). Changes to the LCWRA assessment would increase the numbers in the support group from 6.4 to 6.9 per cent (para.4.9).

The revised Schedules thus appear centrally as the product of the internal *Review* and *CMA* honing, rather than Harrington. The process whereby they came into being has been set out at some length, not only as background. The view taken in this commentary is that, while decision-makers and tribunals must focus on the wording of the Schedules, light can be thrown on particular activities and descriptors both by consideration of the reports that led to them and by consideration, where appropriate, of Upper Tribunal and other court decisions on the predecessors of the current WCA; the AWT/PCA from the incapacity benefits regime and from the pre-March 28, 2011 version of the WCA (see pp.1080–1114, paras 9.457–9.489).

The second Harrington report was published in November 2011: *An Independent Review of the Work Capability Assessment – year two*. This reported that "The WCA has, in my view, noticeably changed for the better. However there is still further to go" (p.7 para.5). The recommendations in the second report were aimed at improving the fairness and effectiveness of the assessment by better communications and sharing of information between all parts of the system, increasing and improving the transparency of the assessment, ensuring quality decisions were made and monitoring the impact of recommendations from the Independent Reviews. For the Government's Response, see Cm 8229 (also November 2011).

A year later the picture was very much the same. The third Harrington report was published in November 2012: *An Independent Review of the Work Capability Assessment – year three*. It reported that "real progress has been made but the pace and scope of the improvements has been slower than the Review would have hoped" (p.8 para. 6). The main areas where further changes were needed were continuing to improve communications with claimants and within DWP Operations, improve the face-to-face assessment and establishing quality dialogue between DWP and First-tier Tribunals. In addition, Harrington advocated keeping the Decision Maker central to the assessment process (and providing them with all the further documentary evidence they need to get the decision "right first time") and stressed the need to continually monitor changes to the WCA and to complete work that was under way on the descriptors. For the Government's Response, see Cm 8474 (also November 2012).

A number of relatively minor changes were made on October 29, 2013 to clarify the drafting of the descriptors and to align the Schedules in these Regulations with those in the ESA Regulations 2013 applicable to "new style" ESA (on which see Part XIII of this volume).

Dr Paul Litchfield conducted the final two reviews. His first was *An Independent Review of the Work Capability Assessment – year four* (December 2013). Dr Litchfield acknowledged at the outset that "the length and complexity of the process contributes to dissatisfaction and negative perceptions surrounding the assessment. People need to feel that they are being treated fairly when dealing with an organisation and it is their perception that drives attitudes and behaviours more than any objective assessment of what has happened" (p.7 para.3). On the WCA itself, he recommended that the DWP review its use of WCA scores, place less emphasis on the number attained and simply use the calculation to determine whether the threshold for benefit has been reached. Further recommendations were designed to improve objectivity, improve decision making and simplify the process. Other changes were suggested with a view to addressing the needs of claimants with mental health conditions. The Government did not publish its response until March 2014 (Cm 8843).

The last report was published in November 2014: *An Independent Review of the Work Capability Assessment – year five* (for the Government's Response see Cm 9014, February 2015). This fifth report contained a total of 33 further recommendations. The report recognised the difficulties created by the frequent changes to the WCA, noted the marked increase in the proportion of claimants being allocated to the support group and yet again emphasised the need to address negative perceptions of the WCA and to improve decision-making standards. The importance of meeting the needs of claimants with mental health problems and/or learning disabilities was also reiterated. The report also set out a number of principles which it recommended should be taken into account it was decided to undertake a fundamental redesign of the WCA, as had been recommended by the House of Commons Work and Pensions Committee in its report *Employment and Support Allowance and Work Capability Assessments* (HC 302, 2014).

Meanwhile the HC Public Accounts Committee has noted how the DWP has increasingly used third-party contractors to provide health and disability assessments *Contracted out health and disability assessments*, 33rd Report of 2015–16, HC 727). In 2005, the Department awarded a contract to Atos Healthcare (Atos) for Incapacity Benefit and, from 2008, ESA assessments. After Atos requested to exit the ESA contract early, the Centre for Health and Disability Assessments (CHDA), a wholly-owned subsidiary within MAXIMUS, took over ESA assessments from March 2015. The Committee noted that the DWP and its contractors have reduced the backlogs that previously existed; outstanding ESA assessments fell from 724,000 in early 2014 to 410,000 in August 2015. However, the Committee also considered that contractors' performance still does not meet claimants', the Department's and taxpayers' expectations, in particular with continuing concerns about the quality of assessments. Thus ESA assessments still take on average 23 weeks. In addition, a significant proportion of the assessment reports sampled by contractors (ranging from 7 per cent to 20 per cent) do not meet the contractual standard required and yet the DWP only returns less than 1 per cent of all assessment reports to contractors because they cannot be used to make a decision. As the DWP increases the number of assessments to be completed by contractors, the Committee states it must learn from past experience to ensure contractors are set challenging but realistic targets against which they are held to account. In addition, the Committee considered the DWP also needs to develop a competitive market for health and disability assessments to ensure that there are sufficient credible bidders for contracts as they come up for renewal.

For the latest and comprehensive Parliamentary report, see HC Work and Pensions Committee, *PIP and ESA Assessments*, Seventh Report of Session 2017-19 (HC 829, February 2018) and *PIP and ESA Assessments: claimant experiences*, Fourth Report of Session 2017-19 (HC 355, January 2018); the Government's response has been published by the Committee as its Eighth Special Report, *PIP and ESA assessments: Government Response to the Committee's Seventh Report of 2017–19*.

The structure of the current Sch.2: As with its predecessor, Sch.2 has two Parts. Part   **9.398** I deals with physical disabilities. Part II covers the mental, cognitive and intellectual function assessment.

Part I (physical disabilities) now contains only ten activities, rather than the eleven in the original Sch.2. They cover: mobilising; standing and sitting; reaching; picking up and moving or transferring by the use of the upper body and arms; manual dexterity; making oneself understood; understanding communication; navigation and maintaining safety; continence (absence or loss of control) other than enuresis; and consciousness during waking moments. The coverage and formulation of the activities and descriptors in the Schedule very much reflects the favoured principle of taking into account adaptations to condition and the use of suitable aids (e.g. walking stick, manual wheelchair, guide dog). This is on the basis that by account-ing for any aids or adaptations which an individual may successfully and reasonably use to mitigate the disabling impact of their condition, their actual capability can the better be determined, and was thought to be consistent with the principle that as few people should be written off from re-engagement with work as possible merely because of their condition (*Review*, para.3.2). "Bending or kneeling" (Activity 3 in the original Sch.2) has been dropped. It was considered that activities 1–3 in the original Sch.2 (walking; standing and sitting; bending or kneeling) provided a sig-nificant level of overlap, whereby an individual (e.g. a wheelchair user) could score in each activity for what was in the modern workplace essentially the same disability, thus affording an inaccurate assessment of the individual's true level of functional limitation. "Bending or kneeling" was seen as:

> "an unnecessary requirement for the workplace. This is highlighted by the fact that wheelchair users who may be capable of work, may also be unable to bend or kneel. Changes to the [other] two activities [walking/mobilising; standing and sitting] mean that Bending or Kneeling is redundant as an activity. The removal of this activity is also in line with active encouragement in the workplace not to bend forward when lifting for health and safety reasons" (*Review*, para.4.3.1, p.19).

Activity 10 of the original Sch.2 (continence other than enuresis) has been short-ened and simplified and is now Activity 9 in the new Sch.2.

Part II of Sch.2 (mental, cognitive and intellectual function assessment) contains seven activities rather than the ten in the original WCA. They cover: learning tasks; awareness of everyday hazards; initiating and completing personal action; coping with change; getting about; coping with social engagement due to cognitive impair-ment or mental disorder; appropriateness of behaviour with other people, due to cognitive impairment or mental disorder. It was thought that this revision and reduction removed unnecessary complexities and overlaps.

II. The importance of the amendments effected on January 28, 2013

As reg.2 of the amending instrument makes clear (see para.9.554, below), these   **9.399** apply to all claims made on or after January 28, 2013 and to most decisions made on or after that date, whether the claim was made before that date or not. For a six month period, however, some cases where questionnaires were sent out before that date remained subject to the unamended regime, on which see the 2012/13 edition of this volume.

The amendments relevant to the application of this Schedule concern the assess-ment process (reg.19(4), (5)); the wording of activities 1, 6, 7, 8, 9; and descriptors 2(b), (c), 5(d), 9(b) and 15(a).

As regards the assessment process, reg.19(4) now provides that in assessing someone's capability to perform the activities in Pt 1 of this Schedule (physical disabilities) the person is to be assessed as if fitted with or wearing any prosthesis with which that person is normally fitted or normally wears, or, as the case may be, wearing or using any aid or appliance which is normally, or could reasonably be expected to be, worn or used. In addition, reg.19(5) brings in the requirement—familiar from the IB regime—that Pt 1 of this Schedule (physical disabilities) must be linked to incapability arising from a specific bodily disease or disablement or as a direct result of treatment provided by a registered medical practitioner for such a disease or disablement. Similarly it introduces the requirement that Pt 2 of this Schedule (mental, cognitive and intellectual function assessment) must be linked to incapability arising from a specific mental illness or disablement or as a direct result of treatment provided by a registered medical practitioner for such an illness or disablement. Under the previous wording of the paragraph (still applicable to some cases after January 28, 2013—see reg.2 of the amending instrument, below, para.9.554), there was no such link (*KP* v *SSWP (ESA)* [2011] UKUT 216 (AAC); *KN* v *SSWP (ESA)* [2011] UKUT 229 (AAC); *RM* v *SSWP (ESA)* [2011] UKUT 454 (AAC); *AH* v *SSWP (ESA)* [2011] UKUT 333 (AAC)).

The changes to particular activities and descriptors are reflected in the commentary to each of them.

III Order of treatment in this commentary

9.400
In the nature of things, this is a lengthy annotation to a Schedule which lies at the heart of determining the key question whether a claimant for ESA has limited capability for work. It aims to identify and highlight key issues and concerns and to indicate which features of a burgeoning case law on the AWT/PCA and the original WCA remain of significance and assistance: (a) in approaching what is in essence a similar task to those earlier regimes (matching a claimant's health condition to a range of activities and descriptors and assigning a score); and (b) more specifically in interpreting and applying any similarly worded terms of the activities and descriptors in the revised LCWA. The commentary is sub-divided as follows:
[A]   Approaching the interpretation of the Schedule as a whole.
[B]   Interpreting specific activities and descriptors: Pt I: physical disabilities.
[C]   Approaching Pt II: mental, cognitive and intellectual function assessment.

[A] Approaching the interpretation of the Schedule as a whole

9.401
Evidence and attention to detail: Decision-makers must pay very close attention to the precise wording of the activities and descriptors and to the matter of appropriate evidence to ground their findings (*CSIB/12/96*). Cases must be decided in the light of the totality of the evidence, medical or otherwise, including that from the claimant (*CIB/15663/1996*). His evidence does not require corroboration unless self-contradictory or improbable (*R(I) 2/51*). Differing medical opinions and reports must carefully be appraised, without rigid preconceptions on whether the report of the examining health professional is always to be preferred as more disinterested and informed than that of the claimant's GP or consultant, or vice versa (contrast *CIB/13039/1996* and *CIB/3968/1996* with *CIB/17257/1996*; *CW* v *SSWP (ESA)* [2011] UKUT 386 (AAC), para.24). Both types of evidence can, from different perspectives, prove valuable (*CIB/17257/1996*; *CIB/21/2002*). A tribunal is not *bound to* decide in the same way as any particular doctor certifies; when faced with a conflict of medical opinion, they are at liberty to prefer, giving reasons, one view rather than another (*R(S) 1/53*; *CSIB/684/1997*; *CSIB/848/1997*; *CIB/309/1997*; *R. v Social Security Commissioner Ex p. Dobie* (QBD, October 26, 1999)—but cf. *CIB/17257/1996*). But that does not warrant underestimating a DWPMS personal capability assessment report, which is based on a more intensive and detailed clinical examination and history-taking than the invalidity benefit system (*CIB/15663/1996*). To prefer a DWPMS doctor's report on the grounds that it is more detailed is not, as such, irrational (*R. v Social Security Commissioner Ex p. Dobie*, QBD (October 26, 1999)). A tribunal should not reject a claimant's appeal on the basis that he was "not a reliable or credible witness" without

giving reasons for that finding (*CSIB/459/1997*). It should be made clear that the claimant's evidence has been considered, what account has been taken of it, and, if rejected, why it has been rejected (*CIB/309/1997*; *CW v SSWP (ESA)* [2011] UKUT 386 (AAC), para.24). Nor should a tribunal simply record acceptance of the DWPMS doctor's findings; rather it should make and record its own findings on the descriptors (*CSIB/459/1997*; *CIB/4232/2007*). The correct approach is to weigh all the evidence in the context of the case (*CIB/3620/1998); CIB/2308/2001*, para.20; *FR v SSWP (ESA)* [2015] UKUT 151 (AAC), paras 9–12). In *CIB/3074/2003* Commissioner Bano allowed the claimant's appeal because the tribunal had dismissed the appeal "on the basis of a formulaic endorsement of the examining medical practitioner's report", rather than looking at it in the light of its nature and the evidence as a whole. Although a tribunal cannot conduct a physical examination of the claimant, it can use all its senses, including ocular observation of the claimant during the hearing, when considering whether the LCWA is satisfied (*R1/01(IB) (T)*; *R4/99 (IB)*) and a tribunal medical member can properly look at x-rays put in evidence (*R(IB) 2/06*). Getting a claimant to roll up his trouser leg so that the tribunal could ascertain whether he had muscle wastage was impermissible (*MA v SSWP (ESA)* [2015] UKUT 290 (AAC), paras 14-19). Tribunals should also consider carefully evidence that the medical examination was perfunctory. Where a claimant criticises as inadequate a WCA examination, it would, however, be extremely unusual to use in such a case the tribunal's power to exclude otherwise admissible evidence on the basis that its admission would be unfair; but where, as usual, the report of that examination is admitted, questions about the adequacy of the report and the examination are relevant to the weight that the tribunal should accord to the report (*JM v SSWP (IB)* [2010] UKUT 386 (AAC), paras 18, 19). Equally, where the health practitioner's report disputes the claimant's account of his disabilities in his questionnaire, natural justice requires that tribunals hear the claimant's oral evidence about his condition, before deciding which account to prefer (*CIB/5586/1999*). Tribunals should be wary of adviser/representative revision of the picture painted by the claimant's questionnaire answers and the health professional's report, and should look for supporting evidence where such statements differ significantly from the claimant's original own assessment of his or her condition (*CIB/2913/2001*).

The issue of the claimant's credibility arose in *KN v SSWP (ESA)* [2016] UKUT 521 (AAC). Judge Gray held that the fact that a claimant did not make a complaint to the organisation responsible for the HCP did not undermine his or her credibility if the report and/or examination is subsequently criticised on any appeal: "There is no legal requirement for a complaint to be made in tandem with an appeal, and it seems to me wholly wrong to use the absence of such a complaint as a significant credibility pointer" (at para.24).

Now that assessments are carried out by a wider range of HCPs, consideration has been given to the weight that should be placed on their evidence, particularly in mental health cases, where the particular experience of the HCP lies in a non-mental health field.

In *(1) ST, (2) GF v SSWP (ESA)* [2014] UKUT 547 (AAC); [2015] AACR 23, a panel of three Upper Tribunal judges categorically rejected Judge Mark's comments in *JH v SSWP (ESA)* [2013] UKUT 269 (AAC), para.22—which it saw as *obiter*—as

> "wrong if and to the extent that they purport to create a rule of law or starting point that observations on mental health descriptors by HCP physiotherapists are of no probative value whatsoever or are highly likely or likely to have little probative value and thus should be accorded no or little weight by the decision maker and the First-tier tribunal" (para.33).

Instead the proper approach is that the probative value of an HCP physiotherapist's report is a matter for the decision maker or tribunal dealing with the case, just as it is with other reports and evidence.

The panel so held, firstly, because the legislation makes no distinction between an HCP's ability to deal with mental health descriptors as opposed to physical ones. It merely requires approval by the Secretary of State and registration with the appropriate regulatory body. So any such rule as Judge Mark's would frustrate the statutory framework (para.34). The panel's second rationale noted the difference between the LCW assessment (how a condition affects the claimant's functional capacity) and "a medical examination carried out as part of a process of diagnosis and treatment" (para.35), a distinction acknowledged in Professor Harrington's *First Review* of the ESA process. The panel thus considered that the medical examination carried out by a HCP for the LCW did not require that HCP to be a medical specialist in all the physical and mental problems that might be exhibited by a particular claimant. To require the HCP to be such a specialist "would create insurmountable problems for the assessment process" since many claimants have a variety of problems which might then require assessment in a particular case by several HCPs rather than one (para.35).

What is required, however, is that the HCP have an informed understanding of the claimant's medical conditions and the difficulties flowing from them. This requires adequate training and supervision. The panel had received detailed information on the current training process (see paras 11-19)—something not available to Judge Mark in *JH*—and, while not commenting on that programme, did observe that none of the independent reviews of the ESA assessment process had criticised the performance of physiotherapists relative to HCPs from other disciplines and that training for HCPs on mental health problems was being reviewed with the aim of increasing the knowledge of all HCPs (para.36).

There is, therefore, no need for a tribunal to adjourn for further particulars on the qualifications of the HCP in a particular case. The specialist tribunal with its medical member must "make its own findings having regard to all the evidence before it" (para.37). The correct starting point was that identified by Judge Ovey in an incapacity benefit appeal (*JF v SSWP (IB)* [2011] UKUT 385 (AAC) at para.25:

"...the report is prepared by an HCP who has been trained (whether as part of the training as an HCP or through other training) at least to the level thought appropriate by the Department of Work and Pensions for carrying out examinations where mental health issues are raised. In other words the selection and training procedures ought to have produced an HCP who can conduct a mental health examination competently. It follows that evidence that the HCP has not undergone separate specialist training should not of itself have any effect on the weight which the tribunal attaches to the report. . ."

The panel held that the weight to be accorded to any report "addressing the functional impact of any medical condition on a claimant" is a matter for the specialist tribunal which should consider

"(a) the level of the author's expertise (for example, an HCP or a consultant psychiatrist) and (b) the knowledge of the claimant possessed by the author (for example, knowledge gained from a one-off assessment or that gained as a treating clinician). Additionally the date of the evidence, its comprehensiveness, and its relevance to the issues the tribunal has to determine are also key matters for the tribunal to consider. Importantly the tribunal should explain its reasoning for attaching weight to one type or piece of evidence rather than to another" (para.38 of *ST/GF*).

In *ST v SSWP (ESA)* [2012] UKUT 469 (AAC), Judge Wright held that with respect to a decision to supersede an award of benefit on the basis of a new work capability assessment, natural justice and the right to a fair trial under art.6(1) ECHR required that the Secretary of State make available to the tribunal the previous work capability assessment (ESA85). In *CA v SSWP (ESA)* [2013] UKUT 442 (AAC), Judge Ward stated that it was likely to be an exceptional case in which a change in descriptors would exempt the Secretary of State from that duty, since a previous WCA assessment, particularly one close in time and where the condition in question is not said to be changing can prove of evidential value and assist the tribunal to assess the robustness of the latest assessment at issue, by giving a picture of the claimant's history and considering the descriptors thought by the previous HCP then to be relevant. It is ultimately for the tribunal what to make of that previous assessment. The scope and extent of the obligation of Secretary of State for Work and Pensions to produce previous medical reports, or records of them, in every case has now been considered by a three-judge panel of the Upper Tribunal in *FN v SSWP (SA)* [2015] UKUT 670 (AAC); [2016] AACR 24 (formerly *CSE/422/2013, CSE/435/2013* and *CSE/19/2014)*. The panel broadly agreed with decisions such as *JC v DSD (IB)* [2011] NICom 177; [2014] AACR 30 and also both *ST v SSWP (ESA)* [2012] UKUT 469 (AAC) and *AM v SSWP (ESA)* [2013] UKUT 458 (AAC). The three-judge panel stressed that the previous adjudication history and associated evidence is not *always* relevant to an employment and support allowance appeal and that, even if the Secretary of State has not produced all the information and evidence that he should have produced with his response to an appeal, it does not necessarily follow that the First-tier Tribunal's decision will be wrong in law and liable to be set aside:

> "79. ... We can envisage a situation where a First-tier Tribunal considers that it has sufficient relevant evidence before it to determine the issues arising in the appeal without the requirement to call for evidence which is missing because the Secretary of State has failed in his duty to provide it.
> 80. ... Our view is that the first choice for the tribunal should not be to adjourn but to get on with the task of determining the issues arising in the appeal when satisfied that it has the necessary relevant evidence before it. It might be the case that having weighed and assessed the appellant's oral evidence, the tribunal might be satisfied that the evidence is credible, should be accepted and the appeal be allowed ..."

In *CA v SSWP (ESA)* [2016] UKUT 523 (AAC) the claimant had failed a previous WCA, not appealed that decision and claimed and received JSA for nine months before making a further (and again unsuccessful) ESA claim. This time she appealed the adverse WCA decision, but did not mention the previous ESA assessment. Judge Lane, dismissing the further appeal, held that the FTT had not failed in its inquisitorial duty:

> "15. Tribunals in the Social Entitlement Chamber are alert to legal and evidential matters that are relevant but which would be obscure to a layman. They are accustomed to being proactive in a way that would be foreign in other Chambers. But, as *FN* establishes, their proactivity is not boundless. A tribunal cannot pull a rabbit out of a hat unless it is given a hat to work with. The hat, in this case, is evidence from the appellant that there has been no change in their medical condition or disablement since a previous award or assessment."

See further the commentary in Vol III of this series to the Social Security and Child Support (Decisions and Appeals) Regulations 1999 (SI 1999/991) reg.6(2) (g) and (r) (Supersession of decisions) and to Tribunal Procedure (First-tier Tribunal) (Social Entitlement Chamber) Rules 2008 (SI 2008/2685) r.24(1)–(5) (Responses).

Where the claimant has complained about a medical examination and no response to that has been received by the tribunal, or any relevant medical report is not before the tribunal, it is appropriate to consider whether to adjourn., but it does not follow that it must adjourn (*SA v SSWP (ESA)* [2013] UKUT 616 (AAC), per Judge Mark):

> "It needs to consider all the matters in issue in the complaint, the likelihood of their being resolved or at least further illuminated by the report, the relevance of the complaints to the matters before it and the likely relevance of any possible response by ATOS in addition to any other relevant matters. Having consid-

ered all relevant matters it needs to decide whether it was better to proceed or to adjourn in order to deal with the case fairly and justly in accordance with the overriding objective in rule 2 of the Tribunal Procedure (First-tier Tribunal) (SEC) Rules 2008 (see further *MA v SoS* [2009] UKUT 221 (AAC)). It also needs to give reasons for its decision."

The computerised medical examination report is the end product of the system. In that report statements or phrases can be produced mechanically by the software, which produces relevant phrases from its memory bank, and, unless the examining health professional using it is very careful, the statements in the report may not necessarily represent actual wording chosen and typed in by him. This generates an increased risk of accidental mistakes or discrepancies being left undetected in the final product of the process. The need for careful appraisal of the computerized report has been stressed by Commissioners Howell and Williams (*CIB/511/2005; CIB/476/2005; CIB/1522/2005; CIB/0664/2005; CIB/3950/2007; CIB/1006/2008*). It is submitted that reports under the revised WCA ought to be scrutinized even more carefully because further glitches might have crept in during the necessary software revision undertaken in a relatively short period of time.

9.402 Section 7 of the Electronic Communications Act 2000 has no application to the computerised report form (*R(IB) 7/05*).

In *NH v SSWP (ESA)* [2014] UKUT 114 (AAC), concerns about the qualifications of the examining health care professional, a nurse, and the computerized report combined so that Judge Williams had to set aside the decision superceding entitlement which had been upheld by the tribunal:

"this report not only calls into question whether the nurse actually conducted a mental health examination as reported or even read the report she submitted before doing so but also more generally the evidential value of a report conducted or purportedly conducted by a nurse when there is no indication that the nurse had any specific qualifications to conduct that aspect of the examination. Was she aware of the importance in this case of examining the mental health issues? Was she qualified to give the advice she gave about them? If so, why is this report so deficient in that area? It also calls into question the validity of a report produced by a computer programme that allows the operator to delete the whole of the relevant parts of the report which should record results of a clinical physical examination so that there is no "supporting medical evidence" while still generating unqualified opinions about unexamined physical functions for which there is no such evidence" (para.10).

Judge Williams thought the case to be "one of the most disturbing examples of repeated failure fairly to assess the actual medical problems of an appellant that I have seen for some time. Indeed, it is disturbing enough to call aspects of the system itself into question" (para.18).

To reiterate: the first task is to decide from all the evidence in the case which descriptors apply, the second to calculate the scores. Decision-makers and tribunals must in the light of all relevant evidence identify the relevant health condition and consider carefully the full range of activities which may be impaired by it (*CIB/5797/1997; CIB/3589/2004*). Scoring should proceed from top to bottom, so as to properly identify the highest ranking descriptor in the range attached to the particular activity which can properly be said to apply to the claimant (*CIB/5361/1997*; reg.19(6)).

9.403 *The LCWA is not a snapshot—the need for an approach characterized by "reasonableness":* The "sometimes" descriptors in the AWT/PCA were not carried over into ESA, but this merely means that there is no descriptor under which the claimant can score points simply because he is sometimes unable to perform the relevant activity. Their removal did not mean that there was no longer a need for the decision-makers to take into account whether the claimant can perform the relevant activity with some degree of repetition. That need subsists in relation to the WCA descriptors as in relation to its predecessors in the AWT/PCA (*AF v SSWP (ESA)* [2011] UKUT 61 (AAC), para.11; *AG v SSWP (ESA)* [2013] UKUT 77 (AAC), paras.14–18; *SAG v Department for Social Development (ESA)* [2012] AACR 6). Indeed such a requirement seems inherent in any test of capability for work designed to be attuned to the needs of the modern workplace and a level of activity an employer would expect. The Government emphasised that, like the PCA, the LCWA was not intended to be a simple snapshot. The review group whose work led to the original WCA rightly stressed that guidance to decision-makers and to the healthcare professionals involved in the assessments of capacity would indicate the factors to be taken into account in ascertaining whether a claimant can perform a particular function: ability to do it just once is not enough (the person must reliably be able to sustain or repeat the activity); distress, pain, and fatigue involved in carrying out the activity; and the detrimental effects of medication. The *Review* leading to the revised WCA commented:

"Individuals whose conditions fluctuate in an unpredictable manner may provide a more significant challenge in relation to employment as employers are less able to predict and manage their absence.

. . . [T]he WCA has afforded individuals greater opportunity to detail the variations in their condition, specifically in the questionnaire which they are asked to complete. Rather than a yes/no format, the potential responses also include 'it varies', and space is provided for the detailing of the variation.

In the course of the assessment itself, healthcare professionals take into account fluctuations which an individual may experience in their capability. The assessment seeks to identify whether an individual is capable of carrying out an activity reliably and repeatedly for the majority of the time. If an individual is unable to do so, then they are considered unable to carry out the activity at all, and will be awarded points accordingly" (para.4.10.1).

The *CMA* honing report also commented on fluctuating conditions, echoed this last point, and emphasised that:

"Guidance states that if an individual cannot complete an action safely, reliably and repeatedly they should be considered unable to complete it at all. Recognising the challenges associated with assessing fluctuating conditions, there is ongoing work which aims to enhance the training that healthcare professionals (HCPs) receive and ensure that advice in this area is comprehensive.

In recognition, however, of the importance of accurately assessing fluctuating conditions, changes have been suggested to certain descriptors where exertion is a significant component. This ensures that where an individual is unable to do something as a result of exhaustion experienced, rather than discomfort, that is captured in the assessment" (*CMA*, para.2.1).

Those changes to specific descriptors have been embodied in the revised Schedules.

But (save where embodied in specific descriptors and thus as specific legal elements) this approach is not just a matter of guidance. It is submitted that it is embodied in legal rules established by the extensive jurisprudence on approaching the very similar exercise in the PCA. The requirement is for ability to perform the specified activities with "reasonable regularity"; there must be an element of reasonableness in the approach to the question of what someone is or is not capable of doing, including consideration of his ability to perform the activities most of the time (*C1/95(IB)*; *CSIB/17/96*), so that the question becomes whether the claimant would normally be able to perform the stated activity if and when called upon to do so (*CIB/13161/96*; *CIB/13508/96*). The nature of a *specific* working environment and the matter of employability are both irrelevant (*C1/95*; *CIB/13161/96*; *CIB/13508/96*), but there is some relationship between Sch.2 and the work context. In *AS v SSWP (ESA)* [2013] UKUT 587 (AAC), approved by the Northern Ireland Court of Appeal in *O'Neill v Department for Communities* [2018] NICA 29 (a ruling refusing permission to appeal), Judge Wikeley considered in some depth the nature of that relationship, stating that he accepted as correctly made a concession by the Secretary of State's representative.

"that the various activities in Schedule 2 have "a connection with the workplace", albeit that the descriptors are not concerned with any one specific working environment and do not bring in wider questions of employability. This concession properly reflects the direction of policy travel as embodied in legislative change in this area. The first clue is in the change of name; Parliament has approved the shift from the "personal capability assessment" in the incapacity benefit scheme to the "work capability assessment" under the ESA regime. The second clue lies in the drafting of the various activities and individual descriptors, and in particular the amendments which took effect on March 28, 2011 (see further the Explanatory Memorandum to the draft 2011 Regulations, sent to the Social Security Advisory Committee on 13 August 2010). Thus the first three activities in the original Schedule 2 to the ESA Regulations—walking, standing and sitting, bending or kneeling—were seen as providing a high degree of overlap for e.g. wheelchair users, so providing an inaccurate assessment of an individual's true level of functional limitation in the workplace. This resulted in a radical re-writing of the first activity, transforming it from "walking" to "mobilising", the specific inclusion of the "work station" test in the second activity (standing and sitting) and the abolition of the third activity (bending or kneeling) as being both an unnecessary and undesirable requirement in the modern workplace.

It follows that the activities and descriptors in Schedule 2 do not exist in some sort of artificial or parallel universe, entirely divorced from the real world of work. They have to be applied on their own terms, but understood against the backdrop of the modern workplace. In deciding whether a particular descriptor is met, decision makers and tribunals may therefore find it helpful to consider the claimant's ability to undertake the activity in question in a range of different working contexts. However, claimants will not be awarded a defined descriptor simply because they can show that it would apply to them if they were employed to do a particular job in a specific type of working environment.

This is entirely consistent with the well-established principle that decision makers and tribunals must consider whether a claimant can perform a particular activity with a reasonable degree of repetition, sometimes referred to as [the] "reasonable regularity" principle. This principle applies to the ESA scheme just as it did to the previous incapacity benefit regime. As Upper Tribunal Judge Turnbull has explained, "if the effect of performing the activity is likely to be to disable the claimant from performing it for a substantial period, that will need to be taken into account" (see *AF v Secretary of State for Work and Pensions* (ESA) [2011] UKUT 61 at para.11, approved and followed in *SAG v Department for Social Development* (ESA) [2012] AACR 6). Judge Nicholas Paines QC has described the principle in similar terms: "it is implicit in this that a description set out in a descriptor will not fit a claimant who can only perform the relevant task exceptionally or infrequently" *(AG v Secretary of State for Work and Pensions (ESA)* [2013] UKUT 77 (at para.18).

Within the legislative scheme as a whole, this principle only makes sense in the context of the needs of a modern workplace and the level of activity that an employer attuned to the requirements of disability discrimination law can reasonably expect. Plainly, the test is not about a high-pressure working environment, e.g. a call-centre with demanding targets or a factory production line with a fast-moving conveyor belt. Equally, however, the test is not about what the person can do in their own home and entirely in their own time and at their own pace, subject to no external constraints or pressures whatsoever. If reasonable regularity is judged by the latter criterion, then the test has ceased to be a test of "whether a claimant's capability for work is limited by the claimant's physical or mental condition within regulation 19(1) of the ESA Regulations" (paras 18-21).

Judge Wikeley further held that the Court of Appeal decision in *Charlton v SSWP* [2009] EWCA Civ 42 (reported as *R(IB) 2/09*), which in the context of ESA Regs 2008, reg.29 required an examination of the work required, does not assist in interpreting the Sch. descriptors (para.17).

Just as the failure to carry over to the WCA the "sometimes" descriptors which featured in the AWT/PCA did not remove this requirement of a reasonable degree of repetition of performance (see *AF v SSWP (ESA)* [2011] UKUT 61 (AAC), para.11; *SAG v Department for Social Development (ESA)* [2012] AACR 6), so it is submitted that the incorporation into specific descriptors of an "exertion" element does not remove the overall requirement of "reasonable regularity". It must govern the overall approach to assessment.

Where variable, intermittent and sporadic conditions and their impact on earning capacity are involved, difficult questions of judgment in assessing incapacity for work arise where the claimant can sometimes do things but at other times not. Neither the PCA nor the LCWA were designed to be a simple "snapshot". The system aims to assess the claimant's condition over a particular period, taking account of pain and fatigue (*CIB/14587/1996*; *CIB/13161/96*; *CIB/13508/96*), fears for health and the medical advice received by the claimant (*CSIB/12/96*). The questionnaire asks about variability—the claimant's own doctor can include material on this in the MED 4, and examining health care professionals with Medical Services have been trained to conduct examinations with these issues in mind. The structure of the legislative scheme, however, produces a problem. It embodies a test based on an examination on a particular day designed to provide information on, and assessment of, a claimant over a period of time. The "normality" approach as part of "reasonable regularity" deals with one aspect of the problem: the reference in *C1/95(IB)* to a claimant being able to accomplish a task most of the time is to be read as meaning "as and when called upon to do so". On this basis, one looks at the position which normally prevails in the period (see *CSIB/459/1997*, para.13; *CIB/911/1997*, paras 12, 13). The more difficult situation is where it is accepted that the claimant's condition is such that for certain periods he is able to cope satisfactorily with normal activities; the problem of the sporadic or intermittent condition. The problem generated significant disagreement among Commissioners on approach. The authoritative Tribunal of Commissioners' decision is *R(IB) 2/99(T)*, endorsed by a tribunal of Commissioners in Northern Ireland in *R1/02(IB) (T)*. *R(IB) 2/99* concerned the situation where a claimant suffered from a condition causing greater disability on some days than on others. The key question was whether the claimant was incapable of work under the PCA on days on which, if the days were viewed in isolation, he or she might not satisfy that test (para.2). While the Tribunal decision does not prescribe any one approach as *universally* applicable, the central thrust of the decision is to see as justified for the majority of cases, the "broad approach" typified by *CIB/6244/97* rather than the stricter "daily approach" exemplified by *CIB/13161/96* and *CIB/13508/96*. The Tribunal did not, however, find helpful the distinction drawn between "variable" and "intermittent" conditions in *CIB/6244/97*. Moreover, the Tribunal recognised that in some cases at least—generally when looking backwards over a prolonged period in the course of which the claimant has only had "short episodes of disablement" (for example, in the dwindling number of cases where the First-tier Tribunal had to consider matters "down to the date of the hearing", or in "review or overpayment cases")—something akin to the meticulous approach in *CIB/13161/96* and *CIB/13508/96* along the lines of Commissioner Jacobs' approach to intermittent conditions in *CIB/6244/1997* would be appropriate (para.17).

The practical reality is that most cases which fall to be decided by the decision-maker in the Department do not concern entitlement to benefit for a past period. Generally, a decision on the award of benefit is "forward looking" and usually made for an indefinite period. Although the decision-maker must of course consider the period from the medical examination up to the date of his decision, that decision will rarely be concerned with entitlement to benefit for a substantial period in the past. While both the "broad" and the "daily basis" approaches are each consistent with the wording of the legislation, the "broad approach" is "the only approach that can sensibly be applied by a decision-maker, making what is in effect a prospective determination for an extended period" (para.11). The Tribunal considered the broader-based approach adopted in *R(A) 2/74* to the attendance allowance issue— was there a period *throughout* which the claimant could be said to be so severely disabled as to require at night prolonged or repeated attention in connection with

9.404

9.405

bodily functions? The Tribunal decided that such an approach applied equally to incapacity benefit despite its daily basis. It noted (without using those statements to support its construction of the legislation) that such an approach accorded with ministerial statements in Parliament on the introduction of the all work test (for example, that the "all work test" (now the "personal capability assessment") is not a "snapshot"). Nonetheless, the Tribunal stressed that:

> "the words of the legislation cannot be ignored . . . [I]n those cases where relevant descriptors are expressed in terms that the claimant 'cannot', rather than 'sometimes cannot', perform the activity, one should not stray too far from an arithmetical approach that considers what the claimant's abilities are 'most of the time'—the phrase used in *C1/95(IB)*. Nevertheless, we agree that all the factors mentioned by counsel [neither of whom argued for a 'daily basis' approach]—the frequency of 'bad' days, the lengths of periods of 'bad' days and of intervening periods, the severity of the claimant's disablement on both 'good' and 'bad' days and the unpredictability of 'bad' days—are relevant when applying the broad approach. Thus a person whose condition varies from day to day and who would easily satisfy the 'all work test' on three days a week and would nearly satisfy it on the other four days might well be considered to be incapable of work for the whole week. But a person who has long periods of illness separated by periods of remission lasting some weeks during which he or she suffers no significant disablement, might well be considered to be incapable of work during the periods of illness but not to be incapable of work during the periods of remission, even if the periods of illness are longer than the periods of remission. Each case must be judged on its merits and . . . there are some cases where a claimant can properly be regarded as incapable of work both on days when the 'all work test' is clearly satisfied and on other days in between those days and that there are other cases where the claimant can be regarded as incapable of work only on 'bad days' . . ." (para.15).

That ESA is a weekly benefit, coupled with the demise of the "sometimes" descriptors, emphasises the continued authority and propriety of this approach to the LCWA tasks. Hence, as regards forward-looking decisions, claimants whose condition is such as only to satisfy the test on four or five days a month (albeit days of severe disablement) cannot, however unpredictable those days may be, properly be regarded as satisfying the test for the whole month. It thus may be that some claimants who are unemployable nonetheless are seen as "capable of work" under the PCA or the LCWA.

In *R1/02(IB)(T)*, a Northern Ireland tribunal of Commissioners endorsed the "broad brush" approach to variable conditions in *R(IB)2/99(T)*, but also laid emphasis on para.15 of it, set out above, with one reservation. They were unhappy with the phrase "the unpredictability of 'bad' days", commenting that those who decide cases:

> "will simply have to try to determine the likely patterns of functional limitation. Uncertainty as to the possibility of a future recurrence would not of itself usually be enough to satisfy the test which must be satisfied on the balance of probability at the time of the decision maker's decision" (para.26).

Applying para.15 of *R(IB)2/99* in *CIB/2620/2000*, Commissioner Bano held that the case before him (a sufferer from dysmenorrhoea) was one of the minority of cases in which the broad approach could not be applied, one where the claimant could only be considered incapable of work on "bad days".

9.406   *Making and recording decisions*: Setting rigorous standards for tribunals (cf. his approach to activity 3 in *CSIB/12/96*), Commissioner Walker in *CSIB 324/97* stipulated the following approach to making and recording decisions under the "all work" test [the predecessor of the IB PCA]:

> "the best and safest practice is for a tribunal to consider and make findings of fact about, first, the disability or disabilities, be they disease or bodily or mental

problems, from which an individual has been proved on the evidence to suffer. Second, they should consider and make findings of fact about which, if any of the activities set out in the Schedule, are established to be adversely affected by any of those disabilities. Thirdly, and based upon appropriate findings of fact, in the case of each and every activity the tribunal should determine which descriptor best fits the case having regard to the evidence, in their view. Finally, in the reasons, they should explain why a particular activity has been held not to be adversely affected where there was a contention that it was so affected, and why a particular descriptor has been preferred to any other contended for" (para.11).

But that best and safest practice need not necessarily always be followed. For example, where the issue is whether or not the tribunal believes the claimant on a matter fundamental and relevant, if on reasonable grounds the tribunal did not believe the claimant when he alleged that his responses in the questionnaire were not accurate, then the finding that the tribunal did not believe that he had been mistaken when providing those responses covered in reality all the disputed areas raised at the hearing, and it was not necessary to record specific findings of fact on each of the activity questions brought up by the claimant (per Northern Ireland Chief Commissioner Martin in *C46/97(IB)*, drawing with approval on Deputy Commissioner Ramsay's decision in *CIB/16572/96*). In para.5 of *CIB/4497/1998*, Commissioner Rowland sets out useful guidance on the minimum requirements of giving reasons. He noted that:

"a statement of reasons may be adequate even though it could be improved on and, in particular, a failure to observe the 'best and safest practice' recommended in *CSIB 324/97* . . . is not necessarily an error of law . . . What is required by way of reasoning depends very much on the circumstances of the case before the tribunal. Those challenging reasoning must explain its inadequacy and show the significance of the inadequacy."

Where a tribunal has heard oral evidence from a claimant on the effect of his/her condition, it must ensure that, when considering the report of the HCP, it makes clear what it makes of the claimant's evidence, whether that agrees or disagrees with findings in the HCP report (*YD v SSWP (IB)* [2010] UKUT 290 (AAC), para.12). In that case, Judge Turnbull also said that where the claimant has given oral evidence, a tribunal will not necessarily then have to deal with each of the mental health descriptors at issue, "although it may often be desirable to do so" (para.13).

When applying the principles to a particular case, it should be remembered that a First-tier Tribunal has an inquisitorial role (*CIB/14442/96*). It should be cautious about exercising that role when considering mental disablement (*CIB/14202/1996*, see head [C] below). Where the claimant is represented by a competent adviser (e.g. a Welfare Rights officer employed by a "responsible" local authority), a tribunal is entitled to proceed on the basis that the representative will put forward all relevant points on his client's behalf and to know the case that is being made for the client. The tribunal in such a case should not be expected to inquire further into the claimant's case; to require that would be to place an impossible administrative burden on tribunals (*CSIB/389/1998*). Overall, the tribunal's task is rendered easier now in that, because of the SSA 1998, the focus is on matters as at the date of the Secretary of State's decision rather than covering matters in the often lengthy period down to the date of the hearing (see further Vol.III: *Administration, Adjudication and the European Dimension*).

[B] Interpreting specific activities and descriptors: Pt I: physical disabilities

9.407

Note that from January 28, 2013, reg.19(4) provides that in assessing someone's capability to perform the activities in this Part of this Schedule (physical disabilities) the person is to be assessed as if fitted with or wearing any prosthesis with which that person is normally fitted or normally wears, or, as the case may be, wearing or using any aid or appliance which is normally, or could reasonably be expected to be, worn or used. In addition, reg.19(5) brings in the requirement—familiar from the IB regime—that this Part of this Schedule (physical disabilities) must be linked to incapability arising from a specific bodily disease or disablement or as a direct result of treatment provided by a registered medical practitioner for such a disease or disablement.

Activity 1: Mobilising unaided by another person with or without a walking stick, manual wheelchair or other aid if such aid is normally, or could reasonably be, worn or used: On a preliminary note, there are of course important differences in the drafting of the mobility descriptors for ESA and PIP respectively. It follows that what may appear to be inconsistent decisions relating to a particular individual's ability to mobilise under ESA and PIP regimes may be more apparent than real. However, there may be circumstances in which on the facts the FTT needs to consider whether to adjourn to have sight of the relevant PIP reports etc when deciding an ESA appeal: see e.g. *JB v SSWP (ESA)* [2017] UKUT 20 (AAC). On the potential significance of an award of PIP to an ESA appeal concerned with mobilising unaided, see *AG v SSWP (ESA)* [2017] UKUT 413 (AAC), where Judge Hemingway ruled as follows on the comparability (if any) of a PIP award and an ESA award (at para.9):

> "The statutory tests are not the same. One is concerned with standing and moving and the other with mobilising which includes the possible use, where appropriate, of a manual wheelchair. Anyway a tribunal, whatever award has been made in respect of a different benefit, will be entitled to make its own decision with respect to entitlement to the benefit with which it is concerned on the appeal before it. It should not simply ignore the possible relevance of an award of a different benefit but that relevance is likely to be in relation to the possibility of there being further relevant evidence which might not be before the tribunal on the appeal and the appropriateness or otherwise of adjourning to get it."

See also *MH v SSWP (ESA)* [2018] UKUT 194 (AAC) where Judge Poole QC held that the tribunal did not act in error of law by failing to adjourn (or to record its reasons for not adjourning) for evidence about a PIP award, nor in either determining the ESA appeal without having before it that evidence or in failing directly to address the claimant's PIP award in its statement of reasons.

As Judge Rowland noted in *KB v SSWP (ESA)* [2014] UKUT 126 (AAC)

> "The scheme of this legislation is clear. For each of descriptors 1(a), (c) and (d), two questions must be asked. First, can the claimant mobilise more than the relevant distance without stopping. If the answer is "no", the descriptor is satisfied. If the answer is "yes", the second limb must be considered and it must be asked whether the claimant can repeatedly mobilise the relevant distance. Again, if the answer is "no", the descriptor is satisfied. Only if the answer is "yes" to both questions is the descriptor not satisfied so that one must consider the next descriptor" (para.6).

To the same effect see *GC v SSWP (ESA)* [2014] UKUT 117 (AAC), applying *HD v SSWP (ESA)* [2014] UKUT 72 (AAC), a decision on Activity 1 in Sch.3.

The profound change here from the PCA/WCA is from "walking" to "mobilizing" and the removal of the "cannot walk at all" descriptor, thus encompassing adaptation to disability, namely manual wheelchair use. On wheelchair or other aids, the question is whether the wheelchair or other aid "could reasonably be worn or used" or "is normally worn or used". Until the decision of a panel of three Upper Tribunal judges in *SI v SSWP (ESA)* [2014] UKUT 308 (AAC); [2015] AACR 5, there was marked judicial disagreement on the range of factors to be taken into account in determining "reasonableness". Some judges favoured taking account of a broad range (see e.g. *M v SSWP (ESA)* [2012] UKUT 376; *NT v SSWP (ESA)* [2013] UKUT 360 (AAC); *BG v SSWP (ESA)* [2013] UKUT 504 (AAC)). Others saw as pertinent a narrower range of factors, focusing on a predominantly (and sometimes an exclusively) functional approach (see e.g. *TB v SSWP (ESA)* [2013] UKUT 408 (AAC); *AR v SSWP (ESA)* [2013] UKUT 417 (AAC); *MG v Department for Social Development (ESA)* [2013] NI Com 359). In *SI*, the panel of three Upper Tribunal judges held that the approach to be followed was the broader "in all the circumstances" one. The panel considered that

"if a person is in practice precluded from using an aid *for any reason and would on that ground be excluded from part of the job market*, it is unfair to assess his or her entitlement to ESA on the basis that he or she could use the aid" (para.58, emphasis supplied by commentator).

Like Judge Wikeley in *AS v SSWP (ESA)* [2013] UKUT 587 (AAC), the panel saw the LCWA as a functional one related to the circumstances of the modern workplace. Like the "cooking test" for disability benefits the WCA is a "thought experiment" so that the LCWA is applied "on the basis that the notional employer from whom the claimant might obtain employment has a modern workplace and is prepared to make reasonable adjustments in order to enable the claimant to be employed" (para.76).

Given that panel decision, it is submitted that the following factors or circumstances—identified from pre- and post-*SI* case law and *SI* itself—are ones of relevance, but this list is not advanced as an exhaustive one:—

- whether use of a wheelchair rather than crutches was medically suitable and had been suggested by medical personnel (*M v SSWP (ESA)* [2012] UKUT 376)—note, however,in contrast,, in a rare case where the claimant inappropriately used a wheelchair (on the medical evidence he did not need one), the tribunal was entitled to assess his ability to mobilize on the basis of his using the wheelchair (*MA v SSWP (ESA)* [2015] UKUT 290 (AAC), paras 23-31);

- whether or not the claimant had been referred for assessment for an NHS wheelchair as an aid to determining whether a wheelchair would normally be used by someone with the claimant's disabilities (*MG v Department for Social Development (ESA)* [2013] NI Com 359, paras 35–44; *TB v SSWP (ESA)* [2013] UKUT 408 (AAC)—although such a referral is not, however, conclusive of whether a wheelchair could in fact reasonably be used by the particular claimant (*TB*);

- whether in light of the claimant's condition and the availability of wheel chairs by local providers, the claimant would in reality have access to one (*M v SSWP (ESA)* [2012] UKUT 376).

    If a claimant does not have a wheelchair, the panel in *SI* stated that Secretary of State should produce evidence on their availability, but it also considered that this would not in practice be problematic given the Access to Work scheme or similar schemes operated by Jobcentres. The panel were mistaken in that the Access to Work scheme does not cover wheelchairs (*CS v SSWP (ESA)* [2014] UKUT 519 (AAC), para.42). But, as noted in *BG v SSWP (ESA)* [2013] UKUT 504 (AAC), while "it is even possible that inability to afford a wheelchair may be relevant ... it would not normally be so given their relative cheapness and their availability from the NHS and charities where reasonably required" (para.15);

- the claimant's home environment (*M v SSWP (ESA)* [2012] UKUT 376; *BG v SSWP (ESA)* [2013] UKUT 504 (AAC)), but in *SI* the panel thought its importance in this context is lessened by the fact that a manual wheelchair could be kept available at the workplace if the home environment does not enable its storage there. It is submitted that this approach focuses too much on the workplace itself, ignoring the issue of how such a claimant would be able to get to and from the workplace, something inherent as a focus in a number of the Sch.2 descriptors and the approach in *Charlton* to regs. 29 and 35.

The mobilization test is an actual rather than hypothetical test; "if the claimant had a manual wheelchair could he or she reasonably use it". As *SI* and the above factors show, the answer to this is not purely a matter of whether, when in the wheelchair, the claimant can mobilize. But even looking at the issue from a purely functional point of view, as Judge Williams made clear in *AR v SSWP (ESA)* [2013] UKUT 417 (AAC), reasonable use of a wheelchair involves several aspects of functional ability aside from the lower limbs. While there is no longer a "rising from sitting" activity in Sch.2, one must nonetheless consider it in the context of whether a wheelchair can reasonably be used. On a functional analysis, "can a claimant reasonably be expected to use a wheelchair (including getting into and out of it) without the aid of another person if he or she cannot reasonably be expected to handle the wheelchair whilst preparing to get into it, or after getting out of it?" (para.35). Unfortunately, the standard forms (ESA50 and ESA85) do not deal with such issues because they are no longer dealt with elsewhere in the Schedules. Tribunals must be wary of falling into the trap of assuming that every claimant who can reasonably use a wheelchair must thereby be able to propel it for more than 50 metres; this is especially so in a case where there is no evidence that the claimant in question has actually used a wheelchair under his own propulsion. Likewise the mere fact of a forthcoming assessment for wheelchair use is not evidence that a wheelchair could be reasonably used (*SG v SSWP (ESA)* [2018] UKUT 34 (AAC)). Note further that a powered wheelchair cannot be an "other aid" for the purposes of Activity 1; see *WT v SSWP (ESA)* [2016] UKUT 472 (AAC);[2017] AACR 16 at para.20.

Descriptor 1(a) is now coterminous with Activity 1 in Sch.3 on LCWRA. That the activity is now mobilising renders this aspect of the LCWA more difficult to satisfy than under the original WCA. Note that "severe discomfort" in the original Sch.2, thought to be ambiguous, has been replaced by "significant discomfort" as part of the CMA honing. Specific provision is made to deal with fluctuating conditions by including "exhaustion" as factor necessitating "stopping" mobilising and by including as an alternative in each of descriptors (a), (c) and (d), the idea of "cannot repeatedly mobilise . . . within a reasonable timescale".

Insofar as the descriptors deal with "walking" as a form of mobilising, no regard should be paid to the case law on "virtually unable to walk" in DLA (*CSIB/60/1996; LD v SSWP* [2009] UKUT 208 (AAC)). However, that there is an award of the mobility component of DLA or PIP is pertinent as regards an ESA claim in respect of this activity in that the *evidence* underpinning the award of that component can throw light on whether the descriptors for Activity 1 are satisfied, but whether it does so or nor depends on all the circumstances (e.g. the nature and date of the award as compared to the date of the ESA decision), so that a decision to adjourn or not for the DLA papers is similarly dependent on circumstances (*DF v SSWP (ESA)* [2014] UKUT 129 (AAC); *ML v SSWP (ESA)* [2013] UKUT 174 (AAC); [2013] AACR 33; *MI v SSWP (ESA)* [2013] UKUT 447 (AAC); *GC v SSWP (ESA)* [2014] UKUT 117 (AAC) *MA v SSWP (ESA)* [2014] UKUT 185 (AAC); *JC v SSWP (ESA)* [2014] UKUT 257 (AAC)). A tribunal need not do so, however, where that evidence would add nothing of significance to the other evidence before the tribunal, for example, because the claimant's condition has fundamentally altered since that award or because that award was made in respect of a temporary condition (e.g. restrictions on walking due to an operation) no longer pertaining (*JC*, paras 4–7). A tribunal faced with evidence of a claimant's ability or lack thereof to walk to identified local shops known to the tribunal can draw appropriate inferences from the representative walking ability of the claimant having regard to what she regularly accomplished (*LD v SSWP* [2009] UKUT 208 (AAC)).

Unlike its immediate predecessor ("without stopping or severe discomfort"), descriptors (a), (c) and (d) stipulate "without stopping in order to avoid significant discomfort or exhaustion". While there is still no explicit requirement that the "significant discomfort" be caused by walking or otherwise mobilising, it would seem that since the stopping must be to avoid "severe discomfort", the reformulation may cast some doubt on the applicability to these reformulated descriptors of *AW v SSWP (ESA)* [2011] UKUT 75 (AAC), where Judge Ward held that the previous formulation covered a claimant whose discomfort was always there.

"Pausing" is to be equated with "stopping" for the purposes of descriptors (a), (c) and (d) *(GC v SSWP (ESA)* [2014] UKUT 117 (AAC), para.21; *DB v SSWP (ESA)* [2014] UKUT 471 (AAC), para.4). So that if a tribunal found that a claimant paused for a few seconds after 30 metres, it should go on to ask "why?" *(DB*, para.5). In addition a tribunal should not confine consideration merely to mobilising on foot but should also consider possible wheelchair use *(DB*, para.7).

In *DJ v SSWP (ESA)* [2016] UKUT 93 (AAC) Judge Wright was concerned with the terms of descriptor 1(b) before its amendment with effect from January 28, 2013. The issue was whether the words "unaided by another person" in that context were limited to physical aid by another person. Judge Wright concluded that no such limitation was in place as regards the pre-January 2013 version of the regulations (at para.45):

"47. I do accept, however, the Secretary of State's argument that the aid from another person which is (and was) contemplated by activity 1 and descriptor 1(b) in Schedule 2 to the ESA Regs means active aid and does not cover passively standing by waiting to intervene if help were to become needed. It seems to me that this flows both (a) from the word "aid" as a verb, which has clear connotations of actively providing help to the other person rather than just standing by, as well as (b) the aid given by another person which would usually be necessary to help a claimant to carry out an activity when their incapability to do so is a mental restriction. Reassuring and cajoling the claimant so as to aid them to surmount their acute anxiety about using stairs will involve talking to them and perhaps hand movements rather than just standing behind or in front of them doing and saying nothing. The latter is not, in my judgment, another person providing aid to the claimant."

However, in holding that the words "unaided by another person" in descriptor 1(a) were not limited to *physical* aid by another person, Judge Wright specifically left open the question of whether the position was different on the terms of the descriptor *after* January 28, 2013, given the amendments at the same time to reg.19(5) (see para.45).

Activity 1: descriptors (a)(ii), (c)(ii) and (d)(ii): "repeatedly mobilise [X metres] within a reasonable timescale: In *AS v SSWP (ESA)* [2013] UKUT 587 (AAC), Judge Wikeley considered the meaning of this phrase, which he saw as a legislative variant on the case law principle of "reasonable regularity" (para. 28). He regarded as an "excellent starting point" Judge Jacobs's decision in *AH v SSWP (ESA)* [2013] UKUT 118 (AAC) (noted fully in the annotation to Sch.3 activity/descriptor 1 (para.9.398)). From that case, he took two points. First of all, the need, when considering the "reasonable regularity" principle to focus on the particular wording of the descriptors so that in this context the use of "repeatedly in descriptors (a)(ii), (c)(ii) and (d)(ii) meant that the principle did not apply to limb (i) of each of those descriptors (para.27). Secondly, he took the point that it was important "where the legislative text contains irreducible terms, [to apply] the statutory language without any gloss" (para.29). Like Judge Jacobs, he took the view that it was not for the Upper Tribunal to proffer a precise definition of these terms, but considered that in this case the tribunal's findings went beyond the bounds envisaged by case law. The provisions of the Sch. had to be construed "against the background of a working environment" (see para.9.374, above). He continued:

"What might well be a reasonable timescale for the Appellant at home would not necessarily be a reasonable timescale in the workplace. The consequence of the tribunal's approach was to rob the word "repeatedly" of any real meaning, as the tribunal's findings would equally well meet a statutory test predicated on the activity in question being performed only "occasionally ... in the course of a day". Whilst I am not prepared to draw a precise line, I am satisfied that on any reasonable analysis this tribunal's conclusion was the wrong side of the line. The ability to perform a function in a working environment "repeatedly ... within a reasonable timescale" must be something more than "occasionally ... in the course of a day" (para.32).

In *CS v SSWP (ESA)* [2014] UKUT 519 (AAC), Judge White considered descriptor 1(a).He held that although the phrase "on level ground" appears only in para.(a)(i) and is absent from para.(a)(ii), "the only possible interpretation of the repeatability test is that it is on the same terms as the primary test. That is on level ground" (para.30). It is submitted that this interpretation must also govern paras (c) and (d).

A claimant's ability to mobilise *with* significant discomfort or exhaustion should be disregarded for the purposes of Activity 1: see *GL v Secretary of State for Work and Pensions (ESA)* [2015] UKUT 503 (AAC).

A tribunal's fact-finding (and the relevance to that process of a claimant's own estimate as to how far s/he can walk) was in issue in *MM v SSWP (ESA)* [2017] UKUT 236 (AAC). Judge Hemingway held that it is perfectly permissible for a tribunal to attach weight to the claimant's own estimate as to how long in terms of time (usually expressed in minutes) he/she is able to walk for. It is also permissible for a tribunal to extrapolate as to what such an estimate, if reliable, might translate into in terms of distance. However, there is no rule to say that where a time estimate is offered it has to be accepted unless there is something specific to contradict it or to suggest it is unreliable. Further, it may be appropriate for a tribunal to consider whether such an estimate is, or is not, likely to be reliable and to probe this in questioning with a claimant. There may be reason to think that time estimates as to journeys which are undertaken regularly might be more reliable than other estimates. Finally, "the tribunal was not required to make a precise finding as to exactly how many metres the claimant could mobilise for. Absolutely precise findings as to something like that will often, realistically, be simply impossible. All it was required to do was make a finding as to which category the claimant fell into as to the range of distances contained within the relevant set of descriptors" (at para.13).

Fact-finding was also an issue in *GZ v SSWP (ESA)* [2017] UKUT 447 (AAC). There the tribunal, dismissing the claimant's appeal found that she qualified for 6 points for mobilising, making the following finding: "We find that she cannot unaided by another person mobilise more than 200 metres on level ground without stopping in order to avoid significant discomfort or exhaustion, or repeatedly mobilise 200 metres within a reasonable timescale because of significant discomfort or exhaustion." Judge Mesher explained why such a finding, without defining which limb of descriptor 1(d) applied, was inadequate:

"6. That [error of law] is in the form of the tribunal's finding of fact in the middle of paragraph 17 of the statement of reasons which adopted the terms of descriptor 1(d) without saying which of the two alternatives within the descriptor was satisfied. That in my judgment is not good enough as a finding of fact, because of the relationship of descriptor 1(d) with descriptors 1(a) and (c). If the tribunal considered that the claimant fell only within descriptor 1(d)(ii), because she could mobilise for more than 200 metres without stopping but could not achieve 200 metres repeatedly within a reasonable timescale, that would necessarily entail that she did not satisfy 1(c)(i) (because she could mobilise more than 100 metres) and would perhaps make it unlikely that she could satisfy descriptor 1(c)(ii) on the basis of not being able to mobilise 100 metres repeatedly. However, if the tribunal considered that the claimant fell within descriptor 1(d)(i), because she could not mobilise more than 200 metres without stopping, that would not as a matter of logical necessity exclude satisfaction of descriptor 1(c). Thus it might be necessary for a tribunal to explain why it chose descriptor 1(d)(i) rather than 1(c)(i). But more pertinently for the present case, if a claimant can only mobilise without stopping for some distance between 100 metres and 200 metres, that does not exclude the possibility that the claimant, while able to mobilise more than 100 metres without stopping, cannot achieve 100 metres repeatedly within a reasonable timescale and so satisfies descriptor 1(c)(ii). The same could potentially be said in relation to descriptor 1(a)(ii) and 50 metres. As a result, while it may not be necessary to the award of 6 points under descriptor 1(d) to specify which alternative is satisfied, in terms of the required underlying findings of fact on the whole activity of mobilising it is necessary in any statement of reasons to be more specific. It seems to me that there are two ways out where descriptor 1(d) is satisfied. The tribunal can identify the distance that it finds that the claimant can mobilise without stopping in order to avoid significant discomfort or exhaustion without considering the issue of repetition. There can then be a firm factual basis, allied to whatever explanation is appropriate, for not applying descriptor 1(c) or 1(a) and in particular for not applying descriptor 1(c)(ii). Alternatively, if the tribunal is unable to be so specific, it may be sufficient for it to explain that, while not sure precisely how far the claimant can mobilise beyond 100 metres without stopping, it has expressly considered descriptor 1(c)(ii) and is satisfied (and why) that the claimant can repeatedly mobilise 100 metres within a reasonable timescale. The question of what sort of range of estimates would be acceptable would very much depend on the circumstances of particular cases. What in my judgment is plainly not sufficient is to make a finding of fact simply in the terms used in the present case and then to say nothing at all in the statement of reasons about descriptor 1(c)."

Activity 2: standing and sitting: The six scoring descriptors—which differentiated standing and sitting more clearly—in the original WCA have been reduced to three. This represents an amalgamation predicated on the modern workplace requiring an individual to remain at their work station long enough to do their job.   **9.408**

As regards descriptor (a), this looks to "without physical assistance from another person", rather than (as in the PCA) "without the help of another person", so ability to do so with encouragement from another person would preclude a score under this head. Ability only to move between one seated position and another located next to one another by using the seat or back of the chair to deliver the force necessary to move cannot score; the precluded assistance is merely "physical assistance from another person" (compare *(R(IB) 2/03)*.

As regards descriptors (b) and (c), there is now no requirement that the individual can both stand and sit; being able to do one or the other for the requisite length of time will preclude scoring under descriptors (b) and (c) *(MC v SSWP (ESA)* [2012] UKUT 324 (AAC); [2013] AACR 13, paras 4, 5; *EW v SSWP (ESA)* [2013] UKUT 228 (AAC), paras 9, 10), something put beyond any doubt by the addition from January 28, 2013 of sub-para.(iii) to descriptors 2(b) and (c). There is no longer any stipulation about the type of chair (it used to be "a chair with a high back and no arms" or "an upright chair")—this was thought unnecessary given the range of adaptable chairs available and the employers' legal duty to provide one as part of the obligation to make reasonable adjustments to the workplace to accommodate persons with disabilities.

While it should be noted that in *MM v Department for Social Development (ESA)* [2014] NI Com 48 a tribunal of three Northern Ireland Commissioners disagreed with Judge Wikeley's approach in *MC* to the interpretation of Activity 2 descriptors *prior to the January 2013 amendment*, that decision is of persuasive authority only and thus, in terms of judicial precedent, ranks lower than that of Judge Wikeley in *MC* which is directly binding in Great Britain *(CC v SSWP (ESA)* [2015] UKUT 62 (AAC)).

The decision of Judge Ward in *EC v SSWP (ESA)* [2015] UKUT 618 (AAC) considers the conflict in the case law on the pre-March 2011 version of the activity 2 descriptors. Judge Ward held that there were "compelling reasons" to depart from the decision of the Northern Ireland Tribunal of Commissioners in *MM v Department for Social Development (ESA)*. In doing so, he analysed a range of materials which shed light on the issues relevant to the interpretation of the Activity 2 descriptors:

"57. In conclusion, it seems to me that an argument based on informed interpretation, if relying on a committee report, needs to be based on its final form and to take into account other material which Parliament must be taken as having had in mind when approving the legislation. In the light of the totality of the material before me, I accept that the mischief at which the legislation was aimed, on this aspect, included ensuring that people who could remain at a workstation for the requisite period by combining sitting and standing would not get points. Seen against that background, the ambiguity in the use of the 'either … or' construction in the descriptors in activity 2 between 2011 and 2013 would fall to be resolved in accordance with Judge Wikeley's obiter views in *MT*. The Tribunal of Commissioners in *MM* did not have the advantage that I have now had, through oral submissions and subsequent written submissions, of comprehensive examination of the background materials leading up to the making of the Regulations. In those circumstances, while I have applied a test of whether there is a 'compelling reason' to depart from the decision in *MM*, I have concluded that there is. With the benefit of those fuller submissions (which it appears were not made in *MC* or *MT* either) I conclude that a person who can remain at a workstation by a combination of sitting and standing for the requisite period is not entitled to points."

In addition, as regards descriptors (b) and (c), the meaning of "at a workstation" was considered by Judge Mitchell in *LC v SSWP (ESA)* [2015] UKUT 664 (AAC). The judge held that the First-tier Tribunal had erred in law by failing to address whether the claimant could fairly be said to have been capable of performing a job of work while remaining sat "at a workstation" in the light of her evidence that she needed to sit with one leg stretched rigidly out in front of her. Judge Mitchell concluded as follows:

"23. I conclude, therefore, that when descriptors 2(b) and 2(c) refer to a person remaining 'at a workstation' they refer to the person being orientated towards a workstation, whether sitting or standing, in such a manner that they may fairly be described as capable of performing a job of work. I do not think I need to go any further than this in interpreting the descriptor by, for example, attempting to define a workstation. I can leave it to the good sense of tribunals, using their knowledge of everyday life and their specialist expertise, to apply that test.

24. If, therefore, a person needs to sit with a rigidly outstretched leg so that s/he could not fairly be said to be capable of doing a job of work at a workstation, even with the benefits supplied by an adjustable chair, this would not amount to the person remaining sat 'at a work station'.

25. So far as section 20 of the Equality Act 2010 (reasonable adjustments) is concerned, I see no need for tribunals to try and predict how it might operate in a particular case. Attempting to identify the content of any particular reasonable adjustment divorced from a real world case is very difficult and liable to introduce unnecessary confusion and complexity. The question of what is reasonable is informed by two sets of variables: the characteristics of the disabled person and the entity obliged to make the adjustment. What might be reasonable for a small independent trader could well differ from what is required of a well-resourced multinational corporation. Instead, tribunals should simply rely on their own knowledge and expertise in applying the descriptors by envisaging the typical workstations and adjustable chairs with which I suspect we are all familiar."

Note again the replacement of "severe discomfort", thought to be ambiguous, with "significant discomfort" as part of CMA honing, and also the inclusion in descriptors (b) and (c) of "exhaustion" and "for the majority of the time" as one aspect of dealing with fluctuating conditions and the requirement of "reasonable regularity". The degree of discomfort must be such as to require the claimant to move away from the workstation; it is not enough if it merely disrupts, even very significantly, the claimant's concentration at the workstation (*DT v SSWP (ESA)* [2013] UKUT 244 (AAC) in the context of the pre-March 28, 2011 descriptors).

"Standing" does not mean standing stock-still. The normal person (the yardstick for applying the descriptors) does not do so for any length of time. As Commissioner Lloyd-Davies stated in *R(IB) 6/04*:

"The quasi-involuntary movements that most people make in standing for pro-longed periods do not . . . count. Instead the tribunal should concentrate on how long a claimant can stand before needing or having to move around or sit down (usually because of pain in the back or legs)" (para.5).

Activity (3): reaching: this assesses a person's ability to raise their upper limbs   **9.409** above waist height. It also identifies those with very restricted shoulder movement. This is almost identical to the reaching Activity 4 in the original WCA, the only omission being that Activity 4 descriptor (b) ("cannot put either arm behind back as if to put on a coat or jacket"). That was thought inappropriate since, by not requiring ability to put both hands behind the back inadequately identified these limitations. Moreover, it was superfluous as this was not a required function in many workplaces.

Descriptor (b) scores only 9, as opposed to 15 under the AWT/PCA in the IB regime. It does not involve raising the upper arm above head level (*CIB 2811/1995*). In contrast, descriptor (c) ("cannot raise either arm above head height as if to reach for something") requires that more than a minimal amount of the arm must be above head level. Reaching involves a degree of stretching, and involves being able to raise the upper arm above shoulder level and to go at least some way towards straighten-ing the arm in moving it towards a notional object" (*CIB 2811/1995*, para.7) so that a claimant with full elbow flexion could probably achieve the task in (b) but not (c).

Activity 4: picking up and moving or transferring by use of the upper body or arms: **9.410** this is similar to the corresponding activity in the original WCA (Activity 5). Like their immediate predecessor, the formulations avoid previous ambiguity over the meaning of "carry", and make it clear that what is covered is picking up and moving, using the upper body and arms (compare *R(IB) 5/03*). The key difference is that under the original WCA the descriptors variously referred to the use of either hand (descriptors (a) and (b)) or of both hands together (descriptor (c)). They thus assumed only persons with two hands. The Review thought this inappropriate; two hands were not necessarily required to perform the activity:

"For example, an item may be transferred by wedging it against the body, or another limb, to achieve the same outcome. Many amputees chose not to have a prosthetic limb in order to retain the sensation of touch; however they remain able to complete the task" (para.4.3.2, p.23).

The new descriptors thus deliberately make no mention of hands thus rendering *MH v SSWP (ESA)* [2011] UKUT 492 (AAC) inapplicable here (see para.8). But as with its predecessor the wording of the activity (use of the upper body or arms) means that it is thus not sufficient only to focus on problems with arms. Problems with shoulder(s) or neck should also be taken into account (*TO'B v SSWP (ESA)* [2011] UKUT 461 (AAC)), as should the effect on a back condition (*AG v SSWP (ESA)* [2018] UKUT 137 (AAC).

This descriptor has been considered in two other cases, each dealing with whether the task can be achieved by someone with only one good arm, given that the descrip-tor, unlike its predecessors no longer stipulates using both hands together.

In *KH v SSWP (ESA)* [2014] UKUT 455 (AAC), Judge Mark accepted that the change in wording means that the use of both hands together is no longer essential, so that if a person could pick the box up and move it by the use of one arm and the upper body, that is by wedging it under the arm, that would suffice as capability to complete the task. But he rightly cautioned that not everyone can be expected to do that. It would depend on all the circumstances of the claimant's condition so that, in this particular case, he considered that the tribunal was entitled to conclude that this claimant "would reasonably require both arms to perform the task", especially so since the object in question is "bulky" (para.4).

In *MT v SSWP (ESA)* [2014] UKUT 548 (AAC), Judge Hemingway agreed with Judge Mark's approach in *KH*, accepting that in principle the task could sometimes be performed by someone with one arm in the way suggested. But he rightly commented that completion of the task is undoubtedly easier for those with two good arms and that it cannot simply be assumed, given the bulky size of the object in question, that someone with one good arm will be capable of accomplishing it (paras 18, 19). It is dependent on all the circumstances of the case. A tribunal should

> "offer some explanation as to how it concludes (if it does so conclude) that the task can be achieved by a claimant who is incapacitated in the way this appellant says he is. In the passage quoted above, the F-tT has not made it clear whether it thinks the appellant could use his left upper limb at all in attempting the task. On the assumption that it does not think he could, it has not explained how it thinks the task might practically be achieved with the use of the rest of his upper body and his right upper limb. Its finding that he is "resolute" does indicate its view that he has determination but that, of itself, will not always be sufficient for a claimant to overcome physical difficulties and does not, of itself, therefore, represent an adequate explanation for its ultimate conclusion. The task of an F-tT in such a case need not be regarded as an exacting one but the standard required has not, for the above reasons, been reached here" (para.20).

A different issue arose in *MK v SSWP (ESA)* [2016] UKUT 74 (AAC), namely whether the ½ or 1 litre carton full of liquid to be picked up and moved under descriptors 4(a) and (b) respectively is a closed or open carton. Judge Wright concluded that the context necessarily implied that it had to be read as a closed carton, and so spillage in the act of picking up and moving is not relevant. The descriptors are therefore limited to the tasks of "picking up" and "moving" and not the manner in which they are achieved (at para.24). However, this is subject to the following qualification:

> "20. Different considerations might apply where the activity of picking up and moving cannot be completed because the item is dropped or thrown away involuntarily before it is moved or transferred. Then issues of whether the activity can be carried out reliably and repeatedly might come in to play. I would accept that the movement or transfer needs to be to a specific place and cannot involve random and involuntary throwing of the item (even though in one sense it would nonetheless have moved if thrown). This is not, however, to do with manner in which the activity is carried out but whether the activity can in any reasonable sense be done at all."

It follows that "if balance and a steady hand are relevant considerations at all then they fall to be considered under manual dexterity and not picking up and moving" (at para.24).

9.411   *Activity 5: manual dexterity:* As compared with its immediate predecessor, gone are the descriptors dealing with a "star-headed" sink tap and doing up or undoing small buttons. The former was thought to have awarded individuals a disproportionately high number of points for an identified disability which was not necessarily an activity for functioning in the workplace, thus misidentifying affected individuals for ESA purposes. Also removed are the six-point descriptors to make scoring more equitable across the activities. Ability to use a pen and pencil now specifically requires ability to use either "to make a meaningful mark" whereas its predecessor had been interpreted to require ability to use either, with either hand, so as to write in a normal manner. The new formulation arguably requires less ability. Ability to do things with one hand was thought by the *Review* to show capability to perform the specified activity. As regards descriptor (d), use of a keyboard, this jarred with the approach taken by Judge May in *DW v SSWP (ESA)* [2010] UKUT 245 (AAC) where he considered a case where a claimant sometimes could physically use a keyboard using one hand, but was unable to do so using two, thus preventing him using "a shift key to form capital letters or for example the sign '@'" (para.3). The approach in the *Review* would suggest that inability to use the shift key does not score so long as the keyboard can be used with one hand. The insertion from January 28, 2013 of "single-handedly" gives effect to that policy intention.

Taking the interpretation implicit in Judge May's decision in *DW*, Judge Mark in *CL v SSWP (ESA)* [2013] UKUT 434 (AAC) thought that inability to use either a keyboard or a mouse is enough to score points; it was not necessary to show inability to use both. He approved Judge May's approach in *DW*, following *Moyna*, on the need to take a broad view on whether a claimant could or could not satisfy the descriptor, stating that there are no absolutes by reference to which "can" and "cannot" are to be defined. The fact that a claimant could use a mouse or keyboard to a limited extent does not mean that s/he can use it in the way it was intended to be used. He disagreed with this commentator's view in the annotation, above, that the reformulation of the descriptor jarred with Judge May's approach, with the Judge himself being able to use a conventional key board with one hand, but did, however, accept that only being able to use one hand was more difficult, would be slower and that, on a conventional keyboard, combinations of three keys (typically control, alt and delete) – often used for logging on and security or recovery purposes – would not be possible on a conventional keyboard. The principle of "reasonable regularity" may also have relevance (see *KE* v *Department for Social Development (ESA)* [2013] NI Com 59, a decision of Chief Commissioner Mullan, on the previous wording of the descriptor). Since the descriptor now refers to a suitable keyboard or mouse, it is a submitted that for a tribunal properly to decide on this descriptor it needs evidence on the nature of the keyboard or mouse envisaged.

The above interpretation arguably chimes with an approach of reading the words of the Schedule in the context of the "work environment" in the sense that it is looking to ability physically to use a normal or adapted computer although not to test "computer literacy" in the same way as descriptor 5(c) no longer tests ability to write in a meaningful manner. But , as Judge Wright held in *DG v SSWP (ESA)* [2014] UKUT 100 (AAC), that analogy with descriptor 5(c) surely means that descriptor 5(d) can be satisfied with a very low level of ability (e.g. using a mouse alone to insert a check in a tick box); that what is being tested is not overall use of a computer with a mouse; but rather—as with Judge Jacobs' "functional approach" in *GS v SSWP (ESA)* [2010] UKUT 244 (AAC) to the descriptor on doing up or undoing small buttons in the predecessor of the manual dexterity activity and the appropriate inference from the analogy with descriptor 5(c) as regards the use of a pen or pencil to make a meaningful *mark*—a very basic degree of dexterity "in terms of use of a suitable keyboard or mouse [reading the "or" conjunctively rather than disjunctively] (e.g. gripping the mouse and moving it over an icon or box and then using a finger to click on it and using the keyboard to type out letters, numbers or symbols" (para.48). In other words, descriptor 5(d), like 5(c), cannot be satisfied if the claimant can do one of the activities: "the nine points only fall to be awarded … if the claimant cannot do both of the tasks [set out in descriptor 5(d)]; in other words, he can do neither of them" (para.3). Judge Wright preferred the "functional approach" and considered *DW* and *CL* to be wrongly decided and, guided by *R(I)12/75*, declined to follow them (paras 3, 55). He saw this interpretation as consonant with that taken by then Commissioner Howell in *R(IB)3/02* ("bending or kneeling") and (building on that analysis) that by Judge Wikeley in *MC v SSWP (ESA)* [2012] UKUT 324; [2013] AACR 13 ("standing or sitting"). He respectfully disagreed with the view of the Chief Commissioner in Northern Ireland, Judge Martin, in *R1/03 (IB)* that "or" was generally to be read disjunctively and only rarely conjunctively, as not fully reflecting the nuances of the English language and failing to focus adequately on the import of the word "cannot" when used with "or". Underscoring all this, Judge Wright considered that the "conjunctive" interpretation meant that the descriptor properly assessed separately different types of "manual dexterity activities", albeit that there was some "crossover":

"The test of "use of a suitable [keyboard]" or "use of a mouse" focuses on the parts of the hands and fingers that are needed to use such an item. Thus with the suitable [keyboard] it is primarily looking at the power, sense and spacing in the finger or fingers of the hand so as to be able to press the buttons on the keyboard.

Grip plays little or no role. On the other hand, the use of a mouse is likely to involve in part, different manual dexterity functions. The primary function may be to grip and then move the mouse, though the ability to click and click and drag, the cursor may also be important, so the flexing of fingers in the hand gripping the mouse is also likely to be important" (para.50).

In addition, if the legislative purpose had been to test the use of a keyboard with a mouse the descriptor could easily have been worded in that way.

Legally speaking, it is open to tribunal judges at either First-tier or Upper level, to choose which of these conflicting decisions to follow. Which is ultimately to be preferred will eventually be decided by the weight of authority or by one but not the other being reported in the AACR. It may be relevant that the issue was the subject of full argument by one of the parties in *DG* but not in *CL*. Perhaps this is an area requiring decision by a panel of three Upper Tribunal judges.

As Judge Mark notes in *KH v SSWP (ESA)* [2014] UKUT 455 (AAC), the disagreement between himself and Judge Wright remains to be resolved on another occasion. As described above, they disagree on whether scoring under this descriptor requires inability to use both these items of computer equipment (Judge Wright) or inability to use one (Judge Mark). But in *KH*, Judge Mark agrees with Judge Wright that it is not computer literacy that is being tested, but that rather

"what is being tested is the physical ability, so far as manual dexterity is concerned, to use a suitable keyboard or mouse. His description in paragraph 48 of his decision of the test is whether the mouse can be gripped and moved over an icon or box and then clicked and using the keyboard to type out letters, numbers and symbols. Again, I would not dissent from that, subject to questions relating to such matters as reasonable repetition and the effects of, for example, repetitive strain injury, and that the purpose of the so using the mouse or typing out letters etc. is to achieve certain results on the computer they are being used with. It is possible that a person may have sufficient control of the hands to be able to move and click the mouse or type letters but insufficient control to do so with any degree of accuracy or with any regularity or for any reasonable time.

When the descriptor speaks of using a keyboard or mouse, as Judge Wright's examples make clear, the use can only be to achieve results on a computer. It follows that in assessing whether hands are so lacking in dexterity as to score points on this descriptor it must be in relation to the operation of a computer. Why that scores the same number of points as not being able to make a meaningful mark with a pen or pencil is unclear, but what is clear is that even Judge Wright's description of what is required is far more demanding than a physical ability to make a cross on a piece of paper" (paras 10, 11).

In *SM v SSWP (ESA)* [2015] UKUT 617 (AAC) the appellant had been with congenital deformities to both hands, involving the fusion of certain fingers. One of the issues on the appeal was descriptor 5c: "cannot use a pen or pencil to make a meaningful mark with either hand". The claimant's appeal was allowed on a reg.29 point. However, Judge Ward expressed the following view:

"7. It follows that I have received only brief submissions from the parties about descriptor 5 (c). The tribunal found as fact that the claimant could write his signature. It certainly is an issue before me (I am not clear whether it was before the First-tier Tribunal) whether he can do so with reasonable regularity but that is something for the tribunal to which this case is remitted to explore. The claimant's representative draws attention to varies definitions of 'meaningful'. In my view descriptor 5(c) is not concerned with marks that are 'meaningful' in the sense of 'having great meaning, eloquent, expressive' (per Collins dictionary). That is a sense which might be appropriate when 'meaningful' is applied to, for instance, glances, but is not a natural sense when applied to something such as rudimentary as a mark with a pen or pencil. Rather, I consider that it in this context means 'having meaning' as opposed to 'not having meaning'. Further than that I prefer not to go in this case."

And see, to the same effect, Judge Jacobs in *SSWP v LH (ESA)* [2017] UKUT 475 (AAC):

"14. The mark has to be meaningful, so it must be capable of conveying some meaning and, inevitably, be a mark that is directed in the sense of the claimant having a meaning in mind. But that does not make the descriptor a test of intellectual capacity, which is the exclusive province of Part 2 of the Schedule (regulation 19(5)(b)). The level of the claimant's literacy is not in issue. This is a test of physical function, whereas literacy is a mental matter. And the test is limited to the claimant's fingers, hands and wrists, which are not related to literacy.
15. I agree with Judge Ward in *SM* that descriptor 5(c) is not concerned with the content of what is written. The only issue is whether it is meaningful. It has to be capable of conveying meaning. Random doodling or scribbling is not sufficient. It is not, though, necessary to convey any particular meaning. None is specified, so any meaning will do. It might be in the form of words, like a person's name or signature. Or it might be in the form of some symbol, such as a tick that could indicate agreement on a form or a cross that could indicate a vote at an election."

SM v SSWP (ESA) and *SSWP v LH (ESA)* were both followed and endorsed by Judge Wright in *NA v SSWP (ESA)* [2018] UKUT 399 (AAC). As regard descriptor 5(c), the judge stressed that the language of the test requires consideration to be given to the claimant's ability to use both the right and the left hand – so no points are scored if the person can carry out the function with at least one hand. In addition, the statutory test is not whether the person can write a word or a sentence with either hand (as under the old law) but rather the more limited test of not being able to make a meaningful mark with either hand. In that context, the use of the word 'cannot' in the descriptor requires attention to be given to a claimant's functional ability to make a meaningful mark with either hand across a range of potential situations. On the facts of the case, the tribunal's error lay in:

"its failure to consider in the round and across a number of potential or actual situations whether the claimant was unable with his right hand or his left hand to make a meaningful mark with a pen or pencil. For example, could he make the mark of a tick or a cross with either his right or his left hand on a census form or an election card? If he could, even if it was only with one hand, it is not apparent on what basis it could be concluded that he could not make a meaningful mark with either hand" (para.26).

Finally, Judge Mitchell has expressed the view (obiter) that the reference to a £1 coin in descriptor 5(b) includes "the £1 coin in the form in which it exists whenever the assessment is applied in an individual case" (para.26) and so can include the new-style £1 coin: *R v SSWP* [2018] UKUT 326 (AAC).

Activity 6: making self understood through speaking, writing, typing, or other means which are normally, or could reasonably be, used, unaided by another person: The immediate predecessor of this Activity dealt solely with communicating and making oneself understood through speech. The *Review* considered that the activities in the original WCA dealing with speech, hearing and vision, focused too much on the impairment rather than the disability it engendered. To do so was to ignore the adaptations that those with disabilities have made, thereby reducing their level of disability. Hence the removal of the "cannot speak at all" descriptor because that removed the message that those who cannot speak at all or only with very significant pain (see *CIB/4306/1999*) inherently cannot work. The *Review* considered that speech was not the sole mode by which individuals conventionally make themselves understood, so the modes of communicating were broadened to reflect this. The yardstick now is ability to convey a simple message, such as the presence of a hazard, whether at all (descriptor (a)), or to strangers (descriptors (b) and (c)).

"Normally used" means normally used by people in the claimant's situation acting reasonably in all the circumstances (*CIB/14499/1996*).

9.412   *Activity 7: Understanding communication by (i) verbal means (such as hearing or lip reading) alone, (ii)non-verbal means (such as reading 16 point print or Braille) alone, or (iii) a combination of (i) and (ii), in each case using any aid that is normally, or could reasonably be, used, unaided by another person:* The version of Activity 7 in force before January 28, 2013 was analysed by Judge Markus QC in *AT and VC v Secretary of State for Work and Pensions (ESA)* [2015] UKUT 445 (AAC); [2016] AACR 8. However, her decision is also relevant to the current formulation of the descriptors (see para.54). At the outset Judge Markus noted that the terms 'verbal' and 'non-verbal' are confusing 'because both forms of understanding in Activity 7 relate to verbal communications, in that the activity is about understanding words whether written or spoken'. Thus "'verbal' is used to mean 'spoken' and 'non-verbal' is used to mean 'written'" (para.37). Further, the drafting left it ambiguous as to "whether a claimant must be unable to understand or have difficulty in understanding communication by both verbal and non-verbal means in order to satisfy the relevant descriptors, or whether inability/difficulty by only one of those means is sufficient" (para.1).

Judge Markus therefore considered the legislative history of Activity 7 and its antecedents. This led her to conclude "that in order to qualify under a relevant descriptor a claimant need be impaired in either hearing or vision (but not both) or, as amended, in understanding either spoken or written communication (but not both)" (para.48). The current formulation "is not much of an improvement on the previous wording" (para.50), but the judge was satisfied "that the word "alone" was inserted after each of (i) and (ii) with the intention of making clear that it is sufficient if a person is unable to understand a message by either verbal or non-verbal means" (para.51). Judge Markus's decision was followed in the context of the post-January 2013 version of the regulations by Judge Ward in *CM v SSWP (ESA)* [2016] UKUT 242 (AAC) (dealing with the parallel descriptor in a Sch.3 case).

The predecessor of this dealt only with hearing. The reformulation here again, as with Activity 6, reflects the view that the activities in the original WCA dealing with speech, hearing and vision, focused too much on the impairment rather than the disability it engendered, sending an erroneous message that those who cannot hear at all are inherently unable to work. The yardstick now is that the claimant, due to sensory impairment, cannot understand a simple message, such as the location of a fire escape, either at all (descriptor (a)) or from a stranger (descriptors (b) and (c)). As regards reading 16 point print, what is being tested is the ability to understand a message contained in something with that size print.

9.413   *Activity 8: Navigation and maintaining safety, using a guide dog or other aid if either or both are normally, or could reasonably be, used:* The predecessor of this tested vision (visual acuity). The reformulation here again, as with Activity 6, reflects the view that the activities in the original WCA dealing with speech, hearing and vision, focused too much on the impairment rather than the disability it engendered, sending an erroneous message that those who cannot see at all are inherently unable to work. The key disabling features of visual impairment were thought by the *Review* to be inability or reduced ability, due to sensory impairment, to navigate and maintain safety. It was considered that these would be greater in unfamiliar surroundings, hence the gradations in scoring. Note that "crossing the road" is merely an example of "a potentially hazardous task" and not the sole context for descriptor (b) (*CC v SSWP(ESA)* [2015] UKUT 62 (AAC)).

"Normally used" means normally used by people in the claimant's situation acting reasonably in all the circumstances (*CIB/14499/1996*).

The policy intent behind the change in wording from January 28, 2013 was

"that this activity should examine the ability to understand communication sufficiently clearly to be able to comprehend a simple message by either verbal or non-verbal means or both. The descriptors may therefore apply if a claimant has hearing impairment alone, visual impairment alone or a combination of hearing and visual impairment" (Explanatory Memorandum, *http://www.legislation.gov. uk/uksi/2012/3096/pdfs/uksiem_20123096_en.pdf)*

The meaning of "due to sensory impairment" was touched on in *Secretary of State for Work and Pensions v AI (rule 17) (ESA)* [2017] UKUT 346 (AAC). Strictly the decision is not a binding authority as it is a decision consenting to the Secretary of State (SSWP) withdrawing his appeal to the Upper Tribunal on the meaning of "sensory impairment" under descriptor 8(b) in Sch. 2. The claimant had serious balance problems caused by Meniere's disease. The SSWP appealed to the Upper Tribunal on the ground that "sensory impairment" meant a direct impairment of one the five physical senses of sight, hearing, smell, taste and touch. The SSWP subsequently sought the Upper Tribunal's consent to withdraw the appeal, having obtained further expert evidence on the nature of Meniere's disease. However, this specialist evidence may be useful in other cases.

Activity 9: Absence or loss of control whilst conscious leading to extensive evacuation of the bowel and/or bladder, other than enuresis (bed-wetting), despite the wearing or use of any aids or adaptations which are normally, or could reasonably be, worn or used: This is a significant simplification compared to the original WCA and its coverage of "continence", although the new WCA does not use that term. Like its predecessors, this Activity does not directly deal with capability to work, but rather with matters of personal dignity and social acceptability; "the loss of dignity resulting from the associated soiling is considered severe enough to make it unreasonable to expect an individual with severe incontinence to work" (*Review*, p.33). As Judge Mitchell pointed out in *PC v SSWP (ESA)* [2015] UKUT 285 (AAC), descriptor (a) has a different logic to the other LCWA activities and descriptors. They relate directly to ability to perform tasks in the workplace. In contrast descriptor 9(a) is

9.414

> "not about bodily and mental processes used to do work. A monthly incontinence event of the type prescribed is of itself unlikely to have any significant bearing on the performance of work tasks. There must be a different reason for the legislator deciding that anyone within descriptor 9(a) meets the condition of having limited capability for work. I think it is obvious that this is connected to the deeply personal and potentially embarrassing and distressing nature of significant continence problems" (para.30).

That is why the focus is on absence or loss of control, rather than mere urgency. The frequency of urination experienced by a diabetic because of the condition or medication is to be distinguished from urgency leading to a loss of control (*NH v SSWP (ESA)* [2011] UKUT 82 (AAC)). As regards descriptor (b) the requirement from January 28, 2013 is that the claimant is *for the majority of the time* at risk of loss of control. Note that it deals with "risk" and not the materialisation of that risk; there can be a risk without it ever materialising or doing so on only a few occasions (*NH v SSWP (ESA)* [2011] UKUT 82 (AAC); *KB v SSWP (ESA)* [2014] UKUT 126 (AAC); *DG v SSWP (ESA)* [2015] UKUT 370 (AAC), paras 15–17)). The aspect of being unable to control the full voiding of the bladder essentially involves asking:

> "no more than, if the appellant starts to urinate, will he be able to stop before his bladder is completely empty? The tribunal is most likely to be able to arrive at a reasoned conclusion on this by applying its expert knowledge to the surrounding evidence including the ESA50, GP and medical reports provided by the appellant or obtained by the tribunal, ESA85 (particularly the typical day) and lifestyle" (*NH v SSWP (ESA)* [2011] UKUT 82 (AAC), para.14).

In *NL v SSWP (ESA)* [2017] UKUT 397 (AAC), allowing the claimant's appeal, Judge Rowland considered it possible that the tribunal had:

> "placed too much weight on the distinction between urgency and incontinence. The word 'continence', which at one time featured in the Schedules, no longer does so: the question is simply whether the claimant loses control, or is at risk of

doing so, to the extent that he requires, or would require, cleaning and a change of clothing. Moreover, the words 'evacuation' of the bowel and 'voiding' of the bladder in descriptor 9(a)(i) need to be read in the light of descriptor 9(a)(ii) and I agree with the Secretary of State that the revised WCA Handbook (5 July 2016) accurately describes their effect –

> 'The descriptors relate to a substantial leakage of urine or faeces – such that there would be a requirement for the person to have a wash and change their clothing' (para.6)."

Judge Rowland added that "Descriptor 9(b) is satisfied when the claimant has only rare occasions of such a substantial leakage but is, for the majority of the time, at risk of having one unless able to reach a toilet quickly" (para.7).

An important starting point for these descriptors is that the "absence or loss of control" experienced must be "whilst conscious", on which see *CL v SSWP (ESA)* [2019] UKUT 39 (AAC). There Judge West held (at para.28) that:

> "a claimant who loses control of his bowel or bladder whilst in a state of altered, as opposed to lost, consciousness, cannot score points under the descriptors linked to activity 9. If a person has lost consciousness, it clearly cannot be said that that person is "conscious" for the purposes of activity 9. A person who is in a state of altered consciousness, as a claimant may be when experiencing a seizure and possibly for a time in its aftermath, equally cannot be said to be "conscious" within the meaning of activity 9."

In *NH*, approved in *CP v SSWP (ESA)* [2011] UKUT 507 (AAC), Judge Lane sets out a number of helpful questions in para.14. That the yardstick is now "extensive evacuation of the bowel and/or voiding of the bladder" precludes, as did its predecessor, application of IB decisions bringing dribbling and leaking within the "loss of control" rubric (see e.g. *CSIB/880/2003*). Sufferers of stress incontinence may thus find it difficult to score. The necessary extent of the disability is measured by the need for "cleaning and a change of clothing". "Change of clothing" does not require a complete change since that would rarely be a consequence even of considerable levels of incontinence (*EM v SSWP (ESA)* [2014] UKUT 34 (AAC), paras 22, 23). Sanitary pads do not constitute "clothing" for this purpose. Nor, in this context, do disposable pants. In *EM*, Judge Mark said:

> "In practical terms, bearing in mind that the activity is dealing with matters of personal dignity and social acceptability, it appears to me that almost any change of clothing would count for this purpose since the soiled clothing would then have to be retained in the workplace for the rest of the day by the person who has soiled him or herself with the real risk of the clothing in question being seen or smelled by others in the workplace. If, however, pants are disposable, then in my view it would be likely to be the responsibility of the employer to ensure that there were facilities for them to be disposed of. Further it does not appear to me to have been intended that a change of disposable protective sanitary wear was to be relevant, since that would normally be needed in the event of the sort of accident contemplated by the descriptor. For those reasons, I would not consider that in most, if not all, circumstances a change of such wear was properly to be included in a change of clothing" (para.23).

Descriptor (a), through sub-para.(ii), recognises that the impact on the individual of such a need for cleaning and a change of clothing "is just as great where it results from leaking of a collecting device rather than loss of control of bladder or bowels". The precise scope of "collecting device" remains untested—does it include incontinence pads, or just catheter bags or stoma bags? The scope of "aids or adaptations" is not wholly clear; as Judge Mark noted in *EM*, the aids and adaptations envisaged might be thought mainly to cover internal devices, such as an artificial valve manually operated to open and close the bladder, which control such opening and closing or the evacuation of the bowel thus not embracing "sanitary pads and similar devices" since they "do not affect control over the evacuation of the bowel or the voiding of the bladder but only the consequences of such an event occurring" (para. 20). However, the wider wording ("aids or adaptations which are normally, or could reasonably be worn or used") suggests the terms are not so limited, so that "sanitary pads are aids which affect a claimant's ability to perform an activity in that their use may result in there being no need for a change of clothing" (para.20). In *PC v SSWP (ESA)* [2015] UKUT 285 (AAC), Judge Mitchell agreed with Judge Mark that "the aids and adaptations encompassed ...are limited" (para.20) to "those which prevent or minimise a loss of control" (para.38). A bucket thus cannot amount to an aid or adaptation. Nor can it amount to an "aid or appliance" for purposes of descriptors (a) and (b):

> "A bucket cannot reasonably be used in any workplace, apart from perhaps an incredibly unusual one like a one-person lighthouse, to deal with incontinence. That would run counter to, and undermine, the purpose of the continence activity and descriptors. It would be impossible to maintain dignity in those circumstances. The range of permissible aids and appliances must be restricted to achieve that aim and discounted if use in the workplace would be likely to expose an individual to the indignity against which these descriptors are designed to protect. But this does not mean that a less intrusive receptacle than a bucket must be discounted, if it can be used by a person without that associated indignity. I have no idea whether such things exist" (para.39).

Nor is a bucket a "toilet" (ibid).

As with all its predecessors, applying these descriptors involves intrusive scrutiny of the lives of claimants, embracing intimate and embarrassing areas affecting a claimant's dignity. It is necessary to appreciate the nature of the problems of sufferers, the varied nature and disabling effects of irritable bowel syndrome (IBS) (see *CIB/14332/96*) the role of diet (*CSIB/889/1999*), and the nature and role of various urinary or fecal collecting devices. It is also necessary to define and apply carefully the terms used in the descriptors.

Aids or adaptations "normally used" means if the aid or adaptation in question is normally used by people in the claimant's situation acting reasonably in all the circumstances (*CIB/14499/1996*). In *LB* v *SSWP (ESA)* [2013] UKUT 352 (AAC), Judge Mark considered the use of aids or adaptations. He thought that the DWP guidance to decision-makers in Memo DMG 24/12, issued after Judge Levenson's decision in *RP* v *SSWP* [2011] UKUT (ESA) 449 (AAC) (noted in the annotation to reg.19(4) (see para.9.49), embodied a non-exhaustive set of useful matters to be considered in cases, but stressed, as does the guidance itself, that those set out are not the only factors which may be relevant. Judge Mark summarized the relevant parts of the guidance thus:

> "In relation to those physical descriptors which specifically refer to the use of aids, including continence, it observes that decision makers should apply the test in a way that displays consistency between the work capability assessment as a whole and the assessment of each descriptor in particular (para.6). It goes on to state that the decision maker should establish whether the claimant normally uses an aid or appliance, and if not, whether the use of it has been prescribed or advised. If a claimant does not have an aid or appliance which they have been prescribed or advised to use, the decision maker should establish whether it would help the claimant, why they are not using one and whether the explanation is reasonable.
>
> The guidance goes on to state that the decision maker must consider all the circumstances in deciding whether it would be reasonable to assess the claimant as using an aid that they have not been prescribed or that they have not been advised to use. Factors identified include whether (1) the claimant possesses the aid or appliance; (2) the claimant was given specific medical advice about managing their condition, and it is reasonable for them to continue to follow that advice; (3) the claimant would be advised to use an aid or appliance if they raised it with the

appropriate authority such as a GP or occupational therapist; (4) if it is medically reasonable for them to use an aid or appliance; (5) the health condition or disability is likely to be of short duration; (6) an aid or appliance is widely available; (7) an aid or appliance is affordable in the claimant's circumstances; (8) the claimant is able to use and store the aid or appliance; and (9) the claimant is unable to use an aid or appliance due to their physical or mental health condition" (paras 11, 12).

He noted that the HCP had not carried out the recommended enquiries. Nor had the tribunal done so. It had referred to the claimant's urine well which he kept in his car as "an aid which he used". But this failed to address the fact it was only of use in the car and even there did not always prove adequate because he could not get to it in time or was not in a suitably quiet place to use it. It could not reasonably be expected to be used in non-private places (para.20). As regards the possible use of pads—which the claimant did not use because he felt shame at the continence problem at his age—Judge Ward stressed that while they could deal with post-urinary dribbling (which does not count for scoring purposes anyway), he was less clear how they could deal adequately with extensive evacuation of the bladder. Moreover—as an additional factor not mentioned in the DWP guidance—the tribunal should consider whether their use might actually exacerbate the problem of "accidents" where the claimant could reach a toilet in time "because they might increase the time required for the claimant to prepare himself to urinate" (para.22).

The descriptors should be applied bearing in the context of the claimant's personal circumstances and any mobility problems experienced by the claimant (*EM v SSWP (ESA)* [2014] UKUT 34 (AAC); *FR v SSWP (ESA)* [2015] UKUT 151 (AAC)). In *EM*, Judge Mark highlighted the error in the then guidance in the DWP Medical Services Handbook which stated that mobility problems should be ignored as regards this descriptor since those problems were dealt with elsewhere in Sch.2. He considered that

"This statement is wholly misguided both in relation to the descriptor as it was at the time of the decision and as it now is. In descriptor 9(a)(i) the only question is whether at least once a month the claimant experiences loss of control leading to extensive evacuation of the bowel and/or voiding of the bladder sufficient to require cleaning and a change of clothes. The fact that this is because the claimant is unable to reach a toilet in time because of other physical problems is irrelevant, as one would expect bearing in mind that the purpose of the descriptor is to deal with questions of personal dignity and social acceptability. This is made even clearer, if that were possible, by the wording of descriptor 9(b) where the question is whether there is a risk of loss of control if not able to reach a toilet quickly. Loss of control at least once a month because the claimant cannot reach a toilet quickly plainly qualifies for 15 points if the other requirements are met" (para.25).

The guidance in that handbook has been revised to take account of *EM* (see *FR v SSWP (ESA)* [2015] UKUT 151 (AAC), para.21). Rightly so, since, as Judge Grey QC put it in *FR*:

"The effect of the "loss of control" set out in descriptor 9 must be assessed in the light of an individual's personal circumstances. If, as a result of limited mobility, he or she is more adversely affected than someone who has greater mobility and an associated ability to better manage the effects of any threatened loss of control, this should be taken into account by the decision-maker. The alternative would be to divorce the assessment of this activity and the descriptors from the reality of an individual's ability to cope with their condition and to replace an assessment which is claimant-centred with one based on (here) the ability of a 'hypothetical', reasonably mobile individual to reach toilets. The activity seeks to assess the likelihood of loss of personal dignity and shame in the workplace associated with significant 'accidents'. It should make no difference whether soiling may occur because an individual's restricted mobility slows down the process of reaching a toilet, or because the loss of control is comparatively rapid. The effect on the individual and their ability to work is the same" (para.19).

For mobilising difficulties to be relevant to Activity 9 and its descriptors, however, there must exist an underlying problem of bowel or bladder functioning; mobilising difficulties alone are not enough. there must be a disease or disablement affecting the control mechanisms of bowel or bladder (*PC v SSWP (ESA)* [2015] UKUT 285 (AAC). paras 33-36, 45; *DG v SSWP (ESA)* [2015] UKUT 370 (AAC), para.18).

For a successful reasons challenge, see *VH v SSWP (ESA)* [2018] UKUT 290 (AAC) (at paras.15 and 16).

Activity 10: Consciousness during waking moments: The focus here is on "involuntary   **9.415** episodes of lost or altered consciousness" which result in "significantly disrupted awareness or concentration". If experienced at least once a week, 15 points are scored and thus limited capability for work established. If experienced at least once a month, six points are scored. With no reference now being made to "epileptic or similar seizures" and the descriptors referring to "significantly disrupted awareness or concentration", the strict and narrow approach in *R(IB) 2/07(T)* is no longer warranted. It cast doubt on earlier authorities on "altered consciousness", finding *CSIB/14/1996*, which had given hope to those who suffered severe headaches, to have been wrongly decided. *R(IB) 2/07(T)* required alteration of consciousness such that the sufferer was "incapable of any deliberate act". In *BB v SSWP (ESA)* [2011] UKUT 158 (AAC); [2012] AACR 2, Judge Ward considered that the Tribunal of Commissioners decision in *R(IB) 2/07(T)*, insofar as it created a test of severity of an episode of altered consciousness should be seen purely as a decision of the previous IB regime. The ESA regime, by providing a statutory yardstick of "results in significantly disrupted awareness or concentration", rendered inapplicable to ESA the test of being "incapable of any deliberate act" (para.14), and the matter of the meaning of the statutory phrase in the ESA regime should be considered "untrammeled as regards the extent of the effects of the episode" by *R(IB) 2/07(T)* (para.15).

In *CB v SSWP (ESA)* [2015] UKUT 287 (AAC), Judge Rowley considered "lost consciousness" self-explanatory in most cases. As regards "altered consciousness", she adopted the proposition set out in the Training and Development Handbook for HCPs, while recognizing that that work is in no way binding on decision-makers or tribunals:

> "'Altered consciousness' implies that, although the person is not fully unconscious, there is a definite clouding of mental faculties resulting in loss of control of thoughts or actions" (PC, para. 10).

The matter of giving substance to the concepts "lost or altered consciousness resulting in significantly disrupted awareness or concentration" and applying them to the facts of disputed cases is very directly the task of the tribunal in the light of all the evidence. In the context of the similarly-worded activity 11 in the Sch. in force at March 27, 2011, *RA v SSWP (ESA)* [2010] UKUT 301 (AAC) considered that the transient and immediate effects of consuming alcohol should not count towards meeting the descriptors of this activity (para.10). Moreover alcohol dependence did not raise issues here since it ranked as a "mental condition" and not, as required, a physical disease or disablement (para.18). In that same context, in *AB v SSWP (ESA)* [2012] UKUT 151 (AAC) Judge Jacobs held that the effects of sleep apnoea were not covered. It takes effect only when asleep and not during waking moments, thus not directly affecting capability for work. Although sleep so interrupted because of the condition does, however, mean that a sufferer may be unrefreshed, tired and liable to fall asleep during the day because of natural tiredness, Judge Jacobs considered that this, even where due to a medical condition could not properly be described as involuntary but rather something subject to control, something we all experience. Nor did he consider it properly describable as disrupting awareness or concentration in this context.

In *JG* v *SSWP (ESA)* [2013] UKUT 496 (AAC), Judge Mark considered the case of a claimant whose drowsiness was a direct side effect of his Parkinson's medication. Applying ESA Regs 2008, reg.19(5)(c), it arose as a direct result of treatment by a medical practitioner for that disease. As tiredness induced by medication, it was thus distinguishable from the "natural tiredness" considered by Judge Jacobs in *AB* v *SSWP (ESA)* [2012 UKUT 151 (AAC). As regards Judge Jacobs's comments on "natural tiredness" in that case, Judge Ward agreed that in general it was something one can control and cannot in the context of descriptor (a) be described as "involuntary", but stated further that

> "[i]t would not, however, be true of somebody suffering from narcolepsy, nor would it be true of somebody who has been administered a sedative designed to cause them to fall asleep, or which has that consequence. There will be occasions when the tiredness or drowsiness is so extreme that voluntary control is lost. Whether there are occasions when the claimant's medication results in such occasions, and if so, how frequently this occurs, is a matter for the tribunal to determine. ... [T]he descriptor clearly refers both to lost and altered consciousness. Sleep is a form of lost consciousness just as much as a state induced by an epileptic fit. A person is not awake if they have lost consciousness and the reference to 'remaining conscious during waking moments' or, as here, 'consciousness during waking moments' is plainly concerned with involuntary loss of consciousness of any type. I can see no difference between losing consciousness due to narcolepsy and losing consciousness due to any other cause. ... [D]rug induced drowsiness can, if severe enough, amount to or result in an involuntary episode of lost or altered consciousness resulting in significantly disrupted awareness or concentration. It is for the tribunal to investigate the cause, nature and extent of the problem and to determine whether there are occasions when the side effects of the claimant's medication have that effect on him, and if so, how frequently they occur" (paras 9–11).

In a Northern Ireland decision, *DM* v *Department for Social Development (ESA)* [2013] NI Com 17, following Judge Jacobs in *AB*, Commissioner Stockman considered that the "correct approach to the activity excludes considerations of periods of normal sleep. Falling asleep during the day does not equate to loss of consciousness" (para.24). *SY v SSWP (ESA)* [2016] UKUT 378 (AAC) confirms that falling asleep during the day due to the effects of a medical condition does not amount to "an involuntary episode of lost or altered consciousness" for the purpose of descriptors (a) or (b) of Activity 10.

[C] Approaching and interpreting specific descriptors: Pt II: mental, cognitive and intellectual function assessment

9.416   The terms of the activities and descriptors in Pt II are so different from those in the PCA that no specific IB case law on the PCA descriptors and activities can readily be made relevant. Not so, however, IB case law on the general approach to be taken, namely that, while a tribunal has an inquisitorial function, it should be cautious about exercising it when considering mental disablement (*CIB/14202/1996*), unless the matter has been raised beforehand and there is in addition some medical or other evidence on the point (*R(IB) 2/98*). Now that assessments are carried out by a wider range of HCPs, consideration has been given to the weight that should be placed on their evidence, particularly in mental health cases, where the particular experience of the HCP lies in a non-mental health field. In *JH v SSWP (ESA)* [2013] UKUT 269 (AAC), the claimant was assessed in a 15-minute interview by a HCP who was a physiotherapist. Judge Mark thought that when dealing with mental health problems:

> "the opinion of the physiotherapist as to the conclusions to be drawn have no probative value whatsoever. This is because the physiotherapist has no professional expertise in mental health matters. Although the strict rules of evidence do not

apply, a tribunal can only take into account evidence that has probative value" (para.22).

He thought that in such cases the disability analyst should have mental health qualifications. But he further noted that even where that is the case, "tribunals should beware of placing too much weight on such reports, based as they are on a very short interview with a claimant and without access to medical records" (para.23). In *ST & GF v SSWP (ESA)* [2014] UKUT 547 (AAC); [2015] AACR 23, a panel of three Upper Tribunal judges categorically rejected Judge Mark's comments—which it saw as *obiter*—as

> "wrong if and to the extent that they purport to create a rule of law or starting point that observations on mental health descriptors by HCP physiotherapists are of no probative value whatsoever or are highly likely or likely to have little probative value and thus should be accorded no or little weight by the decision maker and the First-tier tribunal" (para.33).

Instead the proper approach is that the probative value of an HCP physiotherapist's report is a matter for the decision maker or tribunal dealing with the case, just as it is with other reports and evidence.

The panel so held, firstly, because the legislation makes no distinction between an HCP's ability to deal with mental health descriptors as opposed to physical ones. It merely requires approval by the Secretary of State and registration with the appropriate regulatory body. So any such rule as Judge Mark's would frustrate the statutory framework (para.34). The panel's second rationale noted the difference between the LCW assessment (how a condition affects the claimant's functional capacity) and "a medical examination carried out as part of a process of diagnosis and treatment" (para.35), a distinction acknowledged in Professor Harrington's *First Review* of the ESA process. The panel thus considered that the medical examination carried out by a HCP for the LCW did not require that HCP to be a medical specialist in all the physical and mental problems that might be exhibited by a particular claimant. To require the HCP to be such a specialist "would create insurmountable problems for the assessment process" since many claimants have a variety of problems which might then require assessment in a particular case by several HCPs rather than one (para.35).

What is required, however, is that the HCP have an informed understanding of the claimant's medical conditions and the difficulties flowing from them. This requires adequate training and supervision. The panel had received detailed information on the current training process (see paras 11-19)—something not available to Judge Mark in *JH*—and, while not commenting on that programme, did observe that none of the independent reviews of the ESA assessment process had criticised the performance of physiotherapists relative to HCPs from other disciplines and that training for HCPs on mental health problems was being reviewed with the aim of increasing the knowledge of all HCPs (para.36).

There is, therefore, no need for a tribunal to adjourn for further particulars on the qualifications of the HCP in a particular case. The specialist tribunal with its medical member must "make its own findings having regard to all the evidence before it" (para.37). The correct starting point was that identified by Judge Ovey in an incapacity benefit appeal (*JF v SSWP (IB)* [2011] UKUT 385 (AAC) at para.25:

> ". . .the report is prepared by an HCP who has been trained (whether as part of the training as an HCP or through other training) at least to the level thought appropriate by the Department of Work and Pensions for carrying out examinations where mental health issues are raised. In other words the selection and training procedures ought to have produced an HCP who can conduct a mental health examination competently. It follows that evidence that the HCP has not undergone separate specialist training should not of itself have any effect on the weight which the tribunal attaches to the report. . ."

The panel held that the weight to be accorded to any report "addressing the functional impact of any medical condition on a claimant" is a matter for the specialist tribunal which should consider:

"(a) the level of the author's expertise (for example, an HCP or a consultant psychiatrist) and (b) the knowledge of the claimant possessed by the author (for example, knowledge gained from a one-off assessment or that gained as a treating clinician). Additionally the date of the evidence, its comprehensiveness, and its relevance to the issues the tribunal has to determine are also key matters for the tribunal to consider. Importantly the tribunal should explain its reasoning for attaching weight to one type or piece of evidence rather than to another" (para.38 of *ST & GF*).

In *JS v SSWP (ESA)* [2011] UKUT 243 (AAC), Judge Ward, following *R(DLA) 2/01* and *R(DLA) 3/01*, held that evidence coming into existence after the date of the decision could be relied on so far as relevant to showing the circumstances pertaining at the date of the decision. Accordingly, here, where there was evidence of a recent diagnosis of depression, of recent weight loss, low weight and a very low body mass index (BMI), the tribunal in the exercise of its inquisitorial jurisdiction ought to have followed this up to see if this was a symptom of untreated depression or, at the very least, to have made clear in its reasons what it made of this evidence. There is only a very limited carry-over of case authorities on the original LCWA, given the degree of revision of activities and descriptors undertaken in the amending Regulations.

From January 28, 2013 reg.19(5) requires that incapability to perform the activities in this Part of this Schedule (mental, cognitive and intellectual function assessment) must be linked to incapability arising from a specific mental illness or disablement or as a direct result of treatment provided by a registered medical practitioner for such an illness or disablement. Under the previous wording of the paragraph (still applicable to some cases after January 28, 2013—see reg.2 of the amending instrument, below, para.9.554), there was no such link (*KP v SSWP (ESA)* [2011] UKUT 216 (AAC); [2012] AACR 5; *KN v SSWP (ESA)* [2011] UKUT 229 (AAC); *RM v SSWP (ESA)* [2011] UKUT 454 (AAC); *AH v SSWP (ESA)* [2011] UKUT 333 (AAC)), but the specific language of activities 16 and 17 then as now specifically required causation by cognitive impairment or mental disorder.

The revised LCWA contains only seven activities rather than the ten in the original LCWA. This revision and reduction were designed to remove unnecessary complexities and overlaps and prevent double scoring.

9.417   *Activity 11: Learning tasks*: This aims to identify individuals who have difficulty learning new tasks. The equivalent in the original LCWA covered learning and comprehension but the latter was considered superfluous by the *Review* on the basis that understanding how to do something was built in to the process of retaining that knowledge. The complexity of the task affords the necessary gradation between descriptors. Note that the instances given in each descriptor (setting an alarm clock (descriptors (a) and (b)); operating a washing machine to clean clothes (descriptor (c)) are merely examples.

See by analogy the guidance from Judge Rowley on this activity in the context of Sch.3 in *Secretary of State for Work and Pensions v AT (ESA)* [2017] UKUT 338 (AAC). Note also her observation that "the words 'due to cognitive impairment or mental disorder' do not appear in the descriptors for that activity, presumably because the activity falls under Part 2 of Schedule 2 which is headed 'mental, cognitive and intellectual function assessment.' In my judgment, nothing turns on the difference" (at para.9).

See also *TM v SSWP (ESA)* [2018] UKUT 9 (AAC), dealing with descriptor 11c, where Judge Wikeley observed (at para. 22) that "The method by which the person learns the task in question is irrelevant. They may be able to do so by reading the information booklet. They may be able to do so by having the necessary steps being demonstrated to them. The route is irrelevant. As [the Secretary of State's representative] neatly puts it, 'Reading a manual is just one way of learning to use something, show and tell is another'."

Activity 12: Awareness of everyday hazards (such as boiling water or sharp objects):   **9.418**
The focus here is on significant risk of injury to people or damage to property or possessions (rather than, as originally proposed, on risk of significant injury or significant damage). "Everyday hazards" means commonplace or ordinary hazards that are similar in kind to boiling water and sharp objects; it does not extend to social hazards, e.g. the risk of financial exploitation or sexual abuse that a vulnerable claimant with low social intelligence may face because of her suggestibility (*RR v SSWP (ESA)* [2018] UKUT 143 (AAC). The gradation between descriptors flows from the level of supervision required to manage the risk (supervision needed for: majority of time (15); frequently (9); occasionally (6)). The requisite "reduced awareness of the risks of everyday hazards" could stem from learning difficulties, affected concentration and self-awareness, or the effects of medication (*Review*, para.4.4.2).

Activity 13: Initiating and completing personal action (which means planning, organiza-   **9.419**
tion, problem solving, prioritizing or switching tasks): The overall intention of the Activity is to assess someone's capability to carry out routine activity. Note the meaning of "personal action" set out in the Activity itself. This part of the revised LCWA seeks to combine in one activity disabilities covered by three activities in the original LCWA: memory and concentration; execution of tasks; initiating and sustaining personal action. This was done because the original three were perceived by the *Review* as each identifying the same disability, namely, the inability to complete a task. The amalgamation thus precludes the double or triple scoring available under the former LCWA. The descriptors focus on completion of at least two sequential tasks, since it was unlikely that in a work context an individual would only be required to undertake a single task. The gradation between descriptors (b) and (c) turns on how often verbal prompting from another is needed to complete the personal action ((b) "most of the time"; (c) "frequent"). The *Review* specifically stated that:

> "if the time it takes an individual to complete a task means it cannot be executed reliably and repeatedly, then they will be considered unable to do so" (p.45).

Conditions potentially involving this Activity were thought to be lapses in memory and concentration, due to fatigue, depression or neurological impairment, apathy, obsessive compulsive behaviours, overwhelming fear or delusions.

In *MW v SSWP (ESA)* [2014] UKUT 112 (AAC), a case of a claimant with obsessive compulsive disorder, Judge Rowland held that the tribunal had erred in law:

> "It neither addressed the consequences of the claimant's need constantly to check that what he had done was right nor paid sufficient attention to the precise language of the legislation. The main consequence of the claimant's disorder was that everything took much longer, but there is also evidence that, for instance, turning gas hobs on and off when cooking had resulted a build-up of gas and in him being a danger to himself to the extent that his mother had taken over his cooking from him. The material features of the legislation are, first, that it is not enough that the claimant can initiate and complete personal actions – he or she must be able to do so "reliably"—and, secondly, a finding that a person can sometimes reliably initiate or complete actions may rule out descriptor 13(a)—at least on a literal construction of that descriptor—but it leaves open the possibility of either of descriptors 13(b) or 13(c) being satisfied since those descriptors are satisfied if the claimant cannot reliably initiate or complete at least two [personal] actions "for the majority of the time" or "frequently".
>
> The word "reliably" makes it unnecessary to go as far as is argued on behalf of the claimant and hold that a person is to be treated as not being able to initiate and complete actions at all if he or she can do so only with excessive delay. The Secretary of State is right to argue that one should consider separately whether there is a difficulty in initiating an action and whether there is a difficulty in

completing it and that in this case the difficulty lay in completing actions, although arguably the difficulty in completing the first action creates a difficulty in initiating the second. In any event, the practical point is that, if compulsive behaviour means that it takes an excessive amount of time to complete at least two actions, it can be said that the claimant cannot "reliably" complete them. The First-tier Tribunal did not consider whether that was, at least frequently, so in this case or, if it did, it gave inadequate reasons for its conclusion" (paras 6, 7).

Activity 13 was further considered by Judge Jacobs in *MP v Secretary of State for Work and Pensions (ESA)* [2015] UKUT 458 (AAC), where he noted it was "neither necessary nor appropriate to define 'personal action'. They are ordinary words that have to be given their normal meaning" (see *Moyna v Secretary of State for Work and Pensions* [2003] 1 W.L.R. 1929 at [24]). Accordingly, "At the risk of stating the obvious, it means something undertaken by someone on their own" (para.23). Judge Jacobs held that the tribunal "must apply common sense in deciding what constitutes an action. It is possible to render the legislation redundant by splitting an action into its component parts. The definition of Activity 13 recognises this by referring to 'tasks' as components of a single action" (para.28). See further the analysis at paras.30–41, including this passage at paras 34–35:

"34. The tribunal's decision on Activity 13 must relate only to actions that involve all these tasks. This does not mean that the tribunal must find evidence of an action involving all those tasks that the claimant cannot complete. It may be that there will be evidence from, say, dressing that shows the claimant being unable to plan by selecting appropriate clothing to wear outdoors, which can be put together with evidence from, say, cooking, that shows the claimant being unable to prioritise tasks. This specific evidence may have to be supplemented by inferences drawn from the nature of the claimant's condition or other factors.

35. This does not mean that the action considered need necessarily be complicated, so long as the tribunal takes all potential tasks into account. Take dressing as an example. Most of the time dressing may simply be routine. It may even involve nothing more than putting on the clothing selected and laid out by the claimant's partner. But it can require planning (deciding what to wear), organising (assembling the different items required), problem solving (finding an alternative item of clothing for something that is in the wash), prioritising (deciding whether it is more important to get dressed or to wash a particular item of clothing) or switching tasks (going to iron a shirt to wear). To put it differently. The tribunal must always be sure that the evidence on which it relies actually demonstrates an ability to undertake all the tasks required by the activity."

See, for a successful reasons challenge, *VH v SSWP (ESA)* [2018] UKUT 290 (AAC) (at paras.17–20).

9.420 *Activity 14: Coping with change:* This assesses ability to cope with change. The focus in descriptors (b) and (c) is now on whether the change is "planned" or "unplanned", rather than "expected", "unexpected" or "unforeseen". Decision-makers and tribunals should look at all the evidence about the person's daily life.

In mental health descriptor cases the context of a particular piece of evidence can be very important (see *PD v SSWP (ESA)* [2012] UKUT 255 (AAC)). In *GC v SSWP (ESA)* [2013] UKUT 405 (AAC) work-related stress had been the reason the claimant left his previous job as a driver. Being required to change his planned-out driving route part way through a shift, caused him stress, made him bad-tempered, such that he had to leave that job. The decision reflects Judge Ward's important reminder that different people have different abilities to cope with change.

On the evidence Judge Ward found the claimant's ability to cope with change very low and that he satisfied descriptor (c) and had limited capability for work.

What does "cope" mean? In *GC v SSWP (ESA)* [2013] UKUT 405 (AAC), Judge Ward considered it to be "a word of general application. It significance in the present context is well expressed by a definition given in the Oxford English Dictionary (Online Edition) of 'To manage, deal (competently) with, a situation or problem'. It seems to me that a variety of human behaviours and responses may be indicative of a failure to "cope" in such a sense. Among them may be stress reactions and discomfort sufficient to require the intervention of another in circumstances where such intervention would not normally be expected" (para.6).

Activity 15: Getting about: The differential here between descriptors is one of familiarity. That was thought in the *Review* to ensure the work-related nature of the activity, since the workplace would be a familiar environment. From January 28, 2013, descriptor (a) reads: "cannot get to any place outside the claimant's home with which the claimant is familiar", rather than to "any specified place" thus attempting to make clear that the need is based on most places a claimant cannot get to rather than a single specified place, and aiming to give effect to a policy intention that this activity is to reflect inability to travel unaccompanied by someone for those individuals that are severely affected by a mental health condition (e.g. agoraphobia). "Any place outside the claimant's home" means more than simply beyond their front door. According to Judge Bano in *PC v Secretary of State for Work and Pensions (ESA)* [2015] UKUT 531 (AAC):

9.421

"For my part, I do not consider that putting out the bins or going outside to have a cigarette amounts to 'getting about', even if there is a chance of meeting a neighbour or visitor to the building when doing so. In my judgment, descriptor 1 of Activity 15 requires an investigation of whether a claimant can go to a place outside the immediate vicinity of their home, and that in order to satisfy the descriptor it is not necessary for a claimant to establish that he or she cannot go beyond their front door" (para.8).

The other descriptors refer to "any specified place" or a "specified place", just as did those in Activity 18 in the original LCWA. This phraseology was considered in *DW v SSWP (ESA)* [2011] UKUT 79 (AAC). There, Judge Turnbull dealt with the case of a claimant, suffering from a stress-related illness brought about because of the circumstances of her dismissal from her previous employment, who was found by the tribunal to be fearful of seeing anyone involved with her former employment or reminders of it, such as vans or lorries and who would be unable to visit her employer's premises at all or, at best, accompanied. He took the view that this could not bring her within descriptors 18(a) (as originally worded) or 18(b):

"the words 'cannot get to any specified place . . .' in 18(a) . . . clearly mean that there is no place with which the claimant is familiar (or would be familiar with if she went out) which she could get to on her own. The words 'is unable to get to a specified place . . . without being accompanied by another person on each occasion' in 18(b) . . . mean that the claimant always needs to be accompanied when getting to a familiar place" (para.15).

Evidence that a claimant had gone unaccompanied to familiar places and accompanied to an unfamiliar one where she was trembling and sweating cannot support a finding that she could go unaccompanied to an unfamiliar place (*LM v SSWP (ESA)* [2013] UKUT 552 (AAC)). See also *MC v SSWP (ESA)* [2015] UKUT 646 (AAC), discussed in the commentary to reg.19 above.

In *AB v SSWP (ESA)* [2016] UKUT 96 (AAC) the issue was whether, if a claimant undertakes a journey by taxi, is that claimant "accompanied" by the taxi driver. Judge Hemingway held that "if a claimant can only undertake a journey to an unfamiliar place by taxi because of a requirement of undertaking the journey in the presence of another person or because the assistance of that other person is required, then that journey is, for the purposes of the relevant descriptor, an accompanied one" (at para.12). The tribunal had therefore erred in law by assuming that a journey in a taxi would be an unaccompanied journey without enquiring into whether the presence of the taxi driver was essential or important to the appellant's ability to make a journey to a specified place with which he was unfamiliar.

See also *TM v SSWP (ESA)* [2018] UKUT 9 (AAC), where Judge Wikeley accepted a concession by the Secretary of State that reg.19(4) limits consideration of aids and appliances to the *physical health* descriptors in Part 1 of Sch.2. and so in the context of activity 15 the FTT should not have considered the claimant's ability to navigate by a mobile phone app.

9.422   *Activity 16: Coping with social engagement due to cognitive impairment or mental disorder:* The primary aim here is to assess functional capability in terms of social contact with the ability to get around being dealt with by other activities. The gradation between descriptors (a), on the one hand, and (b) and (c), on the other, is that the latter two look to inability to engage with strangers, the former with anyone ("social contact is always precluded"). The *Review* thought familiarity an appropriate measure in relation to the workplace. That between (b) and (c) turns on whether that engagement is "never possible" (descriptor (b)) or "not possible for the majority of the time" (descriptor (c)). The preclusion of engagement (descriptor (a)) or the difficulty of engagement (descriptors (b) and (c)) must in each case be "due to difficulty relating to others or significant distress experienced by the individual being assessed for LCW". Contact which involves or would involve "significant distress" must be excluded from consideration" (*DW v SSWP (ESA)* [2014] UKUT 20 (AAC), para.4).

What does "cope" mean? In *GC v SSWP (ESA)* [2013] UKUT 405 (AAC), Judge Ward considered it to be:

> "a word of general application. It significance in the present context is well expressed by a definition given in the Oxford English Dictionary (Online Edition) of 'To manage, deal (competently) with, a situation or problem'. It seems to me that a variety of human behaviours and responses may be indicative of a failure to "cope" in such a sense. Among them may be stress reactions and discomfort sufficient to require the intervention of another in circumstances where such intervention would not normally be expected" (para.6).

In *LM v SSWP (ESA)* [2013] UKUT 552 (AAC), Judge Mark considered that descriptor (b) is satisfied if for the majority of the time, social engagement is always precluded (paras 12, 13). As regards descriptors (a) and (b) he could not read "always" as "often" or "for the majority of the time" (the term in descriptor (c)), but rather as "persistently or repeatedly". To say otherwise would have the odd result that a claimant could not satisfy descriptors (a) and (b) but, because of ESA Regs 2008, reg.34(2) would satisfy descriptor 13 in Sch.3 (see para.15). Judge Mark continued:

> "the tribunal is required to form an overall picture of the claimant's ability to engage in social conduct over a period and it does not appear to me that occasional very limited engagement in such conduct need prevent a tribunal concluding that overall the claimant is always unable to do so. To take an extreme example, a person in a coma who surfaces occasionally and is able to engage briefly during that period with familiar and unfamiliar persons before lapsing into unconsciousness should nevertheless be found in this context always to be unable to engage in social contact" (para.16).

He awarded the claimant points under descriptor (b).

See also, however, the annotation to reg.34(2) and the decision of the Court of Session in *SSWP v Brade* [2014] CSIH 39 XA81/13 (May 1,2014); [2014] AACR 29.

The precise scope of "social", of "engagement" and of "contact" has troubled Upper Tribunal Judges and generated different opinions. It has therefore recently been considered by a panel of three Upper Tribunal Judges, but to understand the panel's judgment it is necessary to first take on board the conflicting decisions.

In *KB v SSWP (ESA)* [2013] UKUT 152 (AAC), noted in the annotation to Sch.3, activity and descriptor 13 (see para.9.425), as regards "social engagement" and "social contact", Judge Parker, accepting the approach advanced by the Secretary of State's representative, thought "social" to be "a simple reference to relations with other human beings" carrying no connotations of "leisure, pleasure or mutuality", so that a tribunal could properly look at evidence about business visits or contacts with professionals, as well as with friends, relatives and strangers. It was not tied to contact in an informal setting (see paras 15–17). Judge Ward disagreed with this in *AR v SSWP (ESA)* [2013] UKUT 446 (AAC). It rendered "social" virtually otiose, placing the focus purely on "engagement with others". It also jarred with the ordinary meaning of the word in the Concise Oxford Dictionary, a meaning Judge Ward thought closer to the legislator's intention. Looking at the legislative history, he considered that the difficulties faced by those with autistic spectrum disorder were very much in mind. Material from the National Autism Society showed the difficulties faced in understanding the rules on social contact and distinguishing a "true friend" from a "pretend friend". Accordingly, in Judge Ward's view,

> "social contact in this sense is not the same as contact for business or professional purposes. If one goes to a medical examination, or a tribunal hearing, the rules are firmly established by the process and/or the person conducting it, and are typically clearly defined, often in writing. If the person being examined or whose case it is does not respond in a way that a person without disability might, the person conducting it may because of their professional responsibilities be expected within generous limits to accommodate the non-conforming response and certainly not, as it were, to take a poorer view of, or attempt to avoid further contact with, the person because of it. That is precisely what is lacking in the social sphere, where people are free to interact on their own terms and to accept the behaviour of another or to reject it, and largely do so on the basis of the sort of unwritten rules to which the National Autism Society guidance makes reference, an inability to respect which could, in the words of the descriptor, be an indication of "difficulty relating to others" (para.18).

In *LM v SSWP (ESA)* [2013] UKUT 552 (AAC), Judge Mark cited this paragraph and gave it qualified support, stating that while he agreed that

> "merely attending a medical examination or tribunal hearing does not establish an ability to engage in social contact, but it does not follow that in the course of that examination or hearing the party will not demonstrate an ability to respond appropriately and engage in limited social contact despite the distress that the meeting is causing and that such contact causes. The fact that a person is not so far along the autistic spectrum as to be wholly unable to engage in social contact does not mean that a person might not experience significant distress if required to engage in such contact. A tribunal needs to assess the ability to engage in social contact, which can be in any context, the extent to which a person has the capacity so to engage, the distress it causes when engagement occurs and the impact of that distress on the ability so to engage" (para.18).

In *JM v SSWP (ESA)* [2014] UKUT 22 (AAC), Judge Gray endorsed Judge Ward's **9.423** view and added "the observation that because for the important purpose of benefit entitlement, or indeed in order to effect treatment for a mental health condition, one may be able to summon up reserves to attend such an appointment that may not be sufficient in relation to a test which is of the ability to perform an activity reliably and repeatedly" (para.16).

In *AP v SSWP (ESA)* [2013] UKUT 293 (AAC), Judge Turnbull considered descriptor (c). He accepted that

> "difficulty, from a mental point of view, in simply getting alone to the destination does not fall to be taken into account under activity 16 (unless the difficulty getting there is itself due to problems with engaging in social contact (e.g. on public transport)). In other words, a claimant does not qualify for points under activity 16(c) merely because he could not put himself in most of the situations

where he might engage in social contact with someone unfamiliar, because he could not leave the house unaccompanied in order to do so" (para.11).

"The difficulty with others" aspect of the descriptor envisaged the situation in which it is the need to engage with others which caused the problem. In contrast, however, the alternative—"significant distress experienced by the individual"—did not, in his view,

> "require that it is the need to interact with others which per se causes the distress. … the wording is satisfied whatever the immediate cause of the distress may be, provided that it is due to cognitive impairment or mental disorder, and that it is sufficiently severe and occurs on sufficient occasions to prevent the claimant engaging with others "for the majority of the time."
>
> Thus, if the effect of having to leave his home unaccompanied, or to enter unfamiliar buildings, is to cause distress which prevents the claimant then being able to engage with someone unfamiliar, … 16(c) could apply, even if the claimant would have been perfectly capable of engaging with that unfamiliar person if he had been accompanied by friend or family, or if he had been in familiar surroundings.
>
> Thus, the Claimant in the present case was not in my judgment prevented from satisfying 16(c) merely because it was not the process of interacting with unfamiliar persons per se which caused her difficulty" (paras 12–14).

In *SSWP v LC (ESA)* [2014] UKUT 268 (AAC), Judge Williams agreed with Judge Ward's comments on "social contact" in *AR v SSWP (ESA)* [2013] UKUT 446 (AAC) and with Judge Mark's "persuasive analysis" of the meaning of "always" in *LM v SSWP (ESA)* [2013] UKUT 552 (AAC). Judge Williams considered that it "can be read as meaning "every day" but not "every moment", something important where the problems of a claimant are variable. His construction of "always" was, however, made without knowing of the decision of the Court of Session in *SSWP v Brade* [2014] AACR 29 (see annotation to ESA Regs 2008 reg.34(2)), and reads "always" somewhat more narrowly than the Court of Session which saw it as connoting "cannot 'for the majority of the time' engage". In addition, his decision was made before that in *JC v SSWP (ESA)* [2014] UKUT 352 (AAC); [2015] AACR 6 in which a panel of three Upper Tribunal Judges considered this activity and the case law on it, in particular the conflicting approaches of Judge Parker in *KB v SSWP (ESA)* [2013] UKUT 152 (AAC) and Judge Ward in *AR*, above. Insofar as other decisions are at variance with that of the Three-Judge Panel, *JC* is the authoritative decision to be followed.

In *JC*, the panel considered it "common ground" that the phrases "coping with social engagement" in the definition of the activity and "engagement in social contact" in the definition of the descriptor have the same meaning (para.6). It accepted the submission that "the Activities and their descriptors are intended to assess whether a person is able to engage with others for the purpose of work" (para.16). It also agreed with Judge Wikeley's comments in para.19 of his decision in *AS v SSWP (ESA)* [2013] UKUT 587 (AAC) that the activities and descriptors must be "applied on their own terms, but understood against the backdrop of the modern workplace" (para.16). The panel took the view that the differences between Judges Parker and Ward were less than appeared at first sight (para.22). Like Judge Ward it disagreed with Judge Parker that "social" simply meant "relations with other human beings" and did not "carry connotations of leisure and pleasure", but, unlike Judge Ward, did not accept that Parliament's intention was directed only at the difficulties in communication experienced by these with Autistic Spectrum Disorder (ASD) or similar difficulties, although it agreed that Parliament would have had the difficulties of those with ASD in mind (para.25). Instead, the causes "referred to in the Activities and their Descriptors" when read in the context of other relevant provisions in the legislation "show that the intention was not so confined but was directed to the possible impact of a wider range of impairments or disorders" (para.26). The panel saw the words of the definitions in the Activities and Descriptors at issue as a whole and the underlying statutory purposes as being "the most important factors that determine the nature and quality of the behaviour and communications covered by the Activities and their descriptors" (para. 27). Applying these factors requires decision-makers and tribunals to consider the following:

"(i) the range of meanings in common usage of the individual words that are used and so of "coping", "engagement", "social" and "contact" in the context of their combined effect,

(ii) the causes referred to in the Activities for the problems with coping with and engaging in social contact,

(iii) the causes referred to in the Descriptors and their link with the relevant cognitive impairment or mental disorder, and

(iv) the underlying purposes of the legislation and so of the assessments" (para.27).

Given the underlying purposes (whether a person is able to engage with others for the purpose of work and the context of the modern workplace), the panel could not endorse limitation to

"the nature and quality of the contact or engagement . . . to contact for pleasure or leisure or characterised by friendliness, geniality or companionship and so the choices that that involves [since such a limitation] would be surprising because that limitation (a) would exclude aspects of communication in the workplace, and (b) would not take proper account of the distinction in the descriptors between communication with people with whom the claimant is familiar and all communication. Indeed, it seems to us that points (a) and (b) dictate that the tests in the Activities and their Descriptors extend to contact for the purposes of work and so to contact with other characteristics and purposes that involve different degrees of choice or no choice because they relate to a structured situation or professional relationship (e.g. doctor and patient, lawyer and client)" (para.28).

On that basis the panel agreed with Judge Parker and the Secretary of State that, taken in isolation, "social" is a reference to "with other human beings" (para.29). However, since "social" is not isolated but qualifies "engagement" or "contact", this left open

"the nature and quality of the "engagement" or "contact" that is precluded or not possible for the given reasons and thus the assessment of what "engagement or contact with other people" the claimant can cope with due to his cognitive impairment or mental disorder" (para.30).

Key elements here, viewing "coping" and "engagement" in the context of the statutory purposes underlying assessment, were ones of "reciprocity, give and take, initiation and response" (para.32). These can be demonstrated not only by contact characterised by friendliness, geniality or companionship but also "without those elements (and the choices they involve) being present" such as "is often the case in the workplace and elsewhere", although those other contexts might also sometimes display them (para.32). The panel usefully pointed to examples which could equally demonstrate "the necessary degree of reciprocity, give and take, initiation and response": buying a ticket or groceries; contact with a medical examiner or other professional; conversation with a stranger on a park bench or elsewhere; or contact with the First-tier Tribunal itself (para.33). The panel saw the issues, fact finding and value judgements involved as eminently suitable for the First-tier Tribunal, and in the view of the panel:

9.424

"it is open to a decision maker to base his decision on an example or examples chosen from a wide range of situations. Whether the evidence and findings relating to the claimant's communications with others and behaviour in the chosen example or examples have the necessary degree of reciprocity, give and take, initiation and response raises issues of fact and degree and of judgment having regard to all the circumstances relating to them. As with other such issues, the authorities show that it is not practical or appropriate to identify the statutory criterion by reference to abstract examples or by reference to a general classification or description other than the statutory test" (para.34).

The proper approach for a tribunal in each case is to consider and determine how

"The nature and quality of the examples of communications and behaviour they take into account (and thus the reciprocity, give and take, initiation and response shown thereby) would, for the reasons given in the Activities and their Descriptors, be likely to be an effective barrier to the claimant working" (para.35).

The panel accepted that, because the conceptual test thus set out involves value judgments, this leaves "room for different decision-makers applying the right approach in the right way to reach different answers" (para.36 read with paras 9–12).

Good decision-making here involves carrying out the necessary fact-finding "separately from, although with an eye to, the value judgements that have to be applied to those findings" so as to identify and particularise "by reference to primary facts, the situations and events that will be taken into account and so the bedrock of the decision" (para.38). To reach their decision the tribunal must

"address and decide whether those findings show that:

(i) the claimant has cognitive impairment or mental disorder,
(ii) a causative link between that impairment or disorder and his difficulty relating to others or significant distress, and
(iii) a causative link between that difficulty and distress and a preclusion for all of the time or an impossibility for a majority of the time of contact with all other people, or those who are unfamiliar to the claimant, that has the necessary degree of reciprocity, give and take, initiation and response.

In addressing whether the contact with other people has the necessary nature and quality the tribunal should consider in each individual case how the nature and quality of the communications and behaviour would impact on the ability of the individual to work and so whether or not it would be an effective barrier to him working" (paras 38–39).

As regards the first case under appeal, the panel considered that the tribunal had erred in law in that it may not have understood or applied the statutory test correctly. It had seemed to be concerned about the claimant being able to be helped by someone. The panel did not consider that a person could properly be regarded "as able to engage in social contact if she or he can do so only if accompanied by someone, at least without further explanation as to how it is envisaged that that might be realistic in the workplace" (para.45). The matter was remitted for decision by another tribunal to be decided in light of the guidance proffered by the panel's decision. The panel found no error of law in the second case under appeal (paras 49–60).

9.425   *Activity 17: Appropriateness of behaviour with other people, due to cognitive impairment or mental disorder:* This was revised to remove some of the more negative phraseology of its predecessor, to find more "neutral" terms than "bizarre" or "outbursts". Gradation between descriptors is set in terms of the frequency of the episodes of the relevant behaviour: (a) "on a daily basis"; (b) "frequently"; (c) "occasionally". The episodes must in each case be "uncontrollable". In each case, the behaviour must be "aggressive or disinhibited". A key standard in each descriptor is whether this behaviour "would be unreasonable in any workplace".

As regards descriptor (a), in *WT v SSWP (ESA)* [2013] UKUT 556 (AAC), Judge

Ward considered the meaning of "on a daily basis". While this was a decision dealing with identical wording in Sch.3, activity/descriptor 14, Judge Ward also applied it to descriptor (a), its "mirror descriptor". Rather than merely deploy a dictionary definition, he took the "mischief" approach to interpretation and reasoned thus:

"The mischief that the descriptor must be intended to remedy is the creation of an unsafe or otherwise unacceptable work environment for co-workers. The way in which the avoidance of that is accomplished is to exclude from the workplace those who, due to their mental health condition exhibit certain behaviour. If on virtually every day that they were at work they displayed such behaviour, would the fact that there were very rare days on which they did not prevent them from falling within the meaning of the descriptor? To answer "yes" to that question would not be to address the mischief. The descriptor must, then, be interpreted more widely than literally every day.

I fortify myself in this view because the ordinary meaning of the words "on a daily basis" seem to me to connote a lesser test than "every day". The phrase is not confined to events which happen literally every day. Someone might be said to read a particular newspaper on a daily basis even though there were periods when they did not, such as where they were abroad on holiday when it was not available. Walking the dog on a daily basis is an activity which may be interrupted by the ill-health of either dog or walker, but a short break would not change the very regular nature of the activity or make that description inapt.

The words "on a daily basis", then, in the context of schedule 3 descriptor 14, and its mirror descriptor under schedule 2, regulation 17 (a), means certainly more than for the majority of the time, that being the regulation 34 (2) test, and must mean more than frequently, that being the test of periodicity in regulation 17(b), but it does not mean literally every day or even on every working day. The essence is of this being an enduring position; one which is happening regularly, constantly or continually. It is for the tribunal to find the facts as to the frequency of the behaviour set out in the descriptor, and then apply this approach to those facts with their usual common sense" (paras 40-42).

As regards descriptor (c), in *KE v SSWP (ESA)* [2013] UKUT 370 (AAC), Judge Williams noted that "the incidence [of disinhibited behaviour] is at a lower level of occurrence but at a higher level of intensity than the previous test, although the underlying issue manifested by these forms of conduct is the same" (para.17). It now attracts three more points than its predecessor (9 rather than 6). The claimant had several times been required to leave the Jobcentre because of abusive and insulting things he said rather than did, "a classic form of disinhibited behaviour". As regards the criterion "unreasonable in any workplace, Judge Williams thought a Jobcentre unlikely to "apply a lower test than an employer would be expected to apply" (para.18).

In *WC v SSWP (ESA)* [2014] UKUT 363, Judge Rowley commended to tribunals considering descriptors under this Activity the following list of questions constituting a "methodical approach":

"(a) Does the claimant have cognitive impairment or mental disorder?

(b) If so, does that cause the claimant to behave in the way described by the descriptor, namely:

    (i) Does the claimant have episodes of aggressive or disinhibited behaviour?
    (ii) Are any such episodes uncontrollable?
    (iii) How often do they occur (noting the words of the descriptor: "on a daily basis," "frequently," "occasionally,").
    (iv) Would such behaviour be unreasonable in any workplace?" (para.10).

Judge Rowley, adopting Judge Gray's observations in the quotation from *WT*, considered that the relevant behaviour could include "sufficiently serious verbal aggression" since its use "may well create an unacceptable work environment for co-workers, or indeed others with whom the person exhibiting the behaviour may come into contact in the workplace. It would be wrong to say that such conduct can never be enough to satisfy activity 17. Further, in my view it is not necessary for the claimant to have been involved in a fight or argument for activity 17 to apply. There may be examples where his or her behaviour has been aggressive or disinhibited but has not led to another person responding by fighting or arguing. Indeed, in many cases when faced with such behaviour, some people's natural reaction is to walk away. That does not necessarily make the aggressive or disinhibited behaviour any less serious, nor does it necessarily render it any more acceptable to co-workers or others in the workplace. In each case it will be for the tribunal to consider the evidence, find the facts and decide, in the light of those findings, whether a particular claimant's behaviour, whether physical or verbal, is sufficient to satisfy the relevant criteria" (para.16).

Moreover, since the wording of Activity 17 applies to "any workplace", he rejected as an "unnecessary gloss" on that wording the submission of the Secretary of State that "the claimant's behaviour would have to be considered unacceptable in an average workplace such as a call centre" (para.18).

It is vital to note that under ESA Regs 2008, reg.19(2), (5) incapability of performing the activity in respect of any descriptor in Pt 2 of Sch.2 must arise from a specific mental illness or disablement. Alcohol misuse in itself is not such a disablement. To rank as disablement the misuse of alcohol must rank as "alcohol dependency" in terms of the "constellation of markers" found in quotations from *R(DLA) 6/06* in the Three-Judge Panel's decision in *JG v SSWP (ESA)* [2013] UKUT 37 (AAC); [2013] AACR 23. Accordingly, in *DR v SSWP (ESA)* [2014] UKUT 188 (AAC); [2014] AACR 38, Judge May held that the tribunal were right to hold that the descriptors did not apply. Moreover, he was persuaded that

"the volume of alcohol the claimant is said to drink on a daily basis would not in itself amount to the disinhibited behaviour referred to in descriptors 17(a) in Schedule 2 and 14 in Schedule 3. I see the force in Mr Webster's submission that disinhibited behaviour requires the context of an inhibition. I cannot see, and it has not been established, what the inhibition in this case is and how the drinking of a certain volume of alcohol amounts in itself to disinhibited behaviour. Disinhibited behaviour may result as a consequence of drinking specific quantities of alcohol but that is not the basis upon which the claimant's argument is put. Mr Orr seeks to widen "disinhibition" beyond the scope of what the statutory provisions can bear. The activity for both descriptors relates to the appropriateness of behaviour "with" other people, which suggests that the descriptor is intended to be applied in respect of behaviour which is more than the passive drinking of alcohol" (para.8).

                           Regulation 34(1)

ASSESSMENT OF WHETHER A CLAIMANT HAS LIMITED CAPABILITY FOR   **9.426**
WORK-RELATED ACTIVITY

Activity	*Descriptors*
[² 1. Mobilising unaided by another person with or without a walking stick, manual wheelchair or other aid if such aid is normally, or could reasonably be, worn or used.]	Cannot either: (a) mobilise more than 50 metres on level ground without stopping in order to avoid significant discomfort or exhaustion; or (b) repeatedly mobilise 50 metres within a reasonable timescale because of significant discomfort or exhaustion.
2. Transferring from one seated position to another.	Cannot move between one seated position and another seated position located next to one another without receiving physical assistance from another person.
3. Reaching.	Cannot raise either arm as if to put something in the top pocket of a coat or jacket.
4. Picking up and moving or transferring by the use of the upper body and arms (excluding standing, sitting, bending or kneeling and all other activities specified in this Schedule).	Cannot pick up and move a 0.5 litre carton full of liquid.
5. Manual dexterity.	[³Cannot press a button (such as a telephone keypad) with either hand or cannot turn the pages of a book with either hand.]
[² 6. Making self understood through speaking, writing, typing, or other means which are normally, or could reasonably be, used, unaided by another person.]	Cannot convey a simple message, such as the presence of a hazard.
[² 7. Understanding communication by: (i) verbal means (such as hearing or lip reading) alone, (ii) non-verbal means (such as reading 16 point print or Braille) alone, or (iii) a combination of (i) and (ii), using any aid that is normally, or could reasonably be, used, unaided by another person.]	Cannot understand a simple message [³,such as the location of a fire escape due to sensory impairment [³...] .
[² 8. Absence or loss of control whilst conscious leading to extensive evacuation of the bowel and/or voiding of the bladder, other than enuresis (bed-wetting), despite the wearing or use of any aids or adaptations which are normally, or could reasonably be, worn or used.]	At least once a week experiences: (a) loss of control leading to extensive evacuation of the bowel and/or voiding of the bladder; or (b) substantial leakage of the contents of a collecting device sufficient to require the individual to clean themselves and change clothing.

Activity	Descriptors
9. Learning tasks.	Cannot learn how to complete a simple task, such as setting an alarm clock, due to cognitive impairment or mental disorder.
10. Awareness of hazard.	Reduced awareness of everyday hazards, due to cognitive impairment or mental disorder, leads to a significant risk of: (a) injury to self or others; or (b) damage to property or possessions such that [³ the claimant requires] supervision for the majority of the time to maintain safety.
11. Initiating and completing personal action (which means planning, organisation, problem solving, prioritising or switching tasks).	Cannot, due to impaired mental function, reliably initiate or complete at least 2 sequential personal actions.
12. Coping with change.	Cannot cope with any change, due to cognitive impairment or mental disorder, to the extent that day to day life cannot be managed.
13. Coping with social engagement, due to cognitive impairment or mental disorder.	Engagement in social contact is always precluded due to difficulty relating to others or significant distress experienced by the [³ claimant].
14. Appropriateness of behaviour with other people, due to cognitive impairment or mental disorder.	Has, on a daily basis, uncontrollable episodes of aggressive or disinhibited behaviour that would be unreasonable in any workplace.
15. Conveying food or drink to the mouth.	(a) Cannot convey food or drink to the claimant's own mouth without receiving physical assistance from someone else; (b) Cannot convey food or drink to the claimant's own mouth without repeatedly [³ stopping or] experiencing breathlessness or severe discomfort; (c) Cannot convey food or drink to the claimant's own mouth without receiving regular prompting given by someone else in the claimant's physical presence; or (d) Owing to a severe disorder of mood or behaviour, fails to convey food or drink to the claimant's own mouth without receiving: (i) physical assistance from someone else; or (ii) regular prompting given by someone else in the claimant's presence.

Activity	Descriptors
16. Chewing or swallowing food or drink.	(a) Cannot chew or swallow food or drink;
	(b) Cannot chew or swallow food or drink without repeatedly stopping, experiencing breathlessness or severe discomfort;
	(c) Cannot chew or swallow food or drink without repeatedly receiving regular prompting given by someone else in the claimant's presence; or
	(d) Owing to a severe disorder of mood or behaviour, fails to:
	(i) chew or swallow food or drink; or
	(ii) chew or swallow food or drink
	without regular prompting given by someone else in the claimant's presence.]

Amendments

1. Employment and Support Allowance (Limited Capability for Work and Limited Capability for Work-Related Activity) (Amendment) Regulations 2011 (SI 2011/228) reg.4(2) (March 28, 2011).

2. Employment and Support Allowance (Amendment) Regulations 2012 (SI 2012/3096) reg.5(2) (January 28, 2013, subject to application, transitional and savings provisions in reg.2 of this amending instrument, para.9.554).

3. Social Security (Miscellaneous Amendments) (No.3) Regulations 2013 (SI 2013/2536) reg.13(34) (October 29, 2013).

Definitions

"claimant"—see WRA 2007 s.24(1).

General Note

Establishing limited capability for work-related activity might be said to be the central condition of entitlement to support component. The assumption behind ESA is that the vast majority of claimants, if given the right support, are in fact capable of some work. Government anticipates that only some 10 per cent of claimants (those with more severe health conditions) will be entitled to the support component and so not be subject to work-related activity conditionality requirements. Entry to this protected support group depends on it being established—generally through a work-related activity assessment (LCWRA) of a more stringent nature than the LCWA covered by reg.19 and Sch.2—that the claimant has limited capability for work-related activity: the LCWRA is thus the second element in the revised Work Capability Assessment.

Entry to the support group is based on someone demonstrating that they have a severe level of functional limitation. Until January 28, 2013, this was established when by reason of the claimant's physical or mental condition, at least one of the range of descriptors in this revised Sch.3 to the ESA Regs applies to the claimant. From that date, reg.34(3A) provides that in deciding which descriptor applies, incapability must arise in respect of descriptors 1 to 8, 15(a), 15(b), 16(a) and 16 (b), from a specific bodily disease or disablement or as a direct result of treatment provided by a registered medical practitioner for such a disease or disablement (para.

9.427

(3A)(a), (c)(i)). Similarly, as regards descriptors 9 to 14, 15(c), 15(d), 16(c) and 16 (d), incapability must arise from a specific mental illness or disablement; or as a direct result of treatment provided by a registered medical practitioner for such an illness or disablement (para.(3A)(b), (c)(i)). Note that for some cases after January 28, 2013, for a six month period, the previous version of reg.34 can be applicable (see reg.2 of the amending instrument, below, para.9.554). Under both original and amended forms of reg.34, assessment has to take account of prostheses, aids and appliances (para.(3)). It is submitted here that the key elements of IB case law and ESA case law which carry across into interpreting and applying the provisions in Sch.2 on the revised LCWA will also apply here: decide in the light of the totality of the evidence, making a careful appraisal of differing medical reports; the need for careful attention to detail; the concept of reasonable regularity (the test is not a snapshot); relevant factors of pain, discomfort and of fears for the claimant's health; and the need carefully to approach conditions which vary and fluctuate. But here reg.34(2) makes clear that a:

> "descriptor applies to a claimant if that descriptor applies to the claimant for the majority of the time or, as the case may be, on the majority of the occasions on which the claimant undertakes or attempts to undertake the activity described by that descriptor."

This, in broad terms appears to put on a statutory footing for the LCWRA assessment, the "reasonable regularity" test approved for incapacity benefit in *R(IB) 2/99* and by analogy applicable to ESA assessments (*EH v SSWP (ESA)* [2011] UKUT 21 (AAC), para.31). In considering issues under Sch.3, a tribunal should also consider the full ESA85 report and not simply the section stating the EMP's opinion on the Sch.3 issues, as well as other applicable medical evidence with respect to the claimant (*EH v SSWP (ESA)* [2011] UKUT 21 (AAC), paras 27–30, 41–44). The focus, as in Sch.2, should be on "the claimant's functional ability to perform the particular aspect of the activity covered by a descriptor" (*EH v SSWP (ESA)* [2011] UKUT 21 (AAC), para.38, approving Judge Jacobs's in *GS v SSWP (ESA)* [2010] UKUT 244 (AAC), para.14). On the importance of a consistent approach to the descriptors under Sch.2 and Sch.3 respectively, see *SSWP v JL (ESA)* [2018] UKUT 291 (AAC).

9.428   There is no scoring system and the criteria are deliberately more stringent than in the LCWA. In Committee, the Minister for Employment and Welfare Reform explained both characteristics:

> "The levels of functional limitation used in the descriptors for determining limited capability for work-related activity are greater because we intend to place in the support group only the minority of customers who are so severely impaired that it would not be reasonable to require them to undertake work-related activity . . . People with less severe functional limitations across a range of descriptors might score highly and be inappropriately included in the support group when they might benefit from work-related activity . . . A number of case studies were provided in the background information, which hon. Members will find helpful. [See DWP, *Welfare Reform Bill: Draft Regulations and Supporting Material* (January 2007), pp.13–17.] Under the revised PCA, someone with a moderate learning disability would score 50 points. They would be significantly above the 15-point threshold, but we clearly would not wish to put even someone with 50 points into the support group automatically, because we are determined to ensure that the new system does not write off people with learning disabilities. The technical groups considered all the options. A crude points-based system would have unintended consequences." (*Hansard*, Standing Committee A, October 19, 2006 (afternoon), col.120 (Mr Jim Murphy MP)).

In *CD v SSWP (ESA)* [2012] UKUT (AAC) 289; [2013] AACR 12, Judge Levenson considered the relationship between the terms of descriptors in Sch.2 and the correlative provision in Sch.3, albeit in the context of the Schedules as at March 27, 2011:

"Irrespective of what the Minister told the relevant committee, looking at the wording of the legislation and regulations I cannot find any support for the Secretary of State's argument that a person qualifying under Sch.3 must inevitably be more severely impaired than one who qualifies under Sch.2. The claimant's reference to the reaching descriptors [now Sch.2 para.3(a); Sch.3, para.3] is persuasive on this point" (para.21).

In *CN v SSWP (ESA)* [2014] UKUT 286 (AAC), Judge Markus applied *CD v SSWP (ESA)* [2012] UKUT 289 (AAC); [2013] AACR 12 to find erroneous in law a tribunal decision finding the claimant not to have limited capability for work-related activity when it had accepted that he had limited capability for work without reviewing the basis on which the decision-maker had proceeded (he had used the "old" pre January 2011Sch.2), since that limited capability was not disputed. Judge Markus accepted that there are more substantial differences in wording between the two relevant descriptors in this case than between those in issue in *CD*, but was of the opinion that a claimant who fell within old activity 16(a) would fall within new activity 13(a) in the current version of Sch.2 and so would also fall within activity 11 in Sch.3. Moreover a person who satisfies activity 17(a) under the old Sch.2 must satisfy activity 12 of the current Sch.3, as long as the inability is due to cognitive impairment or mental disorder.

There is an equivalent of the "exceptional circumstances" provision applicable to the limited capability for work question, considered above. A claimant who does not pass the LCWRA can nonetheless be treated as having the requisite limited capability for work-related activity grounding membership of the support group where, by reason of the specific disease or bodily or mental disablement from which s/he suffers, "there would be a substantial risk to the mental or physical health of any person if the claimant were found not to have limited capability for work-related activity" (reg.35(2)).

There were only 11 activities in the original Sch.3. They covered walking or moving on level ground; rising from sitting and transferring from one seated position to another; picking up and moving or transferring by means of the upper body and arms; reaching; manual dexterity; continence; maintaining personal hygiene; eating and drinking (conveying food or drink to the mouth and chewing or swallowing it); learning or comprehension in the completion of tasks; personal action (planning, organisation, problem solving, prioritising or switching tasks); and communication. The terms of the descriptors were also more stringent than in the LCWA, to avoid removing too many people from the group which affords incentive to engage in work-related activity and thus denying them the opportunity to take steps to make real their fundamental right to work. Thus, as regards walking, the single descriptor (since amended) could only be met where a claimant could not "walk" more than 30 metres without repeatedly stopping, experiencing breathlessness or severe discomfort. "Walk" covered walking with a walking stick, other aid or crutches, each if normally used; and embraced the claimant moving by manually propelling a wheelchair. That on rising from sitting etc, required in effect that the claimant fulfilled two of the 15 point descriptors in the LCWA. Most, with counterparts in the LCWA, were couched in terms equivalent to the more difficult of their 15 point descriptors. That original Sch.2 will apply to all decisions made before March 28, 2011 and also beyond that date where ESA questionnaires had before that date been sent out to claimants or notified persons under the Migration Regulations (transferees from IB, IS (incapacity based) or SDA. But that concession on questionnaires sent out before March 28 will cease after six months (September 28, 2011) (see reg.2 of the amending Regulations).

Those meeting the LCWRA test (or satisfying the "exceptional circumstances" provision) were placed in the support group and received the support component without having to satisfy work-related activity conditions, although they could

voluntarily participate in those programmes. Their position could be reviewed periodically or where there had been a change of circumstances in the claimant's physical or mental condition or it was thought that a previous determination was made in
ignorance of or a mistake as to some material fact (reg.34(4), (5)). The threshold for
membership of the support group was high; many claimants in receipt of the middle
and higher rates of Disability Living Allowance (DLA) may not meet it. Those who
fail to establish limited capability for work-related activity instead receive the work-
related activity component.

Under the revised LCWRA assessment the subject of this commentary, now comprising 16 activities, the threshold remains high, and the same basic rules on
the support group continue to apply. But Government anticipated that the
revisions and reformulations effected by the *Review* and *CMA* honing (see
further the commentary to Sch.2, above) would mean a slight expansion of the
numbers allocated to the support group because of a relaxed mobility descriptor (Activity 1 now aligns its requisite distance at 50 metres, as opposed to 30
metres, the same as its highest scoring LCWA counterpart), changes to the
mental function assessment and the addition of another sensory impairment-
related support group (*Review*, para.5.2). As regards Activities 1–15, each activity
and single descriptor corresponds to descriptor (a) (usually the highest scoring
but always the one hardest to satisfy) in the corresponding Activity in the LCWA
in the revised Sch.2, above. Consequently, it is submitted that any case law on
corresponding terms in those revised Sch.2 descriptors is applicable to those in
Sch.3, as effective from March 28, 2011. Note, however, that the numbering
does not correspond as between Schs 2 and 3. Thus in Sch.3 (LCWRA), there
is no equivalent of Sch.2 (LCWA) activity 8 (Navigation and maintaining safety,
using a guide dog or other aid if normally used), activity 10 (Consciousness
during waking moments) or activity 15 (getting about). Similarly, there is in
Sch.2 (LCWA) itself, no equivalent of Sch.3 (LCWRA) multi-descriptor activities 15 (conveying food or drink to the mouth) or 16 (Chewing or swallowing
food or drink). Instead, persons covered by those activities in the terms set out
in Sch.3 (LCWRA) are from March 28, 2011 treated as having limited capability
for work under ESA Regs, reg.20(g).

On the need to interpret the terms of both this Sch and Sch.2 against the background of a working environment, see the annotation to Sch.2 *(Approaching the
Interpretation of the Schedule as a whole) (the LCWA is not a snapshot—the need for an
approach characterized by "reasonableness").*

Interpreting specific activities and descriptors

9.429 *Activity 1: "Mobilising unaided by another person with or without a walking stick, manual
wheelchair or other aid if such aid can reasonably be used":* This descriptor contains
two tests. As Judge Williams put it in *HD v SSWP (ESA)* [2014] UKUT 72 (AAC):

> "the "cannot either" ... "or" wording is properly interpreted as meaning "one or
> the other of (a) and (b)". In other words, a claimant who can satisfy the Secretary
> of State or a tribunal that he or she cannot mobilise to the level of one or other of
> (a) and (b) is entitled to be regarded as meeting the descriptor as a whole even if
> he or she can mobilise to the extent that the other is met" (para.4, citing para.15
> of his decision granting leave to appeal).

The Secretary of State accepted that interpretation (*ibid.*, para.5) to the same effect
see *GC v SSWP (ESA)* [2014] UKUT 117 (AAC), applying *HD*, and *KB v SSWP
(ESA)* [2014] UKUT 126 (AAC), both decisions on Activity 1 in Sch.2. In *AH v
SSWP (ESA)* [2013] UKUT 118 (AAC); [2013] AACR 32, Judge Jacobs pointed
up the difference in wording between descriptors 1(a) and 1(b). With 1(a), he saw
it as impossible to read into it "the need for regularity" (para.14). In contrast the
wording of 1(b), taking due account also of reg.34(2), demands mobilising "repeatedly", without "significant discomfort or exhaustion" and within a "reasonable
timescale". Judge Jacobs saw these as "normal words in everyday use" and as being
coloured by their context. But he saw

"no reason why they should have a different meaning just because they appear in Schedule 3. The purpose of that Schedule is to identify claimants who are not required to take part in work-related activity. But it does so by reference to the nature and extent of their disabilities, not by reference to work-related activity itself. The effect of coming within Schedule 3 may differ from the effect of coming within Schedule 2, but the criteria for classifying claimants are the same. I am not going to attempt to define what these words mean. That would be wrong. It would be the wrong approach to statutory interpretation and would trespass impermissibly into the role of the First-tier Tribunal. It is not for the Upper Tribunal to give more specific content to the law than the language used in the legislation. The Upper Tribunal will not decide that 'repeatedly' means five times, ten times or any other number. Nor will the Upper Tribunal decide that 'reasonable timescale' means five seconds, five minutes or any other time.
The correct approach was explained by Lord Upjohn in *Customs and Excise Commissioners* v *Top Ten Promotions Ltd* [1969] 1 WLR 1163, at 1171:

'It is highly dangerous, if not impossible, to attempt to place an accurate definition upon a word in common use; you can look up examples of its many uses if you want to in the Oxford Dictionary but that does not help on definition; in fact it probably only shows that the word normally defies definition. The task of the court in construing statutory language such as that which is before your Lordships is to look at the mischief at which the Act is directed and then, in that light, to consider whether as a matter of common sense and every day usage the known, proved or admitted or properly inferred facts of the particular case bring the case within the ordinary meaning of the words used by Parliament.'

The key to applying the words of Activity 1 lies in making findings of fact relevant to those words that are as specific as the evidence allows. And, if the claimant is present at the hearing, the tribunal should ensure that it obtains evidence that is sufficient to that purpose. Just to take one example: the tribunal should have probed Mr H's evidence that he 'could not repeatedly do 50 metres'. How far could he walk before stopping? What made him stop? How did he feel? How soon could he proceed? How often could he repeat that process? This was particularly important in this case, because of the content of Mr H's evidence to the tribunal. At least as it was recorded by the judge—the record of proceedings does not have to be verbatim—his evidence was expressed in the language of the Schedule. The tribunal had to obtain evidence that would allow it to assess Mr H's answers by reference to that language. It could not do that if the evidence repeated that language. The tribunal would at least need to know what Mr H meant by 'repeatedly', as he might not be using it in the same way as in Activity 1" (paras 18–21).

As regards "could reasonably be … used", Upper Tribunal Judges are divided on the permissible range of matters to examine, and the issue of the proper approach to take is to be decided by a tribunal of three Upper Tribunal Judges. See further the annotation to Sch.2, Activity 1, above.

Activity 7: "understanding communication"; Descriptor "cannot understand a simpler message such as the location of a fire escape due to sensory impairment": In *AT and VC v SSWP (ESA)* [2015] UKUT 445 (AAC); [2016] AACR 8, Judge Markus QC was "satisfied that Activity 7 in Schedule 3 was intended to correspond with the highest descriptor in Activity 7 of Schedule 2" (para.53). Furthermore, as with Sch.2, Activity 7 (both in its current and previous formulations: see para 54) "applied to a claimant who was unable to communicate by either verbal means or non-verbal means and it was not necessary for the claimant to be unable to communicate by both means" (para.53). Judge Markus's decision was followed in the context of the post-January 2013 version of the regulations by Judge Ward in *CM v SSWP (ESA)* [2016] UKUT 242 (AAC). **9.430**

Activity 9: "learning tasks"; Descriptor: "Cannot learn how to complete a simple task, such as setting an alarm clock, due to cognitive impairment or mental disorder: See the **9.431** following guidance from Judge Rowley on this activity in *Secretary of State for Work and Pensions v AT (ESA)* [2017] UKUT 338 (AAC):

> *"cannot learn"*
> 3. The activity is concerned with a claimant's ability to "learn" a new task, i.e. their ability to absorb, understand and retain information. As the WCA Handbook recognises, different people learn in different ways. They may prefer to watch a visual demonstration, have verbal instruction or read instructions. An inability to learn using one method would not generally lead to an overall inability to learn a new task if another way could be employed.
>
> *"how to complete a simple task"*
> 4. "Simple task" is not defined. It would be inappropriate for me to offer any further definition, save perhaps to note the obvious - a simple task is one which is easy and straightforward. It is unlikely to involve more than one or two steps.
>
> *"such as setting an alarm clock"*
> 5. The words "such as" are important. They confirm that the illustration given – of setting an alarm clock – is merely an example. Other instances may need to be considered by decision makers and tribunals. Further examples are listed in the WCA Handbook:
>
> > "Brushing teeth. This would involve remembering to put toothpaste onto a brush and brushing all areas of teeth.
> > Washing. This would involve the ability to use soap/shower gel and wash their body.
> > Brushing hair.
> > Turning on the television/using basic functions on the TV remote control.
> > Getting a glass of water."

Judge Rowley also stressed the further fundamental requirement that the inability to learn a simple task be "due to cognitive impairment or mental disorder", as reinforced by the requirements of reg.34(6)(b).

9.432 *Activity 12: "coping with change": Descriptor: "Cannot cope with any change, due to cognitive or mental disorder, to the extent that day to day life cannot be managed":* In *CH v SSWP (ESA)* [2013] UKUT 207 (AAC), Judge Fordham held that

> "the word 'any' brings in changes of differing degree of significance. An individual will fail if, the majority of the time: (a) they cannot cope with significant change but (b) they can cope with less significant change. That is the consequence of the word 'any' in descriptor 12. An individual will succeed if, the majority of the time they cannot cope with 'any' change, even a less significant change. It is not of itself fatal that the claimant can sometimes cope with a change" (para.7).

9.433 *Activity 13: "coping with social engagement due to cognitive impairment or mental disorder"; Descriptor: "engagement in social contact is always precluded due to difficulty relating to others or significant distress experienced by the individual":* In *KB v SSWP* (ESA) [2013] UKUT 152 (AAC), Judge Parker considered the relationship between this wording (the requisite of "always") and the stipulation in reg.34(2) that "a descriptor applies to a claimant if that descriptor applies to the claimant for the majority of the time or, as the case may be, on the majority of the occasions on which the claimant undertakes or attempts to undertake the activity described by that descriptor". Having looked at definitions of "always" in the *Concise Oxford Dictionary*, Judge Parker concluded that neither this activity and descriptor, nor its counterpart in Activity 16 of Sch.2 set out an "all or nothing test". Rather "always" here

> "means 'repeatedly' or 'persistent' or 'often'. A 'majority' may be constituted by events which happen only on 50.1% of the possible occasions, but a greater frequency is required by the use of the word 'always'. It is a question of degree, but a fact finding tribunal is eminently suited to applying these subtle nuances of dif-

ference in a common sense way. It suffices to say in the present case, that because a claimant attends one tribunal hearing, and his GP accepts that he comes to the surgery very occasionally, does not *necessarily* entail the conclusion, as the tribunal clearly considered that it did, that it 'cannot be said that engagement in social contact is always precluded'" (para.14).

Judge Fordham took much the same approach in *CH v SSWP (ESA)* [2013] UKUT 207 (AAC) (para.8).

As regards "social engagement" and "social contact", Judge Parker, accepting the approach advanced by the Secretary of State's representative, thought that "social" to be "a simple reference to relations with other human beings" carrying no connotations of "leisure, pleasure or mutuality", so that a tribunal could properly look at evidence about business visits or contacts with professionals, as well as with friends, relatives and strangers. It was not tied to contact in an informal setting (see paras 15–17). What conduct constitutes the necessary "contact" or engagement" is

"a matter of fact and degree, likewise eminently suitable for consideration by a tribunal as a matter of common sense having regard to all the circumstances. At one end of the scale, if a claimant sat silently throughout his tribunal hearing then, outwith exceptional circumstances, a reasonable tribunal could hold that this did not amount to the necessary 'contact' or 'engagement'; similarly, monosyllabic responses in such a context is a borderline scenario. However, where, as here, the claimant communicated with the tribunal on an extensive basis, according to the record, then a conclusion that such did not amount to any 'social engagement' or 'social contact' would have been irrational" (para.18).

See also the annotation to Sch.2, Activity 16 for Judge Mark's narrower view that "always" did not mean "often" (*LM v SSWP (ESA)* [2013] UKUT 553 (AAC)), and for Judge Ward's disagreement with Judge Parker's interpretation of "social" (*AR v SSWP (ESA)* [2013] UKUT 446 (AAC)) and Judge Mark's qualified support for Judge Ward's approach (*LM v SSWP (ESA)* [2013] UKUT 553 (AAC)). See also, however, the annotation to reg.34(2) and the decision of the Court of Session in *SSWP v Brade* [2014] CSIH 39 XA81/13 (May 1, 2014); [2014] AACR 29.

See further the annotation to Sch.2, Activity 16 and in particular the decision of the three-judge panel in *JC v SSWP (ESA)* [2014] UKUT 352 (AAC); [2015] AACR 6, which follows Judge Parker on the meaning of "social", identifies the key elements of "engagement" and "coping" as "reciprocity, give and take, initiation and response", and identifies the conceptual test to be applied and the decision-making process to be followed for its application by tribunals.

Activity 14: Appropriateness of behaviour with other people, due to cognitive impairment or mental disorder: descriptor: Has, on a daily basis, uncontrollable episodes of aggressive or disinhibited behaviour that would be unreasonable in any workplace.

In *WT v SSWP (ESA)* [2013] UKUT 556 (AAC), Judge Ward considered the meaning of "on a daily basis". Rather than merely deploy a dictionary definition, he took the "mischief" approach to interpretation and reasoned thus:

"The mischief that the descriptor must be intended to remedy is the creation of an unsafe or otherwise unacceptable work environment for co-workers. The way in which the avoidance of that is accomplished is to exclude from the workplace those who, due to their mental health condition exhibit certain behaviour. If on virtually every day that they were at work they displayed such behaviour, would the fact that there were very rare days on which they did not prevent them from falling within the meaning of the descriptor? To answer "yes" to that question would not be to address the mischief. The descriptor must, then, be interpreted more widely than literally every day.

I fortify myself in this view because the ordinary meaning of the words "on a daily basis" seem to me to connote a lesser test than "every day". The phrase is not confined to events which happen literally every day. Someone might be said to read a particular newspaper on a daily basis even though there were periods when they did not, such as where they were abroad on holiday when it was not available. Walking the dog on a daily basis is an activity which may be interrupted by the ill-health of either dog or walker, but a short break would not change the very regular nature of the activity or make that description inapt.

The words "on a daily basis", then, in the context of schedule 3 descriptor 14, and its mirror descriptor under schedule 2, regulation 17 (a), means certainly more than for the majority of the time, that being the regulation 34 (2) test, and must mean more than frequently, that being the test of periodicity in regulation 17(b), but it does not mean literally every day or even on every working day. The essence is of this being an enduring position; one which is happening regularly, constantly or continually. It is for the tribunal to find the facts as to the frequency of the behaviour set out in the descriptor, and then apply this approach to those facts with their usual common sense" (paras 40–42).

It is vital to remember that under ESA Regs 2008 reg.34(6)(b), incapability of performing the activity in respect of this descriptor must arise from a specific mental illness or disablement. Alcohol misuse in itself is not such a disablement. To rank as disablement the misuse of alcohol must rank as "alcohol dependency" in terms of the "constellation of markers" found in quotations from *R(DLA) 6/06* in para.44 of the Three-Judge Panel's decision in *JG v SSWP (ESA)* [2013] UKUT 37 (AAC); [2013] AACR 23 (see annotation to ESA Regs 2008 reg.19) Accordingly, in *DR v SSWP (ESA)* [2014] UKUT 188 (AAC); [2014] AACR 38, Judge May held the tribunal were right to hold that the descriptor did not apply. Moreover, he was persuaded that:

> "the volume of alcohol the claimant is said to drink on a daily basis would not in itself amount to the disinhibited behaviour referred to in descriptors 17(a) in Schedule 2 and 14 in Schedule 3. I see the force in Mr Webster's submission that disinhibited behaviour requires the context of an inhibition. I cannot see, and it has not been established, what the inhibition in this case is and how the drinking of a certain volume of alcohol amounts in itself to disinhibited behaviour. Disinhibited behaviour may result as a consequence of drinking specific quantities of alcohol but that is not the basis upon which the claimant's argument is put. Mr Orr seeks to widen "disinhibition" beyond the scope of what the statutory provisions can bear. The activity for both descriptors relates to the appropriateness of behaviour "with" other people, which suggests that the descriptor is intended to be applied in respect of behaviour which is more than the passive drinking of alcohol" (para.8).

Activity 16: Chewing or swallowing food or drink: In *WC v SSWP (ESA)* [2015] UKUT 304 (AAC); [2016] AACR 1, Judge Wikeley held that (given that one cannot "chew" drink) "this phrase means, in effect, and adding words to ensure clarity of meaning", "cannot *either* chew *and* swallow food or *swallow* drink" (para. 1). That decision was considered by Judge Jacobs in *IC v SSWP (ESA)* [2015] UKUT 615 (AAC), where the specific question that arose was whether a claimant can satisfy either descriptor 16a or 16b on account of the difficulties he experiences as a result of his false teeth. Judge Jacobs held that there was simply no evidence that activity 16 could apply on the facts of the instant case, given the requirements of reg.34(6)(b); thus there was no evidence that the claimant's difficulties with his false teeth arose from a specific bodily disease or disablement or from treatment (para.13). Judge Jacobs continued, without deciding, to consider whether false teeth are and aid or appliance (within reg.34(3)(b)) or a prosthesis (within reg.35(3)(a)) (para.14). Judge Jacobs stressed further the importance of applying the statutory test, rather than a substitute test, and gave the following guidance:

> "16. This brings me to another way to frame the issue, which is to concentrate on the food rather than the chewing. As I put it in my preliminary observations: what sort of food is envisaged by the descriptor? Again, there is a range of possibilities.

It is not necessary to be able to eat any food, from the most tender to the toughest. That would set too demanding a standard. But liquidised food is a liquid, more akin to a drink than food, and does not require chewing.

17. A third, and better, way to frame the issue is to take the whole expression and ask: what is involved in chewing food? That at least preserves the immediate context. It makes the expression as a whole the object of the enquiry, rather than its individual components. It does not, though, produce any clear answer.

18. On any formulation, it is important to remember the context, which is a test of whether a claimant's capability for work and for work-related activity is restricted sufficiently to qualify for an employment and support allowance. The disability need not have a direct effect on the performance of work or work-related activity, as feeding oneself is not going to be involved in either case. So the scope of the Activity cannot be calibrated by its effect in those contexts. Nevertheless the effect of satisfying a descriptor in terms of benefit entitlement indicates that the disability should be significant. It must be such that 'it is not reasonable to require' the claimant to undertake work or the activity, to use the language of section 8(1) and 9(1) of the Welfare Reform Act 2007. The passage in the WCA Handbook reflects that, although it is not presented (and must not be taken) as a comprehensive statement of the physical conditions that can lead to the disabilities in Activity 16(a) and (b)."

Regulations 67(1)(a) and (2) and 68(1)(a) and (b)

SCHEDULE 4

AMOUNTS

PART 1

PRESCRIBED AMOUNTS

1. The weekly amounts specified in column (2) in respect of each person or couple specified in column (1) are the weekly amounts specified for the purposes of regulations 67(1) and 68 (prescribed amounts and polygamous marriages).

9.434

(1) Person or Couple			*(2)* Amount		
(1)		*Single claimant—*	(1)		
	(a)	who satisfies the conditions set out in section 2(2) [^{12} ...] or 4(4) [^{12}...] of the Act [^{13} or who is a member of the work-related activity group];		(a)	[^{10}£73.10];
	(b)	aged not less than 25;		(b)	[^{10}£73.10];
	(c)	aged less than 25.		(c)	[^{10}£57.90];
(2)		Lone parent [^{6} or a person who has no partner and who is responsible for and a member of the same household as a young person]—	(2)		
	(a)	who satisfies the conditions set out in section 4(4) [^{12}...] of the Act [^{13} or who is a member of the work-related activity group and satisfies the conditions set out in Part 2 of Schedule 1 to the Act];		(a)	[^{10}£73.10];
	(b)	aged not less than 18;		(b)	[^{10}£73.10];
	(c)	aged less than 18.		(c)	[^{10}£57.90];
(3)		*Couple—*	(3)		
	(a)	where both members are aged not less than 18;		(a)	[^{10}£114.85];
	(b)	where one member is aged not less than 18 and the other member is a person under 18 who—		(b)	[^{10}£114.85];

(1) *Person or Couple*		(2) *Amount*
	(i) [³ if that other member had not been a member] of a couple, would satisfy the requirements for entitlement to income support other than the requirement to make a claim for it; or	
	(ii) [³ if that other member had not been a member] of a couple, would satisfy the requirements for entitlement to an income-related allowance; or	
	(iii) satisfies the requirements of section 3(1)(f)(iii) of the Jobseekers Act (prescribed circumstances for persons aged 16 but less than 18); or	
	(iv) is the subject of a direction under section 16 of that Act (persons under 18: severe hardship);	
(c)	where the claimant satisfies the conditions set out in section 4(4) [¹² . . .] of the Act [¹³ or the claimant is a member of the work-related activity group and satisfies the conditions set out in Part 2 of Schedule 1 to the Act] and both members are aged less than 18 and—	(c) [¹⁰£114.85];
	(i) at least one of them is treated as responsible for a child; or	
	(ii) had they not been members of a couple, each would have qualified for an income-related allowance; or	
	(iii) had they not been members of a couple the claimant's partner would satisfy the requirements for entitlement to income support other than the requirement to make a claim for it; or	
	(iv) the claimant's partner satisfies the requirements of section 3(1)(f)(iii) of the Jobseekers Act (prescribed circumstances for persons aged 16 but less than 18); or	
	(v) there is in force in respect of the claimant's partner a direction under section 16 of that Act (persons under 18: severe hardship);	
(d)	where both members are aged less than 18 and—	(d) [¹⁰£87.50];
	(i) at least one of them is treated as responsible for a child; or	
	(ii) had they not been members of a couple, each would have qualified for an income-related allowance; or	
	(iii) had they not been members of a couple the claimant's partner satisfies the requirements for entitlement to income support other than a requirement to make a claim for it; or	
	(iv) the claimant's partner satisfies the requirements of section 3(1)(f)(iii) of the Jobseekers Act (prescribed circumstances for persons aged 16 but less than 18); or	
	(v) there is in force in respect of the claimant's partner a direction under section 16 of that Act (persons under 18: severe hardship);	
(e)	where the claimant is aged not less than 25 and the claimant's partner is a person under 18 who—	(e) [¹⁰£73.10];

(1)		(2)
Person or Couple		*Amount*

(i) would not qualify for an income-related allowance if the person were not a member of a couple;

(ii) would not qualify for income support if the person were not a member of a couple;

(iii) does not satisfy the requirements of section 3(1)(f)(iii) of the Jobseekers Act (prescribed circumstances for persons aged 16 but less than 18); and

(iv) is not the subject of a direction under section 16 of that Act (persons under 18: severe hardship);

(f) where the claimant satisfies the conditions set out in section 4(4) [¹²...] of the Act [¹³ or the claimant is a member of the work-related activity group and satisfies the conditions set out in Part 2 of Schedule 1 to the Act] and the claimant's partner is a person under 18 who—   (f) [¹⁰£73.10];

(i) would not qualify for an income-related allowance if the person were not a member of a couple;

(ii) would not qualify for income support if the person [¹ were] not a member of a couple;

(iii) does not satisfy the requirements of section 3(1)(f)(iii) of the Jobseekers Act (prescribed circumstances for persons aged 16 but less than 18); and

(iv) is not the subject of a direction under section 16 of that Act (persons under 18: severe hardship);

(g) where the claimant satisfies the conditions set out in section 4(4) [¹²...] of the Act [¹³ or the claimant is a member of the work-related activity group and satisfies the conditions set out in Part 2 of Schedule 1 to the Act] and both members are aged less than 18 and paragraph (c) does not apply;   (g) [¹⁰£73.10];

[¹ (h) where the claimant is aged not less than 18 but less than 25 and the claimant's partner is a person under 18 who—   (h) [¹⁰£57.90];

(i) would not qualify for an income-related allowance if the person were not a member of a couple;

(ii) would not qualify for income support if the person were not a member of a couple;

(iii) does not satisfy the requirements of section 3(1)(f)(iii) of the Jobseekers Act (prescribed circumstances for persons aged 16 but less than 18); and

(iv) is not the subject of a direction under section 16 of that Act (persons under 18: severe hardship);]

(i) where both members are aged less than 18 and paragraph (d) does not apply.   (i) [¹⁰£57.90].

PREMIUMS

9.435   2. Except as provided in paragraph 4, the weekly premiums specified in Part 3 of this Schedule are, for the purposes of regulation 67(1)(b) and 68(1)(c), to be applicable to a claimant who satisfies the condition specified in paragraphs 5 to 8 in respect of that premium.

3. An enhanced disability premium in respect of a person is not applicable in addition to a pensioner premium.

4.—(1) For the purposes of this Part of this Schedule, once a premium is applicable to a claimant under this Part, a person is to be treated as being in receipt of any benefit—
  (a) in the case of a benefit to which the Social Security (Overlapping Benefits) Regulations 1979 applies, for any period during which, apart from the provisions of those Regulations, the person would be in receipt of that benefit; and
  (b) for any period spent by a person in undertaking a course of training or instruction provided or approved by the Secretary of State under section 2 of the Employment and Training Act 1973, or by [³ Skills Development Scotland] or Highlands and Islands Enterprise under section 2 of the Enterprise and New Towns (Scotland) Act 1990, or for any period during which the person is in receipt of a training allowance.
[⁷ (2)   For the purposes of the carer premium under paragraph 8, a claimant is to be treated as being in receipt of a carer's allowance by virtue of sub-paragraph (1)(a) only if and for so long as the person in respect of whose care the allowance has been claimed remains in receipt of—
  (a) attendance allowance;
  (b) the care component of disability living allowance at the highest or middle rate prescribed in accordance with section 72(3) of the Contributions and Benefits Act; [⁸ . . .]
  (c) the daily living component of personal independence payment at the standard or enhanced rate in accordance with section 78(3) of the 2012 Act] [⁸ ; or
  (d) armed forces independence payment.]

Pensioner premium

9.436   5. The condition is that the claimant or the claimant's partner has attained the qualifying age for state pension credit.

Severe disability premium

9.437   6.—(1) The condition is that the claimant is a severely disabled person.
(2) For the purposes of sub-paragraph (1), a claimant is to be treated as being a severely disabled person if, and only if—
  (a) in the case of a single claimant, a lone parent [⁶ , a person who has no partner and who is responsible for and a member of the same household as a young person] or a claimant who is treated as having no partner in consequence of sub-paragraph (3)—
    (i) the claimant is in receipt of the care component [⁷ , the daily living component] [⁸ , armed forces independence payment] [⁵ or attendance allowance];
    (ii) subject to sub-paragraph (4), the claimant has no non-dependants aged 18 or over normally residing with the claimant or with whom the claimant is normally residing; and
    (iii) no person is entitled to, and in receipt of, [¹¹ a carer's allowance or has an award of universal credit which includes the carer element] in respect of caring for the claimant;
  (b) in the case of a claimant who has a partner—
    (i) the claimant is in receipt of the care component [⁷ , the daily living component] [⁸ , armed forces independence payment] [⁵ or attendance allowance];
    (ii) the claimant's partner is also in receipt of the care component [⁷ , the daily living component] [⁸ , armed forces independence payment] or attendance allowance or, if the claimant is a member of a polygamous marriage, all the partners of that marriage are in receipt of the care component [⁷ , the daily living component] [⁸ , armed forces independence payment] or attendance allowance; and
    (iii) subject to sub-paragraph (4), the claimant has no non-dependants aged 18 or

over normally residing with the claimant or with whom the claimant is normally residing, and,

either a person is entitled to, and in receipt of, a carer's allowance [¹¹ or has an award of universal credit which includes the carer element] in respect of caring for only one of the couple or, in the case of a polygamous marriage, for one or more but not all the partners of the marriage or, as the case may be, no person is entitled to, and in receipt of, such an allowance [¹¹ or has such an award of universal credit] in respect of caring for either member of the couple or any partner of the polygamous marriage.

(3) Where a claimant has a partner who does not satisfy the condition in sub-paragraph (2)(b)(ii) and that partner is blind or severely sight impaired or is treated as blind or severely sight impaired that partner is to be treated for the purposes of sub-paragraph (2) as if the partner were not a partner of the claimant.

(4) For the purposes of sub-paragraph (2)(a)(ii) and (b)(iii) no account is to be taken of—

(a) a person receiving attendance allowance, [⁷ the daily living component] [⁸ , armed forces independence payment] or the care component;

(b) subject to sub-paragraph (7), a person who joins the claimant's household for the first time in order to care for the claimant or the claimant's partner and immediately before so joining the claimant or the claimant's partner was treated as a severely disabled person; or

(c) a person who is blind or severely sight impaired or is treated as blind or severely sight impaired.

(5) For the purposes of sub-paragraph (2)(b) a person is to be treated—

(a) as being in receipt of attendance allowance or the care component if the person would, but for the person being a patient for a period exceeding 28 days, be so in receipt;

(b) as being entitled to, and in receipt of, a carer's allowance [¹¹ or having an award of universal credit which includes the carer element] if the person would, but for the person for whom the person was caring being a patient in hospital for a period exceeding 28 days, be so entitled and in receipt [¹¹ of carer's allowance or have such an award of universal credit] .

[⁷(c) as being in entitled to, and in receipt of, the daily living component if the person would, but for regulations under section 86(1) (hospital in-patients) of the 2012 Act, be so entitled and in receipt.]

(6) For the purposes of sub-paragraph (2)(a)(iii) and (b), no account is to be taken of an award of carer's allowance [¹¹ or universal credit which includes the carer element] to the extent that payment of such an award is backdated for a period before the date on which the award is first paid.

(7) Sub-paragraph (4)(b) is to apply only for the first 12 weeks following the date on which the person to whom that provision applies first joins the claimant's household.

(8) In sub-paragraph (2)(a)(iii) and (b), references to a person being in receipt of a carer's allowance [¹¹ or as having an award of universal credit which includes the carer element] are to include references to a person who would have been in receipt of that allowance [¹¹ or had such an award] but for the application of a restriction under section [⁴ 6B or] 7 of the Social Security Fraud Act 2001 (loss of benefit provisions).

(9) [¹¹ (a)] In this paragraph—

[⁹ "blind or severely sight impaired" means certified as blind or severely sight impaired by a consultant ophthalmologist and a person who has ceased to be certified as blind or severely sight impaired where that person's eyesight has been regained is, nevertheless, to be treated as blind or severely sight impaired for a period of 28 weeks following the date on which the person ceased to be so certified;]

"the care component" means the care component of disability living allowance at the highest or middle rate prescribed in accordance with section 72(3) of the Contributions and Benefits Act.

[¹¹ (b) A person has an award of universal credit which includes the carer element if the person has an award of universal credit which includes an amount which is the carer element under regulation 29 of the Universal Credit Regulations 2013.]

Enhanced disability premium

7.—(1) Subject to sub-paragraph (2), the condition is that—   9.438

(a) the claimant's applicable amount includes the support component; [⁷ ...]

(b) the care component of disability living allowance is, or would, but for a suspension of benefit in accordance with regulations under section 113(2) of the Contributions and Benefits Act or, but for an abatement as a consequence of hospitalisation, be payable at the highest rate prescribed under section 72(3) of that Act in respect of—

(i) the claimant; or

> > (ii) the claimant's partner (if any) who is aged less than the qualifying age for state pension credit [7 ; [8 . . .]

[8 (c) the daily living component is, or would, but for regulations made under section 86(1) (hospital in-patients) of the 2012 Act, be payable at the enhanced rate under section 78(2) of that Act in respect of—

> > (i) the claimant; or
> > (ii) the claimant's partner (if any) who is aged less then the qualifying age for state pension credit"]; or

> (d) armed forces independence payment is payable in respect of—
> > (i) the claimant; or
> > (ii) the claimant's partner (if any) who is aged less than the qualifying age for state pension credit.]

(2) An enhanced disability premium is not applicable in respect of—
> (a) a claimant who—
> > (i) is not a member of a couple or a polygamous marriage; and
> > (ii) is a patient within the meaning of regulation 69(2) and has been for a period of more than 52 weeks; or
> (b) a member of a couple or a polygamous marriage where each member is a patient within the meaning of regulation 69(2) and has been for a period of more than 52 weeks.

Carer premium

9.439 8.—(1) Subject to sub-paragraphs (2) and (4), the condition is that the claimant or the claimant's partner is, or both of them are, entitled to a carer's allowance under section 70 of the Contributions and Benefits Act.

(2) Where a carer premium is awarded but—
> (a) the person in respect of whose care the carer's allowance has been awarded dies; or
> (b) in any other case the person in respect of whom a carer premium has been awarded ceases to be entitled to a carer's allowance, the condition for the award of the premium is to be treated as satisfied for a period of 8 weeks from the relevant date specified in sub-paragraph (3).

(3) The relevant date for the purposes of sub-paragraph (2) is—
> (a) where sub-paragraph (2)(a) applies, the Sunday following the death of the person in respect of whose care a carer's allowance has been awarded or the date of death if the death occurred on a Sunday; or
> (b) in any other case, the date on which the person who has been entitled to a carer's allowance ceases to be entitled to that allowance.

(4) Where a person who has been entitled to a carer's allowance ceases to be entitled to that allowance and makes a claim for an income-related allowance, the condition for the award of the carer premium is to be treated as satisfied for a period of 8 weeks from the date on which—
> (a) the person in respect of whose care the carer's allowance has been awarded dies; or
> (b) in any other case, the person who has been entitled to a carer's allowance ceased to be entitled to that allowance.

Persons in receipt of concessionary payments

9.440 9. For the purpose of determining whether a premium is applicable to a person under paragraphs 6, 7 and 8, any concessionary payment made to compensate that person for the non-payment of any benefit mentioned in those paragraphs is to be treated as if it were a payment of that benefit.

Persons in receipt of benefit

9.441 10. For the purposes of this Part of this Schedule, a person is to be regarded as being in receipt of any benefit if, and only if, it is paid in respect of the person and is to be so regarded only for any period in respect of which that benefit is paid.

PART 3

WEEKLY AMOUNT OF PREMIUMS SPECIFIED IN PART 2

11.—   9.442

Premium	Amount
(1) Pensioner premium for a person to whom paragraph 5 applies who—	(1)
(a) is a single claimant and—	(a)
(i) [¹² . . .];	(i) [¹² . . .];
(ii) is entitled to the support component; or	(ii) [¹⁴ £55.60];
[¹² (iii) is not entitled to the support component;]	(iii) [¹⁴ £94.15];
(b) is a member of a couple and—	(b)
(i) [¹² . . .]	(i) [¹² . . .];
(ii) is entitled to the support component; or	(ii) [¹⁴ £101.85];
[¹² (iii) is not entitled to the support component;]	(iii) [¹⁴ £140.40];
(2) Severe disability premium—	(2)
(a) where the claimant satisfies the condition in paragraph 6(2)(a);	(a) [¹⁴ £65.85];
(b) where the claimant satisfies the condition in paragraph 6(2)(b)—	(b)
(i) if there is someone in receipt of a carer's allowance or if the person or any partner satisfies that condition only by virtue of paragraph 6(5);	(i) [¹⁴ £65.85];
(ii) if no-one is in receipt of such an allowance.	(ii) [¹⁴ £131.70].
(3) Carer premium.	(3) [¹⁴ £36.85] in respect of each person who satisfies the condition specified in [¹ paragraph 8(1)].
(4) Enhanced disability premium where the conditions in paragraph 7 are satisfied.	(4)(a) [¹⁴ £16.80] in respect of each person who is neither—
	(i) a child or young person; nor
	(ii) a member of a couple or a polygamous marriage, in respect of whom the conditions specified in paragraph 7 are satisfied;
	(b) [¹⁴ £16.80] where the claimant is a member of a couple or a polygamous marriage and the conditions specified in [¹ paragraph 7] are satisfied in respect of a member of that couple or polygamous marriage.

Regulation 67(3)

PART 4

[¹² THE COMPONENT]

9.443   **12.** [¹² ...].

13. The amount of the support component is [¹⁵ £37.65].

AMENDMENTS

1. Employment and Support Allowance (Miscellaneous Amendments) Regulations 2008 (SI 2008/2428) reg.14 (October 27, 2008).

2. Social Security (Miscellaneous Amendments) Regulations 2009 (SI 2009/583) reg.10(2) (April 6, 2009).

3. Social Security (Miscellaneous Amendments) (No.4) Regulations 2009 (SI 2009/2655) reg.11(1) and (16) (October 26, 2009).

4. Social Security (Loss of Benefit) Amendment Regulations 2010 (SI 2010/1160) reg.12(1) and (3) (April 1, 2010).

5. Social Security (Miscellaneous Amendments) (No.3) Regulations 2011 (SI 2011/2425) reg.23(14) (October 30, 2011).

6. Social Security (Work-focused Interviews for Lone Parents and Partners) (Amendment) Regulations 2011 (SI 2011/2428) reg.5(5) (October 30, 2011).

7. Personal Independence Payment (Supplementary Provisions and Consequential Amendments) Regulations 2013 (SI 2013/388) reg.8 and Sch., para.40(1) and (5) (April 8, 2013).

8. Armed Forces and Reserve Forces Compensation Scheme (Consequential Provisions: Subordinate Legislation) Order 2013 (SI 2013/591) art.7 and Sch., para.37(1) and (5) (April 8, 2013).

9. Universal Credit and Miscellaneous Amendments (No. 2) Regulations 2014 (SI 2014/2888) reg.3(7)(a) (November 26, 2014).

10. Welfare Benefits Up-rating Order 2015 (SI 2015/30) art.11(1) and Sch.4 (April 6, 2015).

11. Universal Credit and Miscellaneous Amendments Regulations 2015 (SI 2015/1754) reg.19 (November 4, 2015).

12. Employment and Support Allowance and Universal Credit (Miscellaneous Amendments and Transitional and Savings Provisions) Regulations 2017 (SI 2017/204) reg.2(1) and (4) (April 3, 2017).

13. Employment and Support Allowance (Miscellaneous Amendments and Transitional and Savings Provision) Regulations 2017 (SI 2017/581) reg.7(1) and (4) (June 23, 2017, subject to the transitional and savings provision in reg.10).

14. Social Security Benefits Up-rating Order 2019 (SI 2019/480) art.27(2) and Sch.8, para.1 (April 8, 2019).

15. Social Security Benefits Up-rating Order 2019 (SI 2019/480) art.27(4) (April 8, 2019).

GENERAL NOTE

9.444   See the commentary to reg.67 and to Sch.2 to the IS Regs.

With effect from April 8, 2019, claimants who are transitionally entitled to work-related activity component of ESA (i.e., who fall within paras 2 to 7 of Sch. 2 to the Employment and Support Allowance and Universal Credit (Miscellaneous Amendments and Transitional and Savings Provisions) Regulations 2017 (see below) and who are also entitled to the pensioner premium, receive a weekly premium of £65.10 for a single claimant or £111.35 for a member of a couple: see art.27(3) and Sch.8, para.2 of SI 2019/480.

Those who are awarded the support component (except for some in-patients) also become entitled to have the enhanced disability premium included in their applicable amount when their entitlement to IRESA is calculated (see paras.7(1)(a) and (2)). In

1326

some cases, this will mean that claimants who were previously only entitled to CESA (*i.e.,* because they were excluded from IRESA by the means test) become entitled to IRESA for the first time. For some of the procedural issues to which this can give rise, see *DJ v Secretary of State for Work and Pensions (ESA)* [2015] UKUT 342 (AAC). Note, in particular, that ESA is a single benefit and it is not necessary for someone who is already entitled to CESA to make a fresh claim to receive IRESA.

Regulation 69

SCHEDULE 5

SPECIAL CASES

PART 1

AMOUNTS PRESCRIBED FOR THE PURPOSES OF SECTION 4(2) OF THE ACT

Claimants without accommodation

1. A claimant who is without accommodation.
1. The amount applicable to the claimant under regulation 67(1)(a). **9.445**

Members of religious orders

2. A claimant who is a member of, and fully maintained by, a religious order.
2. Nil.

Prisoners

3. A claimant
(a) except where sub-paragraph (b) applies, who is a prisoner;
(b) who is detained in custody pending trial or sentence following conviction by a court.

3.
(a) Nil;
(b) only such amount, if any, as may be applicable under regulation 67(1)(c) and the amount of nil under regulation 67(3). **9.446**

Specified cases of temporarily separated couples

4. A claimant who is a member of a couple and who is temporarily separated from the claimant's partner where—
(a) one member of the couple is—
  (i) not a patient but is residing in a care home, an Abbeyfield Home or an independent hospital; or
  (ii) resident in premises used for the rehabilitation of alcoholics or drug addicts; or
  (iii) resident in accommodation provided under section 3 of and Part 2 of the Schedule to, the Polish Resettlement Act 1947 (provision of accommodation in camps); or
  (iv) participating in arrangements for training made under section 2 of the Employment and Training Act 1973 or section 2 of the Enterprise and New Towns (Scotland) Act 1990 or attending a course at an employment rehabilitation centre established under that section of the 1973 Act, where the course requires the person to live away from the dwelling occupied as the home; or

4. Either—
(a) the amount applicable to the claimant as a member of a couple under regulation 67(1); or

       (v)   in a probation or bail hostel approved for the purpose by the Secretary of State; and

  (b)   the other member of the couple is—

  (i)   living in the dwelling occupied as the home; or

  (ii)   a patient; or

  (iii)   residing in a care home, an Abbeyfield Home or an independent hospital.

  (b)   the aggregate of the claimant's applicable amount and that of the claimant's partner assessed under the provisions of these Regulations as if each of them were a single claimant or [³ , a lone parent or a person who has no partner and who is responsible for and a member of the same household as a young person], whichever is the greater.

Polygamous marriages where one or more partners are temporarily separated

9.447   5. A claimant who is a member of a polygamous marriage and who is temporarily separated from a partner, where one of them is living in the home where the other member is—

  (a)   not a patient but is residing in a care home, an Abbeyfield Home or an independent hospital; or

  (b)   resident in premises used for the rehabilitation of alcoholics or drug addicts; or

5.   Either—

  (a)   the amount applicable to the members of the polygamous marriage under regulation 68; or

  (b)   the aggregate of the amount applicable for the members of the polygamous marriage who remain in the home under regulation 68 and the amount applicable in respect of those members not in the home calculated as if each of them were a single claimant or [³ , a lone parent or a person who has no partner and who is responsible for and a member of the same household as a young person], whichever is the greater.

  (c)   attending a course of training or instruction provided or approved by the Secretary of State where the course requires the person to live away from home; or

  (d)   in a probation or bail hostel approved for the purpose by the Secretary of State.

Couple where one member is abroad

9.448   6. Subject to paragraph 7, a claimant who is a member of a couple where one member of the couple is temporarily absent from the United Kingdom.

6.   For the first 4 weeks of that absence, the amount applicable to them as a couple under regulation 67(1) or 69, as the case may be, and thereafter, the amount applicable to the claimant in Great Britain under regulation 67(1) or 69, as the case may be, as if the claimant were a single claimant [³ , a lone parent, or as the case may be a person who has no partner and who is responsible for and a member of the same household as a young person].

Couple or member of couple taking child or young person abroad for treatment

7.— (1) A claimant who is a member of a couple where either—

   (a) the claimant or the claimant's partner is; or

   (b) both the claimant and the claimant's partner are, absent from the United Kingdom in the circumstances specified

  (2) in sub-paragraph (2).

For the purposes of sub-paragraph (1)

   (a) the specified circumstances are—

in respect of a claimant, those in regulation 153(1)(a), (b), (c)(ii), (d) and (e);

   (b) in respect of a claimant's partner, as if regulation 153(1)(a), (b), (c)(ii), (d) and (e) applied to that partner.

7. For the first 26 weeks of that absence, the amount applicable to the claimant under regulation 67(1) or 69, as the case may be and, thereafter, if the claimant is in Great Britain the amount applicable to the claimant under regulation 67(1) or 69, as the case may be, as if the claimant were a single claimant [³ , a lone parent, or as the case may be a person who has no partner and who is responsible for and a member of the same household as a young person].

        9.449

Polygamous marriages where any member is abroad

8. Subject to paragraph 9, a claimant who is a member of a polygamous marriage where one or more members of the marriage are temporarily absent from the United Kingdom.

8. For the first 4 weeks of that absence, the amount applicable to the claimant under regulation 68 and 69, as the case may be, and thereafter, if the claimant is in Great

Britain the amount applicable to the claimant under regulations 68 and 69, as the case may be, as if any members of the polygamous marriage not in the United Kingdom were not a member of the marriage.

        9.450

Polygamous marriage: taking child or young person abroad for treatment

9.—(1) A claimant who is a member of a polygamous marriage where one or more members of the marriage is absent from the United Kingdom in the circumstances specified in sub-paragraph (2).

(2) For the purposes of sub-paragraph (1) the specified circumstances are—

   (a) in respect of a claimant, those in regulation 153(1)(a), (b), (c)(ii), (d) and (e);

   (b) in respect of a claimant's partner or partners, as the case may be, as if regulation 153(1)(a), (b), (c)(ii), (d) and (e) applied to that partner or those [¹ partners].

9. For the first 26 weeks of that absence, the amount applicable to the claimant under regulations 68 and 69, as the case may be, and thereafter, if the claimant is in Great Britain the amount applicable to the claimant under regulations 68 and 69, as the case may be, as if any member of the polygamous marriage not in the United Kingdom were not a member of the marriage.

        9.451

Partner of a person subject to immigration control

10.

   (a) A claimant who is the partner of a person subject to immigration control.

10.

   (a) The amount applicable in respect of the claimant only under regulation 67(1)(a) any amount which may be applicable to

the claimant under regulation 67(1)(b) plus the amount applicable to the claimant under regulation 67(1)(c) or, as the case may be, regulation 69.

        9.452

(b) Where regulation 68 (polygamous marriages) applies and
the claimant is a person—

(i) who is not subject to
immigration control within the
meaning of section 115(9) of
the Immigration and Asylum
Act; or

(ii) to whom section 115 of that
Act does not apply by virtue
of regulation 2 of the Social
Security (Immigration and
Asylum) Consequential
Amendments Regulations
2000; and

(iii) who is a member of a couple
and one or more of the
person's partners is subject to
immigration control within
the meaning of section 115(9)
of that Act and section 115
of that Act applies to that
partner or those partners for
the purposes of exclusion from
entitlement to income-related
allowance.

(b) the amount determined in
accordance with that regulation
or regulation 69 in respect of the
claimant and any partners of the
claimant who are not subject to
immigration control within the
meaning of section 115(9) of the
Immigration and Asylum Act and
to whom section 115 of that Act
does not apply for the purposes of
exclusion from entitlement to an
income-related allowance.

Person from abroad

9.453   11. Person from abroad.   11.   Nil.

PART 2

AMOUNTS PRESCRIBED FOR THE PURPOSES OF SECTIONS 2(1) AND 4(2) OF THE ACT

[² Persons serving a sentence of imprisonment detained in hospital

9.454   12. A person serving a sentence of   12. The amount applicable under regula-
imprisonment detained in hospital.   tion 67(2) and the amount of nil under
regulation 67(3).

Patients]

9.455   13. Subject to paragraph 12, a single claimant   13. The amounts applicable under
who has been a patient for a continuous period   regulation 67(1)(a), (c) and (2) and
of more than 52 weeks or, where the claimant is   the amount of nil under regulation
one of a couple, [⁴ each] member of the couple   67(3).
has been a patient for a continuous period of
more than 52 weeks.

Person in hardship

9.456   14. A claimant who is a person in hardship.   14. The amount to which the claimant
is entitled under regulation 67(1)(a)
and (2) or 68(1)(a) is to be reduced
by 20%.

AMENDMENTS

1. Employment and Support Allowance (Miscellaneous Amendments)
Regulations 2008 (SI 2008/2428) reg.15 (October 27, 2008).

2. Social Security (Persons Serving a Sentence of Imprisonment Detained in Hospital) Regulations 2010 (SI 2010/442) reg.5(4) (March 25, 2010).

3. Social Security (Work-focused Interviews for Lone Parents and Partners) (Amendment) Regulations 2011 (SI 2011/2428) reg.5(6) (October 30, 2011).

4. Social Security (Miscellaneous Amendments) (No. 3) Regulations 2013 (SI 2013/2536) reg.13(1) and (35) (October 29, 2013).

GENERAL NOTE

See the commentary to reg.67 and to Sch.7 to the IS Regs.   9.457

REGULATIONS 67(1)(c), 68[¹(1)](d)

SCHEDULE 6

HOUSING COSTS

Housing costs

1.—(1) Subject to the following provisions of this Schedule, the housing costs applicable to   9.458
a claimant are those costs—
   (a) which the claimant or, where the claimant has a partner, that partner is, in accordance
        with paragraph 4, liable to meet in respect of the dwelling occupied as the home which
        the claimant or that claimant's partner is treated as occupying; and
   (b) which qualify under [³² paragraph 18].
(2) In this Schedule—
   [²⁶ . . .]
"housing costs" means those costs to which sub-paragraph (1) refers;
   [²⁶ . . .]
   [³² . . .]
(3) For the purposes of this Schedule a disabled person is a person—
   [¹³ (a) (i) in respect of whom the main phase employment and support allowance is
               payable to the claimant or to a person living with the claimant; or
          (ii) where they are the claimant or a person living with the claimant, in respect of
               whom there would be entitlement to an employment and support allowance [²⁸
               . . .], but for the application of section 1A of the Act (duration of contributory
               allowance);]
   (b) who, had that person in fact been entitled to income support, would have satisfied
        the requirements of paragraph 12 of Schedule 2 to the Income Support Regulations
        (additional condition for the disability premium);
   (c) aged 75 or over; [²⁰ ...]
   (d) who is disabled or severely disabled for the purposes of section 9(6) of the Tax Credits
        Act (maximum rate) [²⁰ ; or
   (e) who is entitled to an award of universal credit [²⁹ and has limited capability for work or
        limited capability for work and work-related activity as construed in accordance with
        regulations 39 and 40 of the Universal Credit Regulations 2013.]]
   [¹⁴ (3A) For the purposes of this Schedule a claimant is a "work or training beneficiary" on
any day in a linking term where the claimant—
   (a) had limited capability for work–
          (i) for more than 13 weeks in the most recent past period of limited capability for
               work; or
          (ii) for 13 weeks or less in the most recent past period of limited capability for work
               where the claimant became entitled to an award of an employment and support
               allowance by virtue of a conversion decision which took effect from the com-
               mencement of the most recent past period of limited capability for work;
   (b) ceased to be entitled to an allowance or advantage at the end of that most recent past
        period of limited capability for work; and
   (c) became engaged in work or training within one month of so ceasing to be entitled.
(3B) A claimant is not a work or training beneficiary if—
   (a) the most recent past period of limited capability for work was ended by a determina-
        tion that the claimant did not have limited capability for work; and

1331

(b) that determination was on the basis of a limited capability for work assessment.

(3C) In sub-paragraphs (3A) and (3B)—

"allowance or advantage" means any allowance or advantage under the Act or the Contributions and Benefits Act for which entitlement is dependent on limited capability for work;

"conversion decision" has the meaning given in regulation 5(2)(a) of the Employment and Support Allowance (Transitional Provisions, Housing Benefit and Council Tax Benefit) (Existing Awards) (No.2) Regulations 2010;

"linking term" means a period of 104 weeks from the first day immediately following the last day in a period of limited capability for work;

"most recent past period of limited capability for work" means the period of limited capability for work which most recently precedes the period in respect of which the current claim is made, including any period of which that previous period is treated as a continuation by virtue of regulation 145(1) (linking rules); and

"work" means work, other than work under regulation 45 (exempt work), for which payment is made or which is done in expectation of payment.]

(4) For the purposes of sub-paragraph (3), a person will not cease to be a disabled person on account of that person being disqualified for receiving benefit or treated as not having limited capability for work by virtue of the operation of section 18(1) to (3) of the Act.

Remunerative work

9.459   2.—(1) Subject to [¹sub-paragraphs (2) to (8)], a [¹non-dependant (referred to in this paragraph as "person")] is to be treated for the purposes of this Schedule as engaged in remunerative work if that person is engaged, or, where the person's hours of work fluctuate, is engaged on average, for not less than 16 hours a week, being work for which payment is made or which is done in expectation of payment.

(2) Subject to sub-paragraph (3), in determining the number of hours for which a person is engaged in work where that person's hours of work fluctuate, regard is to be had to the average of hours worked over—

(a) if there is a recognisable cycle of work, the period of one complete cycle (including, where the cycle involves periods in which the person does no work, those periods but disregarding any other absences);

(b) in any other case, the period of 5 weeks immediately prior to the date of claim, or such other length of time as may, in the particular case, enable the person's weekly average hours of work to be determined more accurately.

(3) Where no recognisable cycle has been established in respect of a person's work, regard is to be had to the number of hours or, where those hours will fluctuate, the average of the hours, which that person is expected to work in a week.

(4) A person is to be treated as engaged in remunerative work during any period for which that person is absent from work referred to in sub-paragraph (1) if the absence is either without good cause or by reason of a recognised, customary or other holiday.

(5) A person is not to be treated as engaged in remunerative work on any day on which the person is on maternity leave, paternity leave [²⁵, shared parental leave] or adoption leave or is absent from work because the person is ill.

(6) For the purposes of this paragraph, in determining the number of hours in which a person is engaged or treated as engaged in remunerative work, no account is to be taken of any hours in which the person is engaged in an employment or a scheme to which regulation 43(1) (circumstances under which partners of persons entitled to an income-related allowance are not to be treated as engaged in remunerative work) applies.

(7) For the purposes of sub-paragraphs (1) and (2), in determining the number of hours for which a person is engaged in work, that number is to include any time allowed to that person by that person's employer for a meal or for refreshment, but only where that person is, or expects to be, paid earnings in respect of that time.

[¹(8) A person is to be treated as not being engaged in remunerative work on any day in which that person falls within the circumstances prescribed in regulation 43(2) (circumstances in which partners of claimants entitled to an income-related allowance are not to be treated as engaged in remunerative work).

(9) Whether a claimant or the claimant's partner is engaged in, or to be treated as being engaged in, remunerative work is to be determined in accordance with regulations 41 or 42 (meaning of "remunerative work" for the purposes of paragraph 6(1)(e) and (f) of Schedule 1 to the Act) as the case may be.]

Previous entitlement to other income-related benefits

3.—(1) Where the claimant or the claimant's partner was in receipt of, or was treated   **9.460**
as being in receipt of, an income-based jobseeker's allowance or income support not more
than 12 weeks before one of them becomes entitled to an income-related allowance or,
where the claimant or the claimant's partner is a person to whom paragraph 15(2) or (13)
(linking rules) refers, not more than 26 weeks before becoming so entitled and—
    (a) the applicable amount for that income-based jobseeker's allowance or income support
         included an amount in respect of housing costs [32 under paragraph 16 of Schedule 2]
         to the Jobseeker's Allowance Regulations or, as the case may be, [32 paragraph 17 of
         Schedule 3] to the Income Support Regulations; and
    (b) the circumstances affecting the calculation of those housing costs remain unchanged
         since the last calculation of those costs,
the applicable amount in respect of housing costs for an income-related allowance is to be
the applicable amount in respect of those costs current when entitlement to an income-based
jobseeker's allowance or income support was last determined.
    (2) Where a claimant or the claimant's partner was in receipt of state pension credit not
more than 12 weeks before one of them becomes entitled to [¹an income-related allowance]
or, where the claimant or the claimant's partner is a person to whom paragraph 15(2) or (13)
(linking rules) refers, not more than 26 weeks before becoming so entitled, and—
    (a) the appropriate minimum guarantee included an amount in respect of housing costs [32
         under paragraph 13 of Schedule 2] to the State Pension Credit Regulations 2002; and
    (b) the circumstances affecting the calculation of those housing costs remain unchanged
         since the last calculation of those costs,
the applicable amount in respect of housing costs for an income-related allowance is to be the
applicable amount in respect of those costs current when entitlement to state pension credit
was last determined.
    (3) Where, in the period since housing costs were last calculated for an income-based job-
seeker's allowance, income support or, as the case may be, state pension credit, there has been
a change of circumstances, other than a reduction in the amount of an outstanding loan, which
increases or reduces those costs, the amount to be met under this Schedule must, for the purposes
of the claim for an income-related allowance, be recalculated so as to take account of that change.

Circumstances in which a person is liable to meet housing costs

4. A person is liable to meet housing costs where—   **9.461**
    (a) the liability falls upon that person or that person's partner but not where the liability
         is to a member of the same household as the person on whom the liability falls;
    (b) because the person liable to meet the housing costs is not meeting them, the claimant
         has to meet those costs in order to continue to live in the dwelling occupied as the
         home and it is reasonable in all the circumstances to treat the claimant as liable to
         meet those costs;
    (c) in practice the claimant shares the housing costs with other members of the house-
         hold none of whom are close relatives either of the claimant or the claimant's partner,
         and—
         (i)   one or more of those members is liable to meet those costs; and
         (ii) it is reasonable in the circumstances to treat the claimant as sharing responsibil-
               ity.

**Circumstances in which a person is to be treated as occupying a dwelling as the
home**

5.—(1) Subject to the following provisions of this paragraph, a person is to be treated as   **9.462**
occupying as the home the dwelling normally occupied as the home by that person or, if that
person is a member of a family, by that person and that person's family and that person is not
to be treated as occupying any other dwelling as the home.
    (2) In determining whether a dwelling is the dwelling normally occupied as the claimant's
home for the purposes of sub-paragraph (1) regard must be had to any other dwelling occupied by the claimant or by the claimant and that claimant's family whether or not that other
dwelling is in Great Britain.
    (3) Subject to sub-paragraph (4), where a claimant who has no partner is a full-time student
or is on a training course and is liable to make payments (including payments of mortgage interest or, in Scotland, payments under heritable securities or, in either case, analogous payments)
in respect of either (but not both) the dwelling which that claimant occupies for the purpose of

attending the course of study or the training course or, as the case may be, the dwelling which that claimant occupies when not attending that course, that claimant is to be treated as occupying as the home the dwelling in respect of which that claimant is liable to make payments.

(4) A full-time student is not to be treated as occupying a dwelling as that student's home for any week of absence from it, other than an absence occasioned by the need to enter hospital for treatment, outside the period of study, if the main purposes of that student's occupation during the period of study would be to facilitate attendance on that student's course.

(5) Where a claimant has been required to move into temporary accommodation by reason of essential repairs being carried out to the dwelling normally occupied as the home and that claimant is liable to make payments (including payments of mortgage interest or, in Scotland, payments under heritable securities or, in either case, analogous payments) in respect of either (but not both) the dwelling normally occupied or the temporary accommodation, that claimant must be treated as occupying as the home the dwelling in respect of which that claimant is liable to make those payments.

(6) Where a claimant is liable to make payments in respect of two (but not more than two) dwellings, that claimant must be treated as occupying both dwellings as the home only—

(a) where that claimant has left and remains absent from the former dwelling occupied as the home through fear of violence in that dwelling or of violence by a former member of the claimant's family and it is reasonable that housing costs should be met in respect of both that claimant's former dwelling and that claimant's present dwelling occupied as the home;

(b) in the case of a couple or a member of a polygamous marriage where a partner is a fulltime student or is on a training course and it is unavoidable that that student, or they, should occupy two separate dwellings and reasonable that housing costs should be met in respect of both dwellings; or

(c) in the case where a claimant has moved into a new dwelling occupied as the home, except where sub-paragraph (5) applies, for a period not exceeding four benefit weeks from the first day of the benefit week in which the move occurs if that claimant's liability to make payments in respect of two dwellings is unavoidable.

(7) Where—

(a) a claimant has moved into a dwelling and was liable to make payments in respect of that dwelling before moving in;

(b) that claimant had claimed an income-related allowance before moving in and either that claim has not yet been determined or it has been determined but an amount has not been included under this Schedule and if the claim has been refused a further claim has been made within four weeks of the date on which the claimant moved into the new dwelling occupied as the home; and

(c) the delay in moving into the dwelling in respect of which there was liability to make payments before moving in was reasonable and—

(i) that delay was necessary in order to adapt the dwelling to meet the disablement needs of the claimant or any member of the claimant's family;

(ii) the move was delayed pending [¹⁵ local welfare provision or] the outcome of an application for a social fund payment under Part 8 of the Contributions and Benefits Act to meet a need arising out of the move or in connection with setting up the home in the dwelling, and—

(aa) a member of the claimant's family is aged five or under;

(bb) the claimant is a person in respect of whom the main phase employment and support allowance is payable;

(cc) the claimant's applicable amount includes a pensioner premium;

(dd) the claimant's applicable amount includes a severe disability premium; or

(ee) a child tax credit is paid for a member of the claimant's family who is disabled or severely disabled for the purposes of section 9(6) of the Tax Credits Act; or

(iii) the claimant became liable to make payments in respect of the dwelling while that claimant was a patient or was in residential accommodation,

that claimant is to be treated as occupying the dwelling as the home for any period not exceeding four weeks immediately prior to the date on which that claimant moved into the dwelling and in respect of which that claimant was liable to make payments.

(8) This sub-paragraph applies to a claimant who enters residential accommodation—

(a) for the purpose of ascertaining whether the accommodation suits that claimant's needs; and

(b) with the intention of returning to the dwelling which that claimant normally occupies as the home should, in the event, the residential accommodation prove not to suit that claimant's needs, and while in the accommodation, the part of the dwelling which that claimant normally occupies as the home is not let or sub-let to another person.

(9) A claimant to whom sub-paragraph (8) applies is to be treated as occupying the dwelling that the claimant normally occupies as the home during any period (commencing on the day that claimant enters the accommodation) not exceeding 13 weeks in which the claimant is resident in the accommodation, but only in so far as the total absence from the dwelling does not exceed 52 weeks.

(10) A claimant, other than a claimant to whom sub-paragraph (11) applies, is to be treated as occupying a dwelling as the home throughout any period of absence not exceeding 13 weeks, if, and only if—

(a) that claimant intends to return to occupy the dwelling as the home;
(b) the part of the dwelling normally occupied by that claimant has not been let or sub-let to another person; and
(c) the period of absence is unlikely to exceed 13 weeks.

(11) This sub-paragraph applies to a claimant whose absence from the dwelling that that claimant normally occupies as the home is temporary and—

(a) that claimant intends to return to occupy the dwelling as the home;
(b) the part of the dwelling normally occupied by that claimant has not been let or sub-let; and
(c) that claimant is—
  (i) detained in custody on remand pending trial or, as a condition of bail, required to reside—
      (aa) in a dwelling other than the dwelling that claimant occupies as the home; or
      (bb) in premises approved under section 13 of the Offender Management Act 2007,
      or, detained pending sentence upon conviction;
  (ii) resident in a hospital or similar institution as a patient;
  (iii) undergoing or, as the case may be, that claimant's partner or dependant child is undergoing, in the United Kingdom or elsewhere, medical treatment or medically approved convalescence, in accommodation other than residential accommodation;
  (iv) following, in the United Kingdom or elsewhere, a training course;
  (v) undertaking medically approved care of a person residing in the United Kingdom or elsewhere;
  (vi) undertaking the care of a child whose parent or guardian is temporarily absent from the dwelling normally occupied by that parent or guardian for the purpose of receiving medically approved care or medical treatment;
  (vii) a claimant who is, whether in the United Kingdom or elsewhere, receiving medically approved care provided in accommodation other than residential accommodation;
  (viii) a full-time student to whom sub-paragraph (3) or (6)(b) does not apply;
  (ix) a claimant other than a claimant to whom sub-paragraph (8) applies, who is receiving care provided in residential accommodation; or
  (x) a claimant to whom sub-paragraph (6)(a) does not apply and who has left the dwelling that claimant occupies as the home through fear of violence in that dwelling, or by a person who was formerly a member of that claimant's family; and
(d) the period of that claimant's absence is unlikely to exceed a period of 52 weeks, or in exceptional circumstances, is unlikely substantially to exceed that period.

(12) A claimant to whom sub-paragraph (11) applies is to be treated as occupying the dwelling that claimant normally occupies as the home during any period of absence not exceeding 52 weeks beginning with the first day of that absence.

(13) In this paragraph—

"medically approved" means certified by a medical practitioner;

"patient" means a person who is undergoing medical or other treatment as an in-patient in a hospital or similar institution;

[³ "period of study" has the meaning given in regulation 131 (interpretation);]

"residential accommodation" means accommodation which is a care home, an Abbeyfield Home or an independent hospital;

"training course" means such a course of training or instruction provided wholly or partly by or on behalf of or in pursuance of arrangements made with, or approved by or on behalf of, Scottish Enterprise, Highlands and Islands Enterprise, a government department or the Secretary of State.

Housing costs not met

9.463   6.—(1) No amount may be met under the provisions of this Schedule—
    (a) in respect of housing benefit expenditure; or
    (b) where the claimant is living in a care home, an Abbeyfield Home or an independent hospital except where the claimant is living in such a home or hospital during a temporary absence from the dwelling the claimant occupies as the home and in so far as they relate to temporary absences, the provisions of paragraph 5(8) to (12) apply to that claimant during that absence.
    (2)–(14) [³² ...]

Apportionment of housing costs

9.464   7.—(1) Where the dwelling occupied as the home is a composite hereditament and—
    (a) before 1st April 1990 for the purposes of section 48(5) of the General Rate Act 1967 (reduction of rates on dwellings), it appeared to a rating authority or it was determined in pursuance of subsection (6) of section 48 of that Act that the hereditament, including the dwelling occupied as the home, was a mixed hereditament and that only a proportion of the rateable value of the hereditament was attributable to use for the purpose of a private dwelling; or
    (b) in Scotland, before 1st April 1989 an assessor acting pursuant to section 45(1) of the Water (Scotland) Act 1980 (provision as to valuation roll) has apportioned the net annual value of the premises including the dwelling occupied as the home between the part occupied as a dwelling and the remainder,
the amounts applicable under this Schedule are to be such proportion of the amounts applicable in respect of the hereditament or premises as a whole as is equal to the proportion of the rateable value of the hereditament attributable to the part of the hereditament used for the purposes of a private tenancy or, in Scotland, the proportion of the net annual value of the premises apportioned to the part occupied as a dwelling house.

(2) Subject to sub-paragraph (1) and the following provisions of this paragraph, where the dwelling occupied as the home is a composite hereditament, the amount applicable under this Schedule is to be the relevant fraction of the amount which would otherwise be applicable under this Schedule in respect of the dwelling occupied as the home.

(3) For the purposes of sub-paragraph (2), the relevant fraction is to be obtained in accordance with the formula—

$$\frac{A}{A + B}$$

where—
A is the current market value of the claimant's interest in that part of the composite hereditament which is domestic property within the meaning of section 66 of the Act of 1988;
B is the current market value of the claimant's interest in that part of the composite hereditament which is not domestic property within that section.

(4) In this paragraph—
"composite hereditament" means—
    (a) as respects England and Wales, any hereditament which is shown as a composite hereditament in a local non-domestic rating list;
    (b) as respects Scotland, any lands and heritages entered in the valuation roll which are part residential subjects within the meaning of section 26(1) of the Act of 1987;
"local non-domestic rating list" means a list compiled and maintained under section 41(1) of the Act of 1988;
"the Act of 1987" means the Abolition of Domestic Rates Etc. (Scotland) Act 1987;
"the Act of 1988" means the Local Government Finance Act 1988.

(5) Where responsibility for expenditure which relates to housing costs met under this Schedule is shared, the amounts applicable are to be calculated by reference to the appropriate proportion of that expenditure for which the claimant is responsible.

Existing housing costs

9.465   8.—[²⁶ ...]

[²⁶ Housing costs]

9.466   9.—(1) Subject to the provisions of this Schedule, the [²⁶ ...] housing costs to be met in any particular case are—

    (a) where the claimant has been entitled to an employment and support allowance for a continuous period of 39 weeks or more, an amount—

        (i) [³² . . .]

        (ii) equal to any payments which qualify under paragraph 18(1)(a) to (c);

    (b) in any other case, nil.

  (2) [³² . . .]

  (3) Where a claimant or that claimant's partner ceases to be in receipt of or treated as being in receipt of income support, income-based jobseeker's allowance or state pension credit and one of them becomes entitled to an income-related allowance in a case to which [¹paragraph 3] applies, the eligible capital for the time being owing is to be recalculated on each anniversary of the date on which the housing costs were first met for whichever of the benefits concerned the claimant or that claimant's partner was first entitled.

  (4)–(7)[²⁶ . . .]

General exclusions from [²⁶ paragraph 9]

  10.—(1) [²⁶ Paragraph 9] will not apply where—   **9.467**

    (a) [⁷ the claimant or the claimant's partner] has attained the qualifying age for state pension credit;

    (b) the housing costs are payments—

        (i) under a co-ownership agreement;

        (ii) under or relating to a tenancy or licence of a Crown tenant; or

        (iii) where the dwelling occupied as the home is a tent, in respect of the tent and the site on which it stands.

  (2) In a case falling within sub-paragraph (1), the housing costs to be met are—

    (a) where paragraph (a) of sub-paragraph (1) applies, an amount—

        (i) [³² . . .]

        (ii) equal to the payments which qualify under paragraph 18;

    (b) where paragraph (b) of sub-paragraph (1) applies, an amount equal to the payments which qualify under paragraph 18(1)(d) to (f).

The calculation for loans

  11. [³² . . .]   **9.468**

General provisions applying to [²⁶ . . .] housing costs

  12.—[³² . . .]   **9.469**

The standard rate

  13.—[³² . . .]   **9.470**

Excessive Housing Costs

  14.—[³² . . .]   **9.471**

Linking rule

  15.—(1) [⁹ . . .] for the purposes of this Schedule—   **9.472**

    (a) a claimant is to be treated as being in receipt of an income-related allowance during the following periods—

        (i) any period in respect of which it was subsequently determined that that claimant was entitled to an income-related allowance; and

        (ii) any period of 12 weeks or less or, as the case may be, 52 weeks or less, in respect of which that claimant was not in receipt of an income-related allowance and which fell immediately between periods in respect of which—

            (aa) that claimant was, or was treated as being, in receipt of an income-related allowance;

            (bb) that claimant was treated as entitled to an income-related allowance for the purpose of sub-paragraph (9) or (10); or

            (cc) (i) above applies;

    (b) a claimant is to be treated as not being in receipt of an income-related allowance during any period other than a period to which (a)(ii) above applies in respect of which it is subsequently determined that that claimant was not so entitled;

    (c) where—

        (i) the claimant was a member of a couple or a polygamous marriage; and

    (ii) the claimant's partner was, in respect of a past period, in receipt of an income-related allowance for that claimant's partner and the claimant; and

    (iii) the claimant is no longer a member of that couple or polygamous marriage; and

    (iv) the claimant made a claim for an income-related allowance within 12 weeks or, as the case may be, 52 weeks, of ceasing to be a member of that couple or polygamous marriage,

the claimant must be treated as having been in receipt of an income-related allowance for the same period as the claimant's former partner had been or had been treated, for the purposes of this Schedule, as having been;

(d) where the claimant's partner's applicable amount was determined in accordance with paragraph 1(1) (single claimant) or paragraph 1(2) [¹² (lone parents etc.)] of Part 1 of Schedule 4 (prescribed amounts) in respect of a past period, provided that the claim was made within 12 weeks or, as the case may be, 52 weeks, of the claimant and that claimant's partner becoming one of a couple or polygamous marriage, the claimant is to be treated as having been in receipt of an income-related allowance for the same period as the claimant's partner had been or had been treated, for the purposes of this Schedule, as having been;

(e) where the claimant is a member of a couple or a polygamous marriage and the claimant's partner was, in respect of a past period, in receipt of an income-related allowance for that claimant's partner and the claimant, and the claimant has begun to receive an income-related allowance as a result of an election by the members of the couple or polygamous marriage, that claimant is to be treated as having been in receipt of an income-related allowance for the same period as that claimant's partner had been or had been treated, for the purposes of this Schedule, as having been;

(f) where the claimant—

    (i) is a member of a couple or a polygamous marriage and the claimant's partner was, immediately before the participation by any member of that couple or polygamous marriage in an employment programme specified in regulation 75(1)(a)(ii) of the Jobseeker's Allowance Regulations, in the Intensive Activity Period specified in regulation 75(1)(a)(iv) of those Regulations, in receipt of an income-related allowance and the claimant's applicable amount included an amount for the couple or for the partners of the polygamous marriage; and

    (ii) has, immediately after that participation in that programme, begun to receive an income-related allowance as a result of an election under regulation 4(3) of the Social Security (Claims and Payments) Regulations 1987 by the members of the couple or polygamous marriage,

the claimant is to be treated as having been in receipt of an income-related allowance for the same period as that claimant's partner had been or had been treated, for the purposes of this Schedule, as having been;

(g) where—

    (i) the claimant was a member of a family of a person (not being a former partner) entitled to an income-related allowance and at least one other member of that family was a child or young person;

    (ii) the claimant becomes a member of another family which includes that child or young person; and

    (iii) the claimant made a claim for an income-related allowance within 12 weeks or, as the case may be, 52 weeks, of the date on which the person entitled to an income-related allowance mentioned in paragraph (i) above ceased to be so entitled,

the claimant is to be treated as being in receipt of an income-related allowance for the same period as that person had been or had been treated, for the purposes of this Schedule, as having been.

(2) [⁹ . . .]

(3) For the purposes of this Schedule, where a claimant has ceased to be entitled to an income-related allowance because that claimant or that claimant's partner is—

(a) participating in arrangements for training made under section 2 of the Employment and Training Act 1973 or section 2 of the Enterprise and New Towns (Scotland) Act 1990; or

(b) attending a course at an employment rehabilitation centre established under that section, the claimant is to be treated as if that claimant had been in receipt of an income-related allowance for the period during which that claimant or that claimant's partner was participating in such arrangements or attending such a course.

(4) For the purposes of this Schedule, a claimant who has ceased to be entitled to an income-related allowance because—

(a) that claimant or that claimant's partner was participating in an employment programme specified in regulation 75(1)(a)(ii) of the Jobseeker's Allowance Regulations, in the

Intensive Activity Period specified in regulation 75(1)(a)(iv) of those Regulations or in an employment zone scheme; and

(b) in consequence of such participation the claimant or the claimant's partner was engaged in remunerative work or had an income [¹¹ equal to or] in excess of the claimant's applicable amount as prescribed in Part 9,

will be treated as if the claimant had been in receipt of an income-related allowance for the period during which that claimant or that claimant's partner was participating in that programme or activity.

(5) Where, for the purposes of sub-paragraphs (1), (3) and (4), a claimant is treated as being in receipt of an income-related allowance, for a certain period, that claimant will, subject to sub-paragraph (6), be treated as being entitled to an income-related allowance for the same period.

(6) [³² . . .]

(7) For the purposes of this Schedule, in determining whether a claimant is entitled to or to be treated as entitled to an income-related allowance, entitlement to a contribution-based jobseeker's allowance immediately before a period during which that claimant or that claimant's partner is participating in an employment programme specified in regulation 75(1)(a)(ii) of the Jobseeker's Allowance Regulations, in the Intensive Activity Period specified in regulation 75(1)(a)(iv) of those Regulations is to be treated as entitlement to an income-related allowance for the purposes of any requirement that a claimant is, or has been, entitled to an income-related allowance for any period of time.

(8) For the purposes of this Schedule, sub-paragraph (9) applies where a claimant is not entitled to an income-related allowance by reason only that the claimant has—

(a) capital exceeding £16,000; or
(b) income [⁹ equal to or] exceeding the applicable amount which applies in that claimant's case; or
[⁹ (bb) an amount of contributory allowance payable in respect of a claimant under section 2 that is equal to, or exceeds, the applicable amount in the claimant's case; or]
(c) both capital exceeding £16,000 and income exceeding the applicable amount which applies in that claimant's case.

(9) A claimant to whom sub-paragraph (8) applies is to be treated as entitled to an income-related allowance throughout any period of not more than 39 weeks which comprises only days—

(a) on which that claimant is entitled to a contributory allowance, a contribution-based jobseeker's allowance, statutory sick pay or incapacity benefit; or
(b) on which that claimant is, although not entitled to any of the benefits mentioned in paragraph (a) above, entitled to be credited with earnings equal to the lower earnings limit for the time being in force in accordance with regulation 8A or 8B of the Social Security (Credits) Regulations 1975.

[¹² (10) Subject to sub-paragraph (11), for the purposes of this Schedule, a claimant is to be treated as entitled to an income-related allowance throughout any period of not more than 39 weeks following the refusal of a claim for an income-related allowance made by or on behalf of the claimant, if the claimant is a person to whom sub-paragraph (8) applies and who is—

(a) a lone parent;
(b) a person who has no partner and who is responsible for and a member of the same household as a young person; or
(c) a person who is described in paragraph 4 or 5 of Schedule 1B of the Income Support (General) Regulations (person caring for another person).]

(11) Sub-paragraph (10) will not apply in relation to a claimant mentioned in that sub-paragraph who, during the period referred to in that sub-paragraph—

(a) is engaged in, or is treated as engaged in, remunerative work or whose partner is engaged in, or is treated as engaged in, remunerative work;
[¹(b) is in full-time education and in receipt of disability living allowance [¹⁸ , armed forces independence payment] [¹⁶ or personal independence payment];]
(c) is temporarily absent from Great Britain, other than in the circumstances specified in regulation 152 or 153(1)(c)(ii) (temporary absence from Great Britain).

(12) In a case where—

(a) sub-paragraphs (9) and (10) apply solely by virtue of sub-paragraph (8)(b); and
(b) the claimant's income includes payments under a policy taken out to insure against the risk that the policy holder is unable to meet [³² any payment which qualifies under paragraph 18],

sub-paragraphs (9) and (10) will have effect as if for the words "throughout any period of not more than 39 weeks" there will be substituted the words "throughout any period that payments are made in accordance with the terms of the policy".

(13) This sub-paragraph applies—

(a) to a person who claims an income-related allowance, or in respect of whom an income-related allowance is claimed and who—

  (i) received payments under a policy of insurance taken out to insure against loss of employment, and those payments are exhausted; and

  (ii) had a previous award of an income-related allowance where the applicable amount included an amount by way of housing costs; and

(b) where the period in respect of which the previous award of an income-related allowance was payable ended not more than 26 weeks before the date the claim was made.

(14) Where sub-paragraph (13) applies, in determining—

(a) [²⁶ . . .]

(b) for the purposes of paragraph 9(1) whether a claimant has been entitled to an income-related allowance for a continuous period of 39 weeks or more,

any week falling between the date of the termination of the previous award and the date of the new claim is to be ignored.

(15) In the case of a claimant who is a work or training beneficiary, the references in sub-paragraphs (1)(a)(ii), (1)(c)(iv), (1)(d) and (1)(g)(iii) to a period of 12 weeks is to be treated as references to a period of 104 weeks.

(16) For the purposes of sub-paragraph (1)(a)(ii), (1)(c)(iv), (1)(d) and (1)(g)(iii), the relevant period will be—

(a) 52 weeks in the case of a person to whom sub-paragraph (17) applies;

(b) subject to sub-paragraph (15), 12 weeks in any other case.

(17) This sub-paragraph applies, subject to sub-paragraph (18), in the case of a claimant who, on or after 27th October 2008, has ceased to be entitled to an income-related allowance because that claimant or that claimant's partner—

(a) has commenced employment as an employed earner or as a self-employed earner or has increased the hours in which that claimant or that claimant's partner is engaged in such employment;

(b) is taking active steps to establish that claimant or that claimant's partner in employment as an employed earner or as a self-employed earner under any scheme for assisting persons to become so employed which is mentioned in regulation 19(1)(r)(i) to (iii) of the Jobseeker's Allowance Regulations; or

(c) is participating in—

  (i) a New Deal option;

  (ii) an employment zone programme; or

  (iii) the self-employment route; or

  (iv) the Intensive Activity Period specified in regulation 75(1)(a)(iv) of the Jobseeker's Allowance Regulations,

and, as a consequence, that claimant or that claimant's partner was engaged in remunerative work or had income [¹¹ equal to or] in excess of the applicable amount as prescribed in Part 9.

(18) Sub-paragraph (17) is only to apply to the extent that immediately before the day on which the claimant ceased to be entitled to an income-related allowance, that claimant's housing costs were being met in accordance with paragraph [²⁶ . . .] 9(1)(a) or would have been so met but for any non-dependant deduction under paragraph 19.

(19) For the purpose of determining whether the linking rules set out in this paragraph apply in a case where a claimant's former partner was entitled to state pension credit, any reference to an income-related allowance in this Schedule is to be taken to include also a reference to state pension credit.

(20) Where a person is one to whom regulation 6(5) of the Income Support Regulations (persons not treated as engaged in remunerative work) applies, the period prescribed in paragraph (6) of that regulation is not to be included for the purposes of any linking rule or for determining whether any qualifying or other period is satisfied.

Loans on residential property

9.473   **16.**—[³² . . .]

Loans for repairs and improvements to the dwelling occupied as the home

9.474   **17.**—[³² . . .]

[³² Housing costs]

9.475   **18.**—(1) Subject to the deduction specified in sub-paragraph (2) and the reductions applicable in sub-paragraph (5), there are to be met under this paragraph the amounts, calculated on a weekly basis, in respect of the following housing costs—

(a) payments by way of rent or ground rent relating to a long tenancy;
(b) service charges;
(c) payments by way of rentcharge within the meaning of section 1 of the Rentcharges Act 1977;
(d) payments under a co-ownership scheme;
(e) payments under or relating to a tenancy or licence of a Crown tenant;
(f) where the dwelling occupied as the home is a tent, payments in respect of the tent and the site on which it stands.

(2) Subject to sub-paragraph (3), the deductions to be made from the weekly amounts to be met under this paragraph are—
(a) where the costs are inclusive of any of the items mentioned in paragraph 6(2) of Schedule 1 to the Housing Benefit Regulations 2006 (payment in respect of fuel charges), the deductions prescribed in that paragraph unless the claimant provides evidence on which the actual or approximate amount of the service charge for fuel may be estimated, in which case the estimated amount;
(b) where the costs are inclusive of ineligible service charges within the meaning of paragraph 1 of Schedule 1 to the Housing Benefit Regulations 2006 (ineligible service charges) the amounts attributable to those ineligible service charges or where that amount is not separated from or separately identified within the housing costs to be met under this paragraph, such part of the payments made in respect of those housing costs which are fairly attributable to the provision of those ineligible services having regard to the costs of comparable services;
(c) any amount for repairs and improvements, and for this purpose the expression "repairs and improvements" has [³² the meaning in sub-paragraph (6)].

(3) Where arrangements are made for the housing costs, which are met under this paragraph and which are normally paid for a period of 52 weeks, to be paid instead for a period of 53 weeks, or to be paid irregularly, or so that no such costs are payable or collected in certain periods, or so that the costs for different periods in the year are of different amounts, the weekly amount will be the amount payable for the year divided by 52.

(4) Where the claimant or a member of the claimant's family—
(a) pays for reasonable repairs or redecorations to be carried out to the dwelling they occupy; and
(b) that work was not the responsibility of the claimant or any member of the claimant's family; and
(c) in consequence of that work being done, the costs which are normally met under this paragraph are waived,
then those costs will, for a period not exceeding 8 weeks, be treated as payable.

(5) Where in England and Wales an amount calculated on a weekly basis in respect of housing costs specified in sub-paragraph (1)(e) includes water charges, that amount is to be reduced—
(a) where the amount payable in respect of water charges is known, by that amount;
(b) in any other case, by the amount which would be the likely weekly water charge had the property not been occupied by a Crown tenant.

[³² (6) For the purposes of sub-paragraph (2)(c), "repairs and improvements" means any of the following measures undertaken with a view to maintaining the fitness of the dwelling for human habitation or, where the dwelling forms part of a building, any part of a building containing that dwelling—
(a) provision of a fixed bath, shower, wash basin, sink or lavatory, and necessary associated plumbing, including the provision of hot water not connected to a central heating system;
(b) repairs to existing heating system;
(c) damp proof measures;
(d) provision of ventilation and natural lighting;
(e) provision of drainage facilities;
(f) provision of facilities for preparing and cooking food;
(g) provision of insulation of the dwelling occupied as the home;
(h) provision of electric lighting and sockets;
(i) provision of storage facilities for fuel or refuse;
(j) repairs of unsafe structural defects;
(k) adapting a dwelling for the special needs of a disabled person; or
(l) provision of separate sleeping accommodation for persons of different sexes aged 10 or over but under the age of 20 who live with the claimant and for whom the claimant or the claimant's partner is responsible.]

Non-dependant deductions

9.476   **19.**—(1) Subject to the following provisions of this paragraph, the following deductions from the amount to be met under the preceding paragraphs of this Schedule in respect of housing costs are to be made—

(a) in respect of a non-dependant aged 18 or over who is engaged in any remunerative work, [34 £100.65];

(b) in respect of a non-dependant aged 18 or over to whom paragraph (a) does not apply, [34 £15.60].

(2) In the case of a non-dependant aged 18 or over to whom sub-paragraph (1)(a) applies because that non-dependant is in remunerative work, where the claimant satisfies the Secretary of State that the non-dependant's gross weekly income is—

(a) less than [34 £143.00], the deduction to be made under this paragraph will be the deduction specified in sub-paragraph (1)(b);

(b) not less than [34 £143.00] but less than [34 £209.00], the deduction to be made under this paragraph will be [34 £35.85];

(c) not less than [34 £209.00] but less than [34 £272.00], the deduction to be made under this paragraph will be [34 £49.20];

(d) not less than [34 £272.00] but less than [34 £363.00], the deduction to be made under this paragraph will be [34 £80.55];

(e) not less than [34 £363.00] but less than [34 £451.00], the deduction to be made under this paragraph will be [34 £91.70].

[32 (2A) Where a non-dependant deduction is being made under the Loans for Mortgage Interest Regulations 2017, the amount of the deduction under sub-paragraph (1) or (2) is to be reduced by an amount equal to that non-dependant deduction.]

(3) Only one deduction is to be made under this paragraph in respect of a couple or, as the case may be, the members of a polygamous marriage, and where, but for this sub-paragraph, the amount that would fall to be deducted in respect of one member of a couple or polygamous marriage is higher than the amount (if any) that would fall to be deducted in respect of the other, or any other, member, the higher amount is to be deducted.

(4) In applying the provisions of sub-paragraph (2) in the case of a couple or, as the case may be, a polygamous marriage, regard will be had, for the purpose of sub-paragraph (2), to the couple's or, as the case may be, all the members of the polygamous marriage's, joint weekly income.

(5) Where a person is a non-dependant in respect of more than one joint occupier of a dwelling (except where the joint occupiers are a couple or members of a polygamous marriage), the deduction in respect of that non-dependant is to be apportioned between the joint occupiers (the amount so apportioned being rounded to the nearest penny) having regard to the number of joint occupiers and the proportion of the housing costs in respect of the dwelling occupied as the home payable by each of them.

(6) No deduction is to be made in respect of any non-dependants occupying the dwelling occupied as the home of the claimant, if the claimant or any partner of the claimant is—

[24 (a) certified as blind or severely sight impaired by a consultant ophthalmologist, or who is within 28 weeks of ceasing to be so certified;]

(b) receiving in respect of that claimant or that claimant's partner either—

(i) an attendance allowance; [17 . . .]

(ii) the care component of the disability living allowance [17 ; [19 . . .]

(iii) the daily living component] [19 ; or

(iv) armed forces independence payment].

(7) No deduction is to be made in respect of a non-dependant—

(a) if, although the [1 non-dependant] resides with the claimant, it appears to the Secretary of State that the dwelling occupied as the non-dependant's home is normally elsewhere;

(b) if the non-dependant is in receipt of a training allowance paid in connection with youth training;

(c) if the non-dependant is a full-time student during a period of study or, if the non-dependant is not in remunerative work, during a recognised summer vacation appropriate to the non-dependant's course;

(d) if the non-dependant is aged under 25 and in receipt of income support, an income-based jobseeker's allowance or an income-related allowance [28 and they are still in the assessment phase in accordance with regulation 4];

(e) in respect of whom a deduction in the calculation of a rent rebate or allowance falls to be made under regulation 74 of the Housing Benefit Regulations 2006 (non-dependant deductions);

[¹(f) to whom, but for paragraph (5) of regulation 71 (definition of non-dependant) para-   **9.477**
graph (4) of that regulation would apply;]
  (g) if the non-dependant is not residing with the claimant because the non-dependant has
been a patient for a period in excess of 52 weeks, or is a prisoner, and for these purposes—
      (i) "patient" has the meaning given in paragraph 5(13) and "prisoner" has the
meaning given in regulation 69(2) (special cases); and
      (ii) in calculating a period of 52 weeks as a patient, any two or more distinct periods
separated by one or more intervals each not exceeding 28 days is to be treated
as a single period; [²¹ ...]
  (h) if the non-dependant is in receipt of state pension credit; [²¹ or
  (ha) if the non-dependant is aged less than 25 and is entitled to an award of universal credit
which is calculated on the basis that the non-dependant does not have any earned
income;]
[²² (7ZA) For the purposes of sub-paragraph (7)(b)]
    "youth training" means—
      (i) arrangements made under section 2 of the Employment and Training Act 1973
or section 2 of the Enterprise and New Towns (Scotland) Act 1990; or
      (ii) arrangements made by the Secretary of State for persons enlisted in Her
Majesty's forces for any special term of service specified in regulations made
under section 2 of the Armed Forces Act 1966 (power of Defence Council to
make regulations as to engagement of persons in regular forces),
    for purposes which include the training of persons who, at the beginning of their train-
ing, are under the age of 18.
[²¹ (7A) For the purposes of sub-paragraph (7)(ha), "earned income" has the meaning given
in regulation 52 of the Universal Credit Regulations 2013.]
(8) In the case of a non-dependant to whom sub-paragraph (2) applies because that nonde-
pendent is in remunerative work, there is to be disregarded from that non-dependant's gross
income—
  (a) any attendance allowance [¹⁷ , disability living allowance [¹⁹ , armed forces independence payment] or personal independence payment] received by that non-
dependant;
  (b) any payment made under [⁵ or by] the Macfarlane Trust, the Macfarlane (Special
Payments) Trust, the Macfarlane (Special Payments) (No. 2) Trust, the Fund, the
Eileen Trust [⁴ , MFET Limited] [¹⁰ , the Skipton Fund, the Caxton Foundation]
[³⁰, the Scottish Infected Blood Support Scheme] [³³, an approved blood scheme]
[³¹, the London Emergencies Trust, the We Love Manchester Emergency Fund] or
[¹ the Independent Living Fund (2006)] which, had that non-dependant's income
fallen to be calculated under regulation 104 (calculation of income other than earnings), would have been disregarded under paragraph 22 of Schedule 8 (income in
kind); and
  (c) any payment which, had that non-dependant's income fallen to be calculated under
regulation 104 would have been disregarded under paragraph 41 of Schedule 8 (payments made under certain trusts and certain other payments);
[³³ (d) any payment made under or by a trust, established for the purpose of giving relief and
assistance to disabled persons whose disabilities were caused by the fact that during
their mother's pregnancy she had taken a preparation containing the drug known as
Thalidomide, and which is approved by the Secretary of State.]

**Continuity with income support, an income-based jobseeker's allowance or state
pension credit**

20.—(1) For the purpose of providing continuity between income support, an income-   **9.478**
based jobseeker's allowance or state pension credit and an employment and support
allowance—
  (a) [²⁶. . .]
  (b) had the award of an employment and support allowance been an award of income
support or an income-based jobseeker's allowance and the housing costs which would
then have been met would have included an additional amount met in accordance
with paragraph 7 of Schedule 3 to the Income Support Regulations or, as the case may
be, paragraph 18(1)(b) of Schedule 2 to the Jobseeker's Allowance Regulations (add
back), an amount equal to that additional amount must be added to the housing costs
to be met under this Schedule, but that amount must be subject to the same qualifications and limitations as it would have been had the award been of income support or
an income-based jobseeker's allowance; and

(c) subject to paragraph 15(20), for the purposes of any linking rule or for determining whether any qualifying or other period is satisfied, any reference to an employment and support allowance in this Schedule must be taken also to include a reference to income support, an income-based jobseeker's allowance or state pension credit.

(2) [³² . . .]

AMENDMENTS

1. Employment and Support Allowance (Miscellaneous Amendments) Regulations 2008 (SI 2008/2428) reg.16 (October 27, 2008).

2. Social Security (Housing Costs Special Arrangements) (Amendment and Modification) Regulations 2008 (SI 2008/3195) reg.2(1)(a) and (2) (January 5, 2009).

3. Social Security (Miscellaneous Amendments) (No.4) Regulations 2009 (SI 2009/2655) reg.11(17)(a) (October 26, 2009).

4. Social Security (Miscellaneous Amendments) (No.2) Regulations 2010 (SI 2010/641) reg.12(3)(e) (April 6, 2010).

5. Social Security (Miscellaneous Amendments) (No.2) Regulations 2010 (SI 2010/641) reg.12(5)(d) (April 6, 2010).

6. Social Security (Miscellaneous Amendments) (No.4) Regulations 2009 (SI 2009/2655) reg.11(17)(b) (April 12, 2010).

7. Social Security (Miscellaneous Amendments) (No.3) Regulations 2010 (SI 2010/840) reg.9(18) (June 28, 2010).

8. Social Security (Housing Costs) (Standard Interest Rate) Amendment Regulations 2010 (SI 2010/1811) reg.2(1)(d) and (2) (October 1, 2010).

9. Social Security (Miscellaneous Amendments) Regulations 2011 (SI 2011/674) reg.16(11) (April 11, 2011).

10. Social Security (Miscellaneous Amendments) (No.3) Regulations 2011 (SI 2011/2425) reg.23(8) (October 31, 2011).

11. Social Security (Miscellaneous Amendments) (No.3) Regulations 2011 (SI 2011/2425) reg.23(15) (October 31, 2011).

12. Social Security (Work-focused Interviews for Lone Parents and Partners) (Amendment) Regulations 2011 (SI 2011/2428) reg.5(7) (October 31, 2011).

13. Employment and Support Allowance (Duration of Contributory Allowance) (Consequential Amendments) Regulations 2012 (SI 2012/913), reg.9(4) (May 1, 2012).

14. Employment and Support Allowance (Amendment of Linking Rules) Regulations 2012 (SI 2012/919), reg.5(8) (May 1, 2012).

15. Social Security (Miscellaneous Amendments) Regulations 2013 (SI 2013/443), reg.9(4) (April 2, 2013).

16. Personal Independence Payment (Supplementary Provisions and Consequential Amendments) Regulations 2013 (SI 2013/388), reg.8 and Sch., Part 2, para.40(6)(a) (April 8, 2013).

17. Personal Independence Payment (Supplementary Provisions and Consequential Amendments) Regulations 2013 (SI 2013/388), reg. 8 and Sch., Part 2, para.40(6)(b) (April 8, 2013).

18. Armed Forces and Reserve Forces Compensation Scheme (Consequential Provisions: Subordinate Legislation) Order 2013 (SI 2013/591), art.7 and Sch., para.37(6)(a) (April 8, 2013).

19. Armed Forces and Reserve Forces Compensation Scheme (Consequential Provisions: Subordinate Legislation) Order 2013 (SI 2013/591), art.7 and Sch., para.37(6)(b) (April 8, 2013).

20. Universal Credit (Consequential, Supplementary, Incidental and Miscellaneous Provisions) Regulations 2013 (SI 2013/630) reg.37(7)(a) (April 29, 2013).

21. Universal Credit (Consequential, Supplementary, Incidental and Miscellaneous Provisions) Regulations 2013 (SI 2013/630) reg.37(7)(b) (April 29, 2013).

22. Social Security (Miscellaneous Amendments) (No.3) Regulations 2013 (SI 2013/2536) reg.13(36) (October 29, 2013).

23. Social Security (Miscellaneous Amendments) Regulations 2014 (SI 2014/591) reg.10(3) (April 28, 2014).

24. Universal Credit and Miscellaneous Amendments (No. 2) Regulations 2014 (SI 2014/2888) reg.3(7)(b) (November 26, 2014).

25. Shared Parental Leave and Statutory Shared Parental Pay (Consequential Amendments to Subordinate Legislation) Order 2014 (SI 2014/3255) art.20(8) (December 31, 2014).

26. Social Security (Housing Costs Amendments) Regulations 2015 (SI 2015/1647) reg.4 (April 1, 2016).

27. Social Security Benefits (Adjustment of Amounts and Thresholds) Regulations 2016 (SI 2016/242) reg.7(3) (April 11, 2016).

28. Employment and Support Allowance and Universal Credit (Miscellaneous Amendments and Transitional and Savings Provisions) Regulations 2017 (SI 2017/204) regs 2(1) and (5) (April 3, 2017).

29. Employment and Support Allowance and Universal Credit (Miscellaneous Amendments and Transitional and Savings Provisions) Regulations 2017 (SI 2017/204) reg.7(1) and Sch.1, para.15 (April 3, 2017).

30. Social Security (Scottish Infected Blood Support Scheme) Regulations 2017 (SI 2017/329) reg.8(1) and (3)(d) (April 3, 2017).

31. Social Security (Emergency Funds) (Amendment) Regulations 2017 (SI 2017/689) reg.8(1) and (3) (June 19, 2017).

32. Loans for Mortgage Interest Regulations 2017 (SI 2017/725) reg.18 and Sch.5, para.1(c) (April 6, 2018).

33. Social Security (Infected Blood and Thalidomide) Regulations 2017 (SI 2017/870) reg.8(1) and (3) (October 23, 2017).

34. Social Security Benefits Up-rating Order 2019 (SI 2019/480) art.27(5) (April 8, 2019).

DEFINITIONS

"Abbeyfield Home"—see reg.2(1).
"armed forces independence payment"—*ibid.*
"attendance allowance"—*ibid.*
"care home"—*ibid.*
"Caxton Foundation"—*ibid.*
"child"—ibid.
"child support maintenance"—see reg.2(2).
"claimant"—see reg.83(1).
"couple"—see reg.2(1).
"Crown tenant"—*ibid.*
"daily living component"—*ibid.*
"dwelling occupied as the home"—*ibid.*
"Eileen Trust"—*ibid.*
"family"—*ibid.*
"full-time student"—*ibid.*
"the Fund"—*ibid.*
"housing benefit expenditure"—*ibid.*
"independent hospital"—*ibid.*
"the Independent Living Fund (2006)"—*ibid.*
"local welfare provision "—*ibid.*
"Macfarlane (Special Payments) Trust"—*ibid.*
"Macfarlane (Special Payments) (No. 2) Trust"—*ibid.*
"Macfarlane Trust"—*ibid.*
"maintenance assessment"—see reg.2(2).
"maintenance calculation"—*ibid.*
"MFET Limited"—see reg.2(1).
"non-dependant"—see reg.71.

"partner"—see reg.2(1).
"period of study"—*ibid.*
"personal independence payment"—*ibid.*
"polygamous marriage"—*ibid.*
"shared parental leave"—*ibid.*
"Skipton Fund"—*ibid.*
"training allowance"—*ibid.*
"universal credit"—*ibid.*
"water charges"—*ibid.*
"young person"—*ibid.*

GENERAL NOTE

9.479–9.483   Sch. 6 is similar to Sch.3 to the IS Regulations/Sch.2 to the JSA Regulations 1996 (where there are differences between those Schedules Sch.6 generally adopts the income support model) and, in common with those schedules has been heavily amended to restrict its scope following the abolition of benefit payments for mortgage interest and their replacement by repayable loans: see, generally, the commentary to Sch.3 to the IS Regulations in Vol.II and the Loans for Mortgage Interest Regulations in Vol.V.

The differences from Sch. 3 before those changes are set out in full on pp.1331-3 of Vol.I of the 2017-18 edition. Those that remain relevant following the changes are as follows:

• *Paragraph 2* defines when a non-dependant will be treated as in remunerative work for the purposes of Sch.6. This paragraph is necessary because the definition of remunerative work in regs 41 and 42 only applies to the claimant and the claimant's partner and does not apply for the purposes of Sch.6 (see the definition of "remunerative work" in reg.2(1)). See also para.2(9) which specifically provides that whether a claimant or a claimant's partner is engaged in, or is to be treated as engaged in, remunerative work is to be determined in accordance with regs 41 or 42.

• There is no equivalent to para.2(2) of Sch.3 (which relates to trade disputes).

• *Paragraph 15(20)* of this Schedule provides that any period during which a claimant qualifies for a "housing costs run-on" under reg.6(5) of the Income Support Regulations does not count for the purpose of any linking rules or determining whether any qualifying or other period is satisfied under this Schedule.

• There is no waiting period for housing costs if either the claimant's partner or the claimant has reached the qualifying age for state pension credit (para.10(1)(a)) this is the same rule as for JSA (see para.8(1)(a) of Sch.2 to the JSA Regulations 1996) and reflects the fact that it is possible to claim ESA or JSA if a claimant is under pensionable age (WRA 2007 s.1(3)(c), Jobseekers Act s.1(2)(h)), whereas the cut-off in the case of income support is the qualifying age for state pension credit (s.124(1)(aa) SSCBA).

Regulations 96(2), 98(2)

SCHEDULE 7

SUMS TO BE DISREGARDED IN THE CALCULATION OF EARNINGS

9.484   1.—(1) In the case of a claimant who has been engaged in remunerative work as an employed earner or, had the employment been in Great Britain, would have been so engaged—

   (a) any earnings, other than items to which sub-paragraph (2) applies, paid or due to be paid from that employment which terminated before the first day of entitlement to an income-related allowance;

   (b) any earnings, other than a payment of the nature described in [² sub-paragraph (2)(a) or (b)(ii)], paid or due to be paid from that employment which has not been terminated where the claimant is not—

       (i) engaged in remunerative work; or

      (ii) suspended from employment.

  (2) This sub-paragraph applies to—

[² (a) any payment of the nature described in—

       (i) regulation 95(1)(e) (earnings of employed earners), or

      (ii) section 28, 64 or 68 of the Employment Rights Act 1966 (guarantee payments, suspension from work on medical or maternity grounds); and]

   (b) any award, sum or payment of the nature described in—

       (i) regulation 95(1)(g) or (i); or

      (ii) section 34 or 70 of the Employment Rights Act 1996 (guarantee payments and suspension from work: complaints to employment tribunals),

including any payment made following the settlement of a complaint to an employment tribunal or of court proceedings.

  2.—(1) In the case of a claimant to whom this paragraph applies, any earnings (other than a payment of the nature described in [² paragraph 1(2)(a) or (b)(ii)] which relate to employment which ceased before the first day of entitlement to an income-related allowance whether or not that employment has terminated.

  (2) This paragraph applies to a claimant who has been engaged in part-time employment as an employed earner or, had the employment been in Great Britain, would have been so engaged; but it does not apply to a claimant who has been suspended from employment.

  3. If the claimant's partner has been engaged in remunerative work as an employed earner or, had the employment been in Great Britain, would have been so engaged, any earnings paid or due to be paid on termination of that employment by way of retirement but only if—

   (a) on retirement the partner is entitled to a retirement pension under the Contributions and Benefits Act; or

   (b) the only reason the partner is not entitled to a retirement pension under the Contribution and Benefits Act is because the contribution conditions are not satisfied.

  [⁷ **3A.** If the claimant's partner has been engaged in remunerative work as an employed earner or, had the employment been in Great Britain, would have been so engaged, any earnings paid or due to be paid on termination of that employment by way of retirement but only if—

   (a) on retirement the partner is entitled to a state pension under Part 1 of the Pensions Act 2014; or

   (b) the only reason the partner is not entitled to a state pension under Part 1 of the Pensions Act 2014 is because the partner does not have the minimum number of qualifying years.]

  4. In the case of a claimant who has been engaged in remunerative work or part-time employment as a self-employed earner or, had the employment been in Great Britain, would have been so engaged and who has ceased to be so employed, from the date of the cessation of the claimant's employment any earnings derived from that employment except earnings to which regulation 92(2) (royalties etc.) applies.

  5. In the case of a claimant who is undertaking work which falls within one of the categories in regulation 45(2) to (4) any earnings derived from that work which do not exceed the limits specified for that work of £20 in regulation 45(2) or, as the case may be, [⁴ 16 x National Minimum Wage] in regulation 45(3) or (4).

  [³ **5A.** In the case of a claimant who receives a payment to which regulation 92(2) applies, £20, except where regulation 45(2) to (4) applies to the claimant, in which case the amounts specified in paragraph 6 shall apply, but only up to a maximum of £20.]

  6. Where regulation 45(2) to (4) applies to the claimant and that claimant's earnings are less than—

   (a) in a case to which regulation 45(2) applies, £20;

   (b) in a case to which regulation 45(3) and (4) applies, [⁴ 16 x National Minimum Wage], the earnings of the claimant's partner are to be disregarded to the extent that the claimant's earnings are less than £20 or, as the case may be, [⁴ 16 x National Minimum Wage], but only up to a maximum of £20.

7.—(1) In a case to which this paragraph applies, £20; but notwithstanding regulation 83 (calculation of income and capital of members of claimant's family and of a polygamous marriage), if this paragraph applies to a claimant it will not apply to the claimant's partner except where, and to the extent that, the earnings of the claimant which are to be disregarded under this paragraph are less than £20.

(2) Subject to sub-paragraph (3), this paragraph applies in the case of a claimant to whom regulation 40(2)(a), (b) or (e), 43(1)(a), (d), (e) or (f), or (2) or 45(5) applies.

(3) Where a claimant is doing the work set out in regulation 40(2)(b) and is also undertaking any of the categories of work set out in regulation 45(2) to (4), this paragraph applies only to the extent that the claimant's earnings are less than the limit of—

(a) £20 set out in regulation 45(2); or

(b) [⁴ 16 x National Minimum Wage] set out in regulation 45(3) and (4),

as the case may be.

(4) This paragraph applies, in a case where the claimant's partner is in part-time employment and paragraph 6 does not apply.

8. Notwithstanding the foregoing provisions of this Schedule, where two or more payments of earnings of the same kind and from the same source are to be taken into account in the same benefit week, because it has not been practicable to treat the payments under regulation 93(1)(b) (date on which income treated as paid) as paid on the first day of the benefit week in which they were due to be paid, there is to be disregarded from each payment the sum that would have been disregarded if the payment had been taken into account on the date on which it was due to be paid.

9. Any earnings derived from employment which are payable in a country outside the United Kingdom for such period during which there is a prohibition against the transfer to the United Kingdom of those earnings.

10. Where a payment of earnings is made in a currency other than sterling, any banking charge or commission payable in converting that payment into sterling.

11. Any earnings which are due to be paid before the date of claim and which would otherwise fall to be taken into account in the same benefit week as a payment of the same kind and from the same source.

[⁵ **11A.**—(1) In the case of an income-related employment and support allowance, where earnings to which sub-paragraph (2) applies (in aggregate with the claimant's other income (if any) calculated in accordance with this Part) exceed the applicable amount (calculated as specified in section 4(2) and (3) of the Act) less 10 pence, the amount of those earnings corresponding to that excess.

(2) This sub-paragraph applies to earnings, in so far as they exceed the amount disregarded under paragraph 7, derived by the claimant's partner from employment as a member of any [⁶ ...] reserve force prescribed in Part 1 of Schedule 6 to the Social Security (Contributions) Regulations 2001 in respect of annual continuous training for a maximum period of 15 days in any calendar year [⁶ or in respect of training in the claimant's first year of training as a member of a reserve force for a maximum of 43 days in that year.]]

12. In the case of a claimant who—

(a) has been engaged in employment as a member of any [⁶ ...] reserve force prescribed in Part 1 of Schedule 6 to the Social Security (Contributions) Regulations 2001; and

(b) by reason of that employment has failed to satisfy any of the conditions for entitlement to an income-related allowance other than paragraph 6(1)(a) of Schedule 1 to the Act (income not in excess of the applicable amount),

any earnings from that employment paid in respect of the period in which the claimant was not entitled to an income-related allowance.

13. In the case of a person to whom paragraph (5) of regulation 6 of the Income Support Regulations applies, any earnings.

14. In this Schedule—

"part-time employment" means, if the person were entitled to income support, employment in which the person is not to be treated as engaged in remunerative work under regulation 5 or 6(1) and (4) of the Income Support Regulations (persons treated, or not treated, as engaged in remunerative work);

"remunerative work", for the purposes of this paragraph and paragraphs 1, 3 and 4, has the meaning prescribed in regulation 5, except for paragraphs (3B) and (4) of that regulation, of the Income Support Regulations.

AMENDMENTS

1. Social Security (Miscellaneous Amendments) (No.3) Regulations 2009 (SI 2009/2343) reg.5(4) (October 1, 2009).

2. Social Security (Miscellaneous Amendments) (No.4) Regulations 2009 (SI 2009/2655) reg.11(18) (October 26, 2009).

3. Social Security (Miscellaneous Amendments) (No.3) Regulations 2010 (SI 2010/840) reg.9(19) (June 28, 2010).

4. Social Security (Miscellaneous Amendments) Regulations 2011 (SI 2011/674) reg.16(12) (April 11, 2011).

5. Social Security (Miscellaneous Amendments) (No.2) Regulations 2012 (SI 2012/2575) reg.5(3) (November 5, 2012).

6. Social Security (Members of the Reserve Forces) (Amendment) Regulations 2015 (SI 2015/389) reg.4(4)(a) (April 6, 2015).

7. Pensions Act 2014 (Consequential, Supplementary and Incidental Amendments) Order 2015 (SI 2015/1985) art.31(3) (April 6, 2016).

DEFINITIONS

"benefit week"—see reg.2(1).
"couple"—*ibid.*
"employed earner"—*ibid.*
"family"—*ibid.*
"first year of training"—*ibid.*
"National Minimum Wage"—*ibid.*
"partner"—*ibid.*
"polygamous marriage"—*ibid.*

GENERAL NOTE

Paragraphs 1–4
Paragraphs 1 to 4 are similar to paras 1 to 3 of Sch.8 to the Income Support Regulations/paras 1 to 4 of Sch.6 to the JSA Regulations 1996. They contain the earnings disregards on the termination of "remunerative work" (defined in para.14) and on the stopping of "part-time employment" (also defined in para.14) before the claim, as well as on the cessation of self-employment. Note that the definitions of "remunerative work" and "part-time employment" largely (but not entirely) import the income support tests.

9.485

Paragraphs 5–7
The disregards in these paragraphs are different from those in Sch.8 to the Income Support Regulations/Sch.6 to the JSA Regulations 1996 because of the different rules for the effect of work on entitlement to ESA (see regs 40–46 for these rules).

The earnings limit for "exempt work" under reg.45(2) is £20. From April 11, 2011 the earnings limit for such work under reg.45(3) or (4), rather than being a set amount, is 16 x the national minimum wage (rounded up to the nearest 50p or £1, as the case may be—see reg.45(9A)). This change was introduced so as to avoid the need to amend the regulations each time the national minimum wage changes. At the current rate of the national minimum wage (in April 2019) the earnings limit for exempt work under reg.45(3) or (4), after taking account of the rounding up, is £131.50 (see the note to the out-dated definition of "National Minimum Wage" in reg.2(1)).

9.486

Paragraph 5 disregards earnings from exempt work up to the relevant limit. In addition, if the claimant's earnings from such work are less than the relevant limit, his partner's earnings are ignored to the extent of the spare amount below the relevant limit, subject to a maximum of £20 (para.6).

Under para.7 earnings from the following attract a £20 disregard:

(i) work undertaken by the claimant as a councillor, as a member of the Disability Living Allowance Advisory Board (abolished on February 7, 2013 by the Public Bodies (Abolition of the Disability Living Allowance Advisory Board) Order 2013, arts 1(2) and 3) or as a tribunal member with a disability qualification, during an emergency to protect another person, property or livestock, or while receiving assistance in pursuing self-employment under a government scheme;

(ii) work undertaken by the claimant's partner as a childminder, as a councillor, as a part-time fire-fighter, auxiliary coastguard, part-time member of a lifeboat crew or member of the Territorial army, or where the partner is receiving assistance under the "self-employment route" (defined in reg.2(1)), or is not to be treated as in remunerative work under one of the categories in reg.43(2);

(iii) part-time employment (defined in para.14) undertaken by the claimant's partner where the disregard under para.6 does not apply.

9.487   But note that a couple cannot have a total disregard of more than £20.

Note also that if a claimant who is working as a member of the Disability Living Allowance Advisory Board (now abolished, see above) or as a tribunal member with a disability qualification is also doing work that counts as exempt work under reg.45(2) to (4), the disregard under para.7 only applies to the extent that his earnings are less than the relevant limit for that exempt work.

Paragraph 5A

9.488   This provides for a £20 disregard to apply to royalties, copyright payments and public lending right payments. The wording of para.5A is not exactly clear but it seems that the intent is that if a disregard in respect of exempt work already applies, the disregard under para.5A will depend on the amount by which the claimant's earnings fall below the relevant permitted work earnings limit, subject to the £20 maximum (see DMG, para.50468).

Paragraph 11A

9.489   Under para.11A earnings of a claimant's partner as a member of a reserve force from training (i) for a maximum of 43 days in the first year of training (see the definition of "first year of training" in reg.2(1)); or (ii) for a maximum of 15 days' annual continuous training in any calendar year are disregarded to the extent that they would have the effect of reducing entitlement to income-related ESA to less than 10p per week. This disregard is in addition to the £20 disregard of a partner's earnings as a member of a reserve force in para.7(2).

Note that the additional words added at the end of para.11A(2) on April 6, 2015 refer to "the *claimant's* first year of training as a member of a reserve force". However, it seems likely that this is intended to refer in this context to the claimant's *partner's* first year of such training.

The purpose of para.11A is to enable entitlement to ESA to continue while a claimant's partner is attending such training (note that a claimant's partner is not treated as in remunerative work for the purposes of ESA if s/he is engaged in employment as a member of a reserve force: see reg.43(1)(e)(vi)). See also reg.91(4A) for the periods that earnings from such training are taken into account. The relevant period begins on the date that the earnings are treated as paid under reg.93 (see reg.91(4B)).

Paragraphs 8-12

9.490   Paragraphs 8 to 12 are similar to paras 10 to 13 and 15A of Sch.8 to the Income Support Regulations/paras 13–16 and 19 of Sch.6 to the JSA Regulations 1996.

SCHEDULE 8

SUMS TO BE DISREGARDED IN THE CALCULATION OF INCOME OTHER THAN EARNINGS

1. Any amount paid by way of tax on income which is taken into account under regulation 104 (calculation of income other than earnings).

9.491

[[19] **1A.** Any payment in respect of any travel or other expenses incurred, or to be incurred, by the claimant in respect of that claimant's participation in [[23] a scheme prescribed in regulation 3 of the Jobseeker's Allowance (Schemes for Assisting Persons to Obtain Employment) Regulations 2013] or the Mandatory Work Activity Scheme.]

2. Any payment in respect of any expenses incurred, or to be incurred, by a claimant who is—

    (a) engaged by a charitable or voluntary organisation; or

    (b) a volunteer,

if the claimant otherwise derives no remuneration or profit from the employment and is not to be treated as possessing any earnings under regulation 108(3) (notional income).

[[5] **2A.** Any payment in respect of expenses arising out of the [[32] claimant participating as a service user].]

3. In the case of employment as an employed earner, any payment in respect of expenses wholly, exclusively and necessarily incurred in the performance of the duties of the employment.

4. In the case of a payment under Parts 11 to 12ZB of the Contributions and Benefits Act or any remuneration paid by or on behalf of an employer to the claimant who for the time being is unable to work due to illness or maternity or who is taking paternity leave [[35] shared parental leave] or adoption leave—

    (a) any amount deducted by way of primary Class 1 contributions under the Contributions and Benefits Act;

    (b) one-half of any sum paid by the claimant by way of a contribution towards an occupational or personal pension scheme.

5. In Northern Ireland, in the case of a payment under Parts 11 to 12ZB of the Social Security Contributions and Benefits (Northern Ireland) Act 1992, or any remuneration paid by or on behalf of an employer to the claimant who for the time being is unable to work due to illness or maternity or who is taking paternity leave [[35] shared parental leave] or adoption leave—

    (a) any amount deducted by way of primary Class 1 contributions under that Act;

    (b) one-half of any sum paid by way of a contribution towards an occupational or personal pension scheme.

6. Any guardian's allowance.

7.—(1) Any child tax credit.

(2) Any child benefit.

[[12] [[16] (3) Any increase in respect of a dependent child or dependent young person under section 80 or 90 of the Contributions and Benefits Act.]]

8. Any mobility component of disability living allowance [[27] or the mobility component of personal independence payment].

9. Any concessionary payment made to compensate for the non-payment of—

    (a) any payment specified in paragraph 8 or 11;

    (b) an [[1]income-related] employment and support allowance, income support [[31] , universal credit] or [[1] an income-based jobseeker's allowance].

10. Any mobility supplement or any payment intended to compensate for the non-payment of such a supplement.

11. Any attendance allowance [[28] , the care component of disability living allowance or the daily living component].

12. Any payment to the claimant as holder of the Victoria Cross or George Cross or any analogous payment.

13.—(1) Any payment—
(a) by way of an education maintenance allowance made pursuant to—
   (i) regulations made under section 518 of the Education Act 1996;
   (ii) regulations made under section 49 or 73(f) of the Education (Scotland) Act 1980; or
   (iii) directions made under section 73ZA of the Education (Scotland) Act 1980 and paid under section 12(2)(c) of the Further and Higher Education (Scotland) Act 1992; [22 . . .]
(b) corresponding to such an education maintenance allowance, made pursuant to—
   (i) section 14 or section 181 of the Education Act 2002; or
   (ii) regulations made under section 181 of that Act [22 ; or
(c) in England, by way of financial assistance made pursuant to section 14 of the Education Act 2002.]
(2) Any payment, other than a payment to which sub-paragraph (1) applies, made pursuant to—
(a) regulations made under section 518 of the Education Act 1996;
(b) regulations made under section 49 of the Education (Scotland) Act 1980; or
(c) directions made under section 73ZA of the Education (Scotland) Act 1980 and paid under section 12(2)(c) of the Further and Higher Education (Scotland) Act 1992;
in respect of a course of study attended by a child or a young person or a person who is in receipt of an education maintenance allowance [22 or other payment] made pursuant to any provision specified in sub-paragraph (1).

14. Any payment made to the claimant by way of a repayment under regulation 11(2) of the Education (Teacher Student Loans) (Repayment etc.) Regulations 2002.

15.—(1) Any payment made pursuant to section 2 of the Employment and Training Act 1973 (functions of the Secretary of State) or section 2 of the Enterprise and New Towns (Scotland) Act 1990 (functions in relation to training for employment etc.) except a payment—
(a) made as a substitute for an employment and support allowance [12 or a jobseeker's allowance];
(b) of an allowance referred to in section 2(3) of the Employment and Training Act 1973 or section 2(5) of the Enterprise and New Towns (Scotland) Act 1990;
(c) intended to meet the cost of living expenses which relate to any one or more of the items specified in sub-paragraph (2) whilst a claimant is participating in an education, training or other scheme to help the claimant enhance that claimant's employment prospects unless the payment is a Career Development Loan paid pursuant to section 2 of the Employment and Training Act 1973 and the period of education or training or the scheme, which is supported by that loan, has been completed; or
(d) made in respect of the cost of living away from home to the extent that the payment relates to rent for which housing benefit is payable in respect of accommodation which is not normally occupied by the claimant as that claimant's home.
(2) The items specified in this sub-paragraph for the purposes of sub-paragraph (1)(c) are food, ordinary clothing or footwear, household fuel, rent for which housing benefit is payable, or any housing costs to the extent that they are met under regulation 67(1)(c) or 68(1)(d) (housing costs), of the claimant or, where the claimant is a member of a family, any other member of the claimant's family, or any council tax or water charges for which that claimant or member is liable.

[17 **15A.** Any payment made to the claimant in respect of any travel or other expenses incurred, or to be incurred, in complying with a requirement to undertake work-related activity.]

16.—(1) Subject to sub-paragraph (2) and paragraph 41, any relevant payment made or due to be made at regular intervals.
(2) Sub-paragraph (1) is not to apply to a payment which is made by a person for the maintenance of any member of that person's family or of that person's former partner or of that person's children.
(3) In this paragraph, "relevant payment" means—
(a) a charitable payment;
(b) a voluntary payment;
(c) a payment (not falling within sub-paragraph (a) or (b) above) from a trust whose funds are derived from a payment made in consequence of any personal injury to the claimant;

   (d) a payment under an annuity purchased—
        (i) pursuant to any agreement or court order to make payments to the claimant; or
       (ii) from funds derived from a payment made,
     in consequence of any personal injury to the claimant; or
   (e) a payment (not falling within sub-paragraph (a) to (d) above) received by virtue of any agreement or court order to make payments to the claimant in consequence of any personal injury to the claimant.

17. Subject to paragraphs 39 and 40, £10 of any of the following, namely—
   (a) a war disablement pension (except insofar as such a pension falls to be disregarded under paragraph 10 or 11);
   (b) a war widow's pension or war widower's pension;
   (c) a pension payable to a person as a widow, widower or surviving civil partner under any power of Her Majesty otherwise than under an enactment to make provision about pensions for or in respect of persons who have been disabled or have died in consequence of service as members of the armed forces of the Crown;
   (d) a guaranteed income payment [³ and, if the amount of that payment has been abated to less than £10 by a [⁶ pension or payment falling within article 31(1)(a) or (b) of the Armed Forces and Reserve Forces (Compensation Scheme) Order 2005], so much of [⁶ that pension or payment] as would not, in aggregate with the amount of [⁶ any] guaranteed income payment disregarded, exceed £10];
   (e) a payment made to compensate for the non-payment of such a pension or payment as is mentioned in any of the preceding sub-paragraphs;
   (f) a pension paid by the government of a country outside Great Britain which is analogous to any of the pensions or payments mentioned in sub-paragraphs (a) to (d) above;
[³⁹ (g) a pension paid by a government to victims of National Socialist persecution;]
   (h) any widowed mother's allowance paid pursuant to section 37 of the Contributions and Benefits Act;
   (i) any widowed parent's allowance paid pursuant to section 39A of the Contributions and Benefits Act.

18. Where a claimant receives income under an annuity purchased with a loan which satisfies the following conditions—
   (a) that the loan was made as part of a scheme under which not less than 90% of the proceeds of the loan were applied to the purchase by the person to whom it was made of an annuity ending with that person's life or with the life of the survivor of two or more persons (in this paragraph referred to as "the annuitants") who include the person to whom the loan was made;
   (b) that the interest on the loan is payable by the person to whom it was made or by one of the annuitants;
   (c) that at the time the loan was made the person to whom it was made or each of the annuitants had attained the age of 65 [⁴⁹ or, if it was higher at that time, pensionable age];
   (d) that the loan was secured on a dwelling in Great Britain and the person to whom the loan was made or one of the annuitants owns an estate or interest in that dwelling; and
   (e) that the person to whom the loan was made or one of the annuitants occupies the accommodation on which it was secured as that person's home at the time the interest is paid,
the amount, calculated on a weekly basis equal to—
        (i) where, or insofar as, section 369 of the Income and Corporation Taxes Act 1988 (mortgage interest payable under deduction of tax) applies to the payments of interest on the loan, the interest which is payable after deduction of a sum equal to income tax on such payments at the applicable percentage of income tax within the meaning of section 369(1A) of that Act;
       (ii) in any other case the interest which is payable on the loan without deduction of such a sum.

19. Any payment made to the claimant by a person who normally resides with the claimant, which is a contribution towards that person's living and accommodation costs, except where that person is residing with the claimant in circumstances to which paragraph 20 or 21 refers.

20. Where the claimant occupies a dwelling as the claimant's home and the dwelling is also occupied by another person and there is a contractual liability to make payments to the claimant in respect of the occupation of the dwelling by that person or a member of that person's family—   **9.492**

(a) where the aggregate of any payments made in respect of any one week in respect of the occupation of the dwelling by that person or a member of that person's family, or by that person and a member of that person's family, is less than £20, the whole of that amount; or

(b) where the aggregate of such payments is £20 or more per week, £20.

21. Where the claimant occupies a dwelling as the claimant's home and the claimant provides in that dwelling board and lodging accommodation, an amount, in respect of each person for whom such accommodation is provided for the whole or any part of a week, equal to—

(a) where the aggregate of any payments made in respect of any one week in respect of such accommodation provided to such person does not exceed £20, 100% of such payments; or

(b) where the aggregate of any such payments exceeds £20, £20 and 50% of the excess over £20.

22.—(1) Subject to sub-paragraphs (2) and (3), except where regulation 104(8)(b) (provision of support under section 95 or 98 of the Immigration and Asylum Act including support provided by virtue of regulations made under Schedule 9 to that Act in the calculation of income other than earnings) or regulation 107(3)(a) (notional income) applies, any income in kind;

(2) The exception under sub-paragraph (1) will not apply where the income in kind is received from the Macfarlane Trust, the Macfarlane (Special Payments) Trust, the Macfarlane (Special Payments) (No.2) Trust, the Fund, the Eileen Trust[8, MFET Limited][20, the Skipton Fund, the Caxton Foundation][40, the Scottish Infected Blood Support Scheme] [42, an approved blood scheme][41, the London Emergencies Trust, the We Love Manchester Emergency Fund] or [1the Independent Living Fund (2006)].

(3) The first exception under sub-paragraph (1) will not apply where the claimant is the partner of a person subject to immigration control and whose partner is receiving support provided under section 95 or 98 of the Immigration and Asylum Act including support provided by virtue of regulations made under Schedule 9 to that Act and the income in kind is support provided in respect of essential living needs of the partner of the claimant and the claimant's dependants (if any) as is specified in regulations made under paragraph 3 of Schedule 8 to the Immigration and Asylum Act.

(4) The reference in sub-paragraph (1) to "income in kind" does not include a payment to a third party made in respect of the claimant which is used by the third party to provide benefits in kind to the claimant.

23.—(1) Any income derived from capital to which the claimant is or is treated under regulation 117 (capital jointly held) as beneficially entitled but, subject to sub-paragraph (2), not income derived from capital disregarded under paragraph 1, 2, 4 to 8, 10 or 16 of Schedule 9.

(2) Income derived from capital disregarded under paragraph 2 or 4 to 8 of Schedule 9 but only to the extent of—

(a) any mortgage repayments made in respect of the dwelling or premises in the period during which that income accrued; or

(b) any council tax or water charges which the claimant is liable to pay in respect of the dwelling or premises and which are paid in the period during which that income accrued.

(3) The definition of "water charges" in regulation 2(1) is to apply to sub-paragraph (2) with the omission of the words "in so far as such charges are in respect of the dwelling which a person occupies as the home".

24. Any income which is payable in a country outside the United Kingdom for such period during which there is prohibition against the transfer to the United Kingdom of that income.

25. Where a payment of income is made in a currency other than sterling, any banking charge or commission payable in converting that payment into sterling.

26.—(1) Any payment made to the claimant in respect of a child or young person who is a member of the claimant's family—

(a) pursuant to regulations under section 2(6)(b), 3 or 4 of the Adoption and Children Act 2002 or in accordance with a scheme approved by the Scottish Ministers under section 51A of the Adoption (Scotland) Act 1978 (schemes for payment of allowances to adopters) [18 or in accordance with an adoption allowance scheme made under section 71 of the Adoption and Children (Scotland) Act 2007 (adoption allowances schemes)];

(b) which is a payment made by a local authority in pursuance of section 15(1) of, and paragraph 15 of Schedule 1 to, the Children Act 1989 (local authority contribution to a child's maintenance where the child is living with a person as a result of a [³³ child arrangements] order) [⁷, or in Scotland section 50 of the Children Act 1975 (payments towards maintenance of children)];

(c) which is a payment made by an authority, as defined in Article 2 of the Children (Northern Ireland) Order 1995, in pursuance of Article 15 of, and paragraph 17 of Schedule 1 to, that Order (contributions by an authority to child's maintenance);

(d) in accordance with regulations made pursuant to section 14F of the Children Act 1989 (special guardianship support services).

(2) Any payment, other than a payment to which sub-paragraph (1)(a) applies, made to the claimant pursuant to regulations under section 2(6)(b), 3 or 4 of the Adoption and Children Act 2002.

27. In the case of a claimant who has a child or young person—

(a) who is a member of the claimant's family; and

(b) who is residing at an educational establishment at which that child or young person is receiving relevant education,

any payment made to that educational establishment, in respect of that child or young person's maintenance by or on behalf of a person who is not a member of the family or by a member of the family out of funds contributed for that purpose by a person who is not a member of the family.

[¹³ **28.** Any payment made to the claimant with whom a person is accommodated by virtue of arrangements made—

(a) by a local authority under—

[⁴⁴(i) section 22C of the Children Act 1989 (ways in which looked after children are to be accommodated and maintained,]

[⁴³(ia) section 81(2) of the Social Services and Well-being (Wales) Act 2014 (ways in which looked after children are to be accommodated and maintained),]

(ii) section 26 of the Children (Scotland) Act 1995 (manner of provision of accommodation to child looked after by local authority), or

(iii) regulations 33 or 51 of the Looked After Children (Scotland) Regulations 2009 (fostering and kinship care allowances and fostering allowances); or

(b) by a voluntary organisation under section 59(1)(a) of the 1989 Act (provision of accommodation by voluntary organisations).]

29. Any payment made to the claimant or the claimant's partner for a person ("the person concerned"), who is not normally a member of the claimant's household but is temporarily in the claimant's care, by—

(a) a health authority;

(b) a local authority but excluding payments of housing benefit made in respect of the person concerned;

(c) a voluntary organisation;

(d) the person concerned pursuant to section 26(3A) of the National Assistance Act 1948;

[³⁰ (da) a clinical commissioning group;

(db) the National Health Service Commissioning Board; [³⁶...]]

(e) [³⁰...]

(f) a Local Health Board established under section 16BA of the National Health Service Act 1977 or by an order made under section 11 of the Health Service (Wales) Act [³⁶ or

(g) the person concerned where the payment is for the provision of accommodation in respect of the meeting of that person's needs under section 18 or 19 of the Care Act 2014 (duty and power to meet needs for care and support) [⁴³ or under section 35 or 36 of the Social Services and Well-being (Wales) Act 2014 (duty and powers to meet care and support needs of an adult)].]

[⁴⁵**29A.**— Any payment made to a claimant under section 73(1)(b) of the Children and Young People (Scotland) Act 2014 (kinship care assistance).]

30.—(1) Any payment made by a local authority in accordance with—

(a) section 17, 23B, 23C or 24A of the Children Act 1989;

(b) section 12 of the Social Work (Scotland) Act 1968; [⁴³...]

[³⁸ (c) section 22, 26A, 29 or 30 of the Children (Scotland) Act 1995 (local authorities' duty to promote welfare of children, duty to provide continuing care and provision of advice and assistance to certain [⁴³ young persons); or

(d) the following sections of the Social Services and Well-being (Wales) Act 2014—
  (aa) section 37 or 38, but excluding any direct payment made in accordance with regulations made under section 51 of that Act, or
  (bb) section 109, 110, 114 or 115.]]

(2) Subject to paragraph (3), any payment (or part of a payment) made by a local authority in accordance with section 23C of the Children Act 1989 [³⁸ or section 22, 26A or 29 of the Children (Scotland) Act 1995 (local authorities' duty to promote welfare of children, duty to provide continuing care and provision of advice and assistance for certain young persons] to a person ("A") which A passes on to the claimant.

(3) Sub-paragraph (2) applies only where A—
  (a) was formerly in the claimant's care; and
[³⁸ (b) is aged 18 or over or, in the case of a payment or part of a payment made in accordance with section 26A of the Children (Scotland) Act 1995, aged 16 or over, and]
  (c) continues to live with the claimant.

[⁴⁶**31.** Any payment received under an insurance policy taken out to insure against the risk of being unable to maintain repayments on a loan which qualifies under Part 1 of Schedule 1 to the Loans for Mortgage Interest Regulations 2017 (legacy benefit claimants and SPC claimants) and used to meet such repayments.]

32.—(1) Except where paragraph 31 (or 33) applies, and subject to sub-paragraph (2), any payment made to the claimant which is intended to be used and is used as a contribution towards—
  (a) any payment due on a loan if secured on the dwelling occupied as the home which does not qualify under [⁴⁶Part 1 of Schedule 1 to the Loans for Mortgage Interest Regulations];
[⁴⁶(b) any charge which qualifies in accordance with paragraph 18 of Schedule 6 (housing costs) to these Regulations or any interest payment on a loan which qualifies under Part 1 of Schedule 1 to the Loans for Mortgage Interest Regulations, to the extent that the charge or payment is not met under these Regulations or by loan payments (as the case may be)];
  (c) any payment due on a loan which qualifies under [⁴⁶Part 1 of Schedule 1 to the Loans for Mortgage Interest Regulations] attributable to the payment of capital;
  (d) any amount due by way of premiums on—
    (i) an insurance policy taken out to insure against the risk of being unable to make the payments referred to in (a) to (c) above; or
    (ii) a policy of insurance taken out to insure against loss or damage to any building or part of a building which is occupied by the claimant as the claimant's home;
  (e) the claimant's rent in respect of the dwelling occupied by the claimant as the home but only to the extent that it is not met by housing benefit; or the claimant's accommodation charge but only to the extent that the actual charge exceeds the amount payable by a local authority in accordance with Part 3 of the National Assistance Act 1948 [³⁶ or Part 1 of the Care Act 2014 (care and support) [⁴³ or Part 4 of the Social Services and Well-being (Wales) Act 2014 (meeting needs) other than direct payments made in accordance with regulations made under section 50 or 52 of that Act]].

(2) This paragraph does not apply to any payment which is treated as possessed by the claimant by virtue of regulation 107(3)(c).

[⁴⁶(3) In this paragraph—
  (a) "Loans for Mortgage Interest Regulations" means the Loans for Mortgage Interest Regulations 2017;
  (b) "loan payments" has the meaning given in the Loans for Mortgage Interest Regulations.]

33.—(1) Subject to sub-paragraph (2), any payment received under an insurance policy, other than an insurance policy referred to in paragraph 31, taken out to insure against the risk of being unable to maintain repayments under a regulated agreement as defined for the purposes of the Consumer Credit Act 1974 or under a hire-purchase agreement or a conditional sale agreement as defined for the purposes of Part 3 of the Hire-Purchase Act 1964.

(2) A payment referred to in sub-paragraph (1) is to only be disregarded to the extent that the payment received under that policy does not exceed the amounts, calculated on a weekly basis which are used to—
  (a) maintain the repayments referred to in sub-paragraph (1); and
  (b) meet any amount due by way of premiums on that policy.

34.—(1) Subject to sub-paragraphs (2) and (3), in the case of a claimant residing in a care home, an Abbeyfield Home or an independent hospital, any payment, except a charitable or voluntary payment disregarded under paragraph 16 made to the claimant which is intended to be used and is used to meet the cost of maintaining the claimant in that home or hospital.

(2) This paragraph does not apply to a claimant for whom accommodation in a care home, an Abbeyfield Home or an independent hospital is provided by

[³⁶ (a)   a local authority under section 26 of the National Assistance Act 1948; or
     (b)   a person other than a local authority under arrangements made with the person by a local authority in the exercise of the local authority's functions under section 18 or 19 of the Care Act 2014 (duty and power to meet needs for care and support) [⁴³ or under section 35 or 36 of the Social Services and Well-being (Wales) Act 2014 (duty and powers to meet care and support needs of an adult)].]

(3) The amount to be disregarded under this paragraph is not to exceed the difference between—
     (a)   the claimant's applicable amount; and
     (b)   the weekly charge for the accommodation.

35. Any social fund payment made pursuant to Part 8 of the Contributions and Benefits Act.

[²⁵ **35A.** Any local welfare provision.]

36. Any payment of income which under regulation 112 (income treated as capital) is to be treated as capital.

37. Any payment under Part 10 of the Contributions and Benefits Act (pensioner's Christmas bonus).

38. Any payment which is due to be paid before the date of claim which would otherwise fall to be taken into account in the same benefit week as a payment of the same kind and from the same source.

39. The total of a claimant's income or, if the claimant is a member of a family, the family's income and the income of any person which the claimant is treated as possessing under regulation 83(3) (calculation of income and capital of members of claimant's family and of a polygamous marriage) to be disregarded under regulation 133(2)(b) and 134(1)(c) (calculation of covenant income), regulation 137(1) and (2) (treatment of student loans), regulation 138(3) (treatment of payments from access funds) and paragraph 17 is in no case to exceed £20 per week.

40. Notwithstanding paragraph 39 where two or more payments of the same kind and from the same source are to be taken into account in the same benefit week, there is to be disregarded from each payment the sum which would otherwise fall to be disregarded under this Schedule; but this paragraph is to apply only in the case of a payment which it has not been practicable to treat under regulation 93(1)(b) (date on which income is treated as paid) as paid on the first day of the benefit week in which it is due to be paid.

41.—(1) Any payment made under [⁹ or by] the Macfarlane Trust, the Macfarlane (Special Payments) Trust, the Macfarlane (Special Payments) (No. 2) Trust ("the Trusts"), the Fund, the Eileen Trust[⁸, MFET Limited][²⁰, the Skipton Fund, the Caxton Foundation][⁴⁰, the Scottish Infected Blood Support Scheme] or [¹the Independent Living Fund (2006)].

(2) Any payment by or on behalf of a person who is suffering or who suffered from haemophilia, or who is or was a qualifying person which derives from a payment made under [⁹ or by] any of the Trusts to which sub-paragraph (1) refers and which is made to or for the benefit of—
     (a)   that person's partner or former partner from whom that person is not, or where that person has died was not, estranged or divorced or with whom that person has formed a civil partnership that has not been dissolved or, where that person has died, had not been dissolved at the time of that person's death;
     (b)   any child who is a member of that person's family or who was such a member and who is a member of the claimant's family; or
     (c)   any young person who is a member of that person's family or who was such a member and who is a member of the claimant's family.

(3) Any payment by or on behalf of the partner or former partner of a person who is suffering or who suffered from haemophilia or who is or was a qualifying person provided that the partner or former partner and that person are not, or if either of them has died were not, estranged or divorced or, where the partner or former partner and that person have formed a civil partnership, the civil partnership has not been dissolved or, if either of them has died, had not been dissolved at the time of the death, which derives from a payment made under [⁹ or by] any of the Trusts to which sub-paragraph (1) refers and which is made to or for the benefit of—

(a) the person who is suffering from haemophilia or who is a qualifying person;

(b) any child who is a member of that person's family or who was such a member and who is a member of the claimant's family; or

(c) any young person who is a member of that person's family or who was such a member and who is a member of the claimant's family.

(4) Any payment by a person who is suffering from haemophilia or who is a qualifying person, which derives from a payment under [⁹ or by] any of the Trusts to which sub-paragraph (1) refers, where—

(a) that person has no partner or former partner from whom that person is not estranged or divorced or with whom that person has formed a civil partnership that has not been dissolved, nor any child or young person who is or had been a member of that person's family; and

(b) the payment is made either—

(i) to that person's parent or step-parent; or

(ii) where that person at the date of the payment is a child, a young person or a full-time student who has not completed full-time education and had no parent or step-parent, to that person's guardian,

but only for a period from the date of the payment until the end of two years from that person's death.

(5) Any payment out of the estate of a person who suffered from haemophilia or who was a qualifying person, which derives from a payment under [⁹ or by] any of the Trusts to which sub-paragraph (1) refers, where—

(a) that person at the date of that person's death (the relevant date) had no partner or former partner from whom that person was not estranged or divorced or with whom that person had formed a civil partnership that had not been dissolved, nor any child or young person who was or had been a member of that person's family; and

(b) the payment is made either—

(i) to that person's parent or step-parent; or

(ii) where that person at the relevant date was a child, a young person or a full-time student who had not completed full-time education and had no parent or step-parent, to that person's guardian,

but only for a period of two years from the relevant date.

(6) In the case of a person to whom or for whose benefit a payment referred to in this paragraph is made, any income which derives from any payment of income or capital made under or deriving from any of the Trusts.

(7) For the purposes of sub-paragraphs (2) to (6), any reference to the Trusts is to be construed as including a reference to the Fund, the Eileen Trust[⁸, MFET Limited], the Skipton Fund[²¹, the Caxton Foundation][⁴⁰, the Scottish Infected Blood Support Scheme] and the London Bombings Relief Charitable Fund.

42. Any payment made by the Secretary of State to compensate for the loss (in whole or in part) of entitlement to housing benefit.

43. Any payment made to a juror or a witness in respect of attendance at a court other than compensation for loss of earnings or for the loss of a benefit payable under the benefit Acts.

44. Any payment in consequence of a reduction of council tax under section 13 [²⁶ , section 13A] or section 80 of the Local Government Finance Act 1992 (reduction of liability for council tax).

45.—(1) Any payment or repayment made—

(a) as respects England, under regulation 5, 6 or 12 of the National Health Service (Travel Expenses and Remission of Charges) Regulations 2003 (travelling expenses and health service supplies);

(b) as respects Wales, under regulation 5, 6 or 11 of the National Health Service (Travelling Expenses and Remission of Charges) (Wales) Regulations 2007;

(c) as respects Scotland, under regulation 3, 5 or 11 of the National Health Service (Travelling Expenses and Remission of Charges) (Scotland) (No. 2) Regulations 2003 (travelling expenses and health service supplies).

(2) Any payment or repayment made by the Secretary of State for Health [⁴⁷ and Social Care], the Scottish Ministers or the Welsh Ministers which is analogous to a payment or repayment mentioned in sub-paragraph (1).

46. Any payment made to such persons entitled to receive benefits as may be determined by or under a scheme made pursuant to section 13 of the Social Security Act 1988 in lieu of vouchers or similar arrangements in connection with the provision of those benefits (including payments made in place of healthy start vouchers, milk tokens or the supply of vitamins).

47. Any payment made either by the Secretary of State for Justice or by the Scottish Ministers under a scheme established to assist relatives and other persons to visit persons in custody.

48. Any payment (other than a training allowance) made, whether by the Secretary of State or by any other person, under the Disabled Persons (Employment) Act 1944 to assist disabled persons to obtain or retain employment despite their disability.

49. Any supplementary pension under article 23(2) of the Naval, Military and Air Forces Etc. (Disablement and Death) Service Pensions Order 2006 (pensions to widows, widowers or surviving civil partners) and any analogous payment made by the Secretary of State for Defence to any person who is not a person entitled under that Order.

[³ **50.**–(1) If the claimant is in receipt of any benefit under Part 2, 3 or 5 of the Contributions and Benefits Act, any increase in the rate of that benefit arising under Part 4 (increases for dependants) or section 106(a) (unemployability supplement) of that Act, where the dependant in respect of whom the increase is paid is not a member of the claimant's family.

(2) If the claimant is in receipt of any pension or allowance under Part 2 or 3 of the Naval, Military and Air Forces Etc. (Disablement and Death) Service Pensions Order 2006, any increase in the rate of that pension or allowance under that Order, where the dependant in respect of whom the increase is paid is not a member of the claimant's family.]

51. In the case of a pension awarded at the supplementary rate under article 27(3) of the Personal Injuries (Civilians) Scheme 1983 (pensions to widows, widowers or surviving civil partners), the sum specified in paragraph 1(c) of Schedule 4 to that scheme.

52.—(1) Any payment which is—   **9.493**
   (a) made under any of the Dispensing Instruments to a widow, [¹widower or surviving civil partner] of a person—
      (i) whose death was attributable to service in a capacity analogous to service as a member of the armed forces of the Crown; and
      (ii) whose service in such capacity terminated before 31st March 1973; and
   (b) equal to the amount specified in article 23(2) of the Naval, Military and Air Forces Etc. (Disablement and Death) Service Pensions Order 2006.

(2) In this paragraph "the Dispensing Instruments" means the Order in Council of 19th December 1881, the Royal Warrant of 27th October 1884 and the Order by His Majesty of 14th January 1922 (exceptional grants of pay, non-effective pay and allowances).

53. Any payment made [⁴. . .] under section 12B of the Social Work (Scotland) Act 1968 [¹⁰ , or under sections 12A to 12D of the National Health Service Act 2006 (direct payments for health care)] [³⁶ or under sections 31 to 33 of the Care Act 2014 (direct payments)] or under regulations made under section 57 of the Health and Social Care Act 2001 (direct payments) [⁴³, or in accordance with regulations made under section 50 or 52 of the Social Services and Well-being (Wales) Act 2014 (direct payments)].

54.—(1) Any payment specified in sub-paragraph (2) to a claimant who was formerly a student and who has completed the course in respect of which those payments were made.
(2) The payments specified for the purposes of sub-paragraph (1) are—
   (a) any grant income and covenant income as defined for the purposes of Chapter 10 of Part 10;
   (b) any student loan as defined in Chapter 10 of Part 10;
   (c) any contribution as defined in Chapter 10 of Part 10 which—
      (i) is taken into account in ascertaining the amount of a student loan referred to in paragraph (b); and
      (ii) has been paid.

55.—(1) Subject to sub-paragraph (2), in the case of a person who is receiving, or who has received, assistance under the self-employment route, any payment to the person—
   (a) to meet expenses wholly and necessarily incurred whilst carrying on the commercial activity;
   (b) which is used or intended to be used to maintain repayments on a loan taken out by that person for the purposes of establishing or carrying on the commercial activity, in respect of which such assistance is or was received.
(2) Sub-paragraph (1) is to apply only in respect of payments which are paid to that person from the special account as defined for the purposes of Chapter 5 of Part 10.

56. Any payment made with respect to a person on account of the provision of after-care under section 117 of the Mental Health Act 1983 or section 25 of the Mental Health (Care and Treatment) (Scotland) Act 2003 or the provision of accommodation or welfare services to which Part 3 of the National Assistance Act 1948 refers or to which the Social Work (Scotland) Act 1968 refers, [³⁶ or the provision of care and support under Part 1 of the Care Act 2014 (care and support)] [⁴³, or the provision of care and support in respect of an adult under Part 4 of the Social Services and Well-being (Wales) Act 2014 (duty and powers to meet care and support needs of an adult)] which falls to be treated as notional income under paragraph (6) of regulation 107 (payments made in respect of a person living in a care home, an Abbeyfield Home or an independent hospital).

57.—(1) Any payment of a sports award except to the extent that it has been made in respect of any one or more of the items specified in sub-paragraph (2).

(2) The items specified for the purposes of sub-paragraph (1) are food, ordinary clothing or footwear, household fuel, rent for which housing benefit is payable or any housing costs to the extent that they are met under regulation 67(1)(c) or 68(1)(d) (housing costs), of the claimant or, where the claimant is a member of a family, any other member of the claimant's family, or any council tax or water charges for which that claimant or member is liable.

(3) For the purposes of sub-paragraph (2) "food" does not include vitamins, minerals or other special dietary supplements intended to enhance the performance of the person in the sport in respect of which the award was made;

58. Where the amount of a subsistence allowance paid to a person in a benefit week exceeds the amount of income-based jobseeker's allowance that person would have received in that benefit week had it been payable to that person, less 50p, that excess amount.

59. In the case of a claimant participating in an employment zone programme, any discretionary payment made by an employment zone contractor to the claimant, being a fee, grant, loan or otherwise.

[¹¹ **60.**—(1) Any payment of child maintenance made or derived from a liable relative where the child or young person in respect of whom the payment is made is a member of the claimant's family, except where the person making the payment is the claimant or the claimant's partner.

(2) In sub-paragraph (1)—

"child maintenance" means any payment towards the maintenance of a child or young person, including any payment made voluntarily and payments made under—
(a) the Child Support Act 1991;
(b) the Child Support (Northern Ireland) Order 1991;
(c) a court order;
(d) a consent order;
(e) a maintenance agreement registered for execution in the Books of Council and Session or the sheriff court books;
"liable relative" means a person listed in regulation 119 (interpretation) other than a person falling within sub-paragraph (d) of that definition.]

61. In the case of a person to whom paragraph (5) of regulation 6 of the Income Support Regulations (persons not treated as in remunerative work) applies, the whole of that person's income.

62. Any discretionary housing payment paid pursuant to regulation 2(1) of the Discretionary Financial Assistance Regulations 2001.

63.—(1) Any payment made by a local authority or by the Welsh Ministers, to or on behalf of the claimant or the claimant's partner relating to a service which is provided to develop or sustain the capacity of the claimant or the claimant's partner to live independently in the claimant's or the claimant's partner's accommodation.

(2) For the purposes of sub-paragraph (1) "local authority" includes, in England, a county council.

64. Any housing benefit to which the claimant is entitled.

65. [²⁴ . . .]

[²⁹ **66.** Any armed forces independence payment.]

[³⁴ **67.** Any direct payments within the meaning of section 49 of the Children and Families Act 2014 made to a claimant.]

[⁴⁰ **68.** Any bereavement support payment under section 30 of the Pensions Act 2014 except any such payment which is disregarded as capital under paragraph 11(1)(d) or 60 of Schedule 9.]

[⁴⁸ **69.** Any payment of carer's allowance supplement made under section 81 of the Social Security (Scotland) Act 2018.]

[⁵⁰ **70.** Any early years assistance given in accordance with section 32 of the Social Security (Scotland) Act 2018.]

AMENDMENTS

1. Employment and Support Allowance (Miscellaneous Amendments) Regulations 2008 (SI 2008/2428) reg.18 (October 27, 2008).
2. Employment and Support Allowance (Miscellaneous Amendments) Regulations 2008 (SI 2008/2428) reg.20(10) (October 27, 2008).
3. Social Security (Miscellaneous Amendments) (No.7) Regulations 2008 (SI 2008/3157) reg.11(3) (January 5, 2009).
4. Social Security (Miscellaneous Amendments) Regulations 2009 (SI 2009/583) reg.10(9) (April 6, 2009).
5. Social Security (Miscellaneous Amendments) (No.4) Regulations 2009 (SI 2009/2655) reg.11(19)(a) (October 26, 2009).
6. Social Security (Miscellaneous Amendments) (No.4) Regulations 2009 (SI 2009/2655) reg.11(19)(b) (October 26, 2009).
7. Social Security (Miscellaneous Amendments) (No. 4) Regulations 2009 (SI 2009/2655) reg.11(19)(c) (October 26, 2009).
8. Social Security (Miscellaneous Amendments) (No. 2) Regulations 2010 (SI 2010/641) reg.12(3)(f) (April 6, 2010).
9. Social Security (Miscellaneous Amendments) (No. 2) Regulations 2010 (SI 2010/641) reg.12(5)(e) (April 6, 2010).
10. Social Security (Miscellaneous Amendments) (No. 2) Regulations 2010 (SI 2010/641) reg.12(7) (April 6, 2010).
11. Social Security (Miscellaneous Amendments) (No. 4) Regulations 2009 (SI 2009/2655) reg.11(19)(d) (April 12, 2010).
12. Social Security (Miscellaneous Amendments) (No. 3) Regulations 2010 (SI 2010/840) reg.9(20) (June 28, 2010).
13. Social Security (Miscellaneous Amendments) (No. 5) Regulations 2010 (SI 2010/2429) reg.11(4)(a) (November 1, 2010).
14. Social Security (Miscellaneous Amendments) (No. 5) Regulations 2010 (SI 2010/2429) reg.11(4)(b) (November 1, 2010).
15. Social Security (Miscellaneous Amendments) (No. 5) Regulations 2010 (SI 2010/2429) reg.11(4)(c) (November 1, 2010).
16. Social Security (Miscellaneous Amendments) Regulations 2011 (SI 2011/674) reg.16(13) (April 11, 2011).
17. Employment and Support Allowance (Work-related Activity) Regulations 2011 (SI 2011/1349) reg.19 (June 1, 2011).
18. Adoption and Children (Scotland) Act 2007 (Consequential Modifications) Order 2011 (SI 2011/1740) art.1 and Sch.1, para.47(4) (July 15, 2011).
19. Social Security (Miscellaneous Amendments) (No. 2) Regulations 2011 (SI 2011/1707) reg.4(8)(b) and (9) (August 5, 2011).
20. Social Security (Miscellaneous Amendments) (No. 3) Regulations 2011 (SI 2011/2425) reg.23(8) (October 31, 2011).
21. Social Security (Miscellaneous Amendments) (No. 3) Regulations 2011 (SI 2011/2425) reg.23(9) (October 31, 2011).
22. Social Security (Miscellaneous Amendments) (No. 3) Regulations 2011 (SI 2011/2425) reg.23(16) (October 31, 2011).
23. Jobseeker's Allowance (Schemes for Assisting Persons to Obtain Employment) Regulations 2013 (SI 2013/276) reg.15(b) (February 12, 2013).
24. Council Tax Benefit Abolition (Consequential Provision) Regulations 2013 (SI 2013/458) reg.3 and Sch.1 (April 1, 2013).

25. Social Security (Miscellaneous Amendments) Regulations 2013 (SI 2013/443) reg.9(5)(a) (April 2, 2013).

26. Social Security (Miscellaneous Amendments) Regulations 2013 (SI 2013/443) reg.9(5)(b) (April 2, 2013).

27. Personal Independence Payment (Supplementary Provisions and Consequential Amendments) Regulations 2013 (SI 2013/388) reg.8 and Sch., Pt 2, para.40(7)(a) (April 8, 2013).

28. Personal Independence Payment (Supplementary Provisions and Consequential Amendments) Regulations 2013 (SI 2013/388) reg.8 and Sch., Pt 2, para.40(7)(b) (April 8, 2013).

29. Armed Forces and Reserve Forces Compensation Scheme (Consequential Provisions: Subordinate Legislation) Order 2013 (SI 2013/591) art.7 and Sch., para.37(7) (April 8, 2013).

30. National Treatment Agency (Abolition) and the Health and Social Care Act 2012 (Consequential, Transitional and Saving Provisions) Order 2013 (SI 2013/235) art.11 and para.116(3) of Part 1 of Sch.2 (April 1, 2013).

31. Universal Credit (Consequential, Supplementary, Incidental and Miscellaneous Provisions) Regulations 2013 (SI 2013/630) reg.37(8) (April 29, 2013).

32. Social Security (Miscellaneous Amendments) (No.3) Regulations 2013 (SI 2013/2536) reg.13(37) (October 29, 2013).

33. Child Arrangements Order (Consequential Amendments to Subordinate Legislation) Order 2014 (SI 2014/852) art.16 (April 22, 2014).

34. Special Educational Needs (Consequential Amendments to Subordinate Legislation) Order 2014 (SI 2014/2103) art. 27(1) (September 1, 2014).

35. Shared Parental Leave and Statutory Shared Parental Pay (Consequential Amendments to Subordinate Legislation) Order 2014 (SI 2014/3255) art.20(9) (December 31, 2014).

36. Care Act 2014 (Consequential Amendments) (Secondary Legislation) Order 2015 (SI 2015/643) art.2 and Sch., para.29(3) (April 1, 2015).

37. Children and Young People (Scotland) Act 2014 (Consequential Modifications) Order 2016 (SI 2016/732) art.8(2) (August 5, 2016).

38. Social Security (Income-Related Benefits) Amendment Regulations 2017 (SI 2017/174) reg.7 (March 20, 2017).

39. Social Security (Scottish Infected Blood Support Scheme) Regulations 2017 (SI 2017/329) reg.8(3)(e) (April 3, 2017).

40. Pensions Act 2014 (Consequential, Supplementary and Incidental Amendments) Order 2017 (SI 2017/422) art.31(4) (April 6, 2017).

41. Social Security (Emergency Funds) (Amendment) Regulations 2017 (SI 2017/689) reg.8(3)(e) (June 19, 2017).

42. Social Security (Infected Blood and Thalidomide Regulations 2017 (SI 2017/870) reg.8(3)(e) (October 23, 2017).

43. Social Services and Well-being (Wales) Act 2014 and the Regulation and Inspection of Social Care (Wales) Act 2016 (Consequential Amendments) Order 2017 (SI 2017/901) art.13(4) (November 3, 2017).

44. Social Services and Well-being (Wales) Act 2014 and the Regulation and Inspection of Social Care (Wales) Act 2016 (Consequential Amendments) Order 2017 (SI 2017/901) art.27(3) (November 3, 2017).

45. Social Security and Child Support (Care Payments and Tenant Incentive Scheme) (Amendment) Regulations 2017 (SI 2017/995) reg.7(4) (November 7, 2017).

46. Loans for Mortgage Interest Regulations 2017 (SI 2017/725) Sch.5, as amended by Loans for Mortgage Interest and Social Fund Maternity Grant (Amendment) Regulations 2018 (SI 2018/307) reg.2(18)(b) (April 5, 2018).

47. Secretaries of State for Health and Social Care and for Housing, Communities and Local Government and Transfer of Functions (Commonhold Land) Order 2018 (SI 2018/378) Sch., para.21(o) (April 11, 2018).

48. Social Security (Scotland) Act 2018 (Consequential Modifications) Order 2018 (SI 2018/872) art.7 (September 3, 2018).

49. Social Security (Miscellaneous Amendments No.5) Regulations 2017 (SI 2017/1187) reg.8 (December 6, 2018).

50. Social Security (Scotland) Act 2018 (Best Start Grants) (Consequential Modifications and Saving) Order 2018 (SI 2018/1138) art.10(2) (December 10, 2018).

DEFINITIONS

"Abbeyfield Home"—see reg.2(1).
"adoption leave"—*ibid.*
"approved blood scheme"—*ibid.*
"armed forces independence payment"—*ibid.*
"benefit week"—*ibid.*
"board and lodging"—*ibid.*
"care home"—*ibid.*
"Caxton Foundation"—*ibid.*
"child"—*ibid.*
"claimant"—see reg.83(1).
"claimant participating as a service user"—see reg.2(8).
"daily living component"—see reg.2(1).
"dwelling occupied as the home"—*ibid.*
"Eileen Trust"—*ibid.*
"employed earner"—*ibid.*
"employment zone"—*ibid.*
"family"—*ibid.*
"the Fund"—*ibid.*
"guaranteed income payment"—*ibid.*
"Immigration and Asylum Act"—*ibid.*
"independent hospital"—*ibid.*
"the Independent Living Fund (2006)"—*ibid.*
"local welfare provision"—*ibid.*
"the London Bombings Relief Charitable Fund"—*ibid.*
"the London Emergencies Trust"—*ibid.*
"Macfarlane (Special Payments) Trust"—*ibid.*
"Macfarlane (Special Payments) (No. 2) Trust"—*ibid.*
"Macfarlane Trust"—*ibid.*
"Mandatory Work Activity Scheme"—*ibid.*
"MFET Limited"—*ibid.*
"occupational pension scheme"—*ibid.*
"ordinary clothing or footwear"—*ibid.*
"partner"—*ibid.*
"payment"—*ibid.*
"personal independence payment"—*ibid.*
"personal pension scheme"—*ibid.*
"qualifying person"—*ibid.*
"Scottish Infected Blood Support Scheme"—*ibid.*
"self-employment route"—*ibid.*
"shared parental leave"—*ibid.*
"Skipton Fund"—*ibid.*
"sports award"—*ibid.*
"subsistence allowance"—*ibid.*
"training allowance"—*ibid.*
"universal credit"—*ibid.*
"voluntary organisation"—*ibid.*
"week"—*ibid.*
"the We Love Manchester Emergency Fund"—*ibid.*
"young person"—*ibid.*

GENERAL NOTE

9.494   This is similar to Sch.9 to the Income Support Regulations/Sch.7 to the JSA Regulations 1996 (subject to some reordering and minor adjustments in the wording). See the notes in Vol.II where there is no specific note about a provision below.

Under para.7(3), inserted on June 28, 2010 and substituted on April 11, 2011, child dependency increases that are still being paid with carer's allowance, retirement pension, incapacity benefit, severe disablement allowance or widowed parent's allowance are disregarded. This is because income payable to or in respect of a child is not taken into account in ESA as it does not include any entitlement for children.

The amendment to para.15(1)(a), also made on June 28, 2010, means that a training allowance paid as a substitute for JSA is also not disregarded. Under the previous form of para.15(1)(a) only a training allowance paid as a substitute for ESA was not disregarded.

Note para.15A (inserted with effect from June 1, 2011) which provides for an income disregard of travel and other expenses paid in connection with undertaking work-related activity. For the capital disregard, see para.32A of Sch.9.

Paragraph 17

9.495   The amendment to sub-para.(g) in 2017 deals belatedly with the discrimination identified by Judge Williams in *MN v Bury Council and SSWP (HB)* [2014] UKUT 187 (AAC), holding that compensation pension payments made by the Dutch Government to victims of National Socialist persecution should be treated in the same way as payments made under schemes administered by the Governments of Germany and Austria for the purposes of calculating entitlement (in that case) to working age housing benefit.

Paragraph 53

With effect from April 1, 2014, the disregard in para.53 is modified by art.2 of, and para.14 of the Schedule to, the Social Care (Self-directed Support) (Scotland) Act 2013 (Consequential Modifications and Savings) Order 2014 (SI 2014/513) so that the words "as a direct payment as defined in section 4(2) of the Social Care (Self-directed Support) (Scotland) Act 2013" are substituted for the words "under section 12B of the Social Work (Scotland) 1968". However, under art.3 of the Order, this modification does not apply if a payment is made under s.12B of the 1968 Act on or after April 1, 2014.

Paragraph 67

9.496   This provides for an income disregard of payments under s.49 of the Children and Families Act 2014 (personal budgets and direct payments). Under s.49, parents of a child/young person with an education, health and care plan ("an EHC plan") will have the option of a personal budget, through which they will have control over how some of the provision in the EHC plan will be delivered. EHC plans will gradually replace special educational needs statements and learning disability assessments in England.

Paragraph 68

The initial one-off lump sum payment of the new (from April 2017) and controversial bereavement support payment and any arrears of monthly payments included in the first monthly payment are disregarded as capital under paras 11(1) and 60 of Sch.9 for 52 weeks. Paragraph 68 disregards other monthly payments as income other than earnings. In so far as arrears retain their character as income rather than capital (see the notes to para.7 of Sch.10 to the Income Support Regulations in Vol. II of this series) they would be disregarded under para.68.

Paragraph 70

Since the Scottish early years assistance, including the best start grants that came into operation on December 10, 2018, will take the form of lump sum payments, it would probably not constitute income in any event and need this disregard. The payments are disregarded as capital by para.63 of Sch.9.

Regulation 111(2)

SCHEDULE 9

CAPITAL TO BE DISREGARDED

1. The dwelling occupied as the home but, notwithstanding regulation 83 (calculation of income and capital of members of claimant's family and of a polygamous marriage), only one dwelling is to be disregarded under this paragraph.

9.497

[¹⁰ **1A.** Any payment in respect of any travel or other expenses incurred, or to be incurred, by the claimant in respect of that claimant's participation in [¹⁵ a scheme prescribed in regulation 3 of the Jobseeker's Allowance (Schemes for Assisting Persons to Obtain Employment) Regulations 2013] or the Mandatory Work Activity Scheme, but only for 52 weeks beginning with the date of receipt of the payment.]

2. Any premises acquired for occupation by the claimant which that claimant intends to occupy as the home within 26 weeks of the date of acquisition or such longer period as is reasonable in the circumstances to enable the claimant to obtain possession and commence occupation of the premises.

3. Any sum directly attributable to the proceeds of sale of any premises formerly occupied by the claimant as the home which is to be used for the purchase of other premises intended for such occupation within 26 weeks of the date of sale or such longer period as is reasonable in the circumstances to enable the claimant to complete the purchase.

4. Any premises occupied in whole or in part by—
(a) a partner or relative of a single claimant or any member of the family as the home where that person [⁵ has attained the qualifying age for state pension credit] or is incapacitated;
(b) the former partner of a claimant as the home; but this provision is not to apply where the former partner is a person from whom the claimant is estranged or divorced or with whom the person formed a civil partnership that has been dissolved.

5. Where a claimant has ceased to occupy what was formerly the dwelling occupied as the home following the claimant's estrangement or divorce from, or dissolution of the claimant's civil partnership with, the claimant's former partner, that dwelling for a period of 26 weeks from the date on which the claimant ceased to occupy that dwelling or, where that dwelling is occupied as the home by the former partner who is [¹⁴ a lone parent or a person who has no partner and who is responsible for and a member of the same household as a young person,] for as long as it is so occupied.

6. Any premises where the claimant is taking reasonable steps to dispose of those premises, for a period of 26 weeks from the date on which the claimant first took such steps, or such longer period as is reasonable in the circumstances to enable the claimant to dispose of those premises.

7. Any premises which the claimant intends to occupy as the home, and in respect of which that claimant is taking steps to obtain possession and has sought legal advice or has commenced legal proceedings, with a view to obtaining possession, for a period of 26 weeks from the date on which the claimant first sought such advice or first commenced such proceedings whichever is earlier, or such longer period as is reasonable in the circumstances to enable the claimant to obtain possession and commence occupation of those premises.

8. Any premises which the claimant intends to occupy as the home to which essential repairs or alterations are required in order to render them fit for such occupation, for a period of 26 weeks from the date on which the claimant first takes steps to effect those repairs or alterations, or such longer period as is reasonable in the circumstances to enable those repairs or alterations to be carried out and the claimant to commence occupation of the premises.

9. Any future interest in property of any kind, other than land or premises in respect of which the claimant has granted a subsisting lease or tenancy, including sub-leases or sub-tenancies.

10.—(1) The assets of any business owned in whole or in part by the claimant and for the purposes of which that claimant is engaged as a self-employed earner or, if the claimant has ceased to be so engaged, for such period as may be reasonable in the circumstances to allow for disposal of any such asset.

(2) The assets of any business owned in whole or in part by the claimant where that claimant—

(a) is not engaged as self-employed earner in that business by reason of some disease or bodily or mental disablement; but

(b) intends to become engaged (or, as the case may be, re-engaged) as a self-employed earner in that business as soon as the claimant recovers or is able to become engaged, or reengaged, in that business,

for a period of 26 weeks from the date on which the claim for an income-related allowance is made, or is treated as made, or, if it is unreasonable to expect the claimant to become engaged or re-engaged in that business within that period, for such longer period as is reasonable in the circumstances to enable the claimant to become so engaged or re-engaged.

(3) In the case of a person who is receiving assistance under the self-employment route, the assets acquired by that person for the purpose of establishing or carrying on the commercial activity in respect of which such assistance is being received.

(4) In the case of a person who has ceased carrying on the commercial activity in respect of which assistance was received as specified in sub-paragraph (3), the assets relating to that activity for such period as may be reasonable in the circumstances to allow for disposal of any such asset.

11.—(1) Subject to sub-paragraph (2), any arrears of, or any concessionary payment made to compensate for arrears due to the non-payment of—

(a) any payment specified in paragraph 8, 10 or 11 of Schedule 8 (other income to be disregarded);

(b) an income-related allowance, an income-related benefit or an income-based jobseeker's allowance [[18], universal credit], child tax credit or working tax credit;

(c) any discretionary housing payment paid pursuant to regulation 2(1) of the Discretionary Financial Assistance Regulations 2001,

[[23](d) bereavement support payment under section 30 of the Pensions Act 2014,] but only for a period of 52 weeks from the date of the receipt of the arrears or of the concessionary payment.

(2) In a case where the total of any arrears and, if appropriate, any concessionary payment referred to in sub-paragraph (1) relating to any one of the specified payments, benefits or allowances, amounts to £5,000 or more (referred to in this sub-paragraph and in sub-paragraph (3) as the "relevant sum") and is—

[[30] (a) paid in order to rectify, or to compensate for—

(i) an official error as defined in regulation 1(2) of the Social Security and Child Support (Decisions and Appeals) Regulations 1999, or

(ii) an error on a point of law; and]

(b) received by the claimant in full on or after 14th October 2001,

sub-paragraph (1) is to have effect in relation to such arrears or concessionary payment either for a period of 52 weeks from the date of receipt, or, if the relevant sum is received in its entirety during the award of an income-related allowance, for the remainder of that award if that is a longer period.

(3) For the purposes of sub-paragraph (2), "the award of an income-related allowance" means—

(a) the award either of an income-related allowance, income support [[18], universal credit] or of an income-based jobseeker's allowance in which the relevant sum (or first part thereof where it is paid in more than one instalment) is received; and

(b) where that award is followed by one or more further awards which in each case may be either of an income-related allowance, income support [[18], universal credit] or of an income-based jobseeker's allowance and which, or each of which, begins immediately after the end of the previous award, such further awards until the end of the last such award, provided that for any such further awards the claimant—

(i) is the person who received the relevant sum;

(ii) is the partner of the person who received the relevant sum, or was that person's partner at the date of that person's death; [[18] ...]

(iii) in the case of a joint-claim jobseeker's allowance, is a joint-claim couple either member or both members of which received the relevant sum [[18]; or

(iv) in a case where universal credit is awarded to the claimant and another person as joint claimants, either the claimant or the other person, or both of them, received the relevant sum].

12. Any sum—

(a) paid to the claimant in consequence of damage to, or loss of, the home or any personal possession and intended for its repair or replacement; or

(b) acquired by the claimant (whether as a loan or otherwise) on the express condition that it is to be used for effecting essential repairs or improvements to the home,

and which is to be used for the intended purpose, for a period of 26 weeks from the date on which it was so paid or acquired or such longer period as is reasonable in the circumstances to enable the claimant to effect the repairs, replacement or improvements.

13. Any sum—

(a) deposited with a housing association as defined in section 1(1) of the Housing Associations Act 1985 or section 338(1) of the Housing (Scotland) Act 1987 as a condition of occupying the home;

(b) which was so deposited and which is to be used for the purchase of another home, for the period of 26 weeks or such longer period as is reasonable in the circumstances to complete the purchase.

14. Any personal possessions except those which had or have been acquired by the claimant with the intention of reducing that claimant's capital in order to secure entitlement to an employment and support allowance, a jobseeker's allowance or to income support or to increase the amount of those benefits.

15. The value of the right to receive any income under an annuity and the surrender value (if any) of such an annuity.

9.498

16. Where the funds of a trust are derived from a payment made in consequence of any personal injury to the claimant or the claimant's partner, the value of the trust fund and the value of the right to receive any payment under that trust.

17.—(1) Any payment made to the claimant or the claimant's partner in consequence of any personal injury to the claimant or, as the case may be, the claimant's partner.

(2) But sub-paragraph (1)—

(a) applies only for the period of 52 weeks beginning with the day on which the claimant first receives any payment [[2]in consequence of that personal injury];

(b) does not apply to any subsequent payment made to the claimant in consequence of that injury (whether it is made by the same person or another);

(c) ceases to apply to the payment or any part of the payment from the day on which the claimant no longer possesses it;

(d) does not apply to any payment from a trust where the funds of the trust are derived from a payment made in consequence of any personal injury to the claimant.

(3) For the purpose of sub-paragraph (2)(c), the circumstances in which a claimant no longer possesses a payment or a part of it include where the claimant has used a payment or part of it to purchase an asset.

18. The value of the right to receive any income under a life interest or from a life rent.

19. The value of the right to receive any income which is disregarded under paragraph 9 of Schedule 7 or paragraph 24 of Schedule 8 (earnings or other income to be disregarded).

20. The surrender value of any policy of life insurance.

21. Where any payment of capital falls to be made by instalments, the value of the right to receive any outstanding instalments.

22.—(1) Any payment made by a local authority in accordance with—

(a) section 17, 23B, 23C or 24A of the Children Act 1989;

(b) section 12 of the Social Work (Scotland) Act 1968; [[27] ...]

[[21] (c) section 26A, 29 or 30 of the Children (Scotland) Act 1995 (local authorities' duty to provide continuing care and provision of advice and assistance for certain [[27] young persons); or

(d) the following sections of the Social Services and Well-being (Wales) Act 2014—
  (aa) section 37 or 38, but excluding any direct payment made in accordance with regulations made under section 51 of that Act, or
  (bb) section 109, 110, 114 or 115.]]

(2) Subject to paragraph (3), any payment (or part of a payment) made by a local authority in accordance with section 23C of the Children Act 1989 [²¹ or section 26A or 29 of the Children (Scotland) Act 1995 (local authorities' duty to promote welfare of children, duty to provide continuing care and provision of advice and assistance for certain young persons)] to a person ("A") which A passes on to the claimant.

(3) Sub-paragraph (2) applies only where A—
  (a) was formerly in the claimant's care; and
[²¹ (b) is aged 18 or over or, in the case of a payment or part of a payment made in accordance with section 26A of the Children (Scotland) Act 1995, aged 16 or over, and]
  (c) continues to live with the claimant.

23. Any social fund payment made pursuant to Part 8 of the Contributions and Benefits Act.

[¹⁶ **23A.** Any local welfare provision.]

24. Any refund of tax which falls to be deducted under section 369 of the Income and Corporation Taxes Act 1988 (mortgage interest payable under deduction of tax) on a payment of relevant loan interest for the purpose of acquiring an interest in the home or carrying out repairs or improvements in the home.

25. Any capital which under regulation 105 or 137 (capital treated as income or treatment of student loans) is to be treated as income.

26. Where a payment of capital is made in a currency other than sterling, any banking charge or commission payable in converting that payment into sterling.

27.—(1) Any payment made under [⁷or by] the Macfarlane Trust, the Macfarlane (Special Payments) Trust, the Macfarlane (Special Payments) (No. 2) Trust ("the Trusts"), the Fund, the Eileen Trust[⁶, MFET Limited][¹, the Independent Living Fund (2006)], the Skipton Fund[¹², the Caxton Foundation][²², the Scottish Infected Blood Support Scheme] [²⁵, an approved blood scheme][²⁴, the London Emergencies Trust, the We Love Manchester Emergency Fund] or the London Bombings Relief Charitable Fund.

(2) Any payment by or on behalf of a person who is suffering or who suffered from haemophilia or who is or was a qualifying person, which derives from a payment made under [⁷ or by] any of the Trusts to which sub-paragraph (1) refers and which is made to or for the benefit of—
  (a) that person's partner or former partner from whom the person is not, or where that person has died was not, estranged or divorced or with whom the person has formed a civil partnership that has not been dissolved or, where that person has died, had not been dissolved at the time of that person's death;
  (b) any child who is a member of that person's family or who was such a member and who is a member of the claimant's family; or
  (c) any young person who is a member of that person's family or who was such a member and who is a member of the claimant's family.

(3) Any payment by or on behalf of the partner or former partner of a person who is suffering or who suffered from haemophilia or who is or was a qualifying person provided that the partner or former partner and that person are not, or if either of them has died were not, estranged or divorced or, where the partner or former partner and that person have formed a civil partnership, the civil partnership has not been dissolved or, if either of them has died, had not been dissolved at the time of the death, which derives from a payment made under [⁷ or by] any of the Trusts to which sub-paragraph (1) refers and which is made to or for the benefit of—
  (a) the person who is suffering from haemophilia or who is a qualifying person;
  (b) any child who is a member of that person's family or who was such a member and who is a member of the claimant's family; or
  (c) any young person who is a member of that person's family or who was such a member and who is a member of the claimant's family.

(4) Any payment by a person who is suffering from haemophilia or who is a qualifying person, which derives from a payment under [⁷ or by] any of the Trusts to which sub-paragraph (1) refers, where—
  (a) that person has no partner or former partner from whom the person is not estranged or divorced or with whom the person has formed a civil partnership that has not been

dissolved, nor any child or young person who is or had been a member of that person's family; and

(b) the payment is made either—

    (i) to that person's parent or step-parent; or

    (ii) where that person at the date of the payment is a child, a young person or a full-time student who has not completed full-time education and had no parent or step-parent, to that person's guardian,

but only for a period from the date of the payment until the end of two years from that person's death.

(5) Any payment out of the estate of a person who suffered from haemophilia or who was a qualifying person, which derives from a payment under [⁷ or by] any of the Trusts to which sub-paragraph (1) refers, where—

(a) that person at the date of that person's death (the relevant date) had no partner or former partner from whom the person was not estranged or divorced or with whom the person had formed a civil partnership that had not been dissolved, nor any child or young person who was or had been a member of that person's family; and

(b) the payment is made either—

    (i) to that person's parent or step-parent; or

    (ii) where that person at the relevant date was a child, a young person or a full-time student who had not completed full-time education and had no parent or step-parent, to that person's guardian,

but only for a period of two years from the relevant date.

(6) In the case of a person to whom or for whose benefit a payment referred to in this paragraph is made, any capital resource which derives from any payment of income or capital made under or deriving from any of the Trusts.

(7) For the purposes of sub-paragraphs (2) to (6), any reference to the Trusts is to be construed as including a reference to the Fund, the Eileen Trust[⁶, MFET Limited], the Skipton Fund[¹², the Caxton Foundation] [²², the Scottish Infected Blood Support Scheme] [²⁵, an approved blood scheme] [²⁴, the London Emergencies Trust, the We Love Manchester Emergency Fund] or the London Bombings Relief Charitable Fund.

28. The value of the right to receive an occupational or personal pension.

29. The value of any funds held under a personal pension scheme.

30. The value of the right to receive any rent except where the claimant has a reversionary interest in the property in respect of which rent is due.

31. Any payment in kind made by a charity or under the Macfarlane Trust, Macfarlane (Special Payments) Trust, the Macfarlane (Special Payments) (No. 2) Trust, the Fund, the Eileen Trust[⁶, MFET Limited] [¹¹, the Skipton Fund, the Caxton Foundation] [²², the Scottish Infected Blood Support Scheme] [²⁵, an approved blood scheme] or [²the Independent Living Fund (2006)].

32. Any payment made pursuant to section 2 of the Employment and Training Act 1973 or section 2 of the Enterprise and New Towns (Scotland) Act 1990, but only for the period of 52 weeks beginning on the date of receipt of the payment.

[⁹ **32A.** Any payment made to the claimant in respect of any travel or other expenses incurred, or to be incurred, in complying with a requirement to undertake work-related activity but only for 52 weeks beginning with the date of receipt of the payment.]

33. Any payment made by the Secretary of State to compensate for the loss (in whole or in part) of entitlement to housing benefit.

34. Any payment made to a juror or a witness in respect of attendance at a court other than compensation for loss of earnings or for the loss of a benefit payable under the benefit Acts.

35. Any payment [²in consequence of a reduction] of council tax under section 13 [¹⁷ , section 13A] or, as the case may be, section 80 of the Local Government Finance Act 1992 (reduction of liability for council tax), but only for a period of 52 weeks from the date of the receipt of the payment.

36. Any grant made to the claimant in accordance with a scheme under section 129 of the Housing Act 1988 or section 66 of the Housing (Scotland) Act 1988 (schemes for payments to assist local housing authorities and local authority tenants to obtain other accommodation) which is to be used—

(a) to purchase premises intended for occupation as the claimant's home; or

(b) to carry out repairs or alterations which are required to render premises fit for occupation as the claimant's home,

for a period of 26 weeks from the date on which the claimant received such a grant or such longer period as is reasonable in the circumstances to enable the purchase, repairs or alterations to be completed and the claimant to commence occupation of those premises as the claimant's home.

37.—(1) Any payment or repayment made—

(a) as respects England, under regulation 5, 6 or 12 of the National Health Service (Travel Expenses and Remission of Charges) Regulations 2003 (travelling expenses and health service supplies);

(b) as respects Wales, under regulation 5, 6 or 11 of the National Health Service (Travelling Expenses and Remission of Charges) (Wales) Regulations 2007;

(c) as respects Scotland, under regulation 3, 5 or 11 of the National Health Service (Travelling Expenses and Remission of Charges) (Scotland) (No. 2) Regulations 2003 (travelling expenses and health service supplies);

but only for a period of 52 weeks from the date of receipt of the payment or repayment.

(2) Any payment or repayment made by the Secretary of State for Health [29 and Social Care], the Scottish Ministers or the Welsh Ministers which is analogous to a payment or repayment mentioned in sub-paragraph (1); but only for a period of 52 weeks from the date of receipt of the payment or repayment.

38. Any payment made to such persons entitled to receive benefits as may be determined by or under a scheme made pursuant to section 13 of the Social Security Act 1988 in lieu of vouchers or similar arrangements in connection with the provision of those benefits (including payments made in place of healthy start vouchers, milk tokens or the supply of vitamins) but only for a period of 52 weeks from the date of receipt of the payment.

[4 **38A.** Any payment made under Part 8A of the Social Security Contributions and Benefits Act 1992 (entitlement to health in pregnancy grant).]

39. Any payment made either by the Secretary of State for Justice or by the Scottish Ministers under a scheme established to assist relatives and other persons to visit persons in custody, but only for a period of 52 weeks from the date of receipt of the payment.

40. Any arrears of supplementary pension which is disregarded under paragraph 49 of Schedule 8 (sums to be disregarded in the calculation of income other than earnings) or of any amount which is disregarded under paragraphs 51 or 52 of that Schedule, but only for a period of 52 weeks from the date of receipt of the arrears.

41. Any payment (other than a training allowance) made, whether by the Secretary of State or by any other person, under the Disabled Persons (Employment) Act 1944 to assist disabled persons to obtain or retain employment despite their disability.

42. Any payment made by a local authority under section 3 of the Disabled Persons (Employment) Act 1958 [27or under Part 4 of the Social Services and Well-being (Wales) Act 2014] to homeworkers assisted under the Blind Homeworkers' Scheme.

9.499

43.—(1) Any sum to which sub-paragraph (2) applies and—

(a) which is administered on behalf of a person by the High Court or the County Court under Rule 21.11(1) of the Civil Procedure Rules 1998 or by the Court of Protection;

(b) which can only be disposed of by order or direction of any such court; or

(c) where the person concerned is under the age of 18, which can only be disposed of by order or direction prior to that person attaining age 18.

(2) This sub-paragraph applies to a sum which is derived from—

(a) an award of damages for a personal injury to that person; or

(b) compensation for the death of one or both parents where the person concerned is under the age of 18.

44. Any sum administered on behalf of a person in accordance with an order made under section 13 of the Children (Scotland) Act 1995, or under Rule 36.14 of the Ordinary Cause Rules 1993 or under Rule 128 of the Ordinary Cause Rules, where such sum derives from—

(a) an award of damages for a personal injury to that person; or

(b) compensation for the death of one or both parents where the person concerned is under the age of 18.

45. Any payment to the claimant as holder of the Victoria Cross or George Cross.

46. In the case of a person who is receiving, or who has received, assistance under the self-employment route, any sum which is acquired by that person for the purpose of establishing or carrying on the commercial activity in respect of which such assistance is or was received but only for a period of 52 weeks from the date on which that sum was acquired.

47.—(1) [²Any payment of a sports award] for a period of 26 weeks from the date of receipt of that payment except to the extent that it has been made in respect of any one or more of the items specified in sub-paragraph (2).

(2) The items specified for the purposes of sub-paragraph (1) are food, ordinary clothing or footwear, household fuel, rent for which housing benefit is payable or any housing costs to the extent that they are met under regulation 67(1)(c) or 68(1)(d) (housing costs), of the claimant or, where the claimant is a member of a family, any other member of the claimant's family, or any council tax or water charges for which that claimant or member is liable.

(3) For the purposes of sub-paragraph (2) "food" does not include vitamins, minerals or other special dietary supplements intended to enhance the performance of the person in the sport in respect of which the award was made.

48. In the case of a claimant participating in an employment zone programme, any discretionary payment made by an employment zone contractor to the claimant, being a fee, grant, loan or otherwise, but only for the period of 52 weeks from the date of receipt of the payment.

49. Any arrears of subsistence allowance paid as a lump sum but only for the period of 52 weeks from the date of receipt of the payment.

50. Where an ex-gratia payment of £10,000 has been made by the Secretary of State on or after 1st February 2001 in consequence of the imprisonment or internment of—
  (a) the claimant;
  (b) the claimant's partner;
  (c) the claimant's deceased spouse or deceased civil partner; or
  (d) the claimant's partner's deceased spouse or deceased civil partner,
by the Japanese during the Second World War, £10,000.

51. In the case of a person to whom paragraph (5) of regulation 6 of the Income Support Regulations (persons not treated as in remunerative work) applies, the whole of the claimant's capital.

52.—(1) Any payment—
  (a) by way of an education maintenance allowance made pursuant to—
    (i) regulations made under section 518 of the Education Act 1996;
    (ii) regulations made under section 49 or 73(f) of the Education (Scotland) Act 1980;
    (iii) directions made under section 73ZA of the Education (Scotland) Act 1980 and paid under section 12(2)(c) of the Further and Higher Education (Scotland) Act 1992; [¹³ . . .]
  (b) corresponding to such an education maintenance allowance, made pursuant to—
    (i) section 14 or section 181 of the Education Act 2002; or
    (ii) regulations made under section 181 of that Act [¹³ ; or
  (c) in England, by way of financial assistance made pursuant to section 14 of the Education Act 2002.]
  (2) Any payment, other than a payment to which sub-paragraph (1) applies, made pursuant to—
  (a) regulations made under section 518 of the Education Act 1996;
  (b) regulations made under section 49 of the Education (Scotland) Act 1980; or
  (c) directions made under section 73ZA of the Education (Scotland) Act 1980 and paid under section 12(2)(c) of the Further and Higher Education (Scotland) Act 1992,
in respect of a course of study attended by a child or a young person or a person who is in receipt of an education maintenance allowance [¹³ or other payment] made pursuant to any provision specified in sub-paragraph (1).

53.—(1) Subject to sub-paragraph (2), the amount of any trust payment made to a claimant or a member of a claimant's family who is—
  (a) a diagnosed person;

(b) the diagnosed person's partner or the person who was the diagnosed person's partner at the date of the diagnosed person's death;

(c) a parent of a diagnosed person, a person acting in the place of the diagnosed person's parents or a person who was so acting at the date of the diagnosed person's death; or

(d) a member of the diagnosed person's family (other than that person's partner) or a person who was a member of the diagnosed person's family (other than that person's partner) at the date of the diagnosed person's death.

(2) Where a trust payment is made to—

(a) a person referred to in sub-paragraph (1)(a) or (b), that sub-paragraph will apply for the period beginning on the date on which the trust payment is made and ending on the date on which that person dies;

(b) a person referred to in sub-paragraph (1)(c), that sub-paragraph will apply for the period beginning on the date on which the trust payment is made and ending two years after that date;

(c) a person referred to in sub-paragraph (1)(d), that sub-paragraph will apply for the period beginning on the date on which the trust payment is made and ending—

    (i) two years after that date; or

    (ii) on the day before the day on which that person—

        (aa) ceases receiving full-time education; or

        (bb) attains the age of 20,

whichever is the latest.

(3) Subject to sub-paragraph (4), the amount of any payment by a person to whom a trust payment has been made, or of any payment out of the estate of a person to whom a trust payment has been made, which is made to a claimant or a member of a claimant's family who is—

(a) the diagnosed person's partner or the person who was the diagnosed person's partner at the date of the diagnosed person's death;

(b) a parent of a diagnosed person, a person acting in the place of the diagnosed person's parents or a person who was so acting at the date of the diagnosed person's death; or

(c) a member of the diagnosed person's family (other than that person's partner) or a person who was a member of the diagnosed person's family (other than that person's partner) at the date of the diagnosed person's death,

but only to the extent that such payments do not exceed the total amount of any trust payments made to that person.

(4) Where a payment as referred to in sub-paragraph (3) is made to—

(a) a person referred to in sub-paragraph (3)(a), that sub-paragraph will apply for the period beginning on the date on which that payment is made and ending on the date on which that person dies;

(b) a person referred to in sub-paragraph (3)(b), that sub-paragraph will apply for the period beginning on the date on which that payment is made and ending two years after that date;

(c) a person referred to in sub-paragraph (3)(c), that sub-paragraph will apply for the period beginning on the date on which that payment is made and ending—

    (i) two years after that date; or

    (ii) on the day before the day on which that person—

        (aa) ceases receiving full-time education; or

        (bb) attains the age of 20,

whichever is the latest.

(5) In this paragraph, a reference to a person—

(a) being the diagnosed person's partner;

(b) being a member of the diagnosed person's family; or

(c) acting in the place of the diagnosed person's parents,

at the date of the diagnosed person's death will include a person who would have been such a person or a person who would have been so acting, but for the diagnosed person residing in a care home, an Abbeyfield Home or an independent hospital on that date.

(6) In this paragraph—

"diagnosed person" means a person who has been diagnosed as suffering from, or who, after that person's death, has been diagnosed as having suffered from, variant Creutzfeldt-Jakob disease;

"relevant trust" means a trust established out of funds provided by the Secretary of State in respect of persons who suffered, or who are suffering, from variant Creutzfeldt-Jakob disease for the benefit of persons eligible for payments in accordance with its provisions;

"trust payment" means a payment under a relevant trust.

54. The amount of a payment, other than a [³ war disablement pension, war widow's pension or war widower's pension], to compensate for the fact that the claimant, the claimant's partner, the claimant's deceased spouse or deceased civil partner or the claimant's partner's deceased spouse or deceased civil partner—

    (a) was a slave labourer or a forced labourer;

    (b) had suffered property loss or had suffered personal injury; or

    (c) was a parent of a child who had died,

during the Second World War.

55.—(1) Any payment made by a local authority or by the Welsh Ministers, to or on behalf of the claimant or the claimant's partner relating to a service which is provided to develop or sustain the capacity of the claimant or the claimant's partner to live independently in the claimant's or the claimant's partner's accommodation.

(2) For the purposes of sub-paragraph (1) "local authority" includes, in England, a county council.

56. Any payment [²⁰ made as a direct payment under Part 1 of the Care Act 2014 (care and support) or] made under [⁴ . . .] regulations made under section 57 of the Health and Social Care Act 2001 or under section 12B of the Social Work (Scotland) Act 1968[⁸, or under sections 12A to 12D of the National Health Service Act 2006 (direct payments for health care)[²⁷, or in accordance with regulations made under section 50 or 52 of the Social Services and Well-being (Wales) Act 2014 (direct payments)]].

57. Any payment made to the claimant pursuant to regulations under section 2(6)(b), 3 or 4 of the Adoption and Children Act 2002.

58. Any payment made to the claimant in accordance with regulations made pursuant to section 14F of the Children Act 1989 (special guardianship support services).

[¹⁹ **59.** Any direct payments within the meaning of section 49 of the Children and Families Act 2014 made to a claimant.]

[²³ **60.** Any bereavement support payment in respect of the rate set out in regulation 3(2) or (5) of the Bereavement Support Payment Regulations 2017 (rate of bereavement support payment), but only for a period of 52 weeks from the date of receipt of the payment.]

[²⁶ **61.** Any payment made under or by a trust, established for the purpose of giving relief and assistance to disabled persons whose disabilities were caused by the fact that during their mother's pregnancy she had taken a preparation containing the drug known as Thalidomide, and which is approved by the Secretary of State.]

[²⁸[³¹ **62.** Any payment made to a claimant under section 73(1)(b) of the Children and Young People (Scotland) Act 2014 (kinship care assistance).]]

[³¹ **63.** Any early years assistance given in accordance with section 32 of the Social Security (Scotland) Act 2018.]

AMENDMENTS

1. Employment and Support Allowance (Miscellaneous Amendments) Regulations 2008 (SI 2008/2428) reg.8(8) (October 27, 2008).

2. Employment and Support Allowance (Miscellaneous Amendments) Regulations 2008 (SI 2008/2428) reg.19 (October 27, 2008).

3. Social Security (Miscellaneous Amendments) (No.7) Regulations 2008 (SI 2008/3157) reg.11(4) (January 5, 2009).

4. Social Security (Miscellaneous Amendments) Regulations 2009 (SI 2009/583) reg.10(10) (April 6, 2009).

5. Social Security (Equalisation of State Pension Age) Regulations 2009 (SI 2009/1488) reg.44 (April 6, 2010).

6. Social Security (Miscellaneous Amendments) (No.2) Regulations 2010 (SI 2010/641) reg.12(3)(g) (April 6, 2010).

7. Social Security (Miscellaneous Amendments) (No.2) Regulations 2010 (SI 2010/641) reg.12(5)(f) (April 6, 2010).

8. Social Security (Miscellaneous Amendments) (No.2) Regulations 2010 (SI 2010/641) reg.12(7) (April 6, 2010).

9. Employment and Support Allowance (Work-related Activity) Regulations 2011 (SI 2011/1349) reg.20 (June 1, 2011).

10. Social Security (Miscellaneous Amendments) (No.2) Regulations 2011 (SI 2011/1707) reg.4(10)(b) and (11) (August 5, 2011).

11. Social Security (Miscellaneous Amendments) (No.3) Regulations 2011 (SI 2011/2425) reg.23(8) (October 31, 2011).

12. Social Security (Miscellaneous Amendments) (No.3) Regulations 2011 (SI 2011/2425) reg.23(9) (October 31, 2011).

13. Social Security (Miscellaneous Amendments) (No.3) Regulations 2011 (SI 2011/2425) reg.23(16) (October 31, 2011).

14. Social Security (Work-focused Interviews for Lone Parents and Partners) (Amendment) Regulations 2011 (SI 2011/2428) reg.5(8) (October 31, 2011).

15. Jobseeker's Allowance (Schemes for Assisting Persons to Obtain Employment) Regulations 2013 (SI 2013/276) reg.15(b) (February 12, 2013).

16. Social Security (Miscellaneous Amendments) Regulations 2013 (SI 2013/443) reg.9(6)(a) (April 2, 2013).

17. Social Security (Miscellaneous Amendments) Regulations 2013 (SI 2013/443) reg.9(6)(b) (April 2, 2013).

18. Universal Credit (Consequential, Supplementary, Incidental and Miscellaneous Provisions) Regulations 2013 (SI 2013/630) reg.37(9) (April 29, 2013).

19. Special Educational Needs (Consequential Amendments to Subordinate Legislation) Order 2014 (SI 2014/2103) art.27(2) (September 1, 2014).

20. Care Act 2014 (Consequential Amendments) (Secondary Legislation) Order 2015 (SI 2015/643) art.2 and Sch., para.29(4) (April 1, 2015).

21. Children and Young People (Scotland) Act 2014 (Consequential Modifications) Order 2016 (SI 2016/732) art.8(3) (August 5, 2016).

22. Social Security (Scottish Infected Blood Support Scheme) Regulations 2017 (SI 2017/329) reg.8(3)(c) (April 3, 2017).

23. Pensions Act 2014 (Consequential, Supplementary and Incidental Amendments) Order 2017 (SI 2017/422) art.31(5) (April 6, 2017).

24. Social Security (Emergency Funds) (Amendment) Regulations 2017 (SI 2017/689) reg.8(3)(f) (June 19, 2017).

25. Social Security (Infected Blood and Thalidomide Regulations 2017 (SI 2017/870) reg.8(3)(f) (October 23, 2017).

26. Social Security (Infected Blood and Thalidomide Regulations 2017 (SI 2017/870) reg.8(5) (October 23, 2017).

27. Social Services and Well-being (Wales) Act 2014 and the Regulation and Inspection of Social Care (Wales) Act 2016 (Consequential Amendments) Order 2017 (SI 2017/901) art.13(5) (November 3, 2017).

28. Social Security and Child Support (Care Payments and Tenant Incentive Scheme) (Amendment) Regulations 2017 (SI 2017/995) reg.7(5) (November 7, 2017).

29. Secretaries of State for Health and Social Care and for Housing, Communities and Local Government and Transfer of Functions (Commonhold Land) Order 2018 (SI 2018/378) Sch., para.21(o) (April 11, 2018).

30. Social Security (Treatment of Arrears of Benefit) Regulations 2018 (SI 2018/932) reg.7 (September 11, 2018).

31. Social Security (Scotland) Act 2018 (Best Start Grants) (Consequential Modifications and Saving) Order 2018 (SI 2018/1138) art.10(3) (December 10, 2018).

DEFINITIONS

"Abbeyfield Home"—see reg.2(1).
"approved blood scheme"—*ibid.*

"care home"—*ibid.*
"Caxton Foundation"—*ibid.*
"child"—*ibid.*
"claimant"—see reg.83(1).
"dwelling occupied as the home"—see reg.2(1).
"Eileen Trust"—*ibid.*
"employment zone"—*ibid.*
"family"—*ibid.*
"the Fund"—*ibid.*
"independent hospital"—*ibid.*
"the Independent Living Fund (2006)"—*ibid.*
"local welfare provision"—*ibid.*
"the London Bombings Relief Charitable Fund"—*ibid.*
"the London Emergencies Trust"—*ibid.*
"lone parent"—*ibid.*
"Macfarlane (Special Payments) Trust"—*ibid.*
"Macfarlane (Special Payments) (No. 2) Trust"—*ibid.*
"Macfarlane Trust"—*ibid.*
"Mandatory Work Activity Scheme"—*ibid.*
"MFET Limited"—*ibid.*
"occupational pension"—*ibid.*
"ordinary clothing or footwear"—*ibid.*
"partner"—*ibid.*
"payment"—*ibid.*
"personal pension scheme"—*ibid.*
"policy of life insurance"—*ibid.*
"qualifying person"—*ibid.*
"relative"—*ibid.*
"Scottish Infected Blood Support Scheme"—*ibid.*
"self-employed earner"—*ibid.*
"self-employment route"—*ibid.*
"single claimant"—*ibid.*
"Skipton Fund"—*ibid.*
"sports award"—*ibid.*
"subsistence allowance"—*ibid.*
"training allowance"—*ibid.*
"universal credit"—*ibid.*
"the We Love Manchester Emergency Fund"—*ibid.*
"young person"—*ibid.*

GENERAL NOTE

This is similar to Sch.10 to the Income Support Regulations/Sch.8 to the JSA **9.500**
Regulations 1996 (subject to some reordering and minor adjustments in the
wording). See the notes in Vol.II where there is no specific note about a provision
below.

Paragraphs 47 to 49 of Sch.10 to the Income Support Regulations have not been
reproduced in this Schedule as they are no longer relevant.

Note that in para.14 the disregard of the value of personal possessions does not
apply if they have been acquired in order to reduce capital so as to gain entitlement
to, or increase the amount of, ESA, *JSA or income support.* This avoids the question
that might otherwise have arisen on a claimant transferring from income support (or
JSA) to ESA whether, if the acquisition had only been for the purposes of income
support (or JSA), the disregard in para.14 applies.

Note that under para.32A payments of travel or other expenses paid in connection with undertaking work-related activity that count as capital are disregarded but
only for 52 weeks from the date of receipt. For the income disregard see para.15A
of Sch.8.

Paragraph 31

9.501   Note that there has been no amendment to para.31 equivalent to that made with effect from June 19, 2017 in para.27(1) and (7).

Paragraph 56

9.502   With effect from April 1, 2014, the disregard in para.56 is modified by art.2 of, and para.14 of the Schedule to, the Social Care (Self-directed Support) (Scotland) Act 2013 (Consequential Modifications and Savings) Order 2014 (SI 2014/513) so that the words "as a direct payment as defined in section 4(2) of the Social Care (Self-directed Support) (Scotland) Act 2013" are substituted for the words "under section 12B of the Social Work (Scotland) 1968". However, under art.3 of the Order, this modification does not apply if a payment is made under s.12B of the 1968 Act on or after April 1, 2014.

Paragraph 59

9.503   This provides for a capital disregard of payments under s.49 of the Children and Families Act 2014 (personal budgets and direct payments). See further the note to para.67 of Sch.8 which provides for an income disregard of such payments.

Paragraph 60

9.504   The initial one-off lump sum payment of the new (from April 2017) and controversial bereavement support payment is disregarded as capital under this provision for 52 weeks from the date of receipt. The insertion of sub-para.(d) into para.11(1) secures the disregard as capital of payments of arrears of monthly payments, also for 52 weeks from the date of receipt. In so far as arrears of monthly payments retain their character as income rather than capital (see the notes to para.7 of Sch.10 to the Income Support Regulations in Vol.II of this series) they would be disregarded under para.68 of Sch.8.

Paragraph 62

9.505   This paragraph has now formally been given its correct number. See the note to para.74 of Sch.10 to the Income Support Regulations (Vol.II) for payments under s.73 of the Children and Young People (Scotland) Act 2014.

Paragraph 63

9.506   Scottish early years assistance, including the best start grants in operation from December 10, 2018, is also disregarded as income by para.70 of Sch.8.

The Employment and Support Allowance Regulations 2008

(SI 2008/794) (AS AMENDED)

SCHEDULES 2 AND 3, AS IN FORCE AT MARCH 27, 2011.

9.507   These govern all decisions made on or before that date. The degree to which these provisions cover some decisions taken after that date is set out in regulation 2 of the Employment and Support Allowance (Limited Capability for Work and Limited Capability for Work- Related Activity) (Amendment) Regulations 2011 (SI 2011/228), set out in para.9.365 in the previous edition of this volume. The provisions may still be relevant in a very small number of appeals. For their text see the previous edition of this Volume as updated by the 2012/13 Supplement

The Employment and Support Allowance
(Transitional Provisions) Regulations 2008

(SI 2008/795) (as amended)

ARRANGEMENT OF REGULATIONS

1. Citation, commencement and interpretation.
2. Claim for existing award.
3. Claim by person entitled or potentially entitled to existing award.
4. Claim for period before appointed day.
5. Transitional protection in relation to the Jobseekers Act 1995.

9.508

The Secretary of State for Work and Pensions in exercise of the powers conferred by section 25(2)(b) and (c) and 29 of, and paragraphs 1(1), 2 and 3(b), (c) and (d) of Schedule 4 to, the Welfare Reform Act 2007, makes the following Regulations which are made by virtue of, or consequential on, the provisions of the Welfare Reform Act 2007 and which are made before the end of a period of 6 months beginning with the coming into force of those provisions.

Citation, commencement and interpretation

1.—(1) These Regulations may be cited as the Employment and Support Allowance (Transitional Provisions) Regulations 2008. *9.509*

(2) This regulation and regulations 2, 3 and 4 shall come into force on 27th July 2008.

(3) Regulation 5 shall come into force on 27th October 2008.

(4) In these Regulations "income support on the grounds of disability" means income support awarded to a person to whom regulation [¹ . . .] 13(2)(b) or (bb) of, or paragraph 7(a) or (b), 10, 12 or 13 of Schedule 1B to, the Income Support (General) Regulations 1987 (prescribed categories of person) applies.

AMENDMENT

1. Employment and Support Allowance (Miscellaneous Amendments) Regulations 2008 (SI 2008/2428) reg.42 (October 27, 2008).

DEFINITION

"income support on the grounds of disability"—see para.(4).

GENERAL NOTE

This regulation entered into force on July 27, 2008, three months before the main ESA scheme became operative. *9.510*

Claim for existing award

2.—(1) A claim for incapacity benefit, severe disablement allowance or income support on the grounds of disability, whenever made, in respect of a period which begins on or after the appointed day, is to be treated as a claim for an employment and support allowance. *9.511*

(2) Paragraph (1) does not apply to

(a) [²a claim made in respect of a period commencing before 31st January 2011] for incapacity benefit or severe disablement allowance relating to a period of incapacity for work which is one of two periods treated as one period of incapacity for work under section 30C(1)(c) of the Contributions and Benefits Act (linking rules);

(b) [²a claim made in respect of a period commencing before 31st January 2011] made by a welfare to work beneficiary in accordance with regulation 13A of the Social Security (Incapacity for Work) (General) Regulations 1995 (welfare to work beneficiary); [¹ . . .]

(c) [²a claim made in respect of a period commencing before 31st January 2011] for income support on the grounds of disability where—

   (i) the claimant was previously entitled to income support on the grounds of disability, for a period of 4 or more consecutive days, and

   (ii) the claimant ceased to be entitled to income support on the grounds of disability not more than 8 weeks before the commencement of the period in respect of which the current claim is made;

[¹(d) a claim for income support on the grounds of disability made by a claimant who is entitled to incapacity benefit or severe disablement allowance; or

(e) a claim for incapacity benefit made by a claimant who is entitled to income support on the grounds of disability.]

(3) Paragraph (1) does not apply insofar as a claim is treated as a claim for severe disablement allowance, maternity allowance or carer's allowance under regulation 9(1) of and Part 1 of Schedule 1 to, the Social Security (Claims and Payments) Regulations 1987 (claims treated as claimed in addition or in the alternative).

AMENDMENTS

1. Employment and Support Allowance (Transitional Provisions) (Amendment) Regulations 2008 (SI 2008/2783) reg.2 (October 26, 2008).

2. Employment and Support Allowance (Transitional Provisions, Housing Benefit and Council Tax Benefit) (Existing Awards) (No. 2) Regulations 2010 (SI 2010/1907) reg.23 (October 1, 2010).

DEFINITIONS

"appointed day"—see WRA 2007 s.29, Sch.4, para.11.
"claimant"—see WRA 2007 s.24(1).
"incapacity benefit"—see WRA 2007 s.29, Sch.4, para.11.
"income support on the grounds of disability"—see reg.1(4).
"severe disablement allowance"—see WRA 2007 s.29, Sch.4, para.11.

GENERAL NOTE

9.512   This regulation entered into force on July 27, 2008, three months before October 27, 2008, the "appointed day" when WRA 2007 s.1 and the main ESA provisions became operative (see WRA 2007 s.29 Sch.4 para.11, and the Welfare Reform Act 2007 (Commencement No.6 and Consequential Provisions) Order 2008 (SI 2008/787) art.2(4).

It deals with claims for one or more of the benefits in the already existing incapacity benefits' regime: incapacity benefit; severe disablement allowance (limited, of course, only to those entitled to it immediately before April 6, 2001) and "income support on the grounds of disability". This last covers claims for income support by someone to whom regulation 13(2)(b) or (bb) of, or para.7(a) or (b), 10, 12 or 13 of Sch.1B to, the Income Support (General) Regs 1987 (prescribed categories of person) applies (that is someone claiming IS as a person incapable of work; as a disabled or deaf student; or as a blind person).

Paragraph (1) provides that a claim for any such benefit made on or after October 27, 2008 (the "appointed day") is to be treated as one for ESA. To this there are within reg.2 three classes of exception:

(1) Where a claim (made in respect of a period before January 30, 2011) for one of those benefits which is "linked" to a previous entitlement (para.(2)(a)–(c)).

This covers claims for IB or SDA linked to a previous period of incapacity for work by the standard eight week "linking rule" in SSCCBA 1992, s.30C(1)(c) (a period extendible by regs under s.30C(3)) (sub-para.(a)). It also embraces an IB claim by a "welfare to work beneficiary" under the Incapacity for Work Regs, reg.13A (the "104 week" rule) (sub-para.(b). It also covers an incapacity/disability-based claim for IS satisfying the four consecutive days "continuity rule" which ended not more than eight weeks prior to the claim now at issue (sub-para.(c)).

9.513

(2) Where a person entitled to incapacity benefit or severe disablement allowance claims income support on the grounds of disability and a person who is entitled to income support on the grounds of disability claims incapacity benefit (para.(2)(d), (e)).

Memo DMG 40/08 gives an example (IB entitlement enabling IS claim):

"Sue has been in receipt of IB for several years. She is not entitled to IS because her partner Mark is in remunerative work. Mark is made redundant in November 2008, and Sue claims IS on the grounds of disability. The DM makes a determination that Sue's claim is not treated as a claim for ESA, and decides the claim for IS accordingly."

(3) Where a claim is treated as a claim for severe disablement allowance, maternity allowance or carer's allowance under reg.9(1) of and Pt 1 of Sch.1 to, the Social Security (Claims and Payments) Regs 1987 (claims treated as claimed in addition or in the alternative).

See further the commentary to that regulation in Vol.III.

Claim by person entitled or potentially entitled to existing award

3.—(1) A person who is entitled to an existing award is excluded from making a claim for an employment and support allowance.

9.514

(2) A claim for an employment and support allowance made by a person who would be entitled to an existing award if that person made a claim described in regulation 2(2), is to be treated as a claim for that award.

DEFINITION

"existing award"—see WRA 2007 s.29 Sch.4 para.11.

GENERAL NOTE

This regulation entered into force on July 27, 2008, three months before October 27, 2008, the "appointed day" when WRA 2007 s.1 and the main ESA provisions became operative (see WRA 2007 s.29 Sch.4 para.11, and the Welfare Reform Act 2007 (Commencement No.6 and Consequential Provisions) Order 2008 (SI 2008/787), art.2(4).

9.515

Paragraph (1) deals with claims for ESA by someone entitled to an "existing award", that is, one or more of the benefits in the already existing incapacity benefits' regime: incapacity benefit; severe disablement allowance (limited, of course, only to those entitled to it immediately before April 6, 2001) and "income support on the grounds of disability" (WRA 2007 s.29, Sch.4, para.11). This last covers claims for income support under by someone to whom 13(2)(b) or (bb) of, or para.7(a) or (b), 10, 12 or 13 of Sch.1B to, the Income Support (General) Regs 1987 (prescribed categories of person) applies (that is someone claiming IS as a person incapable of work; as a disabled or deaf student; or as a blind person).

Paragraph (1) provides that someone so entitled cannot be entitled to ESA. That and an existing award are mutually exclusive.

Paragraph (2) extends that preclusion to those who claim ESA but would be entitled to an "existing award" (IB, SDA or incapacity/disability-based IS, as the case may be) if they made a "linked" claim for it as envisaged by reg.2(2).

Paragraph (1) receives some consideration in *CG v SSWP (ESA)* [2011] UKUT 167 (AAC), principally in terms of it setting out arguments advanced by the Secretary of State on its application (see para.2 of the decision). Judge May considered that he did not need to comment on those arguments since he was able to decide the appeal on another basis. In this case the claimant had appealed a decision denying him ESA as no longer having limited capability for work on re-assessment. The tribunal upheld that decision of the Secretary of State but purported also to allow an appeal in respect of Incapacity Benefit/credits, that success invalidating any ESA claim. Judge May held that this was outside the jurisdiction of the tribunal and it had thus erred in law. What the tribunal should have done was to determine the ESA appeal before them on the basis as to whether there were any grounds for the Secretary of State to supersede the existing award of ESA and in the event that they were so satisfied to then determine the ESA appeal on its merits, that is, whether the claimant satisfied the conditions for ESA. It would then be for the Secretary of State to determine what he wished to do in the light of that decision.

In *SSWP v C'OC (ESA)* [2011] UKUT 447 (AAC), Judge Wikeley agreed with submissions made by the Secretary of State largely following the lines of the approach taken by Judge May in *CG v SSWP (ESA)* [2011] UKUT 167 (AAC). Here there was no entitlement to an existing award because there had within the previous six months been a disallowance of incapacity benefit following a PCA (ESA Regs 2008 reg.30(2)). Moreover the claimant's appeal was against a supersession decision whereas the First-tier tribunal had focussed on the original decision of the Secretary of State to award ESA, a decision not under appeal, so that the tribunal thus acted outside its jurisdiction.

Claim for period before appointed day

9.516   **4.** Where—

   (a)   (i) before the appointed day a person purports to make a claim, or
         (ii) on or after the appointed day a person makes a claim,
         for an employment and support allowance for a period beginning before the appointed day; and

   (b)   it appears to the Secretary of State that the person would be entitled to incapacity benefit or income support on the grounds of disability if that person made a claim for it in accordance with section 1(1) (a) of the Administration Act, the purported claim or claim may be treated by the Secretary of State as a claim in the alternative for incapacity benefit or income support on the grounds of disability.

"appointed day"—see WRA 2007 s.29 Sch.4 para.11.
"incapacity benefit"—see WRA 2007 s.29 Sch.4 para.11.
"income support on the grounds of disability"—see reg.1(4).

GENERAL NOTE

This regulation entered into force on July 27, 2008, three months before October   **9.517**
27, 2008, the "appointed day" when WRA 2007 s.1 and the main ESA provisions
became operative (see WRA 2007 s.29, Sch.4, para.11, and the Welfare Reform
Act 2007 (Commencement No.6 and Consequential Provisions) Order 2008 (SI
2008/787) art.2(4).

It deals with a claim for ESA made before October 27, 2008 (the "appointed day)
or after that but for a period prior to the appointed day. No entitlement to ESA can
arise until October 27, 2008. So such a claim can either be rejected or, under this
regulation, instead treated by the Secretary of State as a claim in the alternative for
incapacity benefit or income support on the grounds of disability (IS as a person
incapable of work; as a disabled or deaf student; or as a blind person). But it can
only be so treated if the Secretary of State is satisfied that he would have been entitled to one of those benefits has a claim been made for it.

Transitional protection in relation to the Jobseekers Act 1995

5. In relation to a person who—   **9.518**
(a) is entitled to an existing award; or
(b) would be entitled to an existing award if that person made a claim
described in regulation 2(2),
the Jobseekers Act 1995 shall continue to have effect as if paragraphs 12(2),
(5)(b) and (6) of Schedule 3 to the Welfare Reform Act 2007 had not come
into effect.

DEFINITIONS

"existing award"—see WRA 2007 s.29 Sch.4 para.11.

GENERAL NOTE

An "existing award" is an award of one or more of the benefits in the already   **9.519**
existing incapacity benefits' regime: incapacity benefit; severe disablement
allowance (limited, of course, only to those entitled to it immediately before
April 6, 2001) and "income support on the grounds of disability" (WRA 2007
s.29, Sch.4, para.11). This last covers claims for income support under by
someone to whom reg.6(4)(a) or 13(2)(b) or (bb) of, or para.7(a) or (b), 10, 12
or 13 of Sch.1B to, the Income Support (General) Regs 1987 (prescribed categories of person) applies (that is someone claiming IS as a person incapable of
work; as a disabled worker; as a disabled or deaf student; or as a blind person).
This regulation deals with those entitled to an existing award or who would be if
they claimed it in respect of a "linked" period under reg.2(2). It provides that in
respect of them the Jobseekers Act 1995 continues to have effect as if the changes
effected by the specified provisions in WRA 2007 Sch.3 had never taken effect.
In short, read the relevant Jobseekers Act provisions as laid out in the 2008/09
edition of Vol.II.

The Social Security (Housing Costs Special Arrangements) (Amendment and Modification) Regulations 2008

(SI 2008/3195) *(as amended)*

Made by the Secretary of State for Work and Pensions under ss. 123(1)(a), 135(1), 137(1) and 175(1) and (3) and (4) of the Social Security Contributions and Benefits Act 1992, ss. 4(5), 35(1) and 36(2) and (4) of the Jobseekers Act 1995, ss. 2(3)(b), 17(1) and 19(1) of the State Pension Credit Act 2002, and ss. 4(2)(a) and (3), 24(1) and 25(2), (3) and (5) of the Welfare Reform Act 2007.

REGULATIONS REPRODUCED

9.520   1.   Citation, commencement and interpretation

PART 2

MODIFICATIONS RELATING TO CERTAIN CLAIMANTS WHO ARE ENTITLED TO A RELEVANT BENEFIT ON 4ᵀᴴ JANUARY 2009

3.   Application
4.   Modification of the Employment and Support Allowance Regulations
7.   Saving

PART 3

MODIFICATIONS RELATING TO CERTAIN PERSONS WHO CLAIM A RELEVANT BENEFIT AFTER 4ᵀᴴ JANUARY 2009

8.   Application and interpretation
9.   Modification of the Employment and Support Allowance Regulations

GENERAL NOTE

9.521   The modifications to the rules for housing costs for income-related ESA made by these Regulations only apply to certain claimants. See the note to Sch.6 to the ESA Regulations.

The modifications relating to waiting periods made by these Regulations were revoked on April 1, 2016 by the Social Security (Housing Costs Amendments) Regulations 2015 (SI 2015/1647), subject to a saving provision in reg.8 of those Regulations: see below. However, the modifications which concern the capital limit for eligible loans (together with the time limit for receipt of housing costs in the case of JSA) continue in effect.

Citation, commencement and interpretation

1.— (1) These Regulations may be cited as the Social Security (Housing Costs Special Arrangements) (Amendment and Modification) Regulations 2008.

9.522

(2) Regulations 4 to 6, in so far as they relate to a particular person, come into force on the first day of the first benefit week to commence for that person on or after 5th January 2009.

(3) The remaining provisions of these Regulations come into force on 5th January 2009.

(4) In these Regulations—

"benefit week" has the same meaning as in—

(a) regulation 2(1) of the Employment and Support Allowance Regulations, where the relevant benefit is an employment and support allowance;

[(b) and (c)omitted as not relating to ESA]

"housing costs" has the same meaning as in paragraph 1(1) (housing costs) of—

(a) Schedule 6 to the Employment and Support Allowance Regulations, where the relevant benefit is an employment and support allowance;

[(b) and (c) omitted as not relating to ESA]

"relevant benefit" means—

(a) an employment and support allowance;

(b) income support;

(c) a jobseeker's allowance;

"the Employment and Support Allowance Regulations" means the Employment and Support Allowance Regulations 2008;

[Remaining definitions omitted as not relating to ESA]

PART 2

MODIFICATIONS RELATING TO CERTAIN CLAIMANTS WHO ARE ENTITLED TO A RELEVANT BENEFIT ON 4TH JANUARY 2009

Application

3.—(1) This Part applies in relation to a person who—

9.523

(a) is entitled to a relevant benefit on 4th January 2009; and

(b) on or after that date falls within paragraph (3) or (4).

(2) This Part ceases to apply in relation to a person who makes a further claim to the same, or claims another, relevant benefit after 4th January 2009.

(3) A person falls within this paragraph if, apart from these Regulations, the housing costs to be met in the benefit week that includes 4th January 2009 would be nil in that person's case because [¹ that person] has not been entitled to the relevant benefit concerned for the period mentioned in sub-paragraph (1)(a) in any of the following provisions—

(a) paragraph 8 (existing housing costs) or paragraph 9 (new housing costs) of Schedule 6 to the Employment and Support Allowance Regulations;

[(b) and (c) omitted as not relating to ESA]

(4) A person falls within this paragraph if [¹ that person] has been entitled to a relevant benefit for a continuous period, which includes 4th January 2009, for at least 8 weeks but less than 26 weeks under any of the provisions mentioned in paragraph (5) as in force apart from these Regulations.

(5) The provisions are—

(a) paragraph 8(1)(b) (existing housing costs) or paragraph 9(6) (new housing costs) of Schedule 6 to the Employment and Support Allowance Regulations;

[(b) and (c) omitted as not relating to ESA]

AMENDMENT

1. Social Security (Housing Costs Special Arrangements) (Amendment) Regulations 2009 (SI 2009/3257) reg.2 (January 5, 2010).

Modification of the Employment and Support Allowance Regulations

9.524   **4.** Schedule 6 (housing costs) to the Employment and Support Allowance Regulations applies in relation to a person to whom this Part applies as if—

(a) [¹ . . .]

(b) [¹ . . .]

(c) in paragraph 12(4) (general provisions applying to new and existing housing costs) the reference to "£100,000" were to "£200,000";

(d) [¹ . . .]

AMENDMENT

1. Social Security (Housing Costs Amendments) Regulations 2015 (SI 2015/1647), reg.7(1) (April 1, 2016). Note that the revocation of these paragraphs is subject to the saving provision in reg.8 of SI 2015/1647. See p.1378 for this saving provision.

Saving

9.525   **7.**[¹ . . .]

AMENDMENT

1. Social Security (Housing Costs Amendments) Regulations 2015 (SI 2015/1647), reg.7(1) (April 1, 2016). Note that the revocation of this regulation is subject to the saving provision in reg.8 of SI 2015/1647. See p.1378 for this saving provision.

PART 3

MODIFICATIONS RELTING TO CERTAIN PERSONS WHO CLAIM
A RELEVANT BENEFIT AFTER 4ᵀᴴ JANUARY 2009

Application and interpretation

9.526   [¹ **8.**—(1) This Part applies on and after 5th January 2010 to a person ("C") who—

(a) claims a relevant benefit after 4th January 2009; and

(b) satisfies any of the following conditions.

(2) The first condition is that Part 2 applied to C at any time.

(3) The second condition is that this Part (as it has effect on and after 5th January 2010) applied to C in relation to a previous award.

(4) The third condition is that—

(a) neither C nor C's partner has been awarded a relevant benefit as the result of an earlier claim (whether the award was made before or on or after 5th January 2009);

(b) neither C nor C's partner is in receipt of state pension credit before the date on which C's claim is made or treated as made; and

(c) C does not fall to be treated under a linking rule as being in continuous receipt of the benefit to which C's claim relates in respect of a period which begins on or before 4th January 2009 and which ends immediately before the date on which C's claim is made or is treated as made.

(5) The fourth condition is that—

(a) C is not in receipt of a relevant benefit immediately before the date on which a claim made by C after 4th January 2009 is made or treated as made;

(b) neither C nor C's partner is in receipt of state pension credit before that claim is made or treated as made;

(c) C or C's partner was awarded a relevant benefit as the result of a claim made or treated as made before that claim; and

(d) C does not fall to be treated under a linking rule as being in continuous receipt of a relevant benefit during the period which falls immediately between the date on which a claim to which this provision relates is made or treated as made and the last period to occur before that date in respect of which C was in receipt of a relevant benefit (whether as a single person or as a member of a couple or polygamous marriage).

(6) The fifth condition is that—

(a) C or C's partner is in receipt of state pension credit before the date on which any claim for a relevant benefit made by C or C's partner after 4th January 2009 is made or treated as made; and

(b) none of the following provisions apply in relation to any such claim—

(i) paragraph 3(2) (previous entitlement to other income-related benefits) of Schedule 6 (housing costs) to the Employment and Support Allowance Regulations;

(ii) paragraph 1A(1A) (previous entitlement to income-based jobseeker's allowance, income-related employment and support allowance or state pension credit) of Schedule 3 (housing costs) to the Income Support Regulations;

(iii) paragraph 1A(1ZA) or (1B) (previous entitlement to income support, income-related employment and support allowance or state pension credit) of Schedule 2 (housing costs) to the Jobseeker's Allowance Regulations.

(7) In this regulation—

a "linking rule" means a provision of—

(a) paragraph 15 (linking rule) of Schedule 6 (housing costs) to the Employment and Support Allowance Regulations,

(b) paragraph 14 (linking rule) of Schedule 3 (housing costs) to the Income Support Regulations, or (as the case may be)

(c) paragraph 13 (linking rule) of Schedule 2 (housing costs) to the Jobseeker's Allowance Regulations;
"partner" has the same meaning as in regulation 1(3) (citation, commencement and interpretation) of the Jobseeker's Allowance Regulations.]

AMENDMENT

1. Social Security (Housing Costs Special Arrangements) (Amendment) Regulations 2009 (SI 2009/3257) reg.4 (January 5, 2010).

Modification of the Employment and Support Allowance Regulations

9.527   9. Schedule 6 (housing costs) to the Employment and Support Allowance Regulations applies in relation to a person to whom this Part applies as if—
  (a) [¹ . . .]
  (b) [¹ . . .]
  (c) [¹ . . .]
  (d) [¹ . . .]
  (e) [¹ . . .]
  (f) in paragraph 12 (general provisions applying to new and existing housing costs)—
     (i) [¹ . . .]
     (ii) [¹ . . .]
     (iii) in sub-paragraph (4), the reference to "£100,000" were to "£200,000";
  (g) [¹ . . .]
  (h) [¹ . . .]
  (i) [¹ . . .]

AMENDMENT

1. Social Security (Housing Costs Amendments) Regulations 2015 (SI 2015/1647), reg.7(1) (April 1, 2016). Note that the revocation of most of this regulation (with the exception of para.(f)(iii)) is subject to the saving provision in reg.8 of SI 2015/1647: see below.

The Employment and Support Allowance (Transitional Provisions, Housing Benefit and Council Tax Benefit) (Existing Awards) (No. 2) Regulations 2010

(SI 2010/1907) (*as amended*)

COMING INTO FORCE IN ACCORDANCE WITH REGULATION 1(2) AND (3)

ARRANGEMENT OF REGULATIONS

PART 1

GENERAL

9.528   1.   Citation and commencement
  2.   Interpretation
  3.   Persons to whom these Regulations apply

PART 2

CONVERSION DECISIONS

4.   The notice commencing the conversion phase
5.   Deciding whether an existing award qualifies for conversion
6.   Application of certain enactments for purpose of making conversion decisions
7.   Qualifying for conversion
8.   Amount of an employment and support allowance on conversion
9.   Determining entitlement to a transitional addition
10. Transitional addition: incapacity benefit or severe disablement allowance
11. Transitional addition: income support
12. Regulations 10 and 11: supplementary
13. The effective date of a conversion decision
14. Conversion decision that existing award qualifies for conversion
15. Conversion decision that existing award does not qualify for conversion

PART 3

AFTER THE CONVERSION PHASE

16. Application of other enactments applying to employment and support allowances
17. Changes of circumstances before the effective date
18. Reducing the transitional addition: general rule
19. Reducing the transitional addition: increases for dependent children
20. Reducing the transitional addition: increases for adult dependants
21. Termination of transitional addition

PART 4

MISCELLANEOUS

22. Disapplication of certain enactments following conversion decision
23. Treatment of claims until coming into force of regulation 24
24. Revocation of transitional claims provisions
25. Amendment of the 2008 Regulations
26. Consequential amendments
27. Amendments to legislation relating to Housing Benefit and Council Tax Benefit

SCHEDULES

SCHEDULE 1 — Modification of enactments: making conversion decisions
SCHEDULE 2 — Modification of enactments: after the conversion phase
SCHEDULE 3 — List of regulations that apply after the conversion phase
SCHEDULE 4 — Consequential amendments
SCHEDULE 5 — Amendments to legislation relating to Housing Benefit and Council Tax Benefit

The Secretary of State for Work and Pensions makes the following Regulations in exercise of the powers conferred by sections 123(1)(d) and (e), 135(1), 137(1) and

175(1), (3) and (4) of the Social Security Contributions and Benefits Act 1992, section 79(4) of the Social Security Act 1998, paragraphs 4(4) and (6), 20(1) and 23(1) of Schedule 7 to the Child Support, Pensions and Social Security Act 2000, sections 22, 24, 25(2), (3) and (5), 28(2) and 29 of, and paragraph 2 of Schedule 2 and paragraphs 1(1), 3(b), 7 and 8(1) of Schedule 4 to, the Welfare Reform Act 2007.

The Secretary of State has not referred these Regulations to the Social Security Advisory Committee as it appears to the Secretary of State that by reason of urgency it is inexpedient to do so.

The Secretary of State has not undertaken consultation with organisations appearing to the Secretary of State to be representative of the authorities concerned, as it appears to the Secretary of State that by reason of urgency it is inexpedient to do so.

GENERAL NOTE

Introduction

9.529   These Regulations establish the framework within which most current awards of incapacity benefit, income support on the basis of incapacity or disability, or severe disablement allowance will be either be converted to awards of ESA or terminated.

From February 28, 2011 the DWP has been conducting a phased reassessment of claimants with such awards. The process began at the target rate of 1,000 claimants per week. That target then increased to 7,000 claimants per week from April 4, 2011 and to 11,000 per week from May 9, 2011.

Legislative history

9.530   The Regulations are in the same terms as the Employment and Support Allowance (Transitional Provisions, Housing Benefit and Council Tax Benefit) (Existing Awards) Regulations 2010 (SI 2010/875) ("the former Regulations"). However, on March 10, 2010, when the former Regulations were made, paras 7 and 8 of Sch.4 to the Welfare Reform Act 2007 ("the Act")—which were listed in the preamble as being among the powers under which they were said to have been made—had not been brought into force. To regularise matters:

- those paragraphs were brought into force with effect on July 27, 2010 by the Welfare Reform Act 2007 (Commencement No. 12) Order 2010 (SI 2010/1905) ("the Commencement Order");

- the former Regulations were revoked by the Employment and Support Allowance (Transitional Provisions, Housing Benefit and Council Tax Benefit) (Existing Awards) (Revocation) Regulations 2010 (SI 2010/1906) with effect from August 27, 2010, before they came into force; and

- the present Regulations were made in the same terms as the former Regulations under powers which, as a result of the Commencement Order, the Secretary of State now possesses.

The Regulations have subsequently been amended by the Employment and Support Allowance (Transitional Provisions, Housing Benefit and Council Tax Benefit) (Existing Awards) (No. 2) (Amendment) Regulations 2010 (SI 2010/2430) with effect from November 1, 2010, by the Social Security (Miscellaneous Amendments) (No. 3) Regulations 2011 (SI 2011/2425) with effect from October 30, 2011 and by the Social Security (Miscellaneous Amendments) Regulations 2012 (SI 2012/757) April 1, 2012. They will be further amended with effect from May 1, 2012 by reg.10 of the Employment and Support Allowance (Duration of Contributory Allowance) (Consequential Amendments) Regulations 2012 (SI 2012/913).

Personal scope

9.531   By reg.3, the Regulations apply to any person who, on or after October 1, 2010, is entitled to an "existing award". That phrase is not defined in the Regulations. However, by virtue of s.11 Interpretation Act 1978, the definition in para.11 of Sch.4 to the Act applies. That provision defines "existing award" as meaning an award of incapacity benefit, an award of severe disablement allowance and an award of income support made to a person who falls within certain income support pre-scribed categories, namely:

- certain "eligible persons" (namely, those qualifying young persons who satisfy reg.13(2)(b) or (bb) of the Income Support Regulations), persons who are, or are treated as, incapable of work (i.e., those who satisfy paras 7(a) or (b) of Sch.1B to the Income Support Regulations);

- disabled students, deaf students and blind persons (i.e. those who satisfy, respectively, paras 10, 12 or 13 of Sch.1B);

- disabled workers (i.e. those to whom the former reg.6(4)(a) of the Income Support Regulations continues to apply by virtue of reg.4(3)–(4) and (7)–(8) of SI 2009/3228: see Vol.II).

However, under reg.4(5), the conversion process does not apply to anyone who will reach pensionable age before April 6, 2014 (i.e. men born before April 6, 1949 and women born before April 6, 1952).

It is possible for a person to have two existing awards (as where an award of incapacity benefit or severe disablement allowance is "topped up" by income support). However, for ease of exposition, this note is written as if there is only one existing award in any case. Where there are two such awards, what is said below applies to both of them).

The conversion process

The notice

The conversion of existing awards to awards of ESA is governed by Pt 2 of the   9.532
Regulations. Under reg.4 the Secretary of State may give notice to any person who is entitled to an existing award informing him or her that, depending on the satisfaction of certain conditions, that award is either to be converted to an award of ESA or terminated. The issue of such a notice turns the person who is entitled to an existing award into a "notified person" (reg.4(2) and begins the "conversion phase" (reg.4(4)).

The terms of reg.4 have proved problematical. For example, reg.4(3) provides that the notice must inform the recipient of various matters. Those include (reg.4(3) (a)) the fact that the existing award is to be converted into an award of an employment and support allowance if "certain conditions" are satisfied and (reg.4(3)(c)) the requirements that must be met in order to satisfy those conditions. However, the phrase "certain conditions" is not defined and there is no indication of the level of detail in which the requirements that the claimant has to meet must be specified so as to comply with reg.4(3)(c). Moreover, reg.4(3)(b) requires the notice to include the information that "if those conditions are not satisfied, the existing award will not be converted and will terminate". The original version of the standard form notice used by the Department (Form IBM01) did not include an express statement of that fact, although (as the Upper Tribunal held at para.43 in the *JM* case: see below) it could have been inferred from the notice as a whole. It was unclear whether that failure, or a failure to comply with regs 4(3)(a) and (c) invalidated the notice.

Those issues have now been considered by a Three-Judge Panel of the Upper Tribunal in *JM v Secretary of State for Work and Pensions (ESA)* [2013] UKUT 234 (AAC); [2014] AACR 5. The Upper Tribunal decided:

- that where the claimant is in Great Britain, reg.4(3)(a) and (b) have the effect that the phrase "certain conditions" refers only to the condition in s.1(3) (a) of the Welfare Reform Act 2007 (i.e. having limited capability for work) (para.37);
- that reg.4(3)(c) does no more than require that it must be made clear to claimants that, in order to qualify for employment and support allowance, they must satisfy the requirement of having limited capability for work (para.40);

- that the standard form notice did comply with the requirements of reg.4(3) in cases where the claimant was in Great Britain and that it was unnecessary to decide in the cases before the Upper Tribunal whether it would be adequate when a claimant was absent from Great Britain, or was for some reason not bound to satisfy the basic conditions in s.1(3)(b), (c) and (f) of the Welfare Reform Act 2007 (para.45);

- that a notice under reg.4 is "issued" when it is generated *and* sent out by, or on behalf of, the Secretary of State (para.58). Generating the notice without sending it out does not amount to issuing it (para.48); and

- that any breach of reg.4 due to form IBM01 being inadequate on the grounds that Form IBM01 does not contain the information required by reg.4 and so does not comply with it or due to it not being sent or received does not result in any subsequent conversion decision being invalid (para.69).

To the extent that it holds that a failure to send a notice under r.4 does not invalidate the subsequent conversion decision, it is suggested that the Upper Tribunal's decision in *JM* goes too far. The consequences of a failure to meet the information requirements in reg.4(3) and the consequences of not sending the notice at all (and therefore not "issuing" it for the purposes of regs 4(1), (2) and (4)–(6)) are not necessarily the same, but the decision proceeds on the basis that they are.

The Upper Tribunal's reasoning starts from the principle that "the answer to the question whether a breach of a statutory provision has the effect of invalidating subsequent decisions depends on whether it was the legislator's intention that it should have that effect" (para.59). That is clearly correct. The Tribunal then quotes with approval from the opinion of Lord Steyn at para.23 of the decision of the House of Lords in *R. v Soneji* [2005] UKHL 49; [2006] 1 A.C. 340 to the effect that "this is a question of statutory construction and that the emphasis ought to be on the consequences of non-compliance, and posing the question whether Parliament can fairly to be taken to have intended total invalidity" (internal quotation marks omitted).

Although, the Upper Tribunal does not refer to the passage, Lord Steyn makes clear at para.15 that the above approach involves imputing an intention to the legislator rather than identifying what the actual intention was:

> "In framing the question in this way it is necessary to have regard to the fact that Parliament *ex hypothesi* did not consider the point of the ultimate outcome. Inevitably one must be considering objectively what intention should be imputed to Parliament."

Adopting that approach, the Upper Tribunal decides that the legislator did not intend a breach of reg.4 to lead to total invalidity by considering the consequences that would follow were such a breach to invalidate the conversion process and concluding that the legislator cannot have intended those consequences.

Soneji was a case in which, as Lord Steyn described it at para.14 of his opinion, "[p]arliament casts its commands in imperative form without expressly spelling out the consequences of a failure to comply". That is why what is acknowledged to be "a question of statutory construction", which would normally be resolved by looking at the words the legislator had used, has to be resolved by having regard to the consequences of non-compliance and then imputing an intention to the legislator: the question has only arisen because the words used by the legislator do not cover the point.

Whether the failure to comply with the information requirements in reg.4(3) invalidates the notice is just such a question. The legislator has not said anything relevant and the Upper Tribunal's decision that, in the absence of prejudice to the claimant, a breach of reg.4(3) does not invalidate the notice is entirely justified.

However, whether a failure to *issue* the notice by sending it to the claimant invalidates the subsequent process is not the sort of question that was considered in *Soneji*. The legislator has provided expressly for the consequences that flow from the issue of the notice. It is inherent in that provision that the same consequences do *not* flow from the non-issue of the notice. In those circumstances, there is no need to impute an intention to the legislator from the consequences of non-compliance: the legislator's intention can be ascertained in the usual way from the words the legislator has chosen to use.

Specifically, the legislator has said that:

- the issue of the notice to a claimant brings him or her within the definition of "a notified person" (reg.4(2));

- the Secretary of State's power to make a conversion decision arises "in relation to the existing award or awards to which a *notified person* ('P') is entitled" (reg.5(1) added emphasis); and

- the issue of the notice to a notified person begins the conversion phase in relation to that person, with effect from the date of issue (reg.4(4)).

For the Upper Tribunal to hold that those circumstances arise even when a notice has not been issued is, with respect, to ignore what the legislator has said.

There is also the larger point that the legislator chose to make regulations under which the conversion process is initiated by the issue of a notice, even though there was no requirement in the empowering legislation to do so. He could, for example, have provided for the process to be commenced by a (non-appealable) decision rather than the issue of a notice. The regulations show an intention that the issue of the notice is to have consequences. In addition to the examples given above, reg.4(6) provides that a notice issued to a claimant with two existing awards shall "*have effect in relation to both such awards*" (added emphasis) (reg.4(6)). The consequence of the Upper Tribunal's decision (*pace* para.64) is that the issue of the notice has no effect: the conversion phase begins, the claimant becomes a "notified person" and the Secretary of State acquires the power to issue a conversion decision in respect of the claimant's existing awards, whether the notice is issued or not.

It is unclear whether the decision in *JM* is binding on this particular point. On the one hand, the point was raised by the decision of the First-tier Tribunal in the second of the appeals before the Upper Tribunal. On the other, it had been established by the time of the Upper Tribunal's decision that notices had been generated—and therefore, on a balance of probabilities, sent (see para.70)—in all the cases before it (paras 11, 13 and 17). On that basis, it could be said that the point was one the Upper Tribunal did not need to decide.

Even if it is not actually binding, the decision of a Three-Judge Panel is a very strong persuasive authority. Nevertheless, for the reasons given above, it is suggested that the better view is that the Secretary of State has no power to make a conversion decision unless he has first sent a notice under reg.4(1) to the claimant. If that is correct, the Upper Tribunal's view (at para.70) that "it is not actually necessary for a finding to be made [i.e., by the First-tier Tribunal hearing an appeal against a conversion decision] as to whether a notice was in fact sent", and that the Secretary of State did not therefore need routinely to provide evidence of the issue of the notice, is also mistaken.

In *SSWP v PD (ESA)* [2014] UKUT 549 (AAC); [2015] AACR 24, a three-judge panel of the Upper Tribunal considered a challenge to the *vires* of the Regulations on the ground that it was incompatible with s.17 of the Social Security Act 1998, (which provides that decisions about benefits are to be "final", subject to revision, supersession and appeal).

The First-tier Tribunal had held that, by virtue of s.17 of the 1998 Act, the decision to award income support to the claimant was final and could not be brought to an end by the Secretary of State save by way of a supersession under s.10 of that Act, which would be subject to an appeal under s.12 of that Act. The termination of an award under the 2010 Regulations was not such a supersession and those Regulations could not have the effect of amending the 1998 Act because the enabling provisions in the 2007 Act under which the Regulations were made were not in

9.533

the clear terms required to enable subordinate legislation to amend primary legislation. Accordingly, it held the 2010 Regulations to be ultra vires.

The Upper Tribunal rejected that reasoning stating:

> "16.   It is a crucial part of the claimant's case and the reasoning of the First-tier Tribunal that the 2010 Regulations operate so as to amend the 1998 Act, without the 2007 Act having authorised such an amendment. Reliance is placed on *R. (Totel Limited) v First-tier Tribunal (Tax Chamber)* [2012] EWCA Civ 1401; [2013] QB 860 in which Moses LJ, with whom Lord Neuberger MR and Arden LJ agreed, said at [29] that "provided the power conferred by one statute to amend the provisions of another by delegated legislation is clear and express so that it is plain that Parliament understood the nature and scope of the power it was conferring on the executive, there is no reason in principle why the statute should not do so." . . .
>
> 17.   However, we agree with the Secretary of State that regulation 15(2) of the 2010 Regulations, made under paragraph 7(1)(b) of Schedule 4 to the 2007 Act, does not purport to amend the 1998 Act. It is a transitional provision made under a broad power to "make provision for the termination of existing awards". It provides—at least on the Secretary of State's analysis and the primary argument advanced by the claimant—for the termination of existing awards otherwise than by way of revision or supersession and thus implies an exception to the general rule in section 17(1) of the 1998 Act, but express amendment of the 1998 Act is not required for the provision to have that effect. One Act often has to be read subject to a second, later, Act. Moreover, it would be surprising if an express amendment were to be made to an Act so as to make it clear that a provision in it was subject to transitional provisions in either that Act or a later Act. Transitional provisions often operate through the modification of other legislation and are often, although not always, transitory in nature. (Indeed, it is to be noted that one of the regulation-making powers cited in the preamble to the 2010 Regulations is section 28(2) of the 2007 Act, which provides that regulations "may make provision consequential on this Part amending or repealing any provision of . . . an Act passed on or before the last day of the Session in which this Act is passed".)"

The Regulations are therefore *intra vires*.

The conversion decision

9.534   The decision maker then makes a "conversion decision" under reg.5, i.e. s/he decides whether the notified person ("P") satisfies the basic conditions of entitlement to ESA under s.1(3) of the Act (except, of course, the condition in s.1(3)(f) that s/he should not be entitled to income support). That process involves carrying out a work capability assessment. If P does satisfy those conditions then, by virtue of reg.7, the existing award qualifies for conversion. Otherwise, it does not.

Once a conversion decision has been made, the legislation under which the notified person was entitled to an existing award ceases to apply to him or her: see reg.22.

The Secretary of State then notifies P of the conversion decision under reg.5(5).

Existing awards that qualify for conversion

9.535   Where the existing award is to be converted to an award of ESA, that notice must specify how much ESA is to be paid and the effective date (determined in accordance with reg.13) from which it will be paid (reg.5(3)).

Regulation 6 provides that specified legislation is to apply (in a modified form where Schs 1 and 2 so provide) for (among other things) the purposes of enabling the Secretary of State to make a conversion decision. That legislation includes Pt 1 of the Act and the Employment and Support Allowance Regulations. The effect is that, once notice has been given under reg.4, the normal work capability assessment procedures apply. So, for example, if—without good cause—a notified person fails to return the ESA50 questionnaire or to attend for a medical examination, the Secretary of State may determine that s/he does not have limited capability for work (i.e. in accordance with, respectively, regs 21(1)(b) and 22 or reg.23 of the

Employment and Support Allowance Regulations). Such a decision will then lead to a decision that the notified person's existing award does not qualify for conversion.

The amount of the converted award of ESA is determined by reg.8 and may include a "transitional addition" calculated under regs 9 to 12. In broad terms, the transitional addition is calculated as the difference (if any) between the amount of the existing award (or awards) and the amount that would otherwise be payable by way of ESA. The effect should be that no claimant whose existing award qualifies for conversion should be worse of as a result of the conversion process. However, under regs 18–21, any transitional addition reduces by the amount of any increase in ESA rates after the conversion decision (e.g. as a result of annual up-rating). The effect is that the combined amount of the basic ESA award (including the appropriate component) and the transitional addition will remain the same until the ESA award has increased to a level which exceeds that combined amount (i.e. thereby reducing the transitional addition to nil).

In some cases, conversion to ESA will make a claimant better off. Those who are awarded the support component (except for some in-patients) also become entitled to have the enhanced disability premium included in their applicable amount when their entitlement to IRESA is calculated (see paras.7(1)(a) and (2) of Sch.4 to the ESA Regulations). That increase in the applicable amount will have the effect that some claimants who were previously only entitled to (contributory) incapacity benefit (i.e., because they were excluded from IS by the means test) become entitled to IRESA and well as CESA. In such circumstances, a claim for IRESA is not necessary. The Secretary of State's duty (at Step 1 of reg.8(1)) to "determine ... the amount (if any) of [ESA] to which the notified person would be entitled" if that person had claimed ESA, "must encompass consideration of both the contributory amount and the income-related amount": see *DJ v Secretary of State for Work and Pensions (ESA)* [2015] UKUT 342 (AAC) at para.28 and generally.

The failure of the Department always to treat ESA as a single benefit consisting of two components also led to a dispute about the application of the anti-test-case rule in SSA 1998, s.27. Because of a Departmental error, an estimated 75,000 claimants were migrated to CESA rather than IRESA and were therefore not awarded any premiums to which they may have been entitled and which are only paid as part of IRESA.

The Secretary of State accepted that the mistake was made but initially took the view that the unitary nature of ESA was only established by the decision of the Upper Tribunal (Judge Rowland) in *LH v SSWP (ESA)* [2014] UKUT 480 (AAC); [2015] AACR 14 and that, accordingly, s.27 had the effect that arrears were only payable from October 21, 2014 (the date on which *LH* was promulgated). In Scotland, the Upper Tribunal (Judge Gamble) supported that view of s.27 in *SK v SSWP (ESA)* [2018] UKUT 267 (AAC). The decision in *SK* was appealed to the Court of Session sub nom. *Kerr v Secretary of State for Work and Pensions*. In England and Wales, CPAG commenced judicial review proceedings challenging the decision to limit arrears. However, on July 18, 2018, following the publication that day of a critical report by the House of Commons Committee of Public Accounts (HC 975), the Secretary of State announced to the House of Commons in a written statement (HCWS877) that full arrears (i.e., back to the date of conversion to ESA) would be paid to all affected claimants.

Subsequently in *DS v SSWP* [2018] UKUT 270 (AAC), the Secretary of State accepted formally that the unitary nature of ESA was not established by the decision in *LH v SSWP (ESA)* [2014] UKUT 480 (AAC); [2015] AACR 14 and that *SK v SSWP* (ESA) was therefore in error of law. The three-judge panel of the Upper Tribunal in *DS* issued a consent order including a declaration to that effect.

Note that the combined effect of ss.2 and 4 of the Act as modified by paras 3 and 4 of Sch.1, Step 1 of reg.8(1) and reg.12(5) (taken together with either reg.10(4)(b) (where the existing award consisted of incapacity benefit or severe disablement allowance) or reg.11(4)(c) (where the existing award consisted of income support)) is that a notified person who whose existing award qualifies for conversion becomes entitled to the work-related activity component or support component (depending on whether s/he is found to have limited capability for work-related activity) from the effective date of the conversion decision. This is in contrast to the rule where entitlement to ESA is based on a claim for that benefit (in which case, entitlement to the appropriate component starts at the beginning of the 14th week of the person's continuous period of limited capability for work (see reg.7(40) of the Social Security and Child Support (Decisions and Appeals) Regulations 1999 (SI 1999/991) in Vol.3)). This is unaffected by the abolition of the work-related activity component with effect from April 3, 2017 because the Employment and Support Allowance and Universal Credit (Miscellaneous Amendments and Transitional and Savings Provisions) Regulations 2017 (SI 2017/204), reg.7(2) and Sch.1, Pt.1, para.4 establish transitional protection from that change for all holders of existing awards who subsequently become notified persons: see further the General Note to SI 2017/204 below.

Where the existing award qualifies for conversion it takes effect as a single award (i.e. even if there were two existing awards before conversion) of ESA at the rate specified in the conversion decision (reg.14(1)). The exception is where P would continue to be entitled to income support other than on the basis of incapacity for work or disability. In such a case P can elect (before the effective date) to remain on income support (reg.14(2A)) subject (in certain cases) to the loss of the disability premium (reg.14(2B)).

Existing awards that do not qualify for conversion

9.536   In cases where P does not satisfy the conditions of entitlement to ESA, and therefore the existing award does not qualify for conversion, that award comes to an end immediately before the effective date (reg.15(2)). The conversion phase ends on the same day (reg.5(6)(a)) but that circumstance has no significance in cases where the existing award is not converted to ESA. Again there is an exception for people who remain entitled to income support other than on the basis of incapacity for work or disability (reg.15(2A) and (2B)).

Revision and supersession during the conversion phase

9.537   Regulation 17 contains detailed rules for taking into account relevant changes in circumstances and other "relevant events" which occur before the effective date of the conversion decision. Effectively, the decision-maker must treat the conversion decision as if it had not been made, and then revise or supersede the decision making the existing award so as to reflect the change in circumstance. He must then decide whether to convert the revised or superseding decision.

Right of appeal

9.538   There is a right of appeal against the conversion decision. That right is conferred by reg.16(1) and Sch.2, para.5, which modify the list of decisions against which an appeal lies in Sch.3 of the Social Security Act 1998 by inserting a new para.8E. It is important to note, however, that the appeal is against the conversion decision under reg.5 and not against the Secretary of State's decision to begin the process by serving a notice under reg.4. So a notified person cannot argue that s/he should not have been subjected to the conversion process at all (or at any particular time). However, for the reasons given above, the right of appeal appears to be broad enough to allow the appellant to assert that the notice was invalid and that the Secretary of State therefore had no power to make a conversion decision.

A person who has made and is pursuing an appeal against a conversion decision made on the basis that he or she does not have limited capability for work is entitled to ESA at the basic rate while the appeal is pending: see the modifications to regs 30 and 147A of the ESA Regulations made by paras 10 and 15 of Sch.2 and to reg.3 of the Social Security (Claims and Payments) Regulations 1987 by para.18 of Sch.2 and the commentary to reg.147A.

Other changes

9.539   Schedules 1 and 2 set out a large number of modifications to other legislation. The existence of those modifications is noted at the appropriate places in these books and their text is set out below.

The modifications in Sch.1 apply during the conversion phase for the purposes of enabling the Secretary of State to make a conversion decision to revise any such decision before the effective date (see reg.6(1)).

The modifications in Sch.2 apply after the conversion phase for the purposes of revising or superseding conversion decisions on or after the effective date and for "enabling any other matter to be determined in connection with any person's entitlement or continuing entitlement to an award of an employment and support allowance by virtue of these Regulations" (see reg.16(1)).

9.540

Regulations 6(3) and 16(3) have the effect that, for the purposes of revising and superseding decisions and appeals, "the conversion decision is to be treated as if it were a decision as to a person's entitlement to an employment and support allowance which had been made on a claim". This is necessary because, in conversion cases, there will not actually have been a claim for ESA. Under ss.9 and 10 Social Security Act 1998, the Secretary of State may only revise (and, sometimes may only supersede) decisions under s.8, which empowers the Secretary of State to decide (among other things) "any *claim* for a relevant benefit" (emphasis added).

Finally Schs 4 and 5 make consequential amendments. Those in Sch.4 have been incorporated into the text of the amended legislation elsewhere in these books. Those in Sch.5 relate to housing benefit and council tax benefit and are therefore beyond the scope of this publication.

PART 1

GENERAL

Citation and commencement

1.—(1) These Regulations may be cited as the Employment and Support Allowance (Transitional Provisions, Housing Benefit and Council Tax Benefit) (Existing Awards) (No.2) Regulations 2010.

9.541

(2) Subject to paragraph (3), these Regulations come into force on 1st October 2010.

(3) Regulations 24 (revocation of transitional claims provisions) and 25(2) (amendment of the 2008 Regulations) and [¹ paragraphs 1A and 2] of Schedule 4 (consequential amendments to the 2008 Regulations) come into force on 31st January 2011.

AMENDMENT

1. Employment and Support Allowance (Transitional Provisions, Housing Benefit and Council Tax Benefit) (Existing Awards) (No.2) (Amendment) Regulations 2010 (SI 2010/2430) reg.2 (November 1, 2010).

Interpretation

2.—(1) In these Regulations—

9.542

"the 2007 Act" means the Welfare Reform Act 2007;

"the 2008 Regulations" means the Employment and Support Allowance Regulations 2008;

"benefit week" has the same meaning as in the 2008 Regulations;

"contributory allowance" means an employment and support allowance to which a person is entitled by virtue of these Regulations which was based on an award of incapacity benefit or severe disablement allowance to which the person was entitled;

"conversion decision", in relation to a notified person, has the meaning given in regulation 5(2);

"effective date", in relation to a conversion decision, is to be construed in accordance with regulation 13;

"enactment" includes an enactment contained in subordinate legislation (within the meaning of the Interpretation Act 1978);

"income-related allowance" means an employment and support allowance to which a person is entitled by virtue of these Regulations which was based on an award of income support to which the person was entitled;

"notified person" has the meaning given in regulation 4(2);

"pensionable age" has the meaning given by the rules in paragraph 1 of Schedule 4 to the Pensions Act 1995;

"relevant deduction", in relation to a person, includes such of the following deductions as fall to be made in relation to the person—

(a) any deduction made under any of the following provisions of the Social Security (Claims and Payments) Regulations 1987—

   (i) regulation 34A (deductions of mortgage interest which shall be made from benefit
and paid to qualified lenders),

  (ii) regulation 34B (deductions of mortgage interest which may be made from benefits and paid to qualified lenders in other cases), or

 (iii) regulation 35 (deductions which may be made from benefit and paid to third parties);

(b) any deduction made under the Community Charges (Deductions from Income Support) (No.2) Regulations 1990 (deductions which may be made from benefit for meeting sums due in respect of community charges);

(c) any deduction made under the Fines (Deductions from Income Support) Regulations 1992 (deductions which may be made from an offender's benefit);

(d) any deduction made under the Council Tax (Deductions from Income Support) Regulations 1993 (deductions which may be made from benefit for meeting sums due in respect of council tax);

(e) any deduction in respect of overpayment recovery or recovery of social fund loans made under any of the following provisions of the Administration Act—

   (i) section 71 (overpayments-general),

  (ii) section 74 (income support and other payments), or

 (iii) section 78 (recovery of social fund awards).

(2) A requirement under these Regulations to give a notice (or to notify) is a requirement to give notice in writing; and for that purpose—

(a) a message sent by electronic communication shall be treated as a notice given in writing; and

(b) electronic communication has the meaning given in section 15(1) of the Electronic Communications Act 2000.

(3) For the purposes of these Regulations, the conversion phase, in relation to any person entitled to an existing award or awards, is the period which—

(a) begins in accordance with regulation 4(4); and

(b) ends in accordance with regulation 5(6).

(4) In these Regulations, any reference to Step 1, 2 or 3, in relation to any person, is to be construed in accordance with regulation 8.

MODIFICATION

In cases where universal credit has come into force (see the General Note, above), reg.2 is modified. For a list of the modifying provisions see the General Note (para.9.538 above). For the text of the modification, see the text of Sch.4 to SI 2013/983 in Pt. IV of Vol.V.   **9.543**

Persons to whom these Regulations apply

[¹ **3.** In these Regulations, regulations 4 to 22 apply to any person who, on or after 1st October 2010, is entitled to an existing award.]   **9.544**

AMENDMENT

1. Employment and Support Allowance (Transitional Provisions, Housing Benefit and Council Tax Benefit) (Existing Awards) (No.2) (Amendment) Regulations 2010 (SI 2010/2430) reg.3 (November 1, 2010).

PART 2

CONVERSION DECISIONS

The notice commencing the conversion phase

4.—(1) Subject to paragraph (5), the Secretary of State may at any time issue a notice to any person who is entitled to an existing award.   **9.545**

(2) Any person to whom such a notice is issued is referred to in these Regulations as a notified person.

(3) The notice must inform the notified person—

(a) that an existing award is to be converted into an award of an employment and support allowance if certain conditions are satisfied;

(b) that, if those conditions are not satisfied, the existing award will not be converted and will terminate by virtue of these Regulations;

(c) of the requirements that must be met in order to satisfy those conditions; and

(d) of such other matters as the Secretary of State considers appropriate.

(4) The issue of the notice to a notified person begins the conversion phase in relation to that person, with effect from the date of issue.

(5) No notice may be issued to any person—

(a) who reaches pensionable age at any time before 6th April 2014; or

(b) at any time when payment of the existing award to the person is subject to adjustment under regulation 4 of the Social Security (Transitional Payments) Regulations 2009 (adjustment of subsequent payments following an adjusting payment of benefit).

(6) Where a person is entitled to—

(a) an existing award of incapacity benefit or severe disablement allowance; and

(b) an existing award of income support,

the notice issued to the person under this regulation shall have effect in relation to both such awards.

MODIFICATION

In cases where universal credit has come into force (see the General Note, above), reg.4 is modified. For a list of the modifying provisions see the General Note (para.9.538 above). For the text of the modification, see the text of Sch.4 to SI 2013/983 in Pt. IV of Vol.V.

Deciding whether an existing award qualifies for conversion

9.546   **5.**—(1) In relation to the existing award or awards to which a notified person ("P") is entitled, the Secretary of State must, except where paragraph (8)(a) applies, make a conversion decision in accordance with these Regulations.

(2) A conversion decision is—

(a) a decision that P's existing award or awards qualify for conversion into an award of an employment and support allowance in accordance with regulation 7 (qualifying for conversion); or

(b) a decision that P's existing award or awards do not qualify for conversion into an award of an employment and support allowance.

(3) A notice of a conversion decision under paragraph (2)(a) must specify the amount of an employment and support allowance to which P is entitled on the effective date (subject to any relevant deductions).

(4) The amount referred to in paragraph (3) is to be determined in accordance with regulation 8 (amount of an employment and support allowance on conversion).

(5) The Secretary of State must notify P of the Secretary of State's conversion decision.

(6) The conversion phase ends in relation to P—

(a) immediately before the effective date of the conversion decision notified to P; or

(b) if earlier, when P's entitlement to the award or awards to which the notice under regulation 4 (notice commencing the conversion phase) relates otherwise ceases to be subject to conversion (because entitlement to the award has terminated or for some other reason).

(7) The effective date of any conversion decision is to be determined in accordance with regulation 13 (effective date of a conversion decision).

(8) In the event that P's entitlement to an existing award ceases to be subject to conversion (for example, because P's entitlement to an award of income support has ceased to fall within paragraph (c) of the definition of "existing award" in paragraph 11 of Schedule 4 to the 2007 Act)—

(a) before a conversion decision is made, the Secretary of State must notify P that the conversion phase has ended without a conversion decision being made; or

(b) after the making of a conversion decision but before its effective date, the Secretary of State must notify P that the conversion decision shall not come into effect.

(9) On the giving of a notice under paragraph (8)(b), the conversion decision to which it relates shall lapse with immediate effect.

MODIFICATION

In cases where universal credit has come into force (see the General Note, above), reg.5 is modified. For a list of the modifying provisions see the General Note (para.9.538 above). For the text of the modification, see the text of Sch.4 to SI 2013/983 in Pt.IV of Vol.V.

Application of certain enactments for purpose of making conversion decisions

6.—(1) The enactments listed in paragraph (2) apply, subject to the modifications specified in Schedule 1, for the purposes of—

   (a) enabling the Secretary of State to make in relation to any person a conversion decision under this Part; and

   (b) providing for the revision [¹ or supersession] of such decisions at any time before the effective date.

(2) The listed enactments are—

   (a) Part 1 of the 2007 Act;

   (b) the 2008 Regulations;

   (c) regulation 32(1) and (1A) of the Social Security (Claims and Payments) Regulations 1987 (information to be given);

   (d) Chapter 2 of Part 1 of the Social Security Act 1998 (social security decisions and appeals); and

   (e) the Social Security and Child Support (Decisions and Appeals) Regulations 1999.

(3) In the application of the enactments listed in paragraph (2)(d) and (e), the conversion decision is to be treated as if it were a decision as to a person's entitlement to an employment and support allowance which had been made on a claim.

9.547

AMENDMENT

1. Social Security (Miscellaneous Amendments) (No.3) Regulations 2011 (SI 2011/2425) reg.27(2) (October 30, 2011).

MODIFICATION

In cases where universal credit has come into force (see the General Note, above), reg.6(2) is modified. For a list of the modifying provisions see the General Note (para.9.538 above). For the text of the modification, see the text of Sch.4 to SI 2013/983 in Pt IV of Vol.V.

Qualifying for conversion

7. [¹ (1)] [¹ Subject to [² paragraphs (2) and (3)]], for the purposes of regulation 5(2)(a)] (deciding whether an existing award qualifies for conversion), an existing award or awards to which a notified person [¹ ("P")] is entitled qualify for conversion into an award of an employment and support allowance [¹ under these Regulations] only if [¹ P] satisfies the basic conditions set out in section 1(3)(a) to (d) and (f) of the 2007 Act.

[¹ (2) Where P is entitled to an award of an employment and support allowance under the 2007 Act and it has been determined in respect of that entitlement that P—

   (a) has limited capability for work, or

   (b) is to be treated as having limited capability for work, other than by virtue of regulation 30 of the 2008 Regulations,

9.548

in relation to the conversion of P's existing award, P is to be taken as having satisfied the condition set out in section 1(3)(a) of the 2007 Act (limited capability for work).]

[² (3) Where P would be entitled to an award of an employment and support allowance under the 2007 Act but for the application of section 1A of that Act (duration of contributory allowance) and it had been determined in respect of the entitlement that had ceased that P—

(a) had limited capability for work; or

(b) was to be treated as having limited capability for work, other than by virtue of regulation 30 of the 2008 Regulations,

in relation to the conversion of P's existing award, P is to be taken as having satisfied the condition set out in section 1(3)(a) of the 2007 Act (limited capability for work).]

AMENDMENTS

1. Employment and Support Allowance (Transitional Provisions, Housing Benefit and Council Tax Benefit) (Existing Awards) (No.2) (Amendment) Regulations 2010 (SI 2010/2430) reg.4 (November 1, 2010).

2. Employment and Support Allowance (Duration of Contributory Allowance) (Consequential Amendments) Regulations 2012 (SI 2012/913) reg.10(2) (May 1, 2012).

MODIFICATION

In cases where universal credit has come into force (see the General Note, above), reg.7 is modified. For a list of the modifying provisions see the General Note (para.9.538 above). For the text of the modification, see the text of Sch.4 to SI 2013/983 in Pt IV of Vol.V.

Amount of an employment and support allowance on conversion

9.549   **8.** [¹ (1)] For the purposes of regulation 5(3), the amount of an employment and support allowance to which a notified person is entitled shall be determined as follows.

Step 1

Determine in accordance with Part 1 of the 2007 Act and the 2008 Regulations the amount (if any) of an employment and support allowance to which the notified person would be entitled if, on a claim made by that person—

(a) it had been determined that the person was entitled to an award of an employment and support allowance; and

(b) the assessment phase had ended.

Step 2

Determine in accordance with regulations 9 to 12—

[¹ (a)] whether the notified person is entitled to a transitional addition; and

[¹ (b)] if so, the amount of the transitional addition.

Step 3

Aggregate the amounts (if any) which result from Steps 1 and 2.

[¹ (2) In a case to which regulation 7(2) applies (cases where a person is already entitled to an award of an employment and support allowance), a determination that the person has, or does not have, limited capability for work-related activity made in respect of the person's current entitlement to an award of an employment and support allowance is to be treated as having been made for the purposes of Step 1.]

AMENDMENT

1. Employment and Support Allowance (Transitional Provisions, Housing Benefit and Council Tax Benefit) (Existing Awards) (No.2) (Amendment) Regulations 2010 (SI 2010/2430) reg.5 (November 1, 2010).

MODIFICATION

In cases where universal credit has come into force (see the General Note, above), reg.8(1) is modified. For a list of the modifying provisions see the General Note (para.9.538 above). For the text of the modification, see the text of Sch.4 to SI 2013/983 in Pt IV of Vol.V.

9.550

Determining entitlement to a transitional addition

9.—(1) In relation to any notified person whose existing award or awards qualify for conversion into an employment and support allowance—
   (a) the person's entitlement (if any) to a transitional addition; and
   (b) the amount of any such transitional addition,
are to be determined in accordance with regulation 10(2) (transitional addition: incapacity benefit or severe disablement allowance) or 11(2) (transitional addition: income support).

9.551

(2) The amount of transitional addition to which a notified person is entitled is subject to reduction in accordance with regulations 18 to 20.

(3) The entitlement of a notified person to any transitional addition terminates in accordance with regulation 21 (termination of transitional addition).

MODIFICATION

In cases where universal credit has come into force (see the General Note, above), reg.9(1) is modified. For a list of the modifying provisions see the General Note (para.9.538 above). For the text of the modification, see the text of Sch.4 to SI 2013/983 in Pt IV of Vol.V.

9.552

Transitional addition: incapacity benefit or severe disablement allowance

10.—(1) This regulation applies to any notified person who is entitled to an existing award of incapacity benefit or severe disablement allowance (and for these purposes it is irrelevant whether the person is also entitled to any existing award of income support).

9.553

(2) In any case falling within paragraph (1)—
   (a) the notified person shall be entitled to a transitional addition if Amount A exceeds Amount B; and
   (b) the amount of transitional addition to which the notified person is entitled under this paragraph shall be equal to the amount of any such excess.

(3) Amount A is the amount of the weekly rate of the existing award applicable to the notified person.

(4) To calculate Amount B—

(a) take the amount prescribed under paragraph (2) of regulation 67 of the 2008 Regulations (prescribed amounts for purpose of calculating a contributory allowance) which is applicable to the notified person; and

(b) add the amount of the applicable component determined in accordance with regulation 12(5).

(5) In paragraph (3), the reference to the weekly rate of an existing award applicable to the notified person is to—

[¹ (a) in the case of incapacity benefit, the weekly rate payable—

(i) under section 30B(2), (6) or (7) (subject to any deduction made in accordance with section 46(3) of the Pension Schemes Act 1993) of the Contributions and Benefits Act (incapacity benefit: rate),

(ii) under section 40(5) or 41(4) of that Act (long-term incapacity benefit for widows and for widowers),

(iii) under section 80, 81 or 86A of that Act (incapacity benefit: beneficiary's dependent children; restrictions on increase – child not living with beneficiary etc; and increases for adult dependants),

(iv) by virtue of regulation 11(4) of the Social Security (Incapacity Benefit) (Transitional) Regulations 1995 (former sickness benefit), or

(v) by virtue of regulations 17(1) (transitional awards of long-term incapacity benefit) or 17A (awards of incapacity benefit in cases where periods of interruption of employment and periods of incapacity for work link) of those Regulations; or]

(b) in the case of severe disablement allowance, the weekly rate payable under [¹ sections 68(7), 69(1) and 90] of the Contributions and Benefits Act (as they have effect by virtue of article 4 of the Welfare Reform and Pensions Act 1999 (Commencement No.9 and Transitional and Savings Provisions) Order 2000).

[¹ (6) Subject to paragraph (7), in determining the weekly rate of incapacity benefit or severe disablement allowance for the purposes of paragraph (5) the following amounts shall be disregarded–

(a) any relevant deduction within the meaning of regulation 2(1) (interpretation); and

(b) any other deduction relating to the existing award which is made by virtue of the Contributions and Benefits Act, the Administration Act or any other Act which is amended by Schedule 3 to the 2007 Act, the Social Security (Incapacity for Work) Act 1994 or by virtue of regulations made under those Acts.

(7) Where any of the enactments referred to in paragraph (6)(b) provide for an additional amount of incapacity benefit or severe disablement allowance to be payable in prescribed circumstances (such as an increase for an adult dependant) but that additional amount is reduced or not payable in relation to P (such as where the dependant has earnings in excess of the standard amount of an increase), in determining the weekly rate of incapacity benefit or severe disablement allowance, only the reduced additional amount (if any) is to be taken into account.]

AMENDMENT

1. Employment and Support Allowance (Transitional Provisions, Housing Benefit and Council Tax Benefit) (Existing Awards) (No.2) (Amendment) Regulations 2010 (SI 2010/2430) reg.6 (November 1, 2010).

MODIFICATION

9.554

In cases where universal credit has come into force (see the General Note, above), reg.10 is modified. For a list of the modifying provisions see the General Note (para.9.538 above). For the text of the modification, see the text of Sch.4 to SI 2013/983 in Pt IV of Vol.V.

Transitional addition: income support

9.555

11.—(1) This regulation applies to any notified person who is entitled to an existing award of income support (and for these purposes it is irrelevant whether the person is also entitled to any existing award of incapacity benefit or severe disablement allowance).

(2) In any case falling within paragraph (1)—

(a) the notified person shall be entitled to a transitional addition if Amount C exceeds Amount D; and

(b) the amount of transitional addition to which the notified person is entitled under this paragraph shall be equal to the amount of any such excess.

(3) To calculate Amount C—

(a) take the notified person's weekly applicable amount under regulation 17 or 18 of, and Schedule 2 to, the Income Support (General) Regulations 1987 (applicable amounts);

(b) disregard any amount determined in accordance with (as the case may be) regulation 17(1)(e) or 18(1)(f) of, and Schedule 3 to, those Regulations (housing costs); and

(c) disregard any amount included in the person's applicable amount—

 (i) under regulation 17(1)(b), (c) or (d) of those Regulations in respect of a child or young person who is a member of the notified person's family, or

 (ii) under regulation 18(1)(b), (c), (d) or (e) of those Regulations in respect of a child or young person who is a member of the same household as the notified person,

as those provisions have effect by virtue of regulations 1 and 7 of the Social Security (Working Tax Credit and Child Tax Credit) (Consequential Amendment) Regulations 2003.

(4) To calculate Amount D—

(a) take the amount prescribed under regulation 67(1) or 68(1) of the 2008 Regulations (prescribed amounts for purpose of calculating an income-related allowance) which is applicable to the notified person;

(b) disregard any amount determined in accordance with (as the case may be) regulation 67(1)(c) or 68(1)(d) (housing costs) of the 2008 Regulations; and

(c) add the amount of the applicable component determined in accordance with regulation 12(5) of these Regulations.

MODIFICATION

9.556   In cases where universal credit has come into force (see the General Note, above), reg.11 is modified. For a list of the modifying provisions see the General Note (para.9.538 above). For the text of the modification, see the text of Sch.4 to SI 2013/983 in Pt IV of Vol.V.

Regulations 10 and 11: supplementary

9.557   **12.**—(1) This regulation has effect for the purposes of applying regulations 10 and 11 in relation to any notified person.

(2) Subject to paragraphs (3) and (4)—

(a) Amounts A and C are to be calculated in respect of the benefit week which ends immediately before the effective date of the notified person's conversion decision; and

(b) Amounts B and D are to be calculated in respect of the benefit week the first day of which is the effective date of the notified person's conversion decision.

(3) Where—

(a) by virtue of an order made under section 150 of the Administration Act (annual up-rating of benefits), there is an increase in—

    (i) the weekly rate which, in accordance with regulation 10(3) (transitional addition: incapacity benefit or severe disablement allowance), is to be used to calculate Amount A, or

    (ii) the applicable amount which, in accordance with regulation 11(3) (transitional addition: income support), is to be used to calculate Amount C; and

(b) that increase takes effect from any day in the benefit week referred to in paragraph (2)(b), the calculation of Amount A or C is to be made using the increased weekly rate or applicable amount (as the case may be).

(4) Where—

(a) there is a change of circumstances in relation to a notified person which, but for subparagraph (b), would have resulted in an increase or decrease of the weekly rate or applicable amount referred to in paragraph (3)(a)(i) or (ii); and

(b) that increase or decrease would have taken effect from any day in the benefit week referred to in paragraph (2)(b), the calculation of Amount A or C is to be made using the weekly rate or applicable amount (as the case may be) which would have been payable in respect of the existing award if it had not been subject to conversion under these Regulations.

(5) The "applicable component", in relation to the notified person, means—

(a) the work-related activity component, if it has been determined in accordance with the enactments applied by regulation 6 (application of certain enactments for purpose of making conversion decisions) that the notified person does not have and is not to be treated as having limited capability for work-related activity; or

(b) the support component, if it has been determined in accordance with those enactments that the notified person has or is to be treated as having limited capability for work-related activity.

MODIFICATION

In cases where universal credit has come into force (see the General Note, above), reg.12 is modified. For a list of the modifying provisions see the General Note (para.9.538 above). For the text of the modification, see the text of Sch.4 to SI 2013/983 in Pt IV of Vol.V.

9.558

The effective date of a conversion decision

13.—(1) For the purposes of determining the date on which a conversion decision takes effect in relation to any notified person—

9.559

   (a) take the date on which the person is notified of the conversion decision; and

   (b) unless paragraph (2) applies, determine the first complete fortnightly period in respect of which the person's existing benefit is payable after that date, and the effective date of the person's conversion decision is the first day of the benefit week immediately following the end of the fortnightly period referred to in sub-paragraph (b).

(2) Where existing benefit is payable to the notified person in respect of a period other than a fortnight—

   (a) determine the second complete benefit week in respect of which the person's existing benefit is payable after the date on which the person is notified of the conversion decision; and

   (b) the effective date of the person's conversion decision is the first day of the benefit week immediately following the end of that second complete benefit week.

(3) "Existing benefit", in relation to a notified person, means the benefit in respect of the person's existing award or awards.

MODIFICATION

In cases where universal credit has come into force (see the General Note, above), reg.13(3) is modified. For a list of the modifying provisions see the General Note (para.9.538 above). For the text of the modification, see the text of Sch.4 to SI 2013/983 in Pt IV of Vol.V.

9.560

Conversion decision that existing award qualifies for conversion

14.—(1) [¹ Subject to paragraph (2A), paragraphs (2) to (6)] apply in any case where the conversion decision is a decision that a notified person's ("P") existing award or awards qualify for conversion into an employment and support allowance.

9.561

(2) On the effective date of the conversion decision—

   (a) P's existing award; or

   (b) both of P's existing awards (as the case may be),

are by virtue of this paragraph converted into, and shall have effect on and after that date as, a single award of an employment and support allowance of such amount as is specified in the conversion decision.

   [¹ (2A) Where P—

   (a) has an existing award of income support;

   (b) would, on the effective date of P's conversion decision, remain entitled to income support (by virtue of another provision of the Income Support (General) Regulations 1987) were P not a person to whom regulation 6(4)(a) or 13(2)(b) or (bb) of, or paragraph 7(a) or (b), 10, 12 or 13 of Schedule 1B(c) to, those Regulations (persons incapable of work or disabled) applied; and

(c) notifies the Secretary of State before the effective date of P's conversion decision that P wishes to remain entitled to income support on that date, paragraph (2B) applies instead of paragraphs (2) and (4).

(2B) Where paragraph (2A) applies, any entitlement of P to one or both of—

(a) an existing award of incapacity benefit or severe disablement allowance; or

(b) a disability premium by virtue of paragraph 12(1)(b) of Schedule 2 to the Income Support (General) Regulations 1987 (additional condition for the higher pensioner and disability premiums),

shall terminate immediately before the effective date of P's conversion decision.]

[¹ (3) In a case to which regulation 7(2) applies (cases where a person is already entitled to an award of an employment and support allowance), any entitlement of P to an award of an employment and support allowance by virtue of the 2007 Act shall terminate immediately before the effective date of P's conversion decision.

(4) Where, immediately before the effective date of the conversion decision, any relevant deduction was made from the existing award or awards, or from an award of an employment and support allowance which terminates in accordance with paragraph (3), an equivalent deduction shall be made from the award of an employment and support allowance to which P is entitled by virtue of these Regulations.

(5) Where, immediately before the effective date of the conversion decision, P is entitled to be credited with any earnings under regulation 8B(2)(a) of the Social Security (Credits) Regulations 1975 (credits for incapacity for work), P shall not be entitled to be so credited under that regulation on or after that date.

(6) Where—

(a) paragraph (2) applies,

(b) P is a member of a joint-claim couple, and

(c) immediately before the effective date of that conversion decision that couple was entitled to a disability premium by virtue of paragraph 20H(1)(b) or (d) of Schedule 1 to the Jobseeker's Allowance Regulations 1996 (additional conditions for higher pensioner and disability premium: severe disablement allowance or incapacity benefit), paragraph 20H(1)(ee) of that Schedule (limited capability for work) shall be treated as satisfied in relation to that couple on the effective date of that conversion decision.

(7) In this regulation—

(a) paragraphs (2) to (6) are subject to regulation 17 (changes of circumstances before the effective date); and

(b) "joint-claim couple" has the same meaning as in section 1(4) of the Jobseekers Act 1995.]

9.562   AMENDMENT

1. Employment and Support Allowance (Transitional Provisions, Housing Benefit and Council Tax Benefit) (Existing Awards) (No.2) (Amendment) Regulations 2010 (SI 2010/2430) reg.7 (November 1, 2010).

MODIFICATION

In cases where universal credit has come into force (see the General Note, above), reg.14 is modified. For a list of the modifying provisions see the General Note (para.9.538 above). For the text of the modification, see the text of Sch.4 to SI 2013/983 in Pt IV of Vol.V.

Conversion decision that existing award does not qualify for conversion

15.—(1) [¹ Subject to paragraphs (2A) and (4), paragraphs (2), (3) and (6) apply] in any case where the conversion decision is a decision that a notified person's ("P") existing award or awards do not qualify for conversion into an employment and support allowance.

9.563

(2) P's entitlement to one or both of—

(a) an existing award of incapacity benefit or severe disablement allowance; or

(b) an existing award of income support (being an award made to a person incapable of work or disabled),

shall terminate by virtue of this paragraph immediately before the effective date of P's conversion decision.

[¹ (2A) Where P–

(a) has an existing award of income support, and

(b) would, on the effective date of P's conversion decision, remain entitled to income support (by virtue of another provision of the Income Support (General) Regulations 1987) were P not a person to whom regulations 6(4)(a) or 13(2)(b) or (bb) of, or paragraph 7(a) or (b), 10, 12 or 13 of Schedule 1B to, those Regulations (persons incapable of work or disabled) applied, P's existing award of income support shall only terminate under paragraph (2)(b) if P notifies the Secretary of State before the effective date of P's conversion decision that P does not wish to remain entitled to income support on that date.

(2B) Where paragraph (2A) applies, and P's existing award of income support does not terminate under paragraph (2)(b), any entitlement of P to a disability premium by virtue of paragraph 12(1)(b) of Schedule 2 to the Income Support (General) Regulations 1987 (additional condition for the higher pensioner and disability premiums) shall terminate immediately before the effective date of P's conversion decision.]

(3) Where, immediately before [¹ the effective date of P's conversion decision], P is entitled to be credited with any earnings under regulation 8B(2)(a) of the Social Security (Credits) Regulations 1975 (credits for incapacity for work), P shall not be entitled to be so credited under that regulation on or after that date.

(4) Paragraph (5) applies where—

(a) a conversion decision within the meaning of regulation 5(2)(b) ("the earlier conversion decision") is made by virtue of either of the following provisions of the 2008 Regulations (as they apply by virtue of regulation 6)–

(i) regulation 22(1) (failure to provide information or evidence requested in relation to limited capability for work), or

(ii) regulation 23(2) (failure to attend for a medical examination to determine whether the claimant has limited capability for work); and

(b) after P is notified of the earlier conversion decision, the Secretary of State is satisfied (or where the conversion decision is appealed to the

First-tier Tribunal, that tribunal determines) that P had good cause for failing to–

    (i) provide the information requested, or

    (ii) attend for or submit to the medical examination for which P was called.

(5) Where this paragraph applies—

(a) the earlier conversion decision is treated as never having been made;

(b) any entitlement of P–

    (i) to an existing award which was terminated by virtue of paragraph (2), or

    (ii) to be credited with earnings which was terminated by virtue of paragraph (3),

    shall be reinstated with effect from the effective date of the earlier conversion decision;

(c) the Secretary of State must make a conversion decision ("the new conversion decision") in accordance with regulation 5 (deciding whether an existing award qualifies for conversion) in relation to the existing award or awards to which P is entitled;

(d) the notice issued under regulation 4 (notice commencing the conversion phase) has effect in relation to that existing award or those existing awards; and

(e) with the exception of regulation 4 (notice commencing the conversion phase), the remaining provisions of this Part, including this regulation, apply to the new conversion decision.

[¹ (6) Where—

(a) paragraph (2) applies; and

(b) P is a member of a joint-claim couple,

any entitlement of that couple to a disability premium by virtue of paragraph 20H(1)(b) or (d) of Schedule 1 to the Jobseeker's Allowance Regulations 1996 (additional conditions for higher pensioner and disability premium: severe disablement allowance or incapacity benefit) shall terminate immediately before the effective date of P's conversion decision.

(7) In this regulation—

(a) paragraphs (2), (2A), (3) and (6) are subject to regulation 17 (changes of circumstances before the effective date); and

(b) "joint-claim couple" has the same meaning as in section 1(4) of the Jobseekers Act 1995.]

AMENDMENT

1. Employment and Support Allowance (Transitional Provisions, Housing Benefit and Council Tax Benefit) (Existing Awards) (No.2) (Amendment) Regulations 2010 (SI 2010/2430) reg.8 (November 1, 2010).

MODIFICATION

9.564   In cases where universal credit has come into force (see the General Note, above), reg.15 is modified. For a list of the modifying provisions see the General Note (para.9.538 above). For the text of the modification, see the text of Sch.4 to SI 2013/983 in Pt IV of Vol.V.

PART 3

Application of other enactments applying to employment and support allowances

16.—(1) The enactments listed in paragraph (2) apply, subject to the modifications specified in Schedule 2, for the purposes of—

(a) providing for the revision or supersession of any person's conversion decision at any time on or after that decision's effective date; and

(b) enabling any other matter to be determined in connection with any person's entitlement or continuing entitlement to an award of an employment and support allowance by virtue of these Regulations.

[¹ (1A) Where—

(a) a person makes a claim for an employment and support allowance subsequent to the termination of that person's entitlement to an employment and support allowance by virtue of these Regulations; and

(b) the period of limited capability for work in relation to that claim would link, by virtue of regulation 145(1) of the 2008 Regulations, to a period of limited capability for work in respect of which an award was made by virtue of these Regulations,

that person's entitlement to an award of an employment and support allowance shall be determined in accordance with these Regulations.]

(2) The listed enactments are—

(a) Part 1 of the 2007 Act;

(b) Chapter 2 of Part 1 of the Social Security Act 1998 (social security decisions and appeals);

(c) any other Act which is amended by Schedule 3 to the 2007 Act;

(d) the Social Security (Recovery of Benefits) Act 1997; and

(e) the following regulations—

    (i) this Part of these Regulations,

    (ii) the 2008 Regulations, and

    (iii) the Regulations listed in Schedule 3 to these Regulations (being regulations consequentially amended by regulations made under Part 1 of the 2007 Act).

(3) In the application of those enactments, the conversion decision is to be treated as if it were a decision as to a person's entitlement to an employment and support allowance which had been made on a claim.

9.565

AMENDMENT

1. Social Security (Miscellaneous Amendments) Regulations 2012 (SI 2012/757) reg.21 (May 1, 2012).

MODIFICATION

In cases where universal credit has come into force (see the General Note, above), reg.16 is modified. For a list of the modifying provisions see the General Note (para.9.538 above). For the text of the modification, see the text of Sch.4 to SI 2013/983 in Pt IV of Vol.V.

9.566

Changes of circumstances before the effective date

9.567   **17.** Where, on or after the effective date of any person's conversion decision, the Secretary of State is notified of any change of circumstances or
other relevant event which occurred before that date [¹ and which would
have been relevant to the existing award or awards], the Secretary of State—
[¹ (a) must treat any award—

       (i) converted by virtue of regulation 14(2) (conversion decision
          that existing award qualifies for conversion), or

     (ii) terminated by virtue of regulation 14(2B)(a) (termination of an
          existing award of incapacity benefit or severe disablement allow-
          ance where entitlement to award of income support continues),
          regulation 14(3) (termination of award of an employment and
          support allowance where that entitlement already exists) or
          regulation 15(2) (termination of existing awards which do not
          qualify for conversion),

    as if that award had not been converted or terminated;

 (b) must treat any entitlement to be credited with earnings terminated by
     virtue of regulation 14(5) or 15(3) as if it had not been terminated;

 (c) must treat any entitlement to a disability premium terminated by
     virtue of regulations 14(2B)(b), 15(2B) or 15(6) as if it had not been
     terminated;]

[¹ (d)] must take account of the change of circumstances or other relevant
     event for the purposes of determining whether to revise or supersede
     a decision ("the earlier decision") relating to the award or awards in
     respect of which the conversion decision was made;

[¹ (e)] in an appropriate case, must revise or supersede the earlier decision;

[¹ (f)] if any earlier decision is revised or superseded, must determine
     whether to revise [² or supersede] the conversion decision made in
     relation to P; and

[¹ (g)] in an appropriate case, must revise [² or supersede] that conversion
     decision.

AMENDMENTS

    1. Employment and Support Allowance (Transitional Provisions, Housing Benefit
and Council Tax Benefit) (Existing Awards) (No.2) (Amendment) Regulations
2010 (SI 2010/2430) reg.9 (November 1, 2010).
    2. Social Security (Miscellaneous Amendments) (No.3) Regulations 2011 (SI
2011/2425) reg.27(3) (October 30, 2011).

MODIFICATION

9.568   In cases where universal credit has come into force (see the General Note, above),
reg.17 is modified. For a list of the modifying provisions see the General Note
(para.9.538 above). For the text of the modification, see the text of Sch.4 to SI
2013/983 in Pt IV of Vol.V.

Reducing the transitional addition: general rule

9.569   **18.**—(1) The amount of any transitional addition to which a person is
entitled by virtue of these Regulations shall be reduced (but not below nil)
by a sum equal to the aggregate amount of all relevant increases which
occur on or after the effective date in the amount payable to the person by
way of an employment and support allowance.

(2) For the purposes of paragraph (1), a relevant increase is—

(a) in relation to a person entitled to a contributory allowance, an increase in any amount applicable to the person under regulation 67(2)(a) or (3) of the 2008 Regulations; and

(b) in relation to a person entitled to an income-related allowance, an increase in any amount applicable to the person under regulation 67(1)(a) or (b) or (3) or 68(1)(a), (b) or (c) of the 2008 Regulations, which is not excluded by paragraph (3).

(3) In relation to any person, the excluded increases are—

(a) any increase applicable to the benefit week the first day of which is the effective date of the person's conversion decision; and

(b) any increase resulting from the reversal (on appeal or otherwise) of any decision made by the Secretary of State that a person who was previously entitled to the support component has become entitled to the work-related activity component.

MODIFICATION

In cases where universal credit has come into force (see the General Note, above), reg.18 is modified. For a list of the modifying provisions see the General Note (para.9.538 above). For the text of the modification, see the text of Sch.4 to SI 2013/983 in Pt IV of Vol.V.   9.570

Reducing the transitional addition: increases for dependent children

19.—(1) Paragraphs (2) and (3) apply to any person ("T") who—   9.571

[¹ (a) on the day before the effective date of T's conversion decision, was entitled in connection with an existing award of incapacity benefit or severe disablement allowance to an increase under–

(i) in the case of incapacity benefit, section 80 of the Contributions and Benefits Act (beneficiary's dependent children), or

(ii) in the case of severe disablement allowance, section 90 of that Act (beneficiaries under sections 68 and 70), as those sections have effect by virtue of article 3 of the Tax Credits (Commencement No. 3 and Transitional Provisions and Savings) Order 2003; and]

(b) on and after the effective date, is entitled by virtue of these Regulations to an employment and support allowance which includes an amount by way of a transitional addition.

(2) The amount of the transitional addition shall be reduced in accordance with paragraph (3) on the termination, on or after the effective date, of T's entitlement to child benefit in respect of the child or qualifying young person—

(a) for whom; or

(b) for whose care by an adult dependant,

T was entitled to the increase referred to in paragraph (1)(a).

[¹ (3) The amount of the transitional addition shall be reduced (but not below nil) by a sum equal to the amount of the increase referred to in paragraph (1)(a) payable to T on the day before the effective date, in respect of the child or qualifying young person in relation to whom child benefit terminated.]

AMENDMENT

1. Employment and Support Allowance (Transitional Provisions, Housing Benefit and Council Tax Benefit) (Existing Awards) (No.2) (Amendment) Regulations 2010 (SI 2010/2430) reg.10 (November 1, 2010).

Reducing the transitional addition: increases for adult dependants

9.572   **20.**—(1) Paragraphs (2) and (3) apply to any person ("T") who—

(a) on the day before the effective date of T's conversion decision, was entitled in connection with an existing award of incapacity benefit or severe disablement allowance to an increase under—

(i) section 86A of the Contributions and Benefits Act (incapacity benefit: increases for adult dependants), or

(ii) section 90 of the Contributions and Benefits Act (adult dependants of beneficiaries in receipt of severe disablement allowance); and

(b) on and after the effective date, is entitled by virtue of these Regulations to an employment and support allowance which includes an amount by way of a transitional addition.

(2) The amount of the transitional addition shall be reduced in accordance with paragraph (3) on the occurrence, on or after the effective date, of any of the following events—

(a) the death of the adult dependant in respect of whom T was entitled to the increase referred to in paragraph (1)(a);

(b) the permanent separation of T and that adult dependant;

(c) the termination of the entitlement of either T or that adult dependant to child benefit; or

(d) the award to that adult dependant of a personal benefit (within the meaning of the Social Security (Overlapping Benefits) Regulations 1979) which is equal to or more than the amount which, on the day before the effective date, was the amount of the increase referred to in paragraph (1)(a) to which T was entitled.

[¹ (3) The amount of the transitional addition shall be reduced (but not below nil) by a sum equal to the amount which, on the day before the effective date, was the amount of the increase referred to in paragraph (1)(a) payable to T.]

AMENDMENT

1. Employment and Support Allowance (Transitional Provisions, Housing Benefit and Council Tax Benefit) (Existing Awards) (No. 2) (Amendment) Regulations 2010 (SI 2010/2430) reg.11 (November 1, 2010).

Termination of transitional addition

9.573   **21.**—(1) Any entitlement to a transitional addition which a person ("T") may have by virtue of these Regulations terminates on whichever is the earlier of—

(a) the reduction in accordance with regulations 18 to 20 (reducing the transitional addition: general rule and increases for dependent children and adult dependants) of the amount of the transitional addition to nil;

(b) subject to [¹ paragraphs (2), (3) [² , (3A)] and (4)], the termination

1412

in accordance with the enactments applied by regulation 16 of T's entitlement to [¹ an employment and support allowance (entitlement to which arises from sections 1(2)(a) or 1(2)(b) of the 2007 Act), or to a contributory allowance or to an income-related allowance]; and

(c) 5th April 2020.

(2) Nothing in paragraph (1)(b) prevents reinstatement of a person's entitlement to a transitional addition following the reversal on appeal of any determination which results in [¹ a termination of the person's entitlement to which that provision refers].

[¹ (3) Any termination by virtue of paragraph (1)(b) of T's entitlement to a transitional addition under regulation 10(2)(a) (transitional addition: incapacity benefit or severe disablement allowance) shall instead have effect as a suspension of that entitlement in Case 1.

[² (3A) Any termination of T's entitlement to a transitional addition under regulation 10(2)(a) (transitional addition: incapacity benefit or severe disablement allowance) shall instead have effect as a suspension of that entitlement in Case 1A.]

(4) Any termination by virtue of paragraph (1)(b) of T's entitlement to a transitional addition under regulation 11(2)(a) (transitional addition: income support) shall instead have effect as a suspension of that entitlement in Case 1 or Case 2.

(5) Case 1 is where—

(a) on a subsequent claim made by T for an employment and support allowance, a period of limited capability for work is treated under regulation 145(1) [³ . . .] of the 2008 Regulations (linking rules) as a continuation of an earlier period of limited capability for work;

(b) T's entitlement to an allowance which is referred to in paragraph (1)(b) ("T's old entitlement") was in respect of that earlier period; and

[³ (c) in respect of that earlier period, it was terminated–

(i) other than by virtue of a determination that T did not have, or was treated as not having, limited capability for work, or

(ii) by virtue of a determination that the claimant did not have, or was treated as not having, limited capability for work, and, in respect of that subsequent claim, it is determined that T has, or is treated as having, limited capability for work, other than under regulation 30 of the 2008 Regulations.]

[² (5A) Case 1A is where—

(a) T was previously entitled to a contributory allowance;

(b) entitlement to that previous allowance terminated by virtue of section 1A of the 2007 Act (duration of contributory allowance);

(c) on a subsequent claim made by T for an employment and support allowance, a period of limited capability for work is treated under regulation 145(1) of the 2008 Regulations (linking rules) as a continuation of an earlier period of limited capability for work; and

(d) it is determined in relation to the subsequent claim that T has, or is treated as having, limited capability for work-related activity.]

(6) Case 2 is where—

(a) the reason for terminating T's entitlement to an employment and support allowance arising from section 1(2)(b) of the 2007 Act (financial position), or to an income-related allowance, as the case may be, was that the condition set out in paragraph 6(1)(f) of Schedule 1 to the 2007 Act (no entitlement to income-related allowance where other member of a couple engages in remunerative work) had ceased to be satisfied in T's case;

(b) the condition referred to in sub-paragraph (a) is subsequently satisfied;

(c) T again becomes entitled to an allowance which is referred to in sub-paragraph (a); and

(d) that entitlement commences before the end of the 12 week period which begins with the date of termination of T's old entitlement.

(7) In Cases 1 [² , 1A] and 2, the amount of the transitional addition or additions, as the case may be, to which T becomes entitled from the commencement of T's subsequent entitlement to an allowance which is referred to in paragraph (1)(b) is to be determined by reference to the amount of the transitional addition or additions, as the case may be, to which T was entitled on the termination of T's old entitlement, subject to any subsequent adjustment of that amount that would have been made under this Part.]

AMENDMENT

1. Employment and Support Allowance (Transitional Provisions, Housing Benefit and Council Tax Benefit) (Existing Awards) (No.2) (Amendment) Regulations 2010 (SI 2010/2430) reg.12 (November 1, 2010).

2. Employment and Support Allowance (Duration of Contributory Allowance) (Consequential Amendments) Regulations 2012 (SI 2012/913) reg.10(3) (May 1, 2012).

3. Employment and Support Allowance (Amendment of Linking Rules) Regulations 2012 (SI 2012/919) reg.6 (May 1, 2012).

PART 4

MISCELLANEOUS

Disapplication of certain enactments following conversion decision

9.574 **22.** Where a conversion decision has been made in relation to any person, the following enactments shall not apply to that person with effect from the conversion decision's effective date—

(a) sections 30A, [¹ 30C,] 40 or 41 of the Contributions and Benefits Act (incapacity benefit);

(b) section 68 of the Contributions and Benefits Act (as it has effect by virtue of article 4 of the Welfare Reform and Pensions Act 1999 (Commencement No. 9, and Transitional and Savings Provisions) Order 2000);

(c) regulation 13(2)(b) or (bb) of, or paragraph 7(a) or (b), 10, 12 or 13 of Schedule 1B to, the Income Support (General) Regulations 1987(**c**) (prescribed category of persons for the purposes of entitlement on grounds of incapacity or disability);

(d) the Income Support Transitional Regulations 1987; and

(e) the Incapacity Benefit Transitional Regulations 1995.

AMENDMENT

1. Employment and Support Allowance (Transitional Provisions, Housing Benefit and Council Tax Benefit) (Existing Awards) (No. 2) (Amendment) Regulations 2010 (SI 2010/2430) reg.13 (November 1, 2010).

MODIFICATION

In cases where universal credit has come into force (see the General Note, above), reg.22 is modified. For a list of the modifying provisions see the General Note (para.9.538 above). For the text of the modification, see the text of Sch.4 to SI 2013/983 in Pt IV of Vol.V.

Treatment of claims until coming into force of regulation 24

23. [Amends sub-paragraphs (a), (b) and (c) of regulation 2(2) of the Employment and Support Allowance (Transitional Provisions) Regulations 2008 (claim for existing award).]

9.575

[¹ Termination of entitlement to the disability premium for persons incapable of work: income support

23A.—(1)-(3) [Amend para.12 of Sch.2 to the Income Support (General) Regulations 1987 (additional condition for the higher pensioner and disability premiums)]

9.576

(4) Where a person—

(a) is or becomes entitled to an award of income support, and

(b) is a person to whom paragraph 7(a) or (b) of Schedule 1B to the Income Support (General) Regulations 1987 (persons incapable of work) applies, paragraphs 12(1)(b), 12(1A) and 12(5) of Schedule 2 to the Income Support (General) Regulations 1987 continue to apply to that person as if paragraphs (2) and (3) of this regulation had no effect.]

AMENDMENT

1. Employment and Support Allowance (Transitional Provisions, Housing Benefit and Council Tax Benefit) (Existing Awards) (No. 2) (Amendment) Regulations 2010 (SI 2010/2430) reg.14 (November 1, 2010).

Revocation of transitional claims provisions

24. [Amends reg.2(2) of the Employment and Support Allowance (Transitional Provisions) Regulations 2008.]

9.577

Amendment of the 2008 Regulations

25.—(1) [Revokes Regulation 31 of the 2008 Regulations (claimant who claims jobseeker's allowance to be treated as not having limited capability for work)]

9.578

(2) [Amends regulation 144(2)(a) of the 2008 Regulations (which sets out exceptions from the requirement to serve a period of waiting days at the beginning of a period of limited capability for work)].

Consequential amendments

26. Schedule 4 (which makes amendments consequential on these Regulations) has effect.

9.579

Amendments to legislation relating to Housing Benefit and Council Tax Benefit

27. Schedule 5 (which makes amendments to legislation relating to Housing Benefit and Council Tax Benefit) has effect.

9.580

SCHEDULES

SCHEDULE 1

Regulation 6(1)

9.581

MODIFICATION OF ENACTMENTS: MAKING CONVERSION DECISIONS

PART 1

MODIFICATION OF PART 1 OF THE 2007 ACT

[¹ **1**]. Any reference to a claimant is to be read as if it were a reference to a notified person.

[² **2**. Section 1 is to be read as if—

(a) for subsection (2), there were substituted—

"(2) Subject to the provisions of this Part, a notified person is entitled to an employment and support allowance if the person satisfies the basic conditions and—

(a) is entitled to an existing award of incapacity benefit or severe disablement allowance;

(b) is entitled to an existing award of income support and satisfies the conditions set out in Part 2 of Schedule 1, unless subsection (2)(c) applies; or

(c) is entitled to an existing award of income support by virtue of–

(i) regulation 13(2)(b) or (bb) of the Income Support (General) Regulations 1987 (circumstances in which persons in relevant education may be entitled to income support), or

(ii) paragraph 10 (disabled students) or 12 (deaf students) of Schedule 1B to those Regulations,

and satisfies the conditions set out in Part 2 of Schedule 1, with the exception of the condition in paragraph 6(1)(g).";and

(b) subsection (3)(e) were omitted.]

[¹ **3**]. Section 2 is to be read as if, in subsections (2)(a) and (3)(a), references to the assessment phase were to the conversion phase.

[¹ **4**]. Section 4 is to be read as if, in subsections (4)(a) and (5)(a), references to the assessment phase were to the conversion phase.

[¹ **5**]. Section 5 does not apply.

[¹ **6**]. Schedule 1 to the 2007 Act is to be read as if—

(a) paragraphs 1 to 5 were omitted; and

(b) in paragraph 6, after sub-paragraph (1), there were inserted—

"(1A) Paragraphs (1B) and (1C) apply in relation to any person ("P") whose existing award of income support is subject to conversion under the Employment and Support Allowance (Transitional Provisions, Housing Benefit and Council Tax Benefit) (Existing Awards) (No. 2) Regulations 2010 ("the 2010 Regulations").

(1B) In determining for the purposes of paragraph (1)(a) whether P's income exceeds the applicable amount, any amount to which P may become entitled by way of a transitional addition under Part 2 of the 2010 Regulations shall be disregarded.

(1C) But where—

(a) P's existing award would qualify for conversion under Part 2 of the 2010 Regulations but for the fact that the condition set out in paragraph (1)(a) is not satisfied in P's case; and

(b) P would otherwise be entitled to an amount of transitional addition under Part 2 of the 2010 Regulations as a result of carrying out Step 2, the condition set out in paragraph (1)(a) shall be treated as having been satisfied and the amount of an employment and support allowance which applies to P as a result of Step 1 shall be nil.".

PART 2

MODIFICATION OF THE 2008 REGULATIONS

9.582

[¹ **7**]. Any reference to a claimant is to be read as if it were a reference to the notified person.

[¹ **8**]. Part 2 (which makes provision about the assessment phase) does not apply.

[¹ **9**]. Part 3 (which makes provision about contribution conditions which do not apply by virtue of modifications contained in these Regulations) does not apply.

[¹ **10**]. Regulation 30 (which provides for payment of the allowance pending determination of limited capability for work) does not apply.

[² **10A.** In the case of a person who is entitled to an existing award of income support and who is a person to whom paragraph (1) of regulation 6 of the Social Security (Habitual Residence) Amendment Regulations 2004 applies, regulation 70 (special cases: supplemental – persons from abroad) is to be read as if–

(a) the word "or" at the end of paragraph (4)(k) were omitted; and

(b) at the end of paragraph (4)(jj) the word "or" and the following sub-paragraph were added–

"(l) a person who is entitled to an existing award of income support where that person is a person to whom paragraph (1) of regulation 6 of the Social Security (Habitual Residence) Amendment Regulations 2004 applies".]

[¹ **11**]. Regulation 75 (payments treated as not being payments to which section 3 of the 2007 Act applies) is to be read as if—

(a) the existing provisions were renumbered as paragraph (1);

(b) at the end of that paragraph there were added—

"(g) any pension payment or PPF periodic payment which is made to a notified person and which falls within paragraph (2)."; and

(c) after that paragraph there were added—

"(2) This paragraph applies to any pension payment or PPF periodic payment made to the notified person where, immediately before the effective date of the person's conversion decision, section 30DD(1) of the Contributions and Benefits Act (incapacity benefit: reduction for pension payments and PPF periodic payments)—

(a) did not apply to the notified person by virtue of regulation 26 of the Social Security (Incapacity Benefit) Regulations 1994 (persons whose benefit is not to be reduced under section 30DD(1)); or

(b) was not treated as applying to the notified person by virtue of—

(i)   regulation 19(1)(c) or (2)(c) of those Regulations (persons formerly entitled to severe disablement allowance); or

(ii) article 3 of the Welfare Reform and Pensions Act 1999 (Commencement No.9, and Transitional and Savings Provisions) Order 2000 (transitional provision in relation to incapacity benefit).".

[¹ **12**]. Regulation 144 (requirement to serve a period of waiting days at the beginning of a period of limited capability for work) does not apply.

PART 3

MODIFICATION OF OTHER SECONDARY LEGISLATION

Social Security (Claims and Payments) Regulations 1987

[¹ **13**]. Regulation 32 of the Social Security (Claims and Payments) Regulations 1987 (information to be given and changes to be notified) is to be read as if it were modified so as to enable the Secretary of State to require from any person entitled to an existing award—   **9.583**

(a) under paragraph (1), information or evidence for determining whether [² . . .] an existing award should be converted into an award of an employment and support allowance; and

(b) under paragraph (1A), information or evidence in connection with payment of benefit in the event that an existing award is converted into an award of an employment and support allowance.

AMENDMENT

1. Employment and Support Allowance (Transitional Provisions, Housing Benefit and Council Tax Benefit) (Existing Awards) (No. 2) (Amendment) Regulations 2010 (SI 2010/2430) reg.15 (November 1, 2010).

2. Employment and Support Allowance (Transitional Provisions, Housing Benefit and Council Tax Benefit) (Existing Awards) (No. 2) (Amendment) Regulations 2010 (SI 2010/2430) reg.16 (November 1, 2010).

MODIFICATION

In cases where universal credit has come into force (see the General Note, above), Sch.1 is modified. For a list of the modifying provisions see the General Note (para.9.538 above). For the text of the modification, see the text of Sch.4 to SI 2013/983 in Pt IV of Vol. V.   **9.584**

SCHEDULE 2 **Regulation 16(1)**

MODIFICATION OF ENACTMENTS: AFTER THE CONVERSION PHASE

PART 1

9.585 MODIFICATION OF PART 1 OF THE 2007 ACT

[¹ 1]. Any reference to a claimant is to be read as if it were a reference to a person in relation to whom a conversion decision has been made under these Regulations.

[¹ 2]. Section 1 (employment and support allowance) is to be read as if—

[² (a) for subsection (2), there were substituted—

"(2) Subject to the provisions of this Part, a person is entitled to an employment and support allowance if the person satisfies the basic conditions and—

(a) in accordance with Part 2 of the Employment and Support Allowance (Transitional Provisions, Housing Benefit and Council Tax Benefit) (Existing Awards) (No. 2) Regulations 2010, the effect of the conversion decision that was made in relation to the person was to convert the person's existing award or awards into a single award of an employment and support allowance;

(b) that conversion decision has come into effect; and

(c) where–

　(i) the effect of that conversion decision is that the person is entitled to an income-related allowance, or

　(ii) the effect of that conversion decision is that the person is entitled to a contributory allowance and the person subsequently becomes entitled to an income-related allowance,

the person also satisfies the conditions set out in Part 2 of Schedule 1 (conditions relating to financial position), except for the condition in paragraph 6(1)(g) in the case of a person who, before that conversion decision was made, had been entitled to an existing award of income support by virtue of regulation 13(2)(b) or (bb) of the Income Support (General) Regulations 1987 (circumstances in which persons in relevant education may be entitled to income support), or paragraph 10 (disabled students) or 12 (deaf students) of Schedule 1B to those Regulations.";
and]

(b) for subsection (7), there were substituted—

"(7) In this Part—

"contributory allowance" means an employment and support allowance to which a person is entitled by virtue of the Employment and Support Allowance (Transitional Provisions, Housing Benefit and Council Tax Benefit) (Existing Awards) (No. 2) Regulations 2010 which was based on an award of incapacity benefit or severe disablement allowance to which the person was entitled; and

"income-related allowance" means an employment and support allowance to which a person is entitled by virtue of the Employment and Support Allowance (Transitional Provisions, Housing Benefit and Council Tax Benefit) (Existing Awards) (No. 2) Regulations 2010 which was based on an award of income support to which the person was entitled.".

[⁴ 2A.—(1) In relation to awards of an employment and support allowance to persons previously entitled to existing awards, the application of section 1A (duration of contributory allowance) is modified in accordance with sub-paragraph (2).

(2) Section 1A is to be read as if there were substituted—

"1A.—(1) The period for which a person is entitled to a contributory allowance shall not exceed, in the aggregate, the relevant maximum number of days in any period for which his entitlement is established by virtue of the Employment and Support Allowance (Transitional Provisions, Housing Benefit and Council Tax Benefit) (Existing Awards) (No. 2) Regulations 2010.

(2) In subsection (1) the "relevant maximum number of days" is—

(a) 365 days, or

(b) if the Secretary of State by order specifies a greater number of days, that number of days.

(3) The fact that a person's entitlement to a contributory allowance has ceased as a result of subsection (1) does not prevent his being entitled to a further allowance if he satisfies the first and second conditions set out in Part 1 of Schedule 1.

(4) In calculating for the purposes of subsection (1) the length of the period for which a person is entitled to a contributory allowance, the following are not to be counted—
(a) days in which the person is a member of the support group, and
(b) days not falling within paragraph (a) in respect of which the person is entitled to the support component referred to in section 2(1)(b).
(5) In calculating for the purposes of subsection (1) the length of the period for which a person is entitled to a contributory allowance, days occurring before the coming into force of this section are to be counted (as well as those occurring afterwards).".]

[¹ 3]. Section 2 (amount of contributory allowance) is to be read as if—
(a) in subsection (1)(a), after the words "such amount" there were inserted ", or the aggregate of such amounts,"; and
(b) except for the purposes of applying regulation 147A of the 2008 Regulations (claimants appealing a decision), in subsections (2)(a) and (3)(a), references to the assessment phase were to the conversion phase.

[¹ 4]. Section 4 (amount of income-related allowance), except for the purposes of applying regulation 147A of the 2008 Regulations as modified by paragraph 15 of this Schedule, is to be read as if, in subsections (4)(a) and (5)(a), references to the assessment phase were to the conversion phase.

[² 4A. Schedule 1 to the 2007 Act (employment and support allowance: additional conditions) is to be read as if, in paragraph 6, after sub-paragraph (1), there were inserted—

"(1A) Paragraphs (1B) and (1C) apply where any person ("P") is entitled by virtue of the Employment and Support Allowance (Transitional Provisions, Housing Benefit and Council Tax Benefit) (Existing Awards) (No. 2) Regulations 2010 ("the 2010 Regulations") to an employment and support allowance which is attributable to an income-related allowance.
(1B) In determining for the purposes of paragraph 6(1)(a) whether P's income exceeds the applicable amount, the amount of any transitional addition to which P is entitled under the 2010 Regulations shall be disregarded.
(1C) Where—

(a) P ceases to satisfy the condition set out in sub-paragraph (1)(a); but
(b) otherwise remains entitled to an amount by way of a transitional addition under the 2010 Regulations,

the condition set out in sub-paragraph (1)(a) shall be treated as satisfied in P's case and the amount of income-related allowance to which P is entitled shall be the amount of the transitional addition."]

PART 2

MODIFICATION OF OTHER PRIMARY LEGISLATION

Social Security Act 1998

[¹ 5]. Schedule 3 to the Social Security Act 1998 (decisions against which an appeal lies) is   **9.586**
to be read as if, after paragraph 8D, there were inserted—

"Conversion of certain existing awards into awards of an employment and support allowance
8E. A conversion decision within the meaning of the Employment and Support Allowance (Transitional Provisions, Housing Benefit and Council Tax Benefit) (Existing Awards) (No. 2) Regulations 2010."

Social Security Contributions and Benefits Act 1992

[¹ 6]. Section 44B of the Social Security Contributions and Benefits Act 1992 (deemed   **9.587**
earnings factors: 2010-11 onwards) is to be read as if, after subsection (5), there were inserted—

"(5A) In determining whether Condition C is satisfied in relation to any pensioner, the following entitlements of the pensioner to an earnings factor credit may be aggregated if the weeks to which they relate comprise a continuous period—

(a) any entitlement arising by virtue of-
(i) section 44C(3)(c) below (eligibility for earnings factor enhancement in respect of a week in which severe disablement allowance was payable), or

      (ii) section 44C(3)(d) below (eligibility for earnings factor enhancement in respect of a week in which long-term incapacity benefit was, or would have been, payable); and

   (b) where an award of severe disablement allowance or long-term incapacity benefit was converted into an award of an employment and support allowance by virtue of the Employment and Support Allowance (Transitional Provisions, Housing Benefit and Council Tax Benefit) (Existing Awards) (No. 2) Regulations 2010, any entitlement arising by virtue of regulation 5A(2)(ba) of the Additional Pension and Social Security Pensions (Home Responsibilities) (Amendment) Regulations 2001 (earnings factor credits eligibility for pensioners to whom employment and support allowance was payable).".

[² "Income Tax (Earnings and Pensions) Act 2003

9.588

6A. The Income Tax (Earnings and Pensions) Act 2003 is to be read as if—

   (a) in section 660(1) (taxable benefits: UK benefits), in Table A–

      (i) in the first column, after the entry for "Contributory employment and support allowance", there were inserted a new entry "Contributory employment and support allowance (including any transitional addition to which a person is entitled in connection with that award)",

      (ii) in the second column, corresponding to the entry inserted by sub-paragraph (i), there were inserted "WRA 2007",

     (iii) in the third column, corresponding to the entry inserted by sub-paragraph (i), there were inserted "Section 1(2) (as modified and applied by the Employment and Support Allowance (Transitional Provisions, Housing Benefit and Council Tax Benefit) (Existing Awards) (No. 2) Regulations 2010 ("the 2010 Regulations"))", and

     (iv) under the text inserted in the second and third columns by sub-paragraphs (ii) and (iii), there were inserted "Any provision made for Northern Ireland which corresponds to section 1(2) of WRA 2007 (as modified and applied by any provision made for Northern Ireland which corresponds to those contained in the 2010 Regulations)";

   (b) in section 661(1) (taxable social security income), after "contributory employment and support allowance" there were inserted "contributory employment and support allowance (including any transitional addition to which a person is entitled in connection with that award),"; and

   (c) in section 677(1) (UK social security benefits wholly exempt from tax), in Table B–

      (i) in the first column, after the entry for "Income-related employment and support allowance", there were inserted a new entry "Income-related employment and support allowance (including any transitional addition to which a person is entitled in connection with that award)",

      (ii) in the second column, corresponding to the entry inserted by sub-paragraph (i), there were inserted "WRA 2007",

     (iii) in the third column, corresponding to the entry inserted by sub-paragraph (i), there were inserted "Section 1(2) (as modified and applied by the Employment and Support Allowance (Transitional Provisions, Housing Benefit and Council Tax Benefit) (Existing Awards) (No. 2) Regulations 2010 ("the 2010 Regulations"))", and

     (iv) under the text inserted in the second and third columns by sub-paragraphs (ii) and (iii), there were inserted "Any provision made for Northern Ireland which corresponds to section 1(2) of WRA 2007 (as modified and applied by any provision made for Northern Ireland which corresponds to those contained in the 2010 Regulations)".]

PART 3

MODIFICATION OF THE 2008 REGULATIONS

9.589

[¹ **7**]. Any reference to a claimant is to be read as if it were a reference to a person in relation to whom a conversion decision has been made under these Regulations.

[¹ **8**]. Part 2 (which makes provision about the assessment phase) does not apply, except for the purposes of applying regulation 147A of the 2008 Regulations.

[¹ **9**]. Part 3 (which makes provision about contribution conditions which do not apply by virtue of modifications contained in these Regulations) does not apply.

[³ (10) Regulation 30 (conditions for treating a claimant as having limited capability for work until a determination about limited capability for work has been made) is to be read as if, for paragraph (3), there was substituted—

"(3) Paragraph (2)(b) does not apply where a claimant has made and is pursuing an appeal against a conversion decision that embodies a determination that the claimant does not have limited capability for work and that appeal has not yet been determined by the First-tier Tribunal.".]

[¹ 11]. Regulation 45 (exempt work) is to be read as if, for the definition of "specified work" in paragraph (10), there were substituted—

""specified work" means—

(a) work done in accordance with paragraph (4); [² or]

(b) work done in accordance with regulation 17(4)(a) of the Social Security (Incapacity for Work) (General) Regulations 1995; [² . . .].

[¹ 12]. Regulation 67 (prescribed amounts) is to be read as if—

(a) in paragraph (1), after sub-paragraph (c) there were added—

"(d) the amount of any transitional addition to which the person is entitled under regulation 11 of the Employment and Support Allowance (Transitional Provisions, Housing Benefit and Council Tax Benefit) (Existing Awards) (No. 2) Regulations 2010.";

(b) in paragraph (2), for the words from "is the amount" to the end, there were substituted

"are such of the following amounts as may apply in the person's case—

"(a) the amount determined in accordance with paragraph 1(1) of Schedule 4; and

(b) the amount of any transitional addition to which the person is entitled under regulation 10 of the Employment and Support Allowance (Transitional Provisions) (Existing Awards) Regulations 2010.".

[¹ 13]. Regulation 68 (polygamous marriages) is to be read as if, in paragraph (1), after subparagraph (d) there were added—

"(e) the amount of any transitional addition to which the person is entitled under regulation 11 of the Employment and Support Allowance (Transitional Provisions, Housing Benefit and Council Tax Benefit) (Existing Awards) (No. 2) Regulations 2010.".

[¹ 14]. Regulation 75 (payments treated as not being payments to which section 3 of the 2007 Act applies) is to be read subject to the same modifications as are specified in paragraph 38 of Schedule 1 to these Regulations.

[¹ 15]. In its application to a person who has made and is pursuing an appeal against a conversion decision which embodies a determination that the person does not have limited capability for work, Regulation 147A (claimants appealing a decision) is to be read as if there were substituted—

"Claimants appealing a decision

147A.—(1) This regulation applies where a person has made and is pursuing an appeal against a conversion decision which embodies a determination that the person does not have limited capability for work.

[² (1A) A person to whom this regulation applies who has made and is pursuing an appeal against a conversion decision in respect of an existing award of incapacity benefit or severe disablement allowance shall be treated as having satisfied the conditions in Part 1 of Schedule 1 to the Act (contributory allowance: conditions relating to national insurance).]

(2) Subject to paragraph (3), where this regulation applies, a determination of limited capability for work by the Secretary of State under regulation 19 shall not be made until the appeal is determined by the First-tier Tribunal.

(3) Paragraph (2) does not apply where either—

(a) the claimant suffers from some specific disease or bodily or mental disablement from which the claimant was not suffering when entitlement began; or

(b) a disease or bodily or mental disablement from which the claimant was suffering at that date has significantly worsened.

(4) Where this regulation applies and the Secretary of State makes a determination—

(a) in a case to which paragraph (3) applies (including where the determination is not the first such determination) that the claimant does not have, or by virtue of regulation 22 or 23 is to be treated as not having, limited capability for work; or

(b) subsequent to a determination that the claimant is to be treated as having limited capability for work by virtue of a provision of these Regulations other than regulation 30, that the claimant is no longer to be so treated, this regulation and regulation 30 apply as if that determination had not been made.

(5) Where this regulation applies and—

(a) the claimant is entitled to an employment and support allowance by virtue of being treated as having limited capability for work in accordance with regulation 30;

(b) neither of the circumstances in paragraph (3) applies or, subsequent to the application of either of those circumstances, the claimant has been determined not to have limited capability for work; and

(c) the claimant's appeal is dismissed, withdrawn [³ , struck out or has been discontinued in accordance with the provisions of regulation 33(10) of the Social Security and Child Support (Decisions and Appeals) Regulations 1999 (notice of appeal)],

the claimant is to be treated as not having limited capability for work [³ with effect from the day specified in paragraph (5A).]

[³ (5A) The day specified for the purposes of paragraph (5) is the first day of the benefit week following the date on which the Secretary of State either—

(a) receives the First-tier Tribunal's notification that the appeal is dismissed, withdrawn or struck out, or

(b) discontinues action on an appeal in the circumstances to which regulation 33(10) of the Social Security and Child Support (Decisions and Appeals) Regulations 1999 (notice of appeal) applies.]

(6) Where a claimant's appeal is successful, any entitlement to which this regulation applies shall terminate [³ from the first day of the benefit week following the date on which the Secretary of State receives the First-tier Tribunal's notification of that decision.]

[¹ 16]. Schedule 5 (prescribed amounts in special case) is to be read as if any reference to the amount—

(a) applicable to a person under regulation 67(1)(a); or

(b) to which a person is entitled under regulation 67(1)(a),

included the amount of any transitional addition to which the person is entitled under regulation 67(1)(d) (see modification made by paragraph 52(a) of this Schedule).

PART 4

MODIFICATION OF OTHER SECONDARY LEGISLATION

Social Security (Claims and Payments) Regulations 1987

9.590   [¹ 17]. The Social Security (Claims and Payments) Regulations 1987 are to be read subject to the modifications set out in paragraphs [² 18 to 22] of this Schedule.

[¹ 18]. Regulation 3 (claims not required for entitlement to benefits in certain cases) is to be read as if—

(a) after the words "was made" in paragraph (j)(ii), there were inserted—

"[² ...]

[² (k) the beneficiary–

(i) has made and is pursuing an appeal against a conversion decision made by virtue of the Employment and Support Allowance (Transitional Provisions, Housing Benefit and Council Tax Benefit) (Existing Awards) (No. 2) Regulations 2010 which embodies a determination that the beneficiary does not have limited capability for work; or

(ii) was entitled to an employment and support allowance by virtue of the Employment and Support Allowance (Transitional Provisions, Housing Benefit and Council Tax Benefit) (Existing Awards) (No. 2) Regulations 2010 and has made and is pursuing an appeal against a later decision which embodies a determination that the beneficiary does not have limited capability for work;"; and

(b) after paragraph [² (k)], there were added—

"[² (l)] in the case of an employment and support allowance where the beneficiary is entitled to an existing award which is subject to conversion under the Employment and Support Allowance (Transitional Provisions, Housing Benefit and Council Tax Benefit) (Existing Awards) (No. 2) Regulations 2010.".

[¹ 19]. In regulation 26C (employment and support allowance) any reference to an employment and support allowance includes any transitional addition to which the beneficiary is entitled under the Employment and Support Allowance (Transitional Provisions, Housing Benefit and Council Tax Benefit) (Existing Awards) (No. 2) Regulations 2010.

[¹ 20]. Regulation 32(1B) (information to be given and changes to be notified) is to be read as if—

(a) the word "or" at the end of sub-paragraph (a) were omitted; and

(b) after that sub-paragraph, there were inserted—

"(ab) the amount of any transitional addition to which the beneficiary is entitled under the Employment and Support Allowance (Transitional Provisions, Housing Benefit and Council Tax Benefit) (Existing Awards) (No. 2) Regulations 2010; or".

[¹ 21]. Schedule 9 (deductions from benefit and direct payments to third parties) is to be read as if—

(a) in paragraph 1 (interpretation)—

(i) in sub-paragraph (3), after the words ""employment and support allowance" means", there were inserted "(subject to sub-paragraph (4))", and

(ii) after sub-paragraph (3), there were added—

"(4) In the application of sub-paragraph (3) to a beneficiary whose award of an employment and support allowance is by virtue of the Employment and Support Allowance (Transitional Provisions, Housing Benefit and Council Tax Benefit) (Existing Awards) (No. 2) Regulations 2010 ("the 2010 Regulations"), any reference to an employment and support allowance includes any transitional addition to which the beneficiary is entitled under those Regulations.

(5) Where a specified benefit awarded to a beneficiary is subject to conversion under the 2010 Regulations and—

(a) immediately before the effective date of the conversion decision made in relation to the beneficiary, any deduction is being made in accordance with this Schedule from sums payable to the beneficiary by way of the specified benefit; and

(b) with effect from that date, the award of specified benefit is converted into an award of an employment and support allowance under the 2010 Regulations, any deduction falling within paragraph (a) shall have effect as a deduction from the employment and support allowance to which the beneficiary is entitled.".

(b) in paragraph 8—

(i) in sub-paragraph (4), for paragraph (a)(iv), there were substituted—

"(iv) in the case of an employment and support allowance, the applicable amount for the family as is awarded under the provisions specified in sub-paragraph (5); or", and

(ii) after sub-paragraph (4) there were added—

"(5) The specified provisions are—

(a) where the person is entitled to an employment and support allowance by virtue of the Employment and Support Allowance (Transitional Provisions, Housing Benefit and Council Tax Benefit) (Existing Awards) (No. 2) Regulations 2010 ("the 2010 Regulations")—

(i) paragraph (1)(a), (b) and (d) of regulation 67 (prescribed amounts); or

(ii) paragraph (1)(a), (b), (c) and (e) of regulation 68 (polygamous marriages), of the Employment and Support Allowance Regulations (as modified by paragraphs [² 12 and 13] of Schedule 2 to the 2010 Regulations); and

(b) in any other case, paragraph (1)(a) and (b) of regulation 67 or paragraph (1)(a) to (c) of regulation 68 of the Employment and Support Allowance Regulations.".

[¹ 22]. Schedule 9B (deductions from benefit in respect of child support maintenance and payment to persons with care) is to be read as if—

(a) in paragraph (1) (interpretation), the existing provision becomes sub-paragraph (1); and

(b) there were added—

"(2) In the application of this Schedule to a beneficiary whose award of an employment and support allowance is by virtue of the Employment and Support Allowance (Transitional Provisions, Housing Benefit and Council Tax Benefit) (Existing Awards) (No. 2) Regulations 2010 ("the 2010 Regulations"), any reference to an employment and support allowance includes any transitional addition to which the beneficiary is entitled under those Regulations.

(3) Where a specified benefit awarded to a beneficiary is subject to conversion under the 2010 Regulations and—

(a) immediately before the effective date of the conversion decision made in relation to the beneficiary, any deduction is being made in accordance with this Schedule from sums payable to the beneficiary by way of the specified benefit; and

(b) with effect from that date, the award of specified benefit is converted into an award of an employment and support allowance under the 2010 Regulations, any deduction falling within paragraph (a) shall have effect as a deduction from the employment and support allowance to which the beneficiary is entitled.".

[² Community Charges (Deductions from Income Support) (Scotland) Regulations 1989

22A. Regulation 1 of the Community Charges (Deductions from Income Support) (Scotland) Regulations 1989 (citation, commencement and interpretation) is to be read as if, after paragraph (2), there were inserted—

"(2A) In the application of these Regulations to a debtor whose entitlement to an employment and support allowance is by virtue of the Employment and Support Allowance (Transitional Provisions, Housing Benefit and Council Tax Benefit) (Existing Awards) (No. 2) Regulations 2010 ("the 2010 Regulations"), any reference to an employment and support allowance includes any transitional addition to which the debtor is entitled under those Regulations.

(2B) Where a debtor's award of income support is subject to conversion under the 2010 Regulations and—

(a) immediately before the effective date of the conversion decision made in relation to the debtor, any deduction is being made under these Regulations from sums payable to the debtor by way of income support; and

(b) with effect from that date, the award of income support is converted into an award of an employment and support allowance under the 2010 Regulations, any deduction falling within sub-paragraph (a) shall have effect as a deduction from the employment and support allowance to which the debtor is entitled."]

Community Charges (Deductions from Income Support) (No. 2) Regulations 1990

[¹ 23]. Regulation 1 of the Community Charges (Deductions from Income Support) (No. 2) Regulations 1990 (citation, commencement and interpretation) is to be read as if, after paragraph (2), there were inserted—

"(2A) In the application of these Regulations to a debtor whose entitlement to an employment and support allowance is by virtue of the Employment and Support Allowance (Transitional Provisions, Housing Benefit and Council Tax Benefit) (Existing Awards) (No. 2) Regulations 2010 ("the 2010 Regulations"), any reference to an employment and support allowance includes any transitional addition to which the debtor is entitled under those Regulations.

(2B) Where a debtor's award of income support is subject to conversion under the 2010 Regulations and—

(a) immediately before the effective date of the conversion decision made in relation to the debtor, any deduction is being made under these Regulations from sums payable to the debtor by way of income support; and

(b) with effect from that date, the award of income support is converted into an award of an employment and support allowance under the 2010 Regulations, any deduction falling within sub-paragraph (a) shall have effect as a deduction from the employment and support allowance to which the debtor is entitled.".

Fines (Deductions from Income Support) Regulations 1992

[¹ 24]. Regulation 1 of the Fines (Deductions from Income Support) Regulations 1992 (citation, commencement and interpretation) is to be read as if, after paragraph (2), there were inserted—

"(2A) In the application of these Regulations to an offender whose entitlement to an employment and support allowance is by virtue of the Employment and Support Allowance (Transitional Provisions, Housing Benefit and Council Tax Benefit) (Existing Awards) (No. 2) Regulations 2010 ("the 2010 Regulations"), any reference to an employment and support allowance includes any transitional addition to which the offender is entitled under those Regulations.

(2B) Where an offender's award of income support is subject to conversion under the 2010 Regulations and—

(a) immediately before the effective date of the conversion decision made in relation to the offender, any deduction is being made under these Regulations from sums payable to the offender by way of income support; and

(b) with effect from that date, the award of income support is converted into an award of an employment and support allowance under the 2010 Regulations, any deduction falling within sub-paragraph (a) shall have effect as a deduction from the employment and support allowance to which the offender is entitled.".

Council Tax (Deductions from Income Support) Regulations 1993

[¹ **25**]. Regulation 1 of the Council Tax (Deductions from Income Support) Regulations 1993 (citation, commencement and interpretation) is to be read as if, after paragraph (2), there were inserted—

"(2A) In the application of these Regulations to a debtor whose entitlement to an employment and support allowance is by virtue of the Employment and Support Allowance (Transitional Provisions, Housing Benefit and Council Tax Benefit) (Existing Awards) (No. 2) Regulations 2010 ("the 2010 Regulations"), any reference to an employment and support allowance includes any transitional addition to which the debtor is entitled under those Regulations.

(2B) Where a debtor's award of income support is subject to conversion under the 2010 Regulations and—

(a) immediately before the effective date of the conversion decision made in relation to the debtor, any deduction is being made under these Regulations from sums payable to the debtor by way of income support; and

(b) on that date, the award of income support is converted into an award of an employment and support allowance under the 2010 Regulations, any deduction falling within sub-paragraph (a) shall have effect as a deduction from the employment and support allowance to which the debtor is entitled.".

[² *Social Security and Child Support (Decisions and Appeals) Regulations 1999*

25A.—(1) Regulation 3 of the Social Security and Child Support (Decisions and Appeals) Regulations 1999 (revision of decisions) is to be read as if—

(a) in the case of a revision of a decision to award jobseeker's allowance made following the reinstatement of an existing award in accordance with regulation 15(5) of the Employment and Support Allowance (Transitional Provisions, Housing Benefit and Council Tax Benefit) (Existing Awards) (No. 2) Regulations 2010 ("the 2010 Regulations"), the words "within one month of the date of notification of the original decision" in paragraph (1)(a) were omitted;

(b) in the case of a conversion decision where there has been a change of circumstances to which regulation 12(4) of the 2010 Regulations (calculation of transitional addition) applies, paragraph (9)(a) were omitted; and

(c) in paragraph (9)(a), for "in the case of an advance award under regulation 13, 13A or 13C of the Claims and Payments Regulations" there were substituted, "in the cases of an advance award under regulation 13, 13A or 13C of the Claims and Payments Regulations or a conversion decision within the meaning of regulation 5(2)(a) of the 2010 Regulations".

(2) Regulation 6(2)(a)(i) of those Regulations (supersession of decisions) is to be read as if for "in the case of an advance award under regulation 13, 13A or 13C of the Claims and Payments Regulations or regulation 146 of the Employment and Support Allowance Regulations" there were substituted "in the cases of an advance award under regulation 13, 13A or 13C of the Claims and Payments Regulations or regulation 146 of the Employment and Support Allowance Regulations or a conversion decision within the meaning of regulation 5(2)(a) of the 2010 Regulations".]

Additional Pension and Social Security Pensions (Home Responsibilities) (Amendment) Regulations 2001

[¹ **26**]. Regulation 5A of the Additional Pension and Social Security Pensions (Home Responsibilities) (Amendment) Regulations 2001 (earnings factor credits eligibility for pensioners to whom employment and support allowance was payable) is to be read as if—

    (a) the word "or" at the end of paragraph (2)(b) were omitted; and
    (b) after that paragraph (2)(b), there were inserted—

"(ba) that allowance was an employment and support allowance to which the pensioner was entitled by virtue of the Employment and Support Allowance (Transitional Provisions, Housing Benefit and Council Tax Benefit) (Existing Awards) (No. 2) Regulations 2010 and either—

    (i) long-term incapacity benefit or severe disablement allowance was payable to the pensioner immediately before its conversion into an employment and support allowance in accordance with those Regulations; or
    (ii) the condition in sub-paragraph (b) was satisfied; or ".

[³ Social Security (Habitual Residence) Amendment Regulations 2004

27. Regulation 6 of the Social Security (Habitual Residence) Amendment Regulations 2004 (transitional arrangements and savings) is to be read as if—

    (a) in paragraph (1)—
        (i) sub-paragraphs (a), (b) and (d) were omitted, and
        (ii) for sub-paragraph (c) there were substituted—
    "(c) is entitled to an employment and support allowance by virtue of—
        (i) the Employment and Support Allowance (Transitional Provisions, Housing Benefit and Council Tax Benefit) (Existing Awards) (No. 2) Regulations 2010, or
        (ii) regulation 30 of the Employment and Support Allowance Regulations (conditions for treating a claimant as having limited capability for work until a determination about limited capability for work has been made) in the circumstances where the person has made and is pursuing an appeal against a conversion decision made under the Employment and Support Allowance (Transitional Provisions, Housing Benefit and Council Tax Benefit) (Existing Awards) (No. 2) Regulations 2010 which embodies a determination that the person does not have limited capability for work,
    and immediately before the effective date of the conversion decision made in respect of that person, was entitled to a specified benefit in respect of a period which was continuous with a period of entitlement to the same or another specified benefit which included 30th April 2004;"; and
    (b) in paragraph (4), before sub-paragraph (a) there were inserted—
    "(za) "conversion decision" and "effective date" have the same meanings as in regulation 2(1) of the Employment and Support Allowance (Transitional Provisions, Housing Benefit and Council Tax Benefit) (Existing Awards) (No. 2) Regulations 2010;".]

AMENDMENTS

1. Employment and Support Allowance (Transitional Provisions, Housing Benefit and Council Tax Benefit) (Existing Awards) (No. 2) (Amendment) Regulations 2010 (SI 2010/2430) reg.15 (November 1, 2010).

2. Employment and Support Allowance (Transitional Provisions, Housing Benefit and Council Tax Benefit) (Existing Awards) (No. 2) (Amendment) Regulations 2010 (SI 2010/2430) reg.17 (November 1, 2010).

3. Social Security (Miscellaneous Amendments) (No. 3) Regulations 2011 (SI 2011/2425) reg.27(4) (October 30, 2011).

4. Employment and Support Allowance (Duration of Contributory Allowance) (Consequential Amendments) Regulations 2012 (SI 2012/913) reg.10(4) (May 1, 2012).

MODIFICATION

In cases where universal credit has come into force (see the General Note, above),   **9.591**
Sch.2 is modified. For a list of the modifying provisions see the General Note
(para.9.538 above). For the text of the modification, see the text of Sch.4 to SI
2013/983 in Pt IV of Vol.V.

SCHEDULE 3   **Regulation 16(2)(e)(iii)**

LIST OF REGULATIONS THAT APPLY AFTER THE CONVERSION PHASE   **9.592**

The regulations referred to in regulation 16(2)(e)(iii) are—
    The Social Security (Benefit) (Married Women and Widows Special Provisions)
    Regulations 1974
    The Social Security (Benefit) (Members of the Forces) Regulations 1975
    The Social Security (Airmen's Benefits) Regulations 1975
    The Social Security (Mariners' Benefits) Regulations 1975
    The Social Security (Credits) Regulations 1975
    The Social Security (Medical Evidence) Regulations 1976
    The Social Security (Overlapping Benefits) Regulations 1979
    The Statutory Sick Pay (General) Regulations 1982
    The Statutory Maternity Pay (General) Regulations 1986
    The Income Support (General) Regulations 1987
    The Social Security (Claims and Payments) Regulations 1987
    The Social Fund (Recovery by Deductions from Benefits) Regulations 1988
    The Social Security (Payments on account, Overpayments and Recovery) Regulations
    1988
    The Social Fund Cold Weather Payments (General) Regulations 1988
    The Community Charges (Deductions from Income Support) (No.2) Regulations
    1990
    The Child Support (Maintenance Assessment Procedure) Regulations 1992
    The Child Support (Maintenance Assessments and Special Cases) Regulations 1992
    The Fines (Deductions from Income Support) Regulations 1992
    The Council Tax (Deductions from Income Support) Regulations 1993
    The Jobseeker's Allowance Regulations 1996
    The Social Security Benefits (Maintenance Payments and Consequential
    Amendments) Regulations 1996
    [¹ The Employment Protection (Recoupment of Jobseeker's Allowance and Income
    Support) Regulations 1996]
    The Child Support Departure Direction and Consequential Amendments Regulations
    1996
    The Social Security and Child Support (Decisions and Appeals) Regulations 1999
    The Social Security (Immigration and Asylum) Consequential Amendments
    Regulations 2000
    The Social Fund Winter Fuel Payment Regulations 2000
    The Child Support (Maintenance Calculations and Special Cases) Regulations 2000
    The Child Support (Variations) Regulations 2000
    The Child Support (Maintenance Calculation Procedure) Regulations 2000
    The Social Security (Crediting and Treatment of Contributions, and National
    Insurance Numbers) Regulations 2001
    The Children (Leaving Care) Social Security Benefits Regulations 2001
    The Social Security (Loss of Benefit) Regulations 2001
    The State Pension Credit Regulations 2002
    The Social Security (Jobcentre Plus Interviews for Partners) Regulations 2003
    The Age-Related Payments Regulations 2005
    [² The Social Security (Habitual Residence) Amendment Regulations 2004]
    The Social Fund Maternity and Funeral Expenses (General) Regulations 2005

AMENDMENTS

    1. Employment and Support Allowance (Transitional Provisions, Housing Benefit
and Council Tax Benefit) (Existing Awards) (No. 2) (Amendment) Regulations
2010 (SI 2010/2430) reg.18 (November 1, 2010).

2. Social Security (Miscellaneous Amendments) (No. 3) Regulations 2011 (SI 2011/2425) reg.27(5) (October 30, 2011).

3. Employment and Support Allowance (Repeat Assessments and Pending Appeal Awards) (Amendment) Regulations 2015 (SI 2015/437) reg.7 (March 30, 2015). It is a requirement of the amending instrument, and not an editorial error, that the figure "10" at the beginning of the amended paragraph is in brackets and is not in bold type.

MODIFICATION

9.593   In cases where universal credit has come into force (see the General Note, above), Sch.3 is modified. For a list of the modifying provisions see the General Note (para.9.538 above). For the text of the modification, see the text of Sch.4 to SI 2013/983 in Pt IV of Vol.V.

SCHEDULE 4   **Regulation 26**

9.594   CONSEQUENTIAL AMENDMENTS

[Amends paragraph 8(4) of Sch.9 to the Social Security (Claims and Payments) Regulations 1987; regulations 55(4) and 55A(1) of, and paragraph 20H of Schedule 1 to, the Jobseeker's Allowance Regulations 1996; and regulation 2(3) of the Employment and Support Allowance (Transitional Provisions) Regulations 2008. The amendments have been incorporated in the text of those regulations.]

SCHEDULE 5   **Regulation 27**

9.595   AMENDMENTS TO LEGISLATION RELATING TO HOUSING BENEFIT AND COUNCIL TAX BENEFIT

Omitted as not within the subject matter of these books.

The Employment and Support Allowance (Work-Related Activity) Regulations 2011

(SI 2011/1349) (as amended)

In accordance with section 26(1)(b) of the Welfare Reform Act 2007, and section 8(3) of the Welfare Reform Act 2009, a draft of this instrument was laid before Parliament and approved by a resolution of each House of Parliament.

The Secretary of State for Work and Pensions makes the following Regulations in exercise of the powers conferred by sections 9 and 10 of the Social Security Act 1998, and sections 11, 12(1) and (2), 13, 14, 15, 16, 17(3)(b), 24(1) and 25 of the Welfare Reform Act 2007.

In accordance with section 173(1) of the Social Security Administration Act 1992, the Secretary of State has obtained the agreement of the Social Security Advisory Committee that proposals in respect of these Regulations should not be referred to them.

Arrangement of Regulations

Part 1

General

1.   Citation and commencement   **9.596**
2.   Interpretation

Part 2

Work-related activity

3.   Requirement to undertake work-related activity
4.   Directions about work-related activity
5.   Notification of work-related activity and action plans
6.   Requirement to undertake work-related activity at a particular time not to
          apply
7.   Reconsideration of action plans
8.   Failure to undertake work-related activity

Part 3

Contracting Out

9.   Contracting out

Part 4

Amendments to the ESA Regulations

10.   Amendment to regulation 2(1) of the ESA Regulations (interpretation)
11.   Revocation of regulations relating to work-focused health-related assess-
          ments
12.   Amendment to regulation 56 of the ESA Regulations (notification of inter-
          view)
13.   Amendment to regulation 57 of the ESA Regulations (taking part in a work-
          focused interview)
14.   Revocation of regulation 58 of the ESA Regulations (action plans)
15.   Substitution of regulation 61 of the ESA Regulations (failure to take part in
          a work-focused interview)
16.   Amendment to regulation 62 of the ESA Regulations (contracting out
          certain functions relating to work-focused interviews)
17.   Amendment to regulation 63 of the ESA Regulations (reduction of employ-
          ment and support allowance)
18.   Amendment to regulation 64 of the ESA Regulations (cessation of reduction)
19.   Amendment to Schedule 8 to the ESA Regulations
20.   Amendment of Schedule 9 to the ESA Regulations

PART 5

AMENDMENT TO THE SOCIAL SECURITY AND CHILD SUPPORT (DECISIONS AND
APPEALS) REGULATIONS 1999

21.   Amendment to the Social Security and Child Support (Decisions and
Appeals) Regulations 1999

PART 1

GENERAL

Citation and commencement

9.597   **1.** These Regulations may be cited as the Employment and Support
Allowance (Work-Related Activity) Regulations 2011 and shall come into
force on 1st June 2011.

GENERAL NOTE

9.598   For an instructive analysis of the complications and difficulties in challenging
decisions made under the conditionality regime introduced into ESA by these regulations see *LM v SSWP (ESA)* [2016] UKUT 360 (AAC).

Interpretation

9.599   **2.**—(1) In these Regulations—
"the Act" means the Welfare Reform Act 2007;
"the ESA Regulations" means the Employment and Support Allowance
Regulations 2008;
"action plan" means an action plan issued in accordance with regulation
5;
"carer's allowance", "child", [¹ ...] "medical treatment" and "working
day" have the meaning given in regulation 2(1) of the ESA
Regulations.
(2) For the purpose of these Regulations where a written notice is given
by sending it by post it is taken to have been received on the second working
day after posting.

AMENDMENT

1. Social Security (Work-focused Interviews for Lone Parents and Partners)
(Amendment) Regulations 2011 (SI 2011/2428) reg.7 (October 31, 2011).

PART 2

WORK-RELATED ACTIVITY

Requirement to undertake work-related activity

9.600   **3.**—(1) The Secretary of State may require a person who satisfies the
requirements in paragraph (2) to undertake work-related activity as a con-

dition of continuing to be entitled to the full amount of employment and
support allowance payable to that person.

(2) The requirements referred to in paragraph (1) are that the person—

(a) is required to take part in, or has taken part in, one or more work-
focused interviews pursuant to regulation 54 of the ESA Regulations;

(b) is not a lone parent who is responsible for and a member of the same
household as a child under the age of [¹ 3];

(c) is not entitled to a carer's allowance; and

(d) is not entitled to a carer premium under paragraph 8 of Schedule 4
to the ESA Regulations.

(3) A requirement to undertake work-related activity ceases to have effect
if the person becomes a member of the support group.

(4) A requirement imposed under paragraph (1)—

(a) must be reasonable in the view of the Secretary of State, having
regard to the person's circumstances; and

(b) may not require the person to—

(i) apply for a job or undertake work, whether as an employee or
otherwise; or

(ii) undergo medical treatment.

(5) A person who is a lone parent and in any week is responsible for and
a member of the same household as a child under the age of 13, may only
be required to undertake work-related activity under paragraph (1) during
the child's normal school hours.

AMENDMENT

1. Income Support (Work-Related Activity) and Miscellaneous Amendments
Regulations 2014 (SI 2014/1097) reg.15 (April 27, 2014).

GENERAL NOTE

Regulation 3 provides that the Secretary of State may require certain ESA claim-   9.601
ants (who fall within para.(2)) to undertake work-related activity as a condition
of continuing to be entitled to be paid their full ESA. However, by para.(4)(a)
the requirement imposed under para.(1) "must be reasonable, in the view of the
Secretary of State, having regard to the person's circumstances". Further, a claimant who fails to comply with such a requirement must show "good cause" within five
working days of notice of such failure (see reg.8(1)). In *LM v SSWP (ESA)* [2016]
UKUT 360 (AAC) Judge Wright ruled as follows (at para.37):

". . . satisfaction of regulation 8 of the ESA 2011 Regs requires the Secretary of
State's decision maker, and the First-tier Tribunal on an appeal from such a decision to be satisfied, in a case or where the issue arises, that the requirement was
reasonable on the circumstances of the claimants case, as a claimant cannot 'fail'
to meet a requirement where there was in law no lawful requirement."

Furthermore, in accordance with normal principles, later evidence as to what a
claimant's circumstances were "obtaining at [that] time", even if not known to the
decision maker at the time of the decision, could still be taken into account under
s.12(8)(b) of the Social Security Act 1998. As to whether issues arise for determination under regulation 3 (reasonable requirement) or reg.8 (good cause), this will
depend on all the circumstances. According to Judge Wright (at para.43):

". . . If a claimant in his or her appeal letter or at the appeal hearing says the
requirement was not reasonable having regard to his circumstances (or some such
words, the exact statutory wording obviously does not need to be used) then the

First-tier Tribunal will need to determine that issue in deciding the appeal. On the other hand, an appeal written by a welfare rights officer which focuses solely on arguing that the reasons given within the five days amount to good cause and where the surrounding evidence does not suggest that the particular requirement was other than a reasonable one for the particular appellant, would probably not be an appeal giving rise to an issue under regulation 3(4)(a) to be determined."

Directions about work-related activity

9.602   **4.**—(1) The circumstances in paragraph (2) are the circumstances prescribed for the purposes of section 15(1)(a) of the Act.

(2) The circumstances referred to in paragraph (1) are that—

(a) the person has been identified by the Secretary of State as having a barrier to work and in the view of the Secretary of State has refused to address that barrier; and

(b) the Secretary of State considers that the activity specified in the direction given under section 15(1) of the Act is a prerequisite to the person's ability to obtain or remain in work.

Notification of work-related activity and action plans

9.603   **5.**—(1) The Secretary of State must notify a person of a requirement to undertake work-related activity by including the requirement in a written action plan given to the person.

(2) The action plan must specify—

(a) the work-related activity which the person is required to undertake; and

(b) any other information that the Secretary of State considers appropriate.

General Note

9.604   As to what is required by the provision that "the action plan must *specify*" (emphasis added) see the discussion by Judge Wright in *LM v SSWP (ESA)* [2016] UKUT 360 (AAC) at paras 31 and 34(i), although the point did not need to be resolved in the particular circumstances of that appeal.

Requirement to undertake work-related activity at a particular time not to apply

9.605   **6.** The Secretary of State may determine that a requirement as to the time at or by which work-related activity is to be undertaken is not to apply, or is to be treated as not having applied, if in the view of the Secretary of State it would be, or would have been, unreasonable to require the person to undertake the activity at or by that time.

General Note

9.606   For a provisional analysis of the scope and effect of reg.6 in the decision-making and appellate contexts, and whether decisions under regulation 6 are appealable, see the discussion by Judge Wright in *LM v SSWP (ESA)* [2016] UKUT 360 (AAC) at paras 13–17, although the point did not need to be resolved in the particular circumstances of that appeal (see paras 29 and 35).

Reconsideration of action plans

7.—(1) A person may request reconsideration of an action plan.   9.607

(2) On receipt of a request the Secretary of State must reconsider the action plan.

(3) A decision of the Secretary of State following a request must be in writing and given to the person.

Failure to undertake work-related activity

8.—(1) A person who is required to undertake work-related activity but   9.608
fails to do so must show good cause for the failure within 5 working days of the date on which the Secretary of State gives notice of the failure.

(2) The Secretary of State must determine whether a person who is required to undertake work-related activity has failed to do so and, if so, whether the person has shown good cause for the failure.

(3) [*¹Omitted.]*

AMENDMENT

1. Employment and Support Allowance (Sanctions) (Amendment) Regulations 2012 (SI 2012/2756) reg.7(2) (December 3, 2012, in respect of failures on or after that date (see reg.1 of the amending regs.)).

PART 3

CONTRACTING OUT

Contracting out

9.—(1) Any function of the Secretary of State specified in paragraph (2)   9.609
may be exercised by, or by employees of, such person (if any) as may be authorised by the Secretary of State.

(2) The functions are—

(a) any function under—

   (i) regulation 3 (requirement to undertake work-related activity);

   (ii) regulation 5 (notification of work-related activity and action plans);

   (iii) regulation 6 (requirement to undertake work-related activity not to apply);

   (iv) regulation 7 (reconsideration of action plans);

(b) any function under [¹regulation 64(1)(c) and (1A)(b)] of the ESA Regulations (decisions in relation to cessation of reduction);

[¹(c) any function relating to a compliance condition under regulation 63(11) (compliance condition: notifications and agreements).]

AMENDMENT

1. Employment and Support Allowance (Sanctions) (Amendment) Regulations 2012 (SI 2012/2756) reg.7(3) (December 3, 2012, in respect of failures on or after that date (see reg.1 of the amending regs.)).

PART 4

AMENDMENTS TO THE ESA REGULATIONS

9.610   *Amendments to regs 2(1), 56, 57. 58, 61–64 and Schs 8 and 9 of the ESA Regulations effected by regs 10, 12–13 and 15–20 of this SI have been taken into account in preparing the text of those Regs in this Volume.*

The revocation of regs 47–49, 51–53 and 58 of the ESA Regulations effected by regs 11 and 14 of this SI have been taken into account in preparing the text of those Regs in this Volume.

PART 5

AMENDMENT TO THE SOCIAL SECURITY AND CHILD SUPPORT (DECISIONS AND APPEALS) REGULATIONS 1999

Amendment to the Social Security and Child Support (Decisions and Appeals) Regulations 1999

9.611   **21.** *The amendment effected to regulation 1(3) of the Social Security and Child Support (Decisions and Appeals) Regulations 1999 (interpretation) ("failure determination"), has been taken into account in Vol. III: Administration, Adjudication and the European Dimension.*

The Employment and Support Allowance (Amendment) Regulations 2012

(SI 2012/3096)

9.612   The Secretary of State for Work and Pensions makes the following Regulations in exercise of the powers conferred by sections 8(1), (2), (3) and (5), 9(1), (2) and (3), 24(1) and 25(2) and (5) of, and paragraphs 1 and 9 of Schedule 2 to, the Welfare Reform Act 2007.

In accordance with section 173(1)(b) of the Social Security Administration Act 1992, the Secretary of State has obtained the agreement of the Social Security Advisory Committee that proposals in respect of these Regulations should not be referred to them.

REGULATIONS REPRODUCED

1.   Citation, commencement and interpretation
2.   Application, transitional and savings provisions

Citation, commencement and interpretation

9.613   **1.**— (1) These Regulations may be cited as the Employment and Support Allowance (Amendment) Regulations 2012 and come into force on 28th January 2013.

1434

(2) In these Regulations—

"the ESA Regulations" means the Employment and Support Allowance Regulations 2008; and

"the commencement date" means the date on which these Regulations come into force.

Application, transitional and savings provisions

2.—(1) Subject to paragraphs (2) and (3), these Regulations apply to—

(a) a person who makes a claim for an employment and support allowance on or after the commencement date (including a claim in respect of any period beginning before that date);

(b) a person who made a claim for an employment and support allowance before the commencement date in respect of whom a determination is made on or after that date—

    (i) as to whether that person has or is to be treated as having limited capability for work under Part 5 of the ESA Regulations, or

    (ii) as to whether that person has or is to be treated as having limited capability for work-related activity under Part 6 of those Regulations;

(c) a person who is entitled to an employment and support allowance immediately before the commencement date in respect of whom, on or after that date—

    (i) the Secretary of State determines afresh under regulation 19(7) of the ESA Regulations whether the person has or is to be treated as having limited capability for work;

    (ii) the Secretary of State determines afresh under regulation 34(4) of the ESA Regulations whether the person has or is to be treated as having limited capability for work-related activity; and

(d) a notified person within the meaning of regulation 4 of the Employment and Support Allowance (Transitional Provisions, Housing Benefit and Council Tax Benefit) (Existing Awards) (No.2) Regulations 2010 in respect of whom a determination is made on or after the commencement date as to whether that person—

    (i) has or is to be treated as having limited capability for work under Part 5 of the ESA Regulations, or

    (ii) is to be treated as having limited capability for work-related activity under Part 6 of those Regulations.

(2) Where a person has been issued with a questionnaire which relates to the provisions of Schedule 2 of the ESA Regulations as they had effect immediately before the commencement date, regulation 5 does not apply for the purposes of making a determination on or after that date as to that person's limited capability for work under Part 5 of the ESA Regulations and, for those purposes, the provisions of Schedule 2 of the ESA Regulations are to continue to apply in respect of that person as they had effect immediately before the commencement date.

(3) Where a person has been issued with a questionnaire which relates to the provisions of Schedule 3 of the ESA Regulations as they had effect immediately before the commencement date, regulation 6 does not apply for the purposes of making a determination on or after that date as to that per-

9.614

son's limited capability for work under Part 6 of the ESA Regulations and, for those purposes, the provisions of Schedule 3 of the ESA Regulations are to continue to apply in respect of that person as they had effect immediately before the commencement date.

(4) The provisions of paragraphs (2) to (3) do not apply to any determination made in respect of a person on or after 28th July 2013.

DEFINITIONS

"the commencement date"—see reg.1(2).
"the ESA Regulations" —see reg.1(2).

GENERAL NOTE

9.615   This sets the scope of application of the various changes to the ESA Regs effected on January 28, 2013 and taken account of in the text and commentary to those Regulations. Basically, the amended provisions apply to all claims on or after that date and to most decisions on ESA entitlement taken on or after that date (para. (1)). For a six month "period of grace", however, ending on July 28, 2013, those issued with questionnaires based on one or other of the pre-January 28 Schs to those Regulations will have their assessment governed by the relevant pre-January 28 Sch. (paras (2)-(4)).

The Social Security (Housing Costs Amendments) Regulations 2015

(SI 2015/1647)

9.616   *Made by the Secretary of State for Work and Pensions under ss.123(1)(a), 135(1), 137(1) and 175(1), (3) and (4) of the Social Security Contributions and Benefits Act 1992, ss.4(5), 35(1) and 36(2) and (4) of the Jobseekers Act 1995, ss.4(2)(a), 24(1) and 25(2), (3) and (5) of the Welfare Reform Act 2007 and ss.11(4) and (5)(b), 40, 42(1), (2) and (3) of, and para.1 of Sch.6 to, the Welfare Reform Act 2012.*

[In force April 1, 2016]

Saving provision

9.617   **8.**—(1) This regulation applies to a person ("P") where, for the purpose of determining whether P's entitlement to a relevant benefit includes an amount for housing costs, the Secretary of State determines that P is entitled or required to be treated as entitled to one or more relevant benefits for a continuous period which includes 31st March 2016.

(2) Where this regulation applies to P, the provisions of—

(a) Schedule 6 to the Employment and Support Allowance Regulations 2008;

(b) Schedule 3 to the Income Support (General) Regulations 1987; and

(c) Schedule 2 to the Jobseeker's Allowance Regulations 1996,

as modified by the Social Security (Housing Costs Special Arrangements) (Amendment and Modification) Regulations 2008 are to have effect in relation to P as if the amendments made by regulations 2 to 4 of these Regulations and the revocation made by regulation 7(1) had not been made.

(3) Where this regulation applies to P, the provisions of Schedule 5 to the Universal Credit Regulations 2013 are to have effect in relation to P as if

the amendments made by regulations 5 and 6 of these Regulations had not been made.

(4) In this regulation, "relevant benefit" means—

(a) an employment and support allowance under Part 1 of the Welfare Reform Act 2007;

(b) income support under the Income Support (General) Regulations 1987;

(c) a jobseeker's allowance under the Jobseeker's Allowance Regulations 1996; and

(d) universal credit under Part 1 of the Welfare Reform Act 2012.

GENERAL NOTE

See the notes to the Social Security (Housing Costs Special Arrangements) **9.618** (Amendment and Modification) Regulations 2008 above and to Sch. 6 to the ESA Regulations.

The Employment and Support Allowance and Universal Credit (Miscellaneous Amendments and Transitional and Savings Provisions) Regulations 2017

(SI 2017/204)

In Force April 3, 2017

The Secretary of State for Work and Pensions makes the following **9.619** Regulations in exercise of the powers conferred by sections 12(1), 17(4), 18(3), 19(2)(d), 25(a) and 42(3)(a) of the Welfare Reform Act 2012 and sections 15(4) and (5) and 34(1) of the Welfare Reform and Work Act 2016.

In accordance with section 173(5)(b) of the Social Security Administration Act 1992, this instrument contains only regulations made by virtue of, or consequential upon, sections 15, 16, 17 and 34 of the Welfare Reform and Work Act 2016 and is made before the end of the period of 6 months beginning with the coming into force of those sections.

In accordance with section 176(1) of the Social Security Administration Act 1992 the Secretary of State has consulted with organisations appearing to him to be representative of the authorities concerned.

GENERAL NOTE

Parts 1–3 of, and Sch.1 to, these Regulations, taken together with ss.15–17 of the **9.620** Welfare Reform and Work Act 2016, abolish the work-related activity component of ESA (and the LCW element of universal credit) with effect from April 3, 2017 and make a number of consequential amendments. However, for ESA, the abolition is subject to the transitional and savings provisions in Sch.2, Pt.1, to which effect is given by reg.2. Part 2 of the Schedule contains equivalent provisions for universal credit and is reproduced in Vol.V.

Under Pt.1 of Sch.2, claimants who are found to have—or are treated as having—limited capability for work, but not limited capability for work-related activity, continue to be entitled to the work-related activity component in the following circumstances:

- A claim for ESA is made before April 3, 2017 and that claim results in an award of ESA (para.2).

Paragraph 2 does not contain any conditions about when, or by whom, the award is made, so an award that does not include the support component made by the FTT or UT in (say) April 2018 on a claim made before April 3, 2017 will entitle the claimant to the work-related activity component. Nor is there any condition about the date from which the award of ESA must be effective. This leads to consequences that may not have been intended. For example, C claims ESA on March 31, 2017 at a time when she is a person subject to immigration control. However, she is granted indefinite leave to remain with effect from April 10, 2017 and, on April 17, 2017, the Secretary of State decides the claim and awards ESA, Para.2 appears to require that the award should include the work-related activity component because C "has made . . . a claim for ESA before 3rd April 2017 and that claim [has resulted] in an award of ESA" even though the award will be effective from April 10, 2017, a week after the work-related activity component was otherwise abolished.

- A claim for ESA is made after April 3, 2017, but the resulting period of limited capability for work is treated as having begun before that date under the linking rules in reg.145 of the ESA Regulations or reg.86 of the ESA Regulations 2013 (para.3), which provide that any such period which is separated from another by 12 weeks or less is to be treated as a continuation of the earlier period.

- A person with an "existing award" (i.e., of incapacity benefit, severe disablement allowance or income support on the basis of incapacity or disability: see WRA 2007, Sch.4, para.11) becomes a notified person under reg.4 of SI 2010/1907 (para.4). The consequence is that any claimant who is migrated from one of those benefits to ESA, but who is not awarded the support component, will be entitled to the work-related activity component.

- A claim for ESA is made after April 3, 2017 but is treated as covering a period before that date by virtue of reg.19 of the Claims and Payments Regulations or reg.28 of the Claims and Payments Regulations 2013, with the result that benefit becomes payable before April 3, 2017 (para.5).

- A claim for ESA is made after April 3, 2017 but the first day of the claimant's assessment phase began before 3rd April 2017 by virtue of reg.5 of the ESA Regulations or reg.6 of the ESA Regulations 2013 (para.6).

It is difficult to see what para.6 adds to para.3 (see the second bullet point above). A claimant's assessment phase can only begin sooner than the date of claim by virtue of reg.5 or reg.6 if the current period of limited capability for work is treated as a continuation of an earlier period under reg.145 of the ESA Regulations or reg.86 of the ESA Regulations 2013. In those circumstances, the work-related activity component continues in existence by virtue of para.3, so that para.6 appears to be otiose.

- A claimant who was entitled to ESA before April 3, 2017 becomes entitled to maternity allowance immediately after the award of ESA ends and then re-claims ESA within 12 weeks after entitlement to maternity allowance ends.

Citation and commencement

9.621   **1.** These Regulations may be cited as the Employment and Support Allowance and Universal Credit (Miscellaneous Amendments and Transitional and Savings Provisions) Regulations 2017 and come into force on 3rd April 2017.

PART 4

CONSEQUENTIAL, TRANSITIONAL AND SAVINGS PROVISIONS

Consequential, transitional and savings provisions

7.—(1)[Omitted]   9.622
(2) Schedule 2 contains transitional and savings provisions.

Regulation 7(2)

SCHEDULE 2

TRANSITIONAL AND SAVINGS PROVISIONS

PART 1

EMPLOYMENT AND SUPPORT ALLOWANCE: TRANSITIONAL AND SAVINGS PROVISIONS

Transitional and savings provisions: General

1.—(1) The amendments made by regulations 2 and 3, paragraphs 1 to 9   9.623
of Schedule 1 and by section 15(1) to (3) of the Welfare Reform and Work
Act 2016 (which amend sections 2 and 4 of the Welfare Reform Act 2007)
do not apply where any of the circumstances in paragraphs 2 to 7 apply.
(2) In this Part—
"assessment phase" has the same meaning as in the Welfare Reform Act
    2007;
[¹ "claim"] means [¹ . . .] a claim for an employment and support allow-
    ance [¹ made] in accordance with regulations 4ZC, 4G, 4H and 4I
    of the Social Security (Claims and Payments) Regulations 1987 or
    regulations 13 to 17 of the Universal Credit, Personal Independence
    Payment, Jobseeker's Allowance and Employment and Support
    Allowance (Claims and Payments) Regulations 2013;
"employment and support allowance" means an allowance under Part 1
    of the Welfare Reform Act 2007;
"ESA Regulations 2008" means the Employment and Support Allowance
    Regulations 2008;
"ESA Regulations 2013" means the Employment and Support Allowance
    Regulations 2013.

Claimants who have made a claim for employment and support allowance before 3rd April 2017

2. The first circumstance is where the claimant has made or is treated as   9.624
having made a claim for an employment and support allowance before 3rd
April 2017 and that claim results in an award of employment and support
allowance.

Claimants who had been found to have limited capability for work before 3rd April 2017

9.625   3. The second circumstance is where the claimant's period of limited capability for work began on or after 3rd April 2017 and is treated as a continuation of an earlier period of limited capability for work which began before 3rd April 2017 by virtue of—

(a) regulation 145 of the ESA Regulations 2008; or

(b) regulation 86 of the ESA Regulations 2013.

Claimants on Incapacity Benefits who have or will become notified persons

9.626   4. The third circumstance is where the claimant [¹ has been,] is or becomes a notified person within the meaning of regulation 4 of the Employment and Support Allowance (Transitional Provisions, Housing Benefit and Council Tax Benefit) (Existing Awards) (No. 2) Regulations 2010 and a determination is effective as to whether that person—

(a) has or is to be treated as having limited capability for work under Part 5 of the ESA Regulations 2008;

(b) has or is to be treated as having limited capability for work under Part 5 of the ESA Regulations 2013;

(c) has or is to be treated as having limited capability for work-related activity under Part 6 of the ESA Regulations 2008; or

(d) has or is to be treated as having limited capability for work-related activity under Part 6 of the ESA Regulations 2013.

Claimants where their award becomes payable before 3rd April 2017

9.627   5. The fourth circumstance is where the claimant becomes entitled to an employment and support allowance before 3rd April 2017 by virtue of—

(a) regulation 19(1) and paragraph 16 of Schedule 4 to the Social Security (Claims and Payments) Regulations 1987; or

(b) regulation 28 of the Universal Credit, Personal Independence Payment, Jobseeker's Allowance and Employment and Support Allowance (Claims and Payments) Regulations 2013.

Claimants where their assessment phase begins before 3rd April 2017

9.628   6. The fifth circumstance is where the first day of the claimant's assessment phase began before 3rd April 2017 by virtue of—

(a) regulation 5 of the ESA Regulations 2008; or

(b) regulation 6 of the ESA Regulations 2013.

Claimants where they have been entitled to maternity allowance

9.629   7. The sixth circumstance is where—

(a) a claimant was entitled to a maternity allowance under section 35 of the Social Security Contributions and Benefits Act 1992 and the end of that award is within 12 weeks beginning with the date that the claim for an employment and support allowance is made; and

(b) immediately prior to their entitlement to a maternity allowance beginning the claimant was previously entitled to an employment and support allowance before 3rd April 2017.

AMENDMENT

1. Employment and Support Allowance (Miscellaneous Amendments and Transitional and Savings Provision) Regulations 2017 (SI 2017/581) reg.9 (June 23, 2017).

The Employment and Support Allowance (Miscellaneous Amendments and Transitional and Savings Provision) Regulations 2017

(SI 2017/581)

In Force June 23, 2017

ARRANGEMENT OF REGULATIONS

1.   Citation and commencement   9.630
2-9.   *[Omitted]*
10.   Transitional and savings provision

The Secretary of State for Work and Pensions makes the following Regulations in exercise of the powers conferred by sections 15(4) and (5) and 34(1) of the Welfare Reform and Work Act 2016.

In accordance with section 173(5)(b) of the Social Security Administration Act 1992, this instrument contains only regulations made by virtue of, or consequential upon section 15 of the Welfare Reform and Work Act 2016 and is made before the end of the period of 6 months beginning with the coming into force of this section.

In accordance with section 176(1) of the Social Security Administration Act 1992 the Secretary of State has consulted with organisations appearing to him to be representative of the authorities concerned.

GENERAL NOTE

These Regulations make a number of technical amendments to clarify issues that **9.631** have arisen in relation to the abolition of the work-related activity component with effect from April 3, 2017 (see SI 2017/204 above). The amendments made by regs 2-9 have been incorporated in the appropriate places in the text. Reg.10 provides that—unsurprisingly—the amendments made by regs 2-8 do not apply to those who have transitional protection from the changes in SI 2017/204. Reg.9 has not been included in that transitional and savings provision because it makes technical amendments to the extent of that transitional protection given by SI 2017/204 Sch.2, Pt.1.

Citation and commencement

1. These Regulations may be cited as the Employment and Support **9.632** Allowance (Miscellaneous Amendments and Transitional and Savings Provision) Regulations 2017 and come into force on 23rd June 2017.

Transitional and savings provision

10. The amendments made by regulations 2 to 8 of these Regulations **9.633** do not apply where any of the circumstances in paragraph 2 to 7 of

Schedule 2 (transitional and savings provisions) to the Employment and Support Allowance and Universal Credit (Miscellaneous Amendments and Transitional and Savings Provisions) Regulations 2017, as amended by regulation 9 of these Regulations apply.

PART X

INDUSTRIAL INJURIES AND PRESCRIBED DISEASES

The Social Security (Claims and Payments) Regulations 1979

(SI 1979/628) (*as amended*)

ARRANGEMENT OF REGULATIONS

PART I

GENERAL

1.	Citation and commencement	10.1
2.	Interpretation	
3.–23.	*Revoked*	

PART IV

SPECIAL PROVISIONS RELATING TO INDUSTRIAL INJURIES BENEFIT ONLY

24.	Notice of accidents
25.	Obligations of employers
26.	Obligations of claimants for, and beneficiaries in receipt of, disablement benefit
27.–32.	*Revoked*

SCHEDULES

Schedule 4—Particulars to be given of accidents

The Secretary of State for Social Services, in exercise of powers conferred upon him by sections 45(3), 79 to 81, 88 to 90, 146(5) and 115(1) of, and Schedule 13 to, the Social Security Act 1975 and paragraphs 9(1)(a) and (c) of Schedule 13 to, the Social Security (Consequential Provisions) Act 1975 and of all other powers enabling him in that behalf, hereby makes the following regulations, which consolidate the regulations hereby revoked and which accordingly by virtue of sections 139(1) and 141(2) of the Social Security Act 1975—and paragraphs 20 of Schedule 15 and 12 of Schedule 16—are not subject to the requirements of section 139(1) and 141(2) of that Act for prior reference to the National Insurance Advisory Committee and the Industrial Injuries Advisory Council respectively:—

GENERAL

Citation and commencement

10.2   1. These regulations may be cited as the Social Security (Claims and Payments) Regulations 1979 and shall come into operation on 9th July 1979.

Interpretation

10.3   2.—(1) In these regulations, unless the context otherwise requires—
"the Act" means the Social Security Act 1975;
"approved place" means a place approved by the Secretary of State for the purpose of obtaining payment of benefit;
"benefit order" means an order for the payment of a weekly sum on account of benefit to which regulation 16 applies or of a weekly instalment of a gratuity;
"claim for benefit" includes an application for a declaration that an accident was an industrial accident and an application for the review of an award or a decision for the purpose of obtaining any increase of benefit mentioned in Schedule 1 to these regulations but does not include any other application for the review of an award or a decision and the expression "claim benefit" and every reference to a claim shall be construed accordingly;
[³ "health care professional" means—
(a) a registered medical practitioner,
(b) a registered nurse,
(c) an occupational therapist or physiotherapist registered with a regulatory body established by an Order in Council under section 60 of the Health Care Act 1999, or
(d) a member of such other profession, regulated by a body mentioned in section 25(3) of the National Health Service Reform and Health Care Professions Act 2002, prescribed by the Secretary of State in accordance with powers under section 39(1) of the Social Security Act 1998.]
[¹ . . .]
"instrument of payment" means a serial order, benefit order, or any other instrument whatsoever which is intended to enable a person to obtain payment of benefit;
"serial order" means one of a series of orders, including benefit orders, for the payment of a sum on account of benefit which is or has been contained in a book of such orders;
"unemployment benefit office" means any office or place appointed by the Secretary of State for the purpose of claiming unemployment benefit;
and other expressions have the same meaning as in the Act.
[²(1A) The provision in paragraph (1) for the interpretation of the words "claim for benefit" shall not be taken to preclude the application of the regulations to a claim for attendance allowance expressed as

an application for review of an earlier determination but which discloses
no grounds on which such a determination could be reviewed.]

(2) Unless the context otherwise requires, any reference in these regulations to—

   (a) a numbered section is a reference to the section of the Social Security
Act 1975 bearing that number;

   (b) a numbered regulation is a reference to the regulation bearing that
number in these regulations and any reference in a regulation to a
numbered paragraph is a reference to the paragraph of that regulation bearing that number;

   (c) any provision made by or contained in an enactment or instrument
shall be construed as a reference to that provision as amended or
extended by any enactment or instrument and as including a reference to any provision which it re-enacts or replaces, or which may
re-enact or replace it, with or without modification.

(3) For the purposes of the provisions of these regulations relating to the
making of claims every increase of benefit mentioned in Schedule 1 to these
regulations shall be treated as a separate benefit.

(4) The provisions of Schedule 1 and 2 to these regulations shall have
effect; and the following provisions of these regulations shall, in relation
to any particular benefit, have effect subject to any provisions in those
Schedules affecting that benefit.

AMENDMENTS

1. Social Security Act 1998 (Commencement No.8, and Savings and
Consequential and Transitional Provisions) Order 1999 (SI 1999/1958) Sch.4
para.1 (July 4, 1999)
2. Social Security (Attendance Allowance) Amendment Regulations 1980 (SI
1980/1136) reg.6(1) (August 25, 1980).
3. The Social Security (Miscellaneous Amendments) (No. 2) Regulations 2007,
(SI 2007/1626) (July 3, 2007).

GENERAL NOTE

Most of the rules relating to claims and payments can now be found in the Claims **10.4**
and Payments Regulations 1987. The only surviving part of these regulations relates
to specific aspects of claims and payments in industrial injuries cases.

Regulations 3–23 revoked. **10.5**

PART IV

SPECIAL PROVISIONS RELATING TO INDUSTRIAL INJURIES BENEFIT ONLY

Notice of accidents

24.—(1) Every employed earner who suffers personal injury by accident **10.6**
in respect of which benefit may be payable shall give notice of such accident
either in writing or orally as soon as is practicable after the happening thereof.

Provided that any such notice required to be given by an employed earner
may be given by some other person acting on his behalf.

(2) Every such notice shall be given to the employer, or (if there is more than one employer) to one of such employers, or to any foreman or other official under whose supervision the employed earner is employed at the time of the accident, or to any person designated for the purpose by the employer, and shall give the appropriate particulars.

(3) Any entry of the appropriate particulars of an accident made in a book kept for that purpose in accordance with the provisions of regulation 25 shall, if made as soon as practicable after the happening of an accident by the employed earner or by some other person acting on his behalf, be sufficient notice of the accident for the purposes of this regulation.

(4) In this regulation—

"employer" means, in relation to any person, the employer of that person at the time of the accident and "employers" shall be construed accordingly; and

"employed earner" means a person who is or is treated as an employed earner for the purposes of industrial injuries benefit.

(5) In this regulation and regulation 25, "appropriate particulars" mean the particulars indicated in Schedule 4 to these regulations.

Obligations of employers

10.7   25.—(1) Every employer shall take reasonable steps to investigate the circumstances of every accident of which notice is given to him or to his servant or agent in accordance with the provisions of regulation 24 and, if there appear to him to be any discrepancies between the circumstances found by him as a result of his investigation and the circumstances appearing from the notice so given, he shall record the circumstances so found.

(2) Every employer who is required to do so by the Secretary of State shall furnish to an officer of the Department within such reasonable period as may be required, such information and particulars as shall be required—

    (a) of any accident or alleged accident in respect of which benefit may be payable to, or in respect of the death of, a person employed by him at the time of the accident or alleged accident; or

    (b) of the nature of and other relevant circumstances relating to any occupation prescribed for the purposes of Chapter V of Part II of the Act in which any person to whom or in respect of whose death benefit may be payable under that Chapter was or is alleged to have been employed by him.

(3) Every owner or occupier (being an employer) of any mine or quarry or of any premises to which any of the provisions of the Factories Act 1961 applies and every employer by whom 10 or more persons are normally employed at the same time on or about the same premises in connection with a trade or business carried on by the employer shall, subject to the following provisions of this paragraph—

    (a) [¹ keep readily accessible a means (whether in a book or books or by electronic means), in a form approved by the Secretary of State, by which a person employed by the employer or some other person acting on his behalf may record the appropriate particulars (as defined in regulation 24) of any accident causing personal injury to that person; and

(b) preserve every such record for the period of at least 3 years from the date of its entry.]

AMENDMENT

1. Social Security (Claims and Payments) Amendment (No. 3) Regulations 1993 (SI 1993/2113) reg.2 (September 27, 1993)

Obligations of claimants for, and beneficiaries in receipt of [¹. . .] disablement benefit

26.—(1) Subject to the following provisions of this regulation, every claimant for, and every beneficiary in receipt of [¹. . .] disablement benefit shall comply with every notice given to him by the Secretary of State which requires him either—

    (a) to submit himself to a medical examination by a medical [²[⁴ health care professional approved by the Secretary of State] who has experience in the issues specified in regulation 12(1) of the Social Security and Child Support (Decisions and Appeals) Regulations 1999] for the purpose of determining the effects of the relevant accident or the treatment appropriate to the relevant injury or loss of faculty; or

    (b) to submit himself to such medical treatment for the said injury or loss of faculty as is considered appropriate in his case by the medical practitioner in charge of the case [². . .]

(2) Every notice given to a claimant or beneficiary requiring him to submit himself to medical examination shall be given in writing and shall specify the time and place for examination and shall not require the claimant or beneficiary to submit himself [² to examination before the expiration of the period of 6 days beginning with the date of the notice or such shorter period as may be reasonable in the circumstances]

(3) Every claimant and every beneficiary who, in accordance with the foregoing provisions of this regulation, is required to submit himself to a medical examination or to medical treatment—

    (a) shall attend at every such place and at every such time as may be required; and

    (b) may, in the discretion of the Secretary of State, be paid such travelling and other allowances (including compensation for loss of remunerative time) as the Secretary of State may with the consent of the Minister for the Civil Service determine.

(4) [³. . .]

10.8

AMENDMENTS

1. Social Security (Abolition of Injury Benefit) (Consequential) Regulations 1983 (SI 1983/186) reg.11 (April 6, 1983).

2. Social Security Act 1998 (Commencement No.8, and Savings and Consequential and Transitional Provisions) Order 1999 (SI 1999/1958) Sch.4 para.2 (July 4, 1999).

3. Social Security Act 1998 (Commencement No.8, and Savings and Consequential and Transitional Provisions) Order 1999 (SI 1999/1958) Sch.4 para.2(c) (July 4, 1999).

4. The Social Security (Miscellaneous Amendments) (No. 2) Regulations 2007, (SI 2007/1626) (July 3, 2007)

10.9   *Regulations 27–30 revoked.*

10.10   *Regulation 31 omitted*

10.11   *Regulation 32 revoked*

10.12   *Schedules 1–3 revoked.*

SCHEDULE 4   **Regulations 24 and 25**

PARTICULARS TO BE GIVEN OF ACCIDENTS

10.13   (1) Full name, address and occupation of injured person;
(2) Date and time of accident;
(3) Place where accident happened;
(4) Cause and nature of injury;
(5) Name, address and occupation of person giving the notice, if other than the injured person.

10.14   *Schedule 5 revoked.*

The Social Security (General Benefit) Regulations 1982

(SI 1982/1408) (*as amended*)

ARRANGEMENT OF REGULATIONS

PART II

PROVISIONS RELATING TO BENEFIT OTHER THAN INDUSTRIAL INJURIES BENEFIT

10.15   9.   *Omitted.*
           10.   Disqualifications to be disregarded for certain purposes.

PART III

PROVISIONS RELATING TO INDUSTRIAL INJURIES BENEFIT ONLY

Principles of assessment

           11.   Further definition of the principles of assessment of disablement and prescribed degrees of disablement.

Disablement benefit

           14.   Amount of disablement gratuities.
           15.   Weekly value of gratuity for purposes of reduction of increase of disablement benefit during hospital treatment.

16. Earnings level for the purposes of unemployability supplement under section 58 of the Act.

Increase of disablement benefit

17. Circumstances in which, for the purposes of section 60, a beneficiary may be treated as being incapable of following an occupation or employment notwithstanding that he has worked thereat.
18. Payments in respect of special hardship where beneficiary is entitled to a gratuity.
19. Increase of disablement pension for constant attendance.
20. Determination of degree of disablement for constant attendance allowance.
21. Condition for receipt of increase of disablement pension for constant attendance under section 61 while receiving medical treatment as an inpatient.
22. Treatment of distinct periods of hospital in-patient treatment as continuous for the purposes of section 62 of the Act.

Industrial death benefit

Regulations 23–37 omitted.

Adjustment of benefit for successive accidents

38. Adjustment of benefit for successive accidents where a disablement gratuity is payable.
39. Adjustment of increase of benefit in respect of successive accidents.

Disqualification for receipt of benefit, suspension of proceedings on claims and suspension of benefit

40. Disqualification for receipt of benefit, suspension of proceedings on claims and suspension of payment of benefit.

Payments under the act to certain persons who contracted diseases or who were injured before 5 July 1948

Regulations 42–45 omitted.

Regulation 46 revoked.

PART IV

47. Revocation and transitional provisions.

SCHEDULES

Schedule 1—Provisions for the purpose of which disqualifications under the Act are to be disregarded.
Schedule 2—Prescribed degrees of disablement.
Schedule 3—Scale of disablement gratuities.

Schedule 4—Rate of disablement pension payable in lieu of disablement gratuity in accordance with regulation 18.

Schedules 5–9 Omitted.

SCHEDULES

Schedule 2—Prescribed degrees of disablement.

The Secretary of State for Social Services, in exercise of the powers conferred upon him by sections 50(4), 56(7), 57(5), 58(3), 60(4) and (7), 61(1), 62(2), 67(1), 68(2), 70(2), 72(1) and (8), 74(1), 81(6), 82(5) and (6), 83(1), 85(1), 86(2) and (5), 90(2), 91(1), 119(3) and (4) and 159(3) of and paragraphs 2, 3 and 6 of Schedule 8, paragraphs 1 and 8 of Schedule 9 and Schedule 14 of the Social Security Act 1975 and all other powers enabling him in the behalf, hereby makes the following regulations, which only consolidate the regulations hereby revoked, and which accordingly, by virtue of paragraph 20 of Schedule 3 to the Social Security Act 1980, are not subject to the requirements of section 10 of that Act for prior references to the Social Security Advisory Committee and by virtue of section 141(2) and paragraph 12 of the Schedule 16 of the Social Security Act 1975, do not require prior reference to the Industrial Injuries Advisory Council.

PART I

GENERAL

10.16   *For regs 1-4 see Vol.III: Administration, Appeals and the European Dimension.*

PART II

PROVISIONS RELATING TO BENEFIT OTHER THAN INDUSTRIAL INJURIES BENEFIT

Payment of benefit and suspension of payments pending a decision on appeals or references, arrears and repayments

10.17   **9.** *Omitted.*

Disqualifications to be disregarded for certain purposes

10.18   **10.**—(1) Subject to paragraph (2), where a person of any class mentioned in column (1) of Schedule 1 to these regulations would be entitled to the benefit set opposite that class in column (2) of that Schedule but for the operation of any provision of the Act disqualifying him for the receipt of that benefit, that person shall be treated as if entitled to that benefit for the purpose of the provisions of the Act set opposite thereto in column (3) of the said Schedule and of any regulations made thereunder. (2) For the purposes of determining whether the condition contained in section 79(1) of the Act (which makes a claim a condition of any person's right to any benefit) is satisfied, a person who would be entitled to any benefit but for the operation of any provision of the Act disqualifying him for the receipt of it, and who ceases to be so disqualified within a period of 3 months from the commencement of the disqualification, shall be treated as if entitled to it.

PART III

PROVISIONS RELATING TO INDUSTRIAL INJURIES BENEFIT ONLY

Principles of assessment

Further definition of the principles of assessment of disablement and prescribed degrees of disablement

11.—(1) Schedule [6] to the [SSCBA 1992] (general principles relating to the assessment of the extent of disablement) shall have effect subject to the provisions of this regulation.

(2) When the extent of disablement is being assessed for the purposes of section [103], any disabilities which, though resulting from the relevant loss of faculty, also result, or without the relevant accident might have been expected to result, from a cause other than the relevant accident (hereafter in this regulation referred to as "the other effective cause") shall only be taken into account subject to and in accordance with the following provisions of this regulation.

(3) [¹ Subject to paragraphs (5A) and (5B)] an assessment of the extent of disablement made by reference to any disability to which paragraph (2) applies, in a case where the other effective cause is a congenital defect or is an injury or disease received or contracted before the relevant accident, shall take account of all such disablement except to the extent to which the claimant would have been subject thereto during the period taken into account by the assessment if the relevant accident had not occurred.

(4) [¹ Subject to paragraphs (5A) and (5B)] any assessment of the extent of disablement made by reference to any disability to which paragraph (2) applies, in a case where the other effective cause is an injury or disease received or contracted after and not directly attributable to the relevant accident, shall take account of all such disablement to the extent to which the claimant would have been subject thereto during the period taken into account by the assessment if that other effective cause had not arisen and where, in any such case, the extent of a disablement would be assessed at not less than 11 per cent. if that other effective cause had not arisen, the assessment shall also take account of any disablement to which the claimant may be subject as a result of that other effective cause except to the extent to which he would have been subject thereto if the relevant accident had not occurred.

(5) [¹ Subject to paragraphs (5A) and (5B)] any disablement to the extent to which the claimant is subject thereto as a result both of an accident and a disease or two or more accidents or diseases (as the case may be), being accidents arising out and in the course of, or diseases due to the nature of, employed earners' employment, shall only be taken into account in assessing the extent of disablement resulting from one such accident or disease being the one which occurred or developed last in point of time.

[¹ (5A) Where—
(a) a person has an award of industrial injuries disablement benefit in respect of the disease specified in paragraph D1 of Part I of Schedule 1 to the Social Security (Industrial Injuries) (Prescribed

Diseases) Regulations 1985 (in this paragraph and in paragraph (5B) referred to as "disease D1"); and

(b) by virtue of either paragraph (3) or (4) that award takes account of disablement resulting from the effects of chronic bronchitis or emphysema, not being chronic bronchitis or emphysema prescribed in paragraph D12 of Part I of Schedule 1 to the Social Security (Industrial Injuries) (Prescribed Diseases) Regulations 1985 (in this paragraph and paragraph (5B) referred to as "disease D12"); and

(c) after the date on which the award referred to in sub-paragraph (a) of this paragraph was made the person becomes entitled to industrial injuries disablement benefit in respect of disease D12,

then, during any period when such disablement benefit is payable in respect of disease D12, paragraphs (3), (4) and (5) shall not apply to the assessment in respect of disease D1 for the purpose of assessing the extent of disablement resulting from disease D12.

(5B) Where—

(a) a person has an award of industrial injuries disablement benefit in respect of the disease D12; and

(b) by virtue of either paragraph (3) or (4) that award takes account of disablement resulting from the effects of pneumoconiosis, not being disease D1; and

(c) after the date on which the award referred to in sub-paragraph (a) of this paragraph was made the person becomes entitled to industrial injuries disablement benefit in respect of disease D1,

then, during any period when such disablement benefit is payable in respect of disease D1, paragraphs (3), (4) and (5) shall not apply to the assessment in respect of disease D12 for the purpose of assessing the extent of disablement resulting from disease D1.]

(6) Where the sole injury which a claimant suffers as a result of the relevant accident is one specified in column 1 of Schedule 2 to these regulations, whether or not such injury incorporates one or more other injuries so specified, the loss of faculty suffered by the claimant as a result of that injury shall be treated for the purposes of section [103] of, and Schedule [6] to, the Act as resulting in the degree of disablement set against injury in column 2 of the said Schedule 2 subject to such increase or reduction of that degree of disablement as may be reasonable in the circumstances of the case where, having regard to the provisions of the said Schedule [6] to the Act and to the foregoing paragraphs of this regulation, that degree of disablement does not provide a reasonable assessment of the extent of disablement resulting from the relevant loss of faculty.

(7) For the purposes of paragraph (6) where the relevant injury is one so specified in the said column 1 against which there is set in the said column 2 the degree of disablement of 100 per cent. and the claimant suffers some disablement to which he would have been subject whether or not the relevant accident had occurred, no reduction of that degree of disablement shall be required if [² the Secretary of State or, as the case may be,] [³ the First-tier Tribunal] is satisfied that, in the circumstances of the case, 100 per cent is a reasonable assessment of the extent of disablement from the relevant loss of faculty.

(8) For the purposes of assessing, in accordance with the provisions of Schedule [6] to the [SSCBA 1992], the extent of disablement resulting from

the relevant injury in any case which does not fall to be determined under paragraph (6) or (7), [² the Secretary of State or, as the case may be,] [³ the First-tier Tribunal] may have such regard as may be appropriate to the prescribed degrees of disablement set against the injuries specified in the said Schedule 2.

AMENDMENTS

1. Social Security (Industrial Injuries) (Prescribed Diseases) Amendment (No. 2) Regulations 1993 (SI 1993/1985) reg.7 (September 13, 1993).
2. Social Security Act 1998 (Commencment No.8, and Savings and Consequential and Transitional Provisions) Order 1999 (SI 1999/1958) (July 5, 1999).
3. Tribunals, Courts and Enforcement Act 2007 (Transitional and Consequential Provisions) Order 2008 (SI 2008/2683) art.6(1) and Sch.1 para.25 (November 3, 2008).

GENERAL NOTE

This regulation provides for the assessment of the extent of disablement in cases where a disability is due both to the relevant accident and another cause; and it also introduces Sch.2 to the Regs which sets out the prescribed degrees of disablement. S.57 of, and Sch.8 to, the SSA 1975 have been replaced by s.103 of, and Sch.6 to the SSCBA 1992. The purpose of reg.11 was explained in these terms by Judge Parker in *AR v SSWP (II)* [2016] UKUT 111 (AAC):   **10.20**

"10. The provisions of regulation 11 of the general benefit regulations (regulation 11) set out the formula for assessing disablement where there is more than one cause of it; except for regulation 11(5), it is concerned with other causes which are not industrial ones. (Schedule 2 to the prescribed diseases regulations modifies regulation 11 so that it always covers prescribed diseases as well as accidents as appropriate.). The objective is an assessment based solely on that disablement to which any relevant accident or prescribed disease has subjected a claimant, to prevent double-counting; but also to ensure that a claimant is compensated for any greater disablement due to the interaction of the effects of two accidents or diseases i.e. where a claimant's total disablement is more than a simple sum of the two separate disablements considered individually: for example, the loss of vision of one eye is 30% but total loss of sight is 100%."

For an illustration of the operation of these rules and a framework of questions for approaching these matters, see the decision of Commissioner Williams in *CI/2930/2005*, noted in the commentary to SSCBA 1992 s.103 (disablement pension).

For an illustration of the complexities of applying the "multiple effective cause" provisions of this reg., see *CI/3745/2006*. The Schedule to the decision also contains useful evidence from the medical adviser to the DWP (Dr Reed) on PD A8 (tenosynovitis) and PD A12 (carpal tunnel syndrome).

For consideration of the current form BI 118A and the need to consider the connection factor arising out of two injuries both due to the same relevant accident, something not considered in *R(I)1/95*, see *CI/3384/2006*.

In *KW v SSWP (II)* [2012] UKUT 181 (AAC), Judge Parker considered the case of a claimant appealing an assessment in relation to PD A14 where assessment decisions had earlier been made with respect to other industrial accidents. Judge Parker rightly regarded proper identification of the date of onset of the disease under appeal, as being as critical to establish the correct chronology for purposes of applying reg.11. She noted, applying Prescribed Diseases Regs, reg.6(2)(b) and *CI/6027/1999*, that the date of onset is that date the claimant first suffered from the loss of faculty after July 4, 1948, that is, when the disease reached the extent necessary to fit the statutory prescription and that, applying *R(I) 4/96*, that could be before the claimant had worked the 10 years necessary to satisfy the prescribed occupation. That would in the claimant's case be when osteoarthritis of the knee first existed as a matter of fact in his case, something that was not an easy issue to resolve. But how reg.11 applied would depend on whether that date of onset preceded or came after the other industrial accidents. Judge Parker noted that use

"of regulation 11(4) almost certainly falls out of the analysis, except in the very rare instance when a later effective non-industrial cause of disability, which also results from an earlier relevant accident or disease, actually arises after the 'accident or disease being the one which occurred or developed last in point of time.' Where, as here, there is a string of industrial accidents and diseases under consideration for a new exercise of assessment and aggregation, only regulation 11(3) and (5) will usually be applicable" (para.25).

See further on para.(1) *AR v SSWP (II)* [2016] UKUT 111 (AAC).

Paragraph (2)

10.21   Adjudicating medical authorities used to distinguish between conditions that were regarded as "partly relevant" ("O pre" or "O post") and those that were regarded as merely "connected" ("C"). The former were those conditions considered to have more than one cause and the latter were those conditions considered to be quite separate from the one arising from the relevant accident but which were nonetheless thought to have some effect on the disability arising from the condition caused by the relevant accident. That approach (and Form BI 113 Accident) which reflected it has been criticised in *R(I) 4/94* and *R(I) 1/95*. Any contributory factor is either to be included in the relevant loss of faculty or else is an "other effective cause" within para.(2), in which case it is taken into account under paras (3), (4) or (5).

Paragraph (3)

10.22   This makes provision for a case where the "other effective cause" is either a congenital defect or is an injury or disease received or contracted *before* the relevant accident. In *R(I) 13/75*, the Commissioner said:

"In the context of regulation [11(3)] I do not think that 'congenital' should receive its primary meaning, which is 'begotten' or 'born with'; see Shorter Oxford English Dictionary. In my view, the word is used in this regulation in a rather wider sense. I think that it must be taken to mean 'inherent' or 'constitutional,' this is to say that it refers to a defect which is a natural constituent of the person's make-up whether physical or mental. Since Dr. Wright [a principal medical officer of the Department of Health and Social Security] stated that a functional overlay is 'a manifestation of constitutional mental make-up,' I cannot hold that it is not covered by the phrase 'congenital defect' in regulation [11(3)]."

Disablement due to the "other effective cause" must be taken into account except to the extent to which the claimant would have been disabled if the relevant accident had not occurred. Usually this is done by making an assessment of the full extent of disablement resulting from the condition and then applying an "offset" in respect of disablement which would have been present even if the relevant accident had not occurred (*CI/2746/2002*, para.5). There should be no offset in respect of a mere *predisposition* to hysteria (*R(I) 2/74*), functional overlay (*R(I) 13/75*), detachment of retina (*R(I) 3/76*) or development of multiple sclerosis (*R(I) 1/81*). In *R(I) 1/81*, it was held that

"constitutional liability to develop the disease cannot have been a 'disability' because it was wholly symptomless. Such liability corresponds with the statutory concept of 'loss of faculty,' that is to say it is a potential cause of disability but not itself a disability."

The Commissioner emphasised that the assessment was an assessment of disablement and not an assessment of loss of faculty. However, it does not follow that there can never be an offset in respect of a condition which was symptomless before the relevant accident. An adjudicating authority might legitimately apply an offset if a pre-existing, and previously symptomless, condition could have been expected to produced disability at some time even if the accident had not occurred. Nevertheless, such reasoning must be clear, and a tribunal which fails to record good reasons for applying an offset in a case where a claimant has asserted that he or she had no symptoms before the relevant accident is liable to find its decision set aside on appeal (*CI/34/93*). On the other hand, there are some conditions, such as arthritis, from which many older people suffer. That is not a ground for an offset. Rather, it is a ground for not including the effects of the arthritis, to the extent to which other people of the same age would suffer from them, in the assessment of total disability at all. That is because that assessment should be made by comparing the claimant "with a person of the same age and sex whose physical and mental condition is normal" (SSCBA 1992 Sch.6, para.1(a)). There is no reason why an adjudicating authority should not make an assessment which is tapered to take account of the fact that the claimant would have become increasingly disabled even if the accident had not occurred. Whether that is done by increasing an offset over the period of assessment or by simply reducing the total assessment of disablement depends on whether or not the increasing disability is something from which the "normal" person would suffer. In a case where the assessment of total disablement is 100 per cent, see para.(7).

Where the "other effective cause" is a different type of condition or an injury   **10.23** to a different part of the body, it is conventional to talk of a "connection factor" which is expressed as an increase of the disablement resulting from the relevant accident. Like an "offset", a "connection factor" is not a statutory concept, but both concepts are useful ways of explaining decisions. Use of the concepts enables a claimant to be told the proportion of his or her total disablement that is attributable to the relevant accident (*R(I) 2/74, R(I) 1/95*). A claimant ought to know the assessment of the total disablement to which he or she is thought to be subject, as well as the assessment of the disablement attributed to the relevant accident. In *R(I) 1/95*, it was observed that

> "[a]n inability to lift moderate weights with one hand may not be particularly significant when the claimant can use the other hand instead, but it is obviously a substantial handicap if the claimant has only the one hand and cannot be provided with a functional artificial limb".

The "connection factor" represented that additional degree of disablement from which the claimant would not have suffered but for the relevant accident, over and above the degree of disablement suffered by a person who had a fully functional second hand. The same result is reached if the claimant's total disablement is assessed and there is an "offset" in respect of the disablement from which he would have suffered had the relevant accident not occurred. Ideally, both the "connection factor" and the "offset" should be assessed so that it is quite clear that reg.11(3) has been applied correctly (*R(I) 1/95*). In *R(I) 23/61*, the claimant had a pre-existing disability arising from a defective forefinger and then lost a thumb in the relevant accident. The Commissioner said that:

> "where the medical authorities are dealing with an injury to a hand, the possibility of a connection factor is so obvious, or at any rate will seem so obvious to the claimant, that it is essential that they should satisfy themselves specifically whether or not there is any other defect in the hand which might bring the case within regulation [11(3)] and should give a clear decision on it one way or the other."

In *Murrell v Secretary of State for Social Services* (reported as an appendix to *R(I) 3/84*), a blind man who suffered an injury to his elbow, which resulted in a loss of sensation in his hand rendering him unable to read braille, had the 15 per cent assessment in respect of the elbow injury increased by a further 15 per cent to take account of the extra disability arising from that injury because of his pre-existing blindness. The Court of Appeal thought that the increase was rather on the low side.

The fact that the claimant is entitled to a disablement pension under the war pensions scheme in respect of the previous injury is not a ground for reducing the assessment in respect of the later one (*R(I) 1/79*).

Paragraph (4)

10.24   This applies where the "other effective cause" arises *after* the relevant accident. The paragraph is in two parts. First, account must be taken of all disablement "to the extent to which the claimant would have been subject thereto . . . if *that other effective cause* had not arisen". Thus, a claimant who has lost his right forefinger in an industrial accident and then loses his right hand in a non-industrial accident continues to be entitled to an assessment based on the loss of the forefinger, not-withstanding that he or she would have lost it in the second accident even if the first had not occurred. Secondly, effect is given to the "connection factor", but only in a case where the disablement from which the claimant would have suffered would have been at least 11 per cent without the "other effective cause" arising. In such a case, account must be taken of all disablement to which the claimant is subject "*except* to the extent to which he would have been subject thereto if *the relevant accident* had not occurred". In the example given above concerning the loss of a forefinger followed by the loss of the rest of the hand, no increase would be awarded under the second part of the paragraph because the claimant would have been just as disabled after the second accident even if the first had never occurred. However, an assessment may be increased where a subsequent injury results in greater dis-ablement than it normally would because of the effects of the relevant accident. In *R. v Medical Appeal Tribunal Ex p. Cable* (reported as an appendix to *R(I) 11/66* and decided under earlier legislation), a man who had lost the sight of one eye in an industrial accident was held by the Court of Appeal to be entitled to the benefit of the "connection factor" when he lost the sight of the other as the result of a non-in-dustrial disease. If the assessment of total disablement is 100 per cent, adjudicating medical authorities must bear in mind paras (7) and (8) when considering the "con-nection factor" under this para.

Paragraph (5)

10.25   Where a person suffers disablement as a result of two or more industrial accidents or prescribed diseases, it may be appropriate simply for the adjudication officer to aggregate the resulting disablements under s.103(2) of the SSCBA 1992 (if all the causes were accidents) or reg.15A of the Prescribed Diseases Regs 1985. However, the total disablement resulting from the two accidents may be greater than the aggregate of the individual disablements; the loss of two eyes is more than twice as disabling as the loss of one eye. Effect must be given to that "connection factor" in assessing the extent of disablement resulting from the latest accident or disease for which it is relevant (*R(I) 3/91*). See further on para.(5) *AR v SSWP (II)* [2016] UKUT 111 (AAC).

Paragraph (6)

10.26   This introduces Sch.2 which sets out the prescribed degrees of disablement. The degree of disablement may be increased or reduced "as may be reasonable in the circumstances of the case" if the prescribed degree of disablement "does not provide a reasonable assessment of the extent of disablement". Thus a right-handed person who loses his or her right hand might be assessed as more disabled than a left-handed person would be, at least at the beginning of the period of assessment. It would also seem appropriate to make a higher assessment in a case where a person has had a limb amputated and has not yet been fitted with an arti-ficial limb. The disabling effect of any unusual amount of pain must also be taken into account, a statement approved by Commissioner Williams in *CI/2553/2001*, para.17.

In *R(I) 4/04*, Commissioner Jacobs considered entries 26–28 dealing with amputations in lower limbs and, in particular, the need for a tribunal to specify where the measurement of the stump began and ended. What is assessed is the loss of function consequent upon anatomical loss, rather than the latter itself. The legislation does not specify the start and end points for measurement, but the length of the stump must be related to the likely disablement that will result. Given the possibility of fitting a prosthesis, the length of the stump is likely to relate to the effectiveness of that prosthesis. He concluded that

"In a perfect world, the precise measurement would not matter. The tribunal would take account of the Scheduled assessments as a whole. It would realise that the length of the stump would affect the effectiveness of the prosthesis, which would affect the claimant's disablement. It would take account of the Scheduled assessment only as a starting point. It would adjust this as authorised by regulation 11(6). This process of adjustment, with a focus on disablement, would counteract any variation between adjudicating authorities on the precise way in which the measurement was taken.

But life, in my experience, is not always perfect. This analysis presupposes an impossible degree of precision on a matter that is imprecise and impressionistic. In practice, tribunals begin their assessment of disablement with the Scheduled assessment, if there is one. That is the proper approach under regulation 11(6). Despite the infinite flexibility that regulation 11(6) allows in theory, the reality is that the starting point of the Scheduled assessment will affect the outcome.

Disablement depends on the effectiveness of the prosthesis. That depends on the length of bone rather than soft tissue. So, it is obvious that it is only the supporting bone that should be measured. The key bone is the tibia, not the fibula. As the tibia is the inner of the two bones in the lower limb, the measurement should be made on the inner surface of the remaining stump, not the outer. So far, the Secretary of State's guidance does no more than put those conclusions into medical language. All that remains is the position of the leg when the measurement is taken. The Secretary of State recommends that the knee be flexed, which obviously is the best way to obtain the precise measurement required. In conclusion, therefore, the Secretary of State's guidance agrees with the measurement that can be deduced by normal interpretive principles from the legislation" (paras 23–25).

Paragraph (7)
In a case where the assessment of total disablement is 100 per cent, "not because that in fact is the proper figure, but because the law permits no greater figure" a smaller offset or even no offset at all in respect of a pre-existing injury might be reasonable (*R(I) 34/61*). That reflects the fact that an assessment of 100 per cent does not imply total disability.

10.27

Paragraph (8)
In a case where there is no prescribed degree of disablement, the adjudicating authority "may have such regard as may be appropriate" to the Schedule (see *R(I) 1/04* and *R(I) 5/95*). This is necessary in the interests of consistency and fairness as between claimants. Both the unified tribunal and the Commissioners now have jurisdiction over medical and non-medical matters. A Commissioner, allowing an appeal on a point of law, can now take his or her own decision on the facts rather than remitting it to another tribunal. Commissioner Williams did so in *CI/1307/1999* giving a staged assessment of disablement in respect of post-traumatic stress disorder. The decision considers the medical aspects of the claimant's case found to be an industrial accident in *CI/15589/1996*, noted in the annotation to "accident" to SSCBA 1992, s.94. In paras 15–17, Commissioner Williams distinguished "diagnosis" and "disablement" decisions. The former is essentially "a ques-

10.28

tion of medical expertise". A "disablement" decision in contrast is not dissimilar to the tasks performed by judges in assessing common law damages or in applying the tariff of the Criminal Injuries Compensation Authority. In assessing disablement for industrial injuries benefits, however, that Criminal Injuries tariff is not an appropriate yardstick. Instead, supplementing SSCBA 1992 s.103 and Sch.6, regard should be had also to this regulation and Sch.2 to these Regulations. Nonetheless, the import of para. 37 of the decision is that exercise of the Commissioner's power to decide on the facts, rather than remitting to another tribunal, may well be rare. Even so, the decision contrasts markedly with the traditional view of such matters as ones for medical rather than legal judgment (see, for example, Commissioner Howell in *CI/636/93*). That assessment of disablement is ultimately a matter of judgment for the tribunal which hears and sees the evidence was stressed by a Tribunal of Commissioners in *R(I)2/06*. That decision also elaborates on the nature of an error of law, and on the difference between that and a disputed judgment of degree on a question of fact. It also proffers guidance on reference to Sch.2 in non-prescribed cases, on consideration of the judicial guidelines on the assessment of damages in civil personal injury cases, on cross-reference to other schemes such as that for criminal injuries, and on the status of official departmental guidance such as the Medical Assessment Framework (MAF). See further the annotation to SSCBA 1992 Sch.6.

[¹. . .] Disablement benefit

10.29   *Regulations 12 and 13 revoked by SI 1983/186 reg.13 (April 6, 1983)*

Amount of disablement gratuities

10.30   **14.**—(1) Where the extent of a claimant's disablement is assessed at any of the degrees of disablement severally specified in column 1 of Schedule 3 to these regulations, the amount of any disablement gratuity payable shall—

>   (a) if the period taken into account by that assessment is limited by reference to the claimant's life or is not less than 7 years, be the amount calculated as the percentage of the maximum disablement gratuity (specified in paragraph 2 of Part V of Schedule 4 to the Act) which is shown in column 2 of Schedule 3 to these regulations as being appropriate to that degree of disablement;

>   (b) in any other case, be the amount calculated as such a percentage of the maximum disablement gratuity as bears the same proportion to the percentage shown in column 2 of Schedule 3 to these regulations as being appropriate to that degree of disablement as the period taken into account by the assessment bears to a period of 7 years, a fraction of 5 pence being, for this purpose, treated as 5 pence.

[¹ (1A) Paragraph (1) applies in relation to cases where the claim for benefit was made before 1st October 1986.]

(2) For the purposes of this regulation, whenever such maximum disablement gratuity is altered by virtue of the passing of an Act or the making of an up-rating order, corresponding variations in the scale of gratuities payable under this regulation shall be payable only where the period taken into account by the assessment of the extent of disablement in respect of which the gratuity is awarded begins on or after the date of coming into operation of the provision altering the amount of the maximum disablement gratuity.

AMENDMENT

1. Social Security (Industrial Injuries and Diseases) Miscellaneous Provisions Regulations 1986 (SI 1986/1561) reg.7 (October 1, 1986).

Weekly value of gratuity for purposes of reduction of increase of disablement benefit during hospital treatment

15. For the purpose of reducing the weekly rate of disablement pension   10.31
payable by virtue of section 62 to a person awarded a disablement gratuity wholly or partly in respect of the same period, the weekly value of the gratuity shall be the weekly rate of disablement pension which would be payable to that person in lieu thereof in accordance with regulation 18(2) if that regulation applied to his case.

Earnings level for the purpose of unemployability supplement under section 58 of the Act

[¹**16.**—(1) For the purposes of section 58(3) (earnings level that does   10.32
not disqualify for unemployability supplement) the prescribed amount of earnings in a year is determined as follows–
(a) multiply the National Minimum Wage by 16;
(b) where the amount determined by the calculation in sub-paragraph
   (a) would, but for this sub-paragraph, include an amount of—
     (i) less than 50p, the amount determined under sub-paragraph (a)
        shall be rounded up to the nearest 50p, or
     (ii) less than £1 but more than 50p, the amount determined under
        sub-paragraph (a) shall be rounded up to the nearest £1; and
(c) multiply the amount resulting from sub-paragraph (a) or (b) by 52.
(2) In this regulation "National Minimum Wage" means the rate of the national minimum wage specified in regulation 11 of the National Minimum Wage Regulations 1999 (rate of the national minimum wage).]

AMENDMENT

1. Social Security (Miscellaneous Amendments) Regulations 2011 (SI 2011/674) reg.2 (April 11, 2011).

Increase of [¹. . .] Disablement Benefit

Circumstances in which, for the purposes of section 59A, a beneficiary may be treated as being incapable of following an occupation or employment notwithstanding that he has worked thereat

17.—(1) For the purposes of [² section 59A (reduced earnings allow-   10.33
ance)], when it is being determined whether a beneficiary has at all times since the end of [² the period of 90 days referred to in section 57(4) been incapable of following his regular occupation or employment of an equivalent standard which is suitable in his case, and in determining that question only, the fact that since the end of that period of 90 days] such beneficiary had worked at that occupation or any such employment (as the case may be)—
(a) for the purpose of rehabilitation or training or of ascertaining
   whether he had recovered from the effects of the relevant injury;
   or

(b) before obtaining surgical treatment for the effects of the said injury;
shall be disregarded in respect of the periods specified in the next following paragraph.

(2) The periods during which the beneficiary worked at his regular occupation or at employment of equivalent standard, which shall be disregarded
in accordance with the provision of the preceding paragraph, shall be—

    (a) in any case to which sub-paragraph (a) of that paragraph applies—

        (i) any period during which he worked thereat for any of the said
purposes with the approval of the Secretary of State or on the
advice of a medical practitioner, and

       (ii) any other period or periods during which he worked thereat for
any of the said purposes and which did not exceed six months
in the aggregate, and

    (b) in any case to which sub-paragraph (b) of that paragraph applies—

        (i) any period during which he worked thereat and throughout
which it is shown that having obtained the advice of a medical
practitioner to submit himself to such surgical treatment he was
waiting to undergo the said treatment in accordance therewith,
and

       (ii) any other period during which he worked thereat and through-
out which is shown that he was in process of obtaining such
advice.

AMENDMENTS

1. Social Security (Abolition of Injury Benefits) (Consequential) Regulations
1983 (SI 1983/186) reg.13 (April 6, 1983).
2. Social Security (Industrial Injuries and Diseases) Miscellaneous Provisions
Regulations 1986 (SI 1986/1561) reg.7 (October 1, 1986).

GENERAL NOTE

10.34   The regulation permits both the fact of work and the period for which it has been
undertaken to be disregarded where the claimant seeks to establish entitlement to
reduced earnings allowance under the "continuous condition", so long as the work
is undertaken for either of the purposes specified in the regulation. (See generally,
R(I)1/51, R(I)35/55, R(I)35/58.)

If the claimant relies upon the purpose in para.(1)(a), the extent of the qualifying
period depends upon whether the return to work is upon the advice of a medical
practitioner or with the approval of the Secretary of State—without such authorisation the period (or aggregate periods) may not exceed six months. "Rehabilitation",
means getting better (*R(I)69/53*), but "ascertaining the results of the relevant
injury" has been more widely interpreted to mean discovering whether the claimant
can still do the job (*R(I)1/69*). The "advice" of the doctor referred to in the paragraph does not have to be specifically directed to value of a resumption of work, but
there must be something which the claimant can point to in the general advice he
receives which is relevant to one of the specified purposes—the "general approval
and consent of his doctor" (*R(I)93/53*), or "in allowing the claimant to continue at
work while in receipt of treatment the doctor must be taken to have advised him to
remain at work" (*R(I)69/53*).

If the claimant relies upon the purpose in para.(1)(b), the periods he may use
depend upon whether he has actually received advice on surgical treatment, or
is in the process of obtaining it. Note that, in this paragraph, the advice must be
much more clear and the doctor must have given a specific opinion that surgical
treatment should be carried out—further, the claimant must intend to give up
work and undergo the treatment as soon as it can be arranged (*R(I)81/53*). The

claimant can only avail himself of this paragraph if he has been seeking advice "throughout" the period he has been working, or he has been waiting for the treatment "throughout" the period, and he is not entitled to delay unduly in seeking treatment. He must use "reasonable zeal and expedition" to secure the treatment (*R(I)35/57*).

Payments in respect of special hardship where beneficiary is entitled to a gratuity

18.—(1) Where in any case a beneficiary is entitled to or has received a disablement gratuity, such beneficiary shall as respects that gratuity have the like rights to payments in respect of special hardship as he would have had by way of increase of disablement pension under section 60 if the disablement gratuity had been a disablement pension payable during the period taken into account by the assessment.

(2) A beneficiary who is entitled as respects a disablement gratuity to payments in respect of special hardship by virtue of the preceding paragraph shall, if he makes an application in that behalf at any time before that gratuity or any part thereof has been paid to him, be entitled, subject to the proviso to section 57(6), to a disablement pension in lieu of such gratuity for any part of the period taken into account by the assessment during which he may be entitled to an increase of such pension in respect of special hardship under section 60, and the weekly rate of such pension shall be determined in accordance with Schedule 4 of these regulations.

(3) For the purposes of paragraph (2) and notwithstanding the provisions of regulation 14(2) whenever the weekly rate of such pension is altered consequent upon the passing of an Act or the making of an uprating order, such variation shall have effect as from the date on which the provision varying the amount of the disablement pension specified in paragraph 3 of Part V of Schedule 4 to the Act comes into force, whether the period taken into account by the assessment began before or after that date.

(4) Where a pension has been payable under paragraph (2) in lieu of a gratuity for any period and the beneficiary ceases to be entitled to an increase of such pension under the provisions of section 60, the amount of that gratuity shall be treated as reduced by the amounts which have been paid to the beneficiary by way of such pension, other than an increase thereof under the said section 60 and, subject to the provisions of these regulations, the balance (if any) shall then be payable accordingly.

GENERAL NOTE

This regulation will only continue in force to cover those claimants who were in receipt of special hardship allowance under this regulation as at October 1, 1986. A claimant in that group became entitled to reduced earnings allowance on that day and will remain so entitled under this regulation until either the period of assessment has expired or the assessment is reviewed, or until reduced earnings allowance has ceased to be payable (whichever is the earlier). See the Social Security (Industrial Injuries and Diseases) Miscellaneous Provisions Regulations 1986 (SI 1986/1561) reg.7(5), (6).

Increase of disablement pension for constant attendance

19. The amount by which the weekly rate of disablement pension may be increased under [section 104 of the Social Security Contributions and

10.35

10.36

10.37

Benefits Act 1992] where constant attendance is required by a beneficiary as a result of the relevant loss of faculty shall—

  (a) where the beneficiary (not being a case to which paragraph (b) of this regulation relates) is to a substantial extent dependent on such attendance for the necessities of life and is likely to remain so dependent for a prolonged period, be the amount specified in paragraph [2](a) of Part V of Schedule 4 to the Act (unless the attendance so required is part-time only, in which case the amount shall be such sum as may be reasonable in the circumstances) or, where the extent of such attendance is greater by reason of the beneficiary's exceptionally severe disablement, a sum not exceeding one and a half times the amount specified in paragraph [2](a) of Part V of the said Schedule, a fraction of five pence being for this purpose treated as five pence;

  (b) where the beneficiary is so exceptionally severely disabled as to be entirely, or almost entirely, dependent on such attendance for the necessities of life, and is likely to remain so dependent for a prolonged period and the attendance so required is whole-time, be the amount specified in paragraph [2](b) of Part V of Schedule 4 to the Act.

Determination of degree of disablement for constant attendance allowance

10.38

20.—(1) For the purpose of determining whether a person is entitled to an increase by way of constant attendance allowance under section 61 or to a corresponding increase by virtue of section 159(3)(b) of the Act or section 7(3)(b) of the Industrial Injuries and Diseases (Old Cases) Act 1975 of any other benefit, the Secretary of State shall, in a case where that person is subject to disabilities in respect of which payments of two or more of the descriptions set out in the next following paragraph of this regulation fall to be made, determine the extent of that person's disablement by taking into account all such disabilities to which that person is subject.

(2) The payments which may be taken into account are those of the following descriptions:—

  (a) payments by way of disablement pensions under the Act;

  (b) weekly payments to which that person is or has been at any time after 4 July 1948 entitled in respect of injury or disease being payments by way of compensation under the Workmen's Compensation Acts or under any contracting-out scheme duly certified thereunder;

  (c) payments to which that person is or has been at any time after 4 July 1948 entitled as a former constable or fireman on account of an injury pension under or by virtue of any enactment in respect of an injury received or disease contracted by that person before 5 July 1948 or in respect of his retirement in consequence of such an injury or disease;

  (d) payments by way of benefit under the Industrial Injuries and Diseases (Old Cases) Act 1975; and

  (e) payments of personal benefit by way of disablement pension or gratuity under any Personal Injuries Scheme or Service Pensions Instrument or 1914–18 War Injuries Scheme.

(3) In sub-paragraph (2)(e) the expressions "personal benefit", "disablement pension", "Personal Injuries Scheme" and "Service Pensions Instrument" have

the meanings which are assigned to them by the Social Security (Overlapping Benefits) Regulations 1979 for the purposes of those regulations.

Condition for receipt of increase of disablement pension for constant attendance under section 61 while receiving medical treatment as an in-patient

21.—(1) For the purposes of section 61 (increase of disablement pension in respect of the need of constant attendance), subject to paragraph (2) it shall be a condition for the receipt of an increase of disablement pension under the said section 61 for any period in respect of any person that during that period he is not receiving, or has not received, free in-patient treatment, and for this purpose a person shall be regarded as receiving or having received free in-patient treatment if he would be so regarded for the purposes of the Social Security (Hospital In-Patients) Regulations 1975.

(2) Where a person was entitled to an increase of disablement pension under the said section 61 in respect of the period immediately before he commenced to undergo any treatment mentioned in paragraph (1), that paragraph shall not apply in respect of the first 4 weeks of any continuous period during which he is undergoing such treatment.

(3) For the purposes of paragraph (2), 2 or more distinct periods separated by an interval not exceeding 28 days, or by 2 or more such intervals, shall be treated as a continuous period equal in duration to the total of such distinct periods and ending on the last day of the later or last such period.

10.39

Treatment of distinct periods of hospital in-patient treatment as continuous for the purposes of section 62 of the Act

22. For the purposes of section 62 (increase of disablement benefit during hospital treatment) a person who receives medical treatment as an in-patient for 2 or more distinct periods separated by an interval of less than a week in each case shall be treated as receiving such treatment continuously from the beginning of the first period until the end of the last.

10.40

GENERAL NOTE

Section 62 of the Social Security Act 1975 has been replaced by para.10 of Sch.7 to the Social Security Contributions and Benefits Act 1992.

10.41

Regulations 23–37 omitted.

10.42

Adjustment of Benefit for Successive Accidents

Adjustment of benefit for successive accidents where a disablement gratuity is payable

38.—(1) In a case where—
(a) a person who is entitled, as a result of an accident, to a disablement pension (hereafter in this paragraph referred to as an "existing pension") which is payable in respect of an assessment for a period which is limited by reference to that person's life, becomes as a result of any other accident, entitled to an award as a result of an assessment of disablement in respect of which a disablement gratuity would, but for this regulation, be payable; and

10.43

   (b) the aggregate amount of the assessment in respect of the existing pension and of the assessment in respect of which such disablement gratuity would be payable would, if it were the amount of the assessment of the extent of the disablement resulting from any one accident suffered by that person, have entitled him to receive a disablement pension at a higher rate than the rate of such existing pension;

then, if at any time before his claim for disablement benefit is determined, he so elects, that person shall be entitled to a disablement pension in lieu of the said disablement gratuity at a rate equal to the difference between the said higher rate and the rate of the existing pension.

(2) In a case in which a person who is entitled as a result of any accident to a disablement pension would but for the provisions of this paragraph become entitled in respect of any other accident to a disablement gratuity (not being a case in which he is entitled to a disablement pension in lieu of such gratuity)—

   (a) if the assessment in respect of which such pension is payable to him amounts to not less than 100 per cent, such person shall not be entitled to receive any disablement gratuity in respect of such other accident;

   (b) in any other case, such person shall not be entitled to receive, by way of disablement gratuity in respect of such other accident, an amount exceeding that which would be payable in respect of an assessment equal to the difference between 100 per cent. and the percentage of the assessment in respect of which such pension is payable to him.

(3) For the respective purposes of the two preceding paragraphs of this regulation—

   (a) references to an existing pension within the meaning of paragraph (1) and to any disablement pension in paragraph (2) respectively shall include references to all such pensions which may be payable to the person concerned, and references to the amount of the assessment in respect of which, and the rate at which, any such pension is payable shall include references to the aggregate amount of the assessments in respect of which or the aggregate of the rates at which all such pensions are payable as aforesaid;

   (b) the extent by which an assessment is increased by virtue of the provisions of section 62 of the Act (increase of disablement benefit during hospital treatment) shall be disregarded;

   (c) for the purposes of paragraph (1)(a) a person shall be deemed to be entitled to a disablement pension and to an award as described in the said sub-paragraph from the respective dates of commencement of the periods taken into account by the assessments relating to such pension and to such award.

Adjustment of increase of benefit of successive accidents

10.44   **39.**—(1) Where a person who is entitled to a disablement pension in respect of any accident suffered by him—

   (a) has received, or is entitled to, a disablement gratuity in respect of any other accident; and

   (b) as a result of the loss of faculty in respect of which he has received, or is entitled to that gratuity, is incapable of work and is likely to remain permanently so incapable;

the provisions of section 58 (increase of disablement pension by way of unemployability supplement) shall apply as if that loss of faculty resulted from the accident in respect of which such disablement pension is payable.

(2) Where a person—

(a) would be entitled to a disablement pension in respect of any accident but for the provisions of section 91(1)(a) (limitations on the aggregate weekly rates of benefit payable for the same period in respect of successive accidents); and

(b) by reason only of those provisions, is unable to satisfy the conditions for the receipt of an increase of that pension by way of unemployability supplement under section 58;

the provisions of the said section 58 shall apply as if such disablement pension were payable to that beneficiary.

(3) At any time at which the sum total of the several assessments in respect of two or more accidents suffered by any person amounts to not less than 100 per cent during the continuance of the periods respectively taken into account thereby, the weekly rate of any disablement pension which is payable to him may be increased in accordance with the provisions of section 61 if he requires constant attendance as a result of the loss of faculty resulting from any one or more of such accidents, whether or not that pension is payable in respect of an assessment of 100 per cent or in respect of that loss of faculty.

(4) A beneficiary who has suffered two or more accidents shall not be entitled at any time to more than one of each of the following increases of benefit, that is to say—

(a) by way of unemployability supplement under section 58;

(b) in respect of the need of constant attendance under section 61;

(c) in respect of a child, under section 64;

(d) in respect of an adult dependant, under section 66.

Disqualification for Receipt of Benefit and Suspension of Benefit Pending Appeals etc.

Disqualification for receipt of benefit, suspension of proceedings on claims and suspension of payment of benefit

40.—(1)[¹. . .]

(2) If, without good cause—

(a) a claimant fails to furnish to the prescribed person any information required for the determination of the claim or of any question arising in connection therewith; or

(b) a beneficiary fails to give notice to the prescribed person of any change of circumstances affecting the continuance of the right to benefit or to the receipt thereof, or to furnish as aforesaid any information required for the determination of any question arising in connection with the award; or

(c) a claimant for, or a beneficiary in receipt of, disablement benefit fails to comply with any requirement of regulation 26 of the Social Security (Claims and Payments) Regulations 1979 (obligations of claimants for, and beneficiaries in receipt of [¹. . .] disablement benefit);

10.45

he shall, subject to the following provisions of this regulation, if the [² determining authority] so decide, be disqualified for receiving any benefit claimed in respect of the period of such failure.

(3) If a claimant or beneficiary wilfully obstructs, or is guilty of other misconduct in connection with any examination or treatment to which he is required under regulation 26 of the Social Security(Claims and Payments) Regulation 1979 to submit himself, or any proceedings under the Act for the determination of his right to benefit or to the receipt thereof, he shall, subject to the provisions of this regulation, be disqualified for receiving any benefit claimed for such period as the [² determining authority] shall determine.

(4) In any case to which any of the foregoing paragraphs of this regulation relates, proceedings on the claim or payment of benefit, as the case may be, may be suspended for such period as the [² determining authority] may determine.

(5) Nothing in this Regulation providing for the disqualification for the receipt of benefit for any of the following matters, that is to say—
  (a) [¹. . .]
  (b) for failure to comply with the requirements of regulation 26 of the Social Security (Claims and Payments) Regulation 1979;
  (c) for obstruction of, or misconduct in connection with, medical examination or treatment;
shall authorise the disentitlement of a claimant or beneficiary to benefit for a period exceeding six weeks on any disqualification.

(6) No person shall be disqualified for receiving any benefit for refusal to undergo a surgical operation not being one of minor character.

(7) A person who would be entitled to any benefit but for the operation of any of the foregoing provisions of this regulation shall be treated as if he were entitled thereto for the purpose of any rights or obligations under the Act (whether of himself or any other person) which depend on his being so entitled other than the right to payment of that benefit.

AMENDMENTS

1. Social Security (Abolition of Injury Benefit) (Consequential) Regulations 1983 (SI 1983/186) reg.13 (April 6, 1983).
2. Social Security Act 1998 (Commencement No. 12 and Consequential and Transitional Provisions) Order 1999 Sch.3 para.3 (November 29, 1999).

10.46   *Regulation 41 revoked by the Social Security (Claims and Payments)*

10.47   *Regulations 1987 (SI 1987/1968), reg.48 (April 11, 1988).*

10.48   *Regulations 42–45 omitted.*

10.49   *Regulation 46 was revoked by the Social Security Benefits Up-rating Regulations 1992 (SI 1992/469) reg.7 (April 6, 1992).*

10.50   *Regulation 47 omitted.*

PROVISIONS FOR THE PURPOSE OF WHICH DISQUALIFICATION UNDER THE ACT ARE TO BE
DISREGARDED

Class of person (1)	Class of Benefit for which person is disqualified (2)	Section of the Act for the purposes of which disqualification is to be disregarded (3)	Subject matter (4)	10.51
	Widow's allowance	25(3)	Period for which a widowed mothers allowance is payable (being a period for which she is not entitled to widow's allowance	
A widow	Widow's allowance or widowed mother's allowance	26(3)	Period for which a widow's pension is payable (Being a period for which she is not entitled to a widow's allowance or a widowed mother's allowance	
	Widowed mother's allowance	26(1)(b)	Widow's pension for certain widows ceasing to be entitled to widowed mother's allowance	
The husband of a widow	Category A retirement pension	24(1)(a)	Widow's allowance for the widow of a husband who at the date of his death was not entitled to a Category A retirement pension	

In this Schedule "widowed mother's allowance" and "widow's pension" include benefit
under section 39(4) corresponding to a widowed mother's allowance and a widow's pension
respectively

SCHEDULE 2   **Regulation 11**

PRESCRIBED DEGREES OF DISABLEMENT

Description of injury	Degree of disablement per cent	10.52
1. Loss of both hands or amputation at higher sites	100	
2. Loss of a hand and a foot	100	
3. Double amputation through leg or thigh, or amputation through leg or thigh on one side and loss of other foot	100	
4. Loss of sight to such an extent as to render the claimant unable to perform any work for which eyesight is essential	100	
5. Very severe facial disfiguration	100	
6. Absolute deafness	100	
7. Forequarter or hindquarter amputation	100	

Amputation cases—upper limbs (either arm)

8.	Amputation through shoulder joint	90
9.	Amputation below shoulder with stump less than 20.5 centimetres from tip of acromion	80
10.	Amputation from 20.5 centimetres from tip of acromion to less than 11.5 centimetres below tip of olecranon	70
11.	Loss of a hand or of the thumb and four fingers of one hand or amputation from 11.5 centimetres below tip of olecranon	60
12.	Loss of thumb	30
13.	Loss of thumb and its metacarpal bone	40
14.	Loss of four fingers of one hand	50
15.	Loss of three fingers of one hand	30
16.	Loss of two fingers of one hand	20
17.	Loss of terminal phalanx of thumb	20

Amputation cases—lower limbs

18.	Amputation of both feet resulting in end-bearing stumps	90
19.	Amputation through both feet proximal to the metatarso-phalangeal joint	80
20.	Loss of all toes of both feet through the metatarso-phalangeal joint	40
21.	Loss of all toes of both feet proximal to the proximal inter-phalangeal joint	30
22.	Loss of all toes of both feet distal to the proximal inter-phalangeal joint	20
23.	Amputation at hip	90
24.	Amputation below hip with stump not exceeding 13 centimetres in length measured from tip of great trochanter	80
25.	Amputation below hip and above knee with stump exceeding 13 centimetres in length measured from tip of great trochanter, or at knee not resulting in end-bearing stump	70
26.	Amputation at knee resulting in end-bearing stump or below knee with stump not exceeding 9 centimetres	60
27.	Amputation below knee with stump exceeding 9 centimetres but not exceeding 13 centimetres	50
28.	Amputation below knee with stump exceeding 13 centimetres	40
29.	Amputation of one foot resulting in end-bearing stump	30
30.	Amputation through one foot proximal to the metatarso-phalangeal joint	30
31.	Loss of all toes of one foot through the metatarso-phalangeal joint	20

Other injuries		*Degree of disablement per cent*
32.	Loss of one eye, without complications, the other being normal	40
33.	Loss of vision of one eye, without complications or disfigurement of the eyeball, the other being normal	30

Loss of:
A Fingers of right or left hand

	Index finger—	
34.	Whole	14
35.	Two phalanges	11
36.	One phalanx	9
37.	Guillotine amputation of tip without loss of bone	5
	Middle finger—	
38.	Whole	12
39.	Two phalanges	9
40.	One phalanx	7
41.	Guillotine amputation of tip without loss of bone	4
	Ring or little finger—	
42.	Whole	7
43.	Two phalanges	6
44.	One phalanx	5
45.	Guillotine amputation of tip without loss of bone	2

B Toes of right or left foot

Great toe—
46. Through metatarso-phalangeal joint 14
47. Part, with some loss of bone 3

Any other toe—
48. Through metatarso-phalangeal joint 3
49. Part, with some loss of bone 1

Two toes of one foot, excluding great toe—
50. Through metatarso-phalangeal joint 5
51. Part, with some loss of bone 2

Three toes of one foot, excluding great toe—
52. Through metatarso-phalangeal joint 6
53. Part, with some loss of bone 3

Four toes of one foot, excluding great toe—
54. Through metatarso-phalangeal joint 9
55. Part, with some loss of bone 3

GENERAL NOTE

See the notes to reg.11.   10.53

SCHEDULE 3   **Regulation 14**

SCALE OF DISABLEMENT GRATUITIES

Degree of disablement (1)	(1) Appropriate proportion of maximum disablement gratuity (as specified in paragraph 2 of PartV of Schedule 4 to the Act (2)	10.54
	per cent	
1 per cent	10	
2 per cent	15	
3 per cent	20	
4 per cent	25	
5 per cent	30	
6 per cent	35	
7 per cent	40	
8 per cent	45	
9 per cent	50	
10 per cent	55	
11 per cent	60	
12 per cent	65	
13 per cent	70	
14 per cent	75	
15 per cent	80	
16 per cent	85	
17 per cent	90	
18 per cent	95	
19 per cent	100	

[Schedule 4 saved for certain purposes by regulation 7(5) and (6) of The Social Security (Industrial Injuries and Diseases) Miscellaneous Provisions Regulations 1986, SI 1986/1561.]

RATE OF DISABLEMENT PAYABLE IN LIEU OF DISABLEMENT GRATUITY IN ACCORDANCE WITH REGULATION 18

10.55   Where the degree of disablement is as specified in column (1) of the following table, the weekly rate of the pension shall be determined in accordance with column (2) of that table:

Degree of disablement (1)	*Rate of pension (2)*
less than 20 per cent but not less than 16 per cent	the appropriate weekly amount of disablement pension payable in respect of a degree of disablement of 20 per cent as specified in paragraph 3 of Part V of Schedule 4 to the Act;
less than 16 per cent but not less than 11 per cent	75 per cent of the appropriate weekly amount of disablement pension payable in respect of a degree of disablement of 20 per cent as specified in the said paragraph 3:
less than 11 per cent but not less than 6 per cent	50 per cent of the appropriate weekly amount of disablement pension payable in respect of a degree of disablement of 20 per cent as specified in the said paragraph 3:
less than 6 per cent	25 per cent of the appropriate weekly amount of disablement pension payable in respect of a degree of disablement of 20 per cent as specified in the said paragraph 3: a fraction of a penny, being for this purpose treated as a penny.

10.56   *Schedules 5–9 omitted*

The Social Security (Industrial Injuries) (Prescribed Diseases) Regulations 1985

(SI 1985/967) (*as amended*)

ARRANGEMENT OF REGULATIONS

PART I

GENERAL

10.57   1.   Citation, commencement and interpretation.

(SI 1985/967) (as amended)

PART II

PRESCRIPTION OF DISEASES AND PRESUMPTION AS TO THEIR ORIGIN

2. Prescription of diseases and injuries and occupations for which they are prescribed.
3. Sequelae or resulting conditions.
4. Presumption that a disease is due to the nature of employment.

PART III

DATE OF ONSET AND RECRUDESCENCE

5. Development of disease.
6. Date of onset.
7. Recrudescence.
8. Workmen's compensation cases.
9. Re-employment of pneumoconiotics and special provisions for benefit (workmen's compensation cases).

PART IV

APPLICATION OF SECTIONS 94 TO 107 OF THE SOCIAL SECURITY CONTRIBUTIONS AND BENEFITS ACT 1992 AND SECTIONS 8 TO 10 OF THE SOCIAL SECURITY ADMINISTRATION ACT 1992 AND OF REGULATIONS MADE THEREUNDER

10. Definition of "relevant disease".
11. Application of sections 94 to 107 of the Social Security Contributions and Benefits Act 1992 and sections 8 to 10 of the Social Security Administration Act 1992.
12. Application of Claims and Payments Regulations and Benefit Regulations.
13. Benefit not payable in cases covered by the Industrial Injuries and Diseases (Old Cases) Act 1975.
14. Diseases contracted outside Great Britain.
14A. Modification of paragraph 11(1) of Schedule 7 to the Social Security Contributions and Benefits Act 1992.
15. Assessment of extent of disablement.
15A. Aggregation of percentages of disablement.
15B. Rounding.
16. *Omitted.*
17. Special provisions as to determination of regular occupation in relation to persons claiming reduced earnings allowance.
18. Exception from requirements as to notice.
19. Provisions as to medical examination.

PART V

SPECIAL PROVISIONS AS TO PNEUMOCONIOSIS, BYSSINOSIS, OCCUPATIONAL DEAFNESS AND CERTAIN OTHER DISEASES

Section A—Benefit

20. Special conditions for disablement benefit for pneumoconiosis, byssinosis and diffuse mesothelioma.

1473

20A. Diffuse mesothelioma—prescribed loss of faculty.
20B. Primary carcinoma of the lung and angiosarcoma of the liver—special conditions and prescribed loss of faculty
21. Pneumoconiosis—effects of tuberculosis.
22. Pneumoconiosis—effects of emphysema and chronic bronchitis.
23. Reduced earnings allowance—special provision for pneumoconiosis cases.
24. Special requirement for pneumoconiosis claimants in unscheduled occupation cases.
25. Time for claiming benefit in respect of occupational deafness.
26. Claims in respect of occupational deafness.
27. Further claims in respect of occupational deafness.
28. Availability of disablement benefit in respect of occupational deafness.
29. Period to be covered by assessment of disablement in respect of occupational deafness.
30. *Revoked.*
31. *Revoked.*
32. *Revoked.*
33. *Revoked.*
34. Assessment of extent of disablement and rate of disablement benefit payable in respect of occupational deafness.
35. Commencement date of period of assessment in respect of occupational deafness.
36. Time for claiming benefit in respect of occupational asthma.
37.–38.*Revoked.*
39. Suspension from employment.
40. Conditions of suspension.
41.–42.*Revoked.*

PART VI

TRANSITIONAL PROVISIONS AND REVOCATION

43. Transitional provisions regarding relevant dates.
44. Transitional provisions regarding dates of development and dates of onset.
45. *Omitted.*

SCHEDULES

Schedule 1.—Part I: List of prescribed diseases and the occupations for which they are prescribed.
Part II: Occupations for which pneumoconiosis is prescribed.
Schedule 2.—Modifications of sections 94 to 107 of the Social Security Contributions and Benefits Act 1992 and sections 8 to 10 of the Social Security Administration Act 1992 in their application to benefit and claims to which these regulations apply.
Schedule 3.—Assessment of the extent of occupational deafness.
Part I.—Claims to which regulation 34(1) applies.
Part II.—Claims to which regulation 34(2) applies.
Part III.—Formula for calculating binaural disablement.
Schedule 4.—Prescribed diseases and relevant dates for the purposes of regulation 43.
Schedule 5.—Transitional provisions regarding dates of development and dates of onset.
Schedule 6.—*Omitted.*

The Secretary of State for Social Services, in exercise of powers conferred by sections 76, 77, 78, 113 and 155 of and Schedule 20 to the Social Security Act 1975, and of all other powers enabling him in that behalf, and for the purpose only of consolidating regulations hereinafter revoked, after consultation with the Council of Tribunals in so far as is required by section 10 of the Tribunals and Inquiries Act 1971, hereby makes the following regulations:

PART I

GENERAL

Citation, commencement and interpretation

1.—(1) These regulations may be cited as the Social Security (Industrial Injuries) (Prescribed Diseases) Regulations 1985 and shall come into operation on 31st July 1985.

(2) In these regulations, unless the context otherwise requires—

"the Act" means the [Social Security Contributions and Benefits Act 1992];

[¹ "the 1998 Act" means the Social Security Act 1998;]

"the Workmen's Compensation Acts" means the Workmen's Compensation Acts 1925 to 1945, or the enactments repealed by the Workmen's Compensation Act 1925, or the enactments repealed by the Workmen's Compensation Act 1906;

"the Adjudication Regulations" means the Social Security (Adjudication) Regulations 1984;

"the Benefit Regulations" means the Social Security (General Benefit) Regulations 1982;

"the Claims and Payments Regulations" means the Social Security (Claims and Payments) Regulations 1979;

[¹ . . .]

"asbestosis" means fibrosis of the parenchyma of the lungs due to the inhalation of asbestos dust;

"asbestos textiles" means yarn or cloth composed of asbestos or of asbestos mixed with any other material;

"coal mine" means any mine where one of the objects of the mining operations is the getting of coal (including bituminous coal, cannel coal, anthracite, lignite, and brown coal);

"diffuse mesothelioma" means the disease numbered D3 in Part I of Schedule 1 to these regulations;

"employed earner" means employed earner for the purposes of industrial injuries benefit and the term "employed earner's employment" shall be construed accordingly;

"foundry" means those parts of industrial premises where the production of metal articles (other than pig iron or steel ingots) is carried on by casting (not being diecasting or other casting in metal moulds), together with any part of the same premises where any of the following processes are carried on incidentally to such production, namely, the drying and subsequent preparation of sand for moulding (including the reclamation of used moulding sand), the preparation of moulds and cores, knock-out operations and dressing or fettling operations;

"grindstone" means a grindstone composed of natural or manufactured

10.58

sandstone and includes a metal wheel or cylinder into which blocks of natural or manufactured sandstone are fitted;

[² "knock out and shake out grid" means a grid used for mechanically separating moulding sand from mouldings and castings;]

"a local office" means any office appointed by the Secretary of State as a local office for the purposes of the Act or of these regulations;

[³ . . .]

"medical board" has the same meaning as in regulation 30 of the Adjudication Regulations;

[¹ "medical practitioner" means a medical practitioner who has experience in the issues specified in regulation 12(1) of the Social Security and Child Support (Decisions and Appeals) Regulations 1999;]

[⁴ "metal" for the purposes of the disease number A10 in Part I of Schedule 1 to these Regulations, does not include stone, concrete, aggregate or similar substances for use in road or railway construction;]

"mine" includes every shaft in the course of being sunk, and every level and inclined plane in the course of being driven, and all the shafts, levels, planes, works, tramways and sidings, both below ground and above ground, in and adjacent to and belonging to the mine, but does not include any part of such premises on which any manufacturing process is carried on other than a process ancillary to the getting or dressing of minerals or the preparation of minerals for sale;

"occupational asthma" means the disease numbered D7 in Part I of Schedule 1 to these regulations;

"occupational deafness" means the disease numbered A10 in Part I of Schedule 1 to these regulations;

"the old regulations" means the Social Security (Industrial Injuries) (Prescribed Diseases) Regulations 1980, as amended by the Social Security (Industrial Injuries) (Prescribed Diseases) Amendment Regulations 1980, the Social Security (Industrial Injuries) (Prescribed Diseases) Amendment Regulations 1982 and the Social Security (Industrial Injuries) (Prescribed Diseases) Amendment (No. 2) Regulations 1982;

"prescribed disease" means a disease or injury prescribed under Part II of these regulations, and references to a prescribed disease being contracted shall be deemed to include references to a prescribed injury being received;

[³ "primary carcinoma of the lung" means the diseases numbered D8, [⁷ D8A,] D10 and D11 in Schedule 1 to these Regulations;]

"the Secretary of State" means the Secretary of State for Social Services;

"silica rock" means quartz, quartzite, ganister, sandstone, gritstone and chert, but not natural sand or rotten rock;

[² "skid transfer bank" means the area of a steel mill where the steel product is moved from the area of its formation to the finishing area;]

"special medical board" has the same meaning as in regulation 30 of the Adjudication Regulations;

[⁵ "specially qualified adjudicating medical practitioner" means a specially qualified adjudicating medical practitioner appointed by virtue of section 62 of the Social Security Administration Act 1992;]

"tuberculosis" in the description of the disease numbered B5 in Part I of Schedule 1 to these regulations means disease due to tuberculosis infection, but when used elsewhere in these regulations in connection with pneumoconiosis means tuberculosis of the respiratory system only;

and other expressions have the same meanings as in the Act.

(3) Unless the context otherwise requires, any reference in these regulations—

(a) to a numbered section or Schedule is to the section of or, as the case may be, the Schedule to the Act bearing that number; and

(b) to a numbered regulation is a reference to the regulations bearing that number in these regulations, and any reference in a regulation to a numbered paragraph is a reference to the paragraph of that regulation bearing that number; and

(c) to any provision made by or contained in any enactment or instrument shall be construed as including a reference to any provision which it re-enacts or replaces, with or without modification.

[⁶ (4) In these Regulations, any reference to death benefit shall be taken as including also a reference to any benefit in respect of which contribution conditions are taken as having been satisfied in accordance with paragraph 10 of Schedule 3 to the Social Security Act 1986.]

AMENDMENTS

1. Social Security Act 1998 (Commencement No. 8, and Savings and Consequential and Transitional Provisions) Order 1999 (SI 1999/1958) Sch.8 para.1 (July 5, 1999).

2. Social Security (Industrial Injuries) (Prescribed Diseases) Amendment Regulations 1994 (SI 1994/2343) reg.2 (October 10, 1994).

3. Social Security (Industrial Injuries) (Prescribed Diseases) Amendment Regulations 1993 (SI 1993/862) reg.2 (April 19, 1993).

4. Social Security (Industrial Injuries) (Prescribed Diseases) Amendment Regulations 1990 (SI 1990/2269) reg.2 (December 13, 1990).

5. Social Security (Industrial Injuries and Adjudication) Regulations 1993 (SI 1993/861) reg.17 (April 19, 1993).

6. Social Security (Industrial Injuries) (Miscellaneous Amendment) Regulations 1988 (SI 1988/553) reg.5 (April 11, 1988).

7. Social Security (Industrial Injuries) (Prescribed Diseases) Amendment Regulations 2006 (SI 2006/586) reg.2(1) (April 6, 2006).

PART II

PRESCRIPTION OF DISEASES AND PRESUMPTION AS TO THEIR ORIGIN

Prescription of diseases and injuries and occupations for which they are prescribed

2.—For the purposes of [sections 108–110] of the Act—   10.59

(a) subject to [¹ the following paragraphs] of this regulation and to regulation 43(3), (5) and (6), each disease or injury set out in the first column of Part I of Schedule 1 hereto is prescribed in relation to all persons who have been employed on or after 5th July 1948 in employed earner's employment in any occupation set against such disease or injury in the second column of the said Part;

(b) pneumoconiosis is prescribed—

    (i) in relation to all persons who have been employed on or after 5th July 1948 in employed earner's employment in any occupation set out in Part II of the said Schedule; and

    (ii) in relation to all other persons who have been so employed in any occupation involving exposure to dust and who have not worked at any time (whether in employed earner's employment or not) in any occupation in relation to which pneumoconiosis is prescribed by virtue of regulations (apart from this sub-paragraph) in force—

        (i) in the case of any claim for disablement benefit or a claim for death benefit in respect of the death of a person to whom disablement benefit has been awarded in respect of pneumoconiosis, on the date of the claim for disablement benefit;

        (ii) in the case of a claim for death benefit in respect of the death of any other person, on the date of the death of that person;

(c) occupational deafness is prescribed in relation to all persons who have been employed in employed earner's employment—

    (i) at any time on or after 5th July 1948; and

    (ii) for a period or periods (whether before or after 5th July 1948) amounting in the aggregate to not less than 10 years in one or more of the occupations set out in the second column of paragraph A10 of Part I of Schedule 1 to these regulations [⁴. . .]

[² (d) the disease specified in paragraph D12 of Part I of Schedule 1 is not prescribed in relation to persons to whom regulation 22 applies.]

[³ (e) cataract is not prescribed unless the person was employed in employed earner's employment in an occupation set out in the second column of paragraph A2 of Part I of Schedule 1 to these regulations for a period or periods amounting in aggregate to not less than 5 years.]

AMENDMENTS

1. Social Security (Industrial Injuries) (Prescribed Diseases) Amendment Regulations 2000 (SI 2000/1588) reg.2(2) (July 10, 2000).
2. Social Security (Industrial Injuries) (Prescribed Diseases) Amendment (No. 2) Regulations 1993 (SI 1993/1985) reg.2 (September 13, 1993).
3. Social Security (Industrial Injuries) (Prescribed Diseases) Amendment Regulations 2000 (SI 2000/1588) reg.2(3) (July 10, 2000).
4. Social Security (Industrial Injuries) (Prescribed Diseases) Amendment Regulations 2005 (SI 2005/324) reg.2(1) (March 14, 2005).

DEFINITIONS

"employed earner's employment"—see SSCBA 1992 s.95, and note.
"pneumoconiosis"—see SSCBA 1992 s.122(1), above.

GENERAL NOTE

10.60   This regulation links with Sch.1 to the Regulations (below) to establish a list of diseases, and a list of the occupations in respect of which they are prescribed. It is not enough to suffer from a disease which happens to be in the list, it must have been linked to the occupation. Each disease is prescribed only in relation to claimants who have been employed in the occupations described in the Schedule. That is a significant limitation. It is also necessary for the occupation to have caused the disease but that is usually presumed under reg.4.

    On July 5, 1999, AOs' functions with respect to industrial injuries benefits and the making of an industrial accident declaration were transferred to the Secretary of State (SSA 1998 ss.1, 8 and Commencement Order No. 8). He may, however, refer certain issues for report to a medical practitioner who has experience of the issues. The issues so referable are.

(a) the extent of a personal injury for the purposes of s.94

(b) whether the claimant has a prescribed industrial disease and the extent of resulting disablement; and

(c) whether, for disablement benefit purposes, the claimant has a disablement and its extent (Decisions and Appeals Regulations 1999 reg.12).

Decisions on industrial injuries benefits and on the matter of an industrial accident declaration, are appealable to a "unified" appeal tribunal composed of a legally qualified member and up to two medically qualified members (SSA 1998 ss.4, 12, Schs 2 and 3; Decisions and Appeals Regulations 1999 reg.36(2)). Like the Secretary of State, that tribunal is competent to deal with both the medical and non-medical aspect of industrial injuries matters. Note, however, that whether a claimant is an employed or self-employed earner, and whether a specific employment is, or is not, employed earner's employment is to be decided not by the Secretary of State, but by officers of the Board of Revenue and Customs (Social Security Contributions (Transfer of Functions, etc.) Act 1999, s.8(1)). Accordingly, such decisions are not matters of appeal for the "unified" appeal tribunal but rather for appeal to the tax appeal Commissioners (*ibid.*, s.11). Such decisions and appeals are regulated by the Social Security Contributions (Decisions and Appeals) Regulations 1999 (SI 1999/1027).

The key point from all this for industrial injuries matters, is that the distinction between medical issues (the disablement questions) and non-medical issues—previously crucial as demarcating the respective jurisdictions of MATs and SSATs—is no longer relevant.

Regulation 2 requires persons to have been "employed in" an occupation prescribed as relevant for the disease in question in Sch.1 to the regulations. Para.(c) (occupational deafness) further requires the employment in the relevant occupation to have been for a period or periods amounting in the aggregate to not less than 10 years. *R(I) 2/79(T)*, an occupational deafness case, makes it clear that

"the focus of the regulations is directed to the work done rather than to the contractual obligation to do it. The benefit is for disablement incurred whilst working in any of the prescribed occupations and undergoing exposure to noise whilst so working." (para.15).

At the time that case was considered, an otherwise very similar regulation required 20 years' employment. The Tribunal of Commissioners said that to compute the relevant period, one should use this actual work test. However, one cannot look to whether the person worked on every available day. Normal breaks (weekends, holidays, short-term absences for sickness or absenteeism, short-term interruptions for industrial trouble) should be ignored in the sense of not breaking the period of employment. In contrast, abnormal interruptions would break the period of employment and not count towards the 20-year requirement. What, then, was an abnormal interruption? The Commissioners thought it undesirable to lay down an inflexible rule as to what constituted an abnormal interruption, considering the matter to be one of fact and degree in each case. But they considered that an abnormal interruption "should be a substantial or prolonged period of absence from work" and thought "that it would be a most exceptional case where it could be said that a man had been working during a continuous break in actual work of three calendar months or more for whatever reason" and opined that "such periods of absence should normally be excluded from the computation of the period of 20 years." (see especially paras 19, 20). The same approach had to be taken to determining when a person was last employed in a relevant occupation for the purposes of time limits on claims (see further annotation to reg.25, below).

10.61 Where an employed earner works for less than half the time in a prescribed occupation, he or she cannot be said to be working "wholly or mainly" in that occupation during the whole period of employment. However, there may have been parts of the period of employment during which the claimant was working for most of the time in a prescribed occupation and other parts when he or she was not. It is therefore wrong, on a claim in respect of occupational deafness, to look at the whole period of employment and consider whether the claimant was working "wholly or mainly" in a prescribed occupation throughout that period. The question is whether the parts of the period (or periods) of employment during which the claimant was working in a prescribed occupation total in the aggregate to not less than 10 years (*CI/1446/98*).

Special provision is made for pneumoconiosis and occupational deafness. In respect of pneumoconiosis, para.(b)(ii) gives potential entitlement to a group of people who do not work in the specific occupations for which the disease is prescribed in Pt II of the Schedule. Note that this group do not have the benefit of the presumption that the prescribed disease resulted from employment in the specified occupation (see reg.4, below), and the claimant bears the burden of proving that the disease results from being employed, "in any occupation involving exposure to dust". This means that the exposure to dust must be in excess of that met with in ordinary life (*R(I) 40/57*). The requirement was most recently considered in *R(I) 1/85*, which dealt with the same phrase in relation to the prescribed disease D4 (Inflammation of the mucous membrane etc.).

The amendment inserting para.(e) (cataract) is subject to a transitional provision in reg.7(2) and (3) of the amending instrument such that it

"shall not apply in the case of a person—

    (a) who had an assessment of disablement in respect of the relevant disease for a period up to the date 3 months after the commencement date; or

    (b) in respect of whom a decision in relation to a relevant disease on a claim for disablement benefit made before or within 3 months after the commencement date is revised or superseded after that date under section 9 or 10 of the Social Security Act 1998 resulting in an assessment;

during any period when there is in respect of him a continuous assessment of disablement in respect of that disease, and for this purpose two or more assessments, one of which begins on the day following the end of a preceding assessment, shall be treated as continuous." (reg.7(2)).

Nor will it apply

"in the case of a person—

    (a) who had an assessment of disablement in respect of the relevant disease for a period which ended before or within 3 months after the commencement date;

    (b) who suffers a further attack of that relevant disease before or within 3 months after the commencement date;

    (c) who makes a claim for disablement benefit in respect of that disease after the commencement date; and

    (d) in respect of whom it is decided under regulation 7 of the principal Regulations (recrudescence) that the further attack is a recrudescence of that disease." (reg.7(3))

The commencement date is July 10, 2000 and "relevant disease" means the disease referred to in the amendment, or the regulation amended by the amendment (reg.7(4)).

Sequelae or resulting conditions

10.62 **3.**—Where a person—

(a) is or was in employed earner's employment and a disease is or was prescribed under the Act and these regulations in relation to him in such employment; and

(b) is suffering from a condition which, in his case, has resulted from that disease;

the provisions of [sections 108–110] of the Act and of these regulations shall apply to him as if he was suffering from that disease, whether or not the condition from which he is suffering is itself a prescribed disease.

GENERAL NOTE

Disablement resulting from a condition which is not prescribed but which has resulted from a prescribed disease is to be included in any assessment.

In *CI/5972/99*, Commissioner Howell held that a tribunal erred in law when, in respect of someone who was a carrier of viral hepatitis (having had an attack of it in the past) they merely recorded that he was not suffering from the disease. They ought to have considered (as the AMA had) whether he suffered from a sequela of the disease.

10.63

[¹Presumption that a disease is due to the nature of employment

4.—(1) Where a person has developed a disease which is prescribed in Part I of Schedule 1 in paragraphs A3(a), A4, A5, A6, A7, A8, A11, B1(a), B3, B4(a), B9, B10, B11, B12, B14, B15, C3, C24A, D4 or D7, that disease shall, unless the contrary is proved, be presumed to be due to the nature of that person's employed earner's employment if—

(a) that employment was in any occupation set against that disease in the second column of that Part; and

(b) the person was so employed on, or at any time within one month immediately preceding, the date on which, under these Regulations, that person is treated as having developed the disease.

(2) Where a person has developed a disease which is prescribed in Part I of Schedule 1 in paragraphs A1, A2, A3(b), A10, A13, A14, B2, B6, B8B, B13, C17, C18, C22(a), C24, C31, C32, [² C34,]D2, D3, D6, D8, D8A, D9, D10, D11, D12 or D13, that disease shall, unless the contrary is proved, be presumed to be due to the nature of that person's employed earner's employment if that employment was in any occupation set against that disease in the second column of that Part.

(3) Where a person in relation to whom tuberculosis is prescribed in paragraph B5 of Part I of Schedule 1 in respect of the occupation set out in sub-paragraph (a) in the second column of the entry relating to that disease, develops that disease, that disease shall, unless the contrary is proved, be presumed to be due to the nature of that person's employed earner's employment if the date on which, under these Regulations, that person is treated as having developed the disease is—

(a) not less than six weeks after the date on which that person was first employed in that occupation; and

(b) not more than two years after the date on which that person was last so employed in that occupation.

(4) Where a person has developed a disease which is prescribed in Part I of Schedule 1 in paragraphs B1(b), B4(b), B7 and B8A, that disease shall, unless the contrary is proved, be presumed to be due to the nature of that person's employed earner's employment if—

10.64

    (a) that employment was in any occupation set against that disease in the second column of that Part; and

    (b) that person was so employed—

       (i) on the date on which, under these Regulations, that person is treated as having developed the disease; or

      (ii) on a date at any time within—

          (aa) in the case of B1(b) or B8A, two months;

          (bb) in the case of B7, six months; or

          (cc) in the case of B4(b), twelve months

immediately preceding the date on which, under these Regulations, that person is treated as having developed the disease.

(5) Where a person in relation to whom carpal tunnel syndrome is prescribed in paragraph A12 of Part I of Schedule 1 in respect of the occupation set out in sub-paragraph (b) in the second column of the entry relating to that disease, develops that disease, it shall, unless the contrary is proved, be presumed to be due to the nature of that person's employed earner's employment if that person was employed in that occupation on the date, or at any time within one month immediately preceding the date, on which under these Regulations that person is treated as having developed the disease.

(6) Where a person in relation to whom primary neoplasm of the epithelial lining of the urinary tract is prescribed in paragraph C23 of Part I of Schedule 1 in respect of the occupation set out in sub-paragraph (a), (b) or (e) in the second column of the entry relating to that disease, develops that disease, it shall, unless the contrary is proved, be presumed to be due to the nature of that person's employed earner's employment.

(7) Where a person in relation to whom pneumoconiosis is prescribed in regulation 2(b)(i) develops pneumoconiosis, the disease shall, unless the contrary is proved, be presumed to be due to the nature of that person's employed earner's employment if that person has been employed in either of the occupations set out in Part II of Schedule 1 for a period or periods amounting in aggregate to not less than 2 years in employment which either was employed earner's employment or would have been employed earner's employment if it had taken place on or after 5th July 1948.]

AMENDMENTS

1. Social Security (Industrial Injuries) (Prescribed Diseases) Amendment Regulations 2015 (SI 2015/87) reg.2 (March 16, 2015).

2. Social Security (Industrial Injuries) (Prescribed Diseases) Amendment Regulations 2017 (SI 2017/232) reg.2 (March 30, 2017).

GENERAL NOTE

10.65   Each paragraph of this important regulation establishes a presumption that a prescribed disease specified in the particular paragraph is due to the nature of a scheduled occupation provided that the conditions set out in the particular paragraph applicable are met. In each case, the presumption applies "unless the contrary is proved" on the balance of probabilities (*R(I) 38/52*). If a prescribed disease in Part I of Sch.1 is not listed in any of these paragraphs of this regulation no such presumption applies.

    The operation of reg.4 was the subject of detailed analysis by IIAC in its report *Presumption that a disease is due to the nature of employment: the role of rebuttal in claims assessment* (Cm 9030, March 2015). IIAC identified a number of problems posed by the existing formulation of the rule and canvassed various possibilities for reform, including the notion of in effect operating two schedules of prescribed diseases. In one schedule the presumption that the disease is due to the nature of the employment would follow directly from its prescription. In the other decision-makers would be able to gather further information and evidence as necessary. In the end, having weighed the various advantages and drawbacks of competing models for reform, the Council made no actual recommendation for any amendment to the legislative scheme, but expressed the firm view that "rebuttal is, and should only be, used sparingly" (para. 93).

PART III

DATE OF ONSET AND RECRUDESCENCE

Development of disease

5.—[¹(1)] If on a claim for benefit under [sections 108 to 110] in respect of a prescribed disease a person is found to be or to have been suffering from the disease, or to have died as the result thereof, the disease shall, for the purposes of such claim, be treated as having developed on a date (hereafter in these regulations referred to as "the date of onset") determined in accordance with the provisions of the next two following regulations.   **10.66**

[¹ (2) Where a person claims benefit under Part V of the Contributions and Benefits Act and it is decided that he is not entitled on the basis of a finding that he was not suffering from a prescribed disease, the finding shall be conclusive for the purpose of a decision on a subsequent claim of that kind in respect of the same disease and the same person.]

AMENDMENT

1. Social Security, Child Support and Tax Credits (Miscellaneous Amendments) Regulations 2005 (SI 2005/337) reg.5 (March 18, 2005).

GENERAL NOTE

In *R(I) 5/04* (at para.20) Commissioner Howell had decided that neither reg.5 nor reg.6 had any operation where the claimant was *not* found to be suffering from a prescribed disease. There was not what he called a "negative date of onset" where a person was found not to be suffering from the disease on the first claim made. The effect of *R(I) 5/04* was reversed by the Social Security, Child Support and Tax Credits (Miscellaneous Amendments) Regulations 2005 (SI 2005/337), which introduced the new reg.5(2). The amended version of reg.5(2) was considered by Judge Ovey in *PH v SSWP (II)* [2016] UKUT 94 (AAC). The issue raised there was whether the words "a finding that he was not suffering from a prescribed disease" mean only a finding that the person did not have a particular disease or whether they extend to a finding that a person has the disease but is not a person in relation to whom it is prescribed (e.g. because some time limit in the terms of prescription has not been satisfied). Judge Ovey concludes that reg.5 (and reg.6) "only need to be applied once it has been determined that the disease in respect of which the claim has been made is prescribed in relation to the claimant's occupation" (at para.22). See further regs.6 and 7 below.   **10.67**

Date of onset

6.—(1) For the purposes of the first claim in respect of a prescribed disease suffered by a person, the date of onset shall be determined in accordance with the following provisions of this regulation, and, save as   **10.68**

1483

provided in regulation 7, that date shall be treated as the date of onset for the purposes of any subsequent claim in respect of the same disease suffered by the same person, so however that—

(a) [¹ . . .] any date of onset determined for the purposes of that claim shall not preclude fresh consideration of the question whether the same person is suffering from the same disease on any subsequent claim for or award of benefit; and

(b) if, on the consideration of a claim, [² the degree of disablement is assessed at less than one per cent.], any date of onset determined for the purposes of that claim shall be disregarded for the purposes of any subsequent claim.

(2) Where the claim for the purposes of which the date of onset is to be determined is—

(a) a claim for sickness benefit made by virtue of section [102] of the Act by a person to whom regulation 8(1) applies (except in respect of pneumoconiosis, byssinosis, diffuse mesothelioma, occupational deafness, occupational asthma, [³ primary carcinoma of the lung] [⁴, bilateral diffuse pleural thickening or [⁵chronic obstructive pulmonary disease]]) the date of onset shall be the first day on which the claimant was incapable of work as the result of the disease on or after 5th July 1948;

(b) a claim for disablement benefit (except in respect of occupational deafness), the date of onset shall be the day on which the claimant first suffered from the relevant loss of faculty on or after 5th July 1948; and the date of onset so determined shall be the date of onset for the purposes of a claim for sickness benefit made by virtue of section [102] of the Act in respect of pneumoconiosis, byssinosis, diffuse mesothelioma, occupational asthma, [³ primary carcinoma of the lung][³, bilateral diffuse pleural thickening or [⁵chronic obstructive pulmonary disease]];

(c) a claim for disablement benefit in respect of occupational deafness, the date of onset shall be the day on which the claimant first suffered from the relevant loss of faculty on or after 3rd February 1975; or, if later—

(i) 3rd September 1979 in the case of a claim made before that date which results in the payment of benefit commencing on that date, and

(ii) in any other case, the date on which such claim is made as results in the payment of benefit; or

(d) a claim for death benefit, the date of onset shall be the date of death.

AMENDMENTS

1. Social Security Act 1998 (Commencement No.8, and Savings and Consequential and Transitional Provisions) Order 1999 (SI 1999/1958) Sch.8 para.2 (July 5, 1999).

2. Social Security (Industrial Injuries) (Prescribed Diseases) Amendment Regulations 1989 (SI 1989/1207) reg.2 (August 9, 1989).

3. Social Security (Industrial Injuries) (Prescribed Diseases) Amendment Regulations 1993 (SI 1993/862) reg.4 (April 19, 1993).

4. Social Security (Industrial Injuries) (Prescribed Diseases) Amendment (No.2) Regulations 1993 (SI 1993/1985) reg.4 (September 13, 1993).

5. Social Security (Industrial Injuries) (Prescribed Diseases) Amendment Regulations 2015 (SI 2015/87) reg.5 (March 16, 2015).

GENERAL NOTE

This is an important provision because, under Sch.2, references in the Act to the date of the relevant accident must, in disease cases, be construed as references to the date of onset. It is also important when reduced earnings allowance is being claimed because the claimant's "regular employment" is the employment he had at that date (*CI/285/49*). Under para.(1), once there has been a claim for benefit, the date of onset established for the purposes of that claim applies for any future claim in respect of the same disease unless disablement is assessed at less than 1 per cent. Reg.7 deals with the distinction between fresh attacks of a disease and recrudescence of an earlier attack.

In *R(I) 4/96*, Commissioner Goodman makes the important point that the date of onset of a prescribed disease for a particular claimant and the date from which payment of disablement benefit can be paid on or after the disease has been prescribed (added to the Schedule) are not necessarily coincidental. So where prescribed disease D12 (miners' bronchitis etc.) was added from September 13, 1993, disablement benefit was only payable from that date, despite the fact that the date of onset (the date from which the claimant suffered from it) was much earlier. Unless the contrary is clearly indicated in the particular prescription (and it was not here), the insertion into the Schedule of a new prescribed disease is not retrospective so as to enable the payment of disablement benefit (subject to showing good cause for delay in claiming) from the date of onset.

Paragraph (2)(b)
In *CI/17220/1996*, as regards a case where the claimant first began to suffer from a disease in 1945, Commissioner Levenson held that the "obvious way" to read para. (2)(b) of reg.6

> "is that the date of onset is the 5 July 1948 or any later date on which the claimant first suffers from the relevant loss of faculty if the claimant is not suffering from the relevant loss of faculty on 5 July 1948. In other words, if a claimant begins to suffer from the relevant loss of faculty before 5 July 1948, this provision deems the date of onset to be 5 July 1948. In the present case, this interpretation avoids a potentially unfair result and is also in keeping with the notion in regulation 5 of the disease being treated as having developed on the date of onset. In the present case the date of onset is 5 July 1948. The disease is treated as having developed on that date. This is also the date on which, for the purposes of section 108(1) of the Social Security Contributions and Benefits Act 1992 the disease developed. Accordingly since it developed after 4 July 1948, industrial injuries benefit is payable in an appropriate case. The adjudication officer and the tribunal, without spelling it out, assumed in effect that regulation 6(2)(b) meant that the claimant had to have first suffered from the disease on a date later than 4 July 1948. That was the principal error of law by the tribunal" (para.12).

The matter of the date of onset in respect of PD A11 (vibration white finger) was considered by Commissioner Williams in *CI/6027/1999*. On a first claim, the relevant provision is reg.6(2)(b), so that the date of onset is the date when there first is a "relevant loss of faculty". Citing *CSI/382/2000* in support, as well as the agreement of the parties on the point, he agreed that the date of onset is the date when the disease reached the extent necessary to meet the prescribed amount of disablement set down in the schedule of prescription. That prescription contains an "annual test"—it reads "episodic blanching, occurring throughout the year". Commissioner Williams asked:

> "How is that test to be applied? In cases of doubt, the question is from what date it is more probable than not that the disease has reached the necessary extent, applying the 'annual test' prospectively (that is, it will from that date meet the test), not retrospectively. There may be doubt at a particular date whether there is blanching *episodically throughout the year,* as there appears to have been in this case in 1991. It might be argued that it cannot be finally decided that someone has the prescribed disease until at least a year of episodic blanching to the minimum physical extent has occurred, so that in one sense you can only

10.69

10.70

prescribe the disease some months after the date of onset. In my view, the law does not require this because it is looking to certainty rather than probability. PD A11 is well known to be a disease that does not improve. Onset should be judged on the balance of probabilities without waiting a year. The 'date of onset' is the date that the disease probably first reaches the relevant levels and causes disablement. This part of the test for PD A11 is to be stated as 'this probably will be episodic throughout the year'. It is not a test that 'this definitely has been episodic throughout the past year'. But once it is clear that the proper test is applied, determining the date of onset is a question of fact, not of law, and is not for appeal to a Commissioner. It is of the nature of probability decisions that some will be shown by later events to be wrong. There are mechanisms for dealing with that elsewhere in social security legislation." (para.13).

10.71   The Secretary of State appealed against this decision. In *Whalley v Secretary of State for Work and Pensions* [2003] EWCA Civ 166 (reported as *R(I) 2/03*), the Court of Appeal allowed the appeal, but on grounds that do not concern the principles stated above. The appeal was successful on other grounds: that one cannot claim REA without claiming disablement benefit; and that a decision by a tribunal determining the date of onset for a PD, whether given in respect of disablement benefit or REA, as the case may be, binds a later tribunal considering the issue for either benefit. Where there was a refusal by a tribunal of a claim for disablement benefit on the ground that the claimant did not have PD A11 at the date of the decision, a later decision maker, faced with a new claim for that benefit or for REA, cannot specify a date of onset for the disease which is prior to the refusal of the first claim. See also *CI/2531/2001*, para.15:

"if a person makes a claim or successive claims for disablement benefit (and, by the same token, reduced earnings allowance, which depend on establishing the same loss of faculty) in respect of occupational deafness, the 'date of onset' can never be earlier than that of the *first* such claim which results in the actual payment of benefit; and the date so determined is also, by regulation 6(1), to be treated as the date of onset for the purposes of each subsequent claim" (*per* Commissioner Howell).

10.72   *Whalley* has also been applied in *R(I) 2/04* (Commissioner Rowland), *CI/226/2001*, *R(I) 5/04*). With the support of the Secretary of State's representative, Commissioner Howell applied in *CI/3463/2003*, his decision in *CI/5270 & 5271/2002* (now reported as *R(I) 5/04*) that *Whalley* reasoning does not apply to decisions made under the Social Security Act 1998 processes. He could not better the summary of the position as stated in his submission by that representative:

"The effects of finality for the purposes of section 17 of the SS Act 1998 was considered by the Commissioner in *CI/5270/02*. In that case it was held that following the introduction of DMA, decisions on diagnosis were not freestanding but were a question of fact embodied in a decision of the Secretary of State under section 8(1) of the Act on entitlement to benefit. In paragraph 17 the Commissioner stated *'In the absence of such express provision, an earlier finding made under the 1998 Act machinery on such a question cannot fall within the modified statutory form of the principle of* res judicata *which now applies to social security decisions under section 17'.*
The Secretary of State accepts the reasoning in decision *CI 5270/02* and submits that provided no claim had been made under the previous legislation where section 60 of the SS Admin Act [1992] did provide for finality on the question of the date of onset, then that question [*sc. the previous negative diagnosis*] is a matter of fact and not final for the purposes of section 17 of the SS Act 1998."

Commissioner Rowland in *R(I) 2/04* considered the remarks in *Whalley* to have been obiter. Moreover, the reasoning applied on the basis of the decision-making processes prior to the SSA 1998, so that the demise of the earlier provisions on finality of an MAT's decision, means that the binding nature of a decision on a date of onset of a PD for disablement benefit purposes flows from the terms of reg.6, now under consideration (para.14), a view endorsed by Commissioner Howell in *CI/5270 & 5271/2002* (paras16–18). On that basis the proper way to seek to challenge the earlier decision on date of onset, where the earlier decision found that the claimant was suffering from the prescribed disease, would be by way of seeking a supersession of that decision under SSA 1998, s.10, and appealing against the supersession decision or a refusal to supersede *(R(I) 2/04,* para.19). However, where the earlier decision on a first claim for disablement benefit was a negative one—the claimant was found not to be suffering from the claimed PD, there is nothing in the new decision-making and adjudication scheme or in reg.6 to make a diagnosis decision binding for any subsequent claim *(R(I) 5/04,* paras 18–22), so that the appeals tribunal had erred, having found that the claimant was, contrary to an earlier decision of the Secretary of State, suffering from carpal tunnel syndrome (PDA12), in setting the date of onset as the limited by the date of that earlier decision.

In the Northern Ireland decision *C1/04–05 (REA),* applying *Whalley,* Commissioner Brown held that where a tribunal had in 2002 determined the date of onset for a prescribed disease, that decision bound a later tribunal in respect of any subsequent claim in respect of the same disease.

Judge Ovey in *PH v SSWP (II)* [2016] UKUT 94 (AAC) confirms that para. (2)(b) clearly requires the identification of a particular day as the date of onset; thus a tribunal's finding that a claimant developed a condition "in 2006" was insufficiently precise to be a date of onset. In effect, such a finding simply meant the tribunal had decided that the claimant fell at the first hurdle because on its finding, whatever the exact date on which the symptoms of carpal tunnel syndrome had first developed, it was long after the claimant had ceased to be employed. In those circumstances no purpose would be served by determining the date of onset for the purposes of regs. 5 and 6 and on the facts of the case the tribunal had not purported to do so.

Paragraph (2)(c)

10.73

It was clear from *McKiernon v Secretary of State for Social Services (The Times,* November 1, 1989), that reg.6(2)(c) was originally ultra vires. As a result, s.77(2) of the SSA 1975 (now s.109 of the SSCBA 1992) was amended by para.4(2) of Sch.6 to the SSA 1990. Para.4(3) of Sch.6 to the 1990 Act provided that reg.6(2)(c) should be taken always to have been validly made. An argument that the 1990 Act failed to have the desired effect was rejected in *Chatterton v Chief Adjudication Officer* CA, *R(I)1/94).*

Recrudescence

10.74

7.—(1) [¹ Where in respect of a prescribed disease other than pneumoconiosis, byssinosis, diffuse mesothelioma, occupational deafness, occupational asthma, [² primary carcinoma of the lung][³, bilateral diffuse pleural thickening or [⁶chronic obstructive pulmonary disease]], a person's disablement has been assessed at not less than one per cent. and he] suffers from another attack of the same disease, or dies as a result thereof, then—

(a) if the further attack commences or the death occurs during a period taken into account by [¹ that assessment] (which period is in this regulation referred to as a "relevant period") the disease shall be treated as a recrudescence of the attack to which the relevant period relates, unless it is otherwise determined in the manner referred to in the following sub-paragraph;

(b) if the further attack commences or the death occurs otherwise than during a relevant period, or if it is determined [⁴. . .] that the disease was in fact contracted afresh, it shall be treated as having been so contracted.

(2) For the purposes of paragraph (1), a further attack of a prescribed disease shall be deemed to have commenced on the date on which the person concerned was first incapable of work or first suffered from the relevant loss of faculty, whichever is earlier, as a result of that further attack.

(3) Where, under the foregoing provisions of this regulation, a disease is treated as having been contracted afresh, the date of onset of the disease in relation to the fresh contraction shall be the date on which the person concerned was first incapable of work or first suffered from the relevant loss of faculty, whichever is earlier as a result of the further attack, or in the event of his death, the date of death.

(4) Where, under the provisions aforesaid, a disease is treated as a recrudescence, any assessment of disablement in respect of the recrudescence during a period taken into account by a previous assessment of disablement shall be by way of [5 a supersession of the assessment relating to the relevant period].

(5) This regulation shall not apply in relation to a claim for sickness benefit made by virtue of section [102] of the Act except where such a claim is made by a person to whom regulation 8(1) applies.

AMENDMENTS

1. Social Security (Industrial Injuries) (Prescribed Diseases) Amendment Regulations 1989 (SI 1989/1207) reg.3 (August 9, 1989).
2. Social Security (Industrial Injuries) (Prescribed Diseases) Amendment Regulations 1993 (SI 1993/862) reg.5 (April 19, 1993).
3. Social Security (Industrial Injuries) (Prescribed Diseases) Amendment (No. 2) Regulations 1993 (SI 1993/1985) reg.4 (September 13, 1993).
4. Social Security (Industrial Injuries) (Prescribed Diseases) Amendment Regulations 2003 (SI 2003/270) reg.3 (March 17, 2003).
5. Social Security and Child Support (Miscellaneous Amendments) Regulations 2000 (SI 2000/1596) reg.2 (June 19, 2000).
6. Social Security (Industrial Injuries) (Prescribed Diseases) Amendment Regulations 2015 (SI 2015/87) reg.5 (March 16, 2015).

Workmen's compensation cases

10.75   **8.**—(1) If under the foregoing provisions of this Part of these regulations a date of onset has to be determined for the purposes of a claim for benefit in respect of a prescribed disease, other than pneumoconiosis or byssinosis, suffered by a person to whom compensation under the Workmen's Compensation Acts has been awarded or paid in respect of the same disease and, at the date of such claim for benefit, or, if it is a claim for death benefit, at the date of death—

(a) that person was in receipt of weekly payments in respect of such compensation; or

(b) any liability or alleged liability for such compensation had been redeemed by the payment of a lump sum, or had been the subject of a composition agreement under the provisions of the said Acts;

the disease in respect of which the claim is made shall be treated for the purposes of these regulations as a recrudescence of the disease in respect of which such compensation was awarded or paid and not as having developed on or after 5th July 1948 unless it is determined [2 . . .] that the disease was in fact contracted afresh.

(2) If it is determined as provided in the foregoing paragraph that the disease was contracted afresh, or if compensation is not being or has not been paid as provided in sub-paragraph (a) or (b) thereof, the date of onset shall be determined in accordance with regulations 5 to 7 as if no compensation under the Workmen's Compensation Acts has been paid in respect of that disease.

(3) If the date of onset has to be determined as aforesaid in respect of

pneumoconiosis or byssinosis suffered by a person to whom compensation has been awarded or paid in respect of the same disease or in respect of whose death compensation has been awarded or paid under the provisions of any scheme made under the provisions of the Workmen's Compensation Acts relating to compensation for silicosis, asbestosis, pneumoconiosis or byssinosis, the disease in respect of which the claim is made shall (subject to the provisions of regulation 9(2)(b)) be treated for the purposes of these regulations as not having developed on or after 5th July 1948.

(4) If, after the date of a claim for benefit in respect of a prescribed disease, the claimant receives a weekly payment of compensation in respect of that disease under the Workmen's Compensation Acts which he was not receiving at the date of such claim, or if the amount of any such weekly payment which he was receiving at that date is increased, then any decision on any [1 issue] arising in connection with that claim, if given before the date of, or in ignorance of the fact of, the receipt of such weekly payment or increased weekly payment, may be [1 revised or superseded] as if it had been given in ignorance of a material fact, and on such [1 revision or supercession] the [1 issue] may be decided as if the claimant had been in receipt of such weekly payment or increased weekly payment at the date of the claim, and the foregoing provisions of this regulation shall apply accordingly.

(5) For the purposes of this regulation, a person shall be deemed to be, or to have been, in receipt of a weekly payment of compensation if—

(a) he is or was in fact receiving such payment; or
(b) he is or was entitled thereto under an award or agreement made under the Workmen's Compensation Acts.

(6) This regulation shall apply to compensation under any contracting out scheme duly certified under the Workmen's Compensation Acts as it applies to compensation under those Acts.

AMENDMENTS

1. Social Security Act 1998 (Commencement No. 8, and Savings and Consequential and Transitional Provisions) Order 1999 (SI 1999/1958) Sch.8 para.3 (July 5, 1999).
2. Social Security (Industrial Injuries) (Prescribed Diseases) Amendment Regulations 2003 (SI 2003/270) reg.4 (March 17, 2003).

Re-employment of pneumoconiotics and special provisions for benefit (workmen's compensation cases)

9.—(1) Where a person—   10.76

(a) has been certified by a medical board under the provisions of any scheme made under the provisions of the Workmen's Compensation Acts to be suffering from silicosis or pneumoconiosis not accompanied in either case by tuberculosis and has been awarded or paid compensation under the provisions of any such scheme, and by reason of such certification has been suspended from employment in any industry or process or in any particular operation or work in any industry, and

(b) wishes to start work in employed earner's employment in any occupation involving work underground in any coal mine, or the working or handling above ground at any coal mine of any minerals extracted therefrom, or any operation incidental thereto, being an occupation

in which he is allowed by certificate of the medical board under the
provisions of the scheme to engage,
he shall, before starting any such work, submit himself under arrangements
made or approved by the Secretary of State for medical examination by a
[¹ medical practitioner].

(2) Where a person submits himself for medical examination in accordance with the provisions of the foregoing paragraph, the provisions of the
Act and the regulations made thereunder shall apply to him subject to the
following modifications:—

[¹ (a) A medical practitioner shall provide a report to the Secretary of State
to enable him to determine at what degree the extent of disablement
resulting from pneumoconiosis should be assessed in his case.]

(b) Where the extent of disablement has been determined in his case in
accordance with the provisions of the foregoing sub-paragraph by [¹ the
Secretory of State or an appeal tribunal], and he starts any such work
as is mentioned in the foregoing paragraph, the provisions of regulation
38(a) (periodical examinations) shall apply to him as if he were making
a claim for benefit in respect of pneumoconiosis, and the provisions of
regulation 8(3) (pneumoconiosis shall in certain cases be treated as not
having developed on or after 5th July 1948) shall cease to apply to him
as from the date of starting such work.

(c) If, after having started work as aforesaid, he makes a claim at any
time for disablement benefit in respect of pneumoconiosis, the extent
of disablement in his case shall be assessed as if, [¹ to the extent
decided by the Secretary of State or an appeal tribunal] given under
sub-paragraph (a) of this paragraph, his disabilities resulting from
pneumoconiosis were contracted before the date of onset and were
not incurred as the result of the relevant loss of faculty.

(d) A person to whom a disablement pension is payable in respect of an
assessment made in accordance with the provisions of the last foregoing
sub-paragraph and who requires constant attendance shall, if the sum
of that assessment and the assessment made in his case in accordance
with the provisions of sub-paragraph (a) of this paragraph is not less
than 100 per cent., have the like right to payments in respect of the need
of such constant attendance as if the disablement pension were payable
in respect of an assessment of 100 per cent.

(3) Where a person to whom sub-paragraph (a) of paragraph (1) applies
has started any such work as is mentioned in sub-paragraph (b) thereof
without having submitted himself for medical examination in accordance
with the provisions of that paragraph, he may nevertheless, at any time
whilst he is engaged in any such work, so submit himself for medical examination, and the provisions of the foregoing paragraph shall, if he continues
thereafter to be engaged in any such work, apply to him as if he had started
that work immediately after the medical examination.

(4) The Secretary of State, in making or approving any such arrangements
for medical examination of any person as are mentioned in paragraph (1) shall,
as far as possible, co-ordinate those arrangements with any arrangements for
medical examination of that person made or approved under Part V of these
regulations or under the Workmen's Compensation Acts.

AMENDMENT

1. Social Security Act 1988 (Commencement No. 8, and Savings and Consequential and Transitional Provisions Order 1999 (SI 1999/1958) Sch.8 para.4 (July 5, 1999).

PART IV

APPLICATION OF [SECTIONS 94 TO 107 OF THE SOCIAL SECURITY CONTRIBUTIONS AND BENEFITS ACT 1992 AND SECTIONS 8 TO 10 OF THE SOCIAL SECURITY ADMINISTRATION ACT 1992] AND OF REGULATIONS MADE THEREUNDER

Definition of "relevant disease"

10.—In this Part of these regulations, unless the context otherwise requires, the expression "relevant disease" means, in relation to any claim for benefit in respect of a prescribed disease, the prescribed disease in respect of which benefit is claimed, but does not include any previous or subsequent attack of that disease, suffered by the same person, which, under the provisions of Part III of these regulations, is or has been treated—   **10.77**

(a) as having developed on a date other than the date which, under the said provisions, is treated as the date of onset for the purposes of the claim under consideration;

(b) as a recrudescence of a disease for which compensation has been paid or awarded under the Workmen's Compensation Acts.

Application of [sections 94 to 107 of the Social Security Contributions and Benefits Act 1992 and sections 8 to 10 of the Social Security Administration Act 1992]

11.—The provisions of [sections 94 to 107 of the Social Security Contributions and Benefits Act 1992 and sections 8 to 10 of the Social Security Administration Act 1992] which relates to industrial injuries benefit and sickness benefit made by virtue of section 50A of the Act shall, in relation to prescribed diseases, be subject to the following provisions of this Part of these regulations, and, subject as aforesaid, to the additions and modifications set out in Schedule 2 hereto.   **10.78**

GENERAL NOTE

Section 50A of the Social Security Act 1975 has been replaced by s.102 of the Social Security Contributions and Benefits Act 1992.   **10.79**

Application of Claims and Payments Regulations and Benefit Regulations

12.—(1) Save in so far as they are expressly varied or excluded by, or are inconsistent with, the provisions of this Part of these regulations or of regulation 25 or 36, the Claims and Payments Regulations and the Benefit Regulations shall apply in relation to prescribed diseases as they apply in relation to accidents.   **10.80**

(2) Save as provided in this Part of these regulations or where the context

otherwise requires, references in the aforesaid regulations to accidents shall be construed as references to prescribed diseases, references to the relevant accident shall be construed as references to the relevant disease, references to the date of the relevant accident shall be construed as references to the date of onset of the relevant disease, and in regulation 17 of the Benefit Regulations (increase of disablement pension in cases of special hardship), the reference to the effects of the relevant injury shall be construed as a reference to the effects of the relevant disease.

Benefit not payable in cases covered by the Industrial Injuries and Diseases (Old Cases) Act 1975

10.81   **13.**—Benefit shall not be payable by virtue of the provisions of these regulations in respect of the incapacity, disablement or death of any person as a result of any disease, if an award of benefit under the provisions of any Scheme made under the Industrial Injuries and Diseases (Old Cases) Act 1975 (not being an award which is subsequently [[1] revised or superseded so as to terminate entitlement]) has at any time been made in respect of any attack of the disease suffered by him, or in respect of his death.

AMENDMENT

1. Social Security Act 1998 (Commencement No.8 and Savings and Consequential and Transitional Provisions) Order 1999 (SI 1999/1958) Sch.8 para.5 (July 5, 1999).

Diseases contracted outside Great Britain

10.82   **14.**—For section 50(5) (accidents happening outside Great Britain) there shall be substituted the provision that, subject to the provisions of sections 129, 131 and 132, for the purpose of determining whether a prescribed disease is, or, under the provisions of Part II of these regulations is to be presumed to be, due to the nature of the person's employed earner's employment, that person shall be regarded as not being or as not having been in employed earner's employment during any period for which he is or was outside Great Britain, and accordingly benefit shall not be payable in respect of a prescribed disease which is due to the nature of employment in an occupation in which the person has only been engaged outside Great Britain.

GENERAL NOTE

10.83   Sections 50(5), 129, 131 and 132 of the Social Security Act 1975 have been replaced by ss.94(5), 117, 119 and 120 of the Social Security Contributions Act 1992.

[[1] Modification of paragraph 11(1) of Schedule 7 to the Social Security Contributions and Benefits Act 1992

10.84   **14A.**—The provisions of paragraph 11(1) of Schedule 7 to the Social Security Contributions and Benefits Act 1992 shall be modified by adding after the words "(the day on which section 3 of the Social Security Act 1990 came into force)" the words

"and a person shall not be entitled to reduced earnings allowance—

(i) in relation to a disease prescribed on or after 10th October 1994 under section 108(2) above; or

(ii) in relation to a disease prescribed before 10th October 1994 whose prescription is extended on or after that date under section 108(2) above but
only in so far as the prescription has been so extended".]

AMENDMENT

1. Social Security (Industrial Injuries) (Prescribed Diseases) Amendment
Regulations 1994 (SI 1994/2343) reg.3 (October 10, 1994).

Assessment of extent of disablement

15.—For the purposes of paragraph 1(b) of Schedule 8 (disabilities to be   **10.85**
taken into account in assessing the extent of the claimant's disablement)
and of regulation 11 of the Benefit Regulations (which further defines the
principles of assessment of disablement), an injury or disease other than
the relevant disease shall be treated as having been received or contracted
before the relevant disease if it was received or contracted on or before the
date of onset, and as having been received or contracted after the relevant
disease if it was received or contracted after that date.

GENERAL NOTE

Sch.8 to the Social Security Act 1975 has been replaced by Sch.6 to the Social   **10.86**
Security Contributions and Benefits Act 1992.

Aggregation of percentages of disablement

[¹ **15A.**—(1) After the extent of an employed earner's disablement result-   **10.87**
ing from the relevant disease has been determined, the [² Secretary of State]
shall add to the percentage of that disablement the assessed percentage of
any present disablement of his resulting from—
  (a) any accident after 4th July 1948 arising out of and in the course of
      his employment, being employed earner's employment, or
  (b) any other relevant disease due to the nature of that employment and
      developed after 4th July 1948,
and in respect of which a disablement gratuity was not paid to him under
the Act after a final assessment of disablement.

(2) In determining the extent of an employed earner's disablement for
the purposes of section 57 of the Act there shall be added to the percentage
of disablement resulting from any relevant accident the assessed percentage
of any present disablement of his resulting from any disease or injury prescribed for the purposes of Chapter V of Part II of the Act, which was both
due to the nature of the employment and developed after 4th July 1948,
and in respect of which a disablement gratuity was not paid to him under
the Act after a final assessment of his disablement.

(3) This regulation is subject to the provisions of regulation 15B(3).]

AMENDMENTS

1. Social Security (Industrial Injuries and Diseases) Miscellaneous Provisions
Regulations 1986 (SI 1986/1561) reg.3(2) (October 1, 1986).
2. Social Security Act 1998 (Commencement No.8, and Savings and
Consequential and Transitional Provisions) Order 1999 (SI 1999/1958) Sch.8,
para.6 (July 5, 1999).

10.88   Section 57 of the SSA 1975 has been replaced by s.103 of the SSCBA 1992.

Rounding

10.89   [¹ **15B.**—(1) Subject to the provisions of this regulation, where the assessment of disablement is a percentage between 20 and 100 which is not a multiple of 10, it shall be treated—

(a) if it is a multiple of 5, as being the next higher percentage which is a multiple of 10; and

(b) if it is not a multiple of 5 as being the nearest percentage which is a multiple of 10,

and where it is 14 per cent, or more but less than 20 per cent. it shall be treated as 20 per cent.

(2) In a case to which regulation 15A (aggregation of percentages of disablement) applies, paragraph (1) shall have effect in relation to the aggregate percentage and not in relation to any percentage forming part of the aggregate.

(3) [² Where an assessment or a reassessment] states the degree of disablement due to occupational deafness as less than 20 per cent. that percentage shall be disregarded for the purposes of regulation 15A and this regulation.]

AMENDMENTS

1. Social Security (Industrial Injuries and Diseases) Miscellaneous Provisions Regulations 1986 (SI 1986/1561) reg.3(2) (October 1, 1986).
2. Social Security (Industrial Injuries) (Prescribed Diseases) Amendment Regulations 1990 (SI 1990/2269) reg.2(3) (December 13, 1990).

10.90   *Regulation 16 omitted.*

[¹ Special provisions as to determination of regular occupation in relation to persons claiming reduced earnings allowance

10.91   **17.**—Where a person who has been assessed as at least one per cent. disabled in respect of a prescribed disease establishes that he has abandoned any occupation as a result of the relevant disease at any time after having been employed in employed earner's employment in any occupation prescribed for that disease but before the first day in respect of which he was so assessed, then for the purpose of determining his right to, or the rate of, reduced earnings allowance under section 59A, any occupation he has so abandoned may be treated as his regular occupation for the purposes of that section.]

AMENDMENT

1. Social Security (Industrial Injuries and Diseases) Miscellaneous Provisions Regulations 1986 (SI 1986/1561) (October 1, 1986).

GENERAL NOTE

10.92   This regulation simply permits the claimant's regular occupation (see SSCBA 1992 Sch.7 para.11 (formerly SSA 1975 s.59A), above, and note thereto) to include a job he may have been forced to give up because of the effects of the relevant pre-scribed disease. In other circumstances, an occupation abandoned by the claimant may be disregarded for the purposes of determining his regular occupation *(R(1) 5/52)*.

Exception from requirements as to notice

18.—Regulation 24 of the Claims and Payments Regulations (giving of notice of accidents in respect of which benefit may be payable) shall not apply in relation to prescribed diseases.

10.93

Provisions as to medical examination

19.—Those provisions of section 89(1) and (2) which relate to the obli-gation of claimants to submit themselves to medical examination for the purpose of determining the effect of the relevant accident shall apply also to medical examinations for the purpose of determining whether a clai-mant or beneficiary is suffering or has suffered from a prescribed disease, and regulation 26 of the Claims and Payments Regulations shall be con-strued accordingly.

10.94

GENERAL NOTE

Section 89(1) and (2) of the SSA 1975 have been replaced by s.9(1) and (2) of the SSAA 1992.

10.95

PART V

SPECIAL PROVISIONS AS TO PNEUMOCONIOSIS, BYSSINOSIS, OCCUPATIONAL DEAFNESS AND CERTAIN OTHER DISEASES

Section A—Benefit

Special conditions for disablement benefit for pneumoconiosis, byssinosis and diffuse mesothelioma

20.—[¹ (1) On a claim for disablement pension in respect of pneumo-coniosis, [⁴ or] byssinosis [⁴ . . .], section 57(1) shall apply as if for "14 per cent." there was substituted "1 per cent.".

10.96

(1A) Where on a claim for disablement pension in respect of pneumo-coniosis [⁴ or] byssinosis [⁴ . . .] the extent of the disablement is assessed at one per cent. or more, but less than 20 per cent., disablement pension shall be payable at the 20 per cent. rate if the resulting degree of disablement is greater than 10 per cent. and if it is not at one-tenth of the 100 per cent. rate, with any fraction of a penny being for this purpose treated as a penny.

(1B) Where immediately before 1st October 1986 a person is entitled to a disablement pension on account of pneumoconiosis [⁴ or] byssinosis [⁴ . . .] and in determining the extent of his disablement other disabilities were taken into account in accordance with regulation 11 of the Social Security (General Benefit) Regulations 1982, disablement pension shall continue to be payable on or after 1st October 1986 at the weekly rate applicable to the degree of disablement determined on the last assessment made before 14th October 1986 until—

(a) [³ on a reassessment of the extent of disablement or in consequence of an application for revision or supersession the degree of disablement is assessed either as less than 1 per cent. or as equal to or more than that determined on that last assessment, or

(b) the other disability ceases to exist.]

(2) Section 78(4)(b), in so far as it provides that disablement benefit shall not be payable in respect of byssinosis unless the claimant is found to be suffering from loss of faculty which is likely to be permanent, shall not apply.

(3) Notwithstanding paragraph 4(a) of Schedule 8 (period to be taken into account by an assessment of the extent of the claimant's disablement), the period to be taken into account by an assessment of the extent of the claimant's disablement in respect of byssinosis, if not limited by reference to the claimant's life, shall not be less than one year.

[² (4) On a claim for disablement pension in respect of diffuse mesothelioma—

(a) section 103(6) of the Social Security Contributions and Benefits Act 1992 shall apply as if for the words "after the expiry of the period of 90 days (disregarding Sundays) beginning with the day of the relevant accident" there were substituted the words, "the day on which he first suffers from a loss of faculty due to diffuse mesothelioma";

(b) paragraph 6(1) of Schedule 6 to the Social Security Contributions and Benefits Act 1992 shall apply as if the words "beginning not earlier than the end of the period of 90 days referred to in section 103(6) above and in paragraph 9(3) of that Schedule and" were omitted.]

AMENDMENTS

1. Social Security (Industrial Injuries and Diseases) Miscellaneous Provisions Regulations 1986 (SI 1986/1561) reg.3(3) (October 1, 1986).

2. Social Security (Industrial Injuries) (Miscellaneous Amendments) Regulations 1997 (SI 1997/810) reg.5 (April 9, 1997).

3. Social Security Act 1998 (Commencement No.8, and Savings and Consequential and Transitional Provisions) Order 1999 (SI 1999/1958) Sch.8 para.7 (July 5, 1999).

4. Social Security (Industrial Injuries) (Prescribed Diseases) Amendment Regulations 2002 (SI 2002/1717) reg.2(2) (July 29, 2002).

GENERAL NOTE

10.97   Sections 57(1) and 78(4)(b) of the SSA 1975 have been replaced by ss.103(1) and 110(4) of the SSCBA 1992. Sch.8 para.4(a) has been replaced by Sch.6 para.6(2)(a).

Disablement benefit is still payable in respect of pneumoconiosis or byssinosis even if the extent of disablement is less than 1 per cent. The amount of disablement benefit payable is calculated under para.(1A) or (1B). An assessment of disablement in respect of byssinosis must be for at least one year. Para.(4) removes the usual 90-day waiting period for disablement benefit in cases where the claim is in respect of diffuse mesothelioma but makes it clear that there can be no entitlement until the disease results in a loss of faculty. Repeated assessments are seldom to be expected once the condition produces symptoms and so assessments should take into account anticipated deterioration in the claimant's condition. Thirty per cent of sufferers die within six months of the onset of symptoms. With effect from July 29, 2002, impaired function of the pleura, pericardium or peritoneum function caused by diffuse mesothelioma constitutes a loss of faculty for which the resultant degree of disablement is to be taken as 100 per cent (reg.20A, below).

[¹ Diffuse mesothelioma—prescribed loss of faculty

20A.—(1) For the purposes of paragraph 1 of Schedule 6 to the Social Security Contributions and Benefits Act 1992 (which provides for the assessment of the extent of disablement for the purposes of industrial injuries disablement benefit), the loss of faculty set out in paragraph (2) below is prescribed under sub-paragraph (d) of that paragraph 1 (loss of faculty from which the resulting disabilities are to be taken as amounting to 100 per cent. disablement).

(2) The loss of faculty referred to in paragraph (1) above is impaired function of the pleura, pericardium or peritoneum function caused by diffuse mesothelioma.]

10.98

AMENDMENT

1. This reg. was inserted by Social Security (Industrial Injuries) (Prescribed Diseases) Amendment Regulations 2002 (SI 2002/1717) reg.2(3) (July 29, 2002).

GENERAL NOTE

The effect of this new regulation is that impaired function of the pleura, pericardium or peritoneum caused by diffuse mesothelioma is a loss of faculty from which the resulting disabilities are to be taken as amounting to 100 per cent disablement for purposes of assessment of disablement under SSCBA 1992 Sch.6.

10.99

[¹Primary carcinoma of the lung and angiosarcoma of the liver–special conditions and prescribed loss of faculty

20B.—(1) This regulation applies to a claim for disablement pension made in respect of the diseases prescribed in paragraphs C4, C22(b), C24(a), D8, D8A, D10 and D11 of Part 1 of Schedule 1.

(2) On a claim to which this regulation applies—

(a) section 103(6) of the Social Security Contributions and Benefits Act 1992 (entitlement after expiry of 90 days) shall apply as if for the words "after the expiry of the period of 90 days (disregarding Sundays) beginning with the day of the relevant accident" there were substituted the words "the day on which that person first suffers from a loss of faculty due to primary carcinoma of the lung or bronchus or angiosarcoma of the liver"; and

(b) paragraph 6(1) of Schedule 6 to the Social Security Contributions and Benefits Act 1992 (period to be taken into account by an assessment) shall apply as if the words "beginning not earlier than the end of the period of 90 days referred to in section 103(6) above and in paragraph 9(3) of that Schedule and" were omitted.

(3) On a claim to which this regulation applies, the loss of faculty prescribed for the purposes of sub-paragraph (d) of paragraph 1 of Schedule 6 to the Social Security Contributions and Benefits Act 1992 (assessment of the extent of disablement) is lung impairment caused by primary carcinoma of the lung or bronchus, or impairment caused by angiosarcoma of the liver.]

10.100

1. This regulation was inserted by Social Security (Industrial Injuries) (Prescribed Diseases) Amendment Regulations 2015 (SI 2015/87) reg.3 (March 16, 2015).

GENERAL NOTE

10.101   The effect of this regulation, on a claim for disablement pension in respect of the diseases set out in para.(1), is twofold.

Firstly, entitlement in respect of such a claim may arise from the first day a person suffers from a loss of faculty due to one of those diseases.

Secondly lung impairment caused by primary carcinoma of the lung or bronchus, or impairment caused by angiosarcoma of the liver, rank as loss of faculty from which the resulting disabilities are to be taken as amounting to 100 per cent disablement.

Pneumoconiosis—effects of tuberculosis

10.102   **21.**—Where any person is found to be suffering from pneumoconiosis accompanied by tuberculosis, the effects of the tuberculosis shall be treated for the purposes of Chapter V of Part II of the Act and of these regulations as if they were effects of the pneumoconiosis.

GENERAL NOTE

10.103   Chapter V of Part II of the SSA 1975 has been replaced by ss.108-110 of the SSCBA 1992.

Pneumoconiosis—effects of [³chronic obstructive pulmonary disease]

10.104   **22.**—(1) [¹ Except] in the circumstances specified in paragraph (1A),] where any person is disabled by pneumoconiosis or pneumoconiosis accompanied by tuberculosis to an extent which would, if his physical condition were otherwise normal, be assessed at not less than 50 per cent., the effects of [³any chronic obstructive pulmonary disease] from which that person is found to be suffering shall be treated for the purposes of Chapter V of Part II of the Act and of these regulations as if they were effects of the pneumoconiosis.

[¹ (1A) The circumstances referred to in paragraph (1) are that the person is entitled to industrial injuries disablement benefit on account of the disease set out in paragraph D12 of Part I of Schedule 1.]

(2) Where, on a claim for death benefit, the question arises whether the extent of a person's disablement resulting from pneumoconiosis or from pneumoconiosis accompanied by tuberculosis would, if his physical condition were otherwise normal, have been assessed at not less than 50 per cent.—

    (a) if there has been no assessment of disablement resulting from pneumoconiosis or from pneumoconiosis accompanied by tuberculosis made during the person's life, or if there is no such assessment current at the time of death, [² that issue shall be determined by the Secretary of State];

    (b) if there is an assessment of disablement resulting from pneumoconiosis or from pneumoconiosis accompanied by tuberculosis current at the time of the person's death, that [² issue] shall be treated as having been determined by the decision of the [² Secretary of State or, as the case may be, appeal tribunal] as the case may be, which made such assessment.

AMENDMENTS

1. Social Security (Industrial Injuries) (Prescribed Diseases) Amendment (No. 2) Regulations 1993 (SI 1993/1985) reg.5 (September 13, 1993).
2. Social Security Act 1998 (Commencement No. 8, and Savings and Consequential and Transitional Provisions) Order 1999 (SI 1999/1958) Sch.8 para.8 (July 5, 1999).
3. Social Security (Industrial Injuries) (Prescribed Diseases) Amendment Regulations 2015 (SI 2015/87) reg.5 (March 16, 2015).

GENERAL NOTE

Chapter V of Part II of the SSA 1975 has been replaced by ss.108-110 of the SSCBA 1992.

10.105

Reduced earnings allowance—special provision for pneumoconiosis cases

[¹ **23.**—Where a beneficiary in receipt of a disablement pension in respect of pneumoconiosis receives advice from [² the Secretary of State] that in consequence of the disease he should not follow his regular occupation unless he complies with certain special restrictions as to the place, duration or circumstances of his work, or otherwise, then for the purpose of determining whether he fulfils the conditions laid down in [Schedule 7 of the 1992 Act] (reduced earnings allowance) and for that purpose only—

10.106

(a) the beneficiary shall be deemed, unless the contrary is proved by evidence other than the aforesaid advice—
   (i) to be incapable of following his regular occupation and likely to remain permanently so incapable, and
   (ii) to be incapable of following employment of an equivalent standard which is suitable in his case;
(b) where the beneficiary has ceased to follow any occupation to which the aforesaid special restrictions were applicable, the fact that he had followed such an occupation in the period between the date of onset of the disease and the date of the current assessment of his disablement, or for a reasonable period of trial thereafter, shall be disregarded.]

AMENDMENTS

1. Social Security (Industrial Injuries and Diseases) Miscellaneous Provisions Regulations 1986 (SI 1986/1561) reg.6 (October 1, 1986).
2. Social Security Act 1998 (Commencement No.8, and Savings and Consequential and Transitional Provisions) Order 1999 (SI 1999/1958) Sch.8 para.9 (July 5, 1999).

[¹ Special requirement for pneumoconiosis claimants in unscheduled occupation cases

24.—(1) A claim for disablement benefit in respect of pneumoconiosis by a person in relation to whom the disease is prescribed by virtue of regulation 2(b)(ii) shall be referred by the Secretary of State to a medical practitioner

10.107

for a report, unless the Secretary of State is satisfied on reasonable grounds that the claimant is not suffering or has not suffered from pneumoconiosis, in which case he may decide the claim without such a report.

(2) The provisions of paragraph (1) of this regulation shall apply to an appeal tribunal and a Commissioner as they apply to the Secretary of State.]

AMENDMENT

1. Social Security Act 1998 (Commencement No.8, and Savings and Consequential and Transitional Provisions) Order 1999 (SI 1999/1958) Sch.8 para.10 (July 5, 1999).

Time for claiming benefit in respect of occupational deafness

10.108

25.—(1) Regulation 14 of the Claims and Payments Regulations (time for claiming benefit) shall not apply in relation to occupational deafness except in relation to a claim for sickness benefit payable by virtue of section [102].

(2) Subject to regulation 27(1)(c), disablement benefit, or sickness benefit payable by virtue of section [102] of the Act, shall not be paid in pursuance of a claim in respect of occupational deafness which is made later than 5 years after the latest date, before the date of the claim, on which the claimant worked [1 in employed earner's employment] in an occupation prescribed in relation to occupational deafness [3 . . .]

AMENDMENTS

1. Social Security (Industrial Injuries) (Prescribed Diseases) Amendment Regulations 2000 (SI 2000/1588) reg.3 (July 10, 2000).
2. Social Security Act 1998 (Commencement No.8, and Savings and Consequential and Transitional Provisions) Order 1999 (SI 1999/1958) Sch.8 para.11 (July 5, 1999).
3. Social Security (Industrial Injuries) (Prescribed Diseases) Amendment Regulations 2005 (SI 2005/324) reg.2(2) (March 14, 2005).

GENERAL NOTE

10.109

Note that para.4(3) of Sch.6 of the SSA 1990 (effective from July 13, 1990) provides that reg.25, and any former regulations which it directly or indirectly re-enacts with or without amendment, shall be taken to be, and always to have been, validly made. *R(I) 1/92* applied in *CI/276/1988* and *CSI/22/91*, and *CSI/84/89* and *R(I) 1/94* (affirmed by the Court of Appeal in *Chatterton v Chief Adjudication Officer*, July 8, 1993) (reported as *R(I) 1/94*), all hold that the validation effected by para.4(3) of Sch.6 of the SSA 1990 (which entered into force on July 13, 1990) operates retrospectively, thus transforming initially invalid decisions (the Court of Appeal had held reg.25 ultra vires in *McKiernon v Secretary of State for Social Security*) into valid determinations. Furthermore, in *Chief Adjudication Officer v McKiernon*, also decided on July 8, 1993, the Court of Appeal upheld the CAO's appeal against Commisioner Goodman's decision in *R(I) 2/94*. The entry into force of para.4(3), notwithstanding its retrospective operation, was a change of circumstances enabling the AO to review an SSAT's decision that Mr McKiernon had good cause for his late claim so that his claim was timeous.

The regulation prevents disablement benefit or sickness benefit (payable only because of industrial disease) being paid in pursuance of a claim in respect of occupational deafness which is made later than five years after the latest date on which the claimant *worked in* a prescribed occupation, unless further conditions are met including a condition of *employment in* the occupation for a period or aggregate of periods amounting to not less than 10 years. The exemption afforded by those further conditions was revoked with effect from March 14, 2005 by reg.2 of the Social Security (Industrial Injuries) (Prescribed Diseases) Amendment Regulations 2005 (SI 2005/324). *CI/16/91* follows *R(I) 2/79* (see above, notes to reg.2) in holding that in dealing with both time periods one looks to "the work actually done rather than the contractual obligation to do it, so that, for example, time off work through ill-health was not time spent working in the occupation for the purposes of the relevant legislation" (*CI/16/91*, para.5). So, in *CI/16/91*, although the claimant's employment had been terminated on May 11, 1985, he had been on the sick from April 25, 1984. His claim was made in June 1989. Because the focus for the five-year period had to be on when he last *worked*, the Commissioner held that he ceased work in the prescribed occupation on April 25, 1984, and his claim was time-barred by reg.25.

In *CI/286/95*, Commissioner Howell held that "worked in an occupation" in lines four and five of reg.25(2) was *not* to be construed as if it read "worked *in employment earner's employment* in an occupation". He saw no absurdity in a claimant

"being able to claim more than 5 years after ceasing to be an employed earner but within 5 years of stopping his actual work [albeit in self-employment] in a listed occupation which gives rise to exposure to noise. Before he can get the benefit, the question whether his disease is due to the nature of his employment as an employee still has to be determined."

He therefore saw nothing inconsistent with the purpose of the legislation or rendering reg.25(2) ultra vires, in reading it in the way he and the SSAT had done (*ibid.*) Commissioner Howell's approach was followed by Commissioner Walker in *CSI/89/96*. The amendments numbered 2 to para.(2), requiring work in employed earner's employment, reverse the effect of *CI/286/95* and *CSI/89/96*, noted immediately above. The amendment is the subject of a transitional provision in reg.7(1) of the amending instrument such that it "shall not apply in relation to a claim made within 3 months after the commencement date and the amendments made by regulations 2(3), 5 and 6 shall not apply where the date of onset of the relevant disease is prior to the commencement date and the claim is made within 3 months after that date".

Claims in respect of occupational deafness

26.—Where it appears that a person who has made a claim for sickness benefit by virtue of section [102] of the Act in respect of occupational deafness— 10.110

(a) may be entitled to disablement benefit, and
(b) has not previously made a claim for disablement benefit in respect of occupational deafness or such a previous claim has been disallowed,

such a claim for sickness benefit may also be treated as a claim for disablement benefit.

GENERAL NOTE

A claim for sickness benefit on the ground of occupational deafness may be treated as a claim for disablement benefit if the claimant has not already made an unsuccessful claim. This paragraph would seem to apply even if the claimant would have satisfied the contribution conditions. 10.111

Further claims in respect of occupational deafness

27.—(1) In the event of disallowance of a claim for disablement benefit or sickness benefit made by virtue of section [102] of the Act in respect of 10.112

occupational deafness because the claimant has failed to satisfy the minimum hearing loss requirement prescribed in column 1 of paragraph A10 of Part I of Schedule 1 hereto, disablement benefit or sickness benefit made by virtue of section [102] of the Act shall not be paid in pursuance of a further claim in respect of occupational deafness made by or on behalf of that claimant unless—

(a) it is a claim made after the expiration of three years from the date of a claim which was disallowed because the claimant was not suffering from occupational deafness; or

(b) it is a claim made after the expiration of three years from the date of a reassessment by [¹ the Secretary of State or an appeal tribunal] of the extent of the claimant's disablement at less than 20 per cent; or

(c) if the claimant would otherwise be precluded by regulation 25(2) from making a further claim after the expiration of three years from the date of the disallowed claim or from the date of a reassessment by the Secretary of State or an appeal tribunal of the extent of his disablement at less than 20 per cent., as the case may be, it is the first claim made since that date and within five years from the latest date, before the date of the claim, on which he worked [² in employed earner's employment] in any occupation specified in column 2 of paragraph A10 of Part I of Schedule I hereto.

[¹ (2) A claim to be paid benefit by virtue of paragraph (1)(c) may be disallowed by the Secretary of State, an appeal tribunal or a Commissioner ("the determining authority") without reference to a medical practitioner where the determining authority is satisfied by medical evidence that the claimant is not suffering from occupational deafness.]

AMENDMENTS

1. Social Security Act 1998 (Commencement No.8, and Savings and Consequential and Transitional Provisions) Order 1999 (SI 1999/1958) Sch.8 para.12 (July 5, 1999).

2. Social Security (Industrial Injuries) (Prescribed Diseases) Amendment Regulations 2000 (SI 2000/1588) reg.4 (July 10, 2000).

GENERAL NOTE

10.113   The amendment, numbered 2 in the list above, requiring work in employed earner's employment, reverses the effect of *CI 286/95* and *CSI 89/96*, noted in the annotation to reg.25, above. The amendment is the subject of a transitional provision in regulation 7(1) of the amending instrument, reproduced later in this volume.

Availability of disablement benefit in respect of occupational deafness

10.114   **28.**—Where a person is awarded disablement benefit in respect of occupational deafness, section 57(4) (period for which disablement benefit is not available) shall not apply.

GENERAL NOTE

10.115   In occupational deafness cases, the date of onset of the disease is deemed to be no earlier than the date of claim (see reg.6(2)(c)) and so the usual 90-day qualifying period does not apply. Section 57(4) of the SSA 1975 has been replaced by s.103(6) of the SSCBA 1992.

Period to be covered by assessment of disablement in respect of occupational deafness

[¹**29.**—Paragraph 6(1) and (2) of Schedule 6 to the Social Security Contributions and Benefits Act 1992 shall be modified so that in respect of occupational deafness, the period to be taken into account by an assessment of the extent of a claimant's disablement shall be the remainder of the claimant's life.]

10.116

AMENDMENT

1. Social Security (Industrial Injuries) (Prescribed Diseases) Amendment (No.2) Regulations 2003 (SI 2003/2190) reg.2(2) (September 22, 2003).

Supersession of a decision in respect of occupational deafness

30.—[¹ . . .].

10.117

REVOCATION

1. Social Security (Industrial Injuries) (Prescribed Diseases) Amendment (No.2) Regulations 2003 (SI 2003/2190) reg.2(3) (September 22, 2003).

Requirement for leave of appeal tribunal

31.—[¹ . . .].

10.118

REVOCATION

1. Social Security (Industrial Injuries) (Prescribed Diseases) Amendment (No.2) Regulations 2003 (SI 2003/2190) reg.2(3) (September 22, 2003).

No appeal against a decision of disablement in respect of occupational Deafness

32.—[¹ . . .].

10.119

REVOCATION

1. Social Security (Industrial Injuries) (Prescribed Diseases) Amendment (No.2) Regulations 2003 (SI 2003/2190) reg.2(3) (September 22, 2003).

Cases in which reassessment of disablement in respect of occupational deafness is final

33.—[¹ . . .].

10.120

REVOCATION

1. Social Security (Industrial Injuries) (Prescribed Diseases) Amendment (No.2) Regulations 2003 (SI 2003/2190) reg.2(3) (September 22, 2003).

Assessment of extent of disablement and rate of disablement benefit payable in respect of occupational deafness

34.—(1) Subject to the provisions of Schedule [6] and regulations made thereunder and the following provisions of this regulation, the first assessment of the extent of disablement in respect of occupational deafness made in pursuance of a claim made before 3rd September 1979 by a person to

10.121

whom disablement benefit in respect of occupational deafness is payable for a period before 3rd September 1979 [¹ shall be the percentage calculated by—

    (a) determining the average total hearing loss due to all causes for each ear at 1, 2 and 3 kHz frequencies; and then by

    (b) determining the percentage degree of disablement for each ear in accordance with Part I of Schedule 3; and then by

    (c) determining the average percentage degree of binaural disablement in accordance with the formula set out in Part III of Schedule 3.]

(2) Except in any case to which paragraph (1) applies and subject to the provisions of Schedule [6] and regulations made thereunder and the following provisions of this regulation, the extent of disablement in respect of occupational deafness [¹ shall be the percentage calculated by—

    (a) determining the average total hearing loss due to all causes for each ear at 1, 2 and 3 kHz frequencies; and then by

    (b) determining the percentage degree of disablement for each ear in accordance with Part II of Schedule 3; and then by

    (c) determining the average percentage degree of binaural disablement in accordance with the formula set out in Part III of Schedule 3.]

(3) In [¹ . . .] Schedule 3 hereto "better ear" means that ear in which the claimant's hearing loss due to all causes is the less and "worse ear" means that ear in which the claimant's hearing loss due to all causes is the more.

[¹ (3A) For the purposes of determining the percentage degree of disablement in Parts I and II of Schedule 3 to these Regulations, any fraction of an average hearing loss shall, where the average hearing loss is over 50 dB, be rounded down to the next whole figure.]

(4) The extent of disablement in respect of occupational deafness may be subject to such increase or reduction of the degree of disablement as may be reasonable in the circumstances of the case where, having regard to the provisions of Schedule 8 and to regulations made thereunder, that degree of disablement does not provide a reasonable assessment of the extent of disability resulting from the relevant loss of faculty.

[² (5) Where on re-assessment of the extent of disability in respect of occupational deafness the average sensorineural hearing loss over 1, 2 and 3 kHz frequencies is not 50 dB or more in each ear, or where there is such a loss but the loss in one or each ear is not 50 dB or more due to occupational noise, the extent of disablement shall be assessed at less than 20 per cent.]

(6) Where the extent of disablement is reassessed at less than 20 per cent. disablement benefit [³ or reduced earnings allowance] shall not be payable.

(7) In the case of a person to whom disablement benefit by reason of occupational deafness was payable in respect of a period before 3rd September 1979—

    (a) if no assessment of the extent of his disability has been made, [⁴ revised or superseded] on or after that date, the rate of any disablement benefit payable to him shall be the rate payable for the degree of disablement assessed in accordance with paragraph (1), but

    (b) if such an assessment has been made, [⁴ revised or superseded] in respect of a period commencing on or after that date and before 3rd October 1983, the rate of any disablement benefit payable to him shall be either—

        (i) the rate which would be payable if an assessment were made in accordance with paragraph (2), or

(ii) the rate which was payable immediately before the first occasion on which such [⁴ revision or supercession] took place,
whichever is the more favourable to him.

(8) Where in the case of a person to whom disablement benefit by
reason of occupational deafness was payable in respect of a period before 3rd
September 1979 the extent of his disability is reassessed and the period taken
into account on reassessment begins on or after 3rd October 1983 and—

(a) immediately before that date, by virtue of paragraph (7) the rate at
which disablement benefit was payable to him was higher than the
rate which would otherwise have been payable, or,

(b) the reassessment is the first reassessment for a period commencing
after 3rd September 1979,

the rate of disablement benefit payable to him shall be whichever of the
rates specified in paragraph (9) is applicable.

(9) The rate of disablement benefit payable in the case of a person to
whom paragraph (8) applies shall be—

(a) if the current rate appropriate to the extent of his disability as reassessed is the same as or more than the rate at which disablement
benefit was payable immediately before the beginning of the period
taken into account on reassessment, the current rate, or

(b) if the current rate is less than the rate at which disablement benefit
was payable immediately before the beginning of the period taken
into account on reassessment, the lower of the following rates—

(i) the rate at which benefit would have been payable if the reassessment of the extent of his disability had been made in accordance with paragraph (1), or

(ii) the rate at which benefit was payable immediately before the
beginning of the period taken into account on reassessment.

AMENDMENTS

1. Social Security (Industrial Injuries) (Prescribed Diseases) Amendment
Regulations 1989 (SI 1989/1207) reg.4 (October 16, 1989).

2. Social Security (Industrial Injuries and Adjudication) Miscellaneous
Amendment Regulations 1986 (SI 1986/1374) reg.3 (September 1, 1986).

3. Social Security (Industrial Injuries and Diseases) Miscellaneous Provisions
1986 (SI 1986/1561) reg.6 (October 1, 1986).

4. Social Security Act 1998 (Commencement No.8, and Savings and
Consequential and Transitional Provisions) Order 1999 (SI 1999/1958) Sch.8
para.16 (July 5, 1999).

GENERAL NOTE

This regulation and Sch.3 govern the assessment of disablement in occupational   **10.122**
deafness cases. Note, however, that paras (1) and (2) are expressed to be subject
to Sch.6 to the Social Security Contributions and Benefits Act 1992 and regulations made thereunder, including reg.11 of the Social Security (General Benefit)
Regulations 1982.

Paragraph (1) of this regulation and Pt 1 of Sch.3 only apply to the first
assessment of disablement in respect of claims made before September 3, 1979.
Therefore, virtually all assessments are now made under para.(2) of this regulation and Pt 2 of Sch.3 which is less generous. The percentage degree of disablement for each ear is calculated separately and the formula in Pt 3 of Sch.3 is then
applied to give an overall percentage of disablement. However, note that para.(4)
of this regulation enables an adjudicating medical authority to depart from the

Schedule if the result of applying the Schedule is to give an unreasonable assessment. A tribunal should first assess according to the Schedule and then give a reason for departing from that assessment (*R(I) 1/89*). Para.(5) applies only on a reassessment.

Paras (7)–(9) are transitional and apply to a person who was in receipt of disablement benefit before September 3, 1979. If there has been no assessment since that date, entitlement to disablement benefit is calculated under the more favourable provisions of para.(1). If there was an assessment between that date and October 3,1983, disablement benefit is payable either at the rate which would be payable on an assessment calculated under para.(2) or at the rate payable immediately before the review or variation took place, whichever is the more favourable. In view of inflation, the latter option is unlikely to be more favourable. If there has been an assessment on or after October 3, 1983, it will be usual for the claimant to receive the rate appropriate to an assessment under para.(2). However, if that rate is lower than the rate payable immediately before the beginning of the period taken into account on the reassessment, the lower of the two rates mentioned in para.(9)(b) is payable instead. The greater the lapse of time since the review or variation, the less favourable will be the latter option.

The 1989 amendments removed the requirement that hearing loss should be measured by pure tone audiometry as opposed to evoked response audiometry or any other test. In *R(I) 2/98*, it was held that those amendments (in particular, the introduction of para.(3A)) are procedural and so operate retrospectively in respect of periods before October 16, 1989.

Commencement date of period of assessment in respect of occupational deafness

10.123   **35.**—Notwithstanding Schedule [¹ . . .] [8], the period to be taken into account by an assessment of the extent of disablement in respect of occupational deafness shall not commence before 3rd February 1975.

AMENDMENT

1. Social Security Act 1998 (Commencement No.8, and Savings and Consequential and Transitional Provisions) Order 1999 (SI 1999/1958) Sch.8 para.17 (July 5, 1999).

GENERAL NOTE

10.123A   Note that Sch.8 of the SSA 1975 has been replaced by Sch.6 of the SSCA 1992.

Time for claiming benefit in respect of occupational asthma

10.124   **36.**—(1) Subject to paragraphs (2) and (3), disablement benefit and sickness benefit payable by virtue of section 50A shall not be paid in pursuance of a claim in respect of occupational asthma which is made later than 10 years after the latest date, before the date of the claim, on which the claimant or, as the case may be, the person in respect of whom the claim is made worked [¹ in employed earner's employment] in an occupation prescribed in relation to occupational asthma.

(2) Paragraph (1) shall not apply to any claim made before 29th March 1983 by or in respect of a person who ceased on or after 29th March 1972 to [¹ work in employed earner's] employment in an occupation prescribed in relation to occupational asthma.

(3) Paragraph (1) shall not apply to any claim made by or in respect of a person who has at any time been found to be suffering from asthma

as a result of an industrial accident and by virtue of that finding has been awarded disablement benefit either for life or for a period which includes the date on which the aforesaid claim is made.

(4) Subject to paragraphs (5) and (6), industrial death benefit shall not be paid in pursuance of a claim in respect of occupational asthma where the person in respect of whose death the benefit is being claimed died more than 10 years after the latest day on which he worked [¹ in employed earner's employment] in an occupation prescribed in relation to occupational asthma.

(5) Paragraph (4) shall not apply to any claim made in respect of the death of a person who died before 29th March 1983 and who on or after 29th March 1972 had not worked [¹ in employed earner's employment] in an occupation in relation to occupational asthma.

(6) Paragraph (4) shall not apply to any claim made in respect of the death of a person who had at any time been found to be suffering either from asthma as a result of an industrial accident or from occupational asthma and by virtue of that finding had been awarded disablement benefit either for life or for a period which included the date of his death.

(7) Regulation 14 of the Claims and Payments Regulations (time for claiming benefit) shall not apply to a claim in respect of occupational asthma made before 29th March 1983.

AMENDMENT

1. Social Security (Industrial Injuries) (Prescribed Diseases) Amendment Regulations 2000 (SI 2000/1588) reg.5 (July 10, 2000).

GENERAL NOTE

Note that s.50A of the SSA 1975 has been replaced by s.102 of the SSCA 1992. **10.125**

It was clear from *McKiernon v Secretary of State for Social Services* (*The Times*, November 1, 1989), that reg.36 was originally ultra vires. As a result, s.77(2) of the Social Security Act 1975 (now s.109(2) of the Social Security Contributions and Benefits Act 1992) was amended by para.4(2) of Sch.6 to the Social Security Act 1990. Para.4(3) of Sch.6 to the 1990 Act provided that reg.36 should be taken always to have been validly made. See the note to reg.25.

In *CSI/89/96* Commissioner Walker followed the approach of Commissioner Howell in *CI/286/95* (see annotations to reg.25, above) in holding that "worked in an occupation" in para.(1) is not limited to employed earner's employment but can embrace self-employment so that "so long as within 10 years of the date of claim the claimant has been exposed to a sensitizing agent by his self-employment his claim may be sound in law" (para.7). The amendments, requiring work in employed earner's employment in a prescribed occupation, reverse the effect of *CI/286/95* and *CSI/89/96*. The amendment is the subject of a transitional provision in reg.7(1) of the amending instrument reproduced later in this volume.

Initial examinations

37.—[¹ . . .]. **10.126**

REVOCATION

1. Social Security (Industrial Injuries) (Prescribed Diseases) Amendment Regulations 1994 (SI 1994/2343) reg.5 (October 10, 1994).

The Social Security (Industrial Injuries) (Prescribed Diseases) Regulations 1985

Periodical examinations

10.127   **38.**—[¹ . . .]

REVOCATION

1. Social Security (Industrial Injuries) (Prescribed Diseases) Amendment Regulations 1994 (SI 1994/2343) reg.5 (October 10, 1994).

Suspension from employment

10.128   **39.**—A certificate of suspension issued under the provisions of either regulation 43 or regulation 44 of the National Insurance (Industrial Injuries) (Prescribed Diseases) Regulations 1959 (regulations revoked with effect from 27th November 1974 by regulation 7(1) of the National Insurance (Industrial Injuries) (Prescribed Diseases) Amendment (No. 2) Regulations 1974) and in force immediately before 27th November 1974 shall continue in force subject to and in accordance with the provisions of regulation 40 of these regulations.

Conditions of suspension

10.129   **40.**—(1) A certificate of suspension issued under the provisions of either regulation 43 or regulation 44 of the National Insurance (Industrial Injuries) (Prescribed Diseases) Regulations 1959, and remaining in force by virtue of the last preceding regulation, shall suspend the person to whom it relates from further employment in any occupation in relation to which pneumoconiosis is prescribed, with such exceptions and subject to such conditions (if any) as may be specified in the certificate.

(2) [¹ The Secretary of State] may at any time revoke or vary a certificate of suspension on the application of the person to whom it relates, but unless so revoked or varied such certificate shall remain in force throughout the life of such person.

(3) No person who has been suspended from employment may engage or continue in employment, and no employer may employ or continue to employ any such person, in any occupation in relation to which pneumoconiosis is prescribed, except in accordance with the terms of the certificate of suspension in his case.

AMENDMENT

1. Social Security Act 1998 (Commencement No.8, and Savings and Consequential and Transitional Provisions) Order 1999 (SI 1999/1958) Sch.8 para.18 (July 5, 1999).

Duties of employers

10.130   **41.**—[¹ . . .].

REVOCATION

1. Social Security (Industrial Injuries) (Prescribed Diseases) Amendment Regulations 1994 (SI 1994/2343) reg.5 (October 10, 1994).

Fees for initial and periodical examination

10.131   **42.**—[¹ . . .].

1508

REVOCATION

1. Social Security (Industrial Injuries) (Prescribed Diseases) Amendment Regulations 1994 (SI 1994/2343) reg.5 (October 10, 1994).

PART VI

TRANSITIONAL PROVISIONS AND REVOCATION

Transitional provisions regarding relevant dates

43.—(1) Subject to paragraph (2) the "relevant date", in relation to each disease set out in the first column of Schedule 4 hereto, is the date set against the disease in the second column of that Schedule.

(2) Where a disease set out in the first column of Schedule 4 hereto was prescribed in relation to any person by regulations which came into operation on a date earlier than the date set against that disease in the second column of that Sch., the "relevant date" in relation to such disease is such earlier date on which the disease was prescribed in relation to the person in question.

(3) It shall be a condition of a person's right to benefit in respect of any disease set out in Schedule 4 that he was—

(a) incapable of work, or

(b) suffering from a loss of faculty,

as a result of that disease on or after the relevant date.

(4) The "relevant date" in relation to byssinosis—

(a) in the case of a person employed in an occupation involving work in any room in which the weaving of cotton or flax or any other process which takes place between, or at the same time as, the winding or beaming and weaving of cotton or flax is carried on in a factory in which any or all of those processes are carried on is 3rd October 1983;

(b) in any other case, is 6th April 1979 except that where the disease was prescribed in relation to any person by regulations which came into operation on a date earlier that 6th April 1979 the relevant date is that earlier date.

(5) Byssinosis is not prescribed in relation to any person if neither of the following conditions is satisfied, namely:—

(a) that he was suffering from a loss of faculty as a result of bysinnosis on or after the relevant date;

(b) that he has been employed in employed earner's employment in any occupation mentioned in regulation 2(c) of the old regulation for a period or periods (whether before or after 5th July 1948) amounting in the aggregate to five years.

(6) Notwithstanding that a person does not satisfy paragraph (3) infection by leptospira is prescribed in relation to any person if he is or has been either incapable of work or suffering from a loss of faculty as a result of infection by—

(a) leptospira icterohaemorrhagiae in the case of a person employed in employed earner's employment before 7th January 1980 in any occupation involving work in places which are or are liable to be, infested by rats, or

10.132

(b) leptospira canicola in the case of a person so employed in any occupation involving work at dog kennels or the care or handling of dogs.

(7) A person who, immediately before 3rd October 1983, was in receipt of benefit in respect of a disease or injury which was prescribed by virtue of the old regulations, or who makes a claim for benefit in respect of a prescribed disease after 2nd October 1983 where the date of onset of the disease or injury was before 3rd October 1983, shall be treated for the purpose only of determining whether the disease or injury is in relation to him a prescribed disease by virtue of the occupation in which he is or was engaged as if the old regulations were still in force and these regulations had not come into operation, if that would be more favourable to him.

Transitional provisions regarding dates of development and dates of onset

10.133   **44.**—Where a claim for benefit has been made before 6th April 1983 or a date of onset is determined which is before 6th April 1983 or a claim for injury benefit is made after 5th April 1983 for a day falling or a period beginning before 6th April 1983, these regulations shall take effect subject to the provisions of Schedule 5.

10.134   *Regulation 45 omitted.*

SCHEDULES

SCHEDULE 1   **Regulations 2 and 4**

PART I

LIST OF PRESCRIBED DISEASES AND THE OCCUPATIONS FOR WHICH THEY ARE PRESCRIBED

10.135

Prescribed disease or injury	Occupation
	Any occupation involving:
A. Conditions due to physical agents [1 [28 A1 Leukaemia (other than chronic lymphocytic leukaemia) or primary cancer of the bone, bladder, breast, colon, liver, lung, ovary, stomach, testis or thyroid.]	[28 Exposure to ionising radiation where the dose is sufficient to double the risk of the occurrence of the condition.]
A2. [2 . . .] cataract.	[2 Frequent or prolonged exposure to radiation from red-hot or white-hot material.].
	Any occupation involving:
[27A3 (a) Dysbarism, including decompression sickness and barotrauma; (b) Osteonecrosis.]	Subjection to compressed or rarefied air or other respirable gases or gaseous mixtures.
[25A4. Task-specific focal dystonia of the hand or forearm.	Prolonged periods of handwriting, typing or other repetitive movements of the fingers, hand or arm.]
A5. Subcutaneous cellulitis of the hand [19 . . .]	Manual labour causing severe or prolonged friction or pressure on the hand.
A6. Bursitis or subcutaneous cellulitis arising at or about the knee due to severe	Manual labour causing severe or prolonged external friction or pressure at

Prescribed disease or injury	Occupation
or prolonged external friction or pressure at or about the knee [19 . . .]	or about the knee.
A7. Bursitis or subcutaneous cellulitis arising at or about the elbow due to severe or prolonged external friction or pressure at or about the elbow [19 . . .]	Manual labour causing severe or prolonged external friction or pressure at or about the elbow.
A8. Traumatic inflammation of the tendons of the hand or forearm, or of the associated tendon sheaths.	Manual labour, or frequent or repeated movements of the hand or wrist.
[19 A9. *Omitted.*]	*Omitted.*]
[3 A10. Sensorineural hearing loss amounting to at least 50 dB in each ear, being the average of hearing losses at 1, 2 and 3 kHz frequencies, and being due in the case of at least one ear to occupational noise (occupational deafness).]	[16 The use of, or work wholly or mainly in the immediate vicinity of the use of, a—
	(a) band saw, circular saw or cutting disc to cut metal in the metal founding or forging industries, circular saw to cut products in the manufacture of steel, powered (other than hand powered) grinding tool on metal (other than sheet metal or plate metal), pneumatic percussive tool on metal, pressurised air arc tool to gouge metal, burner or torch to cut or dress steel based products, skid transfer bank, knock out and shake out grid in a foundry, machine (other than a power press machine) to forge metal including a machine used to drop stamp metal by means of closed or open dies or drop hammers, machine to cut or shape or clean metal nails, or plasma spray gun to spray molten metal;
	(b) pneumatic percussive tool:—to drill rock in a quarry, on stone in a quarry works, underground, for mining coal, for sinking a shaft, or for tunnelling in civil engineering works;
	(c) vibrating metal moulding box in the concrete products industry, or circular saw to cut concrete masonry blocks;
	(d) machine in the manufacture of textiles for:—weaving man-made or natural fibres (including mineral fibres), high speed false twisting of fibres, or the mechanical cleaning of bobbins;
	(e) multi-cutter moulding machine on wood, planing machine on wood, automatic or semi-automatic lathe on wood, multiple cross-cut machine on wood, automatic shaping machine on wood, double-end tenoning machine on wood, vertical spindle moulding machine (including a high speed routing machine) on wood, edge banding machine on wood, bandsawing machine (with a blade width of not less than 75 millimetres) on wood, circular sawing machine on wood including one operated by moving the blade towards the material being cut, or chain saw on wood;

Prescribed disease or injury	Occupation
	(f) jet of water (or a mixture of water and abrasive material) at a pressure above 680 bar, or jet channelling process to burn stone in a quarry;
	(g) machine in a ship's engine room, or gas turbine for:—performance testing on a test bed, installation testing of a replacement engine in an aircraft, or acceptance testing of an Armed Service fixed wing combat aircraft;
	(h) machine in the manufacture of glass containers or hollow ware for:—automatic moulding, automatic blow moulding, or automatic glass pressing and forming;
	Any occupation involving:
	(i) spinning machine using compressed air to produce glass wool or mineral wool;
	(j) continuous glass toughening furnace;
	(k) firearm by a police firearms training officer; or
	(l) shot-blaster to carry abrasives in air for cleaning.]

A11.

[20(a) Intense blanching of the skin, with a sharp demarcation line between affected and non-affected skin, where the blanching is cold-induced, episodic, occurs throughout the year and affects the skin of the distal with the middle and proximal phalanges, or distal with the middle phalanx (or in the case of a thumb the distal with the proximal phalanx), of—

(i) in the case of a person with 5 fingers (including thumb) on one hand, any 3 of those fingers, or

(ii) in the case of a person with only 4 such fingers, any 2 of those fingers, or

(iii) in the case of a person with less than 4 such fingers, any one of them or, as the case may be, the one remaining finger,

where none of the person's fingers was subject to any degree of cold-induced, episodic blanching of the skin prior to the person's employment in an occupation described in the second column in relation to this paragraph, or

(b) significant, demonstrable reduction in both sensory perception and manipulative dexterity with continuous numbness or continuous tingling all present at the same time in the distal phalanx of any finger (including thumb) where none of the person's fingers was subject to any degree of reduction in sensory perception, manipulative

(a) the use of hand-held chain saws [21 on wood]

(b) the use of hand-held rotary tools in grinding or in the sanding or polishing of metal, or the holding of material being ground, or metal being sanded or polished, by rotary tools; or

(c) the use of hand-held percussive metal-working tools, or the holding of metal being worked upon by percussive tools, in riveting, caulking, chipping, hammering, fettling, or swaging; or

(d) the use of hand-held powered percussive drills or hand-held powered percussive hammers in mining, quarrying, demolition, or on roads or footpaths, including road construction; or

(e) the holding of material being worked upon by pounding machines in shoe manufacture.

Prescribed disease or injury	Occupation

dexterity, numbness or tingling prior to
the person's employment in an occupation
described in the second column in relation
to this paragraph,
where the symptoms in paragraph (a) or
paragraph (b) were caused by vibration.]

[⁷A12. Carpal tunnel syndrome.]

Any occupation involving:

[¹⁹ (a) The use, at the time the symptoms first
develop, of hand-held powered tools
whose internal parts vibrate so as to
transmit that vibration to the hand, but
excluding those tools which are solely
powered by hand; or

(b) repeated palmar flexion and dorsiflexion of
the wrist for at least 20 hours per week for
a period or periods amounting in aggregate
to least 12 months in the 24 months prior

to the onset of symptoms, where
"repeated" means once or more often in
every 30 seconds.]

[¹⁷ A13. Osteoarthritis of the hip.

Work in agriculture as a farmer or farm
worker for a period of, or periods which
amount in aggregate to, 10 years or more.]

[²³A14. Osteoarthritis of the knee.

Work underground in a coal mine for a period
of, or periods which amount in aggregate to,
at least 10 years in any one or more of the
following occupations:
(a) before 1st January 1986 as a coal miner; or
(b) on or after 1st January 1986 as a—
   (i)   face worker working on a non-
      mechanised coal face;
   (ii) development worker;
   (iii) face-salvage worker;
   (iv) conveyor belt cleaner; or
   (v) conveyor belt attendant.
"A non-mechanised coal face" means a coal
face without either powered roof supports or
a power loader machine which simultaneously
cuts and loads the coal or without both.]
[²⁵Work wholly or mainly fitting or laying
carpets or floors (other than concrete floors)
for a period of, or periods which amount in
aggregate to, 20 years or more.]

Any occupation involving:

B. Conditions due to biological agents
[²⁷B1
(a) Cutaneous anthrax;
(b) Pulmonary anthrax.]

(a) Contact with anthrax spores, including
contact with animals infected by anthrax; or
(b) handling, loading, unloading or transport
of animals of a type susceptible to
infection with anthrax or of the products
or residues of such animals.]

B2. Glanders.

Contact with equine animals or their carcases.

B3. Infection by leptospira.

(a) Work in places which are, or are liable to
be, infested by rats, field mice or voles, or
other small mammals; or
(b) work at dog kennels or the care or
handling of dogs; or
(c) contact with bovine animals or their meat
products or pigs or their meat products.

Prescribed disease or injury	Occupation
[²⁷B4 (a) Cutaneous larva migrans; (b) Iron deficiency anaemia caused by gastrointestinal infection by hookworm.] B5. Tuberculosis.	[¹⁷Contact with a source of ankylostomiasis.] [²⁷B5 Contact with a source of tuberculosis while undertaking— (a) work in a hospital, mortuary in which post mortems are conducted, or laboratory; or (b) work in any other workplace.]
B6. Extrinsic allergic alveolitis [²⁸. . .]	Exposure to moulds or fungal spores or heterologous proteins [²⁸ or any other biological substance that causes extrinsic allergic alveolitis] by reason of employment in: (a) agriculture, horticulture, forestry, cultivation of edible fungi or malt-working; or (b) loading or unloading or handling in storage mouldy vegetable matter or edible fungi; or (c) caring for or handling birds; or (d) handling bagasse; [¹⁹ or (e) work involving exposure to metalworking fluid mists.] [²⁸; or (f) any other workplace]
B7. Infection by organisms of the genus brucella.	Contact with— (a) animals infected by brucella, or their carcases or parts thereof, or their untreated products; or (b) laboratory specimens or vaccines of, or containing brucella.
[¹⁷ B8A. Infection by hepatitis A virus. B8B. Infection by hepatitis B or C virus.	Contact with raw sewage. Contact with— (a) human blood or human blood products; or (b) any other source of hepatitis B or C virus.]
B9. Infection by Streptococcus suis.	Contact with pigs infected by Streptococcus suis, or with the carcases, products or residues of pigs so infected.
[⁸ B10. (a) Avian chlamydiosis.	Contact with birds infected with chlamydia psittaci, or with the remains or untreated products of such birds.
B10. (b) Ovine chlamydiosis.	Contact with sheep infected with chlamydia psittaci, or with the remains or untreated products of such sheep.
B11. Q fever.	Contact with animals, their remains or their untreated products.] *Any occupation involving:*
[⁹ 12. Orf.	Contact with sheep, goats or with the carcasses of sheep or goats.
B13. Hydatidosis. [¹⁷ B14. Lyme disease.	Contact with dogs.] Exposure to deer or other mammals of a type liable to harbour ticks harbouring Borrelia bacteria.
B15. Anaphylaxis.	[²⁹ Contact] with products made with natural rubber latex.]

C. Conditions due to chemical agents

[¹⁰ C1. (a) Anaemia with a haemoglobin concentration of 9g/dL or less,	The use or handling of, or exposure to the fumes, dust or vapour of, lead or a

Prescribed disease or injury	*Occupation*
and a blood film showing punctate basophilia; (b) peripheral neuropathy; (c) central nervous system toxicity.]	compound of lead, or a substance containing lead.
[¹⁰ C2. Central nervous system toxicity characterised by parkinsonism.]	The use or handling of, or exposure to the fumes, dust or vapour of, manganese or a compound of manganese, or a substance containing manganese.
[²⁵C3.(a) Phossy Jaw.	Work involving the use or handling of, or exposure to, white phosphorus.
C3. (b) Peripheral polyneuropathy or peripheral polyneuropathy with pyramidal involvement of the central nervous system, caused by organic compounds of phosphorus which inhibit the enzyme neuropathy target esterase.	Work involving the use or handling of, or exposure to, organic compounds of phosphorus.]
[¹⁰C4. Primary carcinoma of the bronchus lung.	Exposure to the fumes, dust or vapour of or arsenic, a compound of arsenic or a substance containing arsenic.
C5A. Central nervous system toxicity characterised by tremor and neuropsychiatric disease.	Exposure to mercury or inorganic compounds of mercury for a period of, or periods which amount in aggregate to, 10 years or more.
C5B. Central nervous system toxicity characterised by combined cerebellar and cortical degeneration.	Exposure to methylmercury.
C6. Peripheral neuropathy.	The use or handling of, or exposure to, carbon disulphide (also called carbon disulfide).
C7. Acute non-lymphatic leukaemia.	Exposure to benzene.]
C8. [¹⁰ . . .]	[¹⁰ . . .]
C9. [¹⁰ . . .]	[¹⁰ . . .]
C10. [¹⁰ . . .]	[¹⁰ . . .]
C11. [¹⁰ . . .]	[¹⁰ . . .]
[¹⁰ C12. (a) Peripheral neuropathy; (b) central nervous system toxicity.	Exposure to methyl bromide (also called bromomethane).]
[¹⁰ C13. Cirrhosis of the liver.	Exposure to chlorinated naphthalenes.]
C14. [¹⁰ . . .]	[¹⁰ . . .]
C15. [¹⁰ . . .]	[¹⁰ . . .]
[¹⁰ C16. (a) Neurotoxicity; (b) cardiotoxicity.	Exposure to the dust of gonioma kamassi.
	Any occupation involving:
C17. Chronic beryllium disease.	Inhalation of beryllium or a beryllium compound.
C18. Emphysema.	Inhalation of cadmium fumes for a period of, or periods which amount in aggregate to, 20 years or more.
C19. (a) Peripheral neuropathy; (b) central nervous system toxicity.	Exposure to acrylamide.
C20. Dystrophy of the cornea (including ulceration of the corneal surface) of the. eye.	Exposure to quinone or hydroquinone.
C21. Primary carcinoma of the skin.	Exposure to arsenic or arsenic compounds, tar, pitch, bitumen, mineral oil (including paraffin) or soot.

Prescribed disease or injury	Occupation
C22. (a) Primary carcinoma of the mucous membrane of the nose or paranasal sinuses; (b) primary carcinoma of the bronchus or lung.	Work before 1950 in the refining of nickel involving exposure to oxides, sulphides or water-soluble compounds of nickel.
C23. Primary neoplasm of the epithelial lining of the urinary tract.	(a) The manufacture of 1-naphthylamine, 2-naphthylamine, benzidine, auramine, magenta or 4-aminobiphenyl (also called biphenyl-4-ylamine); (b) work in the process of manufacturing methylene-bis-orthochloroaniline (also called MbOCA) for a period of, or periods which amount in aggregate to, 12 months or more; (c) exposure to 2-naphthylamine, benzidine, 4-aminobiphenyl (also called biphenyl-4-ylamine) or salts of those compounds otherwise than in the manufacture of those compounds; (d) exposure to orthotoluidine, 4-chloro-2-methylaniline or salts of those compounds; or (e) exposure for a period of, or periods which amount in aggregate to, 5 years or more, to coal tar pitch volatiles produced in aluminium smelting involving the Soderberg process (that is to say, the method of producing aluminium by electrolysis in which the anode consists of a paste of petroleum coke and mineral oil which is baked in situ).]
[^18^C24. (a) Angiosarcoma of the liver; or (b) osteolysis of the terminal phalanges of the fingers; or (c) sclerodermatous thickening of the skin of the hand; or (d) liver fibrosis, due to exposure to vinyl chloride monomer.	Exposure to vinyl chloride monomer in the manufacture of polyvinyl chloride.
C24A. Raynaud's phenomenon due to exposure to vinyl chloride monomer.	Exposure to vinyl chloride monomer in the manufacture of polyvinyl chloride before 1st January 1984.]
	Any occupation involving:
[^10^C25. Vitiligo.	The use or handling of, or exposure to, paratertiary-butylphenol (also called 4-tert-butylphenol), paratertiary-butylcatechol (also called 4-tert-butylcatechol), para-amylphenol (also called p-pentyl phenol isomers), hydroquinone, monobenzyl ether of hydroquinone (also called 4-benzyloxyphenol) or mono-butyl ether of hydroquinone (also called 4-butoxyphenol).
C26. (a) Liver toxicity; (b) kidney toxicity.	The use or handling of, or exposure to, carbon tetrachloride (also called tetrachloromethane).
C27. Liver toxicity.	The use or handling of, or exposure to, trichloromethane (also called chloroform).]

Prescribed disease or injury	Occupation
C28. [¹⁰ . . .]	[¹⁰ . . .]
[¹⁰ C29. Peripheral neuropathy.	The use or handling of, or exposure to, n-hexane or n-butyl methyl ketone.
C30. (a) Dermatitis; (b) ulceration of the mucous membrane or the epidermis.	The use or handling of, or exposure to, chromic acid, chromates or dichromates.]
[²⁴C31. Bronchiolitis obliterans.	The use or handling of, or exposure to, diacetyl (also called butanedione or 2,3-butanedione) in the manufacture of— (a) diacetyl; or (b) food flavouring containing diacetyl; or (c) food to which food flavouring containing diacetyl is added.
C32. Carcinoma of the nasal cavity or associated air sinuses (nasal carcinoma).	(a) The manufacture of inorganic chromates; or (b) work in hexavalent chrome plating]
[²⁷C33 Chloracne.	Exposure to a substance causing chloracne.]
[²⁸ C34 Extrinsic allergic alveolitis.	Exposure to airborne isocyanates; or to any other chemical substance that causes extrinsic allergic alveolitis.]

D. Miscellaneous Conditions

Prescribed disease or injury	Occupation
D1. Pneumoconiosis.	*Any occupation—* (a) set out in Part II of this Schedule; (b) specified in regulation 2(b)(ii).
D2. Byssinosis.	Work in any room where any process up to and including the weaving process is performed in a factory in which the spinning or manipulation of raw or waste cotton or of flax, or the weaving of cotton or flax, is carried on.
D3. Diffuse mesothelioma (primary neoplasm of the mesothelium of the pleura or of the pericardium or of the peritoneum).	[¹¹ Exposure to asbestos, asbestos dust or any admixture of asbestos at a level above that commonly found in the environment at large.]
[⁷ D4. Allergic rhinitis which is due to exposure to any of the following agents— (a) isocyanates; (b) platinum salts; (c) fumes or dusts arising from the manufacture, transport or use of hardening agents (including epoxy resin curing agents) based on phthalic	Exposure to any of the agents set out in column 1 of this paragraph.]
anhydride, tetrachlorophthalic anhydride, trimelliticanhydride or triethylene-tetramine; (d) fumes arising from the use of rosin as a soldering flux; (e) proteolyticenzymes; (f) animals including insects and other arthropods used for the purposes of research or education or in laboratories; (g) dusts arising from the sowing, cultivation, harvesting, drying, handling, milling, transport or storage of barley, oats, rye, wheat or maize, or the handling, milling, transport or	*Any occupation involving:*

Prescribed disease or injury	Occupation

storage of meal or flour made
therefrom;
(h) antibiotics;
(i) cimetidine;
(j) wood dust;
(k) ispaghula;
(l) castor bean dust;
(m) ipecacuanha;
(n) azodicarbonamide;
(o) animals including insects and other
    arthropods or their larval forms, used
    for the purposes of pest control or
    fruit cultivation, or the larval forms
    of animals used for the purposes
    of research, education or in laboratories;
(p) glutaraldehyde;
(q) persulphate slats or henna;
(r) crustaceans or fish or products arising
    from these in the food processing
    industry;
(s) reactive dyes;
(t) soya bean;
(u) tea dust;
(v) green coffee bean dust;
(w) fumes from stainless steel welding.]
[[17] (x) products made with natural
rubber latex.]

**D5. Non-infective dermatitis of external
origin [[7] . . .] (excluding dermatitis due to
ionising particles or electro-magnetic
radiations other than radiant heat).**

Exposure to dust, liquid or vapour or any
other external agent capable of irritating
the skin (including friction or heat but
excluding ionising particles or electro-
magnetic radiations other than radiant
heat).

**D6. Carcinoma of the nasal cavity or
associated air sinuses (nasal carcinoma).**

(a) Attendance for work [[29] at a workplace]
    where wooden goods [[29] or products
    made wholly or partially of wood] are
    manufactured or repaired; or
(b) attendance for work in a building used
    for the manufacture of footwear or
    components of footwear made wholly or
    partly of leather or fibre board; or
(c) attendance for work at a place used
    wholly or mainly for the repair of footwear
    made wholly or partly of leather or fibre
    board, [[29]; or
(d) exposure to wood dust in the course of
    the machine processing of wood.]

Any occupation involving:

**D7. Asthma which is due to exposure to
any of the following agents:**
  (a) isocyanates;

  (b) platinum salts;
  (c) fumes or dusts arising from the
     manufacture, transport or use of
     hardening agents (including epoxy
     resin curing agents) based on
     phthalic anhydride,
     tetrachlorophthalic anhydride,
     trimelliticanhydride or
     triethylenetetramine;

Exposure to any of the agents set out in
column 1 of this paragraph.

Prescribed disease or injury	Occupation
(d) fumes arising from the use of rosin as a soldering flux;	
(e) proteolyticenzymes;	
[12(f) animals including insects and other arthropods used for the purposes of research or education or in laboratories];	
(g) dusts arising from the sowing, cultivation, harvesting, drying, handling, milling, transport or storage or barley, oats, rye, wheat or maize, or the handling, milling, transport or storage of meal or flour made therefrom;	
[12(h) antibiotics;	
(i) cimetidine;	
(j) wood dust;	
(k) ispaghula;	
(l) castor bean dust;	
(m) ipecacuanha;	
(n) azodicarbonamide];	
[9(o) animals including insects and other arthropods or their larval forms, used for the purposes of pest control or fruit cultivation, or the larval forms of animals used for the purposes of research, education or in laboratories;	
(p) glutaraldehyde;	
(q) persulphate slats or henna;	
(r) crustaceans or fish or products arising from these in the food processing industry;	
(s) reactive dyes;	
(t) soya bean;	
(u) tea dust;	
(v) green coffee bean dust;	
(w) fumes from stainless steel welding;	
[17(wa) products made with natural rubber latex;]	
(x) any other sensitising agent] (occupational asthma).	
[18D8. Primary carcinoma of the lung where there is accompanying evidence of asbestosis.	(a) The working or handling of asbestos or any admixture of asbestos; or (b) the manufacture or repair of asbestos *Any occupation involving:* textiles or other articles containing or composed of asbestos; or (c) the cleaning of any machinery or plant used in any of the foregoing operations and of any chambers, fixtures and appliances for the collection of asbestos dust; or (d) substantial exposure to the dust arising from any of the foregoing operations.
D8A. Primary carcinoma of the lung.	Exposure to asbestos in the course of— (a) the manufacture of asbestos textiles; or (b) spraying asbestos; or (c) asbestos insulation work; or

Prescribed disease or injury	Occupation
	(d) applying or removing materials containing asbestos in the course of shipbuilding, where all or any of the exposure occurs before 1st January 1975, for a period of, or periods which amount in aggregate to, five years or more, or otherwise, for a period of, or periods which amount in aggregate to, ten years or more.]
[¹⁸D9. Unilateral or bilateral diffuse pleural thickening [²⁸. . .] .]	(a) The working or handling of asbestos or any admixture of asbestos; or (b) the manufacture or repair of asbestos textiles or other articles containing or composed of asbestos; or (c) the cleaning of any machinery or plant used in any of the foregoing operations and of any chambers, fixtures and appliances for the collection of asbestos dust; or (d) substantial exposure to the dust arising from any of the foregoing operations.

[¹⁵D10. [¹³ Primary carcinoma of the lung.]	(a) Work underground in a tin mine; or
	(b) exposure to bis (chloromethyl) ether produced during the manufacture of chloromethyl methyl ether; or
	(c) exposure to zinc chromate, calcium chromate or strontium chromate in their pure forms [²⁶; or
	(d) employment wholly or mainly as a coke oven worker:
	   (i) for a period of, or periods which amount in aggregate to, 15 years or more; or
	   (ii) in top oven work, for a period of, or periods which amount in aggregate to, 5 years or more; or
	   (iii) in a combination of top oven work and other coke oven work for a total aggregate period of 15 years or more where one year working in top oven work is treated as equivalent to 3 years in other coke oven work.]

	Any occupation involving:
[¹³ D11. Primary carcinoma of the lung where there is accompanying evidence of silicosis.	Exposure to silica dust in the course of— (a) the manufacture of glass or pottery; tunnelling in or quarrying (b) sandstone or granite; (c) mining metal ores; (d) slate quarrying or the manufacture of artefacts from slate; (e) mining clay; (f) using siliceous materials as abrasives; (g) cutting stone; (h) stonemasonry; or (i) work in a foundry.]
[¹¹D12. Except in the circumstances specified in regulation 2(d)— [²⁷chronic obstructive pulmonary disease.]	[²³ Exposure to coal dust (whether before or after 5th July 1948) by reason of working—

Prescribed disease or injury	Occupation
where there is [²³ . . .] evidence of a forced expiratory volume in one second (measured from the position of maximum inspiration with the claimant making maximum effort) which is—	(a) underground in a coal mine for a period or periods amounting in aggregate to at least 20 years;
[¹⁴(i) at least one litre below the Appropriate mean value predicted, obtained from the following prediction formulae which give the mean values predicted in litres—	(b) on the surface of a coal mine as a screen worker for a period or periods amounting in aggregate to at least 40 years before 1st January 1983; or
ii. For a man, where the measurement is made without back-extrapolation, (3.62 x Height in metres)– (0.031 x Age in years)—1.41; or, where the measurement is made with back-extrapolation,(3.71 x Height in metres)— (0.032 x Age in years)—1.44;	(c) both underground in a coal mine, and on the surface as a screen worker before 1st January 1983, where 2 years working as a surface screen worker is equivalent to 1 year working underground, amounting in aggregate to at least the equivalent of 20 years underground.
ii. For a woman, where the measurement is made without back-extrapolation, (3.29 x Height in metres)-(0.029 x Age in years)-1.42; or, where the measurement is made with back-extrapolation, (3.37 x Height in metres)— (0.030 x Age in years)— 1.46; or]]	Any such period or periods shall include a period or periods of incapacity while engaged in such an occupation.]
(ii) less than one litre. [²⁷The value of one litre in (i) and (ii) shall be construed as fixed and shall not vary by virtue of any treatment or treatments.]	
[²² D13. Primary carcinoma of the nasopharynx.	Exposure to wood dust in the course of the processing of wood or the manufacture or repair of wood products, for a period or periods which amount in aggregate to at least 10 years.]

PART II　　　　　　　**Regulations 2, 4, 38 and 40**

OCCUPATIONS FOR WHICH PNEUMOCONIOSIS IS PRESCRIBED

10.136

1.—Any occupation involving—
  (a) the mining, quarrying or working of silica rock or the working of dried quartzose sand or any dry deposit or dry residue of silica or any dry admixture containing such materials (including any occupation in which any of the aforesaid operations are carried out incidentally to the mining or quarrying of other minerals or to the manufacture of articles containing crushed or ground silica rock);
  (b) the handling of any of the materials specified in the foregoing sub-paragraph in or incidental to any of the operations mentioned therein, or substantial exposure to the dust arising from such operations.
2.—Any occupation involving the breaking, crushing or grinding of flint or the working or handling of broken, crushed or ground flint or materials containing such flint, or substantial exposure to the dust arising from any such operations.
3.—Any occupation involving sand blasting by means of compressed air with the use of quartzose sand or crushed silica rock or flint, or substantial exposure to the dust arising from sand and blasting.
4.—Any occupation involving work in a foundry or the performance of, or substantial exposure to the dust arising from, any of the following operations:—

    (a) the freeing of steel castings from adherent siliceous substance;

    (b) the freeing of metal castings from adherent siliceous substance—

        (i) by blasting with an abrasive propelled by compressed air, by steam or by a wheel; or

       (ii) by the use of power-driven tools.

    5.—Any occupation in or incidental to the manufacture of china or earthenware (including sanitary earthenware, electrical earthenware and earthenware tiles), and any occupation involving substantial exposure to the dust arising therefrom.

    6.—Any occupation involving the grinding of mineral graphite, or substantial exposure to the dust arising from such grinding.

    7.—Any occupation involving the dressing of granite or any igneous rock by masons or the crushing of such materials, or substantial exposure to the dust arising from such operations.

    8.—Any occupation involving the use, or preparation for use, of a grindstone, or substantial exposure to the dust arising therefrom.

    9.—Any occupation involving—

    (a) the working or handling of asbestos or any admixture of asbestos;

    (b) the manufacture or repair of asbestos textiles or other articles containing or composed of asbestos;

    (c) the cleaning of any machinery or plant used in any foregoing operations and of any chambers, fixtures and appliances for the collection of asbestos dust;

    (d) substantial exposure to the dust arising from any of the foregoing operations.

    10.—Any occupation involving—

    (a) work underground in any mine in which one of the objects of the mining operations is the getting of any mineral;

    (b) the working or handling above ground at any coal or tin mine of any minerals extracted therefrom, or any operation incidental thereto;

    (c) the trimming of coal in any ship, barge, or lighter, or in any dock or harbour or at any wharf or quay;

    (d) the sawing, splitting or dressing of slate, or any operation incidental thereto.

    11.—Any occupation in or incidental to the manufacture of carbon electrodes by an industrial undertaking for use in the electrolytic extraction of aluminium from aluminium oxide, and any occupation involving substantial exposure to the dust arising therefrom.

    12.—Any occupation involving boiler scaling or substantial exposure to the dust arising therefrom.

AMENDMENTS

    1. Social Security (Industrial Injuries) (Prescribed Diseases) Amendment Regulations 2000 (SI 2000/1588) reg.6(1) and (2) (July 10, 2000).

    2. Social Security (Industrial Injuries) (Prescribed Diseases) Amendment Regulations 2000 (SI 2000/1588) reg.6(1) and (3) (July 10, 2000).

    3. Social Security (Industrial Injuries) (Prescribed Diseases) Amendment Regulations 1989 (SI 1989/1207) reg.4 (October 16, 1989).

    4. Social Security (Industrial Injuries) (Prescribed Diseases) Amendment (No.2) Regulations 1987 (SI 1987/2112) reg.2 (January 4, 1988).

    5. Social Security (Industrial Injuries) (Prescribed Diseases) Amendment Regulations 1994 (SI 1994/2343) reg.4 (October 10, 1994).

    6. Social Security (Industrial Injuries and Diseases) (Miscellaneous Amendments) Regulations 1996 (SI 1996/425) reg.5(4) (March 24, 1996).

    7. Social Security (Industrial Injuries and Diseases) (Miscellaneous Amendments) Regulations 1996 (SI 1996/425) reg.5 (March 24, 1996 with savings, see reg.7 below).

    8. Social Security (Industrial Injuries) (Prescribed Diseases) Amendment Regulations 1989 (SI 1989/1207) reg.6 (August 9, 1989).

    9. Social Security (Industrial Injuries) (Prescribed Diseases) Amendment Regulations 1991 (SI 1991/1938) reg.2 (September 26, 1991).

    10. Social Security (Industrial Injuries) (Prescribed Diseases) Amendment Regulations 2003 (SI 2003/270) reg.5 (March 17, 2003).

    11. Social Security (Industrial Injuries) (Miscellaneous Amendments) Regulations 1997 (SI 1997/810) reg.6 (April 9, 1997).

12. Social Security (Industrial Injuries and Adjudication) Miscellaneous Amendment Regulations 1986 (SI 1986/1374) reg.3 (September 1, 1986).

13. Social Security (Industrial Injuries) (Prescribed Diseases) Amendment Regulations 1993 (SI 1993/862) reg.6 (April 19, 1993).

14. Social Security (Industrial Injuries) (Prescribed Diseases) Amendment Regulations 2000 (SI 2000/1588) reg.6(1) and (4) (July 10, 2000).

15. Social Security (Industrial Injuries) (Prescribed Diseases) Amendment Regulations 1987 (SI 1987/335) reg.2 (April 1, 1987).

16. Social Security (Industrial Injuries) (Prescribed Diseases) Amendment (No.2) Regulations 2003 (SI 2003/2190) reg.3 (September 22, 2003).

17. Social Security (Industrial Injuries) (Prescribed Diseases) Amendment Regulations 2005 (SI 2005/324) reg.3 (March 14, 2005).

18. Social Security (Industrial Injuries) (Prescribed Diseases) Amendment Regulations 2006 (SI 2006/586) reg.3 (April 6, 2006).

19. Social Security (Industrial Injuries) (Prescribed Diseases) Amendment Regulations 2007 (SI 2007/811) reg.2 (April 6, 2007).

20. Social Security (Industrial Injuries) (Prescribed Diseases) Amendment (No. 2) Regulations 2007 (SI 2007/1753) reg.2(1), (2) (October 1, 2007).

21. Social Security (Industrial Injuries) (Prescribed Diseases) Amendment (No. 2) Regulations 2007 (SI 2007/1753) reg.2(1), (3) (October 1, 2007).

22. Social Security (Industrial Injuries) (Prescribed Diseases) Amendment Regulations 2008 (SI 2008/14) reg.2 (April 7, 2008).

23. Social Security (Industrial Injuries) (Prescribed Diseases) Amendment Regulations 2009 (SI 2009/1396) reg.2 (July 13, 2009).

24. Social Security (Industrial Injuries) (Prescribed Diseases) Amendment Regulations 2011 (SI 2011/1497) reg.2 (July 18, 2011).

25. Social Security (Industrial Injuries) (Prescribed Diseases) Amendment Regulations 2012 (SI 2012/647) reg.2 (March 30, 2012).

26. Social Security (Industrial Injuries) (Prescribed Diseases) Amendment (No.2) Regulations 2012 (SI 2012/1634) reg.2 (August 1, 2012).

27. Social Security (Industrial Injuries) (Prescribed Diseases) Amendment Regulations 2015 (SI 2015/87) reg. 4(2) (March 16, 2015).

28. Social Security (Industrial Injuries) (Prescribed Diseases) Amendment Regulations 2017 (SI 2017/232) reg.3 (March 30, 2017).

29. Social Security (Industrial Injuries) (Prescribed Diseases) Amendment Regulations 2018 (SI 2018/769) reg.2(2) (September 28, 2018).

GENERAL NOTE

I. The structure of this annotation
10.137
This annotation examines first some general matters pertaining to the whole of this Sch., dealing with prescribed industrial diseases. It then examines the prescribed diseases by category. The diseases in the Schedule are divided into four categories according to cause and are given letters and numbers for identification:

A1–14 Conditions due to physical agents;

B1–15 Conditions due to biological agents;

C1–33 Conditions due to chemical agents;

D1–13 Miscellaneous conditions.

Within each category, particular diseases will be treated in a depth consistent with the case law on that disease.

II. General matters
10.138
The diseases listed in the Schedule are there because there is some discernible link between the disease and the occupation for which it is prescribed. The power to prescribe diseases is exercised by the Secretary of State, normally upon the advice

of the Industrial Injuries Advisory Council which investigates occupational diseases and reports upon them, as well as keeping the Industrial Injuries scheme generally under review. The Secretary of State exercises his power under the SSCBA 1992, s.108(2) (formerly SSA 1975, s.76(2)) and must be satisfied that the disease is a risk of the occupation and not a common risk, and also that the attribution of particular cases to the nature of the employment can be established or presumed with reasonable certainty.

The system for decision-making and appeals for claims to industrial injuries benefits has undergone several reforms over the years. However, one constant throughout this period of change is that the question of whether a claimant is an employed or self-employed earner, and whether a specific employment is, or is not, employed earner's employment, is to be decided not by the Secretary of State, but by officers of HMRC (Social Security Contributions (Transfer of Functions, etc.) Act 1999 s.8(1)). Accordingly, such decisions are not matters of appeal for the FTT Social Entitlement Chamber but rather for appeal to the FTT Tax Chamber. Such decisions and appeals are regulated by the Social Security Contributions (Decisions and Appeals) Regs 1999 (SI 1999/1027).

Historically, for all other industrial injuries matters, there was a distinction between medical issues (the disablement questions), decided by the medical adjudicating authorities, including on appeal the former MAT, and non-medical issues, decided by insurance officers (and later adjudication officers), with appeals to the former SSAT (or its predecessor). However, on July 5, 1999, the functions of adjudication officers with respect to industrial injuries benefits and the making of industrial accident declarations were transferred to the Secretary of State (SSA 1998, ss.1, 8 and Commencement Order No. 8). He or she may, however, refer certain issues for report to a medical practitioner (now a health care professional) who has experience of the issues. The issues so referable are: (a) the extent of a personal injury for the purposes of s.94; (b) whether the claimant has a prescribed industrial disease and the extent of the resulting disablement; and (c) whether, for disablement benefit purposes, the claimant has a disablement and its extent (Decisions and Appeals Regs 1999 reg.12(1)).

After 1999 decisions by the Secretary of State on industrial injuries benefits, including those on prescribed industrial diseases, and on the matter of an industrial accident declaration, were appealable to the so-called "unified" appeal tribunal, composed of a legally qualified member and up to two medically qualified members (SSA 1998 ss.4, 12, Schs 2 and 3). Like the Secretary of State, that tribunal was competent to deal with the both the medical and non-medical aspect of industrial injuries matters. Since November 3, 2008, and as a result of the Tribunals, Courts and Enforcement Act 2007, the FTT Social Entitlement Chamber has assumed these appellate functions.

The key point from all this for industrial injuries matters is that the historic distinction between medical issues and non-medical issues – previously crucial as demarcating the respective jurisdictions of MATs (col.1 of the Schedule) and SSATs (col.2 of the Schedule) – is no longer relevant. Consequently, issues relating to the interpretation and application of any of the words in the Schedule, whether in col.1 or 2, are now within the remit of the FTT. Both the FTT and the Upper Tribunal now have jurisdiction over both medical and non-medical matters. So, an Upper Tribunal judge, allowing an appeal on a point of law, can now take his or her own decision on the facts rather than remitting it to another tribunal. Commissioner Williams did so in *CI/1307/1999* giving a staged assessment of disablement in respect of post traumatic stress disorder. The decision considers the medical aspects of the claimant's case found to be an industrial accident in *CI/15589/1996*, noted in the annotation to "accident" to SSCBA 1992, s.94(1). In paras 15–17, Commissioner Williams distinguished "diagnosis" and "disablement" decisions. The former is essentially "a question of medical expertise". A "disablement" decision in contrast is not dissimilar to the tasks performed by judges in assessing common law damages or in applying the tariff of the Criminal Injuries Compensation Authority. In assessing disablement for industrial injuries benefits, however, that Criminal Injuries tariff is not an appropriate yardstick. Instead, supplementing SSCBA 1992 s.103 and Sch.6, regard should be had also to reg.11 and Sch.2 to the General Benefit Regulations, above. Nonetheless, the import of para.37 of the decision is that exercise of the Commissioner's (and now the Upper Tribunal's) power to decide on the facts, rather than remitting to another tribunal, may well be rare. Even so, the decision contrasts markedly with the traditional view of such matters as ones for medical rather than legal judgment (see, for example, Commissioner Howell in *CI/636/93*). Note that the suitability of cross-reference to Sch.2 was also advocated in *R(I) 5/95*, where Commissioner Rowland stated that "assessment of disablement should be brought into line with those prescribed in the Schedule", with assessment also reflecting any intermittent or episodic character of the disablement (para.16).

In *R(I) 4/96*, Commissioner Goodman makes the important point that the date of onset of a prescribed disease for a particular claimant and the date from which payment of disablement benefit can be paid on or after the disease has been prescribed (added to the Schedule), are not necessarily coincidental. So where prescribed disease D12 (miner's bronchitis etc.) was added from September 13, 1993, disablement benefit was only payable from that date, despite the fact that the date of onset (the date from which the claimant suffered from it) was much earlier. Unless the contrary is clearly indicated in the particular prescription (and it was not here), the insertion into the Schedule of a new prescribed disease is not retrospective so as to enable the payment of disablement benefit (subject to showing good cause for delay in claiming) from the date of onset.

It is worth noting that the significance of some of the less serious prescribed diseases has been diminished by the abolition of injury benefit and the subsequent restrictions placed upon disablement benefit by the raising of the qualifying level to 14 per cent. Now, unless the disease is serious enough to bring an assessment of 14 per cent or more or, if the assessment is 1 per cent or more, lasts more than the ninety days which is the waiting period for reduced earnings allowance (see SSCBA 1992, Sch.7, para.11, above), the claimant will rely on incapacity benefits rather than an industrial benefit. (Different provision is made for claimants suffering from pneumoconiosis, byssinosis, or diffuse mesothelioma, where title to disablement benefit is established on an assessment of 1 per cent or more, Prescribed Diseases Regulations, reg.20, above.)

The occupations in respect of which the diseases are prescribed are commonly defined by prefacing the cause of the disease with the words "Any occupation involving". The occupations in the Schedule will be considered separately, as appropriate, but the general phrase is applicable to most of the diseases and occupations and is dealt with first.

Any occupation involving: The word "occupation" is not a term of art, it merely con- **10.139** notes the activities of an employed earner under his contract of employment (*R(I) 3/78*). Once some involvement with the prescribed cause of the disease, as a result of employment, has been established, the employment is likely to be accepted as giving rise to entitlement (*R(I) 4/53*) unless the involvement is so trivial or negligible that it can be discounted (*R(I) 8/57*). It is still important for the decision-maker or tribunal to consider carefully whether the occupation is prescribed for the disease—the fact that there is an outbreak of a prescribed disease in one factory is irrelevant to the question of whether the disease is prescribed for a particular employee or group of employees in the factory (*R(I) 2/77*). It is not the frequency of the disease which is significant, but the description of the occupation for which it is prescribed.

Although a claim for disablement benefit may be described as being in respect of a particular disease, there is nothing in the legislation to suggest that a separate claim has to be made in respect of each disease. Accordingly, if a tribunal find that a claimant is not suffering from the prescribed disease in respect of which he claimed but may be suffering from another prescribed disease, they should make a finding in respect of that other disease (*R(I) 6/94*). That may require an adjournment unless the parties are content for the new issue to be considered straightaway. It does not matter whether the diagnosis question is determined before or after the Secretary of State has decided whether the disease is prescribed in relation to the claimant (*CI/13664/96*). The more convenient course should be followed.

10.140   *The proper approach to interpretation of the definitions of the prescribed occupations:* In *Secretary of State for Social Security v Davies* (reported as part of *R(I) 2/01*, and noted further in the commentary on PD A11 [vibration white finger]), the Court of Appeal thought that, given the purpose of this compensation scheme, it would be wrong to give the words too narrow a definition (per Rix L.J. [para.23], Mummery L.J. expressly concurring [para. 36]). In para.35 of that case, Mummery L.J. quoted with approval from Commissioner Levenson in the decision under appeal:

> "The Industrial Injuries Disablement Benefits Scheme was designed to compensate workers for industrial injuries and for contracting prescribed diseases, and the definitions of prescribed occupation should not be artificially narrowed. I do not see why a person doing essentially the same job in a city as is being done by a person in a forest should be denied that compensation" (*CI/729/1998*, para.15).

This approach is not to be confined to its specific context (*CI/2668/2002*, per Commissioner Williams).

Many cases make it clear that one can look for guidance to the relevant report of the IIAC recommending prescription (*Davies; R(I) 2/01; R(I) 4/99; R(I) 3/97; R(I) 3/95; R(I) 2/85; R(I) 5/83; R(I) 11/81(T); R(I) 15/75(T); CI/1884/2004; CI/2668/2002; CI/3261/2000; CI/808/95; CI/22/91*). The reports can be used to help resolve ambiguity or problems with the drafting of regulations, but, naturally, what each decision takes from the exercise varies.

The focus should be on the work the claimant does (did) rather than on the contractual obligation to do it (*R(I) 2/79(T)*); on the activity of the employee, rather than the generic description of the employer's activity(ies) (*CI/2668/2002*, para.16); on what the claimant does rather than on how the job is labelled (*CI/2668/2002*, para.18).

As Judge Wikeley stressed in *DM v SSWP (II)* [2010] UKUT 318 (AAC), while the statutory words of prescription are always the starting point, a purposive approach had to be taken to them. "Any occupation involving" is not "a term of art" but requires a focus on the work activities performed rather than on the precise terms of the contract of employment ("the actual working test"), a proposition supported by *Davies*, above: *R(I)2/79(T)* and *R(I) 3/78*.

III. Prescribed Diseases: Category A: Conditions due to physical agents

A1 (Leukaemia (other than chronic lymphatic leukaemia) or cancer of the bone, female breast, testis or thyroid)

10.141   PD A1 was first reformulated in 2000, subject to transitional provisions in reg.7(2) and (3) of the Social Security (Industrial Injuries) (Prescribed Diseases) Amendment Regulations 2000 (SI 2000/1588). In that formulation PD A1 only covered leukaemia or female breast cancer and cancer of the bone, testis or thyroid.

However, the terms of prescription were extended with effect from March 30, 2017, so as to cover leukaemia or primary cancer of the bone, bladder, breast, colon, liver, lung, ovary, stomach, testis or thyroid (Social Security (Industrial Injuries) (Prescribed Diseases) Amendment Regulations 2017 (SI 2017/232) reg.3). The addition of the six further cancers for which benefit should be payable under PD A1 follows the recommendation by IIAC (see IIAC, *Cancers due to ionising radiation*, Cm 9208, February 2016). IIAC's other proposals were also accepted, namely that the prescription of breast cancer be extended to men, and that the terms of prescription be simplified to read "Any occupation involving: Exposure to ionising radiation where the dose is sufficient to double the risk of the occurrence of the condition".

A2 (Cataract)

The revision of PD A2 is subject to the same transitional provision noted under PD A1, above.

10.142

A4 (Task-specific focal dystonia)

Until April 6, 2007, the terms of prescription referred to "Hand or forearm cramp—writer's cramp". From that date, it referred to "Task-specific focal dystonia". This was recommended as valuable updating and clarification by the IIAC in its report *Completion of the review of the scheduled list of prescribed diseases*, Cm 7003 (January 2007), para.28, referring back to its 2006 report on *Work Related Upper Limb Disorders*, Cm. 6868 (July 2006), para.78.

10.143

In *SSWP v CS (II)* [2010] UKUT 198 (AAC); [2011] AACR 5, Judge Howell held that "task-specific focal dystonia" was limited to conditions affecting the hard and forearm, as those Reports indicated, and so did not cover the work-related cervical dystonia from which the claimant suffered. The wording of the current terms of prescription (effective March 30, 2012) makes that clear beyond doubt.

The occupation must involve *prolonged* periods of handwriting, etc. What amounts to prolonged periods must be a matter of fact for the Secretary of State/ tribunal, but remember to look at the nature of the job in assessing whether it displays the requisite characteristics. In *R(I) 3/97*, Commissioner Rice held that the words "other repetitive movements of the hand or arm" in A4 are to be read *ejusdem generis* (as of the same kind or nature) with "handwriting" and "typing", not at large to include repetitive movements of whatever kind and not so as to "be available at large to all those engaged in repetitive work" (para.10). So that in that case the tribunal did not err in law in finding that it did not cover the appellant analytical chemist whose laboratory bench work primarily involved the filtration and titration of chemicals. The tribunal had found that while the finger, hand and wrist movements were repetitive and carried out over a prolonged period they did not have the intensity or frequency comparable to handwriting or typing.

In *CI/349/2001*, Commissioner Angus considered the case of a cleaner who spent

"a significant part of her working day in prolonged periods of handling the large Swiffer and the floor buffer, each involving repetitive movements of her wrists, and in prolonged periods of cleaning tables involving repetitive movements of the wrists and hands. There is also other cleaning and maintenance work such as cleaning glue off the sinks and repairs to the fabric of the school buildings which involve her in repetitive movements of the arm, wrist or hand. The A4 prescription does not mention movements of the wrist but, as the wrist is the joint between the arm and the hand, movement of the wrist involves the movement of either the hand or the arm in relation to the other. The question is whether the movements of her fingers, hands or arms which the claimant makes in the course of those prolonged periods of activity amount to 'other repetitive movements of the fingers, hand or arm' within the meaning of the prescription in the Schedule to the Regulations" (para.24).

The Commissioner decided that her occupation was not one prescribed under A4, but reached his conclusion

"for slightly different reasons from those given by the tribunal and by the author of *R(I) 3/97*. I respectfully agree with the Commissioner who decided that the *ejusdem generis* rule is an aid to the interpretation of the Schedule 1 prescription of the occupation relevant to A4. However, apart from their involving repetitive movements of the fingers, hand or arm, there is little in common between the activities of handwriting and typing which is apparent from the face of the prescription. Because they are interpreting a regulation based code of law Commissioners and, I think tribunals, have always been entitled to go behind the text of the regulations and examine the background papers to ascertain what is the purpose of any particular provision which is under consideration. The Commissioner who decided *R(I) 3/97* looked at the report by the Industrial Injuries Advisory Council which considered the need to replace the prescriptions of telegraphist's cramp, writer's cramp and twister's cramp, which were prescribed in paragraphs 28, 29 and 30 of Schedule 1 to the 1947 Industrial Injuries and Prescribed Diseases Regulations, and the relevant occupations with one prescribed disease and relevant occupation which would cover all those who suffered from hand and arm cramps as a result of working in employments involving the use of the fingers, hands or arms. The Commissioner quoted most of paragraph 32 and all of paragraph 33 of the Committee's report in which two paragraphs the need for a new prescription which would embrace the three cramps and relevant occupations which were then prescribed as well as the cramps experienced by those engaged in the occupations involving the use of keyboards which were then proliferating. He did not quote the first sentence of paragraph 32 which identifies the characteristic which is common to all the occupations which the Committee had in mind. That sentence is as follows:—

'These diseases are characterised by spasm or other disordered action of muscles used in the performance of duties involving rapid and finely controlled movements of the hand of a repetitive nature.'

Therefore, the activity which the Committee had in mind when it devised the current prescription of the occupation relevant to A4 is movement of the hands and arms which are approximately as rapid, as finely controlled and as repetitive as the movements employed by somebody operating a typewriter or writing by hand. I do not think that there is any likelihood of the hand and wrist movements described by the claimant having the degree of rapidity, fineness of control and repetitiveness of the hand movements of a typist or somebody writing with a pen or a pencil. I take Mr Crawford's point that the twister in the textile industry would not be repairing broken yarns with the degree of repetitiveness with which a typist would be striking the keys of a typewriter but on a machine which could have as many as 70 pairs of bobbins the breaks in the yarn would be fairly frequent and I have no doubt that as the twister would be constrained to keep the pauses in the winding to a minimum the hand movements employed to repair the breaks, in particular the movements of the thumb and forefinger, would be very rapid and, to make effective joins, would be very finely controlled". (para.25).

A5 (subcutaneous cellulitis of the hand), A6 (bursitis or subcutaneous cellulitis (knee)), A7 (bursitis or subcutaneous cellulitis (elbow))

10.144   Until April 6, 2007, the terms of prescription for these referred in brackets respectively to "Beat hand", "Beat knee" and "Beat elbow". From that date, those terms were deleted on the recommendation of the IIAC as "outdated"; the term "used to denote repeated trauma at work, is not widely used or understood in modern clinical practice, being a historical description confined to the field of occupational medicine" (see *Completion of the review of the scheduled list of prescribed diseases*, Cm 7003 (January 2007), para.28, referring back to its 2006 report on *Work Related Upper Limb Disorders*, Cm. 6868 (July 2006), para.78).

Refer back to the definition of "an occupation involving" and note that manual labour of the type described need only be one of the incidents of the prescribed occupation. Hence, the category of jobs in which manual labour is incidental includes not only those which require "muscle", but also those where some physical or bodily work is required. Note also that the pressure on the hand, knee or elbow need only be prolonged *or* severe. These three diseases are good examples of the scheme taking account of the development of an injury by process over a period which would prevent the claimant from showing that it had been caused by accident, but compare *R(I) 11/74*. See also *R(I) 78/54* and *R(I) 60/51*. In *R(I)*

5/98, dealing with A6 (Beat knee), Commissioner Rice held that the prescribed occupation is to be interpreted in the context of the disease covered. Thus it covers not any kind of friction or pressure, but only the type of friction or pressure that causes beat knee. A medical report before him identified the key feature of beat knee as

"direct pressure and/or friction to the knee and immediate vicinity, for example just above or below the knee. This pressure or friction must be applied directly to the skin to cause cellulitis, or directly to the skin overlying the bursa" (para.7).

The anatomical parts affected are superficial, not within the knee joint itself (para.8). In this case, the damage to the claimant's knee through the consistent use of the brake pedal when operating his crane did not result in that sort of friction or pressure; the process involved repeated flexing and extending of the knee, with most of the action taking place at the ankle joint (*ibid*). Similarly in *CI/268/95* (noted in (1997) 4 J.S.S.L. D88). Commissioner Hoolahan held the tribunal decision erroneous in law: in looking at whether the claimant had been involved in any occupation within the A7 prescription (Beat elbow), it had failed to consider whether her work (as a cleaner in a social club) involved severe or prolonged "external" friction or pressure (para.6).

A8 (tenosynovitis)
    For useful evidence from the medical adviser to the DWP (Dr Reed) on PD A8   **10.145**
(tenosynovitis), see the Sch. to *CI/3745/2006*.

A10 (Occupational deafness)
    The revision from September 22, 2003 of the occupations in respect of which   **10.146**
occupational deafness is prescribed, based largely on the IIAC Report on the pre-scription of occupational deafness (Cm 5672, November 2002), means that this commentary is now relevant only to those whose claim for disablement based on occupational deafness was made, or treated as made, on or after that date. See further IIAC's Position Paper no.38, *Noise, occupational deafness and Industrial Injuries Disablement Benefit* (September 2017).
    For claims made, or treated as made, before September 22, 2003, please see the commentary in the 2003 edition of this volume, as updated by the relevant pages of the Supplement 2003/2004.
    In PD A10 occupational deafness is defined as

"Sensorineural hearing loss amounting to at least 50dB in each ear, being the average of hearing losses at 1, 2 and 3 kHz frequencies, and being due in the case of at least one ear to occupational noise."

CI/4567/1999 (now reported as *R(I)6/02*) contains useful material on a variety of tests measuring hearing loss.
    In *CI/2012/2000*, Commissioner Jacobs said, rightly, that *CI/4567/1999* (now reported as *R(I)6/02*) neither is, nor purports to be, authority that ERA (evoked response audiometry), a form of assessment of hearing loss, is always to be preferred to PTA (pure tone audiometry), another form of assessment of hearing loss (para.16).
    ERA "is a record of a person's brain activity in response to sound" (para.12), which is not dependent on the claimant to acknowledge that sound has been heard (and therefore not contingent on his honesty). However, the claimant's behaviour can affect other brain activity and render it more difficult to interpret the results (para.14). Adults are usually tested by cortical or slow vertex ERA. Young children are usually tested by another type, brainstem ERA so that the results are not affected by the anaesthetic or sedative administered to keep the child quiet and still during the test process (para.15).
    PTA is cheap and fairly easy to administer. It is the starting point for all assessments by tribunals and the Secretary of State, but depends upon the claimant acknowledging when a sound (produced at different levels by the PTA equipment) has been heard (para.10).

10.147   The Commissioner advances the following approach for tribunals:

"a tribunal . . . has to weigh the evidence as a whole in order to determine the level of the claimant's sensorineural hearing loss. There is no rule that one type of evidence is always to be preferred to another. The evidence must be considered as a whole. The tribunal may conclude that one type of evidence is preferable to another, but that must be a judgment reached after considering the merits of all the evidence" (para.16).

There was in this case no error of law in the tribunal refusing to order, at public expense, brainstem ERA.

In *CI/1/2002*, without citing Commissioner Jacobs's decision in *CI/2012/2000*, like him Commissioner Williams also concludes that *CI/4567/1999* (now reported as *R(I)6/02*) is not authority that CERA (cortical evoked response audiogram) is always to be preferred to PTA (pure tone audiometry). Noting that Prescribed Diseases Regulations, reg.34 gives precise details about testing and assessment but not the method of testing, Commissioner Williams stated that the matter is one for the experts on the tribunal using their expertise to decide. In the decision under appeal before him, the tribunal had relied on that expertise to conclude that in that case CERA would not be more reliable than PTA. However, the Commissioner noted that declining to order a CERA test on the basis of cost might be a denial of a fair hearing under the HRA 1998/ECHR.

Useful information and guidance—which cannot be binding on decision makers, tribunals or the Upper Tribunal—on both PTA and CERA can be found in the IIAC Report on the prescription of occupational deafness (Cm 5672, November 2002). See para.117 (audiometric testing) and App.6 (guidance on obtaining cortical evoked response audiometry). The IIAC recommended that PTA should be retained as the most appropriate routine assessment method for use in the benefit scheme. Where testing is not repeatable, or response to conversational voice seems better or worse than the audiogram would suggest, use of CERA should be considered. In any event, the IIAC recommended that methods of testing should be kept under review.

10.148   Tribunals can have regard to the Department's guidelines and its rather rough and ready conversational voice testing in its *Industrial Injuries Handbook for Adjudicating Medical Authorities*, so long as it was remembered that this was guidance and not statutorily prescribed. The Tables in the Handbook could be taken on board but only as part of a proper disablement assessment (*CI/5029/2002*, per Commissioner Fellner).

The wide range of occupations for which this disease is prescribed led to a significant number of Commissioners' decisions on the interpretation of the various parts of the Schedule relating to the disease. All, however, can only be authoritative today insofar as they deal with equivalent wording.

The expression which prefaces the reformulated occupations in column (2), *"wholly or mainly in the immediate vicinity of,"* was considered in *R(I)2/85*. That decision held that it was not necessary that the claimant should spend the majority of his time near the specified tools whilst they are in use, and that it was sufficient that the tools were in use more than a negligible amount whilst he was in the vicinity. But the formulation now requires work wholly or mainly in the immediate vicinity *of the use of* a specified tool or piece of equipment, removing the authority of that statement. Note also *CI/226/91* (para.7), citing *Fawcett Properties v Buckingham CC* [1961] A.C. 636 at 669 where Lord Morton said that mainly "probably means more than half". In *R(I)7/76* it was held that whether the claimant was in the vicinity should be determined by the distance from him to the specified tools, taking into account walls, screens etc., but not measuring the level of residual noise at the claimant's workplace. An employee working in an exceptionally noisy factory may, therefore, be exposed to far greater noise than is acceptable but not entitled to benefit because he is not working near enough to the machines making the noise—

"Whether an occupation involves work in the immediate vicinity of the designated plant is a question of fact in each case. I think it is to be answered first by ascertaining the locations, that is to say the area within which the designated plants (which from their nature cover considerable areas) are situated, and the area of the claimant's activities. The question whether the area of work is in the immediate vicinity of the plant then depends in my opinion on the weight to be given to the particular circumstances. The distance at which one area lies from the other may itself be decisive of the question. A second factor may be the physical separation of one area from the other because of intervening buildings . . . A further factor, as here . . . may be the presence of walls and screening, substantially dividing, enclosing or demarking the two areas lying at a distance apart, though under the same factory roof."

See also *R(I) 8/85* where the distance factor was held to be significant. In *CI/245/1991*, Commissioner Goodman stated that the notion of "working in the immediate vicinity" of percussive tools involved consideration of the physical proximity to the use of such tools and not just the noise level, so that the claimant's non-use of ear muffs or protectors supplied by his employer was legally irrelevant to the issue. The Commissioner concluded that the percussive tools were in constant and daily use and that the claimant worked in the immediate vicinity in his job as storeman, his store being separated from that work area only by a wire mesh (paras 10–13).

The original (see above) specified occupations were, broadly speaking, foundries, shipyards and mines and quarries. Whilst the occupations have been changed and widened, the Schedule still refers in paras A10(a) and (b) to the use of, or work wholly or mainly in the immediate vicinity of the use of, a pneumatic percussive tool. The nature of such a tool has been considered in *R(I) 5/76* (an "impact wrench" or "screwing up machine"); *R(I) 8/76* (a computer-controlled burning and marking machine); *R(I) 1/80* (a rivet gun); *R(I) 3/80* (upright pedestal grinder); *R(I) 13/80* (machine mounted vertical spindle surface grinder); *R(I) 6/83* (press set into the ground and operating on compressed air). Whether a particular tool is pneumatic is a question of fact, and it is necessary to look at the essential nature of the tool and determine its driving force (*R(I) 6/83*). But what constitutes a "tool"? The general trend of decisions has been to give the word "tool" a more technical meaning and, as a result, include some machines in the category of tools. A printing press, though pneumatic and percussive was held not to be a "tool" in *CI/17/93*. The test for "tool" was there said to be whether the machine now alleged to be a "tool" is now used to carry out a task traditionally carried out by what everyone would recognise as a hand-held tool. If there is no "recognisable previous identity as a hand-held tool" it is a machine and not a "tool" (*CI/17/93*, para.3. citing *R(I) 6/83*, para.6). In *Appleby v CAO* (reported as *R(I) 5/99*, judgment of June 29, 1999), the Court of Appeal stated that while the test propounded by Commissioner Sanders in *CI/17/93* was "useful", it was not "an exclusive test", particularly as regards new processes where the existence of a sufficiently manual input may enable the alleged tool to qualify. A useful starting point is whether the implement in question is classified in the trade or industry as a machine tool. In *Appleby*, the Court held the electrodes on the spot welding machine qualified as pneumatic, percussive tools; they banged the metal to be welded to ensure a tight fit before emitting the necessary electrical charge, and were, therefore, the mechanical equivalent of the hand held hammer used in the past when welding was effected by hammering together two pieces of preheated metal. The Court, obiter, was provisionally of the opinion that the spot welding machine had sufficient manual input to qualify as a "tool".

The number of paras has been reduced from 23 to 11, and occupations once in separate paras have been regrouped and reworded to simplify matters to aid understanding and administration (IIAC Report, para.105, and App.4). The revision, however, has added occupations but not removed any previously prescribed, since the IIAC "had no evidence that any of the occupations and processes already prescribed have disappeared, ceased to be a hazard to hearing, or fundamentally altered to the extent that their removal from the list would be appropriate" (para.95).

10.149

10.150   *Paragraph (a)*: "metal founding or forging industries": the IIAC saw no need to clarify "forging", considering it an understandable term with a definite meaning in industry (para. 101). The prescription covers the use of powered grinding tools on metal, but not hand-powered ones. On "tool" and "pneumatic percussive tool", see the discussion preceding coverage of this particular para. As regards "metal", note that despite common parlance referring to a metalled road, reg.1(2) provides that "metal" for the purposes of disease A10, does not include stone, concrete, aggregate or similar substances for use in road or railway construction. However in *CI/37/1988* the Commissioner accepted that "on metal" could include the use of pneumatic drills to break up reinforced concrete where the drill would from time to time strike the metal reinforcing rods. But in *CI/540/1994*, where the momentary or occasional contact with a metal reinforcing rod was minimal, the claim was unsuccessful. The ruling in *CI/540/1994* was held in *CI/13238/1996* to apply in respect of noise from drills striking metal reinforcing rods in concrete road structures in a claim by a foreman asphalter.

Note that the terms "foundry", "skid transfer bank" and "knock out and shake out grid" are each specifically defined in reg.1(2), above.

The term "metal nails" has a wider meaning than ordinary nails driven with a hammer; it can include any piece of wire or metal used for holding things together (*R(I)5/83*). In *CI/808/95*, Commissioner Mesher agreed

"with the view expressed by the Commissioner in para.9 of *R(I)5/83*, supported by reference in that case to the report of the Industrial Injuries Advisory Council, that the prescription in paragraph A10(f) [the equivalent of A10(a) formulation 'machine to cut or shape or clean metal nails'] relates to the process of making nails. Thus the crucial question is whether what results from the operation of the claimant's machine can be called a nail in the extended sense described by the Commissioner in *R(I)5/83* [a piece of wire or metal used for holding things together]. One must ask what the product is used for. I conclude that its use in the manufacture of tyres is such that it cannot be called a nail. It does not hold things together in the way in which a nail or rivet holds things together. It does not hold one part of the tyre to another part of the tyre by connecting the two together." (para.9, words in square brackets added.)

The rubber-coated wire cut by the claimant's machine was used to reinforce the rubber moulding of the tyre.

There was brief consideration in *CI/246/1988* of the features of plasma spray gun to spray molten metal, but unfortunately the matter was not pursued very far since the materials deposited by the gun in the case were silica and quartz, neither of which is a metal.

10.151   *Paragraph (b)*: On "pneumatic percussive tool", see the discussion preceding commentary on para (a).

"Underground" means properly underground, with an earth ceiling, and does not include a deep trench which is open to the air, even though the drilling operation is going on below ground level (*R(I)4/84*). It means "underneath the natural surface of the earth". It did not therefore embrace the claimant who was not but may have been working on the floor or below floor level in a prepared building, not under a natural roof (*CI/550/89*, para.6). A tunnel like the Mersey Tunnel is properly encompassed by the term "underground", although the inclusion in para.(b) of "for tunnelling in civil engineering works" in any event provides protection (*CI/13238/1996*).

In *CI/550/89*, Commissioner Heald decided, referring indirectly to *CI/308/1989* (now reported as *R(I)2/92*, noted below) on the meaning of "wood", that "rock" in sub-para. (c) means "rock in its natural state . . . and not in the form of a cement aggregate, at which stage the material which was originally rock, no doubt, had changed its nature and formed part of the cement mix." (para.5). Whether the same is true of "stone", so as to not to cover solid products (e.g. paving slabs, bricks or blocks) made from reconstituted crushed or powdered stone is unclear. The inclusion of new para.(c) will help some of those who work cutting concrete masonry blocks (e.g. builders).

Paragraph (c): none of the terms in this prescription is defined. Nor does there appear to be any case law on its previous partial manifestation as PD A10(q). Its expansion will help some of those who work cutting concrete masonry blocks (e.g. builders). **10.152**

Paragraph (d): This covers the use of machines in the manufacture of textiles. This includes "weaving", but the para is not confined to "weaving". **10.153**

On "weaving", *CSI/65/94* applying *R(I) 13/81* was authority that deafness from working with noisy knitting machines does not come within A10(d) because "knitting" is not "weaving". Commissioner Mitchell reached his decision "with regret" and like the Commissioner in *R(I) 13/81* expressed the hope that an anomaly might be rectified by amending the paragraph, since the evidence in the case showed that the knitting machines at the claimant's place of work were just as noisy as weaving machines. This has now been done as regards the process of "high speed false twisting of fibres" after the IIAC recommending it in its 2002 Report which largely formed the basis for these revised prescriptions. The IIAC accepted that there was enough evidence that high speed false twisting is a process that can take place prior to both knitting and weaving, and one which produces yarn for both of these areas of fabric manufacture.

In *CI/2879/1995*, Commissioner Goodman gave some consideration to the phrase "the high speed false twisting of fibres". He set aside the tribunal decision as erroneous in law on the basis that they had failed to consider whether the claimant's occupation from May 6, 1987 to August 12, 1988 (one bringing her within a five-year period prior to the 1994 claim) met the description. But, approving an argument founded on para.12 of *R(I) 13/81*, he held that the tribunal was entitled to rely on a definition from a research fellow in a University Department of Textile Industries in conjunction with factual information supplied by the employer on the basis that where words are used in legislation with reference to particular trades or businesses and have a particular meaning within that trade or business, the words in the legislation should be construed in the light of that meaning (para.17). The material before the tribunal and letters before the Commissioner from an officer in the Health and Safety Executive and from another expert in the same University Department all confirmed that "false twisting", a technique rather than a process, involved machines operating at speeds in revolutions per minute varying according to whether dealing with staple yarns (a few tens of thousands per minute) or filament yarns (850,000 per minute in 1968, up to 7 million per minute today). Some suggested "false twisting" was limited to synthetic yarns. But, in setting out that material and in remitting the matter back to the tribunal because factual "loose ends" precluded him giving the decision, Commissioner Goodman stressed that the prescription "high speed" is not expressed as being a minimum of revolutions a minute, nor is the word "fibres in any way qualified to limit it to artificial fibres" (para.18). The prescription now explicitly covers man-made and natural fibres, and includes mineral fibres.

The prescription also covers the "mechanical cleaning of bobbins". It was reworded from the former prescription in the old PD A10(e), "mechanical bobbin cleaning" to clarify that what is prescribed is the mechanical cleaning of bobbins, rather than the cleaning of mechanical bobbins (IIAC, Cm 5672, 2002, para. 103)

Paragraph (e): This covers various machines and saws used to work with wood—In *R(I) 2/92* Commissioner Rice considered the meaning of "wood" in a previous occupational prescription in respect of occupational deafness. The claimant had worked in the newspaper print industry near machines cutting newsprint. The Commissioner supported the view of the dissenting chairman in the tribunal that this particular prescribed occupation "refers to wood in [the] accepted sense of the word, not to a material of which wood may be a constituent part. The prescribed occupation . . . clearly refers to working of wood or similar material such as chipboard, and not to the newsprint industry." Commissioner Rice stated that although "newsprint **10.154** is derived from wood, it is not the same as wood. It has undergone a metamorphosis, and in its changed form as newsprint it has become an entirely different material. It follows that the claimant cannot satisfy the relevant statutory requirements," (para.7). *R(I)2/92* (then *CI/309/1989*) was approved and applied in *CI/175/90* (noted below, notes to D7). It was also followed in *CI/43/92*, where Commissioner Rice held that "logs of toilet paper and kitchen paper" had, like newsprint, undergone a metamorphosis and could not be regarded as "wood," (para.6).

The rewording of the prescription to cover the use of specific machines or saws on wood removes the need to argue over issues such as the meaning of "forestry", which the IIAC Report saw as in need of clarification (paras.99, 100). It recommended that prescription cover the *regular* use of chainsaws. Note that this was not carried into the prescription.

The prescription has been reworded on HSE advice to cover all circular sawing machines, including those operated by moving the blade towards the material to be cut (para.104).

10.155   *Paragraph (f)*: Removal of references to "water-jetting industry" (see *CI/2286/2002* and *CI/5331/2002*) helps clarify the scope of the prescription which is now confined (i) to the use of a jet of water (or a mixture of water and abrasive) above a specified pressure of 680 bar (10,000 psi)(much higher than the "at least 3000 psi" formulation used by the Secretary of State to denote "high pressure" in the previous prescription (see *CI/5331/2002*, paras 2 and 18), and (ii) to jet channelling process to burn stone in a quarry. The IIAC was concerned in its proposed revision to clarify that it intended to include only those water-jetting processes in which high pressure was used on a commercial basis, and where an employee would be put at regular and frequent risk of exposure to high levels of noise likely to damage hearing (para.97). In setting the 10,000 psi level evidence was taken from HSE experts on the level of pressure likely to be hazardous to hearing and produce disablement (para.98).

10.156   *Paragraph (g)*: this covers a machine in a ship's engine room or gas turbine, provided that it use covers the specified testing. The meaning of "ship's engine room" was considered in *R(I)2/97* where the Commissioner saw it as "clearly limited to engine rooms on ships, and does not extend to engine rooms on land, regardless of the nature of the engines located there". So, in that case, the fact that the claimant worked in an engine room providing power to a building and the engines in the room were of a type that could be used to power ships, was immaterial. So was the fact that had he been on a ship and rendered deaf by working with the self-same engines, his claim would have succeeded; the occupation has to be a prescribed one (*ibid*., paragraph11).

The Commissioner in so deciding on the appropriate interpretation, made use of a report on Occupational Deafness by the Industrial Injuries Advisory Council. In *CSI/248/2003*, Commissioner Parker considered the meaning of "ship". After reviewing a number of statutory definitions and case law from a variety of legal subject areas, she accepted:

"for the present purpose the value of generally applying the Merchant Shipping Act [1995] definition of a ship (' "ship" includes every description of vessel used in navigation') and how that definition was interpreted in *Perks* [a tax case, a decision of the Court of Appeal found at [2001] EWCA Civ 1228]

The fact finding tribunal must therefore ask itself what is the design and capability of any particular structure and whether 'navigation' in the sense of 'movement across water' (and not requiring 'conveying persons and cargo from place to place') *is a significant part of the function of the structure in question.* The significance of the navigation is an issue of degree on the facts of a particular case and can be overturned by an appellate court only if the conclusions are perverse.

As Carnwath J. noted in *Perks*, the test has enabled the courts to include structures of very specialised kinds within the scope of the definition of 'ship', and to exclude cases where it was considered that the function of 'moving across the seas' was minimal or non-existent" (paras 57—59).

The tribunal to which the case was remitted

"having first found on what type of structures, and when, the claimant worked during the relevant period, must then consider with respect to each whether 'movement across water' was a significant part of its particular function. If the claimant worked only on the North Alwyn, and it is, as the Secretary of State suggests, a huge, fixed platform once set up in its location, it must be doubtful if this would constitute a ship. However, as always, everything depends on the facts found having regard to the evidence" (para.65).

See also *CSI/524/1999*, where the rig had propellers to enable it to move and to turn in bad weather. But, even if the rig at issue in *CSI/248/2003* were a "ship", the question remained whether the claimant, who drove a crane on the rig, worked in the ship's engine room. The Commissioner thought that:

"as a ship is not inevitably self-propelled, then, having regard to the underlying purpose for prescribing the occupation set out in paragraph A(10), it seems inevitable that to constitute a ship's engine room rather than *any* engine room, the engine room in question must provide power *for the ship*. It is insufficient that a claimant works in an engine room, even if integrated with the ship, where the engine of the structure on which he works provides power to that particular structure only, rather than to the ship.

So the question here is whether the claimant works in an engine room of a crane, such a crane being located on a ship, which in no substantial way differs from the engine room of a land crane; alternatively, does his engine room on the crane provide power beyond the crane and for the ship?" (paras 74, 75).

The remainder of the prescription gives aid and comfort to others who work with gas turbines for various specified forms of engine testing.

Paragraph (h): This applies to machines used for certain specified matters in the manufacure of glass containers and hollow war. *R(I) 4/99* remains authority for the proposition that the whole of the prescription is confined to glass manufacture. In that case, considering similar wording in para.(w) of the then prescription, the claimant was a clay worker in the pottery industry. He operated a "forming machine, used in the manufacture of ceramic (pottery) hollow ware, but not glass hollow ware" (para.4). The Commissioner rejected the argument of the claimant's representative that "hollow ware" was not confined to glass, but included metal and ceramics. Taking account of the Industrial Injuries Advisory Council Report [Cm. 817 (1994)], which had led to the introduction of para.(w)) in order to interpret ambiguous wording in the legislative prescription, Commissioner Goodman came to the conclusion that the:

10.157

"prescription is . . . confined to glass manufacture. The words, '. . . forming machines used in the manufacture of glass containers or hollow ware' do in my view read in such a way that the adjective 'glass' applies not only to 'containers' but also to 'hollow ware'. That is the natural meaning of the sentence and it also coincides with the fact that the rest of sub-paragraphs (i) and (ii) and (iii) of paragraph (w) are all clearly confined to the manufacture of various kinds of glass (save 'mineral wool' in sub-paragraph (ii)). The report of the Advisory Council leads to the same conclusion and I am entitled to look at its contents in view of the ambiguity introduced in [sub-] paragraph (i) of paragraph (w) by the use of the word 'or' between 'glass containers' and 'hollow ware'. Overall, therefore, I am satisfied that the tribunal arrived at the correct decision and that the prescribed occupation in paragraph (w) of Paragraph A10 is not intended to apply to any kind of hollow ware except that made of glass. I must therefore dismiss the claimant's appeal accordingly" (para.13).

10.158   *Paragraph (k)*: this was recommended for prescription since evidence from the HSE supported the view that the level of exposure to noise in this situation was at least as high as in the occupations already prescribed (IIAC Report, Cm 5672, 2002, para. 94) Note that cases might also fit (as single incidents or small series of incidents producing deafness) as accidents within SSCBA 1992, s. 94(1). See further *CI/5029/2002* on assessment of disablement in respect of deafness arising from accident in connection with police firearms training.

10.159   *Paragraph (l)*: this was recommended for prescription since evidence from the HSE supported the view that the level of exposure to noise in this situation was at least as high as in the occupations already prescribed (IIAC Report, Cm 5672, 2002, para.94)

A11 (Vibration white finger)

10.160   In *R(I) 2/95*, the form of prescription of prescribed disease A11 was upheld as *intra vires*.

In *R(I) 3/02*, Commissioner Jacobs noted that the legal definition of vibration white finger in referring only to "blanching" is narrower than the medical one, which also takes on board sensory effects. He held that the legal definition only restricted those cases of vibration white finger that are to be subject to an assessment of disablement for purposes of disablement benefit. However, once a case thus comes within that definition because of blanching, when it comes to the loss of faculty causing the claimant's disabilities it is proper then to look to the broader medical concept and include the sensory effects (see paras 17, 22).

Despite suggestions from the Industrial Injuries Advisory Council in Cm.2844 (May 1995) that this should be represcribed as hand-arm vibration syndrome, vibration white finger remains prescribed only in respect of its vascular effect (blanching) and not its neurological effect. But in stressing that in *R(I) 1/02*, Commissioner Williams endorsed the approach in *R(I) 3/02* that

"once there is episodic blanching of the relevant extent, the neurological effect of the disease will be relevant to compensation as well as the vascular effects" (para.10).

10.161   The Tribunal of Commissioners in *R(I) 2/06* approved the principle in *R(I) 3/02* as "correct, and now well-settled" (para.53). It also stressed that assessment of disablement is ultimately a matter of judgment for the tribunal which hears and sees the evidence. That Tribunal decision also elaborates on the nature of an error of law, and on the difference between that and a disputed judgment of degree on a question of fact. It also proffers guidance on reference to Sch.2 in non-prescribed cases, on consideration of the judicial guidelines on the assessment of damages in civil personal injury cases, on cross-reference to other schemes such as that for criminal injuries, and on the status of official departmental guidance such as the Medical Assessment Framework (MAF). See further the annotation to SSCBA 1992, Sch.6.

The terms of prescription of the prescribed disease or injury PD A11 were altered, subject to a transitional provision (Social Security (Industrial Injuries) (Prescribed Diseases) Amendment (No.2) Regulations 2007 (SI 2007/1753) reg.3), with effect from October 1, 2007 so as to add sensorineural symptoms to the description of the disease and a proviso that both sets of symptoms are caused by vibration. It also provides that the prescription shall not cover blanching of the skin or sensorineural symptoms prior to employment in a prescribed occupation. Without renaming PD A11 as "hand-arm vibration syndrome" as there recommended, the changes in some degree reflect ones put forward by the Industrial Injuries Advisory Council in reports in Cm. 2844 (May 1995) and Cm. 6098 (July 2004), and reiterated in its review of the list of prescribed diseases in Cm. 7003 (January 2007) (see paras 38, 39), although the Explanatory Note to the amending regulations makes no mention of any of these reports. The change may also reflect the impact of *R(I) 3/02* as regards taking on board sensory effects in ascertaining loss of faculty, and *R(I) 1/02* in seeing them as relevant to compensation as well as the vascular effects. On limitations on the scope of the preclusive transitional provision, see *DG v SSWP* [2009] UKUT 41 (AAC), noted further in the commentary to the provision. On the need carefully to consider whether the tribunal is applying the "old" or the "new" blanching provision, see *SR v SSWP* [2009] UKUT 39 (AAC).

In *CI/4874/2001*, Deputy Commissioner McLachlan stressed the need to keep separate the issues, on the one hand, whether the claimant has the disease [the col.1 matter] (and the consequent degree of disablement) and, on the other, the question of causation [the col.2 matter]. He stated

> "It is misleading to say that 'the question of blanching . . . has to be considered in the context of vibration induced damage . . .'. The blanching must be considered first, and if the required degree of blanching is established attention should then be turned to causation" (para.10).

In *R(I) 3/04*, Commissioner Mesher ruled the matter of occupational cause to be irrelevant to the diagnosis question. He accepted that "blanching" means more than the normal paleness in the extremities experience on exposure to cold, where there is a reduction of the blood supply to the peripheral arteries in order to protect the system as a whole. He was not, however, prepared to limit "blanching" to intense whiteness, the profound deathly white referred to in the medical paper by Dr Reed, The Blood and Nerve Supply to the Hand, which the Commissioner embodied in an appendix to his decision. That was characteristic but the meaning of "blanching" was not restricted to that, and was rather a matter to be decided in particular cases by tribunals and medical decision makers. Nor was circumferential blanching a requisite, preferring here Commissioner Rowland in *CI/3596/2001* to Commissioner Henty in *CI/1807/2002*. Indeed Commissioner Mesher rejected Commissioner Henty's view that Commissioner Rowland's decision had been given *per incuriam*. He noted that the matter of the Cold Water Provocation Test in the Department's Notes on the Diagnosis of Prescribed Diseases (NDPD) had successfully been challenged in *R. (on the application of the National Association of Colliery Overmen, Deputies and Shotfirers) v Secretary of State for Work and Pensions* [2003] EWHC 607 (Admin). There Pitchford J. found irrational the Secretary of State's refusal to revise the NDPD guidance and required him to amend it to reflect the correct intention behind the words used, namely that a positive result could have diagnostic value but a negative one should be treated as having none (paras 107–109).

In *CI/1720/2001*, Commissioner Rowland gives some guidance to tribunals on the manner of questioning those who claim to suffer from vibration white finger, suggesting that they avoid closed questioning and too technical language (paras 12–14).

In *CI/1763/2002*, having consulted Commissioner Jacobs who gave the decision in *CI/14532/1996* (now *R(I) 3/02*), Commissioner Mesher stressed that they were both agreed that

> "there cannot be an automatic and mechanical rule, without examination of the particular circumstances of each case, that Stage 2 on the Taylor Pelmear Scale means that PD A11 cannot be diagnosed. Stage 2 covers blanching during winter. But it is possible for someone to in addition experience blanching during the summer (thus going towards throughout the year as the prescription requires) without quite reaching Stage 3 on the Scale which requires 'extensive blanching with frequent episodes in summer as well as in winter'" (see paras 11–13 of *CI/1763/2002*).

10.162

Although not mentioned in the Tribunal of Commissioners' decision *CI/535/2005*, that approach is consistent with the tenor of that Tribunal decision and in particular its rejection of the view that there can be produced a ready template for decisions on the assessment of disablement. See further commentary to SSCBA 1992, Sch.6.

In *CI/421/2006*, Commissioner Turnbull held that a claimant refused permission to stand outside the tribunal for a short while in cold weather the better to support his claim that he suffered from vibration white finger was denied natural justice. The Commissioner also suggested that since this claimant had also requested that the last tribunal conduct a Cold Water Provocation Test, it might be wise to offer one at the new hearing. Although a negative result from such a test did not disprove vibration white finger, a positive result could assist a claimant whose history or symptoms were inconclusive (citing *R. (on the application of NACODS) v Secretary of State for Work and Pensions* [2003] EWHC 607, paras 41, 43). The result of any diagnostic test, however, had to be considered in the light of the history and clinical findings in the case.

10.163   In *CI/3596/2001*, Commissioner Rowland accepted that the prescription of PD A11 does not require circumferential blanching. While blanching only of the palmar side of the fingers might be atypical, it suffices to meet the terms of the prescription, the relevant question when determining whether the claimant is suffering from a prescribed disease (para.4). Its atypical nature might, however, in some cases be a basis for doubting the history given by the claimant or for deciding that it was not due to the nature of his/her employment, and might give some indication as to the degree of disablement (para.5).

The words "in forestry" in **sub-para.(a)** were replaced with the broader term "on wood" with effect (subject to a transitional provision) from October 1, 2007, thus giving effect to recommendations of the Industrial Injuries Advisory Council on the confusion generated by "in forestry" (see Cm. 6098 (July 2004), paras. 67, 78 and Cm. 7003 (January 2007), para.38). Happily, the case law on the meaning and scope of "in forestry", which had itself effected a broadening of the term (see below), is thus now only relevant to claims in respect of a period of assessment which relates to a claim made, or having effect, before the date these 2007 Regulations came into force or to a renewed break-out of a condition for which a claim was made before their entry into force. The change brings PD A11 into line with PD A10 where the broader term "on wood" has been applied since September 22, 2003. For the meaning of "wood", see the annotation to PD A10 (e). For the text of the transitional provision see the Social Security (Industrial Injuries) (Prescribed Diseases) Amendment (No. 2) Regulations 2007 (SI 2007/1753).

As indicated above, the meaning of "forestry" (now relevant to claims linked to periods prior to October 1, 2007), has been the subject of dispute, but case law gradually broadened the concept. In *CI/3924/1997*, Commissioner Rice considered it. The term "forestry" is also used in prescribed disease A10(i) and decisions *R(I) 5/96* (formerly *CI/362/94*) and *CI/319/94* on it in that context were cited in argument. Commissioner Rice used the same Shorter Oxford English Dictionary definition as in those cases: "the science and art of forming and cultivating forests, management of growing timber", the latter part of the definition being applicable to the case before Commissioner Rice. Here the claimant was employed by an urban local authority as an "arborist–tree surgeon". The Commissioner, deploying dictionary definitions, took "arborist" as someone who studies trees and, in the absence of a dictionary definition, took "tree-surgeon" as someone who cuts, trims or otherwise prunes trees. But an "arborist–tree surgeon" is not necessarily a forester and a restrictive meaning was given to the prescription:

"He may be concerned . . . with trees which form no part of a forest and do not qualify as growing timber. They may, for example, simply be ornamental trees designed to improve the appearance of a city such as Liverpool. Where they are grown merely to enhance the scenery e.g. along the roadways or in strategic parts of the city or in parks, they clearly do not form part of a forest, nor are they normally 'growing timber' cultivated as a crop for eventual sale for commercial use. Of course when an ornamental tree reaches maturity, it may well be sold off for such a use, but that is not the primary purpose for which it was cultivated. It was merely an incidental consequence of the decorative purpose for which it was initially planted and nurtured" (para.6).

The matter was remitted to a new tribunal to consider the matter again in line with that interpretation in the light of the evidence, old and new, before them. The label attached to the claimant's department "Forestry Department" was not conclusive of its activities nor, if an accurate description of them, would it necessarily apply to all employees in the Department (para.7). Recently in *R(I) 2/01*, Commissioner Levenson took the view that "forestry" should be given a broader, ordinary non-technical meaning. He doubted that the approach in the decisions above, which followed those noted in respect of prescribed disease A10(i), accorded with the approach of the IIAC in its report on the prescription of vibration white finger (Cmnd.8350 (1981)). He declined to follow *R(I) 5/96* and the other cases (see paras 8–15). He considered that prescribed occupations should not be "artificially narrowed" (para.15). Accordingly, he held that the tribunal did not err in law in holding that the claimant who had pruned and felled trees in parks, schools and on highways for a city council had used chain saws in "forestry".

10.164

Commissioner Levenson's comments and broader approach were endorsed by the Court of Appeal in *Davis v Secretary of State for Social Security* (January 12, 2001) reported as *R(I) 2/01*. Rix L.J. stated:

"It seems to me that while the words 'in forestry' in the statutory phrase are plainly intended as some form of limitation, it would be wrong to give to those words too narrow a definition when one considers the purpose of the statute, which was to provide compensation for those who suffered the prescribed disease as result of their occupation. There is great danger that, if too narrow a definition is adopted, then the very persons who fall within the purpose of the statutory protection would fall outside the definition. If, for instance, the requirement was that the work had to be done within a forest properly so-called, which was one part of Miss Lieven's definition of forestry, then someone who spent all his time in the use of chain saws, pruning or cutting down trees in large ornamental estates, or other amenity areas of the countryside which contained extensive woods, but which perhaps may not have been 'forest', would find themselves outside the statutory protection. Again, if the requirement was that the trees concerned, whether in a forest or not, had to be grown for some commercial or industrial purpose, as distinct from some amenity or leisure purpose, or simply the beauty or health of the environment, a similar result would follow.

In the present case, Miss Lieven was ultimately prepared to adopt the dictionary definition, including the words 'management of growing timber', but nevertheless she submitted that to fall within the words 'in forestry' a claimant would either have to work in a forest, or in the commercial production of growing timber.

In my judgment, that is to narrow the meaning of 'in forestry' both by going beyond the dictionary definition which has been adopted in all the previous decisions as well as in the current one, and by doing so in a way which is neither justified by that definition nor justified by the purpose of the statute. Various examples were canvassed in the course of argument. It is not necessary to make a decision in respect of any of them. Decisions of this kind are ultimately always for the tribunal, provided it founds itself on a proper understanding of the statute. But, for instance, the case of an employee of Railtrack who was involved constantly in the management of growing timber beside the railway, by means of pruning or felling it, is an example where, speaking for myself, I could well understand a tribunal deciding, on the particular facts before it, that his work fell within the phrase 'in forestry'.

In my judgment the words 'in forestry' are perfectly adequately defined by the expression 'the management of growing timber', and there is no need to cut down those words any further by requiring that growing timber should be in any particular kind of area, whether described as a forest or parkland or whatever, or should be grown for any particular purpose. Moreover, I would accept that the work of clearing away growing timber is part of its management.

The fact that the statutory phrase has to be taken as a whole, namely 'any occupation involving . . . the use of hand-held chain saws in forestry' suggests that the words 'in forestry' mean no more than 'in or in connection with forestry', and are intended to express a sense of scale about the occupation involved. The words 'occupation involving' are very wide words indeed and raise, of course, the possibility that the occupation may involve the use of hand-held chain saws in only an incidental way. By putting in the words 'in forestry', in my judgment the legislators intended to exclude the use of handheld chain saws in only an incidental way, as might occur in occupations which had nothing to do with forestry (as for instance, might very frequently occur in the case of those who are in occupation merely as gardeners and make some occasional use of a hand-held chain saw)."

The clear implication is disapproval of the approach and result in *CI/3284/97* and *R(I) 5/96*.

10.165 In *CI/373/89* Commissioner Mitchell stated with respect to **sub-para.(b)**:

"The most obvious application of the words of prescription in issue in this case is to occupations involving the holding of material in the form of a work-piece which is being ground by rotary tools. Transmission of vibration to the operator in such a process is as direct and obvious as the immediate application of the words used. The question is whether those words also cover the operation spoken to by the claimant and Mr. Alford [a consulting engineer familiar with the Churchill type machine at issue] and carried out several times daily between operations on workpieces. On the evidence before me I have no doubt that the dressing or resurfacing of the side of the grinding wheel by the manual use of the carborundum stone against it involves appreciable grinding away of the carborundum stone itself progressively from the corners at the end until it becomes too small and is discarded after about one to two weeks. That process of course also involves the transmission of substantial vibration as found by the tribunal. The stone therefore imparts a measure of grinding but also suffers grinding in its own turn and that to a marked extent. I have come to the conclusion that this operation comes within the prescription of an occupation involving 'the holding of material being ground . . . by rotary tools.' (para.14 words in square brackets added by annotator)

'Grinding' in para.(b) is not limited to grinding of 'metal'. In *CSI 987/00*, Deputy Commissioner Sir Crispin Agnew of Lochnaw Bt Q.C. considered the case of a claimant who had worked as a labourer to electricians. His work had involved cutting raggles in concrete walls with a grinder and then hammering and chiselling them out so that the electricians could insert conduits. Occasionally this would involve him striking the metal reinforcing rods in the concrete walls. The Deputy Commissioner rejected "the Secretary of State's submission that grinding relates to metal and that the only metal ground was the occasional action of cutting metal rods with a grinder" (para.15). Instead the Deputy Commissioner considered

"that 'grinding' can be on any 'material', whereas 'sanding or polishing' can only be on 'metal'. I reach this construction of the provision having regard to (i) the use of the word 'in' before 'grinding' and again before 'the sanding or polishing of metal' which suggests that the task of grinding is separate from the task of sanding or polishing of metal and (ii) the fact that the later part of the provision refers to the 'holding of material being ground' and 'the metal being sanded or polished'. Had the intention been that prescription (b) should only apply to the grinding, sanding or polishing of metal, I would have expected the word 'metal' to be used rather than 'material'. 'Material' is a word that can be applied to any substance and not just to metal" (para.16).

Grinding concrete was the grinding of material and was therefore within PD A11(b).

In *CI/22/91* Commissioner Johnson considered whether the claimant's employment fell within the description in **sub-para.(c)**:

"the use of hand-held percussive metal-working tools, or the holding of metal being worked on by percussive tools in riveting, caulking, chipping, hammering, fettling or swaging".

He considered that the 57lb hammer used by the claimant was a hand-held percussive tool used to hammer metal, and continued:

"However, I have to consider whether the words 'metal-working' have any special significance, and also whether 'hammering' should be given its ordinary or has some special meaning in the context of paragraph (c). Certainly the [Industrial Injuries] Advisory Committee recommended that 'prescription should be in terms of the use of certain specified tools in certain specified occupations' . . .; broadly speaking that would appear to be the scheme of Schedule 1, although a number of occupations are very widely defined, for example A5–A8 inclusive, which specify 'manual labour' involving certain movements, and the conditions prescribed under B, C and to a great extent D, depend more on contact with biological or chemical agents than work in any particular industry.

10. So far as prescribed disease A11 is concerned, (a) is restricted to forestry and (e) to shoe manufacture, (d) covers mining, quarrying, demolition and road construction, which is a much wider category, as is (b), specifying the grinding, sanding or polishing of metal, which must take place in a variety of different trades. Looking at it as a whole it cannot be said that any very clear pattern emerges. In my view the 57Lb hammers used by Mr D were 'metal-working tools' as they were used for the purpose of working upon metal objects, whether ships' propellers, crane buckets or friction bands, or on the superstructure of the crane itself. I have also considered whether the word 'hammering' (in the description 'riveting, caulking, chipping, hammering, fettling or swaging') should be given some specialised meaning such as, for example, in the sense of producing a 'hammered' finish to a piece of metal, but I can see no justification for giving 'hammering' anything other than its normal everyday meaning. In my judgment, although the words denote particular processes, the one thing they have in common is not some particular trade or industry, but the fact that they all involve striking metal with metal, with consequent vibration." (paras 9, 10).

"Fettling" means "to remove excess moulding material and casting irregularites from a cast component" (a dictionary definition adopted in *CI/141/93*).

In *CI/207/2004*, Commissioner Williams considered the particular tasks involved in a bedding industry process involving using an automatic staple gun (what the claimant knew as a "rammer") to fix the metal of the bed springs to the bounding metal strip that holds the bed springs together and thus to the wooden base of the bed (known as a Bonnell base). He held that the rammer was a metal-working tool. In *Secretary of State v Westgate* [2006] EWCA Civ 725 (reported as *R(I) 1/06*) the Court of Appeal rejected this view and allowed the Secretary of State's appeal. The Court held that his interpretation was not within the range of reasonable interpretations of that statutorily undefined term. For the Court of Appeal, a metal-working tool is one that "works metal" (para.5). The process involved in the rammer for fixing the metal of the bed springs to the wooden frame was no more working metal than was the act of banging a nail into a wal or driving a bolt through a hole—such processes involve "working with metal" rather than "working metal" (para.6).

A12 (Carpal tunnel syndrome)

10.166   For useful evidence from the medical adviser to the DWP (Dr Reed) on PD A12 (carpal tunnel syndrome), see the Schedule to *CI/3745/2006*.

In *R(I) 3/95* Commissioner Heggs considered the meaning of "hand-held vibrating tool" for the purposes of the prescription of occupation in respect of prescribed disease A12 (carpal tunnel syndrome) as worded prior to March 24, 1996 "the use of hand-held vibrating tools"). The Commissioner said:

> "There is no statutory definition of the expression and the words can be given an extremely wide or narrow interpretation. Mrs Cleave [the claimant's representative] submitted that any vibrating tool falls within the terms of prescribed disease A12 if it can be shown that any part of it is supported or held by the hand of the operator. That is an attractive argument which would afford benefit to a wide category of claimants who could establish that they had sustained carpal tunnel syndrome from the use of vibrating equipment. The expression is however susceptible to the narrower interpretation that the expression 'hand-held' is descriptive of the actual tool in function and not the use made of the tool by the claimant. On this construction as submitted by Mr Jones [the AO's representative] it therefore applies only to the particular kind of vibrating tool which is portable and held manually. It does not extend to the use of tools of any kind in which some part of the operation may involve hand steadying or control. I am entitled to have regard to the Report of the Industrial Injuries Advisory Council (see paragraph 15 of the Tribunal of Commissioners decision *R(I) 11/81* where *Black–Clawson International Ltd v Papierweke–Walhof–Ascheffenburg AG* [1975] A.C. 591 was applied). In my view the Report supports the narrower interpretation because it refers to 'grip required to use such tools—many of which are cumbersome' and that 'other forceful and repetitive movement of the wrist is not sufficient to prescribe carpal tunnel syndrome in any other occupational category'. Accordingly I conclude that the narrower interpretation is that which must apply." (para.14).

That approach was followed by Commissioner May in *CSI/82/94*. This concept of "hand-held" as denoting portability does not necessarily mean that it covers only lightweight tools; as *R(I) 2/96* makes clear, provided the element of portability is there it can cover heavier tools. In *R(I) 2/96*, the claimant worked for a bus company and had to clean the garage floor and inspection pit with a heavy rotary scrubbing or buffing machine which had to be gripped tightly to steer it and to hold in the clutch. Pressure also had to be applied to it in order to remove stubborn patches of oil from the garage floor. As Commissioner Goodman noted:

> "There is no doubt that these machines vibrate considerably, that they have to [be] tightly held, gripped and steered about and that the kind of machine that the claimant was using was heavy in nature, though it could be lifted about by two people and to that extent was portable" (para.6).

10.167   In a decision supplementing rather than dissenting from the emphasis in *R(I) 3/95*, he held that the machine came within the prescription as a "hand-held vibrating tool", but cautioned that "there being a substantial factural element in [his] decision, that it is not necessarily a precedent for other types of machine or tool" (para.11). In the original *CI/15408/1995*, in March 1996, Commissioner Rice followed *CI/160/94*, and decided the appeal against the claimant, holding that the buffing machine operated by her was not a hand-held vibrating tool within the meaning of the legislative prescription. But his decision was given in ignorance of two of Commissioner Goodman's decisions on ostensibly similar machines: *R(I) 2/96* (a concrete floor scrubber) and *CI/514/94* (a floor buffer). When he became aware of those decisions, Commissioner Rice set aside his decision and the appeal was reheard before Commissioner Henty. The product is a new decision *R(I) 6/98*. Commissioner Henty's decision reviews all the pertinent authorities. The decision is in favour of the claimant and follows the *ratio* of Commissioner Goodman's decisions. Its effect is that the approach to "hand-held" in the quotation from *CI/160/94* is seen as correct in so far as it prevents static, fixed machines of the type at issue in that case (on which hands merely rested) being within the prescription. The requirement of "portability" in that approach was seen as *obiter* (not necessary for that decision). Having reviewed the relevant cases and the relevant report of the Industrial Injuries Advisory Council on the prescription of carpal tunnel syndrome (March 1992). Commissioner Henty gave his reasoned opinion on what he found a very difficult question:

"All the previous decisions I have referred to are in agreement that a fixed machine, which requires the application of the hand to operate it, is not 'a hand-held tool'. However, it does not seem to me that there is much difference in fact between (i) a tool which vibrates and requires, during its operation, to be carried by hand either continuously or intermittently; and (ii) a tool which vibrates and, in its operation, requires to be moved either continuously or intermittently and that motion is provided by the energy of the operator. I exclude self-propelled machines. As I have pointed out, a buffing machine is self-supporting and is not mounted on some support. It is therefore clearly different from the fixed tools in *CI/160/94* and *CI/156/94* [both of which concerned fixed sewing machines]. For instance, a portable electric drill vibrates and, when in use, it has to be moved and firmly grasped by hand, and the operator, when drilling, is required to exert considerable pressure. In the same way, an industrial buffing machines vibrates, and, when in use, it has to be moved by the operator backwards and forwards, manoeuvred and guided, requiring a firm grasp, and the firmer the grasp, the more keenly will any vibration be transmitted. I have, therefore, come to the conclusion that an industrial buffing machine is within the definition of a hand-held vibrating tool . . ." (para.14).

He was assisted in so concluding by the fact that when the opportunity was taken to effect a legislative modification to the prescription to vitiate the effect of *CI/227/94* (below), no step was taken to remedy any dissatisfaction with Commissioner Goodman's decisions on hand-held, thus indicating acceptance of the effect of those decisions (*ibid.*). The previous form of prescription was wider covering use of "hand-held vibrating tools". "Vibrating tool" was held to mean nothing more than a tool which vibrates, so that any hand-held tool (powered or not) fell within the description (*CI/227/94*, para.4). So in *CI/227/94*, it covered a hammer and punch used for making marks on metal. There was no need for an independent vibration source within the tool (*CI/227/94; CI/136/95*). On the prescription as then worded, as the Court of Appeal put it in *Janicki v Secretary of State for Social Security* [2001] I.C.R.1220 (reported in *R(I) 1/01*), if the tool vibrates because of necessary contact with something else (in that case the sewing machine on which the heavy cutters held by the claimant had to rest to be used), the source of the vibration was immaterial. The occupational description was, however, altered to its current wording—"hand-held powered tools whose internal parts vibrate so as to transmit that vibration to the hand, but excluding those that are solely powered by hand—with effect from March 24, 1996. That new wording does not affect the cases on "hand-held". But it precludes the application of *CI/227/94, CI/136/95* and *Janicki* if the period under consideration falls after that date, unless the claimant's case is covered by the transitional provision noted at the end of this note, preserving for certain cases the old wording of the prescription. Similarly precluded by the new wording is the approach taken by Commissioner Howell in *CI/474/95* that the requirements are satisfied even when the source of the vibration is the force applied by the operator rather than the mechanism of the tool. Under the former wording, Commissioner Hoolahan held in *R(I) 8/98* that a bus steering wheel, which transmitted vibrations to the driver was not within the prescription: the wheel did not contain within itself "a source of vibration—it merely transmits vibration from something else" (para.16). The change in wording (from merely "hand-held vibrating tools" to "hand-held powered tools whose internal parts vibrate so as to transmit that vibration to the hand") further prevents such a claim succeeding.

10.168   A challenge to the validity of the prescription of disease A12 (carpal tunnel syndrome), because it is prescribed only for those whose occupations involved the use of certain tools, was rejected in *CI/5009/97*.

Paragraph (b) was added to the list of occupations with effect from April 6, 2007 on the recommendation of the IIAC, because its review found evidence "that flexing and extending of the wrist, when repeated over much of the work time, was associated with a more than doubling of risk of CTS" (see *Work Related Upper Limb Disorders*, Cm. 6868 (July 2006), para.46). Appendix 2 to that report contains a useful diagram of the action involved. That Appendix is reproduced in *FR v SSWP* [2008] UKUT 12 (AAC); *R(I) 2/09*. In that decision, Judge Jacobs stressed that it is the nature and direction of the movement involved in dorsiflexion and palmar flexion, rather than the degree of movement, which are important. In that case and in *CI/1961/2008*, it was stressed that the IIAC Report is an appropriate aid to applying C23(b), even though the terms of prescription in it are not exactly the same as that recommended by the IIAC.

A13 (Osteoarthritis of the hip)

10.169   The prescription of osteoarthritis of the hip in relation to work in agriculture as a farmer or farm worker for a period of, or periods which amount in aggregate to, 10 years or more, was added to the Schedule with effect from March 14, 2005. Its prescription is subject to a transitional provision in reg.3 of the inserting regulations— Social Security (Industrial Injuries) (Prescribed Diseases) Amendment Regulations 2005 (SI 2005/324)—set out at the end of this section of the book: the prescription does not apply to a period of assessment relating to a claim made before March 14, 2005. The prescription implements the recommendations of IIAC as set out in their report on *Osteoarthritis of the Hip* (Cm 5977). The disease is common in the population at large, but the IIAC considered that the evidence now made it clear that in farmers and farmworkers there is a raised incidence of the disease sufficiently high that a clear association can be made between that occupation and the condition, even though there is still some uncertainty about exactly what aspect of farming is responsible. The Council thought that it would be most appropriate to prescribe for farmers whose work can be classified according to the Office of National Statistics Standard Occupational Classification 2000, "5111 farmers", "9111 farm workers" or "1211 farm managers", and who have been employed as employed earners in this capacity for 10 years or longer in aggregate. This definition was more restrictive than ones used in the field research, but the Council believed that it provided a workable definition of a level exposure for which the epidemiological evidence of a doubling (or greater) of risk is robust.

On accepted authority in prescribed diseases requiring work for particular periods, the focus should be on the work done rather than the contractual obligation to do it (*R(I) 2/79* and *CI/16/91*—see commentary to regs. 2 and 25, above).

On "agriculture", see *CI/56/95*, noted in the commentary to B6, below.

A14 (Osteoarthritis of the knee) (coal miners and related occupations)

10.170   This prescribed disease was inserted with effect from July 13, 2009. It is not subject to any transitional provision. This new prescription essentially implements, with one change (the inclusion of "face-salvage worker" which IIAC had subsumed within "faceworker"), the recommendations of the Industrial Injuries Advisory Council in its report, *Osteoarthritis of the knee in coal miners* (Cm 7440) (August 2008). The IIAC recommended that:

"The diagnosis of OA knee for the purposes of the IIDB Scheme should be based on knee pain, swelling, stiffness and restricted movement and if possible x-ray evidence of Stage 3 to 4 on the Kellgren-Lawrence scale; but should also be accepted in those who are on a surgical waiting list for knee replacement or have had a knee replacement previously" (para.71).

The IIAC had:

"identified direct research evidence of a greater than doubled risk of osteoarthritis of the knee in miners and indirect evidence of an excess risk of the disorder associated with occupational kneeling and squatting while undertaking heavy manual tasks (such as lifting or shovelling), activities traditionally undertaken by miners. The evidence suggests that the qualifying excess risk would arise after 10 or more years in aggregate of everyday occupational kneeling or squatting while undertaking heavy physical manual work.

The coal mining industry has undergone many changes which have decreased the extent to which miners have been exposed to such employment conditions, notably the closure of many mines by 1986. However, we have received evidence that the relevant exposure circumstances will still have occurred after 1986 in certain categories of miner, such as faceworkers working non-mechanised coal faces" (p.4, Chairman's letter to Secretary of State)

See further paras 27–68 (the evidence and its evaluation). The two figures on p.10 show the contrast between a normal knee-joint and one affected by osteoarthritis.

Extrapolating from a wide range of case authorities, Judge Wikeley in *DM v SSWP (II)* [2010] UKUT 198 (AAC) has provided "some initial guidance on the interpretation and application of the relevant rules" in a context in which, while it was clear that the claimant (described by himself and the Coalboard Enquiry Service as an underground face electrician) had worked underground for at least 10 years, the question was whether he had done so in any of the relevant prescribed occupations. It was important to do so because there had been some 40,000 claims in the past year in respect of PD A14, many of which would generate appeals, and a significant number of which would turn on the issue now before him (para.4).

The statutory words of prescription are the starting point, but a purposive approach has to be taken to them. "Any occupation" is not "a term of art" but requires a focus on the work activities performed rather than on the precise terms of the contract of employment ("the actual working test") (paras 19–30).

PD A14 provides two sets of relevant occupations dealing with the coal industry.   **10.171**
The first deals with periods before January 1, 1986. The second deals with periods on or after that date. The qualifying period might be all before that date, all after, or one spanning a period either side of that date. It need not have been in a single occupation (the words used are "at least 10 years in one or more of the following occupations"). The requisite occupation for periods before January 1, 1986 is working underground as a "coal miner", this term not being defined in social security legislation. Judge Wikeley, stressing the need to avoid an unduly restrictive construction, thought the new tribunal (whose decision it would be) might well have little difficulty in concluding that this claimant was a "coal miner" (para.34). Drawing by analogy on the definition in the now-repealed Stannaries Act 1887, as giving a flavour of what "coal miner" covered, he thought a tribunal might reasonably take the view that the term covered:

"anyone working in or about a coal mine, in a skilled, semi-skilled or unskilled 'blue collar' capacity, but not, for example, a 'white collar' colliery manager, mining engineer or mining surveyor" (para.35).

But he also considered it impossible and unwise to attempt an exhaustive or comprehensive definition, referring here to the "elephant test"—difficult to describe but knowing it when you see it (para.36). "Underground" might usefully if colloquially be summed up as "down the pit" (paras 37–38).

The second set of relevant occupations cover the period on or after January 1, 1986 as a: (i) face worker on a non-mechanised coal face; (ii) development worker; (iii) face-salvage worker; (iv) conveyor belt cleaner; or (v) conveyor belt attendant. Again, the focus must be on what the claimant was actually doing in the periods relied on, and not on the contract of employment. Nor can simple reliance be placed on the claimant's pay grade or the label on his wage packet. The matter is ultimately one of fact for the tribunal (paras 61–63). But the question is whether in the period 1986 onwards the claimant:

> "actually worked *in* one of the relevant occupations, and not whether he worked *in conditions similar to or indeed even identical to* those experienced by the listed occupations" (para.65).

10.172   PD A14 (dealing with the coal industry) requires working underground in the relevant occupation(s) for a period, or aggregate periods, of ten years. As Judge Wikeley noted, this could pose problems where the claimant has moved from pit to pit or work underground is interspersed with work above ground or where, indeed, there was no work done at all because of a prolonged industrial dispute. He referred the new tribunal to which the appeal was remitted to the helpful guidance in *R(I) 3/78* and *R(I) 2/79(T)* on computing periods of work in scheduled occupations, remembering that the focus is to be "on what the claimant actually did" (paras 39–40).

Although PD A14 was inserted because the risk of osteoarthritis because of kneeling and squatting, there was, however, no requirement in the terms of prescription (which he saw as clear and unambiguous) that the claimant's work underground involved periods of kneeling and squatting, prolonged or otherwise (paras 41–48, 54).

In *MD v SSWP (II)* [2011] UKUT 137 (AAC), Judge Wikeley held that, where a tribunal found that the osteoarthritis was due to degenerative causes, the correct wording of the decision should be to indicate that the claimant has PD A14 but is not entitled to benefit because the causation test is not met (see paras 20–21).

In *JL and DO v SSWP (II)* [2011] UKUT 294 (AAC); [2012] AACR 15, Judge Ward considered whether it made any difference where a claimant's osteoarthritis resulted in knee replacement surgery. He held that, where the original loss of faculty was osteoarthritis of the knee, the knee replacement surgery did not break the chain of causation so as to substitute a new cause of ongoing loss of faculty. The relevance of the knee replacement surgery went rather to the stage of assessment of the degree of disablement.

In *GV v SSWP (II)* [2012] UKUT 208 (AAC); [2013] AACR 3 Judge Wikeley considered whether "patella-femoral osteoarthritis" fell within "osteoarthritis of the knee". He concluded that its did, following the broader definition of "the knee" supported by medical dictionaries, even though the IIAC Report suggested a narrower approach excluding the patella. He did so because case authorities (e.g. *R(I) 15/75* and *R(I) 4/99*) show that "if the statutory meaning is clear and unambiguous then IIAC's reports cannot be mined for material to qualify or alter the legislative language" (para.36). Moreover, the patella femoral joint was used more for walking on inclined terrain, kneeling and squatting, functions associated with underground mining and, although the Judge made no mention of them since the claimant had been a coal miner, carpet fitters and other layers of non-concrete floors. Accordingly, Judge Wikeley, regarded the statutory expression "osteoarthritis of the knee" to be unambiguous, noting that if the legislative intention had been only to cover more limited parts of the knee joint, those responsible for drafting the legislation could have said so, but had not (para.37).

A14 (Osteoarthritis of the knee) (carpet fitters and other layers of non-concrete floors)

10.173   This occupation was added from March 30, 2012. It is not subject to any transitional provision. This new prescription implements the recommendations of the Industrial Injuries Advisory Council (IIAC) in its report *Osteoarthritis (OA) of the knee in carpet fitters and carpet and floor layers* (Cm. 7964) (November 2010), but puts the Council's intention that layers of concrete floors were not included into specific statutory wording. The IIAC:

> "concluded that the evidence in carpet fitters or carpet and floor layers is sufficient to recommend that OA of the knee be added to the list of prescribed diseases for those who have worked in these occupations for at least 20 years in aggregate.

There is insufficient evidence (direct or indirect), however, to support prescription of OA of the knee in other groups of construction workers." (p.4,
Chairman's letter to the Secretary of State)."

The Council thus intended:

"the work activities of qualifying claimants to include some or all of the following:
installing linoleum, carpet or vinyl floorings; removal of old flooring; installing
of underlay; installing of skirting board; and the associated preparatory work.
Having taken additional ergonomic advice from the HSE, the Council considers
that workers who lay parquet floors and wooden floors should also be covered by
the terms of prescription, but not workers whose main activity is to lay concrete
floors" (para.68, referring back to para.38).

The exclusion with respect to laying of concrete floors doubtless reflects that most
are laid largely by standing and spreading poured concrete rather than bending or
kneeling. The IIAC is to keep under review the matter of OA of the knee in other
construction workers.
    As with OA and the coal industry, the IIAC thought that for the purposes of the
scheme:

"a diagnosis of OA of the knee should be based on knee pain, swelling, stiffness and
restricted movement and, if possible, X-ray evidence of Stage 3-4 on the Kellgren-
Lawrence scale, but should also be accepted in those who are on a surgical waiting
list for knee replacement or have had a knee replacement previously" (para.6).

The two figures on p.10 of the Report show the contrast between a normal knee-
joint and one affected by osteoarthritis.
    On constructing the requisite 20-year period, see *R (I) 3/78, R (I) 2/79 (T)* and
DM v SSWP (II) [2010] UKUT 198 (AAC).
    On the relevance of knee replacement surgery, see *JL and DO v SSWP (II)*
[2011] UKUT 294 (AAC), noted in the commentary to PD A14 *(Osteoarthritis of
the knee) (coal miners and related occupations)*, above.
    "Patella-femoral osteoarthritis" falls within "osteoarthritis of the knee" (*GV
v SSWP* [2012] UKUT 208 (AAC) noted in the commentary to PD A14
(Osteoarthritis of the knee) (coal miners and related occupations), above.

IV. Prescribed Diseases Category: B. Conditions due to biological agents
    The IIAC in their report on Conditions due to Biological Agents (Cm 5997) in   10.174
November 1993 updated the references for each prescribed disease, and reviewed
the prescribed occupations in each case.

B1 (cutaneous anthrax; pulmonary anthrax)
    These occupational terms of prescription were added to the Schedule with effect   10.175
from March 14, 2005, subject to a transitional provision in reg.3 of the inserting
regulations—Social Security (Industrial Injuries) (Prescribed Diseases) Amendment
Regulations 2005 (SI 2005/324)—set out at the end of this section of the book: the
prescription does not apply to a period of assessment relating to a claim made before
March 14, 2005. The prescription implements the recommendations of IIAC as set
out in their report on Conditions due to Biological Agents (Cm 5997). The IIAC
stated

"Anthrax is a zoonotic disease (i.e. a disease passed from animals to humans)
caused by the bacterium *Bacillus anthracis*. Generally, humans contract anthrax
by exposure to infected herbivorous animals or their products. Bacterial spores
enter the human body via the skin (cutaneous anthrax), the lungs (pulmonary
anthrax) or the gut (intestinal anthrax). Cutaneous anthrax is the most common
type of infection in humans, accounting for approximately 95% of all cases. It is
characterised by an itchy skin lesion (or papule) which becomes a vesicle. This
vesicle bursts forming a characteristic eschar (sloughed off dead tissue), with

surrounding oedema and lymphangitis. This form of anthrax is readily treatable with antibiotics, but if left untreated can lead to death in a small proportion of cases. Pulmonary anthrax accounts for around 5% of human infections and has a high fatality rate. It is characterised by flu-like symptoms, which may lead to respiratory failure and death in a few days. Intestinal anthrax is rare, and is usually found outside the UK where infected meat may be eaten. Septicaemia and meningitis are possible complications of all forms of anthrax infection. Anthrax is common in livestock from parts of Turkey, Sudan and Pakistan" (para.44).

The IIAC recommended clarification of the prescription to go beyond exposure to infected herbivorous animals or their products (the previous prescription). The report acknowledged the potential for infection in other circumstances therefore the prescription has been widened to include any work involving contact with anthrax spores (see paras 45–48).

Originally the disease prescribed was "anthrax". With effect from March 16, 2015 only cutaneous anthrax and pulmonary anthrax are prescribed, reflecting the rarity of intestinal anthrax.

B3 (infection by leptospira)

10.176
This is prescribed in respect of rather wider occupations than may at first appear, with successful claims both by a building site labourer (*R(I) 20/52*) and by a surface worker at a mine (*R(I)531/92*) based on the fact that their work environment was "infested" with rats.

B4 ((a) Cutaneous larva migrans; (b) Iron deficiency anaemia caused by gastrointestinal infection by hookworm.)

10.177
The disease was originally prescribed as "ankylostomiasis" in the workmen's compensation legislation. Wider terms of occupational prescription were added to the Schedule with effect from March 14, 2005, subject to a transitional provision in reg.3 of the inserting regulations—Social Security (Industrial Injuries) (Prescribed Diseases) Amendment Regulations 2005 (SI 2005/324)—set out at the end of this section of the book: the prescription does not apply to a period of assessment relating to a claim made before March 14, 2005. Those terms of occupational prescription remain unchanged. They implement the recommendations of the IIAC as set out in their report on *Conditions due to Biological Agents (Cm 5997)*.The IIAC recommended alteration of the occupational prescription to reflect the fact that contact with sources of ankylostomiasis is not restricted to work in mines (paras 62–67). The change in wording of the disease prescription merely makes the prescription more specific since, as described by the IIAC, ankylostomiasis is

"a zoonotic disease caused by nematodes called hookworms, with the commonest types to infect humans being *Ancylostoma duodenale* and *Necator americanus*. The adult hookworms live, and lay eggs, in the intestines of humans and animals (in particular, dogs and cats). Infected humans or animals excrete the eggs in their faeces. In conditions of poor hygiene, the eggs develop into larvae which contaminate the soil. The larvae can enter the body via cuts in the skin or, if food is grown in the soil, may be swallowed and then penetrate the stomach wall. The larvae then make their way through the blood vessels to the lung. They are coughed up and swallowed, so completing their life cycle as adult hookworms in the intestine.

Individuals infected with hookworms may exhibit acute ankylostomiasis, characterised by skin eruptions that occur at the site of larval entry. Chronic ankylostomiasis is characterised by fatigue caused by anaemia from iron deficiency due to loss of blood into the tissues and gut. Other symptoms of chronic ankylostomiasis include vague abdominal pains and, occasionally, a cough and sore throat. In severe cases, cardiac complications from larval migration can occur, such as endomyocardial fibrosis" (paras 63–64).

B5 (tuberculosis)

This is prescribed for a very wide range of occupations in which contact with a source of infection is involved. It was considered recently by Commissioner Williams in *CI/3625/2003*. There would seem to have been no other cases since 1960 and the pre-1960 cases were of limited assistance given changes in the terms of prescription. In *CI/3625/2003*, Commissioner Williams found that

10.178

> "Mr W fails to make out the case that his employment is prescribed in relation to bovine tuberculosis, prescribed disease B5. I do so without looking too closely at the details of the school and its catchment area, or his job as a senior teacher at that school. I do so because he puts the risk down to contact not with infected children or their families or home settings, but with a professional colleague who was not known to be infected, and not to contact with infected cows or badgers or individuals but with a tick on that colleague's clothing. The tribunal found that Mr W had not satisfied it that the infection from which he was suffering was tick-borne. In other words, he failed to establish a source of infection. There is sound evidence for that and I accept that finding. That answers the question. But even if—hypo-thetically—I found that Mr W was right and X did carry an infectious tick, and that tick had bitten Mr W and caused bovine tuberculosis, what was it about his *employment* that put him at this risk? Why was he at risk as a teacher from that tick, in a different way to any member of X's family, friends or any other contacts or, in the words of section 108, otherwise than 'as a risk common to all persons'. I find no such additional risk. On either analysis, Mr W fails to establish that his occupation was prescribed for prescribed disease B5 in the bovine form." (para.22).

B6 (extrinsic allergic alveolitis)

This was considered by Commissioner Angus in *CI/56/95*. There the claimant was an electrician by trade, whose work was said to have brought him into contact with the agents which cause the disease (e.g. he had had to clean mouldy material out of machinery in the food processing industry before repairing it and had spent some considerable time working on the wiring and cabling of a chicken farm among feathers and chicken muck and had had to handle the birds). The Commissioner, remitting the matter to another SSAT, stated that the new tribunal should first find as a fact whether the claimant had been exposed to "moulds or fungal spores or heterologous proteins". If he had, the SSAT should consider whether such exposure was by reason of his employed earner's employment in any of the activities set out in heads (a)–(d) of the prescription. These are not a list of particular trades. Rather the decision on whether the claimant's occupation (here electrician) comes within those specified is decided by reference to the work done bringing him into contact with the relevant agents. One looks to

10.179

> "whether he has been exposed to the specified agents by reason of his participation in one of the specified activities . . . in so far as that activity or those activities fell within the scope of his employed earner's employment as indicated for him by his employer" (para.12).

As to the meaning of "agriculture" in head (a), the Commissioner deployed a dictionary definition: "the science or occupation of cultivating land and rearing crops and livestock; farming" (Collins English Dictionary, cited in para.15). Where the claimant's employer was not a farmer then:

> "in order to establish whether or not the [claimant] is employed in agriculture it would be necessary to enquire into the nature and organisation of the employer's business and the nature and pattern of the duties assigned to the claimant. Just as an electrician could be regarded as employed in agriculture because he was employed full-time by a farmer, a company of electrical engineers who specialised in servicing agricultural customers might be said to be engaged in agriculture. Alternatively a firm which had no particular tendency to specialise in agricultural customers might have assigned an employee to duties so involved with farming that the employee could be said to be engaged in agriculture" (para.15).

As to (b), the tribunal would have to be satisfied that as regards any handling of mouldy vegetable matter when cleaning out machines, the matter in question was "in storage". As to (c), the question would be did his employers expect him to "handle" birds (paras 18, 19).

Paragraph (e) was added with effect from April 6, 2007, subject to a transitional provision set out in the amending regulations at the end of this part of the book. The IIAC recommended this. It considered there was little doubt that exposure to aerosolised mists of metal working fluid has been the cause of occupational occurrences of EAA (see *Extrinsic Allergic Alveolitis*, Cm 6867 (July 2006), para.39).

The new open occupational category of "(f) any other workplace" was added with effect from March 30, 2017 (see Social Security (Industrial Injuries) (Prescribed Diseases) Amendment Regulations 2017 (SI 2017/232) reg.3). This amendment, which enables exposure to other biological agents that can cause extrinsic allergic alveolitis (EEA), was part of a package of recommendations made by IIAC in its report *Extrinsic allergic alveolitis: isocyanates and other occupational causes*, Cm 9247 (April 2016). IIAC's report has also resulted in the addition of the expression "or another biological substance that causes extrinsic allergic alveolitis" in the terms of prescription. In the same vein the reference to "including farmer's lung" has been dropped from the nomenclature of B6. Furthermore, IIAC's report has resulted in the creation of a new PD C34, designed to recognise that exposure to the chemical vapour of isocyanates can cause EAA, a prescription which includes a new open category of exposure to other chemical agents that can cause EAA.

B8A Infection by hepatitis A virus and B8B (infection by hepatitis B or C virus)

10.180   Prescription of viral hepatitis was originally rather restricted but, after modifications to the Schedule in 1983, is now prescribed for occupations involving any contact with human blood or a source of the disease. The current terms of prescription were substituted with effect from March 14, 2005, subject to a transitional provision in reg.3 of the inserting regulations—Social Security (Industrial Injuries) (Prescribed Diseases) Amendment Regulations 2005 (SI 2005/324)—set out at the end of this section of the book: the prescription does not apply to a period of assessment relating to a claim made before March 14, 2005. The prescription implements the recommendations of IIAC as set out in their report on Conditions due to Biological Agents (Cm 5997) (see paras 88–120). In particular, the Council reviewed hepatitis A infection in sewage workers and found evidence that the risk is more than doubled in those working with raw sewage, although overall sewage workers do not have a significantly increased risk of disease. In relation to hepatitis C, the Council thought some subgroups of health workers to be at elevated risk. Furthermore, HCV infection is the most commonly reported occupationally acquired blood-borne disease in England and Wales. In view of the uncertainty about the risk in some subgroups of health workers and the similar mode of transmission to hepatitis B, the Council thought that prescription of both hepatitis B and C should continue, with wording similar to the present prescription, for all those in contact with blood or body fluids.

B14 (Lyme disease)

10.181   This was prescribed from March 14, 2005, subject to a transitional provision in reg.3 of the inserting regulations—Social Security (Industrial Injuries) (Prescribed Diseases) Amendment Regulations 2005 (SI 2005/324)—set out at the end of this section of the book: the prescription does not apply to a period of assessment relating to a claim made before March 14, 2005. The prescription implements the recommendations of IIAC as set out in their report on Conditions due to Biological Agents (Cm 5997) (see paras 195–201). Since Lyme disease (a tick borne disease with musculo-skeletal, cardiac and neurological effects) was first considered by IIAC in 1990, enough evidence of occupational risk had accumulated to warrant prescription. The high incidence of the disease in deer hunters and forestry workers suggested a clear occupational risk in respect of exposure to *Borrelia*.

B15 (Anaphylaxis)

This was prescribed from March 14, 2005, subject to a transitional provision in reg.3 of the inserting regulations—Social Security (Industrial Injuries) (Prescribed Diseases) Amendment Regulations 2005 (SI 2005/324)—set out at the end of this section of the book: the prescription does not apply to a period of assessment relating to a claim made before March 14, 2005. The prescription implements the recommendations of IIAC as set out in their report on Conditions due to Biological Agents (Cm 5997) (see paras 261–271). "Anaphylaxis is a life-threatening IgE-mediated allergic Type I hypersensitivity reaction due to contact of a sensitised individual with an allergenic protein. Common allergens which can provoke anaphylactic shock include drugs, insect stings, latex and certain food ingredients, such as nuts. Initial exposure to the allergen induces specific IgE antibody. Subsequent contact can provoke an anaphylactic reaction. An anaphylactic-like (anaphylactoid) reaction can occur during first exposure to certain drugs; but these are a manifestation of a toxic, rather than an allergic, reaction to the drug. Anaphylactic shock is due to a sudden massive release of histamine and other mediators from basophils into the bloodstream. These trigger constriction of the airways and swelling of tissue (angioedema), resulting indifficulty breathing, and dilatation of blood vessels, leading to shock and pulmonary oedema. Other symptoms of anaphylaxis include urticarial skin rash and gastrointestinal reactions, such as vomiting, abdominal cramps and diarrhoea. The onset of anaphylaxis can be very rapid, with symptoms occurring within minutes of contact with the allergen" (*ibid.*, para.261). A precipitating exposure at work could ground a claim through the accident route where loss of faculty lasting beyond 90 days, rather than death, ensued. The Committee recommended prescription of anaphylaxis and its sequelae that result from allergy to natural rubber latex in healthcare workers.

10.182

The prescription criteria for PD B15 were originally limited to "employment as a healthcare worker having contact with products made with natural rubber latex". However, many occupations outside the healthcare sector can also involve regular exposure to latex products. IIAC found a similar causal connection in other occupational roles with latex allergy only rarely acquired outside the workplace. IIAC therefore recommended that the prescription for this disease be expanded to include any occupation involving contact with products made with natural rubber latex (see IIAC, *Extending the terms of prescription for latex anaphylaxis*, Cm 9498 (September 2017) p.11). The expansion of this prescription will extend coverage to e.g. police officers, vehicle mechanics, hairdressers, and workers from the food industry amongst others. It also provides parity with other similar diseases within the scheme, such as occupational asthma and rhinitis, which both prescribe any occupation that involves exposure to the listed agents.

V. Prescribed Diseases: Category C: Conditions due to chemical agents

The prescriptions underwent very substantial revision from March 17, 2003, subject to a transitional provision in reg.6 of the amending regulations: the Social Security (Industrial injuries) (Prescribed Diseases) Amendment Regulations 2003 (SI 2003/270). The text of the transitional provision is reproduced later in this volume. For the text of the prescriptions prior to March 17, 2003, and annotations thereto, see the 2002 edition of this volume.

10.183

Prescribed Diseases C8, C9, C10, C11, C14, C15 and C28 were removed. New formulations were substituted for all or part of Diseases C1, C2, C4, C5A and 5B, C6, C7, C12, C13, C16–27, C29 and C30. The changes largely follow the recommendations of the IIAC in its report reviewing the prescription of conditions due to chemical agents (*Cm. 5395 (February 2002)*). These changes were recommended reflecting the fact that many of the "C" diseases were prescribed in the early days of the scheme and there was need to reflect advances in scientific knowledge as well as to bring the wording and terminology used up to date. The removals from the list were based on the view that the very few claims that have been made for these diseases in the past could have been dealt with more appropriately under the accident provisions of the industrial injuries scheme.

Although the chemical agents in C23(c) are primarily encountered in the manufacture of dyes, that does not mean that they cannot be encountered elsewhere. In *SSWP v JS* [2008] UKUT 35 (AAC), Judge Williams upheld a tribunal decision that a claimant who had worked in a coke works was entitled on the evidence to conclude that he had probably suffered relevant exposure.

10.184 A new C24 was substituted, and C24A added, with effect from April 6, 2006 (see Social Security (Industrial Injuries) (Prescribed Diseases) Amendment Regulations 2006 (SI 2006/586), reg.3). They cannot, however be applied to a period of assessment prior to that date (*ibid.*, reg.4)). These changes implement the recommendations of the IIAC as set out in their report *Vinyl Chloride Monomer-Related Diseases* (Cm 6645). As regards C24A, the totality of the evidence led the IIAC to "conclude that an association exists between VCM exposure and Raynaud's phenomenon in the absence of osteolysis in the digits, and also between VCM exposure and scleroderma in the absence of osteolysis in the digits". That evidence indicated that the increased frequency of these conditions enabled attribution to exposure to VCM in the individual case. Consistent evidence showed that the inhalation of VCM in PVC production workers causes a characteristic clinical triad of osteolysis of the terminal phalanges, scleroderma and Raynaud's phenomenon, but that not all three are invariably present together (see para.16). As regards reformulating C24, the IIAC considered the term acro-osteolysis too confusing in that it refers both to a specific condition and to a syndrome the features of which may vary from one person to another. The term should be dropped. Osteolysis of the finger-tips, Raynaud's phenomenon and scleroderma should each be prescribed independently. The IIAC were not prepared to extend coverage to liver tumours other than angiosarcoma. Nor could exposure to PVC itself warrant prescription (para.17).

Prior to April 6, 2006, C 24 prescribed separately: angiosarcoma of the liver; liver fibrosis; and acro-osteolysis. The prescription of acrosteloysis, however, required that it be characterised by (i) lytic destruction of the terminal phalanges, (ii) in Raynaud's phenomenon, the exaggerated vasomotor response to cold causing intense blanching of the digits, and (iii) sclerodermatous thickening of the skin. It was thus open to a strict, literal interpretation that all three aspects (i)–(iii) had to be present. In *CI/1884/2004*, taking on board the IIAC report that had led to that 2003 prescription, Commissioner Williams specifically rejected this interpretation, holding instead that it "must be read disjunctively. The test is met if an individual can show that he (or she) has worked in a prescribed occupation and has thereafter evidenced any one of the three physical conditions listed" (para.38).

The prescription of bronchiolitis obliterans (PD C31) was recommended by the Industrial Injuries Advisory Council (IIAC) in its report *Bronchiolitis Obliterans and Food Flavouring Agents*, Cm. 7439 (July 2008).This is an uncommon but disabling respiratory disease characterised by fixed airway obstruction, whereby fibrous tissue narrows or blocks the bronchioles in the lung. It can be potentially severe, resulting in lung transplantation in some patients. The IIAC concluded that a causal relationship between bronchiolitis obliterans and exposure to food flavouring agents was likely, and was supported by: (a) evidence of the clustering of cases of this rare disease in several factories where exposures to diacetyl were shared in common; (b) the development of fixed airways obstruction in the absence of other explanations (e.g. emphysema); (c) a demonstrated dose response relationship between exposure to food flavouring agents and the onset of symptoms and declining lung function; and (d) experiments demonstrating pulmonary damage in animals exposed to diacetyl. The IIAC considered there to be "strong evidence of an association between work in diacetyl production or use of diacetyl as a food flavouring agent and the development of bronchiolitis obliterans" (*Summary*, para.3). Diagnosis of the disease is relatively complicated, based on clinical features, lung function tests, chest radiographs and computed tomography scans. A distinguishing feature from bronchitis and emphysema is a relatively rapid onset of symptoms (within weeks or months) following diacetyl exposure, as compared to the much slower progression of symptoms associated with the development of chronic airways disease. Cases in which benefit is sought are likely to have had extensive clinical investigations to confirm diagnosis. Diagnosis should normally be based upon prior hospital investigations, with confirmatory evidence of diagnosis being sought from the appropriate source(s).

Prescription of nasal carcinoma (PD C32) was recommended by the Industrial Injuries Advisory Council (IIAC) in its report, *Chromium and Sino-Nasal Cancer*, Cm. 7740 (December 2009). Sino-nasal cancer, a rare disease in the United Kingdom encompassing cancers of the inside of the nose and of the paranasal sinuses has for some time been prescribed in relation to exposure to wood dust and leather working (PD D6), in respect of which there is strong evidence of an increased risk. Following processing, chromium as metal exists in several forms, principally metallic chromium (chromium 0), trivalent chromium (chromium III), and hexavalent chromium (chromium VI). Evidence was considered relating to a number of industries in which exposure to these different forms of chromium occurred, namely chromate production, chrome plating, chromium pigment production, stainless steel welding and the leather and tanning industries. Positive associations, where the risk was more than doubled, were most clearly evident in workers involved in chromate production and chrome plating. 10.185

The form of prescription of C3(a) and C3(b) became effective on March 30, 2012. It is not subject to any transitional provision. It flows from the Secretary of State implementing, in narrower terms after considering further research, recommendations of the IIAC made in its 2002 Report on Category C diseases (*Conditions due to chemical agents* Cm. 5395, paras 47–58), the progress in research on which had been regularly checked by the IIAC (see *Completion of the review of the scheduled list of prescribed diseases*, Cm.7003 (January 2007), para.51).

C33 (Chloracne) was prescribed with effect from March 16, 2015. Its prescription is not subject to any transitional provision and implements recommendations made by the IIAC in its report, *Occupational Chloracne* (Cm 8670, July 2013). Chloracne is a rare but systemic disease caused by systemic exposure to certain halogenated aromatic hydrocarbons called 'chloracnegens'. Its most prominent clinical manifestation is skin involvement and leads to disfigurement of the face. It can be severely disabling and can have enduring effects, sometimes over several years or decades after exposure has ceased. The IIAC intended "prescription to relate to the skin manifestations of chloracne" but it also recognised "that psychological sequelae may accompany skin disfigurement and may comprise an important component of the resulting disablement" (para.30).

C34 (extrinsic allergic alveolitis or EEA) was prescribed with effect from March 30, 2017 (see Social Security (Industrial Injuries) (Prescribed Diseases) Amendment Regulations 2017 (SI 2017/232) reg.3). EEA has been a longstanding 'B' prescribed disease (see B6) in respect of biological agents (commonly referred to as farmer's lung). The addition of EEA as C34 in the 'C' list reflects IIAC's recommendation that the vapour of isocyanates, i.e. chemical exposure, be added to the qualifying terms of exposure for EEA. The prescribed employments are also expressed by way of an open category, a measure designed to facilitate more rapid recognition of new chemical causes of EEA: see IIAC, *Extrinsic allergic alveolitis: isocyanates and other occupational causes* (Cm 9247, April 2016).

VI. Prescribed Diseases: Category D: Miscellaneous conditions

D1 (pneumoconiosis)

D1 (pneumoconiosis) has already been considered in the note to reg.2, above, in respect of its prescription for all occupations involving exposure to dust. There is also a separate section of the Schedule which lists specific occupations for which the disease is prescribed. The diagnosis of pneumoconiosis (prescribed disease D1) was considered in *R(I) 1/96* where the Commissioner held that to say that minimal coalworker's pneumoconiosis "is insufficient radiologically for him to be eligible for industrial injuries benefit" is wrong in law. Pneumoconiosis is defined in s.122(1) 10.186

of the SSCBA 1992 as "fibrosis of the lungs due to silica dust, asbestos dust or other dust, and includes the condition of the lungs known as dust-reticulation". Either the claimant has fibrosis due to dust or he does not. The International Labour Organisation's "International Classification of Radiographs of Pneumoconiosis" is a diagnostic aid but the radiological category does not determine the diagnosis.

In *R(I) 7/98*, the Commissioner held that the definition of pneumoconiosis in s.122 of the SSCBA 1992, "fibrosis of the lungs due to silica dust, asbestos dust, or other dust, and includes the condition of the lungs known as dust-reticulation", carried the implication that dust-reticulation was to be regarded as a form of fibrosis of the lungs whether or not it would otherwise always be medically described as constituting such fibrosis. The statutory definition dates back to 1943. In *R(I) 3/03*, a Tribunal of Commissioners considered its interpretation and application in the light of developments in medical understanding and terminology, especially as they affect post mortem evidence of the effects of coal dust. Those changes meant that the medical evidence often does not reflect this statutory language. The key issue, however, was not changes in terminology, but whether the evidence showed that the statutory definition was met. As regards coal dust, tribunals cannot simply rely on "coal workers pneumoconiosis" in post mortem reports or death certificates as conclusive of the question: is the statutory definition met? This is because experts differ in their use of the term and whether it necessarily includes fibrosis. Moreover, such a statement represents only one doctor's opinion, which has to be assessed in the light of the evidence as a whole. In particular, where the phrase is found in a post mortem report, it represents only a provisional conclusion that might well be changed if microscopic examination reveals contrary findings.

The question as to what constitutes "dust reticulation" was addressed in *S (in the name of S, deceased) v SSWP* [2016] UKUT 485 (AAC), where Judge Mitchell concluded as follows (at para.96):

> "dust reticulation involves structural changes to lung tissue due to the accumulation of dust in widely distributed foci throughout the lungs. Nodularities need not be present nor is a medical diagnosis of fibrosis required and, it follows, scarring need not be present either. In the living, it is difficult to see how dust reticulation may be found in the absence of X-ray or scanning evidence but, for the deceased, post-mortem evidence may also demonstrate the existence of dust reticulation."

Judge Mitchell also made the following observation about the way in which the earlier decision of a Tribunal of Commissioners in *R(I) 3/03* had been reported:

> "41. I think it is clear that, here, the Commissioners were simply describing the agreed medical evidence put before them. The Commissioners did not express disagreement with the evidence but that was not to be expected. They had to deal with the appeal as presented to them. Despite that, the headnote to the reported decision states that the Tribunal of Commissioners held "the term "dust reticulation" is no longer used and is unlikely to be of practical significance in pneumoconiosis cases". My respectful view is that this was potentially misleading. The Tribunal of Commissioners did not hold that the "dust reticulation" element of the statutory definition could be ignored, as the Secretary of State's first submission on this appeal seemed to assert. Such an interpretation would be contrary to the language used by the Tribunal of Commissioners elsewhere in its reasons as well as the decision of Commissioner Mitchell Q.C. which the Tribunal itself referred to and relied on."

D2 (byssinosis)

10.187   D2 (byssinosis) is prescribed for cotton and flax workers. It is neither necessary that the claimant should be employed exclusively in the room within the scheduled description (*R(I) 17/56*), nor that fine distinctions should be drawn in determining the meaning of "room" (*R(I) 26/58*).

D3 (diffuse mesothelioma)

D3 (diffuse mesothelioma) and D4 (inflammation or ulceration of nose etc.) are   **10.188**
both prescribed, in part, in respect of occupations involving exposure to dust. The
meaning of "dust" was considered by the Commissioner in *R(I) 1/85* where he
defined it as earth or other solid matter in minute particles so as to be easily raised and
carried by the wind. The occupational prescription in D3 was altered to its present
wording with effect from April 9, 1997. In *CI/13232/1996*, Commissioner Rowland
considered the meaning of the earlier wording (see p.938 of Bonner, Hooker and
White, *Non-Means Tested Benefits: The Legislation* (1996)) and in particular the prescription "any occupation involving . . . (d) substantial exposure to the dust arising
from any of the foregoing operations". The case concerned a claimant employed as
a cooper on premises adjacent to those of another firm which handled asbestos whose
extraction/ventilation equipment spewed out asbestos dust over his workplace. The
Commissioner held that the Prescribed Diseases Regulations focus on the nature
of the claimant's employment rather than on the nature of the employer's business,
so that here the claimant had only to show that he was employed in an occupation
involving something listed in col.2 of the Schedule. Commissioner Rowland stated:

"It is true that paragraph (a), (b) and (c) are unlikely to be satisfied in the case
of any claimant who is not working for an employer whose business necessarily
involves work with asbestos and the overwhelming majority of cases to which
paragraph (d) applies will also arise where the nature of the employer's business
involves working with asbestos. However there is nothing in the language of the
Regulations so to restrict it. I can see no reason for distinguishing between the
present claimant and, say, a clerical worker employed in the neighbouring firm of
asbestos processors. Neither was engaged in a type of work which could normally
involve exposure to asbestos dust but in both cases the particular location of their
employment caused them to be exposed to dust. It is difficult to see any practical
reason or any reason of principle why the clerical worker should be entitled to
disablement benefit and the present claimant should not." (para.8)

The revision of the prescription's wording to the broader formulation in the current
text essentially endorses the validity of that approach, but clearly a claimant whose
employment exposes him to asbestos, asbestos dust or any admixture of asbestos
must show that such exposure was at a level above that commonly found in the
environment at large.

D4 (allergic rhinitis)

D4 (allergic rhinitis), has, since March 24, 1996, attracted the presumption that   **10.189**
a prescribed disease is due to the nature of a scheduled occupation, provided that
the claimant was employed in that occupation at the date of onset of the disease, or
at any time within one month preceding the date of onset. See, on the consequences
of this, *R(I) 7/02*, noted in the commentary to reg.3, above.

D4(x)—allergic rhinitis due to exposure to products made with natural rubber   **10.190**
latex- was added from March 14, 2005, subject to a transitional provision in
reg.3 of the inserting regulations—Social Security (Industrial Injuries) (Prescribed
Diseases) Amendment Regulations 2005 (SI 2005/324)—set out at the end of
this section of the book: the prescription does not apply to a period of assessment
relating to a claim made before March 14, 2005. The prescription implements the
recommendations of IIAC as set out in their report on Conditions due to Biological
Agents (Cm 5997) (see paras 252–260 on latex allergy). It is prevalent in healthcare workers, especially laboratory workers, nurses and physicians, but it should be
noted that the terms of the prescription are in no way confined to those groups.
Indeed the IIAC noted that individuals may encounter latex in many circumstances, including as part of their work: medical and surgical procedures; dentistry;
laboratory work; latex processing and product manufacture; food preparation; dishwashing and cleaning; use and manufacture of condoms; use and manufacture of
actors' masks; use and manufacture of sports equipment; use and manufacture of

balloons and rubber bands, such as during teaching and nursery school work; and scene of the crime work (para.253).

D5 (non-infective dermatitis)

10.191   D5 (non-infective dermatitis) was a very common source of claims for injury benefit but it is, perhaps, less likely to give rise to claims for disablement benefit. No presumption is made in favour of the claimant. It is for him to prove that the disease was due to the nature of his employment, and that his occupation falls within the terms of the Schedule (see note to reg.4, above).

D6 (nasal carcinoma)

10.192   D6(a) was considered by Commissioner Goodman in *R(I) 4/98*. He concluded that

> "it is not legitimate to extend to the claimant (who in the course of his work as a painter came into contact for many years with quantities of respirable dust) the protection of sub-paragraph (a) of paragraph D6 because the wording of it does not justify it. I accept as correct in law Miss Lieven's submission that subparagraph (a) covers only buildings where, as part of the nature of the building, the manufacture or repair [of wooden goods] is carried out e.g. a factory or warehouse. It could not be said that the dwelling-houses and Royal Ordnance Factory buildings in or near which the claimant worked came within such a description . . . The intention of sub-paragraph (a), as is evidenced by the above cited Industrial Injuries Advisory Council's Report, was merely to extend the existing prescription for work on the manufacture or repair of wooden furniture to wooden goods generally. No further extension to all those who have in their work inhaled wood dust was intended nor is, in my view, shown by sub-paragraph (a)." (para.13).

In September 2017 IIAC recommended that the prescription for PD D6 (nasal carcinoma) be extended to include a new para.(d), namely "exposure to wood dust in the course of the machine processing of wood" (see IIAC, *Nasal carcinoma and occupational exposure to wood dust*, Cm 9499), p.39). This recommendation was implemented with effect from September 28, 2018, along with amendments to para.(a). The original occupational prescription under para.(a) was any occupation involving "attendance for work in or about a building where wooden goods are manufactured or repaired". However, according to the Department some tribunals have placed a narrow interpretation on the meaning of "building", effectively restricting coverage to claimants working in premises which exist to manufacture or repair wooden goods. This had the effect of placing outside the scope of benefit e.g. the carpenter who is exposed to wood dust during the fitting out of shops or on a construction site. The terms of prescription were therefore amended by replacing the words "in or about a building" with "at a workplace" and for completeness, included the manufacture or repair of "products made wholly or partially of wood".

D7 (occupational asthma)

10.193   D7 prescribes asthma in relation to a number of occupations. In D7(f) the words "used for the purpose of research or education or in laboratories" set the environment for the whole of the sub-para., so the claimant's appeal in *CI/383/92* (which is not to be reported) was disallowed because he had only worked with prawns (regarded as animals, being anthropods) in the food processing industry (see para.7).

Sub-paragraphs (o)–(x) of D7 (occupational asthma) were added with effect from September 26, 1991 (see SI 1991/1938). In *CI/175/90*. Commissioner Hallett considered whether the claimant could bring himself within sub-para.(j) because of his exposure to paper dust in the printing industry. Applying *CI/308/1989* (reported as *R(I) 2/92*), he concluded that the term "wood dust" had to be construed as an ordinary expression in the English language, that paper, while derived from wood was a different substance, so that the majority of the SSAT had been correct in regarding paper dust as different from wood dust. Nor did the claimant's exposure

1556

to printing mist help him, since the evidence showed that the inks forming the mist did not contain isocyanates, so that he did not fall within sub-para.(a) either. His claim failed. Cigarette smoke, while an irritant for those with asthma, appears not to be regarded by medical opinion as a sensitising agent within para.(x), any other "sensitising agent" *(CI/73/94)*. One view is that sensitising agent has to read *ejusdem generis* (of a kind or nature) with the agents listed in paras (a)–(w) *(CI/73/94)*. Another is that there is no such restriction on the term: para.(x) catches any agent so long as it is sensitising *(CI/4987/1995)*. In any case the first question should be whether the identified agent relied on by the claimant is a "sensitising agent" *(CI/2543/2002)*. He set out a "triage" approach to help cope with the difficulties of deciding whether something is a "sensitising agent", an approach agreed with and adopted by Commissioner Williams in *CI/564/2005*: there are agents known to be sensitising agents, agents known not to be sensitising agents, and cases where it is not known whether the agent is a sensitising agent. In *CI/3729/2005* Deputy Commissioner White found this a helpful approach. He decided that cardboard dust was not a sensitising agent. He also held (applying *R(I)2/92*) that it was not the same as wood dust and could not fall within D7(j).

In *R(I) 8/02*, Commissioner Howell considered the case of a bus driver claiming that the diesel fumes, dust and particulates he had inhaled during his work constituted "any other sensitising agent". The Commissioner stated:

"Taking into account the terms of the report of the Industrial Injuries Advisory Council dated August 28, 1990 which led to these extra provisions being introduced (Cm 1244, October 1990) from which it is quite clear that the expression 'sensitising agent' when used medically in this context means a chemical agent which actually *causes* a person to develop an asthmatic condition when inhaled at work, the tribunal were in my judgment quite correct in directing themselves that the question they had to consider on the evidence in the claimant's case was whether it had been shown that the diesel fumes, particulates, dust and so forth he inhaled while driving his bus had been the actual cause of his asthmatic condition, rather than merely irritating his chest and making it worse.

As the tribunal correctly recorded, the evidence before them on this issue consisted first of medical advice obtained by the department that diesel exhaust and other vehicle fumes and dust of the kind to which a person is exposed in heavy traffic, while they would certainly act as irritants, would not operate as 'sensitisors' or causative agents for occupational asthma in the way required by the regulations making this a prescribed disease. In addition there were medical reports by three separate doctors on behalf of the claimant himself at pages 35 to 41 which as the tribunal correctly recorded in their statement of reasons at page 46 did not at any point report or state that his asthma had actually been *caused* by exposure to diesel fumes, though they all agreed that it was made much worse by his continuing to work as a bus driver and that it would be a great deal better for him to move to another job" (paras 4, 5).

It would appear that asbestos is not a sensitising agent for purposes of D7 *(CI/2393/02*, paras 7, 8).

There is expert evidence that the chromium element in cement is a sensitising agent *(CI/564/2005)*.   **10.194**

Latex constitutes "any other sensitising agent" and falls within D7(x) *(CI/3565/2004)*. This is important as regards cases occurring before the specific prescription of occupational asthma due to exposure to products made with natural rubber latex in D7(wa).

D7(wa)—occupational asthma due to exposure to products made with natural rubber latex—was added from March 14, 2005, subject to a transitional provision in reg.3 of the inserting regulations—Social Security (Industrial Injuries) (Prescribed Diseases) Amendment Regulations 2005 (SI 2005/324)—set out at the end of this section of the book: the prescription does not apply to a period of assessment relating to a claim made before March 14, 2005. The prescription implements the recommendations of IIAC as set out in their report on Conditions due to Biological Agents (Cm 5997) (see paras 252–260 on latex allergy). It is prevalent in healthcare workers, especially laboratory workers, nurses and physicians, but it should be noted that the terms of the prescription are in no way confined to those groups. Indeed the IIAC noted that Individuals may encounter latex in many circumstances, including as part of their work: medical and surgical procedures; dentistry; laboratory work; latex processing and product manufacture; food preparation; dishwashing and cleaning; use and manufacture of condoms; use and manufacture of actors' masks; use and manufacture of sports equipment; use and manufacture of balloons and rubber bands, such as during teaching and nursery school work; and scene of the crime work (para.253).

D8 and D8A *(primary carcinoma of the lung: asbestos)*

10.195   A new D8 was substituted, and D8A added, with effect from April 6, 2006 (see Social Security (Industrial Injuries) (Prescribed Diseases) Amendment Regulations 2006 (SI 2006/586), reg.3). This implements IIAC recommendations in their report *Asbestos-Related Diseases* (Cm 6553). The Council recommended removing from D8 the requirement for the presence of diffuse pleural thickening because recent evidence indicates its unreliability as a marker of asbestos exposure (para.65). D8A (Primary carcinoma of the lung—with no requisite element of asbestosis) was added because the IIAC's literature review found evidence of a greater than doubled risk for lung cancer in the following groups of workers who have experienced substantial occupational asbestos exposure: workers in asbestos textile manufacture; asbestos sprayers; asbestos insulation workers, including those applying and removing asbestos-containing materials in shipbuilding and gas mask manufacturers (para.62). The requirement of exposure for the requisite number of years prior to 1975 reflects the IIAC view that the risk fell after the introduction of the 1969 Asbestos Regulations (para.63). The reformulation cannot apply to any period of assessment prior to April 6, 2006 (reg.4 of the Amendment Regs as further amended by SI 2006/769, reg.2).

In *SSWP v ER (II)* [2012] UKUT 204 (AAC), Judge May considered the position of a claimant suffering from the prescribed disease, who had as a scaffolder worked in close proximity to others working with asbestos to insulate pipes, but who was not directly himself employed in using asbestos to insulate pipes. The issue was whether his medical condition fell within the terms of the prescription in PD 8A. While Commissioner May agreed that the wording of the prescription could arguably be read as covering those who, like the claimant, had worked in close proximity to asbestos insulation workers for the required periods of time, he nonetheless considered that he was entitled to read the terms of prescription more narrowly in light of the recommendations in the IIAC Report which indicated that there was no intention to widen the range of occupations covered. He stated that this was

> "not a case where the label of what the claimant did was different from what he actually did. It is accepted that his job did not involve participating in the activities referred to in the regulation. The report in my view is concerned with active involvement and in interpreting the regulation in that way this is fatal to the assertion that a claimant satisfied that he was in an occupation to which the prescribed disease applied. To determine otherwise would be to artificially widen the statutory language. The Secretary of State's appeal accordingly succeeds" (para.14).

SSWP v ER (II) [2012] UKUT 204 (AAC) was followed in *SSWP v EK (deceased) (II)* [2016] UKUT 458 (AAC), also involving a stager who had erected scaffolding in shipyards and contracted lung cancer but who was found to fall outside the terms of the prescription. For a further example of the fine lines that may have to be drawn in applying the terms of PD D8a, see *PC v SSWP (II)* [2017] UKUT 409 (AAC), in which Judge Jacobs held that an engineer installing fire alarm systems, whose work involved some cutting, drilling and disturbance of asbestos lagging, was not working in a prescribed occupation: "The work of cutting and drilling does not come within the prescription, as it is not lagging work. It is work related to the preparation for installing the cables. It was not lagging or preparatory to lagging" (at para.10). In so finding, Judge Jacobs followed *SSWP v ER (II)* [2012] UKUT 204 (AAC) and *SSWP v EK (II) (deceased)* [2016] UKUT 458 (AAC).

D9 *(pleural thickening)*

The reformulation of disease D9 from the same date as the amendments to D8 and D8A noted immediately above (i.e. as from April 6, 2006) implemented the IIAC recommendation that the requirement for measurements of pleural thickening be replaced by one involving costophrenic angle on plain chest radiographs (paras 70, 72(a)). However, following a further IIAC report, the definition of diffuse pleural thickening (DPT) for the purpose of D9 has now been modernised by removing the requirement for "obliteration of the costophrenic angle" from the terms of prescription (with effect from March 30, 2017: see Social Security (Industrial Injuries) (Prescribed Diseases) Amendment Regulations 2017 (SI 2017/232) reg.3). This change was made because the radiographic criterion in the former definition was potentially restrictive, since it implied to medical specialists diagnostic assessment by means of a chest radiograph. In practice, however, advances in medical imaging mean that most claimants are now investigated using a computerised tomography (CT) scan. The difficulty identified by IIAC was that some claimants who are disabled with demonstrable DPT on CT scanning fail to meet the criteria for prescription based on a traditional chest X-ray. In addition, many more claimants nowadays are likely to present medical evidence to support their claim in the form of evidence from CT imaging rather than conventional X-rays. See IIAC, *Diffuse pleural thickening*, Cm 9346 (April 2016).

10.196

D10 *(primary carcinoma of the lung: tin, etc)*

The insertion of para.(d) into PD D10 (primary carcinoma of the lung)to include employment wholly or mainly as a coke oven worker implements the recommendations of the IIAC in its report *Lung cancer in coke oven workers* Cm 8163 (September 2011). The IIAC identified evidence of a greater than double the risk of lung cancer associated with work involving coke ovens. For top oven workers, this occurred after only five years of employment (see para.(d)(ii) of the new entry), and for other oven workers, the after 15 years of employment (see para.(d)(i) of the new entry). Since the IIAC realised that workers could in the course of their employment move between top oven work and other oven tasks, yet fail separately to meet either of the five year or 15-year thresholds, it recommended that both periods could combined with each year of top oven work equating to three years of other oven work (see para.(d)(iii) of the new entry).

10.197

The DWP anticipates that the amendment will result in successful claims from some 65 people a year who have worked as coke oven workers for the specified number of years.

D12 *(chronic obstructive pulmonary disease)*

As regards PD D12 (chronic obstructive pulmonary disease), the disease was originally prescribed for certain categories of coal miners in terms of the discrete conditions of chronic bronchitis, emphysema or both (see further N. Wikeley, (1994) *Journal of Social Security Law* 23 and (1997) 26 *Industrial Law Journal* 283). The terms of the PD were recast in 2015, on the recommendation of IIAC, with the aim of better reflecting current medical practice, which is to use the umbrella term chronic obstructive pulmonary disease (COPD) rather than the specific underlying disorder (IIAC, *Effects of treatment and the medical assessment of Chronic Bronchitis ad Emphysema (PD D12, Chronic Obstructive Pulmonary Disease*, Cm 8906, July 2014, at para.48).

10.198

An ongoing matter of controversy has been the measurement of lung function for the purposes of PD D12. In *CI/126/2002* Commissioner Angus noted that in some circumstances a spirometric test can be inaccurate. He stated:

"In assessing the evidential value of the subsequent spirometry it would have been necessary to take into account whether or not the claimant's lung function might have been enhanced by medication. In assessing disablement it is legitimate to base the assessment on what the claimant can do when he has taken medication but for the purposes of diagnosis it is the unassisted function which is relevant" (para.16).

10.199 Commissioner Williams followed this in *CI/2683/2004*. He stressed that the regulations did not require a spirometry test—the diagnosis question must be considered in the light of all relevant evidence, including any such test—and that the focus must be on the claimant's condition as at the date of the original decision. He considered that

"tribunals should have in mind that individuals may or may not have been given guidance and may or may not have acted on it. They should therefore, to ensure fairness, directly check any necessary facts about pre-test medication if they conduct a test. They may also need to check that the medical adviser took appropriate note and account of any relevant medicaments when performing the original test. They should, at least in marginal cases, consider the possible effects of medication when forming a view about the conclusions to be drawn from the "accompanying evidence" (para.29).

The implications of the Commissioner's decision in *CI/2683/2004* were considered by IIAC, at the request of the DWP, in its 2014 report on *Effects of treatment and the medical assessment of Chronic Bronchitis and Emphysema (PD D12, Chronic Obstructive Pulmonary Disease* (Cm 8906, July 2014). In particular, the Council addressed the issue of how, and to what extent, an allowance should be made in the interpretation of spirometry for claimants for PD D12 who use bronchodilator treatments (i.e. drugs aimed at dilating the airways and relieving airflow obstruction). There was concern that *CI/2683/2004* in practice led to arbitrary and sometimes variable offsets being applied by medical advisors in respect of PD D12 claimants taking such treatments.

IIAC furthermore noted that responses to treatments are variable and unpredictable between individuals, and that any effects in cases of COPD (in contrast to cases of asthma) are likely to be small. The Council accordingly concluded that it was not possible to recommend a scientifically valid adjustment factor that would encompass the very wide variety of different treatments now used in the management of COPD while still remaining equitable to individual claimants. In addition, when PD D12 had originally been prescribed, the Council had highlighted that it would be impractical to take account of factors such as work location, job title, actual exposures to coal dust and lifetime smoking habits. In the same way, the Council concluded that it would be impractical to apply an offset to the one litre loss of FEV_1 threshold according to an individual claimant's medical treatment; it was both "beyond the science and beyond the resources of the Scheme to be this exact" (at para.6).

Consequently IIAC recommended that the effects of treatments should be disregarded when interpreting spirometric evidence during medical assessments for PD D12. This accounts for the amendment in force from March 16, 2015 to the effect that the value of 1 litre in the statutory test "shall be construed as fixed and shall not vary by virtue of any treatment or treatments" (see Social Security (Industrial Injuries) (Prescribed Diseases) Amendment Regulations 2015 (SI 2015/87)).

Disease D12 is subject to a transitional provision in reg.9 of the Social Security (Industrial Injuries) (Prescribed Diseases) Amendment (No.2) Regulations (SI 1993/1985) below. Furthermore, the amendment numbered "15" on the appropriate mean value and the prediction formula is subject to a transitional provision in reg.7(2) of the Social Security (Industrial Injuries) (Prescribed Diseases) Amendment Regulations 2000 (SI 2000/1588), reproduced later in this volume.

The prescription of D12 with effect from September 13, 1993 is not retrospec-

tive so as to enable payment of disablement benefit, for a period prior to prescription, to a claimant whose date of onset of the disease precedes that date and
continues to suffer from it (see *R(I) 4/96*, noted in the notes to reg.6, above).

In *CI/1160/2004*, Commissioner Angus held   **10.200**

"that paragraph D12 of Schedule 1 to the Regulations is not irrational. On the
matter of its application to smokers, as Mr Heath said, the fact that smokers who
suffer from coal dust retention might be compensated for having contracted a
coal dust related disease which they might have contracted in any case does not
exclude any non-smoker with coal dust related emphysema or bronchitis from
compensation under the legislation. As regards the use of the 1 litre drop in lung
function as the prescribed decisive indicator of PD D12, Dr. A's opinion that it
can result in the disease not being diagnosed in short men who have a disabling
reduction in lung function due to the retention of coal dust has to be respected.
It is an opinion which may well be shared by other chest physicians: but the D12
prescription is based on the equally respectable opinions of the members of the
Industrial Injuries Advisory Council and the Secretary of State cannot be accused
of irrationality in relying upon their opinion to devise the prescription" (para.26).

He also rejected the view that it was legally challengeable as discriminatory against
short men.

The amendments effected from March 24, 1996 to prescribed diseases A12
(an alteration of terms), D4 (ability to benefit from the reg.4 presumption) and D5
(an alteration of its terms to reflect the newly prescribed disease C30) are subject
to a transitional provision in reg.7 of the Social Security (Industrial Injuries and
Diseases) (Miscellaneous Amendments) Regulations 1996 (SI 1996/425), below.

D13 (primary carcinoma of the nasopharynx)

A new prescribed disease D13 (primary carcinoma of the nasopharynx) (naso-   **10.201**
pharyngeal cancer) was added with effect from April 7, 2008 by reg.2 of the Social
Security (Industrial Injuries) (Prescribed Diseases) Amendment Regulations 2008 (SI
2008/14). The prescription, in respect of a number of occupations involving working
with wood or wood products, reflects the recommendations of the Industrial Injuries
Advisory Council in its report *Nasopharyngeal cancer due to exposure to wood dust* Cm
7162 (July 2007). Those suffering from this rare disease must have worked in the relevant occupations for a period or periods of at least 10 years in the aggregate. A list (not
necessarily exhaustive) of the occupations at risk can be found in App.2 of the report.

SCHEDULE 2   **Regulation 11**

MODIFICATIONS OF [SECTIONS 94 TO 107 OF THE SOCIAL SECURITY
CONTRIBUTIONS AND BENEFITS ACT 1992 AND SECTIONS 8 TO 10 OF THE
SOCIAL SECURITY ADMINISTRATION ACT 1992] IN THEIR APPLICATION TO BENEFIT
AND CLAIMS TO WHICH THESE REGULATIONS APPLY

In [sections 94 to 107 of the Social Security Contributions and Benefits Act 1992 and sec-   **10.202**
tions 8 to 10 of the Social Security Administration Act 1992] references to accidents shall be
construed as references to prescribed diseases and references to the relevant accident shall be
construed as references to the relevant disease and references to the date of the relevant accident shall be construed as references to the date of onset of the relevant disease.

ASSESSMENT OF THE EXTENT OF OCCUPATIONAL DEAFNESS

PART I

CLAIMS TO WHICH REGULATION 34(1) APPLIES

10.203

[¹*Average of hearing losses (dB) due to all causes at 1, 2 and 3 kHz frequencies*]	*Degree of disablement per cent.*
50–52 dB	20
53–57 dB	30
58–62 dB	40
63–67 dB	50
68–72 dB	60
73–77 dB	70
78–82 dB	80
83–87 dB	90
88 dB or more	100

PART II

CLAIMS TO WHICH REGULATION 34(2) APPLIES

10.204

[¹*Average of hearing losses (dB) due to all causes at 1, 2 and 3 kHz frequencies*]	*Degree of disablement per cent.*
50–53 dB	20
54–60 dB	30
61–66 dB	40
67–72 dB	50
73–79 dB	60
80–86 dB	70
87–95 dB	80
96–105 dB	90
106 dB or more	100

PART III

FORMULA FOR CALCULATING BINAURAL DISABLEMENT

10.205

$$\frac{(\text{Degree of disablement of better ear} \times 4) + \text{degree of disablement of worse ear}}{5}$$

AMENDMENT

1. Social Security (Industrial Injuries) (Prescribed Diseases) Amendment Regulations 1989 (SI 1989/1207) reg.4 (October 16, 1989).

SCHEDULE 4   **Regulation 43**

PRESCRIBED DISEASES AND RELEVANT DATES FOR THE PURPOSES OF REGULATION 43

Description of disease or injury	*Relevant date*
10.206 A3. Dysbarism, including decompression sickness, barotrauma and osteonecrosis.	Except in the case of a person suffering from decompression sickness employed in any occupation involving subjection to compressed or rarefied air, 3rd October 1983.

Description of disease or injury	Relevant date
A11. Episodic blanching, occurring throughout the year, affecting the middle or proximal phalanges or in the case of a thumb the proximal phalanx, of— (a) in the case of a person with 5 fingers (including thumb) on one hand, any 3 of those fingers, or (b) in the case of person with only 4 such fingers, any 2 of those fingers, or (c) in the case of a person with less than 4 such fingers, any one of those fingers or, as the case may be, the one remaining finger (vibration white finger).	1st April 1985.
B1. Anthrax	In the case of a person employed in an occupation involving the loading and unloading or transport of animal products or residues, 3rd October 1983.
B3. Infection by leptospira.	(a) In the case of a person employed in an occupation in places which are or are liable to be infested by small mammals other than rats, field mice or voles, 3rd October 1983; (b) in the case of a person employed in an occupation in any other place mentioned in the second column of paragraph B3 of Part I of Schedule 1 above, 7th January 1980.
B5. Tuberculosis.	In the case of a person employed in an occupation involving contact with a source of tuberculosis infection, not being an employment set out in the second column of paragraph 38 of Part I of Schedule 1 to the old regulations, 3rd October 1983.
B6. Extrinsic allergic alveolitis (including farmer's lung).	In the case of a person suffering from extrinsic allergic alveolitis, not being farmer's lung, employed in any occupation set out in the second column of paragraph B6 of Part I of Schedule 1 above, or in the case of a person suffering from farmer's lung, employed in any occupation involving exposure to moulds or fungal spores or heterologous proteins by reason of employment in cultivation of edible fungi or maltworking, or loading or unloading or handling in storage edible fungi or caring for or handling birds, 3rd October 1983.
B7. Infection by organisms of the genus brucella.	In the case of a person suffering from infection by organisms of the genus brucella, not being infection by Brucella abortus, or employed in an occupation set out in the second column of paragraph B7 of Part I of Schedule 1 above, not being an occupation set out in the second column of paragraph 46 of Part I of Schedule 1 to the old regulations, 3rd October 1983.

1563

Description of disease or injury	Relevant date
B8. Viral hepatitis.	In the case of a person employed in any occupation involving contact with human blood or human blood products, or contact with a source of viral hepatitis, 3rd December 1984.
B9. Infection by Streptococcus suis.	3rd October 1983.
[¹ B10. (a) Avian chlamydiosis.	9th August 1989.
B10. (b) Ovine chlamydiosis.	9th August 1989.
B11. Q fever.	9th August 1989.]
C3. Poisoning by phosphorus or an inorganic compound of phosphorus or poisoning due to the anti-cholinesterase or pseudo anti-cholinesterase action of organic phosphorus compounds.	In the case of a person suffering from poisoning by an inorganic compound of phosphorus or poisoning due to the pseudo anti-cholinesterase action or organic phosphorus compounds, 3rd October 1983.
C18. Poisoning by cadmium.	In the case of a person employed in an occupation involving exposure to cadmium dust, 3rd October 1983.
C23. Primary neoplasm (including papiloma, carcinoma-in-situ and invasive carcinoma) of the epithelial lining of the urinary tract (renal pelvis, ureter, bladder and urethra).	In the case of a person employed in an occupation involving work in a building in which methylene-bis-orthochloroaniline is produced for commercial purposes, 3rd October 1983.
C24. (a) Angiosarcoma of the liver; (b) osteolysis of the terminal phalanges of the finger; (c) non-cirrhotic portal fibrosis.	(a) In the case of a person suffering from angiosarcoma of the liver or osteolysis of the terminal phalanges of the fingers, 21st March 1977; (b) in the case of a person suffering from non-cirrhotic portal fibrosis, 3rd October 1983.
C25. Occupational vitiligo.	15th December 1980.
[²C26. Damage to the liver or kidneys due to exposure to Carbon Tetrachloride.	4th January 1988.
C27. Damage to the liver or kidneys due to exposure to Trichloromethane (Chloroform).	4th January 1988.
C28. Central nervous system dysfunction and associated gastro-intestinal disorders due to exposure to chloromethane (Methyl Chloride).	4th January 1988.
C29. Peripheral neuropathy due to exposure to n-hexane or methyl-p-butyl ketone.	4th January 1988.
D3. Diffuse mesothelioma.	In the case of a person suffering from primary neoplasm of the pericardium, 3rd October 1983.
D6. Carcinoma of the nasal cavity or associated air sinuses (nasal carcinoma).	In the case of a person employed in an occupation involving attendance for work in or about a building where wooden goods (other than wooden furniture) are manufactured or where wooden goods are repaired, 3rd October 1983.
D7. Occupational asthma.	[³ (a) In the case of a person suffering from asthma due to exposure to any of the following agents:

Description of disease or injury	Relevant date
	(i)isocyanates;
	(ii) platinum salts;
	(iii) fumes or dusts arising from the manufacture, transport or use of hardening agents (including epoxy resin curing agents) based on phthalic anhydride, tetrachlorophthalic anhydride, trimellitic anhydride or triethylenetetramine;
	(iv) fumes arising from the use of rosin as a soldering flux;
	(v) proteolytic enzymes;
	(vi) animals or insects used for the purposes of research or education or in laboratories;
	(vii) dusts arising from the sowing, cultivation, harvesting, drying, handling, milling, transport or storage of barley, oats, rye, wheat or maize, or the handling, milling, transport or storage of meal or flour made therefrom,
	29th March 1982;
	(b) In the case of a person suffering from asthma due to exposure to any of the following agents:
	(i) animals including insects and other anthropods used for the purposes of research or education or in laboratories;
	(ii) antibiotics;
	(iii) cimetidine;
	(iv) wood dust;
	(v) ispaghula;
	(vi) castor bean dust;
	(vii) ipecacuanha;
	(viii) azodicarbonamide,
	1st September 1986.]
D8. Primary carcinoma of the lung where there is accompanying evidence of one or both of the following— (a) asbestosis; (b) bilateral diffuse pleural thickening.	1st April 1985.
D9. Bilateral diffuse pleural thickening.	1st April 1985.
[⁴ D10. Lung cancer.	1st April 1987.]

AMENDMENTS

1. Social Security (Industrial Injuries) (Prescribed Diseases) Amendment Regulations 1989 (SI 1989/1207), reg.6 (August 9, 1989).

2. Social Security (Industrial Injuries) (Prescribed Diseases) Amendment (No. 2) Regulations 1987 (SI 1987/2112), reg.3 (January 4, 1988).

3. Social Security (Industrial Injuries and Adjudication) Miscellaneous Amendment Regulations 1986 (SI 1986/1374), reg.3 (September 1, 1986).

4. Social Security (Industrial Injuries) (Prescribed Diseases) Amendment Regulations 1987 (SI 1987/335), reg.2 (April 1, 1987).

SCHEDULE 5

Regulation 44

TRANSITIONAL PROVISIONS REGARDING DATES OF DEVELOPMENT AND DATES OF ONSET

10.207 1.—In this Schedule the "date of development" has the meaning attributed to it by regulations 5, 6, 7 and 56 of the old regulations.

2.—Where a claim for benefit has been made before 6th April 1983, a date of development shall be determined and regulation 16 of the old regulations shall apply as if the old regulations were still in force.

3.—Where a claim for benefit is made after 5th April 1983 and a date of onset is determined which is before 6th April 1983, regulation 16 of the old regulations shall apply as if the old regulations were still in force.

4.—Where in pursuance of a claim made before 6th April 1983 a date of development has been determined and an award of benefit has been made these regulations shall have effect in relation to that claim and any subsequent claim made by or on behalf of the same person in respect of the same disease (except where under regulation 7 the disease is treated as having been contracted afresh) as if references to the date of onset were references to that date of development.

5.—Subject to paragraph 6, where a claim for injury benefit for a day falling or a period beginning before 5th April 1983 is made after 6th April 1983 and no date of development or date of onset which can be treated as such for the purposes of that claim has already been determined, for the purposes only of determining the date on which the injury benefit period (if any) is to begin, a date of development shall be determined, so however that if it is later than 5th April 1983 no injury benefit period shall begin and injury benefit shall not be payable.

6.—There shall be no entitlement, in the following cases, to benefit for any day which is earlier than the date specified:—

    (a) in the case of a person who is or has been suffering from
- (i) viral hepatitis : 2nd February 1976
- (ii) angiosarcoma of the liver : 21st March 1977
- (iii) osteolysis of the terminal phalanges of the fingers : 21st March 1977
- (iv) carcinoma of the nasal cavity or associated air sinuses (nasal carcinoma) : 8th August 1979
- (v) occupational vitiligo : 15th December 1980
- [¹ (vi) occupational asthma arising otherwise than as described at (vii) below : 29th March 1982;
- (vii) occupational asthma which is due to exposure to antibiotics, cimetidine, wood dust, ispaghula, castor bean dust, ipecacuanha or azodicarbonamide : 1st September 1986;]

    (b) in the case of a person who is or has been suffering from byssinosis but who has not been employed in employed earner's employment in any occupation mentioned in regulation 2(c) of the old regulations for a period or periods (whether before or after 5th July 1948) amounting in the aggregate to 5 years : 6th April 1979;

    (c) in the case of a person who is or has been suffering from infection by leptospira but neither is nor has been either incapable of work or suffering from a loss of faculty as a result of infection by—
- (i) leptospira icterohaemorrhagiae in the case of a person employed in employed earner's employment in any occupation involving work in places which are, or are liable to be, infested by rats, or
- (ii) leptospira canicola in the case of a person employed in employed earner's employment in any occupation involving work at dog kennels or the care or handling of dogs : 7th January 1980.

AMENDMENT

1. Social Security (Industrial Injuries and Adjudication) Miscellaneous Amendment Regulations 1986 (SI 1986/1374), reg.2 (September 1, 1986).

10.208 *Schedule 6 omitted.*

The Social Security (Industrial Injuries and Diseases) Miscellaneous Provisions Regulations 1986

(SI 1986/1561) (as amended)

ARRANGEMENT OF REGULATIONS

PART II

2.   Regular occupation for the purposes of Reduced Earnings Allowance.   10.209
3–10. *Omitted.*

PART IV

11.   Unemployability Supplement and Reduced Earnings Allowance.
12.   *Omitted.*
13.   *Revoked.*
14.   Claims for disablement benefits made before 1st October 1986.

The Secretary of State for Social Services, in exercise of the powers set out in the Schedule below, and of all other powers enabling him in that behalf, by this instrument, which contains only provisions consequential upon section 39 of the Social Security Act 1986, makes the following regulations:

PART II

MISCELLANEOUS PROVISIONS RELATING TO INDUSTRIAL INJURIES AND DISEASES

Regular occupation for the purposes of Reduced Earnings Allowance

2.—(1) Employed earner's employment in which a claimant was engaged   10.210
when the relevant accident took place but which was not his regular occupation shall be treated for the purposes of section 59A of the 1975 Act (reduced earnings allowance) as if it had been his regular occupation where the claimant, at the time the relevant accident took place, had no regular occupation but was pursuing a course of full-time education, either by attendance at a recognised educational establishment or, if the education is recognised by the Secretary of State in accordance with section 2(1A) of the Child Benefit Act 1975, elsewhere.

(2) In determining for the purpose of paragraph (1) whether a person was pursuing a course of full-time education, any temporary interruption of that education not exceeding a period of 6 months, or such longer period as the Secretary of State may in any particular case determine, shall be disregarded.

GENERAL NOTE

10.211   This provision permits students and others in full-time education to establish a regular occupation for the purposes of Reduced Earnings Allowance. Formerly, a vacation job would not have been regarded as a regular occupation. For commentary on SSCBA 1992 s.142(2), see above. Section 59A of the SSA 1975 has been replaced by para.11 of Sch.7 to the SSCBA 1992 while s.2(1A) of the CBA 1975 has been replaced by s.142(2) of the SSCBA 1992.

10.212   *Regulations 3–7 omitted.*

PART IV

TRANSITIONAL PROVISIONS

10.213   *Regulations 8–10 omitted.*

Unemployability Supplement and Reduced Earnings Allowance

10.214   **11.**—A reduced earnings allowance under section 59A of the 1975 Act and an unemployability supplement shall not be payable for the same period.

GENERAL NOTE

10.215   Section 59A of the SSA 1975 has been replaced by para.11 of Sch.7 to the SSCBA 1992.

10.216   *Regulation 12 omitted.*

10.217   *Regulation 13 revoked.*

Claims for disablement benefit made before 1st October 1986

10.218   **14.**—Where a claim for disablement benefit is made before 1st October 1986, that claim shall be determined as though—
   (a) paragraph 3(1) of Schedule 3 to the 1986 Act had not been enacted,
   (b) paragraph 3(2) had been enacted to the extent only of inserting sub-section (1B) of section 57 of the 1975 Act but omitting the words "Subject to paragraph (1C)" and the words from "and where it is" to the end of the subsection.

GENERAL NOTE

10.219   This still has some effect because a claim is not finally determined until there is a final assessment of disablement. Where there has been a series of provisional assessments following a claim made before October 1, 1986, further awards of disablement benefit are made as though s.57 of the 1975 Act (now s.103 of the SSCBA 1992) had not been significantly amended. This means that a weekly disablement pension is awarded only if disablement is assessed as at least 20 per cent but that a disablement gratuity is payable if disablement is assessed at anything from 1 per cent to 19 per cent (see SSCBA 1992 Sch.7 para.9).

The Social Security (Industrial Injuries) (Reduced Earnings Allowance and Transitional) Regulations 1987

(SI 1987/415) *(as amended)*

ARRANGEMENT OF REGULATIONS

PART I

GENERAL

1.   Citation, commencement and interpretation.   10.220

PART II

REDUCED EARNINGS ALLOWANCE

2.   Determination of the probable standard of remuneration.
3.   Awards at the maximum rate.
4.   Awards following relevant change of circumstances.

PART III

TRANSITIONAL

5.   Claims before 6th April 1987.
6.   Awards for special hardship made before 1st October 1986.
7.   Abatement of Reduced Earnings Allowance.
8.   *Omitted.*
9.   Offsetting prior payment of gratuity against subsequent award.

The Secretary of State for Social Services, in exercise of the powers conferred by section 59A(10) of and Schedule 20 to the Social Security Act 1975 and sections 84(1) and 89(1) of the Social Security Act 1986, and of all other powers enabling him in that behalf, by this instrument, which is made before the end of the period of 12 months from the commencement of the enactments under which it is made, makes the following Regulations:

PART I

GENERAL

Citation, commencement and interpretation

10.221   **1.**—(1) These regulations may be cited as the Social Security (Industrial Injuries) (Reduced Earnings Allowance and Transitional) Regulations 1987 and shall come into force on 6th April 1987.

(2) In these regulations—

"the Act" means the [Social Security Contributions and Benefits Act 1992];

"the 1986 Act" means the Social Security Act 1986.

(3) Unless the context otherwise requires, any reference in these regulations to a numbered regulation is a reference to the regulation bearing that number in these regulations and any reference in a regulation to a numbered paragraph is a reference to the paragraph of that regulation bearing that number.

GENERAL NOTE

10.222   The reference in square brackets was added by the annotator to make the regulations more "user friendly" in the light of the consolidating legislation.

PART II

REDUCED EARNINGS ALLOWANCE

Determination of the probable standard of remuneration

10.223   **2.**—(1) On any award of reduced earnings allowance except the first award made in respect of a relevant accident or a disease prescribed in accordance with [sections 108 to 110] of the Act, a person's probable standard of remuneration shall be determined in accordance with the following provisions of this regulation or, if applicable, of regulation 3.

(2) On the second award made in respect of an accident or disease, a person's probable standard of remuneration in any employment shall be determined in the same manner as on the first award.

(3) On a third or subsequent award made in respect of an accident or disease, a person's probable standard of remuneration in an employment shall be determined—

(a) if applicable, in accordance with paragraphs (4)–(8) of this regulation or with regulation 3, or

(b) otherwise in the same manner as on the first award.

(4) Where at the time of the award a person's regular occupation has ceased to exist, his probable standard of remuneration in the regular occupation shall be determined in accordance with paragraph (6).

(5) Where at the time of the award either—

(a) a person is not employed, or

(b) he is employed but the employment is not suitable in his case, and

(c) there has been no relevant change of circumstances since the last previous award, the probable standard of remuneration in any employed earner's employment which is suitable in his case and which he is likely to be capable of following shall be determined in accordance with paragraph (6).

(6) For the purposes of paragraphs (4) and (5) a person's probable standard of remuneration shall be determined by reference to the standard determined for the purposes of the last previous award of reduced earnings allowance [¹ adjusted by a percentage equal to any percentage change] in the level of relevant occupational groups.

(7) For the purposes of paragraph (6) and regulation 3(1)—

  (a) the relevant occupational group is the number specified in data relating to earnings published from time to time by the Department of Employment which is the nearest to, respectively,

      (i) the person's regular occupation,

      (ii) any employed earner's employments which are suitable in his case and which he is likely to be capable of following; and

  (b) the [¹ percentage change] in the level of earnings shall be determined by reference to the movement in average gross weekly earnings of full-time employees on adult rates in the relevant occupational group where pay was not affected by absence; and

  (c) a [¹ percentage change] for any year shall be applied to a determination of the probable standard of remuneration on an award made for a period commencing on or after the first Wednesday in the February of the year following the year to [¹ which the change relates].

(8) For the purposes of paragraph (4), a person's regular occupation has ceased to exist where—

  (a) his former employer has ceased to trade in the locality, or

  (b) the work the person did at his former place of employment no longer exists or has changed to such a degree that the work amounts to a different occupation,

and there is in the person's locality no employer providing work similar to that in which he was engaged.

AMENDMENT

1. Social Security (Industrial Injuries) (Miscellaneous Amendments) Regulations 1988 (SI 1988/553) reg 4 (April 11, 1988).

GENERAL NOTE

This regulation provides a mechanism for the determination of the probable standard of remuneration as required by SSCBA 1992, Sch.7, para.11(10) and (13), formerly SSA 1975, s.59A(8) and (10). Formerly, the tribunal would have to make a calculation based on information supplied to it on wage rates in individual jobs. This necessitated a great deal of research and information-gathering and this new provision provides a standard method of calculation by reference to published data relating to the earnings of relevant occupational groups.   **10.224**

The first award of reduced earnings allowance

The regulation does not apply to the first award when the calculation is made by reference to actual earnings in employments which would be suitable for the claimant and which he would be capable of following.   **10.225**

The second award
The same procedure is adopted as for the first award.

The third and subsequent awards

10.226   On the third and later awards the tribunal should first establish whether paras (4) to (8) of the regulation apply to the claimant. If not, the same procedure is adopted as for the first and second awards. Paras (4) and (5) apply the standardised calculation to the following claimants—

(a) those whose regular occupation has ceased to exist; or

(b) those who are unemployed at the time of the award, or employed in an unsuitable employment,

and in respect of whom there has been no relevant charge of circumstances since the last award.

The workings of the regulation have been briefly considered in unreported decision *CI/203/1989*. Take care to look also at regs 3 and 4, below, before applying the standard calculation set out in para.(6).

The standard calculation

10.227   Paragraph 6 requires that the standard of remuneration be determined by reference to the percentage change in the level of remuneration in relevant occupational groups, a phrase defined in para.7. That para. also directs the precise calculation of the percentage and fixes the date from which the annual standard change shall be applicable.

Awards at the maximum rate

10.228   **3.**—(1) Where on the second or subsequent award of reduced earnings allowance in respect of an accident or disease the award—

(a) is made at the maximum rate payable under [paragraph 11(10) of Schedule 7] of the Act, or

(b) would have been made at that rate but for paragraph 5(3) of Schedule 3 to the 1986 Act or regulation 8,

then, but subject to paragraph (2), on any award thereafter the probable standard of a person's remuneration in any employment shall be determined as being the same standard as that determined for the purpose of the last previous award of reduced earnings allowance increase by a percentage equal to any percentage increase in the level of earnings for the relevant occupational groups.

(2) This regulation does not apply where—

(a) on an award, reduced earnings allowance would be payable at a rate below the maximum rate payable under [paragraph 11(10) of Schedule 7] of the Act otherwise than by virtue of paragraph 5(3) of Schedule 3 to the 1986 Act or regulation 8; or

(b) there has been a relevant change in the person's circumstances since the last previous award.

Awards following relevant change of circumstances

10.229   **4.**—An award of reduced earnings allowance following a relevant change of circumstances shall be treated for the purpose of Part II of these regulations as the first such award.

GENERAL NOTE

What constitutes a relevant change of circumstances was discussed by Commissioner Walker in *CI/203/1989*. He was considering the case of a person who had been made redundant and concluded that redundancy did constitute a relevant change of circumstances. The Commissioner said,

"... the phrase means no more than that if at the time of making an award there are circumstances different from those obtaining at the time of the making of the previous award, and which differences may have some bearing upon the calculation then there is a relevant change for the purposes of the regulation."

The significance of a change of circumstances is, of course, that it takes the calculation outside the ambit of reg.2 since the award will then be treated as the first award.

10.230

PART III

TRANSITIONAL

Claims before 6th April 1987

5.—Regulations 2 and 3 shall not apply to any award of reduced earnings allowance where the claim which resulted in that award was made before 6th April 1987.

10.231

Awards for special hardship made before 1st October 1986

6.—Any award made before 1st October 1986 of an increase in disablement pension under section 60 of the [Social Security Act 1975] (increase of disablement benefit for special hardship) shall be treated for the purposes of regulations 2 and 3 as an award of reduced earnings allowance.

10.232

Abatement of Reduced Earnings Allowance

7.—(1) For the purposes of paragraph 5(3) of Schedule 3 to the 1986 Act paragraph 5 of that Schedule shall be treated as having come into force on 6th April 1987.

(2) Paragraph 5(3) of Schedule 3 to the 1986 Act shall be modified by the substitution, in head (c), of the words "a reduced earnings allowance under section 59A" for the words "an increase under section 60" and by the substitution of the words "allowance was payable" for the words "increase was payable."

10.233

Regulation 8 omitted.

10.234

Offsetting prior payment of gratuity against subsequent award

9.—For the purpose of offsetting any amount paid by way of gratuity under an award which is subsequently varied on appeal or revised on review, regulation 85 of the Social Security (Adjudication) Regulations 1984 shall

10.235

have effect after 5th April 1987 as if made under section 53(5)(b) of the 1986 Act.

GENERAL NOTE

10.236   Amendments effected by the following regulations have been incorporated in the text above.

Regulations
Social Security (Industrial Injuries) (Miscellaneous Amendments) Regulations 1988 (SI 1988/553).

The Social Security (Industrial Injuries) (Regular Employment) Regulations 1990

(SI 1990/256) (*as amended*)

ARRANGEMENT OF REGULATIONS

10.237   1.   Citation, commencement and interpretation.
2.   Meaning of "regular employment".
3.   Circumstances in which a person over pensionable age is to be regarded as having given up regular employment.

Whereas a draft of this instrument was laid before Parliament in accordance with the provisions of section 29(2)(e) of the Social Security Act 1989 and approved by a resolution of each House of Parliament:

Now, therefore, the Secretary of State for Social Security, in exercise of the power conferred by section 59B(7) and (8) of and Schedule 20 to the Social Security Act 1975, and of all other powers enabling him in that behalf, by this instrument, which is made before the end of the period of 6 months beginning with the coming into force of the aforesaid section 59B(7) and (8), makes the following Regulations:

Citation, commencement and interpretation

10.238   **1.**—(1) These Regulations may be cited as the Social Security (Industry Injuries) (Regular Employment) Regulations 1990 and shall come into force on 1st April 1990.

(2) [¹. . .]

AMENDMENT

1. Social Security (Industrial Injuries and Diseases) (Miscellaneous Amendments) Regulations 1996/425 reg.6(2) (March 24, 1996).

[¹Meaning of "regular employment"

10.239   **2.**—For the purposes of paragraph 13 of Schedule 7 to the Social Security Contributions and Benefits Act 1992, "regular employment" means gainful employment—

(a) under a contract of service which requires a person to work for an average of 10 hours or more per week in any period of five consecutive weeks, there being disregarded for this purpose any week when the contract subsists during which he is absent from that employment

1574

in circumstances where such absence is permitted under the contract (for example in the case of sickness or taking leave); or

(b) which a person undertakes for an average of 10 hours or more per week in any period of five consecutive weeks.]

AMENDMENT

1. Social Security (Industrial Injuries and Diseases) (Miscellaneous Amendments) Regulations 1996 (SI 1996/425) reg.6(3) (March 24, 1996).

GENERAL NOTE

In *R(I) 2/93*, Commissioner Hoolahan noted in passing that this provision does *not* require a person to return to regular employment within five weeks of leaving his previous employment; the five weeks can begin any time in the future (para.10).   10.240

As regards "average", see *CI/3225/2004*. There Commissioner Levenson, deploying para.(b), used "rolling five week averages" as a convenient way of assessing continuing entitlement and determined that this claimant had not given up regular employment. The Commissioner stated:

"It has never been doubted that the word 'average' refers to the arithmetic mean. The use of the phrase 'any period of five consecutive weeks' means that weeks after a particular job comes to an end can be included, and that weeks in which no work is done or expected to be done can also be included. In so deciding, I agree with the conclusions of the Commissioner in paragraphs 20 to 22 of *CI/2517/2001*. Further, I see no reason why a five week period under consideration cannot include some weeks calculated with reference to regulation 2(a) and some calculated with reference to regulation 2(b). Although 2(b) can only be assessed or calculated retrospectively, because it must be established for those purposes whether gainful employment has in fact been undertaken, future weeks can be considered from any particular vantage point (para.12)."

[¹ Circumstances in which a person over pensionable age is to be regarded as having given up regular employment

3.—Unless he is entitled to reduced earnings allowance for life by virtue of paragraph 12(1) of Schedule 7 to the Social Security Contributions and Benefits Act 1992, a person who has attained pensionable age shall be regarded as having given up regular employment at the start of the first week in which he is not in regular employment after the later of—   10.241

(a) the week during which this regulation comes into force; or

(b) the week during which he attains pensionable age.]

AMENDMENT

1. Social Security (Industrial Injuries and Diseases) (Miscellaneous Amendments) Regulations 1996 (SI 1996/425) reg.6(3) (March 24, 1996).

GENERAL NOTE

This regulation came into force on March 24, 1996, the date on which it was inserted by the Social Security (Industrial Injuries and Diseases) (Miscellaneous Amendment) Regulations 1996. In decisions reported as *R(I) 2/99* and affirmed in *Plummer v Hammond*, Commissioner Howell held that it removed entitlement to REA and replaced it with retirement allowance for life with effect from March 31, 1996 (the beginning of the week after March 24, 1996) even in the case of two ladies who had attained pensionable age prior to March 24 and had in normal parlance given up (but not retired from) regular employment because of incapacity   10.242

long before either April 10, 1989 (the date in SSCBA 1992 Sch.7 para.13(1)) or March 24, 1996 (the date reg.3 came into force). The two ladies would not otherwise have been deprived of REA by para.13(1) because of the fact that they had as at October 1, 1989 been long out of work so that they could not be said to have "given up" regular employment on any day on or after that date as para.13(10)(b) as supplemented by the original 1990 regulations required, "gives up" bearing its ordinary natural meaning (*R(I) 2/93, R(I) 3/93*). Reg.3 did, however, deprive them of it and transfer them to retirement allowance by, albeit artificially, regarding them as having given it up. See in particular paras 37, 38 and 40–49.

The case is very useful in charting the bumpy and twisting path of attempts to make entitlements to REA cease on retirement, and makes clear that reg.3 is *intra vires* the rule making power in SSCBA 1992 Sch.7 13(8).

Since both ladies had attained the age of 65 before the regulation deprived them of REA, "the condition linked to pensionable age in paragraph 13(1) has no discriminatory effect", rendering it unnecessary in their case to consider any possible application of Council Dir. 79/7: see *Vol.III: Administration Appeals and the European Dimension.*

10.243   That this can work harshly in respect of persons whose work is seasonal is shown in *SSWP v NH (II)* [2010] UKUT 84 (AAC). Here the claimant did seasonal work in a museum from March to October 2007, when the contract ended. In August 2007 he became 65. He next worked from March 11, 2008 at the museum. Judge Paines, agreeing in part with Judge Howell in *CI/16202/96* (applied in *CI/2517/01*) and partly with Judge Levenson in *CI/3224/04*, took the following approach to reg.3 read with reg.2:

"the question becomes, for the purposes of regulation 3 when read with regulation 2(a), whether the claimant was in employment under a contract (with, to put it loosely, average contractual hours of ten or more); for the purposes of regulation 2(b) the question is whether the claimant was in fact in gainful employment which he undertook for an average of ten hours measured over five consecutive weeks.

Viewing the questions in that way, it seems to me to be impossible to hold that a person is 'in' employment under a contract for the purposes of regulation 2(a) at a point in time at which the contract has ceased. In that regard I find Judge Howell's reasoning . . . compelling.

As far as regulation 2(b) is concerned, I agree with Judge Howell that it embraces both casual employment and self-employment. It is in addition self-evident that the employment or self-employment does not need to be full-time. The Regulations regard a person as being 'in employment' in a week provided at least that he performs enough hours of casual or self-employed work to maintain the required ten-hour average; that is so despite the fact that, if the work is casual, the claimant will probably not be in an employment relationship except during the hours that he performs it. It is against that background that I address the question whether for the purposes of regulation 2(b) there is (as Judge Howell suggested) an implicit requirement that the claimant must perform *some* work in each week.

I do not consider that there is such an implicit requirement. The question to be answered is whether, in the week under examination, the claimant is 'in' employment undertaken for an average of ten hours per week measured over five consecutive weeks. Where a claimant remains in the habit of taking employment, and moreover the five-week rolling average of ten hours' work per week is maintained, I do not find it necessary to hold that he is no longer in employment in a particular week merely because he performs no hours of work in that week.

If it were otherwise, a self-employed person could not take a week off without being regarded as giving up employment for the purposes of the Regular Employment Regulations. I find it impossible to conclude that, despite specifically providing for employees' holiday and other permitted absences to be disregarded for the purposes of the contractual hours calculation under regulation

2(a), the Regulations require self-employed persons to forego time off in order to avoid deemed giving up of employment. As a matter of language I have no difficulty in regarding a self-employed person taking time off as remaining 'in' self-employment. Similarly, I would regard a person as remaining 'in' self-employment even if no customers come his way in a particular week. Likewise I would regard a person who remains in the habit of taking casual employment as remaining 'in' casual employment during a week in which (whether because of a wish to take time off or because of the unavailability of work) he does not actually perform any work. This seems to me to be consistent with Judge Rowland's approach in R(JSA) 1/03 to the concept of 'gainful employment' when used in the JSA Regulations; the same term is used in regulation 2 of the Regular Employment Regulations).

It seems to me to be a matter of giving the concept of being 'in' (for example) casual employment or self-employment its natural meaning. Following this approach, a casual employee or self-employed person will be regarded as giving up regular employment if he decides no longer to take work, or if his average hours fall below ten. The approach seems to me to be consistent with Judge Powell's approach in CI/2517/01, where the nurse's single week without agency work was not regarded as triggering regulation 3" (paras 21–26).

Consequently, reg.2(a) could not apply once the contract had ended in October 2007. Nor could he avail himself of reg.2(b) because there was no suggestion that he undertook or planned to undertake any employment in the weeks immediately following October 30. Whereas, if his job at the museum had been all year round, rather than seasonal, he would have retained entitlement to REA while he continued working. Judge Lane noted the more flexible treatment of seasonal workers under JSA.

The Social Security (Industrial Injuries) (Prescribed Diseases) Amendment (No. 2) Regulations 1993

(SI 1993/1985) *(as amended)*

ARRANGEMENT OF REGULATIONS

1.	Citation, commencement and interpretation.	10.244
2.–8.	*Omitted.*	
9.	Transitional provision with respect to claims for prescribed disease D12.	

The Secretary of State for Social Security, in exercise of the powers conferred by sections 108(2) and (4), 109(2) and (3), 110(1) and (2), 122(1) and 175(1) and (3) of and paragraph 2 of Schedule 6 to the Social Security Contributions and Benefits Act 1992 and sections 5(1)(a) and (b), 58(1)(b) and 189(1) and (4) of the Social Security Administration Act 1992, and of all other powers enabling him in that behalf, after reference to the Industrial Injuries Advisory Council hereby makes the following Regulations:

Citation, commencement and interpretation

1.—(1) These Regulations may be cited as the Social Security (Industrial Injuries) (Prescribed Diseases) Amendment (No. 2) Regulations 1993 and shall come into force on 13th September 1993.   10.245

(2) In these Regulations "the principal Regulations" means the Social Security (Industrial Injuries) (Prescribed Diseases) Regulations 1985.

10.246   *Sections 2–8 omitted.*

Transitional provision with respect to claims for prescribed disease D12

10.247   **9.**—(1) In this regulation—

"prescribed disease D12" means the disease bearing that number and listed in Part I of Schedule 1 to the principal Regulations (chronic bronchitis and emphysema);

"relevant claim" means a claim for benefit in respect of prescribed disease D12; and

"relevant date" means 13th September 1993 or the date upon which the claimant in question first satisfies the conditions specified in Schedule 1 to the principal Regulations in respect of prescribed disease D12, whichever is the later.

(2) The provisions of the Social Security (Claims and Payments) Regulations 1987 shall apply in relation to a relevant claim subject to the following provisions of this regulation.

(3) A person who is aged not less than 70 on 13th September 1993 may make a relevant claim at any time in the period beginning with 13th September 1993 and ending with 28th February 1994, and if so made the claim shall be treated as having been made on the relevant date.

(4) A person who is aged less than 70 on 13th September 1993 and who, on the date the claim is made, has an award of attendance allowance at the higher rate under section 65(3) of the Social Security Contributions and Benefits Act 1992 or of the care component of disability living allowance at the highest rate under section 72(4) of that Act, may make a relevant claim at any time in the period beginning with 13th September 1993 and ending with 28th February 1994, and if so made the claim shall be treated as having been made on the relevant date.

(5) A person who does not fall within either of paragraphs (3) and (4) above may not make a relevant claim before 1st March 1994, but if such a person, or a person falling within paragraph (4) above who has not previously made a relevant claim, makes a relevant claim in the period beginning with that day and ending with 31st August 1994 that claim shall be treated as having been made on the relevant date.

The Social Security (Industrial Injuries and Diseases) (Miscellaneous Amendments) Regulations 1996

(SI 1996/425)

ARRANGEMENT OF REGULATIONS

10.248   1.   Citation and commencement.
2   *Revoked*
3–6.   *Omitted.*
7.   Transitional provisions

The Secretary of State for Social Security, in exercise of the powers conferred by sections 108(2), 109(2) and (3), 113(1)(b), 122(1) and 175(1), (3) and (4) of, and sub-paragraphs (8) and (9) of paragraph 13 of Schedule 7 to, the Social Security Contributions and Benefits Act 1992 and sections 5(1)(k), 27(1)(b) and 189(1) and (4)(b) of the Social Security Administration Act 1992, and of all other powers enabling him in that behalf, after reference to the Industrial Injuries Advisory Council, hereby makes the following Regulations:

Citation and commencement

1. These Regulations may be cited as the Social Security (Industrial Injuries and Diseases) (Miscellaneous Amendments) Regulations 1996 and shall come into force on 24th March 1996.

10.249

Sections 2–6. omitted.

10.250

Transitional provisions

7.—(1) The amendments made by regulation 5 of these Regulations ("the relevant amendments") to the terms in which each of the prescribed diseases A12, D4 and D5 ("the relevant disease") is prescribed shall not apply in the cases specified in the following provisions of this regulation, and in this regulation "commencement date" means the date on which these Regulations come into force.

10.251

(2) The relevant amendments shall not apply in the case of a person—

(a) who had an assessment of disablement in respect of the relevant disease for period which includes commencement date; or

(b) in respect of whom a decision in relation to a relevant disease on a claim for disablement benefit made before commencement date is reviewed on or after that date under section 47 of the Social Security Administration Act 1992 (reviews of medical decisions) which results in an assessment for a period which includes commencement date;

during any period where there is in respect of him a continuous assessment of disablement in respect of that disease which began before commencement date, and for this purpose two or more assessments one of which begins on the day following the end of a preceding assessment shall be treated as continuous.

(3) The relevant amendments shall not apply in the case of a person who makes a claim for disablement benefit in respect of the relevant disease before commencement date which results in an assessment of disablement, where the date of onset of that disease is earlier than commencement date, during any period when there is in respect of him a continuous assessment of disablement in respect of that disease which began not later than 91 days (excluding Sundays) after commencement date, and for this purpose two or more assessments one of which begins on the day following the end of a preceding assessment shall be treated as continuous.

(4) The relevant amendments shall not apply in the case of a person—

(a) who had an assessment of disablement in respect of the relevant disease for a period which ended before commencement date;

(b) who suffers a further attack of that relevant disease before commencement date;

(c) who makes a claim for disablement benefit in respect of that disease after commencement date; and

(d) in respect of whom it is decided, under regulation 7 of the Social Security (Industrial Injuries) (Prescribed Diseases) Regulations 1985 (recrudescence) that the further attack is a recrudescence of that disease.

The Social Security (Industrial Injuries) (Prescribed Diseases) Amendment Regulations 2000

(SI 2000/1588)

ARRANGEMENT OF REGULATIONS

10.252
1. Citation, commencement and interpretation.
2. Amendment of regulation 2 of the principal Regulations.
3. Amendment of regulation 25 of the principal Regulations.
4. Amendment of regulation 27 of the principal Regulations.
5. Amendment of regulation 36 of the principal Regulations.
6. Amendment of Schedule 1 to the principal Regulations.
7. Transitional provision.

The Secretary of State for Social Security, in exercise of the powers conferred by sections 108(2) and (4), 109(2) and (3), 122(1) and 175(1) to (4) of the Social Security Contributions and Benefits Act 1992 and of all other powers enabling him in that behalf, after reference to the Industrial Injuries Advisory Council, hereby makes the following Regulations:

Citation, commencement and interpretation

10.253   **1.**—(1) These Regulations may be cited as the Social Security (Industrial Injuries) (Prescribed Diseases) Amendment Regulations 2000 and shall come into force on 10th July 2000.

(2) In these Regulations, "the principal Regulations" means the Social Security (Industrial Injuries) (Prescribed Diseases) Regulations 1985.

Amendment of regulation 2 of the principal Regulations

10.254   **2.**—*Incorporated in text of principal Regulations.*

Amendment of regulation 25 of the principal Regulations

10.255   **3.**—*Incorporated in text of principal Regulations.*

Amendment of regulation 27 of the principal Regulations

10.256   **4.**—*Incorporated in text of principal Regulations.*

Amendment of regulation 36 of the principal Regulations

10.257   **5.**—*Incorporated in text of principal Regulations.*

Amendment of Schedule 1 to the principal Regulations

10.258   **6.**—*Incorporated in text of principal Regulations.*

Transitional provision

7.—(1) The amendments made by regulations 3 and 4 shall not apply   10.259
in relation to a claim made within 3 months after the commencement
date and the amendments made by regulations 2(3), 5 and 6 shall not
apply where the date of onset of the relevant disease is prior to the
commencement date and the claim is made within 3 months after that
date.

(2) The amendments made by regulations 2(3) and 6 shall not apply in
the case of a person—

(a) who had an assessment of disablement in respect of the relevant
disease for a period up to the date 3 months after the commencement
date; or

(b) in respect of whom a decision in relation to a relevant disease on a claim
for disablement benefit made before or within 3 months after the commencement date is revised or superseded after that date under section
9 or 10 of the Social Security Act 1998 resulting in an assessment;

during any period when there is in respect of him a continuous assessment
of disablement in respect of that disease, and for this purpose two or more
assessments, one of which begins on the day following the end of a preceding assessment, shall be treated as continuous.

(3) The amendments made by regulations 2(3) and 6(2) and (3) shall not
apply in the case of a person—

(a) who had an assessment of disablement in respect of the relevant
disease for a period which ended before or within 3 months after the
commencement date;

(b) who suffers a further attack of that relevant disease before or within
3 months after the commencement date;

(c) who makes a claim for disablement benefit in respect of that disease
after the commencement date; and

(d) in respect of whom it is decided under regulation 7 of the principal
Regulations (recrudescence) that the further attack is a recrudescence of that disease.

(4) In this regulation—

"commencement date" means the date on which these Regulations come
into force; and

"relevant disease" means the disease referred to in the amendment, or
the regulation of the principal Regulations which is amended by the
amendment.

The Social Security (Industrial Injuries) (Prescribed Diseases) Amendment Regulations 2003

(SI 2003/270)

ARRANGEMENT OF REGULATIONS

1.   Citation, commencement and interpretation.   10.260
2.   Amendment of regulation 4 of the principal Regulations.

3.   Amendment of regulation 7 of the principal Regulations.
4.   Amendment of regulation 8 of the principal Regulations.
5.   Amendment of Schedule 1 to the principal Regulations.
6.   Transitional provision.

The Secretary of State for Work and Pensions, in exercise of the powers conferred on him by sections 108(2) and (4), 109(2) and (3), 122(1) and 175(1) to (4) of the Social Security Contributions and Benefits Act 1992 and of all other powers enabling him in that behalf, after reference to the Industrial Injuries Advisory Council, hereby makes the following Regulations:

Citation, commencement and interpretation

10.261   **1.**—(1) These Regulations may be cited as the Social Security (Industrial Injuries) (Prescribed Diseases) Amendment Regulations 2003 and shall come into force on 17th March 2003.

(2) In these Regulations "the principal Regulations" means the Social Security (Industrial Injuries) (Prescribed Diseases) Regulations 1985.

Amendment of regulation 4 of the principal Regulations

10.262   **2.**—*Incorporated in text of principal Regulations.*

Amendment of regulation 7 of the principal Regulations

10.263   **3.**—*Incorporated in text of principal Regulations.*

Amendment of regulation 8 of the principal Regulations

10.264   **4.**—*Incorporated in text of principal Regulations.*

Amendment of Schedule 1 to the principal Regulations

10.265   **5.**—*Incorporated in text of principal Regulations.*

Transitional provision

10.266   **6.**—(1) Regulations 2 and 5 shall not apply—

(a) to a period of assessment which relates to a claim which is made before the commencement date;

(b) to a period of assessment which relates to a claim which is made within 3 months after the commencement date in respect of a period which began before the commencement date; or

(c) where a person suffers from an attack of a disease and under regulation 7 of the principal Regulations (recrudescence) the attack is a recrudescence of a disease for which a claim was made before the commencement date (or within 3 months after the commencement date in respect of a period which began before the commencement date).

(2) For the purposes of this regulation—

(a) "commencement date" means the date on which these Regulations come into force;

(b) the date on which a claim is made is the date on which the claim is made or treated as made in accordance with the Social Security (Claims and Payments) Regulations 1987; and

(c) a period of assessment which begins on the day following the end of a preceding period of assessment, shall be treated as a continuation of the preceding period of assessment.

The Social Security (Industrial Injuries) (Prescribed Diseases) Amendment (No. 2) Regulations 2003

(SI 2003/2190)

ARRANGEMENT OF REGULATIONS

1.   Citation, commencement and interpretation.   10.267
2.   Amendment of the principal Regulations.
3.   Amendment of Schedule 1 to the principal Regulations.
4.   Transitional provision.

The Secretary of State for Work and Pensions, in exercise of the powers conferred on him by sections 108(2), 109(2), 122(1) and 175(1) to (4) of the Social Security Contributions and Benefits Act 1992 and sections 9(1), 10(3) and 79(1), (3) and (4) of the Social Security Act 1998 and of all other powers enabling him in that behalf, being satisfied of the matters referred to in section 108(2)(a) and (b) of that Act of 1992 and after reference to the Industrial Injuries Advisory Council, hereby makes the following Regulations:

Citation, commencement and interpretation

1.—(1) These Regulations may be cited as the Social Security (Industrial   10.268
Injuries) (Prescribed Diseases) Amendment (No.2) Regulations 2003 and shall come into force on 22nd September 2003.

(2) In these Regulations "the principal Regulations" means the Social Security (Industrial Injuries) (Prescribed Diseases) Regulations 1985.

Amendment of the principal Regulations

2.—*Incorporated in text of principal Regulations.*   10.269

Amendment of Schedule 1 to the principal Regulations

3.—*Incorporated in text of Schedule 1 to the principal Regulations.*   10.270

Transitional provision

4.—(1) Regulation 3 shall not apply to a period of assessment which   10.271
relates to a claim which is made before the commencement date.

(2) A provisional assessment of the extent of a claimant's disablement due to occupational deafness, which is in force immediately before the commencement date, shall, from the commencement date, have effect for the remainder of the claimant's life.

(3) For the purposes of this regulation—

(a) "commencement date" means the date on which these Regulations come into force;

(b) the date on which a claim is made is the date on which the claim is made or treated as made in accordance with the Social Security (Claims and Payments) Regulations 1987.

GENERAL NOTE

10.272   This principally protects those whose claims in respect of hearing loss were made, or treated as made, before the date of the change [September 22, 2003] (para.(1) read with (3)(b). But note also the provision in para.(2), which turns a provisional assessment of disablement due to occupational deafness, in force on September 21, 2003, into one for life as from September 22, 2003 ("commencement date"—see para.(3)(a)).

The Social Security (Industrial Injuries) (Prescribed Diseases) Amendment Regulations 2005

(SI 2005/324)

10.273   The Secretary of State for Work and Pensions, in exercise of the powers conferred upon him by sections 108(2), 122(1) and 175(1) to (4) of the Social Security Contributions and Benefits Act 1992 and section 5(1)(a) of the Social Security Administration Act 1992 and of all other powers enabling him in that behalf, being satisfied of the matters referred to in section 108(2) (a) and (b) of the Social Security Contributions and Benefits Act and after reference to the Industrial Injuries Advisory Council, hereby makes the following Regulations:

Citation, commencement and interpretation

10.274   **1.**—(1) These Regulations may be cited as the Social Security (Industrial Injuries) (Prescribed Diseases) Amendment Regulations 2005 and shall come into force on 14th March 2005.

(2) In these Regulations "the principal Regulations" means the Social Security (Industrial Injuries) (Prescribed Diseases) Regulations 1985.

Amendment of regulations 2 and 25 of the principal Regulations

10.275   **2.**—*Incorporated in text of the principal Regulations.*

Amendment of Schedule 1 to the principal Regulations

10.276   **3.**– *Incorporated in text of Schedule 1 to the principal Regulations*

Transitional provision

10.277   **4.**—Regulation 3 shall not apply to a period of assessment which relates to a claim which is made before the date on which these Regulations come into force.

The Social Security (Industrial Injuries) (Prescribed Diseases) Amendment Regulations 2007

(SI 2007/811)

10.278   The Secretary of State for Work and Pensions makes the following Regulations in exercise of the powers conferred by sections 108(2), 122(1) and 175(1) to (4) of the Social Security Contributions and Benefits Act 1992.

The Secretary of State is satisfied of the matters referred to in section 108(2)(a) and (b) of that Act.

In accordance with section 172(2) of the Social Security Administration Act 1992, reference has been made to the Industrial Injuries Advisory Council.

Citation and commencement

1. These Regulations may be cited as the Social Security (Industrial Injuries) (Prescribed Diseases) Amendment Regulations 2007 and shall come into force on the 6th April 2007.

10.279

Amendment of Schedule 1 to the Social Security (Industrial Injuries) (Prescribed Diseases) Regulations 1985

2. — *Incorporated in text of Schedule 1 to the principal Regulations.*

10.280

Transitional provision

3. Regulation 2 shall not apply to a period of assessment which relates to a claim made before the date on which these Regulations come into force.

10.281

The Social Security (Industrial Injuries) (Prescribed Diseases) Amendment (No.2) Regulations 2007

(SI 2007/1753)

ARRANGEMENT OF REGULATIONS

1.   Citation, commencement and interpretation
2.   Amendment of Schedule 1 to the principal Regulations
3.   Transitional provision

10.282

The Secretary of State for Work and Pensions makes the following Regulations in exercise of the powers conferred by sections 108(2), 122(1) and 175(1), (3) and (4) of the Social Security Contributions and Benefits Act 1992.

He is satisfied of the matters referred to in section 108(2)(a) and (b) of that Act.

In accordance with section 172(2) of the Social Security Administration Act 1992 he has referred proposals to make these Regulations to the Industrial Injuries Advisory Council.

Citation, commencement and interpretation

1. —(1) These Regulations may be cited as the Social Security (Industrial Injuries) (Prescribed Diseases) Amendment (No. 2) Regulations 2007 and shall come into force on 1st October 2007.

(2) In these Regulations "the principal Regulations" means the Social Security (Industrial Injuries) (Prescribed Diseases) Regulations 1985.

10.283

Amendment of Schedule 1 to the principal Regulations

2. *Incorporated into the text of Schedule 1 to the principal Regulations.*

10.284

Transitional provision

10.285 **3.** —(1) Regulation 2 shall not apply to a question relating to the blanching of a claimant's fingers where—

(a) the question arises in connection with a period of assessment which relates to a claim which is made—
(i) before the commencement date, or
(ii) within 3 months after the commencement date in respect of a period which began before the commencement date, or
(b) a person suffers from an attack of a disease and under regulation 7 of the principal Regulations (recrudescence) the attack is a recrudescence of a disease for which a claim was made before the commencement date or within 3 months after the commencement date in respect of a period which began before the commencement date.

(2) For the purposes of this regulation—
(a) "commencement date" means the date on which these Regulations come into force; and
(b) a period of assessment which begins on the day following the end of a preceding period of assessment, shall be treated as a continuation of the preceding period of assessment.

GENERAL NOTE

10.286 Regulation 2 added sensorineural symptoms to the description of PD A11 with effect from October 1, 2007. There can clearly be no claim on the basis of such symptoms for any period prior to that date. This transitional provision, preventing claims within a three month period after that date, only prevents claims being made which raise a question of the blanching of a claimant's fingers, so that a claimant whose case is based on the new sensory condition does not have to wait until that three month period is over but can claim in respect of it for periods on or after October 1, 2007 (*DG v SSWP* [2009] UKUT 41 (AAC), paras 5-8).

The Industrial Injuries Benefit (Injuries arising before 5th July 1948) Regulations 2012

(SI 2012/2743) (AS AMENDED)

ARRANGEMENT OF REGULATIONS

1. Citation, commencement and interpretation
10.287 2. Payment of industrial injuries benefit where compensation or benefits were previously payable under Schedule 8 to the Contributions and Benefits Act
3. Claims made but not determined before 5th December 2012

SCHEDULE

The Secretary of State for Work and Pensions makes the following Regulations in exercise of the powers conferred by section 64(3) of the Welfare Reform Act 2012

Citation, commencement and interpretation

1.—(1) These Regulations may be cited as the Industrial Injuries Benefit   10.288
(Injuries arising before [15th July] 1948) Regulations 2012 and come into
force on December 5, 2012.

(2) In these Regulations "the Contributions and Benefits Act" means the
Social Security Contributions and Benefits Act 1992

Payment of industrial injuries benefit where compensation or benefits were previously payable under Schedule 8 to the Contributions and Benefits Act

2. Where, before the commencement of section 64 of the Welfare   10.289
Reform Act 2012 (injuries arising before 5th July 1948), compensation or
benefits were payable to any person under a provision of Schedule 8 to the
Contributions and Benefits Act (industrial injuries and diseases (old cases))
mentioned in column (1) of the table in the Schedule to these Regulations,
the rate or amount of industrial injuries benefit payable to that person is the
corresponding rate or amount set out in column (2) of that table.

Claims made but not determined before 5th December 2012

3. Any claim for compensation or benefits that was made in accordance   10.290
with section 111 of, and Schedule 8 to, the Contributions and Benefits
Act but which was not determined before the coming into force of these
Regulations, is to be treated as a claim for industrial injuries benefit.

SCHEDULE

RATES OF INDUSTRIAL INJURIES BENEFIT CORRESPONDING   10.291
TO COMPENSATION OR BENEFIT PREVIOUSLY PAYABLE UNDER
SCHEDULE 8 TO THE CONTRIBUTIONS AND BENEFITS ACT

(1) Compensation or benefit payable before 5th December 2012 under Schedule 8 to the Contributions and Benefits Act	*(2) Corresponding rate or amount of industrial injuries benefit payable under the Contributions and Benefits Act from 5th December 2012*
Incapacity allowance Major incapacity allowance under paragraph 2(6)(b) of Schedule 8	The rate applicable for 100% degree of disablement as specified in column (2) of the table in Part 5 of Schedule 4
Lesser incapacity allowance under paragraph 2(6)(c) of Schedule 8 payable at the weekly rate of £4.85, £13.15 or £22.05	The rate applicable for 20% degree of disablement as specified in column (2) of the table in Part 5 of Schedule 4
Lesser incapacity allowance under paragraph 2(6)(c) of Schedule 8 payable at the weekly rate of £31.95 or £45.90	The rate applicable for 30% degree of disablement as specified in column (2) of the table in Part 5 of Schedule 4
Lesser incapacity allowance under paragraph 2(6)(c) of Schedule 8 payable at the weekly rate of £58.45	The rate applicable for 40% degree of disablement as specified in column (2) of the table in Part 5 of Schedule 4

Total disablement benefit Allowance in respect of total disablement under paragraph 6(2)(a) of Schedule 8	The rate applicable for 100% degree of disablement as specified in column (2) of the table in Part 5 of Schedule 4
Partial disablement allowance Allowance in respect of disablement which is not total under paragraph 6(2)(b) of Schedule 8	The rate applicable for 40% degree of disablement as specified in column (2) of the table in Part 5 of Schedule 4
Unemployability supplement Unemployability supplement in accordance with paragraph 6(4)(a) or 7(2)(c)(i) of Schedule 8	Unemployability supplement at the rate specified in paragraphs 5 and 6 of Part 5 of Schedule 4
Exceptionally severe disablement allowance Exceptionally severe disablement allowance in accordance with paragraph 6(4)(b) or paragraph 7(2)(c)(iii) of Schedule 8	Exceptionally severe disablement allowance at the rate specified in paragraph 3 of Part 5 of Schedule 4
Constant attendance allowance Increase of allowance in respect of constant attendance in accordance with paragraph 6(4)(b) or of disablement pension under paragraph 7(2)(c)(iii) of Schedule 8	Constant attendance allowance at the rate specified in paragraph 2 of Part 5 of Schedule 4
Increase of benefit or disablement pension for a child dependant Increase of benefit for a child dependant in accordance with paragraph 6(4)(c) or of disablement pension for a child dependant in accordance with [¹paragraph 7(2)(c)(ii)] of Schedule 8	Child dependency increase at the rate specified in paragraph 7 of Part 5 of Schedule 4
Increase of benefit or disablement pension for an adult dependant Increase of benefit for an adult dependant in accordance with paragraph 6(5) or of disablement pension for an adult dependant in accordance with [¹paragraph 7(2)(c)(ii)] of Schedule 8	Adult dependency increase at the rate specified in [¹paragraph 8] of Part 5 of Schedule 4
Payment of a capital sum Payment of a capital sum or sums in accordance with paragraph 6(6) of Schedule 8	A sum or sums of an amount or aggregate amount not exceeding £300

AMENDMENT

1. Industrial Injuries Benefit (Injuries arising before July 5, 1948) (Amendment) Regulations 2012 (SI 2012/2812) reg.2 (December 4, 2012).

(SI 2013/2540)

The Industrial Injuries Benefit (Employment Training Schemes and Courses) Regulations 2013

(SI 2013/2540)

ARRANGEMENT OF REGULATIONS

1. Citation, commencement and interpretation.
2. Employment training scheme and employment training course.
3. Employer.
4. Payment of industrial injuries benefit where payments were previously payable under section 11(3) of the Employment and Training Act.
5. Outstanding claims.

10.292

The Secretary of State for Work and Pensions makes the following Regulations in exercise of the powers conferred by sections 95A, 122(1) and 175(1), (3), (4) and (5) of the Social Security Contributions and Benefits Act 1992 and section 66(3) of the Welfare Reform Act 2012.
In accordance with section 172(2) of the Social Security Administration Act 1992 reference has been made to the Industrial Injuries Advisory Council.

10.293

Citation, commencement and interpretation

1.—(1) These Regulations may be cited as the Industrial Injuries Benefit (Employment Training Schemes and Courses) Regulations 2013.

(2) They come into force on 31st October 2013.

(3) In these Regulations—

"the Employment and Training Act" means the Employment and Training Act 1973;

"the Contributions and Benefits Act" means the Social Security Contributions and Benefits Act 1992;

"the Jobseekers Act" means the Jobseekers Act 1995.

10.294

Employment training scheme and employment training course

2. The following descriptions of employment training scheme and employment training course are prescribed for the purposes of section 95A(1) of the Contributions and Benefits Act—

(a) an employment training scheme or employment training course provided pursuant to arrangements made by or on behalf of the Secretary of State or the Scottish or Welsh Ministers under section 2 of the Employment and Training Act (arrangements for the purpose of assisting persons to select, train for, obtain and retain employment);

(b) an employment training scheme or employment training course which constitutes, or participation in which forms part of, a scheme of a description prescribed under section 17A of the Jobseekers Act (schemes for assisting persons to obtain employment: "work for your benefit" schemes etc.);

(c) an employment training scheme or employment training course in which a person participates pursuant to—

(i) a requirement to undertake work-related activity imposed under regulations under section 13 of the Welfare Reform Act 2007; or

10.295

(ii) a work preparation requirement within the meaning of section 6C of the Jobseekers Act, section 11C of the Welfare Reform Act 2007 or section 16 of the Welfare Reform Act 2012.

Employer

10.296   **3.** The persons prescribed for the purposes of section 95A(2) of the Contributions and Benefits Act are any persons providing an employment training scheme or employment training course of a description prescribed under regulation 2 above.

Payment of industrial injuries benefit where payments were previously payable under section 11(3) of the Employment and Training Act

10.297   **4.** Where, before section 66 of the Welfare Reform Act 2012 (trainees) came into force for all purposes, payments were payable to a person in consequence of an injury or disease under section 11(3) of the Employment and Training Act (power to make payments in respect of trainees equivalent to social security benefits in respect of employees), that person is entitled to equivalent payments of industrial injuries benefit.

Outstanding claims

10.298   **5.** Any claim for payments in consequence of an injury or disease under section 11(3) of the Employment and Training Act, which was made but not determined before section 66 of the Welfare Reform Act 2012 came into force for all purposes, is to be treated as a claim for industrial injuries benefit.

PART XI

VACCINE DAMAGE PAYMENTS

The Vaccine Damage Payments Regulations 1979

(SI 1979/432) (*as amended*)

ARRANGEMENT OF REGULATIONS

PART I

GENERAL

1.   Citation, commencement and interpretation.   11.1

PART II

CLAIMS

2.   Claims to be made to the Secretary of State in writing.
3.   Information to be given when making a claim.
4.   Obligations of disabled person.
5.   Vaccinations to be treated as carried out in England.
5A. Circumstances prescribed in relation to cases of damage through contact.
6.   Claims made prior to the passing of the Act.

PART III

REVIEW BY TRIBUNALS

7–10. *Revoked.*

PART IV

DECISIONS REVERSING EARLIER DECISIONS

11. Decisions reversing earlier decisions made by the Secretary of State or appeal tribunals.
12. Procedure by which a decision may be made under section 31A of the Act on the Secretary of State's own initiative.

The Secretary of State for Social Services in exercise of powers conferred on him by sections 2(5), 3(1)(b), 4(1), 5(2), 7(5) and 8(3) of the Vaccine Damage Payments Act 1979 and of all other powers enabling him in that behalf, hereby makes the following regulations:

PART I

GENERAL

11.2

Citation, commencement and interpretation

1.—(1) These regulations may be cited as the Vaccine Damage Payments Regulations 1979 and shall come into operation on 6th April 1979.

(2) In these regulations, unless the context otherwise requires—

"the Act" means the Vaccine Damage Payments Act 1979;

"hearing" means oral hearing;

"medical practitioner" means registered medical practitioner;

"payment" means a payment under section 1(1) of the Act;

[¹ . . .].

(3) Any notice required to be given to any person under the provisions of these regulations may be given by being sent by post to that person at his ordinary or last known address.

AMENDMENT

1. Social Security and Child Support (Decisions and Appeals), Vaccine Damage Payments and Jobseeker's Allowance (Amendment) Regulations 1999 (SI 1999/ 2677) reg.2 (October 18, 1999).

PART II

CLAIMS

Claims to be made to the Secretary of State in writing

11.3

2.—(1) Every claim for payment shall be made in writing to the Secretary of State on the form approved by him, or in such other manner, being in writing, as he may accept as sufficient in the circumstances of any particular case or class of cases.

(2) Any person who has made a claim in accordance with the provisions of this regulation may amend his claim, at any time before a decision has been given thereon, by notice in writing delivered or sent to the Secretary of State, and any claim so amended may be treated as if it had been so amended in the first instance.

Information to be given when making a claim

11.4

3.—Every person who makes a claim shall furnish such certificates, documents, information and evidence for the purpose of determining the claim as may be required by the Secretary of State.

Obligations of disabled person

11.5

4.—(1) Subject to the following provisions of this regulation, every disabled person in respect of whom a claim has been made under section

1594

3 of the Act shall comply with every notice given to him or, where he is not the claimant, to the claimant by the Secretary of State which requires such disabled person to submit himself to a medical examination either by a medical practitioner appointed by the Secretary of State or by [¹ an appeal] tribunal for the purposes of determining whether he is severely disabled as a result of vaccination against any of the diseases to which the Act applies.

(2) Every notice given under the preceding paragraph shall be given in writing and shall specify the time and place of examination and shall not require the disabled person to submit himself to examination before the expiration of the period of fourteen days beginning with the date of the notice or such shorter period as may be reasonable in the circumstances.

AMENDMENT

1. Social Security and Child Support (Decisions and Appeals), Vaccine Damage Payments and Jobseeker's Allowance (Amendment) Regulations 1999 (SI 1999/2677) reg.3 (October 18, 1999).

Vaccinations to be treated as carried out in England

5.—(1) Vaccinations given outside the United Kingdom and the Isle 11.6 of Man to serving members of Her Majesty's forces or members of their families shall be treated for the purposes of the Act as carried out in England where the vaccination in question has been given as part of medical facilities provided under arrangements made by or on behalf of the service authorities.

(2) For the purposes of section 2(5) of the Act—

(a) "serving members of Her Majesty's forces" means a member of the naval, military or air forces of the Crown or of any women's service administered by the Defence Council;

[¹ (b) a person is a member of the family of a serving member of Her Majesty's forces if—

    (i) he is the spouse or civil partner of that serving member,

    (ii) he and that serving member live together as husband and wife or as if they were civil partners, or

    (iii) he is a child whose requirements are provided by that serving member.]

AMENDMENT

1. Vaccine Damage Payments (Amendment) Regulations 2005 (SI 2005/3070) reg.2 (December 5, 2005).

Circumstances prescribed in relation to cases of damage through contact

[¹ **5A.**—The circumstances prescribed for the purposes of section 1(3) 11.7 of the Vaccine Damage Payments Act 1979 (Act to have effect with respect to a person severely disabled as a result of contracting a disease through contact with a third person who was vaccinated against it) are that:—

(1) the disabled person has been in close physical contact with a person who has been vaccinated against poliomyelitis with orally administered vaccine;

(2) that contact occurred within a period of sixty days beginning with the fourth day immediately following such vaccination; and

(3) the disabled person was, within the period referred to in paragraph (2) of this regulation, either—

(a) looking after the person who has been vaccinated, or

(b) himself being looked after together with the person who has been vaccinated.]

AMENDMENT

1. Vaccine Damage Payments (Amendment) Regulations 1979 (SI 1979/1441) reg.2 (December 13, 1979).

Claims made prior to the passing of the Act

11.8   **6.**—(1) A claim made before the passing of the Act in connection with the non-statutory scheme of payments for severe vaccine damage established by the Secretary of State for Social Services in anticipation of the passing of the Act and which has not been disposed of at the commencement of the Act shall be treated as a claim falling within section 3(1) of the Act.

(2) Any information and other evidence furnished and other things done before the commencement of the Act in connection with any such claim made before the passing of the Act shall be treated as furnished or done in connection with a claim falling within section 3(1) of the Act.

PART III

REVIEW BY TRIBUNALS

11.9   *Regulations 7–10 were revoked by the Social Security and Child Support (Decisions and Appeals) Regulations 1999 (SI 1999/991) reg.59 and Sch.4 (October 18, 1999). For previous text, see Rowland, Medical and Disability Appeals Tribunal: The Legislation 1998.*

[¹ PART IV

DECISIONS REVERSING EARLIER DECISIONS

Decisions reversing earlier decisions made by the Secretary of State or appeal tribunals

11.10   **11.**—(1) The Secretary of State may make a decision under 3A(1) of the Act which reverses a decision of his, made under section 3 of the Act, or of an appeal tribunal, made under section 4 of the Act—

(a) pursuant to an application in the circumstances described in paragraph (2) below; or

(b) except where paragraph (3) applies, on his own initiative.

(2) The circumstances referred to in paragraph (1)(a) above are—

(a) the application is made in writing and contains an explanation as to why the applicant believes the decision in respect of which the application is made to be wrong; and

(b) where the application is in respect of a decision of the Secretary of State, the application is made [²at any time after notification of that decision was given but before a decision of an appeal tribunal has been made]; or

(c) where the application is in respect of a decision of an appeal tribunal, the application is made before whichever is the later of—

   (i) the date two years after the date on which notification of that decision was given; or

   (ii) the date six years after the date on which notification of the decision of the Secretary of State which was appealed was given.

(3) This paragraph applies where—

(a) less than 21 days have elapsed since notice under regulation 12 below was given; or

(b) more than six years have elapsed since the date on which notification of that decision was given except where it appears to the Secretary of State that a payment was made in consequence of a misrepresentation or failure to disclose any material fact.

(4) Where the Secretary of State has made a decision under section 3A(1) of the Act, he shall notify—

(a) the disabled person (if he is alive) to whom the decision relates; and

(b) if the disabled person is not a claimant, the claimant who made the claim in respect of that disabled person,

of that decision and the reasons for it.

AMENDMENTS

1. Social Security and Child Support (Decisions and Appeals), Vaccine Damage Payments and Jobseeker's Allowance (Amendment) Regulations 1999 (SI 1999/2677) reg.4 (October 18, 1999).
2. Social Security, Child Support, Vaccine Damage and Other Payments (Decisions and Appeals) (Amendment) Regulations 2013 (SI 2013/2380) reg.2(1), (2) (October 28, 2013).

[¹Consideration of reversal before appeal

11A.— (1) This regulation applies in a case where—
                                                                     11.11

(a) the claimant's address is not in Northern Ireland;

(b) the Secretary of State gives a person written notice of a decision; and

(c) that notice includes a statement to the effect that there is a right of appeal to the First-tier Tribunal in relation to the decision only if the Secretary of State has considered an application for a reversal of the decision.

(2) In a case to which this regulation applies, a person has a right of appeal under section 4 of the Act in relation to the decision only if the Secretary of State has considered whether to reverse the decision under section 3A of the Act.

(3) The notice referred to in paragraph (1) must inform the person that, where the notice does not include a statement of the reasons for the decision, he may, within one month of the date of the notice, request that the Secretary of State provide him with written reasons.

(4) Where written reasons are requested under paragraph (3), the Secretary of State must provide them within 14 days of receipt of the request or as soon as practicable afterwards.

(5) Where, as the result of paragraph (2), there is no right of appeal against a decision, the Secretary of State may treat any purported appeal as an application for a reversal of the decision under section 3A of the Act.]

AMENDMENT

1. Social Security, Child Support, Vaccine Damage and Other Payments (Decisions and Appeals) (Amendment) Regulations 2013 (SI 2013/2380) reg.2(1), (3) (October 28, 2013).

[¹Procedure by which a decision may be made under section 3A of the Act on the Secretary of State's own initiative

11.12   **12.**—Where the Secretary of State on his own initiative proposes to make a decision under section 3A of the Act reversing a decision ("the original decision") of his or of an appeal tribunal he shall give notice in writing of his proposal to—

(a) the disabled person (if he is alive) to whom the original decision relates; and

(b) the claimant in relation to the original decision where he is not the disabled person.]

AMENDMENT

1. Social Security and Child Support (Decisions and Appeals), Vaccine Damage Payments and Jobseeker's Allowance (Amendment) Regulations 1999 (SI 1999/2677) reg.4 (October 18, 1999).

The Vaccine Damage Payments (Specified Disease) Order 1990

(SI 1990/623)

ARRANGEMENT OF ORDER

11.13   1.   Citation and commencement.
         2.   Addition to the diseases to which the Vaccine Damage Payments Act applies.

The Secretary of State for Social Security, in exercise of the powers conferred by section 1(2)(i) of the Vaccine Damage Payments Act 1979 and of all other powers enabling him in that behalf, hereby makes the following Order:

Citation and commencement

11.14   **1.**—This Order may be cited as the Vaccine Damage Payments (Specified Disease) Order 1990 and shall come into force on 9th April 1990.

Addition to the diseases to which the Vaccine Damage Payments Act applies

11.15   **2.**—Mumps is specified as a disease to which the Vaccine Damage Payments Act 1979 applies.

The Vaccine Damage Payments (Specified Disease) Order 1995

(SI 1995/1164)

ARRANGEMENT OF ORDER

1.   Citation and commencement.   11.16
2.   Addition to the diseases to which the Vaccine Damage Payments Act applies.

The Secretary of State for Social Security, in exercise of powers conferred by section 1(2)(i) of the Vaccine Damage Payments Act 1979(a) and of all other powers enabling him in that behalf, hereby makes the following Order:

Citation and commencement

1.—This Order may be cited as the Vaccine Damage Payments (Specified Disease) Order 1995 and shall come into force on 31st May 1995.   11.17

Addition to the diseases to which the Vaccine Damage Payments Act applies

2.—Haemophilus influenza type b infection is specified as a disease to which the Vaccine Damage Payments Act 1979 applies.   11.18

The Vaccine Damage Payments (Specified Disease) Order 2001

(SI 2001/1652)

ARRANGEMENT OF ORDER

1.   Citation and commencement.   11.19
2.   Addition to the diseases to which the Act applies.
3.   Modification of conditions of entitlement.

The Secretary of State for Social Security, in exercise of the powers conferred upon him by sections 1(2)(i) and 2(2) of the Vaccine Damage Payments Act 1979 and of all other powers enabling him in that behalf, hereby makes the following Order:

Citation, commencement and interpretation

1.—(1) This Order may be cited as the Vaccine Damage Payments (Specified Disease) Order 2001 and shall come into force on 30th May 2001.   11.20

(2) In this Order, "the Act" means the Vaccine Damage Payments Act 1979.

Addition to the diseases to which the Act applies

2.—Meningococcal Group C is specified as a disease to which the Act applies.   11.21

Modification of conditions of entitlement

11.22   **3.**—The condition of entitlement in section 2(1)(b) of the Act (age or time at which vaccination was carried out) shall be omitted in relation to vaccination against Meningococcal Group C.

The Vaccine Damage Payments (Specified Disease) Order 2006

(SI 2006/2066)

ARRANGEMENT OF ORDER

11.23   1.   Citation and commencement.
         2.   Addition to the diseases to which the Vaccine Damage Payments Act 1979 applies.

The Secretary of State for Work and Pensions makes the following Order in exercise of the power conferred by section 1(2)(i) of the Vaccine Damage Payments Act 1979.

Citation and commencement

11.24   **1.** This Order may be cited as the Vaccine Damage Payments (Specified Disease) Order 2006 and shall come into force on 4th September 2006.

Addition to the diseases to which the Vaccine Damage Payments Act 1979 applies

11.25   **2.** Pneumococcal infection is specified as a disease to which the Vaccine Damage Payments Act 1979 applies.

The Vaccine Damage Payments (Specified Disease) Order 2008

(SI 2008/2103)

ARRANGEMENT OF ORDER

11.26   1.   Citation, commencement and interpretation
         2.   Addition to the diseases to which the Act applies
         3.   Modification of conditions of entitlement
         The Secretary of State for Work and Pensions makes the following Order in exercise of the powers conferred by sections 1(2)(i) and 2(2) of the Vaccine Damage Payments Act 1979.

Citation, commencement and interpretation

11.27   **1.**—(1) This Order may be cited as the Vaccine Damage Payments (Specified Disease) Order 2008 and shall come into force on 1st September 2008.

(2) In this Order, "the Act" means the Vaccine Damage Payments Act 1979.

Addition to the diseases to which the Act applies

2. Human papillomavirus is specified as a disease to which the Act applies.   **11.28**

Modification of conditions of entitlement

3. The condition of entitlement in section 2(1)(b) of the Act (age or time at which vaccination was carried out) shall be omitted in relation to vaccination against human papillomavirus.   **11.29**

The Vaccine Damage Payments (Specified Disease) Order 2009

(SI 2009/2516)

ARRANGEMENT OF ORDER

1.   Citation, commencement and interpretation   **11.30**
2.   Addition to the diseases to which the Act applies
3.   Modification of conditions of entitlement

The Secretary of State for Work and Pensions makes the following Order in exercise of the power conferred by sections 1(2)(i) and 2(2) of the Vaccine Damage Payments Act 1979(1).

Citation, commencement and interpretation

1.—(1) This Order may be cited as the Vaccine Damage Payments (Specified Disease) Order 2009 and comes into force on 10th October 2009.   **11.31**
(2) In this Order, "the Act" means the Vaccine Damage Payments Act 1979.

Addition to the diseases to which the Act applies

2. Influenza caused by the pandemic influenza A (H1N1) 2009 virus is specified as a disease to which the Act applies.   **11.32**

Modification of conditions of entitlement

3. The condition of entitlement in section 2(1)(b) of the Act (age or time at which vaccination was carried out) shall be omitted in relation to vaccination against influenza caused by the pandemic influenza A (H1N1) 2009 virus.   **11.33**

GENERAL NOTE

This Order was revoked with effect from September 1, 2010 by the Vaccine Damage Payments (Specified Disease) (Revocation and Savings) Order 2010 (SI 2010/1988), below. Influenza caused by the pandemic influenza A (H1N1) 2009 virus ("swine flu") thus ceases from that date to be one of the specified diseases to which the Act applies. Article 4 of that Revocation and Savings Order ensures, however, that protection under the Act remains applicable to anyone who received the vaccination against "swine flu" prior to September 1, 2010.   **11.34**

The Vaccine Damage Payments (Specified Disease) (Revocation and Savings) Order 2010

(SI 2010/1988)

ARRANGEMENT OF ORDER

11.35   1., 2. Citation, commencement and interpretation.
3. Revocation.
4. Savings.
The Secretary of State for Work and Pensions makes the following Order in exercise of the power conferred by sections 1(2)(i) and 2(2) of the Vaccine Damage Payments Act 1979.

Citation, commencement and interpretation

11.36   **1.** This Order may be cited as the Vaccine Damage Payments (Specified Disease) (Revocation and Savings) Order 2010 and comes into force on 1st September 2010.

11.37   **2.** The "2009 Order" means the Vaccine Damage Payments (Specified Disease) Order 2009.

Revocation

11.38   **3.** Subject to article (4), the 2009 Order is revoked.

Savings

11.39   **4.** The 2009 Order shall continue to apply to any vaccination administered prior to the date this Order comes into force.

The Vaccine Damage Payments (Specified Disease) Order 2015

(SI 2015/47)

ARRANGEMENT OF ORDER

11.40   1.   Citation, commencement and interpretation
2.   Additions to the list of diseases to which the Act applies
3.   Modification of conditions of entitlement

The Secretary of State for Health, in exercise of the powers conferred by sections 1(2)(i) and 2(2) of the Vaccine Damage Payments Act 1979, makes the following Order.

Citation, commencement and interpretation

11.41   **1.**—(1) This Order may be cited as the Vaccine Damage Payments (Specified Disease) Order 2015 and comes into force on 28th February 2015.

(2) In this Order, "the Act" means the Vaccine Damage Payments Act 1979.

Additions to the list of diseases to which the Act applies

2.—(1) Subject to paragraph (2), the following are specified as diseases   **11.42**
to which the Act applies—
(a) rotavirus; and
(b) influenza, other than influenza caused by a pandemic influenza virus.
(2) Paragraph (1)(b) does not affect any entitlement which arises under
the Vaccine Damage Payments (Specified Disease) Order 2009 (addition
of influenza caused by the pandemic influenza A (H1N1) 2009 virus) and
references in this Order to pandemic influenza are to be interpreted accordingly.

Modification of conditions of entitlement

3. The conditions of entitlement in section 2(1) of the Act have effect   **11.43**
subject to the following modifications—
(a) in relation to vaccination against rotavirus, in sub-paragraph (ii) of
    section 2(1)(a), for "5th July 1948" substitute "1st July 2013";
(b) in relation to vaccination against influenza, other than influenza
    caused by a pandemic influenza virus, in sub-paragraph (ii) of
    section 2(1)(a), for "5th July 1948" substitute "1st September
    2013";
(c) in relation to vaccination against rotavirus or influenza, other than
    influenza caused by a pandemic influenza virus, for paragraph (b) of
    section 2(1) substitute—
"(b) that the vaccination was carried out at a time when the person to
    whom it was given was under the age of eighteen; and".

The Vaccine Damage Payments (Specified Disease) Order 2016

(SI 2016/454)

ARRANGEMENT OF ORDER

1.   Citation, commencement and interpretation   **11.44**
2.   Additions to the list of diseases to which the Act applies
3.   Modifications of conditions of entitlement
    The Secretary of State for Health, in exercise of the powers conferred by sections
1(2)(i) and 2(2) of the Vaccine Damage Payments Act 1979, makes the following
Order:

Citation, commencement and interpretation

1.—(1) This Order may be cited as the Vaccine Damage Payments   **11.45**
(Specified Disease) Order 2016 and comes into force on 29th April 2016.
(2) In this Order, "the Act" means the Vaccine Damage Payments Act
1979.

Additions to the list of diseases to which the Act applies

2.— The following are specified as diseases to which the Act applies—   **11.46**

    (a) Meningococcal Group W; and

    (b) Meningococcal Group B.

Modification of conditions of entitlement

11.47   **3.**— The conditions of entitlement in section 2(1) of the Act have effect subject to the following modifications—

    (a) in relation to vaccination against Meningococcal Group W, in sub-paragraph (ii) of section 2(1)(a), for "5th July 1948" substitute "1st August 2015";

    (b) in relation to vaccination against Meningococcal Group B, in sub-paragraph (ii) of section 2(1)(a), for "5th July 1948" substitute "1st September 2015";

    (c) in relation to vaccination against Meningococcal Group W, in paragraph (b) of section 2(1), for "eighteen" substitute "twenty-six".

GENERAL NOTE

11.48   Note that in relation to Meningococcal Group W, the condition of entitlement in s.2(1)(b) of the 1979 Act that the vaccination was carried out when the person to whom it was given was under the age of 18 is modified. For this vaccine the maximum age is raised such that the person to whom this vaccination was given was under the age of 26 at the time the vaccination was carried out. The reason for this change is that vaccination against Meningococcal Group W is also recommended for first time university and college entrants who have missed the adolescent booster. There is no change to the alternative condition of entitlement that the vaccination was carried out at the time of an outbreak within the United Kingdom or on the Isle of Man.

The Vaccine Damage Payments Act 1979 Statutory Sum Order 2007

(SI 2007/1931)

ARRANGEMENT OF ORDER

11.49   1.   Citation and commencement

    2.   Statutory sum for the purposes of the Vaccine Damage Payments Act 1979

    3.   Revocation

A draft of the following Order was laid before Parliament in accordance with section 1(4A) of the Vaccine Damage Payments Act 1979 and approved by resolution of each House of Parliament:

The Secretary of State for Work and Pensions with the consent of the Treasury, in exercise of the powers conferred by section 1(1A) of the Vaccine Damage Payments Act 1979, makes the following Order:

Citation and commencement

11.50   **1.** This Order may be cited as the Vaccine Damage Payments Act 1979 Statutory Sum Order 2007 and shall come into force on 12th July 2007.

Statutory sum for the purposes of the Vaccine Damage Payments Act 1979

2. For the purposes of the Vaccine Damage Payments Act 1979 the statutory sum is £120,000.

11.51

Revocation

3. The Vaccine Damage Payments Act 1979 Statutory Sum Order 2000 is hereby revoked.

11.52

GENERAL NOTE

This Order entered into force on July 12, 2007. It raised the statutory sum from £100,000 to £120,000.

11.53

PART XII

MESOTHELIOMA LUMP SUM PAYMENTS

The Mesothelioma Lump Sum Payments (Claims and Reconsiderations) Regulations 2008

(SI 2008/1595)

ARRANGEMENT OF REGULATIONS

1.	Citation, commencement and interpretation	12.1
2.	Making a claim	
3.	Time for making a claim	
4.	Reconsideration	
4A.	Late application for reconsideration	
4B.	Reconsideration before appeal	
5.	Appeal treated as reconsideration	
6.	Appeals	

The Secretary of State for Work and Pensions in exercise of the powers conferred by section 48(1) to (3), 49(2), 50(4) and 53(2) of the Child Maintenance and Other Payments Act 2008 makes the following Regulations.

GENERAL NOTE

See generally the annotations to ss.48–51 of the Child Maintenance and Other Payments Act 2008 above.   12.2

Citation, commencement and interpretation

1.—(1) These Regulations may be cited as the Mesothelioma Lump Sum   12.3
Payments (Claims and Reconsiderations) Regulations 2008 and shall come into force on 1st October 2008.

(2) In these Regulations—
"claim" means a claim under section 46(1) of the Child Maintenance and Other Payments Act 2008;
"mesothelioma" means diffuse mesothelioma.

Making a claim

2.—(1) Subject to paragraph (2), a claim must be made in writing, signed   12.4
by or on behalf of the person making the claim, on a form approved by the Secretary of State and accompanied by the documents specified in the form.

(2) A claim may be made in such other manner, being in writing, as the Secretary of State may accept as sufficient in the circumstances of any particular case.

Time for making a claim

3.—(1) A claim by a person who has been diagnosed with mesothelioma   12.5
before the coming into force of these Regulations must be made within 12 months from the date on which these Regulations come into force.

(2) A claim by any other person with mesothelioma must be made within 12 months from the date on which that person was first diagnosed with mesothelioma.

(3) A claim by a dependant must be made within 12 months from the

date of death of the person who, immediately before death, had mesothelioma.

(4) Where the Secretary of State considers there was good cause for the claim not being made within the 12 month time limit referred to in paragraphs (1) to (3), he may extend the time limit for such period as he considers appropriate in the circumstances, provided that the time limit is not extended for a death or diagnosis which occurred more than 12 months before the date these Regulations come into force.

Reconsideration

12.6   **4.**—(1) An application made to the Secretary of State for reconsideration of a determination that a payment should or should not be made must—

  (a) be made within one month of the date of notification of the determination, [¹ . . .]

[¹ (aa) where a written statement is requested under regulation 4B(3) (reconsideration before appeal) and is provided within the period specified in sub-paragraph (a) above, be made within 14 days of the expiry of that period,

  (ab) where a written statement is requested under regulation 4B(3) (reconsideration before appeal) and is provided after the period specified in sub-paragraph (a) above, be made within 14 days of the date on which the statement is provided, or

  (ac) be made within such longer period as may be allowed under regulation 4A (late application for reconsideration), and].

  (b) specify the ground for the request and give such other relevant information as the Secretary of State may require in order to deal adequately with the reconsideration.

(2) The Secretary of State may, at any time, in writing, institute a reconsideration of a determination that a payment should or should not be made.

AMENDMENT

1. Social Security, Child Support, Vaccine Damage and Other Payments (Decisions and Appeals) (Amendment) Regulations 2013 (SI 2013/2380) reg.5(2) and (3) (October 28, 2013).

[¹ Late application for reconsideration

12.7   **4A.** —Where, in a case to which regulation 4B (reconsideration before appeal) applies, the Secretary of State considers there was good cause for not applying for reconsideration of a determination within the time limit specified in regulation 4(1) (reconsideration), he may extend the time limit for such period as he considers appropriate in the circumstances.]

AMENDMENT

1. Social Security, Child Support, Vaccine Damage and Other Payments (Decisions and Appeals) (Amendment) Regulations 2013 (SI 2013/2380) reg.5(4) (October 28, 2013).

[¹ Reconsideration before appeal

12.8   **4B.** —(1) This regulation applies in a case where—

(a) the Secretary of State gives a person written notice of a determination made on a claim; and

(b) that notice includes a statement to the effect that there is a right of appeal to the First-tier Tribunal in relation to the determination only if the Secretary of State has, on an application, decided whether to reconsider the determination.

(2) In a case to which this regulation applies, a person may appeal against the determination only if the Secretary of State has decided on an application whether to reconsider the determination under section 49 of the Child Maintenance and Other Payments Act 2008 ("the 2008 Act").

(3) The notice referred to in paragraph (1) must inform the person—

(a) of the time limit specified in regulation 4(1) for making an application for reconsideration of the determination; and

(b) that, where the notice does not include a statement of the reasons for the determination ("written reasons"), he may, within one month of the date of notification of the determination, request that the Secretary of State provide him with written reasons.

(4) Where written reasons are requested under paragraph (3)(b), the Secretary of State must provide them within 14 days of receipt of the request or as soon as practicable afterwards.

(5) Where, as the result of paragraph (2), there is no right of appeal against a determination made on a claim, the Secretary of State may treat any purported appeal as an application for reconsideration of the determination under section 49 of the 2008 Act.]

AMENDMENT

1. Social Security, Child Support, Vaccine Damage and Other Payments (Decisions and Appeals) (Amendment) Regulations 2013 (SI 2013/2380) reg.5(4) (October 28, 2013).

Appeal treated as reconsideration

5.—(1) Where a person appeals against a determination made by the Secretary of State on a claim, the Secretary of State may treat the appeal as an application for reconsideration under section 49 of the Child Maintenance and Other Payments Act 2008.

(2) [¹ . . .]

(3) [¹ . . .]

12.9

AMENDMENT

1. Social Security, Child Support, Vaccine Damage and Other Payments (Decisions and Appeals) (Amendment) Regulations 2013 (SI 2013/2380) reg.5(5) (October 28, 2013).

GENERAL NOTE

The repeals of paras (2) and (3) are subject to the transitional and savings provisions in Social Security, Child Support, Vaccine Damage and Other Payments (Decisions and Appeals) (Amendment) Regulations 2013 (SI 2013/2380) reg.8(1), such that the amendments do not apply in any case where the notice of the decision to which the appeal relates was posted to the appellant's last known address before October 28, 2013.

12.10

[¹ **Appeals**

12.11   **6.** [² . . .]

AMENDMENTS

1. Mesothelioma Lump Sum Payments (Claims and Reconsiderations) (Amendment) Regulations 2008 (SI 2008/2706) reg.4 (November 3, 2008).
2. Social Security, Child Support, Vaccine Damage and Other Payments (Decisions and Appeals) (Amendment) Regulations 2013 (SI 2013/2380) reg.5(5) (October 28, 2013).

GENERAL NOTE

12.12   The repeals of reg.6 is subject to the transitional and savings provisions in Social Security, Child Support, Vaccine Damage and Other Payments (Decisions and Appeals) (Amendment) Regulations 2013 (SI 2013/2380) reg.8(1), such that the repeal does not apply in any case where the notice of the decision to which the appeal relates was posted to the appellant's last known address before October 28, 2013.

The Mesothelioma Lump Sum Payments (Conditions and Amounts) Regulations 2008

(SI 2008/1963)

ARRANGEMENT OF REGULATIONS

12.13   1.   Citation, commencement and interpretation
2.   Disqualifying payments
3.   Disregarded payments
4.   Presence in the United Kingdom
5.   Amount of lump sum payment
6.   Amendment of Pneumoconiosis etc. (Workers' Compensation) (Payment of Claims) Regulations 1988

The Secretary of State for Work and Pensions in exercise of the powers conferred by section 1(1) of the Pneumoconiosis etc. (Workers' Compensation) Act 1979 and sections 46(3) and 47 of the Child Maintenance and Other Payments Act 2008 makes the following Regulations.

Citation, commencement and interpretation

12.14   **1.**—(1) These Regulations may be cited as the Mesothelioma Lump Sum Payments (Conditions and Amounts) Regulations 2008.
(2) These Regulations shall come into force on 1st October 2008.
(3) In these Regulations—
"the Act" means the Child Maintenance and Other Payments Act 2008;
"claim" means a claim under section 46(1) of the Act;
"deceased" means a person who, immediately before death, had diffuse mesothelioma;
"mesothelioma" means diffuse mesothelioma;
"payment" includes a payment in money or money's worth or in kind.

Disqualifying payments

2.—(1) The following payments are prescribed for the purposes of   12.15
section 47(1)(a), (2)(a) and (3)(e) of the Act (payments which, if made in
consequence of diffuse mesothelioma, prevent the conditions provided for
in section 47(1)(a) and (2)(a) from being fulfilled)—
  (a) payment under the Naval, Military and Air Forces Etc. (Disablement
      and Death) Service Pensions Order 2006;
  (b) payment under the Armed Forces and Reserve Forces (Compensation
      Scheme) Order 2005;
[¹ (c) payment from any government department, authority, body cor-
      porate or employer exempted from insurance by or under section
      3 of the Employers' Liability (Compulsory Insurance) Act 1969
      or Article 7 of the Employers' Liability (Defective Equipment and
      Compulsory Insurance) (Northern Ireland) Order 1972];
  (d) payment under the UK Asbestos Trust established on 10th October
      2006, for the benefit of certain persons suffering from asbestos-
      related diseases;
  (e) payment under the EL Scheme Trust established on 23rd November
      2006, for the benefit of certain persons suffering from asbestos-
      related diseases.
  (2) The following payments are prescribed for the purposes of section
47(1)(b) and (2)(b) of the Act (payments eligibility for which prevents the
conditions provided for in section 47(1)(b) or (2)(b) from being fulfilled)—
  (a) payment under the Naval, Military and Air Forces Etc. (Disablement
      and Death) Service Pensions Order 2006;
  (b) payment under the Armed Forces and Reserve Forces (Compensation
      Scheme) Order 2005.

AMENDMENT

  1. Social Security (Miscellaneous Amendments) (No.3) Regulations 2008 (SI
2008/2365) reg.5 (October 1, 2008).

Disregarded payments

3. A payment made in error and which in consequence is liable to be   12.16
repaid in accordance with a statutory provision or rule of law, is to be disregarded for the purpose of section 47(1)(a) or (2)(a) of the Act (conditions
of entitlement).

Presence in the United Kingdom

4.—(1) In the case of a person with mesothelioma it is a condition of   12.17
entitlement that the person was in the United Kingdom at a time when and
place where that person was exposed to asbestos.
  (2) In the case of a dependant it is a condition of entitlement that the
deceased was in the United Kingdom at a time when and place where the
deceased was exposed to asbestos.

GENERAL NOTE

  See the commentary to s.47 of the Child Maintenance and Other Payments Act   12.18
2008 for discussion as to the possibly ultra vires nature of this provision.

Amount of lump sum payment

12.19   **5.**—(1) The amount of a payment made under section 46(2) of the Act to a person with mesothelioma shall be determined in accordance with Table 1 of the Schedule.

(2) In Table 1 of the Schedule, the reference to the age of the person is a reference to—

(a) the age at which the person was first diagnosed with mesothelioma; or

(b) where the age at which the person was first diagnosed with mesothelioma is unknown, the age at which the person made the claim.

(3) The amount of a payment made under section 46(2) of the Act to a dependant shall be determined in accordance with Table 2 of the Schedule.

(4) In Table 2 of the Schedule, the reference to the age of the person with mesothelioma is a reference to the age of that person at death.

Amendment of Pneumoconiosis etc. (Workers' Compensation) (Payment of Claims) Regulations 1988

12.20   **6.** At the end of regulation 3 of the Pneumoconiosis etc. (Workers' Compensation) (Payment of Claims) Regulations 1988 (payments to persons disabled by disease), add—

"(5) Where—

(a) a payment is made to a person under section 46 of the Child Maintenance and Other Payments Act 2008 (the mesothelioma payment) in respect of diffuse mesothelioma,

(b) subsequently it is determined that the same person is entitled to a payment under section 1(1) of the Act in respect of the same diffuse mesothelioma,

the amount payable under paragraph (1) shall be reduced by the amount of the mesothelioma payment.".

SCHEDULE   **Regulation 5**

12.21   **[¹ Table 1**
Amount of lump sum payment to person with mesothelioma

Age of person with mesothelioma at first diagnosis or, if unknown, date of claim	Payment £
37 and under	92,259
38	90,465
39	88,675
40	86,885
41	85,091
42	83,300
43	82,407
44	81,506
45	80,614

Age of person with mesothelioma at first diagnosis or, if unknown, date of claim	Payment £
46	79,717
47	78,821
48	76,318
49	73,810
50	71,298
51	68,793
52	66,278
53	64,489
54	62,700
55	60,912
56	59,112
57	57,322
58	52,666
59	48,006
60	43,355
61	38,695
62	34,038
63	31,170
64	28,301
65	25,440
66	22,572
67	19,707
68	19,123
69	18,537
70	17,961
71	17,378
72	16,798
73	16,302
74	15,797
75	15,314
76	14,828
77 and over	14,334";

Table 2
Amount of lump sum payment to dependant

Age of person with mesothelioma at death	Payment £
37 and under	48,013
38	46,980
39	45,950
40	44,921
41	43,891
42	42,861
43	41,875
44	40,881
45	39,902
46	38,917
47	37,934
48	36,725
49	35,512
50	34,306
51	33,100
52	31,892
53	30,901
54	29,919
55	28,934
56	27,942
57	26,960
58	24,233
59	21,497
60	18,768
61	16,034
62	13,299
63	12,518
64	11,743
65	10,949
66	10,167
67 and over	7,949]

AMENDMENT

1. Mesothelioma Lump Sum Payments (Conditions and Amounts) (Amendment) Regulations 2019 (SI 2019/369) reg.2 (April 1, 2019).

The Diffuse Mesothelioma Payment Scheme Regulations 2014

(SI 2014/916)

ARRANGEMENT OF REGULATIONS

Introductory

1. Citation   12.22
2. Commencement and ceasing to have effect
3. Interpretation
4. Establishment of the scheme

Scheme administrator

5. General duties of the scheme administrator

Eligibility

6. First diagnosis of diffuse mesothelioma and specified payments
7. Circumstances in which a person is to be treated as unable to bring an action

Applications and procedure

8. The application
9. Time limit for making an application
10. Power of scheme administrator to obtain additional documents or evidence
11. Request to applicants to provide additional documents or evidence
12. Duty of applicants
13. Request to third parties to provide documents
14. Withdrawal of an application by person with diffuse mesothelioma
15. Notice for a person to cease to be an eligible dependant

Determination of applications

16. Determination of applications
17. Imposing conditions on the making of a payment
18. Notice of a determination

Payments

19. Payment
20. Circumstances in which a person may be required to repay

Reviews and appeals

21. Review at the request of an applicant
22. Review initiated by the scheme administrator
23. Other circumstances in which a review may be held
24. Conduct of the review
25. Appeal

Scheme administrator's functions to help people bring proceedings

26. Circumstances in which scheme administrator may help people to bring proceedings

Review of these Regulations

27. Review of these Regulations by the Secretary of State

SCHEDULE 1 First diagnosis of diffuse mesothelioma
SCHEDULE 2 Specified Payments
SCHEDULE 3 Information and other material in support of an application
SCHEDULE 4 Amount of Scheme Payments

The Secretary of State makes the following Regulations in exercise of the powers conferred by section 1 and section 17(4) of the Mesothelioma Act 2014.

In accordance with section 17(2)(a) of that Act, as these are the first regulations under section 1, a draft has been laid before Parliament and approved by a resolution of each House of Parliament.

GENERAL NOTE

12.23 The Diffuse Mesothelioma Payment Scheme Regulations 2014, which came into force on April 6, 2014, provide the detail which is largely absent from the Mesothelioma Act 2014. Their purpose is defined by reg.4, namely to "establish the Diffuse Mesothelioma Payment Scheme for making payments to eligible people with diffuse mesothelioma and eligible dependants under sections 2 and 3 of the Act." Although applications were accepted from April 2014, the first payments were expected to be made from July 2014, once the new compensation rates set out in the amended Sch.4 to the Regulations are in force. The Department for Work and Pensions estimates that there will be around 28,500 deaths from diffuse mesothelioma in the United Kingdom between July 2012 and March 2024. The Department's best estimate is that in the absence of the new scheme about 10 per cent (2,900) of these cases will be unable to trace either their employer or their employer's insurer. With the new scheme in place, and once behavioural changes have been factored in, the estimate is that there will be approximately 3,900 claimants and 3,500 awards made over a 10-year period (DWP, *Mesothelioma Payment Scheme: Impact Assessment*, March 2014). The DWP estimates that around 90 per cent of claims will be successful, in line with civil compensation claims for mesothelioma. However, where awards are refused, there is the possibility of review and then appeal to the First-tier Tribunal (see regs 21–25).

Note that HMRC may disclose information held by them to a person who applies for a payment under the Diffuse Mesothelioma Payment Scheme, on the basis that he or she is eligible for such a payment under s.3, for use in connection with the application (Deregulation Act 2015 s.85(1)(c)). Note also that in addition, and with effect from July 31, 2017, s.77 of the Digital Economy Act 2017 enables HMRC to share the name and address of an employer and associated reference numbers with the Employer Liability Tracing Office (ELTO) for the purpose of assisting with such claims. ELTO is a non-profit making company that maintains a database of insurance policies to enable employees to trace former or current employers and their insurers in order to obtain compensation for workplace injuries. It is anticipated that access to this information will help to improve the quality of the ELTO databases.

Citation

1.—These Regulations may be cited as the Diffuse Mesothelioma Payment Scheme Regulations 2014.

12.24

Commencement and ceasing to have effect

2.—(1) These Regulations, apart from regulation 7(2)(c), come into force on the day after the
day on which they are made.

12.25

(2) Regulation 7(2)(c) comes into force when sections 4 to 7 (relevant persons) of the Third
Parties (Rights against Insurers) Act 2010 come into force.

(3) Regulation 7(2)(a) and (b) cease to have effect when regulation 7(2)(c) comes into force.

Interpretation

3.—In these Regulations—
    "the Act" means the Mesothelioma Act 2014;
    "applicant" unless the context requires otherwise, means a person who makes an application(1) on the basis that they are eligible under sections 2 or 3 of the Act;
    "relevant deduction" means a deduction of—

12.26

(a) the amount of the recoverable benefit which is deducted by virtue of—
    (i) section 8A of the Social Security (Recovery of Benefits) Act 1997, or
    (ii) article 10A of the Social Security (Recovery of Benefits) (Northern Ireland) Order 1997; or

(b) the amount of a lump sum payment which is recovered under regulations made under—
    (i) section 1A of the Social Security (Recovery of Benefits) Act 1997, or
    (ii) article 3A of the Social Security (Recovery of Benefits) (Northern Ireland) Order 1997.

Establishment of the scheme

12.27   **4.**—These Regulations establish the Diffuse Mesothelioma Payment Scheme for making payments to eligible people with diffuse mesothelioma and eligible dependants under sections 2 and 3 of the Act.

Scheme administrator

General duties of the scheme administrator

12.28   **5.**—(1) The scheme administrator must provide such information in connection with the operation of the scheme as the scheme administrator considers appropriate.

(2) Information provided under paragraph (1) may, in particular, relate to—

    (a) the procedure for making an application;

    (b) the medical evidence likely to be required to support a diagnosis of diffuse mesothelioma;

    (c) any other evidence likely to be required to establish that a person is eligible under section 2 or 3 of the Act for a payment under the scheme;

    (d) the determination of an application;

    (e) reviews and appeals.

(3) The scheme administrator must—

    (a) in considering an application, apply the normal civil standard of proof (the balance of probability) when deciding all matters of fact which require evidence to establish them;

    (b) make the application forms available on request free of charge; and

    (c) take all steps it considers reasonable to publicise the scheme.

(4) The scheme administrator must ensure that a sufficient number of persons with appropriate training and qualifications are available to decide the matters likely to arise in determining an application.

GENERAL NOTE

12.29   Gallagher Bassett, the claims-handling company which originally won the Government contract to administer the scheme, has been replaced with effect from April 1, 2018 by TopMark Claims Management Ltd (see its dedicated website at *http://www.mesoscheme.org.uk*).

Eligibility

First diagnosis of diffuse mesothelioma and specified payments

12.30   **6.**—(1) For the purposes of sections 2 and 3 of the Act (eligible people with diffuse mesothelioma and eligible dependants) and of these Regulations—

    (a) the meaning of "first diagnosed" is to be determined in accordance with Schedule 1 to these Regulations; and

    (b) "specified payment" means a payment specified in Schedule 2 to these Regulations.

The claimant must have been first diagnosed with the disease on or after July 25,   12.31
2012 (Mesothelioma Act 2014, s.2(1)(b)). The meaning of "first diagnosed" must
be determined in accordance with Schedule 1 to the Regulations. In summary, this
means that a health care professional must have made a diagnosis of diffuse mesothelioma and either the victim or a "connected person" has been officially advised
of that diagnosis. There are detailed provisions in Schedule 1 defining precisely how
the date of such diagnosis is to be determined, depending on whether it is communicated orally, by letter or by e-mail.

Circumstances in which a person is to be treated as unable to bring an action

7.—(1) For the purposes of section 18(3) of the Act, the circumstances   12.32
in which a person is not to be treated as able to bring an action are that an
employer against whom the person is able to bring an action in respect of
diffuse mesothelioma can be found or does exist, but—
   (a) that employer is a person whose circumstances are such that they fall
       within any of the relevant provisions; and
   (b) no other employer or insurer can be found or exists against whom
       the person can maintain an action for damages.
(2) In this regulation "relevant provisions" means—
   (a) section 1 of the Third Parties (Rights against Insurers) Act 1930;
   (b) section 1 of the Third Parties (Rights Against Insurers) Act (Northern
       Ireland) 1930;
   (c) sections 4 to 7 of the Third Parties (Rights against Insurers) Act
       2010;
   (d) section 130 of the Health and Social Care Act 2012 and any regula-
       tions made under that section;
   (e) articles 41 to 43 of the Water and Sewerage Services (Northern
       Ireland) Order 2006; or
   (f) section 17 of the Energy Act (Northern Ireland) 2011.

Applications and procedure

The application

8.—(1) Any application must be made in writing to the scheme adminis-   12.33
trator in such format as the scheme administrator may approve.
   (2) An application must contain or be accompanied by such information
or other material as the scheme administrator may reasonably require for
the purposes of enabling the scheme administrator to determine whether
the applicant is eligible under section 2 or 3 of the Act for a payment under
the scheme.
   (3) The scheme administrator may, in particular, require an applicant
to provide the information or other material which is specified in Part 1 of
Schedule 3 to these Regulations.
   (4) Part 2 of Schedule 3 sets out the key issues that must be addressed by
the information and other material required under Part 1 of that Schedule.
   (5) The scheme administrator may require the applicant to provide evidence in support of the application, including in particular evidence dealing
with matters specified in Part 3 of Schedule 3.
   (6) Unless paragraph (7) applies, the application must also contain a

statement signed by the applicant that the applicant believes the matters stated as facts in the application to be true.

(7) Where the applicant is unable to sign the statement on account of the applicant's physical or mental condition, a person other than the applicant may sign the statement on the application stating that the person who signs it believes the matters stated as facts in the application to be true.

Time limit for making an application

12.34   **9.**—(1) The application by a person applying on the basis that they are eligible under section 2 of the Act (eligible people with diffuse mesothelioma) must be sent so that it is received by the scheme administrator—

(a) before the end of the day that is 3 years after the date on which the applicant was first diagnosed with diffuse mesothelioma; or

(b) if the applicant was diagnosed with diffuse mesothelioma on or after 25th July 2012 but before these Regulations came into force, before the end of the day that is 3 years after the day on which these Regulations came into force.

(2) The application by a person applying on the basis that they are eligible under section 3 of the Act (eligible dependants) must be sent so that it is received by the scheme administrator—

(a) before the end of the day that is 3 years after the date on which the person with diffuse mesothelioma was first diagnosed with the disease; or

(b) if the person with diffuse mesothelioma died on or after 25th July 2012 but before these Regulations came into force, before the end of the day that is 3 years after the day on which these Regulations came into force.

(3) The scheme administrator may extend the time limits in paragraph (1) or (2) by a further period where the scheme administrator considers that there was good reason for the failure to make the application before the end of the periods mentioned in those paragraphs and for any delay since then in making the application.

Power of scheme administrator to obtain additional documents or evidence

12.35   **10.**—Before making a determination of an application, the scheme administrator may—

(a) in accordance with regulation 11, request an applicant to provide such additional documents or evidence in support of the application as the scheme administrator may reasonably require for the purposes of determining the application;

(b) in accordance with regulation 13, request a person other than the applicant to provide specified documents where it appears to the scheme administrator that the document is reasonably required for the purposes of determining the application.

Request to applicants to provide additional documents or evidence

12.36   **11.**—(1) A request for any additional documents or evidence ("requested material") which is made under regulation 10(a) must—

(a) be made in writing; and

(b) specify such period, which must not be less than 14 days from the date of the written request, as is reasonable in all the circumstances within which the requested material is to be provided.

(2) Where any requested material is not provided within the specified period, the scheme administrator must—

(a) send a written notice to the applicant reminding the applicant of the request; and

(b) specify a further reasonable period, which must not be less than 7 days from the date of the written notice, within which the requested material is to be provided.

(3) On the expiry of that further period, the scheme administrator must determine the application on the basis of all the information relating to the application which is then before the scheme administrator whether or not the requested material has been provided.

(4) Any material which the scheme administrator receives after the application is determined is to be treated as a request made by the applicant for a review of the determination under regulation 21.

(5) If, in all the circumstances, the scheme administrator is satisfied that it is appropriate to do so, the scheme administrator may meet the reasonable costs of the applicant which are incurred in obtaining any requested material.

Duty of applicants

12.—(1) As soon as reasonably practicable, an applicant must inform the scheme administrator of—   12.37

(a) any matter that comes to the applicant's attention which may be relevant to the question whether the applicant is eligible under section 2 or 3 of the Act for a payment under the scheme; and

(b) any change in the applicant's address for correspondence.

(2) An applicant must, so far as reasonably practicable, provide any other assistance to the scheme administrator which the scheme administrator requests in connection with the consideration of the application.

Request to third parties to provide documents

13.—(1) A request which is made under regulation 10(b) for a person   12.38
other than the applicant to provide any document may be made following a request made by an applicant to the scheme administrator or on the scheme administrator's own initiative.

(2) The request must be made in writing and must specify—

(a) the document or documents to be produced; and

(b) such period, which must not be less than 14 days from the date of the written request, as is reasonable in all the circumstances within which any specified document is to be produced.

(3) Where any requested document is not produced within the specified period, the scheme administrator must—

(a) send a written notice to the person reminding the person of the request; and

(b) specify a further reasonable period, which must not be less than 7 days from the date of the notice, within which the requested document is to be produced.

(4) The scheme administrator may apply to the court for an order under paragraph (5) where the person has failed to produce a requested document within the further period referred to in paragraph (3).

(5) A court may make an order requiring a person to produce any document requested if it considers it appropriate to do so.

(6) "Court" means—

(a) in England and Wales or Northern Ireland a county court or the High

(b) in Scotland the sheriff or the Court of Session.

Withdrawal of an application by person with diffuse mesothelioma

12.39   **14.**—An application which is made by a person with diffuse mesothelioma may be withdrawn by the applicant at any time before a payment under the scheme is made to the applicant.

Notice for a person to cease to be an eligible dependant

12.40   **15.**—(1) For the purposes of section 3(3) of the Act (which makes provision for a person who does not want a payment under the scheme to cease to be an eligible dependant), notice is given by a person in accordance with the scheme if it is given in writing to the scheme administrator at any time before a payment under the scheme is made to that person.

(2) On receipt of a notice sent by a person in accordance with paragraph (1), the scheme administrator must send a written acknowledgement to the person confirming receipt of the notice.

Determination of applications

Determination of applications

12.41   **16.**—(1) In making a determination the scheme administrator must—

(a) refuse to make a payment in a case where the scheme administrator determines that the applicant does not meet the conditions in sections 2 or 3 of the Act;

(b) decide to make a payment of an amount set out in the second column of the table in Schedule 4 to these Regulations (Amount of Scheme Payment) which corresponds with the age of the person with diffuse mesothelioma in the first column of that Schedule.

(2) Where the scheme administrator makes a determination under paragraph (1)(b) it must—

(i) take account of any conditions imposed under regulation 17;

(ii) take account of any relevant deduction; and

(iii) ensure that where there are two or more eligible dependants, the amount for each of them is the amount for a single eligible dependant divided by the number of eligible dependants.

(3) In this regulation and Schedule 4, the age of the person with diffuse mesothelioma means—

(a) their age at the date of first diagnosis; or

(b) where the application is made by their dependant under the circumstances mentioned in section 3(2) of the Act (where a person has been diagnosed with diffuse mesothelioma following his or her death), the date of death of the person.

Imposing conditions on the making of a payment

12.42   **17.**—(1) Where the scheme administrator decides to make a payment under the scheme the scheme administrator—

(a) may impose one or more conditions on the making of the payment for the purpose of ensuring that the payment is used for the applicant's benefit; and

(b) if it considers that it would be in the interests of the applicant to do so, may impose such conditions as the scheme administrator considers are appropriate for that purpose.

(2) Conditions which may be imposed include—

(a) requiring that a trust be established on such terms or in accordance with such arrangements as the scheme administrator may direct for the purpose of administering the amount to be paid to it under the scheme;

(b) before any payment is made, requiring an application to be made for the appointment of a deputy, guardian or controller.

(3) The conditions imposed must not be such that they result in the payment being made in a form other than that of the lump sum provided for in regulation 19(2).

(4) If, in all the circumstances, the scheme administrator considers it appropriate to do so, the scheme administrator may—

(a) meet the whole or part of any reasonable costs incurred in complying with any condition imposed under this regulation;

(b) provide such advice or other assistance as the scheme administrator considers necessary in order to ensure that the payment under the scheme is used for the benefit of the applicant.

(5) The scheme administrator may vary or remove a condition imposed under paragraph (1) where the scheme administrator considers the circumstances so require.

(6) In this regulation—

(a) "deputy" has the meaning given in section 16(2)(b) of the Mental Capacity Act 2005;

(b) "guardian" has the meaning given in section 57 of the Adults with Incapacity (Scotland) Act 2000;

(c) "controller" has the meaning given by Article 101 of the Mental Health (Northern Ireland) Order 1986.

Notice of a determination

18.—(1) The scheme administrator must send a written notice which states the determination which has been made in the applicant's case—   12.43

(a) to each applicant; or

(b) if the applicant has died, to the personal representatives of the applicant.

(2) Where a payment is refused under regulation 16(1)(a), the notice must state—

(a) the reasons for the determination;

(b) that the applicant may request a review of the decision; and

(c) the period within which such a request is to be made and the procedure for making it.

(3) Where a payment is to be made under the scheme to an applicant, the notice must state—

(a) the amount awarded to the applicant;

(b) where an amount is to be paid to more than one person, the name of the other persons and the amount awarded to each of them;

(c) whether any relevant deduction has been made from the amount awarded to the applicant and, if so—
  (i) the total amount of all relevant deductions made, and
  (ii) in relation to each relevant deduction, the nature of the deduction and its amount;
(d) whether any conditions are to be imposed (see regulation 17), the nature of the conditions and the reasons for imposing them;
(e) that the applicant may, by a written notice sent to the scheme administrator, request a review of the decision; and
(f) the period within which such a request is to be made and the procedure for making it.

Payments

Payment

12.44
19.—(1) This regulation applies where a determination has been made to make a payment under the scheme to an applicant.
(2) The payment must be made in a lump sum.
(3) Subject to any conditions imposed under regulation 17, the payment—
(a) may be made to the applicant by such means as the scheme administrator may determine; and
(b) must be made either at the same time as the sending of the notice under regulation 18 or as soon afterwards as is reasonably practicable.
(4) Where an applicant dies before a payment is made under the scheme (including an applicant who dies before a determination to make the payment is made), any payment which is to be made under the scheme must, where the condition in paragraph (5) is met, be made to the applicant's personal representatives.
(5) The condition is that any document that is by law sufficient evidence of the grant of—
(a) probate of the will of a deceased applicant,
(b) letters of administration of the estate of a deceased applicant, or
(c) confirmation as executor of the deceased applicant, has been provided to the scheme administrator.

GENERAL NOTE

12.45
Payments must be made by way of a lump sum, and be paid to the applicant, subject to any conditions under reg.17. The award must be the appropriate age-related payment for the individual concerned according to the tariff set out in Sch.4 to the Regulations. This sets out a sliding scale, with the youngest victims being eligible for the highest level of award. A victim's age is determined by reference to their age at the date of first diagnosis or, where the application is made post-mortem by an eligible dependant, the date that the victim died (reg.16(3)). The sliding scale is intended to reflect the fact that the average amount awarded in a personal injuries claim through the courts reduces as the victim's age increases. This in turn recognises that older mesothelioma victims would in any event have a shorter life expectancy, relative to their younger peers, had they not contracted the disease. In addition, older mesothelioma victims are more likely to be retired and so be on lower incomes (with claims for loss of earnings being minimal or non-existent). The simple age-based tariff, modelled on the 1979 Act, has the further advantage of facilitating the speedy and efficient handling of claims.

When the Bill was first published, the Government's proposal was that awards under Sch.4 to the Regulations would be set at 70 per cent of average civil awards. This feature of the new scheme was bitterly attacked by victims' support groups, who argued that sufferers should receive full 100 per cent compensation. Insurers argued that the 70 per cent cap was needed as that would limit the total cost of the scheme to an amount equal to 3 per cent of EL gross written premiums, a figure which was considered to be affordable without passing on the costs to current employers. Following further negotiations with the insurance industry, the Government announced, during the Bill's progress through the House of Lords, an increase in the compensation rate from 70 per cent to 75 per cent. Amendments to require compensation payments to be set at 100, 90 or even 80 per cent of civil awards of damages were pressed to the vote but were all defeated during the Bill's progress.

In the Lords, the Opposition argued that as a matter of principle nothing less than 100 per cent would suffice: "One hundred per cent of the tariff is justice; anything less is not" (Lord McKenzie, HL Debs Vol 747, c.821 (July 17, 2013)). Similar sentiments were voiced in the Commons: "Sufferers feel 100% of the injury, and the industry took 100% of the premiums" (Right Hon Mr N. Brown MP, HC Debs Vol 577, c.598 (March 17, 2014)). The Government's argument, on the other hand, supported by the insurance lobby, was that setting the tariff below that of civil damages provided an incentive for all other avenues for redress to be explored first and helped ensure the long-term sustainability of the scheme.

In the event, and shortly before the new scheme went live, the Government announced that the levels of payments under Schedule 4 were to be increased, as a result of savings made through running a competitive open tender process for the appointment of the scheme administrator. Thus two days after the original Regulations were published in April 2014, amending regulations were issued which substituted an entirely new Sch.4, providing for somewhat higher levels of payments (on average by about £8,000 in each case), to take effect from July 2014. As a result the highest award was then set at a ceiling of £216,896 (£203,788 under the original Regulations), where the victim was aged 40 or under. The rates for awards then reduced by about £3,000 a year until the sufferer was aged 90 or over, at which point awards were fixed at £69,649 (originally £65,734). This meant that in practice the tariff payment rates were set at 80 per cent of average civil compensation awards, whilst still keeping within the 3 per cent target for the levy on insurers.

The levels of awards were then increased again for all those who were first diagnosed with diffuse mesothelioma on or after February 10, 2015, or their eligible dependants. The effect of the 2015 changes was to increase the amount of payment to 100% of average civil damages. This increase was apparently made possible because the numbers of people applying to the Scheme were lower than estimated. One of the reasons for that may be ELTO's increasing ability to trace historic employers' liability insurance policies. That in turn has led to savings in the administration costs of the Scheme and this has allowed for payment levels for successful applicants to be increased. To date there has been no further uplift since 2015.

Circumstances in which a person may be required to repay

20.—(1) The scheme administrator may require a person who received a payment under the scheme to repay the whole of the amount of a payment under the scheme which has been received in any case where the scheme administrator is satisfied that relevant evidence shows that— 12.46

    (a) the payment was made in error; or

    (b) whether fraudulently or otherwise, any person has misrepresented or failed to disclose a material fact and the determination to make the payment was made in consequence of the misrepresentation or failure; or

(c) the applicant was for any other reason not eligible under section 2 or 3 of the Act to receive a payment under the scheme.

(2) The scheme administrator may require a person who received a payment to repay a specified part of the amount of a payment under the scheme in any case where the scheme administrator is satisfied that relevant evidence shows that—

(a) the amount paid exceeds the amount payable in accordance with Schedule 4; or

(b) the amount payable to each of a number of persons who are eligible under section 3 of the Act was calculated on the basis of an error (either as to the number of such persons or otherwise).

(3) The scheme administrator must send a written notice to the person required to make the repayment which states—

(a) the amount required to be repaid;

(b) the reasons why the payment was not properly made; and

(c) that an applicant, or if the applicant has died, the personal representatives of the applicant, may request a review of the decision.

(4) In paragraph (2), "specified" means specified by the scheme administrator in the notice under paragraph (3).

(5) In paragraphs (1) and (2), references to "relevant evidence" are to evidence which—

(a) is relevant to the question whether an applicant was eligible under section 2 or 3 of the Act for a payment under the scheme; and

(b) is received by the scheme administrator only after a determination to make a payment in accordance with regulation 19 has been made.

Reviews and appeals

Review at the request of an applicant

12.47

21.—(1) An applicant may request a review of a determination—

(a) notified to the applicant in accordance with regulation 18(1); or

(b) notified in accordance with regulation 20(4).

(2) No review may be sought on grounds that relate to any matter referred to in regulation 18(3)(c).

(3) A request for a review of a determination must—

(a) be in writing;

(b) specify the grounds on which a review is sought; and

(c) be received by the scheme administrator not later than one month after the date of the written notice of the determination.

(4) The scheme administrator may extend the time limit in paragraph (3)(c) by a further period where the scheme administrator considers that there was good reason for the failure to request the review before the end of that initial period and for any delay since then in requesting a review under this regulation.

(5) In a case where a person makes an application and then dies, the reference in this regulation or in any of regulations 22 to 25 to an applicant is to be read as if it were a reference to the applicant's personal representatives.

Review initiated by the scheme administrator

22.—(1) Where the scheme administrator receives information after a determination is made which calls the determination into question, the scheme administrator—   12.48

(a) may decide on its own initiative to conduct a review of any determination referred to in regulation 21(1); and

(b) must notify the applicant in writing of the review and the reasons for it.

(2) The grounds on which a review under this regulation may be held include that—

(a) whether fraudulently or otherwise, any person has misrepresented or failed to disclose a material fact and the determination to make a payment under the scheme or to require a repayment was made in consequence of the misrepresentation or failure;

(b) the determination to make any such payment or require any such repayment was based on a mistake as to a material fact;

(c) there was an error or omission which affected the substance of the determination whether to make a payment under the scheme or the amount of any payment made; or

(d) there was an error or omission which affected the substance of the determination whether to require a repayment or the amount of any repayment required.

(3) The applicant may submit written representations to the scheme administrator about the scheme administrator's decision to conduct a review and about any information on which the decision to conduct a review was based.

(4) Any representation which is made under paragraph (3) must be sent so that it is received by the scheme administrator not later than one month after the date of the scheme administrator's notice of the review under paragraph (1)(b).

(5) The scheme administrator may extend the time limit in paragraph (4) by a further period where the scheme administrator considers that there was good reason for the failure to submit written representations before the end of that initial period and for any delay since then in submitting written representations.

Other circumstances in which a review may be held

23.—(1) Where a notice of an appeal which is made by an applicant to the First-tier Tribunal is received by the scheme administrator before a request for a review under regulation 21 is received—   12.49

(a) that notice is to be treated for all purposes as if it were a request for a review; and

(b) the scheme administrator must delay referring the case to the First-tier Tribunal until the review has been completed.

(2) The scheme administrator must notify the applicant in writing of the matters specified in paragraph (1)(a) and (b).

(3) The applicant may submit written representations to the scheme administrator about the grounds on which the applicant is dissatisfied with the determination which is appealed against.

(4) Any representation which is made under paragraph (3) must be sent

so that it is received by the scheme administrator not later than one month after the date of the scheme administrator's notice under paragraph (2).

(5) The scheme administrator may extend the time limit in paragraph (4) by a further period where the scheme administrator considers that there was good reason for the failure to submit written representations before the end of that initial period and for any delay since then in submitting written representations.

(6) Where the determination made on review is that a payment under the scheme is to be made to the applicant, the case is not to be referred to the First-tier Tribunal unless, on being notified of the determination in accordance with regulation 24(4)(b), the applicant sends a notice in writing to the scheme administrator to indicate that the applicant does not accept the determination made on review.

Conduct of the review

12.50

24.—(1) The scheme administrator must ensure that, in conducting a review, no member of the scheme administrator's staff who had any involvement in the determination that is subject to review under any of regulations 21 to 23 is be involved in making the determination of the review.

(2) Regulations 10 to 13 apply in relation to a review of a determination as they apply in relation to the original determination.

(3) The determinations that may be made on a review are—

(a) to confirm the original determination; or

(b) to make any other determination which the scheme administrator has power to make under regulation 16.

(4) The scheme administrator must—

(a) ensure that the review is carried out as soon as reasonably practicable; and

(b) send the applicant written notice of the result of the review.

(5) The notice under paragraph (4)(b) must—

(a) state that the original determination has been confirmed or state the terms of any new determination which has been made in the applicant's case;

(b) give reasons for the determination made on the review;

(c) in the case of a new determination that a payment under the scheme is to be made to the applicant, specify the details required by regulation 18(3)(a) to (f);

(d) state that the applicant may appeal to the First-tier Tribunal against the determination made on review; and

(e) state the period within which such an appeal is to be made and provide information as to how to make such an appeal.

(6) Nothing in this regulation prevents a determination notified to an applicant in accordance with regulation 18(1) or 20(3) from being confirmed on review for reasons that differ in any respect from the reasons given in relation to that determination.

Appeal

12.51

25.—(1) An applicant may appeal to the First-tier Tribunal from a determination which has been reviewed under regulation 24(3).

(2) An appeal under this regulation is to be conducted in accordance with the Tribunal Procedure (First-tier Tribunal) (Social Entitlement Chamber) Rules 2008.

Circumstances in which scheme administrator may help people to bring proceedings

26.—(1) The circumstances in which the scheme administrator may help a person to bring relevant proceedings under section 10 of the Act (power of scheme administrator to help people bring proceedings) are that— 12.52

(a) a payment under the scheme was made to a person who, on the basis of the information then available, was eligible under section 2 or 3 of the Act;

(b) since the payment was made, further information has become available which indicates that there is a reasonable prospect of bringing an action for damages in relevant proceedings; and

(c) the scheme administrator considers that it would in all the circumstances be appropriate to provide help to any person in bringing such proceedings.

(2) In considering whether it is appropriate to provide help to any person to bring relevant proceedings, the scheme administrator must have regard, in particular, to—

(a) the person's prospects of success in bringing the proceedings;

(b) the level of compensation likely to be awarded in those proceedings;

(c) the aggregate amount of the payments specified in paragraph (3) that is likely to be payable to the Secretary of State in the event that any damages were to be awarded in such proceedings; and

(d) the overall balance between—

    (i) the amount of the payment referred to in paragraph (1)(a); and

    (ii) the costs of providing help to the person to bring relevant proceedings added to the amount referred to in sub-paragraph (c).

(3) The payments are—

(a) a payment under section 6 of the Social Security (Recovery of Benefits) Act 1997 (payment in respect of recoverable benefit) in respect of the period since the payment referred to in paragraph (1)(a) was made;

(b) a payment under article 8 of the Social Security (Recovery of Benefits) (Northern Ireland) Order 1997 (payment in respect of recoverable benefit) in respect of that period;

(c) a payment under regulation 10 of the Social Security (Recovery of Benefits) (Lump sum Payments) Regulations 2008 (payment in respect of recoverable lump sum payments) which was not recovered from the payment referred to in paragraph (1)(a);

(d) a payment under regulation 10 of the Social Security (Recovery of Benefits) (Lump sum Payments) Regulations (Northern Ireland) 2008 (payment in respect of recoverable lump sum payments) which was not recovered from the payment referred to in paragraph (1)(a).

Review of these Regulations by the Secretary of State

27.—(1) The Secretary of State must— 12.53

(a) carry out an annual review of these Regulations;

(b) set out the conclusions of that review in a report; and

(c) publish the report.

(2) The report must in particular—

(a) set out the objectives intended to be achieved by the scheme; and

(b) assess the extent to which those objectives have been achieved over the reporting period.

(3) The first report under this regulation must be published on or before 30th November 2015.

(4) Reports under this regulation are afterwards to be published at intervals not exceeding 13 months.

(5) In this regulation "reporting period" in any year means a period beginning with 6th April in one year and ending with 5th April in the next.

SCHEDULE 1   REGULATION 6

First diagnosis of diffuse mesothelioma

12.54   1. In this Schedule—

"P" means a person with diffuse mesothelioma;

"connected person", in relation to P, means—

(a) any person who, with P's agreement, is acting on P's behalf; or

(b) any personal representative of P;

"health care professional" means—

(a) a registered medical practitioner;

(b) a registered nurse working in a clinical nurse specialist role in relation to patients with cancer;

(c) a member of a multi-disciplinary team for the diagnosis and treatment of patients with cancer which includes one or more persons mentioned in paragraph (a) or (b) of this definition.

Application by a person with diffuse mesothelioma

12.55   2. For the purposes of section 2 of the Act—

(a) a person ("P") is to be taken as having been "first diagnosed" with diffuse mesothelioma where both of the conditions set out in paragraph 3 are met; and

(b) the date of first diagnosis is to be determined in accordance with paragraphs 4 and 5.

3. The conditions referred to in paragraph 2(a) are—

(a) that a diagnosis of diffuse mesothelioma in relation to P is made by a health care professional; and

(b) that either P or a connected person is advised of the diagnosis by a health care professional (whether by the health care professional who made the diagnosis or by a different one).

4. (1) The date of P's first diagnosis is to be determined as follows.

(2) Where the advice that P has diffuse mesothelioma is given orally, the date of first diagnosis is the date shown in P's clinical notes as being the date on which P or a connected person was advised of the diagnosis.

(3) Where the advice that P has diffuse mesothelioma is given in writing, the date of first diagnosis is—

(a) if the advice is contained in a letter, the date shown on the letter;

(b) if the advice is sent by electronic communication, the date on which the communication was sent.

(4) Where no date can be determined in accordance with sub-paragraph (2) or (3), or there is reason to doubt the accuracy of the date so determined, the date of first diagnosis is to be determined by such other evidence as the scheme administrator considers appropriate.

5. (1) In determining whether the conditions set out in paragraph 3 have been met, the scheme administrator may make further enquiries to determine whether the disease that has been diagnosed is in fact diffuse mesothelioma in any case where—

(a) the scheme administrator considers that there is reason to doubt whether the disease that has been diagnosed is diffuse mesothelioma; or

(b) P or a connected person was advised by a healthcare professional that P's diagnosis is of anything other than diffuse mesothelioma (including a diagnosis of mesothelioma without explanation of its extent).

(2) Where, as a result of the further enquiries, the scheme administrator is satisfied that the diagnosis was one of diffuse mesothelioma, the date of first diagnosis is to be determined in accordance with the provisions of paragraph 4.

(3) Where, as a result of the further enquiries, a substituted diagnosis is made in relation to P which is one of diffuse mesothelioma, the date of first diagnosis is whichever of the following occurs first—

(a) the date on which P is advised of the substituted diagnosis;

(b) the date on which a connected person is advised of the substituted diagnosis;

(c) the date on which the scheme administrator is advised of the substituted diagnosis.

Application by a dependant of a person with diffuse mesothelioma

6. For the purposes of section 3 of the Act, P who has died is to be taken as having been "first diagnosed" with diffuse mesothelioma as follows.   **12.56**

7. If the conditions set out in paragraph 3 were met before P's death, the date of first diagnosis is to be determined in accordance with the provisions of paragraph 4.

8. (1) In any other case, P is to be taken as having been "first diagnosed" with diffuse mesothelioma where either of the conditions set out in sub-paragraph (2)(a) or (b) is met and the date of first diagnosis is to be determined in accordance with sub-paragraph (3).

(2) The conditions referred to in sub-paragraph (1) are—

(a) that a diagnosis of diffuse mesothelioma in relation to P is made following a post-mortem examination; or

(b) that, following P's death, a diagnosis of diffuse mesothelioma in relation to P is confirmed in writing by a health care professional without carrying out a post-mortem examination.

(3) The date of P's first diagnosis is the date shown on the report of the post-mortem examination or the date shown on the health care professional's written confirmation of the diagnosis (as the case may be).

SCHEDULE 2   REGULATION 6

SPECIFIED PAYMENTS

Payment under the Naval, Military and Air Forces Etc. (Disablement and Death) Service   **12.57**
Pensions Order 2006.

Payment under the Armed Forces and Reserve Forces (Compensation Scheme) Order 2011.

A compensation payment from any government department.

A compensation payment from an authority, body corporate or employer exempted from insurance by or under the compulsory insurance legislation.

Payment under the UK Asbestos Trust established on 10th October 2006, for the benefit of certain persons suffering from asbestos-related diseases.

Payment under the EL Scheme Trust established on 23rd November 2006, for the benefit of certain persons suffering from asbestos-related diseases.

Payment under a scheme established under section 213 of the Financial Services and Markets Act 2000 (the Financial Services Compensation Scheme).

SCHEDULE 3   REGULATION 8

INFORMATION AND OTHER MATERIAL IN SUPPORT OF AN APPLICATION

PART 1

THE APPLICATION

1. An applicant may be required to state whether the applicant is—   **12.58**

(a) the person with diffuse mesothelioma;

12.59

(b) a person who is a dependant of a person who has died with diffuse mesothelioma.

2. An applicant within paragraph 1(a) or (b) may be required to provide, in relation to the person with diffuse mesothelioma—

(a) the person's name and national insurance number;

(b) the person's date of birth;

(c) the date the person was first diagnosed with diffuse mesothelioma;

(d) the name of all employers of the person;

(e) a description of the arrangements under which the person was engaged by each employer;

(f) a statement of the kind of activities carried on by the person whilst working for each employer and the place where those activities were carried on;

(g) an indication as to whether the application relies on the person with diffuse mesothelioma having been exposed to asbestos as a result of the relevant employer's negligence or breach of statutory duty (or both);

(h) an explanation of why the application relies on the relevant employer's negligence or breach of statutory duty (or both);

(i) a statement that no action for damages has been brought against the relevant employer or any insurer with whom the relevant employer maintained employers liability insurance at the time of the person's exposure to asbestos, in respect of the disease;

(j) an explanation of why it is alleged the applicant is unable to bring an action against any employer or any insurer with whom such an employer maintained employers' liability insurance;

(k) a statement that the person has not received damages or a specified payment in respect of the disease;

(l) a statement that the person is not eligible to receive a specified payment.

12.60

3. An applicant within paragraph 1(b) may also be required to provide—

(a) the name of the applicant;

(b) their date of birth;

(c) a statement of the applicant's relationship to the deceased;

(d) where relevant, a statement of the name of each person who is in the same degree of relationship to the deceased as the applicant;

(e) a statement that no one has brought an action for damages under the fatal accidents legislation, or on behalf of the deceased's estate, against the relevant employer or any insurer with whom the relevant employer maintained employers' liability insurance at the time of the person's exposure to asbestos;

(f) an explanation of why it is alleged that no one is able to bring an action under the fatal accidents legislation, or on behalf of the deceased's estate, against any employer of the deceased or any insurer with whom such an employer maintained employers' liability insurance;

(g) a statement that no one has received damages or a specified payment in respect of the disease;

(h) a statement that no one is eligible to receive a specified payment.

PART 2

KEY ISSUES

12.61

4. The key issues to be addressed by the information and other material required under Part 1 of this Schedule, are—

(a) establishing that the person with diffuse mesothelioma was employed by a relevant employer;

(b) establishing that the person with diffuse mesothelioma was exposed to asbestos during the period of the person's employment;

(c) establishing that the exposure to asbestos resulted from a relevant employer's negligence or breach of statutory duty (or both);

(d) explaining why no action for damages in respect of the disease can be brought against any employer or any insurer with whom such an employer maintained employers' liability insurance;

(e) where the application is made by a person who is a dependant of a person who has died with diffuse mesothelioma—

(i) establishing that the person qualifies as a dependant of the deceased for the purposes of section 3(1) of Pneumoconiosis etc. (Workers' Compensation) Act 1979;

(ii) explaining why no one is able to bring an action for damages under the fatal accidents legislation, or on behalf of the deceased's estate, against any employer or any insurer of such an employer.

PART 3

SUPPORTING EVIDENCE

5. Supporting evidence that may be required in relation to an application includes—   **12.62**
  (a) medical evidence which confirms the person has been diagnosed with diffuse mesothelioma (see Schedule 1);
  (b) witness statements (whether made by the person with diffuse mesothelioma or by others);
  (c) the details of any investigation in contemplation of litigation which has been carried out on behalf of the applicant (including any report made by a relevant expert);
  (d) the details of all steps taken to find any relevant insurer and the results of any search for a relevant insurer that has been carried out;
  (e) a copy of any decision published by the Technical Committee which relates to a person named in the application as a relevant employer or an insurer of that employer.
6. (1) Any witness statement that is provided must be signed by the person making the statement and verified by a statement of truth.
(2) "Statement of truth" means a statement that the person making the witness statement believes the matters stated as facts in the witness statement to be true.

SCHEDULE 4   REGULATION 16

AMOUNT OF SCHEME PAYMENTS

[¹ Table 1

Age of the person with diffuse mesothelioma (see regulation16(3))	Scheme Payment	12.63
40 and under	£271,120	
41	£267,439	
42	£263,758	
43	£260,078	
44	£256,396	
45	£252,715	
46	£249,034	
47	£245,353	
48	£241,671	
49	£237,990	
50	£234,309	
51	£230,628	
52	£226,946	
53	£223,265	
54	£219,584	
55	£215,903	
56	£212,221	
57	£208,540	
58	£204,859	
59	£201,179	
60	£197,498	
61	£193,816	
62	£190,135	
63	£186,454	
64	£182,773	

65	£179,091
66	£175,410
67	£171,729
68	£168,048
69	£164,366
70	£160,685
71	£157,004
72	£153,323
73	£149,641
74	£145,960
75	£142,279
76	£138,599
77	£134,918
78	£131,236
79	£127,555
80	£123,874
81	£120,193
82	£116,511
83	£112,830
84	£109,149
85	£105,468
86	£101,786
87	£98,105
88	£94,424
89	£90,743
90 and over	£87,061]

AMENDMENT

1. Diffuse Mesothelioma Payment Scheme (Amendment) Regulations 2015 (SI 2015/367), reg.2 (March 31, 2015).

The Diffuse Mesothelioma Payment Scheme (Levy) Regulations 2014

SI 2014/2904

ARRANGEMENT OF REGULATIONS

12.64
1. Citation, commencement and interpretation
2. The requirement to pay a share of the total amount of the levy
3. The reference period
4. Determination of relative market share and amounts
5. Information and publication
6. Recovery of the payment amount

Citation, commencement and interpretation

12.65   **1.** (1) These Regulations may be cited as the Diffuse Mesothelioma Payment Scheme (Levy) Regulations 2014.

(2) These Regulations come into force on 28th November 2014.

(3) In these Regulations—

"a financial year" means the 12 month period ending with the 31st March in any year;

"individual gross written premium" means the sum, before commission and the cost of reinsurance are taken out, of all employers' liability insurance premiums written in a calendar year by an individual active insurer;

"reference period" has the meaning given in regulation 3;

"the payment amount" means the share of the total amount of the levy that an active insurer is required to pay;

"the scheme" means the Diffuse Mesothelioma Payment Scheme established by the Diffuse Mesothelioma Payment Scheme Regulations 2014;

"total amount of the levy" means an annual sum decided by the Secretary of State under section 13 of the Mesothelioma Act 2014 in each financial year with a view to meeting the costs of the scheme;

"total gross written premium" means the sum, before commission and the cost of reinsurance are taken out, of all employers' liability insurance premiums written in a calendar year by all active insurers.

The requirement to pay a share of the total amount of the levy

2. (1) An active insurer is required to pay a share of the total amount of the levy based on that insurer's relative market share in the reference period as determined in accordance with regulation 4.

(2) The requirement in paragraph (1) is a requirement—

(a) to pay the Secretary of State the payment amount specified in the notice under regulation 5(1) in accordance with the notice under regulation 5(2); and

(b) subject to details given in a notice under regulation 5(2)(a), to pay the payment amount by the end of a financial year in respect of which the Secretary of State decides the total amount of the levy.

12.66

DEFINITIONS

"a financial year"—see reg.1(3).
"reference period"—see reg.1(3).
"the payment amount"—see reg.1(3).
"total amount of the levy"—see reg.1(3).

The reference period

3. (1) The reference period is a 12 month period ending on 31st December falling in a financial year.

(2) The reference period for the payment amount for the first financial year ends on 31st December 2014.

(3) In this regulation the "first financial year" means the year ending 31st March 2015.

12.67

DEFINITIONS

"a financial year"—see reg.1(3).
"reference period"—see reg.1(3).
"the payment amount"—see reg.1(3).

Determination of relative market share and amounts

12.68

4. (1) An active insurer's relative market share in the reference period is determined in accordance with paragraph (2) and the payment amount an active insurer must pay is determined in accordance with paragraphs (3) to (5).

(2) For the purpose of these Regulations, relative market share in the reference period is to be treated as if it were the same as the relative market share for the calendar year two years before the reference period.

(3) The payment amount an active insurer must pay in a financial year is to be determined by multiplying the total amount of the levy for that financial year by the figure for their relative market share for the calendar year two years before the reference period.

(4) In this regulation "relative market share for the calendar year two years before the reference period" means A divided by B where—

    (a) "A" equals the individual gross written premium for that calendar year;

    (b) "B" equals the total gross written premium attributable to the active insurer whose individual gross written premium has been ascertained for the purpose of "A".

(5) In paragraph (4) where "A" cannot be ascertained, an active insurer's relative market share for the calendar year two years before the reference period is nil.

DEFINITIONS

"a financial year"–see reg.1(3).
"individual gross written premium"–see reg.1(3).
"reference period"–see reg.1(3).
"the payment amount"–see reg.1(3).
"total amount of the levy"–see reg.1(3).
"total gross written premium"–see reg.1(3).

Information and publication

12.69

5. (1) The Secretary of State must notify active insurers in writing of the payment amount due from them.

(2) The Secretary of State must also notify active insurers in writing of—

    (a) the date or dates in the financial year by which the payment amount is required; and

    (b) details of how the payment amount can be made.

(3) The Secretary of State must give active insurers sufficient information to enable them to determine how the payment amount in their case was calculated.

(4) In particular the Secretary of State may give each active insurer information concerning—

    (a) the basis on which they are considered to be an active insurer;

    (b) the action the Secretary of State may take if the payment amount is not made in accordance with the notice under paragraphs (1) and (2).

(5) The Secretary of State must publish annually the costs of the scheme and must in particular publish information on—

    (a) the costs of payments made under the scheme;

    (b) the costs of administering the scheme; and

(c) any costs incurred by the Secretary of State in establishing a body to administer the scheme.

DEFINITIONS

"a financial year"–see reg.1(3).
"the payment amount"–see reg.1(3).
"the scheme"–see reg.1(3).

Recovery of the payment amount

6. If the payment amount notified to an active insurer is not paid in accordance with the notices under regulation 5(1) and (2), the payment amount, or any part of it, which has not been paid, is recoverable as a debt due to the Secretary of State. 12.70

DEFINITIONS

"the payment amount"–see reg.1(3).

PART XIII

"NEW STYLE" EMPLOYMENT AND SUPPORT ALLOWANCE

STATUTES AND REGULATIONS

Important preliminary note
The provisions set out in this new Section of this book apply only to those cases and areas in which universal credit has been introduced. On this see the new *Vol. V: Universal Credit*, Pt 3 dealing with transition and the key Welfare Reform Act 2012 Commencement Orders. These make the amendments operational from various dates on or after April 29, 2013. See further the initial GENERAL NOTE to the Employment and Support Allowance Regulations 2013 (SI 2013/379), below.

Welfare Reform Act 2012

(2012 c.5)

33. Abolition of benefits   13.1

Abolition of benefits

33. — (1) The following benefits are abolished—   13.2
(a) . . . ;
(b) income-related employment and support allowance under Part 1 of
    the Welfare Reform Act 2007;
(c) . . . ;
(d) . . . ;
(e) . . . ;
(f) . . . .
(2) In subsection (1)—
(a) . . . ;
(b) "income-related employment and support allowance" means an
    employment and support allowance entitlement to which is based on
    section 1(2)(b) of the Welfare Reform Act 2007.

DEFINITIONS

"income-related employment and support allowance"—see subs.(2)(b).

GENERAL NOTE

This abolishes IRESA in those cases and areas in which universal credit is opera-   13.3
tional. On this see the new *Vol. V: Universal Credit*, Part IV dealing with transition
and the key Welfare Reform Act 2012 Commencement Orders. These make the
amendments operational from various dates on or after April 29, 2013.

See further the initial General Note to the Employment and Support Allowance
Regulations 2013 (SI 2013/379), below.

Welfare Reform Act 2007

(2007 c.5) (AS AMENDED)

Most of the provisions of this Act set out earlier in this book (paras 1.747-   13.4
1.906) apply to cases and areas in which universal credit is operational in
exactly the same way as in other areas and cases. Some provisions—set out
below—have been repealed and others amended.

SECTIONS REPRODUCED
(In Amended Form Applicable Only To "New Style" ESA)

13.5   1.   Employment and support allowance
            1A.   Duration of allowance
            1B.   Further entitlement after time-limiting
            2.   Amount of allowance
            3.   Deductions from allowance: supplementary
            4.   *Repealed*
            5.   *Repealed*
            6.   *Repealed*

WRA 2007 ss.7-10 apply to "new style" ESA in exactly the same way as to "old style" ESA. For text see the first Section of this book (Statutes).

WRA 2007 ss.11-16 and the italic heading preceding them ("Conditionality") are substituted by ss.11-11K:

Work-related requirements

11.   Work-related requirements
11A.   Claimant commitment
11B.   Work-focused interview requirement
11C.   Work preparation requirement
11D.   Persons subject to no work-related requirements
11E.   Persons subject to work-focused interview requirement only
11F.   Persons subject to work preparation and work-focused interview requirement
11G.   Connected requirements
11H.   Imposition of requirements
11I.   Compliance with requirements
11J.   Sanctions
11K.   Delegation and contracting out
        . . . . . .
16A.   *Repealed*

Miscellaneous

17. Income and Capital: General
18. Disqualification
    WRA 2007 s.19 applies to "new style" ESA in exactly the same way as to "old style" ESA. For text see the first Section of this book (Statutes).
20. Relationship with statutory payments
    WRA 2007 ss.21 and 22 apply to "new style" ESA in exactly the same way as to "old style" ESA. For text see the first Section of this book (Statutes).
23. Repealed

General

24. Interpretation of Part 1
    WRA 2007 s.25 applies to "new style" ESA in exactly the same way as to "old style" ESA. For text see the first Section of this book (Statutes).

26. Parliamentary control
27. Financial provisions relating to Part 1
    WRA 2007 s.28 applies to "new style" ESA in exactly the same way as to "old style" ESA. For text see the first Section of this book (Statutes).
29. *Repealed*
    WRA 2007 ss.30–63: omitted as not relevant to either form of ESA.
    WRA 2007 ss.64–71 apply to "new style" ESA in exactly the same way as to "old style" ESA. For text see the first Section of this book (Statutes).

SCHEDULES

Schedule 1—Employment and support allowance: additional conditions
    Part 1
    Part 2 *(repealed)*
Schedule 2—Employment and support allowance: supplementary provisions
Schedule 3—Consequential amendments relating to Part 1
Schedule 4—*repealed.*
Schedule 5—Omitted
Schedule 6—Omitted
Schedule 7—Omitted

An Act to make provision about social security; to amend the Vaccine Damage Payments Act 1979; and for connected purposes.

[3rd May 2007]

PART 1

EMPLOYMENT AND SUPPORT ALLOWANCE

Entitlement

Employment and support allowance

1.—(1) An allowance, to be known as an employment and support allow-   13.6
ance, shall be payable in accordance with the provisions of this Part.

(2) Subject to the provisions of this Part, a claimant is entitled to an employment and support allowance if he satisfies the basic conditions and [^{3}. . .]—

(a) the first and the second conditions set out in [^{3}. . .] Schedule 1 (conditions relating to national insurance) or the third condition set out in [^{3}. . .] that Schedule (condition relating to youth), [^{3}. . .]

[^{3}. . .].

(3) The basic conditions are that the claimant—

(a) has limited capability for work,

[^{2}(aa) has accepted a claimant commitment,]

(b) is at least 16 years old,

(c) has not reached pensionable age,

(d) is in Great Britain, [^{3}and]

1645

(e) is not entitled to income support, and

(f) is not entitled to a jobseeker's allowance [³. . .].

[¹(3A) After the coming into force of this subsection no claim may be made for an employment and support allowance by virtue of the third condition set out in [³. . .] Schedule 1 (youth).]

(4) For the purposes of this Part, a person has limited capability for work if—

(a) his capability for work is limited by his physical or mental condition, and

(b) the limitation is such that it is not reasonable to require him to work.

(5) An employment and support allowance is payable in respect of a week.

(6) In subsection (3)—

[³. . .];

"pensionable age" has the meaning given by the rules in paragraph 1 of Schedule 4 to the Pensions Act 1995.

[³. . .].

(6A) [³. . .].

(7) [³. . .].

AMENDMENTS

1. Welfare Reform Act 2012 s.53 (May 1, 2012).

2. Welfare Reform Act 2012 s.54(1), (2) (various dates on or after April 29, 2013).

3. Welfare Reform Act 2012 s.33(3), Sch.3 para.23, s.147 and Sch.14 Pt 1 (various dates on or after April 29, 2013).

DEFINITIONS

"claimant"—see s.24(1).

"pensionable age" —see subs.(6).

GENERAL NOTE

13.7   This sets out the key conditions of entitlement to "new style" ESA. The first key difference with WRA 2007 s.1, as set out earlier in the volume, applicable to "old style" ESA (comprising both CESA and IRESA), is the deletion of all references to CESA and IRESA, so that "new style" ESA is designed to be a contribution-based benefit only. Although subs.(2)(a) refers to access to "new style" ESA through the third condition in Sch.1 (the condition relating to youth), that route was barred to new claimants claiming on or after May 1, 2012, so, when read with s.1A limiting title to ESA to 365 days for those not in the support group, that route is unlikely to cover many claimants.

The second key difference between "new style" and "old style" ESA, is that title to the former is dependent upon the claimant accepting a "claimant commitment", an addition to the "basic conditions" applicable in respect of "old style" ESA (subs. (3)(aa)). A "claimant commitment" is a record of the responsibilities of a claimant entitled to "new style" ESA. See further s.11A, below.

[¹Duration of [². . .] allowance

13.8   **1A.**—(1) The period for which a person is entitled to [²an employment and support allowance] by virtue of the first and second conditions set out in [². . .] Schedule 1 shall not exceed, in the aggregate, the relevant maximum number of days in any period for which his entitlement is established by reference (under the second condition set out in [². . .] Schedule 1) to the same two tax years.

(2) In subsection (1) the "relevant maximum number of days" is—

(a) 365 days, or

(b) if the Secretary of State by order specifies a greater number of days, that number of days.

(3) The fact that a person's entitlement to [²an employment and support allowance] has ceased as a result of subsection (1) does not prevent his being entitled to a further such allowance if—

(a) he satisfies the first and second conditions set out in [². . .] Schedule 1, and

(b) the two tax years by reference to which he satisfies the second condition include at least one year which is later than the second of the two years by reference to which (under the second condition) his previous entitlement was established.

(4) The period for which a person is entitled to [²an employment and support allowance] by virtue of the third condition set out in [². . .] Schedule 1 (youth) shall not exceed—

(a) 365 days, or

(b) if the Secretary of State by order specifies a greater number of days, that number of days.

(5) In calculating for the purposes of subsection (1) or (4) the length of the period for which a person is entitled to [²an employment and support allowance], the following are not to be counted—

(a) days in which the person is a member of the support group,

(b) days not falling within paragraph (a) in respect of which the person is entitled to the support component referred to in section 2(1)(b), and

(c) days in the assessment phase, where the days immediately following that phase fall within paragraph (a) or (b).

(6) In calculating for the purposes of subsection (1) or (4) the length of the period for which a person is entitled to [²an employment and support allowance], days occurring before the coming into force of this section are to be counted (as well as those occurring afterwards).]

AMENDMENTS

1. Welfare Reform Act 2012 s.51 (May 1, 2012).

2. Welfare Reform Act 2012 s.33(3) and Sch.3 para.26(a), s.147 and Sch.14 Pt 1 (various dates on or after April 29, 2013).

DEFINITIONS

"relevant maximum number of days"— see subs.(2).

GENERAL NOTE

This is essentially the same as WRA 2007 s.1A as applicable to "old style" ESA, **13.9** the amendments merely replacing the term "contributory allowance" with "an employment and support allowance", since, with the abolition of IRESA in universal credit areas, "new style" ESA has only one form. The other amendments delete references to later provisions not needed with "new style" ESA.

[¹Further entitlement after time-limiting

1B.—(1) Where a person's entitlement to [²an employment and support **13.10** allowance] has ceased as a result of section 1A(1) or (4) but—

(a) the person has not at any subsequent time ceased to have (or to be treated as having) limited capability for work,

(b) the person satisfies the basic conditions, and

(c) the person has (or is treated as having) limited capability for work related activity,

the claimant is entitled to an employment and support allowance by virtue of this section.]

(2) [³*Repealed.*]

AMENDMENTS

1. Welfare Reform Act 2012 s.51 (May 1, 2012).
2. Welfare Reform Act 2012 s.33(3) and Sch.3 para.26(b) (various dates on or after April 29, 2013).
3. Welfare Reform Act 2012 s.147 and Sch.14 Pt 1 (various dates on or after April 29, 2013).

DEFINITIONS

"basic conditions"—see s.1(3), above.

GENERAL NOTE

13.11   This has the same effect as s.1B as applicable to "old style" ESA, the amendments merely replacing the term "contributory allowance" with "an employment and support allowance", since, with the abolition of IRESA in universal credit areas, "new style" ESA has only one form.

Amount of [¹ . . .] allowance

13.12   **2.**—(1) [¹The amount payable by way of an employment and support allowance] in respect of a claimant shall be calculated by—

(a) taking such amount as may be prescribed;

(b) if in his case the conditions of entitlement to the support component [² . . .] are satisfied, adding the amount of that component; and

(c) making prescribed deductions in respect of any payments to which section 3 applies.

(2) The conditions of entitlement to the support component are—

(a) that the assessment phase has ended;

(b) that the claimant has limited capability for work-related activity; and

(c) that such other conditions as may be prescribed are satisfied.

(3) [² . . .]

(4) Regulations may—

(a) prescribe circumstances in which paragraph (a) of subsection (2) [² . . .] is not to apply;

(b) prescribe circumstances in which entitlement under subsection (2) [² . . .] is to be backdated;

(c) make provision about the amount of the component under subsection (2) [² . . .].

(5) For the purposes of this Part, a person has limited capability for work related activity if—

(a) his capability for work-related activity is limited by his physical or mental condition; and

(b) the limitation is such that it is not reasonable to require him to undertake such activity.

AMENDMENTS

1. Welfare Reform Act 2012 s.33(3) and Sch.3 para.26(a), s.147 and Sch.14 Pt 1 (various dates on or after April 29, 2013).
2. Welfare Reform and Work Act 2016 s.15(2) (April 3, 2017).

DEFINITIONS

"assessment phase"—see s.24(2), (3).
"claimant"—see s.24(1).
"limited capability for work-related activity"—see subs.(5).
"prescribed"—see s.24(1).
"regulations"—see s.24(1).
"work-related activity"—see ss.24(1), 13(7), below.

GENERAL NOTE

This has the same effect as WRA 2007 s.2 as applicable to "old style" ESA, the amendments merely replacing the term "contributory allowance" with "an employ-ment and support allowance", since, with the abolition of IRESA in universal credit areas, "new style" ESA has only one form.   **13.13**

Deductions from [¹. . .] allowance: supplementary

3.—(1) This section applies to payments of the following kinds which are payable to the claimant—   **13.14**
- (a) pension payments,
- (b) PPF periodic payments, and
- (c) payments of a prescribed description made to a person who is a member of, or has been appointed to, a prescribed body carrying out public or local functions.

(2) Regulations may—
- (a) disapply section 2(1)(c), so far as relating to pension payments or PPF periodic payments, in relation to persons of a prescribed description;
- (b) provide for pension payments or PPF periodic payments of a pre-scribed description to be treated for the purposes of that provision as not being payments to which this section applies;
- (c) provide for sums of a prescribed description to be treated for the purposes of this section as payable to persons as pension payments or PPF periodic payments (including, in particular, sums in relation to which there is a deferred right of receipt);
- (d) make provision for the method of determining how payments to which this section applies are, for the purposes of section 2, to be related to periods for which a person is entitled to [²an employment and support allowance].

(3) In this section—
"pension payment" means—
- (a) a periodical payment made in relation to a person under a personal pension scheme or, in connection with the coming to an end of an employment of his, under an occupational pension scheme or a public service pension scheme,
- (b) a payment of a prescribed description made under an insurance policy providing benefits in connection with physical or mental illness or disability, and
- (c) such other payments as may be prescribed;

"PPF periodic payment" means—

(a) any periodic compensation payment made in relation to a person, payable under the pension compensation provisions as specified in section 162(2) of the Pensions Act 2004 (c.35) or Article 146(2) of the Pensions (Northern Ireland) Order 2005 (S.I. 2005/255) (NI 1) (the pension compensation provisions), and

(b) any periodic payment made in relation to a person, payable under section 166 of the Pensions Act 2004 or Article 150 of the Pensions (Northern Ireland) Order 2005 (duty to pay scheme benefits unpaid at assessment date etc.).

(4) For the purposes of subsection (3), "occupational pension scheme", "personal pension scheme" and "public service pension scheme" each have the meaning given by section 1 of the Pension Schemes Act 1993 (c.48), except that "personal pension scheme" includes—

(a) an annuity contract or trust scheme approved under section 620 or 621 of the Income and Corporation Taxes Act 1988 (c.1), and

(b) a substituted contract within the meaning of section 622(3) of that Act, which is treated as having become a registered pension scheme by virtue of paragraph 1(1)(f) of Schedule 36 to the Finance Act 2004 (c.12).

AMENDMENTS

1. Welfare Reform Act 2012 s.147 and Sch.14 Pt 1 (various dates on or after April 29, 2013).

2. Welfare Reform Act 2012 s.33(3) and Sch.3 para.26 (c) (various dates on or after April 29, 2013).

DEFINITIONS

"claimant"—see s.24(1), below.
"occupational pension scheme"—see subs.(4).
"pension payment"—see subs.(3).
"personal pension scheme"—see subs.(4).
"PPF periodic payment"—see subs.(3).
"prescribed"—see s.24(1), below.

GENERAL NOTE

13.15   This has the same effect as WRA 2007 s.3 as applicable to "old style" ESA, the amendments merely replacing the term "contributory allowance" with "an employment and support allowance", since, with the abolition of IRESA in universal credit areas, "new style" ESA has only one form.

Amount of income-related allowance

13.16   **4.** [¹. . .].

AMENDMENT

1. Repealed by Welfare Reform Act 2012 s.147 and Sch.14 Pt 1 ((various dates on or after April 29, 2013).

Advance award of income-related allowance

13.17   **5.** [¹. . .].

AMENDMENT

1. Repealed by Welfare Reform Act 2012 s.147 and Sch.14 Pt 1 ((various dates on or after April 29, 2013).

Amount payable where claimant entitled to both forms of allowance

6. [¹. . .].   13.18

AMENDMENT

1. Repealed by Welfare Reform Act 2012 s.147 and Sch.14 Pt 1 (various dates on or after April 29, 2013).

WRA 2007 ss.7-10 apply to "new style" ESA in exactly the same way as to   13.19
"old style" ESA. For text see the first Part of this book (Statutes).

WRA 2007 ss.11-16 and the italic heading preceding them ("Conditionality")   13.20
are substituted as follows:

[¹ Work-related requirements

Work-related requirements

11. — (1) The following provisions of this Part provide for the Secretary   13.21
of State to impose work-related requirements with which persons entitled
to an employment and support allowance must comply for the purposes of
this Part.

(2) In this Part "work-related requirement" means—

(a) a work-focused interview requirement (see section 11B);

(b) a work preparation requirement (see section 11C).

(3) The work-related requirements which may be imposed on a person
depend on which of the following groups the person falls into—

(a) persons subject to no work-related requirements (see section 11D);

(b) persons subject to work-focused interview requirement only (see section 11E);

(c) persons subject to work-focused interview and work preparation requirements (see section 11F).]

AMENDMENT

1. Welfare Reform Act 2012 s.57(1), (2) (various dates on or after April 29, 2013).

DEFINITIONS

"work-focused interview requirement"—see s.11B(1).

"work-related requirement"—see subs.(2).

"work preparation requirement"—see s.11C(1).

GENERAL NOTE

For "new style" ESA, the imposition of "work-related" requirements by the   13.22
Secretary of State replaces "conditionality" applicable to "old style ESA". The idea
behind both is to provide deterrents to ensure that benefit recipients meet specified
responsibilities, which vary according to the group into which the person falls (see
subs.(3)), but are designed to enhance ability ultimately to return to the labour

market. Unless completely exempt (see s.11D), a person entitled to "new style" ESA must comply with the requirements validly imposed. Failure for no good reason to comply is punished by a sanction in the form of a reduction of ESA for a period (see ss.11I and 11J).

"Work-related requirements" consist of a work interview requirement (see s.11B) and/or one a number of work preparation requirements (see s.11C). Some claimants cannot be subject to any work-related requirements (see s.11D). Others may be subject only to a work interview requirement (see s.11E). The remainder can be subject to both a work interview requirement and work preparation requirements (see s.11F). All those entitled to ESA can be required to meet the "connected requirement" of participation in an interview for a purpose(s) related to the imposition of a work-related requirement, verification of compliance with any imposed or assisting the subject of the requirement to comply with it (see s.11G).

[¹Claimant commitment

13.23   **11A.** — (1) A claimant commitment is a record of the responsibilities of a person entitled to an employment and support allowance in relation to the award of the allowance.

(2) A claimant commitment is to be prepared by the Secretary of State and may be reviewed and updated as the Secretary of State thinks fit.

(3) A claimant commitment is to be in such form as the Secretary of State thinks fit.

(4) A claimant commitment is to include—

(a) a record of the requirements that the person must comply with under this Part (or such of them as the Secretary of State considers it appropriate to include),

(b) any prescribed information, and

(c) any other information the Secretary of State considers it appropriate to include.

(5) For the purposes of this Part a person accepts a claimant commitment if, and only if, the claimant accepts the most up-to-date version of it in such manner as may be prescribed.]

AMENDMENT

1. Welfare Reform Act 2012 s.57(1), (2) (various dates on or after April 29, 2013).

DEFINITIONS

"prescribed"—see s.24(1).

GENERAL NOTE

13.24   The "claimant commitment" is a feature of "new style" ESA, "new style" JSA and UC. On the background to it, its nature and how (if at all) a claimant may challenge it, see further the annotations to Welfare Reform Act 2012 s.14 in *Vol. V: Universal Credit*. As regards "new style" JSA, this section defines the "claimant commitment" and is amplified by ESA Regs 2013 regs 44 (date and method of acceptance) and 45 (exceptions).

A "claimant commitment" is thus a record of the responsibilities of someone entitled to "new style" ESA in relation to an award in such form as the Secretary of State thinks fit, drawn up by him and reviewed and updated as he thinks fit. It must include such of the claimant's commitments as the Secretary of State thinks appropriate, any information prescribed by regulations, and such further information as the Secretary of State thinks appropriate. It is thus in some ways redolent of the jobseeker's agreement in "old style" JSA in that it is something imposed by the Secretary of State rather than something into which a claimant enters voluntarily.

[¹Work-focused interview requirement

11B. — (1) In this Part a "work-focused interview requirement" is a requirement that a person participate in one or more work-focused interviews as specified by the Secretary of State.

(2) A work-focused interview is an interview for prescribed purposes relating to work or work preparation.

(3) The purposes which may be prescribed under subsection (2) include in particular that of making it more likely in the opinion of the Secretary of State that the person will obtain paid work (or more paid work or better-paid work).

(4) The Secretary of State may specify how, when and where a work-focused interview is to take place.]

13.25

AMENDMENT

1. Welfare Reform Act 2012 s.57(1), (2) (various dates on or after April 29, 2013).

DEFINITION

"prescribed"—see s.24(1).
"work-focused interview requirement"—see subs.(1).

GENERAL NOTE

This section must be read with s.11D and ESA Regs 2013 reg.46 which specify those persons subject to no work-related requirements, who thus cannot be subjects of a work-focused interview requirement with which this section deals. This section is further amplified by ESA Regs 2013 reg.46 (purposes of a work-focused interview).

13.26

Imposition of a work-focused interview requirement means that its subject must participate in such number of work-focused interviews as the Secretary of State requires (subs.(1)). Such interviews are ones for prescribed purposes relating to work or work preparation, the central purpose is one of enhancing the likelihood of the claimant obtaining paid work, more paid work or better paid work (subss. (2), (3)). On the purposes of such an interview, see ESA Regs 2013 reg.46. The Secretary of State stipulates how, when and where a work-focused interview is to take place (subs.(4)).

[¹Work preparation requirement

11C — (1) In this Part a "work preparation requirement" is a requirement that a person take particular action specified by the Secretary of State for the purpose of making it more likely in the opinion of the Secretary of State that the person will obtain paid work (or more paid work or better-paid work).

(2) The Secretary of State may under subsection (1) specify the time to be devoted to any particular action.

(3) Action which may be specified under subsection (1) includes in particular—

(a) attending a skills assessment;
(b) improving personal presentation;
(c) participating in training;

13.27

(d) participating in an employment programme;

(e) undertaking work experience or a work placement;

(f) developing a business plan;

(g) any action prescribed for the purpose in subsection (1).

(4) The action which may be specified under subsection (1) includes taking part in a work-focused health-related assessment.

(5) In subsection (4) "work-focused health-related assessment" means an assessment by a health care professional approved by the Secretary of State which is carried out for the purpose of assessing—

(a) the extent to which the person's capability for work may be improved by taking steps in relation to their physical or mental condition, and

(b) such other matters relating to their physical or mental condition and the likelihood of their obtaining or remaining in work or being able to do so as may be prescribed.

(6) In subsection (5) "health care professional" means—

(a) a registered medical practitioner,

(b) a registered nurse,

(c) an occupational therapist or physiotherapist registered with a regulatory body established by an Order in Council under section 60 of the Health Act 1999, or

(d) a member of such other profession regulated by a body mentioned in section 25(3) of the National Health Service Reform and Health Care Professions Act 2002 as may be prescribed.]

AMENDMENT

1. Welfare Reform Act 2012 s.57(1), (2) (various dates on or after April 29, 2013).

DEFINITIONS

"health care professional"—see subs.(6).

"prescribed"—see s.24(1).

"work-focused health-related assessment"—see subs.(5).

"work preparation requirement"—see subs.(1).

GENERAL NOTE

13.28   This section must be read with s.11D and ESA Regs 2013 reg.47, which together set out those persons who cannot be subject to any work related requirement at all, and with ESA Regs 2013 reg.48 which, in stipulating which persons can be subject only to a work-focused interview requirement, exempt those persons from the work-preparation requirements with which this section deals.

Work-preparation requirements require their subject to take particular actions specified by the Secretary of State as in his opinion are likely to enhance the likelihood of that claimant obtaining paid work, more paid work or better paid work (subs.(1)). An inclusive (i.e. not exhaustive) list of such actions is set out in subs. (3) and (4) and there is power to set out further ones in regulations (subs.(3)(g), although as yet this power has not been exercised. The time to be spent on each action will also be stipulated by the Secretary of State (subs.(2)).

Although s.11H(2) provides that in considering whether to impose a work-focused interview requirement the Secretary of State must have regard to such matters as may be prescribed, as yet it appears that none have been prescribed.

[¹Persons subject to no work-related requirements

11D.—(1) The Secretary of State may not impose any work-related requirement on a person falling within this section.

13.29

(2) A person falls within this section if—

(a) the person has limited capability for work and work-related activity,

(b) the person has regular and substantial caring responsibilities for a severely disabled person,

(c) the person is a single person responsible for a child under the age of 1,

(d) the person is of a prescribed description.

(3) Where a person falls within this section, any work-related requirement previously applying to the person ceases to have effect.

(4) In this section—

"regular and substantial caring responsibilities" has such meaning as may be prescribed;

"severely disabled" has such meaning as may be prescribed.]

AMENDMENT

1. Welfare Reform Act 2012 s.57(1), (2) (various dates on or after April 29, 2013).

DEFINITIONS

"limited capability for work"—see ss.24(1), 1(4).
"limited capability for work-related activity"—see ss.24(1), 2(5).
"prescribed"—see s.24(1).
"regular and substantial caring responsibilities"—see subs.(4); ESA Regs 2013 reg.47(2), (3).
"severely disabled"—see subs.(4); ESA Regs 2013 reg.47(5).

GENERAL NOTE

This section, together with ESA Regs 2013 reg.47, sets out those who are exempt from the imposition of any work-related requirement (subs.(1), (2)).

13.30

Some claimants will fall permanently within one of the exempt groups and thus never be subject to such requirements. Others, as their condition improves or relevant circumstances change (e.g. the single parent as their child gets older) may move out of the exempt group and can then be subject to such requirements. Others, subject to such requirements because not in an exempt category, may find that their condition worsens or relevant circumstances change (e.g. a child is born to a single parent or the claimant has taken on regular and substantial caring responsibilities for a severely disabled person) so that they then fall into an exempt category, in which case any work-related requirement previously applying to them ceases to have effect (subs.(3)).

Subs.(2) sets out four exempt categories. Firstly, it exempts persons falling within the "support" group as having limited capability both for work and work-related activity (para. (a)). Secondly, it protects from imposition of work-related requirements those having regular and substantial caring responsibilities for a severely disabled person (para. (b)), those key terms being defined in ESA Regs 2013 reg.47(2), (3) (regular and substantial caring responsibilities) and 47(5) (severely disabled). Thirdly, it exempts single parents having responsibility for a child under the age of one (para.(c)). Finally, it exempts those of a "prescribed description", currently those groups listed in ESA Regs 2013 reg.47(1).

[¹Persons subject to work-focused interview requirement only

13.31

11E —(1) A person falls within this section if—

(a) the person is a single person responsible for a child who is aged at least 1 and is under a prescribed age (which may not be less than 3), or

(b) the person is of a prescribed description.

(2) The Secretary of State may, subject to this Part, impose a work-focused interview requirement on a person entitled to an employment and support allowance who falls within this section.

(3) The Secretary of State may not impose a work preparation requirement on a person falling within this section (and, where a person falls within this section, a work preparation requirement previously applying to the person ceases to have effect).]

AMENDMENT

1. Welfare Reform Act 2012 s.57(1), (2) (various dates on or after April 29, 2013).

DEFINITIONS

"prescribed"—see s.24(1).
"work-focused interview requirement"—see s.11B(1).
"work preparation requirement"—see s.11C(1).

GENERAL NOTE

13.32   This section, together with ESA Regs 2013 reg.48 sets out those who, while not exempt from the imposition of all work-related requirements under s.11D, can be subject only to the work-focused interview requirement, thus affording such person exemption from the imposition of any work-preparation requirement. Since someone might not at the outset of the "new style" ESA award have been in one of the categories protected by this section and have thus been the subject of a work-preparation requirement any such requirement will cease to have effect if later in the currency of the award that person falls into one or more of the protected categories.

Subs.(1) stipulates two protected categories. Firstly, it protects a single person responsible for a child aged at least one and below three (the prescribed age set in ESA Regs 2013 reg.48(1)). Secondly, it exempts from work preparation requirements anyone of a prescribed description, currently those listed in ESA Regs 2013 reg.47(1).

Although s.11H(2) provides that in considering whether to impose a work-focused interview requirement the Secretary of State must have regard to such matters as may be prescribed, as yet it appears that none have been prescribed.

[¹Persons subject to work preparation and work-focused interview requirement

13.33   **11F**— (1) A person who does not fall within section 11D or 11E falls within this section.

(2) The Secretary of State may, subject to this Part, impose a work preparation requirement or work-focused interview requirement on a person entitled to an employment and support allowance who falls within this section.]

AMENDMENT

1. Welfare Reform Act 2012 s.57(1), (2) (various dates on or after April 29, 2013).

DEFINITIONS

"work-focused interview requirement"—see s.11B(1).
"work preparation requirement"—see s.11C(1).

GENERAL NOTE

This section stipulates that anyone entitled to "new style" ESA not protected by ss.11D or 11E, above, can be subject to a work-focused interview requirement, to a work-preparation requirement or to both such requirements.

13.34

[¹Connected requirements

11G —(1) The Secretary of State may require a person entitled to an employment and support allowance to participate in an interview for any purpose relating to—

13.35

(a) the imposition of a work-related requirement on the person;

(b) verifying the person's compliance with a work-related requirement;

(c) assisting the person to comply with a work-related requirement.

(2) The Secretary of State may specify how, when and where such an interview is to take place.

(3) The Secretary of State may, for the purpose of verifying a person's compliance with a work-related requirement, require the person to—

(a) provide to the Secretary of State information and evidence specified by the Secretary of State in a manner so specified;

(b) confirm compliance in a manner so specified.

(4) The Secretary of State may require a person to report to the Secretary of State any specified changes in their circumstances which are relevant to—

(a) the imposition of work-related requirements on the person;

(b) the person's compliance with a work-related requirement.]

AMENDMENT

1. Welfare Reform Act 2012 s.57(1), (2) (various dates on or after April 29, 2013).

DEFINITION

"work-related requirement"—see s.11(2).

GENERAL NOTE

This section deals with the processes surrounding the imposition of work-related requirements, with monitoring compliance with them and with assisting those subject to them with compliance with them. The processes can involve participation in an interview with respect to such matters (subs.(1), (2)), providing specified information and evidence or simply confirmation of compliance as part of verification of compliance (subs.(3)), and reporting specified changes of relevant circumstances (subs.(4)).

13.36

[¹Imposition of requirements

11H.—(1) Regulations may make provision—

13.37

(a) Where the Secretary of State may impose a requirement under this Part, as to when the requirement must or must not be imposed;

(b) where the Secretary of State may specify any action to be taken in relation to a requirement under this Part, as to what action must or must not be specified;

(c) where the Secretary of State may specify any other matter in relation to a requirement under this Part, as to what must or must not be specified in respect of that matter.

(2) Where the Secretary of State may impose a work-focused interview requirement, or specify a particular action under section 11C(1), the Secretary of State must have regard to such matters as may be prescribed.

(3) Where the Secretary of State may impose a requirement under this Part, or specify any action to be taken in relation to such a requirement, the Secretary of State may revoke or change what has been imposed or specified.

(4) Notification of a requirement imposed under this Part (or any change to or revocation of such a requirement) is, if not included in the claimant commitment, to be in such manner as the Secretary of State may determine.

(5) Regulations must make provision to secure that, in prescribed circumstances, where a person has recently been a victim of domestic violence—

  (a) a requirement imposed on that person under this Part ceases to have effect for a period of 13 weeks, and

  (b) the Secretary of State may not impose any other requirement on that person during that period.

(6) For the purposes of subsection (5)—

  (a) "domestic violence" has such meaning as may be prescribed;

  (b) "victim of domestic violence" means a person on or against whom domestic violence is inflicted or threatened (and regulations under subsection (5) may prescribe circumstances in which a person is to be treated as being or not being a victim of domestic violence);

  (c) a person has recently been a victim of domestic violence if a prescribed period has not expired since the violence was inflicted or threatened.]

AMENDMENT

1. Welfare Reform Act 2012 s.57(1), (2) (various dates on or after April 29, 2013).

DEFINITIONS

"domestic violence"—see subs.(6)(a); ESA Regs 2013 reg.49(5).
"prescribed"—see s.24(1).
"regulations"—see s.24(1).
"victim of domestic violence"—see subs.(6)(b).
"week"—see s.24(1).
"work-focused interview requirement"—see s.11B(1).

GENERAL NOTE

13.38   Subs.(1) and (5) enable regulations to be made on a variety of matters concerned with the imposition of work-related requirements on those who can be subject to them. To date, the only one made appears to be ESA Regs 2013 reg.48—made pursuant to subs.(5)— dealing with the respite period afforded recent victims of domestic violence.

Although subs.(2) provides that in considering whether to impose a work-focused interview requirement the Secretary of State must have regard to such matters as may be prescribed, as yet it appears that none have been prescribed.

Work-related requirements imposed or particular action specified can be revoked or changed (subs.(3)). If not embodied in the claimant commitment (see s.11A), the imposition of requirements or their revocation or alteration is to be made in such manner as the Secretary of State determines (subs.(4)).

[¹Compliance with requirements

13.39   **11I.** — Regulations may make provision as to circumstances in which a person is to be treated as having—

(a) complied with or not complied with any requirement imposed under this Part or any aspect of such a requirement, or

(b) taken or not taken any particular action specified by the Secretary of State in relation to such a requirement.]

AMENDMENT

1. Welfare Reform Act 2012 s.57(1), (2) (various dates on or after April 29, 2013).

DEFINITIONS

"regulations"—see s.24(1).

GENERAL NOTE

This is comparable to WRA 2012, s.25, as regards UC, and Jobseekers Act 1995 s.6I, as regards "new style" JSA. The comparator provisions have resulted in UC Regs 2013 regs 94–97 and JSA Regs 2013 regs 11–13. In contrast, this section has produced no amplifying regulations.

13.40

[¹Sanctions

11J.—(1) The amount of an award of an employment and support allowance is to be reduced in accordance with this section in the event of a failure by a person which is sanctionable under this section.

(2) It is a failure sanctionable under this section if a person—

(a) fails for no good reason to comply with a work-related requirement;

(b) fails for no good reason to comply with a requirement under section 11G.

(3) Regulations are to specify—

(a) the amount of a reduction under this section, and

(b) the period for which such a reduction has effect.

(4) Regulations under subsection (3)(b) may provide that a reduction under this section in relation to any failure is to have effect for—

(a) a period continuing until the person meets a compliance condition specified by the Secretary of State,

(b) a fixed period not exceeding 26 weeks which is—

  (i) specified in the regulations, or

  (ii) determined in any case by the Secretary of State, or

(c) a combination of both.

(5) In subsection (4)(a)"compliance condition" means—

(a) a condition that the failure ceases, or

(b) a condition relating to future compliance with a work-related requirement or a requirement under section 11G.

(6) A compliance condition specified under subsection (4) (a) may be—

(a) revoked or varied by the Secretary of State;

(b) notified to the person in such manner as the Secretary of State may determine.

(7) A period fixed under subsection (4) (b) may in particular depend on either or both the following—

(a) the number of failures by the person sanctionable under this section;

(b) the period between such failures.

(8) Regulations may provide—

(a) for cases in which no reduction is to be made under this section;

13.41

(b) for a reduction under this section made in relation to an award that is terminated to be applied to any new award made within a prescribed period of the termination;

(c) for the termination or suspension of a reduction under this section.]

AMENDMENT

1. Welfare Reform Act 2012 s.57(1), (2) (various dates on or after April 29, 2013).

DEFINITIONS

"compliance condition"—see subs.(5).
"prescribed"—see s.24(1).
"regulations"—see s.24(1).
"week"—see s.24(1).
"work-related requirement"—see s.11(2).

GENERAL NOTE

13.42 There is no direct sanction for failing to comply with a claimant commitment (see s.11A). Instead failure "for no good reason" (see below) to comply with a work-related requirement or with a connected requirement under s.11G is sanctionable under this section (subss.(1), (2)).

The sanction consists of reduction of an ESA award for a period, the amount and the period being determined by regulations (subs.(3)). As regards period, such regulations may provide that a reduction under this section in relation to any failure is to have effect (i) for a period continuing until the person meets a compliance condition specified by the Secretary of State or (ii) for a fixed period of not more than 26 weeks set by regulations, or determined in any case by the Secretary of State, or (iii) for a period combining (i) and (ii). (subs.(4)). The length of period (ii) (the fixed period) can depend on the number of failures by the person sanctionable under this section, the period between them, or both (subs.(7)). As regards period (i), a compliance condition is one requiring that the failure cease and/or one relating to future compliance with a work-related requirement or with a connected requirement under s.11G (subs.(5), (6)). The regulations in question are ESA Regs 2013 regs 50–53, 58–60.

Under subs.(8)(c), regulations can provide for the termination or suspension of a reduction. On its termination see ESA Regs 2013 reg.57. On its suspension see ESA Regs 2013 reg.56. Subs.(8)(b) empowers regulations to enable the unexpired reduction period in respect of an award of ESA that is terminated to be applied to a subsequent award of ESA within a prescribed period. The product is ESA Regs 2013 reg.55.

Although subs.(8)(a) empowers regulations to specify cases in which no reduction is to be made, this power has not yet been exercised as regards "new style" ESA, although the comparator powers as regards UC and "new style" JSA have been.

"for no good reason"
13.43 Exactly what this means is as yet unclear and will only ultimately be clarified through appeals against sanctions. This term is used both here and as regards UC (WRA 2012 ss.26, 27, see *Vol. V: Universal Credit*, Pt 2) and "new style" JSA (see Jobseekers Act 1995 ss.6J, 6K in Vol.II). In contrast, "old style" JSA deploys the term "without a good reason" while "new style" ESA in the ESA Regs 2013 refers to "without good cause" as regards failures to provide information or attend for or participate in a medical examinations, as do the comparable provisions with respect to "old style" ESA in the ESA Regs 2008.

Despite the variations in terminology, the common idea behind each is that in certain circumstances failures are to be "excused", not to be punished with a sanction. It may be that, despite differences in wording, there will be a commonalty of interpretation, with decision-makers and tribunals seeing their application as requiring consideration of all relevant circumstances but also containing a large element of judgment according to the individual facts of particular cases. Such has been the case with concepts such as "good cause" or "just cause" (see annotations to Jobseekers Act 1995 s.19 as applicable to "old style" JSA in Vol.II). It may be that "for no good reason" will, as with the previously familiar concept of "just cause", be seen to require a balancing between the interests of the claimant and those of the community of contributions payers and taxpayers which finance the benefit in question. The problem, however, remains that decision-makers and tribunals will see the use of different terminology as requiring a different approach; if the approach was meant to be the same as in the past, why deploy different, and arguably more restrictive, words? The phrase "for no good reason" might be read as suggesting that something has been done or not done capriciously or arbitrarily, without any real thought or application of reason. It could therefore be argued that it is easier for a claimant to show that s/he did not act for no good reason and on that basis that the balancing of interests mentioned above could not be applicable. It would be enough that the claimant acted or failed to act rationally in the light of his or her own interests. It can of course be objected that this approach does not give proper weight to the identification of what is a good reason. It is to be hoped that a priority for the Upper Tribunal in dealing with UC, "new style" ESA and "new style" JSA will be the resolution of this ambiguity caused by using different phraseology to that deployed to deal with similar issues in the past.

[¹Delegation and contracting out

11K.—(1) The functions of the Secretary of State under sections 11 to 11I may be exercised by, or by the employees of, such person as the Secretary of State may authorise for the purpose (an "authorised person").

13.44

(2) An authorisation given by virtue of this section may authorise the exercise of a function—

(a) wholly or to a limited extent;

(b) generally or in particular cases or areas;

(c) unconditionally or subject to conditions.

(3) An authorisation under this section—

(a) may specify its duration;

(b) may be varied or revoked at any time by the Secretary of State;

(c) does not prevent the Secretary of State or another person from exercising the function to which the authorisation relates.

(4) Anything done or omitted to be done by or in relation to an authorised person (or an employee of that person) in, or in connection with, the exercise or purported exercise of the function concerned is to be treated for all purposes as done or omitted to be done by or in relation to the Secretary of State or (as the case may be) an officer of the Secretary of State.

(5) Subsection (4) does not apply—

(a) for the purposes of so much of any contract made between the authorised person and the Secretary of State as relates to the exercise of the function, or

(b) for the purposes of any criminal proceedings brought in respect of anything done or omitted to be done by the authorised person (or an employee of that person).

(6) Where—

(a) the authorisation of an authorised person is revoked, and

(b) at the time of the revocation so much of any contract made between the authorised person and the Secretary of State as relates to the exercise of the function is subsisting,

the authorised person is entitled to treat the contract as repudiated by the Secretary of State (and not as frustrated by reason of the revocation).]

AMENDMENT

1. Welfare Reform Act 2012 s.57(1), (2) (various dates on or after April 29, 2013).

DEFINITIONS

"authorised person"—see subs.(1).

GENERAL NOTE

13.45   This section gives the Secretary of State wide powers to delegate the exercise of certain of his/her functions to others and to contract them out to public or private sector providers. The functions, however, are only those in ss.11 to 11I, and so do not embrace the imposition of sanctions covered by s.11J.

Hardship payments

13.46   **16A.** [¹. . .]

AMENDMENT

1. Repealed by Welfare Reform Act 2012 s.147 and Sch.14 Pt 5 (various dates on or after April 29, 2013).

13.47   *WRA 2007 s.17 applies to "new style" ESA in exactly the same way as to "old style" ESA. For text see the first Section of this book (Statutes). Note that it forms one of the "parent Act" bases for ESA Regs 2013 in terms of regulations on the calculation of income in terms of earnings from employed earner's employment and from self-employment. To date, capital is irrelevant as regards CESA and "new style" ESA.*

Disqualification

13.48   **18.**—(1) Regulations may provide for a person to be disqualified for receiving an employment and support allowance, or treated for such purposes as the regulations may provide as not having limited capability for work, if—

(a) he has become someone who has limited capability for work through his own misconduct,

(b) he remains someone who has limited capability for work through his failure without good cause to follow medical advice, or

(c) he fails without good cause to observe any prescribed rules of behaviour.

(2) Regulations under subsection (1) shall provide for any such disqualification, or treatment, to be for such period not exceeding 6 weeks as may be determined in accordance with Chapter 2 of Part 1 of the Social Security Act 1998 (c. 14).

(3) Regulations may prescribe for the purposes of subsection (1)—

(a) matters which are, or are not, to be taken into account in determining whether a person has good cause for any act or omission;

(b) circumstances in which a person is, or is not, to be regarded as having good cause for any act or omission.

(4) Except where regulations otherwise provide, a person shall be disqualified for receiving [¹an employment and support allowance] for any
period during which he is—
  (a) absent from Great Britain, or
  (b) undergoing imprisonment or detention in legal custody.

AMENDMENT

  1. Welfare Reform Act 2012 s.33(3) and Sch.3 para.26 (d) (various dates
on or after April 29, 2013).

DEFINITIONS

  "limited capability for work"—see s.1(4).
  "prescribed"—see s.24(1).
  "regulations"—see s.24(1).
  "week"—see s.24(1).

GENERAL NOTE

  This has the same effect as WRA 2007 s.18 as applicable to "old style" ESA, the   **13.49**
amendment merely replacing the term "contributory allowance" with "an employment and support allowance" in subs.(4), since, with the abolition of IRESA in
universal credit areas, "new style" ESA has only one form.

Subsection (1)-(3)
  The relevant regulation for "new style" ESA is ESA Regs 2013 reg.93, which has   **13.50**
the same effect as ESA Regs 2008 reg.157. No use has yet been made for either type
of ESA of the rule-making power in subs.(3).

Subsection (4)
  The relevant regulations for "new style" ESA are ESA Regs 2013 regs 88–92,   **13.51**
which have the same effect as ESA Regs 2008 regs 151–155.

  WRA 2007 s.19 applies to "new style" ESA in exactly the same way as to "old style"   **13.52**
ESA. For text see the first Section of this book (Statutes).

Relationship with statutory payments

  20.—(1) A person is not entitled to an employment and support allow-   **13.53**
ance in respect of a day if, for the purposes of statutory sick pay, that day–
  (a) is a day of incapacity for work in relation to a contract of service, and
  (b) falls within a period of entitlement (whether or not it is a qualifying
      day).
  (2) Except as regulations may provide, a woman who is entitled to statutory maternity pay is not entitled to [¹an employment and support allow-
ance] in respect of a day that falls within the maternity pay period.
  (3) Regulations may provide that–
  (a) an amount equal to a woman's statutory maternity pay for a period
      shall be deducted from [¹an employment and support allowance] in
      respect of the same period,
  (b) a woman shall only be entitled to [¹an employment and support
      allowance] if there is a balance after the deduction, and
  (c) if there is such a balance, a woman shall be entitled to [¹an employ-
      ment and support allowance] at a weekly rate equal to it.
  (4) Except as regulations may provide, a person who is entitled to

statutory adoption pay is not entitled to [¹an employment and support allowance] in respect of a day that falls within the adoption pay period.

(5) Regulations may provide that–

(a) an amount equal to a person's statutory adoption pay for a period shall be deducted from [¹an employment and support allowance] in respect of the same period,

(b) a person shall only be entitled to [¹an employment and support allowance] if there is a balance after the deduction, and

(c) if there is such a balance, a person shall be entitled to [¹an employment and support allowance] at a weekly rate equal to it.

(6) Except as regulations may provide, a person who is entitled to [² statutory shared parental pay] is not entitled to [¹ an employment and support allowance] in respect of [² a day that falls within a period in respect of which statutory shared parental pay is payable].

(7) Regulations may provide that–

(a) an amount equal to a person's [² statutory shared parental pay for a period] shall be deducted from [¹an employment and support allowance] in respect of the same period,

(b) a person shall only be entitled to [¹an employment and support allowance] if there is a balance after the deduction, and

(c) if there is such a balance, a person shall be entitled to [¹an employment and support allowance] at a weekly rate equal to it.

(8) In this section–

[³ . . .]

"the adoption pay period" has the meaning given in section 171ZN(2) of that Act;

"the maternity pay period" has the meaning given in section 165(1) of that Act.

AMENDMENTS

1. Welfare Reform Act 2012 s.33 and Sch.3 para.26(e) (various dates on or after April 29, 2013).
2. Children and Families Act 2014 c. 6 Sch.7 para.73(2) and (3) (June 30, 2014)
3. Children and Families Act 2014 c. 6 Sch.7 para.73(4) (April 5, 2015).

DEFINITIONS

"the additional paternity pay period"—see subs.(8).
"the adoption pay period"—see subs.(8).
"Contributions and Benefits Act"—see s.65.
"entitled"—see s.24(1).
"the maternity pay period"—see subs.(8).

GENERAL NOTE

13.54   This has the same effect as WRA 2007 s.20 as applicable to "old style" ESA, the amendments merely replacing the term "contributory allowance" with "an employment and support allowance", since, with the abolition of IRESA in universal credit areas, "new style" ESA has only one form.

13.55   *WRA 2007 ss.21 and 22 apply to "new style" ESA in exactly the same way as to "old style" ESA. For text see the first Part of this book (Statutes).*

Recovery of sums in respect of maintenance

23. [¹ . . .]   **13.56**

AMENDMENT

1. Repealed by Welfare Reform Act 2012 s.147 and Sch.14 Pt 1 (various dates on or after April 29, 2013).

General

Interpretation of Part 1

24.—(1) In this Part—   **13.57**
"claimant" means a person who has claimed an employment and support allowance;
[¹. . .];
"employment" and "employed" have the meanings prescribed for the purposes of this Part;
"entitled", in relation to an employment and support allowance, is to be construed in accordance with—
(a) the provisions of this Act,
(b) section 1 of the Administration Act (entitlement dependent on making of claim), and
(c) section 27 of the Social Security Act 1998 (c. 14) (restrictions on entitlement in certain cases of error);
[¹. . .];
[¹. . .];
"limited capability for work" shall be construed in accordance with section 1(4);
"limited capability for work-related activity" shall be construed in accordance with section 2(5);
"period of limited capability for work" has the meaning prescribed for the purposes of this Part;
"prescribed" means specified in, or determined in accordance with, regulations;
"regulations" means regulations made by the Secretary of State;
"week" means a period of 7 days beginning with a Sunday or such other period of 7 days as may be prescribed;
"work-related activity" has the meaning given by section 13(7).
(2) For the purposes of this Part, the assessment phase, in relation to a claimant, is the period—
(a) beginning, subject to subsection (3), with the first day of the period for which he is entitled to an employment and support allowance, and
(b) ending with such day as may be prescribed.
(3) Regulations may prescribe circumstances in which the assessment phase is to begin with such day as may be prescribed.
(3A) [². . .]
(3B) [². . .]
(4) For the purposes of this Part, a person is a member of the support group if he is a person in respect of whom it is determined that he has, or is to be treated as having, limited capability for work-related activity.

AMENDMENT

1. Repealed by Welfare Reform Act 2012 s.147 and Sch.14 Pt 1 (various dates on or after April 29, 2013).

2. Repealed by Welfare Reform Act 2012 s.147 and Sch.14 Pt 5 ((various dates on or after April 29, 2013).

DEFINITIONS

"Administration Act"—see s.65.
"Contributions and Benefits Act"—see s.65.

GENERAL NOTE

13.58   This has the same effect as WRA 2007 s.24 as applicable to "old style" ESA, save that the amendments made remove definitions of "contributory allowance" and "income related allowance" since, with the abolition of IRESA in universal credit areas, "new style" ESA has only one form. Similarly, paras (3A) and (3B) are removed as relevant only to IRESA.

The definition of "income support" is also removed consequent on the abolition of that benefit in universal credit areas.

Parliamentary control

13.59   **26.**—(1) None of the following regulations shall be made unless a draft of the statutory instrument containing them has been laid before, and approved by a resolution of, each House of Parliament—

(a) regulations under section 2(2)(c) or (3)(c)[5 . . .];

[4 (aa) the first regulations under section 11D(2)(d)or 11J;]

[6 (b) . . .];

(c) regulations which by virtue of section 19(1) are to have effect for a limited period.

[1, 3 . . .]

(2) A statutory instrument that—

(a) contains regulations made under this Part, and

(b) is not subject to a requirement that a draft of the instrument be laid before, and approved by a resolution of, each House of Parliament, shall be subject to annulment in pursuance of a resolution of either House of Parliament.

[2(3) A statutory instrument containing an order under section 1A shall be subject to annulment in pursuance of a resolution of either House of Parliament.]

AMENDMENT

1. Welfare Reform Act 2009 s.11 and Sch.3 para.8(4) (November 12, 2009).

2. Welfare Reform Act 2012 s.51(3) (March 20, 2012 (regulation-making purposes); May 1, 2012 (all other purposes)).

3. Welfare Reform Act 2012 s.147 and Sch.14 Pt 6 para.1 (May 8, 2012).

4. Welfare Reform Act 2012 s.57(6) (February 25, 2013).

5. Welfare Reform Act 2012 s.147 and Sch.14 Pt 1 (various dates on or after April 29, 2013).

6. Welfare Reform Act 2012 s.147 and Sch.14 Pt 5 (various dates on or after April 29, 2013).

GENERAL NOTE

This has the same effect as regards "new style" ESA as WRA 2007 s.26 as applicable to "old style" ESA, save that references to rule making powers applicable to IRESA have been removed, coterminous with the abolition of IRESA in universal credit areas.

13.60

Financial provisions relating to Part 1

27.—(1) There shall be paid out of the National Insurance Fund [¹any sums payable relating to Part 1 by way of employment and support allowance].

13.61

(2) There shall be paid out of money provided by Parliament—

(a) [² . . .]

(b) any administrative expenses of the Secretary of State or the Commissioners for Her Majesty's Revenue and Customs in carrying this Part into effect.

(3) The Secretary of State shall pay into the National Insurance Fund sums estimated by him to be equivalent in amount to sums recovered by him in connection with payments of [¹employment and support] allowance.

(4) [² . . .].

AMENDMENTS

1. Welfare Reform Act 2012 s.33 and Sch.3 para.25 (various dates on or after April 29, 2013).

2. Welfare Reform Act 2012 s.147 and Sch.14 Pt 1 (various dates on or after April 29, 2013).

GENERAL NOTE

Apart from the removal of provisions relevant only to IRESA, given its abolition in universal credit areas, this has the same effect as WRA 2007 s.27 as regards "old style" ESA.

13.62

WRA 2007 s.28 applies to "new style" ESA in exactly the same way as to "old style" ESA. For text see the first Section of this book (Statutes).

13.63

Transition relating to Part 1

29. [¹ . . .]

13.64

AMENDMENT

1. Welfare Reform Act 2012 s.147 and Sch.14 Pt 1 (various dates on or after April 29, 2013).

WRA 2007 ss.30–63: omitted as not relevant to either form of ESA

13.65

WRA 2007 ss.64–71 apply to "new style" ESA in exactly the same way as to "old style" ESA. For text see the first Section of this book (Statutes).

13.66

SCHEDULES

SCHEDULE 1   **section 1**

EMPLOYMENT AND SUPPORT ALLOWANCE: ADDITIONAL CONDITIONS

PART 1
[⁴ . . .]
Conditions relating to national insurance

13.67   1.—(1) The first condition is that—
   (a)   the claimant has actually paid Class 1 or Class 2 contributions in respect of one of
         the last [²two] complete tax years ("the base tax year") before the beginning of the
         relevant benefit year,
   (b)   those contributions must have been paid before the relevant benefit week, and
         [²(c)the claimant's earnings determined in accordance with sub- paragraph (2) must
         be not less than the base tax year's lower earnings limit multiplied by 26.]
      [²(2) The earnings referred to in sub-paragraph (1)(c)are the aggregate of—
   (a)   the claimant's relevant earnings for the base tax year upon which primary Class 1
         contributions have been paid or treated as paid, and
   (b)   the claimant's earnings factors derived from Class 2 contributions.
      (3) Regulations may make provision for the purposes of sub- paragraph (2)(a)for determin-
ing the claimant's relevant earnings for the base tax year.
      (3A) Regulations under sub-paragraph (3) may, in particular, make provision—
   (a)   for making that determination by reference to the amount of a person's earnings for
         periods comprised in the base tax year;
   (b)   for determining the amount of a person's earnings for any such period by—
         (i)   first determining the amount of the earnings for the period in accordance with
               regulations made for the purposes of section 3(2) of the Contributions and
               Benefits Act, and
         (ii) then disregarding so much of the amount found in accordance with sub- para-
               graph (i) as exceeded the base tax year's lower earnings limit (or the prescribed
               equivalent).]
      (4) Regulations may—
   (a)   provide for the condition set out in sub-paragraph (1) to be taken to be satisfied in the
         case of [³persons—
         (i)   who] have been entitled to any prescribed description of benefit during any
               prescribed period or at any prescribed time [³or
         (ii) who satisfy other prescribed conditions]
   (b)   with a view to securing any relaxation of the requirements of that condition in relation
         to persons who have been [³entitled as mentioned in paragraph (a)(i)], provide for
         that condition to apply in relation to them subject to prescribed modifications.
      (5) In sub-paragraph (4), "benefit" means—
      [⁶(za) universal credit;]
   (a)   any benefit within the meaning of section 122(1) of the Contributions and Benefits
         Act,
   (b)   any benefit under Parts 7 to 12 of that Act,
   (c)   credits under regulations under section 22(5) of that Act,
   [¹(ca) credits under section 23A of that Act,]
   (d)   [⁵an employment and support allowance], and
   (e)   working tax credit.

13.68   2.—(1) The second condition is that—
   (a)   the claimant has in respect of the last two complete tax years before the beginning of
         the relevant benefit year either paid or been credited with Class 1 or Class 2 contribu-
         tions or been credited with earnings, and
   (b)   the earnings factor derived as mentioned in sub-paragraph (2) must be not less in each
         of those years than the year's lower earnings limit multiplied by 50.
      (2) The earnings factor referred to in sub-paragraph (1)(b) is the aggregate of the claimant's
earnings factors derived—
   (a)   from so much of his earnings as did not exceed the upper earnings limit for the year
         and upon which primary Class 1 contributions have been paid or treated as paid or
         from earnings credited, and

(b) from Class 2 contributions.

(3) Where primary Class 1 contributions have been paid or treated as paid on any part of a person's earnings, sub-paragraph (2)(a) shall have effect as if such contributions had been paid or treated as paid on so much of the earnings as did not exceed the upper earnings limit for the year.

3.—(1) For the purposes of paragraphs 1 and 2—

13.69

(a) "benefit year" means a period which is a benefit year for the purposes of Part 2 of the Contributions and Benefits Act or such other period as may be prescribed for the purposes of this Part of this Schedule;

(b) "Class 1 contributions", "Class 2 contributions" and "primary Class 1 contributions" have the same meaning as in the Contributions and Benefits Act (see section 1 of that Act);

(c) "earnings" shall be construed in accordance with sections 3, 4 and 112 of that Act;

(d) "earnings factor" shall be construed in accordance with sections 22 and 23 of that Act;

(e) "lower earnings limit" and "upper earnings limit" shall be construed in accordance with section 5 of that Act and references to the lower or upper earnings limit of a tax year are to whatever is (or was) the limit in force for that year under that section;

(f) "relevant benefit year" is the benefit year which includes the beginning of the period of limited capability for work which includes the relevant benefit week;

(g) "tax year" means the 12 months beginning with 6th April in any year.

(2) Regulations may provide for sub-paragraph (1)(f) to have effect in prescribed circumstances with prescribed modifications in the case of—

(a) a person who has previously ceased to be entitled to [⁵an employment and support allowance];

(b) a person who has made a claim for an employment and support allowance in connectionwith which he failed to satisfy one or both of the conditions in paragraphs 1 and 2.

Condition relating to youth

4.—(1) The third condition is that—

13.70

(a) the claimant was under 20 or, in prescribed cases, 25 when the relevant period of limited capability for work began,

(b) he is not receiving full-time education,

(c) he satisfies such conditions as may be prescribed with respect to residence or presence in Great Britain (or both),

(d) there has been a day in the relevant period of limited capability for work—

(i) which was a day on which he was aged at least 16, and

(ii) which was preceded by a period of 196 consecutive days throughout which he had limited capability for work.

(2) In sub-paragraph (1), "relevant period of limited capability for work" means the period of limited capability for work which includes the relevant benefit week.

(3) Regulations may prescribe circumstances in which sub-paragraph (1)(a)does not apply in the case of a person who has previously ceased to be entitled to an employment and support allowance to which he was entitled by virtue of satisfying the condition set out in sub-paragraph (1).

(4) Regulations may make provision about when, for the purposes of sub-paragraph (1)(b), a person is, or is not, to be treated as receiving full-time education.

"Relevant benefit week"

5.—In this Part of this Schedule, "relevant benefit week" means the week in relation to which the question of entitlement to an employment and support allowance is being considered.

13.71

AMENDMENT

1. Pensions Act 2007 Sch.1 para.11 (September 27, 2007).

2. Welfare Reform Act 2009 s.13 (November 1, 2010).

3. Welfare Reform Act 2009 s.13(5) (November 29, 2011).

4. Welfare Reform Act 2012 s.147 and Sch.14 Pt 1 (various dates on or after April 29, 2013).

5. Welfare Reform Act 2012 s.33(3) and Sch.3 para.26 (f) (various dates on or after April 29, 2013).

6. Welfare Reform Act 2012 s.31 and Sch.2 para.65 (April 29, 2013).

13.72   "the base tax year"—see para.1(1) (a).
"benefit"—see para.1(5).
"benefit year"—see para.3(1) (a) .
"Class 1 contributions"—see para.3(1) (b).
"Class 2 contributions"—see para.3(1) (b).
"Contributions and Benefits Act"—see s.65.
"earnings"—see para.3(1) (c).
"earnings factor"—see para.3(1) (d).
"entitled"—see s.24(1).
"limited capability for work"—see s.1(4).
"lower earnings limit"—see para.3(1) (e).
"primary Class 1 contributions"—see para.3(1) (b).
"regulations"—see s.24(1).
"relevant benefit week"—see para.5.
"relevant benefit year"—see para.3(1) (f).
"relevant period of limited capability for work"—see para.4(2).
"tax year"—see para.3(1) (g).
"upper earnings limit"—see para.3(1)(e).
"week"—see s.24(1).

GENERAL NOTE

13.73   See commentary to WRA 2007 Sch.1 Pt 1 in the first Section of this book.

13.74   *Part 2 of Sch.1, dealing with IRESA, was repealed in universal credit areas by the Welfare Reform Act 2012 s.147 and Sch.14 Pt 1 with effect from various dates on or after April 29, 2013.*

[¹ SCHEDULE 1A   Section 15A

PERSONS DEPENDENT ON DRUGS ETC.

13.75   [² Repealed.]]

AMENDMENTS

1. Welfare Reform Act 2009 s.11 and Sch.3 para.7 (November 12, 2009).
2. Welfare Reform Act 2012 ss.60(2), 150(2) (b) (May 8, 2012).

SCHEDULE 2   Section 22

EMPLOYMENT AND SUPPORT ALLOWANCE: SUPPLEMENTARY PROVISIONS

Limited capability for work

13.76   **1.**—Regulations may make provision—
(a) for a person to be treated in prescribed circumstances as having, or as not having, limited capability for work;
(b) for the question of whether a person has limited capability for work to be determined notwithstanding that he is for the time being treated by virtue of regulations under sub-paragraph (a) as having limited capability for work;
(c) for the question of whether a person has limited capability for work to be determined afresh in prescribed circumstances.

Waiting days

13.77   **2.**—Except in prescribed circumstances, a person is not entitled to an employment and support allowance in respect of a prescribed number of days at the beginning of a period of limited capability for work.

Periods of less than a week

3.—Regulations may make provision in relation to—
    (a) entitlement to an employment and support allowance, or
    (b) the amount payable by way of such an allowance, in respect of any period of less than a week.

13.78

Linking periods

4.—(1) Regulations may provide for circumstances in which a period of limited capability for work which is separated from another period of limited capability for work by not more than a prescribed length of time is to be treated for the purposes of this Part as a continuation of the earlier period.

    (2) Regulations may provide, in relation to periods which are linked by virtue of regulations under sub-paragraph (1), that a condition which was satisfied in relation to the earlier period is to be treated for the purposes of this Part as satisfied in relation to the later period.

13.79

[² Exemption

4A. Regulations may prescribe circumstances in which a person may be entitled to employment and support allowance without having accepted a claimant commitment.]

13.80

Presence in Great Britain

5.—Regulations may make provision for the purposes of this Part as to the circumstances in which a person is to be treated as being, or not being, in Great Britain.

13.81

[³. . .] Entitlement in case of absence from Great Britain

6.—Regulations may provide that in prescribed circumstances a claimant who is not in Great Britain may nevertheless be entitled to [⁴ an employment and support allowance].

13.82

[³. . .] Modification in relation to employment on ships etc.

7.—(1) Regulations may modify any provision of this Part, so far as relating to [⁴ an employment and support allowance], in its application to any person who is, has been, or is to be—
    (a) employed on board any ship, vessel, hovercraft or aircraft,
    (b) outside Great Britain at any prescribed time or in any prescribed circumstances, or
    (c) in prescribed employment in connection with continental shelf operations.
    (2) Regulations under this paragraph may, in particular, provide—
    (a) for any provision of this Part to apply even though it would not otherwise apply;
    (b) for any such provision not to apply even though it would otherwise apply;
    (c) for the taking of evidence, in a country or territory outside Great Britain, by a consular official or other prescribed person;
    (d) for enabling the whole, or any part, of [⁴ an employment and support allowance] to be paid to such of the claimant's dependants as may be prescribed.
    (3) In this paragraph, "continental shelf operations" has the same meaning as in section 120 of the Contributions and Benefits Act.

13.83

Income-related allowance: entitlement in case of absence from Great Britain

8. [³ *Repealed*].

13.84

Limited capability for work-related activity

9.—Regulations may make provision—
    (a) for a person to be treated in prescribed circumstances as having, or as not having, limited capability for work-related activity;
    (b) for the question of whether a person has limited capability for work-related activity to be determined notwithstanding that he is for the time being treated by virtue of regulations under sub-paragraph (a) as having limited capability for work-related activity;
    (c) for the question of whether a person has limited capability for work-related activity to be determined afresh in prescribed circumstances.

13.85

Effect of work

13.86   10.—Regulations may prescribe circumstances in which a person is to be treated as not entitled to an employment and support allowance because of his doing work.

Treatment of allowance as "benefit"

13.87   11.—Regulations may provide for—
　　(a)　an employment and support allowance,
　　(b)　[³ *repealed*],
　　(c)　[³ *repealed*],
to be treated, for prescribed purposes of the Contributions and Benefits Act, as a benefit, or a benefit of a prescribed description.

Attribution of reductions in cases where allowance taken to consist of two elements

13.88   12. [³ *Repealed*].

Treatment of information supplied as information relating to social security

13.89   13.—Information supplied in pursuance of regulations under any of sections 8, 9 and 11 to 13 [¹, or under any paragraph of Schedule 1A other than paragraph 8,] shall be taken for all purposes to be information relating to social security.

Advance claims

13.90   14.—This Part shall have effect with prescribed modifications in relation to cases where a claim to an employment and support allowance is by virtue of regulations under section 5(1)(c) of the Administration Act (advance claims) made, or treated as if made, for a period wholly or partly after the date on which it is made.

Members of the forces

13.91   15.—(1) Regulations may modify—
　　(a)　any provision of this Part, or
　　(b)　any corresponding provision made for Northern Ireland, in its application to persons who are or have been members of Her Majesty's forces.
　(2) For the purposes of this paragraph, Her Majesty's forces shall be taken to consist of prescribed establishments and organisations in which persons serve under the control of the Defence Council.

AMENDMENT

　1. Welfare Reform Act 2009 s.11 and Sch.3 para.8(5) (November 12, 2009).
　2. Welfare Reform Act 2012 s.54(6) (February 25, 2013).
　3. Welfare Reform Act 2012 s.147 and Sch.14 Pt 1 (various dates on or after April 29, 2013).
　4. Welfare Reform Act 2012 s.33(3) and Sch.3 para.26(g) (various dates on or after April 29, 2013).

DEFINITIONS

　"Administration Act"—see s.65.
　"continental shelf operations"—see para.7(3).
　"Contributions and Benefi ts Act"—see s.65.
　"employed"—see s.24(1).
　"employment"—see s.24(1).
　"entitled"—see s.24(1).
　"Her Majesty's forces"—see para.15(2).
　"limited capability for work-related activity"—see s.2(5).
　"period of limited capability for work"—see s.24(1).
　"prescribed"—see s.24(1).
　"regulations"—see s.24(1).

"week"—see s.24(1).
"work-related activity"—see ss.24(1), 13(7).

GENERAL NOTE

With the removal of references to CESA and IRESA, this is much the same as the text of WRA 2007 Sch.2 as applicable to "old style" ESA and readers should refer to the commentary there for the effect of the provisions. However, as applicable to "new style" ESA, the relevant regulations are not the ESA Regs 2008 referred to in that commentary but the corresponding provisions of the ESA Regs 2013, set out below: **13.91.1**

Para. (2) (waiting days)
ESA Regs 2013 reg.85.   **13.92**

Para. (3) (periods of less than a week)
ESA Regs 2013 regs 98–102.   **13.93**

Para. (4) (linking periods)
ESA Regs 2013 reg.86   **13.94**

Para. (5) (presence in Great Britain)
ESA Regs 2013 reg.12 (condition relating to youth—residence or presence).   **13.95**

Para. (6) (entitlement when absent from Great Britain)
ESA Regs 2013 regs 88–92.   **13.96**

Para. (7) (modification of ESA for those employed on ships etc)
There is now only one form of ESA, but, apart from the reference to CESA, the annotation to the provision in the first section of this book is fully applicable to "new style" ESA.   **13.97**

Para. (10) (effect of work)
Ignore references to IRESA and see now ESA Regs 2013 regs 37–40.   **13.98**

Para. (14) (advance claims)
See Universal Credit, Personal Independence Payment, Jobseeker's Allowance and Employment and Support Allowance (Claims and Payments) Regulations 2013 (SI 2013/380) reg.34 in *Vol. V: Universal Credit*.   **13.99**

Para. (15) (members of Her Majesty's forces)
ESA Regs 2013 reg.92 and Sch.1.   **13.100**

SCHEDULE 3   Section 28

CONSEQUENTIAL AMENDMENTS RELATING TO PART 1

Insofar as the provisions in this Schedule amend legislation contained in the main volumes and have themselves been further amended or repealed, these amendments and repeals have been taken into account in preparing the legislative text.   **13.101**

13.102   AMENDMENT

     1. The whole Schedule was repealed by Welfare Reform Act 2012 s.147 and Sch.14 Pt 1 (various dates on or after April 29, 2013).

The Employment and Support Allowance Regulations 2013

(SI 2013/379) (*as amended*)

ARRANGEMENT OF REGULATIONS

PART 1

General

13.103   1.   Citation, commencement and application
        2.   Interpretation
        3.   Further interpretation
        4.   Rounding of fractions

PART 2

The assessment phase

        5.   The end of the assessment phase
        6.   The assessment phase – previous claimants
        7.   Circumstances where the condition that the assessment phase has ended before entitlement to the support component arises does not apply

PART 3

Conditions of entitlement

        8.   Conditions relating to national insurance and relevant earnings
        9.   Relaxation of the first contribution condition
      10.   Condition relating to youth – claimants aged 20 or over but under 25
      11.   Condition relating to youth – previous claimants
      12.   Condition relating to youth – residence or presence
      13.   Condition relating to youth – full-time education
      14.   Modification of the relevant benefit year

PART 4

Limited Capability for Work

15. Determination of limited capability for work
16. Certain claimants to be treated as having limited capability for work
17. Information required for determining capability for work
18. Failure to provide information in relation to limited capability for work
19. Claimant may be called for a medical examination to determine whether the claimant has limited capability for work
20. Matters to be taken into account in determining good cause in relation to regulations 18 or 19
21. Hospital patients
22. Claimants receiving certain treatment
23. Claimant to be treated as having limited capability for work throughout a day
24. Night workers
25. Exceptional circumstances
26. Conditions for treating a claimant as having limited capability for work until a determination about limited capability for work has been made
27. Certain claimants to be treated as not having limited capability for work
28. Claimants to be treated as not having limited capability for work at the end of the period covered by medical evidence
29. Additional circumstances where claimants are to be treated as having limited capability for work

PART 5

Limited Capability for Work-related Activity

30. Determination of limited capability for work-related activity
31. Certain claimants to be treated as having, or not having, limited capability for work-related activity
32. Relevant linked cases – limited capability for work-related activity
33. Information required for determining capability for work-related activity
34. Failure to provide information in relation to work-related activity
35. Claimant may be called for a medical examination to determine whether the claimant has limited capability for work-related activity
36. Matters to be taken into account in determining good cause in relation to regulations 34 or 35

PART 6

Effect of work on entitlement to an Employment and Support Allowance

37.   A claimant who works to be treated as not entitled to an employment and support allowance
38.   Claimants who are treated as not entitled to any allowance at all by reason of regulation 37(1) are to be treated as not having limited capability for work
39.   Exempt work
40.   Effect of work on entitlement to an employment and support allowance where claimant is receiving certain treatment

PART 7

Claimant responsibilities

41.   Interpretation
42.   Application of regulations where there is dual entitlement
43.   Sanction ceases to apply to employment and support allowance
44.   Claimant commitment – date and method of acceptance
45.   Claimant commitment – exceptions
46.   Purposes of a work-focused interview
47.   Claimants subject to no work-related requirements
48.   Claimants subject to work-focused interview requirement only
49.   Victims of domestic violence

PART 8

Sanctions

50.   Interpretation
51.   General principles for calculating reduction periods
52.   Low-level sanction
53.   Lowest-level sanction
54.   Start of the reduction
55.   Reduction period to continue where award of employment and support allowance terminates
56.   Suspension of a reduction where a fraud sanction applies
57.   Termination of a reduction
58.   Amount of reduction for each benefit week
59.   Daily reduction rate
60.   Lower daily reduction rate
61.   Sanctions where universal credit ends and the person is entitled to an employment and support allowance

PART 9

Amounts of Allowance

62. Prescribed amounts
63. Special cases
64. Permanent health insurance
65. Financial Assistance Scheme
66. Councillor's allowance
67. Deductions for pension payment and PPF payment
68. Payments treated as not being payments to which section 3 applies
69. Deductions for councillor's allowance
70. Date from which payments are to be taken into account
71. Date from which a change in the rate of the payment takes effect
72. Calculation of payment made other than weekly
73. Effect of statutory maternity pay on an employment and support allowance
74. Effect of statutory adoption pay on an employment and support allowance
75. *Revoked*
75A. Effect of statutory shared parental pay on an employment and support allowance

PART 10

Income and earnings

76. Calculation of earnings derived from employed earner's employment and income other than earnings
77. Calculation of earnings of self-employed earners
78. Date on which income is treated as paid
79. Calculation of weekly amount of income
80. Earnings of employed earners
81. Calculation of net earnings of employed earners
82. Earnings of self-employed earners
83. Calculation of net profit of self-employed earners
84. Deduction of tax and contributions for self-employed earners

PART 11

Supplementary provisions

85. Waiting days
86. Linking period
87. Claimants appealing a decision
88. Absence from Great Britain
89. Short absence
90. Absence to receive medical treatment

91.   Absence in order to receive NHS treatment
92.   Absence of member of family of member of Her Majesty's forces

PART 12

Disqualification

93.   Disqualification for misconduct etc
94.   Meaning of "person in hardship"
95.   Treating a claimant as not having limited capability for work
96.   Exceptions from disqualification for imprisonment
97.   Suspension of payment of an employment and support allowance during
       imprisonment

PART 13

Periods of less than a week

98.   Entitlement for less than a week – amount of an employment and support
       allowance payable
99.   Relevant week
100.   Modification in the calculation of income
101.   Reduction in certain cases
102.   Payment of an employment and support allowance for days of certain treat-
       ment

SCHEDULE 1 — Her Majesty's Forces
  PART 1 — Prescribed establishments and organisations
  PART 2 — Establishments and organisations of which Her Majesty's forces
do not consist
SCHEDULE 2 — Assessment of Whether a Claimant has Limited Capability for
Work
  PART 1 — Physical Disabilities
  PART 2 — Mental, cognitive and intellectual function assessment
SCHEDULE 3 — Assessment of whether a claimant has limited capability for
work-related activity

13.104   The Secretary of State for Work and Pensions makes the following
Regulations in exercise of the powers conferred by sections 2(1)(a) and (c)
and (4)(a)and (c), 3(1)(c), (2)(b)and (d)and (3), 8(1) to (3), (4)(a) and
(b), (5) and (6), 9(1) to (3) and (4)(a)and (b), 11A(5), 11B(2) and (3),
11D(2)(d), 11E(1), 11H(5) and (6), 11J(3), (4) and (8), 17(1), (2) and
(3)(a)and (b), 18(1), (2) and (4), 20(2) to (7), 24(1), (2)(b) and (3) and
25(2) to (5) of, and paragraphs 1(3) and (4), 3(2) and 4(1)(a) and (c), (3)
and (4) of Schedule 1 and paragraphs 1 to 4A, 5, 6, 9 and 10 of Schedule 2
to, the Welfare Reform Act 2007, sections 5(1A), 189(4) to (6) and 191 of
the Social Security Administration Act 1992, section 21(1)(a) of the Social
Security Act 1998 and paragraphs 2(3) and 3 of Schedule 5 to the Welfare
Reform Act 2012.

The Social Security Advisory Committee has agreed that the proposals in respect of these Regulations should not be referred to it.

A draft of these Regulations has been laid before Parliament in accordance with section 26(1) of the Welfare Reform Act 2007 and approved by a resolution of each House of Parliament.

GENERAL NOTE

These regulations govern eligibility for "new style ESA". This is a wholly contribution-based benefit for those who have a health condition or disability which limits their capability for work. Those entitled to it whose "resources" are insufficient to meet "needs" will have to seek a top-up through Universal Credit (UC). In the longer term, when the UC scheme is fully rolled out, the result will be a simpler system, since there will then be only one income-related benefit—UC—for persons of working age, rather than the current system of several income-related benefits each for different categories of claimant and administered by different authorities: IS, IBJSA and IRESA (by DWP/JobCentres), tax credits (by HMRC) and housing benefit (by local authorities). But until the UC scheme is fully rolled out, UC is an additional benefit rather than a benefit replacing all those other income related benefits. The roll-out of UC is slow and complicated. As the commentators to Vol.V in this series, *Universal Credit*, put it: **13.105**

"it is inherent in the design of UC that it overlaps with each of the older benefits it is eventually intended to replace. That overlap means that, in addition to the complication of the old and new systems existing side-by-side (including having two different and mutually exclusive benefits both called JSA and two called ESA), it is also necessary to have legislation defining which set of rules applies to any particular claimant at any given time. That legislation is to be found first, in the Universal Credit (Transitional Provisions) Regulations ("the Transitional Provisions Regulations") which create a "Pathfinder Group" of claimants who, depending on where they live, may have to claim UC rather than one of the "legacy" benefits and, second, in a series of Commencement Orders that, even by the high standards set by past social security legislation, are bewilderingly complex."

By December 12, 2018, all gateway areas (otherwise known as 'live service' areas, the successors to the areas designated for the Pathfinder Group) had been converted into 'full service' areas for purposes of UC. The effect is that most new claimants must now claim UC rather than one of the former legacy benefits.

New claimants may now only claim IRESA in two narrowly-defined sets of circumstances. The first exception covers frontier workers, e.g. claimants who live in the Republic of Ireland but work in Northern Ireland. The second exception covers claimants who are (or have been in the last month) entitled to a legacy benefit where their award includes the severe disability premium and who have not been given a 'migration notice' that they will be transferred to UC. However, existing awards of IRESA continue for the time being unless and until a change in circumstances results in 'natural migration' to UC. The entitlement of all claimants who remain on old-style ESA (either or both CESA and IRESA) continues to be governed by the WRA 2007 and the ESA Regs 2008, as set out in Parts I and IX of this volume. However, UC claimants can only claim new-style ESA in its exclusively contributory form and are governed by the WRA 2007 and the ESA Regs 2013.

These 2013 Regulations are both a consolidation of and a rewrite of the already existing ESA Regulations 2008 (as amended to correct some unintended textual errors and to provide greater alignment with these 2013 Regulations and so as somewhat to align a "new style ESA" claimant commitments and sanctions' regime with those applicable to new style JSA and UC. **13.106**

Most of the key rules on "new style ESA" remain the same in terms of effect as those applicable to CESA in the ESA Regulations 2008, but the DWP considers that in drawing up the ESA Regulations 2013 "opportunities have been taken to make simplifications and improvements". In addition, the regulations specific to IRESA are not carried into the 2013 Regulations. This means that material may be differently distributed within the same-numbered regulation in these ESA Regulations 2013 as compared to the ESA Regulations 2008, or be found in a differently numbered one. In addition, in the ESA Regulations 2013, there is a regime of claimant commitments and sanctions analogous in some respects to those applicable to UC and "new style JSA".

Conversion to ESA from IB, IS on the basis of incapacity or disability and SDA is ongoing. It is governed by the ESA (Existing Awards) (No.2) Regs 2010 (SI 2010/1907). These apply to "new style" ESA with modifications made by art.9 and Sch.4 of the Welfare Reform Act 2012 (Commencement No.9 and Transitional and Transitory Provisions and Commencement No.8 and Savings and Transitional Provisions (Amendment)) Order 2013 (SI 2013/983). See further the General Note to the ESA (Existing Awards) (No. 2) Regs 2010 in Pt IX of this book.

PART 1

General

Citation, commencement and application

13.107   **1.**—(1) These Regulations may be cited as the Employment and Support Allowance Regulations 2013.

(2) They come into force on 29th April 2013.

(3) They apply in relation to a particular case on any day on which section 33(1)(b) of the Welfare Reform Act 2012 (abolition of income-related employment and support allowance) is in force and applies in relation to that case.

GENERAL NOTE

Paras 2, 3.

13.108   Although these regulations entered into force on April 29, 2013, they do not as yet apply to all claimants. They will only do so once there has been a full rolling out

13.109   of Universal Credit and consequent total abolition of IRESA. An important step on the way to this goal was the conversion of all UC 'gateway' or 'live service' areas to 'full service' areas by December 12, 2018, meaning that most new claimants must now claim UC rather than one of the former legacy benefits. New claimants may now only claim IRESA in very narrowly-defined circumstances (see General Note above). Existing awards of IRESA continue for the time being unless and until the claimant has a change in circumstances that results in 'natural migration' to UC. The DWP-instigated process of 'managed migration' of existing claimants of legacy benefits (such as IRESA) is scheduled to take place between 2020 and 2023, subject of course to further timetabling changes. A pilot was due to commence in July 2019.

Interpretation

13.110   **2.**—In these Regulations—

"the Act" means the Welfare Reform Act 2007;

"advanced education" means education for the purposes of—

(a) a course in preparation for a degree, a diploma of higher education, a higher national diploma, a higher national diploma of the Business and Technology Education Council or the Scottish Qualifications Authority, or a teaching qualification; or

(b) any other course which is of a standard above ordinary national diploma, a diploma of the Business and Technology Education Council or a higher or advanced higher national certificate of the Scottish Qualifications Authority or a general certificate of education (advanced level);

"benefit week" means a period of seven days ending on such day as the Secretary of State may direct, but for the purposes of calculating any payment of income "benefit week" means the period of seven days ending on—

(a) the day before the first day of the first period of seven days which—

    (i) ends on such day as the Secretary of State may direct; and

    (ii) follows the date of claim for an employment and support allowance; or

(b) the last day on which an employment and support allowance is paid if it is in payment for less than a week;

"carer's allowance" means an allowance under section 70 of the Contributions and Benefits Act;

"child" means a person under the age of 16;

"Claims and Payments Regulations 2013" means the Universal Credit, Personal Independence Payment, Jobseeker's Allowance and Employment and Support Allowance (Claims and Payments) Regulations 2013;

"close relative" means a parent, parent-in-law, son, son-in-law, daughter, daughter-in-law, step-parent, step-son, step-daughter, brother, sister or, if any of the preceding persons is one member of a couple, the other member of that couple;

"confinement" has the meaning given to it by section 171(1) of the Contributions and Benefits Act;

"councillor" means—

(a) in relation to England and Wales, a member of a London borough council, a county council, a county borough council, a district council, a parish or community council, the Common Council of the City of London or the Council of the Isles of Scilly; and

(b) in relation to Scotland, a member of a council constituted under section 2 of the Local Government etc. (Scotland) Act 1994;

"councillor's allowance" means—

(a) in England, an allowance under or by virtue of—

    (i) section 173 or 177 of the Local Government Act 1972; or

    (ii) a scheme made by virtue of section 18 of the Local Government and Housing Act 1989,

other than such an allowance as is mentioned in section 173(4) of the Local Government Act 1972;

(b) in Wales, an allowance under or by virtue of a scheme made by virtue of section 18 of the Local Government and Housing Act 1989 other than such an allowance as is mentioned in section 173(4) of the Local Government Act 1972; or

(c) in Scotland, an allowance or remuneration under or by virtue of—

    (i) a scheme made by virtue of section 18 of the Local Government and Housing Act 1989; or

    (ii) section 11 of the Local Governance (Scotland) Act 2004;

[[1,2]"couple" means—

(a) two people who are married to, or civil partners of, each other and are members of the same household; or

(b) two people who are not married to, or civil partners of, each other but are living together as a married couple;]

"Decisions and Appeals Regulations 1999" means the Social Security and Child Support (Decisions and Appeals) Regulations 1999;

"Decisions and Appeals Regulations 2013" means the Universal Credit, Personal Independence Payment, Jobseeker's Allowance and Employment and Support Allowance (Decisions and Appeals) Regulations 2013;

"descriptor" means, in relation to an activity specified in column (1) of Schedule 2, a descriptor in column (2) of that Schedule which describes a person's ability to perform that activity;

"employed earner" is to be construed in accordance with section 2(1)(a) of the Contributions and Benefits Act;

"employment" includes any trade, business, profession, office or vocation; and "employed" has a corresponding meaning;

"enactment" includes an enactment comprised in, or in an instrument made under, an Act of the Scottish Parliament or the National Assembly of Wales;

"family" means—

(a) a couple;

(b) a couple and a member of the same household for whom one of them is or both are responsible and who is a child or a young person;

(c) a person who is not a member of a couple and a member of the same household for whom that person is responsible and who is a child or a young person;

"first contribution condition" means the condition set out in paragraph 1(1) of Schedule 1 to the Act;

"First-tier Tribunal" has the meaning given by section 3(1) of the Tribunals, Courts and Enforcement Act 2007;

"health care professional" means—

(a) a registered medical practitioner;

(b) a registered nurse; or

(c) an occupational therapist or physiotherapist registered with a regulatory body established by an Order in Council under section 60 of the Health Act 1999;

"Health Service Act" means the National Health Service Act 2006;

"Health Service (Wales) Act" means the National Health Service (Wales) Act 2006;

"Income Support Regulations" means the Income Support (General) Regulations 1987;

"limited capability for work assessment" means the assessment described in regulation 15(2) and in Schedule 2;

"Medical Evidence Regulations" means the Social Security (Medical Evidence) Regulations 1976;

"medical treatment" means medical, surgical or rehabilitative treatment (including any course or diet or other regimen), and references to a person receiving or submitting to medical treatment are to be construed accordingly;

"member of Her Majesty's forces" means a person, other than one mentioned in Part 2 of Schedule 1, who is—

(a) over 16 years of age; and
(b) a member of an establishment or organisation specified in Part 1 of that Schedule, but does not include any such person while absent on desertion;
[⁴ "member of the work-related activity group" means a claimant who has or is treated as having limited capability for work under either—
(a) Part 5 of the Employment and Support Allowance Regulations 2008 other than by virtue of regulation 30 of those Regulations; or
(b) Part 4 of these Regulations other than by virtue of regulation 26;]
"National Minimum Wage" means the rate of the national minimum wage specified in regulation 11 of the National Minimum Wage Regulations 1999 (rate of the national minimum wage);
"net earnings" means such earnings as are calculated in accordance with regulation 81;
"occupational pension scheme" has the meaning given by section 1 of the Pension Schemes Act 1993;
"part-time employment" means, if the claimant were entitled to income support, employment in which the claimant is not to be treated as engaged in remunerative work under regulation 5 or 6(1) and (4) of the Income Support Regulations (persons treated, or not treated, as engaged in remunerative work);
"partner" means—
(a) where a claimant is a member of a couple, the other member of that couple; or
(b) where a claimant is a husband or wife by virtue of a polygamous marriage, the other party to the marriage or any spouse additional to either party to the marriage;
"payment" includes a part of a payment;
"pay period" means the period in respect of which a claimant is, or expects to be, normally paid by the claimant's employer, being a week, a fortnight, four weeks, a month or other shorter or longer period as the case may be;
"period of limited capability for work" means, except in regulation 3(2), a period throughout which a person has, or is treated as having, limited capability for work under these Regulations, and does not include a period which is outside the prescribed time for claiming as specified in regulation 28 of the Claims and Payments Regulations 2013;
"permanent health insurance payment" means any periodical payment arranged by an employer under an insurance policy providing benefits in connection with physical or mental illness or disability, in relation to a former employee on the termination of that person's employment;
"personal pension scheme" means—
(a) a personal pension scheme as defined by section 1 of the Pension Schemes Act 1993;
(b) an annuity contract, trust scheme or substituted contract which is treated as having become a registered pension scheme by virtue of paragraph 1(1)(f) of Schedule 36 to the Finance Act 2004;
(c) a personal pension scheme which is treated as having become a registered pension scheme by virtue of paragraph 1(1) (g) of Schedule 36 to the Finance Act 2004;
"polygamous marriage" means any marriage entered into under a law which permits polygamy where—

(a) either party has for the time being any spouse additional to the other party; and

(b) the claimant, the other party to the marriage and the additional spouse are members of the same household;

"qualifying young person" has the meaning given by section 142 of the Contributions and Benefits Act (child and qualifying young person);

"relative" means close relative, grand-parent, grand-child, uncle, aunt, nephew or niece;

"second contribution condition" means the condition set out in paragraph 2(1) of Schedule 1 to the Act;

"self-employed earner" is to be construed in accordance with section 2(1)(b) of the Contributions and Benefits Act;

"state pension credit" means a state pension credit under the State Pension Credit Act 2002;

"Tax Credits Act" means the Tax Credits Act 2002;

"terminally ill", in relation to a claimant, means the claimant is suffering from a progressive disease and death in consequence of that disease can reasonably be expected within six months;

"training" means—

(a) training in pursuance of arrangements made under section 2(1) of the Employment and Training Act 1973 or section 2(3) of the Enterprise and New Towns (Scotland) Act 1990; or

(b) any training received on a course which a person attends for 16 hours or more a week, the primary purpose of which is the teaching of occupational or vocational skills;

"training allowance" means an allowance (whether by way of periodical grants or otherwise) payable—

(a) out of public funds by a Government department or by or on behalf of the Secretary of State, Skills Development Scotland, Scottish Enterprise, Highlands and Islands Enterprise [³ . . .] or the Welsh Ministers;

(b) to a person for that person's maintenance or in respect of a member of that person's family; and

(c) for the period, or part of the period, during which the person is following a course of training or instruction provided by, or in pursuance of arrangements made with, that department or approved by that department in relation to that person or provided or approved by or on behalf of the Secretary of State, Skills Development Scotland, Scottish Enterprise, Highlands and Islands Enterprise, or the Welsh Ministers,

but does not include an allowance paid by any Government department to or in respect of a person by reason of the fact that that person is following a course of full-time education, other than under arrangements made under section 2 of the Employment and Training Act 1973 or section 2 of the Enterprise and New Towns (Scotland) Act 1990, or is training as a teacher;

"voluntary organisation" means a body, other than a public or local authority, the activities of which are carried on otherwise than for profit;

"week" means a period of seven days except in relation to regulation 22;

"working tax credit" means a working tax credit under section 10 of the Tax Credits Act;

"young person" is a person who, except where section 6 of the Children (Leaving Care) Act 2000 (exclusion from benefits) applies, falls within the definition of qualifying young person in section 142 of the Contributions and Benefits Act (child and qualifying young person).

AMENDMENTS

1. Marriage (Same Sex Couples) Act 2013 (Consequential Provisions) Order 2014 (SI 2014/107), reg.2, Sch.1 para.55 (March 13, 2014). (England and Wales only: see art.1(4)).
2. Marriage and Civil Partnership (Scotland) Act 2014 and Civil Partnership Act 2004 (Consequential Provisions and Modifications) Order 2014 (SI 2014/3229) art.29 and Sch.6 para.23 (December 16, 2014: throughout the United Kingdom: see art.3(1)).
3. Deregulation Act 2015 (Consequential Amendments) Order 2015 (SI 2015/971) Art.2 and Sch.3 para.26 (May 26, 2015).
4. Employment and Support Allowance and Universal Credit (Miscellaneous Amendments and Transitional and Savings Provisions) Regulations 2017 (SI 2017/204) reg.3(2) (April 3, 2017).

GENERAL NOTE

"couple" 13.111

This definition, initially applicable only in England and Wales, is now applicable throughout the United Kingdom, reflecting the different pace of legal acceptance of civil partnerships and same sex marriage in the various parts of the United Kingdom.

Under the Marriage (Same Sex Couples) Act 2013 (Consequential and Contrary Provisions and Scotland) Order 2014 (SI 2014/560) art.5, effective from March 13, 2014, a same sex marriage in England and Wales was treated as a civil partnership in Scotland. That provision was revoked by the Marriage (Same Sex Couples) Act 2013 (Consequential and Contrary Provisions and Scotland) and Marriage and Civil Partnership (Scotland) Act 2014 (Consequential Provisions) Order 2014 (SI 2014/3168) art.4, with effect from December 16, 2014, no longer being necessary since Scotland's acceptance of same sex marriage. Northern Ireland, however, has no same sex marriage legislation. Hence, the Marriage (Same Sex Couples) Act 2013, s.10(3) and Sch.2 para.2 provided that from March 13, 2014 a same sex marriage in England and Wales was to be treated as a civil partnership in Northern Ireland. Similarly, art.6 of the Marriage and Civil Partnership (Scotland) Act 2014 and Civil Partnership Act 2004 (Consequential Provisions and Modifications) Order 2014 (SI 2014/3229) stipulates that a same sex marriage in Scotland is from December 16, 2014 to be treated in Northern Ireland as a civil partnership.

Further interpretation

3.—(1) In these Regulations, any reference to the claimant's family is to be construed as if it included in relation to a polygamous marriage a reference to any partner and any child or young person who is a member of the claimant's household. 13.112

(2) For the purposes of paragraph 4 of Schedule 1 to the Act (condition relating to youth), "period of limited capability for work" means a period throughout which a person has, or is treated as having, limited capability for work.

(3) For the purposes of paragraph 5 of Schedule 1 to the Act, "week" means a period of seven days.

DEFINITIONS

"child"—see reg.2.
"partner"—see reg.2.
"period of limited capability for work"—see para.(2).
"week"—see para.(3).
"young person"—see reg.2.

Rounding of fractions

13.113   **4.**— For the purposes of these Regulations—

(a) where any calculation under these Regulations results in a fraction of a penny, that fraction is, if it would be to the claimant's advantage, to be treated as a penny, but otherwise it must be disregarded;

(b) where an employment and support allowance is awarded for a period which is not a complete benefit week and the applicable amount in respect of the period results in an amount which includes a fraction of a penny, that fraction is to be treated as a penny.

DEFINITIONS

"benefit week"— see reg.2.

GENERAL NOTE

13.114   As with ESA Regs 2008 reg.3, fractions are always rounded in favour of the claimant.

PART 2

The assessment phase

The end of the assessment phase

13.115   **5.**—(1) Subject to paragraphs (2) and (3) and regulation 6, the assessment phase in relation to a claimant ends on the last day of [¹ the relevant period]

(2) Where paragraph (3) applies, the assessment phase is to end when it is determined whether the claimant has limited capability for work.

(3) This paragraph applies where, at the end of [¹ the relevant period]—

(a) the claimant has not been assessed in accordance with a limited capability for work assessment; and

(b) the claimant has not been treated as having limited capability for work in accordance with regulation 16, 21, 22 or 25.

[¹(4) In this regulation, "the relevant period" means the period of 13 weeks beginning with—

(a) the first day of the assessment phase as determined under section 24(2)(a) of the Act; or

(b) where that day immediately follows an extended period of sickness, the first day of the extended period of sickness.

(5) In paragraph (4), "extended period of sickness" means a period in which the claimant was—

(a) entitled to a jobseeker's allowance; and

(b) treated as capable of work or as not having limited capability for work under regulation 55ZA of the Jobseeker's Allowance Regulations 1996 or regulation 46A of the Jobseeker's Allowance Regulations 2013 (extended period of sickness).]

AMENDMENT

1. Jobseeker's Allowance (Extended Period of Sickness) Amendment Regulations 2015 (SI 2015/339) reg.5 (March 30, 2015).

DEFINITIONS

"the assessment phase"—see WRA 2007 s.24(2).
"claimant"—see WRA 2007 s.24(1).
"extended period of sickness"—see para.(5).
"limited capability for work"—see WRA 2007 s.1(4).
"limited capability for work assessment"—see reg.2(1).
"the relevant period"—see para.(4).
"week"—see reg.2(1).

GENERAL NOTE

Same effect as ESA Regs 2008 reg.4. In para.(3) (b), the renumbered regs compare with equivalent ones in the ESA Regs 2008 as follows:　　　　　　　**13.116**

2013 Regs	2008 Regs	Coverage
16	20	Certain claimants to be treated as having limited capability for work
21	25	Hospital patients
22	26	Claimants receiving certain treatment
25	29	Exceptional circumstances

There is no equivalent in the ESA Regs 2013 of ESA Regs reg.33(2) which dealt with ability to treat as having limited capability with respect only to IRESA, a benefit abolished in the cases and areas in which these 2013 Regulations apply.

The assessment phase – previous claimants

6.—(1) Where the circumstances in paragraph (2) apply in relation to a claimant, the assessment phase—　　　　　　　**13.117**
- (a) begins on the first day of the period for which the claimant was previously entitled to an employment and support allowance; and
- (b) subject to paragraphs (3), (4) and (5), ends on the day when the sum of the period for which the claimant was previously entitled to an employment and support allowance and the period for which the claimant is currently entitled to such an allowance is 13 weeks.

[¹(1A) For the purposes of paragraph (1), any period when the claimant was—
- (a) entitled to a jobseeker's allowance; and
- (b) treated as capable of work or as not having limited capability for work under regulation 55ZA of the Jobseeker's Allowance Regulations 1996 or regulation 46A of the Jobseeker's Allowance Regulations 2013,

is to be treated as a period when the claimant was previously entitled to an employment and support allowance.]
(2) The circumstances are that—

(a) all of the following apply—
  (i) the claimant's current period of limited capability for work is to be treated as a continuation of an earlier period of limited capability for work under regulation 86;
  (ii) the claimant was entitled to an employment and support allowance in the earlier period of limited capability for work;
  (iii) the assessment phase had not ended in the previous period for which the claimant was entitled to an employment and support allowance; and
  (iv) the period for which the claimant was previously entitled was no more than 13 weeks;
(b) all of the following apply—
  (i) the claimant's current period of limited capability for work is to be treated as a continuation of an earlier period of limited capability for work under regulation 86;
  (ii) the claimant was entitled to an employment and support allowance in the earlier period of limited capability for work;
  (iii) the previous period of limited capability for work was terminated by virtue of a determination that the claimant did not have limited capability for work;
  (iv) the period for which the claimant was previously entitled was no more than 13 weeks; and
  (v) a determination is made in relation to the current period of limited capability for work that the claimant has or is treated, other than under regulation 26, as having limited capability for work; or
(c) all of the following apply—
  (i) the claimant's current period of limited capability for work is to be treated as a continuation of an earlier period of limited capability for work under regulation 86;
  (ii) the claimant was entitled to an employment and support allowance in the earlier period of limited capability for work;
  (iii) in relation to the previous award of an employment and support allowance, a determination was made that the claimant had limited capability for work or was treated, other than under regulation 26, as having limited capability for work; and
  (iv) the period for which the claimant was previously entitled was no more than 13 weeks.

(3) Where paragraph (4) applies, the assessment phase is to end when it is determined whether the claimant has limited capability for work.

(4) This paragraph applies where, on the day referred to in paragraph (1) (b)—
(a) the claimant has not been assessed in accordance with a limited capability for work assessment; and
(b) the claimant has not been treated as having limited capability for work in accordance with regulation 16, 21, 22 or 25.

(5) Where a person has made and is pursuing an appeal against a decision of the Secretary of State that embodies a determination that the claimant does not have limited capability for work—
(a) paragraphs (3) and (4) do not apply; and
(b) paragraph (1) does not apply to any period of limited capability for work to which regulation 87(2) applies until a determination of

limited capability for work has been made following the determination of the appeal by the First-tier Tribunal.

AMENDMENT

1. Jobseeker's Allowance (Extended Period of Sickness) Amendment Regulations 2015 (SI 2015/339) reg.5 (March 30, 2015).

DEFINITIONS

"the assessment phase"—see WRA 2007 s.24(2).
"claimant"—see WRA 2007 s.24(1).
"limited capability for work"—see WRA 2007 s.1(4).
"limited capability for work assessment"—see reg.2(1).
"week"—see reg.2(1).

GENERAL NOTE

This is the equivalent of ESA Regs 2008 reg.5. On the 2008 equivalents of the renumbered regs in para.(4) (b), see the Table in the annotations to reg.6, above. Reg.86 referred to in para.(2) (a) (i), (b) (i) and (c)(i) is the equivalent of reg.145(1) of the ESA Regs 2008. Reg.26 referred to in para.(2) (b) (v) is the equivalent of reg.30 of the ESA Regs 2008. Reg.87(2) in para.(5) (b) corresponds to reg.147A(2) of the ESA Regs 2008.

13.118

Circumstances where the condition that the assessment phase has ended before entitlement to the support component ['. . .] arises does not apply

7.—(1) Subject to paragraph (4), section 2(2)(a) ['. . .] of the Act does not apply where—

13.119

    (a) a claimant is terminally ill and has either—
        (i) made a claim expressly on the ground of being terminally ill; or
        (ii) made an application for supersession or revision in accordance with the Decisions and Appeals Regulations 1999 or the Decisions and Appeals Regulations 2013 which contains an express statement that the claimant is terminally ill;
    (b) the case is a relevant linked case;
    (c) the case is one where—
        (i) the claimant's entitlement to an employment and support allowance commences within 12 weeks of the claimant's entitlement to income support coming to an end;
       (ii) in relation to that entitlement to income support, immediately before it ended, the claimant's applicable amount included the disability premium by virtue of their satisfying the conditions in paragraphs 11 and 12 of Schedule 2 to the Income Support Regulations; and
      (iii) that entitlement to income support ended only by virtue of the coming into force, in relation to the claimant, of the Social Security (Lone Parents and Miscellaneous Amendments) Regulations 2008; or
    (d) a claimant is entitled to an employment and support allowance by virtue of section 1B of the Act (further entitlement after time-limiting).

(2) For the purposes of paragraph (1) (b) a relevant linked case is a case

mentioned in paragraph (3) where a period of limited capability for work is to be treated as a continuation of an earlier period of limited capability for work under regulation 86.

(3) For the purposes of paragraph (2), the cases are as follows—

(a) case 1 is where—

  (i) the claimant was entitled to an employment and support allowance (including entitlement to a component under section 2(2) [1. . .] of the Act [1 or they were a member of the work-related activity group]) in the earlier period of limited capability for work; and

  (ii) the previous period for which the claimant was entitled to an employment and support allowance was terminated other than by virtue of a determination that the claimant did not have limited capability for work;

(b) case 2 is where—

  (i) the claimant was entitled to an employment and support allowance in the earlier period of limited capability for work;

  (ii) the previous period for which the claimant was entitled to an employment and support allowance was 13 weeks or longer;

  (iii) the previous period for which the claimant was entitled to an employment and support allowance was terminated by virtue of a determination that the claimant did not have, or was treated as not having, limited capability for work; and

  (iv) it is determined in relation to the current period of limited capability for work that the claimant has limited capability for work or is treated, other than under regulation 26, as having limited capability for work;

(c) case 3 is where—

  (i) the claimant was entitled to an employment and support allowance in the earlier period of limited capability for work;

  (ii) the previous period for which the claimant was entitled to an employment and support allowance was 13 weeks or longer;

  (iii) the previous period for which the claimant was entitled to an employment and support allowance was terminated before it could be determined whether the claimant had limited capability for work or was treated, other than under regulation 26, as having limited capability for work; and

  (iv) it is determined in relation to the current period of limited capability for work that the claimant has limited capability for work or is treated, other than under regulation 26, as having limited capability for work; and

(d) case 4 is where—

  (i) the claimant was entitled to an employment and support allowance (including entitlement to a component under section 2(2) ['. . .] of the Act [1 or they were a member of the work-related activity group]) in the earlier period of limited capability for work;

  (ii) the previous period for which the claimant was entitled to an employment and support allowance was terminated because it was determined that the claimant did not have limited capability for work or was treated as not having limited capability for work; and

  (iii) it is determined in relation to the current period of limited capability for work that the claimant has limited capability for work or is treated, other than under regulation 26, as having limited capability for work.

(4) Paragraph (1) (b) does not apply to any period of limited capability for work to which regulation 87(2) applies until the determination of limited capability for work has been made following the determination of the appeal by the First-tier Tribunal.

AMENDMENT

1. Employment and Support Allowance and Universal Credit (Miscellaneous Amendments and Transitional and Savings Provisions) Regulations 2017 (SI 2017/204) reg.3(3) (April 3, 2017).

DEFINITIONS

"claimant"—see WRA 2007 s.24(1).
"entitled"—see WRA 2007 s.24(1).
"limited capability for work"—see WRA 2007 s.1(4).
"period of limited capability for work"—see reg.2(1).
"relevant linked case"—see paras (2)(b), (3).
"terminally ill"—see reg.2(1).
"the assessment phase"—see WRA 2007 s.24(2).

GENERAL NOTE

This is the equivalent of reg.7 of the ESA Regs 2008. 13.120
Reg.86 referred to in para.(2) is the equivalent of reg.145(1) of the ESA Regs 2008. Reg.26 referred to in para.(3) (b), (c) and (d) is the equivalent of reg.30 of the ESA Regs 2008. Reg.87(2) in para.(4) corresponds to reg.147A(2) of the ESA Regs 2008.

PART 3

Conditions of entitlement

Conditions relating to national insurance and relevant earnings

8.—(1) A claimant's relevant earnings for the purposes of paragraph 1(2) 13.121
(a) of Schedule 1 to the Act (employment and support allowance: conditions relating to national insurance) are the total amount of the claimant's earnings equal to the lower earnings limit for the base tax year.

(2) For the purposes of paragraph (1), earnings which exceed the lower earnings limit are to be disregarded.

GENERAL NOTE

See reg.7A of the ESA Regs 2008. 13.122

Relaxation of the first contribution condition

9.—(1) A claimant who satisfies any of the conditions in paragraph (2) is 13.123
to be taken to satisfy the first contribution condition if—
   (a) the claimant paid Class 1 or Class 2 contributions before the relevant benefit week in respect of any one tax year; and
   (b) the claimant has—

> > > (i) earnings equal to the lower earnings limit in that tax year on which primary Class 1 contributions have been paid or treated as paid which in total, and disregarding any earnings which exceed the lower earnings limit for that year, are not less than that limit multiplied by 26; or
> >
> > > (ii) earnings factors in that tax year derived from Class 2 contributions multiplied by 26.
> >
> > (2) The conditions referred to in paragraph (1) are that the claimant—
> >
> > (a) was entitled to a carer's allowance in the last complete tax year immediately preceding the relevant benefit year;
> >
> > (b) had been—
> >
> > > (i) engaged in qualifying remunerative work (which has the meaning given by Part 1 of the Tax Credits Act) for a period of more than two years immediately before the first day of the period of limited capability for work; and
> >
> > > (ii) entitled to working tax credit where the disability element or the severe disability element of working tax credit specified in regulation 20(1)(b) or (f) of the Working Tax Credit (Entitlement and Maximum Rate) Regulations 2002 was included in the award;
> >
> > (c) in respect of any week in any tax year preceding the relevant benefit year—
> >
> > > (i) is entitled to be credited with earnings or contributions in accordance with regulation 9D of the Social Security (Credits) Regulations 1975 (credits for certain periods of imprisonment or detention in legal custody); or
> >
> > > (ii) would have been so entitled had an application to the Secretary of State been made for the purpose of that regulation; or
> >
> > (d) in respect of any week in the last complete tax year preceding the relevant benefit year, is entitled to be credited with earnings in accordance with regulation 9E of the Social Security (Credits) Regulations 1975 (credits for certain spouses and civil partners of members of Her Majesty's forces).

DEFINITIONS

"benefit week"—see reg.2(1).
"carer's allowance"—see reg.2(1).
"claimant"—see WRA 2007 s.24(1).
"Class 1 contributions"—see WRA 2007 s.1, Sch.1 Pt 1 para.3(1)(b).
"Class 2 contributions—see WRA 2007 s.1, Sch.1 Pt 1 para.3(1)(b).
"earnings"—see WRA 2007 s.1, Sch.1 Pt 1 para.3(1)(c).
"earnings factor"—see WRA 2007 s.1, Sch.1 Pt 1 para.3(1)(d).
"first contribution condition"—see reg.2(1); WRA 2007 Sch.1 para.1(1).
"lower earnings limit"—see WRA 2007 s.1, Sch.1 Pt 1 para.3(1)(e).
"period of limited capability for work,"—see reg.2(1).
"primary Class 1 contributions"—see WRA 2007 s.1, Sch.1 Pt 1 para.3(1)(b).
"relevant benefit year"—see WRA 2007 s.1, Sch.1 Pt 1 para.3(1) (f).
"tax year"—see WRA 2007 s.1, Sch.1 Pt 1 para.3(1)(g).
"week"—see reg.2(1).

GENERAL NOTE

13.124   See reg.8 of the ESA Regs 2008.

Condition relating to youth – claimants aged 20 or over but under 25

10.—(1) For the purposes of paragraph 4(1)(a) of Schedule 1 to the   13.125
Act, a claimant who satisfies the conditions specified in paragraph (2) falls
within a prescribed case.

(2) The conditions are that the claimant—

(a) registered on a course of—

    (i) full-time advanced or secondary education; or

    (ii) training,

at least three months before attaining the age of 20; and

(b) not more than one academic term immediately after registration
attended one or more such courses in respect of a period referred to
in paragraph (3).

(3) The period mentioned in paragraph (2) (b) is a period which—

(a) began on or before a day at least three months before the day the
claimant attained the age of 20; and

(b) ended no earlier than the beginning of the last two complete tax
years before the relevant benefit year which would have applied if
the claimant was entitled to an employment and support allowance
having satisfied the first contribution condition and the second
contribution condition.

(4) For the purposes of this regulation a claimant is to be treated as
attending a course on any day on which the course is interrupted by an
illness or domestic emergency.

(5) In this regulation—

"full-time" includes part-time where the person's disability prevents
attendance at a full-time course;

"secondary education" means a course of education below a course of
advanced education by attendance—

(a) at an establishment recognised by the Secretary of State—

    (i) as being a university, college or school; or

    (ii) as comparable to a university, college or school;

(b) at an establishment that is not mentioned in paragraph (a) where the
Secretary of State is satisfied that the education is equivalent to that
given in an establishment recognised—

    (i) as being a university, college or school; or

    (ii) as comparable to a university, college or school.

(6) A claimant is to be treated as not having limited capability for work on
a day which is not, for the purposes of paragraph 4(1)(d)(ii) of Schedule 1
to the Act (period of 196 consecutive days preceding the relevant period of
limited capability for work), part of a period of consecutive days of limited
capability for work.

Definitions

"advanced education"—see reg.2(1).

"claimant"—see WRA 2007 s.24(1).

"first contribution condition"—see reg.2(1); WRA 2007 Sch.1 para.1(1).

"full-time"—see para.(5).

"relevant benefit year"—see WRA 2007 s.1, Sch.1 Pt 1 para.3(1) (f).

"secondary education"—see para.(5).

"second contribution condition"—see reg.2(1); WRA 2007 Sch.1 para.2(1).

"tax year"—see WRA 2007 s.1, Sch.1 Pt 1 para.3(1) (g).

"training"—see reg.2(1).

13.126   This is the same as ESA Regs 2008 reg.9.

Condition relating to youth – previous claimants

13.127   **11.**—(1) Paragraph 4(1)(a) of Schedule 1 to the Act does not apply to a claimant—

(a) who has previously ceased to be entitled to an employment and support allowance to which the claimant was entitled by virtue of satisfying the condition set out in paragraph 4(1) of Schedule 1 to the Act;

(b) whose previous entitlement had not been ended by a decision which embodied a determination (other than a determination in the circumstances applicable to a claimant under paragraph (2)(a)) that the claimant did not have limited capability for work;

(c) in relation to whom regulation 86 (linking rules) does not apply;

(d) who is aged 20 or over or, where regulation 10 would otherwise apply to the person, aged 25 or over; and

(e) to whom paragraph (2) applies.

(2) This paragraph applies to a claimant—

(a) whose previous entitlement to an employment and support allowance ended only with a view to that person taking up employment or training;

(b) whose earnings factor from an employment or series of employments pursued in the period from the end of the previous entitlement to the beginning of the period of limited capability for work, was below the lower earnings limit multiplied by 25 in any of the last three complete tax years before the beginning of the relevant benefit year; and

(c) who—

(i) in respect of the last two complete tax years before the beginning of the relevant benefit year has either paid or been credited with earnings equivalent in each of those years to the year's lower earnings limit multiplied by 50, of which at least one such payment or credit, in the last complete tax year, was in respect of the disability element or severe disability element of working tax credit; or

(ii) makes a claim for an employment and support allowance within the period of 12 weeks after the day on which the last employment referred to in sub-paragraph (b) ceased.

DEFINITIONS

"claimant"—see WRA 2007 s.24(1).
"earnings factor"—see WRA 2007 s.1, Sch.1 Pt 1 para.3(1) (d).
"employment"—see reg.2(1).
"limited capability for work"—see WRA 2007 s.1(4).
"lower earnings limit"—see WRA 2007 s.1, Sch.1 Pt 1 para.3(1)(e).
"period of limited capability for work"—see reg.2(1).
"relevant benefit year"—see WRA 2007 s.1, Sch.1 Pt 1 para.3(1)(f).
"tax year"—see WRA 2007 s.1, Sch.1 Pt 1 para.3(1)(g).
"training"—see reg.2(1).
"week"—see reg.2(1).
"working tax credit"—see reg.2(1).

This is the same as ESA Regs 2008 reg.10. The equivalent in the 2008 Regs of reg.86 (linking rules) referred to in para.(1) is reg.145.

13.128

Condition relating to youth – residence or presence

12.—(1) The conditions prescribed for the purposes of paragraph 4(1) (c) of Schedule 1 to the Act as to residence and presence in Great Britain are that the claimant—

(a) is ordinarily resident in Great Britain;

(b) is not a person subject to immigration control within the meaning of section 115(9) of the Immigration and Asylum Act 1999 or is a person to whom paragraph (3) applies;

(c) is present in Great Britain; and

(d) has been present in Great Britain for a period of, or for periods amounting in aggregate to, not less than 26 weeks in the 52 weeks immediately preceding the relevant benefit week.

13.129

(2) For the purposes of paragraph (1), a claimant is to be treated as being resident and present in Great Britain where the claimant is absent from Great Britain by reason only of being—

(a) the spouse, civil partner, son, daughter, father, father-in-law, mother or mother-in-law of, and living with, a member of Her Majesty's forces who is abroad in that capacity;

(b) in employment prescribed for the purposes of paragraph 7(1)(c) of Schedule 2 to the Act in connection with continental shelf operations; or

(c) abroad in the capacity of being an aircraft worker or mariner.

(3) This paragraph applies where a person is—

(a) a member of a family of a national of an European Economic Area state;

(b) a person who is lawfully working in Great Britain and is a national of a State with which the European Union has concluded an agreement under Article 217 of the Treaty on the Functioning of the European Union providing, in the field of social security, for the equal treatment of workers who are nationals of the signatory State and their families;

(c) a person who is a member of a family of, and living with, a person specified in subparagraph (b) ; or

(d) a person who has been given leave to enter, or remain in, the United Kingdom by the Secretary of State upon an undertaking by another person or persons pursuant to the immigration rules within the meaning of the Immigration Act 1971 to be responsible for that person's maintenance and accommodation.

(4) A person is to be treated as having satisfied the residence or presence conditions in paragraph (1) throughout a period of limited capability for work where those conditions are satisfied on the first day of that period of limited capability for work.

(5) In this regulation—

"aircraft worker" means a person who is, or has been, employed under a contract of service either as a pilot, commander, navigator or other member of the crew of any aircraft, or in any other capacity on board any aircraft where—

   (a) the employment in that other capacity is for the purposes of the aircraft or its crew or of any passengers or cargo or mail carried on that aircraft; and

   (b) the contract is entered into in the United Kingdom with a view to its performance (in whole or in part) while the aircraft is in flight, but does not include a person who is in employment as a member of Her Majesty's forces;

"mariner" means a person who is, or has been, in employment under a contract of service either as a master or other member of the crew of any ship or vessel, or in any other capacity on board any ship or vessel where—

   (a) the employment in that other capacity is for the purposes of that ship or vessel or its crew or any passengers or cargo or mail carried by the ship or vessel; and

   (b) the contract is entered into in the United Kingdom with a view to its performance (in whole or in part) while the ship or vessel is on its voyage, but does not include a person who is in employment as a member of Her Majesty's forces.

(6) In the definition of "mariner" in paragraph (5), "passenger" means any person carried on a ship or vessel except—

   (a) a person employed or engaged in any capacity on board the ship or vessel on the business of the ship or vessel; or

   (b) a person on board the ship or vessel either in pursuance of an obligation to carry shipwrecked, distressed or other persons, or by reason of any circumstance that neither the master nor the owner nor the charterer (if any) could have prevented or forestalled.

DEFINITIONS

   "aircraft worker"—see para.(5)).
   "benefit week"—see reg.2(1).
   "claimant"—see WRA 2007 s.24(1).
   "continental shelf operations"—see WRA 2007 s.22, Sch.2, para.7(3).
   "employment"—see reg.2(1).
   "family"—see reg.2(1).
   "member of Her Majesty's forces"—see reg.2(1).
   "mariner"—see para.(5).
   "passenger"—see para.(5).
   "period of limited capability for work"—see reg.2(1).
   "prescribed"—see WRA 2007 s.24(1).
   "week"—see reg.2(1).

GENERAL NOTE

13.130   This is the same as ESA Regs 2008 reg.11.

Condition relating to youth – full-time education

13.131   **13.**—(1) For the purposes of paragraph 4(1)(b)of Schedule 1 to the Act, a claimant is to be treated as receiving full-time education for any period during which the claimant—

   (a) is at least 16 years old but under the age of 19; and

   (b) attends a course of education for 21 hours or more a week.

(2) For the purposes of paragraph (1)(b), in calculating the number of hours a week during which a claimant attends a course, no account is to be

taken of any instruction or tuition which is, in the opinion of the Secretary of State, not suitable for persons of the same age who do not have a disability.

(3) In determining the duration of a period of full-time education under paragraph (1) any temporary interruption of that education may be disregarded.

(4) A claimant who is 19 years of age or over is not to be treated for the purposes of paragraph 4(1) (b) of Schedule 1 to the Act as receiving full-time education.

DEFINITIONS

"claimant"—see WRA 2007 s.24(1).
"week"—see reg.2(1).

GENERAL NOTE

This is exactly the same as ESA Regs 2008 reg.12.   13.132

Modification of the relevant benefit year

14.—(1) Where paragraph (2) applies, paragraph 3(1)(f) of Schedule 1   13.133
to the Act has effect as if the "relevant benefit year" were any benefit year which includes all or part of the period of limited capability for work which includes the relevant benefit week.

(2) This paragraph applies where a claimant has made a claim for employment and support allowance but does not satisfy—

(a) the first contribution condition;
(b) the second contribution condition; or
(c) either contribution condition,

but would satisfy both of those conditions if the modified definition of "relevant benefit year" provided in paragraph (1) applied.

DEFINTIONS

"claimant"—see WRA 2007 s.24(1).
"first contribution condition"—see reg.2(1); WRA 2007 s.1, Sch.1 para.1(1).
"period of limited capability for work"—see reg.2(1).
"relevant benefit year"—see para.(1).
"second contribution condition"—see reg.2(1); WRA 2007 s.1, Sch.1 para.2(1).

GENERAL NOTE

This is exactly the same as ESA Regs 2008 reg.13.   13.134

PART 4

Limited Capability for Work

Determination of limited capability for work

15.—(1) For the purposes of Part 1 of the Act, whether a claimant's capa-   13.135
bility for work is limited by the claimant's physical or mental condition and,

if it is, whether the limitation is such that it is not reasonable to require the claimant to work is to be determined on the basis of a limited capability for work assessment of the claimant in accordance with this Part.

(2) The limited capability for work assessment is an assessment of the extent to which a claimant who has some specific disease or bodily or mental disablement is capable of performing the activities prescribed in Schedule 2 or is incapable by reason of such disease or bodily or mental disablement of performing those activities.

(3) Subject to paragraph (6), for the purposes of Part 1 of the Act a claimant has limited capability for work if, by adding the points listed in column (3) of Schedule 2 against each descriptor listed in that Schedule which applies in the claimant's case, the claimant obtains a total score of at least—

    (a) 15 points whether singly or by a combination of descriptors specified in Part 1 of that Schedule;

    (b) 15 points whether singly or by a combination of descriptors specified in Part 2 of that Schedule; or

    (c) 15 points by a combination of descriptors specified in Parts 1 and 2 of that Schedule.

(4) In assessing the extent of a claimant's capability to perform any activity listed in Part 1 of Schedule 2, the claimant is to be assessed as if—

    (a) fitted with or wearing any prosthesis with which the claimant is normally fitted or normally wears; or, as the case may be,

    (b) wearing or using any aid or appliance which is normally, or could reasonably be expected to be, worn or used.

(5) In assessing the extent of a claimant's capability to perform any activity listed in Schedule 2, it is a condition that the claimant's incapability to perform the activity arises—

    (a) in respect of any descriptor listed in Part 1 of Schedule 2, from a specific bodily disease or disablement;

    (b) in respect of any descriptor listed in Part 2 of Schedule 2, from a specific mental illness or disablement; or

    (c) in respect of any descriptor or descriptors listed in—

        (i) Part 1 of Schedule 2, as a direct result of treatment provided by a registered medical practitioner for a specific physical disease or disablement; or

        (ii) Part 2 of Schedule 2, as a direct result of treatment provided by a registered medical practitioner for a specific mental illness or disablement.

(6) Where more than one descriptor specified for an activity applies to a claimant, only the descriptor with the highest score in respect of each activity which applies is to be counted.

(7) Where a claimant—

    (a) has been determined to have limited capability for work; or

    (b) is to be treated as having limited capability for work under regulation 16, 21, 22 or 25, the Secretary of State may, if paragraph (8) applies, determine afresh whether the claimant has or is to be treated as having limited capability for work.

(8) This paragraph applies where—

    (a) the Secretary of State wishes to determine whether there has been a relevant change of circumstances in relation to the claimant's physical or mental condition;

(b) the Secretary of State wishes to determine whether the previous determination of limited capability for work or that the claimant is to be treated as having limited capability for work, was made in ignorance of, or was based on a mistake as to, some material fact; or

(c) at least three months have passed since the date on which the claimant was determined to have limited capability for work or to be treated as having limited capability for work.

DEFINITIONS

"claimant"—see WRA 2007 s.24(1).
"descriptor"—see reg.2(1).
"limited capability for work"—see WRA 2007 s.1(4).
"limited capability for work assessment"—see para.(2).

GENERAL NOTE

This replicates ESA Regs 2008 reg.19.

13.136

In para.(7)(b), the renumbered regs compare with equivalent ones in the ESA Regs 2008 as follows:

2013 Regs	2008 Regs	Subject Matter
16	20	Certain claimants to be treated as having limited capability for work
21	25	Hospital patients
22	26	Claimants receiving certain treatment
25	29	Exceptional circumstances

There is no equivalent in the ESA Regs 2013 of ESA Regs 2008 reg.33(2) which dealt with ability to treat as having limited capability with respect only to IRESA, a benefit abolished in the cases and areas in which these 2013 Regulations apply.

Certain claimants to be treated as having limited capability for work

16.—(1) A claimant is to be treated as having limited capability for work if—

13.137

(a) the claimant is terminally ill;

(b) the claimant is—

(i) receiving treatment for cancer by way of chemotherapy or radiotherapy;

(ii) likely to receive such treatment within six months after the date of the determination of capability for work; or

(iii) recovering from such treatment, and the Secretary of State is satisfied that the claimant should be treated as having limited capability for work;

(c) the claimant is—

(i) excluded or abstains from work pursuant to a request or notice in writing lawfully made or given under an enactment; or

(ii) otherwise prevented from working pursuant to an enactment,

by reason of it being known or reasonably suspected that the claimant is infected or contaminated by, or has been in contact with a case of, a relevant infection or contamination;

(d) in the case of a pregnant woman, there is a serious risk of damage to her health or to the health of her unborn child if she does not refrain from work;

(e) in the case of a pregnant woman, she—
  (i) is within the maternity allowance period (which has the meaning it has in section 35(2) of the Contributions and Benefits Act); and
  (ii) is entitled to a maternity allowance under section 35(1) of the Contributions and Benefits Act;
(f) in the case of a pregnant woman whose expected or actual date of confinement has been certified in accordance with the Medical Evidence Regulations, on any day in the period—
  (i) beginning with the first date of the 6th week before the expected week of her confinement or the actual date of her confinement, whichever is earlier; and
  (ii) ending on the 14th day after the actual date of her confinement,
if she would have no entitlement to a maternity allowance or statutory maternity pay were she to make a claim in respect of that period;
(g) the claimant meets any of the descriptors at paragraph 15 or 16 of Schedule 3 in accordance with regulation 30(2), (3) and (6) where applicable; or
(h) the claimant is entitled to universal credit and it has previously been determined that the claimant has limited capability for work on the basis of an assessment under Part 5 of the Universal Credit Regulations 2013.

(2) In this regulation, "relevant infection or contamination" means—
(a) in England and Wales—
  (i) any incidence or spread of infection or contamination, within the meaning of section 45A(3) of the Public Health (Control of Disease) Act 1984 in respect of which regulations are made under Part 2A of that Act (public health protection) for the purpose of preventing, protecting against, controlling or providing a public health response to, such incidence or spread; or
  (ii) tuberculosis or any infectious disease to which regulation 9 of the Public Health (Aircraft) Regulations 1979 (powers in respect of persons leaving aircraft) applies or to which regulation 10 of the Public Health (Ships) Regulations 1979 (powers in respect of certain persons on ships) applies; and
(b) in Scotland, any—
  (i) infectious disease within the meaning of section 1(5) of the Public Health etc (Scotland) Act 2008, or exposure to an organism causing that disease; or
  (ii) contamination within the meaning of section 1(5) of that Act, or exposure to a contaminant, to which sections 56 to 58 of that Act (compensation) apply.

DEFINITIONS

"claimant"—see WRA 2007 s.24(1).
"confinement"—see reg.2(1).
"Contributions and Benefits Act"—see WRA 2007 s.65.
"limited capability for work"—see WRA 2007 s.1(4).
"maternity allowance period" —see para.(1)(e)(i).
"Medical Evidence Regulations"—see reg.2(1).
"relevant infection or contamination"—see para.(2).
"terminally ill"—see reg.2(1).
"week"—see reg.2(1).

(SI 2013/379 reg.16) (as amended)

GENERAL NOTE

This is much the same as ESA Regs 2008 reg.20.

Information required for determining capability for work

17.—(1) Subject to paragraphs (2) and (3), the information or evidence required to determine whether a claimant has limited capability for work is—

   (a) evidence of limited capability for work in accordance with the Medical Evidence Regulations (which prescribe the form of doctor's statement or other evidence required in each case);

   (b) any information relating to a claimant's capability to perform the activities referred to in Schedule 2 as may be requested in the form of a questionnaire; and

   (c) any such additional information as may be requested.

(2) Where the Secretary of State is satisfied that there is sufficient information to determine whether a claimant has limited capability for work without the information specified in paragraph (1)(b), that information must not be required for the purposes of making the determination.

(3) Paragraph (1) does not apply in relation to a determination whether a claimant is to be treated as having limited capability for work under any of regulations 16 (certain claimants to be treated as having limited capability for work), 21 (hospital in-patients) and 22 (claimants receiving certain treatment).

13.138

DEFINITIONS

"claimant"—see WRA 2007 s.24(1).
"limited capability for work"—see WRA 2007 s.1(4).
"Medical Evidence Regulations"—see reg.2(1).

GENERAL NOTE

This corresponds to ESA Regs 2008 reg.21.

13.139

Failure to provide information in relation to limited capability for work

18.—(1) Where a claimant fails without good cause to comply with the request referred to in regulation 17(1)(b), that claimant is, subject to paragraph (2), to be treated as not having limited capability for work.

(2) Paragraph (1) does not apply unless—

   (a) the claimant was sent a further request at least three weeks after the date of the first request; and

   (b) at least one week has passed since the further request was sent.

13.140

DEFINITIONS

"claimant"—see WRA 2007 s.24(1).
"limited capability for work"—see WRA 2007 s.1(4).
"week"—see reg.2(1).

GENERAL NOTE

This is the same as ESA Regs 2008 reg.22.

13.141

1701

Claimant may be called for a medical examination to determine whether the claimant has limited capability for work

13.142   **19.**—(1) Where it falls to be determined whether a claimant has limited capability for work, that claimant may be called by or on behalf of a health care professional approved by the Secretary of State to attend for a medical examination.

(2) Subject to paragraph (3), where a claimant fails without good cause to attend for or to submit to an examination mentioned in paragraph (1), the claimant is to be treated as not having limited capability for work.

(3) Paragraph (2) does not apply unless—

(a) written notice of the date, time and place for the examination was sent to the claimant at least seven days in advance; or

(b) that claimant agreed to accept a shorter period of notice whether given in writing or otherwise.

DEFINITIONS

"claimant"—see WRA 2007 s.24(1).
"health care professional"—see reg.2(1).
"limited capability for work"—see WRA 2007 s.1(4).

GENERAL NOTE

13.143   This is the same as ESA Regs 2008 reg.23.

Matters to be taken into account in determining good cause in relation to regulations 18 or 19

13.144   **20.** The matters to be taken into account in determining whether a claimant has good cause under regulation 18 (failure to provide information in relation to limited capability for work) or 19 (failure to attend a medical examination to determine limited capability for work) include—

(a) whether the claimant was outside Great Britain at the relevant time;

(b) the claimant's state of health at the relevant time; and

(c) the nature of any disability the claimant has.

DEFINITION

"claimant"—see WRA 2007 s.24(1).

GENERAL NOTE

13.145   This corresponds to ESA Regs 2008 reg.24.

Hospital patients

13.146   **21.**—(1) A claimant is to be treated as having limited capability for work on any day on which that claimant is undergoing medical or other treatment as a patient in a hospital or similar institution [¹on any day], or which is a day of recovery from that treatment.

(2) The circumstances in which a claimant is to be regarded as undergoing treatment falling within paragraph (1) include where the claimant is attending a residential programme of rehabilitation for the treatment of drug or alcohol addiction.

(3) For the purposes of this regulation, a claimant is to be regarded as undergoing treatment as a patient in a hospital or similar institution

only if that claimant has been advised by a health care professional to stay [¹for a period of 24 hours or longer] following medical or other treatment.

(4) For the purposes of this regulation, "day of recovery" means a day on which a claimant is recovering from treatment as a patient in a hospital or similar institution as referred to in paragraph (1) and the Secretary of State is satisfied that the claimant should be treated as having limited capability for work on that day.

AMENDMENT

1. Social Security (Miscellaneous Amendments) (No.2) Regulations 2013 (SI 2013/1508) reg.5(1), (2) (July 29, 2013).

DEFINITIONS

"claimant"—see WRA 2007 s.24(1).
"day of recovery"—see para.(4).
"limited capability for work"—see WRA 2007 s.1(4).
"medical treatment"—see reg.2(1).

GENERAL NOTE

This is the same as ESA Regs 2008 reg.25.   13.147

Claimants receiving certain treatment

22.—(1) Subject to paragraph (2), a claimant receiving—   13.148
  (a) regular weekly treatment by way of haemodialysis for chronic renal failure;
  (b) treatment by way of plasmapheresis; or
  (c) regular weekly treatment by way of total parenteral nutrition for gross impairment of enteric function,
is to be treated as having limited capability for work during any week in which that claimant is engaged in receiving that treatment or has a day of recovery from that treatment.

(2) A claimant who receives the treatment referred to in paragraph (1) is only to be treated as having limited capability for work from the first week of treatment in which the claimant undergoes no fewer than—
  (a) two days of treatment;
  (b) two days of recovery from any of the forms of treatment listed in paragraph (1) (a) to (c); or
  (c) one day of treatment and one day of recovery from that treatment,
but the days of treatment or recovery from that treatment or both need not be consecutive.

(3) For the purpose of this regulation "day of recovery" means a day on which a claimant is recovering from any of the forms of treatment listed in paragraph (1) (a) to (c) and the Secretary of State is satisfied that the claimant should be treated as having limited capability for work on that day.

DEFINITIONS

"claimant"—see WRA 2007 s.24(1).
"day of recovery"—see para.(3).
"limited capability for work"—see WRA 2007 s.1(4).
"week"—see reg.2(1).

GENERAL NOTE

13.149   This replicates ESA Regs 2008 reg.26.

Claimant to be treated as having limited capability for work throughout a day

13.150   **23.** A claimant who, at the commencement of any day has, or after that develops, limited capability for work as determined in accordance with the limited capability for work assessment is to be treated as having limited capability for work on that day.

DEFINITIONS

"claimant"—see WRA 2007 s.24(1).
"limited capability for work"—see WRA 2007 s.1(4).
"limited capability for work assessment"—see reg.2(1).

GENERAL NOTE

13.151   This is identical to ESA Regs 2008 reg.27.

Night workers

13.152   **24.**—(1) Where a claimant works for a continuous period which extends over midnight into the following day, that claimant is to be treated as having limited capability for work on the day on which the lesser part of that period falls if that claimant had limited capability for work for the remainder of that day.

(2) Where, in relation to a period referred to in paragraph (1), the number of hours worked before and after midnight is equal—

(a) if the days in question fall at the beginning of a period of limited capability for work, the claimant is to be treated as having limited capability on the second day; and

(b) if the days in question fall at the end of a period of limited capability for work, the claimant is to be treated as having limited capability for work on the first day.

DEFINITIONS

"claimant"—see WRA 2007 s.24(1).
"limited capability for work"—see WRA 2007 s.1(4).
"period of limited capability for work"—see reg.2(1).

GENERAL NOTE

13.153   This replicates ESA Regs 2008 reg.28.

Exceptional circumstances

13.154   **25.**—(1) A claimant who does not have limited capability for work as determined in accordance with the limited capability for work assessment is to be treated as having limited capability for work if paragraph (2) applies to the claimant.

(2) Subject to paragraph (3), this paragraph applies if—

(a) the claimant is suffering from a life-threatening disease in relation to which—

(i) there is medical evidence that the disease is uncontrollable, or uncontrolled, by a recognised therapeutic procedure; and

(ii) in the case of a disease that is uncontrolled, there is a reasonable cause for it not to be controlled by a recognised therapeutic procedure; or

(b) the claimant suffers from some specific disease or bodily or mental disablement and, by reason of such disease or disablement, there would be a substantial risk to the mental or physical health of any person if the claimant were found not to have limited capability for work.

(3) Paragraph (2)(b) does not apply where the risk could be reduced by a significant amount by—

(a) reasonable adjustments being made in the claimant's workplace; or

(b) the claimant taking medication to manage the claimant's condition where such medication has been prescribed for the claimant by a registered medical practitioner treating the claimant.

(4) In this regulation "medical evidence" means—

(a) evidence from a health care professional approved by the Secretary of State; and

(b) evidence (if any) from any health care professional or a hospital or similar institution, or such part of such evidence as constitutes the most reliable evidence available in the circumstances.

DEFINITIONS

"claimant"—see WRA 2007 s.24(1).
"limited capability for work"—see WRA 2007 s.1(4).
"limited capability for work assessment"—see reg.2(1).
"medical evidence"—see para.(4).

GENERAL NOTE

This replicates ESA Regs 2008 reg.29.   13.155

Conditions for treating a claimant as having limited capability for work until a determination about limited capability for work has been made

26.—(1) A claimant is, if the conditions set out in paragraph (2) are met,   13.156
to be treated as having limited capability for work until such time as it is determined—

(a) whether or not the claimant has limited capability for work;

(b) whether or not the claimant is to be treated as having limited capability for work otherwise than in accordance with this regulation; or

(c) whether the claimant falls to be treated as not having limited capability for work in accordance with regulation 18 (failure to provide information in relation to limited capability for work) or 19 (failure to attend a medical examination to determine limited capability for work).

(2) The conditions are—

(a) that the claimant provides evidence of limited capability for work in accordance with the Medical Evidence Regulations; and

[¹(b) in relation to the claimant's entitlement to any benefit, allowance or advantage which is dependent on the claimant having limited capability for work, it has not been determined—

(i) in the last determination preceding the date of claim for an employment and support allowance, that the claimant does not have limited capability for work; or

(ii) within the 6 months preceding the date of claim for an employment and support allowance, that the claimant is to be treated as not having limited capability for work under regulation 22 or 23,

unless paragraph (4) applies;]

[¹(3) Paragraph 2(b) does not apply where a claimant has made and is pursuing an appeal against a relevant decision of the Secretary of State, and that appeal has not yet been determined by the First-tier Tribunal.]

(4) This paragraph applies where—

(a) the claimant is suffering from some specific disease or bodily or mental disablement from which the claimant was not suffering at the time of that determination;

(b) a disease or bodily or mental disablement from which the claimant was suffering at the time of that determination has significantly worsened; or

(c) in the case of a claimant who was treated as not having limited capability for work under regulation 18 (failure to provide information), the claimant has since provided the information requested under that regulation.

[¹(5) In this regulation a "relevant decision" means—

(a) a decision that embodies the first determination by the Secretary of State that the claimant does not have limited capability for work; or

(b) a decision that embodies the first determination by the Secretary of State that the claimant does not have limited capability for work since a previous determination by the Secretary of State or appellate authority that the claimant does have limited capability for work.

(6) In this regulation, "appellate authority" means the First-tier Tribunal, the Upper Tribunal, the Court of Appeal, the Court of Session, or the Supreme Court.]

AMENDMENT

1. Employment and Support Allowance (Repeat Assessments and Pending Appeal Awards) (Amendment) Regulations 2015 (SI 2015/437) reg.4 (March 30, 2015).

DEFINITIONS

"appellate authority"—see para.(6).
"claimant"—see WRA 2007 s.24(1).
"limited capability for work"—see WRA 2007 s.1(4).
"Medical Evidence Regulations"—see reg.2(1).
"relevant decision"—see para.(5)

GENERAL NOTE

13.157   This corresponds to ESA Regs 2008 reg.30.

Certain claimants to be treated as not having limited capability for work

13.158   **27.**—(1) A claimant who is or has been a member of Her Majesty's forces is to be treated as not having limited capability for work on any day which is recorded by the Secretary of State as a day of sickness absence from duty.

(2) A claimant is to be treated as not having limited capability for work on

any day on which the claimant attends a training course in respect of which the claimant is paid a training allowance or premium pursuant to arrangements made under section 2 of the Employment and Training Act 1973 or section 2(3) of the Enterprise and New Towns (Scotland) Act 1990.

(3) Paragraph (2) is not to apply—

(a) for the purposes of any claim to an employment and support allowance for a period commencing after the claimant ceased attending the training course in question; or

(b) where any training allowance or premium paid to the claimant is paid for the sole purpose of travelling or meal expenses incurred or to be incurred under the arrangements made under section 2 of the Employment and Training Act 1973 or section 2(3) of the Enterprise and New Towns (Scotland) Act 1990.

(4) A claimant is to be treated as not having limited capability for work where—

(a) it has previously been determined, within the six months preceding the date of claim for employment and support allowance, on the basis of an assessment under Part 5 of the Universal Credit Regulations 2013 that the claimant does not have limited capability for work; and

(b) it appears to the Secretary of State that—

(i) the determination was not based on ignorance of, or mistake as to, a material fact; and

(ii) there has been no relevant change of circumstances in relation to the claimant's physical or mental condition since the determination.

DEFINITIONS

"claimant"—see WRA 2007 s.24(1).
"limited capability for work"—see WRA 2007 s.1(4).

GENERAL NOTE

This is much the same as ESA Regs 2008 reg.32.   13.159

Claimants to be treated as not having limited capability for work at the end of the period covered by medical evidence

28.—(1) Where the Secretary of State is satisfied that it is appropriate   13.160
in the circumstances of the case, a claimant may be treated as not having limited capability for work if—

(a) the claimant has supplied medical evidence;

(b) the period for which medical evidence was supplied has ended;

(c) the Secretary of State has requested further medical evidence; and

(d) the claimant has not, before whichever is the later of either the end of the period of six weeks beginning with the date of the Secretary of State's request or the end of six weeks beginning with the day after the end of the period for which medical evidence was supplied—

(i) supplied further medical evidence; or

(ii) otherwise made contact with the Secretary of State to indicate that they wish to have the question of limited capability for work determined.

(2) In this regulation "medical evidence" means evidence provided under regulation 2 or 5 of the Medical Evidence Regulations.

GENERAL NOTE

13.161   This is the same as ESA Regs 2008 reg.32A

Additional circumstances where claimants are to be treated as having limited capability for work

13.162   **29.** For the purposes of paragraph 4(1)(d)(ii) of Schedule 1 to the Act, a claimant is to be treated as having limited capability for work on any day in respect of which that claimant is entitled to statutory sick pay.

GENERAL NOTE

13.163   This is exactly the same as ESA Regs 2008 reg.33(1).

PART 5

Limited Capability for Work-related Activity

Determination of limited capability for work-related activity

13.164   **30.**—(1) For the purposes of Part 1 of the Act, where, by reason of a claimant's physical or mental condition, at least one of the descriptors set out in Schedule 3 applies to the claimant, the claimant has limited capability for work-related activity and the limitation must be such that it is not reasonable to require that claimant to undertake such activity.

(2) A descriptor applies to a claimant if that descriptor applies to the claimant for the majority of the time or, as the case may be, on the majority of the occasions on which the claimant undertakes or attempts to undertake the activity described by that descriptor.

(3) In determining whether a descriptor applies to a claimant, the claimant is to be assessed as if—

(a) the claimant were fitted with or wearing any prosthesis with which the claimant is normally fitted or normally wears; or, as the case may be

(b) wearing or using any aid or appliance which is normally, or could reasonably be expected to be, worn or used.

(4) Where a determination has been made about whether a claimant—

(a) has limited capability for work-related activity;

(b) is to be treated as having limited capability for work-related activity; or

(c) is to be treated as not having limited capability for work-related activity,

the Secretary of State may, if paragraph (5) applies, determine afresh whether the claimant has or is to be treated as having limited capability for work-related activity.

(5) This paragraph applies where—

(a) the Secretary of State wishes to determine whether there has been a relevant change of circumstances in relation to the claimant's physical or mental condition;

(b) the Secretary of State wishes to determine whether the previous determination about limited capability for work-related activity or about treating the claimant as having or as not having limited capability for work-related activity, was made in ignorance of, or was based on a mistake as to, some material fact; or

(c) at least three months have passed since the date of the previous determination about limited capability for work-related activity or about treating the claimant as having or as not having limited capability for work-related activity.

(6) In assessing the extent of a claimant's capability to perform any activity listed in Schedule 3, it is a condition that the claimant's incapability to perform the activity arises—

(a) in respect of descriptors 1 to 8, 15(a), 15(b), 16(a)and 16(b)—

    (i) from a specific bodily disease or disablement; or

    (ii) as a direct result of treatment provided by a registered medical practitioner for a specific physical disease or disablement; or

(b) in respect of descriptors 9 to 14, 15(c), 15(d), 16(c)and 16(d)—

    (i) from a specific mental illness or disablement; or

    (ii) as a direct result of treatment provided by a registered medical practitioner for a specific mental illness or disablement.

DEFINITIONS

"the Act"—see reg.2(1).
"claimant"—see WRA 2007 s.24(1).
"descriptor"—see reg.2(1).
"limited capability for work-related activity"—see WRA 2007 s.2(5).
"work-related activity"—see WRA 2007 ss.24(1), 13(7).

GENERAL NOTE

This corresponds to ESA Regs 2008 reg.34.　　　　　　　　　　　　　　13.165

Certain claimants to be treated as having, or not having, limited capability for work-related activity

31.—(1) A claimant is to be treated as having limited capability for work-　　13.166
related activity if—

(a) the claimant is terminally ill;

(b) the claimant is—

    (i) receiving treatment for cancer by way of chemotherapy or radiotherapy;

    (ii) likely to receive such treatment within six months after the date of the determination of capability for work-related activity; or

    (iii) recovering from such treatment,

and the Secretary of State is satisfied that the claimant should be treated as having limited capability for work-related activity;

(c) in the case of a woman, she is pregnant and there is a serious risk of damage to her health or to the health of her unborn child if she does not refrain from work-related activity; or

(d) the claimant is entitled to universal credit and it has previously been determined that the claimant has limited capability for work and work-related activity on the basis of an assessment under Part 5 of the Universal Credit Regulations 2013.

(2) A claimant who does not have limited capability for work-related activity as determined in accordance with regulation 30(1) is to be treated as having limited capability for work-related activity if—

(a) the claimant suffers from some specific disease or bodily or mental disablement; and

(b) by reason of such disease or disablement, there would be a substantial risk to the mental or physical health of any person if the claimant were found not to have limited capability for work-related activity.

(3) A claimant is to be treated as not having limited capability for work-related activity where—

(a) it has previously been determined, within the six months preceding the date of claim for employment and support allowance, on the basis of an assessment under Part 5 of the Universal Credit Regulations 2013 that the claimant does not have limited capability for work and work-related activity; and

(b) it appears to the Secretary of State that—

(i) the determination was not based on ignorance of, or mistake as to, a material fact; and

(ii) there has been no relevant change of circumstances in relation to the claimant's physical or mental condition.

DEFINITIONS

"claimant"—see WRA 2007 s.24(1).
"limited capability for work-related activity"—see WRA 2007 s.2(5).
"terminally ill"—see reg.2(1).
"work-related activity"—see WRA 2007 ss.24(1), 13(7).

GENERAL NOTE

13.167   This is the same as ESA Regs 2008 reg.35.

Relevant linked cases – limited capability for work-related activity

13.168   **32.** A claimant is to be treated as having limited capability for work-related activity where—

(a) they fall within case 1, as defined in regulation 7(3)(a); and

(b) in respect of the earlier period of limited capability for work referred to in regulation 7(3)(a)(i), they had been entitled to a support component under section 2(2) of the Act.

GENERAL NOTE

13.169   This corresponds to ESA Regs 2008 reg.35A.

Information required for determining capability for work-related activity

13.170   **33.**—(1) Subject to paragraph (2), the information or evidence required to determine whether a claimant has limited capability for work-related activity is—

(a) any information relating to the descriptors set out in Schedule 3 as may be requested in the form of a questionnaire; and

(b) any such additional information as may be requested.

(2) Where the Secretary of State is satisfied that there is sufficient information to determine whether a claimant has limited capability for work-

1710

related activity without the information specified in paragraph (1)(a), that information must not be required for the purposes of making the determination.

DEFINTIONS

"claimant"—see WRA 2007 s.24(1).
"limited capability for work-related activity"—see WRA 2007 s.2(5).
"work-related activity"—see WRA 2007 ss.24(1), 13(7).

GENERAL NOTE

This is the same as ESA Regs 2008 reg.36.   13.171

Failure to provide information in relation to work-related activity

34.—(1) Where a claimant fails without good cause to comply with the   13.172
request referred to in regulation 33(1)(a), the claimant is, subject to paragraph (2), to be treated as not having limited capability for work-related activity.
   (2) Paragraph (1) does not apply unless—
   (a) the claimant was sent a further request at least three weeks after the date of the first request; and
   (b) at least one week has passed since the further request was sent.

DEFINITIONS

"claimant"—see WRA 2007 s.24(1).
"limited capability for work-related activity"—see WRA 2007 s.2(5).
"week"—see reg.2(1).
"work-related activity"—see WRA 2007 ss.24(1), 13(7).

GENERAL NOTE

This corresponds to ESA Regs 2008 reg.37.   13.173

Claimant may be called for a medical examination to determine whether the claimant has limited capability for work-related activity

35.—(1) Where it falls to be determined whether a claimant has limited   13.174
capability for work-related activity, that claimant may be called by or on behalf of a health care professional approved by the Secretary of State to attend for a medical examination.
   (2) Subject to paragraph (3), where a claimant fails without good cause to attend for or to submit to an examination mentioned in paragraph (1), the claimant is to be treated as not having limited capability for work-related activity.
   (3) Paragraph (2) does not apply unless—
   (a) written notice of the date, time and place for the examination was sent to the claimant at least seven days in advance; or
   (b) the claimant agreed to accept a shorter period of notice whether given in writing or otherwise.

DEFINITIONS

"claimant"—see WRA 2007 s.24(1).
"health care professional"—see reg.2(1).
"limited capability for work-related activity"—see WRA 2007 s.2(5).
"work-related activity"—see WRA 2007 ss.24(1), 13(7).

GENERAL NOTE

13.175   This is the same as ESA Regs 2008 reg.38.

Matters to be taken into account in determining good cause in relation to regulations 34 or 35

13.176   **36.** The matters to be taken into account in determining whether a claimant has good cause under regulation 34 (failure to provide information in relation to work-related activity) or 35 (failure to attend a medical examination to determine limited capability for work-related activity) include—
     (a) whether the claimant was outside Great Britain at the relevant time;
     (b) the claimant's state of health at the relevant time; and
     (c) the nature of any disability the claimant has.

DEFINITION

     "claimant"—see WRA 2007 s.24(1).

GENERAL NOTE

13.177   This corresponds to ESA Regs 2008 reg.39.

PART 6

Effect of work on entitlement to an Employment and Support Allowance

A claimant who works to be treated as not entitled to an employment and support allowance

13.178   **37.**—(1) Subject to the following paragraphs, a claimant is to be treated as not entitled to an employment and support allowance in any week in which that claimant does work.
     (2) Paragraph (1) does not apply to—
     (a) work as a councillor;
     (b) duties undertaken on either one full day or two half-days a week as a member of the First-tier Tribunal where the member is eligible for appointment to be such a member in accordance with article 2(3) of the Qualifications for Appointment of Members to the First-tier Tribunal and Upper Tribunal Order 2008;
     (c) domestic tasks carried out in the claimant's own home or the care of a relative;
     (d) duties undertaken in caring for another person who is accommodated with the claimant by virtue of arrangements made under any of the provisions referred to in paragraph (7) or where the claimant is in receipt of any payment specified in that paragraph;
     (e) any activity the claimant undertakes during an emergency to protect another person or to prevent serious damage to property or livestock; or
     (f) any of the categories of work set out in regulation 39(1) (exempt work).
     (3) This regulation is subject to regulation 40 (effect of work on entitlement to an employment and support allowance where claimant is receiving certain treatment).

(4) A claimant who does work to which this regulation applies in a week which is—

    (a) the week in which the claimant first becomes entitled to a benefit, allowance or advantage on account of the claimant's limited capability for work in any period; or

    (b) the last week in any period in which the claimant has limited capability for work or is treated as having limited capability for work, is to be treated as not entitled to an employment and support allowance by virtue of paragraph (1) only on the actual day or days in that week on which the claimant does that work.

(5) Regulation 86 (linking rules) does not apply for the purposes of calculating the beginning or end of any period of limited capability for work under paragraph (4).

(6) The day or days in a week on which a night worker works, for the purposes of paragraph (4), are to be calculated by reference to regulation 24 (night workers).

(7) The payments and provisions mentioned in paragraph (2)(d) are—

    (a) any payment made to the claimant with whom a person is accommodated by virtue of arrangements made—

        (i) by a local authority under section 22C(2), (3), (5) or (6)(a) or (b) of the Children Act 1989 (provision of accommodation and maintenance for a child whom the local authority is looking after);

        (ii) by a local authority under section 26 [² or 26A] of the Children (Scotland) Act 1995 (manner of provision of accommodation to child looked after by local authority [² and duty to provide continuing care]);

        (iii) by a local authority under regulations 33 or 51 of the Looked After Children (Scotland) Regulations 2009 (fostering and kinship care allowances and fostering allowances); or

        (iv) by a voluntary organisation under section 59(1)(a) of the 1989 Act (provision of accommodation by voluntary organisations);

[² (aa) any payment made to the claimant under section 73(1)(b) of the Children and Young People (Scotland) Act 2014 (kinship care assistance);]

    (b) any payment made to the claimant or the claimant's partner for a person ("the person concerned"), who is not normally a member of the claimant's household but is temporarily in the claimant's care, by—

        (i) the National Health Service Commissioning Board;

        (ii) a local authority but excluding payments of housing benefit made in respect of the person concerned;

        (iii) a voluntary organisation;

        (iv) the person concerned pursuant to section 26(3A) of the National Assistance Act 1948;

        (v) a clinical commissioning group established under section 14D of the Health Service Act;

        (vi) a Local Health Board established by an order made under section 11 of the Health Service (Wales) Act. [¹; or

        (vii) the person concerned where the payment is for the provision of accommodation in respect of the meeting of that person's needs under section 18 or 19 of the Care Act 2014 (duty and power to meet needs for care and support).]

(8) In this regulation—

"week" means a week in respect of which a claimant is entitled to an employment and support allowance;

"work" means any work which a claimant does, whether or not that claimant undertakes it in expectation of payment;

"work as a councillor" includes any work which a claimant undertakes as a member of any of the bodies referred to in section 177(1) of the Local Government Act 1972 or section 49(1) or (1A) of the Local Government (Scotland) Act 1973(a), of which the claimant is a member by reason of being a councillor.

AMENDMENTS

1. Care Act 2014 (Consequential Amendments) (Secondary Legislation) Order 2015 (SI 2015/643) art.2, Sch para.42 (April 1, 2015).

2. Social Security and Child Support (Care Payments and Tenant Incentive Scheme) (Amendment) Regulations 2017 (SI 2017/995), regs 9(2) and 15(2) (November 7, 2017).

DEFINITIONS

"claimant"—see WRA 2007 s.24(1).
"entitled"—see WRA 2007 s.24(1).
"relative"—see reg.2(1).
"week"—see para.(8) and reg.2(1).
"work"—see para.(8).
"work as a councillor"—see para.(8).

GENERAL NOTE

13.179   This has much the same effect as ESA Regs 2008 reg.40.

Claimants who are treated as not entitled to any allowance at all by reason of regulation 37(1) are to be treated as not having limited capability for work

13.180   **38.**—(1) Where a claimant is treated as not entitled to an employment and support allowance by reason of regulation 37(1), the claimant is to be treated as not having limited capability for work.

(2) Paragraph (1) applies even if—

(a) it has been determined that the claimant has or is to be treated as having, under any of regulations 16 (certain claimants to be treated as having limited capability for work), 21 (hospital in-patients), 22 (claimants undergoing certain treatment) and 25 (exceptional circumstances), limited capability for work; or

(b) the claimant meets the conditions set out in regulation 26(2) for being treated as having limited capability for work until a determination is made in accordance with the limited capability for work assessment.

GENERAL NOTE

13.181   This is much the same as ESA Regs 2008 reg.44.

Exempt work

39.—(1) The categories of work referred to in regulation 37(2)(f) are—   **13.182**

(a) work for which the total earnings in any week does not exceed £20;

(b) work for which the total earnings in any week does not exceed 16 multiplied by the National Minimum Wage, subject to paragraph (4), and which—

    (i) is part of the claimant's treatment programme and is done under medical supervision while the claimant is an in-patient, or is regularly attending as an out-patient, of a hospital or similar institution; or

    (ii) is supervised by a person employed by a public or local authority or by a voluntary organisation or community interest company engaged in the provision or procurement of work for persons who have disabilities;

(c) work which is done for less than 16 hours a week, for which total earnings in any week does not exceed 16 multiplied by the National Minimum Wage, subject to paragraph (4); [¹...]

(d) work done in the course of receiving assistance in pursuing self-employed earner's employment whilst participating in a programme provided, or in other arrangements made, under section 2 of the Employment and Training Act 1973 (functions of the Secretary of State) or section 2 of the Enterprise and New Towns (Scotland) Act 1990 (functions in relation to training for employment etc);

(e) work done where the claimant receives no payment of earnings and where the claimant is—

    (i) engaged by a charity or voluntary organisation; or

    (ii) a volunteer,

and where the Secretary of State is satisfied in either of those cases that it is reasonable for the claimant to do the work free of charge;

(f) work done in the course of participating in a work placement approved in writing by the Secretary of State before the placement starts.

(2) The number of hours for which a claimant is engaged in work is to be determined—

(a) where no recognisable cycle has been established in respect of a claimant's work, by reference to the number of hours or, where those hours are likely to fluctuate, the average of the hours, which the claimant is expected to work in a week;

(b) where the number of hours for which the claimant is engaged fluctuate, by reference to the average of hours worked over—

    (i) if there is a recognisable cycle of work, the period of one complete cycle (including, where the cycle involves periods in which the claimant does no work, those periods but disregarding any other absences);

    (ii) in any other case, the period of five weeks immediately before the date of claim or the date on which a superseding decision is made under section 10 of the Social Security Act 1998 (decisions superseding earlier decisions), or such other length of time as may, in the particular case, enable the claimant's average hours of work to be determined more accurately.

(3) For the purposes of determining the number of hours for which a claimant is engaged in work, that number is to include any time allowed to that claimant by the claimant's employer for a meal or for refreshment, but only where that claimant is, or expects to be, paid earnings in respect of that time.

(4) Where the amount determined by the calculation in paragraph (1) (b)or (c) would, but for this paragraph, include an amount of—

(a) less than 50p, that amount is to be rounded up to the nearest 50p; or

(b) less than £1 but more than 50p, that amount is to be rounded up to the nearest £1.

(5) Part 10 applies for the purposes of calculating any income which consists of earnings under this regulation.

(6) In this regulation—

[¹. . .]

"volunteer" means a person who is engaged in voluntary work otherwise than for a relative, where the only payment received or due to be paid to the person by virtue of being so engaged is in respect of any expenses reasonably incurred by the person in connection with that work;

[¹. . .]

"work placement" means practical work experience with an employer, which is neither paid nor undertaken in expectation of payment.

(7) [¹. . .]

AMENDMENTS

1. Employment and Support Allowance (Exempt Work & Hardship Amounts) (Amendment) Regulations 2017 (SI 2017/205) reg.4 (April 3, 2017).

DEFINITIONS

"the Act"—see reg.2(1).
"claimant"—see WRA 2007 s.24(1).
"Contributions and Benefits Act"—see WRA 2007 s.65.
"employment"—see reg.2(1).
"relevant benefit"—see para.(6).
"self-employed earner"—see reg.2(1).
"voluntary organisation"—see reg.2(1).
"volunteer"—see para.(6).
"week"—see reg.2(1).
"work period"—see para.(6).
"work placement"—see para.(6).

GENERAL NOTE

13.183   This corresponds to ESA Regs 2008 reg.45.

Effect of work on entitlement to an employment and support allowance where claimant is receiving certain treatment

13.184   **40.** Where a claimant who is entitled to an employment and support allowance and is treated as having limited capability for work by virtue of regulation 22 works on any day during a week when the claimant is receiving certain treatment mentioned in regulation 22 or recovering from that treatment, that work is to have no effect on the claimant's entitlement to the employment and support allowance.

DEFINITIONS

"claimant"—see WRA 2007 s.24(1).
"entitled"—see WRA 2007 s.24(1).
"limited capability for work"—see WRA 2007 s.24(1).
"week"—see reg.2(1), WRA 2007 s.24(1).

GENERAL NOTE

This is the same as ESA Regs 2008 reg.46.   13.185

PART 7

Claimant responsibilities

Interpretation

41.—(1) In this Part—   13.186
"responsible carer", in relation to a child, means—
(a) a person who is the only person responsible for the child; or
(b) a person who is a member of a couple where—
  (i) both members of the couple are responsible for the child; and
  (ii) the person has been nominated by the couple jointly as responsible for the child;
"responsible foster parent", in relation to a child, means—
(a) a person who is the only foster parent in relation to the child; or
(b) a person who is a member of a couple where—
  (i) both members of the couple are foster parents in relation to the child; and
  (ii) the person has been nominated by the couple jointly as the responsible foster parent.
(2) The nomination of a responsible carer or responsible foster parent for the purposes of paragraph (1) may be changed—
(a) once in a 12 month period, beginning with the date of the previous nomination; or
(b) on any occasion where the Secretary of State considers that there has been a change of circumstances which is relevant to the nomination.
(3) Only one person may be nominated as a responsible carer or a responsible foster parent.
(4) The nomination applies to all of the children for whom the claimant is responsible.

DEFINITIONS

"child"—see reg.2(1).
"claimant" see WRA 2007 s.24(1).
"couple"—see reg.2(1).
"responsible carer"—see para.(1).
"responsible foster parent"—see para.(1).

GENERAL NOTE

Compare Universal Credit Regs 2013 regs 85, 86.   13.187

Application of regulations where there is dual entitlement

13.188
42.—(1) This regulation applies where a person is entitled to universal credit and an employment and support allowance.

(2) The work-related requirements under sections 11B to 11I of the Act and regulations 46 to 49 of these Regulations do not apply to such a person.

(3) Reductions relating to the award of an employment and support allowance under section 11J of the Act and regulations 50 to 60 of these Regulations do not apply to such a person.

GENERAL NOTE

13.189
This provides that where a person is entitled to UC and ESA, the work-related requirements and sanctions regime applicable to ESA does not apply. The person will instead be subject to the comparable UC regime. See Universal Credit Regs 2013, regs.83–104.

Sanction ceases to apply to employment and support allowance

13.190
43.—(1) This regulation applies where—
(a) a person is entitled to an employment and support allowance;
(b) there is a reduction relating to the award of the employment and support allowance under section 11J of the Act;
(c) the person becomes entitled to universal credit; and
(d) the person remains entitled to an employment and support allowance.

(2) Any reduction relating to the award of the employment and support allowance is to cease being applied to the award of the employment and support allowance.

GENERAL NOTE

Where an ESA reduction in place and the person then becomes entitled to UC as well as ESA, the ESA reduction ceases to apply. The person will instead be dealt with under the UC regime. See Universal Credit Regs 2013, regs.84–114.

Claimant commitment—date and method of acceptance

13.191
44.—(1) For the purposes of section 1(3)(aa) of the Act, a claimant who has accepted a claimant commitment within such period after making a claim for an employment and support allowance as the Secretary of State specifies is to be treated as having accepted that claimant commitment on the first day of the period in respect of which the claim is made.

(2) In a case where an award of an employment and support allowance may be made without a claim, a claimant who accepts a claimant commitment within such period as the Secretary of State specifies is to be treated as having accepted a claimant commitment on the day that would be the first day of the first benefit week in relation to the award.

(3) The Secretary of State may extend the period within which a claimant is required to accept a claimant commitment or an updated claimant commitment where the claimant requests an extension and the Secretary of State considers that the request is reasonable.

(4) A claimant must accept a claimant commitment by one of the following methods, as specified by the Secretary of State—
(a) electronically;
(b) by telephone; or
(c) in writing.

DEFINITIONS

"benefit week"—see reg.2(1).

GENERAL NOTE

This provides for a claimant commitment accepted within a period after the claim   **13.192**
to be backdated to the first day of the claim period (para.(1). As regards an award of
ESA without a claim, acceptance of a claimant commitment within a period can be
attributed to the first day of the first benefit week of the award (para.(2). A period
can be extended by the Secretary of State where the claimant reasonably requests an
extension (para.(3)).The commitment must be accepted electronically, in writing or
by telephone, whichever is specified by the Secretary of State (para.(4)).

Claimant commitment—exceptions

45. A claimant may be entitled to an employment and support allowance   **13.193**
without having accepted a claimant commitment if the Secretary of State
considers that—
  (a) the claimant cannot accept a claimant commitment because they
      lack capacity to do so; or
  (b) there are exceptional circumstances in which it would be unreason-
      able to expect the person to accept a claimant commitment.

GENERAL NOTE

This allows the Secretary of State to release the claimant from the requirement to   **13.194**
accept a claimant commitment as a condition of receiving ESA where the Secretary
of State considers that exceptional circumstances pertain in which it would be
unreasonable to expect acceptance or where the claimant lacks capacity to accept a
claimant commitment,

Purposes of a work-focused interview

46. The purposes of a work-focused interview are any or all of the follow-   **13.195**
ing—
  (a) assessing the claimant's prospects for remaining in or obtaining work;
  (b) assisting or encouraging the claimant to remain in or obtain work;
  (c) identifying activities that the claimant may undertake that will make
      remaining in or obtaining work more likely;
  (d) identifying training, educational or rehabilitation opportunities for
      the claimant which may make it more likely that the claimant will
      remain in or obtain work or be able to do so;
  (e) identifying current or future work opportunities for the claimant that
      are relevant to the claimant's needs and abilities.

GENERAL NOTE

This sets out the purposes of a work-focused interview. Compare ESA Regs 2008   **13.196**
reg.55 and Universal Credit Regulations 2013 reg.93.

Claimants subject to no work-related requirements

47.—(1) A claimant falls within section 11D of the Act (persons subject   **13.197**
to no work-related requirements) if they are a claimant who—
  (a) has caring responsibilities for one or more severely disabled persons
      for at least 35 hours a week but does not meet the conditions of enti-
      tlement to a carer's allowance;

(b) is the responsible foster parent of a child under the age of one;

(c) is an adopter and it is 52 weeks or less since—

    (i) the date on which the child was placed with the claimant; or

    (ii) if the claimant requested that the 52 weeks should run from a date within 14 days before the child was expected to be placed, that date;

(d) has been enrolled on, been accepted for or is undertaking, a full-time course of study or training which is not a course of advanced education and—

    (i) is under the age of 21, or is 21 and reached that age whilst undertaking the course; and

    (ii) is without parental support;

(e) is entitled to an employment and support allowance which is payable at a nil rate;

(f) is pregnant and it is 11 weeks or less before her expected week of confinement; or

(g) was pregnant and it is 15 weeks or less since the date of her confinement.

(2) Subject to paragraph (3), for the purposes of section 11D of the Act, a person has regular and substantial caring responsibilities for a severely disabled person if the person—

(a) satisfies the conditions for entitlement to a carer's allowance; or

(b) would satisfy those conditions but for the fact that their earnings have exceeded the limit prescribed for the purposes of that allowance.

(3) A person does not have regular and substantial caring responsibilities for a severely disabled person if the person derives earnings from those caring responsibilities.

(4) Paragraph (2) applies whether or not the person has made a claim for a carer's allowance.

(5) In this regulation—

"adopter" means a person who has been matched with a child for adoption and who is, or is intended to be, the responsible carer for the child, but excluding a person who is a foster parent or close relative of the child;

"matched with a child for adoption" means an adoption agency has decided that the person would be a suitable adoptive parent for the child;

"severely disabled" has the meaning in section 70 of the Contributions and Benefits Act;

"without parental support" means the person is not being looked after by a local authority and—

(a) has no parent (in this definition, "parent" includes any person acting in the place of a parent);

(b) cannot live with their parents because the person is estranged from them or there is a serious risk—

    (i) to the person's physical or mental health; or

    (ii) that the person would suffer significant harm if the person lived with them; or

(c) is living away from their parents, and neither parent is able to support the person financially because that parent—

    (i) has a physical or mental impairment;

    (ii) is detained in custody pending trial or sentence upon conviction or under a sentence imposed by a court; or

    (iii) is prohibited from entering or re-entering Great Britain.

DEFINITIONS

    "adopter"—see para.(5).
    "carer's allowance—see reg.2(1).
    "close relative" —see reg.2(1).
    "matched with a child for adoption"—see para.(5).
    "parent" —see para.(5).
    "severely disabled"—see para.(5).
    "without parental support"—see para.(5).

GENERAL NOTE

This specifies the persons who under s.11D of the WRA 2012 are not subject to any work-related requirements. Compare Universal Credit Regulations 2013 reg.89.   **13.198**

Claimants subject to work-focused interview requirement only

48.—(1) For the purposes of section 11E(1)(a) of the Act (claimant is the responsible carer for a child aged at least one and under a prescribed age) the prescribed age is [¹three].   **13.199**

(2) A claimant falls within section 11E of the Act (claimants subject to work-focused interview requirement only) if—

  (a) the claimant is the responsible foster parent in relation to a child aged at least one;

  (b) the claimant is the responsible foster parent in relation to a qualifying young person and the Secretary of State is satisfied that the qualifying young person has care needs which would make it unreasonable to require the claimant to comply with a work preparation requirement;

  (c) the claimant is a foster parent, but not the responsible foster parent, in relation to a child or qualifying young person and the Secretary of State is satisfied that the child or qualifying young person has care needs which would make it unreasonable to require the claimant to comply with a work preparation requirement;

  (d) the claimant is a foster parent who—

    (i) does not have a child or qualifying young person placed with them, but intends to; and

    (ii) fell within sub-paragraph (a) within the past eight weeks; or

  (e) the claimant has become a friend or family carer in relation to a child within the past 12 months and is also the responsible carer in relation to that child.

(3) In paragraph (2) (e), "friend or family carer" means a person who is responsible for a child, but is not the child's parent or step-parent, and has undertaken the care of the child in the following circumstances—

  (a) the child has no parent or has parents who are unable to care for the child; or

  (b) it is likely that the child would otherwise be looked after by a local authority because of concerns in relation to the child's welfare.

AMENDMENT

1. Income Support (Work-Related Activity) and Miscellaneous Amendments Regulations 2014 (SI 2014/1097), reg.17 (April 27, 2014).

DEFINITIONS

"child"—see reg.2(1).
"friend of family carer"—see para.(3).
"qualifying young person"—see reg.2(1).

GENERAL NOTE

13.200   This lists for the purposes of s.11E of the WRA 2007 the persons who are to be subject only to a work-focused interview requirement. Compare Universal Credit Regulations 2013 reg.91, as amended.

Victims of domestic violence

13.201   **49.**—(1) Where a claimant has recently been a victim of domestic violence and the circumstances set out in paragraph (3) apply—

(a) a requirement imposed on that claimant under sections 11 to 11G of the Act ceases to have effect for a period of 13 consecutive weeks starting on the date of the notification referred to in paragraph (3)(a); and

(b) the Secretary of State must not impose any other such requirement on that claimant during that period.

(2) A person has recently been a victim of domestic violence if a period of six months has not expired since the violence was inflicted or threatened.

(3) The circumstances are that—

(a) the claimant notifies the Secretary of State, in such manner as the Secretary of State specifies, that domestic violence has been inflicted on or threatened against the claimant by a person specified in paragraph (4) during the period of six months ending on the date of the notification;

(b) this regulation has not applied to the claimant for a period of 12 months before the date of the notification;

(c) on the date of the notification the claimant is not living at the same address as the person who inflicted or threatened the domestic violence; and

(d) as soon as possible, and no later than one month, after the date of the notification the claimant provides evidence from a person acting in an official capacity which demonstrates that—

(i) the claimant's circumstances are consistent with those of a person who has had domestic violence inflicted on or threatened against them during the period of six months ending on the date of the notification; and

(ii) the claimant has made contact with the person acting in an official capacity in relation to such an incident, which occurred during that period.

(4) A person is specified in this paragraph if the person is—

(a) where the claimant is, or was, a member of a couple, the other member of the couple;

(b) the claimant's grandparent, grandchild, parent, parent-in-law, son, son-in-law, daughter, daughter-in-law, step-parent, step-son, step-daughter, brother, step-brother, brother-in-law, sister, step-sister or sister-in-law; or

(c) where any of the persons listed in sub-paragraph (b) is a member of a couple, the other member of that couple.

(5) In this regulation—

[¹"coercive behaviour" means an act of assault, humiliation or intimidation or other abuse that is used to harm, punish or frighten the victim;

"controlling behaviour" means an act designed to make a person subordinate or dependent by isolating them from sources of support, exploiting their resources and capacities for personal gain, depriving them of the means needed for independence, resistance or escape or regulating their everyday behaviour;

"domestic violence" means any incident, or pattern of incidents, of controlling behaviour, coercive behaviour, violence or abuse, including but not limited to—

(a) psychological abuse;

(b) physical abuse;

(c) sexual abuse;

(d) emotional abuse;

(e) financial abuse,

regardless of the gender or sexuality of the victim;]

"person acting in an official capacity" means a person who is a member of a profession regulated by a body mentioned in section 25(3) of the National Health Service Reform and Health Care Professions Act 2002, a police officer, a registered social worker, the claimant's employer, a representative of the claimant's trade union or any public, voluntary or charitable body which has had direct contact with the claimant in connection with domestic violence;

"registered social worker" means a person registered as a social worker in a register maintained by—

[² (a) the Health and Care Professions Council;]

[³ (b) Social Care Wales;]

(c) the Scottish Social Services Council; or

(d) the Northern Ireland Social Care Council.

AMENDMENTS

1. Social Security (Miscellaneous Amendments) (No.2) Regulations 2013 (SI 2013/1508 reg.5(1), (3) (October 29, 2013).

2. Universal Credit and Miscellaneous Amendments Regulations 2014 (SI 2014/597) reg.4(1), (2) (April 28, 2014).

3. Social Security (Social Care Wales) (Amendment) Regulations 2017 (SI 2017/291), reg.4 (April 1, 2017).

DEFINITIONS

"coercive behaviour"—see para.5.
"controlling behaviour"—see para.5.
"couple"—see reg.2(1).
"domestic violence"—see para.5.
"person acting in an official capacity"—see para.5.
"registered social worker"—see para.5.

The Employment and Support Allowance Regulations 2013

GENERAL NOTE

13.202 This enables recent victims (v) of domestic violence to obtain a "breathing space" during which work-related requirement already imposed are lifted and others can not be imposed. Compare Universal Credit Regulations 2013 reg.98 and JSA Regs 1996, reg.14A.

Domestic violence is defined in para.(5). The reg covers both its infliction and it being threatened. V is a recent victim if no more than 6 months have elapsed since domestic violence was inflicted or threatened (para.2).

V can obtain this 13 week period of respite commencing with V's notification to the Secretary of State so long as V provides within one month of the notification evidence from a person acting in an official capacity confirming that the claimant is indeed such a victim in the last six months and has been in contact with that person about an incident of domestic violence. The claimant must not be living on the date of notification at the same address as the person who inflicted or threatened the domestic violence. The person inflicting or threatening the domestic violence must be someone specified in para.(4) (covering a very wide range of "family" members or relatives). There can only be one respite period in any 12 months (para.(3)(b)).

PART 8

Sanctions

Interpretation

13.203 **50.** For the purposes of this Part—

[¹ "current sanctionable failure" means a failure of the following kinds in relation to which the Secretary of State has not yet determined whether the amount of an award of benefit is to be reduced—

(a) a sanctionable failure,

(b) a JSA sanctionable failure, or

(c) a UC sanctionable failure;]

"JSA sanctionable failure" means a failure by a claimant which is sanctionable under section 6K of the Jobseekers Act 1995;

"low-level sanction" means a reduction of an employment and support allowance in accordance with section 11J of the Act for a sanctionable failure by the claimant to comply with—

(a) a work-focused interview requirement imposed under section 11F(2) of the Act (persons subject to work preparation requirement and work-focused interview requirement);

(b) a work preparation requirement imposed under section 11F(2) of the Act; or

(c) a requirement under section 11G of the Act (connected requirements);

"lowest-level sanction" means a reduction of an employment and support allowance in accordance with section 11J of the Act for a sanctionable failure by the claimant to comply with a requirement imposed under section 11E(2) of the Act (persons subject to work-focused interview requirement only);

"reduction period" means the number of days for which a reduction in the amount of an award of an employment and support allowance is to have effect;

1724

[¹ "relevant failure" means—

(a) a sanctionable failure giving rise to a low-level sanction,

(b) a UC sanctionable failure giving rise to a sanction under section 27 of the Welfare Reform Act 2012 to which regulation 104 of the Universal Credit Regulations 2013 applies, or

(c) a JSA sanctionable failure giving rise to a sanction under section 6K of the Jobseekers Act 1995 to which regulation 21 of the Jobseeker's Allowance Regulations 2013 applies;]

"sanctionable failure" means a failure which is sanctionable under section 11J of the Act;

"total outstanding reduction period" means the total number of days for which no reduction has yet been applied for all of the claimant's low-level sanctions, lowest-level sanctions and reductions to which regulation 61 applies;

"UC sanctionable failure" means a failure by a claimant which is sanctionable under section 26 or 27 of the Welfare Reform Act 2012.

AMENDMENT

1. Social Security (Jobseeker's Allowance, Employment and Support Allowance and Universal Credit) (Amendment) Regulations 2016 (SI 2016/678) reg.7(2) (July 25, 2016).

General principles for calculating reduction periods

51.—(1) Subject to paragraphs (3) and (4), the reduction period is to be determined in relation to each sanctionable failure in accordance with regulations 52 and 53.   13.204

(2) Reduction periods are to run consecutively.

(3) Where the reduction period calculated in relation to a sanctionable failure in accordance with regulation 52 or 53 would result in the total outstanding reduction period exceeding 1095 days, the number of days in the reduction period in relation to that failure is to be adjusted so that 1095 days is not exceeded.

(4) In determining the reduction period in relation to a sanctionable failure, a previous sanctionable failure, UC sanctionable failure or JSA sanctionable failure is to be disregarded if it—

(a) [¹ . . .]

(b) gave rise to a reduction under these Regulations, the Universal Credit Regulations 2013 or the Jobseeker's Allowance Regulations 2013.

AMENDMENT

1. Social Security (Jobseeker's Allowance, Employment and Support Allowance and Universal Credit) (Amendment) Regulations 2016 (SI 2016/678) reg.7(3) (July 25, 2016).

DEFINITIONS

"JSA sanctionable failure"—see reg.50.
"reduction period"—see reg.50.
"sanctionable failure"—see reg.50.
"total outstanding reduction period"—see reg.50.
UC sanctionable failure—see reg.50.

13.205   This deals with the general principles applicable to sanctionable failures with respect to work-related requirements as regards ESA under s.11J of the WRA 2007. Sanctions consist of periods for which ESA is reduced. The reduction period is to be set in accordance with regs 52, 53 below (para.1). Reduction periods run consecutively (para.(2) That is subject to the general overall three-year limit in para.(3): a reduction in accordance with regs 52 and 53 cannot take over three years (1095 days) in length the total outstanding reduction period for all the claimants low-level or lowest level sanctions (whether under ESA, JSA or UC) and those under reg.61. This drafting is somewhat opaque. The idea appears to be that if adding a new reduction period to the end of what is likely to be a chain of reduction periods would take the total days in the chain over 1095 days the new reduction period must be adjusted to make the total 1095 days in all.

Para.(4) purports to stipulate when previous sanctionable failures or ones sanctionable under UC and JSA are to be ignored. However, the July 2016 amendment to para.(4) appears to create an absurdity. Before that amendment, the purpose of para.(4) was to disregard previous sanctionable failures giving rise to a reduction in benefit that occurred in the 13 days immediately before the date of the current sanctionable failure. Yet the clear words of reg.7(3) of the amending regulations omit only sub-para.(a) of para.(4), leaving the opening words and sub-para.(b) in place. Because the form of para.(4) is to require the disregarding of the identified sanctionable failures, the result is that the remaining words require the disregarding of *all* previous sanctionable failures that gave rise to a reduction in benefit *at any point* in the process of determining the length of the reduction period for the current sanctionable failure. If that is right, then in the new tables (see e.g. reg.54) only the first entry (and so the shortest sanction), i.e. where there has been no previous relevant sanctionable failure, could ever be applied. See further by analogy the more detailed analysis in Vol.II of this series, commenting on reg.18(4) of the JSA Regulations 2013.

Low-level sanction

13.206   **52.** The reduction period for a low-level sanction is the total of—
(a) the number of days beginning with the date of the sanctionable failure and ending with—
   (i) the day before the date on which the claimant meets a compliance condition specified by the Secretary of State;
   (ii) the day before the date on which the claimant falls within section 11D of the Act;
   (iii) the day before the date on which the claimant is no longer required to take a particular action specified as a work preparation requirement by the Secretary of State under section 11C(1) or 11F(2) of the Act; or
   (iv) the day on which the award of an employment and support allowance is terminated,
whichever is soonest; and
[¹ (b) in the circumstances described in the first column of the following table, the number of days set out in the second column.

Circumstances applicable to claimant's case	Number of days
Where there has been no previous relevant failure by the claimant	7 days
Where there have been one or more previous relevant failures by the claimant and the date of the most recent previous relevant failure is not within 365 days beginning with the date of the current sanctionable failure	7 days

Where there have been one or more previous relevant failures by the claimant and the date of the most recent previous relevant failure is within 365 days, but not within 14 days, beginning with the date of the current sanctionable failure and the reduction period applicable to the most recent previous relevant failure is—

(a) 7 days	14 days
(b) 14 days	28 days
(c) 28 days	28 days

Where there have been one or more previous relevant failures by the claimant and the date of the most recent previous relevant failure is within 14 days beginning with the date of the current sanctionable failure and the reduction period applicable to the most recent previous relevant failure is—

(a) 7 days	7 days
(b) 14 days	14 days
(c) 28 days	28 days.]

AMENDMENT

1. Social Security (Jobseeker's Allowance, Employment and Support Allowance and Universal Credit) (Amendment) Regulations 2016 (SI 2016/678) reg.7(4) (July 25, 2016).

DEFINITIONS

"compliance condition"—see WRA 2007 s.11J(5).
"JSA sanctionable failure" —see reg.50.
"low-level sanction" —see reg.50.
"reduction period" —see reg.50.
"sanctionable failure" —see reg.50.
"UC sanctionable failure" —see reg.50.

GENERAL NOTE

This regulation deals with the period of reduction of ESA in respect of a low-level   **13.207**
sanction. See also, reg.54 on when the period takes effect.

This regulation specifies the reduction period as the sum of two periods. Under para (a) the first period begins on the day of the sanctionable failure and ends on whichever is the earliest of the days identified in para. (a)(i)(iv) which apply in the particular case. Sub-para.(i)in effect means the day before the one on which the claimant does what the Secretary of State wants in terms of work-related requirements (remedies the failure). Sub-para. (ii) sets the end of this first period as the day before that on which the claimant becomes exempt from work-related requirements under s.11D of the WRA 2007 read with reg.47, above. Sub-para. (iii) envisages this first period ending where the claimant is no longer required to take a particular action as a work preparation requirement under s.11C(1) of 11F(2) of the WRA 2007 Finally, sub-para. (iv) sees the end of the first period as the day on which an ESA award is terminated.

Para. (b) sets the second period at varying lengths (7, 14 or 28 days) depending on whether the failure was a first, second or subsequent offence (whether with respect to ESA, JSA or UC) in the 364 days preceding the failure in question. Note, however, that sanctionable failures attracting a JSA, ESA or UC reduction occurring in the 13 days before the sanctionable failure in question are to be disregarded (reg.51(4)).

Lowest-level sanction

13.208   **53.** The reduction period for a lowest-level sanction is the number of days beginning with the date of the sanctionable failure and ending with—

(a) the day before the date on which the claimant meets a compliance condition specified by the Secretary of State;

(b) the day before the date on which the claimant falls within section 11D of the Act; or

(c) the day on which the claimant's award of an employment and support allowance is terminated, whichever is soonest.

DEFINITIONS

"compliance condition"—see WRA 2007 s.11J(5).
"lowest-level sanction"—see reg.50.
"sanctionable failure"—see reg.50.

GENERAL NOTE

13.209   This deals with the reduction period in respect of a lowest-level sanction. Such a sanction is in respect of a failure by the claimant to comply with a requirement imposed under section 11E(2) of the Act (persons subject to work-focused interview requirement only). The period ends on whichever is the earliest of the days specified in paras (a), (b) or (c) as is applicable to the particular case. Para. (a) specifies this as the day before that on which the claimant complies with the condition. Para. (b) sets it as the day before that on which the claimant becomes exempt from work-related requirements under s.11D of the WRA 2007 read with reg.47 above. Para. (c) deals with the case where an award of ESA is terminated.

Start of the reduction

13.210   **54.** A reduction period determined in relation to a sanctionable failure takes effect from—

(a) where the claimant has not been paid an employment and support allowance for the benefit week in which the Secretary of State determines that the amount of the award of employment and support allowance is to be reduced under section 11J of the Act, the first day of that benefit week;

(b) where the claimant has been paid an employment and support allowance for the benefit week referred to in paragraph (a), the first day of the first benefit week for which the claimant has not been paid an employment and support allowance; or

(c) where the amount of the award of the employment and support allowance for the benefit week referred to in paragraph (a) or (b) is already subject to a reduction because of a previous sanctionable failure, the first day in respect of which the amount of the award is no longer subject to that reduction.

DEFINITIONS

"benefit week"—see reg.2.
"reduction period"—see reg.50.
"sanctionable failure"—see reg.50

GENERAL NOTE

13.211   This regulation deals with the matter of when a reduction period is to be given effect.

Reduction period to continue where award of employment and support allowance terminates

55.—(1) Where an award of an employment and support allowance ter-   13.212
minates while there is an outstanding reduction period—
  (a) the period continues to run as if a daily reduction were being applied;
       and
  (b) if the claimant becomes entitled to a new award of an employment
       and support allowance before the period expires, that new award
       is subject to a reduction for the remainder of the total outstanding
       reduction period.
  (2) Paragraph (3) applies where—
  (a) an award of an employment and support allowance terminates before
       the Secretary of State determines that the amount of the award is to
       be reduced under section 11J of the Act in relation to a sanctionable
       failure; and
  (b) that determination is made after the claimant becomes entitled to a
       new award of an employment and support allowance.
  (3) Where this paragraph applies—
  (a) the reduction period in relation to the sanctionable failure referred
       to in paragraph (2) is to be treated as having taken effect on the day
       before the previous award terminated;
  (b) that reduction period is treated as having continued to run as if a
       daily reduction were being applied; and
  (c) if the new award referred to in paragraph (2)(b) begins before that
       reduction period expires, that new award is subject to a reduction for
       the remainder of the total outstanding reduction period.

DEFINITIONS

"reduction period"—see reg.50.
"sanctionable failure"—see reg.50.
"total outstanding reduction period"—see reg.50.

GENERAL NOTE

If an award of ESA terminates while there is an outstanding reduction period,   13.213
subsequent days count as if an actual reduction of benefit were being applied (thus
reducing the days outstanding in the period), so that on any further claim for ESA
the claimant is subject to the reduction only for the remainder of the period, if any
(para.(1)). If an award of ESA terminates before the Secretary of State has made
a decision about a reduction for a sanctionable failure, but a new award is in place
by the time the decision is made, the reduction period starts as if the decision had
been made on the day before the previous award terminated, so that the new award
of ESA will be reduced for the remainder of the total outstanding reduction period
(paras (2), (3)).

Suspension of a reduction where a fraud sanction applies

56.—(1) A reduction in the amount of an award of an employment and   13.214
support allowance in accordance with section 11J of the Act is to be suspended for any period during which section 6B or 7 of the Social Security
Fraud Act 2001 applies to the award.
  (2) The reduction ceases to have effect on the day on which that period
begins and has effect again on the day after that period ends.

Termination of a reduction

13.215　**57.**—(1) A reduction in the amount of an award of an employment and support allowance under section 11J of the Act is to be terminated where, since the date of the most recent sanctionable failure which gave rise to such a reduction, the claimant has been in paid work—

(a) for a period of at least 26 weeks; or

(b) for more than one period where the total of those periods amounts to at least 26 weeks.

(2) The termination of the reduction has effect—

(a) where the date on which paragraph (1) is satisfied falls within a period of entitlement to an employment and support allowance, from the beginning of the benefit week in which that date falls; or

(b) where that date falls outside a period of entitlement to an employment and support allowance, from the beginning of the first benefit week in relation to any subsequent award of an employment and support allowance.

(3) The claimant is in paid work for the purposes of paragraph (1) where their weekly earnings are at least equal to 16 multiplied by the national minimum wage which would apply for a person of the claimant's age under the National Minimum Wage Regulations 1999.

DEFINITIONS

"benefit week"—see reg.2.
"in paid work"—see para.(3).
"sanctionable failure"—see reg.50

GENERAL NOTE

13.216　Any reduction for any level of sanction or sanctions terminates where since the date of the most recent sanctionable failure the claimant has been in paid work for at least 26 weeks, not necessarily consecutive, with weekly earnings at least equal to 16 multiplied by the national minimum wage applicable to a person of the claimant's age under the National Minimum Wage Regulations 1999 (paras (1), (3)). Para.(2) sets out the time the termination takes effect dependent on whether or not the day the 26 week period is up falls within or outside a period of entitlement to ESA. If within, termination takes effect from the beginning of the benefit week in which there fell the completion of the 26 week period. If outside, it takes effect from the beginning of the first benefit week of any subsequent ESA award.

Amount of reduction for each benefit week

13.217　**58.** Where it has been determined that an award of an employment and support allowance is to be reduced in accordance with section 11J of the Act, the amount of the reduction for each benefit week in respect of which a reduction has effect is to be calculated as follows.

Step 1
Take the number of days—
(a) in the benefit week; or
(b) if lower, in the total outstanding reduction period,
and deduct any days in that benefit week or total outstanding reduction period for which the reduction is suspended in accordance with regulation 56.

Step 2
Multiply the number of days produced by step 1 by the daily reduction rate.

Step 3
Deduct the amount produced by step 2 from the amount of the award of employment and support allowance for the benefit week.

<small>DEFINITIONS</small>

"benefit week"—see reg.2.
"daily reduction rate"—see regs 59(1), 60.
"total outstanding reduction period"—see reg.50

<small>GENERAL NOTE</small>

This provides the means of calculating for each benefit week the amount of reduc- 13.218
tion depending on whether the claimant's case fits within reg.58(1) (daily reduction rate) or reg.60 (lower daily reduction rate)

Daily reduction rate

59.—(1) The daily reduction rate for the purposes of regulation 58 is, 13.219
unless regulation 60 applies, the amount prescribed for the claimant under regulation 62(1) or, where applicable, regulation 63(2), multiplied by 52 and divided by 365.
(2) The amount of the daily reduction rate is to be rounded down to the nearest 10 pence.

<small>GENERAL NOTE</small>

Unless the lower daily reduction rate in reg.60 applies, the daily reduction rate 13.220
is the weekly prescribed amount appropriate for the particular claimant under reg.62, or if the claimant is a special case within reg.62, the weekly amount there prescribed. The pertinent prescribed amount is then multiplied by 52 and divided by 365 to produce the daily reduction rate. The daily rate must be rounded down to the nearest 10 pence.

Lower daily reduction rate

60.—(1) The daily reduction rate is 40% of the rate applicable 13.221
under regulation 59(1) if, at the end of the benefit week, the claimant falls within—
 (a) section 11E of the Act;
 (b) section 11D(2)(c) of the Act; or
 (c) regulation 47(1)(b), (c), (f) or (g).
(2) The daily reduction rate is nil if, at the end of the benefit week, the claimant falls within section 11D(2)(a) of the Act.

<small>DEFINITIONS</small>

"benefit week"—see reg.2.

<small>GENERAL NOTE</small>

If at the end of the benefit week the claimant falls within s.11E (person subject 13.222
only to work-focused interview requirement) or s.11D(2) (c) (someone subject

to no work-related requirements as a single person responsible for a child aged less than one) of the Welfare Reform Act 2007, the daily reduction rate is instead 40 per cent of the daily reduction rate determined under reg.58(1). Similarly if at the end of the benefit week the claimant falls with reg.47(1)(b) (responsible foster parent of a child aged under one), (1)(c) (an adopter in the first year of the adoption), (1)(f) (pregnant with 11 weeks or less to confinement), or (1)(g) (was pregnant and it is 15 weeks or less since confinement). If, however, the claimant falls within s.11D(2)(a) of the 2007 Act (as someone with limited capability for work and work related activity—a member of the support group) the reduction rate is nil.

Sanctions where universal credit ends and the person is entitled to an employment and support allowance

13.223   **61.**—(1) This regulation applies where—
(a) a person ceases to be entitled to universal credit;
(b) there is a reduction relating to the person's award of universal credit under section 26 or 27 of the Welfare Reform Act 2012; and
(c) the person is entitled to an employment and support allowance.
(2) Any reduction relating to the award of the universal credit is to be applied to the award of the employment and support allowance.
(3) The period for which the reduction relating to the award of employment and support allowance is to have effect is the number of days which apply to the person under regulation 102, 103, 104 or 105 of the Universal Credit Regulations 2013 minus any such days which—
(a) have already resulted in a reduction in the amount of universal credit; or
(b) fall after the date on which the person ceases to be entitled to universal credit and before the date on which the person becomes entitled to an employment and support allowance.
(4) The daily reduction rate for the reduction relating to the award of employment and support allowance is—
(a) the amount referred to in regulation 60(1) where, on the date the claimant becomes entitled to an employment and support allowance, the claimant falls within—
　(i) section 11E of the Act;
　(ii) section 11D(2)(c) of the Act; or
　(iii) regulation 47(1)(b), (c), (f) or (g);
(b) zero where the claimant falls within section 11D(2)(a) of the Act; or
(c) the amount referred to in regulation 59(1) in all other cases.
(5) The amount of the reduction of the claimant's award of an employment and support allowance is the number of days arrived at under paragraph (3) multiplied by the daily reduction rate referred to in paragraph (4).

GENERAL NOTE

13.224   Where someone subject to a UC sanction ceases to be entitled to UC and becomes entitled to ESA, the remaining reduction period applicable to the UC award carries over to reduce the ESA award. The remaining reduction period is calculated by deducting from the period imposed as regards UC (i) the days for which UC has been in consequence reduced and (ii) the days between the cessation of entitlement to UC and the beginning of entitlement to ESA. Para.(4) identifies the appropriate daily reduction rate according to whether the claimant falls within reg.61 (paras (4)(a)and (b)) or reg.59(1) (para.(4)(c)).

PART 9

Amounts of Allowance

Prescribed amounts

62.—(1) Subject to regulation 63 (special cases) the amount prescribed for the purposes of the calculation of the amount of a claimant's employment and support allowance under section 2(1)(a) of the Act is— **13.225**
   (a) where the claimant satisfies the conditions set out in section 2(2) of the Act [³ or the claimant is a member of the work-related activity group and satisfies the conditions set out in Part 1 to Schedule 1 to the Act], [¹ £73.10]; or
   (b) where the claimant does not satisfy the conditions set out in section 2(2) of the Act [³ or the claimant is a member of the work-related activity group and satisfies the conditions set out in Part 1 to Schedule 1 to the Act] —
      (i) where the claimant is aged not less than 25, [¹ £73.10]; or
      (ii) where the claimant is aged less than 25, [¹ £57.90].
   [² (2) Subject to regulation 63 the amount of the support component is [⁴ £38.55].]

GENERAL NOTE

This sets the prescribed amounts of ESA, for claimants who are not special cases under reg.63. Where the assessment phase has ended, the weekly rate is £73.10, to which will be added a further £38.55 support component if the claimant has limited capability for work and work-related activity (members of the support group). **13.226**

Where the assessment phase has not yet ended for the claimant, the rate of basic ESA depends on age: £73.10 for those aged 25 or over; £57.90 for those under 25.

AMENDMENTS

1. Welfare Benefits Up-rating Order 2015 (SI 2015/130) art.12 (April 6, 2015).
2. Employment and Support Allowance and Universal Credit (Miscellaneous Amendments and Transitional and Savings Provisions) Regulations 2017 (SI 2017/204) reg.3(4) (April 3, 2017).
3. Employment and Support Allowance (Miscellaneous Amendments and Transitional and Savings Provision) Regulations 2017 (SI 2017/581) reg.8 (June 23, 2017).
4. Social Security Benefits Up-rating Order 2019 (SI 2019/480) art.28(1) (April 8, 2019).

Special cases

63.—(1) The amount prescribed for the purposes of the calculation of the amount of a claimant's employment and support allowance under section 2(1)(a) of the Act in respect of a claimant who— **13.227**
   (a) satisfies either of the conditions in paragraphs (3) or (4); or
   (b) has been a patient for a continuous period of more than 52 weeks,
   is the amount applicable under regulation 62(1) and the amount of nil under regulation 62(2).

(2) The amount prescribed for those purposes in respect of a claimant who is a person in hardship, is the amount to which the claimant is entitled—

(a) under regulation 62(1) reduced by 20%; and

(b) under regulation 62(2).

(3) The first condition mentioned in paragraph (1) (a) is that—

(a) the claimant is being detained under section 45A or 47 of the Mental Health Act 1983 (power of higher courts to direct hospital admission; removal to hospital of persons serving sentences of imprisonment etc); and

(b) in any case where there is in relation to the claimant a release date within the meaning of section 50(3) of that Act, the claimant is being detained on or before the day which the Secretary of State certifies to be that release date.

(4) The second condition mentioned in paragraph (1) (a) is that the claimant is being detained under—

(a) section 59A of the Criminal Procedure (Scotland) Act 1995 (hospital direction); or

(b) section 136 of the Mental Health (Care and Treatment) (Scotland) Act 2003 (transfer of prisoners for treatment of mental disorder).

(5) In this regulation—

"patient" means a person (other than a prisoner) who is regarded as receiving free in-patient treatment within the meaning of regulation 2(4) and (5) of the Social Security (Hospital In- Patients) Regulations 2005;

"prisoner" means a person who—

(a) is detained in custody pending trial or sentence on conviction or under a sentence imposed by a court; or

(b) is on temporary release in accordance with the provisions of the Prison Act 1952 or the Prisons (Scotland) Act 1989,

other than a person who is detained in hospital under the provisions of the Mental Health Act 1983 or, in Scotland, under the provisions of the Mental Health (Care and Treatment) (Scotland) Act 2003 or the Criminal Procedure (Scotland) Act 1995.

(6) For the purposes of this regulation—

(a) except where sub-paragraph (b) applies, a person is a "person in hardship" if they satisfy regulation 94; and

(b) where a person satisfies regulation 94 for more than six weeks, they are a "person in hardship" only for the first six weeks.

DEFINITIONS

"patient"—see para.(5).

"person in hardship"—see para.(5).

"prisoner"—see para.(5).

GENERAL NOTE

13.228   This sets the prescribed amounts of ESA awards for claimants who are special cases either as patients, certain persons detained under specified provisions of the applicable mental health legislation, persons in hardship and some remand prisoners or ones on temporary release.

Permanent health insurance

64. For the purposes of sections 2(1)(c) and 3(3) of the Act (deductions from an employment and support allowance) "pension payment" is to include a permanent health insurance payment.

13.229

DEFINITIONS

"pension payment"—see WRA 2007 s.3(3).
"permanent health insurance payment"—see reg.2.

GENERAL NOTE

This is the same as ESA Regs 2008 reg.72(1).

13.230

Financial Assistance Scheme

65.—(1) For the purposes of sections 2(1)(c) and 3(3) of the Act (deductions from an employment and support allowance) "pension payment" is to include a Financial Assistance Scheme payment.

(2) In this regulation "Financial Assistance Scheme payment" means a payment made under the Financial Assistance Scheme Regulations 2005.

13.231

DEFINITIONS

"Financial Assistance Scheme payment"—see para.(2).
"pension payment"—see WRA 2007 s.3(3).

GENERAL NOTE

This replicates ESA Regs 2008 reg.72A.

13.232

Councillor's allowance

66. For the purposes of section 3(1)(c) of the Act—
(a) a councillor's allowance is a payment of a prescribed description; and
(b) the prescribed bodies carrying out public or local functions are—
  (i) in relation to England and Wales, a London borough council, a county council, a county borough council, a district council, a parish or community council, the Common Council of the City of London or the Council of the Isles of Scilly; and
  (ii) in relation to Scotland, a council constituted under section 2 of the Local Government etc. (Scotland) Act 1994.

13.233

DEFINITIONS

"councillor"—see reg.2.
"councillor's allowance"—see reg.2.

GENERAL NOTE

This is the same as ESA Regs 2008 reg.73.

13.234

Deductions for pension payment and PPF payment

67.—(1) Where—
(a) a claimant is entitled to an employment and support allowance in respect of any period of a week or part of a week;
(b) there is—

13.235

(i) a pension payment;

(ii) a PPF periodic payment; or

(iii) both of the payments specified in paragraphs (i) and (ii),

payable to that person in respect of that period (or a period which forms part of that period or includes that period or part of it); and

(c) the amount of the payment, or payments when taken together, exceeds—

(i) if the period in question is a week, £85; or

(ii) if that period is not a week, such proportion of £85 as falls to be calculated in accordance with regulation 79(1) or (5) (calculation of weekly amount of income),

the amount of that allowance is to be reduced by an amount equal to 50% of the excess.

(2) For the purposes of regulations 67 to 72 "payment" means a payment or payments, as the case may be, referred to in paragraph (1)(b).

DEFINITIONS

"claimant"—see WRA 2007 s.24(1).
"payment"—see para.(2).
"pension payment"—see WRA 2007 s.3(3); regs 64, 65.
"PPF periodic payment"—see WRA 2007 s.3(3).

GENERAL NOTE

13.236   This is the same as ESA Regs 2008 reg.74.

Payments treated as not being payments to which section 3 applies

13.237   **68.** The following payments are to be treated as not being payments to which section 3 of the Act applies—

(a) any pension payment made to a claimant as a beneficiary on the death of a member of any pension scheme;

(b) any PPF periodic payment made to a claimant as a beneficiary on the death of a person entitled to such a payment;

(c) where a pension scheme is in deficit or has insufficient resources to meet the full pension payment, the extent of the shortfall;

(d) any pension payment made under an instrument specified in section 639(2) of the Income Tax (Earnings and Pensions) Act 2003;

(e) any guaranteed income payment (which means a payment made under article 15(1)(a) or 29(1)(a) of the Armed Forces and Reserved Forces (Compensation Schemes) Order 2011);

(f) any permanent health insurance payment in respect of which the employee had contributed to the premium to the extent of more than 50%.

DEFINITIONS

"claimant"—see WRA 2007 s.24(1).
"guaranteed income payment"—see para.(e).
"pension payment"—see WRA 2007 s.3(3); regs 64, 65.
"permanent health insurance payment"—see reg.2.
"PPF periodic payment"—see WRA 2007 s.3(3).

GENERAL NOTE

13.238   This is much the same as ESA Regs 2008 reg.75

Deductions for councillor's allowance

69.—(1) Where the net amount of councillor's allowance to which a   13.239
claimant is entitled in respect of any week exceeds 16 multiplied by the
National Minimum Wage, subject to paragraph (3), an amount equal to the
excess is to be deducted from the amount of an employment and support
allowance to which that claimant is entitled in respect of that week, and only
the balance remaining (if any) is to be payable.

(2) In paragraph (1) "net amount", in relation to any councillor's allowance to which a claimant is entitled, means the aggregate amount of the
councillor's allowance or allowances, or remuneration to which that claimant is entitled for the week in question, reduced by the amount of any
payment in respect of expenses wholly, exclusively and necessarily incurred
by that claimant, in that week, in the performance of the duties of a councillor.

(3) Where the amount determined by the calculation in paragraph (1)
would, but for this paragraph, include an amount of—

(a) less than 50p, that amount is to be rounded up to the nearest 50p; or

(b) less than £1 but more than 50p, that amount is to be rounded up to
the nearest £1.

DEFINITIONS

"councillor's allowance"—see reg.2.
"net amount"—see para.(2).

GENERAL NOTE

This is the same as ESA Regs 2008 reg.76.   13.240

Date from which payments are to be taken into account

70. Where regulation 67(1) or 69(1) applies, a deduction must have   13.241
effect, calculated where appropriate in accordance with regulation 79(1) or
(5), from the first day of the benefit week in which the payment or councillor's allowance is paid to a claimant who is entitled to an employment and
support allowance in that week.

DEFINITIONS

"benefit week"—see reg.2.
"claimant"—see WRA 2007 s.24(1).
"councillor's allowance"—see reg.2.
"payment—see reg.67(2).

GENERAL NOTE

This corresponds to ESA Regs 2008 reg 77. The annotation there refers to   13.242
reg.94(1) and (6) of those Regs. The equivalent provisions in these 2013 Regulations
are reg.79(1), (5).

Date from which a change in the rate of the payment takes effect

71. Where a payment or councillor's allowance is already being made   13.243
to a claimant and the rate of that payment or that allowance changes, the
deduction at the new rate must take effect, calculated where appropriate
in accordance with regulation 79(1) or (5), from the first day of the benefit

week in which the new rate of the payment or councillor's allowance is paid.

DEFINITIONS

"benefit week"—see reg.2.
"claimant"—see WRA 2007 s.24(1).
"councillor's allowance"—see reg.2.
"payment—see reg.67(2).

GENERAL NOTE

13.244   This is the equivalent of ESA Regs 2008 reg.78. The annotation there refers to reg.94(1) and (6) of those Regs. The equivalent provisions in these 2013 Regulations are reg.79(1), (5).

Calculation of payment made other than weekly

13.245   **72.**—(1) Where the period in respect of which a payment or councillor's allowance is paid is otherwise than weekly, an amount calculated or estimated in accordance with regulation 79(1) or (5) is to be regarded as the weekly amount of that payment or allowance.

(2) In determining the weekly payment, where two or more payments are payable to a claimant, each payment is to be calculated separately in accordance with regulation 79(1) or (5) before aggregating the sum of those payments for the purposes of the reduction of an employment and support allowance in accordance with regulation 67.

DEFINITIONS

"benefit week"—see reg.2.
"claimant"—see WRA 2007 s.24(1).
"councillor's allowance"—see reg.2.
"payment—see reg.67(2).

GENERAL NOTE

13.246   This is the equivalent of ESA Regs 2008 reg.79. The annotation there refers to reg.94(1) and (6) of those Regs. The equivalent provisions in these 2013 Regulations are reg.79(1), (5). The deduction rule (then in reg.74) is now in reg.67.

Effect of statutory maternity pay on an employment and support allowance

13.247   **73.**—(1) This regulation applies where—
(a) a woman is entitled to statutory maternity pay and, on the day immediately preceding the first day in the maternity pay period, she—
   (i) is in a period of limited capability for work; and
   (ii) satisfies the conditions of entitlement to an employment and support allowance in accordance with section 1(2)(a) of the Act; and
(b) on any day during the maternity pay period—
   (i) she is in a period of limited capability for work; and
   (ii) that day is not a day where she is treated as not having limited capability for work.

(2) Where this regulation applies, notwithstanding section 20(2) of the Act, a woman who is entitled to statutory maternity pay is to be entitled to

an employment and support allowance in respect of any day that falls within the maternity pay period.

(3) Where by virtue of paragraph (2) a woman is entitled to an employment and support allowance for any week (including part of a week), the total amount of employment and support allowance payable to her for that week is to be reduced by an amount equivalent to any statutory maternity pay to which she is entitled in accordance with Part 12 of the Contributions and Benefits Act for the same week (or equivalent part of a week where entitlement to an employment and support allowance is for part of a week), and only the balance, if any, of the employment and support allowance is to be payable to her.

DEFINITIONS

"the Act"—see reg.2.
"Contributions and Benefits Act"—see WRA 2007 s.65.
"maternity pay period"—see WRA 2007 s.20(8); SSCBA 1992 s.165(1).
"week"—see reg.2.

GENERAL NOTE

This is the same as ESA Regs 2008 reg.80.   13.248

Effect of statutory adoption pay on an employment and support allowance

74.—(1) This regulation applies where—   13.249
(a) a claimant is entitled to statutory adoption pay and, on the day immediately preceding the first day in the adoption pay period, she—
  (i) is in a period of limited capability for work; and
  (ii) satisfies the conditions of entitlement to an employment and support allowance in accordance with section 1(2)(a) of the Act; and
(b) on any day during the adoption pay period—
  (i) that claimant is in a period of limited capability for work; and
  (ii) that day is not a day where that claimant is treated as not having limited capability for work.

(2) Where this regulation applies, notwithstanding section 20(4) of the Act, a claimant who is entitled to statutory adoption pay is to be entitled to an employment and support allowance in respect of any day that falls within the adoption pay period.

(3) Where by virtue of paragraph (2) a claimant is entitled to an employment and support allowance for any week (including part of a week), the total amount of employment and support allowance payable to that claimant for that week is to be reduced by an amount equivalent to any statutory adoption pay to which that claimant is entitled in accordance with Part 12ZB of the Contributions and Benefits Act for the same week (or equivalent part of a week where entitlement to an employment and support allowance is for part of a week), and only the balance, if any, of the employment and support allowance is to be payable to that claimant.

DEFINITIONS

"the Act"—see reg.2.
"adoption pay period"—see WRA 2007 s.20(8).

"claimant"—see WRA 2007 s.24(1).
"Contributions and Benefits Act"—see WRA 2007 s.65.
"week"—see reg.2.

General Note

13.250   This replicates ESA Regs 2008 reg.81.

Effect of additional statutory paternity pay on an employment and support allowance

13.251   **75.** — [¹. . .].

Revocation

1. Shared Parental Leave and Statutory Shared Parental Pay (Consequential Amendments to Subordinate Legislation) Order 2014 (SI 2014/3255) art.30 (1), (2) (April 5, 2015).

[¹Effect of statutory shared parental pay on an employment and support allowance

13.252   **75A.**—(1) This regulation applies where—
  (a) a claimant is entitled to statutory shared parental pay and, on the day immediately preceding the first day in the shared parental pay period the claimant—
    (i) is in a period of limited capability for work; and
    (ii) satisfies the conditions of entitlement to an employment and support allowance in accordance with section 1(2)(a) of the Act; and
  (b) on any day during the statutory shared parental pay period—
    (i) that claimant is in a period of limited capability for work; and
    (ii) that day is not a day where that claimant is treated as not having limited capability for work.

(2) Where this regulation applies, notwithstanding section 20(6) of the Act, a claimant who is entitled to statutory shared parental pay is to be entitled to an employment and support allowance in respect of any day that falls within the shared parental pay period.

(3) Where by virtue of paragraph (2) a person is entitled to an employment and support allowance for any week (including part of a week), the total amount of such benefit payable to that claimant for that week is to be reduced by an amount equivalent to any statutory shared parental pay to which that claimant is entitled in accordance with Part 12ZC of the Contributions and Benefits Act for the same week (or equivalent part of a week where entitlement to an employment and support allowance is for part of a week), and only the balance, if any, of the employment and support allowance is to be payable to that claimant.

(4) In this regulation "statutory shared parental pay period" means the weeks in respect of which statutory shared parental pay is payable to a person under section 171ZY(2) of the Social Security Contributions and Benefits Act 1992.]

Amendment

1. Shared Parental Leave and Statutory Shared Parental Pay (Consequential Amendments to Subordinate Legislation) Order 2014 (SI 2014/3255) art.30 (1), (3) (December 31, 2014).

DEFINITIONS

"the Act"—see reg.2(1).
"claimant"—see WRA 2007, s.24(1).
"contributory allowance"—see WRA 2007 s.1(7).
"Contributions and Benefits Act"—see WRA 2007 s.65.
"statutory shared parental pay period"—see para.(4).
"week"—see reg.2(1).

GENERAL NOTE

This is the same as ESA Regs 2008 reg.82A.   13.253

PART 10

Income and earnings

Calculation of earnings derived from employed earner's employment and income other than earnings

76.—(1) Earnings derived from employment as an employed earner and   13.254
income which does not consist of earnings are to be taken into account over
a period determined in accordance with the following provisions of this
regulation and at a weekly amount determined in accordance with regulation 79 (calculation of weekly amount of income).

(2) Subject to the following provisions of this regulation, the period over
which a payment is to be taken into account is to be—

(a) where the payment is monthly, a period equal to the number of
weeks beginning with the date on which the payment is treated as
paid and ending with the date immediately before the date on which
the next monthly payment would have been treated as paid whether
or not the next monthly payment is actually paid;

(b) where the payment is in respect of a period which is not monthly, a
period equal to the length of the period for which payment is made;

(c) in any other case, a period equal to such number of weeks as is
equal to the number obtained (see paragraph (9)) by applying the
formula—

$$\frac{E}{J}$$

where—

E is the net earnings;

J is the amount of an employment and support allowance which
would be payable had the payment not been made;

and that period is to begin on the date on which the payment is treated as
paid under regulation 78 (date on which income is treated as paid).

(3) Where—

(a) earnings are derived from the same source but are not of the same
kind; and

(b) but for this paragraph, the periods in respect of which those earnings
would fall to be taken into account overlap, wholly or partly,

those earnings are to be taken into account over a period equal to the aggregate length of those periods, and that period is to begin with the earliest date on which any part of those earnings would be treated as paid under regulation 78.

(4) In a case to which paragraph (5) applies, earnings under regulation 80 (earnings of employed earners) are to be taken into account in the following order of priority—

(a) earnings normally derived from the employment;

(b) any payment to which paragraph (1)(b) or (c) of that regulation applies;

(c) any payment to which paragraph (1)(j) of that regulation applies;

(d) any payment to which paragraph (1)(d) of that regulation applies.

(5) Where earnings to which regulation 80(1)(b) to (d) applies are paid in respect of part of a day, those earnings are to be taken into account over a period equal to a day.

(6) Any earnings to which regulation 80(1)(j) applies which are paid in respect of, or on the termination of, part-time employment, are to be taken into account over a period of one week.

(7) For the purposes of this regulation the claimant's earnings are to be calculated in accordance with regulations 80 and 81.

(8) For the purposes of paragraph 10 of Schedule 2 to the Act (effect of work), the income which consists of earnings of a claimant is to be calculated on a weekly basis by determining the weekly amount of those earnings in accordance with regulations 77 to 84.

(9) For the purposes of the number obtained as mentioned in paragraph (2)(c), any fraction is to be treated as a corresponding fraction of a week.

DEFINITIONS

"the Act"—see reg.2.
"claimant"— see WRA 2007 s.24(1).
"employed earner"—see reg.2.
"employment"—see reg.2.
"net earnings"—see reg.2.
"week"—see reg.2.

GENERAL NOTE

13.255   This has affinities with ESA Regs 2008 reg.91, save with respect to the formula in para.(2)(c) of this regulation.

Calculation of earnings of self-employed earners

13.256   **77.**—(1) Where a claimant's income consists of earnings from employment as a self-employed earner, the weekly amount of the claimant's earnings is to be determined by reference to the claimant's average weekly earnings from that employment—

(a) over a period of one year; or

(b) where the claimant has recently become engaged in that employment or there has been a change which is likely to affect the normal pattern of business, over such other period as may, in any particular case, enable the weekly amount of the claimant's earnings to be determined more accurately.

(2) For the purposes of this regulation the claimant's earnings are to be calculated in accordance with regulations 82 to 84.

DEFINITIONS

"claimant"—see WRA 2007 s.24(1).
"self-employed earner"—see reg.2.

GENERAL NOTE

This is much the same as ESA Regs 2008 reg.92(1), (3).   13.257

Date on which income is treated as paid

78. A payment of income to which regulation 76 (calculation of earnings   13.258
derived from employed earner's employment and income other than earnings) applies is to be treated as paid—
  (a) in the case of a payment which is due to be paid before the first
      benefit week pursuant to the claim, on the date on which it is due to
      be paid;
  (b) in any other case, on the first day of the benefit week in which it is
      due to be paid or the first succeeding benefit week in which it is prac-
      ticable to take it into account.

DEFINITIONS

"benefit week"—see reg.2.
"claimant"— see WRA 2007 s.24(1).
"employed earner"—see reg.2.
"employment"—see reg.2.

GENERAL NOTE

This is the equivalent of ESA Regs 2008 reg.93(1).   13.259

Calculation of weekly amount of income

79.—(1) For the purposes of regulation 76 (calculation of earnings   13.260
derived from employed earner's employment and income other than earnings) and regulations 64 to 72 (deductions from employment and support
allowance), subject to paragraphs (2) to (5), where the period in respect of
which a payment is made—
  (a) does not exceed a week, the weekly amount is to be the amount of
      that payment;
  (b) exceeds a week, the weekly amount is to be determined—
       (i) in a case where that period is a month, by multiplying the
           amount of the payment by 12 and dividing the product by 52;
      (ii) in a case where that period is three months, by multiplying the
           amount of the payment by four and dividing the product by 52;
     (iii) in a case where that period is a year and the payment is income,
           by dividing the amount of the payment by 52;
      (iv) in any other case, by multiplying the amount of the payment
           by seven and dividing the product by the number equal to the
           number of days in the period in respect of which it is made.
  (2) Where a payment for a period not exceeding a week is treated under
regulation 78(a) (date on which income is treated as paid) as paid before
the first benefit week and a part is to be taken into account for some days
only in that week (the relevant days), the amount to be taken into account

for the relevant days is to be calculated by multiplying the amount of the payment by the number of relevant days and dividing the product by the number of days in the period in respect of which it is made.

(3) Where a payment is in respect of a period equal to or in excess of a week and a part thereof is to be taken into account for some days only in a benefit week (the relevant days), the amount to be taken into account for the relevant days is to be calculated by multiplying the amount of the payment by the number of relevant days and dividing the product by the number of days in the period in respect of which it is made.

(4) Except in the case of a payment which it has not been practicable to treat under regulation 78(b) (date on which income is treated as paid) as paid on the first day of the benefit week in which it is due to be paid, where a payment of income from a particular source is or has been paid regularly and that payment falls to be taken into account in the same benefit week as a payment of the same kind and from the same source, the amount of that income to be taken into account in any one benefit week is not to exceed the weekly amount determined under paragraph (1)(a) or (b) of the payment which under regulation 78(b) is treated as paid first.

(5) Where the amount of the claimant's income fluctuates and has changed more than once, or a claimant's regular pattern of work is such that the claimant does not work every week, the foregoing paragraphs may be modified so that the weekly amount of the claimant's income is determined by reference to the claimant's average weekly income—

(a) if there is a recognisable cycle of work, over the period of one complete cycle (including, where the cycle involves periods in which the claimant does no work, those periods but disregarding any other absences);

(b) in any other case, over a period of five weeks or such other period as may, in the particular case, enable the claimant's average weekly income to be determined more accurately.

DEFINITIONS

"benefit week"—see reg.2.
"claimant"—see WRA 2007 s.24(1).

GENERAL NOTE

13.261   This equates to ESA Regs 2008 reg.94 (1)–(3), (5), (6).

Earnings of employed earners

13.262   **80.**—(1) Subject to paragraphs (2) and (3), "earnings" means, in the case of employment as an employed earner, any remuneration or profit derived from that employment and includes—

(a) any bonus or commission;

(b) any payment in lieu of remuneration except any periodic sum paid to a claimant on account of the termination of the claimant's employment by reason of redundancy;

(c) any payment in lieu of notice;

(d) any holiday pay except any payable more than four weeks after the termination or interruption of employment;

(e) any payment by way of a retainer;

(f) any payment made by the claimant's employer in respect of expenses not wholly, exclusively and necessarily incurred in the performance of the duties of the employment, including any payment made by the claimant's employer in respect of—

    (i) travelling expenses incurred by the claimant between the claimant's home and place of employment;

    (ii) expenses incurred by the claimant under arrangements made for the care of a member of the claimant's family owing to the claimant's absence from home;

(g) any award of compensation made under section 112(4) or 117(3)(a) of the Employment Rights Act 1996 (the remedies: orders and compensation, enforcement of order and compensation);

(h) any payment made or remuneration paid under [¹section] 28, 34, 64, 68 [¹or] 70 of the Employment Rights Act 1996 (right to guarantee payments, remuneration on suspension on medical or maternity grounds, complaints to employment tribunals);

(i) any such sum as is referred to in section 112(3) of the Contributions and Benefits Act (certain sums to be earnings for social security purposes);

(j) where a payment of compensation is made in respect of employment which is part-time employment, the amount of the compensation;

(k) the amount of any payment by way of a non-cash voucher which has been taken into account in the computation of a person's earnings in accordance with Part 5 of Schedule 3 to the Social Security (Contributions) Regulations 2001.

(2) "Earnings" are not to include—

(a) subject to paragraph (3), any payment in kind;

(b) any remuneration paid by or on behalf of an employer to the claimant in respect of a period throughout which the claimant is on maternity leave, paternity leave[²,] adoption leave (which means a period of absence from work on ordinary or additional adoption leave under section 75A or 75B of the Employment Rights Act 1996)[², shared parental leave under section 75E or 75G of that Act] or is absent from work because the claimant is ill;

(c) any payment in respect of expenses wholly, exclusively and necessarily incurred in the performance of the duties of the employment;

(d) any occupational pension (which means any pension or other periodical payment under an occupational pension scheme but does not include any discretionary payment out of a fund established for relieving hardship in particular cases);

(e) any lump sum payment made under the Iron and Steel Re-adaptation Benefits Scheme;

(f) any payment in respect of expenses arising out of the claimant participating as a service user;

[¹ (g) any bounty paid at intervals of at least one year and derived from employment as—

    (i) a part-time fire-fighter in a fire brigade maintained in pursuance of the Fire and Rescue Services Act 2004;

    (ii) a part-time fire-fighter employed by a fire and rescue authority under that Act;

    (iii) a part-time fire-fighter employed by the Scottish Fire and Rescue Service established under section 1A of the Fire (Scotland) Act 2005;

     (iv) an auxiliary coastguard in respect of coast rescue activities;
     (v) a person engaged part-time in the manning or launching of a lifeboat;
     (vi) a member of any territorial or reserve force prescribed in Part 1 of Schedule 6 to the Social Security (Contributions) Regulations 2001.]

(3) Paragraph (2)(a) is not to apply in respect of any non-cash voucher referred to in paragraph (1)(k).

(4) In this regulation—

"compensation" means any payment made in respect of, or on the termination of, employment in a case where a claimant has not received or received only part of a payment in lieu of notice due or which would have been due to the claimant had that claimant not waived the right to receive it, other than—

(a) any payment specified in paragraph (1)(a) to (i);
(b) any payment specified in paragraph (2)(a) to (f);
(c) any redundancy payment within the meaning of section 135(1) of the Employment Rights Act 1996;
(d) any refund of contributions to which that person was entitled under an occupational pension scheme; and
(e) any compensation payable by virtue of section 173 of the Education Reform Act 1988;

"paternity leave" means a period of absence from work on ordinary paternity leave by virtue of section 80A or 80B of the Employment Rights Act 1996 or on additional paternity leave by virtue of section 80AA or 80BB of that Act.

(5) The reference in paragraph (2)(f) to a person participating as a service user is to—

(a) a person who is being consulted by or on behalf of—
     (i) a body which has a statutory duty to provide services in the field of health, social care or social housing; or
     (ii) a body which conducts research or undertakes monitoring for the purpose of planning or improving such services, in the person's capacity as a user, potential user, carer of a user or person otherwise affected by the provision of those services; or
(b) the carer of a person consulted under sub-paragraph (a).

AMENDMENTS

1. Universal Credit and Miscellaneous Amendments Regulations 2014 (SI 2014/597) reg.4(1), (5) (April 28, 2014).
2. Shared Parental Leave and Statutory Shared Parental Pay (Consequential Amendments to Subordinate Legislation) Order 2014 (SI 2014/3255) art.30 (1), (4)(a) (December 31, 2014).

DEFINITIONS

"claimant"—see WRA 2007 s.24(1).
"compensation"—see para.(4).
"employed earner"—see reg.2.
"employment"—see reg.2.
"part-time employment"—see reg.2.
"paternity leave"—see para.(4).
"person participating as a service user"—see para.(5).

GENERAL NOTE

This is much the same as ESA Regs 2008 reg.95.   **13.263**

Calculation of net earnings of employed earners

81.—(1) For the purposes of regulation 76 (calculation of earnings   **13.264**
derived from employed earner's employment and income other than earnings) the earnings of a claimant derived from employment as an employed
earner to be taken into account are the claimant's net earnings.

(2) For the purposes of paragraph (1) net earnings are to be calculated
by taking into account the gross earnings of the claimant from that employment less—
  (a) any amount deducted from those earnings by way of—
      (i) income tax;
      (ii) primary Class 1 contributions under section 6(1)(a) of the
           Contributions and Benefits Act;
  (b) one-half of any sum paid by the claimant in respect of a pay period by
      way of a contribution towards an occupational or personal pension
      scheme.

DEFINITIONS

"claimant"—see WRA 2007 s.24(1).
"employed earner"—see reg.2.
"occupational pension scheme"—see reg.2.
"pay period"—see reg.2.
"personal pension scheme"—see reg.2.

GENERAL NOTE

Compare ESA Regs 2008 reg.96(1), (3).   **13.265**

Earnings of self-employed earners

82.—(1) Subject to paragraph (2), "earnings", in the case of employ-   **13.266**
ment as a self-employed earner, means the gross receipts of the employment and include any allowance paid under section 2 of the Employment
and Training Act 1973 or section 2 of the Enterprise and New Towns
(Scotland) Act 1990 to the claimant for the purpose of assisting the claimant in carrying on the claimant's business.

(2) "Earnings" do not include—
  (a) where a claimant is involved in providing board and lodging accom-
      modation for which a charge is payable, any payment by way of such
      a charge;
  (b) any award made by one of the Sports Councils named in section
      23(2) of the National Lottery etc Act 1993 out of sums allocated to
      it for distribution under that section.
(3) In this regulation, "board and lodging" means—
  (a) accommodation provided to a person or, if the person is a member
      of a family, to that person or any other member of that person's
      family, for a charge which is inclusive of the provision of that
      accommodation and at least some cooked or prepared meals which
      both are cooked or prepared (by a person other than the person to
      whom the accommodation is provided or a member of that person's

family) and are consumed in that accommodation or associated premises; or

(b) accommodation provided to a person in a hotel, guest house, lodging house or some similar establishment, except accommodation provided by a close relative of the person or any other member of the person's family, or other than on a commercial basis.

DEFINITIONS

"board and lodging"—see para.(3).
"claimant"—see WRA 2007 s.24(1).
"self-employed earner"—see reg.2.

GENERAL NOTE

13.267   This is the same as ESA Regs 2008 reg.97.

Calculation of net profit of self-employed earners

13.268   **83.**—(1) For the purposes of regulation 77 (calculation of earnings of self-employed earners), the earnings of a claimant to be taken into account are to be—

(a) in the case of a self-employed earner who is engaged in employment on that self-employed earner's own account, the net profit derived from that employment;

(b) in the case of a self-employed earner whose employment is carried on in partnership or is that of a share fisherman within the meaning of the Social Security (Mariners' Benefits) Regulations 1975, that self-employed earner's share of the net profit derived from that employment less—

(i) an amount in respect of income tax and of National Insurance contributions payable under the Contributions and Benefits Act calculated in accordance with regulation 84 (deduction of tax and contributions for self-employed earners); and

(ii) one half of any contribution paid in the period that is relevant under regulation 77 (calculation of earnings of self-employed earners) in respect of a personal pension scheme.

(2) For the purposes of paragraph (1)(a) the net profit of the employment, except where paragraph (8) applies, is to be calculated by taking into account the earnings of the employment over the period determined under regulation 77 less—

(a) subject to paragraphs (4) to (6), any expenses wholly and exclusively defrayed in that period for the purposes of that employment;

(b) an amount in respect of—

(i) income tax; and

(ii) National Insurance contributions payable under the Contributions and Benefits Act, calculated in accordance with regulation 84 (deduction of tax and contributions for self-employed earners); and

(c) one half of any contribution paid in the period that is relevant under regulation 77 in respect of a personal pension scheme.

(3) For the purposes of paragraph (1)(b), the net profit of the employment is to be calculated by taking into account the earnings of the employment over the period determined under regulation 77 less, subject to

(SI 2013/379 reg. 83) (as amended)

paragraphs (4) to (6), any expenses wholly and exclusively defrayed in that period for the purpose of that employment.

(4) Subject to paragraph (5), a deduction is not to be made under paragraph (2)(a) or (3) in respect of—

(a) any capital expenditure;

(b) the depreciation of any capital asset;

(c) any sum employed or intended to be employed in the setting up or expansion of the employment;

(d) any loss incurred before the beginning of the period determined under regulation 77 (calculation of earnings of self-employed earners);

(e) the repayment of capital on any loan taken out for the purposes of the employment;

(f) any expenses incurred in providing business entertainment.

(5) A deduction is to be made under paragraph (2)(a) or (3) in respect of the repayment of capital on any loan used for—

(a) the replacement in the course of business of equipment or machinery; and

(b) the repair of an existing business asset except to the extent that any sum is payable under an insurance policy for its repair.

(6) The Secretary of State must refuse to make a deduction in respect of any expenses under paragraph (2)(a) or (3) where the Secretary of State is not satisfied that the expense has been defrayed or, having regard to the nature of the expense and its amount, that it has been reasonably incurred.

(7) A deduction—

(a) is not to be made under paragraph (2)(a) or (3) in respect of any sum unless it has been expended for the purposes of the business;

(b) is to be made under paragraph (2)(a) or (3) in respect of—

(i) the excess of any Value Added Tax paid over Value Added Tax received in the period determined under regulation 77;

(ii) any income expended in the repair of an existing asset except to the extent that any sum is payable under an insurance policy for its repair;

(iii) any payment of interest on a loan taken out for the purposes of the employment.

(8) Where a claimant is engaged in employment as a child minder the net profit of the employment is to be one-third of the earnings of that employment, less—

(a) an amount in respect of—

(i) income tax; and

(ii) National Insurance contributions payable under the Contributions and Benefits Act, calculated in accordance with regulation 84 (deduction of tax and contributions for self-employed earners); and

(b) one half of any contribution paid in respect of a personal pension scheme.

(9) Notwithstanding regulation 77 (calculation of earnings of self-employed earners) and the foregoing paragraphs, the Secretary of State may assess any item of a claimant's income or expenditure over a period other than that determined under regulation 77 as may, in the particular case, enable the weekly amount of that item of income or expenditure to be determined more accurately.

(10) Where a claimant is engaged in employment as a self-employed

1749

earner and that claimant is also engaged in one or more other employments as a self-employed or employed earner, any loss incurred in any one of the claimant's employments is not to be offset against the claimant's earnings in any other of the claimant's employments.

DEFINITIONS

"claimant"—see WRA 2007 s.24(1).
"employment"—see reg.2.
"personal pension scheme"—see reg.2.
"self-employed earner"—see reg.2.

GENERAL NOTE

13.269   This is much the same as ESA Regs 2008 reg.98.

Deduction of tax and contributions for self-employed earners

13.270   **84.**—(1) Subject to paragraph (2), the amount to be deducted in respect of income tax under regulation 83(1)(b)(i), (2)(b)(i) or (8)(a)(i) (calculation of net profit of self-employed earners) is to be calculated on the basis of the amount of chargeable income and as if that income were assessable to income tax at the basic rate [², or in the case of a Scottish taxpayer, the Scottish basic rate,] of tax less only the [² personal reliefs to which the claimant is entitled under Chapters 2, 3 and 3A of Part 3 of the Income Tax Act 2007 as are] appropriate to the claimant's circumstances.

(2) If the period determined under regulation 77 is less than a year, the earnings to which the basic rate [², or the Scottish basic rate,] of tax is to be applied and the amount of the personal reliefs deductible under paragraph (1) are to be calculated on a pro rata basis.

(3) The amount to be deducted in respect of National Insurance contributions under regulation 83(1)(b)(i), (2)(b)(ii) or (8)(a)(ii) is to be the total of—

(a) the amount of Class 2 contributions payable under [¹ section 11(2) or, as the case may be, (8)] of the Contributions and Benefits Act at the rate applicable at the date of claim except where the claimant's chargeable income is less than the amount specified in section 11(4) of that Act ([¹ small profits threshold]) for the tax year in which the date of claim falls; but if the assessment period is less than a year, the amount specified for that tax year is to be reduced pro rata; and

(b) the amount of Class 4 contributions (if any) which would be payable under section 15 of that Act (Class 4 contributions recoverable under the Income Tax Acts) at the percentage rate applicable at the date of claim on so much of the chargeable income as exceeds the lower limit but does not exceed the upper limit of profits applicable for the tax year in which the date of claim falls; but if the assessment period is less than a year, those limits are to be reduced pro rata.

(4) In this regulation—

"assessment period" means the period mentioned in regulation 77 over which the weekly amount of the claimant's earnings is to be determined; "basic rate" has the same meaning as in the Income Tax Act 2007 (see section 989 of that Act);

"chargeable income" means—

(a) except where paragraph (b) applies, the earnings derived from the employment less any expenses deducted under paragraph (2)(a) or, as the case may be, (3) of regulation 83;

(b) in the case of employment as a child minder, one-third of the earnings of that employment.

[² "Scottish basic rate" means the rate of income tax of that name calculated in accordance with section 6A of the Income Tax Act 2007;

"Scottish taxpayer" has the same meaning as in Chapter 2 of Part 4A of the Scotland Act 1998]

AMENDMENTS

1. Social Security (Miscellaneous Amendments No. 2) Regulations 2015 (SI 2015/478) reg. 38 (April 6, 2015).

2. Social Security (Scottish Rate of Income Tax etc.) (Amendment) Regulations 2016 (SI 2016/233) reg.8 (April 6, 2016).

DEFINITIONS

"claimant"—see WRA 2007 s.24(1).
"Contributions and Benefits Act"—see WRA 2007 s.65.

GENERAL NOTE

This is much the same as ESA Regs 2008 reg.99.   13.271

PART 11

Supplementary provisions

Waiting days

85.—(1) The number of days prescribed for the purposes of paragraph 2   13.272
of Schedule 2 to the Act (days during which a person is not entitled to an employment and support allowance at the beginning of a period of limited capability for work) is [¹ seven].

(2) Paragraph 2 of Schedule 2 to the Act does not apply where—

(a) the claimant's entitlement to an employment and support allowance commences within 12 weeks of the claimant's entitlement to income support, incapacity benefit, severe disablement allowance, state pension credit, a jobseeker's allowance, a carer's allowance, statutory sick pay or a maternity allowance coming to an end;

(b) the claimant is terminally ill and has—

(i) made a claim expressly on the ground of being terminally ill; or

(ii) made an application for supersession or revision in accordance with the Decisions and Appeals Regulations 1999 or the Decisions and Appeals Regulations 2013 which contains an express statement that the claimant is terminally ill;

(c) the claimant has been discharged from being a member of Her Majesty's forces and three or more days immediately before that discharge were days of sickness absence from duty, which are recorded by the Secretary of State; or

(d) the claimant is entitled to an employment and support allowance by virtue of section 1B of the Act (further entitlement after time-limiting).

DEFINITIONS

"claimant"—see WRA 2007 s.24(1).
"a member of Her Majesty's forces"—see reg.2(1).
"terminally ill"—see reg.2(1).

GENERAL NOTE

13.273   This is the same as ESA Regs 2008 reg.144.

Linking period

86. Any period of limited capability for work which is separated from another such period by not more than 12 weeks is to be treated as a continuation of the earlier period.

DEFINITIONS

"claimant"—see WRA 2007 s.24(1).
"week"—see reg.2.

GENERAL NOTE

13.274   This is the same as ESA Regs 2008 reg.145.

Claimants appealing a decision

13.275   **87.**—[¹(1) This regulation applies where a claimant has made and is pursuing an appeal against a relevant decision of the Secretary of State as defined in regulation 26.]

(2) Subject to paragraph (3), where this regulation applies, a determination of limited capability for work by the Secretary of State under regulation 15 must not be made until the appeal is determined by the First-tier Tribunal.

(3) Paragraph (2) does not apply where either—
(a) the claimant suffers from some specific disease or bodily or mental disablement from which the claimant was not suffering when entitlement began; or
(b) a disease or bodily or mental disablement from which the claimant was suffering when entitlement began has significantly worsened.

(4) Where this regulation applies and the Secretary of State makes a determination—
(a) in a case to which paragraph (3) applies (including where the determination is not the first such determination) that the claimant does not have or, by virtue of regulation 18 or 19, is to be treated as not having limited capability for work; or
(b) subsequent to a determination that the claimant is to be treated as having limited capability for work by virtue of a provision of these Regulations other than regulation 26, that the claimant is no longer to be so treated, this regulation and regulation 26 have effect as if that determination had not been made.

(5) Where this regulation applies and—
(a) the claimant is entitled to an employment and support allowance

1752

by virtue of being treated as having limited capability for work in accordance with regulation 26;

(b) neither of the circumstances in paragraph (3) applies, or, subsequent to the application of either of those circumstances, the claimant has been determined not to have limited capability for work; and

(c) the claimant's appeal is dismissed, withdrawn or struck out,

the claimant is to be treated as not having limited capability for work with effect from the day specified in paragraph (6).

(6) The day specified for the purposes of paragraph (5) is the first day of the benefit week following the date on which the Secretary of State receives the First-tier Tribunal's notification that the appeal is dismissed, withdrawn or struck out.

(7) Where a claimant's appeal is successful, subject to paragraph (8), any finding of fact or other determination embodied in or necessary to the decision of the First-tier Tribunal or on which the First-tier Tribunal's decision is based is to be conclusive for the purposes of the decision of the Secretary of State, in relation to an award made in a case to which this regulation applies, as to whether the claimant has limited capability for work or limited capability for work-related activity.

(8) Paragraph (7) does not apply where, due to a change of circumstances after entitlement began, the Secretary of State is satisfied that it is no longer appropriate to rely on such finding or determination.

AMENDMENT

1. Employment and Support Allowance (Repeat Assessments and Pending Appeal Awards) (Amendment) Regulations 2015 (SI 2015/437) reg.4 (March 30, 2015).

DEFINITIONS

"claimant"—see WRA 2007 s.24(1).
"First-tier Tribunal"—see reg.2.

GENERAL NOTE

This is essentially the same as ESA Regs 2008 reg.147A.   13.276

Absence from Great Britain

88.—(1) A claimant who is entitled to an employment and support allow-   13.277
ance is to continue to be so entitled during a period of temporary absence from Great Britain only in accordance with regulations 89 to 92.

(2) A claimant who continues to be entitled to an employment and support allowance during a period of temporary absence is not disqualified for receiving that allowance during that period under section 18(4) of the Act.

DEFINITIONS

"claimant"—see WRA 2007 s.24(1).

GENERAL NOTE

This is identical to ESA Regs 2008 reg.151.   13.278

Short absence

13.279   **89.** A claimant is to continue to be entitled to an employment and support allowance during the first four weeks of a temporary absence from Great Britain if—

(a) the period of absence is unlikely to exceed 52 weeks; and

(b) while absent from Great Britain, the claimant continues to satisfy the other conditions of entitlement to that employment and support allowance.

DEFINITIONS

"claimant"—see WRA 2007 s.24(1).
"week"—see reg.2.

GENERAL NOTE

13.280   This is identical to ESA Regs 2008 reg.152.

Absence to receive medical treatment

13.281   **90.**—(1) A claimant is to continue to be entitled to an employment and support allowance during the first 26 weeks of a temporary absence from Great Britain if—

(a) the period of absence is unlikely to exceed 52 weeks;

(b) while absent from Great Britain, the claimant continues to satisfy the other conditions of entitlement to that employment and support allowance;

(c) the claimant is absent from Great Britain only—

(i) in connection with arrangements made for the treatment of the claimant for a disease or bodily or mental disablement directly related to the claimant's limited capability for work which commenced before leaving Great Britain; or

(ii) because the claimant is accompanying a dependent child (which means any child or qualifying young person who is treated as the responsibility of the claimant or the claimant's partner, where that child or young person is a member of the claimant's household) in connection with arrangements made for the treatment of that child for a disease or bodily or mental disablement; and

(d) those arrangements relate to treatment—

(i) outside Great Britain;

(ii) during the period whilst the claimant is temporarily absent from Great Britain; and

(iii) by, or under the supervision of, a person appropriately qualified to carry out that treatment.

(2) In this regulation, "appropriately qualified" means qualified to provide medical treatment, physiotherapy or a form of treatment which is similar to, or related to, either of those forms of treatment.

DEFINITIONS

"appropriately qualified"—see para.(2).
"child"—see reg.2.
"claimant"—see WRA 2007 s.24(1)
"dependent child"—see para.(1) (c) (ii)

"partner"—see reg.2.
"qualifying young person"—see reg.2.

GENERAL NOTE

This is the same as ESA Regs 2008 reg.153.

13.282

Absence in order to receive NHS treatment

91. A claimant is to continue to be entitled to an employment and support allowance during any period of temporary absence from Great Britain if—

13.283

(a) while absent from Great Britain, the claimant continues to satisfy the other conditions of entitlement to that employment and support allowance; and

(b) that period of temporary absence is for the purpose of the claimant receiving treatment at a hospital or other institution outside Great Britain where the treatment is being provided—

    (i) under section 6(2) of the Health Service Act (Performance of functions outside England) or section 6(2) of the Health Service (Wales) Act (Performance of functions outside Wales);

    (ii) pursuant to arrangements made under section 12(1) of the Health Service Act (Secretary of State's arrangements with other bodies), section 10(1) of the Health Service (Wales) Act (Welsh Ministers' arrangements with other bodies), paragraph 18 of Schedule 4 to the Health Service Act (joint exercise of functions) or paragraph 18 of Schedule 3 to the Health Service (Wales) Act (joint exercise of functions); or

    (iii) under any equivalent provision in Scotland or pursuant to arrangements made under such provision.

DEFINITIONS

"claimant"—see WRA 2007 s.24(1).

GENERAL NOTE

This is the same as ESA Regs 2008 reg.154.

13.284

Absence of member of family of member of Her Majesty's forces

92.—(1) A claimant is to continue to be entitled to an employment and support allowance during any period of temporary absence from Great Britain if the claimant is a member of the family of a member of Her Majesty's forces and temporarily absent from Great Britain by reason only of the fact that the claimant is living with that member.

(2) In this regulation "member of the family of a member of Her Majesty's forces" means the spouse, civil partner, son, daughter, step-son, step-daughter, father, father-in-law, step-father, mother, mother-in-law or step-mother of such a member.

DEFINITIONS

"claimant"—see WRA 2007 s.24(1).
"member of Her Majesty's forces"—see reg.(2) and Sch.1.
"member of the family of a member of Her Majesty's forces"—see para.(2).

13.285   This corresponds to ESA Regs 2008 reg.155.

PART 12

Disqualification

Disqualification for misconduct etc

13.286   **93.**—(1) Subject to paragraph (3), paragraph (2) applies where a claimant—
- (a) has limited capability for work by reason of the claimant's own misconduct, except in a case where the limited capability is due to a sexually transmitted disease;
- (b) fails without good cause to attend for or submit to medical or other treatment (excluding vaccination, inoculation or surgery which the Secretary of State considers is major) recommended by a doctor with whom, or a hospital or similar institution with which, the claimant is undergoing medical treatment, which would be likely to remove the limitation on the claimant's capability for work;
- (c) fails without good cause to refrain from behaviour calculated to retard the claimant's recovery to health; or
- (d) is, without good cause, absent from the claimant's place of residence without informing the Secretary of State where the claimant may be found.

(2) A claimant referred to in paragraph (1) is to be disqualified for receiving an employment and support allowance for such period not exceeding six weeks as the Secretary of State may determine in accordance with Chapter 2 of Part 1 of the Social Security Act 1998.

(3) Paragraph (2) does not apply where the claimant—
- (a) is disqualified for receiving an employment and support allowance by virtue of regulations made under section 6B or 7 of the Social Security Fraud Act 2001; or
- (b) is a person in hardship.

(4) In this regulation, "doctor" means a registered medical practitioner, or in the case of a medical practitioner practising outside the United Kingdom, a person registered or recognised as such in the country in which the person undertakes medical practice.

DEFINITIONS

"claimant"—see WRA 2007 s.24(1).
"doctor"—see para.(4).
"medical treatment"—see reg.2.
"person in hardship"—see reg.94.
"week"—see reg.2.

GENERAL NOTE

13.287   This has the same effect as ESA Regs 2008 reg.157.

Meaning of "person in hardship"

94.—(1) A claimant is a "person in hardship" if the claimant— 13.288
 (a) has informed the Secretary of State of the circumstances on which the claimant relies to establish that fact; and
 (b) falls within paragraph (2), (3) or (5).
 (2) A claimant falls within this paragraph if—
 (a) she is pregnant;
 (b) a member of the claimant's family is pregnant;
 (c) the claimant is single and aged less than 18; or
 (d) the claimant is a member of a couple and both members are aged less than 18.
 (3) Subject to paragraph (4), the claimant falls within this paragraph if the claimant or the claimant's partner—
 (a) has been awarded an attendance allowance, the care component or the daily living component;
 (b) has claimed attendance allowance, disability living allowance or personal independence payment and the claim has not been determined;
 (c) devotes what the Secretary of State considers is a considerable portion of each week to caring for another person who—
  (i) has been awarded an attendance allowance, the care component or the daily living component; or
  (ii) has claimed attendance allowance, disability living allowance or personal independence payment and the claim has not been determined; or
 (d) has attained the qualifying age for state pension credit, which has the meaning given in section 1(6) of the State Pension Credit Act 2002.
 (4) A claimant to whom paragraph (3)(b) or (3)(c)(ii) applies is a person in hardship only for 26 weeks from the date of the claim unless the claimant is a person in hardship under another provision of this regulation.
 (5) The claimant falls within this paragraph where the Secretary of State is satisfied, having regard to all the circumstances and, in particular, the matters set out in paragraph (6), that unless an employment and support allowance is paid, the claimant, or a member of the claimant's family, will suffer hardship.
 (6) The matters referred to in paragraph (5) are—
 (a) the resources which are likely to be available to the claimant and the claimant's family and the length of time for which they might be available; and
 (b) whether there is a substantial risk that essential items, including food, clothing and heating, will cease to be available to the claimant or a member of the claimant's family, or will be available at considerably reduced levels and the length of time for which this might be so.
 (7) In this regulation—
"attendance allowance" means—
 (a) an attendance allowance under section 64 of the Contributions and Benefits Act;
 (b) an increase of disablement pension under section 104 or 105 of that Act;

(c) [¹*omitted*]
(d) [¹*omitted*];
(e) a payment by virtue of article 14, 15, 16, 43 or 44 of the Personal Injuries (Civilians) Scheme 1983 or any analogous payment;
(f) any payment based on the need for attendance which is paid as an addition to a war disablement pension (which means any retired pay or pension or allowance payable in respect of disablement under an instrument specified in section 639(2) of the Income Tax (Earnings and Pensions) Act 2003);

"care component" means the care component of disability living allowance at the highest or middle rate prescribed under section 72(3) of the Contributions and Benefits Act;

"daily living component" means the daily living component of personal independence payment at the standard or enhanced rate referred to in section 78 of the Welfare Reform Act 2012;

"disability living allowance" means a disability living allowance under section 71 of the Contributions and Benefits Act;

"personal independence payment" means an allowance under Part 4 of the Welfare Reform Act 2012.

AMENDMENT

1. Social Security (Miscellaneous Amendments) (No.2) Regulations 2013 (SI 2013/1508) reg.5(1), (4) (October 29, 2013).

DEFINITIONS

"attendance allowance"—see para.(7).
"care component"—see para.(7).
"claimant"—see WRA 2007 s.24(1).
"Contributions and Benefits Act"—see WRA 2007 s.65.
"daily living component"—see para.(7).
"disability living allowance"—see para.(7).
"family"—see reg.2.
"person in hardship"—see para.(1).
"personal independence payment"—see para.(7).

GENERAL NOTE

13.289   This has the same effect as ESA Regs 2008 reg.158.

Treating a claimant as not having limited capability for work

13.290   **95.** The claimant is to be treated as not having limited capability for work if the claimant is disqualified for receiving an employment and support allowance during a period of imprisonment or detention in legal custody if that disqualification is for more than six weeks.

DEFINITIONS

"claimant"—see WRA 2007 s.24(1).
"week"—see reg.2.

GENERAL NOTE

13.291   This has the same effect as ESA Regs 2008 reg.159(1).

Exceptions from disqualification for imprisonment

96.—(1) Notwithstanding section 18(4)(b) of the Act, a claimant is not   13.292
disqualified for receiving an employment and support allowance for any
period during which that claimant is undergoing imprisonment or detention in legal custody—

(a) in connection with a charge brought or intended to be brought
against the claimant in criminal proceedings;

(b) pursuant to any sentence of a court in criminal proceedings; or

(c) pursuant to any order for detention made by a court in criminal proceedings,

unless paragraph (2) applies.

(2) This paragraph applies where—

(a) a penalty is imposed on the claimant at the conclusion of the proceedings referred to in paragraph (1); or

(b) in the case of default of payment of a sum adjudged to be paid on
conviction, a penalty is imposed in respect of such default.

(3) Notwithstanding section 18(4)(b) of the Act, a claimant ("C") is not
to be disqualified for receiving an employment and support allowance, for
any period during which C is undergoing detention in legal custody after
the conclusion of criminal proceedings if it is a period during which C is
detained in a hospital or similar institution in Great Britain as a person
suffering from mental disorder unless C satisfies either of the following
conditions.

(4) The first condition is that—

(a) C is being detained under section 45A or 47 of the Mental Health
Act 1983 (power of higher courts to direct hospital admission;
removal to hospital of persons serving sentences of imprisonment
etc); and

(b) in any case where there is in relation to C a release date within the
meaning of section 50(3) of that Act, C is being detained on or before
the day which the Secretary of State certifies to be that release date.

(5) The second condition is that C is being detained under—

(a) section 59A of the Criminal Procedure (Scotland) Act 1995 (hospital direction); or

(b) section 136 of the Mental Health (Care and Treatment) (Scotland)
Act 2003 (transfer of prisoners for treatment of mental disorder).

(6) For the purposes of this regulation—

(a) "court" means any court in the United Kingdom, the Channel
Islands or the Isle of Man or in any place to which the Colonial
Prisoners Removal Act 1884 applies or any naval court-martial,
army court-martial or air force court-martial within the meaning
of the Courts-Martial (Appeals) Act 1968 or the Courts-Martial
Appeal Court;

(b) "hospital or similar institution" means any place (not being a prison,
a young offender institution, a secure training centre, secure accommodation in a children's home [¹, a place at which a secure accommodation service within the meaning of Part 1 of the Regulation
and Inspection of Social Care (Wales) Act 2016 is being provided]
or a remand centre, and not being at or in any such place) in which
persons suffering from mental disorder are or may be received for
care or treatment;

(c) "penalty" means a sentence of imprisonment or detention under section 90 or 91 of the Powers of Criminal Courts (Sentencing) Act 2000, a detention and training order under section 100 of that Act, a sentence of detention for public protection under section 226 of the Criminal Justice Act 2003 or an extended sentence under section 228 of that Act or, in Scotland, under section 205, 207 or 208 of the Criminal Procedure (Scotland) Act 1995;

(d) in relation to a person who is liable to be detained in Great Britain as a result of any order made under the Colonial Prisoners Removal Act 1884, references to a prison must be construed as including references to a prison within the meaning of that Act;

(e) criminal proceedings against any person must be deemed to be concluded upon that person being found insane in those proceedings so that the person cannot be tried or that person's trial cannot proceed.

(7) Where a claimant outside Great Britain is undergoing imprisonment or detention in legal custody and, in similar circumstances in Great Britain, the claimant would, by virtue of this regulation, not have been disqualified for receiving an employment and support allowance, the claimant is not disqualified for receiving that allowance by reason only of the imprisonment or detention.

AMENDMENT

1. Social Security and Child Support (Regulation and Inspection of Social Care (Wales) Act 2016) (Consequential Provision) Regulations 2018 (SI 2018/228) reg.15(2) (April 2, 2018).

DEFINITIONS

"claimant"—see WRA 2007 s.24(1).
"court"—see para.(6) (a).
"hospital or similar institution"—see para.(6)(b).
"penalty"—see para.(6)(c).
"prison"—see para.(6)(d)

GENERAL NOTE

13.293   This has the same effect as ESA Regs 2008 reg.160.

Suspension of payment of an employment and support allowance during imprisonment

13.294   **97.**—(1) Subject to the following provisions of this regulation, the payment of an employment and support allowance to any claimant—

(a) which is excepted from the operation of section 18(4)(b) of the Act by virtue of the provisions of regulation 96(1), (3) or (7); or

(b) which is payable otherwise than in respect of a period during which the claimant is undergoing imprisonment or detention in legal custody, is suspended while that claimant is undergoing imprisonment or detention in legal custody.

(2) An employment and support allowance is not to be suspended while the claimant is liable to be detained in a hospital or similar institution, as defined in regulation 96(6), during a period for which in the claimant's case, the allowance is or would be excepted from the operation of section 18(4)(b) by virtue of the provisions of regulation 96(3).

(3) Where, by virtue of this regulation, payment of an employment and support allowance is suspended for any period, the period of suspension is not to be taken into account in calculating any period under the provisions of regulation 55 of the Claims and Payments Regulations 2013 (extinguishment of right to payment if payment is not obtained within the prescribed time).

DEFINITIONS

"claimant"—see WRA 2007 s.24(1).
"hospital or similar institution"—see reg.96(6).

GENERAL NOTE

This has the same effect as ESA Regs 2008 reg.161.   **13.295**

PART 13

Periods of less than a week

Entitlement for less than a week – amount of an employment and support allowance payable

98.—(1) This regulation applies where the claimant is entitled to an   **13.296**
employment and support allowance for a part-week and this regulation is subject to the following provisions of this Part.
(2) The amount payable by way of an employment and support allowance in respect of a part-week is to be calculated by applying the formula—

$$(N \chi X)/7$$

where—
X is the amount calculated in accordance with section 2(1) of the Act;
N is the number of days in the part-week.
(3) In this Part—
"part-week" means an entitlement to an employment and support allowance in respect of any period of less than a week; and
"relevant week" means the period of seven days determined in accordance with regulation 99.

DEFINITIONS

"claimant"—see WRA 2007 s.24(1).
"part-week"—see para.(3).
"relevant week"—see para.(3).

GENERAL NOTE

This has much the same effect as ESA Regs 2008 reg.165.   **13.297**

Relevant week

13.298   **99.**—(1) Where a part-week—

(a) is the whole period for which an employment and support allowance is payable, or occurs at the beginning of an award, the relevant week is the period of seven days ending on the last day of that part-week; or

(b) occurs at the end of an award, the relevant week is the period of seven days beginning on the first day of the part-week.

(2) Where a claimant has an award of an employment and support allowance and that claimant's benefit week changes, for the purpose of calculating the amounts of an employment and support allowance payable for the part-week beginning on the day after the last complete benefit week before the change and ending immediately before the change, the relevant week is the period of seven days beginning on the day after the last complete benefit week.

DEFINITIONS

"benefit week"—see reg.2.
"claimant"—see WRA 2007 s.24(1).
"part-week"—see reg.98(3).
"relevant week"— see reg.98(3).

GENERAL NOTE

13.299   This has the same effect as ESA Regs 2008 reg.166.

Modification in the calculation of income

13.300   **100.** For the purposes of regulation 98 (entitlement for less than a week – amount of an employment and support allowance payable), a claimant's income is to be calculated in accordance with regulations 76 to 84 subject to the following changes—

(a) any income which is due to be paid in the relevant week is to be treated as paid on the first day of that week;

(b) any widow's benefit, training allowance, widowed parent's allowance, [¹ bereavement support payment under section 30 of the Pensions Act 2014], carer's allowance and any increase in disablement pension payable in accordance with Part 1 of Schedule 7 to the Contributions and Benefits Act (unemployability supplement) which is payable in the relevant week but not in respect of any day in the part-week is to be disregarded;

(c) where the part-week occurs at the end of the claim—
(i) any income; or
(ii) any change in the amount of income of the same kind,
which is first payable within the relevant week but not on any day in the part-week is to be disregarded;

(d) where only part of the weekly balance of income is taken into account in the relevant week, the balance is to be disregarded.

AMENDMENT

1. Pensions Act 2014 (Consequential, Supplementary and Incidental Amendments) Order 2017 (SI 2017/422) art.44 (April 6, 2017).

"carer's allowance"—see reg.2.
"claimant"—see WRA 2007 s.24(1).
"training allowance"—see reg.2.
"week"—see reg.2.
"part-week"—see reg.98(3).
"relevant week"— see reg.98(3).

GENERAL NOTE

This has the same effect as ESA Regs 2008 reg.167.   13.301

Reduction in certain cases1

101.—(1) Where a disqualification is to be made in accordance with   13.302
regulation 93 in respect of a part-week, the amount referred to in paragraph
(2) is to be payable by way of an employment and support allowance in
respect of that part-week.

(2) The amount mentioned in paragraph (1) is—

(a) one seventh of the employment and support allowance which would
have been paid for the part-week if—

  (i) there was no disqualification under regulation 93; and

  (ii) it was not a part-week; multiplied by

(b) the number of days in the part-week in respect of which no disqualification is to be made in accordance with regulation 93.

DEFINITIONS

"claimant"—see WRA 2007 s.24(1).
"part-week"—see reg.98(3).
"relevant week"— see reg.98(3).

GENERAL NOTE

This has the same effect as ESA Regs 2008 reg.168.   13.303

Payment of an employment and support allowance for days of certain treatment

102.—(1) Where a claimant is entitled to an employment and support   13.304
allowance as a result of being treated as having limited capability for work
in accordance with regulation 22, the amount payable is to be equal to one
seventh of the amount of the employment and support allowance which
would be payable in respect of a week in accordance with section 2(1) of
the Act multiplied by N.

(2) In paragraph (1), N is the number of days in that week on which the
claimant was receiving treatment referred to in regulation 22 or recovering
from that treatment, but does not include any day during which the claimant does work.

SCHEDULE 1

HER MAJESTY'S FORCES

Regulation 2

PART 1

PRESCRIBED ESTABLISHMENTS AND ORGANISATIONS

13.305

1. Any of the regular naval, military or air forces of the Crown.
2. Royal Fleet Reserve.
3. Royal Navy Reserve.
4. Royal Marines Reserve.
5. Army Reserve.
6. Territorial Army.
7. Royal Air Force Reserve.
8. Royal Auxiliary Air Force.
9. The Royal Irish Regiment, to the extent that its members are not members of any force falling within paragraph 1.

PART 2

ESTABLISHMENTS AND ORGANISATIONS OF WHICH HER MAJESTY'S FORCES DO NOT CONSIST

13.306

10. Her Majesty's forces are not to be taken to consist of any of the establishments or organisations specified in Part 1 of this Schedule by virtue only of the employment in such establishment or organisation of the following persons—

(a) any person who is serving as a member of any naval force of Her Majesty's forces and who (not having been an insured person under the National Insurance Act 1965 and not having been a contributor under the Social Security Act 1975 or not being a contributor under the Contributions and Benefits Act) locally entered that force at an overseas base;

(b) any person who is serving as a member of any military force of Her Majesty's forces and who entered that force, or was recruited for that force outside the United Kingdom, and the depot of whose unit is situated outside the United Kingdom;

(c) any person who is serving as a member of any air force of Her Majesty's forces and who entered that force, or was recruited for that force, outside the United Kingdom, and is liable under the terms of engagement to serve only in a specified part of the world outside the United Kingdom.

GENERAL NOTE

13.307   This is the same as ESA Regs 2008 Sch.1.

SCHEDULE 2 **Regulation 15(2) and (3)**

ASSESSMENT OF WHETHER A CLAIMANT HAS LIMITED CAPABILITY FOR WORK

PART 1

PHYSICAL DISABILITIES   13.308

(1) Activity			(2) Descriptors	(3) Points
1. Mobilising unaided by another person with or without a walking stick, manual wheelchair or other aid if such aid is normally or could reasonably be worn or used.	1	(a)	Cannot, unaided by another person, either: (i) mobilise more than 50 metres on level ground without stopping in order to avoid significant discomfort or exhaustion; or (ii) repeatedly mobilise 50 metres within a reasonable timescale because of significant discomfort or exhaustion.	15
		(b)	Cannot, unaided by another person, mount or descend two steps even with the support of a handrail.	9
		(c)	Cannot, unaided by another person, either: (i) mobilise more than 100 metres on level ground without stopping in order to avoid significant discomfort or exhaustion; or (ii) repeatedly mobilise 100 metres within a reasonable timescale because of significant discomfort or exhaustion.	9 6
		(d)	Cannot, unaided by another person, either: (i) mobilise more than 200 metres on level ground without stopping in order to avoid significant discomfort or exhaustion; or (ii) repeatedly mobilise 200 metres within a reasonable timescale because of significant discomfort or exhaustion.	
		(e)	None of the above applies.	0
2. Standing and sitting.	2	(a)	Cannot move between one seated position and another seated position which are located next to one another without receiving physical assistance from another person.	15
		(b)	Cannot, for the majority of the time, remain at a work station: (i) standing unassisted by another person (even if free to move around); (ii) sitting (even in an adjustable chair); or (iii) a combination of paragraphs (i) and (ii),	

(1) Activity		(2) Descriptors	(3) Points
		(for more than 30 minutes, before needing to move away in order to avoid significant discomfort or exhaustion.	9
		(c) Cannot, for the majority of the time, remain at a work station:	6
		(i) standing unassisted by another person (even if free to move around);	
		(ii) sitting (even in an adjustable chair); or	
		(iii) a combination of paragraphs (i) and (ii),	
		for more than an hour before needing to move away in order to avoid significant discomfort or exhaustion.	
		(d) None of the above applies.	0
3. Reaching.	3	(a) Cannot raise either arm as if to put something in the top pocket of a coat or jacket.	15
		(b) Cannot raise either arm to top of head as if to put on a hat.	9
		(c) Cannot raise either arm above head height as if to reach for something.	6
		(d) None of the above applies.	0
4. Picking up and moving or transferring by the use of the upper body and arms.	4	(a) Cannot pick up and move a 0.5 litre carton full of liquid.	15
		(b) Cannot pick up and move a one litre carton full of liquid.	9
		(c) Cannot transfer a light but bulky object such as an empty cardboard box.	6
		(d) None of the above applies.	0
5. Manual dexterity.	5	(a) Cannot press a button (such as a telephone keypad) with either hand or cannot turn the pages of a book with either hand.	15
		(b) Cannot pick up a £1 coin or equivalent with either hand.	15
		(c) Cannot use a pen or pencil to make a meaningful mark with either hand.	9
		(d) Cannot single-handedly use a suitable keyboard or mouse.	9
		(e) None of the above applies.	0
6. Making self understood through speaking, writing, typing, or other means which are normally or could reasonably be used, unaided by another person, to strangers.	6	(a) Cannot convey a simple message, such as the presence of a hazard.	15
		(b) Has significant difficulty conveying a simple message	15
		(c) Has some difficulty conveying a simple message to strangers.	6
		(d) None of the above applies.	0
7. Understanding communication by: (i) verbal means (such as hearing or lip reading) alone;	7	(a) Cannot understand a simple message, such as the location of a fire escape, due to sensory impairment.	15
		(b) Has significant difficulty understanding a simple message from a stranger due to sensory impairment.	15

(1) Activity		(2) Descriptors			(3) Points
(ii) non-verbal means (such as reading 16 point print or Braille) alone; or		(c)		Has some difficulty understanding a simple message from a stranger due to sensory impairment.	6
(iii) a combination of sub-paragraphs (i) and (ii), using any aid that is normally or could reasonably be used, unaided by another person.		(d)		None of the above applies.	0
8. Navigation and maintaining safety using a guide dog or other aid if either or both are normally used or could reasonably be used.	8	(a)		Unable to navigate around familiar surroundings, without being accompanied by another person, due to sensory impairment.	15
		(b)		Cannot safely complete a potentially hazardous task such as crossing the road, without being accompanied by another person, due to sensory impairment.	15
		(c)		Unable to navigate around unfamiliar surroundings, without being accompanied by another person, due to sensory impairment.	9
		(d)		None of the above applies.	0
9. Absence or loss of control whilst conscious leading to extensive evacuation of the bowel and/or bladder, other than enuresis (bedwetting), despite the wearing or use of any aids or adaptations which are normally or could reasonably be worn or used.	9	(a)		At least once a month experiences: (i) loss of control leading to extensive evacuation of the bowel and/or voiding of the bladder; or (ii) substantial leakage of the contents of a collecting device sufficient to require cleaning and a change in clothing.	15
		(b)		The majority of the time is at risk of loss of control leading to extensive evacuation of the bowel and/or voiding of the bladder, sufficient to require cleaning and a change in clothing, if not able to reach a toilet quickly.	6
		(c)		Neither of the above applies.	0
10. Consciousness during waking moments.	10	(a)		At least once a week, has an involuntary episode of lost or altered consciousness resulting in significantly disrupted awareness or concentration.	15
		(b)		At least once a month, has an involuntary episode of lost or altered consciousness resulting in significantly disrupted awareness or concentration.	6
		(c)		Neither of the above applies.	0

PART 2

MENTAL, COGNITIVE AND INTELLECTUAL FUNCTION ASSESSMENT

(1) Activity			(2) Descriptors	(3) Points
11. Learning tasks.	11	(a)	Cannot learn how to complete a simple task, such as setting an alarm clock.	15
		(b)	Cannot learn anything beyond a simple task, such as setting an alarm clock.	9
		(c)	Cannot learn anything beyond a moderately complex task, such as the steps involved in operating a washing machine to clean clothes.	6
		(d)	None of the above applies.	0
12. Awareness of everyday hazards (such as boiling water or sharp objects).	12	(a)	Reduced awareness of everyday hazards leads to a significant risk of: (i) injury to self or others; or (ii) damage to property or possessions, such that the claimant requires supervision for the majority of the time to maintain safety.	15
		(b)	Reduced awareness of everyday hazards leads to a significant risk of: (i) injury to self or others; or (ii) damage to property or possessions, such that the claimant frequently requires supervision to maintain safety.	9
		(c)	Reduced awareness of everyday hazards leads to a significant risk of: (i) injury to self or others; or (ii) damage to property or possessions, such that the claimant occasionally requires supervision to maintain safety.	6
		(d)	None of the above applies.	0
13. Initiating and completing personal action (which means planning, organisation, problem solving, prioritising or switching tasks).	13	(a)	Cannot, due to impaired mental function, reliably initiate or complete at least two sequential personal actions.	15
		(b)	Cannot, due to impaired mental function, reliably initiate or complete at least two sequential personal actions for the majority of the time.	9

(1) Activity		(2) Descriptors	(3) Points
	(c)	Frequently cannot, due to impaired mental function, reliably initiate or complete at least two sequential personal actions.	6
	(d)	None of the above applies.	0
14. Coping with change. 14	(a)	Cannot cope with any change to the extent that day to day life cannot be managed.	15
	(b)	Cannot cope with minor planned change (such as a prearranged change to the routine time scheduled for a lunch break), to the extent that, overall, day to day life is made significantly more difficult.	9
	(c)	Cannot cope with minor unplanned change (such as the timing of an appointment on the day it is due to occur), to the extent that, overall, day to day life is made significantly more difficult.	6
	(d)	None of the above applies	0
15. Getting about. 15	(a)	Cannot get to any place outside the claimant's home with which the claimant is familiar.	15
	(b)	Is unable to get to a specified place with which the claimant is familiar, without being accompanied by another person.	9
	(c)	Is unable to get to a specified place with which the claimant is unfamiliar without being accompanied by another person.	6
	(d)	None of the above applies.	0
16. Coping with social engagement due to cognitive impairment or mental disorder. 16	(a)	Engagement in social contact is always precluded due to difficulty relating to others or significant distress experienced by the claimant.	15
	(b)	Engagement in social contact with someone unfamiliar to the claimant is always precluded due to difficulty relating to others or significant distress experienced by the claimant.	9
	(c)	Engagement in social contact with someone unfamiliar to the claimant is not possible for the majority of the time due to difficulty relating to others or significant distress experienced by the claimant.	6
	(d)	None of the above applies.	0

(1) Activity	(2) Descriptors	(3) Points
17. Appropriateness of behaviour with other people, due to cognitive impairment or mental disorder.	17 (a) Has, on a daily basis, uncontrollable episodes of aggressive or disinhibited behaviour that would be unreasonable in any workplace.	15
	(b) Frequently has uncontrollable episodes of aggressive or disinhibited behaviour that would be unreasonable in any workplace.	15
	(c) Occasionally has uncontrollable episodes of aggressive or disinhibited behaviour that would be unreasonable in any workplace.	9
	(d) None of the above applies.	0

GENERAL NOTE

13.309   This Sch. is the same as ESA Regs 2008 Sch.2, as amended.

SCHEDULE 3   **Regulation 30(1)**

13.310   Assessment of whether a claimant has limited capability for work-related activity

Activity	Descriptors
1. Mobilising unaided by another person with or without a walking stick, manual wheelchair or other aid if such aid is normally or could reasonably be worn or used.	1. Cannot either: (a) mobilise more than 50 metres on level ground without stopping in order to avoid significant discomfort or exhaustion; or (b) repeatedly mobilise 50 metres within a reasonable timescale because of significant discomfort or exhaustion.
2. Transferring from one seated position to another.	2. Cannot move between one seated position and another seated position located next to one another without receiving physical assistance from another person.
3. Reaching.	3. Cannot raise either arm as if to put something in the top pocket of a coat or jacket.
4. Picking up and moving or transferring by the use of the upper body and arms (excluding standing, sitting, bending or kneeling and all other activities specified in this Schedule).	4. Cannot pick up and move a 0.5 litre carton full of liquid.
5. Manual dexterity.	5. Cannot press a button (such as a telephone keypad) with either hand or cannot turn the pages of a book with either hand.
6. Making self understood through speaking, writing, typing, or other means which are normally, or could reasonably be, used unaided by another person.	6. Cannot convey a simple message, such as the presence of a hazard.

Activity	Descriptors

7. Understanding communication by:
  (i) verbal means (such as hearing or lip reading) alone;
  (ii) non-verbal means (such as reading 16 point print or Braille) alone; or
  (iii) a combination of subparagraphs (i) and (ii), using any aid that is normally, or could reasonably, be used unaided by another person.
	7. Cannot understand a simple message, such as the location of a fire escape, due to sensory impairment.

8. Absence or loss of control whilst conscious leading to extensive evacuation of the bowel and/or voiding of the bladder, other than enuresis (bed-wetting), despite the wearing or use of any aids or adaptations which are normally or could reasonably be worn or used.	8. At least once a week experiences
	  (a) loss of control leading to extensive evacuation of the bowel and/or voiding of the bladder; or
	  (b) substantial leakage of the contents of a collecting device
	sufficient to require the individual to clean themselves. and change clothing.

9. Learning tasks.	9. Cannot learn how to complete a simple task, such as setting an alarm clock, due to cognitive impairment or mental disorder.

10. Awareness of hazard.	10. Reduced awareness of everyday hazards, due to cognitive impairment or mental disorder, leads to a significant risk of:
	  (a) injury to self or others; or
	  (b) damage to property or possessions
	such that the claimant requires supervision for the majority of the time to maintain safety.

11. Initiating and completing personal action (which means planning, organisation, problem solving, prioritising or switching tasks).	11. Cannot, due to impaired mental function, reliably initiate or complete at least two sequential personal actions.
12. Coping with change.	12. Cannot cope with any change, due to cognitive impairment or mental disorder, to the extent that day to day life cannot be managed.
13. Coping with social engagement, due to cognitive impairment or mental disorder.	13. Engagement in social contact is always precluded due to difficulty relating to others or significant distress experienced by the claimant.
14. Appropriateness of behaviour with other people, due to cognitive impairment or mental disorder.	14. Has, on a daily basis, uncontrollable episodes of aggressive or disinhibited behaviour that would be unreasonable in any workplace.

15. Conveying food or drink to the mouth.	15 (a) Cannot convey food or drink to the claimant's own mouth without receiving physical assistance from someone else;
	  (b) Cannot convey food or drink to the claimant's own mouth without repeatedly stopping or experiencing breathlessness or severe discomfort;
	  (c) Cannot convey food or drink to the claimant's own mouth without receiving regular prompting given by someone else in the claimant's presence; or

Activity	Descriptors
	(d) Owing to a severe disorder of mood or behaviour, fails to convey food or drink to the claimant's own mouth without receiving: (i) physical assistance from someone else; or (ii) regular prompting given by someone else in the claimant's presence.
16. Chewing or swallowing food or drink. 16	(a) Cannot chew or swallow food or drink; (b) Cannot chew or swallow food or drink without repeatedly stopping or experiencing breathlessness or severe discomfort; (c) Cannot chew or swallow food or drink without repeatedly receiving regular prompting given by someone else in the claimant's presence; or (d) Owing to a severe disorder of mood or behaviour, fails to: (i) chew or swallow food or drink; or (ii) chew or swallow food or drink without regular prompting given by someone else in the claimant's presence.

GENERAL NOTE

13.311   This Sch. is the same as ESA Regs 2008 Sch.3, as amended.

INDEX

LEGAL TAXONOMY
FROM SWEET & MAXWELL

This index has been prepared using Sweet and Maxwell's Legal Taxonomy. Main index entries conform to keywords provided by the Legal Taxonomy except where references to specific documents or non-standard terms (denoted by quotation marks) have been included. These keywords provide a means of identifying similar concepts in other Sweet & Maxwell publications and online services to which keywords from the Legal Taxonomy have been applied. Readers may find some minor differences between terms used in the text and those which appear in the index. Suggestions to *sweetandmaxwell.taxonomy@thomson.com*.

(All references are to paragraph number)

Abatement
 deeming benefit, 3.48–3.49
 reduced earnings allowance, 10.233
"Abbeyfield Home"
 employment and support allowance, 9.4
Absence abroad
 see **Persons abroad**
Absence of loss of control
 see **Descriptors for incapacity**
Accidents
 persons abroad, 3.135
Accrual rates
 see **Physical disabilities pensions**
Action plans
 generally, 1.761–1.762
 work-focused interviews, 9.156
 work-related activities
  generally, 9.603–9.604
  reconsideration, 9.607
Acute non-lymphatic leukaemia
 generally, 10.135
"Additional pensions"
 see also **Category A retirement pensions**
 accrual rates for purposes of s 45(2)(d), 1.535–1.545
 amount, 1.516
 calculation
  contributions equivalent premium paid or treated as paid, where, 6.31
  earnings factor credits eligibility, 6.35–6.37
  earnings partly from employment with contracted-out scheme membership, 6.32
  earnings partly from employment with scheme membership, 6.33
  other cases of mixed forms of contracted-out employment, 6.34
  preclusion from regular employment, 6.38
 Regulations, 6.29–6.38

 contracted-out employment, 1.521–1.532
 contributions equivalent premium paid or treated as paid, where, 6.31
 disabled persons' tax credit, and, 1.107–1.128
 earnings factor credits eligibility
  pensioners to whom ESA was payable, 6.35
  pensioners to whom s 1A of 2007 Act, 6.37
  persons entitled to UC, 6.36
 generally, 1.104–1.105
 mixed forms of contracted-out employment, 6.34
 modifications to provisions, 1.111
 other cases, 1.533–1.534
 preclusion from regular employment, 6.38
 prescribed maximum, 6.74–6.79
 reduction, 1.109–1.110
 surplus earning factor, 1.517–1.520
 working families' tax credit, and, 1.107–1.128
Adjustment (benefits)
 hospital in-patients, 3.77–3.78
 incapacity benefit
  hospital in-patients, 3.77–3.78
  persons abroad, 3.109–3.117
 industrial injuries benefit
  overlapping benefits, 3.89–3.90
  persons abroad, 3.131
  successive accidents, 1.413–1.415
 overlapping benefits
  dependency benefits, 3.91–3.98
  jobseekers allowance, 3.102
  part week, for, 3.99
  personal benefits, 3.86–3.90
  priority, 3.100
 Regulations
  hospital in-patients, 3.74–3.79
  overlapping benefits, 3.86–3.104
Adopted children
 child benefit, 1.629

Adoption leave
definition, 3.22
employment and support allowance, 9.4
Adoption pay
see **Statutory adoption pay**
Adult dependants
adjustment of benefits
overlapping benefits, 3.93
apportionment of pension payments,
3.61
contribution to cost, 3.64–3.65
earnings rules, 3.58–3.60
fluctuating earnings, 1.324–1.326
incapacity benefit
generally, 1.308
reduced contributions, 1.309–1.311
relevant earnings, 1.314–1.316
restriction, 1.312–1.313
increase of benefits
abolition, 1.888
Regulations, 3.58–3.65
statutory provisions, 1.297–1.326
persons residing together, 3.149–3.153
Regulations (1977)
apportionment of pension payments,
3.61
contribution to cost, 3.64–3.65
earnings rules, 3.58–3.60
relevant earnings, 1.314–1.316
retirement pensions
husband, 1.303–1.305
person with care of children,
1.306–1.307
wife, 1.299–1.302
short-term benefits, 1.297–1.298
trade disputes, 1.320–1.323
unemployability supplement
generally, 1.588
introduction, 1.599
Advance payments
employment and support allowance
generally, 9.338–9.339
statutory provisions, 1.741–1.742,
1.828
Advanced education
see **Further education**
Age addition
hospital in-patients, 3.77–3.78
persons abroad, and, 3.129–3.130
rate, 1.511
retirement pensions, 1.289–1.291
widows' benefits, 6.122
Air crew
employment and support allowance, 9.5
generally, 1.450–1.451
Allergic rhinitis
generally, 10.135
prescribed occupations, 10.191
Allocation (contributions)
increases for spouse, 3.46–3.47
Alveolitis
generally, 10.135
prescribed occupations, 10.179

Anaemia
generally, 10.135
Anaphylaxis
generally, 10.135, 10.182
Angiosarcoma
generally, 10.135
liver, of the, 10.100
Ankylostomiasis
generally, 10.135, 10.177
Anthrax
generally, 10.135, 10.175
Appeals
mesothelioma
First-tier Tribunal, to, 1.873–1.874
procedure, 12.11–12.12
Social Security Commissioner, to,
1.875–1.876
'new style' ESA, 13.275–13.276
occupational deafness, 10.118–10.119
vaccine damage payments, 1.16–1.17
Apprentices
child benefit, 1.629
contribution credits, 2.18–2.19
Appropriateness of behaviour
see **Descriptors for incapacity**
Approved training
see **Contribution credits**
Armed forces
credits for spouses and civil partners,
2.40–2.43
generally, 1.447–1.449
'new style' ESA
absence from Great Britain of member
of family, 13.284–13.285
limited capability for work,
13.158–13.159
prescribed establishments and
organisations, 13.305–13.307
personal independence payments
excluded persons, 4.260
residence, 4.205
vaccine damage payments, 11.6
**Armed Forces and Reserve Forces
Compensation Scheme**
employment and support allowance, 9.4
Armed forces independence payments
employment and support allowance, 9.4
overlapping benefits, 3.82
Artificial prosthesis
see **Mobility component**
Arrested development
see **Mobility component**
Asbestosis
generally, 10.135
prescribed occupations, 10.195
Assessment
see also **Assessment (disablement)**
'new style' ESA
duration, 13.115–13.116
general note, 13.116
generally, 13.115–13.116
previous claimants, 13.117–13.118
terminally ill claimants, 13.119–13.120

personal independence payments
  ability to carry out activities,
    4.174–4.176
  consultation to determine if claimant
    has ability to carry out activities,
    4.186–4.187
  daily living activities, 4.172–4.173,
    4.230
  definitions, 4.230–4.231
  information or evidence required for
    determining ability to carry out
    activities, 4.184–4.185
  matters to be taken into account in
    determining good reason,
    4.188–4.189
  miscellaneous, 4.232–4.238
  mobility activities, 4.172–4.173, 4.231
  redetermination of ability to carry out
    activities, 4.190–4.191
  scoring, 4.177–4.183

Assessment (disablement)
  accident, 1.399
  aggregation of percentages, 10.87–10.88
  checklist of questions, 1.398
  connected conditions, 10.21
  connection factor, 10.22
  constant attendance allowance
    comment, 1.582
    generally, 1.571
  differences of expert medical opinion,
    1.401
  disablement benefit
    comment, 1.578–1.581
    generally, 1.570
  dominant hand, 1.577
  employed earner, 1.399
  extent, 10.85–10.86
  generally, 1.395–1.405
  loss of physical or mental faculty, 1.400
  method
    comment, 1.574–1.576
    generally, 1.568
  miscellaneous provisions, 1.568–1.582
  multiple industrial accidents, 10.25
  other effective cause, 10.22–10.24
  partly relevant conditions, 10.21
  prescribed degrees of disablement
    generally, 10.52–10.53
    introduction, 10.26–10.28
  principles, 10.19–10.28
  resulting disablement, 1.402
  rounding of percentages, 10.89
  severe disablement allowance, 1.569

Asthma
  generally, 10.135
  prescribed occupations, 10.193–10.194
  time limits for claims, 10.124–10.125

Attendance allowance
  see also **Non-contributory benefits**
  adjustment
    medical expenses paid from public
     funds, 4.26–4.27
    persons abroad, 3.132

  care home residents
    exemption, 4.24–4.25
    generally, 4.21–4.22
    relevant patients, 4.30
    terminally ill, 4.23
  Christmas bonus, 1.464–1.467
  employment and support allowance, and,
    9.4
  entitlement
    care home residents, 4.20–4.25
    extension of qualifying period,
     4.10–4.11
    generally, 1.153–1.157
    hospital in-patients, 4.19–4.20
    person residing in GB to whom EU
     Regulation applies, 4.6–4.7
    person residing in EEA state or
     Switzerland, 4.8
    private nursing home residents,
     4.20–4.25
    refugees, 4.9
    renal failure sufferers, 4.14–4.18
    residence, 4.4–4.5
    terminally ill, 1.165–1.167
  excluded persons, 1.168–1.171
  extension of qualifying period, 4.10–4.11
  hospital in-patients
    exemption, 4.24–4.25
    generally, 4.19–4.20
    relevant patients, 4.30
  medical expenses paid from public funds
    exemption, 4.27
    generally, 4.26
  national insurance numbers, 4.3
  person residing in GB to whom EU
    Regulation applies, 4.6–4.7
  person residing in EEA state or
    Switzerland, 4.8
  persons abroad, 3.132
  private nursing home residents
    exemption, 4.24–4.25
    generally, 4.21–4.22
    relevant patients, 4.30
    terminally ill, 4.23
  rate, 1.158–1.164, 1.511
  refugees, 4.9
  renal failure sufferers, 4.14–4.18
  residence, 4.4–4.5
  terminal illness
    generally, 1.165–1.167
    Regulations, 4.23

Attention and supervision
  see **Care component**

Avian chlamydiosis
  generally, 10.135

Awareness of everyday hazards
  see **Descriptors for incapacity**

Barotrauma
  generally, 10.135

Bathing
  see **Personal independence payments**

Beat elbow
  generally, 10.135, 10.144

Beat hand
generally, 10.135, 10.144
Beat knee
generally, 10.135, 10.144
"Benefit week"
computation of earnings, 3.4
employment and support allowance, 9.4
Benefits for the aged
see **Elderly persons**
Bereavement allowance
contribution conditions
general note, 1.504–1.505
miscellaneous provisions, 1.486
contribution credits
generally, 2.5
starting credits, 2.6–2.7
generally, 1.81–1.82
home responsibilities protection,
2.49–2.50
rate, 6.155
Bereavement benefits
contribution credits, 2.25–2.26
rate, 6.152–6.155
Bereavement payment
abolition, 1.68
contribution conditions, 1.485
generally, 1.67–1.68
persons abroad, 3.120–3.121
Bereavement support payment
contribution condition, 1.1006
duration, 6.219–6.220
entitlement, 1.1005
excluded persons, 6.225
general note, 1.1008–1.1009
generally, 1.1005
higher rate, 6.223
introduction, 1.68
period for which payable, 6.219–6.220
persons entitled
higher rate, 6.223
standard rate, 6.224
territory, 6.227
prisoners, and
generally, 1.1007
Regulations, 6.225–6.226
proof of death, 1.1016–1.1018
proof of valid marriage, 1.1010–1.1015
rate, 6.221–6.222
Regulations (2017)
citation, 6.218
commencement, 6.218
general provisions, 6.219–6.220
remand in custody, 6.226
specified territory, 6.227
standard rate, 6.224
statutory provisions, 1.1005–1.1018
validity of marriage, 1.1010–1.1015
Beryllium
generally, 10.135
Binaural disablement
see **Occupational deafness**
Biological agents
see **Industrial diseases**

Blanching
generally, 10.135
vibration white finger, 10.160–10.165
Board and lodging
see **Lodgings**
Bowel
personal independence payments, 4.246
Bronchitis
generally, 10.135
pneumoconiosis, and, 10.104–10.105
prescribed occupations, 10.198
transitional provision, 10.247
Brucella organism
generally, 10.135
Budgeting
see **Personal independence payments**
Bursitis
generally, 10.135, 10.144
Byssinosis
generally, 1.425–1.430
prescribed diseases, 10.135
prescribed occupations, 10.187
special conditions, 10.96–10.97
Calculation of earnings
see **Computation (earnings)**
Cancer
generally, 10.141
Capable of work
see **Incapacity for work**
**Capital (employment and support
allowance)**
calculation
generally, 9.273–9.274
in the UK, 9.277–9.278
income treated as capital,
9.275–9.276
outside the UK, 9.279–9.280
claimant's partner, of, 9.216–9.217
diminishing notional capital rule,
9.283–9.284
disregards, 9.497–9.506
in the UK, 9.277–9.278
income treated as capital, 9.275–9.276
jointly held capital, 9.285–9.286
limit, 9.271–9.272
notional capital
diminishing capital rule, 9.283–9.284
generally, 9.281–9.284
outside the UK, 9.279–9.280
Regulations, 9.271–9.287
statutory provision, 1.769–1.770
tariff income from capital, 9.287–9.288
treated as income, 9.261–9.262
Carcinoma
generally, 10.135–10.135
prescribed occupations, 10.201
special conditions, 10.100–10.101
Cardiotoxicity
generally, 10.135
Care component
see also **Disability living allowance**
age limits, 1.247
'attention and supervision', 1.207

attention for a significant portion of the day, 1.220–1.221
'attention in connection with bodily functions', 1.208–1.219
care home residents
  exemption, 4.61–4.62
  generally, 4.57–4.59
  relevant persons, 4.60, 4.122
children, 1.240–1.243
conditions
  cooking test, 1.222–1.227
  day, 1.228–1.233
  introduction, 1.198–1.219
  lowest rate, 1.220–1.221
  night, 1.234–1.239
continual supervision, 1.231–1.233
cooking test, 1.222–1.227
day conditions
  continual supervision, 1.231–1.233
  frequent attention throughout the day, 1.228–1.230
  introduction, 1.228
defined phrases
  'attention and supervision', 1.207
  'attention in connection with bodily functions', 1.208–1.219
  'for any period throughout which', 1.199
  'requires', 1.204–1.206
  'so severely disabled mentally or physically', 1.200–1.203
'for any period throughout which', 1.199
frequent attention throughout the day, 1.228–1.230
generally, 1.196–1.249
hospital in-patients
  exemption, 4.61–4.62
  generally, 4.53–4.56
  relevant persons, 4.60, 4.122
lowest rate conditions
  attention for a significant portion of the day, 1.220–1.221
  cooking test, 1.222–1.227
  introduction, 1.220
medical expenses paid from public funds
  exemption, 4.64
  generally, 4.63
national insurance numbers, 4.33
night conditions
  awake at frequent intervals for purpose of watching over, 1.239
  awake for prolonged period, 1.239
  generally, 1.234–1.236
  prolonged or repeated attention, 1.237–1.238
persons aged 65 or over
  entitlement, 4.40–4.44, 4.102–4.115
  generally, 1.278–1.280
persons residing in GB to whom EU Regulation applies, 4.36–4.37
persons residing in EEA state or Switzerland, 4.38
prescribed circumstance, 4.65–4.66

private nursing home residents
  exemption, 4.61–4.62
  generally, 4.57–4.59
  relevant persons, 4.60, 4.122
qualifying period
  generally, 1.244–1.245
  regulations, 4.47–4.48
rates
  generally, 1.246
  regulations, 4.45
refugees, 4.39
renal failure sufferers, 1.248, 4.49–4.52
'requires', 1.204–1.206
'so severely disabled mentally or physically', 1.200–1.203
'terminally ill', 1.247
Care expenses
computation of earnings, and, 3.36
Care homes
attendance allowance
  exemption, 4.24–4.25
  generally, 4.21–4.22
  relevant patients, 4.30
  terminally ill, 4.23
disability living allowance
  exemption, 4.61–4.62
  generally, 4.57–4.59
  relevant persons, 4.60, 4.122
employment and support allowance, 9.4
personal independence payments
  generally, 1.926–1.927
  Regulations, 4.226–4.227
Carer premium
employment and support allowance
  generally, 9.439
  weekly amount, 9.442
Carers
contribution credits,
  additional period of allowance, 2.80–2.81
  applications, 2.83–2.86
  definitions, 2.72
  disqualification, 2.81–2.82
  'engaged in caring', 2.76–2.77
  'foster parent', 2.74–2.75
  general note, 2.71
  generally, 1.51–1.52
  imprisonment, and, 2.81–2.82
  limit on award of child benefit, 2.78–2.79
  provision of information, 2.85
  residence in GB, and, 2.81–2.82
  time limits for applications, 2.86
  transitional provision, 2.73
Carer's allowance
  see also **Non-contributory benefits**
adjustment of allowance
  overlapping benefits, 3.97
  persons abroad, 3.134
carers, 4.129–4.132
Christmas bonus, and, 1.464–1.467
contribution credits, 2.12–2.13
election of recipient, 4.137

employees, 4.138–4.141
employment and support allowance, 9.4
entitlement
    caring, 4.129
    election of recipient, 4.137
    employment, persons in, 4.138–4.141
    full-time education, persons in,
        4.133–4.135
    gainful employment, 4.138–4.141
    persons aged 65 or over, 4.151–4.154
    persons residing in GB to whom EU
        Regulation applies, 4.146–4.147
    persons residing in EEA state or
        Switzerland, 4.148–4.149
    prescribed persons, 4.136
    refugees, 4.150
    residence, 4.142–4.145
    severely disabled persons, 4.128–4.129
full-time education, persons in,
    4.133–4.135
general note, 4.124
generally, 1.178
increases for dependants
    abolition, 1.888
    generally, 1.317–1.319
multiple claimants
    election of recipient, 4.137
national insurance numbers, 4.127
overlapping benefits, 3.97
persons abroad, 3.134
persons aged 65 or over
    generally, 4.153
    men attaining 65 before October 1994,
        4.154
    treated as entitled, 4.151
    women attaining 65 before October
        1994, 4.152
persons residing in EEA state or
    Switzerland, 4.148–4.149
persons residing in GB to whom EU
    Regulation applies, 4.146–4.147
persons residing together, 3.149–3.153
prescribed persons, 4.136
rate
    generally, 1.511
    increases for dependants, 1.513
refugees, 4.150
severely disabled persons
    carers, 4.129–4.132
    generally, 4.128
Carpal tunnel syndrome
generally, 10.135, 10.166–10.168
Cataract
generally, 10.135, 10.142
Category A retirement pensions
see also **Contributory benefits**
additional pension
    accrual rates for purposes of s 45(2)(d),
        1.535–1.545
    amount, 1.516
    calculation, 6.29–6.38
    contracted-out employment,
        1.521–1.532

    generally, 1.104–1.105
    prescribed maximum, 6.74–6.79
    other cases, 1.533–1.534
    reduction, 1.109–1.110
    surplus earning factor, 1.517–1.520
age addition
    generally, 1.289–1.291
    rate, 1.511
adult dependant's addition
    husband's pension, 1.303–1.305
    person with care of children,
        1.306–1.307
    wife, 1.299–1.302
contribution conditions
    see also **Contribution conditions**
    earnings factors, 1.49
    general note, 1.504–1.505
    generally, 1.48
    miscellaneous provisions, 1.486
contribution credits
    generally, 2.5
    starting credits, 2.6–2.7
contributor attains pensionable age after
        April 6, 2010, 1.506
deemed earnings factors
    credits, 1.103
    generally, 1.99–1.101
    years 2010–2011 onwards, 1.102
deferral, 6.4–6.6
earnings factors
    conditions, and, 1.47
    credits, 1.103
    generally, 1.99–1.102
gender recognition, 1.693–1.694
generally, 1.97–1.98
home responsibilities protection, 2.49–2.50
hospital in-patients, 3.77–3.78
incapacity addition, 1.112–1.113
increases for dependants
    adults, 1.297–1.307
    child, 1.292–1.296
    husband, 1.303–1.305
    person with care of children,
        1.306–1.307
    wife, 1.299–1.302
increase where entitlement is deferred
    generally, 1.136–1.138
    miscellaneous provisions, 1.546–1.560
increase where entitlement to shared
        additional pension is deferred
    generally, 1.144
    miscellaneous provisions, 1.561–1.567
persons residing together, 3.149–3.153
pre-1975 beneficiaries and contributors,
        6.134–6.135
rate
    age addition, 1.511
    increases for dependants, 1.512
spouse's contributions, 1.114–1.116
state second pension
    credits, 1.103
    generally, 1.99–1.101
    years 2010–2011 onwards, 1.102

supplemental provisions, 1.135
widow's pension, 6.103–6.105
Category B retirement pensions
see also **Contributory benefits**
age addition
  generally, 1.289–1.291
  rate, 1.511
civil partners
  former, 1.119–1.120
  generally, 1.117–1.118
  survivors, 1.127–1.128
contribution conditions
  earnings factors, 1.49
  general note, 1.504–1.505
  generally, 1.48
  miscellaneous provisions, 1.486
contribution credits
  generally, 2.5
  starting credits, 2.6–2.7
date of commencement, 1.125
deferral, 6.4–6.6
divorcees, 1.119–1.120
entitlement by reference to benefits under
  ss 39A or 39B, 1.123–1.124
former civil partners, 1.119–1.120
gender recognition, 1.129, 1.695–1.696
general, 1.125
home responsibilities protection,
  2.49–2.50
hospital in-patients, 3.77–3.78
increases for dependants
  child, 1.292–1.296
increase where entitlement is deferred
  generally, 1.136–1.138
  miscellaneous provisions, 1.546–1.560
increase where entitlement to shared
  additional pension is deferred
  generally, 1.144
  miscellaneous provisions, 1.561–1.567
married people
  divorcees, 1.119–1.120
  generally, 1.117–1.118
  special provision, 1.130–1.131
  spouse changed gender, where, 1.129,
    1.695–1.696
  survivors, 1.132–1.133
pre-1975 beneficiaries and contributors,
  6.134–6.135
rate
  age addition, 1.511
  generally, 1.509
  increases for dependants, 1.512
spouses
  divorcees, 1.119–1.120
  generally, 1.117–1.118
  special provision, 1.130–1.131
  spouse changed gender, where, 1.129,
    1.695–1.696
  survivors, 1.132–1.133
supplemental provisions, 1.135
survivors
  civil partners, 1.127–1.128
  spouses, 1.132–1.133

widowers
  attained pensionable age before 6 April
    2010, who, 1.127–1.128
  generally, 1.121–1.122
  Regulations, 6.101–6.102
widows
  attained pensionable age before 6 April
    2010, who, 1.127–1.128
  generally, 1.121–1.122
  Regulations, 6.101–6.102
Category C retirement pensions
see also **Non-contributory benefits**
adult dependant's addition
  person with care of children,
    1.306–1.307
  wife's pension, 1.299–1.302
age addition
  generally, 1.289–1.291
  rate, 1.511
child dependant's addition
  dependency, and, 3.54–3.55
  generally, 1.292–1.294
  restrictions, 1.295–1.296
gender recognition, 1.700–1.701
generally, 1.287–1.288
hospital in-patients, 3.77–3.78
increases for dependants
  adults, 1.297–1.307
  child, 1.292–1.296
  person with care of children,
    1.306–1.307
  wife, 1.299–1.302
persons residing together, 3.149–3.153
rate
  age addition, 1.511
  increases for dependants, 1.512
widow's pension
  divorced woman of man over 65 in
    1948, for, 6.112–6.113
  entitlement conditions, 6.106–6.107
  widow of man over 65 in 1948, for,
    6.110–6.111
Category D retirement pensions
see also **Non-contributory benefits**
age addition
  generally, 1.289–1.291
  rate, 1.511
generally, 1.287–1.288
hospital in-patients, 3.77–3.78
rate
  age addition, 1.511
  generally, 1.511
  increases for dependants, 1.512
widow's pension, 6.108–6.109
Cellulitis
generally, 10.135
Central nervous system toxicity
generally, 10.135
Change of circumstances
reduced earnings allowance,
  10.229–10.230
Channel Islands
persons abroad, and, 3.137

Chemical agents
see **Industrial diseases**
Child benefit
adopted children, 1.629
apprentices, 1.629
care, 1.629
child in care, 1.629
child in detention, 1.629
child in full-time education, 1.629
civil partnership, 1.629
detention, 1.629
employed trainees, 1.629
entitlement, 1.463
exclusions
apprentices, 1.629
child in care, 1.629
child in detention, 1.629
employed trainees, 1.629
imprisoned child, 1.629
married child, 1.629
severely disabled child, 1.629
tax exempt persons, 1.629
full-time education, 1.629
imprisoned child, 1.629
increases for dependants, and
persons entitled treated as not entitled, 3.52–3.53
persons not entitled treated as entitled, 3.50–3.51
married child, 1.629
persons exempt from tax, 1.629
severely disabled child, 1.629
tax exempt persons, 1.629
widowed mother's allowance, 6.118–6.119
widowed parent's allowance, 6.120
Child dependants
adjustment of benefits, 3.91–3.92
contribution to cost, 3.54–3.55
dependency, and, 3.54–3.55
employment and support allowance, 9.5
generally, 1.292–1.294
increases of benefits, 1.292–1.296
overlapping benefits, 3.91–3.92
reduced contributions, 1.309–1.311
relevant earnings, 1.314–1.316
restrictions, 1.295–1.296
unemployability supplement, 1.586–1.587
Child maintenance
see **Maintenance**
Child Maintenance and Other Payments Act 2008
arrangement of sections, 1.856
commencement, 1.857
general note, 1.857–1.858
general provisions, 1.859–1.882
Child support
employment and support allowance
date on which to be treated as paid, 9.305
disregard of payments, 9.306
generally, 9.222
treatment, 9.303
weekly amount, 9.304

Child tax credit
employment and support allowance, 9.4
Childcare costs
computation of earnings, and, 3.35
Child's special allowance
see also **Contributory benefits**
adjustment
persons abroad, 3.120–3.121
conditions
earnings factors, 1.49
general note, 1.507
generally, 1.48
miscellaneous provisions, 1.488
dependency, and, 3.54–3.55
earnings factors, 1.49
generally, 1.145
increases for dependants
generally, 1.292–1.296
relevant earnings, 1.314–1.316
persons abroad, and, 3.120–3.121
pre-1975 beneficiaries and contributors, 6.136
Chlamydiosis
generally, 10.135
Christmas bonus
definitions, 1.467
generally, 1.464–1.465
supplementary provisions, 1.466
Chronic beryllium disease
generally, 10.135
Chronic bronchitis
generally, 10.135
pneumoconiosis, and, 10.104–10.105
prescribed occupations, 10.198
transitional provision, 10.247
Chronic obstructive pulmonary disease
prescribed occupations, 10.198–10.200
Cirrhosis
generally, 10.135
Civil partners
retirement pensions
former, 1.119–1.120
generally, 1.117–1.118
survivors, 1.127–1.128
Civil Partnership Act 2004
consequential amendments
Order, by, 6.156–6.163
Civil partnerships
child benefit, 1.629
"Claimant commitment"
'new style' ESA
date of acceptance, 13.191–13.192
exceptions, 13.193–13.194
generally, 13.23–13.24
introduction, 13.7
method of acceptance, 13.191–13.192
Regulations, 13.191–13.194
Claimants
computation of earnings, 3.4
Claims
claimants' obligations, 10.8
computation of earnings, 3.4
definitions, 10.3

employers' obligations, 10.7
meaning, 3.4
notice of accidents, 10.6
particulars of accidents, 10.13
personal independence payments
  generally, 1.932–1.933
  payment after an interval, for,
    4.198–4.199
  reaching relevant age, after, 4.216–4.217
pre-October 1986
  disablement benefit, 10.218–10.219
  reduced earnings allowance, 10.232
vaccine damage payments, and
  armed forces, members of, 11.7
  disabled person's obligations, 11.5–11.6
  generally, 11.3
  pre-scheme, 11.8
  required information, 11.4
Class 3 contributions
appropriation, 2.56
crediting, 2.57
Clerical errors
vaccine damage payments, and, 1.22
Clinical commissioning groups
computation of earnings, 3.4
"Close relative"
computation of earnings, 3.4
employment and support allowance, 9.4
Cohabitation
generally, 3.149–3.153
Completion of tasks
see **Descriptors for incapacity**
Computation (earnings)
see also **Earnings**
care charges, 3.36
child care charges, 3.35
definitions, 3.4–3.5
disregards
  care charges, 3.36
  child care charges, 3.35
  generally, 3.33–3.34
employed earners
  date of payment, 3.18
  disregards, 3.33–3.36
  generally, 3.14–3.17
  introduction, 3.13
  net earnings, 3.24–3.26
  relevant earnings, 3.22–3.23
  weekly sums, 3.19–3.21
fractional sums, 3.12
general provisions, 3.6–3.7
introductory provisions
  calculation of earnings, 3.6–3.7
  notional income, 3.8–3.11
  rounding of fractions, 3.12
national insurance contributions, 3.31
net income
  employed earners, 3.24–3.26
  self-employed earners, 3.29–3.30
notional income
  determination methods, 3.11
  generally, 3.8–3.9
  unascertainable earnings, 3.10

Regulations
  definitions, 3.4–3.5
  employed earners, 3.13–3.26
  general provisions, 3.6–3.7, 3.33–3.38
  notional income, 3.8–3.11
  rounding of fractions, 3.12
  self-employed earners, 3.27–3.31
relevant earnings
  employed earners, 3.22–3.23
  self-employed earners, 3.28
rounding of fractions, 3.12
self-employed earners
  disregards, 3.33–3.36
  generally, 3.27
  national insurance contributions, 3.31
  net profit, 3.29–3.30
  relevant earnings, 3.28
  tax, 3.31
transitional provisions, 3.32
weekly sums, 3.19–3.21
"Concessionary payments"
employment and support allowance
  definition, 9.4
  generally, 9.440
Concrete masonry blocks
see **Occupational deafness**
Conditionality
see **Work-related requirements**
Conditions (entitlement)
bereavement allowance
  general note, 1.504–1.505
  generally, 1.486
bereavement payment, 1.485
child's special allowance
  general note, 1.507
  generally, 1.488
contribution-based employment and
    support allowance
  additional conditions, 1.806–1.810,
    9.22–9.32
  assessments, 1.747–1.752
  basic conditions, 1.710–1.721
contributory allowance
  definition, 1.710
  further entitlement after time-limiting,
    1.724–1.725
  generally, 1.722–1.723
definitions, 1.490
earnings factors, 1.49
employment and support allowance
  additional, 1.806–1.813
  assessments, 1.747–1.754
  conditionality, 1.755–1.768
  generally, 1.710–1.721
  Regulations, 9.20–9.42
general note
  coverage, 1.491–1.500
  division of responsibility, 1.492–1.495
  generally, 1.501–1.507
  satisfaction in early years, 1.508
generally, 1.48
income-based employment and support
    allowance

additional conditions, 1.811–1.813,
    9.33–9.42
assessments, 1.747–1.752
basic conditions, 1.710–1.721
income-related allowance
    definition, 1.710
maternity allowance
    general note, 1.503
    generally, 1.484
miscellaneous provisions, 1.482–1.490
retirement pensions
    general note, 1.504–1.505
    generally, 1.486
satisfaction in early years
    general note, 1.508
    generally, 1.489
short-term incapacity benefit
    general note, 1.501–1.502
    generally, 1.483
    satisfaction in early years, 1.508
unemployment benefit, 1.482
vaccine damage payments, and, 1.6–1.8
widowed mother's allowance
    general note, 1.504–1.505
    generally, 1.486
widowed parent's allowance
    general note, 1.504–1.505
    generally, 1.486
widow's pension
    general note, 1.504–1.505
    generally, 1.486
Connected conditions
  see **Assessment (disablement)**
Connection factor
  see **Assessment (disablement)**
Consciousness during waking moments
  see **Descriptors for incapacity**
Constant attendance allowance
assessment of disablement, and
    comment, 1.582
    generally, 1.571
generally, 1.406–1.408
increases, 10.37–10.41
Continental shelf
generally, 1.456–1.457
persons abroad, and, 3.136
Contract of service
  see **Contracts of employment**
Contracted out schemes
additional pension, and, 1.521–1.532
Contracting out
'new style' ESA, 13.44–13.45
'old style' ESA
    generally, 1.766–1.767
    work-focused interviews, 9.163–9.164
    work-related activity, 9.609
Contracts of employment
categories of earners, 1.40
meaning, 1.460
Contribution-based employment and
    support allowance
  see also **Employment and support**
    allowance ('old style')

additional conditions
    generally, 1.806–1.810
    introduction, 1.715
    national insurance, 9.20–9.22
    'relevant benefit year', 9.31–9.32
    youth, 9.23–9.30
amount
    deductions, 1.733–1.737
    generally, 1.726–1.732
    prescribed minimum, 1.745–1.746
basic conditions, 1.710–1.721
contribution credits, 2.5
contributions, and, 2.55
credits, 2.3
deductions
    councillors' allowances, 9.195–9.196,
      9.201–9.202
    date from which change in rate takes
      effect, 9.205–9.206
    date from which taken into account,
      9.203–9.204
    financial assistance scheme payments,
      9.193–9.194
    generally, 1.733–1.737
    non-weekly amounts, 9.207–9.208
    pension payments, 9.197–9.200
    permanent health insurance payments,
      9.191–9.192
    PPF periodic payments, 9.197–9.200
entitlement
    additional conditions, 1.806–1.810,
      9.22–9.32
    assessments, 1.747–1.752
    basic conditions, 1.710–1.721
    general, 1.715
    introduction, 1.711–1.714
    meaning, 2.3
    national insurance conditions,
      9.20–9.22
    'new style' ESA , and, 13.7
    overlapping benefits, and, 3.86
    relevant benefit year, 9.31–9.32
    supplementary provisions, 1.820–1.821
youth conditions
    claimants aged 20 or over but under 25,
      9.23–9.24
    full-time education, 9.29–9.30
    previous claimants, 9.25–9.26
    residence or presence, 9.27–9.28
Contribution-based jobseeker's
    allowance
contribution credits, 2.5
Contribution conditions
bereavement allowance
    general note, 1.504–1.505
    generally, 1.486
bereavement payment, 1.485
child's special allowance
    general note, 1.507
    generally, 1.488
coverage, 1.491–1.500
credits
  see also **Credits**

definitions, 2.3
generally, 2.4–2.43
definitions, 1.490
division of responsibility, 1.492–1.495
earnings factors, 1.49
general note
  coverage, 1.491–1.500
  division of responsibility, 1.492–1.495
  generally, 1.501–1.507
  satisfaction in early years, 1.508
generally, 1.48
home responsibilities protection,
  2.49–2.50
maternity allowance
  general note, 1.503
  generally, 1.484
miscellaneous provisions, 1.482–1.490
retirement pensions
  general note, 1.504–1.505
  generally, 1.486
satisfaction in early years
  general note, 1.508
  generally, 1.489
short-term incapacity benefit
  general note, 1.501–1.502
  generally, 1.483
  satisfaction in early years, 1.508
unemployment benefit, 1.482
vaccine damage payments, and, 1.6–1.8
widowed mother's allowance
  general note, 1.504–1.505
  generally, 1.486
widowed parent's allowance
  general note, 1.504–1.505
  generally, 1.486
widow's pension
  general note, 1.504–1.505
  generally, 1.486
Contribution credits
adoption pay period, 2.36–2.37
apprenticeship, termination of, 2.18–2.19
approaching pensionable age, 2.32–2.33
approved training, 2.10–2.11
bereavement allowance, 2.6–2.7
bereavement benefits, 2.25–2.26
carer's allowance, 2.12–2.13
carers, for
  additional period of allowance,
    2.80–2.81
  applications, 2.83–2.86
  definitions, 2.72
  disqualification, 2.81–2.82
  'engaged in caring', 2.76–2.77
  'foster parent', 2.74–2.75
  general note, 2.71
  generally, 1.51–1.52
  imprisonment, and, 2.81–2.82
  limit on award of child benefit,
    2.78–2.79
  provision of information, 2.85
  residence in GB, and, 2.81–2.82
  time limits for applications, 2.86
  transitional provision, 2.73

civil partners of armed forces personnel,
  2.40–2.43
contribution-bases jobseeker's allowance,
  2.29
custodial detention, 2.38–2.39
definitions, 2.3
disability element of working tax credit,
  2.14–2.15
education, and, 2.18–2.19
foster carers
  generally, 2.4–2.5
  imprisonment, 2.38–2.39
incapacity benefit
  generally, 2.31
  official error, following, 2.27
incapacity for work, 2.23–2.24
jury service, 2.34–2.35
maternity allowance, 2.8
maternity grant, 2.9
maternity pay period, 2.36–2.37
parents, for
  additional period of allowance,
    2.80–2.81
  applications, 2.83–2.86
  definitions, 2.72
  disqualification, 2.81–2.82
  'engaged in caring', 2.76–2.77
  'foster parent', 2.74–2.75
  generally, 1.51–1.52
  general note, 2.71
  imprisonment, and, 2.81–2.82
  limit on award of child benefit,
    2.78–2.79
  provision of information, 2.85
  residence in GB, and, 2.81–2.82
  time limits for applications, 2.86
  transitional provision, 2.73
persons approaching pensionable age,
  2.32–2.33
persons entitled to universal credit,
  2.31
relevant benefits, 2.5
retirement pensions
  generally, 2.6–2.7
  official error, following, 2.28
short-term incapacity benefit, 2.31
sickness benefit, 2.8
spouses of armed forces personnel,
  2.40–2.43
state pension, and, 1.673–1.674
termination of bereavement benefits,
  2.25–2.26
termination of education, 2.18–2.19
termination of training, 2.18–2.19
unemployment, 2.20–2.22
unemployment benefit, 2.8
universal credit recipients, 2.31
widowed mother's allowance, 2.6–2.7
widowed parent's allowance, 2.6–2.7
widow's pension, 2.6–2.7
working tax credit, 2.16–2.17
Contribution to cost
  see **Dependants**

Contributions
categories of earners, 1.37–1.40
earner, 1.41–1.43
earnings
  meaning, 1.41–1.43
  payments treated as, 1.44–1.45
remuneration, 1.44–1.45
"Contributory allowance"
definition, 1.710
further entitlement after time-limiting,
  1.724–1.725
generally, 1.722–1.723
Contributory benefits
adjustment
  hospital in-patients, 3.77–3.78
  persons abroad, 1.454–1.455
calculation of earnings
  disregards, 3.33–3.36
  employed earners, 3.13–3.26
  fractional sums, 3.12
  generally, 3.6–3.7
  notional income, 3.8–3.11
  rounding of fractions, 3.12
  self-employed earners, 3.27–3.31
child's special allowance, 1.145
conditions
  earnings factors, 1.49
  general note, 1.491–1.508
  generally, 1.48
  miscellaneous provisions, 1.482–1.490
disqualification, 1.434–1.441
earnings, 1.431–1.433
earnings factors, 1.49
graduated retirement benefit, 1.148–1.150
hospital in-patients, 3.77–3.78
incapacity benefit, 1.55
maternity allowance
  curtailment, 5.16–5.22
  earnings, 5.11–5.15
  entitlement, 5.3–5.8
  generally, 1.56–1.65
  work abroad, 5.8
meaning, 1.47
persons abroad, and, 1.454–1.455
rate, 1.509
retirement pensions
  category A, 1.97–1.116
  category B, 1.117–1.128
  generally, 1.95–1.96
  increase where entitlement deferred,
    1.136–1.138
  shared additional pension, 1.139–1.144
  special provisions, 1.130–1.133
  supplemental provisions, 1.135
special cases
  airmen, 1.450–1.451
  continental shelf operations,
    1.456–1.457
  Crown employment, 1.444–1.446
  Her Majesty's forces, 1.447–1.449
  mariners, 1.450–1.451
  married women, 1.452–1.453
  persons abroad, 1.454–1.455

  polygamous marriages, 1.458–1.459
  seafarers, 1.456–1.457
suspension, 1.434–1.441
types, 1.47
unemployment benefit, 1.54
widowers' benefits
  bereavement allowance, 1.81–1.82
  bereavement payment, 1.67–1.68
  long-term incapacity benefit, 1.89–1.94
  rates, 1.83–1.84
  retirement pensions, 1.121–1.122,
    1.127–1.128
  widowed parent's allowance, 1.79–1.80
widows' benefits
  bereavement allowance, 1.81–1.82
  bereavement payment, 1.67–1.68
  long-term incapacity benefit, 1.86–1.88
  retirement pensions, 1.121–1.122,
    1.127–1.128
  widowed mother's allowance, 1.70–1.73
  widowed parent's allowance, 1.79–1.80
  widows' payment, 1.67
  widow's pension, 1.74–1.78
**Contributory employment and support
  allowance**
  see **Contribution-based employment
    and support allowance**
Conversion decisions
after conversion phase
  application of other enactments,
    9.565–9.566
  change of circumstances before effective
    date, 9.567–9.566
  reduction of transitional addition,
    9.569–9.572
  termination of transitional addition,
    9.573
amount of ESA on conversion,
  9.549–9.550
appeals, 9.538
change of circumstances before effective
  date, 9.567–9.566
decisions, 9.545–9.562
definitions, 9.542–9.543
determining whether existing award
  qualifies
  application of certain enactments, 9.547
  generally, 9.546
disabled students and workers, 9.531
disapplication of enactments, 9.574
effective date, 9.559–9.560
eligible persons, 9.531
existing award
  meaning, 9.531
  non-qualifying, 9.536
  qualifying awards, 9.535
existing award does not qualify for
  conversion, that, 9.563–9.564
existing award qualifies for conversion,
  that, 9.561–9.562
general note
  conversion process, 9.532–9.539
  introduction, 9.529

legislative history, 9.530
personal scope, 9.531
Universal Credit cases, 9.540
legislative history, 9.530
meaning, 9.534
miscellaneous provisions, 9.575–9.580
modification of other legislation
after conversion phase, 9.585–9.591
general note, 9.539–9.540
making conversion decisions,
9.581–9.584
non-qualifying awards, 9.536
notice
general note, 9.532–9.533
generally, 9.545
personal scope, 9.531
persons affected, 9.544
process
appeals, 9.538
decision, 9.534
non-qualifying awards, 9.536
notice, 9.532–9.533
qualifying awards, 9.535
revision of decision, 9.537
supersession of decision, 9.537
qualifying existing awards
general note, 9.535
generally, 9.546
reduction of transitional addition
general rule, 9.569–9.570
increases for adult dependants, 9.572
increases for dependent children, 9.571
Regulations applying after conversion
phase, 9.592–9.593
relevant persons, 9.544
revision, 9.537
supersession, 9.537
termination of entitlement to disability
premium, 9.575
termination of transitional addition, 9.573
transitional addition
entitlement, 9.551–9.552
incapacity benefit, and, 9.553–9.554
income support, and, 9.555–9.556
reduction, 9.569–9.572
severe disablement allowance,
9.553–9.554
supplementary provisions, 9.557–9.558
termination, 9.573
Universal Credit cases, 9.540
Cooking test
see **Care component**
Co-ownership
employment and support allowance, 9.4
Coping with change
see **Descriptors for incapacity**
**Coping with social engagement/
situations**
see **Descriptors for incapacity**
Corneal dystrophy
generally, 10.135
Correction of errors
see **Clerical errors**

Councillors
see also **Councillors' allowances**
employment and support allowance, 9.4
Councillors' allowances
'new style' ESA
deduction, 13.239–13.240
generally, 13.233–13.234
'old style' ESA
calculation of income, 9.227–9.228
deduction, 9.201–9.202
generally, 9.195–9.196
meaning, 9.4
"Couple"
computation of earnings, 3.4
dependency, 3.72
Cramp
generally, 10.135
industrial injuries, 10.143
Credits
see **Contribution credits**
Crown employees
generally, 1.444–1.446
"Crown property"
computation of earnings, 3.4
Crown tenancies
employment and support allowance, 9.4
Curtailment
see **Maternity allowance**
Custody
child benefit, 1.629
contribution credits, 2.38–2.39
disqualification from benefit, 1.438
employment and support allowance,
9.378–9.379
Cutaneous larva migrans
generally, 10.135, 10.177
"Daily living activities"
assessment of ability to carry out,
4.174–4.176
bathing, 4.245
budgeting decisions, 4.254
consultation to determine if claimant has
ability to carry out, 4.186–4.187
definition, 1.943
descriptors, 4.232, 4.239–4.254
dressing, 4.247
evidence required for determining ability,
4.184–4.185
face to face engagement, 4.251–4.253
food preparation, 4.239–4.240
generally, 1.917–1.918
health condition monitoring, 4.242–4.244
incontinence, 4.246
information required for determining
ability, 4.184–4.185
introduction, 1.910
matters to be taken into account in
determining good reason,
4.188–4.189
nutrition, 4.241
reading signs, 4.250
redetermination of ability to carry out,
4.190–4.191

scoring, 4.177–4.178
therapy management, 4.242–4.244
toilet needs, 4.246
understanding signs, 4.250
undressing, 4.247
verbal communication, 4.248–4.249
washing and bathing, 4.245
Daily living component
definition, 1.943
employment and support allowance, 9.4
generally, 1.909–1.911
introduction, 1.906
overlapping benefits, 3.82
Date of development
see **Date of onset**
Date of onset
industrial injury benefits
determination, 10.66–10.73
transitional provisions, 10.133, 10.207
occupational deafness, 10.114–10.115
Day conditions
see **Care component**
Decisions reversing earlier decisions
see **Vaccine damage payments**
Decompression sickness
industrial injuries, 10.135
Deemed earnings factors
see **Category A retirement pension**
Deeming benefit
see **Dependants**
Deafness
appeals, 10.118–10.119
assessment of extent
binaural disablement, 10.205
generally, 10.121–10.122
relevant claims, 10.203–10.204
claims, 10.110–10.111
date of onset, 10.114–10.115
duration of assessment
commencement date, 10.123
generally, 10.116
further claims, 10.112–10.113
prescribed occupations
cutting concrete masonry blocks,
10.152
firearms training, 10.158
glass container manufacturer, 10.157
introduction, 10.146–10.149
metal founding/forging, 10.150
pneumatic percussive tool, 10.151
ships engine room, 10.156
shot-blasters, 10.159
textile manufacturing, 10.153
water jets, 10.155
weaving, 10.153
wood working, 10.154
reassessment of disablement, 10.120
supercession of decision, 10.117
time limits for claims, 10.108–10.109
Deductions
'new style' ESA
councillor's allowance, 13.239–13.240
exempt payments, 13.237–13.238

pension payments, 13.235–13.236
PPF payments, 13.235–13.236
statutory basis, 13.14–13.15
'old style' ESA
councillors' allowances, 9.195–9.196,
9.201–9.202
date from which change in rate takes
effect, 9.205–9.206
date from which taken into account,
9.203–9.204
financial assistance scheme payments,
9.193–9.194
non-weekly amounts, 9.207–9.208
pension payments, 9.197–9.200
permanent health insurance,
9.191–9.192
PPF periodic payments, 9.197–9.200
Deferred pensions
gender recognition, 1.698–1.699
generally, 1.136–1.138
miscellaneous provisions, 1.546–1.560
Regulations
election provisions, 6.10–6.13
generally, 6.4–6.6
shared additional pension
generally, 1.144
miscellaneous provisions, 1.561–1.567
Department for Work and Pensions
change of name, 1.1073
Department of Social Security
change of name, 1.1073
Dependants
adjustment
hospital in-patients, 3.77–3.78
overlapping benefits, 3.91–3.102
persons abroad, 3.138–3.141
adult dependants
apportionment of pension payments,
3.61
contribution to cost, 3.64–3.65
earnings rules, 3.58–3.60
incapacity benefit, 1.308
reduced contributions, 1.309–1.311
restriction, 1.312–1.313
retirement pensions, 1.299–1.307
short-term benefits, 1.297–1.298
allocation of contributions, 3.46–3.47
calculation of earnings
disregards, 3.33–3.36
employed earners, 3.13–3.26
fractional sums, 3.12
generally, 3.6–3.7
notional income, 3.8–3.11
rounding of fractions, 3.12
self-employed earners, 3.27–3.31
carer's allowance, 1.317–1.319
child benefit
persons entitled treated as not entitled,
3.52–3.53
persons not entitled treated as entitled,
3.50–3.51
child dependants
contribution to cost, 3.54–3.55

generally, 1.292–1.294
reduced contributions, 1.309–1.311
relevant earnings, 1.314–1.316
restrictions, 1.295–1.296
child's special allowance
generally, 1.292–1.296
relevant earnings, 1.314–1.316
conditions
allocation of contributions,
3.46–3.47
deeming rules, 3.48–3.49
family fund test, 3.44–3.45
generally, 3.42–3.43
contribution to cost
adult dependants, 3.64–3.65
child dependants, 3.54–3.55
deeming benefit
abatement, 3.48–3.49
disability living allowance, 1.327–1.329
disqualification
see also **Disqualification (benefits)**
generally, 1.434–1.441
earnings, 1.431–1.433
family fund test, 3.44–3.45
fluctuating earnings, and, 1.324–1.326
generally, 3.42–3.43
hospital in-patients, 3.77–3.78
incapacity benefit
child dependants, 1.292–1.296
generally, 1.308
reduced contributions, 1.309–1.311
relevant earnings, 1.314–1.316
maintenance, 3.42–3.43
maternity allowance
generally, 1.297–1.298
reduced contributions, 1.309–1.311
relevant earnings, 1.314–1.316
mesothelioma, 1.859
overlapping benefits
adult dependant, 3.93
carer's allowance, 3.97
child dependant, 3.91–3.92
more than one dependant, 3.98
part week, for, 3.99
personal benefits payable, 3.94–3.95
priority, 3.100
severe disablement allowance, 3.97
training allowance, 3.96
person with care of children
generally, 3.62–3.63
retirement pension, 1.306–1.307
persons abroad, and
child dependants, 3.140–3.141
generally, 3.138–3.139
persons maintaining, 1.442–1.443
pneumoconiosis scheme, 1.32
rate, 1.512
Regulations (1977)
adult dependants, 3.58–3.65
child dependants, 3.54–3.55
dependency, 3.42–3.53
increase of benefits, 3.66–3.73
relevant earnings

apportionment of pension payments,
3.61
generally, 1.314–1.316
retirement pensions
adults, 1.297–1.307
child, 1.292–1.296
husband, 1.303–1.305
person with care of children,
1.306–1.307
reduced contributions, 1.309–1.311
relevant earnings, 1.314–1.316
wife, 1.299–1.302
severe disablement allowance,
1.317–1.319
special cases
airmen, 1.450–1.451
continental shelf operations,
1.456–1.457
Crown employment, 1.444–1.446
Her Majesty's forces, 1.447–1.449
mariners, 1.450–1.451
persons abroad, 1.454–1.455
polygamous marriages, 1.458–1.459
seafarers, 1.456–1.457
short-term benefits, 1.297–1.298
suspension, 1.434–1.441
trade disputes, effect of, 1.320–1.323
transitional provision, 3.69
unemployability supplement
generally, 1.586–1.588
introduction, 1.599
'widowed mother's allowance
generally, 1.297–1.307
relevant earnings, 1.314–1.316
Dermatitis
generally, 10.135
prescribed occupations, 10.191
Descriptors for incapacity
see also **Employment and support
allowance**
absence of loss of control, 9.414
amendments effected on January 28,
2013, 9.399
appropriateness of behaviour, 9.425
attention to detail, 9.401–9.402
awareness of everyday hazards, 9.418
background, 9.394
consciousness during waking moments,
9.415
coping with change, 9.420
coping with social engagement,
9.422–9.424
decision-making, 9.406
evidence, 9.401–9.402
general note, 9.394–9.406
getting about, 9.421
initiating and completing personal action,
9.419
interpretation of Schedule
decision-making and recording, 9.406
evidence, 9.401–9.402
reasonableness, 9.403–9.405
learning tasks, 9.417

lists
  mental, cognitive and intellectual
      function, 9.393
  physical disabilities, 9.393
making self understood, 9.411
manual dexterity, 9.411
mental, cognitive and intellectual function
  appropriateness of behaviour, 9.425
  awareness of everyday hazards, 9.418
  coping with change, 9.420
  coping with social engagement,
      9.422–9.424
  generally, 9.416
  getting about, 9.421
  initiating and completing personal
      action, 9.419
  learning tasks, 9.417
mobilising unaided, 9.407
navigation and maintaining safety, 9.413
physical disabilities
  absence of loss of control, 9.414
  consciousness during waking moments,
      9.415
  making self understood, 9.411
  manual dexterity, 9.411
  mobilising unaided, 9.407
  navigation and maintaining safety,
      9.413
  picking up and moving or transferring,
      9.410
  reaching, 9.409
  repeatedly mobilise, 9.407
  standing and sitting, 9.408
  understanding communication, 9.412
picking up and moving or transferring,
    9.410
preliminary note, 9.392
reaching, 9.409
reasonableness, 9.403–9.405
record of decisions, 9.406
repeatedly mobilise, 9.407
revisions to Schedule 2, 9.395–9.397
standing and sitting, 9.408
structure of Schedule 2, 9.398
understanding communication, 9.412
Detained persons
personal independence payments
  generally, 1.930–1.931
  Regulations, 4.226–4.227
Detention
child benefit, 1.629
contribution credits, 2.38–2.39
disqualification from benefit, 1.438
employment and support allowance,
    9.378–9.379
**Diffuse Mesothelioma Payment Scheme
    2014**
see also **Mesothelioma**
additional documents or evidence
  duty of applicants, 12.37
  request to applicants, 12.36
  request to third parties, 12.38
  scheme administrator's powers, 12.35

administration
  assistance to people to bring
      proceedings, 12.52
  duties of administrator, 12.28–12.29
  initiation of review, 12.48
  powers of administrator, 12.35
  statutory basis, 1.954
appeals
  general, 12.51
  statutory basis, 1.953
applications
  additional documents, 12.35–12.38
  contents, 12.58–12.62
  dependant of person with diffuse
      mesothelioma, by, 12.55
  determination, 12.41–12.43
  general, 12.33
  key issues, 12.61
  notice for person to cease to be eligible
      dependant, 12.40
  person with diffuse mesothelioma, by,
      12.55
  statutory basis, 1.952
  supporting evidence, 12.62
  time limits, 12.34
  withdrawal, 12.39
assistance to people to bring proceedings
  general, 12.52
  statutory basis, 1.956
circumstances in which person is to be
      treated as unable to bring an
      action, 12.32
conditions on payments, 12.42
definitions
  Regulations, 12.26
  statute, 1.960
dependant of person with diffuse
      mesothelioma
  applications, 12.55
  eligibility, 1.949–1.950
determination of applications
  conditions on payments, 12.42
  general, 12.41
  notice, 12.43
eligibility
  dependants, 1.949–1.950
  duty of applicants, 12.37
  first diagnosis, 12.30–12.31
  person with diffuse mesothelioma,
      1.948
  statutory basis, 1.948–1.950
  unable to bring an action, 12.32
establishment
  generally, 12.27
  statutory basis, 1.947
exclusion of payments under other
      legislation, 1.958
first diagnosis
  general, 12.54
  introduction, 12.30–12.31
general note, 12.23–12.23A
key issues, 12.61
levy

definitions, 12.65
determination of relative market share
    and amounts, 12.66
information, 12.67
publication, 12.67
recovery of payment amount, 12.70
reference period, 12.67
Regulations, 12.64–12.70
requirement to pay a share of total
    amount, 12.66
notice for person to cease to be eligible
    dependant, 12.40
notice of determination, 12.43
payments
    amount, 12.63
    conditions on making, 12.42
    general, 12.44–12.45
    recovery, 12.46
    statutory basis, 1.951
procedure
    general, 12.33–12.43
    statutory basis, 1.952
recovery of payments
    general, 12.46
    statutory basis, 1.957
Regulations
    conditions and amounts, 12.21–12.63
    levy, 12.64–12.70
Regulations 2014
    arrangement, 12.21
    citation, 12.24
    commencement, 12.25
    definitions, 12.26
    general note, 12.23–12.23A
    general provisions, 12.27–12.53
    introduction, 12.22
    review, 12.53
    schedules, 12.54–12.63
repayment
    general, 12.46
    statutory basis, 1.957
requested material, 12.36
reviews
    conduct, 12.50
    initiation by scheme administrator,
        12.48
    other circumstances, 12.49
    request of applicant, 12.47
    statutory basis, 1.953
specified payments
    general, 12.57
    introduction, 12.30–12.31
statutory basis
    citation, 1.963
    commencement, 1.961
    definitions, 1.960
    eligibility, 1.948–1.950
    establishment of scheme, 1.947
    extent, 1.962
    general note, 1.945–1.946
    payments, 1.951
    procedure, 1.952
    recovery of payments, 1.956–1.957

relationship with other legislation,
    1.958
reviews and appeals, 1.953
scheme administration, 1.954
supporting evidence, 12.62
unable to bring an action, 12.32
withdrawal of applications, 12.39
Diffuse Mesothelioma Scheme 2008
appeals against determinations
    First-tier Tribunal, to, 1.873–1.874
    Social Security Commissioner, to,
        1.875–1.876
conditions of entitlement, 1.861–1.863
'dependant', 1.859
determination of claims
    appeals, 1.873–1.876
    generally, 1.864–1.867
    reconsideration, 1.868–1.872
'diffuse mesothelioma', 1.859
general note, 1.857–1.858
general provision, 1.859–1.860
minors, 1.877–1.878
persons lacking capacity, 1.877–1.878
reconsideration of determinations,
    1.868–1.872
recovery of benefits, and, 1.881–1.882
regulations, 1.879–1.880
self-employed, 1.857–1.858
time limits, 1.865–1.866
Diptheria
see also **Vaccine damage payments**
appeals, 1.16–1.17
conditions of entitlement, 1.8–1.11
determination of claims, 1.12–1.18
error correction, 1.22
finality of decisions, 1.23–1.24
fraudulent statements, 1.27
generally, 1.2–1.7
payment, 1.19–1.21
setting aside decisions, 1.22
Disability element
working tax credit, 2.14–2.15
Disability living allowance
see also **Non-contributory benefits**
abolition, 1.935–1.936
care component
    care home residents, 4.57–4.62
    generally, 1.196–1.249
    hospital in-patients, 4.53–4.56
    medical expenses paid from public
        funds, 4.63–4.64
    prescribed circumstance, 4.65–4.66
    private nursing home residents,
        4.57–4.62
    qualifying period, 4.47–4.48
    renal failure sufferers, 4.49–4.52
care home residents
    exemption, 4.61–4.62
    generally, 4.57–4.59
    relevant persons, 4.60, 4.122
entitlement
    care component, 4.47–4.66
    generally, 1.190–1.195

mobility component, 4.67–4.100
persons aged 65 or over, 4.40–4.44
persons residing in GB to whom EU
        Regulation applies, 4.36–4.37
persons residing in EEA state or
        Switzerland, 4.38
refugees, 4.39
residence, 4.34–4.35
hospital in-patients (care component)
    exemption, 4.61–4.62
    generally, 4.53–4.56
    relevant persons, 4.60, 4.122
hospital in-patients (mobility component)
    adjustment, 4.100
    exemption, 4.99
    generally, 4.97–4.98
invalid vehicle scheme
    generally, 1.275–1.277
    Regulations, 4.101, 4.116–4.121
medical expenses paid from public funds
    exemption, 4.64
    generally, 4.63
mobility component
    artificial prosthesis, 4.90
    arrested development, 4.91
    assessment of degree of disablement,
        4.88
    double amputees, 4.86
    entitlement, 4.69–4.96
    exertion, 4.85
    generally, 1.250–1.274
    inability to walk, 4.76–4.84
    incomplete physical development,
        4.91
    invalid carriages, 1.275–1.277, 4.101
    hospital in-patients, 4.97–4.100
    oxygen requirement, 4.85
    physical condition, 4.71–4.75
    physical disablement, 4.71–4.75
    physical restraint, 4.92–4.94
    qualifying period, 4.67–4.68
    virtually unable to walk, 4.84
national insurance numbers, 4.33
persons aged 65 or over
    entitlement, 4.40–4.44, 4.102–4.115
    generally, 1.278–1.280
persons residing in GB to whom EU
        Regulation applies, 4.36–4.37
persons residing in EEA state or
        Switzerland, 4.38
private nursing home residents
    exemption, 4.61–4.62
    generally, 4.57–4.59
    relevant persons, 4.60, 4.122
rate, 4.45
refugees, 4.39
renal failure sufferers, 4.49–4.52
supplementary provisions,
        1.281–1.285
Disability premiums
employment and support allowance
    generally, 9.437–9.438
    weekly amount, 9.442

Disability working allowance
increases for dependants, and,
        1.327–1.329
Disabled persons' tax credit
additional pensions, 1.107–1.128
"Disablement"
accident, 1.399
aggregation of percentages, 10.87–10.88
assessment of extent
    comment, 1.574–1.576
    generally, 1.568
checklist of questions, 1.398
connected conditions, 10.21
connection factor, 10.22
constant attendance allowance
    comment, 1.582
    generally, 1.571
differences of expert medical opinion,
        1.401
disablement benefit
    comment, 1.578–1.581
    generally, 1.570
dominant hand, 1.577
employed earner, 1.399
extent, 10.85–10.86
generally, 1.395–1.405
loss of physical or mental faculty, 1.400
method
    comment, 1.574–1.576
    generally, 1.568
miscellaneous provisions, 1.568–1.582
multiple industrial accidents, 10.25
other effective cause, 10.22–10.24
partly relevant conditions, 10.21
prescribed degrees of disablement
    generally, 10.52–10.53
    introduction, 10.26–10.28
principles, 10.19–10.28
resulting disablement, 1.402
rounding of percentages, 10.89
severe disablement allowance, 1.569
Disablement benefit
see **Industrial injuries disablement
        benefit**
Disablement gratuity
amount, 10.30
generally, 1.591
introduction, 1.599
rate, 1.515
special hardship payments, 10.35
weekly value, 10.31
Disablement pension
see also **Industrial injuries benefits**
adjustment
    persons abroad, 3.131
aggregation of percentages, 10.87–10.88
assessment of disablement
    aggregation of percentages,
        10.87–10.88
    connected conditions, 10.21
    connection factor, 10.22
    extent, 10.85–10.86
    generally, 1.395–1.405

miscellaneous provisions, 1.568–1.582
multiple industrial accidents, 10.25
other effective cause, 10.22–10.24
partly relevant conditions, 10.21
prescribed degrees, 10.26–10.28
principles, 10.19–10.28
rounding of percentages, 10.89
connected conditions, 10.21
connection factor, 10.22
constant attendance
  assessment of disablement, 1.568, 1.582
  generally, 1.406–1.408
  increases, 10.37–10.41
exceptionally severe disablement, 1.409–1.411
generally, 1.395–1.405
hospital treatment, during
  generally, 1.592
  introduction, 1.599
increases
  constant attendance, 1.406–1.408, 10.37
  generally, 1.406–1.411
  hospital treatment, during, 1.592
  multiple industrial accidents, 10.25
  other effective cause, 10.22–10.24
  partly relevant conditions, 10.21
  persons abroad, 3.131
  persons residing together, 3.149–3.153
  prescribed degrees, 10.26–10.28
  rate, 1.514–1.515, 10.55
  rounding of percentages, 10.89
Disqualification (benefits)
absence abroad
  see also **Persons abroad**
  generally, 1.437
generally, 1.434–1.436
imprisonment, 1.438
'new style' ESA
  claimant not having limited capability for work, 13.290–13.291
  exemptions, 13.292–13.293
  imprisonment, and, 13.292–13.295
  misconduct, for, 13.286–13.287
  'person in hardship', 13.288–13.289
  Regulations, 13.286–13.295
  statute, 13.48–13.52
'old style' ESA
  exceptions for imprisonment, 9.376–9.379
  generally, 9.361–9.367
  'person in hardship', 9.368–9.373
  statutory provisions, 1.771–1.773
  treating claimant as not having limited capability for work, 9.374–9.375
reciprocal agreements, 1.439–1.441
Domestic violence
'new style' ESA, 13.201–13.202
Double amputees
see **Mobility component**
Dressing
see **Personal independence payments**

Drug addiction
jobseeker's allowance, 1.885
'new style' ESA, 13.75
'old style' ESA, 1.814
Dysbarism
industrial injuries, 10.135
Dystrophy of cornea
generally, 10.135
"Earner"
categories, 1.37–1.40
meaning, 1.41–1.43
Earnings
calculation
  disregards, 3.33–3.36
  employed earners, 3.13–3.26
  fractional sums, 3.12
  generally, 3.6–3.7
  notional income, 3.8–3.11
  rounding of fractions, 3.12
  self-employed earners, 3.27–3.31
calculation (employed earners)
  date of payment, 3.18
  generally, 3.14–3.17
  introduction, 3.13
  net earnings, 3.24–3.26
  notional income, 3.8–3.11
  relevant earnings, 3.22–3.23
  rounding of fractions, 3.12
  weekly sums, 3.19–3.21
definition, 3.4
disregards
  care charges, 3.36
  child care charges, 3.35
  generally, 3.33–3.34
earnings factors
  conditions, and, 1.47
  credits, 1.103
  deemed, 1.99–1.102
  generally, 1.97–1.98
employed earners
  date of payment, 3.18
  disregards, 3.33–3.36
  generally, 3.14–3.17
  introduction, 3.13
  net earnings, 3.24–3.26
  relevant earnings, 3.22–3.23
  weekly sums, 3.19–3.21
fractional sums, 3.12
generally, 3.6–3.7
maternity allowance
  average weekly amount, 5.15
  specified payments, 5.11–5.13
  specified period, 5.14
meaning
  definition, 3.4
  generally, 1.431–1.433
  termination payments, 1.41–1.43
notional income
  determination methods, 3.11
  generally, 3.8–3.9
  unascertainable earnings, 3.10
payments treated as, 1.44–1.45
rounding of fractions, 3.12

self-employed earners
  disregards, 3.33–3.36
  generally, 3.27
  national insurance contributions, 3.31
  net profit, 3.29–3.30
  relevant earnings, 3.28
  tax, 3.31
unemployability supplement
  generally, 1.589
  introduction, 1.599
Education
  carer's allowance, 4.133
  child benefit, 1.629
  contribution credits, 2.18–2.191
  employment and support allowance,
    9.39–9.40
Elderly persons
  see also **Non-contributory benefits**
  carer's allowance
    generally, 4.153
    men attaining 65 before October 1994,
      4.154
    treated as entitled, 4.151
    women attaining 65 before October
      1994, 4.152
  disability living allowance
    entitlement, 4.40–4.44, 4.102–4.115
    generally, 1.278–1.280
  retirement pensions
    age addition, 1.289–1.291
    category C, 1.287–1.288
    category D, 1.287–1.288
Emergencies
  industrial injuries benefit, 1.383–1.387
Emphysema
  generally, 10.135
  pneumoconiosis, and, 10.104–10.105
  prescribed occupations, 10.198
  transitional provision, 10.247
"Employed earner"
  calculation of earnings
    date of payment, 3.18
    disregards, 3.33–3.36
    generally, 3.14–3.17
    introduction, 3.13
    net earnings, 3.24–3.26
    notional income, 3.8–3.11
    relevant earnings, 3.22–3.23
    rounding of fractions, 3.12
    weekly sums, 3.19–3.21
  carer's allowance
    generally, 1.156
    Regulations, 4.138–4.141
  date of payment, 3.18
  definition
    categories of earners, 1.33, 1.460
    computation of earnings, 3.4
  disregards
    care charges, 3.36
    child care charges, 3.35
    generally, 3.33–3.34
  employment and support allowance
    calculation, 9.233–9.234

  generally, 9.241–9.242
  net earnings, 9.243–9.244
generally, 3.14–3.17
introduction, 3.13
net earnings, 3.24–3.26
'new style' ESA
  deduction of tax and contributions,
    13.270–13.271
  earnings, 13.262–13.263
  generally, 13.254–13.255
  net earnings, 13.264–13.265
'old style' ESA
notional income
  determination methods, 3.11
  generally, 3.8–3.9
  unascertainable earnings, 3.10
relevant earnings, 3.22–3.23
rounding of fractions, 3.12
weekly sums, 3.19–3.21
Employed trainees
  see **Trainees**
Employees
  see **Employed earners**
Employers' transport
  see **Industrial injuries benefit**
**Employment and support allowance
  ('new style')**
  see also **Employment and support
    allowance ('old style')**
  absence from Great Britain
    generally, 13.277–13.278
    medical treatment, for, 13.281–13.282
    member of family of service personnel,
      13.284–13.285
    NHS treatment abroad, for,
      13.283–13.284
    short period, 13.279–13.280
  additional conditions
    national insurance, 13.67–13.69
    'relevant benefit week', 13.71
    youth, 13.70
  adoption pay, and, 13.249–13.250
  amounts
    adoption pay, 13.249–13.250
    councillor's allowance, 13.233–13.234,
      13.239–13.240
    dates from which change in rate takes
      effect, 13.243–13.244
    dates from which payment to be taken
      into account, 13.241–13.242
    deductions, 13.235–13.240
    exempt payments, 13.237–13.238
    Financial Assistance Scheme,
      13.231–13.232
    general, 13.12–13.13
    income-related, 13.16
    maternity pay, and, 13.247–13.248
    paternity pay, and, 13.251–13.253
    payment other than weekly,
      13.245–13.246
    pension payments, 13.235–13.236
    permanent health insurance,
      13.229–13.230

PPF payments, 13.235–13.236
prescribed sums, 13.225–13.226
Regulations, 13.225–13.253
SAP, and, 13.249–13.250
SMP, and, 13.247–13.248
SPP, and, 13.251–13.253
special cases, 13.227–13.228
statutory basis, 13.12–13.13
appeals against decisions, 13.275–13.276
armed forces
    absence from Great Britain of member
        of family, 13.284–13.285
    limited capability for work,
        13.158–13.159
    prescribed establishments and
        organisations, 13.305–13.307
assessment phase
    duration, 13.115–13.116
    general note, 13.116
    generally, 13.115–13.116
    previous claimants, 13.117–13.118
    terminally ill claimants, 13.119–13.120
claimant commitment
    date of acceptance, 13.191–13.192
    exceptions, 13.193–13.194
    generally, 13.23–13.24
    introduction, 13.7
    method of acceptance, 13.191–13.192
    Regulations, 13.191–13.194
claimant responsibilities
    claimant commitment, 13.191–13.194
    definitions, 13.186–13.187
    domestic violence, where,
        13.201–13.202
    dual entitlement, 13.188–13.189
    exempt persons, 13.197–13.198
    no work-related requirements, where,
        13.197–13.198
    persons only subject to interview
        requirement, 13.199–13.200
    purpose of work-focused interviews,
        13.195–13.196
    sanction ceases to apply, 13.190
compliance with requirements,
        13.39–13.40
conditions of entitlement
    national insurance, 13.121–13.124
    'relevant benefit year', 13.133–13.134
    relevant earnings, 13.121–13.124
    youth, 13.125–13.132
connected requirements, 13.35–13.36
consequential amendments, 13.101
contracting out, 13.44–13.45
contribution-based benefit, as, 13.7
councillor's allowance
    deduction, 13.239–13.240
    generally, 13.233–13.234
dates from which change in rate takes
        effect, 13.243–13.244
dates from which payment to be taken
        into account, 13.241–13.242
deductions
    councillor's allowance, 13.239–13.240

exempt payments, 13.237–13.238
pension payments, 13.235–13.236
PPF payments, 13.235–13.236
statutory basis, 13.14–13.15
definitions
    Regulations, 13.110–13.112
    statute, 13.57–13.58
delegation, 13.44–13.45
disqualification
    claimant not having limited capability
        for work, 13.290–13.291
    exemptions, 13.292–13.293
    imprisonment, and, 13.292–13.295
    misconduct, for, 13.286–13.287
    'person in hardship', 13.288–13.289
    Regulations, 13.286–13.295
    statute, 13.48–13.52
domestic violence, and, 13.201–13.202
drug dependency, 13.75
duration, 13.8–13.9
effect of work on entitlement
    claimants receiving regular treatment,
        13.184–13.185
    exempt work, 13.182–13.183
    generally, 13.178–13.179
    limited capability for work, and,
        13.180–13.181
    Regulations, 13.178–13.185
employed earner's income
    deduction of tax and contributions,
        13.270–13.271
    earnings, 13.262–13.263
    generally, 13.254–13.255
    net earnings, 13.264–13.265
entitlement
    amount, 13.12–13.13
    conditions, 13.121–13.134
    duration, 13.8–13.9
    generally, 13.6–13.7
    time-limiting, after, 13.10–13.11
failure for no good reason
    'for no good reason', 13.43
    generally, 13.41–13.42
'family', 13.111
Financial Assistance Scheme, and,
        13.231–13.232
financial provisions, 13.61–13.63
'for no good reason', 13.43
general note
    Regulations, 13.105–13.106
    statute, 13.4
hardship payments, 13.46
'health care professional', 13.111
Her Majesty's Forces, 13.305–13.307
hospital in-patients, 13.146–13.147
imposition of requirements, 13.37–13.38
imprisonment, and
    disqualification, 13.292–13.293
    suspension of payment,
        13.294–13.295
income
    date on which treated as paid,
        13.258–13.259

deduction of tax and contributions,
13.270–13.271
earnings of employed earners,
13.262–13.263
employed earner's earnings,
13.254–13.255, 13.262–13.265
other than earnings, 9.233–9.234,
9.259–9.270
self-employed earners earnings,
13.256–13.257, 13.270–13.271
tax deduction, 13.270–13.271
weekly amount, 13.260–13.261
income-related
absence from Great Britain, 13.84
advance award, 13.17
amount, 13.16
infectious persons, 13.137
limited capability for work
additional circumstances,
13.162–13.163
assessment, 13.308–13.309
claimants receiving regular treatment,
13.148–13.149
claimants treated as having, 13.137
cognitive function, 13.308–13.309
contaminated persons, 13.137
determination, 13.135–13.136
excepted claimants, 13.158–13.159
exceptional circumstances,
13.154–13.155
failure to provide required information,
13.140–13.141
good cause, and, 13.144–13.145
hospital in-patients, 13.146–13.147
infectious persons, 13.137
information required, 13.138–13.141
intellectual function, 13.308–13.309
limited capability at start of day,
13.150–13.151
medical examinations, 13.142–13.143
mental function, 13.308–13.309
night workers, 13.152–13.153
physical disabilities, 13.308–13.309
pregnant women, 13.137
Regulations, 13.135–13.163
required information, 13.138–13.141
service personnel, and, 13.158–13.159
supplementary provisions,
13.308–13.309
terminally ill claimants, 13.137
training courses, and, 13.158–13.159
treatment of claimant at end of period
covered by evidence,
13.160–13.161
treatment of claimant pending
determination, 13.156–13.157
limited capability for work-related activity
assessment, 13.310–13.311
claimants treated as having,
13.166–13.167
determination, 13.164–13.165
failure to provide required information,
13.172–13.173

good cause, and, 13.176–13.177
information required, 13.170–13.173
medical examinations, 13.174–13.175
pregnant women, 13.166–13.167
Regulations, 13.164–13.177
relevant linked cases, 13.168–13.169
required information, 13.170–13.173
supplementary provisions,
13.310–13.311
terminally ill claimants, 13.166–13.167
linking period, 13.273–13.274
maternity pay, and, 13.247–13.248
medical examinations
limited capability for work,
13.142–13.143
limited capability for work-related
activity, 13.174–13.175
medical treatment
absence from Great Britain,
13.281–13.284
definition, 13.111
periods of less than a week, 13.304
member of family of service personnel,
13.284–13.285
national insurance condition
generally, 13.121–13.122
relaxation, 13.123–13.124
'relevant benefit year', 13.133–13.134
statutory basis, 13.67–13.69
night workers
limited capability for work,
13.152–13.153
occupational pension schemes, 13.14
Parliamentary control, 13.59–13.60
'part-time employment', 13.111
'partner', 13.111
paternity pay, and, 13.251–13.253
'pay period', 13.111
pension payments
Regulations, 13.235–13.236
statutory basis, 13.14
periods of less than a week
amount payable, 13.296–13.297
medical treatment, and, 13.304
modification in calculation of income,
13.300–13.301
reduction in certain cases,
13.302–13.303
relevant week, 13.298–13.299
permanent health insurance
definition, 13.111
generally, 13.229–13.230
persons dependent on drugs, 13.75
persons subject to no work-related
requirements, 13.29–13.30
'polygamous marriage', 13.111
PPF periodic payments
definition, 13.14
generally, 13.235–13.236
pregnant women
limited capability for work, 13.137
limited capability for work-related
activity, 13.166–13.167

prescribed sums, 13.225–13.226
recovery of sums, 13.56
reduction of
    amount for each benefit week,
        13.217–13.218
    continuation of period, 13.212–13.213
    daily rate, 13.219–13.222
    definitions, 13.203
    fraud, and, 13.214
    low-level sanction, 13.206–13.207
    lower daily rate, 13.221–13.222
    lowest-level sanction, 13.208–13.209
    principles for calculating periods,
        13.204–13.205
    Regulations, 13.203–13.224
    start, 13.210–13.211
    suspension, 13.214
    termination, 13.215–13.216
    universal credit ends, where,
        13.223–13.224
Regulations
    definitions, 13.110–13.112
    general note, 13.105–13.106
    general provisions, 13.115–13.304
    rounding of fractions, 13.113–13.114
    schedules, 13.305–13.311
'relevant benefit week', 13.71
relevant earnings condition
    generally, 13.121–13.122
    relaxation, 13.123–13.124
'relevant benefit year', 13.133–13.134
relevant sections, 13.5
requirements
    compliance, 13.39–13.40
    connected, 13.35–13.36
    exempt persons, 13.29–13.34
    imposition, 13.37–13.38
    work-focused interview, 13.25–13.26
    work preparation, 13.27–13.28
    work-related, 13.21–13.22
'responsible carer', 13.186–13.187
'responsible foster parent', 13.186–13.187
rounding of fractions, 13.113–13.114
rule-making powers, 13.59–13.60
sanctions
    amount of reduction for each benefit
        week, 13.217–13.218
    continuation of reduction period,
        13.212–13.213
    daily reduction rate, 13.219–13.222
    definitions, 13.203
    'for no good reason', 13.43
    fraud, and, 13.214
    generally, 13.41–13.42
    low-level sanction, 13.206–13.207
    lower daily reduction rate,
        13.221–13.222
    lowest-level sanction, 13.208–13.209
    principles for calculating reduction
        periods, 13.204–13.205
    Regulations, 13.203–13.224
    start of the reduction, 13.210–13.211
    statutory basis, 13.41–13.43

suspension of reduction, 13.214
termination of reduction,
        13.215–13.216
universal credit ends, where,
        13.223–13.224
self-employed income
    deduction of tax and NICs,
        13.270–13.271
    'earnings', 13.266–13.267
    generally, 13.256–13.257
service personnel
    absence from Great Britain of member
        of family, 13.284–13.285
    limited capability for work,
        13.158–13.159
    prescribed establishments and
        organisations, 13.305–13.307
short period of absence, 13.279–13.280
statutory adoption pay, and
    generally, 13.249–13.250
    introduction, 13.53–13.54
statutory maternity pay, and
    generally, 13.247–13.248
    introduction, 13.53–13.54
statutory paternity pay, and
    generally, 13.251–13.253
    introduction, 13.53–13.54
supplementary provisions
    absence from Great Britain,
        13.82–13.84, 13.96
    advance claims, 13.89, 13.99
    armed forces personnel, 13.90, 13.100
    effect of work, 13.86, 13.98
    employment on ships, 13.83, 13.97
    exemption, 13.80
    information supplied as to social
        security, 13.89
    limited capability for work, 13.76
    limited capability for work-related
        activity, 13.85
    linking periods, 13.79, 13.94
    periods of less than a week, 13.78,
        13.93
    presence in Great Britain, 13.81–13.82,
        13.95
    reductions, 13.88
    Regulations, 13.272–13.285
    service personnel, 13.90, 13.100
    waiting days, 13.77, 13.92
terminally ill claimants
    limited capability for work, 13.137
    limited capability for work-related
        activity, 13.166–13.167
    'terminally ill', 13.111
'training', 13.111
training courses
    limited capability for work,
        13.158–13.159
'training allowance', 13.111
transition, 13.64–13.66, 13.102
treatment as benefit, 13.87
'voluntary organisation', 13.111
waiting days, 13.272–13.273

work-focused interview requirement
  generally, 13.25–13.26
  persons only subject to, 13.31–13.32
  purpose, 13.195–13.196
work preparation requirement
  generally, 13.27–13.28
  persons subject to, 13.33–13.34
work-related requirements
  connected requirements, 13.35–13.36
  exempt persons, 13.29–13.30
  generally, 13.21–13.22
  interview requirement, 13.25–13.26
  persons only subject to interview
    requirement, 13.31–13.32
  persons subject to preparation
    requirement, 13.33–13.34
  preparation requirement, 13.27–13.28
youth condition
  full-time education, 13.131–13.132
  generally, 13.125–13.126
  presence in Great Britain,
    13.129–13.130
  previous claimants, 13.127–13.128
  'relevant benefit year', 13.133–13.134
  residence, 13.129–13.130
  statutory basis, 13.70
**Employment and support allowance
  ('old style')**
absence from country, 1.834
action plans
  generally, 1.761–1.762
  Regulations, 9.156
additional conditions
  contributory allowance, 1.806–1.810
  income-related allowance, 1.811–1.813
  introduction, 1.715
additional conditions (contributory
  allowance)
  claimants aged 20 or over but under 25,
    9.23–9.24
  conversion decisions, 1.806
  full-time education, 9.29–9.30
  introduction, 1.715
  national insurance, as to, 1.806,
    1.807–1.808, 9.20–9.22
  previous claimants, 9.25–9.26
  relevant benefit week, 1.806
  relevant benefit year, 9.31–9.32
  residence or presence, 9.27–9.28
  youth, as to, 1.806, 1.809–1.810,
    9.23–9.30
additional conditions (income-related
  allowance)
  claimants not treated as receiving
    education, 9.37–9.38
  claimants treated as receiving
    education, 9.35–9.36
  courses of study, 9.39–9.40
  disability living allowance, and,
    9.41–9.42
  'education', 9.33–9.34
  generally, 1.811–1.813
  introduction, 1.715

advance awards
  generally, 9.338–9.339
  statutory provisions, 1.741–1.742,
    1.828
amendments
  Regulations (2017), 9.619–9.629
amount
  components, 9.443–9.444
  contributory allowance, 1.726–1.732
  deductions, 9.191–9.208
  entitlement to both allowances, where,
    1.743–1.744
  income-related allowance, 1.738–1.740
  persons from abroad, 9.187–9.188
  polygamous marriages, 9.183–9.184
  premiums, 9.435–9.442
  prescribed amounts, 9.179–9.190,
    9.434
  Regulations, 9.179–9.215
  statutory payments, 9.209–9.215
appeals against decision, and,
  9.342–9.348
armed forces, and, 9.390–9.391
assessment phase
  claimants appealing against decision,
    9.15
  duration, 9.11–9.12
  general note, 9.10
  generally, 9.11–9.12
  national insurance, and, 9.18–9.19
  previous claimants, 9.13–9.14
  relevant earnings, and, 9.18–9.19
  terminally ill claimants, 9.16–9.17
assessments
  limited capability for work, 1.747–1.749
  limited capability for work-related
    activity, 1.750–1.752
  report to Parliament, 1.753–1.754
basic conditions, 1.710–1.721
capital
  calculation, 9.273–9.280
  claimant's partner, of, 9.216–9.217
  diminishing notional capital rule,
    9.283–9.284
  disregards, 9.497–9.506
  generally, 1.769–1.770
  in the UK, 9.277–9.278
  income treated as, 9.275–9.276
  jointly held capital, 9.285–9.286
  limit, 9.271–9.272
  notional capital, 9.281–9.284
  outside the UK, 9.279–9.280
  Regulations, 9.271–9.287
  tariff income from capital, 9.287–9.288
capital treated as income, 9.261–9.262
carer premiums
  generally, 9.439
  weekly amount, 9.442
child maintenance, 9.290
child support
  date on which to be treated as paid,
    9.305
  disregard of payments, 9.306

generally, 9.222
treatment, 9.303
weekly amount, 9.304
claimants aged 20 or over but under 25,
   9.23–9.24
claimants appealing against decision,
   9.342–9.348
claimants not treated as receiving
   education, 9.37–9.38
claimants receiving regular treatment,
   9.145–9.146
claimants treated as receiving education,
   9.35–9.36
complete relief, 9.130
components, 9.443–9.444
conditionality
   see also **Conditionality**
   contracting out, 1.766–1.767
   Regulations, 9.147–9.178
   work-focused health-related
      assessments, 1.755–1.756
   work-focused interviews, 1.757–1.758
   work-related activity, 1.759–1.760
conditions
   additional conditions, 1.806–1.813,
      9.20–9.42
   assessments, 1.747–1.754
   basic conditions, 1.710–1.721
   contributory allowance, 1.806–1.810
   generally, 1.710–1.721
   income-related allowance, 1.811–1.813
conditions (contributory allowance)
   additional conditions, 1.806–1.810,
      9.20–9.32
   basic conditions, 1.710–1.721
conditions (income-related allowance)
   additional conditions, 1.811–1.813,
      9.33–9.42
   basic conditions, 1.710–1.721
contracting out, 1.766–1.767
contributions, and, 2.55
contributory allowance
   see also **Contribution-based**
      employment and support
      allowance
   amount, 1.726–1.732
   conditions, 1.806–1.810, 9.20–9.32
   deductions, 1.733–1.737
   general, 1.715
   supplementary provisions, 1.820–1.821
contribution credits, 2.5
conversion of other benefits to
   see also **Conversion decisions**
   after conversion phase, 9.565–9.573
   decisions, 9.545–9.564
   definitions, 9.542–9.543
   disapplication of enactments, 9.574
   general note, 9.529–9.539
   generally, 1.806
   miscellaneous provisions, 9.575–9.580
   relevant persons, 9.544
councillors' allowances
   deduction, 9.201–9.202

income, as, 9.227–9.228
   meaning, 9.195–9.196
courses of study, 9.39–9.40
credits, and, 2.3
de minimis principle, and, 9.131–9.132
deductions (contributory allowance)
   councillors' allowances, 9.195–9.196,
      9.201–9.202
   date from which change in rate takes
      effect, 9.205–9.206
   date from which taken into account,
      9.203–9.204
   financial assistance scheme payments,
      9.193–9.194
   non-weekly amounts, 9.207–9.208
   pension payments, 9.197–9.200
   permanent health insurance,
      9.191–9.192
   PPF periodic payments, 9.197–9.200
deemed entitlement, 1.778–1.779
deferral of requirement
   work-focused interviews, 9.157–9.158
definitions
   general, 1.799
   Part I, 1.784–1.785
   Regulations, 9.4–9.5
descriptors
   see also **Descriptors for incapacity**
   general note, 9.394–9.406
   lists, 9.393
   mental, cognitive and intellectual
      function, 9.416–9.425
   physical disabilities, 9.407–9.415
   preliminary note, 9.392
disability living allowance, and, 9.41–9.42
disability premiums
   generally, 9.437–9.438
   weekly amount, 9.442
disqualification
   exceptions for imprisonment,
      9.376–9.379
   generally, 9.361–9.367
   'person in hardship', 9.368–9.373
   statutory provisions, 1.771–1.773
   treating claimant as not having limited
      capability for work, 9.374–9.375
drugs-dependent claimants, 1.814
education, 9.39–9.40
effect of work on entitlement
   claimants receiving regular treatment,
      9.145–9.146
   complete relief, 9.130
   de minimis principle, and, 9.131–9.132
   exempt work, 9.141–9.144
   general, 9.127–9.132
   limited capability for work, and,
      9.139–9.140
   partial relief, 9.129
   partners of claimants not to be treated
      as in work, 9.137–9.138
   'remunerative work', 9.133–9.136
   trivial amounts of work, 9.131–9.132
employed earner's earnings

calculation, 9.233–9.234
generally, 9.241–9.242
net earnings, 9.243–9.244
enhanced disability premiums
generally, 9.438
weekly amount, 9.442
entitlement
both allowances, to, 1.743–1.744
deemed, 1.778–1.779
generally, 1.710–1.721
exempt work, 9.141–9.144
financial assistance scheme payments,
9.193–9.194
full-time education, 9.29–9.30
general note, 1.711–1.714
hardship payments
amount, 9.174
circumstances in which treated as in
hardship, 9.172
entitlement, 9.171
generally, 1.768
introduction, 9.4
matters to be taken into account, 9.173
housing costs
generally, 9.179–9.182
Regulations, 9.458–9.483, 9.616–9.618
incapacity benefit, and, 1.711
income
calculation, 9.229–9.236
capital treated as, 9.261–9.262
child maintenance, 9.220–9.221
child support, 9.222
claimant's partner, of, 9.216–9.217
councillors' allowances, 9.227–9.228
date on which treated as paid,
9.237–9.238
disregards, 9.484–9.496
employed earner's earnings,
9.233–9.234, 9.241–9.244
generally, 1.769–1.770
liable relative payments, 9.220–9.221
notional income, 9.263–9.270
other than earnings, 9.233–9.234,
9.259–9.270
participants in exempt work,
9.225–9.226
participants in self-employment route,
9.218–9.219, 9.251–9.258
pension payments, 9.227–9.228
polygamous marriage, and,
9.216–9.217
PPF periodic payments, 9.227–9.228
Regulations, 9.229–9.270
self-employed earners earnings,
9.235–9.236, 9.245–9.250
students 9.223–9.224
weekly amount, 9.239–9.240
income-related allowance
see also **Income-based employment
and support allowance**
advance award, 1.741–1.742
amount, 1.738–1.740
conditions, 1.811–1.813, 9.33–9.42

general, 1.715
supplementary provisions, 1.822
income support, and, 1.711
jobseekers' allowance, and, 1.716
liable relative payments
date on which to be treated as paid,
9.300–9.301
definitions, 9.289–9.290
disregard of payments, 9.293–9.294
generally, 9.220–9.221
period over which to be taken into
account, 9.295–9.298
treatment, 9.291–9.292
weekly amount, 9.299–9.300
limited capability for work
additional circumstances, 9.100–9.102
claimants receiving regular treatment,
9.68–9.69
claimants treated as having, 9.51–9.53
definition, 1.716–1.717
descriptors, 9.392–9.425
determination, 9.43–9.50
effect of work on entitlement, and,
9.139–9.140
excepted claimants, 9.97–9.98
exceptional circumstances, 9.74–9.90
failure to provide required information,
9.56–9.57
generally, 1.747–1.749
good cause, and, 9.62–9.63
hospital in-patients, 9.64–9.67
jobseeker's allowance, and, 9.96
limited capability at start of day,
9.70–9.71
medical examinations, 9.58–9.61
night workers, 9.72–9.73
pregnant women, 9.51–9.53
reasonable adjustments in workplace,
9.90
Regulations, 9.43–9.102
required information, 9.54–9.55
supplementary provisions, 1.815
terminally ill claimants, 9.51–9.53
training courses, and, 9.97–9.98
treatment of claimant at end of period
covered by evidence, 9.99
treatment of claimant pending
determination, 9.91–9.95
limited capability for work-related activity
claimants treated as having,
9.107–9.117
descriptors, 9.426–9.428
determination, 9.103–9.106
failure to provide required information,
9.121–9.122
generally, 1.750–1.752
good cause, and, 9.125–9.126
interpreting activities and descriptors,
9.429–9.433
medical examinations, 9.123–9.124
pregnant women, 9.107–9.117
Regulations, 9.103–9.126
relevant linked cases, 9.118

required information, 9.119–9.120
terminally ill claimants, 9.107–9.117
linking rules
  generally, 9.336–9.337
  statutory provisions, 1.818, 1.832
maintenance, and, 1.782–1.783
membership of household, 9.359–9.360
mental, cognitive and intellectual function
  appropriateness of behaviour, 9.425
  awareness of everyday hazards, 9.418
  coping with change, 9.420
  coping with social engagement,
    9.422–9.424
  generally, 9.416
  getting about, 9.421
  initiating and completing personal
    action, 9.419
  learning tasks, 9.417
  preliminary note, 9.392
national insurance
  generally, 1.806, 1.807–1.808
  Regulations, 9.18–9.22
national insurance numbers
  general, 9.6–9.7
introduction, 2.55
'national minimum wage', 9.5
'non-dependant', 9.189–9.190
Northern Ireland, 1.797–1.798
notional income
  calculation, 9.269–9.270
  deprivation of income, 9.263–9.264
  due to be paid, 9.265–9.266
  other income, 9.267–9.268
  paid to third party, 9.265–9.266
overlapping benefits, and, 3.86
overview, 1.711–1.714
partial relief, 9.129
participants in exempt work, 9.225–9.226
participants in self-employment route
  calculation, 9.218–9.219
  definitions, 9.251–9.252
  generally, 9.251–9.258
  gross receipts, 9.253–9.254
  tax, 9.257–9.258
partners of claimants not to be treated as
  in work, 9.137–9.138
payment below prescribed minimum,
  1.745–1.746
pension payments
  calculation of income, 9.227–9.228
  deductions from allowance,
    9.197–9.200
pensioner premiums
  generally, 9.436
  weekly amount, 9.442
periods of less than a week
  amount of allowance, 9.381–9.382
  generally, 1.817, 1.831
  modification to income calculation,
    9.385–9.386
  reduction, 9.387–9.389
  relevant week, 9.383–9.384
permanent health insurance, 9.191–9.192

persons from abroad, 9.187–9.188
persons starting or returning to work,
  9.159–9.160
physical disabilities
  absence of loss of control, 9.414
  consciousness during waking moments,
    9.415
  making self understood, 9.411
  manual dexterity, 9.411
  mobilising unaided, 9.407
  navigation and maintaining safety,
    9.413
  picking up and moving or transferring,
    9.410
  preliminary note, 9.392
  reaching, 9.409
  repeatedly mobilise, 9.407
  standing and sitting, 9.408
  understanding communication, 9.412
pilot schemes, 1.774–1.775
polygamy
  calculation of income, 9.216–9.217
  generally, 9.183–9.184
PPF periodic payments, 9.197–9.200
premiums
  generally, 9.435–9.441
  weekly amount, 9.442
prescribed amounts
  generally, 9.179–9.182
  housing costs, 9.458–9.483
  list, 9.434–9.457
  'non-dependant', 9.189–9.190
  persons from abroad, 9.187–9.188
  polygamous marriages, 9.183–9.184
  schedule, 9.434
  special cases, 9.185–9.186
presence in Great Britain, 1.819, 1.833
previous claimants, 9.13–9.14, 9.25–9.26
reasonable adjustments in workplace, 9.90
recovery
  generally, 9.340–9.341
  statutory provision, 1.782–1.783
reduction of allowance
  cessation, 9.168–9.170
  generally, 9.165–9.167
  hardship payments, 9.171–9.174
Regulations
  definitions, 9.4–9.5
  general provisions, 9.09–9.389
  generally, 1.711–1.714
  introductory provisions, 9.1–9.9
  schedules, 9.390–9.506
  statutory provision, 1.786–1.787
relevant benefit week, 1.806
relevant benefit year, 9.31–9.32
'remunerative work', 9.133–9.136
residence or presence, 9.27–9.28
rounding of fractions, 9.8–9.9
self-employed earners, 9.245–9.250
service user group, 9.4
severe disability premiums
  generally, 9.437
  weekly amount, 9.442

statutory adoption pay, and
  generally, 1.776–1.777
  Regulations, 9.211–9.212
statutory maternity pay, and
  generally, 1.776–1.777
  Regulations, 9.209–9.210
statutory paternity pay, and
  generally, 1.776–1.777
  Regulations, 9.213
statutory provisions
  conditionality, 1.755–1.768
  definitions, 1.784–1.785
  entitlement, 1.710–1.754
  financial provisions, 1.790–1.791
  miscellaneous, 1.769–1.783
  Northern Ireland, 1.797–1.798
  Parliamentary control, 1.788–1.789
  regulations, 1.786–1.787
  schedules, 1.806–1.855
  transitional provisions, 1.795–1.796
statutory shared parental pay
  Regulations, 9.214–9.215
students
  access fund payments, 9.322–9.323
  changes during summer vacation,
    9.332–9.333
  covenant income, 9.312–9.315
  definitions, 9.308–9.309
  disregard of amounts, 9.316–9.319
  disregard of contributions, 9.326–9.327
  fee loans, 9.324–9.325
  further disregard, 9.328–9.329
  generally, 9.223–9.224
  grant income, 9.310–9.311
  income treated as capital, 9.330–9.331
  student loans, 9.320–9.321
  weekly amount, 9.299–9.300
suspension of payment
  imprisonment, 9.378–9.379
temporary absence from GB
  armed forces personnel, 9.358–9.359
  generally, 9.350–9.351
  medical treatment, for, 9.354–9.355
  receive NHS treatment, to,
    9.356–9.357
  short absence, 9.352–9.353
terminally ill claimants, 9.16–9.17
transitional provisions
  generally, 1.795–1.796
  Regulations (2008), 9.508–9.519
  Regulations (2017), 9.619–9.629
trivial amounts of work, 9.131–9.132
urgent cases, 9.380
waiting days
  generally, 9.334–9.335
  statutory provisions, 1.816, 1.830
work, and
  claimants receiving regular treatment,
    9.145–9.146
  complete relief, 9.130
  de minimis principle, and, 9.131–9.132
  exempt work, 9.141–9.144
  general, 9.127–9.132

limited capability for work, and,
    9.139–9.140
  partial relief, 9.129
  partners of claimants not to be treated
    as in work, 9.137–9.138
  'remunerative work', 9.133–9.136
  trivial amounts of work, 9.131–9.132
work capability assessment
  introduction, 1.748
  limited capability for work, for,
    1.747–1.749, 9.43–9.102
  work-focused health-related assessment,
    for, 1.755–1.756, 9.147
  work-related activity, for, 1.750–1.752,
    9.103–9.126
work-focused health-related assessments
  Regulations, 9.147
  statutory provisions, 1.755–1.756
work-focused interviews
  action plans, 1.761–1.762, 9.156
  contracting-out functions, and,
    9.163–9.164
  deferral of requirement, 9.157–9.158
  failure to take part, 9.161–9.162
  generally, 1.757–1.758
  notification, 9.152–9.153
  persons starting or returning to work,
    9.159–9.160
  purposes, 9.150–9.151
  Regulations, 9.148–9.164
  requirement to take part, 9.148–9.149
  statutory provisions, 1.757–1.758
  taking part, 9.154–9.155
work or training beneficiaries, 9.349
work-related activity
  abolition, 1.1071–1.1072, 9.619–9.629
  action plans, 9.603–9.604
  contracting-out functions, and, 9.609
  deferral of requirement, 9.605–9.606
  directions, 1.763–1.764, 9.602
  failure to take part, 9.608
  generally, 1.759–1.760
  notification, 9.603–9.604
  reconsideration of action plans, 9.607
  Regulations, 9.596–9.611
  requirement to undertake, 9.600–9.601
youth
  generally, 1.806, 1.809–1.810
  Regulations, 9.23–9.30
**Employment and Support Allowance
  Regulations 2008**
see also **Employment and support
  allowance ('old style')**
amendments to
  2011, 9.610
  2012, 9.612–9.615
  2015, 9.616–9.618
  2017, 9.619–9.629, 9.630–9.633
arrangement of, 9.1
citation, 9.3
commencement, 9.3
definitions, 9.4–9.5
general provisions

amount of allowance, 9.179–9.215
assessment phase, 9.09–9.19
capital, 9.271–9.288
child maintenance, 9.289–9.303
child support, 9.304–9.307
conditionality, 9.147–9.178
conditions of entitlement, 9.20–9.42
deductions from allowance,
  9.191–9.208
disqualification, 9.361–9.379
effect of work on entitlement,
  9.127–9.146
employed earners, 9.241–9.244
income, 9.229–9.270
income and capital, 9.216–9.333
liable relative payments, 9.289–9.303
limited capability for work, 9.43–9.102
limited capability for work-related
  activity, 9.103–9.126
membership of household, 9.359–9.360
miscellaneous, 9.334–9.348
participants in self-employment route,
  9.251–9.258
periods of less than a week,
  9.381–9.389
prescribed amount, 9.179–9.190
reduction of allowance, 9.165–9.174
self-employed earners, 9.245–9.250
statutory payments, 9.209–9.215
students, 9.308–9.333
temporary absence, 9.350–9.358
urgent cases, 9.380
work-focused health-related assessment,
  9.147
work-focused interviews, 9.148–9.164
work or training beneficiaries, 9.349
national insurance numbers, 9.6–9.7
rounding of fractions, 9.8–9.9
schedules
  amount of allowance, 9.434–9.444
  disregarded capital, 9.497–9.506
  disregarded income, 9.484–9.496
  Her Majesty's Forces, 9.390–9.391
  housing costs, 9.458–9.483
  limited capability for work,
    9.392–9.425
  limited capability for work-related
    activity, 9.426–9.433
  special cases, 9.445–9.457
Employment and Support Allowance
  Regulations 2013
see also Employment and support
  allowance ('new style')
amendments to
  2017, 9.619–9.629
arrangement of, 13.103
citation, 13.107–13.109
commencement, 13.107–13.109
definitions, 13.110–13.112
general note, 13.105–13.106
general provisions
  amount of allowance, 13.225–13.253
  assessment phase, 13.115–13.120

claimant responsibilities,
  13.186–13.202
conditions of entitlement,
  13.121–13.134
disqualification, 13.286–13.295
effect of work on entitlement,
  13.178–13.185
income, 13.254–13.271
limited capability for work,
  13.135–13.163
limited capability for work-related
  activity, 13.164–13.177
periods of less than a week,
  13.296–13.304
sanctions, 13.203–13.224
supplementary provisions,
  13.272–13.285
rounding of fractions, 13.113–13.114
schedules
  Her Majesty's Forces, 13.305–13.307
  limited capability for work,
    13.308–13.309
  limited capability for work-related
    activity, 13.310–13.311
Employment and Support Allowance
  (Transitional Provisions)
  Regulations 2008
amendment, 9.578
arrangement of, 9.508
citation, 9.509
commencement, 9.509–9.510
definitions, 9.509
general provisions, 9.511–9.519
Employment and Support Allowance
  (Transitional Provisions, etc)
  (Existing Awards) (No.2))
  Regulations 2010
application, 9.544
arrangement of, 9.528
citation, 9.541
commencement, 9.541
consequential amendments,
  9.578–9.580
definitions, 9.542–9.543
general note, 9.529–9.539
general provisions, 9.545–9.577
schedules, 9.581–9.595
Universal Credit cases, 9.540
Employment and Support Allowance
  (Work-Related Activity)
  Regulations 2011
arrangement of, 9.596
citation, 9.597
commencement, 9.597
definitions, 9.599
general note, 9.598
general provisions, 9.600–9.611
Employment at sea
  see Continental shelf, Seafarers
Employment training schemes
  see Industrial injuries benefit
Engine room
  see Occupational deafness

"Enhanced disability premium"
employment and support allowance
generally, 9.438
weekly amount, 9.442
"Enhanced rate"
daily living component, 1.909–1.911
mobility component, 1.912–1.916
overlapping benefits, 3.82
personal independence payments
daily living component, 1.909
mobility component, 1.912
terminal illness, 1.921–1.922
Episodic blanching
generally, 10.135
Equality
pensions, 1.653–1.667
Errors
see **Clerical errors**
Evidence
personal independence payments
generally, 4.184–4.185
matters to be taken into account in
determining good reason,
4.188–4.189
Exertion
see **Mobility component**
Extrinsic allergic alveolitis
generally, 10.135, 10.179
Face to face engagement
see **Personal independence payments**
False statements
vaccine damage payments, and, 1.27
Family fund test
see **Dependants**
Farmer's lung
generally, 10.135, 10.179
Finality (decisions)
vaccine damage payments, and, 1.19
Financial Assistance Scheme
'new style' ESA, 13.231–13.232
'old style' ESA, 9.193–9.194
Firearms
occupational deafness, and, 10.158
Flexible working
industrial injuries benefit, 1.360–1.362
"Fluctuating earnings"
increases for dependants, 1.324–1.326
unemployability supplement
generally, 1.590
introduction, 1.599
Food preparation
see **Personal independence payments**
For any period throughout which
see **Care component**
Forestry
vibration white finger, and,
10.160–10.165
Foster carers
contribution credits,
additional period of allowance,
2.80–2.81
applications, 2.83–2.86
definitions, 2.72

disqualification, 2.81–2.82
'engaged in caring', 2.76–2.77
'foster parent', 2.74–2.75
general note, 2.71
generally, 1.51–1.52
imprisonment, and, 2.81–2.82
limit on award of child benefit,
2.78–2.79
provision of information, 2.85
residence in GB, and, 2.81–2.82
time limits for applications, 2.86
transitional provision, 2.73
home responsibilities, 2.48
Fractional sums
see **Earnings**
Fraud
vaccine damage payments, and, 1.27
Full-time students
carer's allowance, 4.133
child benefit, 1.629
Further education colleges
employment and support allowance, 9.4
**Gastrointenstinal infection by
hookworm**
generally, 10.135, 10.177
Gender recognition
application of provisions, 1.682
certification, 1.677–1.678
definitions, 1.681
general note, 1.680
introductory, 1.683
long-term incapacity benefit,
1.690–1.691
occupational pensions
equivalent benefits, 1.707–1.708
general note, 1.704
guaranteed minimum, 1.705–1.706
state pension, 1.692
state retirement pensions
Category A, 1.693–1.694
Category B, 1.695–1.696
Category C, 1.700–1.701
deferment of, 1.698–1.699
graduated, 1.702–1.703
shared additional, 1.697
widowed mother's allowance,
1.684–1.685
widowed parent's allowance, 1.688–1.689
widow's pension, 1.686–1.687
Gender Recognition Act 2004
see also **Gender recognition**
arrangement of sections, 1.676
commencement, 1.676
definitions, 1.681
general note, 1.677–1.678
general provisions, 1.679–1.680
schedules, 1.682–1.708
Getting about
see **Descriptors for incapacity**
Glanders
generally, 10.135
Glass container manufacturers
see **Occupational deafness**

"Good cause"
limited capability for work, 9.62–9.63
limited capability for work-related activity,
    9.125–9.126
Good reason
see **Personal independence payments**
Graduated retirement benefit
see also **Contributory benefits**
alteration of rates, 6.18
generally, 1.148–1.150
increase where pensioner's deceased
    spouse has deferred entitlement,
choice, 6.61
elections, 6.67–6.70
generally, 6.62
transitional provisions, 6.65–6.66
introduction, 6.16
lump sum where pensioner's deceased
    spouse has deferred entitlement,
calculation, 6.64
choice, 6.61
elections, 6.67–6.70
entitlement, 6.63
rounding, 6.71–6.72
transitional provisions, 6.65–6.66
modification of regulations,
generally, 6.20
modified regulations, 6.26–6.28
preservation of existing rights,
generally, 6.19
relevant provisions of NIA 1965,
    6.24–6.25
uprating, 6.18
Gratuities
reduced earnings allowance,
    10.235–10.236
Guaranteed minimum pension
effect of payments and contributions on
    benefits, 1.644–1.650
persons abroad, and, 3.125
Guardian's allowance
see also **Non-contributory benefits**
entitlement, 1.286
persons abroad, 3.120–3.121
rate, 1.511
Haemophilus influenza type b
see also **Vaccine damage payments**
appeals, 1.16–1.17
conditions of entitlement, 1.8–1.11
determination of claims, 1.12–1.18
error correction, 1.22
finality of decisions, 1.23–1.24
fraudulent statements, 1.27
generally, 1.2–1.7
payment, 1.19–1.21
setting aside decisions, 1.22
updating Order, 11.16–11.18
Hardship
reduced earnings allowance, 10.232
Hardship payments
'new style' ESA, 13.46
'old style' ESA
    amount, 9.174

circumstances in which treated as in
    hardship, 9.172
entitlement, 9.171
generally, 1.768
introduction, 9.4
matters to be taken into account, 9.173
Health condition monitoring
see **Personal independence payments**
Hepatitis
generally, 10.135, 10.180
Her Majesty's forces
see **Armed forces**
Hip
industrial diseases, 10.135
Home responsibilities protection
generally, 2.49–2.50
Hookworm
generally, 10.135, 10.177
Hospital in-patients
see **In-patients**
Households
employment and support allowance,
    9.359–9.360
Housemaid's knee
industrial injuries, 10.144
Housing costs element
employment and support allowance
amendments (2015), 9.616–9.618
apportionment, 9.464
continuity with other benefits, 9.478
costs not met, 9.463
definitions, 9.458
excessive e costs, 9.471
excluded costs, 9.463
existing and new costs, 9.465–9.469
generally, 9.179–9.182
liability of person to meet, 9.461
linking rule, 9.472
loans, 9.468
miscellaneous provisions, 9.458–9.483
new costs, 9.466–9.469
non-dependent deductions,
    9.476–9.477
occupying a dwelling as the home, 9.462
other costs, 9.475
previous entitlement to other income
    benefits, 9.460
remunerative work, 9.459
repair and improvement loans, 9.474
residential property loans, 9.473
standard rate, 9.470
Human papillomavirus
see also **Vaccine damage payments**
appeals, 1.16–1.17
conditions of entitlement, 1.8–1.11
determination of claims, 1.12–1.18
error correction, 1.22
finality of decisions, 1.23–1.24
fraudulent statements, 1.27
generally, 1.2–1.7
payment, 1.19–1.21
setting aside decisions, 1.22
updating Order, 11.26–11.29

Hydatidosis
generally, 10.135
Illegal employment
see **Industrial injuries benefit**
Imprisonment
child benefit, 1.629
contribution credits, 2.38–2.39
disqualification from benefit, 1.438
'new style' ESA
disqualification, 13.292–13.293
suspension of payment, 13.294–13.295
'old style' ESA, 9.378–9.379
Inability to walk
see **Mobility component**
Incapacity benefit
see also **Contributory benefits**
adjustment
hospital in-patients, 3.77–3.78
persons abroad, 3.109–3.117
adult dependants, 1.308
child dependants
dependency, and, 3.54–3.55
generally, 1.292–1.294
restrictions, 1.295–1.296
conditions
earnings factors, 1.49
general note, 1.491–1.508
generally, 1.48
miscellaneous provisions, 1.482–1.490
conversion to ESA
see also **Conversion decisions**
after conversion phase, 9.565–9.573
decisions, 9.545–9.564
definitions, 9.542–9.543
disapplication of enactments, 9.574
general note, 9.529–9.539
miscellaneous provisions, 9.575–9.580
relevant persons, 9.544
credits
generally, 2.31
official error, following, 2.27
dependants' increases
generally, 1.308
reduced contributions, 1.309–1.311
earnings factors, 1.49
employment and support allowance, and,
1.711
generally, 1.55
hospital in-patients, 3.77–3.78
increases for dependants
child dependants, 1.292–1.296
generally, 1.308
reduced contributions, 1.309–1.311
relevant earnings, 1.314–1.316
long-term
Christmas bonus, 1.464–1.467
post-employment or training, 1.92–1.94
widowers' benefits, 1.89–1.91
widows' benefit, 1.86–1.88
maternity pay, and, 1.638–1.640
persons abroad
generally, 3.109–3.110
grounds, 3.111–3.117

persons residing together, 3.149–3.153
rate
generally, 1.509
increases for dependants, 1.512
short term benefit
conditions, 1.48–1.49
contribution credits, 2.31
increases for dependants, and,
1.297–1.298
statutory sick pay, 1.630–1.637
widowers' benefits
generally, 1.89–1.91
post-employment or training, 1.92–1.94
widows' benefits
generally, 1.86–1.88
post-employment or training, 1.92–1.94
Incapacity for work
see also **Descriptors**
contribution credits, 2.23–2.24
employment and support allowance
definition, 1.716–1.717
generally, 1.747–1.749
supplementary provisions, 1.815
widow's pension, 6.92
Incapacity suffered during day
see **Limited capability for work**
Income ('new style' ESA)
date on which treated as paid,
13.258–13.259
deduction of tax and contributions,
13.270–13.271
earnings
employed earners, 13.262–13.263
self-employed earners, 13.256–13.257
employed earner's earnings
deduction of tax and contributions,
13.270–13.271
'earnings', 13.262–13.263
generally, 13.254–13.255
net earnings, 13.264–13.265
other than earnings, 9.233–9.234,
9.259–9.270
self-employed earners earnings
deduction of tax and NICs,
13.270–13.271
'earnings', 13.266–13.267
generally, 13.256–13.257
tax deduction, 13.270–13.271
weekly amount, 13.260–13.261
Income ('old style' ESA)
calculation
employed earner's earnings,
9.233–9.234
generally, 9.229–9.333
other than earnings, 9.233–9.234
self-employed earners earnings,
9.235–9.236
capital treated as, 9.261–9.262
child maintenance, 9.290
child support
date on which to be treated as paid,
9.305
disregard of payments, 9.306

generally, 9.222
treatment, 9.303
weekly amount, 9.304
claimant's partner, of, 9.216–9.217
councillors' allowances, 9.227–9.228
date on which treated as paid,
    9.237–9.238
disregards
    calculation of earnings, 9.484–9.490
    calculation of income other than from
        earnings, 9.491–9.496
employed earner's earnings
    calculation, 9.233–9.234
    generally, 9.241–9.242
    net earnings, 9.243–9.244
generally, 1.769–1.770
liable relative payments
    date on which to be treated as paid,
        9.300–9.301
    definitions, 9.289–9.290
    disregard of payments, 9.293–9.294
    generally, 9.220–9.221
    period over which to be taken into
        account, 9.295–9.298
    treatment, 9.291–9.292
    weekly amount, 9.299–9.300
notional income
    calculation, 9.269–9.270
    deprivation of income, 9.263–9.264
    due to be paid, 9.265–9.266
    other income, 9.267–9.268
    paid to third party, 9.265–9.266
other than earnings
    calculation, 9.233–9.234
    capital treated as income, 9.261–9.262
    generally, 9.259–9.260
    notional income, 9.263–9.270
participants in exempt work, 9.225–9.226
participants in self-employment route
    calculation, 9.218–9.219
    definitions, 9.251–9.252
    generally, 9.251–9.258
    gross receipts, 9.253–9.254
    tax, 9.257–9.258
pension payments, 9.227–9.228
polygamous marriage, and, 9.216–9.217
PPF periodic payments, 9.227–9.228
Regulations, 9.229–9.270
self-employed earners earnings
    calculation, 9.235–9.236
    generally, 9.245–9.246
    net profit, 9.247–9.248
    tax and national insurance, 9.249–9.250
students 9.223–9.224
weekly amount, 9.239–9.240
**Income-based employment and support
    allowance**
see also **Employment and support
    allowance**
abolition, 13.1–13.3
additional conditions
    claimants not treated as receiving
        education, 9.37–9.38

claimants treated as receiving
    education, 9.35–9.36
courses of study, 9.39–9.40
disability living allowance, and,
    9.41–9.42
'education', 9.33–9.34
generally, 1.811–1.813
introduction, 1.715
advance award, 1.741–1.742
amount
    generally, 1.738–1.740
    prescribed minimum, 1.745–1.746
basic conditions, 1.710–1.721
contributions, and, 2.55
credits, and, 2.3
entitlement
    additional conditions, 1.811–1.813,
        9.33–9.42
    basic conditions, 1.710–1.721
general, 1.715
introduction, 1.711–1.714
national insurance numbers, and, 2.55
'new style' ESA
    absence from Great Britain, 13.84
    advance award, 13.17
    amount, 13.16
overlapping benefits, and, 3.86
supplementary provisions, 1.822
Income support
conversion to ESA
    see also **Conversion decisions**
    after conversion phase, 9.565–9.573
    decisions, 9.545–9.564
    definitions, 9.542–9.543
    disapplication of enactments, 9.574
    general note, 9.529–9.539
    miscellaneous provisions, 9.575–9.580
    relevant persons, 9.544
generally, 1.711
Incomplete physical development
see **Mobility component**
Incontinence
personal independence payments, 4.246
Industrial death benefit
Christmas bonus, and, 1.464–1.467
generally, 1.597
introduction, 1.599
persons abroad, and, 3.131
Industrial diseases
allergic rhinitis, 10.189–10.190
asbestosis, 10.195
asthma, 10.193–10.194
beat elbow, hand and knee, 10.144
biological agents, conditions due to
    introduction, 10.137–10.140
    list, 10.135
    prescribed occupations, 10.174–10.182
bursitis, 10.144
byssinosis
    generally, 1.425–1.430
    prescribed occupations, 10.187
    special conditions, 10.96–10.97
cancer, 10.141

carcinoma of the lung
  asbestos, 10.195
  tin, etc, 10.197
carcinoma of the nasopharynx, 10.201
carpal tunnel syndrome, 10.166–10.168
cataract, 10.142
chemical agents, conditions due to
  introduction, 10.137–10.140
  list, 10.135
  prescribed occupations,
    10.183–10.184
chronic bronchitis, 10.198
chronic obstructive pulmonary disease,
    10.198–10.200
cramp, 10.143
date of development
  generally, 10.66–10.67
  transitional provisions, 10.133, 10.207
date of onset
  determination, 10.68–10.73
  transitional provisions, 10.133,
    10.207
dermatitis, 10.191
diffuse mesothelioma
  generally, 10.96–10.97
  prescribed occupations, 10.188
emphysema, 10.198
generally, 1.416–1.421
housemaid's knee, 10.144
inflammation of nose, 10.188
leukaemia, 10.141
lung cancer, 10.197
miscellaneous conditions
  allergic rhinitis, 10.189–10.190
  asbestosis, 10.195
  asthma, 10.193–10.194
  byssinosis, 10.187
  carcinoma, 10.201
  chronic bronchitis, 10.198
  chronic obstructive pulmonary disease,
    10.198–10.200
  diffuse mesothelioma, 10.188
  emphysema, 10.198
  inflammation of nose, 10.188
  introduction, 10.137–10.140
  list, 10.135
  lung cancer, 10.197
  nasal carcinoma, 10.192
  nasopharyngeal cancer, 10.201
  non-effective dermatitis, 10.191
  occupational asthma, 10.193–10.194
  pleural thickening, 10.196
  pneumoconiosis, 10.186
  ulceration of nose, 10.188
nasal carcinoma, 10.192
nasopharyngeal cancer, 10.201
non-effective dermatitis, 10.191
occupational asthma
  prescribed occupations, 10.193–10.194
  time limits for claims, 10.124–10.125
occupational deafness
  appeals, 10.118–10.119
  assessment of extent, 10.121–10.122

claims, 10.110–10.111
  date of onset, 10.114–10.115
  duration of assessment, 10.116
  further claims, 10.112–10.113
  prescribed occupations, 10.146–10.159
  reassessment of disablement, 10.120
  supercession of decision, 10.117
  time limits for claims, 10.108–10.109
persons abroad, and, 3.135
physical agents, conditions due to
  cancer, 10.141
  carpal tunnel syndrome, 10.166–10.168
  cataract, 10.142
  housemaid's knee, 10.144
  introduction, 10.137–10.140
  leukaemia, 10.141
  list, 10.135
  occupational deafness, 10.146–10.159
  vibration white finger, 10.160–10.165
  writer's cramp, 10.143
pleural thickening, 10.196
pneumoconiosis
  chronic bronchitis, effect of,
    10.104–10.105
  emphysema, effect of, 10.104–10.105
  generally, 1.425–1.430
  prescribed occupations, 10.136,
    10.186
  reduced earnings allowance, 10.106
  special conditions, 10.96–10.97
  tuberculosis, effect of, 10.102–10.103
  unscheduled occupation cases, 10.114
prescribed occupations
  biological agents, conditions due to,
    10.135, 10.174–10.182
  chemical agents, conditions due to,
    10.135, 10.183–10.184
  general matters, 10.138–10.140
  introductory note, 10.137
  miscellaneous conditions, 10.135,
    10.186–10.201
  physical agents, conditions due to,
    10.135, 10.141–10.168
  pneumoconiosis, 10.186
recrudescence, 10.74
relevant dates
  generally, 10.132
  list, 10.206
respiratory diseases, 1.425–1.430
subcutaneous cellulitis, 10.135
supplementary provisions, 1.422–1.424
suspension from employment
  conditions, 10.129
  generally, 10.128
tenosynovitis, 10.145
tuberculosis, 1.425–1.430
ulceration of nose, 10.188
vibration white finger
  forestry, 10.160–10.165
  generally, 10.160–10.165
  metal grinding, 10.160–10.165
  percussive metal tools, 10.160–10.165
writer's cramp, 10.143

Industrial Injuries Benefit (Employment Training Schemes and Courses) Regulations 2013
arrangement of, 10.292
citation, 10.294
commencement, 10.294
definitions, 10.294
general provisions, 10.295–10.298
Industrial Injuries Benefit (Injuries arising before July 5, 1948) Regulations 2012
arrangement of, 10.287
citation, 10.288
commencement, 10.288
definitions, 10.288
general provisions, 10.289–10.290
schedule, 10.291
Industrial injuries benefits
accident, 1.337–1.347
accidents abroad, 1.364
adjustment
  overlapping benefits, 3.89–3.90
  persons abroad, 3.131
  successive accidents, 1.413–1.415
airmen, 1.450–1.451
arising out of and in course of employment
  arising in course of, 1.354–1.356
  arising out of , 1.351–1.353
  introduction, 1.350
airmen, 1.450–1.451
arising before July 5, 1948
  generally, 1.902–1.903
  Regulations, 10.288–10.291
armed forces, 1.447–1.449
assessment of disablement
  aggregation of percentages, 10.87–10.88
  connected conditions, 10.21
  connection factor, 10.22
  extent, 10.85–10.86
  generally, 1.395–1.405
  miscellaneous provisions, 1.568–1.582
  multiple industrial accidents, 10.25
  other effective cause, 10.22–10.24
  partly relevant conditions, 10.21
  prescribed degrees, 10.26–10.28
  principles, 10.19–10.28
  rounding of percentages, 10.89
breach of regulation, earner acting in, 1.374–1.376
calculation of earnings
  generally, 3.5–3.12
  disregards, 3.33–3.36
  employed earners, 3.13–3.26
  fractional sums, 3.12
  generally, 3.6–3.7
  notional income, 3.8–3.11
  rounding of fractions, 3.12
  self-employed earners, 3.27–3.31
cause, 1.348–1.349
claimants' obligations, 10.8
claims pre-October 1986

disablement benefit, 10.218–10.219
reduced earnings allowance, 10.232
claims and payments
  claimants' obligations, 10.8
  definitions, 10.3
  employers' obligations, 10.7
  notice of accidents, 10.6
  particulars of accidents, 10.13
continental shelf operations, 1.456–1.457
Crown employment, 1.444–1.446
date of development
  generally, 10.66–10.67
  transitional provisions, 10.133, 10.207
date of onset
  determination, 10.68–10.73
  transitional provisions, 10.133, 10.207
disablement
  aggregation of percentages, 10.87–10.88
  connected conditions, 10.21
  connection factor, 10.22
  extent, 10.85–10.86
  generally, 1.395–1.405
  miscellaneous provisions, 1.568–1.582
  multiple industrial accidents, 10.25
  other effective cause, 10.22–10.24
  partly relevant conditions, 10.21
  prescribed degrees, 10.52–10.53
  principles, 10.19–10.28
  rounding of percentages, 10.89
disablement benefit
  assessment of disablement, 1.578–1.581
  claimants' obligations, 10.8
  generally, 1.570
  increase, 10.33–10.34
disablement gratuity
  amount, 10.30
  generally, 1.591
  introduction, 1.599
  rate, 1.515
  weekly value, 10.31
disablement pension
  see also **Disablement pension**
  constant attendance, 1.406–1.408
  exceptionally severe disablement, 1.409–1.411
  generally, 1.395–1.405
  hospital treatment, during, 1.592
  increases, 1.406–1.411
  rate, 1.514–1.515
disease contracted outside UK, 10.82–10.83
disqualification
  see also **Disqualification (benefits)**
  generally, 1.434–1.441
doubt as to circumstances of accident, 1.363
earnings, 1.431–1.433
elements of scheme
  accident, 1.337–1.347
  accidents abroad, 1.364
  arising out of and in course of employment, 1.350–1.356

cause, 1.348–1.349
doubt as to circumstances of accident,
    1.363
employed earner, 1.335
flexible working, 1.360–1.362
generally, 1.330–1.334
incapacity for work, 1.365
normal working day, 1.357
recreational activity, 1.359
sick leave, workers on, 1.360–1.362
suffers personal injury, 1.336
taking a break, 1.358
emergency situations, 1.383–1.387
employed earner, 1.335
employers' obligations, 10.6
employer's transport, travelling in
effect, 1.380–1.382
generally, 1.377–1.378
introduction, 1.379
employment training schemes
generally, 1.366–1.368
Regulations, 10.292–10.298
exceptionally severe disablement,
    1.409–1.411
flexible working, 1.360–1.362
general provisions
another's misconduct, 1.388–1.393
earner acting in breach of regulation,
    1.374–1.376
emergency situations, 1.383–1.387
employment training schemes,
    1.366–1.368
entitlement, 1.330–1.365
illegal employment, 1.373
relevant employers, 1.372
relevant employment, 1.369–1.371
travelling in employer's transport,
    1.377–1.382
Her Majesty's forces, 1.447–1.449
illegal employment, 1.373
incapacity for work, 1.365
industrial death benefit
generally, 1.597
introduction, 1.599
persons abroad, and, 3.131
initial medical examination
employers' duties, 10.130
fees, 10.131
generally, 10.122
mariners, 1.450–1.451
married women, 1.452–1.453
meaning, 1.460
medical examination
employers' duties, 10.130
fees, 10.131
generally, 10.94–10.95
initial, 10.122
periodical, 10.127
misconduct of another, 1.388–1.393
notice of accidents, 10.5
normal working day, 1.357
overlapping benefits
dependency benefits, 3.91–3.98

jobseekers allowance, 3.102
part week, for, 3.99
personal benefits, 3.86–3.90
priority, 3.100
particulars of accidents, 10.12
periodical medical examination
employers' duties, 10.130
fees, 10.131
generally, 10.127
persons abroad, and
Regulation, 3.131
statutory provision, 1.454–1.455
polygamous marriages, 1.458–1.459
prescribed diseases
see also **Prescribed diseases**
generally, 1.416–1.421
prescription of diseases, 10.59–10.61
presumption as to origin, 10.64–10.65
respiratory diseases, 1.425–1.430
resulting conditions, 10.62–10.63
supplementary provisions, 1.422–1.424
transitional provisions, 10.234, 10.239
prescribed occupations
generally, 10.59–10.61
list, 10.135–10.201
presumption as to origin, 10.64–10.65
prescription of diseases, 10.59–10.61
presumption as to origin, 10.64–10.65
prior to July 5, 1948
generally, 1.902–1.903
Regulations, 10.288–10.291
rate, 1.514–1.515
recreational activity, 1.359
recrudescence, 10.74
reduced earnings allowance
abatement, 10.233
background, 1.600–1.601
change of circumstances, 10.229–10.230
generally, 1.593–1.594
introduction, 1.599
maximum rate, 10.228
pre-October 1986 claims, 10.232
probable standard of remuneration,
    10.223–10.227
qualifying conditions, 1.602–1.620
rate, 1.621
regular occupation, 10.210–10.211
special hardship, 10.232
transitional provisions, 10.231–10.236
unemployability supplement,
    10.214–10.215
regular employment
meaning, 10.239–10.240
persons aged 65 or over, 10.241–10.243
regular occupation, 10.91–10.92
relevant disease, 10.77
relevant employers, 1.372
relevant employment, 1.369–1.371
resulting conditions, 10.62–10.63
retirement allowance
generally, 1.595–1.596
introduction, 1.599
qualifying conditions, 1.622–1.627

seafarers, 1.456–1.457
sequelae, 10.62–10.63
sick leave, workers on, 1.360–1.362
sickness benefit, 1.394
special cases
    airmen, 1.450–1.451
    continental shelf, employment on,
        1.456–1.457
    Crown employment, 1.444–1.446
    Her Majesty's forces, 1.447–1.449
    mariners, 1.450–1.451
    married women, 1.452–1.453
    persons abroad, 1.454–1.455
    polygamous marriages, 1.458–1.459
    seafarers, 1.456–1.457
special provisions
    byssinosis, 10.96–10.97
    diffuse mesothelioma, 10.98–10.99
    occupational asthma, 10.124–10.125
    occupational deafness,
        10.108–10.123
    pneumoconiosis, 10.96–10.107
special hardship, 10.247
successive accidents, 1.413–1.415
suffers personal injury, 1.336
suspension, 1.434–1.441
suspension from employment
    conditions, 10.129
    generally, 10.128
taking a break, 1.358
trainees, 1.904
transitional provisions
    date of development, 10.133
    date of onset, 10.133
    disablement claims pre-October 1986,
        10.218–10.219
    reduced earnings allowance,
        10.231–10.236
    relevant dates, 10.132
unemployability supplement
    availability, 1.583
    duration, 1.584
    earnings level, 10.32
    fluctuating earnings, 1.590
    generally, 1.583–1.590
    increase, 1.585
    increase for adult dependents, 1.588
    increase for dependent children,
        1.586–1.587
    introduction, 1.599
    rate, 1.584
    reduced earnings allowance,
        10.214–10.215
    relevant earnings, 1.589
    time qualifications, 1.412
workmen's compensation cases
    generally, 10.75
    re-employment of pneumoconiotics,
        10.76
Industrial injuries disablement benefit
assessment of disablement, and
    comment, 1.578–1.581
generally, 1.570

claimants' obligations, 10.8
increase, 10.33–10.34
Inflammation of nose
industrial diseases, 10.188
Influenza
see also **Vaccine damage payments**
appeals, 1.16–1.17
conditions of entitlement, 1.8–1.11
determination of claims, 1.12–1.18
error correction, 1.22
finality of decisions, 1.23–1.24
fraudulent statements, 1.27
generally, 1.2–1.7
payment, 1.19–1.21
setting aside decisions, 1.22
updating Order, 11.40–11.43
Influenza caused by H1N1 virus
see **Swine flu**
Initial medical examinations
see **Medical examinations**
**Initiating and completing personal
    action**
see **Descriptors for incapacity**
In-patients
attendance allowance
    exemption, 4.24–4.25
    generally, 4.19–4.20
    relevant patients, 4.30
disablement pension
    generally, 1.592
    introduction, 1.599
increase in benefits for dependants,
        3.77–3.78
limited capability for work,
        9.64–9.67
'new style' ESA, 13.146–13.147
personal independence payments
    generally, 1.928–1.929
    Regulations, 4.226–4.227
Invalid care allowance
see **Carer's allowance**
Invalid carriages
see also **Disability living allowance**
definition, 3.4
generally, 1.275–1.277
Regulations
    entitlement, 4.116–4.121
    generally, 4.101
    persons aged 65 and over, 4.105
Invalid Vehicle Scheme
see **Invalid carriages**
Iron deficiency anaemia
generally, 10.135, 10.177
Jobseeker's allowance
drugs-dependent claimants, 1.885
limited capability for work, 9.96
overlapping benefits, 3.102
Jury service
contribution credits, 2.34–2.35
Kidney toxicity
generally, 10.135
Learning tasks
see **Descriptors for incapacity**

Leptospira
generally, 10.135, 10.176
Leukaemia
generally, 10.135, 10.141
Liable relative payments
employment and support allowance
date on which to be treated as paid,
9.300–9.301
definitions, 9.289–9.290
disregard of payments, 9.293–9.294
generally, 9.220–9.221
period over which to be taken into
account, 9.295–9.298
treatment, 9.291–9.292
weekly amount, 9.299–9.300
**Limited capability for work ('new style
ESA')**
additional circumstances, 13.162–13.163
assessment, 13.308–13.309
claimants receiving regular treatment,
13.148–13.149
claimants treated as having, 13.137
cognitive function, 13.308–13.309
contaminated persons, 13.137
determination, 13.135–13.136
excepted claimants, 13.158–13.159
exceptional circumstances,
13.154–13.155
failure to provide required information,
13.140–13.141
good cause, and, 13.144–13.145
hospital in-patients, 13.146–13.147
infectious persons, 13.137
information required, 13.138–13.141
intellectual function, 13.308–13.309
limited capability at start of day,
13.150–13.151
medical examinations, 13.142–13.143
mental function, 13.308–13.309
night workers, 13.152–13.153
physical disabilities, 13.308–13.309
pregnant women, 13.137
Regulations, 13.135–13.163
required information, 13.138–13.141
service personnel, and, 13.158–13.159
supplementary provisions, 13.308–13.309
terminally ill claimants, 13.137
training courses, and, 13.158–13.159
treatment of claimant at end of period
covered by evidence,
13.160–13.161
treatment of claimant pending
determination, 13.156–13.157
**Limited capability for work ('old style
ESA')**
absence of loss of control, 9.414
additional circumstances, 9.100–9.102
amendments effected on January 28,
2013, 9.399
appropriateness of behaviour, 9.425
assessment (post-March 27, 2011)
general note, 9.394–9.406
lists, 9.393

mental, cognitive and intellectual
function, 9.416–9.425
physical disabilities, 9.407–9.415
preliminary note, 9.392
assessment (pre-March 28, 2011)
definition, 1.716–1.717
general note, 9.507
generally, 1.747–1.749
supplementary provisions, 1.815
attention to detail, 9.401–9.402
awareness of everyday hazards, 9.418
background, 9.394
claimants receiving regular treatment,
9.68–9.69
claimants treated as having, 9.51–9.53
consciousness during waking moments,
9.415
coping with change, 9.420
coping with social engagement,
9.422–9.424
decision-making, 9.406
definition, 1.716–1.717
determination, 9.43–9.50
evidence, 9.401–9.402
excepted claimants, 9.97–9.98
exceptional circumstances, 9.74–9.90
failure to provide required information,
9.56–9.57
generally, 1.747–1.749
getting about, 9.421
good cause, and, 9.62–9.63
hospital in-patients, 9.64–9.67
initiating and completing personal action,
9.419
interpretation of Schedule
decision-making and recording, 9.406
evidence, 9.401–9.402
reasonableness, 9.403–9.405
jobseeker's allowance, and, 9.96
learning tasks, 9.417
limited capability at start of day,
9.70–9.71
lists
mental, cognitive and intellectual
function, 9.393
physical disabilities, 9.393
making self understood, 9.411
manual dexterity, 9.411
medical examinations, 9.58–9.61
mental, cognitive and intellectual function
appropriateness of behaviour, 9.425
awareness of everyday hazards, 9.418
coping with change, 9.420
coping with social engagement,
9.422–9.424
generally, 9.416
getting about, 9.421
initiating and completing personal
action, 9.419
learning tasks, 9.417
mobilising unaided, 9.407
navigation and maintaining safety, 9.413
night workers, 9.72–9.73

physical disabilities
  absence of loss of control, 9.414
  consciousness during waking moments, 9.415
  making self understood, 9.411
  manual dexterity, 9.411
  mobilising unaided, 9.407
  navigation and maintaining safety, 9.413
  picking up and moving or transferring, 9.410
  reaching, 9.409
  standing and sitting, 9.408
  understanding communication, 9.412
picking up and moving or transferring, 9.410
pregnant women, 9.51–9.53
preliminary note, 9.392
reaching, 9.409
reasonable adjustments in workplace, 9.90
reasonableness, 9.403–9.405
record of decisions, 9.406
Regulations
  additional circumstances, 9.100–9.102
  claimants receiving regular treatment, 9.68–9.69
  claimants treated as having, 9.51–9.53
  definition, 1.716–1.717
  determination, 9.43–9.50
  excepted claimants, 9.97–9.98
  exceptional circumstances, 9.74–9.90
  failure to provide required information, 9.56–9.57
  generally, 1.747–1.749
  good cause, and, 9.62–9.63
  hospital in-patients, 9.64–9.67
  jobseeker's allowance, and, 9.96
  limited capability at start of day, 9.70–9.71
  medical examinations, 9.58–9.61
  night workers, 9.72–9.73
  pregnant women, 9.51–9.53
  reasonable adjustments in workplace, 9.90
  required information, 9.54–9.55
  terminally ill claimants, 9.51–9.53
  training courses, and, 9.97–9.98
  treatment of claimant at end of period covered by evidence, 9.99
  treatment of claimant pending determination, 9.91–9.95
repeatedly mobilise, 9.407
required information, 9.54–9.55
revisions to Schedule 2, 9.395–9.397
standing and sitting, 9.408
statutory provisions
  definition, 1.716–1.717
  generally, 1.747–1.749
  supplementary provisions, 1.815
structure of Schedule 2, 9.398
terminally ill claimants, 9.51–9.53
training courses, and, 9.97–9.98

treatment of claimant at end of period covered by evidence, 9.99
treatment of claimant pending determination
  continued entitlement to ESA, 9.95
  generally, 9.91–9.95
  'new claim', 9.93
  relevant circumstances, 9.93
  'repeat claim', 9.94
understanding communication, 9.412
work capability assessment
  general note, 9.394–9.406
  lists, 9.393
  mental, cognitive and intellectual function, 9.416–9.425
  physical disabilities, 9.407–9.415
  preliminary note, 9.392
Limited capability for work-related activity ('new style ESA')
assessment, 13.310–13.311
claimants treated as having, 13.166–13.167
determination, 13.164–13.165
failure to provide required information, 13.172–13.173
good cause, and, 13.176–13.177
information required, 13.170–13.173
medical examinations, 13.174–13.175
pregnant women, 13.166–13.167
Regulations, 13.164–13.177
relevant linked cases, 13.168–13.169
required information, 13.170–13.173
supplementary provisions, 13.310–13.311
terminally ill claimants, 13.166–13.167
Limited capability for work-related activity ('old style ESA')
claimants treated as having, 9.107–9.117
descriptors, 9.426–9.434
determination, 9.103–9.106
failure to provide required information, 9.121–9.122
generally, 1.750–1.752
good cause, and, 9.125–9.126
lone parents of children under 7, 1.884
medical examinations, 9.123–9.124
pregnant women, 9.107–9.117
post-March 27, 2011
  general note, 9.434
  list, 9.426
  preliminary note, 9.392
Regulations, 9.103–9.126
relevant linked cases, 9.118
required information, 9.119–9.120
statutory provisions
  generally, 1.750–1.752
  supplementary provisions, 1.823
terminally ill claimants, 9.107–9.117
Linking rules
'new style' ESA, 13.273–13.274
'old style' ESA
  generally, 9.336–9.337
  statutory provisions, 1.818, 1.832

Liver fibrosis
generally, 10.135
Liver toxicity
generally, 10.135
Living together
see **Cohabitation**
"Local welfare provision"
employment and support allowance, 9.4
Lodgings
computation of earnings, 3.4
employment and support allowance, 9.4
Lone parents
computation of earnings, 3.4
work-related activity assessment, 1.884
"Long-term benefit"
gender recognition, 1.690–1.691
meaning, 1.47
Long-term incapacity benefit
Christmas bonus, and, 1.464–1.467
widowers' benefits
generally, 1.89–1.91
post-employment or training, 1.92–1.94
widows' benefit
generally, 1.86–1.88
post-employment or training, 1.92–1.94
Lowest rate conditions
see **Care component**
Lump sum payments (mesothelioma)
amount
generally, 12.19
payment to dependent, 12.20
payment to person affected, 12.20
appeals against determinations
First-tier Tribunal, to, 1.873–1.874
procedure, 12.11–12.12
Social Security Commissioner, to,
1.875–1.876
claims
definitions, 12.3
procedure, 12.4
time limits, 12.5
conditions of entitlement
disqualifying payments, 12.15
disregarded payments, 12.16
generally, 1.861–1.863
presence in the UK, 12.17
determination of claims
appeals, 1.873–1.876
generally, 1.864–1.867
procedure, 12.6–12.12
reconsideration, 1.868–1.872
disqualifying payments, 12.15
disregarded payments, 12.16
general note, 1.857–1.858
general provision, 1.859–1.860
minors, 1.877–1.878
persons lacking capacity, 1.877–1.878
presence in the UK, 12.17
reconsideration of determinations
generally, 1.868–1.872
procedure, 12.6–12.10
recovery of benefits, and, 1.881–1.882
regulations, 1.879–1.880

Lung carcinoma
generally, 10.135
prescribed occupations, 10.197
special conditions, 10.100–10.101
Lyme's disease
generally, 10.135, 10.181
Maintenance
employment and support allowance,
9.290
Making self understood
see **Descriptors for incapacity**
Manual dexterity
see **Descriptors for incapacity**
Mariners
see **Seafarers**
**Marriage and Civil Partnership
(Scotland) Act 2014**
consequential amendments
Order, by, 6.156–6.163
Married child
see **Child benefit**
Married persons
see **Spouses**
Married women
generally, 1.452–1.453
Maternity allowance
see also **Contributory benefits**
adjustment of benefits
persons abroad, 3.109–3.117
appropriate weekly rate, 1.62–1.63
average weekly amount, 5.15
contribution conditions
general note, 1.503
generally, 1.484
contribution credits, 2.8
curtailment, 5.16–5.22
earnings
average weekly amount, 5.15
specified payments, 5.11–5.13
specified period, 5.14
entitlement
appropriate weekly rate, 1.62–1.63
disqualification, 5.4
generally, 1.56–1.61
modified period, 5.5
workers abroad, 5.8
increases for dependants
abolition, 1.888
generally, 1.297–1.298
reduced contributions, 1.309–1.311
relevant earnings, 1.314–1.316
national insurance numbers, 5.3
participating wife or civil partner of self-
employed earner, 1.63–1.64
persons abroad
employed overseas, 5.8
generally, 3.109–3.110
grounds, 3.111–3.117
rate
appropriate weekly rate, 1.62–1.63
specified payments
aggregation, 5.13
average weekly amount, 5.15

employed earners, for, 5.11
self-employed earners, for, 5.12
specified period, 5.14
work abroad
employed overseas, 5.8
generally, 3.109–3.110
grounds, 3.111–3.117
Maternity leave
definition, 3.22
Maternity pay
contribution credits, 2.36–2.37
'new style' ESA, 13.247–13.248
relationship with other benefits,
1.638–1.640
Measles
see also **Vaccine damage payments**
appeals, 1.16–1.17
conditions of entitlement, 1.8–1.11
determination of claims, 1.12–1.18
error correction, 1.22
finality of decisions, 1.23–1.24
fraudulent statements, 1.27
generally, 1.2–1.7
payment, 1.19–1.21
setting aside decisions, 1.22
Medical examinations
'new style' ESA
limited capability for work,
13.142–13.143
limited capability for work-related
activity, 13.174–13.175
limited capability for work,
9.58–9.61
limited capability for work-related
activity, 9.123–9.124
industrial injuries benefit
employers' duties, 10.130
fees, 10.131
generally, 10.94–10.95
initial, 10.122
periodical, 10.127
initial examination
employers' duties, 10.130
fees, 10.131
generally, 10.122
periodical examination
employers' duties, 10.130
fees, 10.131
generally, 10.127
Medical expenses
attendance allowance
exemption, 4.27
generally, 4.26
disability living allowance
exemption, 4.64
generally, 4.63
Medical treatment
'new style' ESA
absence from Great Britain,
13.281–13.284
definition, 13.111
periods of less than a week, 13.304
personal independence payments, 4.203

Meningococcal Group C
see also **Vaccine damage payments**
appeals, 1.16–1.17
conditions of entitlement, 1.8–1.11
determination of claims, 1.12–1.18
error correction, 1.22
finality of decisions, 1.23–1.24
fraudulent statements, 1.27
generally, 1.2–1.7
payment, 1.19–1.21
setting aside decisions, 1.22
updating Order, 11.19–11.22
Mesothelioma
see also **Diffuse Mesothelioma Payment
Scheme, Mesothelioma (lump
sum payments)**
disablement benefit
generally, 10.96–10.97, 10.135
prescribed occupations, 10.188
special conditions, 10.98–10.99
scheme of last resort
definitions, 12.26
eligibility, 12.30–12.32
establishment of scheme, 12.27
general note, 12.23–12.23A
payments, 12.44–12.46
procedure, 12.33–12.43
reviews and appeals, 12.47–12.53
scheme administrator, 12.28–12.29
statutory basis, 1.944–1.963
Mesothelioma Act 2014
see also **Diffuse Mesothelioma Payment
Scheme**
arrangement, 1.944
citation, 1.963
commencement, 1.961
definitions, 1.960
eligibility, 1.948–1.950
establishment of scheme, 1.947
extent, 1.962
general note, 1.945–1.946
payments, 1.951
procedure, 1.952
purpose, 1.944
recovery of payments, 1.956–1.957
relationship with other legislation, 1.958
reviews and appeals, 1.953
scheme administration, 1.954
Mesothelioma (lump sum payments)
amount
generally, 12.19
payment to dependent, 12.20
payment to person affected, 12.20
appeals against determinations
First-tier Tribunal, to, 1.873–1.874
procedure, 12.11–12.12
Social Security Commissioner, to,
1.875–1.876
claims
definitions, 12.3
procedure, 12.4
time limits, 12.5
conditions of entitlement

disqualifying payments, 12.15
disregarded payments, 12.16
generally, 1.861–1.863
presence in the UK, 12.17
determination of claims
appeals, 1.873–1.876
generally, 1.864–1.867
procedure, 12.6–12.12
reconsideration, 1.868–1.872
disqualifying payments, 12.15
disregarded payments, 12.16
general note, 1.857–1.858
general provision, 1.859–1.860
minors, 1.877–1.878
persons lacking capacity, 1.877–1.878
presence in the UK, 12.17
reconsideration of determinations
generally, 1.868–1.872
procedure, 12.6–12.10
recovery of benefits, and, 1.881–1.882
regulations, 1.879–1.880
**Mesothelioma Lump Sum Payments
(Claims and Considerations)
Regulations 2008**
see also **Mesothelioma (lump sum
payments)**
arrangement of, 12.1
citation, 12.3
commencement, 12.3
definitions, 12.3
general provisions, 12.4–12.12
**Mesothelioma Lump Sum Payments
(Conditions and Amounts)
Regulations 2008**
see also **Mesothelioma (lump sum
payments)**
arrangement of, 12.13
citation, 12.14
commencement, 12.14
definitions, 12.14
general provisions, 12.15–12.20
schedule, 12.20
Metal founding/forging
see **Occupational deafness**
Metal grinding
see **Vibration white finger**
MFET Limited
employment and support allowance, 9.4
Minors
mesothelioma, 1.877–1.878
"Miscellaneous conditions"
allergic rhinitis, 10.189–10.190
asbestosis, 10.195
asthma, 10.193–10.194
byssinosis, 10.187
carcinoma, 10.201
chronic bronchitis, 10.198
chronic obstructive pulmonary disease,
10.198–10.200
diffuse mesothelioma, 10.188
emphysema, 10.198
inflammation of nose, 10.188
introduction, 10.137–10.140

list, 10.135
lung cancer, 10.197
nasopharyngeal cancer, 10.201
non-effective dermatitis, 10.191
'occupation', 10.139
occupational asthma, 10.193–10.194
pleural thickening, 10.196
pneumoconiosis, 10.186
ulceration of nose, 10.188
Mobilising unaided
see **Descriptors for incapacity**
"Mobility activities"
assessment of ability to carry out,
4.174–4.176
consultation to determine if claimant has
ability to carry out, 4.186–4.187
definition, 1.943
descriptors, 4.233, 4.255–4.259
evidence required for determining ability,
4.184–4.185
generally, 1.917–1.918
information required for determining
ability, 4.184–4.185
introduction, 1.910
journey planning, 4.256–4.257
matters to be taken into account in
determining good reason,
4.188–4.189
moving around, 4.258–4.259
redetermination of ability to carry out,
4.190–4.191
scoring, 4.179–4.180
Mobility component
disability living allowance
entitlement, 4.69–4.96
generally, 1.250–1.274
in-patients, 4.97–4.100
invalid vehicle scheme, 1.275–1.277
persons aged 65 or over, 1.278–1.280
qualifying period, 4.67–4.68
rate, 4.45
personal independence payment
definition, 1.943
generally, 1.912–1.916
introduction, 1.906
**Mobility component (disability living
allowance)**
artificial prosthesis, 4.90
arrested development, 4.91
assessment of degree of disablement, 4.88
double amputees, 4.86
entitlement
artificial prosthesis, 4.90
arrested development, 4.91
assessment of degree of disablement,
4.88
double amputees, 4.86
exertion, 4.85
generally, 4.69–4.96
inability to walk, 4.76–4.84
incomplete physical development, 4.91
oxygen requirement, 4.85
physical condition, 4.71–4.75

physical disablement, 4.71–4.75
physical restraint, 4.92–4.94
virtually unable to walk, 4.75–4.84
exertion, 4.85
generally, 1.250–1.274
hospital in-patients
adjustment, 4.100
exemption, 4.99
generally, 4.97–4.98
inability to walk, 4.76–4.84
incomplete physical development, 4.91
in-patients
adjustment, 4.100
exemption, 4.99
generally, 4.97–4.98
invalid vehicle scheme
generally, 1.275–1.277
Regulations, 4.101, 4.116–4.121
national insurance numbers, 4.33
oxygen requirement, 4.85
persons aged 65 or over
entitlement, 4.40–4.44, 4.102–4.115
generally, 1.278–1.280
persons residing in GB to whom EU
Regulation applies, 4.36–4.37
persons residing in EEA state or
Switzerland, 4.38
physical condition, 4.71–4.75
physical disablement, 4.71–4.75
physical restraint, 4.92–4.94
qualifying period, 4.67–4.68
rate, 4.45
refugees, 4.39
virtually unable to walk
generally, 1.253
Regulations, 4.75–4.84
Mobility supplement
see **War pensioner's mobility
supplement**
Multiple industrial accidents
see **Assessment (disablement)**
Mumps
see also **Vaccine damage payments**
appeals, 1.16–1.17
conditions of entitlement, 1.8–1.11
determination of claims, 1.12–1.18
error correction, 1.22
finality of decisions, 1.23–1.24
fraudulent statements, 1.27
generally, 1.2–1.7
payment, 1.19–1.21
setting aside decisions, 1.22
updating Order, 11.13–11.15
Nasal carcinoma
prescribed occupations, 10.192
Nasopharyngeal cancer
prescribed occupations, 10.201
National insurance contributions
see also **Contribution credits**
Class 3
appropriation, 2.56
crediting, 2.57
treatment, 2.62–2.64

collection, 2.65
generally, 2.1–2..78
jobseeker's allowance, 2.65A
late paid
generally, 2.58
no consent, connivance or negligence,
where, 2.58
through ignorance or error, 2.61
'new style' ESA
generally, 13.121–13.122
relaxation of condition, 13.123–13.124
'relevant benefit year', 13.133–13.134
statutory basis, 13.67–13.69
paid under arrangement, 2.66
payment, 2.65
retrospective earnings, 2.60
treatment, 2.58–2.66
National insurance numbers
application for allocation, 2.67
attendance allowance, 4.3
carer's allowance, 4.127
disability living allowance, 4.33
employment and support allowance
general, 9.6–9.7
introduction, 2.55
maternity allowance, 5.3
widowed mother's allowance, 6.121
widow's pension, 6.88
National minimum wage
employment and support allowance, 9.5
Navigation and maintaining safety
see **Descriptors for incapacity**
Neoplasm
generally, 10.135
Nervous system toxicity
generally, 10.135
"Net earnings"
computation of earnings, 3.4
Net profits
computation of earnings, 3.4
Neuropathy
generally, 10.135
Neurotoxicity
generally, 10.135
Night conditions
see **Care component**
Night workers
limited capability for work
'new style' ESA, 13.152–13.153
'old style' ESA, 9.72–9.73
Non-contributory benefits
adjustment
hospital in-patients, 3.77–3.78
persons abroad, and, 1.454–1.455
aged, for the
see also **Elderly persons**
age addition, 1.289–1.291
category C pensions, 1.287–1.288
category D pensions, 1.287–1.288
attendance allowance
see also **Attendance allowance**
entitlement, 1.153–1.157
excluded persons, 1.168–1.171

rate, 1.158–1.164
    terminal illness, 1.165–1.167
benefits for the aged
    see also **Elderly persons**
    age addition, 1.289–1.291
    category C pensions, 1.287–1.288
    category D pensions, 1.287–1.288
calculation of earnings
    disregards, 3.33–3.36
    employed earners, 3.13–3.26
    fractional sums, 3.12
    generally, 3.6–3.7
    notional income, 3.8–3.11
    rounding of fractions, 3.12
    self-employed earners, 3.27–3.31
carer's allowance
    see also **Carer's allowance**
    carers, 1.153–1.155
    entitlement, 1.176–1.189
    increases for dependants, 1.317–1.319
    rate, 1.511–1.513
disability living allowance
    see also **Disability living allowance**
    care component, 1.196–1.249
    generally, 1.190–1.195
    invalid carriages, 1.275–1.277
    mobility component, 1.250–1.274
    persons aged 65 or over, 1.278–1.280
    supplementary provisions, 1.281–1.285
disqualification
    see also **Disqualification (benefits)**
    generally, 1.434–1.441
    earnings, 1.431–1.433
guardian's allowance
    see also **Guardian's allowance**
    generally, 1.286
hospital in-patients, 3.77–3.78
invalid care allowance
    see also **Carer's allowance**
    generally, 1.178
meaning, 1.151–1.152
persons abroad, and, 1.454–1.455
rate, 1.511
severe disablement allowance
    see also **Severe disablement
        allowance**
    generally, 1.172–1.175
special cases
    airmen, 1.450–1.451
    continental shelf, employment on,
        1.456–1.457
    Crown employment, 1.444–1.446
    Her Majesty's forces, 1.447–1.449
    mariners, 1.450–1.451
    married women, 1.452–1.453
    persons abroad, 1.454–1.455
    polygamous marriages, 1.458–1.459
    seafarers, 1.456–1.457
suspension, 1.434–1.441
types, 1.151–1.152
"Non-dependant"
    employment and support allowance,
        9.189–9.190

Non-infective dermatitis
    generally, 10.191
Northern Ireland
    employment and support allowance,
        1.797–1.798
Notices of accidents
    see **Industrial injuries benefit**
Notional capital
    diminishing capital rule, 9.283–9.284
    generally, 9.281–9.284
Notional income
    determination methods, 3.11
    employment and support allowance
        calculation, 9.269–9.270
        deprivation of income, 9.263–9.264
        due to be paid, 9.265–9.266
        other income, 9.267–9.268
        paid to third party, 9.265–9.266
    generally, 3.8–3.9
    unascertainable earnings, 3.10
Nursing homes
    attendance allowance
        exemption, 4.24–4.25
        generally, 4.21–4.22
        relevant patients, 4.30
        terminally ill, 4.23
    disability living allowance
        exemption, 4.61–4.62
        generally, 4.57–4.59
        relevant persons, 4.60, 4.122
Nutrition
    personal independence payments, 4.241
    pleural thickening, 10.196
Occupational asthma
    prescribed occupations, 10.193–10.194
    time limits for claims, 10.124–10.125
Occupational deafness
    appeals, 10.118–10.119
    assessment of extent
        binaural disablement, 10.205
        generally, 10.121–10.122
        relevant claims, 10.203–10.204
    claims, 10.110–10.111
    cutting concrete masonry blocks, 10.152
    date of onset, 10.114–10.115
    duration of assessment
        commencement date, 10.123
        generally, 10.116
    firearms training, 10.158
    further claims, 10.112–10.113
    glass container manufacturer, 10.157
    introduction, 10.146–10.149
    masonry blocks cutting, 10.152
    metal founding/forging, 10.150
    pneumatic percussive tool, 10.151
    prescribed occupations
        cutting concrete masonry blocks,
            10.152
        firearms training, 10.158
        glass container manufacturer, 10.157
        introduction, 10.146–10.149
        metal founding/forging, 10.150
        pneumatic percussive tool, 10.151

ships engine room, 10.156
shot-blasters, 10.159
textile manufacturing, 10.153
water jets, 10.155
weaving, 10.153
wood working, 10.154
reassessment of disablement, 10.120
ships engine room, 10.156
shot-blasters, 10.159
supercession of decision, 10.117
textile manufacturing, 10.153
time limits for claims, 10.108–10.109
water jets, 10.155
weaving, 10.153
wood working, 10.154
Occupational pensions
computation of earnings, 3.4
gender recognition
equivalent benefits, 1.707–1.708
general note, 1.704
guaranteed minimum, 1.705–1.706
'new style' ESA, 13.14
Offsetting prior gratuity
see **Reduced earnings allowance**
Offshore installations
generally, 1.456–1.457
Orf
generally, 10.135
Osteoarthritis
industrial diseases
generally, 10.135
hip, 10.169
knee, 10.170–10.173
Osteolysis
generally, 10.135
Osteonecrosis
industrial injuries, 10.135
Other effective cause
see **Assessment (disablement)**
Overlapping benefits
adjustment of dependency benefits
adult dependant, 3.93
carer's allowance, 3.97
child dependant, 3.91–3.92
more than one dependant, 3.98
part week, for, 3.99
personal benefits payable, 3.94–3.95
priority, 3.100
severe disablement allowance, 3.97
training allowance, 3.96
adjustment of personal benefits
carer's allowance, 3.97
earnings-related supplements, 3.88
generally, 3.86–3.87
industrial injuries benefits, 3.89–3.90
part week, for, 3.99
priority, 3.100
relevant benefits, 3.104
severe disablement allowance, 3.97
carer's allowance, 3.97
industrial injuries benefits, 3.89–3.90
jobseekers allowance, 3.102
training allowance, 3.96

severe disablement allowance, 3.97
widows' benefit, and, 3.84–3.85
Ovine chlamydiosis
generally, 10.135
Oxygen requirement
see **Mobility component**
Parkinsonism
generally, 10.135
Participants in self-employment route
see **Employment and support
allowance**
Particulars of accidents
see **Industrial injuries benefit**
Part-time employment
'new style' ESA, 13.111
Partly relevant conditions
see **Assessment (disablement)**
Partners
computation of earnings, 3.4
'new style' ESA, 13.111
Paternity leave
definition, 3.22
"Pay period"
'new style' ESA, 13.111
'old style' ESA, 3.4
Payments
claimants' obligations, 10.8
computation of earnings, 3.4
definitions, 10.3
employers' obligations, 10.7
notice of accidents, 10.6
other than industrial injuries benefits,
10.17
particulars of accident, 10.13
vaccine damage
generally, 1.16
pre-scheme, 1.17
Pension income
'new style' ESA
Regulations, 13.235–13.236
statutory basis, 13.14
'old style' ESA
calculation of income, 9.227–9.228
deductions, 9.197–9.200
Pension schemes
computation of earnings, 3.4
gender recognition
Category A, 1.693–1.694
Category B, 1.695–1.696
Category C, 1.700–1.701
deferment, 1.698–1.699
graduated, 1.702–1.703
occupational pensions, 1.704–1.708
widow's pension, 1.686–1.687
payments and contributions on benefits,
1.644–1.650
pre-1975 beneficiaries and contributors,
6.126–6.151
Pension sharing
appropriate weekly rate, 1.1053–1.1056
appropriate weekly reduction,
1.1062–1.1065
consequential amendments, 1.988

creation of state scheme debits and credits
  activation of benefits, 1.672
  definitions, 1.675
  generally, 1.673
  shareable rights, 1.671
  transferor in new state pension scheme, 1.674
  generally, 1.985–1.986
  reduction in sharer's section 4 pension, 1.976
  shared additional pension, 1.143
  transitional provision, 6.211–6.213
  up-rating state pension, 1.1057–1.1061
Pensionable age
  contribution credits, 2.32–2.33
  equalisation, 1.653–1.669
  increase, 1.1003
  periodic review, 1.1004
  'persons approaching pensionable age', 2.32–2.33
Pensioner premiums
  employment and support allowance
    generally, 9.436
    weekly amount, 9.442
Pensions Act 1995
  amendments
    Pensions Act 2014, by, 1.1003
  arrangement of sections, 1.652
  general provisions, 1.653–1.655
  schedule, 1.656–1.669
Pensions Act 2014
  see also **State retirement pension**
  arrangement of, 1.964
  citation, 1.1024
  commencement
    generally, 1.1022–1.1023
    Order No 4, 6.164–6.166
  consequential amendments, 1.1019
  extent, 1.1021
  final provisions, 1.1019–1.1024
  general note, 1.966
  general provisions
    bereavement support payment, 1.1005–1.1018
    option to boost old retirement pensions, 1.1002
    pensionable age, 1.1003–1.1004
    state pension, 1.965–1.1001
  Orders
    pension sharing on divorce, 6.211–6.213
    transitional provision, 6.214–6.217
  regulations and orders, 1.1020
  schedules, 1.1025–1.1070
  transitional provisions, 6.214–6.217
Pensions Schemes Act 1993
  arrangement of sections, 1.642
  general note, 1.643
  general provisions, 1.644–1.650
Percussive metal tools
  see **Vibration white finger**
Periodical medical examinations
  see **Medical examinations**

Peripheral neuropathy
  generally, 10.135
Permanent health insurance
  'new style' ESA
    definition, 13.111
    generally, 13.229–13.230
  'old style' ESA, 9.191–9.192
Person responsible for child
  see **Dependants**
Personal independence payments
  ability to carry out activities, 4.174–4.176
  absence from Great Britain
    generally, 4.202
    receive medical treatment, to, 4.203
    special cases, in, 4.204
  age-related provisions, 4.214–4.219
  'aid or appliance', 4.235–4.236
  'aided', 4.235
  armed forces
    excluded persons, 4.260
    residence, 4.205
  assessment
    ability to carry out activities, 4.174–4.176
    claims, of, 4.304–4.306
    consultation to determine if claimant has ability to carry out activities, 4.186–4.187
    daily living activities, 4.172–4.173, 4.232
    definitions, 4.230–4.231
    information or evidence required for determining ability to carry out activities, 4.184–4.185
    matters to be taken into account in determining good reason, 4.188–4.189
    miscellaneous, 4.232–4.238
    mobility activities, 4.172–4.173, 4.233
    redetermination of ability to carry out activities, 4.190–4.191
    scoring, 4.177–4.183
  'assistance', 4.237
  attendance allowance, 1.153
  bathing, 4.245
  budgeting decisions, 4.254
  care home residents
    generally, 1.926–1.927
    Regulations, 4.226–4.227
  carer's allowance, 3.176
  carrying out activities, 1.917–1.918
  change of circumstances, 4.297–4.298
  claims
    assessment, 4.304–4.306
    death before of after, 4.290–4.291
    defective, 4.282–4.283
    definitions, 4.262
    determination procedure, 4.292–4.293
    excluded persons, 4.271
    express intention not to make, 4.286–4.287
    failure to provide information, 4.284–4.285

Index

further opportunity, 4.278–4.279
generally, 1.932–1.933
invitations to persons entitled to DLA,
4.263–4.265
notification inviting person, 4.272–4.275
payment after an interval, for,
4.198–4.199
persons entitled to DLA, by,
4.263–4.268
persons unable to act, 4.315–4.318
persons under 16, by, 4.269–4.270
reaching relevant age, after,
4.216–4.217
suspension of DLA when none made,
4.276–4.277
termination of DLA for failure to make,
4.280–4.281
transitional provisions, 4.261–4.322
withdrawal, 4.288–4.289
'condition', 4.235
consultation to determine if claimant has
ability to carry out activities
generally, 4.186–4.187
matters to be taken into account in
determining good reason,
4.188–4.189
contributions credits, 2.72
daily living activities
assessment of ability to carry out,
4.174–4.176
bathing, 4.245
budgeting decisions, 4.254
consultation to determine if claimant
has ability to carry out,
4.186–4.187
definition, 1.943
descriptors, 4.232, 4.239–4.254
dressing, 4.247
evidence required for determining
ability, 4.184–4.185
face to face engagement, 4.251–4.253
food preparation, 4.239–4.240
generally, 1.917–1.918
health condition monitoring,
4.242–4.244
incontinence, 4.246
information required for determining
ability, 4.184–4.185
introduction, 1.910
matters to be taken into account in
determining good reason,
4.188–4.189
nutrition, 4.241
reading signs, 4.250
redetermination of ability to carry out,
4.190–4.191
scoring, 4.177–4.178
therapy management, 4.242–4.244
toilet needs, 4.246
understanding signs, 4.250
undressing, 4.247
verbal communication, 4.248–4.249
washing and bathing, 4.245

daily living component
definition, 1.943
generally, 1.909–1.911
introduction, 1.906
definitions
general Regulations, 4.170
transitional provision Regulations,
4.262
detainees
generally, 1.930–1.931
Regulations, 4.226–4.227
disability living allowance, 1.192
disabled persons
badges for motor vehicles, 4.321–4.322
dressing, 4.247
employment and support allowance, 9.4
enhanced rate
daily living component, 1.909
mobility component, 1.912
entitlement
care home residents, 1.926–1.927
detainees, 1.930–1.931
generally, 1.905–1.907
hospital in-patients, 1.928–1.929
persons of pensionable age,
1.923–1.924
prisoners, 1.930–1.931
terminal illness, 1.921–1.922
UK is not competent state, 1.925
evidence required for determining ability
generally, 4.184–4.185
matters to be taken into account in
determining good reason,
4.188–4.189
extension of fixed term period,
4.294–4.296
extinguishment of rights under DLA
scheme, 4.299–4.303
face to face engagement, 4.251–4.253
food preparation, 4.239–4.240
generally, 1.905–1.908
good reason, 4.188–4.189
health condition monitoring, 4.242–4.244
HM forces
excluded persons, 4.260
residence
hospital in-patients
generally, 1.928–1.929
Regulations, 4.226–4.227
incapable persons, 4.315–4.318
incontinence, 4.246
information required for determining
ability
generally, 4.184–4.185
matters to be taken into account in
determining good reason,
4.188–4.189
invitations to claim, 4.263–4.265
matters to be taken into account in
determining good reason,
4.188–4.189
medical treatment, 4.203
mobility activities

assessment of ability to carry out, 4.174–4.176
consultation to determine if claimant has ability to carry out, 4.186–4.187
definition, 1.943
descriptors, 4.233, 4.255–4.259
evidence required for determining ability, 4.184–4.185
generally, 1.917–1.918
information required for determining ability, 4.184–4.185
introduction, 1.910
journey planning, 4.256–4.257
matters to be taken into account in determining good reason, 4.188–4.189
moving around, 4.258–4.259
redetermination of ability to carry out, 4.190–4.191
scoring, 4.179–4.180
mobility component
  definition, 1.943
  generally, 1.912–1.916
  introduction, 1.906
nutrition, 4.241
overlapping benefits, 3.82
payability in certain circumstances
  care home residents, 4.220–4.221
  detainees, 4.226–4.227
  hospital in-patients, 4.222–4.225
  periods of residence, 4.228–4.229
  prisoners, 4.226–4.227
periods of residence, 4.228–4.229
persons of pensionable age
  generally, 1.923–1.924
  Regulations, 4.313–4.314
persons residing in EEA state to whom relevant EU Regulation applies
  generally, 4.210–4.211
  refugees, 4.212
persons to whom relevant EU Regulation applies, 4.208–4.209
persons unable to act, 4.315–4.318
'physically or mentally' disabled, 1.910
prescribed conditions
  generally, 1.906
  Regulations, 4.200–4.201
prescribed date
  claims for payment after an interval, 4.198–4.199
  generally, 4.196–4.197
presence in Great Britain
  absence from Great Britain, 4.202–4.204
  armed forces, 4.205
  generally, 1.906
  introduction, 1.908
  persons residing in EEA state to whom relevant EU Regulation applies, 4.210–4.211
  persons to whom relevant EU Regulation applies, 4.208–4.209

prescribed conditions, 4.200–4.201
refugees, 4.212
Regulations, 4.200–4.212
serving members of HM forces and family members, 4.205
terminal illness, 4.206–4.207
prisoners
  generally, 1.930–1.931
  Regulations, 4.226–4.227
'prompting', 4.237
qualifying benefit, 1.435
rate, 4.213
reading signs, 4.250
receiving medical treatment, 4.203
redetermination of ability to carry out activities, 4.190–4.191
refugees, 4.212
Regulations
  age-related provisions, 4.214–4.219
  arrangement of, 4.161–4.168
  assessment, 4.172–4.191
  citation, 4.169
  commencement, 4.169
  definitions, 4.170
  general provisions, 4.172–4.229
  payability in certain circumstances, 4.220–4.229
  presence, 4.200–4.212
  rate, 4.213
  required period condition, 4.192–4.199
  residence, 4.200–4.212
  schedule, 4.230–4.259
  transitional provisions, 4.261–4.322
required benefit condition
  claims after an interval, 4.198–4.199
  daily living component, 1.911, 4.192–4.193
  further provision, 1.919–1.920
  introduction, 1.906
  mobility component, 1.915, 4.194–4.195
  prescribed date, 4.196–4.199
  Regulations, 4.192–4.199
residence
  absence from Great Britain, 4.202–4.204
  armed forces, 4.205
  generally, 1.906
  introduction, 1.908
  persons residing in EEA state to whom relevant EU Regulation applies, 4.210–4.211
  persons to whom relevant EU Regulation applies, 4.208–4.209
  prescribed conditions, 4.200–4.201
  refugees, 4.212
  Regulations, 4.200–4.212
  serving members of HM forces and family members, 4.205
  terminal illness, 4.206–4.207
revision of award, 4.218–4.219
scoring
  daily living activities, 4.177–4.178

further provisions, 4.181–4.183
mobility activities, 4.179–4.180
serving members of HM forces and family
members
excluded persons, 4.260
residence, 4.205
standard rate
daily living component, 1.909
mobility component, 1.912
supersession of award, 4.218–4.219
'supervision', 4.238
temporary absence from GB, 4.311–4.312
terminal illness
generally, 1.921–1.922
residence, 4.206–4.207
therapy management, 4.242–4.244
toilet needs, 4.246
transitional provisions, 4.261–4.322
UK is not competent state, 1.925
'unaided', 4.236
understanding signs, 4.250
undressing, 4.247
verbal communication, 4.248–4.249
washing and bathing, 4.245
**Personal Independence Payment
(Transitional Provisions)
Regulations 2013**
arrangement of, 4.261
citation, 4.262
commencement, 4.262
definitions, 4.262
general provisions , 4.256–4.322
Persons abroad
accidents abroad, 3.135
age addition, 3.129–3.130
attendance allowance, 3.132
bereavement payment, 3.120–3.121
carer's allowance, 3.134
Channel Islands, 3.137
child's special allowance, 3.120–3.121
Continental Shelf operations, 3.136
contributory benefits, 1.454–1.455
dependant's benefits
child dependants, 3.140–3.141
generally, 3.138–3.139
dependants, increases for, 1.454–1.455
disablement benefit, 3.131
disqualification from benefit, 1.437
guaranteed minimum pension, 3.125
guardian's allowance, 3.120–3.121
incapacity benefit
generally, 3.109–3.110
grounds, 3.111–3.117
industrial death benefit, 3.131
industrial injury benefits
Regulations, 3.131
statutory provision, 1.454–1.455
maternity allowance
employed overseas, 5.8
generally, 3.109–3.110
grounds, 3.111–3.117
'new style' ESA
generally, 13.277–13.278

medical treatment, for, 13.281–13.282
member of family of service personnel,
13.284–13.285
NHS treatment abroad, for,
13.283–13.284
short period, 13.279–13.280
non-contributory benefits, 1.454–1.455
payment of benefits, and, 3.143
personal independence payments
generally, 4.202
receive medical treatment, to, 4.203
special cases, in, 4.204
prescribed disease contracted abroad,
3.135
retirement pensions, 3.120–3.121
severe disablement allowance
employed overseas, 5.8
generally, 3.109–3.110
grounds, 3.111–3.117
state maternity allowance
generally, 3.109–3.110
grounds, 3.111–3.117
temporary absence
generally, 3.111
SoS's certificate, 3.112–3.117
unemployability supplement
generally, 3.109–3.110
grounds, 3.111–3.117
uprating of benefit
awards between 1985 and 1991, 3.145
generally, 3.122
ordinarily resident, 3.123–3.124
widows' benefit, 3.120–3.121
"Persons aged 65 or over"
carer's allowance
generally, 4.153
men attaining 65 before October 1994,
4.154
treated as entitled, 4.151
women attaining 65 before October
1994, 4.152
disability living allowance
entitlement, 4.40–4.44, 4.102–4.115
generally, 1.278–1.280
retirement pensions
age addition, 1.289–1.291
category C, 1.287–1.288
category D, 1.287–1.288
Persons approaching pensionable age
see **Pensionable age**
Persons elected as councillors
see **Councillors**
"Persons from abroad"
employment and support allowance,
9.187–9.188
Persons lacking capacity
mesothelioma, 1.877–1.878
"Persons residing together"
generally, 3.149–3.153
Phosphorus poisoning
generally, 10.135
"Physical agents"
cancer, 10.141

carpal tunnel syndrome, 10.166–10.168
cataract, 10.142
housemaid's knee, 10.144
introduction, 10.137–10.140
leukaemia, 10.141
list, 10.135
occupational deafness
  cutting concrete masonry blocks,
    10.152
  firearms training, 10.158
  glass container manufacturer, 10.157
  introduction, 10.146–10.149
  metal founding/forging, 10.150
  pneumatic percussive tool, 10.151
  ships engine room, 10.156
  shot-blasters, 10.159
  textile manufacturing, 10.153
  water jets, 10.155
  weaving, 10.153
  wood working, 10.154
vibration white finger
  forestry, 10.160–10.165
  generally, 10.160–10.165
  metal grinding, 10.160–10.165
  percussive metal tools, 10.160–10.165
writer's cramp, 10.143
Physical condition
  see **Mobility component**
Physical disabilities
absence of loss of control, 9.414
consciousness during waking moments,
  9.415
making self understood, 9.411
manual dexterity, 9.411
mobilising unaided, 9.407
navigation and maintaining safety,
  9.413
picking up and moving or transferring,
  9.410
preliminary note, 9.392
reaching, 9.409
standing and sitting, 9.408
understanding communication, 9.412
Physical disablement
  see **Mobility component**
Physical restraint
  see **Mobility component**
Picking up and moving
  see **Descriptors for incapacity**
Pilot schemes
employment and support allowance,
  1.774–1.775
Pilots
generally, 1.450–1.451
Pleural thickening
generally, 10.135
prescribed occupations, 10.196
Pneumatic percussive tool
  see **Occupational deafness**
Pneumococcal infection
  see also **Vaccine damage payments**
appeals, 1.16–1.17
conditions of entitlement, 1.8–1.11

determination of claims, 1.12–1.18
error correction, 1.22
finality of decisions, 1.23–1.24
fraudulent statements, 1.27
generally, 1.2–1.7
payment, 1.19–1.21
setting aside decisions, 1.22
updating Order, 11.23–11.25
Pneumoconiosis
chronic bronchitis, and, 10.104–10.105
definition, 1.460–1.461
'dependants', 1.32
emphysema, effect of, 10.104–10.105
generally, 1.425–1.430
prescribed occupations, 10.135, 10.136,
  10.186
reduced earnings allowance, 10.106
special conditions, 10.96–10.97
tuberculosis, and, 10.102–10.103
unscheduled occupation cases, 10.107
Pneumoconiosis etc. (Workers'
  Compensation) Act 1979
arrangement of sections, 1.31
citation, 1.33
commencement, 1.33
extent, 1.33
general note, 1.34
general provisions, 1.32
Poisoning
generally, 10.135
Poliomyelitis
  see also **Vaccine damage payments**
appeals, 1.16–1.17
conditions of entitlement, 1.8–1.11
determination of claims, 1.12–1.18
error correction, 1.22
finality of decisions, 1.23–1.24
fraudulent statements, 1.27
generally, 1.2–1.7
payment, 1.19–1.21
setting aside decisions, 1.22
Polygamy
computation of earnings, 3.4
contributory benefits
  generally, 1.458–1.459
  Regulations, 3.156–3.158
definition, 3.4
'new style' ESA, 13.111
non-contributory benefits
  generally, 1.458–1.459
  Regulations, 3.156–3.158
'old style' ESA
  calculation of income, 9.216–9.217
  prescribed amount, 9.183–9.184
retirement pension for women, 3.158
"PPF periodic payments"
'new style' ESA
  definition, 13.14
  generally, 13.235–13.236
'old style' ESA
  calculation of income, 9.227–9.228
  deductions, 9.197–9.200
  definition, 1.733

"Pre-1975 beneficiaries and contributors"
generally, 6.126–6.151
Pregnancy
'new style' ESA
limited capability for work, 13.137
limited capability for work-related activity, 13.166–13.167
'old style' ESA
limited capability for work, 9.51–9.53
limited capability for work-related activity, 9.107–9.117
Premiums
employment and support allowance
generally, 9.435–9.441
weekly amount, 9.442
"Prescribed degrees of disablement"
generally, 10.52–10.53
introduction, 10.26–10.28
Prescribed industrial diseases
see **Industrial diseases**
"Presence in Great Britain"
attendance allowance, 4.4–4.5
carer's allowance, 4.142–4.145
disability living allowance, 4.34–4.35
employment and support allowance, 1.819, 1.833
personal independence payments
absence from Great Britain, 4.202–4.204
armed forces, 4.205
generally, 1.905
introduction, 1.908
persons residing in EEA state to whom relevant EU Regulation applies, 4.210–4.211
persons to whom relevant EU Regulation applies, 4.208–4.209
prescribed conditions, 4.200–4.201
refugees, 4.212
Regulations, 4.200–4.212
serving members of HM forces and family members, 4.205
terminal illness, 4.206–4.207
mesothelioma lump sum payments, 12.17
Pressure
see **Stress**
Primary carcinoma
generally, 10.135
prescribed occupations, 10.201
special conditions, 10.100–10.101
Priorities
overlapping benefits, 3.100
Prisoners
disqualification from benefit, 1.434–1.441
personal independence payments
generally, 1.930–1.931
Regulations, 4.226–4.227
Private nursing homes
see **Nursing homes**
Probable standard of remuneration
see **Reduced earnings allowance**

Public authorities
employment and support allowance, 9.4
Q fever
generally, 10.135
Qualifying young person
see **Young persons**
Rate of Bereavement Benefits Regulations 2010
arrangement of, 6.152
citation, 6.153
commencement, 6.153
general provisions, 6.154–6.155
Rate of payment
age addition, 1.511
attendance allowance, 1.158–1.164, 1.511
bereavement allowance, 6.155
carer's allowance, 1.513
Category A retirement pensions
increases for dependants, 1.512
Category B retirement pensions
generally, 1.509
increases for dependants, 1.512
Category C retirement pensions
increases for dependants, 1.512
Category D retirement pensions
generally, 1.511
increases for dependants, 1.512
contributory benefits, 1.509
dependants, 1.512
disabled living allowance, 4.45
disablement pension, 1.514–1.515
guardian's allowance, 1.511
incapacity benefit
generally, 1.509
increases for dependants, 1.512
industrial injuries benefit, 1.514–1.515
non-contributory benefits, 1.511
reduced earnings allowance 1.621
retirement pension
Category B, 1.509
Category C, 1.511
Category D, 1.511
increases for dependants, 1.512
severe disablement allowance
generally, 1.511
increases for dependants, 1.513
successive accidents benefit, 1.515
unemployability supplement
generally, 1.515, 1.583
introduction, 1.599
widowed mother's allowance
generally, 1.77–1.78
increases for dependants, 1.512
Regulations, 6.154
widowed parent's allowance
generally, 1.83–1.85
increases for dependants, 1.512
Regulations, 6.155
widowers' pension
generally, 1.77–1.78
industrial injuries benefit, 1.515
Regulations, 6.155
widow's pension

generally, 1.77–1.78
industrial injuries benefit, 1.515
Regulations, 6.154
Raynaud's phenomenon
generally, 10.135
Reaching
see **Descriptors for incapacity**
Reconsideration
see **Reviews**
Recovery of benefits
mesothelioma, 1.881–1.882
'new style' ESA, 13.56
'old style' ESA
generally, 9.340–9.341
statutory provision, 1.782–1.783
Recrudescence
see **Industrial injuries benefit**
Reduced earnings allowance
see also **Industrial injuries benefits**
abatement, 10.233
amount, 1.618–1.619
background, 1.600–1.601
change of circumstances, 10.229–10.230
conditions of entitlement
basic concepts, 1.605–1.606
duration, 1.617
generally, 1.602–1.620
incapacity, 1.611
regular occupation, 1.607–1.612
duration, 1.617
generally, 1.593–1.594
incapacity, and, 1.611
introduction, 1.599
maximum rate, 10.228
offsetting prior gratuity, 10.235–10.236
pneumoconiosis, 10.106
pre-October 1986 claims, 10.232
probable standard of remuneration,
10.223–10.227
rate, 1.621
regular occupation
deeming regulations, 1.613
employment of equivalent standard,
1.610
generally, 1.607
incapacity, 1.611
prospects of advancement, 1.609
Regulations, 10.210–10.211
result of loss of faculty, 1.612
subsidiary occupations, 1.608
special hardship, 10.232
transitional provisions, 10.231–10.236
unemployability supplement,
10.214–10.215
notification, 9.175–9.176
Reduction of benefits
'new style' ESA
amount for each benefit week,
13.217–13.218
continuation of period, 13.212–13.213
daily rate, 13.219–13.222
definitions, 13.203
fraud, and, 13.214

low-level sanction, 13.206–13.207
lower daily rate, 13.221–13.222
lowest-level sanction, 13.208–13.209
principles for calculating periods,
13.204–13.205
Regulations, 13.203–13.224
start, 13.210–13.211
suspension, 13.214
termination, 13.215–13.216
universal credit ends, where,
13.223–13.224
'old style' ESA
cessation, 9.168–9.170
generally, 9.165–9.167
hardship payments, 9.171–9.174
Refugees
attendance allowance, 4.9
carer's allowance, 4.150
disability living allowance, 4.39
personal independence payments, 4.212
Regular employment
see **Industrial injuries benefit**
Regular occupation
see **Reduced earnings allowance**
"Relevant benefit week"
'new style' ESA, 13.71
"Relevant earnings limit"
computation of earnings, 3.4
Remuneration
meaning, 1.44–1.45
Renal failure
attendance allowance, 4.14–4.18
disability living allowance, 4.49–4.52
Repeatedly mobilise
see **Descriptors for incapacity**
Required benefit condition
personal independence payments
claims after an interval, 4.198–4.199
daily living component, 1.911,
4.192–4.193
further provision, 1.919–1.920
introduction, 1.905
mobility component, 1.915,
4.194–4.195
prescribed date, 4.196–4.199
Regulations, 4.192–4.199
Requires
see **Care component**
Residence
attendance allowance
generally, 4.4–4.5
person to whom EU Regulation applies,
4.6–4.7
carer's allowance, 4.142–4.145
disability living allowance, 4.34–4.35
Great Britain, in
attendance allowance 4.4–4.7
carer's allowance, 4.142–4.145
disability living allowance, 4.34–4.35
personal independence payments
absence from Great Britain,
4.202–4.204
armed forces, 4.205

generally, 1.905
introduction, 1.908
persons residing in EEA state to whom
    relevant EU Regulation applies,
    4.210–4.211
persons to whom relevant EU
    Regulation applies, 4.208–4.209
prescribed conditions, 4.200–4.201
refugees, 4.212
Regulations, 4.200–4.212
serving members of HM forces and
    family members, 4.205
terminal illness, 4.206–4.207
Residing together
    see **Cohabitation**
Respiratory diseases
industrial injury benefit, 1.425–1.430
"Resulting conditions"
industrial injuries, and, 10.62–10.63
Retirement allowance
    see also **Industrial injuries benefits**
generally, 1.595–1.596
introduction, 1.599
qualifying conditions, 1.622–1.627
Retirement annuity contracts
computation of earnings, 3.4
Retirement pensions
    see **State retirement pension**
Reviews (claims)
mesothelioma payments
    generally, 1.868–1.872
    procedure, 12.6
vaccine damage payments, 11.9
Revision
conversion decisions, 9.537
disability living allowance
    persons aged 65 and over, 4.102–4.115
personal independence payments,
    4.218–4.219
Rhinitis
generally, 10.135
prescribed occupations, 10.189–10.190
Rotavirus
    see also **Vaccine damage payments**
appeals, 1.16–1.17
conditions of entitlement, 1.8–1.11
determination of claims, 1.12–1.18
error correction, 1.22
finality of decisions, 1.23–1.24
fraudulent statements, 1.27
generally, 1.2–1.7
payment, 1.19–1.21
setting aside decisions, 1.22
updating Order, 11.40–11.43
"Rounding of fractions"
contributory benefits, 3.12
'new style' ESA, 13.113–13.114
'old style' ESA, 9.8–9.9
Rubella
    see also **Vaccine damage payments**
appeals, 1.12–1.17
conditions of entitlement, 1.8–1.11
determination of claims, 1.12–1.18

error correction, 1.22
finality of decisions, 1.23–1.24
fraudulent statements, 1.27
generally, 1.2–1.7
payment, 1.19–1.21
setting aside decisions, 1.22
Sanctions
'new style' ESA
    amount of reduction for each benefit
        week, 13.217–13.218
    continuation of reduction period,
        13.212–13.213
    daily reduction rate, 13.219–13.222
    definitions, 13.203
    'for no good reason', 13.43
    fraud, and, 13.214
    generally, 13.41–13.42
    low-level sanction, 13.206–13.207
    lower daily reduction rate,
        13.221–13.222
    lowest-level sanction, 13.208–13.209
    principles for calculating reduction
        periods, 13.204–13.205
    Regulations, 13.203–13.224
    start of the reduction, 13.210–13.211
    statutory basis, 13.41–13.43
    suspension of reduction, 13.214
    termination of reduction,
        13.215–13.216
    universal credit ends, where,
        13.223–13.224
Sclerodermatous thickening
generally, 10.135
Scoring
    see **Personal independence payments**
Seafarers
    see also **Continental shelf**
generally, 1.450–1.451
Self-employed workers
calculation of earnings
    disregards, 3.33–3.36
    generally, 3.27
    national insurance contributions, 3.31
    net profit, 3.29–3.30
    notional income, 3.8–3.11
    relevant earnings, 3.28
    rounding of fractions, 3.12
    tax, 3.31
computation of earnings, 3.4
definition
    categories of earners, 1.33, 1.460
    computation of earnings, 3.4
disregards
    care charges, 3.36
    child care charges, 3.35
    generally, 3.33–3.34
employment and support allowance
    calculation, 9.235–9.236
    generally, 9.245–9.246
    net profit, 9.247–9.248
    tax and national insurance, 9.249–9.250
generally, 3.27
mesothelioma, 1.857–1.858

national insurance contributions, 3.31
net profit, 3.29–3.30
'new style' ESA
    deduction of tax and NICs,
        13.270–13.271
    'earnings', 13.266–13.267
    generally, 13.256–13.257
notional income
    determination methods, 3.11
    generally, 3.8–3.9
    unascertainable earnings, 3.10
relevant earnings, 3.28
rounding of fractions, 3.12
tax, 3.31
Self-employment
employment and support allowance
    calculation, 9.218–9.219
    definitions, 9.251–9.252
    generally, 9.251–9.258
    gross receipts, 9.253–9.254
    tax, 9.257–9.258
Self-employment route
see **Self-employment**
Sensorineural hearing loss
generally, 10.135
"Sequelae"
industrial injuries, and, 10.62–10.63
Service personnel1
credits for spouses and civil partners,
        2.40–2.43
generally, 1.447–1.449
'new style' ESA
    absence from Great Britain of member
        of family, 13.284–13.285
    limited capability for work,
        13.158–13.159
    prescribed establishments and
        organisations, 13.305–13.307
personal independence payments
    excluded persons, 4.260
    residence, 4.205
vaccine damage payments, 11.6
"Service user group"
employment and support allowance,
        9.4
Setting aside (decisions)
vaccine damage payments, 1.18
Severe disablement allowance
see also **Non-contributory benefits**
adjustment of
    overlapping benefits, 3.97
    persons abroad, 3.109–3.117
assessment of disablement, 1.569
conversion to ESA
    see also **Conversion decisions**
    after conversion phase, 9.565–9.573
    decisions, 9.545–9.564
    definitions, 9.542–9.543
    disapplication of enactments, 9.574
    general note, 9.529–9.539
    miscellaneous provisions, 9.575–9.580
    relevant persons, 9.544
generally, 1.172–1.173

overlapping benefits, 3.97
persons abroad, 3.109
persons residing together, 3.149–3.153
rate
    generally, 1.511
    increases for dependants, 1.513
Regulations, 4.160
Severe disablement premium
employment and support allowance
    generally, 9.437
    weekly amount, 9.442
Severely disabled persons
carer's allowance
    carers, 4.129–4.132
    generally, 4.128
child benefit, 1.629
vaccine damage payments
    see also **Vaccine damage payments**
    appeals, 1.12–1.17
    conditions of entitlement, 1.8–1.11
    determination of claims, 1.12–1.18
    error correction, 1.22
    finality of decisions, 1.23–1.24
    fraudulent statements, 1.27
    generally, 1.2–1.7
    payment, 1.19–1.21
    setting aside decisions, 1.22
Shared additional pensions
gender recognition, 1.697
generally, 1.139–1.140
increase where entitlement deferred
    generally, 1.144
    miscellaneous provisions, 1.561–1.567
    new state scheme pension credit, because
        of, 1.141–1.142
    pension sharing, 1.143
    reduction, 1.143
Ships
occupational deafness, and, 10.156
"Short-term benefit"
meaning, 1.47
Short-term incapacity benefit
conditions
    see also **Contribution conditions**
    earnings factors, 1.49
    general note, 1.501–1.502
    generally, 1.48
    miscellaneous provisions, 1.483
    satisfaction in early years, 1.508
contribution credits
    further conditions, 2.31
    generally, 2.5
increases for dependants, and,
        1.297–1.298
Shot-blasters
see **Occupational deafness**
Sick pay
overview, 1.373
relationship with other benefits,
        1.630–1.635
Sickness benefits
contribution credits, 2.8
occupational deafness, 10.110–10.111

Smallpox
see also **Vaccine damage payments**
appeals, 1.12–1.17
conditions of entitlement, 1.8–1.11
determination of claims, 1.12–1.18
error correction, 1.22
finality of decisions, 1.23–1.24
fraudulent statements, 1.27
generally, 1.2–1.7
payment, 1.19–1.21
setting aside decisions, 1.22
So severely disabled mentally or physically
see **Care component**
Social Security and Family Allowances (Polygamous Marriages) Regulations 1975
arrangement of, 3.154
citation, 3.155
commencement, 3.155
definitions, 3.155
general provisions, 3.156–3.158
Social Security (Attendance Allowance) Regulations 1991
arrangement of, 4.1
citation, 4.2
commencement, 4.2
definitions, 4.2
general provisions, 4.3–4.29
schedules, 4.30
Social Security Benefit (Computation of Earnings) Regulations 1996
arrangement of, 3.1
citation, 3.2–3.3
commencement, 3.2–3.3
definitions, 3.4–3.5
general provisions
    employed earners, 3.13–3.26
    self-employed earners, 3.27–3.31
introductory provisions
    calculation of earnings, 3.6–3.7
    notional income, 3.8–3.11
    rounding of fractions, 3.12
schedules
    calculation of earnings, 3.33–3.38
transitional provisions, 3.32
Social Security Benefit (Married Women and Widows Special Provisions) Regulations 1974
general provisions, 2.51–2.53
Social Security (Carer's Allowance) Regulations 1976
arrangement of, 4.123
citation, 4.125
commencement, 4.125
definitions, 4.126
general note, 4.124
general provisions, 4.127–4.158
schedules, 4.159
Social Security (Claims and Payments) Regulations 1979
arrangement of sections, 10.1
citation, 10.2

commencement, 10.2
definitions, 10.3
general note, 10.4
general provisions, 10.5–10.11
schedule, 10.12–10.14
Social Security (Consequential Provisions) Act 1992
general note, 1.641
Social Security Contributions and Benefits Act 1992
amendments to
    Order, by, 6.156–6.163
    Pensions Act 1995, by, 1.653–1.668
application, 1.471–1.472
arrangement of sections, 1.35
citation, 1.481
commencement, 1.481
definitions
    age, 1.472–1.473
    Parts I–VI, 1.460–1.462
    Part X, 1.467
    references to Acts, 1.474
    territorial waters, 1.470–1.471
general provisions
    Christmas bonus, 1.464–1.467
    child benefit, 1.463
    contributions, 1.36–1.43
    contributory benefits, 1.47–1.150
    dependants, increases for, 1.292–1.329
    incapacity for work, 1.469
    industrial injuries benefits, 1.330–1.430
    miscellaneous, 1.431–1.459
    non-contributory benefits, 1.151–1.292
miscellaneous provisions
    interpretation, 1.470–1.474
    short title, etc., 1.481
    subordinate legislation, 1.475–1.480
schedules
    additional pension, 1.516–1.545
    child benefit, 1.629
    contribution conditions, 1.482–1.508
    disablement assessment, 1.568–1.582
    increase of pension on deferred entitlement, 1.546–1.567
    industrial injuries benefits, 1.583–1.627
    rates of benefits, 1.509–1.515
    statutory maternity pay, 1.638–1.640
    statutory sick pay, 1.630–1.637
subordinate legislation
    Parliamentary control, 1.478–1.480
    Regulations, orders and schemes, 1.475–1.477
Social Security (Contribution Credits for Parents and Carers) Regulations 2010
arrangement of, 2.69
citation, 2.70
commencement, 2.70
definitions, 2.72
general note, 2.71
general provisions, 2.74–2.86
transitional provisions, 2.73

Index

Social Security (Crediting and Treatment of Contributions, and National Insurance Numbers) Regulations 2001
arrangement of, 2.54
citation, 2.55
commencement, 2.55
definitions, 2.55
general provisions, 2.56–2.68
Social Security (Credits) Regulations 1975
arrangement of, 2.1
citation, 2.2
commencement, 2.2
definitions, 2.3
general provisions, 2.4–2.43
schedule, 2.45–2.46
transitional provisions, 2.44
Social Security (Deferral of Retirement Pensions) Regulations 2005
arrangement of, 6.1
citation, 6.2
commencement, 6.2–6.3
definitions, 6.2
general provisions, 6.4–6.7
miscellaneous provisions, 6.8–6.14
Social Security (Dependency) Regulations 1977
arrangement of, 3.39
citation, 3.40
commencement, 3.40
definitions, 3.40–3.41
general provisions
  adult dependants, 3.58–3.65
  child dependants, 3.54–3.55
  dependency, 3.42–3.53
  increase of benefits, 3.66–3.68
schedules
  increase of benefits, 3.72–3.73
transitional provisions, 3.69–3.71
Social Security (Disability Living Allowance) Regulations 1991
arrangement of, 4.31
citation, 4.32
commencement, 4.32
definitions, 4.32–4.33
general provisions
  care component, 4.47–4.66
  generally, 4.34–4.46
  invalid vehicle scheme, 4.101
  mobility component, 4.67–4.100
schedules
  invalid vehicle scheme, 4.116–4.121
  persons aged 65 or over, 4.102–4.115
  relevant persons, 4.122
Social Security (General Benefit) Regulations 1982
arrangement of, 10.15
general provisions
  disablement benefit, 10.30–10.41
  disqualification, 10.45
  other than industrial injuries benefits, 10.17–10.18

principles of assessment, 10.19–10.28
successive accidents, 10.43–10.44
miscellaneous provisions, 10.49
schedules, 10.51–10.56
Social Security (Graduated Retirement Benefit) Regulations 2005
arrangement of, 6.39
citation, 6.40
commencement, 6.40
definitions, 6.40
general provisions, 6.41–6.44
schedules, 6.45–6.73
Social Security (Graduated Retirement Benefit) (No.2) Regulations 1978
arrangement of, 6.15
citation, 6.17
commencement, 6.17
definitions, 6.17
general note, 6.16
general provisions, 6.18–6.20
revocations, 6.21
schedules, 6.22–6.28
Social Security (Hospital In-Patients) Regulations 2005
arrangement of, 3.74
citation, 3.76
commencement, 3.76
general provisions, 3.77–3.78
introduction, 3.75
revocations, 3.79
Social Security (Housing Costs Special Arrangements) Regulations 2008
arrangement of, 9.520
citation, 9.522
commencement, 9.522
definitions, 9.522
general note, 9.521
general provisions, 9.523–9.527
Social Security (Incapacity for Work) Act 1994
generally, 1.651
Social Security (Industrial Injuries) (Prescribed Diseases) Regulations 1985
amendments to
  1986, 10.209–10.219
  1990, 10.237–10.243
  1993, 10.244–10.247
  1996, 10.248–10.251
  2000, 10.252–10.259
  2003, 10.260–10.266
  2003 (No 2), 10.267–10.272
  2005, 10.273–10.277
  2007, 10.278–10.281
  2007 (No 2), 10.282–10.286
arrangement of, 10.57
citation, 10.58
commencement, 10.58
definitions, 10.58
general provisions
  date of onset, 10.66–10.76
  miscellaneous, 10.77–10.95
  generally, 10.244–10.247

prescription of disease, 10.59–10.65
recrudescence, 10.74
reduced earnings allowance,
    10.220–10.236
regular employment, 10.237–10.243
special conditions, 10.96–10.131
miscellaneous provisions, 10.209–10.219
schedules
    dates of development and onset, 10.207
    modification of Acts, 10.202
    occupational deafness, 10.203–10.205
    prescribed diseases and occupations,
        10.135–10.201
    relevant dates, 10.206
transitional provisions, 10.132–10.133
Social Security (Industrial Injuries)
    (Reduced Earnings Allowance)
    Regulations 1987
arrangement of, 10.220
citation, 10.221
commencement, 10.221
definitions, 10.221–10.222
general provisions, 10.223–10.236
Social Security (Maternity Allowance)
    Regulations 1987
arrangement of, 5.1
citation, 5.2
commencement, 5.2
definitions, 5.2
general provisions, 5.3–5.5
Social Security (Maternity Allowance)
    (Earnings) Regulations 2000
arrangement of, 5.9
citation, 5.10
commencement, 5.10
definitions, 5.10
general provisions, 5.11–5.15
Social Security (Maternity Allowance)
    (Work Abroad) Regulations 1987
arrangement of, 5.1
citation, 5.2
commencement, 5.2
definitions, 5.2
general provisions, 5.6–5.8
Social Security (Maximum Additional
    Pension) Regulations 2010
arrangement of, 6.74
citation, 6.75
commencement, 6.75–6.76
definitions, 6.77
general provisions, 6.78–6.79
Social Security (Overlapping Benefits)
    Regulations 1979
arrangement of, 3.80
citation, 3.81
commencement, 3.81
definitions, 3.82–3.83
general provisions
    adjustment of dependency benefits,
        3.91–3.103
    adjustment of personal benefits,
        3.84–3.90
schedules

adjustment of personal benefits,
    3.104–3.105
Social Security Pensions (Home
    Responsibilities) Regulations 1994
arrangement of, 2.47
citation, 2.48
commencement, 2.48
definitions, 2.48
general provisions, 2.49–2.50
Social Security (Personal Independence
    Payment) Regulations 2013
arrangement of, 4.161–4.168
citation, 4.169
commencement, 4.169
definitions, 4.170
general provisions
    age-related provisions, 4.214–4.219
    assessment, 4.172–4.191
    payability in certain circumstances,
        4.220–4.229
    presence, 4.200–4.212
    rate, 4.213
    required period condition, 4.192–4.199
    residence, 4.200–4.212
schedule, 4.230–4.259
Social Security (Persons Abroad)
    Regulations 1975
arrangement of, 3.106
citation, 3.107
commencement, 3.107
definitions, 3.107–3.108
general provisions, 3.109–3.144
schedule, 3.145
Social Security (Persons Residing
    Together) Regulations 1977
arrangement of, 3.146
citation, 3.147
commencement, 3.147
definitions, 3.147–3.148
general provisions, 3.149–3.153
Social Security (Retirement Pensions
    etc.) (Transitional Provisions)
    Regulations 2005
arrangement of, 6.80
citation, 6.81
commencement, 6.81–6.82
definitions, 6.81
general provisions, 6.83–6.84
Social Security (Severe Disablement
    Allowance) Regulations 1984
generally, 4.160
Social Security (Widows' Benefit and
    Retirement Pensions) Regulations
    1979
amendments to, 6.7
arrangement of, 6.85
citation, 6.86–6.87
commencement, 6.86–6.87
definitions, 6.86–6.87
general provisions,
    retirement pensions, 6.88–6.113
    widows' benefit, 6.114–6.109
schedule, 6.124–6.125

**Social Security (Widows' Benefit,
    Retirement Pensions and Other
    Benefits) (Transitional)
    Regulations 1979**
arrangement of, 6.127
citation, 6.128
commencement, 6.128–6.129
definitions, 6.130
general provisions, 6.131–6.150
long title, 6.126
schedule, 6.151
Special hardship
    see **Reduced earnings allowance**
Spouses
retirement pensions
    generally, 1.117–1.118
    special provision, 1.130–1.131
    spouse changed gender, where, 1.129,
        1.695–1.696
    survivors, 1.132–1.133
Standing and sitting
    see **Descriptors for incapacity**
State pension
    see also **State retirement pension**
amount
    full rate, 1.969–1.970
    reduced rate, 1.969
    Regulations, 6.169
    transitional rate, 1.973
background, 1.96
based on contributions of others,
    1.975–1.976
categories, 1.96
contracting-out
    abolition for salary related schemes,
        1.1001
creation, 1.965
debits and credits, 1.673–1.674
deferral
    calculating weeks, 1.993
    effect, 1.991–1.992
    generally, 1.989–1.990
    overseas residents, 1.996–1.997
    prisoners, 1.994–1.995
    Regulations, 6.172–6.182
    supplementary, 1.993
definitions
    general, 1.999
    'old state pension', 1.998
    Regulations, 6.168
effective date, 1.96
entitlement
    based on contributions of others,
        1.975–1.976
    full rate, 1.967–1.968
    reduced rate, 1.967–1.968
    transitional rate, 1.971–1.972
full rate
    amount, 1.969–1.970
    entitlement, 1.967–1.968
    Regulations, 6.169
gender recognition, 1.692
generally, 1.965–1.1001

graduated retirement benefit, 6.184–6.189
inheritance of
    additional old state pension,
        1.975–1.976
    amount, 1.1034–1.1037
    choice, 1.977
    deferral amount, 1.1043–1.1047
    deferred old state pension, 1.978–1.979
    graduated retirement benefit,
        1.980–1.981
    up-rating, 1.1038–1.1042
legislative scheme, 1.96
minimum qualifying period, 6.182
national insurance credits, 6.194–6.210
'old state pension', 1.998
option to boost old retirement pensions,
    1.1002
overseas residents
    generally, 1.996–1.997
    Regulations, 6.190–6.193
pension sharing on divorce
    appropriate weekly rate, 1.1053–1.1056
    appropriate weekly reduction,
        1.1062–1.1065
    consequential amendments, 1.988
    generally, 1.985–1.986
    reduction in sharer's section 4 pension,
        1.976
    up-rating, 1.1057–1.1061
pensionable age
    increase to 67, 1.1003
    periodic review, 1.1004
policy statement, 1.96
postponement
    calculating weeks, 1.993
    effect, 1.991–1.992
    generally, 1.989–1.990
    overseas residents, 1.996–1.997
    prisoners, 1.994–1.995
    Regulations, 6.172–6.182
    supplementary, 1.993
prisoners
    generally, 1.994–1.995
    Regulations, 6.170–6.171
rate
    full, 1.967–1.970
    reduced, 1.967–1.969
    transitional, 1.971–1.974
reduced rate
    amount, 1.969
    basic amount, 1.1052
    elections, 1.1048–1.1051
    entitlement, 1.967–1.968
Regulations
    deferral, 6.172–6.182
    definitions, 6.168
    full rate, 6.169
    graduated retirement benefit,
        6.184–6.189
    minimum qualifying period, 6.182
    national insurance credits, 6.194–6.210
    overseas residents, 6.190–6.193
    prisoners, 6.170–6.171

shareable state scheme rights, 1.674
survivor's pension
  choice, 1.977
  inheritance of additional old state
    pension, 1.975–1.976
  inheritance of deferred old state
    pension, 1.978–1.979
  inheritance of graduated retirement
    benefit, 1.980–1.981
  inherited amount, 1.1034–1.1037
  inherited deferral amount,
    1.1043–1.1047
  up-rating, 1.1038–1.1042
suspension
  calculating weeks, 1.993
  effect, 1.991–1.992
  generally, 1.989–1.990
  overseas residents, 1.996–1.997
  prisoners, 1.994–1.995
  Regulations, 6.172–6.182
  supplementary, 1.993
transitional rate
  amount, 1.973
  backdating, 1.974
  based on contributions of others,
    1.975–1.976
  calculating amount, 1.1025–1.1031
  entitlement, 1.971–1.972
  pension sharing on divorce,
    1.985–1.988
  recalculation, 1.974
  up-rating, 1.1032–1.1033
women who have had reduced rate
  election, 1.982–1.984
State pension credit
  Christmas bonus, 1.464–1.467
State Pension Regulations 2015
  see also **State pension**
  amendments to other legislation, 6.183
  arrangement of, 6.167
  citation, 6.168
  commencement, 6.168
  definitions, 6.168
  general provisions
    deferral of state pension, 6.172–6.182
    full rate of state pension, 6.169
    graduated retirement benefit,
      6.184–6.189
    minimum qualifying period, 6.182
    national insurance credits, 6.194–6.210
    overseas residents, 6.190–6.193
    prisoners, 6.170–6.171
  schedule, 6.211
State retirement pension
  see also **Contributory benefits,**
      Graduated retirement benefit,
      State pension
  abolition, 1.966
  adjustment of
    hospital in-patients, 3.77–3.78
    persons abroad, 3.120–3.121
  child dependant's addition, 3.54–3.55
  category A

additional pension, 1.104–1.111
  deemed earnings factor, 1.99–1.102
  deferral, 6.4–6.6
  earnings factor credits, 1.103
  generally, 1.97–1.98
  incapacity addition, 1.112–1.113
  increase where entitlement deferred,
    1.136–1.138
  increases for dependants, 1.299–1.306
  spouse's contributions, 1.114–1.116
  supplemental provisions, 1.135
category B
  civil partners, 1.117–1.120,
    1.127–1.128
  date of commencement, 1.125
  deferral, 6.4–6.6
  divorcees, 1.119–1.120
  entitlement by reference to benefits
      under ss 39A or 39B,
      1.123–1.124
  former civil partners, 1.119–1.120
  general, 1.125
  increase where entitlement deferred,
    1.136–1.138
  married person, 1.117–1.118,
    1.129–1.133
  married person whose spouse changed
      gender, 1.129
  supplemental provisions, 1.135
  surviving civil partners, 1.127–1.128
  surviving spouse, 1.132–1.133
  widowers, 1.121–1.122, 1.127–1.128
  widows, 1.121–1.122, 1.127–1.128
category C
  generally, 1.287–1.288
  increases for dependants, 1.299–1.306
category D, 1.287–1.288
Christmas bonus, and, 1.464–1.467
conditions
  earnings factors, 1.49
  general note, 1.504–1.505
  generally, 1.48
  miscellaneous provisions, 1.486
contribution credits
  generally, 2.5
  official error, following, 2.28
  starting credits, 2.6–2.7
creation, 1.965
deferral
  election provisions, 6.10–6.13
  generally, 6.4–6.6
effect of Pensions Act 2014, 1.966
gender recognition
  Category A, 1.693–1.694
  Category B, 1.695–1.696
  Category C, 1.700–1.701
  deferment, 1.698–1.699
  graduated, 1.702–1.703
  shared additional, 1.697
  occupational pensions, 1.704–1.708
  widow's, 1.686–1.687
general note, 1.966
generally, 1.95–1.96

hospital in-patients, 3.77–3.78
increase where entitlement is deferred
    generally, 1.136–1.138
    miscellaneous provisions, 1.546–1.560
increase where entitlement to shared
        additional pension is deferred
    generally, 1.144
    miscellaneous provisions, 1.561–1.567
increase where pensioner's deceased
        spouse has deferred entitlement
    generally, 6.52
    introduction, 6.51
increase where pensioner's entitlement is
        deferred
    calculation of increment, 6.48
    generally, 6.47
    introduction, 6.46
increase where treated as receiving
        pension at nominal weekly rate
    calculation of increment, 6.58
    generally, 6.57
    introduction, 6.56
increase where pensioner's deceased
        spouse has deferred entitlement
    calculation of increment, 6.54
    generally, 6.53
    introduction, 6.51
increases for dependants
    adults, 1.297–1.307
    child, 1.292–1.296
    husband, 1.303–1.305
    person with care of children,
        1.306–1.307
    reduced contributions, 1.309–1.311
    relevant earnings, 1.314–1.316
    wife, 1.299–1.302
legislative scheme, 1.96
lump sum where pensioner's entitlement
        is deferred
    calculation of increment, 6.50
    generally, 6.49
    introduction, 6.46
lump sum where treated as receiving
        pension at nominal weekly rate
    calculation of increment, 6.60
    generally, 6.59
    introduction, 6.56
pension sharing, 1.143
persons abroad, 3.120–3.121
persons residing together, 3.149–3.153
polygamous marriages, 3.158
pre-1975 beneficiaries and contributors,
        6.126–6.151
qualifying period, 6.182
rate
    Category B, 1.509
    Category C, 1.511
    Category D, 1.511
    increases for dependants, 1.512
replacement, 1.965–1.1001
scheme of legislation, 1.96
shared additional pension
    generally, 1.139–1.140

increase where entitlement deferred,
        1.144
new state scheme pension credit,
        because of, 1.141–1.142
pension sharing, 1.143
reduction, 1.143
transitional provisions, 6.83–6.84
State second pension
see also **State pension**
abolition, 1.643
credits, 1.103
general note, 1.643
generally, 1.98
years 2010–2011 onwards, 1.102
Statutory adoption pay
contribution credits
    'adoption pay period', 2.36–2.37
    'new style' ESA, 13.249–13.250
    'old style' ESA
        generally, 1.776–1.777
        Regulations, 9.211–9.212
Statutory maternity allowance
see **Maternity allowance**
Statutory maternity pay
contribution credits, 2.36–2.37
'new style' ESA
    generally, 13.247–13.248
    introduction, 13.53–13.54
'old style' ESA
    generally, 1.776–1.777
    Regulations, 9.209–9.210
relationship with other benefits,
        1.638–1.640
Statutory paternity pay
'new style' ESA
    generally, 13.251–13.253
    introduction, 13.53–13.54
'old style' ESA
    generally, 1.776–1.777
    Regulations, 9.213
Statutory shared parental pay
curtailment, 5.16–5.22
generally, 1.776–1.777
Regulations, 9.214–9.215
Statutory sick pay
overview, 1.373
relationship with other benefits,
        1.630–1.637
Streptococcus suis infection
generally, 10.135
Students
carer's allowance, 4.133
employment and support allowance
    access fund payments, 9.322–9.323
    changes during summer vacation,
        9.332–9.333
    covenant income, 9.312–9.315
    definitions, 9.308–9.309
    disregard of amounts, 9.316–9.319
    disregard of contributions, 9.326–9.327
    fee loans, 9.324–9.325
    further disregard, 9.328–9.329
    generally, 9.223–9.224

grant income, 9.310–9.311
income treated as capital, 9.330–9.331
student loans, 9.320–9.321
weekly amount, 9.299–9.300
Subcutaneous cellulitis
generally, 10.135, 10.144
"Successive accidents"
adjustment of benefits, 10.43–10.44
generally, 1.413–1.415
rate, 1.515
Supersession
conversion decisions, 9.537
decisions
occupational deafness, 10.117
personal independence payments,
4.218–4.219
disability living allowance
persons aged 65 and over, 4.102–4.115
personal independence payments,
4.218–4.219
"Surplus earning factor"
additional pension, and, 1.517–1.520
Surviving spouses
retirement pension, 1.132–1.133
Suspension (benefits)
employment and support allowance
imprisonment, 9.378–9.379
industrial injuries benefits
certificate, 10.128
conditions, 10.129
generally, 1.434–1.441
other than industrial injuries benefits,
10.12
Swine flu
see also **Vaccine damage payments**
appeals, 1.16–1.17
conditions of entitlement, 1.8–1.11
determination of claims, 1.12–1.18
error correction, 1.22
finality of decisions, 1.23–1.24
fraudulent statements, 1.27
generally, 1.2–1.7
payment, 1.19–1.21
setting aside decisions, 1.22
updating Order, 11.30–11.39
Task-specific focal dystonia
industrial injuries, 10.143
Tax exempt persons
see **Child benefit**
Temporary absence
employment and support allowance
armed forces personnel, 9.358–9.359
generally, 9.350–9.351
medical treatment, for, 9.354–9.355
receive NHS treatment, to,
9.356–9.357
short absence, 9.352–9.353
generally, 3.111
SoS's certificate, 3.112–3.117
Tenosynovitis
generally, 10.145
Terminal illness
attendance allowance, 1.165–1.167

care component, 1.246
'new style' ESA
limited capability for work, 13.137
limited capability for work-related
activity, 13.166–13.167
'terminally ill', 13.111
'old style' ESA
assessment phase, 9.16–9.17
limited capability for work, 9.51–9.53
limited capability for work-related
activity, 9.107–9.117
personal independence payments
generally, 1.921–1.922
residence, 4.206–4.207
Tetanus
see also **Vaccine damage payments**
appeals, 1.16–1.17
conditions of entitlement, 1.8–1.11
determination of claims, 1.12–1.18
error correction, 1.22
finality of decisions, 1.23–1.24
fraudulent statements, 1.27
generally, 1.2–1.7
payment, 1.19–1.21
setting aside decisions, 1.22
Textile manufacturing
see **Occupational deafness**
Therapy management
see **Personal independence payments**
Toilet needs
see **Personal independence payments**
Trade disputes
increases for dependants, and,
1.320–1.323
Trainees
child benefit, 1.629
industrial injuries benefit, 1.904
Training
adjustment of benefits, 3.96
credits
generally, 2.10–2.11
termination, 2.18–2.19
'new style' ESA
definition, 13.111
limited capability for work,
13.158–13.159
'old style' ESA, 9.97–9.98
overlapping benefits, 3.96
Training allowance
see **Overlapping benefits**
Tuberculosis
see also **Vaccine damage payments**
appeals, 1.16–1.17
conditions of entitlement, 1.8–1.11
determination of claims, 1.12–1.18
error correction, 1.22
finality of decisions, 1.23–1.24
fraudulent statements, 1.27
generally, 1.2–1.7
industrial diseases, and, 10.135
industrial injury benefit, 1.425–1.430
payment, 1.19–1.21
pneumoconiosis, and, 10.102–10.103

prescribed occupations, 10.178
setting aside decisions, 1.22
Ulceration of nose
generally, 10.188
Unable to walk
see **Mobility component**
Understanding communication
see **Descriptors for incapacity**
Undressing
see **Personal independence payments**
Unemployability supplement
adjustment of benefits
hospital in-patients, 3.77–3.78
persons abroad, 3.109–3.117
availability, 1.583
Christmas bonus, and, 1.464–1.467
duration, 1.584
earnings level, 10.32
fluctuating earnings, 1.590
generally, 1.583–1.590
hospital in-patients, 3.77–3.78
increase
adult dependents, 1.588
dependent children, 1.586–1.587
generally, 1.585
introduction, 1.599
persons abroad
generally, 3.109–3.110
grounds, 3.111–3.117
persons residing together, 3.149–3.153
rate, 1.515, 1.584
reduced earnings allowance,
10.214–10.215
relevant earnings, 1.589
statutory sick pay, 1.630–1.637
time qualifications, 1.412
Unemployment
contribution credits, 2.20–2.22
Unemployment benefits
contribution conditions, 1.482
contribution credits, 2.8
generally, 1.54
Universal credits
contribution credits, 2.31
conversion to ESA, 9.540
duration of 'new style' ESA, 13.9
reduction of 'new style' ESA,
13.223–13.224
Uprating (benefits)
persons abroad
generally, 3.122–3.124
1985 to 1991 awards, 3.145
Urgent cases
employment and support allowance,
9.380
Vaccine damage payments
amount
generally, 1.2–1.7
updating Order, 11.49–11.53
appeals, 1.16–1.17
armed forces personnel, 11.6
claims
armed forces, members of, 11.6
disabled person's obligations, 11.6–11.7
generally, 11.3
pre-scheme, 11.8
required information, 11.4
conditions of entitlement, 1.8–1.11
decisions reversing earlier decisions
generally, 1.12
Regulations, 11.10–11.12
determination of claims
appeals, 1.16–1.17
reconsideration, 1.17
reversal, 1.12
error correction, 1.22
finality of decisions, 1.23–1.24
fraudulent statements, 1.27
generally, 1.2–1.7
Orders
amount, 11.49–11.53
specified diseases, 11.44–11.48
statutory sum, 11.49–11.53
payment
generally, 1.18
pre-scheme, 1.19
pre-scheme claims
generally, 1.19
procedure, 11.8
prescribed circumstances, 11.7
reconsideration, 1.17
reviews, 11.9
service personnel, 11.6
setting aside decisions, 1.22
specified diseases
generally, 1.2–1.7
haemophilus influenza type B,
11.16–11.18
human papillomavirus, 11.26–11.29
influenza, 11.40–11.43
influenza (H1N1), 11.30–11.39
meningococcal group C, 11.19–11.22
mumps, 11.13–11.15
Order (2016), 11.44–11.48
pneumococcal infection, 11.23–11.25
rotavirus, 11.40–11.43
swine flu, 11.30–11.39
statutory sum
generally, 1.2–1.7
updating Order, 11.49–11.53
transitional claims, 1.6–1.7
Vaccine Damage Payments Act 1979
arrangement of sections, 1.1
citation, 1.30
extent, 1.30
financial provisions, 1.29
general provisions, 1.2–1.23
miscellaneous provisions
fraudulent statements, 1.27
Regulations, 1.25–1.26
**Vaccine Damage Payments Regulations
1979**
arrangement of, 11.1
citation, 11.2
commencement, 11.2
general provisions

claims, 11.3–11.8
decisions reversing earlier decisions,
    11.10–11.12
reviews, 11.9
interpretation, 11.2
Vaccine Damage Payments (Specified
    Disease) Order 2006
arrangement of, 11.23
citation, 11.23
commencement, 11.23
general provisions, 11.25
Verbal communication
  see **Personal independence payments**
Vibrating tools"
  see **Carpal tunnel syndrome**
Vibration white finger
forestry, 10.160–10.165
generally, 10.160–10.165
metal grinding, 10.160–10.165
percussive metal tools, 10.160–10.165
Viral hepatitis
generally, 10.135, 10.180
Virtually unable to walk
  see **Mobility component**
Vitiligo
generally, 10.135
Voidable marriages
generally, 1.458–1.459
Voluntary organisations
computation of earnings, 3.4
'new style' ESA, 13.111
"Waiting days"
'new style' ESA, 13.272–13.273
'old style' ESA
  generally, 9.334–9.335
  statutory provisions, 1.816, 1.830
War disablement pension
Christmas bonus, and, 1.464–1.467
War pensioner's mobility supplement
Christmas bonus, and, 1.464–1.467
War widow's pension
Christmas bonus, and, 1.464–1.467
Washing and bathing
  see **Personal independence payments**
Water jets
  see **Occupational deafness**
Weaving
  see **Occupational deafness**
"Weekly amount of income"
employment and support allowance,
    9.239–9.240
Weeks
computation of earnings, 3.4
dependency, 3.72
Welfare Reform Act 2007
  see also **Employment and support**
    allowance ('old style')
amendments, 1.886–1.887
arrangement of sections, 1.709
citation, 1.805
commencement, 1.803–1.804
consequential amendments, 1.792–1.794
definitions

general, 1.799
Part I, 1.784–1.785
extent, 1.802–1.802A
financial provisions
general, 1.800
Part I, 1.790–1.791
general note, 13.4
general provisions, 1.710–1.783
'new style' ESA
  additional conditions, 13.67–13.74
  consequential amendments, 13.101
  definitions, 13.57–13.58
  drug dependency, 13.75
  entitlement, 13.6–13.56
  financial provisions, 13.61–13.63
  general note, 13.4
  Parliamentary control, 13.59–13.60
  Regulations, 13.103–13.311
  relevant sections, 13.5
  supplementary provisions,
    13.76–13.100
  transition, 13.64–13.66, 13.102
Northern Ireland, 1.797–1.798
Parliamentary control, 1.788–1.789
regulations, 1.786–1.787
repeals, 1.801
schedules, 1.806–1.855
transitional provisions, 1.795–1.796
Welfare Reform Act 2009
arrangement of sections, 1.883
citation, 1.895
commencement, 1.894
extent, 1.893
financial provisions, 1.892
general provisions, 1.884–1.890
repeals, 1.891
revocations, 1.891
schedule, 1.896
Welfare Reform Act 2012
amendments, 1.937
arrangement of sections, 1.897–1.901
consequential provision, 1.938
definitions, 1.943
general provisions
  abolition of benefits, 13.1–13.3
  disability living allowance, 1.935–1.936
  industrial injuries, 1.902–1.904
  personal independence payments,
    1.905–1.934
regulations, 1.941–1.942
supplementary provision, 1.938
transitional provision, 1.939–1.940
Welfare Reform and Pensions Act 1999
arrangement of sections, 1.670
definitions, 1.675
general provisions, 1.671–1.674
Welfare Reform and Work Act 2016
general provision, 1.1071–1.1072
Whooping cough
  see also **Vaccine damage payments**
appeals, 1.16–1.17
conditions of entitlement, 1.8–1.11
determination of claims, 1.12–1.18

error correction, 1.22
finality of decisions, 1.23–1.24
fraudulent statements, 1.27
generally, 1.2–1.7
payment, 1.19–1.21
setting aside decisions, 1.22
Widowed mother's allowance
adjustment of benefits
  hospital in-patients, 3.77–3.78
  overlapping benefits, 3.84–3.85
child benefit, 6.118–6.119
Christmas bonus, and, 1.464–1.467
contribution conditions
  see also **Contribution conditions**
  earnings factors, 1.49
  general note, 1.504–1.505
  generally, 1.48
  miscellaneous provisions, 1.486
contribution credits
  generally, 2.5
  starting credits, 2.6–2.7
deaths before 9 April 2001, 1.71–1.73
gender recognition, 1.684–1.685
generally, 1.71–1.73
home responsibilities protection,
  2.49–2.50
hospital in-patients, 3.77–3.78
increases for dependants
  generally, 1.297–1.307
  rate, 1.512
  relevant earnings, 1.314–1.316
national insurance numbers, 6.121
pre-1975 beneficiaries and contributors,
  6.134–6.135
rate
  generally, 1.77–1.78
  increases for dependants, 1.512
  Regulations, 6.154
Widowed parent's allowance
child benefit, 6.120
Christmas bonus, and, 1.464–1.467
contribution conditions
  see also **Contribution conditions**
  earnings factors, 1.49
  general note, 1.504–1.505
  generally, 1.48
  miscellaneous provisions, 1.486
contribution credits
  generally, 2.5
  starting credits, 2.6–2.7
gender recognition, 1.688–1.689
generally, 1.79–1.80
home responsibilities protection,
  2.49–2.50
rate
  generally, 1.83–1.85
  increases for dependants, 1.512
  Regulations, 6.155
Widowers' benefits
adjustment of benefits
  hospital in-patients, 3.77–3.78
bereavement allowance, 1.81–1.82
bereavement payment, 1.67–1.68

hospital in-patients, 3.77–3.78
long-term incapacity benefit
  generally, 1.89–1.91
  post-employment or training, 1.92–1.94
rate
  generally, 1.515
  Regulations, 6.155
retirement pensions, 1.121–1.122,
  1.127–1.128
widowed parent's allowance
  generally, 1.79–1.80
  rate, 1.83–1.85
Widows' benefits
see also **Contributory benefits**
adjustment of benefits
  hospital in-patients, 3.77–3.78
  overlapping benefits, 3.84–3.85
  persons abroad, 3.120–3.121
age addition, 6.122
bereavement allowance
  generally, 1.81–1.82
  Regulations, 6.155
bereavement payment, 1.67–1.68
conditions
  see also **Contribution conditions**
  earnings factors, 1.49
  general note, 1.491–1.508
  generally, 1.48
  miscellaneous provisions, 1.482–1.490
contribution credits
  widowed parent's allowance, 2.6–2.7
  widow's pension, 2.6–2.7
gender recognition, 1.686–1.687
hospital in-patients, 3.77–3.78
long-term incapacity benefit
  generally, 1.86–1.88
  post-employment or training, 1.92–1.94
persons abroad, and, 3.120–3.121
retirement pensions , 1.121–1.122,
  1.127–1.128
widow of man over 65 in 1948, for
  corresponding to widowed mother's
    allowance, 6.116
  corresponding to pension, 6.114–6.115
  restrictions, 6.117
widowed mother's allowance
  see also **Widowed mother's allowance**
  adjustment of, 3.84–3.85
  child benefit, 6.118–6.119
  generally, 1.70–1.74
  increases for dependants, 1.297–1.307
  national insurance numbers, 6.121
  rate, 1.77–1.78
widowed parent's allowance
  see also **Widowed parent's allowance**
  child benefit, 6.120
  generally, 1.79–1.80
  rate, 1.83–1.85
widows' payment, 1.66
widow's pensions
  see also **Widow's pensions**
  days of increment, 6.93–6.96
  election not to receive, 6.89–6.91

entitlement conditions, 6.101–6.109
generally, 1.74–1.76
incapacity for work, 6.92
national insurance numbers, 6.88
rate, 1.77–1.78
rate where second contribution
    condition not satisfied,
    6.97–6.100
Widows' payments
see **Bereavement payment**
Widow's pension
adjustment of benefits
    hospital in-patients, 3.77–3.78
Category A, under, 6.103–6.105
Category B, under, 6.101–6.102
Category C, under
    divorced woman of man over 65 in
        1948, for, 6.112–6.113
    entitlement conditions, 6.106–6.107
    widow of man over 65 in 1948, for,
        6.110–6.111
Category D, under, 6.108–6.109
Christmas bonus, and, 1.464–1.467
contribution conditions
    see also **Contribution conditions**
    earnings factors, 1.49
    general note, 1.504–1.505
    generally, 1.48
    miscellaneous provisions, 1.486
contribution credits
    generally, 2.5
    starting credits, 2.6–2.7
days of increment
    enhancement period, 6.96
    generally, 6.93–6.95
election not to receive
    generally, 6.89–6.90
    post-election provisions, 6.91
entitlement conditions
    Category A, 6.103–6.105
    Category B, 6.101–6.102
    Category C, 6.106–6.107
    Category D, 6.108–6.109
gender recognition, 1.686–1.687
generally, 1.74–1.76
home responsibilities protection,
    2.49–2.50
hospital in-patients, 3.77–3.78
incapacity for work, 6.92
national insurance numbers, 6.88
pre-1975 beneficiaries and contributors,
    6.134–6.135
rate
    generally, 1.77–1.78
    industrial injuries benefit, 1.515
    Regulations, 6.154
    second contribution condition not
        satisfied, where, 6.97–6.100
Wood working
see **Occupational deafness**
Work capability assessments
introduction, 1.748
limited capability for work, and

additional circumstances, 9.100–9.102
claimants receiving regular treatment,
    9.68–9.69
claimants treated as having, 9.51–9.53
definition, 1.716–1.717
descriptors, 9.393–9.425
determination, 9.43–9.50
excepted claimants, 9.97–9.98
exceptional circumstances, 9.74–9.90
failure to provide required information,
    9.56–9.57
generally, 1.747–1.749
good cause, and, 9.62–9.63
hospital in-patients, 9.64–9.67
jobseeker's allowance, and, 9.96
limited capability at start of day,
    9.70–9.71
medical examinations, 9.58–9.61
night workers, 9.72–9.73
pregnant women, 9.51–9.53
reasonable adjustments in workplace,
    9.90
Regulations, 9.43–9.102
required information, 9.54–9.55
supplementary provisions, 1.815
terminally ill claimants, 9.51–9.53
training courses, and,, 9.97–9.98
treatment of claimant at end of period
    covered by evidence, 9.99
treatment of claimant pending
    determination, 9.91–9.95
work-focused health-related assessments,
    and
    Regulations, 9.147
    statutory provisions, 1.755–1.756
work-related activity, and
    claimants treated as having,
        9.107–9.117
    descriptors, 9.426–9.428
    determination, 9.103–9.106
    failure to provide required information,
        9.121–9.122
    generally, 1.750–1.752
    good cause, and, 9.125–9.126
    interpreting activities and descriptors,
        9.429–9.433
    medical examinations, 9.123–9.124
    pregnant women, 9.107–9.117
    Regulations, 9.103–9.126
    relevant linked cases, 9.118
    required information, 9.119–9.120
    terminally ill claimants, 9.107–9.117
Work-focused health-related
    assessments
Regulations, 9.147
statutory provisions, 1.755–1.756
Work-focused interviews
action plans
    generally, 9.156
    statutory provisions, 1.761–1.762
contracting-out functions, and,
    9.163–9.164
deferral of requirement, 9.157–9.158

failure to take part, 9.161–9.162
generally, 1.757–1.758
'new style' ESA
  generally, 13.25–13.26
  persons only subject to, 13.31–13.32
  purpose, 13.195–13.196
notification, 9.152–9.153
persons starting or returning to work,
  9.159–9.160
purposes, 9.150–9.151
Regulations, 9.148–9.164
requirement to take part, 9.148–9.149
statutory provisions
  action plans, 1.761–1.762
  generally, 1.757–1.758
taking part, 9.154–9.155
"Work for your benefit"
work-related activity assessment, 1.884
"Work or training beneficiaries"
generally, 9.349
Work preparation requirements
'new style' ESA
  generally, 13.27–13.28
  persons subject to, 13.33–13.34
Work-related activities
abolition
  generally, 1.1071–1.1072
  Regulations, 9.619–9.629
action plans
  generally, 9.603–9.604
  reconsideration, 9.607
claimants treated as having, 9.107–9.117
contracting-out functions, and, 9.609
deferral of requirement, 9.605–9.606
descriptors, 9.426–9.428
determination, 9.103–9.106
directions, 1.763–1.764, 9.602
failure to provide required information,
  9.121–9.122
failure to take part, 9.608
generally, 1.759–1.760
good cause, and, 9.125–9.126
interpreting activities and descriptors,
  9.429–9.433
limited capability for
  claimants treated as having,
    9.107–9.117
  descriptors, 9.426–9.434
  determination, 9.103–9.106
  failure to provide required information,
    9.121–9.122
  generally, 9.426–9.434
  good cause, and, 9.125–9.126
  introduction, 1.750–1.752
  lone parents of children under 7, 1.884
  medical examinations, 9.123–9.124
  pregnant women, 9.107–9.117
  Regulations, 9.103–9.126
  relevant linked cases, 9.118
  required information, 9.119–9.120
  statutory provisions, 1.750–1.752
  supplementary provisions, 1.823
  terminally ill claimants, 9.107–9.117

medical examinations, 9.123–9.124
notification, 9.603–9.604
pregnant women, 9.107–9.117
reconsideration of action plans, 9.607
Regulations
  abolition, 9.619–9.629
  general, 9.596–9.611
  limited capability, 9.103–9.126
relevant linked cases, 9.118
requirement to undertake, 9.605–9.606
terminally ill claimants, 9.107–9.117
Work-related activity assessment
see **Limited capability for work-related
    activity**
**Work-related requirements ('new style'
    ESA)**
connected requirements, 13.35–13.36
exempt persons, 13.29–13.30
generally, 13.21–13.22
work-focused interviews
  generally, 13.25–13.26
  persons only subject to, 13.31–13.32
  purpose, 13.195–13.196
work preparation
  generally, 13.27–13.28
  persons subject to, 13.33–13.34
**Work-related requirements ('old style'
    ESA)**
see also **Employment and support
    allowance ('old style')**
Administration Act modifications,
  9.177–9.178
contracting out, 1.766–1.767
notification, 9.175–9.176
reduction of allowance
  cessation, 9.168–9.170
  generally, 9.165–9.167
  hardship payments, 9.171–9.174
Regulations
  hardship payments, 9.171–9.174
  notification, 9.175–9.176
  reduction of allowance, 9.165–9.170
  work-focused health-related
    assessments, 9.147
  work-focused interviews, 9.148–9.164
statutory provisions
  action plans, 1.761–1.762
  contracting out, 1.766–1.767
  directions, 1.763–1.764
  hardship payments, 1.768
  work-focused health-related
    assessments, 1.755–1.756
  work-focused interviews, 1.757–1.758
  work-related activity, 1.759–1.760
work-focused health-related assessments
  Regulations, 9.147
  statutory provisions, 1.755–1.756
work-focused interviews
  action plans, 1.761–1.762, 9.156
  contracting-out functions, and,
    9.163–9.164
  deferral of requirement, 9.157–9.158
  failure to take part, 9.161–9.162

generally, 1.757–1.758
notification, 9.152–9.153
persons starting or returning to work,
    9.159–9.160
purposes, 9.150–9.151
Regulations, 9.148–9.164
requirement to take part, 9.148–9.149
statutory provisions, 1.757–1.758
taking part, 9.154–9.155
work-related activity
    directions, 1.763–1.764
    generally, 1.759–1.760
Working families' tax credit
additional pensions, 1.107–1.128
Working tax credit
contribution credits, 2.16–2.17
disability element, 2.14–2.15
Workmen's compensation
generally, 10.75

re-employment of pneumoconiotics,
    10.76
"Writer's cramp"
industrial injury benefit, 10.135, 10.143
"Year of assessment"
computation of earnings, 3.4
Young persons
care, in, 1.629
detention, in, 1.629
"Youth condition"
'new style' ESA
    full-time education, 13.131–13.132
    generally, 13.125–13.126
    presence in Great Britain,
        13.129–13.130
    previous claimants, 13.127–13.128
    'relevant benefit year', 13.133–13.134
    residence, 13.129–13.130
    statutory basis, 13.70